THE
TONY EVANS
BIBLE
COMMENTARY

Advancing God's Kingdom Agenda

REFERENCE

NASHVILLE, TENNESSEE

Tony Evans Bible Commentary
Copyright © 2019 by Holman Bible Publishers
Nashville, Tennessee. All Rights Reserved.

Some material in the Bible book introductions was previously published in the *Holman Illustrated Bible Commentary*, 2013, by B&H Publishing Group. Used by permission.

Unless otherwise noted, all Scripture quotations are taken from the Christian Standard Bible®, Copyright © 2017 by Holman Bible Publishers. Used by permission. Christian Standard Bible® and CSB® are federally registered trademarks of Holman Bible Publishers.

The interior of the *Tony Evans Bible Commentary* was designed and typeset by 2K/DENMARK, Højbjerg, Denmark. Proofreading was provided by Peachtree Publishing Services, Peachtree City, Georgia.

ISBN: 978-0-8054-9942-1

BISAC: REL00605/RELIGION/Biblical Commentary/General

Printed in the United States
5 6 7 — 22 21 20
LSC

TONY EVANS BIBLE COMMENTARY

ACKNOWLEDGMENTS

A work of this magnitude requires an enormously committed support system. *The Tony Evans Bible Commentary* (and its companion *The Tony Evans Study Bible*) has been years in the making. It is for this reason I wish to express my heartfelt gratitude to all who enabled this project to reach its completion.

First of all, I want to thank the B&H Publishing family for their hard work. This includes Trevin Wax who oversaw the publishing of this work. I am also grateful for the investment of time and energy given by the managing editor, Chris Cowan, with whom I spent countless hours critiquing, constructing, and reviewing the content of my exposition of every paragraph of God's Holy Word. Thanks also to B&H's editorial and production team, including J. D. Green, Lloyd Mullens, Garry Fulton, Dustin Curtis, and Bethany McShurley for the wonderful and professional way they put this project together. And I want to thank Jeremy Howard for his vision as we started this project a decade ago.

A special thanks goes to my good friend Phil Rawley for his hard work and tremendous contribution with regard to certain elements of content. Thanks also go to Jeff Godby and 2K/DENMARK for their design and typesetting expertise, as well as to Dylan Geril and Vijay Prabhaker, who handled video and audio production.

I am also very grateful to my longtime executive assistant, Mrs. Sylvia Stewart, for the endless time and effort she put into keeping up with all the administrative duties connected with this project amidst all her other responsibilities. My appreciation goes to Mrs. Heather Hair, who helped to strategize, organize, and manage all the moving parts of this work during this multi-year process in an efficient and excellent way.

Finally, I want to express my deepest, heartfelt gratitude to my wife and ministry partner Lois Evans for her unending love, patience, support, and encouragement that made this legacy work possible.

DR. TONY EVANS

Dr. Tony Evans is the founder and senior pastor of Oak Cliff Bible Fellowship in Dallas, is founder and president of The Urban Alternative, served as chaplain of the NBA's Dallas Mavericks and the NFL's Dallas Cowboys, and is author of over one hundred books, booklets, and Bible studies. The first African American to earn a doctorate of theology from Dallas Theological Seminary, he has been named one of the 12 Most Effective Preachers in the English-Speaking World by Baylor University.

Dr. Evans holds the honor of writing and publishing the first full-Bible commentary and study Bible by an African American.

His radio broadcast, *The Alternative with Dr. Tony Evans*, can be heard on more than 1,300 US outlets daily and in more than 130 countries.

Dr. Evans launched the Tony Evans Training Center in 2017, an online learning platform providing quality seminary-style courses for a fraction of the cost to any person in any place. The goal is to increase biblical literacy and to advance God's kingdom agenda not only among lay people but also among those Christian leaders who cannot afford or find the time for formal ongoing education.

For more information, visit TonyEvans.org.

INTRODUCTION

This commentary is based on a simple yet profound biblical worldview: the glory of God through the advancement of his kingdom. This is the unifying theme of Scripture, from Genesis through Revelation. The concept of God's kingdom is what ties all of the Bible together. When this central point of connectivity is lost to the reader, it is easy for Scripture to seem like a series of disconnected stories, events, personalities, and doctrines that do not strategically and thematically connect to one another.

The word *kingdom* means "rule" or "authority." When linked to God, it refers to the rule of God in both heaven and earth encompassing both eternity and time. It is therefore comprehensive in nature. This kingdom is composed of a ruler (God), subjects (angels and people), a realm (creation), and regulations (laws).

The Bible unfolds how God's kingdom operates in the affairs of the world and how God receives glory through his kingdom rule, even when that rule is being opposed by both angels and human beings. While God's kingdom rule takes various forms with varying laws through varying administrations (i.e., dispensations), it nonetheless maintains its central goal of bringing God glory whether through blessing or judgment.

The *kingdom agenda*, then, is the visible manifestation of the comprehensive rule of God over every area of life. God's kingdom agenda is carried out through four covenantal spheres: the individual, the family, the church, and the government (i.e., nations). A covenant is a divinely created relational bond through which God administrates his kingdom program. It establishes a legal relationship in the spiritual realm that is to be lived out in the physical realm. To operate and function underneath the umbrella of God's kingdom covenants and guidelines is to position the specific covenantal relationship (i.e., individual, family, church, government) to experience God's greatest involvement and benefits within that covenantal sphere. Conversely, to operate outside of and in opposition to God's kingdom covenant is to experience the negative consequences of not being aligned and covenantally covered.

This commentary is designed to reflect this kingdom perspective through an exposition of each of the sixty-six books of the Holy Scriptures. My goal is that this work will serve as a valuable study resource for serious students of the Bible by combining exegesis, exposition, and exhortation that creates a relevant kingdom mindset.

As you use this study tool, remember:

A. Study the Scriptures with a view to meeting with God, not just learning about him.

B. Study the Scriptures by routinely asking, "What should I do in light of what I have learned?"

C. Study the Scriptures in their context in order to be accurate in your understanding of what the biblical authors are saying.

D. Study the Scriptures in prayer and in dependency on the Holy Spirit to open up your mind and heart to the meaning and contemporary relevancy and application of the text.

E. Study the Scripture with a kingdom mindset, seeking to identify God's rule over every area of life.

While nothing can be added to or subtracted from God's inerrant Word, it is my sincere hope that this tool will aid you in your understanding and application of the Bible to your life. For additional study notes, articles, and supporting materials, see also *The Tony Evans Study Bible: Advancing God's Kingdom Agenda*. Most importantly, it is my prayer that your reading, studying, and obedience to the written Word will lead you into a deeper, more intimate relationship with the living Word, Jesus Christ, as kingdom disciples as you live all of life under his kingdom rule.

Cradled within the depths that define our humanity lies an unyielding fascination with kingdom. No matter what color, creed, or culture we examine, we find with even the most cursory glance into the accounts passed down by either pen or by tongue something intertwined with kingdom. Whether it be the great kings and rulers of Scripture such as David or Solomon, or whether it be Caesar, Alexander the Great, Charlemagne, Tutankhamun, and the like, these lives somehow captivate us, intriguing our imaginations.

Even rulers who did not hold the official title of "king" have left their legacies, for good or for bad, to enthrall us. There is Napoleon, the dominator of continental Europe, who possessed a formidable intellect and superior military mind. There is Khan, the evil and brutal ruler, who conquered most of the world during his time. There are the Pharaohs, most of whom possessed strength and skill to such a degree that for many centuries they progressed their nation beyond the others in academics, engineering, medicine, and writing. Then there are also the Monarchs spanning over sixteen hundred years of history, in one form or fashion, beginning humbly as the Angles, moving to Aengla Land, and eventually becoming what we know today as England.

Stories of conquerors, conquests, rebellions, and conspiracy mesmerize us. We tell them to our children in fairy tales riddled with kings, queens, princes, princesses and kingdoms. We read about them in history books, mythology, fables, legends, and fiction. We flock to movies to watch the rise or fall of power connected to a kingdom in epic adventures. Inevitably, we portray the king, or the prince, as reputedly handsome—when he is a good king. We portray him as sinister and ugly when he is bad.

Queens and princesses play a role in our fascination as well. From Cinderella to Nefertiti to Elizabeth I, we hold in highest regard that special strength of a woman who both utilizes and maintains her nobility in the face of constant and devastating betrayal and opposition in order to produce a greater good for her kingdom and her subjects.

The life of a king or a queen is often envied. Yet, that envy is naïve. Any true historian knows the utter fragility that comes with absolute power. As the playwright Shakespeare once wrote, "Uneasy lies the head that wears the crown." Kings, queens, and rulers frequently function in a culture of conflict, and even violence. Those around them might swear an oath of total allegiance while they simultaneously plot their destruction, or even their death.

As a result, history reminds us again and again, through what may seem like the same story just set on a different stage, that kings and rulers often resort to brute force and extreme taxation to protect their own personal interests and power. While uprisers such as the Scottish William Wallace (best known for being portrayed in the film *Braveheart*) could wind up hung and quartered in a meat factory, it wasn't only the uprisers who needed to fear the virtual paranoid wrath that sometimes appeared in a king. No one was safe when it came to the possibility of usurping his role, as we see with poisoning of family members and even the gruesome, bloody beheading of wives with Henry VIII.

Nowhere in any story of a king or in any story of a kingdom do we read about the ruler himself sacrificing his own greatest treasure simply for the benefit of others. Sure sacrifices were made. Lives were lost. But this always happened toward the aim of preserving power, rather than yielding it— that is, except for one instance. The true King of the Bible gave up his own Son, Jesus Christ, in order that those who believe on him—his death, burial, and resurrection—would be restored to the place of both fellowship and dominion with their king, something they had lost in the battle in the garden.

THE UNUSUAL KINGDOM

It is not unusual that this unusual action occurred by this very unusual king because his is an even more unusual kingdom. Jesus spoke of it plainly when he told Pilate that the ways of his kingdom do not reflect the ways of the kingdoms on earth, "My kingdom is not of this world." He said, "If my kingdom were of this world, my servants would fight, so that I wouldn't be handed over to the Jews. But as it is, my kingdom is not from here" (John 18:36).

When his followers asked him to tell them who is the greatest in this very unusual kingdom, Jesus pulled a child close and replied, "Therefore, whoever humbles himself like this child—this one is the greatest in the kingdom of heaven" (Matt 18:4). Then rather than requiring the pomp and circumstance typical of a king, he instructed his subjects on how he would like to be approached as their Ruler and Lord: "And whoever welcomes one child like this in my name welcomes me" (18:5).

This is a kingdom without borders, and a kingdom without time. To try and apply the rules, precepts, and writs of this world to this very unearthly kingdom would be similar to giving a football linebacker a horse and a polo stick and instructing him to get on with it and play. Neither the rules of this earth nor its tools govern the rules of God's kingdom. As King, he determines the way it is both to operate and function.

In his kingdom, neither race nor gender delineate inequality. In his kingdom, power goes to the weak who recognize their weakness and humbly look to him. Forgiveness reigns preeminently, and the amount of money matters less than the heart that offers it, as we see in the case of the widow and her gift (Luke 21:1-4). Significance, in this unusual kingdom, is connected to service. Hope comes through helping others who may need it as well.

That is not to say there are no battles to fight or wars to win in this kingdom, or that this is a kingdom of rainbows, waterfalls, and unending bliss. There is a vile enemy still lurking and still seeking to dethrone the King because his kingdom is the greatest of all. Its origin lies in eternity past, and it will last forever.

In fact, before there ever was an earth at all, there was a kingdom. It existed solely in the heavenlies, and it was a place of glory, majesty, and beauty. Yet treason was committed in an attempt to steal the seat of power, and those caught in an attempt to lay siege to the throne were repudiated—kicked down into darkness, which would later be sculpted and called Earth. Satan, the leader of this primeval rebellion, now uses charm, deception, distraction, temptation, lust, pride, apathy, and evil to try and establish a rival kingdom whose subjects aim to defeat the subjects of the one, true King.

In the chancery known as the Holy Spirit, the story of this unique kingdom has been preserved for us, its subjects—followers of the Lord Jesus Christ—in what we call the Bible. Throughout Scripture, chroniclers—inspired by the Spirit—recorded, encouraged, equipped, lamented, and presented the history, rules, redemption, and purpose of our King and his kingdom. Unfortunately, today, many of us are living as followers of a King whom we also seek to dethrone, though perhaps not outrightly, through subtle ways of complacency, autonomy, independence, or just simply through a lack of a connection to him, his Word, and his covenants. As a result, we experience what anyone in any kingdom living apart from the rules of the King would. In our personal lives, homes, churches, communities, and our nation, we feel the chaos that comes from rebellion.

This is because in a kingdom, life is to be lived under the rule and authority of the King. The blessings of the covenantal charter of our King in his Word, imbued with the authority he gives us through his covenants, along with his promises and loyal love, come when we live all of our life under God. It comes when we live our lives on target with his goals and purposes as a kingdom disciple.

The unifying central theme throughout the Bible is the glory of God and the advancement of his kingdom. The conjoining thread from Genesis to Revelation—from beginning to end—is focused on one thing: God's glory through advancing his kingdom.

When you do not have that theme, the Bible becomes disconnected stories that are great for inspiration but seem to be unrelated in purpose and direction. The Bible exists to share God's movement in history toward the establishment and expansion of his kingdom. Understanding this theme increases the relevancy of this ancient book to your day-to-day living, because the kingdom is not only then, it is now.

Throughout the Bible, the kingdom of God is his rule, his plan, his program. God's kingdom is all-embracing. It covers everything in the universe. In fact, we can define the kingdom as God's comprehensive rule over all creation. It is the rule of God (theocracy) and not the rule of man (homocracy) that is paramount.

Now if God's kingdom is comprehensive, so is his kingdom agenda. The kingdom agenda, then, may be defined as *the visible demonstration of the comprehensive rule of God over every area of life.* The Greek word the Bible uses for kingdom is *basileia*, which basically means "rule" or "authority." Included in this definition is the concept of power. So when we talk about a kingdom, we're talking first about a king or a ruler. We are talking about someone who is in charge. Since there is a ruler, there also have to be "rulees," or kingdom subjects. In addition, a kingdom includes a realm—that is, a domain over which the king rules. Finally, if you're going to have a ruler, rulees, and a realm, you also need kingdom regulations, guidelines that govern the relationship between the ruler and the subjects. These are necessary so that the rulees will know whether they are doing what the ruler wants.

God's kingdom operates through his covenant. *A covenant is a divinely created relational bond through which God reveals himself and administers his kingdom program.* The four biblical covenantal spheres through which the kingdom operates are the individual, family, church, and community (or government).

Individual: The individual realm refers to each of us singularly as his kingdom disciple. A kingdom disciple can be defined as *a believer in Christ who takes part in the spiritual developmental process of progressively learning to live all of life under the lordship of Jesus Christ.* The goal of a kingdom disciple is to have a transformed life that transfers the values of the kingdom of God so that they replicate themselves in the lives of others. The result of such replication is God's exercising his rule from heaven to history through his kingdom disciples. Discipleship is the missing key to a life of authority under God. But surrender to Christ's lordship and obedience to his rule of love are the grooves

and edges which make up that key, which (when used rightly) will unlock the power to bring heaven to bear on earth.

Family: The family realm refers to familial units, both immediate and extended. This can also include variations on family due to death or adoption. The foundation of a family involves a husband and wife. A kingdom marriage is defined as *a covenantal union between a man and a woman who commit themselves to function in unison under divine authority in order to replicate God's image and expand his rule in the world through both their individual and joint callings.* Kingdom parenting can be defined as *the responsibility to intentionally oversee the generational transfer of a comprehensive Christian worldview so that children learn to consistently live all of life under God's divine authority.*

Church: The local church is the context and environment God has created to transform Christians into what we were created and redeemed to be: fully devoted followers of Jesus Christ. It is the spiritually redeemed body of believers that are to legislate the values of the kingdom of God from heaven to earth. A kingdom church can be defined as *a group of believers who covenant together to disciple its members in order to model and transfer heaven's values in history.* Discipleship is that process of the local church that seeks to bring believers from spiritual infancy to spiritual maturity so that they are then able to repeat that process with someone else.

Community: The community includes the multiple layers of society through which God works to establish order and ensure the freedoms and rights of all are carried out. This is obtained through biblical justice, which can be defined as *the equitable and impartial application of the rule of God's moral law in society.* Whether exercising itself through economic, political, social, or criminal justice, the one constant is the understanding and application of God's moral law within the social realm. It is the division of the sacred and the secular that has led to the cultural disintegration we are now experiencing (2 Chr 15:3-6). It was never the Creator's desire to have such a separation exist in his world. From Genesis to Revelation, it is inextricably clear that the spiritual and the social are always to be integrated if life is to be lived the way God intended.

The more these four covenantal spheres are properly connected to God and each other, the more ordered society will be. The less they are connected, the more conflict and chaos will occur.

It is my desire and prayer that this commentary be used by God to guide, equip, strengthen, inspire, and inform you of all you need to fully experience both his power and his peace as you live under his rule. May it also awaken an even greater desire to discover more about our Lord himself as you explore his kingdom, anytime and anywhere.

Scan this code with your mobile device or follow this link for videos of Tony Evans teaching on the Kingdom Agenda.

www.bhpublishinggroup.com/qr/te/67-01

Scan these codes with your mobile device or follow these links for additional audio messages of Tony Evans teaching on the Kingdom Agenda.

KINGDOM AGENDA SERMONS

www.bhpublishinggroup.com/qr/te/67-02

KINGDOM LIFE SERMONS

www.bhpublishinggroup.com/qr/te/67-03

KINGDOM FAMILY SERMONS

www.bhpublishinggroup.com/qr/te/67-04

KINGDOM SOCIETY SERMONS

www.bhpublishinggroup.com/qr/te/67-05

The Bible is a book unlike any other book. It is, in fact, a whole library of books, all bound together in one volume. These individual books were written by many different authors over an extended period of time. What makes the Bible so unique, though, is that its many human authors were all inspired by its one divine author—God himself! The Greek word Paul uses for "inspired by God" means "God-breathed." These words that carry God's breath are words that can change and transform our lives. Paul reminds us that all of Scripture "is inspired by God and is profitable for teaching, for rebuking, for correcting, for training in righteousness" (2 Tim 3:16).

If we want to understand who God is, what his purposes are, and how he has made Himself known to the human race, we cannot afford to ignore the Bible. Whenever you purchase a complicated gadget it is usually accompanied by a set of instructions—a manufacturer's handbook. Without this handbook you'll find yourself having to guess at how it works. In a sense, the Bible is the "manufacturer's handbook" for life. The one who created us has plans and purposes for us. If we don't know the content of his manufacturer's handbook, we won't know his plans and purposes, nor will we know how to live as he intends.

Still, many people put little effort into reading the Bible. Sometimes the problem is just laziness or a wrong set of priorities. But that isn't the only reason. The Bible *can* be a difficult book to understand. While its most important teachings are understandable by a child, there is much in the pages of Scripture that is not easy to grasp without some extra effort and help.

That's where a study Bible comes in handy. It will provide you with some background material and theological explanation that will bring biblical truths into sharper focus. But don't count on the study Bible to do all the work for you. If you want to get the most out of the Scripture you need to learn to read it for yourself and learn to interpret it by giving careful focus to the passage you are reading and by comparing what you learn there with the rest of what the Bible teaches.

What follows are some things you can do to help you get the most out of your biblical study.

READ CAREFULLY

Though the Bible is an exciting book, you can't read it in the same way you'd read a thrilling novel. If you race through the pages you will miss much of what it has to offer. Good Bible reading begins with reading slowly and carefully, and it is a good idea to have a pen and paper handy to jot down the things you observe. Or maybe you'll want to write in the margins of your Bible. Mark down the things that inspire, challenge, or puzzle you. If there is a key verse or key idea you discover, you might want to underline it. You can make a study Bible your own by recording *in* it the things you are learning *from* it.

As you read, pay close attention to words like *if*, *then*, and *therefore*, which will help you understand the relationships between the concepts it teaches. These little words may reveal requirements and expectations that you need to keep in mind. Many of the Bible's promises, for example, are conditional. There are things you are expected to do if that promise is to become real in your life. And in the New Testament letters, the word *therefore* is often a signal that what went before is the doctrinal basis on which a truth can be embraced and applied.

Read and read again. You might even try reading aloud as a way of forcing yourself to slow down and take in every thought. Above all, don't be in a hurry. Read slowly and think about what each sentence and paragraph means. Don't just hunt for an inspiring nugget of truth. Let every sentence speak to you!

ASK QUESTIONS

One of the common characteristics of children is that they are almost insatiably curious. They ask lots of questions, which can sometimes become exhausting for their parents. But it is the way they learn new things. One of the problems with adults is that they often stop asking questions as they grow older. So be more like a curious child as you read the Bible. Don't assume you already know what it says. Keep your curiosity high and keep your heart and mind open. One great way to do this is by cross-examining the passage you are reading in order to make sure you are noticing all it has to say. See if you can answer these questions: *who*, *what*, *where*, *when*, *why*, and *how*? Exploring the answers to these questions will open new depths of understanding.

PAY ATTENTION TO THE CONTEXT

Paying attention to *context* is extremely important if you want to accurately understand what the Bible is saying. Some people just search its pages for an individual verse that speaks to their need of the moment, without paying much attention to the verses that surround it. Reading this way is like treating the Bible as a fortune cookie or as a collection of inspirational memes. As you read the Bible, sometimes a verse will stand out and engage your heart in a very personal way. But when that happens, it's important to see how that verse relates to the verses around it. If you don't pay attention to the context, you are in danger of trying to make the Bible say something that it doesn't actually say.

Every verse of the Bible is part of a chapter, and every chapter is part of a book, and every book of the Bible is part of one larger God-inspired message that unfolds across its pages. Many people don't realize that the Bible wasn't originally written in chapters and verses. Each book was one continuous text contained in a scroll, and it was not until the late Middle Ages that someone came up with the idea of dividing it into chapters and verses to make it more convenient for readers and as a tool for helping people locate specific passages they wanted to remember. You should keep that in mind before pulling a verse out of its context and applying it to your life.

As you read, pay attention to the immediate context of the neighboring verses and try to understand the main point that the biblical writer is making. Ask yourself how it fits in the context of the entire book. You should notice if the passage you are reading is part of a larger story or a larger argument and who is speaking or being spoken to. There are, for example, places in the Bible that contain the words of Satan or of a godless leader, and we don't want to treat those in the same way we'd treat the words of Jesus!

As we study the Bible, it is important to keep our focus upon the main points and the most important teachings, and not allow ourselves to be sidetracked too much by secondary issues. Make sure you understand the big picture through your *telescope* before you pull out your *microscope* to examine the details! The Bible isn't a puzzle book or a coded message, so don't look for complicated symbols and secret meanings. Ask yourself what it meant to the original readers and how that applies to you today.

BE READY TO OBEY

Applying what we read in the Bible to our daily lives is the highest purpose of Bible study. We don't study it so that we can win theological arguments or impress people with our knowledge. We read it so that God can use it to transform our lives. Therefore, we should read the Bible with humility and an open heart, being ready to be challenged and changed by God's Word. We should read it with an open mind, not assuming we already know what it means. The more you read the Bible, the more new and fresh truths you will discover in its pages. It is inexhaustible.

The Bible speaks with God's own authority, so the proper response to such authority is obedience. James 1:23 tells us that the Bible is a mirror in which we can catch an honest glimpse of ourselves. As you read, you can perceive where you are falling short, where you are making improper compromises, where you are following your own desires instead of God's best, and where you are placing your cultural prejudices over God's truth. So, as you read Scripture, hear—and then obey.

PRAY

Since the Bible is a spiritual book, it must be approached spiritually. You approach studying the Bible spiritually by bathing your study in prayer. In this way, the Holy Spirit can illuminate your mind regarding the meaning and application of its truth to your life (1 Cor 2:9-16; Eph 6:18).

THE BIG STORY AND ALL THE LITTLE ONES

The Bible is filled with history, biographies, miracles, prophecies, songs, poems, letters, and practical teaching. Each element deserves your time and attention, and each book contains wisdom and guidance for your life. But as you read and study, you should never lose sight of the big over-arching story of the Bible, which is the story of God's redemptive love and his desire to be present with his people. It is a story about a King who will go to any lengths to invite his people into relationship with him and to join him in advancing his kingdom agenda in history.

The Old Testament tells the story of how that relationship grew and changed over time. It focuses upon the story of Israel, a people specially chosen by God to establish and advance his kingdom for his glory. He worked with his people in different ways through each of the covenants he made with them. The New Testament contains the fulfillment of these promises and covenants in the person of Jesus Christ, who is God in the flesh.

The Bible tells a story with a big narrative arc, and that arc points toward God's increasingly intimate dealings with his people. That's why it is important to pay attention to where you are in the big story as you read through the Bible.

The Pentateuch (Genesis–Deuteronomy) tells of the creation of the universe, the fall of humanity, the calling of Abraham to be the father of a chosen people, God's deliverance of his people from slavery through Moses, and the giving of the law as a sign of the covenant God made with his people. These five books are the foundation for everything that follows in the establishing and expansion of God's kingdom.

The Historical Books (Joshua–Esther) record the many victories and failures of Israel. It is often not a pretty story! The historical books record the conquest of the land God had promised, the era of the judges, the rise of the monarchy, and the constant struggles against the temptations toward idolatry and immorality. They also tell of how Israel underwent a civil war and was divided into a northern kingdom (Israel) and a southern kingdom (Judah). This led to destruction and exile. The last few books reveal what happened when the Israelites finally emerged from exile.

The Poetical Books (Job–Song) were written at various times during the history of Israel, though the lion's share were penned during the high points of the monarchy under David and Solomon, who are traditionally considered to be the authors of much that is in these books. Job struggles with the question of why there is suffering in the lives of good people. Psalms is a book of songs, praises, and prayers. Proverbs offers bite-sized nuggets of wisdom for living, Ecclesiastes centers on the meaning of a truly good and purposeful life. The Song of Songs reflects upon human and divine love. Since poetry is less straightforward than prose, these books take a different path to revealing important truths about God and our walk with him.

The Prophetic Books (Isaiah–Malachi) record the stories and messages of the men God raised up to challenge Israel for its unfaithfulness, injustice, and hypocrisy. The prophets challenged the status quo and pointed toward the future with hope. They gestured toward a time when God will powerfully intervene in history and make himself known. Included in these books are prophecies of the coming Messiah, as well as the coming realization of the kingdom of God upon the earth.

The Gospels (Matthew–John) give us four different, but complementary, perspectives on the life of Jesus. We see in them the story of the one who embodies the kingdom of God and who offers a path to salvation based upon his love, his sacrifice, and his grace. The Gospels also record Jesus's kingdom teaching and his establishment of the church through his disciples.

Acts is the story of the early church, focusing especially on the ministries of Peter and Paul. It shows how the power of the Holy Spirit was unleashed upon God's people so that they could bear witness to the truth—by miracles, healings, and especially by the powerful proclamation of the good news of Jesus Christ and his kingdom program.

The Epistles (Romans–Jude) are a collection of letters that the apostle Paul and other early church leaders wrote to inspire, instruct, and encourage the church—as well as to challenge false teachings that were beginning to creep into the early congregations. These letters give us a picture of the early Christian communities and offer practical advice about living the life of faith.

Revelation is the last book of the New Testament, and the last book of the Bible. Unquestionably the most complex and difficult biblical book to interpret, it has spawned a variety of different interpretations. But the central message is clear: A day is coming when God will defeat all the powers of darkness and establish his eternal worldwide kingdom with his people. This is the great and grand hope of Revelation.

As you read and study each book of the Bible, remember that the big story is one of God's love and redemption, and his desire to dwell with and in his people. The King is establishing a kingdom where he can rule in every heart, and where his grace will be the basis for relationship. Every page of the Bible is, in some way, pointing toward this ultimate hope.

Scan this code with your mobile device or follow this link for videos of Tony Evans leading you on an overview of the Old Testament.

www.bhpublishinggroup.com/qr/te/67-07

Scan this code with your mobile device or follow this link for videos of Tony Evans leading you on an overview of the New Testament.

www.bhpublishinggroup.com/qr/te/67-06

Knowing key terms and sound doctrine matters as we come to know God in all of his of triune fullness as Father, Son, and Holy Spirit, as far as we can with our finite minds. God wants us to know him. Paul prayed "that the God of our Lord Jesus Christ, the glorious Father, would give you the Spirit of wisdom and of revelation in the knowledge of him" (Eph 1:17). Knowing God is the foundation of the wisdom we need to live victorious and abundant Christian lives (Prov 9:10). Below are explanations of key terms and a selection of doctrinal topics from God's Word, as well as relevant Scripture for each.

Baptism: *The ordinance of water baptism is an outward testimony of an inward reality— the salvation of a soul by the blood of Christ and the baptism of that person into the body of Christ by the Holy Spirit, formally initiating the life of discipleship.*

Because water baptism is symbolic of this inner, spiritual work, it was never intended to have saving power in itself. The primary meaning of baptism for the believer is public identification with Christ in his death, burial, and resurrection, pictured by the immersion of the believer in the waters of baptism. Baptism inaugurates the formal beginning of the believer's life of discipleship (Matt 28:19; Rom 6:1-4; 1 Cor 12:13; Col 2:12; 1 Pet 3:21).

Biblical Justice: *The equitable and impartial application of the rule of God's moral law in society.*

Biblical justice provides society with a divine frame of reference from which to operate. The word *justice* in Scripture means to prescribe the right way. Biblical justice is not a man-made, socially imposed, top-down system ultimately leading to the negation of freedom. Biblical justice promotes freedom by emphasizing accountability, equality, and responsibility in providing a spiritual underpinning in the personal and social realms. Biblical justice must always be coupled with righteousness (Gen 18:19; Ps 7:6; 9:16; 11:7; 33:5; 89:14; Matt 12:18-20).

Blessing: *The capacity to experience, enjoy, and extend the goodness and favor of God in your life.*

A blessing is not merely what God does for you or to you. A blessing is also what God is able to do through you in order to similarly bring a blessing to others. Christians who want God to bless them must be willing for God to bless others through them. We must align ourselves under the fundamentals of God's covenant to be in a position to receive the blessings he has promised. Living in God's kingdom brings blessings, but these blessings are often contingent upon living for his kingdom and underneath his authority (Gen 1:28; Luke 6:38; Acts 20:35; Gal 3:14; Eph 1:3; 1 Pet 3:9).

Calling: *The customized life purpose God has ordained and equipped you to accomplish in order to bring him the greatest glory and achieve the maximum expansion of his Kingdom.*

As followers of Jesus and subjects in God's kingdom, believers have been placed on earth to carry out God's will according to their personal gifts and his plan for each life. Your calling is unique to you and will often involve an intersection of your past experiences, passions, gifts, skills, position, and personality when God ushers you into its fulfillment (Acts 13:36; Gal 2:20; Eph 2:10; Phil 2:12-13).

Church: *The spiritually redeemed body of believers that is to legislate the heavenly values of the kingdom of God on earth.*

The church is built and God's kingdom is advanced by faithful believers who serve Christ to the best of their ability. God designed the church to be the epicenter of culture, and the church's strength or weakness is a major determining factor in the success or failure of human civilization, since the church alone possesses the keys of the kingdom and its authority. A church also provides a community in which spiritual gifts are to be used for the benefit of others, and a place where believers partake in worship, study, fellowship, and outreach (Matt 16:18-19; Acts 2:42-47; Eph 1:22; 2:11-22; 3:10; Col 1:18-24).

Confession: *To acknowledge to God and others, as appropriate, that what God calls a sin we also call a sin in our own lives, thoughts, and actions.*

Every misery we encounter is related to sin to some extent—whether it is our own sin, someone else's sin, or just the evil, sinful world in which we live. But God's mercy and grace extend beyond our sin through the blood of Christ. When God sees our pain, he feels and experiences it with us. But grace must precede mercy because God can't help us with our pain until he first deals with our sin. That's why we are told to confess our sins. Confession of your sin enables God to extend his mercy to you (Prov 28:13; Eph 2:1-5; Jas 5:16; 1 John 1:9).

Covenant: *A divinely created relational bond through which God reveals himself and administers his kingdom program that's designed to bring his greatest blessing to human beings who operate under its guidelines.*

A biblical covenant involves far more than a contract. In a biblical covenant, you enter into an intimate relationship with another person or persons. Jesus's blood has established the new covenant under which you are to align your life in order to receive its full covenantal blessings, covering, and protection. There must be covenantal alignment under the lordship of Jesus Christ in order to experience his kingdom presence, power, authority, provision, and covering (Deut 29:9; 1 Cor 10:16; Heb 8:6; 9:15; 12:24).

Dispensations: *Divisions of time that can be defined as progressive stages in God's revelation, each consisting of a distinct stewardship or rule of life.*

Since each dispensation is distinct and identifiable—such as Innocence, Law, Grace, and Kingdom—there are different characteristics, administrations, jurisdictions and judgments in each period. Dispensationalism recognizes the movement of God in redemption history and identifies how he related to people in the time in which they lived with the divine revelation that he had communicated to them (Matt 5:21-22; John 1:17; Acts 17:31-32; 1 Cor 9:17; Eph 1:10; 3:2; Col 1:25).

Election: *The sovereign prerogative of God to choose individuals, families, groups, and nations to serve his kingdom purposes as he so wills.*

Election is specifically related to service, usefulness, and blessings—not individual salvation. Jesus died for all human beings without exception and desires for all to be saved (Rom 9:10-13; 1 Tim 2:4; 4:10; Heb 2:9; 2 Pet 3:8-11; 1 John 2:2).

Eternal Life: *The never-ending reality of growing in our experiential knowledge of God while abiding in his unabated presence forever.*

It's important to see that Jesus did not define eternal life solely in terms of its length. Eternal life certainly means that we are going to live forever. But there's much more to it than that. Even the lost will exist forever. The eternal life that God gives is a quality of life that Jesus defined as knowing God the Father and God the Son. This is personal, intimate knowledge, and it begins the moment we trust Christ (John 4:13-14; 10:27-30; 17:2-3; 2 Pet 1:2-3).

Eternal Security: *The clear teaching of Scripture that those who come to know Christ as their Savior enter into an eternal relationship with God that guarantees their eternal security.*

God's power is able to keep believers from falling because it is up to him, not to us, to make good on the Bible's guarantee of eternal life for true believers in Christ. Simply put, the doctrine of eternal security means that our redemption in Christ Jesus is permanent (John 10:27-30; Rom 8:31-39; Eph 1:13-14; 1 Tim 2:10-13; 1 John 5:11-13).

Evangelism: *Sharing the good news of Christ's substitutionary death and resurrection and his free offer of forgiveness of sin and eternal life to all who come to him by faith to receive it.*

Every believer is called to share the gospel with every lost person possible, both at home and abroad. The act of sharing your faith is not reserved for ministers or evangelists. Jesus has given believers the task of telling others about him and the gospel of saving grace as we go about our daily lives. It can be as simple as doing a kind act for someone in need and then asking to pray with them afterwards while sharing the gospel, or it could be more elaborate (Mark 16:15; Acts 1:8; 21:8; 2 Cor 5:18-21; Eph 4:11; 2 Tim 4:5).

Faith: *Acting like God is telling the truth; acting like it is so even when it is not so in order that it might be so simply because God said so.*

Faith is the opposite of sight, acting and judging things based solely on what we can see and perceive with our human senses. Faith always involves your feet. It is an action of your life, not merely words from your lips. A person can feel like they lack faith but still be full of faith if they choose to obey what God has revealed to do or say. Faith is not merely a feeling; it is an action in response to God's revealed will (Rom 4:17; 2 Cor 5:7; Eph 2:8-9; Heb 11:1-3, 6).

Fellowship: *Intimate communion with God and his people as they share the life and love of Christ with one another.*

Biblical fellowship is not just coffee and donuts in Sunday school, or a meal in the fellowship hall. Fellowship is the sharing of our lives and sharing the life and love of Christ with other believers. The Bible teaches that Christians are bonded together in a relationship of unity as members of one another. In fact, those who withdraw from the community of believers will find their relationship with God limited by their failure to participate in the fellowship of the saints. (Acts 2:42; Rom 12:5; 1 Cor 11:29; Heb 10:25; 1 John 1:5-9).

Forgiveness: *The decision to no longer credit an offense against an offender with a view to executing personal vengeance.*

There are two basic categories of forgiveness: (1) *Unilateral forgiveness* is the decision to release someone from an offense who is either unable or unwilling to repent in order that the offended person is set free. Give to the Lord that situation in which someone misunderstood you, misread your motives, hurt you, or sinned against you. Forgive the people involved if that's needed, and rest your case with God, realizing that he knows your heart. (2) *Transactional forgiveness* is the decision to release someone from an offense who repents of his or her sin, thus

opening up the opportunity for reconciliation (Matt 6:12, 14-15; 18:21-35; 2 Cor 2:10; Eph 4:32; Col 3:12-13).

Freedom: *The release from illegitimate bondage so that you can choose to exercise responsibility in maximizing all that you were created to be.*

The freedom that is actualized through a kingdom perspective, that of embracing God's sovereignty, generates a faith more powerful than any human weapon or system of philosophy could ever produce. It accesses God's grace in such a way so as to grant a freedom that is not dependent upon externals. Authentic biblical freedom releases people from sin and illegitimate bondage to righteousness so that they can serve God and others as they fulfill his will for their lives (John 8:32-36; 2 Cor 3:17; Gal 5:1-4).

God: *The eternally perfect uncreated Creator, Sustainer, and Ruler of all things who is one in essence but exists in three coequal persons: Father, Son, and Holy Spirit (the Trinity).*

God exists before time and will exist beyond time. He sits outside of the confines of our finite humanity. He is the great "I AM," dependent upon no one. Within him lies all wisdom, knowledge, and understanding. His multiplicity of attributes comprise a sovereign and supreme being exhibiting an array of emotion, power, authority, and gentleness unlike any other. The many declarations in Scripture that God exists as a triune being have made the doctrine of the Trinity a central tenet of true, biblical faith (Gen 1:26; Matt 3:16-17; 28:19; 2 Cor 13:14).

Grace: *The inexhaustible goodness of God which he freely bestows upon human beings, which is undeserved, unearned, and unable to be repaid.*

Grace is God's unmerited favor. It is by grace that we are saved, and it is grace that is to serve as a believer's motivation for righteous living and good works. Our gratitude for God's grace provides the impetus for obedience, worship, and fellowship with the Lord. Personal power and strength become perfected as we experience a greater level of God's grace. We are to grow in our understanding of grace and are also called to extend grace to one another as a reflection of God's grace in our own lives (John 1:16; Rom 3:24; 5:15; 2 Cor 12:9; Eph 1:7-8; 2:8-9, 1 Pet 4:10; 2 Pet 3:18).

Grace over Law: *The grace of God saves us totally apart from any merit of our own, overcoming the power of the law to condemn.*

As Christians we often tend to get our Bible doctrines confused and start mixing truths that were never meant to be mixed. The Christians in Galatia got sidetracked because a group of people called the Judaizers had confused them about the relationship between the gospel of grace and the works of the law. Their message was that people needed to add law-keeping to grace to truly be saved and sanctified. But Paul wrote that salvation and sanctification is by grace through faith from first to last. The demands of the law are met as believers grow in grace (Rom 1:17; 3:20; 8:1-4; 11:6; Gal 2:21; 5:1-4; Eph 2:8-9; Titus 2:11, 12).

Hierarchy: *A covenantally authorized functional order that operates within a particular alignment and chain of command.*

The triune God perfectly illustrates this concept. Although the Father, Son, and Holy Spirit are equally God, the Son obeys and glorifies the Father, and the Spirit only speaks what the Father and Son tell him to say. Likewise, the Spirit's calling is not to glorify himself but rather to glorify the Son. Based on the activity in the Trinity, God has established a hierarchy in human relationship as well. Hierarchy does not delineate value or equality; rather, it establishes an order for effective kingdom function (John 5:19; 16:14; 17:4; 1 Cor 11:3; Heb 13:17).

Hope: *Confident expectation about the future based on the character and promises of God.*

Local churches are to be centers of hope in every community where they minister. The church is supposed to be a little bit of heaven a long way from home. It is to be that place where the values of eternity operate in history—a place where weary people can go to find truth, acceptance, equality, freedom, safety, forgiveness, justice, and hope. Jesus is working to bring glory to himself and hope to mankind in fulfillment of his kingdom purposes and provisions (Jer 29:11-14; Matt 5:13-14; Rom 5:3-5; Heb 10:23; 1 Pet 3:15

Hypostatic Union: *Two natures (divine and human) in one person (Jesus Christ) unmixed forever.*

This is the term theologians use to describe the perfect union of Christ's divine and human natures, both in their fullness without any confusion. Christ's undiminished deity and perfect humanity are united forever in one person. Jesus was no less God when he became a perfect man. He was fully human but without sin. Jesus is the God-man, united forever in heaven. He is unique—God in the flesh (John 1:1, 14; Luke 2:52; Phil 2:5-8; Heb 2:14).

Inheritance: *The temporal and eternal blessings and privileges afforded to faithful Christians for the enjoyment of all the rights and benefits of the King and his kingdom.*

Believers are heirs of the kingdom promises to Abraham, having already been blessed by the King with all spiritual blessings (Eph 1:3). We only receive a portion of the rights and benefits of our inheritance in the present age. But when Jesus comes, we will receive our full inheritance based on our obedience, faithfulness, and fulfillment of God's will for our lives (Rom 4:13-16; 8:17; Eph 1:3, 14, 18; Col 1:12; 3:24; Heb 9:15; 1 Pet 1:4).

Joy: *The feeling and expression of the inner celebration and satisfaction of the soul that transcends circumstances.*

Joy is the overflow of life, the stability inside despite chaos on the outside. The influence of the first-century church was so powerful in society that it brought great joy to the entire city of Samaria when Philip took the gospel there (Acts 8:8). The Holy Spirit's task is to make real in the lives of true believers the comfort and confidence of their security in Christ (Neh 8:10; Luke 2:10-11; John 15:11; Rom 14:17; Phil 1:25; 1 Pet 1:8-9).

Justification: *Justification is a legal term that means to acquit, to find the defendant not guilty.*

In the New Testament, it means to declare the former defendant righteous. A basic definition of biblical justification is a judicial act by which God declares righteous those who believe in Jesus Christ. The picture is a courtroom in which we stand condemned by our sin. But justification is a pardon from a death penalty. On the cross, Jesus announced that the price for sin had been paid in full. Justification comes from God alone. The opposite of justification is condemnation (John 19:30; Rom 3:19-24; 5:1, 8-9; 8:33).

Kingdom: *The sovereign and comprehensive rule of God over all of his creation.*

The Bible declares that God's kingdom is the entire universe, which includes the earth and all of its inhabitants (Ps 24:1). The job of the Holy Spirit is to bring people to recognize God's right to rule as King and to submit to his authority. Jesus told the apostles that God will indeed establish his earthly kingdom someday, but in his own time. In the meantime, God has decided to set up his own kingdom communities. This community is called the church, brought into being by the Holy Spirit in order to exercise God's kingdom authority in history (1 Chr 29:11; Ps 115:3; Dan 4:34-35; Matt 6:33; 16:18-19; 1 Thess 2:12; Heb 12:28).

Kingdom Agenda: *The visible manifestation of the comprehensive rule of God over every area of life.*

We are called to align our lives underneath God's over-arching rule. His kingdom rule needs to remain at the forefront of our thinking in order to fully penetrate our choices and decisions thus bringing about the full realization of his covenantal blessings and authority. It transcends the politics of men and offers the solutions of heaven, removing the division humanity often erects between the sacred and the secular. This agenda is manifested through the four covenantal spheres of the individual, family, church, and community—which includes civil government (Ps 128:1-6; Matt 6:10, 33; John 18:36; Col 1:13; 4:11; Rom 13:1-7).

Kingdom Authority: *The sovereign and comprehensive rule of God over all of his creation.*

Kingdom authority is the divinely authorized right and responsibility delegated to disciples to act on God's behalf in spiritually ruling over his creation under the lordship of Jesus Christ. Believers are given authority to rule in God's kingdom under his direction and in accordance with his will and purposes. We gain access to this authority through living under the comprehensive rule of God in our lives. While authority is offered through

Christ, it is not always accessed. There is a process to entering into the complete realization and execution of the divine mission for our individual lives, families, church, nation, and world (Gen 1:26-28; Deut 4:28-37, Dan 4:34-37; Matt 25:14-30; 28:18-20; Phil 3:14-20).

Kingdom Citizen: *A visible, verbal follower of Jesus Christ who consistently applies the principles of heaven to the concerns of the culture.*

Kingdom citizens have an obligation to fully utilize and fulfill their assigned tasks through the use of God-given resources and abilities for the benefit of society. Spiritual ministry and social responsibility work hand-in-hand. When the two are properly connected and integrated, people become productive citizens of society while also becoming prepared for life in eternity (Jer 29:7; Matt 5:13-16; Rom 13:1-7; Gal 6:10; 1 Tim 2:1-3; 1 Pet 2:17).

Kingdom Disciple: *A believer who takes part in the spiritual developmental process of progressively learning to live all of life under the lordship of Jesus Christ.*

This process of growth from spiritual infancy to spiritual maturity enables the believer to become increasingly more like Christ. Kingdom discipleship is designed to be replicated again and again until Jesus has many brothers and sisters who look, act, and think like him (Matt 28:18-20; Rom 8:29, 2 Cor 3:17-18; 2 Tim 1:13; 2:2).

Kingdom Man: *A male who is consistently living under the rule of God and lordship of Jesus Christ over every area of his life.*

A kingdom man accepts his responsibilities under God and faithfully carries them out. When this man is faithful, God will move even pagan powers and other forces and circumstances on earth to support his kingdom man doing his kingdom business. Jesus is the perfect example of a kingdom man in his earthly ministry (Gen 18:19; Exod 34:23-24; John 17:4; 19:30; 1 Cor 11:3; Phil 3:7-14).

Kingdom Marriage: *A covenantal union between a man and a woman who commit themselves to function in unison under divine authority in order to replicate God's image and expand his rule in the world through both their individual and joint callings.*

God established marriage and created the first family. A man and a woman together were to reflect God's image, which is unity in diversity—God the Father, the Son, and the Holy Spirit. The marriage union most fully expresses who God truly is, and it is the most comprehensive manifestation of his image on earth as well as the foundation for a stable society. Paul uses the sacred covenant of marriage to illustrate both the bond and function between Christ and his church (Gen 1:26-28; 2:22-25; Mal 2:10-17; Matt 19:3-10, Eph 5:22-23).

Kingdom Parenting: *The responsibility to intentionally oversee the generational transfer of a comprehensive Christian worldview so that children learn to consistently live all of life under God's divine authority.*

Parents are to train children in the biblical principles of a kingdom worldview. Through consistent time in imparting truths from God's Word to their children, parents disciple their children in spiritual growth. Kingdom parents leave a legacy and inheritance not only for their children but also for their children's children. Children are to be "like young olive plants around your table"—indicating a regular pattern of purposeful development. Parents are also to encourage their children and lovingly correct them when they disobey (Deut 6:4-9; Psalm 128:3; Prov 13:22; 22:6; Eph 6:1-4; Col 3:20-21).

Kingdom Prayer: *The divinely authorized methodology to access heavenly authority for earthly intervention.*

Prayer links us to a heavenly realm we are unfamiliar navigating. Prayer is the God given communication link between heaven and earth, time and eternity, the finite and the infinite. Simply put, it is relational communication with God (Luke 18:1; Phil 4:4-7; 1 Thess 5:17; 1 Tim 2:1-2).

Kingdom Single: *An unmarried Christian who has committed to fully and freely maximizing his or her completeness under the rule of God and the Lordship of Jesus Christ.*

According to the apostle Paul, being single is a very good thing (1 Cor 7:26). In fact, a kingdom single is in the best possible spiritual position. Singlehood is a unique platform and position provided to you for great enjoyment, accomplishment, discovery, exploration, freedom, meaning and spiritual fellowship as well as eternal impact (1 Cor 6:17-20; 7:20, 25-40; Phil 4:11-13).

Kingdom Steward: *A believer who faithfully oversees, protects, and expands the assets God has given him or her to manage on his behalf.*

A kingdom steward carries out the divinely ordained responsibility of faithfully managing God's assigned resources (time, talent, and treasures) in such a way that they bring him glory and expand his kingdom rule in the world. Stewardship is the responsibility to protect and expand the possessions of another, which for believers means recognizing that everything we have is a gift from God for which we are accountable as his stewards or managers (Matt 25:14-30; Luke 16:9-13; 19:11-27; 1 Cor 4:2; 16:2; Titus 1:7; 1 Pet 4:10).

Kingdom Woman: *A female who is consistently living under the rule of God and lordship of Jesus Christ over every area of her life.*

A kingdom woman has been uniquely tasked with the purpose of not only living out her own calling but also providing a strong help (*ezer kenegdo*) in the home and to her husband. In addition, she is to utilize her spiritual gifts and exercise her delegated positions of leadership for the benefit of the church and society. She models strength, diligence, charity, compassion, entrepreneurism, and dedication to those placed within her sphere of influence (Prov 31:10-31; Luke 8:2-3; Rom 16:1-2; 1 Cor 11:1-10; Eph 5:22-24, 33; 2 Tim 3:10-11; 1 Pet 3:1-6).

Local Church/Membership: *A local church is called an* ekklesia, *meaning a body of "called out ones" taken from the world and joined to Jesus Christ in a living union, a body of which he is the head.*

Many of the references to the church in the New Testament refer to a specific local church, or a group of local assemblies, whether in Rome, Corinth, Ephesus, etc. Every Christian becomes a member of the universal church at salvation, but is also exhorted to become a functioning, faithful member of a biblically sound local church. The role of the local church is to exercise the authority of the kingdom in history (Matt 16:18-19; 1 Cor 1:2; 2 Cor 1:1; 1 Thess 1:1; 2 Thess 1:1; Heb 10:25).

The Lord's Supper: *Also known as communion, the Lord's Supper is one of the two ordinances (along with baptism) given by Jesus Christ to his church through which believers publicly proclaim their association with and surrender to him through his death, burial, and resurrection.*

The Lord's Supper was instituted by Jesus on the night before his crucifixion, as he observed the Jewish Passover with his disciples. Jesus transformed the elements by teaching that the bread represented his body which would soon be broken to atone for sin and that the cup represented the "new covenant" in his blood—the promise of the Passover lamb being fulfilled in the salvation he provided. In communion, the believer can experience the unique spiritual presence of Christ as well as accesses his authority in a unique way over the spiritual realms of darkness (Luke 22:14-23; 1 Cor 10:16; 11:23-29).

Lordship: *The recognition of and submission to the rule of Christ over the life of a believer.*

Believers in Jesus Christ are called to bring every area of life under Christ's rule and lordship. Only as a believer acknowledges and submits to the lordship of Christ can the power and authority of God's kingdom be made visible in history. God explicitly states that it is his determined purpose to bring all of history under the rule of Jesus Christ. There must be covenantal alignment under the lordship of Jesus Christ in order to experience his kingdom power, authority, provision, and covering (Rom 14:6-9; 1 Cor 8:5-6; Eph 1:9-10; Phil 2:9-11; Col 1:13).

Love: *The decision to compassionately, righteously, and sacrificially seek the well-being of another.*

Love is not first and foremost an emotion. Love is a decision. We are to choose love even when we do not feel like loving because we are called to love others as God has loved us. Our relationship with Christ is first and foremost one of love. Out of our intimate abiding with him, we are to extend love to those around us. It is by the mark of love

that people are to recognize us as followers of Christ (John 3:16; 13:35; Rom 5:5; 1 Cor 13:1-8; 1 John 3:1; 4:10-11, 19-20).

Mercy: *The expression of God's steadfast love that relieves misery and does not give all that the sinner deserves.*

Believers can praise God that even though they were once destined for death as members of Satan's kingdom, God saved them by his mercy. Biblical justice also comes tempered with the potential for mercy toward the offender. The cross of Jesus Christ is the greatest example of this appeal for mercy. While on the cross, Jesus asked his Father to forgive those who were killing him. Through the parable of the two slaves who owed money, Jesus teaches that this principle of mercy that he offers us should govern how we treat others (Lam 3:22; Matt 5:7; 18:21-34; Eph 2:4-5; Heb 4:16).

Offices of Christ: *The three major offices or categories of leaders for God's people, Israel, in the Old Testament were prophet, priest, and king.*

Each office was a separate calling and duty. Each of these offices was a type and a foretaste of the coming Messiah, Jesus Christ, who now fulfills all three offices. Christ is the prophet we need to instruct us in the things of God. He is also our great high priest who redeemed us by offering his own body as the final and full sacrifice for sin. Christ is also our glorious, coming King, ruling over all things now from heaven he awaits his triumphant return to earth (Deut 18:15; Luke 4:24; Acts 3:22; Heb 4:14-16; Rev 19:16).

Original Sin: *The entrance of sin into the human race through Adam's sin in the garden of Eden.*

When Adam fell by disobeying God and eating from the tree of the knowledge of good and evil, his spirit died and his soul became contaminated by sin. His nature was changed and became corrupted, separated from God and in need of forgiveness and redemption. Since Adam is the father of the human race, every child of Adam is born in sin with what theologians call the Adamic nature (Gen 2:15-17; 3:6-7; Ps 51:5; Rom 5:12-14; Eph 2:1-3).

Peace: *Well-being, contentment, and wholeness produced through an abiding faith in and relationship with God.*

Peace does not mean that you will have no troubles. Peace means that God's provision of his presence will lighten the stress those troubles produce. Peace is the umbrella in the storm, calming nerves and covering you from the results of worry. Peace comes through prayer and also through keeping your mind fixed on the truth of God's Word. Peace is the order and calm the Holy Spirit brings into the life of a believer despite external circumstances (John 14:27; Rom 14:17; Eph 2:14-17; Phil 4:4-6).

Rapture: *The split-second moment when Christ will return in the air to take his people, the church, home to be with him forever.*

This is one of the themes of prophecy in the Bible. The Christians at Thessalonica were shaken because they feared they would never see their dead loved ones again. Paul wrote to assure them with the truth of the church's rapture when the church is taken out of the world. The world will not realize the restraining and sanctifying influence of the church until God raptures his church and all of hell breaks loose on the earth in the tribulation (1 Thess 4:13-18; 2 Thess 2:7; Titus 2:13).

Reconciliation: *The restoration of a previously broken relationship based on repentance and forgiveness.*

Reconciliation involves removing the hostility between parties and restoring peace and harmony in a relationship. It means that the wall separating the hostility has been broken down; the breach has been healed. Jesus accomplished our reconciliation with God when He died on the cross for our sins. This should encourage believers to be reconciled with one another (Matt 5:24; Luke 12:58; Rom 5:10; 2 Cor 5:18-19; Eph 2:11-22; 2:14-16).

Redemption: *To deliver through the payment of a price.*

Christ's death was the price God demanded to redeem us from slavery to sin. God never skips sin. Someone has to pay the price—either you or an acceptable substitute. On the cross Jesus said, "It is finished" (John 19:30), meaning, "paid in full." All the requirements necessary to pay for our redemption were put up by Jesus Christ on the cross (Mark 10:45; 1 Cor 6:20; Gal 1:4; Eph 1:7-11 Titus 2:14; 1 Pet 1:18-19).

Repentance: *The inner resolve and determination to turn away from a sin that is manifested by an external change in behavior coupled with appropriate restitution.*

When a person bows to Jesus in repentance and submission, He becomes Lord of that person's life. Christ's death removed the barrier keeping sinners from being reconciled to a holy God, thus freeing God to save any and everyone who believes. We are still responsible to come to Christ in faith to be saved and in repentance to be in fellowship with him, but Christ's death makes that avenue open and available to all (Mark 1:15; Luke 13:1-5; 19:1-10; Rom 2:4; 2 Cor 7:10).

Resurrection: *To become alive again from the dead.*

Six distinct resurrections are mentioned in Scripture. In the order of their occurrence they are the resurrection of Jesus Christ; the resurrection of an unnamed number of believers in Jerusalem who were resurrected when Christ arose from the grave; the resurrection of the church at the rapture; the resurrection of Old Testament saints at Christ's second coming; the resurrection of tribulation believers; and the resurrection of the wicked for judgment (Matt 27:52-53; John 20:1-10; 1 Thess 4:13-18; Rev 20:5; 20:11-15).

Righteousness: *The divine standard God has established for mankind's actions and attitudes to be acceptable to him.*

The vast difference between God and mankind is that he is righteous in his character and we are not. Since perfect righteousness on our part is required to enter God's presence, Jesus Christ lived a perfectly sinless, righteous life and died on the cross for the payment of our sins. As a result, God could bestow on those who trust in Christ through faith his own righteousness as a gift of grace. We are then to live out God's righteous standards in our daily lives (Rom 1:18-21; 3:10-22; 9:30; 2 Cor 5:21; Phil 1:9-11; 1 Tim 6:11; Heb 12:14).

Sanctification: *The process of the believer's growth in Christ.*

Positional sanctification was accomplished for every believer at the moment of salvation by receiving Christ's righteousness (the same root word as "sanctify"). *Progressive* sanctification is the growth process by which believers seek to become more like Christ in their decisions and lifestyle. *Entire* or *ultimate* sanctification will only be achieved when we stand perfect before Christ in glory (1 Cor 1:2; 1 Thess 4:3; 5:22-23; 2 Thess 2:13).

Sanctions: *The negative and positive consequences of obedience and disobedience.*

The progress or regression of our lives, families, churches, and society is directly tied to divine sanctions operating in history. Sanctions, both positive and negative, are one of the distinctions of a spiritual covenant. This is the cause and effect relationship that is built into history. Sin brings destruction, and righteousness brings blessing (Deut 30:15-20; 2 Chr 15:3-6; Mal 2:13-16; 1 Cor 11:23-32).

Sin: *The failure of man to measure up to God's perfect standard of righteousness, whether in thought, word, or deed.*

Human beings are sinners by nature—their sin inherited from the first Adam—as well as sinners by personal choice. The human heart has been thoroughly corrupted by sin, leaving people without Christ in a state of total depravity—a doctrine that means we have nothing within ourselves to commend us to God. To sin is to "miss the mark," to fall short of God's standard of righteousness and perfection. The result, or punishment, for sin is death, which is removed only by the saving grace of Jesus Christ (Jer 17:9; Rom 3:10-12, 23; 5:19; 6:23; 11:32).

Sovereignty/Providence: *The sovereignty of God means that he exercises his prerogative to do whatever he pleases with his creation. His providence is the outworking of God's eternal plan for mankind and all of his creation.*

Providence is the invisible and mysterious hand of God at work in the details of history to bring to pass his sovereign will. God's providence includes every part of creation, from the inanimate world to individuals and entire nations. In his righteous, wise, and loving providence, God is bringing to pass his eternal purposes for his glory and our eternal good (Ps 22:28; 24:1; 66:7; 103:19; Rom 8:28).

Spiritual Warfare: *The cosmic conflict waged in the invisible spiritual realm but simultaneously fleshed out in the visible physical realm, which our enemy the devil uses when he seeks to defeat us.*

Satan seeks to discourage and distract us from the real battle and convince us that we have to fight him physically rather than spiritually. Yet while Satan may have power, he does not have authority. The victory in spiritual warfare rests in the authority of Christ made available to believers through the weapons of warfare. When it comes to spiritual warfare and the issue of our victory, the matter has already been settled. Jesus Christ defeated the devil and all of his forces on the cross, and nothing can cancel out that victory. We are not fighting for victory, but from a position of victory. Satan is a defeated foe (1 Cor 2:11; 2 Cor 10:3-5; Eph 6:10-18; Col 2:15; 1 Pet 5:8-9; Rev 12:10-11).

Stronghold: *A sin or circumstance that illegitimately holds a person in spiritual bondage; a negative, destructive pattern of thinking or actions used by Satan to promote a recurrence of sin in our lives.*

God says these strongholds have to be destroyed, which means he didn't build them. Once a stronghold is built, it gives our enemy Satan a place from which to launch further attacks against our minds and a fortification from which to repel our attempts to dislodge him. But the Word of God gives us the weapons to tear down these satanic fortresses (Rom 12:2; 2 Cor 10:3-5; 6:7; Eph 6:10-18).

Substitutionary Atonement: *Christ's death was a blood atonement as a sacrificial substitution, in our place, to satisfy the demands of the law in order to appease a holy God for the payment of sin.*

God has always required the shedding of blood to atone for sin. This requirement of blood goes all the way back to Eden, when God killed an animal to cover Adam and

Eve after they sinned. The animal's death temporally satisfied God's requirement and substituted for their deaths. Jesus didn't die just to leave us a good example or to show us how to bear up under suffering. Our guilt was transferred to him; therefore, he took the death stroke that should have fallen on us for all eternity (Gen 3:21; 2 Cor 5:21; Heb 9:12-14; 1 Pet 2:24).

Total Depravity: *Every facet of human nature has been polluted, defiled, and contaminated by sin.*

This is the inborn corruption we inherited as children of Adam, which means there is nothing within us to commend us to a holy God. We are sold into sin—unable to save ourselves, and totally dependent on God's grace in Christ, which he offers to all mankind (Jer 17:9; Rom 1:29 3:23; Phil 2:15; 2 Tim 3:8; 2 Pet 2:19).

Truth: *The absolute standard by which reality is measured. It is God's view on every subject.*

Absolute truth cannot be perceived by human beings apart from the revelation of God. The Bible is the sole repository and determiner of absolute truth, and God guarantees the truth of every word he has given in Scripture. The believer is dependent on the ministry of the Holy Spirit as the illuminator of Scripture in order to understand and obey what God has revealed to us (Num 23:19; Ps 19:1-10; John 17:17, 2 Tim 3:7).

Universal Church: *The church is revealed in the New Testament as the body and bride of Christ through whom God is accomplishing his purposes in this present age.*

The church is that company of redeemed people called out from the world and joined together in one living union by the baptism and indwelling of the Holy Spirit. As such, the universal church refers to every believer from the church's birthday on the day of Pentecost to the future rapture, when Christ will come for his church and take his people out of the world (Matt 16:18; Acts 2:1-4; Eph 1:22-23; 3:10; Col 1:18).

Unlimited Atonement: *This refers to the universal extent of Christ's atoning death.*

The Bible teaches that Christ's sacrifice is sufficient for all mankind, even though not every person is saved. Sin has to be atoned for, because God is too holy to ignore sin, and too loving to let us plunge headlong into hell. Atonement is paying what must be paid— the penalty of death—to settle God's righteous claim against us. And the only death that satisfied this demand was that of Christ on the cross for all sin for all mankind without exception (John 3:16, 36; Rom 5:15-17; 2 Cor 5:15; 1 Tim 2:6; Heb 2:9; 1 John 2:2).

Worship: *The recognition of God for who he is, what he has done, and what we are trusting him to do.*

The job of believers as worshipers is to praise and exalt the glory of our great God and his Son, the Lord Jesus Christ. God fills all of the universe and eternity. There is no lack in him that requires us to magnify him so that He becomes bigger. Rather, worship recognizes and extolls how big he truly is. Magnifying God is when we focus our praise and worship on him. We see him for the great and awesome God that he is; he is bigger than our problems and circumstances. That's the power worship has. It changes us by changing our perspective of God. Worship is to be the lifestyle of the believer (Ps 29:2; 66:4; Matt 4:10; John 4:23; Rom 12:1; Phil 2:9-11).

The word *doctrine* means "teaching" or "instruction." Applied to the study of the Scriptures, another word for doctrine is "truth," the gathering together in a systematic way of all that God's infallible, inerrant Word says about a given subject.

While the Bible contains all the truth God wants us to know about himself, these teachings are not arranged in an alphabetic, systematic way because the Bible is not a textbook. The challenge is to organize the truths of God's Word in a way that clearly communicates what the Bible teaches on any subject it addresses. This process is called *systematic theology* and is needed because we cannot turn to any one portion of Scripture to find the full biblical revelation on any subject. So it's important to bring together the Bible's teachings on any doctrine so that they can be studied in an orderly way.

This is the purpose of this section, which summarizes the major doctrines of systematic theology. I have dealt with this at length in my Understanding God series (Moody Publishers) and in detail in my book, *Theology You Can Count On* (Moody, 2008).

23:19; Mal 3:6), either in his person or in his purposes, although he can and does change in his methods. Therefore, we can trust his promises and eternal love for us (Jer 31:3; Jas 1:17).

4. God is a triune being. The Bible makes it inextricably clear that there is only one true God, and he is one (Deut 6:4; Isa 45:5; 1 Cor 8:4). However, this one God exists in three co-eternal and co-equal—yet distinct—persons: Father, Son, and Holy Spirit. They are unified in their essence, yet each has a different function in the Godhead.

We use the words *Trinity* or *Triune* to speak of the unity of this three-in-one God, although these words themselves do not appear in Scripture. But the truth of the divine Trinity appears throughout the Bible. In Matt 28:18-20, Jesus used the singular "name" of the Father, Son, and Holy Spirit, a strong proof of both the unity and the "threeness" of God.

The Trinitarian nature of God is also demonstrated in that the Father (Gal 1:1, 3; Eph 1:2-3), the Son (John 20:28), and the Holy Spirit (Acts 5:3-4) are each called God.

THEOLOGY PROPER

Virtually all studies on theology begin with this subject, which is so-called because it focuses on God the Father. These truths will help you grasp the greatness of our God. (See the Doctrinal Outlines for more detail.)

1. God is an eternal, transcendent being. God has no beginning or end (Ps 90:1-2). He told Moses, "I AM WHO I AM" (Exod 3:14). God exists prior to, above, and distinct from his creation (Isa 40:18-25). God is distinct in his person (Ps 50:21) and in his thoughts (Isa 55:8-9).

2. God is a spirit being. God in his essence is pure spirit (John 4:23-24a). He is immaterial in that he does not have a body; therefore, God is invisible (John 1:18).

3. God is an immutable being. Immutability means not having the ability to change. God cannot, does not, and will not change (Num

CHRISTOLOGY

Christology consists of what the Bible teaches about Jesus Christ in his person and work. (See further under "Christology" in the Doctrinal Outlines.) Jesus is unique, the only "one-of-a-kind" Son of God (John 3:16) who is both fully God and man, perfect in both natures without any mixture, division, or confusion.

Jesus made a clear claim to his pre-existence and divine nature as God (John 10:30), a statement his hearers understood so well that they tried to stone him for making himself equal with God (10:33). The prophecy of his birth also included a claim to his eternal existence (Mic 5:2). Isaiah called Jesus Christ "Eternal Father" or "Father of eternity" (Isa 9:6).

Fully divine, Jesus also became a man in his birth, or incarnation. He was born as no other person has been born, because he was born of a virgin (Isa 7:14; 9:6; Matt 1:22-23). The apostle Paul tied these prophecies together in Gal 4:4. Jesus is also unique in his death and resurrection.

PNEUMATOLOGY

The formal name for study of the person and ministry of the Holy Spirit is derived from the Greek word *pneuma*, which means "breath" or "spirit." He is the Third Person of the Trinity, co-equal and co-eternal with the Father and Son. (See the Doctrinal Outlines for more detail.)

The Holy Spirit's unique role is to make the truth of God's Word and the reality of his presence a living experience in the lives of Christians. The Spirit is active on every page of Scripture, from his work in creation (Gen 1:2) to his invitation to salvation and eternity with Jesus in heaven (Rev 22:17).

Two of the Holy Spirit's most important ministries have already been accomplished. He was the life-giving force in Jesus's virgin birth (Luke 1:35), protecting the Savior from the contamination of human sin inherited through one's father. The Spirit inspired the writers of God's Word so that what was written is infallible, inerrant, and wholly trustworthy, protected from human contamination (1 Pet 1:20-21).

The Holy Spirit's primary roles today include glorifying Christ (John 16:14), indwelling believers for the power to do what God has called us to do (Acts 1:8), and convicting unbelievers of their sin and coming judgment (John 16:7-11).

SOTERIOLOGY

Salvation is the miracle by which a lost person is granted forgiveness and given eternal life through the death and resurrection of Christ. The term *soteriology* comes from the Greek word *sōtēr*, which means "savior."

1. Sin: the need for salvation. The Bible declares that all of us are under the curse and penalty of sin (Rom 3:23; 6:23) because we have failed to measure up to God's demands of perfection. We inherited a sin nature from Adam (Rom 5:12). Our sin debt is so great, we cannot pay it ourselves which is why the sinless Son of God had to die for our sins on the cross.

2. Justification: the verdict of salvation. The Greek word translated "justify" means to announce a favorable verdict in a courtroom, or to declare righteous. Justification is a judicial act by which God declares righteous those who believe in Jesus Christ. The Bible is clear that justification comes from God alone, for "God is the one who justifies" (Rom 8:33). Every person ever born is lost in sin and needs to be justified through Christ's redemptive sacrifice (Rom 3:23-24). Justification is a gift of God's grace. We have nothing to offer God to make us acceptable to him.

3. Regeneration: the miracle of salvation. Regeneration is the process by which God implants new spiritual life, his very life, in the heart of a sinner who believes on Jesus Christ for salvation. The Bible describes regeneration as a new birth (John 3:1-8), a spiritual resurrection (Rom 6:4-5), and a new creation (2 Cor 5:17). Salvation not only brings such a complete change that we are born again spiritually and raised from the dead, but we are also completely remade people.

4. Security: the assurance of salvation. Our assurance of salvation is bound up in the promise of the gospel and the finished work of Christ (John 5:24; 10:27-30). John built a powerful case for our security (1 John 5:11-13), concluding with this assuring statement: "I have written these things to you who believe in the name of the Son of God so that you may know that you have eternal life" (5:13).

There is certainty in our salvation. Jesus never brought anyone from spiritual death to eternal life only to let that person fall back under God's judgment.

BIBLIOLOGY

This doctrine involves the study of God's Word. The Bible is unique among all other books and so-called sacred writings, because it alone is the very Word of God (Isa 55:10-11).

1. The Bible is truth. God's Word is pure, unadulterated truth (Ps 12:6). God declares that when he speaks, everything he says is true (Isa 45:19). Jesus also affirmed the absolute truth of Scripture (John 17:17).

2. The Bible is authoritative. Christ said that the Bible carries the imprint of his divine authority (Matt 24:35). The authority of God's Word is a settled issue in heaven (Ps 119:89).

3. The Bible is Holy Spirit-inspired: The Spirit inspired the writing of Scripture to protect it from contamination by human ideas or opinions (2 Pet 1:20-21). So it is accurate to say that God himself is the author of the Bible, and the result is pure truth from him.

ECCLESIOLOGY

The doctrine of the church comes from the Greek word *ekklēsia*, which means "assembly" or "called out ones." From this term we can formulate a definition of the church as a special called-out assembly of people, chosen by God to become part of what Paul called both the body and the bride of Christ (1 Cor 12:12-31; Eph 5:22-27, 32). The Bible also makes it clear that the church is God's family (Rom 1:13; 16:1; Heb 2:11). Thus, the church consists of people; it is not merely an organization or a building.

The church is the most important entity on earth in terms of God's program for this age. God has commissioned the church alone to be his representative agency. And the church alone has been granted the authority to bring the realities of God's kingdom program to bear on history since it has been given the keys of the kingdom (i.e., heavenly authority to be utilized on earth, Matt 16:18-19).

Jesus prophesied the coming of the church during a critically important time of teaching with the apostles (Matt 16:13-19). This passage is unmistakably clear that the church is built on Christ, not Peter or any other apostle. Jesus said it is "my church." Both Paul and Peter agreed that Christ alone is the church's "cornerstone" (Eph 2:20; 1 Pet 2:6).

The universal church is made up of all believers from the church's birthday at Pentecost (Acts 2) to the future day when Christ will rapture his church (1 Thess 4:13-18) from the world. But the universal church is visibly expressed and functions through the many local churches where believers assemble to carry out the mandates Christ gave to his people and live out the principles of the Christian life.

The church is the apex of God's eternal plan for mankind (Eph 3:1-21). It is the means by which God will demonstrate to the angelic realm—including both holy angels and Satan and his demons—his infinite wisdom in choosing weak, lesser creatures like us to manifest his glory and carry out his kingdom program.

ANGELOLOGY

This doctrine deals with angelic beings, both the holy (elect) angels and the evil ones (Satan and his demonic realm). Angels are not eternal but were created by God as part of his original creation (Col 1:16). This verse also teaches the important truth that angels were not created for themselves, but for Christ and for God's divine purposes. Angels were created to give God endless worship around his throne (Ps 148:2). This is important because a heresy that arose in the early church was the worship of angels (Col 2:18). Although angels are far more glorious and powerful than human beings, they were also created to be "ministering spirits" (Heb 1:14) to serve God and his people.

Angels are spirit beings, although they can take on a human appearance in order to accomplish a specific, God-given mission on earth. An example of this is when the angels visited Abraham and destroyed Sodom (Genesis 18–19; see also Heb 13:2). The word *angel* means "messenger," which provides a basic understanding of their ministry. As God's creation, angels also possess intellect, emotion, and will—the fundamental attributes of personhood.

Since angels do not reproduce (Mark 12:25) and do not die, the number of angels God created is the same number of those who exist now. We aren't told their numbers, but they are said to exist in unimaginable numbers (Deut 33:2; Rev 5:11).

The first category of angels are those called holy who stayed true to God and did not follow Satan in his rebellion. Satan, formerly known as Lucifer (Isa 14:12, KJV) or "morning star," heads the second category, the evil angels known as demons. This includes one-third of the angels who followed Lucifer when he tried to usurp God's throne because he wanted to be worshiped as God (Rev 12:4) and build his own demonic kingdom to rival the righteous kingdom of God (Isa 14:13-14; Col 1:13).

Satan's evil character was formed the moment his pride led him to rebel against God and seek to establish his own kingdom (Isa 14:12-15). He was transformed from the most beautiful of all God's creatures into the prince of darkness, kicked out of heaven to earth, falling with the speed of lightning (Luke 10:18).

Lucifer was also given some new names. *SATAN* means "adversary, opposer." *DEVIL* means "*accuser*" or "*slanderer*." He was defeated the moment he challenged God, was defeated again at the cross (Col 2:15), will one day be confined during Christ's millennial reign, and then judged and sent forever to hell (Matt 25:41, Rev 20: 7-10).

In the meantime, Satan and his demons have access to earth to deceive the world and carry out spiritual warfare against believers (Eph 6:10-12). Satan has also been granted temporary access to heaven, to accuse believers before God (Job 1:6; 2:1-2). But Jesus is our defense attorney to counter those accusations with his blood (1 John 2:2).

ESCHATOLOGY

The study of Bible prophecy is so-named because it is derived from a compound of two Greek words meaning "last things." It's astounding to realize that God has chosen to reveal his plan for the future ahead of time—not to satisfy our curiosity or so we can guess at dates for Christ's return, but as a stimulus to holy living (2 Pet 3:1-15). The Scriptures set forth several major events that are yet to come on God's prophetic timetable:

1. *The rapture of the church.* The rapture will be instantaneous and could occur at any moment. It will end the church age as Christ comes in the clouds to take his church home to be with him (1 Thess 4:13-18). This is the "blessed hope" we look forward to as God's people (Titus 2:13). After the rapture, believers will appear before the judgment seat of Christ to receive or lose rewards based on their faithfulness or lack thereof (2 Cor 5:10).

2. *The tribulation.* The joy of the rapture for believers will usher in a time of unprecedented judgment, terror, and suffering on the unbelieving world left behind, as the Antichrist and his false prophet take center stage.

Jesus prophesied the tribulation (Matt 24:4-28), and the book of Revelation (particularly chapters 4–18) chronicles its unfolding. Although this seven-year period will begin peacefully as the Antichrist makes a peace treaty with Israel, at the midpoint he will break this treaty and reveal himself in all of his evil. The second half of the tribulation will be a literal "hell on earth" for those who have to endure it.

3. *Christ's second coming and millennial kingdom.* At his triumphant return, Christ will defeat Satan, the Antichrist, and all the forces of evil (Rev 19:11-21). He will then bind Satan and establish his glorious one-thousand-year reign on the throne in Jerusalem as Israel's Messiah (Rev 20:1-2).

4. *The great white throne judgment and the eternal state.* The great white throne judgment (Rev 20:11-15) is the last event before God brings in the eternal state. This is a judgment for those who have rejected Christ. Their eternal doom is announced and carried out. But for believers, our judgment for sin is past and the bliss of our eternal life in heaven is described in Revelation 21–22. We will forever be with the Lord.

*Scan this code with your mobile device or follow this link for *videos* of Tony Evans providing an overview of theology.*

God possesses a number of attributes or essential qualities that are inherent in his essential being. These attributes are eternally held by the Triune God and are true of each member of the Trinity—God the Father, God the Son, and God the Holy Spirit.

Because human beings are uniquely created in God's image (Gen 1:26), we share some of his attributes such as love and anger. These are called God's *communicable* attributes. But God also possesses divine attributes that belong to him alone, known as his *incommunicable* attributes. These include perfections such as his eternality and absolute holiness.

The study below reviews these attributes of God as Father, Son, and Holy Spirit. Because each person of the Trinity displays these attributes, the study below includes verses that speak to all three Persons, rather than separating each member of the Trinity into a separate list.

1. The Transcendence of God: God is before, above, and totally distinct or transcendent from his creation. God is unique, one of a kind. No comparison can be made between God and any portion of his creation because there is nothing or no one to compare him to (Is 6:1; 40:18; 55:8-9).

2. The Infinity of God: God is eternal with no limitations except those imposed by his own nature. He is not bound by the succession of events. Jesus claimed eternality in his dealings with the Jews. The Bible also calls the Holy Spirit "eternal" (Ps 90:2; John 8:56-58; Heb 9:14).

3. The Self–Existence of God: God does not depend on anyone or anything outside of himself for his life. He has the ground of existence in himself. God is independent in his Being and in everything else—his virtues, decrees, and works. He also causes everything in creation to depend on him (Ps 50:12; Jer 10:10-13).

4. The Self-Sufficiency of God: God is totally and absolutely complete within himself. Jesus claimed his self-sufficiency in predicting his death, making it clear that he retained complete control over his life (Ps 23:1-6; John 10:17-18; Acts 17:24-25).

5. The Holiness of God: God's intrinsic and transcendent purity is the standard of righteousness to which the whole universe must conform. God's holiness is the key to understanding everything else about Him; this attribute infiltrates all the other attributes. Jesus is called holy, and the Holy Sprit's very name reveals his divine character (Isa 6:1-3; Luke 1:35; Acts 1:8; 4:27-30; 1 Pet 1:13-19; Rev 4:8).

6. The Sovereignty of God: God rules and controls all of his creation, including human affairs. God sits on the universe's throne as Lord. Everything that happens comes about because he either directly causes it or permits it to occur. Nothing enters into history or could ever exist outside of history that does not come under God's absolute control (Job 23:13; 42:2; Ps 115:3; 135:6; Dan 4:28-37).

7. The Glory of God: God's glory is the visible manifestation of his attributes. The word translated "glory" in the Old Testament means "to be weighted, to be heavy." When we discuss God's glory, we mean someone with an awesome reputation because he has awesome splendor (Exod 33:12-23; Ps 29:3; Luke 2:9; 1 Tim 6:15-16; Rev 21:23).

8. The Omniscience of God: God has intuitive knowledge of all things both actual and potential. This word is a compound of two words: *omni*, which means "all," and *science*, which has to do with knowledge. There is absolutely nothing God doesn't know (Ps 139:1-6; 147:5; Isa 40:13-14; Heb 4:13).

9. The Omnipresence of God: God's complete essence is fully present in all places at all time. There is no place in creation where God does not exist in all his divine fullness. God's presence is in the sphere of immensity and infinitude. *Infinitude* (or infinity) means that which is without limit. *Immensity* refers to that which cannot be contained (1 Kgs 8:26-27; Ps 139:7-12).

10. The Omnipotence of God: God is all-powerful. But his omnipotence involves more than just raw power. Rather, it involves the exercise of his prerogative to use his unlimited power to reflect his divine glory and accomplish his sovereign will. The unlimited power of deity is also ascribed to Jesus and to the Holy Spirit (Ps 62:11; 147:5; Matt 19:26; Rom 1:4; 1 Cor 2:4; Eph 3:8-21).

11. The Wisdom of God: God has the unique ability to so interrelate his attributes that he accomplishes his predetermined purposes by the best means possible. God's ability to use his attributes in perfect wisdom is unique because no one else can accomplish this (Exod 31:1-5; Dan 2:19-20; Rom 11:33; 16:27; Jas 3:13-18).

12. The Goodness of God: This attribute describes the collective perfections of God's nature and benevolence of his acts. God is good by nature and good in what he does. The goodness of God is the standard by which anything called good must be judged. Jesus was also called "good teacher" (Ps 107:1-15; 119:68; Mark 10:17-18; Jas 1:17).

13. The Wrath of God: God's wrath is his necessary, righteous retribution against sin. God's wrath is not an easy subject to consider, but it is as integral to his nature as any of his other perfections. The Bible has more to say about God's wrath than about his love. God's wrath against sin arises by necessity because of the justice of his law and the righteousness of his character. God must judge sin, although he takes no pleasure in punishing the unrighteous (Exod 34:7; Deut 32:41; Ezek 33:11; Rom 5:8-9; 11:22).

14. The Love of God: God's love is his joyful self-determination to reflect the goodness of his will and glory by meeting the needs of mankind. God did not become love after he made the world and mankind. God's love is eternal. In and of himself, God is love. God's love is also inextricably tied to his own glory (John 3:16; Rom 5:8; Eph 1:4-6; 1 John 4:7-21).

15. The Grace of God: Grace is God's inexhaustible supply of goodness that does for mankind what they could never do for themselves. God has supplied every true believer with a magnificent provision of grace. We can't earn it and we don't deserve it, but he has made it abundantly available to all mankind in general (common grace) and to believers in particular. God's endless supply of grace also means that it is sufficient for our every need (2 Cor 9:8; 12:9; Eph 2:1-10; 1 Tim 4:10; Heb 4:16).

16. The Veracity of God: God is always reliable and completely truthful. He cannot lie. The first challenge Satan made against God was to question his truthfulness to Eve (Gen 3:1-5). Jesus Christ and the Holy Spirit are also called true and "the truth" (Num 23:19; Heb 6:16-18; 1 John 4:6; 5:20).

17. The Immutability of God: The immutability of God means he never alters his purposes or changes his nature. Immutability means not having the ability to change. As the eternal Son of God, Jesus also does not change (Mal 3:6; Heb 12:17; 13:8; Jas 1:17).

THE UNIQUENESS OF SCRIPTURE

There is no other book in history that can be compared with the Bible. It is not merely human words about God; it is the very Word of God to humanity. It is in fact the voice of God in print, and as such Scripture is of divine origin and in a class by itself.

The Bible is composed of sixty-six books, divided into two testaments. There are thirty-nine books in the Old Testament and twenty-seven books in the New Testament. The Bible was written over a period of 1,500 years by almost forty different authors who were unified in the central purpose of perfectly communicating the truth of God to humanity so that he could be glorified and his Kingdom advanced. The ultimate uniqueness of Scripture is that it is *alive* and is able to pierce into the deepest depths of a person's life, emotions, and thoughts (Heb 4:12-13) and to transform the lives of those who respond to its message.

THE AUTHORITY OF SCRIPTURE

Many Christians live their lives according to their own set of laws because they do not respect God or acknowledge his rule over every area of their lives. Just as a driver should fear the authority of a police officer (i.e., take the officer seriously) whether they see him or not, Christians show true reverence for God by how they acknowledge his authority. As it turns out, God has infused his authority into the truth of Scripture.

Scripture is authoritative because it is truth (John 17:17). Truth is the absolute standard by which reality is measured. It's God's view on every subject. In Scripture, God has made truth knowable (John 8:32). Since God cannot lie (Heb 6:18) and since his Word is eternally settled in heaven (Ps 119:89), then his Word can be completely trusted (Pss 12:6; 18:30).

Christian doctrine has developed over the centuries but not out of thin air or out of the imaginations of men gone by. These doctrines we hold dear were articulated from Scripture itself. For those of us who take Scripture seriously, we affirm the divine authority of the Bible: *Sola Scriptura*—that is, by Scripture alone.

Since God's nature is perfectly true (1 John 5:20) then his Word is inerrant. Inerrancy means that the original autographs of Scripture are completely true concerning everything about which they speak and were completely recorded without error down to the most minute detail (Matt 5:17-18). Therefore, Scripture is binding on every aspect of our lives (John 10:35).

What can we say, then, about Scripture? It is divine in its authority. It is the absolute final authority for all matters of our lives. We can live under God's perfect rule, trusting that he has given us the governance we need through the pages of Scripture.

THE REVELATION OF SCRIPTURE

Imagine going to a play, sitting while the curtain is closed waiting for the performance, and then watching the curtain open to reveal the scene. If you go to a play, you receive a program in which you can read about that play, but you're waiting for the curtain to open because you want to see it on display. That's revelation.

In theology, revelation refers to the initiative of God to disclose or reveal himself to humanity (Heb 1:1-3) so that we could know what otherwise we would not know or understand. Since he is totally unique and distinct from his creation (Isa 55:10-11), revelation is needed for finite people to understand and properly relate to an infinite God. God has revealed his eternal attributes in general revelation (i.e., nature/creation, Rom 1:19-20), and he has also revealed himself in special revelation through the living Word, Jesus Christ (John 1:1, 14), and the written Word of Scripture.

It is in this special revelation that we find God revealing to humanity his true nature, done primarily through the pages of the Bible (Ps 19:1-6; Rom 1:18-20; 2:14-16; John 1:14-18; Acts 17:24-34). All creation can plainly see *that* he exists, but those who have been illuminated by the Holy Spirit can begin to see *who* he really is.

THE INSPIRATION OF SCRIPTURE

Inspiration refers to the process by which God oversaw the composition of Scripture so that its message was perfectly recorded (2 Tim 3:16) without error through the instrumentality and personalities of human authors. Human authors were perfectly guided by the Holy Spirit in the writing of every word of Scripture (2 Pet 1:19-21). In the same way that the Holy Spirit used humanity's instrumentality in the birth of the living Word (the incarnation) keeping the sin nature of Mary from being transferred to Jesus, he likewise kept sin and error from being transferred from the human authors in the writing of Scripture.

Hebrews 4:12 tells us that Scripture is the "living and effective" Word from God, one that is able to pierce the very soul and spirit and to discern our thoughts and intentions. In other words, the Bible is no empty collection of stories about people who lived long ago. Rather, in its pages, we encounter the living God, and its words are enlivened by the Spirit of God. When we open the Bible, we are not just opening a book, we are opening ourselves up to the discerning, piercing voice of God that calls forth an active response from us.

By studying inspiration we seek to understand the origin of Scripture, the process of faithfully recording God's revelation about himself, and how these inspired ("living and effective") Scriptures are uniquely authoritative in the life of the believer.

THE CANONICITY OF SCRIPTURE

We might think that the Holy Scriptures always existed in the perfectly convenient form that we find today, yet the process was more complex than that. The journey through time and culture to compile our Bible has always been a *divine process* in which the Holy Spirit supervised both its writing and development.

Canonicity refers to the principles and processes of recognizing which writings were the inspired books to be included in the Bible. Jesus stated that the whole Old Testament was Scripture (Luke 24:27). He also prophesied that the Holy Spirit would disclose to the apostles the truths that would become New Testament Scripture (John 16:13-15).

While it may seem uncomfortable at first to dissect the manner in which all sixty-six books came to be recognized as God's Word, you will find that the hand of God was present at every turn, guiding this process through the church. The same God who inspired holy men to record every word exactly as he wanted it also oversaw the process by which the books were assembled into the complete and authoritative collection of Scripture.

THE INTERPRETATION OF SCRIPTURE

Perhaps you have heard the popular phrase, "Something got lost in translation." When people use that phrase, what they mean is that what someone says isn't always understood by the one who receives the message. If this is true with people who speak the same language in the same society, then you can only imagine the complexities in communication that can occur when we study a more complex subject matter such as the Holy Scriptures. With the Word of God, ultimately the Lord is the originator, or encoder, of his message, and we are the decoder, the person tasked with understanding the message that is being communicated.

Interpretation refers to meaning—what is the text actually saying. It seeks to understand what the author was saying to the audience to whom he was speaking, and then, relate that meaning to us today. Interpretation is a *science* since words have meaning and language follows certain rules of grammar and composition that can be observed and cataloged.

Interpretation is also an *art* as we seek to understand and match the meaning of words from one language, culture, and context to another. Thus, God wants us to be diligent in our study of his Word so that we will understand what the biblical authors were communicating in their day and how his eternal truth relates to us today (Ezra 7:10; 2 Tim 2:15; 3:16-17).

THE ILLUMINATION OF SCRIPTURE

Illumination refers to the Holy Spirit's work of personally enlightening the human mind to the understanding and application of biblical truth (1 Cor 2:9-16) for the purpose of bringing spiritual conviction to unbelievers (John 16:7-11) and transforming believers into the image of Christ (2 Cor 3:17-18). Through the *process* of illumination, you and I are able not only to grasp the truths of God but to internalize and live out his precepts.

There is a danger in speaking of illumination as a lightbulb moment, such that spiritual insight into the Scriptures may seem like something that is instantaneous. Thomas Edison, the inventor of the lightbulb, famously stated that the genius behind his inventions was "one percent inspiration and ninety-nine percent perspiration." Similarly, there is a process at work that brings the experience of the illumination of God's Word to the heart and mind of the Christian. This process of illumination finds its origin in the Holy Spirit, yet it also involves the responsiveness of the believer. We must be careful, though, not to think that spiritual illumination will come through our study alone. Spiritual insight is also founded on the Holy Spirit working within us.

THE SUFFICIENCY OF SCRIPTURE

Sufficiency refers to the comprehensive nature of Scripture in its ability to address every area of life. It is therefore the standard by which all of life is understood and evaluated. Scripture also possesses the power to address what it proclaims (Isa 55:11) both in creation (Ps 33:6) and in every aspect of our daily lives (Ps 19:7-14).

Paul writes in 2 Tim 3:16-17, "All Scripture is inspired by God and is profitable for teaching, for rebuking, for correcting, for training in righteousness, so that the man of God may be complete, equipped for every good work." That means we do not need to rely on extra knowledge, wisdom, or insight to do what God wants us to do. We have been fully equipped for living abundantly in his kingdom based on the truth he has provided in the pages of the Bible.

Scan this code with your mobile device or follow this link for videos of Tony Evans helping you to dig deeper into the study of bibliology.

www.bhpublishinggroup.com/qr/te/67-11

NAMES OF GOD, JESUS, AND THE HOLY SPIRIT

NAMES OF GOD
Elohim-God (Gen 1:1)
  – The strong creator
Jehovah-LORD (Gen 2:4)
  – The self-existing One
Adonai-LORD /Master (Gen 15:2)
  – The Headship Name

THE COMPOUND NAMES OF THE LORD GOD
"Jehovah El and Jehovah Elohim"
Jehovah El Elohim (Josh 22:22)
  – The LORD God of Gods
Jehovah Elohim (Gen 2:4; 3:9-13, 21)
  – The LORD God
Jehovah Elohe Abothekem (Josh 18:3)
  – The LORD God of Your Fathers
Jehovah El Elyon (Gen 14:22)
  – The LORD, the Most High God
Jehovah El Emeth (Ps 31:5)
  – LORD God of Truth
Jehovah El Gemuwal (Jer 51:56)
  – The LORD God of Recompenses
Jehovah Elohim Tsebaoth (Ps 59:5; Isa 28:22)
  – LORD God of Hosts
Jehovah Elohe Yeshuathi (Ps 88:1)
  – LORD God of My Salvation
Jehovah Elohe Yisrael (Ps 41:13)
  – The LORD God of Israel

THE COMPOUND NAMES OF GOD
"El, Elohim, and Elohe"
Elohim (Gen 1:1)
  – God
Elohim Bashamayim (Josh 2:11)
  – God in Heaven
El Bethel (Gen 35:7)
  – God of the House of GOD
Elohe Chaseddi (Ps 59:10)
  – The God of My Mercy
Elohe Yisrael (Gen 33:20)
  – God, the God of Israel
El Elyon (Gen 14:18; Ps 78:56; Dan 3:26)
  – The Most High God
El Emunah (Deut 7:9)
  – The Faithful God
El Gibbor (Isa 9:6)
  – Mighty God
El Hakabodh (Ps 29:3)
  – The God of Glory

El Hay (Josh 3:10; Jer 23:36; Dan 3:26)
  – The Living God
El Hayyay (Ps 42:8)
  – God of My Life
Elohim Kedoshim (Josh 24:19)
  – Holy God
El Kanna (Exod 20:5)
  – Jealous God
El Kanno (Josh 24:19)
  – Jealous God
Elohe Mauzi (Ps 43:2)
  – God of My Strength
Elohim Machase Lanu (Ps 62:8)
  – God Our Refuge
Eli Maelekhi (Ps 68:24)
  – God My King
El Marom (Mic 6:6)
  – God Most High
El Nekamoth (Ps 18:47)
  – God that Avengeth
El Nose (Ps 99:8)
  – God that Forgave
Elohenu Olam (Ps 48:14)
  – Our Everlasting God
Elohim Ozer Li (Ps 54:4)
  – God My Helper
El Rai (Gen 16:13)
  – God Seest Me
Elsali (Ps 42:9)
  – God, My Rock
El Shaddai (Gen 17:1,2, Ezek 10:5)
  – Almighty God
Elohim Shophtim Ba-arets (Ps 58:11)
  – God that Judgeth in the Earth
El Simchath Gili (Ps 43:4)
  – God My Exceeding Joy
Elohim Tsebaoth (Ps 80:7; Jer 35:17; 38:17)
  – God of Hosts
Elohe Tishuathi (Ps 18:46; 51:14)
  – God of My Salvation
Elohe Tsadeki (Ps 4:1)
  – God of My Righteousness
Elohe Yakob (Ps 20:1)
  – God of Israel
Elohe Yisrael (Ps 59:5)
  – God of Israel

THE COMPOUND NAMES OF JEHOVAH
Jehovah (Exod 6:2,3)
  – The LORD

Adonai Jehovah (Gen 15:2)
– Lord God

Jehovah Adon Kol Ha-arets (Josh 3:11)
– The LORD, the Lord of All the Earth

Jehovah Bore (Isa 40:28)
– The LORD Creator

Jehovah Chereb (Deut 33:29)
– The LORD ... the Sword

Jehovah Eli (Ps 18:2)
– The LORD My God

Jehovah Elyon (Gen 14:18-20)
– The LORD Most High

Jehovah Gibbor Milchamah (Ps 24:8)
– The LORD Mighty In Battle

Jehovah Maginnenu (Ps 89:18)
– The LORD Our Defense

Jehovah Goelekh (Isa 49:26; 60:16)
– The LORD Thy Redeemer

Jehovah Hashopet (Judg 11:27)
– The LORD the Judge

Jehovah Hoshiah (Ps 20:9)
– O LORD Save

Jehovah Immeka (Judg 6:12)
– The LORD Is with You

Jehovah Izuz Wegibbor (Ps 24:8)
– The LORD Strong and Mighty

Jehovah-jireth (Gen 22:14)
– The LORD Shall Provide

Jehovah Kabodhi (Ps 3:3)
– The LORD My God

Jehovah Kanna Shemo (Exod 34:14)
– The LORD Whose Name Is Jealous

Jehovah Keren-Yishi (Ps 18:2)
– The LORD the Horn of My Salvation

Jehovah Machsi (Ps 91:9)
– The LORD My Refuge

Jehovah Magen (Deut 33:29)
– The LORD the Shield

Jehovah Makkeh (Ezek 7:9)
– The LORD that Smiteth

Jehovah Mauzzam (Ps 37:39)
– The LORD Their Strength

Jehovah Mauzzi (Jer 16:19)
– The LORD My Fortress

Ha-Melech Jehovah (Ps 98:6)
– The LORD the King

Jehovah Melech Olam (Ps 10:16)
– The LORD King Forever

Jehovah Mephalti (Ps 18:2)
– The LORD My Deliverer

Jehovah Mekaddishkem (Exod 31:13)
– The LORD that Sanctifies You

Jehovah Metsudhathi (Ps 18:2)
– The LORD My High Tower

Jehovah Moshiekh (Isa 49:26; 60:16)
– The LORD Your Savior

Jehovah Nissi (Exod 17:15)
– The LORD My Banner

Jehovah Ori (Ps 27:1)
– The LORD My Light

Jehovah Uzzi (Ps 28:7)
– The LORD My Strength

Jehovah Rophe (Exod 15:26)
– The LORD (our) Healer

Jehovah Roi (Ps 23:1)
– The LORD My Shepherd

Jehovah Sabaoth (Tsebaoth) (1 Sam 1:3)
– The LORD of Hosts

Jehovah Sali (Ps 18:2)
– The LORD My Rock

Jehovah Shalom (Judg 6:24)
– The LORD (our) Peace

Jehovah Shammah (Ezek 48:35)
– The LORD Is There

Jehovah Tsidkenu (Jer 23:6)
– The LORD Our Righteousness

Jehovah Tsuri (Ps 19:14)
– O LORD My Strength

NAMES OF JESUS

Alpha and Omega (Rev 22:13)
Advocate (1 John 2:1)
Anointed One (Luke 4:18)
Apostle and High Priest (Heb 3:1)
Author and Finisher of Our Faith (Heb 12:2)
Authority (Matt 28:18)
Bread of Life (John 6:35)
Beloved (Matt 3:17)
Bridegroom (Matt 9:15)
Chief Cornerstone (Ps 118:22)
Christ (John 11:27)
Christ the Lord (Luke 2:11)
Chosen One (Luke 9:35)
Deliverer (1 Thess 1:10)
Door (John 10:9)
Everlasting Father (Isa 9:6)
Faithful and True (Rev 19:11)
Freedom Maker (John 8:36)
Good Shepherd (John 10:11)
Great High Priest (Heb 4:14)
Head of the Church Body (Eph 1:22)
Helper (John 14:16)
Hope (1 Tim 1:1)
Servant (Acts 4:29-30)
I Am (John 8:58)
Immanuel (Isa 7:14)
Gift from God (2 Cor 9:15)
Jesus of Nazareth (Acts 10:38)
Judge (Acts 10:42)
King of the Jews (Matt 27:37)
King of Kings (Rev 17:14)
Last Adam (1 Cor 15:45)

Lamb of God (John 1:29)
Light of the World (John 8:12)
Lion of the Tribe of Judah (Rev 5:5)
Lord of All (Phil 2:9-11)
Master (Luke 5:5)
Mediator (1 Tim 2:5)
Messiah (John 1:41)
Mighty God (Isa 9:6)
Mighty One (Isa 60:16)
Morning Star (Rev 22:16)
Prince of Peace (Isa 9:6)
Peace (Eph 2:14)
Prophet (Mark 6:4)
Rabbi (John 3:26)
Redeemer (Job 19:25)
Resurrection and the Life (John 11:25)
Risen Lord (1 Cor 15:3-4)
Rock (1 Cor 10:4)
Sacrifice for Our Sins (1 John 4:10)
Savior (John 4:42)
Son of David (Matt 9:27)
Son of God (Matt 14:33)
Son of Man (Mark 9:31)
Son of the Most High (Luke 1:32)
Supreme Creator (1 Cor 1:16-17)
The Almighty (Rev 1:8)
Way (John 14:6)
Word of Life (John 1:1)
Word of God (Rev 19:13)
True Vine (John 15:1)
Truth (John 8:32)
Victorious One (Rev 3:21)
Wonderful Counselor (Isa 9:6)

NAMES OF THE HOLY SPIRIT

Ruah qadesow – Holy Spirit (Is 63:10)

Ruah qadse a – Holy Spirit (Ps 51:11)

Ruah Elohim – Spirit of God (Gen 1:2)

Nismat Ruah hayyim – The Breath of the Spirit of Life (Gen 7:22)

Ruah YHWH – Spirit of YHWH (Isa 11:2)

Ruach hakmah ubinah – Spirit of Wisdom (Isa 11:2)

Ruah esah ugeburah – Spirit of Counsel and Might (Isa 11:2)

Ruah daat weyirat YHWH – Spirit of Understanding and Fear of YHWH (Isa 11:2)

Pneumatos Hagiou – Holy Spirit (Matt 1:18)

Pneumati Theou – Spirit of God (Matt 12:28)

Ho Paraclētos – The Intercessor (John 16:7)

Pneuma tēs Alētheias – Spirit of Truth (John 16:13)

Pneuma – Spirit (John 3:8)

Pneumatos – Spirit (John 3:8)

Breath of the Almighty (Job 33:4)

Comforter (John 14:16)

Eternal Spirit (Heb 9:14)

Free Spirit (Ps 51:12)

God (Acts 5:3)

Good Spirit (Neh 9:20)

His Spirit (Eph 2:22)

Lord (2 Thess 3:5)

My Spirit (Gen 6:3)

Power of the Highest (Luke 1:35)

Spirit (Matt 4:1)

Spirit of the Lord God (Isa 61:1)

Spirit of the Lord (Isa 11:2)

Spirit of God (1 Cor 2:11)

Spirit of the Father (Matt 10:20)

Spirit of Christ (Rom 8:9)

Spirit of the Son (Gal 4:6)

Spirit of life (Rom 8:2)

Spirit of grace (Zech 12:10)

Spirit of prophecy (Rev 19:10)

Spirit of adoption (Rom 8:15)

Spirit of wisdom (Isa 11:2)

Spirit of counsel (Isa 11:2)

Spirit of might (Isa 11:2)

Spirit of understanding (Isa 11:2)

Spirit of knowledge (Isa 11:2)

Spirit of the fear of the Lord (Isa 11:2)

Spirit of truth (John 14:17)

Spirit of holiness (Rom 1:4)

Spirit of revelation (Eph 1:17)

Spirit of judgment (Isa 28:6)

Spirit of burning (Isa 4:4)

Spirit of glory (1 Pet 4:14)

Seven Spirits of God (Rev 1:4)

The most important study one can embark on is the study of God. The Lord says through the prophet Jeremiah, "The wise person should not boast in his wisdom; the strong should not boast in his strength; the wealthy should not boast in his wealth. But the one who boasts should boast in this: that he understands and knows me—that I am the Lord, showing faithful love, justice, and righteousness on the earth, for I delight in these things" (Jer 9:23-24). To grow in experiential knowledge of God should be the primary pursuit of every believer since this knowledge affects all of life in time and for eternity.

I. THE KNOWLEDGE OF GOD

A. The Concept of Knowing God
  I. It involves the acquisition of accurate facts about God (John 17:17; 2 Tim 3:16-17)
  II. It involves a saving encounter with God (John 3:3; 1 John 5:20)
  III. It involves an ongoing intimacy with God (2 Pet 1:5-8; 3:18)
  IV. It involves personal experiences with God (Jas 1:2-5; 1 Pet 1:6-7; 5:10)

B. The Possibility of Knowing God
  I. God commands us to know Him (Jer. 9:23-24)
  II. God desires to be known intimately (Exod 33:11; Ps 25:14)
  III. God has prescribed a way to know him (Acts 2:40-47)
    – Worship
    – Fellowship
    – Education
    – Outreach
  IV. God has limitations on what can be known about him (Isa 40:12-14; 45:15; Deut 29:29)
  V. God has given believers the Holy Spirit to reveal the things of God (John 16:13-15; 1 Cor 2:10)

C. The Importance of Knowing God
  I. It is the only way a person can escape judgment and enter into eternal life (John 17:3)
  II. It is the only way a person can truly know themselves (Isa 6:5)
  III. It is the best way of having an accurate knowledge of the world (Rom 1:20; Col 1:15-17)
  IV. It is essential for personal holiness (Jer 9:23-24)
  V. It enables people to be strong as they face the challenges of life (Dan 11:32)
  VI. It generates the true worship of God (Rom 11:33-36)

II. THE REVELATION OF GOD

A. Naturalistic Arguments for God's Existence
  I. Argument of Cause-Effect (Cosmological): For every effect there must be a cause. Thus, there must be a powerful cause for the existence of the universe. This argument does not prove that the cause is the Christian's God, but it does prove that the cause is powerful.
  II. Argument of Purpose (Teleological): There is definite order and design in the universe (seasons, earth rotating on axis, planets revolving around the sun, etc.). Thus, the first cause must be intelligent (just as a watch proves there must exist a watchmaker).
  III. Argument from the nature of man (Anthropological): Man's conscience, moral nature (sense of right and wrong), intelligence, and mental capacities have to be accounted for. His Creator must thus bear these same qualities of

personhood. Personal existence must have a personal source.

IV. Argument from the idea of God (Ontological): Man has the idea of a most perfect being (where did that idea come from given the imperfections of man and the universe). Since a most perfect being who does not exist is not as perfect as one who does exist, there must be a God.

B. **Biblical Arguments for God's Existence**
   I. General revelation (that which is universally available in creation to all mankind)
      – Creation reveals God's glory and power (Ps 19:1)
      – Creation reveals God's supremacy and divine nature (Rom 1:20)
      – Creation reveals God's providential control of nature (Acts 14:17)
      – Creation reveals God's goodness (Matt 5:45)
      – Creation reveals God's intelligence (Acts 17:24-29)
      – Creation reveals God's existence (Acts 17:24-28)
      – Man's conscience universally affirms the existence of God (Rom 1:19)
   II. Special revelation (that which is limited to Jesus Christ and the Bible)
      – Jesus Christ is the supreme and final revelation of God to man (Heb 1:1-2)
      – Jesus Christ "exegetes" (explains) the person of God (John 1:18)
      – Jesus Christ reveals the glory of God (John 1:14)
      – Jesus Christ reveals the power and wisdom of God (1 Cor 1:24)
      – Jesus Christ reveals the grace of God (Titus 2:11)
      – Jesus Christ reveals the love of God (Rom 5:8)
      – The Bible assumes and does not seek to prove the existence of God (Gen 1:1; Ps 14:1; Heb 11:6)
      – The Bible is the inerrant revelation of God (2 Tim 3:16-17)

III. THE TRIUNITY OF GOD

A. **The Definition of the Trinity**: Trinity is a theological term (not a biblical one) used to describe the biblical teaching of the nature of God. There is one God who exists in three co-equal persons who are one in essence yet distinct in personality. Thus, God is three in one.

B. **The Delineation of Trinity**
   I. There is only one true God (Deut 6:4; Isa 44:6; John 17:3; 1 Cor 8:4)
   II. There is plurality in God (Gen 1:26-27; Isa 48:16; 63:7-10)
      – The Father is recognized as God (John 6:27; 1 Pet 1:2)
      – Jesus Christ is recognized as God (John 1:1, 14, 18; Titus 2:13; Heb 1:8)
      – The Holy Spirit is recognized as God (Acts 5:3-4; 1 Cor 3:16)
   III. These three are distinct persons.
      – The Father and the Son are distinct persons (John 5:20, 32, 37; 17:5)
      – The Father and the Son are distinct from the Spirit (John 14:16; 15:26)
   IV. These three are unified (Matt 28:19; 3:12-16; 2 Cor 13:14)

C. **The Work of the Trinity**
   I. The Trinity works together to provide salvation (John 6:63; 1 Cor 6:19-21; Eph 1:7-9)
   II. The Trinity works together in the revelation of God's truth (John 1:17-18; 16:13)
   III. The Trinity works together in prayer (John 14:14; Eph. 1:6; 2:18; 6:18)
   IV. The Trinity works together in creation (Gen 1:1-3,26; Col 1:16)

V. The Trinity works together in confirmation (Matt 3:16-17)

D. The Praise of the Trinity
   I. The Father glorifies the Son (John 6:37-40; Eph 1:4)
   II. The Son honors the Father (John 5:19, 30-31; 12, 28)

III. The Spirit honors the Son (John 15:26; 16:8-10,14)

E. The Essence of the Trinity: All three members of the trinity possess the attributes or perfection of deity.

Jesus Christ is unique in history; he is fully God and fully man. His deity is from all eternity because he is the Son of God. But he also chose to leave heaven and come to earth as a man to save us and establish God's promised kingdom on earth. Jesus partook of human nature in his earthly ministry as the "Son of Man." This was Jesus's favorite title for himself during his ministry. At his birth, his incarnation, Jesus became flesh and blood, fully identifying with humanity, without relinquishing his divine attributes.

I. THE PERSON OF JESUS CHRIST

A. **Christ's Pre-Existence as the Eternal Son of God**
  I. Jesus is the Second Person of the Trinity, co-eternal and co-equal with God the Father and the Holy Spirit (John 1:1-2; 8:58; Heb 1:2-4)
  II. Jesus clearly claimed to be God when he declared, "I and the Father are one" (John 10:30 see also John 5:17-18)
  III. Jesus is also the co-Creator with God the Father (John 1:3, Col 1:16-17)
  IV. Jesus made pre-incarnate appearances in the Old Testament (Gen 18:1-3; Josh 5:13-15; Judg 13:3, 9–18)
  V. The prophet Micah declared that Jesus has no beginning; his existence reaches into eternity past (Mic 5:2)
  VI. Jesus is also designated "Eternal Father" (Isa 9:6) or "Father of eternity"

B. **Christ's Incarnation as the Unique God/Man**
  I. Jesus was born in Bethlehem to the virgin Mary, fulfilling biblical prophecy (Isa 7:14; Matt 1:22-23; Luke 1:26-35)
  II. Jesus's was born without sin because he was conceived by the Holy Spirit, avoiding the contamination of sin through a human father (Luke 1:35; 3:23; Rom 5:12)
  III. Jesus took on human flesh with its frailties and limitations, except for sin (John 1:14)
  IV. Jesus experienced the range of human emotions, further proof that his incarnation was not merely a mirage; he did not simply appear to be a man. He became tired and thirsty (John 4:6-7); he wept at the grave of Lazarus; he felt compassion for people (Matt 9:36); he experienced exultant joy (Luke 10:21)

II. THE WORK OF JESUS CHRIST

A. **His Ministry on Earth**
  I. Jesus preached the gospel and called people to repentance (Matt 4:17; Luke 4:18, 43-44; 13:1-6)
  II. Jesus called the twelve apostles to himself, then trained and commissioned them for ministry (Matt 10:1-4; Luke 5:1-11; John 1:35-51)
  III. Jesus died on the cross as the atonement for our sins (John 19:17-30; Rom 5:6-8; 1 Cor 15:3)
  IV. Jesus was buried in Joseph's tomb, and his body was guarded by Roman soldiers, proving that he died (Matt 27:57-66; 1 Cor 15:4)
  V. Jesus rose bodily on the third day, triumphing over the devil, sin, and the grave (John 20:1-9; 1 Cor 15:4, 55-57; Col 2:15; Heb 2:14; 1 John 3:8)
  VI. The risen Christ appeared to hundreds of people (Matt 28:16-20; Luke 24:13-43; John 20:10–18; 1 Cor 15:5–8)
  VII. Christ ascended back to the Father's right hand in heaven (John 20:17; Acts 1:11; Eph 4:8-10)

B. **His Present Ministry in Heaven and Future Return**
   I. Christ is in heaven today fulfilling his ministry as our great high priest, interceding with God for believers (Heb 4:14-16; 7:25; 1 John 2:2)
   II. Christ will come in the clouds *for* his saints at the rapture, and return to the earth in power and glory *with* his saints to judge the earth and assume his millennial kingdom throne (1 Thess 4:13-18; Rev 19:11–20:4).

C. **The Importance of Knowing Christ**
   I. The knowledge of Christ begins with the acquisition of accurate facts about him (Matt 16:13-17; John 17:3, 6-8)

   II. It continues as the Holy Spirit convicts of sin and the need for salvation (John 3:3, 7; 16:8-11)
   III. It brings the sinner to a saving encounter with Christ by faith (Acts 9:1-19; 16:30-31)
   IV. It grows as the believer becomes conformed to the image of Christ through a life of holiness, fellowship with Christ, and obedience to Christ (John 14:15, 23; 1 Cor 1:9; 2 Cor 3:17-18; 1 Pet 1:15-16; 2 Pet 1:5-8; 3:18; 1 John 1:3b)
   V. It will continue at the rapture of the church when believers see Christ face-to-face (1 Thess 4:13-18: 1 John 3:2)
   VI. It will culminate in Jesus's kingdom rule with his saints (Rom 8:17; Rev 19:11-6)

The Holy Spirit is not merely an addendum to the Christian faith. He is at the heart and core of it. He is not merely a force or an influence but rather the third Person of the Trinity to whom we must personally relate. Therefore, if we are going to live the victorious Christian life, it is critical that we understand the person and ministry of the Holy Spirit.

I. THE PERSON OF THE HOLY SPIRIT

A. **The Holy Spirit's eternality as the Third Person of the Triune God**
   I. The Holy Spirit is co-eternal and co-equal with God the Father and Jesus Christ (Matt 28:19; Acts 5:1-9; 2 Cor 13:14)
   II. The Holy Spirit is thus a person, not merely a force or influence. He displays intellect, emotion, and will—the fundamental attributes of personhood (Rom 8:27; 1 Cor 2:10-13; 12:11; Eph 4:30)

B. **The Bible's Proof of the Holy Spirit's Deity and Personhood**
   I. Jesus used personal pronouns for the Holy Spirit (John 15:26; 16:13)
   II. The Spirit refers to himself in the first person and can speak his thoughts to others, which only a person can do (Acts 13:2)
   III. The Holy Spirit expresses emotions (Eph 4:30)

II. THE WORK OF THE HOLY SPIRIT

A. **His Ministry in the Old Testament (before the Incarnation of Christ)**
   I. The Holy Spirit was the active agent in creation (Gen 1:2)
   II. The Spirit came upon believers at specific (limited) times for specific tasks, but did not permanently indwell them (Exod 31:1-11; 35:30-31; Num 11:16-17; 25-26; Judg 3:10; 6:34; 11:29; 13:25; 14:6, 19; 15:14)
   III. The Spirit inspired the authors of the Old Testament to record God's Word without error (2 Pet 1:19-21)

B. **His Ministry in the New Testament**
   I. The Holy Spirit was the active agent in Christ's virgin birth, his incarnation (Matt 1:18; Luke 1:26-35)
   II. The Spirit came in answer to Jesus's promise to give birth to the church on the day of Pentecost (John 14:16-17; 15:26; Acts 1:8; 2:1-4)
   III. The Spirit is the active Agent in the salvation of every believer (John 3:5-8)
   IV. Beginning at Pentecost, the Spirit baptizes every believer into the church, the body of Christ (1 Cor 12:13)
   V. The Spirit permanently indwells every believer in the church age (John 14:16-17; Rom 8:9-11)
   VI. The Spirit is the divine teacher of God's Word as the Spirit of truth (John 14:26; 16:12-13, 15; 1 Cor 2:10-13)
   VII. The Spirit empowers Christians for service, equips them with his sovereignly given gifts, and sends them out in ministry (Acts 13:1-2; Rom 15:13; 1 Cor 12:1-11; 2 Cor 3:6)
   VIII. The Spirit is sent to glorify Christ (John 16:14)
   IX. The Spirit convicts the world of sin, righteousness, and judgment (John 16:7-11)
   X. The Spirit inspired the authors of the New Testament to record God's Word without error (2 Pet 1:19-21)

Spiritual growth is offered to every true believer, resulting in an ever-increasing experience of the abundant life Christ died to supply (John 10:10). Yet while it is offered, it is not automatic. Spiritual growth requires your participation for it to take place.

Spiritual growth may be defined as that transformational process by which we allow the indwelling Christ to increasingly express himself in and through us. This, then, enables us to bring God greater glory as we also experience more of his power and presence in our own lives. As you mature spiritually, you gain access to the kingdom benefits that result from living as a fully committed kingdom disciple.

The process of spiritual growth occurs through feeding the seed you were supplied by the Holy Spirit at the moment of your conversion so that you may, as Peter wrote, "grow up into your salvation" (Eph 4:15; 1 Pet 2:2; 2 Pet 1:2-11; 3:18). In so doing, you progressively learn to let Christ live his life through you, as you abide with him in an intimate relationship (John 15:5; Gal 2:20.)

Information about the Christian faith is critical, because our faith has specific content. But it is also critical that this information gets connected to the living reality of Jesus Christ if you are going to experience spiritual growth. God will transform you as you make him your focus, thus reflecting his glory and becoming more like him (Rom 8:29; 2 Cor 3:17-18).

THE ESSENTIALS OF SPIRITUAL GROWTH

1. Conversion: The Foundation of Spiritual Growth. Conversion, or salvation, is the process whereby God deposits within every believer a new nature that is from him and is, therefore, perfect. When you receive Christ, everything becomes new at the core of your being, giving you the disposition and the capacity to know and serve God rather than serving sin and self.

God's will for a believer is spiritual growth, to the end that what is on the inside becomes visible on the outside. God often applies the heat and the pressure to bring about this release. That's why our greatest times of spiritual growth are almost always our times of greatest trial. Lasting spiritual growth comes about through internal transformation, not just external reformation. Paul wrote, "I say then, walk by the Spirit and you will certainly not carry out the desire of the flesh" (Gal 5:16).

We think that if we can just stop fulfilling the lust of the flesh, then we can begin walking in the Spirit. But it's just the opposite. The Holy Spirit working on the inside produces spiritual victory on the outside. All that we need to walk in victory and grow in Christ is already present within us (2 Pet 1:3).

2. Identity: The Key to Spiritual Growth. The moment you placed your faith in Christ alone for salvation, God implanted a new nature deep within your being. This new nature, also called the new birth, is the reference point for your identity. But when God gave you this new nature, through which you are now alive spiritually, he also put to death your old nature. This death occurred on the cross of Jesus Christ, when he died for the sins of the world. This is why your identity as a Christian begins at the cross.

The truth of this is expressed so clearly in Gal 2:20, which contains all we need to know about our identity as believers in one power-packed capsule. If you can absorb and apply the truth of this verse, you are well on your way to growing spiritually, because your identity is the key to your spiritual development.

Our old self is dead and gone, crucified with Christ on the cross and buried with him when he was buried in the tomb (Rom 6:4). Since that's true, we had better be looking for our identity somewhere else. A key step in spiritual growth and our identity with Christ is coming to grips with the fact of our death to sin and the old life.

3. Sin: The Hindrance to Spiritual Growth. Sin's impact on our lives is not by accident, since we have three formidable enemies arrayed against us. These include the world (an evil system, 1 John 5:19), the flesh (our evil desires, Rom 7:14-15), and the devil (an evil spiritual being, Rev 12:9). They join forces in a well-planned campaign to use sin to block our spiritual development.

But we are not alone, because Jesus has overcome the world (John 16:33; 1 John 4:4), God has given us victory over our evil desires (Rom 7:25), and he has stripped the devil of his power through Jesus's death on the cross (Heb 2:14). That's why it's so important that you grow in Christ. The more you grow spiritually, the more the Spirit dominates the flesh rather than the flesh defeating us and thwarting the Spirit's work in your life. When we confess our sins to God, we have the tremendous promise of his forgiveness and cleansing (1 John 1:9).

4. Grace: The Environment of Spiritual Growth. A failure to understand and grow in grace (i.e., God's unmerited favor) inevitably results in faulty development and stunted spiritual growth. Christians who do not learn to function under grace are underdeveloped saints. This failure is the single greatest cause of spiritual regression.

Read Eph 2:4-5 and notice especially the last sentence: "You are saved by grace!" This is the key. Do you understand that if you know Christ as your Savior, you are saved not because of your decision or anything else you did, but because God took the initiative to reach down and save you by grace? Salvation is God's work from beginning to end. Similarly, it is by grace that you need to live the Christian life after you are saved (2 Pet 3:18). God's promise of abundant grace is found in 2 Cor 9:8, a verse you ought to memorize if you haven't already done so.

5. Faith: The Action of Spiritual Growth. Faith is so important to our spiritual growth because it is the mechanism God has given us whereby we can tap into the spiritual realm that is above and beyond the world of our five senses. Living by faith is so crucial that spiritual growth is impossible without it, because the absence of faith means we are displeasing rather than pleasing to God (Heb 11:6).

In other words, faith and spiritual growth are inextricably woven together. A life of faithfulness to God demands that we live by faith, just as we were saved by faith. Biblical faith is a settled confidence in the person and the promises of God as revealed in his Word. Faith trusts in the integrity of God because it believes that God has told the truth about unseen realities. Faith also transports us to a supernatural realm that transcends our senses—a truth Paul prayed we would grasp (Eph 3:14-21). Practically speaking, faith is acting like God is telling the truth.

6. The Holy Spirit: The Enabler for Spiritual Growth. Only as we are empowered by the indwelling Holy Spirit will we produce what our lives are supposed to produce. The Holy Spirit is God's supernatural gift to make experiential, alive, and real the new beings we have become. The Spirit is the heart and soul of a growing, flourishing Christian life, and if we don't get plugged in to him, we will continue to stagnate and remain stunted in our spiritual development. The Spirit is the most active member of the Godhead when it comes to the matter of spiritual growth.

The issue for believers is not how much of the Spirit we have, but how much he has of us. Ephesians 5:14-17 tell us that it is possible to be a Christian, and yet be asleep spiritually as well as unwise and foolish. This is why Paul issued the familiar command of Scripture: "Don't get drunk with wine, which leads to reckless living, but be filled by the Spirit" (Eph 5:18). We are to live our lives from a spiritual perspective (Rom 8:1-13; Gal 5:16-18).

7. Scripture: The Food of Spiritual Growth. In refuting the devil's temptation, Christ explicitly stated the connection between spiritual health and the Word of God (Matt 4:4). Given the essential part the Word plays in our spiritual growth, it is unfortunate today that the Bible has been reduced to a menu to be studied rather than a nourishing meal to be enjoyed and consumed.

When learning the Scriptures becomes merely an academic exercise, we can actually increase in biblical knowledge while regressing in spiritual understanding. Jesus told the people of his day that while they were diligent to search the Scriptures, their study didn't do them any good because it did not lead them to believe in him (John 5:39-40).

We need to be absolutely clear that the Bible is the inspired, inerrant revelation of God (Isa 55:8-9; Matt 5:17-18; 2 Tim 3:16). But its purpose is not just to give us information for our heads, but food for the new nature to feed upon so that spiritual growth can be maximized (1 Pet 2:2). What milk is to a baby's body, the Word of God is to the soul. It is the food that fuels healthy spiritual growth.

8. Prayer: The Access of Spiritual Growth. Prayer is that which causes all the parts of the Christian life to relate properly to one another, because prayer is the primary means by which we relate to and communicate with God (Matt 6:5-7).

God has made us in such a way that the power of the Holy Spirit flows along the wires of prayer, which makes prayer absolutely vital to our spiritual growth. Prayer is so important that the Bible tells us, "Pray constantly" (1 Thess 5:17). The Holy Spirit understands prayers that we can't express adequately, and makes sense of thoughts that we don't even understand ourselves, because he knows the language of prayer and can interpret it for us (Rom 8:26).

We need to pray constantly because prayer is the link between the physical and the spiritual worlds. And since the spiritual world controls the physical world, getting connected to and accessing the authority of the spiritual world affects your functioning in the physical world.

9. The Church: The Context of Spiritual Growth. The church is the most exciting entity that God has placed on this earth, because it is the life-support system for individual Christians. God never meant for us to grow spiritually in isolation from other believers. Spiritual growth is a group project, which should be good news to you because it means you don't have to do it all yourself.

The Bible uses a number of terms to illustrate this community, corporate aspect of the church. One of these terms is the family. One of Paul's synonyms for salvation is adoption, the act by which God places all believers into his family (Gal 4:5; Eph 1:5).

The great thing about God's adoption program is that no believer is left out. The church is not just a classroom for spiritual instruction, but a living and growing organism to enhance our spiritual development. The book of Ephesians especially teaches the importance of the church to the spiritual development of its members (Eph 2:19-22; 4:11-16; see also Heb 10:23-25).

10. Giving: The Generosity of Spiritual Growth. Everything we have, including the breath in our lungs, is a gift from God (Jas 1:17).

Our giving is part of what the Bible calls our stewardship—the fact that we are merely managers of God's possessions and called to handle them wisely (2 Cor 4:4). But before we can understand this responsibility, we need to be reminded that we have *been given* everything, including the money God entrusted to us. So anything we give back to God is just returning to him a small part of what he has given to us.

A steward is a manager who oversees the property of another. God owns everything (Ps 24:1), yet he has given each of us time, talents, and treasures to manage for him until he returns (Matt 25:14-30). A key text on the stewardship of giving is (2 Cor 9:6-7). It teaches that the person who gives little will receive little, and the person who gives generously will receive much. Tithing, as well as using resources to carry out good works, gives tangible evidence that we recognize God as our source and that we take him seriously (Deut 14:23). It also testifies that we recognize and are submitted to the priesthood of Jesus Christ (Heb 7:1-25).

11. Trials: The Test of Spiritual Growth. A lot of people don't want to hear that trials are necessary for Christians, but it's true. Scripturally, a trial comes as an adverse set of circumstances in your life, either permitted or created by God, to develop you spiritually.

Each part of this definition is important, because we don't want to gloss over or deny that a trial is an adversity. Trials are not easy to handle. But God is behind our trials, which means we are not the victims of random fate. And because God is in control, our trials have a good purpose, which is to grow and mature us spiritually.

Christians can even rejoice in the middle of a trial (Jas 1:2) because we know trials are opportunities for us to grow into spiritual maturity. Spiritual maturity is the process of our becoming more like Jesus Christ (Gal 4:19). God assures that he will successfully guide us through our trials when we look to him in the midst of them (1 Cor 10:13).

12. Temptation: The Battle of Spiritual Growth. We need to be clear that the temptation to sin we face in the Christian life is not from God (Jas 1:13-14). God won't cause you to sin, and the devil can't make you sin. Satan can offer you a temptation and make it look inviting, but he cannot force you to sin. You have to cooperate.

The devil's power is influence and deception, not coercion. Jesus experienced all of our temptations without sinning (Heb 4:15). So don't let the devil put you on a guilt trip for being tempted. Your response determines whether a temptation becomes sin. The problem with sin is that the devil uses false advertising. Sin almost never comes with a sticker that says, "Warning: Will Cause Death." Sin looks attractive, and its price seems reasonable. But it always costs more than the advertised price. Satan's goal is to use sin to break our fellowship with God.

13. Calling: The Ministry of Spiritual Growth. Your calling is the customized life purpose that God has shaped, fashioned, and equipped for you, in order to expand his kingdom and bring himself greater glory (Jer 29:11).

Ephesians 2:10 also deals with our calling, which is to produce "good works" that bless and help others and glorify God (Matt 5:16). So your calling is not just what you do for a living, but your divinely preplanned service for God that is your response to the great grace he has shown you in salvation (Rom 12:1-8). God has a calling that is tailor-made for you (Acts 13:36).

14. Obedience: The Response of Spiritual Growth. The connection between the new nature that God put within us at salvation and our obedience to him is so vital that I want to establish it first.

God announced in Jeremiah 31:31-34 that someday he would relate to human beings in a new way called the new covenant. This covenant is not based on law and animal sacrifice, but on the once-and-for-all sacrifice of Jesus Christ. The main feature of the new covenant is this: "I will put my teaching within them and write it on their hearts" (v. 33). The fact that these desires are built-in, or internal, is crucial, because it revolutionizes our understanding of obedience.

Not only has God given us his law, but when he made us new creations in Christ, he also gave us the internal desire to obey his law by walking in his ways (Phil 2:12-13). Jesus called our obedience his "yoke," which he also said is the source of rest for those who are weary (Matt 11:28-30). Obedience activates the word and work of God in our lives (Jas 1:19-25).

15. Maturity: The Goal of Spiritual Growth. Paul challenged the often infantile Corinthians to grow up (1 Cor 14:20). Spiritual maturity is the ability to consistently view and live life from the perspective of the Spirit rather than the flesh, with the result that we maximize our God-given capacity to bring him glory.

In other words, mature Christians consistently see things that human eyes can't see. They hear things that the most acute hearing on earth cannot detect. And they have thoughts that they did not originate on their own because the Holy Spirit is helping them think God's thoughts. The Holy Spirit is free to send his message clearly and directly to the spiritually mature (see Heb 5:11-14).

The promise to a person who is listening to the Spirit is that he or she will "understand what has been freely given to us by God" (1 Cor 2:12). This puts you in another world from the mass of people (1 Cor 2:14). A mature believer is worlds removed from the understanding of the unsaved person. Mature believers have transformed lives that reflect and transfer the values of the kingdom of God (2 Cor 3:17-18).

Scan this code with your mobile device or follow this link for videos of Tony Evans as he disciples you to grow in spiritual maturity.

TOPICAL INDEX

Creation longs to be redeemed - Rom 8:22
Creation will be restored - Rev 21:1-5

DEATH

The great enemy - Rev 20:14
A result of the Fall - Gen 2:15-17
Mortality of humanity - Heb 9:27; Jas 4:14
Defeated at the cross - 1 Cor 15:55-57
Death of Jesus - 1 Pet 3:18
Physical vs spiritual death - Gen 2:17; John 14:6;
    Rom 6:23
Grief and mourning - John 11:32-38

DOUBT

Faith when facing doubt - Ps 73
Doubt hinders prayer - Jas 1:6-8
Combatting doubt when facing difficult
    circumstances - Ps 69:1-3
Combatting doubt with God's Word
    - Acts 17:11-12

END TIMES

The Antichrist - Rev 13:1-18
The abomination of desolation - Dan 12:1-13;
    Matt 24:15;
Rapture - 1 Thess 4:13-17
Return of Christ - Acts 1:11
New heaven and new earth - Rev 21:1
Resurrection of the dead - 1 Cor 15:1-58
Judgement seat of Christ - 2 Cor 5:10
The great tribulation - Matt 24:1-54
The millennium - Rev 20:1-15
The fate of the devil - Rev 20:10
The fate of death - Rev 20:14
The end of sin - Rev 21:4
Timing - Matt 24:36; 2 Thess 2:3-12

ETERNAL LIFE

Eternal life begins at conversion - John 4:13-14
God is the God of the living - Mark 12:24-27
Eternal life is a free gift - Rom 6:23
Eternal life is found through faith in Jesus -
    John 3:16
Eternal life is spent with Christ - Luke 23:43,
    2 Cor 5:6-8
Eternal life is the knowledge of God - John 17:3

EVANGELISM

Commanded by Jesus - Matt 28:19-20; Acts 1:8
Evangelism spreads the gospel beyond all
    barriers - Acts 1:8
Gift of evangelism - Eph 4:11
Who should evangelize? - 1 Pet 3:15

Cross-cultural ministry - Acts 17:22-34
Responsibility of all believers – 2 Cor 5:18-20

FAILURE

Failure and the anger of the Lord - Ps 106:7-43
Peter's denial of Christ - Matt 26:69-75
Failure as a result of pride - Gen 11:3-8
Failure as a result of disobedience
    - Num 14:40-45
God helps us through failure - Ps 37:23-24
Encouragement through failures
    - John 21:12-17
Jesus will finish working in you - Phil 1:6

FAITH

Faith defined - Heb 11:1
Faith leads to salvation - Eph 2:8-9
Faith means trusting God's ways - Isa 55:8-9
God's faithfulness - 1 Cor 1:9
Faith and works - Rom 4:1-5; Jas 2:14-26
Examples of faith - Heb 11:1-40
Rewards of faith - Heb 11:32-40
Faith should be childlike - Matt 18:3
Focus of faith – Heb 12:1-2
The power of faith – Matt 21:21-22; 1 Pet 1:5
Walking by faith – 2 Cor 5:7

FALL

The occurrence of the fall - Gen 3:1-7
The curse of the fall - Gen 3:8-24
The reversal of the fall - Rev 22:1-5
The fall led to death - 1 Cor 15:22
The fall separated mankind from God
    - Eph 4:18
The fall planted evil in the hearts of all people
    – Eph 2:1-3
The condemnation of the fall – Rom 5:18-19

FAMILY

Family roles - Col 3:18-21
Raising children - Prov 22:6
Honor parents - Exod 20:12
Family as a picture of the church
    - Eph 2:19; 5:22-33
Fighting for the family - Neh 4:14
Providing for the family - 1 Tim 5:4, 8

FEAR

Source of fear - Gen 3:10
Fear of God - Ps 111:10
Commands not to be afraid - Phil 4:6
God is our refuge - Ps 46:1-2
We do not have a spirit of fear - 2 Tim 1:7

Fear is the opposite of love - 1 John 4:8
Bring your fears to God – Ps 34:4-5; 56:3-4

FORGIVENESS

God forgives us - Ps 103:12
Forgiving others - Matt 18:21-35
Confession leads to forgiveness - 1 John 1:9
Forgiveness brings fellowship with God -
    Ps 85:2
Jesus has the authority to forgive sins -
    Matt 9:1-8
Christians should forgive others - Eph 4:32
Petition for forgiveness – Ps 51:1-19
Blessedness of forgiveness – Ps 32:1-7

GOD

Glory - Ps 8:1
Immutability - 1 Sam 15:29
Omnipresence - Ps 139:7-12
Omniscience - Matt 10:30; 1 John 3:20
Omnipotence - Matt 19:26
Wisdom of God - Rom 11:33
Goodness - Ps 34:8
Graciousness - Titus 2:11
Mercy - Eph 2:4-5
Wrath - Rom 12:19
Love - 1 John 4:8

GOD'S WILL

Discerning God's will - John 7:17
God's timing is perfect - Ps 37:34
God's will is beyond our understanding - Isa 55:9
Growing in holiness demonstrates the will of
    God - Rom 12:2
Submitting to God's will - Jas 4:13-17

GOVERNMENT

Leaders are placed by God - Rom 13:1-7
Governments wield power to enforce law
    - Rom 13:4
Governments will overextend their authority
    - 1 Sam 8:10-18
Governments are subject to God - Rom 13:1-7
Pray for those in leadership - 1 Tim 2:1-2
Earthly governments are temporary - Isa 9:6-7;
    Rev 19:15-16
God is sovereign over government – Isa 40:23;
    Prov 21:1
Submitting to government – 1 Pet 2:13-15

GRACE

God's grace is sufficient - 2 Cor 12:9
Grace is the means of salvation - Eph 2:8-9

Grace is the perfection of the law - John 1:17
Grace is a gift - Rom 11:6
Grace is essential to the health of a church
    - Acts 13:43
Grace and peace - 1 Cor 1:3; Gal 1:3; Eph 1:2;
    Phil 3
Grace is essential to the gospel - Titus 2:11-14
Grace is the foundation of spiritual growth
    - 2 Pet 3:18

HEAVEN

The dwelling place of God - Matt 6:9
Where the stars reside - Gen 1:1; Ps 19:1-4
Third heaven - 2 Cor 12:2-4
Heavenly citizenship - Phil 3:20
Free of the curse - Rev 21:4
Worship of God - Rev 22:1-5
Prepared by Jesus – John 14:1-3

HELL

Eternal separation from God - Matt 25:46
Characterized by fire - Mark 9:43
Second death - Rev 2:11
Outer darkness – Matt 13:41-42
For fallen angels - Matt 25:41; 2 Pet 2:4
The final dwelling of death and the devil
    - Rev 19:20, 20:13-14
The second death – Rev 20:14-15

HOLY SPIRIT

Member of the Trinity – Matt 28:19
The Spirit proceeds from the Father and the
    Son - John 15:26; Gal 4:6
Role in salvation - Acts 2:38; Gal 5:16-26
Baptism of the Holy Spirit - Acts 1:4-5
Filling of the Holy Spirit - Eph 5:18
Illumination of the Holy Spirit - 1 Cor 2:10-16
Seals the believer - Eph 4:30
Fruit of the Spirit - Gal 5:22-23
Source of life - Rom 8:11
The Holy Spirit was active in creation - Gen 1:2
The Holy Spirit intercedes on our behalf
    - Rom 8:26
The Holy Spirit can be resisted - Acts 7:51

INDIVIDUAL

God deals with individuals - Eph 4:7
God loves individuals - Luke 15:4-7
God has a plan for your life - Phil 1:9-11
Salvation is provided to individuals
    - John 3:16
Each person will give an individual account
    before God - 1 Cor 3:10-15

The resurrection is promised to individual people - John 5:25-30

ISRAEL

Given the law - Exod 19
God's chosen people - Deut 7:6
Settled in the promised land - Josh 1:4
As a national identity - Exod 19:5-6
Jacob was renamed Israel - Gen 32:28
The civil war - 2 Sam 2:12-32
Jerusalem the capital - 2 Chr 6:5-6
The Babylonian exile - 2 Kgs 25:21
The Assyrian exile - 2 Kgs 18:11
Coronation of Saul, the first king - 1 Sam 10
Building of Solomon's temple - 1 Kgs 6
Destruction of the first temple - Ezra 5:12
Rebuilding of the temple - Ezra 3:8-13
Restoration of the nation - Isa 43:4-6;
 Ezek 39:25-29

JESUS CHRIST

Jesus is divine - John 1:1; Titus 2:13
Jesus is human - Rom 1:3-4; Gal 4:4
Jesus has power - Mark 4:35-41
Jesus has all authority - Matt 28:18
Jesus's death, burial and resurrection
 - John 19–21; 1 Cor 15:12-20
Spoke in parables - Matt 13:10-17
Sermon on the Mount - Matt 5–7
Second Coming - Acts 1:11; Rev 19:11-19
The union of Jesus's two natures - Phil 2:5-11
He is the eternal God - Col 1:17; 2:9; Heb 1:3
Our great high priest - Heb 7:25; Heb 4:14-16

JUSTICE

God is just - Deut 32:4
God's laws are just – Ps 19:7-9; 111:7-8
God's laws are to be applied impartially
 - Num 15:16; Deut 1:17; Rom 2:11
Justice is to be applied in society - Ps 72:1-2; 4;
 Amos 5:21-24
God requires men to do justice – Mic 6:8;
 Zech 7:9-10
Justice is to be connected to righteousness
 - Ps 89:14; Amos 5:24
Justice for the orphan, widow, and alien
 - Deut 10:17-19

KINGDOM

God's kingdom agenda - Ps 128:1-6
Jesus proclaimed the kingdom - Mark 1:14-15
The kingdom must be prioritized - Matt 6:33-34
The kingdom is not of this world - John 18:36
The kingdom has a King - John 18:37
The kingdom brings order to chaos
 - Gen 1:1-3; Isa 32:1-4
The kingdom glorifies its King - Rom 11:36
The kingdom has subjects - Matt 25:34-40
The kingdom is unshakeable - Heb 12:28
The kingdom operates by covenants
 - Exod 19:5-6
The mysteries of the kingdom - Matt 13:24-50
Paul proclaimed the kingdom - Acts 28:23, 30-31
The disciples proclaimed the kingdom
 - Luke 9:1-2
The church possesses the keys to the kingdom
 - Matt 16:18-19
The kingdom covenant of dominion
 - Gen 1:26-28; Ps 8:3-6

LOVE

God is love - 1 John 4:8
We are to love one another - John 13:34
We are to love God - Deut 6:5
God loves the world - John 3:16
Love exists between the persons of the Trinity
 - John 17:24; 1 John 4:7-14
Love described - 1 Cor 13:1-13
Love your enemies - Matt 5:44
Time to love - Eccl 3:8
Love casts out fear - 1 John 4:18

MEN

A man provides for his family - 1 Tim 5:8
A man loves his wife - Eph 5:25
A man disciplines his children in love - Eph 6:4
A man should be strong and firm in the faith
 - 1 Cor 16:13
Men of exceeding moral character should
 lead the church well - 1 Tim 3:1-10
A man is under divine authority
 - Exod 34:23-24; 1 Cor 11:3
Men are to be the foundation of the family
 - Exod 18:19
Men are to lead in prayer - 1 Tim 2:8

MARRIAGE

Marriage should reflect Christ and the church
 - Eph 5:22-33
Marriage was created before the fall
 - Gen 2:24
Marriage is permanent until death
 - Matt 19:3-9; Rom 7:1-3; 1 Cor 7:39
Marriage does not exist in heaven
 - Luke 20:34-38
God hates divorce - Mal 2:16

Sexual activity should only happen within marriage - Prov 5:15-20

Marriage is between a man and a woman - Gen 2:24

Husbands and wives have unique roles in marriage - Eph 5:22-33

Husbands and wives are to be unified in prayer - 1 Cor 7:5; 1 Pet 3:7

MERCY

God has mercy on people - Ps 86:15

Mercy is a spiritual virtue - Matt 5:7; Luke 6:36

Jesus's throne dispenses mercy - Heb 4:14

Mercy given can be received - Matt 5:7; Jas 2:13

Mercy should be given to others - Jude 22-23

MONEY

The love of money - Eccl 5:10; 1 Tim 6:10

The worship of money - Matt 6:24

Treasure in heaven - Matt 6:19-21

Money and contentment - 1 Tim 6:6-8

Money and temptation - 1 Tim 6:9

Money and pride - 1 Tim 6:17-19

Danger of greed - Luke 12:13-21

Money and stewardship - Matt 25:14-30; Luke 19:11-27

The power to make wealth - Deut 8:17-18; Isa 48:17

Making friends with money - Luke 16:1-13

Financial sowing and reaping - Luke 6:38; 2 Cor 9:6-10

Slavery of debt - Prov 22:7

Priority of giving - Prov 3:9-10; Ps 50:14-15, 23; Luke 6:38; 1 Cor 16:2

PATIENCE

God is patient with us - 2 Pet 3:9

We are to be patient with others - Gal 5:22-23

We are to be patient in times of tribulation - Rom 12:12; Jas 5:7-8

Patience is developed through trials - Jas 1:3-4

Joy should accompany patience - Col 1:9-12

God is the source of patience - Rom 15:5

Patience is a fruit of the spirit – Gal 5:22

Patience in ministry - 2 Cor 6:6; 2 Tim 4:2

PEACE

A unique kind of peace comes from God - Phil 4:7

God's kingdom will usher in permanent peace between people - Isa 2:4

Peace should exist among Christians - 2 Cor 13:11

Christ is our peace - Eph 2:14

Jesus gives us inner peace - Mat 11:28-30

Peace in the midst of tribulation - John 16:33

The peace of God - Phil 4:6-7

Peace with God - Rom 5:1

PRAYER

Prayer brings the peace of God - Phil 4:6-7

God listens to our prayers - Ps 34:17-18

God answers prayer - Ps 50:15; 91:15; Jer 33:3; Matt 7:7

People should pray together - Acts 2:42

People can pray alone - Dan 6:10

Prayer can be brief and wordless - Neh 2:4-5

Jesus's instructions on prayer - Matt 6:5-15

A person's attitude and relationships affect the efficacy of prayer - Jas 4:1-3; 1 Pet 3:7

Power of prayer - Eph 3:14-20; Jas 5:16-18

The seasons for unanswered prayer - Jas 1:5-7; 4:1-5

Praying in faith - Jas 1:5-7; 5:13-15

REPENTANCE

Humility accompanies repentance - 2 Chr 7:14

Repentance and the kingdom - Matt 3:2

Unrepentance brings the wrath of God - Rom 2:4-5

National repentance - Joel 1:14

Baptism of repentance - Mark 1:4

Repentance from dead works - Heb 67:1

All should repent - Acts 17:30

RECONCILIATION

People should be reconciled to God - Rom 5:10; 2 Cor 5:20

People should be reconciled to each other - Matt 5:24

Racial reconciliation - Zeph 3:9; Eph 2:11-22; Gal 2:11-20

Global reconciliation - Rev 7:9

Believers have the ministry of reconciliation - 2 Cor 5:18-19

RESURRECTION

Resurrection of the body - 1 Cor 15:42-45

Resurrection of Christ - 1 Cor 15:3-4

OT references to the resurrection - Dan 12:2

God is the God of the living - Mark 12:24-27

Jesus will raise the dead - John 5:25-29

Resurrection at the rapture - 1 Thess 4:16

Resurrection at the white throne judgement - Rev 20:11-15

SALVATION

Need for salvation - Rom 6:23; Eph 2:1-3
Cure for sin - Rom 7:24-25; 8:1-3
Justification - Rom 3:21-31
Sanctification - Rom 5:9-10; Jas 1:19-21
Glorification - Col 3:4
Regeneration - Titus 3:5
Free gift - Rom 3:24; 6:23
Security - John 10:27-29; Rom 8:31-39
Salvation belongs to the Lord - Ps 3:8
Helmet of salvation - Eph 6:17

SATAN

Satan fell from heaven - Isa 14:12-17;
    Luke 10:18;
Satan deceived Eve - Gen 3:1-7
The ruler of this world - John 12:31
The deceiver - Rev 12:9
The accuser - Zech 3:1; Rev 12:10
Frustrates the work of God's Word
    - Mark 4:15
Father of lies - John 8:44
Tempts Jesus - Matt 4:1-11
Hell prepared for - Matt 25:41

SIN

Original sin - Ps 51:5
Separates man from God - Isa 59:2
Harms interpersonal relationships
    - 1 Cor 6:9-11
Leads to death - Rom 5:12; 6:23
Entered the world at the fall - Rom 5:12
God forgives sin - Eph 4:32
Jesus became sin for us - 2 Cor 5:21
Sin is universal - Ecc 7:20; Rom 3:10-12; 6:23
Confession is the remedy for sin - 1 John 1:9
Christ died for us in our sin - Rom 5:8
Christ died for our sins - 1 Cor 15:3

SPIRITUAL GIFTS

The variety of gifts - Rom 12:4-8; 1 Cor 12:4-11
The sovereign distribution of gifts
    - 1 Cor 12:11, 18
The servanthood of spiritual gifts
    - 1 Pet 4:10-11
The purpose of spiritual gifts - Rom 1:11;
    Eph 4: 8-16
The importance of each spiritual gift
    - 1 Cor 12:14-31
The unity of spiritual gifts - 1 Cor 12:25-26
The abuse of spiritual gifts - 1 Cor 14:1-40
The motivation behind spiritual gifts
    - 1 Cor 13:1-13

SPIRITUAL GROWTH

Bearing good fruit - Matt 3:8-10
Seek first the kingdom of God - Matt 6:33
God will complete the work he started in you
    - Phil 1:6
Fruit of the Spirit - Gal 5:22-23
A theology of spiritual growth - 2 Pet 1:2-11
The role of the Word of God - 2 Tim 2:15
Help others grow in their faith
    - 2 Tim 4:11-15
God is the source of spiritual growth
    - 1 Cor 3:7
Grow in grace - 2 Pet 3:18
Grow in the Word - 1 Pet 2:2

SPIRITUAL WARFARE

The armor of God - Eph 6:10-16
God is our protection – Ps 91:1-16
The enemy seeks to destroy us - 1 Pet 5:8
God's Word is powerful - Heb 4:12
God provides a way to escape temptation of
    the devil - 1 Cor 10:13
Jesus has overcome the world - John 16:33
Jesus was tempted and came through
    victorious - Matt 4:1-11
Overcoming the devil - Rev 12:11
The cross defeated the demonic realm
    - Col 2:15

TRIALS

The purpose of trials - Jas 1:2-4
Trials test our faith - 1 Pet 1:7
The expectation of trials - 1 Pet 4:12
The ministry of trials - 2 Cor 1:3-11
The victory over trials - John 16:33
Entering the kingdom through tribulation
    - Acts 14:22

TRINITY

God has a triune name - Matt 28:19
Jesus spoke of the other two persons of the
    Trinity as distinct - John 14:26
The Spirit proceeds from the Father and the
    Son - John 15:26; Rom 8:9
All three members of the Godhead were
    active in creating the world - Gen 1:1-2;
    Col 1:16
God speaks in the first person plural -
    Gen 1:26; Isa 6:8
Trinitarian formats are used throughout the
    New Testament - 2 Cor 13:14
All three members were involved in Jesus
    baptism - Luke 3:22

Trinitarian construction can be found in the
   Old Testament - Isa 42:1

UNITY

The blessing of unity - Ps 133:1-3
The preservation of unity - Eph 4:3
The condemnation of disunity - 1 Cor 1:10-13
The condemnation of racial disunity
   - Num 12:1-10; Gal 2:11-20
The unity of the body - 1 Cor 12:7-26
The power of unity - Acts 4:24-31
The mindset of unity - Rom 15:5-6; Phil 1:27
The goal of unity - Eph 4:11-16
The prayer for unity - John 17:20-23

WOMEN

First at the resurrection - John 20:11-18
Role in the church - Rom 16:1-2; 1 Tim 3:11;
   1 Cor 11:5
Role in marriage - Eph 5:22-33
Jesus ministered to women - Luke 10:38-42;
   John 4:1-38

Importance to the ministry of Jesus
   - Luke 8:1-3
Provided political and military leadership
   - Judg 4–5

WORSHIP

Worship is reserved only for God - Luke 4:8
Continuous worship in heaven - Rev 4:1-11
Worship should be continuous on earth
   - Phil 4:4
Worship glorifies God - Ps 86:9
Creation sings praises to God - Isa 55:12
Worship includes singing - Isa 12:5
Worship includes music and instruments
   - Ps 150
Our lives should be an act of worship -
   Rom 12:1
Worship is a community event - Ps 95:1-6;
   Eph 5:19
Worship is a private event – Eph 5:19
Worship is to be in spirit and truth
   - John 4:24

OLD TESTAMENT

GENESIS

INTRODUCTION

Author

THOUGH THE BOOK OF GENESIS IS anonymous (no author is listed), ancient Jewish and Christian traditions held that Moses authored the first five books of the Bible—referred to as the *Pentateuch* ("five vessels") or the *Torah* (a Hebrew word for "law" or "instruction"). That Moses stood behind these five books is attested to in both the Old and the New Testaments (see Neh 8:1; Mark 12:26).

Assuming Mosaic authorship does not prevent us from accepting that others would have provided some editorial additions later—for example, the details of Moses's death in Deuteronomy 34:5-12 and the mention of the city Dan in Genesis 14:14, which would not have been named until the time of the judges (see Judg 18:29). Thus, though many critical scholars today reject Mosaic authorship, we have good reason to accept the biblical tradition that Moses wrote the Pentateuch. For Genesis in particular, Moses probably used written sources and put them together to form this book.

Historical Background

Genesis covers the lengthy period from the creation of the heavens and the earth (1:1) to the death of Joseph, the son of Jacob, in Egypt (50:26). It includes an account of the origin of humankind and another of the origin of the nation of Israel. The rest of the Bible is dependent on the history and

theology of Genesis. It is foundational for all that follows. Here we have the creation of the universe, man and woman made in the image of God, the mandate for humans to rule the earth, the first marriage, Satan's opposition to humanity, the fall of humanity into sin, God's promise to defeat Satan through the seed of the woman, Noah and the flood, the tower of Babylon, God's covenant with Abraham, the faith of Abraham, the sacrifice of Isaac, the introduction to the twelve sons of Jacob (that is, Israel), the story of Joseph, and more.

Message and Purpose

Genesis is the book of beginnings. It is critical because it sets the stage for the rest of Scripture. The best way to understand Genesis is through its personalities, beginning with the first couple: Adam and Eve. God gave his dominion covenant to humankind, to rule on God's behalf on earth as a reflection of his dominion over all. This set the stage for the fall, when Adam and Eve sinned against God, bringing earth under the temporary control of Satan. But the episode recording the entrance of sin is also embedded with the prophecy of a Redeemer (3:15)—Jesus Christ who will defeat Satan and restore God's kingdom rule over all.

In the meantime Genesis records the angelic conflict being waged on earth to such an extent that God destroyed the earth with a flood and began again with Noah to establish his kingdom rule—for Genesis introduces us to a kingdom concept. The world after the flood also rebelled against God at Babylon, and God judged the people for trying to establish unity without him.

Then God called one man, Abraham, through whom he would reestablish his kingdom regime. Beginning with chapter 12, Genesis traces the history of Abraham and his family as God lays the foundation of his kingdom through the nation of Israel.

www.bhpublishinggroup.com/qr/te/01_00

Outline

GENESIS

I. FROM ADAM TO ABRAHAM (1:1–11:9)

➤ A. Creation, Marriage, and the Fall into Sin (1:1–5:32) ☙

1:1 The Bible is not the only religious book that talks about the origins of the universe. It is, however, the most audacious. Most ancient creation accounts chronicle a struggle between good and evil forces, with the earth popping up as a sort of accidental by-product of struggle. In these other accounts, the gods who created the world did so out of some prior material. The gods crafted, but they could not truly create.

The creation story in Scripture is altogether different: **In the beginning God created the heavens and the earth.** What we see here is creation *ex nihilo*—that is, out of nothing. God did not need raw material to make his universe. He creates by divine decree. With a mere word he made everything—both spiritual and physical. This establishes that God existed before time and space and, therefore, exists in the realm outside of both.

1:2 The Hebrew phrase translated **formless and empty** connotes a desolate, uninhabitable place. Why would the author describe God's new universe like this? Some believe God intended to show us his progressive approach through creation. The following verses certainly do show God using a process.

But it seems that something else has happened between verses 1 and 2, because disorder and darkness do not reflect the character of God. Someone else arrived on the scene, and his name is Satan. We get few details

of Satan's fall in this chapter (Ezek 28 and Isa 14 provide more), but it appears that his rebellion plunged the earth into darkness (see Luke 10:18). Fortunately for humanity, even when Satan is active, God has a plan to save. **The Spirit of God was hovering over the surface of the waters**, ready to bring order out of chaos.

1:3-5 The creation story is arranged according to seven days, although God takes the seventh day off. (If anyone deserved the break, he did.) On day one, God began by creating light, then separating that light from the darkness. Based on the apostle John's testimony (see John 1:1-2), we know that the word that God spoke here is actually Jesus Christ. Even as early as Genesis 1, the eternal Son of God was seeking to re-create and restore his planet. His illuminating light dispels the darkness and reveals the plan of God to blinded eyes.

God also established, from the very beginning, his authority over the created world. He made the light, but he also *named* it: **God called the light "day," and the darkness he called "night"** (1:5). By naming the parts of his creation, God expressed sovereign rule over them. Even the concept of light, which is fundamental to our created world, only exists because God, the King, daily sustains it.

1:6-8 On day two, God began to separate the sky from the earth. He placed some **water above the expanse** (1:7), which will later be the basis of rain and our earthly water cycle. God created the atmosphere of our planet so that life here is possible.

1:9-13 On the third day, God **gathered into one place** (1:9) all of the water, essentially pulling the land up to create the continents. He then created vegetation, **according to ... kinds** (1:12), showing that God has an order and plan to everything. As with the previous days, God gave names to these new creations, establishing his rule and reign over them. He also recognized that these things were **good** (1:10, 12)—a common refrain throughout this first chapter. Even though humanity wasn't even on the scene of this story yet, and the world was still in need of restoration, God's word boldly declared, "What I am doing in this world is both powerful and *good.*"

1:14-19 Day four confuses many: here God created the **lights in the expanse of the sky** (1:14)—the sun and moon and stars— but just a few verses earlier, on day one, God had created light and darkness. So what was emanating light for the first three days? God himself was (see Rev 22:5). On day four, God handed over that responsibility to a group of celestial representatives, so that they would **provide light on the earth** (1:17) and **serve as signs for seasons and for days and years** (1:14). This too he declared **good** (1:18).

1:20-23 God filled the sky and the seas on day five. Just as he populated the ground with plants (1:11-13), he also made birds and fish **according to their kinds** (1:21). What is unique here is that he blessed them with a commission to **be fruitful, multiply, and fill the ... earth** (1:22). God created a built-in desire and capacity for his creation to reproduce.

1:24-25 Day six is the last day of God's creative week, and he made land animals after the same pattern of the plants, birds, and fish. The creatures were made **according to their kinds** (1:24), and their very existence was **good** (1:25). The threefold taxonomy of animals here reflects the Jewish way of categorizing animals. You find **livestock** (1:24), domesticated animals like cows, sheep, and goats. Then there are **creatures that crawl** (1:24), or the tiny things we would generally call insects, rodents, and lizards. All the rest are **wildlife of the earth** (1:24). Those wildlife, by the way, would include the creatures we call dinosaurs.

1:26-30 The end of day six breaks the pattern. Until this point, God had simply spoken and the created world sprang into being. But here God demonstrated his creative genius with his crowning achievement: **Let us make man in our image**, visibly mirroring God's spiritual nature, **according to our likeness**, visibly mirroring God's functional actions (1:26). "Let us" is a hint at the Trinity: God the Father, God the Son, and God the Spirit agreed together to make the first human family, and that family was supposed to reflect truths about God. Like the Trinity, humanity has unity in diversity. **God ... created him** [that is, humans] **in the image of God** (1:27), so every human reflects the unity of God. But he also **created them male and female** (1:27), so our differences reflect the diversity of the Trinity too, since we were designed to mirror the Creator. This also lays the groundwork for upholding the importance of heterosexual marriage as the foundation of the family in fulfilling God's kingdom agenda in history.

We humans are to rule the world on God's behalf, and we are to reproduce for his glory (1:28). The more we image-bearers reproduce and fill the earth, the more his image goes out. Just as God handed over responsibility to the sun, so that it would shine *for God,* God handed over responsibility to us, so that we would govern and rule and steward his world *for him.* This is God's world, but he's put it in our hands and said, "Let them rule."

Notably, God's promise of blessing followed man's fulfillment of this dominion mandate. Thus, failure to do so robs mankind of the experience of God's favor. We must also note that while man was given the authority to rule over creation, that didn't include ruling over other people.

1:31 For the first time in this chapter, God declared his world not merely good, but **very good indeed**. Humanity reflected the beauty and complexity of God like no other part of creation could.

2:1-3 Most take days off because we get tired and need a break. Not God. He **rested on the seventh day** (2:2), not because he was weary, but because he wanted to provide us a model. If even God, who "does not slumber or sleep" (Ps 121:4), took an entire day off to enjoy the fruit of his work, we too should take time to stop our labors and focus on him.

2:4-7 Chapter 1 of Genesis describes creation in broad strokes. In chapter 2, the author decides to zoom in, focusing not on the human race but a specific person—Adam. The word *Adam*, in Hebrew, refers to that which comes from the ground, because **the Lord God formed the man out of the dust from the ground** (2:7). With the introduction of the name "Lord" (Yahweh) with "God" (Elohim) in these verses, God introduced himself relationally to his creation. God made Adam from the same ground that he was to oversee. God also breathed into Adam **the breath of life** (2:7).

This combination is astounding: Adam was, at one and the same time, a piece of dirt and the bearer of God's own breath. This should keep us from thinking of ourselves either too highly or too lowly. God made us out of the most mundane material imaginable, so we shouldn't be conceited. But God also infused us with his Spirit, which gives us tremendous value. Like Adam, we are all a fusion of the divine and the dusty.

2:8-15 God placed Adam in **a garden in Eden** (2:8) and gave him a job. Adam was **to work** the garden **and watch over it** (2:15). Before Adam had a wife, he had a place to live, a job, and a relationship with the living God. (Real men are defined by God's calling.)

Adam's calling was unique, but we can all learn about our calling through Adam's, because he was not just our shared ancestor; he was also the prototype for all humanity. God asked Adam to work a specific garden, cultivating it, working the ground, and bringing out the hidden potential of all that God had made.

He was also to guard and protect that which was under his responsibility. Since the only threat in existence was Satan, this reinforces the view that Satan's fall had already occurred. This introduces the angelic conflict and the fact that man was created to demonstrate God's greater glory to the angelic realm as he managed God's creation on his behalf (see Ps 8:4-6; Eph 3:10; 6:10-12).

It is the same with us. Each of us has a "garden," a God-given sphere of responsibility that God has placed within our care. Whether we are working in business, staying at home caring for children, or serving the Lord professionally in ministry, God wants us to make his global purpose apparent in our local situations. God won't do the work for you; he wants to do the work with and through you.

2:16-17 Eve hadn't made her grand entrance yet, because God had something else to give Adam first—his word. **The Lord God commanded the man** and expected him to obey (2:16). Many men today hate the idea of others telling them what to do. That kind of independence may make someone *feel* like a man, but God measures manhood by a person's ability to submit to the rule of God. A man hasn't arrived at biblical manhood if he won't let God tell him what to do.

The commandment was simple, though it may have struck Adam as odd: **You are free to eat from any tree of the garden, but you must not eat from the tree of the knowledge of good and evil** (2:16-17). Freedom, then, is a divinely ordained right—not a humanly determined one. Biblical freedom is the responsibility and opportunity to choose to maximize one's calling under God. God gave Adam a tremendous amount of freedom, allowing him to enjoy whatever God provided. But biblical freedom, as opposed to our culture's ideas of freedom, has healthy limits. The fundamental issue at work in this passage is this: Would man live by divine revelation or human reason? To eat the forbidden fruit meant man would seek right and wrong independently of God. In creating the man first, God was highlighting that he holds men ultimately responsible and accountable for the expansion of his kingdom program (see Gen 3:9; Exod 34:23-24; Rom 5:14-19; 1 Cor 15:21).

Just as the rules in a football game help the players and fans enjoy the game, boundaries in our spiritual walk help us live the way God intended. When we misuse that freedom, the consequences are severe. Just one bite, God warned, and **you will certainly die** (2:17). Ignoring God's boundaries can feel liberating, but it always ends in death. This is true for individuals, families, and nations.

2:18 Throughout chapter 1, God kept saying of his creation, "It is good." Yet when God saw Adam by himself, he responded this way: **It is not good for the man to be alone**. So he promised to make **a helper corresponding to him**. The Hebrew phrase *ezer kenegdo* means an essential collaborator not a maid. As strong as a man is, no man has it all; he needs someone to make up for his deficiencies, especially since he was minus ribcage. A wife is there to be a man's counterpart, equal to him and adding what he lacks, as she fulfills her biblical role. The moment a man says he doesn't need her, he contradicts God.

2:19-20 The solution to Adam's isolation was preceded by a parade. After promising to make him a wife, God brought by the animals. Adam, exercising the authority God gave him, **gave names to all the livestock, to the birds of the sky, and to every wild animal** (2:20). "Bear . . . gorilla . . . elephant . . . anteater," he said. But then he noticed something. For every Mr. Elephant, there was a Mrs. Elephant. Mr. Gorilla had his Mrs. Gorilla. But for Adam, **no helper was found corresponding to him** (2:20). There was a Mr. Adam, but no other half.

2:21-22 God lovingly addressed Adam's need, putting Adam to sleep and creating a woman out of one of Adam's ribs. The English translations don't usually make it clear, but the word used for God creating the woman is much different than the one used for making Adam (2:7). God formed Adam, but he *fashioned* Eve. When God made man, he took some dirt and threw it together; when he made woman, he took his time.

Not only did God fashion the woman, but he also brought Adam and Eve together. He **brought her to the man** (2:22), as if playing matchmaker. Just like Adam, Eve had a relationship with God before she had a relationship with her husband. (Women who place their hands in God's hand can trust him to place them in the hands of the right men.)

2:23-25 When their marriage took place, Adam broke out into a little song. The Hebrew poem here, **This one, at last, is bone of my bone and flesh of my flesh** (2:23) is—I think—Adam's way of saying, "*That's* what I'm talking about!" And Adam—*ish* in Hebrew—gives his wife his name. **This one will be called "woman"** (2:23), he says, the Hebrew word for "woman" being *isha*. Together, **they become one flesh** (2:24), which is to say they share a unity of

purpose while retaining their uniqueness as individuals. This is a pattern for all married couples. As Jesus would later say about this passage, "what God has joined together, let no one separate" (Mark 10:9). In a culture characterized by abandoned mothers, easy divorce, and broken homes, God offers a better way. And the man is to lead in accepting the responsibility for leaving and cleaving.

3:1 The text doesn't say it here directly, but **the serpent** that showed up to tempt Adam and Eve was the devil, Satan, in disguise. He approached **the woman** on purpose, because he knew that Eve did not hear the command of God firsthand; only Adam did. Adam was supposed to lead his family by making sure that both he and Eve knew God's commands and walked in them. The serpent sought to reverse the divinely ordained roles in the family by bypassing the man and appealing to the woman. This is a reminder that role reversal leads to chaos.

Importantly, Satan omitted God's relational name *LORD* (Yahweh) when speaking with Eve. This indicates that he doesn't mind religion as long as there's no relationship with the Lord God driving it. Notice Satan's tactics. There was only one restriction that God gave, but that's the only restriction the devil wanted to discuss. Not only that, but he also intentionally misrepresented God, implying that God had commanded, **You can't eat from any tree in the garden.** One of Satan's oldest lies, as alluring today as it was then, is this: *God is holding out on you.* Thus, Satan questioned the goodness of God.

3:2-3 Eve answered the initial attack well enough, pointing out that God allowed them to **eat the fruit from the trees in the garden** (3:2), but that they should not eat from the tree of the knowledge of good and evil. If they did, they would die (3:3). Adam had emphasized to Eve that she was not even to touch it (3:3).

3:4-5 Satan became bolder here, revealing two more of his classic lies. The first is that sin carries no consequences. **You will not die**, he told Eve (3:4). Every one of us has felt that lie, since it's at the heartbeat of every act of sin. God tells us not to cross a line—because the consequences are disastrous—and we pretend like he's all talk. The second lie is that humans can become equal to God. As Satan said, **When you eat the fruit your eyes will be opened and you will be like God, knowing good and evil** (3:5). The irony is that God intended for us to be like him, sharing in his reign and ruling over his world. But Satan tempted Adam and Eve to try to *take God's place*, kicking him off the throne altogether.

3:6 We see another lie of Satan as Eve contemplated the fruit. She sized it up and concluded **that the tree was good for food and delightful to look at**, so she took a bite. Our culture expresses this lie this way: "If it feels good, do it!" The results of buying the lie are just as tragic today as they were for Adam and Eve.

By the way, notice that Adam **was with her** this whole time. God had given him the task of protecting the garden and leading his wife, and here he was standing next to Eve while the snake laid a heavy line on her. Sitting there in silence, Adam became the responder instead of the leader, and literally all hell broke loose as a result. His failure to help his wife live in obedience to God's word had tragic consequences.

3:7-8 God promised that eating from the tree would lead to death, and he was right. The manifestation of that death was emotional, spiritual, relational, environmental, and ultimately physical. Adam and Eve **knew they were naked** and **sewed fig leaves together** for clothing (3:7). They had been naked up to this point—and unashamed. But suddenly they were full of shame and guilt, so their nakedness was a mark of emotional death, rather than life. Fear crept in too, another sign of emotional death. When they heard God approaching, they **hid from the Lord God among the trees of the garden** (3:8). The spiritual relationship that nourished them and should have brought them their greatest joy had become a terror to them.

3:9-13 God never asks questions because he doesn't know the answer. So when he called to Adam, **Where are you?** (3:9), he wasn't losing a game of hide-and-seek. He was calling Adam to task, because Adam was the accountable one. He was the leader, and he had failed. I suspect that God is calling out to many men with the same question today. To those men abandoning their families, sitting

passively in their relationships, and wasting their lives, God says, "Where are you?" It's time to stop acting like little boys; step up to be the men God created you to be. Kingdom men accept responsibility under God.

3:14-19 We see the seeds of death grow further as God issued punishments for Adam's and Eve's sin. Their rebellion led to relational death, as God promised that the relationship between men and women would become a battle rather than a partnership (3:16). We even see economic death, as God promised that work would become **painful labor** rather than the fruitful process he intended (3:17). And while Adam and Eve would not drop dead on the spot, their coming biological death was now guaranteed (3:19). They were like flowers cut off from the plant. The process of physical death had begun.

3:20-24 In response to all of this, God did something gracious. He **drove the man out** of the garden, placing a **cherubim** with a **flaming, whirling sword** at the entrance (3:24). This was the kindest thing God could have done. If Adam and Eve had eaten of the tree of life in their sinful state, they would have been locked into that sinful state and its consequences forever. God also provided redemptive covering for them through the slaying of an animal (3:21).

4:1-5 Even though Adam and Eve were exiled from the garden, God continued to bless them. **With the Lord's help** (4:1), Eve gave birth to two sons—Cain and Abel. Both sons grew up hearing stories about God, so both knew that they should bring offerings to their Creator. In **the course of time** (4:3), both boys came ready to worship. But while **the Lord had regard for Abel and his offering** (4:4), **he did not have regard for Cain and his offering** (4:5).

What made the difference between the two offerings? We get a clue from the sort of offerings they brought: Cain offered **produce** from the ground, but we know that the ground was under the curse. This suggests Cain had aligned himself with the curse. The apostle John points this out, calling Cain "evil" even before he killed his brother (see 1 John 3:12). Abel, on the other hand, was exercising dominion over the animals, as

God had commanded (Gen 1:28), as well as offering the required sacrifice of shed blood (see Heb 9:22). True worship must be what God will receive, not merely what we want to give. So God rejected Cain and accepted Abel, because one was evil and the other righteous.

4:5-7 Because God rejected his offering, Cain became both **furious** and **despondent** (4:5)— mad and sad at the same time. That makes for a dangerous combination. God gave Cain an opportunity to break out of his emotional funk, reminding him that if he did **what is right**, he would **be accepted** (4:7). The cure for emotional problems is found in spiritual realignment.

4:8-16 Rather than listening to God's counsel and choosing to worship according to God's pattern, Cain nursed his negative emotions until they manifested as murder (4:8). There is an eerie familiarity in what follows, echoing the interaction between God and Adam after the fall. Like Adam, Cain sinned. God asked him a question, not so that he could get information, but so that he could give Cain a chance to accept responsibility for his actions. Like Adam, the son shirked that responsibility, brushing off what he'd done (4:9). And just as he did with Adam, God punished Cain. This time, instead of the ground merely becoming cursed, it **will never again give you its yield**, God said, making Cain a **restless wanderer on the earth** (4:12). Cain was cast out, not just from the garden, like his father, but **from the LORD's presence** altogether (4:16).

4:17-24 What follows Cain's punishment is the tale of two families, a theme that shows up repeatedly throughout Genesis. Unfortunately, Cain's murderous ways infected his family line. By the time we get to his great-great-great-grandson, we find a man *bragging* about his own violence. **I killed a man for wounding me**, Lamech boasted (4:23). Notice too that Lamech was talking to **his wives**—*plural* (4:23). God's perfect design is only four chapters old, and already we find people reveling in bloodshed and flouting his design for marriage.

4:25–5:32 In contrast to Cain's line, God raised up another family tree. **In place of Abel** God granted Eve a son named **Seth** (4:25). Seth

typified the same type of worship as his deceased brother Abel, because in connection with Seth, **people began to call on the name of the LORD** (4:26). The prideful way of worship, Cain's way (see Jude 11), points to itself. The humble way of worship, Abel and Seth's way, calls out to God. It is no surprise, then, that when God wanted to choose an obedient servant, hundreds of years later, that servant— Noah—would come from Seth's line (5:28-32).

❧ B. The Flood *(6:1–8:22)* ❧

6:1-4 The Nephilim (6:4), described only here in the Bible, were demonized men, whose sexual intimacy with women led to a demonized society. They had given themselves over to powers of darkness so fully, it seems, that they became **powerful men** (6:4). Yet their dark powers were no match for the Creator God, who looked down and decreed that **their days will be 120 years** (6:3). God would only take so much evil, so he announced a 120-year window for people to repent, after which judgment would come.

6:5-7 We have fallen a long way from Genesis 3. What began with Adam and Eve's sin, grew in Cain's murderous ways, and bore fruit in Lamech's boastful violence is now in full bloom throughout the entire human race. God looked on the earth and saw **that every inclination of the human mind was nothing but evil all the time** (6:5). People had become comprehensively corrupt, manufacturing evil at the highest possible level. This pained God (6:6), and it moved him to action. God's Spirit would no longer shield men from his just judgment, as he issued a decree of total destruction (6:7).

6:8-13 In the midst of this corrupt and violent generation, **Noah . . . found favor with the LORD** (6:8). He was exceptional because he walked with God. In the same way, all believers should be exceptions in the midst of their own sinful generations.

6:14–7:5 God revealed his plan to Noah: **I am bringing a flood . . . to destroy every creature under heaven with the breath of life**

in it (6:17). The only escape would be through the ark that God commanded Noah to build, a flat-bottomed vessel enormous enough to preserve both human and land animal life. God intended to start over, so this judgment was not total.

Noah was to **bring into the ark two of all the living creatures** so that their kinds would be spared (6:19). God made a distinction between the clean and unclean animals, though. Of the clean animals, Noah was to take with him **seven pairs** (7:2-3), rather than just one. These were for Noah and his family to eat after exiting the ark and—as we will see at the end of this story—for Noah to sacrifice to God in worship. In all this, Noah obeyed God completely, doing **everything that the LORD commanded him** (7:5). Obedience in the midst of evil should be the supreme goal and desire of God's people.

7:6-22 After all the preparations, and after 120 years of God waiting for people to repent, the flood finally began. Only **Noah, his sons, his wife, and his sons' wives entered the ark** (7:7), while every other human was wiped out. The water came from above as well as below (see 7:11-12), raining down while the subterranean waters broke loose from underneath. The result was a flood that affected the whole earth, lasing **forty days and forty nights** (7:12). Just as God had promised, the flood destroyed all life on land (7:21-22).

7:23-24 Only **Noah was left, and those that were with him in the ark** (7:23). Yet not a drop of this judgment was more extensive than it needed to be. Great was the sin, so also was God's just judgment. Sitting on that boat while **the water surged on the earth 150 days** (7:24), Noah's family acted as a living reminder that the God who fiercely judges sin is the same one who, through our faith, mercifully delivers us from it.

8:1-14 Just as God had done in the original creation, so here God gathered the waters together to reveal dry land (8:1, 3, 13-14). Eventually Noah's ark came to rest **on the mountains of Ararat** (8:4), inaugurating a new beginning for mankind.

8:15-22 God wanted Noah to know about this new beginning. The flood was not merely a purge of evil, but a chance to return to God's original goal. So we see a repetition of some of the blessings of chapter 1, as the animals—and people—were commissioned to **spread over the earth and be fruitful and multiply** (8:17). Noah, overflowing with thanks for the way that God had saved him, made an offering of some of the clean animals (8:20). When he saw Noah's worship, God was pleased and promised to **never again curse the ground because of human beings** (8:21). God would providentially preserve the earth and its ecology for the sake of humanity.

His promise, however, was larger than this. God's promise gives us hope that when we respond to him in faith, he can renew something that has been lost. He can restore that which has been destroyed, rebuilding that which lies broken because of our sin.

⇒ C. A New Beginning—And a Dead End (9:1–11:9) ⇐

9:1 God recommissioned Noah with the command to **be fruitful and multiply and fill the earth**—the commission given originally to Adam and Eve. The judgment of the flood, it is important to remember, was not God abandoning his original purposes, but resetting the scene so that his original purposes could go forth.

9:2-6 Humanity was now free to eat meat for the first time. The only restriction God placed on this was to avoid eating meat **with its lifeblood in it** (9:4). Raw meat was off limits because it represented life (see Lev 17:11). God also added another new command about lifeblood, this one about people: **Whoever sheds human blood, by humans his blood will be shed** (9:6).

This is the basis of capital punishment, and it is grounded in the fact that **God made humans in his image** (9:6). Humans uniquely reflect God's image and nature, so taking innocent human life is unthinkable and requires retribution, since at its core murder is an attack on God.

9:7-11 God made a new covenant with Noah, promising **that never again will every creature be wiped out by floodwaters** (9:11). God won't wipe out every creation *with a flood* again, but he still reserves the right to wipe it out *some other way*. A second judgment is indeed coming, one not carried along by waves but by flames (see 2 Pet 3:7).

9:12-17 God established his covenants with signs, physical pictures to encourage us and remind us of his faithfulness. The sign God gave here is the rainbow (9:13). What is significant about the rainbow (and the covenant) is that it required nothing from humans. Generally covenants are two-party agreements: I do this; you do that. But God simply said, **Whenever ... the bow appears in the clouds, I will remember my covenant** (9:14-15). God keeps his promises toward us unconditionally, even in the face of our sin. If he didn't, no covenant between us would last.

9:18-19 All humanity has its origin in Adam and the three sons of Noah: **Shem, Ham, and Japheth** (9:18; also see Acts 17:26). This is an appropriate foundation for gaining a proper biblical basis for racial identity. Because all races stem from the same root, it is absurd for any group to claim superiority over another. God intended to reestablish the human race through the three sons of Noah; therefore, God legitimized all races over which each son stood as head and over which Noah presided as father. This is especially true since Scripture says that God blessed Noah and his sons, and the command to repopulate the earth was comprehensive and equally applied to each of them (see 9:1). Each son is associated with nations of peoples, as is recorded in the "Table of Nations" in Genesis 10. All races can take pride in the fact that it was God's intention that each unique group exist, survive, and function as nations of peoples, without any one group or ethnicity being superior in nature to any other.

9:20-23 It's difficult to end well, as Noah's life shows us. He **became drunk, and uncovered himself inside his tent** (9:21). Noah's sinful drunkenness provided the setting for another sinful act. Ham, one of Noah's three

sons, **saw his father naked**. But rather than covering his nakedness and removing his father's shame, Ham ridiculed his father to his brothers (9:22). His brothers covered their father, but Ham's spiteful words created a ripple effect, leading to the curse on Ham's son, **Canaan**.

9:24-29 Canaan's line would continue in unrighteousness and oppression, following in the footsteps of Ham's example (9:24-25). And God's plan to bless the world would now focus instead on Shem's descendants, while Canaan's descendants would be removed from that plan (9:26-27).

Since Ham was the father of black people (see below on 10:6), and since his descendants were cursed to be **slaves** because of his sin against Noah (9:25-27), some have argued that Africans and their descendants are destined to be servants, and should accept their status as slaves in fulfillment of biblical prophecy. Due to this "curse of Ham" theory, there existed a myth of inferiority with apparent biblical roots in Christian history and culture. This theological basis provided the raw material necessary to convince slaves during the antebellum slave era that to resist their assigned inferior status was to resist the will of God. It was also used to give slavery a perceived biblical approval for slave owners and traders. This myth became an authoritative one because it was rooted in a purported theology, and slave owners used this twisted belief system to sustain a perverted sociology.

Yet even as slavery was ultimately abolished, this false theology, coupled with the legal status of American segregation in the early twentieth century, did nothing to ameliorate the already culturally inflicted and discolored perception of black people in the minds of many white Christians. Unfortunately, this contributed to the establishing and continuation of a distorted myth of black inferiority in the American Christian psyche.

This interpretation of the "curse of Ham" is incorrect due to multiple reasons. Bear in mind that the Bible says Canaan, Ham's son, was cursed, not Ham himself. Thus, only one of Ham's four sons was cursed. How then could all black people everywhere be cursed? The Bible also places limitations on curses—only three or four generations at most (Exod 20:5). Moreover, the curse that Canaan and his descendants would be slaves found its most obvious fulfillment in the ongoing defeat and subjugation of Canaan by Israel (see Josh 9:23; 1 Kgs 9:20-21). The descendants of Ham's other sons—Cush, Mizraim, and Put (Gen 10:6)—have continued to this day as national peoples in Ethiopia (Cush), Egypt (Mizraim), and Libya (Put). In fact, founders of the first two great civilizations, Sumer (Mesopotamia) and Egypt, descended from Ham.

God says that curses based on disobedience only extend to three or four generations at most and are reversed when people repent and turn again to obedience (Exod 20:5-6). This is certainly sufficient to negate the Christian endorsement of the American enslavement of black Christians as well as any lingering myth of superiority or inferiority based on race.

10:1-32 It can be helpful to think of Genesis like a movie. The author wants us to know the main characters, but he also fast-forwards through other sections of the plot to move us from one key scene to the next. So even though a lot happened between Seth and Noah, the author fast-forwards by using a genealogy (5:1-32). Here he does it again, fast-forwarding from Noah to the next big scene at the famous tower of Babylon (11:1-9).

As we skip through these centuries, however, we see God populating the earth and creating the multitude of nations. Japheth's descendants spread out to the north and west (10:2-5); Ham's descendants migrated to the area of Mesopotamia (10:6-20); Shem and his descendants became ancestors of the Jewish people (10:21-31). Even though God would focus his redemptive plan through one line (Shem's), this chapter reveals that God is a God of all nations. He cares for them all and has a plan to redeem people from every people group.

Noah's son Ham had four **sons: Cush, Mizraim, Put, and Canaan** (10:6). Cush was the progenitor of the Ethiopian people. This is validated by the fact that the names Cush and Ethiopia are used interchangeably in the Scriptures. Mizraim was the progenitor of the Egyptian people, who are understood

in Scripture to have been a Hamitic people, and thus African (see also Ps 78:51; 105:23, 26-27; 106:21-22). Put was the progenitor of Libya. Canaan was the progenitor of the Canaanites, one of the most problematic foes of God's chosen people, the Israelites.

In 10:8-12 (see also 11:2), we find a particularly important and powerful person named **Nimrod**, the descendant of **Cush**, who ruled in **the land of Shinar**. Nimrod eventually became the father of two of the greatest empires in the Bible and in world history, Assyria and Babylon. He was the first great leader of a world civilization. Nimrod's presence and accomplishments confirm the unique and early leadership role black people played in world history. Unfortunately, he also led the world away from God.

11:1-2 A key, but subtle, theme hinges on this word **east** (11:2). When God pushed Adam and Eve out of the garden, he sent them east (3:24). When Cain was removed from God's presence after killing his brother, the text says he too went east (4:16). "East" represents a journey away from God. So when we see the people gather at **a valley in the land of Shinar**, in **the east** (11:2), the author is telling us that the next scene will move humanity further away from God.

11:3-4 The people at Babylon/Babel made a declaration of independence—not from another nation, but from God himself. **Let us build ourselves a city and a tower with its top in the sky. Let us make a name for ourselves** (11:4). To build a city was to build civilization. To build a tower was to build a religious order. Both would be man-centered, not God-centered, efforts. They were adopting a form of humanism.

Instead of pursuing God's agenda—multiplying and filling the earth—they wanted to do everything to *prevent* being **scattered throughout the earth** (11:4). In a sense, they wanted what most teenagers today want: independence (with all of its benefits) while still retaining all the perks of living at home under parental provision. This scene shows humanity telling God, "Keep putting food on my table and clothes on my back, but don't tell me what to do. Keep blessing me, but don't instruct me."

11:5 The people at Shinar wanted to build "a tower with its top in the sky" (11:4), reaching all the way up to heaven. What happened next? God **came down to look over the city and the tower** (11:5). The people thought they could use man-made religion and technology (brick and mortar) to build their own physical and spiritual world. But God had to stoop down to even see what they were doing. It doesn't matter how high you climb; the only way you can reach God is if he comes down to you.

11:6-7 If they have begun to do this … then nothing they plan to do will be impossible for them (11:6). God was not threatened by what humanity was doing. He wasn't fearful that humanity was suddenly an unstoppable force. Rather he recognized that unified sinful humanity had enormous potential to sour God's creation. Left unchecked, their unified language would only make it easier for evil to proliferate on the earth. So in order to put the brakes on that, God decided to disunify them and **confuse their language so that they will not understand one another's speech** (11:7). God interrupted their plans to communicate.

11:8-9 The result of this language shake-up was twofold. First, the people **stopped building the city** (11:8). Without the benefit of easy communication, the great nation they were building was left unfinished. (I see in this a warning to any country: if we pursue the blessing of God without the instruction of God, we may not be allowed to finish as a civilization.) Second, God's original purpose was accomplished: all the people—now speaking precursors of Arabic and German and Swahili and not having a clue what the other guys were saying—were forced to scatter **throughout the earth** (11:9). If God intended for his people to multiply and fill the earth, they *would*.

II. ABRAHAM (11:10–24:67)

⮞ A. Father Abraham and His Rocky Faith Journey (11:10–14:24) ⮜

11:10-32 The end of chapter 11 is another fast-forward, as the author transitions from the failure of Babel to the next move in God's redemptive plan. We get a closer look at the line of Shem, which was already highlighted in 10:21-31, and watch God handing down the blessing from Shem to Abraham (11:10-26). God was still keeping his program going, despite the evil that needed to be addressed in the world. Life and longevity were declining, but God was establishing his purposes through the genealogical record.

The genealogy slows down as it approaches **Abram**, whose name means *exalted father* (11:27-32). We pick up the action as Abram's father, **Terah**, was moving his family from **Ur of the Chaldeans** (a wealthy city in Mesopotamia) **to go to the land of Canaan**, the promised land (11:31). Terah, however, stopped short in the land of **Haran**—modern day northern Syria (11:31). Abram's trip to the promised land would have to wait until Terah's death (11:32).

12:1-3 When God saw the wickedness in Noah's day, he reestablished his plan by choosing one faithful man. We see the same pattern happening here with Abram. God's desire was still to fill the earth with his glory and bless **all the peoples** (12:3), but he began that mission by calling one individual. Thus, God commanded Abram to leave his **land**, his **relatives**, and his **father's house** to go to a new land (12:1).

Abram had to act in faith, because he did not know where God was leading him. He only knew that if he would obey, God would respond by making him **into a great nation**, making his **name great**, and even using him to bring **blessing** to others (12:2). God was advancing his kingdom agenda through Abram.

12:4-7 Abram obeyed God's command, leaving Haran with **his wife Sarai, his nephew Lot**, and all of the other **people** (12:5) who were stepping out in faith with Abram. When he arrived **at the oak of Moreh** (12:6), most likely a Canaanite worship center, God promised to **give this land** to Abram's **offspring** (12:7). Abram's faith in action had led to further illumination.

This is God's pattern: not only does obedience lead to blessing, but it also leads to greater clarity of God's will, purpose, and direction in our lives. God speaks in concert with our obedience, not with our rebellion.

12:7-9 Abram responded to God's promise by building two altars to the true God—one at the oak of Moreh and another in Bethel (see 12:7-8). These altars represented public declarations of faith in the midst of a pagan environment. We may not build stone altars today, but we too should make public declarations of our faith in God—even when our society wants nothing to do with him.

12:10 Abram began his journey of faith well, obediently leaving Haran, traveling to Canaan, and making declarations of allegiance to God along the way. But his faith soon gave way to fear. A **famine** caused Abram and his family to travel to **Egypt** for food. This was a bad move because God had made it clear that he wanted Abram in Canaan, not Egypt. The moment Abram assessed the situation from a human perspective, he made a decision that threatened to jeopardize God's program.

12:11-15 While in Egypt, Abram's fear grew. He worried that someone might see Sarai's beauty and kill him to get her (12:11-12). So he hatched a plan to save his skin. Sarai was to say that she was Abram's **sister** (12:13)—which, according to 20:12, was half true. Abram may have reasoned that any serious suitor would have to ask him for permission to marry Sarai, which would give them enough time to escape. But not just *any* suitor showed interest. Pharaoh himself wanted Sarai for a wife, so he bypassed the normal conventions and welcomed her right into the palace (12:15).

12:16 The immediate outcome of this little drama was that Abram got fabulously wealthy. But at what cost? No amount of money could make up for the fact that Abram was ready to give up his wife and abandon the promise of God for mere self-preservation.

12:17-20 This odd story demonstrates God's commitment to his kingdom program and promises. He sent **severe plagues** to Pharaoh's household (12:17), which immediately signaled to the people involved that they had been deceived. Pharaoh, whose position of power would have allowed him to do nearly anything, acted with more integrity than Abram in giving Sarai back without punishing the couple in any way (12:18-20).

13:1-7 Having been sent away from Egypt, Abram and his family journeyed **to the Negev** (13:1), then **from the Negev to Bethel** (13:3), gradually making their way back toward the land of promise. By this point Abram had become **rich in livestock, silver, and gold** (13:2), but so had his nephew Lot (13:5). Had the men's wealth just been in silver and gold, they would have had no problem. But their herds were too vast for any one area (13:6). There simply wasn't enough water and pasture for all of their livestock.

13:8-9 Abram recognized that he and Lot had to separate. Surprisingly, though, Abram chose to preserve relationship over keeping the economic upper hand. He allowed Lot to pick his plot of land first (13:9). This was an incredibly generous decision: in that culture, as head of the household, Abram had every right to make the first choice himself. But he had faith in God's promise and provision, so he was able to defer to Lot.

13:10-13 Lot looked at the two options and **saw that the entire plain of the Jordan as far as Zoar was well watered everywhere** (13:10). He saw the material wealth in front of him, but failed to see what he should have—that it couldn't last. God was going to judge the region soon, because **the men of Sodom were evil, sinning immensely against the LORD** (13:13). Yet Lot chose to get close to sin for the material gain and beauty of a moment, journeying **eastward** toward Sodom and Gomorrah (13:11). In Genesis, moving *east* was always a bad sign, and that is precisely the direction in which Lot was headed.

13:14-17 Earlier, Lot lifted up his eyes and saw only what can be seen with the physical senses. Here, however, God lifted up Abram's eyes to see the spiritual promise of God (13:14). The great lesson for Israel—and for us—here is that we must get God's perspective on our situations, not relying on our own. We perceive only the temporary; God sees the eternal.

What God offered to Abram was long-term: **I will give you and your offspring forever all the land that you see** (13:15). Moreover, God seemed to increase his promise, now telling Abram that his descendants would multiply so dramatically that they would be as innumerable as **the dust of the earth** (13:16). Best of all, Abram wouldn't have to do anything to make this happen. **I will give it to you** (13:17), God plainly told him. The beautiful part of obeying God is that you don't have to take what's yours; he gives it to you freely.

13:18 Abram moved his tent **near the oaks of Mamre at Hebron**, building there another **altar to the Lord**. He heard God's promise and received it, worshiping God because of his word and finding security in that word. Unlike he'd done during his time in Egypt, Abram was now moving by faith, not by sight, which would be the foundation not only of *his* obedience but also of the obedience that God wants for all who follow him (see 2 Cor 5:7).

14:1-12 It wasn't long before Lot's location led him to trouble. War broke out among five Canaanite kings (14:8-9) and four kings from the east (14:1-2), and Lot was caught in the scuffle. In the process of conquering the five Canaanite kings, the eastern armies took spoils from the region—including Lot and his family (14:12).

14:13-16 Word reached Abram that Lot had been captured (14:13-14), so he **assembled his 318 trained men** to go get his nephew back (14:14). (If you're going to take 318 men against the armies of four kings, they had better be "trained"!) With them, Abram pursued the armies **as far as Hobah to the north of Damascus** (14:15)—that means he covered about 240 miles, by night, without a single army vehicle. And sure enough, **he brought back . . . his relative Lot and his goods, as well as the women and the other people** (14:16).

The only explanation for such a victory was God fulfilling his word to Abram—that those who hurt Abram were hurting God, and God himself would defend Abram. God wants to be our protector when circumstances have raided our lives and stolen our joy, our hope, our tomorrows. He can lead a rescue mission to bring them back.

14:17-18 Abram's daring military venture released a lot more than Lot and his family. Several kings were freed, and one of them came to thank Abram. His name was **Melchizedek, king of Salem**, called a **priest to God Most High** (14:18). *Melchizedek* means "King of Righteousness," and *Salem* means "peace." (The city of *Jerusalem*, for instance, means "city of peace.") So this person is also the King of Peace.

The peculiar thing about him is that he's both a king and a priest. Kings rule over the people, while priests stand between the people and God. No Jew ever occupied both offices. This is why the author of Hebrews says that Jesus was a priest and a king in "the order of Melchizedek" (Heb 5:10). Jesus is the true and permanent King of Righteousness and Peace, and he is the great high priest who bridged the gap between God and humanity. Melchizedek is a prototype of the Son of God.

14:19 Melchizedek blessed Abram in the name of **God Most High, Creator of heaven and earth**. This name for God, *El Elyon*, emphasizes his power and might. Literally, it's a superlative, meaning "God, the highest." It comes up in this context because God wanted to emphasize his control. He wanted Abram to know that the kings were never in charge of the situation; he was. The kings thought they were high until *El Elyon* got into the fight. With *El Elyon*, an army of 318 can overpower the armies of multiple kings. With *El Elyon* in your life, the "kings" of sin, darkness, and temptation don't stand a chance.

14:20 We see the first tithe here, as **Abram gave** Melchizedek **a tenth of everything**. The order here is crucial. Abram only gave Melchizedek his tithe *after* Melchizedek had blessed him (14:19-20). In other words, Abram did not give to get God's blessing; he gave because he had already been blessed by

God. His giving was a response to what God had done. Since Jesus came in "the order of Melchizedek," the tithe is still valid today as believers respond to the goodness of God in their lives (see Heb 7:1-17).

14:21 Apparently the king of Sodom liked the sight of Melchizedek getting a tenth of Abram's spoils, so he moved in to cut a deal with Abram too: **Give me the people, but take the possessions for yourself.** In other words, he wanted to make this a fifty-fifty split. But the king of Sodom had been on the losing end of this battle. He was one of the captives that Abram set free, yet he was trying to negotiate to make it look like he had something to do with the victory.

14:22-24 Abram responded by putting the king of Sodom in his place. He told the king that he would be keeping his own spoils (thank you very much), and wouldn't touch even **a thread or sandal strap or anything that belongs to** him, because Abram wanted to make sure the king could never say, I **made Abram rich** (14:23). The victory was God's, and so God alone deserves the glory. This is a subtle reminder not to compromise with the world for the sake of economic or political gain.

➣ B. From Abram to Abraham: A Covenant Renewed (15:1–17:27) ≪

15:1-3 About ten years had passed since Abram first picked up and moved his family toward Canaan (12:1-4). Back then, God promised Abram great blessing, his own land, and a multitude of children. But Abram still had no kids—a fact that he felt compelled to point out to God (15:2-3). His faith was starting to falter.

15:4-5 God renewed his covenant with Abram by insisting that **one who comes from [his] own body** would inherit his wealth (15:4). He also added some specificity to the promise: whereas previously he had said Abram would simply become "a great nation" (12:2), now he fleshed that out by pointing to the stars. **Count the stars, if you**

are able (15:5). *That's* how many descendants you'll have. Abram felt old and barren, and God knew it. But if God was powerful enough to create billions of stars out of nothing, he would be powerful enough to create new life from an old man. And he's powerful enough to create new life in you, too.

15:6 While looking up at the night sky, in spite of all the obstacles still before him, Abram believed God's promise. God saw this faith and **credited it to him as righteousness.** The apostle Paul would pick up on this verse in Romans 4:3, using Abram as an example of how faith works. God spoke to Abram, and Abram took him at his word. That's the essence of faith. Because of this faith, God chose to count Abram's faith as righteousness. That's the result of faith.

15:7-21 Abram believed but still wanted more details about how all of this would come to pass. He asked, **Lord God, how can I know that I will possess** this land? (15:8). God then asked Abram to perform what seemed to be a bizarre ritual. He told Abram to get **a three-year-old cow, a three-year-old female goat, a three-year-old ram, a turtledove, and a young pigeon** (15:9). Abram did so and cut each animal in half (15:10). Then Abram fell asleep (15:12).

These strange details are important to what happened next. God renewed his covenant with Abram, giving a few more specifics about the promised land (15:18-21) and letting Abram know about Israel's future exile in Egypt (15:13-16). The key detail, though, is that God alone—in the form of **a smoking fire pot and a flaming torch**—passed through the path of the torn animals (15:17).

Covenants like this one were supposed to have two people involved. Both parties to the covenant were supposed to walk between the slain animals, signaling that if either one broke their side of the agreement, he would suffer a fate like that of the animals. God's covenant, then, was radically unique: Abram wasn't even awake when it was made, so he couldn't walk the covenant out. God walked through for both of them, promising to bear the fatal burden if *either* of them broke the covenant. Centuries later, after mountains of human sin had accumulated, the Son of God bore the covenant penalty on the cross of Calvary.

16:1-4 Even after hearing the promise of God again—and believing it—Abram and Sarai found it difficult to know how they would produce a child. After all, both of them were old, pushing the century mark, and the promise was still unfulfilled.

So Sarai did what many of us do when we don't like God's timing: she produced a scheme to help God out. It was the custom of the day for a servant to act as a surrogate when the wife of the household couldn't conceive. Sarai, therefore, took **Hagar, her Egyptian slave**, and offered **her to her husband . . . as a wife** (16:3). Abram quietly acquiesced to the plan (16:4), passively making the same mistake Adam did in allowing his wife to overrule the word and will of God.

16:4-6 Abram and Sarai's scheme seemed successful when **Hagar . . . became pregnant** (16:4). But her pregnancy was hardly the panacea that Sarai hoped for. (After all, encouraging your man to sleep with another woman will never lead to a happy family life.) And so, Hagar's pregnancy, rather than causing celebration, only incited Sarai's jealousy and rage. **Sarai mistreated her so much that she ran away** (16:6). Just as with Adam and Eve, the consequences of sin were immediately present in interpersonal conflict.

16:7-11 Hagar was now a pregnant single woman without a place to lay her head. But God met her in her place of despair. Through the **angel of the LORD** (16:7), he guided her back to Abram and Sarai (16:9). He also promised that the child in her womb would be a son (16:11). Not only that, but also God called his name **Ishmael**, which means "God hears" (16:11). Even though the people closest to her had turned on her and she felt completely alone, God himself came close to Hagar, reassuring her that he had heard her despair. God is near to the brokenhearted, and he hears their cries (see Ps 34:18). This gives hope to any single mother who reaches out to God.

16:12 Ishmael, Hagar's promised son, would be **like a wild donkey**, which is not to be taken as a compliment in any era or culture.

His descendants would be unruly, bringing conflict into the household of God for generations to come. The Ishmaelites would be a consistent nemesis for the Jews, with their **hand . . . against everyone.** Sarai's earthly act, though intended to serve a spiritual purpose, only led to more conflict, crisis, and enmity. The only safe way to fulfill the purposes of God is through living in obedience to the revealed will of God.

16:13-16 In spite of the negative promises about Ishmael's future, Hagar still recognized that God had met her in her place of despair. So she named the LORD who spoke to her: "You are El-roi" (16:13), meaning "The God who sees." What greater comfort can there be than to know that God hears, sees, and cares?

17:1 Abram was **ninety-nine years old.** Twenty-four years had passed since God first promised him a son, a promise that looked increasingly impossible if Sarai was to be the mother. But God assured Abram, **I am God Almighty.** He is full of power. Abram, then, didn't need to worry about the fulfillment of the promise. All he needed to do was to fulfill his obligation to God: **Live in my presence and be blameless.**

17:2-3 God repeated his covenant to Abram again, promising to **multiply** him **greatly** (17:2). Abram responded in the only appropriate way: he **fell facedown** before God (17:3). This represented both fear and faith, a combination that God honored by revealing more of his plan.

17:4-8 Name changes in the Bible are always important, because names carry meaning and identity. God changed Abram's name, even before the promise was fulfilled, from **Abram** to **Abraham** (17:5). *Abram* means "exalted father," but *Abraham* means "father of a multitude" because he would become **the father of many nations** (17:5). The promise had grown.

Notice, however, that nothing had changed in Abram's life, except that he had gotten older, faltering in his faith along the way. What was unlikely at age seventy-five was now downright unthinkable at age ninety-nine. And God didn't do anything to change the circumstances. Instead, he changed Abram's name to fit his own promise. Some of us are walking through life thinking we need a new circumstance, when what we need is a new name. God may not do anything to fix our situation, but he can always change our name to fit his purposes.

17:9-14 The sign of God's renewed covenant with Abraham was that every male **must circumcise the flesh of [his] foreskin** (17:11). This painful procedure underscores the commitment God expected from those in covenant with him. Even though God was the primary agent in the covenant, his people were responsible to sacrifice in order to enter that agreement.

Circumcision had two unique areas of significance. First, it was a signal that men would carry the covenant, as we see this promise pass from Abraham to his son Isaac, to his son Jacob, and so on. Second, circumcision was to be a perpetual reminder to the people that God intended to remove impurity from their midst. Removing the male foreskin helped to prevent disease, and God used the practice to prefigure how his kingdom would operate: it would be purged of impurity and would pursue holiness.

17:15-16 Just as Abram received a new name from God (Abraham), so too did Sarai. By God's command, **Sarai** became **Sarah**, meaning "princess" (17:15). With this new name comes a renewed promise, that **she will produce nations; kings of peoples will come from her** (17:16).

17:17-22 Abraham found this as difficult to believe as we would, since he was pushing one hundred and Sarah was ninety. **He laughed** (17:17) because he couldn't take God seriously, so God decided to have a little fun with Abraham. He repeated the promise of Sarah bearing a son, but added, **you will name him Isaac** (17:19)—the name *Isaac* meaning "he laughs." For the rest of his life, every time Abraham would say his son's name, he would be reminded that he had laughed at the miracle God had promised. God always gets the last laugh.

17:23-27 Abraham immediately obeyed the command to circumcise himself and his men,

on that very day (17:23). Considering what the procedure entailed, I think this was nothing short of a miraculous act of faith. For believers today, circumcision no longer operates as the sign of God's kingdom. It has been replaced by baptism, the sign of the new covenant. Baptism serves as a sign that we are operating in accordance with God's covenant and allowing his kingdom rule to govern our lives.

❧ C. Sodom and Lot (18:1–19:38) ❧

18:1-2 Soon after Abraham's covenant of circumcision, he was visited by what appeared to be **three men standing near him** (18:2). But the text makes it clear that it was actually **the LORD** and two angels (18:1; 19:1). Like Old Testament appearances of the "angel of the LORD" or the "commander of the LORD's army" (see Josh 5:13-15; Judg 2:1-5; 13:1-23), this was a "Christophany," a preincarnate but visible manifestation of the Second Person of the Trinity.

18:3-8 Abraham did not realize at the time who these visitors were; nevertheless, he hurried to show them hospitality (18:3-4). God had decided to visit with Abraham, personally confirming what he had already promised many times. The picture here is a surprisingly intimate one: God sat and ate with Abraham for half a day, fellowshipping with him and surrounding his promise with his presence.

18:9-12 Every time God interacted with Abraham, he reminded him of the same promise. This time, though, the promise got more specific. **I will certainly come back to you in about a year's time**, God said, **and your wife Sarah will have a son!** (18:10). Sarah, who had her ear to the tent door, overheard this audacious promise. **She laughed to herself**—scoffed—at the silliness of the idea (18:12). Evidently Abraham had failed to pass along the lesson he had just learned about the folly of laughing at God.

18:13-15 God, of course, knew that Sarah was laughing, whether he heard it directly or not (18:13). In response, he asked the most important question of faith: **Is anything impossible for the LORD?** (18:14). In other words,

Sarah, did you forget who you are dealing with here? Do you think it's *hard* for a God who made billions of stars from literally nothing to make an old lady a mother?

Most of our faith problems go back to how we answer this question. We look at the facts and say, "I must be too old, too weak, too messed up. God can't work in *this* situation." But God invites us to look past the facts and see his face, to let the facts be swallowed up in faith. *Is anything impossible for the Lord?* No!

18:16-21 God had not just come to reinforce his promise to Abraham. He had come on a mission of judgment toward Sodom and Gomorrah, which he shared with Abraham as they prepared to leave (18:16, 20). He would **go down to see if what they have done justifies** the judgment planned (18:21), which some interpreters think means that God actually needed on-the-ground intelligence. But as the fully omniscient God, of course, he already had all the information he needed. He just wanted to make it plain that the coming destruction was just. The presence of God and his angels—and the way they were to be treated—would further verify that **the outcry against Sodom and Gomorrah** was **immense**, and that **their sin** was **extremely serious** (18:20). It consisted of gross immorality, violence, and oppression of the poor (see Ezek 16:49-50).

18:18-19 In the midst of this mess, God makes a beautiful statement about his vision for kingdom fathers, men who represent God, the ultimate Father. Kingdom fathers are **chosen** (18:19). If you're a man and you're a Christian, God has selected and elected you for a reason. You have a world-altering destiny that God intends you to fulfill (18:18).

A kingdom father also bears the responsibility to **command his children and his house after him to keep the way of the** **LORD** (18:19). Specifically, fathers are to teach and model before their children the duel responsibilities of righteousness (obedience to God's moral standards) and justice (the equitable and impartial application of God's moral law in society). God intends for men to lead their families. Our generation's fundamental problem is family breakdown, which has lead to a generation of children with few men to follow. So our youth either follow fools or

they follow themselves (which can turn out to be the same thing). God intends to use his men to represent him in the building of strong families and the raising of kingdom kids; that may be a weighty responsibility, but it's also a thrilling opportunity. Don't let it pass you by.

It would be in fulfilling his family responsibility that Abraham would see God's national promises fulfilled. This again highlights the crucial role that family plays in expanding God's kingdom agenda and building a stable society.

18:22-26 With the destruction of Sodom and Gomorrah imminent, God paused, yet again, to allow them another chance. This time Abraham would be a part of the forbearing process. Abraham appealed to God's justice, by saying, **Will you really sweep away the righteous with the wicked?** (18:23). What follows is a peculiar scene that sounds akin to the kind of haggling you would hear in a fruit market. Abraham was attempting to "talk God down," and surprisingly enough, God played along. **Will you . . . sweep away the righteous . . . if there are fifty righteous people in the city?** (18:23-24) Abraham asked. God responded, If I find fifty righteous people in the city of Sodom, I will spare the whole place for their sake (18:26).

18:27-33 The negotiation continued. For **forty-five** (18:28)? For **forty** (18:29)? **Thirty** (18:30)? **Twenty** (18:31)? Even just **ten** (18:32)? Each time God responded to Abraham's compassionate intercession by granting him his request. God was not only allowing, but was also *encouraging* Abraham to keep asking for more.

This entire scene corresponds with what we read in Matthew 5:13-16, where Jesus talks of believers as the "salt of the earth" and "light of the world." Our job, as members of God's kingdom, is to act as a preserving influence in a dark and dying world. Note that God would have spared the entire city if there had been just *ten* believers there! Righteous people, even a small minority of them, can promote righteousness in such a way that the entire society benefits (see Jer 29:7).

19:1-5 The text shifts from Abraham's conversation to the angels' journey into Sodom, and immediately we see a contrast in the "hospitality" that these angels are offered. Yes, Lot **prepared a feast and baked unleavened bread for them** (19:3), but it was not long before **the men of the city of Sodom, both young and old**, began pounding on Lot's door (19:4), demanding to release the men so they could **have sex with them** (19:5). The outcry against Sodom, it seems, took only a few hours to prove its claims. Sodom had descended into such a den of sin that visitors to the city could not be left in public alone for even a few hours without fear of being raped (19:3, 5).

19:6-8 Initially, we might view Lot sympathetically. After all, he saw two men in danger and brought them in. He took a great risk in doing so. What he does next, however, shows how much of Sodom's wicked culture he had absorbed. In his attempt to protect his angelic guests, Lot offered to give the lustful, riotous crowd his **two daughters** so that they could be raped instead (19:8). We are (and should be) repulsed by such an offer, which reveals Lot's moral ties to Sodom as well as his failure to believe that God would protect him. This contrast becomes all the more plain once the angels themselves strike the crowd with blindness (19:10-11), thankfully preventing Lot from following through on his disgusting plan.

19:9-14 With the mob beating down Lot's door, the angels decided to reveal God's plan to Lot. **We are about to destroy this place**, they warned (19:13). If **you have anyone else here**—anyone you want to rescue—now is the time to get them out (19:12). Lot tried, but was met with confusion and laughter from his daughters' husbands-to-be when he extended the invitation for them to leave town with him (19:14). There is no more dangerous place to be than hearing the warnings of God and shrugging them off as if they are a joke.

19:15-29 The potential sons-in-law refused to leave Sodom because they did not believe God's wrath was real. But even Lot, the reason for this rescue mission, **hesitated** to leave when the time came (19:16). The angels had to drag him, his wife, and his daughters out of the city by hand because they were all too attached to it. They had become

comfortable in a society that rejected God and his laws. Lot's wife showed the most hesitance—and received the due punishment for it. Even though the angels strictly warned them, **Don't look back and don't stop anywhere on the plain** (19:17), Lot's wife paused to look back, and instantly **became a pillar of salt** (19:26). She thus became a permanent monument of the consequences of disobedience and worldliness. Only because of God's promise to Abraham were Lot and his two daughters—a mere three people out of the entire city—saved from destruction (19:29).

The story of Sodom's destruction, while it clearly shows God's judgment against homosexuality, offers a much larger warning. In Luke 17:32 Jesus charged us to remember not the evil men of Sodom, but "Lot's wife," because our chief temptation is to become too attached to this world. Jesus teaches us to be in the world, working for the good of our neighbors, but not attached to the world in sinful ways, contaminated by its rebellion against God.

19:30-38 The conclusion to Lot's story is a pitiful one. His daughters, with their fiancés now dead, were so concerned about their marriage prospects that they devised a scheme to get Lot drunk and have sex with him (19:31-32). The plan worked, and **both of Lot's daughters became pregnant by their father** (19:36). However, as with every scheme cooked up in the minds of sinful man, this "success" would eventually turn out to be a disaster. The two sons these daughters produced, **Moab** and **Ben-ammi**, would become the patriarchs of the Moabites and Ammonites, ongoing enemies of God's people. When we try to solve God's "problems" for him, we only create more problems for ourselves.

D. Isaac: Birth, Sacrifice, and Quest for a Wife (20:1–24:67)

20:1-18 If you feel like you've heard this story before, you have. In Genesis 12:10-20, Abraham, fearing for his life, lied to Pharaoh about Sarah. He said she was his sister rather than his wife. God revealed Abraham's deception then, preventing Pharaoh from doing anything rash. In the end, Abraham left Egypt with more resources than when he had arrived.

Years later, Abraham, finding himself in a similar position—this time with the King Abimelech—decided to pull the same stunt. **Abraham said about his wife Sarah, "She is my sister"** (20:2). And even though Sarah was ninety years old, she was apparently still quite attractive. The king immediately brought her to himself (20:2). Before anything could happen, however, God approached Abimelech in a dream, giving him news of the real relationship between Abraham and Sarah (20:6-8). This is the first time we see Abraham called **a prophet** (20:7). Abraham, in spite of his sin, was still God's spokesman. But it seems intentional that God uses that word *now*, when Abraham is failing to act uprightly. Once again it is an unbelieving king, not Abraham, who does the virtuous and right thing. Abraham, the prophet, should be humiliated for being rebuked by a heathen king.

Abraham's actions before Abimelech were more dangerous than he probably realized. God had just promised to open Sarah's womb and let her conceive. The promise of a child, which Abraham and Sarah had been waiting on for twenty-five years, was on the cusp of fulfillment, but Abraham nearly threw it away. God himself had to intervene dramatically, threatening death to Abimelech (20:7) and closing the wombs of Abimelech's entire household (20:18) to keep his covenant intact.

21:1-7 It had taken twenty-five years, and the promise often seemed in doubt, but sure enough, **the LORD did for Sarah what he had promised** (21:1). She **became pregnant and bore a son to Abraham** (21:2). Abraham and his wife demonstrated their faith by naming the boy Isaac, just as God had told them (21:3). The name *Isaac*, we will remember, means "he laughs." But whereas the laughter of Abraham and Sarah had previously been scoffing and doubtful, with the fulfillment of the promise it transformed into the laughter of joy. Sarah herself recognized that everyone who heard her story would **laugh with [her]** (21:6), for what shows off the hilariously generous grace of God more than a couple

in their nineties having their first child? The grace of God often seems so absurd.

21:8-13 Isaac's birth might have transformed his parents' mocking into laughter, but his presence precipitated another instance of mocking. Ishmael—**the one Hagar the Egyptian had borne to Abraham** (21:9)—began to mock his half-brother Isaac. Clearly the tension between Hagar and Sarah had not fully dissipated, as the feud passed from mother to son. Sarah saw Ishmael as a threat to her son's inheritance (21:10). In this God saw an opportunity to remove Ishmael from the household, so there would be no threat to the promised seed. But while God shared Sarah's concern that Ishmael **not be a coheir with . . . Isaac** (21:10), he did not share her animosity toward Ishmael. He reassured Abraham that he would **also make a nation** of Ishmael **because he is [Abraham's] offspring** (21:13).

The apostle Paul uses this separation of Ishmael and Isaac in Galatians 4:21-31 to illustrate the difference between flesh and Spirit, law and grace. When the legitimate heir (that is, Spirit and grace) comes, there is no longer need for the illegitimate (that is, the flesh and law). In fact, the two cannot coexist. So the flesh must be removed if believers are to experience freedom and the enjoyment of the promise of God.

21:14-21 Hagar was sent into the wilderness for the second time, this time with her son Ishmael (21:14). As before, Hagar assumed that she would soon die. Out of water and unable to bear to watch her young son die of thirst, **she left the boy under one of the bushes** (21:15) and went a distance away to await their deaths. But *Ishmael* means "he hears," and just as God did before, **God heard the boy crying** (21:17). He provided a well (21:19), meeting their physical needs, and renewed the promise to **make [Ishmael] a great nation** (21:18), giving them spiritual hope for the journey ahead. Again God shows compassion for a single mother in distress.

21:22-32 Abraham's blessings continued to increase, which led to a new covenant with the powerful King Abimelech. Abimelech would receive some of Abraham's **flocks**

and herds (21:27). In return, Abraham would retain rights to the well in **Beer-sheba** (21:30-31), which means "Well of the Oath."

21:33-34 Planting trees, as Abraham did here (21:33), was not a common part of most Old Testament covenants. But the symbol was an important one, as it signified that Abraham intended to coexist in the land with other nations. This **tamarisk tree in Beer-sheba** (21:33) would be a sign of peace, security, and the appropriate kind of godly compromise. Abraham was doing what all believers should do: pursuing peace with his unbelieving neighbors without compromising his kingdom principles. The tree would also be a symbol of longevity, as Abraham anticipated that he (and his descendants) would stay on the land. This is why he refers to God as **the Everlasting God** (21:33) in this context.

22:1-2 By this point in the narrative, the promised son, Isaac, had become a young man. Abraham's dream had come true, but into this paradise God suddenly said, **Take your son ... and offer him ... as a burnt offering** (22:2). The author says this was God's way of testing Abraham (22:1), and what a devastating test it was! In its most basic terms, this test was a choice between God's blessing and God himself. Would Abraham obey God and respond in faith, even though God's new command was just as baffling—and even *more* painful—than any command he had previously been given?

The command is fraught with apparent contradictions. God's command seemed to contradict God's promises. How could God command murder? And how could such an action be explained to Sarah?

22:3 How would Abraham respond? The answer is given in that little clause, **Abraham got up early in the morning**. God told Abraham to give up the one blessing in his life that he treasured most—a legitimate son. Abraham's response was to obey immediately. He may not have understood *how* God would provide, but he knew *that* God would provide. So he avoided the counterfeits of partial obedience and delayed obedience (which are both really disobedience anyway), following God boldly into the unknown.

22:4-6 When Abraham and Isaac reached the mountain, Abraham told his servants, **The boy and I will go over there to worship; then we'll come back to you** (22:5). Somehow Abraham believed that he would be coming back down the mountain *with Isaac*. The book of Hebrews helps us understand what was going on in his head. The writer notes that Abraham "considered God to be able even to raise someone from the dead" (Heb 11:19). Abraham knew God's promise that Isaac would continue the line of blessing, but he also knew that God had commanded him to sacrifice Isaac. The only conclusion he could draw was that God would bring him back from death.

Abraham's belief in resurrection seems odd, especially when we realize that there had been no recorded instances of resurrection to this point. But don't forget: Abraham had already seen God's resurrection power. Sarah's womb had been "dead" for twenty-five years; Abraham himself was past the age for bearing children, too. The author of Hebrews says that in terms of reproduction, the couple was "as good as dead" (Heb 11:12). Yet from this death God brought new life. Abraham may not have had a front row seat to a literal resurrection, but he knew that the same resurrecting power that brought Isaac into the world would somehow keep him in it.

22:7-8 The situation began to get awkward when Isaac noticed the lack of an animal (22:7). Abraham responded by reassuring Isaac that **God himself** would **provide the lamb for the burnt offering** (22:8). Abraham knew he was in a situation that he couldn't fix. What he'd been asked to do felt like a contradiction, but instead of unraveling the contradiction himself, he decided to wait on God. Therefore, when God puts you in a contradiction that has no apparent solution, he alone must be trusted to resolve it.

22:9-12 When the moment of truth finally came, **Abraham reached out and took the knife to slaughter his son** (22:10). Thankfully, **the angel of the Lord called** out to him before he made the cut (22:11). Then this individual said something strange. **Now I**

know, he said, **that you fear God, since you have not withheld your only son from me** (22:12).

Many Bible students scratch their heads at this, because it sounds like God legitimately didn't know how Abraham would act. But God knows everything factual and potential. He hasn't, however, personally *experienced* everything he knows. For example, he knows all about sin, but he has never personally experienced committing sin (and never will). God had not yet experienced Abraham's obedience. He delights in experiencing what he already knows to be the case, just as a wife delights in experiencing the love that her husband proclaims. God wants to *feel* our commitment. This is why he became a man—so that he could sympathize with our weaknesses.

22:13 At the same time God stopped Abraham from sacrificing Isaac, **Abraham looked up and saw a ram caught in the thicket by its horns.** God's timing is funny like that. The ram must have been there the entire time, but Abraham didn't notice it until God wanted to reveal it. The answer to Abraham's problem was already supplied, but it was only revealed when Abraham took his step of obedience and faith. While Abraham walked up one side of the mountain with his problem, God had arranged it so that up the other side of the mountain was coming his answer. Please note, however, that God didn't reveal the answer until obedience was complete.

22:14 Abraham fittingly named the place *Yahweh-yireh*, which means **The LORD Will Provide.** Abraham believed that God was a provider before, but something about this event made that head knowledge turn into heart knowledge.

22:15-19 Abraham would have been content to walk back down the mountain and call this a win. But God wasn't done. He showed up again, repeating and expanding his promise to Abraham. **I will indeed bless you and make your offspring as numerous as the stars ... and the sand on the seashore** (22:17), and **all the nations of the earth will be blessed by your offspring** (22:18).

This sounds familiar. But then God takes it a step further. The author of Hebrews points out that [in verse 16] God makes an oath: **By myself I have sworn** (see Heb 6:13-18). What's the difference between an oath and a promise? God's promise is what he is going to do when all conditions have been met. It's a guarantee. But God's oath means that he's *ready* to do it. You may have to wait for a promise, but the oath means that the promise is well on its way to fulfillment. It is because of these two realities (promise and oath) that it is impossible for God to lie (see Heb 6:13-18). His veracity assumes both.

22:20-24 This short, seemingly incidental genealogy contains one name that should stick out to us—**Rebekah** (22:23). If Abraham's line was to continue, just as God had promised (and now sworn), then Isaac would require a wife. Rebekah would soon be that wife.

23:1 Sarah died at the age of 127 **years**, which may seem like a random detail. However, I see God's gracious provision here. Sarah was ninety years old when Isaac was born—not only too old to have children, but also too old to spend any significant time with them. And yet God gave Sarah almost four decades with her son. Even the span of our short lives rests in the hands of a God who cares about these details.

23:2-20 Why all this talk about a burial plot? Remember where Abraham was—**in Kiriath-arba (that is, Hebron) in the land of Canaan** (23:2). Abraham was in the land of promise, and saw in his wife's death the opportunity to seize the firstfruits of God's promise. This explains why he insisted upon paying **the full price** for his burial plot (23:9, 13), rather than receiving it as a gift, as Ephron and the other local leaders desired (23:6, 11). Abraham knew he could hold no lasting right to a *gifted* grave. An actual sale, on the other hand, with an exchange of money (23:15) and a company of witnesses (23:16), would give him a toehold in possessing the land of Canaan.

24:1-4 Abraham had begun to inherit the promises of God by this point. He had fathered Isaac, who had become grown. And with the burial plot in Kiriath-arba, he officially owned property in Canaan, God's promised land. But God had not just promised a little land and a few descendants to him. He promised descendants as numerous as the stars and as plentiful as sand. So it became crucial for Abraham to find Isaac a wife.

He commissioned **the elder of his household** (24:2), essentially his chief of staff, to go to his **land** and **family to take a wife for . . . Isaac** (24:4). Abraham wanted to be sure that Isaac stayed true to the one true God, and he remembered the lesson of Lot—who became far too comfortable surrounded by godless people in a heathen culture. Rather than let Isaac get entangled in the same net with the Canaanites, Abraham looked to his homeland for Isaac's wife. This decision was so serious that he made the servant pledge an oath by putting **[his] hand under [Abraham's] thigh** (24:2)—an intimate action commonly used in those days to affirm sacred oaths.

24:5-9 Eliezer had some questions. What if **the woman is unwilling** to leave (24:5)? Should Isaac move to be near her instead? Abraham redoubled his intentions for Isaac to remain in the promised land (24:6), reminding Eliezer that God himself promised to **give this land to [his] offspring** (24:7). He had faith that God would oversee the journey so that Eliezer would find the right wife. Too many today lack that faith when it comes to finding a spouse. Only those who are committed to God and remain confident in God can expect to receive their romantic counterpart from God.

24:10-14 The servant stepped out in faith and prayed for God to reveal the right mate for Isaac. The key piece of prayer is the specific request for **the girl** to whom he would say, **Please lower your water jug so that I may drink** to respond by saying, **Drink, and I'll water your camels also** (24:14). This would be an act of tremendous hospitality. It was customary in those days to offer water to strangers. It was incredibly rare, however, to offer to water a stranger's animals. Eliezer's entourage was not small either. He had brought **ten of his master's camels** (24:10), and camels can drink up to twenty-five gallons of water.

24:15-21 To bring enough water for all the camels would have required Rebekah to haul water back and forth from the well for hours. And yet without any prodding, after offering water to Abraham's servant, she also offered to **draw water for [his] camels until they have had enough to drink** (24:19). Not only that, but she also **hurried to the well** to do it (24:20). Rebekah showed herself to be a woman with a servant's heart and a bodybuilder's strength!

24:22-33 Rebekah may have been a perfect match in terms of character, but Eliezer was still wondering whether she was from the right family. After all, he had been given specific orders to take a wife from Abraham's clan (24:4). Imagine his relief and thrill when Rebekah introduced herself as **the daughter of Bethuel son of Milcah, whom she bore to Nahor** (24:24). It may seem odd to us, but it was comforting to Eliezer to realize that Rebekah was Isaac's cousin.

24:34-48 We should not overlook the faithfulness of the servant throughout this story; he kept his mission in front of him at all times. He had obviously rehearsed the instructions given to him by Abraham so frequently that he was able to recount the entire interaction, in extreme detail, at a moment's notice. This lengthy retelling proves how serious his task was. It also shows that marriage relationships are much more important than a bride and groom might think. The purpose of marriage is not simply personal happiness, but kingdom fulfillment.

24:49-59 The moment of truth came when the servant plainly asked Rebekah's family whether they would bless the marriage (24:49). Laban and Bethuel acknowledged that **this is from the Lord**, who had orchestrated the entire event (24:50). Interestingly, Rebekah too approved of the marriage (24:58), even though she had never seen Isaac. Rebekah was spiritual enough to submit her entire future to a husband she didn't even know, because she was convinced God was at work.

24:60 Rebekah's family sent her out with a blessing that ought to sound familiar: **May**

your offspring possess the city gates of their enemies. There is no indication that the family knew of the promise to Abraham, which was phrased in precisely the same way (22:17). What may at first seem a coincidence is further proof of God's involvement.

24:61-67 Just as Rebekah showed faith in agreeing to marry Isaac, Isaac also trusted God (and his father) with this match. Rebekah had her face covered with a **veil** (24:65) until the moment of the wedding, so Isaac needed to believe that the woman God had chosen would not only fit what he needed but would also be appealing to him. Apparently she was, because even though Isaac was grieving **his mother's death**, Rebekah was able to bring him comfort and love (24:67).

III. JACOB (25:1–36:43)

A. Jacob the Deceiver and Esau the Impulsive (25:1–28:9)

25:1-6 The author mentions Abraham taking **another wife** (25:1) without seeming to comment on whether Sarah was still living when he did or the ethics surrounding the decision. Importantly, although God's established order was for marriage to be between one man and one woman (2:21-24), polygamy crept in early. Though the Old Testament does not condemn polygamy as frequently as we might expect, we see strong hints—even here—that the practice was problematic. Isaac, after all, was the son of promise, so Abraham **gave everything he owned to Isaac** (25:5). The **sons of his concubines** were only given a few gifts and sent eastward (25:6)—**the East,** as we will recall, being a recurring negative symbol throughout Genesis.

25:7-10 When Abraham **took his last breath and died** (25:8), it brought together his two previously estranged sons. Together they **buried him in the cave of Machpelah** (25:9) **...with his wife Sarah** (25:10). But the family strife had hardly been buried with the patriarch.

25:11-18 We find another genealogy here, which often indicates a shift in the plot. In this case, the author wants to confirm God's promise to Isaac (25:11), contrasting that with Ishmael. Even though Ishmael would have a lineage of his own (25:12-26) and would live a lengthy life (25:17), the story leaves him behind and moves toward Isaac and his descendants.

Names sometimes referred to the actual skin tone of dark-complexioned people. For example, **Kedar** (25:13) means "to be dark." Thus, the Kedarites are a dark-skinned people.

25:19-23 Isaac and Rebekah encountered a problem similar to Abraham and Sarah's: Rebekah was unable to have children (25:21). We aren't given as much insight into Rebekah's struggle as we got with Sarah's, but note that they could not conceive for *twenty* years (25:20, 26). When God answered Isaac's prayer to let her conceive, though, he did so in duplicate! As Rebekah began to wonder why her pregnancy was so active (25:22), God answered, **Two nations are in your womb; two peoples will come from you and be separated** (25:23). Even before their births, Jacob and Esau were battling one another, foreshadowing the coming conflict between their two nations, Israel and Edom. God also let Rebekah know another surprising detail about these twins. Unlike the custom of the day, in which the older son would get the birthright and the blessing, **the older [would] serve the younger** (25:23).

25:24-26 The twins were finally born. The older was **covered with** red **hair like a fur coat, and they named him Esau** (25:25). He was also called *Edom* (see 25:30), which is the Hebrew word for "red." The younger **came out grasping Esau's heel with his hand.** So they **named** him **Jacob,** which means, "he grasps the heel" (25:26). Jacob's name is an important one, because it can also mean, "he strives" or "he deceives." Both meanings prove prophetic over the course of his life—the deception part coming into play in just the next few verses.

25:27-28 Personality differences are an enormous factor in the conflict between Jacob and Esau. Esau was outgoing, while Jacob was a homebody (25:27). By itself this may not have been a problem, but it apparently led the parents to choose favorites. **Isaac loved Esau** because he was a "man's man," and **Rebekah loved Jacob** because he loved spending time at home (25:28). Isaac and Rebekah were as much to blame as anyone in the feud between the boys.

25:29-34 One day, as Esau arrived famished from a day of hunting, he made an incredibly foolish trade. Esau gave his inheritance to Jacob in exchange for a bowl of food. We see here the character flaws of both sons. Jacob, quick to seize upon Esau's hunger, immediately decided to squeeze him for all he was worth: **Sell me your birthright** (25:31). He even made sure to put Esau on the hook by having him swear an oath (25:33). Jacob's "grasping" and deceiving ways are on full display here.

Esau, on the other hand, proved to be impulsive and shortsighted. When faced with the prospect of losing his double inheritance, he reasoned, **I'm about to die** (from hunger), **so what good is a birthright to me?** (25:32). In other words, he settled for temporary satisfaction over hanging on to something much more spiritually valuable. This is why the author says **Esau despised his birthright**, because he considered it so insignificant that a single bowl of **lentil stew** became more important to him (25:34).

The author of Hebrews cautions his readers to avoid being an "immoral or irreverent person like Esau" (Heb 12:16). Heed the warning: never let physical satisfaction take precedence over spiritual priorities. Whenever you do, you are despising that which is more valuable. Our generation, saturated with lies about sex, needs this warning now more than ever. Don't be the impulsive fool that Esau was, throwing away your future for momentary pleasure.

26:1-11 If this short account sounds familiar, it should. Isaac's father Abraham tried the

same trick with Sarah (twice!)—with similar results. The context is similar: Isaac, like Abraham, was facing **famine** (26:1). Because of the famine, he moved into the region ruled by **Abimelech** (26:2). Out of fear for his life (26:9), he lied to Abimelech by calling his wife his **sister** (26:7), but Abimelech soon learned the truth (26:8). And just as before, a ruler both scolded a man in this family for his deception and warned his own people not to touch the woman involved (26:10). Once more, we see God's commitment to keep his covenant, since it would be necessary that the line of descent remain uncontaminated.

It is ironic that in the midst of a scene of Isaac's fear and unfaithfulness, we find a repetition of God's covenant to him. Isaac, like Abraham, was promised **lands . . . offspring as numerous as the stars**, and a blessing that would be for **all the nations of the earth** (26:3-4). This promise—personal, national, and international—was unconditionally made to Abraham and passed on to Isaac despite his faithlessness.

26:12-22 God's hand was on Isaac, so when he **sowed seed in that land . . . he reaped a hundred times what was sown** (26:12). His flocks also multiplied greatly (26:13-14). Unfortunately, the Philistines of the area grew envious of Isaac's success, so they attempted to sabotage Isaac by stopping **up all the wells** (26:15). In an agrarian society, wells indicated dominion. Owning one meant that you essentially governed the surrounding area. Rather than quarrel over specific wells, however, Isaac avoided conflict by constantly moving and digging new wells (26:19-21). Eventually God provided an uncontested well—and, by extension, a space for Isaac to **be fruitful in the land** (26:22).

26:23-25 As God continued to provide for Isaac, he also reminded him of the promise. **I will bless you and multiply your offspring**, God told Isaac, adding a new promise: **Do not be afraid, for I am with you** (26:24). God knew fear was a problem for Isaac, so while he confirmed his promise he also confirmed his presence. In response, Isaac did what we all should do, demonstrating faith by fresh worship. He **called on the name of the LORD** (26:25).

26:26-33 Abimelech recognized that God was with Isaac, so he sought to make a treaty with him (26:28-29). This is a partial fulfillment of the promise to Abraham and Isaac that the Gentiles would share in the blessings of God's people. Abimelech even referred to God as **the Lord** (26:29), using God's covenant name. He had grown in his understanding of God through his association with Isaac—just as people today are meant to grow closer to God because of the witness of his people.

26:34-35 Meanwhile, even though God had been blessing Isaac, Esau was making **life bitter for Isaac and Rebekah** (26:35) by marrying two **Hethite** women (26:34). Rebellion against his parents' wishes further illustrates why Esau was not fit to carry on the covenant. Rather than allowing his father to help him choose an acceptable spouse, he followed his own impulses and took not just one wife, but two from the idolatrous nations around him.

27:1-4 As Isaac grew older and anticipated his death, he decided to impart his blessing to Esau. Jacob may have already stolen the birthright—the physical inheritance—but Esau still had the chance to inherit his father's blessing—the more important spiritual inheritance. The blessing represented the umbrella of God's operation in the family line, so that no matter what showers and storms were going on around them, they were under cover.

Isaac began the ritual of passing on his blessing by calling **his older son Esau** to him and requesting **a delicious meal . . . so that [he could] bless [him] before [he died]** (27:1, 4). Isaac preferred Esau's wild game and wanted him to hunt for an animal that they could share during this sacred time.

27:5-17 Esau went to the field to hunt some game (27:5), just as his father had ordered, but his mother, Rebekah, had other plans. Calling in Jacob, she hatched a plot: Jacob would **go to the flock**, pick out **two . . . young goats**, and mom would **make them into a delicious meal** for Isaac (27:9). Then Isaac, whose "eyes were so weak that he could not see" (27:1), would be deceived and bless Jacob rather than Esau. When Jacob objected,

Esau is a hairy man, but I am a man with smooth skin (27:11), his mother revealed the rest of her plan. She would take **the skins of the young goats** and put them on Jacob's **hands and the smooth part of his neck** (27:16). Evidently Esau was *so* hairy that the feel (and odor! cf. 27:27) of a dead goat was a sufficient disguise.

27:18-25 When Jacob approached his father Isaac, the ruse almost didn't work because of Jacob's unique **voice** (27:22). But when **Jacob came closer**, the hairy hands and neck did the trick (27:22-23). All the while Jacob was lying, adopting the name of Esau (27:19). Three times, in fact, Isaac asked Jacob if he was *really* Esau, and without a hesitation, Jacob the deceiver assured him (27:19, 21-22, 24). Worst of all, Jacob even used God's name in vain, explaining that he was able to find the goat so quickly because **the Lord your God made it happen** (27:20).

27:26-27 The transfer of blessing always included meaningful touch, which is why Isaac implored Jacob to **come closer and kiss [him]** (27:26). Touch symbolized identification and intimacy.

27:28 Isaac passed on his most valuable possession, the blessing he had received from his father Abraham, to Jacob. **May God give to you—from the dew of the sky and from the richness of the land—an abundance of grain and new wine**. In other words, heaven is going to rain down everything you need to get the promises of God fulfilled, son. The agricultural metaphor is a vivid one: it doesn't matter how hard you work on the land if God doesn't send the rain. Far too many of us are working hard to make something of our lives without the blessing that can only come raining down from heaven. We don't need to work harder; we need to put ourselves in a position to receive God's blessing.

27:29 Isaac repeated the classic covenant that he had received from his father: **those who curse you will be cursed, and those who bless you will be blessed**. The center of God's blessing would now rest on Jacob, as deceptive as he was. But Isaac actually goes back further than Abraham, to Adam. In saying, **May peoples serve you and nations bow in worship to you,** Isaac was recalling the original kingdom authority given to Adam and Eve. With the blessing comes the responsibility to use our God-given authority, skills, talents, gifts, and opportunities—in whatever "garden" he has placed us—to lead in a way that honors God.

27:30-34 The plot thickens because just as **Jacob had left the presence of his father Isaac, his brother Esau arrived from his hunting** (27:30). By the time Isaac has realized what happened, the blessing cannot be revoked (27:33). Esau's response is simultaneously pitiful and tragic. **He cried out with a loud and bitter cry** (27:34), probably loud enough for Jacob, who wasn't far off, to overhear. This was a gut-wrenching wail from a man who realized that his entire future had been snatched out of his hands.

27:34-38 Esau's insistence on receiving some blessing from his father mirrors the heart cry of so many in our society: **Bless me too, my father** (27:34)! Esau shouted with increasing desperation (27:38). How many young people today, whether they know how to articulate it or not, are crying out for their fathers simply to speak a simple word of blessing into their lives?

27:39-41 In the end, Esau received a word from his father, but it was far from a blessing. Rather than receiving "from the dew of the sky and from the richness of the land" (27:28), Esau was told that his **dwelling place** would be **away from the richness of the land** and **away from the dew of the sky** (27:39). No wonder, then, that **Esau held a grudge against Jacob,** plotting to kill him (27:41).

27:42-46 Jacob's mother, Rebekah, ever the eavesdropper, found out about Esau's murderous intent in time to hatch another plot. Jacob would **flee at once** to Rebekah's **brother Laban in Haran** (27:43), hiding out there until Esau's rage could cool (27:44-45). As a positive side effect of this plan, she reasoned, Jacob would also be more inclined to marry someone within their clan—rather than the **Hethite girls** that had been making Rebekah's life so miserable (27:46).

28:1-2 Isaac, in rare agreement with his wife, sent Jacob out with a commission against marrying **a Canaanite girl** (28:1). Instead, Jacob was charged to **marry one of the daughters of Laban** (28:2), a near kinsman—just as Isaac had gotten his wife Rebekah through this interconnected family line. Even in the midst of Jacob's deception, God was at work to keep the line of succession pure.

28:3-5 Isaac reiterated the promise God had made, first to his father, then to him. God would bless Jacob and make him **fruitful and multiply** (28:3), giving his **offspring the blessing of Abraham** so that he would **possess the land** (28:4). Isaac knew that more was at stake than merely keeping Isaac alive. God had a larger plan in store for Jacob.

28:6-9 Poor Esau, attempting to placate and please his father (and possibly get back some of the blessing), tried to emulate what Jacob was doing. So he **went to Paddan-aram** (28:7) to get a wife, avoiding the **Canaanite women** that his **father Isaac disapproved of** (28:8). Yet **Esau went to Ishmael and married** (28:9). This was *closer* to the pure line, but still not the line itself. Clearly Esau still didn't get the basics of God's promise. He did what made sense to him based on what he knew, never realizing that this wasn't a righteous action that God wanted.

⤜ *B. A Holy God, a Beautiful Woman, and a Deceptive Uncle (28:10–29:29)* ⤐

28:10-12 Jacob, now a fugitive on the run, found himself at an ordinary place. His circumstances were so grim that the only pillow he had was a rock (28:11). Yet in this ordinary place, in these dire circumstances, he would soon have an extraordinary experience. That night, **he dreamed** that **a stairway was set on the ground with its top reaching the sky, and God's angels were going up and down on it** (28:12). Jacob was watching divine activity at work even in a messy human situation. Prior to this dream, all he could see was the mess. But God opened his eyes to a spiritual reality that transformed his viewpoint.

28:13 Not only were there angels marching up and down this stairway, but also the Lord was **standing there beside [Jacob]**. God, you see, was watching over Jacob, even before Jacob had begun dreaming. Now Jacob got to *see* it.

28:14-15 Jacob didn't just get a vision from God. He also got a word from God. The word for Jacob was a confirmation of the promise to Abraham and Isaac: **Your offspring will be like the dust of the earth, and . . . all the peoples on earth will be blessed through you** (28:14). This is the first time Jacob heard that promise from God himself. It wasn't new information, but the information became real because he finally realized that it was God's promise. God often does something similar for us, confirming what we may have heard a thousand times— through hymns, or preaching, or reading the Bible—but for whatever reason, he illuminates that word so that we hear the Spirit speaking *to us*.

28:16 When **Jacob awoke from his sleep**, he immediately recognized what had happened. **Surely the LORD is in this place**, he concluded, **and I did not know it.** The place had not changed. It was still just a desert with only a rock for a pillow. But in that place, God showed up. He showed up to Jacob in his brokenness and weariness, because he needed Jacob to come to the end of himself before he could begin relying on God.

28:17 We know Jacob had a fresh encounter with God because **he was afraid**—no longer afraid of Esau, but afraid of the one true God. A lesser fear had been driven out by a greater fear, because the power of God overruled the power of Esau.

28:18-22 Jacob had fallen asleep in "a certain place" (28:11), but having seen God, he woke up and gave the place a sacred name—**Bethel** (28:19). What had been a dark place became a sacred space. Nothing had changed in Jacob's circumstances. All that had changed was Jacob getting a fresh vision of God. And that transformed everything. The pagan city of **Luz** suddenly became **Bethel**, literally the "house of God" (28:19). Jacob **poured oil on top of** the very same stone that had been his rough pillow (28:18), making it the cornerstone of an altar to God (28:22). And Jacob **made a vow** (28:20) to God, promising to **give to [him] a tenth** (28:22). He sanctified this dark location, recognizing the supernatural at work, invisibly, right there in the gritty and tough natural world.

29:1-8 Jacob, now with a fresh vision of God, **resumed his journey** toward his clan (29:1), looking for a bride. Through providential circumstances, he met **Rachel**, a woman of Laban's household, part of his extended family (29:5-6). The scene is similar to that of Isaac and Rebekah's meeting: Rachel, like Rebekah, proved her industrious character by leading her sheep (29:9) even while the other shepherds were lazily lounging about (29:8).

29:9-12 Jacob, upon seeing Rachel, showed his own industrious spirit. He jumped up, **rolled the stone from the opening and watered his uncle Laban's sheep** (29:10). The stones covering wells in those days were intentionally large, meant to be moved by several men. But Jacob, smitten with love upon seeing the beautiful Rachel (29:17), shifted the thing over all on his own. Rachel, too, seemed immediately taken with Jacob, because she **ran**—not a common action back then—**and told her father** (29:12).

29:13-20 What follows the meeting between Jacob and Rachel is testimony both to Jacob's devotion and Laban's deceit. Laban rushed to Jacob, **hugged him and kissed him**, and **took him to his house** (29:13), acknowledging him as **my own flesh and blood** (29:14). On the surface, Laban seemed to treat Jacob like close family. Yet when Jacob requested to marry his beloved daughter, Laban deceived him. Still penniless at this point, Jacob agreed to **work for . . . seven years** to afford a dowry for Laban's **younger daughter Rachel** (29:18). Laban agreed (29:19), and the years flew by for Jacob, **because of his love for her** (29:20).

29:21-25 On the honeymoon, however, Jacob experienced the shock of his life. **Laban** had taken **his daughter Leah and gave her to Jacob, and he slept with her** (29:23). Jacob's surprise at seeing Leah's face in dawn's light is captured in what has to be the most profound understatement in the Bible: **When morning came, there was Leah**! Leah, indeed! Understandably upset by the trick, Jacob confronted Laban (29:25).

29:26 Apparently aware of some of Jacob's history with Esau, Laban replied that it was **not the custom . . . to give the younger daughter in marriage before the firstborn.** The statement was intentionally chosen to remind Jacob of his own trickster past. Laban had out-tricked his nephew under the very same scenario that Jacob had manipulated his older brother Esau. The younger and the older had been swapped, except this time Jacob was on the short end of the trick. He was experiencing what the apostle Paul calls the law of sowing and reaping (see Gal 6:7-8). A person reaps what he sows; or, as we would say it, what goes around comes around. Our actions, righteous or unrighteous, will always bear fruit in keeping with the roots.

29:27-29 Jacob, realizing that he had no basis for "righteous" anger, accepted the marriage to Leah (29:27-28). But he was still in love with Rachel, so he agreed to marry her too for the dowry of *another* seven years of labor (29:27-30). One wonders whether these "flew by" as quickly as the first seven!

↣ C. Jacob Multiplies, Struggles with God, and Meets Esau Again
(29:30–33:20) ↢

29:30-35 Difficulties caused by Laban's actions continued as Jacob's family began to grow. Leah and Rachel, competing for Jacob's affection, began a race to produce children. Their sons would ultimately become the patriarchs of the twelve tribes of Israel, but that complex family tree was born out of conflict.

The conflict began because Jacob **loved Rachel more than Leah** (29:30). God, recognizing that **Leah was unloved, . . . opened her womb** before Rachel's (29:31). The names of Leah's sons reflected her marital situation. The first she named **Reuben**, which sounds

like "has seen my affliction" (29:32) in the Hebrew language in which Genesis was written. Even in the loveless relationship with her husband, she expressed faith in God, believing that he knew the reality of her circumstances. When she conceived again, she named the second son **Simeon**, which sounds like "has heard" (29:33). Again, Leah knew that God had loved her even though Jacob had not. With the third son, **Levi**, whose name sounds like "attached to" in Hebrew, Leah hoped that Jacob would develop an attachment to her (29:34). But he wouldn't, so with son number four, **Judah**, which sounds like "praise," Leah turned her full attention to God, saying, **This time I will praise the LORD** (29:35). Her marital circumstance had not changed, but she chose to praise God *despite* her challenges.

30:1-8 Rachel was also having family difficulties, because her sister was bearing children while she wasn't. **She envied her sister** and felt like she was dying inside (30:1). Jacob **became angry with Rachel** and didn't offer much reassurance, other than the true—but rather cold—reminder that God **has withheld offspring from you** (30:2). So Rachel did what Sarah had done, seeking a human solution to her problem. She offered to Jacob her servant Bilhah as a surrogate mom, who would have kids on her behalf (30:3-4). The plan worked, resulting in two sons—**Dan** and **Naphtali** (30:6-8).

30:9-13 Not to be outdone, Leah responded in kind, offering *her* servant Zilpah to Jacob as a surrogate (30:9). Her human solution worked as well as Sarah's, and two more sons—**Gad** and **Asher**—entered the mix (30:11-13).

30:14-24 The sisters' manipulative competition for Jacob's affection continued, this time leading to Reuben's involvement. Finding **some mandrakes in the field** (30:14), which were fruits believed to help women conceive, Reuben brought them to his mother Leah, who agreed to share some with Rachel in exchange for another night with Jacob (30:15). Leah conceived again—and again—bearing **Issachar** and **Zebulun** (30:18, 20). Then Rachel finally had her first child, **Joseph** (30:22-24).

The drama between Rachel and Leah, which rivals anything modern soap operas could produce, reveals God's ability to graciously meet our needs in all things. In spite of the sisters' human (and sinful) approaches to fixing their situations, God still blessed and provided for them. Their sinful tactics continued to make matters confusing and painful, but God was gracious to mitigate against the damage.

30:25-36 Jacob had arrived in Laban's house poor and alone. But by this point God had multiplied him tremendously, so he desired to return to his **homeland** (30:25). Laban, however, knew how beneficial Jacob was to his business; he wanted to strike a deal for Jacob to stay (30:27-28). So Jacob offered to stay if only he could have the **speckled or spotted . . . dark-colored sheep among the lambs** and goats (30:32). These were considered less valuable, so Laban immediately accepted the deal (30:34). He separated the flock to protect his investment (30:36), thinking he had, once again, gotten the better of Jacob.

30:37-43 No husbandry manual teaches that animals that breed in the sight of peeled branches (30:38) produce speckled offspring. Jacob was attempting to selectively breed speckled sheep, but God was the one supernaturally guiding the process. In the end, **the weak sheep belonged to Laban and the stronger ones to Jacob** (30:42), and Jacob **became very rich** (30:43). This is a reminder that it doesn't matter how good a deal seems in human terms; the man on whose side God stands will have the better deal.

31:1-3 Jacob's continued success became an annoyance to Laban, which Jacob recognized (31:2). God was using the conflict to call Jacob **back to the land of [his] fathers and to [his] family** (31:3). God often does this, allowing conflicts to create new directions in our lives, breaking off relationships with those who are not moving toward him so that we can pursue him with greater focus.

31:4-16 Jacob revealed his plans to his wives, letting them know that God himself had commanded him to **get up, leave this land, and return to [his] native land** (31:13). Rachel and Leah responded by following Jacob's leadership (31:16), proving that the best way for a man to lead his wife is by communicating where God is leading him.

31:17-35 Jacob rallied his family and his flocks and left, **not telling [Laban] that he was fleeing** (31:20). Laban didn't realize what had happened until three days later (31:22), but as soon as he did, he rushed after Jacob (31:23). A week later the two parties met, and Laban scolded Jacob for sneaking away, taking his **daughters away like prisoners of war** (31:26). What had most irked Laban, however, was the disappearance of his household gods (31:30), which Rachel had stolen on their way out of town (see 31:19). Perhaps she took them because she, like her father, believed they brought good luck. Perhaps she was just paying her father back for the terrible way he had treated her and Jacob. Either way, her theft was risky, and she was only able to cover it up by stashing the idols under a saddle, sitting on it, and explaining that she was having her **period** (31:35) and therefore couldn't rise.

31:36-55 Jacob, unaware that Rachel really had committed this crime, went on a counter-attack against Laban. He chronicled all of the ways that he had worked hard for Laban while Laban only took advantage of him (31:38-41). Laban remained unmoved, responding, **the daughters [you took] are my daughters, the sons, my sons; and the flocks, my flocks** (31:43)—which was not true, as he had given the daughters in marriage and agreed to give Jacob the speckled flocks. But realizing that he couldn't weasel his way out of this situation, Laban tried to limit the loss, proposing that a **covenant** be made between them (31:44). The terms of the covenant were meant to keep Jacob and Laban apart (31:52), and God was at work through Laban's covenant to finally end the connection between the two men.

32:1-2 Having come out of a crisis with Laban and about to enter another potential crisis with his brother Esau, Jacob was in need of divine help. God sent **angels** to meet Jacob and assure him of God's presence and protection (32:1). The battle before him, like the battle behind him, would be primarily spiritual in nature, so before addressing anything physical, God wanted to reveal to Jacob his own spiritual authority.

32:3-8 Jacob sent messengers . . . to his brother Esau (32:3) in an attempt to **seek** Esau's **favor** and reestablish their broken relationship (32:5). Imagine Jacob's surprise and dread, then, when a messenger returned with news that Esau was **coming to meet [him]—and he has four hundred men with him** (32:6). Jacob assumed, reasonably so, that Esau was out for vengeance.

32:9-12 Jacob's fear drove him to plead with God for deliverance (32:11). His short prayer is a model for the way we should pray, too: he approached God with humility (32:10), reminded God of his promises (32:9), and asked God to act in accordance with those promises (32:12).

32:13-23 Jacob prayed, but he also devised a plan. He **took part of what he had** and sent it ahead as a gift for Esau (32:13), hoping to soothe his wrath. And in case the first gift didn't do the trick, he arranged for a couple more, just to be sure (32:19-20). Jacob still wasn't confident that God would answer the prayer he had just prayed!

32:24-25 On the night before his big confrontation with his supposedly murderous brother, Jacob was suddenly jumped by **a man** who **wrestled with him until daybreak** (32:24). An all-night wrestling match will make you weary enough, but with one touch of **Jacob's hip socket** this mysterious stranger **dislocated his hip** (32:25). If Jacob had been unable to best Esau physically before this fight, now he couldn't even run from him. He was alone, afraid, and completely broken—just where God wanted him to be.

32:26-28 In the middle of the fight, Jacob struck up a conversation. **Bless me** (32:26), he demanded, because he realized that this physical altercation was about something much bigger. The wrestler responded by asking, **What is your name** (32:27)? Jacob

responded with the identity he had for himself: I'm a trickster and a jiver, which is what the name **Jacob** means. But the man responded, **Your name will no longer be Jacob**, but **it will be Israel** (32:28). In other words, he said, you don't operate by schemes anymore. Now you'll be identified by the fact that you've wrestled with God.

32:29 Jacob, now Israel, responded by asking for the name of the wrestler. But the man responded with a scoff, **Why do you ask my name?** Think about it: this man had just given Jacob the name "Israel" because he had **struggled with God** (32:28). With *God!* Jacob had been given the name of the wrestler already.

32:30-32 Just like he had done when he woke from his dream of the ladder to heaven, Jacob responded to God's presence with the shock that **[his] life has been spared** (32:30). And yet his life would never be the same, because he was now **limping because of his hip** (32:31). This suggests that any man God blesses will possess a limp. God will create something in that person's life that makes him despair of his own strength and lean on the Lord's instead. Jacob's limp, in fact, was so significant to his blessing that when the author of Hebrews mentioned Jacob's demonstration of faith, he mentioned Jacob's walking "staff" (see Heb 11:21). It's as if out of all the colorful scenes in Jacob's life, the writer of Hebrews wanted to say, "In the end, Jacob was a man who was forced to lean on God."

33:1-7 As **Esau** and his army of **four hundred men** approached, Jacob **bowed to the ground seven times** (33:3), humbling himself before Esau. To Jacob's surprise, Esau **ran to meet him, hugged him, threw his arms around him, and kissed him** (33:4). Something had changed in Esau so that he no longer sought vengeance, but reconciliation.

33:8-11 Jacob had sent a bevy of gifts to Esau to prevent Esau from attacking. But considering Esau's forgiving mood, it seemed that the gifts might prove unnecessary (33:9). But Jacob insisted that Esau share in his blessing,

because God [had] been gracious (33:11). This suggests that we become truly generous, not when we give out of compulsion, but when we realize that God has given us all we possess.

33:12-17 Fearing a possible change of heart, Jacob avoided traveling any further with Esau. Using his **children** and his **flocks** as an excuse (33:13), he appealed to Esau to **go ahead** while Jacob himself would **continue on slowly** (33:14). Once Esau was out of sight and **on his way back to Seir** (33:16), Jacob changed directions and **went to Succoth**, which was in exactly the opposite direction (33:17).

33:18-20 Jacob **arrived safely at Shechem in the land of Canaan** (33:18) and, like Abraham, **set up an altar there** (33:20). He acknowledged that God had indeed brought him back to the land of promise.

✸ D. The Defilement of Dinah and the Return to Bethel (34:1–36:43) ✵

34:1-4 **Dinah**, the only daughter of Jacob, **went out to see some of the young women of the area** (34:1), likely desiring to know how they lived. But during her visit, a man named **Shechem**, the son of **the region's chieftain . . . took her and raped her** (34:2). Adding insult to injury, he then decided that **he loved the young girl** (34:3) and wanted to marry her (34:4).

34:5-7 **Jacob heard that Shechem had defiled his daughter Dinah** (34:5) and that Shechem desired to marry her (34:8), but his response was surprisingly mute (34:5). Instead, it was **Jacob's sons** who became **deeply grieved and very angry**, rightly calling Shechem's actions an **outrage** that **should not be done** (34:7).

34:8-24 Shechem's father Hamor seemed unaware of Jacob's sons' rage, because he pursued the marriage deal further, presenting intermarriage between the two families as a profitable situation for everybody involved (34:10). Jacob's sons, taking after their

father's old ways, **answered Shechem and his father Hamor deceitfully** (34:13), plotting to take Shechem down by surprise. They required Shechem, Hamor, and all of their men to be **circumcised**, allegedly to make the marriage pure (34:14-16). Hamor and company considered this a small price to pay for a bride (34:19) and all of Jacob's **possessions** (34:23), so they eagerly agreed (34:24).

34:25-31 But Jacob's sons had no interest at all in a deal. The circumcision they required was a ruse to weaken the men, and **when they were still in pain**, two of Dinah's brothers, **Simeon and Levi**, avenged their sister's honor and slaughtered all the men of the town (34:25). They **plundered the city** as well (34:27), leaving Hamor's people devastated (34:29). Jacob, thinking of his long-term prospects in the land, was not pleased with the attack. He feared retribution from the other Canaanites in the area, who were much more numerous than they (34:30).

Most of the men in this story respond in ways that show little faith in God: Shechem violated God's just laws and did violence to an innocent woman; Jacob didn't trust that God would maintain his family in the land like he had promised; and Jacob's sons used a sacred symbol of the covenant with God as a trick to murder far more people than were guilty.

35:1 The violence of Simeon and Levi (34:25) had Jacob terrified for his life. In the midst of this fear, God showed up with a new command: **Get up! Go to Bethel and settle there**. God's timing is never accidental. He spoke to Jacob in the middle of a family crisis because he knew Jacob was desperate enough to listen. Sometimes we should thank God for putting us flat on our backs, because only then are we facing the right direction.

35:2 Jacob experienced a personal revival, which spilled over into a family revival. After completely abdicating his leadership role during the Dinah debacle, he finally manned up. In Jacob's revival, we see the three steps that anyone can follow when returning to God.

First, he said, **get rid of the foreign gods that are among you**. Rachel, Jacob's favorite wife, had snatched some of her father's household gods. For the last twenty years, apparently, those idols had been in Jacob's household. Jacob announced it was time to make a clean break and put them away for good. Second, he said, **purify yourselves.** This is an extension of the first point. Get the idols out of your life, and remove the sin from your midst, too. Third, **change your clothes.** Changing garments symbolizes a reorienting of life. For instance, when a judge puts on his robe, he's not an ordinary man anymore; he has authority. In revival, God expects us to change our position, reorienting ourselves so that God's authority can flow through us.

35:3 Jacob's revival hinged on the specific place of Bethel. God told him to go, so Jacob felt he **must get up and go to Bethel** to **build an altar there to the God who answered** in his **day of distress**. Bethel was the location where Jacob met God the first time. Over twenty years before, when Jacob was on the run from Esau, God appeared to Jacob— promising to protect him, multiply him, and bring him *back* to Bethel. Jacob had known, then, that he was supposed to go back to that spot, but for two decades he had detoured. The good news was that God didn't abandon Jacob even when Jacob got off track. Jacob acknowledged, **[God] has been with me everywhere I have gone.**

35:4-5 A few verses earlier, Jacob had cowered in fear because of what his enemies might do to him. But when he set out for Bethel, suddenly **a terror from God came over the cities around them** (35:5). What had changed? Jacob had stepped up to be the leader God called him to be. He led his family in revival. He listened to the voice of God. And in response, the same people he had been fearing turned to run.

35:6-15 When Jacob arrived and **built an altar** in Bethel (35:7), **God appeared to Jacob again** and **blessed him** (35:9). The blessing and promise are nearly identical to those given to Jacob when he first arrived at Bethel. Jacob would be **fruitful and multiply** into **an assembly of nations** and would inherit

the **land** (35:11-12). Most importantly, God repeated his promise to change Jacob's name to **Israel** (35:10), a symbol of a new identity and a new direction. God had not changed. The promise had only lain dormant until Jacob returned to a place where God could pull it off.

35:16-18 God finally answered Rachel's prayer for a second son. She gave birth and named him **Ben-oni**, which means "Son of My Sorrow," because she was dying (35:18). Jacob renamed the child **Benjamin**, which means "Son of the Right Hand," as an indication of the place the boy would have in Jacob's heart.

35:19-26 Benjamin's special status was not merely a matter of Jacob's preference. Since Benjamin was born **on the way to Ephrath** (35:19), that made him the only son to be born inside of the promised land. To remind us of this distinction, the author recaps the full list of Jacob's sons, which would become the patriarchs of the twelve tribes of Israel (35:23-26). Except for Benjamin, all of them **were born to [Jacob] in Paddan-Aram** (35:26).

Almost as an aside, the author stops to point out that **Reuben went in and slept with his father's concubine Bilhah** (35:22). Though Bilhah was not his mother, this was still an egregious sin similar to incest. While Reuben might have thought that no harm would come from his sexual sin, **Israel heard about it** (35:22). And Reuben's momentary thrill would thus become the very reason that Reuben would not inherit the covenant. This reminds us that no sin is committed in secret. In the end, everything comes to light.

35:27-29 I love the reunion we see here at Isaac's death. Isaac, thought to be on death's doorstep twenty years prior, finally passed away after living for **180 years** (35:28). But unlike the last time Isaac expected his death, when his sons were conniving against each other to steal his blessing, this time **Esau and Jacob buried him** together in cooperation (35:29).

36:1-43 A major shift in the narrative is about to take place. This is indicated by means of the extended genealogy. The author gives the genealogical record of **Esau** as a way of closing the book on Esau and his family, just as he had done for Cain in chapter 4, Noah's sons in chapter 10, Lot in chapter 19, and Ishmael in chapter 25. As God had promised, Esau's descendants would grow into a nation of his own—**the Edomites in the mountains of Seir** (36:9). This, however, was a nation forged after the flesh, with a series of **kings** (36:31-43) who promoted their own agendas.

IV. JOSEPH (37:1–50:26)

➢ A. Joseph the Dreamer and Judah the Hypocrite (37:1–38:30) ⬿

37:1-4 Jacob's family dysfunction continued into the next generation. This should not surprise any discerning reader. The cause of the problem in chapter 37 is a familiar one—favoritism. **Israel** (that is, Jacob) **loved Joseph more than his other sons** because Joseph was the son of his favorite wife, Rachel (37:3). Joseph was the eleventh of twelve boys, which made the favoritism sting his older brothers who surely felt passed up. So when Jacob **made a robe of many colors for** Joseph (37:3), which was a garment symbolizing the privilege of the firstborn, the sibling rivalry erupted. Joseph's brothers **hated him and could not bring themselves to speak peaceably to him** (37:4).

37:5-9 To make matters worse, Joseph had a chip on his own shoulder because he had received some notable dreams. In the first, Joseph's sheaf of grain **stood up**, while his brothers' **sheaves gathered around it and bowed down to** it (37:7). In the second dream, **the sun, moon, and eleven stars**—that is, Joseph's father, mother, and eleven brothers—**were bowing down to** him (37:9). Joseph, being an immature seventeen-year-old, was foolish enough to brag about these dreams to his brothers, who **hated him even more because of his dream** (37:8).

37:10-11 The interesting fact about Joseph's dreams, which we aren't told at this point in the story, is that they were prophetic. Jacob asked, **Am I ... and your brothers really going to come and bow down to the ground before you** (37:10)? Actually, *yes*, Jacob, you will. God had given Joseph these dreams, and he wanted to lead Joseph to a grand destiny. But Joseph would have a lot of unexpected detours in his life before he got to that point. *Without* the detours, however, Joseph would never have been prepared to walk in his God-given destiny. (Keep that in mind the next time God brings an unexpected detour into your life.)

37:12-20 Joseph's first detour came courtesy of his own family. One day, when Jacob had sent Joseph to check on his brothers (37:13-14), **they saw him in the distance** and **plotted to kill him** (37:18). (You may think you have family drama; but it doesn't get much worse than your brothers literally plotting to end your life.) Joseph's brothers couldn't stand his dreams, so they wanted to ensure that they would never come true. **Let's kill him**, they decided, and then **we can say that a vicious animal ate him** (37:20).

37:19-24 Fortunately for Joseph, eldest brother **Reuben** stepped in to save his life. He reasoned with them, **Throw him into this pit in the wilderness**, thinking that he could return later to **rescue [Joseph] from them** (37:22). When Joseph arrived, **they stripped off [his] robe** and **threw him into the pit**, which was **empty** and **without water** (37:23-24). This is a reminder that God sometimes allows us to be stripped of what we love most, because he knows that things have to get worse for us before we can walk into our true destiny.

37:25-28 Joseph's fortunes had changed in a moment. He was living large, like royalty, until his brothers **sold him for twenty pieces of silver** to traveling **Ishmaelites** (37:27-28). Just like that, he became a slave. Little did he know that God was orchestrating something much bigger than he could imagine.

37:29 Reuben, it seems, wasn't with the brothers when they sold Joseph into slavery. So when he **returned to the pit and saw that Joseph was not there, he tore his clothes** in despair. He had managed to save Joseph's life, but couldn't protect him completely.

37:30-32 Together Joseph's older brothers decide to cover up their evil actions with deceit. They **took Joseph's robe, slaughtered a male goat, and dipped the robe in its blood** (37:31). They then presented the robe to their father Jacob (37:32). There is a certain level of irony here, since Jacob had used goat skins to deceive his brother years before; now Jacob is deceived by animal evidence. Jacob's deceptive character had been transferred to his sons.

37:33-35 Recognizing Joseph's robe, Jacob assumed that Joseph had been killed, and he **mourned for his son many days** (37:33-34). He even **refused to be comforted** by his other children when they tried to cheer him (37:35), showing that Jacob's depression affected the entire family.

37:36 Just when God surely seemed absent from the perspective of Joseph and Jacob, we get a hint that he was up to something in the middle of this family disaster. God, we will soon discover, intended to bring Jacob and his sons to Egypt in order to protect them from a coming famine, and Joseph's recent departure placed him **in Egypt**, in the house of **Potiphar, an officer of Pharaoh** in preparation for that time. God was setting the stage to bring about Joseph's destiny, even when no human was aware of it.

38:1-2 Much of the rest of Genesis focuses on Joseph. But to remind us of the line of succession, the author briefly steps away from his story to focus on one of Joseph's brothers. **Judah** would eventually become the son to inherit the promise and blessing of Abraham, but at this point in the story he was just another conniving member of a dysfunctional family. For instance, it was Judah who came up with the idea of selling Joseph as a slave (37:26-27). The following narrative further reveals Judah's deeply flawed character.

Judah married **the daughter of a Canaanite named Shua** (37:2), which was an inauspicious start. Not only had Judah married one of the pagan Canaanites, but he also appeared to have given the marriage no thought at all. He saw a woman he wanted; he went for her. Such impulsive lust would soon get Judah into trouble.

38:3-10 Judah's wife had three sons—Er, Onan, and Shelah. The eldest son, Er, married a woman named **Tamar** (38:6). Unfortunately, Er **was evil in the LORD's sight, and the LORD put him to death** (38:7), leaving Tamar with no husband and no children. The custom of the day in situations such as this was for the next living brother of the deceased to marry the widow. The first son from this marriage, then, would legally belong to the deceased older brother, providing him an heir and preserving his name (see Deut 25:5-10). **Onan**, the brother in line for this task, was fine with taking Tamar as his wife, but because he **knew that the offspring would not be his**, he intentionally avoided getting her pregnant (38:9). In other words, he was using Tamar for sexual gratification while refusing his responsibility to her and his brother. God was neither pleased nor deceived by this, **so he put him to death also** (38:10).

38:11-15 Tamar, now a widow twice over and still childless, was in a tough position. Legally she could expect to marry **Shelah**, the third son. But Judah seemed to blame *Tamar* for the death of his other two sons, and he refused to arrange the marriage (38:11, 14). Knowing that the only way to secure inheritance rights for herself was to produce offspring, Tamar took matters into her own hands. She **took off her widow's clothes, veiled her face**, and posed as a prostitute (38:14-15). Apparently Tamar knew Judah's lustful ways, and so she planned to lure him.

38:16-23 Wages, whether for prostitution or any other transaction, were often given in pledges in those days. Judah agreed to pay the supposed prostitute with **a young goat** (38:17), and as a guarantee that he would follow through with this, he left his **signet ring** and his **staff** (38:18). Both would have had markings uniquely identifying Judah as their owner. So when Judah was unable to retrieve his belongings, he knew he was liable to **become a laughingstock** (38:23). His lack of impulse control had given someone the power to blackmail him.

38:24-26 When it became obvious that Tamar was pregnant, Judah responded with self-righteous hypocrisy, **Bring her out . . . and let her be burned to death!** (38:24). Yet with excellent timing and a thick sense of irony, Tamar responded by sending his missing pledge to him, and asking, **Whose signet ring, cord, and staff are these** (38:25)? The question she posed to Judah bears a resemblance to the question Judah and his brothers posed to their father Jacob after faking Joseph's death: *Do you recognize these?* (See Gen 37:32.) Thus, Judah the deceiver was deceived in kind. He immediately recognized his guilt, knowing that Tamar had acted desperately because he refused to give her as a wife to his **son Shelah** (38:26).

38:27-30 Tamar gave birth to **twins**, and just as with Jacob and Esau, the older of these two (**Zerah**, 38:30), would serve the younger (**Perez**, 38:29). Thus the line of Judah, which was the covenant line, was preserved and continued, even in the midst of sinful circumstances. God's program will not be thwarted. He never accepts or condones sin, but he can still *use* sin to sovereignly accomplish his kingdom plan.

➢ B. From Rags to Riches in Egypt
(39:1–41:57) ❧

39:1-2 At the same time that Judah was proving his own immorality, younger brother Joseph was showing the opposite characteristic of purity. Joseph's circumstances, though, started off much more grim than Judah's. He **had been taken to Egypt** as a slave. But because **the LORD was with Joseph . . . he became a successful man** in the house of **Potiphar, an officer of Pharaoh and the captain of the guards** (39:1-2). He may have been a slave, but God was with him. Joseph's life proves the lesson taught by the sponge: when you fill a sponge with water and then

add pressure, water comes out. Joseph was so full of God's presence that when life squeezed him, evidence of his dedication to God oozed out. And **he became a successful man** (39:2).

39:3 Notice that Potiphar didn't just see Joseph's good work ethic. He **saw that the LORD was with him.** That suggests Joseph didn't mind telling Potiphar about the Lord because how else would Potiphar have known about him?

39:4-5 Because Joseph knew that God was with him, he became the best employee in Potiphar's house. Potiphar **placed all that he owned under his authority**, and **the LORD's blessing was on all that he owned, in his house and in his fields** (39:4-5). Joseph thus shows us how we should all conduct ourselves when working with and for non-Christians. We should be the most punctual, most productive, most trustworthy, most honest employees in our companies. Knowing God is with us should make us stand out dramatically.

39:6-7 Joseph grew so central to Potiphar's enterprise that Potiphar essentially gave him the keys to his estate (39:6). Things were beginning to look up for Joseph. But then Potiphar's wife started to meddle. Seeing that **Joseph was well-built and handsome** (39:6), she wanted to seduce him. Her advances weren't subtle, either. **Sleep with me** (39:7), she said, cutting straight to the point.

39:8-9 Joseph responded to Potiphar's wife's solicitation wisely. His reaction is a sort of template for how we should resist temptation, sexual or otherwise. First, he saw that the consequences of sin would be damaging. Potiphar had placed all of his possessions under Joseph's **authority** (39:8). To sleep with his master's wife would ruin that trust and surely lead to harsh consequences. More importantly, he recognized that what makes sin sinful is that it is an **immense evil** committed **against God** (39:9). People who love God don't need to be told to avoid sin; they instinctively hate sin because they don't want to pierce the heart of the One who chose them and set his affection on them.

39:10-20 Unfortunately, Potiphar's wife was relentless. She **spoke to Joseph day after day**, even though he kept rejecting her advances (39:10). Then one day, when no one was around, **she grabbed him by his garment** and gave her trademark line, **Sleep with me** (39:12). Joseph bolted, which was the right move. But, in doing so, he **left his garment with her** (39:13). So Potiphar's wife flipped the script and spun a story about Joseph trying to rape her (39:14-18). This created a no-win situation for Joseph: no one else witnessed the event; his garment in her possession served as evidence; he was a foreigner; and most importantly, she was the boss's wife. The resulting fallout was as predictable as it was unjust: Potiphar **heard the story his wife told him** (39:19), grew furious, and had [Joseph] **thrown into prison** (39:20).

39:21-23 Joseph's situation seemed even worse than when he'd showed up in Egypt. Back then he was a slave, but at least he had a job. Now he was in prison. Nevertheless, in the midst of a horrid situation, **the LORD was with Joseph** (39:21). God wasn't surprised by anything that happened to him. And before long, Joseph had gained such a good reputation that **the warden put all the prisoners ... under Joseph's authority** (39:22), making the prisoner the warden! This is just the kind of thing God can do when we trust him in our detours. He may not take us out of jail at our request, but he will come and join us in it. And living with God's presence in the middle of jail offers a truer freedom than living without God anywhere else ever could.

40:1-2 In prison, Joseph came into contact with two other prisoners—**the chief cupbearer and the chief baker** (40:2). Since both the cupbearer and the baker handled Pharaoh's food and drink, perhaps Pharaoh was concerned about an assassination attempt, since capital punishment was on the table (40:18-19, 22).

40:3-4 . It just so happened that the cupbearer and baker were put **in custody in the house ... where Joseph was confined** (40:3). But what at first looks like a strange coincidence might have been intentional. It was **the captain of the guards** who **assigned Joseph** to these two men (40:4), and this term, "captain of the guards," is different than the one used for the warden running the prison (see 39:21). That means it could refer to Potiphar. If that is the case, it's possible Potiphar did not believe the charge his wife had brought against Joseph. Not only would that mean that he refrained from executing Joseph but also that he, knowing well Joseph's managerial skills, personally placed other prisoners under Joseph's control.

40:5-7 When we're suffering, we tend to be self-absorbed. But God intends to use our suffering for the sake of others. Joseph could have been having a pity party while he waited on God to minister to him. Instead, he noticed that the cupbearer and baker **looked distraught** (40:6). He expressed concern for their emotional well-being, asking, **Why do you look so sad today** (40:7)? Even in his misery, Joseph was making time to minister to the hurting (see 2 Cor 1:3-7). And unbeknownst to him, by serving during his own suffering, Joseph was putting himself back on the path toward future blessing.

40:8 The problem for these two prisoners was the same—troubling **dreams**. Joseph immediately recognized that God was at work in arranging his encounter with the pair. He displayed confidence in God by reminding them that only **God** could interpret dreams. Most striking, however, is his confidence that God *would use* him to reveal the dreams' meanings. In our suffering, a common temptation is to stop believing that God will use *us*. Joseph's example prompts us not to fall into that wrong thinking.

40:9-13 The cupbearer relayed his dream first. Standing in front of a vine with three branches, he took some of the grapes from the vine, **squeezed them into Pharaoh's cup, and placed the cup in Pharaoh's hand** (9:10-11). This turned out to be good news for the cupbearer, as Joseph said the dream meant he would be restored to his position in just **three days** (40:12-13).

40:14-15 Joseph was no fool, so he tried to use the connections he had to get himself out of prison. **When all goes well for you,**

he told the cupbearer, **show kindness to me by mentioning me to Pharaoh, and get me out of this prison** (40:14). Joseph pointed out that he and the cupbearer were both wrongly convicted (40:15), so he must have been hopeful that his favor would soon lead to release.

40:16-19 The baker went next, explaining a dream in which **three baskets of white bread were** on his head, with **birds** swooping down to eat the bread (40:16-17). The verdict for the baker wasn't favorable: in **three days** Pharaoh would hang the baker and the birds would **eat the flesh** off of his body (40:19).

40:20-23 Three days later, everything happened **just as Joseph had explained** (40:22). Pharaoh **restored the chief cupbearer** to his original position (40:21) and **hanged the chief baker** (40:22). For a moment, it looked like Joseph was about to get his "get-out-of-jail-free card." **Yet the chief cupbearer did not remember Joseph** (40:23). Joseph's detour, then, wasn't quite finished. This is how our circumstances go at times, too. Victory appears to be right on the horizon, then suddenly life takes a hard left and the joy we thought was coming disappears. Through his experiences, however, Joseph continued to trust God. Though people may leave us and forget us, God never will.

41:1 Between Joseph interpreting the dreams of the prisoners and his next chance to get out of jail, **two years** had passed. We know that Joseph was "thirty" when Pharaoh let him out of jail (41:46), which means there was a gap of thirteen years between Joseph's initial dream and him living out his destiny. At the close of chapter 40, Joseph was twenty-eight years old and had been in a detour for eleven years already. Sitting in his dingy dungeon, he waited and waited for the knock on the door that would announce his freedom. But for two years, that knock never came.

Joseph's life hadn't panned out as he had intended, but God was still up to something. While Joseph waited for God to act in the prison, God was at work in someplace unexpected: the king's bedroom. **Pharaoh had a dream** that he couldn't figure out.

41:2-8 In the king's dream, seven sick cows were eating seven healthy cows (41:2-4), and seven ugly heads of grain were eating seven healthy heads of grain (41:5-7). Pharaoh didn't understand the vision, **so he summoned all the magicians of Egypt and all its wise men.** Though he called in the professionals, **no one could interpret** the dreams for him (41:8).

This is a reminder that when God is setting something up for his glory, he won't let human wisdom come up with an answer. As the apostle Paul would say centuries later, "God has chosen what is foolish in the world to shame the wise, and God has chosen what is weak in the world to shame the strong" (1 Cor 1:27). If we're wise in the ways of the world, we may climb certain ladders of success; but eventually we'll come across problems that only godly wisdom can solve. I'd rather be a fool to the world with God's wisdom in my heart than the other way around.

41:9-14 The wise men couldn't interpret the dreams, but their discussion was overheard by the **cupbearer** (41:9). The light bulb finally went off for him, and he realized he had left the interpreter of dreams languishing in prison. So the cupbearer told Pharaoh all about Joseph and his gift for dream interpretation, and **Pharaoh sent for Joseph** (41:10-14). For two years Joseph had waited, but when God was ready to move, he moved in a hurry. Sometimes when it seems that God isn't doing anything at all, he will change our circumstances in a heartbeat. Of course, God *is* active all along. We simply aren't aware of it, until it's time for his purpose to be revealed—at a time when our development has been completed (see Ps 105:17-19).

41:15-16 Pharaoh told Joseph his predicament, and Joseph's reply shows that he had been letting God work on him during his imprisonment. **It is God who will give Pharaoh a favorable answer** (41:16). Few people would have cried foul if Joseph took sole credit for his dream interpretation gift. In fact, Pharaoh seemed to assume that the power was within Joseph (41:15). But Joseph was keeping God at the center of his life and central to his conversation. God's presence had been his constant companion, so God's preeminence was always on his mind.

41:17-31 Pharaoh recounted the two dreams to Joseph (41:17-24), who explained that both **dreams mean the same thing** (41:25). God was about to send **seven years of great abundance** (41:29) to Egypt—symbolized by the seven fat cows and seven healthy heads of grain—followed by **seven years of famine** (41:30)—symbolized by the thin cows and ugly grain. The famine would be so severe, Joseph warned, that **the abundance in the land** would **not be remembered because of the famine** (41:31).

41:32 Here Joseph pointed out a principle that is often true throughout Scripture—when God intends to do something, he will confirm his Word with two or three witnesses. In this case, **since the dream was given twice to Pharaoh**, Joseph knew **the matter [had] been determined by God**. Similarly, we may often wonder which way God is leading us. But when we feel Scripture speaking to our hearts and our brothers and sisters in Christ start to back up that message in unison, we can be sure that God is confirming his plan by repeating it.

41:33-36 Pharaoh had only asked Joseph for a little dream interpretation. Joseph dutifully gave it, but then he kept right on going, advising Pharaoh on how to handle the impending crisis. Joseph's plan was to **take a fifth of the harvest of the land** during the rich years and to stockpile it as **a reserve for the land during the seven years of famine** (41:34-36). To make this massive undertaking work, though, someone savvy would have to oversee the task (41:33).

41:37-45 Pharaoh immediately recognized that Joseph was the man for the job. Not only did he have wisdom to see things spiritually, but he could also make right conclusions based on that wisdom (41:39). This led Pharaoh to elevate Joseph to become his second-in-command (41:40). With that privilege came enormous benefits: Joseph had an entire team of servants dedicated to helping him (41:43). He was given symbols of his exalted position—**a signet ring** with which he could sign in Pharaoh's name as well as beautiful **linen garments** and **gold** jewelry (41:42). He was even given **a wife** (41:45).

What a sudden change of circumstances! In a single day, he went from rags to riches, from the pit to the palace.

41:46-49 The **seven years of abundance** came (41:47), just as Joseph had predicted. So he began storing **all the excess food in the land of Egypt** to prepare for the coming famine (41:48). Evidently he excelled at this, because he soon had **stored up grain in such abundance . . . that he stopped measuring it because it was beyond measure** (41:49).

41:50-52 Even though Joseph had been given an Egyptian wife and an Egyptian name (41:45), and even though it had been thirteen years since he had seen his family, he did not forget his heritage. When his wife gave birth to two sons, Joseph gave them Hebrew names. The first, **Manasseh**, sounds like the Hebrew verb for "forget," because God made Joseph **forget** his **hardship** (41:51). The second, **Ephraim**, sounds like the word "fruitful," because God made him **fruitful in the land** of his **affliction** (41:52). Pharaoh may have been the hand that pulled Joseph out of prison, but Joseph looked past that hand to the loving arm of God, who was guiding him all along.

41:53-57 After the seven years of plenty, **the seven years of famine began, just as Joseph had said** (41:54). In Egypt alone there was food, so Egypt became the breadbasket of the world—and Joseph was in charge of selling food to people from **every land** (41:57), including the land where his family lived.

❧ C. Family Reunion (42:1–47:31) ❧

42:1-5 The famine extended to the land of Canaan, where Jacob and his sons still lived (42:5). Hearing that there was grain in Egypt, Jacob sent his sons to **go down there and buy some** so that they would **not die** (42:2). Jacob, however, **did not send Joseph's brother Benjamin with his brothers** (42:4) because he didn't trust the brothers to protect him. He had already lost Joseph under suspicious circumstances, and he refused to lose the other son of his beloved Rachel.

42:6-17 When Joseph's brothers arrived in Egypt **and bowed down before him** (42:6), he immediately recognized them, but **they did not recognize him** (42:8). Joseph also saw in their actions the fulfillment of his **dreams** so many years before (42:9). After twenty years, Joseph had finally been exalted over all of his brothers. To test them and draw out more information, Joseph accused them four times of being **spies** sent to **see the weakness of the land** (42:9, 12, 14, 16).

In an ironic twist, Joseph detained his brothers in a prison, just as they had done in throwing him into a cistern (42:16-17). We aren't sure what all of Joseph's motives were: was he paying his brothers back? Trying to orchestrate contact with his younger brother? Attempting to drive his brothers to repent? Perhaps it was some combination of these. What we *do* know is that God was working through Joseph to bring the brothers to a place where he could use them. God was driving them to a place of repentance, which would ultimately lead to restoration.

42:18-24 After letting his brothers languish in prison for three days, Joseph kept Simeon in custody and sent the others home, charging them to return with Benjamin (42:19-20, 24). At this point, the brothers began to realize their guilt. **Trouble has come to us**, they said to one another. **We saw [Joseph's] deep distress when he pleaded with us, but we would not listen** (42:21). They had ignored Joseph's cry for help, and they saw that they were reaping a similar response during *their* cry for help against unjust accusations. Joseph, who was present while they discussed this, was able to understand their Hebrew language (though they didn't realize it). Hearing his brothers express remorse overwhelmed him to the point of tears (42:23-24).

42:25-28 Joseph sent his brothers back to Canaan **with grain**, just as they had requested, but he also secretly put **each man's silver** back in **his sack**, and gave them **provisions for their journey** (42:25). When the brothers noticed that their money had been returned, **their hearts sank**, because now it *really* looked like they were spies up to no good (42:28).

42:29-38 Returning home without their brother Simeon, Jacob's sons relayed **all that had happened to them** (42:29). When they mentioned the demand of **the lord of the country** that they must **bring back** their **youngest brother**, however, Jacob grew stubborn (42:33-36). He said, **Joseph is gone, and Simeon is gone** (42:36). With two sons lost, Jacob had no desire to see something happen to Benjamin, his youngest. Even with Reuben swearing on the lives of his *own* two sons (42:37), Jacob dug in his heels: **My son will not go down with you**, lest you ... **bring my gray hairs down to Sheol in sorrow** (42:38). God had begun to mold the hearts of Jacob's sons, but Jacob was proving to be tougher clay.

43:1-7 As the famine dragged on, Jacob's family soon **used up the grain they had brought back from Egypt** (43:2). Jacob instructed his sons to go get more, prompting Judah to remind him of Joseph's words: **You will not see me again unless your brother is with you** (43:3). Jacob, greatly upset, began to wonder about the mysterious man with whom they were dealing in Egypt. He asked, **Why did you tell the man that you had another brother?** (43:6). Jacob was finding himself in a position of helplessness—the exact place where God wanted him. Often it's when we have nowhere else to turn that we are finally willing to look to God for deliverance.

43:8-9 **Judah** stepped up to take responsibility for Benjamin: **If I do not bring him back ... I will be guilty before you forever** (43:9). Interestingly, Judah was the man who spearheaded the conspiracy to sell Joseph into slavery in the first place. He was the impulsive man who slept with his own daughter-in-law and then hypocritically demanded her death. But clearly this was not the *same* Judah making so selfless a vow. God had been softening his heart over the last twenty years, shaping him into the sort of vessel that he could use.

43:10-14 Jacob reluctantly agreed to send his sons, Benjamin in tow, back to Egypt. He suggested that they take valuable local gifts—**a little balsam and a little honey, aromatic**

gum and resin, pistachios and almonds (43:11)—to curry favor with Egypt's demanding leader. He also sent **twice as much silver** as before (43:12), thus replacing the returned silver that Joseph could have claimed was stolen and providing money for more grain. But even though he sent them out with a prayer and a blessing, Jacob was patently pessimistic. He assumed that Benjamin would die (43:14).

43:15-23 When Joseph's brothers returned, they were taken to Joseph's personal house, a turn of events that hardly inspired any confidence in them (43:16-18). Approaching Joseph's **steward**, they attempted to clear up the misunderstanding about the money (43:19-22). But the steward replied, **Your God and the God of your father must have put treasure in your bags** (43:23). This suggests that Joseph's faith must have spread to his staff, because here was an Egyptian servant invoking the name of the God of the Hebrews! Apparently Joseph had been talking about the Lord from the time he was a slave in Potiphar's house right up until the present moment of prosperity. This begs the question, Are you speaking up about God in every moment of your life—in the moments of adversity as well as in the moments of prosperity?

43:24-31 Simeon was delivered to his brothers, and together they prepared for the meal (43:24-25). When Joseph saw **Benjamin** for the first time, he couldn't contain his **emotion for his brother, and he was about to weep** (43:30). Knowing that to do so would cause suspicion, though, Joseph rushed away until he could regain **composure** (43:31).

43:32-34 It must have been a shock to Joseph's brothers to see that in the seating arrangements, **they were seated ... in order by age, from the firstborn to the youngest** (43:33). How could this Egyptian ruler have known their birth order?

44:1-12 As Joseph's brothers left Egypt, Joseph arranged for one final test. He had his steward put his **cup, the silver one, at the top of the youngest one's bag** (44:2). In this move, he was framing Benjamin for theft

to see whether his brothers would defend him. The steward, following Joseph's orders, overtook his brothers and charged them with stealing **the cup** of his **master** (44:5). The brothers denied it, but of course, when the bags were searched, **the cup was found in Benjamin's sack** (44:12). The penalty for such an act would have been Benjamin becoming Joseph's **slave** (44:10).

44:13-16 The immediate response of Benjamin's brothers indicates that they were no longer the heartless, cruel, deceitful men they had once been. When Benjamin was exposed as the thief, **they tore their clothes** (44:13), showing intense grief. Not only did they grieve, but they also refused to abandon Benjamin to his plight. The steward would have been content to return with Benjamin, but the brothers **each ... loaded his donkey and returned to the city** (44:13), signaling to their youngest sibling that they were in the mess together. Even when Joseph repeated his intentions to imprison only Benjamin, they offered themselves as willing **slaves** in solidarity (44:16).

44:17-34 Joseph kept up his poker face for a while, insisting that Benjamin must stay as his **slave** (44:17). At this point, **Judah** once again moved to the forefront. He had already stepped up to lead his brothers by promising their father to bring Benjamin back alive (44:32). At this point he led them by giving an impassioned plea for Joseph to show mercy, both for Benjamin's sake and for the sake of his **father** Jacob (44:34).

The pinnacle of Judah's appeal—the proof that he had truly experienced a change of heart—was the staggering offer he made to **remain here as [his] lord's slave, in place of the boy** (44:33). Once Judah had been so bereft of virtue that he thought nothing of sacrificing his brother's life for his own convenience; now he was willing to lay down his own life so another brother could be free. The character transformation was complete, and God was ready to carry out the next step in his plan.

45:1-3 Joseph couldn't take the suspense any longer, so he commanded, **Send everyone away from me** (45:1). Then, alone with his brothers, he revealed his identity (which may have included revealing his circumcision and, thus, confirming his descent from Abraham). He also asked about their **father** (45:3). Joseph had been thinking about this moment for weeks, so he was ready to have the reunion. But his brothers weren't as prepared! They sat in stunned silence, **terrified in his presence** (45:3). Joseph, the brother they had intended to kill, was now standing before them with all the power in the world. And to their surprise, he was extending not vengeance but mercy. (May we follow his example.)

45:4-8 Joseph displayed varsity-level maturity next. Though he'd been imprisoned by his brothers without cause, he was able to see the hand of God in that evil thing the brothers had done. He said, **God sent me ahead of you to preserve life** (45:5). The terrible string of events had all led Joseph to his position of privilege just in time to save the lives of tens of thousands, and he had noticed the connection (45:7-8).

Think about it: had Joseph gotten his way at any point along this journey, he might have stopped God's plan. Had he not been sold into slavery, he wouldn't have been in Egypt. Had he not been falsely accused in Potiphar's house, he wouldn't have been in the jail. Had he not been in the jail, he wouldn't have met Pharaoh's servants. Had the cupbearer remembered him and had him released earlier, he wouldn't have been in a place where he could be easily summoned to interpret Pharaoh's dream. If any *one* of the links in this chain were broken, famine would have overtaken the land, killing countless people, including Joseph and the rest of his family. All the promises God had made to Abraham, Isaac, and even Jacob would've come to nothing.

Joseph's entire life demonstrated the truth that Paul declared, "All things work together for the good of those who love God, who are called according to his purpose" (Rom 8:28). When God doesn't intervene in your life the way you want and in the moment you want, it may be that he is working, behind the scenes, to accomplish in his perfect timing something so much bigger and so much better than you could ever imagine.

45:9-13 Joseph told his brothers to **return quickly** to their **father** and give him the news (45:9). He invited Jacob to **settle in the land of Goshen** with all of his **children ... grandchildren, flocks, herds**, and everything else (45:10). Thus Jacob and also Joseph's brothers came under Joseph's authority and care, just as God had long ago promised Joseph that they would.

45:14-15 Full of emotion, Joseph and his brothers were reunified. Both Joseph and **Benjamin wept** (45:14), and Joseph proved his renewed intimacy with his brothers by offering each one a kiss (45:15). It had taken twenty-two years, but Joseph and his brothers were finally reconciled.

45:16-23 The reunion was so exciting that even **Pharaoh** wanted to get involved. Out of gratitude to Joseph, he offered his entire family the best of the land of Egypt and **the richness of the land** (45:18). He also arranged for their transportation, so that the large caravan could make the long journey with all of their belongings (45:19-21). Jacob's family, seemingly on the cusp of starvation, had become fabulously wealthy in a moment.

45:24 Just before the journey, Joseph gave his brothers one command: **Don't argue on the way**. The unity they had just achieved had taken decades to accomplish, and Joseph did not want to see it undone by quarrels over who was most responsible for the negative events of the past. He encouraged his brothers to move forward in their newfound unity rather than peering backward into the sinful disputes that had fractured their lives. We too are quick to resurrect old quarrels and remind each other of past sins, but God speaks to us a bold word of encouragement through this story: you are all fellow travelers and fellow sinners; don't argue on the way through life.

45:25-28 Jacob, the last family member to learn about Joseph, **was stunned** and **did not believe** the report at first (45:26). But eventually the testimony of his sons, combined with the phenomenal gifts sent from Egypt, convinced him. And his **spirit ... revived**

(45:27). God's plan, when hidden from our eyes, can often lead us to despair. But if we can hold out until God is prepared to reveal what he is doing, our spirits will be revived. Who knows what reunions, reconciliations, and renewals God has in store for those who trust him?

46:1-7 Even though Jacob would have been thrilled to travel to Egypt and see Joseph, there must have been a question in the back of his mind: *What about the promised land?* Would God bring his people back to Canaan if they left, en masse, for Egypt? Knowing Jacob's anxieties, God appeared to Jacob in a vision to reassure him. The journey to Egypt would fulfill part of his promise, making Jacob **into a great nation there** (46:3). At the appointed time, God would bring them **back** (46:4). And in the meantime, God promised to be with Jacob for the journey (46:4). Armed with God's presence and a renewal of God's promise, Jacob was able to make the trek with hope.

46:8-27 What follows here is a list of Jacob's descendants at the time of his journey to Egypt. Each of Jacob's sons had a bundle of sons of their own, so that the entire family numbered **seventy persons** (46:27). God's promise to make Abraham's descendants as numerous as the stars in the sky was already on its way to fruition. This was an enormous family by any measure. But the specific number seventy would have been significant as well. In Hebrew culture, the number seven indicated completion and fullness. In pointing out that Jacob had a family of seventy, the author hints to us that Jacob's family was fulfilling the promise that God had made.

46:28-30 After an absence of twenty-two years, Joseph was reunited with his father Jacob. Joseph **threw his arms around him, and wept for a long time** (46:29). Jacob was overcome with emotion as well, exclaiming that he was **ready to die now because** he had **seen** Joseph's face (46:30). This reunion once again confirmed to Jacob that God's promises were good and dependable, even when circumstances had seemed to threaten them.

46:31-34 Joseph gave his family a brief lesson in cross-cultural communication, helping them know how to interact with Pharaoh. Specifically, he encouraged them to emphasize not only that they were shepherds—**since all shepherds are detestable to Egyptians**—but also that they had **raised livestock from** their **youth** (46:34). Joseph hoped to acquire for his family the land near Goshen, which was suitable for raising sheep and cattle.

47:1-6 Joseph's family met Pharaoh; they asked to **settle in the land of Goshen**; and Pharaoh agreed (47:4-6). God had sent Joseph ahead to save his family and prepare a place for them; here God was fulfilling his promise and settling Jacob's family in the land.

47:7-12 Jacob's brief audience with Pharaoh hints at the fulfillment of another aspect of God's covenant with Abraham. The promise had three parts: (1) multiplying Abraham's offspring, (2) giving them the promised land, and (3) blessing all the families of the earth through them (see Gen 12:1-3). Jacob's family had already settled in the land. They had multiplied phenomenally. Here **Jacob blessed Pharaoh** as a firstfruits fulfillment of God's intention to bless all the nations of the world (47:7) through this line.

The direction of this blessing is staggering, and it displays Jacob's deep faith. Pharaoh sat on his throne, thinking that he was ruling over the world. *He* should have been the one bestowing blessings. But Jacob knew better: Jacob saw that in God's economy, he had the greater wealth; in God's kingdom, he had the true position of privilege.

47:13-26 As the famine dragged on, **the land of Egypt and the land of Canaan were exhausted** (47:13). Under Joseph's authority, the people were saved from starvation and Pharaoh's treasury was filled to the brim with **silver** (47:14). Eventually the people of the region ran out of money, so Joseph began to barter for their livestock. In short order, all of **the horses, the flocks of sheep, the herds of cattle, and the donkeys** in the entire region belonged to Joseph (47:17). The famine dragged on for years more, so the people then began to offer their very **land** in exchange for food (47:19). In the end, because of Joseph's wisdom, he **acquired all the land in Egypt for Pharaoh** (47:20), asking in return only that the people provide a tax of a **fifth** of their produce, a practice that held for hundreds of years (47:24, 26).

47:27-31 As Jacob neared death, he charged Joseph, **Do not bury me in Egypt** (47:29). He remembered the promises of God and wanted his bones to rest where his ancestors' did—in the promised land (47:30). Joseph, swearing with a solemn oath, agreed to Jacob's request (47:31).

❧ D. The Blessings of Jacob and the Promises of God (48:1–50:26) ❧

48:1-12 The time came for Jacob's life to end. Joseph brought **his two sons, Manasseh and Ephraim** (48:1), so that Jacob would give them a final blessing (48:9). Recalling the special place that Rachel, Joseph's mother, held in his life, Jacob decided to double Joseph's inheritance accordingly. In saying that **Ephraim and Manasseh belong to [him] just as Reuben and Simeon do** (48:5), Jacob expressed his desire for each son to receive a portion of the inheritance equal to that of the other true brothers. Thus the twelve portions became thirteen, and Joseph—once again the son of honor—would receive the double portion usually reserved for the firstborn.

It is important to remember that Manasseh and Ephraim were born to Joseph while he was in Egypt. Yet Jacob made it clear that both were to be treated as though they were Jacob's sons; therefore, they were to receive an inheritance in the promised land. The claim to the inheritance of Jacob was not a matter of skin color, but instead a matter of lineage. The critical question was, "Who was your father?" not "What color is your skin?"

48:13-20 Joseph positioned his two sons so that **Manasseh**, the older, would receive the more prominent blessing from Jacob's **right hand** (48:13). Much to Joseph's shock and disagreement (48:17-18), Jacob switched his hands so that **Ephraim**, the younger, would receive the **firstborn** blessing (48:14). It is

amusing that Joseph, of all people, would be surprised by this departure from worldly tradition. His father and grandfather were the younger brothers, receiving the blessing and inheritance in place of the firstborn sons in their households. And Joseph himself had *ten* brothers older than he, yet God raised him to a position of distinction. Jacob was simply continuing the pattern of reversal that God had used all throughout the history of the Jewish patriarchs, proving that God's ways are not ours.

Jacob was the first person in Scripture to say that **God . . . has been my shepherd all my life** (48:15). Hundreds of years later, King David would expand on this imagery in writing Psalm 23, but David certainly didn't invent the idea. Jacob had spent decades tending sheep—feeding them, cleaning them, defending them against predators, binding them up when they were injured, searching for them when they wandered. He knew how much tenderness and devotion it required to care for sheep. And by the end of his life, Jacob had come to see God through that light. He realized that in all of his wanderings, God had been tenderly and devotedly providing for him, defending him, healing him, and searching for him.

Jacob bestowed on Ephraim and Manasseh two blessings, reminding us of the wonderful chance that God offers grandparents today to speak hope and life into their own offspring's lives. The lesser blessing, that **they grow to be numerous within the land** (48:16), is the sort of blessing that we all inherently want. It's a prayer for material prosperity. And God, in his faithfulness, would be quick to answer Jacob's prayer. But the greater blessing that Jacob gave was that **they be called by [his] name and the names of [his] fathers Abraham and Isaac** (48:16). Material blessings come and go; in the end, we can't actually keep any of them. But to be included in the family of God is a blessing that bears fruit for eternity.

48:21-22 Before calling in the rest of the brothers, Jacob reminded Joseph once again of God's promise. Even though the family would grow numerous in Egypt, God would deliver them **back to the land of their fathers** (48:21). Israel was supposed to interpret their coming years in Egypt as only a detour, much like Joseph's. God had not changed their final destination. He would deliver them to Canaan.

49:1-2 Jacob then called his sons to his bedside to tell them about **the days to come** (49:1). Jacob's blessing was distinct from that of Isaac and Abraham before him. Isaac and Abraham passed on God's promise to their children, but Jacob went beyond that. He issued prophetic words about the future of each son, reflecting the destinies that their tribes would live out.

49:3-4 The first three sons were rejected from being able to lead the messianic line. **Reuben**, Jacob's **firstborn** (49:3), would have been the most natural candidate for the job, but he disqualified himself by defiling his **father's bed** (49:4). Years earlier, Reuben had slept with one of his father's concubines (35:22). That one adulterous decision came back to haunt him, keeping him from carrying the torch of God's messianic promise.

49:5-7 Jacob said of the next two brothers, **Simeon and Levi** (49:5), that they were men of anarchy and violence. **In their anger they kill men, and on a whim they hamstring oxen** (49:6), Jacob said, remembering their deceitful attack against the inhabitants of Shechem (34:24-29). They may have consoled themselves that they were doing right because they defended the honor of their sister, but Jacob recognized that their motives were mixed. They responded in violence because they cherished violence.

49:8-10 Joseph was Jacob's favorite, and I think he would have been Jacob's personal choice to continue the messianic line. But God had chosen Judah—in spite of his failings—to father the line of kings leading to Christ, as **the scepter will not depart from Judah or the staff from between his feet until he whose right it is comes** (49:10). He would be the new leader of his brothers, full of power and majesty **like a lion** (49:8-9). From Judah would come the kingly line of David and Solomon and all of their descendants. More importantly, Jesus would be called the "Lion from the tribe of Judah"

(Rev 5:5). He is the one **whose right it is** to carry the scepter throughout eternity, **and the obedience of the peoples belongs to him** (Gen 49:10).

49:11-12 The **wine** and **milk** imagery that Jacob chose to express Judah's reign (and, by extension, Jesus's reign) was meant to communicate richness and plenty. As the biblical storyline would clarify later, these promises would be fulfilled in part in the promised land, but they would await final fulfillment in the millennial kingdom of Jesus in the age to come.

49:13 Jacob continued going down the line, addressing his two sons by Leah, Zebulun and Issachar. **Zebulun will live by the seashore and will be a harbor for ships**, indicating the future trade of this son's descendants. When the people of Israel would return to the promised land and apportion the land, the tribe of Zebulun would be given land near the ocean, and they would make their living on the sea.

49:14-15 Issachar, whose tribal inheritance was not far from Zebulun's, would not fare well during the return to Canaan. Issachar **leaned his shoulder to bear a load and became a forced laborer** (49:15), a prophecy about the tribe's approach to the native inhabitants of the promised land. Even though Issachar had strength enough to drive the people out as God promised (49:14), they grew comfortable living alongside them. And what began as a seemingly harmless partnership between the groups eventually led to Issachar's slavery.

49:16-17 Jacob, finishing the blessings for the sons of Leah, moved on to the sons from his concubines. **Dan**, which sounds like the Hebrew word for "has judged," **will judge his people as one of the tribes of Israel** (49:16). In their best moments, the people of Dan were to provide justice for the rest of the nation. In reality, however, they proved to be treacherous, like **a snake by the road, a viper beside the path, that bites the horses' heels so that its rider falls** (49:17). During Israel's conquest of the promised land, Dan quickly gave up on the land to which God had called them (see Judg 2:3-4), leaving the land to the Philistines. Worse than that, Dan appears to be the first tribe to plummet into full-scale idolatry during that same time (see Judg 18).

49:18 In the midst of his blessings, Jacob interrupted himself to remind his sons of their need to follow the Lord and be dependent on him. Even with so many of God's promises fulfilled, Jacob knew that he still needed to **wait for [God's] salvation.** In this life, Christians never graduate from faith, and faith is seen in those moments when we hope for what is unseen.

49:19-21 Jacob's other three sons by concubines—**Gad, Asher,** and **Naphtali**—were given rapid-fire prophecies. Gad would **be attacked by raiders** (49:19), indicating the constant conflict that the tribe would experience. *Asher,* whose name means "blessed," would live a life worthy of the name, with rich food and **royal delicacies** (49:20). Naphtali would be a free people, dwelling in the mountains to the north (49:21).

49:22-26 Last of all, Jacob came to the sons of Rachel. Unsurprisingly, Jacob spent a great deal of time blessing his favorite son Joseph. As in his life, so in his tribe's future, Joseph would be **a fruitful vine beside a spring** (49:22), not only succeeding for his own sake, but also blessing the lives of others. Joseph's tribe would continue to be one of the most prosperous of the twelve, victorious in battle and overflowing with **blessings** (49:25-26).

49:27-28 Jacob concluded his blessing with the youngest son, **Benjamin.** Though Jacob favored Benjamin personally, it appears that the future of this tribe would be a mixed one. Jacob characterized the Benjaminites like **a wolf** that **tears his prey** and **divides the plunder** (49:27). They would be a tribe with a violent spirit, which was seen perhaps most vividly in their two most famous descendants. King Saul, Israel's first king, was a Benjaminite; so too was the persecutor-turned-apostle Paul.

49:29-33 Jacob understood that he was **about to be gathered to [his] people** (49:29)—that is, he was about to die. So he instructed Joseph to bury him, not in Egypt, but in the land of promise, **with [his] fathers in the cave in the field of Ephron the Hethite** (49:29). Notably, he finally gave honor to his first wife, **Leah,** asking to be buried with her (49:31) rather than with his beloved Rachel. In death Leah found the honor that so often eluded her in life.

50:1-13 Jacob died and was buried as he had requested. Joseph arranged it all, ensuring that Jacob was embalmed after the style of Egyptian royalty (50:3). The entire nation mourned for Jacob **seventy days** (50:3), a phenomenal show of respect that proves how dearly beloved Joseph was among the Egyptians. **When the days of mourning were over** (50:4), Joseph obeyed his father's dying wishes, bringing his body back to the land of Canaan for burial (50:5). The funeral procession was **very impressive** (50:9), which is an understatement: with **all Pharaoh's servants, the elders of his household, and all the elders of the land of Egypt** joining with **all Joseph's family** (50:7-8), the scene would have been jaw-dropping. In fact, it was such a spectacular caravan that **the Canaanite inhabitants of the land** renamed one of their cities because of it (50:11).

50:14-15 Joseph's brothers had happily received the gifts and the land from their younger brother, but Jacob's death proved that they were still uneasy with the entire situation. **After Joseph buried his father** (50:14), his brothers realized that one of the last impediments to Joseph taking any vengeance on them had just disappeared. Perhaps, they thought, **Joseph is holding a grudge against us.** Maybe he was merely waiting to strike until after their father was gone. If so, **he will certainly repay us for all the suffering we caused him** (50:15).

50:16-18 The brothers were scared, so they did what many of us do in our fear: they lied. They sent a message to Joseph, claiming that their father had said, **Please forgive your brothers' transgression and their sin** (50:17). They even reverted to the same posture they assumed when they first came to Egypt, bowing down before Joseph and saying, **We are your slaves** (50:18).

50:19-20 Joseph held the highest position in the world—other than Pharaoh, and Pharaoh would certainly have looked the other way if he had acted against his treacherous brothers. Now his father was dead, so there was no one else who would have pleaded with him to stop. Yet Joseph responded with one of the most profound statements of faith in the entire Bible. **You planned evil against me; God planned it for good** (50:20).

We often give people too much credit. Yes, what Joseph's brothers did was horribly wrong. But even through their sinful actions God was orchestrating something bigger than they were. They had small-scale evil intentions, but God was overriding their evil for eternal good. Joseph recognized that the detours of his life were part of God's providential plan. How could he possibly respond in anger when God had used their terrible acts to deliver him to such a lofty position? Please note the order: evil, God, good. When we experience unjust evil, we must look for God who is able to bring about incredible good.

50:21 Joseph responded to his brothers with forgiveness, promising to **take care** of them and their **children**. The very brothers who threw him in the pit, **he comforted . . . and spoke kindly to**. Joseph had discovered the secret of forgiving your enemies: you need the right view of God. Throughout his tumultuous journey, Joseph believed that God was with him and guiding him to an intentional destiny. And if God was guiding the process *then*, Joseph was content to let God guide it *now*.

Vengeance belongs to God, and the longer we cherish an unforgiving attitude in our hearts, the more we harm ourselves. Unforgiveness acts like a leash that keeps snapping us back, painfully, to the past. Only when we choose to let God be the God of vengeance (and take ourselves off that lofty throne) does the leash disappear, allowing us to march forward toward the destiny God has in store for us. God's destiny for us will always bring blessing and benefit to others.

50:22-26 Joseph ended his days in peace, living among his brothers (50:22) and watching his family grow (50:23). When the time came for him to die, he remembered the promises made to his forefathers, that God would bring him **to the land he swore to give to Abraham, Isaac, and Jacob** (50:24). Thus he made his brothers promise **to carry [his] bones** to the promised land (50:25).

And that's exactly what they did. Years later, after the Lord rescued the people of Israel from Egyptian slavery, entered a covenant with them, disciplined them in the wilderness for their sins, made them victorious in battle, and delivered the promised land to them, the Israelites buried Joseph (see Exod 13:19; Josh 24:32).

EXODUS

INTRODUCTION

Author

THE BOOK OF EXODUS, LIKE THE other books of the Pentateuch (the first five books of the Bible) names no particular author. Early Jewish and Christian tradition, however, affirmed that Moses was the writer. In several places, the book indicates that Moses wrote down God's instructions (see Exod 17:14; 24:4; 34:27-28). Thus, though the book is formally anonymous, there is every reason to accept the tradition that it was written by the main character in its storyline: Moses.

Historical Background

Exodus opens where the book of Genesis ends—with the death of Joseph in Egypt in about 1805 BC (see Gen 50:22-26). But by Exodus 1:8, the narrative has skipped forward three hundred years to the period of the Israelites' enslavement in Egypt. The first half of the book describes how Moses led the Israelites out of Egypt through the initiative and miraculous deliverance of God. The second half explains how God entered into a covenant relationship with Israel (in spite of their sins), gave them his law, and established the tabernacle.

Scholars debate the year of the exodus. But many conservative scholars arrive at a date of 1446 BC. In 1 Kings 6:1, the author indicates that Solomon began constructing the temple in the fourth year of his reign, which was "in the four hundred eightieth year after the Israelites came out of the land of Egypt." Since this date

is determined to be 966 BC, the math brings us to the year 1446 BC for Israel's sojourn out of Egypt. If this is correct, then the Pharaoh who enslaved the Israelites would have been Thutmose III. The Pharaoh during the exodus would have been his son, Amenhotep II.

Message and Purpose

Exodus is the continuation of Genesis in that we see within it the fulfillment of God's promise to Abraham to make of him a great nation (Gen 12:2), the nation of Israel. To accomplish this, God brought the people of Israel—Abraham's biological descendants—out from bondage in Egypt through the deliverance of Moses and the plagues that he called down on the Egyptians. Exodus shows how God kept Pharaoh from continuing to oppress the Israelites and from destroying them.

The book also shows how God moved the people of Israel into the wilderness to begin the process of developing them into the nation he wanted them to become. This is a reminder that after deliverance comes development. It was in the wilderness, in fact, that Israel would learn to walk with God, trust him, and receive their national constitution, the Ten Commandments. These familiar rules were guidelines God gave the Israelites regarding how they were to relate to him and to each other.

God also gave strict guidelines for constructing the tabernacle and placing it at the very center of the Israelite camp in the wilderness. This was to teach the people that he was to be at the very heart of their worship and their lives. Thus, Exodus is a book about what it means to worship God and keep him at the center of life. These principles are at the heart of kingdom living.

www.bhpublishinggroup.com/qr/te/02_00

EXODUS

I. PREPARING ISRAEL'S DELIVERER (1:1–4:31)

1:1-7 Jacob (also called Israel), his sons, and all of their families had come to dwell in Egypt to escape the famine that had spread as far away as Canaan. This **fruitful** clan of **seventy** Israelites **multiplied ... so that the land was filled with them** (1:5-7). By the time of the exodus, the people of Israel consisted of "six hundred thousand able-bodied men . . . besides their families" (12:37). God was fulfilling his kingdom promise to Abraham to give him numerous descendants (see Gen 13:16). The people of Israel were becoming the nation God had promised.

1:8-10 After Joseph and all of his brothers died, **a new king** ascended to the throne in Egypt. This pharaoh **did not know about Joseph** and had no appreciation for his achievements on behalf of Egypt (1:8). As he saw the **Israelite people** multiplying all around him, he became alarmed, fearing that they might align with Egypt's enemies in a time of **war** (1:9-10).

1:11 Pharaoh decided to exploit the Israelites for their economic potential. He **assigned taskmasters** over them and oppressed them **with forced labor**. Importantly, years before this, God had told Abraham that one day his offspring would be enslaved by another nation for four hundred years (see Gen 15:13-14). It had finally come to pass: the people of Israel were now slaves. But God had also promised that he would judge the nation that mistreated them and that Abraham's descendants would plunder their oppressors. How that would happen would soon unfold.

1:12-14 As it turned out, **the more [Egypt] oppressed [the Israelites], the more they multiplied** (1:12). In spite of Pharaoh's ill-treatment, their numbers only continued to rise. This tells us that in the midst of their suffering, God was blessing them. Yet the Egyptians **came to dread** them, and Pharaoh treated them **ruthlessly** (1:12-14).

1:15-17 Pharaoh decided to use an even more wicked method of population control. He told the **Hebrew midwives** to **kill** any **son** that the **Hebrew women** delivered (1:15-16). But the midwives refused to obey **the king of Egypt.** Why? They **feared God** (1:17). Though Pharaoh had the power to execute them, these defenseless women knew God held ultimate power, and they acted on that knowledge.

1:18-21 When the king demanded an explanation for their disobedience to his command, the midwives lied, saying that they routinely arrived at the births too late (1:18-19). They decided to lie to this wicked king—who didn't deserve the truth—in order to prevent the murder of innocent children made in God's image. For their actions, **God was good to the midwives** and **gave them families** (1:20-21). And the Israelites **multiplied** even more (1:20). The principle here is that when God's people are faced with only two sinful options (in this case, lying and murder), we are to choose that which brings God the greater glory.

1:22 Being foiled in his second attempt to control the Israelites' numbers was the last straw for **Pharaoh.** He **commanded all his**

people to throw every son born to the Hebrews into the Nile. With this decree, the stage was set for the rise of Moses. God had blessed his people, which led to a problem, which led to more blessing, which led to worse problems, which led to preparation for God's ultimate deliverance. This is a reminder that many times God will allow blessings in our lives that will actually lead to some suffering, which will in turn lead to even greater blessings for his kingdom purposes. We, however, must patiently wait for him to work things out.

2:1-4 A woman from the **family of Levi** had a **son.** She saw that **he was beautiful** and **hid him for three months,** trusting God over the power of Pharaoh's edict (2:1-2; see Heb 11:23). When she could hide him no longer, the woman placed her son in a **basket** in the **Nile** River. She hoped that, in the providence of God, this body of water in which the babies were being drowned would serve as a means of deliverance for her child (2:3). And the baby boy's **sister** Miriam watched to see what God would do (2:4).

2:5-9 When **Pharaoh's daughter** arrived to **bathe** in the river, she found the **basket** with the Hebrew baby inside and **felt sorry for him** (2:5-6). (God had intervened on behalf of his people.) The boy's **sister** then offered to find a Hebrew mother to **nurse the boy,** and Pharaoh's daughter agreed (2:7-8). One moment the baby was under the threat of death, the next moment his mother was being paid by Pharaoh's daughter to raise him (2:9). This is the sovereignty of God at work.

God, I find, demonstrates amazing providential care when people operate according to his kingdom agenda. In the remarkable provision of the Lord, all of these women—the midwives, the mother, the sister, and even Pharaoh's daughter—were used by God to cover and care for a child whom God would use to bring about his kingdom purposes.

2:10 When the boy **grew older,** the mother **brought him to Pharaoh's daughter, and he became her son.** Then **she named him Moses.** An Israelite child who was supposed to have been executed under royal orders was now being raised in the royal household—"educated in all the wisdom of the Egyptians" (Acts 7:22). In divine irony, the future prophet of God who would bring plagues upon Egypt and lead slaves to freedom was being nurtured right under the enemy oppressor's nose.

2:11-15 After **Moses had grown up,** he **observed** the oppression of **his own people** (2:11). At some point along the way, notwithstanding his advantages, Moses decided to identify with the Hebrews and help them. One day, when he noticed an Egyptian beating a Hebrew, Moses killed the Egyptian and **hid** his body (2:11-12). But **the next day,** when he tried to break up a fight between **two Hebrews,** one asked, **Who made you a . . . judge over us?** (2:13-14). They rejected Moses's attempts at peacemaking and deliverance. "He assumed his people would understand that God would give them deliverance through him, but they did not" (Acts 7:25). Moses had miscalculated.

Then the Hebrew asked Moses if he planned to kill him like he **killed the Egyptian** (2:14). And **Moses became afraid** when he realized that his actions had become **known.** When Pharaoh finally caught wind of things, he **tried to kill Moses** (2:14-15), and that did it. **Moses** had to run for his life, fleeing to **Midian** (2:15), which was in modern Saudi Arabia on the east side of the Gulf of Aqaba.

Moses's life story could now be summed up in two words: murder and rejection. He went from a privileged upbringing to going on the lam. One moment he had Pharaoh for a step-granddad; the next moment he was being hunted like a fox. Moses was well-intentioned in trying to help his native people, but impulsive. This is a reminder that we shouldn't attempt to do the right things in the wrong way. Moses needed not just secular training and not just the stories about his ancestors that he'd likely heard. The man needed God's perspective on his situation. Eventually, in God's timing, he would get it.

2:16-22 In Midian, Moses came to the defense of the **daughters** of **the priest** there (2:16-17), who is called by several names in

Scripture: **Reuel** (2:18), Jethro (3:1), and Hobab (Judg 4:11). As a result of Moses's kindness, this father invited him to **dinner** and eventually gave him **his daughter Zipporah** as a wife (2:18-21). She bore Moses a **son whom he named Gershom**, and Moses became a shepherd in Midian (2:22). Talk about downsizing! Moses had gone from living as Pharaoh's protégé to working as a desert herdsman. But in reality God was supernaturally working behind the scenes to prepare the deliverer of his people. Sometimes, to accomplish his purposes through you, God has to take you low before he will take you high.

What's true in basketball is also true in life. Unfortunately, life has its missed shots. The crucial question is: will you *rebound* so that you can shoot again? The key to spiritual victory is spiritual *resiliency*.

2:23 After many years, **the king of Egypt died**. But things didn't improve for the Israelites. Their **labor** was so **difficult** that they **groaned** to God. They were desperate. Note the connection here: their bitter bondage forced them to cry out. Sometimes this is just the kind of thing it takes to get us to call on God. Some Christians ask why God is allowing them to go through such difficult circumstances. The answer might be this: because it forces you to turn your focus upward and to take God seriously.

2:24-25 **God heard . . . and God remembered his covenant with Abraham, with Isaac, and with Jacob** (2:24). The God of heaven and earth listened to his people's cries. He paid attention. Why? The answer hinges on one word: covenant. The Lord had made an agreement with Abraham to make his descendants a mighty nation and to give them a mighty land (see Gen 12:3). This agreement is what God promised to fulfill. Now the cry of the Israelites connected with God's word of promise. And even while they were crying out, God was preparing a deliverer.

3:1 By this time, Moses was an eighty-year-old man (see Acts 7:23, 30), working for **his father-in-law**. He likely had come to accept this as his lot in life. But things changed dramatically when he **came to Horeb, the mountain of God**, which is another name

for Mount Sinai (see Exod 3:12; 19:20; Deut 1:19)—the place where God would soon enter into a covenant with the nation of Israel.

3:2-3 After forty years of dealing with the consequences of his actions, Moses was about to have a fresh encounter with God. **Then the angel of the LORD appeared to him in a flame of fire . . . . [A] bush was on fire but was not consumed** (3:2). Clearly, that's not normal. But that shouldn't be surprising, for the Lord says, "My thoughts are not your thoughts, and your ways are not my ways" (Isa 55:8). Moses's ordinary day was about to be invaded by God's extraordinary plan. Moses saw the bush and decided to investigate (3:3). God often reveals his special presence in the contradictions of life.

3:4-5 When Moses responded to what God was doing, God spoke (3:4). Once Moses was listening, God began with a command: **Remove the sandals from your feet, for the place where you are standing is holy** (3:5). Moses was standing on about a quarter of an inch of sandal sole. But in the presence of a holy God, that's too much. He needed to humble himself. He also needed to be reminded of where he came from. Man was made "out of the dust from the ground" (Gen 2:7). By removing his sandals, then, Moses meekly identified with his humble beginnings.

3:6-10 When he realized who was speaking to him, Moses **hid his face because he was afraid to look at God** (3:6). In other words, he took God seriously. At that point, the Lord told Moses that he had seen **the misery of [his] people in Egypt**. He was not unaware of their **sufferings** but had heard their cries (3:7, 9). Therefore, he said, **I have come down to rescue them** (3:8). But God doesn't merely determine the ends, he also determines the means. He was ready to rescue his people, and he now explained to Moses how he would: **I am sending you to Pharaoh so that you may lead my people, the Israelites, out** (3:10).

Moses may have thought that his life was nearly over as he passed time with the sheep as an octogenarian. But the Lord was still preparing him. He gave Moses forty years of uptown training in Egypt, followed by forty years of downtown training in the wilderness. That's what was necessary to get this shepherd ready to lead the sheep of Israel out of Egypt and into the promised land. Of course, Moses's sojourn in the wilderness was the consequence of his murder of an Egyptian too (2:11-15). But God can bring a miracle out of a mess.

3:11-12 By the time God singled out Moses to lead his people out of Egypt, gone was the bold and brash man who murdered an Egyptian and expected his fellow Hebrews to look up to him. Instead of jumping at the chance to deliver Israel, he asked God, **Who am I that I should go to Pharaoh and that I should bring the Israelites out of Egypt?** (3:11). Moses had been humbled. And notice how the Lord responded: **I will certainly be with you** (3:12). God did *not* tell Moses, "Cheer up and believe in yourself." Instead he promised him his divine presence. Moses's greatest need (and ours too) was not self-confidence; he needed God-confidence.

Here, too, God revealed his purpose in setting his people free: **When you bring the people out of Egypt, you will all worship [me] at this mountain** (3:12). In other words, God wasn't freeing the Israelites so they could sit around and be lazy. He was freeing them so that they could do what they had been created for: he wanted them to worship him as the one true God. Whenever God delivers you *from* something, he also delivers you *to* something—himself.

3:13 But how was Moses going to convince Israel of this? If he showed up and said he was supposed to be their deliverer, they would want to know who signed off on his job description. On whose authority was Moses operating? **What is his name?**

3:14-15 To this God responded: **I AM WHO I AM. . . . Say to the Israelites: I AM has sent me to you. . . . The LORD, the God of your fathers . . . has sent me to you** (3:14-15). "I AM" is the English translation of the first-person singular Hebrew verb meaning "to be." It could also be rendered, "I WILL BE WHAT I WILL BE" or "I CAUSE TO BE WHAT I CAUSE TO BE." By describing himself this way, God was affirming his self-existence and

self-sufficiency. He depends on nothing and no one. He is the Creator and Sustainer of all.

The name "LORD" is related etymologically to this Hebrew verb. Instead of the first-person singular form ("I AM"), "LORD" represents the third-person singular form (thus, "HE IS"). In Hebrew, it is represented by four consonants without any vowels: YHWH. We don't know for certain how this was pronounced because the Jews feared pronouncing the sacred name, but it may have been said this way: "Yahweh."

Later Hebrew scribes added vowels guiding readers to say the Hebrew word *adonai* (that is, "Lord") whenever they saw the word YHWH, which led early translators to write it "Jehovah." When the ancient Greek translation of the Old Testament (that is, the Septuagint) translated the divine name YHWH, it rendered it with the Greek word *kurios*, "Lord." This influenced the New Testament authors to do the same and influenced subsequent generations of Christians (as well as Bible translators) to render the divine name in the Old Testament as "LORD."

Many people claim to believe in a generic "God." But Moses was to tell the Israelites that he had been sent by the one true God—"the LORD," the God of their fathers. He alone is "the God of Abraham, Isaac, and Jacob," and he is the Father of our Lord Jesus Christ. He is the personal, all-powerful God who is responsible for all that exists, and he sovereignly directs all things to accomplish his kingdom purposes. Though the world is ever-changing, HE IS. If Moses needed assurance about following and obeying the One who was sending him, he got exactly what he needed.

3:16-18 Moses was to tell the Israelites that their God, **the LORD**, was intimately aware of their plight **in Egypt** and had come to deliver them to **a land flowing with milk and honey** (3:16-17). God promised that they would listen to his words. Then Moses was to stand before **the king of Egypt** and tell him to let the people go **into the wilderness** to worship the Lord (3:18).

3:19-22 But God made it clear that Pharaoh would not consent to this (3:19). So God would respond with miraculous displays of divine power to compel the king to release Israel (3:20). The Lord would also see to it that the Israelites didn't leave Egypt **empty-handed** (3:21). In fact, after all the suffering linked to the coming plagues, the Egyptians would gladly give Israel riches just to get rid of them. As a result, the Israelites would **plunder the Egyptians** (3:22). In a sense, they would receive the back wages they deserved.

Thus, Moses and the Israelites were to act in faith, trusting that the self-sufficient God who had revealed himself to them would be everything they could ever need. He is all we need too.

4:1-9 Moses was still nervous. He asked, **What if they won't believe me?** (4:1). Therefore, the Lord literally filled his hands with reason for confidence. When he told Moses to **throw** his shepherd's **staff** on the **ground**, it miraculously **became a snake** (4:2-3). When he picked it up, it turned into a staff again (4:4). The Lord assured his servant that, with the aid of such miracles, the people of Israel would believe that **the God of Abraham . . . Isaac, and . . . Jacob** had **appeared to** him (4:5). If the Israelites failed to believe this **sign**, God would use additional supernatural signs to convince them (4:6-9).

4:10 This still wasn't good enough for Moses. He said, **Please, Lord, I have never been eloquent . . . because my mouth and my tongue are sluggish.** Whether Moses had a speech impediment, was a poor public speaker, or simply didn't want to go, he argued, "Lord, you need someone else to be your mouthpiece!"

4:11 God's response to Moses is for all those who come up with excuses for why they are unable to obey the Lord's will: **Who placed a mouth on humans? Who makes a person mute or deaf, seeing or blind? Is it not I, the LORD?** When God commanded Moses to speak to Pharaoh on his behalf, God was not unaware of Moses's weaknesses. Similarly, when he calls you to kingdom service, he knows about your fears and your shortcomings.

This, in fact, is a reminder that God didn't choose you to serve him because he desperately needed your qualities on his team. He

chose you so that you could reflect his glory to the world. Paul told the Corinthians, "Consider your calling: Not many were wise from a human perspective, not many powerful. . . . Instead, God has chosen what is foolish in the world to shame the wise, and God has chosen what is weak in the world to shame the strong . . . so that no one may boast in his presence" (1 Cor 1:26-29).

4:12 Moses's lack of eloquence was inconsequential to the Lord. He didn't care about Moses's resume. God had the man he wanted. **Go! I will help you speak and I will teach you what to say**, he said. Ultimately, the exodus of God's people from Egypt wouldn't depend on Moses but on God. If God promises to inject his heavenly presence into your earthly reality, that's all you need.

4:13-17 All of the excuses Moses offered for why he shouldn't be the deliverer led to this final outburst: **Please, Lord, send someone else** (4:13). That's when **the LORD's anger burned** (4:14). The truth was out: Moses simply didn't want to go. But God wasn't taking "No" for an answer. He said that Moses's brother **Aaron** would do the actual talking. God would speak to Moses, Moses would speak to Aaron, and Aaron would convey the message to Pharaoh (4:14-16). It was time for Moses to take courage, trust God, and start walking. Though he initially fought it, he was destined to be God's kingdom man.

4:18-20 The Lord informed Moses that those who had **wanted to kill** him were **dead** (4:19). The previous Pharaoh had been succeeded by his son. So Moses gathered **his wife and sons** and began the journey to Egypt (4:20).

4:21 The LORD instructed Moses to perform the miracles he had given him **power** to accomplish, yet God would **harden** Pharaoh's **heart** so that he wouldn't **let the people go.** Note, however, that God didn't harden Pharaoh's heart until Pharaoh first hardened himself. When Pharaoh repeatedly refused to listen (7:22; 8:15, 32) God told him, in a sense, "Have it your way." He only hardened his heart further (9:12) in order to use Pharaoh's rebellion for his greater glory and to achieve his kingdom purpose.

4:22-23 Moses was to tell Pharaoh that the Lord said, **Israel is my firstborn son** (4:22). In other words, the ethnic group that the king was abusing wasn't just some random group; Creator God saw them as his son, making himself their *Father*. Moreover, Israel was his *firstborn son*. The firstborn held a position of honor and privilege in the ancient Near East. Pharaoh had enslaved those to whom God demanded that he show respect. If the king of Egypt refused to honor God's firstborn son, he would pay a high price for his rebellion: his own **firstborn son** (4:23).

4:24-26 Suddenly, out of the blue, this happened: **The Lord confronted [Moses] and intended to put him to death** (4:24). Why was God ready to execute the one whom he had chosen to deliver his people? Moses's wife's actions (4:25), which at first glance seem rather bizarre, provide the answer.

As a descendent of Abraham (see Gen 17:1-27), Moses was to circumcise his son. He, however, had failed to lead his family and demonstrate his commitment to God's covenant. Moses was to serve as God's representative to lead God's firstborn son—that is, the Israelites—to worship him, but he hadn't even fulfilled his basic obligation toward his own firstborn. Fathers, the Lord calls us to lead our families in following Christ (see Eph 6:4). Wives are to help, but God has laid the responsibility at our feet.

Since Moses had been negligent in his covenant commitment, **Zipporah** circumcised their son and deflected God's judgment (4:25-26)—thus, saving her husband's life. This suggests that many a life is saved as godly mothers obey the Lord when their husbands fail to do so. Though wives are called to submit to their husbands, this submission is limited. A women's highest commitment is to God, not her husband. Wives, should these two commitments conflict, you are to serve the Lord.

4:27-31 Moses had a happy reunion with his brother **Aaron** and told him all that the Lord **had commanded him to do** (4:27-28). They gathered **the elders of the Israelites**, explained everything, and **performed the signs** (4:29-30). Then, **the people believed** (4:31), just as God had promised (3:18). Once the descendants of Israel knew God's mercy on their **misery**, they **worshiped** (4:31). News of God's deliverance should always lead his people to praise.

II. THE DELIVERER CONFRONTS PHARAOH (5:1–11:10)

5:1-2 The moment of confrontation arrived. Moses and Aaron stood before Pharaoh and said, **This is what the Lord, the God of Israel, says: Let my people go, so that they may hold a festival for me** (5:1). Pharaoh could have avoided a tremendous amount of grief if he had heeded this simple request. Instead he refused to **obey** the Lord because he didn't **know** him (5:2). He didn't recognize him as a deity among Egypt's pantheon.

5:3-9 They repeated the request, emphasizing that they were under the Lord's authority and that he might become angry and punish them if they didn't obey (5:3). But instead of relenting, Pharaoh accused Moses and Aaron of enabling the people to be idle (5:4-5). So he decided to put the enslaved people in their place and prevent any further unruliness. He commanded the Egyptian **overseers** and Israelite **foremen** not to **supply** the Israelites with **straw** to make **bricks** but to let them **gather** it themselves and still produce the same quantity of bricks (5:6-8). That, he reasoned, would keep the lazy **slackers** busy and would prevent further whining about worshiping the Lord (5:8-9).

5:10-18 The news was delivered to the Israelites, and they **scattered throughout the land . . . to gather stubble for straw** (5:10-12). When they failed to make their quota, **the Israelite foremen . . . were beaten** (5:14). They cried out to Pharaoh about the injustice, but he just laid blame on their desire to **sacrifice to** the Lord (5:15-18).

5:19-21 Upon leaving Pharaoh's presence, **the Israelite foreman . . . confronted Moses and Aaron** (5:19-20). They angrily blamed the brothers for making matters worse and called on God to **judge** them (5:21). If the Hebrews hadn't wanted Moses for a deliverer in the past (2:13-14), they certainly didn't want him now.

5:22-23 Moses fell into despair. The people blamed him, so he shifted the blame to God: **Why have you caused trouble for this people? And why did you ever send me?... You haven't rescued your people at all** (5:22-23). In other words, he accused God of having made matters worse and having failed to keep his promise. One has to wonder what Moses was expecting when he and Aaron had audience before Pharaoh that first time. Hadn't God told him that Pharaoh's heart would be hard, that their freedom would be won only by God's mighty power, and that it would be a fight to the death?

6:1-5 Nevertheless, the Lord recognized the strain Moses was under and did not rebuke him. Everything that had happened up to now was merely prologue. Things were about to get exciting. **Now**, God said, **you will see what I will do to Pharaoh** (6:1). He reminded Moses that he had revealed himself to the patriarchs, though they had not known him **by [his] name 'the Lord'** (6:3). He had **established a covenant with them to give them the land of Canaan** (6:4). In recent days he had **heard the groaning** of the people, that is their blood descendants, and **remembered** his **covenant** (6:5).

When the Bible says that God "remembers," it doesn't mean that he called to mind something that he had previously forgotten. It means that, based on a covenant promise he made, he's ready to act to fulfill his obligation. In God's perfect timing, the season of deliverance had come for Israel.

6:6 The Lord was going to **rescue** Israel **from slavery**. His **outstretched arm** refers to his supernatural power that would invade history to such an extent that people would still be talking about what happened in Egypt thousands of years later. If Pharaoh had immediately let the people go, the Israelites might have attributed their deliverance to Pharaoh's kindheartedness or to Moses's eloquence. Instead, as the following chapters

demonstrate, there could be no doubt in the minds of future generations that it was the Lord who had rescued his people from Egypt with his outstretched arm. He alone would deserve all of the glory because only he could write the story that was about to unfold.

6:7-8 Importantly, God wasn't setting the Hebrews free so that they could spend their days as their own masters. He was setting them free for a relationship. They would be his people, and he would be their God in the land he had promised (6:7-8). In the future, the people of Israel, too, would know him as **the Lord [their] God, who brought [them] out from the forced labor of the Egyptians** (6:7; see 20:2).

6:9-13 In spite of what Moses relayed to the people, they refused to listen **because of their broken spirit and hard labor** (6:9). Moses's first real attempt to deliver them, after all, had only led to increased labor. So when God told Moses to speak to Pharaoh a second time, Moses was again reluctant (6:10-12). He asked, **If the Israelites will not listen ... how will Pharaoh?** (6:12). Again, Moses pointed to his lack of eloquence as if that would somehow lead to the downfall of God's plan. But God intended to deliver the people through his outstretched arm (6:6), not through Moses's eloquence. So he **gave** Moses and Aaron **commands** (6:13).

6:14-25 The story is interrupted briefly by a listing of **the heads of their fathers' families** (6:14). Since the Levites would be responsible for the tabernacle and the descendants of Aaron would be responsible for priestly duties, this genealogy helps establish that **Aaron** and **Moses** were descended from **Levi**, Jacob's third son (6:16-20). **Reuben** and **Simeon** are named first here (6:14-15) because they were Jacob's first and second sons.

The name **Phinehas** means "the Negro" or "Nubian," a dark-skinned people (also see 1 Chr 9:20). Phinehas was the son of **Eleazar** and his wife, a daughter of **Putiel** (6:25). This is interesting, because when Phinehas was born, Israel was already established as a separate commonwealth, although it was in transit. Therefore, at least some of the citizens within the commonwealth of Israel were giving birth to children whose names characterized them as Nubian or Negroes. Thus, the children of Israel must have been heterogeneous.

Putiel's name provides us with a possible understanding of who his people were. The first three letters of Putiel's name appear to have a lexical/etymological link to Put, one of the sons of Ham. Where the name Put is used in the Old Testament, it usually names African peoples (see also Jer 46:9; Ezek 27:10; 30:5; 38:5). This would certainly explain how Phinehas was born a Nubian in the midst of a Semitic congregation.

6:26 –7:2 The statement that **it was this Aaron and Moses whom the Lord told** to lead the Israelites out of Egypt (6:26) means that these two had the right family credentials for the work God had assigned them.

7:3-5 Here we see further evidence that because of **Pharaoh's** already hard **heart**, the Lord would **harden** it further (7:3; see commentary on 4:21). Since Pharaoh would refuse to **listen**, God would **stretch out [his] hand against Egypt** in judgment and **put [his] hand into Egypt** to deliver his people (7:4-5). This is a reminder that all people will experience the hand of God one way or another—either its hardness or its mercy.

7:6-7 Moses and Aaron . . . did just as the Lord commanded them (7:6). There's no better commendation a person can receive than this. Those who do likewise will hear the Lord Jesus say, "Well done, good and faithful servant!" (Matt 25:23).

Notice that these two brothers began their ministry at age **eighty** and **eighty-three** (7:7). For the godly saint devoted to the King's agenda, the senior years can be the most fruitful.

7:8-13 To persuade Pharaoh of the Lord's power, the messengers first cast Moses's **staff** before the king (7:8-9). When **it became a serpent**, Pharaoh was not impressed and had his **sorcerers** do the same **by their occult practices** (7:9-11). But lest Pharaoh think that his magic and the Lord's supernatural power were on equal footing, **Aaron's**

staff **swallowed their staffs** (7:12). Nevertheless, **Pharaoh's heart was hard** (7:13). In the core of his being, he was rebellious against the will of God.

7:14-18 Thus, the first of God's plagues—which were essentially divine curses—began. As the king stood **by the bank of the Nile**, Moses and Aaron warned him that the Lord would **turn** the river **to blood**, and the **water** would be undrinkable (7:15-18). That which was a source of life for Egypt would become a source of death.

7:19-24 At God's command, Aaron took Moses's divinely empowered staff **in the sight of Pharaoh and his officials** and **struck the water in the Nile** (7:19-20). All the water **turned to blood** and the Egyptians **could not drink** it (7:20-21). Once again, Egypt's **magicians . . . did the same thing by their occult practices**, probably by some sort of sleight of hand—but clearly on a much smaller scale (7:22). But even if they were able to mimic God's miracle, they were unable to reverse it. The Egyptians thus had to dig for water, while the Nile ran polluted and stank for a week (7:24). Still, Pharaoh's **heart** was stone; he simply walked away from the first clear evidence of God's hand at work against him (7:23). Pharaoh suffered from the greatest of all sins: pride. He refused to submit to divine authority.

8:1-7 The next time Moses and Aaron appeared before Pharaoh, it was the same message from the Lord: **Let my people go, so that they may worship me** (8:1). This time the king's refusal would lead to a **plague** of **frogs** all over the land (8:2). With a wave of Moses's staff, there were frogs in the **bed**, frogs in the **ovens**, and frogs in the **kneading bowls** (8:3-6). They were everywhere. Yet once again, Pharaoh's **magicians** imitated this sign (8:7). Ridding the land of them would've demonstrated genuine spiritual power, but this they couldn't do.

8:8-14 This time, Pharaoh said, **Appeal to the Lord to remove the frogs. . . . Then I will let the people go** (8:8). But notice Moses's cunning reply: **You may have the honor of choosing. When should . . . the frogs be**

taken away? (8:9). This move would prevent Pharaoh from claiming that their coming and going was a freak act of nature; it was an act of God (8:10-11). When **Moses cried out to the LORD for help**, he answered. However, the frogs didn't merely hop away. They **died**, producing a wretched stench (8:12-14).

8:15 When Pharaoh saw there was relief, he hardened his heart again. This is a warning to us all. When struggles are intense, we tend to cry to God for relief. Yet, as soon as the relief comes, we can easily fall back into business as usual.

Importantly, while the Lord could have wiped this arrogant Pharaoh off the map, he gave him many chances to repent. God's kindness was intended to lead the king to repentance (see Rom 2:4), but Pharaoh wasn't interested in God's good gift.

8:16-19 Plague number three came without warning. God caused **the dust of the land** to become swarms of **gnats throughout ... Egypt. People and animals** were covered with them (8:17). On this occasion, Egypt's sorcerers were unable to replicate the plague by their magic arts (8:18). For the first time, they realized they were in over their heads and confessed to Pharaoh, **This is the finger of God.** But not only did Pharaoh fail to listen to Moses and Aaron. Now he **would not listen to** his own spiritual advisors (8:19).

8:20-23 Soon the Lord announced the fourth plague to Moses: **swarms of flies** were coming. They would fill the **houses** of the people of Egypt (8:21). But this time God expressly declared that he would **give special treatment** to his people in **the land of Goshen** (8:22). He would **make a distinction** between the Israelites and the Egyptians by permitting **no flies** in the land of his people (8:22-23). By announcing the plague in advance and preventing the flies from swarming in a particular geographical area, God was giving all involved further proof that his power alone was behind the ecological disasters suddenly falling on Egypt.

8:24-27 Pharaoh decided he would try to strike a compromise and offered to let the people go to **sacrifice** to God **within the**

country of Egypt (8:25). But Moses wouldn't haggle. If the Israelites remained in Egypt, the Egyptians would **stone** them because they would **detest** their sacrifices (8:26). The worship that the true God found acceptable clashed with the religious practices of pagan Egypt.

8:28-32 Pharaoh relented, asking that the Israelites not travel **very far** and that Moses **appeal** to the Lord on his behalf (8:28). Moses agreed but warned Pharaoh against acting **deceptively** (8:29). When Moses prayed, God answered, and every last fly departed, which had to be a welcome relief (8:30-31). Nevertheless, **Pharaoh hardened his heart**, marching further toward destruction (8:32).

9:1-7 Again God demanded the Egyptian king, **Let [his] people go, so that they may worship** (9:1). Refusal would bring about **a severe plague** on the Egyptian **livestock in the field** (9:3). Yet the Lord would again **make a distinction** between Israel and Egypt; the livestock of the former would live while that of the latter would die (9:4). To this point, there had been no destruction of property or bodily suffering as a result of Pharaoh's obstinacy—unless you equate having frogs hopping on your pillow as a painful experience. But all of that leniency was about to change. The death of the livestock would have been a severe blow to the Egyptian economy. Nevertheless, when Pharaoh saw that none of the **Israelite livestock** was harmed, he remained unmoved (9:7).

9:8-12 Next God directed Moses and Aaron to **take handfuls of furnace soot** and toss it in the air before Pharaoh. It would become **dust** over the land and would cause **festering boils** on both man and beast (9:8-9). With this sixth plague, painful physical suffering visited the Egyptians. Even Pharaoh's **magicians could not stand before Moses** because they were covered with boils (9:11). Yet Pharaoh was defiant, unmoved by the misery of his own subjects. Therefore, the Lord removed all restraint and gave the king over to his own destructive habits. God finally "supersized" the hardness of Pharaoh's heart (see commentary on 4:21).

9:13-14 Before unleashing his seventh curse against Pharaoh and his people, God warned him once more to release the Israelites. If not, he would send **all [his] plagues against** Egypt, so that the nation would know that **there is no one like [the Lord] on the whole earth** (9:14). Don't miss that with each plague, God was giving Pharaoh an opportunity to humble himself and repent even while he was demonstrating his sovereign power over his creation. But though he extended grace, God would increase the pressure until Pharaoh finally confessed that the Lord was God, and that he (Pharaoh) was not.

9:15 Through his intermediaries God said to Pharaoh, **By now I could have stretched out my hand and struck you . . . and you would have been obliterated**. Notice what he does here. It's as if Egypt's king is a petulant child who has talked back to his father one too many times, earning this response: "Do you understand whom you're talking to, young man?" Except, in the biblical case, the situation is incredibly magnified. Parents have limited authority over their children. God has complete, righteous authority over all his creatures. Pharaoh *thought* he could oppose God and prevent him from accomplishing his will. In reality, the king's life hung by a thread. He existed only by God's mercy.

9:16 I **have let you live for this purpose**, God continued, **to show you my power and to make my name known on the whole earth**. Christians often quote the gracious promise of Romans 8:28: "We know that all things work together for the good of those who love God, who are called according to his purpose." But there's a flipside to that reality: All things can work together for the bad of those who hate God and who resist his purposes.

Make no mistake: God is the sovereign King of the universe, and he will accomplish his kingdom purposes. He has given each person the freedom to cooperate with him or to oppose him. Would Pharaoh submit to God, or would he be run over by God's sovereignty tires? God *will* be glorified—through us or in spite of us.

If you cooperate with the sovereignty of God, it does not mean you won't experience hardship and suffering. Rather, it means you can be assured that the good, bad, and ugly of your life will be put into God's blender, ultimately bringing you to the place where he wants you to be. If, by contrast, you rebel against the all-powerful God, understand that you have not escaped his sovereignty. God will still do exactly what he wants. You, however, will be on the wrong side of his sovereignty and will remove yourself from the covering of his blessing.

9:17-21 Because of Pharaoh's willfulness, plague number seven was coming. The Lord was about to **rain down the worst hail** Egypt had ever experienced (9:17-18). Yet once more God tempered judgment with mercy and urged the man to bring all the **livestock** (that had survived the fifth plague) into the **shelters**. (Perhaps the Egyptians had traded with the Israelites for their animals or had bartered with other nations to restock.) **Every person and animal** outside when the **hail** fell would be killed (9:19). By this time, there were some of **Pharaoh's officials who feared the word of the LORD** and brought their livestock in (9:20). But others followed the example of their king (9:21).

9:22-26 A severe hailstorm mixed with lightning fell on the land, killing **both people and animals** (9:23-25). But God again spared **the land of Goshen, where the Israelites were** (9:26). This distinction makes it clear that this was not the work of Mother Nature, a fictitious figure often wrongly credited with the marvels of the natural world; it was the work of Father God, the true Creator and sustainer of all.

9:27-30 Pharaoh confessed his guilt and the Lord's righteousness (9:27). He begged Moses to pray for him and vowed to let Israel **go** (9:28). On the surface, it appeared that the man was changing. Moses therefore promised to appeal to the Lord, and the hail would stop (9:29). But God had given Moses spiritual insight into Pharaoh's heart. Before the meeting ended, Moses told him, **I know that you still do not fear the LORD God** (9:30). Indeed, the king of Egypt was willing to say what was necessary to cause a change in his wretched circumstances. But there had been no spiritual change in his heart.

9:31-35 Even in the midst of all this devastation, God had been merciful to Egypt. **The flax and the barley were destroyed**, but **the wheat and the spelt** were preserved because they were not yet in season (9:31-32). God's judgment was severe, but he had not wiped out the entire food supply. Shockingly, Pharaoh saw this as opportunity to persist in rebellion. When the plague was lifted, Pharaoh **hardened his heart** and held tight to his slaves (9:34-35).

10:1-2 God told Moses that he had further **hardened** Pharaoh's **heart** (see commentary on 4:21) so that he could perform his **miraculous signs** (10:1). But the Lord wanted Israel to realize that the miracles weren't merely for the Egyptians—they were also for their sake. Israelites in the generations to come were to tell their children and grandchildren how the Lord had powerfully judged their enemies, so that they might **know** and revere **the LORD** (10:2). The same general concept holds true today. Christian parents are to pass on their faith to their children, so that they might know, trust in, and live in light of the grace and power of God (see Eph 6:4).

10:3 God asked Pharaoh through Moses, **How long will you refuse to humble yourself before me?** Of course, God knew the answer. Pharaoh *would* eventually humble himself. There was no question about that. But how much destruction and sorrow would he bring on himself and his people before he finally gave in? Make no mistake, Pharaoh. The true King will get his way. The only question is whether a person will submit to his agenda and experience his blessing or resist it and experience misery.

10:4-7 Plague number eight was **locusts** that would **cover the . . . land** (10:4-5). What few crops had escaped the hail would be devoured (10:5). At this news, Pharaoh's advisors had had enough. They urged the king to release the Israelites: **How long must this man be a snare to us? . . . Don't you realize yet that Egypt is devastated?** (10:7). Their

words are a reminder that even as Pharaoh continued to puff himself up, his nation was crumbling all around him. Sometimes a leader's arrogance—whether he rules a nation or a home—prevents him from seeing what everyone around him can see. Pharaoh was running Egypt into the ground.

10:8-11 Again Pharaoh attempted a compromise. Though Moses informed him that the entire nation must go to offer sacrifices to the Lord, the king refused and said that only the able-bodied men could go. This was a shrewd move because he knew that these husbands and fathers would certainly not run off and leave their wives and children behind (10:8-11). "If you think I'm going to give you anything more than that," Pharaoh told Moses in essence, **you're heading for trouble** (10:10). But he was blind to the fact that he was a player in a game that he was destined to lose.

10:12-20 So Moses **stretched out his staff**, and **an east wind** blew the **locusts** into town (10:12-13). There had never been anything in Egypt that was an ominous as that cloud of marching, chewing soldiers (10:14). They consumed every plant until **nothing green was left** (10:15). Things got so bad that once again Pharaoh admitted his sin, asked for forgiveness, and begged that Moses pray to God to remove the locusts (10:16-17). In response, Moses prayed, God blew away the insects, and Pharaoh—as expected—again refused to let Israel go (10:18-20).

10:21-23 Pharaoh was given no warning about the ninth plague. The Lord simply brought darkness on **the land of Egypt for three days** (10:22). It was so bad, so oppressive and complete, that the Egyptians didn't move during that time. But, miraculously, **the Israelites had light where they lived** (10:23).

10:24-29 Pharaoh again made a half-hearted attempt to submit by letting the Israelite **families** go but demanding that the **flocks and herds . . . stay behind** (10:24). But Moses would not compromise. He knew partial obedience to God is disobedience. Moses insisted that all the livestock had to go too because the people would not know exactly what was needed until they arrived in the wilderness (10:25-26). Pharaoh was so filled with rage at this that he warned Moses not to appear before him again: **for on the day you see my face, you will die** (10:28). Moses agreed (10:29).

11:1 God told Moses, **I will bring one more plague on Pharaoh . . . . After that, he will let you go from here.** Importantly, God could have freed the Israelites with only one plague—or none. But he had planned to use ten from the beginning, to demonstrate conclusively his sovereign authority and power to the whole earth.

11:2-3 Earlier, when God called Moses in the wilderness to be the deliverer of his people, he promised that Israel would "plunder the Egyptians" when they departed (3:22). That promise was about to become a reality.

Moses was to tell the Israelites to **ask their neighbors for silver and gold items** because **the LORD gave the people favor** (11:2-3). After years of slavery, Israel was receiving its just wages.

11:4-10 The final curse against Pharaoh and Egypt would be a plague on the firstborn. The Lord would **go throughout Egypt, and every firstborn male** would **die**—whether human or livestock (11:4-5). The **anguish** in Egypt would be severe (11:6), but again God would make a **distinction** so that no harm would befall his people Israel (11:7). As a result, the Egyptians would beg the Israelites to leave.

When Moses had communicated this information to Pharaoh, he left his presence **fiercely angry** (11:8). An unarmed Hebrew issued an ultimatum to the most powerful ruler in the land and then stormed out of his palace.

III. THE DELIVERANCE OF ISRAEL (12:1–15:21)

12:1-2 Exodus 12 describes the greatest of Israel's annual festivals: Passover. By faithfully putting this ritual into practice, the Israelites would be protected by God from the plague on the firstborn and delivered from Egyptian bondage. Then, every year afterwards, they were to celebrate the Passover to remember how God had saved them. The month in which Passover was to be held would be **the first month** of the Jewish calendar year (12:2). It includes portions of our months March and April. In Canaan the month was called Abib; in Babylonia it was called Nisan.

12:3-13 Each family was to **select an animal** (12:3). The sheep or goat was to be **a year-old male** and **unblemished** (12:5). It was to be selected on the **tenth day** of the month and slaughtered at **twilight** on the **fourteenth** (12:3, 6). At that point, the Israelites were to take its blood and place it on the **doorposts and the lintel** of their **houses** (12:7). They were also to be **dressed for travel** and to hurriedly **eat the meat . . . roasted . . . along with unleavened bread and bitter herbs**

(12:8, 11). This was **the LORD's Passover** (12:11). The name of the festival arises from the fact that the Lord would **pass through the land . . . and strike every firstborn male** (12:12), but he would **pass over** homes bearing the **distinguishing mark** of **blood** (12:13).

Passover foreshadowed the coming of the Lord Jesus Christ and his atoning death on the cross. To make sure his followers didn't miss the connection, Paul told the church in Corinth, "Christ our Passover lamb has been sacrificed" (1 Cor 5:7). It was through the events of the first Passover that Israel was set free from slavery. Through placing faith in Christ's substitutionary death, we likewise are set free from slavery to sin (see Rom 6:17-18). And as people covered by "the blood of the lamb," we will conquer Satan (see Rev 12:11). "In him we have redemption through his blood, the forgiveness of our trespasses, according to the riches of his grace" (Eph 1:7). Don't miss that we are redeemed from sin "with the precious blood of Christ" (1 Pet 1:19). God had our salvation, too, in mind on that fateful night in Egypt.

12:14-20 This day was to be a lasting **memorial** for Israel to **celebrate** as **a permanent statute** (12:14). They were to **observe the Festival of Unleavened Bread** for **seven days** and **remove yeast** from their houses (12:15-20). Yeast, sometimes called "leaven," is often symbolic of sin in the Bible (see Luke 12:1; 1 Cor 5:6-8). Moreover, eating unleavened bread would remind the Israelites of their hasty exodus out of Egypt because their deliverance happened so quickly that there was no time to use yeast to allow the bread to rise before they hit the road.

12:21-28 Once Moses received the Lord's instructions about **the Passover**, he relayed them to **all the elders of Israel** (12:21). The festival would be a time of sober remembrance and celebration. But it would also provide a teaching tool for future generations. When Jewish **children** asked their parents the meaning of the feast, the parents were to explain how God had judged Egypt and delivered his people (12:26-27).

When the Israelites heard what God planned to do on their behalf, the people **knelt low and worshiped** and **did just as the Lord had commanded** (12:27-28). The appropriate response to divine deliverance is always worship and obedience.

12:29-30 The stage was set; the preparations were made. **At midnight the Lord struck every firstborn male in the land** (12:29). There was a **loud wailing** throughout Egypt because there wasn't a household that didn't awaken to at least one corpse within it (12:30). Pharaoh had led his nation to cruelly enslave Israel and rebelliously despise Israel's God. As a result, Egypt was drinking the fury of the cup of God's wrath.

12:31-36 Finally, Pharaoh had endured enough. He said, **Get out immediately from among my people** (12:31). He released all of the Israelites and all of their animals, just as the Lord had said he would (12:31-32; cf. 3:19-20). The Egyptians did everything they could to hurry the Israelites **quickly** on their way, giving them **silver . . . gold . . .** and **clothing** (12:33-34). **In this way [the Israelites] plundered the Egyptians** (12:36; see commentary on 11:2-3).

12:37-39 **Six hundred thousand able-bodied men** left Egypt in the exodus (12:37). With women and children, the people of Israel would have numbered over two million. The Lord had certainly blessed the original seventy descendants of Jacob who had come to Egypt (1:5). The **mixed crowd** indicates that non-Israelites accompanied them (12:38). Marriages to Egyptians, much like those of Joseph and Eleazar, would have produced dark-skinned offspring such as Phinehas (see 6:25), as well as a merging of the bloodlines between Nubians and Semites.

12:40-42 The Israelites' **430 years** there had finally come to an end (12:40-41), just as the Lord had promised Abraham that they would (Gen 15:13-14). Therefore, the Hebrews were to always remember this night **in honor of the Lord** (12:42).

12:43-51 These verses provide further instructions regarding the Passover, outlining who may and may not partake of it. Note that, regarding the sacrifice, the Israelites were not permitted to **break any of its bones** (12:46). According to the New Testament, this was also fulfilled in Jesus Christ, the true Passover Lamb (see commentary at 12:3-13). When Jesus was crucified, the soldiers did not break his legs—which was a typical tactic used to hasten the death of a crucifixion victim—because Jesus was already dead when they broke the legs of those killed alongside him. The apostle John saw that action as a fulfillment of Exodus 12:46 (see John 19:31-36).

13:1-10 Since God had destroyed all of the firstborn males of Egypt and spared the firstborn of Israel, he declared that the Israelites were to **consecrate**, or dedicate, to him their own **firstborn** (13:2). Moses reminded the people to **remember this day**, the day God had delivered them **out of the place of slavery** (13:3). They were to celebrate it in the years to come, even after they had entered the promised land. They were also to teach its meaning (13:5, 9).

13:11-13 When the Israelites arrived in **the land of the Canaanites**, every firstborn male—man and animal—was to be presented to the Lord (13:11-12). The people were to **redeem every firstborn** son by offering a sacrifice from their flocks. They were also to redeem every firstborn **donkey** with a sacrifice. If they did not redeem the donkey, they were to **break its neck** (13:13).

13:14-16 With these actions too came opportunities for the Israelites to teach their children truths about God and what he had done for them (13:14). The redemption of the firstborn was a reminder that God had spared Israel's firstborn when he killed Egypt's (13:15). Similarly, the acts of baptism and the Lord's Supper provide Christian parents visual pictures to help them instruct their children about the redemptive work of God through Jesus Christ. Taking advantage of such opportunities is part of how we "Bring [children] up in the training and instruction of the Lord" (Eph 6:4).

13:17-22 When the Israelites departed Egypt, God did not lead them down the nearest road because it led to **the land of the Philistines**. To go immediately from slavery to battle might discourage the people and cause them to **return to Egypt** (13:17). Though the departing Israelites had assumed **battle formation**, God knew they were not ready to face opposition. So he led them **toward the Red Sea along the road of the wilderness**—that is, into the Sinai Peninsula (13:18). God led his people with **a pillar of cloud** by day and **a pillar of fire** by night (13:21). In keeping with Joseph's wishes (see Gen 50:24-25), **Moses took the bones of Joseph with him** so that they could bury him in the land God had promised to Abraham, Isaac, and Jacob (13:19).

14:1-4 At this point, the Lord had Moses change the direction of the Israelites (14:1-2). He did this so that Pharaoh would hear of it and become convinced that they were **wandering around the land in confusion** (14:3). In other words, God's judgment on Egypt was not yet complete. One more time he would **harden Pharaoh's heart** and **receive glory** through Pharaoh's foolish rebellion against his clear will. Then the Egyptians would know once and for all that **[he is] the LORD** (14:4).

14:5-9 Pharaoh acted just as the Lord predicted. When he learned of the seemingly erratic actions of the Israelites, he asked, **What have we done? We have released Israel from serving us** (14:5). Then he took **six hundred . . . chariots**, sped after the people in hot pursuit, and **caught up with them . . . by the sea** (14:6-9).

14:10 When the Israelites caught sight of their pursuers, they **were terrified and cried out to the LORD for help.** Clearly, they thought themselves in a no-win situation. And true, they seemed to be caught between a rock and a hard place—between the sea and the Egyptian army. But what they were failing to grasp was that God was sovereignly directing the whole encounter. God, in fact, had orchestrated an apparent disaster. And he often does similar things in our lives today. Sometimes he will place his people in a dilemma, so that he can be glorified as he teaches us more about himself and accomplishes his purposes in our lives.

14:11-12 Out of the Israelites' fear rose some fussing. The hero who had delivered them from slavery quickly became an object of their scorn. They asked, **Is it because there are no graves in Egypt that you have taken us away to die in the wilderness?** (14:11). In other words, they felt they'd been better off living as slaves **than to die in the wilderness** (14:12).

14:13-14 Just as the people started to panic—caught between death by drowning and death by Egyptian will—Moses declared, **Don't be afraid. Stand firm and see the LORD's salvation. . . . The LORD will fight for you, and you must be quiet** (14:13-14). Though their fear made them want to run, the Lord told them to "stand firm." You too *can* choose not to fear by fulfilling your obligation as one under the protection of God— by acting in spite of your fear.

Notice that God didn't give Israel a plan of attack. He told them to "see [his] salvation" because "[he would] fight for [them]." Their eyes were on the Egyptians and the sea, which means they were looking in the wrong places. They needed to shift their attention away from their fears in order to recognize that the Lord would indeed fight on their behalf. This is a reminder that when you're boxed in by a dilemma, you must trust in the Lord. Look with the eyes of faith to see him working through your circumstances.

14:15-20 God called Moses to **stretch** his **staff . . . over the sea** and **divide it** so that the people could walk **through the sea on dry ground** (14:16). Meanwhile God would **harden the hearts of the Egyptians** (14:15; see commentary on 4:21; 9:8-12) so that they would chase the Israelites into the sea. Once again, God's plan was to bring himself **glory** through the actions of those who'd initially set themselves against him (14:17-18). While the Israelites prepared to march toward the sea, **the angel of God**—who had been leading them with **the pillar of cloud**—now **stood behind them** as a guardian, preventing the Egyptians from overtaking them (14:19-20).

14:21-22 Moses did as God commanded, **the LORD drove the sea back**, and **the Israelites went through . . . on dry ground** (14:21-22). God, then, worked two miracles. Not only did he split the sea in half, but he also dried the ground so they could walk through without getting all muddy. This was a surprise level of provision they never would have expected, even given the dramatic escape route provided. It suggests that we too should look for the lavish, unexpected miracles that often accompany the bigger, more obvious ways that God works to help us as we face crises. Thanking him for such things gives him the glory that he deserves.

14:23-25 Moses had told the Israelites, "The LORD will fight for you" (14:14). And they were about to see him in action. As **the Egyptians set out in pursuit**, God threw them **into confusion** and **caused their chariot wheels to swerve** (14:23-25). Pharaoh's forces, having just survived the plagues, immediately realized what was happening: **The LORD is fighting for [the Israelites]**. And they knew what they should do in response: **Let's get away from Israel**, they said (14:25).

14:26-28 Finally, the Lord was ready to deliver the knockout punch. He again told Moses to **stretch out [his] hand over the sea** (14:26).

And as the Egyptians tried to escape, the Lord caused the sea to flow back into its **normal** position (14:27). **The water . . . covered the chariots and horsemen** and **the entire army. . . . Not even one of them survived** (14:28). The Egyptian king who had defied the God of creation had his army wiped out by God's creation.

14:29-31 Israel, however, walked to safety at the other side of the sea (14:29). When they **saw the great power that the LORD used against the Egyptians, the people feared the LORD** (14:31). Likewise, when you receive deliverance from a crisis, you should remember that the correct response to it is to fear the Lord. Take him and his work on your behalf seriously. Give him the praise he's due and submit to his agenda.

15:1-5 In a response of praise for this miraculous exodus, **Moses and the Israelites sang this song to the LORD.** They said, God is **highly exalted** because of his triumph over Pharaoh's army, casting **the horse and its rider into the sea** (15:1). They had seen for themselves that the God of their fathers—of Abraham, Isaac, and Jacob—had come to save his people (15:2). The **elite** troops of Egypt were no match for their God: **the LORD is a warrior** (15:3-4).

15:6-10 Scripture often speaks of God accomplishing actions with his **right hand** as a way of referring to his mighty **power**. Like a boxer with a devastating right hook, the Lord **shattered the enemy** (15:6). The song's poetic imagery emphasizes God's **great majesty.** His **burning wrath** reduced the opposition to **stubble** (15:7), and the mere breath of his **nostrils** transformed the **sea** into a weapon of mass destruction (15:8, 10).

15:11-12 The song asks, **Who is like you among the gods?** The answer is obvious. The Lord is one of a kind. He alone is **glorious in holiness** and to be **revered with praises** (15:11). The Egyptian "gods" had proven powerless to stop him because they were imaginary.

15:13-18 The final verses of the song look to the future. God **will lead** the people whom he has just **redeemed** (15:13). The enemies who stand in their way will be filled with **anguish** and **terror and dread** when they hear how the mighty Egyptians fared under his actions on Israel's behalf (15:14-16). The Lord will **plant** Israel securely like a mighty tree in the land **prepared** for them (15:17). All they needed to do was follow their King—who **will reign forever** (15:18).

15:19-21 Once again, God's miraculous deliverance of Israel is emphasized (15:19). It's little wonder why the exodus is still celebrated by Israel and is so frequently mentioned in the pages of the Old Testament. The song continues: Moses's sister **Miriam** (the first woman to be identified in Scripture as a **prophetess**) sang to the **women** of Israel (15:20-21). Interestingly, Micah 6:4 speaks of Miriam along with her brothers Moses and Aaron as playing a role in the deliverance of the people. This is a reminder that even in the early biblical witness, women were not marginalized but were critically involved in the kingdom program of God. Thus, the church must celebrate and encourage the ministry of women.

IV. DIVINE PROVISION (15:22–18:27)

15:22-24 From the Red Sea, Israel traveled **three days in the wilderness** (15:22). Don't miss that the only way they could reach their destination was by going through the wilderness. This is a strong indicator that although you may sometimes experience "wilderness" moments in your life, you are not necessarily outside of God's will. Sometimes modern believers, too, must pass "through the wilderness" to get where God wants us to be.

The Israelites' main problem at this point in the story was that they could find no **water** (15:22). When the people finally encountered some, they discovered that **it was bitter**, so they **could not drink** it. Their reaction, given all that God had done for them to this point, should raise our eyebrows. They **named** the place **Marah** (which is Hebrew for "bitter") (15:23) and **grumbled to Moses** (15:24).

Only a mere three days had passed since the Red Sea miracle. But, unfortunately, it doesn't take long for the human heart to move from thanksgiving to complaining—from tambourine shaking in praise (15:20) to fist waving in hostility (15:24). What makes this reaction truly ironic is that their previous crisis had involved a water problem for which there had been no visible solution in sight. Here, when confronted by another water problem with no visible solution in view, they immediately forecast doom for themselves. Yet these people had clearly seen what God could do with water! (Absolutely whatever he wants.) We doubt what God can do only because we forget what God has done.

15:25 Moses prayed, and God instructed him to throw **a tree . . . into the water**. As a result, **the water became drinkable**. Of course, this is not an orthodox method of water purification. But neither was cutting the sea in two an orthodox method of allowing people to cross to the other side. Don't miss God's purpose in allowing this water problem: **He tested them** through it.

Students do poorly when they fail to study something their instructor says will appear on their test. The Lord had expected Israel to learn from the Red Sea event. Demonstrating that miraculous deliverance before their eyes, in fact, was his way of telling them, "This is going to be on the test! Remember it. Be ready to draw on this knowledge and apply it in the future." The Israelites had failed to trust a God who had proven himself completely trustworthy. They thus earned an F when the pop quiz of bitter water was placed before them.

15:26 After the test, God explained a statute for the Israelites (15:25): **If you will carefully obey the LORD your God . . . I will not inflict any illnesses on you that I inflicted on the Egyptians. For I am the LORD who heals you.**

There are some who try to stretch the promise of this verse too far, advocating a "health and wealth" gospel that assures all believers that they will be disease free and rich too if only they trust in Christ. They say that you shouldn't become sick if you are truly saved. But this is unbiblical thinking that adds to what God was saying. The illnesses that God would prevent in ancient Israel and the healing that he would provide did not prevent them from deteriorating with age or even from contracting a virus or getting involved in an accident. We live in a fallen world, and these things inevitably happen.

Nevertheless, sometimes people suffer maladies—physical, mental, or emotional ones—because, like the Egyptians, they live in rebellion against God and operate from an unbiblical worldview. God promised Israel that, if they trusted him and followed his instructions, they wouldn't suffer as Egypt had. Instead, he would be their healer as they encountered sickness.

Importantly, some believers suffer—not due to age or germs—but because they are living outside of the will of God. To them, the Great Physician says in effect, "Take your medicine—obey my Word. For I am the Lord who heals you."

15:27 The Lord directed Israel to an oasis in the wilderness where **twelve springs** of water flowed and **seventy date palms** grew. Once again, he showed his power over water and provided for their needs.

16:1-3 As it turned out, the people of Israel remained quick to forget what God could do. In the **second month** after leaving Egypt, they began what would be a habitual pattern: grumbling **against Moses and Aaron** (16:1-2). But since these brothers were the Lord's chosen servants, ultimately Israel's grumbling was directed against the Lord. When food ran low, they complained about how good they had it in Egypt (16:3). How sad that Egyptian slavery with a full belly looked better to them than God-supplied freedom with a little hunger along the way.

16:4-5 God was going to provide for them, but with his provision would be another **test.** He would **rain bread from heaven,** and they were only to **gather** what they would consume each day. **On the sixth day,** they were to gather enough for two days. Now, these were fairly simple instructions God gave for the people to follow. Yet a rebellious heart will ignore even simple instructions.

16:6-12 Moses and Aaron explained to the people that Israel's complaints against them were really **complaints** against the Lord (16:6-7, 9). They were simply leading under God's authority. The pair also explained to the Israelites that the Lord would provide them with **bread** in the **morning** and **meat** in the **evening** (16:8, 12). Faced with such provision, the people would surely know that theirs was the God who had **brought** them **out of the land of Egypt** (16:6, 12).

16:13-20 In the **evening quail . . . covered the camp,** and **in the morning** God caused his heavenly bread to appear **on the ground** (16:13-14). Moses relayed God's instructions about gathering only enough for each day—**two quarts per individual** (16:16). None of the food was to be kept overnight (16:19). Nevertheless, some of the Israelites attempted to hoard it. And in the morning, the leftovers **bred worms and stank** (16:20).

16:21-30 Moses explained why it was necessary to gather two days' worth on the sixth day. The seventh day was **a holy Sabbath to the Lord** (16:23, 29-30), which was a hint of a commandment to come (20:8-11). The people were not to gather on that day; therefore, they wouldn't **find any in the field** (16:25). But just as sure as some ignored the instruction about gathering too much, others ignored the instruction about not gathering on the Sabbath. As they went out to gather food, **they did not find any** (16:27). Needless to say, Moses was angry (16:20), and the Lord was angry too (16:28).

Through his instructions God was teaching the Israelites the principle that he provides for his people one day at a time. God's mercies "are new every morning" (Lam 3:22-23). Jesus articulates this kingdom provision in the Lord's Prayer: "Give us today our daily bread" (Matt 6:11). But will we trust him to provide and receive it in the way he prescribes?

16:31-36 Since the Israelites had never seen the unusual **substance** (16:31) before, they asked, "What is it?" (16:15), which in Hebrew is the word **manna**. So that's what they called it (16:31). Moses commanded them to preserve **two quarts** of manna in **a container** so that future **generations** could see it (16:32-33). Eventually it would be placed in the ark of the covenant (16:34; cp. Heb 9:4). Israel would eat manna every day for **forty years** until they entered **the land of Canaan** (16:35; cp. Josh 5:12).

17:1-4 The people of Israel journeyed on. At their next campsite, there was **no water** (17:1). Now, you would think that they would have learned by then that God is able to provide. But instead they **complained to Moses** and tested the Lord (17:2). Rather than trusting the Lord who had delivered them and provided for them, they simply tested his patience. They were so upset, in fact, that they even threatened to **stone** Moses! (17:4).

17:5-7 In spite of Israel's fickleness, God graciously told Moses to take his **staff** and **hit the rock at Horeb** (17:5-6). When he did, water miraculously gushed out for the people to drink. Moses **named the place Massah** (or "Testing") **and Meribah** (that is, "Quarreling"), because Israel had faithlessly **tested the LORD** there (17:7). Though God provided for them in spite of their sin, the Israelites were setting themselves on a path of habitual disobedience that would lead to sorrow and disappointment. Eventually, their stubborn tendency to refuse to trust God would lead him to forbid that generation from entering the land at all (see Num 14:20-23).

Later, the author of Psalm 95 would warn God's people not to test the Lord like the Israelites of Moses's day (see Ps 95:7-11). Still later, the author of Hebrews warned Christians about the same thing, pointing to Psalm 95 (see Heb 3:7-19). It's important to remember that all these things "were written for our instruction" (1 Cor 10:11).

17:8 With the water crisis solved, another crisis arose. The people of **Amalek** arrived to attack Israel (17:8). Amalek was a grandson of Esau, brother of Jacob, who was a patriarch of the Israelites (see Gen 36:12). Both the Israelites and the Amalekites, then, could trace their ancestries back to Isaac and to Abraham. But that family connection didn't matter: Amalek wanted war.

17:9 Moses recognized that Israel had no option but to stand her ground. So he commanded **Joshua** to **select some men** for battle. What would Moses do while Joshua led the troops? He would **stand on the hilltop with God's staff in [his] hand**. Moses had a simple shepherd's staff. But he knew God had sanctified it; previously he had used it to perform the miraculous (see 14:16, 21-22, 26-28). And once again God was going to work through the natural to perform the supernatural.

17:10-11 As the battle raged in the field below him, **Moses held up his hand**, holding his staff high. As long as he did this, **Israel prevailed.** But whenever he lowered his tired hands for a rest, **Amalek prevailed** (17:11). What was happening down below, then, was inextricably tied to what Moses was doing on the mountain. Moses was engaging in spiritual intercession while the people were fighting. This tells us that both military force and spiritual commitment were needed. This is a reminder that we must avoid the extremes of thinking that either we'll simply pray and let God take care of the life battles we face or that we must assume all responsibility and solve each problem in our human capacities alone. To prevail against enemy attack, you must *both* make contact with heaven *and* take responsibility for your actions.

17:12-13 Eventually, Moses grew tired. So they gave him a **stone** to sit on. Then **Aaron and Hur** stood on either side of their leader and **supported his hands** (17:12). By doing so, they helped keep God's staff held high, and Joshua was able to defeat Amalek (17:13). Moses was a godly leader and servant of the Lord. But he couldn't do the work he'd been assigned alone. Just as sure as Joshua couldn't fight the Amalekites by himself, Moses couldn't engage in spiritual warfare by himself.

You, too, need others in your life—brothers and sisters in the Lord—who will be there to help you spiritually when times get heavy. So put aside your pride, and let others "lift up your hands" when you're overwhelmed by the trials of life.

17:14 God promised Moses that he would **blot out the memory of Amalek under heaven.** Because of the Amalekites' wicked hostility toward their kin Israel, the Lord planned to eradicate them. He would later command King Saul to accomplish their demise. But because of Saul's disobedience, the prophet Samuel would have to finish the job (see 1 Sam 15:1-3, 32-33). The Amalekites' story reminds us that while God is patient in bringing his wrathful judgment, he never forgets to mete it out.

17:15-16 Then **Moses built an altar and named it, "The LORD Is My Banner"** (17:15). A banner is a sign or a flag. People hold or display these as a visible testament to their commitment. Spectators at sporting events, for instance, often hold or wave banners to indicate which team they're pulling for— that is, where their allegiance lies. Moses wanted to remind Israel to give the Lord their allegiance, for he alone could defeat their crises and give them victory.

18:1-12 During the journey, the Israelites passed near the home of **Moses's father-in-law Jethro** (18:1). **Moses's wife** and **sons** had been staying with him—probably as a means of protection during Moses's confrontation with Pharaoh (18:2-3). So they came to **meet** with Moses (18:5-7). Moses explained to Jethro **all that the LORD had done** on behalf of his people, and Jethro declared, **Blessed be the LORD . . . who rescued you** (18:8-10). Jethro was **the priest of Midian** (18:1). We know he had become a follower of the true God because he **brought a burnt offering and sacrifices to God** (18:12). Jethro was a Kenite (see Judg 1:16), part of the Canaanite tribes (see Gen 15:19) who descended from Ham of African descent. At that time, the Kenites had settled in the land of Midian.

18:13-16 Jethro observed how Moses was handling the daunting task of judging the people. **From morning until evening,** they would stand waiting to bring their disputes before Moses, so that he could **judge** them, render **a decision,** and **teach them God's statutes**

(18:13-16). But remember: When Israel left Egypt, there were *six-hundred thousand men* (12:37)—and that didn't include the women and children! This job we see outlined here, then, was hardly an easy task for Moses to do by himself. And Jethro recognized it.

Even at a large church, with multiple staff members, it can be difficult to schedule a counseling appointment with one of the pastoral staff. Church members might have to wait days or weeks. So imagine what Moses was dealing with. And be patient with your leaders who work hard to shepherd the hearts of the people.

18:17-18 Jethro made a wise observation: **What you're doing is not good. . . . You will certainly wear out both yourself and these people . . . because the task is too heavy for you. You can't do it alone.** In other words, this man said to his son-in-law, "Have you lost your cotton-pickin' mind? This job's too big for one guy!"

People were standing in line all day to wait for a chance for one man to hear their cases and render verdicts. And Moses rightly wanted to help the people because they came to him "to inquire of God" (18:15). This tells us that his heart was right, but his plan in this case was bad. Moses was a good and capable man, but he wasn't God. Both he and the people were going to "wear out" physiologically and psychologically if he didn't get some help, because Moses couldn't do it all—and the people couldn't wait forever for justice.

18:19-20 Jethro offered Moses some helpful advice (18:19). He encouraged Moses to be the mediator—**to represent the people before God** and **teach them the way to live** (18:19-20). In other words, he counseled Moses to pray to God for the people and to teach God's laws. But he warned him that he could not be the sole person responsible for helping each and every person to apply God's laws to their specific situations. While Moses could provide the people with a spiritual framework, they would need more than Moses alone to help them fill in the details of how to apply it.

18:21 Jethro encouraged Moses to **select** men who were **God-fearing, trustworthy, and [who hated] dishonest profit.** This strongly suggests that the priority in enlisting spiritual leadership should be identifying those who are living in a godly manner and are biblically focused in their dealings. When Paul listed qualifications for church leaders, in fact, the lists consisted primarily of character qualities (see 1 Tim 3:1-12; Titus 1:6-9). Moses needed to identify leaders who loved God, knew his law, and submitted to it in their own lives. Such men could then lead groups of people, tackling their issues in bite-sized chunks, and teaching them how to apply the Word of God to their lives.

18:22-23 Such a team of leaders could **judge the people at all times.** Moses could continue to judge **every major case,** but the leaders could **judge every minor case** (18:22) in his stead. That translated to no more waiting in line all day for the people and no more heavy burden of playing judge and teacher having to be carried by Moses alone. This way, Moses could **endure,** and the people could **go home satisfied** (18:23).

Here I see a reminder to the church that pastors cannot bear the burdens of the church alone. Wise, Word-centered church lay leaders must share the load. By dividing the work in this way, more Christians can be trained to think biblically about life, and they in turn can help their brothers and sisters in Christ to think and live biblically. This is how the body of Christ is built up. It was never intended to be a one-man job.

18:24-27 **Moses listened** to his father-in-law's advice and chose leaders to serve in the young nation's new judicial system (18:25-26). Then Jethro returned to his home (18:27). In this story God used a Gentile man to provide wise counsel for the effective administration of the entire Jewish nation.

V. SINAI AND THE TEN COMMANDMENTS (19:1–20:21)

19:1-4 Three months after the exodus from Egypt, Israel arrived at **the mountain** in the **Sinai Wilderness** where God had first appeared to Moses (19:1-2). The Lord had promised Moses that Israel would worship him at this very spot (3:12).

19:5-6 On the mountaintop Moses was commanded to tell the people of Israel, **If you will carefully listen to me and keep my covenant, you will be my own possession out of all the peoples** (19:5). The Lord, then, was about to enter into a covenant with Israel as a whole. A biblical covenant is a spiritually created bond. For example, marriage between a husband and wife is a covenant. God intended to enter a binding relationship with Israel—making them his "own possession." If they kept the covenant stipulations, the end result would be their blessing: "Observe the words of this covenant and follow them, so that you will succeed in everything you do" (Deut 29:9).

God is a King with an agenda. His goal is that his kingdom will be manifested in history through the lives of those who submit to his rule and thus experience his authority and blessing. The kingdom agenda, then, is the visible manifestation of the comprehensive rule of God over every area of life. Covenants are the instrument through which God's kingdom operates. If Israel would operate under the covering of his covenant, they would be his **kingdom of priests** and his **holy nation** (19:6), experiencing the benefits and privileges that his kingdom offers.

As recorded in Old Testament history, however, the sinful people of Israel would repeatedly break God's covenant and forfeit his blessings. Only God's Son Jesus Christ, born in human flesh, descended from the Israelite people, perfectly kept the laws of the covenant and offered himself as an atoning sacrifice for sinners. By the shedding of his own blood, he established a new covenant. All those who trust in Christ's sacrifice receive full atonement for sins, are indwelt by the Holy Spirit, and have fellowship with God. As members of the new covenant, Christians now have the capacity to obey God, so that they may experience his authority and deliverance in their daily circumstances.

19:7-15 Moses presented to **the elders of the people** what God had said, and **all the people** agreed to enter into a covenant with him (19:7-8). So the Lord commanded the people to observe three-days of purification to prepare and **consecrate** themselves (19:10-11). Then they were to observe **boundaries** around the mountain. Anyone—**animal or human**—who touched the mountain of God's presence would be put to death (19:12-13). These regulations were meant to help reveal to Israel how special and holy this event was to be.

19:16-25 When God revealed his presence on the mountain, **all the people in the camp shuddered.** With his arrival there was **thunder and lightning**, a dark **cloud**, and a deafening **trumpet sound** (19:16). Moses went up the mountain to speak with God and then descended to bring God's words to the people (19:20-21). The people were to remain at the mountain's base (19:21-25). Just as God's presence had made the ground holy when Moses first encountered him (3:5), so now the mountain was holy for the same reason. All of this was a vivid reminder of the glory of God and of the great chasm that exists between a holy God and sinful people.

20:1-2 The centerpiece of God's covenant with Israel was what we call the Ten Commandments. They reflect and reveal God's righteousness. They present the minimum standards of righteousness that God set for his people—I say *minimum* standards because Jesus showed that the sin problem people face is not limited to external sins but even warps internal attitudes (see Matt 5:21-30). If God's people were to please him, they had to keep his commands.

The Ten Commandments also have a restraining purpose because humans are fallen creatures who need some basic legal guidelines if they are to function in steady consideration of one another. Since people have a propensity to do whatever suits them in the moment, God's commandments establish boundaries to restrain evil. Thus, following the commandments gives people protection from themselves and from one another. Laws promote order in society and prevent chaos.

The commandments also have a redemptive purpose. Contrary to popular opinion, you can't get to heaven by obeying the Ten Commandments because you can't keep them perfectly all the time. But as Paul says, the law shows us that we are sinners (see Rom 7:7-13) in the same way that a mirror can show you what's wrong with your hair. The law was designed to show you that you can't satisfy God's perfect standards and that you need a Savior (see Gal 3:19-24).

In the preamble to the Ten Commandments, God established his identity and his relationship to Israel: I **am the LORD your God, who brought you out of the land of Egypt, out of the place of slavery** (20:2). Israel, then, was about to enter a covenant relationship with the God of heaven and earth because of what he had done for them. This is a principle that is still at work in the New Testament era. Under the *new* covenant, Christ died so that those who trust him might "no longer live for themselves, but for the one who died for them and was raised" (2 Cor 5:15). The believer's motivation for obeying God's laws, then, is not to earn salvation (we can't). Rather, we obey because we want to please the One who delivered us from hell and judgment.

20:3 Do not have other gods besides me. This rule means you are to treat no other person, place, or thing in your life like God. He is *not* to be your *chief* God; he is to be your *only* God. Sometimes business contracts have exclusivity clauses. Such a clause requires that the persons entering the agreement engage in an *exclusive* relationship with each other—having no competing loyalties and no competing contractual obligations that could in any way hinder their own partnership. The first commandment is an exclusivity clause. The Lord alone is to be God in your life.

Notice that this is the first commandment. You can't get this one wrong and expect to proceed to the other nine with success. A baseball player might hit an inside-the-park homerun, getting around every base before the other team can throw him out. But if he actually missed tagging first base, it doesn't matter if he touched second, third, and home. He's still out. If there is ever anything in your life other than God that you look to or depend on as your source of well-being, satisfaction, or deliverance, then you are serving another god. Get commandment one wrong, and you'll fail at obeying all the rest.

Notice too that there is an implicit promise in the first commandment. Though you are not to have any other gods besides him, you *are* to have him. False gods can do nothing. But the Lord is self-existing, all-powerful, all knowing, and full of grace and mercy to help weak and unworthy sinners. He alone is able to save from hell, deliver from crises, and bless with his kingdom promises. Why would you rather serve anyone or anything else?

20:4-6 Do not make an idol for yourself (20:4). The previous commandment told us not to have other gods (20:3). This one warns against approaching the true God in the wrong way. Making an idol is attempting to create a visible representation of the invisible God. Any such attempt will always misrepresent him. No matter how beautiful the picture we might create to represent him is, it's no substitute for reality.

If we look to an idol, we are looking to something other than God. Idols, no matter the physical form they take, can never connect heaven with earth. They can never offer aid. All they do, in fact, is arouse God's jealousy: **I, the Lord your God, am a jealous God**, he says (20:5). However, jealousy in God is not sinful. Think of it as the righteous and loving jealousy of a husband who is zealous for the faithfulness of his wife and wants to keep her and their marriage from harm.

In his indictment of idolatry in Romans 1, Paul mentions images of birds and animals. And with that in mind, we might assume we have no idolatry problems if we don't worship creatures or bow to statues. But importantly, the first idol in Paul's list is "mortal man" (Rom 1:23). This is a warning that should you start thinking of a person as your primary source of blessings and contentment, you have made that person an idol.

Not all idols, however, are physical. Elsewhere, Paul mentions several sinful desires—sexual immorality, impurity, lust, evil desire, and greed—and calls these things "idolatry" (Col 3:5). Gratifying such things frequently becomes the ruling influence in a person's life. A person who seeks to satisfy one of those desires, in fact, often will do and sacrifice anything to serve his idol.

There is only one legitimate representation of God and therefore only one legitimate means of accessing him. I'm talking about the Word who became flesh, the God-Man (see John 1:1-2, 14). "[Jesus Christ] is the image of the invisible God" (Col 1:15)—the only true representation of God. Jesus told his disciples, "I am the way, the truth, and the life. No one comes to the Father except through me. . . . The one who has seen me has seen the Father" (John 14:6, 9). We cannot approach God through an idol, but through Jesus Christ alone.

20:7 Do not misuse the name of the Lord your God. In the Bible, a person's name is a reflection of who he is; it speaks of his character and reputation. God is rightly concerned about the glory of his name. He does not want it defamed or abused, but valued and honored. We are not to use his name casually or carelessly, but seriously and reverently. Too often, however, we use frivolous phrases like, "Thank God," or, "I swear to God." At its core, this kind of flippancy is treating God's name insignificantly; it is saying that *he* is insignificant.

Think about it this way. Forgery is the unauthorized use of someone's name. If you sign someone else's name to a document in order to obtain something, you have illegally used that individual's name—their identity. So if you say, "God told me to do this," you'd better be sure he did. Otherwise, you're forging God's name to drive your own agenda. Most people are zealous to protect their reputations. Imagine how the righteous God of the universe feels about the way his name is used.

We are to honor the Lord's name as holy (see Matt 6:9). How? By exalting his name (see Ps 34:3)—by praising him and declaring to the world who he is and what he has done: "Ascribe to the Lord the glory due his name" (Ps 29:2). Give God his due; he deserves the best you have to offer. Live all of life "in the name of the Lord," seeking to honor him in everything (1 Sam 17:45). If you "wear" his name as you ought, you will live a life of righteousness, honor, and love.

Finally, honor Jesus, for God has given him "the name that is above every name" (Phil 2:9). We are to confess the name of Jesus and submit to him as Lord. When we honor God's Son, we honor God's name.

20:8-11 Remember the Sabbath day, to keep it holy (20:8; see 31:12-17). The Sabbath day concept is predicated on what God did at creation. He made the world **in six days; then he rested on the seventh** (20:11). Clearly, the all-powerful God didn't "rest" because he was tired. Rather, he rested so that he could enjoy what he had done: "God saw all that he had made, and it was very good indeed" (Gen 1:31). Likewise, after six days of work, we are also called to rest and enjoy the fruit of our labor. This is a valuable means of helping ourselves to avoid becoming so busy and preoccupied that we forget what God has done too.

God also made the Sabbath so that his people would be reminded of his sovereignty. **The seventh day is a Sabbath to the LORD** (20:10). He is in charge; we live under his rule. He is the One who brought order out of chaos (Gen 1:1-2).

The author of Hebrews, writing to Christians, reminds us that "a Sabbath rest remains for God's people" (Heb 4:9). But the early Christians did not gather for worship on the Jewish Sabbath—Saturday, the official seventh day of the week. They gathered for worship on Sunday, the first day of the week, because it was on that day that Jesus was raised from the dead. He is "Lord of the Sabbath" (Matt 12:8), and he promises rest for his weary people (see Matt 11:28). Though we in the New Testament era are not tied down to keeping a specific Sabbath day (see Col 2:16), there remains a principle of Sabbath rest for the people of God. We willingly "enter" that rest by faith, trusting God and living obediently in accordance with our faith (see Heb 3:18–4:3, 11).

20:12 Honor your father and your mother. The family is the foundational unit of society. Parents have the responsibility to raise their children to know the Lord and to follow him. Children have the responsibility to honor their parents, willingly receiving wisdom and instruction from them. The parent-child relationship, in fact, represents a chain of command: God the Father is in charge; we, his children, are not. When you disregard the order of the family relationship, you bring harm to yourself.

To "honor" your parents means to respect and value them. How this is done will depend on a child's stage in life. Young children and teenagers living under their parents' authority are to obey them in all things (unless doing so dishonors God). Even Jesus obeyed his parents (see Luke 2:51). But adult children, too, who are no longer in their parents' home or under their authority still owe their parents honor. This might show up in the form of spending time with them, praising their merits, and providing physical or financial assistance (see 1 Tim 5:8, 16). Even children whose parents have neglected, abandoned, or abused them are called to honor them spiritually by praying for them and forgiving them, "just as God also forgave . . . in Christ" (Eph 4:32).

The apostle Paul says this "is the first commandment with a promise" (Eph 6:2-3), a blessing from God: **so that you may have a long life in the land.** If you honor your father and mother, then, God promises his special care in your life—he can bring heavenly realities into your earthly history.

20:13 Do not murder. This commandment doesn't forbid all killing. God authorized Israel to go to war against their enemies. Scripture also authorizes self-defense (see Exod 22:2-3) and capital punishment by governing authorities (see Gen 9:6; Rom 13:1-4). It specifically prohibits *murder*— any unauthorized killing of an individual, whether or not its premeditated. This includes the taking of one's own life in suicide. Abortion is also prohibited by this commandment, because the Bible makes clear that an unborn baby is a person, not mere tissue (see Exod 21:22-24; Ps 139:13-16; Jer 1:5; Luke 1:41-44).

The reason murder is forbidden is because all humans are uniquely made in the image of God (see Gen 1:26-27; 9:6). At creation, humans were set apart to reflect God like no other creatures on earth could do. Therefore, a murderous attack against a human being is an attack against the Creator.

If you have never murdered, though, it doesn't mean you're in the clear. Jesus explained that keeping this commandment is actually a minimum standard. To express or harbor unrighteous anger toward another person is not just sin—it is murder committed in the heart (see Matt 5:21-22). Moreover, even cursing someone is an attack on the image of God, which all human beings share (see Jas 3:9). In putting this high standard into practice, it helps to remember that "Human anger does not accomplish God's righteousness" (Jas 1:20). Instead, we must "leave room for God's wrath, because it is written, 'Vengeance belongs to me; I will repay,' says the Lord" (Rom 12:19).

20:14 Do not commit adultery. Sexual gratification has become our culture's drug of choice. It is even used as the chief means of selling a product. As a result of this perversion of sexuality, a good gift of God is routinely cheapened and defiled. God created sex as a wonderful blessing to be shared by a husband and wife within the boundaries of a marriage covenant. Sex was intended to inaugurate and renew that covenant, that "one flesh" union (see Gen 2:24). Adultery—that is, sexual intercourse involving at least one married person—is a defiling of that covenant bond. Think of sex like a fire, with marriage serving as a living room fireplace. If you allow sex to blaze outside of its intended boundary, you just might burn down your own home. In any case, you will unleash destruction.

Those who have sex according to their own personal parameters—whether that includes committing adultery or engaging in fornication or homosexuality—will experience God's judgment (see Rom 1:24-32; Heb 13:4). That's because sexual sin is primarily a sin against God (see Gen 39:9). But understand that sexual immorality defiles humans like no other sin can: "The person who is sexually immoral sins against his own body" (1 Cor 6:18). A Christian's body, Scripture teaches, is the temple of the Holy Spirit. It also reminds us, "You are not your own" (1 Cor 6:19). God calls us to holiness, because he is holy. So instead of indulging in sexual immorality, we are to pursue sanctification (see 1 Thess 4:3). Believers are to become more and more like Jesus.

This commandment, too, however, is meant as a minimum standard. Jesus upped the ante: "Everyone who looks at a woman lustfully has already committed adultery with her in his heart" (Matt 5:28). Thus, lustful thoughts and engaging in voyeurism by viewing pornography are all condemned. Jesus's remedy to indulging in such sins, in fact, is to cut off the hand and gouge out the eye that constantly leads you into those traps (see Matt 5:29-30). Obviously, he wasn't teaching self-mutilation because, once again, lust is a matter of the heart. Rather, he uses hyperbole to instruct us to take drastic, decisive measures to avoid sexual sin before it's too late. Nonetheless, to those who have fallen into these traps, Jesus offers forgiveness and hope: "Neither do I condemn you. Go, and from now on do not sin anymore" (John 8:11).

20:15 Do not steal. To steal is to take what belongs to someone else without the right or permission to do so. We typically think of stealing in terms of pocketing money or making off with possessions, but theft can take a variety of forms: kidnapping, plagiarism, accepting praise or credit that should have gone to another, not paying taxes, accepting a paycheck without earning it, and even withholding wages count. Theft also happens when we rob God by not contributing tithes (see Mal 3:8-10).

Ultimately, everything belongs to the Lord (see Ps 24:1). He grants ownership and stewardship rights to individuals. Stealing is a rejection of this fact. It's also a sign of discontentment regarding what God has provided. If you fail to see God as your source, you'll be tempted to steal, essentially proclaiming that you are your own source.

Even career thieves, however, can be forgiven. To one repentant thief, Jesus said, "Today you will be with me in paradise" (Luke 23:43). The ex-thief is not only commanded to "no longer steal" but also "to do honest work with his own hands, so that he has something to share" (Eph 4:28). When Zacchaeus repented, he returned what he had stolen with interest and gave to the poor as well (see Luke 19:8). Such passages are a reminder that rather than being self-interested, we are to be motivated by love of neighbor so that we can provide for those who are in need. God blesses you, in fact, so that you can bless others.

20:16 Do not give false testimony against your neighbor. The old childhood rhyme about "sticks and stones" being unable to do harm is wrong. Words do hurt. Proverbs 18:21 says, "Death and life are in the power of the tongue." James 3:8 says that the tongue is "a restless evil, full of deadly poison." Many people have been emotionally scarred or have had their reputations damaged by careless or intentionally harmful words. Lies and slanderous accusations can even end a life.

On rare occasions a lie might be justified. God blessed the Hebrew midwives when they lied to Pharaoh (1:15-21). They were motivated by fear of the Lord, refused to be accomplices to murder, and knew that Pharaoh didn't deserve the truth. But the lie this commandment confronts is "bearing false testimony" against another person—whether damaging a reputation through gossip, causing them material loss, or saying something untrue that results in a death. In short, it's an intentional attempt to hurt someone through falsehood. Such actions imitate the devil who is "a liar and the father of lies" (John 8:44). Christians, by contrast, are to "[put] away lying" and "[speak] the truth in love" (Eph 4:15). Our words are to build others up rather than tear them down (see Eph 4:29).

20:17 Do not covet. Coveting is a passionate longing to possess something that is not yours. Advertisers spend an inordinate amount of time trying to make us dissatisfied with our lives, so that they can make us covetous enough to spend money on their products. A covetous person is materialistic. He considers the physical more important than the spiritual and assumes that his life consists in "the abundance of his possessions" (Luke 12:15). He is thus never satisfied. He fails to trust God to provide for him and assumes God is holding out on him.

The antidote for covetousness is contentment. Contentment begins with trusting that God is good and that he withholds nothing good "from those who live with integrity" (Ps 84:11). When you truly believe God's promise

that he "will never leave you or abandon you," then you are able to be satisfied with what you have (see Heb 13:5).

20:18-20 After God concluded the Ten Commandments, the people were terrified. There was **thunder and lightning**, the blaring of a **trumpet**, and **smoke**. So the people **stood at a distance**, where they may have felt a certain degree of safety (20:18). The voice of God was frightening to them. That's why they wanted to hear from Moses and not directly from God (20:19). Moses's response sounds like doubletalk: **Don't be afraid, for God has come to test you, so that you will fear him and will not sin** (20:20). How can he tell them, "Don't be afraid," and "Fear," at the same time?

We must understand what it means to "fear God." It does not mean to be scared of him. It means being so gripped by his greatness that we hold him in the highest esteem. To fear God is to respect him and take him seriously. The concept, in fact, is similar to how we ought to think of electricity. We're not to be so scared of electricity that we're unwilling to plug anything in. But neither should we go around sticking screwdrivers into outlets. Electricity is awesome and beneficial, but it must be treated with respect.

God wanted to test the people, so that they would fear him and not sin. Similarly, God tests you because he wants you to worship him by choice, not simply by mandate. He wants you to say "no" to sin and "yes" to him because you have a healthy fear of him.

20:21 The people remained standing at a distance. This tells us that the people were driven by the wrong kind of fear. If they had feared God rightly, their perspective would have drawn them to him. But since they were afraid of God, their wrong perspective only served to drive them away from him. In this I see a deep truth. When we come close to God, he will confront our sins and our idols. And that can be scary if we want to hang onto them. The people had already complained about wanting to return to Egypt (14:12; 16:3), so they kept their distance because they didn't want the Lord confronting their evil desires. If you are keeping God at an arm's length, it's time to ask why.

VI. THE DIVINE COVENANT (20:22–24:18)

20:22-23 The people had heard God speak to them; they saw and heard a display of his glory (20:22). So the Lord commanded them not to make **gods . . . to rival** him (20:23). No gods of their own creation, of course, could rival what they had just witnessed (though they would soon forget this; see 32:1-35).

20:24-26 The one true God deserves appropriate worship. So the people were to make altars for sacrifices to deal with their impurity and sin. The altars were to be made of earth or uncut stones (20:24-25)—natural materials that were untouched by human hands and that reflected God's holy handiwork alone. There were also not to be steps leading to the altar, in order to avoid any chance of them witnessing any indecent exposure in a time predating underclothes (20:26).

21:1 The next three chapters provide various laws and **ordinances** that were specific applications of the more general Ten Commandments. They showed Israel examples of how the commandments were to function and would provide a framework for resolving problems and disputes in the nation.

21:2-11 An Israelite, for instance, might sell himself into slavery—that is, indentured servitude—for various reasons, such as paying off debt or surviving financial calamity. He would serve a period of **six years** and then go free, unless he elected to stay in permanent servitude out of **love** for his master and family (21:2-5). Since slaves were in a vulnerable position, provisions were made to ensure their proper treatment, especially in cases involving female slaves (21:7-11).

21:12-14 The laws dealing with personal injury (21:12-36) begin with the most serious of injuries—homicide (21:12-14). The **death** penalty was prescribed for intentional homicide only. In the event of unintentional homicide, the person could **flee** to an appointed place (21:12, 14)—what would become known as a "city of refuge." Someone guilty of involuntary

manslaughter, then, could go to one of these sanctuary cities for protection from those who would seek retribution (see Num 35:9-34; Deut 4:41-43; 19:1-13; Josh 20:1-9). But there was no refuge or sanctuary for someone guilty of premeditated murder.

21:15-17 Should parents exercise their authority legitimately, they were to be respected and honored. Physical or verbal abuse against one's parents was a capital crime (21:15, 17). Kidnapping was also a capital offense (21:16). Human trafficking of any kind was not to be tolerated.

21:18-19 Personal injuries not resulting in death still required compensation to the **injured** party.

21:20-27 Owners had the right to punish slaves, but such measures were not to involve violence. If a slave was struck and died, **the owner** was to be **punished** (21:20). Permanent physical harm to the slave resulted in his or her freedom and loss of the owner's investment (21:26-27). Such laws limiting a slave owner's power and respecting the rights of slaves were unprecedented and unique to Israel in the ancient Near East.

Compensation was mandatory for accidentally causing a premature birth, even if no injury resulted (21:22). Clearly, then, an unborn infant is considered a person with basic rights. Negligence resulting in injury or death to an unborn baby incurred consequences.

The stipulation in 21:23-24 is commonly referred to by the Latin expression *lex talionis*, the "law of retaliation." The idea behind **life for life, eye for eye, tooth for tooth**, etc. was to limit punishment given. The legal process was meant to provide fair punishment and to prevent escalation of hostilities. Penalties were to match and not exceed the damage done to the victim.

21:28-36 Owners were accountable for any injuries or deaths caused by their animals (21:28-32, 35-36). **Compensation** (21:27) must be made. If his animal had a history of causing harm and he refused to restrain it, **the owner** would pay with his life (21:29).

22:1-4 Thieves had to make compensation—**full restitution** (22:3). The high cost of repayment (22:1, 4) was meant to deter future thieves. If a thief was **caught in the act** at night and killed, the homeowner was guiltless (22:2). During daylight hours, however, the owner would be guilty if he killed a thief (22:3).

22:5-6 In an agrarian society, devastation to a man's crops could render him destitute. Therefore, if a man's field was damaged through the negligence of another, **restitution** was to be made.

22:7-15 These verses provide regulations regarding settling disputes over personal property—particularly when a man borrowed or was otherwise in possession of his neighbor's goods or animals.

22:16-17 Promiscuity was recognized as harmful to families and not tolerated. If a man seduced and slept with a **virgin**, he had to pay **the bridal price for her to be his wife** (22:16)—regardless of whether or not the father chose to give his daughter to him in marriage (22:17).

22:18-20 These verses stipulate additional capital crimes: sorcery, bestiality, and sacrifices made to false gods. Essentially, sorcery and idolatry were rejections of the first two commandments (20:3-4). Bestiality is a form of immorality that not only rejects marriage between a husband and wife as the proper framework for sexual intercourse (20:14), but also rejects God's created order and the distinction between humanity and animals. According to biblical classifications, man is no mere mammal.

22:21-27 Every society has its vulnerable. Israel was expected to care for these classes of people, seeing that they were not oppressed. The Israelites were to remember that they too were once **resident aliens** in Egypt; therefore, they were not to **oppress** resident aliens in their own land (22:21). God promised

to hear the **cry** of the **widow** and the **fatherless** if they were mistreated; thus, their oppressors would not go unpunished (22:22-24). Loans of money or goods to fellow Israelites were to help the **poor** not to harm them by making their situations worse. Israelites were not to **charge** them **interest** or to take their life's necessities as **collateral** (22:25-27).

22:28-31 The people were not to curse God or one of his appointed leaders (22:28). They were also not to defraud God by withholding their **offerings** and **firstborn**—which belonged to him (22:29-30). Israel was the Lord's **holy people**. So they were to eat **meat** only in prescribed ways (22:31).

23:1-9 These ordinances call for impartial justice. The Israelites were to deal honestly and fairly with all people. No one was to be treated with **favoritism**—not even the poor (23:3). And no one was to be treated with injustice—not even an enemy's animal (23:4-5). Injustice, false accusations, bribes, and oppression are to have no place among God's people (23:6-9).

23:10-13 Israel was to observe a variety of Sabbaths and festivals. The law regarding a weekly Sabbath of rest for people and animals (23:12; see 20:8-11) was expanded to Sabbatical years to provide **rest** for the land and food for the poor (23:10-11). It was a reminder that God owned the land; they were stewards on his behalf.

23:14-19 The people were also to celebrate **three** festivals every year in honor of the Lord (23:14, 17). **The Festival of Unleavened Bread** was held in conjunction with the Passover and commemorated the exodus from Egypt (23:15; see commentary in 12:1-20). **The Festival of Harvest** (23:16), also known as the "Festival of Weeks" or "Pentecost," took place after the wheat harvest, seven weeks after the Festival of Unleavened Bread. **The Festival of Ingathering** took place **at the end of the year** (23:16). Each was a reminder of God's provision for his people.

The practice of boiling **a young goat in its mother's milk** may have been a pagan custom (23:19) that the Lord didn't want his people to adopt.

23:20-26 Here the Lord stressed the need for obedience. He would provide **an angel** to guide and deliver the Israelites, but they must **listen to him** and **obey him** (23:20-22). When the people arrived in the promised land, they were to **wipe out** their enemies and **demolish** their objects of worship (23:23-24). If they were careful to do all these things, the Lord would grant them blessing and health (23:25-26).

23:27-33 God thoughtfully promised to **drive** the Israelites' enemies out of the land gradually—or else **the land would become desolate** (23:27-30). He also prescribed the borders of the promised land: they would extend from **the Red Sea** in the east to **the Mediterranean Sea** in the west, and from **the wilderness** in the south to **the Euphrates River** in the north (23:31). Israel was to make no **covenant** with the inhabitants of the land or with **their gods** (23:32). Failure to drive them out of the land would result in them being a **snare** to the Israelites. Their idolatrous beliefs and practices would lure Israel, leading God's people to **sin** (23:33). They needed the regulation of God's laws if they were to enjoy God's blessings—and that meant no compromising with their enemies and no idolatry.

24:1-2 God's covenant with Israel was inaugurated with a ceremony. Moses, Aaron, Aaron's sons, and seventy elders of the people were called to **approach the Lord** (24:1-2). This suggests that worship is not something we initiate. It begins with a divine invitation.

24:3 After the invitation, Israel received God's revelation. Moses **told the people all the commands of the Lord**. This is a reminder that the only reason we can truly know God is because he chooses to make himself known to us. We learn about him because he decides to tell us.

We need God's revelation. But the proclamation of the Word of God is not a mere opportunity for note taking. It's a call to respond to God. The people said, **We will do everything that the Lord has commanded**. Hearing from God is necessary, but it is not sufficient. We must respond to him with trust

and obedience, or else his Word has fallen on deaf ears. Scripture says, "Be doers of the word and not hearers only, deceiving yourselves" (Jas 1:23).

24:4-8 Next Moses built **an altar** with **twelve pillars** representing **the twelve tribes of Israel** (24:4). They then made **offerings** and **sacrificed** to the Lord so that they might have **fellowship** with him (24:5). Moses took **the blood of the covenant** and **splattered it** on **the altar** and **on the people** to consecrate them (24:6-8).

The sacrifice and offering that God requires of his people today is called "a sacrifice of praise" (Heb 13:15). He wants us to present our "bodies as a living sacrifice" (Rom 12:1). In other words, you are to worship him with your words and your deeds—not merely on Sunday but every day. He's the King, and he deserves it.

The reason we no longer need to offer bloody sacrifices to have fellowship with God is because the ultimate sacrifice has been made. Jesus Christ obtained our eternal redemption "not by the blood of goats and calves, but by his own blood" (Heb 9:12). Through his atoning sacrifice, the Son of God inaugurated a new covenant—one that provides complete forgiveness of your sins and grants you a new heart, so that you have the capacity to obey him if only you'll place faith in him (see commentary on Heb 8:8-13).

24:9-11 Then Moses, Aaron, his sons, and the elders went up, and **they saw the God of Israel. . . . God did not harm** them, and **they ate and drank** (24:9-11). This means that the Lord let them see something of his glory in a manner similar to what Moses would later experience in a more dramatic fashion (see 33:18-23; 34:5-8).

Many people want to experience God; they want him to show up in their experiences. Israel, we must note, only saw God when they worshiped at his invitation, responded to his revelation, and received the blood of his consecration. If you want to experience God, then, trust in the consecrating blood of Jesus, worship him in spirit and truth, and respond to his Word with obedience.

24:12-18 God summoned Moses to the mountaintop so that he could give him the stone tablets containing the law and commandments that God himself had written for the people (24:12). Moses temporarily turned over leadership to Aaron and Hur, as Joshua accompanied him up the mountain (24:13-14). A cloud representing God's glory covered the mountain (24:15-16). After six days, Moses saw God's glory was like a consuming fire (24:17). He remained there forty days and forty nights (24:18).

VII. RIGHT WORSHIP AND WRONG WORSHIP (25:1–34:35)

25:1-7 The following chapters provide the instructions God gave Moses for constructing the tabernacle, preparing its furnishings, outfitting the priests, and consecrating everything for the Lord's service. Through these details, God was showing his people how they were to worship him rightly. First, the Israelites were given an opportunity to make an offering of precious materials so that everything for the tabernacle could be constructed and prepared (25:2-7). Back when Israel departed Egypt, God gave the people favor with the Egyptians. As a result, they gave the Israelites whatever they wanted, and "they plundered the Egyptians" (12:36). This story gives us a wonderful insight into God's ways: he knows how to take the wealth of his enemies and use it for his kingdom purposes.

25:8-9 The Israelites were to make a tabernacle and all its furnishings (25:9). The tabernacle or sanctuary would be a tent where God could make his presence known and would dwell among his people (25:8). The tabernacle could be taken down and reassembled as the people traveled from place to place. Eventually, after Israel settled in the promised land and found rest from their enemies, the tabernacle would be replaced by a temple (see 1 Kgs 6:1).

25:10-22 The first piece of furniture for the tabernacle was the ark made of acacia wood (25:10). It was to be overlaid with pure gold and was to have poles inserted through its side rings so that the priests could carry the ark without touching it (25:11-15). The lid or cover was referred to as the mercy seat (25:17). On top of it were two golden cherubim—glorious angelic beings facing each other (25:18-20). Inside the ark, Moses was to place the tablets of the testimony (25:16, 21)—that is, the two stone tablets on which God wrote the Ten Commandments (see 24:12). Thus, the ark was also called the ark of the testimony. Above the mercy seat was where God manifested his presence (25:22). Israel viewed the ark as God's throne on earth; he was enthroned above the mercy seat between the cherubim (see 1 Sam 4:4; 2 Sam 6:2; Ps 80:1; 99:1; Isa 37:16).

25:23-30 A table was also to be constructed of acacia wood and overlaid with pure gold (25:23-24). On it the priests were to put the Bread of the Presence (25:30). This consisted of twelve flat loaves of bread, one representing each of the twelve tribes; it was to be eaten by the priests. The bread was to be replaced every Sabbath and demonstrated God's provision (see Lev 24:5-9). The bread foreshadowed someone who would arrive on the scene later in history: the true "bread of God" is his Son Jesus, "the bread of life." Whoever comes to him will never be hungry (see John 6:33, 35).

25:31-40 The lampstand was made of seventy-five pounds of pure, hammered gold (25:31, 39). It was to have six branches—with three branches on each side—and a total of seven lamps (25:32, 37). It was to be kept burning every night by the priests with olive oil supplied by the Israelites (see 27:20-21; Lev 24:2-4). This too foreshadowed Christ. Jesus declared, "I am the light of the world. Anyone who follows me will never walk in the darkness but will have the light of life" (John 8:12).

26:1-14 Chapter 26 describes the tabernacle itself in extreme detail. Ten curtains were to enclose the structure, each made of finely spun linen and beautifully colored yarn, with a design of cherubim worked in (26:1). As with the ark, visual representations of the angelic beings were included to give the tabernacle the appearance of heavenly glory. God provided exacting instructions regarding the material and length of the curtains, as well as their loops and clasps (26:2-13). Then a layered covering was made for the top (26:14).

26:15-30 These verses explain how the framing of the tabernacle was to be constructed. The Israelites were to build the tabernacle based on the plan that God had shown to Moses on the mountain (26:30). This was not a structure that came out of man's imagination. God's instructions were precise and purposeful.

26:31-37 A curtain was to be made to separate the holy place, which contained the table and the lampstand, from the most holy place, which contained the mercy seat on the ark (26:31-35). Only the high priest could pass through the curtain into the most holy place—and only once per year on the Day of Atonement (see Lev 16:1-34; Heb 9:7). When Christ died on the cross, the curtain separating the most holy place in the temple was torn (shockingly) in two by an unseen hand (see Matt 27:51). This symbolized that Jesus had gained for his people full and eternal access to God's holy presence. No other sacrifice would ever be needed.

27:1-8 The next item to be made was the altar, which would be used for sacrificing burnt offerings to the Lord (27:1). It was to be overlaid with bronze, and all its utensils were to be made of bronze (27:2-3). As with everything else having to do with the tabernacle, it was to be made as it was shown ... on the mountain (27:8). God's word was to be followed exactly.

27:9-19 These verses describe the rectangular courtyard for the tabernacle. The height of the hangings constructing its walls prevented anyone from seeing inside them. One couldn't simply waltz into God's presence. There was only one gate for entrance (27:16).

27:20-21 The Israelites were to bring pure oil from crushed olives as fuel for the lampstand (27:21; see 25:31-40).

28:1-5 God chose the descendants of Levi to care for and transport the tabernacle and all its furnishings (see Num 1:50). From the Levites, God chose Aaron and his descendants to serve as Israel's priests (28:1). They were to have holy garments appropriate to their holy role (28:2). Skilled artisans were to make the garments—a breastpiece, an ephod, a robe, a specially woven tunic, a turban, and a sash (28:2-4)—based on God's specific instructions in 28:6-43.

28:6-14 The ephod was an artistically embroidered vest-like garment that the priest was to wear (28:6-8). It would include two onyx stones engraved with six of the names of Israel's sons on each, since the priest would be representing the twelve tribes in his ministerial duties (28:9-11). Aaron was to carry their names on his two shoulders before the Lord as a reminder of God's covenant with his people (28:12).

28:15-28 There was also to be an embroidered breastpiece attached to the ephod (28:15-28). It was to include four rows of three precious gemstones (28:17-20), each one engraved with one of the names of the twelve tribes (28:21).

28:29-30 As with the onyx stones on the ephod (28:6-14), the gemstones for each tribe reflected the fact that the priest was representing and interceding for the nation. He bore the names of Israel's sons over his heart (28:29). The reason it was called the breastpiece for decisions was because it included the Urim and Thummim (28:29-30). It is not clear exactly what these items were or exactly how they were used. But they were used for decision-making when Israel needed an answer from the Lord. Though Moses heard directly from the Lord, the priests were to discover God's will through use of the Urim and Thummim (see Num 27:18-21; 1 Sam 14:41-42; 28:5-6; Ezra 2:63).

28:31-35 The priest's robe was made entirely of blue yarn (28:31). It included gold bells attached to its lower hem (28:33-34). That way, others could hear the bells and know that the priest was ministering **before the Lord** (28:35).

28:36-38 The priest would also wear a **turban** with a **pure gold medallion** fastened to it. Engraved on the medallion was Holy to the Lord (28:36-37). The priest was set apart for God's service. He was to **bear the guilt** with regard to Israel's **holy offerings** (28:38). The only high priest who would be perfectly holy and able to perfectly intercede for his people, however, would be Jesus Christ (see Heb 7:26-28).

28:39-43 The final garments for the priests included tunics, sashes, and headbands. Such artistically woven items of beautiful material set apart **Aaron's sons** and gave **them glory and beauty** (28:40). Those who were to minister in the name of a glorious God were to be dressed gloriously. All of these stipulations and requirements had to be carried out so that the priests did not **incur guilt and die** (28:43).

29:1-42 Moses was to engage in an elaborate seven-day ceremony to consecrate Aaron and his sons to the priestly office. This included ceremonial washing (29:4), dressing them in the priestly **garments** (29:5-9), **anointing** with oil (29:6), sacrificial offerings (29:10-28, 35-42), and an ordination meal (29:31-34). The blood from one of the slaughtered rams was to be placed on Aaron and his sons—on **the right earlobes, on the thumbs of their right hands, and on the big toes of their right feet** (29:20). Thus, the whole body would be consecrated to the Lord's service—their ears to hear God's Word, their hands to do his work, and their feet to walk in his ways.

29:43-46 Through all of this, the Lord would **consecrate the tent of meeting and the altar**, as well as **Aaron and his sons . . . as priests** (29:44). Incredibly, through the priestly ministry in the tabernacle, the Lord would **dwell among the Israelites and be their God** (29:45), and Israel would know him as **the Lord their God, who brought them out of the land of Egypt** (29:46). In this way, God would bring his rule to the nation of Israel.

30:1-10 An additional altar was to be constructed—**an altar for the burning of incense** (30:1). It was to be overlaid with **pure gold** (30:2-5) and placed **in front of the curtain** leading into the most holy place where the **ark of the testimony** was kept (30:6). Aaron was to **burn fragrant incense** twice a day on it in the **morning** and at **twilight** (30:7-8). **The atonement ceremony** (30:10) is a reference to the Day of Atonement (see Lev 16).

The ministry of the priests was holy, sacred, and serious. No **unauthorized incense** was to be offered (30:9). Sadly, soon Aaron's sons Nadab and Abihu would pay the price for presenting "unauthorized fire before the Lord" (see Lev 10:1-2). Our God is not to be trifled with.

30:11-16 Each of the men of Israel—**twenty years old or more**—were to **pay a ransom** to the Lord (30:12, 14). This served two purposes. First, it served as an **atonement** for their lives and prevented **plague** from coming on them should they disobey (30:12, 15-16). Second, the money was used to maintain **the tent of meeting** (30:16).

30:17-21 The **bronze basin** was used as a reservoir for water so that the priests could perform their ritual washing before approaching to minister in the tabernacle.

30:22-33 Nothing about the way worship was to be carried out at the tabernacle was left to human ingenuity. God carefully described the ingredients for the **holy anointing oil** (30:22-25). Anything that didn't meet these specific requirements would be considered "unauthorized incense" (30:9). The **tent of meeting**, all its furnishings, and all its **utensils** were to be anointed with it (30:26-29). Then **Aaron and his sons** were to be anointed too so that they could serve as **priests** (30:30). This oil was holy and not to be used for any other purpose (30:31-32). Anyone who used the holy anointing oil for anything else would be **cut off** (30:33). The things of God were to be held with the highest regard.

30:34-38 As with the anointing oil, God provided specific instructions for making the **incense** (30:34-35). It would be **holy** and used only in the tabernacle (30:35-36). Anyone who mixed a batch of the sacred incense for his own use would be **cut off from his people** too (30:38).

31:1-11 The Lord **appointed** two men **by name** to lead the work of constructing the tabernacle, its furnishings, and the priestly garments: **Bezalel** and **Oholiab** (31:2-11). This tells us that God not only provided precise instructions for everything needed, but he also endowed men with wisdom and skill to do the work. God also provides the means to accomplish what he calls you to do.

31:12-17 These verses remind Israel of the commandment to **observe the Sabbath** (31:14; see 20:8-11). It was a day when no work was to be done, in honor of the Lord. To reject this holy day was to reject holy God. Thus, anyone who ignored the command was to be **put to death** (31:15).

31:18 When the Lord **finished speaking** to Moses, he gave him the two **stone tablets** with the Ten Commandments, **inscribed by the finger of God.** These were to be placed inside the ark of the covenant (25:16). The law of God was attributed to the hand of God because it was the very Word of God.

32:1 Moses was on the mountain receiving instructions from the Lord for a long time—"forty days and forty nights," in fact (see 24:18). Apparently, that was too long for the Israelites. They were impatient and had had enough waiting. They showed contempt for the one whom God used to deliver them from slavery: **this Moses . . . we don't know what has happened to him.** They also demanded that Aaron make them an idol to lead them in Moses's place as well as the Lord's—which was a rejection of the first two commandments (20:3-4) and a repudiation of their vow to obey the Lord (24:7).

32:2-4 Tragically, Aaron listened to them and told them to bring him **gold,** and he **fashioned it . . . into an image of a calf** (32:4). This is a significant choice because the Egyptians and the Canaanites, the native inhabitants of the land promised to Israel, were known for their deities shaped as calves. Thus, Israel

had scorned the great "I AM" (3:14) who had rescued them, and they worshiped instead a false god of the nations. A statue of gold received the praise that was owed to God alone (32:4).

32:5-6 Aaron said they would have **a festival to the LORD** (32:5), and the people **offered burnt offerings** and **presented fellowship offerings** (32:6). Don't miss that they called this idol "the Lord" as they made sacrifices that the real Lord had prescribed. Religious syncretism always results in false religion. If you mix idolatry with Christianity, you no longer have Christianity.

The people sat down to eat and drink, and got up to party (32:6). Clearly, this was no innocent celebration they were having. Rejection of the true God was its foundation, and the party likely incorporated corrupt cultic practices from other nations, including things like drunkenness and immorality. Paul quotes this verse when he warns the Corinthians, "Don't become idolaters" (1 Cor 10:7).

32:7-10 On the mountain for days in God's presence, Moses was ignorant of what was happening. God informed Moses that **[Moses's] people** (notice he didn't say "my people") had **acted corruptly** and **quickly** forsook God for idol worship (32:7-8). The Lord declared that they were a **stiff-necked people,** and he intended to **destroy them** (32:9-10). He would, after all, be able to make Moses **into a great nation** instead (32:10).

32:11-14 Rather than embrace the idea of being the patriarch of a nation absent the existing Israelites, Moses pleaded with God not to destroy Israel (32:11). He appealed not to any merit on their part, but to God's reputation and his character. First, Moses said the **Egyptians** would ridicule God's name and claim that he had **brought** Israel **out** only to **kill them** (32:12). Second, he reminded the Lord of his promise to the patriarchs, **Abraham, Isaac, and Israel,** to make their **offspring** into a great nation (32:13). And as a result of Moses's intercession, **the LORD relented** and did not wipe out the Israelites (32:14).

This brings us to an important point. God himself says that he does not change (see Mal 3:6). Yet he also declares that he may choose to relent and not bring threatened judgment upon a people should they change their ways (see Jer 18:8; 26:3). In other words, he might relent if the people repent or, as here, in response to intercessory prayer.

The Lord is relational; he interacts with his people. Moses didn't tell God anything he didn't already know. Instead Moses appealed to God based on what he knew about the glory of his name and his faithfulness to his promises. This suggests that when we relate to an aspect of God's character, he is free to change with regard to his actions without changing at all in character. That is, he is free to make a change in how he will interact with his people. God's relenting from destroying Israel didn't imply that he'd changed his attitude toward their sin. In fact, though he didn't obliterate them, he did hold them accountable for their wickedness (32:27-28, 33-35). God thus upheld his reputation, remained faithful to his Word, and displayed his grace.

32:15-20 Moses descended the mountain holding the **two tablets**, engraved with **God's writing** (32:15-16). **Joshua**, who had accompanied Moses up the mountain (see 24:13), heard the noise in the Israelite camp below and assumed that enemy attack had to be the source of it. But Moses knew better (32:17-18). When Moses saw **the calf** and the people **dancing**, he erupted in anger and smashed **the tablets** as an expression of frustration that Israel had (so quickly!) broken the covenant God had made with them (32:19). Then he **burned** and **ground** the calf to **powder** and forced the Israelites to **drink** their sin (32:20).

32:21-24 Moses questioned his brother **Aaron**, the high priest. He was supposed to lead Israel to know and follow God but instead had **led them into . . . a grave sin** (32:21). Rather than fessing up, Aaron merely shifted the blame to the people, as if they forced him to do it (32:22-23). Then he made this ridiculous claim: **When I threw** the gold **into the fire, out came this calf** (32:24). He thus falsely implied that the idol was supernaturally formed.

32:25-29 Moses saw that the people were out of control (32:25). Though he had confronted them with their sin, many

were unrepentant. So he called out, **Whoever is for the LORD, come to me** (32:26). When the Levites gathered around him in response, Moses sent them to act out God's judgment on those who persisted in their idolatry and immorality (32:27). As a result, **three thousand men** soon **fell dead** (32:28).

Sin is no joke. It brings death (see Gen 3:17; Rom 6:23; Jas 1:15). Sometimes it may result in untimely physical death. But if one does not receive God's grace through Jesus Christ, it will result in the second death, which is much worse: eternal judgment in the lake of fire (see Rev 20:14-15).

32:30-32 The next day, Moses reminded the people of their sin and declared his intention to intercede with God for them (32:30). Scripture follows this with another remarkable example of intercessory prayer. Moses confessed the sin of the people and pleaded for their forgiveness. If God would not forgive them, Moses asked that God might destroy him instead of them (32:31-32). He was willing to lay down his life for this ungrateful, sinful people.

32:33-35 In response to Moses's prayer, God vowed to hold the people **accountable for their [own] sin** (32:34). Though he would not destroy the nation, he addressed their sin by inflicting **a plague** (32:35).

Even though Moses faithfully prayed and interceded for Israel, God would not allow him to take their sin upon himself and be punished in their place. Moses was himself a sinner, so he could not bear the sin of others. But one day a holy and righteous man would come—the God-Man, Jesus Christ. Without sin himself, Jesus would be able to bear and take away the sin of the world (see John 1:29; 2 Cor 5:21; Heb 7:26-27; 9:14).

33:1-3 Next the Lord commanded Moses to lead the people to the promised land and vowed that he would **drive out** their enemies (33:1-2). But, because of the people's sin, God said he would **not go up with** them, otherwise he **might destroy** them (33:3). Thus, God would not dwell among his people any longer; the tabernacle would not be the place of his presence (25:8).

This sobering passage tells us that it's possible to receive blessings (like **a land flowing with milk and honey,** 33:3) yet lack God's presence. Since knowing God—and not merely receiving his blessings—is the goal of a believer's life, we should be grieved at the thought of doing life without him.

33:4-6 The people **mourned** and took off **their jewelry** they had obtained from the Egyptians (12:35-36), knowing that some of that very wealth had been misused to make the golden calf (32:2-4). Removing it was a sign of remorse.

33:7-11 Moses **took a tent and pitched it outside the camp** to meet with God (33:7). The tent of meeting was to be in the midst of the Israelite camp (see Num 2:2). The fact that Moses pitched his tent outside the camp indicated that God was serious about his threat not to go with them to the promised land (33:3). Nevertheless, God had not completely abandoned them yet. **When Moses entered the tent,** the **cloud**—representing God's presence—descended, and **the LORD** spoke **with Moses** (33:9, 11).

At that point, **anyone who wanted to consult the LORD would go to the tent of meeting that was outside the camp** (33:7). So God's presence was still available. To take advantage of it, though, the people had to leave the camp and make their way to a special place.

This trek they made is a reminder that God makes his blessed presence available to anyone who makes the effort to seek him. We must, however, be willing to break away from the noise of the crowd if we want to hear what God has to say to us through his Word and his Spirit.

The LORD would speak with Moses face to face, just as a man speaks with his friend (33:11). "Face to face" is a figure of speech that means "openly and honestly." To be friends with God requires openness and honesty. That's why the Bible opposes worldliness (see 1 Cor 3:2-3). To be worldly is to take on the values of the world system that leaves God out of the life equation. But, remember: "Friendship with the world is hostility toward God" (Jas 4:4). While we are to be in the world where we can reach

out in love to those who do not yet know God, we are not to be "of the world" (see John 17:14-15). This is because if you are a friend to the world's sinful ways, you will not come to God openly and honestly. God invites you to be his friend—to speak with him face to face.

33:12-17 The Lord knew Moses, and Moses had found favor with him (33:12). But Moses wasn't satisfied with their relationship. He wanted more of God. Though he had experienced the burning bush incident, the opening of the Red Sea, seeing water gush from the rock, and had eaten bread from heaven, all of that was yesterday's news. He wanted to know God more. He wanted a fresh, deeper knowledge of him. So Moses said to the Lord, **Please teach me your ways, and I will know you** (33:13). Moses was like a hungry man who'd sat down to an elegant meal. He wasn't satisfied to nibble on an appetizer and to sample the soup. He wanted to *feast* on all the Lord offers.

The problem for many Christians is that they're either not hungry for spiritual things at all or they hunger for the wrong things, things like emotional highs and purely academic knowledge about Scripture. This is one reason why God may bring difficulties into your life; he wants to help reorient your hunger so that you'll crave a deeper connection with him. Whatever your circumstances, pray for true spiritual hunger, because God will satisfy those who hunger for him (see Matt 5:6).

Moses understood what the psalm writer said: "As a deer longs for flowing streams, so I long for you, God. I thirst for God, the living God" (Ps 42:1-2). This should be the attitude of every believing heart. God doesn't want mere churchgoers. He wants people who are hungry and thirsty to know him. That, in fact, is the meaning of eternal life—to know God: "This is eternal life: that they may know you, the only true God, and the one you have sent—Jesus Christ" (John 17:3).

Moses again interceded for Israel. He said to God, **Consider that this nation is your people** (33:13). Because of Moses's concern, God reversed his previous threat (see commentary on 33:1-4) and agreed that his **presence** would accompany them to the promised land (33:14; see commentary on 32:11-14). Moses made his position clear: **If your presence does not go . . . don't make us go up from here** (33:15). He had no faith in his people's ability to thrive without the Lord.

Moses knew that to be in God's presence is *everything*. In fact, he would rather be in the desert with God than in the promised land without him. He would have agreed with the psalmist: "Better a day in your courts than a thousand anywhere else" (Ps 84:10). This brings to mind a question we all face. What do we want more, if we have to choose between God's presence and God's blessing? Far too many Christians choose the latter. Nothing compares to knowing that the Lord walks beside you.

33:18 Moses wanted still more. He said to the Lord, **Please let me see your glory** (33:18). In other words, Moses wanted to see a visible manifestation of the invisible God. He wanted God to "go public" for him and provide an observable display of his glorious deity. Are you satisfied with listening to a sermon and singing a few songs to God? Or do you constantly long to see more of God in your life, to grasp a greater sense of God's glory?

33:19-20 The Lord graciously replied to Moses's request. He promised to show him a manifestation of his glory. God would let his **goodness** pass before Moses while God proclaimed his own name, **the LORD** (33:19). But even though he would be allowed that remarkable encounter, Moses couldn't see God's **face, for humans cannot see [his] face and live** (33:20).

This means that while God would let Moses see a portion of his glory, he would not show him his face—not the essence of his being. To be exposed to the unfiltered glory of God on this side of eternity would be like entering a nuclear reactor or traveling to the sun; the divine holiness would consume us.

33:21-23 God's **glory** would pass by Moses while he stood on a **rock** (33:21-22). God said to him, **I will put you in the crevice of the rock and cover you with my hand until I have passed by. Then I will take my hand away, and you will see my back** (33:22-23). In other words, the Lord was limiting Moses's

exposure to his glory for Moses's own welfare. He could not be subjected to anything more than a glimpse of the back of God's glory. Yet, as a result of even this limited exposure, his face would literally shine with the wonder of the encounter and the sacredness of speaking to the Lord (34:29-35).

Of course, God, who is spirit (see John 4:24) has no body, so he has no back—just as he has no arm (see commentary on 6:6). This is anthropomorphic language, or the use of human concepts to explain a spiritual reality. God's "arm" refers to his power. God's "back" refers to the amount of glory that Moses was able to handle. (Think of it like the exhaust that's left behind when a high-flying jet passes overhead.)

No one has ever seen God in all his glory, but the Son of God has revealed him (John 1:18). Jesus, in fact, told his disciples, "The one who has seen me has seen the Father" (John 14:9). One day, believers will see Jesus Christ in all his glory, as the apostle John did late in the biblical story (see Rev 1:12-16). Until then, we keep walking with God by faith.

34:1-4 God commanded Moses to **cut two stone tablets like the first ones** that he had smashed (see 32:19). He promised to **write** the Ten Commandments on these (34:1). Moses was to bring them with him the next day when he ascended the mountain (34:2). **No one** was to accompany him, neither man nor beast (34:3). So Moses did **just as the LORD had commanded him** (34:4).

34:5-7 Then, as promised (33:19-23), God **proclaimed his name** and **passed in front** of Moses (34:5). He proclaimed his glorious attributes, the marvelous divine nature. He said, **The LORD is a compassionate and gracious God, slow to anger and abounding in faithful love and truth** (34:6). He is rich in mercy and kindness. **But,** he continued, **he will not leave the guilty unpunished** (34:7).

This tells us that God's love is not permissive. It's a holy love. He is righteous and cannot overlook sin. That, in fact, is what makes the gospel such good news. In the cross of Christ, God's justice and God's love met. He satisfied his own righteous demands, so that he could show grace to those who come to his Son in repentance and faith.

34:8-9 As God's glory passed by, Moses had the appropriate response. He **immediately knelt low** and **worshiped** (34:8). Then he pleaded once again that the Lord would **forgive** the Israelites, **accept** them as his own, and **go** with them to the promised land (34:9).

34:10-17 In spite of Israel's sin, God vowed to stay true to the **covenant** (34:10). He promised to **perform** further **wonders** and **drive out** the wicked inhabitants of the land he was giving them (34:10-11). Israel's job was to **observe** what God commanded (34:11). They were not to **make a treaty with the inhabitants of the land** or intermarry with them (34:12, 15-16). **The LORD is jealous for his reputation**, so his people should be too and must never **bow down to another god** (34:14).

34:18-26 These verses repeat a number of the Lord's commands and instructions, especially those regarding the firstborn and festivals. Of special note is that all of the **males** were to meet with the Lord three times per year. Don't miss that if the men would take their rightful place under God's kingdom rule, he would protect the whole nation (34:23-24).

34:27 God had Moses **write down** the **words** of the **covenant** that he gave him. This lends strong support to the view that Moses is the author of the book of Exodus (as well as the entire Pentateuch).

34:28-35 Moses spent **forty days and forty nights** in the Lord's presence, writing down the Word of God (34:28). When he finally descended the mountain, **he did not realize that the skin of his face shone as a result of speaking with the LORD** (34:29). In other words, God had rubbed off on him. I know

this because Scripture declares, "God is light" (1 John 1:5). And Jesus said, "I am the light of the world" (John 8:12). Moreover, in the new creation, there will be no need for light from the sun, because God glory will provide light (see Rev 21:23; 22:5). When Moses spent extended, uninterrupted time in God's presence, he began to glow. What's even more interesting is that others observed it before Moses knew it was happening (34:29-30).

God wants to transform you too, and he wants others to see the transformation. But first, you have to be hungry for him. When a person has lost his physical appetite, it's typically because he's either sick or has been snacking on junk food between meals. The same is often true in terms of spiritual matters. We eat Christian doughnuts and religious french fries, taking in a little gospel music and adding a little Christian lingo to our vocabularies as if that's what a life with Jesus is all about. We reduce Christianity to a matter of tradition, and then we wonder why we don't hunger for God. We need extended, uninterrupted time with him. We need to go much deeper in our commitment.

Paul reminds the Corinthians that the old covenant, which was written on stone and brought death (because the law can't save), made Moses's face glorious. So how much more glory does the new covenant, written on believers' hearts in this era marked by Christ's saving death and resurrection, bring through the ministry of the Spirit? (see 2 Cor 3:7-10). As believers, we are transformed into the image of Christ by the Spirit of God as we peer into his Word (2 Cor 3:17-18). God is supposed to rub off on us more than he rubbed off on Moses, whose glory faded (2 Cor 3:13). We are to "shine like stars in the world" as a result of Christ's transforming influence in our lives (Phil 2:15).

VIII. CONSTRUCTING THE TABERNACLE (35:1-40:38)

35:1-3 With instructions in hand for constructing the tabernacle and its furnishings, Moses was ready to relay everything to the Israelites so that the work could begin. But first he reminded them of the Sabbath. **Six**

days of **work** were to be followed by **a Sabbath of complete rest to the LORD** (35:2).

35:4-29 Moses called the Israelites to give sacrificially: **Let everyone whose heart**

is willing bring items needed for building the tabernacle, he said (35:5-8). He told them about all of the tabernacle furnishings that God had commanded them to build (35:10-19; see 25:1–28:43). In response to Moses's exhortation, **everyone whose heart was moved and whose spirit prompted him came and brought an offering to the Lord** (35:21). This means the people gave willingly, not out of compulsion—which is the kind of giving that God loves (see 2 Cor 9:7).

35:30–36:7 Moses informed the Israelites that God had chosen **Bezalel** and **Oholiab** by name to lead **all the skilled people** to construct the sanctuary (35:30–36:1; see 31:1-6). Then **Moses summoned Bezalel, Oholiab,** and the others to commission them in their work. **The Lord had placed wisdom** in their **hearts** (36:2). Now, as good stewards under God, it was time to use their divine gifts for his service.

Don't miss that the people gave sacrificially for the work on the tabernacle. In fact, Moses had to order the people to stop giving, because there was **more than enough** (36:6-7). (How often do churches today have to give an order like that?)

36:8-38 If you compare these verses to 26:1-37, you'll notice that virtually all of this section is repeat. The point of that redundancy is to show that those who built the tabernacle did not improvise. They followed God's instructions word for word. Everything that God said to do, they did.

37:1–38:20 These verses indicate that the skilled workers also made everything related to the tabernacle exactly as God command-ed. The description of each item repeats the instructions Moses received from God. Each item was constructed according to the divine plan: **the ark** (37:1-9; cp. 25:10-22), **the table** (37:10-16; cp. 25:23-30), **the lampstand** (37:17-24; cp. 25:31-40), **the altar of incense** (37:25-28; cp. 30:1-5), **the altar of burnt offering** (38:1-7; cp. 27:1-8), **the bronze basin** (38:8; 30:17-21), and **the courtyard** (38:9-20; cp. 27:9-19).

38:21-30 At Moses's command, those building the tabernacle took an **inventory** of all the materials that were donated and used

(38:21). This was clearly a vast and expensive project. Tons of **gold**, **silver**, and **bronze** were incorporated (38:24-31). But God is worth every penny spent in his service. The Lord took the wealth Israel plundered from wicked Egypt and used it to accomplish his kingdom work (see 11:2; 12:35-36).

39:1-31 Just as they did with the tabernacle and its furnishings (see commentary on 36:8-38; 37:1–38:20), the skilled artisans made the priestly garments exactly in accordance with God's instructions: **the ephod** (39:2-7; see 28:6-14), **the breastpiece** (39:8-21; see 28:15-28), **the robe** (39:22-26; see 28:31-35), and the other garments (39:27-31; see 28:36-43).

39:32-43 It's one thing to work hard on an assignment; it's another thing for your completed work to withstand close scrutiny. Whether a student has written a paper or an employee has finished a project, there comes a time when an assessment of the effort must be made. The paper must be graded by the teacher; the project must be evaluated by the boss. When the Israelites had finished all of the work, Moses began his inspection (39:33). Moses knew that God was holy; therefore, the tabernacle, its furnishings, and the priestly garments had to meet the divine specifications precisely. When he had **inspected all the work**, Moses was pleased, and he **blessed** the workers (39:43).

If you are a Christian, you should serve the Lord with excellence in whatever work he has assigned you. The all-knowing God sees all you do, and he knows all of your thoughts and motives. He did not spare his own Son to save you (see Rom 8:32), and he sealed you with his promised Holy Spirit (see Eph 1:13). So why would you offer to him anything but your very best?

40:1-33 Finally, it was the moment of truth. God commanded Moses to **set up the tabernacle ... on the first day of the first month** (40:1-2). As God instructed (40:3-15), so Moses **did** (40:16-33). Everything was put in its proper place and anointed with oil. Then Aaron and his sons were dressed in their garments and anointed for their priestly duties. Moses followed the divine plan without deviation. He did everything **just as the Lord**

had commanded him (40:16, 19, 21, 23, 25, 27, 29, 32). That's a good habit to adopt.

40:34-35 When everything was in place, the cloud of God's glory descended and filled the tabernacle (40:34). God had promised to dwell among his people. When they obediently followed his agenda, he came and took up residence among them. In fact, Moses couldn't even enter the tent because it was bursting with the glory of the LORD (40:35).

The same thing would happen later when Solomon built the temple: "The cloud filled" it, and there was no room for the priests to perform their ministry (see 1 Kgs 8:10-11). Importantly, when the Son of God took on flesh and came into the world, he "dwelt [literally, in Greek, "tabernacled"] among us" and displayed "his glory" (John 1:14). All those who trust in him receive the Holy Spirit to dwell within them. As a believer, "you are God's temple," and "the Spirit of God lives in you" (1 Cor 3:16). And if the Spirit of God lives within you, there's no room for anyone else but him.

40:36-38 When the glory cloud was in the tabernacle, Israel stayed put. When the cloud lifted, Israel went wherever the cloud led them (40:36-37; see Num 9:15-23). Thus, the book of Exodus ends with God's people following his direction, as he led a nation of former slaves to the promised land.

LEVITICUS

INTRODUCTION

Author

THE BOOK IS ANONYMOUS; NO AUthor's name is included. However, evidence from the Bible (see Rom 10:5), as well as ancient Jewish and Christian traditions, points to Moses as the author of Leviticus—and of the Pentateuch (the first five books of the Old Testament) in general. As the book demonstrates, Moses was the Lord's intermediary, making his revelation known to the people of Israel (see 1:1; 4:1; 5:14; 6:1, 8). Clearly, the author was familiar with the events recorded in Leviticus, so there is no reason to doubt that this writer was Moses.

Historical Background

From the time the Israelites arrived at Mount Sinai (see Exod 19:1-2) until they departed (see Num 10:11-13) was about one year. In that time, Moses received the Lord's covenant, constructed the tabernacle, and received all of the instructions recorded in Leviticus and in the early chapters of Numbers. The repeated expression found throughout the book, "The LORD spoke to Moses" (see 4:1; 5:14), leaves no doubt that Leviticus contains divine revelation—not the ideas of Moses. The title of the book derives from the attention it gives to the duties of the Levites who were charged with the ministry of the tabernacle.

Message and Purpose

Leviticus is one of the most neglected and yet powerful books in the Bible. It establishes the guidelines by which God is to be known and worshiped. It is far more relevant to us than many realize.

The book distinguishes between the profane, the common, and the holy. Here's an illustration that may help to explain the differences between those concepts. When you have dirty dishes in your sink, they are profane. That is, they are unacceptable to use until they have been cleaned. Profane things in our lives are completely unacceptable to God because they bring dirt before him. The common dishes, by contrast, are those you use every day. There's nothing wrong with them; they just aren't special. And should we treat God as common, we don't hold him in the high regard his holiness deserves and demands.

Think about what's holy in relation to the china dishes secured behind the glass doors in the hutch in the dining room. These are the ones we only bring out on special occasions for honored guests. That picture gives insight into how Leviticus teaches us to treat God—the Holy One who is like no other. We are to relate to God and worship him as our unique, one-of-a-kind Lord, and King of his kingdom. He deserves only the best.

VIDEO | INTRO

www.bhpublishinggroup.com/qr/te/03_00

Outline

LEVITICUS

I. APPROACHING A HOLY GOD THROUGH SACRIFICE (1:1–7:38)

ᴥ A. Regulations for the Burnt Offering (1:1-17) ᴥ

1:1 The opening words of Leviticus give us the context we need to understand the importance of Israel getting their worship of God right; after all, his character is pure holiness. Moses recorded the moment when God revealed to him the regulations for proper worship: **Then the Lord summoned Moses and spoke to him from the tent of meeting**, the tabernacle. Moses did not sit down with the priests and Levites to brainstorm a worship program that they thought would please God. The regulations contained in Israel's book of worship came from the Lord himself.

1:2-9 In keeping with God's perfect holiness, the **burnt offering** was to be perfect—an **unblemished** animal (1:3). The burnt offering was the most frequent of Israel's offerings, to be offered by God's priests every morning and evening (see 6:8-13). But its frequency in no way diminished its importance. The burnt offering could also be a voluntary offering brought by an individual in dedication or praise to God, which is the kind of offering spoken of here. The worshiper brought the offering and laid his hand on the animal's head to signify that it was his substitute to make **atonement for** his sin (1:3-4). The offerer then skinned and cut up the animal for burning by the **priests**, who

also sprinkled its **blood** on the **altar** (1:5-9). This was a messy affair. Atoning for sin is serious business.

The burnt offering was unique in that the entire sacrifice was consumed as **a fire offering of a pleasing aroma to the Lord** (1:9). The Hebrew word for the burnt offering means "to ascend." The smoke from the fire ascended into God's nostrils, so to speak, and pleased him. This was critical for Israel because pleasing a holy God by performing acceptable worship in his presence was a life-and-death matter to his people, as we will soon learn from the deaths of Aaron's sons who violated God's commands and paid the ultimate price for doing things their own way (10:1-3). God's pleasure with and acceptance of the sacrifice also gave the worshiper the assurance that he, despite being a sinner, was accepted and forgiven in God's holy presence.

1:10-17 One other feature of the burnt offering worth noting is that no Israelite was left out of giving it, no matter how poor he was. The most expensive offering came from the cattle herd (1:3), with a sheep or goat being next in order of cost (1:10). But those who could not afford either of these animals could offer **turtledoves or young pigeons** (1:14). Actually, poor people could bring birds for other offerings as well, which is what happened at Jesus's birth when Joseph and Mary presented birds at the temple for his dedication (see Luke 2:21-24). They did this because the law of Moses in Leviticus 12:2-8 specified that the mother of a newborn was to offer both a burnt offering and a sin offering for her cleansing.

forever. (This covenant will be fulfilled when Jesus takes the throne of David at his second coming and rules in his millennial kingdom.)

✻ B. Regulations for the Grain Offering (2:1-16) ✺

2:1-16 Leviticus doesn't specify when the Israelites were to bring a **grain offering** to the Lord at the tabernacle, except for the period known as **firstfruits** at harvest time (2:12-16). These offerings provided a way for the people of Israel to recognize and confess their dependence on God for their food and their very lives. We learn from Numbers 28 that these offerings were, like the burnt offering, to be made every morning and at twilight.

The grain offerings were the only bloodless sacrifices, but they were still holy to the Lord. They were to be free of **yeast or honey** (2:11). These could be offered as **firstfruits** but not offered **on the altar** (2:12). We know from other passages of Scripture that yeast was often used as a symbol of sin (see 1 Cor 5:8).

Most of the chapter deals with the various elements that could be offered and the various ways the priests could prepare a grain offering. The portion to be offered to God included these instructions: **The priest will take a handful of fine flour and oil from it, along with all its frankincense, and will burn this memorial portion of it on the altar, a fire offering of a pleasing aroma to the LORD** (2:2). The incense increased the fragrance of the aroma that would rise. The remainder of the offerings—**the holiest part**—belonged to **Aaron and his sons** (2:3,10). In payment for their ministry, the consecrated priests were allowed to eat these offerings.

All of the grain offerings were to include **the salt of the covenant with your God** (2:13). Salt was a symbol of permanence; it was something that the ancients believed could not be destroyed even by fire. The concept of "a covenant of salt" appears in Numbers 18:19 and in 2 Chronicles 13:5, the latter referring to the permanence of God's covenant with David to establish his throne

✻ C. Regulations for the Fellowship Offering (3:1-17) ✺

3:1-17 This was another largely voluntary sacrifice the Israelites could bring to the Lord at the tabernacle. Many of the specifics of its preparation and offering are similar to those of the burnt offering (1:1-17). The distinctive element of the fellowship offering is that the worshiper shared in it by eating the meat of the sacrifice (7:11-35; cf. Deut 12:7), except for the fat portions, which the priests burned on the altar as **a fire offering of a pleasing aroma to the LORD** (3:5).

If the worshiper brought an offering from the flock instead of the herd, the sacrifice could be either a **male or female** (3:6). Birds were excluded from this offering since they were so small that nothing would be left to eat. The worshiper, his family, and friends were invited to eat the fellowship meal consisting of the meat returned to them by the priests.

That this was a fellowship offering indicates that it was to be a festive meal as an expression of the offerer's joy in experiencing communion with God. The fact that the fellowship offering is often mentioned in conjunction with the burnt offering (as in Ex 20:24 and 24:5) reinforces the picture of a worshiper first offering a sacrifice to atone for his sins—an offering given entirely to the Lord—and then presenting a fellowship offering in praise and gratitude.

The prohibition on eating any of the fat portions of the fellowship offering is explicitly stated: **All fat belongs to the LORD** (3:16). Various explanations for this have been offered, including the suggestion that since the fat is the choicest part of the animal, God alone is worthy of it. But the Bible never says exactly why the fat was to be reserved for burning. The prohibition against eating **blood** (3:17) was established in God's covenant with Noah because in the blood is the life of an animal (see Gen 9:4).

❧ D. Regulations for the Sin Offering
(4:1–5:13) ❧

4:1 Establishing an offering to atone for the sins of God's people was an absolute necessity in order for a holy God to interact with sinful humans. That God himself had to initiate this is obvious from the opening phrase: **The Lord spoke to Moses.** Making a way for sinners to be made right with him has always been important to God. Interestingly, the natural human reaction for dealing with sin is to hide, as Adam and Eve did in the garden after they sinned (see Gen 3:8).

4:2 Israel's sin offering provided forgiveness and atonement for sins committed **unintentionally against any of the Lord's commands.** This is a broad statement that covers all kinds of situations, although in 5:1-6 the Lord gave four specific examples of unintentional sins needing atonement. Should you wonder about intentional sins committed in deliberate rebellion against God, know that the only atonement for them was the death of the offender.

4:3 The structure of chapter 4 outlines the **sin offering** requirements for four groups in Israel's camp (the nation was still in the wilderness when Moses received the law). These groups were **the anointed priest** (4:3), "the whole community of Israel" (4:13), leaders (4:22), and "the common people" (4:27). The word *common*, of course, had nothing to do with their intrinsic value to God. Rather, it was a recognition of their diverse positions within the community and the potential impact their sins would have on the nation. This difference applied to the cost of the animals (or grain in the case of extreme poverty) that were required for the sacrifice and the ritual of applying the blood to achieve atonement.

With this in mind, we can see why the sins of **the anointed priest** were the first that needed to be atoned for. The entire sacrificial system would grind to a halt if the high priest, which is probably the more precise way to refer to the "anointed priest," was carrying unforgiven sin that would disqualify him from ministering before the Lord. His sin

would bring guilt on the entire nation, so his sacrifice had to be **a young, unblemished bull**, the costliest animal for an Israelite.

4:4 The priest would **lay his hand on the bull's head**, signifying that this animal was bearing his sin. He was then to **slaughter it before the Lord**, catching the creature's blood in a bowl. The phrase "before the Lord" occurs ten times in chapter 4 alone, and many times afterward. This means that through these rituals people were constantly being reminded that their sin was first and foremost an offense against the holy God they worshiped; thus, it was him they needed to satisfy. David showed he understood this truth when he was finally forced to face his sins of adultery with Bathsheba and the murder of her husband Uriah. David cried out to God in his prayer of confession: "Against you—you alone—I have sinned and done this evil" (Ps 51:4).

4:5-12 **The anointed priest** who sinned took the **blood** of the sacrifice into the tabernacle, dipped his finger in the bowl, and sprinkled that blood **seven times** (4:5-6) in front of the veil that separated the holy place from the most holy place. He then applied blood to **the horns of the altar of fragrant incense**, pouring out the rest at the base of **the altar of burnt offering** (4:7). The **fat** of the sacrifice was burned as a further offering to the Lord, and the rest of the carcass was taken away and **burned** (4:8-12). Many of these procedures were the same for other offerings, but it's important to note that the priest had to be first in line for cleansing and forgiveness so he could serve effectively before the Lord in handling the people's sin offerings.

4:13 The second set of sin offering procedures is for **the whole community of Israel**. This signals a logical progression because if the congregation as a whole was under God's displeasure for sin, nothing good was going to happen at the individual level. Similarly, in the church, God's people need to keep short their sin accounts with the Lord, so that we can move ahead as one to advance his kingdom on earth. And even though the church is not given a formal ritual for corporate confession in Scripture, it is very appropriate for a local body of believers to acknowledge where they have fallen short and to seek God's forgiveness through Jesus Christ.

4:14-21 The purification from sin for the community involved bringing a **young bull** (4:14) instead of a full-grown one. **The elders of the** community, as the congregation's leaders and representatives, laid their **hands on the bull's head** in confession of sin and acknowledgment that the bull was being offered in place of the people (4:15). The bull was **slaughtered** and **burned** in a way similar to the previous procedures, and the result was **atonement** and forgiveness of sins (4:15-21).

4:22-26 A **leader** who sinned unintentionally was to bring an **unblemished male goat as his offering** (4:22-23). Such a person could have been either a tribal leader or an official in one of the clans of a particular tribe. When the goat was slaughtered, **the priest** applied some of its blood **to the horns of the altar of burnt offering** (4:25).

4:27-35 If one of the **common people** in the Israelite community sinned **unintentionally**, he could bring an **unblemished female goat** or **lamb** for his sin offering (4:27-28, 32); these options were less costly for the average person to purchase. The ritual for atonement, however, was the same as for the leader (4:29, 33-35). No one who sinned in ignorance and offended Israel's holy God was left without a remedy—but addressing the offense always required the shedding of blood.

5:1-4 The four conditions mentioned in these verses could be categorized as sins of omission or neglect. The first instance involved a person failing to speak up about something he knew in a particular case—that is, withholding information by not testifying (5:1). The fourth instance is similar to the first. This has to do with **swear[ing] rashly to do what is good or evil** (5:4). God took it very seriously when one of his people made a vow (see Lev 27). That's why Scripture says, "When you make a vow to God, don't delay fulfilling it, because he does not delight in fools. Fulfill what you vow. Better that you

do not vow than that you vow and not fulfill it" (Eccl 5:4-5).

The other two offenses in this section concern touching something that made an Israelite **unclean** (5:2-3). This refers to ceremonial defilement that disqualified the offender from participating in worship and made him guilty before God. The things outlined here may sound like minor offenses to us, but God was using them to teach his people the important difference between being clean and unclean—between being holy and profane.

5:5-13 A **female lamb or goat** (5:6) was an acceptable sacrifice if the person could afford one. In cases of more severe poverty, the offering could be **two turtledoves or two young pigeons** (5:7) or even **two quarts of fine flour** (5:11). A person's financial ability or inability in no way lessened the guilt that needed to be atoned for.

❧ E. Regulations for the Guilt Offering (5:14–6:7) ❧

5:14-19 The **guilt offering** was like the sin offering in several ways, since both of them required atonement for a guilty party through the blood of a sacrifice. However, this offering introduced the concept of **restitution** when one sinned against "any holy thing" or defrauded his neighbor (5:16; 6:2-3). The sacrifice required was an **unblemished ram** (5:15). A fine was added to this offering in recognition that a wrong had been done against God or the injured party (5:16).

The opening section here deals with offenses against God in regard to his **holy things** (5:15) or his **commands** (5:17). The offense against "any holy thing" could involve anything from mishandling the portion of a sacrifice that was meant for the priest, to failure to give God the tithe, to not keeping a vow. Since the offense was against God, the extra penalty was paid to his representative, **the priest** (5:16). In both of these instances the sin was done **unintentionally** or out of ignorance (5:15, 17), but, again, this did not excuse the guilty party once he became aware of his sin.

6:1-7 These verses address regulations for the guilt offering when a person deceives or **defrauds his neighbor**, specifically with regard to property (6:2-3). Not only did the guilty person have to make **full restitution** for the **item**, he also had to pay the owner an additional **fifth of its value** (6:4-5). Having to pay back the full value plus twenty percent was a strong deterrent to crime. And make no mistake about it. If the principles of biblical justice were implemented in our society today, we wouldn't have prisons full to overflowing. The aim of biblical justice is always a cessation of the crime coupled, when possible, with restitution to the victim.

Regardless of the application, in fact, biblical restitution was always specific to the offended victim. Once full restitution was made, the sin was forgiven by God and the clear implication is that the two human parties involved would put the matter behind them and move on. Instead of this justice and closure in our current cultural system, however, we have offenders warehoused in prisons where they learn to be better criminals while their victims must seek restitution by other means, which all too often ends with nothing being restored.

Another crucial principle of biblical justice that speaks to a crying need in our legal system today is the concept that a person's offense was both against God and against the victim, a fellow human being with a name and a family, rather than merely being a crime against some vague entity such as society or the state. We talk about people paying their debt to society; but in most cases, it wasn't a society or the state that had its property taken by fraud or theft or some other crime. And it isn't society or the state that suffers loss while the offender is locked away and cannot repay his victim even if he wants to.

≫ F. Priestly Regulations for the Five Offerings (6:8–7:38) ≪

This section deals with the same five offerings found in 1:1–6:7, but this time it is the priests who are addressed. This is something of a supplement to the instructions for the offerings prescribed previously; it gives the priests information on how to handle the elements of each of these sacrifices. The order here is slightly different, but the same five offerings are covered.

6:8-13 God told Moses to **command Aaron and his sons** (6:8-9). Already the people had been instructed in how to present their sacrifice to atone for a wrongdoing. But the priests were charged with actually handling the sacrifices as God prescribed. If they were negligent, there were consequences for them as well as for the offender who was counting on them to do things in the right way. As the teachers of the law in Israel, the priests were also responsible to instruct the Israelites in the proper offerings to bring so they could deal with sin and live as a holy people before the Lord.

The instructions to the priests in handling the **burnt offering** (6:9) are relatively brief since none of the sacrifice was allowed to be eaten—it was all consumed by fire on the altar as a sweet aroma to God. The priest's main responsibilities were to make sure the fire on the altar was kept **burning** at all times, to slaughter and prepare the burnt offering the right way (see 1:1-17), and to properly **remove** its **ashes** (6:10-13).

6:14-23 Next came the priestly regulations for handling the **grain offering** (6:14). This section is longer both because part of the grain offering was to be eaten and because it includes a description of the priest's own grain offering (6:19-23). Only a **memorial portion** (6:15) of the grain was burned; the rest was to be roasted and consumed by the priests in a specific way—without leaven (yeast) and **in the courtyard of the tent of meeting** (6:16). The entire offering was designated as **especially holy** (6:17).

Since the grain offering in 6:19-23 was brought by the priest himself and presented before the Lord, however, he was not allowed to eat any of it. The reference to the day that the priest is **anointed** (6:20) suggests that this was a praise offering for God's mercy in providing a mediator between him and his people and ensuring the continuation of the priestly line through Aaron's descendants.

For New Testament believers, by virtue of his sinless life, atoning death, and resurrection, Jesus Christ is our ever-living, merciful high priest (see Heb 4:14-16).

6:24-30 The third section of priestly instructions concerns the **sin offering** (6:25). Whatever **touches** the **flesh** of the sin offering **will become holy** (6:27). Furthermore, the washing of clothing spattered with the sacrificial blood and the smashing or cleansing of a **pot** in which the meat was **boiled** were prescribed (6:27-28). The portion of the meat the priests were allowed to eat had to be consumed **in the courtyard of the tent of meeting** (6:26). The exception was a sin offering whose blood was brought into the tabernacle **to make atonement in the holy place**. This had to be completely burned (6:30).

7:1-6 The priests' regulations for the **guilt offering** (7:1) include several new elements: the place where it was to be offered, the parts of the sacrificial animal to be burned, and the fact that **any male among the priests** could eat the remaining meat (7:3-6). The fact that the guilt offering is called **especially holy** twice is another reminder both of the purity of Israel's God and of the holy behavior he expected from his covenant people (7:1, 6).

7:7-10 These verses work like a pause to summarize the parts of the offerings that went to the priests as their food, since they would not have lands and crops of their own given the way the promised land was to be distributed among the tribes. God's provision for his servants is a biblical principle that can be traced from the law of Moses to the church today (see 1 Cor 9:1-12; 1 Tim 5:17-18).

7:11-21 The **fellowship sacrifice** (7:11) was unique as the only offering in which the person bringing it was allowed to eat a portion of the sacrifice—usually as part of a celebration meal with family and friends. This may help explain the additional verses (7:22-38) devoted to this offering, which include instructions not only to the priests but to the congregation as well. The name of this offering explains its purpose. The worshiper sought to draw near to God by making a sacrifice either in **thanksgiving** as a testimony to God's goodness (7:12-15), or as an offering in fulfillment of a **vow**, or simply as a **freewill offering** (7:16-18).

The fellowship sacrifice also included various leavened and unleavened **cakes** and **wafers** (7:12). The meat of the thanksgiving sacrifice had to be **eaten** the same day it was offered (7:15), while the meat from the vow fulfillment and freewill offerings could be carried over to a second day (7:16). In no case was any meat to be eaten on **the third day** (7:17-18). A violation would result in the nullification of the sacrifice, and the offender would **bear his iniquity** (7:18). The same was true for anyone who ate the fellowship sacrifice while being **unclean** (7:19-21).

7:22-27 Next came the strict prohibition against eating either the **fat** or the **blood** of any animal (7:22-27). God had set aside the fat portion of the offerings, the choicest part of the animals, as his alone (see commentary on Lev 3:1-17), reminding the Israelites that their great God deserved their best. The prohibition against eating blood was in recognition that "the life of a creature is in the blood" (Lev 17:11). Since life itself is a creation of God, and since blood (the stuff of life) was used as the means of atonement for sin, it was not an appropriate source of nutrition for the Israelites. The complete absence of blood in any meat is still a requirement for observant Jews today, who will not eat meat unless it is certified as having been slaughtered in a kosher manner.

7:28-36 It's clear that God wanted the nation to know he had made provision for the priests. Their portion of the fellowship sacrifice was the breast and the right thigh. The **breast** was **presented as a presentation offering before the Lord** (7:30), a ritual in which the offerer held the breast in his hands while the priest placed his own hands under those of the worshiper. Together they lifted the piece to symbolize that it belonged to the Lord, who then graciously gave it back **to Aaron and his sons** to eat (7:31). **The right thigh** was given to the officiating priest (7:33). The Lord meant this to be their **permanent portion throughout their generations** (7:36).

7:37-38 This long section of Leviticus wraps up with a summary statement about the various offerings. Connecting these instructions to the giving of the law on **Mount Sinai** firmly established their authority as coming from the **Lord** through **Moses** (7:38). These verses also set the stage for the next section, a narrative describing the anointing of Aaron and his sons to the priesthood.

II. THE ORDINATION AND SERVICE OF ISRAEL'S PRIESTS (8:1–10:20)

A. The Ordination Ceremony
(8:1-36)

8:1 With Israel's sacrifices described and instituted, the nation now needed a consecrated priesthood to administer them before the Lord. God chose Moses's brother Aaron and his sons for this holy assignment and gave Moses specific instructions for the priests' anointing and ordination to ministry. The importance of this section is marked by the opening statement: **The Lord spoke to Moses.** Everything concerning the priests' consecration was to be done according to divine revelation.

8:2-5 The ordination was to be a public ceremony. God told Moses to bring Aaron and his sons along with everything needed for the ceremony and to **assemble the whole community at the entrance to the tent of meeting** (8:2-3). Moses obeyed and made it clear to **the community** that this was **what the Lord . . . commanded** (8:4-5).

8:6-9 The service began with a ceremonial washing of Aaron and his sons, symbolizing the fact that they as sinful humans were intrinsically unclean and needed to be purified before they could minister before a holy God (8:6). Once the priests were washed, Moses dressed Aaron in the high priest's garments, including a tunic undergarment and a beautiful **breastpiece** with its twelve precious stones representing the twelve tribes of Israel (8:8; see Exod 28:15-30). This symbolized the fact that the high priest carried the people close to his heart and represented them when he ministered before the Lord.

Next the **Urim and Thummim** were placed in a pouch on the breastpiece (8:8; see Exod 28:30). We assume these were two named stones that were used to determine God's will in circumstances when the people needed special guidance. But actually, nothing is said in Scripture about their specific purpose or usage. Aaron's **turban** was also magnificent, featuring a **gold medallion** (8:9).

8:10-13 Moses then took the **anointing oil** and **sprinkled** the **altar** and everything else in the **tabernacle** that needed to be consecrated for the priests' use (8:10-11). This was followed by the anointing of Aaron (8:12-13)—which wasn't done by dabbing a mere drop of oil on his forehead. In the Psalms, David referred to the "fine oil on the head, running down on the beard, running down Aaron's beard onto his robes" (Ps 133:2). Aaron was thoroughly anointed to serve the Lord. Moses also dressed **Aaron's sons** in their priestly garb (8:13).

8:14-21 Oil played an important part in the consecration of Israel's priests, but it was not enough by itself. Blood was required to atone for sin, so the next steps in the ordination process were offerings to purify Aaron and his sons, and even the altar, from the contamination of sin. The **sin offering** (8:14-17) was made for atonement. Moses applied the blood to the altar and dealt with the rest of the sacrifice as God had instructed previously (see 4:1-35), except that in this case the blood was applied to the altar of burnt offering instead of the altar of incense. Next came the **burnt offering** (8:18-21), which was completely consumed on the altar as **a pleasing aroma, a fire offering to the Lord** (8:21), symbolizing the offerer's complete dedication to God.

8:22-24 The third offering was called the **ordination** offering, which completed the purification that Aaron and his sons needed to be able to serve as priests (8:22). It involved a unique element that was not part of the people's offerings: the application of the blood to the **right earlobe**, the right **thumb**, and the right **big toe** of both Aaron and his sons (8:23-24). These parts of the body could have been chosen because they stood for the activities of hearing, doing, and walking (or obeying)—all of which needed to be consecrated to the Lord's use.

8:25-30 Moses also put a portion of the offering into the hands of Aaron and his sons, which they then **presented** before the Lord **as a presentation offering** (8:27). These parts of the sacrifice were then burned, in keeping with God's command. Moses's final act of consecration was to sprinkle **Aaron and his sons** with the oil and **blood** (8:30).

8:31-36 Once the required sacrifices were made, the priests had one more requirement to fulfill: they were to eat an ordination meal **at the entrance to the tent of meeting** (8:31). The food came from the parts of the ordination ram and the consecrated bread that were not burned. The priests also had to observe a seven-day confinement period, during which they could not leave the area around the tabernacle under penalty of death (8:33-35). The priests apparently offered and ate the same sacrifice each day during the seven days, at the end of which they were fully ordained to serve the Lord.

✣ B. The Beginning of the Priestly Ministry (9:1-24) ✣

This chapter makes it clear that Israel's worship program got off to the best start possible. The priests functioned flawlessly in presenting the sacrifices both for themselves and for the people, and when it was all done the awesome glory of God appeared to everyone.

9:1-7 On **the eighth day** following the seven days the priests spent in separation, the people brought the required sacrifices to the tabernacle—**sin offering** and **burnt offering, fellowship offering** and **grain offering**—as Moses had commanded (9:1-4). Everyone stood in front of the altar (9:5) as Moses turned to Aaron and gave him the go-ahead to officially begin Israel's sacrificial system. He said, **Approach the altar and sacrifice your sin offering and your burnt offering; make atonement for yourself and the people. Sacrifice the people's offering and make atonement for them, as the LORD commanded** (9:7).

9:8-14 Appropriately, Aaron's first sacrifices were a **sin** and a **burnt offering** for **himself** to atone for his sin and signal his complete consecration to the Lord (9:8-14). It's important to point out the irony here in that Aaron was instructed to offer a **calf** (9:8) as his sin offering, a glaring reminder that he had made the golden calf idol in the wilderness in disobedience to God (see Exod 32). Regardless, the people were now assured that Aaron's sin had been forgiven and that he was authorized to serve as their high priest.

9:15-24 Aaron was then ready to offer the sin, burnt, and fellowship offerings the people had brought. These sacrifices atoned for their sin, symbolized their complete dedication to God, and provided a way for sinful humans to have fellowship with a holy God. The sacrifices made it possible for God to dwell among his people without contaminating his holiness or having to judge the people for their sins. Such forgiveness and fellowship is what the Israelites needed then; it's also what we still need today.

God demonstrated his acceptance of their worship by his appearance in the cloud of **glory** and the consuming **fire**. The people **shouted and fell facedown** (9:23-24). This was not only a response of worship but also of godly fear. They knew God's fire could just as easily have consumed them as it did a sacrifice. Tragically, the fire of God's wrath would soon render judgment on disobedience (10:1-3).

As believers whose sins have been forgiven once-for-all by Christ's death on the cross, we are truly in a privileged position today. The writer to the Hebrews says that God's awesome, holy presence was so terrifying in the days of Moses that even he trembled in fear (see Heb 12:18-24). Incredibly, we can come into God's presence with assurance and joy, and even share in his holiness, through the atoning death and resurrection of Christ.

❧ C. The Tragic Sin of Nadab and Abihu (10:1-20) ❦

10:1-3 At the inauguration of Israel's sacrificial system, **Nadab and Abihu,** Aaron's two oldest sons, **presented unauthorized fire before the Lord, which he had not commanded them to do** (10:1). It's not clear exactly how they erred, but clearly the fire they presented was somehow contrary to what God had commanded. The point is that Nadab and Abihu knew better. They did not sin in ignorance. And as a result, **fire came from the Lord,** and Aaron's sons **died** (10:2). Afterwards Moses reminded Aaron that it was critical for all the people to understand the Lord's **holiness.** Aaron didn't attempt a reply; he made no excuses for his sons' sin (10:3).

It's critical for God's people to understand that the Lord isn't our pal or our buddy. He's our God. He is "holy, holy, holy" (Isa 6:3; Rev 4:8)—the pure, perfect, and powerful Creator of the universe. When he issues a command, he means for it to be obeyed.

10:4-7 Sadly, Aaron had to watch as two of his cousins carried his sons' corpses **outside the camp** (10:4). In other words, the sin of Nadab and Abihu led them from the place of God's presence to a place that came to symbolize being rejected and discarded. And that wasn't all. Aaron and his surviving sons, **Eleazar and Ithamar,** were forbidden to mourn for the dead (10:6-7).

10:8-11 The priesthood and Israel's worship had to go on, so Moses issued a fresh set of instructions to Aaron. This included helping the people to **distinguish between the holy and the common, and the clean and the unclean,** which Nadab and Abihu had failed to do and thus paid the price (10:10).

10:12-20 Moses also reminded Aaron and his remaining sons to eat the **portions** of the people's offerings that had been designated for the priests (10:12-15). At this point it wouldn't be surprising if Aaron and his sons showed reluctance to carry on with the sacrifices, for fear of displeasing the Lord and sharing the fate of Nadab and Abihu. Sure enough, **Eleazar and Ithamar** burned a part of the sin offering they were supposed to have eaten (10:16-18). Moses was **angry** (10:16) about this, but **Aaron** explained that their mistake was due either to fear of offending the Lord or maybe grief (10:19). **Moses** accepted the explanation, and God obviously forgave Aaron's sons since they were not struck down (10:20).

III. THE LAWS OF CLEANNESS AND UNCLEANNESS (11:1–15:33)

❧ A. Laws of Clean and Unclean Animals (11:1-23) ❦

11:1-7 This section of Leviticus dispels any doubt that God cared about the everyday, routine lives of his people in relation to his requirement that they live holy lives before him. Nothing could be more routine than daily meals, but the Israelites were commanded to take great care in what they ate, or even touched, because God had designated some animals and activities as clean and others as unclean.

Much speculation surrounds the reasons behind Israel's dietary restrictions. It's clear from this list that in part God used them to set Israel apart from the pagan nations around them. There may also have been health reasons for the distinctions. In addition, some of the animals listed, including pigs, were used in pagan religious ceremonies of the day. But the main source of the distinction between the two categories of animals is simply the revealed will of God.

A land animal was considered unclean or clean—and therefore forbidden or edible—based on whether it had **divided hooves** and chewed **cud** (11:3). Animals that met the standard in only one of these ways were unclean. Thus, the Jews were prohibited from eating pork because the pig had a divided hoof but did not chew the cud. Even though the prohibition against pork is probably the most well-known of the Jewish dietary restrictions, the text does not seem to single out pigs as any more **unclean** (10:7) than other unclean animals.

11:9-23 For animals **in the water**, the standard for cleanness was whether they had **fins and scales** (11:9). God used the word **abhorrent** in relation to unclean fish, birds, and insects (11:10-13, 20, 23), meaning they were to be especially detestable to the Jews. The **birds** listed are birds of prey (11:13-19), which would be clearly prohibited because they ate flesh that still had the blood in it—something forbidden to the Israelites. The clean **insects** that could be eaten included the **locust, katydid, cricket, and grasshopper** (11:20-22).

B. Avoiding Defilement from Unclean Animals (11:24-47)

11:24-32 The **carcasses** of all animals were considered unclean, except for those sacrificed properly in worship, which also meant that their blood had been drained. Death in any form caused uncleanness and isolation from the Israelite community, and the goal of all cleansing was to be able to approach the holy God of Israel and worship him acceptably.

The second half of chapter 11 deals with the procedures the Israelites needed to follow if they, their clothing, or the things in their households—**any item of wood, . . . leather, sackcloth, or any implement used for work** (11:32)—were made unclean by contact with an unclean animal or the carcass of any animal, whether it was clean or unclean in life. The uncleanness meant the person had to go outside the camp **until evening** (11:31) and then wash his clothes

so that he could be made clean and restored to the community.

11:33-40 This was also the case for the item of clothing or household item rendered unclean by contact with an unclean animal. A **clay pot** so contaminated, however, had to be broken (11:33), and an unclean **oven or stove** had to **be smashed** (11:35). Even contact with the carcasses of clean animals defiled a person, if the animals died in any way other than in the rituals of worship.

11:41-47 God repeated the prohibition against eating or touching unclean animals and gave the reason: **For I am the LORD your God, so you must consecrate yourselves and be holy because I am holy** (11:41-44). To make sure they did not miss the point, he repeated himself: **You must be holy because I am holy** (11:45).

Holiness is still a requirement for God's people today. Of course, we cannot make ourselves holy. Sinners are made acceptable to God only through the atoning sacrifice of Jesus Christ when they place their faith in him. But after coming to saving faith in Christ, we are called to live lives that please him. The New Testament, in fact, is filled with commands about walking in holiness and honoring the Lord with lives dedicated to his service (see Rom 12:1; 1 Thess 4:7; 1 Pet 1:15-16; 2 Pet 3:11). God is holy, and he calls his people to be like him.

C. Laws Concerning Childbirth (12:1-8)

12:1-8 The birth of a child was a cause for rejoicing in Israel, even as it is today. It wasn't a child's birth that made the mother unclean, but the flow of blood that followed the birth. It's important to see here, then, that the mother's ceremonial uncleanness was not because of sin. She needed only ritual **purification** after delivery (12:4), for which the proper sacrifice was prescribed, so she could enter the tabernacle and worship God again. Her time of purification was twice as long for a girl as for a boy, for which no reason is given (12:4-5).

A male child was to be circumcised **on the eighth day** after birth (12:3), after his mother had observed seven days of ceremonial uncleanness. Then when her full time of separation from the sanctuary was complete, she was instructed to take a **burnt offering** and a **sin offering** to the tabernacle—again, not to atone for any sin she had committed just by giving birth, but for her purification. The specified sacrifices were **a year-old male lamb for a burnt offering, and a young pigeon or a turtledove for a sin offering** (12:6), or in the case of the mother's poverty, **two turtledoves or two young pigeons** (12:8) would do. This, in fact, was the offering Joseph and Mary made at the temple for her purification after Jesus was born (see Luke 2:21-24). Even giving birth to the sinless Son of God did not exempt Mary from obeying the law of Moses concerning purification after childbirth.

➢ D. Laws for Diagnosing Skin Diseases (13:1-46) ≪

13:1-8 A serious disease on the skin (13:1) that might be infectious is a threat to any community in which people live in close proximity. This was definitely the case among the Israelites who lived in the wilderness in a time before germs were understood and hospitals could help contain them. Removing from the community a person who had a disease that could spread to others had obvious benefits. Yet the real thrust of chapters 13-15 is not the medical implications of these conditions, but the fact that many of them made the sufferer ceremonially unclean and thus excluded him or her from the presence of God. This doesn't mean, however, that God necessarily assigned moral blame to people with skin diseases. Nonetheless, they had to undergo a period of hoped-for healing, followed by a ceremony to be purified before the Lord.

Verses 1-8 deal with conditions such as **a swelling, scab, or spot on the skin** (13:2). The swelling could refer to a discoloration of the skin, and the scab could refer to a rash. These were the most common kinds of skin problems at that time and could include

psoriasis or eczema. The question is often asked whether any of the diseases described in this chapter could be Hansen's disease, the modern name for the Bible's dreaded "leprosy" condition that destroys tissue and makes the victim more or less a permanent outcast from society. Hansen's disease in the ancient world was progressive and incurable. We can't say for sure whether it is included in this chapter, but the text seems to be dealing with more manageable conditions such as psoriasis or even acne.

The process for the priestly diagnosis of these skin diseases followed a pattern. The symptoms of the problem were described; the priest made his initial inspection, taking note of what he observed. He then declared the person clean or unclean. If the person was declared to be clean on the first inspection, nothing more was done. If the priest was unsure of the condition, the person was isolated for seven days and then re-examined to see if the priest could make a decision on the sufferer's cleanness or uncleanness at that point.

Uncleanness required a seven-day period of isolation. The unclean person was then re-examined and either declared clean or told to stay in isolation. The ritual for cleansing involved washing the **clothes** (13:6), after which the person was clean and could rejoin the community and, even more importantly, regain access to the tabernacle to offer sacrifices and maintain fellowship with God.

13:9-17 This section describes another range of conditions. Note that if a person's skin turns **totally white** over his **entire body**, he is pronounced **clean** (13:12-13). This symptom actually refers to a condition known as leucoderma, which cannot be passed from one person to another. **Raw flesh**, by contrast, indicated a much more serious problem (13:10, 14-16). **Raw flesh is unclean; this is a serious skin disease** (13:15). Thus, a person with a condition involving it had to go the priest for examination.

13:18-28 Visible skin problems resulting from a **boil** or a **burn** (13:18, 24) were dealt with next. The priest followed the same steps to diagnose possible uncleanness in those instances. An issue became a possible problem when there was inflammation, color change in the skin, or a spread of the condition. The best outcome in both cases was when the spot turned out to be just the **scar** from the boil or burn (13:23, 28).

13:29-37 The next category involved conditions on **the head or chin** (13:29). Key here was determining how deep the problem went—whether only skin deep or below the skin. If the problem was **deeper than the skin**, the priest pronounced the person **unclean** (13:30). If there was doubt about the depth of the problem, the afflicted person had to be isolated the prescribed seven days—and again, depending on whether the problem spread, the process of isolation and re-examination could go for several rounds. The person might be required to **shave** his hair, except for the affected area, allowing the priest to better determine if it had spread (13:33).

13:38-44 The reference to **white spots** (13:38) may be another indication of leucoderma (see commentary on 13:9-17). It was a harmless condition and not contagious, so the person with this condition was **clean** (13:39). You might smile to discover that being **bald** was also included in a chapter on skin diseases (13:40-44). However, baldness itself did not make a man unclean (13:40-41); the presence of a **skin disease** on the scalp did (13:42-44).

13:45-46 Many today find these long descriptions of skin problems and other potentially unclean conditions tedious. But verses 45-46 are a sobering reminder that such "tedious" details were necessary because failure to keep God's holy standards in even matters such as these could have a life-altering impact on people. A person with an infectious skin disease had **his clothes torn and his hair hanging loose** (13:45). This alone would make the person repulsive to the eyes of others. But he also had to **cover his mouth and cry out, "Unclean, unclean!"** (13:45), signaling that he could potentially spread the infection he carried. Worse, he had to **live alone in a place outside the camp** (13:46). The holy standards of God, the well-being of the community, and a person's life and family were at stake when disease was found within

the camp. To banish a person from the camp and the tabernacle was significant, so it was vital that the correct diagnosis was made. With this background in mind, imagine the joy and gratitude overflowing from those Jesus healed from skin diseases (see Luke 17:11-19). He made a way for even those who'd once thought themselves hopelessly unclean to find total physical restoration. And that's a picture of what he can do for people spiritually, too.

☞ E. Laws for Diagnosing Mildew
(13:47-59) ☜

13:47-59 Like people, clothing and other garments could be rendered unclean by the appearance of something abnormal on them. Here that something is described as **mildew** (13:47). This was not just a spot on the surface of a fabric, but a contamination that went deep to the core of the piece, into its **warp or weft** (13:48), signaling that the problem had intertwined itself with the fabric and could not be cleansed away by washing. The procedure for diagnosis and resulting quarantine isolation efforts were similar to those for skin diseases—except that fabrics that could not be declared clean were burned (13:50-52). If, after washing, a questionable spot had faded, the affected part alone was to be cut out and burned (13:56). As always, the objective was for the priest to be able to pronounce the affected item **clean or unclean** (13:59).

☞ F. Laws for Cleansing Skin Diseases
(14:1-32) ☜

14:1 The importance and solemn nature of the ritual to restore a person cured of a skin disease was indicated by yet another repetition of the words, **The Lord spoke to Moses.** Following these procedures allowed the person to again enjoy fellowship with the Lord and the community.

14:2-9 The cleansing process involved several stages. A person who believed he had been cured of his disease would send for the priest, who would go **outside the camp and examine him** (14:2). If the priest verified that the cleansing had taken place, he took **two ... birds, ... slaughtered** one, and caught its blood in a **pot** (14:4-5). Then the priest performed a unique ceremony. **The live bird together with ... cedar wood, scarlet yarn, and hyssop** were dipped into the blood, which was then sprinkled **seven times** on the patient. The **live bird** was then released, probably as a symbol of the person's cleansing and release from his isolation (14:6-7). (Seeing that bird fly away had to be a happy moment for one who had been in isolation for days or even weeks.)

Now pronounced **clean**, the person was allowed to **enter the camp**, but only after washing his clothes, bathing, and shaving off all his hair (14:7-8). He then had to sit outside his tent for another seven days, at the end of which he washed his clothes, bathed, and shaved off his hair again—even his **eyebrows** (14:9). Of course, a person who looked like this was a dramatic illustration to passersby that his life was beginning over. He could resume his life (14:8-9).

14:10-20 Though the person was clean again, there were sacrifices to be offered on **the eighth day** as part of his restoration (14:10). They included the various types of sacrifices presented earlier in the book, such as the grain, guilt, burnt, and sin offerings (14:10-20). The priest took some of the **blood** of the guilt offering and anointed the cleansed person's **right ear**, right **thumb**, and the **big toe of his right foot** (14:14), and then he did the same with **oil** (14:17). The similarity between this and the consecration ceremony for the priests outlined in chapter 8 cannot be a coincidence. It must have symbolized that just as the priests had been fully consecrated and were ready to bring sacrifices to God, so was this cleansed person. Even the remaining oil from this ceremony was poured **on the head** of the worshiper (14:18), also in imitation of the priests' ordination ceremony.

14:21-32 Here too provision was made for a poor person, who was to bring **whatever he could afford** (14:22). Otherwise, the requirements and ritual were the same for all. Once

again, we see the significance of the mediating role of the **priest**—making **atonement** in order to reconcile God and humanity (14:31-32). This is what our great high priest Jesus came to do (see Heb 10:10-21).

✒ G. Laws for Cleansing Mildew (14:33-57) ✒

14:33-57 The regulations for this section are, in many ways, the same as those for cleansing mildew from garments (13:47-59). Since the Israelites were living in tents when these instructions were given, the regulations for examining a house (and either cleansing it or tearing it down) were for future use, when they took possession of **the land of Canaan** (14:34). The priest was to inspect the house to determine if it was unclean. Contamination required a period of quarantine, re-examination, and then necessary steps were to be followed if the mildew had spread (14:36-53). This is another reminder of how seriously God wanted his people to take the difference between cleanness and uncleanness, between the holy and unholy. Even in the case of houses, the cleansing ritual described earlier for people (14:4-7) was to be conducted (14:48-53).

✒ H. Laws of Uncleanness Concerning the Body (15:1-33) ✒

15:1-18 In chapter 15, the subject of cleanness and uncleanness is further covered through laws regarding what to do for periodic discharges for both men and women. Following the principle that something unclean touching something clean makes the clean unclean, the opening section on a man's **discharge** reveals that every person and thing he came into contact with during this time became unclean (15:2-15). The people he contacted could be cleansed by bathing; they would then **remain unclean until evening** (15:5-11).

Interestingly, the man with such a discharge was not sent outside the camp as were those with skin diseases. Some argue that this was because the discharge was not infectious. Others say the lack of an isolation period indicated that God was mostly concerned with the man's ceremonial uncleanness. Once the discharge had stopped and the man had waited **seven days**, he could **wash** and be clean, and then offer the sacrifices of **cleansing** (15:13-15). The second example was male semen **emission**, possibly during intercourse (15:16-18). The emission brought uncleanness to the man and the **woman** (15:18) involved.

15:19-24 A woman's monthly menstruation also resulted in her being unclean. The stipulations for **her bed** (15:21) and other objects she touched, or for the person who came in contact with her, were generally the same as those for a man with a discharge. The exception is that the man who came in contact with her flow—like the woman (15:19)—was unclean for **seven days** (15:24).

15:25-30 The final case was that of a woman with a chronic discharge of blood. She was considered **unclean** during her entire illness (15:25). This scenario brings to mind the New-Testament-era woman who had suffered from bleeding for twelve years before she touched Jesus and was healed (see Matt 9:20-22). According to the law, she should not have touched Jesus. And this may explain why she came "with fear and trembling" when Jesus called her forward (Mark 5:33). But no contamination, of course, could make Jesus unclean!

15:31-33 These verses provide a summary and signal the close of the discussion on uncleanness. God's regulations were to **keep the Israelites from their uncleanness, so that they do not die by defiling [God's] tabernacle that is among them** (15:31). God's holiness, and his demand for holiness from his people, gave these laws life-and-death importance.

IV. THE DAY OF ATONEMENT (16:1-34)

16:1-10 The Day of Atonement was the most solemn day on Israel's calendar. The emphasis in this chapter is on the necessity of sin being atoned for so that God's people may be forgiven and reconciled to him. The ministry of the high priest was crucial in facilitating this. God set the regulations for the Day of Atonement in the context of priestly disobedience and made it inextricably clear to Aaron that he must follow the Lord's commands to the letter (16:1-2).

Aaron was the central figure in this drama of redemption. He could not enter whenever he wanted into **the holy place behind the curtain** where the **ark** of the covenant was. If he did, he would **die**. Why? Because, the Lord said, **I appear** there **in the cloud above the mercy seat**—the gold cover over the ark (16:2). In other words, this small cubicle in the tabernacle, and later the temple, literally housed the glorious, holy presence of God. Thus, God alone would decide who could enter his throne room and under what circumstances it could happen. In keeping with God's demand for purity, Aaron had to first offer

sacrifices for himself and his family (16:3-6). Verses 7-10 then give a general overview of the day's rituals before the detailed instructions begin.

16:11-15 Aaron entered and left the most holy place three times during the day's sacrifices and rituals (16:12-15). The first time was to burn **fragrant incense** before the Lord (16:12-13). The second time was to get some of **the bull's blood** from his sin offering and sprinkle it **against the east side of the mercy seat** and **before the mercy seat seven times** (16:14). His third entrance into the most holy place was to bring the blood of **the male goat for the people's sin offering** and sprinkle it on and in front of the **mercy seat** (16:15).

16:16-19 Once Aaron had purified **the most holy place in this way** for all the Israelites' sins, he was to **do the same for the tent of meeting** itself (16:16). As this purification was taking place, nobody else was allowed into the tabernacle from the time Aaron entered until he had **made atonement for himself, his**

household, and the whole assembly of Israel (16:17). The congregation of Israel—who also had to cleanse and prepare themselves for this solemn day (see 16:29, 31)—would know all was well when Aaron emerged to **make atonement** for the **altar** of burnt offering with the **blood** of the sacrifices (16:18-19).

16:20-22 The ritual involving the **live male goat** was another unique feature of the Day of Atonement. Aaron was to **lay both his hands on the head of the live goat and confess over it** all the **sins** of the people. In this way he ceremonially transferred the nation's sins to the goat, which was sent into the wilderness—symbolizing the removal of their sins from the camp. The Hebrew word for this goat, *azazel*, has generated some speculation. The traditional interpretation of the term is "scapegoat," which fits the context since the goat was to bear the nation's sins. But the term could also refer to a rocky precipice— off of which the goat was pushed to its death. Regardless, redemption was illustrated by the transferring of sins to this live animal.

For believers in Jesus Christ, this offers strong encouragement. Since our sins too have been sent away, so to speak, we cannot lose our salvation. The scapegoat isn't coming back tomorrow to return to us all the sins we thought were gone. If you have trusted Jesus Christ as your Savior, your sins have been removed "as far as the east is from the west" (Ps 103:12).

Watching the goat being led away served as a vivid illustration to the Israelites that their sins had been removed and fully atoned for. Yet, it's important to remember that this ritual had to be repeated annually (see Lev 16:34). Only through Christ do sinful people have a sacrifice that was offered "once for all time" and lasts "forever" (Heb 10:10-14).

16:23-33 Following this ceremony, Aaron returned to the tent of meeting to change out of his special clothing and **bathe** again. He then offered the **burnt offering** that made atonement for his sins and those of the people (16:23-24). The unused parts of the offering were **brought outside the camp and burned** (16:27). The author of Hebrews alludes to the practice and says this was also true of Jesus Christ who "suffered outside the gate" of the city (Heb 13:11-12). Therefore, Christians should identify with their Lord and "go to him outside the camp." In other words, we must be willing to bear "his disgrace" (Heb 13:13).

16:34 The Day of Atonement was to be established as an annual event. With it came a once-a-year sacrifice of atonement for Israel's sins, officiated by the high priest alone. It was needed to **make atonement for the Israelites . . . because of all their sins**. When Jesus offered himself as our great high priest, he made atonement for our sins once and for all (see Heb 10:10). The Day of Atonement was fulfilled in him.

V. ISRAEL'S HOLINESS CODE: LIVING BEFORE A HOLY GOD (17:1–26:46)

A. Laws Concerning Eating Meat and Blood (17:1-16)

17:1-6 Beginning with chapter 17, the focus of Leviticus turns to the subject of how God's people were to be holy in their everyday lives. For this reason, these chapters are often called Israel's "Holiness Code."

The LORD spoke to Moses and gave him instructions for **Aaron, his sons, and all the Israelites** (17:1-2). The first command was a prohibition against sacrificing animals anywhere except at the **tabernacle**. Sacrifices were to be performed by the Lord's authorized priest in the proper way (17:3-4). This not only insured the proper worship of Israel's holy God, but also prevented the Israelites from joining in the detestable practice of offering sacrifices to the false gods of the nations around them. Although not explicitly stated, another benefit of bringing animals to the tabernacle was ensuring that the needs of God's priests were met, since they consumed some sacrifices.

17:7-9 Apparently some Israelites had been offering sacrifices to **goat-demons**, which the Lord considered an act of spiritual prostitution (17:7). Israel was his people, his bride, and must therefore remain committed to him alone. Anyone who offered a sacrifice without bringing it to **the tent of meeting to sacrifice it to the LORD** was guilty of a heinous sin and was to be **cut off from his people** (17:8-9; see also 17:4, 10, 14).

17:10-12 The second prohibition was against eating blood. This had already been stated earlier (3:17; 7:26-27), but these verses give the reason that eating it was forbidden: **the life of a creature is in the blood, and I have appointed it to you to make atonement on the altar for your lives, since it is the lifeblood that makes atonement.** (17:11).

This prohibition established among the people a deeper respect for life in general as well as a respect for blood as the means of atonement that God required for the forgiveness of sins. Blood is not merely *a* means of atonement but *the* means of atonement. That's why the author of Hebrews insisted that "without the shedding of blood there is no forgiveness" (Heb 9:22). The animal was to die as a substitute for the sinner. But ultimately all of these sacrificial animals were only shadows of the much more important sacrifice that was to come. They pointed to the Savior who fulfilled Israel's sacrificial system (see Heb 9:25-26). Jesus is the Lamb of God who takes away the sin of the world (John 1:29, 36; Rev 5:6; 7:10, 14; 12:11).

17:13-16 The final verses deal with the handling of any animal that was to be eaten. If it was hunted and killed, the blood had to be drained and covered **with dirt** (17:13). If a person ate an animal that had died of natural causes or had been killed by another animal, that person was **unclean until evening** and had to ceremonially **bathe** (17:15).

⤳ B. Laws Regulating Sexual Relations (18:1-30) ⤝

18:1-5 The prohibitions in this chapter protect the sanctity of marriage and family. God left no doubt about the importance of sexual purity in his sight. His regulations for sexual relations are introduced with, **I am the LORD your God** (18:1-2). What's the connection between his identity as their God and the Israelites' sex lives? Since they were his people, Israel's sexual practices were to be completely different from those of the land where they came from (**the land of Egypt, where [they] used to live**) and where they were going (**the land of Canaan, where** God was taking them). No matter where they lived, God's people were to follow his holy **statutes** rather than pagan **customs** (18:3-5). The same principle is true today. The Lord designed sex, so he gets to decide the parameters in which it is to happen. Importantly, we can trust that engaging in it his way will always bring us the most joy and will save us from the devastating consequences that follow sexual immorality.

18:6-30 Understand that the various sinful, incestuous family sexual relations described in 18:7-18 were not merely chosen at random. **All these things** had been practiced by the Canaanite inhabitants of the land (18:24). Such regulations as **you are not to come near any close relative for . . . intercourse** (18:6) were necessary and relevant even in Paul's day. The prohibition against having sex with **your father's wife** (18:8), for instance, was flaunted in the church at Corinth, so Paul rebuked the church for allowing a member to have an illicit relationship with his stepmother (see 1 Cor 5:1-5).

Verse 19 stands alone in the sense that it doesn't prohibit illicit relations but speaks to a situation in marriage—the wife's menstrual period—during which intercourse was forbidden. Later Jewish tradition not only forbade sexual relations during this time but for seven days afterward. This had to do with the issue of blood and ceremonial uncleanness. The prohibitions in verses 18:20, 22-23 shift the focus to sinful sexual relations outside the family: adultery, homosexuality, and bestiality. Today's smug, modern society hasn't advanced past practicing these ancient sins. Instead, it celebrates them.

The command **not to sacrifice any . . . children in the fire to Molech**, the pagan god of the Ammonites, is a reminder of the great depravity that humans are capable of (18:21). Religious fervor sometimes drove ancient peoples to sacrifice their own children to appease the "gods"—who were really demons in disguise (see Ps 106:37; 1 Cor 10:20). Today child sacrifice is more likely to take place at the altar of sexual freedom. The abortion industry has slaughtered millions. (The church of Jesus Christ must not be silent against the murder of the unborn.)

God takes sexual offenses very seriously. The Canaanites had **defiled themselves by all these things**, and God was about to make the land **vomit out its inhabitants** as a result (18:24-25). In our age of political correctness, this move sounds harsh because so many people hold to such a low view of God. To them, he is just a tame god of their own creation whose role is to affirm their lifestyle choices—whether they are based on Scripture or not. Our true Creator, however, is a holy and righteous God who considers sin **detestable** (18:26). This is the God with whom we are confronted.

As a result of the Canaanites' sins, God was giving the Canaanite land to the Israelites. But lest the Israelites get careless, God warned his people that if they engaged in practices similar to the evil things already happening in the land, he would vomit *them* out of it too (18:28). Tragically, this is exactly what would happen. First the northern kingdom of Israel would be carried into captivity by Assyria in 722 BC. Then the southern kingdom of Judah would be taken captive by Babylon in 587–586 BC.

⤜ C. Laws Concerning Everyday Life
(19:1-37) ⤛

19:1-2 The regulations in this chapter are wide-ranging. But woven throughout these verses are the principles of the Ten Commandments as applied to everyday life. In addition, God says, **I, the LORD your God, am holy** (19:2), and we see here the constant refrain, "I am the LORD" or "I am the LORD your God" throughout the chapter. This means Leviticus 19 does not stray from the central theme of the book: the holiness of Israel's God and, thus, the personal holiness

he requires of those who desire to worship and follow him.

The people of Israel were not merely to offer sacrifices but were to lead righteous lives. Many people have the mistaken notion that keeping religious laws or performing rituals is all it takes to please God. But Leviticus 19 makes it clear that holy living in every aspect of life is what our holy God requires. This is his kingdom agenda for his people, and it's what provides access to his blessings. His holy character is the standard by which both human righteousness and sin are measured.

19:3-8 God's standards for his people include **respect** for **mother and father**, keeping the **Sabbaths**, and rejecting **idols** (19:3-4). Each of these principles was included in the Ten Commandments. By keeping these, the Israelites would honor God, honor his authorities in the family, and honor his special day of worship. This suggests that getting things right in our churches and families leads to getting things right in our societies. Verses 5-8 also relate to worship, reinforcing the command concerning how to handle the meat that was presented in sacrifice.

19:9-10 Repeatedly in Scripture, God expresses and demonstrates his concern for **the poor** (19:10). It's a concern his people should share. The poor are to be treated fairly, with dignity and justice. Notice that the command was to leave part of **the harvest** (19:9) for the poor to glean. The Israelites were not to greedily wring every penny of profit out of the fields; they were to leave some produce behind as provision for the less fortunate.

There is a crucial, timeless principle here. In Scripture, extending charity included providing an opportunity to work. God's people were told to leave a portion in their fields, so that the poor could gather it for themselves. People thus could turn poverty into productivity in response to the charitable opportunities provided. This is much more helpful to someone who has fallen on hard times than simply lining up for a check from the government. If a person *can* work, then biblically he is expected *to* work (see 2 Thess 3:10). Gleaning provided the opportunity for the poor to help themselves. And the harder a poor person worked, the more productive that person became. This gave him or her the opportunity to maximize personal God-given potential and live with dignity. In the book of Ruth, Naomi and her daughter-in-law benefited from this system (see Ruth 2).

19:11-18 Treating the poor in this way was one example of exercising biblical justice. Other examples follow. God's people are not to **steal . . . swear falsely . . . oppress** their neighbor . . . defraud workers of their **wages** . . . hinder the **deaf** and **blind** . . . render unjust decisions . . . **give preference** to one group over another . . . spread **slander** . . . **harbor hatred** against a brother . . . or **take revenge** (19:11-18). In other words, they are to follow this principle: **love your neighbor as yourself** (19:18). As both Jesus and Paul pointed out, all of Scripture is summed up in the commands to love God and neighbor (see Mark 12:31; Gal 5:14).

19:19-37 The regulations in these verses cover a wide array of circumstances, all of which were intended to establish and set apart the Israelites as God's holy people. These included prohibitions against occult practices such as **divination** and **witchcraft** and consulting **mediums** and **spiritists** (19:27, 31). Saul, Israel's first king, would stray so far from following God that he would ignore these commands and turn to the world of the occult for guidance (see 1 Sam 28:3-25)!

Not only are God's people to respect children and the poor (18:21; 19:9-10), they are also to respect the elderly. The exhortation to **rise in the presence of the elderly and honor the old** (19:32) is still needed today. In a culture that worships youthfulness, we need to be reminded that "gray hair is a glorious crown" (Prov 16:31). Godly older men and women have experience, maturity, and wisdom that young people can ignore, but only to their own peril. The aged deserve your respect and honor. Make time for them.

When the Lord commanded his people to love their neighbors as themselves (19:18), that included **the alien** as well as **the native-born among [them]**. They were **to love [them]** . . . **for [once the Israelites] were aliens in the land of Egypt** (19:34). Therefore, they were to consider the foreign-born peoples among them as their own brothers and sisters—and treat them accordingly. Many foreigners attached themselves to Israel as the nation moved through the wilderness and settled in Canaan, and they were to be treated well.

❧ D. Laws for Offenses Requiring the Death Penalty (20:1-27) ❧

20:1-6 The Israelites were to avoid the following conduct as they prepared to enter Canaan, where abominations against God were common. To engage in these practices in Israel, in fact, was to incur the death penalty. To give one's **children to Molech** (20:2-5) no doubt meant to burn them as a child sacrifice (see 18:21). Such false worship was **defiling** to God's **sanctuary** and **profaning** to his **holy name** (20:3). (On turning to **mediums or spiritists** (20:6), see the commentary on 19:19-37.)

20:7-8 Here the Israelites were told, **Consecrate yourselves and be holy, for I am the LORD your God. Keep my statutes and do them; I am the LORD who sets you apart** (20:7-8). Once again, then, we get a restatement of the central thesis of Leviticus: God is holy, and this requires holiness from his people. When a person or object was sanctified or set apart, he or it was separated from the common and ordinary, and made special and unique.

Many of us have "sanctified" places in our homes. When I was growing up, for example, our living room was off limits most of the time. We weren't allowed to play there; it was set apart for special times or guests.

If Leviticus teaches anything, it is that God has set apart his people for his use and glory. Yet, God's people are also to **consecrate** themselves and **be holy** (20:7). This paradox points to what we could call the dynamic tension of the Christian life. We are set apart by God, in the sense of being his chosen people, at the moments we are saved. But we are also to set ourselves apart every day in the decisions and choices we make. That's where God's blessings are found. In other words, sanctification (becoming more like

Jesus) is not some passive process whereby we simply go through our days expecting God to rubber stamp our choices and bless us. He sanctifies, but he also calls us to sanctify ourselves by choosing to live according to his holy standards.

20:9-27 Moses turned to consider offenses against the family, with honor for parents at the head of the topical list (20:9). As in chapter 18, prohibitions are provided to prevent sexual immorality. **Adultery**, incest, homosexuality, bestiality (20:10-21)—all these were forbidden and incurred death if committed. Such were the sinful practices of the Canaanites, and such practices are still with us today.

Living as God's holy people in an unholy world has never been simple. As a result of their sin, **the nations** were being driven from the land by God (20:23). If God's people followed in the tracks of the Canaanites, they would be expelled from the land too (20:22). But if Israel desired to live in the land—*and stay in the land*—they had **be holy**, because **the LORD** is **holy**, and he had **set [them] apart from the nations** as his own (20:26).

➤ E. Laws Concerning the Priests and Their Sacrifices (21:1–22:33) ❧

21:1-15 Defilement was a significant matter of concern for Israel's priests, who ministered in the holy presence of God. Their requirements for holiness were more stringent than those for the congregation because they presented **the fire offerings to the LORD** (21:6).

A priest would be defiled by contact with a **dead** body. The only exception made was for members of **his immediate family** (21:1-4). The prohibitions against making **bald spots**, shaving **the edge of their beards**, and making **gashes on their bodies** (21:5) had to do with pagan rituals. The reputations of a priest's wife and daughters were also relevant to his fitness to serve in the sanctuary (21:7-9).

If the laws for Israel's priests were more stringent than those for the congregation at large, then the laws for the high priest (that is, **the priest who is highest among his brothers**) were more stringent still (21:10-15). He

was forbidden to show any signs of mourning even for his parents (21:11-12), and he could only **marry** a **virgin**, so as not to risk corruption to **his bloodline** (21:13-15).

21:16-24 Priests were also restricted from their service based on various physical defects and deformities. We must read these verses in their context to understand why. Moses was not making a statement about the value of such persons; they were no less human beings who bear God's image. Rather, he was emphasizing the necessity for priests to represent wholeness in serving a holy God. Priests with physical limitations, then, could not perform the ceremonies. However, they were not shunned but were provided for (21:22).

22:1-16 The priests were responsible **to deal respectfully with the holy offerings** in order not to **profane** God's **holy name** (22:2). This extended to the way they ate them. Once again the repeated refrain from God emphasizes the serious nature of things: **I am the LORD who sets them apart** (22:9, 16). The priests had to be ceremonially clean when they presented the Lord's offerings. Any priest who knowingly approached the holy offerings while unclean was to be **cut off** from God's presence (22:3).

God made provision for the needs of the priests through the portions of the people's sacrifices they were permitted to eat. But since these meals consisted of food that had been offered in sacrifice, they were **holy** (22:10). This regulated who could eat at the priest's table alongside him (22:10-16). None of the priest's relatives or friends, but only the family members under his roof, were to eat from it. This is because it wasn't right for non-priests to live off the offerings of the congregation. If a mistake was made and an Israelite ate a **holy offering in error**, he was to **add a fifth to its value and give the holy offering to the priest** (22:14).

22:17-33 The animals the priests presented for sacrifice were to be **unblemished** and free from **defect** (22:18-25). The chapter's concluding statement includes a reminder of God's grace that preceded the Israelites being set apart as his people: God is **the one**

who brought you out of the land of Egypt to be your God (22:33). The Israelites needed no higher reason to honor and obey God by living holy lives—and neither do we. If you are a Christian, remember that God sacrificed his own Son to save you from his righteous judgment. Why would you choose any other path but to live for him?

⋙ F. Laws Concerning Festivals and Other Special Occasions (23:1–25:55) ⋘

23:1-3 In Leviticus 23 the emphasis is on Israel's holy days and festivals—**the times of the LORD** that they were to **proclaim as sacred assemblies** (23:2). The first day mentioned is the weekly **Sabbath**, which was Israel's foundational holy day. This was to be a time of **complete rest** and **a sacred assembly** (23:3).

23:4-5 The festivals or **sacred assemblies** (23:4) that God commanded Israel to observe celebrated his provision for the nation in various ways. Perhaps the most well-known is the **Passover** (23:5), commemorating the night God delivered Israel from bondage in Egypt. The Israelites were to apply the blood of a sacrificial lamb to the lintels and doorposts of their homes on that occasion. Then the death angel "passed over" their houses and struck down the firstborn of the Egyptians, sparing Israel's sons. From that point forward the Passover was to be a permanent observance (see Exod 12:1–13:16). Jesus celebrated it with his disciples before his crucifixion (see Luke 22:7-15), and he fulfills it because he is "our Passover lamb" (1 Cor 5:7).

23:6-8 Connected to the Passover was the **Festival of Unleavened Bread**, during which the people were to **eat unleavened bread** for **seven days** (23:6; see Exod 12:17-20). This was to serve as a reminder that they had "left . . . Egypt in a hurry" (Deut 16:3), having no time to put leaven (yeast) in their bread dough to make it rise.

23:9-14 During the week of the Festival of Unleavened Bread, the Israelites were to **bring the first sheaf of** their barley **harvest to the** priest (23:10). This custom became known as the Feast of Firstfruits, honoring God for the firstfruits of the spring barley harvest. Before they could eat from the crop, the people had to give an **offering** to **God** (23:14), acknowledging his provision and signaling their ongoing trust in his future provision. In the New Testament, Paul describes the risen Lord Jesus as the "firstfruits" of those who have died (1 Cor 15:20). His resurrection is the promise that all those who trust in him will also be raised to life when he comes (see 1 Cor 15:22-23).

23:15-22 After **seven complete weeks starting from the day after the Sabbath, the day [they] brought the sheaf of the presentation offering** (thus, **fifty days** after the Feast of Firstfruits), the Israelites were to celebrate the Festival of Weeks (23:15-16). Seven weeks from that day brought the people to late spring and the wheat harvest. Thus, the offerings included **bread . . . as firstfruits to the LORD** (23:17). Later Jewish tradition connected the Festival of Weeks to the giving of the law at Mount Sinai. The festival also became known as "Pentecost" from the Greek word for "fiftieth." This, along with Passover and the Feast of Shelters, was one of the three "pilgrim feasts," for which God required the attendance of every Jewish man in Jerusalem. It was at Pentecost, when thousands of Jewish pilgrims were in Jerusalem, in fact, that the first disciples of Christ would receive the Holy Spirit, thus marking the church's birthday (see Acts 2:1-4).

23:23-25 On **the first day** of **the seventh month**, the people held a **scared assembly** with **rest, commemoration, and trumpet blasts** (23:24). This became known as the Festival of Trumpets—modern day Rosh Hashanah, the Jewish New Year. In the Old Testament, trumpet blasts called God's people to worship or to war. In the New Testament, trumpet blasts are said to precede the rapture (see 1 Thess 4:16-17) and God's end time acts of judgment (see Rev 8).

23:26-32 Ten days after the Festival of Trumpets was **the Day of Atonement** (23:27). The high priest was to enter the most holy place on that day to make atonement for the sins of the people (see Lev 16). But the people themselves were **not to do any work** (23:28, 31) and were to **practice self-denial** under threat of severe penalty (23:27, 29, 32). For those who trust in Christ, he is the once-for-all "atoning sacrifice" for sins (Rom 3:25; 1 John 4:10).

23:33-36 Lastly, there was **the Festival of Shelters** (or "Tabernacles" or "Booths"), which was observed for **seven days** (23:34). It was named for the temporary structures the Israelites were to build and live in during the festival to commemorate God's provision for them during the years when they lived in **shelters** in the wilderness after he brought them **out of . . . Egypt** (23:42-43). John records an occasion when Jesus was in Jerusalem for the Festival of Shelters (see John 7:2, 10). During the festival, the Jews would perform a ritual in which they poured out water before the Lord to commemorate his water miracles during the exodus. It was likely during this tradition that Jesus cried out, "If anyone is thirsty, let him come to me and drink. The one who believes in me . . . will have streams of living water flow from deep within him." This "living water" was the Holy Spirit (John 7:37-39).

24:1-4 Chapter 24 turns to the responsibilities of the priests in the tabernacle. The first of these duties was **to keep the lamp burning** (24:2). This is a reference to **the pure gold lampstand in the Lord's presence** (24:4). This lamp stood in the holy place of the tabernacle, and the Lord commanded that the priest **continually tend** to it with olive **oil** (24:1, 4). Jesus, who was foreshadowed by this lamp, would later say of himself, "I am the light of the world" (John 8:12). You'll never have to worry about his light going out.

24:5-9 The second of these priestly duties was to bake **twelve loaves** of bread for **every Sabbath** and arrange them on the **pure gold table before the Lord** (24:5-8). These twelve loaves represented the twelve tribes, and the bread was known as "the Bread of the Presence" (Exod 25:30). It was set out each week as a reminder that the twelve tribes of Israel were always in the Lord's presence, and perhaps reminding them too that the

first of their grain harvest belonged to the Lord. The priests were to eat the bread that was replaced by the new loaves each week. Bread was a common staple in the Israelite diet. To live, you ate bread. Thus later in history, when Jesus said, "I am the bread of life" (John 6:35), his meaning was clear: Come to me if you want to live.

24:10-12 The seriousness of God's holiness is here demonstrated in a dramatic way through the story of a man **who cursed and blasphemed the Name** (24:10-11). The "Name" of course refers to God's name, "Yahweh" (typically rendered in English Bibles as "Lord" in small caps). In a fit of anger, this man lost his temper and cursed God's name. Evidently this transgression had not occurred before, since no one knew what to do about it. The people **put him in custody** until **Moses** could seek **the Lord's decision** (24:11-12).

24:13-23 The Lord spoke, and he did not hesitate: **Bring the one who has cursed to the outside of the camp and have all who heard him lay their hands on his head; then have the whole community stone him** (24:13-14). The witnesses put their hands on the man's head as a sign that their testimony was true, and the people **stoned him** to death (24:23). This was a lasting reminder to the community that blasphemy was not to be tolerated.

Between the pronouncement of the offender's sentence and its execution, the Lord gave a series of laws often called the *lex talionis,* or law of retaliation (24:17-22). The principle here is that the punishment should fit the crime. This concept of proportionate justice is woven into our own legal code today, and few people seem to have a problem with it. But these laws, including such detailed instructions as **fracture for fracture, eye for eye, tooth for tooth** (24:20), have been so twisted, misapplied, and ridiculed over the course of history that their original wisdom and purpose have almost been lost. Importantly, they were not an invitation for individuals to exact private vengeance; they were statutes to be administered by the duly appointed leaders of the community. These regulations actually prevented excessive revenge by limiting the response to the severity of the crime. The penalty for cursing your covenant God was the severest of all.

25:1-7 The subject changes again here as the chapter deals with the special years that Israel was to observe: **the Sabbath year** and the Year of Jubilee (25:8-55). The Sabbath year was to be observed once the people of Israel were living in Canaan and planting crops. They could plant and harvest for six years in succession, but there was to be **a Sabbath of complete rest for the land in the seventh year . . . : [they were] not to sow [a] field or prune [a] vineyard** (25:4). Thus, the land itself enjoyed a Sabbath rest in the seventh year, even as God provided a Sabbath rest for his people every seventh day.

Skipping the harvest for a full year sounds like a risky idea for an agriculturally-dependent people, but remember that the Israelites were not ordinary farmers. They were the people of God who needed constant reminders of their utter dependence on him for everything. Tragically, as time passed, Israel disregarded God's command to observe the Sabbath year—not for a mere decade or two but for 490 years! That's seventy Sabbath years they would neglect to observe, and God would keep count. When he sent them into exile in Babylon, they remained there for seventy years—one year for each Sabbath year they violated (see Lev 26:33-35; 2 Chr 36:20-21). If God's people wouldn't give his land rest, God himself would do it in spite of them. It would be an unforgettable reminder that the land and everything in it ultimately belongs to God.

25:8-12 The principles of spiritual and social justice behind these regulations are foundational. In fact, I believe that anytime these principles are implemented, they will prove transformational for any society.

After **seven sabbatical years**—that is, **seven times seven years**—the **fiftieth year** was the year of **Jubilee**. The Israelites were to **consecrate** this year and **proclaim freedom in the land for all its inhabitants** (25:8-10). All those in servitude were set free and property reverted to its original owners. This was to begin with **the Day of Atonement** (25:9; see Lev 16:1-34; 23:26-32), the

day set aside to atone for the individual and corporate sins of the nation of Israel. The Day of Atonement marked the time when Israel got right with God through the shedding of blood—that is, through the slaying of a sacrifice. In other words, they didn't get to enjoy the Jubilee (i.e., God's involvement in their economy, society, and politics) without first getting their sins addressed by God. Getting right spiritually had to come first.

Many people want God to do things for them without coming to him for atonement (or even recognizing that they need it). They cry out for justice, or ask God to pay this, fix that, or vindicate them, while skipping the very thing that inaugurates God's Jubilee—that is, addressing personal and corporate sin. But God's wrath against sin must always be addressed if we intend to enjoy the blessings of God's aid. This comes through having a relationship with Jesus Christ. But don't miss this: you can't have the benefits of the Messiah without entering a relationship with the Messiah. You can't have deliverance from your problems without the King who delivers.

25:13-34 A primary feature of the Jubilee was the return of all property in Israel to its original owners (25:14-17)—the only exception to this rule involved property in walled cities (25:29-30). This was based on the following principle: **The land is not to be permanently sold because it is [God's], and [the people are] only aliens and temporary residents on [his] land** (25:23). There were occasions when Israelites had to sell their land, or sell themselves into servitude because of poverty. But since they and their land really belonged to God, any such sale was temporary. There was also justice for the land buyer in that he didn't lose out completely when the property reverted to its original owner at Jubilee. The price he paid was based on the number of years since the last Jubilee, which meant that what was being sold to him was actually the crops the land would produce (25:14-17).

Since the land was to enjoy a second consecutive year of rest following the Sabbath year that preceded the Year of Jubilee, the people might have wondered how they would have enough food during that time

(25:20). But God assured them that if they would only obey him, he would provide and **appoint [his] blessing**. The land would produce so abundantly in **the sixth year** (the year before the Sabbath rest) that there would be abundant food during the two years without harvest (25:21-22).

God made it clear that no one could refuse to allow the redemption of land during Jubilee. He said, **You are to allow the redemption of any land you occupy** (25:24). Notice that God did not use the word *own*. Again, the people were only **temporary residents** in his land (25:23). Given this universal requirement, the question would inevitably arise concerning an Israelite who was too poor to redeem his land. He would obviously miss out on its productivity, so he could turn to **his nearest relative** for help (25:25). But if that was not possible, the poor man had to wait until Jubilee to get his land back (25:28).

25:35-55 The rules of Jubilee also concerned the people of Israel who were poor, who had been sold, or who had sold themselves into a form of indentured servitude to pay a debt (25:35-43). The poor were to be treated with respect and hospitality, never taken advantage of or charged interest. If an Israelite did sell himself for service, he was to be treated as **a hired worker or temporary resident** instead of as a slave (25:39-40). His station was only a temporary condition that was to be reversed during the Year of Jubilee, when the indentured man and his family were released to return to their **clan** and **ancestral property** (25:41).

Israelites were not to be **sold as slaves** because they were God's **servants** whom he **brought out of . . . Egypt** (25:42). Foreigners whom the Israelites had purchased were not eligible for release during the Year of Jubilee (25:44-46). They could be held for life and even passed on to future generations as part of an inheritance. Often in ancient Israel foreign peoples became slaves as a result of war. Such refugees might have no other means of subsistence. In contrast to other nations in the ancient Near East, Israel was required to grant protection and justice to slaves (see Exod 21:20-21, 26-27; Deut 23:15-16). Also, see commentary on Eph 6:5-9.

The final section deals with the case of an Israelite who became poor and had to sell himself to **an alien or temporary resident** (25:47). The same rules of release applied: Either a relative of the poor man could pay off his debt and release him, or if the indentured man prospered he could redeem himself. If neither of these was possible, the Israelite was set free during the Year of Jubilee. **For the Israelites are my servants**, God explained. **They are my servants that I brought out of the land of Egypt; I am the LORD** (25:55). Just as the land was God's, so also the people in it were his.

The principles of Jubilee relating to servitude, redemption, and freedom have great meaning to us as believers today. We are God's possession since he bought us back from slavery to sin by the blood of Jesus Christ. We are free from sin and death, but we are servants of God.

✒ G. Laws Concerning Obedience and Disobedience (26:1-46) ✑

26:1-2 This chapter of blessings and cursings for either obedience or disobedience to the law of Moses is similar in form to the ancient treaties between kings and their subjects found in the lands around Israel. In this case, the king is the Lord who lays down the rules to be followed by his subjects in a covenant relationship with him. The basic commands the people were to obey in order to enjoy God's blessings were stated up front: **Do not make idols for yourselves . . . keep my Sabbaths and revere my sanctuary.** Why? **I am the LORD your God** (25:1-2).

26:3-13 What blessings would God provide in return for faithfulness? Abundant **rain** for a rich **harvest** and peace and protection from **enemies** (26:4-8). The land would be so fruitful, in fact, that the people would have to **clear out** the uneaten portions of the previous harvest to make room for the new (26:10). This was all possible because of the greatest blessing of all: God promised to take up his **residence among** the people, **walk among** them, and **be [their] God** (26:11-12). None of this was because they had sought him out—but because he had sought them out. God said, **I am the LORD . . . who brought you out of the land of Egypt, so that you would no longer be their slaves. I broke the bars of your yoke and enabled you to live in freedom** (26:13). This is in line with a well-known New Testament teaching: "We love because [God] first loved us" (1 John 4:19).

26:14-17 But how different life would be if Israel rejected the Lord and his covenant! In that case, God would rain down curses on Israel—literally reversing the blessings God had just laid out for obedience (26:14-20). Sadly, Israel eventually disregarded God's law and covenant and encountered these terrible judgments. The people would experience **wasting disease and fever that [would] cause [their] eyes to fail and [their lives] to ebb away** (26:16). They would also taste defeat at the hands of their enemies instead of enjoying divine protection from them. In fact, things would get so bad that they would **flee** in paranoid terror even when the enemy wasn't after them (26:17).

26:18-22 The curses for disobedience also fell on the land. God warned that he would make the **sky like iron and [the] land like bronze** (26:19), a graphic picture of drought that would produce a famine so severe that the people's efforts to raise crops would be useless (26:18-20). The Lord also would send **wild animals** into the land that would kill people as well as their **livestock** (26:22), a sharp contrast to the promise that God would "remove dangerous animals from the land" (26:6).

26:23-26 Continued disobedience would bring **a sword against** Israel, **to execute the vengeance of the covenant** (26:25). This means God would give them over to their enemies. They would also suffer from **pestilence** (26:25), and food would become so scarce that it would lead to rationing and constant hunger (26:26).

26:27-46 Yet, the consequences for continued disobedience would grow worse. When God's patience with Israel's stubborn unfaithfulness would finally run out and he

would send their enemies against them, conditions would become so desperate in the accompanying siege that the people would resort to cannibalism (29:29); this was a horrifying judgment on persistent idolatry. Eventually, the people would even be exiled from the land (26:33), so it would finally have all of its unfulfilled **Sabbath** rests (26:34-35). But still the Lord's judgment on sin would not be finished. Even in captivity the Israelites who survived all the other disasters would be subjected to fear and would ultimately die in the land of their exile. They would **waste away because of their [sin] . . . and because of their fathers' [sins]** (26:39).

Anyone who feels the Lord was being too harsh in the punishments he threatened should reread the various phrases describing Israel's deliberate and prideful disobedience. Note the "if" clauses (26:14, 15, 18, 21, 23, 27) and the statement about the people rejecting God's **ordinances and [abhorring his] statutes** (26:43). The Israelites would not be innocent bystanders who ignorantly displeased God. They would quickly grow into a nation that established a lengthy pattern of idolatry and hatred toward the God who had rescued them, ignoring his warnings and expecting his blessings anyway.

Thankfully, there would remain a ray of hope amid all the suffering promised. This is an indicator that there is always hope for people who will turn to God in humble sincerity, brokenness, and repentance. If the people experiencing God's judgment were to do this (26:41-42), God would **remember the covenant** and restore them (26:45).

Note the last phrase in 26:39: **because of their fathers' iniquities along with theirs.** It hints at the reality of the generational curse, which I believe is still an operational concept in God's economy and is, in fact, tearing lives and families apart today. A *generational curse* may be defined as a pattern of behavior inherited or passed down from one generation to another due to rebellion against God. Parents pass down to their children their physical traits, including the color and texture of their hair and their basic body build. But just as there are biological traits handed down to our children and even grandchildren through DNA, there are also spiritual characteristics that get passed along—for good or ill.

This verse, then, points to the fact that many of life's problems—addictions, bad habits, and slothfulness to name a few—are like trees in that they have deep roots. Thus, some sins, attitudes, and tendencies get handed down from generation to generation in some families. God made inextricably clear to his people the importance of imparting spiritual truth and love for him to their children and grandchildren by teaching and modeling a godly life to them (see Deut 6:4-9). Likely modeling the wrong things is just as potent. Grandpa's alcoholism or Great-Grandma's explosive temper can and often does show up in their descendants.

The point of trying to identify and frankly discuss any generational curses that might be alive in our families, though, is to break them—not to bemoan what our fathers and mothers did. We often want to blame our sin on our pasts: "Well, you know, my daddy did this; therefore, I . . ." or "My momma used to tell me, so I . . . ." Instead, we need to own up to our iniquity and confess our part in any generational problems that have a hold on us.

God teaches in Leviticus, and other places, that the first step in breaking such a curse is to confess and repent of our participation in it. God called on the Israelites to confess both their sins and the sins of their fathers (26:40), which were not dealt with in their fathers' generation and so continued to poison the stream of Israel's relationship with God. Confession and repentance are a potent remedy.

Many today think that talking about generational sin is a waste of time because what's done is done: Let's just forget the past and move on, they say. But that's not what God says. His people were to repent of their fathers' sins and their own. Taking this radical step can break the chains of iniquity that have shackled generations. It opens the pathway to God's blessings.

VI. REGULATIONS CONCERNING VOWS AND TITHES (27:1-34)

27:1-8 It makes sense that a book which began with the sacrifices the Israelites were obliged to make would conclude with offerings and vows that they were under no obligation to make, but which God took just as seriously (see Eccl 5:4-5). The first category of vows included dedicating a person to the Lord in some special way (27:2-8). These ways are not spelled out, but we have an example later in Scripture of what one might involve. We find it in the story of Hannah, who dedicated her yet-to-be-conceived son Samuel to the Lord: "I will give him to the Lord all the days of his life," she promised (1 Sam 1:11). Had she wished to keep the child upon his birth, she would have been required to pay a price to the tabernacle that was equivalent to the boy's value. The price to release a man in the prime of his productive years from a vow was **fifty silver shekels** (27:3), a high price that represented that many months' wages. There were allowances made for the poor, but even they had to pay something to fulfill their promise to God.

27:9-13 Animals could also be used as payment for a vow, but they also had to be redeemed if the person wanted to withdraw them from being used in sacrifice. The exception was a clean animal that was acceptable **as an offering to the Lord** (27:9). Such animals were holy to God and could not be bought back at any price. The redemption price for even an unclean animal was the animal's value as determined by **the priest**, plus twenty percent (27:11-13).

27:14-29 Property could also be used to make a vow, but here the various rules and calculations were more complicated (27:14-25). According to 27:26-27, no firstborn animals could be redeemed, because **a firstborn already belongs to the Lord.** This principle was established during the first Passover when God spared the firstborn of Israel's sons and livestock while striking down all of Egypt's firstborn, human and animal. From that night onward, every firstborn was the Lord's (see Exod 13:1-2, 11-13).

27:30-34 Leviticus ends with instructions for the giving of the tithe (27:30-33). Vows were voluntary, but tithes were required. **Every tenth of the land's produce . . . belongs to the LORD; it is holy** (27:30). God expected his people to return to him a portion of what he already owned and had graciously lent to them. (When we approach giving with the mindset that everything belongs to God, we realize what a blessing it is that he allows us to give these resources back to him to be used for his glorious purposes.) The Israelites could also **redeem** their tithes, but at the twenty percent markup, so to speak (27:31).

One reason for requiring the tithe was very practical. This was how the priests, the tabernacle, and Israel's entire sacrificial system was funded. But the tithe was also a reminder to the Israelites, and to us today, that even though we might earn our salaries by the sweat of our brows, we are not the originators of our blessings. We must never think that God's blessings are rewards for our labors in the sense that we are entitled to them. "You may say to yourself, 'My power and my own ability have gained this wealth for me,' but remember that the LORD your God gives you the power to gain wealth" (Deut 8:17-18).

NUMBERS

INTRODUCTION

Author

THE BOOK OF NUMBERS IS FOR-
mally anonymous—that is, it
does not indicate the name of
its writer. But ancient Jewish and Christian tradition affirms that Moses was the
author—not only of Numbers but also of
the entire Pentateuch (the first five books
of the Old Testament). We read repeatedly
that "The Lord spoke to Moses" (1:1), and
we are informed that "Moses wrote down"
what God told him (33:2). So, even though
it's likely that a later editor added some
things (such as 12:3) to the text, we have
every reason to trust the claim that Moses
authored the book.

Historical Background

Numbers picks up where Exodus left off—
recounting events that happened one
month later than what is recorded there (see
Exod 40:2; Num 1:1). As the narrative opens,
the Israelites have been free from Egyptian
bondage for one year, have entered into a
covenant with the Lord, and have received
God's law through the hand of his servant
Moses. As a result of Israel's national sin, the
people descended from Israel (Jacob) would
wander in the wilderness for forty years.
Numbers covers the period from their departure from Sinai (1:1) to their arrival "by the
Jordan across from Jericho" (36:13)—that is,
it ends with God's people being on the verge
of entering the promised land.

Message and Purpose

Numbers begins with a focus on the first
generation out of Egypt, acknowledging
their wanderings in the wilderness. It closes with the second generation preparing to
enter the promised land.

As God's people left slavery, they had to
move through the ins and outs of learning to
trust their Deliverer daily. Through all their
experiences, God was teaching them what
it means to walk by faith, to move from the
point of initial deliverance to their destiny as
heirs of the promise. But a major factor on
that journey was the wilderness itself. Living
as nomads called to trust in a God they could
not see for even the daily basics of food and
water was difficult for the people. Though
they obediently followed God through the
wilderness, they consistently displayed a
lack of faith in him at the same time.

Nothing brings out the people's failure to
trust God more than Numbers 14 does. There
the people chose to believe the majority report that said the promised land couldn't be
taken. In doing so, they rejected the report
of Joshua and Caleb, who wisely said they
could take it indeed if only they would believe God. As a result, that faithless generation was sentenced to die in the wilderness.

The rest of the book centers on the second generation of Israelites, who learned
to walk in faith so that they could realize
the destiny their parents had failed to gain:
God's blessings in the promised land that

was prepared for them. Numbers is a great reminder that kingdom benefits can only be secured by faith.

www.bhpublishinggroup.com/qr/te/04_00

Outline

I. Preparing to Travel to the Promised Land (1:1–10:10)
  A. The Numbering and Organization of the Twelve Tribes (1:1–4:49)
  B. Instructions for the Journey (5:1–10:10)

II. Israel on the Journey to the Promised Land (10:11–21:35)
  A. Traveling from Sinai to Kadesh (10:11–15:41)
  B. God's Discipline of the People (16:1–20:13)
  C. Traveling from Kadesh to Moab (20:14–21:35)

III. Israel on the Edge of the Promised Land (22:1–36:13)
  A. God's Faithfulness and Israel's Unfaithfulness (22:1–25:18)
  B. Preparations for Entering the Promised Land (26:1–30:16)
  C. Midianites Defeated and Transjordan Settled (31:1–32:42)
  D. Exhorting a New Generation and Dividing the Land (33:1–36:13)

NUMBERS

I. PREPARING TO TRAVEL TO THE PROMISED LAND (1:1–10:10)

❧ A. The Numbering and Organization of the Twelve Tribes (1:1–4:49) ❧

1:1-16 Once the Israelites were living under a covenant with the Lord, it was time for the people to set out for the promised land of Canaan. But first, over two million souls had to be organized into a coherent and orderly traveling community. As it turned out, the Israelites would also need chastening, cleansing, repentance, and restoration in order to live in the presence of their holy God. The LORD himself got this massive process started with a command to Moses: **Take a census of the entire Israelite community . . . counting the names of every male . . . twenty years old or more by their military divisions—everyone who can serve in Israel's army** (1:1-3). This count assessed Israel's preparedness for war with the native Canaanites as the new nation approached the edge of their promised land.

1:17-43 The twelve tribes listed were all descended from the sons of Jacob (1:20-43), except for **Ephraim** and **Manasseh** (1:32-35), who replaced the tribe of Levi. These two tribes descended from Jacob's son, **Joseph**. The Levites received no land inheritance because they were to serve as the Lord's priests and temple servants.

The order in which each tribe is listed does not follow birth order. Rather, they are listed

according to how they were to arrange themselves within the camp (see 2:1-34).

1:44-46 The census revealed the total number of available fighting men, those **twenty years old or more** (1:45), to be **603,550** (1:46; see Exod 12:37). Thus, the total number of people in this traveling band—including wives and children—would have been over two million strong. Moving so many people in an orderly way must have seemed mind-boggling.

1:47-50 As noted previously, **the Levites** were not included in this count (1:47-49). This is an indicator that even in the event of war, the worship of God was to remain paramount. The Levites were set aside to care for **the tabernacle . . . , all its furnishings, and everything in it** (1:50).

The Israelite camp was laid out in a cross shape, with three tribes grouped on each side of the tabernacle, which was situated in the middle. The Levites camped around the tabernacle within the perimeter of the camp and thus stood between the people and access to God. Even in the physical layout of the Israelite nation on the move, then, the message was clear that the people needed a human mediator to stand between them and God. The ultimate and perfect mediator would come in the Son of God, Jesus Christ, who would die on a cross (see 1 Tim 2:5; Heb 8:6).

1:51-54 Just in case someone missed the message that God's presence could not be approached by just anyone, a warning was given: **Any unauthorized person who comes near** the tabernacle **is to be put to death** (1:51). The Levites' ministry in caring for, transporting, and setting up the tabernacle properly was crucial in God's eyes. Doing it right would prevent his **wrath** from falling **on the Israelite community** (1:53). Here we are told, **The Israelites did everything just as the LORD had commanded Moses** (1:54). So far, so good.

2:1-2 The twelve tribes were to **camp around the tent of meeting at a distance from it** (2:2). This gave the Levites room to camp on the inside perimeter while also illustrating the importance of the Levites' ministry of interceding before God on behalf of the nation. The fact that the Levite men were excused from military service demonstrates how essential their ministerial duties were to God.

2:3-9 The placement of the tribes around the camp, three tribes to a side, generally followed the various groupings of Jacob's sons by his four wives: Leah and Rachel, the daughters of Laban, and their maidservants, Zilpah and Bilhah, respectively (see Gen 29–30). The three tribes on the east side were **Judah . . . Issachar . . . Zebulun** (2:3-9). They were all sons of Jacob by Leah. The east was the direction in which the tabernacle faced. This meant that the tribe of Judah led the way when the nation traveled. It was the appropriate position for the tribe from which kings would come. Judah's leader, **Nahshon son of Amminadab** (2:3), is named in the genealogy of David (Ruth 4:20) and the genealogy of Christ (Matt 1:4).

2:10-17 Next, the tribes on the **south side** of the camp were listed: **Reuben . . . Simeon . . . Gad** (2:10-16). Reuben was Jacob's firstborn through Leah, and Simeon was Leah's second son. Gad was the son of Leah's maidservant Zilpah, but his tribe was assigned in this group to take the place of Levi, Leah's third son whose tribe had other duties (see 1:47-50). When they moved, the tribes were **to move out just as they** camped, **each in his place, with their banners** (2:17).

2:18-24 The **west side** of the camp included the tribes of **Ephraim . . . Manasseh . . . Benjamin.** Ephraim and Manasseh (the sons of Joseph) and Benjamin represented the two sons of Rachel; they were Jacob's youngest sons. Benjamin was not only the baby of the family, but his tribe was also the smallest— later, in fact, it would be almost completely absorbed into the tribe of Judah. After the division of the kingdom of Israel into two parts hundreds of years into the nation's history, the southern kingdom was known as Judah; it is often spoken of in the biblical accounts as if only one tribe lived there.

2:25-34 The last group listed was to camp on the **north side** and **move out last.** These three tribes were **Dan . . . Asher . . . Naphtali** (2:25-31). Dan and Naphtali were the sons of Bilhah, while Asher was the son of Zilpah. Here once again, we read, **The Israelites did everything the LORD commanded** (2:34).

3:1-3 The most important item in the Israelite camp was the tent of meeting—the tabernacle that housed the holy presence of the Lord. So it follows that the most important assignments any Israelite could have were those that pertained to the worship in and care of the structure. Before the nation departed for the promised land, Moses assigned the duties of the tabernacle to the Levites.

While both Moses and Aaron were descendants of Levi, only Aaron and his descendants were chosen by God to serve as priests. The rest of the Levites were commanded to assist the priests as necessary and to care for the tabernacle and its furnishings. The first of the Levites to be listed were Aaron and his four **sons, the anointed priests, who were ordained to serve** (3:3).

3:4 Moses reminded his readers that **Nadab and Abihu,** Aaron's eldest sons who were also priests, had **died in the LORD's presence when they presented unauthorized fire before the LORD in the Wilderness of Sinai, and they had no sons** (see Lev 10:1-2). That left **Eleazar and Ithamar,** who **served as priests under the direction of Aaron their father.**

3:5-10 God told **Moses to bring the tribe of Levi near and present them to the priest Aaron to assist him** (3:5-6). The Levites' duties were explained in general terms in 3:7-10 and given in more detail later in chapter 4. One important warning was attached: These non-priestly Levites were not to have anything to do with the **sanctuary** where the sacrifices were made, on pain of **death** (3:10).

3:11-13 God sovereignly chose the Levites for this service. He declared, **The Levites belong to me, because every firstborn belongs to me** (3:12-13). This is a reference to what happened during the exodus. When God **struck down every firstborn in . . . Egypt**, he **consecrated every firstborn in Israel** to himself (3:13; see Exod 13:2, 15). Thus, he could have claimed every firstborn male in Israel to be set aside for his service at the tabernacle. But instead he chose the Levites to serve **in place of every firstborn Israelite** (3:12).

3:14-26 When it came time to count the Levites and assign them their duties and positions, they were divided according to **Levi's sons by name: Gershon, Kohath, and Merari**, who were also the heads of **clans** (3:17-20). **The Gershonite clans** were placed **on the west side** (3:23). They were responsible for **the tabernacle, the tent, its covering, the screen for the entrance to the tent of meeting, the hangings of the courtyard, the screen for the entrance to the courtyard . . . and the tent ropes** (3:25-26).

3:27-32 Next **the Kohathites** who **camped on the south side** are mentioned (3:29). Their **duties involved** the furnishings of the tabernacle, including **the ark, the table, the lampstand, the altars, the sanctuary utensils . . . and the screen** (3:29-31). Thus, they were charged with the care of the tabernacle's holy objects, which is probably why **Eleazar son of Aaron the priest** was their supervisor (3:32). Interestingly, Moses was also a Kohathite through his father Amram (see Exod 6:18, 20).

3:33-39 The third Levite group consisted of the **Merarite clans** who were **camped on the north side of the tabernacle** (3:35). Their responsibilities were to dismantle, carry, and set up **the tabernacle's** wooden framework and all the other wood and metal connecting items that supported it (3:36-37). That left the **east** side of the tabernacle to be

occupied by **Moses, Aaron, and his sons** the priests (3:38), who had overall responsibility for the ministry of the tabernacle. **The total number** of male Levites **registered** was **22,000** (3:39).

3:40-51 God's redemption of the **firstborn** of all the males in Israel was something he took so seriously that a precise count was made to ensure there were enough Levites to redeem every firstborn male in the camp (3:40-42). The Levite count was 22,000 (3:39), but the firstborn count among the Israelites was **22,273** (3:43). So something had to be done to redeem the extra **273 firstborn Israelites** (3:46). The solution was to take up a collection of **five shekels** of silver for each of the 273 males as their redemption price. This, a total of **1,365 shekels**, was to be given to **Aaron and his sons**. This was done **in obedience to the LORD** (3:47-51).

4:1-8 Those who were to perform service among the Levites had to be **from thirty years old to fifty** (4:3; cf. 4:23, 30). So a census was taken of each of the three Levite clans to identify those who would be responsible for taking down and moving the tabernacle and its articles. As we saw previously, **the Kohathites** bore the responsibility for transporting the **most holy objects**, including **the ark of the testimony** and **the table of the Presence** (4:4-7). These were carefully covered with **leather** and **cloth** wrappings by the priests, and **poles** were inserted through the rings in the ark and the table, so they could be carried without being touched or even seen (see 4:7-8).

4:9-20 The **lampstand . . . gold altar . . . bronze altar** and all their **utensils** were also prepared for travel (4:9-14). Once everything was properly covered and organized, **the Kohathites** could **carry them**. But if they touched any of **the holy objects**, they would **die** (4:15). It was the job of **Eleazar, son of Aaron the priest** to make sure everything was done according to God's command so that the Kohathites did not incur his wrath in their **transportation** duties (4:16-20).

4:21-28 The **Gershonites** were in charge of the cloth and leather parts of the tabernacle, including the **curtains . . . the covering . . . the**

screen for the entrance . . . the hangings of the courtyard . . . along with . . . all the equipment for their service (4:25-26). The leader of this work was Aaron's son **Ithamar** (4:28).

4:29-33 The **Merarites** were the "heavy haulers" among the Levites, transporting the wooden and metal parts of the tabernacle over which the cloth and leather were hung. **Ithamar** also led this group (4:33).

4:34-49 When the census was conducted, there were more than enough Levites to share the work. The number of men qualified to serve were 2,750 registered **Kohathite** men, 2,630 registered **Gershonite** men, and 3,200 registered **Merarite** men (4:34-45). Thus, there was a total of 8,580 Levites in the Lord's service (4:48). Each man's **assignment was as the Lord commanded Moses** (4:49). With that many men assigned to serve the needs of transporting the tabernacle, the work could be shared among them. No one would be overburdened. This cooperative approach should carry over into the church.

⋙ B. Instructions for the Journey
(5:1–10:10) ⋘

5:1-4 If the *organization* of the Israelites traveling to the promised land was important, their *sanctification*—that is, their status as the set-apart people of God—was critical. God had delivered his people out of Egypt, but it was time to get Egypt out of his people. That, however, would prove to be a forty-year process, requiring God's infinite patience and disciplining hand.

God's holiness was manifested in a visible way in the tabernacle, which was in the center of the Israelites' camp and served as the symbol of God's presence in their midst. The people were called to be holy because the Lord is holy (see Lev 19:2). Part of their spiritual holiness was linked to the condition of their bodies and to proper relationships with their fellow covenant members. The regulations of chapter 5 spell out several of these stipulations, isolating as "unclean" anyone among them having **a skin disease, anyone** with **a discharge, or anyone who was**

defiled because of contact with **a corpse** (5:2). Such people had to go **outside the camp** so that they didn't defile the Israelite encampment where the Lord dwelled (5:3-4).

Importantly, the issue here was ceremonial uncleanness, not an inherent spiritual inferiority within the suffering individual or a wholesale rejection of contaminated persons. There were procedures for cleansing and restoring the affected people to the camp with their fellow Israelites (see Lev 13:1-46; 14:1-32; 15:1-32; 22:4-9). Nevertheless, isolating someone with a skin disease that could turn out to be contagious also had health benefits in a large community.

This chapter on regulations for Israel's life and worship is a good place for a reminder that one purpose for the book of Numbers was to warn Moses's readers that as long as Israel obeyed the Lord by living according to his law, the nation would prosper. But the reverse was also true. (And if you know the rest of the story, you know that by the end of the book things went badly for Israel. That they would receive their just desserts is more than a history lesson for us. The principle of faith in God versus unbelief and the consequences belonging to each choice still holds true today.)

5:5-6 The regulation presented here involved a person who committed **any sin against another** (5:6). Since such a sin was some kind of moral or legal violation, serious steps had to be taken to make it right. But even before the offended party was addressed, an important point was made. Everyone needed to be reminded that *any* sin in Israel's kingdom community was ultimately a sin against **the Lord** and made the person **guilty** in his sight (5:6).

We never sin in a vacuum either. Our sin always affects other people—either directly or indirectly. But first and foremost, our sin is always an offense against our Creator. King David understood this. Even though he committed adultery (wronging both Bathsheba and her husband Uriah) and murder (by having Uriah killed), David knew that he had offended God most of all. For it was God who said, "Do not murder," and "Do not commit adultery" (Exod 20:13-14). This is why David prayed, "Against you—you alone—I have sinned and done this evil in your sight" (Ps 51:4).

5:7-10 Make no mistake, however, the offended human victim of sin also has to be compensated. So the Lord instituted the principle of recompense with the repayment of the wrong plus **a fifth** of the **value** of whatever was taken, damaged, or lost (5:7). If there was no one to whom such a payment could be made, it was to go **to the LORD for the priest, along with the atonement ram by which the priest will make atonement for the guilty person** (5:8). In following these instructions carefully, the violator helped ensure that any wrongdoing would be thoroughly purged from among the people.

5:11-14 The rest of this chapter deals with a husband who had **a feeling of jealousy** (5:13-14), suspecting that his wife had committed adultery with another man. Adultery was a sin that could not be tolerated under the Mosaic covenant because, once again, every sin is first a violation against the Lord. The procedure for establishing a wife's guilt or innocence sounds strange to us, but it was prescribed by God himself.

5:15-26 The process began with the husband bringing his **wife to the priest**, along with an **offering** of **barley flour** to deal with possible **guilt** (5:15). The priest would then take **holy water in a clay bowl** and mix it with **dust from the tabernacle floor** to make a **bitter** drink, which the woman would be required to consume after affirming that she was innocent of adultery and accepting a **curse** if she were lying. The words of the cruse would also be written on a **scroll** and then washed off into the mixture the woman had to drink (5:16-24).

5:27-31 If the woman were innocent, no harm would come to her (5:28). But if she were guilty, the curse would supernaturally render her sterile (5:27). Some modern critics of the Bible have pointed to this as an example of how the Bible affirms the oppression of women, but it is actually an example of how God supernaturally protected women in a time before there was any other way to prove their innocence. God was the perfect Judge in these cases; he is also the best witness any defendant could have in a trial.

6:1-8 Serving the Lord at the tabernacle was limited to the priests and other servants who belonged to the tribe of Levi. But any Israelite could consecrate himself or herself to the Lord for a time of special separation and devotion by taking **a Nazirite vow** (6:2). Usually this was done for a limited period of time. In the case of Paul in Acts 18:18, his haircut was the sign that he was ending his vow (see Num 6:18).

But in the case of two famous Old Testament Nazirites, Samuel (see 1 Sam 1:11) and Samson (see Judg 13:5), their vows were lifelong. Interestingly, both vows were made before these boys were born. Samuel's vow was made by his mother Hannah, pledging him to the Lord's service. In Judges, God himself told Samson's parents to make him a Nazirite. Samuel honored his vow, while Samson famously violated his own in several ways and made an unholy mess of his life.

The normal procedure, however, was for the person to make his or her own decision to undertake a Nazirite vow. Three stipulations highlighted the separateness of consecration: abstinence from **wine and beer** or **anything produced by the grapevine**; no cutting of the **hair throughout the time of** the **vow of consecration**, and no going **near a dead body** (6:3-6). By following these guidelines, the Nazirite would be set apart for the Lord's service. He or she would be **holy to the LORD during the time of consecration** (6:8).

6:9-12 If a Nazirite accidentally became defiled, there were rituals prescribed to cleanse him and re-establish his consecration so he could resume his vow. (See commentary on Judg 6:1-8.) Samson, for instance, violated his vows when he scooped honey from a dead lion (see Judg 14:5-9) and when he revealed his secret to Delilah, leading her to cut his hair (see Judg 16:17-19). There is no record that Samson ever tried to undergo the prescribed rituals to reinstate his Nazirite status. But since God was the one who designated Samson as a Nazirite, he graciously restored his Nazirite status with his supernatural strength when his hair began to grow again (see Judg 16:22).

6:13-17 When the period of consecration was over, the Nazirite was to present to the Lord three **unblemished** animals at the tabernacle **as a burnt offering . . . a sin of- fering** and **a fellowship offering** (6:14). The burnt offering symbolized complete conse- cration to God, the sin offering atoned for any sins the Nazirite may have unintention- ally committed during his vow period, and the fellowship offering denoted that he and the Lord were in harmony.

6:18-21 Then the Nazirite would **shave his consecrated head** and throw **the hair** into **the fire** (6:18) on the altar, symbolizing the completion of his vow. The priest would give him **the boiled shoulder from the ram, one unleavened cake from the basket, and one unleavened wafer** (6:19), which the Nazirite would present or wave before the Lord. Then he and the priest would eat the sacrifice to- gether in a meal. With these steps completed, the Nazirite was released from his vow.

6:22-27 This chapter ends with a beautiful priestly blessing designed to place the Lord's **name** on his people (6:27): **May the Lord bless you and protect you; may the Lord make his face shine on you and be gra- cious to you; may the Lord look with favor on you and give you peace** (6:24-26). God's instruction to Moses, **This is how you are to bless the Israelites** (6:22), is similar to Jesus's introduction to the Lord's Prayer for his disci- ples: "You should pray like this" (Matt 6:9). This blessing, then, is a formula that acts as a guide for God's people to bless others.

7:1-6 In chapter 7 Moses took a step back- ward to recall the day when Israel **finished setting up the tabernacle** and **consecrated it and all its furnishings** (7:1). With the tab- ernacle complete and dedicated, **the leaders of Israel . . . brought as their offering be- fore the Lord six covered carts and twelve oxen . . . and presented them in front of the tabernacle** (7:2-3). Moses then presented these gifts to the Levites (7:5-6) for their use in transporting the tabernacle to the prom- ised land.

7:7-8 These carts and oxen were distributed based on the duties of the various Levitical families. **The Gershonites** were given **two carts and four oxen corresponding to their service** (7:7), which involved transporting the

lighter cloth and leather parts of the sacred tent, while **the Merarites** received **four carts and eight oxen corresponding to their ser- vice** (7:8) of carrying the much heavier metal and wooden pieces (see 4:21-33).

7:9 But Moses did not give carts or oxen **to the Kohathites, since their responsibility was service related to the holy objects carried on their shoulders.** These men carried the ark of the covenant and the altars on poles rather than on carts so that no one would touch these sacred objects (see 4:1-20). Later, King David's failure to transport the ark in the right way would cost Uzzah his life when he reached out to steady the ark as it was trans- ported by ox and cart (see 2 Sam 6:1-8).

7:10-11 What follows in the remainder of the chapter is a list of **the dedication gift for the altar** that **the leaders** of each of the twelve tribes brought for **the altar** in the tabernacle (7:10). God called each leader to come on a separate day to **present his offering for the dedication** (7:11) so that each gift could be honored and celebrated individually.

7:12-83 The presentation of gifts began with **Nahshon . . . from the tribe of Judah** (7:12), the tribe that led the way when Israel moved out. His generous offering consisted of **one silver dish . . . one silver basin . . . one gold bowl . . . one young bull, one ram, and one male lamb a year old . . . one male goat . . . and two bulls, five rams, five male goats, and five male lambs a year old** (7:13-17). The leaders of the other eleven tribes fol- lowed suit, coming on each of the next eleven days in the same order as the arrangement of the tribes encamped around the tabernacle (7:18-83; see 2:3-31). They brought offerings identical to Nahshon's.

7:84-89 After all of the gifts were added up (7:84-88), **Moses entered the tent of meet- ing to speak with the Lord** and heard his **voice speaking to him from above the mercy seat that was on the ark of the tes- timony** (7:89). This was a pivotal moment establishing a new level of communication between God and his people. Moses spoke di- rectly to God in his sanctuary, and God spoke directly to Moses.

8:1-12 The Lord's next set of instructions was for the priests and Levites. First, **Aaron** was to **light** the **seven lamps** in the tabernacle (8:2). Then came the instructions for the cleansing and consecration of the Levites for their service. Their outward purification required them to be sprinkled **with the purification water**, to have their **entire bodies** shaved, and to wash **their clothes** (8:6-7). These steps to **purify themselves** outwardly (8:7) were followed by internal cleansing, accomplished by the offering of one **young bull** as a burnt **offering** and a **second young bull for a sin offering** to atone for unintentional sins (8:8-12).

Once these ceremonies were complete, **the Levites** were brought out to be presented by Aaron to **the entire Israelite community** (8:9). There, **before the LORD**, Aaron was to **have the Israelites lay their hands on them** (8:10) in a service we would recognize today as a form of ordination. It was called **a presentation offering** to the Lord from the Israelites, so that the Levites could **perform the LORD's work** (8:11). Thus, the Levites were a gift to the Lord, and the people were investing them with the authority to execute their ministry. The Levites concluded this solemn ceremony by laying **their hands on the heads of the bulls**. The **sin offering** atoned for sin, and the **burnt offering** symbolized total commitment to God (8:12).

8:13-19 God then made a presentation and gift of his own. He told Moses to **have the Levites stand before Aaron and his sons ... to present them before the LORD as a presentation offering** (8:13). The reason was **to separate the Levites from the rest of the Israelites** so that the Levites would belong to God (8:13-14). As stated earlier (3:11-13; see Exod 13:2, 15), God's special possession of the Levites was based on his redemption of the firstborn of all the males of Israel in the tenth plague of the exodus from Egypt. Instead of calling out every firstborn male from every tribe for his service, God chose the Levites for this sacred task (8:16-18). God then turned around and gave the Levites **exclusively to Aaron and his sons to perform the work for the Israelites at the tent of meeting.** This was to protect the rest of the community from bringing a **plague** upon themselves by

coming in contact with the sacred objects of the **sanctuary** (8:19), thereby defiling themselves and suffering death.

8:20-22 The chapter concludes by affirming that **Moses, Aaron, and the entire Israelite community** obeyed God's commands (8:20). Unfortunately, this will contrast sharply with the whining and rebellion of the Israelites once they hit the road toward Canaan. Even in the face of God's miraculous deliverance, the Israelites often failed to trust God when the going got tough.

8:23-26 The beginning age of tabernacle service for the Levites was **twenty-five**. Nevertheless, the upper limit remained at **fifty years** (8:24-25). The men had to retire from active service at that age, but they could **assist** their fellow Levites by performing lighter duties (8:26). This was a merciful provision that would prevent men who may not be physically able from failing in their duties and simultaneously bringing defilement on the nation.

Earlier, in 4:3, we read that the minimum age for Levitical service was "thirty" years old. This seeming discrepancy is less glaring when we realize that the events in chapter 4 actually happened after the events in 7:1–9:14 (see 7:1). For some reason unknown to us, the age was raised from twenty-five to thirty during that time. Some Bible commentators suggest that this could have happened after the deaths of Nadab and Abihu (3:4; see Lev 10:1-2). If that is the case, it could be that the age was raised to ensure greater spiritual maturity on the part of the priests. Or, it could be that the Levites entered an apprentice phase at age twenty-five and then entered full service at thirty.

9:1-5 God underscored the importance of **the Passover** by commanding Moses to have Israel observe this festival **at its appointed time on the fourteenth day of [the first] month at twilight** (9:2-3). The first Passover was celebrated prior to the exodus from Egypt. It was through the events of the Passover that the Lord delivered his people from slavery. So it was appropriate to celebrate it again in the first month of the nation's **second year** out from Egypt (9:1).

9:6-8 There were some Israelites who had been disqualified from participating in the Passover on the appointed day because of their contact with **a human corpse** (9:6). Such contact brought spiritual defilement on them. They came to Moses to ask, **Why should we be excluded from presenting the LORD's offering at its appointed time ...?** (9:7). This was only the second Passover, so Moses had no precedent from which to answer them. So he instructed them to **wait** while he went before the Lord to see what he would command about the matter (9:8).

9:9-11 God's answer was gracious and provided an ordinance for future generations. Those in a similar situation could wait a month and observe the Passover **in the second month, on the fourteenth day at twilight** (9:11), still keeping all of the required regulations. They wouldn't have to miss out.

9:12-14 Then God dealt with two further cases that Moses didn't anticipate. The first concerned an Israelite who simply skipped the Passover. That person was to be **cut off from his people,** bearing **the consequences of his sin** (9:13), which would have meant banishment or death. Interestingly, in the New Testament era, similar mistreatment of the Lord's Supper by the Corinthians resulted in sickness or death (see 1 Cor 11:28-30). The second case dealt with **an alien** among the Israelites who wanted to **observe the Passover.** Such a person was permitted to do so, as long as it was done **according to the Passover statute and its ordinances** (9:14). Aliens who wanted to become followers of the Lord were to be given the same privilege as native Israelites in this case.

9:15-23 The Israelites had an unmistakable divine GPS guiding them during their entire time in the wilderness, and God's guidance was always reliable. They were guided by the Lord's **cloud** that **covered the tabernacle** (9:15). When the cloud hovered low over the tabernacle, the Israelites remained in camp; when the cloud **lifted,** the Israelites broke camp and followed the cloud until it stopped again over a new location (9:17-18). No matter how long or short a stay between those journeys, Moses recorded that the people **carried out the LORD's requirement and did not set out** (9:19) until he told them to move.

Unfortunately, though, the Israelites as a whole do not obey God much throughout the remainder of the book. A few individuals, including Moses and Aaron, are said later to obey God, but that's it. From this point forward in Numbers, we will hear mostly grumbling and rumbling coming from the tents of Israel.

10:1-10 Keeping over two million people organized required a lot of precision and clear signals, especially in times of danger or war. So God prescribed a series of **blasts** from **trumpets** that would be used to call either the entire congregation or their leaders to rally at the tabernacle **or set out** as needed (10:2-5). These trumpets were blown on all occasions by **the priests** (10:8). The trumpet sound during battle was especially important as a reminder to the Israelites that **the LORD** was going before them and would save them from their **enemies** (10:9). Trumpets also became a key part of Israel's sacrifices and festivals, serving as auditory reminders that the Lord alone was their God (10:10).

II. ISRAEL ON THE JOURNEY TO THE PROMISED LAND (10:11–21:35)

⋙ A. *Traveling from Sinai to Kadesh* (10:11–15:41) ⋘

10:11-13 The momentous day finally arrived when God determined that it was time for his people to collapse their tents, dismantle the tabernacle, and make tracks for the promised land. They had been parked at Sinai for almost a year. So when the time came, God announced the message by lifting **the cloud** that was **above the tabernacle** (10:11). The cloud's first stop en route to Canaan was **in the**

Wilderness of Paran (10:12), a long stretch of barren land.

10:14-17 The order of their march followed the earlier organization (2:3-31), with the tribe of Judah leading the way, followed by the tribes of Issachar and Zebulun. With the east side of the camp now open to accommodate the Israelites' further movement, the tabernacle was then taken down, and the Gershonites and the Merarites set out, transporting the tabernacle (10:17).

10:18-21 The second of the four **divisions** (10:18) of Israel's tribes then marched out with its three tribes—Reuben, Simeon, and Gad—followed by the Levite clan of the Kohathites, who were **transporting the holy objects; the tabernacle was to be set up before their arrival**. Thus, when the ark of the covenant, the altars, and the holy utensils used in worship arrived at the stopping point, the tabernacle would already be ready to house these holy objects.

10:22-28 With all three of the Levite clans on their way with the tabernacle and its furnishings, the final two divisions of the tribes were ready to march. The tribes of Ephraim, Manasseh, and Benjamin set out (10:22-24). Then the final tribes of Dan, Asher, and Naphtali brought up the rear, **serving as** the **rear guard** (10:25-28). Moses summarized what must have been an awe-inspiring sight: **This was the order of march for the Israelites by their military divisions** (10:28).

10:29-32 Moses invited **Hobab**, his **relative by marriage**, to come with the Israelites on their journey and to share in their blessings (10:29). To Moses's disappointment, Hobab preferred to return to his home (10:30). Nevertheless, Moses urged him to come since Hobab knew the region and Moses was hoping to draw on his knowledge for the best routes through a harsh and dangerous land (10:31-32).

10:33-34 The Israelites thus began **a three-day journey with the ark of the LORD's covenant traveling ahead of them . . . to seek a resting place for them** (10:33). The presence of the ark must have been a tremendous

comfort to Moses and all Israel, for it was to serve as the Lord's throne among his people; he dwelled above it, between its decorative cherubim (see 1 Sam 4:4; 2 Sam 6:2; Ps 80:1; 99:1; Is 37:16). Moreover, the Lord showed his presence and guidance through **the cloud** that **was over them by day when they set out from the camp** (10:34).

10:35 Whenever the ark set out, Moses would raise what was essentially a war cry calling on the Lord to scatter his **enemies** and cause those who hated him to **flee from** his **presence**. These words were a reminder to the people of Israel that war laid ahead. They would eventually encounter hostile forces that despised the Lord and, therefore, despised his people. I see here another reminder for Christians: we should not expect acceptance from a world that rejects God. Jesus articulated this to his disciples: "If the world hates you, understand that it hated me before it hated you" (John 15:18).

10:36 When the ark **came to rest**, Moses called to God to **return . . . to the countless thousands of Israel**, essentially making a request for his comforting presence and protection over the people.

11:1-3 Sadly, it didn't take long for the Israelites to forget God's miraculous deliverance and merciful covenant and start **complaining openly . . . about hardship**. They didn't even bother pretending to hide their gripes from him. As a result, God's anger burned. He became, literally, as mad as a fire is hot. In fact, he sent **fire** that **blazed among them and consumed the outskirts of the camp** (11:1). Once again, Moses interceded for his wayward Israelite brothers, praying for grace from their holy God. And so, **the fire died down** (11:2). They named the place **Taberah**, which means, "Blaze" (11:3). (This wouldn't be the last time that a location was named as a result of Israel's rebelliousness.)

11:4-9 The fire had hardly burned out when the **riffraff among them** began complaining about their **craving for other food** (11:4). God had graciously and supernaturally provided **manna** —bread from heaven— for them (11:7-9). But these complainers no longer had an **appetite** for it and couldn't stand to even **look at** it (11:6). They were tired of the Lord's menu. Shockingly, they preferred **the free fish . . . cucumbers, melons, leeks, onions, and garlic** they had back **in Egypt** (11:5).

11:10-15 Family after family was **weeping** like children whining about what they had to eat for dinner. So God was **very angry**, and Moses was **provoked** (11:10). Moses's prayer here shows his tremendous frustration with the people at this point in the journey (11:11-15). He basically said, "Lord, what did I do to make you so mad at me that you loaded me down with this nation of gripers and crybabies?" The people wanted **meat**, but Moses couldn't give it to them (11:12-13). If dealing with this rabble was to be his lot in life, in fact, Moses no longer wanted the job. He preferred that the Lord simply **kill** him (11:15).

This brings us to an important aside. Moses wouldn't be the last ministry leader to be overwhelmed by the spiritual immaturity of those under his care. But he had forgotten one thing: shepherding Israel was *God's project*, not his. Those who lead and feed God's people are under-shepherds; the chief Shepherd is the One who's really in charge (see 1 Pet 5:1-4). And not only is he able to supply his under-shepherds with the resources they need to do the work he has called them to do, but he will reward them for their faithfulness.

11:16-17 Once again, God responded to Moses with grace and mercy. He neither killed Moses (as requested) nor relieved him of leadership. Instead, he did something far better: he provided Moses with help by appointing **seventy . . . elders and officers** to share the leadership load (11:16). They needed to be competent and trustworthy men, but they also needed something even more important: the Holy Spirit. God said he would **take some of the Spirit** who was on Moses and **put the Spirit on** the seventy elders, so that they would be fully equipped to **help** him **bear the burden of the people** (11:17).

11:18-20 God also took action to deal with those who clamored for meat to eat—but not in the way they would have liked. He told

them to **consecrate** themselves **in readiness for** the next day. They had complained, **"Who will feed us meat? We were better off in Egypt"** (11:18). In response, the Lord was going to give it to them. He intended to feed them meat **for a whole month** until it was coming out of their **nostrils**; it would literally make them ill. Why? Because they had **rejected the LORD** (11:20). Notice, however, that the Israelites never claimed that they were rejecting the Lord. Rather, they complained about God's provision. *That's* rejecting the Lord.

11:21-23 Moses was so frustrated at this point that even *he* doubted God's ability to provide a source of meat for so many for so long. Moses was tired, exasperated, and at the end of his rope (11:21-22). His attitude was essentially this: "Lord, these people are such a mess I don't even think *you* can do anything for them!" But God rebuked his prophet in no uncertain terms. The all-powerful Creator is not **weak**. If he promised it, he will do it (11:23).

11:24-30 Moses carried out the consecration service for the seventy elders whom God told him to select (11:24). As God promised, **He took some of the Spirit that was on Moses and placed the Spirit on the seventy elders**. These men **prophesied**, but only on this occasion (11:25). Then **Joshua** learned that two other men—who **had remained in the camp**—were **prophesying**. He reported this to Moses and urged him to **stop them** (11:26-28). But Moses responded by asking a question and shifting his focus. He said, **Are you jealous on my account? If only all the LORD's people were prophets and the LORD would place his Spirit on them!** (11:29).

Joshua had sought to protect Moses from any challenge to his leadership. But Moses demonstrated why God's Word calls him, "a very humble man" (12:3). God provided an answer to Moses's ministry leadership problem, and he didn't miss it. Rather than seeing the men as somehow stealing his glory, Moses saw them as God's blessing intended to bring more glory to God. The more people who know, obey, and teach God's Word, the more the church is edified and God is glorified.

11:31-35 As promised (11:18-20), God's meat delivery service rolled up to the camp right on time. **Quail** started showing up in droves (11:31). **The people were up all that day and night and all the next day gathering** the birds (11:32). (It was grilling time!) Yet **while the meat was still between their teeth, before it was chewed, the LORD's anger burned against the people, and the LORD struck them with a very severe plague** (11:33). God was still providing for his people. But he also brought down his judgment on those **who had craved meat** and whined about what they felt was a lousy menu (11:34; see 11:4-6). The ingrates had craved their way to the grave, so the survivors called the place **Kibroth-hattaavah**, which means "Graves of Craving" (11:34).

12:1 Unfortunately, the criticisms of Moses didn't end with the deaths of the cravers. Things really got ugly when **Miriam and Aaron**, his older siblings, **criticized Moses because of the Cushite woman he married**. Likely this challenge to his legitimate authority was prompted by his marriage to a woman from a region called Cush, which today is Ethiopia. This means the woman that this Jewish forefather married was of African descent; she was a descendant of Noah's son Ham, through Cush (see Gen 10:6). God soundly rejected Miriam and Aaron's reproof by bringing upon Miriam a leprous state, which lasted for seven days to serve as a reminder of her sin. There is no place for racial hatred and division among God's people (Num 12:9-15).

Moses's wife, like her husband, had embraced faith in the One True God (see commentary on Exod 4:24-26). The couple serves as a reminder to us that when it comes to entering the marriage covenant, Christians are to marry "in the Lord"—that is, we are to marry others who share the same faith in God through Jesus Christ that we do (see 1 Cor 7:39). Marriage is to be faith-based—not race-based.

12:2 Apparently Moses had entered what some today would call an interracial marriage, and Miriam and Aaron didn't like it. Maybe they were jealous that their baby brother had been appointed leader of Israel over them. Perhaps they wanted more influential leadership roles. Regardless of what motivated their attack, they used his marriage as an illegitimate means to challenge his authority. They found his wife's ethnic origin to be unacceptable.

12:3-8 The LORD heard what the sister and brother had said about Moses—the man whom God claimed was more humble **than anyone on the face of the earth** (12:3). So he called all three of them to meet him at the **tent of meeting** (12:4). This event was a rough equivalent to what people used to call "a trip to the woodshed." Somebody was in trouble. When the siblings arrived, God told **Aaron and Miriam** to step out front and center so he could brag on Moses (12:4-8).

The thing that distinguished Moses in his leadership was his ability and willingness to submit himself to the will of God. In a word, Moses was **faithful**. Therefore, the Lord had great confidence in his **servant** (12:7) and granted him an intimate relationship (12:8). God spoke with Moses face to face. Jesus promised that those who are faithful in history with the responsibilities God has given them will one day hear their Master say, "Well done, good and faithful servant! You were faithful over a few things; I will put you in charge of many things" (Matt 25:21).

12:9-10 Given God's high opinion of Moses, combined with Miriam and Aaron's criticism of their brother, God was understandably angry with his prophet's persecutors (12:9). His punishment was swift. Since Miriam was the leader of the rebellion—a fact which we can assume because she was named first in the passage, which would not have been the natural order; see 12:1), her **skin suddenly became diseased**—white as **snow** (12:10). Don't miss the appropriateness of the punishment. Miriam had condemned Moses because of the color of his wife's skin. The penalty fit her crime.

12:11-16 Aaron pled with Moses for Miriam's healing, and Moses pled with God, who **answered** his prayer (12:10-14). After **seven days** of exile from **the camp**, Miriam returned (12:15). But an important lesson had been driven home.

This lesson remains important in our own divided culture. Racism in any form is a sin, whether it is based on ethnic origin or the color of one's skin. To judge people on the basis of so-called race is to reject the truth that all human beings are created in God's image. We are all descendants of Adam and Eve.

The cross of Jesus Christ is the answer to hate rooted in perceived differences. The atoning death of Christ tears down the illegitimate divisions that separate humanity. This doesn't mean that the gospel obliterates distinctions like race and ethnicity. Rather, it means that the gospel and the power of the Holy Spirit enable us as believers—no matter where we come from or what we look like—to embrace differences because we share a common commitment to God. Because we have peace with God through Christ, we can have peace with one another and become a part of a whole new race made up of members from every tribe, language, and nation. I'm talking about heaven's new community, the church (see Eph 2:11-17).

13:1-16 Numbers 13 and 14 are two pivotal chapters in the history of God's people. They also provide modern believers with a profound illustration of the consequences of unbelief. In 1 Corinthians 10:6-10, the apostle Paul warned the Corinthians to consider the unfaithfulness of the wilderness generation of Israelites and exhorted them, "These things happened to them as examples, and they were written for our instruction." And the same can be said for other Old Testament books. They are not mere history books; they are historically true spiritual instruction manuals for God's people in all times and places. By reading and heeding them, we can avert God's judgment and enjoy his blessings.

Now that Israel was on the edge of the promised land, God instructed Moses to **send men to scout out the land of Canaan [he was] giving to the Israelites.** Moses was to **send one man ... from each of their ancestral tribes** (13:2). These twelve scouts or spies (13:4-15) included **Caleb** and **Hoshea,** who would become two great heroes in Israel's history (16:6, 8). Bible readers know Hoshea better as **Joshua** (13:16); he would one day fight the battle of Jericho and succeed Moses to lead Israel.

Interestingly, Joshua hailed from the tribe that descended from **Ephraim,** one of two sons of Joseph and his Egyptian wife (13:8; see Gen 41:50-52). The people of Egypt were descended from Noah's son Ham and his grandson Mizraim. This means the Egyptians were a Hamitic, and thus an African people (see commentary on Gen 9:18-29). **Caleb** was the son of Jephunneh the Kenizzite (13:6; see Josh 14:6); the Kenizzites were a part of the Canaanite tribes and also descendants of Ham. Moreover, Caleb also came from the tribe of Judah. Judah, the progenitor of the tribe, fathered twin sons by Tamar, who was a Hamitic descendent (see Gen 38). Thus, Hamitic (that is, dark-skinned) peoples were crucial to the program of God throughout Old Testament history.

13:17-27 Moses's instructions to the scouts contained a number of questions he wanted answered (13:17-20). What was the condition of the land? What were the inhabitants like? How fortified were their cities? The spies did their recon work and brought back the answers, both verbally and visually, supplying **a single cluster of grapes,** along with **some pomegranates and figs** harvested during the **forty days** they were gone (13:23-25). They reported that the land was awesome, figuratively **flowing with milk and honey** (13:27)—just as God had promised (see Exod 3:8, 17).

13:28-33 Nevertheless, all was not well. Though Caleb and Joshua were confident that God could deliver them the land (13:30; 14:6-9, 24, 30, 38), the other ten scouts caved in to fear (13:28-29). After seeing the size of Canaan's tall inhabitants and towering, walled **cities** (13:28-29), **they gave a negative report to the Israelites** and declared, **We can't attack ... because they are stronger than we are** (13:31-32). In spite of Caleb's attempt to quiet the crowd and rally them in favor of taking the land (13:30), the other scouts planted a defeatist mentality in the people's minds (13:33).

It's interesting that when Moses retold the story forty years later, he provided additional information on this scene that we don't have in Numbers. He said to the Israelites, "Then all of you approached me and said,

'Let's send men ahead of us, so that they may explore the land for us and bring us back a report about the route we should go up and the cities we will come to.' The plan seemed good to me, so I selected twelve men from among you, one man for each tribe" (Deut 1:22-23). In other words, this was Israel's idea, which the Lord obviously endorsed (see Num 13:1). This also tells us that initially the Israelites weren't afraid to enter the land; they only wanted to know which way to go and how to deal with the enemies they would encounter. It was only after the scouts, their "brave" leaders, wimped out on them that the people wanted to turn tail and cower in the desert. This is why God dealt with these ten men so severely (see 14:37).

14:1-2 Once the ten scouts gave a fearful report about the land, the negative thinking multiplied rapidly. **The whole community broke into loud cries, and the people wept that night** (14:1). But these were illegitimate and completely unwarranted tears, because they were crying due to unbelief. These wailing people don't deserve our sympathy. The Israelites were crying because of their refusal to move forward in the will of God. They literally preferred death in the land of slavery or death in the wilderness to trusting in God's promises (14:2).

14:3-4 The people sealed their doom by going so far as to accuse God of dragging them out of their comfortable slavery to let them die in the desert (14:3). They cried out, **Let's appoint a leader and go back to Egypt** (14:4). In other words, they had rejected God's deliverance, God's leader, and God's provision. They were cutting themselves off from their only legitimate source.

14:5-10 **Moses and Aaron**, as well as **Joshua** and **Caleb**, tried to stop the madness (14:5-6). The latter two even made an impassioned plea for the Israelites to forget their rebellion and take the promised land God had given them (14:7-8). Though Canaan's inhabitants looked impressive, the Lord had **removed** their **protection** (14:9). The God who had rained down plagues on the Egyptians and destroyed Pharaoh's army in the Red Sea was the same God who would lead the Israelites

to victory over the Canaanites. But even as they spoke, **the whole community threatened to stone them**. They were actually ready to put God's leaders to death! That's when **the glory of the LORD appeared to all the Israelites** (14:10). God had had enough of the nonsense.

14:11-16 Once again, God threatened judgment on Israel for their rebellion. As he had done before (see Exod 32:7-10), God vowed to **destroy them** and make Moses into an even **mightier nation** (14:11-12). But, as before, Moses interceded for the people. He didn't try to excuse Israel's sin, though. Instead, Moses prayed for God to spare them so that he might preserve the glory of his great **fame** among the **nations** (14:13-16).

14:17-19 The Lord had previously displayed his glory to Moses and declared the essence of his character (see Exod 34:5-7). Here Moses quoted the Lord's own words back to him: **The LORD is slow to anger and abounding in faithful love, forgiving iniquity and rebellion. But he will not leave the guilty unpunished** (14:18). Pointing to the truth of God's character, Moses pleaded with him to **pardon** them **in keeping with the greatness of [his] faithful love** (14:19).

I find it helpful to remember that Moses was a human being just like the rest of us. If you wonder why his prayers were answered while yours often are not, you may need to look no further than your desires (that is, what you pray for) and your motives (why you pray). Moses prayed for things consistent with God's character; he was deeply concerned that God be glorified. We are wise to follow his example.

14:20-25 God's Word affirms that "the prayer of a righteous person is very powerful in its effect" (Jas 5:16). We see that in action here as once more, God responded positively to the great intercessory prayer of Moses and pardoned Israel (14:20). He would not forsake the nation. Nevertheless, he swore that he would "not leave the guilty unpunished," which is a move consistent with his character (14:18): **None of the men who have seen my glory and the signs I performed in Egypt and in the wilderness, and have tested me these**

ten times and did not obey me, will ever see the land, God said (14:22-23). Because of their loyalty to God, Caleb and Joshua were exceptions to this (14:24; see 13:30; 14:6-9, 30, 38). But the rest of the Israelites were sentenced to die in the wilderness without ever entering the promised land.

14:26-38 God's verdict provides a beautiful example of poetic justice. In reality, the Israelites had sentenced themselves. In their complaining, they had lamented, "If only we had died in this wilderness!" (14:2). So God said, "You want to perish in this desert you're wandering in? You got it" (14:28-29). And to make sure they wouldn't fail to remember their part in their own demise, the length of time they and their children would still have to wander in the wilderness before that first generation had died off was determined by the length of time the rebels had spent scouting out the land. God said, **You will bear the consequences of your iniquities forty years based on the number of the forty days that you scouted the land, a year for each day** (14:34).

The ten faithless scouts who **spread the negative report** didn't even last that long. They **were struck down by the LORD** (14:37). **Only Joshua . . . and Caleb . . . remained** (14:38).

14:39-43 Once Moses read God's sentence to the people, their response was typical of those who get caught doing wrong and are suddenly "repentant," wanting everything to go back to the way it was before judgment fell, essentially trying to carry on with life as if nothing had happened (14:39-40). They were like children who realized they were in trouble and were now ready to obey to avoid punishment: "Okay, okay. We'll do what you asked us to do. Just don't ground us!" They vowed to attack the inhabitants of the land (14:40). But Moses warned them: **Don't go, because the LORD is not among you** (14:42). This brings up an important principle: Just as you can't be defeated with the Lord at your side, you can't be victorious without him.

14:44-45 Regardless of the warning, the people **dared** to enter the land, **even though the ark . . . and Moses** were not with them

(14:44). They had become too spiritually dull to understand the foolishness of such an action. And as a result, **the Amalekites and Canaanites** thrashed them (14:45).

15:1-16 Once again, God proved gracious to his people in spite of themselves. Though the Israelite generation that had left Egypt would not enter the promised land, their children would. So God provided instructions about making offerings to those who would **enter the land** that he was giving them (15:2). The offerings described in 15:3-16 were not for sin or guilt, but were to be presented as voluntary sacrifices of praise, thanksgiving, and fellowship. They were designed to show the Lord how much the people valued his covenant faithfulness. Whether it was **a burnt offering or a sacrifice, to fulfill a vow, or as a freewill offering, or at [their] appointed festivals** (15:3), these offerings of grain and animals were to be presented precisely as described (15:4-16), so that they would **produce a pleasing aroma for the LORD** (15:3).

15:17-21 The next set of regulations had to do with planting crops and enjoying harvests in the promised land. This was the principle of the firstfruits: **offer a contribution to the LORD when you eat from the food of the land** (15:19). In this case, the offering was **a loaf from your first batch of dough** as a lasting ordinance throughout Israel's **generations** (15:20-21).

15:22-31 Next came the regulations for **sin** offerings covering disobedience to God's **commands** done **unintentionally** (15:22-29). These seem to be sins of omission that **the entire community** could be guilty of without even being aware of it, which nevertheless required **atonement** so that the people might be **forgiven** (15:24-25). Except for offering a **goat** instead of a bull as **a sin offering**, an individual who sinned **unintentionally** followed the same procedure to receive forgiveness as the willful sinner did (15:27-28). The importance of the *unintentional* nature of sin that God would forgive was driven home by the repetition of this word in various forms seven times in these verses. In stark contrast, anyone who sins

defiantly . . . blasphemes the LORD. Such a person is to be **cut off from his people**. His **guilt remains** (15:30-31).

15:32-36 To drive home the point of 15:30-31 in a way the whole nation witnessed and probably never forgot, mention is made of **a man gathering wood on the Sabbath day** (15:32)—in a blatant and defiant violation of a clear command. Those who found him **brought him to Moses** (15:33). The Lord himself pronounced the sentence: **The man is to be put to death. The entire community is to stone him outside the camp** (15:35-36). It isn't hard to imagine the fear of God this execution instilled in the participants.

Defiant sin is no laughing matter. Sometimes the judgment it brings is immediate physical death (see Acts 5:1-11). And without the perpetrator placing faith in the atoning death of Jesus Christ before he or she passes, it will bring God's eternal judgment.

15:37-41 The final instruction of the chapter was particularly appropriate after what had just happened. It was a practical way to help the Israelites **remember and obey** God's holy commandments (15:40). They were to **make tassels for the corners of their garments, and put a blue cord on the tassel at each corner** (15:38). These embellishments were to serve as visible reminders of the people's covenant God, so that they would obey him.

➢ B. God's Discipline of the People
(16:1–20:13) ☙

16:1-2 Notably, the **two hundred and fifty** rebels who caused trouble at this point in the narrative weren't the "riffraff" who had previously complained about food (11:4). They were **prominent Israelite men who were leaders of the community and representatives in the assembly** (16:2). **Korah** was **a son of Levi** (16:1), meaning he was one of the Levites set apart to serve the Lord at the tabernacle. In other words, these men already held positions of great honor when they decided to make a play for further power. This story is a reminder that sin doesn't play favorites; it infects us all—the riffraff and the prominent.

16:3 The men **came** en masse with their charge (16:3), which brings to my mind the way Miriam and Aaron made complaint against Moses earlier (12:2). Korah and his followers claimed to be as holy as Moses and Aaron. Then he delivered this arrogant question: **Why then do you exalt yourselves above the LORD's assembly?** (16:3). The obvious answer was that Moses and Aaron hadn't exalted themselves at all. They had been called and appointed by the Lord.

After all that has happened to this point, one has to wonder if Korah and his followers had been paying any attention at all. Where were they when the people complained against Moses, cried for meat, stuffed themselves on quail, and then died when God struck them with the food still in their mouths in chapter 11? Were they sleeping when Miriam and Aaron challenged Moses's authority and God struck her with leprosy in chapter 12? Were they ill in their beds when the ten spies and the people defied the Lord, refused to take the promised land, and were banished to the wilderness for forty years in chapters 13 and 14? It is mind-blowing that they thought they could pull off a successful rebellion against Moses. Not one of these previous incidents or God's responses, however, penetrated the hard hearts of Korah and his followers. Their accusation even included Aaron, the high priest, suggesting that they were challenging both the religious and governmental leadership of God's kingdom structure.

16:4-7 When **Moses heard** this charge, he knew that, ultimately, Korah and crew were not sinning against him but against the Lord. So **he fell facedown** in worship and prayer before God (16:4). He must have been there long enough to get instructions from God for the event that would take place the next day at the entrance to the tabernacle. The terms were simple. **Korah** and his **followers** were to **take firepans** and **place fire in them and put incense on them before the LORD**. Then **the man the LORD [chose would] be the one . . . set apart** (16:6-7).

16:8-11 Clearly, Moses understood Korah's real motive in making the charges. He wasn't content to serve God by taking care of the **tabernacle** as a Levite. He wanted to usurp the role of a priest, even though God had given that ministry to Aaron and his family alone among the descendants of Levi (16:9-10). God had **brought [Korah] near** (16:10) by sanctifying him for ministry, but that wasn't good enough for him. He wanted the **priesthood as well**, and that meant that Korah and his friends were conspiring **against the LORD** in trying to get it (16:11).

16:12-14 Dathan and Abiram, two of the other prominent leaders who had joined forces with Korah, were so mad at Moses that they refused to answer his call to the meeting (16:12). Their claim was outrageous. In their minds, Egypt—the land in which they had been enslaved—was **a land flowing with milk and honey** (16:13). So not only had Moses yanked them out of their "paradise" in Egypt, he had failed to give them the land that had been promised. They felt Moses had so deceived the people that the only way he could hide his true intention to **kill** everyone **in the wilderness** was to **gouge out the eyes** of the rebels who knew the real truth (16:13-14). In a word, they were delusional.

16:15-17 Such nonsense filled Moses with righteous indignation. Everything Dathan and Abiram said was a lie; he had never wronged any Israelite (16:15); the opposite, in fact, was true: he had cared for and interceded for them. The time for talk was over. Aaron, Korah, and all of Korah's followers were each to **present** their firepans **before the LORD** the next day (16:16-17).

16:18-22 Korah's prominence within the camp is on display here because he was able to assemble **the whole community against** Moses and Aaron **at the entrance to the tent of meeting** (16:19). Yet his popularity did not mean his heart was right or that he was worth following. God was so angry with his faithless people at this point that he threatened once again to rid the earth of them. And he would have done so had not Moses and Aaron fallen **facedown** in intercession again (16:22).

16:18-30 God spared the community, but there would be no reprieve for Korah and his fellow rebels. The **community** at least had enough sense to listen to Moses when he warned them to get **away from the dwellings of Korah, Dathan, and Abiram** (16:23-27). Moses then announced to everyone how they would know **that the LORD** had called him to lead the people (16:28). If the rebels died a natural death, then Moses was an imposter (16:29). But if **the ground [opened] its mouth and [swallowed] them**, it would be an unmistakable sign that Korah had led a rebellion against God (16:30).

16:31-40 What followed was a terrifying scene of judgment. As Moses predicted and through the supernatural work of God, **the earth** consumed **all Korah's people** (16:32). Then it **closed over them, and they vanished from the assembly** (16:33). As for the other troublesome men, **fire** from the Lord **consumed** them (16:35). The **people of Israel** were horrified (16:34). The men's **firepans** were made into **hammered sheets as plating for the altar**, both because they were **holy** and as **a reminder . . . that no unauthorized person outside the lineage of Aaron should approach to offer incense before the LORD** lest he become like Korah and his followers (16:38-40).

16:41-45 That should have been the end of the story. But **the next day the entire Israelite community complained about Moses and Aaron**, accusing *them* of killing **the LORD's people!** (16:41). This outrageous claim serves as witness that humans can be tenacious in their willingness to deny the truth and believe a lie—no matter how obviously the facts are presented to them. God was again angry enough to destroy the nation, but Moses and Aaron **fell facedown** yet one more time, asking God to spare the people (16:45).

16:46-50 God did spare the Israelites to a degree, but sin always has consequences. God sent a **plague** among the accusers. Moses saw it beginning, and sent Aaron with a **firepan** full of **incense** out into the camp to **make atonement for** the people (16:46). He knew it wouldn't be stopped until God's holy wrath was satisfied. Aaron did as he was ordered and **the plague was halted**, but not before 14,700 more rebels had died (16:47-49).

This fresh revelation of God's fierce holiness no doubt put reverential fear in the hearts of the remaining Israelites, so that they might not sin against the Lord. It should have a similar impact on us. The Lord is a holy God. The worst thing you can do in life is fail to take him seriously.

17:1-5 Since Aaron's authority as priest had been challenged, God took a decisive step to make it clear that he had invested only Aaron's family with the priesthood. A leader from each tribe was to bring a staff forward. There would be one **for each ancestral tribe, twelve staffs from all the leaders of their tribes** (17:2). Each tribal leader's name was then written on his staff, with **Aaron's name on Levi's staff** (17:3). Then all the staffs were placed in the tabernacle **in front of the testimony** (17:4). The wooden staff of God's chosen priest would supernaturally **sprout** (17:5).

17:6-11 Moses did as instructed. When he entered the tabernacle the next day, **Aaron's staff . . . had sprouted, formed buds, blossomed, and produced almonds** (17:8). God told Moses to put the rod **back in** the tabernacle (see Heb 9:4) as a sign and a warning to the **rebels** to think twice before they challenged God's leaders again—lest they **die** (17:10).

17:12-13 It seems that the people finally got the point. They were so afraid to approach God after this incident that they wailed to Moses: **We're all lost! . . . Anyone who comes near the LORD's tabernacle will die. Will we all perish?** (17:12-13). It's interesting that we get no mention of Moses trying to soothe their fears. He was probably glad to see the fear of God finally grip their hearts.

18:1 The instructions of this chapter serve as an appropriate follow-up to the sin and judgment of chapter 16. The opening verse was a solemn reminder to Aaron, his **sons** and his **ancestral family** that they carried an awesome responsibility as priests, because they would be **responsible for iniquity against the sanctuary** and **iniquity involving** the **priesthood**. To carry out their duties in any way other than the prescribed manner would invite God's wrath and the penalty of death.

18:2-7 But the Lord reminded Aaron that he had graciously given the Levites to the priests so that they wouldn't be overwhelmed by their duties. The Levites were responsible for caring for and transporting the tabernacle and all its furnishings (18:2-3; see 4:1-33). The Levites were God's **gift** to the priests, while the priesthood itself was his **gift** to Aaron and his descendants (18:6-7).

18:8-20 The Old Testament priesthood was a full-time ministry, so God provided for Aaron and his sons to be supported from **the contributions . . . all the holy offerings of the Israelites** (18:8). Since their daily labor revolved around the tabernacle, the priests and their families were to receive provision for daily life through the offerings made by their fellow Israelites. This included portions of the meat from the **sin . . . guilt** and **presentation offerings**, as well as **all the best of the fresh oil, new wine, and grain, which the Israelites give to the LORD as their firstfruits** (18:9-12). **Everything in Israel . . . permanently dedicated to the LORD** belonged to them (18:14). They were to receive no **inheritance** of **land**, for the Lord was their **portion** (18:20).

In the New Testament era, Paul recognized a ministry principle here that applies today. Ministers of the gospel have a legitimate right to make a living from their work on behalf of the gospel—even though Paul, a tentmaker by trade, had declined to use that right himself. He said to the Corinthians, "Don't you know that those who perform the temple services eat the food from the temple? . . . In the same way, the Lord has commanded that those who preach the gospel should earn their living by the gospel" (1 Cor 9:13-14).

18:21-31 The Levites were also provided for from the Israelites' offerings (18:21-30). God set aside a **tenth** of the Israelites' offerings for the Levites to live on, since they also would **not receive an inheritance among the Israelites** (18:21, 23). But unlike the priests, the Levites had to tithe back to God on their tithe from the people **as an offering to the LORD**—a tenth of the tenth (18:26). And because it was a **consecrated** offering to God, it was to be the **best part of the tenth** (18:29). Once that was done, the Levites could eat of their offerings as their **wage in return for [their] work at the tent of meeting** (18:30-31).

19:1-2 There were many things in the life of the Israelites that had religious symbolism, and death was high on the list. It brought to mind the pervasiveness of sin and its corruption. That's why provision had to be made to cleanse the camp from the contamination that resulted from contact with a human corpse. This entire chapter is devoted to the rituals for cleansing the unclean person and even the priest who officiated at his cleansing ceremony. The priest's ritual uncleanness is just one element that made everything about this ceremony of the **red cow** sacrifice (19:2) different than any other sacrifice God prescribed.

19:3-8 The cow was **brought outside the camp and slaughtered**; notice this did not happen at the altar (19:3). And instead of its parts being separated, the sacrifice was burned intact, along with **cedar wood, hyssop, and crimson yarn** (19:5-6). The priest then had to **wash his clothes and bathe his body in water** before he could re-enter **the camp**, but even then he was **ceremonially unclean until evening**, and **the one who burned the cow** had to do the same thing and also **remain unclean until evening** (19:7-8). Every step of this cleansing ritual underscored that death is the ultimate symbol of sin; it cannot remain in God's presence. It must, by God's prescription, be washed away.

19:9-10 The elaborate process continued. Someone who was **clean** was sent to **gather up the cow's ashes and deposit them outside the camp in a ceremonially clean place**, where they were stored until they would be mixed with **water to remove impurity** (19:9). Then the one who did this had

to go through the same ritual and evening of uncleanness as the priest and the person who burned the cow (19:10).

19:11-13 These procedures were necessary to cleanse anyone who came into contact with a **human corpse**, whatever the reason. That person would be **unclean for seven days** (19:11). He was instructed to wash on **the third day and the seventh day** to be clean again (19:12). And to remind Moses, Aaron, and the entire congregation that these were not just ceremonial regulations with little spiritual ramification, God commanded that anyone who touched a corpse and failed to **purify himself** would defile the tabernacle. That person was to be **cut off from Israel** (19:13).

19:14-18 The practicality of these rules can be seen in the case of someone who died **in a tent** or came upon a dead body **in the open field** (19:14, 16), two places where a nomadic group would spend their time. Some of the **ashes** of the red cow that had been stored were **put . . . in a jar** with **fresh water** added to them (19:17). **A person** who was clean would take **hyssop, dip it in the water, and sprinkle** every item of furniture and everyone in the tent where someone had died, along with anyone who had touched any part of a corpse in the open field (19:18).

19:19-22 After the sprinkling, the person was to **wash his clothes and bathe in water, and he [would] be clean by evening** (19:19). The chapter closes with a timeless spiritual principle that we need to take to heart today: **Anything the unclean person touches will become unclean, and anyone who touches it will be unclean** (19:22). In other words, sin that isn't dealt with contaminates that which is holy; this is a principle to remember.

20:1 There's no indication of it in this verse, but **the first month** referred to here is actually in the fortieth year of Israel's wandering in the wilderness. This means the sentence God pronounced on Moses's generation had been served. We can date this confidently because Numbers 33:38 says Aaron died in that fortieth year, and his death is recorded in 20:22-27.

God had said no one from that generation, save the two faithful spies Joshua and Caleb, would enter Canaan. Sadly, that would include Aaron, Miriam, and even Moses. The nation was back **in Kadesh** where they had rebelled against the Lord and refused to take the promised land. **Miriam died and was buried there.**

Interestingly, we don't know what happened between the second and fortieth year of Israel's wandering. Those years aren't discussed in Scripture.

20:2-13 What we do know is that, unfortunately, the nation's tendency to grumble hadn't changed much during the nearly four decades preceding this written entry. And once again, when **there was no water for the community, . . . they assembled against Moses and Aaron** (20:2). The people's complaint was the same as before. They said in effect, "Why have you brought us out here to die?" (20:3-5). So Aaron and Moses took this concern to the Lord (20:6). In response, God commanded Moses to take his **staff**, gather the people, and **speak to the rock** (20:8). But at this point, Moses lost his temper. It doesn't appear that his anger was directed at God, the faithful Provider. He was frustrated with the people and said, **Must we bring water out of this rock for you?** (20:10). Then he **raised his hand and struck the rock twice with his staff** (20:11).

Don't miss what might at first seem to be only a minor breach of obedience here. Moses totally failed to obey the Lord, striking the rock instead of speaking to it. And equally jarring are his words. He publicly attributed to his own efforts the authority that should have belonged to God alone. The result would be disastrous for God's servant. Particularly because of his high spiritual position, the consequences of his sin would be grave indeed.

The people got their requested refreshment (20:11), but Moses and Aaron lost their opportunity to enter the promised land. God's indictment and sentence must have been painful to hear. He said, **Because you did not trust me to demonstrate my holiness in the sight of the Israelites, you will not bring this assembly into the land I have given them** (20:12). The failure of

Moses and Aaron to honor the Lord in word and deed meant that they, like the rest of the assembly, would die before the younger generation could possess the land they'd heard such good things about. This judgment once again directed attention to the Lord's **holiness**, which the pair had failed to honor. The scene closes with another place along the Israelites' travel route being named because of Israel's sin: **the Waters of Meribah** means "the Waters of Quarreling" (20:13).

⮞ C. Traveling from Kadesh to Moab (20:14–21:35) ⮜

20:14-17 In spite of his failure, Moses would remain Israel's leader for the rest of his life, and he knew the nation needed to press on toward Canaan. Moses hoped for passage through the land of **Edom**. He sent an appeal to Edom's king, essentially signing the spoken query with the name **"your brother Israel"** (20:14), since the Edomites were the descendants of Israelite patriarch Jacob's (that is, Israel's) brother Esau. The two people groups shared common ancestors in Abraham and Isaac. Moses rehearsed the story of Israel from the captivity in Egypt all the way down to the present day (20:15-16). He then humbly asked for permission to go through Edom, promising not to leave the path or even touch any of the Edomites' food or water (20:17).

20:18-21 In spite of Moses's entreaty, the Edomite king turned Moses down cold, even threatening military action if Israel entered his land (20:18). Moses pled with the ruler again, this time offering to pay for any water the millions of people or animals in his company drank while passing through, but the king said no again. Worse, he came out with such a large army to underscore his refusal that the Israelites had no choice but to turn away (20:19-21). (So much for that plea to brotherhood Moses had been counting on.)

20:22-29 The next event of import occurred at Mount Hor **on the border of the land of Edom** (20:23). Aaron and Moses heard Aaron's own death announcement from the

Lord. He was to die because **both he and Moses rebelled against [God's] command at the Waters of Meribah** (20:24). It must have been hard for Aaron's son **Eleazar** to take part in Aaron's burial preparations even before he had died, but that was God's command (20:25-26). The entire nation, in fact, watched as **Aaron's** priestly **garments** were removed and put on Eleazar (20:28). Then when Aaron died, **Moses and Eleazar came down from the mountain, and the entire house of Israel mourned . . . thirty days** (20:28-29). The first generation out of Egypt was rapidly coming to an end: Aaron and Miriam were both gone. Only Moses remained.

21:1-3 The next challenge on the journey was from **the Canaanite king of Arad, who lived in the Negev**, the desert region in the south of what is now called Israel. Instead of letting the Israelites pass, he attacked them and **captured some prisoners** (21:1). Israel, understandably piqued, pledged to **completely destroy** their attacker's **cities** if God gave them victory over this people (21:2). So God made Israel victorious, and **they named the place Hormah**, "Destruction," to commemorate it (21:3).

21:4-6 Moses saw that he could not deliver the people to the edge of the promised land by going straight up from the south after what had happened with Arad and with Edom. So he set out on a longer route, skirting around **Edom** to the east (21:4). But this arduous journey (unsurprisingly) frustrated the Israelites, who resorted to their favorite complaint against God and Moses: **Why have you led us up from Egypt to die in the wilderness?** (21:5). Now, the Lord had mercifully preserved them in the wilderness for forty years. To assume the worst of him at this point was scandalous. So, since they were determined to complain about dying, God gave them something to actually complain about. He **sent poisonous snakes among the people, and they bit them so that many Israelites died** (21:6).

21:7-9 When **the people** confessed their sin, **Moses interceded for** them (21:7). The Lord told him to **make a snake image and mount**

it **on a pole** so that **anyone** who had been **bitten** could look at it and recover (21:8). Moses obeyed, and thus anyone who looked at **the bronze snake** in faith that God would heal them as promised **recovered** (21:9). Much later in history, Jesus compared the lifting up of the bronze snake to his being lifted up on the cross as an antidote for the world's sin problem. It's a wonderful illustration of the necessity of looking to the Lord in faith to be saved (see John 3:14-15).

21:10-20 These verses include a listing of places along the Israelites' journey. **Beer** means "well"; it was there where God told Moses to dig a **well** (21:16). Given the constant lack of water along the way, the people must have found it a joyous moment to have an ongoing water source at their disposal. They were so happy they **sang a song** (21:17-18). Then Israel came to **the Pisgah highlands that overlook the wasteland** (21:20). The name "Pisgah" would later have great importance as the place where God would take Moses to view the promised land before his death (see Deut 34:1).

21:21-23 Before long, two more formidable enemies stood in Israel's way, beginning with **King Sihon of the Amorites** (21:21). As Moses had done with the Edomites (20:14-21), Israel asked for permission to **travel through** Sihon's **land** rather than just setting out across it, vowing not to take anything from his **fields or vineyards** or drinking **any well water** (21:22). But, just like Edom's king, Sihon refused and **gathered his whole army and fought against Israel** (21:23). This was a foolish move.

21:24-32 When attacked, Israel didn't turn away and go quietly. **Israel struck** Sihon and **took possession of his land from the Arnon River to the Jabbok** River (21:24). They even took **the city of King Sihon** (21:26). Don't miss the poem here. It is an ancient Amorite poem of Sihon's conquest of the Moabites (21:21-30). It's included because what Sihon had taken from Moab, Israel wrenched away from Sihon (21:31). (Talk about poetic justice.)

21:33-35 The other king Israel had to confront was **King Og of Bashan, who also came**

out against [Israel] with his whole army (21:33). Og was another Amorite king who presented no threat to Israel because the Lord had already given him and his land into Israel's hands. Og's defeat was a foregone conclusion before he even put on his armor. After the battle, Israel also took possession of his land (21:35).

III. ISRAEL ON THE EDGE OF THE PROMISED LAND (22:1–36:13)

⹂ A. God's Faithfulness and Israel's Unfaithfulness (22:1–25:18) ⹌

22:1 Finally, the Israelites arrived **near the Jordan** River **across from** the city of **Jericho**. This is where the book of Deuteronomy opens, as well as the book of Joshua. But the next several chapters of Numbers follow the actions of two men named Balak and Balaam rather than covering the more famous events that were to come.

22:2-6 Balak son of Zippor was Moab's king (22:4). He had seen what happened to the **Amorites**, and his people were **terrified of the Israelites** (22:2-3). Therefore, the king decided to hire Balaam son of Beor to come and **curse** the people of Israel, so that Moab could **defeat** them (22:6). Balaam was essentially a prophet-for-hire in an area where the false god Baal was worshiped. So Balak **sent messengers to Balaam** with a request: **Please come and put a curse on these people. . . . I know that those you bless are blessed and those you curse are cursed** (22:5-6).

Apparently, Balaam had a reputation for getting results through the words he spoke. But the Lord's reputation is flawless: if he says something will happen, it will happen. This is important to understanding what happened next because God had promised Abraham many years before that he would, "make [him] into a great nation. . . . [He would] bless those who bless [Abraham], and curse anyone who treats [Abraham] with contempt" (Gen 12:2-3). These promises would extend to the Israelites, Abraham's blood descendants. Balak's plan, then, was failed from the start. If God is determined to bless you, no one's words to the contrary can overrule him.

22:7-12 Balak sent **elders of Moab and Midian** to Balaam **with fees for divination in hand** (22:7). It's interesting that although Balaam practiced God-forbidden forms of sorcery, he refused to go with these men until he had received an answer from **the Lord** about it (22:8). The implication seems to be that he intended to do whatever God told him to do, no matter how good the money was—which is exactly what he did at each point in the story. So that night God graciously condescended to appear to this sorcerer, who generally was not committed to living in a manner pleasing to him (see Rev 2:14), and asked, **Who are these men with you?** (22:9). Balaam relayed what he had been asked to do to Israel, and God warned him not to curse his people whom he had blessed (22:10-12).

22:13-20 Balaam obeyed and sent his guests away empty-handed, but Balak wouldn't take no for an answer. He **sent officials again who were more numerous and higher in rank than the others**, with the promise of even greater reward if Balaam would **put a curse on** Israel as asked (22:15-17). But Balaam was still hesitant until he consulted with God again and was told to **go with them**—not to curse Israel, but to do what God told him (22:18-20).

22:21-22 It was while Balaam was on his way to meet Balak that the prophet and his **donkey** encountered God, who was so **incensed** that Balaam **was going** to Moab that he appeared in the road as **the angel of the Lord . . . to oppose him** (22:21-22). We get insight into what motivated this surprising reaction in 2 Peter 2:15. It says, "Balaam . . . loved the wages of wickedness." So it seems that, even though Balaam claimed to follow the Lord's instructions and even did when it suited him, he really was a mercenary prophet at heart.

Though God had given Balaam permission to go with the elders from Moab, God knew that he cared nothing for Israel and that out of greedy motivation the man was prepared to curse Israel for the reward—despite God's instructions.

22:23-30 This duplicity within the prophet led to the curious and humorous scene between an animal with keen spiritual sense and a human being who was as dumb as a rock spiritually. Balaam's **donkey saw the angel . . . standing on the path with a drawn sword in his hand** and was rightly scared off the road. **Balaam**, eager to get to his payday, **hit her to return her to the path** (22:23). After this situation repeated itself twice, God—unexpectedly and supernaturally—opened the donkey's mouth. She asked, **What have I done to you that you have beaten me these three times?** (22:28). Don't miss that what follows is a conversation between a faithful donkey and an unfaithful prophet (22:29-30).

22:31-35 Finally, God **opened Balaam's eyes** to see **the angel of the LORD** who was blocking his path (22:31). As Balaam lay facedown **in worship**, the Lord explained to the prophet that his "dumb" donkey had saved his life (22:31-33). Chagrined, Balaam started getting his thinking straight and offered to turn around and go home (22:34). But God had determined to display his glory to the Moabites and Midianites and to bless his people through Balaam. So he told him to **go with the men**, but to **say only** what God told him to say (22:35).

22:36-41 Balak had been waiting a while for Balaam to show up. He was shaking in his sandals at the sight of the Israelite horde camped in the desert at the edge of his land, ready to devour his culture like a swarm of locusts descending on a barley crop. So he was a little edgy when Balaam finally arrived (22:36-37). Balaam, however, wasn't ruffled by Balak's irritation. He even warned him that he was only going to say what God put in his **mouth** (22:38). Balak ignored this, offered a sacrifice to his false god Baal, and hustled Balaam to a place called **Bamoth-baal**, "the High Places of Baal," (22:40-41). Thus, Balak

was calling on an idol to curse Israel and expected Balaam to serve as his spiritual megaphone.

23:1-3 Once they arrived, Balaam told Balak to **build . . . seven altars . . . and prepare seven bulls and seven rams** (23:1). And when this was done, they offered the sacrifices (23:2). Then Balaam told Balak to stay behind while he went to **a barren hill** to seek the message that the Lord might have him deliver (23:3). Now, this is amazing! Repeatedly Balaam pointed out that he could do nothing without the approval of God—Creator God whom the Israelites worshiped—and yet Balak never objected or complained, "What are you doing consulting with the God of the Israelites? They're the enemies I'm paying you to curse!" Clearly he put little stock in the Lord's say in the matter.

23:4-10 God did meet with Balaam, essentially putting a message in his mouth for **Balak, who was standing there by his burnt offering with all the officials of Moab** (23:4-6) waiting for the prophet to return. Then Balaam delivered the first of his four poetic messages, or oracles, of blessing on Israel. First, he rehearsed why he was there: he'd been summoned to **denounce Israel** (23:7). Yet he asked how anyone could **curse someone God has not cursed** and **denounce someone the LORD has not denounced** (23:7-8). Then he considered Israel's vast numbers, a fact that was likely common knowledge, and said that even to be identified with Israel in **death** was a blessing (23:10).

23:11-12 Clearly, this was not what Balak had in mind when he hired Balaam to curse his enemy! He was stunned to hear what was coming out of the man's mouth and felt betrayed. He said, **I brought you to curse my enemies, but look, you have only blessed them!** (23:11). To this Balaam could only reply, **Shouldn't I say exactly what the LORD puts in my mouth?** (23:12). Now, that should have been the end of Balak's bad idea, the point at which he let the matter go. But he wasn't ready to give up. Surely the money he had promised the prophet would eventually coax him to do as requested.

23:13-17 Balak thought a change of scenery would do Balaam some good (23:13). So the Moabite king took the sorcerer to **Lookout Field on top of [Mount] Pisgah**, where Balak once more **built seven altars, and offered a bull and a ram on each** in hopes of influencing his god to curse Israel (23:14). Once again, Balaam went off alone to seek the Lord, who again **put a message in his mouth** (23:15-16). Surprisingly, this time Balak even asked, **What did the Lord say?**, when the prophet returned (23:17). (He apparently held out hope that the God of the Israelites had finally decided to curse his own people.)

23:18-20 Balaam answered with another poetic blessing on Israel that began with a personalized call that should have made the king catch his breath: **Balak, get up and listen; son of Zippor, pay attention to what I say!** (23:18). Then, under the inspiration of the Holy Spirit, the idolatrous prophet uttered a glorious statement of God's immutable nature (23:19). Because of who God is and the promises he had made, Balaam had been given a command to bless Israel. In other words, since God had decreed blessing for his people, there was nothing Balaam could do. **I cannot change it**, he said (23:20).

23:21-26 Balaam went on to say that since God brought Israel **out of Egypt**, the nation had the strength **of a wild ox**. She was a force against which **no magic curse** or **divination** like the kind of tricks Balak was trying to employ could work against her (23:22-23). When Balaam had finished this speech, Balak basically said to him, "Look, if you can't say something bad about Israel, don't say anything at all!" (23:25). But in this matter Balaam was working for a higher King (23:26).

23:27-30 It seems that Balak was either a slow learner or simply a desperate leader, because he was actually willing to give his plan a third try. He took Balaam to a third location (23:28). **Maybe it will be agreeable to God that you can put a curse on them for me there**, he said (23:27). In the ancient Near East where these men lived, the peoples often believed that certain gods had power over certain geographical areas. This makes it less surprising that Balak thought a new location might somehow change the results he was hearing.

24:1-4 This time Balaam changed the routine by simply looking out over Israel, which was encamped below according to the careful pattern God had laid out (24:1; see commentary on Num 1:47-50). When he saw the vast nation **encamped tribe by tribe, the Spirit of God came on him** (24:2). Then the prophet essentially described the Lord's influence on him. His **eyes** were **opened**, he heard **the sayings of God**, he saw a **vision from the Almighty**, and he fell **into a trance with his eyes uncovered** (24:2-4). In this state Balaam uttered his third oracle, another poetic tribute to God's hand of blessing on Israel.

24:5-7 Though looking down on Israel as a nomadic city of tents, he pictured Israel as a beautiful land of abundance and prosperity (24:6). He also referred to Israel as a **kingdom** (24:7), even though their first king (Saul) would not rule until hundreds of years in the future.

The mention of **Agag** (24:7) is curious. A future king of the Amalekites named Agag would be executed by the prophet Samuel during King Saul's day (see 1 Sam 15). However, in the ancient Near East, kings often carried the same throne name down through the decades—as we see in the case of Egypt's Pharaoh or Philistia's Abimelech. So Amalek's current king probably bore the name Agag, too. Assuming that this is so, we should consider that this wasn't the first prophecy regarding the Amalekites. This nation had attacked Israel after the exodus (see Exod 17:8-16). So the Lord had promised at that time, "I will completely blot out the memory of Amalek under heaven" (Exod 17:14). Balaam, then, now prophesied Israel's future dominance over the Amalekite kingdom.

24:8-9 In the rest of the oracle, Balaam emphasized God's strength in bringing Israel out of **Egypt** and defeating **enemy nations** before them (24:8). The latter was exactly what Balak was afraid of. Balaam concluded with a chilling announcement: **Those who curse [Israel] will be cursed** (24:9). By seeking to curse Israel, King Balak had sealed his own fate.

24:10-14 Finally, Balak had heard enough. He **became furious with Balaam** and sent him home without any payment (24:10-11). Nevertheless, Balaam calmly repeated everything he had said from the beginning about his obligation to say whatever God told him to say (24:12-13). Before the two men parted, Balaam had one more oracle of blessing for Israel and a word of warning for Balak (24:14).

24:15-25 Balaam's final oracle was the most remarkable of all, because it included a prophecy of the coming of Israel's Messiah. Incredibly, he made predictions about the future rising of the **star . . . from Jacob** and a **scepter . . . from Israel**; these are references to the Christ, a descendant of Israel and the "morning star" of Revelation 22:16 (24:17). He also foresaw Israel's victories over **Moab** (Balak's people), the Edomites, and the Amalekites (24:17-20). Then, with his mission complete, Balaam returned home— as did Balak (24:25). The cursing of Israel had failed.

25:1-3 Balaam may have spoken the blessing of the Lord on the Israelites, but his true character surfaced afterward. Balaam was responsible for what we will see happen here in chapter 25. It seems that even though he was unable to curse Israel, Balaam still offered advice to her enemies. We read this in Numbers 31:16: "At Balaam's advice, [the Midianite women] incited the Israelites to unfaithfulness against the LORD in the Peor incident." And later, the risen Lord Jesus would say this about the matter, "You have some there who hold to the teaching of Balaam, who taught Balak to place a stumbling block in front of the Israelites: to eat meat sacrificed to idols and to commit sexual immorality" (Rev 2:14). So, in spite of what Balaam said in chapters 22–24, he was a wicked enemy of the true God and his people.

Don't miss that since Israel's enemies couldn't get the Lord to be unfaithful to his people, they chose to lead his people to be unfaithful to him. And as a direct result of this maneuver, God's people **began to prostitute themselves with the women**

of Moab (25:1). **The women invited them to the sacrifices for their gods, and the people ate and bowed in worship to their gods** (25:2). The Lord had protected his people by refusing to let Balaam curse Israel, but now Israel was essentially cursing the Lord through actions. Therefore, God's **anger burned** (25:3).

25:4-6 The Lord's judgment was swift. He said, **Kill each of the men who aligned themselves with Baal** (25:5).

In light of this obviously public execution and the national **weeping at the entrance to the tent of meeting** that it brought, it is almost beyond comprehension that an Israelite man would dare to march his Midianite girlfriend into camp and into his tent **in the sight of Moses and the whole Israelite community** (25:6). Yet that's exactly what happened. Spurred on by lust, this man dared to flout God and his law in front of everyone.

25:7-13 That was too much for **Phinehas son of Eleazar, son of Aaron the priest** (25:7). He was **zealous** for God's holiness (25:11), so he left the service of repentance at the tabernacle, **took a spear**, ran into the man's **tent, and drove it through both the Israelite man and the woman**. (This is a clear indication that they were having sexual relations when he found them; 25:7-8).

In verse 9 we gain an additional insight into the Lord's wrath against Israel's unfaithfulness. God had apparently sent a **plague** among the people for their sin. Phinehas's righteous action **stopped** the plague, but only after **twenty-four thousand** Israelites died (25:8-9). God praised Phinehas for his zeal and promised a **perpetual priesthood** to **him and his future descendants** (25:12-13). This meant that the Aaronic priesthood would remain with Phinehas and his family.

25:14-15 The **Israelite man** whom Phinehas executed was the son of a **Simeonite** leader; the woman was **the daughter** of a **tribal leader in Midian** (25:14-15). If the men involved in these sins were mostly Simeonites, this could explain the drastic decrease in their number of males from the first census of "59,300" (1:23) to "22,200" (26:14). **Zimri**

(25:14) was from a prominent family and brought great destruction on his people with his blatant sin. Thus, once again Scripture warns that our sin is never committed in a vacuum; it always affects others.

25:16-18 The Moabites and Midianites appeared together in the Balaam narratives because they lived in the same area and were both involved in hiring Balaam to curse Israel (see 22:4, 7). The Israelites didn't attack the Moabites, who were descendants of Abraham through Lot. But the Lord commanded Israel to **attack the Midianites** because they had been involved in inciting the Israelites to worship Baal (25:16-18; see also 31:15-16).

☙ B. Preparations for Entering the Promised Land (26:1–30:16) ☙

26:1-4 By this time most of Moses's generation had died according to God's decree, as Israel prepared to end their wilderness wanderings and enter the promised land. So it was time to take a census of the new generation, counting males **twenty years old or more who can serve in Israel's army** (26:1-2). Israelite soldiers would be needed to battle the inhabitants of Canaan. The census was taken on the east side of the **Jordan** River, across from **Jericho** (26:3). This was the first fortified city Israel would encounter in Canaan, and what happened there would mark Israel's first victory in the long-anticipated conquest (see Josh 6:1-27).

26:5-11 The rest of the chapter is primarily a report of this new census recorded tribe by tribe and family by family. But it also contains several interesting side notes. The first concerns a family among the Reubenites that included **Dathan** and **Abiram**. These were the two men who had joined **Korah's followers** in their rebellion **against the LORD** (26:9; see 16:1-50). **The earth opened its mouth and swallowed them.** Therefore, the pair serves **as a warning sign** (26:10). The follow-up note that **the sons of Korah did not die** (26:11) acknowledges that grace had been extended, allowing Korah's family line to continue. Sons that did not follow his

rebellion would have an inheritance in the promised land.

26:12-56 The census records continued until the total of fighting men was calculated: **601,730** (26:51). This figure was quite close to the original count of "603,550," taken almost four decades earlier (1:46). So even though the exodus generation died off and Israel suffered a number of severe judgments on their way to Canaan, God prospered his people and they were ready to cross the Jordan at full strength. The census was followed by the casting of a **lot** to determine where each tribe's inheritance in the promised land would be located (26:55-56). The actual dividing of the land would come later.

26:57-62 Since the Levites had no land inheritance because of their service to the Lord, they weren't included in that census; they had their own. The three main Levite clans—**Gershonite**, **Kohathite**, and **Merarite** clans were counted (26:57).

Here Moses also included a note about his own family: **Kohath was the ancestor of Amram. The name of Amram's wife was Jochebed, a descendant of Levi, born to Levi in Egypt. She bore to Amram: Aaron, Moses, and their sister Miriam** (26:58-59). He also listed Aaron's family and the number of Levites in the new generation who would eventually be available for service: **23,000, every male one month old or more** (26:60-62).

26:63-65 Chapter 26 is a passage in which names are important. So it's fitting that the chapter ends with two more significant names. Their significance is first enhanced by the historical note that of all those Israelites whom **Moses** had **registered** in the new census, **there was not one ... who had been registered by Moses and the priest Aaron when they registered the Israelites in the Wilderness of Sinai** four decades earlier, because the **LORD** had said to them that they would all die (26:63-65). Only two men of Moses's generation stood firm in faith and were still alive at the new census: **Caleb** and **Joshua** (26:65). These two, who had witnessed the plagues of Egypt and God's every provision in the wilderness, would enter the land.

27:1-2 As the lot was cast to determine where the tribal lands would be located, a problem came up. A man named **Zelophehad** from the tribe of **Manasseh** died without a son but left behind five **daughters** (27:1). Under Israel's laws of inheritance, in which property was reckoned through the male head of the family, these women were facing a bleak future when the nation divided up the promised land. So they approached **Moses, the priest Eleazar, the leaders, and the entire community** at the door of the tabernacle to present their case (27:2).

27:3 The girls' mention that their father died for **his own sin** doesn't necessarily mean that he did something terrible. (His daughters were careful to say he was not part of **Korah's** rebellion.) More likely, they were referring to the fact that he died like most of the members of his generation had, under God's discipline for their collective disbelief.

27:4-11 The question that Zelophehad's daughters brought to Moses and Israel's elders, then, was legitimate: **Why should the name of our father be taken away from his clan? Since he had no son, give us property among our father's brothers**, they implored (27:4). God agreed with their position, and he established a new rule of inheritance that covered this family's dilemma and underscored his care not just for men, but women too (27:5-11).

27:12-14 Now that Israel was on the verge of crossing the Jordan and entering Canaan, it was time for God to appoint Moses's successor. God took Moses to Mount Nebo in the **Abarim range** just across from Jericho where he could look out over **the land that** God had **given the Israelites** (27:12). Seeing the land from afar was the best Moses could hope for, since he and Aaron had **rebelled against** God at **Meribah-kadesh** by angrily striking the rock instead of speaking to it, thereby failing to uphold God's **holiness** before the people by publicly exercising an authority that did not belong to them (27:14; see 20:1-13).

27:15-17 To Moses's credit, he didn't argue for a second chance or lament, "Woe is me." Instead, his immediate thought as death neared was to make a plea that God would give his people a godly, qualified leader who would lead them with courage (27:15-16). He asked for someone to **go out before them** as their military commander, who would also direct them like a tender and caring **shepherd** (27:17).

27:18-20 God had just the man in mind, Moses's trusted lieutenant Joshua—**a man who has the Spirit in him** (27:18). Certainly Joshua was already well-known and certainly well-respected among the Israelites for his close association with Moses, his record of bravery regarding Canaan years before, and his advanced age. All he lacked was the public stamp of approval from the Lord through a ceremony in which Moses would symbolically transfer his mantle of leadership. God commanded Moses to have Joshua **stand before . . . the whole community** for a commissioning service, so that **the entire Israelite community** would **obey him** (27:19-20).

27:21-23 From that point onward, Joshua would work hand-in-hand with **the priest Eleazar**, who would **consult the Lord for him** to determine God's will so Joshua could carry it out (27:21). Moses did as God commanded (27:22), and Israel's future leadership was secured.

28:1-3 Chapters 28–29 include examples of what the new generation of Israelites needed to know as they prepared to conquer Canaan and settle down in the land. These chapters outline various offerings and festivals that had been prescribed before, but needed to be reviewed and established again to ensure that Joshua's generation knew what God expected.

One important element of these offerings was that whether they were daily, weekly (on the Sabbath), monthly, or presented for annual festivals such as Passover or Pentecost, each offering was to be made **at its appointed time** as **a pleasing aroma** to the Lord (28:2). The offering of the sacrificial animals also emphasized to the worshiper (and to those who would read about the offerings) the tremendous offense that sin is to God. Only blood can atone for it and bring the sinner into fellowship with him.

28:4-8 The first of these sacrifices were the daily burnt offerings, requiring **one lamb in the morning and the other lamb at twilight**, along with the specified grain and drink offerings at both times. The burnt offerings had been given to Israel at Sinai as the means by which God would come down to his people, fellowship with them, and be their God as he smelled the aroma of their pleasing sacrifices (see Exod 29:42-46).

28:9-10 Next came the regulations for the weekly **Sabbath** offerings (28:9-10), which involved an entirely new set of animal, grain, and drink offerings in addition to the day's regular burnt offerings. If any Israelite thought worship was cheap or easy, or that the Lord would accept any leftover his followers tossed his way, these regulations were intended to shake him or her into reality. (Tragically, many Christians offer their leftover time, talents, and treasures to the same God who has always demanded the first and best of his people.)

28:11-15 The offerings required on the first day of each month took Israel's worship requirements to a whole new level with the presentation of **two young bulls, one ram**, and **seven male lambs a year old**, in addition to enhanced **grain** and **drink** offerings (28:11-14). These observances became festive occasions called New Moon festivals. Provision was also made for sin with the sacrifice of **one male goat** as **a sin offering** (28:15).

28:16-25 The **Passover** was the holy festival that came **in the first month, on the fourteenth day** to commemorate Israel's freedom from Egyptian bondage (28:16). The people were to **eat unleavened bread . . . for seven days** as their parents and grandparents had on the night of the first Passover so they could leave Egypt in haste. In this instance too there were substantial offerings to be made, like those on the New Moon festivals, except that they were offered every day for **seven days** (28:17-22, 24). And once again, all of these Passover offerings

were in addition to **the regular** (daily) **burnt offering** (28:23).

28:26-31 The final instruction of this chapter concerned the feast of **firstfruits** or **Festival of Weeks**, which occurred fifty days after Passover: this is also called "Pentecost" (28:26). It was a harvest festival that required the same special offerings as a New Moon observance. And although the fact isn't emphasized here, the people were also to bring the firstfruits of their fields to celebrate it—clearly pointing forward to the day when they would take the promised land and establish themselves there.

29:1-6 Next the Lord gave Moses instructions for offerings associated with three more holy observances: the Festival of Trumpets, the Day of Atonement, and the Festival of Shelters. **The first day** of the **seventh month** was a special day that later came to be known as Rosh Hashanah ("the head of the year"). On this date, the Jewish New Year, no **daily work** was allowed. A key feature of the event was the blowing of trumpets (29:1). An offering equal to the regular New Moon offerings was to be made, along with **the monthly and regular burnt offerings** (29:6). Notice that the requirement for acceptable worship never decreases with the addition of special days and even weeks; it always increases.

29:7-11 The Feast of Trumpets was followed by the Day of Atonement ("Yom Kippur" in Hebrew); it was and still is the most sacred day on the Jewish calendar. It was to be a day of confession and mourning for sin. It was also the one day of the year when the high priest entered the most holy place to sprinkle blood on the mercy seat of the ark of the covenant to make atonement for the people (see Lev 16:1-34). It was a day of **self-denial** in the form of fasting (29:7). And on it, a **male goat** was to be sacrificed **for a sin offering** (29:11). Importantly, for believers in Jesus Christ, full atonement for sin was made in his substitutionary death on the cross, which is why such sacrifices as those we read about here no longer need to be offered (see Heb 9:28).

29:12-38 The remainder of the chapter deals at length with the week-long celebration of the Festival of Shelters (or "Tabernacles" or "Booths"). During it, the Israelites were to leave their homes and live in shelters of sticks and greenery as a reminder of their forebearers' years of wilderness wanderings and as a commemoration of God's promised deliverance out of that season. Since this festival lasted longer than most, there were specific instructions for each day's observance. Not surprisingly, the offerings required were huge, since this festival celebrated the end of the harvest year and was designed to express thanksgiving to God.

The first day's offerings were **thirteen young bulls, two rams, and fourteen male lambs a year old**, a **grain offering**, a **male goat as a sin offering**, and the daily **burnt offering** (29:13-16). The offerings for the second day were different in two respects, with **twelve young bulls** being offered instead of thirteen, and **drink offerings** being specified (29:17-18). This reduction in the number of bulls continued at one each day (29:20-32) until **the seventh day**, when **seven bulls** were sacrificed (29:32). The **eighth day** of the festival was like the first in that the Israelites were to **hold a solemn assembly** and refrain from **work** while still presenting the prescribed offerings (29:35).

29:39-40 The chapter concludes with a reminder to the people that making all these sacrifices, and keeping the festivals **at [their] appointed times**, was to be done in addition to the offering of any **vow and freewill offerings** an Israelite worshiper might feel led to bring to God out of gratitude for his goodness or in a desire to make a special promise to him (29:39).

The many offerings and sacrifices required of the Israelites were costly. But the people's contributions to God didn't compare with the grace the Lord had shown the nation by choosing them as his own, redeeming them from bondage, and entering into a covenant relationship with them.

30:1-2 Vows to do something or to abstain from something for the Lord's sake were entirely voluntary. So God was entirely within his rights to demand complete faithfulness from an Israelite who made one. Such a person **must not break his word** (30:2). This admonition alone, in fact, should have been enough to keep people from half-heartedly making promises to the Lord. But many years later, Solomon gave this solemn advice about vows to make sure Israel didn't take their words to God lightly: "God ... does not delight in fools. Fulfill what you vow. Better that you do not vow than that you vow and not fulfill it" (Eccl 5:4-5).

30:3-5 At this point in the text, there's a great example of God's kingdom agenda for the home in operation here. The situation presented involved a woman who was living **in her father's house during her youth** (30:3)—that is, she was not yet an adult and was under parental authority. If such a girl made a vow to the Lord that put her under some obligation, her father had the authority either to let the vow stand—in which case his daughter was bound to it—or to declare it void and **release** her from the obligation (30:4-5). What we see here, then, is a divine protection for an underage woman who spoke rashly. Her daddy got the last word. This was a loving provision. It's also a reminder that Israelite women needed the covering of the covenant through their fathers before their release to the protection and covering of their husbands.

30:6-16 The following case (30:7-8, 10-15) also comes under the umbrella of illustrating the divinely appointed authority in the home. If an unmarried woman was bound by a vow that her father approved, she would carry that vow into her marriage, where her husband had the same choice as her father regarding whether or not she'd have to keep it from that point. If he canceled her vow, the Lord released her from it too (30:6-8). By contrast, **every vow a widow or divorced woman [put] herself under [was] binding**: she would make her own calls (30:9).

Interestingly, a husband had to act on the day he heard about his wife's vow (30:12). If he delayed and then decided later that he didn't want his wife to keep her vow, he became **responsible for her commitment** (30:15) because by that point the vow had been in effect for some time. This is yet another illustration of God warning his people not to make promises to him lightly.

⇝ C. Midianites Defeated and Transjordan Settled (31:1–32:42) ⇜

31:1-2 Moses's last act as leader of the Israelites was to fulfill God' command to **execute vengeance . . . against the Midianites**. When this was complete, Moses would be **gathered to [his] people**—that is, he would breathe his last and be buried (31:2). God's vengeance against the Midianites was going to be fierce because of their part in seducing Israel into the degrading worship of Baal (see 25:1-18).

31:3-6 Israel, however, would need only a fraction of her troops, since God was leading this campaign in a special way. This was to be a limited war. So Moses only called for **one thousand men . . . from each Israelite tribe** to go against Midian (31:4-5). Each tribe had been affected by the sin of Baal worship, so each tribe would be involved in cleansing the source of this sin. **Phinehas son of Eleazar the priest**, who had been zealous for God's holiness in the event to be avenged (25:6-13), accompanied the troops, bringing along **the holy objects and signal trumpets** (31:6).

31:7-12 The Israelites **waged war against Midian, as the LORD had commanded Moses, and killed every male**—that is, every soldier (31:7). One of those killed along with the soldiers and **the Midianite kings** was **Balaam son of Beor**, who suffered the consequences of his sin (31:8; see 31:16; Rom 6:23). But in spite of these victories, the Israelite troops failed to follow the Lord's command. They **took the Midianite women and their dependents captive** as they destroyed the Midianites' dwellings and took **all the spoils of war** (31:9-12).

31:13-18 When **Moses** and **Eleazar** and **all the leaders of the community** went out to meet the returning troops, **Moses became furious with the officers** (31:13-14). He couldn't believe what he saw. Some of the women whom they had captured were the very ones who had **incited the Israelites to unfaithfulness** in the first place (31:15-16).

They had lured Israelite men to commit sexual immorality in worshiping Baal, resulting in the very plague on the people that killed twenty-four thousand Israelites (see 25:1-18). So Moses gave the following command: **Kill every male among the dependents and kill every woman who has gone to bed with a man** (31:17). In other words, those who had not participated in the immorality of the Peor incident were permitted to live (31:18). The execution of the others was a necessary purge of evil lest the Midianites' ways be allowed to further influence—and endanger—God's covenant people.

31:19-24 The soldiers had become ceremonially unclean in carrying out their duties, so they and their captives had to remain **outside the camp for seven days** (31:19). This was necessary so that they could ritually **purify** themselves and their belongings (31:19-20). Items **such as gold, silver, bronze, iron, tin, and lead** (presumably part of the soldiers' plunder) was to **pass through fire** and then be purified **with . . . water**. Those items that could not **withstand fire** were to be purified with water alone (31:22-23). After a week and the washing of clothing, the soldiers could **enter the camp** (31:24).

31:25-30 Next came the counting and dividing of the spoil brought back from Midian. The soldiers who had fought the battle received half of all the bounty, with God requiring a **tribute** of **one out of every five hundred people, cattle, donkeys, sheep, and goats** (31:25-29). The **entire community** received the other half of everything, with the Lord's **tribute** being **one out of every fifty from the [living spoil]** (31:27, 30).

31:31-47 Moses and Eleazar did as the LORD commanded, with the soldiers' shares being described in 31:32-40. Moses also made sure to give **the tribute to the priest Eleazar as a contribution for the LORD** (31:41). Then came the distribution of **the Israelites' half**, which is totaled up in 31:42-47.

31:48-50 The Midianite campaign had been a tremendous success. But the leaders of the troops who had fought had one more blessing to report—and a gift of thanks to offer. They informed Moses that not one of their soldiers was **missing** after the battle. None had been lost (31:49). They recognized how incredible this was and wanted to make a sacrificial offering of thanks to God for his divine protection. So they **presented . . . an offering of the gold articles each man found**—armlets, bracelets, rings, earrings, and necklaces—to make atonement for themselves (31:50).

To suffer no casualties in a battle of this size is unheard of, and these soldiers knew it. Their offering was given entirely of their own freewill, and it was over-the-top generous because they knew more than anyone else what God had done for them and their fellow troops. The "atonement" they spoke of was probably not a reference to some sin, but rather a recognition that God's faithfulness to them was far more than they deserved.

31:51-54 Moses and . . . Eleazar received the gold—all **420 pounds** of it (31:51-52). It was placed in **the tent of meeting as a memorial** to the Lord (31:54). Such an offering recognized that everything the Israelites possessed came from the hand of the Lord and served as a reminder that he is able to supply every need. God loves it when giving is done willingly, cheerfully, and generously (see 2 Cor 9:6-8).

32:1-5 While the Israelites were still camped on the east side of the Jordan River opposite Canaan, the tribes of Reuben and Gad looked around and **saw that the region was a good one for livestock**—of which they had huge numbers (32:1). The territory was firmly in Israel's hands, so these tribes came to Moses and the other leaders with a special request: **Let this land be given to your servants as a possession. Don't make us cross the Jordan** (32:5). In other words, they were happy to stay right where they were while the rest of the tribes entered promised-land proper.

32:6-7 It's not clear whether the **Gadites and Reubenites** had given any thought to how their request would impact their

fellow tribes who had to enter Canaan and do battle. But Moses gave them a quick dose of reality. He asked, **Should your brothers go to war while you stay here?** (32:6). With these words he implicitly questioned their courage. Did they really prefer the land on the east side of the Jordan? Or were they actually trying to avoid plunging into battle in support of their fellow Israelites? Moses's words got more pointed: **Why are you discouraging the Israelites from crossing into the land the LORD has given?** (32:7). He wanted them to recognize that their decision would affect the rest of the nation deeply.

There is a principle here that is applicable to the church. Some people who claim to follow Christ insist that their similar actions—whether they are choosing to worship at home each Sunday when they could just as easily join a local fellowship or deciding not to serve in their churches but only to sit and soak—are not hurting anyone. But sinful choices do affect those around us—whether directly or indirectly. We must take care not to cause our fellow Christians discouragement. A discouraged Christian is an unfruitful Christian.

32:8-15 Moses used the request of the Gadites and Reubenites as an opportunity to offer a quick history lesson. He compared their willingness to forgo the promised land to their ancestors' devastating failure to trust God and enter the land at **Kadesh-barnea** despite seeing the bounty of the land in the grapes from the **Eshcol Valley** (32:8-9). God's **anger burned** as a result of that unfaithfulness (32:10, 13). He'd **made them wander in the wilderness forty years** until that entire generation died (32:13). And now it looked like their children wanted to follow in their wicked footsteps! So Moses didn't hold back. He said, **If you turn back from following [God], he will once again leave this people in the wilderness, and you will destroy all of them** (32:15).

32:16-19 That led these tribal leaders to change tactics. Judging by their reaction and their offer to lead the way in battle, it does appear that they had not thought through all the implications of their plan when they'd proposed it. The leaders of Reuben and Gad asked permission **to build sheep pens** for their **livestock** and **cities for [their] dependents** before they, the fighting men, joined their brothers in battle across the Jordan (32:16). They would stay on the job until the promised land was secure in Israel's hand (32:17-18). Further, they would not expect **an inheritance . . . across the Jordan**; they would be content with their lands in Transjordan (32:19).

32:20-24 Moses was willing to accept their terms (32:20-22), but he strictly warned them of the consequences of failing to stand by their promise. His words are chilling: **If you don't do this, you will certainly sin against the LORD; be sure your sin will catch up with you** (32:23).

Sin's consequences can't be escaped. But through trusting in the atoning sacrifice of Jesus Christ, you will escape God's eternal judgment, that doesn't mean you will escape all the consequences for sin in this life. As Paul reminded the Galatians, "God is not mocked. For whatever a person sows he will also reap" (Gal 6:7).

32:25-32 The Gadites and Reubenites accepted Moses's terms and reaffirmed their intent to leave their dependents and livestock in Gilead, cross the Jordan, and fight (32:25-27). Therefore, since Moses knew he wouldn't still be around by the time all this took place, he instructed **the priest Eleazar, Joshua . . . and the family heads** to give these tribes the land on the east side of the Jordan as their possession—as long as they fulfilled their promise (32:28-29). If they failed, they were to **accept land in Canaan** (32:30).

32:33-42 Then, in anticipation of the fulfillment of their promises, Moses gave Gad and Reuben their inheritance—the former kingdoms **of King Sihon of the Amorites and . . . King Og of Bashan**. But Moses also included another Transjordan group: **half the tribe of Manasseh** in this allotment (32:33). Apparently, they shared a desire to dwell east of the Jordan, since they had defeated a number of enemies there and captured their land (32:39-41).

⇥ D. Exhorting a New Generation and Dividing the Land (33:1–36:13) ⇤

33:1-4 Moses kept a highly detailed travelogue of the Israelites' journey from the time they left **the land of Egypt** (33:1). It began **the day after the Passover** when **the Israelites went out defiantly in the sight of all the Egyptians** as they **were burying every firstborn male** that God had struck (33:3-4).

33:5-36 Not long after that, **Israel traveled from Pi-hahiroth and crossed through the middle of the [Red Sea] into the wilderness** (33:8)—which, unfortunately, would be their home for decades to come. Moving farther down in the text, Moses noted that the Israelites camped in **the Wilderness of Zin (that is, Kadesh)** (33:36), which is a name that would live in infamy for Israel. It was because of their rebellion there that the nation would wander in the wilderness for forty years.

33:37-49 At **Mount Hor**, Moses's brother **Aaron . . . died** at 123 (33:37-39). After mentioning that, Moses noted the opposition of **the Canaanite king** who tried to stop the people's progress, only to be badly defeated (33:40; see Num 21:1-3). Moses also recorded the nation's encampment **in the Abarim range** (33:47); there God allowed Moses to view the promised land from a distance after he was told he would not be permitted to enter (27:12-14).

33:50-52 The remainder of this chapter includes Moses's instructions and exhortation to God's people about entering the promised land. He emphasized the total spiritual depravity of the Canaanites they would encounter, as well as the Lord's command concerning them. The Israelites were to **drive out all the inhabitants of the land . . . destroy all their . . . images, and demolish all their high places** (33:51-52). There could be no compromises. The nation had entered a covenant relationship with the Lord alone, and through their obedience he would judge the Canaanites for many years of extreme wickedness.

33:53-56 Once God's people occupied the land, it was to be divided among them (33:54). Moses's message from the Lord then ended with a stern warning: **But if you don't drive out the inhabitants . . . those you allow to remain will become . . . thorns for your sides; they will harass you in the land where you will live. And what I had planned to do to them, I will do to you** (33:55-56). In other words, if Israel were to disobey their covenant God and fail in their assignment, those inhabitants would prove to be a snare to them. Israel would ultimately adopt their idolatrous ways and fall under God's judgment. If Israel didn't drive out the nations, God would drive out Israel.

Tragically, this warning would prove prophetic. The Israelites would indeed fail to fully dislodge the Canaanites and would suffer all manner of military and spiritual defeats in the centuries ahead. Eventually, after years of covenant unfaithfulness—and years of the Lord's abundant patience—they would be cast from the land in stages.

34:1-15 Before the transition of leadership from Moses to Joshua, the Lord gave Moses essential details about dividing up the land so that there would be no confusion among the tribes. He provided precise boundaries for the land (34:1-15) and identified the leaders from the tribes who would oversee the distribution (34:16-29).

The Lord identified the **southern** (34:3-4), **western** (34:6), **northern** (34:7-9), and **eastern** (34:10-12) borders of the promised land. Each tribe was to receive a portion of the land **by lot**, which was a bit like drawing straws. However, this was a process for only **nine and a half** of the **tribes** (34:13). The other **two and a half tribes** (Reuben, Gad, and half the tribe of Manasseh) would receive—as they had requested—the land on the east side of the Jordan River (34:13-15; see 32:1-42).

34:16-29 Since Moses would not be there to oversee the land distribution, God reiterated that **the priest Eleazar and Joshua** were his chosen leaders in the matter (34:17). God gave Moses the name of **one leader from**

each tribe to distribute the land to help them with this task and to ensure that each tribe was fairly represented (34:18-29).

35:1-5 The tribe of Levi didn't receive a land inheritance because the Lord was their portion—that is, they had been chosen from among all the tribes to serve the Lord at the tabernacle. Nevertheless, they still needed places to live and pasture for their livestock. That's why God instructed Moses to **command the Israelites to give cities out of their hereditary property for the Levites to live in** (35:2). Thus, the Levites were to have dwellings scattered throughout the land of Israel.

Not only did this provide practically for the Levites, but it was also spiritually strategic. If they lived in cities that were dispersed throughout the territories, the Levites were thus accessible to all the people. They were well positioned to "teach the Israelites all the statutes that the LORD [had] given" (Lev 10:11).

35:6-15 Among the **forty-eight** cities for the Levites, **six** were to be designated as **cities of refuge** (35:6-7). As the name implies, these were places where **a person who [killed] someone unintentionally [might] flee . . . until he [stood] trial** (35:11-12). These cities were to be equally divided so that those living throughout the area could access them (35:14).

35:16-29 The cities of refuge were intended to provide sanctuary for those whose actions unintentionally caused death. But there was no refuge for the person who committed premeditated murder. Fittingly, this required the **death** penalty (35:16). The idea behind the descriptions given here is the presence of **hatred** and **malicious intent** (35:17-21). In such cases, **the avenger of blood himself [was] to kill the murderer** (35:19). This individual was a family member of the victim. It was his responsibility to carry out justice.

In the case of an accidental death or an incident of manslaughter—when death was caused **without hostility** and **without malicious intent** (35:22)—the cities of refuge provided a safe haven for the guilty party until the case could be heard and emotions could cool. **The assembly** of the people of Israel would **protect** the person from the avenger and **judge** his case (35:24-25). The defendant, however, had to be brought to court from his city of refuge—which would expose him to the avenger temporarily. If the court ruled for the defendant, he would be safely taken back to his city of refuge, where he was required to live **until the death of the high priest** (35:25) after which he was free to return home. In this mention we see that there was an atoning effect in even the high priest's death in that it signaled a cleansing and forgiveness of past sins in the nation and a fresh start for people who had accidentally taken a life. Importantly, if the person violated the terms of his house arrest by leaving his **city of refuge** before the high priest's death, **the avenger** could kill him without guilt (35:26-28). The wise King Solomon would one day employ a similar precedent in his dealings with Shimei, who'd tried to stone his father, King David (see 1 Kgs 2:36-46).

35:30-32 Another provision to prevent miscarriages of justice was the necessity of multiple witnesses in a murder case so that no one would be **put to death based on the testimony of one** (35:30). Once a murder had been established and the guilty one convicted, however, no amount of money could buy him his life back. The *only* acceptable payment a murderer could make was to forfeit his own life for the death of his victim (35:31). And neither could a person confined to a city of refuge pay a fine to cover his penalty and go back home **before the death of the high priest** (35:32).

35:33-34 At the end of the chapter, we learn the bottom line reason for these ordinances: **Bloodshed defiles the land.** There could be **no atonement** to cleanse the **land . . . except by the blood of the person who shed it** (35:33). As with any other circumstance that resulted in uncleanness or defilement, the reason it could not be tolerated was because the **LORD** himself resided **among the Israelites** (35:34). God is holy; therefore, he requires holiness from his people.

36:1-4 In the final chapter we meet a family we have encountered before, the five daughters of Zelophehad (see 27:1-11). The first time they went to Moses, they were concerned that they would have no inheritance in Israel since their late father had no sons and they, as females, weren't in line to receive any land. Moses had obtained a favorable ruling from God for the girls: If no male could be found, the land should be given to the nearest relatives. It was a good day for the daughters.

This time, it wasn't Zelophehad's girls who raised a concern but **the family heads from the clan** (36:1). The problem they faced was significant for a nation in which a family's land was a sacred grant from the Lord that was never to be permanently sold. (One generation used it and then passed it along to the next, as if it were on lease to a family from God.) The male leaders of the clan to which Zelophehad's daughters belonged realized that if the women married outside of their tribe—while owning their fathers' land—that land would pass to other tribes (36:2-4).

36:5-13 Moses recognized that what they said was **right** (36:5). So he sought the Lord and returned with a ruling for this case that would become a statute for all of Israel. Zelophehad's daughters were free to **marry anyone . . . provided they marry within a clan of their ancestral tribe** (36:6). Furthermore, **no inheritance belonging to the Israelites [was] to transfer from tribe to tribe** (36:7). That meant that Israelite daughters who owned an inheritance were to marry within their own clan (36:8). So **the daughters of Zelophehad** obeyed (36:10-12).

In the book of Numbers, Moses has taken readers from Sinai, where the Lord made his covenant with Israel, to the edge of the land he had sworn to give them. Though the people—including Moses—continued to fall into unfaithfulness, God remained faithful to his promises. He would preserve his people, drive out their enemies, and settle them into the land.

But, in the days to come, he would also be faithful to his greatest promise of all: "A star will come from Jacob, and a scepter will arise from Israel" (24:17). And sure enough, the messianic King, Jesus Christ, came to atone for sin, defeat his enemies, and give the riches of his grace to his people. "Every one of God's promises is 'Yes' in him" (2 Cor 1:20).

DEUTERONOMY

INTRODUCTION

Author

DEUTERONOMY 1:1 TESTIFIES that the book's recorded words were spoken by Moses. Moreover, later biblical books quote from Deuteronomy and attribute the words to Moses (see Matt 19:7; Acts 3:22; Rom 10:19). Surely a final editor added some things, like the account of Moses's death in Deuteronomy 34:5-12, but since Moses was Israel's God-appointed leader who wrote things down at God's command (see Num 33:2), we have no reason to doubt the traditional Jewish and Christian position that Moses is the author of this book.

Historical Background

After the Lord delivered the nation of Israel from Egyptian slavery, he led them to the Sinai Wilderness, entered into a covenant with them, and gave them his law. One year later, they departed Sinai, and God led them to the edge of the promised land. However, because the people feared the inhabitants of Canaan, they refused to take possession of it. Therefore, God caused the Israelites to wander in the wilderness for forty years as punishment for their unbelief in his ability to provide—until every Israelite from that generation had died. At the end of the book of Numbers and the beginning of the book of Deuteronomy, Israel was once again on the edge of the promised land. They were encamped across the Jordan River, not far from the Canaanite city of Jericho. Here Moses reviewed the Lord's covenant and laws with the new generation. The title of the book comes from the Greek translation of the Old Testament (the Septuagint). *Deuteronomy* means "second law" (*deutero nomos*) or "repetition of the law."

Message and Purpose

This fifth and final book of the Pentateuch is Moses's farewell address to the second generation of Israelites, those whose once enslaved parents came out of Egypt on their way to the promised land of Canaan. Deuteronomy is structured like the treaties of that day, in which a king would spell out the laws, standards, and stipulations by which he would rule the vassals, or servants, who made up his nation. God was (in a very real sense) Israel's King, the people of Israel were his servants, and the standards of his kingdom had been spelled out in the covenant he made with them at Sinai.

Moses's message to this new generation of Israelites was that their choice to obey or disobey God's law—to submit to their King or not—would determine the kind of life they would have once they entered Canaan. In fact, the people's obedience to God would be the very thing to bring them the blessings of the covenant that stretched all the way back to Abraham—land, national identity, and a promise of bringing blessing to the other nations. But tied to the choice they faced were curses for disobedience, too. Deuteronomy is thus a covenantal book.

Through it, God tells his people that he will bond with them based on their adherence to the covenant of his kingdom.

www.bhpublishinggroup.com/qr/te/05_00

Outline

DEUTERONOMY

I. THE FIRST ADDRESS BY MOSES —HISTORICAL RECAP (1:1–4:43)

1:1-5 The spotlight in Deuteronomy landed on Moses, but not for his sake. He was speaking on the Lord's behalf as Israel's lawgiver and leader, the man through whom the Lord had liberated his people and revealed his covenant. When the people sinned against the Lord, Moses burned with righteous indignation and was zealous for God's holiness (see Exod 32:17-20). When the Lord threatened Israel with destruction for their sin, Moses interceded for them (see Exod 32:11-14). He had led the people of Israel for forty years, never shrinking back from delivering God's messages to them. And here, as he faced the end of his life, **the words Moses spoke to all Israel** were once again **everything the Lord had commanded him to say to them** (1:1, 3).

Moses began to explain God's **law** to the people (1:5). Why was this review necessary? One reason is the sad historical lead up to his message. Years before, the Israelites had received God's law, departed Mount Sinai, and arrived at Kadesh-barnea. From there they were supposed to enter the promised land and conquer it. But it was now **the fortieth year** since that day (1:3). At Kadesh-barnea, the people had rebelled against the Lord and refused to enter the land. Therefore, God had decreed that everyone from Moses's generation, those twenty years and older, would die in the wilderness for failing to trust him.

So Deuteronomy opens with a new generation of Israelites standing at the edge of the promised land, this time at **Moab** (1:5).

These children of the previous generation needed to hear afresh how Moses's generation had failed to obey God, and what God expected of them as they prepared to lay hold of their inheritance as his people. Only by renewing their faithfulness to God and his covenant could they hope to conquer the land and live there in peace and prosperity.

1:6-8 As he reviewed the nation's history, Moses started at the right place. He said, **The Lord our God** (1:6). This God, the only true God, had redeemed Israel from Egyptian bondage, just as he had promised their ancestor Abraham (see Gen 15:13-14). He had chosen them for himself and entered into a covenant with them—a sacred agreement in which he would be their God and they would be his people. The Lord had delivered them, revealed himself to them, and promised his faithfulness to them. In response, they were to give their faithful obedience to him—and him alone.

When the Lord **spoke** to the Israelites **at Horeb** (which is another name for Mount Sinai, where the Ten Commandments were given), he commanded them to leave and go to **the land** he promised to **Abraham, Isaac, and Jacob and their future descendants** (1:6-8). But notice that even though he had **set the land before** them, Israel still had to **take possession of** it (1:8). This is an important principle for modern believers to embrace. Whatever God promises, he delivers. But laying hold of those promises still requires our obedience. We do not inherit the promises of God by sitting in our easy chairs. We love, work, serve, pray, and fight the good fight of the faith because this is our kingdom role. We follow our King's agenda, trusting that he will follow through with his blessings.

1:9-18 Though Moses was a faithful leader, he couldn't do it all by himself. The people of Israel were too **numerous** for him to bear all of their **troubles, burdens, and disputes** himself (1:9-12). So **leaders** —**wise, understanding, and respected men**—were appointed for every **tribe** to help Moses (1:13-14). Thus, every person in the community would have a place of appeal to obtain a hearing, with Moses ruling only on the most **difficult** cases (1:15-18; see Exod 18:13-27).

1:19-25 The Israelites' journey from Horeb to Kadesh-barnea was anything but easy. They had to cross a **terrible wilderness** (1:19). But once they reached the edge of Canaan, Moses could point to it and say, **See, the LORD your God has set the land before you. Go up and take possession of it ... Do not be afraid** (1:21). It was at that point that they sent twelve scouts—one from each tribe—to **explore the land** (1:22-24). When they returned from their survey, the scouts declared, **The land the LORD our God is giving us is good** (1:25).

1:26-28 But things rapidly went downhill from there. The people **rebelled against the Lord** and **grumbled** when ten cowardly men among the scouts claimed the inhabitants were giants in cities **fortified to the heavens** (1:26-28). They actually had the audacity to claim that God had brought them out of Egypt to let the Amorites slaughter them— because he hated them (1:27). Years later, the Lord would testify, "When Israel was a child, I loved him, and out of Egypt I called my son" (Hos 11:1). But the people of Israel, the very ones for whom he so tenderly and graciously provided, described the *love* of God as *hatred*.

1:29-36 Moses tried to rally the people with the reminder that the Lord would go before them and fight for them, as he had done in Egypt and in the wilderness (1:29-31). But the Israelites' fear had made them deaf and blind to God's goodness. Sadly, they **did not trust** him (1:32). This provoked him to such anger that he **swore an oath** that none of that **evil generation** would enter the **good land** he had promised (1:34-35). Only **Caleb** (1:36) and **Joshua** (1:38), the two scouts who responded faithfully when confronted with seeming obstacles, would receive an inheritance in the promised land.

1:37-38 Even Moses wasn't spared this sad fate. The Lord also prohibited him from entering the land (1:37). Instead of speaking to a rock so that it would provide water (as God commanded), Moses had struck it with his staff, also effectively claiming to share in God's glory for the provision of the water (see Num 20:7-11). In mentioning this incident, Moses wasn't blaming the people for his sin but reminding them that their grumbling had been so contagious that it caused him to sin too (1:37). Joshua, Moses's faithful servant, would lead the people in his place (1:38).

1:39-46 On their first opportunity to do so, the people of Israel refused to enter the land, claiming that their children would be **plunder** for the nations living there (1:39). Ironically, God turned their excuse against them. In reality they would be excluded from the promised land and die in the wilderness, while their children inherited the land (1:39-40). Realizing their error, the people reacted to the sentence by foolishly trying to conquer Canaan. They got thrashed because God wasn't with them (1:41-44). They **returned** to camp in tears (but without any genuine repentance). Because of their rebellious hearts, God ignored their **requests** (1:45). That's a warning to all of us that he wants to be approached with sincere repentance and humility.

2:1 Following the failure at Kadesh, God told the Israelites to turn back and head into the **wilderness**, where they wandered for the next few decades. It had already been well over a year since they had left Egypt, so from this point the nation had to spend "thirty-eight years" wandering around (see 2:14). Moses recalled how they encountered three groups of relatives along the way, whom the Lord told them not to pick a fight with: the Edomites, the Moabites, and the Ammonites. The former group descended from forefather Jacob's (that is Israel's) twin brother Esau. The latter two were related to the patriarch Abraham since they were descended from his nephew Lot.

2:2-7 The first people Israel faced were the Edomites, **the descendants of** the brother of Jacob (2:4). God told the Israelites not to **provoke them**, because he had given their land to them as their **possession** (2:5). If they required any **food** or **water**, they were to pay Edom for it (2:6). As it turned out, though, the Edomites refused to give Israel *anything* or even to allow them to pass through their land (see Num 20:14-21). Nevertheless, God had **blessed** Israel and **watched over** them. Even though they were a nation of over two million people milling around in an **immense wilderness**, the Lord saw to it that they **lacked nothing** for **forty years** (2:7). Through this mention Moses wanted to instill in the new generation the confidence that just as God had been faithful to their parents, so he would be faithful to them.

2:8-12 From the land of Edom, Israel traveled to the territory of **Moab** and received the same command from God not to **provoke** the Moabites, since they were **the descendants of Lot,** Abraham's nephew (2:8-9). Previously, a very tall and impressive-looking people group lived in Moab, but they had been driven out (2:10-12).

2:13-15 Moses then recalled God's command to cross the **Zered Valley** in Moab. He reminded his listeners that the **entire generation of fighting men** had not died in the wilderness from natural causes. On the contrary, **the Lord's hand was against them, to eliminate them from the camp until they had all perished** (2:13-15). This is a solemn reminder that no matter how healthy, wealthy, or powerful you are, you will not succeed if you reject the Lord's will. His hand will be against you. Conversely, if you submit

to his kingdom agenda, his hand will be with you to help you in your circumstances.

2:16-23 When God's judgment on the older generation had been carried out, Israel was ready to move on in preparation for entering the promised land (2:16). Once again, they were to **cross the border of Moab**, thus bringing them near the territory of **the Ammonites** (2:18-19). Like his half-brother Moab, the Ammonite patriarch Ben-ammi was a son of Lot through his daughter (see Gen 19:30-38). Israel was not to **provoke** his descendants either, for God had given them their land (2:19). The land of the Ammonites, too, had been previously inhabited by a **numerous** and **tall** people who had been driven out (2:20-23). This served as a clear message of encouragement to Israel that they could similarly displace the seeming giants that dwelled in the land of Canaan.

2:24-30 The next movement recounted by Moses was the taking of Transjordan (the land east of the Jordan River across from Canaan), beginning with the defeat of the **Amorites' King Sihon** (2:24). Through this victory, God would start making people **tremble** in **fear** because of the Israelites (2:25). Moses had made **an offer of peace to King Sihon** (2:26-29). But the Lord knew in advance that the Amorite king would reject peace with Israel. **God had made his spirit stubborn and his heart obstinate in order to hand him over to** Israel (2:30).

This brings to mind the way God hardened Pharaoh's heart back in Egypt, so that he could display his great power and glory. The hardness of Pharaoh's heart, though, began with Pharaoh. He repeatedly defied God, stubbornly setting his heart against him (see Exod 7:22; 8:15, 32). Finally, God gave Pharaoh what he wanted and hardened his heart even further (see Exod 9:12). Don't think then, that when God made Sihon's heart obstinate, Sihon had been a righteous man previously. He'd been obstinate to begin with. And a day arrived when God used his obstinacy to bring righteous judgment upon him.

2:31 Notice what God told the Israelites in this passage: **I have begun to give Sihon and his land to you. Begin to take**

possession of it. This raises the question, Did God give it to them, or did they have to take possession of it? The answer is both. Though God makes promises to his children, we must obey him to secure those promises. God feeds the birds of the sky (see Matt 6:26), but they don't sit in their nests waiting for a special delivery of worms. They go out and obtain the food that God has provided. This is a lesson for us all.

2:32-37 When King Sihon came out to confront Israel with his army, God **handed him over**, and Israel **defeated** him (2:33). The Amorites were **destroyed**, and Israel took all of their possessions (2:34-35). **There was no city that was inaccessible** (2:36). Compare this victory to what is recorded in 1:28, where the faithless scouts complained that the Canaanite cities were "fortified to the heavens." Moses wanted the new generation, which was about to cross over into Canaan and face those fortified cities, to know that nothing could stand in their way if they gave themselves fully to obeying the Lord's instructions.

3:1-7 Another Amorite king whom the Israelites encountered was **Og of Bashan**. Like Sihon, Og **came out against** Israel **with his whole army to do battle** (3:1). And as in Sihon's case, God had already determined to give the king, **along with his whole army and his land**, into Israel's hands (3:2). Israel **destroyed** all the people and captured all **sixty cities** in Og's kingdom, which also had the same **high walls** as Sihon's (3:4-6). High-walled cities were no barrier when God decided to hand an enemy over to his people. The most spectacular example of that truth would come later at the city of Jericho (see Josh 6:1-21).

3:8-11 Israel defeated Sihon and Og and took possession of their vast lands on the east side of the Jordan (3:8). Then Moses added another parenthetical comment. **King Og** was the last **remnant of the Rephaim**, a people group of gigantic physical size. **His bed was made of iron** and was **13 1/2 feet long and 6 feet wide** (3:11). Clearly, he was no puny king. And his take down testifies to the truth that the Lord is

no puny god. Israel need not worry about the size of the enemies they would have to face. They needed only to remember the size of their God.

3:12-20 Moses then recounted the dividing of the Transjordan among the **Reubenites**, the **Gadites**, and **half the tribe of Manasseh** (3:12-13). These groups had asked to dwell on the east side of the Jordan rather than accompany the other tribes into Canaan (see Num 32:1-42). Yet they promised to send soldiers to help their brothers conquer the promised land before returning home (3:18-20). **Jair**, a member of the tribe of Manasseh, was singled out for his valiant efforts in taking land for his family (3:14).

3:21-22 Next came a discussion regarding the transfer of leadership—something that must have been very difficult for Moses. He reminded Joshua of what he had seen with his **own eyes**. Israel had vanquished the two kings, Sihon and Og, and captured their lands. But there was a larger purpose in their destruction than mere land acquisition: **The LORD [would] do the same to all the kingdoms [they were] about to enter** (3:21). In other words, Moses said, "Don't worry about the enemies in the promised land, Joshua, because you've just seen what God can do to those who oppose him. **Don't be afraid of them, for the LORD your God fights for you**" (3:22). (You too can be courageous to follow God's will for your life because he has your back.)

3:23-25 Since he had disobeyed the Lord, Moses had been forbidden to enter the promised land (see Num 20:1-13), but it seems the encouraging victories he had led in Transjordan may have given him hope that God was open to changing his mind. So Moses, whose intercessory prayers had been effective previously, **begged** God to let him **cross over and see the beautiful land** (3:23-25).

3:26-28 But God's "no" was indeed "no." He, like a parent putting his foot down, said, **That's enough! Do not speak to me again about this matter** (3:26). All he allowed Moses to do was to ascend Mount **Pisgah** and view the land from afar (3:27). Nevertheless, though Moses could not go with them, the Lord continued to provide leadership for his people. **Joshua** (mentioned now for the third time in the book; see also 1:38; 3:21) would lead Israel and **enable them to inherit [the] land** (3:28). To inherit what God was giving them required obedience, and Joshua was the man for the job.

4:1-4 Chapter 4 is an important hinge in Deuteronomy, pivoting from Moses's retracing of Israel's forty-year journey in the wilderness to the lessons the nation needed to learn from this retelling. This chapter transitions to Moses's formal teaching of God's laws and commands, which covers the majority of the book (5:1–26:19). Before this second address begins, Moses finishes his first address to Israel with a strong call to respond to God with obedience.

To the new generation of Israelites, Moses had a message with two simple but powerful points: obey God and worship him alone. In their short time as God's covenant people, Israel had repeatedly failed at this. Moses reminded them of one example with the mention of **Baal-peor** (4:3). This was the infamous incident in which the Israelite men were enticed into physical and spiritual adultery with Moabite and Midianite women, worshiping the false god Baal (see Num 25:1-18; 31:13-16). God **destroyed** every Israelite **who followed Baal of Peor** (4:3). Yet Moses made a clear contrast between that group and his hearers: **But you who have remained faithful to the Lord your God are all alive today** (4:4). Obedience to the Lord brings life and blessings; disobedience brings death and cursing. That's the message of Deuteronomy.

4:5-8 One of the purposes of God's **statutes and ordinances** (4:5) was to teach Israel to be a light to the nations around them. If the Israelites were faithful to follow these commands, **the peoples** surrounding them would marvel at their wisdom and understanding (4:6). After all, their **righteous statutes and ordinances** were without equal (4:8). This pointed not to the greatness of Israel—but to the greatness of their God, who is **near** to his people **whenever we call**

(4:7). This is a wonderful indicator that when you faithfully follow the agenda of your divine King, you will experience the comfort you need, and he will receive the glory he deserves. Moreover, those who don't know him will take notice that there is something different about your approach to life and will seek to learn about it.

4:9 To fulfill their role and live as God's covenant people, Israel dare not **forget the things** they had **seen** and been taught. The human mind has an amazing tendency to forget God's goodness and fall into sin again and again. One of the ways to help the people avoid this pitfall involved them regularly teaching God's ways to their **children** and **grandchildren**—that is, they needed to establish a godly legacy within their homes. Living faithfully as God's people requires that we transmit our faith to our children.

4:10-12 Israel faced the constant temptation to copy the idolatry of the surrounding nations, as they had at Baal-peor. To help the new generation remember the greatness of Israel's God, Moses recounted that fear-inducing experience when God gave them his law at **Horeb** (4:10). The **mountain** was **blazing with fire** and **enveloped in a totally black cloud** (4:11). In the midst of this experience, God **spoke**. Yet the people saw no **form** but only heard a **voice** (4:12). In other words, the people had been given no image to associate with their deity. God did not reveal himself in a physical form; therefore, Israel was not to worship physical images—idols of their own creation.

4:13-14 Instead of revealing an image of himself, the Lord revealed his own character and his will for his people in the form of **the Ten Commandments** (4:13). If Israel were to **cross into and possess** the land, keeping God's Word would be essential to their ability to flourish (4:14). It would show their reverential awe of him, their holy fear. When we fear God, we take him seriously—so much so that we fear disobeying his Word.

4:15-20 Since idolatry had posed such a problem for Israel in the past, and since the land they were entering was filled with it, Moses spent extensive time warning the Israelites against idolatry's consequences (4:15-31). He pointed out that on the day Israel entered a covenant with the Lord, they saw no **form** of the Lord—no shape of a person or animal (4:15). To worship an **idol** in the shape of anything in all creation would only corrupt them; the Lord was not to be represented in such a manner (4:16-19).

4:21-24 Again Moses reminded the people that he wouldn't accompany them into **the good land** (4:21). In his exasperation with the people's complaining, Moses had disobeyed God (see Num 20:1-13). So he knew he wouldn't be there to help them focus their minds and hearts on God when they reached their destination. Instead, he urged them **not to forget the covenant** God had made with them by making **an idol** (4:23). **For the LORD your God is a consuming fire**, he said, **a jealous God** (4:24). Idolatry is spiritual adultery, a theme that will be highlighted throughout much of the Old Testament. Like a faithful husband whose wife has broken the marriage covenant, the Lord expresses a righteous jealousy for his people when they turn from his love and their own promises to cozy up to strangers.

4:25-28 If Israel were to forsake their covenant God for **an idol in the form of anything**, his judgment on them would be severe (4:25-26). Sadly, though, these words of warning would become a prophecy. Eventually, God would indeed **scatter** Israel **among the peoples** of Assyria and Babylon because of their unfaithfulness (4:27).

4:29-31 Yet even in that extreme state of distress, God would not completely abandon his people. Moses said, **You will search for the LORD your God, and you will find him when you seek him with all your heart** (4:29). This, in fact, is a promise that is still available today. Though you may have strayed far from God, if you turn to him in true repentance, he will not hide from you but will allow himself to be found. He is **a compassionate God** who does not forget his **covenant** promises (4:30-31).

4:32-40 Moses invited the Israelites to consider their circumstances. **From the day God created mankind**, had any other people experienced what Israel had? he asked (4:32). Had any other nation **heard God's voice** or been miraculously rescued by him? (4:33-34). Never. Israel had been shown such amazing grace, so that they **would know that the LORD is God; there is no other** (4:35). What should the knowledge of this unique and incomparable God drive his people of all times to do? To **keep his statutes and commands . . . so that [we and our] children after [us] may prosper** (4:40).

4:41-43 The cities of refuge were places where an Israelite **who committed manslaughter** could **flee** for protection until he could receive a trial (4:42; see Num 35:9-29). There were to be a total of six such cities throughout Israel, three on the west side of the Jordan River and three on the east. Since the people already occupied the land to the east of the Jordan, **Moses set apart three cities** there (4:41): **Bezer** in Reuben's territory, **Ramoth** in Gad's, and **Golan** in Manasseh's (4:43).

II. THE SECOND ADDRESS BY MOSES —COVENANT OBLIGATIONS (4:44–26:19)

➣ A. The Ten Commandments and the Greatest Command (4:44–6:25) ☙

4:44–5:2 After summarizing Israel's history since departing Egypt, Moses began to explain the covenant obligations that Israel owed the Lord. In this long section that comprises most of the book of Deuteronomy (4:44–26:19), Moses reviewed for the new generation God's laws and commands. They were to **learn and follow** these **statutes and ordinances** that Israel had received (5:1-2). Notice the imperatives: Learn *and* follow.

Bible study is good and necessary. But if you get no further than acquiring an intellectual knowledge of the Bible, you haven't gone far enough. A football team might have an expert understanding of the rules of the game. But if the coach and players fail to put those rules into practice, the only thing they will obtain will be a losing record.

5:3-4 Moses said, God **did not make this covenant with our fathers, but with all of us who are alive here today** (5:3). But actually, God did make the covenant with their fathers—that is, with the previous generation at Sinai (Horeb). Moses had stated this plainly (4:10-14, 45). In fact, he said it in the previous sentence! (5:2). So this should be viewed as a rhetorical point. In effect Moses was telling those standing before him, "This isn't merely your father's covenant I'm talking about; this is *your* covenant. Your fathers are gone; now *you* are God's covenant partners. He expects obedience from *you*." When God **spoke** with the previous generation of Israelites **from the fire on the mountain** years before (5:4), he was speaking to all future generations.

5:5-6 As Israel's mediator, Moses had stood between them and the Lord to receive his commands for them (5:5). Here he declared those commands once again. The preamble to the commands sets the context for all the rest: **I am the LORD your God, who brought you . . . out of the place of slavery** (5:6). The law was not given for Israel's redemption; they had already been redeemed from Egypt when he gave the law to them. No one is saved by keeping the law, then. Rather, the law provided the means for a redeemed people to express their reciprocal love for the holy God who had saved them.

5:7-21 (See Exod 20:1-17 for commentary on the Ten Commandments.)

5:22-27 When God had given his Ten Commandments, the people had reacted in terror at his fearsome presence. The **loud voice** of the Lord, combined with the **fire, cloud, and total darkness on the mountain** from which he spoke, was too much for them (5:22-23). They had seen God's **glory and greatness**, and surprisingly it hadn't killed them (5:24). But they weren't convinced this would last! They felt sure they would **die** if they heard the Lord's voice any longer (5:25). So they begged Moses to represent them

before God, hear his commands, and relay everything he said: they wanted a buffer. With Moses serving as their mediator, the Israelites promised to **listen and obey** (5:27).

5:28-33 Unfortunately, the Lord recognized that Israel's actual obedience wouldn't prove to be as strong as their words. It would take the new covenant sacrifice of Jesus Christ to make it possible for those who trust him to receive new hearts with the capacity to obey him steadfastly (see Heb 8:7-13). Nevertheless, the Lord agreed to have Moses serve as an intermediary for the people (5:30-31). So Moses urged the new generation to do what the previous generation had promised (see 5:27): **Do as the LORD your God has commanded you . . . so that you may live, prosper, and have a long life in the land you will possess** (5:32-33).

6:1-3 Many years later, King Solomon would write, "The fear of the LORD is the beginning of wisdom" (Prov 9:10). But Moses already knew this truth. Fearing God (reverencing and respecting him) was necessary if Israel was to obey him and **have a long life** (6:2). He therefore urged them to **be careful to follow** God's instructions so that they would **prosper and multiply** (6:3).

6:4-9 These verses are known in Judaism as the *Shema*, which is the Hebrew word that begins 6:4; it means "listen, hear." Moses was calling the people to sit up and take notes on what he was about to say because of how important it was. In fact, Jesus would later call it "the greatest and most important command" (Matt 22:37-39). Moses said, **Listen, Israel: The LORD our God, the LORD is one. Love the LORD your God with all your heart, with all your soul, and with all your strength** (6:4-5). It was vital that the people get this right because if the Israelites were going to survive and thrive in the promised land, the family unit would have to become the primary place where faith in and love for the Lord was modeled and transferred. Parents are to teach God's commandments and statutes regularly to their children in the everyday events of life (6:7-9).

It's good for families to read through devotionals together and have formal teaching times. But such things need to be combined with the powerful witness of a godly lifestyle that incorporates God's Word in each day's routine. Notice how regularly Israel was told to speak of the things of God: **when you sit in your house and when you walk along the road, when you lie down and when you get up** (6:7). That purposeful approach to spiritual training, that effort to welcome the Lord to be part of all aspects of life, is how parents can transfer to their children a biblical worldview so that God is their point of reference as they navigate choices. Such was God's agenda for his kingdom people in Moses's day, and it's still true today. This responsibility doesn't rest with the government, schools, or even ultimately with the church. *The family* carries the primary responsibility for passing along the torch of faith as the church supports parents in the work. The primary role of the home is to foster gospel evangelization and to disciple children.

Many Jews took the command to **bind** God's words on their **forehead** literally (6:8). They wrote Exodus 6:4-9 on tiny scrolls, placed them in small boxes called phylacteries or frontlets, and tied them to their foreheads. This was the practice that Jesus would have in view when he condemned scribes and Pharisees who enlarged their phylacteries in order to draw attention to themselves (see Matt 23:5).

6:10-12 Writing God's Word on their minds and loving him with their entire being would be essential for the Israelites, who were about to enter into a land of instant prosperity. There were abundant **cities . . . houses . . . cisterns . . . vineyards and olive groves** there—none of which Israel had built, filled, dug, or planted (6:10-11). All this new generation of Israelites had to do was take the land and enjoy its riches. (This is a picture of how God's promises, while in our reach, must be grasped with our hands of faith.) But Moses had spent forty years in the wilderness with these people's parents! And he knew the sinful human tendency to **forget** God's past deliverance and provision when times are good (6:12).

6:13-19 Moses warned what would happen if Israel ceased to **fear the LORD** and turned instead to **follow other gods** (6:13-14). In

his anger, the Lord would **obliterate** them (6:15). This taking over of Canaan, then, was no game. Israel was to represent the one true and living God to the surrounding nations. His glory was at stake. So Moses warned them, **Do not test the LORD your God as you tested him at Massah** (6:16).

Massah means "Testing." This was the place where Israel had complained against Moses and the Lord because they had no water (see Exod 17:1-17). How quickly they forgot God's ability to do miraculous things with water, as he had done at the Red Sea. Moses warned the people not to test God as Israel had done at "The Place of Testing," a location that had borne the name of their rebellion since that time. Yet despite this fierce warning, the Israelites could be confident that obedience to God would bring the prosperity and protection he had promised (6:17-19).

6:20-25 Moses then returned to the theme of teaching future generations. When Israelite children would ask their parents what these **decrees, statutes, and ordinances** meant (6:20), the fathers and mothers were to give a God-glorifying answer. (Notice the spiritual responsibility entrusted to them. They were expected to be informed and quick to reply with truth.) The answer began with the Israelites as helpless Egyptian **slaves** (6:21). But God delivered them through **great and devastating signs and wonders** so that he could bring his people into **the land** he had promised (6:22-23). Then he graciously gave Israel his law so they would prosper by being **careful to follow every one of these commands** (6:24-25). This is the kind of teaching that children need today from Christian parents. We must remind them of God's miraculous acts of grace, exhorting them to trust and obey him for the blessings promised.

⮞ B. Remember God's Faithfulness and Obey Him (7:1–11:32) ⮜

7:1-6 Israel's possession of the promised land would include the hard but holy work of destroying the God-hating nations that lived there. Moses could speak of the conquest as if it were an accomplished fact because the

Lord would deliver their enemies into their hands. Though **seven nations more numerous and powerful than** Israel lived there, Israel would **completely destroy them** (7:1-2). Doing so was necessary because of the wicked practices of the Canaanites (see Lev 18:1-30; Deut 18:9-14). In this specific instance of history, God's people were called to execute God's vengeance.

If Israel were to let them live, make a **treaty with them**, or intermarry with them, they would corrupt Israel and turn their hearts **to worship other gods**, provoking God to anger and thereby calling down his wrath on his people (7:2-4). The only safeguard against idolatry's spread was to destroy the Canaanite idols (7:5). The Lord is a holy God; therefore, his people are **a holy people** (7:6) and must live lives of holiness.

7:7-8 God had not set his heart on Israel because they were an especially **numerous** or righteous group (7:7). Rather, he did so because he **loved** them (7:8). This passage reminds us as Christians that we were not saved because we were something special or because we sought God's help. It all began with God's love: "he loved us and sent his Son to be the atoning sacrifice for our sins" (1 John 4:10).

7:9-11 Distinct above every so-called god of the nations, the Lord is the only true God. He is faithful not only to bless those who **love** and obey him, but also to judge those who **hate** and disobey him (7:9-10). Therefore, the only wise thing Israel could do was to keep the commands and ordinances of God that Moses was laying out for them (7:11). This principle is still applicable to us.

7:12-15 The promises for obedience were tremendous. God would keep his **covenant loyalty** with Israel, by loving, blessing, and multiplying his people (7:12-13). Their blessings would also include freedom from **all the terrible diseases** they had suffered in **Egypt** (7:15). God would withhold no good thing from his people.

7:16-24 But the price of blessing was obedience. And the obedience God required of Israel included the destruction of the Canaanites and the rejection of their gods. Knowing that the people harbored a fear of the Canaanites, Moses pointed to what God did to **Pharaoh and all Egypt** in order to rescue his people (7:18-19). Even as seemingly weak Israel prepared to walk into the future God had prepared for them, Pharaoh's mighty chariot army lay at the bottom of the Red Sea. So Moses said, **The Lord your God will do the same to all the peoples you fear. . . . Don't be terrified of them, for the Lord your God, a great and awesome God, is among you** (7:19, 21). The ultimate cure for fear is awareness of the presence and power of God.

7:25-26 The promise of victory was accompanied by a warning not to **covet** and **take** any of the spoils of the defeated Canaanites. Just as the gold in the tabernacle was holy because it was devoted to the Lord's service, so also the **gold** of the Canaanites was **detestable** because it was devoted to **the images** of their gods (7:25). So the possessions of the Canaanites were to be devoted to destruction. Joshua 7:1-26, however, records how an Israelite would disobey this command, cause harm to his fellow Israelites, and pay the ultimate price.

8:1 Moses was a great historian who knew what God's people had been through. He was also a great teacher who wanted his students to go out from his classroom to great success. Moses never tired of telling his listeners that obedience to God was something they needed to take seriously and keep in front of them if they wanted to experience blessings in the land God was giving them.

8:2-4 God's classroom for teaching the Israelites humble dependence on and obedience to him was **the wilderness**, where he tested them to find out if they **would keep his commands** (8:2). At work here is an important spiritual principle. All believers must go through the wilderness of testing before God will let us reach our destiny. Of course, God knew what the Israelites would do; *he* didn't have to test them. But *they* needed to find out if their faith in God would hold strong in a place where they had to depend on him for everything: food, water, clothing, protection. What they needed to learn was that **man does not live on bread alone but on every word that comes from the mouth of the Lord** (8:3). The manna that sustained their lives arrived by God's Word, as did everything good they received. Keeping God's Word and past provision at the forefront of our thoughts in times of testing will bring us spiritual victory.

8:5 Good parents know that their children require discipline in order to become wise and responsible adults. God is the ultimate parent who **disciplines** his children for their own good. The author of Hebrews reminds us, "No discipline seems enjoyable at the time, but painful. Later on, however, it yields the peaceful fruit of righteousness to those who have been trained by it" (Heb 12:11).

8:6-11 In contrast to the hardships of the wilderness, the promised land held out the prospect of abundant water, crops, and minerals. It was a land so rich that when the people enjoyed its bounty they would **bless the Lord** for giving them such a **good land** (8:7-10). But with prosperity comes the temptation to **forget the Lord . . . by failing to keep his commands** (8:11).

8:12-17 The human heart can quickly turn from thanking God for his blessings to puffing itself up with pride (8:12-14). And there's little worse than a person who has come from humble circumstances through the help and mercy of others turning around and forgetting about them and acting like his change of fortune came about by his own merit, essentially claiming, **My power and my own ability have gained this wealth for me** (8:17). Later, Paul told the Romans, "I tell everyone among you not to think of himself more highly than he should" (Rom 12:3). Ultimately, to be prideful is to lie to yourself about yourself. "God resists the proud but gives grace to the humble" (1 Pet 5:5).

8:18 To counter arrogance, Moses made one of the great statements of kingdom economics: **Remember that the Lord your God gives you the power to gain wealth.** In other words, God gives the ability and opportunity necessary for gaining wealth, and

he does so with the specific goal of preparing people to fulfill his kingdom purposes, which include being a blessing to others. God doesn't give us wealth just so that we can lavish it on ourselves. To separate wealth from God, in fact, is a travesty because prosperity is inextricably tied to his kingdom agenda for his people.

8:19-20 The Israelites were warned that if they acted like the Canaanites, God would treat them like Canaanites: **Like the nations the Lord is about to destroy before you, you will perish if you do not obey [him]** (8:20). God doesn't play favorites. He doesn't let his people live as they please.

9:1-3 Moses emphasized the challenge that lay ahead of them on the other side of the Jordan River: the need to **drive out nations greater and stronger than** Israel, whose inhabitants were like giants (9:1-2). But he quickly assured the people that the Lord would act in advance **as a consuming fire**, assuring victory (9:3).

9:4-6 Then Moses cautioned against another kind of spiritual pride: **Do not say to yourself, 'The Lord brought me in to take possession of this land because of my righteousness'** (9:4). On the contrary, God was removing the Canaanites from the land because of their great **wickedness** and **to fulfill the promise he swore to . . . Abraham, Isaac, and Jacob** (9:4-5). In other words, Israel was receiving the promised land because God hates wickedness and keeps his promises. If Israel was tempted to think of themselves as inherently righteous, they needed to nip that idea in the bud. Moses pulled no punches when he said, **You are a stiff-necked people** (9:6).

9:7-12 That last comment led Moses to offer an extended illustration of the Israelites' rebellious nature. He said, **Remember and do not forget** (9:7). Moses wanted to drive home how easy it was for God's people to go off the rails even in the face of his constant mercy and faithfulness. He reminded them of the quintessential example of Israel's sin: the golden calf incident (see Exod 32:1-35). Israel had indulged in idolatry and debauchery, breaking God's commandments while Moses was still on the mountain receiving them (9:8-12).

9:13-21 God was so angry in the calf incident that he threatened to destroy Israel and start over with Moses (9:13-14). Moses was furious too, smashing the tablets of the law on the ground (9:17). He burned the calf, ground it to powder, and put it into Israel's water source to make them drink it (9:21). Then Moses **fell down . . . in the presence of the LORD for forty days and forty nights**, fasting **because of all the sin [the people] committed** (9:18). He interceded for them. An unrighteous people owed their preservation to the prayers of a righteous man and the mercy of a gracious God. Israel's story consisted of rebellion, divine anger, intercession by Moses, divine grace, repeat. They'd not been chosen for their inherent goodness: we haven't been either.

9:22-29 Moses was just getting warmed up. He mentioned Israel's rebellions at several other stops along the way to the promised land (9:22-23). Then, for good measure, he added, **You have been rebelling against the LORD ever since I have known you** (9:24). In spite of this, Moses **prayed** for them, appealing to God's promises to the patriarchs, his reputation among the nations, and his grace (9:26-29).

10:1-5 Continuing his lesson on the events at Sinai and beyond, Moses told the Israelites how God led him to replace the **stone tablets** of the law that had been broken and to make an **ark** to put them in. Moses did exactly as the Lord commanded him.

10:6-9 These verses refer to the events of Aaron's death and the succession of his son **Eleazar** to the high priesthood (10:6). Moses reminded the people that the Lord **set apart the tribe of Levi** to assist the priests with the work of carrying **the ark of the LORD's covenant** (10:8).

10:10-13 Moses then resumed his narrative of his second stint of **forty days and forty nights** on Mount Sinai (10:10). God heard Moses's prayer and agreed **not to annihilate** Israel (10:10). Then it was time for the nation to move on to **possess** Canaan (10:10-11). But doing so successfully, and living there in prosperity under God's blessing, would require that the people **fear the LORD**. What does a person do who "fears" the Lord? He walks in his ways, loves him, and worships him (10:12). Such a person takes God seriously—so seriously that he does what God says. To do so is **for [his] own good** (10:13).

10:14-22 God was worthy of Israel's complete devotion because he is the Lord of creation to whom everything belongs (10:14). And yet, out of all the nations on the earth, he **had his heart set on** Israel's **fathers and loved them**, choosing them in his sovereign love and election (10:15). The only appropriate response the people of Israel could make was to **circumcise** their **hearts**—that is, to bow in submission to God and be **stiff-necked** no longer (10:16; see 9:6). The God of Israel is **the God of gods and Lord of lords**, the God of justice, love, and mercy who calls his people to show these same qualities to others (10:17-19). Moses's heartbeat was for God's people to **fear** and **worship him** because of who he is and what he had done for them (10:20-22).

11:1 Therefore—in light of all that the Lord had done for Israel—Moses called them to **love** God and **keep** his **commands**. For God's people, there is no such thing as professing sincere love for God without obeying him. And the Israelites had the added motivation of the promise that obedience to God would bring untold blessing and prosperity on them in the land he was giving them as their inheritance. In other words, they were promised internal strength and external abundance.

11:2-7 All of Israel's history had been for the purpose of learning God's **discipline**. One reason the generation about to enter the promised land needed to learn the lessons from it was that their **children** had not **experienced** or seen the Lord's discipline as they had lived it (11:2). This mention could refer not only to the children in their tents at that time, but to future generations who would need to learn the lessons of faith (see 11:18-21).

Moses delivered a brief history lesson beginning with Israel's deliverance from Egypt, where God's **greatness, strong hand, and outstretched arm** decimated **Pharaoh** and his **army** (11:2-4). Then he singled out the sin of **Dathan and Abiram**, who joined in the rebellion of Korah. On that terrifying day, **the earth opened its mouth and swallowed them** (11:6; see Num 16:1-35), a judgment Moses said his hearers had witnessed firsthand (11:7).

11:8-9 This was a huge contrast to the bright future that awaited Israel in Canaan if they would love and obey God with all their hearts. Moses may have singled out Dathan and Abiram as examples of disobedience because they blamed Moses for dragging them out of Egypt—"a land flowing with milk and honey" (Num 16:13). This was a deliberate dig at God's promise to lead his people to **a land flowing with milk and honey** (11:9). If you refer to a land in which you were enslaved as a land of blessing, your moral compass is defective.

11:10-17 Moses compared Egypt with Canaan, reminding his hearers that Egypt had to be **irrigated by hand** in order for anything to grow (11:10). By contrast, Canaan was **watered by rain from the sky** (11:11). But this didn't come from the hand of a fictional Mother Nature, but from the hand of Father God (11:12). So if Israel was careful to **obey . . . love . . . and worship** the Lord, they could count on him to care for the land and bless their produce (11:13-15). For an agrarian society, that's everything. But if they turned to **worship** false **gods** that couldn't help them, they would find that their **produce** wouldn't grow (11:16-17)—a devastating situation.

11:18-25 The antidote to forgetfulness and idolatry was stated in 6:4-9 and is repeated here in 11:18-21. Israel needed to **imprint** God's **words** on their **hearts and minds,** and **teach them** to their **children** every day in all circumstances (11:18-19). Should they fail in this, they would trip and fall. Should they do it faithfully, their **days** would be **many in the land** (11:21), God would **drive out** their enemies (11:23), and **no one** would **be able to**

stand against them (11:25). God was providing them with the perfect means to achieve guaranteed results. This is a pattern worth following.

11:26-32 The choices God gave Israel boiled down to two clear options: **a blessing** for obedience and **a curse** for disobedience (11:26-28). These choices would be made visible and audible later when the nation came to **Mount Gerizim** and **Mount Ebal** in Canaan. There they would **proclaim** the **blessings** and the **curse** (11:29-30; see 27:1–28:68; Josh 8:30-35). Like a parent teaching a child an important lesson yet again, Moses cautioned the Israelites to **be careful to follow all the statutes and ordinances** set before them (11:32).

⇲ C. True Worship and False Worship (12:1–13:18) ⇲

12:1-4 Another concern loomed large in Moses's mind—and with good reason. As Israel entered the land God had promised, they would see the various Canaanite worship centers, which were typically erected **on the high mountains, on the hills, and under every green tree** (12:2). These sites contained **sacred pillars** and **Asherah poles** honoring the Canaanite god and goddess of fertility, Baal and Asherah (12:3). Moses knew that the people might be intrigued by forms of worship that sought divine favor for fertile crops and livestock. This kind of perverted worship often included sexual symbols and immoral sexual acts. The Israelites had fallen for such debauchery before (see Num 25:1-9). But Israel was not to **worship** the Lord **this way** (12:4).

12:5-7 Instead, Israel was to worship at **the place** God would choose **to put his name for his dwelling** (12:5). Rather than permitting worship on any high place or under any green tree, God intended to centralize Israel's worship. The ultimate fulfillment of this would be at the temple in Jerusalem. Until that was built, the divinely ordained place for worship was the tabernacle. This was the place where Israel would bring **burnt**

offerings and sacrifices and rejoice in God's presence (12:6-7).

12:8 What they were *not* to do was what they were doing—everyone [was] doing whatever [seemed] right in his own sight. Previously God had commanded the people to "do what [was] right in [God's] sight" (Exod 15:26). This highlights a great divide. Will we follow the destructive path that looks good to our faulty eyes? Or will we follow the path of life that God sees and reveals to us?

12:9-14 Moses repeated what he had just said in 12:5-7. When the Israelites entered the land, they were to worship only in the place where the Lord chose to have his name dwell (12:10-11, 14). That location would be the only appropriate place to offer worship and sacrifice—in contrast to all the sacred places (12:13). In other words, God's people must not worship at the "sacred places" where the Canaanites worshiped their false deities. The Canaanites thought that by worshiping in all the "right" places throughout the land, they could compel or convince the gods to act on their behalf. But Israel didn't need to guess or discover the right hilltop on which to worship the Lord. He would reveal it. Unfortunately, Israel's sad history demonstrates that they did indeed seek to worship "on every high hill and under every green tree" (1 Kgs 14:23; cp. 2 Chr 28:4).

12:15-16 Though animals could only be sacrificed in one place, this did not prevent Israelite fathers from hunting animals for family meals (12:15). Animals could be eaten freely without needing to be brought to the central sanctuary. But one thing was prohibited: the people were not [to] eat the blood [but to] pour it on the ground like water (12:16).

Consuming blood was strictly prohibited "because the life of every creature is its blood" (Lev 17:14) and "without the shedding of blood there is no forgiveness" (Heb 9:22). Therefore, it was sacred. This prohibition pointed to the ultimate blood sacrifice, "for it is impossible for the blood of bulls and goats to take away sins" (Heb 10:4). By Jesus's own blood, he has "obtained eternal redemption" (Heb 9:12).

12:17-28 Any animals and produce to be presented to God in sacrifice had to be brought to the tabernacle to be offered and eaten in the presence of the LORD (12:17-18).

The instructions that follow here (12:21-28) may strike us as unnecessary repetition (see 12:15-19). But we must remember Moses's purpose—for both his immediate audience and future readers—of driving home the absolute necessity of fearing and obeying God. Given the sinful human tendency to forget, any good teacher of God's Word knows the value of repetition, as illustrated by the apostle Peter: "I will always remind you about these things, even though you know them. . . . I think it is right, as long as I am in this bodily tent, to wake you up with a reminder (2 Pet 1:12-13).

12:29-32 Moses's concern over the Israelites' vulnerability to idolatry also led him to repeat the warning he had given them at the beginning of this chapter (see 12:1-4). He knew that once the people became curious and asked, How did these nations worship their gods?, they would be hooked into thinking, I'll also do the same (12:30). Therefore Moses warned them that false worship is no harmless sin. What we worship drives how we live: as part of their idolatry, the Canaanites burned their sons and daughters in the fire to their gods (12:31). Worldview matters. Ideas have consequences.

13:1-3 Some might assume that if a self-proclaimed prophet is able to perform a miraculous sign or wonder (13:1), then he must be the real deal. But Satan and his followers have performed and will perform false miracles in order to lead people astray (see Exod 7:11-12; Matt 24:24; 2 Thess 2:9; Rev 13:11-4). Moses said the test of a true prophet is not his *magic* but his *message*. No matter what a prophet, magician, or soothsayer did to dazzle the Israelites, Moses said in effect, "It's his theology that matters." If a person said, Let us follow other gods, Israel was not to listen to him under any circumstances—no matter what astonishing signs he performed (13:2-3).

13:3-4 The Lord would permit apparent wonder workers to appear because he was testing the Israelites—to see if they would love God, **keep** his laws, **worship him**, and **remain faithful to him** (13:3-4). The Lord does the same to us today. Though he never tempts us, he does permit us to encounter temptation in order to test our faithfulness and reveal what is in our hearts.

13:5 A false **prophet or dreamer** who attempted to lead Israel astray was to face **death** because to entice God's people to follow idols is to urge **rebellion against the Lord**. Idolatry was not to be tolerated.

False doctrine is not to be tolerated in the church either. Though the church does not have authority to carry out capital punishment, it does have the authority (and responsibility) to carry out church discipline and exclude people from church membership who propagate false teachings about the essentials of the faith and seek to lead Christians astray.

13:6-11 Sadly, the temptation to fall into idolatry could come from an intimate source, like a person's **brother . . . son . . . daughter . . . wife** or **closest friend** (13:6). The issue of Israel's love for God and the nation's moral and spiritual purity was so paramount that it superseded even love of family (see Matt 10:37). The sin in such a case was the same as that committed by the false prophet overtly enticing people to **worship other gods** (13:6). So not only was the offense to incur the death sentence, but the family member whom the offender tried to lead away from the Lord was to cast the first stone **to put him [or her] to death** (13:8-9). The resulting fear that would fall on those who heard about it was for a good purpose: **they [would] no longer do anything evil like [that]** (13:11). The death sentence was meant as a powerful deterrent.

13:12-17 Idolatry among God's people had the potential to infect an entire **city** in Israel (13:12-13), so if anyone was found guilty of tolerating it, **the inhabitants of [such a] city** were to be struck down **with the sword**, and the city was **not to be rebuilt** (13:14-16).

Unfortunately, though, Israel failed to carry out these steps over the centuries as its people fell steadily captive to the allure of the false religions around them. In time,

even Jerusalem itself would be declared by prophet after prophet to be a stronghold of idolatry. Degrading worship practices were even carried out in secret in the rooms of the temple. Yet most of the nation's kings and people failed to listen, much less work to purge the evil from their midst.

13:18 Moses told the people that the only way to avoid having God's judgment fall on the nation was to keep his commands and to do **what is right in the sight of the Lord**. When we adopt a spiritual perspective on life—God's perspective—we see that his way is always best. Following God's Word points us to the best path for our good and for his glory.

⮞ D. Food, Tithes, the Sabbath Year, and Pilgrim Festivals (14:1–16:17) ⬿

14:1-2 Moses warned the Israelites against following the gods of the nations. He also warned them against following their various religious practices. God had given Israel very explicit instructions regarding how they were to worship him. The relevant portions of Exodus, Leviticus, Numbers, and Deuteronomy provide explicit details. Therefore, an Israelite had no excuse if he chose to depart from God's way and engage in unapproved spiritual activities.

The Lord prohibited Israel from practicing the mourning rituals of the nations. They were not to **cut** themselves or **make a bald spot on** their **head on behalf of the dead** (14:1). Such customs were banned because they were part of the Canaanite religions and were thus unfit for God's **holy people** (14:2).

14:3-21 A major day-to-day aspect of Israel's covenant with God involved keeping the nation's food laws. Why God permitted some foods and prohibited others has been long debated. Some say God gave these lists of prohibited animals out of concern for the Israelites' health. They point out, for example, that **pigs** (14:8) can carry diseases and that **vultures** (14:12) feed on rotting flesh. This is a popular argument, but Scripture does not give health concerns as justification for the prohibition. Furthermore, Jesus would later declare all foods clean (see Acts 10:9-15).

Another explanation for the food laws was that the prohibited animals were used in false religious rites and thus were out of bounds for the Israelites. But the evidence for this is lacking as well. While the custom of boiling **a young goat in its mother's milk** *may* have been a Canaanite religious practice that was forbidden to Israel for that reason (14:21), the bull was a significant symbol in the religions of the ancient Near East that was nonetheless permitted in Israel's sacrifices.

We have only one clear reason why God declared some food clean and some unclean for Israel: **You are a holy people belonging to the LORD your God** (14:21). The food laws, then, were another way of setting Israel apart from the other nations to be the unique people of God.

14:22-29 The laws of the tithe, or **tenth** (14:22), were another way of reminding the Israelites that everything they had came from God's gracious hand. They were to bring their tithes from their crops and livestock to the central sanctuary and **eat** part of them in a communal meal of rejoicing before **the Lord** (14:23-26). Part of the uneaten tithe provided for the needs of the Levites (14:27). Every third year, the entire tithe was stored away for **the Levite . . . the resident alien, the fatherless, and the widow** (14:28-29). If the Israelites were faithful in this way, the Lord would **bless** them **in all the work of** their **hands** (14:29).

God's kingdom agenda for his people's money is the opposite of the world's advice. According to the world, hoarding our money leads to prosperity. But God says that giving is the way of blessing (see 2 Cor 9:6-8). God does not call us to give generously to him so that he can make us rich, however. That's the so-called "prosperity gospel," which only results in prosperity for its preachers.

Giving to God first is crucial because it shows how much you value him, and it expresses your faith in his ability and willingness to provide for you. When Israel gave the Lord their tithe, they were *not* saying that ten percent belonged to God while the

other ninety percent belonged to them. Instead, giving a tenth to God was their way of acknowledging that *everything* they had was from God.

Giving to God is a test of our faith. Israel lived in an agrarian society, so the people were dependent on their harvest to survive. When they gave God the first portion of their crops, they were trusting him to bless them and provide for their needs so that they could feed their families and be charitable to others. The Lord calls followers of Jesus to put this principle into practice today.

15:1-3 The instructions about giving in 14:22-29 led Moses to a related subject, the seventh or Sabbath year, in which **debts** were cancelled (15:1). That sounds like an impossible way to run a country to us, but it was part of God's original plan and will for Israel. Though a **creditor** could collect a debt from a **foreigner**, he was to **forgive** what he had **lent** to his fellow Israelites (15:2-3). This is a reminder that God's kingdom does not operate according to the principles by which the banker downtown conducts business.

15:4-6 If the people would **obey** these principles of generosity, the Lord would **bless** them **in the land**, and he would ensure that there would be **no poor among** them (15:4-5). Moreover, if they were financially obedient, God would guarantee that Israel would **lend to** and **rule** nations, but they would never **borrow** from or be ruled by those lands (15:6). Sadly, history would show that Israel was unfaithful to God's economic commands. Too often the church similarly fails to exercise biblical justice by taking action that helps the oppressed, transforms communities, and empowers the poor through opportunities.

15:7-11 Moses continued the emphasis on compassion and generosity. God commanded the Israelites to help the **poor** who were **among** them. They were not to be **hardhearted or tightfisted** (15:7). But God also knew the human heart's tendencies, so he had Moses add a stern warning. If someone realized that **the seventh year**, the **year of canceling debts** was **near**, and therefore chose not to give to a **poor brother** in need, that cheapskate would stand **guilty** in God's eyes (15:9).

What at first seems a harsh judgment toward someone who hadn't robbed anyone, but had only held on to his own money lest he make a poor investment boils down to this. God commanded his people to trust him and to be generous. This is an important kingdom principle. Giving to others as God commands is crucial because it shows how much you value him, and it expresses your faith in his ability and willingness to provide. The Sabbath year with its debt forgiveness and care for the poor was not really about financial transactions; it was a test of whether God's people would trust him even when doing so didn't make sense on the ledger. Furthermore, to provide for someone in need is the fulfillment of the second most important commandment: "love your neighbor as yourself" (Lev 19:18; Mark 12:28-31).

Don't suppose that 15:11 contradicts 15:4. Verse 4 was a statement of God's will for his people if they obeyed. Verse 11 is a sad mention of what God knew would become reality because of sin. He thus required his people to be generous toward the needy.

15:12 Commands regarding the Sabbath year continue in 15:12-18. A **fellow Hebrew** who was too poor to repay his debts could sell himself to his debtor as an indentured servant. But **in the seventh year** he was to be set free (see Lev 25:39-42).

15:13-18 Furthermore, the newly released servant was to be set up with everything he needed to make a successful fresh start (15:13-14). A Hebrew, that is an Israelite, was to **give generously** to his former servant based on how the Lord had **blessed** him (15:14). He was also to **remember** that he was once worse off than an indentured servant—he was **a slave in the land of Egypt** (15:15). To any Israelite who considered it too much of a financial hardship to lose a valuable worker and have to give him a generous severance package on the seventh year, Moses gave this reminder: getting **six years** of hard work without having to pay **a hired worker** is a good deal (15:18). Nevertheless, if a servant loved his situation, provision

was made for him to stay with the **family** he served **for life** (15:16-17).

Sadly, Israel would fail to keep the sabbatical years and the rules surrounding the Year of Jubilee that are discussed in this passage and elsewhere (see Lev 25:1-55). And since the Lord warned them that if they rejected his commands and rebelled against his way, he would cast them out of the land so that the land could enjoy its Sabbath rests (see Lev 26:33-35), that is exactly what would happen (see 2 Chr 36:20-21).

15:19-23 The following verses deal with giving up possessions to the Lord. Moses had just mentioned the Israelites' slavery in Egypt (15:15), so they knew well that **every firstborn male** among their animals belonged to God (15:19). These creatures, the best of the herds and flocks, were to be brought to the sanctuary for sacrifice. Those which had a **defect** could be eaten at home like any other animal, provided the **blood** was properly drained first (15:20-23).

16:1-4 There were three festivals on Israel's annual worship calendar that required all males to make a pilgrimage to the central sanctuary. The first was **Passover**, the seven-day festival celebrating God's deliverance of the people **out of Egypt** (16:1). On it, they were to sacrifice **a Passover animal from the herd or flock** and **eat unleavened bread with it**, in remembrance that they **left the land of Egypt in a hurry** (16:2-3). In this way, they would **remember** for the rest of their lives the day God set them free (16:3). The command to eat unleavened bread was so serious that there was to be **no yeast . . . anywhere** in their **territory** during those days (16:4). The word "yeast" is frequently representative of sin in Scripture.

16:5-7 The command for the men to appear before the Lord at the tabernacle and later the temple in Jerusalem was underscored by the corollary that a Passover celebration was prohibited in any town in Israel except **the place where the LORD . . . chooses to have his name dwell** (16:6)—which would eventually be Jerusalem. The first Passover and the liberation from Egypt were considered the birth of Israel as a nation, so requiring Passover to be observed as a national holiday reinforced the importance of this festival and God's deliverance. The **tents** would have been those erected by the worshipers as temporary quarters during the festival (16:7).

16:8-11 The next national gathering was the **Festival of Weeks** (16:10), also known as Pentecost (from the Greek term meaning "fiftieth"), which occurred fifty days after the festival of Firstfruits. This was a joyful celebration of God's abundant provision in the harvest and was marked by a **free-will offering** given **in proportion to how the LORD** had blessed them throughout the year (16:10). There was a joyful communal meal at the central sanctuary that was to include the Levites and the marginalized (16:11).

16:12-15 The third pilgrim festival was the **Festival of Shelters**, also known as the Festival of Tabernacles or Booths (16:13). This was a seven-day observance in which the Israelites were commanded to build and live in temporary shelters as a reminder of God's care for them during their wilderness wanderings (see Lev 23:42-43). It also celebrated God's provision in the fall harvest.

16:16-17 Moses's summary of these festivals reminded the men that, as the heads of their families, they were to lead the way in worshiping the Lord (16:16). (This principle carries over into our time.) They were also to bring a **gift** in keeping with their **means** and reflecting how the Lord had blessed them (16:17).

❧ E. Leaders *(16:18–18:22)* ❧

16:18-20 Biblical Israel was a theocracy, meaning that the country had a form of government in which God served as the nation's King. This meant that the nation's civil leaders, its **judges and officials**, were charged with judging the people with **righteous judgment** (16:18)—just as the Lord would. As a nation in covenant with God, Israel was accountable to the law of Moses,

the statutes and commands that God had given the people through his servant Moses. To break God's holy requirements by, for example, accepting **a bribe** to pervert justice could cause Israel to forfeit **the land** God was giving them (16:19-20). God's leaders—those of yesterday and today—are not to pursue selfish gain but to **pursue . . . justice alone** (16:20).

16:21–17:1 The theocratic nature of Israel's government is clearly seen in these verses. Moses suddenly seemed to change subjects from the duties of judges to forbidden forms of worship. But the two topics were intricately related because in Israel, even the civil rulers were responsible for guarding the nation's purity of worship and punishing offenders. Moses put the leaders on alert to watch for violations of true worship (16:21–17:1).

Israel was the only theocracy ever ordained by God. And as much as some believers might wish it were so in America, this country is not a theocracy. More importantly, our kingdom calling as the church is not to make it so. Nevertheless, we can (and should) call our civil leaders to account based on the righteous standards of God's Word. If they refuse to acknowledge the objective standards of justice and righteousness set by the Creator, we can seek to replace them with leaders who will.

17:2-5 Since the proper worship of God was the most serious issue in Israel, judging the cases of those accused of violating it was a serious matter. Moses had already established a system of justice in the wilderness to hear and rule on cases, so what he laid out here was not entirely new. An accusation of false worship that came to the attention of the authorities needed to be **thoroughly** investigated (17:2-4). If the accusations proved true, the guilty party was to be put to **death** (17:5).

17:6-7 The accused could not be condemned on hearsay or the testimony of just one person. He or she could only be executed **on the testimony of two or three witnesses** (17:6), who not only had to stand by their testimony but also had to take the lead **in putting** the guilty person **to death** and purging the evil from Israel (17:7).

17:8-13 As for cases that a local judge felt were too difficult for him to decide, Moses instructed the people to set up something of a supreme court at the central sanctuary in the promised land. There the case would be heard by both the religious and civil leaders, **the Levitical priests** and **the judge who [presided in a given] time** (17:9). Their verdict would be final. Moses emphasized this by stating repeatedly that the parties involved in the case must do **exactly** as instructed, without exception (17:10-11). The leaders were ruling on God's behalf, so judgment had to be followed. No appeals would be heard. Anyone who failed to listen to **the priest** or **the judge** would pay the consequence: death (17:12).

17:14-20 Next God provided instructions for that momentous day when Israel would become a monarchy. That switch in governmental approach, however, wouldn't mean that God ceased to be Israel's King. Rather, the divine King would rule through a human king. The Lord would still bless the nation, as long as the king obeyed him and upheld his law. Israel's history demonstrates that their kings were, for the most part, failures. It would require God himself coming in human flesh to be the King that Israel needs.

In its early years in the promised land, Israel would be ruled by judges and priests. But the book of Judges reveals how imperfectly that system would work. Eventually, Israel would clamor for a king **like all the nations around** them (17:14; see 1 Sam 8:4-5).

In advance of that day, Moses specified that Israel's king had to be an Israelite and not **a foreigner** (17:15). Moreover, **he must not acquire many horses**—which would require going **back to Egypt** in violation of God's command (17:16). He was also not to **acquire many wives** or **acquire very large amounts of silver and gold** (17:17). And, most importantly, he was to **write a copy of this instruction for himself** and **read from it all the days of his life** so that he would not **turn from this command** (17:18-20).

Later, King Solomon would be called the wisest man who ever lived. Nevertheless, in his sinfulness, Solomon broke all of these commandments for kings by accumulating horses in the thousands, seven hundred wives who led his heart astray, and wealth that could not be counted. (Just because a person has access to wisdom doesn't guarantee he'll use it.)

18:1-8 Levitical priests (18:1) were those men in the tribe of Levi set apart by the Lord to offer sacrifices and administer other duties in the tabernacle (and later in the temple). Not all Levites were priests—only those who were the descendants of Aaron. The others were also consecrated to serve God by assisting the priests with the tabernacle and its furnishings.

Since the Levitical priests received no inheritance of land, they were to be supported by a portion of **fire offerings** brought by the Israelites (18:1). They were also to receive **the firstfruits** of their produce and flocks (18:4). If a Levite wanted to go to the central sanctuary to serve, he was entitled to a part of the sacrifices there along with whatever **he [might]** have **received from the sale of the family estate** (18:6-8). Though the Levites did not receive land inheritance like the other tribes, they were given cities to live in throughout Israel, along with pasturelands for their animals (see Num 35:1-5).

18:9-11 Moses turned immediately from teaching about true worship to warning about that which is false. The various demonically inspired **customs** of the **nations** mentioned here were intended to influence or manipulate the gods to act in favor of the person seeking their help (18:9). The most horrific practice of the nations was to **sacrifice** one's child **in the fire** to the gods (18:10). In 2 Kgs 3:26-27, we find an example of this being practiced.

The rest of the forbidden occult practices can be summarized in three basic categories, beginning with **divination** (18:10). Divination is an attempt to get secret knowledge by interpreting omens or looking to astrology. Lest you think of this as an ancient practice, many people today get up every morning and read their horoscopes before they make any decisions—yet they refuse to seek the guidance of the God who made them, which is found in the Scriptures.

The second category is magic, which includes **sorcery** and **spells** (18:10-11). This is not to be confused with the art of illusion practiced by entertaining magicians, like those we see today. Moses was talking about witchcraft, through which humans attempt to accomplish in the spiritual realm what human power alone can't pull off.

The third category is spiritism, which involves the attempt to get in touch with spiritual intermediaries by contacting the **dead** or going into some kind of trance or hypnotic state to talk with a spirit guide or some other being on "the other side" (18:11). Holding séances and playing with Ouija boards are modern expressions of spiritism.

18:12-14 All of these practices are **detestable** to God. These religious acts were the very reason that God was **driving out the nations** and giving their land to Israel (18:12). Therefore, God called his people to be **blameless** and not follow the ways of the world (18:13-14).

18:15 In this verse we find a wonderful prophecy: **The LORD your God will raise up for you a prophet like me from among your own brothers. You must listen to him**. Here Moses told the people that the Lord would provide another mediator after he was gone—an in-between person who would speak on God's behalf and help the people to access God. But the Israelites who listened to Moses couldn't have fathomed how God would fulfill this prophecy.

Centuries later, Jesus Christ would rise up from among his brothers, fully human (see John 1:14; Heb 2:14-18). But God the Father also declared him to be fully divine, his own "beloved Son," and commanded the disciples to "Listen to him!" (Matt 17:5). The apostle Peter declared that Moses's words were fulfilled in Jesus (see Acts 3:22-23). He is our perfect mediator: "There is one God and one mediator between God and humanity, the man Christ Jesus" (1 Tim 2:5).

18:16-19 Previously, when God gave Moses the law, the people were so terrified by God's **voice** and his **fire** that they thought they would **die** (18:16). And so, God said he would send them a mediator. God warned that he would **hold accountable whoever** did not **listen** to this prophet, the Messiah (18:18-19). Indeed, there are serious consequences to ignoring Christ: it's a matter of life and death.

18:20-22 God also gave Israel a measuring stick to hold up against any prophet who claimed to speak in his name. The Lord assured them that if someone claimed to be his **prophet**, and yet his **message** did **not come true**, he was most certainly *not* a prophet. Rather than **be afraid of** such a false prophet (18:22), Israel was to put him to death (18:20).

➢ F. Relationships and Daily Life
(19:1–26:19) ❦

19:1-3 There were numerous regulations covering every aspect of life that Moses wanted to review with the Israelites before he sent them over the Jordan into Canaan. These chapters cover a wide range of them, beginning with his command to establish **three cities** (19:2) as "cities of refuge" (see Num 35:6-34; Josh 20:1-9). A person who committed **manslaughter** (19:3) could flee to one of these cities and be safe from the victim's relative who was bent on revenge.

19:4-13 Moses then offered an example of someone causing an accidental death without harboring any previous hatred toward that person (19:4-5). By having the three cities spaced throughout the land, Israel allowed the person who committed manslaughter a city of refuge within a close enough distance that he could get to it before being overtaken. By contrast, someone who had clearly hated his **neighbor** and killed him in cold blood was to be given no refuge. That person was to be put to death in order to **purge from Israel the guilt of shedding innocent blood** (19:11-13).

19:14 Moving a **neighbor's boundary marker** was a serious offense. To do so was to encroach upon someone else's rightful property, essentially stealing land that God himself had allotted to the tribes of Israel (see Exod 20:15). Anyone who dared take land that God had given as a gift to someone else was under God's curse (see 27:17).

19:15-21 Moses had already established the principle that **the testimony of two or three witnesses** was necessary for a suspect to be condemned (19:15). But there must have been cases in which only one witness was available. And if a sole witness insisted on bringing a case to Israel's leaders at the central sanctuary, he needed to know that he was as much on trial as the accused since his charge could not be corroborated. In such cases, both parties were to **stand in the presence of the Lord before the priests and judges in authority** (19:16). If the witness proved to be **a liar**, his punishment was severe: **Do not show pity: life for life, eye for eye, tooth for tooth, hand for hand, and foot for foot** was the rule used to discipline him (19:18-21).

This command has often been referred to by the Latin expression *lex talionis*—that is, the "law of retaliation." This means that the punishment was to fit the crime. This, however, has been misunderstood and criticized over the years as sanctioning revenge, when in fact God intended it to do exactly the opposite. This was not street justice but was administered by God-ordained authorities, and it *limited* the punishment to fit the crime. In other words, if someone knocked out your tooth, you couldn't bust out three or four of his in response. Through this law, God wisely prevented both leniency and excess punishment in his legal system.

20:1-4 Moses's next message for Israel concerned how to conduct themselves during war, especially in the forthcoming battles for the promised land. This message was as much for General Joshua as it was for the people and their military commanders. It seems that every army Israel met was **larger than** they were in number, and yet God constantly commanded and assured his people, **Do not be afraid of them, for the Lord your God . . . is with you** (20:1).

The priest was to lead the way into battle and give the troops a divine pep talk beforehand, reminding them not to fear the enemy because the Lord would **fight** against their **enemies** and give Israel **victory** (20:2-4). This exhortation was extremely important. The

previous generation of Israelites died in the wilderness because they had succumbed to fear of Canaan's inhabitants and failed to trust that God would provide for them (see Num 13:1–14:45). Therefore, the current generation needed to learn from the mistake of their ancestors.

We too often fail to follow the Lord and do as his Word commands because we fear the world—what they will think of us or do to us. Instead, we must trust that our King will provide the means to accomplish the kingdom agenda that he commands of us.

20:5-9 God permitted soldiers exemption from a given battle if they met any one of four conditions. The first three were related: if they had built a **house** and hadn't been able to live in it yet; if they planted a new **vineyard** whose **fruit** they had not enjoyed; or if they were **engaged** and waiting to be **married** (20:5-7). Each of these involves a lack of fulfillment in pursuing one of life's basic pleasures. They may have been chosen by God to illustrate the ways in which he intended his people to enjoy the good land he was giving them. The fourth exemption involved a soldier with a **cowardly** heart. He was sent home, not for his own sake, but so that he wouldn't demoralize **his brothers**, which could have disastrous consequences (20:8).

20:10-14 Israel's approach to war was not indiscriminate, as Moses's instructions make clear. Enemy cities outside the promised land were to be offered terms of **peace**, which they could accept on the condition of becoming **forced laborers** of Israel (20:10-11). Refusing the offer, however, led to **siege**, the death of all a city's men, and the taking of their goods **as plunder** (20:12-14).

20:15-20 But no such offer of peace was to be made to the Canaanites. Israel was to **completely destroy** every **living thing** among them (20:16-17). Otherwise, survivors would teach the Israelites **to do all the detestable acts they [did] for their gods** and cause the people to **sin against the Lord** (20:18). This matter was crucially important because Israel had already demonstrated a propensity to adopt the false religious practices of the surrounding nations (see Num 25:1-18). Also,

Israel was to refrain from the common practice in ancient warfare of punishing a defeated enemy by decimating its land (20:19-20). After all, Canaan was to be Israel's possession.

21:1-9 No detail of Israel's life escaped God's notice and concern, as Moses's address makes clear. The cold case of an unsolved **murder** (21:1) required a sacrifice because life was precious to God and because the victim's blood had to be atoned for. So God instituted the unique ceremony described in these verses to satisfy his holiness and **purge** the land of the **innocent blood** spilled (21:9).

21:10-14 The next item involved an Israelite soldier who wanted to marry a woman **among the captives** from one of the cities outside of Canaan (21:11). The woman was allowed to undergo a certain physical and spiritual ritual to separate her from her old life, including a month-long period of mourning **for her father and mother** (21:12-13)—either because they had been killed or in recognition of the fact that she would not be going back to them. A provision was also made for divorce if the husband was not pleased with his wife, but he could **not sell her** or mistreat her in any way (21:14). Though other nations often brutally mistreated women during times of war, this law provided a woman of a subjugated country with protection if a soldier wanted her for a bride.

21:15-17 Discussion of marriage to a foreign captive led to another marriage issue, the case of polygamy and fathering sons by more than one wife. Polygamy was tolerated in Old Testament times, but it was never God's standard for marriage—which was to be between one man and one woman (see Gen 2:22-24). Importantly, the culturally accepted practice of taking more than one wife *always* led to problems among God's people. (See, for example, the experiences of grief that polygamy brought into the lives of Jacob, David, and Solomon.) Jealousy was just one of those problems; it could cause one wife to push her son forward as the favorite, even if he were not the firstborn. Nevertheless, fathers were strictly forbidden to play that game and were commanded to give their **firstborn** sons **two shares of** their estates, because those

sons—whether or not their mothers held their fathers' hearts—had **the rights of the firstborn** (21:17).

21:18-21 Next Moses dealt with another difficult family situation. It's important to understand that this passage isn't advocating the death penalty for mere juvenile delinquency. The son in view here was not a teenager who had been acting foolishly once in a while or fell into sassy speech on occasion. This was a son who, though his parents would **discipline him**, refused to repent of his rebellion (21:18). Instead, his **stubborn and rebellious** nature mirrored that of Egypt's hard-hearted Pharaoh, and it even included his being known as **a glutton and a drunkard** (21:20). Such rebellion was a capital offense in God's eyes, because left unpunished it would destroy Israel's home life and eventually the entire covenant community. The bottom line here is that this young man refused to submit to the Lord as his King and to his parents as his God-ordained authority. The **elders** of the parents' city were to recognize the seriousness of this sin and **stone** the rebel themselves to **purge the evil** from Israel (21:20-21). Once again, Scripture uses the threat of capital punishment as a deterrent.

21:22-23 These verses describe a sentence reserved for those who received **the death penalty**. Their bodies were hung **on a tree**—probably as a warning to others not to repeat whatever offense had led to their demise (21:22). But interestingly, the **corpse** could not be left there **overnight** because **anyone hung on a tree is under God's curse**. To leave them there would **defile the land** (21:23). Undergoing God's curse is what Jesus Christ did for us. But he died for our wrongs, not his. He redeemed us by his death on the cross—being hung on a tree—and enduring God's curse against sin in our place (see Gal 3:13).

22:1-4 Moses continued in chapter 22, teaching on a wide variety of subjects. Clearly, the command to care for a **brother Israelite's ox or sheep** or any other possession that was **lost** (22:1-3) was a practical way to live out the command to "love your neighbor as yourself" (Lev 19:18).

22:5 The prohibition against a **woman** wearing **male clothing** and vice versa is a reminder of the gender distinctions that God designed. Men and women equally share in bearing the image of God, but he has designed them to be distinct from and complementary toward one another (see Gen 1:27). The gender confusion that exists in our culture today is a clear rejection of God's good design.

In many places, homosexuality and transgenderism are aggressively promoted by the government and school systems. Whenever a nation's laws no longer reflect the standards of God, that nation is in rebellion against him and will inevitably bear the consequences. When that happens, the people of God should promote his kingdom agenda through biblically based kingdom political involvement and sincere love for others. This is to be done not by violent revolution from the top down, but by social transformation based on spiritual principles that work from the bottom up. What God wants from his people is not revolution, but transformation.

22:6-8 The command to leave a **mother** bird behind while taking her **chicks or eggs** (22:6-7) is not much different than what a farmer does today in gathering the eggs and leaving the mother hen to guarantee a continual food supply. The command to build a **railing** (22:8) around the flat roofs of Israelite houses to keep someone from falling off was another example of neighbor love. Both promote the application of wisdom in daily life.

22:9-11 The common theme in these verses is the mixing of unlike things. Teaching the Israelites to recognize distinctions would help them see the importance of being holy and distinct in a sinful world. Paul uses a similar idea to **Do not plow with an ox and a donkey together** (22:10) when he warns believers not to enter into partnership with unbelievers: "Don't become partners with those who do not believe" (2 Cor 6:14). The verb Paul uses can be literally rendered, "unequally yoked," which is exactly what God prohibited the Israelites from doing—unequally yoking an ox and a donkey together. Though believers must live in this fallen world, God wants us to live lives that are holy and separate from the wickedness around us.

22:12 The **tassels** mentioned here served as visual reminders to obey God's laws (see Num 15:37-41).

22:13-21 The chapter ends with instructions for violations of the marriage covenant. These statutes defended the sanctity of marriage, the purity and innocence of virginity, and the honor of a woman's reputation. Remember that Moses's purpose in his final messages to the Israelites was to exhort them to renew their commitment to faithfulness to God's covenant before entering the promised land. One of the ways they were to express faithfulness to God was by honoring the covenant of marriage. The same is true for us.

Given human sinfulness, God knew there would be marital problems. So he gave Moses regulations to be applied in the case of a husband who came to **hate** his wife, accused her of **shameful conduct**, and gave her **a bad name** by claiming she wasn't a virgin when he married her (22:13-14). If this were true, she was to come under the death penalty (22:20-21). Sexual immorality of any kind was forbidden. But if her parents could prove her pre-marital purity by providing **evidence of her virginity**, her husband was given a stiff fine by **the city elders** and prohibited from ever divorcing his wife (22:15-19). Being prepared to show evidence of virginity was a customary practice that perhaps involved a blood-stained cloth from the wedding night.

22:22-24 Marriage is a sacred creation of God meant to be revered as holy. Adultery by married people was a capital offense under the Mosaic law, and an engaged woman was treated the same way as a married woman in a case in which sex was consensual. Israel's violations of her covenant with God were described as spiritual "adultery" (see Hos 2:2), another indicator that God holds marital fidelity in high regard.

22:25-30 Rape too was a capital offense if the victim was **engaged**. If she wasn't, the perpetrator had to pay the victim's father a fine, marry the woman, and live with her for the rest of his life to provide for her because he stole her virginity (22:25-29).

In verse 30 Moses prohibited a man from marrying his stepmother (22:30). Note Paul's application of this principle in his letter to the Corinthians (see 1 Cor 5:1).

23:1-8 The prohibition that is included here against a eunuch participating in worship when the people gathered at the tabernacle (23:1) was not a matter of the person's sin; it was a ceremonial rule meant to teach Israel the need for perfection before the Lord. The ban on people of **illegitimate birth** would have meant primarily those born of a union between an Israelite and a non-Israelite (for instance, a Canaanite). Their ban was permanent, which is the practical meaning behind the idea of **the tenth generation** (23:2). The Ammonites and Moabites were also barred because of their cruel treatment of the Israelites during their travels in the wilderness and because the Moabites hired **Balaam** to **curse** Israel (23:3-6). Israel's **brother** the Edomites and even the Egyptians, however, were to be treated decently (23:7-8).

23:9-14 Throughout the Pentateuch, we've seen many times how seriously God took every detail of his people's lives—even their camp hygiene. There was a righteous way to be cleansed from **bodily emission** (23:10-11) and to dispose of daily waste (23:12-14) in order to keep the camp ceremonially clean so that holy God could dwell among his people.

23:15-16 The Lord wanted a particular group—fugitive slaves—to feel welcome in the Israelite camp. These were most likely slaves who had **escaped** (23:15) from the nations surrounding Israel. The righteous thing to do was to give these people sanctuary rather than returning them to their masters, even letting them **live** (23:16) where they wished in the cities to which they fled.

23:17-18 Cult prostitution involving both genders was prevalent in Canaan, so Moses had to continually warn Israel not to be tempted by this heinous evil or patronize a Canaanite **cult prostitute** (23:17). Furthermore, they were not to bring a **prostitute's wages ... into the house of the LORD** (23:18). Such wicked forms of "worship"—whether one was visiting a cult prostitute or acting as one—were contrary to the sexual ethic the Lord had established.

23:19-20 The law's command to Israel to "love your neighbor as yourself" (Lev 19:18) came into focus again in the matter of charging **interest on** a loan. God did not allow an Israelite to charge interest to a fellow **Israelite**, although it was acceptable to charge interest to **a foreigner** (23:19-20).

23:21-23 Vows to God were completely voluntary, but once made they were to be kept, or else it was **counted against** the person as **sin** (23:21).

23:24-25 An Israelite could also love his neighbor by not taking advantage of his **vineyard** or **standing grain**. It was acceptable to pluck **grapes** or **heads of grain** to eat while on a neighbor's property, but this did not give anyone license to show up with a **sickle** and a **container** and start harvesting (23:24-25).

24:1-5 **Divorce** was not part of God's ideal for marriage, even though he permitted it here. Jesus told his disciples that this concession was made because of the hardness of the Israelites' hearts—that is, their refusal to submit to divine standards (see Matt 19:8). God allowed for divorce when the husband found **something indecent** about his wife, that is, something unacceptable. This protected the woman and freed her to remarry (24:1). Better by far was the mandate that Israel should help a newly married couple get off to a good start by giving the husband **one year** off from service in **the army**. This would allow the couple time to adjust to their life together and prevent a new bride from losing her husband in war before having a chance to enjoy married life and possibly conceive (24:5).

24:6-7 In ancient Israel, there were no refrigerators or freezers in which to store food, no closets full of extra clothes, no heaters to turn on at night when the weather got cold, no banks or ATMs. A man worked each day, got paid each evening, and bought or harvested his food for that night's dinner. So taking his **grindstones or even the upper millstone as security for a debt** was cruel because it meant that he couldn't prepare his daily bread (24:6).

Even worse was **kidnapping** a fellow Israelite to enslave or sell him, an offense rightly punishable by death (24:7). This is a stiff warning against human trafficking.

24:8-9 A **serious skin disease** was a matter of great concern, since it required the affected person to be quarantined and to endure extensive procedures with **the Levitical priests** in order to be pronounced clean again (24:8; see Lev 13:1-46; 14:1-32). Moreover, Moses reminded the people what **God did to Miriam** when she opposed Moses's leadership (24:9). Her skin became "diseased, resembling snow" (Num 12:10).

24:10-13 If anything was to mark the people of God, it was compassion for those in need—a trait in short supply both then and now. God was even concerned about the dignity of an Israelite debtor, who was to be spared the humiliation of having his lender barge into **his house**, scoop up whatever he wanted for his **security** on **the loan**, and walk out with the debtors' neighbors watching (24:10-11). If the debtor was **a poor man** who had nothing to offer but the **garment** he needed to sleep in at night to keep warm, the lender was told to return it to him by **sunset**, an act of kindness that God **counted as righteousness** (24:12-13).

24:14-22 Continuing this focus on compassion, Moses pointed out that workers deserved their **wages** in a timely manner— even more so if they were poor and had no other way to eat. God held employers liable if they cheated their workers (24:14-15). Out of a similar emphasis on compassion, **fathers** and **children** did not have to answer for each other's sins (24:16). Moreover, a widow or resident alien was not to be denied justice simply because of personal powerlessness (24:17). The repeated motivation for the Israelites to obey these laws was that they were once slaves in Egypt (24:18, 22). Of all the peoples who should understand the pain of injustice, it was the Israelites. Therefore, they were commanded to care for the three most vulnerable groups within their society: **the resident alien, the fatherless, and the widow** (24:19-21).

This leads us to an important side note. Know that if you have been comforted by God, he expects you to share that comfort

with others who have experienced similar suffering. "He comforts us in our affliction, so that we may be able to comfort those who are in any kind of affliction, through the comfort we ourselves receive from God" (2 Cor 1:4). Your experience of God's blessings should lead you to bless others.

25:1-4 The theme of justice in Israel continued with the demand that when **a dispute between men** was heard in **court**, the **judges** would hand down a ruling that ensured acquittal for the **innocent** and punishment for **the guilty**, in keeping with the seriousness of the offense **but** not going beyond it (25:1-3). God even cared about justice being offered to the animals that served the Israelites (25:4), as an example of the fact that "he who threshes should thresh in hope of sharing the crop" (see 1 Cor 9:4-12).

25:5-10 Israel also had a law that provided a way for a man who died without a male heir to keep from having his name **blotted out from Israel**. If brothers lived **on the same property** and one died **without a son**, the living brother was to marry the widow and raise up a son for his brother (25:5-6). If the brother refused to do his duty, the widow could haul him before the **elders of his city** and subject him to a humiliating ritual that would leave him with a disgraceful nickname (25:7-10).

25:11-12 This points to the fact that having and raising children was highly valued in ancient Israel. "Sons are indeed a heritage from the LORD, offspring, a reward. Like arrows in the hand of a warrior are the sons born in one's youth. Happy is the man who has filled his quiver with them" (Ps 127:3-5). Thus, harming a man's reproductive ability incurred a severe penalty.

25:13-16 Justice and honesty in business were not options for Israel: they were required. To use **differing weights** on a scale for buying and selling merchandise was dishonest, greedy, and deceptive to one's neighbor (25:13-14). The Lord demanded an **honest weight** (25:15). Anything less was **detestable** to him (23:16). The Israelites should not be tempted to put a "thumb on the scales," so to speak, when God had promised to prosper them in everything they did if only they would honor and obey him.

25:17-19 In case Israel needed to be reminded of what happened to people who mistreated God's chosen ones, Moses left a stern command for Israel to annihilate **the Amalekites** (25:17) for the shameful way they had treated the weakest among God's people in the wilderness (25:18). God didn't even want a **memory of Amalek** left anywhere on earth (25:19).

26:1-3 Moses frequently called his hearers to remember what God had done for them and to do the things he required of them once they entered the promised land. One of these requirements was the joyful bringing of the **first of all the land's produce** to the Lord at the central sanctuary. This offering of the firstfruits of their **harvest** was an opportunity for the people to remind themselves and declare publicly that God had indeed given them the land as promised and that the produce was the proof (26:2-3).

26:4-11 After presenting their firstfruits offering, the people would recite a saying in which they recounted their history and struggles from the days of Jacob to the day they stood before the Lord. Jacob, or Israel, was the **wandering Aramean**, which is a reference to his father Abraham's years in Aram on his way to Canaan. Jacob married Rachel, who was from the Aramean side of his family. Jacob's family was small when he **went down to Egypt** under Joseph's protection, but the Israelites **became a great, powerful, and populous nation** whom **the Egyptians . . . oppressed** (26:5-6). When the Israelites cried out to God, he delivered them and brought them to **a land flowing with milk and honey** (26:7-9). The firstfruits

ceremony gave each family the opportunity to **bow down** in gratitude to the Lord and rejoice along with **the Levites** and **the resident aliens** who also were blessed by God's gracious hand (26:10-11).

26:12-15 There is debate as to whether the tithe prescribed here to be brought **in the third year** was the regular third-year tithe Moses had already taught about (see Deut 14:28-29), a one-time offering like the firstfruits offering above, or a second tithe to be made every third year. This was for the **Levites, resident aliens, fatherless children and widows**—those who had no other means of support (26:12). The worshiper was to declare that he was giving the whole tithe and not holding anything back (26:13-14). Based on this confession, he could pray for God's blessing on his **people** and his **land** (26:15).

26:16 At the conclusion to this lengthy message about Israel's covenant obligations to the Lord, Moses called for the people's complete commitment to the Lord and obedience to his **statutes and ordinances** as contained in his covenant. But their obedience was not to be grudging or mechanical. As people who were called to love the Lord their God with all of their being, they were to obey him willingly and fully, **heart** and **soul**.

26:17-19 The people responded by affirming that the Lord was their God and that they would **walk in his ways, keep his statutes, commands, and ordinances, and obey him** (26:17). God responded with his covenant promise that if his people would **keep all his commands**, he would **elevate** them **to praise, fame, and glory above all the nations** and make them **a holy people** to himself (26:18-19). Nothing else could compare.

III. THE THIRD ADDRESS BY MOSES—BLESSINGS, CURSES, AND FINAL EXHORTATION (27:1–30:20)

27:1-8 In these chapters Moses identified the blessings and curses that would fall on Israel for keeping or despising the Lord's covenant. **Moses and the elders . . . commanded**

the people to conduct a covenant renewal ceremony that included writing the **law** on **large stones** covered **with plaster** (27:1-3). These stones were to be set up on **Mount**

Ebal, located about thirty-five miles north of Jerusalem, where the Israelites were also commanded to **build an altar of stones** and **offer burnt** and **fellowship offerings** to the Lord (27:4-7). The burnt offerings were completely consumed, symbolizing complete commitment to the Lord, while the fellowship offerings were eaten in a communal meal that expressed thanksgiving to God and joy in his presence.

27:9-10 Moses described the unusual form of this ceremony, which Joshua later carried out (see Josh 8:30-35). Moses's statement, **This day you have become the people of the LORD your God** (27:9), doesn't mean the Israelites weren't God's people before this point. Rather, at this crucial moment in their history, as they were ready to enter the land God had given them, they had recommitted themselves to obey his covenant by drawing a new line in the sand and stepping across it, so to speak.

27:12-13 To confirm that renewal in an unmistakable way, Moses commanded the people to divide themselves into two groups of six tribes between **Mount Gerizim** and **Mount Ebal** (27:12-13) to hear the blessings and curses read. Moses designated the Levites to read the curses to the people. These sobering warnings are listed in the rest of this chapter.

27:14-26 Twelve curses were given, with a summary curse being made at the end. Moses had issued stern warnings before, but in this ceremony the people would affirm that they understood each point through following it with an "Amen!" (27:15-26). They were pledging their obedience before God on each point and also giving him permission to bring down on them the curse attached to committing the sin described.

There's a new element introduced here that seems to tie these curses together: the fact that these sins could all be done **in secret** (27:15; also **secretly**, v. 24). A person could dishonor his parents behind the closed doors of their home, move **his neighbor's boundary marker** at night (27:17), mistreat **a blind person** or the powerless without everyone else knowing about it (27:18-19), or commit sexual sins or murder without being found

out (27:20-25). Nevertheless, the omniscient (all-knowing) and omnipresent (everywhere present) God would see what was done and judge the offender. Any Israelite tempted to commit so-called secret sins, then, was warned that God would not let him go unpunished.

The last verse here pronounced a sentence no Israelite—or anyone else for that matter—could escape: **Anyone who does not put the words of this law into practice is cursed** (27:26). As Israel would learn in the hard and bitter years ahead, they would prove incapable of perfectly keeping God's law. That's because the law doesn't give one the power to obey. It simply points out your shortcomings without granting you the ability to overcome them. In this way, the law is like a mirror—it shows what you look like but doesn't clean you up. The law is intended to show people our need for a Savior (see Gal 3:10-14).

28:1-6 Chapter 28 lays out for Israel the divine blessings for obedience to the covenant and the divine curses for disobedience. The chapter is hugely imbalanced: fourteen verses are devoted to blessings and fifty-four to curses. (Clearly God knew the tendency of his people to disobey.)

Nevertheless, the promised blessings for keeping the covenant were spectacular. God would bring a state of prosperity to every area of life if the Israelites would **faithfully obey** and be **careful to follow all his commands** (28:1). Not only would God exalt Israel **far above all the nations of the earth**, but his blessings would overwhelm them (28:1-2). Moses elaborated on that with a panoramic statement that covered every aspect of daily life (28:3-6).

28:7-14 Israel's blessings would affect the nations around them. Those lands that were their **enemies** would not be able to stand up against them (28:7). As a result of God's obvious favor on Israel, all nations **[would] see that** Israel bears **the LORD's name** and **stand in awe** (28:10). And while Israel would be a lender nation, she would not be a debtor one (28:12). In others words, God would see to it that Israel was honored in the eyes of the nations—so that *God* was honored in the eyes of the nations. All peoples would know that Israel's blessings came from the Lord, the Creator of all.

God's blessing would also extend to the Israelites' crops, children, and **livestock** (28:8, 11-12). This summary blessing provides a wonderful picture: Israel would be **the head and not the tail** among the nations, moving always **upward and never downward** if the people would be **careful to follow** God's commands (28:13). By living under God's authority and according to his agenda, you too get to live as the "head" rather than the "tail," experiencing God's blessings instead of being wagged this way and that as a result of sinful choices and their fallout.

28:15 Transitional words are important in Bible study. They are like flags signaling that an important change in thought, a conclusion, or a needed action step is coming. Here we see one of those transitional words: **But**. It's a sad word because it was followed by a barrage of curses that are gruesome in their detail. If Israel would **not obey the Lord**, they would be overtaken, not by blessings, but by **curses**. Unfortunately, future generations of Israelites would live to see these curses imposed.

28:16-25 It would have been bad enough if the curses had stopped with 28:15-19, which reversed the blessings of 28:3-6. But that described only the beginning of the terrible national fallout of living in opposition to the Lord. Israel would find itself encountering a stark reversal of their fortunes among the nations. Instead of remaining victorious, the people would **be defeated** by their **enemies**. Instead of being held in awe by the surrounding lands, Israel would be **an object of horror to all the kingdoms of the earth** (28:25).

28:26-29 Disobedience would also cause God to **afflict** the people with the physical and mental plagues he inflicted on **Egypt** when he delivered Israel from slavery (28:27-29; see also 28:60). In other words, if God's people chose to live as his enemies, he would treat them as such.

In the centuries to come, the curses were to have a teaching purpose, because when the people found themselves in an awful mess, they could see in God's promises a clear reminder that it was because they had failed to obey their good God in times of prosperity. Moses's desire was that future generations would read these words and commit themselves to avoiding the sins of their ancestors.

28:30-68 The worst horrors among the coming curses were the siege and the exile of Israel, two terrible judgments that would eventually come true (28:52, 63-64). The idea of exile is first mentioned in 28:36-37. But the real horrors associated with it are found in 28:49-57.

In the distant future, the **nation from far away** that would **swoop down on** Jerusalem **like an eagle** (28:49) would be Babylon under King Nebuchadnezzar. Babylon was **a ruthless nation, showing no respect for the old and not sparing the young** (28:50). Its army would besiege Jerusalem until its people resorted to the unimaginable degradation of cannibalism on their own children as all human compassion and dignity melted under the madness of hunger (28:53; see Lam 2:20; 4:10). The same thing would happen even earlier when the Arameans laid siege to the city of Samaria (see 2 Kgs 6:24-29).

Moses spared no detail in showing how disobedience to God would cause his people to be abandoned to the depths of depravity. But even then he wasn't done. The chapter ends with another powerful list of curses (28:58-68). Israel would endure **plagues** and **sicknesses** (28:59-61), their numbers would dwindle (28:62-63), they would be scattered among the nations (28:64), and they would find **no peace** (28:65). Such destruction would come upon them because they forgot the Lord and worshiped false gods. Therefore, the Lord would give them what they wanted: indeed they would **worship other gods**, make-believe deities with no power to hear them, let alone help them (28:64). And as a result, the Israelites would find themselves where they were before God had rescued them—as **slaves** (28:68).

Moses couldn't have been more clear. Faithfulness to God's covenant would grant the people of Israel everything. Rejection of the covenant would cost them everything. Neither the generation to whom he spoke or all those to follow could say they hadn't been warned.

29:1 Here the Israelites were reminded that **the words of the covenant** came *from* the Lord *through* Moses. The covenant was initiated by God, and God set the covenant parameters. This was his covenant, and he called the shots. But this covenant was mediated through Moses, who was the Lord's chosen representative. To reject Moses was to reject God, because Moses spoke God's words to the people. When Miriam complained about Moses's leadership, God struck her with diseased skin (see Num 12:1-10). When the Israelites complained about Moses and wanted to appoint a new leader, they were actually despising God (see Num 14:1-12).

As members of God's kingdom and participants in the new covenant, Christians are called to live under God's covenant in obedience to the covenant mediator, Jesus Christ. To reject Christ is to reject God.

29:2-4 Once again, Moses provided an important review of Israel's history. He reminded them of **everything the LORD did in Egypt to Pharaoh** (29:2). But before continuing Moses made a powerful observation: **Yet to this day the LORD has not given you a mind to understand, eyes to see, or ears to hear** (29:4). This was a sad recognition that even as the people stood there on the plains of Moab with all of God's miraculous deliverance and sustaining power in their memories, they had not yet fully grasped the spiritual significance of what he'd done. They would not operate according to the instructions of God's covenant and receive its blessings without it.

29:5-8 Moses continued by reviewing God's provision during their **forty years in the wilderness** (29:5) and their conquests in the Transjordan, as if to say, "Don't you remember, don't you see, don't you understand that God has provided for you to this point and can be trusted with your future?" His approach reminds us that history is not self-interpreting. An unbeliever could look at Israel's history and conclude that they were simply a resourceful and lucky people. But Moses provided the divine perspective on

their experiences—that is, the only reliable perspective. Every blessing, provision, and victory Israel received was from the Lord.

If you recognize that a similar truth governs your own life story, you will understand your utter dependence on God. If you don't grasp it, it won't be long before you believe in your own self-sufficiency, operate outside of his covenant, and find yourself living as the "tail" rather than the "head" (see 28:13).

29:9 In light of all the Lord had done for them, the Israelites were to **follow** his **covenant**. Why? **So that [they would] succeed in everything [they did]**. If Israel wanted success—victory over enemies, fruitful harvests and families, the ability to overcome their circumstances—covenant faithfulness was necessary.

God's covenants are designed to benefit his people. As members of the new covenant, Christians trust in Jesus Christ for forgiveness of sins. But, as his people, we are also called to live by the principles of and under the cover of his covenant. If you operate within God's covenant, you will experience the flow of his power. If you operate outside of it, you will not receive the covenant benefits but will be subject to being oppressed by sin, the world, and Satan. God's covenant is like an umbrella. It doesn't stop the rain from falling, but it keeps you from getting wet if you keep it over your head. The umbrella doesn't change your circumstances, but it keeps those circumstances from adversely affecting you.

29:10-15 The Israelites were **standing** with Moses **before the LORD** to **enter into the covenant** with him (29:10-12). Previously, these people's parents had entered God's covenant and failed to receive the promised land because of their disobedience. Now this new generation was being given an opportunity. God was going to fulfill what he **promised** to **Abraham, Isaac, and Jacob**—their forefathers (29:13). Nevertheless, it would require Israel's obedience to take hold of what God had promised. The Lord also looked ahead to generations yet unborn, calling on his listeners to obey God not only for their blessings but also for the sake of their children and grandchildren (29:14-15).

29:16-18 Moses couldn't put a period after the blessings, however. Another harsh warning was added for any man, woman, clan, or tribe who turned from the Lord to idolatry—a reminder of how even a small **root** of sin among the people could bear **poisonous and bitter fruit** (29:18) that would bring God's judgment.

The author of Hebrews made reference to this verse when he warned his readers to make sure that "no root of bitterness [sprung] up" among them (Heb 12:15). When one of God's people experiences trying circumstances, he needs the encouragement and comfort of the rest of the body of Christ. Otherwise difficulties can make people bitter and cause them to turn to sin, eventually poisoning the entire fellowship of believers.

29:19-21 Lest any Israelite **consider himself exempt** from this warning (29:19), he needed to know that such selfish thinking could lead to the ruin of the whole land—as well as bringing **every curse written in** Deuteronomy down on his head as God blotted out **his name under heaven** (29:20). Nothing can be hidden from God, and he would have no trouble picking out and punishing an individual guilty of such thoughts (29:21).

29:22-28 To make his point more graphic, Moses described the destruction of Israel for idolatry in terms of the land becoming **a burning waste of sulfur and salt . . . like . . . Sodom and Gomorrah** (29:23). The nations around Israel that knew it was supposed to be the object of God's favor would be shocked at such devastation and would ask how it could happen (29:24). The answer would be that Israel had forsaken its covenant with the true God and worshiped and served false gods, leading to its destruction and exile (29:25-28).

29:29 As was the case for Israel, it's impossible for us to know everything there is to know about God. Paul declares, "Oh, the depth of the riches both of the wisdom and of the knowledge of God! How unsearchable his judgments and untraceable his ways!" (Rom 11:33). The Lord is infinite and transcendent. Whatever knowledge he chooses to keep from us is beyond our ability to obtain. Nevertheless, he has **revealed** to us everything that we need to know. God's Holy Word contains all that we (**and our children**) need in order to understand, trust, and obey him.

30:1-10 Moses had pleaded with great passion for his hearers to maintain faithfulness to the Lord once they crossed the Jordan and took possession of the promised land. But he also foresaw their future apostasy and even exile from the land (30:1). So he gave them a promise of future regathering and blessing that his immediate audience and later generations of Israelites must have wondered about in terms of its fulfillment. This first half of the chapter is a prophecy, the interpretation of which requires that the full lens of Scripture be used. Moses was speaking about Israel's full spiritual restoration and material blessing in the kingdom age, which will not come about until the return of Jesus Christ in his millennial kingdom. In other words, we're still waiting for it.

But at that time God will give the people of Israel new hearts to **obey him** (30:2, 6), and they will believe in Jesus as their Messiah. They will enjoy a time of blessing in Christ's millennial kingdom greater than the nation has ever known before (30:5). All the blessings that Moses had recited to the nation will be realized when the people of Israel become circumcised in heart to **love** God as he has commanded them to do (30:6). It will be God's great delight to bless his people with abundant **prosperity** when they return to him wholeheartedly and obey him (30:9-10).

30:11-15 Moses spent almost the entire book of Deuteronomy explaining God's law and urging the people of Israel to obey it. He could do this because the law was not some hard-to-understand code they couldn't figure out, or a strange teaching they were hearing for the first time (30:11). It was not a buried treasure they had to search for before reaping its benefits (30:12-13). Instead, Moses argued, God's law was **very near** to them, something he had graciously made known to them (30:14). And they knew the consequences for obedience and disobedience: **life and prosperity** or **death and adversity** (30:15).

30:16-20 So Moses told the people once more the requirements for life—to **love** God, **walk in his ways**, and **keep his commands** (30:16). And he also declared once again the warning of judgment for disobedience (30:17-18). Then came this charge: **Choose life so that you and your descendants may live** (30:19). In other words, Moses argued, no other decision made sense: God himself is the **life** of his people. He is the only one who could **prolong** their **days** in the promised land (30:20). Therefore, to experience the favor of God, his people must choose obedience to divine revelation over their own autonomous human reason.

IV. THE TRANSITION FROM MOSES TO JOSHUA (31:1–34:12)

31:1-5 Moses's messages were over. He had come to the end of his leadership. Even though he was **120 years old** (31:1), his age was not what would prevent him from entering the promised land (see Num 20:1-13). But Moses didn't dwell on that. He knew the important thing was that the Lord would **cross ahead** of Israel, clearing the way before them (31:3). Under the leadership of **Joshua**, Israel would defeat their enemies because God would **deliver them over** (31:3-5).

31:6-8 Moses then gave the Israelites an exhortation that became God's rallying call later to Joshua: **Be strong and courageous** (31:6; see Josh 1:6-7, 9, 18). Then Moses turned and said those same words to Joshua (31:7). If you're wondering why God had to tell Joshua so many times to be strong and courageous, it's because he knew the human tendency to be **afraid** and **discouraged** when facing giants (31:8).

31:9-13 Moses wrote down this law and gave it to the priests, with the command to have it read **aloud** (publicly) every seventh year when the nation gathered in Jerusalem for the **Festival of Shelters** (31:9-10). The seventh year was the Sabbatical year when debts were forgiven and slaves were freed (see 15:1-23), making it an important time already. The Festival of Shelters was one of three annual pilgrim festivals requiring all Israelite men to go to the central sanctuary. On this occasion, however, they were commanded to bring their families. A public reading of the law would have the benefits of review and education: the people would **listen and learn to fear the LORD** through hearing it (31:12). In addition, the **children who [did] not [yet] know the law** would be taught **to fear the LORD** (31:13).

31:14-15 Joshua had been publicly commissioned as God's choice for Moses's successor (see Num 27:18-23). Here, as the time for Moses's death approached, God ratified his choice a final time with another commissioning service at the tabernacle. The appearance of the glory of God in **a pillar of cloud** (31:15) would have provided all the confirmation that Israel needed: Joshua was God's man.

31:16-30 But the Lord also gave heartbreaking news to Moses. After he died, Israel would **soon prostitute themselves with the foreign gods** in the land of Canaan. They would **abandon** God and **break the covenant** that Moses had spent so much time explaining (31:16). Therefore, God would **abandon them and** would **hide [his] face from them** (31:17). God also gave Moses a **song** whose purpose was to remind his people of the reason for the **troubles and afflictions** they would encounter, showing them the path to forgiveness by means of his grace (31:19-21). Moses must have left this meeting with mixed emotions: sadness over the future sin of God's people, joy in knowing that his legacy would continue through the writing down of the covenant, and righteous anger over the Israelites' **rebellious and stiff-necked** nature that would lead them to spiritual disaster (31:27).

32:1-12 Then Moses proceeded to recite the song to the entire assembly of Israel (31:30). The "Song of Moses" is an incredible teaching instrument that traces God's deal-ings with the nation. As if in a courtroom, Moses called the **heavens** and the **earth** as witnesses to the truth of what he was about to say, beginning with his testimony to **the greatness of our God** whose **work is per-fect** (32:1-4). In contrast to God's greatness and faithfulness to Israel, his people **acted corruptly toward him** by becoming **a de-vious and crooked generation**—it was a wretched way to repay the love and kindness he had shown them (32:5-12).

32:13-18 The Lord had **nourished** Israel throughout their journey (32:13-14). But once the people enjoyed these blessings, **Jeshurun** (a term of affection for Israel meaning "Upright One") **became fat, bloat-ed, and gorged**, like a rebellious, stupid an-imal that kicks at the master who feeds it even as it chews what he's provided (32:15). Israel treated God with utter contempt and scorn by abandoning him for **different gods** who were actually **demons** (32:16-17). They forgot **the God who gave birth to** them (32:18). The Lord was a kind and devoted Father, but his ungrateful children hated him.

32:19-21 Israel's flagrant disobedience pro-voked God's righteous anger and judgment. This statement is ominous: **I will hide my face from them** (32:20). When the God who alone made you and sustains you turns his back on you, there is absolutely no hope. We see a similar phrase used in the book of Esther when Queen Esther revealed that Haman had plotted to kill her and the Jews. Once King Ahasuerus passed sentence on Haman, "they covered Haman's face" (Esth 7:8) to hide the king's face from him. This symbolized that he was out of appeals.

32:22-27 God's anger is compared to a raging **fire** (32:22). His judgment would come in the form of **disasters** such as **pestilence and bitter plague . . . wild beasts . . . venom-ous snakes . . . the sword** and **terror** that would take the lives of everyone, includ-ing **the infant and the gray-haired man** (32:23-25). Israel's record of apostasy was already so great that the nation deserved to be cut off completely by their enemies. But

God stopped short of doing that lest Israel's enemies wrongfully concluded that their power—and not God himself—had defeat-ed God's people (32:26-27). The Lord would make sure that the nations understood: Is-rael hadn't been vanquished because their God was weak. On the contrary, Israel was vanquished *by* their holy God.

32:28-29 You have to wonder what Moses's hearers were thinking when they heard him say, **Israel is a nation lacking sense with no understanding at all** (32:28). They could consider the example of their parents' gen-eration—those who had been buried in the wilderness because they failed to trust God and blew their chance to enjoy the prom-ised land. But perhaps this new generation thought to themselves that they wouldn't be like that. If so, they would have benefit-ed from Paul's warning to the Corinthians: "Whoever thinks he stands must be careful not to fall" (1 Cor 10:12).

32:30-33 We all would like to think that we'll do better than those who have gone before us. But we would be wiser to recog-nize that we are prone to failure and pray to the Lord, "Do not bring us into temptation, but deliver as from the evil one" (Matt 6:13). In the case of arrogant Israel, apostasy was in their future to such a tragic degree that the Lord would give them up (32:30) because they had become as sinful as **Sodom** and **Gomorrah** (32:32).

32:34-47 Moses concluded his song with a word of deliverance for Israel after God's fierce judgment had run its course. God would take **vengeance** on Israel's enemies once he saw that the nation had come to the end of its **strength** and turned back to him (32:34-36). But Israel had to learn a hard les-son first—the futility of depending on false **gods** for **help** in their time of disaster (32:37-38). Only then would they be ready to come back in repentance to the Lord, who **alone** could **heal** them (32:39). Then he would rise up in **vengeance on** his **adversaries** (32:41) and **purify his land and his people** (32:43). Moses taught the people these **words** of life to help ensure their blessing in the promised land (32:44-47).

32:48-52 On that same day, Moses was given instructions regarding where he was to go to die. **From a distance** (32:48-52), and out of God's mercy, he would be able to view the promised land's extent.

33:1-5 The blessing Moses gave in this chapter served as something of a last will and testament. It was modeled on the blessing Jacob imparted to each of his sons, the patriarchs of Israel's tribes, who shared their names (see Genesis 49). One difference is that the tribe of Simeon is omitted and Joseph is counted as one, although his two sons Manasseh and Ephraim are mentioned. Judging from the statement in 34:1, it seems Moses pronounced his blessing to the people before making the final climb up Mount Nebo. It was appropriate for Moses to bless the children of Israel as their "father" who was present at the nation's birth in the exodus of Egypt. He recalled God's majesty in his appearance at Sinai and his guidance through the wilderness years (33:2-5). Then he spoke of the future.

33:6-11 First, Moses asked that **Reuben**, the tribe descended from Israel's eldest son by that name, would **live . . . though his people become few** (33:6). **Judah**, the tribe from which Jesus would be born, had led the way in Israel's march through the wilderness and would continue to lead into the promised land, needing God's **help** for victory in battle (33:7). **Levi** was also a significant tribe, providing Israel with its priests and counting Moses and Aaron among its members. The Levites were the faithful ones who **kept** God's **word** and **maintained** his **covenant** by teaching his **ordinances** and **instruction** (33:8-10). Thus, Moses asked that Levi be protected from **his adversaries and enemies** (33:11).

33:12-25 Benjamin (33:12) and Joseph (33:13-17), the patriarchs of the tribes bearing their names, were Jacob's youngest and favorite sons through his beloved Rachel. **Benjamin** is called **the LORD's beloved** who **rests on** God's **shoulders**, which is a picture of great peace that brings to mind a shepherd carrying a lamb (33:12). **Joseph** was the most blessed of all of Jacob's sons and was a type of Christ (that is, a foreshadowing of Christ) in that he was the redeemer of his family in a situation that would've ended in their deaths. Moses prayed that God would bless Joseph with great material prosperity (33:13-16). The blessing on Joseph's **land** (33:13) was realized by his sons, **Manasseh** and **Ephraim** (33:17), since his portion among his brothers was given to his offspring (see Gen 48). The blessings continued with the tribes of **Zebulun** and **Issachar** (33:18-19), **Gad** and **Dan** (33:20-22), **Naphtali** and **Asher** (33:23-25).

33:26-29 Moses concluded his blessing on the tribes of Israel with his final words of praise to **the God of Jeshurun** (33:26; on "Jeshurun," see 32:15). There was no word of warning or coming judgment here, just a magnificent picture of Israel's majestic God who held them in his **everlasting arms** and stood ready to **destroy** their enemies (33:27). If only Israel would love and serve him faithfully, God would see to it that his people lived **securely** and **untroubled in a land of grain and new wine** where even God's **skies drip with dew** and Israel's enemies **cringe before** them (33:28-29).

34:1-4 With those words said, Moses walked up **Mount Nebo** to his funeral, as an anonymous writer recorded here as an epilogue to the story (34:1). God graciously **showed him all the land** of Israel, which suggests that what he saw required a supernatural extension of his vision (34:1-3). Even though Moses would not be allowed to enter Canaan, God affirmed his promise to **Abraham, Isaac, and Jacob** to give it to their **descendants**, the Israelites (34:4).

34:5-12 Moses **died there** on Mount Nebo and was buried by the Lord **in the land of Moab**, even though he was **not weak** and had not lost his **vitality** (34:5-7). After a **mourning** period of **thirty days**, the Israelites prepared to move into Canaan under **Joshua**, whom God **filled with the spirit of wisdom** for his huge task (34:8-9). The closing tribute to Moses ends this book and demonstrates the truth that **no prophet** like him ever arose again in Israel—a prophet **whom the LORD knew face to face** and who performed **mighty acts of power and terrifying deeds . . . in the sight of all Israel** (34:10-12).

Nevertheless, one day a new kind of prophet—an even better one—would arise (see 18:15; Acts 3:22-23). He would be a man—but far more than a man (see John 1:1-14). He would be the Son of God (see Matt 3:17). Though God knew Moses face to face, yet God's glory would truly shine in the face of Jesus Christ (see 2 Cor 4:6). Moses was faithful in God's household, but the Son would be worthy of more honor, in the same way that a builder has more honor than the house (see Heb 3:2-3). For the law came through Moses, but grace and truth would come through Jesus Christ (see John 1:17).

JOSHUA

INTRODUCTION

Author

THE BOOK OF JOSHUA IS ANONY-mous; no author is identified in the text. It's certainly possible that Joshua himself wrote much of it. If he did not, then the book was penned by someone who both knew him and had access to his testimony and deeds. Regardless of whether or not Joshua was personally involved in its authorship, the book was clearly completed after his death, given the final words in 24:29-33.

Historical Background

The events in Joshua take place after the death of Moses (Josh 1:1), who appointed Joshua as his successor in obedience to the Lord (see Num 27:15-23; Deut 34:9). The people of Israel had come out of Egypt, entered into a covenant with God, spent forty years in the wilderness for their disobedience, and were now on the verge of crossing the Jordan River and entering the promised land (Josh 1:2-4). According to 1 Kings 6:1, "the fourth year" of King Solomon's reign over Israel (966 BC) happened 480 years after the Israelites had departed Egypt. Allowing for the forty years Israel spent in the wilderness, that would mean the book of Joshua opens in approximately 1400 BC—that is, fourteen hundred years before the birth of Christ.

Message and Purpose

The book of Joshua shows how God was faithful to fulfill his covenant with Israel to give them the land of Canaan. It also shows the participation of the people in the fulfillment of that plan as they conquered what God had already said he would give them. Israel had experienced a forty-year delay in

claiming the promised land because of the disobedience of Moses's generation. But now the new generation would see that indeed God was faithful to his promises every step of the way—from the parting of the Jordan River, to making the sun stand still, to collapsing the walls of Jericho.

The lesson of Joshua for us is twofold: God is faithful to keep his Word, and we are to participate in his kingdom work through our obedience to him. Joshua refused to succumb to the pressures around him, and he challenged God's people to do the same. May we declare with Joshua, "As for me and my family, we will worship the LORD" (24:15).

www.bhpublishinggroup.com/qr/te/06_00

Outline

I. Entering the Promised Land (1:1–5:12)
  A. Joshua Assumes Command (1:1-18)
  B. The Faith of Rahab (2:1-24)
  C. Crossing the Jordan (3:1–5:12)
II. Claiming the Promised Land (5:13–12:24)
  A. Victory at Jericho (5:13–6:27)
  B. Defeat and Victory at Ai (7:1–8:35)
  C. Deceived by Gibeon (9:1-27)
  D. Victory throughout the Land (10:1–12:24)
III. Dividing the Promised Land (13:1–21:45)
IV. Serving God in the Promised Land (22:1–24:33)

JOSHUA

I. ENTERING THE PROMISED LAND (1:1–5:12)

❧ A. Joshua Assumes Command
(1:1-18) ❧

1:1-2 The LORD spoke to Joshua son of Nun . . . **"Moses my servant is dead. Now . . . prepare to cross over the Jordan [River]"** (1:1-2). Moses had been the greatest human leader Israel had ever known, but Moses was gone; he was yesterday's news. Israel had to stop looking back to the leeks and garlic of Egypt (see Num 11:4-6) and the good old days when Moses had led and instead look ahead to the milk and honey and new leadership of the promised land (Exod 3:7-8). It was time to move on.

It's important to remember the past: we should appreciate the good and learn from the bad. But in the walk of faith, you can't live on nostalgia; you can't live with your eyes on the rearview mirror of your life. You've got to face forward.

1:3-6 **I have given you every place where the sole of your foot treads. . . . No one will be able to stand against you . . . Be strong and courageous** (1:3-6). In other words, he reminded Joshua that the promised land—Israel's inheritance—was already given to them. That didn't mean, however, that they were to sit and do nothing and wait for the local inhabitants to simply abandon Canaan to them. Actions of faith were required to make literal what God had already made legal. The enemies of God would resist, but they would fail—provided that Israel was "strong and courageous" (1:7, 9, 18).

This is an example of the intersection of God's sovereignty and human responsibility. God makes promises, but we are called to obey in order to secure them. Consider a parent who pays for a child's education. If the child doesn't go to class or study, it is not the promise of a free education that will inevitably fail. The problem is that the promise wasn't embraced.

God's process for every believer mirrors his process for Israel: he offers deliverance, development, and destiny. *Deliverance* is salvation—what happens when we trust in Jesus Christ. *Development* is the process of sanctification; it's like our time in the wilderness as we experience God's trials to test and grow our faith. *Destiny* is what God has planned for us, eternal life in heaven and the rewards that come with it. God's promises are a sure thing, but much of the timing depends on us. Will we say yes to deliverance? Are we willing to grow in our faith? Are we committed to living in light of eternity? We are called to pursue God's promises, reaching out to touch heaven through acts of faith while our feet still walk on this broken ground.

1:7-9 Next God said, **Observe carefully the whole instruction my servant Moses commanded you . . . so that you will have success wherever you go** (1:7). Success for Israel, then, involved obtaining their inheritance. To do this, they had to stay tightly tethered to God's Word.

Ultimately, success for a Christian is not rising to popularity, power, prosperity, or position. Success is fulfilling your God-given purpose in life. To do that, you (like Israel) must **meditate on** Scripture and **carefully observe everything written in it** (1:7-8). To meditate on something is to roll it over and over in your mind in much the same way that a cow chews its cud. When you do, the Word of God is driven deeply into your soul so that your actions can be driven by God's perspective rather than your feelings or cultural opinion.

1:10-15 After receiving instructions from the Lord, Joshua told the people in effect to "get ready to rumble" (1:10-11). Specifically he told **the Reubenites, the Gadites, and half the tribe of Manasseh,** who had already received their **inheritance . . . on the east side of the Jordan,** to help the other tribes claim their land. Joshua challenged them to reject selfishness and to **battle** alongside their **brothers** so that everyone could obtain the **rest** (i.e., the experience of God's promise) that God had provided (1:12-15).

1:16-18 To this the people responded, **Everything you have commanded us we will do** (1:16). They had accepted the fact that the baton had been passed from **Moses** to Joshua (1:17). They were fully on board with the stated plan. All they wanted was for their leader to **be strong and courageous** (1:18). In other words, they wanted him to obey the Lord. Believers must expect the same of their church leaders. They are to be followed inasmuch as they follow God.

⮞ B. The Faith of Rahab (2:1-24) ⮜

2:1 The acquisition of the promised land began with Joshua dispatching two **spies** to determine the best military approach to use in the days ahead. In particular, they were to **scout** the city of **Jericho**—the first major city the people would encounter upon crossing the Jordan River. When the spies entered Jericho, they chose to hide in the red light district and stayed with **a prostitute named Rahab.** (It could be that Rahab was running an inn for travelers. If so, staying there would have helped the spies to look inconspicuous.) Importantly, these men were in town for righteous purposes—not for wickedness.

2:2-7 Somehow **the king of Jericho** learned of the presence of the **Israelite men** within the gates of his city and demanded that Rahab turn them in (2:2-3). But Rahab put him off by engaging in some righteous risky business: she hid the men and lied to the authorities (2:4-7).

2:8-12 Rahab's actions in this chapter raise a significant ethical question: When is it acceptable to lie? Rahab was confronted with two sinful options, lying or abetting the execution of God's representatives, and she chose the option that would bring the most glory to God—protecting his people. She then told the spies that Jericho had **heard** of how the Lord had miraculously protected the Israelites from their enemies and that therefore, the people were terrified (2:8-11). In this, she encouraged them. Yet it's clear by what we see in this story that neither the king nor his people were planning to surrender to the plans of the Lord regarding their homeland.

Rahab was different. She confessed that the LORD . . . is God in heaven above and on earth below and showed **kindness** to his people (2:11-12). In other words, she expressed personal faith in the true God's ability to work on behalf of those aligned with him and acted on it. This required her to shelter God's people and work against his enemies, in much the same way that the Hebrew midwives had frustrated the murderous plans of Pharaoh in Exodus 1:15-21.

2:13-21 Trusting that Israel would successfully conquer Jericho, Rahab hid the spies and asked them to **spare** her and her family on the day when they sacked the city (2:13). This they promised to do—as long as she tied a **scarlet cord** in the window of her **house,** which was in **the wall of the city**. If she did that, both she and her **family** would be saved (2:14-20). Remarkably, though Jericho's walls would soon fall down (6:20), this woman's house that was constructed within them was left standing (6:22-23). Rahab submitted in faith to God's program. As a result, she came under the covering of Israel, and her family did too.

2:22-24 The spies returned to Joshua and **reported everything** (2:22-23). They were confident that **the LORD [had] handed over**

the entire land to [them] as promised (2:24). Why were they so certain? Much of it came down to the words and actions of an unlikely ally, the prostitute named Rahab.

This woman's background and significance in God's kingdom plan cannot be overstated. Hers is a story that provides hope to us all. It's a beautiful reminder that God's grace can meet us where we are and use us to accomplish his purposes. Throughout Scripture, Rahab is repeatedly identified by her occupation as a *prostitute* (2:1; 6:17, 22, 25)—even in the New Testament (Heb 11:31; Jas 2:25). In the Bible, repetition is emphasis. God wants us to understand that, no matter how wretched our pasts, he can do great things through anyone who righteously connects to him through faith. In God's providence, Rahab would become a link in the family chain leading to Jesus Christ (see Matt 1:5).

❧ C. Crossing the Jordan (3:1–5:12) ❧

3:1-4 It was time to move. **The ark of the covenant of the Lord** would lead the way (3:3). Back when the Israelites left Egypt, God's presence led them—first in a "cloud" by day and then in a "pillar of fire" by night (see Exod 13:21-22). Since God is invisible, he manifested his presence for them in these ways. But when Israel crossed the Jordan, God's presence would be manifested by the golden ark of the covenant, a box containing the tablets of the Ten Commandments that was covered by the "mercy seat," which had two cherubim on it. It was above the mercy seat and between the cherubim that God promised to meet with Moses (see Exod 25:22). Since the Israelites understood the Lord to be "enthroned between the cherubim" (1 Sam 4:4; 2 Kgs 19:15), in fact, this was a visual reminder that Israel's King would personally lead them into the promised land.

3:5-6 Joshua called the people to make spiritual preparation for divine manifestation, to **consecrate** themselves (3:5). Most people wouldn't dream of walking into the presence of the president of the United States without first taking a shower and dressing appropriately—though a human leader is

a sinner just like the rest of us. How much more, then, should we prepare ourselves spiritually if we want to encounter the divine presence of God? Joshua told Israel to clean up and prepare because God was about to blow their minds.

3:7-13 God spoke to Joshua and provided instructions for the priests and the people. The **priests** were to carry **the ark** out in front of the tribes (3:8, 11). The Lord would stop the **water** of the Jordan River from **flowing** so that the soldiers and people could cross—but only after the priests stepped into the river (3:12-13). Why not stop the waters first? Because God wanted to see faith in action before he provided the miracle. God's purpose for accomplishing such wonders was plain: **You will know that the living God is among you and that he will certainly dispossess before you** the inhabitants of the land (3:10). Dividing the waters of the Jordan would be God's way of demonstrating to Israel that he was alive and with them, so that they would be prepared for the challenges ahead. God sometimes does wondrous things in our lives too, so that when we meet a challenge in the future we will *remember* his power.

3:14-17 When the people broke camp they could see that not only was there a river in the way, but it was overflowing **its banks** (3:15). The waters were as broad and deep as they could be: there was no hope of wading or even swimming across. But as soon as the priests' feet hit the water, the people were able to cross because **the water flowing downstream . . . was completely cut off** (3:15-16). And even more amazingly, the Lord also quick dried the earth where the river had been. No feet stuck in the mud; no cart wheels bogged down. **Israel crossed on dry ground** (3:17). This was no freak act of nature. It was an act of God.

4:1-3 God commanded Joshua to have **twelve men from the people, one man for each tribe** take **twelve stones** from the riverbed and carry them to their new camp. These were to be memorial stones. A memorial is used to help people remember important events and individuals in history. The national park service, for instance, manages sites with memorials of significant people, places, or battles from American history. The football and baseball halls of fame have memorials to special athletes and their achievements. Even the church has memorials. The greatest of these is Communion, a special ceremony through which we remember the accomplishment of the sacrificial death of Christ (see 1 Cor 11:23-26).

4:4-7 God wanted the people to remember what he did at the Jordan and to pass on that remembrance to future generations. When **in the future** the people's children and grandchildren saw the stones and asked, **What do these stones mean to you?** (4:6), parents would be able to point to the rocks, taking advantage of an opportunity for spiritual formation in their children (4:7). They were to tell them the history of God's work on their behalf.

We must not only remember the times in our lives when God has shown up, stepped into a difficult situation, or done something extraordinary. We must also give testimony about them.

4:8-9 The Israelites did exactly as God commanded (4:8). But Joshua also set up a second memorial of his own. He took **twelve stones** and set them up **in the middle of the Jordan where the priests ... were standing** (4:9). Knowing that the rocks stood there, long after the river covered them over, would encourage Joshua in later years that nothing could stand in Israel's path with the Lord leading the way. When the book of Joshua was completed, those stones the priests had placed (and those under the water) were **still there** (4:9), silent reminders of the mighty power of Israel's great God.

4:10-18 After all the people had crossed the riverbed (4:10-13), God told Joshua to command the **priests** carrying the ark **to come up from the Jordan** (4:16). When they did, the water returned to its place (4:17-18). **On that day the LORD exalted Joshua** so that Israel **revered** Joshua **as they had revered Moses** (4:14), through whom God had worked to part the Red Sea four decades prior. God wanted all Israel to know: Joshua is my man. Follow him.

4:19-24 The people **camped at Gilgal** (4:19), where Joshua reminded the Israelites to use the memorial **stones** to bear witness to their **children** about the amazing works of God (4:21-23). But ultimately this testimony wasn't merely for the benefit of the people of God. They were to report God's deeds **so that all the peoples of the earth** (including you and me) **[might] know that the LORD's hand is mighty, and so that [they would] always fear the LORD** (4:24). God's people, past and present, are to work to spread his fame and glory throughout the earth.

5:1-9 When the **kings** of the land heard what God had done at the river, they were terrified and **their courage failed** (5:1), which is much in line with Rahab's earlier report to the spies (2:9-11). But before the Israelites were to engage in battle, God told Joshua to have the men **circumcised** (5:3).

Circumcision was the sign of the covenant between God and the descendants of Abraham (see Gen 17:9-14). The practice made them physically different from the surrounding peoples. Even though the men who had come **out of Egypt** had been circumcised, their children had not (5:4-6). So it was time to rectify the problem. **The entire nation** (that is, the males within it) was **circumcised** and stayed **in the camp until they recovered** (5:8).

Circumcision is a painful procedure for an adult male to undergo, and it requires a period of healing. During that time, then, the men would have been physically vulnerable to attack. But, by coming under the covenant as instructed, they were spiritually protected by divine covering. So what appeared to be negative was actually a positive.

What did God mean when he said, **Today I have rolled away the disgrace of Egypt from you?** (5:9). In Egypt, the Israelites had been slaves. And even in the wilderness, many Israelites were longing to return there. But in the men's submission to the act of circumcision, this disgrace had been rolled back. It signaled that they were finally, truly free.

One of the great spiritual truths of the New Testament is that believers in Jesus Christ are free from slavery to sin (8:34-36). Though it lures us, we don't have to submit to it. Yet throughout our lifetimes, the devil works to deceive us, to cause us to think and act like we're still slaves to his will. He works to keep us from believing the truth of our freedom from sin, because the one who believes that he's truly free might actually start acting like it. If you find yourself falling for his tricks, it's time to ask the Lord to "roll away" the disgrace of your past so that you can move forward in victory.

5:10-12 While camping on **the plains of Jericho**, Israel **observed the Passover**, remembering their deliverance from Egyptian slavery (5:10). During the celebration, **they ate . . . from the produce of the land** (5:11). That may sound like a throw-away statement until you read the follow up: **And the day after . . . the manna ceased** (5:12). For

the last forty years during their wanderings in the wilderness, God had provided manna—bread from heaven—for them to eat (see Exod 16). But once God brought them to the promised land, their manna days were over. Thus, from this point forward, if they were going to eat, they would have to act on his promises.

Here I see an application to a person's spiritual development. Babies have to be fed. But if you're spoon-feeding your twelve-year-old, there's a serious problem! Similarly, as you grow in Christian maturity, God expects you to exercise more and more responsibility for your spiritual growth. It's good to receive instruction in the Scriptures. But we will remain spiritual infants unless we put into practice what we're learning by trusting God and acting on his promises.

II. CLAIMING THE PROMISED LAND (5:13–12:24)

❧ A. *Victory at Jericho* (5:13–6:27) ❦

5:13 The Israelites were on the plains of Jericho, in sight of the impregnable walled city. Joshua knew God had given them the land of Canaan, but fortress cities like Jericho stood in the way of takeover. Perhaps while he was pondering that very thing, Joshua noticed **a man standing in front of him with a drawn sword**. Obviously, this stranger wasn't merely out for a stroll. He was armed for a fight. So in light of that, Joshua logically wanted to know whose side he was on. He asked, **Are you for us or for our enemies?**

5:14-15 The man replied, **Neither**. His allegiance belonged not to Jericho or Israel, but to heaven. He said, **I have . . . come as commander of the LORD's army**. Who was he? Well, God directs legions of angels to do his will, and this mighty warrior commanded them all. It's important to observe this as an earthly manifestation of the Son of God before his incarnation as a man. Why? First, when he recognized that he was outranked by the visitor, **Joshua bowed with his face to the ground in worship** (5:14). We are to worship God alone, and angels

rightly reject worship (see Rev 19:10; 22:9). This stranger accepted it as his due. Though Joshua didn't understand the Trinitarian nature of God (that is, the fact that God is one in three persons), he clearly recognized that this was a visible manifestation of the divine presence. Second, **the commander** told Joshua to **remove [his] sandals** because he was standing on **holy** ground (5:15). If these words sound familiar, it's because we have heard them before. As the man who had taken Moses's place, Joshua was having his own burning bush moment, complete with the command to remove his shoes (see Exod 3:1-6). Holy ground is God-occupied space. Only God can turn an ordinary place into sacred territory.

In the next moments, God would give Joshua a divine strategy for defeating Jericho (6:1-5). But don't miss the order of events leading up to the fight: Joshua faced a stronghold, God revealed himself, and Joshua worshiped. The strategy for victory would come only after worship had occurred.

6:1-2 The next chapter opens with the reminder that **Jericho was strongly fortified** (6:1). As Rahab had told the spies (2:9-11), the people of Jericho were terrified of the

Israelites and their God. So as the invaders drew near, the city's occupants weren't letting anyone get in or out of their defensive wall of protection. But the Lord told Joshua, **I have handed Jericho, its king, and its best soldiers over to you** (6:2). This meant that though the battle hadn't even occurred yet, Jericho had already lost according to God. Though it had not yet happened in history, the victory had been declared in eternity. God wanted Joshua to be assured of this because he was about to give him a battle plan that wouldn't make sense.

6:3-5 God commanded Joshua to have **seven priests carry seven ram's-horn trumpets.** They and all the men were to **march around the city** . . . **one time** every day for **six days.** Then **on the seventh day**, they were to march **seven times** (6:3-4). After the final lap around the city, the priests were to **blow the trumpets** and the men were to shout. Then the **wall** would **collapse** in such a way that the invaders could go **straight** in and take care of business (6:4-5).

You'd have to be asleep not to notice the repetition of the number "seven" in these verses. In Scripture, seven is the number of completion. God created the world in six days and rested on the seventh. The seven churches of Revelation represent all churches. As Revelation continues, the seven seals are opened, the seven trumpets sound, and the seven bowls are poured out—all indicating the completion of God's work.

So in these instructions God was emphasizing to Joshua that he must follow the instructions completely if he wanted God to bring down his problem supernaturally. Don't miss that truth.

6:6-25 A careful reading of 6:6-15 reveals that Joshua and the people did exactly what the Lord told them to do. We don't know what the people of Jericho thought about this seven-day parade, but Israel was faithful to obey God. On the seventh day, **the priests blew the trumpets** and Joshua ordered, **Shout!** (6:16). Show time! And at that moment, **the wall collapsed.** Immediately thereafter, **the troops advanced into the city, each man straight ahead** (6:20). God had turned the barrier that stood in their way into a pathway

of stepping-stones leading to their goal. But he didn't do it without their involvement. The author of Hebrews says, "By faith the walls of Jericho fell" (Heb 11:30). To be a person of faith, then, doesn't mean sitting around doing nothing. It requires acting on that faith—trusting that what God says, he will do. By faith, Israel followed divine instruction and saw supernatural results.

Because she was faithful in protecting God's people, **Rahab the prostitute** was rescued as promised, along with her whole family (6:17, 22-23, 25). Many years later, the author of Hebrews would single her out for her faith (see Heb 11:31). But because the inhabitants of Jericho defied God with their wickedness (see Deut 12:29-31; 20:16-18), they were put to death (6:21). The Israelites were not to take any of the things that were **set apart** for this **destruction** (6:18). Everything of value in the city was either to be destroyed or preserved for **the LORD's treasury** (6:19)—a prohibition that will be very important to the events of chapter 7.

6:26-27 Joshua placed a **curse** on Jericho. Whoever sought to rebuild the city would do so at the cost of his own children (6:26). This prophetic curse would be fulfilled centuries later (see 1 Kgs 16:34).

➤ B. Defeat and Victory at Ai
(7:1–8:35) ❦

7:1 Chapter 7 shows Israel's move from the thrill of victory to the agony of defeat. Joshua had commanded the Israelites, "Keep yourselves from the things set apart, or you will be set apart for destruction" (6:18). He was warning the people not to take articles in the city (whether they be of silver, gold, bronze, or iron) because such things were to be "dedicated" for "the treasury of the LORD's house" (6:19, 24). In other words, if anyone messed with restricted items, God would mess with him. Unfortunately, one Israelite thought he could ignore the warning. He tried to get away with stealing from God.

The first verse reveals the guilty party's identity. Then the remainder of the chapter describes the consequences of his sin. After the battle of Jericho, **Achan son of Camri ... took some of what was set apart.** Therefore, **the LORD's anger burned against the Israelites.** But if Achan was the lone thief, why was God angry with the whole nation? Why does the passage say **the Israelites ... were unfaithful?** This is a reminder of the corporate nature of the people of God. The Israelites were like a football team in one sense. Thus, if one player committed an infraction of the rules, the entire team was penalized.

Importantly, God still expects his people to function as a team. Paul says the church is a *body*: "If one member suffers, all the members suffer with it; if one member is honored, all the members rejoice" (1 Cor 12:26). This, in fact, is why the author of Hebrews urges us to "encourage each other daily ... so that none of [us are] hardened by sin's deception" (Heb 3:13).

7:2-5 Unaware of what Achan had done, Joshua and the Israelites prepared for their next battle. Given how successfully things had gone against Jericho, the men who scouted **Ai** reported that the enemy forces were few in number. They thus advised, **Don't wear out all our people there** (7:3). In other words, they confidently said, "We've got this under control; just send a few troops, and the job will be done." Yet *Israel* was soundly defeated, and **thirty-six** Israelite men were killed (7:4-5).

7:6-12 After this, **Joshua tore his clothes and fell facedown to the ground** and **put dust on** his head as signs of mourning (7:6). Then he cried out to the Lord in confusion. Why had God failed to give them victory? (7:7-9). God told Joshua to **stand up** and made it clear that the failure happened because the people had **violated [the] covenant that [he] appointed for them** (7:10-11). Earlier, at Mount Sinai, the Lord had made a covenant with Israel—a divinely orchestrated agreement. Under it, he would be their God and deliver them, provided that they obeyed his instructions. By taking **some of what was set apart**, they had **stolen** from God and **deceived** him (7:11). Joshua would have to deal with the sin in order for God to reverse their circumstances and fight for them again (7:12).

7:13-15 Joshua announced that the people were to **consecrate themselves**—that is, dedicate themselves to God—and present themselves **tribe by tribe** (7:13-14). God would then begin the process of identifying the guilty party—by **tribe**, then by **clan**, then by **family**, then by **man** (7:14). The thief he revealed was then to be executed for his sin against God (7:15). Why reveal the guilty party through such a lengthy process? First, it demonstrated to everyone the seriousness of this sin, which had affected the entire nation. Second, it allowed the people to see that God really did know each of them and their deeds intimately. And third, it gave Achan the opportunity to come clean as he watched the events unfold.

7:16-26 Joshua began the process of elimination. God selected the tribe of **Judah** and worked his way to smaller groups until **Achan** was identified as the culprit (7:16-18). At that point Achan finally confessed that he had **coveted** some of the restricted items, **took them**, and **concealed** them in his **tent** (7:20-21). Once the items were recovered (7:22-23), Joshua pronounced sentence on Achan and his children—who were apparently co-conspirators in his sin—and had them put **to death** (7:24-26) in accordance with the Lord's command (7:15). Then Joshua made another pile of memorial stones (see 4:8-9) to remind the people of the seriousness of rebelling against the Lord (7:26).

Some may consider this judgment too severe. But we must be careful not to soft-pedal Achan's sin. He willfully violated God's covenant with Israel, disobeyed a clear prohibition, stole what belonged to the Lord, brought a curse on the nation, and was responsible for the deaths of thirty-six innocent men! And he invited all of those consequences simply so that he could enrich himself with a few trinkets. The lesson here is this: be careful not to take your own sin lightly. Though God does not call down fire and brimstone today (see Gen 19:24-25), he still shows his wrath against sin by letting people experience the consequences of their sinful choices (see Rom 1:18-32).

8:1-2 Once the sin had been dealt with, God commanded Joshua to **attack Ai** because he had **handed over ... the king of Ai, his**

people, city, and land (8:1). As with Jericho (see 6:2), God had given a promise in the spiritual realm that Israel would need to actualize in the earthly realm. However, notice that this time they were to employ a different strategy. God didn't instruct them to march around the city and blow trumpets. This time they were to use a military tactic. Israel was to set an ambush (8:2).

This is a reminder that we must not presume to know God's plan for a given situation. His strategies are diverse, so God's people need to stay close to him in order to make sure we do as he wants. God's ways are not our ways (see Isa 55:8).

8:3-8 Joshua briefed the troops on God's plan and prepared the attack (8:3). One group was to lie in ambush behind the city (8:4). Another group was to approach the city from the front and then pretend to run scared when Ai's troops came out of the city to confront their invaders (8:5-6). Then the first group would emerge from the shadows and seize the city and burn it (8:7-8).

8:9-29 Joshua and his men executed the plans flawlessly, and the people of Ai fell for the ruse (8:12-14). As a result, Ai was destroyed and the king's body was hung on a tree. At evening, Joshua ordered the Israelites to take down the king's body (8:24-29). It's easy to pass by that statement and not recognize its significance. Earlier God had commanded Israel that if they executed a guilty person by hanging him on a tree, "[They were] not to leave his corpse on the tree overnight but [were] to bury him." To disobey the Lord in this would be to "defile the land [their] God [was] giving" (Deut 21:22-23). So here we see that Joshua was not only a talented military tactician, he was also a godly leader. He understood the dangers of disobeying God's Word (see chapter 7) and was not about to ignore it. His faithfulness to the Word of God, in fact, would continue throughout his life.

8:30-35 The victory over Israel's enemies at Ai didn't end with a party. It ended with a covenant ceremony and the public reading of the Word of God. In Deuteronomy 27, Moses had instructed the people what they were

to do upon entering the land across the Jordan. They were to build an altar of stones on Mount Ebal, write the law of Moses on them, offer sacrifices, and read aloud the blessings and curses of the law (see Deut 27:2–28:68). So, now that they were in the land, Joshua obeyed all of these instructions. While Moses had prepared the people for the land, Joshua had brought them into the land

Israel's future experience there, though, would depend on the people's response to God. Whether they lived or died, whether they prospered or went hungry, whether they experienced blessing or cursing depended on their choices. Would they serve God or themselves? Like Adam and Eve, our shared first parents, the people of Israel were given the freedom to choose. Moses had admonished them to "choose life so that [they] and [their] descendants [might] live" (Deut 30:19). But only by heeding God's covenant commands could Israel maximize what the promised land had to offer them. Similarly, by choosing God's way, you will maximize the purpose God has for your life and the blessings he intends.

C. Deceived by Gibeon (9:1-27)

9:1-2 Joshua and the people had made a name for themselves. But mostly, it was God's reputation and fame that had become well-known (see 9:9). Once the kings of the land heard what his people Israel had done to Jericho and Ai, . . . they formed a unified alliance to fight against Joshua and Israel.

9:3-13 Not everyone was up for a fight, though. When the inhabitants of Gibeon heard the news about the two fallen cities, they were scared. They wanted to live and knew their chances were poor. So they acted deceptively (9:3-4), pretending they had traveled from a distant land—that is, from outside the promised land—to make a treaty with Israel (9:6). At first, Joshua and the leaders were skeptical of the Gibeonites' claims; maybe these people lived just down the block (9:7-8). But the Gibeonites were prepared to deal with such questions. Before leaving home, they had put on raggedy **clothing** and **sandals** to make it look like they had journeyed a great distance. They also carried **provisions** that appeared to be old and depleted (9:4-5). So in effect they said to Joshua, "See our worn out clothes? Look at this moldy bread; it was hot out of the oven when we started. You can trust us." (9:11-13).

In the midst of all their lies, the Gibeonites did say one thing that was true: They had come to make a treaty **because of the reputation of the LORD [Israel's] God. For [they had] heard of his fame** (9:9). This is a reminder that when God does amazing things through you, people will take notice. And they might even try to get in on the blessings.

9:14-15 Joshua decided the Gibeonites' story sounded legitimate. He saw the tattered clothes, shabby sandals, cracked wineskins, and crumbly bread with his own eyes. **So Joshua . . . made a treaty to let them live, and the leaders . . . swore an oath to them** (9:15). There was just one problem: Israel **did not** first pause to **seek the LORD's decision** (9:14). When Scripture drops insightful statements like that, make sure you don't miss the point being made. Even though Israel had interrogated and inspected the travelers, they failed to consult God as they decided what to do with them.

Israel relied solely on what their eyes saw and their ears heard. And because they did not seek God's perspective on the situation, they allowed themselves to be deceived into doing exactly what God had commanded them not to do (see Deut 7:1-2). In a word, God's people had been flimflammed. This is a reminder that Satan can deceive you into sinning, too. He can lure you into doing things that compromise the promises you've made to God. So since you can only see what you see, you need to maintain a spiritual connection to the one who sees what you cannot. You need to know what God's Word says and ask him to help you live by it one moment at a time.

9:16-20 Three days later, Israel learned the truth. **The Gibeonites were their neighbors,** living only a few miles down the road (9:16). And although **the community**

grumbled against Israel's **leaders** over what happened, there was nothing they could do. They had **sworn an oath** and could not retaliate against the Gibeonites (9:18-19). They had taken a *self-maledictory oath*—that means that if they were to break their promise of peace, judgment would fall upon them. Oaths are a serious thing in the Bible and are not to be taken lightly.

9:21-27 Thus, the Israelites had to deal with the consequences. But so did the Gibeonites. Since they had practiced deception, they would become Israel's servants: **woodcutters and water carriers for the whole community** and **for the LORD's altar** (9:21-23, 27). They had heard of the Lord's reputation and fame (9:9); from this point forward, they would be made to work for him (9:27).

> ⇢ *D. Victory throughout the Land*
> *(10:1–12:24)* ⇠

10:1-5 The treaty between Israel and Gibeon had a ripple effect. The Amorite king of **Jerusalem** heard about **Jericho**, **Ai**, and now **Gibeon**, and he became greatly alarmed (10:1-2). Gibeon wasn't a tiny village but a major **city** whose **men were warriors** (10:2). If a significant city like that teamed up with the Israelite invaders, it was only a matter of time before Jerusalem would be attacked. So its king **joined forces** with four other **Amorite kings** and **besieged Gibeon** (10:3-5). They determined to put a stop to Israel's growing strength before all the peoples of the land fell like dominos before her God.

10:6-8 When the kings attacked, **the men of Gibeon** knew it was time to cash in on their treaty with Israel. They sent a message to **Joshua** and got right to the point: **save us!** (10:6). So Joshua gathered **his troops** and listened to the Lord, who told him, **Do not be afraid of them, for I have handed them over to you** (10:7-8). Thus, once again we see a biblical principle repeated in the book of Joshua. Those who want to see God acting in a situation are called to demonstrate faith in him by obeying him. God promised Joshua that Israel would defeat the Amorite kings. But the victory wouldn't happen unless Joshua and Israel stepped out in obedience with swords in hand.

10:9-11 God didn't cause the walls to topple, as at Jericho. He didn't devise an ambush as at Ai. This time, when Joshua and his men confronted their enemies, **the LORD threw them into confusion** and **threw large hailstones on them from the sky** (10:10-11). Now, if God throws anything, he's not going to miss. If he threw a baseball, we would call it a strike. So this was a dark day indeed for the men allied against him. But notice that this miraculous intervention on behalf of his people didn't happen until God saw the Israelites' faith in action. The hailstones didn't fall until the army marched. And when those on earth were obedient, heaven intervened in history.

I like that God didn't tell Joshua what he planned to do in this case. All Joshua and Israel needed to know was what God required of them. Sometimes Christians declare that they're waiting on God to act in their situations. But they don't realize that God is often waiting on them to obey him before he will.

10:12-13 As Israel's battle against the five Amorite kings raged, Joshua prayed and the Lord replied with one of the most amazing miracles in the Bible. Joshua was committed to finishing the work God had given him, but he needed more daylight to complete the job. So he prayed that the **sun** and **moon** would **stand still**, and **the sun stopped** in the sky for **almost a full day** (10:12-13).

Sometimes people who are critical of the Bible will claim that passages like this prove that the Bible is fictional. After all, they argue, science shows us that the sun is already "standing still." It's the earth that's moving—spinning on its axis and orbiting around the sun. But this is an absurd objection. When people today talk about the sun rising and setting, they don't mean that they think the sun is literally moving up and down in the sky or that the sun is orbiting the earth. They're simply using the language of observation. This passage is written in the same way, describing the way things appeared.

10:14-15 Clearly, this was a miracle that required numerous supporting miracles. If the earth slowed its rotation, it would be catastrophic—unless the author of creation was multi-tasking behind the scenes to keep everything in order. And that's what happened. Mother Nature is answerable to Father God.

Yet, even more amazing is that **the LORD listened to a man** (10:14) regarding such an outlandish request. Joshua was dedicated to accomplishing the will of God—radically so. Therefore, when he boldly asked for divine drastic measures, God was willing to literally move—or in this case pause—heaven and earth. For those who are committed to making God's agenda their own, even the wildest prayer requests just might be granted.

10:16-27 Following the super long day of battle, **the five defeated kings** tried to hide, but they couldn't escape (10:16). Joshua had **the military commanders** place their **feet on the necks of these kings** (10:24)—a pose illustrating the triumph of Israel and the subjugation of her enemies. Then they were **executed** (10:26).

We see this imagery of the victor's feet on the enemy's head expressed repeatedly in the Bible, beginning with the promise that the "offspring" of the woman would "strike" the serpent's "head" (Gen 3:15). In Psalms, the Lord instructs his Messiah, "Sit at my right hand until I make your enemies your footstool" (Ps 110:1). In the New Testament, both Jesus and Paul emphasize that indeed the Christ will be victorious in this way (see Matt 22:43-44; 1 Cor 15:24-25). But what is true of the King will also be true of the faithful members of his kingdom: "The God of peace will soon crush Satan under your feet" (Rom 16:20). So keep walking with Jesus. The devil may be spiritually attacking you now (see Eph 6:10-18), but he's destined to have your foot on his head.

10:28-43 These verses chronicle the conquest of the southern part of the promised land by Joshua and Israel. One city after another was defeated until **Joshua conquered the whole region** (10:40). The point is that God made good on his promise, just as he had said, "I have given you every place where the sole of your foot treads.... No one will be able to stand against you" (1:3, 5).

But this was a conditional promise. God would deliver the land only if Joshua and the people were faithful to do what he commanded. We know this is the case by looking at what happened to the previous generation. They wandered in the wilderness for forty years and died there because they sinfully refused to pursue what God had promised (see Num 13–14). So if you want to enjoy the purposes God has for your life, you must trust him and follow through on what he asks of you. His promises are guaranteed—but not automatic. Remember, "Without faith it is impossible to please God, since the one who draws near to him must believe that he exists and that he rewards those who seek him" (Heb 11:6).

11:1-5 With the southern portion of the promised land conquered, it was time to turn the Israelites' attention north. And the kings of the northern cities were fully aware of which way the wind was blowing. So they banned together until **their armies** were **a multitude as numerous as the sand on the seashore** (11:4), and they prepared to **attack Israel** (11:5). God's people were about to face vast combined forces, the likes of which they had never seen.

11:6-15 Yet God told Joshua, **Do not be afraid of them** (11:6). This command appears often in Scripture—and for good reason. When the Lord tells his people not to be afraid, it's because there's something to be afraid of! In this case, Israel was grossly outnumbered. But God is the sole being who is able to counteract and overcome whatever strikes fear into the hearts of humans. He assured Joshua that

by that **time tomorrow**, all their enemies would **be killed** (11:6). So, with faith in the power and promises of God, Joshua and the troops struck down their enemies—just as the Lord said (11:7-15).

11:16-23 The conquest of the land as a whole, however, didn't happen overnight. **Joshua waged war with all these kings for a long time** (11:18). **No city made peace with the Israelites except ... Gibeon** (11:19; see 9:1-27). Why? Because **it was the LORD's intention to harden their hearts, so that they would engage Israel in battle** (11:20). As a result, Israel defeated the peoples and **took the entire land** (11:23).

The Bible has a lot to say about God hardening the hearts of sinners. The first occurrence of this expression is in the book of Exodus where we read that God hardened Pharaoh's heart (see Exod 9:12; 10:27; 11:10). But it's important to recognize that God only hardened Pharaoh's heart after Pharaoh first hardened it himself (see Exod 7:22; 8:15, 32). God does not harden the hearts of people who are seeking him, but of those who are defiantly rejecting him. The Canaanites were not struggling to do right but were determined to do wrong. When people reach that point of willful rebellion, God will further harden their hearts to accomplish his purposes.

12:1-24 Chapter 12 offers a list of all the kings defeated by Israel in the promised land. Future generations would read it and know that these stories were not fairy tales; they were history. The name of each king provides confirmation to readers of how heaven has acted in earth's history to punish hardened sinners and bring about God's agenda for his people.

III. DIVIDING THE PROMISED LAND (13:1–21:45)

13:1-7 There was still much land that remained for the Israelites to acquire (13:1-6), and **Joshua** had become very **old** by this point (13:1). Nevertheless, God promised to drive out the remaining peoples before Israel (13:6). Therefore, in light of God's promise,

Israel was to **divide** the promised land **as an inheritance** among the **tribes** (13:7).

13:8-33 So each tribe was apportioned its land. **Half of the tribe of Manasseh**, the **Reubenites**, and the **Gadites** had already received their portions on the **east** side of the **Jordan** River (13:8). Back before the nation had crossed the Jordan, these tribes were commanded to help their brothers and sisters take possession of their own lands (see 1:12-15). The inheritance of the Reubenites (13:15-23), the Gadites (13:24-28), and half the tribe of Manasseh (13:29-31) had been assigned to each tribe just as Moses had promised.

The only tribe that did not receive an inheritance of land was that of **Levi** (13:14, 33). This is because the Levites had been chosen by God to perform the work of maintaining the tabernacle (and later the temple) and providing priests to do the work of ministry. When the Israelites brought offerings to the Lord, a portion would be given to the Levites, to provide for them (see Num 18:8-32). Instead of a parcel of land, **the LORD** himself, **the God of Israel, was their inheritance** (13:33). Because of their special purpose and calling, they had a special relationship with God.

14:1-6 The following chapters (through chapter 21) chronicle the division of the land among the tribes, providing specific details of cities and borders that were apportioned to each. This way, there would be no cause for disputes. Relevant details were recorded for posterity. All was done **as the LORD** had **commanded** (14:5).

14:6-8 As the book of Joshua describes the division of the land among the tribes of Israel, it also includes an account of a special man and his inheritance. **Caleb** was from the tribe of **Judah**. He **approached Joshua** to remind him of **what the LORD promised** concerning him (14:6). Many years previously, Caleb and Joshua had been two of the twelve spies whom Moses had sent to scout out the land of Canaan (see Num 13:1-25). Though all twelve men had brought back a good report of the land, all but Joshua and Caleb said the land was full of terrible warriors and fortified cities that would be impossible to conquer (see Num 13:26-33). Caleb and Joshua, by contrast, insisted that God had not sent them to debate the land but to take the land. They **brought back an honest report**, but the other ten **caused the people to lose heart** (Josh 14:7-8).

As a result, Israel rebelled against God and Moses, God swore that he wouldn't permit that generation to enter the promised land, and Israel wandered in the wilderness for forty years until nearly all of that first generation out of Egypt dropped dead (see Num 14:1-38). The author of the letter to the Hebrews tells us that God did not let the people enter the land—his "rest"—because of their unbelief and disobedience (see Heb 4:3).

14:9-15 Only two adults in that group survived the punishment, the faithful spies. Caleb was promised an **inheritance** in the land, because he **followed the LORD [his] God completely** (14:9). In other words, Caleb didn't follow the crowd. He stood by his convictions without compromise. That was **forty-five years** ago. Caleb was now an **eighty-five**-year-old man, but he was **still as strong** as was when Moses had sent him out (14:10-11). So he asked Joshua to **give** him the land that had been promised to him (14:12). **Joshua blessed Caleb** and gave him his inheritance (14:13).

Caleb's story reminds us that when people around us make problems sound bigger than God, we don't have to succumb to popular opinion; we can take God at his Word. Of course, this doesn't mean you should ignore problems; they may be significant. But no matter what you face, you can take courage in the knowledge that God is sovereign over your problems and those of your peers. Caleb walked faithfully with God, and God remembered him. He can do the same for you as you choose to be influenced not by those who say God can't make a way but by the knowledge that there is nothing too big for him.

15:1-63 Chapter 15 focuses on the inheritance of the tribe of **Judah**. The borders of Judah, which is the name by which the area would be called, are described (15:1-12), and **the cities** of Judah are named (15:20-63). As the biblical storyline unfolds, Judah will become more and more prominent. This is because in Genesis, Israelite forefather Jacob (Israel) prophesied that a kingly dynasty would arise from his son Judah, eventually resulting in the Messiah (see Gen 49:9-10). This prophecy would first become a reality when God had the prophet Samuel anoint a young shepherd named David to be king of Israel (see 1 Sam 16:1-13). Though in Joshua's day, the tribe of **Judah could not drive out the Jebusites who lived in Jerusalem** (Josh 15:63), King David would not only defeat the Jebusites; he would claim Jerusalem as his capital (see 2 Sam 5:6-9).

Within this chapter we also learn something further about Caleb (15:13-19; see 14:6-15). He personally drove the inhabitants out and took possession of his land (15:13-15). Caleb also looked after **his daughter Achsah** and gave her a portion of land for her own inheritance, her **blessing** (15:17-19).

In the Old Testament, much is made of the family inheritance and passing down the favor of God from one generation to the next. In God's economy, the family is the foundation of society. Thus, in Israel the family was the basis for passing down not only the physical blessings but also the spiritual heritage (see Deut 6:4-9). In the New Testament too, fathers are exhorted to raise their children "in the training and instruction of the Lord" (Eph 6:4).

The family is under attack today. Satan is passionate about undermining and redefining this unit because he wants to stop the blessings and favor of God from being passed on generationally. Many people have been harmed because of what they experienced in their families, and they in turn pass on these bad habits and sins to their own children. Christian parents—and especially fathers—must determine to pass on to the next generation not a legacy of brokenness and spiritual compromise but one of blessing and training in God's Word.

16:1-10 The tribe of Joseph was actually divided into two tribes descended from Joseph's two sons, **Ephraim and Manasseh** (16:4). Those descended from Ephraim received their own **inheritance** in the land (16:5-8). **However, they did not drive out the Canaanites who lived in Gezer. So the Canaanites** would continue to live in Ephraim's territory as **forced laborers** (16:10). Why does Scripture tell us this? Because the Canaanites and their idolatrous religious practices would slowly work against Israel like a cancer, as we will learn in the

book of Judges. In growing negligent to drive out the enemy as instructed, Israel was setting itself up for a fall.

17:1-13 Next **the tribe of Manasseh,** who was **Joseph's firstborn** (17:1), received its allotment of land (17:7-11). (Half of Manasseh had already received a portion of land on the east side of the Jordan; see 13:29-31.) But, like Ephraim (16:10), Manasseh didn't drive out the Canaanites completely from its portion (17:12-13). That lack of perseverance left another thorn in Israel's side, a problem that would fester in the years ahead.

In the midst of these verses, we're told about five **daughters** of a man named **Zelophehad** who **had no sons** (17:3). **They came before the priest Eleazar, Joshua ... and the leaders** to remind them of what the Lord had commanded concerning their family (17:4). Since a land inheritance was to be passed down from fathers to sons, these daughters would have received no inheritance. Others would have owned their father's land, and their father's name would have been forgotten. But years earlier, these daughters had wisely implored Moses to allow them an inheritance within the territory of Manasseh (see Num 27:1-4). When Moses asked the Lord about the matter, the Lord told him to give the daughters "their father's inheritance" (see Num 27:5-7). Furthermore, God commanded, "When a man dies without having a son, transfer his inheritance to his daughter" (Num 27:8). **In keeping with the LORD's instruction** in Moses's day, the leaders under Joshua faithfully gave the women their **inheritance** (17:4-5).

17:14-18 Since Joseph's descendants (Ephraim and Manasseh) were so numerous, they asked Joshua for more land (17:14). When Joshua directed them to an additional portion of land, however, the people were fearful of the Canaanites there (17:15-16). But Joshua, ever the courageous leader, encouraged them that they could **drive out the Canaanites** (17:18). Whereas these people saw their own vast numbers as a problem, Joshua saw a strength: working together they could clear additional land and rid it of their enemies.

18:1-10 All of Israel gathered at **Shiloh** and **set up the tent of meeting**—that is, the tabernacle, the place where they would meet with God and offer sacrifices (18:1). Though **the land had been subdued before them** and several tribes had been allotted their territory by this point, there were still **seven tribes** that had not received **their inheritance** (18:1-2). So Joshua reprimanded them and basically said, "Look, this land isn't going to divide up itself. You've got work to do" (18:3). He told them to appoint **three men from each tribe** to **survey the land** and **divide it into seven portions** (18:4-5). After that, Joshua would **cast lots** and assign each remaining tribe its land (18:6). The people obeyed, and the remaining land was **distributed** (18:9-10).

Once again we're reminded here that even though God's promises may be within our reach, they may not be in our hands. God had promised Israel the land, but the people still had to do the work of taking it. Similarly, God feeds the birds of the sky (see Matt 6:26), but they still have to hunt for their worms. God has a purpose for your life, but you must walk with him by faith to see that purpose become a reality.

18:11–19:48 After the land was surveyed, lots were cast, and the land was divided, the remaining tribes could take possession of their territories. "Casting lots" was something like rolling dice, but Israel understood that nothing happens by chance (see Prov 16:33). By casting lots, Joshua was acknowledging that it was God's decision to decide which tribe received which section. The remainder of chapter 18 and all of chapter 19 describe the allotment to the remaining seven tribes called **Benjamin** (18:11-28), **Simeon** (19:1-9), **Zebulun** (19:10-16), **Issachar** (19:17-23), **Asher** (19:24-31), **Naphtali** (19:32-39), and **Dan** (19:40-48).

19:49-51 Finally, Joshua received his personal inheritance. Like a good leader, he made sure that all the people had received their territories before settling down in his own. Joshua was from the tribe of Ephraim, so the Lord gave him **the city of Timnath-serah in the hill country of Ephraim** (19:50). With their leader now in

his new home, Israel **finished dividing up the land** (19:51).

20:1-6 God had told Moses in Numbers 35:9-34 that Israel was to establish **cities of refuge** when they entered the land. The time had come for Joshua to **select** them (20:1-2). If an Israelite were to **accidentally** kill someone, a relative of the victim might want to avenge his loved one. Thus, **the one who committed manslaughter** (20:5) could flee to one of the cities of refuge, which would be positioned throughout Israel.

The accused would stand **at the entrance of the city gate** and state his case to the city elders (20:4). The gate of the city was where the elders met to adjudicate legal cases. Once they heard his story, they were to provide him a safe place to live until his case could be decided. If **the avenger of blood**—the relative of the deceased—came looking for him, the elders were not to hand him over (20:5). For this protection, however, the man would have to stay in the city **until he [stood] trial** and **until the death of the high priest** currently serving. After that, the man would be able to **return home** (20:6). God thus established a mechanism for protecting an individual who had accidentally killed someone without premeditation from vigilantism.

20:7-9 The Israelites established six cities of refuge throughout the land. These were positioned so that no matter where one lived in Israel, there was a refuge within reasonable traveling distance.

21:1-3 As discussed previously, the tribe of Levi received no land allotment. Since they served the Lord in the work of ministry, he was to be **their inheritance** (21:3). Nevertheless, the Levites still needed places to live. So the heads of the Levite families approached the high priest, Joshua, and the Israelite leaders to remind them of what **the Lord commanded through Moses** (21:1-2; see Num 35:1-8). Within the lands divided among their brothers, the Levites were to receive **cities with their pasturelands** (21:3). Thus, by living in cities scattered throughout the territories of the various tribes, the Levites would have access to all of the people so that they could fulfill their duty to "teach the Israelites all the statutes that the LORD [had] given to them through Moses" (Lev 10:11).

21:4-8 The Levites received a total of forty-eight cities. Twenty-three went to **the Kohathite clans**, the descendants of Levi's second son, with thirteen of those cities going to the descendants of **Aaron** who served as priests (21:4-5). Thirteen cities went to **Gershon's** clans, the descendants of Levi's first son (21:6). And twelve cities went to **Merari's** clans, the descendants of Levi's third son (21:7).

21:9-42 The cities of the **Kohathite clans** were in **Judah**, **Simeon**, and **Benjamin** (21:9-19). Since the **descendants of . . . Aaron** had to perform their priestly duties in the temple, it made sense for them to be close to Jerusalem (21:13). The **clans of Kohath's descendants** were given cities in **Ephraim**, **Dan**, and **Manasseh** (21:20-26). The **descendants of Gershon** received cities in **Manasseh**, **Issachar**, **Asher**, and **Naphtali** (21:27-33). The **descendants of Merari** lived in **Zebulun**, **Reuben**, and **Gad** (21:34-40).

21:43-45 In fulfillment of his promises, **the LORD gave Israel all the land he had sworn**, and he **gave them rest on every side** (21:43-44). This leads to the central affirmation of the book of Joshua: **None of the good promises the LORD had made to the house of Israel failed. Everything was fulfilled** (21:45).

Hundreds of years prior, God had promised a pilgrim named Abram that he would give the land of Canaan to his offspring (see Gen 12:1-7). Though it had taken many years and there were delays for various reasons, God was faithful in keeping that word. When Jacob (Israel) and his sons (the tribal heads of the groups discussed in this chapter) had to flee Canaan because of a famine, God was faithful. When the Israelites were enslaved in the land of Egypt, God was faithful. When the people wandered in the wilderness because of their unfaithfulness, God was faithful.

We live in a world full of broken promises. But the author of Hebrews says, "Let us hold on to . . . our hope without wavering, since he who promised is faithful" (Heb 10:23). Many people make promises they have no intention of keeping. Others mean well, but their fallen humanity or unexpected circumstances prevent them from fulfilling their promises. But not one of God's promises has ever failed; he does not disappoint. Every one of God's promises is "Yes" in Jesus Christ (2 Cor 1:20).

We are called to declare our trust in the God who is faithful to always keep his word. And that declaration of trust, that confession, requires action. God's promises are available to you, but you must lay hold of them. God promised that the walls of Jericho would fall. But the Israelites had to march around the city by faith before it would happen (see Heb 11:30). When they acted in faith, God was faithful to act.

IV. SERVING GOD IN THE PROMISED LAND (22:1–24:33)

22:1-8 With the land acquired and at rest, Joshua sent the tribes of Reuben, Gad, and the half tribe of Manasseh back to their homes on the east side of the Jordan (22:1-5). They had faithfully crossed the Jordan with their brothers to help them conquer the land (see 1:12-15). Now that the work was done, **Joshua blessed them and sent them on their way** (22:6). But he challenged them to **carefully obey the command and instruction that Moses the LORD's servant gave** them (22:5). In other words, he said, "Even though you're

departing from your brothers, you hold tight to God."

22:9-12 When the two-and-a-half tribes returned to their homes across the river, the first thing they did was build **a large, impressive altar** (22:10). But when the rest of Israel on the west side of the Jordan heard about it, they were deeply concerned. An altar was a place of worship, a place to sacrifice to a god. But the only acceptable place for Israel to worship was in Shiloh at the tabernacle, the tent of meeting. So as far as the rest of Israel was concerned, idolatry was brewing in the east among their brothers, and they didn't want to pay the price when God's resulting wrath visited the entire nation. Therefore, **the entire Israelite community assembled at Shiloh to go to war against them** (22:12).

22:13-20 The concerned tribes **sent Phinehas son of Eleazar the priest** and a delegation of **leaders** to meet with **the Reubenites, Gadites, and half the tribe of Manasseh** to ask them in essence, "What were you thinking?" (22:13-16). Before attacking their kinsmen in battle, they wanted an explanation for why they had built a competing altar. They reminded them of past instances of sin—for which there was *corporate* judgment, such as when some of the Israelites worshiped Baal **of Peor** (22:17; see Num 25:1-15) and when **Achan** stole items that had been set apart for God (22:20; see Josh 7:1-26). In each instance, God's anger had fallen on the entire **community** (22:17, 20). So if the two-and-a-half tribes were to rebel against God **today**, everyone would pay for it **tomorrow** (22:18).

The delegation was ready to go to any length to make things right with God and avoid war with their brothers. They even told them to move in with them on the west side of the Jordan if there was a problem with their land on the east side (22:19). In other words, they would rather be crowded together than experience the wrath of God.

22:21-29 When the tribes on the east side of the Jordan heard this accusation, they cried out, **The Mighty One, God, the Lord! The Mighty One, God, the Lord!** (22:21-22). This repetition of three different Hebrew names for God was a way of making an extreme oath. **May the Lord himself hold us accountable if we intended** to do wrong, they swore. They confessed that they had no intent of using their **altar** for worship of any kind (22:23). Instead, they had established it as a replica of the true altar at Shiloh, to bear witness to future generations that all the tribes on the east side of the Jordan were true Israelites who worshiped the Lord like their brothers did. They had built it out of fear that the children of those on the west side might raise questions one day about

whether those to the east were legitimate tribes of Israel, since the Jordan River divided them (22:24-29). In other words they said to their accusers, "You've misunderstood our motives entirely. We wanted to put a reminder in place—visible to all—that those of us to the east are committed to the same God as you are."

22:30-34 After this explanation, the delegation of tribes from the west breathed a sigh of relief (22:30-31). Then they returned home and shared the good news with the rest of the tribes (22:33). Disaster had been averted.

There are two important lessons to be learned from the wise actions of these leaders. The first is this: Don't act hastily. Proverbs says, "The one who gives an answer before he listens—this is foolishness and disgrace for him" (Prov 18:13). Instead of immediately going on the offensive and starting a war, the western tribes wisely paused first to ask the others to explain themselves. Too often, couples, friends, families, or co-workers go on the attack when they feel offended instead of first seeking clarity over the issue of concern. The second lesson is this: Take a stand. Though we don't want to be hasty about confronting our Christian brothers when we fear they are stepping into sin, nevertheless, we must not compromise. These leaders didn't want anything to stand in the way of their family's relationship with the Lord. Believers must not ignore sin either. The only way we can experience God's blessing together is when we deal with sin biblically and honestly.

23:1-5 Chapters 23 and 24 include Joshua's farewell address to Israel. He knew his death was approaching, and he wanted to exhort the people one last time. Many years had passed since **the Lord had given Israel rest from all the enemies around them**, and Joshua was now an **old** man (23:1). He reminded the people that they had seen with their own eyes what God had done for them. He said, **It was the Lord your God who was fighting for you** (23:3). He was the one who'd ultimately **destroyed** the nations (23:4). Yes, it was true that the Israelites did the fighting. But they were only victorious because God had worked through them.

23:6-8 In light of what God had accomplished through them, Joshua commanded them to **be very strong**. What does that look like? First, they were to **continue obeying all that is written in the book of the law of Moses, so that [they would] not turn from it to the right or left** (23:6). This is a reminder to us not to add to God's Word or take away from it (see Rev 22:18-19). God doesn't need your help revising Scripture; he knew exactly what he wanted to say when he put together his Word. Your job is to believe what you find in it and, with the help of the Holy Spirit, to obey it. The second way to "be very strong" is to **be loyal to the LORD** (23:8) by not compromising with the world. We have to live *in* the world, but we're not to be *of* the world (see John 17:11, 16). In other words, don't embrace the world's value system. God's people are to be distinct and reflect his character. As John the apostle says, "Do not love the world or the things in the world. If anyone loves the world, the love of the Father is not in him" (1 John 2:15).

23:9-11 Next Joshua said, **The LORD has driven out great and powerful nations before you. . . . One of you routed a thousand** (23:9-10). This tells us that when God fights for us, we don't need to worry about the number of folks working against us. If you're on God's team, the odds are always in your favor. So, as Joshua said, **diligently watch yourselves! Love the LORD your God!** (23:11). To follow God is not merely adhering to rules and regulations; it's about accepting and cultivating relationship. He loves you, and he calls you to love him as well.

23:12-13 Joshua next exhorted the Israelites not to **intermarry** with the surrounding peoples (23:12). We must be clear about what he meant and why. He wasn't prohibiting marriage between couples of differing skin tones and ethnicities. Joseph and Moses both had interracial marriages in that sense (see Gen 41:45; Exod 2:16, 21; Judg 1:16), and the Bible never condemns these. All people groups descend from Adam and Eve and are of equal worth (see Gen 3:20; Acts 17:26).

There is no scriptural prohibition against marrying someone of another *race*. But there is a prohibition against marrying someone

of another *religion*—that is, marrying someone who believes in and worships other gods rather than the one true God. The apostle Paul said that Christians should marry "in the Lord" (1 Cor 7:39). So if you're a believer seeking a spouse, you need to marry someone who is going in the same direction spiritually. And this is the reasoning behind God's intermarriage prohibition to Israel. As Moses had told the previous generation, if the Israelites were to intermarry with the peoples of the land, "they [would] turn [their] sons away from [God] to worship other gods. Then the LORD's anger [would] burn against [them], and he [would] swiftly destroy [them]" (Deut 7:4). So Joshua was repeating this warning.

23:14-16 In saying, **I am now going the way of the whole earth**, Joshua knew that he was about to die, and he knew these would be his final words to Israel. So he reminded them that **not one promise** of God had **failed** (23:14). But to enjoy those promises in the land, the people would be required to give God their loyalty and commitment. They'd need to move together with God, not perfectly (which was impossible) but purposefully. Unfortunately, the next book of the Bible, Judges, shows Israel failing to walk with God, repenting, being rescued, and failing again cyclically. In time, they would lose the land and the blessings that God had for them as a result. Don't follow their example.

24:1-13 Chapter 24 continues Joshua's farewell address to Israel, which began in chapter 23. As Joshua's exhortation continued, he gave the people a history lesson. Now that they were in the promised land, Joshua reminded them of how they got there, taking them all the way back to Abraham's story that began in Genesis 12. The speaker here is Joshua, but the message is from God. Notice that throughout the rehearsal of Israel's history, God insisted that *he* was the star of the show and the performer of the action: **I took** (24:3), **I gave** (24:3-4, 13), **I sent** (24:5, 12), **I defeated** (24:5), **I brought** (24:5-6, 8), **I did** (24:7), **I handed** (24:8), **I annihilated** (24:8), **I would not listen** (24:10), **I rescued** (24:10). In summary, God was telling them, "You got from slavery to here because of me. When you sinned and were unfaithful, I came through. I never bailed on you, and my promises never failed. Yes, there were things you had to do, but I enabled you to succeed all the way."

In saying, **I gave you a land you did not labor for** (24:13), God reminded the Israelites that they were living in homes they hadn't built, eating food they hadn't grown, and sitting under shade trees they hadn't planted. Now that doesn't seem like a big deal at first given the way our culture buys and sells houses and ready-made meals. But in Bible times, if you wanted a home, you built it. If you wanted to eat, you grew or raised it. And if you wanted a luxury like a shade tree, you couldn't just transplant a sapling from the local nursery. That God gave his people a land so well-equipped was a *big* deal.

Importantly, he used the unrighteous to get all this ready for them. The Canaanites did all the work, enjoying the fruit of their labors up until the day God evicted them for their wickedness. This reminds us that even the ungodly are God's ungodly—not by relationship but by sovereignty. Similarly, even the devil is God's devil, because he can only do what God permits. Israel needed to remember that they were like turtles on fence posts, which hadn't gotten to their safe place by their own power.

What should believers in Jesus Christ learn from this? Whatever blessings we have received, we should give him all the thanks and praise.

24:14 So how was Israel to respond to this gracious provision from God? They were to **Fear the Lord and worship him in sincerity and truth**. To "fear" God means to take him seriously, rather than having a mere casual relationship with him and trying to keep him on the periphery of life. They were also to **Get rid of the gods [their] fathers worshiped**. While this was likely a reference to the false gods mentioned in the Old Testament story to this point, an idol isn't merely a statue before which someone bows. An idol is any unauthorized person, place, or thing that a person looks to as a source of purpose, promise, or provision. Therefore, an idol can be money, power, popularity, sex, influence, or a person, and

the list goes on. You have only one ultimate source to meet your needs—God. Look to nothing else, take him seriously, and serve him.

24:15 In this verse Joshua laid all his cards on the table. He said, **Choose for yourselves today: Which will you worship? . . . As for me and my family, we will worship the Lord**. Joshua spoke like a kingdom man. He couldn't control the hearts of the people of Israel, but he knew whose agenda he himself would follow and who would lead his home. He was determined to serve the Lord. He called the Israelites to make the same crucial decision.

24:16-20 In response to Joshua's bold declaration, the people replied, **We will certainly not abandon the Lord to worship other gods! . . . We too will worship the Lord, because he is our God** (24:16-18). To this, however, Joshua responded, **You will not be able to worship the Lord** (24:19).

Now that response may seem a little odd. Why challenge them to follow the Lord and then call them liars when they promise to do it? Joshua said this because he recognized the danger of not putting your money where your mouth is. Talk is cheap, but actions prove our words. Frankly, Joshua didn't believe they were serious, so he doubled down. He warned, **He is a jealous God. . . . If you abandon the Lord and worship foreign gods, he will turn against you** (24:19-20). Indeed, God is jealous—righteously jealous— for his people, just as an honorable husband would be righteously jealous if he saw his wife acting inappropriately with another man. It isn't enough to agree with truth; you must act on that truth.

24:21-22 The people responded to Joshua and insisted that they got the point: **No! . . . We will worship the Lord** (24:21). Therefore, Joshua told them, **You are witnesses against yourselves that you have chosen to worship the Lord**. To this Israel replied, **We are witnesses** (24:22). So be it. By publicly vowing to worship God, the people of Israel had made a self-maledictory oath. If they were to fail in their pledge of fidelity, their own words would call down a curse on them and justify the judgment of God. They had testified against themselves in advance.

24:23 Since the people had promised to walk the talk, Joshua admonished them: **Get rid of the foreign gods . . . among you.** This tells us that Joshua was aware of inconsistencies between what the people claimed and how they lived.

God will not tolerate idols. If you have an idol in your life that you are unwilling to renounce (see commentary on 24:14), then you have, in effect, rejected God's help and blessings in your situation. Many people ask God why he's not working in their circumstances, while they're hugging their idol of choice at the same time. They don't stop to consider that God's inactivity may be a result of the fact that like many in Israel, they aren't willing to lay down the competition.

24:24-28 On that day Joshua made a covenant for the people (24:25). A covenant is a divinely sanctioned bond. It's a declaration of legal relationship in the spiritual realm. Through a covenant, God provides a "covering" for individuals, families, and nations. For example, when a husband honors his marriage covenant with his wife, God provides a covering—an umbrella—of blessing. So Joshua **recorded** this agreement **in the book of the law of God** (24:26). He also set up **a large stone** as a **witness** (24:26-27). Previously, Joshua had set up memorial stones to remind Israel of what God had done for them (see 4:1-9) and to remind them of the

seriousness of sinning against God (7:26). This time, however, the memorial stone was to point them to their agreement to worship God. Every time they passed by it, the stone would silently whisper, "Do **not deny your God**; practice what you preach" (24:27).

24:29-31 After challenging Israel to follow their God, Joshua **died** at the ripe old **age of 110.** How would he be remembered? As **the LORD's servant** (24:29). And as a testimony to his faithfulness, we are given this insight: **Israel worshiped the LORD throughout Joshua's lifetime** (24:31). Unfortunately, as the book of Judges will reveal, that pattern would soon change.

24:32-33 Many years before, when Joseph was about to die in Egypt, he made the sons of Israel—his brothers—vow to carry his remains to the land God swore to give to Abraham, Isaac, and Jacob, and bury them there (see Gen 50:24-26). So, when Moses led the Israelites out of Egypt, he "took the bones of Joseph with him" (Exod 13:19). But now that Israel was in the land that God had promised, they buried **Joseph's bones** (24:32).

Though he would not live to see the outcome of the promise, Joseph believed that God would keep his word to his family. And if you think about it, Christians are essentially called to do the same thing. We wait for entry into the divine promised land where God will dwell among his people forever. So with that truth ever in view, walk with God and trust him for what he has planned for your life. Because none of his promises fail.

JUDGES

INTRODUCTION

Author

THE AUTHOR OF THE BOOK OF Judges is unknown. The date of composition is also uncertain. The most we can say is that it was probably composed after the rise of Israel's monarchy, given the book's repeated refrain, "In those days, there was no king in Israel" (17:6; 18:1; 19:1; 21:25).

Historical Background

Judges covers a period of about three hundred years, explaining what happened in the promised land between its conquest under Joshua and the rise of the monarchy under Saul and David. The title of the book comes from the title given to the leaders who arose during this period to give Israel deliverance from their enemies (2:16). These were dark years of religious compromise and moral decay for the descendants of Jacob. There was no divine standard operating in the nation because the people had quickly forgotten the rules of the covenant they had made with God in Moses's day and reaffirmed in his successor's. Thus, "Everyone did whatever seemed right to him" (17:6; 21:25). And that caused countless problems. (It always does.)

Message and Purpose

The book of Judges is about cycles—cycles of disobedience, discipline, repentance, and deliverance. The Israelites' disobedience brought God's discipline. But in each instance that the people repented, God raised up a judge to bring about deliverance.

The generation after Joshua did not remain faithful to God, which led to cultural decline and horrific sin. Judges shows what happens to a society when it drifts away from following God and living in respect of his moral standards. Yet Judges also offers hope: it shows how even in the darkest days God can use men and women to accomplish his plan—even though they are flawed themselves. The book serves as a warning that disaster will ultimately befall a people who reject God's kingdom rule over them, and it emphasizes the necessity of repentance before God will intervene to deliver and restore them to a place of blessing.

VIDEO   INTRO

www.bhpublishinggroup.com/qr/te/07_00

Outline

I. Victory and Compromise (1:1-36)
II. The Cycle of Judgment (2:1–3:6)
III. The Judges (3:7–16:31)
  A. Othniel, Ehud, and Shamgar (3:7-31)
  B. Deborah and Barak (4:1–5:31)
  C. Gideon and Abimelech (6:1–9:57)
  D. Tola, Jair, and Jephthah (10:1–12:7)
  E. Ibzan, Elon, Abdon, and Samson (12:8–16:31)
IV. The Corruption of the Levites (17:1–21:25)
  A. Micah's Priest (17:1–18:31)
  B. Outrage in Benjamin (19:1–21:25)

JUDGES

I. VICTORY AND COMPROMISE (1:1-36)

1:1-2 After the death of Joshua, the Israelites got off to a good start. They **inquired of the Lord** regarding their next military steps. Joshua had led them into the promised land and brought about the general defeat of **the Canaanites** (1:1). Now it was up to the people to carry out the mopping-up operations. They wisely asked the Lord for direction, since the man who had given them direction was no longer with them. This was the right way to begin their season of transition. And it reminds me of an important truth: when we have uncertainty, we must inquire of the Lord. As the people did in this case, approach him with specific prayers—if you want specific answers.

1:3-10 In response to God's guidance, **the men of Judah fought against Jerusalem, captured it, put it to the sword, and set the city on fire** (1:8). In Scripture, fire is used as a means of judgment to remove all evil. In time, Jerusalem would become Israel's capital and the holy city of God.

1:11 Then **they marched against the residents of Debir**, which was also called **Kiriath-sepher**. *Debir* comes from the Hebrew word that means "word," and *Kiriath-sepher* means "The City of the Scribe." This was the town where the records of the Canaanites were held; it was the repository for details about their history, culture, and background. To destroy Debir would be to destroy their history and their culture. The Canaanites would defend this city vigorously.

1:12-15 **Caleb** was one of the two faithful spies who had survived from Moses's time. Like Joshua, he was permitted to enter the promised land (see Num 13:1–14:9; 14:36-38; 26:65; 32:10-12). He said, **Whoever attacks and captures Kiriath-sepher, I will give my daughter Achsah . . . as a wife** (1:12). Now, that's a tall order for a father to make: "If you want this girl, I've got to see you fight and succeed." The high value that he placed on his daughter is a reminder that every father ought to have high standards regarding the man who wants to marry his daughter. Fathers need to look for kingdom men for their daughters: leaders and providers committed to loving their wives and future children.

Othniel rose to the challenge: he captured the city and became Caleb's son-in-law. In time he would also become Israel's first judge (1:13; see 3:9).

1:16-18 As a result of God's command to "go" (see 1:2), **Judah captured Gaza and its territory** (1:18). The Lord had promised Judah victory in battle; they could be assured of the outcome. But they still had to fight.

If God promises something, you can count on it. But that doesn't mean you don't have to exert faith and effort to obtain it. Jesus said that God feeds the birds (Matt 6:26), but you don't see birds on branches with their mouths open toward heaven. They know they've got to leave the branch and obtain what God has provided. God promises us spiritual victory—provided we fight in the power of the Spirit with the Word of God as our sword.

1:19-20 The LORD was with Judah in their battles and enabled them to take possession of the hill country, but they could not drive out the people who were living in the valley because those people had iron chariots (1:19). Why wasn't Judah fully victorious? Some time later, God would defeat iron chariots easily (4:12-16), so apparently that wasn't the problem. The problem was that the Israelites' faith on the hill outmatched their faith in the valley (1:19). God was with them in both places, but they allowed what seemed to them an insurmountable problem in the valley to limit their faith in God.

When you're following the will of God, don't despair when circumstances are daunting. The God on the hill is the same God in the valley. Remember what Caleb said earlier when the Israelites feared entering Canaan altogether. He kept his eyes on God's promise and declared, "We can certainly conquer it!" (Num 13:30). Don't let the size of your problem become bigger than the size of your God.

1:21-36 These verses record a sad shift in Israel's victory record that would lead to problems for years to come. The Benjaminites did not drive out the Jebusites (1:21). Then Manasseh failed to take possession of Beth-shean. . . . they made the Canaanites serve as forced labor but never drove them out completely (1:27-28). Then Ephraim failed to drive out the Canaanites who were living in Gezer (1:29). And so it continued: Zebulun failed to drive out the residents of Kitron (1:30). Asher and Naphtali failed to drive out the residents of the land (1:31, 33). Get the picture?

All of this marks the beginning of a cycle of compromise, a cycle of partial obedience. Perhaps they excused their failure with thoughts like: "Hey, the Canaanites could be beneficial to us. There's no need to get rid of all of them." But in Deuteronomy 7:1-6 God had commanded them to fully remove the Canaanites and destroy their idols because he knows that "a little leaven leavens the whole batch of dough" (1 Cor 5:6). Just as sure as a small cancer will metastasize, leaving pockets of Canaanites within the promised land would grow into a major problem. Though the Israelites may have thought that doing so would be in their best interest, it would turn into their worst nightmare.

II. THE CYCLE OF JUDGMENT (2:1–3:6)

2:1-2 The angel of the LORD is a Christophany—that is, a preincarnate manifestation of the Son of God showing up in the Old Testament's narrative. We can conclude this because the angel claimed to have brought them out of Egypt and led them into the promised land (2:1). Clearly, these were the actions of God himself. Previously, in Joshua 5, the "angel" showed up as the commander of the Lord's army (Josh 5:13-15). There he allowed Joshua to worship him and said that his presence caused the ground to be holy— just as God had said to Moses (Exod 3:5). No mere angel would say such things.

The visitor rebuked the Israelites because they had not obeyed him, and the key word he used was covenant (2:1). A covenant is a bond—entering one is like being glued together with that other party. God had made a covenant with Israel, and one of its stipulations was that they were not to make a covenant with the inhabitants of Canaan. Instead, they were to destroy their altars and gods (2:2). To make a treaty with Canaan, in fact, was to make a covenant with their gods. The native inhabitants of Canaan were not mere people; they were people wholeheartedly connected to a worldview that contradicted the God who had delivered Israel. This is the principle behind the Paul's words: "Don't become partners with those who do not believe" (2 Cor 6:14). Being a partner is a bond of equality. But there can be no true equality between one who worships the true Creator and one in league with his competition.

2:3 The angel warned the people that their disobedience was going to come back on them: I will not drive out these people before you. They will be thorns in your sides, and their gods will be a trap for you. In other words, Israel's disobedience to God's clear order would boomerang back to slap them. Similarly, if the thing or person with whom you choose to bond is contrary to God, it will lead you astray and cause you harm.

2:4-5 The people wept and **offered sacrifices** in response to the heavenly visitor's words. They repented and asked for forgiveness for their failure to do what they'd been told to do.

2:6-10 Here the author presses rewind on the narrative to tell us that **the people [had] worshiped the LORD throughout Joshua's lifetime** (2:7). After Joshua **died** (2:8), things went downhill. When his generation passed away, **another generation rose up who did not know the LORD or the works he had done for Israel** (2:10). Tragically, parents had failed to transfer their faith in God to their children. And the resulting generational spiritual breakdown would bring about decline in the culture. This is a sharp warning for us: When the family breaks down, civilization breaks down with it. We need to take seriously the spiritual development of our children, because not only do they depend on it, society is banking on it.

Amazingly, the majority of these Israelites didn't know the works that God had done for their nation in the past. So they were ignorant about what he could do for them. Repeatedly Moses had told the Israelites to teach their children the ways of God to avoid this very situation (Deut 6:4-7). While children may not see the benefit of spiritual training as it's offered—or even want it—one day they're going to need it.

2:11 When the transfer of faith from parents to children failed, **the Israelites did what was evil in the LORD's sight. They worshiped the Baals**. Baal was a dominant idol among the Canaanites. To them, he was the god of fertility—though he was really a god of *futility*. Baal was said to look after the fertility of soil, farm animals, and humans. An idol is any person, place, thing, or thought that you look to as your source—of meaning, provision, deliverance, and fulfillment. The Israelites had lost faith in God as their source and began to look to the natural realm.

2:12-13 They **abandoned** God and **followed other gods from the surrounding peoples** (2:12). This tells us that not only did the Israelites fail to rub off on the culture, they had allowed their enemies' culture to rub off on them. This should make us ask: What ungodly aspects of today's culture are rubbing off on our children? Are they buying into cultural lies because we've failed to transfer our faith to them?

2:14-15 When the Israelites left God, God **handed them over to marauders** and **sold them to the enemies around them** (2:14). Since they submitted to the evil system, God allowed that system to rule them. Understand that when you and I wander from serving the true God, false humanistic worldviews will fill the vacuum, taking his place in our hearts and ultimately wielding control over us.

As a result of Israel's unfaithfulness, God's anger burned against them: **Whenever the Israelites went out, the LORD . . . brought disaster on them** (2:15). Now from the people's perspective, the bad things that happened to them might have just seemed like bad luck, but in reality God himself was working against them. If God is against you, it doesn't matter what you have going for you. And if God is for you, it doesn't matter who is against you (see Rom 8:31). It's your obedience to his Word that will make all the difference.

2:16-19 These verses provide a summary of the book of Judges. Israel sinfully departed from the Lord, their enemies oppressed them, the Lord felt sorry for them when they cried for help, he raised up a deliverer, the deliverer defeated their enemies, the deliverer died, and Israel returned to their idols. Every time this cycle repeated, the people grew more wicked.

2:20-23 During the years covered in the book of Joshua, God drove out the Canaanites, opened doors, and made things happen. But in this era of Israel's history, God said, **Because this nation has violated my covenant that I made with their fathers and disobeyed me, I will no longer drive out before them any of the nations Joshua left when he died** (2:20-21).

Here we get some insight into God's mysterious ways. He said that he would leave Israel a problem—some Canaanites within their borders—specifically **to test Israel** (2:22). A *test* is a negative reality that God allows in your life so that *you* can see how serious (or lacking) your spiritual devotion to him is. God already knows how you'll respond to such tests; he's not shocked by you reaction. But he uses a test to validate or invalidate your commitment. A divine test, then, is a blessing because it enables you to know the strength of your commitment to the Lord. But how will you respond should you learn that your commitment was merely a house of cards?

3:1-6 This is a list of **the nations** (3:1) that God left in the land **to test Israel, to determine if they would keep the LORD's commands** (3:4). Such testing also served **to teach the future generations of the Israelites how to fight in battle** (3:2). But at their core these skirmishes were to be spiritual battles fought on a physical battlefield. The only way the Israelites could wage such a spiritual war was by obeying God's Word and relying on his help. But instead, **they settled among the Canaanites**, merged their families, and even **worshiped their gods** (3:5-6). The Israelites received an "F" on their spiritual report card.

There's an important lesson here for us. According to Paul, "The weapons of our warfare are not of the flesh. . . . We demolish arguments and every proud thing that is raised up against the knowledge of God" (2 Cor 10:4-5). Every day a spiritual battle rages around us in the heavenly realm, and we are participants in it by default. So when you encounter difficult people or trying situations or are tempted to bend God's rules, know that "our struggle is not against flesh and blood, but against the rulers, against the authorities, against the cosmic powers of this darkness, against evil, spiritual forces in the heavens" (Eph 6:12). Satan doesn't want you to be aware of the spiritual realm because he doesn't want you to know how to fight spiritual battles. But if you lose the spiritual battle, you lose every other battle.

III. THE JUDGES (3:7–16:31)

➤ A. Othniel, Ehud, and Shamgar (3:7-31) ➤

3:7-11 Because God's covenant people, the Israelites, **did what was evil** and **worshiped the Baals and the Asherahs** (3:7), God let their enemies rule them. When did God start to help them? When **the Israelites cried out to the LORD** (3:9). "Crying out" speaks of a prayer of desperation. It means that the people had come to the end of themselves and knew they needed divine intervention. That's why God let things get so bad in the first place—so that they would take him seriously and call on him. Unfortunately, it took them **eight years** to come to their senses (3:8). How long does it take you to cry out to the Lord when you experience difficulties?

That God raised up **a deliverer to save** them (3:9) means that he appointed them a judge or savior. A *judge* was basically a civil ruler whom God selected to deliver his people and take vengeance against his enemies. **The Spirit of the LORD came on** a man named Othniel in order to supernaturally enable him to fulfill the task (3:10). He was so successful that **the land had peace for forty years** (3:11). Don't miss that it was the Israelites' desperate cry to God that turned eight years of slavery into forty years of victory.

If you find yourself experiencing year after year of defeat, it's time to cry out to God. Disconnect from serving any idols in your life—including the idol of self—and throw yourself completely on God's mercy. Don't merely pray for help. Recommit yourself to God's agenda and to fully following him, asking him to bring you to a place of victory.

3:12-14 By the time Othniel died (3:11), Israel had gotten used to God's goodness and again forgot about him. So after forty years of God-given peace, they **again did what was evil** (3:12). This time God handed the Israelites to King Eglon of Moab, and he possessed the

City of Palms, which was Jericho (3:13). They **served** Eglon for **eighteen years** (3:14). So not only were the Israelites being plagued from the Canaanites within their borders, surrounding nations were picking on them too.

3:15 Once again, **the Israelites cried out to the LORD**. Why wait eighteen years to do so? Sometimes we can stray so far from God that we're not conscious of how far we've gone or how long we've been gone. We can get so used to being a slave that we don't even look to the divine deliverer. Yet when they finally called to him, God **raised up** another judge, a human **deliverer**.

3:16 Ehud made himself a **double-edged sword**—that is, one that was sharp on both sides. Such a weapon can make significant work of an enemy. The author of Hebrews describes the living Word of God as being "effective and sharper than any double-edged sword" (Heb 4:12). It will pierce the conscience and the heart, exposing motives and sin, laying its hearers bare to the penetrating gaze of an omniscient God.

3:17-26 Ehud delivered **the tribute to King Eglon . . . who was an extremely fat man**, and he told him, **I have a secret message for you** (3:17, 19). Since Ehud had lavished him with a gift, Eglon was interested to hear whatever **message from God** Ehud had to share (3:20). He was completely caught off guard when Ehud took his sword and **plunged it into Eglon's belly** (3:21). The message from God was thus delivered: the Lord did not appreciate the king oppressing his people. By the time Eglon's servants discovered their **dead** ruler, Ehud had **escaped** (3:24-26).

3:27-30 Ehud led the tribe of **Ephraim** into battle against **the Moabites**, and God used him to turn eighteen years of slavery into a respite of **eighty years** of **peace** (3:27-30). In this story we see not only that God providentially directed the course of history but was also involved in the small details. For instance, it was significant that Ehud was left-handed. It kept the sword on "his right thigh" safe from detection because no one would've expected a sword to be hidden there (3:16, 21). We tend to look for evidence

of God at work in the major events and fail to notice how the little things fit together to make major events possible. So keep your eyes open for how God orders minor details before he provides deliverance.

3:31 After Ehud, **Shamgar son of Anath became judge. He also delivered Israel, striking down six hundred Philistines with a cattle prod**. There's only one further mention of Shamgar later in Judges. It says, "In the days of Shamgar son of Anath, in the days of Jael, the main roads were deserted because travelers kept to the side roads" (5:6). That means that insecurity and volatility were so great in this man's day that people had deserted the streets and kept to the back roads to avoid attack. Philistine thugs made life rough.

We can conclude that Shamgar was a farmer because his only weapon was a cattle prod, a pole with a sharp point on the end used to goad livestock into moving. How do you kill six hundred Philistines with one cattle prod? Probably gradually and consistently over time, rather than all at once. If so, Shamgar was an ordinary man who was dissatisfied with the Philistine oppression and used what he had to do something about it. With God's help, he turned his ordinary cattle prod into something extraordinary.

You don't need extraordinary resources or gifts to be used of the Lord, to make a difference in the culture. You just need to be faithful with what the Lord has given you. Think about the gifts God has provided you. Consider where God has placed you. You may have more than you think—when you open yourself to obeying his prompting and to embracing opportunities.

⮞ B. Deborah and Barak (4:1–5:31) ⮜

4:1-3 Again Israel began the cycle of walking away from God. So the Lord handed them over to **King Jabin of Canaan** (4:2). After Israel had been **harshly oppressed** for **twenty years**, they finally **cried out to the LORD** for help (4:3).

4:4-5 Here we're introduced to **Deborah, a prophetess** and female judge (4:4). She was a leader in the civil arena. A prophet or prophetess is a person who communicates God's will about a specific scenario. He or she tells others how they ought to respond in accordance with God's Word. Interestingly, God would speak through Deborah to call a man to lead the coming military battle.

4:6-7 Deborah **summoned Barak**, who was **from Kedesh in Naphtali**, to lead Israelite men against **Jabin's army** (4:6-7). Kedesh was a Levitical city (see Josh 21:1-3, 32), which suggests that Barak was a Levite. Deborah understood that Israel needed spiritual deliverance from their social reality, and it would come in the form of a literal battle.

Through Deborah, God told Barak what he was going to do and what he wanted Barak to do. This brings to mind Paul's insight, which says that we are "working together with [God]" (2 Cor 6:1). God sovereignly works to accomplish his purposes, but he expects our participation in the spiritual battles we face. Too often believers are waiting for God to act, when he is actually waiting for us to step up.

4:8-9 Notice Barak's hesitance. He replied to Deborah, **If you will not go with me, I will not go** (4:8). Though Deborah agreed to his request, she informed him that **a woman** would **receive** the **honor** for the victory ahead (4:9). In other words, Barak was going to miss out on blessing because he balked at obeying God's command to assume leadership. Make no mistake: if God can't find the right man to take care of a task, he will find a good woman. Many women have had to act because the men who should have been leading the way chose passivity.

4:10-16 Sisera, King Jabin's commander, had his **nine hundred iron chariots** (4:13) lined up against Barak and his **ten thousand men** (4:10). Deborah told Barak, **Go! This is the day the LORD has handed Sisera over to you** (4:14). In other words, she was saying, "The victory is in your reach, Barak, but it's just not yet in your hand. You must *act* to obtain it." And when he did, the world got to see what can happen when the human and the divine work together: **the LORD threw Sisera . . . into a panic before**

Barak's assault. God guaranteed the victory, but Barak had to respond in obedience.

4:17-21 Sisera ran to the tent **of Heber the Kenite**, because Sisera's king, Jabin, was at **peace** with Heber (4:17). Unknown to Sisera, however, Heber's wife Jael had decided to align herself with the Lord and his people. She gave Sisera some warm **milk** and a **blanket**, welcoming him as if he were a guest who could find safe refuge with her and allowed him to fall asleep (4:18-20). Once he was cozy, Jael **took a tent peg** and **hammered [it] into his temple** (4:21). Jael knew that Sisera and Jabin were wicked enemies of God's people, and she recognized that a wife is not to follow her husband into rebellion against the Lord. So when given the opportunity to fight back against the enemies of Israel, Jael took action on behalf of God.

4:22-24 When Barak arrived, Sisera was already **dead** (4:22). As Deborah had prophesied in 4:9, a woman, Jael—"most blessed of women" (5:24) was given credit for his demise. From that day forward, as God and Israel worked together, **the power of the Israelites continued to increase . . . until they destroyed** Jabin altogether (4:24). God and man working in partnership against their common enemy is the principle behind spiritual warfare.

5:1-11 Deborah and Barak . . . sang a song of victory and praise. Clearly, even though Israel fought valiantly, the Lord is the hero of the song. The **leaders** led, **the people** volunteered to fight, and the **warriors** performed **righteous deeds** (5:2, 9, 11). But **the LORD** deserved the **praise** and blessings because of his **righteous acts** (5:2-3, 9, 11). He made Israel victorious.

Deborah is significant because she was **a mother in Israel** (5:7). Paul says that a woman "will be saved through childbearing" (see commentary on 1 Tim 2:15). He's saying that mothers experience spiritual victory in their unique role of raising children to submit to God's kingdom and battle the forces of darkness in his name. Mothers, don't take your role lightly, because motherhood is a noble role through which God works to undermine Satan's work. And on this day motherhood saved Israel.

5:12-31 After recounting the battle (5:12-23), the song praises **Jael** as the **most blessed of women** (5:24). Though her husband was at peace with Jabin and Sisera (4:17), Jael knew Sisera was the enemy of God's people (5:25-27). Thus, when she killed Sisera, she saved her husband, because he had thought it no big deal to be in league with someone aligned against God's people. As a result, **the land had peace for forty years** (5:31).

✷ C. Gideon and Abimelech
(6:1–9:57) ✷

6:1-6 Sadly, over time Israel again **did what was evil**, so the Lord **handed them over to Midian** (6:1). The oppression grew so bad that they had to hide in **caves** (6:2). Their enemies destroyed their **crops** and wasted the land until the people of Israel were **poverty-stricken** (6:3-6). This happened because God was no longer covering them since they had departed from his covenant. It's a reminder that when we stray from the Lord, he will sometimes allow a crisis in our lives to compel our return.

6:7-10 The **Israelites cried out** to the Lord again in a desperate appeal for divine intervention (6:7). But before God delivered them this time, he wanted to make some things clear. God reminded them through **a prophet** of all he had done for them by delivering them from **slavery** in **Egypt**, providing them with a **land** to live in, and conquering the people and **gods** who opposed them (6:8-10). Yet, in spite of all the Lord's kindness to them, they continued to do "what was evil" in his sight (6:1). They **did not obey** him (6:10), and it had cost them as he had warned (see Deut 28:15-25).

6:11-12 Normally **wheat** is threshed in a place that catches a breeze so that the chaff is blown away. But Gideon was **threshing wheat in the winepress in order to hide it from the Midianites** (6:11). Thus, things were bleak, and Gideon was hiding. That's

why it's so surprising that the heavenly visitor said to him, **The LORD is with you, valiant warrior** (6:12). Indeed, Gideon's success as a warrior would be dependent on whether or not the Lord was with him.

6:13 Gideon was perplexed. If God was with Israel, **why [had] all this happened?** Though Gideon had heard about the Lord's deliverance of Israel from Egypt, he felt that they had since been **abandoned**. Gideon could only see his own circumstances and not the big picture. Yes, God had saved Israel from Egypt, but he had saved them for a covenant relationship with him. They "did not obey" him (6:10) and were now suffering the covenant consequences.

6:14-16 Gideon had been minding his own business. (Always leave room for divine interruptions, because God does not always tell you up front when he wants to take you in a direction you didn't plan to go.) Then God told him to **deliver Israel from the grasp of Midian** (6:14). Hiding in a winepress threshing wheat, Gideon certainly wasn't expecting a call to war. After all, he was young and came from an inadequate **family** (6:15). He couldn't understand why God had chosen him. But God responded to Gideon just as he had responded to Moses's concerns of inadequacy years prior: **I will be with you** (6:16; see Exod 3:11-12). The key to accomplishing an impossible task is always walking in the presence of God.

6:17-21 Gideon must have thought he was dreaming when the Lord tapped him to defend Israel. Perhaps that's why he wanted some proof, **a sign**, that God was **speaking** (6:17). So he **prepared** an offering, and the visitor told him to put the **meat**, **bread**, and **broth** on a **stone** (6:19-20). Then the **angel of the LORD** caused the offering to be **consumed by fire**, and he **vanished from** Gideon's sight (6:21). Gideon wanted a sign that God was really speaking to him; miraculous proof doesn't get much better than that.

6:22-24 When Gideon realized whom he had been chatting with, he said, **Oh no, LORD GOD! I have seen the angel of the LORD face to face!** (6:22). Likely he had in mind the

Lord's words to Moses, "You cannot see my face, for humans cannot see me and live" (Exod 33:20). But in response to Gideon's fear, the Lord assured him that he would live (6:23). It's clear, then, that Gideon did not see the full, unshielded expression of God's glory. As a result of the encounter, Gideon built an altar, and called it The Lord Is Peace (6:24).

6:25-27 Gideon's first task as judge was to tear down the altar of Baal that belonged to his father and cut down the Asherah pole beside it (6:25). It took two bulls and ten of his male servants to tear down the altar, so it was obviously a major presence on his father's property. There's a principle at work here: Don't expect God to do something *outside* of your home if you're not willing to get things right *inside* your home. In spite of Gideon's courageous action, he was afraid (6:27), but his fear didn't lead to disobedience.

6:28-32 In the morning, the men of the city observed what had happened and discovered that Gideon was responsible (6:28-29). So they told Joash, Gideon's father, to give him up for execution (6:30). That provides a clear picture of just how bad idolatry had become in Israel—these people wanted to kill a man who had torn down an idol and erected in its place an altar for the God who had rescued them from Egypt. Perhaps Gideon's father saw the irony in that when he argued that Baal, if he was real, didn't need them to fight his battles (6:31). Surely, he said in effect, a god can defend himself! Thus, by God's grace Gideon earned a reputation as Jerubbaal, "Baal Fighter" (6:32).

6:33-35 When the three nations who had been victimizing Israel (6:33) gathered to descend on her again, the Spirit of the Lord enveloped Gideon (6:33-34). So he blew the ram's horn and four Israelite tribes rallied behind him (6:34-35). Things happened quickly after that, bringing to mind the truth that when God is ready to move in your circumstance, change can happen in a moment.

6:36-38 Gideon had heard God's promise of deliverance (6:14-16), but he was afraid. He wanted further assurance. So he said, I will put a wool fleece here on the threshing

floor. If dew is only on the fleece, and all the ground is dry, I will know that you will deliver Israel by my strength (6:37). Now, we would expect the dew to cover not just an object resting on the ground, but the ground itself. So Gideon was asking God to interrupt the natural order of things with a deviation from the usual, which is the definition of a miracle. God compassionately responded to his request: in the morning, Gideon wrung dew out of the fleece though the surrounding earth was dry (6:38).

6:39-40 Gideon was like the man who told Jesus, "I do believe; help my unbelief!" (Mark 9:24). Though he'd had a divine visit and God did as Gideon requested (6:38), that wasn't enough for Gideon. This time, he asked for the reverse as a sign: dry fleece and wet ground (6:39). God responded mercifully (6:40).

7:1-3 The time to fight had arrived. And while Gideon could certainly have used some encouraging words from the Lord, God had a surprise for him. He said, You have too many troops (7:2). Now, we just read in 6:5 that the Midianites were "without number" and "like a great swarm of locusts." So if anything, Gideon probably was hoping for more warriors to join his army. But God was thinking of his own glory and the good of his people. God knew that if Israel fought with superior numbers, they might elevate themselves over him and say, My own strength saved me (7:2). So, to keep them from proudly trusting in themselves, God reduced their number by more than half (7:3). Though his ways may puzzle you at times, God wants you to live life his way so that he gets all the glory.

7:4-8 Yet again God said there were too many (7:4). So Gideon led them to water, and God said, Separate everyone who laps water with his tongue like a dog. Do the same with everyone who kneels to drink (7:4-5). Through this, God chose the three hundred men who took water in their hands, stood, and lapped it from their hands (7:6-7). They were alert to what was happening around them. And since what was to follow was a holy war, they needed to be standing alert, fully committed even when eating or drinking. Gideon kept only **three hundred troops** (7:8).

7:9-15 God promised that he had **handed** the Midianites over to Gideon (7:9), but he also offered him some "insider information." He told him to go near the enemy's camp and **listen**. What he heard would encourage him **to attack** (7:10-11). Sure enough, Gideon overheard a conversation about a dream in which **a loaf of barley bread** rolled down into the Midianite camp and destroyed it (7:13). A Midianite soldier interpreted the dream to mean that **God [had] handed the entire Midianite camp over** to Gideon (7:14). That was all Gideon needed to hear (7:15).

7:15-25 When Gideon got the boost of encouragement needed, he first **bowed in worship**, no doubt thanking God for it (7:15). Gideon then **divided the three hundred men into three** groups, and they circled the camp in the middle of the night (7:16; see 7:12). Then each man shattered a clay pitcher, uncovered a torch, blew a trumpet, and shouted, **A sword for the LORD and for Gideon!** (7:20). The noise startled the Midianites from sleep. They assumed they were being overrun by a superior force. In fact, God created such confusion among the enemy that they began fighting one another (7:22). As a result, they were completely defeated, and their leaders were executed (7:23-25).

God calls us to follow his agenda, even when it doesn't make sense. He wants you to watch and see what he can do in response to your obedience and faith. When God is ready to move, it doesn't matter how big your "enemy" is. The Midianites were shattered by the power of God working through the people of God in the midst of dark circumstances. Let the church take notice. Even when we don't understand things and think the odds are against us, God calls us to do what he says—individually and collectively—and then watch him work.

8:1-3 The men of Ephraim were upset that they were called at the end of the battle, rather than at the beginning (8:1). But Gideon told them the mopping-up operations were also important, and they were assuaged for the moment (8:2-3).

8:4-9 Gideon and his little army soon grew weary from chasing the Midianite kings, **Zebah and Zalmunna**. So they asked the men of the city of Succoth, **Please give some loaves of bread to the troops** (8:5). Yet while Gideon was a brother to the men of Succoth, they weren't willing to risk siding with him against God's enemies—whom Gideon hadn't actually caught yet (8:6). Frustrated by this lack of support, Gideon promised that when he had dealt with God's enemies, **I will tear your flesh with thorns and briers** (8:7). When **the men of Penuel** proved similarly disinclined to help, Gideon promised to **tear down** their **tower** (8:8-9).

8:10-21 With the Lord's help, Gideon routed what was left of Midian's army and captured the two kings (8:10-12). On the way home, he whipped the leaders of Succoth and tore down the tower and killed the men of Penuel—as promised (8:13-17).

8:22-23 In response to Gideon's victory, the Israelites said, **Rule over us, you as well as your sons and your grandsons, for you delivered us from the power of Midian**. Gideon was already the deliverer God provided, but the Israelites wanted more: they wanted a king. But God didn't intend them to be like other nations. He did not want them to have a monarchy until they had learned to live under him: **the LORD will rule over you** (8:23). When men do not know how to be ruled properly under God, they are willing to be ruled improperly by man because man will seek to become a god.

8:24-27 Gideon rejected their request to be their king, and that's good (8:23). Yet he asked each of them to give him **an earring** of gold (8:24). With these he made **an ephod**, and it became a spiritual trap for Israel, for Gideon, and for his family (8:27). An ephod was a priestly article that fit like a vest. There was only one official ephod; it was to be used only by a Levitical priest in the tabernacle (see Exod 28:6-14). Thus Gideon chose to make something that he shouldn't have to use in a place where such a thing didn't belong. In doing so, he assumed an illegitimate position of religious authority that had not been assigned to him. And as the Israelites looked to him and his ephod to be a spiritual guide, they were unfaithful to God's program.

8:28-31 Israel **had peace for forty years** (8:28). But, unfortunately, **Gideon had seventy sons ... since he had many wives** (8:28, 30). Things didn't go as smoothly under Gideon's leadership as they might have. Whenever you see polygamy in the Bible, you've got a messy situation that contrasts with God's stated his design for marriage (see Gen 2:23-24). As if Gideon's "many wives" aren't alarming enough, he also had a **concubine** (that's a mistress), and he named their son **Abimelech**, which means—get ready for this—"My Father Is King" (8:31). It seems that the power Gideon got from acting like a priest had gone to his head, and he was setting the stage for a dynasty. That's just the kind of overreach that can happen when someone is given unlimited power without accountability. Every leader needs limits and advisors to hold him in check.

8:32-35 Eventually Gideon **died**, and immediately **the Israelites turned and prostituted themselves by worshiping** false gods (8:32). Not only did the Israelites fail to remember that ultimately it was God who had delivered them from their enemies, but they didn't even respect Gideon's family for all he had done for them (8:34-35).

As a result, they'd started worshiping **Baal-berith**, "Baal of the covenant" (8:33). In other words, they were practicing religious syncretism: they were mixing faiths, worshiping Baal and mixing it with God's covenant with them. This is much like what happened when a previous generation made a golden-calf idol and called it the one who brought Israel up from Egypt (see Exod 32:4-5). Such compromises can only lead to death.

9:1-6 Gideon's polygamous ways led to a series of complicated events. His son **Abimelech**, having aspirations to rule, decided to get rid of Gideon's other **seventy** sons—the competition (9:2). He hired **worthless men** to kill all of them—though one escaped (9:4-5). Don't miss that this deed was carried out **on top of a large stone** (9:5). Since such stones were used as altars, we are to understand that this was human sacrifice. The man

literally sacrificed his family for political power. And the local citizens **proceeded to make** him their **king** (9:6)!

These horrible events were set in motion when the people departed from God with their syncretistic religious practices. It's a chilling reminder that when we compromise with idolatry—even just a little—it is fatal. Satan often tempts people to consume his spiritual poison by camouflaging it with truth. Without godly discernment, rooted in God's Word, you won't know what you're believing and following until you're spiritually sick.

9:7-21 Gideon's youngest son, **Jotham**, who had escaped the slaughter, stood on **Mount Gerizim**, the place of blessing (see Deut 11:29), when he received the news that Abimelech had been named king (9:7). He told the people a parable about how the trees were looking for a leader to rule over them. Each tree they asked said, "No," because the work they were already doing was honoring God and benefitting people. But finally, in their desperation to be ruled, the trees asked the bramble—a thornbush to lead them. Importantly, the bramble is unproductive and is a symbol of the curse (see Gen 3:18). To be called a bramble was no compliment; to have put one in leadership was stupid.

The bramble effectively said, "If you don't let me rule over you like I want to rule over you, I will destroy you." That was Jotham's warning that Abimelech planned to rule the people with totalitarian authority, which is an illegitimate use of rule, biblically speaking. He wouldn't share power with God; he'd simply destroy anyone who opposed him. Having given his warning, **Jotham fled** for his life (9:21).

9:22-24 God sent **an evil spirit between Abimelech and the citizens of Shechem** (9:22-23). Notice who did the action in that sentence. God and the devil do not battle as equals. God is sovereign; Satan is not. God can use the devil to mess up a situation that is offensive to his will.

9:25-41 God created chaos and conflict in Israel. The citizens of Shechem used to be Gideon's friends, but now **they cursed** his son **Abimelech**, their chosen monarch (9:27). A man named **Gaal** seized power and taunted Abimelech, but Zebul, the ruler of the city, **secretly sent messengers to Abimelech** and told him to set an **ambush** for Gaal (9:31-32). Unresolvable madness was taking over Israel, and people were taking sides. This is precisely what happens when God uses the devil like a tool to deal with evil.

9:42-49 Abimelech caught most of **the people of Shechem** outside the gate and slaughtered them (9:42-45). Meanwhile, their local leaders holed up in the **temple of El-berith**, meaning "God of the Covenant," because they thought their god would protect them. When Abimelech set **fire** to the temple and everyone died, there could be no doubt that this so-called deity was powerless (9:46-49). Thus, Jotham's curse: "May fire come from Abimelech and consume the citizens of Shechem" (9:20) was fulfilled. But this was only the first half of the curse. The fulfillment of the second half would see that Abimelech was destroyed, too.

9:50-55 What goes around comes around—maybe not today and maybe not tomorrow, but one day. Abimelech, continuing his rampage, went to destroy **Thebez** (9:50). As the people of that town huddled on the roof of their tower for protection against the invasion, Abimelech approached. Then, **a woman** above **threw the upper portion of a millstone on Abimelech's head and fractured his skull** (9:53). As Abimelech realized the severity of his injuries, he called on his right hand man to kill him so that the people could not say that he had been killed by **a woman** (9:54). Nevertheless, though his armor bearer obeyed his request, Scripture reports the truth of his embarrassing end. Once again in the book of Judges, a woman brings an end to a godless man (see 4:17-22; 5:24-27).

9:56-57 Why did this all happen? Because **God brought back Abimelech's evil** on his own head (9:56). God did not forget that the man had slain his seventy brothers. **God also brought back to the men of Shechem all their evil** in helping him to do it and naming that wicked man king. Thus, **the curse of**

Jotham son of Jerubbaal came upon them (9:57). That righteous man, Jotham, had gone to the place of blessing and called on God to show justice, and—in his perfect timing—God dealt justly with the situation.

֎ D. Tola, Jair, and Jephthah
(10:1–12:7) ֍

10:1-5 Judge Tola's name means "worm." We know little about him other than that **he was from Issachar** and **judged Israel twenty-three years** (10:1-2). Tola was followed by Jair, who had **had thirty sons** (10:4). That high number suggests that he, like Gideon, was a polygamist trying to build a dynasty.

After sharing how long each of these judges judged, the author notes their deaths (10:2, 5). This signals to the reader that no human judge could serve as the people's permanent source of deliverance. While God works through people, we have only one ongoing source—the living and true God.

10:6-7 With Tola and Jair gone, the Israelites repeated the cycle that is so central to the book of Judges. **They worshiped . . . the gods** of the surrounding peoples. **They abandoned the Lord** (10:6). And, right on cue, God **sold them to the Philistines and the Ammonites** (10:7). At work here is a sobering spiritual principle. If you demand to worship false gods, God will eventually let you be ruled by your preferences.

10:8-14 After they had suffered terribly **for eighteen years** (10:8), the Israelites finally **cried out to the Lord** and confessed their sin (10:10). When their enemies had oppressed them in the past, God had delivered them every time. Yet clearly, they had not learned or grown. This time he said, **I will not deliver you again. Go and cry out to the gods you have chosen. Let them deliver you** (10:11-14). If God is finished with you, then where will you appeal in an oppressive situation? To whom will you go for deliverance? If the people were honest with themselves, they had to realize that there was no one else to whom they could go for deliverance.

10:15-16 Desperate for help, the Israelites said, **We have sinned. Deal with us as you see fit; only rescue us today!** And to try to show repentance, **they got rid of the foreign gods among them and worshiped the LORD** (10:15-16). Now, here we have an interesting switch. Previously, when they said, "We have sinned," the people kept the gods in their back pockets. They'd been all talk and no action. But when they said, "We've sinned, please deliver us," *and* they got rid of their gods, God was willing to act on their behalf (10:16).

What happened here? In verse 14 God said, "I will not deliver you again." Yet when they repented, God did something he had said he wasn't going to do. When our actions realign us with God's will, doors of blessing can open to us that were previously closed. Confessing our sins through repentance and getting back on track through action is key. Confession is acknowledging sin, but repentance is turning away from it. And it's the combination that God desires.

The Bible says that God does not change his mind (see Num 23:19; 1 Sam 15:29). So why does it seem that he did so here? Though God's being and moral character do not change, he can change in his relationship with humans based on how they relate to him. And when he does this, he is still being consistent with himself because he has promised to show mercy, grace, and forgiveness to those who truly repent and believe.

This passage also says something else about God: he expresses emotions. The Bible speaks of his anger, sadness, grief, and joy. While we express similar emotions because we are made in God's image, sin has distorted our feelings. Yet God is perfect, and his emotions are too. He couldn't bear to see Israel hurting anymore. So he chose to prepare a new deliverer.

11:1-11 Jephthah the Gileadite was a **valiant warrior, but he was the son of a prostitute** (11:1). Why did the author tell us that detail about his parentage? Because as the man's story unfolds, we'll see that your background doesn't determine your usefulness to God. Rahab the harlot, for instance, cast herself on the mercy of the Lord and ended up being in the lineage of Jesus Christ (see Josh 1:21;

6:22-23; Matt 1:5). So although Jephthah's family drove him out and he lived in another country for a while, he was still of worth to God's kingdom plan. When his kinsmen wanted to draft him to lead them militarily (11:4-6), Jephthah agreed. He also made them vow to God to make him their leader if he agreed to defeat the Ammonites (11:9-10). His days of living as an outcast were over.

11:12-28 First Jephthah tried to work things out with the Ammonites through negotiation. The king of the Ammonites said, **When Israel came from Egypt, they seized my land** (11:13). But Jephthah explained what had really happened. When Israel asked to pass through the same general area when they came out of Egypt, **Sihon king of the Amorites** wouldn't let them and attacked Israel instead (11:19-20). So the Lord helped Israel defeat Sihon's people and gave them their land (11:21-23). **But the king of the Ammonites would not listen to Jephthah's message** (11:28).

11:29-31 The Spirit of the LORD came on Jephthah (11:29). This was a supernatural endowment to fulfill a particular task. Jephthah was so intent on defeating Israel's enemy that he wanted to let God know that he was serious about following through on the job. He vowed that if God handed over the Ammonites to him, he would offer the first thing that walked out of his home as a **burnt offering** to the Lord (11:30-31).

11:32-40 God gave Jephthah victory (11:32-33), and when he came home, **there was his daughter, coming out to meet him with tambourines and dancing!** (11:34). Who knows what he was expecting to walk out when he made the vow, but it was his only child, his daughter. If it had been an animal, he would have sacrificed it on the altar, but since it was a person, she would be dedicated to the Lord's service for the rest of her life (Ps 68:25)—like a nun or a priest. She submitted to her fate, but she wept over her **virginity** (11:36-37). She would not be able to marry and have a family.

Jephthah's condition for leading this army was to be made the leader of Gilead (11:9). Clearly he had aspirations to be king, to build a family dynasty. But until the Israelites were willing to look to God as their King, he didn't want them to have a human king, because unless a government is accountable to God, men in power will act like gods. Consider Gideon, Abimelech, Jephthah (and, later, Saul): God blocked any dynasty that would be man-centered and not God-centered. So when Jephthah's daughter, his only offspring, came out of his house to meet him, his dynasty plans were thwarted. Though God calls us to obey governing authorities (see Rom 13:1), we are to give our ultimate allegiance to him because he is sovereign (see Acts 5:29).

12:1-6 Just as in the days of Gideon, **the men of Ephraim** were upset because they hadn't been called into the battle right away (12:1; see 8:1). This time the dispute resulted in Israel's tribes fighting each other. And ultimately, **forty-two thousand** Israelites were killed because of wounded pride (12:6). The Bible highlights pride as one of the chief sins. Pride means thinking more of yourself than you ought, and it's the very thing that led to Satan's fall. He wanted to be like God—that is, he wanted to be more than he was created to be (see Ezek 28:14-17). All of us fight pride on different levels, but to battle against it successfully, you must remember that (1) God hates pride and (2) you're not him.

12:7 Jephthah judged Israel six years, and then he **died**. Thus, another flawed Israelite judge delivered the people and then passed from the scene.

➤ E. Ibzan, Elon, Abdon, and Samson (12:8–16:31) ❧

12:8-15 After Jephthah, **Ibzan judged Israel seven years**, then he **died** (12:9-10). Elon **judged Israel ten years**, then he **died** (12:11-12). Abdon **judged Israel eight years**, then he **died** (12:14-15). This brings us to a sobering reality: unless Christ comes first, we're all going to die. And how we will be remembered will come down to the choices we make: will we, like these judges, serve God or something else?

If you want to be a doctor, but you don't want to go to medical school, then you don't really want to be a doctor, because you're not doing what is necessary to achieve what you want. Similarly, if you want to reign with Christ, you have to trust and follow Christ in the here and now.

13:1-3 Again the Israelites **did what was evil in the LORD's sight, so the LORD handed them over to the Philistines forty years** (13:1). At this point the author introduces us to a man named **Manoah**, whose **wife was unable to conceive** (13:2). Her barrenness was outside of her control, but it was fully under the control of the sovereign God of heaven. He was getting ready to do something remarkable in her life. **The angel of the LORD** appeared to her and said, **You will . . . give birth to a son** (13:3). And that son, that miracle, would be Israel's next deliverer.

When you are discouraged and can't seem to see your way past a difficult time, seek God and ask him what he's up to behind the scenes. He won't necessarily remove the source of your discouragement. But he never does anything without a reason. Your trying circumstances may be an opportunity for God to work remarkably in your life and conform you to the likeness of Christ.

13:4-5 This promised boy would grow up and **begin to save Israel** from the Philistines' **power** (13:5). And with this role came a job requirement not made of the other judges: the angel instructed Manoah's wife to rear the child under the **Nazirite** vow. As explained in Numbers 6:1-21, this meant that he was not to drink wine or beer or cut his hair (13:5). But remarkably, the angel told the woman **not to drink wine or beer, or to eat anything unclean** while she was pregnant (13:4). That meant that her son was to be consecrated to God as a Nazirite even in the womb. This is wonderful evidence that personhood begins at conception.

Every moral issue we face in our culture has a spiritual component to it. Abortion, for instance, is a spiritual matter because it's the destruction of a person created in the image of God. Throughout his Word, God condemns those who shed innocent blood (see Prov 6:16-17), and no blood is more innocent than a child in the womb.

13:6-14 Even though the heavenly visitor was talking directly to her, the woman showed her respect for her husband when she **went and told [him]** what happened (13:6). At the news, Manoah prayed that the angel would **come again** (13:8). He wanted confirmation that the marvelous report he'd heard was true, and God graciously granted it. The angel came again, confirmed what he had said, and provided further details (13:13-14).

13:15-18 Presumably, Manoah thought he was talking to a mere man sent from the Lord, so he said, **Please stay here, and we will prepare a young goat for you** (13:15). The visitor agreed to stay, but said he wouldn't eat anything. It would be more appropriate for the couple to offer **a burnt offering** (13:16). At this, Manoah asked for the man's name, and he replied, **It is beyond understanding** (13:18).

This cryptic statement is a reminder that while we often think we understand what he is going to do in our lives, the Lord likes to shock us with his marvelous ways. So don't put God in a box. He can unpredictably bust right past all your preconceived ideas.

13:19-23 When Manoah put the burnt offering on a rock as requested, the visitor **did something miraculous**: he ascended in the **flame** and went up **to the sky**. Manoah and his wife **fell facedown on the ground** at the sight (13:19-20). Suddenly, Manoah was terrified and said, **We're certainly going to die ... because we have seen God!** (13:22). He rightly equated the angel of the Lord with God.

This is another Old Testament Christophany—a pre-incarnate but visible manifestation of Christ (see 2:1-2). Jesus Christ, the second Person of the Trinity, is the manifestation of God in history. The eternal Father, who existed before time and who initiated it, routes his activity in time through Jesus. Just as the sun is the center of our solar system, the Son is the center of God's working in history. He has "first place in everything" (Col 1:18).

13:24-25 Manoah's wife named her child **Samson**. God **blessed him**, and **the Spirit of the LORD began to stir him**, readying Samson for the work prepared for him.

14:1-4 For a man set apart for God's service since birth, Samson made some questionable life decisions—ultimately proving that God can use a person in spite of himself. **Samson went down to Timnah and saw a young Philistine woman there** (14:1). He told his parents to arrange a marriage with her. His parents tried to speak wisdom into his life by telling him he should not marry someone who was not a part of God's people. But they didn't know that his interest in this particular woman **was from the LORD, who wanted the Philistines to provide an opportunity** for a confrontation (14:4). God threw a curve ball. He would use Samson's fascination with this woman to create an opportunity to deliver his people. God was providentially working uniquely in Samson's circumstances to accomplish his purposes.

Importantly, though, a believer is not to use this passage to justify marrying an unbeliever. Samson's parents were right. The Lord had warned his people not to intermarry with the surrounding nations because they didn't worship the One True God (see Deut 7:1-3). And similarly, believers should not be partners with unbelievers (see 2 Cor 6:14). Christians should marry only Christians. A couple that is unequally yoked is likely to run into trouble.

14:5-9 On the way to Timnah where his bride-to-be lived, Samson was attacked by a young lion, and **the Spirit of the LORD came powerfully on him, and he tore the lion apart with his bare hands** (14:6). This was a clear sign that indeed he had been elected and empowered by God for a supernatural purpose. But later, when he discovered that **bees** had made a hive in the **carcass**, Samson blatantly ignored the law of Moses regarding unclean foods and took some of the **honey** (14:8-9).

14:10-14 At **a feast** probably intended to serve as his engagement party, Samson decided to pose a **riddle** to the **Philistines** (14:10-12). The prize for answering the riddle within a week would be **thirty changes of clothes** (14:12). (In biblical days, an additional set of clothing was a sign of honor and dignity.) Samson, his recent kill and the accompanying honey on his mind, said, **Out of the eater came something to eat, and out of the strong came something sweet** (14:14). When the Philistines couldn't figure out the meaning, they became furious.

14:15-20 The men threatened to kill Samson's bride (who, remember, was one of their own) and her family unless she got Samson to tell her the answer and share it with them (14:15). Frightened, **she wept** in front of Samson for **seven days**, and finally he couldn't take it anymore **because she had nagged him so much** (14:17). So he told her the answer. Later, when the Philistine men parroted the answer (14:18), Samson knew how they had obtained it. **The Spirit of the LORD came powerfully on him**, and he **killed thirty** Philistine men in another town, giving their clothes to these men to keep the deal he'd struck (14:19). After that, he returned home—without his wife (14:19-20).

15:1-8 Some time later, Samson brought about further destruction on the Philistines. He wanted to visit his wife, but **her father would not let him enter** her room. He had given her to another man because he assumed Samson was not happy with her (15:1-2). Samson was enraged by this news. Since the Philistines had interfered with his family "harvest"—his plan to start a family with this woman—he decided to interfere with their harvest. He destroyed their crops by catching **three hundred foxes**, tying their **tails** together with rope and **torches**, setting them on fire, and releasing them into their fields (15:3-5). In response, the Philistines killed **Samson's wife** and her father (15:6). And Samson, in turn, avenged the murders with his bare hands (15:8).

15:9-13 While Samson hid in a cave, the Philistines attacked a town in Judah to pay Samson back. To pacify the Philistines, **three thousand men of Judah** went to arrest Samson, saying that he had brought trouble on them by riling up the Philistine oppressors

(15:11). (Don't miss the irony here. They chose to hand over the man God had sent to save them *from* the Philistines *to* the Philistines.) Samson went along with them, but only after they promised that they would not kill him themselves (15:12-13).

15:14-17 When the Philistines saw the bound Samson approaching, they shouted. But in that moment, **the Spirit of the LORD came powerfully on** Samson (15:14). This was bad news for the Philistines: If you're fighting against someone, you don't want the Spirit of the Lord to come powerfully on him! Since Samson was empowered by God's Spirit, his enemies were outnumbered. The **ropes** used to tie him up were nothing, given his strength (15:14). **He found a fresh jawbone of a donkey . . . and killed a thousand men with it** (15:15). The empowerment of the Lord allowed him to do what would've otherwise been impossible.

15:18-20 When Samson finished executing judgment on the Philistines, **he became very thirsty and called out to the LORD** (15:18). The Lord graciously responded by making a spring there to restore his strength. So Samson called it, "Spring of the One Who Cried Out" (15:19). And he **judged Israel twenty years** (15:20).

Whenever the Spirit of the Lord came on Samson, supernatural activity followed. In the Old Testament, the Spirit of the Lord came on people specifically related to certain events. Since New Testament times, however, the Spirit of the Lord comes to indwell every believer (see Eph 1:13-14; Rom 8:9). In other words, on this side of the cross the supernatural presence of God is not related to the Spirit coming on believers, but to the fullness of the Spirit at work within us. The Spirit "came powerfully on" Samson for supernatural purposes. And this same Spirit is in us today.

One reason that we don't see more of the Holy Spirit's supernatural activity in our time is that we often fail to "walk by the Spirit" (Gal 5:16). That is, we are so busy doing life the world's way that we fail to honor his presence in our lives. By contrast, we should "be filled by the Spirit" (Eph 5:18), which essentially means living under his control.

16:1 Samson's personal choices become even more concerning at this point in the narrative. **Samson went to Gaza, where he saw a prostitute and went to bed with her.** Now, for years the people of Israel had "prostituted themselves with other gods" (2:17; 8:27, 33). They had blatantly compromised with the surrounding culture and betrayed the Lord. And by this season of his life, Samson the leader was openly living in a way that reflected what Israel had been doing. This trend would be his downfall.

16:2-3 The Philistines in Gaza discovered Samson was with the prostitute and thought they had him trapped. They guarded the town's exit. But when Samson was ready to leave, he simply **took hold of the doors of the city gate along with the two gateposts, and pulled them out, bar and all. He put them on his shoulders and took them to the top of the mountain overlooking Hebron** (16:3). You or I couldn't carry these massive doors a block's distance on level ground! This scene serves as proof that though Samson was outside of the will of God in what he was doing, God had not left him—*yet.*

16:4-5 Samson was in a downward spiral when Delilah entered his life, and he **fell in love with** her (16:4). It is not clear whether Delilah was a Philistine woman, but her loyalties lay with them and their **silver.** The **Philistine leaders** asked her to **persuade** Samson to confide in her about **where his great strength [came] from,** so that they could **overpower him, tie him up, and make him helpless.** They promised her a great deal of money for her aid (16:5).

16:6-17 Three times Delilah tried to learn his secret, while the Philistines lay waiting to ambush him (16:6-14). Each time Samson gave her a false story about the source of his strength. But she steadily wore him down. In the end, Delilah used the very trick Samson's bride had once employed when she betrayed him to the Philistines. She pleaded, **How can you say, "I love you" . . . when your heart is not with me?** (See 14:15-20). And she accused him of mocking her (16:15). Of course, if she really loved *him*, she wouldn't set him up like this. In the end, **because she nagged him day**

after day . . . until she wore him out, he finally told **her the whole truth** (16:16-17). If his hair were cut, he would lose his strength and become **like any other man** (16:17).

16:18-20 Delilah didn't waste time. She had Samson's head shaved while he slept **on her lap** (16:19). And since the Philistine leaders were waiting in the shadows and had **brought the silver with them** (16:18), she was free to count her dirty money while the deed was done.

Once Samson had been made helpless, we read these sad, pitiful words: **When he awoke from his sleep, he said, "I will escape as I did before and shake myself free." But he did not know that the LORD had left him** (16:20).

Samson let his relationship with Delilah take priority over his commitments to God, and it cost him dearly. This is evidence that no human relationship, no matter how close, is to trump your relationship with the Lord.

16:21 Samson's sin cost him tremendously. The Philistines **gouged out** Samson's **eyes,** put him in **shackles,** and set him to work in **prison.** In other words, the enemies of God were suddenly in control of his every move. This is a reminder that when God is no longer in a life's equation, Satan controls the situation.

16:22 Here we get a hint that God wasn't done with Samson yet. Why else would we need to be told that his hair, which was the secret to his strength, had begun to **grow back**? His hair's return was an outward symbol that he was inwardly repentant and turning back to God. His repentance would become apparent in his upcoming prayer to the Lord (16:28).

Sometimes God has to take you as low as you can possibly go to get your undivided attention. Samson was at the bottom. But his hair was growing back.

16:23-24 As Samson ground grain in the prison, **the Philistine leaders gathered together to offer a great sacrifice to their god Dagon** (16:23). They were ready to celebrate that their god had **handed over** their enemy to them (16:24). But there was a problem with their reasoning: Dagon hadn't handed

Samson over to them at all; God had. Thus, the battle between Samson and his tormentors was not merely personal or political but theological.

When we are in a conflict, we should retreat as quickly as we can to the spiritual nature of the battle, as young David would do years later when facing off against this same people group and their champion, Goliath (see 1 Sam 17:45-47). David heard the challenge the man made in defiance of God and quickly realized that the battle to be fought was spiritual in nature, even though it would be played out in the physical arena. He saw it as a conflict between the god of the Philistines and the true God. We must do the same, recognizing that our conflicts are spiritual and theological, not merely physical or emotional.

16:25-31 The Philistines were **in good spirits** at their party. They called for Samson to amuse them, and **they had him stand between the pillars** of the temple (16:25). In

doing so, they set themselves up for destruction. **The temple was full of men and women . . . and about three thousand [people] were on the roof** (16:27). Samson, aware of this, prayed that God would strengthen him one last time, so that he might bring down the roof on the Philistines (16:28). **He pushed with all his might, and the temple fell on the leaders and all the people in it**. Thus, Samson killed more of Israel's oppressors that day than he had killed all the rest of his days (16:30).

Unfortunately, Samson had yielded to the idolatrous culture around him and made sinful choices. Nevertheless, in Hebrews 11:32-33 Samson is included in the "Hall of Faith," alongside upright Old Testament people like Daniel. And that inclusion ought to birth hope in every heart. While Samson was not even close to being a perfect man, he got this right: he *believed* God could use him to accomplish his will. Therefore, let us trust God, submit to his agenda for our lives, and give him everything we have.

IV. THE CORRUPTION OF THE LEVITES (17:1–21:25)

To fully appreciate the depth of depravity seen in this next section, we must remember that the priests of Israel came from the tribe of Levi. Priests and Levites were supposed to steer the people away from idolatry toward the worship of God, teaching them right from wrong (see Lev 10:8-11; Ezek 44:23). But during the time period covered in these final five chapters, there was no divine standard operating in the nation. Everyone simply ignored the rules God had given to Moses and did "whatever seemed right to him" (17:6). And by this point in the nation's history, even the Levites were complicit in the decline and debauchery.

A. Micah's Priest (17:1–18:31)

17:1-3 The first thing we learn about the Ephraimite named **Micah** is that he stole from his own **mother**. She had **1,100 pieces of silver** (that's about twenty-eight pounds!),

and Micah helped himself to it. Only when he heard her **curse** the silver so that it would fail to be an advantage to whoever stole it, did he return her money (17:1-2). (So not only was he a thief, but he was superstitious too.) At his admission, his mother **blessed** him and said, **I personally consecrate the silver to the LORD for my son's benefit to make . . . a silver idol** (17:2-3).

Clearly, we have problems here. She dedicated the silver to the Lord for the express purpose of making an idol. But the Lord had commanded Israel, "Do not make an idol for yourself" (Exod 20:4). That kind of blatant double-mindedness is just what we would expect to develop in a culture that tries to blend the worship of the true God with the world's pagan ways. The Lord demands whole-hearted devotion.

17:4 The woman **took five pounds of silver and gave it to a silversmith**. Don't miss that little detail. While she'd promised the whole twenty-eight pounds would be used in the idol's manufacture, she only gave up part of it. Micah probably learned how to steal from her.

17:5-6 Once the idol was in his house, Micah used both an **ephod** to determine God's will and **household idols** to determine the pagan gods' preferences. Then he made one of his own sons **to be his** personal **priest** (17:5). Micah was from the tribe of Ephraim, and only Levites could be priests. Thus, this was a further flagrant disregard for God's commands.

It's not surprising that the author of Judges says, **In those days there was no king in Israel; everyone did whatever seemed right to him** (17:6). The people had completely forgotten that the Lord was to be their King. So there was no divine standard operating in Israel. Everyone followed his own standard, his own god.

17:7-12 Next we are introduced to **a young man, a Levite from Bethlehem**, and he was looking for **a place** to stay (17:7-8). Micah invited him to be his personal **priest** for **four ounces of silver a year** and living expenses (17:10). The Levite **agreed to stay with the man** (17:11). And while only another priest could consecrate a priest, **Micah consecrated the Levite** (17:12). This tells us that while Micah was an idolater, the Levite was just as far away from God's standards of holiness in his thinking and practices. He accepted the role of personal priest for a price (17:6).

17:13 Micah was convinced that having a Levite of his own was a sign of the Lord's blessing: **Now I know that the LORD will be good to me, because a Levite has become my priest**. Yet this mixture of worshiping the true God with idols and substituting right doctrine for warped would contribute to a whole series of terrible events. It most certainly was *not* a sign of God's blessing.

If you attend church and half-heartedly worship the Lord, but then you go home to your idols—those things that you look to as your source of satisfaction and deliverance—you have an unholy mixture in your life, too. The Lord clearly commands us, "Do not have other gods besides me" (Exod 20:3). So know that should you worship and pray to the true God while counting on an idol, you undermine yourself and prevent your prayers from being answered. God will not accept partial allegiance.

18:1 In those days, there was no king in Israel. There was no governing authority to bring God's rule to bear on the nation. That's how the book ends as well (21:25).

And since people were pretty much doing whatever they liked, **the Danite tribe** decided to look **for territory to occupy**. The problem was that the tribe of Dan had failed to conquer what they were supposed to have conquered in the power of the Lord (1:34). So they searched for a people weak and helpless enough that they would be able to take their land away.

18:2-6 The Danite scouts found Micah's house, and they asked the Levite about his circumstances (18:2-3). He said concerning Micah, **He has hired me, and I became his priest** (18:4). Impressed, the men asked the priest to inquire of God so that they could know the way to become prosperous and find a new land (18:5). The Levite said to them, **Go in peace. The LORD is watching over the journey you are going on** (18:6). Now, that's the kind of thing he was expected to say—what he was paid to say. The Danites weren't paying him to give them bad news. But in truth, if you only get good news from a preacher, he's not doing his full job.

18:7-10 The scouts found a place called **Laish**, where the people were **unsuspecting**. They had **no alliance with anyone** who would come to their aid (18:7). Thus, it appeared that the Levite had been right that God was watching over their journey and had even provided just the kind of target they'd wanted. Encouraged, they told their brothers, **Come on, let's attack them** (18:9). **God has handed it over** (18:10).

18:11-14 Six hundred Danites set out for Laish. On the way, they came by **Micah's house** (18:11, 13), and the scouts said, **Did you know that there are an ephod, household gods, and a carved image and a silver idol in these houses? Now think about what you should do** (18:14). What they should have done was "destroy" the idols and "drive out" the idol worshiper (see Num 33:52). But given how spiritually dark Israel had become, it doesn't take a genius to figure out what they planned to do.

18:15-21 The Danites **took the carved image, the ephod, the household idols, and the silver idol** (18:17). Concerned, the priest asked, **What are you doing?** (18:18). But the Danites answered, **Keep your mouth shut. Come with us. . . . Is it better for you to be a priest for the house of one person or for you to be a priest for a tribe and family in Israel?** (18:19). In other words, they appealed to his pride and materialism. They said, "We are giving you an opportunity for promotion: leave this house church and come lead our megachurch." And the priest, ever the opportunist, gathered his idols and moved on to his new post (18:20). Thus, a compromised priest who'd been serving in a compromised house was now moving on to serve in a compromised community. Idolatry was spreading.

18:22-26 Micah gathered a few of his neighbors to chase after the Danites. The six hundred Danite soldiers faced them down and asked what the problem was. Micah replied, **You took the gods I had made and the priest, and went away. What do I have left?** (18:24). Now, any god that can be stolen from you is no god at all, but no one involved in this saga seemed to grasp that. And in the end, though Micah begged for pity, the Danites threatened to harm him and his family if he didn't just accept the turn of events and go home (18:25). The Danites, then, were a gang of thugs who treated their brother Israelite with contempt.

18:27-31 Taking Micah's gods with them, the Danite army continued to Laish and killed **a quiet and unsuspecting people** (18:27). They burned and rebuilt the city and named it **Dan** after their patriarch, who was one of the sons of Israel (that is, Jacob; 18:29). It would become the northernmost city in Israel, a fact often acknowledged in the phrase "from Dan to Beersheba (Israel's southernmost city)," which appears throughout the Old Testament. Then **they set up for**

themselves Micah's carved image that he had made, and it was there as long as the house of God was in Shiloh (18:31). Thus, they had created an idolatrous stronghold. And though they still kept the Lord in the equation, used his name, and even inquired of him, they were not truly worshipping the Lord. They were worshiping a god of their own making.

Idolatry is a devastating sin that robs the true God of glory and cuts people off from his help. The Lord will not compete with false gods. You don't have to bow down to a statue of wood or stone to commit idolatry. If you look to anything other than God as your source of meaning, provision, deliverance, and fulfillment, you're looking to an idol. Worship and serve the Creator, not the creation (see Rom 1:25).

❧ B. Outrage in Benjamin
(19:1–21:25) ❧

19:1-9 In this sad chapter we see that the Levites continued to facilitate the compromise of Israel. A **Levite** from **Ephraim** took a **concubine** for himself **from Bethlehem.** Concubines, or mistresses, were typically slaves. Over the course of time, **she was unfaithful to him and left him for her father's house** (19:1-2). After several months, the Levite went searching for her **to speak kindly to her and bring her back** (19:3). The girl's father was glad to see him, so he stayed with them (19:4). On the fourth day, he was preparing to depart with his concubine, but the father-in-law insisted that he stay (19:5). This happened every time he attempted to leave (19:6-9).

19:10-12 Finally, the Levite refused to stay any longer. He traveled as far as **Jebus** (which would one day be called **Jerusalem**, 19:10), and it was getting late. His servant suggested that they stay within its borders for the night, but the Levite insisted, **We will not stop at a foreign city where there are no Israelites. Let's move on to Gibeah**, which was a town in the territory of Benjamin (19:12). Unfortunately, finding a city of Israelites would bring perversion instead of provision.

19:13-21 When they arrived at **Gibeah**, a city of the tribe of Benjamin, **the Levite . . . sat down in the city square, but no one took them into their home to spend the night** (19:15). Hospitality was an important and valued practice in the ancient Near East. It was customary to offer a stranger a place to stay. So the fact that nobody would do even that basic service for his fellow Israelites shows that at this point in history there really was no spiritual standard among the people—and that's a recipe for disaster. Finally, **an old man** who was heading in from a day of hard work in the fields outside town saw the priest and welcomed him into his house. **I'll take care of everything you need**, he said. **Only don't spend the night in the square** (19:20). Clearly, he didn't think it would be safe to camp out in that neighborhood.

19:22 As they were having dinner, **wicked men of the city surrounded the house and beat on the door**. They demanded that the man hand over the Levite: **Bring out the man who came to your house so we can have sex with him!**

Careful Bible readers will notice that this story sounds familiar. In Genesis 19, Abraham's nephew Lot lived in the city of Sodom and welcomed into his home two angels. But the wicked men of the city demanded, "Where are the men who came to you tonight? Send them out to us so we can have sex with them!" (Gen 19:5). The author of Judges wants us to see a sad reality: God's people—who were called to be holy—had become just like the Canaanites whom they had driven out.

19:23-24 The old man defended his guest (19:23), but then he said the unthinkable: **Here, let me bring out my virgin daughter and the man's concubine now. Abuse them and do whatever you want to them. But don't commit this outrageous thing against this man** (19:24). This is horrific! Though he wanted to protect the Levite, he was willing to do so by handing over two defenseless women to a group of rapists! This is a twisted and depraved form of manhood. Even he, apparently among the city's finest given his hospitality, was completely

without conscience with regard to how women should be treated.

19:25-30 The Levite grew so concerned for his own safety that he cruelly delivered his concubine over to be **raped** by these men all night! He slept while she was **abused** (19:25). In the morning **she collapsed at the doorway . . . where her master was** (19:26). Yet, he still showed no remorse. Ready to continue his journey, he said to her callously, **Get up. . . . Let's go** (19:28). And when she didn't respond, he put her on a donkey and carried his dead concubine to his house—where he butchered her (19:28-29). This story is enough to make you ill.

He **cut her into twelve pieces . . . and then sent her throughout the territory of Israel** (19:29). Those who saw the grim deliveries said, **Nothing like this has ever happened . . . since the day the Israelites came out of the land of Egypt** (19:30). This was serious cultural decadence and decline. There was homosexuality, rape, cultural chaos, and mutilation among God's people in the promised land, because there was no divine standard operating.

When people within a nation move away from honoring God, debauchery, decline, and chaos do inevitably set in. It doesn't matter who is in power. Until the spiritual aspect gets rectified and idols are dismissed—specifically among God's people—there will be no God, no King, no divine standard operating within that country that can fix the downhill race into tragedy.

20:1-13 The soldiers of the tribes of Israel **assembled as one body before the Lord at Mizpah** and asked how the terrible matter could have happened (20:1-3). The Levite explained the previous events—though he carefully omitted the fact that he had been wickedly willing to sacrifice his concubine to save himself (20:4-7). When they heard the awful story, the Israelites decided to **attack** Gibeah **to punish them for all the outrage they committed** (20:8-10). Then they sent messengers throughout Benjamin (since Gibeah was in the territory of Benjamin) saying, **Hand over the wicked men in Gibeah so we can put them to death and eradicate evil from Israel** (20:12-13).

The result would be a civil war. **The Benjaminites would not listen to their fellow Israelites** (20:13). They preferred to defend their own evil tribesmen rather than let the instigators face judgment. Their relationship with the town trumped their relationship with the people of God. Their misplaced loyalty should make us ask whether we are willing to endorse what is wrong for the sake of a relationship.

20:14-25 Over **twenty-six thousand** men from Benjamin and Gibeah faced off against **four hundred thousand** men from Israel (20:15-17). The Israelites, perhaps awakening to the fact that they'd need God's help in setting things right within their borders, asked the Lord who should fight Benjamin first. He answered that **Judah** would be **first** (20:18). They did as God told them, but **the Benjaminites came out of Gibeah and slaughtered twenty-two thousand men of Israel on the field that day** (20:21). (Things had gotten so bad that victory wasn't going to come easily.) They wept and asked God if they should attack again. God said, **Fight against them** (20:23). But once more **the Benjaminites came out from Gibeah to meet them and slaughtered an additional eighteen thousand Israelites** (20:25).

20:26-48 Grieved by their losses, Israel decided to get serious about making sure of its repentance before the Lord. This time **the whole Israelite army went to Bethel where they wept and sat before** God. The also **offered burnt offerings and fellowship offerings to the LORD.** With that show of sincerity and humility done, **the Israelites inquired of the LORD** (20:26-27). This time **the LORD defeated Benjamin in the presence of Israel** (20:35).

What changed? In the first two battles they prayed and inquired of God while allowing unaddressed sin to linger in their midst. But before battle number three, they offered a burnt offering to sacrifice for their sins and a fellowship offering to make sure there was harmony between them and the Lord. If you have a request to make of God, make sure you deal with any known sin in your life before expecting him to overrule your circumstances (see Jas 1:19-21).

21:1-14 Disgusted by their brothers' behavior, **the men of Israel had sworn** not to give their daughters to any **Benjaminite in marriage** (21:1). But when they realized how depleted the tribe had become already and that there would be no propagation of the tribe, they **had compassion on their brothers** (21:6). Since the city of **Jabesh-gilead** had not come out to fight against Benjamin, they decided to put the city to death and take **virgins** from the city as wives for the Benjaminites (21:8-14). Thus, in spite of a season of repentance, Israel continued to slide into moral darkness.

21:15-24 Even with the slaughter at Jabesh-gilead there were still Benjaminite men who had no wives. Yet the Israelites had declared, **Anyone who gives a wife to a Benjaminite is cursed** (21:18). So the elders reminded the Benjaminites that there was **an annual festival to the LORD in Shiloh** (21:19). They told them to **hide in the vineyards** and when **the young women of Shiloh** came **to perform the dances**, the Benjaminites were to **leave the vineyards and catch** wives from among them (21:20-21). Apparently, they had reasoned this way: the curse said that no one could *give* them wives, it said nothing about the Benjaminites *catching* wives. Thus, they convinced themselves that they wouldn't be **guilty** (21:22). Fallen human beings are good at justifying their actions and explaining away their guilt.

21:25 In those days there was no king in Israel; everyone did whatever seemed right to him. The book of Judges ends with an indictment against the people of God—who looked nothing like "people of God." They had turned from God to idols, and the Levites had facilitated their departure. There was no spiritual standard in those days, no king to turn the people to God through his example.

Thankfully, this is no longer the case. Though the judges and even the later kings of Israel were always imperfect and often wicked, we now have a Judge and King like no other: Jesus Christ. He alone can turn sinners to the living and true God, making them holy and upright. Will you submit to his kingdom rule over your life?

RUTH

INTRODUCTION

Author

THOUGH ANCIENT JEWISH SOURC-
es attributed the authorship of
Ruth to the prophet Samuel, there
is no mention in the book of the writer's identity. Given the genealogy at the end (4:18-22),
the book was written during or after the reign
of King David, who ruled from 1011–971 BC.

Historical Background

The book is set "during the time of the judges" (Ruth 1:1), which the author of Judges
describes as a sad period in Israel's history
when "there was no king in Israel" and "everyone did whatever seemed right to him"
(Judg 21:25). The period lasted about three
hundred years, from Joshua's death until the
rise of Israel's monarchy. Though we don't
know when the events of the book of Ruth
took place within this frame, "there was a
famine in the land" at the time (Ruth 1:1).

Ruth, the book's namesake, was a Moabitess. The land of Moab was to the west of Judah,
on the far side of the Dead Sea. The people of
Moab were descended from Lot (Abraham's
nephew) and his firstborn daughter (see Gen
19:30-38). Though Ruth was a Gentile descended from these humble circumstances,
she worshiped the God of Israel, married into
God's chosen people, and became the ances-
tress of King David and Jesus Christ.

Message and Purpose

This book is personal, prophetic, and full of
theology. Written during the dark days of the
period of Israel's judges, Ruth centers on a
Gentile woman by that name. Through her experiences, we see the demonstration of God's
providence, grace, love, and redemption.

Ruth was from Moab. Her mother-in-law,
an Israelite named Naomi, was living in Moab
when her husband and two sons (one of them
being Ruth's husband) died. Ruth made a
faith-based decision to go back to Israel
with Naomi because she had adopted the
true God of Israel as her own. In Bethlehem,
Ruth experienced God's providential provision—his invisible hand at work through the
glove of history. She made a connection with
a man named Boaz, who became her "family
redeemer" (2:20). That role was designed to
ensure that a man's lineage continued even if
he had no heirs. The couple's story provides
an illustration of God's love for Gentiles within the framework of his covenant with Israel.

Through Ruth's marriage to Boaz, she became the grandmother of King David, the
ancestor of Jesus Christ. In her story, we see
the lengths to which God went to ensure that
Jesus legally qualified to be Israel's Messiah
and Savior of the world. This is why Ruth's
name appears in Jesus's genealogy (see Matt
1:5). The book of Ruth shows how God can
take messes and make miracles in order to advance his kingdom program, plan, and agenda.

VIDEO   INTRO

www.bhpublishinggroup.com/qr/te/08_00

Outline

I. Disappointment (1:1-22)
II. Service (2:1-23)
III. Hope (3:1-18)
IV. Redemption (4:1-22)

RUTH

I. DISAPPOINTMENT (1:1-22)

1:1-2 The events of this book occurred **during the time of the judges**, a miserable period in Israel's history when a vicious cycle kept repeating itself: the people fell into idolatry, God let their enemies oppress them, they cried out to him for deliverance, he raised up a judge to rescue them, and they fell into idolatry again. As the author of the book of Judges says, "In those days there was no king in Israel; everyone did whatever seemed right to him" (Judg 21:25). Thus, the **famine** that was **in the land** as the book of Ruth opens was likely a result of God judging Israel's idolatry. To get relief from it, a man named **Elimelech**, who was **from Bethlehem in** the tribal territory of **Judah**, took his wife, **Naomi**, and **two sons** and went to stay in the land of **Moab** (1:2).

1:3-5 While they lived in Moab, **Elimelech died**, leaving Naomi a widow (1:3). Her **sons** married **Moabite women** named **Orpah** and **Ruth**, but after only **ten years** in Moab these sons **died**, too (1:4-5). **Naomi was left without her two children and without her husband** (1:5). Thus, things had gone from bad to worse for this descendant of Abraham. In an attempt to escape the peril of famine, Naomi had become a widow and childless. Her circumstances had spiraled down to a point at which she had no way to provide for herself in Moab.

1:6-13 When Naomi heard that the famine back in her native Israel had ended, she determined to return home to **Judah** (1:6-7). She encouraged her daughters-in-law to return to their childhood homes in Moab and prayed

God might **grant** each **a new husband** (1:9). She wanted God to deal kindly with them, a fact that may suggest she felt they had placed themselves under God's covenant covering by marrying Israelite men. In any event, as far as Naomi was concerned, the women would be throwing their lives away to stay with her because she could not provide either with another husband and was more or less destitute herself (1:11-12). As she described it, **The LORD's hand [had] turned against** her (1:13). Yet, it was through her very difficult situation that God was about to work in a big way.

1:14-19 In spite of what Naomi said, Ruth was determined to remain with her. Though Orpah turned back, Ruth said, **Wherever you go, I will go . . . your people will be my people, and your God will be my God** (1:16). She even swore an oath to remain with her mother-in-law for life (1:17). Her commitment was so deep that she preferred widowhood and its challenges to abandoning Naomi and her God—a fact suggesting that she'd probably come to place faith in him at least in part through the woman's witness. In renouncing the idolatry of the Moabites and embracing Israel's God as her own, Ruth had clearly made a complete break with her past. And because **Ruth was determined**, Naomi stopped trying to dissuade her, and the two women returned to **Bethlehem** (1:18-19).

1:20-22 Naomi reentered Israel as a broken and **bitter** woman (1:20; see 1:13). She told the people of her hometown, **the LORD has opposed me, and the Almighty has afflicted**

me (1:21). In other words, in returning to her homeland empty-handed, Naomi felt she had nothing to show for her commitment to her husband or to her God. Nevertheless, she recognized that both good and bad circumstances come through the fingers of the Lord. In his sovereignty, he either causes events or permits them to come to pass. And, while Naomi was truly in despair, it was time for **the barley harvest** (1:22). She could see that God had ended the famine, the very thing that had driven her family off and to their graves. There was hope in the midst of her hopelessness.

II. SERVICE (2:1-23)

2:1-3 Through this story, God was preparing sleepy Bethlehem, hometown to Naomi and the male lead to whom we're introduced here, as the site of his miraculous interruption at a later point in history (see Mic 5:2; Matt 2:1). **Boaz** was a wealthy **relative** of Elimelech (2:1) and, as Matthew 1:5 reveals, the son of Rahab, the same former prostitute who hid Israel's spies and survived the collapse of Jericho because of her faith in God (see Josh 2:1-24; 6:22-25).

Ruth wanted to serve and care for Naomi, so she asked to **go into the fields and gather fallen grain** (2:2). The law of Moses (as if it had been given with Ruth and Naomi in mind) provided for the poor by commanding the Israelites to leave behind some grain at harvest time so that the poor could gather it and have food (see Lev 19:9-10; 23:22; Deut 24:19-21). So, Ruth went **to gather grain behind the harvesters**. Seemingly by chance, though, **she happened to be in the portion of the field belonging to Boaz** (2:3). Of course, nothing happens by chance, and no one just happens to be anywhere. The use of "happened to be" is the author's way of acknowledging the providential working of God in Ruth's life.

2:4-18 When Boaz arrived and learned who the gleaning woman was, he had compassion on her and offered her provision and protection (2:5-9). Ruth couldn't understand why she had **found favor** with him, especially because she was a Moabitess, **a foreigner** to Israel (2:10). Boaz essentially told her that she was simply reaping the blessings of the kind of life she had sown. Her kindness, service to her **mother-in-law**, and decision to take **refuge** under the Lord's provision had brought blessing on her own head (2:11-12). The care Ruth had shown to Naomi would have been especially meaningful to Boaz because Naomi's husband had been his relative.

Because of Ruth's faithful commitment, Boaz pronounced a blessing on her, asking that the Lord—**under whose wings [she had] come for** protection—would provide a spiritual covering for her (2:12). To this, Ruth responded with humble gratitude (2:13). Then, Boaz graciously provided still further help to her—more than the law required—so that she would not have to work as hard to provide for herself and Naomi (2:14-18).

2:19-20 That evening, Naomi was pleased to see how well Ruth had done in her gleaning, but she was shocked when she learned that Boaz was the one to show her such kindness. Immediately, Naomi recognized that this was no chance encounter: the sovereign hand of God had made a connection for them. She informed Ruth that Boaz was **one of [their] family redeemers** (2:20).

As a "family redeemer" (or kinsmen redeemer), Boaz could fulfill the law of levirate marriage (see Deut 25:5-10). This was an ancient provision that meant that if an Israelite man were to die without having a son as an heir to carry on his family name, the man's brother could provide for the deceased by marrying his widow. Then "the first son she [bore would] carry on the name of the dead brother, so his name [would] not be blotted out from Israel" (Deut 25:6).

2:21-23 Given this provision in God's Word and the divine connection that had occurred between Ruth and Boaz, Naomi encouraged Ruth to continue working in Boaz's field (2:22-23). Naomi was right that God had shown kindness to them in their pain and loss. But, he had also stretched his sovereign hand over these circumstances in order to use them for his larger kingdom purposes, something the women would not be able to understand within their lifetimes (4:17-22).

Make no mistake: God can similarly work through your circumstances today to bring about future blessings and even to change the world—whether or not you're able to connect all the dots on this side of eternity.

III. HOPE (3:1-18)

3:1-4 Knowing the hazards Ruth faced in widowhood, Naomi decided to become a matchmaker so that Ruth might have a secure home and future (3:1). She told her to put on her **best** and go to Boaz's **threshing floor** that night. The threshing floor was where the **winnowing** would take place, separating the **barley** from the inedible chaff (3:2-3). During the harvest, Boaz would have spent the night there to prevent theft of his grain. Naomi advised Ruth to **uncover his feet, and lie down** after he **finished eating and drinking** and went to sleep for the night. Once Boaz realized she was there, he would **explain** what she **should do** next (3:3-4).

3:5-9 Ruth agreed to Naomi's instructions and followed them exactly (3:5-6). After a hard day of work and with a full belly, Boaz finally lay down for the night. Then, Ruth approached. With his feet **uncovered**, perhaps feeling the cool of the evening, he woke and **was startled** to find a woman **lying at his feet** (3:7-8). Because it was dark, he asked her to identify herself, and Ruth replied, **I am Ruth, your servant.... Take me under your wing, for you are a family redeemer** (3:9).

Through these words and actions, Ruth was making a marriage proposal. Furthermore, she was requesting that Boaz perform his legal responsibility as a family redeemer (see commentary on 2:19-20). By asking him to take her "under his wing," Ruth was reminding him of the blessing he had pronounced on her previously. Boaz had said to her, "May you receive a full reward from the LORD God of Israel, under whose wings you have come for refuge" (2:12). Ruth was challenging him to become the human expression of that divine covering.

3:10-13 Boaz had been impressed with Ruth initially (2:11-12), but he was even more impressed by her that night. Though Boaz was older and perhaps past his prime, Ruth had **not pursued younger men** (3:10). Clearly, then, this was **a woman of noble character** (3:11), and she had shown honor to Boaz in the highest way she could.

But Boaz was aware of a complication in the circumstances. Even though he was indeed **a family redeemer**, there was another **redeemer** who was **closer** than he (3:12). In other words, this other relative was a nearer relation to Ruth's dead husband, so he qualified to redeem her ahead of Boaz if he chose to do so. But, should the man refuse to raise up an heir for his dead relative, Boaz vowed that he would fulfill the obligation and marry Ruth (3:13). Boaz was a man of honor.

Don't miss the word *redeem* that appears multiple times in verses 12 and 13. Through its use, Boaz is presented as an Old Testament type or picture of Jesus Christ who redeemed or "bought back" sinners from slavery to sin. Through Christ our Redeemer, we are forgiven, set free from sin, made new creations, and have a new relationship with God (see Rom 3:23-24; Gal 3:13-14; 4:4-5; Eph 1:13-14; Col 1:13-14; Heb 9:11-12; Eph 1:13-14). If Boaz were to redeem Ruth, she'd be bought out of slavery to her impoverished circumstances and formally adopted into God's chosen family.

3:14-18 Ruth arose and left **while it was still dark** so that no one would see her and misconstrue the night's events, bringing harm to their reputations (3:14). But, before she left, Boaz gave her a generous provision of **barley** (3:15). Ruth returned home with the food and the news, and Naomi felt confident that Boaz would come through on the matter (3:16-18).

IV. REDEMPTION (4:1-22)

4:1-2 Boaz went to the gate of the town, where business and civic activities were conducted. **Soon the family redeemer Boaz has spoken about came by** (4:1). Thus, the stage was set for the climax of the story. Boaz invited the man to **sit down** with him and asked **ten** of **the town's elders** to join them. These men would serve as witnesses of the legal proceedings that were about to transpire.

4:3-5 Boaz informed the nameless man that the widow **Naomi**, who had recently **returned** from **Moab**, needed money and would be selling a **portion of the field that belonged to (their close relative) Elimelech** (4:3). Thus, because he was the closest relation, the man had first rights to buy the land. **If you want to redeem it, do it**, Boaz pressed. Otherwise, Boaz himself intended to do so, because he was **next** in line (4:4).

When the man jumped at the chance to acquire some new land (4:4), Boaz dropped the other—less appealing—piece of information. If the man redeemed the land, he would also be redeeming the widow Ruth for a wife **to perpetuate the man's name on his property** (4:5). That meant that with the economic acquisition came a social acquisition.

4:6-9 The man's eagerness began to fade once he realized he'd have to take someone else's bride along with the property. Gaining land was one thing; gaining a wife was another. By seeking to preserve his relative's name, he would jeopardize his **own inheritance**. So, he refused his right **of redemption** (4:6).

At that time in Israel, you couldn't sign some legal documents and have them notarized. So, a **legally binding** transaction of this nature was ratified by the custom of a man giving **his sandal** to another party with whom he was doing business (4:7). In front of ten **witnesses**, the man gave Boaz his **sandal**, symbolically granting Boaz the legal right to redeem the **property** and **Ruth** (4:8-9).

4:10 Whereas the man was concerned about ruining his own inheritance (4:6), Boaz's motives were more selfless. He acquired Ruth

and the property out of concern for others— **to perpetuate the deceased man's name on his property, so that his name [would] not disappear among his relatives or from the gate of his hometown**. This sacrifice brings to mind this New Testament principle: "Whoever wants to save his life will lose it, but whoever loses his life because of me will find it" (Matt 16:25). Often, blessings follow when we lay down our priorities for the sake of God's kingdom; selfishness tends to turn off the blessing faucet.

4:11-12 The **elders** served as **witnesses** of the proceedings and pronounced blessings on Boaz and his wife-to-be. They prayed that God would bless Ruth as he had blessed **Rachel and Leah**, who gave birth to many of the fathers of the tribes of Israel (4:11). They also prayed that Boaz's **name** and **house** would become famous in Israel **because of the offspring the LORD [would] give [him] by this young woman** (4:11-12; see also 4:14). Little did they know how famous Boaz would become or how great his offspring would be (see Matt 1:5-17)!

4:13-15 Boaz and Ruth married, and God gave them **a son** whom they named Obed (4:13, 17). The women of the town rejoiced with Naomi and blessed the Lord for how he had provided for this poor woman who had endured great bitterness such a short time ago (4:14-15). In fact, they told Naomi that Ruth was **better** to her **than seven sons** (4:15). Because *seven* was the biblical number of perfection or completion, seven sons would have been a supreme blessing. Yet, by God's grace, Ruth had proved herself to be an even better gift. That's high praise for this noble woman.

For her faithfulness, God had blessed Ruth with a child—even as he would bless Mary many years later with the Son of God (see Luke 1:26-33).

4:16-22 The final verses of the book reveal a genealogy, beginning with Judah's son **Perez** and ending with **David** (4:18-22). It tells us that Ruth and Boaz's son Obed would be grandfather to David, the great king of Israel. The ancient Israelites to whom the author was writing knew of this amazing heritage.

But, what they didn't know was that there was an even greater descendant to come from this bloodline. The kingly line of David would ultimately lead to the Messiah, Jesus Christ (see Matt 1:1-16), who would be born in his ancestral home: Bethlehem. Though Boaz and Ruth were unaware of it, their lives and decisions were part of God's kingdom program. By submitting yourself to the Lord's agenda, you open yourself to his sovereign purposes—not only for your own benefit but potentially for the benefit of generations after you.

1 SAMUEL

INTRODUCTION

Author

THE BOOKS OF 1 AND 2 SAMUEL are named for the prophet who first appears in 1 Samuel and who anointed both Saul and David as king. Ancient Jewish tradition, in fact, attributes at least some of the material to Samuel. Because his death is reported in 1 Samuel 25, it's possible he was responsible for chapters 1–24. Additional Jewish tradition claims that the prophet Gad (who appears in 1 Samuel 22) and Nathan (who appears in 2 Samuel 7, 12) compiled the rest of the books (see 1 Chr 29:29). But, ultimately, the text of 1–2 Samuel does not name any author.

Historical Background

First Samuel follows on the heels of the book of Judges, which chronicles the time period after Joshua's death and before Israel's monarchy. During the time of the judges, the Israelites fell into repeated cycles of disobedience to the Lord, oppression by enemies, and deliverance by God-appointed judges. First Samuel opens in the eleventh century at the end of this period. The initial chapters describe the calling of Samuel to his ministry and the transition to a monarchy beginning with Saul. The final event in 2 Samuel (the building of David's altar at the threshing floor of Araunah) occurred in about 975 BC.

Message and Purpose

The books of 1 and 2 Samuel highlight the life and influences of the prophet Samuel—especially in the early chapters of 1 Samuel, which record his miraculous birth and prophetic calling. Through Samuel's prophetic office, God allowed and established a king in Israel. Though God wanted to be his people's King, they wanted to have a human king like those over other nations. So, he gave them Saul and then later David, the two monarchs who are the main focus of 1–2 Samuel.

These books not only show Samuel's influence over Israel in bringing God's Word to his people, but they also teach some powerful spiritual lessons. We see the consequences of disobedience as Saul's failure to obey God cost him his kingdom rule. But, we also see the emergence of David as the "man after [God's] own heart" (1 Sam 13:14).

In 2 Samuel, David is anointed as king, and God makes a covenant with him to establish his royal line forever—a line through which the Messiah would come. Thus, David is a key figure in God's kingdom agenda—not only for Israel but for the whole world. Second Samuel is about spiritual priorities and obedience, but it is also about grace. When David sinned greatly, God did not take his life. He showed him mercy.

Both books teach us to walk under God's kingdom rule so that we can experience the full benefit of his kingdom blessing as kingdom people.

VIDEO   INTRO

www.bhpublishinggroup.com/qr/te/09_00

Outline

1 SAMUEL

I. SAMUEL AND THE TRANSITION TO THE MONARCHY (1:1–8:22)

A. Samuel's Birth and Early Life
(1:1–3:21)

1:1-5 The first person we meet in this story is **Elkanah**, Samuel's father, who was a descendant of the priestly tribe of Levi (see 1 Chr 6:33-34), even though he is identified here as an **Ephraimite**—which referred to the territory in which he lived rather than his lineage. Samuel would serve as a priest and as Israel's last judge. Elkanah was a godly man, as attested by his faithfulness to go **every year to worship and to sacrifice to the LORD** at the tabernacle in **Shiloh**, north of Jerusalem, where the ark of the covenant was kept (1:3).

But Elkanah had two wives, which was a violation of God's original design for marriage (see Gen 2:18, 21-24). His first wife, **Hannah, was childless**, but deeply **loved** (1:2, 5). **Peninnah**, who was likely younger given cultural practices of the day and her behavior throughout the story, was fruitful (1:2). This became a source of great tension in the household (see 1:6-7). A second wife was sometimes taken in the case of a childless first marriage, but bigamy or polygamy was never God's perfect plan.

In verse 3, the writer also included a brief historical note that would soon become very important for Samuel's service and the nation's future. Israel would soon come out of the tragic and sordid period of the judges, and God was preparing the nation for a new kind of leadership. At the tabernacle in Shiloh, the elderly Eli had turned

over the priestly duties to his sons, **Hophni and Phinehas** (1:3), who would prove to be unworthy. Their gross sins, followed by no real rebuke or discipline from Eli, would lead to severe judgment on Israel. Though Samuel would step in to fill the void, the people would soon cry out for a king and, in response, God would establish the monarchy.

For many years, Hannah had been childless because God had **kept [her] from conceiving** (1:5). Likely Samuel's coming, then, was welcomed as a miracle.

1:6-8 Because the commonly held view of childlessness in ancient Israel was that it was a curse from God, Hannah had to bear the bitter taunting of Peninnah (1:6-7). The related agony didn't last for a few months, but instead went on **year after year**, in spite of Elkanah's attempts to comfort his favorite wife (1:7-8).

1:9-18 Finally, Hannah couldn't take the heartache any longer and went to the tabernacle to pray. **Deeply hurt**, she poured out her heart to God with great anguish. She vowed that if God would **give** her **a son**, she would dedicate him back to God all of **his life** (1:10-11). By promising that **his hair [would] never be cut** (1:11), Hannah was offering to raise him in accordance with the Nazirite vow, which included abstinence from alcohol and untrimmed hair as signs of a person's dedication to God (see Num 6:1-21).

While observing Hannah's intense prayer, **Eli** mistakenly assumed she was **drunk** (1:12-14). But, when Hannah explained her situation,

Eli comforted her with a blessing, and Hannah received it with gratitude (1:15-18).

1:19-20 The phrase, **the LORD remembered** Hannah, is important (1:19). Why? Because the Lord "had kept" her from conceiving (1:6). The inclusion of these parallel truths signals to us that if God causes a problem, only God can fix it. Note the prayer was answered when there was a kingdom purpose for ministry connected to it.

The **birth** of **Samuel** gave Hannah reason to put away her grief (1:20), and his arrival also heralded a gift of incalculable value to Israel. Samuel would be the last of the judges as well as a prophet and priest. He would serve as the great transitional figure from the lawless days of the judges to the relative structure and orderliness associated with Israel's monarchy. The latter period would last from the coronation of Saul in about 1050 BC to the Babylonian captivity in 587–586 BC.

1:21-28 For three years, Hannah nurtured her baby, but never lost sight of her vow to take Samuel back to the tabernacle **to stay there permanently** and serve the Lord (1:22). When he no longer needed nourishment from her, she knew the time had come for her to take little Samuel to Eli. Once there, Hannah reminded Eli of her story and promise and entrusted Samuel to the elderly priest's charge (1:24-28).

2:1-10 Hannah responded to the fulfillment of her vow with a tremendous song of praise to God. The themes of Hannah's song were the holiness, sovereignty, and power of God, displayed among his people and in her own life. The lyrics exalt the Lord for all of God's actions on behalf of his people: He is **holy**, a **rock**, and full **of knowledge** (2:2-3). He **brings death and gives life** (2:6). He **brings poverty and gives wealth** (2:7). **He guards the steps of his faithful ones** (2:9). Those who align themselves with him, then, are on the winning side.

2:11 Elkanah and Hannah went back home, but Samuel stayed at Shiloh and **served the LORD**.

2:12-17 Although Samuel could not have known it at his tender age, he had come to the Lord's service at a difficult time. The situation at Shiloh was terrible and would soon become disastrous. This summary statement sets the scene: **Eli's sons were wicked men; they did not respect the LORD or the priests' share of the sacrifices from the people** (2:12-13). The sacrifices made were holy to the Lord, yet Hophni and Phinehas—descendants of Aaron—stole the choicest parts of the meat for themselves and threatened violence on any worshiper who objected (2:13-16). In this way, they showed **contempt** for God's **offering** (2:17).

2:18-24 By contrast, **Samuel served** the Lord faithfully in the middle of this mess. As a result, God blessed not only him but also his parents (2:18-21). The contrast between a **mere boy** serving the Lord well (2:18) and two grown men functioning as wicked priests couldn't be greater. And, as if their foul actions in the tabernacle weren't bad enough, Hophni and Phinehas also added to their list of sins adultery **with the women who served** at the tabernacle (2:22). Eli, however, did nothing to stop his boys except to scold them. **No, my sons, the news I hear the LORD's people spreading is not good**, he said (2:24). In other words, Eli said, "Now, you boys, stop that," as if one half-hearted rebuke would set them on the right track. But, he never appears to have made an attempt to restrain them or remove them from service.

2:25-26 God's patience eventually wore thin with Hophni and Phinehas. Because they refused to repent, **the LORD intended to kill them** for their iniquity (2:25). Samuel, on the other hand, **grew in stature and in favor with the LORD and with people** (2:26).

2:27-36 God sealed the fate of Eli and his family through the prophecy of a **man of God** who delivered the message (2:27). The judgment was severe because Eli's failure to discipline his sons revealed that, at heart, he despised God's **sacrifices and offerings**, too (2:29). By his actions, Eli had **honored** his **sons more than** God (2:29). Thus, Eli's family would lose its priestly privileges, which were transferred to the family of Zadok later in Israel's history (see 1 Kgs 2:26-27, 35). Eli's **descendants** would **die violently**; his **sons**

would even **die on the same day** (2:33-34). The **faithful priest** whom God promised to **raise up** could have been Zadok himself. He would serve God's king—first David and then Solomon (2:35).

3:1 Samuel may have been in his teens by the time his call from the Lord took place. The word translated **boy** means a young man. It's the same word translated "youth" to describe David when he killed Goliath (see 1 Sam 17:33).

It's important not to skim over the acknowledgement that God didn't reveal himself much in those days, **and prophetic visions were not widespread**. With Eli and his worthless sons in charge of Israel's house of worship and ministry, that's not surprising.

3:2-9 When God was ready to speak, he called Samuel's name one evening. The young man thought it was Eli repeatedly calling him (3:2-6). Finally, Eli realized what was happening and told Samuel how to respond if the call came again (3:8-9). Samuel's lack of understanding of what was happening boiled down to the fact that he did **not yet know the Lord, because the word of the Lord had not yet been revealed to him** (3:7). In God's sovereign plan, however, that was all about to change.

3:10-14 God called again, and this time Samuel responded (3:10). He was given his first charge to deliver a message as God's prophet. The message was one of judgment on Eli and his family for his sons' sins and for Eli's failure to stop them (3:11-14).

3:15-21 It's understandable that Samuel **was afraid to tell Eli the vision** (3:15). But, Eli insisted that he do so anyway. And, when he heard this terrible prophecy, there was nothing Eli could do but resign himself to God's will (3:17-18). Samuel's life and ministry, however, were just getting started. He continued to grow in spiritual power as God **fulfilled everything Samuel prophesied** (3:19). Samuel's authority became known throughout **Israel** as he ministered faithfully at **Shiloh** and God **revealed** himself to Samuel there (3:20-21).

❧ B. The Capture and Restoration of the Ark (4:1–7:17) ❧

4:1-3 The judgment prophesied for Eli and his family didn't stop at their front door. Because Eli was a leader in Israel, the nation suffered along with him. This is a spiritual principle that we see repeatedly in the Old Testament. Moreover, the entire story of 1 Samuel 1–7 also illustrates the kingdom principle that when one aspect of God's kingdom structure fails to meet his standards, his kingdom work suffers. Everything is related. Eli's drastic failure of kingdom responsibility in the family had consequences in the larger spiritual sphere. Because Eli was Israel's spiritual leader as well as the leader of his family, those consequences were disastrous.

When the time came for God to carry out his judgment on the house of Eli, he did it through a familiar avenue in those days: war with the Philistines. These powerful people lived on the eastern shore of the Mediterranean Sea and had been adversaries of Israel since the days of the judges. In fact, they would still be giving Israel a hard time years later, leading a young shepherd to face a giant Philistine with a sling and some rocks (see 1 Sam 17). In the days of Eli, God would use the Philistines as his tool of judgment against Israel.

A day came when **Israel went out to meet the Philistines in battle** (4:1). The Israelites were beaten badly (4:2), and clearly they hadn't been expecting this defeat from the hands of the Lord (4:3). (It's unlikely that Eli had advertised the prophecy against his family.) From the reaction of **the elders of Israel**, it seems that the lame spiritual leadership of Eli and his sons had penetrated the attitudes of the people. Instead of seeking God for the reason Israel had been routed, they simply decided to **bring the ark of the Lord's covenant from Shiloh** (4:3). In other words, they were treating it like a good luck charm that would protect them and guarantee a victory. They mistook the symbol of God's presence and blessing for his true presence and blessing.

4:4-5 Bringing the ark from Shiloh meant that none other than **Hophni and Phinehas** would be carrying it to the battle site (4:4). As they set out with the ark in tow, these wicked priests probably thought they were going as heroes to bring Israel a victory; instead, they were actually going to their own funerals. The Israelites, however, were so encouraged to see the symbol of the Lord's covenant and glory arrive in their midst that their **loud shout** made the earth shake (4:5).

4:6-11 The Philistines knew the history of their enemy, being aware of the **plagues** related to the Israelites' exodus from Egypt. When they **discovered** that **the ark**, God's throne, **had entered the camp**, they assumed they were in serious trouble: Israel's God had come to fight for them (4:6-8). Yet, instead of running away in panic, the Philistine army rallied and inflicted a **slaughter** on the Israelites that included Eli's sons (4:10-11). Worse yet, the Philistines **captured** the ark (4:11). Understand that this wasn't merely a demoralizing military defeat for Israel; this was the judgment of God at work.

4:12-22 Back in Shiloh, Eli was looking down the road toward the battle site, **because he was anxious about the ark of God** (4:13). He perhaps realized that the prophecy against his family was being fulfilled. But, when he'd witnessed the ark being transported from the tabernacle, Eli must have also recognized that God's judgment was going to reach beyond his own house to the entire house of Israel.

The news that **the ark of God [had] been captured** caused Eli to fall **off the chair**, break his **neck**, and die (4:17-18). But even then, God wasn't finished. **The wife** of Eli's son **Phinehas** also died giving birth to a son. With her last breaths, she **named** him **Ichabod** because **the glory [had] departed from Israel** (4:19-22). This means that the glory of God left the tabernacle with the ark because the Israelites had misused it and defamed God's glory.

5:1 The Philistines left the battle with their prize, **the ark of God**, and brought it to **Ashdod**, one of the five cities in their confederation (the others were Ashkelon, Gaza, Gath, and Ekron; see 1 Sam 6:16-17). To crush an enemy, strip him of his god, and bring it back home to display as a trophy was the ultimate symbol of victory for an ancient army. It also was a statement that the winner's god was stronger than the loser's god. But, the Philistines may also have had another strong motive for taking the ark back to their land. Because they knew the stories of how the ark had brought Israel such great and miraculous victories when they battled in the promised land, the Philistines may have believed that, by possessing the ark, they would inherit its related power.

The irony in this story is that Israel often operated by faulty theological thinking, too. Many Israelites, for instance, believed that their spiritual condition didn't matter simply because they were God's people. This is what led John the Baptist to later tell the Pharisees and Sadducees not to presume that their Jewish heritage would save them because "God is able to raise up children for Abraham from . . . stones" (Matt 3:9). God cannot be obligated, and he expects obedience from his children. To put this in modern terms, merely showing up to church on Sunday morning won't save you or give you God's blessings. You need to repent and place saving faith in Jesus.

5:2-5 Merely possessing the ark didn't do the Philistines any good. They placed it in the **temple** of their god **Dagon** to demonstrate his power over the Lord and to give Dagon's worshipers incentive to gloat over their victory (5:2). But nobody mocks God and gets away with it. By **early the next morning**, the Lord had humiliated Dagon in his own house. The Philistines' idol had **fallen . . . before the ark** as if in both humiliation and worship (5:3). Though they put Dagon back on his feet, the same thing happened the next morning. This time, **Dagon's head and both of his hands were broken off** (5:4). In that time period, severing the head and hands of an enemy was often done in battle, meaning these were trophies of victory. The message was clear: Dagon was nothing before the Lord.

5:6-8 The people of Ashdod were **terrified** of the Lord in the coming days—not only because he had defeated their god but because he afflicted them **with tumors** (5:6). This could be a reference to anything from boils to something like the bubonic plague. Once the leaders of Ashdod had had enough, **they called** a city council meeting (5:8). What was the outcome? They decided it was time to share the ark with their Philistine brothers in **Gath** (5:8).

5:9-12 Gath was situated about twelve miles from Ashdod, so it's hard to believe the people there had not heard about Ashdod's troubles because of the ark. Nevertheless, they received it, and the same problems experienced by their countrymen started immediately among them. Everybody in Gath was **afflicted** with **tumors** (5:9).

Gath thus decided to send the ark to the city of **Ekron**. But the people of Ekron said, "No way!" (5:10). The ark of God had become a deadly hot potato that none of the Philistines wanted to handle. Everyone realized that keeping it could mean nothing but more bad news for them—perhaps even death (5:12). They decided that if they didn't do something drastic, no one would survive. The people of Ekron **called all the Philistine rulers** and demanded that they **send the ark of Israel's God away ... to its place** (5:11).

6:1-3 All of this punishment at the hands of the Lord happened over the course of **seven months** (6:1). **The Philistines summoned the priests and the diviners** to figure out an appropriate way to send the ark **back to** Israel (6:2). These pagan leaders had seen ample evidence that the God of Israel was a powerful deity who needed to be appeased. So, they proposed returning the ark with a **guilt offering** to remove **his hand** of affliction from the people (6:3).

6:4-6 The mention of rodents in this passage suggests God had sent mice to cause the tumors that had afflicted the Philistines, because the guilt offering was to include **five gold tumors and five gold mice** (6:4). The key statement here is that the Philistines were to **give glory to Israel's God** so that he might stop **oppressing [them]** (6:5). This is a reminder that God *will* ultimately receive glory even from his enemies. Importantly, the Philistine religious leaders also had

enough sense not to repeat the mistake of **the Egyptians and Pharaoh** who had decided to **harden** their **hearts** against **Israel**, resulting in their defeat (6:6).

6:7-9 In spite of the decent decisions they made regarding the ark, the Philistines were still pagans who wondered if they had just hit a run of bad luck unrelated to their prize. So, they devised a test for returning it that they believed would prove whether these events were from the hand of **the LORD** or had simply happened **by chance** (6:9). They took **two milk cows** away from their nursing **calves** and hitched them up to a **new cart** (6:7). They placed the ark on the cart with the **guilt offering** inside another box alongside it and sent both off **toward Beth-shemesh** on the border of Israel (6:8-9).

6:10-12 The idea behind the Philistines' plan was that the cows' maternal instincts, and their unfamiliarity with a yoke, would naturally cause them to want to throw off their restraints and turn back toward their bawling babies. So, if they didn't fight the yoke and turn back, but went straight, the Philistines would know that the God of Israel had caused their troubles. Sure enough, as **the Philistine rulers** followed the cart all the way to the border of Israel, **the cows ... never strayed to the right or to the left** (6:12). Thus, the Lord again proved himself to be the true God.

6:13-18 As much as the people of the Philistine cities had come to dread the ark, the Israelites in **Beth-shemesh** rejoiced at its arrival—at first (6:13). Because the cart carrying the ark stopped at a perfect place to serve as an altar, the people did the right thing in using the cart and the **cows as a burnt offering to the LORD** (6:14). They also did the right thing in calling for **the Levites** to handle the ark's removal from the cart. That was a crucial step, in fact, because only the priestly leaders were consecrated to deal with the Lord's holy things. They offered the Lord **sacrifices** (6:15).

6:19-21 Joy was short-lived when **seventy** people of Beth-shemesh **looked inside the ark** and were struck dead (6:19). Keep in mind that, under normal circumstances, the ark was to be kept in the tabernacle, screened off from view (see Exod 40:21). And, as a result of what happened, the people—like the Philistines—became afraid and asked the residents of **Kiriath-jearim** to take charge of the ark (6:21). This tells us that God's people were, in one sense, as spiritually insensitive as the Philistines.

7:1-3 The ark stayed in **Kiriath-jearim** for **twenty years**. In those days, God stirred **the whole house of Israel** to long for him (7:1-2). Samuel knew where the people's repentance had to begin if it were to be truly sincere. The Israelites had become worshipers of false gods whose presence had polluted the land. Baal was the chief deity of the Canaanites, the god of the sky who controlled everything. Ashtoreth was the female fertility deity whose worship involved debauchery. Israel, in worshiping the two, had fallen far from God. So, Samuel commanded the people to **get rid of the foreign gods** and **dedicate** themselves **to the Lord, and worship only him** (7:3).

7:4-6 The people obeyed Samuel and **only worshiped the Lord** (7:4). And, in his first publicly recorded ministry appearance, Samuel led the nation in a service of repentance at **Mizpah**, about seven miles north of Jerusalem. There, the Israelites **fasted** and **confessed** their sins (7:6). God was going to use this demonstration of national repentance and unity to give Israel a resounding victory over their enemies, a fact implying that he accepted their repentance as genuine.

7:7 Apparently the Philistines considered this Israelite gathering a threat to their security. So, they **marched up toward Israel**. The Israelites were immediately struck with fear over this and decided to ask Samuel to intercede with the Lord for them. Israel had not been successful against the Philistines in the past (4:2, 10), so they didn't have high hopes of escaping another whipping.

7:8-14 Israel urged Samuel, the Lord's prophet, to intercede for them and ask the Lord to **save** them (7:8). So, Samuel made an **offering**

and prayed **to the Lord on behalf of Israel, and the Lord answered him** (7:9). God took matters into his own hands.

The offering was still on the fire when the Philistines attacked, but God's thunder sent them **into such confusion** that Israel was able to defeat them (7:10). That day, God became Israel's **Ebenezer**, their "stone of help" (7:12). The Philistines were pushed completely out of **Israel's territory**, and Israel even regained some **cities** and **territories** the Philistines had held (7:13-14).

7:15-17 The closing verses of the chapter summarize Samuel's ministry as Israel's judge, prophet, and religious head. His yearly **circuit** included three cities that had been gathering places for Israel in the hill country of Judah (7:16).

❧ C. Israel's Demand for a King
(8:1-22) ❦

8:1-5 This chapter records a pivotal moment in Israel's history—the establishment of the monarchy, which would be in place from the coronation of Saul in 1051 BC to the destruction of Jerusalem by Nebuchadnezzar and the deportation of Judah's King Zedekiah to Babylon in 587–586 BC. But Samuel's readers needed to know about the rise of Israel's monarchy for its theological as well as its historical reasons, because it profoundly affected the nation's relationship with its sovereign King and Lord.

Israel's demand for a king grew out of frustration over the corruption of Samuel's sons, whom **he appointed . . . as judges over Israel** (8:1). Unfortunately, like Eli's sons had been in the office of priesthood, Samuel's sons were **dishonest** in their office. They **took bribes** and **perverted justice** (8:3). The obvious way to correct the problem would have been to remove these two men from their positions and reform the system. But instead, **all the elders of Israel** took matters into their own hands and asked Samuel to **appoint a king to judge** the nation (8:4-5). They had observed that **all the other nations** had kings, and they had probably wanted one for some time (8:5).

This was a case of family breakdown leading to an appeal for the government to come to society's rescue when the family should have led the way. In this sense, the situation in 1 Samuel 8 is not that different from what we see happening in our own culture today. Many of the problems that government tries to fix are present because the family unit has broken down. Thus, people often want the government to manage affairs that should be in the hands of families. But, when civil government reaches into the other spheres that God has instituted—things like the family or the church—government grows far beyond its divinely authorized scope. This allows government to both confiscate and redistribute what should not be moved. That is exactly what God warned Israel against in 8:10-18 as they insisted on having a human king.

8:6-7 As soon as he heard what the elders wanted, **Samuel considered their demand wrong** (8:6). He did the right thing in taking his distress to the Lord, who confirmed Samuel's deep concern. But, God insisted that the request was not a rejection of Samuel but a rejection of God himself **as their king** (8:7). Israel already had a king—the King of kings in fact—who was also the Lord of all the earth and worthy of worship above all other gods. Israel's rejection of God was nothing new, but still unbelievable. They preferred to be led by a fallible human.

8:8-18 Samuel must have been speechless at God's response, knowing that Israel was standing on thin ground with this sinful request. Nevertheless, God told Samuel to anoint a king, provided that he explain to the nation the **rights of the king who [would] reign over them** (8:9). Samuel did all that the Lord commanded him and communicated everything **to the people** (8:10-18).

Importantly, it wasn't the request for a king per se that was wrong. A king was in God's sovereign plan for his people (see Deut 17:14-15). The issue, then, was more that they merely wanted a human ruler. Rather than being set apart as God's own, they wanted to be like all of the other nations. But, this was not the time of God's perfect choosing, nor were these the right circumstances for the next season of Israel's development. Yet, his people were impatient and unwilling to wait for the Lord's will. The irony is huge.

8:19-22 Sadly, Israel's people **refused to listen to Samuel**, meaning they refused to listen to the Lord (8:19). In the end, the people got their obstinate way, as God granted their desire (8:22). The people's thoughts were focused on the idea that a king would be preferable to being judged by Samuel's crooked sons. And besides, the right king could be the military leader and hero everybody wanted to lead the nation into battle. So, in spite of warnings about the heavy personal and taxation burdens their kings would inflict on them, the people went home in anticipation.

II. THE RISE AND FALL OF KING SAUL (9:1–15:35)

➤ A. Saul's Anointing and Early Successes (9:1–12:25) ✧

9:1-2 God set about the work of controlling the choice of king and the circumstances of his anointing. **Kish** was **a prominent man of** Benjamin's tribe (9:1). Thus, he was a man of leadership and valor. So, **Saul** came from good stock. He was also **impressive** and **a head taller than anyone else** (9:2). These are the kinds of qualities that would inspire confidence in the people. But, as things would

turn out, they were all that Saul had going for him. God was no doubt giving them the kind of king they wanted—someone who looked the part. But later, after the people saw the disaster that was King Saul, God would choose a king for them whose heart was right for the job (16:7).

9:3-6 God providentially arranged the first meeting between Saul and Samuel. The circumstances were fairly mundane. Some of Kish's **donkeys** were lost, so he sent **his son Saul** and some of **the servants** to find them

(9:3). That proved to be a long and futile effort that eventually took the search party to **Zuph** in the hill country of Ephraim near Samuel's hometown of Ramah (9:4-5). Saul wanted to give up the search and go home (9:5). But, one of the servants realized that the Lord's prophet might be able to tell them where to find the lost animals (9:6).

9:7-10 Apparently, it was customary to bring a **gift** when seeking a prophet's advice, and the servant just happened to have a **little silver** on him (9:7-8). So, the search party switched gears to find the prophet, or **seer**, as he was called (9:9-10).

9:11-17 Drama is added to the narrative as Saul and his men learned that Samuel was about to leave for a sacrifice at **the high place** outside of town (9:11-12). In God's sovereign timing, Samuel and Saul met on the road (9:14). Samuel knew immediately that this tall stranger was the future king of Israel because the Lord had revealed to him **the day before** how their meeting would take place (9:15-17). God's specific assignment for Saul was to **save** his people **from the Philistines** who were oppressing them (9:16).

Saul would have early success against the Philistines (14:47), but he would cower in fear with the rest of his army when Goliath defied Israel (17:11). And, in the end, after God had rejected Saul and his life fell apart, he died ingloriously at the hands of the Philistines and brought his family and nation down with him (31:1-10).

9:18-27 Though Saul was still looking for his father's donkeys, Samuel had the kingship of Israel on his mind. His cryptic statement that Saul was the one whom **all Israel** desired caught Saul completely off guard (9:20). He responded that his family's status hardly qualified him for such an honor (9:21). Nevertheless, Samuel made Saul the guest of honor at the banquet held in connection with the worship at the high place. Seating Saul **at the head of the thirty or so men** in attendance probably was a way of getting Saul's name and face out there; it signaled he was a person to notice (9:22). After the meal, Samuel took Saul back to his home in Ramah (9:23-27).

10:1-9 The prophet privately **anointed** Saul as the **ruler over** Israel (10:1). And, to confirm for Saul that he was God's choice, Samuel predicted three signs that Saul would see fulfilled that same day (10:2-8). **When Saul turned around to leave . . ., God changed his heart, and all the signs came about that day** (10:9). The expression "God changed his heart" could refer to the Holy Spirit coming upon Saul in power to accomplish his kingship, just as the Spirit came upon other leaders in the Old Testament for specific purposes.

10:10-16 One evidence of God's power on Saul was his ability to prophesy with **a group of prophets** he encountered, surprising all those who knew him (10:10-11). Their questions were an expression of amazement that Saul, of all people, was now exercising the prophetic gift (10:11-12). When Saul got home, his uncle questioned him about where he had been and what Samuel had said, but Saul said nothing about the **kingship**, a curious omission (10:14-16).

10:17-19 When the time came for Saul's public presentation and anointing as king, **Samuel** called all of Israel together **at Mizpah** (10:17), the place where God had brought about such a great and supernatural victory over the Philistines (see 1 Sam 7:2-13). Samuel began the proceedings in a solemn way, reminding the people of the evil nature of their request for a king. Such a demand was actually a rejection of the Lord who had saved them from their enemies (10:18-19). Nevertheless, God was gracious and did not bring retribution on them for their sin. Instead, as time would reveal, because the people were not wholly devoted to him, God was giving them a king who would be not wholly devoted to him, either.

10:20-24 To make sure there could be no doubt about God's choice, Samuel brought all the **tribes** and **clans** forward. Samuel worked his way down to smaller and smaller groups—probably by casting lots (see Josh 7:16-18)—until **Saul son of Kish was selected** (10:20-21). But Saul, as it turned out, was hiding (10:22)—apparently overcome with either modesty or fear of the glare of the cameras! When he was finally brought before the people, they saw that **he stood a head taller than anyone else** (10:23). He was just the kind of physically impressive king they wanted (10:24).

10:25-27 Samuel **proclaimed to the people the rights of kingship** and then **wrote them on a scroll** before sending everyone **home** (10:25). Saul had made a great first impression, but he would not ultimately measure up to God's standards for a king. And, even before things began to unravel, Samuel suspected that the man he'd presented to Israel was not God's best for his people.

11:1-3 Saul soon met the first test of his reign. **Nahash the Ammonite** and his army **laid siege to Jabesh-gilead**, located about twenty-five miles south of the Sea of Galilee (11:1). The townspeople were so ill-prepared to defend themselves that they agreed to Nahash's humiliating and crippling **treaty** term to **gouge out everyone's right eye** (11:1-2). Nahash was so confident that no one would come to rescue them that he agreed to give them a week to send out an SOS and await response (11:3).

11:4-6 Help would come in the person of Saul. Israel's new king was out plowing, apparently having returned to his former life for the time being. But, when news of the siege at Jabesh-gilead reached his **hometown** of **Gibeah**, the people **wept aloud** (11:4). Saul found out what had happened and was suddenly empowered by **the Spirit of God** and his fierce **anger** (11:6).

11:7-11 Saul took extreme measures to rally Israel's troops to march out against the Ammonites, and a large army responded in the face of Saul's threat (11:7). He led the troops to the Ammonite camp and, using good military strategy, split them **into three divisions**. The defeat of the Ammonites was so complete that the few survivors were completely scattered—**no two of them were left together** (11:11).

A great victory over an enemy that had been menacing Israel solidified Saul's position as king in the eyes of the people (see 8:20). And, according to Samuel's speech in

chapter 12 (see 12:12), that he'd dealt with Nahash, in particular, made Saul's victory even more impressive.

11:12-13 The people were so taken with Saul that they wanted to execute his naysayers (11:12), maybe the same wicked men who had snubbed him at his coronation (see 10:27). But, Saul showed them grace, acknowledging that **the LORD** had **provided deliverance** (11:13). Unfortunately, this was the spiritual high point of Saul's reign. Things would roll downhill.

11:14-15 Saul's victory led the nation to convene at Gilgal (11:14-15), a historic site where the Israelites had first camped after entering the promised land during the conquest under Joshua (see Josh 5:10-12). The purpose of the meeting was two-fold: to confirm Saul as Israel's king and to confirm the people's commitment to him as such. Saul was confirmed **in the LORD's presence**, and Israel **rejoiced greatly** (11:15).

The report here might make it seem that Samuel's earlier distress at the people's sinful demands had been laid to rest, as if all was now well in Israel. But, God's decision to bless Saul as the leader of his people was an act of grace that did not cancel out Israel's sin in seeking a king apart from God's will and timing. Samuel would remind the people of this in his final address to the nation, yet he would also call them to obey and follow the Lord faithfully to enjoy his blessing under their chosen king. Unfortunately, Saul would prove unworthy of his high calling.

12:1-5 Following Saul's victory and the people's obvious enthusiasm for him, Samuel decided it was time for him to step aside and officially hand the reins of political leadership over to Saul. The Israelites were looking to Saul anyway, and Samuel was elderly by this time. Nevertheless, he had a crucial message to share before stepping out of the limelight—although he would continue to play a spiritual leadership role. What he said probably wasn't something the Israelites would want to hear. They were, no doubt, feeling good and had perhaps forgotten about the circumstances of Saul's choice and Samuel's warning. It wasn't the first time the Israelites had suffered from spiritual amnesia, nor would it be the last.

Samuel began his speech by reestablishing the credibility of his long ministry as Israel's judge—an office in which honesty and integrity were essential. In closing the books on this part of his ministry, he wanted the record to show that his judgeship had been honest not only in the people's eyes, but also **before the LORD** (12:3). Samuel put himself in the dock, confident that no one could prove a charge of corruption against him. (All spiritual leaders ought to be able to similarly point to their lives as being "above reproach" [1 Tim 3:2]).

12:6-7 Here, we learn why Samuel wanted to reassert his authority. He switched out of judge mode to speak as a prophet with a message from the Lord. The Israelites would experience God's blessings if they lived righteously, and they would experience his judgment if they failed to obey. Samuel's call to the people to **present** themselves was a reminder that they were **before the LORD** (12:7)—that is, they were in his presence, which meant they had no excuse for not hearing and heeding what Samuel was about to tell them. The great prophet began his message in a pattern that would become a familiar one to the later writing prophets. He gave a recap of God's **righteous acts** (12:7) before outlining the forgetfulness and ingratitude of the people that led them back into the sins from which he had delivered them.

12:8-12 Samuel reviewed the history of the Lord's dealings with Israel. He told of the exodus from **Egypt** and arrival in the promised land, where Israel **forgot the LORD** (12:8-9). This led to oppression by a series of enemies, a cry to the Lord for help, and relief through a series of heroic judges: **Jerubbaal** (Gideon), **Barak, Jephthah, and Samuel** himself (12:11). But, each rescue was followed by a relapse into sin, the latest of which was the demand for **a king** (12:12). This point may have taken some of the collective air out of the Israelites' celebratory sails. They'd rejected their true king.

12:13-15 It seems Samuel also had a word of grace from the Lord, saying essentially, "What's done is done, so let's move forward" (12:13). The Lord was still their God, and he would not abandon his people. If they would **fear the LORD, worship and obey him**, and not **rebel**, then they and the king would be blessed (12:14). But, if they chose to disobey, God's judgment would fall on them like a ton of bricks—just as their **ancestors** had experienced (12:15).

12:16-25 Samuel proposed a sign that would prove his words: a thunderstorm during the **wheat harvest** when rain was rare (12:17). The point of the miracle was to reinforce the sin the people had committed and, thus, the urgency of their need to repent and follow the Lord with all their hearts. The miracle occurred, and the people reacted with repentance (12:19)—just as their ancestors had confessed their sins, pledged their obedience, and cried out for God's help in earlier days. Once again, Samuel promised God's presence if his people would follow and obey him (12:20-22). Samuel also vowed his own faithfulness to continue **to pray** for them (12:23). Finally, he offered a word of blessing for obedience and judgment for disobedience—a judgment that would include an end to the monarchy (12:24-25).

➤ B. Saul's Decline and Rejection
(13:1–15:35) ❦

13:1-5 It didn't take long for Saul's personal and spiritual defects to manifest themselves, to his own destruction and Israel's detriment. He was an impatient and impulsive person who made bad decisions under pressure and then tried to justify himself instead of admitting his wrongs.

As a new king, Saul would need a standing army to meet the military threats he would face—including the Philistines, who continued to be a pain. Saul's son **Jonathan**, introduced here (13:2), was a brave soldier like his father and would eventually become David's friend, protector, and advocate in Saul's court. While Saul was mustering his troops, Jonathan pulled off a raid against a **Philistine**

garrison that brought the huge Philistine army, **as numerous as the sand on the seashore**, to set up camp against Saul (13:3-5).

13:6-12 The Israelites got one look at the enemy horde and **hid** behind or under any rock they could find (13:6). Some **even crossed the Jordan** to the safety of the east side. Saul and his army had gathered **at Gilgal**, the site of their great earlier victory, but now they, too, **were gripped with fear** (13:7). Previously, Saul and Samuel had apparently agreed that the king would wait for Samuel to come and offer the appropriate sacrifices seeking the Lord's help for victory (13:8). But, Saul got tired of waiting and sinned by usurping the priest's role (13:9). Samuel arrived, took in the scene, and asked ominously, **What have you done?** (13:10).

Saul's excuse sounded plausible, at least to him. He was a military commander with a deserting army, a massive enemy who might pounce on him at any moment, and a priest who was nowhere to be found on the last day of their agreed-on waiting period. Besides, Saul claimed, he really wanted God's **favor**, so against his better judgment he'd **forced** himself to do what he knew he shouldn't (13:11). In other words, Saul was clearly hoping that Samuel could see the tight spot he was in and understand. After all, Samuel was the one who was late.

13:13-15 Excuses didn't work, and at this early stage of his reign, Saul forfeited his right to be Israel's king (13:13). Here is an example of the interplay between God's sovereignty and human responsibility. God had already made it abundantly clear that Saul was not his choice, and earlier biblical prophecy foretold that God's king would come from the tribe of Judah (see Gen 49:8-10). But, Saul was still responsible for his actions and could have enjoyed God's blessing on his reign. The writer wanted his readers to see how God was orchestrating circumstances under Saul to usher God's chosen, covenantal ruler, **a man after his own heart** to the throne (13:14).

13:16-23 Saul's response to his rejection is not recorded. He left to face the Philistine threat with only a handful of men (see 3:15), which is why the Philistines were successful in raids against the Israelites in **three**

directions (13:16-18). Another reason for Philistine military superiority was their decision to rid Israel of blacksmiths, lest the Israelites **make swords or spears** (13:19). So, Saul's army had little to work with (13:22).

14:1-3 Saul's son **Jonathan**, who was armed, attempted another daring raid against a **Philistine garrison** (14:1). If successful, it could demoralize the enemy and swing the momentum Israel's way despite the Philistines' military superiority. Meanwhile, Saul was resting with his troops and a priest near his headquarters at **Gibeah** (14:2). The priest, named **Ahijah**, was **wearing an ephod** (14:3), a priestly garment housing the Urim and Thummim, which were objects used to determine God's will in a specific situation (see Exod 28:6-30). Thus, it seems Saul was evidently waiting for some kind of divine guidance—or maybe he was just reluctant to go into battle with so few men.

14:4-14 It didn't make much sense militarily to attack a garrison with only two men, but Jonathan's attitude was right. The Philistines were **uncircumcised men** who were defying the armies of Israel's savior, God (14:6). (David would say essentially the same about Goliath in the near future; see 17:26). Jonathan had confidence in God's ability to deliver his people, so when his armor bearer said in effect, "I'm right behind you," the attack was on (14:7). Jonathan devised a sign to determine the Lord's will. And, when God clarified that he had his blessing, Jonathan and his armor bearer won a great victory (14:8-14).

14:15-23 The report of what Jonathan had just done (see 14:14), combined with **terror** spreading **from God**, threw the Philistines into such a panic that they scattered **in every direction** (14:15-16).

Back in camp, Saul started to seek divine guidance for his own next steps, but canceled that plan and took off after the fleeing enemy (14:18-22). As a result of Jonathan's initiative, **the LORD saved Israel that day** (14:23).

14:24-30 The Israelite army pursued the Philistines so hard that day that Saul refused to let any of his exhausted troops stop to eat, putting a death curse on any man who so much as tasted the **honey** that was **on the ground** all around them (14:24-26). This was another of Saul's foolish, impetuous actions that weakened his troops, just when they had their enemies on the run and needed all their strength. And, just as bad, Saul's foolhardiness almost cost Jonathan his life.

Jonathan had not heard his father's threat and did what a hungry warrior naturally would. He **ate** some of the **honey** and was immediately refreshed (14:27). One of the horrified soldiers told Jonathan what Saul had made the troops swear to, but Jonathan brushed off his father's curse for the troublesome idea it was. It was bad military strategy. If Saul had let his troops eat and maintain their strength, he reasoned, their victory would have been even **greater** (14:28-30).

14:31-35 The consequences of Saul's curse continued. As Israel's army continued to defeat the Philistines, the **exhausted** troops began to eat animals from **the plunder** without draining the blood, a violation of the law of Moses (14:31-33). Saul had enough spiritual sense left to know that this would bring God's disfavor, so he made a provision for proper butchering (14:33-35).

14:36-52 When Saul inquired of the Lord as to whether he should continue pursuing the Philistines, **God did not answer him** (14:37). Saul pursued the problem, and the **Urim** and **Thummim** revealed that Jonathan was the issue (14:38-42). Saul was ready to kill his son for disobeying his order (even though he hadn't heard it until it was too late), but the people rescued him because of the great victory he had won for Israel **with God's help** (14:42-45). Nothing more was said, and Saul did not go back into battle without God's approval (14:46). His strategy during his reign was to attack and defeat kingdoms that posed a threat to Israel (14:47-48).

15:1-3 Whatever shred of credibility Saul's kingship had crumbled with the next major event in chapter 15. Samuel relayed God's instructions to attack **the Amalekites** and **destroy** them (15:2-3). If God's enemies were ranked on a scale of how deeply they had offended him, the Amalekites would be high on that list. God had seen what they did to his

people **as they were coming out of Egypt** (15:2; see Exod 17:8-16). God had promised at that time to eventually "blot out the memory of Amalek under heaven" (Exod 17:14). So, God appointed Saul to complete the Amalekites' destruction, even down to their animals.

15:4-9 Saul gave the **Kenites**, a nomadic people living near the Amalekites, a chance to escape because they had been kind to the Israelites during the exodus (15:6). They were also the people of Moses's father-in-law, Jethro (see Judg 1:16).

Saul set the attack (15:4-5), and may have begun with the intention of obeying God's instructions as delivered through Samuel. But, as the battle raged and the Israelites got the upper hand, Saul apparently got a big head. Though he struck down the Amalekites, he spared **King Agag** and **the best of the . . . animals**. These became spoils of war. In spite of the Lord's explicit command, Saul and his troops **were not willing to destroy** what God said to destroy (15:8-9). To boldly do what God clearly forbids and then to justify yourself is a conscience-searing act.

15:10-11 It is sad but not surprising to read God's words to Samuel regarding Saul's actions: **I regret that I made Saul king** (15:11). Clearly, God is omniscient and knew how his reign would turn out. Nevertheless, he was genuinely grieved by Saul's rebellion against him. Samuel, likewise, was affected. He **became angry and cried out to the LORD all night** (15:11). No one sins in a vacuum. Our disobedience affects God, and it affects people in our lives.

15:12-13 Self-glorification seems to have been Saul's intent in disobeying orders, because when Samuel came to **confront** him, he was told that the king had gone to **Carmel** to **set up a monument for himself** (15:12). When Samuel caught up with Saul at Gilgal, Saul had his story all lined up, and even had the gall to start with his testimony of obedience: **I have carried out the LORD's instructions** (15:13).

15:14-15 Samuel quickly brought Saul back to reality from his world of self-justification. With Samuel's simple question about the noise from the Amalekites's animals—which were supposed to be dead—Saul realized he was in trouble (15:14). But, true to form, he had an excuse ready. The best of the animals were spared **in order to offer a sacrifice to the LORD your God** (15:15). In other words, he said, "I slightly modified God's commands so that I might worship him." But you can't honor God by defying him. You can't glorify the King by rejecting his kingdom agenda.

15:16-21 Samuel didn't want to hear Saul's excuses (15:16). He proceeded to tell Saul what God thought of his actions. He had failed to **obey the LORD** and instead did **what was evil in the LORD's sight** (15:19). At this rebuke, Saul protested his innocence once again: **But I did obey the LORD!** (15:20). He even implied that Samuel and God should be pleased that the animals were going to be used for sacrifices (15:20-21).

15:22-24 The lesson Saul missed was the timeless principle that **to obey is better than sacrifice, to pay attention is better than the fat of rams** (15:22). In other words, the Lord calls people to submit to his agenda, not to attempt to honor him with their own agendas. When Saul failed Obedience 101, it cost him his throne (15:23). So, Saul modified his justification for his actions. He admitted that he had **sinned**, but blamed **the people** for it (15:24). Unfortunately, Saul feared humans more than he feared God.

15:25-29 Saul asked Samuel for forgiveness and begged him to **return** with him to the people to show that Saul had not lost Samuel's support (15:25). That Saul **grabbed** and tore Samuel's **robe** (15:27) shows a desperate man grasping for a straw of hope, but even that became a prophetic sign against him (15:28-29).

15:30-35 When Saul pleaded with Samuel to **honor** him **before the elders**, Samuel eventually agreed (15:30-31). But, it didn't change God's decree, even though Saul would rule for many more years. Samuel's greater mission in returning with Saul was to finish the job this failed king was supposed to have accomplished. He called for **King Agag** and then personally put him to death (15:31-33).

The statement in verse 35 that **Samuel never saw Saul again** does not contradict Saul's appearance before Samuel in 19:24. The verb *see* can also mean "to have regard for, to take notice of." As far as Samuel was concerned, then, his relationship with Saul was over. God had rejected him.

Chapter 15 is strategic for the author's purpose of introducing David and his dynasty in the chapters to follow. It was important to show how Saul's disobedience had disqualified him and his family from the kingship, and that it was the Lord who chose David and his descendants. Through David's line, God would fulfill his covenant promise to send an eternal ruler, his Messiah.

III. DAVID'S ANOINTING
AND HISTORY UNDER SAUL (16:1–28:2)

❧ A. David's Anointing and Service to Saul (16:1-23) ❧

16:1 Samuel's grief over Saul's failure was understandable. But apparently, God felt it had gone on for too long. He roused his elderly prophet to action, giving him the most important assignment of his ministry. He sent Samuel to the home of **Jesse of Bethlehem** because he had **selected a king from his sons**. Saul's replacement was at hand.

16:2-5 Samuel was afraid of Saul's reaction because of the king's suspicious nature and violent temper (16:2). But, God told Samuel to go to Bethlehem to offer a **sacrifice to the LORD** and to **invite Jesse** to join him (16:2-3). Ironically, **the elders** of Bethlehem **trembled** with fear at the sight of Samuel, perhaps expecting him to deliver some message of judgment (16:4). But, Samuel put their minds at ease and called everyone to a **sacrifice** (16:5).

16:6-7 As soon as he looked at Jesse's sons, Samuel began sizing them up. He may have recalled that when Saul was identified as king of Israel he "stood a head taller than anyone else" (10:23). It certainly seems Samuel had physical characteristics in mind when he just looked at Jesse's firstborn **Eliab and said, "Certainly the LORD's anointed one is here"** (16:6). But, as Samuel would find out, God's selection wasn't based on physical **appearance** or stature. People tend to **see what is visible, but the LORD sees the heart** (16:7).

16:8-12 Jesse presented seven of his sons to Samuel. Each time, the Lord said in effect, "Pass that one up" (16:8-10). But, when the **youngest** son, who was out **tending the sheep**, was finally brought before Samuel, **the LORD said, "Anoint him, for he is the one"** (16:11-12). The purpose of David's selection and anointing is clear to us because we know the whole story. But importantly, the text doesn't tell us whether Samuel revealed to Jesse and his sons exactly what he was doing to David that day. They knew that David was being anointed in some ritual way, but they may not have known why.

16:13 Though his father and brothers could see the external anointing happening, they couldn't view the inner reality taking place: **the Spirit of the LORD came powerfully on David from that day forward.** Suddenly, David was not just a man after God's own heart (see 13:14), but was filled with the Holy Spirit. Not only was that the right combination for the king of God's people, it's also the right combination for any kingdom citizen.

In time, King David would be remembered as one of the greatest kings in Israel's history. Notably, David's great-grandmother Rahab was a Canaanite (which indicates that she was of a dark-skinned lineage). David's grandmother was Ruth, a Moabite, from a people who were Canaanites as well, of African descent. Thus, David, one of the heroes of the faith, hailed from mixed Jewish and Hamitic ancestry (see Gen 10:6) and stands as a leader of whom blacks can be proud to call our own.

16:14-23 Though the Spirit of God was with David in a powerful way (16:13), God withdrew his Spirit from Saul and appointed an **evil spirit . . . to torment him** (16:14). This spirit was most likely a demon sovereignly

appointed by God to trouble Saul mentally and emotionally, demonstrating God's power over Satan and his kingdom. God used this both to highlight Saul's utter rejection as king, and to bring David providentially into the royal court (16:15-19). Saul liked David so much that he became the king's **armor-bearer**, as well as the court musician to soothe the king and bring relief from the **evil spirit** (16:20-23). That this problem came **from God** lets the reader know again that God was in control of Saul's demise and David's eventual rise to the throne.

In response to the way God used Satan's kingdom to terrorize Saul, Saul should have responded with repentance for his rebellious acts against the gracious God who had made him king. He needed to turn back to the Lord, asking him to lift his hand of judgment. But sadly, the discipline of God never resulted in repentance from Saul.

Interestingly, these verses also illustrate the warning Samuel had given to the Israelites when they first demanded a king, telling them that the king would press their sons into his service (16:19, 22; see 8:11-12), with the clear implication that there was nothing they could do about it. Saul **loved** David and said that David had **found favor with** him (16:21-22). Unfortunately, as David continued to obey God and began to receive honor in the eyes of the Israelites, he would quickly lose Saul's good opinion.

❧ B. David's Defeat of Goliath
(17:1-58) ❦

17:1-11 Once again, Saul and the Israelite army faced off against their archenemies, **the Philistines** (17:1-2). As the rival troops were squaring off this time, the Philistine **champion named Goliath** appeared in the **ravine between them** (17:3-4). The description of his size (**nine feet, nine inches tall**), armor, and weapons emphasizes the terror his appearance struck in the hearts of Saul and his soldiers (17:4-7, 11). He was without question a horrifying sight.

Goliath **stood and shouted** his dare for a one-on-one, winner-take-all contest against any Israelite (17:8-9). Goliath declared, **I defy** the ranks of Israel, a challenge to which the king of Israel responded with silence (17:10-11). But, Goliath wasn't merely defying Israel and their king; he was defying Israel's God. Though this would be clear to David when he heard the giant's arrogant words (17:26), King Saul was so **terrified** that he missed it (17:11).

Your level of fear can reveal your closeness to God. In general, the more you are afraid, the farther you are from God; the less you are afraid, the closer you are to God. "Perfect love drives out fear" (1 John 4:18).

Saul was singled out in verse 11 by the author for at least two reasons. First, he was Israel's leader, their king and commander. If he lost his courage and confidence, the rest of his army would lose heart, too. The second reason is that Saul stood head and shoulders above all the people—he was *Israel's champion*, the logical choice to represent Israel and go fight Goliath. But, he wanted no part of the action.

17:12-15 The stage was set for David's providential visit to the battle line. His father, Jesse, sent him with provisions for his **three oldest** brothers who were serving in Saul's army. Though David was officially in Saul's service (16:22), he went back and forth to help care for his father's **flock** because Jesse **was already an old man** (17:12, 15).

17:16-22 The Philistine giant had been issuing his challenge **morning and evening for forty days** (17:16). Apparently, the Israelite army had been **marching out to its battle formation** each of these days, **shouting their battle cry** in hopes that Goliath would give up and they could just get on with a conventional battle (17:20).

17:23-27 Goliath **came forward** again and again, and the Israelites **retreated** in terror again and again (17:23-24). But, when **David heard** the Philistine's challenge (17:23), he stood his ground, looked around, and saw that he was alone in his convictions. So, he decided to do something about the situation. David learned that the king had offered a reward for the man who would defeat Goliath; he'd promised to give his own daughter to him in marriage (17:25-27). But, David was more concerned about removing Israel's **disgrace** at the hands of an **uncircumcised Philistine**,

who was defying **the armies of the living God**, than he was by the prize (17:26).

Where the rest of the army saw a terrifying warrior, David saw an "uncircumcised" opponent—that is, someone who was not a part of God's covenant community and, therefore, not under God's covering. In spite of Goliath's size, he lacked the authority and power to which David had access as a covenant member.

17:28-31 David's inquiry provoked the anger of his **oldest brother Eliab** (17:28). It's possible that Eliab was jealous of David's anointing at the hands of Samuel the prophet (see commentary on 16:8-12). But, it's clear that Eliab despised his baby brother as a cocky kid who was showing off and neglecting his duties (17:28). The funny thing is that David's hint that he wasn't afraid of Goliath didn't bother any of the other soldiers. They were more than happy to tell Saul about him and potentially get themselves off the hook (17:31).

17:32-40 At first, when David declared his intent to mop up the battlefield with Goliath, Saul attempted to discourage the young man from throwing his life away (17:32-33). But, David explained how he had repeatedly **killed lions and bears** that had threatened his sheep and that the Lord had **rescued** him every time (17:34-36). David was full of courage, zealous to protect those under his care, and bursting with trust in his covenant God. So, Saul tried to arm David, but the **armor** was too cumbersome (17:38-39). Instead, David went to war armed with **his sling** and a few **smooth stones** and the Creator of the universe on his side (17:40).

17:41-44 When the Philistine saw David, he was thoroughly unimpressed with the **youth** (17:41-42). Then, he threatened to feed him to **the wild beasts** and **cursed David by his gods** (17:43-44). Little did Goliath know that his own taunts had put him under a curse by the only true God (see Gen 12:3).

17:45-47 The giant's threats meant nothing to David, and neither did the Philistine's weapons. This young shepherd confidently faced perhaps the world's most menacing warrior ever with the greatest weapon: **I come against you in the name of the LORD of Armies, the God of the ranks of**

Israel—you have defied him (17:45). In other words, he said, "You've insulted the one true God. And he's mad." In the end, it would be the Philistines—not David—who became food for the wild creatures (17:46).

Don't miss the youth's bold declaration: the battle is the LORD's. He will hand you over to us (17:47). No obstacle is too large and no circumstance is too menacing when you realize that God is sovereign over all.

17:48-52 Goliath, who stood for all that was evil, was a terrifying presence. But, like our enemy, Satan (see 1 Pet 5:8), Goliath was a toothless lion despite his roaring because David was fighting in the Lord's name and strength. In the end, it was no contest. As thousands watched, David slung his stone and Goliath toppled (17:49-50). Then, the future king took the Philistine's own sword and cut off his head (17:51). That sight was enough for the Philistine army. They turned tail and ran, with the Israelites in hot pursuit (17:51-52).

17:53-58 David kept Goliath's weapons for himself and carried the Philistine's head around for a while (17:54, 57). In this trophy, we have a glimpse of what God promised that his Messiah would do to the serpent, the devil: "He will strike your head" (Gen 3:15). As David vanquished the giant, so Christ, the Son of David, will vanquish all his enemies. The chapter ends with Saul seeking to find out the name of David's father so he could properly reward the family of Jesse of Bethlehem (17:58; see 17:25).

The defeat of Goliath was another huge turning point in Israel's history. Saul had failed miserably as king. But, the stories recorded in the rest of 1 Samuel show the wisdom of God's sovereign choice of David to succeed him.

➣ C. David's Service in Saul's Court
(18:1–20:42) ➤

18:1-5 The person who loved David the most was Saul's oldest son and heir, Jonathan. We don't know when Jonathan realized that David, not he, would be Israel's

next king (see 20:14-15). But, even in these early days, he fully supported David by making a covenant of close friendship with him (18:3). If Jonathan did not yet know that God had rejected his father, the events in the chapters that follow would make it abundantly clear.

The fact that Saul kept David with him from the day he defeated Goliath means that David became a permanent leader in the army (18:2). Saul could see that David was a capable and courageous warrior and that the whole army was in awe of him. So, he put David in command of the fighting men. This pleased everyone because God was making David successful in everything (18:5).

18:6-9 Because he had put David in command and sent him to war, one would expect Saul to be pleased with David's success, too. And surely he was pleased—until the people started praising David as more successful than he. The women of Israel sang, Saul has killed his thousands, but David his tens of thousands (18:6-7). And, at the refrain, the fire of Saul's jealousy was ignited: David had been given more credit. So, while the people of Israel admired and loved David, Saul hated him from that day on (18:8-9). The king let his pride take over, ultimately fulfilling the truth of Proverbs 16:18: "Pride comes before destruction, and an arrogant spirit before a fall."

Saul wrongly assumed that David was seeking an opportunity to seize the throne (18:8). But, nothing could be further from the truth. David was God's man and was living in God's timing. God had elevated him from the sheep pasture, and David was determined to leave his destiny in God's hands. In the years to come, he would show tremendous restraint in honoring Saul as "the Lord's anointed" even when Saul was trying to kill him (see 24:1-22).

18:10-16 The next day, God confirmed the sinful path Saul had chosen by sending his appointed evil spirit to torment Saul so powerfully that he began to rave and tried to kill David twice (18:10-11). By now, Saul had recognized that the LORD was with David, and it filled the king with fear (18:12). So, Saul sent David off to battle. David's success and popularity skyrocketed (18:13-16).

18:17-19 Saul tried another course of action to get rid of David. He vowed to give David his **daughter Merab** for a **wife, if [he would] be a warrior for [Saul] and fight the LORD's battles** (18:17). Because Saul had already reneged on his promise to give his daughter in marriage to the warrior who killed Goliath (see 17:25), it's not surprising to learn that he still had no intention of making David his son-in-law. Instead, he expected **the Philistines** to kill him in battle first (18:17). David humbly objected to the offer, not thinking himself worthy of being related to the king (18:18). But, **when it was time** to give his daughter to David, Saul broke his word and gave her to another man (18:19).

The more honorable David acted, the more treacherous Saul became. Sometimes, living righteously and being determined to follow God leads the furnace of contempt and rejection to become even hotter. It doesn't guarantee ease.

18:20-30 When Saul learned that his **daughter Michal loved David**, he devised another plan (18:20). He believed that she would become **a trap for him** (18:21), because of the **bride-price** he intended to demand for her hand in marriage—**a hundred** dead Philistines (18:25). Though in his humility David was again reluctant to **become the king's son-in-law** (18:22-23), he was willing to do it if it meant another opportunity to defeat the Lord's enemies (18:26). When David returned with twice the number of required Philistine trophies, Saul had no choice but to give Michal to him (18:27). The wretched king continued to poison himself with his own bitterness of heart, watching David's star rise as his own faded (18:28-30).

19:1-8 Having tried and failed twice to kill David himself, and having failed to have David die at the hands of the Philistines, Saul took a more direct approach. He **ordered his son Jonathan and all his servants to kill David** (19:1)—no tricks, no subtlety, just a straight order. Jonathan told David to **hide** while he talked with his father to see if he truly intended to have him murdered on sight (19:2-3). Jonathan's defense of David was passionate and apparently hit home with Saul during one of his saner moments (19:4-6). He knew

Jonathan was right, so the king **swore an oath** in God's name that David would not be harmed (19:6). Jonathan believed his father's vow, and David believed Jonathan, so David came back to the court in Saul's hometown of Gibeah. All of Israel benefited from his military leadership (19:7-8).

19:9-17 Soon, that **evil spirit sent from the LORD came on Saul** again, revealing Saul's lack of genuine repentance and his murderous heart (19:9-10). After another attempt on his life, David knew he would never be safe in Saul's presence, oath or not. When he ran to his home that night to hide, **Saul sent agents to David's house** with the order to **kill him** (19:11). But, with Michal's deception of her wicked father, David escaped (19:11-17).

19:18-24 David was desperate, so he departed for the only place where he knew he would be welcome—the home of **Samuel at Ramah** (19:18). When Saul got word of it, he sent his death squad there for David, but then an amazing scene unfolded. Three teams of Saul's **agents** arrived, but were overcome with a spirit of prophecy, which some commentators believe was a power that immobilized them so they could not harm David (19:19-21). When Saul finally went himself, he experienced the same phenomenon, causing him to collapse (20:22-24). Once again, Saul had failed to eradicate David. And, once again, as a result of divine intervention, it was clear that the Lord was with David. Yet, Saul refused to repent.

20:1-4 David fled back **to Jonathan** in despair and frustration (20:1). Jonathan was evidently unaware that his father had sent death squads to hunt down David. It was too much for Jonathan to take in because he still believed in Saul's oath not to harm David (20:2; see 19:6). But, David suggested the real reason Saul had kept his plans from his son: he knew that Jonathan would **be grieved** (20:3). This insight jarred Jonathan with the reality of the situation, and he was ready to help his treasured friend in any way (20:4).

20:5-9 An opportunity presented itself to test Saul's mood toward David. The **New Moon** was a festival that involved special meals, which David would be expected to attend at

Saul's table because he was a member of the king's court. But, David devised a plan whereby he would **hide** for the **two nights** of the festivities (20:5). Meanwhile, Jonathan would say David had been asked to come to **Bethlehem** for **an annual sacrifice** with his **whole clan** (20:6). David and Jonathan agreed that Saul's reaction to David's absence would tell them if David would ever be **safe** again in Saul's service (20:7). David concluded the plan by urging Jonathan to just **kill** him if he was indeed guilty of any wrongdoing—a suggestion that Jonathan dismissed immediately (20:8-9).

20:10-23 Jonathan came up with a plan to alert David about his father's reaction. The plan, laid out in 20:11-23, was very simple. The key verses are 14–16, in which Jonathan expressed to David his awareness that David would not only live, but also inherit the kingdom from Saul someday and see all of his enemies obliterated. There is an element of sadness in Jonathan's words: **if I die, don't ever withdraw your kindness from my household** (20:14-15). By this point, Jonathan clearly understood that his father was under God's judgment. Though he was the king's son, Jonathan knew he would not be king himself. But, instead of expressing jealousy and rage like his father, **he loved** David **as he loved himself** (20:17). He submitted himself to God's will and pledged loyalty to the future king.

20:24-34 Jonathan went to the first night of the celebration (20:25). Saul gave David a pass, assuming there was a ceremonial reason for his absence (20:25-26). But, the next night, Jonathan's answer threw Saul into such an uncontrollable rage that he cursed his son (20:27-30). Saul was furious and thought that Jonathan couldn't see what was so obvious: David posed a huge threat to Jonathan's succession to the throne (20:31). What Saul didn't know was that Jonathan and David had already settled that issue. So, although Saul was king, his son far surpassed him as a kingdom man.

20:35-42 There could no longer be any question in Jonathan's mind about Saul's evil intentions toward David. There was nothing left to do but put the plan into effect with the bad news that David would have to become a fugitive. David bid a tearful goodbye to his beloved friend

(20:41). Jonathan blessed David and reminded him of the covenant the two had made before God: **The LORD will be a witness between you and me and between my offspring and your offspring forever** (20:42; see 18:3).

⇾ D. David's Fugitive Years
(21:1–28:2) ⇽

21:1 Suddenly cut off from family and friends, David was a true fugitive. He left Jonathan at Gibeah and fled south to **Nob**, a priestly sanctuary about one mile north of Jerusalem. **The priest Ahimelech** was apparently suspicious when he saw that David was **alone**, so he **was afraid**.

21:2-6 David lied to the priest by telling him that he and his men were on a secret **mission** for Saul (21:2). He asked that Ahimelech provide them with sustenance—**bread or whatever [could] be found** (21:3). Ahimelech had nothing on hand but the **consecrated bread**, the "Bread of the Presence" that was set apart and could only be eaten by the priests (21:4; see Exod 25:30; Lev 24:5-9). He gave David the day-old **consecrated bread** that had been **removed** and **replaced** with fresh bread (21:6).

The Bread of the Presence was holy and intended for the priests only, but this was an extraordinary circumstance. David was God's chosen future king, who was undergoing unjust persecution and fleeing for his life. So, as long as David and anyone traveling with him met the ceremonial requirements specified by Ahimelech (21:4-5), it was acceptable nourishment. Jesus made this clear to the Pharisees when they criticized Jesus's disciples about picking and eating grain on the Sabbath (see Matt 12:1-8). Jesus compared his disciples' actions to those of David eating the consecrated bread that was technically not lawful to eat. An overly strict interpretation of the law of Moses would have caused the needy to go hungry.

21:7 The story takes a tragic turn here that will come to light later. This event at Nob was witnessed by **Doeg the Edomite, chief of Saul's shepherds**. The Edomites were longtime enemies of Israel, and we learn later that this foreigner had no qualms about massacring God's people. He was in Nob for an unexplained reason; he was **detained before the LORD**. He left immediately to report David's presence at Nob (see 22:9-10).

21:8-10 David unintentionally implicated **Ahimelech** further in his escape by asking the priest to provide him with a weapon (21:8). Ahimelech had the perfect one, **the sword of Goliath**, which David had previously kept after defeating the Philistine (21:9; see 17:54). David took it and, feeling the heat, no longer felt safe anywhere in Israel.

Later, we'll learn that David had a band of men with him in this scene that would eventually grow into a small army of about six hundred (see 23:13; Matt 12:1-4). Yet, militarily, they were no match for Saul and the armies of Israel. So, he and his men rode not just into the territory of their bitter enemies the Philistines, but into **Gath**, the hometown of Goliath, with David wearing the giant's sword. Perhaps David hoped he could enter Gath without being recognized by **King Achish** (21:10).

21:11-15 The king's **servants**, however, recognized David immediately, knew the song the Israelite women had been singing about him, and even referred to him as **the king of the land [of Israel]** (21:11). David knew his life was in danger, **so he pretended to be insane**, acting **like a madman** (21:12-13). The reason Achish didn't kill David may have been because of an ancient superstition against killing an insane person based on the belief that insanity was a divine judgment not to be interfered with. David's act worked as Achish sent him and his men packing (21:14-15).

22:1-5 Realizing there was no hiding place for him among the Philistines, David traveled to **the cave of Adullam**, located about twenty miles southwest of Jerusalem (22:1). When they learned of his whereabouts, David's family joined him there, because their lives would also have been in danger from Saul. And, **every man who was desperate, in debt, or discontented**—that is, those whom we would call the disenfranchised or who had a gripe against the way Saul was running

things—joined up with David (22:2). David then took his family to **the king of Moab** for protection (22:3); that was a good plan because Moab was the home of David's great-grandmother Ruth (see Ruth 4:21-22). Then, David and his men went to a **stronghold** (22:4). But, even there, they weren't safe. So, on the advice of **the prophet Gad**, the fugitives hid in a **forest in the land of Judah** (22:5).

22:6-10 Back in Gibeah, the paranoid Saul royally chewed out his own men for conspiring against him to protect David (22:6-8). Saul's twisted charge that Jonathan was against him and that David was actually waiting **in ambush for** him shows how deranged and dangerous Saul had become (22:8). **Doeg** saw his chance to ingratiate himself with the king, so he reported what he had seen and heard at **Nob** (22:9-10; see 21:7). Doeg's malice, combined with Saul's paranoia, could produce nothing but calamity.

22:11-15 Saul's reaction was tragically predictable. **Ahimelech . . . and his father's whole family** were called to stand trial for treason (22:11-13). But, it was a kangaroo court. The king charged Ahimelech with conspiring with David and claimed that David was waiting **in ambush** to attack at any moment (22:13). Ahimelech made a valiant attempt to defend David's honor and his own innocence. As far as Ahimelech was concerned, he had been merely following the orders of the king's own **son-in-law** and **bodyguard** (22:14-15).

22:16-19 But Ahimelech's explanation and justification didn't matter. Saul had already made up his mind. Ahimelech was guilty by association. Saul condemned the priest and his family to death (21:16). Yet, Saul's **guards** apparently still had enough fear of the Lord in them that they **would not lift a hand to execute the priests of the LORD** (22:17). **Doeg the Edomite**, however, had no such qualms. He not only killed all **eighty-five** priests at Nob, but he also massacred every person and animal in the town (22:18-19).

22:20-23 Only **Abiathar**, a son of Ahimelech, **escaped** and **fled to David** to tell him what happened (22:20-21). Though these murders lay at the feet of Saul (who felt no remorse), David felt **responsible for** them (22:22). Abiathar stayed with David and would later serve in the priesthood when David became king (22:23).

The heading of Psalm 52 indicates that David wrote that psalm when he learned of Doeg's treachery. David knew that God would be faithful to bring down this wicked man, so David trusted and praised God for his steadfast love (see Ps 52:5-9). His example is a reminder that, regardless of how bad things look, we are to worship. God is still on his throne, and he will ultimately right every wrong.

23:1 David did more than merely hide from Saul during his days as a fugitive. He was still a loyal son of Israel and member of the tribe of Judah. So, when the Philistines attacked the Judean town of **Keilah**, about three miles south of Adullam, David was concerned for his countrymen.

23:2-6 But first, **David inquired of the LORD** (23:2), no doubt using the **ephod** that Abiathar the priest had brought with him from Nob (23:6). This was the garment housing the Urim and Thummim, which the priest would use to determine an answer from the Lord. David got a "yes" from God, directing him to **rescue Keilah** (23:2). But, his men were afraid of fighting the Philistines while Saul was seeking to destroy them as well (23:3). So, David **inquired** again and got a second "yes" from the Lord. With this reassurance, David and his men were victorious in battle (23:4-5).

23:7-14 Even this victory did not give David rest. When word spread that Saul knew where David was and had gathered his army to march on Keilah and take him, David suspected that the people there would hand him over to Saul (23:7-12). Indeed, the people of Keilah probably knew what happened to the people of Nob (see 22:11-19), and they wanted no part of protecting David at such a cost. David consulted the Lord again through the **ephod** (23:9). To his credit, David didn't want the blood of Keilah's people on his conscience, and he knew Saul wouldn't hesitate to slaughter them. When God revealed to him that Saul would attack and that the people

of Keilah would hand him over, David and his men fled into to **the wilderness strongholds** (23:13-14).

23:15-16 David had to be at a low point in terms of morale. Even rescuing his own countrymen from enemies hadn't provided him with relief or safety. But, it was at this point that God sent Jonathan to David and **encouraged him in his faith in God** (23:16). Similarly, when other believers are at spiritual low points, Christians are to be faithful Jonathans to them. This is what it is to love your neighbor as yourself.

23:17-18 Jonathan was confident that God would spare David and make him **king over Israel**. Jonathan was looking forward to serving as David's **second-in-command** one day (23:17), but sadly, that would never happen. David and Jonathan renewed the **covenant** they had made previously and parted (23:18; see 18:3). This would be the last time these two friends would see one another.

23:19-23 David and his men were in a desolate wilderness place, but even there, they weren't safe. The **Ziphites**, who lived in a town in the Judean wilderness near where David was hiding, were eager to betray him to Saul. Perhaps they wanted to ingratiate themselves with the king, or maybe they wanted to avoid being accused of knowing where David was and not telling. Regardless, they went to **Saul at Gibeah** with their news (23:19-20). Saul was pleased with the Ziphite informers and asked them to return and be his eyes and ears to report David's whereabouts (23:21-23).

23:24-29 The Ziphite spies did their job so well that David and Saul were soon on the same **mountain**, with Saul just steps away from capturing him (23:26). But, by the providence of God, the Philistines sent a raiding party on Israel, and Saul had to give up the chase (23:27-28). Because of David's heart-stopping escape, the site was named **the Rock of Separation** to commemorate God's deliverance (23:28). But, David also knew better than to stay put. This respite allowed him to move to **En-gedi**, an oasis along the Dead Sea about thirty-five miles southeast of Jerusalem (23:29). There, David and his men hid in a cave, where he would soon prove his innocence once again.

24:1-3 By including the following incident at En-gedi, the author of 1 Samuel clearly intended to show that, even though David was God's anointed choice as king, he refused to take the throne by violence but determined to wait on God's timing. God has a plan for every believer's life. The question is: Will you seek his will for you at any cost: or will you pursue it according to God's agenda and timetable?

When Saul **went to look for David** at En-gedi, he entered a cave **to relieve himself** (24:2-3). In an almost humorous instance of God's providence, Saul chose to do that in the very cave in which David was hiding. The tension couldn't be thicker. Here was David's opportunity. He could rid Israel of its corrupt king and assume his own rightful place on the throne.

24:4-7 But, instead of burying his knife in Saul's back, David only **cut off the corner of Saul's robe** (24:4). David's **conscience** was so sensitive that even that act bothered him (24:5). In spite of his wickedness, Saul was still **the LORD's anointed** (24:6), and David intended to leave him in the hands of the Lord.

24:8-10 When Saul left the cave, he was no doubt shocked to hear David's voice calling to him and then to see him **knelt low** paying **homage** (24:8). Up until now, other people like Jonathan had spoken to Saul in David's defense. But now, David had his own opportunity, and Saul stood speechless. David began with the obvious. If he had really wanted to **harm** Saul, he had just had the perfect opportunity to do it. He said, **the LORD handed you over to me today in the cave** (24:9-10). Though others had urged David to kill Saul, David demonstrated in the clearest way possible that he had no such intensions against **the LORD's anointed** (24:10).

24:11-13 David affectionately called Saul his **father**—which was either a reminder that David was the king's son-in-law or a reference to Saul as David's king. Then, David produced the piece of **robe** to show Saul how close he had come to death. Saul had pursued David unjustly and sought his life, but David had mercifully spared Saul (24:11). If any **vengeance** were to be inflicted on Saul's head, it would come from the hand of God himself, not David (24:12). David's final appeal was to his weak position in comparison to Saul's exalted status as king. In other words, he said, Saul wasn't chasing a legitimate threat to his kingdom, but a poor man with a tiny band of misfits who couldn't do him any harm (24:14).

24:16-21 David's appeal seemed to work. Saul broke into tears (24:16). He said, **You are more righteous than I, for you have done what is good to me though I have done what is evil to you** (24:17). In the hearing of his troops and David's men, Saul confessed his treachery and David's innocence. The facts were plain to everyone. Therefore, Saul blessed David, admitted that David would be king one day, and asked David to pledge not to **wipe out** his family (24:19-21).

24:22 David swore to Saul that he would not, further cementing a promise he had already made to his son Jonathan (see 20:14-17). Interestingly, however, David did not return with Saul and his army to Gibeah. Instead he stayed in **the stronghold** (24:22). Clearly, David was not thoroughly convinced of the sincerity of Saul's repentance—or at least that Saul's sincerity would last. As the reader of 1 Samuel learns, David was wise to doubt the genuineness of Saul's change of heart.

25:1 As chapter 25 opens, Israel is hit with a blow: **Samuel died** (25:1). The prophet who anointed Israel's first king (Saul) and its future king (David) was no more. He was so revered that **all Israel** gathered at his **home in Ramah** to **mourn for him** (25:1). The last of Israel's judges had filled a unique role.

25:2-8 David went to a place called **Maon**, the home of a wealthy man named **Nabal** and his wife, **Abigail**. She was as **intelligent and beautiful** as her husband was **harsh and evil** (25:2-3). Without being under obligation, David and his men provided protection for Nabal's herds (25:7). **So David sent ten young men** to greet Nabal, asking that he might spare some food—whatever he thought fair for David and his men, in light of the safety they had provided for Nabal's flocks and **shepherds** (25:5-8).

25:9-17 True to his nature, Nabal insulted David's men and sent them away empty-handed (25:9-11). To David, such ingratitude and offense deserved vengeance (25:12-13). Thankfully, Nabal had a young servant who valued his own head enough to tell Abigail the whole story, including how David had protected the family's herds and how Nabal had **screamed at** David's messengers (25:14-16). Apparently, Nabal's character was an open topic of discussion in the household because this servant didn't hesitate in pointing it out to the lady of the house: **He is such a worthless fool nobody can talk to him!** (25:17).

25:18-22 Abigail knew her husband, so she knew that the servant was exactly right. In Hebrew, *Nabal* means "fool" or "stupid." The name fit. Abigail had to act fast if she was to prevent a disaster from striking their home. Abigail collected a large supply of provisions and sent them **ahead of** her with a group of servants to meet David (25:18-19). She followed **behind**, ready to intercede for her household and for Nabal. She was as wise as Nabal was foolish, for David intended to kill every male in the household (25:22). If she didn't intercede, innocent lives would be lost and David would come to regret his actions.

25:23-31 Abigail **paid homage to David** as to a king (25:23). She admitted that Nabal's name matched his character. He was a **worthless fool**, and **stupidity [was] all he [knew]** (25:25). She then recalled the ways that God had shown favor to David and protected him from his enemies (25:28-29). Then, she urged David to forget Nabal and his petty **offense** (25:28). One day, David would be Israel's king. On that day, **there [would] not be remorse or a troubled conscience ... because of needless bloodshed**, if David restrained himself from revenge (25:31).

25:32-35 As far as David was concerned, Abigail was worth her weight in gold. Her **discernment** had spared her household and

prevented David from shedding innocent blood. He **blessed** her, **accepted** her gifts, and sent her **home in peace** (25:33, 35).

Abigail is a perfect example of the "wife of noble character" discussed in Proverbs 31:10. She didn't let her fool of a husband prevent her from fearing and obeying the Lord. She was a true kingdom woman. Soon, she would see "the reward of her labor" (Prov 31:31).

25:36-38 This story ends with a twist. Having saved the day, Abigail went home to find a drunken husband who had no idea how close to death he had come (25:36). When Nabal finally **sobered up** and Abigail told him everything, he had a stroke or heart attack—**His heart died and he became a stone** (25:37). He lingered for **ten days** before God **struck Nabal dead** in judgment (25:38).

25:39-44 When David heard of Nabal's death, he took Abigail as his own **wife** (25:41-42). Though his action was clearly intended to honor this godly woman, David was already **married** (25:43-44). Polygamy was never God's ideal for his people. And, in David's case, polygamous marriage would result in horrific family dysfunction (including rape and murder among his children) that would bring him much grief.

26:1-4 In God's providence, the treachery of **the Ziphites** brought Saul within David's reach again (26:1). This was their second betrayal of David to Saul (see 23:19). In spite of his earlier repentance for unjustly pursuing David (see 24:16-21), Saul again brought his troops to catch David in his hiding place (26:2-3). Aware of Saul's movements, David sent out a recon team that located Saul's camp in the wilderness (26:4).

26:5-6 David approached Saul's camp at night and got so close he could see **the place where Saul and Abner ... the commander of his army, were lying down** (26:5). David had two men with him that night, including a soldier named **Abishai**, who would later become one of his mighty men (see 1 Chr 11:20-21). David suddenly got an idea that must have sounded suicidal: let's sneak right into Saul's camp. But, Abishai responded immediately, **I'll go with you** (26:6).

26:7-11 Militarily speaking, two against three thousand didn't make for a good plan. But, this was not a military operation. David made it clear to Abishai that he had no violent intent toward Saul (26:7-11). The author of 1 Samuel wanted us to know that the Lord was leading David on this midnight adventure to demonstrate again that, though he was the legitimate king of Israel, he was not a usurper. David would wait patiently for the Lord's timing, holding to his conviction that it was not his place to strike **the LORD's anointed** (26:9).

26:12-16 David took Saul's **spear and the water jug** by his head. Possessing them would serve as evidence of David's good will and Saul's close brush with death. Taking them was possible because **a deep sleep from the LORD came over** Saul, Abner, and all of their army (26:12). Once David was again at a safe distance from the camp, he called out to Abner and Saul's troops, ridiculing them for failing to protect their king (26:13-16). Abner must have felt as if his pockets had been picked when he awoke to find someone had gotten to the king without his even knowing it. David revealed that he had taken Saul's gear right out from under Abner's nose (26:16). The army commander was publicly humiliated and had nothing to say.

26:17-20 Saul, too, was humiliated. Once again, Saul was shown to be seeking the life of a man who bore him no ill will (see 24:1-22). David protested his innocence before the king (26:18). He called down a curse on those who were troubling him falsely and who had cut him off from worshiping the Lord within Israel (26:19). Finally, he emphasized how ridiculous Saul's pursuit was, for David was nothing more than **a single flea** (26:20).

26:21-25 David's actions and plea again seemed to hit home with Saul, who acknowledged his sin and realized that David could have killed him if he'd desired to. Saul admitted, **I have been a fool!** (26:21). (That's putting it mildly.) Unfortunately, Saul would not reform his ways. There is no point in acknowledging your foolishness if you insist on continuing to walk a foolish road.

Saul promised, **I will never harm you again** (26:21). But, David had heard this promise before. After declaring his innocence before the Lord once again (26:22-24), David **went on his way, and Saul returned home** (26:25). Though there is no further record of Saul hunting David, this may be because David would soon leave Israel (see 27:4). Saul didn't turn over a new leaf to live a God-honoring life, as we will soon see.

27:1-4 David was convinced that he wasn't safe from Saul anywhere in Israel. So, for the second time, he took the drastic step of going **to the land of the Philistines** (27:1)—and right back to **Achish . . . the king of Gath**, no less (27:2; see 21:10-15). It's hard to know what kind of reception David expected in enemy territory, but clearly he believed it couldn't be any worse than the fugitive life he had been living. This risky move may make more sense when we remember that David was responsible for six hundred **men** and their families as well as his own—quite an entourage to try and provide for in a barren wilderness (27:3). With this move by David, Saul **no longer searched for him** (27:4).

27:5-6 By now, Achish and the Philistines had become convinced that David really was a mortal enemy of Saul and could never go back to Israel. This made him a potentially valuable ally in their never-ending war with the Israelites. So, King Achish let David settle among them, in the outlying city of **Ziklag**, located about thirteen miles north of Beersheba in the desert region of the Negev (27:5-6). Achish was making David his vassal, or servant, with David pledging his loyalty and putting him and his men at Achish's service—or so the Philistine king thought.

27:7-11 David had other plans. He wanted to be away from Gath to be out from under the king's close scrutiny so he could operate without being watched all the time. David used Ziklag as his headquarters for the next sixteen months, right up until the death of Saul (27:7). From there, David and his men carried out raids against various desert tribes that were enemies of Israel, including the nation's bitter and ancient foes, **the**

Amalekites (27:8). David made sure that no one survived these raids to go to Gath and report to Achish what he was really doing (27:11). When Achish **inquired** about David's activities, he deceived the king by telling him that he was carrying out raids against his own people in **Judah** (27:10).

27:12–28:2 Achish bought the deception completely, thinking that because David had **made himself repulsive to his people Israel**, he would be Achish's **servant forever** (27:12). As far as Achish was concerned,

David and his men were now loyal comrades of the Philistines, who were obligated to fight with them against the Israelites. So, when the time came for the next battle between these two armies, Achish didn't give David an option. He had to **fight** with the Philistines **against Israel** (28:1). David gave the answer Achish wanted to hear, and the Philistine king made David his **permanent bodyguard** (28:2). Then, like any good drama, the book of 1 Samuel leaves the reader in suspense as attention turns once again to King Saul.

IV. SAUL'S SAD FINAL DAYS AND DEATH (28:3–31:13)

✒ A. Saul Consults a Medium
(28:3-25) ✒

28:3-7 Saul was in a bad place as **the Philistines gathered** their forces to go to war against Israel (28:4). **He was afraid** (28:5). But, he didn't have a military problem alone; he also had a spiritual problem. The Lord's prophet Samuel was now dead, and the Lord refused to respond to Saul's inquiries for guidance (28:6). Previously, **Saul had removed the mediums and spiritists from the land** (28:3) in obedience to the law of Moses: "Do not turn to mediums or consult spiritists, or you will be defiled by them" (Lev 19:31; see also Deut 18:9-12). But now, desperate for supernatural guidance, Saul resorted to that which God had clearly prohibited (28:7). His failure as king over God's people was total.

28:8-13 A medium was someone who consulted the dead to determine the future. Saul didn't care about God's law. He was desperate and wanted answers. So, he **disguised himself** and visited a medium so that she could **consult a spirit for** him (28:8). Because such people had been eradicated in Israel by the king, the woman was concerned that this was a sting operation (28:9). But, Saul promised she would be safe. So, as requested, she called up Samuel from the dead and was as shocked as anyone when the prophet actually appeared.

Immediately, she recognized that her client was King Saul (28:11-12).

28:14-19 Rivers of ink have been spilled by commentators arguing for different views of whether this account was or was not actually a return of Samuel's spirit from the dead. The text presents it as such in a straightforward way, rather than as a demon impersonating Samuel or suggesting the medium merely used her wiles to trick Saul. It's doubtful that Saul would have been fooled by an impersonator, and Samuel's message of judgment on Saul—including his loss of the kingdom to David, his impending death, and Israel's defeat—were exactly what would come to pass. Thus, it would appear that God used an otherwise forbidden means to convey his verdict on a rebellious Saul.

When Saul asked Samuel for help, claiming that **God** had **turned away** from him, Samuel responded in effect, "Of course he has!" (28:15-18). Saul had disobeyed the Lord's clear instructions, and the Lord had **torn the kingship** from Saul's hands (28:17-18). Then, Samuel declared God's final judgment on the house of Saul: **Tomorrow you and your sons will be with me**—that is, dead (28:19).

28:20-25 Samuel's words caused the doomed king to fall **flat on the ground**. He was horrified and **weak** from lack of nourishment (28:20). Even the medium felt sorry for what must have been the pathetic sight of Israel's king practically fainting in abject terror. She tried to persuade Saul to eat and finally got him to take a meal (28:22-25). The entourage finally left and returned to the Israelite camp (28:25). It would be Saul's last night on earth.

◆ B. David's Movements (29:1–30:31) ◆

29:1-5 Saul's fate—and that of his sons and Israel's army—had been sealed by the word of the Lord. The events of chapter 29 actually precede those of chapter 28 chronologically, but the incident with Saul and the medium provides the spiritual setting for Saul's death and Israel's defeat. When the text left David (27:12), he and his six hundred men were facing a dilemma in Philistine territory as they were expected to serve the Philistines militarily against the Israelites.

But, God providentially intervened. **The Philistine commanders asked** King Achish suspiciously, **What are these Hebrews doing here?** Achish was proud to introduce David who, as far as he was concerned, had been a valuable asset since **the day he defected** from Saul (29:3). But, the other commanders had long memories, and they valued their heads. They accused Achish of taking an incredibly dangerous risk in assuming that David would actually fight with them against his own people, instead of turning on them in order to **ingratiate himself with his master,** Saul (29:4). The song sung about David in Israel was still well-known in the land of Philistia (29:5).

29:6-8 There were five Philistine commanders representing the five major cities of their kingdom, of which Achish and Gath were only one. Though Achish believed in David, he was outvoted. So, with great reluctance, Achish called David and gave him the bad news. David was no doubt delighted that he was no longer expected to go to war against Israel. But, he played along with the charade, protesting this decision and emphasizing his past allegiance to the Philistines (29:8).

29:9-11 Achish trusted in David's loyalty, but there was nothing he could do. David and his men were to leave the next day at first

light so that they couldn't interfere with the battle. They returned to **the land of the Philistines** (29:11), specifically to Ziklag, where he and his army would find a tragedy waiting for them that would threaten David's leadership.

30:1-5 At Ziklag, David and his men found nothing but the smoke from a raid by the **Amalekites** who had **burned** the city and **kidnapped the women and everyone in it from youngest to oldest** (30:1-5). The men **wept loudly until they had no strength left** (30:4). Surely, no honorable husband and father can read about the horrifying scene without thinking of his own family and feeling a lump in his throat.

30:6 The deep grief in David's army soon turned to fierce anger against him as **the troops talked about stoning him.** They probably blamed him for the decision to leave Ziklag defenseless as they fled to Gath to escape Saul. **But David found strength in the LORD his God.** He remembered that God had delivered him from lions and bears when he was a young shepherd (17:37), and he had delivered him from the hand of Saul numerous times.

David knew where to turn for help. As he operated in the earthly realm, his true strength and protection lay in the heavenly realm. This raises the question: To whom do you turn first when life's troubles visit you?

30:7-10 David found divine direction when **the priest Abiathar** brought **the ephod** and David **asked the LORD** if a raid on the Amalekites would succeed. The answer was affirmative, including the encouraging message that he would **rescue** all the captives (30:7-8). With that word of assurance, David and his army set out in pursuit. And, when two hundred of his men became too tired to continue chasing the Amalekites, he made an executive decision (30:9-10) that would become important when it came time to divide the spoil after the battle.

30:11-20 David and the rest of his men continued on and met **an Egyptian** slave whose Amalekite master had left him behind when he couldn't keep up with the raiders

(30:11-15). God had providentially placed this man in David's path, for he agreed to **lead** David to the Amalekites (30:15). As a result, David's army arrived at the Amalekite camp at the best possible time. The bad guys were in the worst possible military and physical condition to defend themselves: they were **spread out over the entire area, eating, drinking, and celebrating** (30:16). So, David decimated the Amalekites and **recovered everything** from the smallest lamb to the smallest child (30:18-19). The victorious troops were so ecstatic they shouted, **This is David's plunder!** (30:20).

30:21-25 As David prepared to divide the spoil among his men, he intended to include **the two hundred men** who had become too weary to continue the pursuit (30:21; see 30:9-10). But, **the corrupt and worthless men among those who had gone with David** objected (30:22). They didn't want to share with the two hundred who stayed back **with the supplies** (30:22, 24). In effect, David asked how they could show such unkindness to their brothers in light of the protection they had received from the Lord (30:23). Therefore, his principle of equal sharing became **a law and an ordinance for Israel** (30:25).

30:26 Then, David made another wise and diplomatic move by sending gifts from the plunder **to his friends, the elders of Judah**, his own tribe. These gifts helped to reaffirm David's loyalty to his people after his time among the Philistines. The Egyptian slave had told David that "the territory of Judah" was among the places the Amalekite raiders had looted (30:14). So, in returning the plunder to these Judean cities, David was restoring what they had lost.

30:27-31 Each of the cities mentioned here was in the territories of Judah and Simeon. David's actions helped cement Judah's loyalty to him, because it was the people of Judah who would later crown him as king (see 2 Sam 2:1-4). **Hebron** is worth noting (30:31) because David would be anointed king of Israel there and would rule from Hebron for more than seven years before capturing Jerusalem and moving his capital there (see 2 Sam 5:1-5).

✣ C. Saul's Death at Gilboa (31:1-13) ✣

31:1-3 While the events of chapter 30 were taking place, the tragic battle that Samuel had prophesied (28:19) took place **on Mount Gilboa** between **Israel** and **the Philistines** (31:1). Following a common strategy in ancient warfare, the Philistines focused on Israel's leaders, **Saul and his sons** (31:2). **Jonathan** and two of his brothers were killed, and Saul was **severely wounded** (31:2-3). Saul knew that if the Philistines found him alive, they would subject him to a slow, torturous end.

31:4-7 In an attempt to escape **torture**, Saul commanded **his armor-bearer** to run him through with his sword. But, the armor-bearer was too afraid and unwilling to lift his hand against the king, so he refused Saul's command (31:4). As a result, Saul **fell on his own sword and died** (31:4-6). The battle was going so badly that **when the men of Israel** on both sides of the Jordan River saw that Saul was dead, they **fled** in panic and **abandoned** some **cities** so completely that the Philistines were able to settle **in them** (31:7).

31:8-10 The fact that the Philistines couldn't torture Saul and display him as a trophy while he was alive didn't keep them from dishonoring his body. They beheaded him, pinned his corpse on the wall at **Bethshan**, a few miles from Gilboa, and put his armor in the **temple of** their gods as a sign of the power of their deities over the Lord (31:8-10). Saul's disobedience to God and complete spiritual collapse ended tragically—not just for him and his family, but also for the people of Israel who had insisted that he be their king and who had ignored God's warnings about their choice. Now, their king was dead, his family was decimated, Israel's army was shattered, and the nation had lost part of its territory. Worst of all, the name of the Lord had been dishonored.

Importantly, Saul still could have enjoyed God's blessing if he had chosen to obey the Lord with all of his heart. But, Saul's half-hearted attitude toward God's commands and quickness to excuse himself and blame others revealed the flaws of character that God knew would disqualify him as king. The author of 1 Chronicles summarized Saul's reign this way: "Saul died for his unfaithfulness to the LORD because he did not keep the LORD's word. He even consulted a medium for guidance . . . . So the LORD put him to death and turned the kingdom over to David son of Jesse" (1 Chr 10:13-14).

31:11-13 The people **of Jabesh-gilead** had been rescued from the Ammonites by Saul many years earlier (see 11:1-11), and here they showed their gratitude. **Their brave men** made a dangerous, all-night trip to recover the bodies of Saul and his sons from Beth-shan and dispose of them properly (31:11-13). The people of Jabesh **buried** their bones and observed **seven days** of fasting for Saul and his sons (31:13).

The grief they expressed in this fast was genuine. All Israel could rightly share in it. King Saul's sin and rejection of the Lord's will had brought destruction and shame on the whole kingdom. The nation had reached a low point that only God could lift it out of. As it turned out, he was prepared to do just that through another king, one who was a "man after his own heart" (1 Sam 13:1).

2 SAMUEL

INTRODUCTION

Author

See discussion in 1 Samuel.

Historical Background

See discussion in 1 Samuel.

Message and Purpose

See discussion in 1 Samuel.

Outline

I.   Coronation and Conflicts (1:1–5:5)
II. Jerusalem, the Davidic Covenant, and Military Victory (5:6–10:19)
III. David's Sin and Its Consequences (11:1–14:33)
IV. A Son's Rebellion and Its Consequences (15:1–20:26)
V.   Final Years as King (21:1–24:25)

VIDEO   INTRO

www.bhpublishinggroup.com/qr/te/09_00

2 SAMUEL

I. CORONATION AND CONFLICTS (1:1–5:5)

1:1-4 The opening verses of 2 Samuel pick up right where 1 Samuel left off. This book is devoted to David's forty-year reign as king. It also includes the establishment of the Lord's covenant with David, through which the promised Messiah would come. Despite David's faults and those of his descendants, this was a unilateral, unconditional promise that God would keep. The author of 2 Samuel wants his readers to see the events of David's kingship against the backdrop of the Davidic covenant. He also wanted to encourage them in faithfulness to the Lord—something their ancestors frequently failed to achieve. Although earthly kings often fail, the true King of Israel is always on his throne and will never abandon his people or his promises.

The story continues after David's defeat of **the Amalekites** (see 1 Samuel 30) and his return to **Ziklag** (1:1). Though David and his men were victorious, the Israelite army under King Saul had not been. A straggler appeared at Ziklag with tragic news **from Saul's camp**: Israel's forces had been defeated by the Philistines, and **Saul and his son Jonathan [were] dead** (1:2-4).

1:5-10 The young man who reported this to David gave firsthand details of how he knew Saul and Jonathan were gone, even telling David that he had killed Saul himself at the wounded king's request (1:6-10). He also presented Saul's **crown** and **armband** as gifts to David, Israel's new king (1:10).

1:11-16 It's important to note that the man was lying about his role in Saul's death. The author of 1–2 Samuel has already informed us that Saul committed suicide (see 1 Sam 31:4-6). Moreover, the fact that the man "happened to be on Mount Gilboa" (1:6) at the moment of a major battle is a pretty sketchy story. We don't know if David suspected the man was lying, but he judged the man according to his own testimony. Most likely, he was robbing corpses after the battle (and before "the next day" when "the Philistines came to strip the slain"; see 1 Sam 31:8). When he found Saul dead, he probably saw it as an opportunity to curry favor with the soon-to-be king. He may have thought, "If I say I killed Saul, David will reward me generously!"

Though the man no doubt thought he was bringing David happy news for which he might be rewarded, he didn't realize that he was actually digging his own grave. The man was **the son of a resident alien** (1:13). As such, he was subject to King Saul and should have shown reverence for the king rather than a willingness to take his life. *Strike one.* He was also **an Amalekite** (1:13). The Amalekites had opposed Israel during the exodus, and the Lord had commanded Saul to destroy them all (see 1 Sam 15:1-3). *Strike two.* By his own admission (whether true or not), the man **killed the LORD's anointed** (1:10, 16). David had two opportunities to end Saul's life, but he chose to leave Saul in God's hands (see 1 Sam 24, 26). This Amalekite should have done the same. *Strike three.* So, David had him executed (1:15).

1:17-21 The rest of the chapter shows why David became well-known as a poet and musician in Israel. Many of the Psalms bear his name. The power and emotion in his **lament** are incredible (1:17). David was not only heartsick, but also deeply concerned for the honor of Saul and Jonathan and, ultimately, for the God of Israel. David could not bear the thought **of the uncircumcised** gloating in victory over God's king and army. If the men's deaths were announced in the cities of **Gath** or **Ashkelon, the daughters of the Philistines** would **rejoice**—as the daughters of Israel had rejoiced at the victories of David and Saul (1:20; see 1 Sam 18:7). David even called down a curse on the **mountains of Gilboa**, the place where Saul and Jonathan fell (1:21).

1:22-27 David's tribute to the military prowess of **Saul and Jonathan** was appropriate. Saul had proved to be unfit spiritually to be Israel's king, but he was a brave warrior who led his army in many battles. And Jonathan had proven his own courage, leading daring raids that helped turn the tide (1:22-23). Together, father and son fell **in the thick of battle** (1:25). Nevertheless, they were **mighty** (1:27)

David's expression of grief and brotherly **love** for Jonathan is especially poignant (1:26). These two men had made a covenant of friendship and lifelong loyalty to each other (see 1 Sam 20:14-17, 42; 23:15-18). And their bond was not broken by death, as David would soon go to great lengths to care for and protect Jonathan's crippled son Mephibosheth (see 2 Sam 9).

An era in Israel's history was over, ending in tragedy for the royal family and the nation itself.

2:1-7 With David's period of mourning complete, it was time to look to the future and claim the throne of Israel that was rightly his. He **inquired of the LORD** as to his next step and was told to go **to Hebron**, located about twenty miles south of Jerusalem in the territory of Judah (2:1). There **the men of Judah . . . anointed David king over the house of Judah** (2:4). But, he was not yet king over all of Israel, a fact serving as an early indication of the coming division between the northern territories, which would one day become Israel, and the southern territories, which would be called Judah.

David also learned that **the men of Jabesh-gilead** had **buried Saul** (2:4). Therefore, he promised to show them **the same goodness** they had shown to Saul (2:6). But, he also wanted them to affirm their loyalty to him as their new king (2:7).

2:8-11 The extent of the division between the north and the south became evident when **Abner**, the **commander of Saul's army**, set up Saul's weak son **Ish-bosheth** (whose name meant "man of shame") as king **over all Israel** instead of recognizing David's legitimate rule (2:8-9). As will become clear as the story unfolds, Abner was the real power behind the throne (see 3:6-11). This rebellion against David (and against the Lord) would lead to civil war, with Israelite brother against brother for the **two years** Ish-bosheth reigned over Israel (2:10). David would remain in **Hebron** for **seven years and six months**, until he moved his throne and capital to Jerusalem (2:11; see 5:6-12).

2:12-23 The conflict started in a way very familiar to the readers of 1 Samuel. Just as David and Goliath had fought as representatives of their armies to determine the outcome of the battle between the Israelites and the Philistines (see 1 Sam 17), Abner suggested a similar contest to **Joab**, his counterpart as the commander of David's army (2:12-14). When the contest ended in a tie, a fierce battle broke out, including the dogged pursuit of Abner by **Asahel**, a brother of Joab (2:17-20). Abner tried to make Asahel give up, but Asahel persisted until Abner killed him (2:21-23).

2:24-32 Joab and **Abisahi**, his other brother, took up the pursuit until Abner's army rallied around him. Abner persuaded Joab to stop on the grounds that it would only lead to further bloodshed between **brothers** (2:24-26). Joab called off the chase, which allowed Abner and his army to return to their headquarters at **Mahanaim** (2:27-29). Joab and David's army counted their losses: twenty men in all. But, they had inflicted eighteen times that many casualties on Abner's men (2:30-31). They took Asahel's body and buried it in his hometown of **Bethlehem** and returned to David at Hebron (2:32). But, Joab did not forget what Abner had done to his brother Asahel. He would wait for the right moment to take his revenge.

3:1-5 This **long war** was not just between two rival armies and their commanders, but between two kingdoms—and it's clear that God was blessing **the house of David**, which **was growing stronger** (3:1). The author lists David's first six sons, each born to a different mother (3:2-5). Though acquiring many wives was a practice of ancient kings, it was not to be the practice of Israel's king (see Deut 17:17). At least one of David's marriages was made to form an alliance with a foreign power: **Maacah** was **the daughter of King Talmai of Geshur** (3:3).

The names of three of his sons—**Amnon**, **Absalom**, and **Adonijah** (3:2-4)—will appear later in David's story. Unfortunately, as a consequence of David's own sins of adultery and murder, God's judgment would visit his family and bring the king much grief (see 11:1–12:15). These three sons would themselves commit heinous sins, including incestuous rape, murder, and rebellion.

3:6-11 Things began to change when Ish-bosheth accused Abner of sleeping with Saul's **concubine**, **Rizpah** (3:7). Such an action was considered an attempt to lay claim to a king's throne. Abner flew into a rage and accused Ish-bosheth of calling him a traitor. Abner had so much power that **Ish-bosheth did not dare to respond to Abner because he was afraid of him** (3:11).

3:12-16 Abner then pledged his loyalty to David and offered to make a **covenant** with him (3:12). The king accepted the offer on condition that Abner would bring David his first wife, **Michal** (3:12-13). Michal was Saul's daughter whom he had given to David; later, he gave her to another man while David was a fugitive (see 1 Sam 18:27; 25:44). There had never been a divorce, so Michal was taken from **Paltiel** and given to David, legal son-in-law to Saul and rightful heir to the throne (3:15).

3:17-19 Abner then set about building support for David among **the elders of Israel** (3:17). He reminded them of God's promise

that David was God's chosen **servant** to save his people from **the Philistines** and **all Israel's enemies** (3:18). Abner also approached **the Benjamites**, Saul's own tribe, to get their agreement to back David. Then, he brought the good news of his negotiations to David at **Hebron** (3:19).

3:20-23 David was happy to receive Abner and his entourage; he prepared a **banquet** to host them (3:20). Abner promised to go throughout **all Israel** and unite the people as one under David so that he could be king over the entire nation (3:21). David was obviously pleased, and the author is careful to note three times that David sent Abner on his mission **in peace** (3:21-23). That would become important in light of what was about to happen. When **Joab returned** to Hebron, he was informed of Abner's visit (3:22-23).

3:24-25 Joab was furious that the killer of his brother Asahel had been treated kindly by David. He went to the king to accuse Abner of deceiving him as a spy. It's hard to know for certain what Joab's motives were. Revenge for the death of his brother? Protection of David's throne? Jealousy that Abner might be a rival for command of David's army? Perhaps all of the above.

3:26-27 Assuming Abner was engaging in deceit, Joab left David and concocted some deceit of his own. While **David was unaware**, he sent a message to Abner to come back, probably saying that David wanted to see him again (3:26). When Joab met Abner, he approached **as if to speak to him privately**. Then, he murdered Abner as **revenge for the death of Asahel**, his brother (3:27; see 2:21-23). Joab's other **brother Abishai** was also involved in the plot (see 3:30).

3:28-29 David was grief-stricken at the news of Abner's murder. He had made a covenant with him to bring about peace in Israel and to consolidate his kingdom (see 3:12-13). So, he wanted to avoid the appearance that he had anything to do with Joab's underhanded plot. David declared that he was **forever innocent before the LORD** and pronounced a severe curse on Joab and his descendants.

3:30-35 David showed his genuine grief for Abner in every way possible. Consolidating all of Israel under his rule depended on it. He knew how important it was that the people of Israel understood that he was not gaining the throne through evil means. He commanded mourning for Abner (3:31), **walked behind the coffin** (3:31), **wept** at the **tomb** (3:32), composed **a lament** as he had done for Saul (3:33-34; see 1:17-27), and fasted (3:35).

3:36-39 David's innocence was accepted by **all the troops and all Israel** (3:37). He lamented the violent nature of Joab and his brother, **the sons of Zeruiah**, but he did not discipline them for their deeds (3:38-39). The fact that Zeruiah was David's half-sister may explain his reluctance to take action (see 17:25; 1 Chr 2:16).

4:1-3 The death of Abner spread panic throughout the northern half of Israel where **Ish-bosheth** was king (4:1). He was a weak ruler, and with Abner gone, the people may have feared that David would invade and conquer them. Here the author introduces two **Benjaminites** who had served Saul, **Baanah** and **Rechab** (4:2). But, before completing this account, the author inserts a parenthetical note.

4:4 Mephibosheth was the son of Jonathan, Saul's son and David's trusted friend. When **Saul and Jonathan** were killed by the Philistines, Mephibosheth **was five years old**. When his nanny fled with him in fear, she dropped him, and his **feet** became **crippled**. The author includes this note here to prepare the reader for the later story of David's kindness to Mephibosheth, out of his love for Jonathan (see chapter 9).

4:5-8 Returning to **Rechab and Baanah**, the author tells us that they took matters into their own hands and cold-heartedly assassinated Ish-bosheth. He was defenseless in his bed when they murdered him (4:5-7). That they were evil men with selfish motives becomes even more evident, for they tried to curry favor with David as the new king of Israel. They took **Ish-bosheth's head to David at Hebron**, hoping to be rewarded (4:8).

4:9-12 Little did they know that another man had similarly hoped for the king's approval by eradicating David's rival, but things didn't turn out so well for him (see 1:1-16). David essentially told them, "The last guy who did something like this was indeed rewarded— with death!" (3:10). The cowardly nature of the attack against **a righteous man** horrified David (4:11). There was no evidence that Ish-bosheth was seeking to take David's life. **So David gave orders**, and his men **killed Rechab and Baanah**. Cutting off the killers' **hands and feet**—the parts of their bodies used in the murder—served as a gruesome way of denouncing their wicked actions and warning anyone else who might think of committing a similar act (4:12). Furthermore, David needed to make it clear to all of Israel that he'd had nothing to do with this deed.

5:1-2 God was sovereignly controlling events to bring David to the national throne. **All the tribes of Israel came to David at Hebron**. They acknowledged several important facts that made David the right choice to rule over the nation. First, they were all **flesh and blood** (5:1)—that is, they were members of the twelve tribes of Israel, descendants of Abraham, Isaac, and Jacob. In other words, they were brothers. Second, David was their national military hero, a revered leader. Even back when Saul was king, David had fought Israel's battles. Third and most important, they recognized God's calling and anointing on David, for God had said to him, **You will shepherd my people Israel, and you will be ruler** (5:2).

5:3 Previously, the men of Judah, David's own tribe, had anointed him as king (see 2:4). But now, **all the elders of Israel** came to **Hebron** and **anointed David king over Israel**. It had been a long road since the day God had first commanded Samuel to anoint a young shepherd as the one to replace King Saul (see 1 Sam 16:11-13). David had endured much hardship and persecution. But, through it all, he trusted the Lord and waited on his perfect timing. Though David was by no means perfect (as 2 Samuel will soon reveal), his willingness to obtain God's purpose for him in God's way is a model for others to follow. David was God's kingdom man.

5:4-5 At age **thirty**, David became king, ruling **over Judah seven years and six months** and **thirty-three years over all Israel**, too (5:4-5). Thus, he reigned over God's people for **forty years** (5:4). The Davidic dynasty had begun. And through it, the Son of David, the Messiah, would one day come (Matt 1:1).

II. JERUSALEM, THE DAVIDIC COVENANT, AND MILITARY VICTORY (5:6–10:19)

5:6 Until he was anointed king over all Israel, David had been reigning from Hebron. Now, he set out to conquer a new capital, a city that would become one of the most well-known in history. David did not know at this point that his choice would become the holy city, the place of God's temple. But, God would make that clear in time.

This would be a capital for a united Israel that was past the hostility of the civil war between Saul's house and David's. It would need to be in neutral territory, so David selected a city on the border of the lands of Benjamin and Judah—the tribes of Saul and David.

The Jebusites, one of the Canaanite peoples, didn't think much of Israel's new ruler. In fact, they felt so secure in their mountain stronghold of Jerusalem (formerly, Jebus; see Josh 18:28) that they claimed **the blind and lame** among their people could **repel** David's troops. The city was easily defensible on three sides, an important feature in the ancient world.

5:7-9 The Jebusite fortress seemed impregnable, but David knew there was a way **through the water shaft** under the wall (5:8). According to 1 Chronicles 11:6, Joab found the access and was given the command of David's army. David conquered Jerusalem and **the stronghold of Zion . . . which he named the city of David** (5:7, 9). Verse 9 seems to indicate that David filled in the area between the hills to level the city, or he may have built embankments to protect Jerusalem on the north at its most vulnerable point.

5:10 David became more and more powerful. As king, this was certainly necessary. But, the most significant fact was that **the LORD God of Armies was with him**. Tremendous earthly strength is useless unless heaven is on your side. David was powerful because the heavenly armies were fighting for him—as he would soon learn (see commentary on 5:20-25).

5:11-16 Once David was secure in his capital, other kingdoms had to come to grips with the new force. **King Hiram of Tyre** did it peacefully, sending envoys, supplies, and builders to construct **a palace for David** (5:11). David also **took more concubines and wives** (5:13). This was a violation of God's law (see Deut 17:17) and would lead to grief for him.

5:17-19 Other foreign powers didn't take as kindly to the new king. The Philistines, whom David had battled and deceived for years, were determined to bring him down (5:17-18). But, the Lord made it clear to David that he need not fear. He vowed to **hand the Philistines over** to David (5:19).

5:20-25 In two decisive battles, God gave David victory in radically different ways. In the first battle, the Israelites **burst out against** the Philistines like a roaring **flood** and swept them away (5:20). On the second occasion, the Israelites surprised the enemy from behind. This time, God told David to wait until he heard **the sound of marching in the tops of the balsam trees**. When this happened, he was to attack, **for then the LORD [would] have gone out ahead of [him]** (5:24). In other words, God himself would lead the armies of heaven in the charge against David's enemies.

When God goes before you, you have no need to fear—but you *do* have to follow. God will clear the way before you, but the victory isn't yours unless you do things his way. **David did exactly as the LORD commanded him**, and the battle was won (5:25).

6:1-2 David turned his attention to God's throne—the ark of the covenant. This sacred chest, which **bears the Name, the name of the LORD of Armies who is enthroned between the cherubim** (6:2), had been neglected during Saul's reign. But, unlike Saul, David was zealous for the worship of the Lord. He understood the importance of the ark to Israel's worship and spiritual well-being.

Moreover, David knew that God was the heavenly King who stood behind his own earthly kingship. Therefore, it was essential that God's throne be brought into Israel's capital city. This would not be an everyday event but, rather, a time of great celebration. David himself wrote of the day, "Lift up your heads, you gates! Rise us, ancient doors! Then the King of glory will come in" (Ps 24:7).

6:3-5 David and his troops went to **Abinadab's house**, where the ark was located, and prepared for the journey to Jerusalem (6:3). But, for some inexplicable reason, David disobeyed God's explicit commands regarding how the ark was to be transported. God's throne was to be moved the way God had demanded. The Levites alone were to carry the ark with poles inserted through its rings (see Exod 25:12-15; 37:3-5; Deut 10:8). Instead, David and his men **set the ark of God on a new cart** (6:3). The ark was once transported this way—by the Philistines (see 1 Sam 6:7). But, God's people should have known better. They had God's revealed Word available to them. All their sincere worship (6:5) could not make up for neglecting God's will.

6:6-7 When **the oxen** pulling the cart **stumbled**, a man named **Uzzah**, who was guiding the cart, **reached out** and touched the ark to steady it (6:6). **Then the LORD's anger burned against Uzzah, and God struck him dead ... for his irreverence** (6:7). The Israelites had failed to treat God as holy or "set apart" from his creation. "Holy, holy, holy is the LORD of Armies," the seraphim would declare to Isaiah. "His glory fills the whole earth" (Isa 6:3). Forgetting that was a costly mistake.

6:8-11 David was angry because of the LORD's outburst against Uzzah (6:8). Was David angry with God—a sin for which he later repented? Was he angry with Uzzah for touching the ark? Or, was he angry with himself for being foolish? Whatever the reason, **David feared the LORD that day** (6:9). Even though he sincerely loved God, he had not taken him seriously enough. That day, however, he realized the awesome holiness of the Lord in a new way. And, afraid to proceed, David diverted the ark **to the house of Obed-edom of Gath**, who was mightily **blessed** for the **three months** the ark remained there (6:10-11).

6:12-14 The report of Obed-edom's blessing convinced David that it was time to finish his task of bringing the ark to Jerusalem—this time in the right way. Notice that the author mentions **those carrying the ark of the LORD**. This is no doubt a reference to the Levites transporting the ark properly, in accordance with God's Word. David also offered sacrifices (6:13). The king was now fully following his King's agenda, and he got his praise back on, **dancing with all his might** (6:14).

6:15-20 As David was **leaping and dancing before the LORD**, his wife **Michal** saw him. Apparently, as far as she was concerned, these were not the dignified actions of a king. So, **she despised him** (6:16). When the ark was in its new home and the celebrations were complete (6:17-19), David went home to an angry and embarrassed wife. Three times in this chapter, Michal is referred to as **Saul's daughter** (6:20; also 6:16, 23). By emphasizing this relationship, the author wants us to know that Michal had the same uncaring attitude toward the ark and toward the true worship of God that her father had.

6:21-23 For David, worshiping the Lord from the heart was more important than his appearance before others. The God who had appointed him as **ruler over ... Israel** deserved his praise (6:21). David was willing to **dishonor** and **humble** himself, if God were exalted in the process (6:22).

Will you live life from God's perspective or from your own? Michal viewed the extravagant worship of God from an earthly perspective and considered it vulgar and embarrassing (6:20). As a result, God closed her womb (6:23). David viewed the worship of God from a heavenly perspective, and it brought him tremendous joy. For this, he was **honored** (6:22).

7:1 In chapter 7, we have one of the Bible's watershed moments. David was not simply the next king in line after Saul. He was *the* anointed king of Israel, the Lord's sovereign choice to establish a dynasty through which the promised Messiah, the Lord Jesus Christ, would come. In spite of David's own sins and those of the kings who would follow him, God was about to establish an unconditional covenant that would guarantee the eventual eternal reign of the ultimate Son of David.

Though he was previously a fugitive in the wilderness running from King Saul, David was now a king living in a **palace**. Though David was a courageous and mighty warrior who had slain "his tens of thousands" (1 Sam 18:7), the author makes it clear that **the LORD had given him rest on every side from all his enemies**. All that David had was from God. (That's a truth that too many believers are quick to forget with relation to themselves.)

7:2-3 David was very aware of how God had blessed him. That's what prompted him to visit the Lord's prophet. He told **Nathan** that he felt uneasy living in his **cedar** palace, while **the ark of God** was housed in a mere **tent** (7:2). Sensing the king's zeal for God and knowing that God was with him, Nathan encouraged David to do whatever he had in **mind** (7:3). But, the Lord had other plans.

7:4-10 That night, God gave Nathan a word for David. With regard to building a temple, God's response was essentially, "Thanks, but no thanks." From the time of the exodus to David's day, God had never demanded a **house** from the Israelites. So, there was no need for David to feel sorry for God (7:4-7). Instead, God reminded David that he had taken this shepherd boy from humble beginnings and made him king, even as he took Israel from being a nation of slaves and had planted them in their land (7:8-10). Far from needing provision, God had always been the Provider.

7:11-16 Don't miss the shock value of this statement: **The LORD himself will make a house for you** (7:11). God was engaging in

word play. Instead of David building God a house (that is, constructing a temple for him), God would build David a house (that is, he would raise up a kingly dynasty for him). God promised that he would **establish** the **kingdom** of David's **descendant** (7:12). It was this king who would **build a house** (a temple) for the **name** of the Lord (7:13). God would be his **father**, and the king would be his **son** (7:14). If he rebelled, God would **discipline him**, but his **faithful love** would never depart from him (7:14-15). Thus, the **house and kingdom** and **throne** of David would be **established forever** (7:16).

Clearly, the near-term fulfillment of these promises would be David's son Solomon. God would indeed establish his kingdom, paving the way for Israel's golden age. Solomon would be the one to build the temple. And, when Solomon (and subsequent kings) sinned, God's discipline would fall.

But, ultimately, it would take more than a mere man to fulfill the promises of this Davidic covenant. To have a kingdom and throne established forever, the God-man, Jesus Christ, was needed. The divine Son of God fulfills the Father-Son relationship in the truest sense. As Matthew and Luke show, Jesus in his humanity is a descendent of David and heir to the throne (see Matt 1:1-16; Luke 3:23-38). As the angel proclaimed to Mary, he is "the Son of the Most High, and the Lord God will give him the throne of his father David" (Luke 1:32). "He will reign forever and ever" (Rev 11:15). Jesus will take up his right and rule from David's throne in Jerusalem when he returns in glory to reign in his millennial kingdom. Then, he will rule for all eternity as King of kings and Lord of lords.

7:17-29 When Nathan **reported** all of this to David, the king was overwhelmed. He responded with a prayer of praise and humble worship, recognizing his unworthiness. He asked God, **Who am I . . . that you have brought me this far?** (7:18). (If that isn't the testimony of your own heart, you don't yet see the depth of your sin and the lavish grace and kindness of God.) David also magnified the Lord for doing great things for him, for Israel, and for future generations (7:19-24). Finally, David prayed that God would **fulfill** his **promise** (7:25-29).

In this last part of David's request, we see a reminder that when you don't know what else to pray, you should ask God to fulfill his promises, because "if we ask anything according to his will, he hears us" (1 John 5:14). So, like David, pray that the promises God has made in eternity become a reality in your history.

8:1-2 God had promised that David would have "rest from all [his] enemies" (7:11), and now he set about to accomplish it. David began by defeating and subjugating Israel's ever-present foes to the west, the **Philistines** (8:1). **He also defeated the Moabites**, who lived to the southeast of Israel, and he executed two-thirds of their captive troops. Then, they became **David's subjects** (8:2).

8:3-6 David's expansion of his kingdom continued in every direction. His campaigns in the north included the conquest of **Hadadezer . . . king of Zobah**, whose area lay just north of Damascus (8:3). **When the Arameans of Damascus came to assist King Hadadezer . . . David struck down twenty-two thousand Aramean men** (8:5). David then **placed garrisons in Aram**, a kingdom that would be later known as Syria, and also made these people his **subjects** who paid him **tribute**. The reason for David's unbroken success was unmistakable: **The LORD made David victorious wherever he went** (8:6).

8:7-8 David also took large amounts of plunder from his defeated enemies in the form of the **gold shields of Hadadezer's officers** and **huge quantities of bronze from Betah and Berothai, Hadadezer's cities**, which he took to Jerusalem and added to his royal coffers.

8:9-12 Not every kingdom north of Israel was sad to see David march north and conquer territory. A king named **Toi** ruled over **Hamath**, another Aramean city-state that was about a hundred miles north of Damascus. Toi was so glad **that David had defeated the entire army of Hadadezer** that he sent his son **Joram** to David with expensive gifts to congratulate him on his victory, because **Toi and Hadadezer had fought many wars** (8:9-10). As he did with all his spoil and gifts, **David also dedicated these to the LORD** (8:11).

Notice the pattern: "The LORD made David victorious" (8:6), and David dedicated his spoils to the Lord (8:11). The gracious provision of God should inspire our gratefulness and giving, too.

8:13-14 Turning to the south, David gained widespread fame when he defeated an army of **eighteen thousand Edomites in Salt Valley** (8:13). These were the descendants of Esau and proved to be bitter enemies of the Israelites. David also subjugated the Edomites to make sure they didn't rise up against him again. As before (see 8:6), the author tells us that **the LORD made David victorious wherever he went** (8:14). God's might enabled David's army.

By now David ruled over a kingdom territory promised to Abraham by covenant (see Gen 15:18). But, this was not the fulfillment of the Abrahamic covenant, because David did not occupy *all* of this territory, and Israel did not possess it *permanently*. This covenant will not be fulfilled until Jesus Christ returns to rule in his millennial kingdom.

8:15-18 At this point, David's reign over all of Israel was in its relatively early stages. But, he still needed religious, political, and military leaders to help him in **administering justice and righteousness for all his people** (8:15). **Joab** was military commander (8:16). The priests **Zadok** and **Ahimelech** were from two different priestly lines descended from Aaron (8:17). Ahimelech was from the line of Eli, whose family was cursed because of the sins of Eli's sons, Hophni and Phinehas, and Eli's failure to restrain them. Samuel had said this family line would come to an end (see 1 Sam 3:10-14). The line of Zadok, however, would continue on through the end of the Old Testament. **Benaiah** was the leader of **the Cherethites and the Pelethites**, elite troops of David. His **sons** served as **chief officials** (8:18).

9:1-4 David never forgot his covenant promise of friendship with Saul's son Jonathan. He wanted to honor that promise with **kindness** to **anyone** in Saul's family **for Jonathan's sake** (9:1). **Ziba** had been a **servant** in Saul's house who had kept up with the family (9:2-3). He knew that Jonathan had a crippled son,

Mephibosheth (introduced in 4:4), and Ziba knew that he was living in **Lo-debar** on the opposite side of the Jordan River—possibly in hiding (9:3-4).

9:5-7 David immediately sent for **Mephibosheth**, who bowed down to the ground and **paid homage** to David, perhaps not knowing the fate that awaited him as the heir of the disgraced former king (9:5-6). But, David quickly laid the young man's fears to rest by repeating his covenant promise to Jonathan and assuring Mephibosheth that he was to be the recipient of that blessing. These blessings included all his **grandfather Saul's fields** and a permanent seat at the king's **table** (9:7).

9:8-13 Mephibosheth was understandably grateful and deeply humbled because he knew that he had done nothing to deserve this favor from David's hand (9:8). The change in circumstances came as a result of sheer grace. David also arranged for the administration of Mephibosheth's new estate. He assigned Ziba and his family to manage the grant he had just made to Mephibosheth (9:9-11). The land David had restored was to be cultivated to feed the rest of Mephibosheth's household, while he himself lived in Jerusalem and ate at the royal table with David.

There was no precedent in the ancient world for what David did on behalf of Mephibosheth. But then, there was no king like David, a type and forerunner of Jesus Christ, who took mercy on us as crippled sinners and extended to us his kindness (see Titus 3:4-5).

10:1-2 Chapter 10 begins with another story of David's kindness. This time, however, his kindness was rejected, and he received gross insult in return. David sent a delegation to Ammon, the kingdom directly east of Israel, to express his sympathy at the death of **the king of the Ammonites** (10:1). The late king, **Nahash**, had been an enemy to Saul and Israel many years earlier (see 1 Sam 11:1-10). But, in later years, he had apparently shown some unnamed **kindness to** David. So, David wanted to express his condolences to Nahash's son **Hanun** (10:2).

10:3-5 Hanun had foolish counselors who had no love for Israel or her king. Without evidence, they accused David of sending his delegation as spies to scope out the capital so he could come with his army and **demolish it** (10:3). Unfortunately for Hanun and his people, he listened to his counselors and humiliated David's representatives by shaving their **beards** and exposing their nakedness (10:4). The men were understandably and **deeply humiliated** (10:5). David would not let the insult pass without response.

10:6-10 The Ammonites realized they had become repulsive to David, so they began preparing for war with Israel. Taking on a formidable enemy like David would require extra troops, so Hanun hired tens of thousands of mercenaries **from the Arameans**, and from the smaller kingdoms of **Maacah** and **Tob** (10:6). David **sent Joab and all the elite troops** (10:7). The enemy split their forces, with **the Ammonites** guarding the city while the mercenary troops **were in the field by themselves** (10:8). So, Joab also divided Israel's forces and sent **his brother Abishai** against the Ammonites while he attacked the Arameans (10:10).

10:11-14 Joab and Abishai agreed to help each other if one of their lines faltered and prayed for God's will to **be done** (10:11-12). As a result of their strategy (and God's help; see 8:6, 14), the Arameans **fled** from Joab, and when the Ammonites saw this they lost courage and retreated into their city (10:13-14). Thus, Israel won another great victory, and Joab called off the attack against the Ammonites. He and his forces returned in triumph to **Jerusalem** (10:13-14).

10:15-19 The Arameans, however, couldn't take their whipping, learn their lesson, and go home. Instead, **they regrouped** (10:15). **Hadadezer** called for even more troops and lined up for battle (10:16). This time, David responded in person. **He gathered all Israel** and engaged **the Arameans** in battle (10:17). The outcome was a foregone conclusion. David and Israel not only routed the enemy, but David also killed **Shobach commander of their army**, a devastating psychological blow to the Aramean troops (10:18). At last, the Arameans realized that fighting against David was a hopeless cause, so **they made peace with Israel and became their subjects** (10:19).As a man after God's own heart (see 1 Sam 13:14), David had been a faithful follower of God as a young shepherd, an unjustly persecuted fugitive, and then as a powerful king. God had blessed him with a powerful kingdom and rest from his enemies on every side. David's fame and power were at their height. Unfortunately for David and Israel, it was at this point that he faltered.

III. DAVID'S SIN AND ITS CONSEQUENCES (11:1–14:33)

11:1 In the ancient world, kings had control over the records of their reigns, so they could suppress their failures. But, this is not the case with the biblical records of kings. These chapters are hereby inspiration of the Holy Spirit. They serve as a warning to us (see 1 Cor 10:6, 11), reminding us that none of us is above sin. Even a man after God's own heart like David (see 1 Sam 13:14) can fail to guard his own heart and rebel against God's will. These chapters also help us understand the consequences of the king's sins. David, his family, and his kingdom would suffer much grief and rebellion as a result of his failure to fight off temptation.

The problem began **in the spring when kings march out to war**. Instead of joining his men in battle, David **sent Joab** and his army out while he **remained in Jerusalem**—for unnamed reasons. The author is making it clear from the first verse of the chapter that David should have been elsewhere fulfilling his responsibilities. It's often when we're not doing what we ought to be doing that temptation chooses to pounce.

11:2 David was **on the roof of the palace** one night when **he saw a woman bathing**—a **very beautiful woman**. David was at the height of his reign. He had been walking with God in victory as Israel's anointed king for twenty years. He was Israel's poet and singer who wrote many psalms. But, on that evening, this married man was captivated in all the wrong ways by someone else's wife. This was not an immoral man; this was not a man who wanted to fall. This was a man who put himself in a vulnerable position and let down his guard. The results would be costly.

11:3-4 It didn't take long for David to find out that the woman was **Bathsheba**, the wife of **Uriah the Hethite**, one of David's valued and loyal soldiers (1 Chr 11:26, 41). But, by now, nothing mattered to David except fulfilling his lust, so he **sent messengers to get her, and when she came to him, he slept with her** (11:4). Ultimately, we don't know how Bathsheba felt about this. But, we are given no reason to think that she was trying to seduce David. *He* stayed behind while his troops were fighting battles. *He* strolled on his rooftop when he should have been sleeping. *He* had another man's wife brought to him. David was the king, and his every order was to be obeyed. Bathsheba was a defenseless woman. The blame lies squarely on David.

11:5-8 David may have thought that his one-night-stand could be quickly forgotten. If so, he was wrong. Not long after, David received unexpected news from Bathsheba. Her message said, **I am pregnant** (11:5). The king had made the mistake of his life. But, instead of seeking to stop the damage by repentance, he made it infinitely worse by scheming. David brought **Uriah** back home from the battlefield and encouraged him to go home for a few days and enjoy time with his wife. David assumed that Uriah would take advantage of the opportunity to sleep with her, assume the coming baby was his own, and David would be off the hook (11:6-8).

11:9-13 No matter how hard David tried— even getting Uriah **drunk**—he couldn't get the faithful soldier to sleep with his wife. Uriah was too honorable to do that. He knew his fellow troops were away from their own wives, fighting the nation's battles (11:13).

The contrast between David's underhanded plotting and Uriah's open integrity could not be greater.

11:14-15 David was so desperate to bury his sin that he decided to bury Uriah. This is what sin will do to you, if you refuse to confess it and deal with it. When Uriah didn't do what David wanted, David went from being crafty to being cruel. He sent Uriah back to the battlefront where Israel's soldiers were besieging the Ammoniate capital of Rabbah. Unknowingly, the soldier carried his own death notice with him.

11:16-21 The man after God's own heart grew increasingly cold-hearted. Joab obeyed the king's orders recorded in verse 15, though there is no indication that he knew the reason for the poor man's sentence. As a result, Uriah **died** (11:16-17). Because Joab knew that David would want to know about it right away, he sent a **messenger** with news of the battle (11:18), cautioning him that the king might get mad at such suicidal military strategy (11:18-21). If that were to happen, Joab told the messenger to say, **Your servant Uriah the Hittite is dead also** (11:21). In other words, he was reminding him that the battle tactics had been employed to accomplish the king's desire.

11:22-25 The messenger delivered his news word for word, and David was satisfied (11:22-24). He was so hardened by his sin that he essentially sent this response **to Joab:** "Don't let Uriah's death bother you. You win some; you lose some. Everyone has to die sometime" (11:25). In other words, this godly man had become unrecognizable.

A person who is in moral sin may feel bad about it at first. But, if that sin is not dealt with, eventually the sinner's heart grows calloused. The conviction he should feel over his sin doesn't get through. He becomes spiritually numb, and sins begin to multiply.

11:26-27 Bathsheba **mourned for** her husband Uriah (11:26). Then, she became David's **wife** (11:27).

David, meanwhile, had stained his legacy with adultery and added murder to it. As far as David was concerned, the cover-up was complete following the marriage. Uriah was out of the way. The child would appear legitimate. The matter could be put to rest.

But, David had forgotten about his omniscient and omnipresent God, the one about whom David himself would write, "You understand my thoughts . . . Where can I flee from your presence? . . . Even the darkness is not dark to you" (Ps 139:2, 7, 12). David had acted in secret. But, nothing is hidden from the God who sees and knows all: **The Lord considered what David had done to be evil** (11:27).

12:1-4 The Lord sent **Nathan** the prophet to confront David (12:1). But, instead of simply laying out David's sin and calling for a confession, Nathan let David hang himself. He told a story of injustice. A **rich man** had taken advantage of a **poor man**, callously depriving him of his precious **ewe lamb**. Though the rich man had flocks beyond measure, he slaughtered **the poor man's lamb** and fed it to his guest (12:1-4).

12:5-6 The crime was so obvious and cruel that David jumped to the defense of the injured party. He was **infuriated** and said, **As the Lord lives, the man who did this deserves to die!** Because he has done this thing and shown no pity, he **must pay four lambs for that lamb.** Sadly, though, David had no idea that the tale was a parable of his own actions. The rich man represented David, the poor man represented Uriah, and the ewe lamb represented Bathsheba. David's sin had blinded him. In condemning the rich man, he condemned himself.

12:7-12 Nathan's reply was quick: **You are the man** (12:7). The prophet then recounted how God had blessed David and how David had sinned against God. The Lord had given David everything, including all that had been Saul's, which included Saul's **wives** (12:8), who would become servants of the king and his kingdom because there is no indication that David married them. David had repaid the Lord with wickedness (12:7-9). Then, Nathan pronounced God's judgment: **the sword will never leave your house** (12:10). From that day forward, David's family would be plagued by rape, murder, and rebellion. Part of David's humiliation would include having his **wives** taken from him and given **to another**—we'll later learn it was his own son Absalom—who would **sleep with them in broad daylight** (12:11; see 16:22).

12:13-18 David's eyes were finally opened. He responded as a man of God: **I have sinned against the LORD**. According to the law of Moses, David deserved to die for adultery and murder. Yet, God graciously forgave him and spared his life (12:13). Nevertheless, there would still be serious consequences, beginning with the death of Bathsheba's baby (12:14). The child **became deathly ill** (12:15).

Despite God's pronouncement through Nathan, **David pleaded with God for the boy**, fasting, praying, and hoping that God might change his mind (12:16). The members of his household saw David in such agony of soul that when the baby died, **David's servants were afraid to tell him** because they were afraid he might **do something desperate** (12:18).

12:19-23 David could tell by his servants' **whispering** that the infant had passed away (12:19). Realizing that God's will had been done, he gave up his fast and resumed his life (12:20). His servants were surprised at this sudden change in the king, but he replied that there was no longer any hope that the baby would come back to him because death was final (12:21-23).

12:24-25 Knowing that Bathsheba was also mourning their son, David **comforted** her, and she gave birth to **Solomon**, whose name sounds like the Hebrew word for "peace" (12:24). But, the Lord named him **Jedidiah**, which means "Beloved of the Lord." This was a gracious sign that God had not removed his love from David (12:25).

12:26-31 Joab urged David to come to **Rabbah** and finish the battle—lest Joab win the fight and gain the honor instead of the king (12:26-28). **David assembled all the troops** and finished off **Rabbah**, even taking the **crown** off the king's head (12:29-30). He put the people to forced labor, as he did to **all the Ammonite cities**, then **returned to Jerusalem** (12:31).

13:1-5 The Lord had forgiven David's grievous sins of adultery and murder (12:13), but he had also told David that there would be disastrous related consequences for his family (12:10). In the following chapters, those consequences unfold. David's multiple wives had given him sons and daughters who were half-brothers and half-sisters. Polygamy was about to come back to haunt David.

David's son Amnon became **infatuated with** his half-sister **Tamar**, the full sister of **Absalom** (13:1). Amnon's **shrewd** cousin **Jonadab** offered to help him with his "problem" (13:3). Jonadab suggested a deceitful plan that would enable him to be alone with Tamar. Even worse, he would use David, who was clueless about his intentions, to help him (13:5).

13:6-14 The trap was set. Poor, unsuspecting Tamar was sent by royal request to her "sick" half-brother's bedroom (13:6-7). Once they were alone, she prepared to feed him (13:9-10). But, **he grabbed her** and made his intensions clear (13:11). Tamar struggled and pleaded with him not to **disgrace** her by committing such an **outrage** (13:12). To commit this act would bring **humiliation** on Tamar and cause Amnon to be regarded as **one of the outrageous fools in Israel**. She even suggested that he ask the king to give her to him as a wife instead (13:13). But Amnon couldn't be persuaded; he was dead set on his sin. **He refused to listen to her, and because he was stronger than she was, he disgraced her by raping her** (13:14). Like his father David before him (11:2-4), Amnon was blinded by lust and couldn't see the inevitable consequences of such actions.

13:15-18 True to his low character, **Amnon hated Tamar with such intensity that the hatred he hated her with was greater than the love he had loved her with** (13:15) after he had violated her. Clearly, his "love" was nothing more than self-centered lust. This is confirmed by his response to her afterward. Tamar pleaded with him not to send her away. Because he had robbed her of her virginity by violating her, he ought to marry her. Otherwise, she would likely have no other prospects for marriage. To cast her out would be **much worse than the great wrong** he'd **already done** (13:16). But, Amnon simply **threw her out** (13:17-18). Rather than setting things right, Amnon compounded his sin, just as his father had done.

13:19-22 Tamar **went away** in distress and mourning (13:19). Seeing her grief, Absalom quieted her and told her to keep the incident to herself (13:20). But, David heard of it and **was furious** (13:21). Amazingly, though, the king did nothing to punish Amnon. The reader might wonder at this point if David's moral resolve had been weakened by the knowledge of his own past sexual sin. Regardless, his failure to act was itself an act that spoke volumes. **Absalom**, on the other hand, would act. He **hated Amnon** for disgracing **his sister** (13:22). So, he patiently bided his time, looking for a chance at revenge.

13:23-27 Two years passed, but Absalom had not forgotten. He held a festival in connection with the sheep-shearing, a common practice in those days, and invited David and **all the king's sons** (13:23-24). When David declined, Absalom insisted that the king send all of his sons, including **Amnon**, his first-born (13:25-26).

13:28-36 During the feast, **Absalom's young men** followed their master's orders and killed **Amnon**, while **the rest of the king's sons got up, and each fled on his mule** (13:28-29). Before they arrived home, a false report came to David that all of his sons had been killed, but that was quickly proven false (13:30-33). David was reunited with his remaining sons, and they all **wept very bitterly** (13:35-36).

13:37-39 Absalom fled to the home of his maternal grandfather, King **Talmai** of Geshur (see 3:3), where he stayed for **three years** (13:37-38). **King David longed to go to Absalom, for David had finished grieving over Amnon's death** (13:39). Thus, the stage was set for Absalom's return to Jerusalem. Unfortunately, the consequences of David's sins were only beginning. Things would become worse.

14:1-7 The story of Absalom's return to Jerusalem from his self-imposed exile has as many plot twists as a Hollywood film. David wanted Absalom back, but he couldn't just send for him and pretend everything was fine or the people might think the king didn't take Absalom's crime of murder seriously.

Joab, David's army commander, came up with a reunion plan and persuaded a **wise woman** from **Tekoa**, located about ten miles south of Jerusalem, to carry it out (14:1-3). She pretended to be a **widow** who **had two sons**, one having killed the other (14:4-6). She claimed that **the whole clan** wanted to put the guilty brother **to death for the life of the brother he murdered**. But, if this happened, her **husband's name** would die out (14:7).

14:8-11 David promised to **issue a command** on the woman's behalf to prevent this from happening (14:8). But she pressed on, telling David that she would not hold him or his throne responsible if he failed to stop the revenge killing of her son (14:9). David was patient with her, saying that anyone who did anything would have to answer to him (14:10). But, even that wasn't good enough. We don't know if David saw where this was going, but he agreed to the woman's request to swear by the Lord to protect her son and prevent the shedding of his blood. David vowed, **As the LORD lives . . . not a hair of your son will fall to the ground** (14:11).

14:12-14 With this solemn vow in hand, the woman pulled a Nathan on David, saying in her own way, "You are the man" (see 12:1-7). In speaking **as he did about this matter**, she said, David had **pronounced his own guilt** (14:13). David knew she was right; he was willing to grant clemency to some unnamed murderer while not granting it to his own son.

14:15-24 The woman then tried to make it sound like her real concern was her own case and not David and Absalom (14:15-17). But, David was now wise to her; he figured out that **Joab** was behind it all (14:19-20). Even here, however, David did not get angry at Joab's scheming, realizing that he had the king's interests at heart. David gave Joab permission to bring Absalom back to Jerusalem (14:21). Yet, David wasn't ready for a full reconciliation. His son could come back under one condition: **He may return to his house, but he may not see [David's] face** (14:24). Such a half-hearted attempt at reconciliation was bound to fail.

14:25-26 The author wastes no time building a portfolio on Absalom: **No man in all Israel was as handsome and highly praised as [he]** (14:25). His physical attributes and personality would become important in helping explain how Absalom would be able to easily grab the throne and raise such a large following against his father. Absalom could capture and hold a crowd by his good looks and charm. Unfortunately, he would begin to

believe his own press releases and get a big ego. The text says, **He did not have a single [physical] flaw** (14:25). But, he did develop one fatal character flaw: pride.

14:27-33 After **two years** of not seeing the king, Absalom began to chafe (14:28). He tried to get Joab to intercede with David for him, **but Joab was unwilling** (14:29). So, like a sulky child, he had Joab's barley **field** set **on fire** to get his attention (14:30). Finally, Joab interceded for Absalom and went to the king. **So David summoned Absalom, who came to the king and paid homage with his face to the ground before him. Then the king kissed Absalom** (14:33). Unfortunately, this reunion would prove to be too little too late.

IV. A SON'S REBELLION AND ITS CONSEQUENCES
(15:1–20:26)

15:1-6 Absalom, still disgruntled, knew exactly how to begin his plot to take his father's throne. He didn't need an army. He had charm and good looks—traits any good politician knows how to use to advantage. He also had a shrewd political strategy: identify the shortcomings of the current administration and make promises of better days under his own leadership.

Absalom **would get up early and stand beside the road leading to the city gate**, intercepting anyone coming to Jerusalem to get a hearing on some **grievance to bring before the king for settlement** (15:2). Absalom would sympathize with the people and lament that, though their claims were just, **the king [did] not have anyone to listen to [them]** (15:3). Perhaps the royal courts were jammed or no one cared. Regardless, Absalom showed so much concern that he **stole the hearts of the men of Israel** (15:6). Little did David know that his son was slowly winning the loyalty of the king's subjects.

15:7-10 After **four years** of conniving, Absalom felt confident about moving forward in his rebellion. He asked David for permission to **go to Hebron** (where David had been

anointed king of Judah; see 2:1-4) so that he might **fulfill a vow** (15:7-8). Absalom went with David's blessing, and his plot unfolded quickly (15:9-10). Absalom had arranged for his **agents** to go **throughout the tribes of Israel** announcing, **Absalom has become king in Hebron!** (15:10). The insurrection had begun.

15:11-12 To make matters worse, **two hundred men from Jerusalem** had gone to Hebron with Absalom **innocently**, not knowing about the plot (15:11). But evidently, they quickly went over to Absalom's side, as did **David's adviser Ahithophel**. From that point, things snowballed: **The conspiracy grew strong, and the people supporting Absalom continued to increase** (15:12).

15:13-16 Word of the rebellion reached David, and he instantly realized that this was no minor incident (15:13-14). He ordered an evacuation of his entire household from Jerusalem—to avoid bloodshed and to spare Jerusalem from certain destruction (15:14). David **left behind ten concubines to take care of the palace** (15:16), a note that is sadly important because it would become part of

God's judgment on David for his sins. As Nathan the prophet had foretold, David's wives would be taken from him and given to one who would lie with them in broad daylight (see 12:11-12). Absalom would soon fulfill this prophecy to humiliate David (see 16:20-22).

15:17-23 Even in his agony of soul, David was concerned about a faithful soldier, **Ittai of Gath,** a foreigner and exile (15:19). David urged Ittai to return, but Ittai swore his undying loyalty to David, whether it meant **life or death** (15:20-21). The sight of the king, his household, and troops on the run from Absalom caused **all the people** in the **countryside** to weep **loudly** (15:23). The king of Israel was going into exile.

15:24-29 The priest **Zadok** was there, too. **All the Levites with him were carrying the ark of the covenant of God.** Then, the priest **Abiathar offered sacrifices** (15:24). But, David insisted that they **return the ark of God to the city.** Though the king was going on the run, he was firmly convinced that God's throne should not. **If I find favor with the LORD,** David said, **he will bring me back and allow me to see both it and its dwelling place** (15:25). David was leaving his fate in the hands of his sovereign God (15:26). And, rather than having them flee with him, David asked that Zadok and Abiathar serve him as informers (15:27-29).

15:30-31 David continued his flight, going up **the Mount of Olives, weeping as he ascended. His head was covered, and he was walking barefoot** in grief (15:30). When he learned that his advisor **Ahithophel** had defected to Absalom, **David pleaded** with God that he would thwart Ahithophel's counsel and turn his words **into foolishness** (15:31). Actually, God would go one better than that.

15:32-37 When David reached the top of the Mount of Olives, he found **Hushai the Archite** waiting for him, grieving for his king (15:32). He was another **personal adviser** of David (15:37). The king realized that Hushai would be the perfect person to send back to Jerusalem under the guise of joining the conspiracy and offering his counsel to Absalom. He could **counteract** Ahithophel and

also gather valuable intelligence to send to David through the priests (15:33-36). David now had the eyes and ears he desperately needed in Jerusalem to find out what Absalom's plans were. God was answering David's prayer (15:31).

16:1-2 As David continued his flight east away from Jerusalem and toward the Jordan River, he encountered **Ziba,** the former servant of Saul whom David had appointed to be **servant** to Jonathan's son Mephibosheth (16:1; see 9:1-13). Ziba's arrival was unexpected, so David questioned him about his presence and the many provisions he had brought (16:2). The king had apparently expected to see Mephibosheth himself.

16:3-4 Ziba explained that Mephibosheth was **staying in Jerusalem,** hoping that his grandfather Saul's **kingdom** would be restored to him (16:3). That was disturbing news to David because it meant Ziba was accusing Mephibosheth of treason. David believed Ziba and reversed the decision he'd made earlier concerning Saul's estate (see 9:9). He gave Ziba all that had belonged **to Mephibosheth** (16:4). Later, Mephibosheth would testify that Ziba had slandered him to the king (see 19:24-30).

16:5-8 Another character David encountered was a man from **the family of ... Saul** named **Shimei,** who was **yelling curses** and throwing **stones at David** and his entourage (16:5-6). Shimei called the fleeing king **a man of bloodshed** and a **wicked man** (16:7). Though David had done no violence to Saul or his family, Shimei falsely accused him of being responsible **for all the blood of the house of Saul** (16:8).

16:9 One would think that Shimei would have been a little more cautious, considering that David could have had him executed in a heartbeat. In fact, this is exactly what Abishai suggested: **Why should this dead dog curse my lord the king? Let me go over and remove his head!** But David refused Abishai, and this wasn't the first time. Years ago, Abishai had urged David to kill King Saul when he had the opportunity (see 1 Sam 26:7-11).

16:10-14 David took Shimei's cursing as a rebuke from God, which he needed to hear (16:10). After all, though he was not guilty of Saul's blood, David was indeed guilty of sinful bloodshed (see 11:14-27). Besides, David reasoned, his own son had dethroned him and was seeking his life, which meant he had much bigger issues to worry about than this man yelling curses at him (16:11). After a long, exhausting march, David and his party rested (16:14).

16:15-23 Back in Jerusalem, **Absalom and all the Israelites** arrived in what must have been for him a smug, triumphant parade (16:15). David's former trusted adviser and now traitor **Ahithophel** was at Absalom's side. Getting Ahithophel to switch off of David was a big coup as far as Absalom was concerned because **the advice Ahithophel gave . . . was like someone asking about a word from God**—such was the regard that both David and Absalom had for Ahithophel's advice (16:23). But, God was going to thwart his counsel and use it against Absalom.

David had a few loyal friends who were working undercover in Absalom's court, including **Hushai** (16:18; see 15:31-37), whose devotion to David was such that Absalom was suspicious of him (16:16-17). Therefore, Hushai had to convince Absalom that he was siding with the new king (16:18-19).

When it came time for **advice** on his next step, Absalom turned to Ahithophel who recommended that Absalom publicly take the king's harem as his own (16:20-21). This would do two things. First, it would demonstrate to all that Absalom was claiming the throne. Second, it would humiliate David, ending any possibility of a reconciliation between father and son. So, Absalom followed Ahithophel's advice to the letter (16:22).

17:1-4 The next question was what to do about David and his loyal followers, who were on the run. Ahithophel had a plan for that, too. He asked Absalom for **twelve thousand men** to pursue David that night, while he was **weary and discouraged**, so that he and everyone with him might be thrown into **a panic** and **scatter**. Then, Ahithophel would **strike down** David **and bring all the people back** to Absalom (17:2-3). **Absalom and**

all the elders of Israel liked the plan (17:4), which meant David and his weary followers were in trouble.

17:5-10 In God's providence, Absalom asked to hear Hushai's counsel, too (17:5-6). Hushai no doubt agreed that Ahithophel's advice was sound. That's why, as David's friend, he immediately declared that it was **not good** and sought to undo it (17:7). Hushai's reasons for rejecting Ahithophel's plan for an immediate attack were a stroke of storytelling genius (17:7-12). David and his men had impeccable reputations as **warriors** (17:8). Few, if any, men in Israel would want to face David on the battlefield—especially when his back was against the wall. He and his elite troops were probably **hiding** in **caves**, ready to pounce on Absalom's soldiers (17:9). If this happened, the hearts of even the bravest of Absalom's men would melt like butter (17:10). Hushai did a masterful job of instilling fear.

17:11-14 Having undermined Ahithophel's counsel, Hushai presented an alternate idea. If Absalom would wait until he gathered a large enough army, he could simply overwhelm David with massive numbers and gain a decisive victory. And, appealing to Absalom's ego, Hushai also suggested that the new king **personally** lead his troops into **battle** (17:11). Absalom took the bait. He didn't know that **the LORD had decreed that Ahithophel's good advice be undermined in order to bring about Absalom's ruin** (17:14). This brings to mind the truth that "A king's heart is like channeled water in the LORD's hand: He directs it wherever he chooses" (Prov 21:1).

17:15-20 Even though Hushai had undercut Ahithophel's counsel, Absalom was still a threat. So, **Hushai** told the loyal **priests** in Jerusalem, **Zadok and Abiathar**, to tell David not to **spend the night** at the **Jordan** River, but to **cross over** and keep going. Otherwise, they would **be devoured** by Absalom and his forces (17:15-16). Using their espionage system, the priests got word to their sons **Jonathan and Ahimaaz**, who were staying at **En-rogel** south of Jerusalem, so that they could carry the message to David (17:17). This was incredibly dangerous business, and sure enough, Jonathan and Ahimaaz were spotted by someone who **informed Absalom** (17:18). Yet, because they were hidden by a faithful woman and God spared them, they lived to do their job (17:18-20).

17:21-23 The two brave men delivered the message to David, and his party crossed the Jordan to safety (17:21-22). The opportunity that Ahithophel had sought was gone (17:2-3). The counselor became distraught when he **realized that his advice had not been followed**. As a result, he committed suicide (17:23). This was no overreaction to having his advice rebuffed. Ahithophel could see the writing on the wall. He knew that Absalom was a fool for preferring Hushai's plan. It would only be a matter of time before David regained the throne. And, when that happened, Ahithophel would be executed for rebellion. He preferred to die in his own way.

17:24-29 David **arrived at Mahanaim**, on the east side of the Jordan, just as **Absalom crossed** the river with his army and its new commander **Amasa**, who was related to David and his commander Joab (17:24-25). David had friends near Mahanaim who refreshed and resupplied his **hungry, exhausted, and thirsty** people (17:27-29).

18:1-4 David and his **troops** regrouped after their refreshment, and he organized them for the coming battle with Absalom and the forces of Israel (18:1-2). Being the leader that he was, David announced, **I must also march out with you** (18:2). But that brought an immediate gasp from everyone. They **pleaded** with David, reasoning that if David died their whole cause would be lost (18:3). So the king relented: **I will do whatever you think is best** (18:4). Thus, David would not be on the battlefield when Absalom faced the inevitable consequences of his actions.

18:5 David's rebel son was forefront in his mind. Even on the verge of a battle that would determine his future and the future of his kingdom, David told his three commanders, **Treat the young man Absalom gently**. And, the author makes it clear to the reader that **all the people heard the king's orders to all the commanders about Absalom**.

18:6-9 The battle went well for David's army, with the harsh terrain of the **forest of Ephraim** claiming as many Israelite soldiers as David's troops did (18:6-8). The treacherous nature of the forest, in fact, played a significant role in the battle when Absalom's head—perhaps because of his long hair—became caught in **the tangled branches of a large oak tree**, leaving him suspended in midair (18:9).

18:10-15 One of David's soldiers saw Absalom hanging in the tree and informed Joab, who was stunned that the soldier hadn't killed him (18:10-11). When the man confessed his fear of harming Absalom given David's clear instructions (see 18:5), Joab reacted with disgust (18:12-13). He pushed the soldier aside and ran Absalom through with **three spears**, then allowing his ten **armor-bearers** to finish Absalom off (18:14-15).

18:16-18 Once the leader of the rebellion was dead, **Joab blew the ram's horn** to call his soldiers back from the battle (18:16). He knew that news of Absalom's death would take the steam out of Israel's troops. Joab buried Absalom in a **pit** and raised **a huge mound of stones over him**, but Absalom already had a memorial prepared for himself back in Jerusalem (18:17-18).

18:19-23 Next came the unenviable task of telling David that his son was dead. **Ahimaaz son of Zadok**, one of David's faithful spies who risked his life for the king, asked Joab for permission to take David what he thought would be **good news** (18:19). But, Ahimaaz was too young to know what happened to messengers who brought David that kind of "good" news (see 1:1-16; 4:5-12). The veteran Joab thus said in effect, "Son, you don't know what you're asking. This is *not* good news for David. Let this **Cushite** go instead" (18:20-21). But, Ahimaaz insisted, so Joab relented, and Ahimaaz **outran** the other messenger (18:22-23).

18:24-29 When the **watchman** saw him coming and told the king, David was encouraged at first (18:24-27). Ahimaaz informed him that the rebellion had been stopped, and David asked the fateful question: **Is the young man Absalom all right?** (18:28-29). Clearly,

Ahimaaz knew the answer (see 18:19-20), but he pulled back and blew smoke instead: **I saw a big disturbance, but I don't know what it was** (18:29). Whether he'd planned all along to let the Cushite be the bearer of the bad news or just lost his nerve when King David looked him in the eye, the hanging question would soon be answered.

18:30-33 The Cushite delivered the message that Ahimaaz was unwilling to deliver. Undoubtedly, given the manner in which he announced the news, he assumed that David would be overjoyed at what had happened to this **young man** who rose up against the king **with evil intent** (18:32). He was wrong. David went to his **chamber** and **wept**, overwhelmed with grief. He cried, **My son Absalom! My son, my son Absalom! If only I had died instead of you** (18:33). David's kingdom had been spared, but his rebel son had not.

19:1-4 When he learned that **the king** was **weeping** and **mourning over Absalom**, Joab knew he had to do something (19:1). Because of the king's grief, **the troops** felt as if they had been **humiliated** in defeat and could not rejoice in the **victory** (19:2-3). Thousands of brave men had just put their lives on the line to save David, his family, and his throne. Likely many had died. Although a parent's grief over the death of a child—even an estranged one—is understandable, David was on the verge of communicating the wrong message to his supporters.

19:5-8 Joab wasn't bashful about speaking his mind to the king. He laid out the facts with no sugarcoating. Joab chastised him: **Today you have shamed all your soldiers . . . by loving your enemies and hating those who love you** (19:5-6). In other words, David would have a serious morale and loyalty problem on his hands if he didn't pull himself together. Joab warned, **Go out and encourage your soldiers. . . . If you don't go out, not a man will remain with you tonight**. This would be a turn of events **worse** than all the previous **trouble** (19:7). Realizing that Joab was right, David ended his mourning and made an appearance **in the city gate** (19:8).

19:9-10 With Absalom dead, the northern tribes of Israel faced a dilemma. They had rallied behind Absalom, but with the throne now empty, they had to ask whether they should invite David to return. Opinions were divided. Some of the people argued that David had been an effective leader in the past and should be restored. But, others were hesitant, possibly because they had backed Absalom and worried about reprisals.

19:11-12 David sensed that the place to start in recovering his throne was with **Judah**. If any tribe was going to **restore the king**, it should be his own (19:11). If Judah delayed, it would send the wrong message to the nation. So, David chided **the elders of Judah** through his representatives, **Zadok and Abiathar**, saying that **all Israel** was talking about bringing him back to Jerusalem (19:11-12). David's own tribe, then, shouldn't be in the embarrassing position of being **the last to restore the king** (19:12).

19:13 David vowed to make **Amasa** the **commander** of the **army** in place of **Joab**. Because Absalom had appointed Amasa over his army, David was demonstrating that he bore no animosity toward those who had sided with Absalom. Furthermore, the demotion of Joab was no doubt a response to Joab's execution of Absalom—something he'd done against the king's order. Though David obviously didn't intend to kill Joab for his actions, neither did he intend to let him retain his position.

19:14-15 This gesture **won over all the men of Judah, and they unanimously sent word** to David to come back and resume the throne (19:14). Then, Judah came out in force to **escort** David as he came to the **Jordan** River to cross over on his way back to Jerusalem (19:15).

19:16-23 On his return, David was met by a variety of characters. The first mentioned is Shimei, the descendant of Saul who had cursed David so violently on his retreat that Abishai wanted to cut off his head (see 16:5-9). In fact, when **Shimei** begged for forgiveness, **Abishai** once again asked the king if he could slay Shimei (19:16, 19-21). But, David granted him a stay of execution (19:23; but see 1 Kgs 2:8-9). There would be no killing on that day.

Shimei had **a thousand men from Benjamin with him**, showing that Saul's tribe was attempting to link itself with Judah now that David was fully in control of the throne again (19:17). Shimei said he was **the first one of the entire house of Joseph** to come and welcome David back (19:20). This was a reference to the large tribe of Ephraim, Joseph's son, standing for the northern tribes of Israel as a whole.

19:24-30 Another familiar face who showed up was Mephibosheth's servant **Ziba**, who crossed the Jordan with his family and servants to meet David's needs (see 19:17-18). Later, came **Mephibosheth** himself, who pleaded his case with David, telling him that he had not sought the kingship when David fled but that Ziba had **slandered** him (19:24-28). Given the competing claims between Mephibosheth and Ziba, David divided the estate between them (19:29).

19:31-39 Barzillai the Gileadite had also come with David **to the Jordan River** to say goodbye (19:31). **A very wealthy man, he had provided for the needs of the king** during his brief exile (19:32). David wanted Barzillai to go to **Jerusalem** with him so he could take care of him, but aged Barzillai wanted to live out his remaining years at home (19:33-37). Nevertheless, Barzillai asked that David take **Chimham**, possibly Barzillai's son, with him and let him enjoy whatever reward David would have given to Barzillai (19:37). David readily agreed (19:38-39).

19:40-43 Still more trouble was brewing. **The men of Israel** accused **Judah** of sneaking down to the Jordan to bring David back without telling them (19:41). The men of Judah shot back that David was one of their own (19:42). But, Israel responded that because they had ten tribes, they had **ten shares in the king**—and thus **a greater claim to David** than Judah did. Moreover, Israel had been **the first to speak of restoring** the king (19:43). Old wounds were being re-opened, and another revolt was brewing. Again, the

author of Samuel shows his readers the roots of the nation's coming bitter division.

20:1-3 A leader was needed to set ablaze the fire of rebellion. Enter **a wicked man, a Benjaminite named Sheba**, who **blew the ram's horn** and called **Israel** to war against Judah (20:1). Thus, the battle lines were drawn (20:2). But, David's first act upon arriving at his palace in Jerusalem was reclaiming his harem of **ten concubines** by whom Absalom had publicly humiliated his father. These poor women lived as well-provided-for **widows** the rest of their lives (20:3).

20:4-7 David turned to the urgent business of putting down Sheba's revolt. But, Joab would insert his cold-hearted brutality in the war preparations. David ordered **Amasa**, his new army commander, to rally Judah's troops and meet David **within three days** (20:4). But, for whatever reason, Amasa failed to make his deadline (20:5). So, David turned to Joab's brother **Abishai** and ordered him to **pursue** Sheba before his revolt got out of hand (20:6-7).

20:8-13 Abishai and his forces met Amasa at **Gibeon**, where **Joab** was also present (20:8). Joab had long been known as a violent man, but it was at this point that he showed his true treachery. He pretended to greet Amasa with a **kiss** of brotherly kindness and then gutted him like an animal (20:9-10). Then, Joab went on after **Sheba** as if nothing had happened. At least the troops of Judah had regard for Amasa, because they had to move his body out of sight before the army would go on (20:11-13).

20:14-22 Once back in his old job as army commander, Joab pursued Sheba to far northern Israel, to the city of **Abel of Bethmaacah**; it was about twenty-five miles north of the Sea of Galilee (20:14). **Joab** and his army **built a siege ramp against the outer wall of the city** and began **battering the wall to make it collapse** (20:15). **A wise woman** of the city **called out** to Joab (20:16), horrified that Joab was trying to destroy a prominent city of Israel (20:18-19). When she learned the reason for Joab's assault and the conditions for his withdrawal, she informed the people of the city, and they **threw** Sheba's **head** down to his enemies (20:20-22). The fact that they so readily agreed to give up Sheba shows that not everyone in Israel had the stomach for another rebellion.

20:23-26 Despite his murder of Amasa, **Joab commanded the whole army of Israel** (20:23). Given all of the rebellion, killing, and intrigue of the past days, perhaps David had decided that enough was enough and therefore kept Joab in his position as a key administrator over the nation. Eventually, however, Joab's murderous spirit would cost him his life (see 1 Kgs 2:28-35).

V. FINAL YEARS AS KING (21:1–24:25)

21:1-3 During David's later years, Israel was plagued by **a famine** that lasted **for three successive years**, which caused David to seek the Lord regarding the reason for it. God responded, **It is due to Saul and to his bloody family, because he killed the Gibeonites** (21:1). This is a reference to an incident not recorded in Scripture, but it clearly violated a covenant Joshua had made with these non-Israelites years before (2:2; see Josh 9:15-21). To lift God's judgment against Israel, David asked the Gibeonites how he could **make atonement** for this wrong and restore the Lord's blessing to Israel (21:3).

21:4-6 The Gibeonites asked that **seven** of Saul's **male descendants** be hanged (21:6). Saul had no doubt killed far more Gibeonites, but the number *seven* was likely chosen as the number of completeness. This would bring full satisfaction for the wrongs Saul and his family had committed against these people. As grim as this seems to us, it is a reminder that sin is a great offense to God.

21:7-14 David agreed to their terms and selected seven men from Saul's family to be executed. Two were sons of Saul's concubine **Rizpah**, and five were sons of his daughter **Merab** (21:8). **David spared** Jonathan's son **Mephibosheth** because of the **oath** he had made (21:7). The seven were **hanged** and their bodies were left out in the open **until the rain poured down from heaven**, signaling the Lord's lifting of the curse and the end of the drought (21:9-10).

Saul's concubine **Rizpah** went to the execution site and spent many days protecting her sons' bodies from scavengers (21:10). When David heard of her devotion, he retrieved **the bones of Saul and his son Jonathan from the citizens of Jabesh-gilead**, gathered up the bones of the seven executed grandsons of Saul, and buried all of them in Saul's ancestral tomb (21:11-14). God accepted the atonement that had been made and **was receptive to prayer for the land** (21:14).

21:15-17 Sometime later, **the Philistines again waged war against Israel**, and David once again led his troops out in battle. But, he was no longer an energetic young warrior, and he soon **became exhausted** (21:15). Then, a great Philistine warrior named **Ishbi-benob** raised his **spear** and **intended to kill David** (21:16). Thankfully, the king was narrowly rescued by **Abishai**. But, it had been too close of a call for David's soldiers. They made him promise not to go into battle again. They said, **You must not extinguish the lamp of Israel** (21:17). They didn't want their aged king dying on the battlefield.

21:18-22 Three more Philistine champions fell in battles with the Israelites (21:18-21). One of these Israelite warriors, **Elhanan**, was said to have killed Goliath of Gath (21:19), which would contradict the report that David killed him (see 1 Sam 17). There could have been two giants named Goliath. Most likely, though, a scribe made an error while copying this passage, because the parallel account in 1 Chronicles 20:5 says that Elhanan killed "the brother of Goliath." Altogether, **four** great Philistines were killed by the Israelite warriors (21:22).

22:1-4 David's song of praise in this chapter is virtually identical to Psalm 18. He wrote it after **the LORD rescued him from the grasp**

of all his enemies and from the grasp Saul (22:1). It was a public declaration of praise to God for his deliverance. As the song opens, David uses one vivid word after another to describe and give glory to his almighty God: **rock ... fortress ... deliverer ... shield ... horn of my salvation ... stronghold ... refuge ... Savior** (22:2-3).

22:5-6 David then elaborated on the dangers from which the Lord had rescued him. He described his troubles as being overwhelmed by **the waves of death** and **the torrents of destruction** (22:5), feeling the **ropes of Sheol** (that is, the grave) entangling him, and being caught in **the snares of death** (22:6). David had faced death multiple times, so he was aware of God's sovereign ability to rescue when all hope seems lost.

22:7-20 David's poetic abilities really took over as he described what happened when he **called to the Lord** for help (22:7). The awesome Creator of the universe shook the earth in response to David's prayer. **He bent the heavens and came down** (22:10). The **Lord** thundered from heaven (22:14). **He hurled lightning bolts and routed** David's enemies (22:15). In other words, David had seen that God would move heaven and earth for the one who trusted in him and sought to honor him. God **rescued** David because **he delighted** in him (22:20).

22:21-30 The theme of David's response to God's gracious deliverance is that God works on behalf of the righteous and thwarts the schemes of the wicked. This doesn't mean that David thought he was perfect and sinless. Clearly he was not—and David knew it. Yet, David sought to honor God over the long haul of his life. When he sinned, he turned to God in repentance, trusting in God to forgive him by means of the sacrificial atonement he had provided for Israel through the tabernacle's system.

David knew the source of his deliverance and his blessings, and he readily acknowledged that the Lord alone was the righteous God who rewarded **righteousness** and judged evil (22:21, 25). David also knew that it was God who empowered him to overcome his enemies.

22:31-51 The final stanza of David's song returns to the theme of God's attributes, tying them to the ways God had worked through them on David's behalf. God was David's protector—**a shield to all who take refuge in him**, as well as a **rock** and **a strong refuge** (22:31-33), the one in whom David could find protection. To underscore his point, David asked two questions in 22:32 to which he and the reader knew the answer: **Who is God besides the Lord? And who is a rock?** There is no solid and immovable rock like the Lord. God was the one who subdued David's **enemies** (22:38-41) and delivered David from harm (22:47-51). If the **king** of Israel looked to God as his **tower of salvation**, surely all of God's people should do the same (22:51).

23:1-4 David's **last words** are also a psalm of praise to God for exalting David from his humble beginnings as a shepherd boy in Bethlehem to the throne of Israel. He was the one chosen and **anointed by the God of Jacob**. To David, **this [was] the most delightful of Israel's songs** (23:1). And, here, he seems to claim divine inspiration for his writings (23:2-3), an idea that is fully expressed in the New Testament, but which the Old Testament prophets claimed in many places when they said things like, "The word of the Lord came to me" (see Jer 1:11; Ezek 6:1). David was also aware that a king who ruled God's people righteously was a special blessing to the land (22:3-4).

23:5-7 The heart of David's reign is the Davidic covenant (see 2 Sam 7:12-16) that will be fulfilled when Jesus Christ returns in glory to reign on David's throne in his coming millennial kingdom (see Luke 1:31-33). David expressed his complete confidence that God would be faithful to his **permanent covenant** (22:5). In contrast, **the wicked are like thorns** that are completely useless and are only good for the fire of God's judgment (23:6).

23:8-39 The remainder of this chapter is devoted to the names and exploits of **David's warriors** (23:8). The stories that follow are better than those credited to any comic book superhero—and they're true.

Interestingly, among all the names, "Joab" is not included. His brothers **Abishai** and **Asahel** are listed, and each is designated as **Joab's brother** (23:18, 24). Joab was certainly a great warrior who was the commander of David's entire army for most of his reign. But, Joab was also an extremely violent and brutal man who did not hesitate to kill his own kinsmen when they got in his way. (On the other hand, his omission from the list may have been due simply to his position as commander, which meant he was over all these men.)

The three men listed in 23:8-12 performed incredible feats of bravery in warfare, rallying Israel from defeat to victory over the Philistines more than once. There were also the **thirty leading warriors** who acted with great bravery and devotion to David (23:13). During a particular battle, the king expressed a wish he probably never dreamed his men would take literally. He said, **If only someone would bring me water to drink from the well at the city gate of Bethlehem!** (23:15). David was being nostalgic about his hometown drinking fountain and likely did not expect anyone to take his wish seriously because the Philistines were camped in Bethlehem as he spoke. Nevertheless, **three of the thirty** did exactly that, risking their lives to draw water **from the well** (23:13, 16). But, David was struck by his conscience over the risk they took, and he poured out the water as an offering to the Lord.

Benaiah was another of David's great warriors. He was famous for going **down into a pit on a snowy day** and killing a **lion** (23:20-21). David wisely put Benaiah **in charge of his bodyguard** (23:23), and later Solomon placed him in command of his own army (see 1 Kgs 2:35).

The remainder of the chapter lists **the Thirty**—David's elite warriors (22:24-39). Interestingly, this list includes **Uriah the Hethite** (22:39). His inclusion underscores the power that sin can have even in the life of a dedicated believer like David when it takes over. Uriah wasn't just a good and loyal soldier. He was one of David's best, a man who had taken a vow to defend the king at the cost of his own life. Ironically, being David's soldier did cost Uriah his life, but his death was to David's great shame (see 2 Sam 11).

24:1-2 The story of David's census is an example of the mysterious interplay between God's sovereignty and human responsibility. Here the text says that **the Lord's anger burned against Israel again, and he stirred up David against them** to take this census (24:1). But, according to 1 Chronicles 21:1, "Satan rose up against Israel and incited David to count the people of Israel." So, who did the action? The Lord or Satan? The answer is both.

God was angry with Israel, apparently because the people had sinned in some way. So, he allowed Satan to tempt David to arrogantly count the size of the troops under his command. This interplay between God and Satan is similar to God allowing Satan to trouble Job (see Job 1:1–2:7). Ultimately, though, it was God who was sovereign over Job's circumstances. Job understood that he had suffered because of "all the adversity the Lord had brought on him" (Job 42:11). Though Satan had meant the adversity for evil, God had meant it for Job's good.

In principle, it isn't sinful for a commander to count his troops in order to know if he has sufficient numbers to go to battle. But, the Lord had made it clear to David that he—not the army—was the source of Israel's strength. Satan had tempted David to meet a legitimate desire (to win Israel's battles) by an illegitimate means (the number of his forces) rather than a legitimate means (relying completely on the Lord).

24:3-10 On this occasion, **Joab** was more spiritually aware than David. He objected to David's order because he saw it for what it was—a needless attempt by David to take pride in and feel secure in his military might instead of trusting the Lord (24:3). But, David overruled Joab, and the count was made (24:4-9). Too late, **David's conscience troubled him** and he confessed to God, **I have sinned greatly in what I've done. . . . I've been very foolish** (24:10).

24:11-13 Sin, even forgiven sin, always has consequences. So, the Lord gave the king a choice of **three** very painful judgments. These three, spelled out to David by **the prophet Gad**, increase in severity from a famine to a **plague**, but decrease in length from **three years** to **three days**. Gad gave David some time to think things over before choosing his punishment (24:13).

24:14-17 David thought through the options and made what he considered the best decision. He had experienced years of fleeing from his enemies, so he knew he would find no mercy from them. Knowing the Lord's **mercies are great**, David placed himself in God's hands (24:14). Therefore, **the LORD sent a plague on Israel**, which resulted in **seventy thousand** deaths (24:15). The plague stopped only when God spared **Jerusalem** in his mercy by saying to his destroying angel, **Enough, withdraw your hand now!** (24:16).

This happened **at the threshing floor of Araunah the Jebusite** (24:16). (In 1 Chronicles, Araunah is known by his alternate name, Ornan; see 1 Chr 21:18-28.) **When David saw the angel striking the people**, he pleaded with God for mercy. He recognized that the sin was his and begged God to let the judgment be against his family alone (24:17). This is a reminder that we never sin in a vacuum. You may think that your sinful choices affect no one but you. But, this is never correct. When we choose to sin, we leave spiritual harm in our wake—whether or not we see the results immediately.

24:18-23 God ordered David to go to **the threshing floor of Araunah** to set up an **altar** so that the plague might be stopped (24:18). David obeyed immediately. When Araunah saw him coming, he **paid homage to the king with his face to the ground** (24:19-20). Once he learned the reason for David's visit, Araunah was more than happy to give him not only the threshing floor, but everything else he needed for the sacrifice (24:22-23).

24:24 David refused the offer, insisting that he would pay for everything at full price (see Chr 21:22, 24). Then, he stated one of the great biblical principles of sacrificial giving: **I will not offer to the LORD my God burnt offerings that cost me nothing.** This should make us ask what we give to the Lord and his kingdom work (prayers, time, service, money, resources) that costs us little in terms of sacrifice.

24:25 David **offered burnt offerings and fellowship offerings**. God was pleased with David's sacrifice, **and the plague on Israel ended**. In God's sovereign plan, he accomplished his will despite David's sin.

The piece of land that David **bought** (24:24) was Mount Moriah, the spot where Abraham once offered his son Isaac to the Lord and where Solomon would one day build the Lord's temple (see Gen 22; 2 Chr 3:1). God allowed Satan's wickedness and David's sin to run their course until what would become Israel's holiest site was selected.

The census was the last recorded act of David in the book of 2 Samuel, showing both the king's vulnerability to sin and his sensitivity to turn to the Lord in repentance. Similarly, God calls all kingdom men and women to be on guard regarding their own vulnerability to sin and to maintain hearts that are sensitive to the Holy Spirit's convicting work.

1 KINGS

INTRODUCTION

Author

THE AUTHOR OF 1–2 KINGS IS UN-known. Though ancient Jewish tradition attributed the books to the prophet Jeremiah, the books themselves are silent with regard to their writer. Clearly, the author was interested in showing how God's people had failed to live up to the requirements of the covenant, particularly as they are laid out in Deuteronomy. The books were completed sometime after the final event they mention: the pardoning of Jehoiachin (see 2 Kgs 25:27-30) in 561 BC. Given the timeframe and the theological emphases, Jeremiah is certainly a good candidate.

Historical Background

First Kings begins with King David's final days, and 2 Kings ends with "the thirty-seventh year of the exile of Judah's King Jehoiachin, in the year Evil-merodach became king of Babylon" (2 Kgs 25:27). Thus, the books take readers from the golden age of Israel's monarchy to the exile of Judah's king, a period spanning four hundred years. Though 1–2 Chronicles cover much of the same ground, 1–2 Kings consider the kings and history of both the northern and southern kingdoms (Israel and Judah), while 1–2 Chronicles focus only on Judah. In 1–2 Kings, readers see the construction of Solomon's temple (960 BC), the split of the nation into two kingdoms (930 BC), the exile of Israel (722 BC), and the exile to Babylon (587 BC).

Message and Purpose

Written to the Jews living in captivity in Babylon, this two-volume work is a history of the united—and then divided—kingdom of Israel. The books describe the reigns of the kings of both Israel and Judah: there were nineteen kings in the northern kingdom (Israel) and twenty kings in the southern kingdom (Judah).

The message of 1–2 Kings was the same message God gave to Moses in Deuteronomy: He would provide blessing for obedience to him and judgment for disobedience. The writer wanted his readers to know that they were in captivity because of disobedience, but obedience to God would bring deliverance. The prophetic ministries of Elijah, Elisha, and Isaiah are highlighted in these books, as these prophets called the people back to God so they could avoid the consequences of rebelling against their covenant with him.

The sweep of history within these works, from David's time through the broken kingdom era, shows us that no human ruler can fulfill God's ultimate demands. It reveals humanity's need for the ultimate King, the final Son of David, who alone could satisfy God's requirements and bring his people deliverance. Reading 1–2 Kings causes us to look forward to the righteous kingdom rule of David's final Son, the Messiah and our Savior.

VIDEO | INTRO

www.bhpublishinggroup.com/qr/te/11_00

Outline

1 KINGS

I. THE UNITED KINGDOM (1:1–11:43)

⇨ A. The Rise of King Solomon
(1:1–2:46) ⇦

1:1-4 By the time the events of 1 Kings began to unfold, David was **advanced in age** and in poor health. He was unable to keep **warm**, no matter how well he was covered (1:1). So the king's servants suggested that they find **a young virgin** who could provide him with warmth and also be **his caregiver** (1:2). The woman they found was **Abishag** (1:3), from the village of Shunem in the tribal territory of Issachar. She fulfilled all of their requirements, including being of **unsurpassed beauty** (1:4). This fact would become important later when Solomon's half-brother Adonijah became attracted to her and used her to make a thinly disguised attempt to usurp the throne (see 2:13-25).

1:5-10 A reason behind the forthcoming trouble in chapter 2 is revealed here. David's family drama that resulted from his past sins continued to plague him all the way to his grave. Seeing the king's great weakness, **Adonijah**, David's fourth son and Solomon's elder, decided the time was right to make his move (1:5). He probably assumed that he was the rightful heir because he was likely the eldest living son. Moreover, there is no record of David publicly declaring his choice of Solomon as his successor prior to this incident.

It seems Adonijah had a lot in common with Absalom (see 2 Sam 15:1-10). First, he **kept exalting himself** and declared, **I will be king!** (1:5). Second, like Absalom, he won

over many followers by his good looks and charm. Even David's military commander **Joab**, his faithful supporter **Abiathar** the **priest** (1:7), as well as Adonijah's **royal brothers and all the men of Judah** sided with Adonijah (1:9).

1:11-21 The prophet **Nathan** and **Bathsheba** soon realized how serious the situation had become (1:11; on David's sin with Bathsheba and its consequences, see 1 Sam 11:1–12:25). They developed a plan to convince David that, unless he acted quickly and decisively, Adonijah would be king (1:12-14). Bathsheba approached and reminded David that he had sworn to crown **Solomon**, their son (1:15-17). (This promise is not mentioned elsewhere, so it may have been a private matter between them.) She also informed him that Adonijah had proclaimed himself king, was winning support, and had not invited Solomon to his banquet (1:18-19). That meant that when David was dead and buried, Solomon and his mother would be treated **as criminals**, enemies of the throne (1:21).

1:22-27 Nathan the prophet came before the king, echoing Bathsheba's report. Then, he essentially asked the king, "Did I miss something? Did you endorse Adonijah without letting us know about it?" (1:24, 27).

1:28-35 Though David was feeble, he wasn't feeble-minded. He would keep his previous promise (1:28-30).

Adonijah had not engaged in armed rebellion, as Absalom had done. So, rather than attack Adonijah and touch off a possible civil war, David reasoned rightly that the majority of the people were still loyal to him and would rally around his chosen successor. So, David ordered his faithful servants to **anoint** Solomon at **Gihon**, declare him **as king** before all the people, and place him on David's **throne** (1:32-35).

1:36-40 When they did just as David commanded, **all the people** rejoiced (1:38-40). Gihon was only about half a mile from where Adonijah and his crowd were celebrating. From there, it wouldn't be hard to hear the noise the people were making (see 1:41).

1:41-48 David's plan had the desired effect. When Adonijah, Joab, and all the guests at the illegitimate coronation banquet **heard the sound of the ram's horn** announcing Solomon's coronation, they knew something big was happening (1:41). When **Jonathan son of Abiathar the priest** showed up, Adonijah felt better for a moment, hoping he was **bringing good news** (1:42). "**Unfortunately not**," Jonathan answered him (1:43)—which is one of the great understatements of Scripture. He then proceeded to tell Adonijah, step-by-step, how David had established Solomon as king of Israel. He'd even bowed in his bed (1:43-48).

1:49-53 At the news, Adonijah's former loyal followers fled like rats from a sinking ship while Adonijah ran to the tabernacle in Jerusalem (1:49). He grabbed **the horns of the altar** as a way of pleading for his life (1:50-51). Solomon granted Adonijah a reprieve—on the condition that he prove himself loyal (1:52). When he stood before Solomon and **paid homage**, the king sent him **home** (1:53). It was an uneasy peace—and it wouldn't last.

2:1-4 As David realized his days were few, he left his final instructions to Solomon for the wise administration of his kingdom. These are divided into two parts: Solomon's walk with the Lord and his dealings with the people who could bring harm to his throne.

The most important thing David said to his son was this: **Be strong and be a man, and keep your obligation to the LORD your God to walk in his ways.** How would Solomon know how to walk in God's ways? By keeping

his **statutes, commands, ordinances, and decrees** that were **written in the law of Moses.** If Solomon were careful to put God's Word at the center of his reign, he would **have success in everything** (2:2-3). David then spoke to Solomon of the covenant God had made with David, granting him an eternal dynasty and establishing his throne forever (see 2 Sam 7:8-16). But, it would require that Solomon and his sons after him **walk faithfully before** God (2:4).

Though Solomon and his descendants would ultimately fail in this and would instead lead the people into idolatry, God would fulfill his own covenant requirements. When the time was right, he would send his perfect Son, born of the line of David. Jesus Christ would fulfill the demands of God's law, offer his life as an atoning sacrifice for sin, and then rise from the dead. He will sit on David's throne and reign forever (see Isa 9:6-7).

2:5-6 David's awareness of his impending death made him remember that there were some outstanding injustices to correct and a faithful family to reward. The first name on his list was **Joab**, who had too long escaped justice for his treacherous, cold-blooded murders of **Abner** and **Amasa**, both of whom he killed **in a time of peace.** Joab's guilt clung to him like the blood of these men that stained his **waistband** and **sandals** (2:5). David had probably withheld Joab's well-deserved death sentence because he had served him loyally. But recently, there'd been a breach in Joab's loyalty when he conspired with Adonijah (1:7, 19). So, David charged Solomon with the responsibility of bringing justice to Joab (2:6).

In the United States, when we have an election, the winners enter office and the losers go do something else. A new government official will typically replace the old guard in his administration with new officials of his choosing. But, that's not how things worked in the ancient world.

Most of us don't know what it's like to live in a monarchy in which the king must always be on guard against the plotting of his enemies who want to assassinate him and usurp his throne. Joab had proved to be fierce and self-serving. His words and actions could not be trusted; he would be a liability to Solomon.

2:7-9 Good things were in store for **the sons of Barzillai the Gileadite**, David's great friend who'd ministered to the king's needs when **Absalom** drove him into exile. Bringing the aged man's family to Solomon's **table** was David's way of charging Solomon with taking care of their needs (2:7).

Another man who had appeared during David's flight from Absalom was **Shimei**, who had **uttered malicious curses** at David (2:8). Though he'd apologized when David returned to retake the throne (see 2 Sam 19:16-22), David didn't trust Shimei but considered him an opportunist. He had to answer for cursing the Lord's anointed (2:9).

2:10-12 David was **buried** in the capital he had established, satisfied that Solomon's **kingship was firmly established** (2:10, 12). King David had **reigned over Israel** a total of **forty years** (2:11).

2:13-17 Adonijah had already proved his willingness to conspire to obtain the throne (2:13). Fading into the background after Solomon spared his life would've been the wise thing to do (see 1:51-53), but he couldn't leave well enough alone.

Adonijah approached Bathsheba for a "peaceful" **talk** (2:13-14). He began by reminding her—cue the sad music—that he and **all Israel expected** him **to be king**, but that it was taken away from him (2:15). Then, he made a request. Adonijah foolishly asked Solomon's mother to approach the king on his behalf and give him **Abishag the Shunammite** as his **wife** (2:17).

2:18-25 Abishag had been David's concubine, though he had not been intimate with her (see 1:1-4). To acquire a woman from a king's harem was to have grounds for claiming the crown (see 2 Sam 3:6-7; 16:21-22). Whether Bathsheba was oblivious to what Adonijah's request meant or understood it all too well, Bathsheba relayed it to the king.

Solomon saw immediately that Adonijah's request was really a plot against the throne. He retorted, **Since he is my elder brother, you might as well ask the kingship for him** (2:22). Because Adonijah had been next in line in the normal succession of kings, marrying Abishag would have given him *two* claims to

the throne in the eyes of Israel's people. As far as Solomon was concerned, then, his brother's request was an act of treason. Adonijah paid for his conspiring with his life (2:25).

There was more going on here, however, than the mere elimination of a rival to Solomon. God was still judging David and his family for his earlier sins of adultery and murder (see 2 Sam 11:1–12:23). Years before, David had pronounced judgment on himself when he thought he was passing judgment on the villain of Nathan's story about a rich man eating a poor man's pet sheep. He'd said, "As the Lord lives, the man who did this deserves to die! Because he has done this thing and shown no pity, he must pay four lambs for that lamb" (2 Sam 12:5).

Don't miss that God had taken David at his word. Up to now, David had paid for his sins with the lives of three "lambs": his sons Amnon (see 2 Sam 13:21-29), Absalom (see 2 Sam 18:9-15), and the unnamed baby boy resulting from his adultery (see 2 Sam 12:15-23). The fourth loss was Adonijah. The lesson is clear: even forgiven sin has consequences.

2:26-27 Solomon also didn't trust **the priest Abiathar** (2:26), who had "conspired with" Adonijah (see 1:7). Though Solomon thought he deserved **death**, he chose to banish Abiathar from the priesthood instead, because he had **carried the ark** of God for King David and had been judged unworthy of continuing the privilege (2:26-27). The author lets us know that this was actually a fulfillment of **the Lord's prophecy ... against Eli's family**, spoken even before David was born (2:27; see 1 Sam 2:27-33). God's wheels of judgment often grind slowly, but he is as faithful to judge as he is to pardon and forgive.

2:28-46 The executions of **Joab** (2:28-35) and **Shimei** (2:36-46) completed Solomon's task of purging the threats to his kingdom.

When Joab heard **the news** about what had happened to his fellow conspirators Adonijah and Abiathar, he realized that his time had come. So he fled to the **tabernacle**, normally a place of refuge, and grabbed **the horns of the altar** in hopes of being spared (2:28)—as Adonijah had done after his failed coup attempt (see 1:50-51). But, Joab was not being sought for his part in that rebellion. Solomon announced that Joab was condemned for murders in David's day, which that king had had no part in (2:31-33). The king didn't want the crimes of Joab to taint David's **throne** and **dynasty** (2:33), so the man of extreme violence was finally executed (2:34).

In Shimei's case, Solomon was initially gracious, allowing him to live as long as he remained **in Jerusalem** (2:36-37). In fact, **Shimei** considered his **sentence** to be **fair** (2:38). But, **three years** later, when his **slaves ran away**, Shimei traveled in pursuit of them (2:39-40). (Clearly, he didn't believe the king would actually follow through on what he'd said.) With Shimei's death, **the kingdom was established in Solomon's hand** (2:46).

✨ B. Solomon's Wisdom, Administration, and Fame (3:1–4:34) ✨

3:1 Solomon undoubtedly felt the weight of governing God's people. Sometime early in his reign, the king **made an alliance with Pharaoh king of Egypt by marrying [his] daughter**. This move showed that Solomon was not hesitant to use marriage as a political strategy, and he would eventually take polygamy and foreign marriages to dizzying heights. In Old Testament times, God tolerated polygamy among his people, but it always cost them because it was outside his will. The king's practice would exact a terrible cost, not just from Solomon but also from the entire nation of Israel.

3:2-3 At this time, the people of Israel **were sacrificing on the high places** (3:2), engaging in a pagan practice they learned from their Canaanite neighbors that was in violation of the Mosaic law (see Lev 17:3-4). Despite following these pagan practices, **Solomon loved the Lord by walking in the statutes of his father David** (3:3).

3:4-9 It was at **Gibeon**—which **was the most famous high place** (3:4)—that Solomon famously asked the Lord for wisdom. God initiated the proceedings by appearing to Solomon with a stunning offer: **What should I give you?** (3:5). Solomon's response

showed that, in one sense, he was already wise beyond his years. (He was about twenty when he became king.) The young man recognized his inadequacies. He had no **experience in leadership**, yet he had been made ruler of a numerous **people** (3:7-8). What he needed was **a receptive heart to judge** and lead them well (3:9). The first step toward becoming a kingdom man is to realize your desperate need for God.

3:10-15 God was so **pleased** that Solomon asked for wisdom (see Jas 1:5), rather than **long life or riches**, that he granted the request—and added to it what Solomon did not ask for: **riches . . . honor . . . and a long life** (3:10-14). But, for these promised blessings to be a reality, Solomon would have to **walk** in the Lord's **ways** and **keep** his **statutes and commands** (3:14). God's promises were sure, *but* they had to be accessed by obedience. Solomon responded to the encounter with worship and feasting (3:15).

3:16-22 The story appearing in this section was clearly intended by the author of 1 Kings to demonstrate the profound wisdom that God had granted Solomon. It helps us see that having wisdom does not involve the mere acquisition of knowledge and understanding. Rather, wisdom is spiritual understanding applied to earthly living. God had given Solomon not just smarts, but also the ability to see the world from a spiritual perspective and apply that perspective to life. The book of Proverbs, written mostly by Solomon, is further demonstration that God had blessed the king with the ability to put spiritual truth into action.

The king served as Israel's one-man supreme court, the last level of appeal in difficult cases. This particular case involved a dilemma between **two women who were prostitutes** (3:16). Each had given birth to a child (3:17-18). The first woman claimed that the child of the second woman had **died because she lay on him** while sleeping (3:19). Then, while it was still night, the second woman placed her **dead son** next to the first woman and took her living son for herself (3:20). When the first woman woke to find the child next to her dead, she recognized that he wasn't her son (3:21). The second woman vigorously denied it and claimed the exact opposite (3:22).

3:23-26 Left without the help of a DNA test, the average judge would be stumped by the case. But, with his God-given insight into the ways of human nature, Solomon knew just what to do. He said to **cut the living boy in two** and give half to each woman! (3:25). And, just as the king knew would happen, the child's true mother begged for the baby's life and was even willing to give him up; the other woman cruelly seconded the king's decision (3:26).

3:27-28 His unique solution to the dilemma rewarded, Solomon gave **the living baby to the first woman** (3:27). The account quickly made the rounds in Israel, so that everyone **stood in awe of the king because they saw that God's wisdom was in him to carry out justice** (3:28). Solomon's reputation as the wisest man who'd ever lived spread quickly, and it brought glory to God.

4:1-19 Solomon also displayed God's wisdom in the way he organized his administration, delegating responsibility for the kingdom's order and efficiency. His top **officials** included **secretaries** (4:1-2), a position that could be comparable to secretary of state. These men would have prepared the official documents that pertained to the administration of Solomon's kingdom. The **court historian** (4:3) was responsible for keeping a record of the court's daily activities. Other officials included the **priests** and the commander of **the army** (4:4). And so it went down the line, as Solomon appointed his kingdom administrators. The king also divided the nation into twelve districts with **twelve deputies**. Each was to provide **food for the king and his household** for **one month out of the year** (4:7).

4:20-21 The people of **Judah and Israel** were **numerous** (in fulfillment of God's promise in Gen 22:17), and Solomon's kingdom was vast. The king exacted **tribute** from the nations under his rule, and they **served** him (4:21). This is a reminder that God is able to take the resources of unbelievers and use them for his kingdom purposes.

4:22-28 The **provisions** required for the king and **everyone who came to [his] table** were staggering (4:22-24, 27). The twelve district **deputies** who were responsible for

supplying the **food** each **month** had a huge assignment on their hands (4:27; see 4:7). Each one must have been glad when he could hand over the responsibility to the next guy! Nevertheless, **they neglected nothing** (4:27), and all of **Judah and Israel lived in safety** under **Solomon's reign** (4:25).

4:29-34 As a result of God's blessing, Solomon was what we would call a Renaissance man. There was no area in which he did not have unsurpassed **wisdom** (4:29). He was an author of **proverbs**, a composer of **songs**, and even a botanist and zoologist (4:32-33). That his wisdom far surpassed **the wisdom of all the people of the East** and **all the wisdom of Egypt** (4:30) was significant because these regions were fabled for their wisdom. In fact, the author flatly declared that there was no real comparison to be made: Solomon **was wiser than anyone**. What's more, Solomon's **reputation** was no secret. **The surrounding nations** came to know and revere the king of Israel (4:31). **Every king on earth** sent **emissaries** to **listen to Solomon's wisdom** (4:34). The kingdom of God was blessing the kingdoms of the world.

A consideration of Solomon's ancestry is instructive. He was David's son by Bathsheba, a Hamitic woman of African descent. We know of her lineage because Bathsheba literally means "the daughter of Sheba." The "Table of Nations" identifies Sheba in the line of Ham, making Sheba a man from an African nation (see Gen 10:7). Solomon's mother (as well as his ancestors Rahab and Ruth; see commentary on 1 Sam 16:13) gave him further roots within the black community. They thus place him as an example of black achievement as well as black history in biblical culture.

➣ C. The Construction and Dedication of the Temple (5:1–8:66) ❦

5:1-5 Though King Solomon was exalted for his unsurpassed, God-given wisdom (4:29-34), the high point of his rule was his construction of the temple in Jerusalem. His **father David** had desired to build a permanent **temple for** the Lord, but he was told no (5:3; see 2 Sam 7:1-17). That assignment would instead fall to this son. When the king received a congratulatory message from **King Hiram of Tyre** (5:1), a Phoenician kingdom just north of Israel, Solomon's plans for temple construction and for enlisting Hiram's assistance got rolling.

5:6-9 The Phoenicians were well-known for their architectural abilities, and the **cedars from Lebanon** to the east of Tyre would provide excellent lumber. So, Solomon offered to pay Hiram to provide **timber** for the temple, and Hiram agreed (5:6-9). In fact, Hiram, who had been a friend of David (5:1), **blessed** the Lord and praised Solomon for his wisdom (5:7).

5:10-12 Tyre and Sidon (another Phoenician city) provided Solomon with **all the cedar and cypress timber he wanted** for the temple's construction (5:10). In return, Hiram asked for huge quantities of **wheat** and olive **oil** to feed his own royal **household**. This arrangement continued **year after year** (5:11). Solomon conducted his negotiations with Hiram in the wisdom God gave him. Instead of simply demanding what he wanted or treating Hiram as an inferior, Solomon was able to secure the wood he needed while maintaining their cordial relationship and ensuring **peace** between the two nations (5:12).

5:13-18 The building project required workers by the tens of thousands. So, Solomon **drafted forced laborers** (5:13). These laborers had to go to Tyre for **one month** at a time, with **two months** home (5:14). Not only did their project require a tremendous amount of timber (5:10-12), but it also required large quantities of **stone** (5:17-18). The sheer scope of Solomon's temple project is overwhelming—even in modern terms.

6:1 This chapter begins with an important chronological statement that allows us to fix several key dates in Israel's history. **Solomon began to build the temple ... in the four hundred eightieth year after the Israelites came out of the land of Egypt, in the fourth year of his reign over Israel**. It is generally agreed that Solomon reigned

from 971 to 931 BC. So, the fourth year of his reign would have been about 966 BC. Going back 480 years from this allows us to arrive at a date for the exodus: 1446 BC.

Solomon's charge to build the temple, Israel's house of worship, was the key feature of his reign. From this point onward, the attitude of Israel and Judah's kings toward the temple, and by extension toward the Lord and his covenant, would be the basis for their evaluation in God's eyes. Additionally, all of these kings, beginning with Solomon, would be compared to David to see whether any of them was the promised Son of David who would fulfill the Davidic covenant in all of its details. In other words, each king would be weighed on whether he could possibly be the messianic king.

Of course, no king would ace this test on all points, leaving the readers of 1 and 2 Kings to look to the future for their Messiah. We will see this spiritual evaluation of the various kings more in 1 and 2 Chronicles, which were written from a perspective that was more interested in how each king measured up to God's standards than in what each did during his reign.

6:2-4 Solomon's temple was not huge in terms of square footage, but its size was the only modest thing about it. Its outer appearance must have been stunning. It featured dressed stones, cedar, and gold. **The portico in front of the temple** was a large, open porch that extended out another **fifteen feet** (6:3)

6:5-10 Among the other descriptions of the temple's features was the construction of a series of storage **side chambers** on three floors of the building (6:5-6, 8, 10). **The temple's construction used finished stones cut at the quarry so that no hammer, chisel, or any iron tool was heard in the temple while it was being built** (6:7). Making sure that each piece was precut so that it would sit perfectly in place would have required amazing skill. Just as the Lord had provided skilled workers to build the tabernacle (see Exod 31:1-11), he provided the same for the construction of his holy temple.

6:11-13 When God spoke to Solomon, he restated his promise to **dwell among** his people in the temple and **not abandon** them (6:13). But, it would require Israel's obedience, with Solomon leading the way (6:12). In short, God wanted to remind the king and all Israel that he was more concerned about their hearts and their obedience to him than he was with the building they were working on. Yet, sadly, as history would reveal, the king would stray from the Lord and the people would follow.

6:14-20 The remainder of this chapter contains a description of the temple's **interior** (6:15). The emphasis is on the temple's most important sections, including the holy place and the **inner sanctuary, the most holy place** (6:16). The former was **sixty feet long**, while the most holy place was a **thirty**-foot cube (6:17, 20). In this **inner sanctuary**, the **ark of the LORD's covenant** would rest (6:19). The ark was considered the throne of God; he was enthroned between the cherubim above its cover, the mercy seat (see 1 Sam 4:4; Isa 37:16). Solomon **overlaid** the most holy place **with pure gold** (6:20). According to 2 Chronicles 3:8, the weight of gold overlaying the most holy place was "forty-five thousand pounds"! Then, Solomon **overlaid the interior of the temple with pure gold**, and he **added the gold overlay to the entire temple** (6:21-22). The one true God deserved a temple of unequaled grandeur.

6:23-38 The **two cherubim** in the inner sanctuary were carved **out of olive wood** and **overlaid . . . with gold** (6:23, 28). Their wings were to stretch out and tower over the ark of the covenant (6:24-27).

As if the magnificence of the temple wasn't enough, Solomon then **overlaid** even **the temple floor with gold** (6:30). The splendor of Solomon's temple staggers the imagination. Everything about it spoke of the majesty of God.

The project was completed in the **eleventh year** of Solomon's reign. Thus, the temple took **seven years** to build (6:38).

7:1-8 It took Solomon almost twice as long to build his **entire palace complex** (7:1) as it took to build the temple. The palace was without question a grand structure. The **House of**

the **Forest of Lebanon** (7:2) was probably so named because cedar from Lebanon was used extensively in its construction (see 5:6). Within the larger complex was also **the Hall of the Throne**, which was explained as the place where Solomon **would judge**; thus, it is further described as **the Hall of Judgment** (7:7). Mention of the house **for Pharaoh's daughter, [Solomon's] wife** finished the insights we get into Solomon's royal residence (7:8).

7:9-12 The author emphasizes how grand the entire complex was by repeating the **costly** nature of the materials (7:9-11). As with the Lord's temple, Solomon spared no expense in the construction of his palace.

7:13-14 Solomon brought a man named **Hiram** to Jerusalem to do the extensive bronze work needed for the temple (7:13). This man was not the king of Tyre (see 5:1-12) but a **widow's son from the tribe of Naphtali**. His **father was a man of Tyre** and **a bronze craftsman**. That he was brought in suggests his skill was beyond anything Solomon could find locally. Hiram set right to work.

7:15-22 Hiram **cast two bronze pillars**, which were incredibly elaborate pieces, each free-standing, with ornate **capitals of cast bronze** on top of each (7:15-17). When these pillars were ready and in place on the portico of the temple, Solomon actually named them: **he set up the right pillar and named it Jachin; then he set up the left pillar and named it Boaz** (7:21). These names, meaning, "He Will Establish" and "In Him Is Strength," respectively, were a testimony to the security and strength that the Lord offered to his people.

7:23-39 Hiram also made a huge **metal** water **basin** with elaborate decorations. It rested on the backs of **twelve oxen** he had sculpted (7:23-25). The basin was so large that it held **eleven thousand gallons** of water (7:26); it would be used by the priests to wash themselves (see 2 Chr 4:6).

Even though they had **wheels** and were movable, the **ten bronze water carts** were also awesome in size and very elaborate (7:27, 32). **Ten bronze basins** were made and placed on **the ten water carts** (7:38). These could be taken wherever they were needed to supply water for rinsing the burnt offerings (see 2 Chr 4:6).

7:40-47 Hiram's work was catalogued without attempt to summarize the amount of bronze used (7:40-46). Instead, **all the utensils** were left **unweighed because there were so many; the weight of the bronze was not determined** (7:47).

7:48-51 The **gold** work completed on the temple and its furnishings was summarized briefly (7:48-50). And, once everything was in its place, the temple was ready for its dedication and use in worship (7:51).

8:1-5 The temple dedication began with the transport and installation of **the ark of the Lord's covenant** from its place on Mount **Zion** (8:1; see 2 Sam 6:17). This was to be a great ceremony to which Solomon called **all the men of Israel**, from **leaders** to representatives of every family (8:1-2). The procession of the ark to the new temple was elaborate and tremendous in scale. They sacrificed so many **sheep, goats, and cattle** that they **could not be counted or numbered** (8:5), suggesting that, once again, Solomon spared no expense.

8:6-8 In contrast with David's first attempt to move the ark as recorded in 2 Samuel 6:1-10, **the ark** was carried the proper way this time, by **the priests** using **poles** attached through rings on the sides of the ark so that no one would touch it (see Exod 25:12-15; Deut 10:8). The ark's journey was complete when the priests set it down in **the most holy place beneath the wings of the cherubim**, which **covered the ark** (8:6-7). They spread their wings over the ark **from above** (8:7). The author even mentions the way the ark's carrying poles extended beyond the holy place, as if no detail about the ark was unimportant (8:8).

8:9 The ark was the centerpiece of the temple. God had promised Moses that he would meet with his people above the mercy seat on top of the ark (see Exod 25:22). The contents of the ark were **the two stone tablets that Moses had put there at Horeb** (Mount

Sinai). These pointed to the fact that the primary concern for Israel was to obey the law of their divine King. (Previously, the **covenant** that God made with Israel at Sinai had often been neglected and disobeyed by the people.) The purpose of the dedication ceremony described was to reiterate that Solomon and Israel still saw themselves as bound to the Lord's covenant, as indeed they were.

8:10-11 Once the ark was in place in the inner sanctuary, **the cloud filled the Lord's temple**; this was a visible symbol of the Lord's presence (8:10). What an awe-inspiring sight that must have been! Interestingly, the same thing had happened when the tabernacle was dedicated in Moses's day (see Exod 40:34). And, just as Moses was unable to enter the tent because the cloud of God's glory filled it, so, too, **the priests were not able to continue ministering, for the glory of the Lord filled the temple** (8:11). When God manifests his glory, all activity must cease. Israel's great King had come to dwell with his people.

8:12-19 Solomon broke the silence by blessing the Lord and the people of Israel. He explained that God's presence was a confirmation that he had **fulfilled** his promises to David **by his power** (8:15). During David's reign, God had **not chosen a city to build a temple in** (8:16). David's **desire** to build a temple for God was good (8:17-18), but God intended that David's **son** would do the work (8:19).

8:20 Everything God had spoken had come to pass. Notice how Solomon articulated it: **The Lord has fulfilled what he promised. . . . I have built the temple for the name of the Lord, the God of Israel.** Importantly, Solomon didn't take all of the credit for himself; the construction of the temple had been planned and promised by God. Nevertheless, God didn't miraculously cause the temple to appear out of thin air; its existence required careful obedience from Solomon. This is divine sovereignty and human responsibility in action.

8:21 The purpose of the temple was to serve as a home for the **ark**. The Lord had intended this end hundreds of years earlier when he **brought** Israel **out of the land of Egypt**. The great moment had finally arrived. Thus, Solomon reminded the people that God had been true to his word of so long ago.

We often expect or even demand God to act immediately. But, God brings about his promises and plans in his perfect timing. He knows what we need; he also knows when we need it.

8:22 After reviewing God's faithfulness, Solomon offered a long prayer of intercession for himself and the people (8:22-53). He dramatically **stood before the altar . . . in front of the entire congregation . . . and spread out his hands toward heaven**. What he said next became one of the greatest affirmations of the person and work of God in Scripture.

8:23 Solomon began by acknowledging the Lord's uniqueness among the false gods that surrounded Israel. He said, **There is no God like you**. The nations beyond Israel's borders boasted of their powerful gods, but those pretenders were all talk and no action. The Lord, by contrast, demonstrated that he alone is God because he kept **the gracious covenant** that he had made with the children of Israel. So, not only did he make promises, he also acted to keep them.

8:24-26 One of the promises God had made to David was that he would **never fail to have a man . . . on the throne of Israel**. Solomon was living proof that God had begun to fulfill that promise. But, in order for that promise to continue, it would require that David's sons **take care to walk before** the Lord in faithfulness (8:25). Unfortunately, as the books of 1–2 Kings and 1–2 Chronicles bear witness, the sons of David who reigned on his throne after him frequently failed.

Ultimately, God himself would fulfill the requirements in the person of his Son, Jesus Christ. As a descendent of David, he would qualify to sit on the throne (see Matt 1:1; Rom 1:3; Rev 22:16). And, as the sinless and eternal Son of God, he alone can fulfill God's promise to "establish the throne of his kingdom forever" (2 Sam 7:13).

8:27 Next, Solomon extolled the transcendence of God—the truth that God is beyond creation and cannot be contained by it. He

asked, **Will God indeed live on earth**? In spite of the fact that Solomon had **built** a temple for God to "dwell" in, the king was not so naïve as to think that the Lord of heaven and earth actually needed a home and could be confined to it. Not even heaven itself can **contain** him! Solomon knew that when the transcendent Creator manifested his presence to his people in the cloud of glory (8:10-11), it was a demonstration of his grace to them.

8:28-30 Understanding that God could not be contained by the temple, Solomon prayed that God would nevertheless fulfill his promise to make his **name** (8:29)—a synonym for his presence and character—dwell there. He asked that the Lord would hear the prayers of his people, which they would pray in the direction of the structure, and that he would **forgive** them (8:30). Solomon's prayer thus established the custom that subsequent Jews would follow of turning toward Jerusalem when they prayed (see 8:48; Dan 6:10).

8:31-32 As was fitting in launching this new era in Israel's history, Solomon presented a number of specific requests to the Lord as part of his prayer. Each request was tied directly to the people's response to the Lord and his temple (8:31-51). Because taking an **oath** before God at his **altar** there was a serious matter (8:31), Solomon asked that God would condemn **the wicked** and reward **the righteous**. He also prayed that **justice** between individual Israelites would be done when they brought their disputes to the Lord there (8:32).

8:33-34 The temple was also to be the place where Israel would seek God's forgiveness for sins that caused them to be **defeated** in battle (8:33). Such defeats could cause Israel to lose a part of the **land** that God **gave their ancestors**. Solomon thus asked that God would **restore** such land when the people repented (8:34). (The readers of 1–2 Kings would have felt a special pain in reading these verses, because they knew God had taken away all the land and sent his people into exile for their disobedience.)

8:35-40 Another form of punishment on sin was drought (8:35). For an agricultural society, adequate **rain** was not simply refreshing, but was also an absolute necessity for survival (8:36). The land, crops, and people were also subject to other disasters that God might send to awaken Israel to sin, such as **pestilence, blight, locust,** and **plague** (8:37).

Solomon knew the Lord would hear and restore those who were truly repentant because God **alone** knows **every human heart** (8:39). By disciplining them for their sin and forgiving them when they repent, God leads his people to take him seriously—to **fear** (that is, to honor and respect) him (8:40).

8:41-43 Solomon's prayer list even included **the foreigner** (8:41), the non-Israelite who attached himself to Israel because of his faith in the Lord. If God would hear such devout followers from other nations and answer their prayers toward the temple, **then all peoples of earth** would **know** and **fear** God (8:42-43).

8:44-45 Though Solomon's empire had become vast and powerful, he knew that victory over **enemies** depended on the blessing and presence of the Lord (8:44). So, he asked that prayers offered by Israelite soldiers in the direction of Jerusalem would be answered with success (8:44-45). The idea of facing Jerusalem in prayer was not a mere magic formula. Instead, it represented Israel's acknowledgement that the God who alone could deliver them dwelled in his temple just as promised.

8:46-51 Solomon's final petition was prophetic. To be driven from the land and deported to an **enemy's country** was the worst fate they could imagine (8:46). At the time, the prospect of this sort of disaster must have seemed completely alien. Yet, this was a real danger that loomed large over Israel's future. Thus, Solomon left Israel with a word of hope that, even in the most disastrous circumstance possible, the God whose temple was in Jerusalem would hear and answer his people's genuine prayers of repentance (8:47-50)—because he had done it before when he brought them out of captivity in **Egypt** (8:51). This same God stands ready to hear your prayers of repentance, as well.

8:52-66 Solomon's benediction restated the heart of his prayer—that the God who **set them apart** as his **inheritance** would hear

his people's prayers. After this, the king **blessed** the people and the Lord (8:53-56). He asked that God would remember his prayer and be glorified among all the people of the earth (8:57-61). Then, the people offered **sacrifices** in the thousands and thus **dedicated the LORD's temple** (8:62-63). **The festival** that followed ran for two weeks (8:65). When the celebration was complete, the people **blessed the king,** and Solomon sent everyone home **with happy hearts for all the goodness that the LORD had done** (8:66).

The worship and joy that Israel experienced in the Lord's presence that day is a picture of what the church should experience on a regular basis. It is also a foretaste of the tremendous joy that we will experience in the ages to come with Jesus Christ as our King.

⇥ D. Solomon's Kingdom, Wealth, and Downfall (9:1–11:43) ⇐

9:1-5 Once again, God spoke to Solomon in a dream (9:1-2; see 3:1-15). He responded to the king's prayers with a promise and a solemn warning. In the first dream, God had promised Solomon wisdom and wealth. This time, he promised to **establish** Solomon's **royal throne** and the kingly line of David **forever**—provided that the king would **walk before** God **with a heart of integrity** (9:4-5).

9:6-9 If Solomon and those who came after him failed to keep God's commands, if they served and worshiped false gods instead of the one true God, the Lord would **reject the temple** and **cut off Israel from the land** (9:6-7). The newly finished structure that stood in all its glory would be decimated (9:8). But, if so, God would make sure that all of the surrounding nations knew why it happened. **Ruin** would come on Israel because they had **abandoned** their God (9:8-9).

Was it really possible that Israel could fall into idolatry after God had manifested his glorious presence? Tragically, it had happened before. The generation that Moses led out of the wilderness, in fact, witnessed the Lord's spectacular signs and wonders over and over again. Yet, they rejected him—over and over again. Sure enough, then, not only would Israel bow down to other gods in the future, but King Solomon himself would do so.

9:10 The remainder of this chapter and the next emphasize the vastness of Solomon's kingdom, his fame, and his tremendous wealth. Solomon ruled forty years. So, when he completed the temple and his palace **at the end of twenty years**, he had reached the midpoint of his reign.

9:11-14 King Hiram of Tyre, who had been a friend of David, supplied Solomon with abundant **cedar and cypress logs and gold for** his building projects. But, Solomon was not as generous toward Hiram. He **gave Hiram twenty towns in the land of Galilee** in northwest Israel, not far from Tyre (9:11). But, Hiram wasn't happy with his gift, calling the towns the **Land of Cabul**, a Hebrew word meaning "Like Nothing" (9:13). In other words, though Hiram had given Solomon **nine thousand pounds of gold** (9:14), Solomon gave him "nothing" in response. In providing this insight, it seems the author was indicating that Solomon's character was beginning to crack.

9:15-23 The record of Solomon's **forced labor** (9:15) shows how he acquired the workers needed to complete the temple and his palace complex. Some of the workers came from his father-in-law, **Pharaoh king of Egypt**, who **captured Gezer** (located about twenty miles west of Jerusalem) and gave it as a **dowry to his daughter** (9:16). Solomon then **rebuilt Gezer**, as well as a number of other cities throughout the land (9:17-19). The slaves he used for all of his construction projects came from **the peoples who remained of** Israel's enemies, that is, **their descendants** (9:20-21). And, while the Israelites weren't consigned to slavery, that doesn't mean Solomon didn't put them to work. They served as his **soldiers** and his **servants** (9:22-23). This heavy burden of labor would prove to be a problem for Solomon's successor (see 12:2-4).

9:24-25 Even though the first seeds of Solomon's downfall were being planted, he was faithful in his early years to offer the required sacrifices **three times a year** (9:25) in obedience to the Lord's command that all males come to Jerusalem annually for the festivals (see Exod 23:14-16).

9:26-28 Interestingly, Solomon was also famous for his navy, for which he needed the expertise of Hiram's sailors, who helped the Israelite seamen on their voyages to acquire **gold** (9:28).

10:1-5 Earlier, we read that Solomon's fame had spread widely (4:34). The story in 10:1-13 serves to illustrate that point. It also shows that God was blessing the peoples of the world through his people, just as he had promised Abraham (Gen 12:3). This was only a small foretaste, though. Ultimately, Israel would fail at this task. True spiritual blessings for all peoples of the earth would eventually come through the true seed (descendent) of Abraham, Jesus Christ (see Gal 3:14, 16, 29).

The **queen of Sheba** visited Solomon's court. She was from an Arabian kingdom that was located in what is modern-day Yemen; her country lay about 1,200 miles from Jerusalem. The queen visited Solomon because of his **fame connected with the name of the LORD**, which is probably a reference to the wisdom that the Lord had given him. She **came to test him with riddles** to see for herself if his abilities lived up to his reputation (10:1). She wasn't exactly a pauper herself, bringing with her **a very large entourage** of expensive and exotic gifts (10:2). But, Solomon's wisdom and wealth were far beyond what she could fathom. By the time she had heard his explanations and seen his glorious kingdom, **it took her breath away** (10:3-5).

10:6-13 The visiting queen admitted that she hadn't believed **the reports** she had heard about Solomon. But, she'd seen that he was the real deal (10:6-7). She then **blessed** the Lord for putting Solomon on his throne for Israel's sake (10:9). She also gave Solomon a mind-boggling treasure of gifts (10:10), and he apparently returned the favor (10:13).

Later, Jesus mentioned the queen of Sheba (also called "the queen of the south") in his condemnation of the scribes and

Pharisees (Matt 12:42). She was willing to travel hundreds of miles to hear Solomon's wisdom. But, while the Son of God far exceeded Solomon in wisdom and glory, the Jewish religious leaders only scoffed at him. According to Jesus, at the final judgment, the queen of Sheba will point her finger at them in condemnation. They will have no excuse for having rejected the Messiah.

10:14-22 The wealth that Solomon acquired **annually** was astounding. Aside from what he obtained through **merchants** and **traders**, he received **twenty-five tons** of gold every year (10:14-15). With this, he **made two hundred large shields . . . [and] three hundred small shields of hammered gold** (10:16-17), which were kept in storage and evidently used for ceremonial purposes only. No expense was spared in making Solomon's impressive **throne** (10:18-20), and even his **drinking cups were gold** (1:21). The king's wealth in gold was so vast that nothing was made of **silver, since it was considered as nothing in Solomon's time** (10:21, see 10:27). Such splendor is hard to imagine.

10:23-29 God kept his promise to make Solomon the wisest and richest man who ever lived (see 3:11-13). He **surpassed all the kings of the world in riches and in wisdom**, and people from all over the world wanted to come to Solomon's court **to hear the wisdom that God had put in his heart** (10:23-24).

Solomon also made Israel a military power by importing **chariots** (10:26), the most advanced weapon of the day. He also imported **horses** from **Egypt** (10:28). With these mentions, the careful Bible reader will note a hint of the creeping pride and inattention to the Lord's commands that would soon bring Solomon down. The Lord had told Moses that when God appointed a king for his people, the king was not to "acquire many horses for himself or send the people back to Egypt to acquire many horses" (Deut 17:16). Moreover, he was also not to "acquire very large amounts of silver and gold for himself" (Deut 17:17). Descriptions like these make us wonder at what

point Solomon began putting his trust in his wealth, his chariots, and his horses instead of in the Lord.

11:1-3 The opening verses in this chapter are some of the saddest in Scripture. No one else in the Bible rose as high as Solomon, and few fell as hard and as low. Solomon began to accumulate **many foreign women** as **wives** and **concubines** (11:1, 3). First, this was a problem because it was contrary to God's original design of one man and one woman being united together (see Gen 1:22-25). Second, marrying women from the surrounding nations was clearly forbidden, for God had warned that such women would **turn** the Israelites' **heart away to follow their gods** (11:2; see Deut 7:3-4). And third, as God had told Moses, the king in particular was "not [to] acquire many wives for himself, so that his heart [wouldn't] go astray" (Deut 17:17). Tragically, Solomon hadn't overlooked these truths merely once or twice but *hundreds* of times. He had **seven hundred wives** and **three hundred . . . concubines**. And, indeed, **they turned his heart away** (11:3).

11:4 The very next verse repeats the indictment: Solomon's **wives turned his heart away to follow other gods**. Interestingly, this happened when he **was old**, suggesting that decades of marrying foreign wives and providing for their false worship had drained Solomon's life of spiritual vitality. Yet, that was no excuse for his sin. **He was not wholeheartedly devoted to the Lord, as his father David had been.**

The comparison to David was inevitable because Solomon was the heir of God's promise to give David an everlasting throne. While David had sinned greatly, too, he had repented. Solomon, however, only continued in his downward slide.

11:5-8 The list of false gods and goddesses that **Solomon followed** and for which he **built** high places is shocking: **Ashtoreth, Milcom,** and **Chemosh** (11:5, 7) were the gods of the surrounding nations. And, Scripture pulls no punches. What the king did was **evil in the Lord's sight** (11:6) because such idols were **abhorrent** (11:7). But, because **all**

his foreign wives burned incense and offered sacrifices to their gods (11:8), Solomon built them places of worship. How ironic that the king who had built the magnificent temple for the one true God was now constructing sites of devotion and veneration for idols! Saying that he did not remain loyal to the LORD (11:6) is a major understatement.

11:9-10 The Lord had appeared to Solomon in dreams twice and made tremendous promises to him (see 3:5-17; 9:1-9). Despite this, the king repaid God's kindness by turning his heart away from him. Needless to say, the LORD was angry (11:9). Though God had specifically warned him, Solomon disregarded him (11:10).

11:11-13 The Lord revealed himself to Solomon one more time—bringing a message of judgment. For his rejection of the Lord, Solomon would have his kingdom torn away and given to another. Though his kingdom no doubt seemed invincible, it would crumble. Solomon's son would retain a portion of the kingdom—one tribe (11:13). But, Solomon's servant would claim the rest (11:11). While God wouldn't let the kingdom split occur until Solomon's son was in power and would still grant him a throne, he did this not because Solomon deserved a reprieve but for the sake of . . . David and for the sake of Jerusalem (11:12-13).

How did Solomon receive this message of judgment? Scripture doesn't tell us, but God's judgment was final.

11:14-22 Solomon didn't have to wonder how God was going to execute his judgment. In his own day, God raised up two foreign enemies and one domestic foe against the kingdom. Hadad the Edomite was a survivor of the slaughter of the Edomites that occurred in David's day, led by Joab, David's brutal army commander who did not relent until he had killed every male in Edom (11:14-16). Hadad had been a boy at the time and a member of the royal house in Edom, Israel's ancient enemy to the southeast that was descended from Esau, Abraham's grandson. Hadad found asylum and a whole lot more in Egypt. He gained the favor of the Pharaoh, who gave him a house, land, and

a wife (11:18-19). But, despite his obvious ease there, Hadad couldn't wait to return to his homeland once he heard that both David and Joab were gone. He was no doubt seething with hatred toward Israel and looking for revenge (11:21-22).

11:23-25 Solomon's second foreign enemy was a man named Rezon. Notice, again, that divine sovereignty was at work: Rezon was raised up by God (11:23). He became the leader of a raiding party in David's day that became a pain in Israel's side throughout Solomon's reign (1:24-25). Rezon eventually became king of Aram and loathed Israel (11:25).

11:26-28 By far, the most significant of Solomon's enemies was the man described as his "servant" (11:11). Capable Jeroboam was from the tribe of Ephraim, the leading tribe in the north (11:26). Solomon had appointed him over the entire labor force of the house of Joseph (11:28). But, eventually, Jeroboam rebelled against Solomon (11:27). The reader must wait until chapter 12 to understand why Jeroboam rebelled—from a *human* perspective. But, from the *divine* perspective, we learn in 11:29-40 that Jeroboam's rebellion was part of God's plan to tear the kingdom apart because of Solomon's sin.

11:29-36 Jeroboam's rise to power was confirmed by a prophetic announcement from Ahijah, who visually demonstrated his message by tearing his cloak into twelve pieces and giving ten pieces to Jeroboam (11:29-31). God told Jeroboam through Ahijah that he would tear the kingdom from Solomon—though not during Solomon's lifetime (11:31, 34). Jeroboam would be given ten of Israel's tribes to rule (11:31, 35). And, for the sake of . . . David and Jerusalem, the Lord would grant one tribe to Solomon's son (11:32, 36). (The missing tribe, that is the tribe that would bring the total to twelve, is Benjamin, who would side with Judah; see 12:21). Ahijah provided God's justification for his judgment: they (led by King Solomon) have abandoned me and bowed down to the false gods of the nations (11:33).

11:37-39 God made a remarkable promise to Jeroboam. Solomon had appointed him over the "labor force of the house of Joseph" (11:28). But, God would appoint him as **king over Israel** (11:37). God even promised to build Jeroboam **a lasting dynasty**—if he would obey him (11:38). Unfortunately, in spite of this prospect and high hopes, Jeroboam would fail royally.

11:40-43 Solomon apparently learned about the prophecy because he **tried to kill Jeroboam**, who fled to the safety of **Egypt** until Solomon died (11:40). This, in fact, is the last recorded act of Solomon. He reigned **forty years** like his father, David (11:42), but sadly he did not remain loyal to the Lord like David had (11:6). Then, **his son Rehoboam** came to power (11:43).

II. THE DIVIDED KINGDOM (12:1–22:53)

❧ A. Rehoboam, Jeroboam, and the Dividing of Israel (12:1–14:31) ❦

12:1 God's judgment on Solomon was exacted during the reign of his son. The previous chapter explained the *what* and the *why* of what happened: the kingdom would be torn from Solomon's son and divided in two because of Solomon's unfaithfulness. This chapter explains the *how*. God used the bad advice Rehoboam received from his younger advisers and his foolishness in listening to carry out his promise.

Following Solomon's death, the people of Israel came together at **Shechem** to make Solomon's son **Rehoboam** their new **king** (12:1). Shechem was an important historical site for the nation. Upon Abraham's arrival in Canaan, God appeared to him there and promised the land to his offspring (see Gen 12:4-7). Later, Jacob settled in Shechem (see Gen 33:18-20). Then, after the exodus from Egypt and the conquest of the promised land, Joseph was buried there (see Josh 24:32). Shechem was located in the valley between Mount Ebal and Mount Gerizim; it was the place where the Israelites under Joshua pledged to keep the law of Moses (see Josh 24:16-22). It was also in the northern part of Israel, making it a good choice for Rehoboam's coronation, which could double as an effort to overcome lingering hostilities between the northern and southern halves of Israel (see 2 Sam 19:40–20:1-2).

12:2-4 It wasn't long before the people called **Jeroboam** back from exile **in Egypt** and made him their spokesman. They approached Rehoboam for relief from the heavy tax and labor load his father had laid on them. Their plea for relief was also a pledge of loyalty if Rehoboam would show some compassion: **lighten your father's harsh service and the heavy yoke he put on us, and we will serve you** (12:4).

12:5-7 Rehoboam asked for **three days** to consider his answer (12:5). To his credit, the king asked for advice from **the elders who had served his father Solomon**, and they answered him wisely (12:6-7). These senior court officials knew that provoking the people would only inflame the divisions that already existed in the nation. They encouraged Rehoboam to be **a servant to [the] people** so that they, in turn, would serve him (12:7). That's pretty sound advice because leaders should serve those whom they have authority over by governing in their best interest. As Jesus said, "whoever leads" should be "like the one serving" (Luke 22:26).

12:8-11 Rehoboam **rejected the advice of the elders** and turned to **the young men**, his attendants who were from his own generation (12:8). These men encouraged Rehoboam to unload on the people rather than pacify them. As far as they were concerned, it was time for the ungrateful and rebellious subjects to learn a lesson by seeing the new king come down even harder on them than Solomon had (12:10-11).

12:12-16 Foolishly, Rehoboam listened to the wicked **advice** of his contemporaries (12:13-14). But, the author wants the reader to understand the truth of Proverbs 21:1:

"A king's heart is like channeled water in the LORD's hand: He directs it wherever he chooses." Thus, he mentions that **this turn of events came from the LORD to carry out his word . . . spoken through Ahijah** his prophet (12:15; see 11:29-39). As anyone should have been able to predict, the people reacted angrily to the news, using a cry that was similar to the battle cry Sheba had given when he rebelled against David (12:16; see 2 Sam 20:1).

12:17-19 This was the prelude to division and civil war. Only **Judah** remained loyal to Rehoboam—along with Benjamin, the small tribe whose territory was next door to them and who remained loyal to the house of David (see 12:21). The extent of Rehoboam's unpopularity in the north was proven when the people stoned to death **Adoram**, his head of **forced labor**, and almost killed **Rehoboam** himself (12:18-19). Thus, what was supposed to have been Rehoboam's coronation (12:1) almost became his assassination (12:18).

12:20 The lines were clearly drawn when the ten northern tribes crowned **Jeroboam** as **king over all Israel**. The land was henceforth divided into the northern kingdom of Israel and the southern kingdom of Judah, each with its own king.

12:21-24 When he returned to **Jerusalem**, Rehoboam prepared for war. He was determined not to allow the north to secede, so he amassed an army from **Judah** and **Benjamin** to defeat the new rival regime (12:21). But, a man named **Shemaiah** came to the king with a message from God. The Lord commanded Judah and Benjamin not to go to war against their **brothers**, and this time Rehoboam wisely **listened** (12:22-24).

12:25-27 Jeroboam set right to work, building up **Shechem** for defense and for his headquarters (12:25). But, despite God's promises to make his kingdom thrive if he would be faithful, the new king was paranoid. Jeroboam rationalized that if the people in the north continued to visit **Jerusalem**—the holy city and site of the **temple**—for worship and religious festivals, their loyalty

would eventually **return to the house of David** and **King Rehoboam** (12:26-27). What's more—they would probably **kill** Jeroboam (12:27). So, Jeroboam decided to solve his theoretical problem himself. And, not only did he fail to look to God for help, but he also eliminated God from the equation entirely.

12:28-30 King Jeroboam **sought advice** from unnamed advisers (12:28). Whoever they were, they were no wiser than the advisors Rehoboam had followed (12:8-16). He decided that the answer to all his problems was idolatry. To prevent the northern tribes from reuniting with Judah, Jeroboam established a rival system of worship to compete with the true worship of God in southern Jerusalem. He made **two golden calves** and set them up in **Dan** and **Bethel** (12:28-29), cities on either end of his northern kingdom.

The author summed up succinctly the effect this had on the people: **This led to sin** (12:30). How could it not? Jeroboam had effectively recapitulated the sin Israel had committed at the foot of Mount Sinai. Back then, while Moses was on the mountain receiving God's law for his people, Israel made a golden calf and worshiped it as the god that had delivered them from Egyptian slavery (see Exod 32:1-6). Jeroboam had apparently learned nothing from his people's history because he did the exact same thing that had gotten them into such trouble (see Exod 32:35)—only he gave the people two golden calves for the price of one!

12:31-33 In addition to endorsing blatant idolatry, Jeroboam built **shrines on the high places**, appointed **priests . . . who were not Levites**, and established **a festival** to compete with the festival in Jerusalem so that the people wouldn't have to travel there—all in direct disobedience to God's commands. The Lord had graciously made Jeroboam king, but Jeroboam "exchanged the truth of God for a lie, and worshiped and served what has been created instead of the Creator" (Rom 1:25). And, he led the people to do the same.

13:1-3 As a result, God's judgment was coming. The message of that judgment came by way of a **man of God . . . from Judah** (13:1).

That insight tells us the man was living under God's authority rather than under Jeroboam's rule. His prophecy is amazing because it named King **Josiah** from **the house of David**, who would someday sacrifice on the altar **the priests of the high places**, whom Jeroboam had appointed and defile it by burning **human bones** on it (13:2). While Josiah would not be born for almost three centuries, he would indeed do exactly what the man of God said he would (see 2 Kgs 23:15-20). The prophet also gave Jeroboam a **sign** that his prophecy would be fulfilled: **The altar will now be ripped apart, and the ashes that are on it will be poured out** (13:3, see 13:5).

13:4-6 Jeroboam didn't want to hear more; he **stretched out his hand** in a kingly gesture of authority and ordered the man of God arrested (13:4). But, God gave Jeroboam an unmistakable lesson in who was really in charge by withering the king's **hand** and destroying **the altar** as prophesied (13:4-5). Suddenly, arresting the prophet didn't seem like such a good idea, so Jeroboam begged the prophet to intercede for him. The man prayed for the king as requested, and God mercifully healed Jeroboam (13:6).

13:7-10 Behind the offer of **reward** made in verse 7, Jeroboam may have been thinking, "Whew! That was close. I need this guy on my side." But, the man had his orders. He was not to associate with Jeroboam and was to go home a different way (13:8-10). In other words, true prophets of God are not for sale. Doing the work of the King is its own reward.

13:11-14 The story that follows served as a graphic object lesson on the need for complete obedience to the word of the Lord; it was a lesson that God wanted Jeroboam and the people of Israel to take to heart. There was an **old prophet** in **Bethel** whose sons informed him of **the man of God** and his prophecy against Jeroboam for his apostasy (13:11). The Bethel prophet rode after the man of God and found him on his way back home (13:13-14). The old prophet may have been jealous over the other prophet's ministry. We simply don't know why he did what he did.

13:15-19 Whatever his motives, the old prophet (like Jeroboam) invited the prophet from Judah to go back to Bethel and eat with him. The man of God knew what God had commanded him, but the old prophet **deceived him**, saying that **the word of the LORD** had come to him and changed God's original command (13:18). The prophet from Judah should have known better than to believe a prophet from Bethel—a place where Jeroboam's idolatry ran rampant. But, he foolishly ignored his charge from the Lord and went back to Bethel (13:19).

13:20-32 At dinner, God's word came upon the old prophet, and he uttered God's judgment on the disobedient prophet (13:20-22). This unusual story continued with the prophet from Judah being killed by **a lion** on his way home (13:23-24). And then, unnaturally, the **lion** and the man's **donkey** remained **standing** still beside **the corpse** (13:24). In other words, this was no accidental death, but the work of God.

While we aren't told whether the old prophet from Bethel knew that his deception would lead to the other prophet's death, he retrieved his body, buried him, **mourned** him, and affirmed that his prophecy would come true (13:30, 32).

13:33-34 All of these events were public knowledge in Bethel, but the lesson was lost on Jeroboam, who **did not repent** (13:33). He continued to appoint false **priests** to serve at **the high places** (13:33). **This was the sin that** would ultimately cause **the house of Jeroboam to be . . . obliterated** (13:34).

14:1-3 The demise of Jeroboam's family and kingdom did not take long to begin. His young son **Abijah** became **sick**, which prompted the king to send his **wife** to see the prophet at **Shiloh**, in an attempt to secure the boy's healing (14:1-2). Ahijah had prophesied Jeroboam's rise to power, so the king hoped for a favorable word on his son. It's not clear why Jeroboam wanted his wife to **disguise** herself (14:2). It could be that he didn't want the people of Israel knowing that his wife was visiting a prophet of the Lord.

14:4-5 Jeroboam's wife took food gifts with her to Ahijah, who was **blind due to his age** (14:4). The great irony is that, despite her disguise and the prophet's blindness, he knew who she was because the Lord had revealed it to him (14:5). God had a message of doom for Jeroboam that he wanted the prophet to deliver. So, in a sense, it was Ahijah who was sent to the king's wife, not vice versa.

14:6-9 The blind and elderly prophet must have stunned his visitor with his greeting: **Come in, wife of Jeroboam!** (14:6). His message was nothing but **bad news** (14:6). God reviewed everything that he had graciously done for Jeroboam, who was not from the royal line but was made a king anyway. God tore the kingdom away from Solomon and gave a portion of it to Jeroboam (14:7-8). But, Jeroboam proved to be so unfaithful, so unlike David, that his wickedness was greater **than all who were before** him (14:9).

14:10-11 Jeroboam had sinned so deeply that God was ready to **bring disaster** on his house. The prophetic picture is graphic: The Lord would **wipe out all** of Jeroboam's male descendants, causing his **house** to be swept away like a pile of **dung** (14:10). Their bodies would be eaten by **dogs** and **birds** (14:11).

14:12-18 As if this insight weren't bad enough, the Lord declared that Jeroboam's son, the one whose healing he was seeking, would **die** (14:12). In fact, when Jeroboam's wife returned home, **the boy died** as she crossed **the threshold of the house** (14:17). He would be the only male member of Jeroboam's house to receive a **proper burial because . . . something favorable to the Lord . . .** had been **found in him** (14:13). The boy's immediate death was a sure sign that the more distant parts of the prophecy would come to pass.

The Lord declared through his prophet that he would **raise up for himself a king over Israel** to **wipe out the house of Jeroboam** (14:14). The readers of 1 Kings would see this fulfillment in the next chapter (15:27-29). God's prophecy was so certain of fulfillment that Ahijah could say, **This is the day** (14:14), even though the pronouncement of Israel's scattering (14:15-16) would not

be fulfilled until 722 BC when the northern kingdom of Israel would be swept off the map by the Assyrians.

14:19-20 Next, the author informs us that the king's deeds were recorded in **the Historical Record of Israel's Kings**, a historical document lost to history (14:19). Jeroboam reigned for **twenty-two** miserable **years** (14:20). His death would usher in a continuing parade of wicked kings that would march the nation all the way to the Assyrian invasion.

14:21-24 When last we saw Rehoboam, his reign in Judah had begun with foolishness (12:1-19). Things didn't improve. During his **seventeen years in Jerusalem** (14:21), Judah (like the northern kingdom) fell into gross idolatry. The people did **what was evil in the Lord's sight**—this would become a familiar refrain throughout the books of 1–2 Kings. The sin in Rehoboam's day was even worse than that of Judah's **ancestors**, a strong indictment considering their history (14:22). **They imitated all the detestable practices of the nations** that God had driven out on their behalf (14:24). And, if Israel wanted to live like idolatrous nations, God would treat them like idolatrous nations.

14:25-31 Rehoboam had been on the throne fewer than five years when **Shishak of Egypt** invaded Judah and threatened Jerusalem (14:25). Though Jerusalem was ultimately spared, Rehoboam still had to pay Shishak a ransom from **the treasuries of the Lord's temple and the treasuries of the royal palace** (14:26) to get the Egyptian king to back off. The mighty kingdom of David and Solomon was no longer on top.

Just as alarmingly, Rehoboam had **war** with Jeroboam during **their reigns** (14:30). At Rehoboam's death, he was succeeded by his son **Abijam** (14:31).

➤ B. The Reigns of Abijam and Asa in Judah (15:1-24) ◄

15:1-8 Rehoboam's son was a chip off the old royal block. **Abijam walked in all the sins his father before him had committed**

(15:3). Instead of being a defender of true worship, as the king was expected to be, he perpetuated idolatrous practices. **He was not wholeheartedly devoted to the LORD his God as his ancestor David had been** (15:3). Yes, David had sinned greatly by committing adultery with the wife of **Uriah** (15:5), but he repented of his deeds. Moreover, he didn't succumb to idolatry as Solomon and his descendants had done. Thus, for Judah's kings, the standard of success was how they compared to David. After all, it was **for the sake of David** that the Lord preserved his royal line (15:4).

Abijam, too, was at **war** with Jeroboam during Abijam's brief reign of **three years** (15:2, 7), an indication that the hostilities between the two kingdoms were at high pitch. When he died, his son reigned in his place (15:8).

15:9-15 Abijam's death brought his son **Asa** to the throne. He was a good king—one of a few such blessings to Judah. **He reigned forty-one years in Jerusalem** (15:10), one more year than either David or Solomon had. He even passed the most important test for a king of Judah: **Asa did what was right in the LORD's sight, as his ancestor David had done** (15:11). Evidence for this assessment is provided. He rid the land of **male cult prostitutes** and **the idols that his fathers had made** (15:12). He even **removed his grandmother ... from being queen mother because** of her idolatry (15:13). Though he didn't remove the **high places**, nevertheless he **was wholeheartedly devoted to the LORD his entire life** (15:14). Asa was a shining light of truth in Judah, pointing the way through the fog of apostasy.

15:16-17 Asa did, however, stumble in his reliance on God. Though the author of 1 Kings does not say so explicitly here, the Chronicler records that Asa was rebuked by the prophet Hanani for seeking help from Aram rather than from the Lord (see 2 Chr 16:7-9).

He was also in continual war with **King Baasha of Israel** (15:16), which revealed a chink in his trust. Baasha started the **war against Judah** by fortifying **Ramah** (15:17), which lay on the border of Israel and Judah and was only four miles north of Jerusalem.

Likely, this was an effort to isolate the southern kingdom and control the traffic between the two nations.

15:18-22 Instead of turning to the Lord for help, Asa emptied **the treasuries of the LORD's temple and ... the royal palace** to persuade **Ben-hadad**, the **king of Aram** (modern-day Syria) to break his **treaty** with Baasha and attack Israel to relieve his pressure on Judah (15:18-19). Ben-hadad agreed to the deal and attacked Israel from the north, taking a good amount of territory and forcing Baasha to withdraw from Ramah (15:20-21). Asa then had Ramah torn down and built his own defensive towns of **Geba** and **Mizpah** with the building materials (15:22).

15:23-24 Overall, Asa was marked by faithfulness to the Lord, as required of a king in David's line. He was succeeded by his son **Jehoshaphat** (15:24), whose reign is not covered until the end of 1 Kings.

➤ C. The Reigns of Five Evil Kings in Israel (15:25–16:28) ❧

15:25-32 Between the accounts of kings Asa and Jehoshaphat of Judah come the stories of five kings of the northern kingdom of Israel. These reigns include that of the wicked King Ahab and his wife Jezebel and their extended clashes with the great prophet Elijah. The reason five straight stories of Israel's kings are given without mention of Judah's kings is that Asa had a long reign of forty-one years (15:10), which spanned the reigns of several kings in Israel.

The first of these kings was **Nadab son of Jeroboam** (15:25-32), who reigned for a brief **two years**. The only noteworthy fact about Nadab was that he **did what was evil in the LORD's sight** (15:25-26). He was assassinated during a battle against the Philistine town of **Gibbethon** by a man named **Baasha**, who became king in Nadab's place (15:27-28). Baasha proceeded to wipe out the entire family **of Jeroboam** (15:29). This was in fulfillment of **the word of the LORD** that he spoke against **Jeroboam** for his own sins and for leading Israel away from God (15:29; see 14:14). Thus, Nadab's death closed the book on Jeroboam.

15:33-34 Baasha, mentioned in the earlier discussion of Asa (see 15:16-22), reigned **twenty-four years** on the throne of Israel **in Tirzah** (15:33), the city where Jeroboam lived (see 14:17). It would serve as the capital for Israel's kings down to the time of Omri (see 16:23). Baasha gained the kingship by assassination, preventing the reader from expecting godliness from him.

In the same way that Judah's kings were compared with David, Baasha and the kings of Israel were compared with **Jeroboam** (15:34; see 14:10-11).

16:1-4 Details of Baasha's doom were delivered by the prophet **Jehu**, through whom God expressed his disgust with the king's sinful ways after God had **raised** him **up from the dust** and put him on the throne (16:1-2). From a human perspective, Baasha had seized the throne. But, from a divine perspective, nothing happens apart from the supernatural, providential working of God.

Baasha was not only an evil king, but he followed the worst example: **Jeroboam** (16:2). Therefore, God declared the same judgment on Baasha that he had pronounced on him. He said, **I will eradicate Baasha and his house**; his descendants would be eaten by **dogs** and **birds** (16:3-4; see 14:10-11). This was a dose of divine irony. The king whom the Lord had raised up to wipe out Jeroboam's family would now have his own family wiped out because he imitated Jeroboam's idolatry and wickedness.

16:5-7 The writer of 1 Kings notes that wicked Baasha's reign included **accomplishments** that he achieved by his **might**, which were **written in the Historical Record of Israel's Kings** (16:5). This kind of thing is repeated in some form in many cases with the kings of Israel. They weren't necessarily unsuccessful from the human standpoint. But, whatever a man accomplishes is of no consequence in God's eyes if he isn't obeying him and living for his glory. So, **Baasha's house** was struck down (16:7).

16:8-14 Baasha's son **Elah** lasted only **two years** before being killed by **Zimri**, one of his army commanders. Zimri assassinated Elah as he was **getting drunk** (16:8-9). Zimri then assumed the throne and executed God's judgment on the rest of **the house of Baasha**, just as **Jehu** the prophet had declared (16:10-13; see 16:1-4).

16:15-19 Zimri may have been a tool in the Lord's hand for judgment, but he was no hero. His reign lasted only **seven days**, making it the shortest in Israel's history (16:15). That week, the army was still besieging the Philistine stronghold of **Gibbethon**, where Baasha had earlier killed King Nadab (see 15:27). Zimri's actions were so unpopular that when word of his murder of Elah reached the army in Gibbethon, its commanders pulled off a coup and **made Omri, the army commander, king over Israel that very day in the camp** (16:16). Omri then led the men back to Tirzah to remove Zimri from the throne. The army **captured** the capital city, and when Zimri saw that he was doomed, **he entered the citadel of the royal palace and burned it down over himself**, dying not just because of his failed attempt to take over, but because he also did **what was evil in the LORD's sight** (16:17-19).

16:20-22 The story of Zimri illustrates how far the northern kingdom had descended into chaos. Following his death, **the people of Israel were divided** (16:21). A man named **Tibni** had the support of **half** the people, while the other half backed Omri. The conflict lasted for six years, but because Omri's followers were stronger (probably because he had the support of the army), they won out. Tibni died in the struggle for the throne, while **Omri became king** (16:22).

16:23-28 Omri was a strong king who ruled for **twelve years**, at the midpoint of which he moved the Israelite capital from **Tirzah** to **Samaria** (16:23-24), where it remained until the northern kingdom was destroyed by Assyria. But he, too, **did what was evil in the LORD's sight**. In fact, **he did more evil than all who were before him** (16:25). (That is a stunning statement given the heinous sins that the kings who came before him had committed!)

The kings of Israel were to walk in the ways of the Lord—that is, to live in ways pleasing to him. But **Omri walked in all the ways of Jeroboam** (16:26).

You might hope that when Omri died (16:28), the wickedness ended in Israel. But, no. His son Ahab would only make things worse.

⇥ D. The Reign of Ahab and the Ministry of Elijah (16:29–22:40) ⇥

16:29-31 Omri's wickedness goes a long way toward explaining the total corruption and evil of his son **Ahab**, who reigned in **Samaria** for **twenty-two years** (16:29). He was more evil **than all who were before him** (16:30), earning him the shameful title of Israel's worst king. For him, walking in **the sin of Jeroboam** wasn't bad enough. So, he also **married Jezebel, the daughter of Ethbaal king of the Sidonians** (or Phoenicians). As a result, Ahab led Israel to worship **Baal** (16:31), the fertility god of the Canaanites.

16:32-33 Jezebel was committed to advancing Baal worship throughout Israel, and Ahab was happy to help. **He set up an altar** and built a **temple** for Baal **in Samaria** (16:32). And, to add to his perverted worship, **Ahab also made an Asherah pole** (16:33). Asherah was a fertility goddess and the mother of Baal. Thus, Ahab succeeded in angering God more than any king who preceded him (16:33). And Jezebel, with Ahab's complicity, led Israel into levels of idolatry that were previously unheard of.

16:34 The chapter ends with a seemingly unrelated account of something that happened **during** Ahab's **reign**. A man named **Hiel** decided to defy the curse God had pronounced through **Joshua** on anyone who tried to rebuild **Jericho** after Joshua destroyed it (see Josh 6:26). The curse was specific: the builder would succeed only at the cost of his **firstborn** and **youngest** sons, a price that Hiel paid. The point of this account may be to illustrate two things. First, neglect of God's Word was rampant during the days of Ahab. Second, just as God's Word was fulfilled in the case of Hiel, it would also be fulfilled in the case of Ahab. Israel's worst king wouldn't escape divine judgment. No matter how many years go by, God doesn't forget.

17:1 Through the end of 1 Kings and the beginning chapters of 2 Kings, two of Israel's most famous prophets will share the stage with the royal main characters. Their names are Elijah and Elisha.

Ahab was a wicked king, and he had a powerful ally in Queen Jezebel. But, God had a match for them in the person of **Elijah the Tishbite** from Gilead. Elijah's name means, "Yahweh is my God." This rugged, rough-dressing prophet waltzed into Ahab's court—seemingly out of nowhere—with a message from the Lord.

Now, God's prophets usually showed up because something was spiritually wrong with God's people, and that problem was usually associated with idolatry. Clearly, then, the spiritual breakdown in Ahab's day had reached monumental proportions. God's prophet stood between the people and God himself as sort of a last appeal before God would have to address the issue directly from heaven. That would mean severe judgment.

Elijah appeared at Ahab's court and boldly announced in God's authority that there would be **no dew or rain** whatsoever, except as he commanded. This was a direct attack at Baal, a fertility god. His worshipers depended on *him* to provide rain to ensure good crops. Elijah would demonstrate that the Lord alone was in control of the natural world. He was their source.

Years before, God had warned the people through Moses to be "careful that you are not enticed to turn aside, serve, and bow in worship to other gods. Then the LORD's anger will burn against you. He will shut the sky, and there will be no rain; the land will not yield its produce, and you will perish quickly from the good land the LORD is giving" (Deut 11:16-17). Once again, the author of 1 Kings, who knew Deuteronomy well, highlights how Israel's unfaithfulness to God's covenant was causing his judgment to fall on their heads. Or, in this case, how it was keeping his blessing of rain from falling on their heads.

17:2-9 Elijah's announcement placed him in danger with the king. So, God told him to leave the city and go to the country where a **wadi** or brook was located. There, he would be fed by **ravens**—which were unclean birds (17:2-3). Importantly, this would make it easier for the prophet to receive help from a Gentile later. Elijah obeyed and was nourished by the birds bringing him food for **a while**, until the stream dried up because of the drought (17:5-7).

Nevertheless, God's provision for his prophet continued and his mission did, too. God sent Elijah to Gentile country, to **Zarephath that belongs to Sidon**, where a Gentile **widow** would **provide for** him (17:9). When God allows his provision to dry up in our lives, it is because he is ready to do a new thing or move us in a new direction.

God was preparing Elijah for the great tests of faith he would soon face on Mount Carmel and afterward. He was teaching his prophet that he could provide whatever was needed both for him and for others. God was also using this opportunity to bring his blessing to a Sidonian household. If the king of Israel, its false prophets, and its people preferred to worship Baal (see chapter 19), the Lord would elicit praise from the mouth of a Gentile woman instead (17:24).

Zarephath was a hot, dry village located in Sidon (modern-day Lebanon). This was the home turf of Jezebel (see 16:31), so, in a sense, God had sent Elijah to the idolatrous "Baal Belt." Elijah was going into enemy territory to demonstrate that the Lord is the true God who alone has power over creation and can even provide in the den of Satan.

17:10-14 Zarephath was suffering from the drought, too. When Elijah entered the town, he met a poor **widow** and asked for a drink of **water** and a **piece of bread** (17:10-11). She got the water, but noted that providing bread was another matter. She and her son were on the verge of starvation. There was only a bit of **flour** and **oil** left. She was about to prepare their last meal; then they would **die** (17:12).

Elijah challenged the widow to act on faith and feed him first with the last of her flour for bread (17:13). She knew that the Lord was his God (17:12), and Elijah was declaring that

the LORD God of Israel would supply her needs if she trusted him (17:14).

17:15-16 The widow believed God's word through Elijah and did as he said. The result was a miraculous provision of food lasting **many days** (17:15). Her **flour jar did not become empty, and the oil jug did not run dry** (17:16). Even in the face of certain death, she acted on faith, trusting in the word of the living God, and he provided. This reinforces a New Testament principle: we should give others the very thing we wish God would give to us (see Luke 6:38).

17:17-21 After this, however, the widow's son **became ill** and died (17:17). Having been exposed to the holiness of God through his miraculous works, she was aware of her own **iniquity**. She believed her sin had come to God's attention through Elijah's presence in her home. Thus, in her mind, God was punishing her for her sin by putting her **son . . . to death** (17:18). Elijah responded by taking the boy **from her arms** and carrying him **to the upstairs room where he was staying**. Then, he **laid him on his own bed** and began to pray (17:19-20).

Elijah's prayer showed that even he did not understand why God had brought about this **tragedy** (17:20). The Lord had sent Elijah to this woman and her son, and he had spared their lives through Elijah. So, why take her son's life? Regardless of the reason, Elijah knew the sovereign God who held all the answers and who had the power to restore life. So, the prophet **stretched himself out over the boy three times** and cried out to God to give the child his **life** back (17:21).

Remembering how God has answered us in one trial can serve as a foundation for trusting him when we enter the next trial. This story also demonstrates that we (like the widow) can piggyback on the spirituality of others when we need God to resurrect something in our lives.

17:22-24 God graciously answered Elijah's prayer, and **the boy's life came into him again** (17:22). Imagine the look on the mother's face when Elijah **brought him down from the upstairs room** and said, **Look, your son is alive** (17:23). That moment confirmed her faith in the Lord as the true God (17:24). The miracle also no doubt strengthened Elijah's faith for the tests he was about to face as he returned to Israel to confront Ahab and the prophets of Baal.

18:1-4 After the drought had lasted **a long time**, God sent Elijah to Ahab to announce that he would **send rain** (18:1). The prophet obeyed, and on the way to **Samaria**, he encountered Ahab's servant **Obadiah** (18:2-3). Obadiah **was in charge of the palace**. But, he was also a faithful believer **who greatly feared the LORD and took a hundred prophets and hid them [from Jezebel] . . . and provided them with food** (18:3-4). Like Joseph, Daniel, and Nehemiah, Obadiah held a position of trust and responsibility in the palace of an unbelieving ruler. Only in Obadiah's case, the ruler was the king of Israel whose queen had **slaughtered** the true **prophets** of the true God (18:4).

18:5-15 In hopes of saving his animals, Ahab had sent Obadiah out looking for any grazing land that might be left after years of drought (18:5-6). It was on this search that Obadiah met Elijah, to his amazement (18:7). Elijah told Obadiah to let Ahab know he was back and wanted to meet him (18:8). But, Obadiah feared that Elijah was pronouncing his death sentence. Ahab had put a price on Elijah's head. If Obadiah told the king that he had found Elijah, and then the prophet failed to appear, surely Ahab would put his servant to death (18:9-14). But, Elijah assured Ahab's servant that he would make an appearance, declaring his confidence in **the LORD of Armies** (18:15).

18:16-17 The two foes met, and Ahab immediately cast the blame for Israel's woes on Elijah. According to Ahab, the prophet was **ruining Israel** (18:17) because he had proclaimed there would be no rain except at his command (see 17:1). In truth, Elijah had spoken on behalf of God. But, Ahab took out his fury on the prophet who represented him. The wicked king wouldn't accept responsibility for his nation's suffering.

18:18-19 But, Elijah was no shy prophet. He boldly spoke the truth. It was Ahab and his **father's family** who were ruining Israel because they had **abandoned** God's **commands and followed the Baals** (18:18). Then, Elijah issued a challenge: **Summon all Israel to meet me at Mount Carmel, along with the 450 prophets of Baal and the 400 prophets of Asherah** (18:19). These numbers indicate the extent to which Jezebel had plunged Israel into gross idolatry. It was time for a faceoff.

King Ahab had integrated idolatry into a system that was supposed to be run on God's agenda because the Israelites were his people. Israel was suffering because of failed leadership. But, Elijah represented another kingdom orientation. He was not tied to the royal family or any political party. He could speak truth to earthly power without being co-opted or compromised. Elijah was an independent who was committed to the truth and didn't care who was in power. He represented an entirely different kingdom with a different agenda.

18:20 Ahab summoned all the Israelites and gathered the prophets at Mount Carmel. He took up Elijah's challenge, which means that he must have been confident of the outcome. Elijah was a powerful prophet, but 950 to 1 were pretty good odds.

This mass gathering set the stage for one of the most important questions in all of Scripture: Who is the true God? The Lord had declared to Israel that he alone was God. Now, the people were going to have to make up their minds. Would they believe in the God of their fathers? Or, would they continue to follow the gods of the nations?

18:21 Elijah asked, **How long will you waver between two opinions?** There is no place for double-mindedness on spiritual matters; you can't have God and the world (see Jas 4:8). Israel was like an intoxicated man who couldn't walk a straight line but weaved from side to side, and Elijah's question implied that Israel's two-timing of God had been going on too long. It was time to choose sides: **If the LORD is God, follow him. But if Baal, follow him.** There is no such thing as neutrality when it comes to the true God and his demand for exclusive worship (see Matt 12:30).

Shockingly, **the people didn't answer** Elijah's impassioned challenge. The people of Israel—the decedents of Abraham, Isaac, and Jacob—couldn't even bring themselves to affirm that the Lord is the one true God! They didn't answer because they had lost all conviction. By failing to choose, they had already made their decision.

18:22-24 When the contestants and the audience had gathered together, Elijah set the terms of the coming battle. On one side, the 450 prophets of Baal would receive a sacrificial bull. On the other side, Elijah—standing alone—would receive the other bull. Each side would prepare its bull on an altar, and each would call on their deity to set their offering ablaze. **The God who answers with fire**, Elijah said, **he is God** (18:24).

Did the people really expect to see a supernatural response that day? Or, did they have no expectations? Regardless, it's unlikely that they thought the out-gunned Elijah would come out on top. They simply responded, **That's fine** (18:24).

18:25-29 The false prophets got to go first. They slaughtered their **bull** and called on **Baal from morning until noon**. But, **no one answered**. So, **they danced around the altar** (18:26). Eventually, they became so desperate for a response that they began shouting and cutting themselves, so that **blood gushed over them** (18:28). Still, the heavens were silent. **No one answered, no one paid attention** (18:29). This is the outcome for those who trust in anyone or anything besides the true God.

While this was happening, Elijah offered sarcastic commentary on the proceedings. He **mocked** both the prophets and their god: **Maybe he's thinking it over**, he said, **maybe he has wandered away. . . . Perhaps he's sleeping!** (18:27). Because Ahab and his prophets had led the people of Israel astray, Elijah wanted to make it clear that their false god and his religion were a lie and a disgrace that had caused the Lord to judge his people. Baal deserved to be mocked.

18:30-31 Finally, Elijah brought a halt to the nonsense and called the people to come to the Lord's altar (18:30). For it, Elijah used **twelve stones** (18:31), representing the twelve tribes of Israel. This was a significant

object lesson to the crowd watching. Even though the nation was divided at this time, they were still the one people of God; they consisted of the descendants of the twelve sons of Jacob. In other words, Elijah was preparing the Israelites to see their God work by calling them to unity.

18:32-35 Elijah's elaborate preparations of the altar were designed to leave no doubt in anyone's mind that the Lord is the only true God. The prophet even worked against himself. By pouring an abundance of **water** on the sacrifice and altar, he was making it impossible for the soggy **wood** and **offering to be burned** (18:33-35). No human could light such a mess.

18:36-37 Elijah prayed. And what a prayer! The heart of Elijah's request was that Israel's God would glorify himself before all of the people that day. What would be the payoff? The people would _know_ that the Lord is God, that Elijah was his prophet, and as a result **their hearts** would be **turned** back to him. A prayer for God to be glorified and for his people to be edified is the kind of prayer that God answers.

18:38-40 God's dramatic response to Elijah's prayer was heightened by the fact that it was now evening (18:36). The perfect time for a divine fireworks display! **Fire fell** from heaven, consuming the **offering, the wood, the stones, and the dust**. The flames even **licked up the water** (18:38). It would have been obvious to everyone present that the supernatural had invaded the natural world; the spiritual had touched the physical; eternity had invaded history. So, the people of Israel responded in the only appropriate way: they fell on their faces and confessed, **The Lord, he is God! The Lord, he is God!** (18:39). And, with the outcome so one-sided, **the prophets of Baal** were shown to be the frauds that they were. Their fate was sealed (18:40).

18:41-46 With the greatness and uniqueness of the Lord vindicated and confessed, it was time to lift the drought and famine from the land (see 18:1). The prophet informed Ahab that **a rainstorm** was approaching and went **to the summit of Carmel** to pray

(18:42). Elijah persisted in his intercession until the Lord answered with **a downpour**. In other words, he took the mental position of a woman in the travail of childbirth as he kept praying. After seven times (the number of completion), the answer came. He even received the bonus blessing of supernatural strength, which enabled him to outrun Ahab's **chariot** to Jezreel (18:43-45). Without a doubt, **the power of the LORD was on Elijah** (11:46). He was on a spiritual mountaintop. But, he was about to enter the valley of the shadow of death.

19:1-2 Though Elijah had won a great victory, he had also ticked off the vicious Queen Jezebel. Her god Baal had been mocked and her **prophets** had been **killed**—all because of this upstart prophet of the Lord (19:1). Therefore, she threatened to make Elijah like her own prophets—that is, dead **by [that] time** the following day (19:2).

19:3-8 This was quite a reversal of fortune for Elijah. He **became afraid and immediately ran for his life**, going deep into Judah's **wilderness** (19:3-4). The irony of Elijah's fear of a godless queen could not be greater, coming on the heels of his greatest victory. But, there he was, exhausted, discouraged, and praying to **die**, when he finally fell asleep (19:4-5).

Even the strongest saints have weaknesses. Spiritual depression strikes when we least expect it—especially following on the heels of spiritual victory. Remember that even Jesus was attacked after his glorious baptism (see Matt 3:16–4:1).

Elijah may have assumed that, after the victory at Carmel, Ahab would lead Israel in returning to the Lord. Perhaps he'd thought that Queen Jezebel would be cast out of the palace, or that she would raise the white flag and surrender. But, neither of those things happened. Ahab was as weak as ever, and Jezebel was as evil as ever. So, Elijah was disillusioned and ready to give up.

But, God knew what Elijah needed. It began with food and rest. An **angel** fed him, let him sleep some more, and then fed him some more (19:5-8). Sometimes, what we need is simply a good meal and a good night's sleep. This gave Elijah the strength he needed to walk **forty days and forty nights to Horeb**,

the **mountain of God** (19:8). Horeb was the ancient name for Mount Sinai, where Moses had met God in the burning bush (see Exod 3:1-2), and where God had entered into a covenant with his people (see Deut 5:2). Just as sure as Elijah needed food and rest, he also needed time in God's presence to get his spiritual feet back under him.

19:9 In a cave at Horeb, **the word of the LORD came to him** (19:9). He asked the prophet, **What are you doing here?** Of course, the obvious answer was, "I'm resting." But, God wasn't asking Elijah what he was *doing* at Horeb, but rather what he was doing *at Horeb*. Why had he fled so far from Israel, where the Lord had called him to minister?

19:10 Elijah was ready with his complaint. He had done everything God had asked of him. But, nothing had changed. In effect, Elijah wailed, "Israel is still in rebellion; your prophets have been killed; and now they're after me!" As far as he knew, he was the last man in Israel who still followed God. His answer could have been construed as saying, "God, your power was great, but it wasn't enough. We won the battle, but we've lost the war."

19:11-14 Elijah's thinking had become foggy; he needed a good dose of truth. God didn't rebuke him, but rather gave him supernatural illumination (19:11-13). Elijah was awed by this encounter, but God had a reason for displaying his power. The message behind it was this: things were well under control. God's power had not diminished. In fact, Elijah didn't need to run and hide because God had more work for him to do. So, God asked him again, **What are you doing here, Elijah?** (19:13). Still not ready to move forward, Elijah voiced his complaint again (19:14).

19:15-21 God had heard enough. Far from being thwarted, the Lord was about to wipe the throne of Israel clean and remove Baal worship from the nation. And, now that Elijah had experienced a spiritual retreat of sorts, God had his next assignment ready. He commanded the prophet to return to the north and **anoint Hazael as king over Aram** and anoint Jehu . . . as king over Israel (19:15).

These men would exact God's vengeance on Israel's sin.

God also told Elijah to **anoint** his successor: **Elisha son of Shaphat** (19:16), indicating that Elijah wasn't as alone as he had feared (19:10). There were other servants of the Lord in the land. In fact, God revealed to his prophet that he had **seven thousand** followers **in Israel** who had **not bowed to Baal** (19:18).

After this word, Elijah **found Elisha** and called him to serve with him, throwing **his mantle over him** as a sign that, in time, he would assume Elijah's role (19:19). Elisha celebrated the Lord's calling on his life; then he **followed Elijah** and **served him** (19:21).

20:1-6 Once Elijah was functioning prophetically again, events began to unfold that would bring about God's judgment on the house of Ahab and on Israel's worship of Baal. **King Ben-hadad of Aram** and his enormous army besieged **Samaria**, Ahab's capital, and made harsh demands. Being badly outnumbered, Ahab agreed to them (20:1-4). Yet, Ahab's concession only made Ben-hadad more greedy. He further demanded that his men be allowed into Samaria to plunder Ahab's **palace** and his **servants' houses**, as well (20:5-6).

20:7-13 Ben-hadad's second demand was too much, so Ahab gathered his advisers, **all the elders of the land** (20:7). They counseled resistance, as did **all the people** (20:8). Therefore, Ahab sent Ben-hadad a resounding, "No," and the armies prepared for war (20:9-12). At this point, an unnamed **prophet** came to Ahab with a promise of victory from the Lord (20:13). Clearly, this encouragement came not because Ahab deserved deliverance or even asked the Lord for help. Rather, the victory over Aram was intended to teach Ahab that the Lord was the true God (20:13). Would Ahab learn the lesson?

20:14-25 The battle proved to be a spectacular success for Israel (20:14-21). Ben-hadad himself barely **escaped** (20:20). But, Israel was not yet done with Aram. The same **prophet** informed Ahab that **the king of Aram** would be back for a new fight the following **spring** (20:22). Sure enough, Ben-hadad's advisers gave him bad advice concerning the power

of the Lord (**their gods are gods of the hill country**), so he planned the next battle for **the plain** where Aram would have an advantage—or so he thought (20:23).

20:26-34 Once again, **the man of God** prophesied victory for Ahab, which would happen in an even more spectacular way than in the previous battle (20:28). Aram's defeat was so complete, in fact, that Ben-hadad's **servants** advised that they should surrender to Israel and throw themselves on Ahab's mercy. Ahab accepted Ben-hadad's surrender and even **made a treaty with him and released him** (20:31-34). God had handed over Ahab's enemy so that Ahab might defeat him and worship God. Instead, Ahab made friends with his enemy and forgot about God.

20:35-36 The final verses of the chapter introduce us to another prophet from God. Before he confronted King Ahab, though, the prophet told **his fellow prophet** to **strike** him (20:35). When **the man refused**, he was **killed** by a **lion** as a means of judgment. This may seem an odd story. But, these men knew each other; they shared the role of divine spokesmen; and the first prophet was speaking **by the word of the LORD** (20:35). So, the second prophet should have known better than to ignore it. God's word is to be obeyed. The consequences for failing to obey can be catastrophic.

20:37-43 The next man was quick to obey. The **wound** the prophet received allowed him to disguise himself with a **bandage** (20:37-38). Then, he approached King Ahab with a story (20:39-40) reminiscent of the tale Nathan told to King David after he had sinned—a tale that was designed to entrap him (see 2 Sam 12:1-10). The point of the story was that Ahab had committed a grave sin in releasing Ben-hadad when God had **set apart** that king **for destruction** (20:42). Because Ahab had failed to carry out the Lord's will, he and Israel would suffer. Ahab, ever the pouter, stormed off for Samaria **resentful and angry** (20:43).

21:1-4 Ahab's habit of pouting when he didn't get what he wanted turned deadly when the king of Israel eyed a **vineyard** belonging to **Naboth the Jezreelite** that was next to Ahab's palace (21:1-2). Ahab offered to trade Naboth **a better vineyard** in exchange for his land or to buy it outright (21:2). But, Naboth refused to sell his ancestral inheritance—rightly so (21:3; see Lev 25:23). As a result, the king went home **resentful and angry** once again and lay on his bed like a spoiled child, refusing to **eat** (21:4).

21:5-16 Enter Jezebel, who assured her husband that she would get Naboth's vineyard for him (21:5-7). The evil queen set in motion a coldhearted plan to have Naboth executed under trumped-up charges (21:8-10). Then, **the wicked men** whom she conspired with carried out her plan to the letter, until Naboth was **stoned to death** (21:13-14). With the evil deed done, Jezebel coldly reported his death to Ahab and presented her weak-willed husband with **the vineyard** he had wanted so much (21:15-16).

21:17-24 God was not about to let this monstrous act go unpunished. So, he called **Elijah** to deliver his **word** of judgment on Ahab (21:17-19). Ahab greeted Elijah as his **enemy**, clearly unconcerned that the Lord's prophet was paying him a visit (21:20). Immediately, Elijah proceeded to spell out Ahab's judgment from the Lord: **I will wipe out all of Ahab's males, both slave and free, in Israel** (21:21). The king's posterity would be utterly destroyed, just as the Lord had done to the houses of **Jeroboam** and **Baasha** (21:22). The same judgment that had been pronounced on these kings, in fact, was now pronounced on Ahab (21:24; see 14:11; 16:4). Elijah also had a word of judgment for **Jezebel**. For slaughtering the Lord's faithful servants over the years, she would finally receive what she deserved: **The dogs [would] eat [her]** (20:23).

21:25-29 Ahab was the worst of many bad kings in Israel, helped along by the incitement of Jezebel (20:25). Yet, when the king heard his sentence, **he tore his clothes, put sackcloth over his body, and fasted** (20:27)—these were physical actions intended to convey his repentance. When God saw Ahab's humility, he relented on destroying his family **during his lifetime** (21:28-29).

Ahab would still die in battle, but he would not see his house destroyed.

22:1-4 The events of chapter 22 set in motion Ahab's last days. After **three years without war between Aram and Israel** (22:1), the godly **King Jehoshaphat of Judah** (about whom we will learn more in 22:41-50) paid Ahab a visit—probably for political reasons. Ahab proposed a joint military campaign between Israel and Judah to retake the Israelite city of **Ramoth-gilead** from the Arameans (22:3-4).

22:5-7 Jehoshaphat agreed to fight as one army with Ahab—on one condition. He wanted to **ask . . . the Lord's will** on the matter (22:5). (This is the reader's first clue that Jehoshaphat was not like Ahab.) The king of Israel agreed and called **about four hundred** false, lying prophets to join them. And, through that act, we can see that Ahab's repentance in 21:27 hadn't brought about true reform in his life. These prophets would say anything Ahab wanted them to say. So, they assured Ahab of victory (22:6). But, Jehoshaphat smelled a rat. He wanted a second opinion—one from **a prophet of the Lord** (22:7).

22:8 Ahab admitted that there remained one such prophet: **Micaiah**. But, Ahab hated him **because he never [prophesied] good about [him], but only disaster**. That answer laid bare the heart of the king. He didn't want to hear the truth; he only wanted to hear what was in his favor. Unfortunately, too many people feel the same way. Are you willing to receive the Word of God when it tells you what you don't want to hear?

22:9-12 After Jehoshaphat rebuked Ahab for his hatred (22:8), Ahab reluctantly sent for **Micaiah** (22:9). As the kings of Israel and Judah waited for him to arrive, Ahab's prophets foretold his victory over Aram. One of them, **Zedekiah**, predicted a glorious triumph (22:11). And to this, all of his fellow lying prophets said, "Amen" (22:12).

22:13-16 Before Micaiah entered the king's presence, he was coached not to disagree with the other prophets. Micaiah disdained this charade; he was God's prophet (22:14). But, when he appeared before Ahab, he said what the king wanted to hear: **March up and succeed. The Lord will hand it over to [you]** (22:15). Ahab recognized that Micaiah was being sarcastic, so he insisted on **the truth** (22:16). And, if Ahab wanted to hear the truth, Micaiah would give it to him.

22:17-23 God's prophet said Israel was **like sheep without a shepherd** (22:17). Their king was a failure, and the Lord was about to do something about it. Micaiah was even given a glimpse into the heavenly throne room to see how God would bring about Ahab's downfall (22:19-22). What's fascinating is that none of the remarkable details were hidden from Ahab. The prophet explained exactly what God planned to do, but the king would still move ahead with his plans despite the warning.

A **lying spirit** volunteered to lead King Ahab astray by telling lies through **his prophets** (22:22). As you process that insight into what took place in the Lord's throne room, note two things. First, God did not lie. He permitted this lying spirit's actions to accomplish his purposes. This is no different than God allowing Satan to act with evil intent so that God can achieve his good kingdom intentions in spite of Satan's plans (see Gen 50:20). Second, God allowed Micaiah to reveal to Ahab that he was being lied to! He said in effect, "Look, Ahab, your 'yes man' prophets are leading you astray." But, while Ahab was being granted divine truth about the lie, it didn't matter. He had not responded positively to truth in the past; this time would be no different.

22:24-28 Like so many of God's faithful prophets, Micaiah was treated violently for speaking the truth (22:24). Then, Ahab had Micaiah thrown in **prison** and fed **bread and water** until his own safe return (22:27). But, Micaiah had the last word: Ahab wouldn't be coming back—at least, not alive (22:28).

22:29-34 Though he had been warned that the battle would end in disaster for him, Ahab went to fight against the king of Aram anyway (22:29). He tried to **disguise** himself in order to steer the enemy's fire away from himself (22:30), but you can't hide from divine judgment. A warrior from Aram shot a random arrow and **struck the king of Israel through the joints of his armor** (22:34). God takes random shots and makes them hit the bullseye.

22:35-40 Ahab died later that day, and the Israelite army scattered (22:35-36). The king's body was taken to **Samaria** and **buried**, and **the dogs licked up his blood** (22:37-38)—just as the Lord had foretold through Elijah (21:19). Ahab was succeeded to the throne by his son **Ahaziah** (22:40).

⤳ E. The Reigns of Jehoshaphat in Judah and Ahaziah in Israel (22:41-53) ⤶

22:41-50 Scripture declares that a few of Judah's kings were good, and **Jehoshaphat** was one of them. He was a reformer like his father, Asa, walking in the Lord's ways (22:41-43, 46). Unfortunately, Jehoshaphat's alliances with Ahab and his son Ahaziah proved to be disastrous (22:44, 48-49). And, for these alliances, Jehoshaphat was rebuked by the Lord (see 2 Chr 19:1-2; 20:35-37). When he died, his son **Jehoram** reigned in his place (22:50).

22:51-53 In **Israel**, Ahab's oldest son had a short and fruitless reign because **he did what was evil in the Lord's sight** (22:51-52). **He walked in the ways of** his parents, Ahab and Jezebel, **and in the ways of Jeroboam** (22:52). Ahaziah learned well from these three bad examples. He embraced their idolatry and wickedness, and he **angered the Lord God of Israel** as they had (22:53).

The story of the kings of Israel and Judah is often a depressing one. But, there are moments when God's goodness and grace come shining through. In spite of the sins of his covenant people, the Lord was committed to fulfilling his kingdom purposes. The story continues in 2 Kings.

2 KINGS

INTRODUCTION

Author

See discussion in 1 Kings.

Historical Background

See discussion in 1 Kings.

Message and Purpose

See discussion in 1 Kings.

www.bhpublishinggroup.com/qr/te/11_00

Outline

I. The Divided Kingdoms of Israel and Judah (1:1–17:41)

A. The Reign of Ahaziah in Israel (1:1-18)

B. The Departure of Elijah and the Ministry of Elisha (2:1–8:15)

C. The Reigns of Two Evil Kings in Judah and Jehu in Israel (8:16–10:36)

D. The Reigns of Good and Evil Kings in Israel and Judah (11:1–16:20)

E. The Reign of Hoshea and Israel's Downfall (17:1-41)

II. The Surviving Kingdom of Judah (18:1–25:30)

A. The Reign of Hezekiah (18:1–20:21)

B. The Reigns of Manasseh and Amon (21:1-26)

C. The Reign of Josiah (22:1–23:30)

D. The Reigns of Judah's Final Kings (23:31–25:30)

2 KINGS

I. THE DIVIDED KINGDOMS OF ISRAEL AND JUDAH (1:1–17:41)

⌁ A. The Reign of Ahaziah in Israel (1:1-18) ⌁

1:1 Having learned at the end of 1 Kings that King Ahaziah of Israel "served Baal" (1 Kgs 22:53), we will soon catch a glimpse of the king's devotion to this abominable god. When Ahaziah's father Ahab died, **Moab**—who had been paying tribute to Israel (see 3:4)—**rebelled**. The international political landscape was changing, leading to an approaching war.

1:2 King Ahab had been an idolater, and his son Ahaziah was a chip off the old block. Even when he suffered a serious **injury** by falling from a window, he sought a word from **Baal-zebub, the god of Ekron**, rather than the Lord. "Baal-zebub" means "Lord of the Flies." With this term, the author was intentionally mocking this false god, by changing the name "Baal-zebul," which means "Lord of Glory," to something less impressive. Ahaziah chose to look to a Philistine idol (Ekron was a Philistine city) for help. And, though the king hadn't inquired of the true God, he was about to receive an answer from him anyway.

1:3-4 The prophet **Elijah the Tishbite** had been a thorn in King Ahab's side. His son Ahaziah was about to get a dose of the same harsh treatment he'd received from the prophet. God told Elijah to intercept the king's **messengers** and deliver to them a question and a

pronouncement. First, he asked Ahaziah why he was seeking advice from a foreign god—as if Israel had no God of their own (1:3). Second, as a result of the king's failure to seek the Lord, Elijah sent him a divine prognosis: he would **certainly die** (1:4).

1:5-12 When the messengers returned and relayed the news (1:5-6), the king only needed a physical description to know exactly who the prophet of doom was: **Elijah the Tishbite** (1:7-8). Apparently, Ahaziah had learned nothing from his father's encounters with Elijah. This was the same prophet who had stood on a mountain and called down fire from heaven (see 1 Kgs 18:30-40). Nevertheless, the king sent **a captain with his fifty men** to take Elijah into custody (1:9).

The captain demanded that this **man of God** come with them (1:9). But, if he was truly a "man of God," why were fifty soldiers trying to arrest him? Given the respect he should've been shown, Elijah said, **If I am a man of God, may fire come down from heaven and consume you and your fifty men**. And, in an instant, they were wiped out (1:10). Unfortunately for captain number two and his men, Ahaziah was not deterred. The second captain made the same demand of Elijah but insisted that he come with them **immediately** (1:11). But, the only thing that happened immediately was a doubling of the body count (1:12).

1:13-15 It seems the king was short on wisdom and long on expendable troops because he sent a third detachment. But, the third captain wasn't as bold as the other two. He **fell on his knees** and **begged** Elijah not to wipe them out (1:13). In light of the captain's humility and recognition that Elijah was truly a **man of God**, the Lord told Elijah to accompany them **to the king** (1:13, 15).

1:16-18 Ahaziah accomplished two things through his efforts to take Elijah into custody: the death of more than a hundred of his men and the opportunity for Elijah to pronounce God's judgment in person. The prophet repeated his earlier prophecy. Ahaziah was an idolater who would not recover from his injury; he would **certainly die** (1:16). And, indeed, **Ahaziah died** in accordance with the Lord's pronouncement. His son **Joram**, who would also prove to be faithless, succeeded him to the throne (1:17).

✒ B. The Departure of Elijah and the Ministry of Elisha (2:1–8:15) ❧

2:1 As the previous chapter revealed, Elijah had lost none of his power, but it was time for him to be taken **up to heaven** and pass on the spiritual baton of prophetic leadership (2:1). Elisha, the man whom God appointed to be Elijah's helper and successor (see 1 Kgs 19:16, 19-21), was aware of this, as the following narrative makes plain.

2:2-3 As the two men were traveling together, Elijah told Elisha to stay in Gilgal because the Lord was sending him **to Bethel** (2:2). But, Elisha refused to abandon his mentor. At Bethel, they encountered some **sons of the prophets**. The phrase doesn't mean "children of the prophets"; instead, it was apparently some sort of school or seminary (a prophet training center). Having divine insight, they asked Elisha whether he knew that God would **take** his **master away** that day. Elisha knew, but he didn't want to talk about it (2:3).

2:4 Elijah's next destination at the Lord's command was **Jericho**. And, once again, he told Elisha to **stay** behind. Was this a test for Elisha? He knew that God was taking Elijah away within hours, and he also knew that he was to be Elijah's successor. Was Elijah

testing his protégé to see if he was ready to accept his divine responsibility? If so, Elisha showed no sign of turning back from his calling. Once again, he declared, **I will not leave you.** Elisha's insistence demonstrated his commitment to accepting the mantle of leadership.

2:5 In Jericho, they visited another community of **the sons of the prophets** (see commentary on 2:2-3). Just like the group in Bethel, they asked Elisha if he knew God was taking Elijah away. Again, perhaps filled with sorrow, Elisha told them to **be quiet**.

2:6-7 For the final time, Elijah told Elisha not to follow him. But, Elisha vowed again to accompany his master and walked with him to the **Jordan** River (2:6). Each one of the locations along their route was a place where God's presence and power had been demonstrated. It seems, then, that Elijah wanted Elisha to review with him key locations memorializing God's acts to build up Elisha's confidence in God's presence and power being with him.

When the pair reached their destination, **fifty men from the sons of the prophets** arrived with them (2:7). They knew it was time for Elijah to depart, so they had traveled to say farewell to Israel's faithful prophet. They would also serve as witnesses to the transfer of prophetic authority.

2:8-9 Elijah then performed his final miracle by parting the Jordan with his **mantle**, a sleeveless outer garment, so he and Elisha could cross over **on dry ground** (2:8). Once there, the elder prophet asked his successor if he had any final requests. So, Elisha boldly asked, **Please, let me inherit two shares of your spirit** (2:9).

This was no random request. Elisha was likely thinking of Deuteronomy 21:17, which states that a "firstborn" son was entitled to "two shares" of his father's estate. Based on God's own testimony (see 1 Kgs 19:16), Elisha was to be anointed prophet in Elijah's "place." Elijah was his spiritual "father" (see 2:12), and Elisha was his heir, so to speak. It was a legitimate request, and Elisha knew he would need an extra dose of divine enablement for the tasks that lay ahead.

2:10-12 Though the request was legitimate, it was not Elijah's to grant. So, he stated the condition for Elisha's plea to be granted. If God chose to honor Elisha's request, he would actually see Elijah **being taken** away by God. And, as they continued along their way, **a chariot of fire** pulled by **horses of fire suddenly appeared**. Elijah climbed aboard and **went up into heaven**.

Though Elijah didn't die, he was still taken away. Elisha grieved the loss of his mentor. It appears he called Elijah both **my father**, a title of respect, and **the chariots and horsemen of Israel**, an acknowledgment that Israel's true strength was not in their army but in this one who faithfully delivered the Word of God (2:12).

2:13-14 When the chariot had faded into the distance, Elisha picked up Elijah's fallen **mantle**, which was the symbol of his authority. As Elijah's successor, he put the mantle to work by striking the **Jordan** with it (2:13). Then, Elisha showed that he knew the true source of power. The power wasn't in him, nor was it in the garment. It was in **the LORD God**. Then, the waters of the river **parted** just as they had for Elijah (2:14).

2:15-18 The sons of the prophets from Jericho recognized that a transfer of authority had taken place, so they showed deference to Elisha (2:15). Nevertheless, they asked to go and search for Elijah (2:16), though it's not clear why. Even though they knew that Elisha had assumed Elijah's role, they may have thought that Elijah would make a landing somewhere after his supernatural flight. (After all, it's not every day that someone rides to heaven in a fiery chariot never to be seen again!) Or, it could be that they thought God would leave his body behind somewhere so that they could bury it.

Whatever the sons of the prophets thought had happened to Elijah, Elisha didn't want them to search (2:16). He knew Elijah was gone. But, they **urged him to the point of embarrassment** (2:17). So, Elisha let them search, but to no avail (2:17-18). Elijah wouldn't be seen again—until several hundred years later when he appeared with Moses on a mountain in Israel, talking with the Son of God (see Matt 17:1-3).

2:19-25 If anyone questioned whether Elisha had received a double dose of divine power as he had requested (2:9), he answered their concerns with amazing demonstrations of power—both for healing and for judgment. First, he provided a miraculous cure for **water** that had turned **bad** (2:19-22). Then, when **some small boys ... jeered at** Elisha, he **cursed** them, and the Lord brought swift judgment on them by means of **two ... bears** (2:23-24). Scholars debate the meaning of the phrase translated "small boys" here; it could refer to young men. Regardless, they mocked God's prophet by saying, **Go up, baldy!** (2:23). Apparently, they wanted Elisha to go away, to "go up" like Elijah had done, never to be seen again.

While what happened to the boys may seem like a harsh judgment, we must remember that this is exactly what God warned Israel about when he made his covenant with them. In Leviticus, the Lord told his people what he would do if they were hostile toward him and refused to obey: "I will send wild animals against you that will deprive you of your children" (Lev 26:21-22). Ultimately, then, this scene is a judgment upon godless parenting. Parents have a responsibility to lead their children to God. Leading children away from him is disastrous for both parents and their offspring.

3:1-9 Joram, another **son of Ahab**, inherited the throne of Israel (3:1). Though he was not as bad as Ahab and Jezebel, he was still **evil in the LORD's sight** (3:2). For some time, **Moab** had been subject to Israel, paying tribute in the form of huge numbers of **lambs** and the **wool** from just as many **rams** (3:4). Mesha, **the king of Moab**, evidently sensed a weakness in Israel with the quick changes in leadership and **rebelled** (3:5). But, Joram gathered his army and asked good **King Jehoshaphat of Judah** to join him in attacking Moab (3:6-7). Jehoshaphat agreed, and **Edom** joined the alliance. But, as the three kings and their armies marched down the eastern shore of the Dead Sea toward Moab, their **water** supply suddenly ran out (3:7-9).

3:10-12 The idol-worshiping **king of Israel** blamed the Lord for their predicament (3:10). But, Jehoshaphat wouldn't let Joram's blasphemous charge stand. So, he called for a **prophet of** God to speak to the dilemma. When he heard that **Elisha . . . who used to pour water on Elijah's hands**—that is, serve Elijah—was available, Joram probably shuddered (3:11). For even if Joram didn't know of Elisha, he surely remembered Elijah—the one who had prophesied judgment and death on both his father Ahab and his brother Ahaziah. But, whatever Joram was thinking, Jehoshaphat was convinced that they needed to hear from this divine spokesman. So, he convinced **the king of Israel** and **the king of Edom** to go with him to visit Elisha (3:12).

3:13-18 Notice how Elisha greeted King Joram of Israel: **What do we have in common? Go to the prophets of your father and your mother!** (3:13). In other words, he said, "You're an idolater, Joram! What are you doing coming to see me? Go ask your idols for advice!" Then, Joram demonstrated that he deserved Elisha's contempt by repeating his accusation against the Lord. The only thing that kept Elisha from showing Joram to the door was his **respect for King Jehoshaphat** (3:14). And, because of that respect, Elisha gave a remarkable prophecy of a miraculous supply of **water** in a dry land that would meet their need (3:16-17). He also informed the three kings that God would **hand Moab over** to them (3:18).

3:20-27 Everything happened just as Elisha predicted. Not only was the **water** supply a miracle in itself, but God also used it to fool the Moabite army into thinking that the ground was soaked in the **blood** of their enemies as if they'd been fighting each other (3:20-23). When they approached to steal the spoils, Moab's army had to flee because Israel attacked and pushed them all the way back to **Kir-hareseth**, Moab's major city (3:24-25). After that, King Mesha was so desperate for help that he committed the heinous sin of sacrificing his **firstborn son** and heir **as a burnt offering on the city wall**. As a result, **great wrath was on the Israelites**, perhaps from Moabites, though the text isn't clear. Then, Israel **withdrew** and **returned to their land** (3:27).

4:1 Just as 1 Kings included an extended narrative of Elijah's ministry (see 1 Kgs 17:1–19:21), so also 2 Kings includes an extended

narrative of that of his successor, Elisha (4:1–8:15). The order in which his miraculous deeds are presented in these chapters may or may not be chronological. The author might have arranged them topically.

At the beginning of Elijah's ministry, he had miraculously provided for a widow and raised a dead boy to life (see 1 Kgs 17:8-24). Elisha was about to do the same. One day, a wife of one of **the sons of the prophets** (see commentary on 2:2-3) **cried out to Elisha** that her **husband** had **died**. Apparently, her debt was great, so **the creditor** was coming to take her **children** as **slaves** to work off what was owed. She was in an economic, emotional, familial, and spiritual crisis. Her destitution may have resulted from the fact that true prophets were not honored in the largely apostate northern kingdom of Israel. In going to Elisha, she was seeking a spiritual solution for her dilemma.

4:2-7 All the widow owned was a single **jar of oil** (4:2). Elisha told her to **borrow** all the **empty containers** from her **neighbors** that she could, which must have sounded like an odd response to what she'd shared (4:3; see 4:1). With that done, she was to begin pouring oil into them (4:4).

Miraculously, the widow soon found that oil **kept pouring** out of the jar until every **container** gathered was **full** (4:5-6). By obeying the Lord's word through Elisha, the widow had enough **oil** to **sell** so that she could **pay** off her **debt** and then **live on** the remaining money (4:7).

This story is a reminder that God's Word does not always seem to make sense to us. But, he's God, and we're not. Blessings—sometimes physical but always spiritual—come when we respond to his Word with faith and obedience.

4:8-9 Elisha ministered to another faithful woman who lived in **Shunem**, a town near Jezreel. She was a **prominent woman** and had a **husband**—unlike the late prophet's poor widow (see 4:1-7). Yet, God was mindful of her faith, too, as well as her desire for a child. She recognized Elisha as a true prophet from the Lord, so she opened her home to this **holy man of God** as a resting place on his travels (4:9).

4:10-13 Elisha was grateful for her hospitality, so he sought a way to reward her. He sent **his attendant Gehazi** to find out what she might want, even if that meant speaking **on [her] behalf to the king or the commander of the army** (4:11-13). That's a remarkable statement given that Elisha was talking about the evil King Joram. So clearly, Elisha had influence even though he spoke for God amid an idolatrous administration. This is a classic example of God's kingdom agenda in operation. He can give his people influence in the civil government when they are faithfully serving him in their primary sphere of spiritual authority.

4:14-17 Elisha's hostess said she was content, but Gehazi noticed that she had **no son**, and her husband was **old**. Thus, she had little chance of motherhood (4:14). So, Elisha promised her a son within a year, a promise that God would fulfill (4:15-17).

For the readers of 1–2 Kings, both those who experienced Babylonian exile and their descendants, this story served as a reminder that God honors faithfulness to him and his covenant. Every person in Israel and Judah, from king (3:13-14) to lowly prophet's widow (4:1-7), was responsible for his or her response to the Lord.

4:18-24 Sometime later, the Shunammite woman's son fell ill while helping his father with the harvest (4:18-19). Then, he tragically **died** in his mother's arms (4:20). She put the boy in Elisha's room and immediately made plans to visit the prophet (4:21-22).

4:25-28 When Elisha saw her coming, he sent **Gehazi** to find out why she had come, but she wouldn't reveal the reason for her visit to Elisha's attendant (4:25-26). The woman knew where her hope for her son lay, and she didn't want to see anyone but Elisha. She **clung to his feet**, and Elisha could see her **anguish** (4:27). Her questions to Elisha are heartbreaking (4:28). Essentially, she asked, "Why would God give me a son that I never asked for, only to take him away?" She was experiencing the mystery of suffering.

4:29-37 Elisha hastily sent **Gehazi** ahead with his **staff** to lay **on the boy's face**, while he and the woman followed behind (4:29-30). However, the staff produced no results (4:31), indicating that this job wasn't going to be easy. So, Elisha **prayed to the Lord**, and he **lay on the boy**, just as Elijah had once done (4:33-34; see 1 Kgs 17:21-22). **The boy's flesh became warm**, but he didn't wake (4:34). After this, Elisha **paced** in the house—perhaps praying more—then **bent down over him again**. This time, the boy's eyes **opened** (4:35). Then, no doubt to her great delight, Elisha gave the woman her son (4:36-37).

For only the second time in the Old Testament, God responded to the prayers of one of his servants and raised someone from the dead. These miracles were foretastes of the power Jesus Christ would wield as he raised people from the dead (see Luke 7:11-17; 8:52-56; John 11:1-44). And, Christ's miraculous resurrections, of course, were just a foretaste of his own resurrection that would serve as a promise of resurrection for all those who believe in him (see John 11:25-26; Acts 26:23; 1 Cor 15:20-23).

4:38-41 Elisha's miracles continued. During a time of **famine**, he was with a group of prophets who had to eat whatever they could find (4:38). So, as Elisha's **attendant** made a stew, he added **many wild gourds** without knowing **what they were** (4:38-39). Evidently, the gourds were poisonous, for the prophets **ate** some and **cried out** in despair: **There's death in the pot** (4:40).

Because the prophets were responsible for communicating God's word to his people, the wild gourd situation was not just a literal dilemma; it shows us the danger of mixing heresy with the truth. When leaders are spiritually sick and contaminated, the people cannot be fed. Notice that only when the substance of flour was added that the food was made edible. Thus, only when the substance of God's truth is poured in and emphasized can the contamination of false religion be overcome. Elisha miraculously cured the stew so that the men could eat (4:41). The Lord graciously provided for his servants in a time of distress.

4:42-44 Another food shortage was solved by the astounding power at work through Elisha. This time, only **twenty loaves of barley**

bread were available to feed **a hundred men** (4:42-43). Nevertheless, Elisha commanded that it be given **to the people to eat.** As the bread was distributed, it multiplied until everyone had enough—and there were even leftovers (4:44). Once again, then, we see a foretaste of the miracles of Jesus, who would feed thousands with only a few loaves and fish and have basketsful left over (see Mark 6:30-44; 8:1-9).

5:1 To this point, we have seen Elisha perform miracles for a lowly widow, a prominent woman, and a school of prophets. But, these were all people from Israel. Could those outside the people of God be recipients of God's grace and power, too? The Lord had promised Abraham that he would bless all the peoples of the earth through him (see Gen 12:3). So, without a doubt, he wanted people from every nation to worship him.

Elijah had ministered to a Sidonian woman (see 1 Kgs 17:8-24), so it's not surprising to see Elisha bringing God's grace to a non-Israelite, as well. Given the amount of unbelief and idolatry that existed in Israel, God was determined to glorify his name—even among the Gentiles. Later, when Jesus was rejected in Jewish Nazareth, he reminded his listeners of God's grace to non-Israelites through Elijah and Elisha (see Luke 4:24-27).

Elisha was about to meet **Naaman,** a mighty and proud **commander of the army for the king of Aram**, a nation that often warred against Israel's evil kings. Naaman was a Gentile who nevertheless experienced God's favor in battle. But, he had a significant problem—the incurable **skin disease** of leprosy.

5:2-3 In the course of his **raids** against Israel, Naaman had brought home **a young girl who served [his] wife** (5:2). It would be the kindness of this girl and her confidence in the God of Israel that would turn Naaman's life around. She told her mistress about a **prophet . . . in Samaria** who could **cure** her husband's **disease** (5:3).

5:4-7 When Naaman explained this to **the king of Aram**, the king sent him to Samaria loaded down with money and a **letter to the king of Israel** that included a simple request:

"Cure my military commander" (5:4-6). Of course, Israel's wicked King Joram had no faith in God, so he had no faith that even the prophet Elisha could fix such an earthly problem by divine power. In fact, Israel's king saw nothing spiritual in the request at all. What he saw was a military disaster waiting to happen. Joram was convinced that Aram's king was simply **picking a fight** through such an outlandish note, and he panicked (5:7). He reasoned that if he told Aram's king that he couldn't heal his commander, Aram would invade. And, instead of laying the letter before the Lord and asking for his guidance and protection, Joram essentially had a nervous breakdown. (For a dramatic contrast to this, see 2 Kgs 19:14-19).

5:8 When Elisha learned of Joram's panic attack and unbelief, he told the king to send Naaman to him so that **he [would] know there [was] a prophet in Israel**. In other words, he said, "You, Israel's king, don't believe in the God of Israel. But, when I finish with this foreign general, he will."

5:9-10 Naaman arrived at **Elisha's house** and **stood at the door** (5:9). If he was expecting the red carpet treatment, he had another thing coming. Elisha didn't even say hello to him! Instead he **sent . . . a messenger** to tell Naaman to **wash seven times in the Jordan** River to be healed (5:10). This means that, though Elisha intended to heal Naaman's physical problem, he also intended to deal with his spiritual problem—his pride.

5:11-12 Naaman's pride manifested itself at once: he **got angry**. He had expected Elisha to **wave his hand** over him in **the name of . . . his God** and **cure** his skin (5:11). In other words, Naaman just wanted a quick fix to his flesh without recognizing that his real problem was his heart. A lot of people today have the same attitude.

Why, Naaman asked in effect, couldn't he simply **wash in** one of his own **rivers**, which were **better than all the waters in Israel**? And then, he stormed off **in a rage** (5:12). This conceited commander wasn't about to be humiliated by some two-bit prophet from a country that he had been routinely beating up. But, Naaman did not yet realize that his victories hadn't been his own doing. They had been gifts from the God whose help he desperately needed (see 5:1).

5:13-14 Previously, one of Naaman's servants—a young Israelite girl—had pointed him toward truth and wisdom (5:2-3). Similarly now, **his servants** who were with him displayed more wisdom that their arrogant master (5:13). If Elisha had given Naaman some significant task to accomplish, surely he would have done it. So, was he really willing to pass up an opportunity to be healed simply because the cure seemed too mundane? Their argument made sense, so Naaman gave in, obeyed Elisha, and **dipped himself in the Jordan seven times**. To his astonishment, **his skin was restored** (5:14).

5:15-16 Naaman had been cured, but he had also been humbled. Notice that when he spoke to Elisha, he referred to himself as **[his] servant**. And, having left in a rage, Naaman now returned with thankfulness. He said, **I know there's no God in the whole world except in Israel**. Elisha had told the king of Israel that this foreign general would soon know there was a prophet in Israel, and Naaman had indeed learned that and much more. He confessed the Lord as the one true God.

To express his gratitude, Naaman offered the prophet **a gift** (5:15). However, Elisha **refused** (5:16). He was God's servant doing God's work. He wanted to make it clear to everyone that his services were not for sale. The king of Aram may have sent his army commander to Israel in order to purchase his healing. But, Naaman left in God's debt—not the other way around.

5:17 Given Elisha's response, Naaman decided to ask Elisha for a gift instead. He wanted to take some of Israel's **soil** back home so that he could build an earthen altar and **sacrifice** to God on it. Previously, he thought the rivers of his homeland were "better than all the waters of Israel" (5:12). But by this point, he'd realized that even Aramean dirt wasn't good enough for erecting an altar for Israel's God. If he were to make **a burnt offering** to the Lord, he would do it on an altar made from the land that the Lord had blessed. And,

from that point forward, Naaman wouldn't **sacrifice to any other god but the Lord**.

5:18-19 Naaman sought God's **pardon** in one **matter** he'd face back home. He wanted the Lord to forgive him for those times when his **king** would bow **in worship** in **the temple of** his god **Rimmon**, leaning on Naaman's **arm** for support so that Naaman had to bow as well (5:18). Elisha laid no further burden on this new believer and bid him to **go in peace** (5:19). Whatever shortcomings there were in Naaman's circumstances, this non-Israelite from an idolatrous land had confessed the Lord alone to be God—unlike the king of Israel and most of his subjects.

5:20-24 The faith of an Aramean commander is immediately contrasted with the duplicity of Elisha's attendant, **Gehazi**, who couldn't bear to see all of the offered money and clothes headed back to Aram (5:20). So, he pursued Naaman and lied his way to **one hundred fifty pounds of silver** and **two** new outfits, which he promptly hid in his **house** (5:21-24).

5:25-27 When Gehazi returned to his duties, Elisha asked an ominous question: **Where did you go?** This leading question is a reminder that you can't escape the gaze of an all-knowing God. Gehazi had been deceptive and had dishonored the Lord. Therefore, his punishment would fit the crime. Elisha pronounced his sentence: **Naaman's** leprosy would **cling to** him and his **descendants forever** (5:25-27). In other words, the faithlessness of this Israelite had earned him the **diseased** skin that the believing Aramean had left behind.

6:1-3 That one of the schools of the prophets in the northern kingdom was growing was no doubt a tribute to Elisha's ministry and **supervision** (6:1). Some of the prophets wanted to **build** a **place** near the **Jordan** because their existing living arrangements were **too small**, so they asked Elisha to go with them (6:2-3).

6:4-7 While felling trees for the structure, one of the prophets watched as his **iron ax head fell into the water**. But, the worst part was that it was **borrowed** (6:5). This student prophet was no doubt poor, making the item difficult to replace. Living as a spokesman for the true God during those dark days in Israel was not a profitable line of work (see 4:1-7). Yet, Elisha's miraculous recovery of the lost tool showed God's concern for even the smallest needs of his people (6:6-7).

6:8-10 Sometime later, **the king of Aram** was **waging war against Israel**. This is most likely a reference to the same king who sent Naaman to Israel (see 5:1). This probably wasn't an all-out war because the Arameans were called "raiders" (6:23), but it was still a serious incursion. Despite Aram's superior forces, Elisha had access to divine intelligence about the schemes of Aram's king. The ruler couldn't make the slightest plan in his tent without Elisha relaying it in detail to **the king of Israel** so he could take appropriate countermeasures (6:9-10).

6:11-14 The king of Aram became so upset that he accused his **servants** of harboring a spy for Israel (6:11). And, when he learned that **Elisha, the prophet in Israel**, was the source of his problems, the king sent **horses, chariots, and massive army** to capture him (6:12-14). Because this was the same prophet who had healed the commander of Aram's army (5:1-19), however, he wouldn't be captured so easily.

6:15-16 When the servant of Elisha saw the horde of enemy forces surrounding their city, he cried out, **Oh, my master, what are we to do?** (6:15). But, Elisha wasn't worried. He could see with eyes of faith and said, **Those who are with us outnumber those who are with them** (6:16). His certainty here bears similarities with the apostle John's exhortation to believers: "The one who is in you is greater than the one who is in the world" (1 John 4:4). When we align ourselves with God, our enemy is always outnumbered.

6:17-23 The Lord answered Elisha's prayer, and his servant saw God's army. There were **horses and chariots of fire all around Elisha** (6:17); it was a wall of divine protection. Heavenly involvement even extended to striking the enemy army **with blindness** and allowing

Elisha to lead them right into Israel's camp (6:18-19). There, King Joram was so excited at the prospect of any easy victory that he must have been jumping up and down like a child as he hollered, **Should I kill them, should I kill them, my father?** (6:21). His term of respect for Elisha was significant, but the sentiment wouldn't last long. Elisha not only refused to allow the slaughter, but he also commanded that a feast be prepared for them (6:22-23). And as a result, the astonished **Aramean raiders** withdrew from Israel (6:23).

In this chapter, we see that God provides for the small concerns of his people (a lost ax head, 6:1-7), as well as the big concerns (6:8-23).

6:24-31 Eventually, **King Ben-hadad of Aram** invaded the northern kingdom again and **laid siege to Samaria** (6:24). Things got so bad that the city was cut off from the outside world and disintegrated into the horrors of cannibalism. One day, **as the king** walked on the city **wall, a woman** told him an appalling tale of feeding on her own **son** for survival (6:25-29). The Lord had warned Israel that such tragedies would befall them if they rejected him as their King (see Deut 28:53-57). Yet, instead of crying out to the Lord in repentance and pleading for salvation at such news, the king breathed murderous threats against Elisha (6:31).

6:32-33 When **the king sent a man** to seize Elisha, the prophet rightly called the king a **murderer** (6:32). The king's **messenger** admitted that the siege and famine was from God (6:33). Yet, if that was really his belief, he should have been humbling himself before God rather than threatening his prophet.

7:1-2 Though the king hadn't sought the Lord, Elisha had a word from the Lord, announcing the end of the siege and of the famine (7:1). **The king's right-hand man** was incredulous because such an abundance of food sounded impossible. Therefore, because of the man's unwillingness to believe, Elisha promised him that he would indeed see the provision, but he wouldn't **eat any of it** (7:2).

7:3-7 The news that the Aramean siege was lifted came not from the king's soldiers, but from **four men** with the incurable **skin disease** of leprosy (7:3). They decided they had nothing to lose by going to the Arameans and throwing themselves on their mercy for some scraps of food. The worst that could happen was that the Arameans would kill them, but they were going to die of starvation anyway (7:3-4). So, they set off for the **camp**, only to find that it was completely abandoned (7:5, 7). The author of 2 Kings informs the readers that **the Lord had caused the Aramean camp to hear the sound of chariots, horses, and a large army**. Assuming that Israel's king had hired foreign warriors to save them, the terrified Arameans fled (7:6-7).

7:8-11 The **diseased men** had a feast and started hauling off the loot when they suddenly had a pang of conscience (7:8). They realized they had to share this **good news** with their fellow Israelites. If they didn't, they knew **punishment [would] catch up with [them]** (7:9). So, they ran back to the city and **reported** what they had found (7:10-11).

7:12-13 In spite of the wonderful report, the king assumed the worst. As far as he was concerned, the men described a trap. He was sure **the Arameans** were actually in hiding, ready to pounce on the people when they came **out of the city** (7:12). Finally, **one of his servants** said basically the same thing the lepers had said: "We're going to die anyway, so please at least send some men out to see whether the report is true" (7:13). Sadly, wisdom had to come from the servants and outcasts because the king of Israel had none.

7:14-20 When **the messengers** investigated, they found that the Arameans had truly abandoned everything—**clothes and equipment** (7:14-15). And soon, in their mad stampede for food, the starving people of Samaria rushed toward the spoils and **trampled** the king's **right-hand man**, who had been put **in charge of the city gate**. Therefore, **he died** just as Elisha, **the man of God**, had **predicted** (7:16-20; see 7:2).

8:1-3 Chapter 8 opens with another story about the Shunammite woman **whose son** Elisha had raised (8:1). Elisha warned the woman about **a seven-year famine** in Israel,

which she and her family avoided by living **as resident aliens in the land of the Philistines**. But, she must have lost her land as a result of the maneuver, because she had to go to the king to appeal for what was hers (8:2-3).

8:4-6 In God's providence, the king of Israel was asking **Gehazi**, Elisha's **attendant**, to tell him **all the great things Elisha has done** (8:4), just as the woman walked in to ask the king to have her property restored. Having just told her tale, **Gehazi** was able to inform **the king** that this was the very **woman** and **son** whom **Elisha** had **restored to life**. The king thus returned to the woman her house and **field**, as well as the **income** her field had generated while she was gone (8:5-6). Obviously, the timing of this encounter happened not by chance, but by divine intervention. There are no chance encounters in your life either: "A person's heart plans his way, but the LORD determines his steps" (Prov 16:9).

You may wonder what Gehazi was doing in the presence of the king in light of the judgment God placed on him and his progeny for his greed (see 5:20-27). One answer is that he must have been restored due to passing a retest God gave him to redeem himself. Sometimes, God gives us retests in order to offer new opportunities to reverse the consequences of our sin.

I think it's likely that Gehazi was one of the diseased men in 7:3-11. If so, as one of these lepers who went into the Aramean camp, he said it would not be good to selfishly consume the bounty in secret (7:9)—which is an offense not unlike the deed that brought about his leprosy in the first place. From experience, then, he knew that concealing the sin of greed would bring punishment.

8:7-8 One of Elisha's last acts as a prophet involved an unusual visit to **Damascus** to see **King Ben-hadad of Aram**, an old enemy of Israel (see 6:24). Ben-hadad **was sick** (8:7). He obviously respected Elisha's ministry and authority, so he had a man named **Hazael** take **a gift** to Elisha and ask him to **inquire of the LORD** about his illness (8:8).

8:9-15 At first glance, Elisha's contradictory answer is confusing. If Ben-hadad were **sure to recover** (8:10), why would the king die?

But, when Hazael asked why Elisha was crying, everything became clear. In time, Hazael himself would assume the throne of Aram and then slaughter Israel's people (8:11-13). Thus, Ben-hadad *would have* recovered from his illness. But, before he could, Hazael would assassinate him, which is exactly what happened (8:14-15).

↣ C. The Reigns of Two Evil Kings in Judah and Jehu in Israel
(8:16–10:36) ↢

8:16-19 For the first time in 2 Kings, the focus shifts to Judah in the south. The first king of Judah described in this chapter was **Jehoram**, who was the son of the godly king **Jehoshaphat** (8:16). Unfortunately, he was condemned as **evil in the LORD's sight** because he was greatly influenced by his wife, who was wicked **Ahab's daughter** (8:18). Thus, the evil of Ahab's legacy flowed, not only through the kings of Israel, but now also through the kings of Judah. Nevertheless, God in his faithfulness preserved **Judah** from destruction **for the sake of his servant David**. The Lord made a covenant promise to **give a lamp to David and his sons forever** in the form of a king to rule on his throne (8:19). Ultimately, the "forever" of this promise will be fulfilled in Jesus Christ.

8:20-29 Jehoram had to deal with the revolt of **Edom** during his eight-year reign, but he could not bring them under control (8:20-22). He was succeeded by his son **Ahaziah**, who **reigned** for only **one year**, and who was equally **evil** (8:25, 27). Like his father, he also came under the influence of **Athaliah**, his mother, the daughter of Ahab (8:26). Ahaziah joined with **Joram** of the northern kingdom **to fight against King Hazael of Aram**, but Joram was wounded and went to Jezreel to **recover**. Ahaziah went to **visit Joram** at Jezreel (8:28-29); it would be a fatal choice.

9:1-4 The time had finally come for the Lord to eradicate the descendants of Ahab and Jezebel from Israel. Years before, God had told Elijah to anoint Jehu as the king of Israel for this stated purpose (see 1 Kgs 19:16-17). But,

the assignment of anointing Jehu actually fell to Elisha, who sent one of his student prophets to meet with **Jehu son of Jehoshaphat** (not Jehoshaphat the former king of Judah) in a private ceremony and **anoint** him as **king over Israel** in place of the wounded King Joram (9:1-3; see 2 Kgs 8:28-29). Elisha warned the young prophet to run for his life after the anointing to **escape** any possible reprisal that his act might generate (9:3).

9:5-10 The young man found Jehu, called him aside into a private room, poured oil on his head, and repeated God's charge: **I anoint you king over the LORD's people, Israel. You are to strike down the house of your master Ahab** (9:5-7). The prophet also predicted the manner of Jezebel's death and the shameful way her body would be left for the **dogs** to **eat** (9:10). These predictions of destruction were consistent with what Elijah had previously announced (see 1 Kgs 21:22-24).

9:11-15 Jehu's fellow soldiers thought the man who had requested an audience with Jehu (and then ran away) was a **crazy person**—but, they weren't buying Jehu's brush-off of the incident (9:11). When he told them the truth, they rallied around him and declared, **Jehu is king!** (9:13).

Meanwhile, the army was **at Ramoth-gilead** with King Joram, fighting against **Aram** (9:14). Jehu told his new subjects not to let anyone leave Ramoth and not to tell Joram in **Jezreel** so that he wouldn't have time to mount a defense before Jehu could get there (9:15).

9:16-20 Jehu had nothing to worry about because God was working his sovereign plan behind the scenes. Jehu made his way to **Jezreel**, where King **Joram** of Israel and **King Ahaziah of Judah** (both members of Ahab's house) were together (9:16). **The watchman . . . on the tower in Jezreel** saw Jehu's rapid approach and told them, **I see a mob!** (9:16-17). Joram sent **a rider** to see if the mob was peaceful (9:17). But, when the **horseman** relayed the question, **Jehu** essentially said, "If you know what's good for you, you'll stop talking and join us" (9:18). This happened a second time before the watchman realized that the leader appeared to be Jehu (9:19-20).

9:21-29 Recognizing that this was serious business—but not concerned enough to flee—Joram and Ahaziah rode out to meet Jehu **at the plot of land of Naboth the Jezreelite** (9:21). It was this very acreage that King Ahab had claimed as his own after Queen Jezebel had Naboth murdered (see 1 Kgs 21:1-16). It would, therefore, be a fitting place for their wicked descendants to be put to death. Joram asked Jehu, **Do you come in peace?** And, when Jehu made his intentions clear, citing the evil deeds fostered by the king's family as the reason behind his coming, Joram and Ahaziah **fled** (9:22-23). But, it was too late. Jehu and his followers shot and killed both of the doomed kings (9:24, 27).

9:30-37 Jehu arrived in Jezreel to carry out one final execution. Queen **Jezebel heard about** what he had done to her son Joram. So, she **painted her eyes** and **fixed her hair** (9:30), probably in mock tribute to Israel's new king. She also derisively called him **Zimri** (9:31), a reference to the man who had killed Israel's king, reigned seven days before killing himself, and was replaced by Ahab's father, Omri (see 1 Kgs 16:9-20). Jezebel was implying that Jehu would meet the same fate.

Jehu didn't bother responding. Instead, he called to two of her servants, rightly assuming they'd be willing to **throw** her to her death. Then, Jehu **rode over her** corpse with his chariot (9:32-33). That done, he went in to eat and ordered her to be buried. But, when the servants went to do so, they found that **dogs** had eaten **Jezebel's flesh** in fulfillment of the prophecy of **Elijah** (9:35-36). Thus, early readers of 2 Kings were being reminded that God called to account those in Israel who failed to keep his law and turned to idols—the very sins for which those readers had been exiled.

10:1-3 Jehu knew that his position wasn't secure as long as there were officials in the kingdom who were still loyal to Ahab's house. Especially concerning were the guardians of Ahab's **seventy** (seventy!) **sons in Samaria** (10:1). So, Jehu penned correspondence to everyone who had connection to the royal house and challenged them to **select the most qualified** son of Ahab to fight him for the **throne** (10:2-3).

10:4-8 These leaders had heard of what happened to Joram, Ahaziah, and Jezebel, and they wanted no part of Jehu's fury. So they promptly agreed to join his side and obeyed his grisly order to slaughter Ahab's **sons** and deliver **their heads** to him (10:4-7). Jehu displayed them **until morning** as silent but effective evidence that he had succeeded in conquering the dynasty of Ahab once and for all. Moreover, any resistance against him was futile (10:8).

10:9-11 The next morning, Jehu stood behind the pile of severed heads and made a speech that put his actions in the proper perspective (10:9-10). The people of **Jezreel** must have been shocked at what they saw and maybe fearful that Jehu's bloody rebellion would bring the fury of Israel's government down on their heads. But, Jehu dismissed that idea and took full responsibility for what he did. The Jezreelites and all of Israel needed to hear that what they were witnessing was God's **word** spoken **against the house of Ahab** being fulfilled. None of his plans **will fail** (10:10).

10:12-17 God's judgment against Ahab's family was not complete yet. Jehu executed **forty-two** members of Ahaziah's family he met on his way to Samaria (10:11-14). Then, he struck down the rest of **the house of Ahab in Samaria . . . according to the word of the LORD spoken to Elijah** (10:17). Judgment is God's work, but Jehu was obedient.

God gave Jehu a companion named **Jehonadab son of Rechab,** who was a zealous follower of the Lord (10:15-16, 23; see Jer 35:6-7, 14-16). This man agreed with Jehu's plan to rid the land of Ahab's influence and Baal worship, so he shook his hand and joined Jehu in his chariot.

10:18-27 When Jehu arrived in Samaria, he arranged the largest house-cleaning of Baal worship since Elijah's contest on Mount Carmel (see 1 Kgs 18). He called **all the prophets . . . servants** and **priests** of Baal to come to a great **sacrifice.** But, **Jehu was acting deceptively,** perhaps because he still wasn't confident of his level of support in Samaria (10:19). In the end, **all of the servants of Baal came** (10:21). They were excited to find that the new king embraced the new "faith" of Israel that they had dedicated themselves to. And, they packed out Baal's temple. When Jehu confirmed that there were no servants of the true God present (10:23), he sprang his trap. The king turned his **eighty men** loose to **kill** all the idolaters, tear down **the temple of Baal**, and heap on it the ultimate disgrace by making it into a **latrine** (10:24-27).

10:28-29 Thus, **Jehu eliminated Baal worship from Israel** (10:28). Yet, in the next verse, we find that he didn't **turn away** from **worshiping the gold calves** that Jeroboam had set up in **Bethel and Dan** (10:29). So, while Jehu eradicated a great demonic evil in the land (Baal) and its human representatives (the house of Ahab and Baal's priests), Jehu nevertheless failed to follow the Lord wholeheartedly. This truth points to the sad reality that Israel would never be fully cleansed of their idolatry. That's why God would eventually bring his judgment on the northern kingdom, ejecting them from their land entirely.

10:30-36 Because of Jehu's obedience in the matter of Ahab, however, God did promise him a dynasty of **four generations** of **sons** who would rule in Israel (10:30). Yet, God also demonstrated his displeasure with the idolatrous northern kingdom by allowing their land to be reduced through conquests by King **Hazael** of Aram during Jehu's reign of **twenty-eight years** (10:32-36).

◈ D. The Reigns of Good and Evil Kings in Israel and Judah
(11:1–16:20) ◈

11:1-3 Jehu had destroyed all of Ahab's family in the north, but this was not the end of Ahab's descendants in the southern kingdom of Judah. None was more dangerous than **Athaliah**, the **mother** of King Ahaziah (whom Jehu killed). Importantly, she was the daughter of Ahab and Jezebel. **She proceeded to annihilate all the royal heirs** when she saw her opportunity to seize the throne (11:1). But, **Jehosheba, who was . . . Ahaziah's sister**, rescued Ahaziah's son (and Athaliah's grandson) **Joash** and, in God's

providence, hid him in the **temple six years** during Athaliah's evil reign (11:2-3).

11:4-8 In the seventh year, the high priest **Jehoiada** decided it was time to act. He gathered a loyal band of men, **showed them** Joash, and planned a coup against Athaliah (11:4). The idea was to split them into three groups to protect **the king's palace**, while also supplying the young king with **protection** when the coup was revealed (11:5-7). Anyone trying to approach their **ranks** was to be **put to death** (11:8).

11:9-16 The men were armed and stationed; everything was ready (11:9-11). That's when **Jehoiada brought out** young Joash, crowned him, and **anointed him**, as the crowd shouted, **Long live the king!** (11:12). The commotion attracted Athaliah to the scene, as Jehoiada had hoped it would. When she saw (no doubt with wide eyes) Joash— whom she'd assumed was as dead as his siblings—she cried out, **Treason! Treason!** (11:14). (Given her treachery in murdering the "royal heirs" (11:1), it's absurd that she would have the gall to accuse others of treason!) But, it was too late for anyone to save her. The **commanders . . . in charge of the army**, who were loyal to the rightful king, seized Athaliah, putting her and her followers to death (11:15-16).

11:17-21 The rest of the chapter makes it clear why nobody grieved over the demise of Athaliah. The people of Judah were obviously tired of her wickedness and devotion to Baal worship, and at this stage in the nation's history, they were still sensitive to the Lord's honor. **Jehoiada** led them in making **a covenant between the Lord, the king, and the people** of renewed faithfulness to God (11:17). **The people** then showed their sincerity by tearing down **the temple of Baal**, smashing **its altars and images to pieces**, and killing **Mattan, the priest of Baal** (11:18). Joash was just **seven years old** when officially installed on his **throne** (11:19, 21).

12:1-3 Joash **reigned forty years in Jerusalem** (12:1), but his rule was a mixed bag. Joash did what was right in God's sight, but only as long as his godly mentor, **the priest**

Jehoiada, was alive to keep him on track (12:2; see 2 Chr 24:15-25). Even then, Joash left intact the idolatrous **high places** where the people of Judah **continued sacrificing and burning incense** (12:3). Even if some worshiped the Lord (rather than false gods) in these places, doing so was still rebellion to his command to worship him at the Jerusalem temple only. So, unfortunately, Joash was a weak ruler whose devotion to God was only outward.

Is your faith superficial? Or, does it go deep down to the heart?

12:4-8 In spite of his failings, Joash did decide to undertake a renovation program for the **temple,** which would have been about one hundred years old by this time and in need of repairs. His plan was to have the priests set aside a part of the **dedicated silver** that they received in offerings from the people to **repair whatever damage** was **found in the temple** (12:4-5). But, that plan didn't work because the priests didn't follow through. So, **by the twenty-third year** of his reign, Joash got exasperated and called **Jehoiada and the other priests** on the carpet for their lack of progress and told them to forget the original plan because he had a new idea (12:6-8).

12:9-16 The king had a box installed by the **altar** with **a hole in its lid.** Instead of the priests receiving silver, it was to be placed in this box (12:9). Then, **the king's secretary and the high priest** would empty the box and give the money to those overseeing the temple repair work (12:10-11). And, everything was done with honesty and **integrity** (12:15).

12:17 In 2 Chronicles 24, we learn of the downfall of Joash. Jehoiada, his spiritual mentor, died. Then, Joash became an apostate, serving false gods and even murdering Jehoiada's son. So, the attack by **King Hazael of Aram** in view here was God's judgment against Joash and Judah because they had abandoned the Lord (see 2 Chr 24:24).

12:18-21 Joash didn't repent or seek the Lord's help; instead, he bought off King Hazael by using the **treasuries** of the **temple** and **the king's palace** (12:18). So, Hazael departed, but the seeds had been sown for

Joash's destruction. His **servants conspired against him** and assassinated him (12:20-21). The king had thought he could escape God's judgment by scheming. But, the only way to escape God's judgment is by turning to God in repentance and faith.

13:1-3 While Joash was on the throne in Judah beginning repairs on the temple, **Jehoahaz son of Jehu** rose to power in **Israel** (13:1). He was the first of the four generations of Jehu's descendants whom God promised would occupy Israel's throne (see 10:30). Sadly, though, none of the four was anything to write home about. Jehoahaz **did what was evil** in God's eyes by following steadfastly in **the sins** of **Jeroboam,** the idolatrous founder of the northern kingdom (13:2). So once again, God used a foreign power (**Aram**) to serve as an instrument of judgment against his rebellious people (13:3).

13:4-8 When the king saw how badly **the king of Aram** was afflicting Israel's people, Jehoahaz **sought the LORD's favor** (13:4). So, God graciously provided **a deliverer** who gave Israel relief from the Arameans (13:5), though the deliverer is not named. After the divine deliverance, however, the people went back to their old idolatrous ways (13:5-6)— which sounds like a page out of the book of Judges. So, God kept Israel weak, allowing them only a pitiful army that could easily have been blown away by an enemy **like dust at threshing** (13:6-7).

13:9-13 **Jehoash** followed Jehoahaz as **king over Israel** and **reigned sixteen years,** but his tenure was like that of his father and grandfather: **he did what was evil** (13:10-11). Little is said about his reign except that he went to **war against** his Jewish brothers in **Judah** (13:12).

13:14 Though there was nothing positive to report about Jehoash's reign, something significant took place while he sat on the throne. Elisha, the man of God, was dying. When the king heard about the prophet's illness, he went to see the him, **wept,** and exclaimed, **My father, my father, the chariots and horsemen of Israel!** (13:14). (This was the same way that Elisha had addressed

Elijah when the latter was taken away in a fiery chariot from heaven; see 2:11-12). Thus, in spite of his flaws, King Jehoash had great respect for the aged prophet before him. The king also recognized that Elisha was his divine lifeline if Israel were to receive any aid during their crisis with Aram.

13:15-17 Though Jehoash was generally ungodly, God had mercy on him. Elisha was a true prophet, and God wanted the king to know that coming to him for help was the right thing to do. Elisha told the king to **get a bow and arrows** (13:15). Then, **Elisha put his hands on the king's hands** and had the king **shoot** an arrow out **the east window**, in the direction of their enemy, Aram (13:16-17). When the king obeyed, Elisha said victory over Aram would be his.

While Elisha declared a victory that had not yet happened, he gave the king God's view of the situation. This is a picture of the natural being sanctified by the supernatural when God places his hands on it. When Jehoash had enough faith to follow Elisha's instructions, the arrow that left his bow was no longer his but, as Elisha said, **the LORD's arrow of victory . . . over Aram** (13:17). In other words, the ordinary became extraordinary when linked to the spiritual. The battle was now a spiritual one—not just a physical one, because the weapons of war were now sanctified.

13:18-19 Unfortunately, Jehoash didn't have the faith to trust God for an even greater victory. God's supernatural power and promises do not negate our responsibility to act in faith. Elisha told Jehoash to **take the arrows** and **strike the ground** (13:18) in order to claim on earth what God had already declared in heaven (see Matt 16:19). It's not clear whether the prophet wanted the king to shoot his arrows into the ground (as he did with the first arrow), or instead to hold them in his hand and hit the ground. Regardless, the king lacked the zeal that Elisha said he should have displayed. Therefore, Israel would experience only a partial victory, rather than a total one, because he refused to use all the resources at his disposal, indicating a lack of faith and commitment. Complete obedience and engagement are needed for complete victory.

13:20-21 Even after he **died and was buried** (13:20), the power of Elisha didn't cease. That's because the power he'd wielded in life was not his own. Sometime later, a dead man was tossed into **Elisha's tomb**. Then, **when he touched** the prophet's **bones**, the dead man came back to life (13:21)!

13:22-25 As Elisha had prophesied, King Jehoash **defeated** Aram **three times**, regaining **cities** that Israel had lost (13:25). God was **gracious** toward Israel, but not because of their goodness. Instead, God was faithful to **his covenant with Abraham, Isaac, and Jacob**, their forefathers. Even after all they had done, he had not yet **banished** Israel **from his presence** (13:23). What a beautiful reminder that the Lord is "slow to anger and abounding in faithful love and truth" (Exod 34:6). But, eventually, his patience would run out; in time, the northern kingdom would be defeated and carried away.

14:1-4 The next change in kingship happened in Judah, where **Amaziah son of Joash** succeeded his father **in Jerusalem** (14:1-2). The statement made in 14:3 is key. It says, **He did what was right in the LORD's sight, but not like his ancestor David. He did everything his father Joash had done.** All the kings of Judah were measured against David, Judah's greatest king who kept God's law and received the promise of the Messiah coming from his line. Amaziah upheld the worship of God as Joash had done, at least in the early years of his reign. Yet, he also left the **high places** standing where the people practiced forbidden worship (14:4).

14:5-7 Amaziah also **killed** the men who had assassinated his **father**. But, importantly, he limited his retribution to that prescribed by **the law of Moses**, an indication of Amaziah's respect for the law (14:5-6).

He experienced a successful battle against Edom when it tried to rebel against Judah's control, seizing the city of **Sela**, which today is the famous rock fortress of Petra in Jordan (14:7).

14:8-10 Amaziah was apparently feeling strong and cocky after the Edomite campaign, so he looked north and challenged

Jehoash in Israel to meet him face to face (14:8). Israel's army was weak after years of being battered by Aram (see the commentary on 13:4-8), so perhaps Amaziah thought this was a good time for Judah to stick it to Israel. Jehoash answered with a parable that ridiculed Judah's strength (14:9). Then, he warned Amaziah in no uncertain terms: You have become overconfident ... stay at home (14:10).

14:11-14 The good advice stung Amaziah's pride. He **would not listen**. He felt he couldn't let it pass because he had issued the initial challenge, so his response was predictable.

When Jehoash saw that Amaziah had no intention of backing off, he **advanced**. The two kings **met face to face at Beth-shemesh**, about fifteen miles west of Jerusalem (14:11). Just as Jehoash had warned, the battle between them was a complete disaster for the southern kingdom. Judah was **routed** and **fled** (14:12). Even worse, Jehoash **captured** Amaziah. Then, he **went to Jerusalem and broke down two hundred yards of** the **wall**, plundered the **temple** and palace **treasuries**, and took **hostages** (14:13-14).

14:15-22 Jehoash's death was recorded for a second time here, probably because of his battle with Amaziah, an insight that fleshes out what was revealed previously in 13:12. Jehoash's **son Jeroboam became king in his place** (14:16). He was the third of the four kings in Jehu's dynasty, as promised to him by the Lord.

Judah's King Amaziah was released after Jehoash's death and lived for **fifteen years**. But, like his father, he, too, became the victim of assassins who followed him to **Lachish** when he tried to get away (14:17, 19). He was succeeded by his son **Azariah** (14:21).

14:23-24 Jeroboam began his reign after the death of his father. He is often referred to as Jeroboam II to distinguish him from the first king of Israel by the same name (mentioned in 14:24). He had reigned with Jehoash for eleven years as co-regent, and altogether **he reigned forty-one years** (14:23)—longer than any king of Israel up to that time. Spiritually, his rule followed the same distressing pattern as those of his immediate ancestors.

14:25-29 Yet, Jeroboam II was a successful military commander who regained much territory that Israel had lost to Aram. A prophecy concerning this restoration of land was made by **Jonah son of Amittai** (14:25). (This is the same Jonah tasked with prophesying to Nineveh; see Jonah 1:1). Again, God intervened on behalf of his people out of his compassion. They had suffered much under Hazael of Aram. By God's grace, Jehoash had begun to reverse this trend (see 2 Kgs 13:22-25) and Jeroboam continued it (14:25-27). He was even able to take **Damascus**, the capital of Aram (14:28). Upon his death, Jeroboam was replaced by his son **Zechariah** (14:29), the fourth and final king in Jehu's dynasty.

15:1-7 Here the author of 2 Kings switches, once again, to the southern kingdom of Judah and the reign of **Azariah** (15:1); his was the second-longest reign of any king on either side of the border. Dismissing his **fifty-two years** with only a few verses may seem odd, especially because he was commended as a king who **did what was right in the LORD's sight**, except for leaving the **high places** intact (which almost all the kings of Judah did; 15:2-4). The only other thing included about Azariah was that God **afflicted** him with a **serious skin disease** (15:5), which required him to live separately in the later years of his reign while his son **Jotham** administered. So, what happened?

Importantly, Azariah was also known as Uzziah (see 15:13, 30). In 2 Chronicles, we find some helpful details about his story. Uzziah was one of the most effective kings of Judah, expanding its territory and following the Lord—until he became proud, usurped the role of the priest, and was struck by God with a skin disease for his arrogance (see 2 Chr 26:1-23). Perhaps God left it to the author of 2 Chronicles to fill in the details of Azariah's reign because 1–2 Chronicles take a special interest in Judah's kings (see the introduction to 1–2 Chronicles).

15:8-15 Up in the northern kingdom, Zechariah's evil reign over **Israel** lasted only six months before a man named **Shallum** assassinated him **publicly** and claimed the throne (15:8-10). The writer is careful to note that

Zechariah's reign fulfilled God's promise to Jehu that **four generations** of his sons would **sit on the throne of Israel** (15:12). The usurper Shallum lasted even less than Zechariah: one **month**. He was replaced by someone who did the same thing to him. **Menahem** took him out and **became king** (15:13-14).

15:16-18 Menahem further demonstrated his brutality by attacking the town of **Tiphsah** because its people **wouldn't surrender**— that is, they wouldn't acknowledge him as king. His murder of **all the pregnant women** and their children was especially barbaric (15:16). It highlights the horror and cruelty of which fallen human beings are capable. It's no surprise that the author describes Menahem's reign as **evil** (15:18). He was a butcher.

15:19-22 Menahem wasn't strong enough to handle an invasion by the Assyrians under **King Pul** in 743 BC. Pul was the throne name of the powerful King Tiglath-pileser III. This is the first mention of Assyria we find in 2 Kings, but it won't be the last. (In time, this foreign power would conquer Israel.) Menahem gave Pul a huge payment in **silver**, both to stop the invasion and to get his **support** as Menahem sought **to strengthen his grasp on the kingdom** (15:19). Menahem's attack on Tiphsah had shown that he was not universally liked, and taxing **each of the prominent men of Israel** to raise the money to pay off the king of Assyria probably did nothing to enhance his popularity (15:20).

15:23-31 Menahem's son **Pekahiah** ascended to the throne and diligently followed the apostasy of **Jeroboam son of Nebat** (15:23-24). He was killed and replaced in yet another military coup by one of his officers, **Pekah** (15:25). His reign of **twenty years** (752–732 BC) was another dark period in Israel (15:27-28) and brought the northern kingdom ever closer to the year of its defeat and deportation by the Assyrians (722 BC). **King Tiglath-pileser of Assyria** invaded Israel again and **captured . . . all the land of Naphtali . . . and deported the people to Assyria** (15:29). This defeat led **Hoshea** to organize **a conspiracy against Pekah**, assassinate him, and claim the throne of Israel

(15:29-30). Thus, with yet another coup, yet another wicked king of Israel was replaced.

15:32-35 Back in Judah, **Jotham** took the throne in place of his father **Uzziah** and reigned for **sixteen years** (15:32-33). Happily, just as the bad kings of Israel followed their predecessors in doing evil, Jotham followed Uzziah (also called Azariah) in doing **what was right**. However, like most of Judah's kings, he failed to destroy Judah's **high places** (15:34-35)—the alternate places of worship that God had forbidden through Moses.

16:1-4 Ahaz son of Jotham was one of the evil kings of Judah (16:1). Not only did he **not do what was right** when compared to **David**, but he actually **walked in the ways of the kings of Israel**—a charge that could not be taken as a compliment (16:2-3). And, as if that weren't bad enough, Ahaz committed the vile act of sacrificing **his son in the fire** (16:3).

Hundreds of years earlier, the Lord had warned the people through Moses not to "imitate the detestable customs" of the nations that the Israelites were driving out of Canaan. The first item on the list of forbidden practices was to "sacrifice [one's] son or daughter in the fire" (Deut 18:9-10). Yet, here was the king of Israel, destroying the most vulnerable members of society. He killed his own son, who was made in God's image (Gen 1:26). And, whereas previous kings of Judah left the high places intact, Ahaz worshiped false gods at **every** shrine he could find (16:4). Make no mistake: left unchecked, false theology leads to corruption and violence. Ahaz was wicked to the core.

16:5-9 Judah came under attack by a joint force from Aram and Israel (16:5). If this trouble was a test of faith for Ahaz, he failed it miserably. He did not call out to God for deliverance. Instead, Judah's king requested deliverance from **King Tiglath-pileser of Assyria**, pledging his allegiance to him if Assyria would only save him from **Aram** and **Israel** (16:7). But, such deliverance doesn't come free. Ahaz had to pay protection money: **silver and gold** from the **temple** and **the king's palace** (16:8).

Once he was paid off, Tiglath-pileser not only attacked and captured Aram's capital of **Damascus**, but also killed King **Rezin** as well (16:9). Judah was delivered—for now. But, in ignoring God, Ahaz was cutting off his nation from the only one who could provide true and lasting deliverance.

16:10-16 Initially, Ahaz was so excited at having the pressure off of him that he **went to Damascus to meet** his new master, **King Tiglath-pileser** (16:10). This was no meeting of equals, however, because Ahaz was now the vassal of the Assyrian king and had to be careful not to do anything to offend him (see 16:18). That may, in fact, be one reason why Ahaz sent back to Jerusalem a **model** and **complete plans** for the **altar** he saw in Damascus so his high **priest Uriah** could build it (16:10-11). Tiglath-pileser probably made it known to Ahaz that he wanted the worship of Assyrian gods to be observed in Judah, at least to some extent. Ahaz was ungodly enough to comply without a whimper of protest.

By the time Ahaz returned to Jerusalem, the altar was **completed**, so he **ascended** its steps and offered a false version of Israel's legitimate **offerings** (16:11-13). Then, Ahaz further offended God by moving the **bronze altar that** Solomon had made, so he could put his new altar in its prominent place (16:14). He also ordered the faithless **priest Uriah** to offer on this abomination of an altar three of Israel's most important offerings: the **burnt offering** symbolizing forgiveness of sin and communion, the **evening grain offering** symbolizing dedication, and the **drink offerings** symbolizing joy poured out before God (16:15).

16:17-20 For reasons not explained, Ahaz also cut other worship items apart, dismantled the **Sabbath canopy they had built in the palace**, and **closed the outer entrance for the king**—all to satisfy his Gentile overlord (16:17-18).

The only good thing that came out of Ahaz's life was his son **Hezekiah**, who would become one of Judah's outstanding kings (16:20). Though Ahaz was truly a wicked ruler, Hezekiah serves as a wonderful example of the fact that our futures are not pre-determined by the character of our parents. Even if your parents didn't follow God, you

can follow a different path—a God-honoring path—by God's grace and your willingness to make a change.

❧ E. The Reign of Hoshea and Israel's Downfall (17:1-41) ❧

17:1-3 **Hoshea** became king of Israel by leading a conspiracy to kill King Pekah (see 15:29-30). He would be the northern kingdom's last leader, and he did not turn from the treacherous path of his predecessors, for he was a ruler who **did what was evil in the LORD's sight** (17:1-2). An attack by **King Shalmaneser of Assyria**, who had succeeded his father Tiglath-pileser III, made Hoshea **his vassal** who **paid him tribute** (17:3).

17:4-6 Hoshea decided to break his vassal agreement with Shalmaneser. Yet, he didn't do it by seeking the Lord's help but by engaging **in a conspiracy** to seek help from **So king of Egypt**. Hoshea was so confident of his plot that he quit paying **tribute** to Shalmaneser. But, Egypt's help was worthless, the plan was discovered, and Hoshea was **arrested** (17:4). His foolishness and refusal to trust God helped to doom his nation, in fact, because Shalmaneser in his fury over Hoshea's treachery **invaded the whole land** and laid siege to Samaria **for three years** (17:5).

When Samaria finally fell, Shalmaneser **deported the Israelites to Assyria** (17:6). This occurred in 722 BC. The northern kingdom had lasted more than two centuries. Twenty kings had sat on its throne—every one of them judged as evil in God's sight.

17:7 The rest of the chapter explains the reasons for this sad ending to the kingdom of Israel. The failure of the kings and the people to keep God's law and their practice of idolatry brought ruin upon them. The writer of 1−2 Kings leaves no doubt in his readers' minds why all these disasters befell God's people: **This ... happened because the people of Israel sinned against the LORD their God who had brought them out of the land of Egypt ... and because they worshiped other gods**. That statement is a summary of everything that follows. The people of Israel and their leaders rejected the God who had rescued them from slavery. They exchanged their living Redeemer for imaginary gods of wood and stone. (Thankfully, as we will see at the close of 2 Kings, he also holds out a flicker of hope because of God's faithfulness to his covenant promises, even in the face of his people's complete lack of obedience.)

17:8-10 The indictment against Israel runs for a number of verses, with the offenses piling up. The Israelites imitated **the customs of the nations** that God had driven out of the promised land—customs that God had explicitly forbidden through Moses (see Deut 18:9). Israel's own **kings** —the men who were to lead the people in holiness and faithfulness—adopted these rebellious ways, and the people followed their lead (17:8). They thought they were doing these things **secretly** while still carrying on the pretense of worshiping God, as if he would be fooled (17:9). But, God is omniscient (that is, all-knowing) and omnipresent (that is, everywhere present). Nothing we do is in secret.

17:11-15 Israel's wickedness angered the Lord (17:11), who like a loving father caring for the well-being of his children, had commanded them time and again, **You must not do this**. But they, instead, **served idols** that could not save them (17:12). This is a critical point, and one that Psalm 115:4-7 drives home. The psalmist wrote this about idol worshipers as well: "Those who make them are just like them" (Ps 115:8). In other words, the people of Israel **followed worthless idols and became worthless themselves** (17:15). Despite God's repeated warnings (17:13), **they would not listen** (17:14). Take note: you become like what you worship.

17:16-17 Of all the customs of the nations that Israel imitated, one was especially horrific: **they sacrificed their sons and daughters in the fire** (17:17). The most vulnerable members of society were put to death by their own parents!

Tragically, this sounds like our own culture in which the appalling practice of abortion is so prevalent. God will not turn a blind eye to the destruction of his image-bearers (see Gen 1:26).

17:18-20 In spite of the author's condemnation of Israel, Judah was not blameless either. After King Solomon died, the nation of Israel had divided into the northern kingdom of Israel and the southern kingdom of Judah. And, though Judah had several godly kings while Israel had none, that kingdom too, experienced great depravity and fell far from God's standards. Thus, the author wants to make it clear that Israel wasn't the only guilty party. He makes a parenthetical comment that **even Judah did not keep the commands of the LORD . . . but lived according to the customs Israel had practiced** (17:19). Though Judah's punishment was yet to come, they would not escape God's righteous wrath. In time, Judah would suffer a fate similar to Israel's.

17:21-23 Back **when the LORD tore Israel from the house of David**, he gave it to **Jeroboam**. But, King Jeroboam spurned God's grace and **caused** Israel **to commit immense sin** (17:21). So, finally, after years of Israel following in the footsteps of Jeroboam, God finally **removed Israel from his presence**—which was no surprise. He had warned the kings and the people of this very thing through **his servants the prophets** for years—but they hadn't listened.

The author helpfully notes that Israel's people were still in Assyria in his **day**, years after their homeland's collapse (17:23).

17:24-26 When rulers in the ancient Near East conquered a nation and took its people into exile, they would often settle peoples from other conquered nations into the newly conquered land. This separation of the people from their lands—and supposedly from their gods—was intended to prevent nationalistic sentiment from arising. Exiling the people and mixing them with other peoples would make them less likely to rebel. Thus, the Assyrians settled all sorts of foreigners **in the cities of Samaria** in place of the Israelites (17:24).

Importantly, these foreigners brought their religions and gods with them, a situation to which God responded by sending **lions among them, which killed some of them** (17:25). These **settlers** quickly realized that the God of the Israelites was someone to be reckoned with, so they asked **the king of Assyria** for help because they didn't know what to do to placate **the god of the land** (17:26). They wanted to take measures to ensure they didn't offend what they believed to be the local god in whose land they were taking up residence.

17:27-33 The Assyrian king had an easy solution to the problem: he would send back a **deported** Israelite priest to **teach** the foreign residents in Israel **how they should fear the LORD** (17:27-28). Now, understand that the priest may have been one of the very people who'd led Israel to worship the golden calves erected by Jeroboam. So, the fact that he taught these unbelievers what the Lord required was no guarantee that he lived by those standards or was above blending in with the people as they made and worshiped **their own gods**, too (17:29). For their part, the new inhabitants didn't mind mixing worship of the Lord with that of their idols (17:33). The scene here is typical of ancient polytheism and syncretism.

17:34 Here, we get a general indictment against the new inhabitants of what had been Israel. The author says, **They are still observing the former practices to this**

day. These verses, then, explain the origin of the syncretistic Samaritan people of Jesus's earthly ministry (see John 4). Many of the Israelites who were still in the land following Israel's overthrow intermarried with the foreign peoples over time until the distinctiveness of Israel's religion was systematically dismantled and replaced by a smorgasbord of religion in which the Lord was just one deity among many. In effect, everything God had done to set his people apart from the nations around them had been undone by the people of the northern kingdom.

17:35-41 Years before, God had **made a covenant with Jacob's descendants** (17:35). He pledged his faithfulness and protection to them, but, in return, they were to be faithful to him. They were to honor him exclusively as their King and live from the perspective of being citizens of his kingdom (17:36-39). Because they'd failed to do this, God kicked them out of the land.

When people from other **nations** came to live in the land—even though they knew what happened to the former inhabitants— they **continued their former practices** (17:40). They taught their offspring to mix worship of the Lord with worship of their **idols** (17:41). What a sad outcome.

II. THE SURVIVING KINGDOM OF JUDAH (18:1–25:30)

❧ A. The Reign of Hezekiah
(18:1–20:21) ❦

18:1-3 Though Judah would eventually fall, too, the southern kingdom was temporarily blessed with the godly reign of **Hezekiah**, a man who was the polar opposite of his evil father, **Ahaz** (18:1). He enjoyed the rare commendation of doing **what was right in the LORD's sight** just as his ancestor David had done (18:3).

18:4-6 Hezekiah was one of the few kings who **removed the high places**—the forbidden places of worship. He also **cut down** the idolatrous **Asherah poles**. Moreover, he destroyed **the bronze snake that Moses**

made centuries before (see Num 21:8-9), which **was called Nehushtan**, meaning a "A Bronze Thing." How sad that this object that God had used to deliver his people had become a thing of worship! For these and other reasons, Hezekiah was hailed as a king set apart from and above the other **kings of Judah** in his faithfulness to God's **commands** (18:5-6; for his other spiritual reforms and activities, see 2 Chr 29–31).

18:7-8 After we've read of the unfaithfulness and vile actions of so many of the kings of Israel and Judah, King Hezekiah is a breath of fresh air. **The LORD was with him, and wherever he went he prospered.** Notice that when Hezekiah honored God, God's presence was with him and gave him success.

And, instead of bowing down in subservience to a foreign power, the king opposed **the king of Assyria and did not serve him** (18:7). He also **defeated the Philistines** (18:8). As this man looked to God as his source of deliverance, God was with him.

18:9-12 The author briefly repeats the earlier account of Assyria conquering the northern kingdom and deporting the Israelites (see 17:3-6) because these events happened during Hezekiah's reign.

18:13-16 Interestingly, the account in 2 Kings 18:13–20:19 very closely parallels Isaiah 36:1–39:8. The Assyrian king whom Hezekiah would deal with was **Sennacherib**, the successor to Shalmaneser, who had conquered Israel. Unfortunately, things did not go well for Judah. **Sennacherib attacked all the fortified cities of Judah and captured them** (18:13), leaving only Jerusalem. And, at that point, Hezekiah may have been thinking that he had badly miscalculated the situation. He admitted to Sennacherib, **I have done wrong**, and offered a ransom to save his people from suffering the same fate as Israel (18:14). The demand made of him was huge, and Hezekiah sent all the **silver** and **gold** he could collect, even stripping the gold from the **temple** (18:15-16). Yet, things were about to get worse. God would circle the Assyrians around Jerusalem to test Hezekiah's faith and to demonstrate his own mighty power to his people.

18:17-18 Either Hezekiah's ransom wasn't enough for Sennacherib or he was looking for a pretext to attack Jerusalem and complete his conquest of Judah anyway, because the Assyrian king sent a delegation and a **massive army** to Jerusalem to demand the city's surrender. This they wanted to deliver to **the king** in person, but they had to settle for speaking to Hezekiah's delegation—although there were people gathered "on the wall," listening in (see 18:26).

18:19-25 Sennacherib's **royal spokesman** (18:19) made what he thought was a slam-dunk case for Hezekiah and his people to open their gates and surrender. First, **Egypt** was a useless ally that would not deliver them (18:21). This was true. Second, he was sure the people of Judah had angered their God by destroying his worship centers—that is, the forbidden **high places and altars** that Hezekiah had demolished (18:22). Of course, Hezekiah had been right to demolish them. But likely, even the king's supporters would question the king's actions in light of what was happening. Third, Sennacherib's spokesman reminded them that Judah's army was too weak to repel the Assyrian army (18:24). Given Hezekiah's attempt to pay off Assyria, this was also probably true. And finally, he claimed that **the LORD** himself had told him to **attack this land and destroy it** (18:25), essentially saying, "Hey, your God is on my side!" This point was a lie, but to the demoralized people of Jerusalem, it certainly may have looked as if he were right. After all, their northern neighbors had fallen to Assyria, and those same cruel conquerors were now at their gates.

18:26-30 The three men's plea for the negotiations to be done **in Aramaic** instead of **Hebrew** was designed to shield the listeners **on the wall** from the threats (18:26). But, the Assyrian spokesman wasn't about to accommodate. He wanted everyone to fear his king's ultimatum. He even loudly threatened them in Hebrew in the most repulsive way imaginable (18:27). Then, he warned the people not to listen to any promises Hezekiah might make about the Lord showing up to **rescue** them (18:30). Given this diatribe, how long would the people of Judah continue to trust their king?

18:31-32 Sennacherib's spokesman offered the people **peace** and prosperity instead of suffering and starvation, if they would simply **surrender** (18:31). Those words may have sounded tempting to the people of Jerusalem, who were about to face a siege and be cut off from the world. The Assyrian also made it clear that deportation **to a land like [their] own** was part of the bargain. He promised them it would be a land of **grain and new wine**, of **olive trees and honey** (18:32). Similarly, Satan tempts believers with offers that sound inviting, but sin never delivers all it promises.

18:33-37 The speech concluded with six rhetorical questions. Their essence was this: **the gods of the nations** had not rescued their followers from **the power of the king of Assyria**. And, neither would **the LORD rescue Jerusalem** (18:33-35). Intimidated by this encounter, Hezekiah's men took their report back to the king **with their clothes torn** in distress (18:37).

19:1-4 When he **heard their report**, King Hezekiah did the same thing that his men did: **he tore his clothes** in grief (19:1). Surely, he wondered how such a terrible turn of events had happened. After all, he had been faithful to God. He had reformed Judah's worship. He had kept the Lord's commands. Previously, God had caused him to prosper (18:5-8). But, at that moment, God seemed silent.

This account, then, is a good reminder that faithfulness to God does not keep you from trials. However, it *does* prepare you to meet those trials. By living life from a divine perspective, you will be equipped to deal with trouble and suffering. To rely on him in the bad times as you've relied on him in the good. And, you will have an opportunity to see God at work.

In spite of his distress, King Hezekiah **went into the LORD's temple** to worship (19:1). In addition, he did what so many of his predecessors had not. He sought a word from the Lord through **the prophet Isaiah** by sending a delegation dressed in **sackcloth** (19:2). They explained to God's prophet the grim situation that Judah was facing, and they informed him that the Assyrian leader had come **to mock the living God** (19:3-4).

19:5-7 Isaiah already knew all of this because God knew all of this. So, he gave **the servants** a message for Hezekiah that began with a command: **Don't be afraid** (19:5-6). This command is repeated often in Scripture. It's God's way of calming his people, filling them with confidence, and assuring them, "I have everything under control. You can trust me." Not only had the Lord heard the blasphemous words of the Assyrian king's lackey (19:6), but he also planned to do something about them. Far from defeating Jerusalem, King Sennacherib would instead **return to his own land** and **fall by the sword** (19:7).

19:8-13 Sennacherib's **royal spokesman** was probably camped at the walls of Jerusalem waiting for an answer from Hezekiah when a report came that the king had **pulled** his army out of **Lachish** and was fighting at **Libnah**, located twenty-five miles southwest of Jerusalem (19:8). Sennacherib **had heard** a report that **King Tirhakah of Cush** was coming out to **fight** him (19:9), causing the Assyrian king to divert his attention from Jerusalem for what he thought was only a short time. So, Sennacherib made sure that Hezekiah knew he would be back, repeating the threats his underling had made earlier (19:10-13).

19:14-19 Hezekiah didn't tear his clothes in anguish when he read the **letter** from Sennacherib. He took it to the temple **and spread it out before** God and **prayed** (19:14-15). Acknowledging his submission to the divine King, Hezekiah began, **LORD God of Israel, enthroned between the cherubim** (19:15). He then reminded God of his unique relationship with Israel as opposed to the purported relationships between conquered peoples and the false gods of the nations Assyria had defeated. He knew that none of the **gods** of the nations had delivered their people because they were **made by human hands** and lacked any power (19:18). But, the Lord is different. He isn't a creation of man; he is the Creator of man. He **made the heavens and the earth** (19:15). Hezekiah saw Sennacherib's letter as an attack on God's character (19:16), and he pleaded with God to vindicate himself and his people (19:19). Hezekiah was reminding him that answering his prayer would bring God great glory. This prayer is a model for believers in distress.

19:20-28 God heard Hezekiah and once again, sent the king his answer through **Isaiah** (19:20). This poetic response ridicules Sennacherib and exalts God's sovereign rule over the nations. The king of Assyria hadn't merely mocked Judah and her king; he had **mocked and blasphemed . . . the Holy One of Israel!** (19:22). While Sennacherib arrogantly assumed his own leadership and might had cut a swath through many nations (19:23-24), he didn't know that his victories were ordained by God as part of his plan drawn up **long ago** (19:25). The big-headed Assyrian king, then, was just a pawn on God's kingdom chessboard. Sennacherib couldn't make a move or have a private thought that God didn't know about, which included any **raging** he did **against** the Lord (19:27). Yet, Sennacherib would find out how insignificant he was because God would put his **hook** in his **nose** and drag him back to Assyria (19:28).

19:29-31 God gave a word of comfort to a king and people facing a seemingly un-avoidable siege and starvation. The people of Jerusalem hadn't been able to go outside the walls to plant crops for fear of the Assyri-ans. But, God's **sign** to Hezekiah was that, for the next two years, the people of Jerusalem would **eat** harvests from the seed that grew **on its own**. In the **third year**, they would be able to **sow and reap, plant vineyards and eat their fruit** (19:29). Judah would not be wiped out. A **remnant** would survive, **bear fruit**, and go outside the walls of **Jerusalem**, for the Lord has great **zeal** for his glory and for his covenant people (19:30-31).

19:32-34 God himself would **defend** Jerusa-lem (19:34) against Sennacherib. He would do this, he said, **for my sake and for the sake of my servant David** (19:34). God would not al-low his plans to be thwarted by some upstart Assyrian king. Nor would he fail to fulfill his promise to David to keep one of his descen-dants on the throne of Jerusalem forever—a promise ultimately culminating in the king-ship of Jesus Christ our Lord.

19:35-37 All it took to rid Hezekiah of his enemy was one stroke from **the angel of the Lord**—a phrase that is often used to in-dicate a pre-incarnate appearance of Jesus Christ in Old Testament times. In an instant **one hundred eighty-five thousand** As-syrian soldiers were **dead** (19:35). And sud-denly, without his army, Sennacherib had no choice but to go back home. Later, his own sons killed him **while he was worshiping in the temple of his god Nisroch** (19:37). The Assyrian king had ridiculed the Lord for being unable to protect Jerusalem. But, in the end, it was Sennacherib's god who was

unable to protect his devoted follower—even in his own temple.

20:1-3 Sometimes biblical authors do not put events in chronological order. Rather, they order events in their narratives to fit their purposes. In this case, it's likely that the ac-count of Hezekiah's illness (20:1-21) actually happened before the previous account of Sennacherib's invasion (18:13–19:37; see 20:6; Isa 38:6).

Hezekiah became **terminally ill** and was advised by God through **the prophet Isaiah** to prepare for his death (20:1). It's one thing when the doctor says your case is terminal. But, when the Lord announces it, there is no possibility of a misdiagnosis. So, it's not hard to sympathize with Hezekiah's fervent prayer and the fact that he **wept bitterly** (20:3).

20:4-6 God was moved by Hezekiah's heart-felt prayer. Isaiah was still in the **inner court-yard** of the palace when God sent him back to tell Hezekiah, **I have heard your prayer; I have seen your tears. Look, I will heal you** (20:4-5). He also promised to deliver Jerusa-lem from **the king of Assyria** (20:6).

God does not lie (see Num 23:19), and he does not change (see Mal 3:6). Yet, he *is* re-lational; he personally relates to his people. His declaration of death for Hezekiah was real. But, God is free to change—not in his character or in his ultimate purposes—but with regard to his actions within his purpos-es. This is a principle articulated repeatedly in Scripture. When God threatens judgment on sin, he is free to show mercy and grace in response to repentance (see Jonah 3:4-10). When he proclaims his intent to do some-thing—sometimes as a test of faith—he is free to alter his actions in response to prayer (see Exod 32:11-14) or obedience (see Gen 22:1-18) because people have adjusted their relationship to him.

20:7-11 Isaiah commanded that a medici-nal **lump of pressed figs** be **applied** to the king's infection (20:7) in order to draw out the poison. This tells us that prayer, medica-tion, and the word of God worked together to bring about his healing. Before that heal-ing, Hezekiah asked for a confirming **sign** from God (20:8), and God graciously granted his request (20:9-11). Signs are never to replace God's word, but they are used to confirm it.

20:12-13 After the account of Hezekiah's faithfulness, the author presents an account of Hezekiah's foolishness.

Assyria was the world power at this time, and (like Judah) Babylon was feeling its pressure. The **letters** and **gift** sent by **Merodach-baladan** of **Babylon** to congratulate Hezekiah were probably also an effort to secure his support in an alliance against Assyria (20:12). As mentioned above (see commentary on 20:1-3), this visit was likely prior to the threatened Assyrian invasion since Hezekiah's **treasuries** that he showed to the Babylonians were full (20:13). When Sennacherib threatened Jerusalem, Hezekiah emptied his treasuries to keep the city safe (see 18:15-16).

20:14-21 Hezekiah's pride (see 2 Chr 32:25-26) led him to show off in front of his visitors, which is why he replied so readily to Isaiah's questions (20:14-15). Because the king didn't think his actions were foolish, he didn't see any reason to hide them. But, the prophet replied to the news with the announcement of Judah's impending Babylonian captivity— even though it was more than one hundred years in the future. Unfortunately, Hezekiah didn't seem bothered by that because he realized he would enjoy **peace and security** himself (20:19). Regardless, Isaiah's prophecy foreshadowed the grief and destruction that awaited Judah in the years ahead.

✈ B. The Reigns of Manasseh and Amon (21:1-26) ✆

21:1-2 The end of Hezekiah's reign brought his son **Manasseh** to the throne; he had served for a time as co-regent with his father. The son was the worst of Judah's kings, ruling for a total of **fifty-five years in Jerusalem** (21:1). Manasseh imitated **the detestable practices of the nations that the LORD had dispossessed before the Israelites** (21:2), meaning that, while he was an Israelite physically, he was a Canaanite spiritually.

21:3-9 A whole list of specifics demonstrate how much further Manasseh went in doing evil than his predecessors in Judah. Manasseh was infected with spiritual disease and plunged the kingdom of Judah into wickedness. Among his despicable acts, he **rebuilt the high places that . . . Hezekiah had destroyed** (21:3). (Other kings of Judah had been rebuked for leaving these idolatrous shrines in place. But, after Hezekiah had the spiritual fortitude to tear them down, his son Manasseh actually erected them again.) Manasseh also reinstituted **Baal** worship and made another **Asherah** pole, **as King Ahab of Israel had done** (21:3). He **built altars** in the temple for worship of the stars, **sacrificed his son in the fire**, and practiced every form of occultism imaginable (21:4-6). Furthermore, he set **the carved image of Asherah . . . in the temple** where God had promised to **establish** his **name** (21:7). And, under such wicked influence, Judah's people **did worse evil than the nations the LORD had destroyed** in order to give **the Israelites** their land (21:9). Like king, like people.

21:10-11 There was nothing left to do but announce God's judgment on Judah. One of the **prophets** who delivered this message of judgment may have been Isaiah, who according to Jewish tradition was sawn in two under Manasseh's orders (see Heb 11:37 for a possible reference to this incident). Comparing Manasseh's evil to that of **the Amorites** (21:11) was one way of putting it in context because they were one of the most morally deficient people groups of Joshua's day.

21:12 God had much more to say about the **disaster** he was going to bring **on Jerusalem and Judah**. Such news would shock everyone who heard it because the people of Jerusalem in particular thought they were bulletproof. Why? Because they lived in God's holy city with his holy temple in their midst. They were confident he would never allow an enemy to destroy it.

21:13-15 God's word of doom on Judah included two names, Samaria and Ahab— references that would have made even the smuggest resident of Jerusalem break out in a cold sweat. He was **measuring** Jerusalem for the same kind of disaster that befell **Samaria**, and he was using **the mason's level** to draw a straight line of destruction on Manasseh the way he did **on the house of Ahab**.

To ensure that his message wasn't missed, the Lord threatened to **wipe Jerusalem clean** like someone does to a **bowl** after it's been used for a meal. He would **abandon** his people **to their enemies** because of their evil.

21:16-26 The **innocent blood that** Manasseh spilled (21:16) certainly included his child sacrifices, but it also possibly included the innocent people he may have eliminated to hold on to power. Manasseh's long legacy of evil continued in his evil son **Amon** (21:19-22), whose brief reign ended in his assassination (21:23-24).

➤ C. The Reign of Josiah (22:1–23:30) ❧

22:1-2 Amon's son **Josiah** was just **eight years old when he became king**, so he obviously needed the help of advisers in his early years (22:1). According to the chronicler, Josiah began seeking the Lord at age sixteen, and four years later began his religious reforms by ridding Judah of the idolatrous mess his grandfather Manasseh had created (see 2 Chr 34:3-7). The statement that Josiah **did what was right in the Lord's sight** and was worthy of comparison with **David** is a testimony to God's grace and the fact that you are not condemned to follow in the footsteps of unfaithful parents.

22:3-7 One of Josiah's greatest reform efforts began when he was twenty-six: repairing the temple in Jerusalem, which had been desecrated by the idolatrous altars and images that Manasseh had placed in it. The procedure is very similar to that used by an earlier reformer, King Joash (see 12:1-16), in that the priests collected the money and gave it to **those who oversee the Lord's temple**, who passed it on **to the workmen . . . to repair**

the damage (22:5). And, like their counterparts in Joash's day, these workers did the work **with integrity** (22:7).

22:8-11 It was during this process that **the high priest Hilkiah . . . found the book of the law** in the **temple** (22:8), which could have been a copy of the entire Pentateuch (that is, the first five books of the Bible). Evidently, Manasseh had made sure the Word of God would not be available to mess up his program of idolatry, and he may have destroyed any other copies. Josiah's **court secretary Shaphan** read the book for himself, then took it to Josiah and **read it** to him (22:8-10). The immediate, earnest response of grief by the king suggests that the law had not been part of Judah's life and worship for a long time (22:11). This is what it looks like when God's Word delivers its convicting power.

22:12-17 Josiah called for five of his top aides and sent them to **inquire of the Lord** and learn how they could appease God's **wrath** against Judah for this neglect of his Word (22:12-13). The king's men went to **the prophetess Huldah**, who sent them back to Josiah with a sad message of **disaster** for Judah. For too long, its people had **abandoned** God to serve **other gods**, provoking Yahweh to **anger** to such a degree that his **wrath** would not **be quenched** (22:14-17).

22:18-20 The Lord's word to Josiah, however, was one of mercy. For his **tender** heart and humility, and his tears of repentance on behalf of himself and his people, Josiah would be spared the coming **disaster** that God would bring on Judah in the form of the Babylonian captivity (22:19-20). (Josiah would die in 609 BC, just four years before Nebuchadnezzar's first invasion of Judah.)

23:1-3 When Josiah learned that God wouldn't bring his judgment on Judah during his reign, the young king could have simply said, "Whew," and returned to business as usual. Instead, Josiah was rightly zealous in his desire to please and glorify the Lord. Josiah was not managing his own kingdom; he was managing *God's* kingdom. So, he wasn't about to be negligent with regard to an opportunity he saw.

Chapter 23 essentially records how Josiah rolled up his sleeves and set about destroying every vestige of false worship in the vicinity and establishing worship of the true and living God. First, the king gathered everybody in Judah at the **temple** where he himself **read in their hearing all the words of the book of the covenant** (23:2). (Revival among God's people always begins with the Word of God.) Then, he led the people in making a new **covenant** promise before God to keep the law they had just heard. And **all the people agreed to** it (23:3). This public and corporate commitment would help the people to stand strong and hold one another accountable.

23:4 With God's Word proclaimed and a fresh commitment of obedience made, Josiah was ready to begin his cleanup campaign. He started in the temple, which Manasseh had turned into a shrine to false gods. **Hilkiah** and other **priests** and temple workers brought out the things used to worship **Baal, Asherah, and all the stars in the sky.** Then, the king **burned them.** His efforts are a reminder that when you identify areas of temptation in your life, you are not merely to throw them in a closet or shove them under a rug. You must eradicate them.

23:5-9 Josiah also eliminated **the idolatrous priests** whom previous kings had allowed to operate **in the cities of Judah,** and he **burned** and beat to **dust** the **Asherah pole** in the temple (23:5-6). He **defiled the high places from Geba** in the far north of Judah to **Beer-sheba** in the far south. Priests who had worshiped at **the high places** could not serve at **the altar** of the rededicated temple (23:8-9).

23:10-15 Even with all of these reforms accomplished, Josiah was only getting started. **He defiled Topheth,** where worshipers of **Molech** practiced child sacrifice. He also eliminated items used to worship the heavenly bodies (23:10-11). The false worship sites Josiah destroyed even included some built centuries before by **King Solomon** after his heart was led astray (23:13; see 1 Kgs 11:1-6). Josiah went so far as to destroy the idolatry at neighboring **Bethel,** tearing down the **altar** and the **high place** that Israel's King **Jeroboam** had built (23:15).

23:16-20 While in Bethel, Josiah saw the **tomb** of the prophet who, many years earlier, had foretold of him and predicted his future actions (23:17; see 1 Kgs 13:2-3). So, the king ordered **his bones** and those of another **prophet** not to be disturbed (23:18). Nevertheless, he completed his purge of idolatry in the former northern kingdom (23:19-20). That Josiah was able to freely move in this region that was part of the Assyrian empire may suggest how weak Assyria was by this time; it was in the waning years of its power.

23:21-23 After proclaiming God's Word to the people (23:2), making a covenant to keep it (23:3), and ridding the land of idolatry (23:4-20), Josiah returned to Jerusalem to celebrate the Lord's **Passover** with obedience—**as written in the book of the covenant** (23:21). Remarkably, such faithful attention to detail had not been seen in the land since **the time of the judges** (23:21-22); that is, since about five centuries earlier! How sad that God's people had neglected his law for so long, yet how good and right it was for Josiah to lead them in reforming their ways.

23:24-27 The author added the note that Josiah also got rid of all the occult practitioners in his kingdom, and anyone or anything else that was **abhorrent** to the Lord, doing everything in accordance with God's Word (23:24). Yet, despite the ultimate commendation Josiah received, that **there was no king like him** before or after him (23:25), God **did not turn** away from his decree to **remove Judah** from his **presence** and allow his **temple** to be destroyed (23:26-27). Josiah was one of Judah's great kings. But, Judah had persisted in sin for a *long* time. A reckoning was coming.

23:28-30 Josiah died in battle at the age of thirty-nine while trying to stop **Pharaoh Neco** of **Egypt** from linking up with the Assyrian army and possibly attacking Judah (23:29). Josiah's death was tragic, but it was also part of God's plan in executing his judgment on Judah. He mercifully removed his faithful king from the scene before pouring out his wrath on his unfaithful people (see

22:19-20). Josiah's son **Jehoahaz** (23:30) and the kings who followed him (three of whom were Josiah's sons!) were hollow shells compared to their godly ancestors.

☞ D. The Reigns of Judah's Final Kings (23:31–25:30) ☜

23:31-33 God didn't put up with the first king in this section's hall of shame for very long. "The common people" had made Jehoahaz king (23:30), which could mean they hoped he would continue the good reign of his father. If that was the case, they were sorely disappointed. Jehoahaz immediately reverted to the **evil** of **his ancestors** (23:32), for which he and Judah paid dearly. Soon, Jehoahaz was **imprisoned** by **Neco**, and Judah was put under a heavy tribute (23:33). To the informed reader, the name **Riblah** has an ominous sound; there, Nebuchadnezzar would set up his headquarters during the destruction of Judah, and he would also execute many of the nation's leaders.

23:34-37 Neco put Jehoahaz's older brother **Eliakim** on the throne in Jerusalem and changed his name to **Jehoiakim** (23:34) as a way of showing that he (that is, Pharaoh) was in charge. The **common people** suffered heavily under the taxation needed to pay the tribute Neco demanded, yet Jehoiakim spent **eleven years** doing **evil in the LORD's sight** (23:35-37).

24:1-7 The name **Nebuchadnezzar** appears for the first time in 2 Kings in connection with his initial attack against Judah in 605 BC, during which he took Daniel of lions' den fame and other captives back to Babylon in the first of three deportations. Nebuchadnezzar had defeated Neco at the famous battle of Carchemish earlier that year, establishing **Babylon** as the next world superpower and bringing Egypt's vassal states under Babylonian control (24:7). Nebuchadnezzar attacked Judah to firm up his control in that region, and **Jehoiakim** submitted to him for **three years** before rebelling (24:1). This rebellion, though, was contrary to God's will for Judah: Nebuchadnezzar was his instrument of judgment on the nation, as **spoken through his servants the prophets**, for all **the sins of Manasseh** (24:2-3). The Lord had had enough (24:4).

24:8-17 Jehoiakim's death brought his son **Jehoiachin** to the throne in Jerusalem for a brief, three-month, **evil** reign (24:8-9). Meanwhile, Nebuchadnezzar had sent troops to besiege **Jerusalem** because of Jehoiakim's rebellion, but, apparently, by the time the Babylonian king arrived in 597 BC, Jehoiakim was gone and Jehoiachin was ruling (24:10-11). Undeterred, Nebuchadnezzar took captive Jehoiachin and many other **officials** and took them to **Babylon**, along with a haul of **treasures**—a total of **ten thousand** people in all (24:12-14), including the prophet Ezekiel. Nebuchadnezzar left another puppet king named **Mattaniah**, a son of Josiah, on the throne in Jerusalem and **changed his name to Zedekiah** (24:17).

24:18-20 Zedekiah was last in the line of evil kings whom God appointed to occupy the throne in Judah's final years. The writer first summed up the result of Zedekiah's reign as the time in which the cup of God's **anger** finally ran over, and he **banished** his people **from his presence** (24:20). In the final chapter of 2 Kings, the story of Zedekiah's rebellion and Judah's downfall unfolds.

25:1-7 Zedekiah's rebellion against Babylon (24:20) was the historical event God used to destroy Judah. Nebuchadnezzar's siege of Jerusalem brought hunger to the people and caused the city's defenders, including Zedekiah, to try and escape **at night** when the Babylonians (**Chaldeans**) broke through into the city in 586 BC (25:1-4). Nevertheless, the invaders easily captured Zedekiah. They took him to Nebuchadnezzar at his field headquarters in **Riblah**, where his fearful sentence was carried out (25:6). There, the king of Judah watched his **sons** get executed before being **blinded**. He was finally taken **to Babylon** in **bronze chains** (25:7).

25:8-21 With the political and military threat against him neutralized, Nebuchadnezzar sent his troops to Jerusalem to destroy everything of importance, including **the walls** (25:10) and the **temple** (25:13-16). They took what was of value that could be carted off and burned the rest. There was no mercy for **Seraiah the chief priest**, an ancestor of the great priest Ezra (25:18; see Ezra 7:1), or for the seventy-one other priests and leaders in Jerusalem. They were arrested, taken to Nebuchadnezzar at Riblah, and executed (25:20-21). Jerusalem was a smoking ruin.

25:22-24 Nebuchadnezzar still needed someone in Judah to govern the poor and the other stragglers he had left behind. So, this time he **appointed Gedaliah**, the grandson of **Shaphan**, who had been one of Josiah's officials (25:22). Gedaliah was apparently a good man, who befriended the prophet Jeremiah (see Jer 39:14). He obviously believed Jeremiah's counsel that the people left in the land should **serve the king of Babylon** so that it might go well for them (25:24; see Jer 39:11-14; 40:6, 9-10). But, there were still those left in Judah who (unwisely) wanted to fight the Babylonians.

25:25-26 A man named **Ishmael** led a band of assassins to murder Gedaliah and his associates, including some Babylonians, **at Mizpah** north of Jerusalem where he had set up his headquarters (25:25). The people then fled to **Egypt** in fear of Nebuchadnezzar's reprisals (25:26).

25:27-30 In spite of all the wicked kings, sordid history, and harsh judgments of God that occupy the pages of 2 Kings, the book ends with a message of hope for its readers in exile—a final reminder of God's promise that he would never completely abandon his people.

The date of the kindness shown to **King Jehoiachin** by Nebuchadnezzar's successor, **Evil-merodach**, moves the history forward to somewhere between 562-560 BC, or in the **thirty-seventh year** of the king's **exile** in Babylon (25:27). Jehoiachin had been imprisoned for a long time, in keeping with the harsh treatment conquered kings usually received in the ancient world. But, he received a pardon, a release, and a place of honor over the other **kings who were with him in Babylon** (25:28). Jehoiachin also **dined regularly** with Evil-merodach and received **a regular allowance . . . for the rest of his life** (25:29-30).

The Babylonian king may have done this to curry favor with the Jews (those who had been imported from Judah), as some historians suggest. But, God was also working his sovereign plan to preserve his people even in captivity. And, his faithful prophets in Babylon reminded the exiles that when the time of their punishment was fulfilled, he would bring them back to their homeland.

1 CHRONICLES

INTRODUCTION

Author

ANCIENT TRADITION CLAIMS that Ezra wrote 1–2 Chronicles. The author must have lived after the Babylonian exile and the return of the Jews to the land of Israel. He also must have had access to historical records and an interest in the reimplementation of the law and the temple. All of this makes Ezra a good candidate. Furthermore, the final verses of 2 Chronicles are the first verses of Ezra. In the end, however, Chronicles does not claim Ezra as author. Thus, the writer will be referred to here as "the chronicler."

Historical Background

First Chronicles begins with extensive genealogies covering the time of Adam to the period of the Jewish nation's return from exile. The book focuses on the reign of David and concludes with David's death and the transition of power to Solomon. Second Chronicles begins with Solomon and follows the reigns of subsequent kings up to the Babylonian exile and the restoration. It covers the same time period as 1–2 Kings except that 2 Chronicles focuses exclusively on the kings of Judah. Chronicles was written after the return from exile, perhaps in the middle of the fifth century BC. Clearly, the chronicler makes use of material from the books of 1–2 Samuel and 1–2 Kings, but he uses it for his own purposes and adds much of his own material.

Message and Purpose

In these books, the chronicler records the history of the southern kingdom of Judah, focusing on the reigns of the Davidic kings, as well as giving attention to the priesthood. Thus, we see in these books the wedding of the kingship and the priesthood, with a focus on the temple as the place of God's presence.

The message of 1–2 Chronicles was one of hope for the readers, who were struggling in Babylonian exile. They were reminded that while God ruled over them as King, he also related to them through the priesthood. God's rule over and relationship with his people are the key aspects of his kingdom identity with them.

These books use the historical ups and downs of the kingdom of Judah to show the need for a leader who could perfectly fulfill the roles of king and priest. Ultimately, this would happen in the Messiah, the Lord Jesus Christ, who would be both King and high priest. He rules us and rescues us.

VIDEO INTRO

www.bhpublishinggroup.com/qr/te/13_00

1 CHRONICLES

I. THE GENEALOGIES (1:1–9:44)

The first nine chapters of 1 Chronicles can be pretty tough sledding. These genealogical lists of hard-to-pronounce names can bog down even the most faithful Bible readers. But, 2 Timothy 3:16-17 says, "All Scripture [yes, even the genealogies] is inspired by God and is profitable for teaching, for rebuking, for correcting, for training in righteousness, so that the man of God may be complete, equipped for every good work."

God does not list names because he ran out of material. He always has purposes in mind. For example, the genealogies of Jesus in Matthew 1:1-17 and Luke 3:23-38 are not mere lists. Matthew's genealogy traces Jesus's lineage through Joseph, his legal father. This established the fact that Jesus Christ had legal right to the throne because his lineage could be traced back to David. Luke's genealogy traces Jesus's line through his mother Mary, while being careful to note that Joseph was not Jesus's birth father (see Luke 3:23). So, even though the purpose of a biblical genealogy may not be immediately obvious, God had a reason for including it. There is a rhyme and reason to even the most seemingly insignificant statements in Scripture.

⇒ A. The Genealogies from Adam to Israel (1:1–2:2) ⇐

1:1-4 The genealogies of 1 Chronicles, the most extensive in the Scriptures, show the development of Israel's theocracy, focusing on the messianic line of David in the tribe of Judah, from which God's promises and Savior would come, and the priestly line of Levi, which was crucial to the ministry of the temple. In this sense, then, the genealogies of 1 Chronicles 1–9 are like a compressed history of Israel. Chapter 1 begins at the dawn of creation with the mention of **Adam** and his descendants (1:1). This served to connect the history of Israel with the very beginning of God's creative work.

1:5-27 There is a valuable lesson for us in this long list of names. God had given Adam what is called the *cultural mandate* in Genesis 1:28: "Be fruitful, multiply, fill the earth, and subdue it." He repeated this command to Noah after the flood (1:4; Gen 9:1) in almost identical language: "God blessed Noah and his sons and said to them, 'Be fruitful and multiply and fill the earth.'" This mandate, by the way, has never been rescinded, and in 1 Chronicles 1:19 we can see the influence of a later generation's disobedience to this command. The writer says that during the lifetime of a man named Peleg, **the earth was divided**. This phrase refers to God confusing the people's language at Babel (Gen 11:7-9) to thwart their plan of huddling together in defiance of his orders and building a man-centered kingdom for themselves.

The lesson behind the repetition of the mandate is that we, as Bible readers, should watch out when God says something twice; we must sit up and listen! After all, Jesus always spoke the truth, but when he wanted his hearers to really focus on what he had to say, he would preface it with "Truly I tell you" (see, for example, John 3:5-6, 11). That's a translation of a repeated word in the original Greek text. It's roughly equivalent to what we say to our kids, "Now, you listen here, young man (or young woman)," when we want to make sure they don't miss what we're about to say. When God repeats himself, we had better take notice. The people of Babel paid for their failure to obey: "The LORD scattered them . . . over the face of the whole earth" (Gen 11:9).

In verse 17, Noah's son **Shem**'s offspring are listed after those of the other sons of this patriarch because Shem's was the godly line through which the Messiah (that is, Jesus) would come. By listing Shem third, the writer was able to end this section of his genealogy with **Abram (that is, Abraham)** (1:27). This set the stage for the introduction of Abraham's line.

1:28-34 Much as he did by listing Shem last in the genealogy of Noah, the writer set the stage for the genealogies of **Isaac** (1:34) and his descendants, including Esau's offspring (1:35-54), by focusing on the son of Hagar (**Ishmael**; 1:29-30) and those of Abraham's concubine **Keturah** first (1:32-33).

1:38-54 Even though Esau's line did not figure prominently in either messianic or Levitical history, he was a grandson of Abraham and the brother of Jacob (also called Israel). Their descendants had a long and often stormy history.

2:1-2 Israel was crucial to the Jewish nation's history; he was the father of Israel's twelve tribes. God changed Jacob's name to Israel after his smack down with the angel that's described in Genesis 32:24-28. It's significant when God changes a person's name; it means he has a new purpose and direction for that person's life.

➢ B. The Genealogies of Israel's Twelve Tribes (2:3–8:40) ➣

2:3-55 The offspring of Jacob's twelve sons eventually formed Israel's tribes. **Judah** (2:4) was not the first son in birth order, but he

became prominent because God promised that Israel's rulers would come from his line; this promise included the Messiah (see Gen 49:10). This is why Judah and his descendants are discussed first and at length from 2:3 all the way through 4:23.

Because Judah is the tribe of King David, we are introduced to **Jesse** and his sons, the last of whom was **David**, in 2:13-15.

3:1-24 David was the nation's most important king, which is why his progeny receive so much attention here (3:1). God made a covenant with David to give him a kingly dynasty—culminating in the Messiah (see 1 Chr 17). Thus, David was not just the head of Judah's royal line, but also the ancestor of Jesus. Chapter 3 especially lists the Davidic kings of Judah (3:10-16) before following the Davidic line after the Babylonian exile (3:17-24).

4:1-23 The writer completes the list of Judah's descendants here. Included is the interesting account of Jabez. According to the Chronicler, **Jabez was more honored than his brothers** (4:9). In other words, Jabez was special; he stood out from the crowd. Importantly, he was not singled out because of some great feat he did for God or because he had overcome great obstacles. Rather, he was lifted above his brothers because of his simple, powerful prayer of faith that moved God to respond. Jabez said, **If only you would bless me, extend my border, let your hand be with me, and keep me from harm, so that I will not experience pain** (4:10).

Much about Jabez is left to speculation, but we know a few things. First, his name means **"pain,"** so something happened surrounding his birth that caused his mother to give Jabez this unusual name (4:9). Now, a name like that is quite a burden to overcome. I believe God wanted us to read about this man in part as a reminder that pain doesn't have to be the last word in our lives.

Second, Jabez realized that he didn't just need *someone* to bless him; he needed the impartation of spiritual favor that comes from God alone. It's interesting that Jabez's request is open-ended instead of specific. Jabez did not try to make a deal with God;

after all, when you do that, you are limited to the terms of your deal. The beautiful thing about just throwing yourself on the mercy of God is that he decides what's in your best interest. Jabez brought God an empty cup and asked him to fill it as he saw fit. That's a prayer of faith. Let God decide what to fill your cup with and how high to fill it.

Third, Jabez wanted God to expand his borders. In essence, he prayed, "God, broaden my frontier." The problem with too many of us is that we are too easily satisfied where we are. We have become complacent with our little plots of land in the kingdom when God wants to use us to expand the influence of his kingdom in history. People who are complacent aren't motivated to ask God for anything, so they don't receive anything from God. Jabez wanted his kingdom influence to grow, and he knew the Lord could deliver.

Fourth, Jabez knew that God was capable of keeping him from harm, from pain. Why did he pray that? I suspect Jabez did not want the blessings he anticipated to become a source of pain by allowing them to disconnect him from God. So he asked God to put a restraining order on the devil, as it were. The more God blesses you, the more Satan sets his sights on you. Success, then, is a great opportunity for failure if we are not alert. After all, the higher you go, the farther you can fall. When received, blessings like those Jabez requested can dull our sense of dependency on God. This man knew Satan would try to use coming blessings as an opportunity to tempt him to become independent from God.

Don't miss that **God granted his request** (4:10). Jabez got what he desired from God because he asked for it. He was like Jacob who said as he wrestled with God: "I will not let you go unless you bless me" (Gen 32:26). Do you pursue God until you see a transformation in your situation?

4:24-43 Simeon was another son of Jacob by his wife Leah (4:24). The most interesting and important historical detail regarding his descendants that's recorded here appears in 42-43: **Five hundred men from these sons of Simeon went** and **struck down the remnant of the Amalekites.**

The Amalekites had been the bitter enemies of God's people since the days of Moses. They attacked Israel without provocation, leading to the famous incident in which Aaron and Hur held up Moses's hands so Israel could prevail against them (see Exod 17:8-13). After the battle, God said, "I will completely blot out the memory of Amalek under heaven" (Exod 17:14). But, when given the chance to blot out the Amalekites when they entered the promised land as the Lord had decreed, King Saul failed in the mission (see 1 Sam 15). Rather than eradicating the Amalekites and everything they owned, Saul kept back the best of the livestock for sacrifice and spared their king, Agag.

About five hundred years after Saul, Queen Esther, a Jewish exile living in Persia, had to take her life in her hands to beg King Xerxes not to allow Haman the Agagite to annihilate her people (Esth 3:1). Haman was likely a descendent of King Agag of Saul's day and, thus, a descendant of the Amalekites whom Israel evidently did not destroy as God commanded. If so, that disobedience almost led to an Old Testament holocaust at the hands of Haman. It appears that Simeon's descendants had attempted to finish the job left incomplete in Saul's day. (Even partial disobedience can have consequences not only for us, but also for those who come after us.)

An interesting insight is provided in 4:40: **rich, good pasture** was found **for some Hamites had lived [in a particular area] previously.** This passage suggests that Hamitic (that is, dark-skinned) people living in Canaan had positively contributed to community life, productivity, and social well-being. This verse refutes the so-called "curse of Ham" (which is really a misunderstanding of Noah's curse of Ham's son Canaan) as applying to an entire race or sub-set of humanity (see commentary on Gen 9:24-29).

5:1-26 Chapter 5 begins with a historical reference. It explains why Reuben, Jacob's firstborn son, fell out of God's favor and was replaced by Judah, whose tribe would be given the honor of becoming the messianic line leading to Jesus. **Reuben defiled his father's bed** (5:1), which is a way of saying he committed adultery with his father's concubine Bilhah (see Gen 35:22; 30:4). Reuben's sin was detestable to God, so Reuben forfeited his birthright to **Joseph** (5:2) for the same reason Esau did earlier: both men cared more about their physical appetites than their spiritual heritage (see Gen 25:32).

The accounts of Esau and Reuben teach an important principle at work in God's kingdom. Through his sovereign power, God can do more with the lesser creatures (in theses cases, Esau's younger brother Jacob and Reuben's younger brother Joseph) than the devil can do with the greater creatures when the lesser are devoted to him.

6:1-81 The line of the priestly tribe of Levi was so important to Israel that the chronicler devoted all of chapter 6 to it. To the original readers, this was a vital record of the priestly descent so the Israelites who'd returned from the Babylonian exile could be assured that the priests serving them were legitimate.

There are some familiar names in this list. **Aaron** was the founder of the priestly line (6:3). **Nadab** and **Abihu** (6:3) were put to death for failing to treat God as holy (see Lev 10:1-3). **Zadok** (6:8) was the high priest who remained loyal to David during the rebellion of Absalom (see 2 Sam 15:24-29).

The chapter also includes a list of the musicians that David put in charge of the music (6:31-46) and identifies the settlements that were given to the Levites (6:54-81).

7:1-40 Chapter 7 lists the descendants of tribal forefathers **Issachar** (7:1-5), **Benjamin** (7:6-12), **Naphtali** (7:13), **Manasseh** (7:14-19), **Ephraim** (7:20-29), and **Asher** (7:30-40).

Of particular interest here is the note about Asher's sons, who had four outstanding qualities: **They were the heads of their ancestral families, chosen men, valiant warriors, and chiefs among the leaders** (7:40). A desperate need in our country and in the church today is for godly, committed men to take up these roles of leadership. A summary of these qualities reveals character traits that seem to be in short supply in this era of weakened manhood.

First, Asher's sons were "heads" of their families. That suggests Asher raised his sons to be leaders. They weren't just hanging around the house, eating and taking up space. Every man, without exception, has been created to be a leader because every man has been created to be the head of a household. A leader knows where he's going and shows others how to join him along the way.

Second, they were "chosen men." That phrase suggests Asher raised his boys to be the cream of the crop. They were the kind of men a father would choose for his daughter to marry, men of high character and strong ethical standards who accepted responsibility.

Third, they were "valiant warriors"—that is, they were men of valor, like those who fought alongside David in his many battles. These guys had a sense of boldness and conviction and were ready to take a stand when a stand needed to be taken. A warrior is a man of courage and conviction who will take risks for a good cause.

Fourth, Asher's sons are described as "chiefs among the leaders." Another word for leader is "prince," and a prince is just a king waiting to happen. Asher's sons were outstanding even among the literal princes of Israel.

8:1-40 Here Benjamin's descendants are spoken of at more length than they received in 7:6-12. This tribe was small, but important, because it was the tribe of Saul, Israel's first king. Benjamin was also closely identified with Judah, so much so that Benjamin was absorbed into Judah and, at times, both tribes were referred to by the latter's name.

The family and tribal connections made in chapters like this one may seem strange to us, but, to the original readers, they were received as part of the rich history of God's sovereign provision for and blessing of his people Israel.

↗ C. The Genealogies of the Returning Exiles and King Saul (9:1-44) ↖

9:1 Here the chronicler reminds the readers of what they were painfully aware: Judah [had been] exiled to Babylon because of their unfaithfulness. At the end of the seventy-year period of exile, however, God had graciously brought them back to the land.

Mentioning the Babylonian captivity in passing as the chronicler did would serve to remind the people of Judah of the gross sin, idolatry, and apostasy that had led to the exile and destruction of the Jerusalem temple and the land of Judah. It was far more than a history lesson, then. It was a powerful reminder that the current generation must live faithfully before their Lord.

9:2-34 Here the chronicler lists those who had returned from Babylonian exile. Now, before the final invasion by Nebuchadnezzar's army and destruction of Jerusalem and the temple, false prophets in Judah had said the captivity would never happen. But, God had insisted through his faithful prophets that it would. And, when it had, the prophet Jeremiah wrote to the captives in Babylon to say this: "Build houses and live in them. Plant gardens and eat their produce. Take wives and have sons and daughters. . . . Multiply there; do not decrease. Pursue the well-being of the city I have deported you to. Pray to the LORD on its behalf, for when it thrives, you will thrive" (Jer 29:4-7). In other words, God was saying to his people, "I have placed you among the Gentiles for a long time. Show them what kingdom people look like when they work and worship and have families and interact with unbelievers. You may not be in my land right now, but you still carry my name." That message sounds very similar to what the church, as God's people bearing witness to him in a pagan culture, should do before God leads us to our own heavenly homeland.

Don't miss that this passage emphasizes the **priests** (9:10-13), **Levites** (9:14-16), **gatekeepers** (9:17-26), and other **servants** of God who officiated in and cared for the **temple** (9:2). The chronicler is greatly concerned with God's law, his holiness, and the purity of worship that he demands, along with the priesthood and its proper functioning. This, then, is one of the places where

we know that the chronicler had a definite theological or spiritual purpose for his work and wasn't merely compiling historical facts. The temple is central to the story in 1–2 Chronicles.

Later, in his treatment of Solomon's reign in 2 Chronicles 1–9, he spends one chapter on Solomon's wisdom, and eight chapters on his preparations, building, and dedication of the temple. A lot of the historical details of Solomon's reign found in 1 Kings are omitted there. Why? Because they did not fit into the author's purpose of focusing on the main achievement of Solomon's reign: the building of the temple.

The tabernacle of Moses's day, a collapsible and moveable tent that Israel carried and set up through the nation's wilderness wanderings, and later the temple itself, were often called *God's house*. The temple was the representative abode of the presence of God among his people. Of course, no building can house God because God is greater than the sum total of his creations. A reference to the temple stood as a symbol of the presence and power of its occupant. We see something similar today when reporters use expressions such as, "The White House said," to note that a comment is either from the President directly or carries his authority.

The chronicler wanted the people to read their history from the divine perspective so they could bring all of life under the lordship of their great Creator God. This is what I call an overarching kingdom agenda. Similarly, God's kingdom agenda for the church is to comprehensively bring every area of life under the lordship of Jesus Christ so that his people live all of life the way God intended.

9:35-44 The final verses of chapter 9 list Saul's descendants and serve as an introduction to chapter 10, which tells the story of Saul's demise and death as the unfaithful and disobedient king who lost his throne and life under God's judgment. Instead of fulfilling the agenda God gave him as king of his people, Saul chose the path of compromise and sinfulness.

II. THE REIGN OF DAVID (10:1–29:30)

Chapter 10 is where the chronicler's narrative begins. He starts with Saul's death and takes us to David's death at the end of 1 Chronicles.

⇨ A. David Anointed as King
(10:1–11:9) ⇦

10:1-14 Saul's entire reign and death, which covered "forty-two years" (1 Sam 13:1) and stretched for twenty-four chapters (1 Sam 8-31) take the chronicler only fourteen verses to sum up. Why did Saul deserve so little attention here from God's viewpoint? **Saul died for his unfaithfulness to the LORD because he did not keep the LORD's word. He even consulted a medium for guidance, but he did not inquire of the LORD. So the LORD put him to death and turned the kingdom over to David** (10:13-14).

Saul's failures include the time he became impatient waiting for Samuel and took it upon himself to make a burnt offering, which was a violation of God's law (see 1 Sam 13:9-14). Another time, he made a rash vow that almost cost his son Jonathan his life (see 1 Sam 14:24-45). And, even though Saul was the biggest and best warrior Israel had (see 1 Sam 9:1-2), he was content to let the Philistine Goliath blaspheme God for forty days without attempting to stop him (see 1 Sam 17). Then, after David killed Goliath and vindicated God's name, Saul hated David for the praise he received (see 1 Sam 18:7-9). All of this was in addition to the fact that his partial obedience in the matter of the Amalekites cost him the kingdom (see commentary on 4:24-43).

The sad, pitiful end of Israel's first king (10:3-9) provides a strong lesson for us and illustrates the difference between living for a kingdom agenda and living for a selfish, personal agenda. Saul's life followed the path of convenience, regardless of God's Word or priorities.

11:1-3 After the fall of Saul's house, **All Israel came together** and acknowledged that David was God's chosen one to **shepherd [his] people Israel . . . and be ruler over them** (11:1-2). So, **they anointed David king over Israel, in keeping with the LORD's word through Samuel** (11:3).

That "all Israel" came to Hebron for the anointing (11:1) was a significant statement of national unity for the readers of 1 Chronicles who had returned from the Babylonian exile. Israel had been divided, tribe against tribe, from the time of Solomon's death until the exile—a period of several hundred years. Now that the people were back in the land, unity was more important than the divisions that had led to years of conflict and suffering.

11:4-9 David needed a centrally located capital for his kingdom and chose **Jerusalem**, which, at that time, was the stronghold of **the Jebusites** (11:4). Though the Jebusites tried to put up a fight, David captured **the stronghold of Zion**, which came to be known as **the city of David** (11:5, 7). In time, the city would house the temple. Thus, Jerusalem would be home to the throne of King David and, more important, to the throne of the King of kings.

What was the source of David's growth in power? **The LORD of Armies was with him** (11:9).

That an Israelite soldier named **Joab** answered David's call to breach the walls of Jerusalem and so became David's commander-in-**chief** shows the man's ability (11:6). But, Joab is a good example of a person who has strong qualities such as leadership, bravery, and loyalty, yet can't control his impulses or his temper. In the end, Joab's violent and deceptive side did him in (see 1 Kgs 2:5-6).

⇨ B. David's Mighty Warriors
(11:10–12:40) ⇦

11:10-47 David was a warrior through and through (22:8), so it's not surprising that he attracted to himself other brave fighters who swore loyalty to him. The exploits of these men sound like something out of a superhero movie, telling us that David had an incredible office staff! The fighting skills and loyalty of **the Three** (11:18) were on display when they **broke through** the Philistines' lines to get David the **drink** he wanted from the **well** at **Bethlehem** (11:15-19). David was grieved when he realized that three of his best men could have been killed just to satisfy a whim he happened to mention, so he poured out the water as an offering to the Lord. **Abishai** and **Benaiah** (11:20, 22) are two names that figure prominently in David's reign and military campaigns. Abishai was **Joab's brother** and the **leader of the Three** (11:20). Benaiah was so fearless **he went down into a pit on a snowy day and killed a lion** (11:22).

The chronicler makes it clear that David and his warriors were not victorious merely because of their brute strength and military cunning. Though they possessed these qualities, **the LORD gave them . . . great victory** (11:14). So, don't pat yourself on the back and forget the true source of your victory, either.

12:1-40 So clear was it to **Amasai, chief of the Thirty**, that God was with David that he and his men pledged their loyalty to him (12:18). How did Amasai come by this insight? After all, at the time described in verses 1-22, David **was still banned from the presence of Saul** (12:1) and was hiding in his desert **stronghold** (12:8, 16). Why and how would Amasai persuade other warriors to join David? The answer is that **the Spirit enveloped Amasai** (12:18)—that is, he received a direct revelation from the Lord who said of David, "This is my man." Small wonder, then, that when all the soldiers gathered to David, it looked **like an army of God** (12:22).

Most of the mighty men listed in chapter 11 were from David's own tribe of Judah. But, according to chapter 12, many fighting men from other Israelite tribes also came to serve David. Among these were the Issacharites, **who understood the times and knew what Israel should do** (12:32). That insight tells us that somebody raised those boys to understand what was happening around them, and they were ready to serve. They're a faithful example of kingdom living.

Parents, teach your children to be observant about the dangerous times we live in and to follow God's path of wisdom. May we raise up followers of Christ of whom it is one day said, "They understood the times and knew what the church should do."

Importantly, **all these warriors** that are featured by the chronicler, as well as **all the rest of Israel**, were united in their purpose **to make David king** (12:38). As a group of football players with diverse roles become a team when united in purpose, so God's people are truly united when his kingdom purposes become theirs. As the apostle Paul affirms, true unity is a spiritual issue (see Eph 4:3).

❧ C. David Brings the Ark to Jerusalem and Desires to Build a Temple (13:1–17:27) ❧

13:1-4 God himself described David as "a man after his own heart" (1 Sam 13:14), and David understood that victory is from God's hand. He said, "The LORD saves, for the battle is the LORD's" (1 Sam 17:47). So, it's not surprising that David urged the people to **bring back the ark** of God (13:3)—the symbol of God's holy presence where he met with his people—to Jerusalem. In the days of Saul, Israel had failed to **inquire of** God (13:3). When the leadership neglected God, the people did, as well. But, David wasn't about to follow Saul's example.

13:5-6 Where had the ark been? The ark had fallen into Philistine hands because God judged Israel's priests for using the ark like a good luck charm (see 1 Sam 2:12–4:22). When it had proved to be way too hot for the Philistines to handle, they'd sent it back to Israel (see 1 Sam 5–6). For many years, it remained in the city of **Kiriath-jearim** (13:5).

13:7-14 This was a moving party with the emphasis on *party*. **David and all Israel were dancing with all their might before God** (13:8). At the center of worship is the celebration of who God is, what he has done, and what we are trusting him to do. As the author of many of the Psalms, David was a worshipping man, so he led the celebration.

But, the story recorded here reminds us that worship must be more than heartfelt.

It must be carried out in the way God prescribes. God had given Israel strict instructions about how to transport the ark. Only the Levites were to carry it and only by using poles inserted through rings in its side (see Exod 25:12-15; 37:3-5; Deut 10:8). Yet, when David transported the ark, it was placed **on a new cart** pulled by oxen (13:7). That detail is important because this was how the godless Philistines had moved the ark when they sent it back to Israel (see 1 Sam 6:7).

God's worshipers aren't free to just make things up as they go along, and the parade didn't end well. **Uzzah**, one of those guiding the cart, **reached out to hold the ark because the oxen had stumbled** (13:9). As a result, **the Lord's anger burned . . . and he struck him dead** (13:10). Through this response, God was reminding David and Israel that he is holy—that is, "separate" or "set apart." He is separate from his creation, unstained by sin, and is the standard of righteousness. We are to approach him as such.

If you were in charge of transporting the President of the United States, you wouldn't have the freedom to simply show up at the White House on horseback and tell the leader of the free world to climb aboard. So, how much more important was it for Israel to submit to the agenda of their holy and transcendent King "who is enthroned between the cherubim" on the ark when it was time to transport it (13:6)?

As a result of **the Lord's outburst against Uzzah**, David was too afraid to take the ark to Jerusalem. He put it in the house of **Obed-edom** instead (13:11-13). There it **remained** until David was ready to do things the right way (13:14; see 15:2-15).

14:1-7 Here, the chronicler hits pause on the story of the ark to emphasize God's blessings on David—perhaps to reassure his readers that God's favor was still on David in spite of his failure. **King Hiram of Tyre** sent builders and materials **to build a palace for** David (14:1). **Then David knew that the Lord had established him as king** (14:2). David's star was shining brightly. Things were going well for this former shepherd boy whom God had taken from the outhouse to the White House, so to speak.

14:8-17 Right in the middle of all of his incredible blessings, David experienced a problem. **When the Philistines heard that David had been anointed king over all Israel, they all went in search of David** (14:8). Similarly, when God blesses you for his purposes, you become the target of the enemy. Yet, when the Philistines threatened David and the people of Israel, God's man was determined **to face them** (14:8).

David knew better than to go it alone, so he **inquired of God** (14:10). To inquire of God—to pray—is to seek heavenly intervention in an earthly situation. It is the established means by which God relates to his people and we relate to him. God has wired the world of his people, in fact, to work through prayer. Thus, David didn't rely on his military might or past victories. He humbly looked to the one who had made him king in the first place.

Think of God's power like the electricity in your home. Your home has been wired for power; that's the way it was built. The electric company will provide your home with all the power you need, but you have to plug in the toaster to get the benefits of that power. You have to flip the switch. Similarly, if you are a Christian, you are wired for divine power. But, unless it is activated through prayer, you'll never see heavenly power working on earth. You've got to flip the switch.

Prayer is calling forth in history what God has determined in eternity. It is a passport to and a point of contact with the heavenly sphere. When David made such contact, the Lord answered with stunning victories over the enemy (14:10-16). As a result, **David's fame spread throughout the lands, and the Lord caused all the nations to be terrified of him** (14:17).

15:1-26 The journey of the ark to Jerusalem resumes here. This time, things were done right. **No one but the Levites** carried the ark (15:2), and they accomplished the task **the way Moses had commanded according to the word of the Lord** (15:15). Note carefully: the Bible—the written Word of God—is no mere book. It's not simply words on a page. It's the authoritative voice of God. If you mix a human viewpoint with the divine viewpoint, the result can be deadly (13:9-10). But, David made sure the priests and Levites **consecrated**

themselves for their holy assignment in the way prescribed (15:14), and he offered sacrifices along the way (15:26). He took what God said seriously, and we should, too.

15:27-29 Here, we see a marriage lesson based on the idea that you will live according to God's priorities or your own. You will either view life from a heavenly perspective or an earthly one.

David had married Michal, a daughter of Saul who was apparently quite a diva. (Saul even chuckled to himself when he gave Michal to David because he hoped she would be a trap to bring him down; see 1 Sam 18:20-21). **As the ark of the covenant of the LORD was entering the city**, Michal saw David **leaping and dancing**. But, instead of worshiping and celebrating with him, **she despised him in her heart** (15:29).

What happened in this passage is why Christians ought not be "partners with" or "unequally yoked" with (as the KJV put it) unbelievers (2 Cor 6:14). A believer's marriage to someone who refuses to place himself or herself under God's kingdom rule will result in having two radically different agendas trying to operate under the same roof. Be careful whom you marry *before* you marry.

16:1-43 Once the ark was in place, David wrote a great hymn to the Lord (16:8-36). It combines portions of three Psalms: 95, 105, and 106. Two aspects of the hymn are worth noting.

First, in it David called God's people to **praise** (16:9, 25, 35-36) and worship (16:28-29) him. Why? Because God provides **salvation** (16:23), **made the heavens** (16:26), and possesses all **glory and strength** (16:28). A policeman deserves honor because of his badge and uniform. Without these, though, he's just another person. God never removes his uniform of divinity. He will always be the glorious Creator and Redeemer; he deserves our praise.

Second, David urges the people to **remember** God's wonderful deeds (16:12, 15) and to **give** him **thanks** (16:8, 34). You're going to encounter plenty of sorrow and difficulty in life. There will be times when you'll want to throw in the towel. And, that's why you have to regularly remember the Lord's goodness

to you. Recall yesterday's blessings to help you through today's hardships. Recalling God's actions in your life will help you cultivate a grateful heart. When you cease giving thanks to the Lord, it's because you've forgotten what he's done for you.

17:1-7 Though all was well with Israel, all was not well in David's heart. He lived in a **cedar house** while the Lord's ark was **under tent curtains** (17:1). He was ashamed and wanted to build a grand temple for God. At first, **Nathan** the prophet gave David the green light for running with that idea (17:2). **But that night**, Nathan received a message from the Lord rejecting David's offer (17:3-4). God had never asked Israel for **a house**, so David didn't need to feel sorry for him (17:5-6). He reminded David that he was the gift-giver and David was the recipient. God had taken a shepherd from the **pasture** and placed him on a throne (17:7).

17:8-15 God also declared that he would **make a name for** David **like that of the greatest on the earth**. He would establish Israel and **subdue all [David's] enemies** (7:8-10). These big promises are a reminder not to place God in a box. He "is able to do above and beyond all that we ask or think" (Eph 3:20).

Even these grand promises weren't enough, though. David had proposed building a house for God. But God said, I **will build a house for you** (17:10). The house God had in mind wasn't composed of bricks and wood. The house he was giving David was actually a royal dynasty. And, not only would David's son build a temple for the Lord (17:11-12), but God would also be a **father** to him and would establish his kingdom **forever** (17:13-14).

The near term referent in these verses is, of course, Solomon; he would build God's temple (see 2 Chr 2:1–7:11). Ultimately, though, this covenant with David couldn't be fulfilled by a mere man. It required a God-man. Only Jesus Christ could fulfill the Davidic covenant and rule as an eternal King. "He ... will be called the Son of the Most High, and the Lord God will give him the throne of his father David" (Luke 1:32), and "he will reign forever" (Rev 11:15).

17:16-27 How could David respond to such promises? The only way you can respond to divine grace—with gratitude and praise.

Though David's origins were humble, the Lord regarded him **as a man of distinction** (17:17). And, in the end, the only opinion of you that matters is God's.

Don't miss David's prayer, **Do as you have promised** (17:23). If you sometimes wonder what to pray, ask God to fulfill the promises he has made to his children. If he promises it, you know it's his will. So, pray that he makes that which is settled in heaven a reality in your earthly history.

➤ D. David Wages War against Israel's Enemies (18:1–20:8) ✦

18:1-17 Chapters 18–20 record a number of David's military campaigns against Israel's enemies. The battles listed here are not necessarily in chronological order, but were probably chosen to demonstrate the greatness of David's rule as he consolidated and expanded his kingdom. According to chapter 18, David defeated the Philistines, Moabites, Arameans, Ammonites, Amalekites, and Edomites. No superpowers stood in his way because **the LORD made David victorious wherever he went** (8:6, 13). With this repeated phrase, the chronicler wants his readers to remember that God was the power behind David's sword.

David not only defeated his enemies, he also plundered them. They **brought** him **tribute** (18:2, 6), and he seized their **gold, silver, and bronze items** (18:7-11). But, these things weren't done so that David could merely accumulate wealth. He **dedicated these to the LORD** (18:11) so that, one day, **Solomon** could use them for constructing the temple (18:8). In other words, David's tribute and plunder served as a good illustration of the principle found in Proverbs 13:22: "the sinner's wealth is stored up for the righteous." A kingdom-minded economic agenda recognizes that God often providentially transfers the resources of the wicked to be used and developed for kingdom purposes.

19:1-19 The battle against **the Ammonites** and their mercenaries demonstrated the need for leaders to have wise counselors. David desired to **show kindness to Hanun**

the Ammonite king (19:1-2). But, the rash Ammonite leaders convinced the king that David's overtures **to console him** concerning his father's death were actually an effort to **spy** (19:2-3). When Hanun treated **David's emissaries** shamefully and prepared for battle (19:4-7), David sent **Joab** and **Abishai** to engage them (19:8-11). And, recognizing that victory comes from the Lord, David's men declared, **May the LORD's will be done** (19:13). The Ammonites and their Aramean mercenaries turned tail and ran (19:14-19).

20:1-8 The beginning of chapter 20 may sound familiar. It hints of the infamous occasion when David stayed in Jerusalem (while his army went to battle) and committed adultery with Bathsheba, which led to the murder of her husband, Uriah (see 2 Sam 11:1-27). Recording those events in detail didn't fit with the chronicler's purpose of showing God's favor to his people through his blessing of David; besides, it was likely well-known. In any event, the Ammonites were, once again, crushed by David's army (20:3). No one stood in the king's way—not even the massive Philistine giants (20:4-8).

➤ E. David Orders a Sinful Census (21:1–22:1) ✦

21:1 Lest you think that because the chronicler omitted the account of David's sin with Bathsheba in chapter 20, he's somehow whitewashing David's history, chapter 21 presents David warts and all. The only perfect hero in Chronicles is God. In this chapter, the chronicler recounts the devastation that resulted from David's pride when he commanded a military census. He isn't covering up David's sins; he's writing with a purpose. There's a significant reason this story is included, as we'll see.

After filling pages and pages with accounts of blessing (the ark brought to Jerusalem, God's covenant with David, David's military victories), the chronicler hits us with this: **Satan rose up against Israel and incited David to count the people of Israel** (21:1). Now, in 2 Samuel 24:1 it says, "The LORD's anger burned against Israel again, and he stirred up David against them to say: 'Go, count the people of Israel and Judah.'" So, what happened? Did God stir David to take a census of the people, or did Satan? The answer is both.

To execute his own judgment on some sin the people of Israel had committed, God allowed Satan to lay a snare for David by tempting him to take pride in the size of his kingdom and in the number of his troops rather than trusting in God. So, God put Satan on a short leash that allowed him permission to work on David. (This is similar to the scene in Job 1–2, in which God permits Satan to do a number on Job for his purposes.)

We can learn about Satan's methods of deception from this incident. Satan likes to mess with our minds, our thoughts. The apostle James, in fact, explains the process by which Satan deceives people. It begins with our desires, which, in David's case, was the desire to know his army's strength. James says, "Each person is tempted when he is drawn away and enticed by his own evil desire" (Jas 1:14). Now, it isn't necessarily sinful for a king and military commander to take stock of his troops so he knows whether he has sufficient strength to meet an enemy or defend the land. But, God wanted David to rely completely on him instead of numbers. After all, God had already demonstrated that he could give Israel victory even over much larger armies. The bottom line is that it did not matter how many fighting men David had.

So, stage one in Satan's deception plan is the arousal of a desire. And, even legitimate desires become a problem when the devil tempts us to meet a legitimate desire in an illegitimate way. That's what the process of temptation is often about, in fact: trying to get us to meet a good need in a bad way. Our legitimate desires are God-given. But, the enemy wants to influence how we decide to satisfy them. Satan wants our desires to master us. And, while he can't make us do anything, he can build castles of desire in our minds that lure us to do wrongful things.

21:2-4 David bought into the temptation presented to him, so he gave this order to Joab: **Go and count Israel from Beer-sheba to Dan and bring a report to me so I can know their number** (21:2). But, Joab was thinking more clearly than his king and replied to David, **May the LORD multiply the number of his people a hundred times over! My lord the king, aren't they all my lord's servants? . . . Why should he bring guilt on Israel?** (21:3). In other words, Joab tried to help David see the sinfulness of his actions, but he was overruled. He had to carry out the census against his own wishes and better judgment (21:4).

21:5-8 Verse 6 informs us that Joab didn't actually complete the census **because the king's command was detestable to him.** More important, it **was also evil in God's sight, so he afflicted Israel** (21:7).

Whereas before, Satan had appealed to David's desires to lead him to sin, the Holy Spirit apparently worked on David's conscience to lead him to repent (see 2 Sam 24:10). He confessed to God: **I have sinned greatly . . . . Now, please take away your servant's guilt, for I've been very foolish** (21:8). To repent means to change one's mind and reverse direction. It's like reversing course when you realize you've been traveling the wrong road. David's *confession* of his sin was what the Lord was waiting for, but it did not eliminate the *consequences* of his sin.

21:9-13 God is faithful to discipline us for our sin—for our good and for his glory. So, through **Gad** the **seer**, God confronted David with three choices of consequences for his actions (21:9-12). Each of the choices was horrific, so David chose to appeal to God's grace. He said, **Let me fall into the LORD's hands because his mercies are very great** (21:13). David knew that though the Lord's discipline can be extremely severe, he doesn't exercise it as with vengeance toward an enemy, but rather as a father toward his children.

21:14-16 God **sent a plague on Israel and seventy thousand Israelite men died** (21:14). **The angel** was wreaking havoc when God **relented** and ended **the destruction** (21:15). When David saw him **with his drawn sword . . . stretched out over Jerusalem**, he and the elders **fell facedown** (21:16). This scene brings us to an important aside: angels in the Bible aren't pictured as sweet cherubs with rosy cheeks. When visible in all their glory, they're overwhelming and fearsome-looking creatures (see Dan 10:5-9; Rev 22:8-9).

21:17 David begged God for mercy. He said, **Wasn't I the one who gave the order to count the people? I am the one who has sinned and acted very wickedly.** In other words, he didn't attempt to excuse his actions or explain them away. He didn't claim he'd made a mistake. David called what he'd done what it was: sin. He accepted full responsibility for it, and he pleaded with God to punish him instead of the people. When the Holy Spirit convicts you of your sin, humbly agree with him.

21:18-19 An insight gained here helps explain why the chronicler included this larger story in God's Word. The rest of the chapter describes how David purchased this piece of property, **the threshing floor of Ornan**, on which to build an **altar** and offer sacrifices to atone for his sin and stop the plague (21:18).

21:20-24 David asked the owner to sell him the piece of land at full price—no favors, no discounts. He said, **Give it to me for the full price, so the plague on the people may be stopped** (21:22). **Ornan** was more than glad to do his part and donate the land (21:23), but his offer only led to David's famous statement, **I insist on paying the full price, for I will not take for the Lord what belongs to you or offer burnt offerings that cost me nothing** (21:24). Now, if our churches were infused with this kind of attitude toward God and Christian service, we would have fewer problems. David understood that sacrifice isn't sacrifice if it doesn't hurt. Likewise, service isn't service if it doesn't cost you something.

21:25–22:1 After David bought the land from Ornan, built an altar, and made offerings to the Lord, God **answered him with fire from heaven** and commanded the angel to **put his sword back into its sheath** (21:25-27). In the midst of this, David immediately recognized the importance of his purchase: **This is the house of the Lord God, and this is the altar of burnt offering for Israel** (22:1). That means that David concluded that this

was where God wanted Israel to build him a temple, a good idea confirmed in 2 Chronicles 3:1, which says, "Solomon began to build the Lord's temple in Jerusalem on Mount Moriah where the Lord had appeared to his father David, at the site David had prepared on the threshing floor of Ornan the Jebusite." In his sovereignty and providence, then, God directed the sinful actions of David into a positive outcome by leading him to the very place, Mount Moriah, where Abraham had offered Isaac (see Gen 22).

Although God allowed the enemy of our souls to lure David into sin, God turned the devil's plan on its head by identifying Israel's holiest site as a result of what happened. The devil is evil and the enemy of God, but he is God's devil in the end. Our awesome God has Satan on a leash. He can take the devil's wicked schemes and turn them around to accomplish his own righteous purposes.

⇒ F. David Makes Temple Preparations and Appoints Leaders (22:2–27:34) ⇐

22:2-5 Even though God did not permit David to build the temple personally, David did everything in his power to ensure that his son would have what he needed to do the job. The chronicler distinguishes himself from the authors of 1–2 Samuel and 1–2 Kings by describing David's significant efforts to acquire the workers and the resources for the temple. He did this to help ensure that **the house [that would] be built for the Lord [would] be exceedingly great and famous and glorious in all the lands** (22:5). David was determined that God's temple would be the best—and that people from every land would know it. Is your service to the Lord marked with this same demand for excellence?

Don't miss the insight that David knew these **lavish preparations** were necessary because Solomon was too **young and inexperienced** to pull off the upcoming building project on his own (22:5). This suggests that David spent his remaining days preparing his son to be a leader. Dads, take note.

22:6-10 A day came when David sent for Solomon to give him the charge **to build** the temple (22:6). He delivered to his son an incredible word of prophecy and promise from God concerning Solomon's future reign (22:7-10). (Talk about being born with a silver spoon in your mouth!) I don't know of anyone in the Bible who got off to a better start than Solomon. He not only inherited the kingdom of Israel, but God himself promised him **rest from all his surrounding enemies** (22:9). Even Solomon's **name** was a daily reminder of God's promise (22:9). "Solomon" is related to *shalom*, the Hebrew word for peace. This man inherited the covenant blessings and promises God had given to David to **establish the throne of his kingdom over Israel forever** (22:10). This means that Solomon was placed in the messianic line, just as he was chosen for the greatest assignment anyone in Israel could ever hope to have: to build a house for the Lord.

22:11-16 After this, David asked that the Lord might grant his son success in constructing the temple. Then, he said to Solomon, **Above all, may the Lord give you insight and understanding when he puts you in charge of Israel so that you may keep the law of the Lord your God. Then you will succeed if you carefully follow the statutes and ordinances the Lord commanded Moses for Israel** (22:11-12).

His father's hope that God would grant him "insight and understanding" obviously had a significant affect on Solomon. Later, when God asked him what he would like most, Solomon requested "wisdom and knowledge" (2 Chr 1:7-10). He knew he couldn't lead God's people without heavenly insight for earthly living. Importantly, David's heart desire for Solomon was the same as God's heart desire for Solomon—that he would walk in the ways of the Lord. This should be the deepest desire of all Christian parents for their children.

Later, after the completion of the temple, the Lord similarly exhorted Solomon about keeping his "statutes" and commands. God promised that he would establish Solomon if he did everything he was commanded. He also warned him that if he turned away from

keeping his law, he would uproot Israel from the land (see 2 Chr 7:17-22). Unfortunately, this warning would one day become a reality. But, at this point in 1 Chronicles, Solomon was just beginning a reign that was full of promise.

David's final word of encouragement for Solomon echoed God's words to Joshua that had been uttered long ago: **Be strong and courageous. Don't be afraid or discouraged** (22:13; see Josh 1:9). Why did he need to say that? Because the natural human tendency is to be afraid in the face of a huge assignment like the responsibility that was being laid on Solomon. And, it wouldn't be long before Solomon lost his father's advice and could no longer draw courage from him, for David would pass away not long after he assumed the throne. We need to remember that the people of Scripture were just that— people. They were human beings with the same fears and emotions we have. So, in the case of Solomon, feeling fearful and uncourageous would be understandable. Yet, the most powerful antidote to fear is knowledge of the Lord's presence. That's why David concluded with the phrase, **May the Lord be with you** (22:16).

22:17-19 After speaking to Solomon, David **ordered all the leaders of Israel to help his son** (22:17). He knew Solomon couldn't go it alone, so David ensured that those who had been loyal to him would be loyal to his son. He exhorted them to **seek the Lord** and **get started building** (22:19). That's perfect advice no matter what endeavor you are about to begin. Seek the Lord—and get started.

23:1 When David was old and full of days, he installed his son Solomon as king over Israel (23:1). He essentially made Solomon his co-regent. Then, with Solomon on the throne, David set about providing for the service of the future temple.

23:2-32 Temple service was to be accomplished by **the Levites**, whom the Lord had set aside to care for and transport the ark, the tabernacle, and all its furnishings (23:2; see Num 1:50; Deut 10:8). Once the temple was built, there would no longer be a need to carry the tabernacle or any of the equipment for its service (23:26). At that point, then, the Levites were to assist the descendants of Aaron (the Levitical family chosen for the priesthood) with the service of the LORD's temple (23:28). So, while the priests offered sacrifices, the Levites not descended from Aaron were responsible for helping with various work in the temple (23:28-32).

The Levites served as Israel's praise and worship team. Their ministry included standing every morning and evening to give thanks and praise to the LORD (23:30). In fact, David assigned four thousand Levites to praise the LORD with . . . instruments (23:5). We know based on how many psalms David wrote that he placed a high value on worship. He wanted to ensure that there were enough Levites—singers and musicians—to praise the Lord twenty-four hours a day.

24:1-31 By including the extensive lists of names seen in this chapter, the chronicler enabled Levites and priests in his day who had returned from exile to know how they fit into the plan of temple service. One of the Levites, a secretary . . . recorded them in the presence of the king and the other leaders (24:6). Service in the Lord's temple was serious business.

How serious was it? As he lists Aaron's sons, the chronicler mentions Nadab and Abihu who died before their father (24:2) because they "presented unauthorized fire before the LORD" (Lev 10:1). Moses had made it clear that these two men didn't give proper regard for God's "holiness" and "glory" (Lev 10:3). In other words, they failed to take God seriously. When you do that, you're taking your life into your own hands. As a result of their sin, Nadab and Abihu had no sons to follow them into the priesthood (24:2).

Each of the different families had their assigned duties for service when they entered the LORD's temple (24:19). This provided enough priests for the continual, round-the-clock worship of the Lord.

25:1-31 The praise and worship leaders are named in this chapter (see 23:5). Notice that the officers of the army were involved

with David in making these appointments (25:1), a reminder that David was both a warrior and a worshiper. This close connection between worship and Israel's military campaigns is obvious as far back as the conquest of Jericho (see Josh 6), when Israel basically defeated the city with praise music, marching around the city walls and blasting trumpets.

Notice that these people were all trained and skillful in music for the LORD (25:7). In other words, they weren't born with musical talent. They had to train and practice to become highly skilled. This was their God-given job, and they did it with excellence.

We are all stewards in God's kingdom. We all have responsibilities and gifts from him. Make the most of yours. One day, you'll give an account for how faithful you were to your king's agenda (see Luke 19:11-26). Life is like a coin. You can spend it anyway you want. But, remember: you only get to spend it once.

26:1-32 This chapter completes David's preparations for the future temple. The gatekeepers (26:1) served as a security detail around the various gates, and they were carefully selected. They cast lots to determine their assignments (26:13). This doesn't mean, however, that the assignments were random. The Lord providentially directs all things. As Solomon would write years later, "The lot is cast in the lap, but its every decision is from the LORD" (Prov 16:33).

There were guards stationed at every watch (26:16). The temple of the Lord was to function twenty-four hours a day, seven days a week. The doors didn't close. This reminds us that worshiping God is full-time work.

Levites were also in charge of the treasuries of God's temple (26:20) and took care of the duties outside the temple as officers and judges over Israel (26:29). This concept of God-appointed spiritual leaders rendering decisions for his people, in fact, is reflected in Paul's rebuke of the Corinthians for not being able to decide disputes among themselves without having to take them downtown to secular judges (see 1 Cor 6:1-8). Civil government has its own sphere of operation in God's creation. But, as Paul reminds us, it's wrong to take church matters to the civil courts.

27:1-34 As a nation, Israel also had civil or secular leaders for other areas of administration besides worship and the functioning of the temple. These included military **commanders** and **their officers** (27:1-15). There were also leaders over the various **tribes of Israel** (27:16-22). A third group had authority over **the king's storehouses**, agriculture, and **herds** (27:25-31). Finally, there were counselors who advised the king on important matters (27:32-34).

God has ordained various forms of government in his creation: self-government, family government, church government, and civil government. The latter is a legitimate sphere within God's world—but it has a limited agenda. Jesus legitimized government, and also limited its reach, in one brilliant statement: "Give, then, to Caesar the things that are Caesar's, and to God the things that are God's" (Matt 22:21).

The biblical role of civil government is to maintain a safe, just, and righteous environment in which freedom can flourish. So, the government is supposed to spend its time and energy removing tyranny from the marketplace and producing harmony in society—in other words, promoting and administering justice, protecting law-abiding citizens, punishing the lawless, and ensuring that fairness operates in such areas as business and racial relationships. Government should work to prevent evil and injustice.

If individuals, families, and churches do their jobs—producing responsible self-government within individual lives—the civil government can focus on what it needs to focus on, rather than having to deal with people who look to the government to do everything for them. If you are expecting the civil government to do for you what God says you are to do for yourself, that is a misuse and misappropriation of government. Plus, if you expect Uncle Sam to do everything for you, you are destined for disappointment, anyway. Moreover, whenever we appeal to the civil government first to deal with a church matter like divorce, we rebel against God's decentralized approach to government and ignore the separate spheres of his governments.

G. David Delivers His Farewell Message and Dies (28:1-29:30)

28:1 The book of 1 Chronicles ends with an incredible display of spiritual leadership and worship. With everything ready for the temple's construction, **David assembled all the leaders of Israel in Jerusalem** for his final charge to them.

28:2-8 David rehearsed what we learned in chapter 17: he'd desired to build a temple for the Lord, but God told him his son would be the temple builder instead. But, David wanted to make something perfectly clear: **The LORD God of Israel chose me out of all my father's family to be king over Israel forever** (28:4). Moreover, God had chosen **Solomon to sit on the throne** after him and to **build** the temple (28:5-6). Notice how many times David said God "chose" him, his tribe, and his son in verses 4-7. This was his way of telling them, "This family's leadership over you is God's doing. Get on board."

The Lord said of Solomon, **I will establish his kingdom forever if he perseveres in keeping my commands and my ordinances as he is doing today** (28:7). Then, David said to the leaders, **observe and follow all the commands of the LORD your God so that you may possess this good land and leave it as an inheritance to your descendants forever** (28:8) Don't miss the emphasis here on the condition for success in God's kingdom: obedience to God and his Word.

28:9-21 **Solomon** was also present at this assembly, so David gave him a similar exhortation (28:9). He said, **Be strong, and do it** (28:10). Of course, this did not mean Solomon was to work in his own strength but rather in dependence on the Lord. David told him, **Be strong and courageous, and do the work. Don't be afraid or discouraged, for the LORD God, my God, is with you. He won't leave you or abandon you until all the work for the service of the LORD's house is finished** (28:20). The temple would be the greatest achievement of Solomon's reign and would require every ounce of his ability and dependence on God.

David handed over to Solomon all of the **plans** for the temple, its furnishings, and the divisions of the priests and Levites (28:11-18). With the help of the Lord, David had been enabled to complete all of the preparations (28:19). Nothing remained but to execute the plans.

29:1-5 David told the Israelites that the task they were about to begin was tremendous. But, he reminded them that **the building [would] not be built for a human but for the LORD** (29:1). In other words, they were not about to erect a skyscraper for the glory of man but a glorious temple for the worship of the living God. It would be worth the effort.

To the best of my ability I've made provision for the house of my God. David had acquired vast amounts of treasures for temple construction (29:2). But, that's not all. Because of his **delight in the house of [his] God**, he also gave his **personal treasures** (29:3). David set the example and gave generously. That's what leaders do.

29:6-9 In response to David's actions, the leaders **gave willingly** and generously (29:6-8). When the people saw this, they **rejoiced** and King David did, too (29:9). This offering was given so spontaneously, so open-handedly, and so willingly that it provided the necessary funds for God's work to be carried out without David even having to pass the plate.

29:10-19 What would drive believers to sacrificially give like this? That's a good question because the attitude of willingness and generosity reflected in this offering is meant to be the norm for God's people—not the exception. The answer to the question is found in David's prayer that followed the offering.

David praised God because he recognized some key truths about giving and gratitude that we sing and talk about in church, but don't always understand. David acknowledged that **everything in the heavens and on earth** belongs to the Lord in the first place (29:11). **Riches and honor come from him** (29:12). When we give to God, then, we are only giving back to him a portion of what he has given to us in the first place. David was rightly offering to God the praise due to him as the first and most abundant giver. If we

as Christians don't understand this principle of stewardship, we won't be inclined to give. God has richly provided everything we have or will have. We should have hearts of generosity and gratitude in response.

When my children were young, there were times when they would ask for money so they could buy me a birthday present. What they didn't realize was that they *needed* me to *bless* me. Now, I was still touched by their desire to give me a gift because their hearts were in the right place. But, you see, I wasn't any better off having received a present that I had paid for. What was meaningful to me was that my kids wanted to bless me out of their hearts of love for me.

David understood this principle clearly: **Everything comes from you, and we have given you only what comes from your own hand** (29:14). He even acknowledged that his people were really just renters, more or less tenant farmers in the land of Israel, which ultimately belonged to God, too (29:15).

In part, the reason he prayed this way was because he understood another principle of giving that we need to embrace. God tests **the heart** (29:17). When it's all said and done, giving is a heart thing. God is looking at the size of our hearts, not our checkbooks. Jesus gave us the best example of this in the story of the widow and her two small coins. He said of her actions, "This poor widow has put more into the treasury than all the others. For they all gave out of their surplus, but she out of her poverty has put in everything she had—all she had to live on" (Mark 12:43-44).

Embracing that everything we have is a gift from God is the genesis of both generosity and thanksgiving. This is why we must approach not only our giving, but also all of life from a kingdom perspective that recognizes that everything we have and are, or will ever have or be, is from God's hand. Like the lights on the dashboard of your car that show what's going on deep down under the hood, your willingness to give generously indicates whether your heart is right.

29:20-25 The people of Israel had their hearts right in 1 Chronicles 29, and it showed. The reaction to David's prayer was spontaneous and joyous. **The whole assembly** broke out into a worship party in which praise and

sacrifices were offered in amazing quantities (29:20-22). That set the perfect stage for David to, once again, bring Solomon before the nation and anoint him as God's chosen ruler (29:22-25).

Don't miss the chronicler's description in 29:23: **Solomon sat on the LORD's throne as king**. This indicates that although Solomon was the king, he was *God's* king, sitting on *God's* throne in *God's* kingdom. His was a stewardship of massive proportions.

The summary statement about Solomon's reign tells the story of his unparalleled blessing from God: **The LORD highly exalted Solomon in the sight of all Israel and bestowed on him such royal majesty as had not been bestowed on any king over Israel before him** (29:25). This insight makes it even more tragic that Solomon would later squander God's blessing (see 1 Kgs 11:1-13).

29:26-30 The final verses of 1 Chronicles summarize David's reign. David was like a lot of great figures from history in that his influence did not end with his death. But, unlike all other kings and leaders, one of David's descendants would have an eternal influence: his greater Son and our Savior, the Lord Jesus Christ. "He will reign on the throne of David and over his kingdom, to establish and sustain it with justice and righteousness from now on and forever" (Isa 9:6-7). David looked forward to that day, and so do we.

2 CHRONICLES

INTRODUCTION

Author

See discussion in 1 Chronicles.

Historical Background

See discussion in 1 Chronicles.

Message and Purpose

See discussion in 1 Chronicles.

www.bhpublishinggroup.com/qr/te/13_00

Outline

2 CHRONICLES

I. THE REIGN OF SOLOMON (1:1–9:31)

The book of 2 Chronicles continues the story of the Davidic monarchy in the southern kingdom of Judah following David's death. It begins with the reign of Solomon (starting about 970 BC) and ends with the reign of Zedekiah, the last king of Judah before the nation's descent into captivity in Babylon in 587–586 BC. This book omits any mention of the northern nation of Israel's kings during the time of the two kingdoms. Clearly, the chronicler's purpose was to focus on David's descendants, the messianic line.

✒ A. Solomon's Wisdom and Wealth (1:1-17) ✑

1:1-6 Following Solomon's accession to the throne, he **strengthened his hold on his kingdom** (1:1). Ancient kings often did that by eliminating disloyal people in the court and addressing threats to their reign—even if such a purge involved getting rid of family members. Solomon was no exception to this rule (see 1 Kgs 1–2), but he also quickly established his worthiness to rule by calling **every leader in all Israel** to accompany him to the **tabernacle** to offer **sacrifices** to the Lord (1:2-6). This is an indication of the chronicler's concern for the proper worship of God by his people, which was always the prerequisite for receiving God's blessing. This matter was especially relevant in the chronicler's day, hundreds of years after Solomon's time, when the people had returned from Babylon and were trying to put the nation and their lives back together.

1:7-17 This scene was clearly a high point of Solomon's reign—and happened at its very beginning. God asked Solomon, **What should I give you?** (1:7). Just imagine receiving this opportunity from the Lord! The sky's the limit. What would you ask for? The new king, acknowledging God's **great and faithful love** (1:8), humbly prayed for **wisdom** to guide God's people (1:10). When God offered him the world on a string, Solomon made the right choice. God was pleased with the request and granted the king **wisdom and knowledge** to **judge** the nation (1:11). Solomon also received abundant **riches, wealth,** and **glory**—greater than that enjoyed by any other king (1:12). We are given just a small sampling of Solomon's wealth in the closing verses of the chapter (1:14-17).

There is a powerful lesson for us right here at the front door of 2 Chronicles. We know from other portions of Scripture that Solomon began to abandon his God-given wisdom as the years passed and came to a bitter end (see 1 Kgs 11:1-43). The kingdom would eventually become divided because of Solomon's unfaithfulness (see 1 Kgs 11:11-13). And, even his great wealth and power became a source of frustration, pain, and regret to him as he explained in great detail in the book of Ecclesiastes. Solomon's life, then, is a sobering reminder of the fleeting nature of worldly fame, wealth, and power when they are not used for the glory of God.

Examples of this truth abound. Consider the legendary boxer Muhammad Ali. In his prime, Ali was easily the most famous athlete on earth. Later in life, however, Ali stated the futility of fame and power in a *Sports Illustrated* article. He took the reporter to the barn on his farm and showed him some mementos of his fabled career, but then, he turned the photos of his most well-known fights to the wall, walked to the door, looked out, and spoke so quietly the writer had to ask the champ to repeat himself. Ali famously said, "I had the world, and it wasn't nothing."

Solomon had wisdom and wealth beyond anyone else's, but, by themselves, they did not guarantee him spiritual success. His many wives and the pursuit of pleasure only led his heart away from the Lord. Few of us will know such fame and fortune in this life. Yet, all of us have a choice regarding whether we will use God's gifts to us for his glory or for our own. Keep this in mind: your personal glory has a limited shelf life.

B. Building the Temple (2:1–5:1)

Beginning in chapter 2, the subject turns to an important focus for the chronicler: the temple of the Lord that was to be built in Jerusalem. Even though the report of the temple's construction and dedication ends at 7:22, the temple and the proper worship of God it represented remain the focus of the chronicler's concern throughout the book. This focus is part of the chronicler's kingdom agenda.

There is good reason for this focus. The sad conclusion of 2 Chronicles is the final deportation of the people into exile for repeated violations of God's law, among which was their stubborn refusal to stop worshiping false gods. No sin could have been more offensive to the God of Israel, whose first commandment forbid the worship of false gods. He said, "Do not have other gods besides me" (Exod 20:3).

2:1-2 The prospect of judgment was far from anyone's mind when Solomon began assembling the materials and manpower needed to build his magnificent temple. His staggering workforce of more than 150,000 included **porters . . . stonecutters**, and **supervisors** (2:2). These were the foreign men living in Israel (2:17-18). Yet, even with this many people working on the project continuously, it took "seven years" to finish the temple (see 1 Kgs 6:37-38).

2:3-6 Solomon turned to **King Hiram of Tyre** for the materials needed for construction. In his letter to Hiram, Solomon diplomatically drew on the friendship Hiram had enjoyed with his **father David** (2:3). His letter praised **the LORD our God**, who is **greater than any of the gods** (2:4-5) and acknowledged that his temple could never **contain** God who reigns over all creation (2:4-6).

2:7-10 Solomon's request turned to the more formal terms as he requested a skilled craftsman to lead the work of adorning and beautifying the temple and also asked for the different kinds of wood and materials to be used in the construction (2:7-9). For Hiram's services, Solomon offered abundant agricultural produce (2:10).

2:11-16 Hiram's response, **Blessed be the LORD God of Israel, who made the heavens and the earth** (2:12), was most likely a courtesy response to Solomon and didn't necessarily reflect Hiram's personal faith in the true God. Hiram sent **Huram-Abi** to serve as **a skillful man** and to accomplish **all kinds of engraving** (2:13-14). Interestingly, he was a half-Israelite, which must have given him some advantage in working with Solomon's craftsmen and in understanding Israel's culture (2:14). With the payment agreed upon by the two kings, Solomon was ready to build his workforce and begin laying the foundation of the temple in **Jerusalem** (2:15-16).

2:17-18 The brief note that the job of the **supervisors** was **to make the people work** makes it clear that these thousands of foreign laborers were far from volunteers. In fact, the increasing harshness with which Solomon extracted what he needed even from his own people, became one of the major issues that led to the secession of Israel's ten northern tribes after his death (10:1-4).

3:1 The record of Solomon's temple construction begins with a very important geographical identifier—its location on **Mount Moriah**. This rise in Jerusalem is the place **where the LORD had appeared to his father David** (see 1 Chr 21:1–22:1), confirming the Lord's will that this was his chosen site. It was also the place where Abraham had offered Isaac in obedience to God (see Gen 22:2); that's the only other place where Moriah is mentioned by name in the Bible.

3:2-17 Solomon initiated the work in **the second day of the second month in the fourth year of his reign** (3:2).

The details of the temple's size, utensils, and furniture that fill these chapters are highlighted by the description of **the most holy place** (3:8), also known as the holy of holies. This was the inner sanctuary containing the ark of the covenant with its lid, or mercy seat. The high priest would enter that room once a year, on the Day of Atonement, to offer a sacrifice for the people's sins. The sight of the two gold **cherubim** standing over the ark, with a combined **wingspan** of **30 feet**, touching each other and the walls of the most holy place, must have been truly awe-inspiring (3:10-13).

4:1-10 The grand size of the **bronze altar** (4:1) is another indication of how magnificent Solomon's temple was. His workers also made a **basin** standing on **twelve** cast **oxen** that **could hold eleven thousand gallons** of water (4:2-5). The priests would ceremoniously wash themselves in this reservoir before performing their religious duties (4:6). In addition to this, there were **basins for washing** the **burnt offering** as well as **lampstands . . . tables**, and **bowls** (4:6-8).

4:11–5:1 Chapter 4 records the completion of the metalwork that **Huram** from Tyre (see 2:13-14) was contracted to do for Solomon (4:11-16). Solomon's wealth and the immensity of the temple made it impossible to calculate the amount of **bronze** used (4:18). Just as impressive is the fact that the rest of the temple's furnishings were made **of pure gold** (4:20). Nothing was too good for the Lord's temple. When the work was finally done and the temple was ready to be furnished, the treasures **David** had previously dedicated for the temple, when combined with those of Solomon, were so great that there was a surplus (5:1).

➢ C. Dedicating the Temple
(5:2–7:22) ⤸

5:2-3 A temple as magnificent as Solomon's deserved a dedication ceremony just as magnificent, and the king did not disappoint. The building was ready for worship, except for its most important piece of furniture: **the ark of the covenant**. That item had been temporarily located in **the city of David, that is, Zion** (5:2), an area of Jerusalem south of Mount Moriah where the new temple stood.

The chronicler noted that this great event occurred during the **festival** in **the seventh month**, which was the Festival of Shelters (or Tabernacles or Booths). This helps explain why **all the men of Israel were assembled in** Jerusalem at the time (5:3). The Festival of Shelters was one of Israel's three pilgrim festivals (along with Passover and Pentecost), during which all men were required to make their pilgrimage to Jerusalem. For that holiday, the people built temporary booths to live in for one week, commemorating the nation's exodus from Egypt when the Israelites became wanderers living in temporary dwellings as the Lord cared for them (see Lev 23:34-43).

5:4-10 Solomon accompanied the procession carrying the **ark** to the temple (5:4-6), just as his father David had done years earlier when the ark was brought into Jerusalem (see 1 Chr 15:25-29). As with all the festivities of this historic day, the procession was enormous in scope. So many sacrifices were offered along the route that they **could not be counted . . . because there were so many** (5:6).

The ark was being carried with **its poles** by Levites (5:7-9)—which was the correct way to transport it that contrasted with David's initial failure and subsequent correction in this regard (see 1 Chr 13:7, 9-10; 15:2, 13-15). The priests carried the **ark**, which contained **the two tablets** of the law that

Moses had put in it (5:10), and placed it in the most holy place, beneath the wings of the towering cherubim (5:7-8).

Would the ark stay there? Well, we know the ark was removed at least once, much later in Judah's history, probably during the debauched reign of Manasseh when he defiled the temple by setting up an idol in it. We know the ark was not in the temple at that time because Manasseh's godly grandson, Josiah, had to order the ark to be brought back to the temple and left there during his restoration (see commentary on 35:1-9).

5:11-14 The joyful worship and praise offered on this glorious day was led by the Levites with instrument and voice (5:11-13). What was their refrain of praise to the Lord? **He is good; his faithful love endures forever** (5:13). What we see translated as the phrase "faithful love" comes from the great Hebrew word that is variously translated in Bible versions as "loving kindness," "loyal love," or "mercy." This is the word for God's enduring love for Israel; it's a reminder of the covenant he made with the nation at Mount Sinai.

The people's praise pleased God, and he manifested his pleasure by filling his temple **with a cloud**, the visible symbol of his presence and **glory** (5:13-14).

Don't overlook this statement in verse 11: **all the priests who were present had consecrated themselves regardless of their divisions.** The priesthood had twenty-four divisions, which rotated the duties the men were required to perform. But, none of that mattered on this day because the people were coming together as one to worship and glorify the Lord. The priestly divisions were legitimate in order to get the work of the temple accomplished, but they were irrelevant in this situation in which God himself was the unified focus. **The trumpeters and singers** thus **joined together to praise and thank the LORD with one voice** (5:13). They exhibited unity in the midst of legitimate diversity. And, when they did, God showed up in a special way. Spiritual *unity* brings God's presence, while *disunity* creates God's absence. This is a vital kingdom perspective for today's church.

Oneness in the body of Christ, though, does not mean everyone is the same anymore than the Father, Son, and Holy Spirit are indistinct persons within the one God. They really are three, yet one. Those who make up the church aren't the same either. We're from different backgrounds and different ethnicities; we have different genders and personalities, and all of those are legitimate distinctions.

But, the oneness God wants from his church has to do with unity of purpose as people who have legitimate differences head toward the same goal line. Oneness means being on the same page spiritually. The devil wants to cause conflict because it creates disunity—and where there is disunity, God's glory won't show up.

6:1-11 Chapter 6 is an account of Solomon's blessing of the people and dedication prayer for the exalted temple where the Lord would **dwell** (6:1-2). After he **blessed the entire congregation** (6:3), the king praised **the LORD** for fulfilling his **promise** to **David** (6:3-4) to choose **Jerusalem** as the city for his own **name** (6:6). While God had not let David build the **temple**, he had promised this honor to his **son** (6:7-9). What he had **promised**, then, had now been **fulfilled** (6:10).

6:12-17 Solomon **stood before the altar** and **knelt down** on a specially made **bronze platform** to pray (6:12-13). The king first praised the Lord **who keeps his gracious covenant** with his people (6:14). Then, he again acknowledged that God had kept his **promise** to **David**: his son was not only on the throne, but also had built the temple (6:15). So, Solomon prayed God would continue to remain faithful, **never** failing to provide a son of David to sit **on the throne** (6:16-17).

The interesting thing is that God's promise to David and his successors could only be enjoyed by those kings who adhered to the Lord. Notice God's words in verse 16: **If only your sons guard their way to walk in my Law** (6:16). As the rest of 2 Chronicles makes clear, many of David's heirs failed at this and proved unworthy of the promise's blessing. But, God's promises can never fail. One day the perfect and divine Son of David, Jesus Christ, will reign on David's throne forever (see Luke 1:32-33).

6:18-21 Here, we find one of the greatest expressions of God's *transcendence* in Scripture: **Even heaven, the highest heaven, cannot contain you, much less this temple I have built** (6:18). God is transcendent. In other words, he is independent of the universe. He is our Creator and sustainer. So, how can humans expect him to dwell in a temple?

The answer is found in the reality that ours is not a God who is aloof from his creation and takes no interest in human affairs. He is not only transcendent, he is also *immanent*—that is, he is present within his creation while remaining distinct from it. And, this is what Solomon knew. That's why he prayed! He asked God to **listen** and **hear** him, so that his **eyes** would **watch over** the **temple** (6:19-20). And, because our big, transcendent God is also close to us, Solomon also asked him to **forgive** his people when they cried out to him (6:21).

6:22-42 With praises and requests as a backdrop, Solomon prayed in great detail (6:22-39) for God's mercy on Israel when the people committed any number of wrongs and returned to the Lord in repentance, seeking forgiveness. This catalog of offenses is punctuated by variations on this recurring prayer: **may you hear in heaven and forgive the sin of your people Israel** (6:25; see also 3:23, 27, 30, 33, 39). The king then concluded his prayer the way it had begun, with the plea that God would remember his **servant David** (6:42).

7:1-3 The close of Solomon's prayer brought down the consuming **fire** of God **from heaven** on **the sacrifices**, and his **glory** cloud **filled the temple** (7:1). **All the Israelites** could do was bow down with their **faces to the ground** in awe and godly fear (7:3).

As glorious as the coming of God's glory was on that day, Ezekiel the prophet would witness the tragic departure of the glory cloud generations later during a time of great apostasy on the part of Judah (see Ezek 10:18). But, importantly, in Ezekiel's vision of a new temple, he saw the glory of God returning (see Ezek 43:4-5).

The arrival and departure of God's glory in his house points to an important lesson for modern Christians. For Israel, the way

things worked in society was determined by the way things worked, or did not work, in the temple. So, in the event that God left the temple, the problems showed up in the streets. Yet, when God returned his manifest presence to the temple, the healing showed up in the streets, as well. God's first concern in his kingdom agenda should be ours. We, however, get all worked up about what is happening, or going to happen, in the White House or the Supreme Court without giving much thought to what is happening, or not happening, in God's church. We must understand that if God doesn't see the church getting things right, it doesn't matter whom we elect to the White House. Both judgment and healing start with the household of God. I believe the reason for our cultural demise is spiritual. And, if a problem is spiritual, its cure must be spiritual. Pursing right relationship with God is our solution.

7:4-7 Solomon offered so many **sacrifices** that the bronze altar couldn't accommodate them all! So, **the courtyard** of the temple was **consecrated**, and the rest of the offerings were made there.

7:8-11 For the next week, Israel celebrated the temple's dedication followed by still another week of observing the Festival of Booths (7:8-9). Then, finally, Solomon sent everyone away **with happy hearts for the goodness the LORD had done** (7:10). **Everything that had entered Solomon's heart to do for the LORD's temple . . . succeeded** (7:11).

7:12-16 God **heard** Solomon's **prayer** (7:12), which indicates that there's always hope if God's people will fall on their knees and pray as the people did at the dedication of Solomon's temple. We need not merely talk about prayer; we must actually pray. And, when we do, we may be able to move the hand of God to bring restoration. Consider God's promise to Solomon: **If I shut the sky so there is no rain, or if I command the grasshopper to consume the land, or if I send pestilence on my people, and my people, who bear my name, humble themselves, pray and seek my face, and turn from their evil ways, then I will hear from heaven, forgive their sin, and heal their land** (7:13-14).

In this hallmark passage, God calls his people to pray. Prayer is an earthly request for heavenly intervention. It is the tool we have been given in order to pull something down out of the invisible and into the visible. Prayer enacts God's hand in history like nothing else because prayer is humanity's relational communication with God.

There are several key elements in 2 Chronicles 7:14 that determine whether a prayer will prove effective. The first element is found in the words "my people, who bear my name." This is a reference to God's covenant people. We can approach God through our new-covenant relationship with his Son.

The second element of prayer that moves God is the heart attitude of those who seek him. God seeks those who "humble themselves." Humble Christians get through to God, for they renounce pride. Humility includes the idea of dependency—the recognition that without the Lord, we can do nothing (see John 15:5). Prayer, in fact, is by its nature an admission of our weakness and need. Many Christians don't pray because they are too proud.

A third element related to prayer's effectiveness is God's call to "seek [his] face." That is, to seek his forgiveness and favor. We saw an example of this kind of prayer in 7:3, where the people of Israel were so overcome by the manifestation of God's presence that they fell on their faces in worship. So, seeking God's face means much more than saying "thank you for this food" or reciting "now I lay me down to sleep." Prayer that moves God comes from a recognition that sin turns his face away from us and turns us away from him. It approaches God on his terms. Prayer is not a process of negotiation. It requires seeking and accepting God's terms of reconciliation. The good news is that God invites us to seek his face. He is open to us.

The fourth and final element of effective prayer is for God's people to "turn from their evil ways." The idea here is of turning away from something that displeases God and turning toward something that pleases him. If we, as God's people, want God to show his face to us, we must turn toward him in repentance. That involves turning our backs on sin—anything that is contrary to his will.

7:17-22 The final words from the Lord recorded in this chapter include his promise of blessing if the king walks in God's ways and judgment for sin if he turns away from keeping God's commands (7:17-20). Many years later, when the inhabitants of Jerusalem were finally uprooted from their land and sent into exile in Babylon, the people would ask, "How could such a calamity fall on us? Aren't we God's people, the object of his favor?" The explanation for God's judgment should have been clear to them: **they abandoned the LORD God of their ancestors who brought them out of the land of Egypt. They clung to other gods and bowed in worship to them and served them. Because of this, he brought all this ruin on them** (7:22).

➤ D. Solomon's Kingdom (8:1–9:31) ❧

8:1-10 Solomon spent the first half of his forty-year reign occupied primarily with building the **temple and his own palace** (8:1). And, once they were complete, he was ready to turn his attention to other matters. His desire to extend his kingdom into foreign lands is evident by his conquest of **Hamath-zobah**, a city in modern-day Syria that was almost three hundred miles north of Jerusalem (8:3). Solomon's **storage cities** (8:4, 6) in the north and south of his territory also give us a sense of the reach of his empire.

Previously, the chronicler reported that Solomon conscripted a large number of conquered people ("resident alien men," 2:17) to work on the temple. These were the **descendants** of the Canaanite peoples whom **the Israelites had not completely destroyed** as God had commanded. **Solomon** had **imposed forced labor on them** then, and they were still being used in this way in the chronicler's day (8:8).

8:11 Here, we find a hint of what helped to bring about Solomon's eventual downfall. He had married **the daughter of the Pharaoh**, a union that may have been as much political as it was personal because it was common for rulers in that day to cement treaties or other agreements through marriage. Pharaoh's daughter, though, was only the first of many foreign women Solomon married. These were "women from the nations about which the LORD had told the Israelites, 'You must not intermarry with them, and they must not intermarry with you, because they will turn you away to follow their gods.' To these women Solomon was deeply attached in love . . . and they turned his heart away [from the Lord]" (1 Kgs 11:1-3).

The key to this destructive influence was the fact that Solomon accommodated his wives' worship of their false gods, while also trying to remain true to the Lord—which was a losing battle. We see a glimpse of this struggle in Solomon's concern for **the places** connected with the holy **ark** of the covenant. David's palace was erected at one of these locations, so Solomon built a separate palace for his Egyptian wife, lest her pagan origin and ways defile David's palace.

8:12-16 Ironically, the hint about Solomon's accommodation to his pagan wife is followed immediately by this report of his great devotion to the Lord. The chronicler notes approvingly that Solomon **followed the daily requirement for offerings according to the commandment of Moses** (8:13). The king also followed **the ordinances of his father David** (8:14) in terms of maintaining the divisions of the priests and Levites that David had instituted. Solomon's diligence in building the temple and establishing its worship was such that there were no deviations from his orders (8:15). Most important of all for the chronicler's purpose, he was able to report that **the LORD's temple was completed** (8:16).

8:17-18 Solomon owned a fleet of commercial ships that brought precious metals, spices, and beautiful woods to Jerusalem. Hiram, the king of Tyre, helped Solomon in this venture by sending him experienced Phoenician sailors (8:18). Trips to such places as **Ophir**, which may have been as far away as east Africa or India, allowed Solomon to tap into incredible resources to enrich his kingdom.

9:1-12 Perhaps the most famous event in Solomon's reign was the visit by **the queen of Sheba** (9:1). Her introduction here may

be a reference to the Sabean peoples of southwestern Arabia. By her report, the wisdom and wealth Solomon possessed was known far and wide. The king's thoughtful answers to her difficult questions and the sight of his wealth **took her breath away** (9:4). Though she had brought some of her own stockpile of wealth to Solomon (9:9), he sent her back with **more than she had delivered** (9:12).

9:13-28 Mention of the queen's visit led the chronicler to a catalog of Solomon's riches. His annual income of **twenty-five tons** of **gold** did not even include the revenue brought in by his commercial navy or the tribute (that is, the taxes) paid to him by lesser rulers (9:13-14). The **two hundred large shields of hammered gold** and **three hundred small shields of hammered gold** (9:15-16) were ornamental rather than military in nature; nevertheless, they must have been a very impressive sight. Solomon also built a **throne** unlike anything that had ever been seen before (9:17-19). The chronicler provides an apt summary of the state of affairs during the heyday of Solomon's reign: [He] surpassed all the kings of the world in riches and wisdom. All the kings of the world wanted an audience with Solomon to hear the wisdom God had put in his heart (9:22-23).

9:29-31 The remaining events of Solomon's reign, from beginning to end (9:29), were recorded in other places now lost to history. In Scripture, we learn much more about him in 1 Kings, but the events acknowledged there were not part of the chronicler's focus and purpose.

Rumblings related to the trouble to come must have been in existence even before this king's death, because we know that many of Solomon's subjects chafed under aspects of his reign. But, it's safe to say that no one in Israel could have foreseen, at the time, that Solomon's death would end Israel's golden age begun under David, pave the way for a bitter division of the nation, and open the floodgates of idolatry. Solomon did not live to see the damage done by his departure from the Lord, but his descendants did.

II. THE DIVIDED KINGDOM AND THE KINGS OF JUDAH (10:1–36:23)

After a period of having a united Israel ruled by Saul, David, and then Solomon, the Israelites would split their tribes into two kingdoms. Israel would be the name of the kingdom of the north, spanning ten tribes, and Judah would be the name of the southern kingdom, which would include the tribes of Judah and Benjamin. Jeroboam would be the first king of the new Israel, and Rehoboam (Solomon's son) would be the first king of Judah. Importantly, the northern kingdom would be ruled entirely by evil kings for more than two hundred years; it would fall to the Assyrians in 722 BC. The southern kingdom of Judah, based in Jerusalem, would be ruled by a mixture of good and evil kings before finally falling to the Babylonians in 587–586 BC.

❧ A. Rehoboam (10:1–12:16) ❧

10:1-3 Solomon's death brought **Rehoboam** to the throne—ironically, he was the only one of what must have been the many sons of Solomon to be named in Scripture. Clearly, Rehoboam was his father's choice. The chronicler also introduces **Jeroboam**, an influential man and one of Solomon's officials (10:1-2; see 1 Kgs 11:26-28). Previously, Jeroboam had rebelled against Solomon, possibly over the king's harsh labor practices and heavy taxation. Solomon had tried to kill Jeroboam, who fled to Egypt (see 1 Kgs 11:40). But, with Solomon dead, Jeroboam felt it was safe to return to Israel (10:2).

Jeroboam's stature among the people is obvious from the fact that they **summoned him** to lead them in bringing their complaints to Rehoboam (10:3). And, as a result of that encounter, what was meant to be Rehoboam's coronation quickly turned into a confrontation in which the people made it inextricably clear to Rehoboam that he could not simply continue the policies of his father without making some major concessions.

10:4-14 Lighten your father's harsh service and the heavy yoke he put on us, and we will serve you (10:4). The statement sounds very much like a loyalty oath conditioned on Rehoboam's willingness to act on their concerns. But, rather than taking immediate, decisive action on the matter, the king asked for **three days** to consult his advisors—both the wise **elders** inherited from his father and his homeys, a group of **young men** like him who were feeling their new power and were itching for a fight (10:5-11).

The elders' advice isn't surprising, given that they had served under Solomon and could see the handwriting on the wall in terms of the trouble Rehoboam was facing if he did not lighten the people's heavy workload. It didn't take a prophet to see that "all Israel" (10:3) had more than the celebration of Rehoboam's assumption of the throne on their minds. The **kind words** the elders advised the king to give may have indicated something stronger than mere gentle comments; it may have suggested that they wanted him to make an alliance with the people in which Rehoboam would commit himself to the asked-for reforms (10:7).

Rehoboam, though, was in no mood for concessions, so **he rejected** the elders' advice and turned to his boys (10:8-9). Their counsel, by contrast, was designed not only to reject the people's demands, but also to serve notice that Rehoboam and his men were clearly in charge (10:10). The **barbed whips** (10:11) with which they threatened the people were particularly vicious whips, something like those used to flog Jesus before his crucifixion. Rehoboam foolishly embraced the advice of fools (10:12-14).

10:15 You might wonder how Rehoboam could be such a fool as to follow advice destined to split the kingdom. However, "destined" is an appropriate word here because the chronicler put all these events in perspective when he said **the turn of events came from God**, who had sovereignly decreed that judgment was to fall on Solomon's house because of his departure from the Lord (see 1 Kgs 11:26-40).

10:16-19 In order to fulfill his promise to David, God allowed Solomon's descendants to hold on to the southern kingdom. Rehoboam's harsh answer, however, infuriated the people from the northern part of Israel. They made their discontent known in a deadly way by stoning the king's labor overseer and almost killing Rehoboam himself (10:18). The **rebellion** was on, and from this point until the fall of the southern kingdom many years later, the name "**Israel**" would no longer designate the chosen nation; it referred only to the northern kingdom consisting of ten tribes (10:19).

It's helpful to recall at this point that the chronicler is not interested in the events or kings of Israel because his focus is on Jerusalem, the temple, and the Davidic kingdom. Even the key prophecy, in which God promised the ten tribes to Jeroboam and offered him an enduring kingdom if he would be faithful to the Lord (see 1 Kgs 11:29-39), does not merit a mention in 2 Chronicles. (And, for the record, Jeroboam would *not* follow the Lord.)

11:1-12 As the northern tribes stormed off to their homes in anger, Rehoboam returned to Jerusalem and mustered his army from the two tribes left to him, **Judah and Benjamin** (11:1). In the years ahead, there would be many bloody conflicts between Israel and Judah—but not this time. God intervened, sending the prophet **Shemaiah** to Rehoboam with this message: **You are not to march up and fight against your brothers. Each of you must return home, for this incident has come from me** (11:2-4). To his credit, the king obeyed the Lord and sent his troops home. But, Rehoboam **fortified** his kingdom, making his defensive perimeter **very strong** (11:5-12).

11:13-16 Another development that strengthened Judah was the defection of the **priests and Levites from** the northern kingdom to Jerusalem because they wanted to worship the Lord in the true way (11:13-14). Jeroboam, meanwhile, **appointed his own priests** and made idols for the people of the

northern kingdom to worship in an attempt to keep them from going south to Jerusalem (11:15). Jeroboam feared that pilgrimages to the temple in Jerusalem would give the northern tribes incentive to go back to King Rehoboam. As a result, **Those from every tribe of Israel who had determined in their hearts to seek the Lord** moved to Judah (11:16).

11:17-23 The chronicler says the refugees added to Judah's strength, both by their numbers (presumably) and **because they walked in the ways of David and Solomon**. Unfortunately, though, Rehoboam's good situation only lasted **three years** (11:17). Like his father, he had many **wives** and children (11:18-21), among whom was **Abijah**, Rehoboam's choice to succeed him as king (11:22). While Rehoboam showed some initial discernment in his rule (11:23), it didn't last long.

12:1-4 Once **Rehoboam had established his sovereignty and royal power**, he led the people in apostasy and **abandoned the law of the Lord** (12:1). In other words, with his throne secure and his military position strong, Rehoboam became spiritually careless. Yet, when God brought the pharaoh **Shishak** against Judah, Rehoboam's **fortified cities** in which he had come to trust were overrun and the Egyptians were soon at the gates of **Jerusalem** (12:2-4).

12:5-11 God sent the prophet **Shemaiah** to Rehoboam again with a message: **You have abandoned me; therefore, I have abandoned you to Shishak** (12:5). Now, at this word, Rehoboam and his leaders **humbled themselves** before God and instead of begging God to turn the Egyptians back and spare Jerusalem, they acknowledged their sin and declared, **The Lord is righteous** (12:6). Thus, God relented from pouring out his **wrath** on Judah (12:7); nevertheless, **Shishak** plundered the **temple** and the **palace** before he withdrew (12:9). Moreover, Judah became Shishak's servant. This was God's punishment intended to help Rehoboam and Judah **recognize the difference between serving [God] and serving the kingdoms of other lands** (11:8). It was a hard lesson.

12:12-16 Rehoboam's reign was a sad mixture of good and evil—of what might have been and what actually was. There was some **good in Judah** (12:12), and Rehoboam rallied after the invasion by the Egyptians to regain some of his former power. But, the summary of his reign was that **Rehoboam did what was evil, because he did not determine in his heart to seek the LORD** (12:14). That is a tragic way to be remembered.

⇝ B. Abijah and Asa (13:1–16:14) ⇜

13:1-12 The chronicler's report of the brief reign of **Abijah** is dominated by the account of his war with **Jeroboam** (13:1-2). Israel's forces outnumbered Judah's two-to-one (13:3). Abijah made a remarkable effort to avoid bloodshed between brothers with his speech to Jeroboam and Israel's forces. In it, he reviewed the events that had brought the two sides into conflict (13:4-12).

Abijah reminded Israel's army that the kingdom rightly belonged to David and his descendants, by virtue of God's eternal **covenant** (13:5). The king also revealed his disdain for Jeroboam's followers, calling them **worthless and wicked men**. According to Abijah, Jeroboam had confronted Rehoboam when the latter was **young, inexperienced, and unable to assert himself against** Jeroboam and his band of rebels (13:7). (Whether this was partially true or just a son's defense of his father, however, Rehoboam had still been responsible for his actions.)

More important, Abijah pointed out that Israel's army was being led by the **golden calves** Jeroboam had made and the false **priests** he had ordained (13:8-9). By contrast, Abijah declared, **As for us, the LORD is our God** (13:10). In other words, he said, his nation of Judah was still faithfully led in worship by the priests and Levites offering sacrifices at the temple in Jerusalem as instructed long ago (13:11). Abijah ended his speech with a plea to Jeroboam not to attack Judah—which he equated to a **fight against the LORD** God. He warned, **you will not succeed** (13:12).

13:13-18 Yet, even as Abijah spoke, Jeroboam's army rose up in **ambush** (13:13). Judah was outnumbered and surrounded, but they responded with worship and **cried out to the LORD** (13:14). As **the priests blew the trumpets**, Judah's soldiers met the men of Israel in battle. Clearly, God heard Judah's cry for help because, according to the chronicler, **God routed Jeroboam and all Israel** (13:14-15). The forces of Judah were victorious **because they depended on the LORD, the God of their ancestors** (13:18).

13:19–14:1 After this event, Jeroboam lost power . . . **the LORD struck him and he died** (13:20). Meanwhile, **Abijah grew strong** (13:21). When he died, his son **Asa became king** in Judah (14:1).

14:2-7 Asa was a faithful king who began well, doing **what was good and right in the sight of the LORD his God** (14:2). He was deliberate about destroying idol worship in Judah and fortifying his territory against future attack (14:3-5). Asa was able to build defenses and his army without interference. We are told plainly that **No one made war with him in those days because the LORD gave him rest** (14:6). This is a reminder that while erecting defensive fortifications against enemy attack is good and wise, peace and safety ultimately come from the Lord. Asa acknowledged this. He said, **The land is still ours because we sought . . . our God** (14:7).

14:8-15 In God's timing, however, Asa's years of peace came to an end when a huge army led by **Zerah the Cushite** attacked Judah at **Mareshah**, located about twenty-five miles southwest of Jerusalem (14:9). Again, Judah led the battle with worship and prayer. Asa called on the Lord, expressing his people's dependence on him and asking God to give them victory. Though the enemy had a **large army**, Asa knew they were like a **mere mortal** compared to the Lord (14:11). And, again, God answered prayer in a big way. He **routed the Cushites** on Judah's behalf, and **the people of Judah carried off a great supply of loot** back to **Jerusalem** (14:12-15).

15:1-6 The next recorded event of Asa's reign was his visit from the prophet **Azariah**, who had been led to him by **the Spirit of God**. Azariah urged the king and the people of **Judah and Benjamin** to continue seeking the Lord (15:1-2). The prophet reinforced his message by reminding Asa of the sad condition God's people had experienced during an earlier age, which many Bible commentators believe to be a reference to the period of the judges (15:3-6). If so, Azariah was speaking of Israel's lowest spiritual point.

Several things from these verses are worth noting. For instance, the description of a society in which **there was no peace for those who went about their daily activities because the residents of the lands had many conflicts** (15:5) sounds much like what we see in our world today. Our culture, too, is experiencing chaos and confusion. But, what ought to grab our attention here is the statement that Judah's situation came about because **God troubled** the people (15:6). God was the author of their lack of peace, although he was not in any way the author of their sin that had provoked his judgment. What was it about this period of Israel's history that caused God to deliver distress? **For many years Israel [had] been without the true God, without a teaching priest, and without instruction** (15:3).

The first problem referenced is the lack of "the true God." This does not mean that God had withdrawn himself from Israel. Even in the days of the judges, there was religious activity happening there. But, while people were offering sacrifices to God, they were not practicing the kind of authentic religion that pleased him or produced the right kind of response from him.

So, what could have caused such ineffectiveness? The answer is suggested in the second problem, that "Israel was without a teaching priest." Without a faithful teacher of spiritual truth, God's people became confused about the nature of God and mixed their true beliefs with the false ones of the surrounding peoples. The priests, then, were doing an inadequate job of providing a divine viewpoint through which the people could interpret all of life and make God-honoring decisions. There was a systemic spiritual failure at the heart of Israel's spiritual leadership that kept the people ill-informed about their responsibility before God and the consequences of failing to meet his demands.

The third problem follows as a natural consequence of the first two. Because the people lacked faithful teaching about the one true God, they were essentially left "without instruction." They didn't know how to apply God's Word to the situations they faced. And, because the divine rules weren't being applied, the people made up their own. One repeated phrase from the book of Judges illustrates this problem perfectly: "Everyone did whatever seemed right to him" (Judg 17:6; 21:25).

Because the basic realities of spiritual conflict and the superior power of the spiritual world haven't changed since the days of the judges in ancient Israel, we can still see the same principle of the visible world being controlled by the invisible world at work today. For God's kingdom people to experience lives that please him and demonstrate his glory in the world, they need knowledge of his kingdom agenda as expressed through his Word. Today, the vehicle on earth through which God teaches his Word and builds up his people is the church of Jesus Christ. Through Christ, believers may know "the only true God" (John 17:3) and "be sanctified by the truth" for earthly living (John 17:18-19).

15:7 As for you, be strong; don't give up, for your work has a reward. These words recall the Lord's admonition to Joshua to be courageous in taking the promised land (see Josh 1:6-9). In light of Israel's prior spiritual degradation, Azariah encouraged Asa to take courage and remember that doing God's work never goes unseen or unrewarded in the long run. As Paul would tell the church in Corinth many years later, "Be steadfast, immovable, always excelling in the Lord's work, knowing that your labor in the Lord is not in vain" (1 Cor 15:58).

15:8-19 God's words through the prophet didn't fall on deaf ears. Asa took the admonition to heart in a dramatic way. **He took courage** and pushed ahead with his reforms, removing **the abhorrent idols** from the land and renovating **the altar** in the Lord's temple (15:8). **When they saw that the Lord his God was with** Asa, many people from the idolatrous northern kingdom of Israel **defected to him** (15:9). This suggests that those whose hearts are devoted to the Lord recognize godly spiritual leadership and initiative when they see it.

A day came when the king **gathered** his subjects together for a service of sacrifice and worship (15:9-15). **They entered into a covenant to seek the LORD God of their ancestors with all their heart** (15:12). The people took this so seriously, in fact, that anyone who failed to pledge faithfulness to Asa's covenant was **put to death** (15:13). The chronicler even records how loudly and enthusiastically the people vowed to follow the Lord; they **rejoiced** (15:14-15). For seeking God wholeheartedly, the people received God's blessing: **He was found by them.** Moreover, he gave them protection from their enemies, **rest on every side** (15:15; see 15:19).

16:1-6 Within these chapters is an important lesson: past spiritual victory does not guarantee future spiritual success. Committing oneself to God's agenda is a day-by-day experience.

Things changed for Asa in the final years of his reign—or, more precisely, he changed in his attitudes and actions during those last years. Despite having sought God's deliverance from the Cushite forces years earlier, Asa panicked and failed to rely on the Lord when **Israel's King Baasha went to war against Judah** (16:1). Perhaps Asa had become complacent during those two decades of peace and spiritual prosperity. But, whatever the reason for Asa's lack of trust, he bribed the pagan king **Ben-hadad** of Aram (which is modern-day Syria) to break his treaty with Israel and attack them so that Baasha would withdraw from threatening Judah (16:2-5). Asa used **silver and gold** from the temple's **treasuries** to pay the bribe, which must have been offensive to the Lord (16:2).

16:7-10 Asa's scheme was a military success but a spiritual failure, a reminder that earthly victory is worthless when it comes at the expense of divine favor. God sent **the seer Hanani** to deliver the news to Asa (16:7). He pointed out that when Asa had **depended on the LORD** in the past, God had come through (16:8). He said God's **eyes** are always

watching; he knows **those who are wholeheartedly devoted to him** (16:9). Yet, instead of falling on his face in repentance before the Lord at this word, Asa reacted like a typical ancient ruler whose actions were called into question. He became enraged at Hanani and **put him in prison.** Then, he took out the rest of his rage on his own people and **mistreated** them (16:10).

16:11-12 An event at the end of Asa's life further marred his early legacy as a godly king. He contracted **a disease in his feet**—probably gout, that left him with severe pain. But, apparently, Asa had become so hardened by that time that **he didn't seek the LORD** for healing **but only the physicians** (16:12). Doing the same is a temptation for us today. We should be grateful for the blessings of doctors and modern medicine. But, ultimately, all healing comes from the Lord. So, visit your physician and take your medication. But, first, pray.

16:13-14 Asa's death provides a good place to remind ourselves of those to whom the chronicler was writing in his day. His audience lived a generation or so after Israel's return from the Babylonian captivity, which had been a crushing blow that fell because the people and their leaders failed to seek the Lord's agenda. The chronicler's choice of events to record from the lives of kings like Asa (who often got things right, though not always) was done purposefully. It reminded God's people of the importance of *complete* faithfulness to him.

✒ C. Jehoshaphat (17:1–20:37) ✒

17:1-6 Asa's son **Jehoshaphat** began his twenty-five-year reign in a strong position, both spiritually and militarily (17:1-2). **The LORD was with** him **because he walked in the former ways of . . . David** (17:3). Jehoshaphat rejected idolatry and followed God's commands (17:3-4, 6). The king's **mind rejoiced in the LORD's ways** (17:6). He believed the words written by his great-great-great-grandfather David: "Take delight in the LORD, and he will give you your heart's desires" (Ps 37:4). Therefore, **the Lord established the kingdom in his hand** (17:5).

17:7-9 One significant detail of this king's reign was the fact that he sent a group of **his officials**, along with **Levites** and **priests**, throughout Judah to teach the people **the Lord's instruction**. This tells us that Jehoshaphat took steps to ensure that God's people did not flounder in ignorance of God's Word; he essentially protected them from confusion and idolatry. Today, this same responsibility is laid on church leaders for the good of their congregations and on parents for the good of their children.

17:10-19 Jehoshaphat had a clear sense of his kingdom priorities. It's why he created an environment in which the ministry of God's Word could flourish. And, as a result of God's Word being honored among the people, God honored Jehoshaphat's kingdom. **The terror of the Lord** fell on the surrounding nations, and they paid **tribute to Jehoshaphat** (17:10-11). This testified to what God told his people in an earlier generation: "I will honor those who honor me" (1 Sam 2:30). Therefore, **Judah** became strong and **fortified** (17:12-19).

18:1-4 Jehoshaphat did make some questionable choices. He made alliances—marital, military, and commercial—with the northern kingdom of Israel, one of which almost cost him his life. Possibly the most glaring was an **alliance** he made with wicked King **Ahab** of Israel **through marriage** when his son married Ahab's daughter (18:1; see 21:6).

Another time, Ahab was engaged in fierce warfare with the Arameans (Syrians) and needed Jehoshaphat's help to take the strategic city of **Ramoth-gilead** (18:2-3), situated about fifty miles northeast of Jerusalem on the east side of the Jordan River. Ahab won Jehoshaphat's pledge to fight alongside Israel. But, to his credit, Jehoshaphat had enough spiritual sensitivity to insist on asking **the Lord's will** first (18:4).

18:5-27 Here is an amazing picture of what it's like to teach and uphold God's Word in a nation lacking spiritual guidance or commitment to truth at any official level. Ahab's **four hundred** false **prophets** desired only

to flatter their master, predicting a favorable outcome for an upcoming battle (18:5, 9-11). But, the faithful prophet **Micaiah** stood alone against the idea. Ahab complained that Micaiah **never** prophesied **good** about him **but only disaster** (18:16-17), suggesting that king wanted "yes men" not "truth-tellers" to counsel him. In any event, when asked to **speak favorably** about the matter at hand, Micaiah declared, **As the Lord lives, I will say whatever my God says** (18:12-13). He spoke about Israel's apostasy and prophesied King Ahab's downfall in battle (18:16, 22, 27).

Micaiah also explained why Ahab's four hundred prophets were wrong. Ahab was under God's judgment, and God was planning his defeat. Amazingly, **a lying spirit** volunteered to **entice** Ahab to attack the Arameans. Though God was not the author of the lie, he permitted the lying spirit to do his work to bring about Ahab's **disaster** (18:18-22). Later, in a similar way, God would permit a "messenger of Satan" to torment Paul in order to humble the apostle and cause him to depend more on the Lord (2 Cor 12:7-10). The main difference between the two instances is that Paul learned from the experience, but Ahab pressed on in his arrogance—even when he was told that his prophets were deceived.

18:28-34 Ahab was unfazed by Micaiah's prophecy of disaster and **went up to Ramoth-gilead** for war (18:28). But, apparently, Ahab decided a little precaution couldn't hurt. He planned to **disguise** himself in battle while Jehoshaphat wore his **royal attire** (18:29). (Surprisingly, Jehoshaphat agreed to the scheme.) Ahab may have thought he could fool God and prevent the prophecy's fulfillment. But, it didn't work. The disguised king was killed when an enemy archer **drew his bow without taking special aim**. Of course, nothing is random in a universe governed by an omniscient (all-knowing) and omnipotent (all-powerful) God. The divinely directed arrow struck Ahab at a weak point in **his armor**, and **he died** (18:33-34). Meanwhile, Jehoshaphat escaped only because God **helped him** (18:31).

19:1-3 Importantly, Jehoshaphat did not escape a stern rebuke from the Lord through

Jehu son of the seer for his foolish decision to side with Ahab (19:2). Though the prophet praised the king for opposing idolatry in the land (19:3), he chastised him for helping **wicked** Ahab and loving **those who hate the LORD** (19:2).

19:4-11 Instead of throwing Jehu in prison, as Ahab had done to Micaiah for his rebuke (18:26), Jehoshaphat took God's message to heart. He responded in faith and obedience by launching a new series of reforms throughout the land. Jehoshaphat **appointed judges** and **priests** to render judgments and hear disputes **in the fear of the LORD, with integrity, and wholeheartedly** (19:5, 8-9).

Though we do not live in Old Testament Israel, our civil government today is accountable to God to do good, too—to act with justice and righteousness (see Rom 13:3-4). The church's responsibility with regard to civil government is to make sure that the state doesn't lose sight of the truth that God rules and that there is a moral standard by which the political realm must operate. The church is to exercise a prophetic role of being a voice for God and his righteous standards. Our government is in desperate need of leaders who can inject righteousness and justice into our political bloodstream, for a society can never rise above the quality of its leadership.

20:1-12 God had one more great test of faith for Jehoshaphat. Word arrived that **the Moabites and Ammonites** were preparing to attack (20:1). **Jehoshaphat was afraid**, but he called a nationwide **fast** and held a service to **seek the LORD** (20:3-4). When all the people had assembled, Jehoshaphat offered a powerful prayer (20:6-12).

He acknowledged that their God ruled over all nations and none could stand against him (20:6). He professed that Abraham's descendants were his **people**, lived in the **land** he gave them, and built a **sanctuary** for his **name** (20:7-8). They trusted in the Lord's promise to **deliver** them when they called to him (20:9). Finally, he surveyed the current threat from an unjust nation and implored God to intervene (20:10-12).

Jehoshaphat knew what to do because he was familiar with King Solomon's prayer given over a century earlier at the temple

dedication (see 6:28-30). He even referred to that prayer in his own intercession (20:8-9) because his crisis was exactly the kind of disaster Solomon had prayed about. Solomon had talked about the Lord going out from his temple and fighting the battles for his people. Jehoshaphat spoke to the Lord about the same thing and in the same terms. God's people were under attack, and the promised land was being threatened. But, Jehoshaphat knew that victory by God's hand had been promised long ago. And, Jehoshaphat knew that God keeps his promises.

This is a powerful example for Christians of how to respond to crises and prevail in God's strength. Though Christians can still be overwhelmed by a crisis situation just like people of the world can, we have the option of looking to the Lord for his intervention and deliverance when we don't know what to do—as Jehoshaphat did when he faced his enemies.

20:13-19 God answered the king's prayer through a man named **Jahaziel**, through whom **the Spirit of the LORD** encouraged the king and the people. Note Jahaziel's declaration: **the battle is not yours, but God's** (20:14-15). In other words, the Lord was telling his people, "I've got this." In fact, even though the king's forces would have to face the enemy, they wouldn't have to fire a single arrow (20:16-17). At this news, Jehoshaphat and all the people **fell down** in worship, while **the Levites** stood up to sing praises to God (20:18-19). Notice: Jehoshaphat and his people won this battle on their faces before him.

20:20-30 The next morning was a continuation of worship. Jehoshaphat urged the people of Judah to **believe in the LORD**, and then he stationed the praise team **in front of the armed forces** to sing of God's **faithful love** (20:20-21). What was the result of this unorthodox battle plan? God caused the enemy forces to turn on each other (20:22-23), and soon all Judah could find on the battlefield were enemy **corpses** (20:24). Jehoshaphat and the people gathered **the plunder** and returned to the temple with rejoicing (20:25-28). As a result, **the terror of God**—not the terror of Jehoshaphat—fell on the surrounding lands, and God gave **rest** to **Jehoshaphat's kingdom** (20:29-30).

Jehoshaphat trusted in his divine King for a supernatural deliverance. You may not be a king facing a national military crisis, but you are just as dependent on spiritual intervention for earthly living as he was. Will you look to the Lord as your deliverer when you don't know what to do? Or, will you trust in your own ingenuity and in human strength? Don't forget: a key lesson in this story is the power of praise.

20:31-37 According to the chronicler, Jehoshaphat **did what was right in the LORD's sight** (20:32). The final incident in Jehoshaphat's reign is recorded briefly, reminding us that this good king still made mistakes. It involved his final alliance with the northern kingdom. The king of Israel by this time was **Ahaziah**, who was **guilty of wrongdoing** (20:35). The two kings joined together in a commercial venture involving a fleet of **ships** sailing **to Tarshish** (20:36). **Eliezer** the prophet rebuked Jehoshaphat for the **alliance**, and the **ships were wrecked** by the hand of the Lord. This effort was another case of light trying to join forces with darkness (20:37).

◈ D. Jehoram, Ahaziah, Queen Athaliah, and Jehoiada (21:1–23:21) ◈

21:1-6 Judah's spiritual and military fortunes took a steep nosedive during the eight-year reign of Jehoshaphat's **firstborn** son, **Jehoram** (21:1-3). His biography reads like those of the evil kings of Israel, and that is not by coincidence. Jehoram not only married King **Ahab's daughter**, but the chronicler says he also **walked in the way of the kings of Israel** and **did what was evil** (21:6). His treachery was plain from the outset, and before he was done, he'd murdered his six younger **brothers** and other members of the royal family whom he considered a threat to his throne (21:4).

21:7 In spite of Jehoram's wickedness, God's promise to the house of David remained. Because of the Lord's **covenant** with **David**,

he was unwilling to cast aside **the house of David**. So, although this particular king was faithless, God would remain faithful to his promise to keep a son of David on the throne **forever** (see 1 Chr 17). God allowed Jehoram to retain his throne, but that didn't mean things would go well for him—just the opposite, in fact. And a day is coming when the perfect son of David—Jesus Christ—will inherit the throne and reign forever.

21:8-11 Jehoram's troubles started when **Edom rebelled** after being under **Judah's control** for years (21:8). Jehoram led his army to bring the rebels back into the fold but found himself **surrounded** by the **Edomites** (21:9). Then, the people of **Libnah** also revolted against Judah.

The chronicler doesn't leave us to guess at the reason Jehoram was plagued with rebellions during his reign. It was **because he had abandoned the LORD, the God of his ancestors** (21:10). Jehoram **built high places**—locations on top of hills or mountains for worshiping pagan gods—and **led Judah astray** (21:11). This is a sobering reminder that we should never underestimate the power of a leader to take people into ungodliness.

21:12-15 The national mess came to the attention of **the prophet Elijah**, who wrote Jehoram **a letter** outlining his doom (21:12). This famous man of God—the same one who stared down King Ahab, faced off against 450 false prophets, and called down fire on Mount Carmel (see 1 Kgs 18:20-40)—delivered a chilling message to the king of Judah. Jehoram had led the nation into idolatry and **killed** his own **brothers** (21:13), so God would strike Jehoram's family and possessions with **a horrible affliction** (21:14). Moreover, the king himself would be personally **struck** by painful and grotesque **illness** (21:15).

21:16-20 The word of the Lord through Elijah came true. **The Philistines and the Arabs** went to war against Judah, carrying off Jehoram's **wives . . . sons**, and **possessions** (21:16-17). The king was also **afflicted** with the foretold excruciating illness for two years before his death (21:18-19).

After such a reign of sin, it comes as no surprise that the people of Judah did not

honor Jehoram at his end (21:19). Rather, he **died to no one's regret**—was buried and forgotten (21:20). What a tragic legacy to leave behind.

22:1-4 Ahaziah was Jehoram's youngest and only surviving son (22:1). Importantly, he was part of the house of Ahab, and the curse on that wicked family continued as Ahaziah followed **evil advice** from **his mother** and **did what was evil in the LORD's sight like the house of Ahab** (22:3-4).

22:5-9 Ahaziah followed the king of Israel into a disastrous battle that ultimately cost Ahaziah his life—but not from battle wounds (22:5-6). As a grandson of Ahab, Ahaziah was under God's judgment that decreed the eradication of Ahab's entire line. Therefore, he was killed by **Jehu . . . whom the LORD had anointed to destroy the house of Ahab** (22:7; see 2 Kgs 9:1–10:17).

22:10-12 The evil queen mother **Athaliah** (daughter of Ahab, wife of Jehoram, and mother of Ahaziah) flew into action when she heard her son Ahaziah was dead. **She proceeded to annihilate all the royal heirs of the house of Judah** so she could usurp the throne (22:10). Yet, God still had some faithful people in Judah, even during this brutal period. Two of these people were **Jehoshabeath** (Ahaziah's sister) and her husband, **the priest Jehoiada**. Jehoshabeath rescued her infant nephew **Joash** from Athaliah's murderous rampage and hid him in the temple for **six years** while Athaliah **reigned** (22:11-12). Jehoiada bided his time and waited for an opportunity to oppose Athaliah effectively.

23:1-11 In the seventh year of Athaliah's reign, Jehoiada made his move. He gathered the priests, Levites, and troops and stationed them in and around the temple to stop any attempt to prevent the coronation of the rightful king, Joash (23:1-7). The plan worked. Soon, Joash was seated on the throne to shouts of **Long live the king!** (23:11).

23:12-15 When Athaliah heard the commotion and realized she was being deposed in a coup, she screamed, **Treason!** (23:12-13),

which must have sounded ridiculous to those who remembered how she had murdered her way to the throne. Wasting no time, **Jehoiada** had the queen executed (22:14-15). In his ironic providence, then, the Lord saw to it that Athaliah's life fulfilled the spiritual principle of "sowing and reaping." What she had sown, she reaped. We do well to remember that "God is not mocked" (Gal 6:7).

23:16-21 Jehoiada set about restoring the proper worship of God in Judah (23:16-19). Under the previous idolatrous rulers, **a temple of Baal** had actually been erected! This was quickly **smashed** to pieces (23:17). Then, Jehoiada and all the officials held a proper coronation for young King Joash, and **all the people . . . rejoiced** (23:21).

❧ E. Joash and Amaziah (24:1–25:28) ❧

24:1-3 Joash's forty-year reign is a good illustration of the stranglehold that idolatry had on the Lord's people generation after generation. **Throughout the time of the priest Jehoiada, Joash did what was right in the LORD's sight** (24:2). Unfortunately, that state of affairs would not last.

24:4-14 For the first part of Joash's reign, Jehoiada apparently provided godly influence. Joash commanded the renovation of **the LORD's temple** (24:4), which had fallen to disrepair. Queen Athaliah had even had **the sacred things** of the temple used to worship false gods (24:7). But, when Joash got serious about restoring the temple, the people of Judah paid the temple **tax** that **Moses** had required and gave generously on top of that (24:8-11). These funds provided for the temple to be fully renovated and for **articles** to be made for worship (24:12-14).

24:15-19 Joash's reign and the worship of God stayed on course as long as Jehoiada lived. But, when **Jehoiada died** (at the ripe age of 130), Joash did a spiritual 180. He **abandoned the temple of the LORD** and worshiped **idols** instead (24:17-18). So, even though Joash had witnessed the devastation and judgment that false worship had brought on Judah, his heart was obviously never fully devoted to the Lord. And, unfortunately, with Jehoiada gone, the vacuum of influence over him was filled by men who steered Joash toward idolatry. Although God sent **prophets** to warn them, the people of Judah **would not listen** (24:19)

24:20-22 Joash's spiritual betrayal was bad enough. But, when God sent **Zechariah son of Jehoiada** to announce his judgment on Judah, Joash coldly ordered Zechariah to be killed by stoning (24:20-21). The chronicler poignantly observes that **King Joash didn't remember the kindness that Zechariah's father Jehoiada had extended to him** (24:22). Instead, he put to death the son of the faithful priest who had preserved Joash's own life as a helpless boy and later placed him on the throne (22:11–23:21).

24:23-27 Silencing the Lord's prophet wouldn't prevent the fulfillment of his words. Within the year, **the LORD handed over** Judah to the invading **Aramean army** because Judah **had abandoned the LORD** (24:23-24). The devastation left Joash wounded, and in the end, his servants **killed him on his bed** because of his treachery against the family of Jehoiada (24:25). Once again, then, the Bible shows that what goes around comes around.

25:1-4 The tragic pattern of early faithfulness followed by later apostasy was repeated by Joash's son **Amaziah**. He began well, doing **what was right in the Lord's sight**—but (the chronicler quickly adds) **not wholeheartedly** (25:1-2). An unusual example of Amaziah's obedience to the law was the way he handled the execution of his father's assassins. He put the conspirators to death, but not their children, because that's what the Mosaic law had stipulated (25:3-4).

25:5-8 Amaziah raised a large army from the men of Judah for battle (25:5). But, he wanted even more troops. So, **he hired one hundred thousand** Israelite **warriors** for **7,500 pounds of silver** (25:6). But, this move displeased God, who had rejected the idolatrous northern kingdom and sent an unnamed prophet to Amaziah, declaring, **the LORD is not with Israel—all the Ephraimites** (25:7). "Ephraim" was a leading tribe of the northern kingdom, so the name was often used to speak of Israel as a whole. The prophet warned the king that if the warriors of Israel joined them, God would cause his forces to **stumble** (25:8).

25:9 To his credit, Amaziah believed the prophet's warning. The king also followed the prophet's instructions not to worry about recouping the money he had paid for the services of the Israelite warriors. **The LORD is able to give you much more than this,** the prophet said. That's a good promise to remember. God doesn't need Satan's help to bless you.

25:10-14 **Amaziah released** the Israelites and had success against his enemies (25:10-12). But, the Israelite soldiers were so ticked off at not getting a crack at some serious plunder that they ransacked several towns in **Judah** and slaughtered **three thousand** people (25:13). Inexplicably, when Amaziah returned from battle, he brought his enemies' false gods back to Jerusalem and **set them up as his gods** and **worshiped before them** (25:14).

25:15-16 Amaziah's idolatry aroused **the LORD's anger**. So, he sent another **prophet** to call the king back to his senses. The utter absurdity of Amaziah's actions is evident in the stinging logic of the prophet's question: **Why have you sought a people's gods that could not rescue their own people from you?** (25:15). His question reveals the stark truth about idolatry: It's insanity. But, by this time, Amaziah was feeling his power and warned the prophet to be quiet or die. The prophet's parting words foretold the king's doom (25:16).

25:17-19 Amaziah apparently traded the wise counsel of God's prophets for foolish **counsel** that advised him to challenge Israel to a fight (25:17). **King Jehoash of Israel** tried to warn Amaziah to back off for his own good. While Amaziah had **defeated Edom**, he had become too big for his britches. Jehoash urged the upstart king of Judah to **stay at home** (25:18-19).

25:20-24 In verse 20, the God-inspired chronicler tells the reader of the spiritual reality that was working the downfall of the king in his earthly stupidity. God was planning Amaziah's defeat because of his idolatry. In other words, the Lord let the stubborn and overconfident king of Judah go into battle and get thrashed (25:21-24).

25:25-28 After forsaking the Lord, Amaziah became very unpopular in Judah, and **a conspiracy was formed against him**. When the king fled, the assassins hunted him down and executed him (25:27). His reign had followed the pattern of his father, Joash, who also had turned away from God in his later years and was assassinated. Theirs is an unfortunate example of the adage, "Like father, like son."

⫷ F. Uzziah and Jotham *(26:1–27:9)* ⫸

26:1-4 Uzziah was just a teenager when he became king. The reference to his installation on the throne is a little unusual. Apparently, his father, Amaziah, was not involved in naming his successor. Instead, **all the people of Judah took Uzziah ... and made him king** (26:1). And, like previous kings of Judah, Uzziah began well: **He did what was right in the LORD's sight** (26:4).

26:5 Uzziah had an older, godly mentor—a man named **Zechariah**, whom the chronicler described as **the teacher of the fear of God**. Like his grandfather Joash (who'd been counseled by Jehoiada), Uzziah followed the Lord as long as his mentor Zechariah was alive. In fact, as long as Uzziah **sought the LORD, God gave him success**. It's not certain that Uzziah's pride and punishment coincided exactly with Zechariah's death, but that may have been the case.

26:6-15 Uzziah enjoyed a number of successes during his fifty-two-year reign. He was successful in battle against **the Philistines**, the longtime enemies of God's people (26:6-7). He became so powerful that another old enemy, **the Ammonites**, paid him **tribute** in submission as the king's fame **spread as far as** Egypt (26:8). He also **built** defensive

towers at several places along the walls of Jerusalem and was extensively engaged in agriculture (26:9-10). Uzziah was a great military leader, too, and even **designed** military **devices** to **shoot arrows and catapult large stones** from the Jerusalem towers (26:11-15). Therefore, it is no surprise that **his fame spread** wide (26:15).

26:16-18 Uzziah's story took a wrong turn when he allowed his power, fame, and prosperity to make him **arrogant**. At first glance, his sin may seem relatively minor compared to the murders, idolatry, and gross immorality of which several other kings of Judah were guilty. However, by usurping the role of the priest **to burn incense** in the temple, Uzziah committed an act of great unfaithfulness to the Lord (26:16). A huge cadre of **brave priests** sought to stop the king before he went too far. **They took their stand against King Uzziah** (26:17-18) and called him out on his foolishness. This took tremendous courage considering that the king could have executed them with a word. They urged him to realize that he would **not receive honor from the LORD** (26:18).

26:19-23 Through the intervention of the priests, the Lord gave Uzziah a chance to repent. He could have humbled himself, honored God, and won the respect of the priests. Instead, **he became enraged**. But, before the king could unleash his anger, God afflicted him with **a skin disease** (26:19). This required that he live **in quarantine** until the day of his death (26:21). In other words, because of his arrogant violation of God's law, Uzziah spent the rest of his days in isolation. (Keep yourself humble before the Lord. Pride will be your undoing.)

27:1-2 Uzziah's son **Jotham** got a head start on ruling because he had to assume the reins of leadership during the years his father was unable to govern (27:1). The chronicler gives Jotham this commendation: **He did what was right in the LORD's sight just as his father Uzziah had done. In addition, he didn't enter the LORD's sanctuary** (27:2). The statement about the temple is an obvious reference to Uzziah's sin, but it appears that Jotham learned from his dad's error. This is another instance of the chronicler using a historical incident to emphasize his message that faithful kings (and the nation under them) would prosper while faithless kings would lead the people into ruin.

Nevertheless, Jotham's reign had its shortcoming. Apparently, though he himself was faithful, he was unable to rid Judah of the idolatry and spiritual unfaithfulness that had plagued God's people for so long. So, while Jotham was following the Lord, **the people still behaved corruptly** (27:2).

27:3-9 Jotham accomplished significant construction projects (27:3-4) and was successful in battle (27:5) **because he did not waver in obeying the LORD his God** (27:6). After a reign of **sixteen years**, Jotham died and left the kingdom to **his son Ahaz** (27:8-9).

Not only did Jotham fail to influence the people to obey the Lord (even though he personally obeyed), but it also seems he failed to influence his son, as well.

⋗ G. Ahaz (28:1-27) ⋞

28:1-4 Ahaz did not follow in the obedient footsteps of his father. In fact, he was so thoroughly corrupted by defection from the Lord and idolatry (28:2, 4) that he actually sacrificed **his children** by burning them in the **detestable practices of the nations** (28:3). This sad story highlights where idolatry leads. As we've seen throughout 2 Chronicles, the worship of false gods leads to godless living: wickedness, treachery, and violence. Ahaz's actions demonstrated idolatry at its worst: it led to the murder of his innocent children.

King Ahaz was notable for another reason, too. About midway through his reign, the northern kingdom of Israel fell to the Assyrians in 722 BC. God had given Israel over to its sin until, finally, his judgment fell on the nation. Ominously, one of the indictments issued against Ahaz was that **he walked in the ways of the kings of Israel** (28:2). Israel was punished soundly for their idolatry with conquest and exile. It was a lesson that Ahaz should have taken to heart— but didn't.

28:5-8 The chronicler doesn't mention the fall of Israel because his focus was on Judah, Jerusalem, and the Davidic kings. Instead, he points out that Israel was one of the nations the Lord used in the earlier part of Ahaz's reign to punish him for his sinfulness. And, as Judah's king committed himself to idol worship, **God handed Ahaz over to the king of Aram**. The Arameans began the onslaught by inflicting a crushing defeat on Ahaz and taking hostages back to their capital of Damascus (28:5). Then, Israel came against Ahaz, resulting in the death of **the king's son** and the capture of **two hundred thousand** people from Judah (28:7-8).

28:9-11 Here, the story takes an unusual turn. Not everyone in the northern kingdom had turned away from the Lord, because a **prophet of the LORD named Oded** met the Israelite army returning from its victory over Ahaz (28:9). When Oded saw all the captives straggling along behind the troops, he raised a strong protest. His speech (28:9-12) was a passionate plea not to make the suffering of Judah worse by reducing **the people of Judah and Jerusalem . . . to slavery** (28:10). He commanded them to release the **captives** to avoid **the LORD's burning anger** (28:11).

28:12-15 Oded's warning of God's wrath on Israel for taking their brothers and sisters into captivity fell on the receptive ears of a group of leaders who insisted that the army do the right thing and release the people (28:12-13). To their credit, the soldiers obeyed and even took some of their plunder to clothe, feed, and otherwise care for **the captives**. Then, the designated soldiers took them **to Jericho** so they could be reunited with their families (28:14-15). Within this turn of events is the ultimate irony: unfaithful Israel listened to the voice of the Lord, while Judah did not— even though their kings were in the line of faithful David.

28:16-21 Ahaz didn't seem to be moved by any of this. Instead of turning to the Lord when his kingdom was under attack by the **Philistines** and the **Edomites**, Ahaz turned to **Assyria for help** (28:16-18). But, this decision was doomed. The Lord brought havoc on Judah because Ahaz **was unfaithful to**

the Lord (28:19). Rather than offering military assistance, the Assyrians **oppressed** Ahaz (28:20). Did that cause Ahaz to turn to God in repentance? No. He stripped the **temple** and the **palace** of their treasures and attempted to pay off the Assyrian king instead. But even this, the chronicler tells us, **did not help him** (28:21).

28:22-23 Idolatry is blinding, a fact highlighted in the next moves of Ahaz. The more he was plagued with trouble, the worse he became spiritually. He became **more unfaithful to the Lord and sacrificed to the gods of Damascus which had defeated him** (28:22-23). Ahaz rationalized that because **the gods of the kings of Aram** helped them, these same gods would also help him if he worshiped them. He didn't understand that each catastrophe he suffered was punishment from the hand of his own God as a result of his disobedience. The idols that he looked to for deliverance were his **downfall** (28:23).

28:24-27 Ahaz locked up the **temple** and established idol worship stations **on every street corner in Jerusalem** (28:24). All of this, of course, only stoked the Lord's anger against him (28:25). In the end, he was refused burial with the other kings in a final statement of his complete unfitness to be identified with the Davidic **kings** before him (28:27).

❧ H. Hezekiah (29:1–32:33) ❧

29:1-2 Had the man's son followed in his footsteps, Ahaz could have served as the poster boy for bad fathers. But, remarkably, his son pulled off one of the greatest revivals in Judah's history. The most important thing that the chronicler could say about **Hezekiah** was that **he did what was right in the Lord's sight just as his ancestor David had done** (29:1-2). This king was worthy of comparison to David!

29:3-7 Hezekiah's revival began **in the first month** of his reign, when he **opened** and **repaired** the temple **doors** (29:3). Having

witnessed firsthand his father's reign, Hezekiah acknowledged the wickedness done by past kings who'd committed evil in God's sight and turned their backs on him (28:6-7). And so, his reforms began in the house of the Lord. He commanded the **Levites** to **consecrate** themselves and the temple (29:4-5). He realized that if Judah was going to turn around, it would have to start by worshiping God as he had commanded.

29:8-9 As a teenager and young adult, Hezekiah must have watched in horror as Judah's enemies battered the nation in wars while unspeakable idolatries were practiced in Jerusalem. Hezekiah knew the reason for these disasters: **The wrath of the Lord was on** his nation. Therefore, God made Judah **an object of terror, horror, and mockery** (29:8). The king had also seen thousands of his fellow Judahites— **sons . . . daughters . . . wives**—carried off into **captivity** (29:9).

29:10-11 Hezekiah determined to do something about the sorry situation. Reopening the temple had been a good start, but Judah also needed a king whose **heart** was devoted to the Lord. Hezekiah, determined to be that king, set about making **a covenant with the Lord, the God of Israel** to turn his **anger** away (29:10). He even challenged the Levites: **don't be negligent now**. God had **chosen** them for their tasks, and they had an opportunity to reverse the damage done in the past (29:11).

29:12-19 The Levites and priests responded readily. **They gathered their brothers together, consecrated themselves,** and went to work cleansing the temple (29:15). The priests also **went to the entrance of the Lord's temple to cleanse it** (29:16). For sixteen days, in fact, they purified the temple and everything associated with it. When they were done, they were able to report to Hezekiah that they had **cleansed the whole temple of the Lord, the altar of burnt offering and all its utensils, and the table for the rows of the Bread of the Presence and all its utensils** (29:18). In other words, everything was ready for the service of re-consecration and worship.

29:20-30 This service included two parts. First, Hezekiah **gathered the city officials** and **went up to the LORD's temple** (29:20). These leaders held a great convocation of sacrifices and music in a joyful experience of worshiping the Lord and seeking his favor on his people once again (29:21-29). This ceremony ended with the king and his officials bowing their heads in worship as the music rang out (20:30).

29:31-36 What followed was apparently a broader service in which the entire **congregation** of Judah was invited to come and share in the worship. The people responded by bringing **sacrifices and thank offerings, and all those with willing hearts brought burnt offerings** (29:31). The response was so great that it overwhelmed the ability of the few priests to prepare all the sacrifices; thus, **the Levites** helped until the work was done (29:32-35). The conclusion of this glorious restoration of faithful worship was joy and satisfaction all around: **Hezekiah and all the people rejoiced . . . for it had come about suddenly** (29:36). Incredibly, Hezekiah accomplished all of this in just one month, after the temple had been padlocked for years.

30:1-5 The restoration of proper worship in the temple led to bigger things for Hezekiah and the people of Judah: the celebration of **the Passover**, which had fallen into neglect for many years (30:1). The date was set for **the second month** on the religious calendar, a month late (30:2), but the reasons were valid. There weren't enough consecrated priests to celebrate the festival, and the people from the far regions needed time to get there (30:3). The invitation went out not only to Judah, the southern kingdom, but also to those in the northern kingdom of Israel, referred to here as **Ephraim and Manasseh** (30:1). This is a reference to those who had not been taken captive by the Assyrians.

30:6-12 Hezekiah's invitation warmly asked those in the north to come to Jerusalem for a united celebration (30:6-7). It even contained a promise—**return** in service to the Lord, and he will **return** your fellow Israelites who have been taken away into captivity (30:8-9).

(Now, that is a promise for the ages: return to God, and he will return to you; see Zech 1:3). But, the people of Israel, except for a few **who humbled themselves**, rejected the invite and **mocked them** (30:10-11), which confirms Gods judgment of them with captivity for their rebellion.

30:13-20 It's obvious from the rest of the chapter that those who didn't come to the Passover were the losers. **A very large assembly of people was gathered in Jerusalem to observe the Festival of Unleavened Bread** (30:13), the seven-day celebration that immediately followed the Passover. The people's hearts were so tuned to the Lord, in fact, that they undertook another purge of **the altars** where false gods were worshiped (30:14)! They celebrated the Passover with such enthusiasm that some of the people who participated were still **ritually unclean** (30:18), a violation that would normally have brought severe judgment. But, because they were doing so with a **heart** to seek the Lord, Hezekiah **interceded for them** and the Lord forgave them (30:18-20).

30:21-25 The Festival of Unleavened Bread that followed the Passover was such a big event in Judah that it took many thousands of animals to provide for all the worshipers (30:22-24). They even took the unprecedented step of extending the festival for another **seven days** (30:23). Through their enthusiasm the people were saying, in effect, "We haven't worshiped like this in our whole lives. This is tremendous!"

30:26-27 The chronicler notes that, indeed, nothing like this had been experienced in Jerusalem **since the days of Solomon son of David** (30:26), which is a clear reference to the importance of the Davidic king's faithfulness to the Lord. The long celebration ended on the best of all possible high points: **the priests and the Levites stood to bless the people, and God heard them, and their prayer came into his holy dwelling place in heaven** (30:27).

31:1-8 All of this was followed by the best of all outcomes in Judah—a spiritual revival that included still another purge of false worship, restoration of the giving of the people (chapter 31), and a miraculous deliverance from the armies of the dreaded Assyrians (chapter 32). **Hezekiah reestablished the divisions of the priests and Levites** that had been set in place to divide the workload in the various aspects of temple worship (31:2). Then came the people's tithes and freewill offerings to support the priests and Levites as they served the Lord (31:4).

Hezekiah set the example by first giving generously and then calling on the people **to give** (31:3-4). They answered, bringing **the best of the grain, new wine, fresh oil, honey, and of all the produce of the field ... in an abundance** (31:5). These offerings began to accumulate **into large piles** as the people spent four months bringing their tithes and gifts to the Lord's house (31:6-7). Then, the Lord received all the praise (31:8).

31:9-21 The rest of this chapter describes how King Hezekiah provided for the proper oversight and use of the people's gifts, making sure that the priests, Levites, and their families were provided for. It concludes with another ringing endorsement of Hezekiah's faithfulness to the Lord in **every deed that he began in the service of God's temple** (31:21). The man was doing things right, and the Lord took careful notice.

32:1-8 The events of chapter 31 are intimately linked with what happened next in Hezekiah's reign because the threat from Assyria came **after these faithful deeds** on Hezekiah's part (32:1). The army of the Assyrian king **Sennacherib** invaded Judah and proceeded to conquer a number of towns on its march toward Jerusalem. Hezekiah did the wisest things he could do in the face of this terrifying threat: he prepared to defend the city (32:2-6) while hoping in the Lord (32:7-8).

Hezekiah worked hard to weaken the enemy, shore up Jerusalem's defenses, and arm his troops, but his ultimate trust was in God. His statement to the people was a ringing declaration of Hezekiah's faith and courage: **Be strong and courageous! Don't be afraid or discouraged before the king of Assyria or before the large army that is with him,**

for there are more with us than with him. He has only human strength, but we have the Lord our God to help us and to fight our battles (32:7-8).

32:9-19 The army of Assyria showed up, and its spokesman went to great lengths to dishearten the people by mocking and insulting the true God. He explained what the Assyrians had done to the other nations, whose gods had failed to protect them. Why should the God of puny Judah be any different (32:13-15)? Sennacherib's servants even shouted **to the people of Jerusalem, who were on the wall, to frighten and discourage them** (32:18).

32:20-23 Hezekiah wisely sought the counsel and support of the great **prophet Isaiah**, and together these godly men **prayed ... and cried out to heaven** (32:20). The Lord took note of the insults of a pagan king and the prayers of his humble people, and he responded. **The Lord sent an angel who annihilated every valiant warrior, leader, and commander in the camp of the king of Assyria** (32:21). Sennacherib went home **in disgrace** and was assassinated by **his own children** (32:21). Hezekiah **was exalted in the eyes of all the nations after that** (32:23). This story is a beautiful reminder that God is sovereign. Fortunes can be reversed in a heartbeat.

32:24-33 Unfortunately, when Hezekiah was exalted, it became a source of temptation to succumb to pride. In the midst of an illness, Hezekiah **prayed** and received **a miraculous sign** from the Lord (32:24). But, Hezekiah then became **proud** and **didn't respond according to the benefit that had come to him**. This means that while God had answered Hezekiah's prayer, Hezekiah was ungrateful. He thought more highly of himself than he should have. So, the Lord disciplined him and the people (32:25). Thankfully, Hezekiah got the message and **humbled himself**. As a result, **the Lord's wrath didn't come ... during Hezekiah's lifetime** (30:26), which is an ominous note that bad times were still coming.

Even in light of his failures, Hezekiah was a great king who died with great honor. But, another hint of the bad times ahead is found in the note that **his son Manasseh** succeeded him (32:33).

✵ I. Manasseh and Amon (33:1-25) ✵

33:1-3 The ultimate low point of Judah's kings who departed from the Lord seems to have been reached with the long reign of **Manasseh**. And, it is evident from the beginning that Manasseh either learned nothing from his godly father, or quickly rejected it once he became king (33:1-2). His actions were a complete reversal of Hezekiah's reforms. In fact, the chronicler reports that Manasseh **rebuilt the high places that his father Hezekiah had torn down and reestablished the altars for the Baals** (33:3). The familiar formula, **he did what was evil in the LORD's sight** (33:2), summarizes all but the last few years of Manasseh's kingship.

33:4-8 It seems there was no form of degrading worship that Manasseh did not embrace and promote. He even **built altars to all the stars in the sky** (33:5). In other words, he worshiped the heavenly bodies rather than the God who created them. He also practiced child sacrifice, using his own sons as offerings to pagan gods in **Ben Hinnom Valley**. Additionally, **he practiced witchcraft, divination, and sorcery, and consulted mediums** (33:6).

But, these abominations weren't enough for Manasseh. He also desecrated God's temple. The king **built altars in the LORD's temple, where the LORD had said, "Jerusalem is where my name will remain forever"** (33:4). Then, he committed the ultimate sin of erecting **a carved image of the idol, which he had made**, right there **in God's temple** (33:7).

33:9 The catalog of evil that Manasseh practiced seemed to include every form of idolatry and abomination he could find. The chronicler's conclusion of Manasseh's sin was that he led Judah to commit **worse evil than the nations the LORD had destroyed** when he gave Israel the promised land. God

had kicked the Canaanites out of the land because of their wickedness. Now, his people, recipients of that land, were worse than the Canaanites!

33:10-13 God could not allow this situation to go unchecked, so he **spoke to Manasseh and his people, but they didn't listen** (33:10). Rather than allowing Manasseh to remain on his throne and afflict the nation further, God disciplined this wicked king. Manasseh was captured by the Assyrians and taken like an animal with **hooks** and **shackles** to **Babylon** (33:11). Finally, in great **distress**, Manasseh **sought** the Lord's **favor** and **humbled himself before the God of his ancestors** (33:12). The Lord was moved by Manasseh's humility, answered his prayer, and returned him to Jerusalem. **So Manasseh came to know that the LORD is God** (33:13).

33:14-17 Upon his restoration, Manasseh tried to undo all of the evils he had done. First, he fortified the city against attack (33:14). Then **he removed** all of the idols and pagan altars that he had erected and reinstituted true worship of **the God of Israel** (33:15-16). In the end, his reforms were limited because **the people still sacrificed at the high places, but only to the LORD their God** (33:17).

33:18-25 Manasseh's death set the stage for the brief and unhappy reign of **his son Amon** (33:18-20). The key to Amon's reign is found in the report that, despite all the evil he did, repeating many of the sins of his father, Amon **did not humble himself before the LORD like his father Manasseh** (33:22-23). On the contrary, **Amon increased his guilt** (33:23). In the end, the king was assassinated, **the common people** executed his killers, and **Josiah** became Judah's child king (33:24-25).

✵ J. Josiah (34:1–35:27) ✵

34:1-2 At the age of **eight**, Josiah could hardly be ready to rule. But, he obviously had a heart for the Lord, a key fact with which the chronicler sought to encourage his readers after the Babylonian captivity. Josiah **did what was right in the LORD's sight and walked in the ways of his ancestor David.** He also merited this praise, which could be said about few other kings of Judah: **He did not turn aside to the right or the left** (34:2).

34:3-7 Josiah's heart for the Lord manifested itself at the age of sixteen when he began **to seek** the Lord in earnest (34:3). And, when he was just twenty, he undertook a purge of all false worship and false worshipers that extended all the way north into the territory of Israel (34:3-7; see 1 Kgs 13:1-3).

34:8-18 It was during extensive and much-needed renovations to the temple (34:8-13) that **the priest Hilkiah found the book of the law of the LORD written by the hand of Moses** (34:14). What happened next is famous in biblical history: **Hilkiah told the court secretary Shaphan, "I have found the book of the law in the LORD's temple," and he gave the book to Shaphan. Shaphan took the book to the king** (34:15-16).

Just imagine it. The book of God's law, "written by the hand of Moses," had been tossed aside in some closet in the temple! Imagine Josiah's shock when Shaphan told him, "Guess what we found."

34:19-28 When he heard the law being read, Josiah **tore his clothes**—a symbolic act indicating great grief and mourning (34:19). He realized how far God's people had fallen from him and how much God's **wrath** was against them for their sin (34:21). The king's men took the book to **the prophetess Huldah**, who confirmed God's intent **to bring disaster** upon Judah for abandoning the Lord. His **wrath** would be **poured out** and would **not be quenched** (34:22-25) However, because Josiah had a tender **heart** and **humbled** himself, God promised that he would not see the **disaster** when it came (34:26-28).

34:29-33 How would you have responded to Huldah's dire predictions (34:22-28)? Would you have been relieved? Would you have thought, "At least I won't have to live through it?" Nothing like that was on Josiah's mind. The king read **the book of the covenant** in the hearing of **all the people** (34:30). Then, he led a **covenant** renewal ceremony in which the king and the people pledged themselves **to follow the LORD** (34:31). Josiah made everyone **agree** to the covenant, removed the **detestable** things from the land, and required the people **to serve the LORD their God** (34:32-33). And, this wasn't a mere ceremony that was later forgotten. During Josiah's reign, Judah **did not turn aside from following the LORD** (34:33).

35:1-9 The temple wasn't the only thing that had fallen into neglect when Josiah came to the throne. It had been many years since Judah had observed the **Passover** (35:1). Josiah made elaborate preparations to correct this problem, including his order to replace **the ark** in the holy of holies (35:3) after it had obviously been removed from the temple again. The king and **his officials . . . donated** extravagantly in preparation for this celebration (35:7-9).

35:10-19 The priests and the Levites faithfully accomplished their duties and the people celebrated (35:10-17). The event was so incredible that the chronicler confessed, **No Passover had been observed like it in Israel since the days of the prophet Samuel. None of the kings of Israel ever observed a Passover like the one that Josiah observed** (35:18). This evaluation is at once both wonderful and tragic. It is wonderful because it demonstrates the intense repentance and devotion to the Lord of this young king. He was going to ensure that God was honored by the nation on his watch. But, it is also tragic that the worship of God had been so neglected.

35:20-27 Although Josiah was a godly king, God's plan to spare him from seeing the destruction of Judah involved his death. Josiah went out to confront **King Neco of Egypt** (35:20). Neco warned Josiah that he did not want to fight him, but Josiah **did not listen** (35:21-22). According to the chronicler, **Neco's words** were **from the mouth of God** (35:22). As a result, Josiah was slain by Neco's **archers** (35:23-24). And, with the death of Judah's last great king, the nation's demise began to unfold quickly.

➤ K. The Final Kings, Exile, and the Decree of Cyrus (36:1-23) ⬧

36:1-3 Jehoahaz became king in place of his father Josiah. The text does not explain why Neco came to Jerusalem and **deposed** the king after only **three months** on the throne, but Neco's control was obvious in that he imposed taxes on the land and installed another son of Josiah as king.

36:4-8 When he placed Jehoahaz's brother **Eliakim** on Judah's throne, **Neco** changed the new king's name to **Jehoiakim**, perhaps to demonstrate again that Egypt was now in charge in Judah. **Jehoahaz** was carried off to Egypt, no doubt to be paraded as Neco's prize and then either imprisoned or worse (36:4). Eliakim would be the first of four puppet kings who reigned in Judah before the exile to Babylon.

Like so many wicked kings before him, Jehoiakim didn't learn anything from God's judgment on his people. **He did what was evil in the sight of the LORD** (36:5). Throughout his reign, Jehoiakim was a puppet whose strings were being pulled by Judah's oppressors—first Egypt, and then Babylon when Nebuchadnezzar drove out the Egyptians in 605 BC and took control of Judah. We learn in 2 Kings 24:1 that Jehoiakim rebelled against the king of Babylon. As a result, **Nebuchadnezzar** took Jehoiakim to **Babylon** in **bronze shackles** and also carried off **articles** from the **temple** (36:6-7). The **detestable** reign of Jehoiakim was over (36:8).

36:9-10 Jehoiakim's son **Jehoiachin** did not fare well at all, due to the **evil** he did in the **LORD's sight** (36:9). **Nebuchadnezzar** carried him off **to Babylon**, too, and made his brother **Zedekiah** king (36:10).

36:11-14 Judah's royal puppet show had one final act, and it lasted a long time. **Zedekiah** was the fourth and last of the pitiful puppet kings who did their part to lead Judah into destruction (36:11-12). He **did not humble himself before the prophet Jeremiah at the LORD's command** and decided to rebel against King Nebuchadnezzar (36:12-13).

36:15-20 The grace of God is truly amazing. In spite of their centuries of unfaithfulness, the Lord **time and time again** sent **messengers** to warn both the king and the people to repent. Why? Because **he had compassion on his people and on his dwelling place** (36:15). God's love for his people is unfathomable.

Sadly, when God's kings and people continued to reject his word, **there was no remedy** (36:16). God handed them over to the Babylonians or **Chaldeans**. They **killed** many of God's people, **burned** the **temple** of the Lord, **tore down Jerusalem's wall**, and **deported** many to Babylon (36:17-20).

36:21 The chronicler adds a final comment regarding God's judgment. The people had failed to observe the **Sabbath rest** of the land. The law had commanded that the land must lie fallow every seventh year (see Lev 25:1-7). Thus, God added one year of captivity for every Sabbath rest the land had missed. The people would be exiled for **seventy years**.

36:22-23 The story of Judah would have closed on this tragic note were it not for this very important word of hope and future restoration. (The chronicler's readers had already witnessed the fulfillment of the promise that God would raise up **King Cyrus of Persia**—the Persians eventually defeated the Babylonians). Cyrus would have mercy on his people and be the human instrument of their restoration to the land of Israel (36:22). In 539 BC, he issued a decree that said the Lord had **appointed** him **to build [God] a temple at Jerusalem in Judah**. Moreover, God's people were free to return to their land (36:23).

EZRA

INTRODUCTION

Author

THOUGH THE BOOKS OF EZRA AND Nehemiah are separate writings in English Bibles, they were regarded as a single book in the Hebrew Bible and were not separated in Hebrew Bibles until the fifteenth century. The early Christian theologian Origen separated Ezra-Nehemiah into two books, and Jerome followed suit with the Latin translation of the Bible, the Vulgate.

Ezra is an anonymous work, but ancient Jewish sources attribute authorship to Ezra. Some scholars believe the book was written by "the chronicler," the author of 1–2 Chronicles, because 2 Chronicles 36:22-23 and much of Ezra 1:1-3 are identical. Thus, Ezra may have authored both 1–2 Chronicles and Ezra.

Historical Background

Ezra was a priest and scribe sent by Artaxerxes the Persian king to Jerusalem in 458 BC (that is, in "the seventh year of King Artaxerxes," Ezra 7:7) to appoint magistrates and judges and to teach God's law in Israel (see Ezra 7:1-28).

Message and Purpose

The book of Ezra is about spiritual restoration. It deals with the restoration of the temple by Israel's people after their return from Babylonian captivity as a result of their persistent disobedience and idolatry. God had made a kingdom promise to them that if they would return to him, he would bring them back to their land.

The priest Ezra led the second group of exiles back to Israel. He focused on reestablishing the temple and its sacrificial system, making it clear that the worship of God's people would only be effective if they dedicated themselves to obeying God's law. He challenged them that if they would get serious with the Lord, they would experience his covenantal blessings. But, this required Israel to stop compromising with God's enemies and to turn from idolatry. Israel needed to be people separated to God to experience his blessings and be restored to his kingdom promises.

The message of Ezra is that when we depart from God, we lose our experience of him. But, when we return to him, he will restore us to fellowship with him.

VIDEO INTRO

www.bhpublishinggroup.com/qr/te/15_00

Outline

I. The Return of the Exiles under Zerubbabel (1:1–6:22)

   A. The Decree of Cyrus (1:1-11)

EZRA

I. THE RETURN OF THE EXILES UNDER ZERUBBABEL
(1:1–6:22)

➣ A. The Decree of Cyrus (1:1-11) ❧

1:1-4 The book of Ezra begins where 2 Chronicles ends (see 2 Chr 36:22-23). Indeed, the sovereign **LORD roused the spirit of King Cyrus** (1:1) to issue a decree to end the Jewish exile and rebuild the temple **in Jerusalem** (1:2-4).

Although this was joyful news, it should not have come as a shock to God's faithful people, for it happened **to fulfill the word of the LORD spoken through Jeremiah** (1:1). Jeremiah had prophesied that the Jews would return to Israel when the seventy years of exile in Babylon that God had decreed for them were fulfilled (see Jer 29:10). Furthermore, the prophet Isaiah had mentioned Cyrus by name, announcing that he would release the Jews and send them home (see Isa 44:28–45:13). These things were foretold far in advance of Cyrus's appearance on the world scene.

The decree of return was voluntary; many Jews who had prospered in Persia after its conquest of Babylon decided to stay put. But, others returned to their homeland. Many Bible commentators see this event as a second exodus of sorts, because in it God's people again were given permission to leave their land of bondage for the promised land and were richly supplied for the journey by the gifts of **the men of that region** (1:4).

1:5 The **LORD's house**, the ruined temple in Jerusalem, needed to be rebuilt. So, this became the priority for **the** returned **family heads of Judah and Benjamin, along with the priests and Levites—everyone whose spirit God had roused**. Notice that God was the initiator. He is to be praised for putting the desire in their hearts. Notice also that the spiritual and civil leaders—the family heads, the priests, the Levites—led the way. During the days of idolatry and moral decay in Judah and Jerusalem before the exile, the spiritual and civil leaders were the prime culprits behind the problems. But, in Ezra's day, the leaders aligned themselves with God's agenda. His kingdom had become their priority. If we are to see lasting change in our churches and culture, we need leaders who will allow the same.

1:6-11 The returnees had everything they needed, from money to the temple vessels that **Nebuchadnezzar had taken** when he destroyed the temple (1:7). These articles were holy and consecrated to the Lord; it had been an abomination to have them housed in a pagan temple. How overjoyed the people must have been when king Cyrus returned these items (1:8-10)!

Bible scholars speculate over the identity of **Sheshbazzar the prince of Judah** (1:8). He seems to be the leader whom King Cyrus designated for the return and temple rebuilding. However, Zerubbabel is the generally acknowledged leader. Sheshbazzar is only mentioned three other times in Ezra (1:11; 5:14, 16), so it's possible he died soon after arriving in Jerusalem and was succeeded by Zerubbabel. In any case, the former was the one in charge of bringing the temple **articles** back to Jerusalem (1:11).

Though the numbers listed in 1:9-10 do not add up to the **5,400** in 1:11, it is possible that the first list includes only the larger and more important items, while the total includes every piece down to the smallest items.

➤ B. The Jews Who Returned to Jerusalem (2:1-70) ❦

2:1-2 The opening verses identify the leaders of this early return; **Zerubbabel** is listed first (2:2).

2:3-70 The list of names here was meant to confirm that the returnees were true Israelites. Many Bible readers might consider the list to be tedious reading, but Ezra 2 would have been a genuine encouragement to the original readers, who were decades removed from this first return in 539 BC and were part of the second return under Ezra. Those readers were faltering in their worship of the Lord–even though they had the temple–and needed to be reminded of their need to follow God with all their hearts. It would have been a blessing to them to read the names of their families and ancestors among those who were willing to leave the safety and the known of Persia to trek back to Israel, to the unknown, and to rebuild the temple out of devotion to the Lord. The reminder of their ancestors' commitment, in fact, would inspire Ezra's readers to renew their own faithfulness to the Mosaic law, as happened in Ezra 9–10.

Because rebuilding the temple and restoring the proper worship of God were primary, Ezra noted that the returnees who were unable to establish their priestly ancestry **were disqualified from the priesthood** until that crucial connection could be verified (2:62-63). When the exiles reached Jerusalem and saw the rubble of the first temple that Nebuchadnezzar had left behind, they dug deep and **gave freewill offerings for the house of God . . . based on what they could give** (2:68-69). When it came to giving in the local church, this was Paul's attitude as well: one

ought to give according to his means (see 1 Cor 16:2; 2 Cor 8:3-4; 9:6-7).

There is a crucial lesson in Ezra 2 that applies to God's kingdom agenda for the church today. This list of God's people includes those who were willing to work to accomplish his will, even if it meant leaving comfort and convenience. Ezra 2 is a membership role, then, of those who were willing to say, "I am not going to sit on the sidelines and reap the benefits of God's house and people. You can count me in."

The church—not just the building, but the people within it—is the New Testament temple. This is why the church is so strategic to the building of God's kingdom in our day. The church is the one entity on earth that offers the presence of God. Furthermore, it has the largest volunteer force potentially of any other institution in the world—with all manner of skills, talents, gifts, and resources at its disposal. And, maybe most important of all, the church is a biblically based, moral institution that still holds to and teaches God's absolute standards.

Therefore, if churches were committed to a heavenly perspective and a kingdom agenda, there would be a massive transformation in our communities that would radiate out to our cities and, ultimately, our world. The church is not just a building in a neighborhood. God's house is where community transformation begins. When churches degenerate to only being places we attend on Sundays, we have stopped being the people of God. Our kingdom calling is to move out into the community with God's transforming power that affects every area of life.

➤ C. The Altar Built and the Temple Begun (3:1-13) ❦

3:1-2 The priest **Jeshua** and **Zerubbabel** the civil leader led the way (3:2). Jeshua was a descendant of Aaron, and Zerubbabel was in David's line; thus, the people were guided by authorized leaders.

Interestingly, the first thing the returning exiles began building was not the temple, but the **altar**, so that they might restore the true worship of God. The altar was necessary **to** offer burnt offerings ... as it is written in the law of Moses (3:2). Because it was the Jews' failure to worship the Lord and serve him only that had led to the destruction of the temple and the Babylonian exile, the returnees knew that the temple had to have priority. And, even before it was rebuilt, the altar itself was. These returnees wanted to make sure they were faithful to the Mosaic covenant and its requirements so that they might worship God rightly—unlike their ancestors.

3:3 Here, the reader is reminded that the Israelites were in hostile surroundings: **they feared the surrounding peoples**. Thus, they could expect opposition, which would come soon enough. Nevertheless, they offered **burnt offerings** to the Lord in spite of their fear. They had come to embrace an important lesson: we are to fear God more than man.

3:4-5 The people **celebrated the Festival of Shelters**, also known as the Feast of Tabernacles or Booths (3:4). During it, they were to erect temporary shelters to remind them of how their ancestors had lived during their forty-year trek through the wilderness after leaving Egypt. For these Israelites who had returned from Babylon to Jerusalem in a second exodus, this celebration was a reminder of God's provision.

3:6-9 With the sacrifices restored, the former exiles gave **money ... food, drink, and oil** to those who supplied the materials and those who would perform the work on the temple (3:7).

The temple's foundation was begun seventy years after Nebuchadnezzar's first deportation of Jews to Babylon in 605 BC. Some Bible scholars count the beginning of work on the temple as the end of the seventy-year Babylonian exile, while others begin the count with the destruction of Jerusalem and the final deportation to Babylon in 586 BC, ending with the completion of the temple in 515.

3:10-13 When the foundation of the temple was laid, the people had a worship party. But, the singing and shouting **with praise and thanksgiving to the LORD** (3:11) was mixed

with equally loud weeping from **the older priests, Levites, and family leaders, who had seen the first temple** (3:12)—Solomon's temple that the Babylonians had destroyed. So, while it was a joy to be building God's temple again, those who remembered what once had been knew it would not achieve its former glory.

✒ D. The Temple's Construction Halted by Opposition (4:1-24) ✒

4:1-5 "The surrounding peoples" (3:3) who did not want to see the Jews rebuild the temple soon made their presence felt. When these **enemies of Judah and Benjamin** heard what was happening, they first tried to fake friendship with the Jews (4:1-2). But, **Zerubbabel** and the other leaders shut this tactic down with a blunt, "Thanks, but no thanks" (4:3). Rebuffed, they thus **discouraged the people** from building and **bribed officials** to **frustrate** the work (4:4-5). (Clearly, they were no friends of the returnees.)

4:6 Reference to Judah's enemies led Ezra to insert a parenthetical account about other trouble (4:6-23); it probably happened before Nehemiah returned and completed rebuilding Jerusalem's walls. Here, the issue was the rebuilding of Jerusalem, with the opposition beginning in the reign of the Persian king **Ahasuerus**, or Xerxes. The **people who were already in the land** were the descendants of the foreigners whom the Assyrians had imported into Samaria after the fall of the northern kingdom of Israel in 722 BC (see 4:10; 4:2). They were pagans who intermarried with the remaining Jews and mixed the worship of the Lord with their idolatry.

4:7-16 There is no record of what happened as a result of the protest to Xerxes. But, during the reign of **King Artaxerxes**, the letter of protest hit home (4:7). Their accusation was that once the Jews finished Jerusalem's walls, they would stop paying tribute, the king would suffer dishonor, and the people of Jerusalem would become a rebellious thorn in his side (4:12-16).

4:17-23 Artaxerxes consulted his royal records and discovered that Jerusalem had, in fact, been the scene of **uprisings . . . rebellions and revolts** in times past (4:19). So, the king issued a decree for the Jews **to stop** their work (4:21-22), which prompted their enemies to use force to halt the construction (4:23). The Jews' enemies knew that if they could neutralize the construction, they could neutralize the temple, the walls, the city, and the community. And, if they were successful in all this, the influence of God's people would be neutralized. In other words, the enemies had an anti-kingdom agenda, and it was successful for a while.

4:24 This verse jumps backward in time, picking up the narrative where Ezra left off at 4:5. Here we learn that the temple work was stopped **until the second year of the reign of King Darius** in 520 BC. This means as much as eighteen years had passed.

E. The Temple's Construction and Completion (5:1–6:22)

5:1-2 It was imperative that the temple be finished if the people of Israel hoped to restore the true worship of God, so it was a blessing when the long delay was interrupted by the ministries of the prophets **Haggai and Zechariah**. They began to call God's people back to the work on his house (5:1). Because the people had also left the Word of God when they abandoned the temple project, Haggai and Zechariah called them back to faithfulness. As a result, the leadership of **Zerubbabel** and **Jeshua** responded, and **the prophets of God were with them** to help (5:2). Once again, the spiritual and civil leaders were renewed in their desire to finish the work God had given.

5:3-5 Trouble soon came again when the regional governor **Tattenai** and his assistants, who were accountable to the Persian king Darius, heard that the work in Jerusalem had resumed and came to investigate. Tattenai was concerned that the Jews in Jerusalem were planning something devious toward the Persian king. So, the governor asked who had given them the order to rebuild the temple. Furthermore, he made it clear he was taking names so he could report the Jewish leaders to King Darius (5:4). Thankfully, though, **God was watching over the Jewish elders**. He kept them from harm so that they could continue the work until a written response arrived from the king (5:5).

5:6-10 Tattenai began his **letter** by acknowledging that the Jews **of the great God in the province of Judah** were making significant progress on the temple, with the work **being done diligently and succeeding through the people's efforts** (5:6-8). In this statement, the regional governor was not making any particular claims about "the great God"; he was simply noting that he was the God of that region. To acknowledge that certain gods had control over certain lands and peoples was a belief very common in the ancient world. With that done, Tattenai reported his actions and his interrogation of the Jews (5:9-10).

5:11-12 The Jewish leaders composed a response to the governor, which Tattenai in turn forwarded to King Darius. They start by identifying themselves: **We are the servants of the God of the heavens and earth** (5:11). (They knew who they were; that's where you have to start. What you do flows from who you are.) They also were honest about their sin and its consequences. Because their ancestors had angered God, **he handed them over to King Nebuchadnezzar** (5:12). In other words, the king of Babylon hadn't defeated them because his gods were more powerful. Rather, the God of Israel and Judah had delivered them into Nebuchadnezzar's hands because of their disobedience.

5:13-17 Far from acting as rebels, the Jewish people in Jerusalem pointed out that they were acting under the orders of an earlier Persian ruler, **King Cyrus**. He had **issued a decree to rebuild the house of God** (5:13). Thus, everything they were doing was completely legal and above board and that was why they could confidently say of their building project, **It has been under construction from that time** (5:16). The Jewish leaders presented their case to Darius and urged him to conduct a **search of the royal archives** to verify their claims (5:17). Royal documents were carefully recorded and preserved, so the Jews were no doubt confident that they were on solid ground.

6:1-5 Chapter 6 is climactic in many ways and concludes the report of the first return of Jewish exiles to Jerusalem under Zerubbabel. **King Darius** ordered the search requested by the Jewish leaders (6:1). Thankfully, the **scroll was found** with Cyrus's edict commanding that **the house of God in Jerusalem ... be rebuilt** (6:2-3), setting in motion a chain of events that led to the temple's completion.

6:6-10 Darius's own decree began with a stern warning to Tattenai and his officials to **stay away from that place** (that is, Jerusalem) and not to do anything to interfere with **the construction of the house of God** (6:6-7). Moreover, he said that **the cost** of the rebuilding was **to be paid in full ... out of the royal revenues from the taxes of the region west of the Euphrates River**—that is, from the taxes collected in the region over which Tattenai served as governor (6:8). Thus, Tattenai was ordered to leave the Jews alone *and* to give them all the funds they needed from his own coffers. Then, Darius also ordered that everything be provided to the Jews so that they could **offer** their **sacrifices** to God (6:9-10). This statement is a reminder that God knows how to take the resources of the wicked to accomplish the work of his kingdom. It's doubtful that Darius was a true believer in Israel's God, but clearly he was happy to have the Jews **pray** on his behalf (6:10).

6:11-12 The king closed his letter with a P.S., warning **any man who [interfered] with this directive** what would happen to him. If anyone hindered the work on the Jerusalem temple, **a beam** would be **torn from his house**, and he would be **impaled on it**. Then, his **house** would be turned **into a garbage dump** for good measure (6:11). Darius's warning to Tattenai couldn't have been more clear. In effect, he said, "Stay away from Jerusalem, quit harassing the Jews, and send them all the money and provisions they need. Cross me, and I'll have you executed." The king concluded with a wish for God to

overthrow anyone who would oppress his people (6:12). This account of God's provision had to be a great encouragement to Ezra's readers; it was evidence of the unending faithfulness of their God.

6:13-15 Tattenai and his officials had no choice but to carry out the king's orders **diligently** (6:13). Darius had put the fear of God into them. The Lord's number one agenda item for his returning people was to erect the temple, and no human agenda could get in the way.

Notice the importance of **the prophesying of Haggai the prophet and Zechariah** to the success of the work (6:14). Allowing God's word to lead the way was necessary to keep the workers from becoming discouraged or losing focus. These prophets faithfully reminded the people of the urgency and importance of their work in God's eyes. Thus, the temple was completed in the spring of 515 BC, twenty-one years after the work had begun (6:15).

6:16-22 The celebration at the temple's completion was quite an affair. Everyone **celebrated the dedication of the house of God with great joy** (6:16). The number of animals sacrificed was incredible (6:17), suggesting that nothing was too good for the Lord.

The former exiles celebrated alongside a second group described as **all who had separated themselves from the uncleanness of the Gentiles of the land in order to worship the LORD, the God of Israel** (6:21). These were perhaps Jews who had stayed in the land when their brothers were exiled, defiling themselves with paganism by intermingling with the nations around Israel.

The **Festival of Unleavened Bread** (6:22) was also observed for seven days to remind the Jews to separate themselves from sin and defilement by removing all leaven (that is, yeast) from their bread and even their houses.

God had reminded his people that he alone is sovereign, no matter what earthly king sits on the throne. He had **changed the ... king's attitude toward them** (6:22), a reminder that "A king's heart is like channeled water in the LORD's hand: He directs it wherever he chooses" (Prov 21:1).

II. THE RETURN OF THE EXILES UNDER EZRA (7:1–10:44)

❧ A. Ezra: the Man and His Commission (7:1-28) ❧

7:1-6 Chapter 7 leaps ahead several decades to the second return under Ezra himself. **During the reign of King Artaxerxes of Persia, Ezra**—the book's namesake—came to Jerusalem in 458 BC (7:1). His genealogy is provided to establish his priestly pedigree and to show that he descended from Aaron (7:1-5). **A scribe** was an expert in **the law of Moses**, capable of interpreting it and teaching it to the people (7:6). This detail would become vital to the next events recorded because though God's people were out of Babylon, there was still a lot of Babylon (idolatry and immorality) in God's people. Ezra's primary ministry in Judah would be resolving this.

Ezra not only had the right credentials, but he also **came up from Babylon** with the full authority of King Artaxerxes of Persia, who **granted [Ezra] everything he requested because the hand of the LORD his God was on him** (7:6). This explanation for Ezra's success, in fact, is the key to all that happened in the return of God's people from exile and the rebuilding of the temple, from the first return under Zerubbabel to Nehemiah's building of the wall around Jerusalem. God's "hand" being on this process is mentioned numerous times in Ezra (7:6, 9, 29; 8:18, 22) and twice in Nehemiah (see 2:8, 18). So, while pagan kings from Cyrus to Artaxerxes had given the Jews all the protection, royal authority, and financial aid they needed, God was the true King behind these human thrones. He arranged events to fulfill his agenda for Israel.

7:10 Another key to Ezra's ministry was that he **had determined in his heart to study the law of the LORD, obey it, and teach its statutes and ordinances in Israel** (7:10). Ezra was the total package. First, he studied God's law. The Word of God is supremely authoritative because its author is the King of creation. If the divine Ruler of the universe has something to communicate to you,

you can bet it's important. Ezra, accepting this, was determined to know God's Word through and through.

Second, he obeyed it. Ezra wasn't content to be a mere academic, studying the Bible while failing to let it affect his beliefs, character, and actions. God wants his Word to guide our decision-making and to set the agenda for our lives, too. Merely knowing it is insufficient; we must live in submission to it.

Third, Ezra taught God's Word to others. It is good and right to study and obey Scripture. But, we mustn't stop there. We must share it with others so that they, in turn, can understand and obey it. Only then will our families, churches, and communities be transformed.

Ezra is a reminder of the importance of godly human leadership within the church. For the church to function at all, someone has to lead. Moreover, such leadership is God's means of building his kingdom in history. Spiritual leadership today comes with the responsibility of advancing God's agenda by helping to facilitate the biblical goals of Christian maturity and ministry effectiveness in the lives of those under one's charge (see Eph 4:11-12). A good leader is someone who knows the way, goes the way, and shows the way, as Ezra did.

7:11-26 Ezra arrived in Jerusalem carrying a written **letter** from **King Artaxerxes** (7:11) giving permission for any Jew in his kingdom to go back **to Jerusalem** (7:13). It also spelled out how the civil authorities in that region were to help the Jews financially (7:15-24). The king's edict focused on what was needed for the Jews to worship **the God of the heavens** (7:12, 21).

This group of returnees showed up with **silver and gold** given by **the king and his counselors** for God's house, plus the offerings of people **throughout the province of Babylon** (7:15-16). These details are astounding! Not only did the king permit the exiles to return to their homeland, but he also ensured that they would not lack the resources needed to restore the temple and the worship of their God.

Though we have no reason to think Artaxerxes was a true follower of the Lord, he recognized the power of "the God of the heavens." He probably believed in multiple gods but clearly wanted, like Darius (see 6:10), to experience the favor of the God of Israel. Thus, he called for obedience to God, **so that wrath [would] not fall on [his] realm** (7:23).

7:27-28 How did Ezra respond to this display of royal support? He exclaimed, **Blessed be the Lord** (7:27). He knew praise was the only appropriate response to God's sovereign provision. Ezra reminded himself and his readers that God was the true power behind the events: he had **put it into the king's mind to glorify the house of the Lord in Jerusalem** (7:27). He also **took courage** to accomplish the work before him because he had been **strengthened by the hand of the Lord** (7:28). When you know your God and experience his powerful work in your life, you will have the confidence and courage to fulfill the ministry he has given you, too.

⮞ B. The Return to Jerusalem
(8:1-36) ⮜

8:1-14 The list Ezra compiled of the Jewish exiles who were willing to return to Jerusalem began with priestly families and descendants of David and was organized by **family heads** (8:1). It was a much smaller group of returnees than the earlier one under Zerubbabel and Jeshua (2:1-67).

8:15-20 When the group assembled for the hazardous, 900-mile journey to Jerusalem initially, Ezra discovered there were **no Levites** among the returnees (8:15). This was a concern because Levites would be needed to do the work of the Lord at the temple and to teach the law of Moses to the people. The exiles would desperately need to understand God's Word if they were to be successful in their resettlement. Therefore, Ezra commissioned a band of eleven men to go to **Iddo, the leader at Casiphia**, an unknown area, with a message **for him and his brothers . . . that they should bring . . . ministers for the house of . . . God** (8:17). In response,

Levites and a large number of **temple servants** signed up for the trip—because **the gracious hand of . . . God was on** Ezra and the group (7:18-20).

8:21-23 The next challenge was the lengthy, dangerous journey itself. Because Ezra had confidently told the king that God would protect his people on their journey, he was **ashamed to ask the king** for a military escort (8:22). Instead, Ezra called the people to **fast** and pray to God, an act of humility and dependence to which the Lord responded (8:21, 23).

The purpose for fasting was the same then as it is in our day. Fasting communicates to God that we are willing to go without a basic necessity for a period of time because we recognize our need for him is even greater. When we need to experience God more deeply or need his answer in a significant way, fasting is a tangible expression of our dependence on him. Though fasting certainly doesn't twist God's arm to respond as we want, it demonstrates to him (and to us) that we are serious about living according to his perspective.

8:24-30 Ezra did something else very important before setting out for Jerusalem. He committed the offering that the exiles were carrying with them into the hands of a group of trustworthy **priests** and **Levites** who would **guard the silver** and **gold** articles and deliver them safely to the temple (8:24-29). This wise move put Ezra above suspicion and delegated this task to those who would have rightful responsibility for the **holy** articles once **in Jerusalem** (8:28-30). Leaders of God's people must be above reproach and call others to fulfill their own ministerial duties.

8:31-34 Ezra summarized the journey back to Jerusalem in one sentence: **We were strengthened by our God, and he kept us from the grasp of the enemy and from ambush along the way** (8:31). God had responded with divine deliverance to the people's humble fasting and prayer (see 8:21-23).

8:35-36 Upon the group's arrival to their new home, three days of rest (8:32) were followed by multiple sacrifices of praise and worship to God. Ezra gave a copy of the king's decree to the leaders in the region, **so that they would support the people and the house of God** (8:36).

❧ C. Sin of the People and Ezra's Confession *(9:1-15)* ❧

9:1-2 The joy of the return was short-lived. Ezra found himself with a crisis on his hands. Some **leaders** of the Jewish community approached Ezra with bad news, really bad news, and then even worse news. The bad news was that the returned exiles were showing how little they had learned from the example of their ancestors because they had not **separated themselves from the surrounding peoples** and their **detestable practices** (9:1). The really bad news was that **the Israelite men** had taken non-Israelite wives, **so that the holy seed [had] become mixed with** that of **the surrounding peoples**. Even worse, **the leaders and officials [had] taken the lead in this unfaithfulness** (9:2).

Such actions had been clearly forbidden by God. After the exodus from Egypt and before Israel entered the promised land, Moses had commanded them not to intermarry with the people groups listed in Ezra 9:1 (see Deut 7:1-3). Why? "Because they will turn your sons away from me to worship other gods. Then the LORD's anger will burn against you, and he will swiftly destroy you" (Deut 7:4). The Israelites of Ezra's day, then, were walking a path that would send them right back into divine judgment.

9:3-4 Ezra dramatically demonstrated his horror and humiliation before the Lord on behalf of his sinful people (9:3). Those who similarly took God seriously—that is, those **who trembled at the words of the God of Israel**—gathered around Ezra as he **sat devastated** (9:4).

Some Christians today, who have grown up in a culture that prizes individualism, might be puzzled at Ezra's response here. After all, Ezra himself wasn't guilty of this sin, so why should he be so concerned? But, Ezra had a right understanding of the *corporate* aspect of being a part of the people of God.

Think of it this way. A faithful offensive lineman may perform a well-executed block. But, if the rest of the offensive line collapses and the quarterback is sacked, the faithful football player is still on the losing end of things because he is part of a *team*. God calls his church a *body*—composed of many parts but functioning as one unit (see 1 Cor 12:12-31). We, as the church, are not merely to look after ourselves but to practice the "one anothers" of Scripture (see John 15:12; Gal 6:2; Eph 4:32; 1 Thess 5:11). God doesn't want Lone Ranger Christians. Our spiritual vitality and growth only come as we serve the Lord *together.* ✦

9:5-7 Like the godly leader he was, Ezra turned to the Lord in prayer. Though he was personally innocent, he readily identified with God's people, his fellow Jews, who had sinned. Ezra **fell on [his] knees and spread out [his] hands to the LORD**, which was a position of deep contrition and repentance (9:5). He was personally **ashamed and embarrassed** to look up to God because of the people's unfaithfulness (9:6).

Unfortunately, such blatant sin among the Israelites was nothing new, but had characterized previous generations who had suffered under the disciplining hand of God as a result (9:7). How could the men of Ezra's generation be so blind and hard-hearted as to ignore their people's history and invite God's judgment once again?

9:8-9 Ezra might have despaired about the future of the restored community except for one wonderful truth about the Lord: He is a God of **grace** (9:8). He had seen fit to **preserve a remnant** of his people and to deliver them from **slavery** once again—not so that they might live for themselves, but so that they might **rebuild the house of . . . God** (9:8-9).

9:10-15 In light of God's abundant grace, there was no excuse for this sin of intermarrying with the unrighteous nations surrounding them. Ezra acknowledged that the people had broken God's clear commands, even quoting them back to God to demonstrate his understanding of how serious this offense was (9:11-12). Ezra knew God had already treated Israel far better than they deserved (9:13). He would be completely justified in sweeping them away and leaving no **survivor** (9:14). So, with all this said, Ezra made no specific request of the Lord. Instead, he threw himself and his people on God's grace. He said, **we are before you with our guilt ... no one can stand in your presence because of this** (9:15).

➤ D. Confession of the People
(10:1-44) ✦

10:1-4 Ezra's distraught condition over the sin of interfaith marriages and his humble, **facedown** repentance drew a large crowd to the open square in front of the temple (10:1). The people joined Ezra in bitter weeping, and, to their credit, were determined to deal with the situation. A man named **Shecaniah** spoke for the group, pledging their support for the painful steps the leader Ezra would have to take to remedy these sinful intermarriages (10:2-4).

The seriousness of the situation is indicated in Shecaniah's use of the word **covenant** to describe the people's earnestness (10:3). A covenant is a promise that binds the parties to its fulfillment. The people had determined **to send away all the foreign wives and their children** (10:3). Clearly, this cleansing would be difficult, but it was necessary to maintain the purity of the restored Israelite community and to avert further spiritual corruption that would bring God's judgment again.

Having said that, I want to clarify that these were unique circumstances in the history of the nation of Israel. The church should not see these events as prescribing a principle for marriages today in which a Christian is married to an unbeliever. Clearly,

a believer is to marry another believer—one who is "in the Lord" (1 Cor 7:39). But, if a person becomes a believer *after* he or she is already married to an unbeliever, Paul gives biblical counsel about such situations in 1 Corinthians 7:12-16.

10:5-8 Soon, the leaders **circulated a proclamation ... that all the exiles should gather at Jerusalem** (10:7). The Israelite men who had entered into such marriages had flouted the Mosaic law's prohibition against unholy unions (see Deut 7:1-4). And sadly, nearly one-quarter of the offenders were priests and Levites who knew God's Word better than anyone. Drastic measures, then, had to be taken. Any offender who did not show up in Jerusalem to appear before Ezra **would forfeit all his possessions** and be excommunicated **from the assembly of the exiles** (10:8).

10:9-16 Ezra took his place of leadership to begin reviewing the cases, but a bone-chilling **heavy rain** made the proceedings miserable to endure (10:9). Then, Ezra called it like it was. He said, **You have been unfaithful** (10:10). And so, a plan was worked out to let leaders in each town judge the offenders among them (10:12-14). The related process took three months to implement fully, but in the end, the cleansing was complete (10:16).

10:18-44 As if to emphasize the seriousness of this sin and its threat to the restored community, the list of Jewish men who had married pagan wives was led by **the priests ... Levites ... singers**, and **gatekeepers** (10:18, 23-24)—those responsible for overseeing the temple and leading Israel to worship the Lord. Only when these leaders had dealt with their sin could the whole assembly move forward in establishing themselves in their land under God's blessing.

NEHEMIAH

INTRODUCTION

Author

THOUGH THE BOOK OF NEHEMIAH is recognized as an anonymous work, it claims to convey "the words of Nehemiah son of Hacaliah" (1:1). This combined with the frequent first-person perspective make clear that much of the content goes back to Nehemiah himself. Thus, we are justified in attributing authorship to him.

Historical Background

Nehemiah was the cupbearer to Artaxerxes the Persian king (see Neh 1:11). Thirteen years after Ezra, in about 445 BC (or "the twentieth year of King Artaxerxes," Neh 2:1), Nehemiah was sent to Jerusalem to rebuild the walls (see Neh 2:1-8) to address the failure of God's people to reestablish what God had intended with regard to their physical, social, political, economic, and family life.

Message and Purpose

Nehemiah led the third return of exiled Jews back to the land of Israel. As cupbearer to the king of Persia, he held an important administrative post in the government. When he received word that the people who had already returned to Jerusalem were in distress, he was greatly disturbed. But, he believed God's promise that when his people repented and returned to him, he would restore their land.

Based on God's Word, Nehemiah began a program of what we today could call "community development" among God's people. With the blessing and help of a pagan king, Nehemiah returned home to rebuild the walls of Jerusalem, the city of God. This demonstrates that even the secular world is subject to God when his people operate according to his kingdom promises and authority.

Nehemiah also provides a study in great leadership. In a mere fifty-two days, Nehemiah led the people, amid opposition, to rebuild Jerusalem's walls. He also called for the development of solid families, for the temple to be the center of life, for the people to live under the covenant promises of God, and for them to become a righteous and just community. The book of Nehemiah is about making wrong things right.

VIDEO   INTRO

www.bhpublishinggroup.com/qr/te/16_00

Outline

NEHEMIAH

I. PRAYING FOR A CHANGE (1:1-11)

1:1 God's method is to work through individuals. He is always looking for someone he can use. **Nehemiah son of Hacaliah** would accomplish in fifty-two days what had not been accomplished in 141 years. His story is a reminder that if you are trying to fix what is broken down, it does not take long—if you put God first.

Nehemiah, a Jew living in the Persian Empire, **was the king's cupbearer** (1:11), a significant role. More than just a food taster, the cupbearer served as chief of staff. King Artaxerxes would've made sure to fill the spot with someone who had a great reputation and could be trusted.

1:2-3 Nehemiah remembered where he came from. When his brother reported, **Jerusalem's wall has been broken down, and its gates have been burned** (1:3), Nehemiah knew that those in his homeland were experiencing insecurity galore because that was a sign of degradation galore. The people who'd returned to Israel had made absolutely no progress in reestablishing what God had intended with regard to their physical, social, political, economic, and family life.

1:4 Nehemiah **wept** and **mourned . . . fasting and praying before the God of the heavens**. He backed away from his personal peace and affluence long enough to ask, "What about those at home who don't enjoy the privileges I know?" Some of us are on our way to heaven and are satisfied. When is the last time you wept over relatives who don't know Christ?

Nehemiah prayed in response to the news he'd received. It sounded like Jerusalem's was a society of broken people. Broken people cannot fix broken walls. This raises the question: is prayer the first thing or the last thing that you do when you see that something is broken? If it's the last thing, then you waste time in everything you do that leaves God out of the equation to fix it. Far too often, we allow other things to push prayer aside rather than allowing prayer to push other things aside.

Nehemiah also fasted. Fasting indicates that you are really serious about your relationship with God. It is being willing to give up something that your body craves in order to gain something your spirit needs.

What wall has crumbled in your personal life? Your family life? Your career? Push everything else aside and connect with God on the matter.

1:5 Prayer is the preamble to action. You can always tell how serious people are about their belief that only God can make the difference by their prayer. Nehemiah began by saying, **Lord, the God of the heavens, the great and awe-inspiring God who keeps his gracious covenant with those who love him and keep his commands**. While most of us would have jumped in and said, "Fix this problem, Lord," Nehemiah reminds us that we should start off reminding ourselves of who our God is and what our God can do!

A woman once said to British evangelist G. Campbell Morgan, "I only take small things to God because I don't want to worry him with the big things." To this he replied, "Lady, anything you bring to God is small." We tend to magnify our problems, when we should magnify God instead. If we rightly see him for who he is, we'll never see our problems as too much for him to handle.

1:6-7 Nehemiah prayed **day and night** (1:6). In 1:1, his prayer began **during the month of Chislev**, and in 2:1 we'll see that he didn't get an answer until "the month of Nisan"—four and a half months later! I am often asked, "How long should I pray for something?" To this I respond, "Until you get an answer." God can say, "Yes," or he can say, "No." Or, he can say nothing, which means, "Wait." Until God says, "Yes" or "No," you pray.

To understand what Nehemiah did in this part of his prayer, we need to know that God places his people in culture as a preservative (see Matt 5:13-14). He works through people to address society at large. But, the sons of Israel, who had a covenant with God, had **sinned** (1:6). Nehemiah included himself in this problem; he identified with Israel and understood his contribution to their woes (1:7). He knew he was in a representative position. A real man says, "I identify with this problem; it is mine."

This man's focus on sin when the wall's state was likely foremost on his mind indicates that deterioration—whether in personal life, family life, or society—can be traced back to sin. And, one of the great failures in our culture is the failure of the church of Jesus Christ to acknowledge its own. The Bible says, "the time has come for judgment to begin with God's household" (1 Pet 4:17). Only then we can address the unrighteous.

1:8-9 This is an awesome line: **Please remember what you commanded your servant Moses** (1:8). Now, we know that God does not forget. So, what Nehemiah was saying, in effect here, was, "Lord, you remembered your word about cursing us: **If you are unfaithful, I will scatter you**. But, remember your other word: **If you return to me . . . I will gather [you]** (1:8-9).

No matter what mess you have created, no matter how far you have gone, God has good news for you. He's in the gathering business. In other words, if you are faithful, he will turn circumstances around. No matter how bad things get, God will honor his word.

1:10 The word **servants** here is a good reminder that God obligated himself to the believing world, so the believing world could get things done for the non-believing world.

1:11 Nehemiah was a layman who had become upper class because he had gotten some unique privileges. It dawned on him that God had positioned him to make a difference. The **man** he referred to was the king. He was getting ready to ask his permission to go back and rebuild Jerusalem.

Now, you don't just ask the king for such a leave of absence if you are his cupbearer, because you are the one who makes sure no one assassinates him. It would be unlikely that he'd let you disappear for months at a time. Nevertheless, Nehemiah intended to ask.

In the church, we often separate our careers from our worship. But, Nehemiah saw his career as a strategic position. King Artaxerxes was an unregenerate man, but he had the power to solve the problem. So, after arming himself with prayer, Nehemiah needed to ask for it. Prayer is the power for action. God can use the unrighteous to fulfill his goal for the righteous.

Perhaps you work for a major organization, but you have not interpreted your "cupbearing" as an opportunity to make a difference for the glory of God. If we are going to rebuild our communities, we need to learn to kingdomize our skills. Any person who uses a computer who then takes time to teach a brother or sister to use that skill so that they can become employed and become a contributing member of society and take care of their family has kingdomized his skill. Ask the Lord to show you how to use your job situation to make a kingdom difference.

Also of note here is the word **today**. Spoiler alert: what Nehemiah would ask would not work out for four and a half months. But, this pause is good news for you if you're waiting for divine intervention: God has not forgotten you; he is working out a network of events. Sometimes, God has to let A go over to Z to get back to T to enter with B so you can have a well-defined alphabet of life. He is dependable and he is faithful. Don't give up, but "Seek first the kingdom of God and his righteousness, and all these things will be provided for you" (Matt 6:33).

II. GOD'S SOVEREIGNTY (2:1-20)

Once, I told my kids to put on their coats because it was going to become cold later in the day. They said it wasn't cold. I explained that I had listened to the weather report for the day and that they should trust me. With some grumbling, they obeyed. When they got out of school that afternoon, it was freezing. (Dad was right again!)

I had inside information on what the circumstances would be hours later. And, we need to know something about God: he knows the weather report. When God speaks to you, you should listen to him even if you feel that you don't need your coat. He has inside information on the "spiritual weather" outlook of your life. Thus, his wisdom and knowledge should be the foundation of your actions.

In this chapter, we'll see a tension between God at work and government at work, and between the sovereignty of God and the responsibility of men. When such tension is brought into balance, rebuilding can occur—not only in your personal life, but in your career and community.

2:1-3 Part of Nehemiah's job was cheering up the king. So, when the king noticed he was sad, Nehemiah was **overwhelmed with fear** (2:2); the king could have executed him for it. The insight into the cupbearer's feelings indicates that you can be walking with God and still be afraid.

After giving respect to the king, Nehemiah spoke frankly: **Why should I not be sad when the city where my ancestors are buried lies in ruins and its gates have been destroyed by fire?** (2:3). He did not identify Jerusalem specifically because he was being shrewd. (In Ezra 4, King Artaxerxes had thought that if Jerusalem were rebuilt the people might stop paying taxes.) Nehemiah avoided the political issue by boiling it down to a personal issue.

In verse 6, we'll learn that "the queen" was there to hear this conversation. God had arranged it so there was a sensitive heart, a feminine touch in the environment. Moreover, history tells us there were revolutions in Syria at this time, so if in addressing

Nehemiah's concerns the king could get his own man on the field, he could have a new citadel to help him keep an ear out for news from there. In other words, God had been putting things in place to help Nehemiah's cause. As Proverbs 21:1 says, "A king's heart is like channeled water in the LORD's hand: He directs it wherever he chooses."

2:4 According to Romans 13:1-7, government is to be God's servant. But, unless God's people are influencing government so that it has a divine standard by which to operate, government won't know which way to go. The reason most governments don't carry out God's agenda, in fact, is because God's people are not influencing them.

We see here Nehemiah's awareness that he was dealing with two kings. He was talking to **the king** of Persia, even as he prayed to **the God of the heavens**. There is *a* king, and there is *the* King. We want to give up when our careers and marriages are not going right because we are looking at *a* king and not *the* King. But, I don't care what you are facing; if you will bring *the* King to bear on it, it does not matter how big *a* king—a boss, a rival, a mess—is.

When our church was meeting at an elementary school, we received a letter stating that we could not meet there any longer because three members of the school board were very upset by our presence. We called the congregation to prayer. We asked for a meeting with the school board. Even on the drive to the meeting, we prayed: "Lord in heaven, this is bigger than us. Give us the right words to say, and reverse the decision." There were supposed to be ten board members at the gathering, but only seven showed. The head of the committee thus said, "Because they aren't here, we'll render a decision without them." As a result, the vote went in our favor. We were blessed that day because we appealed to the God of heaven, and the sovereign Lord heard our cry.

2:5-6 The phrase, **it pleased the king to send me**, may suggest that Artaxerxes saw in his cupbearer's concerns an opportunity to do something for his own kingdom. Before the meeting's close, he not only let Nehemiah go, he also made him the governor of Jerusalem (see 5:14). God was working "all things work together for the good" of his servant (Rom 8:28).

2:7-9 Nehemiah requested **letters** (2:7) for safe passage and goods to finance the rebuilding—a government grant. The Bible says, "the earth is the Lord's, and all that is in it" (1 Cor 10:26), so it's a simple matter for God to dispense wealth when it is going to accomplish his divine agenda. He always pays for his will.

Clearly, Nehemiah had already planned for this conversation. God's sovereignty means he decides what happens. Your planning means you are ready for it whenever it happens. Paul says we are "working together" with God (2 Cor 6:1). Anything you accomplish, then, is because God either scored the points or provided the assist; you never do anything good on your own. "Every good and every perfect gift is from above" (Jas 1:17). Anything you are able to do is because of God's goodness and grace.

The king granted Nehemiah's request because **the gracious hand of** God was on him (2:8). So, if you find success, is it because you came up with a good plan? No. Is it because you are a brilliant individual, a smooth politician, a great businessman? No. It does not matter what you plan if God's hand is not on you. People and families are falling apart, in fact, because they won't let God's hand operate on their behalf.

Plans are made by man, but only God gives the increase. So, while Nehemiah asked for a letter and wood, God also gave him **infantry and cavalry** (2:9). You can know God is in a thing, in fact, when you ask for A and he also gives you B and C. God likes to outdo the request.

2:10 Sanballat and Tobiah ... **were greatly displeased**. Their mention here is a reminder that whenever you are going to do something right, enemies will show up. Satan has an agenda. But remember: "Our struggle is not against flesh and blood, but against ... evil" (Eph 6:12). If you are spending most of your time fighting another person, in fact, you are not fighting the problem. The other person is only a tool, a pawn.

2:11-15 Nehemiah quietly went out and **inspected the walls of Jerusalem that had been broken down** (2:13). Sometimes, that is what a family head has to do. He has to inspect the walls, to look at what is tearing down a home, and to ruminate on how the matter can be addressed. With this job comes the tough task of asking, "Am I contributing to this problem? Am I doing what God wants, or what I want?"

2:16-18 Nehemiah talked to the people: **Come, let's rebuild Jerusalem's wall, so that we will no longer be a disgrace** (2:17). His words suggest that the people of God are often an embarrassment, though we are supposed to be the people of God. To this situation Nehemiah said, "No more!" Thus, **their hands were strengthened to do this good work** (2:18).

2:19-20 Satan showed up again through **Sanballat ... Tobiah**, and **Geshem. They mocked and despised** the workers and said, **What is this you're doing? Are you rebelling against the king?** (2:19). In other words, they suggested this spiritual work was a political issue. But, Nehemiah appealed to a higher source for his vindication: **the God of the heavens** (2:20).

III. PLANNING FOR SUCCESS (3:1-32)

3:1 The **rebuilding** work in this passage is a reminder that no matter what fell apart in your life, God can rebuild it in less time than it took you to mess it up. There is hope for a broken-down life, a broken-down family, a broken-down church, and even a broken-down community when God gets a good person with a good plan going about his kingdom agenda. These people had been living in Jerusalem for years, but they just never linked up to deal with the wall issue. Nehemiah unified them around a common purpose, and suddenly things were getting done.

The devil's task is to keep people in the church from linking up to take on their common spiritual goals. As long as he can keep you disunified, he can keep walls torn down and the gates burned up. But, when Christians realize they have a common enemy, all other problems lessen in their significance. We find power in unity.

This same principle applies to the home. Sometimes, a husband will say, "My wife is different from me." Of course she is! If both marriage partners were the same, one of them would be unnecessary. The main thing a husband has to do in a home is set forth God's agenda for the family. If you don't, everyone will have his or her own agenda. When there is unity, however, there is power.

Importantly, unity is not sameness. Unity is oneness of purpose. That, in fact, is why people have so many meetings over race problems that don't seem to go anywhere. Everyone has their own interests and agenda. The only way you can overcome that is to have a purpose so much bigger than everyone's private focuses that they can march on common ground.

Don't miss that **the high priest** and **his fellow priests** were leading the way in the rebuilding of this community by **rebuilding the Sheep Gate**. What would come through this gate once it was back in repair? The sheep that would be sacrificed in the temple. Thus, they **dedicated** the Sheep Gate—an action that showed their divine perspective on the work.

The mention of these men here brings me to an important point. Whenever people decide they are going to rebuild the community, they must be aware that the most important institution in a community is the church. The values that must be operating in an area in order for it to survive and for businesses to stay within it, has to be set forth by a moral agency. What better agency is there than the church?

Society needs a standard, a measuring rod. The church does not replace a bank or a social entity, but it infiltrates and influences them so they begin to make their decisions based on a proper moral code. The church highlights the standards, the absolutes, the rights and wrongs. The church points to the truth. Thus, churches based on the Word of

God can begin to turn a dilapidated community around when they operate biblically.

3:2 The men of Jericho were commuters, meaning that there is a place in a local church family for people who must commute a long distance to attend. However, people tend to move away from communities where the spiritual needs are greatest. So, while it's okay to commute to your church, make sure you let your godly presence and the strengths that God has given you be felt in your local community where the walls are torn down and the gates are burned.

3:3-8 Even the **goldsmith** and **the perfumer made repairs** (3:8)! Though these men may not have been used to such physical labor, they were willing to use their time and energy to make a difference in the community process. Similarly, when there is a common agenda, you have to take some of your time and energy and get busy with the greater need. Nehemiah called out the wealthy **Tekoites** who chose to be lazy and **did not lift a finger to help** (3:5).

3:9-11 Don't miss that the **ruler of half the district of Jerusalem** made **repairs** (3:9). Some people have the idea—especially if they're considered somebodies in the community—that a church is blessed because they joined. Let us get this straight: you are the privileged one when you are granted membership, by the grace of God, in his church. It is not because of who we are but because the cross of Christ has enough grace that we are let in.

3:12 Shallum's **daughters** made repairs, too. God has called women in his kingdom to have strategic positions of responsibility that must be acknowledged and respected. The strengths of godly women are not to be ignored or bypassed but utilized. Similarly, if your wife has a degree or a skill in a particular field, you're foolish if you don't recognize, honor, and promote that skill, so that your family benefits.

3:13-27 Apparently, there were bachelors on the wall because **Benjamin and Hasshub made repairs opposite their house** (3:23).

The key here is that they weren't working on their *houses* but their *house*. Even though they were single, they found their place on the wall. (And, who knows? They might have run into Shallum's eligible daughters in the process; see 3:12).

This whole passage is full of phrases like "after them" and "next to them," showing how the people combined forces to get the job done. When you have a puzzle, you have protrusions and indentations. The protrusions represent the strengths and the indentations reflect the weaknesses. Your protrusion in a puzzle fits into another piece's indentations, so that you link up. If we link our strengths with someone else's weaknesses and vice versa, then we can put something on display worth looking at.

This massive project was handled in much the same way that you would eat an elephant: in manageable sections. The people in Jerusalem for 150 years had been saying, "The job's too big. All the walls are down!" And, this is just the kind of thing many people say at the thought of addressing their broken marriages, kids, and communities. But, to do that is to look at the whole elephant rather than the small bite on your fork. Taking on the whole world *is* too big, so focus on one thing at a time. When you do, what you thought would take centuries to address might well be accomplished in fifty-two days.

I love that this chapter's lists include men's names. These guys had been there all the time—doing nothing, a reminder that Satan's great victory against spiritual progress in a nation is the removal of men from the spiritual sphere. If you are going to rebuild families and communities, you are going to need men to stop wimping out and making excuses. There is a place for sports and entertainment, but all of that is secondary to what men were created to do. Manhood requires taking responsibility for the challenges you face. Whenever you are being irresponsible, you are not being a kingdom man.

Don't miss that the Tekoites did so well on one wall (3:5) that **they made repairs to another section** (3:27).

3:28 The priests made repairs **each opposite his own house**. Why? First, for the sake of time: they did not have far to go, so they could give more time to getting the work done. Second, this would ensure excellence: if a man is fixing a wall outside of his home, it will be a well-fixed wall. Third, this allowed whole families to get involved. Thus, Nehemiah masterfully gave his craftsman personal investments in the work.

3:29-32 After them . . . And beside him . . . Next to him are all phrases suggesting solidarity and even quality control (3:29-30). Within the church, sometimes you may miss a ministry opportunity, but as soon as you see it, you have to plug it by inviting someone else to come alongside to meet that need. We as believers have all kinds of personalities and all kinds of skills, but many of us have never kingdomized them. God wants you to use your spiritual gift to link up with other Christians and accomplish his divine agenda.

IV. THE FAITH THAT OVERCOMES (4:1-23)

4:1 When you are the most determined to fix your life, your family, your church, or your society, people will show up to tell you why it shouldn't and can't be done. **When Sanballat heard that [they] were rebuilding the wall, he became furious. He mocked the Jews.** There will always be people who'll find it in their self-interest to keep you from succeeding in building what needs to be built in your life because they are threatened by it. That, in fact, was Sanballat's problem. He knew that the prospering of the Jews would be a threat to his own status. But, when you are in the will of God, what is yours is yours—God protects it until you get it.

4:2-3 Sanballat and his friends ridiculed the Jews. The last thing they needed was someone sitting on the sidelines telling them how big the job was and how they really couldn't do it, and Sanballat's critique was partially true! The Jews really were **pathetic**. The original wall had been built by many more people and was more impressive-looking. Tobiah said, **If a fox climbed up what they are building, he would break down their stone wall** (4:2-3), which was an exaggeration, but still discouraging.

People can only criticize you when you are *doing* something. If you are never being criticized, then, it could be that you are just sitting around. When you take a right stand, you are going to be criticized. Some men need to be criticized for being home with their families too much. Some women need to be criticized for prioritizing marriage. Some teenagers need to be criticized for having high moral standards.

4:4-5 Nehemiah did not retaliate. The Lord says, "Vengeance belongs to me; I will repay" (Deut 32:35). When you do the repaying, then, you cancel out divine benefits that may have otherwise been received. Nehemiah called on God to defend his people.

4:6 That **the people had the will to keep working** means it was in their hearts and minds to persevere. When I hear a husband and wife tell me, "We can't make it anymore," I know divorce is in their minds. When a drug addict says, "I can't kick the habit," I know that refusing to try is in his mind. When you say, "I can't keep my morality under control," living below God's standards is in your mind. When you say, "We can't turn the community around," defeat is in your mind. So, the greatest task that God has in people's lives is changing our minds to trust that, with his help, we can do anything. When people come together with this and a will to work at whatever task is ahead, we will get a better end scenario.

4:7-9 Nehemiah's enemies' criticism did not work, so they upped the ante and **plotted** against the Jews (4:8). Thus, everyone **prayed** to God and **stationed a guard** (4:9).

The people's actions here are a reminder that the way you know whether you prayed in faith is by what you do after taking a matter to God. You can't say, "I'm praying that God gives me a job," without going job-hunting in the meantime. When you pray, you are trusting God so much that you feel confident that you *can* do something. Prayer is the preamble to action.

All you need is faith the size of a mustard seed and you can move mountains (see Matt 17:20). So often, our underlying problem is not that we need *great* faith, but that we have a *small* God in our minds. You need a *little* bit of faith in a *big* God, not a *lot* of faith in a *little* God. You and I exercise faith all the time. When you fly, you trust the mechanics, engineers, and pilots. But, why place faith in two or three men to take you to 36,000 feet and not have faith in God who created the resources and natural laws from which the plane was created and is able to fly? Nehemiah knew that the job was big, but he also knew that his God was *bigger*.

4:10-11 The enemies had a conspiracy, but God could hear what was happening in their camp. When Nehemiah prayed, the conspiracy was revealed (4:11), and he set a watch. God can lead you to safety when you did not even know you were in trouble. He sets watch over you and frustrates the plans of the evil one.

4:12-14 Satan wants us to forget the Lord. That's why Nehemiah encouraged the people not to be **afraid** but to **remember the great and awe-inspiring Lord**. Then he said, **Fight for your countrymen, your sons and daughters, your wives and homes** (4:14). The people of God need a shared vision: we, too, are brothers and sisters in arms, facing a shared enemy in the spiritual battle of the cosmos.

4:15-23 Prayer must be balanced with prudence. That's why the workers **held spears, shields, bows, and armor** (4:16), while saying, **Our God will fight for us!** (4:20). They were dependent on God. But, because God had given them weapons, they trusted him to use those means he'd provided to do whatever fighting needed to be done. To use available means without prayer is to be self-sufficient. To pray and not use available means is to be irresponsible. Prudence utilizes the resources that God has given to maximize our ability to do what God has called us to do.

The Bible says God feeds the birds. When was the last time you saw a bird on a branch with his mouth open toward heaven, just waiting for worms to drop? Birds go worm-hunting. So, does God provide the worms? Absolutely, because every worm that any bird finds, God made.

Nehemiah gave the people this big vision in verse 20: "Our God will fight for us!" I like being put in impossible situations because it's then that I will call on God to do the supernatural. So many of us never see such things happen because we do our fighting for ourselves.

Icebergs will never be pushed in the direction of the wind because the current of the water is stronger than the power of the wind, and the water has access to nine-tenths of the iceberg. Most of us react to the winds of life that are blowing against us, when we have the current of God's power available to us. You don't have to go with the wind if you flow with the current. "The one who is in you is greater than the one who is in the world" (1 John 4:4).

V. A CRY FOR JUSTICE AND THE POWER OF PERSEVERANCE (5:1–6:19)

5:1-5 What we see here was a serious family matter (5:1). Some Jews were practicing economic exploitation (5:2-5). It was a time of personal loss because families were involved in corporate activity and, therefore, didn't have the time for agricultural development. Facing growing debt and government taxation, they were forced to seek help. And, profiteering Jews seized the opportunity to make money off misfortunes by charging exorbitant interest rates on loans made to their Jewish brothers. It's unbiblical to charge interest to profit off someone's distress.

5:6-8 Nehemiah said, **We have done our best to buy back our Jewish countrymen who were sold to foreigners, but now you sell your own countrymen, and we have to buy them back** (5:8). So, not only did they have to buy back fellow Jews from sinners, but also from supposed saints. There ought to be a difference between the two groups! Similarly, if a man names the name of Jesus Christ, you ought to be able to trust that you're dealing with someone who is not going to rip you off.

5:9-11 What was happening was a spiritual issue because they were making God look bad in front of **foreign enemies**. They weren't walking **in the fear of . . . God**, and it stained God's reputation in the eyes of outsiders. (5:9). Understand that when you are not responsible for your actions, it makes God look bad. Your job is to make God look good through everything you do.

In essence, Nehemiah told them to give back what they'd stolen with interest (5:11). This highlights a spiritual principle. If you have done sloppy work for someone, go to them, apologize, and make it up to them. This is the principle of restitution, and it applies to romantic relationships, as well. If you have ignored your spouse for five years, go apologize and say, "I want to spend the next five years making it up to you." If you follow up on that promise, you will have the Lord's blessing.

5:12-13 What we see here is called a self-maledictory oath—an oath of impending doom if a person fails to fulfill the contract. Nehemiah's shaking of **the folds of [his] robe** (5:13) meant that such a thing would happen to the people who failed to do as they said. God holds you accountable to your promise.

5:14-19 Nehemiah looked over his career of **twelve years** as governor (5:14) and concluded that he had honored the Word of God. He hadn't done what the **governors who preceded** him had (5:15). He had **devoted [himself] to the construction of [the] wall** (15:16). Just as importantly, he'd led by example.

I love Nehemiah's prayer in verse 19: **Remember me favorably, my God**. It should make you ask, "How is God going to remember me?" When a student violinist receives a standing ovation, he should be mostly concerned with whether his teacher is applauding; after all, only he would know exactly how the piece ought to sound and what it took for the student to play it well. If God is not well pleased with you, you are a dismal failure. So, live in such a way that on judgment day, Jesus Christ stands and says, "Well done, good and faithful servant" (Matt 25:21).

6:1-4 Nehemiah's only remaining task was to install **the doors** (6:1). The last part of a task, however, can be the toughest part of all. He had to persevere, but Nehemiah got some inside information that his enemies **were planning to harm** him (6:2).

Nehemiah knew he couldn't submit to his enemies' request because he was **doing important work** (6:3). He said this because you don't leave something greater to do something lesser. You never leave the will of God. So, why would he leave his work and go down to those who ridiculed the people of God and declared war on them? Before you follow someone, ask: "Is this person taking me away from God's will? What is his character like?"

6:5-9 Nehemiah's enemy sent an **open letter** to sway the public's perception, leading them to think that Nehemiah was just doing his own show—that he wanted **to become their king** (6:6). This turn of events likely scared Nehemiah, so he did what he did best: he prayed. He said, **God, strengthen my hands** (6:9).

When you know you are doing what God wants you to do, but you are ready to quit, you need to go to God. If you are feeling pressure to walk away from a standard or to make compromise because you are worried about what everybody else thinks, you have to say, "I only care what God thinks." The majority must not be allowed to rule you; God rules.

6:10-14 Shemaiah claimed to have a **prophecy** (6:10-12), but many people misuse the name of the Lord as Shemaiah did. Please, be careful what you listen to. Religious terminology does not guarantee legitimacy. Thankfully, Nehemiah knew **that God had not sent him** but that **Tobiah and Sanballat had hired him** (6:12). Shemaiah was trying to get Nehemiah to disobey God out of fear.

6:15-19 You won't arrive at the completion of God's plan for your life without facing your own Sanballats, Tobiahs, and Geshems; without being tempted to fear; without encountering moments in which you can sense that the enemy is trying to destroy you. If you submit to your King's agenda, Satan will never cease trying **to intimidate** you (6:19). Don't fear him. When you finally achieve success, you'll be able to proclaim with Nehemiah, **this task [was] accomplished by our God** (6:16).

VI. REQUIREMENTS FOR A REAL REVIVAL (7:1–8:18)

7:1-2 If a leader wants to keep something going in the right direction, he will need to enlist the help of people who are capable, and leaders in the church must also ensure those workers have brought their lives into submission to the Lord. With this principle in mind, Nehemiah picked a military commander who **was a faithful man who feared God** (7:2). To fear God is not to be terrified of him, but to be rightfully in awe of him. It means taking God seriously. Spiritual leadership that fears God will make a kingdom impact.

7:3 Nehemiah got everyone involved protecting their territory, **some at their posts and**

some at their homes. This is a reminder that the church must be ever vigilant. Later, Paul would warn the Ephesians elders that "savage wolves" would rise up among them and "distort the truth to lure the disciples into following them" (Acts 20:29-31). The pastors and elders of local churches are to protect God's people by teaching what is faithful to God's Word and exposing what deviates from it.

7:4-69 Nehemiah had restructured the community and provided protection and security and welfare, but **there were few people** actually living in Jerusalem (7:4). What they needed was a reinvestment. Nehemiah wanted a census of the people so he could bring families back into the city. **God put it into [his] mind** to do this (7:5), a reminder that when you have a dynamic prayer life and an obedient life, the Spirit of God will move your heart to accomplish his will, too. Nehemiah **found a genealogical record of those who came back first** from exile (7:5); this was exactly what he needed.

7:70-73 God never ordains things that he does not fund. The funding problems our local churches face often come down to management: we, as believers, are not theological with our money. We must remember that all we have is his and give generously.

8:1 When **all the people gathered**, they asked for the preacher. Soaking in the word of God is like taking vitamins. Over the long haul, it provides a sense of well-being. **Ezra** had been preaching among the Jews for fourteen years (Ezra 7:10), creating a spiritual environment, softening the ground with truth, and orienting the people toward a standard. That, in fact, was why Nehemiah had found the people open to the possibility for rebuilding the wall—for family renewal and community development. By this point, the people had seen the miracle God had done in fifty-two days when they obeyed God's word. They wanted to know what else God could do.

8:2-3 Ezra **read out of [God's Word] from daybreak until noon** (that's six hours!) and the people **listened attentively** (8:3). Should you find yourself saying "I can't pay attention to the Word of God for six hours at a time," consider whether you can watch TV for six hours. Or hang out with your friends. You *can* do what you *want* to do. You can do it because, once you perceive a benefit from a thing, "long" becomes "short." The Israelites perceived the value of the Word of God.

8:4-5 Such respect was given to the Word of God that they literally lifted it up. They built a **platform** (8:4). And, when Ezra opened the book, **all the people stood** without being asked because they understood that God was speaking through it (8:5). The Word of God is worthy of your reverence.

8:6 Ezra **blessed the Lord and all the people said, Amen!** *Amen* means, "I agree." They also lifted **their hands** palms up, which is to say, "I am now ready to receive." And, they bowed their heads—that is, they went high and they went low—**with their faces to the ground**. When God shows up, humble yourself.

8:7-8 Translating and giving the meaning is what we call exposition. Nehemiah broke the people into small groups and assigned leaders to them who explained God's Word **so that the people could understand** it (8:8). It is not enough to hear if you don't understand.

8:9 Remarkably, **all the people were weeping as they heard** the Word of God read. They cried when it dawned on them that because of their refusal to hear the Word of God previously, they had gone nearly 150 years without progress.

After you have understood God's Word and wept, you have to dry your eyes and remember that God is good. As Paul says, "Forgetting what is behind and reaching forward to what is ahead, I pursue as my goal the prize promised by God's heavenly call in Christ Jesus" (Phil 3:13-14).

8:10 Nehemiah said, **Do not grieve**. Then, he offered them something in sorrow's place: **the joy of the Lord**. What you focus on governs how you feel. The reason why many of us stay grieved for so *long* is because we stay focused on what is so *wrong*. Rather than finding our chief joy in the Lord, we turn on the TV to escape. We enter into illegitimate relationships to escape. We get involved with drugs or alcohol to escape. If your focus is properly situated on the Lord, however, he will give you his joy; and his joy will give you **strength**.

8:11-12 The Levites said, **Don't grieve**. Why? Because that day was **holy** (8:11). In other words, the people were to remember that God was still on the throne, and he was still taking care of business. Thus, the people of God had **a great celebration, because they had understood the words that were explained to them** (8:12). No party compares to the joy of understanding the gracious Word of God that promises salvation and kingdom blessings to all who will believe.

8:13 The men, **the family heads**, agreed that they had better take their rightful position. They understood that the law of God is hierarchical. If it does not flow through the leadership of the family, it won't get passed down to the kids.

8:14-18 In honor of the Festival of Shelters, everyone **made shelters and lived in them**, and **there was tremendous joy** (8:17). The shelters represented the temporary housing the Israelites erected during their wilderness wanderings. The rejoicing was not over the shelters, but over the renewed obedience to the Word of God, which had been neglected. On this one week a year, they were to be reminded that there was a time when they had nothing, and God had taken care of them.

VII. A CALLING TO TEACH (9:1-38)

9:1-4 At the assembly, they spent **a fourth of the day** reading from God's Word (9:3), with the leaders explaining it (8:7-8). Then, they **spent another fourth of the day in confession and worship** (9:3). Understanding Scripture, then, caused the community to confess their sins before God and to praise him. That, in fact, is why the preaching and teaching of the Word, as well as personal Bible study, are so important. God declares that his Word will prosper in what he sends it to do (see Isa 55:11).

9:5 The Levites began to teach the Israelites their history with God. There were some young people in this group who had not been taught the Word of God, and their fathers had not told them how God chose them and brought them out of the land of Egypt! Maybe some of the fathers didn't even know their own history. Thus, the Levites educated a new generation of fathers and leaders who could then teach their children the plan of God.

9:6-15 Because their ancestor **Abraham** was **faithful**, God gave the land on which Jerusalem was built to **his descendants** (9:7-8). The Levites taught that God showed Israel **the way they should go** (9:12) and **gave them . . . good statutes and commands** (9:13). Similarly, we need a new generation of Christian teachers to enter the classroom to convey such truths to our children.

9:16-21 The Israelites had **refused to listen** to God's servant Moses. But, God was **gracious and compassionate**, and he **did not abandon them** (9:17). Thus, we reflect God's character when we do not abandon our young people who sometimes refuse to listen. Rather, we must be gracious and compassionate. Few qualities are as necessary as patience.

9:22-25 God had given Israel great blessings, and the Levites listed some of them. Among them was the mention that Israel **became prosperous** (9:25), but they failed to teach their descendants to be thankful and grateful to God for all those things. We need to remind our kids (and ourselves) that everything we have is a blessing from God.

9:26-31 When God's people forgot where their blessings came from, they rejected God every way they could until eventually God rejected them. Over and over, God **rescued them**, but they quickly forgot him and returned to their sin (9:27-28).

Teaching sobering truths like these is often frustrating, which is why teachers—which is the capacity in which the Levites served in this chapter—need both an aptness for teaching accompanied by the power of the Holy Spirit as well as the courage to persevere.

9:32-38 The Levites prayed that God would be satisfied with the time that had been served, Judah's seventy years in Babylon. They admitted that God had **acted faithfully**, though they as a people had **acted wickedly** (9:33). They acknowledged it was only fair that they'd been reduced to **slaves in the land** of their **ancestors** (9:36). The leaders of the Jews signed a pledge to listen to and obey him henceforth (9:38).

The fact that they had been able to return to the land at all was a demonstration of God's grace, but in this action they *hoped* that their merciful God would grant them something better. That's what teachers of God's Word are called to offer.

VIII. GOD'S RESOURCES FOR REBUILDING (10:1-39)

10:1-27 The list of those who signed and sealed the pledge to obey God included **Nehemiah**, who had been granted the position of **governor** (10:1), plus twenty-two **priests** (10:2-8), seventeen **Levites** (10:9-13), and forty-four leaders (10:14-27). God brought all these influential people together so they could encourage each other to stick to their convictions. If one Levite began to weaken, a priest might inspire him to carry on. If the governor became downhearted, a leader could come alongside to motivate and invigorate him. God had provided all the resources they needed to fulfill their obligations to him, to get their community back on track.

10:28-29 The rest of the people didn't sign the pledge, but they still **separated themselves** from the ungodly people around them and determined in their hearts **to obey** God's law. The group included **gatekeepers**, who could remind people every time they left the city that they had an obligation to come back and rebuild it. They included **temple servants**, who could tell the Jews every Sabbath day to honor God and his agenda for the sake of their wives and children.

10:30-31 God had told them everything they needed to know to build a solid and secure community, and now they promised to obey his commands. They would not intermarry with the **surrounding peoples** (10:30). They remembered that Solomon had brought wicked, idolatrous ideas into his life and into the nation by marrying women who did not worship the Lord. They, by contrast, would honor God by obeying his commands about the **Sabbath day**, fallow fields, and the year of jubilee (10:31).

10:32-34 The people realized that God had richly blessed them with all the resources they needed, and they could use a portion of it to improve God's **house** (10:32). Likewise, God has provided his people with all the money and talents needed to rebuild our churches and our communities. We have the gospel of Christ and the power of the Holy Spirit. He will bless our submission to his program, but we must step out in obedience and give to access those blessings.

10:35-39 The Jews had a **firstfruits** mentality. They didn't think of themselves first and leave God until second—or last! They made it a priority to bring their offerings to the **LORD's house** (10:35) and not **neglect** it (10:39). They brought their riches: fruit, livestock, bread, grain, wine, and oil. Then, **the storerooms of the treasury** were equipped to fulfill God's kingdom agenda (10:38). This is the mindset our churches need, too. God supplies the resources. Will we commit them to his work?

IX. CHRISTIAN URBAN RENEWAL (II:I-I2:26)

11:1-2 When it came time to decide which families would need to populate the holy city long term, Nehemiah started with **the leaders of the people**. They **stayed in Jerusalem** (11:1). This suggests that real leaders don't assess the political climate first to determine whether they will act on principle. Leaders *lead*. They don't compromise principle for popularity. Leaders determine how things ought to be and move on that knowledge. Christian men lead because they have a responsibility, and that responsibility demands they take initiative.

The rest of the people cast lots for one out of ten to . . . live in Jerusalem (11:1). This tells us that, in a sense, God tithed from the population with the goal that the relocators would make a difference for him in the city and, eventually, duplicate themselves. Over time, as the rest saw that the problems that kept them out of the city initially had been eradicated, they would feel comfortable coming back.

God calls for redevelopment in this story. Our church adopted a local apartment complex. We had to get someone to invade the premises, exert a godly influence there, and duplicate themselves. Nine people who didn't go were tasked with supporting the one who did.

In Jeremiah 29:7, God said, "Pursue the well-being of the city I have deported you to. Pray to the LORD on its behalf, for when it thrives, you will thrive." Within that statement is the idea that a believer has the ability to influence the pagan environment where he lives. Pornography, crime, and drugs are destroying our kids. So, what can you do? In asking God to show you how to build a stable context for life, you will help build a strong family. You can influence your city for Christ.

11:3-36 There's a reason God included the list within this chapter in Scripture. In it, we see that God does not mind recognizing people

who deserve it and condemning people who deserve it—by name. These leaders had the guts to move forward for God.

Most of these names belong to **priests** and **Levites** (11:3) because Nehemiah was establishing a religious base. The religious base of a community ultimately determines its well-being because the way all life issues are handled relates to what people believe about God.

There is a high degree of organization in this list as well as lots of detail. There were **heads of the province** (11:3), people **who did the work at the temple** (11:12), people **who supervised the work outside the house of God** (11:16), and someone **who began the thanksgiving in prayer** (11:17). In your house, your business, or your world—seek organization. God does not work in the midst of disorder. As 1 Corinthians 14:40 says, "Everything is to be done decently and in order." You cannot give chaos to God and say, "Bless it."

12:1-26 These are the priests and Levites who went up with Zerubbabel (12:1). In recording their names here, Nehemiah was saying to the returnees, "Look, you have a hundred-year legacy." Everyone stands on someone's shoulders; many someones enabled you to be where you are.

X. A DEDICATION WORTH CELEBRATING (12:27-47)

12:27-29 The wall was finished in chapter 6, but until now, the walls were right and the people were wrong. For God, the dedication of the people always comes before **the dedication of the wall** (12:27). God never honors things until the people related to the things are right.

The people prepared to celebrate **with thanksgiving and singing** (12:27) because everybody knew that God was behind their success in erecting the structure. Something is wrong with the fan who can sit still in his seat when his team scores the winning goal with one second left on the clock. How can we not praise God for all he has done on our behalf?

That **they sent for the Levites wherever they lived** (12:27) shows that they got religion

back at the center of the nation's life. This detail is important because if you want heaven to intervene in your earthly circumstances, God's kingdom agenda must become your focus.

12:30 After the priests and Levites had purified themselves, they purified the people, the city gates, and the wall. God is absolutely holy—set apart and separate from sinners. He doesn't tolerate wickedness. When we come before his presence, we must conform to his agenda. That means we confess our sins before him and walk by grace in righteousness.

My dog gets dirty and wants to come into my house, but to do that he must conform to my agenda. Because this is our Father's world, and we are dirty sinful people, each of us must be made clean to worship God. If you are a Christian, Jesus Christ sanctified you. You are set apart for God.

12:31-42 There were two choirs on the wall, to the right and to the left. In other words, they were stationed in such a way that they got a panoramic view of what God had done. Moreover, they could reflect on their unity in the flow of movement as they all converged on the house of God.

12:43 The people **rejoiced because God had given them great joy**. Joy is a spiritual tranquility provided by God. When Paul was locked up in chains he said, "Rejoice in the Lord always. I will say it again: Rejoice!" (Phil 4:4). Joy is not circumstantially determined, but rather divinely determined.

According to Nehemiah, **Jerusalem's rejoicing was heard far away**. It had been

a long difficult road, full of peril. But, the people were able to see the hand of God in their past. Their present circumstances weren't perfect, but the God who gave them joy *was*.

12:44-47 When the people got right with God, they prioritized things. They brought in the **contributions** and **tenths** (12:44). If modern believers really understood what the church is and the influence that we could make, there would be no problem getting Christians to serve and give and invest in eternal things. Our thinking must be conformed to the divine perspective, so that our actions follow.

Too many Christians are trying to live in two kingdoms. They are trying to serve God and serve the world order at the same time, and you can't do that. We have a desperate need for people who will put God's kingdom first.

XI. THE CATASTROPHE OF COMPROMISE (13:1-31)

13:1-5 When his people stop compromising, God can turn a **curse into a blessing** (13:2). Sometimes we wonder, "I'm doing A, B, and C; why isn't God blessing me?" The answer just might be that you are compromising on D, E, and F. You may be coming to church on Sunday, but if you are compromising on Monday, you negate what he could have done for you.

The compromise here was letting family relations control spiritual decisions. Eliashib **was a relative of Tobiah** (13:4), archenemy of God. Nehemiah wouldn't even let Tobiah help build the wall, yet Eliashib had let him take up an apartment in the temple! As a priest, Eliashib should have been setting the spiritual temperature for the rest of the people. His actions here are a reminder that, regardless of your love for your family, they are never to have such an influence on you that you make spiritually foolish decisions. Jesus said, "If anyone comes to me and does not hate his own father and mother, wife and children, brothers and sisters . . . he cannot be my disciple" (Luke 14:26). So, if a family member wants you to disobey God, then you have

to make a choice. Jesus said, "I did not come to bring peace, but a sword" (Matt 10:34).

Tobiah was able to move into the temple because the room that normally would hold the tithes of the grain was empty. This supports what Malachi says in Malachi 1:6-14: the priests were disrespecting God and using the house of God for unholy purposes.

13:6-9 In throwing **all of Tobiah's household possessions out of the room** (13:8), Nehemiah made an autocratic decision to cut off a family relationship because it violated the premises of God. Unfortunately, we often want to take years to fix problems. Or, we aren't willing to speak up when we see sin or injustice in the church. If people are rebelling against the principles of God, it's your business to love them enough to turn them around.

13:10-12 The problem presented in verse 10 was a compromise of ministry. The things that mattered to people were put first, and the things of God were last. Thus, **the portions for the Levites had not been given**

(13:10). And, as the ministry went downhill, so the spiritual temperature of the people went downhill. In Malachi 3:8, the prophet asked, "Will a man rob God?" And, indeed, because the people had stolen from God in the matter of the Levites, their lives were cursed. Believers are to "seek first the kingdom of God and his righteousness" (Matt 6:33).

13:13 Nehemiah appointed certain men who **were considered trustworthy**. Overseeing **the storehouses** was a ministry, so reliability was important. We need leaders who won't live one way in the sanctuary and another in the marketplace.

13:14 When Nehemiah asked God to **remember** him, he was asking for help to accomplish God's kingdom agenda in his community.

13:15-22 What we see here was the people's compromise with materialism. In the past, **God brought . . . disaster** on the people because of such unfaithfulness to him (13:18). They were to **keep the Sabbath day holy** (13:22).

Similarly, you ought to use the first day of the week to remind yourself, "I ate last week. My roof is still over my head. I've got clothing." Making time for intentional reflection on the grace of God in your life will result in more consistent obedience and thankfulness.

13:23-24 Within these verses, we see the results of a moral compromise. Jews **had married women from Ashdod, Ammon, and Moab** (13:23). And, that immorality had led their children to learn **the language of Ashdod** instead of the language in which God's law was written (13:24). The problem was not marrying someone of another race or nationality, but rather marrying someone who didn't worship and obey the one true God. The men committed immorality, and their children suffered.

13:25-28 I rebuked them, cursed them, beat some of their men, and pulled out their hair (13:25) is one way of saying that Nehemiah went off on them. He reminded them that when Solomon sinned **in matters like** these, his personal life went downhill, and the nation of Israel split (13:26).

To keep yourself from compromising in terms of sexual purity, in particular, contemplate the significant damage a breach in standards would do to the cause of Christ, to the respect received from your children, and to your relationship with your spouse (current or future). Satan is actively looking for opportunities to bring you down. He studies your game film. He knows your weaknesses.

13:28-31 Nehemiah invited God to remember that although **one of the sons of Jehoiada** had compromised (13:28), Nehemiah had not. Surely, then, God would remember him **with favor** at the day of judgment (13:31).

You too, can live your life from God's perspective, so that you may hear those joyous words, "Well done" (Matt 25:21).

ESTHER

INTRODUCTION

Author

THE AUTHOR OF THE BOOK OF ESther is unknown. The book itself names no writer, and no reliable tradition exists identifying one.

Historical Background

In 587 BC, Jerusalem fell to King Nebuchadnezzar who carried many of the people of Judah into exile in Babylon (see 2 Chr 36:15-21). In 539 BC, Cyrus the Great, the ruler of the Medo-Persian Empire, conquered Babylon and issued a decree permitting exiled people, including the Jews, to return to their homelands (see 2 Chr 36:22-23). Though many Jews returned, others continued to live throughout the Medo-Persian Empire. The events of the book of Esther took place during the reign of King Ahasuerus (Xerxes I); he ruled the empire from 486–465 BC. His son, Artaxerxes I, would later send both Ezra and Nehemiah to Jerusalem (see Ezra 7:11-28; Neh 2:1-8).

Message and Purpose

Esther is unique because it is the only book in Scripture that does not mention the name of God directly. This is because God wanted to use the book to show how his providence (that is, his invisible hand) works behind the scenes to bring about his purposes in history. So, even though God is not on the front page of Esther, his fingerprints are all throughout the book.

Esther's dramatic story unfolds with the people of God, the Jews, living in Persia because of their sin. Through a series of circumstances, the young Jewish woman for whom the book is named is selected as the new queen because of her natural beauty. And yet, her people are threatened with annihilation due to an evil man named Haman. But God, working behind the scenes, brings about his people's deliverance when Esther decides to risk her life to speak up for them to the king and declares, "If I perish, I perish" (4:16).

This book demonstrates that though his methods vary, God is in control. His kingdom promises and purposes cannot be thwarted.

www.bhpublishinggroup.com/qr/te/17_00

Outline

I. Setting the Stage: A New Queen and a Foiled Assassination (1:1–2:23)

II. The Tension Builds: A Threatened Disaster (3:1–5:14)

III. Climax: The God of Reversals (6:1–10:3)

ESTHER

I. SETTING THE STAGE: A NEW QUEEN AND A FOILED ASSASSINATION (1:1–2:23)

1:1-2 Esther opens by giving us its historical context. The book's **events took place during the days of Ahasuerus.** He was king of the Medo-Persian Empire, **ruled 127 provinces from India to Cush** (1:1), and **reigned** over his huge kingdom from his capital in **Susa** (1:2) in what is now southwest Iran.

Ahasuerus is most likely a title (like "president" or "czar") for Xerxes I, the Persian king who ruled from 486–465 BC. The first Medo-Persian king, Cyrus the Great, had issued a decree in 539 BC permitting the Jews to return to their homeland and rebuild the temple (see 2 Chr 36:22-23). By the time Ahasuerus came to power, many Jews had returned to Jerusalem. But, many others had not.

1:3-8 The events that would engulf two Jews named Esther and Mordecai began when Ahasuerus decided to hold **a feast . . . for all his officials** (1:3). But, this was no ordinary party; it was to last **180 days** (1:4)—six months! At the conclusion of this period, **the king held a week-long banquet** where his glory and wealth were on full display for his guests (1:5-6). Moreover, **the royal wine flowed freely** (1:7), meaning there was no limit to the potential for inebriation. Meanwhile, in another location, **Queen Vashti also gave a feast for the women** (1:8).

1:9-12 On the final day of the banquet, **the king was feeling good from wine** (1:10)—that is, he was quite intoxicated. So,

he decided to **show off** his **very beautiful** queen to all his drunken friends (1:11). But, when he sent for Vashti, she **refused to come**. In an instant, Ahasuerus went from feeling good to being **furious** (1:12).

1:13-15 The king consulted the wise men . . . experts in law and justice (1:13) because what had happened wasn't considered a mere marital dispute but a legal matter. A queen had **refused to obey** the king publicly. Ahasuerus needed his legal team to advise him about what he should do with Vashti **according to the law** (1:15).

1:16-18 One of the king's officials agreed that Vashti's actions posed a serious problem. He argued that when word got out, **all the women** of the land would **despise their husbands** (1:16-17). If the queen was allowed to snub the king, **the noble women of Persia and Media** would do the same **to all the king's officials** (1:18). In other words, he said, "She's gotten us all in hot water with our wives, King!"

1:19-20 The official argued that there was only one thing to do: **issue a royal decree.** If such a ruling were **recorded in the laws of Persia and Media**, it could not be **revoked,** a government detail that would later prove important. The decree would forbid Vashti from ever entering **Ahasuerus's presence** and paved the way to give **her royal position** to someone else (1:19). By means of these tough measures, the official insisted, the crisis would be averted and the women of the kingdom would **honor their husbands** (1:20).

1:21-22 Memucan's suggestion was all the king needed to hear. As far as Ahasuerus was concerned, his queen had disrespected him in public, his advisors were in a state of panic, and he needed a plan to prevent things from getting out of hand. So, he **approved the proposal** (1:21) and **sent letters** throughout his kingdom, demanding that **every man should be the master of his own house** (1:22). With that, the king's officials no doubt breathed a sigh of relief. And, the stage was set for the events to follow.

2:1-4 Some time later, four years later to be exact (as we learn in 2:16; see 1:3), **King Ahasuerus's rage had cooled** and **he remembered Vashti** (2:1). But, there was nothing to be done. He had banished her, and the laws of Persia and Media couldn't be altered. So, his **personal attendants suggested** an idea: hold a kingdom-wide beauty contest. Every **beautiful young** virgin would be gathered, and the king could choose his favorite to **become queen instead of Vashti** (2:2-4). Ahasuerus thought this was a great idea; after all, the winner would receive him as the grand prize.

Everything to this point appeared to have nothing to do with the people of God. An arrogant Gentile king threw a six-month bash, got drunk, had marital problems, and sent a search party to find him a new beautiful bride. Yet, these events started a chain reaction that would lead to the potential destruction of God's people, followed by an amazing eleventh hour deliverance through God's providence.

God is sovereign. This, in fact, is one of his chief attributes in Scripture. He has supreme authority over all creation. The Lord "works out everything in agreement with the purpose of his will" (Eph 1:11). "From him and through him and to him are all things" (Rom 11:36). *Providence* is the miraculous and mysterious way that God weaves events together behind the scenes so that his sovereignty over the world is carried out. Though the book of Esther never mentions the name of God, his breathtaking providence in her

life and on behalf of his people couldn't be more obvious.

2:5-7 In the fortress of Susa—the location of Ahasuerus's throne (see 1:2)—**there was a Jewish man named Mordecai** (2:5). He **had been taken into exile** by **Nebuchadnezzar** and was **the legal guardian of his cousin,** a young woman named **Esther** (2:6-7). But, Esther was no ordinary woman. She **had a beautiful figure and was extremely good-looking** (2:7). In fact, Esther and Mordecai only entered the picture of events related to the palace because of Esther's beauty—something outside of their control. Yet, that would give them important roles to play in upcoming events regarding the entire Jewish people.

2:8-11 When the **king's command** was announced, **many young women** were taken to his palace—including **Esther** (2:8). The man who supervised the beauty contest especially liked her, so Esther received a spa package unlike any other woman has ever seen (2:9). At no time, though, did Esther **reveal her ethnicity** because **Mordecai had ordered her not to** do so (2:10). (Apparently, he didn't think she could become queen otherwise because of existing attitudes in the empire against the Jews.)

2:12-13 The text speaks of **each young woman's turn to go to King Ahasuerus.** This was not merely an opportunity to say, "Hello." Rather, the phrase was a euphemism for sleeping with the king, as 2:14 makes clear. **For six months** prior to the event, each candidate for queen received one round of beauty treatments, and during **another six months,** she received a second round (2:12). That's a lengthy preparation for one night with the king.

2:14 When each woman's turn arrived, **she would go in the evening** to the king **and in the morning she would return** to a **second harem.** Unless the king requested her, she'd never go to him again. Though this kind of behavior may have been acceptable in the Gentile world, it was considered scandalous among God's people. A man and woman were only to engage in a "one flesh" union when they had come together as husband and wife (Gen 2:24). Furthermore, the people of Israel were not to marry unbelievers (see Deut 7:3). But sometimes, God allows things to happen of which he doesn't approve in order to accomplish his greater purpose. This could also explain why God kept his name from being mentioned in the book.

2:15 That **Esther gained favor in the eyes of everyone who saw her** implies that God was providentially at work. Every woman was allowed to take whatever she wished "from the harem to the palace" (see 2:13). But, Esther only took what **the king's eunuch . . . suggested**. In other words, she turned down an opportunity to pile up material things for herself. She was different. And, as a result, she set herself apart, and people took notice—including the king.

2:16-18 When Esther was taken to the king, he **loved** her **more than all the other women**. Though much in Esther's story was happening that was inconsistent with God's character, the Jews were his covenant people, and he had promised to cover them. So, Esther **won more favor and approval** than the other women, and the

king **placed the royal crown on her head** (2:17).

2:19-22 One day, **Mordecai was sitting at the King's Gate** (2:19), a fact indicating he worked for the king in some capacity and from that position had told Esther not to inform the king that she was a Jew (2:20). While on duty, Mordecai overheard **two of the king's eunuchs** plotting **to assassinate King Ahasuerus** (2:21). So, he immediately told Esther, and she **reported** the **plot** to the king **on Mordecai's behalf** (2:22). This last piece of information is important because it tells us Esther gave Mordecai credit for uncovering the scheme.

2:23 Once everything **was investigated and verified**, the two eunuchs were executed. And, **the event was recorded in the Historical Record in the king's presence**. That means Mordecai's name was on record as the hero. Yet, like an unseen puppet master pulling the strings, God was the one at work in prolonging the king's life and moving the story of his people forward. Though he may often seem absent in your life, God *is* at work. Trust him where you are because he is doing something bigger than you can imagine.

II. THE TENSION BUILDS: A THREATENED DISASTER (3:1–5:14)

3:1 For reasons unknown, the king honored **Haman . . . the Agagite** and **gave him a higher position than all the other officials**. Jews reading this story would have taken note of the man's background. Haman was a descendent of Agag, leader of the Amalekites, an ancient enemy of Israel. The Amalekites had opposed Israel from the beginning, when they had departed from Egypt under Moses (see Exod 17:8-16), so Ahasuerus's new right-hand man would have hated Jews. Moreover, Mordecai was a "son of Kish, a Benjaminite" (2:5). It was King Saul, son of Kish (1 Sam 9:1-3), who had failed to execute King Agag (see 1 Sam 15:3, 8-9). For Mordecai to honor this Agagite would have been unthinkable, an affront to God.

3:2-6 The king had commanded that **the royal staff** pay **homage** to Haman by bowing down. But, Mordecai refused. To give honor to an enemy of God's people was unacceptable. The rest of the staff warned him, but he wouldn't listen (3:2-4). So, they informed Haman of the actions and the ethnicity of Mordecai (3:4). When Haman learned that Mordecai wouldn't bow, his fragile ego couldn't handle it. **He was filled with rage** (3:5). But, when he learned that Mordecai was a Jew, he was determined to do more than simply kill him. **He planned to destroy all of . . . the Jews, throughout Ahasuerus's kingdom** (3:6). Genocide was the only thing that would satisfy his hatred.

3:7 Haman began to hatch his plot. First, during **the first month** of the year, he cast **the Pur—that is, the lot**. Doing so was like rolling dice. He was determining when he would carry out his wicked plan. The lot fell **on the twelfth month, the month Adar** (3:7; see 3:13). Haman was probably hoping for a sooner date on which to carry out his treachery. But, as Proverbs says, "The lot is cast into the lap, but its every decision is from the LORD" (Prov 16:33). Thus, God sovereignly provided an eleven-month window of grace. Even when Satan rolls the dice, God loads them.

3:8-9 Haman approached the king and told him there was an **ethnic group** in his kingdom that was a problem. They kept **themselves separate**, followed strange **laws**, and refused to **obey** the king's commands. This group, he said, shouldn't be tolerated (3:8). A royal **order** should be issued to destroy them. Haman even offered to pay **375 tons of silver to . . . the royal treasury** to help accomplish the task (3:9). Clearly, Haman was no pauper. And, he was willing to spend his own resources to wipe out the Jews.

3:10-11 The king agreed to the request and gave **his signet ring**—a tool of great power, as we'll see—**to Haman . . . the Agagite, the enemy of the Jewish people** (3:10; see 3:1). In other words, a wicked man with a vendetta held in his hand the authority to kill God's people.

3:12-15 Haman commanded **the royal scribes** to write letters on behalf of the king to the leaders throughout the empire. The letters ordered **the officials to destroy, kill, and annihilate all the Jewish people** and **plunder their possessions**. Each was **sealed with the royal signet ring**, which acted as the king's own signature (3:12-13), and the message **was distributed** throughout the empire (3:14).

While everyone outside the walls of the palace **was in confusion** over this decree, **the king and Haman sat down to drink** (3:15), an ominous insight suggesting there seemed to be no stopping the madness. But, nothing would take place until **the thirteenth day of Adar, the twelfth month** (3:13), because God was at work behind the scenes and controlling the timetable (see 3:7).

4:1-3 Previously, Mordecai had stood firm, unwilling to bow to Haman (3:1-4). But, when he heard of the king's order to exterminate the Jews, **he tore his clothes** and **put on sackcloth and ashes**, symbolizing his great grief and anguish. Then he **cried loudly and bitterly** (4:1). In fact, the same was true of **Jewish people in every province** (4:3). What was happening was an instance of spiritual warfare in the extreme. Satan was seeking to destroy God's covenant people, and Haman was a willing partner in crime. There seemed to be no hope, only pain.

4:4-9 When Esther learned of Mordecai's condition, **she sent clothes** for him **to wear** (4:4). Uninformed of the king's command, she didn't understand what was troubling her cousin. When Mordecai rejected the gift, Esther sent a messenger to him (4:6). Then **Mordecai told him everything** (4:7). He even gave the messenger **a copy of the written decree** that ordered the execution of the queen's people. Mordecai's **command** to Esther was clear: **approach the king, implore his favor, and plead with him personally** on behalf of our **people** (4:8).

Previously, Mordecai had warned Esther to keep her ethnic identity under wraps, possibly because of anti-Semitic atmosphere (2:10). But now, he insisted that she go public. The time had come for God to use her for her ultimate purpose. Esther had been providentially positioned to leverage influence for God's kingdom purposes. And similarly, know that however God blesses you, he does it so that you may be a blessing to others.

4:10-12 There was a hurdle standing in the way of Esther simply obeying Mordecai. It was against the royal law for anyone who hadn't **been summoned** to approach the king unless he extended his **gold scepter** to them. Offenders wouldn't receive a mere slap on the wrist—they'd receive **the death penalty**. And, in spite of the fact that Esther was queen, she had **not been summoned to appear before the king for the last thirty days** (4:11). Five years had passed since their wedding, and apparently the honeymoon was over. Did the royal couple have a falling out? Had the king grown bored with Esther's beauty? The text doesn't tell us. Yet, regardless, Esther knew that if she tried to break their romantic dry spell by entering King Ahasuerus's presence uninvited, she would be risking her life.

Importantly, Esther had forgotten that she had not climbed the ladder of success by herself; she had been placed on top by the goodness of God. We are what we are by the grace of God. Extraordinary experiences and opportunities that we are granted are not merely for our sake, then, but for the sake of God's kingdom agenda. When we lose sight of that, we miss God's kingdom program in history and become useless to him. Jesus told his disciples that God's people are called to be salt in an unsavory world. But, if salt no longer tastes salty, it has lost its purpose (see Matt 5:13).

4:13 Mordecai pressed his order by saying, **Don't think that you will escape the fate of all the Jews because you are in the king's palace.** "You'll be found out," Mordecai warned.

4:14 As if that wasn't bad enough, Esther would lose her opportunity to fulfill the purpose for which God had blessed her. **If you keep silent at this time, relief and deliverance will come to the Jewish people from another place**, Mordecai said. He knew God's Word and character. The Lord had promised to bless *all* the peoples of the earth through Abraham's offspring (see Gen 12:3), so he would not permit his entire people to be wiped out. But, if Esther refused to use her position for kingdom influence, God would still get the job done by some other means—even though Esther and her father's family would **be destroyed**.

This is a reminder that we, as Christians, need to keep our theology straight: God is sovereign and will accomplish his program with or without us. He certainly desires to use you. Yet, no one is indispensable. If you refuse to obey him, he will still carry out his agenda through someone else, and you will have missed an opportunity to serve his kingdom purposes.

Perhaps you have come to your royal position for such a time as this. It was Mordecai's way of saying to Esther, "Don't you see that God has placed you in this situation at this time in history so that you

can have a tremendous kingdom impact?" Similarly, the church of Jesus Christ is called to accomplish kingdom purposes. If a local church is not winning the lost to Christ and discipling them in the faith so that they can have a heavenly influence on earth, it has failed in its calling. *You* have been called to God's kingdom for such a time as this. Whose agenda will you follow?

4:15-17 To her credit, Esther didn't need to hear anymore. She told Mordecai to gather **all the Jews . . . in Susa** to fast for her **for three days**. She would do the same. Then, she would **go to the king**, even though it was **against the law**. Esther knew that to do the right thing would require a risky step of faith. The human king had forbidden her to approach him uninvited. But, her heavenly King had called her to a higher standard. Esther was resolved: **If I perish, I perish** (4:16).

Shadrach, Meshach, and Abednego were commanded to bow down before an idol (Dan 3:1-30). Daniel was told to pray to no one but a human king (Dan 6:1-24). Yet, these men too, all chose to trust God and take risks of faith. Whether they lived to see another day was God's problem. So, what risk of faith is God calling you to make? Are you willing to obey God's Word even when the outcome is uncertain? Even if it might cost you? Don't let the time you have been given pass you by.

5:1-2 On the third day, the moment arrived (5:1). Esther had fasted and no doubt prayed "for three days" prior (4:16). She had been willing to sacrifice her physical craving for food in order to heighten her spiritual awareness because she needed divine insight to know how to proceed. Decked in all her finery, the queen **stood in the inner courtyard**, and **the king was sitting on his royal throne** (5:1). Ahasuerus hadn't requested her, so she was breaking the royal law by approaching. But the unseen, sovereign God was at work: Esther **gained favor in his eyes**. He **extended the gold scepter** toward her, granting her permission to draw near (5:2).

5:3 Not only did the king allow her to approach him, but he also gave her the freedom to request anything—**even half the**

kingdom! Thus, in place of the threat of death, God granted an open door to Esther to set her plan in motion.

5:4-8 The queen invited **the king and Haman** to a **banquet** (5:4). So, King Ahasuerus readily agreed and sent for Haman (5:5). During the meal, he told his wife once more, **Whatever you ask will be given you** (5:6). (At this point, the tension that has been building in the narrative is thick.) Then Esther declared, **This is my petition and request:** come back to dinner again tomorrow (5:7-8). What happened? Why wasn't she willing to follow through? Had she gotten cold feet? Regardless, the wheels of God's providence were turning.

5:9 When Haman left, he was in a good mood. He was the king's right-hand man, and the queen repeatedly invited him to her dinner parties. Nothing could disturb him—nothing except ... **Mordecai**. The man wouldn't **rise or tremble in fear** at Haman's presence. Haman already hated Mordecai,

but this latest show of defiance **filled** him **with rage**. He probably thought, "Doesn't this Jew realize how important I am? The king and queen like nothing better than to spend time with me!"

5:10-13 Haman **controlled himself and went home** (5:10). He informed his friends and his wife about all of his good fortune. He was wealthy and powerful. **The king had honored him and promoted him** above everyone else (5:11). Even the queen loved having him around (5:12). Nevertheless, **none of this** satisfied him because **Mordecai the Jew** was still breathing (5:13).

5:14 The answer to Haman's problem was simple, according to **his wife** and **friends**. All he needed to do was **build a gallows** and influence the king **to hang Mordecai on it**. Then, he could attend Esther's **banquet** and **enjoy** himself with an end to his troubles within reach. Haman couldn't have been more **pleased** with this **advice**, so he started construction.

III. CLIMAX: THE GOD OF REVERSALS (6:1–10:3)

6:1 The night after the queen held her banquet, **sleep escaped the king**. It was the very night on which Haman thought himself on top of the world as a gallows was being constructed for Mordecai. It was a night when God's people needed heaven to intervene in history.

On this particular night, the king had insomnia, even though he should've been sleeping like a baby. The most powerful man in the empire couldn't sleep for a theological reason: "A king's heart is like channeled water in the LORD's hand: He directs it wherever he chooses" (Prov 21:1). God knows how to keep people awake at night in order to accomplish his sovereign program. Thus, the king had someone **read** to him **the book recording daily events**. In other words, he wanted the most boring book in his possession to be read to make him sleepy.

6:2 When the servant opened the book, he came to the **report of how Mordecai had informed on ... the king's eunuchs** who

had **planned to assassinate** the king. On the very night when Haman was plotting Mordecai's death, the king's sleepless night was filled with a bedtime story about how Mordecai had saved his life five years ago. In a universe in which the sovereign God accomplishes his will by his meticulous providence, nothing happens by chance. There are no coincidences. Luck and sovereignty don't mix.

Though God's name does not appear in the book of Esther, his fingerprints are everywhere. Events leading to this moment had all started eight years before with Queen Vashti snubbing King Ahasuerus. Sometimes we think, "God should act right now in my circumstances!" But, we must recognize that God is weaving a whole series of people and events together in history to achieve his kingdom goals. You are a representative of the kingdom whom God desires to use. But, God's kingdom is bigger than you, and his timing is perfect.

6:3 Upon being reminded of Mordecai's faithful service, the king wanted to know how he had been repaid. He asked, **What honor and special recognition had been given?** The answer was, **Nothing.** This man had saved King Ahasuerus's life, but no one had even told him, "Thank you."

6:4-5 The king intended to rectify this oversight right away, but he needed someone to carry out his plan to honor Mordecai. Whom could he use? Who was available? It was the early hours of the morning. At that moment, **Haman was just entering the outer court . . . to ask the king to hang Mordecai** (6:4). The king demanded that Haman **enter** (6:5).

6:6-9 Before Haman had a chance to ask Ahasuerus to kill Mordecai, the king asked him, **What should be done for the man the king wants to honor?** Certain the king was intending to honor him, Haman suggested the man should be decked out in the king's own robe and **a royal crown** while a top official led him around on a **horse** in **the city square**, declaring the king's praise of him (6:7-9). Such actions would publicly position him for a leadership role in the kingdom of Persia.

6:10-11 Ahasuerus thought this was a perfect idea. **Hurry, and do just as you proposed . . . for Mordecai** (6:10). And with those words, the humiliation and downfall of Haman had begun. Imagine the look on Haman's face at that moment. In an instant, his fortunes had changed. Everything good he had intended for himself was done to Mordecai, his nemesis, instead. And Haman himself had to lead around the Jewish man whom he hated, as he shouted to the crowds, **This is what is done for the man the king wants to honor** (6:11).

This scene is a reminder that "with God all things are possible" (Matt 19:26). When circumstances look their bleakest, God can connect what doesn't seem connectable. He can cause roads to intersect that look like they could never meet.

6:12 Haman returned **home** in shame. He had just played cheerleader to the man who had refused to bow to him. Mordecai had refused to honor Haman, and now Haman was forced to honor Mordecai. The day of Mordecai's execution turned out to be the day of his exaltation. And all of this happened because while we sleep, God is at work (see Ps 121:4).

6:13-14 If Haman was hoping for encouragement from his wife and friends, he was disappointed. As far as they were concerned, what had happened was really bad luck that wouldn't end well. **Your downfall is certain** (6:13). At that moment, **the king's eunuch . . . rushed Haman** off to Esther's **banquet.** Haman's fortunes were about to go from bad to worse.

7:1-2 For **the second day** in a row, Esther held a **feast** for **the king and Haman.** This one probably wasn't as enjoyable for Haman as the previous one. He was likely nursing a headache after the morning's embarrassment. Worse, before Haman could even eat a decent meal, the king asked Esther to make her request.

7:3-4 This time, Esther was ready to speak up. But, more to the point, God was ready for her to do so. He'd wanted everything to occur in exactly the right sequence. Even Esther may not have understood why she'd delayed having a difficult conversation the previous day, but as Paul had been restrained by the Holy Spirit (see Acts 16:6-7), so Esther had been restrained. God put her announcement on pause for twenty-four hours so that he could make his final adjustments. The stage was set. Esther's spiritual antennae were poised to follow divine leading. Is your spiritual receiver tuned to pick up heaven's signals?

Hear the passion in Esther's request: **Spare my life** and **spare my people . . . For my people and I have been sold to destruction, death, and extermination** (7:3-4). Surely, this was not something the king expected to hear. How much more shocking was it to Haman?

7:5-6 Who would devise such a scheme? the king demanded to know (7:5). And, at this point, Haman was no doubt looking around frantically for the exit. Esther pointed to the culprit: **The adversary and enemy is this evil Haman** (7:6). In an instant, Haman went from favored dinner guest to public enemy number one. He was rightly **terrified** (7:6).

7:7 The king arose in anger and went out to **the palace garden.** Realizing that he had been duped by Haman into authorizing the destruction of his own queen, Ahasuerus was hot. Haman knew that **the king was planning something terrible for him** out there, so he started **to beg Queen Esther for his life.**

7:8 When **the king returned,** he misunderstood Haman's groveling actions, thinking that he was trying to assault Esther. This wasn't Haman's day. No sooner had the king asked, **Would he actually violate the queen while I am in the house?** than his servants **covered Haman's face.** This tells us he didn't even have an opportunity to explain his actions. The divine Judge was passing sentence on the enemy of his people, and no defense could be given.

7:9 At that moment, **one of the king's eunuchs** walked in to announce that the **gallows** that Haman had prepared **for Mordecai**—the man whom the king had honored that very morning for saving his life—was ready. God's providential orchestration was complete. So, the king gave his command: **Hang [Haman] on it.**

7:10 The outcome of divine intervention couldn't be more ironic. **Mordecai** was honored with the plan that Haman has proposed for himself (6:6-11), and **Haman was hanged … on the gallows he had prepared for Mordecai.** Thus, the apparent power of God's enemies is meaningless. When he moves against them, they will fall by their own wicked designs. "The one who leads the upright into an evil way will fall into his own pit" (Prov 28:10).

8:1-2 The Lord is a God of reversals. Following Esther's intervention, there came a *financial* reversal. **That same day King Ahasuerus awarded Queen Esther the estate of Haman, the enemy of the Jews** (8:1). Thus, everything that Haman owned suddenly belonged to the woman who had bravely called him out. This highlights the truth of Proverbs

13:22: "The sinner's wealth is stored up for the righteous." Then, there was a *political* reversal. Esther **revealed her relationship to Mordecai,** and the king took Haman's **signet ring** and **gave it to Mordecai** (8:1-2). The authority that Haman once held, then, was granted to his rival.

The Lord of heaven and earth can cause things to turn on a dime. No matter how powerful the people and circumstances aligned against you may seem, they have nothing unless God grants it to them. And, if he grants it to them, he can take it away. Just ask Nebuchadnezzar, the man who'd carried Esther's people away from their homeland in the first place (see Dan 4:1-37).

8:3-10 In spite of all this, there was still evil to be undone. The royal decree to annihilate the Jews was still standing. Esther **begged** the king to **revoke** Haman's wicked **plot,** and the king showed her favor (8:3-4). So, Esther asked Ahasuerus to issue a new **royal edict** counteracting the former one (8:5). Then, just as Haman had been given the authority to write orders in the king's name and seal them with **the royal signet ring** (see 3:12), so now Esther and Mordecai were authorized to do the same (8:8-10).

8:11-14 This was a *legal* reversal. The new edict **gave the Jews in each and every city the right to assemble and defend themselves, to destroy, kill, and annihilate** everyone **hostile to them** (8:11). Sadly, the laws of Persia and Media could not be revoked (see 1:19), so the decree Haman had written remained in force. But, that didn't mean the Jewish people had to take it lying down. If anyone sought to harm them, the new decree gave them authority to fight back and **avenge themselves against their enemies** (8:13).

8:15-17 Next came an *emotional* reversal. **The city of Susa,** which was formerly in confusion over the edict against the Jews (3:15), now **rejoiced** (8:15). The mourning of the Jews (4:3) had turned to celebration **with gladness, joy, and honor** (8:16). This led, finally, to a *spiritual* reversal. **Many of the ethnic groups of the land professed themselves to be Jews** (8:17). In other words, many sinners got saved. To profess oneself to be a Jew was to come under the Jewish covenant. To come under the Jewish covenant, one had to accept the Jewish God. Unbelievers had seen the deliverance and favor that God had bestowed on his people, and they wanted his covenant protection, too.

The greatest reversal was still to come, however. Several centuries in the future, Satan would think he had destroyed the Son of God. But, the cross on which Christ was condemned became the path to his victory and glory. Three days later, he arose with "all authority" in heaven and on earth given to him (Matt 28:18). Our God is a God of reversals.

9:1-2 Haman's original edict to slaughter the Jews was to be carried out on a certain day (3:13). So, the new command **went into effect** on the exact same day: **on the thirteenth day of the twelfth month, the month Adar**. Thus, **on the day** when the enemies of the Jews had planned to exterminate them, the Jews were prepared to defend themselves (9:1). As a result, **fear of them fell on every nationality** (9:2).

9:3-10 Mordecai was now a **powerful** man. Every official throughout the empire **aided the Jews because they feared** him (9:3-4). So, when their enemies rose up against them, the Jews fought back and put them to death (9:5). **In the fortress of Susa**, they **killed . . . five hundred men**, including **the ten sons of Haman** (9:6-10).

God had provided the Jews with supernatural deliverance from those who hated them, but his people still had to fight. They couldn't merely sit back and do nothing. The same is true for Christians. We are called to spiritual battle (see 2 Cor 10:3-5; Eph 6:10-18). Yes, God is our Savior and our Deliverer. But, he demands our involvement. We must wage spiritual warfare.

9:11-15 When the king received word of what was happening as a result of his edicts, he asked Esther if she wanted anything (9:11-12). She asked for one more day to finish the job; there were still evil men to be dealt with. Furthermore, she requested that the

corpses of **Haman's ten sons be hung on the gallows** (9:13). This would serve as a public warning to others. Before that second day was spent, **three hundred** more enemies were killed in Susa (9:14-15).

9:16-22 In the other **royal provinces**, the Jews **killed seventy-five thousand** of their enemies (9:16). After this, there was **feasting and rejoicing** (9:17-19). Mordecai **sent letters** throughout the empire, ordering the Jews **to celebrate the fourteenth and fifteenth days of Adar every year** as a **holiday** (9:20-22). For on these days, God had turned their **mourning** into **rejoicing** (9:22).

9:23-28 The Jews called their new holiday **Purim, from the word Pur** (9:26). The term *Pur* refers to **the lot** that Haman had **cast** (like rolling dice) to determine when he would **destroy** the Jews (9:24; see 3:7). Haman had looked to chance to fulfill his wicked desires. The people of God knew that their deliverance had not come by chance but by the providential hand of God; thus, they coopted the term and used it to magnify God.

Believers need to remind themselves, one another, and their children that the circumstances of their lives are not the result of random events. God is orchestrating the events of our lives according to his sovereign plan and for his kingdom purposes.

9:29-32 Queen Esther wrote a **letter** as well to **confirm** Mordecai's **letter about Purim** (9:29). The missives were sent throughout the empire **with assurances of peace and security to all the Jews** (9:30). Esther and Mordecai wanted to ensure that their people never forgot what God had done and never failed to give him glory.

10:1-3 Mordecai the Jew was second only to King Ahasuerus (10:3). He had been **honored** by the king and was **famous among the Jews** (9:2-3). Yet, Mordecai knew that God had providentially raised him. What had happened was not merely for his sake but for the sake of God's kingdom. Therefore, from that day on, he continued **to speak for the well-being of** his people (10:3). May the people of God do the same today.

JOB

INTRODUCTION

Author

THE AUTHOR OF THE BOOK IS UNknown but was likely an Israelite because of his frequent use of God's covenant name, Yahweh (rendered, "the Lord").

Historical Background

Job's story is set in the patriarchal period at a time when wealth was determined by the quantity of livestock and servants one owned. As with other Old Testament patriarchs, Job performed priestly duties for his family (1:5) and lived to a very old age (42:16). The events take place in the country of Uz (1:1), which was located in the northern Arabian Peninsula. The date of the writing is unknown, but Jewish tradition places it during the time of Moses.

Message and Purpose

This book is critical to Scripture because it deals with one of the hardest realities of life: God often seems silent when we are doing our best to please him and yet experience suffering. The question of why comes up again and again in life, even as it did for Job, one of the godliest people in the Bible who had no explanation for why he was suffering so terribly.

In Job, God is engaged in a dialogue with the devil over Job and the pain God allows to come into Job's life. Ultimately, the book reveals God's kingdom authority over life circumstances because not even the devil can do his dirty work without divine permission. As the book unfolds, God reveals things about himself that overwhelm Job. By the end, Job has to repent and bow before God's wisdom—a

wisdom that he cannot understand, but that he knows is best because he trusts God.

One of the key truths to grasp from the book of Job is that we must trust God even when we cannot understand him, even when he is thoroughly confusing to us. The central statement in the book is one of Job's closing comments to God: "I had heard reports about you, but now my eyes have seen you" (42:5).

VIDEO INTRO

www.bhpublishinggroup.com/qr/te/18_00

Outline

JOB

I. JOB'S TRIALS AND SUFFERING (1:1–3:26)

1:1 It did not take the author long to establish what kind of man Job was. **He was a man of complete integrity, who feared God and turned away from evil.** Job did not compromise with evil. He was not perfect; Job himself admitted that he was a sinner (7:21; 9:20). Nevertheless, as a person of integrity, Job practiced fairness and justice in all his dealings. Integrity means being whole and undivided, lacking in hypocrisy or duplicity. In a modern context, Job wouldn't have been someone who acts one way at church and another way in the marketplace.

The man wasn't moral merely for the sake of being moral, however. That he "feared God" speaks volumes. It means he took God seriously and lived his life to honor him. His integrity, in fact, was rooted in his fear of God. That he "turned away from evil" means he actively fled from temptation when he encountered it and took steps to avoid it. A significant example of this is Job's confession near the end of the book: "I have made a covenant with my eyes. How then could I look at a young woman?" (31:1; see commentary).

1:2-5 Job was blessed with ten children, a symbol of God's blessing in the ancient world. And, his material wealth was beyond that of anyone around him—which is even more noteworthy because we already know Job did not acquire his wealth by fraud or deceit. He **was the greatest man among all the people of the east** (1:3).

Job was also the spiritual leader and priest of his family (1:4-5). He was clearly a godly man—which makes the rest of the story tough to fit together from a human standpoint. But, that's the problem with the way many people approach human suffering. If you come to Job with preconceived ideas of what's fair, or with the kind of rigid thinking that says that if A happens, then B must always follow, you'll lose your mind trying to figure out this book. Job's friends would bring this kind of thinking to the table, which would leave them room for only one conclusion: "Job, you must be a big-time sinner, because look at all the terrible things that have happened to you."

1:6-7 The Lord held a heavenly conference for his angels and permitted **Satan** to attend the meeting. This tells us that, for now, God in his wisdom has decided not to completely ban Satan from his presence. (That will happen on a future day when he is judged and thrown into the lake fire; Rev 20:10). On this occasion, Satan had been **roaming through the earth** (1:7), no doubt looking for someone to "devour" (see 1 Pet 5:8).

Up to the moment of his personal sin, Satan was the "shining morning star" (Isa 14:12). Ezekiel's description of him is even more awesome: "You were the seal of perfection, full of wisdom and perfect in beauty" (Ezek 28:12). Satan, it seems, was God's angel in charge. But, he got tired of worshiping God and wanted to be his own god and run his own show. Therefore, every time you try to run your own life, be your own boss, and act like your own god, you are saying in essence, "Satan, I agree with you. I, too, want to ascend to heaven and call my own shots."

1:8-11 It was at this point that things started coming unglued for Job. He would soon suffer in history because of a discussion in eternity. Notice that God took the initiative in the matter: He brought up Job in his conversation with Satan! God praised Job's devotion to him and, for his own reasons, goaded Satan into finding out what he already knew personally—that Job's faith was not superficial or based only on his blessings (1:8).

Satan didn't deny Job's devotion, but he attacked it by asking, **Does Job fear God for nothing?** (1:9). In other words, Satan was the original proponent of the health-and-wealth, name-it-and-claim-it theology we hear today. He was convinced that Job was only in the righteous living game for the blessings. That he only loved God because the money was coming in, his property was extensive, and his family was intact. Take everything away, Satan said to God, and he'll **curse you to your face** (1:10-11).

1:12 Very well, the Lord replied. Satan wanted to show him that Job was a spiritual fake. So, God gave the devil power over all Job owned. The challenge was on, with one restriction: Satan was not allowed to touch Job himself. This divine block tells us this wouldn't be a battle between equals. God drew the line where Satan had to stop; he maintained authority over the evil one. In his grace, God limits our trials. Satan never has free reign. God's goal was to purify and sanctify Job, not to take him out.

1:13-19 As a result of God's sovereign permission and Satan's malicious actions, Job entered the worst day of his life. He received news of four back-to-back calamities. Many people have suffered horrific loss. Few of us have undergone the comprehensive disaster Job experienced in the span of a few minutes. A combination of enemies and natural disasters took his livestock, his servants, and—worst of all—his children.

1:20-21 Job stood up, tore his robe, and shaved his head. He was grief-stricken, as anyone would be. But, it's his next response

that should get our attention: **He fell to the ground and worshiped** (1:20). Job knew where to turn when everything fell apart.

Naked I came from my mother's womb, and naked I will leave this life. This acknowledges that we enter the world naked (with nothing), and the only reason we won't go to the grave naked is because someone else dresses us. Nevertheless, we won't take anything with us. Death is the great equalizer. Rich or poor, we ultimately own nothing,

Amid the loss of his children and his property, Job confessed that everything he had was from God, so God had the right to take it away. He said, **The LORD gives, and the LORD takes away. Blessed be the name of the LORD** (1:21). It's easy to worship God when it's all flowing, when everything's smooth. But, what we truly believe, whom we really love, is demonstrated when the bottom falls out.

1:22 In spite of the catastrophes, **Job did not sin or blame God for anything**. Believing in the sovereignty of God is to believe that whatever comes to you comes as part of his wise purposes for you. It's being convinced that God intends our good and his glory through all (see Rom 8:28).

2:1-8 Round one went to the Lord; Job retained **his integrity** (2:3). But still, Satan wasn't willing to give up. He hinted at his next tactic to undo Job: **A man will give up everything he owns in exchange for his life** (2:4). In other words, Satan suggested that, if pressed, Job's priority would be saving his own skin. Afflict his **flesh and bones**, Satan said, and he'll **curse you**, God (2:5). **Very well**, the Lord said and granted Satan power over Job's body (2:6). And, Satan went and **infected Job with terrible boils** from head to toe (2:7).

2:9-10 At this point, Job's helpmate became a hurt-mate. **Are you still holding on to your integrity?** his wife asked. **Curse God and die!** (2:9). Of course, this was the very thing Satan wanted. Yet, even after he lost his health and had to sit on the garbage heap scraping his sores, Job still understood something we need to grasp. He replied to his wife, **Should we accept only good from God and not**

adversity? Job knew that the Lord was no Santa Claus whose sole purpose is to give us what we want and never to cause us discomfort. He is sovereign. And thus, once again, we're told that **Job did not sin in what he said** (2:10).

As much as we might wish otherwise, trials are inevitable. It's not a question of *if* a believer will suffer but *when* (see John 16:33; Jas 1:2). And those around us will, too. Death, disease, pain, loss, and grief don't come with easy explanations. Yet we, like Job, must be convinced of these essential truths: God is sovereign over all things, and God is good. At times, he allows Satan to test us. But, the good news is that the devil is on a short leash; he can only bring against us what has already passed through God's hands.

2:11-13 Regarding Job's suffering, **Job's three friends** knew only what they had heard. They hadn't seen him yet and were unaware of the test he was undergoing or the Lord's evaluation of Job as a man of "perfect integrity" (1:8; 2:3). They intended to **sympathize with . . . and comfort him** (2:11). However, when they saw him, **they could barely recognize him** (2:12). So, for **seven days and nights**, they grieved with him but spoke no word **because they saw that his suffering was very intense** (2:13). This is a reminder that, sometimes, the best comfort you can provide is your quiet presence and tears.

Remember to "weep with those who weep" (Rom 12:15).

3:1-26 When Job finally spoke, he had plenty to say. He **cursed the day he was born** (3:1). This is a bitter complaint, to be sure, but it's not the bitterness of a former believer who has jettisoned his faith. Rather, after an unknown period of intense suffering, Job's physical, emotional, and spiritual stamina started to crack. He felt so low that he wished he had perished at birth (3:11-19). At least then, he reasoned, he **would be at rest** (3:13). But, as it was, he couldn't even **relax** (3:26).

Job railed against his existence, and began to question God, a theme that we will see repeated in his defenses against the accusations to come. This is a reminder that being a believer doesn't necessarily mean we will never have times of doubt. God, however, is big enough to handle our doubts and will deal with them as long as we keep the lines of communication with him open. Nevertheless, we need to guard against letting our doubts descend into denial of his sovereignty. Notice that Job didn't say, "Look at what Satan has done to me!" He said, **Why is life given to a man . . . whom God has hedged in?** (3:23). Job didn't understand why terrible things had happened to him, but he knew they had come from the hand of his sovereign God.

II. ELIPHAZ'S FIRST SPEECH AND JOB'S RESPONSE (4:1–7:21)

4:1–5:27 Eliphaz was most likely the oldest of Job's three visitors because he spoke first. He began on a soft note, reminding Job that he had been known for his wisdom and counsel while helping **many** people in days past (4:3-4).

The problem was, according to Eliphaz, that Job was not following the advice he had given to others. In general, Eliphaz argued that Job must be suffering because he had sinned. In Eliphaz's mind, that was the only explanation for all that had happened, because he had a rigid belief in the teaching of retribution. That is, he believed the

good guys *always* win, and the bad guys *always* lose. He was the guy who said, "You do A, and B will follow." Thus, Eliphaz asked, **Who has perished when he was innocent?** (4:7).

Now, there is some truth in what Eliphaz told Job—just as there would be some truth in every speech that his friends made. But, while it's true that we reap what we sow (see Gal 6:7-9), it's also true that, *at the end of history*, good will triumph over evil. So, reaping good is not always the case *in history*. Neither is everything that happens to us the result of some sin we have committed (though sometimes it is). Life is too complex for that. To say that wherever there is suffering, you're seeing the result of someone sowing sin is wrong. Sometimes, God permits suffering for his glorious purposes (see John 9:1-3). And Jesus is the perfect example of someone who suffered though he was sinless; he's even the example to follow when we suffer unjustly (see 1 Pet 2:19-23).

Eliphaz was a strict believer in cause-and-effect, and his theology didn't allow for exceptions. His experience-based theory is summed up when he claims, **In my experience, those who plow injustice and those who sow trouble reap the same** (4:8-9). And, because Job's suffering was a cut-and-dried case of sin, Eliphaz felt, Job might as well "'fess up," get it all out on the table, and admit that he deserved what had happened. He should not **reject the discipline of the Almighty** (5:17). Rather, he should just receive God's correction so that God would heal him (5:17-26). It's **true**, Eliphaz insisted. Job just needed to **hear it and understand it** (5:27).

6:1–7:21 Job admitted that he had fallen into despair because he felt he was suffering unjustly. He denied Eliphaz's charges of wrongdoing, however, saying in effect that his extreme pain gave him a right to moan (6:2-3). He felt like God was using him for target practice, firing his **arrows** of judgment at him, though he could not imagine why (6:4). With God seemingly against him, Job saw his situation as hopeless, even though he had not sinned or denied God (6:8-13).

Instead of helping, then, Eliphaz had only added to Job's misery by his accusations. And judging by Job's reference to his **friends** and **brothers** (6:14-15), Job evidently anticipated that he was going to be attacked by Bildad and Zophar, too. His friends had thus become like **streams** of water that **evaporate in warm weather** (6:15, 17); they were all talk and no comfort.

Job challenged Eliphaz to tell him what he had done wrong. He promised that if Eliphaz got it right, he would admit his sin. **Please look at me**, he urged, **I will not lie to your face** (6:28). He wanted Eliphaz to remember that he really was dealing with a man of integrity.

Job lamented the futility, the misery, and the emptiness of life (7:1-5). His own life, he was certain, was short and would soon vanish. He would die, go to his grave, and be forgotten (7:6-10). In fact, he wished God would let him die and leave him **alone** (7:11-16). Job wondered why God would bother to inflict so much pain on a person for no apparent reason. And, Job's challenge to God was essentially, **what have I done** to deserve this? (6:17-21).

In this opening round of speeches, a pattern develops in which Job's friends attack, Job responds by protesting his innocence, and, in the process, he becomes more and more determined to get a fair hearing from God.

III. BILDAD'S FIRST SPEECH AND JOB'S RESPONSE (8:1–10:22)

8:1-22 Bildad, another of Job's friends, confronted him with the same basic accusation as Eliphaz had: Job had sinned against God and was suffering righteous punishment for it. Bildad was big on **justice** (8:3) and appealed to the experience of previous generations (8:8-10). The principle those ancestors taught is that suffering is the result of sin. Thus, **the hope of the godless will perish** (8:13). Therefore, because Job was suffering, he must have acted godlessly. **God does not reject a person of integrity** (8:20), he said. Therefore, if God had rejected him, Job must have lacked integrity. Here, too, we can find truth in the proverbial statements made, but we can't build a rigid system that allows no exceptions. God's ways are mysterious and hidden from us unless he chooses to reveal them: "The hidden things belong to the LORD our God, but the revealed things belong to us and our children forever" (Deut 29:29).

Unlike Eliphaz, who at least started out gently with Job, Bildad lacked discretion and mercy. He hit Job where he hurt the most, focusing on the loss of his children. He said, **Since your children sinned against [God], he gave them over to their rebellion** (8:4). While Bildad had no personal knowledge that Job's children had sinned, he simply assumed it because it fit with his cause-and-effect theology. But, be warned: if you go around offering this sort of harsh counsel to those who are suffering, you need to repent.

Bildad followed this accusation by telling Job that life would be better for him again if Job would just **ask the Almighty for mercy** and start living right (8:5-7). If Job would change his heart, God would change Job's circumstances. That, he asserted, was the only way God would stop afflicting Job and restore him to a life that was **full of prosperity** (8:7). Then, Bildad reminded Job that those who live without God will die like plants without water (8:11-12).

9:1–10:22 Job sought to defend himself by arguing again that he was innocent before God. In fact, Job really wanted to appear before the Lord in court so he could prove his innocence. But, he realized how impossible it would be to win a case against God, noting that **God is wise and all-powerful**. No one who **had opposed him** could come out **unharmed** (9:4).

Job's observations about God display his majesty to us. Some of us need our view of God transformed because the God we claim to believe in is too small. The God of the Bible **removes mountains . . . shakes the earth . . . stretches out the heavens . . .** and **makes the stars** (9:5-9). He is the holy Creator of the universe and holds you in the palm of his hand.

Importantly, **how can a person be justified before God?** (9:2) is a question the Bible answers. If humans are to be justified, God must do it himself (see Rom 3:23-24).

Job was so distraught that he believed that, even if he **were in the right**, God wouldn't **pay attention** (9:15-16). We have to remember that sometimes God is silent. But, don't count his silence as neglect. When God gives us the silent treatment, it's not because he's in a bad mood or careless. It's always because he's trying to teach us something we wouldn't otherwise learn. That doesn't

mean we just **forget** our problems and put on a **smile**; Job knew that (9:27-28). Instead, it means we trust our God who knows what we don't know, can do what we can't do, and never fails.

In the end, Job realized he could not defend himself before God. **He is not a man like me, that I can answer him** (9:32). Thus, Job wished there was someone to mediate between them (9:33). This is an important biblical concept. A mediator is a go-between, someone who can stand between two parties who are at odds with each other and bring them together. Job was struggling and hurting. He was desperate for help as his three friends accused him of sin. But, he knew a human could never effectively argue with God. Job was in no position to plead his case before a transcendent God. Thus, Job wanted an umpire—a judge who could listen impartially to both God and him and make a ruling. Yet, Job knew of no one who could fill this role.

To be an effective mediator between sinners and a holy God, someone would have to be like God and like human beings—knowing how he feels and thinks and how we feel and think, too. The mediator Job wished for would have had to understand Job so he could accurately represent him. Yet, he must be as great as God himself to accurately represent God. In time, this perfect mediator who could stand between humanity and God would become flesh in the person of Jesus Christ.

Jesus is God himself, yet he also knows the human condition intimately because he became human. He has a divine nature and a human nature. He experienced everything we have experienced. We needed a God-man, and only the Lord Jesus Christ uniquely fulfills that requirement. On the cross, Jesus hung between two estranged parties, his Father and the human race, to reconcile us. "For there is one God and one mediator between God and humanity, Christ Jesus, himself human" (1 Tim 2:5). He is the only mediator who can stand between God and us. And he does this every day as our resurrected high priest who lives forever and intercedes for us.

Job continued his answer to Bildad in chapter 10, wondering aloud why God allowed him to live when his days were filled with nothing but pain and agony. He'd become so disillusioned that he believed God would not reveal the charges against him even if he could take God to court (10:1-7). Then, Job asked God an interesting question: why would the **hands** that had so skillfully **shaped** Job want to **destroy** him (10:8)? If God had created him merely to destroy him, Job concluded that it would have been better if he had died at birth (10:18-19). And, out of that place of deep pain, Job said to God, **Leave me alone, so that I can smile a little before I go to a land of darkness and gloom**, which is death (10:20-21).

Job had fallen into a deep pit, and there was no one to lift him up. He needed brothers to give him biblical insight and help him think clearly. He needed believers to walk with him and put their arms around him while he suffered. However, his third so-called friend was about to push Job deeper into the pit.

IV. ZOPHAR'S FIRST SPEECH AND JOB'S RESPONSE (11:1–14:22)

11:1-20 Job's third friend **Zophar** was probably the youngest of the three, which would explain why he spoke last. Zophar has been described as a hardheaded, common sense kind of guy. Unfortunately, he used some of the harshest language against Job yet. Zophar accused Job of **babbling** on and **ridiculing** others, saying he needed someone to **humiliate** him (11:3). He also implied that Job was **worthless** and **stupid** (11:11-12). It's obvious Zophar never took a class on winning friends and influencing people. He was completely insensitive to Job's situation.

Zophar even went so far as to say that **God [had] chosen to overlook** some of Job's sin (11:6). In other words, while Eliphaz and Bildad said Job deserved the suffering he was undergoing, Zophar said, "Job, you're actually getting less punishment than you deserve!" What's interesting is that Zophar shared Job's longing for a hearing before God, but for a different reason. Job was sure God would vindicate him if he could just present his case. Zophar said the opposite would happen; God was letting Job off easy, so if Job were to go to court with God, he would surely be condemned (11:5-6). He felt Job should be thankful things weren't as bad as they could be.

When it came time for Zophar to give Job the pearls of his wisdom to fix the mess he was in, Zophar followed the format established by Eliphaz and Bildad. Because he felt Job's problems were rooted in his sin, all Job had to do was repent and he would see his life restored to its previous state of prosperity and happiness (11:13-20).

Like a good preacher, Zophar had three points in his message to Job concerning the steps he needed to take. First, Job needed to **redirect [his] heart** to God; Job needed to stop living in sin and conduct his life in a righteous way. Second, he needed to **spread out [his] hands** to God in prayer, which is probably a reference to a prayer of repentance (11:13). Third, Job needed to get rid of any **iniquity** he was practicing and not allow any **injustice** to be found in his **tents**—that is, in his life (11:14). These are great steps for someone who needs to deal with sin to follow, but all of them were based on Zophar's false assumption that Job was under God's discipline. Good prescription; bad diagnosis.

As in the cases of Eliphaz and Bildad, Zophar got a few things right. It's true that a life of faith in God requires us to honestly deal with sin and seek to obey and please God. And it's true that God blesses his people with hope, security, and peace. But, Zophar was wrong in not leaving room for God to allow his people to experience suffering— for his glory and for their good—for reasons known only to him.

12:1–14:22 In chapters 12–14, Job responded to Zophar's attack with what was becoming his standard defense. He declared his innocence and talked about God's mysterious and sovereign ways with humanity, while rejecting the charges of his friends and building the case he hoped to present to God in court.

This time, Job began with some thick sarcasm: **No doubt . . . wisdom will die with you!** (12:2). Translation? Zophar, your head is too big; do you think you're God's gift of wisdom? **Ask the animals**, Job said. Let them **instruct you** (12:7). In other words, he wanted him to consider that sometimes God's ways are not an open book. He "moves in a mysterious way," as the great hymn declares. Despite his pain and his growing frustration with his unanswered questions about suffering, Job had his theology straight.

Rather than blaspheming God, Job proclaimed his **wisdom and strength** (12:13). No one can undo what God does. You can't untie the knot God ties. **True wisdom and power belong to him** (12:16). **Counselors . . . kings . . . priests . . . leaders . . . advisers . . . nobles**—none in humanity can compare to him (12:17-21). God **makes nations great, then destroys them** (12:23). Whatever Job's struggles, he knew his God was glorious and almighty.

In saying, **my eyes have seen all this; my ears have heard and understood it** (13:1), Job was sure he could hold his own and more with Eliphaz, Bildad, and Zophar. He continued, **Everything you know, I also know; I am not inferior to you** (13:2). He wanted those boys to know they had nothing on him when it came to knowing and understanding God or how life works. Thus, he could see that his friends used **lies like plaster**. They were just whitewashing over the facts with false assumptions about what a terrible sinner he was. They were **worthless healers** who had no real prescriptions to offer him that would ease his pain (13:4). Their **memorable sayings** were no better than ashes (13:12).

In 13:15 we come to Job's famous declaration: **Even if [God] kills me, I will hope in him**. Other than Jesus himself, Job is the classic biblical example of someone who endured the devil's assaults and yet remained faithful to God. Satan took everything Job had, but Job refused to curse God or abandon his faith. This is the kind of resolute faith we need. A faith that perseveres. The only way to

lay claim to such a faith is to take advantage of what God provides—to put on the "full armor of God" (see Eph 6:13-18).

Job still wanted to **defend** himself before God; he was confident that he would be acquitted (13:15-16). But, because he wasn't being given that opportunity, Job was stuck with debating with his friends and trying to disprove their bad theories. What was Job's ultimate suggestion for them? **Shut up and let that be your wisdom!** (13:5). Eliphaz, Bildad, and Zophar had been at their best when they quietly wept with Job (2:12-13). In Job's advice is a truth that Solomon would write many years later: "Even a fool is considered wise when he keeps silent—discerning, when he seals his lips" (Prov 17:28).

Because Job still had the floor, he pressed ahead with his defense. He was ready to speak out to God and take the consequences even if it meant risking his life. He was willing to take this risk because of the possibility that God might acquit him. He said, **I have prepared my case; I know that I am right** (13:18). Job said he was willing to be quiet if one of his friends could make his charges stick (13:19). But, because Job did not think that was going to happen, he asked God for two things: to end his pain and stop frightening him with **terror** (13:20-21).

Job was so certain of his integrity that he wanted to take his chances. **Call**, he announced to God, **and I will answer** (13:22). "Show me my sins," he begged. "What have I done?" he wanted to know (13:23). But, God didn't show up in the court Job attempted to create, causing Job to ask why God was treating him like an enemy (13:27). In Job's opinion, God's silence was a way of tormenting him as someone would hit a helpless person while he was down.

Part of the value of the book of Job (and also Ecclesiastes) is simply the fact that it's actually in the Bible. Sometimes we think we're the first ones to ask the tough why questions. We look at the suffering and injustice of the world and ask, "How can this be?" But, one of God's most faithful servants, one whom God described as "a man of perfect integrity" (1:8), asked the same and struggled with indescribable grief. Things got so dire that he said, **Anyone born of** woman is short of days and full of trouble (14:1). Truly, life *is* short and filled with grief. But, God is not indifferent to these facts; he himself has entered into our suffering (see 1 Pet 2:24).

Job asked God for relief instead of judgment, for a little rest from the pain. If **a tree** is cut down, it can sprout again. But, if a man dies, he won't **rise again** (14:7-12). As **water** slowly **wears away stone**, Job felt God destroying all his hope, bit by bit (14:19).

V. ELIPHAZ'S SECOND SPEECH AND JOB'S RESPONSE (15:1–17:16)

15:1-35 Eliphaz signaled the mood for the second round of speeches as he began blasting away at Job without a hint of mercy. Job's three accusers must have huddled together before this and said, "Well, we tried the kid gloves approach, and it didn't work. It's time for the gloves to come off. We're going bare-knuckle." They were ticked that Job hadn't just thrown in the towel, admitted their superior wisdom, and begged God and them for forgiveness.

There's a distinct lack of sympathy here. Eliphaz essentially said all of Job's words were useless. His suffering friend had filled **himself with the hot east wind** (15:2). In other words, he thought Job was just a windbag. Then, as if that wasn't insulting enough, Eliphaz hit Job below the belt: he claimed that Job's own words proved he didn't really fear God and was nothing but a hardened sinner (15:4-6)! Even with this, though, old Eliphaz was just getting warmed up. He also accused Job of being so arrogant that he believed he was smarter than anyone else (15:7-10).

To twist the knife with which he had struck Job, Eliphaz called his own speech **God's consolations** that Job should appreciate because Eliphaz had spoken **words that [dealt] gently** with him (15:11). It's possible to become so convinced of your own wisdom that, if it's ever called into question, you simply buckle down and defend yourself rather than reevaluating your words. That's the warning sign that you're arrogant and unteachable.

Finally, to top off his accusations, Eliphaz spelled out in great detail the terrible, well-deserved things that happen to wicked people like Job (15:21-33). He saved his cruelest punch for the end, clearly implying

that Job had lost his children and everything else because he was **godless** and was getting what he deserved (15:34-35).

16:1–17:16 Eliphaz may have thought he had hit Job with a knockout blow, and Job's answer leaves no question that Job was reeling like a fighter who had taken some hard punches but refused to go down. He called his friends **miserable comforters** (16:2). If he were in their place, he said, he would **encourage** with his words and **bring relief** (16:5). Here too, however, the real object of his complaint was God. Though his friends had an atrocious bedside manner, God was the one who had **devastated [his] entire family** (16:7-8). And if that was not bad enough, Job added, **God** was also handing him **over to the unjust** and throwing him **to the wicked** (16:11)—a message that I'm sure his friends got.

In 16:19-21, Job returned to his main desire. He wanted a hearing before God, but he knew he couldn't get a court date on his own. So, he asked again for someone to step in and take his case to heaven. Job wished **that someone might argue for a man with God just as anyone would for a friend** (16:21). He was confident that if God would just give him a hearing, he would come out clean and prove to everyone that he hadn't done anything wrong.

In chapter 17, Job fell into further despair, as part of a pattern that we've seen before: he had desperate hope that God would intervene and end his grief, and then the realization that it wasn't going to happen hit. Job felt he had nothing to look forward to but the relief of **a graveyard** (17:1). He challenged his friends to **try again**, but was convinced there was not a **wise man among** them (17:10). He had no **hope** (17:15).

VI. BILDAD'S SECOND SPEECH AND JOB'S RESPONSE (18:1–19:29)

18:1-21 Bildad took up where Eliphaz left off, telling Job in effect, "Shut up! Do you expect the world to stop just because you're moaning about your situation?" (18:1-4). He then delivered his one-two punch of new accusations against Job for being so **wicked** (18:5-21). According to Bildad, the way you can spot a wicked sinner is that **his strength is depleted** (18:12), **parts of his skin are eaten away** (18:13), he's lost everything (18:15), and he has **no children** or survivor (18:19), thus leaving little mystery about just which person Bildad had in mind.

19:1-29 Job answered with a few twists of his own. The **ten times** Job said his friends had **humiliated** him (19:3) is a Hebrew expression meaning "often." He also told Bildad, **Even if it is true that I have sinned, my mistake concerns only me** (19:4), which is another way of saying, "Who invited you to pass judgment? I didn't ask for you three to come. You showed up on your own and just took over."

Besides inviting his friends to stay out of his business, Job also made a serious accusation: **it is God who has wronged me and caught me in his net** (19:6). In other words, Job said, "I wasn't trying to run away from God, but he dropped his net on me anyway, and now I'm trapped." God had taken everything from him (19:7-12), and everyone had turned against him. His family and friends couldn't stand the sight of him (19:13-18). **Those I love have turned against me**, he lamented (19:19). Even the **friends** who had come to comfort Job instead persecuted him as God was apparently doing (19:21-22).

We might expect a lightning bolt to strike Job at this point. But, God is gracious, and this is where the story takes another unusual turn. Job went from accusing God to praising him (19:25-27)! Hymns and songs of faith have been written from these verses. And what's most amazing about Job's statement of faith here is that he seemed to expect a bodily resurrection (19:26). If so, this would be the earliest evidence of this doctrine in Scripture. Certainly, Job was confident that death would not end his existence, a truth the rest of the Bible affirms.

Importantly, Job's confidence that his **Redeemer lives** (19:25) led him to warn his friends against misinterpreting God and opening themselves up for judgment (19:28-29). Time would prove that Job's warning was legitimate.

VII. ZOPHAR'S SECOND SPEECH AND JOB'S RESPONSE (20:1–21:34)

20:1-29 Zophar blew off Job's warning. He was **upset** and insulted (20:2-3). Zophar reached all the way back to Adam, **from the time a human was placed on earth** (20:4), to prove his point that the wicked only prosper for a little while before they are crushed (20:5). This, then, is an early attempt to answer one of the most puzzling questions God's people have ever faced: why do the wicked prosper and the righteous suffer? Zophar was partly true in saying that the wicked only last for a season and eventually face God's judgment. But, that "season" can seem awfully long when a wicked person enjoys a life of wealth and ease. That, in fact, is why we have to keep a kingdom perspective on life so we don't get caught up in chasing the stuff of earth instead of living for eternity.

Zophar encouraged his audience to envision a wicked, rich person coughing up his wealth rather than enjoying it because God made him choke on it (20:15), and there's no doubt that Zophar was talking about Job. It seems he even accused him of acquiring his wealth illegitimately by oppressing **the poor** (20:19)! And lest Job still be confused about Zophar's point, he finished by saying, in so many words, "Job, God's got an 'inheritance' waiting for you, but it's **a fire** that will **consume** you" (20:26).

21:1-34 It seems Job was more thoughtful in his defense this time, building a strong case against the argument that the wicked always suffer and die prematurely, while the righteous always prosper and live long, happy lives. Job didn't really expect his friends to change their minds or their tune toward him (21:2), even though the mere sight of him in his suffering should have made them **shudder** with horror and be too stunned to say anything (21:5).

Job's complaint that wicked people often prosper reminds me of a similar complaint that would be made centuries later by the psalmist (see Ps 73:1-14). This writer was as eloquent as Job in describing how easy some evil people have it, and what a waste of time that keeping oneself pure before God can seem. But, as soon as he stepped into God's house, his perspective changed drastically (see Ps 73:15-28). Suddenly, he saw things clearly. He realized that evil people who pay no attention to God have one foot in the grave and the other on a banana peel.

Job wasn't quite to that point of peaceful clarity yet. He recounted all the good things that evil people have (21:7-13). **Their children are established** (21:8); **their homes are secure** (21:9); **they spend their days in prosperity** and die **in peace** (21:13). Job couldn't get his mind around this because these were the same people who told God: **Leave us alone! We don't want to know your ways. Who is the Almighty, that we should serve him?** (21:14-15). This is the attitude of those who live for the moment but not for eternity. These are people who care nothing for their Creator's agenda. They have their own.

Had Job's friends really not observed wicked people like this in the world who prosper (21:27-30)? Could they really not grasp the fact that Job was an innocent sufferer? How could they offer him **such futile comfort** (21:34)?

VIII. ELIPHAZ'S THIRD SPEECH AND JOB'S RESPONSE (22:1–24:25)

22:1-30 Job's comforters started a third round of speeches, but Zophar wouldn't speak a third time. Instead, Elihu—a man from whom we have not yet heard—would take over and give a lengthy speech (33:1–37:24).

This time, Eliphaz said that man adds nothing to God, and that God receives no benefit from man (22:2-3). That's good theology. God does not need you or me. We need him, but God is sufficient, complete within himself. He does not need anything in his created order to make him feel better about being God.

Eliphaz wasn't content to leave things on that truth, however. He took his accusations against Job to a new level, mentioning a long list of the sins and crimes he was sure Job had committed. He accused Job of evils such as ripping off his **brothers**, even if it left **them naked** (22:6). He claimed that Job refused to give **water to the thirsty** and **food** to the **famished**, despite the fact that he was **a powerful man** who owned a lot of **land** and could have done something about such needs (22:7-8). Further, Eliphaz asserted that Job also mistreated the two most helpless segments of society, **widows** and **the fatherless** (22:9). And if such charges against Job had been true, it was no wonder Eliphaz was convinced that Job was suffering justly. He was simply getting the sentence a righteous and holy God had handed down.

Eliphaz, therefore, issued an altar call of sorts to Job, calling on him to come forward and repent (22:21-30). All Job had to do was admit that everything his friends said about him was true. Then, Eliphaz was sure, God would restore and forgive him.

23:1–24:25 When it was his turn to speak, Job continued to insist that if a trial were held in heaven's court, God would pay attention to his case and declare him not guilty (23:3-7). The problem, Job had decided was that he didn't know where to find God (23:8-9). Yet, even though he was frustrated in his desire to get a hearing, Job was confident that God knew his heart. He was sure that when God had **tested** him, he would **emerge as pure gold** (23:10).

When you experience trials, you often won't be able to make sense of things. You won't get answers to all of your why questions. And that's why it's crucial that you grasp this truth and don't let go: *God is in control.* He's not only in control of the blessings, he's also in control of the messes. Like Job, you may not be able to figure out where God is, but he knows where you are (23:8-10). We worship him because of what we know that *he* knows.

I have not departed from the commands of [God's] lips; I have treasured the words from his mouth more than my daily food (23:12). Believers who aren't regularly feeding on God's Word are malnourished. It's not enough just to be under the teaching of the Bible weekly in church. We also need to be in the Word daily. When we want to hear from God in his Word more than we want to eat, we are on the way to developing healthy spiritual lives. In this way, Job is a model for us in his hunger for the commands and words of God's mouth. And he foreshadows the one who would one day say, "My food is to do the will of him who sent me and to finish his work" (John 4:34).

Job had his own list of injustices committed not by him but by the wicked against **the poor** and **needy** (24:2-12). **Yet**, he concluded, **God [paid] no attention to this crime** (24:12). Murderers, thieves, and adulterers just seem to have their way (24:13-16).

IX. BILDAD'S THIRD SPEECH AND JOB'S RESPONSE (25:1–31:40)

25:1–27:23 Job 25 is the shortest chapter of the book. (I think Bildad ran out of arguments and just punted.)

But, although Bildad may have been short-winded this round, Job wasn't. He congratulated Bildad on his non-existent achievements that he thought qualified him to tear Job apart (26:1-4). Then, in the rest of chapter 26, he brilliantly highlighted God's majesty and power, ending with his acknowledgement of how little we know of God's greatness (26:5-14). All the fantastic truths he listed are summed up in the statement, **These are but the fringes of his ways** (26:14). As much as we know about the majesty of God from observing his creation, we've only scratched the surface.

In chapter 27, Job returned to his claim of innocence before God, vowing that he would never admit to the charges his friends made against him. He said, **I will never affirm that you are right** (27:5). To do so would mean giving up his **integrity**, which he also vowed to maintain as long as he lived (27:5-6).

Then, Job considered the fate of the wicked. **The godless** man has no **hope** when **God takes away his life** (27:8). So, while the wicked may prosper in this life, an eternal judgment is coming (27:13-23). A lifetime of eighty to ninety years is certainly lengthy. But, in light of eternity, it's a blip on the radar screen. Here and gone. If you won't live for God's agenda in this life, you'll be forced to bow to his agenda in the afterlife—an agenda of everlasting punishment.

28:1-28 Chapter 28 sounds like it came straight out of the book of Proverbs. In it, Job answered the question, How do you find wisdom? In order to obtain **silver** and **gold**, a **miner** does some amazing things. He cuts a **shaft** deep into the ground, probes the foundations of the mountains, and discovers hidden treasures (28:2-11). **But where can wisdom be found?** (28:12). No matter how much gold you have, you can't even buy it (28:12-19). **The price of wisdom is beyond pearls** (28:18). In fact, if you ask, "How much does it cost to buy some wisdom?" the answer will always be, "More than you've got."

Where . . . does wisdom come from? (28:20). How can you find it? Only **God understands the way to wisdom** (28:23). He is its source and exercises wisdom in all he does

(28:24-27). So, how can you be wise? Well, God says, **The fear of the LORD—that is wisdom. And to turn from evil is understanding** (28:28). And it sounds like King Solomon was reading Job when he wrote Proverbs 1:7 and 9:10. To have wisdom and understanding, to know how to live well in a world gone bad, you have to fear the Lord. That is, you have to take God seriously and embrace his kingdom agenda for your life—even when you don't know where it will lead. The good news is that God knows where it leads.

29:1–31:40 In these chapters, Job offered up his final defense. In the process of answering his accusers, Job gave us a picture of his life. By chapter 29 he had been forced into defending himself, so it's not as if he decided to brag for a while. If you want to be a kingdom man or woman—someone who humbly aligns your life under God's authority—pay attention to Job's life.

Job began by reflecting on his relationship with God when he was in his prime (29:1-5). The Lord **watched over** him (29:2), and **God's friendship rested on** his home (29:4). In those days, **the Almighty was still with [him] and [his] children were around [him]** (29:5) as he worked to build and hand down a spiritual legacy for his family as a kingdom man does. With these reflections, Job was not saying that his faith was a dead thing of the past. Rather, he was looking back to happier times. The entire book of Job, in fact, shows that he never lost faith in God.

Then, Job was reminded of the respect he had earned for his godly reputation (29:7-11). When he **went out to the city gate** and took his **seat in the town square**, young and old took notice (29:7-9). Young men stepped aside when Mr. Job showed up. The older men said, "Quiet! Job has something to say." **City officials** and noblemen **blessed** Job and **spoke well of** him (29:9-11). Job didn't demand this respect by puffing out his chest; he earned it by his conduct and character. He influenced his neighborhood for the better. When a kingdom man shows up, a higher standard enters the scene.

Next, we catch a glimpse of specific actions that earned Job such high praise: he was well-known for practicing mercy and justice

(29:12-17). Job was a successful businessman who also compassionate. There was no category of people in need that he neglected. He cared for **the poor . . . the fatherless . . . the dying . . . the widow . . . the blind . . . the lame . . . the needy**, and **the stranger** (29:12-13, 15-16). When **the unjust** attempted to sink **fangs** into the innocent, Job busted their chops (29:17). A kingdom man hurts with people who hurt and helps those who need help. He is an advocate for the weak because his God is the same (see Ps 68:5).

Finally, Job blessed those around him with his wisdom (29:21-25). It's clear from chapter 28 that Job understood wisdom—what it is, where it comes from, and how you get it. When he opened his mouth, **men listened to [him] with expectation** (29:21). Just as the **dew** and **rain** bring refreshment and life, so Job's advice and counsel gave people hope and turned their lives around (29:22-23). Wisdom is the ability to apply God's truth to the practical issues of day-to-day life. The only way to do that is to regularly spend time with God and know his mind on matters. Many today are drinking from the wrong fountain. The counsel of a kingdom man is like fresh water to the thirsty.

But now, Job said sadly, **they mock me** (30:1). Those who'd formerly respected and listened to him made fun of him because of the calamities that had come upon him. This group included not only his friends but **the rabble** of society (30:1-15). In the past, Job himself **grieved for the needy** (30:25). But, in his time of distress, no one came to his aid (20:26).

In 31:1-34, Job presented a long list of sins that he denied committing. In the integrity of his heart, Job declared himself innocent of these vices. Importantly, Job still wasn't claiming perfection. He knew he was a sinner. But, he also knew his suffering hadn't come upon him because of his wickedness. Chapter 31, in fact, is Job's evidence that supports the truth of God's testimony: "No one else on earth is like him, a man of perfect integrity, who fears God and turns away from evil" (1:8).

Job's righteousness wasn't merely concerned with externals. He knew that righteousness begins in the heart and mind. Therefore, he had **made a covenant with**

[his] eyes, so that he might not look at a young woman (31:1). Similarly, if you want to be a godly man, few things are more important—especially in today's culture—than guarding your eyes. Pornography exists in many forms and is easily accessible. That's why you have to be prepared for battle. Job didn't have to face the temptation of pornography. But, he certainly knew what lust was and was confronted with that temptation. So, he made a covenant, a sacred agreement with his eyes, to honor God and the women around him.

Job continued to list the sins that he had avoided: lying, adultery, mistreatment of his servants, oppressing the poor and needy, greed, gloating over an enemy's misfortune, and hiding his sins (31:2-34). And, because Job had not committed them, he entered one final plea of innocence. If he was guilty of wickedness, he summoned God to indict him (31:35-40). Then, Job rested his case.

X. ELIHU'S SPEECH (32:1–37:24)

Like a good theatrical drama, the book of Job has a surprise twist near its end: the appearance of a fourth visitor, Elihu. We're not left in doubt regarding how he felt about the discussion he'd overheard—he was angry (32:2-3, 5). Elihu was angry at Job because he had justified himself rather than God (32:2). Job was right: he wasn't suffering because of his sin. But, he had put God on trial by affirming his own righteousness and implying that God was unjust. Elihu was also ticked off at Job's three friends because they had failed to refute him and yet had condemned him (32:3). They thought God was punishing Job for his sin, but they never proved their case against him; thus, they condemned an innocent man.

Was Elihu a cocky youngster who made some of the same bad arguments as the men he chastised? Did he offer needed criticism of both Job and his friends? Or, did he do a little bit of both? Regardless, he was bursting at the seams by the time he started to weigh in. Likely the youngest man present, he first practiced deference (32:6-7). But, ultimately, wisdom comes from God and does not reside in the old alone (32:8-10). He'd listened to everything that was spoken and was eager to have his say (32:11-22).

Elihu challenged Job: Refute me if you can (33:5). But, in doing so, he was confident that what he was about to say was "the truth, the whole truth, and nothing but the truth" that Job wouldn't be able to contradict. Elihu began by summarizing Job's own argument, showing that he had been taking notes. Elihu said, in effect, "Job, here's what you've been saying. You are innocent before God, but despite this, he has attacked you without cause and treated you like his enemy" (33:8-11). But I tell you that you are wrong in this matter, since God is greater than man (33:12). In other words, Elihu countered that God didn't owe Job an explanation for what he was enduring because God is transcendent. Why do you take him to court for not answering anything a person asks? (33:13). In other words, Elihu said, "Let's not forget who is the Creator and who is the creature here."

Critically, not all suffering is punishment for personal sin. The holy Son of God willingly suffered—the righteous for the unrighteous—to bring us to God (see 1 Pet 3:18). The author of Hebrews encouraged his readers to endure suffering as the Lord's loving discipline (see Heb 12:5-11). Perhaps Elihu had this idea in mind when he said, A person may be disciplined on his bed with pain (33:19)—not because God is judging him for his sin, but because he is refining him for his glorious purposes and helping him avoid future evil.

Elihu upheld the righteousness of God. It is impossible for God to do wrong, and for the Almighty to act unjustly (34:10). To do so would be contrary to God's character. The Lord can do all things—except evil (34:12). After all, how could a wicked god govern the world? (34:17). But, the Righteous One is impartial and judges with equity (34:17-20). No one needs to approach God to have his day in court, for he sees all and knows all (34:21-23). God does not live according to our terms (34:33).

Elihu continued. Humanity's righteousness does not give God anything he doesn't already have, and humanity's unrighteousness does not have an adverse effect on him (35:3-7). Yet, our actions do affect other people who suffer the consequences of our unrighteous actions (35:8-9). How we live and respond to adversity influences others. God provides human beings with **songs in the night** (35:10). He gives us **more understanding than the animals** (35:11). Yet, the animals don't complain to God that they don't see him and can't make their case before him (35:14)!

In alleging **complete knowledge** (36:4), Elihu was not exactly making a modest claim. But, as with Job's miserable comforters, Elihu did speak truth regarding many of God's attributes (and so did Job). For a clear picture, though, we'll need to hear from God himself—who would enter the scene soon enough.

Elihu pointed out that **God is mighty, but he despises no one** (36:5). He is the supreme being, but this does not make him too lofty to show kindness to the lowly. He judges **the wicked** and delivers **the afflicted** (36:6-15). In fact, **God rescues the afflicted by their affliction** (36:15). Here, Elihu returned to the theme of divine discipline. He warned Job not to **turn to iniquity** because this is why he was **tested by affliction** (36:21). To quote the author of Hebrews, "No discipline seems enjoyable at the time, but painful. Later on, however, it yields the peaceful fruit of righteousness to those who have been trained by it" (Heb 12:11). Whatever God intends to teach you through your trials, it is always for your benefit.

Elihu concluded with a consideration of God's glorious might displayed in his creation (36:26–37:24). God shows himself **exalted in power** (37:23). Elihu's questions to Job about how God works his wonders seem to foreshadow God's own coming questions in chapters 38–41. Though Elihu was long-winded, his advice to **stop and consider God's wonders** (37:14) would turn out to be exactly what Job needed.

XI. GOD'S RESPONSE (38:1–41:34)

After each visitor had his say, **the LORD answered Job from the whirlwind** (38:1). In other words, God took over and did a face-to-face with Job that revealed his awesome sovereignty and power, leaving Job flat on the ground. He said, **Who . . . obscures my counsel with ignorant words? Get ready to answer me like a man** (38:2-3). Previously, Job had demanded a hearing with God. So, the lesson here is this: be careful what you wish for.

Don't miss the imbalance of power in this divine confrontation. One night, I encountered a cockroach in my kitchen. Only, this was no ordinary roach. When I moved toward him, he didn't skitter; he didn't run. He sat there as if to say, "*This* is *my* place." I couldn't believe it when the thing wouldn't budge. And that stubborn posture meant he clearly didn't understand who I was, and thus, I squashed that boy flat. Now, what that insect did to me is what autonomous man often does to God. He gets "roachy" on God, digging in his heels or swaggering around like he is someone, like he has power. But, it's suicide to get in God's face because only he has *ultimate* power.

When God spoke up and told Job to stand up and face him, Job's friends were probably as terrified as Job by God's overwhelming presence and were thankful he wasn't speaking to them (not yet, at least). But, instead of rebuking Job for all his supposed sins, God began asking him a series of questions. And every one of them was rhetorical because God wasn't interested in Job's answers. In fact, God knew Job wouldn't be able to answer any of his questions. That was the whole point.

The Lord demanded of Job, **Where were you when I established the earth?** (38:4). Then, for the next two chapters, God asked Job what he knew about creation (38:4–39:30). Job thus got the oral exam of his life. He'd wanted his day in court, and it couldn't have been fun to find himself under cross-examination. How was the world made? What makes the sun rise? Where does the wind come from?

Why do the stars shine? Can you command lightning bolts to strike? Do you provide for the animals of the world? Are you able to create a horse? **Tell me, if you know all this.... Don't you know?... you have lived so long!** (38:18, 21).

Importantly, in a sense, God's questions were an answer to Job's accusations—not that God needed to defend himself or his actions to Job or anyone else. But, as Job pressed God time and again to tell him why he was suffering and why God was punishing him for no reason (at least no reason as far as Job was concerned), Job's attitude became sinful as he began to see his troubles as God's grossly unfair attack on him. So, God used these and the other questions to humble Job and help him see how truly ignorant he was of God's sovereign wisdom and power. Job didn't understand the reason for his suffering. But, God told him, "That's only the tip of the iceberg. There's a lot more you don't understand."

God's grilling of Job brings us to chapter 40, in which Job was finally allowed to speak. The court date hadn't turned out as Job had expected. The Lord had made the most awe-inspiring and irrefutable opening statement ever before pausing to permit Job a chance to reply: **Will the one who contends with the Almighty correct him? Let him who argues with God give an answer** (40:2). Job, however, couldn't answer a single one of God's questions—let alone the whole multitude of them.

Job responded the only way a frail human could: **I am so insignificant. How can I answer you?... I have spoken once, and I will not reply; twice, but now I can add nothing** (40:4-5). Nevertheless, the Lord wasn't finished with him yet: **Would you really challenge my justice? Would you declare me guilty to justify yourself?** (40:8).

This confrontation is a small glimpse of the future. It's one thing to scold God for his handling of our affairs when we can't see or hear him. It's another thing to confront God to his face. Yet, all of us will stand before him face-to-face one day like Job. Job was moved to repentance. Will you shake your fist at God? Or, bow your head in humility?

Within this section, the Lord also directed Job's attention to **Behemoth** and **Leviathan** (40:15–41:34). Clearly, these beasts were the epitome of strength, ferocity, and terror in Job's day. Yet, they were also objects of God's creative power and wisdom. Humanity cannot comprehend all the intricacies of such creatures. How much less, then, can we comprehend the mysteries of God's providential dealings?

XII. JOB'S RESTORATION (42:1-17)

Job was a righteous man. But, even when righteous men are confronted with God's holiness and glory, the response can't be casual. Job was clearly overwhelmed and responded to the Creator's awesome revelation with a new and richer appreciation of God's sovereignty. He said, **I know that you can do anything and no plan of yours can be thwarted.... Surely I spoke about things I did not understand, things too wondrous for me** (42:2-3). Job confessed that he had spoken too soon and in ignorance of who he was dealing with.

Job was filled with genuine sorrow over the things he had said about God's fairness and the accusations he had made against God's character. While he had not committed the blatant sins that his friends accused him of, in the end, God's greatness had exposed his pride and presumption in challenging the Almighty. **I had heard reports about you, but now my eyes have seen you. Therefore, I reject my words and am sorry for them; I am dust and ashes** (42:5-6). In other words, Job said, "I didn't know any of this—until I went through this mess. And now I'm changed."

As a pastor, I've been asked countless times by godly, suffering people, "Why is this happening to me?" I can't answer all of the *why* questions, and neither can anyone else. Importantly, when Job asked why, God answered with a *who*. Job wanted to know the *reasons* behind his suffering. God pulled back the curtain for a glimpse at the incomprehensible *God* behind his suffering.

God sometimes allows us to go through painful and even prolonged suffering to give us a fresh vision of him that goes far beyond what we could have otherwise experienced. So, in the midst of your trials, pray for deliverance. But, pray also that God would use your circumstances to allow you to see him, understand him, and worship him as never before.

Though his questions were not answered, Job wisely repented of his sin before God. But, it was not the kind of repentance Job's friends had demanded. Job didn't repent for secret sins but for questioning God's sovereignty and justice. Job's final confession must have satisfied God, because he turned immediately to the other three men and said to Eliphaz as the oldest, **I am angry with you and your two friends, for you have not spoken the truth about me, as my servant Job has** (42:7).

Now, that had to be a frightening statement to hear from God. Eliphaz and his pals had tried to defend God and his justice, but in the process, they argued that all suffering was the direct result of sin—which wasn't true then and still isn't true today. They had been wrong about Job and—even worse—they had been wrong about God. They had, in fact, misrepresented God. Their failure brings to my mind the words of James: "Not many should become teachers, my brothers, because you know that we will receive a stricter judgment" (Jas 3:1). It's no small thing to teach about God what is false.

Eliphaz, Bildad, and Zophar needed forgiveness from both God and Job. So, the Lord commanded them to offer sacrifices for themselves. What then? **Then my servant Job will pray for you** (42:8). The man they had condemned as a sinner, then, was going to be their intermediary. The one who cried out for a "mediator" (9:33) was going to become one. **I will surely accept his prayer and not deal with you as your folly deserves** (42:8). In other words, these boys would not get what they rightfully had coming to them!

This whole encounter, though, must have been humiliating for these men. Job had spoken the truth about God, and they had not (42:8). Now, this doesn't mean that every word they spoke was a flat-out lie, or that every word Job uttered was spot-on. Rather, Job's friends had made erroneous statements about the character and works of God and had also made false charges against Job. Yet, when humbled, the three friends obeyed, and God accepted Job's prayer (42:10).

In an amazing display of divine grace, God blessed the later part of Job's life more than the first: **The LORD restored [Job's] fortunes and doubled his previous possessions** (42:10). Not only that, but he also blessed him with ten more children (42:13). His family and acquaintances gathered around him and **comforted him concerning all the adversity the LORD had brought on him** (42:11). Notice the clarifying words here: they comforted him regarding the adversity that *God* had brought upon him—not that *Satan* had brought upon him. Thus, remember that whatever part the devil plays in your suffering, know that he can only inflict you with trials that have first passed through the hands of an all-wise, all-powerful, and all-loving God.

In the long run, Job received back everything he had lost and more. We like that part. But, keep in mind the pattern established throughout the book: Job was righteous; he lost everything; he didn't understand; he got a fresh view of God; he responded rightly to this fresh view—and then he got his stuff back. Our temptation is to say, "I don't need a fresh view of anything. I just want my stuff back." But, such a quick fix isn't what we need, and it's not what God promises. He doesn't promise to restore our losses or reward us with material wealth in this life. There's nothing wrong with getting stuff. But, God knows that's not what you need. What you need is him. What you need is a fresh view of his glory.

May God grant to us a fresh vision of God our Father and our Lord Jesus Christ. And may we confess with Job, "Even if he kills me, I will hope in him" (13:15).

PSALMS

INTRODUCTION

Author

THE BOOK OF PSALMS HAS NO single author. King David authored a large number of the one hundred and fifty psalms—almost half. Seventy-three psalms explicitly bear the designation "a psalm of David." Other authors include Asaph (Pss 50; 73–83), the sons of Korah (Pss 42–49; 84–85; 87), Solomon (Pss 72; 127), Moses (Ps 90), Heman the Ezrahite (Ps 88), and Ethan the Ezrahite (Ps 89). Many other psalms are anonymous.

Historical Background

Psalms is a collection of one hundred and fifty works of Hebrew poetry. Our English word "psalms" comes from the Greek word *psalmoi* ("songs"), which is the title of the collection in the Septuagint, the Greek translation of the Old Testament. Given the likely indications of authorship, the psalms were composed from the time of Moses in the fifteenth century BC to some time after the exile in the sixth century BC. Many of the psalms include titles with a variety of information, such as the psalm's historical context or liturgical use in worship. Psalms is divided into five parts: Book I (Pss 1–41), Book II (Pss 42–72), Book III (Pss 73–89), Book IV (Pss 90–106), and Book V (Pss 107–150).

Message and Purpose

Psalms is actually five books of prayers and praises brought together as one. Each was written to be sung in worship to God. The Psalms cover every possible circumstance that life could ever throw at us, which is why there are one hundred and fifty of them. They cover the ins-and-outs and the ups-and-downs of life—touching on physical, financial, emotional, and spiritual needs.

The Psalms were written so the people of God could communicate with him in the midst of all of the circumstances of life. They will shape your ability to talk with God and will teach you about his character, attributes, and kingdom purpose in history. Through using the Psalms, you can even talk with God in the very words of Scripture, singing and praying his Word back to him. So, in the same way that you would pick up a hymnal to sing praises to God, pick up the book of Psalms. It will enhance your prayer life, your praise life, and your approach-to-problems life, in the context of God-centered worship.

VIDEO INTRO

www.bhpublishinggroup.com/qr/te/19_00

Outline

PSALMS

I. BOOK I (PSALMS 1–41)

❧ *Psalm 1* ❧

1:1 This tells how to become **happy**. The word translated "happy" in the CSB can also be rendered "blessed." To be blessed by God is to be happy.

Everyone wants to be blessed, but we should define what that means. For many people, being blessed refers to stuff acquired. Yet, one can have an abundance of stuff and be miserable. So, put simply, *blessing* is the God-given capacity to experience, enjoy, and extend the goodness and favor of God in your life—whatever form God's goodness and favor takes. Paul confesses, "I know both how to make do with little, and I know how to make do with a lot. In any and all circumstances I have learned the secret of being content—whether well fed or hungry, whether in abundance or in need. I am able to do all things through him who strengthens me" (Phil 4:12-13). In other words, he had learned to enjoy God's heavenly goodness regardless of his earthly circumstances.

Interestingly, the psalmist explains what the blessed / happy person does *not* do. First, he **does not walk in the advice of the wicked**. The biblical metaphor of "walking" refers to how one lives. The fastest way to miss your blessing is to take counsel from those who have no regard for God's view on life. Second, he does not **stand in the pathway with sinners**. The blessed person does not hang out with people who will influence him toward sin and away from God. Third, he does not **sit in the company of mockers**. Mockers make light of serious things, sitting in judgment of everyone and everything. Yet, they fail to allow their critical gaze to turn back to themselves. Notice the progression: walking, standing, sitting. The one who is regularly influenced by people with little regard for God finds himself more and more at home with human viewpoints and misses God's blessings.

1:2 What does the blessed person do? He delights **in the Lord's instruction**. To delight in something is to find your joy and pleasure in it. The blessed man or woman finds this in God's Word, meditating **on it day and night**. To this, someone may object, "I have a job and a family. I don't have time to read the Bible day and night!" But, the psalmist doesn't say the blessed person *reads* God's instruction day and night; he says he *meditates* on it.

To meditate on something is to recall, ponder, and interact with it in the mind. When we meditate on God's Word, we mentally chew on it until it becomes a part of us. This, in fact, is why consuming God's Word is often spoken of in terms of eating: "Your words were found, and I ate them. Your words became a delight to me and the joy of my heart" (Jer 15:16; see Ps 119:103; Ezek 3:1-3; Rev 10:9-10).

When we meditate on the Word of God, we think about how it connects to life. We ask ourselves, "How does the Word speak to the circumstances I am currently facing?" The gap between hearing the Word and being blessed is closed with meditation. Considering life from the divine viewpoint and acting in accordance with it brings the tangible experience of blessing.

1:3 The blessed person **is like a tree planted beside flowing streams**. Such trees are not easily swayed; they hold their ground. The "flowing streams" in view are irrigation channels, so regardless of how barren the weather, such a tree is positioned to drink from a continuous source of life.

That the tree **bears its fruit in its season** indicates that the blessed person is productive, maximizing his potential. Importantly, fruit reveals something about the quality of the tree that bears it. If you're not bearing worthwhile fruit, then, it's because there's nothing worthwhile inside of you. Moreover, trees don't eat their own fruit; the fruit exists for the benefit of others. Thus, you know that you're blessed when you are being a blessing.

That the **leaf does not wither** doesn't mean that a blessed person never has negative experiences. Rather, the negative things don't cause him to wither and die. You know you're blessed when you bounce back from life's trials more quickly than you once did.

1:4 The psalmist contrasted the fruitful life of the righteous one who is blessed by God with the worthless life of **the wicked**. Instead of being like mighty and stable trees, the wicked **are like chaff that the wind blows away**. In the ancient process of winnowing, the kernel of grain was separated from the husk. While the kernel fell to the threshing floor to be collected, the worthless husk and other parts—the chaff—blew away in the breeze. The righteous who live by God's Word produce things of eternal value. The wicked and their useless deeds won't last.

1:5-6 The basis of God's **judgment** will be his omniscience, his intimate knowledge of all people—the wicked and the righteous—and all they do. **The wicked will not stand** among **the righteous** on the day when God's just verdict is rendered (1:5). He **watches over the way of the righteous**. But, because they fail to submit to God's authority through his Word, **the way of the wicked** only **leads to ruin** (1:6). Choose wisely which path you will take.

ꙮ *Psalm 2* ꙮ

2:1-3 This is the first messianic psalm, which moves from the lesser King David to his greater son, King Jesus. It celebrates the coronation of the king. Though the psalm includes no title indicating authorship, the New Testament attributes its words to David (see Acts 4:25-26).

The raging of the nations mentioned in verse 1 is **in vain** in that it's a waste of time. Why? Because these **kings** and **rulers** of the world had conspired together to **take their stand . . . against the LORD and his Anointed One** (2:2). And, while a coalition of world powers could threaten humanity, they pose no threat to the God of the universe. At the height of David's power as king, many nations submitted to Israel and paid tribute, and they desired to **tear off their chains** and be free from David's domination (2:3). But, to stand against King David was to stand against God, which is ultimately futile.

How much more is this true of Jesus Christ, the Son of David? He is the true "Anointed One," the Messiah, the Son of God. To reject the Son is to reject the Father (see 1 John 2:23). Gentile and Jewish rulers conspired against Jesus and executed him by crucifixion. Yet, this was all part of God's plan (see Acts 4:25-28) that he might bring salvation to sinners. In the end, then, their plot proved futile; even death could not hold him.

2:4-6 In spite of the rebellion of the nations on earth, God remains **enthroned in heaven**. And the God who created the universe with the mere words of his mouth chuckles at the ridiculous rebels and **ridicules them** (2:4). No one who fails to submit to the Lord's authority, he knows, will escape his **anger** and **wrath** (2:5). He is in control and will respond with judgment for the wickedness of rejecting his **king** (2:6). Ultimately, this will happen when Jesus rules in Jerusalem during his millennial reign.

2:7-9 The interesting statement, **You are my Son; today I have become your Father** (2:7), is first a reminder that the Davidic king was considered God's "son" when anointed and installed on his throne (see 2 Sam 7:12-14). But, this sentence is even truer of Jesus, the heir to the Davidic throne and the only one who can truly be called "the Son of God." Though David possessed a great kingdom and ruled the nations because of the victories God gave him, only King Jesus will receive all **the nations** as his **inheritance** and **the ends of the earth** as his **possession** when he reigns in the millennium (2:8). No nation—however powerful—will be able to stand against him. With his **iron scepter**, he will one day **break** and **shatter** all who oppose him (2:9). Rebellion against the kingdom reign of Messiah is pointless; it is the rebellion of an ant against an elephant.

2:10-11 All **kings** are called to **be wise** and **receive instruction** (2:10). God calls them to **serve** him **with reverential awe** and to **rejoice with trembling** (2:11). If they will humble themselves in submission, they will prosper. To continue prideful revolt is a fool's errand that will result in defeat.

2:12 How can the kings of the earth submit to God during the millennium? By paying **homage** to his **Son**. In Hebrew, to "pay homage" is literally "to kiss" the Son—that is, to submit to his authority and rule. King Jesus is not only to be obeyed but also worshiped just as the Father is worshiped. "Every knee will bow . . . and every tongue will confess that Jesus Christ is Lord, to the glory of God the Father" (Phil 2:10-11). So, why should the nations **perish** in their **rebellion**? They can escape the Son's anger against sin by taking **refuge in him**. Those who do so are **happy** and blessed. The church is to model this satisfaction that will be universal in the millennial kingdom.

⊰ *Psalm 3* ⊱

This **psalm** is ascribed to **David**. It is his cry for deliverance **when he fled from his son Absalom** who sought to seize his throne and drove the king from his palace (see 2 Sam 15:1–16:14).

3:1-2 Verse one is an acknowledgement that many of David's fellow Israelites under the influence of his son had risen up against him. They were convinced that Absalom was too strong for the aging David and that God couldn't deliver him. **There is no help for him in God** (3:2) means that, in their eyes, David's demise was certain.

3:3-4 Regardless of how bleak the circumstances looked, David expresses his confidence in God's deliverance: **You, Lord, are a shield around me** (3:3). Though he recognized the danger of his situation, his focus was not ultimately on his enemies but on God. He cried to the Lord whose earthly throne was on Zion, **his holy mountain** (that is, Jerusalem), where the temple would be built (3:4). God was the source of David's protection; therefore, he believed he would be restored to a place of dignity. God himself would lift his weary **head** (3:3).

3:5-6 Whether David lay down to **sleep** or awoke to a new day, he recognized that God—not his own strength or ability—sustained him (3:5). And, if he couldn't even sustain himself through the daily act of sleeping, how much less could he do so during a rebellious uprising? Trusting in God's sustaining power, David would not fear **thousands** who stood **against** him (3:6). He had a great sense of peace and calm from God in spite of his difficulties. When our circumstances overwhelm us, we are called to look to the same God of peace.

3:7-8 David petitions God to **rise up** and **save** him. He calls on God to override his enemies and subjugate them. To **strike** one's **enemies on the cheek** (3:7) was an insult intended to bring them to their senses and place them into submission—in this case, both to God and to David. David concludes his prayer of deliverance with a Godward focus because **salvation belongs to the Lord** (3:8). He alone determines the time, place, and method of our deliverance.

Importantly, David was not looking out only for himself. He was concerned for God's people; thus, he prays, **may your blessing be on your people** (3:8). When we are illegitimately oppressed, our focus should be on

God. Though we must not ignore the reality of our suffering, we can find peace in the midst of our storms. What you look at will affect how you feel.

⇝ Psalm 4 ⇜

4:1 Answer me when I call, God. David expresses his dependency on the Lord because he is the source of righteousness, the one who vindicated him. Just as God had **freed** him from his past suffering and **affliction**, David knew that God would meet him in the midst of his current trials. He appeals to God to **be gracious to** him, hear his **prayer**, and provide what he needs to face his circumstances.

4:2-5 David warns "the sons of a man" (the literal rendering of CSB's **exalted ones**) to take God seriously; this is what Scripture calls "fearing God." They should not **love what is worthless** or **pursue a lie** (4:2). Rather, they should tremble before God and not allow their anger to cause them to sin against God's anointed king. For God watched over his **faithful** servant David and would **hear** his cries for help (4:3-4). It was thus a better option to **trust** the Lord and offer righteous sacrifices (4:5).

4:6 God alone is the source of blessing. David thus encourages the discouraged around him, those who ask, **Who can show us anything good?** He reminds them that the Lord can revive the countenance. He would illuminate them and show them favor in spite of their adversity.

4:7-8 David celebrates the **joy** that God had placed in his **heart**—more joy than was possible even during the great harvest festival (4:7)—because, in the midst of David's difficulty, God had given him **sleep . . . peace**, and **safety** (4:8). This is a reminder that in times of trial, God often gives proof of his presence. Thus, the follower of God can experience "the peace of God, which surpasses all understanding" and that "will guard your hearts and minds in Christ Jesus" (Phil 4:7). This psalm reminds us that God provides

confidence and encouragement in our suffering. We, in turn, are able to share that confidence and encouragement with others.

⇝ Psalm 5 ⇜

5:1-3 David appeals to the Lord to **consider** his **sighing** and **pay attention** to his **cry** (5:1-2). Though David was king over Israel, he recognizes that he depends on God, the true sovereign **King** over all (5:2). David makes his plea early **in the morning**; he does not delay. The more dangerous, difficult, and desperate the circumstances, the more urgent it is to begin each day seeking God's intervention and watching **expectantly** for him to answer (5:3).

5:4-6 David focuses on God's holiness. He is completely separate from **wickedness** and **evil** (5:4). He is opposed to sin, regardless of the form it takes. Therefore, he opposes **all evildoers** (5:5). We can have confidence that his judgment will fall on **violent and treacherous people** (5:6). David extols God's separateness from evil and his hatred of sin because he wants to appeal to God's righteousness to act on his behalf.

5:7 David praises God for his **faithful love**, his *hesed*—the Hebrew word for God's loyal affection for those underneath his covenant. It was because of this love that David was able to enter the Lord's presence to worship him. David recognizes the unique calling of God on his life and the mission he'd been given. The Lord had promised to give David a royal dynasty, through which the Messiah would come and reign forever (see 2 Sam 7:11-16). God's covenantal loyalty drove David to worship.

5:8-10 David needed guidance to do the right thing, given the **adversaries** he was facing. He recognized that righteousness is found in God alone; therefore, he needed God to **lead** him so that he could operate in sync with what God viewed as right (5:8). In contrast, his foes were unrighteous. He describes their throats as **an open grave**. This means he found their words to be full of deceit with murderous intent. There was **nothing reliable in what** they said (5:9).

He calls on God to **punish them** because their rebellion against him was, ultimately, against God. David also prays that **their own schemes** would be used against them (5:10). Just as God would reverse the actions of Haman against God's people and cause his wicked plot to fall on his own head (see Esth 3–8), David asks that the plots of his enemies would cause their own downfall because they were actually scheming against God.

5:11-12 David was confident that God would act on his behalf and on behalf of his people. He praises God for the blessings and protection he provides for **those who love** him. He urges God's people to **boast about** him and to **shout for joy** as a way of expressing recognition of who God is, what he has done, and what he can be trusted to do (5:11). The one who experiences God's **favor** will be surrounded by God **like a shield** (5:12). There is no safer place to be.

that God **rescue** him before he descends to the grave (**Sheol**), for then it would be too late. In other words, he wants to be able to praise God for his deliverance so that people would see and know that he is a God who hears and delivers. **In death**, there would be no opportunity to do that (6:5).

6:6-7 David confesses his emotional turmoil. His **groaning** was continual, and his **tears** drenched his **bed** (6:6). He was engulfed in sorrow, **eyes . . . swollen from grief**, because of his sins, the actions of his enemies, and the possibility of an untimely death (6:7).

6:8-10 David declares his separation from **all evildoers** (6:8). He was confident that the Lord had **heard** his **weeping** and his **plea for help**; his **prayer** for mercy and deliverance had been accepted (6:8-9). Thus, he looks forward to how God would act on his behalf, **turn back** his **enemies**, and disgrace them for their deeds against God's anointed one (6:10).

⊰ Psalm 6 ≪

6:1 David admits his guilt before God and asked for mercy. To receive mercy is to avoid getting the punishment that you deserve for your sin. In spite of his own, David asks that the Lord not **discipline** him in **wrath**. Like a son appealing to his father, he asks for relief from earned rebuke.

6:2-3 David had sinned, and his spiritual condition had physical and emotional repercussions. His **bones** and soul experienced anguish and **terror** (6:2-3). He asked the Lord **how long** his chastening would continue (6:3). But, notice that in his pain, David does not run *from* God; he runs *to* God. We, too, can go to God for mercy and understanding, even in the context of our sin and failure, because of his loyal love and our covenant relationship with him through Jesus Christ (see 1 John 1:5-9).

6:4-5 David pleads with God on the basis of his covenantal, **faithful love** (6:4). He asks

⊰ Psalm 7 ≪

David **sang** this psalm **to the LORD concerning the words of Cush, a Benjaminite**. The identity of Cush is unclear, but he was likely one of the men of King Saul (who was from the tribe of Benjamin) who hunted David when Saul felt threatened by him.

7:1-2 David prays to God to **rescue** him from his **pursuers** (7:1). **Like a lion** chasing its prey, his enemies (likely King Saul's men) hunted him so that they might pounce and **tear** him **apart** (7:2).

7:3-5 David was willing to be chastised if he had done anything wrong. **If there [was] injustice on [his] hands**, he was willing for his **enemy** to **overtake** him and **trample** him (7:3, 5). This means David wants God to uphold his righteous standards—even if it meant that David himself was punished. In this way, David affirms his integrity. He was confident that he had acted uprightly. It was his enemies who were guilty.

7:6-8 David implores God to **rise up** like the righteous Judge he is, **take [his] seat** on the tribunal, and make things right (7:6-7). He wants God to **vindicate** him and judge him **according to** his **integrity** (7:8).

7:9-11 David affirms that God not only judges human actions but also **examines the thoughts and emotions** (7:9). Nothing escapes the omniscient (all-knowing) and omnipresent (everywhere-present) God. The evil of the wicked does not go unnoticed. He is aware of their deeds, and he **shows his wrath every day** (7:11).

Not all judgment, then, is reserved for the future. On a daily basis, God carries out judgment on the wicked though they don't expect it. Moreover, as Paul tells us, we must "leave room for God's wrath" (Rom 12:19). We are not to take vengeance into our own hands because God is our vindicator, our **shield** (7:10).

7:12-16 God is ready, like a warrior with **sword . . . bow**, and **arrows** to execute judgment on **anyone** who **does not repent** (7:12-13). He routinely causes the wicked schemes of man to result in their own downfall. For instance, the sinner who digs **a pit** for someone else falls into it himself; the evil one who concocts **violence** finds that it comes crashing **on his own head** (7:15-16). Therefore, we must pursue righteousness, or repent when we have failed, so that God can operate on our behalf and we can avoid such ends.

7:17 David thanks the Lord, knowing that he would do what is right, because of **his righteousness**. And, he sings **about the name**—that is, about the character and glory—**of the LORD Most High**. How can we not give voice to God's praise?

⮞ Psalm 8 ⮜

8:1-2 In the Bible, the name reflects the character and reputation of the person. Thus, to praise God's name is to praise God. David considers the Lord's **name** as the most **magnificent** in all **the earth**. It's full of splendor because he has **covered the heavens** with his **majesty** (8:1). Infants and nursing **babies**—that is, those who are humble and dependent (8:2; see Matt 11:25; 18:1-4; 19:14)—are able to experience God's name as **a stronghold** of protection from an **enemy** (8:2).

8:3-4 When David considers the billions of **stars** and galaxies, he stands in awe. This glorious masterpiece is nothing more than **the work of** God's **fingers**, a divine painting **set in place** to be admired (8:3). Yet, the immensity of it causes David to realize just how small he and the rest of humanity are: **what is a human being that you remember him, a son of man that you look after him?** (8:4). Modern man tends to be full of himself because God is so small in his eyes. But, when we see God as he truly is (massive!), we understand how truly miniscule we are.

8:5-8 Though man is small in light of who God is, nevertheless, the Creator made him only a **little less than God and crowned him with glory and honor** (8:5). This means that though you are reduced in size in comparison to God, you are increased in significance in relationship to him.

After Satan rebelled, God created Adam and Eve to have dominion over the earth. He made man **ruler over the works of [his] hands** and **put everything under his feet** (8:6) with the idea that humans would rule on God's behalf. Through us he intended to establish a kingdom that would defeat Satan's kingdom. And, though Adam and Eve and the rest of us fell into sin, God's kingdom program outlined here was fulfilled in Jesus Christ, the God-Man (see Heb 2:6-9). Jesus defeated Satan and provided redemption for humanity through his atoning death on the cross (see Heb 2:14-17). Ultimately, Christ will reign in his millennial kingdom, subjecting all creation to the kingdom of God (see 1 Cor 15:24-28) and vanquishing Satan once and for all (see Rev 20:1-3, 7-10). Until then, Christ's followers are called to exercise authority on earth in his name and model his kingdom rule in obedience to his kingdom agenda (see Matt 28:19-20).

8:9 David concludes as he began. In light of who God is and the kingdom he is establishing, his **name** is to be praised as **magnificent . . . throughout the earth**.

❧ Psalm 9 ❦

9:1-6 David thanks God **with all [his] heart** for all of his **wondrous works**. Regardless of his own power and fame, David chooses to **boast** in God alone (9:1-2). The reason for his praise was that the Lord had vindicated him and **destroyed** his **enemies** (9:3-5). This demonstrated both God's righteousness in judgment (9:4) and his unrivaled power (9:5-6).

9:7-10 The LORD **sits enthroned forever** (9:7). He is the true, eternal King who rules over all. As a result, **he executes judgment on the nations**, acting **with fairness** on behalf of the oppressed and the afflicted (9:8-9). He is the champion of those who are **persecuted**, providing a secure **refuge** for **those who seek** him (9:9-10).

9:11-12 David exhorts those who are **oppressed** to praise the Lord and **proclaim his deeds** on their behalf, for God **remembers** his people. Therefore, his people should remember to glorify him for his deliverance.

9:13-14 He asks God to **consider** his enemies and to protect him from their murderous intentions (9:13). What is his motivation? **So that I may declare all your praises.** David wants to give verbal witness to God's **salvation** so that all Jerusalem would hear and join him in worship (9:14).

9:15-18 David anticipates God's destruction of the **wicked** (9:16). He will cause their malice to return on them like a boomerang. They'll fall **into the pit they made** for others; they'll be snared **in the net they have concealed** for the innocent (9:15). The Lord will simultaneously judge **the wicked** and deliver **the oppressed** (9:17-18); that's a great promise!

9:19-20 Rise up, LORD! (9:19). David calls on God to strike fear in the hearts of the nations (9:19). Whatever power they thought they possessed, they needed a reminder of their own mortality. Therefore, he prays that God would remind them that **they are only humans** subject to the God who created them (9:20).

❧ Psalm 10 ❦

10:1-11 LORD, **why do you stand so far away?** and **Why do you hide in times of trouble?** are questions that struggling believers have asked through the ages (10:1). Indeed, it does sometimes seem that **the wicked** are allowed to prosper and get away with cursing **the LORD** (10:2-3). All this seems to do is to convince evildoers that **there's no God** and, therefore, **no accountability** (10:4). Thus, they are encouraged to continue in their wickedness, believing there will be no **judgments** rendered. He is **secure** in **his ways** (10:5). The evil man just continues to live as he pleases and to afflict **the innocent** (10:6-10). He reasons that God—if there is one—**hides his face and will never see** (10:11).

10:12-15 The psalmist urges God to act against wickedness: **Rise up!** (10:12). He wants God to uphold his glory and name by addressing the rampant wickedness around him. He knows that God is aware of the condition of **the oppressed ... the helpless**, and **the fatherless** (10:12, 14). He longs for the divine Judge to **break the arm of the wicked, evil person** (10:15). The question is: *When* would God take action?

10:16-18 The psalmist concludes with triumphant praise for the Lord, **the King**. He looks by faith to the future, knowing that God alone will reign forever, while **the nations will perish** (10:16). Ultimately, **the oppressed**, the orphan, will be delivered from those who don't follow God (10:17-18). He will eliminate those who cause terror (10:18).

Because we know God's character and his past actions, we can have confidence that he will bring justice at the right time. This should encourage us to pray in faith. Even when we see nothing happening, we can be certain that God doesn't miss a thing and has set the timer for when he will intervene.

ᴥ *Psalm 11* ᴥ

11:1-3 David confesses his confidence in God, who is his **refuge**, his ultimate place of safety. David rebukes the advice of the faint-hearted and the weak who suggest he should run from danger **like a bird** fleeing **to the mountains** to hide (11:1). Indeed, **the wicked** have their **bows** bent and **arrows** pointed, ready to bring down **the upright in heart** (11:2). **When the foundations are destroyed, what can the righteous do?** The people were afraid that due to the proliferation of evil and lawlessness in society, the nation—its social order and institutions—might crumble (11:3). David viewed what was happening from an eternal, heavenly perspective and thus challenged the righteous not to be passive in the midst of a decaying culture; rather, they were to be influential and impactful as salt and light. This is a principle that we, too, should apply (see Matt 5:13-16).

11:4-6 **[God's] eyes watch; his gaze examines everyone** (11:4). David's eternal perspective is revealed. He knows that God is sovereign, ruling from heaven over the affairs of men. He sees the deeds done on earth, **hates the wicked**, and will punish them with **burning coals and sulfur** (11:5-6). A scorching judgment *will* fall on evildoers—in God's appointed time.

11:7 In contrast to the fate of the wicked, **the upright will see** God's **face**. Because he **is righteous**, the Lord **loves** those who perform **righteous deeds**. Those who follow him will ultimately experience his presence and enjoy his blessings.

ᴥ *Psalm 12* ᴥ

12:1-4 David expresses sorrow that the righteous appear to be extinct: **The loyal have disappeared from the human race** (12:1). Instead, they had been replaced by liars (12:2-4). The absence of the righteous had created a void that had been filled by corruption.

Hypocrisy ruled the day. Thus, David appeals to God to address the problem: to **cut off all flattering lips** (12:3).

12:5 God vows to act—to help **the needy** and **the poor**. Final deliverance and justice will take place in his kingdom; nevertheless, there are moments in history when he brings his sovereignty to bear and rights wrongs committed on earth.

12:6-8 David confesses confidence in the perfection of God's words. **Like silver** that has been **refined** in the fire, so **the words** of the living God are **pure** (12:6). He is faithful to keep his promises and to preserve those he loves from those who bring harm by deceptive words (12:7). God's Word will overrule the deeds of the wicked. Though humanity often exalts the **worthless** (12:8), the Lord will prevail.

ᴥ *Psalm 13* ᴥ

13:1-2 David feels forsaken by God and wrestles with thoughts of abandonment. Four times in the first two verses he asks, **How long**. He longed for God to intervene. It appeared that God was allowing David's **enemy** to **dominate** him (13:2). This is a common human experience. When we encounter trying circumstances during an extended period, we can feel abandoned by God and assume that evil is winning.

13:3-4 David calls on God to **answer** and deliver him (13:3). As powerful as David was, as mighty as his army, he realizes that defeat is certain without God's intervention. Do you see things similarly? Do you recognize that your spiritual defeat is certain without the aid of God's strengthening hand?

13:5-6 David has confidence in the Lord's **faithful love**—his commitment to his covenant, to his people, and to his king. Regardless of the actions of his enemy, then, David is determined to **rejoice** over the **deliverance** that he knew God would provide (13:5). Likewise, we should live with expectation in the goodness of God as we wait for him to move in our own situations. He has **treated** us **generously** in the past. Let us **sing** and put our hope in him (13:6).

joy universally and comprehensively. In the meantime, God's people are to model his rule in a sinful world.

✥ Psalm 14 ✥

14:1-3 The fool says in his heart, "There is no God." The "fool" in view here is a person who lives life without regard for God. Either he disbelieves in the existence of God or is convinced that he is not accountable to God for his actions. Day after day, the idea of divine justice is far from his mind. Therefore, his lifestyle is **corrupt** (14:1). There were so many such people around in his day that David pictures God looking **down from heaven on the human race** and finding no one who sought God or lived in wisdom (14:2). **There is no one who does good, not even one** (14:3). Indeed, the entire human race has been corrupted by sin.

These first three verses are quoted by Paul in Romans 3:10-12 when he makes his case for the sinfulness of humanity. Elsewhere he says, "All have sinned and fall short of the glory of God"; therefore, our only hope is the grace of God and "the redemption that is in Christ Jesus" (Rom 3:23-24).

14:4-6 Will evildoers never understand? (14:4). David is amazed that the wicked think they can devour God's people and not experience consequences. They are unaware that God will overwhelm them. They don't realize that **God is with those who are righteous** (14:5), and to attack God's people is to attack him. Though, for a time, **sinners frustrate the plans of the oppressed**, they will not prevail. For the righteous take **refuge** in God (14:6). He will vindicate them. So, take heart, you who follow the Lord. He keeps track of injustices, and he will bring about your deliverance at the right time.

14:7 David longs for the day of **Israel's deliverance**, the day when God would restore **the fortunes of his people**. Ultimately, this will take place when Jesus Christ rules from David's throne in his millennial kingdom. On that day, God will establish justice and

✥ Psalm 15 ✥

15:1-5 David raises very relevant questions: **LORD, who can dwell in your tent? Who can live on your holy mountain?** What are the qualifications for the worship of the true God in his dwelling place? The answer is the one who is aligned with God—**the one who lives blamelessly, practices righteousness, and acknowledges the truth** (15:1-2). One cannot merely profess to love God, but also must actually walk before him in integrity (15:2-3). In other words, to have access to God, one's life must reflect devotion to the two great commandments: love for God and love for people (see Mark 12:28-31).

The righteous one cares for **his neighbor** and **despises** those who do evil (15:3-4). He **honors those who fear** God—those who take God seriously. He **keeps his word whatever the cost** (15:4). No matter what personal harm may come to him, he holds true to his commitments. He does not seek to prosper by ripping off others, nor can he be bribed. Such a person **will never be shaken** (15:5). Because he aligns himself with God, he will have a stable life because God will oversee it.

✥ Psalm 16 ✥

16:1-2 In this passage, David uses three different Hebrew names for God (*Elohim*, *Yahweh*, and *Adonai*) to appeal to God's sovereignty for protection, because he took **refuge in** him (16:1).

I have nothing good besides you (16:2). Can you make this same declaration? Is God your ultimate joy and treasure? Believers need to understand that we only have one *source*: God. Everything else is a *resource*. David understood this, especially during difficult times.

16:3-4 David's delight in God (16:2) expands to **delight** in what God cares about—his

holy people (16:3). Those who are important to God were important to David. **Those who take another god for themselves** experience nothing but **sorrows** (16:4). Not only does idolatry rob God of his glory, but it also brings inevitable grief to those who practice it. An idol is any person, place, thing, or thought that you look to as your source instead of God.

16:5-6 The Levites were the only Israelite tribe that received no portion in the promised land. Instead, because they received the privilege of serving God in the tabernacle / temple, the Lord himself was to be their inheritance (see Num 18:20; Josh 18:7). Likewise, in spite of all that he had received from God, David sees the Lord himself as his **portion** (16:5). Thus, his **boundary lines** had **fallen** in **pleasant places**. In other words, he had great joy in knowing that God—not his possessions—was his true **inheritance** (16:6). Whatever material blessings the Lord grants are not your inheritance either. They are merely bonuses.

16:7-8 David is grateful to take refuge in God's presence. The Lord **counsels**, instructs, and guides him because David was near him (16:7-8). Similarly, Christians are called to remain in Christ (see John 15:1-8). By doing so, we experience stability in an uncertain life and bear fruit. The greater life's challenges, in fact, the more believers should strive to remain in God's presence.

16:9-10 David is confident that the Lord would not **abandon** him **to Sheol** (the grave) or let him **decay** (16:10). If this was the case for King David, how much more is it true of the great Son of David, Jesus Christ? Both Peter and Paul applied this passage to the Messiah, whom God raised from the dead (see Acts 2:24-28; 13:35).

16:11 In your presence is abundant joy; at your right hand are eternal pleasures. Both in history and in eternity, there is unfathomable joy in God's presence. No challenge can overshadow this truth. Thus, believers must make living in God's presence and anticipating an eternal future with him a way of life.

⟿ Psalm 17 ⟾

17:1-5 David petitions God to hear and respond to his prayer for **vindication**, for his **lips** were **free of deceit** (17:1-2). In other words, he had no unaddressed sin in his life that would block God's answers to prayer. David had submitted to divine discipline. God had **tested** and **examined** him (17:3). Therefore, David is confident that no remnant of sin could hinder God from answering his prayer. This man knew his **steps** followed God's **paths** (17:5).

17:6-12 David longs for God to reveal his **faithful love** to him and show himself to be the true **Savior of all who seek refuge** in him (17:6-7). The Lord's protection of his people is described in beautiful imagery: **Protect me as the pupil of your eye; hide me in the shadow of your wings** (17:8). As one is zealous to shield his own eye from danger, so God shelters his servants. As a mother bird lovingly protects her chicks, so the Lord overshadows his own. David's violent enemies surrounded him (17:9-12), so he wisely sought God's covering.

17:13-15 Though the wicked continued to reap benefits in the world (17:14), David is confident in God. Though the judgment on evildoers might be delayed, it would come. In the meantime, David chooses to find his ultimate satisfaction in the **presence** of his God (17:15).

⟿ Psalm 18 ⟾

David wrote Psalm 18 to express his gratitude to God for delivering him **from the grasp of all his enemies**, including King **Saul**. This psalm is also found in 2 Samuel 22.

18:1-3 As the king of Israel, divinely installed on the throne, David had a legal relationship with God. But, the relationship was also one of love: **I love you, LORD, my strength** (18:1). And because the love was reciprocated, David is confident in God as his source of deliverance and **salvation** (18:2).

18:4-6 David describes his situation as equivalent to that of an animal in a trap, **entangled in the snares of death** (18:5). Apart from divine intervention, he is doomed. So, he **called** to the Lord **for help**. And God **heard** (18:6). Sometimes, we can be wrapped up by our negative circumstances and surrounded by hopelessness, but this state simply gives God the unique opportunity to demonstrate that he alone is God—the only solution to our problems. We need only to ask for his aid.

18:7-15 These verses provide a poetic description of God's response to David's plea. The imagery is vivid and powerful: **the earth shook . . . Smoke rose from [God's] nostrils . . . The LORD thundered from heaven . . . he hurled lightning bolts**. As a result of David's cry for divine assistance, the Lord responded via creation. It was as if nature itself erupted on his behalf to bring salvation.

18:16-19 Because David and God shared an intimate relationship, God **delighted in** him and orchestrated a massive intervention to deliver David from his **powerful enemy** (18:17-19). Too many believers don't experience close fellowship with God. As a result of the distance, they don't get to see God work on their behalf in a dramatic way.

18:20-24 God rewarded David **according to [his] righteousness** (18:20, 24). Our faithfulness and obedience to God brings reward, including victory over our circumstances. Never underestimate the blessings that result from living **blameless toward** God (18:23).

18:25-29 God is **faithful . . . blameless**, and **pure** with those who deal the same way with him (18:25-26). He rewards obedience. Conversely, he is **shrewd** and humbles those who are **crooked** and **haughty** (18:26-27). He is just. David knew that with God on his side, he could defeat an enemy and advance against any opposition (18:29). Such should be our mindset, as well.

18:30-45 David rejoices in God's character. He is **perfect** in all his ways. Therefore, his people can trust him to be their **shield** and defender (18:30). David then explains how God equipped, enabled, and strengthened him to battle and be victorious over his enemies (18:32-45). David cried for help; the Lord heard and saved. Though David's enemies **cry for help . . . there is no one to save them** (18:41).

18:46-50 David praises God for delivering him from his enemies—proof that he was the living God and not a lifeless idol. As his **rock** (18:46), God was David's source of security and safety. Remembering his covenant with David to give him a royal dynasty (see 2 Sam 7:11-16), God showed **loyalty to his anointed** king and to **his descendants** (18:50); this blessing would even affect the Gentiles.

❧ Psalm 19 ❧

19:1 The heavens declare the glory of God, and the expanse proclaims the work of his hands. Divine revelation takes two forms: general revelation and special revelation. *Special* revelation consists of the written and living Word of God. In it, God reveals in detail who he is, what he has done, and what he requires of us. Only through the special revelation of Scripture can we know the gospel of Jesus Christ.

General revelation, on the other hand, consists of that which all people everywhere can know about God, even if they have no access to Scripture. For instance, our moral conscience lets us know that we are accountable to our Creator (see Rom 2:14-16). Similarly, creation itself testifies to the existence of the one who made all things for his own glory (see Rom 1:19-21). The heavens "declare" God's glory by confirming that an omnipotent deity exists and has made things that are marvelous in scale and complexity.

19:2-6 God's works of creation **pour out speech** every day (19:2). **Their message** goes out to **the ends of the world** (19:4). As David says in Psalm 14:1, only the fool says in his heart, "There's no God." His existence is inextricably clear from the world he has made. **The sun** serves as a supreme example (19:4) of this truth as **it rises from one end of the heavens and circles to their other end**. This masterpiece dominates the skies for all to see. **Nothing is hidden from its heat** (19:6). Without the sun, in fact, we would cease to exist; thus, it cannot be hanging in the heavens by chance. The Creator is greater than his creation. Atheistic evolution, then, is the worldview of a fool. Every watch demands a watchmaker.

19:7-10 After opening with the idea of general revelation, David moves to the topic of special revelation: the Word of God as recorded in Scripture. He makes declarations about the sufficiency of Scripture to address every aspect of life.

First, **the instruction of the Lord is perfect, renewing one's life.** *Perfect* means "whole" or "complete." In other words, Scripture lacks nothing. Everything you need to know to be what God expects you to be has been revealed in his Word. It can renew you and provide you with abundant life. Second, **the testimony of the Lord is trustworthy, making the inexperienced wise** (19:7). The Bible is reliable. You can bank on it. Those without experience, the simple and foolish, can be trained how to be discerning and can be enabled to make good and wise choices that reflect a divine perspective from reading and trusting it.

Third, **the precepts of the Lord are right, making the heart glad.** The divine principles of the Bible lead a person down the right path. They point out the road we ought to take and promise us blessing for taking it. Fourth, **the command of the Lord is radiant, making the eyes light up** (19:8). In other words, the commandments of God are eye-opening. They illuminate dark situations so that we know how to proceed.

Fifth, **the fear of the Lord is pure, enduring forever.** God reveals himself without contamination or flaw. His Word is unchanging and always relevant. Sixth, **the ordinances of the Lord are reliable and altogether righteous** (19:9). "Ordinances" are judgments or verdicts delivered from a judge's bench. We can be assured that anything that comes from the supreme Judge of the earth is righteous and true.

Seventh, **they are more desirable than gold.** The Bible is more precious than your paycheck. It's more valuable than anything

the world has to offer because it can provide what the world doesn't have. It's **sweeter than honey** (19:10). You don't comprehend the sweetness of God's Word by merely reading it, however. You must *experience* it: "Taste and see that the Lord is good" (34:8).

19:11-14 The words of Scripture warn us of danger and promise us **reward** for **keeping them** (19:11). So, whether our problem is **hidden faults** (those no one but God sees) or **willful sins** (wrongs that we actually plan to do), the Bible can tell us how to be cleansed (19:12-13). The Word of God is sufficient for helping us to make both our external **words** and our internal **meditation . . . acceptable** before God (19:14).

❧ *Psalm 20* ❧

20:1-3 This psalm is the testimony of David and the congregation of Israel on the eve of battle. King and people are gathered in **the sanctuary** in **Zion**, where God manifested his presence, to invoke his **help** against their enemies (20:2). **In a day of trouble**, they petition the Lord to **answer** with victory (20:1) and pray that the **offerings** for the atonement of sin would be acceptable (20:3).

20:4-5 The worshipers ask that God would grant the king's **desires** and **fulfill** his battle plans (20:4). They joyfully anticipate **victory** as the king raises **the banner in the name of [their] God** (20:5). David's victory would be seen as God's victory.

20:6 David expresses assurance that God has answered their request and would grant **victory to his anointed.** The Lord would act with **his right hand**—that is, by demonstrating his great power and strength.

20:7-8 David's confidence was not like the confidence of the Gentile kings **who take pride in chariots** and **horses.** They trusted in their military might and boasted in their armaments. But, the boast of David and his people was this: **We take pride in the name of the Lord our God** (20:7). Regardless of the size of the respective armies of Israel and their enemies, David knew that victory comes ultimately from God. Therefore, he trusted in the Lord's character, reputation, and sovereignty—and expected a great **collapse and fall** of his enemy (20:8). We should follow David's example. As we face the conflicts of life, we can be certain that our God is big enough to deal with them. The greater our focus *on* God, the greater our confidence *in* God.

20:9 The worshipers respond to David's confidence with a petition that God would **give victory to the king**. This is true not only for David, but also for the Son of David, the ultimate King. God's people long for the Messiah to have victory over enemies—both his and ours. So, we follow him by faith, having confidence that he will reign in our circumstances and defeat all opposition.

❧ *Psalm 21* ❧

21:1-6 David affirms God as the source of his **strength** and the foundation of his joy. He praises God for giving him **his heart's desire**, including **victory** over his enemies (21:1-2). The Lord had given him abundant **blessings**, including the preservation of his **life** and the **majesty** that went along with being king, as well as the **joy** of God's **presence** (21:3-6).

21:7 What was the key to David's state of blessing? **The faithful love** (Hebrew: *hesed*), or covenant faithfulness, **of the Most High**. David's stability could not be **shaken**. Because of the intimacy of their relationship, God had the freedom to act on the king's behalf.

21:8-10 Because David's enemies were also God's **enemies**, God's **wrath** would **devour them** and end their hopes of having any **offspring**. When we are closely united to God in a family relationship, our enemies are his.

21:11-13 Regardless of what David's enemies had plotted against him, God would turn their plans against them (21:11-12). The **strength** and power of God are to be forever **exalted** and praised (2:13).

❧ *Psalm 22* ❧

This psalm of David consists of two halves. The first half is a lament (22:1-21a), while the second half shifts to thanksgiving (22:21b-31).

22:1 David cries out because he was experiencing a sense of hopelessness and abandonment. It was this deep sense of being divinely **abandoned** that Jesus would experience and express on the cross (see Matt 27:46). Though these words were true of King David, they were fulfilled truly and fully in the Messiah, David's Son.

22:2-5 Though David was living in a state of despair (22:2), nevertheless he continues to affirm God's **holy** character to declare him worthy of Israel's **praises** (22:3). He rehearses the confidence of previous generations who **trusted** in God and experienced his deliverance (22:4-5). This history lesson serves as a reminder to David—and to us—to continue to trust the Lord in spite of circumstances.

22:6-8 David was enduring constant scorn and ridicule, being **despised** and mocked by others (22:6-7). Those who hated him said, **He relies on the Lord; let him save him; let the Lord rescue him, since he takes pleasure in him** (22:8). These would be the very words used to taunt Jesus as he hung on the cross (see Matt 27:43).

22:9-10 David recalls his history of dependence on the Lord. Even when he was an infant in his mother's **womb** and a newborn, he was completely reliant on God. Thus, he knew he was still dependent on God even as a grown man and king of Israel. Remember to rehearse your history of trusting in God's protection and provision. It will help you trust in him for today and tomorrow.

22:11-18 David's enemies were like beasts— **bulls . . . lions**, and **dogs**—that encircled him and sought to devour him (22:12-13, 16). He was exhausted. His **strength** was gone (22:14-15). The piercing of his **hands** and **feet** and the casting of **lots** for his **clothing** are not elaborated on in Scripture but proved prophetic in that they were fulfilled in Jesus's suffering (22:16, 18; see Matt 27:35; Isa 53:5; Zech 12:10).

22:19-21a David pleads with God to be near and to **rescue** him from those who wish him harm (22:19-20), again comparing his enemies to beasts: **dogs**, lions, and **wild oxen** (22:20-21a). David knows that only the Lord was capable of saving him.

22:21b-26 You answered me! (22:21b). In the midst of his despair and petitions, David knows that God has heard his prayers. Therefore, he celebrates. He proclaims the Lord's name and urges God's people to **praise** . . . **honor**, and **revere him** (22:22-23). Those who have experienced the goodness of God can't help but worship him and exhort others to do the same. David uses his situation to be an encouragement to others. He wants to live in obedience before God's people and urge them to find satisfaction in him (22:25-26).

22:27-31 David anticipates the time when **all the ends of the earth** will **turn to the LORD** (22:27). Though he was chosen by God to serve as king, he recognizes that, ultimately, **kingship belongs to the LORD**. All **the nations** will one day submit to the kingdom of God when the Messiah comes to reign (22:28-29). Then, **a people yet to be born** will hear all peoples **declare his righteousness** (22:31).

⤳ Psalm 23 ⤶

23:1 The LORD is my shepherd. David was familiar with tending sheep. After all, he used to do the job (see 1 Sam 16:11-12; 17:15, 34-37). He knew firsthand what it was for a shepherd to protect and provide for sheep, so he describes his relationship to God in those terms. What David had been for his sheep, God had been to him. Notice that the Lord wasn't a mere generic shepherd to David; he was David's personal shepherd. He calls him "my shepherd." As a result, David confidently confesses, **I have what I need.** Because God had covered all of David's needs, he recognized that he lacked nothing.

Some Christians have trusted God to save them for eternity, but they don't have much confidence that he can provide for them in history. David's beautiful, poetic testimony can help instill in us the confidence that he can. Having declared the Lord to be his shepherd, David proceeds in the remainder of the psalm to explain how God met all his needs.

23:2-3 God met David's *spiritual* needs. Just as a shepherd gives sheep rest in **green pastures** and refreshes them with **quiet waters** (23:2), so God had done spiritually to David. The cares and struggles of this world can leave us exhausted. Such times are opportunities to learn our dependence on the Lord. He provides spiritual refreshment and restoration. He **renews** our life (23:3).

God met David's *directional* needs. **He leads me along the right paths** (23:3). Sheep are prone to wander and become lost; they need guidance. Many cars today have navigational systems. If you deviate from the best route to reach your destination, the system will warn you to return to the right road. Through his Word and his Spirit, God leads us along the right paths in life—and reroutes us when we foolishly become wayward. Why? **For his name's sake** (23:3)—that is, so that others can hear us say, "My God has brought me here."

23:4 God met David's *emotional* needs. Regardless of the **danger** surrounding them, sheep can follow their shepherd without **fear**. He provides **comfort** with his **rod** (used to beat wild animals that attack the sheep) and his **staff** (used to guide the sheep and pull them back from harm). When life takes you **through the darkest valley**, receive consolation knowing that your divine shepherd has power in one hand and grace in the other.

23:5 God met David's *physical* needs. Though **enemies** hovered near, God fed him when he hungered and anointed him **with oil** when he needed healing. Like David, we must recognize that we have one source. There are many *resources*—many channels God may use to provide and care for your physical well being—but you have only one *source*. And God never runs dry. That's why David's **cup** overflowed.

23:6 God met David's *eternal* needs. **Only goodness and faithful love will pursue me all the days of my life.** Shepherds often have sheep dogs that keep the sheep from wandering. The divine shepherd has two sheepdogs named "goodness" and "faithful love." Sometimes, they bark and nip at you when you wander from the fold. But, they do so with the intent of driving you back into fellowship with your shepherd, so that you may eternally **dwell in the house of the Lord**.

Submit to "the great Shepherd of the sheep" (Heb 13:20), our Lord Jesus Christ. He lays down his life for his sheep (see John 10:11), and through his wounds, we are healed (see 1 Pet 2:24). If you have gone astray, return to him (1 Pet 2:25), because he knows his sheep, and they know him (see John 10:14). He will welcome you.

✥ Psalm 24 ✥

24:1-2 David affirms the worldwide scope of God's dominion. **The earth and everything in it ... belong to the Lord** (24:1). The reason God can claim sovereignty over all things is because he is the Creator of all. **He laid** the earth's **foundations** (24:2). Everything exists because God spoke it into existence (see Heb 11:3).

24:3-6 David gives the requirements for the one who wants to be accepted in God's presence (24:3). He or she must have **clean hands and a pure heart** (24:4)—that is, a life that is clean inside and out. This is the one who **will receive blessing** and **righteousness** (24:5). Like **Jacob**, he will wrestle with God (see Gen 32:24-30), but get to see his **face** (24:6).

24:7-10 King David calls for the **gates** of the holy city of Jerusalem to be opened for the triumphal procession of **the King of glory**, the Lord Almighty (24:7). The historical context of this psalm may have been David's return from battle with the ark of the covenant, which was considered the Lord's throne (see Exod 25:22; 1 Sam 4:4; Isa 37:16). Above it was the divine **King**—the **Lord of Armies**—who was **mighty in battle** (24:8, 10) and gave victory to Israel. The Messiah, too, will one day defeat his enemies in the tribulation and establish his millennial kingdom.

Praise is the appropriate response to our great God. He alone can claim victory. We should not enter into his presence for worship in a careless or casual manner. He is the King of glory! If we fail to honor and worship him for who he truly is, it is to our detriment.

✥ Psalm 25 ✥

25:1-3 In this psalm, King David expresses a deep longing for God's intervention in his circumstances. Notice the repetition: He does not want to be **disgraced** before his **enemies** (25:2). He knows that those who wait on God will not be **disgraced**. Instead, treacherous people will (25:3). David is confident that his **trust** in God is justified (25:2). He would experience a reversal. That which he feared would actually fall on his enemies.

25:4-7 David requests divine guidance so that he might walk in God's **ways** (25:4). He trusts in the Lord as the one who delivers (25:5) and calls on him to **remember** his **faithful love** (25:6)—his covenant love—instead of remembering his **sins** (25:7). David appeals to God based on the loyal, loving relationship they shared. The greater his intimacy with God, the greater his dependency on God. The greater his dependency on God, the greater the expectation for intervention and deliverance. This is why our covenant relationship with Christ is so critical. David knows that past sins could interfere with God answering his requests, so he confesses them to position himself for divine favor.

25:8-11 Because of God's character (the fact that he is **good and upright**), **sinners** can learn from him the right **way** to live (25:8). They ought to **humble** themselves and receive his instruction (25:9), rather than proudly assuming they can make it their own way. The Lord's ways are always good and true, and they are experienced by those who come under the cover of **his covenant** (25:10). Again, David asks God to **forgive** his **iniquity** (25:11), which could block the flow of covenant blessings.

25:12-15 Who is the person who fears the LORD? (25:12). To fear God is to take him seriously. This disposition toward God is reflected by our obedience to him. Such a person will **live a good life**, which includes blessings that lead to internal and external prospering (25:13). God rewards **those who fear** him with his inside information—**secret counsel** that is particular to the person and his individual experience of God's **covenant** (25:14). Therefore, David kept his **eyes** focused on the Lord, confident that he would **pull** his **feet out of the net**—that is, deliver him from his enemies (25:15).

25:16-22 Again, David pleads with God to be **gracious** in the midst of the **affliction** brought on by his **enemies** (25:16-19). He petitions the Lord to **guard** him, and he waits on him to act (25:20-21). Yet, the king doesn't want God to rescue him alone but the whole congregation of **Israel** (25:22). This is a reminder that as we pray for ourselves, we ought to look to the needs of fellow believers. Let us ask God to work through our requests so that he might benefit others, as well.

⋙ Psalm 26 ⋘

26:1-2 David calls on the Lord to **vindicate** and exonerate him from false accusations because he has **lived with integrity** (26:1). He invites divine scrutiny of his **heart and mind** (26:2). Only God has access to our inner lives—to our thoughts and motivations. So, to request such an internal examination, David was clearly confident of his uprightness.

26:3-5 He validates his integrity by pointing to his life, his actions. Not only does he **live by** the **truth** of God (26:3), he also avoids association with **the worthless ... hypocrites ... evildoers**, and **the wicked** (26:4-5; see 1:1).

26:6-8 David seeks to address any sin in his life. To **wash** his **hands** is to metaphorically cleanse his life of evil deeds. He also offers the appropriate sacrifices at the **altar** to atone for sin (26:6). This enables him to attend public worship, where God's **glory** was manifested, so that he could give thanks and proclaim God's **wondrous works** (26:7-8). We are called to do the same: confess our sins to God, celebrate the atoning sacrifice of Christ through Communion, and join together corporately with God's people to worship God for who he is, what he has done, and what we are trusting him to do.

26:9-12 The king concludes with his desire to separate himself from evildoers (26:9-10), **live with integrity** (26:11), and **bless the LORD in the assemblies** of God's people (26:12). These are key steps for us to take, too. Do not come under the influence of those who despise God; instead, walk in God's ways with an upright heart, and stay in fellowship with God's covenant people to keep you steady in difficult times.

⋙ Psalm 27 ⋘

27:1-3 David affirms the Lord as the source of his confidence. As his **light** (27:1), God illuminates the darkness that surrounds David. As his **salvation** (27:1), God delivers him physically and spiritually in spite of the adversity he faces (27:2-3).

27:4-6 I have asked one thing from the LORD ... to dwell in the house of the LORD all the days of my life (27:4). David passionately pursues intimate fellowship with God as he worships him in his tabernacle. It was this pursuit of God that bolstered his confidence in him. This great psalmist of Israel knew that, in God's presence, he would experience both divine covering and divine exaltation (27:5-6).

27:7-10 David appeals to God to **be gracious** and hear his **call** (27:7). He wants nothing more than to **seek** the **face** of God (27:8)—that is, to pursue God's presence in order to experience his favor and fellowship. David knows that God is the only one he could truly not do without. If everyone were to abandon him—even his **father and mother** (27:10)—he would not be left void of care. God would fill the gap.

27:11-14 Show me your way (27:11). David wants clear direction and a **level path** so that his enemies would not overpower him (27:11-12). Having received encouragement and comfort from God, David then turns and offers encouragement to others (see 2 Cor 1:3-5): **Wait for the LORD; be strong, and let your heart be courageous** (27:14). "Waiting" on God does not mean being passive; rather, it is an active engagement of life's challenges within the revealed will of God as we hope for his deliverance.

➣ Psalm 28 ☙

28:1-5 David pours out his heart to the Lord in a plea for mercy and **help** (28:1-2). He asks that God not judge him along with **the wicked**, but instead **repay them** as the **evil of their deeds** deserved (28:3-4). People devote themselves to wickedness because they fail to **consider ... the work of [God's] hands** (28:5). They are without excuse and incur his wrath (see Rom 1:18-23).

28:6-8 The king praises God because he **heard** his prayer, served as the source of his **strength** and protection, and enabled him to escape the schemes of the wicked. Praise is the appropriate response to divine intervention in our lives. Whenever God provides some form of deliverance in your circumstances, it ought to prompt fresh praise for his shield of covering amid the evil that surrounds us.

28:9 David concludes with a request for protection of the entire nation. David was the king, the shepherd of God's sheep. Yet, he knew that the Lord is the ultimate shepherd, both for him personally and for Israel. So, he urges God to **shepherd** his **people** and **carry them** through their trials.

➣ Psalm 29 ☙

29:1-2 David calls the **heavenly beings** to praise the Lord by ascribing **glory** to him (29:1-2). Such **worship** is fitting. It is the

adoration **due his name** because of the **splendor of his holiness**, which refers to God's separateness and uniqueness (29:2). He is uncontaminated and in a class by himself. Thus, worship is not merely something created beings do for God; it is something we rightly owe him.

29:3-9 As Psalm 19:1 says, "The heavens declare the glory of God." The creation testifies to the majesty of the Creator. **The voice of the LORD** is the focus of these verses. Clearly, the reference is to a thunderstorm. Such a spectacular display is not the work of so-called Mother Nature, but of Father God. His lightning **flashes flames of fire** and **shatters the cedars of Lebanon** (29:5, 7). Nothing in all of creation is unaffected by such power (29:8-9). Thus, as his people gather to worship him in Jerusalem, they shout, **Glory!** (29:9). We must give the Lord the unique exaltation he deserves.

29:10-11 God has used his creation to judge wickedness, as at **the flood** (29:10; see Gen 7:11-24), and to deliver his people, as at the Red Sea (see Exod 14:15-31). As the Creator of the earth, God is rightly seen as the **King** of the earth, **enthroned** above all he has made (29:10). He exercises final authority. This ought to give his people comfort when we face opposition that's too powerful for us. God has the final word. Regardless of how weak we are, he **gives his people strength**. No matter who curses, he **blesses his people with peace** (29:11)—that is, with completeness and well-being. His overwhelming glory should encourage us and evoke even greater praise.

➣ Psalm 30 ☙

30:1-3 David exalts God for lifting and delivering him from a deep pit—and preventing his **enemies** from celebrating his downfall (30:1). He had apparently suffered from a physical ailment, but God **healed** him and rescued him **from Sheol**, the grave (30:2-3).

30:4-5 He invites the people of God to **sing to the LORD** and **praise** him (30:4). For his **anger**

with his children is temporary. He is eager to reverse course and bring blessing. **Weeping may stay overnight, but there is joy in the morning** (30:5). This should encourage us in repentance. God does not enjoy bringing discipline but prefers to shower us with his grace.

30:6-7 Feeling **secure** and self-assured, David had said of himself, **I will never be shaken** (30:6). In other words, he had become proud and independent from God. This led to divine discipline. God **hid [his] face**, removing his covering and presence (30:7). God hates pride. It was the sin of Satan. Therefore, a prideful heart will always drive him away. "God resists the proud but gives grace to the humble" (1 Pet 5:5).

30:8-10 When experiencing the disciplining divine hand, David humbled himself and **sought favor from** God (30:8). He pleaded with God for forgiveness. After all, if he were to descend to the **Pit** in **death**, he could not **praise** God or **proclaim** his **truth** (30:9). He wanted God's healing and restoration so that he could publicly exalt the God who delivers.

30:11-12 David concludes the psalm, celebrating how God had **removed** the **sackcloth** of his sorrow and replaced it with the clothing of **gladness** (30:11). As a result, David refuses to **be silent** (30:12). How could he be? How can *we* be? When we experience the deliverance of God in whatever form it takes— spiritual, physical, emotional, relational, or financial—let our testimony be the same as David's: **LORD my God, I will praise you forever** (30:12).

❧ *Psalm 31* ❧

31:1-5 David appeals to God for deliverance from oppression. He affirms his complete trust in the Lord because he alone can be described as **a rock of refuge** and **a mountain fortress** (31:2). Such a stronghold would be impregnable to enemy attack. That is what God was to David. There is no safer shelter than living under the Lord's covenant covering, so David is confident that God would

guide him through his troubles (31:3). Like Jesus on the cross, he confessed, **Into your hand I entrust my spirit** (31:3-5; see Luke 23:46).

31:6-8 He expresses his hatred for the worship of **worthless idols** (31:6). Indeed, they are lifeless and powerless. The Lord, on the other hand, was worthy of David's **trust** because of his **faithful love** (31:6-7). Because of God's commitment to his covenant with David, and David's dependence on him, he delivered David from his **enemy** (31:8). Like David, we must reject idolatry in whatever form it takes. God draws near to those who place their confidence in him alone.

31:9-13 David pours out his heart to the Lord regarding his **distress** and **frustration** (31:9). Note the language he uses to describe how he feels and how he has been treated by others: his **life is consumed with grief** and **with groaning**; his **strength has failed** (31:10); he has been **ridiculed** and **forgotten**—not only by enemies but also by friends (31:11-12); he has been hurt by **gossip** (31:13). Let David's transparency before God be an example to you. When you have been wounded by life, take these divinely inspired prayers and make them your own.

31:14-22 In spite of his desperate circumstances, David trusts that God has the **power** to **rescue** him (31:14-15). He knew every aspect of his life was in God's hands, and he anticipated deliverance because of God's character. For those who **fear** God, the **goodness** of God is described as something **stored up** (31:19). He has piled his goodness high and is ready to dispense it to those who take him seriously, honor him, and look to him with expectation. "What no eye has seen, no ear has heard, and no human heart has conceived—God has prepared these things for those who love him" (1 Cor 2:9). **Blessed be the LORD, for he has wondrously shown his faithful love** (31:22).

31:23-24 David exhorts his fellow worshipers—including you and me—to **love** God, **be strong** and **courageous**, and **put** their **hope** in him. God is worthy of this because of who he is and the support he promises to all who look to him. Let this psalm challenge you to know God's character so that you can appeal to that character when you need him most.

❧ Psalm 32 ❧

32:1-2 The apostle Paul writes, "All have sinned and fall short of the glory of God" (Rom 3:23). David knew this to be true—particularly about himself. That's why he could affirm the blessedness of forgiveness from God. What joy to know that God has **forgiven** our **transgression** and **iniquity**.

32:3-5 When David left his sins of adultery and murder unaddressed, it took its toll on him, physically and emotionally. His **bones** ached, his **groaning** filled the air, and his **strength was drained** (32:3-4). His problem was not medical, though, but theological: God's **hand was heavy on [him]** (32:4). Thus, David emphasizes the relationship among unaddressed sin, physical and emotional well-being, and loss of fellowship with God. When he **acknowledged [his] sin**, God granted forgiveness and removed David's **guilt** (32:5).

32:6-7 In light of the mercy David experienced, he calls on all believers to respond the same way regarding their own sin. We should **pray to [God] immediately**. When we are engulfed in **floodwaters** of distress, we need to go to God without delay in confession and repentance (32:6). Those in Noah's day refused to repent, and the flood of judgment took them away. But, Noah responded to God and found himself and his family covered. Likewise, David experienced God as his **hiding place**, a place of protection from **trouble** (32:7).

32:8-11 David uses an illustration to reinforce the foolishness of resisting repentance: **Do not be like a horse or mule ... that must be controlled with bit and bridle** (32:9). Such animals are stubborn; they must be made to do what they don't want to do. Similarly, humans don't naturally confess their sins and repent of them. But, we must see the incentives for doing so: forgiveness from God, intimacy with God, and joy in God. **The**

wicked who refuse to repent will have **many pains**, but **the one who trusts** God will be immersed in his **faithful love** and can **shout for joy** (32:10-11).

So, when you have sinned and the call for repentance comes, don't hold back. Confess your sins specifically, agree with what God says about them, appeal to his grace and mercy for forgiveness, and anticipate the return of the joy of your salvation.

❧ Psalm 33 ❧

33:1-5 Psalm 33 is a call to collective praise of the Creator, a **song** of God's **righteous ones** set to musical accompaniment (33:1-3). God ought to be worshiped musically by his people because he is true and faithful: his **word** is **right** and his **work is trustworthy** (33:4). What does he love? What does he want to see in his people? **Righteousness and justice** (33:5). These two are regularly linked in Scripture. They combine the vertical righteous standing before God and the horizontal just treatment of our neighbors. They are coupled together here because they must not be separate, but rather operate simultaneously.

33:6-11 David expands on the *word* and *work* of God from 33:4. All of creation is a product of his powerful **word** (33:6). **He spoke, and it came into being; he commanded, and it came into existence** (33:9). The Lord merely speaks, and things happen. He simply declares a thing to be, and it is. Such sovereign, creative power should cause everyone everywhere to **fear** and **stand in awe of him** (33:8). By his word, God also controls history. **The counsel** and **plans** of menacing **nations** may strike fear into the hearts of humans (33:10), but they are nothing before God— just a mere "drop in a bucket" (Isa 40:15). **He thwarts** them, but his **counsel** and **plans** are unstoppable (33:10-11).

33:12-19 What a blessing it is to be part of God's elect **people** (33:12)! In his omniscience, he **observes everyone** (33:13). He does not deliver those who are self-sufficient, who rely on their own might or ingenuity (33:16-17). Instead, he rescues those who depend on his **faithful love** in the midst of the most perilous circumstances (33:18-19).

33:20-22 David ends with a reaffirmation of the **trust** and **hope** that he and the people had in the Lord (33:21-22)—which was demonstrated as they waited on him. To **wait for the LORD** (33:20) is not to be idle. It is to refuse to step out of his will to address your situation. By doing this, you can have confidence of experiencing his **faithful love** (33:22).

⇝ Psalm 34 ⇜

The superscription indicates the psalm's historical context. **David** penned it after he had **pretended to be insane in the presence of Abimelech**. This is a reference to the time when David feigned madness to protect himself from being executed by King Achish of Gath (see 1 Sam 21:10-15). "Abimelech," a Hebrew word meaning "my father is king," was apparently a title or another name for Achish.

34:1-3 David vows to **praise** the Lord—not merely when all is well—but **at all times** (34:1), and especially when things are at their worst. Such worship of God will elicit gladness from other believers and encourage them (34:2). David urges these fellow saints to **exalt** God with him (34:3). In other words, he says, "Don't make me praise God by myself. Let's together make him appear as big as he truly is."

34:4-5 Meditating on the perilous situation from which he'd escaped, David reveals that he had **sought** God in the midst of his troubles, and the Lord thus **rescued** him from his **fears** (34:4). We live in a world full of things that incite fear. So, where will we turn when fear strikes? **Those who**, like David, **look to** the Lord will have **joy** (34:5). Faith expressed in prayer is God's antidote for fear (see Phil 4:6-7).

34:6-7 Though David was a mighty warrior, he was at the mercy of King Achish on this particular occasion. He was a mere **poor man** who could only cry to God. And God **saved him** (34:6). Your weakness is not a liability when the Lord is your God. **Those**

who **fear him**—those who give him the honor he deserves—need not fear anything else, because **the angel of the LORD** (that is, the pre-incarnate Christ) will set his battle encampment around them (34:7).

34:8-10 David extends an invitation to **taste and see that the LORD is good**. He invites us to perform a taste test about something he's discovered. *Anything* that is good in your life has its origin in God (see Jas 1:17), so you can trust him to do what only he can do. **Young lions** may hunt for **food** and yet **go hungry**. But, what are we called to do in our need? **Seek the LORD** (34:10). "Seek first the kingdom of God and his righteousness, and all these things will be provided for you" (Matt 6:33). If you align yourself with God, you will be positioned to receive the goodness that he knows you need regardless of the trials that come your way.

34:11-14 What does the **fear of** God look like? (34:11). What is required of someone who wants to experience **what is good**? (34:12). Keep your mouth and actions from **evil** (34:13-14). Instead, **do what is good** and **seek peace** (34:14). The formula is simple. If God is "good" (34:8), and you want "to enjoy what is good" (34:12), then "do what is good" (34:14).

34:15-18 **The righteous**, those who trust the Lord and submit to his kingdom agenda, receive his full attention. His **eyes** see them, **his ears** hear them, he **rescues them from . . . troubles**, and he grants them his presence (34:15, 17-18). As it turns out, **those who do what is evil** also receive God's attention. But, in their case, he sets his **face** against them in order to wipe their **memory . . . from the earth** (34:16). How would you prefer that God take notice of you?

34:19-20 The **righteous** have **many adversities**. In fact, you haven't seen trouble until you've become a Christian because that's when the devil puts his bull's-eye on you. Yet, the Lord has the ability to rescue, no matter the situation. David learned that truth firsthand. That's why he could say, **he protects all his bones; not one of them is broken** (34:32). This promise found ultimate fulfillment when Jesus went to the cross (see John 19:33-36).

34:21-22 David concludes with words that you can bank on: **Those who hate the righteous will be punished** (34:21). Indeed, those who set themselves against God and his people will not escape his retribution. In contrast, those **who take refuge in him will not be punished** (34:22). When you place yourself under God's covering, you're in the safest place in the universe.

⮞ Psalm 35 ⮜

35:1-10 Oppose my opponents . . . fight those who fight me (35:1). David's prayer is an appeal for God's intervention against his enemies who were persecuting him. He wants God to be like a warrior, using his **shields** and **spear** to protect him (35:2-3). He wants his enemies to be **like chaff in the wind** driven away by **the angel of the Lord** (35:5). He hopes they'll be caught in the very **net** that they **hid** for him (35:8-9). If the Lord would save him, David vows to rejoice in the **deliverance** of the God who rescues the **poor** and **needy** (35:9-10).

35:11-18 David laments over those who **repay** his kindness toward them with **evil** (35:12). **When they were sick**, he had mourned, fasted, and prayed for them (35:13-14). But, when David **stumbled**, they gloated and mocked (35:15-16). He thus asks God, **how long will you look on?** (35:17). When would God take action? Yet, he again promises to give public **praise** when his deliverance comes (35:18).

35:19-21 He urges God to prevent the triumph of his foes because they hated him **without cause** (35:19). They were the kind of people who **wink** and make false accusations against those living **peacefully** with others (35:19-20).

35:22-26 You saw it, Lord; do not be silent (35:22). Regardless of the lies people spread, God knows the truth. Thus, David calls on him to be his defender and vindicator (35:23-24). He pictures his enemies as beasts that wanted to growl, **We have swallowed him up!** (35:25). And, because their actions were

so shameful, David longs for God to clothe them **with shame** (35:26).

35:27-28 David desires that the **vindication** he expected from God would lead to continuous **praise** from both God's people and himself. When you experience injustice, let the words of David's inspired psalm help you to pray. Don't fail to give God the praise he is due when he comes through for you.

⮞ Psalm 36 ⮜

36:1-4 David points to two reasons why the **wicked person** turns to ungodliness: **Dread of God has no effect on him**, and he has a **flattering opinion of himself** (36:1-2). In other words, he has a low view of God and a high view of self. He continuously commits sin, and his conscience does not trouble him. He boldly speaks evil and plans evil (36:3-4).

36:5-9 Where does David turn to find relief from the wickedness that surrounds him? He meditates on God, comparing his **faithful love . . . faithfulness . . . righteousness . . . judgments** to the grandest aspects of the created world (36:5-6). As the king of Israel, David was a wealthy man. But, the most **priceless** treasure to which he had access was the **faithful love** of God. The one who benefits from it is like a chick protected under the **wings** of a mother hen (36:7). Those who look to God as their source will experience **the abundance** of his provision and be satisfied (36:8). He is **the wellspring of life** (36:9).

36:10-12 David concludes his prayer with a request that God would provide his protective **love** for those who **know** him in intimate fellowship (36:10). He asks that **the wicked** would not prevail but be defeated by divine judgment (36:11-12).

⮞ Psalm 37 ⮜

37:1-6 David encourages the righteous not to fret over **evildoers**, for they are temporary and will **wither quickly like grass**

under a hot sun (37:1-2). The key to security is to **delight in the** LORD. Then, **he will give you your heart's desires** (37:4). You can expect God's movement in your life when your thinking and desires match his. He desires to bless you more than you want to be blessed, so **commit your way to the** LORD (37:5). If you entrust your entire life to the King's agenda, **he will act** on your behalf with **righteousness** and **justice** (37:5-6).

37:7-15 Our focus should be on God and not on the wicked. We are to **wait expectantly for him** (37:7). Notice that we are not to merely wait, but to wait with expectation—confident that he will respond when our "trust" and "delight" are "in him" (37:3-5). We need **not be agitated** about **evildoers**, for the Lord will deal with them (37:8-10). Remember: vengeance belongs to God; he will repay (Deut 32:35). The Lord knows that the **wicked** person's **day is coming** when he will fall by his own schemes (37:12-15). But, those who look to and submit to God will experience provision and peace (37:9, 11)—and will receive their duly allotted inheritance (see Matt 5:5).

37:16-26 The little that the righteous person has is better than the abundance of many wicked people (37:16). No matter how much the wicked acquire, eventually they will **be broken ... fade away ... destroyed** (37:17, 20, 22). No matter how little the righteous have, however, the Lord **supports** and **watches over** them (37:17-18). **Their inheritance will last forever** (37:18). God will keep their blessings secure until the time is right to dispense them—sometimes in history, but mostly in eternity. He is a loving Father to his people. Even when they fall, he holds them **with his hand** in a gentle but firm grip (37:24). God's **children** will not be **abandoned**. Instead, he is **generous** to them so that they, in turn, **are a blessing** to others (37:25-26).

37:27-40 David further contrasts the righteous and the wicked regarding their eternal destinies. The posterity of the wicked will be wiped out (37:28). Though **a wicked, violent person** seems to be **flourishing** at present, the Lord will uproot him so that he is no longer **found** (37:35-36). His **future ... will be destroyed** (37:38). But, those who **turn away from evil** and **do what is good** will **dwell ... permanently** (37:27, 29). The one who follows God **will have a future** (37:37). Make the Lord your **refuge**, your shelter, and **he will deliver** you (37:39-40).

⮞ Psalm 38 ⮜

38:1-8 David begins the psalm with a cry to God for mercy (38:1). He was experiencing the chastisement of God, which was affecting him physically, spiritually, and emotionally (38:2-8). This divine discipline on David was **because of [his] sin ... iniquities**, and **foolishness**, which he admitted to the Lord (38:3-5).

38:9-12 David's suffering was open and exposed (38:9-10). He looked to God for help because there was no one else to whom he could turn. His suffering caused his **loved ones and friends** to avoid him; it caused his enemies to **threaten** him and **plot treachery** against him (38:11-12).

38:13-20 I put my hope in you, LORD (38:15). David's need was great and his situation was desperate; therefore, God was his only hope. He looked to God to protect him (38:16). He recognized that his **sin** had led to his suffering and that his enemies were too **powerful** for him (38:18-19). Only God could deal with both problems. David was helpless to help himself.

38:21-22 He petitions God not to forsake him but to be quick to save him: **Hurry to help me, my Lord, my salvation** (38:22). In your moments of need, remember that God is your Savior, too. He does not merely provide you with salvation; he *is* your salvation.

⮞ Psalm 39 ⮜

39:1-3 David resolves not to sin through his words (39:1). The book of Proverbs contains much wisdom about how to do this, which is necessary help because James reminds us how hard it is to control the tongue (see Jas 3:1-12). Because David did not want to say anything he would regret, he **kept silent, even from speaking good.** In the long run, however, he took his silence too far; it only **intensified** his **pain** and anguish (39:2-3). We can sin not just with our words but also with our silence. Knowing when to speak and when to withhold something requires wisdom.

39:4-11 David prays that God would help him understand **how short-lived** he was (39:4). In comparison to God, his **life span** was insignificant. **Every human being**, in fact, is nothing but **a vapor** (39:5, 11). In light of such brevity of life (39:4-5) and its uncertainty (39:6), David declares that God is his **hope** and the one who would **rescue** him (39:7-8). David also petitioned God to end his **discipline** and remove the consequences of sin he was enduring (39:10-11).

39:12-13 David asks that God would **not be silent** (39:12)—as David had been earlier when he should have spoken (39:2, 9). He prays that God would **hear** his **cry**, not treat him like a stranger, and show him favor in his remaining days.

☞ *Psalm 40* ☜

40:1-5 David celebrates his past deliverance from trouble. God **heard** his **cry** and responded (40:1). With vivid imagery, David explains how God lifted him from a miry **pit** and set his feet on solid **rock** (40:2). Therefore, he praises God with **a new song**, so that it would motivate others to put their **trust in the Lord**, too (40:3). Such **trust** in God makes one **happy** (40:4). David's psalms arose out of his deep experiences of God, and he desired that others would have rich experiences of him, as well. We ought to keep track of the **wondrous works** that God has accomplished in our lives, so that—like David—we are able to testify confidently that **they are more than can be told** (40:5).

40:6-8 David affirms that God prefers that we commit our lives to him rather than merely offering sacrifices to him. He submits himself to **the scroll** of God's Word, which reveals God's will (40:7). David does not obey

God begrudgingly. He does so willingly and with joy: **I delight to do your will, my God** (40:8). Many people want personal guidance directly from the Lord, yet they skip the guidance available in his revealed Word. You cannot be led in God's personal will for your life if you neglect his revealed will in Scripture.

The author of Hebrews applies these verses to Jesus Christ, who came to fulfill the Father's purposes (see Heb 10:5-7).

40:9-10 David is overwhelmed when he contemplates the attributes of God. He could not **keep [his] mouth closed** (40:9). Thus, to the assembly of God's people, he proclaimed God's **righteousness . . . faithfulness . . . salvation . . . love and truth** (40:10).

40:11-17 He shifts from praise to urgent prayer. His **iniquities** had brought negative consequences upon him, so he pleads with God for **compassion** (40:11-12). David implores God to **rescue** him (40:13), prevent his enemies from triumphing over him (40:14-15), and to **let all who seek [God] rejoice** (40:16). All of these actions brought glory to the God of **salvation** and causes his people to declare, **The Lord is great!** (40:16). This should be our declaration, too.

☞ *Psalm 41* ☜

41:1-3 David highlights the truth that God shows special concern and care for those who are **considerate of the poor** (41:1). Anyone who wants to receive mercy, then, must show mercy. God takes note of such demonstrations of kindness and causes the blessings of mercy to boomerang back to the merciful. He rewards the merciful with protection, security, and restoration (41:2-3; see Jas 1:27; 2:13).

41:4-9 David confesses his sin and sought God's grace (41:4). He is grieved to see his **enemies** taking advantage of his condition, saying he would not survive the consequences of his sin (41:5-8). These who conspired against him included even his **friend in whom [he] trusted.** Though this person had shared close fellowship with David over meals, he **raised his heel against** him

(41:9). Perhaps this is a reference to Ahithophel, David's counselor, who betrayed him by joining Absalom's conspiracy (see 2 Sam 15:12; 16:20–17:4). According to the New Testament, though, the passage was ultimately fulfilled when Judas betrayed his Master, the Son of David (see John 13:18-30).

41:10-13 David wants to see his enemies repaid for their evil (41:10-11). He has confidence in God's support because he had acted with **integrity** (41:12). He concludes with eternal praise for **the LORD God of Israel** (41:13). This closes the first book of the Psalms.

II. BOOK II (PSALMS 42–72)

֎ *Psalm 42* ֍

The titles of Psalms 42 and 44–49 indicate that they are psalms **of the sons of Korah**, who were active in Levitical worship (see 1 Chr 9:17, 19-21; 12:6). Psalm 43 is the only one in this batch without a title. Given this and the fact that the refrain of 42:5 and 11 is repeated in 43:5, it is likely that Psalm 42 and Psalm 43 were originally one.

42:1-3 The psalmist opens with an expression of his deep desire for God: **As a deer longs for flowing streams, so I long for you** (42:1). In the same way that deer search for life-sustaining refreshment, this worshiper pants for God who sustains his life: **I thirst for God** (42:2). The problem, however, is that he remains thirsty. He feels disillusioned by the distance of God. He, therefore, has no appetite; instead, his **tears** were his **food**. Seeing his desperate condition, his enemies mockingly ask, **Where is your God?** (42:3). He is suffering spiritually, physically, and emotionally.

42:4-5 Sometimes, it feels like God has taken a long-distance trip and not informed us of when he'll return. The first thing to do in such circumstances is to draw from past experiences with God. The psalmist recalls times when he joined **the festive procession** to Jerusalem for one of the annual festivals, singing and shouting for joy (42:4). The second thing the psalmist does is to counsel himself with the truth. He asks himself why he is **so dejected** and filled with **turmoil** (42:5). Then, he urges himself, in spite of the darkness, **Put your hope in God** (42:5).

When we walk through dark times, we must follow the psalmist's example. Keep

track of those times when God has come through for you. Store such experiences in your memory bank. It's important to have a history with God so that during the bad times, you can remember the good times to help you persevere. In addition, when God seems absent and uninterested, remember what you know to be true about God. He is faithful and worth hoping in. To hope is to expectantly wait for God to act. Just because you can't see God working doesn't mean he's inactive. Sometimes, like Abraham, you must hope against hope, trusting that God will do what he has promised (see Rom 4:17-21).

42:6-8 The psalmist shifts back to distress: **I am deeply depressed** (42:6). His life is like a seesaw; he's up and then down. He fluctuates between songs and sobs, hope and despair, confidence and collapse, fear and faith. His trying circumstances are like the **roar** of **waterfalls**, like **breakers** and **billows** sweeping over him (42:7). He pictures himself being rocked by an enormous wave, only to be overrun by another as soon as it passes. But, again, he prays for and hopes in God's **faithful love**. His **song** to the Lord would be his comfort **in the night** (42:8). Like a child frightened in the night by a thunderstorm, he longs for his Father's presence—not to stop the thunder and lightning, but to remind him that he isn't alone.

42:9 Why have you forgotten me? The truth is that God hadn't **forgotten** the psalmist, but sometimes it does feel this way.

Importantly, the apostle Paul reminds us that "all things work together for the good of those who love God" (Rom 8:28). Notice he doesn't say that all things *are* good, but that all things *work together for* good. Think of the way God puts the pieces of our situations together for a good end in terms of an automobile assembly plant where the various parts of the car are scattered about. Before the Lord is done taking us through his assembly line, what would seem to be only a confusing mass of pieces is brought together as a finished product. Right now, the pieces of your life may seem unrelated and purposeless. But, God is up to something: he's conforming you "to the image of his Son" (see Rom 8:29).

42:10-11 Though his **adversaries taunt** him (42:10), the psalmist returns to his earlier refrain, repeating words that he needed to hear: **Put your hope in God** (42:11). Even in the dark, then, continue to hope in God. When he doesn't change your situation, keep pursuing him. He is faithful. "Weeping may stay overnight, but there is joy in the morning" (30:5).

⋗ Psalm 43 ⋖

See introductory comments on Psalm 42.

43:1-2 The psalmist cries out to God for vindication and deliverance from his enemies—both corporate and individual. **An unfaithful nation** opposes him and a **deceitful and unjust person** seeks his life (43:1). But, he is despondent ultimately because, though **God** is his **refuge**, God seems to have **rejected** him because his cries go unanswered (43:2). What believer has not felt this way? We want immediate responses to our prayers of distress. When God delays in answering, we feel that he is indifferent toward us.

43:3-4 He calls on the Lord to **send** his **light** and **truth**—that is, divine understanding and revelation—to guide him back to God's temple, his **dwelling place** on his **holy mountain** in Jerusalem (43:3). He longs to be back among God's people, worshiping at **the altar of God** and joyously praising him (44:4). Not only does worship provide much needed nourishment and encouragement, but so does gathering in the presence of fellow worshipers who are trusting God to deliver them, as well.

43:5 The psalmist closes with the same refrain from 42:5 and 11. Though his **soul** is awash in dejection and **turmoil**, he urges himself, **Put your hope in God**. He was determined to continue to put his confidence in God, whom he believed would yet bring deliverance. Like the psalmist, we often have to talk to ourselves in the midst of our despair. We need to remind ourselves that God is worthy of our trust and that we should expect him to answer in a way that will give us a new reason to give him fresh praise.

⋗ Psalm 44 ⋖

44:1-3 The psalmist bears witness to what he and his fellow Israelites had heard from their **ancestors** about the **work** that God **accomplished** on their behalf **long ago** (44:1). He had **displaced** other **nations** and instead planted their family in the land he had promised to Abraham, Isaac, and Jacob (44:2). None of this happened as a result of their own strength, but because God was **favorable toward them** and gave them **victory** by his **right hand** (44:3).

44:4-8 Because of what God had done in the past for their ancestors, the psalmist and those with him could trust their divine **King** to provide continuing **victories** for them (44:4). Though they would have to battle their **enemies**, the psalmist knew that success didn't ultimately come from his **bow** or his **sword** (44:5-6). **Victory** comes from the Lord, in whom they could rightly **boast** and to whom they could offer **praise** (44:7-8).

44:9-16 The nation had experienced defeat at the hands of their enemies. Thus, they felt **rejected** by God (44:9). Just as victory is ultimately from the Lord, so is defeat. They recognized that everything that happened to them was from him: **You make us retreat ... You hand us over ... You sell your people ... You make us an object of reproach ... You make us a joke** (44:10-14). They had become a source of ridicule to their enemies; they were filled with disgrace and shame.

44:17-22 The psalmist and the people believe they had not **forgotten** the Lord or **betrayed** their **covenant** with him (44:17). Therefore, they didn't feel their defeat was deserved. They had not turned from God to idols (44:20). Yet, they were **counted as sheep to be slaughtered** (44:22)—regularly facing the hostility of their enemies. Paul quotes this passage in Romans 8:36 to emphasize the fact that Christians can expect to face suffering and persecution.

44:23-26 The psalmist cries out to God to **wake** from his **sleeping**. In other words, he couldn't imagine that God would intentionally **reject** them or delay in addressing their plight (44:23). He couldn't believe he would ignore their misery. They had **sunk down** and reached their lowest point (44:25), yet they would continue to trust God to deliver them. Just as God had delivered their ancestors because of his strength, not theirs (44:3), so the psalmist pleads with God to **redeem** his people—not because of their worthiness—but because of his **faithful love** (44:26).

When you experience unjust suffering and it seems that God has abandoned you, don't cease trusting him. Remember what he has done in the past, understand that suffering is part of the experience of God's people on this fallen earth, and trust him to deliver you according to his faithfulness.

☞ Psalm 45 ☜

The heading describes this as **a love song**. It's a wedding psalm celebrating the marriage of the king. But, it also applies to the Messiah and his marriage to his people.

45:1-5 The psalmist's **heart** overflows with joy as he pens his song to the king, a **handsome** man, full of gracious speech, and **blessed** by God (45:1-2). The king was also a **mighty warrior**, ready to fight in God's name for **truth, humility, and justice** (45:3-4). Nations fell before him as he went to battle with his **enemies** (45:5).

45:6-7 As God's representative, the king would have a **throne** that would last **forever**

and ever (45:6), which is an allusion to God's covenant with David, which promised that he would never fail to have a descendent on his throne (see 2 Sam 7:11-16). The king was just in the administration of his kingdom, loving **righteousness** and hating **wickedness** (45:7). Hebrews 1:8-9 applies these verses to the Son of God, Jesus Christ. He will rule in his millennial kingdom with perfect justice and righteousness. And, he fulfills God's covenant with David. By virtue of his resurrection from the dead, he will ever live to sit on David's throne.

45:8-12 The king was magnificently arrayed on his wedding day, scented with fragrances, and surrounded by joyful music (45:8). His bride was beside him, **adorned with gold** (45:9). She is urged to pay homage to the king, her **lord**, who honored her for her **beauty** (45:10-11). Glorious gifts would be bestowed on her (45:12).

45:13-17 The **glorious** bride is **led** into **the king's palace** (45:13-15). The psalmist foretells the prosperity of their marriage—which would produce **sons** who would be **princes throughout the land** (45:16). The king would be honored by **all generations**, and **the peoples will praise [him] forever** (45:17). This will ultimately be fulfilled at the marriage of the Lamb when the great King, the Lord Jesus Christ, is united forever with his bride, the church (see Rev 19:6-9). In the meantime, like the bride who forsakes her family to be with the king, believers are to forsake the world now that we are promised to Christ (see Luke 14:26-33).

☞ Psalm 46 ☜

46:1-3 God is our refuge. He is a place of security for his people. He is never too busy but always available **in times of trouble** (46:1). The psalmist imagines the worst possible conditions on earth: earthquakes that topple mountains and cause tsunamis (46:2-3). Yet, even should those worst things happen, **we will not be afraid**, for God is still near to help (46:2).

46:4-7 When the Messiah returns to reign in Jerusalem, **the city of God**, the Creator will be intimately accessible to his people (46:4). God, in the person of the Messiah, will have his throne **within her** and **will help her** (46:5). It will be an Eden-like environment with **a river** in the midst of the city (46:4). No enemies, however strong, will harm her for **the LORD of Armies** is the **stronghold** of his people (46:6-7).

46:8-11 The psalmist encourages and comforts God's people with the knowledge that he would fight their battles and defend them against their enemies (46:8-9). They did not need to worry or strive when faced with challenges or difficulties. The same is true for us. Remember that the Lord is with his people. He is **our stronghold**—our security and strength (46:11).

❧ Psalm 47 ❧

47:1-2 The psalmist calls all nations to rejoice in the worship of God, for he alone is **King over the whole earth**. He is **the Most High**, exalted over everything and everyone in his creation. He is to be feared—that is, taken seriously—by all and paid homage.

47:3-4 God is to be feared specifically because he had subdued nations **under** the **feet** of his people (47:3). He did this when he chose Israel as his special people (47:4), brought them into the promised land, and drove out Canaan's inhabitants before them.

47:5-7 The psalmist exhorts the people to shout with **joy** and **sing praise to God** (47:5-6). He is worthy of all acclamation. As Creator of **the whole earth**, he is its **King** (47:7). Therefore, he deserves to be exalted by his creation and especially by the people to whom he has shown special favor.

47:8-9 All earthly **leaders** will submit to the Lord's sovereign rule (47:9). As Paul testifies in Philippians 2:10-11, one day "every knee will bow . . . and every tongue will confess that Jesus Christ is Lord, to the glory of God

the Father." God's people are to be put into practice now what will eventually be true worldwide: submission to God's kingdom agenda, the visible manifestation of the comprehensive rule of God over every area of life. Those who do not bow voluntarily to Christ and his kingdom now will be forced to do so mandatorily later.

❧ Psalm 48 ❧

48:1-3 **Mount Zion** is a reference to Jerusalem—**the city of our God . . . His holy mountain . . . the city of the great King** (48:1-2). It was there where God dwelled among his people Israel, and in it Solomon constructed God's temple. The city was holy because God was in their midst; it was mighty because **God** was their **stronghold** (48:3).

48:4-8 According to the psalmist, the enemies of God's people were defeated, not because of the strength of Israel's army, but because of the strength of Israel's God. Their enemies **froze with fear** and their **ships** were **wrecked** (48:5, 7). **The LORD of Armies** of angels is their defender. Though God would allow Jerusalem to be decimated by Babylon as a result of Israel's sins, he **will establish it forever** (48:8). The Lord Jesus will rule from Jerusalem during his millennial kingdom. Then, in the new creation, God will dwell with his people forever in the New Jerusalem (see Rev 21:1-27).

48:9-10 The psalmist praises God for his **faithful love**, that is, his loyal love toward those in covenant with him (48:9). **Praise** of God extends **to the ends of the earth**, as he demonstrates his faithfulness and **justice** (48:10).

48:11-14 God's people are to be **glad** and **rejoice** by observing the security he provides for Jerusalem (48:11-13). The psalmist exhorts his audience to be confident that **God . . . will always lead** his people (48:14).

Indeed, we can have this same confidence. God keeps his promises. The same God who made those who first read this passage secure will eternally keep believers who trust him. Nothing "will be able to separate us from the love of God that is in Christ Jesus our Lord" (Rom 8:39).

ᚎ Psalm 49 ᚎ

49:1-4 The psalmist calls all **peoples of the world** to pay special attention to his words (49:1). Those who give ear to the **wisdom** he speaks in the form of a **proverb** or **riddle** will gain **understanding** (49:3-4).

49:5-9 The wicked **trust in their wealth**; they **boast** in their **riches** (49:6). But, though earthly treasure can buy great material possessions, it cannot buy redemption of one's soul from death. Riches **cannot redeem a person or pay his ransom to God** (49:7). Wealth cannot acquire salvation. The cost is too high (49:8). Only one thing can redeem sinful humanity **so that [we] may live forever and not see** death (49:9): the precious blood of the Son of God, Jesus Christ.

49:10-15 Whether one is **wise** or **foolish**, all people **die**. And whether one acquires much or little, his **wealth** will be left **to others** (49:10). It is foolish, then, to think that the possessions and property we amass in this life will cause our names or reputations to endure (49:11-12). In the end, the grave (**Sheol**) is coming for us all (49:14). Yet, for those who trust in God, there is hope. Though we cannot save ourselves, God is mighty to save. **God will redeem me from the power of Sheol, for he will take me** (49:15). In other words, the righteous have the hope of resurrection.

49:16-20 It is foolish to fear or be jealous of the ungodly who gain **wealth** in this life (49:16). **When he dies, he will take nothing at all** (49:17). No matter how much money they accumulate, those who lack spiritual **understanding** will be **like the animals that perish** (49:18-20). This is both a reminder and an encouragement to pursue righteousness above riches. Your life will soon end. The riches you have deposited in heaven will prove far more important in the long run than whatever riches you deposited

on earth (see Matt 6:19-21). Prioritize the spiritual over the material.

ᚎ Psalm 50 ᚎ

50:1-6 The psalmist, Asaph, sets forth God's credentials as the Creator. **From the rising of the sun to its setting**, he rules the world with strength (50:1). He is an all-powerful **judge** (50:3-4). Therefore, his **covenant** people are to listen to him and heed his words (50:5-6).

50:7-15 The Lord warns his people not to let their worship consist of merely outward religious actions—making **sacrifices** and **burnt offerings** (50:8). He owns **the cattle on a thousand hills**; therefore, he doesn't *need* his people to provide them to him (50:9-12). What God desires more than anything in his followers is inward devotion that is reflected in expressing thanks to God and paying **vows** to him (50:14). He urges people to **call on [him] in a day of trouble**, with the result that he would rescue them and they would **honor** him with praise (50:15). Such genuine acts of worship and obedience bring God the greatest glory.

50:16-21 The wicked, past and present, are condemned for their hypocrisy. They make a pretense of reciting God's **statutes** and **covenant**, but they don't truly care (50:16). Instead, they **fling [his] words behind [them]** (50:17). Though they assemble with those who love the Lord, they don't take his word into their hearts. They **make friends with** evil people and use their tongues for **deceit** and slander (50:18-20). They mistake God's patience for his approval. When he keeps **silent** and doesn't immediately bring retribution, they think he is just like them (50:21). They will one day learn the error of their ways.

50:22-23 Hypocrites are admonished to change their actions before it's too late (50:22). They need to re-examine themselves and understand that God withholds his judgment to allow repentance. He thus urges them to approach him with thanksgiving and to adjust their **conduct**. If they do, they will experience his **salvation** from judgment (50:23). Indeed, those who repent of their sins and turn to God in faith can have hope because he abundantly pardons.

❧ Psalm 51 ☙

The heading for this **psalm of David** indicates that he composed it after **the prophet Nathan** confronted him concerning his adultery with **Bathsheba** and the murder of her husband (see 2 Sam 12:1-15), prompting David's repentance.

51:1-3 David appeals to God for forgiving grace and spiritual cleansing based on God's character and **compassion**. He wants God to **blot out** his sin from his memory (51:1). Of course, God can't forget, but David wants his sin erased in the sense that God would not relate to him based on his rebellious actions. The king longs for the Lord's supernatural cleansing because he is unable to wash himself and escape the guilt of his wickedness (51:2). He is tormented by the remembrance of what he had done (51:3)—an indication of his heart's sensitivity toward God.

51:4-6 Though David had clearly wronged Bathsheba and Uriah, he understands that, ultimately, he had **sinned** against God **alone** (51:4). He recognizes that God is the perfect righteous standard by which our actions are judged; therefore, all sin violates his character. All evaluations of right and wrong must be consistent with the standards that he himself has revealed. David knows that he was born, like all humans, with a sin nature: **I was sinful when my mother conceived me** (51:5). This acknowledgement, however, could also suggest that he was the offspring of an illegitimate relationship—a theory supported by the fact that his father Jesse knowingly excluded him from consideration when Samuel asked him to call his sons before him (see 1 Sam 16:1-11). In any case, David needed a radical transformation of his **inner self** so that he might learn **wisdom** and adopt God's perspective on all things (51:6). We need the same.

51:7-9 David pleads for mercy and protection from the legitimate consequences of his sin—he'd earned the death penalty for committing both adultery and murder. Only God could **purify** him, so he requests cleansing with **hyssop** (51:7). This plant had been dipped into the Passover lamb's blood when it was applied to the Israelites' doorframes (see Exod 12:21-23). He longs for God to remove the weight of his **guilt**, which brought him both physical and spiritual grief, and to **blot** it **out** (51:8-9).

51:10-13 When David requests that God give him **a clean heart** and not take away the **Holy Spirit from** him (51:10-11), the king was not concerned about losing salvation. He was not speaking of the indwelling of the Spirit because the Spirit did not indwell Old Testament believers as he does New Testament believers. At issue here is David's desire to fulfill the royal calling God had placed on his life. When he was anointed as king, "the Spirit of the LORD came powerfully on David from that day forward" (1 Sam 16:13). He did not want to lose God's calling and empowerment like his predecessor Saul had (see 1 Sam 16:14). He thus asks God to return to him **the joy of [his] salvation** so that he would be energized to turn other **sinners** to the Lord in repentance, faith, and obedience (51:12-13).

51:14-19 If **God** would deliver him from the **guilt of** his sin, David commits to give God abundant, public praise (51:14). He knew that God doesn't **want** mere external worship and **sacrifice**; he wants a **humbled heart** that is **broken** over personal sin (51:16-17). A casual relationship with sin, in fact, means no authentic worship of God. True worship requires that we give ourselves wholly to God without reserve (see Rom 12:1). When God's people come to him in true repentance, then he will show them favor and accept their worship (51:18-19).

❧ Psalm 52 ☙

Psalm 52 was written by **David** after **Doeg the Edomite** told **Saul** that David had visited and received assistance from Ahimelech the priest. Doeg's actions resulted in the execution of Ahimelech, as well as many other priests and their families (see 1 Sam 21:1-9; 22:9-23).

52:1-4 David calls Doeg the Edomite a **hero** sarcastically because Doeg boasts **about evil** (52:1). He contrasts Doeg's character with the Lord's. Whereas the Lord demonstrates **faithful love**, this wicked man only loves **evil** and **words that destroy** (52:1, 3-4). By means of his **treachery** and **lying** (52:2-3), he caused many innocent people to die.

52:5-7 David is certain that God would judge the wicked, including Doeg, with eternal damnation. He would **bring** the man **down forever** (52:5). His wickedness, then, was only temporary. Because he made **his destructive behavior** his **refuge** instead of God (52:7), Doeg's acts would come crashing down on his own head.

52:8 Not only will God execute justice against the wicked, but he will also vindicate the righteous. David is **like a flourishing olive tree** in the tabernacle in the presence of his God. Why? Because he **[trusts] in God's faithful love**—the one thing in the universe that is "constant" (see 52:1). When you face the wickedness of the world, keep looking to God. Though he permits evil for a time, God will accomplish his purposes, and unrepentant sinners will face his eternal judgment. You, like David, can be firmly rooted in his truth, thriving in spite of the wicked.

52:9 In light of God's faithful love, righteous character, and unfailing justice, David offers **praise . . . in the presence of [God's] faithful people**. Don't fail to thank God, giving public testimony to what he has done so that others may be encouraged to put their **hope** in him.

⮑ *Psalm 53* ⮌

This psalm is almost the same as Psalm 14.

53:1-3 Many people declare, **There's no God.** But, David insists that such a conclusion arises only from the **heart** of a **fool** (53:1). The

reason people believe this lie is because they are corrupt and commit vile deeds. By disbelieving in God and his standards of righteousness, they assume they have absolved themselves of accountability for their actions. Such people do not seek God, so they feel free to become **corrupt** (53:2-3). Nevertheless, God is well aware of their sin; the omniscient Creator sees everything (53:2).

The apostle Paul quotes from these verses in his letter to the Romans as he argues for the universal sinfulness of humanity (see Rom 3:10-12). Apart from God, then, we are all fools. That's why we need to be "declared righteous by faith," so that we can have "peace with God through our Lord Jesus Christ" (Rom 5:1).

53:4-6 These **evildoers** are naïve. They don't **understand** (53:4). They assume they can harm God's people, work against God's program, and prosper in the end. But, God will fill them with **dread** and **shame** when he brings his judgment upon them (53:5). He will also bring his **deliverance** to his people, restoring their **fortunes** during the millennial kingdom of the Lord Jesus Christ. In that day, **Israel** will **be glad** (53:6).

⮑ *Psalm 54* ⮌

The heading of this psalm refers to the time when **David** was **hiding** in the Judean wilderness of Ziph. Some of **the Ziphites** reported this to **Saul** and sought to hand him over to the king (see 1 Sam 23:15-29).

54:1-3 David pleads with God for deliverance from the Ziphites, the **strangers** and **violent men** who sought to **kill** him without provocation (54:3). God's **name** (54:1) represents his character and reputation. David thus appeals to God's attributes of righteousness and faithfulness for protection from those who hated him. Though those who oppose him **do not let God guide them** (54:3), David firmly trusts in God.

54:4-5 David expresses his confidence that the Lord is his **helper** and source of **life** (54:4). He knew that God would bring recompense to his **adversaries**. They would not escape unscathed. **Their evil** deeds against God's anointed one would lead to their annihilation (54:5).

54:6-7 David concludes the psalm by affirming his commitment to **praise** his God who **rescued [him] from every trouble**. He knew the goodness of God by experience, so he vows to worship God and was confident that God would vindicate him. Though we can be certain that we will know hardships in this life, we can also be confident in the God who is able to deliver us from them all.

⟫ Psalm 55 ⟪

55:1-5 David cries out to God with a **plea for help** (55:1). Once again, an enemy threatened him (55:3) so that David was distraught. The descriptions of his suffering emphasize the anxiety he was experiencing. He is **restless and in turmoil**; his **heart shudders**; he is **overwhelmed** by **horror** (55:2, 4-5). Should you ever feel consumed with dread and find yourself reeling from negative emotions, follow David's example. Cry out to God, for he hears.

55:6-8 He longs to have **wings like a dove**—a bird that knows how to find obscure places in which to nest. He wants to **fly away** somewhere inaccessible to those who threatened his life (55:6). Just as we do when living in a state of worry, David desires a **shelter** that would provide him with safety and **rest** (55:6, 8).

55:9-11 David asks the Lord to interfere with his enemies' ability to communicate with one another (55:9), just as the Lord had confused the speech of those building the tower in Babylon (see Gen 11:1-9). David pleads for this because his enemies were full of **violence** ... **strife** ... **oppression**, and **deceit** (55:9, 11).

55:12-15 It's bad enough when harm comes from an **enemy**. But, betrayal at the hands of a **good friend** was more than David **could bear** (55:12-13). Being unjustly hurt by friends or family, in fact, is one of the worst kinds of

pain. David and this **companion** had shared **close fellowship** (55:13-14), yet, at this point, the betrayer sought his life. So, David prays for God's judgment against those who would do **evil** (55:15). Notice, though, that David does not seek revenge himself; he asks that God would bring about his own justice.

55:16-17 David pleads with God for deliverance, crying out to him around the clock, confident that God **hears [his] voice** (55:17). He doesn't utter a calm, respectable prayer; instead, he complains and groans (55:17), being emotionally honest with God. Fear God— take him seriously—but be authentic with him when your life is in turmoil. He already knows your thoughts and anxieties, so there's no point trying to hide them from him.

55:18-21 David comforts himself with the knowledge that no matter how many opposed him, God was **enthroned** as King and would **humiliate them** (55:18-19). The Lord knew about David's **friend** who broke **covenant** with him (55:20). Such actions do not go unnoticed by the God who is always faithful to his own covenant.

55:22-23 Having made his requests known to God, David urges those who read his words to **cast [their] burden on the LORD**. If you do that, in fact, you can trust in the promise that **he will sustain you** (55:22; see 1 Pet 5:7). Place on God's shoulders that which is weighing you down as you wait for him to intervene in your circumstances. Pray to him concerning the **treachery** of the wicked and **trust** him to act on your behalf in accordance with his kingdom program (55:23).

⟫ Psalm 56 ⟪

According to the heading, **David** wrote this psalm with reference to the occasion **when the Philistines seized him in Gath** when he was fleeing from Saul. David pretended to be crazy to prevent the Philistine king from killing him (see 1 Sam 21:1-15; Ps 3).

56:1-4 David calls on God to **be gracious** in light of his **adversaries** who **trample [him]**

all day (56:1-2). In the midst of his fears, David utters a prayer that all of God's children would do well to remember: **When I am afraid, I will trust in you . . . What can mere mortals do to me?** (56:3-4). He realized the importance of having a divine perspective. When fear consumed him, he compared the size of his enemies to the size of his trustworthy God. And doing that changed the equation. Adopting such a perspective, in fact, will transform how you face negative circumstances.

56:5-7 Having acknowledged that wicked humans are nothing in comparison to God, David lays their wicked deeds before the Lord, knowing that they would not **escape**. God would **bring down the nations** who oppose David (55:7).

56:8-9 David was confident that God knew about all of the emotional turmoil he was experiencing. Not only would the wicked not escape God's judgment (56:7), but also David's tears would not escape God's notice. He describes God with beautiful and comforting imagery: He **put** David's **tears** in a **bottle** (55:8). Your God is aware of the details of your suffering. And, in the person of his Son, he took on humanity and suffered for you. Thus, believers can **know** for certain: **God is for [you]** (56:9).

56:10-13 David again expresses **praise** and **trust** in God, knowing that **mere humans** cannot overrule God's plans for him (56:10-11). David looks forward to deliverance when he would **walk before God in the light of life**—experiencing the full reality and presence of God—both in time and in eternity (56:13).

ᘓ Psalm 57 ᘒ

David wrote this psalm in remembrance of the time **he fled before Saul into the cave** (see 1 Sam 24:1-22).

57:1-3 David prays for God's **gracious** intervention, as if he were a baby bird being protected from **danger** under the **wings** of its mother (57:1). He knows that God has a **purpose for** him and trusts him to fulfill it (57:2). His **faithful love and truth** guides David's steps and defends him (57:3).

57:4-6 His circumstances were akin to being **surrounded by lions** that wanted to devour him (57:4). This is likely a reference to his being pursued by Saul, who desperately wanted to strike him down. But, in spite of the trap laid for him, David's enemies **fell into it** (57:6) Therefore, David was determined to exalt God because he had displayed his **glory** in David's trying circumstances (57:5).

57:7-11 David remains steadfast and **confident** in God (57:7), so he can't help but **sing praises**—not only among his own people, but also **among the nations** (57:9). He is in awe of the Lord's **faithful love** and **faithfulness**, which he compares to the grandeur of creation (57:10). David asks that **God** would **be exalted above the heavens** and that his **glory** would be **over the whole earth** (57:11). Having experienced God's deliverance in the past and looking expectantly for his deliverance in the future, David was dominated by a desire to glorify God. This is the disposition we should cultivate within our own hearts. Whatever trying circumstances have come our way, we ought to seek to magnify God in them and through them.

ᘓ Psalm 58 ᘒ

58:1-5 David challenges certain **mighty ones** (that is, unrighteous justices), asking if they **speak righteously** and **judge people fairly** (58:1). Human leaders are supposed to act as God's intermediaries, ruling on his behalf and expressing his own attributes of righteousness and justice. But, these leaders had failed in their accountability before God. David thus compares them to venomous snakes (58:4-5). They were guilty of **injustice** and **violence**, having demonstrated depravity **from birth** (58:2-3).

58:6-8 He pleads with God to execute divine judgment on such evil people, rendering them powerless like defanged lions (58:6).

The imagery continues: He prays they would **vanish** in the ground **like water**, miss the targets at which they aim, and fail to **see the sun** (58:7-8).

58:9-11 The execution of divine justice would be like a whirlwind sweeping away the wicked and bringing great rejoicing to God's people (58:9-10). The judgment of God against evil **is a reward for the righteous** (58:11). The day will finally come when the Lord will set *all* things right. All sin will be punished, either in the cross of Christ, or at the final judgment.

➤ Psalm 59 ✦

David wrote Psalm 59 with reference to the time **when Saul sent agents to watch [David's] house and kill him** (see 1 Sam 19:11-18).

59:1-8 David implores God to **rescue** him from his **enemies** (59:1), who had come to execute him on behalf of King Saul. They waited to **ambush** him, but not because he was guilty of any **rebellion** (59:3). There was, in fact, **no fault** in David (59:4). He was in danger solely because Saul was consumed by jealousy. So, David calls on **the LORD God of Armies** to **help** him (59:4-5). Anyone who opposed David, God's anointed, was opposing God. Therefore, David had confidence that the Lord would **laugh at** their attempts (59:8).

59:9-13 God was David's impregnable fortress, his **stronghold** (59:9). Though his enemies outnumbered him, David was kept safe by divine protection. He asks God to defeat the wicked men (59:11-13)—not merely so that he would be delivered—but so that **people will know throughout the earth that God rules over Jacob** (59:13). He wanted God's glory to be acknowledged everywhere.

It's easy to be consumed with fear and anxiety when confronted with dreadful circumstances. To whom will you look when you are faced with a problem that's too powerful for you? Look to the omnipotent "LORD God of Armies" (59:5). He alone can override your negative circumstances so that "all things work together for the good of those who love God, who are called according to his purposes" (Rom 8:28).

59:14-17 Though his enemies circle him, **snarling like dogs** (59:14), David was determined to **joyfully proclaim [God's] faithful love** every **morning** (59:16). This is a good way to begin your day—looking to God's faithful love to provide you with strength to make it through the next twenty-four hours. The **faithful God** is your **strength** (59:17).

➤ Psalm 60 ✦

Psalm 60 is a reflection on some of King David's battles, points at which he prayed for divine aid to receive victory (see 2 Sam 8).

60:1-5 David prays for a reprieve from some **hardship** that God had brought on his people when he was **angry** with them (60:1, 3). Because God was responsible for the damage, only he could **restore** the nation from its brokenness (60:1). He had called his people to walk under his banner, but then he allowed them to **flee** and experience defeat (60:4). So, David pleads with God to **save** his people from their enemies using his mighty **right hand** (60:5).

60:6-8 From **his sanctuary**, the tabernacle, God answered. All the land is his—from the territory given to his people, to that of their enemies. He gives land to whomever he will. **Judah** is David's tribe, and the Lord calls it his **scepter** (60:7). In other words, it is the tribe from which future kings would come. God affirms that David would triumph. **Moab, Edom,** and **Philistia** were neighboring lands with which Israel was regularly contending. To **throw** a **sandal** at someone is to treat them with contempt. God would defeat Israel's enemies and **shout in triumph over** them (60:8).

60:9-12 David acknowledges that both victory and defeat come from the hand of God. So, he again appeals to God for **aid against the foe, for human help is worthless** (60:11). Only the Lord can provide deliverance. Without him, we cannot succeed; with him, we cannot fail.

❧ Psalm 61 ❧

61:1-2 Overwhelmed, David prays for divine security. Though David is **without strength**, his God is a **rock . . . high above** (61:2). David recognized both his own limitations and God's unconquerable might. Pray for the humility to be able to do the same.

61:3-4 God alone is **a strong tower in the face of the enemy** (61:3). Therefore, David wanted to remain in his presence. God is like a mother hen providing **refuge under the shelter of [his] wings** (61:4). The only wise position from which to operate in life, then, is under the divine covering—an unassailable place of safety from elements and enemies.

61:5-8 David expresses confidence that God heard his prayer. **To those who fear [his] name**, those who take him seriously, God gives a **heritage**, a promised inheritance (61:5). The specific heritage he had promised to David was a royal dynasty. So, David prays that he might prolong his **life** and let his sons remain **enthroned before God forever** (61:6-7) in accordance with God's covenant promise to him (see 2 Sam 7:11-16). Ultimately, God will fulfill this prayer in the Lord Jesus Christ, the Son of David who will reign on David's throne forever.

David asks that God's **faithful love and truth** would **guard him** (61:7)—protecting him from his enemies and circumstances and from his own sinfulness. He concludes with a commitment to **continually sing** the Lord's praises and to daily fulfill his **vows** he had made (61:8). In other words, if God would deliver him, David would ensure that God receives the glory for it.

❧ Psalm 62 ❧

62:1-2 Given what he was facing, David confesses that his sole focus was on the God of his **salvation**. Only such an undistracted, divine focus could give him **rest**, for **God alone** provides David with a **stronghold**—a sure defense against those who attacked him.

62:3-4 David marvels at the attempt of his enemies to oppose him in light of his confidence in God. Did they really think that the king who had God as his stronghold would be as easy to topple as **a tottering fence**? (62:3). They were wicked men who only wanted to **bring [David] down** from his throne. Outwardly **they bless**, but **they curse inwardly** (62:4). The righteous God would take note of such duplicitous scheming against his anointed king.

62:5-8 David repeats his confident words with which he began the psalm (62:1-2). He exhorts his **soul** that **God alone** is his defense and security. With God as his hope, David could **not be shaken** (62:5-6). David's kingdom was dependent on God. Without God's covering of protection, there would be no **salvation** for David, no **glory** (62:7). Therefore, he encourages fellow saints to **pour out [their] hearts before him**, as he was himself doing. Believers have every reason to **trust** God as their ever-present **refuge** (62:8).

62:9-10 Life is transitory. We are **less than a vapor** (62:9). Therefore, David tells us not to put our trust in sinful actions (**oppression** and **robbery**) as a means of providing ourselves with security. For riches are as transitory as life itself. **Wealth** cannot deliver you. **Don't set your heart on it** (62:10). Don't look to the material to do what only the spiritual can do.

62:11-12 God declares that **strength** and **faithful love** belong to him. Because of his faithful love, he has compassion on his people. And because of his strength, he has the power to demonstrate that compassion to them. So, all people should take heed: God will **repay each according to his works** (62:12). Let the believer have confidence; let the unbeliever beware.

❧ Psalm 63 ❧

This **psalm of David** reflects his experience **in the Wilderness of Judah** while he was king (see 63:11)—most likely when he fled Jerusalem during Absalom's rebellion.

63:1-2 His experience in the **dry, desolate** wilderness **without water** prompts David to consider his **thirst**—that of his soul. What he truly thirsts for is not water but **God** (63:1). This thirst had been satisfied when he was able to **gaze on** the **glory** of God in his **sanctuary**, the tabernacle (63:2). But, in the wilderness, David longs for God's glory.

63:3-5 Even in the wilderness, David finds satisfaction, joy, and comfort in praising God. **Better than life** itself is the **faithful love** that God demonstrates toward those who fear him (63:3). When you, like David, realize that God's faithfulness is more important than life-sustaining necessities such as food and water, you, too, will **praise [him] with joyful lips** (63:5). Such genuine worship will sustain you in your own wilderness experiences.

63:6-8 As he lay awake at night, David could have been consumed by his troubles. Instead, he disciplines himself to **meditate on** God, because he is his **helper** (63:6-7). God's **right hand**—a metaphor for his sovereign power—supports David (63:8). David's musings should make you ask where you focus during your times of suffering. To whom do you first turn for help?

63:9-11 Even though David is in the wilderness, chased from his throne and hunted like an animal, he is certain that his enemies would be defeated (63:9-10). This was not self-confidence but God-confidence. In spite of the fact that a rebellion had taken his crown, David believes that the state of affairs was temporary. He is still **the king.** Thus, he would **rejoice in God**, knowing that the **liars** who oppose him would not succeed (63:11). No matter the negative circumstances you face, put your confidence in the one whose love for you is "better than life" (63:3).

➤ Psalm 64 ❧

64:1-4 David cries out to God **in anguish** so that he might protect him **from the scheming of wicked people** (64:1-2). These evildoers attack **the blameless**, those innocent of wrongdoing. Their **words** are like **swords** and **arrows**. They tell lies, lay plans, and ruin reputations (64:3-4). All this they did without being **afraid** of repercussions (63:4).

64:5-6 The wicked encourage one another in their plans to carry out injustice. They are convinced that no one could **see** the **traps** they'd laid (64:5). No one knows the **secret plan** they had **perfected** (64:6).

64:7-8 David predicts divine intervention against his enemies. Though they aim their words like arrows at the innocent (64:4), God himself would launch his own **arrows** and cause their **tongues** to **work against them** (64:7-8). Their evil deeds would return like a boomerang; the destruction they planned for others would cause their own downfall.

64:9-10 Such a visible manifestation of **God's work** would cause **everyone** to **fear** him and give testimony to his glorious deeds (64:9). What does **the righteous** person do when he sees the deliverance of God? He **rejoices in** God, **takes refuge** under his covering, and offers him **praise** (64:10). That was David's hope for the people of God in his day. Likewise, it should be our hope for the people of God today.

➤ Psalm 65 ❧

65:1-4 David celebrates the joy of atonement for sin. He knew that **only [God] can atone for our rebellions** (65:3). When God provides covering for our **iniquities** and forgives our transgressions, it opens the door for **praise** and **prayer** from his people (65:1-3). **How happy** are those who are able to draw **near to** him once God has removed the barrier of sin (65:4).

If David experienced the joy of forgiven sins, even though he had to continue to offer the required sacrifices every year, how much more joy can we experience through Jesus Christ? The sacrifices offered by priests in the temple could not atone for sins once and for all. But, when Jesus offered himself as the one perfect sacrifice for sins, he brought eternal forgiveness and sanctification to those who trust in him (see Heb 10:11-18).

65:5-8 David expresses confidence that God would **answer** the prayers of his people with **awe-inspiring works**—in light of the **salvation** he provides and **the hope** they have placed in him (65:5). The Lord's **power** and **strength** are demonstrated in his sovereignty over creation. **Mountains** and **seas** bow to his will (65:6-7). His supernatural activity causes people to fear, rejoice, and enter fellowship with him (65:8).

65:9-13 David is reminded of the goodness of God as he provides his blessings on **the earth**. By sending rain **showers** and granting growth, his people received a harvest of **grain** (65:9-10, 13). Creation itself is **robed with joy** and shouts **in triumph** at his works (65:12-13).

And, just as creation displays fruitfulness when it receives God's blessings, the same is true for us. When we turn to God in repentance and faith—whether as a new believer or as one who has stepped out of fellowship with God because of sin—we can know the blessing of Christ's atoning work and live a life of fruitfulness (see 1 John 1:9).

☞ Psalm 66 ☜

66:1-4 The psalmist calls on all peoples of the **earth** to **praise** God in song because of his greatness (66:1-2). Our worship should be suitable to the one whom we worship. A great God deserves great praise. The psalmist foretells a day when **the whole earth will worship [God]** (66:4). This is indeed true (see Phil 2:10-11).

66:5-9 The psalmist rehearses **the wonders of God** sovereignly demonstrated when he **turned the sea into dry land** for his people (66:5-6)—both at the Red Sea during the exodus (see Exod 14:15-31) and at the Jordan River as they entered the promised land (see Josh 3:1-17). **The rebellious**—like Pharaoh who spurned God's commands—**should not exalt themselves** (66:7). Even as God supernaturally

used the waters to deliver his people, he also used them to vanquish Pharaoh's army. All **peoples** should **praise** the Lord because he will preserve his own (66:8-9).

66:10-12 God also let his people experience hardship and oppression. In all such things, though, our sovereign God works "for the good of those who love" him (see Rom 8:28). He tests us so that we may be **refined** as **silver** (66:10). He will permit you to encounter negative circumstances so that he can reveal to you his comfort and power.

66:13-15 The psalmist intends to fulfill his **vows** to God in his time of **distress**. He had apparently made his commitment before his troubles began, but he wouldn't let that prevent him from honoring what he had **promised** (66:13-14). His **offerings** and **sacrifice** would continue, as he trusted God to provide for him (66:15).

66:16-20 Come and listen (66:16). He concludes by sharing his praise with the congregation for God's answer to his prayer. The psalmist confesses that this deliverance would not have happened if he had clung to sin in his **heart** (66:18). The principle is clear: honesty and openness before God are essential. Confession and repentance are necessary if our prayers are not to be hindered (see 1 Pet 3:7). But, when we address our personal sin, we open the door to experiencing the **faithful love** of God (66:20).

☞ Psalm 67 ☜

67:1-2 The writer of the psalm prays that **God** would **be gracious** to his people and **bless** them (67:1). But, what is the reason for this request? Is it so that they could enjoy material prosperity? Is it so that they might have glory and power? No, the author has a missional reason. He desires the Lord's favor **so that [his] way may be known on the earth** and **[his] salvation among the nations** (67:2). When God delivers his people and showers them with blessings, his goal is that he would receive glory and that other people would experience salvation and discipleship.

God wants all people everywhere to know him, and this should be our desire, as well. He does not bless you merely for your own sake. He blesses you so that you may be a blessing to others, leading them to put their faith in Jesus Christ, to glorify God, and to live their lives in joyful obedience to him.

67:3-5 He prays that all nations would **praise . . . rejoice . . . shout for joy** over the greatness of God and the justice he establishes. Praise leads to blessing, which results in more praise, which leads to salvation of the lost, which ignites further praise. This circular process ensures that God is exalted more and more.

67:6-7 The psalmist acknowledges how God has blessed them with a bountiful **harvest** (66:7). And once again, he proclaims the purpose of this rich blessing: so that **all the ends of the earth will fear** God (66:7).

God does not bless you so that you can kick back, enjoy your blessings, and be self-absorbed. He blesses you so that you will make his priorities your own. He blesses you so that you will give him public praise and use his blessings in such a way that others will see him for who he is and be compelled to take him seriously.

☞ Psalm 68 ☜

68:1-3 David observes what happens when **God arises.** When the sovereign Lord goes into action, **his enemies scatter** (68:1). Like **smoke**, they are **blown away.** Like **wax**, they melt (68:2). But, these same actions cause **the righteous to rejoice.** When God executes justice on the earth, his people **celebrate** (68:3).

68:4-6 He calls the people to praise God **who rides on the clouds.** He is worthy of worship because he is **a champion of** orphans, **widows**, and the oppressed (68:5-6). Simultaneously, he rains down judgment on **the rebellious** (68:6).

68:7-14 David reminds the people of how the Lord led their ancestors in the **desert** after the exodus from Egypt (68:7). At **Sinai**, he

gave them his law, and he refreshed them in the wilderness (68:8-9). When they entered the promised land, God gave them victory. **The kings of the armies** fled and were **scattered** (68:12, 14). Then, he blessed them with the **spoil** taken from their defeated enemies (68:12-13).

68:15-18 The nations of the world looked with **envy** on Jerusalem, the city on **the mountain** that **God desired for his abode** (68:16). There, he was surrounded by **thousands** of **chariots** (68:17)—emphasizing the fact that he is "the LORD of Armies" (46:7; 59:5). He **ascended** in triumph like a mighty conqueror receiving tribute from those whom he'd defeated (68:18). Paul quotes this verse in Ephesians 4:7-8, emphasizing that when Christ victoriously rose from the dead and ascended to heaven, he rescued those who were captive to Satan and gave them spiritual gifts so that they could serve him and others in his church.

68:19-27 David praises God because **he bears our burdens.** He provides **salvation** for his people and defeats their **enemies** (68:20-23). David describes a victory parade as the Lord, the **King**, triumphantly entered his **sanctuary** with singers and **musicians** (68:24-25). This perhaps describes a procession in which the ark of the covenant was carried into the tabernacle. All the tribes of **Israel** are called to bless the Lord their God (68:26-27).

68:28-35 He asks God to give a fresh demonstration of his power by subduing all peoples so that **kings** from foreign lands would pay **tribute to** him and pay homage (68:28-31). David concludes by exhorting **the kingdoms of the earth** to **praise** God for his power and majesty (68:32-34). In light of what he has done among his people, and in light of our great need for him in the future, let us cry out along with David, **Blessed be God!** (66:35).

☞ Psalm 69 ☜

The New Testament quotes Psalm 69 numerous times. Its references to the wicked are applied to unbelieving Israel (see Rom 11:9-10

[Ps 69:22-23]) and to Judas (see Acts 1:20 [Ps 69:25]). On most occasions, though, the psalm is quoted with reference to Jesus Christ. Like David, Jesus was consumed with zeal for God's house, demonstrating this when he cleansed the temple (see John 2:17 [69:9]). In his passion, Christ fulfilled the psalm, showing that he was the perfect righteous sufferer (see John 15:25 [Ps 69:4]; Rom 15:3 [Ps 69:9]).

69:1-4 David laments his circumstances and calls out to God for salvation. He was overwhelmed, like a man sinking in a miry bog. He couldn't get free and **the water** was about to cover his head (69:1-2). Unable to help himself, he was **looking for [his] God** (69:3). His enemies were **more numerous** than he could count, and they had no legitimate **cause** for persecuting him (69:4).

69:5-12 Although David recognizes he is a sinful man (69:5), he knows that personal sin was not the cause of his plight. He had **endured insults because of [the Lord]** (69:7). He was suffering for righteous reasons, which is the only kind of suffering God wants us to undergo. "For it is better to suffer for doing good, if that should be God's will, than for doing evil" (1 Pet 3:17). His enemies included his own family members, judges **at the city gate**, and **drunkards** (69:8, 12). Thus, he was assailed from every direction, causing him to mourn, fast, and wear **sackcloth** (69:10-11).

69:13-18 David pleads for God's **favor** in accordance with his **faithful love** (69:13, 16). Again, David pictured himself sinking in **mud** with **floodwaters** swallowing him (69:14-15). Such helpless feelings are common to the human experience—regardless of the specific circumstances. So, when you are suffering and don't know what to pray, let David's prayer here be your own.

69:19-21 David knows that his omniscient God was fully aware of the **insults** he had endured (69:19), so he needs his compassion. The reproach David suffered had **broken [his] heart**, and no one extended **sympathy** or comfort (69:20). Instead, they spitefully offer him bitter **food** and **drink** (69:21). This was fulfilled when Jesus was offered vinegar

to quench his thirst on the cross (see Matt 27:34; Luke 23:26; John 19:28-30).

69:22-28 David repeatedly prays that the wickedness of his enemies would turn against them. Notice, however, that David does not seek to avenge himself against his enemies but leaves vengeance to God. Because they have sinned against God, David asks that his **burning anger** would **overtake them** (69:24). He prays that they would be punished both in history (69:22-23, 25) and in eternity (69:28).

69:29-33 In contrast to those who hated him, David was **poor and in pain** (69:29). Anticipating God's delivering hand, David vows to give **praise** and **thanksgiving**, which was more pleasing to God than an abundance of sacrifices (69:30-31). He expresses confidence that God hears **his own**—especially those who are **needy** and imprisoned (69:33).

69:34-36 David calls for the universal praise of God by all creation, in light of his forthcoming deliverance of his people (69:34-35). This would result in security for God's people in the land (69:35-36). Thus, David desires not only short-term rescue but also long-term divine covering.

❧ *Psalm 70* ❧

70:1-3 David petitions God to **hurry** and provide a rapid rescue from **those who wish [him] harm** (70:1-2). He asks that his enemies would be **humiliated** and **retreat in shame** (70:2-3). Our sovereign God is able to cause malice directed at you to return on your adversary's head.

70:4-5 David wasn't concerned about himself alone. Rather, he wants all who **seek** the Lord and **love [his] salvation** to magnify him. Even in the midst of trouble, David cares about God's glorification and the saints' edification. Those who know and have experienced the greatness of God should declare, **God is great!** (70:4). He concludes with another urgent request for rescue. He acknowledges himself as **oppressed and needy**, desperately in need of the one and only **deliverer** (70:5).

❧ Psalm 71 ❧

71:1-8 The psalmist looks to God as his **refuge**, his **rock** and his **fortress** (71:1, 3) because of **the power of the wicked** (71:4). Despite their threats, he continues to **hope** in God, which he had done **from [his] youth** (71:5). Never underestimate the "staying power" of faith when children are taught to know and love the Lord from an early age. The psalmist's **mouth** is **full of praise** (71:8).

71:9-16 He asks that God would continue to sustain him in his **old age** (71:9). Growing physically weak, he requests that the Lord protect him from those who sought to take advantage of him as the years pass (71:10-11). The psalmist prays for God's intervention (71:12-13) and, at the same time, vows that he would continue to **hope** in God and offer **praise** to God **all day long** (71:14-15).

71:17-24 The psalmist emphasizes the longevity of his discipleship. He had learned from God in his **youth** and was **still** proclaiming his **wondrous works** (71:17). Therefore, he prays that God would not **abandon** him when he was **old and gray**. He longs to see **another generation** know and serve the Lord (71:18). Though God had brought **many troubles and misfortunes** into the psalmist's life to strengthen, correct, and develop him (see Jas 1:1-12; Heb 12:4-11), he was confident that God would restore him **once again** (71:20-21). Therefore, his mouth would be filled with **praise** as he anticipated the disgrace of those who meant him **harm** (71:22-24). We can look to God with this same confidence regarding the trials he brings into our lives.

❧ Psalm 72 ❧

This is the first of two psalms ascribed to King **Solomon** (see also Ps 127).

72:1-4 Solomon requests that God would grant **justice** and **righteousness to** the **king** (and his **son** after him), so that he would **judge** with equity for all the **people** (72:1-2). The result would be peace in the land and relief for **the afflicted** (72:3-4).

72:5-7 Solomon longs to have a kingdom in which the people fear God forever, to be a **king** who brings life to **the earth**, and to cause **the righteous** to **flourish** under his rule. Thus, he anticipated the reign of the Messiah, for these things will only be true when the Son of God reigns eternally—beginning with his millennial kingdom.

72:8-11 Solomon desires to see his kingdom stretch to **the ends of the earth**, as his **enemies lick the dust** (72:8-9). This is an allusion to the curse on the serpent; it would "eat dust" all of its days (see Gen 3:14). Those who follow the devil's ways share his fate. Meanwhile, **the kings of** the world will **bring tribute** and **bow in homage** to the king (72:10-11). This is a prophecy that will be fulfilled in the future reign of Christ when "the kings of the earth will bring their glory" into the new Jerusalem (Rev 21:24).

72:12-17 The Messiah's universal reign will be characterized by justice for the **poor** and **afflicted**, as he rescues them from **oppression and violence** (72:12-14). Solomon prays that this King and the people of his kingdom would be **blessed** and **flourish** (72:15-16). He also prays that **all nations** would be **blessed by him** (72:17). God had promised Abraham that all the peoples of the earth would be blessed through him (Gen 12:3). And indeed, through the "seed of Abraham," Jesus Christ, all those who put faith in him are blessed with justification from sin (see Gal 3:7-9, 16).

72:18-20 Solomon concludes with a doxology of praise, blessing **the LORD God** and praying that **the whole earth** would be **filled with his glory** (72:18-19). Thus ends the second book of the Psalter.

III. BOOK III (PSALMS 73–89)

⋟ Psalm 73 ⋞

73:1-5 Asaph begins the psalm with a declaration of the goodness of God to his people (73:1). Yet, in spite of this divine reality, he confesses that his **feet almost slipped** and his **steps nearly went astray** (73:2). He had almost departed from the right path! Why? Because he **envied the arrogant** and **saw the prosperity of the wicked** (73:3). It seems they have **an easy time** and don't experience trouble **like most people** (73:4-5). Asaph was feeling conflict between his theology and his experience. He thus wants to know why the righteous experienced difficulties as the wicked flourished. More than a few Christians have been tempted to think similarly.

73:6-12 Not only do the arrogant seem to live at ease, but they flaunt their wickedness. They wear **pride** like a **necklace** (73:6). **They mock** and **speak maliciously** about others (73:8). They even mock God, speaking **against heaven** and denying that God knows **everything** (73:9, 11). By their lives they proclaim, "Hey, followers of God, why are you wasting your time? I care nothing about him. I live as I please. And I'm doing just fine."

73:13-16 Asaph reveals the conflict that filled his heart: **Did I purify my heart and wash my hands in innocence for nothing?** (73:13). He wants to know if his ethical behavior had been a waste of time. After all, while the wicked person thrives, Asaph had been **afflicted** and **punished** (73:14). In his misery, he wonders if he should have lived as he pleased so that he might at least share in the benefits of the unbelievers. He realizes, though, that he couldn't **say these things aloud** to God's **people**, because such pessimism would drive them *from* God instead of driving them *to* God (73:15). He didn't **understand**; all **seemed hopeless** (73:16).

Notice that Asaph didn't hide his feelings from God. He was honest about his confusion and frustration. When you are upset and feel that God has let you down, bring your struggles to him in prayer. He's not afraid of your concerns; he's not troubled by your disappointments. It is far better to pour out your anger and anxieties to God through prayer than to bury them inside and turn to sin (which Asaph almost did; see 73:2).

73:17-20 Asaph's "until" indicates the turning point. He was filled with envy of the wicked and tempted to follow them, **until [he] entered God's sanctuary. Then [he] understood their destiny** (73:17). When Asaph entered the presence of God, he experienced a fresh vision of his glory and gained an eternal perspective regarding the wicked. He suddenly grasped that God had **put them in slippery places** (73:18). And if they don't turn in repentance and faith, God would see to it that their slick path sent them sliding into hell. They may appear to be cruising along life's highway, they're certain to **come to an end** (73:19).

73:21-23 Asaph finally grasps that **when [he] became embittered**, it caused him to be **stupid** and act like **an unthinking animal toward** God (72:21-22). In the midst of his frustration, he lacked an eternal perspective. When Asaph once again understands God's view of life, he realizes that he is **always with** God, who holds his **right hand** (73:23). Notice who was holding whom. God was holding Asaph, and he wasn't letting go.

73:24-26 Not only did Asaph have God's presence, but he also had his guidance, his **counsel**. God's Word directs us to believe what is true and to live with wisdom. Then, when this life is over, though the wicked are "swept away by terrors" (73:19), God **will take** the righteous **up in glory** (73:24). When Asaph's perspective changes to match this reality, he realizes that he desired nothing but God (73:25). He recognizes that the Lord was everything to him. And, regardless of what temporary pleasures the wicked receive in this life, Asaph has God as his **portion forever** (73:26).

73:27-28 Asaph began this psalm with, "But as for me, my feet almost slipped" (73:2). He finishes with, **But as for me, God's presence is my good** (73:28). So, what happened in between verses 2 and 28? He encountered God in worship. In the presence of God, he found the truth, hope, and strength he needed. As a result, he wants nothing more than to **tell** others **about** God (73:28). Let life's confusion drive you to God, not away from him.

⪼ *Psalm 74* ⪻

74:1-11 Asaph expresses his sense of rejection by God in light of the affliction that God's people, **the sheep of [his] pasture**, were experiencing (74:1). He urges God to **remember** both the **congregation** that he had **redeemed** and **Mount Zion** where he dwelled (74:2). Asaph calls on God to intervene because of the **ruins** in Jerusalem, the destruction that Babylon had wrought on **the sanctuary** (74:3). The invaders had smashed and burned God's **dwelling place** (74:6-7), and **there [was] no longer a prophet** to speak to the people for God and tell them **how long this [would] last** (74:9). Asaph understands that **the enemy** did not simply **mock** the people of God; he mocked God himself (74:10). Therefore, he pleads with God to punish them (74:11).

74:12-23 In spite of the dreadful circumstances of God's people, Asaph confesses that **God** is still **King** (74:12). He has repeatedly demonstrated his sovereign strength over creation (74:13-17), often using creation as a means of delivering his people, as when he **divided the sea** during the exodus (74:13). Thus, God is not without power. So, Asaph emphasizes how **the enemy has mocked the LORD** and implores him **not** to **forget** his **poor people**, the people of his **covenant** (74:18-20). In this way, Asaph prays that God's concern for his own glory would be his motivation for acting. God's name was at stake. Therefore, Asaph appeals, **Rise up, God, champion your cause!** (74:22).

When we pray for intervention in our circumstances, we, too, should desire to see God vindicated and glorified. So, whatever assistance we need, let us be motivated to see God's name lifted high in praise as he brings down the wicked and demonstrates his faithfulness to his people.

⪼ *Psalm 75* ⪻

75:1-5 Asaph expresses **thanks to** God for his nearness to his people in spite of what they were experiencing (75:1). In verses 2-5, God speaks. He has a sovereign timetable according to which he will intervene in human history and bring about his final judgment on earth against the wicked (75:2-3). He thus exhorts those who **boast** in their wickedness and **arrogantly** exalt themselves **against heaven** (75:4-5). Unless they repent, their days are numbered.

75:6-8 God alone **is the Judge: He brings down one and exalts another** (75:7). No one escapes his righteous gaze; therefore, no one will escape his condemnation of pride. "God resists the proud but gives grace to the humble" (1 Pet 5:5). He will pour out his **cup** of judgment on **the wicked**, who will have no choice but to **drink** its contents down (75:8).

75:9-10 Asaph praises the Lord and desires to make his name and deeds known to everyone (75:9). The final words are God's. He vows to **cut off all the horns of the wicked**, but to lift up **the horns of the righteous** (75:10). An animal's horns represent power. Thus, God will act in a way that's consistent with his just and righteous character, vanquishing those who exalt themselves, but establishing those who submit to his kingdom rule and authority.

⪼ *Psalm 76* ⪻

76:1-3 Asaph declares that one of the ways that God makes himself **known** is by destroying **the weapons** of those who make **war** against his people (75:1, 3). He dwells in the midst of **Zion** (75:2), and he wages battles on their behalf against their enemies.

76:4-6 Asaph extols the **resplendent and majestic** God who falls on his enemies, no matter how **brave-hearted** and powerful they are (76:4-5). He destroys them, sending them to **their final sleep** (76:5). This, of course, takes little effort on God's part: a mere **rebuke** and he defeats them (76:6).

76:7-10 God's wrath against the wicked demonstrates his sovereignty. When he displays his anger, no one **can stand before [him]** (76:7). As a result, his people praise him and are moved to fear him (76:7-8), which serves as a deterrent against further evil.

76:11-12 Believers are exhorted to fear **the awe-inspiring** God—that is, to take him seriously—by keeping their **vows** and maintaining their commitment to him (76:11). **He humbles** proud **leaders** so that they might fear him, as well (76:12).

All people will submit to the Lord one day, whether in joy or by coercion (see Phil 2:10-11). He invites us to fear and enjoy him now so that we may experience his blessings. Those who do not will experience his judgment.

➢ *Psalm 77* ☙

77:1-3 Seeking comfort in the midst of his **trouble**, Asaph reaches out to God in prayer. He has faith that the Lord would **hear** him (77:1-2). Yet, comfort alludes him because God has not yet responded; thus, he is affected physically and spiritually. He groans, and his **spirit** is **weak** (76:3). Notice, though, that Asaph continues to pursue God in his despair.

77:4-6 While waiting on God to answer, Asaph searches his own spirit for comfort. Because God kept him awake at night (77:4), he contemplates **past** times when he had experienced God's deliverance and sang in the **night** (77:5-6). He then ponders the fact that he had no current reason for praise, given the nation's circumstances (77:6).

77:7-9 Asaph was confused because it seemed that God had rejected him and his

people by removing from them his **faithful love**, covenantal promises, and graciousness (77:7-9). God's **anger** seemed to have replaced his **compassion** (77:9).

77:13-15 For comfort and assurance, Asaph turns to recalling and meditating on the **holy** God's deliverances in the past. Truly, there is no one **like** him (77:13). God is in a class by himself. He worked **wonders** and **redeemed** Israel **with power** (77:14-15).

77:16-20 Creation itself **trembled** when God acted for his people (77:16). When he rescued Israel from Egypt, he made a **way . . . through the sea** and further demonstrated his power with **storm clouds . . . thunder . . . lightning** (77:17-19). God used **Moses and Aaron** as instruments to lead and deliver his **people like a flock** of sheep (77:20).

By recalling this great redemption of Israel by God's hand, Asaph encourages himself that God would again come to the aid of his people. His delayed response does not mean abandonment. Thus, when God delays in answering our prayers, we need to remember how he cared for us in other times of distress. His footprints of grace from yesterday give us the power to trust him today.

➢ *Psalm 78* ☙

78:1-2 Asaph invites those with spiritual understanding to hear the **instruction** and **wise sayings** that he was about to share. Those without spiritual perception would not be able to interpret and apply the truths he was about to teach; they would remain **mysteries** from their view. Similarly, those who were without spiritual insight and unwilling to receive it would be unable to understand Jesus's parables (see Matt 13:10-17).

78:3-8 The purpose of this psalm was to recount God's faithfulness throughout Israel's history so that **a future generation** would praise God for the **wondrous works he has performed** for his people (78:3-4).

The psalmist begins with the giving of the **law** to **Israel** (78:5). God did this so that they would know what he required of his covenant people. Thus, they could know him and trust him. Asaph wants to challenge his own generation to teach **their children** not to be like their ancestors who were **stubborn and rebellious** (78:6-8). We, too, must learn from the past, imitating the faithful and avoiding the foolishness of the wicked, if we are to experience the goodness of God.

78:9-16 Asaph laments how Ephraim **did not keep God's covenant** (78:9-10). The significant tribe of Ephraim was often used as shorthand for the entire northern kingdom of Israel. **They forgot** the **wondrous works** of God when he rescued the Israelites from slavery in Egypt and supernaturally cared for them **in the wilderness** afterwards (78:11-16).

78:16-33 Though **he brought** them **streams out of stone** and **rained** both **bread** and **meat** on them, the Israelites continued to sin against God **in the desert** (78:16-17, 24, 27). They **tested** him regardless of how much he provided for them (78:18-20) **because they did not believe God or rely on his salvation** (78:22). As a result, **God's anger** caused him to kill many of them (78:31). Nonetheless, they **kept sinning** and experienced further **disaster** (78:32-33).

78:34-39 When God judged them, some of the people made a pretense of repenting (78:34). But, they **were insincere**, confessing with their mouths but demonstrating with their lives that they were still **unfaithful to his covenant** (78:37). Amazingly, though, God **was compassionate** and **atoned for their iniquity** (78:38).

78:40-55 Asaph recalls the plagues that the Lord brought upon **Egypt** (78:43-51)—all of which the people of the exodus had failed to **remember** (78:42). He explains how he brought them to **safety** and settled them in the promised land, **his holy territory** (78:53-54).

78:56-66 Though he brought them to the land of promise, the people continued to rebel against God. They turned to **carved images** instead of to the true and living God (78:58). Therefore, he gave them over to their enemies (78:61-64). Nevertheless, the Lord would

not completely give up his people. In time, he **beat back** their adversaries (78:65-66).

78:67-72 Ultimately, God would choose **the tribe of Judah** and the house of **David** for the messianic line (78:68, 70; see 2 Sam 7:11-16). Thus, the one who shepherded **sheep** (David) would **shepherd** God's **people** in fulfillment of his kingdom purpose (78:70-71). This shepherding role, however, would ultimately be fulfilled by Jesus Christ, the good shepherd (see John 10).

God's people today need to be students of history. Knowing how God has acted in the past can influence how we respond in the future. Divine sovereignty and human responsibility go hand in hand.

✺ Psalm 79 ✺

79:1-4 Asaph laments over the city of **Jerusalem**. God's **holy temple** had been **invaded** and **desecrated** (79:1). Many of the people had been killed and left unburied, their bodies devoured by scavengers (79:2-3). As a result, God's people were an object of scorn among the nations (79:4).

79:5-9 Asaph calls on the Lord not to continue to be **angry** with his people or to **hold** their sins **against them** (79:5, 8). He asks God to be the defender of **Jacob** (that is, Israel) and to execute his justice against the wicked nations that had **devastated** the land God had given them (79:6-7). He begs God to help them **for the glory of [his] name** (79:9). When you need God's intervention, and have dealt with your own sin, appeal to God's glory. As Scripture shows, it's a trusted way to get God's attention.

79:10-13 Asaph is concerned that the nations are asking, **Where is their God?** (79:10). He wants the Lord to show them that he was right there, present with his people. He thus seeks to motivate God to respond to his cry by pointing to the suffering that his people were enduring (79:11). In the Bible, the number *seven* denotes completeness. Thus, a request that God **pay back sevenfold** means that Asaph wants them to experience complete **reproach** for what they'd done (79:12). Such thorough divine deliverance would result in continual **praise** from his people (79:13).

⇒ Psalm 80 ⇐

80:1-3 Asaph requests that God **restore** his battered people (80:3). After all, he was their **Shepherd** and their King, **enthroned between the cherubim** above the ark of the covenant (80:1-2). He prays that God would **make [his] face shine on them** (80:3)—that is, that he would allow his favor and blessing, which had been blocked because of their sin, to return to them.

80:4-7 Asaph recognizes that God was the one responsible for their **tears** (80:5). And, he had **put [them] at odds with [their] neighbors** (80:6). Thus, Asaph wants to know **how long** the Lord's anger would continue (80:4). In verse 7, he repeats the request of 80:3 that God would return his favor upon them and end their despair.

80:8-13 When God delivered his people from **Egypt**, he transplanted them to the land he had promised (80:8-9). For a time, Israel flourished (80:10-11). But then, God removed their protection so that they were oppressed by enemies; they became like an untended vine whose **fruit** could be devoured by animals (80:12-13).

80:14-19 Asaph pleads with God to care for **this vine** of his, which was a reference to his people Israel (80:14)—even though the vine had been **cut down and burned** as a result of the Lord's discipline (80:16). He asks that God rescue his people through **the man at [his] right hand**, the **son of man** (80:17), a reference to the messianic deliverer. In that day, God's people would **call on** him (80:18). Asaph then concludes with the refrain of 80:3 and 7: **Restore us, LORD, God of Armies; make your face shine on us, so that we may be saved** (80:19).

In times when God is correcting us, let us return to him quickly so that his favor can return quickly to us.

⇒ Psalm 81 ⇐

81:1-5 The psalmist, Asaph, calls on God's people to **sing for joy to [him]** (81:1). He urges fellow believers to come to the **feasts** (81:3) in obedience to God's commands and as a reminder of God's work on their behalf.

81:6-10 In the remainder of the psalm, the Lord speaks to his people. He reminds them of how he'd lifted their **burden** when they suffered under Egyptian bondage (81:6). When he'd **tested** them at **Meribah**, they had flunked (81:7; see Exod 17:1-7). He thus admonished them to **listen to** him and put their false gods away (81:8-9). They needed to remember that he was the one who had rescued them from **Egypt**, and he was the one who could provide for them still, who could **fill** their mouths with good things (81:10) as they came to him with great petitions.

One of the quickest ways to sever fellowship with God is to appeal to false gods in time of need. There is only one true God. Loyalty to him is critical if we are to receive all that he wants us to have.

81:11-16 When his people didn't submit to him, God let them follow their own **stubborn hearts**—a dead-end street (81:11-12). If his people would **follow** him, he promised to **subdue their enemies** and shower them with blessings, represented here by **wheat** and **honey** (81:13-16).

Obedience brings blessing, a reversal of fortune, and supernatural provision (see Exod 17:6).

The same is true today. If we want God to reverse our circumstances, we need to place ourselves in a position of submission to his will and kingdom authority.

⇒ Psalm 82 ⇐

82:1-2 In the divine assembly, which is the assembly of the angels, God **pronounces judgment among the gods** (82:1). In this context, "gods" is a way of referring to human rulers, those who are made in God's image and are charged with the responsibility of mirroring God's character and judgments. But, the particular leaders in view had ruled **unjustly** and favored **the wicked** (82:2). They hadn't represented God's way. The courts had failed to reflect God's concern for justice for the poor (see Deut 24:17; Isa 11:4; Jer 22:16).

82:3-5 Therefore, the Lord exhorts these faithless rulers to **provide** true **justice** for those who need it—**the needy** and **the oppressed** (82:3)—those who can't stand up for themselves. A leader's righteousness is demonstrated when such people are rescued and **the power of the wicked** is overthrown (82:4). Yet, the rulers continue to **wander in darkness**, giving no attention to the Lord or his ways (82:5).

82:6-8 Though these rulers, these **gods** (see commentary on 82:1-2), were **sons of the Most High** (82:6), they were not behaving as sons of God. (This verse was quoted by Jesus when the Jewish religious leaders wanted to stone him for declaring himself to be the Son of God; see John 10:34-38.) The rulers had failed to exercise justice and righteousness on God's behalf. As a result, they would **fall like any other ruler** (82:7). The psalmist concludes by calling the true King to **judge the earth**. He alone can bring justice to **the nations** (82:8).

❧ Psalm 83 ❧

83:1-4 Asaph makes a plea to God **not** to **keep silent** but to take action against his **enemies** (83:1-2). They were concocting **schemes against** God's people, his **treasured ones**, in an attempt to **wipe them** off the map (83:3-4). Asaph could appeal to God for help because of Israel's covenant relationship to him. Their enemies were his enemies. Therefore, the battle was his.

There are two principles here for believers to remember. First, every battle is spiritual at root—even if there are other physical, emotional, financial, or political components involved. Second, when you're involved in a righteous spiritual battle, you should verbally transfer the fight to the Lord's hands. If you are operating under his covenant and kingdom rule, ask him for help according to his covenantal, faithful love.

83:5-8 Asaph identifies those who had made **an alliance against** God and his people. These included Israel's relatives: **Edom** (descendants of Jacob's brother Esau) as well as **Moab** and **Ammon** (descendants of Abraham's nephew **Lot**) (83:6-7).

83:9-12 He prays earnestly that God would **deal with** Israel's present enemies just as he had dealt with their past enemies. Each of those Asaph names had oppressed Israel during the days of the Judges (see Judg 4:1-24; 6:1–8:21). They sought to subdue God's people and take the land he had given them, saying, **Let us seize God's pastures for ourselves** (83:12). This, however, was pure foolishness. Though the Lord at times judged Israel by giving its land to others, the land was never *taken* from him. One may as well try to seize a cub from a mother grizzly.

83:13-18 Asaph implores God to **terrify** their enemies and bring them to **shame** (83:15-17), so that—whether in repentance or in despair—they would **know that [God] alone** is **the Most High over the whole earth** (83:18).

❧ Psalm 84 ❧

84:1-4 The psalmist expresses his longing to be in **the courts** of the Lord's **dwelling place**, his **house** (84:1-2, 4)—references to the temple. Ultimately, his desire was to be in God's presence, which should be the longing of all those who love God. He repeatedly refers to God as **Lord of Armies** (84:1, 3; also 84:8, 12), the all-powerful one who commands hosts of unconquerable angelic forces.

84:5-7 The psalmist affirms that blessings come to those who find their **strength** in God alone (84:5). He recharges their spiritual batteries so that **they go from strength to strength** (84:7). Prioritizing God's presence through his Word is a means of finding spiritual refreshment and vigor.

84:8-10 The psalmist prays for God's favor on his **anointed one**, the king who leads his people (84:9). He then expresses the exceeding joy to be found in communion with God. One **day** with him is better than **a thousand** elsewhere. To **stand** at the entrance of God's **house** is better than to **live in the tents of wicked people** (84:10). In other words, the psalmist would rather be found serving God than serving self. Those who have tasted the goodness of God know this to be true.

84:11-12 The Lord's **favor and honor** are available to **those who live with integrity**. His blessings provide both provision and protection, shining on them like the rays of the **sun** and sheltering them like a **shield** (84:11). Thus, the psalmist looks forward to the "pilgrimage" (84:5) to Jerusalem to gather with God's people at his temple to enjoy his presence (84:1-2, 4, 7, 10).

Today, believers have the privilege of enjoying God's presence through his Holy Spirit who dwells in us, making us God's temple—individually and collectively (see Rom 8:9; 1 Cor 3:16; 6:19; Eph 2:21). His presence enables us to experience his provision and protection in our lives.

⇾ Psalm 85 ⇽

85:1-3 The psalmist remembered God's love and **favor** that he had shown to his people by restoring them to their homeland from their Babylonian captivity (85:1). Such a restoration was possible because God **forgave . . . their sin** and removed his **anger** in response to their repentance (85:2-3).

85:4-7 In light of the favor God had shown them in the past, the psalmist petitions him to **show** his covenant people his **faithful love** and **salvation** once again for their present circumstances (85:7). He begs that God might **revive** them so that they could give him glory and **rejoice in [him]** (85:6). Our prayers ought to be similarly God-centered, asking for God's intervention so that we might give him public praise. The steadfastness of his love allows for the continuous flow of his grace and mercy.

85:8-13 His salvation is very near those **who fear him** (85:9). Deliverance is available to those who take God seriously. Such **faithful ones** (85:8) will experience the fullness of God as he brings **faithful love and truth** together and causes **righteousness and peace** to combine in their lives (85:10). The coupling of these blessings will ultimately be established by the Messiah in his earthly kingdom rule. **Earth** and **heaven** (85:11) will be united when Jesus Christ comes to reign as King.

⇾ Psalm 86 ⇽

86:1-5 David appeals to God for help. He affirms his need for God (**I am poor and needy**), his submission to God (**I am faithful**), and his dependence on God (**your servant . . . trusts in you**) (86:1-2). He is confident of God's character and knows the Lord was **kind and ready to forgive** (86:5). Likewise, in your times of need, deal with any known sin in your life and appeal to God's character.

86:6-10 Again, David calls on God to **hear** his **plea** (86:6). Though many **gods** are worshiped in the world, **there is no one like** the true and living God (86:8). He **alone** can perform supernatural **works** and **wonders** (86:8, 10). He is incomparable. Why would we turn to anyone or anything else?

86:11-13 David asks the Lord to **teach** him so that he could have an **undivided mind** to follow him—rather than trying to pursue two conflicting ways to **live** (86:11). This kind of single-minded devotion to God leads to obedience (**I will live by your truth**) and worship (**I will praise you with all my heart**) (86:11-12).

86:14 King David asks for strength to deal with the **arrogant people** who **have attacked [him]**. What made them arrogant? **They [would] not let [God] guide them.** The prideful person lives life from his own limited, distorted viewpoint. The humble person, by contrast, lives life from God's heavenly, righteous viewpoint.

86:15 God is **compassionate and gracious** ... **slow to anger and abounding in faithful love and truth**. For deliverance, then, David appeals to God's righteous character that he revealed to Moses (see Exod 34:6). This God of compassion, grace, faithful love, and truth was available to Moses. He was available to David. And he's available to you.

86:16-17 David wants **a sign** of God's **goodness**, showing that he would deliver him from his **enemies** (86:17), so that all would know that God had worked on his behalf.

❧ Psalm 87 ❧

87:1-3 The psalmist reflects on the **city of God** ... **glorious** Jerusalem, which the Lord loved and where he dwelt in his temple (87:3). This was where God manifested his glory on earth, and it is where Christ will manifest his glory when he returns to set up his millennial kingdom.

87:4-6 When Christ returns to rule on earth from Jerusalem, people from all the nations will come to worship him—including those who were previously enemies of God and his people: **Rahab** (that is, Egypt), **Babylon, Philistia, Tyre, and Cush** (87:4). **Zion** will be the mother city of the earth, full of new citizens who will come to dwell there (87:5-6).

87:7 Celebration, typified by **singers and dancers**, will characterize the Messiah's kingdom rule from Jerusalem. The testimony of God's people in that day will be, **My whole source of joy is in you**. Where else could joy be found?

❧ Psalm 88 ❧

The heading of the psalm indicates that it was composed by **Heman the Ezrahite**.

88:1-9 The psalmist desired divine aid in the midst of his affliction; therefore, he cries to the Lord **day and night** so that his **prayer** might enter his **presence** (88:1-2). His **troubles** were so intense that he felt he was about to go to **Sheol**, the place of the dead (88:3). In a sense, he feels that he was already **lying in the grave**, forsaken by God (88:5). The source of his despair was God's **wrath**, which **overwhelmed** him like violent **waves** crashing on a shore (88:7). Even his **friends** found him **repulsive** and kept their distance from him (88:8). Nevertheless, he would not cease **crying** out to God **all day long** (88:9).

88:10-12 Heman reasons that if God let him die, he couldn't **praise** him for his **faithful love** and **wonders** (88:11-12). He wants God's deliverance so that he could declare his glory on this side of the grave.

88:13-18 Again, he laments his affliction and the inaction of God to answer his prayers (88:13-14). Again, he points to his suffering under the **wrath** of God (88:16). Again, he despairs that loved ones avoided him (88:18). Hopelessness surrounds him. **Darkness is [his] only friend** (88:18). Yet, in spite of his emotional turmoil, he continued to pray.

Sometimes, we must pray through affliction and uncertainty. When God appears unresponsive and our feelings lead us to despair, our faith in God's character and past actions must push us forward.

❧ Psalm 89 ❧

This psalm was written by **Ethan the Ezrahite**, whose great wisdom was compared to that of Solomon (see 1 Kgs 4:30-31).

89:1-4 The psalmist celebrates God's **faithful love** and **faithfulness** (89:1-2), especially as it had been demonstrated in his **covenant** with **David** (89:3). The Lord promised David an eternal kingdom: He would have an **offspring forever** sitting on his **throne** (89:4; see 2 Sam 11-16).

This was not fulfilled by an eternal succession of Davidic kings, but by one Davidic King who lives forever, the resurrected Lord Jesus Christ (see 2 Sam 7:1-19; Acts 2:29-36). He will reign from David's throne in Jerusalem in his millennial kingdom (see Rev 20:4). Though the sons of David would prove unfaithful in their role as kings, this Son of David will never fail.

89:5-14 Ethan praises the unrivaled God. No one **can compare** to him; no one **is like** him (89:6). He is **feared** among the angelic council (89:7). How much more should he be feared by humanity? He scatters his **enemies** by his strength (89:8-10) and sovereignly rules over his creation (89:11-12). He alone is God, known for his **righteousness and justice**, for his **faithful love and truth** (89:14). Let all creation praise him!

89:15-18 Next, Ethan the Ezrahite personalizes his praise. He knows from experience that the Lord is to be adored by those who **walk in the light from [his] face** (89:15)—that is, by those who live in intimate fellowship with him. They **rejoice** in him and enjoy the blessing of having God as their **shield** (89:16, 18).

89:19-29 He returns to praising God for his gracious choosing and anointing of **David** to be the king of Israel (89:19-20). His **covenant with** David would be kept **forever** through his seed, the Messiah (89:28-29). God will give this King his strength, **faithfulness**, and **power** (89:21, 24-25). The Messiah's kingdom will be universal and unconquerable.

89:30-37 God promised to discipline David's **sons** who disobeyed him (89:30-32). Nevertheless, he would not **violate** his **covenant** because he would never **betray** his own

faithfulness (89:33-34). He had **sworn to David** and would **not lie** (89:35). In spite of the failure of the Davidic kings, the Lord assured David that **his offspring [would] continue forever** (89:36). Ultimately, his promises would be kept through Jesus Christ. The sinfulness of humanity, then, can't prevent God from accomplishing his sovereign goals.

89:38-45 The reason the psalmist is anxious to affirm God's faithfulness to his unconditional covenant promise is because it seemed that God had cast off the Davidic line. One after another of David's sons had been unfaithful—until finally God allowed Jerusalem to be overrun and David's **throne** to be overthrown, too (89:38-40, 44). The sins of the kings and the people had resulted in **shame** (89:45). Had God's judgment trumped his promises?

89:46-52 In light of this destruction, the psalmist asks **how long** his judgment would continue (89:46). How long would God hide his favor from his people? He pleads with God not to forget his covenant with **David** (89:49). He reminds the Lord of how his enemies had **ridiculed** him, his **anointed** one, and his people (89:50-51). He insists that God's reputation is at stake and again asks God to **remember** (89:50)—a prayer that is ultimately answered in the coming of Christ.

The psalmist concludes, **Blessed be the Lord forever** (89:52). Thus ends the third book of Psalms.

IV. BOOK IV (PSALMS 90–106)

❧ Psalm 90 ❧

Because this psalm was authored by **Moses**, it is the oldest of all the psalms.

90:1-6 God alone is a place of divine shelter and protection for all those who take **refuge** in him (90:1) because he alone is eternal. Moses compares the glory of the infinite God to the transitory existence of finite humanity (90:2-3). With God, the passing of **a thousand years** is like the passing of a day (90:4).

Human beings, on the other hand, are like **grass** that **withers** (90:5-6). Our time is brief; death comes for all.

90:7-12 Moses recognizes that the transitory nature of humanity's existence is due to sin. Death is God's righteous judgment against man's rebellion (see Gen 3:22-24; Rom 6:23). Whether **sins** are committed in public or in **secret**, all are visible to him and incur his **wrath** (90:7-9). Sin and death have limited the lifespan of human beings; our lives **pass quickly** (90:10). In light of this reality, Moses asks God, **Teach us to number our days carefully so that we may develop wisdom** (90:12).

Let us implore God with this same prayer. Ask the Lord to make the brevity of life sink in to your soul, so that you are convicted to make godly choices during your short stay on earth. Life is like a coin. You can spend it any way you wish, but you can only spend it once.

90:13-15 Moses pleads with God to have **compassion on** his people, showing them his **faithful love** so that they might have **joy** and not sorrow (90:13-14). He wants their years of **adversity** to be matched by years of rejoicing (90:15). He hopes that God's blessings would not be less than his judgment.

90:16-17 Moses concludes with a prayer for God's **favor** on his people (90:17). The brevity of life and the divine anger against sin that Moses considered ought to drive us to God, not away from him. A meaningful life in which God [**establishes**] **the work of our hands** (90:17) comes through wisdom, and wisdom comes from submitting all we are to God for the brief time he gives us.

❧ Psalm 91 ❧

91:1-4 The psalmist expresses the great confidence he has in the security that comes from dwelling **in the shadow of the Almighty**. With him, there is abiding **protection** (91:1). Just like a bird takes refuge under the **wings** of its parent, the believer who lives under the **cover** of God's covenant finds safety (91:4).

91:5-8 God covers his own with his faithfulness 24/7, thus providing them with a shield of protection. Knowledge of this should produce confident trust in God, in spite of the threats and attacks of the wicked (91:5). Regardless of the dangers around them, those who experience the covering that God provides will be cared for and, ultimately, will see **the punishment of the wicked** (91:7-8).

91:9-13 The one who makes God his **refuge** will not experience **harm** because the Lord

has commissioned **his angels** to watch over him (91:9-11). This tells us that believers have angels divinely assigned to protect and strengthen them from spiritual dangers— which are depicted here as wild beasts (91:13). Only in eternity will we know how many dangers, toils, and snares angels have protected us from (see Heb 1:14).

When he tempted Jesus in the wilderness, the devil appealed to 91:11-12, urging Jesus to throw himself from the temple (see Matt 4:5-6) and demonstrating how Scripture can be twisted for selfish purposes. The psalmist wants God's people to understand how he cares for them—not how they can manipulate God to do their bidding.

91:14-16 The psalmist communicates God's promise to **deliver** and **protect** those who set their hearts on him (91:14). Indeed, the believer whose heart is devoted and submitted to the Lord in this way can count on God to **rescue him** and **satisfy him with** the full length of days ordained for him (91:15-16).

❧ Psalm 92 ❧

92:1-4 The psalmist expresses how **good** it is to publicly thank and **praise** the Lord for his **love** and **faithfulness** to his people (92:1-2). **The works** of God in his life cause him to **rejoice** (92:4). The reason there is so little genuine worship among God's people today is because we don't keep track of and call to mind all of God's past deeds in our lives. The blessings of God should inspire his people to praise him for who he is, thank him for what he has done, and trust him for what he will do.

92:5-15 This psalm gives praise to the eternal perspective of the righteous as opposed to the short-lived perspective of **the wicked** who, **like grass**, flourish momentarily and then **perish** (92:5-9). The psalmist knew that, in contrast to this fate, God lifts him up above his **enemies** (92:11). God causes **the righteous** to **thrive** even in their **old age** (92:12-14). As a result, they **declare** the greatness of God (92:15). The goodness of God gives rise to the adoration of God.

ᵜ Psalm 93 ᵜ

93:1-2 The LORD reigns! The psalmist acknowledges that God is a majestic King. And the **strength** of this divine Ruler is seen in the creation that he made and sustains. **The world is firmly established** (93:1). God demonstrated his sovereign control when he brought it into being. Yet, while his **throne** was **established from the beginning**, God himself is **from eternity** (93:2).

93:3-4 The grandeur of creation testifies to the greatness of God. This is seen in the **pounding waves** and **mighty breakers of the sea.** They exist by his will and operate under his control.

93:5 The psalmist concludes with the assurance that God's **testimonies are completely reliable.** His Word is without fault and cannot fail. His authoritative Word reflects his authoritative rule. Because God is sovereign and in a class by himself, whatever he says should be received with delight and obeyed without delay.

ᵜ Psalm 94 ᵜ

94:1-3 The psalmist calls for God—the divine **Judge of the earth**—to unleash his **vengeance** so that he might end the **proud** celebrations of **the wicked** (94:1-3). He wonders **how long** it would be before God sets all things right (94:3). Observe that the concerns of God's people today are the same as the concerns of God's people in the past.

94:4-7 The evil activity of the wicked justifies divine judgment. **Arrogant words** flow from their mouths (94:4); **they oppress** God's **people** (94:5); **the widow** and **the fatherless** receive injustice from their hands (94:6). They commit such heinous deeds because they are convinced that God **doesn't see** or **pay attention** (94:7). They couldn't be more wrong.

94:8-11 The psalmist challenges the wicked to reconsider their faulty thinking. Their thoughts were **stupid** (94:8). God, the one who created **the eye**, could certainly **see** what they were up to (94:9). His all-inclusive knowledge even includes **the thoughts of mankind** (94:11).

94:12-15 The writer finds consolation in reminding himself that the Lord uses **the wicked** as a chastening rod. In other words, evildoers do not have free reign, but God puts them to work to **discipline** his own and accomplish his purposes for them (94:12-13). He will not **abandon** his **people** or allow the wicked to escape **justice** (94:13-15).

Believers today can also find comfort in knowing that our God uses the wicked to fulfill his plans. If we receive his discipline, we will grow spiritually and become more faithful followers of the living God.

94:16-19 God was his only comfort, for God alone could **stand** on his behalf **against evildoers** (94:16). Therefore, when **cares** overwhelmed him to the point that he was ready to throw in the towel, he put his full trust in God, whose **comfort** brought him **joy** (94:18-19). When you are dominated by worry, amp up your confidence in God so that he can relieve the pressure and anxiety you're experiencing.

94:20-23 Though some may trust in **a corrupt throne** that brings harm to **the innocent**, the psalmist would look nowhere else for **protection** but to the Lord (94:20-22). Evil rulers do not realize that their days are limited, but **God will pay them back for their sins** (94:23).

Maintain a divine perspective on life. Take the long view of things. The judgment of God will come in time. Count on him.

ᵜ Psalm 95 ᵜ

95:1-5 Because God is **the rock of our salvation**, believers ought to **shout joyfully** to him corporately (95:1). Our praise is rooted in God's power to save us. He alone is **a great King above all gods** because he is the Creator of all things—**the mountain**

peaks . . . the sea . . . the dry land (95:3-5). When people in the ancient world came into the presence of kings to whom they were subjected, they would bring gifts. When we enter our King's presence, the gift we bring is thanksgiving (95:2) for who he is, what he has done, and what we are trusting him to do.

95:6-7a The psalmist calls God's people to demonstrate their submission to him by bowing before him (95:6), a posture symbolizing the recognition of his sovereignty. Like sheep depend on their shepherd to protect and provide for them, so we, as the people of [God's] pasture, look to him for every good thing we need (95:7a).

95:7b-11 He then urges his readers to listen and obey the Lord's voice (95:7b). He pleads with them not to harden [their] hearts (that is, to willfully reject God), and he reaches into the past to give them an example of what such rejection looks like. At Meribah ("Quarreling") and Massah ("Testing"), Israel complained to God after the exodus, demanding water (95:8; see Exod 17:1-7). But, this was not the end of their rebellion. They continued to test God and eventually refused to enter the promised land (95:9). Therefore, God gave them their wish, swearing, They will not enter my rest (95:11)—that is, they would not experience the blessings that come through a right relationship with him. As a result, that generation would spend forty years in the wilderness and die there (95:10), and their children entered the land instead (see Num 14:11-38).

The author of Hebrews quotes Psalm 95 to warn believers not to miss out on God's "rest"—his blessings and favor—by following a path of unbelief and disobedience (see Heb 4:7-13).

ᴈ Psalm 96 ᴕ

96:1-3 The psalmist exhorts the whole earth to praise the Lord with a fresh, new song (96:1). Such singing should be accompanied by proclamations of his salvation and glorious deeds from days gone by

(96:2). Such worship recognizes the glory that is due to God alone and which should be acknowledged among all peoples of the earth (96:3).

96:4-6 Because only the LORD is God, only he should be praised and feared (96:4). So-called gods are mere idols conjured up by human imagination (96:5). While God revealed his splendor and majesty . . . strength and beauty in his sanctuary—his temple in Jerusalem (96:6)—false gods reveal nothing but their inadequacy.

96:7-9 Again *all* the earth, the families of the peoples, are exhorted to worship the Lord (96:7; see 96:1). This is a reminder that God is not only the God of Israel, but also the God of the Gentiles. He calls the whole earth to tremble before him (96:9). One day, every person will bow to Jesus Christ and confess that he is Lord to the glory of God (see Phil 2:10-11).

96:10-13 God's people are to declare throughout the nations that the LORD reigns (96:10). One day, this glorious truth *will* be universally acknowledged when our Messiah, the Lord Jesus, manifests his glory in his worldwide reign. In those days, all of creation will rejoice and shout for joy (96:11-12). When Christ establishes his kingdom, all will be made right. He is coming to judge the earth . . . with righteousness (96:13).

Just as the psalmist lived in expectation of the coming of the King, so believers today should do the same. May his return motivate our conduct, and may we live in expectation of his intervention in our lives.

ᴈ Psalm 97 ᴕ

97:1 The psalmist's vision for God's rule—like God's own vision—includes all the earth (not merely Israel). All people should rejoice over the reality of God's kingdom rule.

97:2-5 The Lord's awe-inspiring presence is described in vivid imagery. He is surrounded by clouds and total darkness (97:2). He sends **fire** and **lightning** to accomplish his deeds (97:3-4). Creation itself reacts to **the presence of the LORD**, as **mountains melt like wax** before him (97:5). Consider, then, what destruction awaits those who oppose him.

97:6-9 When the Lord returns to rule the earth, **the heavens** will **proclaim his righteousness** and **all the peoples will see his glory** (97:6). There will be no hiding it, nor will there be any hiding from it. Idolaters **will be put to shame** as they are confronted with the reality that the images in which they placed their trust are worthless (97:7). Therefore, God's people should **rejoice** in this knowledge of a certain future. His coming **judgments** give us confidence that the true God is **exalted above all the gods** (97:8-9).

97:10-12 In light of God's sovereign rule and judgment of the wicked, those **who love** him must **hate evil** and obey him. God will position them to experience his delivering power on their behalf as **he rescues them from the power of the wicked** (97:10). Such knowledge causes **light** to dawn in the heart of the **righteous** so that they can see things from God's perspective (97:11).

◈ Psalm 98 ◈

98:1-3 This psalm calls for praise concerning the victorious **wonders** that God has **performed**. It requires **a new song** because there are always fresh reasons to worship God (98:1). What he has done has not been carried out in secret but **in the sight of the nations** (98:2). **All the ends of the earth have seen** God's **faithfulness to the house of Israel** (98:3). In spite of the opposition of their enemies, Israel was repeatedly delivered from obliteration, demonstrating that God was looking after his people.

98:4-8 Having seen God's marvelous deeds, everyone on the planet should give praise to God (98:4). In fact, creation itself is invited to **shout . . . for joy** over the glory of its Creator (98:7-8).

98:9 Now is the time to worship the Lord and receive him as King. For when he comes, he will come **to judge the earth**. Therefore, all peoples are encouraged not to delay. When the Messiah comes to rule on earth with his rod of iron in his kingdom, it will be too late to join him. "Now is the acceptable time; now is the day of salvation!" (2 Cor 6:2).

◈ Psalm 99 ◈

99:1-3 The psalmist praises God, the King who **reigns** (99:1). **He is holy**—that is, unique, separate, and **awe-inspiring** (99:3). He rules from **Zion** where **he is enthroned between the cherubim** above the ark of the covenant (99:1-2). Yet, though his throne is in his temple in Jerusalem, he is not merely the King over Israel. Rather, **he is exalted above all peoples** (99:2).

99:4-5 Because the Lord reigns with **justice** and **righteousness**, all humanity ought to **bow in worship at his footstool**, submitting to his kingdom authority (see Isa 66:1; Matt 5:35). This posture of humility and acknowledgement of his regal authority should be matched by an inward bowing of the heart.

99:6-9 The psalmist recalls God's deeds among Israel's forefathers: **Moses . . . Aaron**, and **Samuel**, ordinary men with an extraordinary God. **They called to the LORD, and he answered** their prayers (99:6). When God communicated to them, **they kept his decrees** (99:7). When God's people sinned, these men prayed, and God forgave them (99:8). Thus, God is to be praised for raising up these men to mediate for his people. And he is to be praised for not giving his people what their sins deserved. Though he **is holy** and **an avenger** of sin (98:8-9), he shows mercy.

For believers today, God has provided the perfect mediator (see 1 Tim 2:5) and the ultimate means to forgive sins. Through Jesus Christ and his atoning death on the cross, God exalts both his holiness and his mercy. The only appropriate response is to **exalt** and **worship** him (99:9).

❧ Psalm 100 ❦

100:1 Let the whole earth shout triumphantly to God! In the Bible, worship is not some sedate event. People are to engage in it with a sense of excitement. You can't worship the Lord without your emotions. It is no mere intellectual exercise. Moreover, worship is for "the whole earth." All peoples are invited to join the celebration. No one is left out. Worship is all that we are responding to all that he is. It is the recognition of God for who he is, what he has done, and what we are trusting him to do.

100:2 The emphasis on emotions continues: **Serve the LORD with gladness.** The sovereign God of the universe has invited you into his presence to serve him. How could anyone receive such a remarkable invitation with disinterest? **Come before him with joyful songs** is a reminder that no one would approach a human king, president, or other ruler with an attitude of indifference. When we come before God, then, we shouldn't slouch, but sing with gusto.

100:3 The LORD is God is a translation of the Hebrew phrase, "Yahweh is Elohim." *Yahweh* is the name of God revealed in his covenant relationship with his people. *Elohim* speaks of power; he is the one who created the heavens and the earth. Thus, the powerful God wants a relationship with you and should be given recognition. **He made us,** after all, and we are his **sheep.** He is our Creator and Sustainer. He is the source of everything we need.

100:4 The people in the psalmist's day were commanded to **enter his gates** and **courts.** Though we do not go to a temple today, we are similarly commanded to enter into his presence. What is the password for entrance? **Thanksgiving** and **praise.** No matter what your circumstances, **give thanks to him and bless his name** because there's always a reason to thank God. And doing so will transform you.

100:5 God **is good** and **faithful.** But, to experience his goodness and **faithfulness,** you

must "taste and see that the LORD is good" (Ps 34:8). So, worship him, trust him, and obey him. You won't be disappointed.

❧ Psalm 101 ❦

101:1-5 In light of God's **faithful love** and his demonstrated **justice** (101:1), King David devotes himself to the Lord through the use of his repeated vow **I will.** He pledges to worship God (101:1), to live with **integrity** (101:2), to avoid sin and **evil** (101:3-4), and to enforce justice under his rule (101:5).

David understood that the quality of his character and leadership had a direct influence on the nation. He took his role as king seriously. He wanted to honor God and bless the people under his reign with justice and righteousness. Whether in the church or in society, leadership based on such principles is a crucial factor in the well-being of those being governed and led.

101:6-8 King David would only have people serving in his administration who displayed **faithful** character and a commitment to God (101:6). Those known for deceit and **lies** would be shown the door (101:7). The destruction of **the wicked** would be a daily priority for him (101:8). In these ways, he would invite God's blessings on himself and on his people.

❧ Psalm 102 ❦

102:1-7 In a great ordeal of affliction, this psalmist cries to God **for help,** begging him to **listen** and **answer** (102:1-2). He chronicles the depth of his despair as he experiences the full range of physical, emotional, and spiritual grief (102:3-5). He is overwhelmed by his loneliness and isolation (102:6-7).

When you are suffering and desperate for God's intervention, let these biblical laments guide you in your prayers. When you don't know what to say, use the inspired words of this psalm.

102:8-11 He was enduring the taunts of his **enemies** and existing in a constant state of mourning (102:8-9). **Ashes** were his food and **tears** were his drink (102:9). Yet, all of this was because he was experiencing the **wrath** of God, by whom he felt abandoned (102:10). His life was wasting away (102:11). Jerusalem had fallen to the Babylonians and lay in ruins. The psalmist and all of God's people were dealing with the consequences of idolatry.

102:12-17 In the midst of his despair, this man expresses his confidence in the reign of God (**you . . . are enthroned forever**), hope in the covenant faithfulness of God (**you will . . . have compassion on Zion**), and trust in the future victory of God (**the nations will fear the name**) (102:12-13, 15). Therefore, the psalmist continues to pray, knowing that the Lord would **pay attention to the prayer of the destitute** (102:17).

102:18-22 The psalmist knows that he wasn't writing these words merely for himself—or even for his contemporaries. He was writing **for a later generation**, for **a people** not yet born who would **praise the LORD** (102:18). Though in the psalmist's day there was sorrow, in the future there would be rejoicing. Not only would the Lord **set free those condemned to die** among his people, but also **peoples and kingdoms** would assemble **to serve** him (102:20-22).

Such worldwide acknowledgement of God's kingdom will be completely fulfilled during the Messiah's millennial kingdom rule. At that time, Jerusalem will be fully restored, and the entire world will recognize the greatness and glory of the Lord Jesus Christ.

102:23-28 In his day, however, the psalmist feels weak and pleads with God for mercy (102:23-24). Though he knew that his own days were transitory, he acknowledged that God is eternal (102:24). Indeed, the Lord existed before creation, and he will outlast it (102:25-26). God **will never end** (102:26-27).

The author of Hebrews quotes 102:25-27 and applies the verses to Jesus Christ (see Heb 1:10-12). Sharing in the divine nature of God the Father, God the Son is likewise everlasting: "Jesus Christ is the same yesterday, today, and forever" (Heb 13:8). And, because God is everlasting, the psalmist knows that he will preserve his **children**.

Thus, believers have a model prayer of suffering and hope, of despair and confidence. Come to God with your complaint, your repentance, your grief, and your hope. He is big enough to deal with them all.

⇲ Psalm 103 ⇱

103:1-2 With **all that is within [him]**, David exhorts his **soul** to **bless the LORD** (103:1). And then he does so again (103:2). He wants to express praise and thanksgiving to God for all he had done—both for David personally and for his people corporately. Such **benefits** from God must not be forgotten or taken for granted (103:2).

103:3-5 The benefits God provides that David highlights include spiritual and physical blessings such as forgiving **iniquity**, healing **diseases**, and demonstrations of his **faithful love and compassion** (103:3-4). For those who are weary, he provides **renewed** vitality (103:5). There are countless reasons to praise God and express our gratitude to him. But, because sinful humans are prone to forget to do so, we must bring the benefits of God continually to our minds.

103:6-10 David praises God's **acts of righteousness and justice** on behalf of the **oppressed** (103:6). He recalls how he'd acted through **Moses** among **the people of Israel** when he rescued them from bondage in Egypt (103:7). David even describes God's character just as God himself had revealed it to Moses: **He is compassionate and gracious, slow to anger and abounding in faithful love** (103:8; see Exod 34:6). Though the Lord had judged the people of Israel for their sins, he had not dealt with them as their sins deserved. They deserved nothing but his wrath, but he extended mercy in the midst of judgment (103:9-10). God yearns for his wayward children to return to him.

103:11-13 How great is God's **faithful love** toward those who take him seriously? It's **as high as the heavens are above the earth** (103:11)—that is, beyond our comprehension. How far does he remove his people's **transgressions** from them? **As far as the east is from the west** (103:12)— that is, forgiven sins are never to be seen again. If this was true when Israel offered God-ordained animal sacrifices that could not, in an ultimate sense, take away sin (see Heb 10:4, 11), how much more is it true of the once-for-all atoning sacrifice of Jesus Christ (see Heb 10:14-18)? David illustrates God's kindness toward those who fear him by picturing **a father** having **compassion on his children** (103:13). Such is how the Lord feels toward those who come to him in repentance and faith.

103:14-18 David underscores the ongoing benefits of God's loyal love for his people by highlighting the weak and temporary nature of man's life. As children of Adam, we are **made of . . . dust** (103:14; see Gen 2:7). The **days** of our lives are like those of **a flower** that blooms for a moment and then **vanishes** (103:15-16). By contrast, **the LORD's faithful love is from eternity to eternity** for those **who fear him**—those **who remember to observe his precepts** (103:17-18).

103:19-22 David concludes by acknowledging God as the sovereign King who **rules over all** and by inviting all creation—heaven and earth—to **bless** him (103:19-20). This review of God's faithfulness toward his people causes David to erupt like a volcano with praise. May the same be true of all believers. Let us take God seriously and declare his praises.

➢ Psalm 104 ☙

104:1-9 The psalmist exhorts himself to **bless** God for his **majesty and splendor** (104:1). Here, the elements of nature are described as the Lord's clothing, **his palace,** and **his chariot** (104:2-3). He is the all-powerful Creator, and the whole universe exists to serve his purposes. Whatever he builds cannot topple; **the earth** that he **established** cannot **be shaken** (104:5). Though his flood **water** once **covered** the earth, he restored **the mountains** and **valleys** to their rightful prominence (104:6-8). The water **will never cover the earth again** (104:9).

104:10-18 God is the one who filled the earth with everything necessary to sustain life. He provides food and drink for animals and humans alike (104:10-15). The earth is suitable for all kinds of life because God made it so.

104:19-23 Yet, his sovereignty is not limited to the earth but extends to the heavens. He created **the moon** and **the sun** (104:19) so that they would establish day and night, seasons and years, providing times and rhythms for **man** (104:23) and beast to function within.

104:24-30 The psalmist praises God for the greatness of his creation, which reveals his unsurpassed **wisdom** (104:24). He designed fabulous **creatures**—both **large and small**—that depend on his provision (104:25). He is sovereign over their lives and deaths (104:29-30).

104:31-35 Having considered all God's marvelous **works,** the psalmist breaks forth in exaltation of God's **glory** (104:31). He sings God's praises and prays that this **meditation** would **be pleasing to him** (104:34). He concludes with a wish that **sinners** would **vanish from the earth** (104:35). Whether through the judgment of God or through faith in Jesus Christ, one day this will be so.

➢ Psalm 105 ☙

105:1-11 The psalmist calls on God's people to **praise** and give **thanks** to him for his **wondrous works** (105:1-2, 5). In light of what he has done, his people should **seek his face always** (105:4). The psalmist recalls the faithfulness of God through his **covenant** with **Abraham . . . Isaac,** and **Jacob** to deliver them **the land of Canaan** as an inheritance (105:8-11).

105:12-41 He traces the history of Israel from the days of **Joseph** (105:17) through the exodus out of **Egypt** (105:37-38). The Lord had made them a great nation by his providential and powerful delivering hand. Israel's story is one that involved the constant supernatural provision and protection of God.

105:42-45 The Lord was faithful to **his holy promise to Abraham** (105:42). And, although Israel was hindered by enemies and by their own sinful rebellion, God gave them the land he had promised—**the lands of the nations** (105:44). What was the reason for all of the Lord's remarkable deeds? That his people **might keep his statutes and obey his instructions** (105:45).

Similarly, God saves us so that we will love and obey him. We are not delivered from sin and death so that we can go our own way. We are rescued for reverence; we are saved to serve.

⇗ Psalm 106 ⇖

106:1-5 The psalmist exhorts God's people to thank God because his **faithful love** is everlasting (106:1). Thus, it's impossible to **praise** him enough and truly give him his **due** (106:1-2). Because of God's character, those who (like him) practice **justice** and **righteousness** are **happy** or blessed (106:3). The psalmist asks God to **remember** and **show favor to** him so that he could benefit from the kindness he shows to the **nation** (106:4-5).

106:6-12 The psalmist acknowledges that Israel had **sinned** in his day as the nation's ancestors had (106:6). Their forefathers **rebelled** against the Lord (106:7). **Yet he saved them for his name's sake** (106:8). In spite of their lack of faith, he delivered them through **the Red Sea** from their **adversary**

(106:9-10). As a result, **they believed his promises and sang his praise** (106:12).

106:13-33 But, their belief only lasted a little while. **They soon forgot his works** (106:13). They **tested God** on numerous occasions, and he punished them severely (106:14-20). He gave them what they wanted, but their selfish cravings ended in sickness (106:15). If not for the intercessory prayer of **Moses**, God **would have destroyed them** for their idolatry (106:23; see Exod 32). Yet, their rebellion continued. Eventually, they refused to enter the promised **land** that he had prepared for them (106:24-25). So, he sentenced them to die in the **desert** (106:26). In spite of all this, they did not repent but turned to idols and even caused Moses to sin (106:28-33).

106:34-46 When their descendants entered the promised land, they did not **destroy** all of their enemies as God had **commanded** (106:34). Instead, they **served** the **idols** of the nations, committing horrific acts, including child sacrifice (106:36-38). Therefore, the Lord let their enemies oppress them (106:41-42). Even though he **rescued them many times**, they refused to learn but continued **to rebel** (106:43). The only thing that prevented Israel from being completely wiped out was **the abundance of [God's] faithful love** (106:45).

106:47-48 The psalmist concludes by praying that God would again **save** his people. Though they had disobeyed like their ancestors, he pleads with God to rescue them so that they might **rejoice in [his] praise** (106:47). Book IV of the Psalms thus concludes.

V. BOOK V (PSALMS 107-150)

⇗ Psalm 107 ⇖

107:1-3 This psalm exhorts God's people to **give thanks** to him for his gracious act of redeeming his people from Babylonian exile and gathering them back in the land. That re-gathering was only partial, however. It will be permanently fulfilled in Messiah's millennial kingdom reign.

107:4-9 The psalmist recalls how God cared for his people in the **wilderness** when they cried out to him (107:4-6). He **rescued them** and **led them** (107:6-7). Thus, the psalmist calls the people of God to thank him **for his faithful love**—the love he expresses toward those in covenant with him (107:8). Such knowledge should cause God's people today to praise him and look to him for deliverance in their own times of trouble.

107:10-16 Next, the psalmist recalls the Babylonian captivity when God's people were carried off to **darkness** and **hard labor** as a result of their rebellion (107:10-12). Yet, in their desperation, when **they cried out to** God, he rescued them from their **gloom** and **chains** (107:13-14). Again, the psalmist urges the people to thank God **for his faithful love** (107:15).

107:17-22 They **suffered** because of their foolish rebellion (107:17). They refused to obey God and **came near** to **death** (107:18). As before, though, he delivered them from **their distress** when they called on him (107:19). The psalmist again offers his repeated refrain: **Let them give thanks to the Lord for his faithful love and his wondrous works for all humanity** (107:21). Clearly, the psalmist has no interest in declaring the virtue of rebellious sinners, but rather in proclaiming the grace and mercy of the covenant-keeping God.

107:23-32 The psalmist continues with praise to God for his sovereign rule over nature. When those on **ships** encountered the ferocity of **stormy wind** and **waves**, they **cried out** to him, and **he stilled the storm** (107:23-29) and took them where they needed to go. What should people do in light of such glorious deeds? By now, the reader of the psalm knows that they should **give thanks** to God **for his faithful love** and **exalt him** (107:31-32). When God delivers us from the overwhelming circumstances of life, we should respond with great praise.

107:33-43 The Lord's power over creation results in **wasteland** becoming **fruitful** (107:34). **Thirsty ground** is satisfied so that **hungry** people can be satisfied (107:33, 36). When his people are oppressed, God **pours contempt on** their oppressors, cares for **the needy**, and ends **injustice** (107:39-42). Whether the opposition is nature or humanity, nothing stands in the way of the sovereign God. Therefore, the **wise** should **pay attention**. Nothing is more valuable in life that the Lord's **faithful love** (107:43). Nothing is wiser than aligning yourself with it.

⮩ Psalm 108 ⮨

108:1-6 David expresses his confidence in God, praising him for his **faithful love** and **faithfulness** (108:1-4). He desires to see God **exalted** and to see him **save** his people (108:5-6). Thus, he worships God for what he has done in the past and for what he hopes he would do in the future.

108:7-13 God answers, declaring his ownership of the territories of Israel (108:7-8) and his power over Israel's enemies (108:9). Yet, David knew that he needed leadership and help. Unless the Lord accompanied David's armies, there was no hope; **human help is worthless** (108:11-12). Without God, we are impotent to achieve anything. **With God we will perform valiantly** (108:13).

⮩ Psalm 109 ⮨

109:1-5 David pleads with God to act (109:1). He is under **attack** by **wicked** people **without cause**; though he has demonstrated **love** toward them, they lie and **accuse** him (109:2-4). **They repay [him] evil for good** (109:5). Yet, though he could have given up in despair, he vows that he would **continue to pray** in spite of his pain (109:4).

109:6-15 David requests divine retribution against the one who unjustly persecutes him. He does not seek vengeance himself, but rather calls for divine vengeance. He trusts in the one who declares, "Vengeance belongs to me; I will repay" (Deut 32:35). He asks that God would ignore the **prayer** of this **wicked person** (109:6-7), take him away from his family (109:9), confiscate his property (109:11), and grant him no **descendants** (109:13).

109:16-20 David did not ask God to do this merely for his own sake, but because the wicked man lived and acted contrary to God's righteous character. He did not love **kindness** but persecuted **the needy** (109:16). He **loved cursing** and hated blessing (109:17). Therefore, he prayed God would bring the man's **cursing** upon himself (109:18-19).

109:21-29 David appeals to God's **faithful love** and asks him to **deal kindly** with him and **help** him (109:21, 26). He is **suffering, wounded . . . weak**, and **an object of ridicule** (109:22-25). In spite of that, he is confident that God could overturn the actions of the wicked. Though people **curse**, God can **bless** (109:28). And David wants his enemies to know that his deliverance is from the **hand** of God, so that he would receive the glory (109:27).

109:30-31 David concludes with public thanks and **praise** to the Lord (109:30). He is confident of God's character; therefore, he anticipates God's intervention. The God who helps **the needy** (109:31) would help David in time of need—and he will do the same for us.

⇾ Psalm 110 ⥢

110:1 David describes a conversation that he was permitted to hear. **The LORD** (Yahweh) spoke to David's **Lord**—that is, to the Messiah. Thus, David overhears God the Father speaking to God the Son, telling him, **Sit at my right hand until I make your enemies your footstool**. To sit at the right hand of a king was a position of privilege and authority. The Father vows to put all of the Son's enemies under his feet. This is an indicator that the promise spoken in the beginning, in which the seed of the woman would vanquish the serpent—"he will strike your head"—will be fulfilled (see Gen 3:15).

Jesus himself claimed that this verse spoke of the Messiah and proved that the Messiah was David's Lord, not merely his descendant (see Matt 22:41-46). The New Testament authors clearly see this verse fulfilled in Jesus, applying it to him numerous times (e.g., Acts 2:34-35; 1 Cor 15:25; Eph 1:20; Heb 1:13). Upon his resurrection and ascension, the Son took his seat at the right hand of God the Father.

110:2-3 God vows to grant his Messiah to **rule over** his **enemies** in his millennial kingdom (110:2). The Messiah's **people will** join him in **battle** against the wicked (110:3), and these believers will share in his righteous rule.

110:4 Not only would the Messiah be a mighty King, but God the Father also vows that the Messiah would be **a priest . . . according to the pattern of Melchizedek**. Just as Melchizedek was both a king and a priest (see Gen 14:18), so the Messiah would occupy both offices.

Moreover, Melchizedek blessed Abraham, and Abraham paid a tithe to Melchizedek (see Gen 14:19-20). According to the author of Hebrews, this shows that Melchizedek's priesthood is superior to the priesthood of the Levites who would descend from Abraham (see Heb 7:1-10). Thus, Jesus—a priest "according to the pattern of Melchizedek"— is superior to the Levitical priests. He has offered a perfect sacrifice to atone for sin, and he lives forever to intercede for us by virtue of his resurrection.

110:5-7 This psalm anticipates the victorious rule of the Messiah with his saints, when he establishes his kingdom on earth. The Messiah will be completely victorious over those who oppose him. He will **crush kings** and **judge the nations** (110:5-6). God the Father has granted universal dominion to the one whom he has designated as the messianic Priest-King: the Lord Jesus Christ.

⇾ Psalm 111 ⥢

111:1-9 To declare **hallelujah** is to bestow boasting and honor on the Lord. The psalmist praises God publicly and wholeheartedly (not merely externally or ritualistically) (111:1). God's mighty **works** are **splendid and majestic**—they are even worthy of being **studied** for both their power and purpose (111:2-3). The psalmist recounts God's **wondrous works** among his **covenant** members, including providing for them, **giving them the inheritance of the nations**, and redeeming them (111:4-9). The

Lord **is holy and awe-inspiring** (111:9). He's in a class by himself.

111:10 In light of the glory of God, the psalmist concludes by describing the disposition that should characterize all true worshipers: **the fear of the Lord**. To take God seriously is the foundation of **wisdom**. To be wise is to have a clear understanding of how to obey God's commands in specific situations. Exercising such wisdom leads us to experience God at a deeper level, which should lead to even more **praise**.

⇾ *Psalm 112* ⇽

112:1-6 The psalmist describes **the person who fears the Lord**. Such a person is not all talk; rather, he takes **delight in [God's] commands** (112:1). He knows that fearing God is about how you live and not merely what you say. The psalmist also recounts the blessings available to those who fear the Lord and describes their godly character (112:2-4). As a result, they will experience goodness and be unshakeable (112:5-6).

112:7-10 The one who fears God **will not fear** circumstances or people because **his heart is confident, trusting in the Lord** (112:7-8). He cares for **the poor**, and God cares for him (112:9). **The wicked one**, on the other hand, sees the activity of those who fear God and is driven to rage. Nevertheless, such rage is impotent; his **desire . . . leads to ruin** (112:10). Thus, we are reminded that, ultimately, the righteous will prosper and the wicked will perish (see Ps 1).

⇾ *Psalm 113* ⇽

Psalms 113–118 are known as the Hallel Psalms (*hallel* is the Hebrew word for "praise"). These were sung by Jews celebrating the Passover.

113:1-4 Give praise . . . praise the name of the Lord . . . let the name of the Lord be praised (113:1-3). This threefold call is a reminder of the obligation his people have to continually extol God's greatness. It's natural to praise that which is worthy of praise. People do it all the time in everyday life. So, how much more natural should it be for those who know the God who saves, the God whose **glory** is **above the heavens**, to offer him such (113:4)?

113:5-9 The Lord is **enthroned on high** (113:5). He is transcendent, yet he is also intimately involved with his creation. He **stoops down** and **raises the poor from the dust** (113:6-7). Those whom society considers as nobodies, then, God lifts up to sit with the somebodies (113:8). He gives **children** to those who are barren, turning mourning to joy (113:9). All this and more should lead God's people to praise him "from the rising of the sun to its setting" (113:3).

⇾ *Psalm 114* ⇽

114:1-2 This psalm celebrates the deliverance God gave his people from **Egypt** (114:1). He made **Judah** his **sanctuary** and **Israel** his **dominion** (114:2)—that is, he became the nation's King and ruled from his temple in Zion (Jerusalem).

114:3-8 The parts of creation are spoken of as if they were alive. **The sea** and **the mountains** retreated from the Lord when he came to rescue his people (11:4-6), highlighting his sovereignty over everything. The **earth** was wise enough to **tremble . . . at the presence of the God of Jacob**, who even brought a drinking **pool** from **the rock** (114:7-8). How can weak and sinful humans do otherwise? A holy dread and awe of our Creator should be the response of those who know the awesome might of God.

⇾ *Psalm 115* ⇽

115:1 Believers who have a correct perception of God and a correct perception of themselves know that God alone deserves **glory**, not **us**. This is because he is the source of **faithful love** (the kindness he provides to those under his covenant covering) and **truth** (the absolute standard by which reality is measured).

115:2-3 The nations in the ancient world had idols, visual representations of the gods they worshiped. Thus, when they looked at Israel—for whom idolatry was forbidden (see Exod 20:4-5)—they asked, **Where is their God?** (115:2). The psalmist answered: **Our God is in heaven and does whatever he pleases** (115:3). In other words, the Lord is not a finite idol, but rather a limitless, transcendent God with the sovereign power to accomplish his will.

115:4-8 The Lord is not like **idols** made of **silver and gold** (115:4). They are impotent—unable to **speak ... see ... smell ... feel ... walk** (115:5-7). Thus, no matter how much you plead with them, they are unable to deliver you. Moreover, **those who make them are just like them** (115:8). You become like that which you worship—a sobering reality. So, be sure you worship the one true God.

115:9-15 The psalmist issues a clarion call to God's people to **trust in the LORD** (115:9-11). All forms of idolatry are to be rejected. Trusting him alone is the only way to access the blessings that he—**the Maker of heaven and earth**—is able to provide (115:12-13, 15).

115:16-18 God has given **the earth** for the benefit of **the human race** (115:16). So, what is it that humankind is to do while we live on it? **Praise the LORD** (115:17). This is not something for **the dead** to do. Here the psalmist is not denying life after death. He is simply saying that submitting to God in praise, faith, and obedience is something we are called to do now. We cannot wait until later. After death, it is too late to make this decision. Only if we **bless** God **now** will we be able to bless him **forever** (115:18).

➢ *Psalm 116* ❧

116:1-4 The psalmist expresses his **love** for God because he listened to and responded

to his prayer (116:1-2). This increases his commitment to **call** on the Lord for the rest of his life (116:2). His circumstances weren't inconsequential. The psalmist faces dire, life-threatening **trouble and sorrow** (116:3). In that context, he appeals to God to save his life (116:4). Prayer is an acknowledgment of our desperate need for God. It is a request for heaven to intervene in history.

116:5-11 He praises God for his grace, righteousness, and compassion. Notice, though, the corporate dimension of his worship. He points out that he is **our God** (116:5), belonging to all of his people. The psalmist then offers testimony of his experience with God in order to encourage the congregation. Though he had been brought low by his difficulties, the Lord had **saved** him (116:6). Therefore, he confidently says, **I will walk before LORD** (116:9). Though his enemies lied to him (116:11), he knew that the battle was not over and that God would have the last word.

116:12-14 In light of the Lord's goodness to him, the psalmist contemplates what he could give back to God (116:12). He mentions two things. First, he would **take the cup of salvation** (his blessings and deliverance) that God had graciously given him and **call on** his **name** (116:13). In other words, he would continue to worship and depend on the God who saves. Why would we turn anywhere but to the one who has proven that he can deliver? Second, he would **fulfill [his] vows to the LORD** (116:14). Obedience is the only appropriate response when God has come through for us.

116:15-19 **The death of [God's] faithful ones** is supremely **valuable in [his] sight** (116:15). He finds great pleasure and joy in fellowship with his children, who go to be with him eternally at death because of their personal relationship with him. Knowing this, the psalmist pledges to continue praising and serving the Lord publicly (116:17-18) so that God's people would be encouraged to do the same.

❧ Psalm 117 ❧

This is the shortest of all the Psalms.

117:1-2 **All nations** and **all peoples** are called to **glorify** and **praise** God (117:1). Though the psalmist was a member of the people of Israel, he recognizes that the God of Israel was the God of the nations. The God who entered into covenant with Israel and demonstrated his **faithful love** to them (117:2) is the Creator of the heavens and the earth. He calls everyone everywhere to come to him in worship.

Paul quotes 117:1 in Romans 15:11, emphasizing the truth that, through the sacrifice of Jesus Christ, the Gentiles can glorify God for his mercy (see Rom 15:7-11). Because of the gospel, Jews and Gentiles are able to come together to worship God for his great salvation.

❧ Psalm 118 ❧

118:1-4 The psalmist calls on **Israel** (all God's people), **the house of Aaron** (all the priests), and **those who fear the Lord** (all who take him seriously) to **give thanks** to him. Why? Because **his faithful love endures forever**. Notice the repetition. The biblical writers weren't able to emphasize important truths with bold typeface or italics like we do today; instead, they used repetition for emphasis. If there's one thing the psalmist wanted us to know, it is this: For those who come under God's covenant covering, his loyal, covenantal love lasts forever. It doesn't get any better than that.

118:5-9 When the psalmist was **in distress,** God delivered him (118:5). If you have access to this kind of divine aid, what is there to **be afraid** of? **What can a mere mortal do to** us (118:6)? Or, as the apostle Paul puts it, "If God is for us, who is against us?" (Rom 8:31). When God is your **helper,** those who **hate** you do not have ultimate power over you (118:7). So, with the psalmist, let us not **trust in humanity** but **take refuge in** God (118:8-9).

118:10-14 Though the psalmist was **surrounded** by enemies, outnumbered and

outmatched, he **destroyed them** (118:10-12). Yet, this was not because of his strength or strategy. Rather, the Lord was his **strength** and **helped** him (118:13-14). Victory is found only in God—as the quote from the victory song of God's deliverance at the Red Sea also highlights (118:14; see Exod 15:2).

118:15-21 How does the psalmist respond to God's deliverance? He responds with **joy** and praise (118:15-16). Because the Lord had preserved his life, the psalmist confesses, **I will live and proclaim what the Lord has done** (118:17). He wants to enter **the gates** of the temple and publicly **give thanks to** God for his **salvation** (118:19-21).

How do you respond to answered prayer? Do you give vocal acknowledgement to God and glorify him so that others may be encouraged to trust him? Or, do you take his blessings and provision for granted?

118:22-26 The psalmist uses a building metaphor to teach an important truth. **The builders rejected a stone** that God had selected. In his sovereign providence, he ensured that this particular stone would **become the cornerstone** (118:22) of a figurative building of his design; it would be the stone on which everything else would be aligned. This imagery is fulfilled in Jesus Christ (see Luke 20:17). He is the Messiah sent by God to his people. He is the **blessed** one **who comes in the name of the Lord** (118:26; see Matt 21:9). But, Israel's religious leaders rejected him and had him put to death. Nonetheless, God vindicated him, raising him from the dead to be the Lord of all. Those with eyes of faith recognize this as **wondrous** (118:23).

118:27-29 The psalmist concludes as he began (see 118:1-4). He gives **thanks** and exalts God for the **faithful love** that he expresses toward his people (118:28-29). Not only is such divine, covenant-based love exactly what we need, but it also **endures forever** (118:29).

❧ Psalm 119 ❧

Psalm 119, the longest chapter in the Psalter (and the longest in the Bible), is an acrostic psalm. Each of its twenty-two stanzas is introduced by a different letter of the Hebrew alphabet, presented in sequence. Each letter is indicated at the beginning of the paragraphs below. The entire psalm is an appreciation for, celebration of, and dependency on the Word of God to enable us to properly negotiate the twists and turns of life.

119:1-8 *Aleph. The blessings of God's word.* The Hebrew word translated here as **happy** (119:1-2) can also mean "blessed." Those **who walk**—that is, live their lives—according to God's Word are blessed (and happy!). This is the same truth affirmed at the beginning of the Psalter (see 1:1-2). This is why God has **commanded** that his people **diligently** keep his **precepts** (119:4). Doing so brings pleasure. Moreover, the one who keeps his **statutes** will **not be ashamed**, but rather have **an upright heart** that brings forth **praise** (119:5-7).

119:9-16 *Beth. The protection from God's word.* Following God's **word** provides safety. This principle is especially critical for those who are **young**—those who are learning to resist temptation and **keep [their] way pure** (119:9). By treasuring the principles of Scripture in our hearts, we train ourselves to love God's ways. Then, when we are confronted by temptation, we are prepared to reject **sin** (119:10-11). If we embrace God's word with our hearts, we will rejoice in it more than **in all riches** (119:14).

119:17-24 *Gimel. The comfort of God's word.* The psalmist requests God's favor—that God would **deal generously with** him and **open [his] eyes** to give him understanding **from [his] instruction** (119:17-18). He needs comfort in the midst of difficult circumstances because **arrogant** men had insulted him and spoken against him (119:21-23). Nevertheless, he is committed to observing God's **decrees**, which he considers his **counselors** (119:24). There is no better teaching and counseling for life.

119:25-32 *Daleth. The strength of God's word.* The psalmist prays to be revived and strengthened by the word. **[His] life is down in the dust,** and he is **weary from grief**

(119:25, 28). The **instruction** of Scripture, however, enables him to avoid the allure of sin and **the way of deceit** (119:29). Therefore, he does not merely read God's **decrees**—he clings to them (119:31).

119:33-40 *He. The commitment to God's word.* He expresses his total dedication to the Lord's **statutes . . . I will always keep them** (119:33). He asks that God would bless such a commitment by turning his **heart** from **dishonest profit** and his **eyes** from **what is worthless** (119:36-37). He desires a life of value, not one of **disgrace** (119:39). Devotion to the word can provide such a life.

119:41-48 *Waw. The instruction of God's word.* Given the covenant relationship that he shares with God, the psalmist asks for his **faithful love**, so that he might be delivered from those who taunt him (119:41-42). As a result, he vows to always **obey [his] instruction** and declare it openly and without shame to those in powerful seats of authority (119:44, 46).

119:49-56 *Zayin. The hope from God's word.* In spite of the **affliction** and **ridicule** he was experiencing, the psalmist had received **hope** through God's **word** (119:49-51). This gave him tremendous **comfort** and freedom (11:50), which further motivated him to **obey [God's] precepts** (119:52, 56). Biblical hope is not mere wishful thinking. It is a confident expectation about the future based on the character of God and his promises.

119:57-64 *Cheth. The obedience to God's word.* The psalmist was surrounded by wickedness, as if **ropes** were **wrapped** around him (119:61). Nevertheless, he was committed to keeping the Lord's **words** and **commands** (119:57, 60). Obedience was a priority. His gratefulness for Scripture was so profound that he woke **at midnight** to thank God for it (119:62). Whom did the psalmist befriend? **All who fear** God and keep his **precepts** (119:63).

119:65-72 *Teth. The discipline of God's word.* The word of God disciplined the psalmist. Previously, he had been **afflicted** and **went astray** into sin (119:67), but the word corrected him and taught him **discernment** so that he could clearly distinguish between right and wrong (119:66). He recognizes this as good treatment from the Lord (119:65, 68), "for the Lord disciplines the one he loves, just as a father disciplines the son in whom he delights" (Prov 3:12). It is good when we are **afflicted** by God so that we can **learn [his] statutes** (119:71).

119:73-80 *Yod. The trust in God's word.* The **hands** of God **formed** the psalmist. Therefore, he trusts his Maker's word. He desires **understanding** so that he could **learn [God's] commands**, and he desires **compassion** so that God's **instruction** would be his **delight** (119:73, 77). The psalmist trusts God to bring **shame** on **the arrogant** and, simultaneously, to keep him from **shame** through a **heart** that was **blameless regarding [God's] statutes** (119:78, 80).

119:81-88 *Kaph. The faithfulness of God's word.* The psalmist was experiencing weakness and distress because of his **persecutors** (119:81-84). He wonders how long he would have to wait for deliverance and vindication (119:84). Nevertheless, he knows the Lord's **commands** are faithful and **true** and that he would act **in accordance with [his] faithful love** (119:86-88). Therefore, the psalmist would **obey [God's] decree** (119:88) while waiting on God to work.

119:89-96 *Lamed. The security of God's word.* God's **word is forever** and **firmly fixed in heaven** (119:89). It will never change and remains relevant to all people in every culture throughout history. The foundation of the word's faithfulness is God's **faithfulness**; his creation and **judgments** are firm (119:90-91). The psalmist knows that he has security through God's **precepts**, so he determines to **never forget** them (119:93).

119:97-104 *Mem. The preciousness of God's word.* To the psalmist, the Lord's **instruction** is not merely something to read but to **love** (119:97). By devouring God's commands, he has become **wiser** (i.e., he had more insight for right living and decision-making) than his **enemies** . . . **teachers**, and **elders** (119:98-100). Thus, the word was **sweet** to

him—**sweeter than honey**—and led him to walk in purity (119:103-104).

119:105-112 *Nun. The illumination of God's word.* The word is a source of light to guide the believer through life. It's **a lamp** directing our **feet** in a dark world (119:105). When the psalmist's **life [was] constantly in danger**, God's **instruction** provided illumination (119:109), helping him to see his circumstances from God's perspective. He was **resolved to obey [the Lord's] statutes** (119:112) so that he could live without stumbling.

119:113-120 *Samek. The reverence for God's word.* The psalmist hates **those who are double-minded** when it came to God's **instruction** (119:113). His devotion to Scripture is not half-hearted; rather, his entire **hope** is in the **word** (119:114). The psalmist is aware of what happens to those who **stray from [God's] statutes**: God rejects them and removes them from the **earth** (119:118-119). Therefore, with deep reverence for the Lord's word, the psalmist confesses, **I tremble in awe of you** (119:120).

119:121-128 *Ayin. The value of God's word.* The psalmist was looking to God for deliverance from his **oppressors** (119:121), those who had **violated [God's] instruction** (119:126). Unlike them, he follows all the precepts of Scripture and hates deceit (119:28). He perceives the richness and value of God's word. He loves the Lord's **commands more than** . . . **the purest gold** (119:127). Indeed, nothing is of greater worth.

119:129-136 *Pe. The wonder of God's word.* The **decrees** of God are **wondrous** because they give **light** and **understanding** (119:129-130). This is why the psalmist prays that God would **be gracious to [him]** and establish his **steps**, so that he would keep his word and not **let any sin dominate [him]** (119:132-133). He wants to experience the wonder of God's shining **face**—that is, his presence—so that he could learn his **statutes** (119:135). He loves the **instruction** of the Lord so much that he sobbed when others disobeyed it (119:136), a fact that should prompt us to ask how we respond to the world's rejection of God's word.

119:137-144 *Tsade. The righteousness of God's word.* The Lord is **righteous**; he is the standard of what is right. Therefore, his **judgments are just**, and his **decrees are righteous** (119:137, 144). If you want to live a life that is pure (see 119:9), then, you need the purity of God's word. Though the standards of this sinful world are constantly in flux, **[God's] righteousness is an everlasting righteousness** (119:142).

119:145-152 *Qoph. The truthfulness of God's word.* Because the psalmist knows that **all [God's] commands are true**, he knows that they are **established** and can never fail (119:151-152). Therefore, he wants the God of such words to intervene on his behalf. Evildoers were **near**, and he needed the Lord to **help** and **save** him (119:146-147, 150). The psalmist continuously finds his **hope** in **[God's] word** (119:147).

119:153-160 *Resh. The deliverance of God's word.* In spite of his **affliction**, the psalmist has not **forgotten** the Lord's **instruction** (119:153). In fact, he confessed, **I love your precepts** (119:159). That's why he had confidence that God would deliver him from his troubles. He knows that **the wicked** who reject God's **statutes** do not experience deliverance because **salvation is far from** them (119:155). Deliverance comes to those who hope in God and in his word.

119:161-168 *Sin / Shin. The joy of God's word.* The promises of Scripture are to the psalmist like a **vast treasure** that made him **rejoice** (119:162). Because of his love for God's instruction, he praises him **seven times a day** (119:164). In the Bible, *seven* is the number of perfection or completion. So, in other words, praise is continually on the psalmist's lips. There is great joy in loving and keeping the word of God. Those who do so experience **abundant peace** and **nothing makes them stumble** (119:165).

119:169-176 *Taw. The praise for God's word.* The psalmist concludes with a plea for God to rescue him from his enemies (119:169-170, 173). What does the follower of God do when he needs help in the midst of trouble? His **lips pour out praise** and his **tongue sings**

(119:171-172). The psalmist longs for God's **salvation** (119:174). What will he do if God lets him **live**? **Praise** him more (119:175). May it be so with us. Let us praise the Lord for his beautiful and powerful word. And let our testimony match the psalmist's final words: **I do not forget your commands** (119:176).

☞ *Psalm 120* ☜

Psalms 120–134 are the songs of ascents, used by Israelite pilgrims traveling up to Jerusalem to participate in the annual feasts.

120:1-4 The psalmist pleads with God to **rescue** him from those who sought to destroy him with their **lying** and deceit—and the Lord **answered** (119:1-2). Then, knowing of his enemies' assured destruction at God's hands, the psalmist speaks to them of God's coming judgment. It would be like **a warrior's sharp arrows with burning charcoal** (119:4).

120:5-7 The psalmist expresses sorrow that he had to dwell among people who pursued **war** when he was a man of **peace** (120:6-7). **Meshech** is a reference to a people who lived far to the north of Israel, while **Kedar** referred to a people who lived to the southeast (120:5). Likely, then, this was his poetic way of saying that he was surrounded by those who were not God's people. But, though he was living amid a culture that despised righteousness, the psalmist looked to God for help and honored God with his obedience.

☞ *Psalm 121* ☜

121:1-2 The psalmist considers **the mountains** of Israel, mighty towers of rock. Such images of strength caused him to ask himself, **Where will my help come from?** (121:1). He concludes that **help comes from of the LORD, the Maker of heaven and earth** (121:2). Indeed, the greatest protection doesn't come from the mountains—but from the one who created the mountains.

121:3-4 The Lord is the **Protector** of his people (121:3). There is no safer place in the universe than being where God wants you to be. He cannot be defeated, and he **does not slumber or sleep** (121:4).

121:5-8 The LORD is a **shelter** (121:5). He protects from all manner of evil, physical and spiritual. He guards his people **from all harm**, whether by **day** or **night**, whether they are **coming** or **going** (121:6-8). Submit yourself to God's kingdom, then, and receive the blessings of his covenantal covering.

⪫ Psalm 122 ⪪

122:1-5 David expresses excitement as he anticipates worshiping with the people of Israel in **the house of the LORD**, the tabernacle in **Jerusalem** (122:1-2). God had given the twelve **tribes** of **Israel** an **ordinance** to obey. They were to appear before him in Jerusalem at the annual festivals that he had established for them so that they might **give** him **thanks** (122:4; see Deut 16:16-17). Not only was Jerusalem the location of the Lord's tabernacle, it was also the city of the king, the location of the **thrones of the house of David** (122:5)— from whose family the Messiah would come.

122:6-9 David vows to **pursue** Jerusalem's **prosperity** (122:9), and he exhorts true worshipers to **pray for** the **peace** and security of that city and its people, his **brothers and friends**. To be devoted to the Lord, in fact, meant to be devoted to the city he had chosen for his king and for the worship of his name. The prayer in view here will, ultimately, be answered under the Messiah's kingdom rule (122:6-8).

⪫ Psalm 123 ⪪

123:1-4 The psalmist looks to God, the King of creation, **the one enthroned in heaven**, for provision and help (123:1). As a servant looks to his master, so the people of Israel looked to the Lord to be favorable toward them (123:2). Though their enemies had

shown them **contempt**, they were confident that God could reverse their circumstances (123:3). Thus, the psalmist prays repeatedly, **show us favor**. If the Lord grants you favor, no one can stand against you.

⪫ Psalm 124 ⪪

124:1-7 To encourage the people of God to trust in his faithfulness in their present circumstances, David recalls God's deliverance in the past. If not for divine intervention at the Red Sea, Israel would have been slaughtered by Pharaoh's army and drowned in the **raging water** (124:2-5). But, God had enabled his people to escape from their captors **like a bird** from a trapper's snare (124:7).

124:8 Reflecting on God's help in the past gave David confidence to declare that God would **help** his people again. As **the Maker of heaven and earth**, he ruled over them. This is a powerful lesson for God's people today. Keep track of the goodness of God in your life. Take note of times when God delivers you from adversity. You'll need to recall these times of blessing to give you confidence in God's faithfulness and power for future troubles.

⪫ Psalm 125 ⪪

125:1-3 This psalm affirms the permanence of **Mount Zion** as an illustration of the security experienced by **those who trust in the LORD** (125:1). Just as **mountains surround Jerusalem**, so also God **surrounds his people**, giving them covering and protection (125:2). The ultimate display of God's protection will appear when the Messiah comes to reign as King from Jerusalem in his millennial kingdom. In that day, **the scepter of the wicked will not remain** and will not cause **the righteous** to turn to **injustice** (125:3).

125:4-5 The psalmist asks God to **do what is good ... to those whose hearts are upright** (125:4)—that is, to those whose hearts trust in God and submit to his kingdom agenda.

What will become of those who prefer **crooked ways** (the paths of sin)? The Lord will judge them **with the evildoers** (125:5). Let all God's people remain loyal to him, turn from wickedness, and travel the path of righteousness.

ᾧ Psalm 126 ᾥ

126:1-3 The psalmist recalls the joy that God's people experienced when he **restored** their **fortunes** upon their return after exile (126:1). They recognized that this was the work of the Lord, resulting in **laughter** and **joy** (126:2).

126:4-6 Thinking of **watercourses in the Negev**, which were streams that overflowed south of Israel during the rainy season, the psalmist longs for an overflow of God's blessing so that they might experience restoration and have their sorrow turned to **joy** (126:4-5). This is an important truth: don't become complacent in your expectations. God is "able to do above and beyond all that we ask or think" (Eph 3:20). In his sovereign grace, God can cause **those who sow in tears** to **reap with shouts of joy** (126:5). He can turn our sorrow into blessing.

ᾧ Psalm 127 ᾥ

This is the second of two psalms by Solomon (see Ps 72).

127:1-2 According to Solomon, all **labor** done independently of God is done **in vain** (127:1) Even seeking to build a home and a family apart from God is a waste because no matter how diligently you apply yourself, your human efforts are limited without God to back them. What we need in our households is his involvement and blessing—combined with our faithful labor. No matter how many books on marriage and parenting you read, or how much advice you receive, all falls short unless your foundation is built on God.

127:3-4 Far from being a burden or inconvenience, children are intended to be received and valued as a gift from the Lord, **a reward** (127:3). They should be treated as a wonderful inheritance and, thus, receive care and training.

Children are **like arrows in the hand of a warrior** (127:4). But, if they are to hit their targets—that is, to fulfill their kingdom purposes—parents must shape them and aim them correctly. Boys and girls must be raised to know the Lord, gaining experiential knowledge of God through watching their moms and dads live in dependence on him.

127:5 The man whose **quiver** is **filled** with such "arrows" **will never be put to shame**. He will send his children into the world so that they honor God and their families. Building the next generation is important kingdom work, so don't presume to engage in it without bringing your parenting under submission to the King's agenda.

ᾧ Psalm 128 ᾥ

God's kingdom agenda is defined as the visible manifestation of the comprehensive rule of God over every area of life. He administers this agenda through spiritually binding relationships called covenants. To bring his rule to bear on your life, God operates through four covenantal spheres. This psalm provides a helpful illustration of these spheres.

128:1-2 The first sphere through which God works is the *individual*. The psalmist declares, **How happy is everyone who fears the LORD, who walks in his ways** (128:1). God's goal is that every person learns to take him seriously and to govern himself or herself under divine rule. We cannot merely keep God on the periphery of our lives but must be willing to embrace commitment and accountability. The Lord will bless those who do so in their fortune (**you will surely eat what your hands have worked for**), their feelings (**you will be happy**), and their future (**it will go well for you**) (128:2).

128:3-4 The next sphere is the *family*. God created the family to be the foundation of civilization. Societal breakdown in the United

States, then, doesn't begin with the White House; it begins in *your* house! Because God designed men to be godly leaders in their homes, he addresses them. To **the man who fears the LORD** (128:4), he says, **Your wife will be like a fruitful vine within your house, your children, like young olive trees around your table** (128:3).

When a husband takes God seriously, becomes a servant leader in his home, and loves his wife sacrificially as Christ loved the church (see Eph 5:25), he encourages his wife to be the fruitful helper that God wants her to be (see Gen 2:20-23). Furthermore, such a man is diligent in his responsibilities as a father. He will gather his children around the table to teach them wisdom, a habit that will result in productive citizens.

128:5-6 The third sphere through which God accomplishes his kingdom purposes is the *church*. The name *Zion* (128:5) was used in the Old Testament to describe either the city of Jerusalem or the holy temple within it. But, in the New Testament, the church is the temple of God (see 2 Cor 6:16; Eph 2:21), and Christians are said to come to worship at "Mount Zion" (Heb 12:22). Thus, for believers, Zion refers to the church, God's people.

Christians are called to be part of God's covenant community. If you've been born again by placing faith in Jesus, you're not an only child but part of a family that calls God "our Father" (Matt 6:9). Thus, in the New Testament, taking an active part in a local church is a normal and expected part of the Christian experience.

Certain blessings can only be received corporately. God wants to **bless** his people, but it comes **from Zion** (128:5). The church of Jesus Christ is like an embassy operating with God's kingdom authority in a foreign land. The church is where the rules of eternity operate at a location in history. We gather together to hear from heaven so that we may live out heaven's viewpoint in the world.

The final sphere is *society*. The psalmist concludes with a desire to see **prosperity** in **Jerusalem** and **peace** in **Israel** (128:5-6). He desires good and comprehensive well-being

(i.e., *shalom* or "peace") for the capital and country where God's people dwelled. We ought to do the same.

Frequently, we expect our own country to be made better from the top down though politics, but God wants to see societies transformed from the bottom up. When God's kingdom agenda is a priority in individuals who are committed to families that are committed to churches that are committed to making a difference in their communities, society is transformed for the better. May it be so with God's people today.

⟩⟩ *Psalm 129* ⟨⟨

129:1-4 The psalmist invites God's people to testify to his mighty deliverance. From the beginning of the nation (Israel's "**youth**"), they were oppressed, but their enemies had **not prevailed against** them (129:2). They had suffered greatly, as if someone had **plowed over** their backs (129:3). Yet, because **the LORD is righteous**, he brings justice to his people and thwarts the intentions of **the wicked** (129:4).

129:5-8 The name *Zion* is frequently used in the Old Testament to speak of the city of Jerusalem or God's holy temple within it. In either case, to **hate Zion** is to hate God. So, the psalmist prays that such people would wind up **in disgrace** (129:5). He asks that they would be **like grass** growing on **rooftops**, which **withers** away because of the lack of soil (129:6). Just as it is wrong to curse when we ought to bless (see Jas 3:9-10), it is wrong to pronounce a **blessing** on the wicked who don't deserve it (129:8).

⟩⟩ *Psalm 130* ⟨⟨

130:1-3 The psalmist cries out to God from **the depths** of his emotional turmoil (130:1). He realizes his desperate situation as his sin is juxtaposed with God's holiness: **If you kept an account of iniquities, LORD, who could stand?** (130:3). When our sin is measured against God's righteousness, we fall short of God's glory (Rom 3:23) and deserve death (Rom 6:23).

130:4 But—praise God—that's not where it ends, because **with [God] there is forgiveness.** The Lord made forgiveness possible through the atoning sacrifices he required of Israel. But, ultimately, these sacrifices are fulfilled in Jesus Christ. By faith in his death on the cross, "we have redemption, the forgiveness of sins" (Col 1:14). God extends such grace not so that it will lead to indulgence but **so that [he] may be revered** and taken seriously.

130:5-6 The psalmist waits for divine deliverance from guilt, like **watchmen** who stay awake all night waiting **for the morning** to come. He looks to God to remove the weight that his sin had laid on him.

130:7-8 In light of God's **faithful love**, the psalmist urges **Israel** (and believers today) to **put [their] hope** in him for the blessings of **redemption** and deliverance (130:7). One day, the Lord **will redeem Israel from all its iniquities** (130:8). They will believe in their Messiah and repent of their rejection of him, and Christ's millennial kingdom will be ushered in.

✥ Psalm 131 ✥

131:1 David understands who he is in light of who God is. Knowing that God alone is exalted and that God hates pride (even in a human king), David rejects a desire to be **proud** or **haughty**. In spite of his royal position, he placed himself humbly under divine rule.

131:2 He affirms his dependence on God; he is like a **child** resting against the bosom of his **mother**. David is confident of the care and protection of the one who watches over him. Regardless of what is happening in the world around you, there is no safer place to be than under the covenant covering of God.

131:3 David concludes by encouraging Israel to **hope in the LORD** with the same

confidence that he had. We do not trust in God merely for ourselves. Rather, our visible trust, demonstrated in our submission to his will, should encourage others to do likewise and find rest in him.

✥ Psalm 132 ✥

132:1-5 The people ask God to **remember David**, both for **the hardships he endured** and for his **vow** to centralize the worship of God in Jerusalem (132:1-2). He brought the ark of the covenant into the city of David (2 Sam 6:12-17), so that he could provide **a dwelling for the Mighty One of Jacob** (132:5). David wanted his throne to be near God's throne.

132:6-9 The people remember when Israel brought the ark from **the fields of Jaar** (that is, Kiriath-jearim). The Philistines had captured it, endured God's wrath, and returned it (see 1 Sam 5:1–7:1). The people long to go to God's **dwelling place** on earth (the temple) and **worship at his footstool** (the ark) (132:7-8). The ark of God's power assured his victory on behalf of his people. They pray for **righteousness** for the **priests** and **joy** for the **faithful** (130:9).

132:10-12 They ask God to be faithful to his covenant promise to David (see 2 Sam 7:11-16) and, thus, **not reject** his descendant, God's **anointed** king (132:10). For the Lord had promised that David's descendants would **sit on [his] throne forever** (132:12). But, rather than through a perpetual succession of Davidic kings, this promise would be fulfilled in the resurrected Son of David who lives forever.

132:13-18 God had **chosen Zion . . . for his home** (132:13), the place of his earthly rule, and he promises to bless its people (132:15-16). In response to their prayers, the Lord vows to be faithful to his promise to David. His **anointed one** will be a source of power and light (132:17). He will vanquish **his enemies** and reign in glory (132:18). Believers today hope in this same Anointed One, and we long for his kingdom (see Luke 1:32-33; Acts 2:30). "Come, Lord Jesus!" (Rev 22:20).

❧ Psalm 133 ❧

133:1 David exalts the glory of **brothers living together in harmony.** Just as it was **good and pleasant** (attractive) when this was true among Israel's tribes then, so it is true of God's people today. When brothers and sisters in Christ gather for worship, it is beautiful. When we come together in peace, love, and unity, it reflects the attitude of Christ (see Phil 2:1-5).

133:2 The unity of God's people is like when the **oil** was poured on **Aaron's** head to anoint him to the priesthood. The oil consecrated him to his God-appointed task, and the unity of God's people brings divine consecration to them. To experience the kingdom work of God in our churches, unity is critical. God will not work amid division and dissension (see John 17).

133:3 The Israelites' unity is also compared to **the dew of** Mount **Hermon**, the tallest mountain in Israel. The atmospheric moisture from Hermon fell **on the mountains of Zion**, bringing refreshment and productivity to the land. Similarly, unity among the people of God frees him to rain down **blessing** on them. This explains why the devil seeks to sow discord among God's people. He wants to block the flow of God's blessings.

❧ Psalm 134 ❧

134:1-3 The psalmist calls on the priests who serve, standing **in the LORD's house at night**, to praise him (134:1). Their uplifted **hands** express not only worship, but also dependency (134:2). He then prays that their Creator—the **Maker of heaven and earth**—would bless his people (134:3).

Through Jesus Christ, believers have been made priests to one another (see 1 Pet 2:9; Rev 1:6). Therefore, these words apply to Christians everywhere. We are called to bless God and serve one another.

❧ Psalm 135 ❧

135:1-7 The palmist calls the priests **who stand in** the temple, **the house of the LORD**, to **praise** and **sing** to him for his goodness and his choosing of Israel as his special **possession** (135:1-4). The Lord is also to be praised for his supremacy over worthless idols and his sovereign power over creation (135:5-7). He is truly incomparable.

135:8-14 God is to be praised for his protection of his covenant people. From his defeat of Egypt during the exodus (135:8-9) to his vanquishing of **many nations** during the conquest of Canaan (135:10-11), God repeatedly delivered his people and then blessed them with **an inheritance** (135:12). No one has a glorious and enduring **reputation** like the Lord (135:13).

135:15-18 Those who trust in **idols** are fools. Though the Lord is the Creator of heaven and earth, **silver and gold** idols are **made by human hands** (135:15). They are lifeless (135:15-17) and—unlike the living God who saves—cannot act on behalf of those who worship them. **Those who make them are just like them** (135:18). This is the powerful principle that you become like what you worship. If you look to what is lifeless and empty as your source, your life will reflect it.

135:19-21 The psalmist concludes with a call to all God's people (**Israel**) and all those who serve as priests and ministers in the temple (the houses of **Aaron** and **Levi**) to bless **the LORD** (135:19-20). The one who **dwells** in his temple on Mount **Zion** in **Jerusalem** is to be praised (135:21).

❧ Psalm 136 ❧

This psalm celebrates the *faithful love* (Hebrew: *hesed*) of God, his steadfast and never-failing love toward his covenant people. It includes a beautiful line repeated throughout: His faithful love endures forever. Probably after the priest sang each verse, the entire congregation would respond by singing this refrain.

136:1-26 The psalmist calls the people to **give thanks to the God of gods** and **the Lord of lords** who alone is sovereign and supreme (136:1-3). He is to be praised for his works of creation (136:4-9), his miraculous redemption of Israel from slavery in Egypt (136:10-15), and his deliverance of his people from their foes and into the land of promise (136:16-24). He is the **God** who rules from **heaven**, the only true King (136:26). Let us give thanks to the faithful love he has shown us through Jesus Christ our Lord.

☞ Psalm 137 ☜

137:1-6 The psalmist recalls the deep sorrow the exiles experienced during their Babylonian captivity. They sat **by the rivers of Babylon** and **wept** (137:1). They **remembered** the glory of **Zion**, while their **captors** mocked them, asking them to **sing . . . the songs of Zion** (137:1, 3). The psalmist wondered how he could sing Zion's songs in a **foreign** land, yet he was determined to remember **Jerusalem**, though it lay in devastation (137:4-6).

137:7-9 The psalmist moves from sorrow for Jerusalem to a desire for justice against his people's oppressors. He longs for God's vengeance against **the Edomites**, who cheered Jerusalem's **destruction**, and against **Babylon**, who carried out the violence (137:7-8). His prayer against the **little ones** (137:9) reflected a desire that his enemy would have no descendants.

☞ Psalm 138 ☜

138:1-6 David vows to **praise** God wholeheartedly, because his **love and truth** are constant (138:1-2). The Lord had **exalted** himself by answering David's prayer (138:2-3). Therefore, Israel's king desires **all the kings on earth** to thank God and **sing of his glory** (138:4-5). For he gives attention to **the humble** but rejects the proud (i.e., those who

believe they can live their lives independently of him) (138:6; see Jas 4:6). Believers should not be ashamed to give public praise to God before all people, whether great or small.

138:7-8 David was confident that God would deliver him from danger with the power of his **right hand** (138:7). He pleads with God to **fulfill** the **purpose** he had for him and not to **abandon** him (138:8). We, too, can be brutally honest with God. Even while you praise him, you can ask him not to let you down—particularly in times of crises—knowing that he will answer for your good and his glory.

☞ Psalm 139 ☜

139:1-4 David contemplates the staggering omniscience of God. Not only does the Lord know everything about the universe, he has also **searched** and **known** his servant (139:1). God knows every last detail about you, too. Nothing escapes his knowledge; nothing catches him off guard. He knows all of your actions, your **thoughts**, and your words (139:2-4). Before **a word is** formed **on [your] tongue**, God knows what you will say (139:4).

139:5-6 In light of this, David concludes, **You have encircled me** and **placed your hand on me** (139:5). In other words, "I'm locked inside your knowledge, God. There's nowhere to run and hide." While the Lord's complete awareness is bad news for the unbeliever, it is glorious news for the believer. It means we are never lost and never forgotten. Though others misunderstand and misread your intentions, God is never confused about you. God understands. How does David respond to such **wondrous knowledge**? He admits that it is **beyond** him; it's unfathomable (139:6). When we comprehend that God can do the incomprehensible, it should cause us to be overwhelmed with worship for him.

139:7-9 Not only is the Lord omniscient, but he is also omnipresent. God is everywhere. David asks, **Where can I flee from your presence?** (139:7). But, of course, no one can escape God. David therefore confesses that wherever he might try to hide—even in **heaven** or **in Sheol** (the grave) or **at the eastern horizon** or **at the western limits** (139:8-9)—he would still bump into God. He inhabits the universe from top to bottom.

139:10-12 Believer, no matter where you are, God's **right hand will hold on to [you]** (139:10). No **darkness** is too dark to **hide** us from his sight (139:11). To him, **the night shines like the day** (139:12). So, regardless of the circumstances you face, remember God is ever-present. Call on the intimate God in your day of distress, knowing that he is right by your side.

139:13-14 In spite of popular opinion, we are not the products of evolution. We are not here by chance. David affirms that God had not only created him, but he had actually **knit him together in [his] mother's womb** (139:13). You, too, are a work of art that God put together by hand. You have been **remarkably and wondrously made** (139:14). No matter the circumstances surrounding your conception, no matter your ethnicity or gender, your existence is intentional. You are not a mistake, for God makes no mistakes. You are created in the image of God (see Gen 1:27) with purpose and meaning. This truth is to be the foundation for a person's self-worth and self-esteem.

139:15-16 David was **not hidden** from God even when he was in his mother's womb (139:15). He thus declares, **Your eyes saw me when I was formless**. This truth is why abortion is so horribly wrong. Divinely given human life exists from the moment of conception. God didn't merely see an embryo or fetus in the womb; he saw *David* ("Your eyes saw *me*").

Moreover, David says, **All my days were written in your book and planned before a single one of them began** (139:16). The Lord similarly knew all of your days from beginning to end. Your existence is no accident. You are part of the divine plan.

139:17-18 David is overwhelmed by but also comforted by God's vast knowledge: **How precious your thoughts are to me** (139:17). No matter his circumstances, David knows that he is in God's presence and intimately

known by him. And the same is true of you. The Lord is aware of every detail of your life. He cares for you, and you are continually on his mind.

139:19-22 Because of David's deep love for the Lord, he hates everything that was in opposition to him (139:21). Thus, he prays for God's judgment on **the wicked** (139:19) in accordance with his holy character. David considers God's **enemies** as his own (139:22).

139:23-24 David concludes by acknowledging that his motives were flawed. But, he also knew that God understood his **heart** through and through. Therefore, he asks God to **search** and **test** him so that he might reveal to him **any offensive** and unrighteous thoughts and intentions (139:23-24). Like David, we do not fully know ourselves, either. So, let us pray that God's Spirit would help us understand ourselves rightly so that we can repent where necessary and enjoy intimate fellowship with him as he leads us **in the everlasting way** (139:24).

☙ *Psalm 140* ❧

140:1-5 David appeals to the Lord to defend him against **violent men** who were stirring up trouble for him, using their venomous **tongues** to turn others against him and ruin his reputation (140:1-3). Their actions toward David were equivalent to setting **a trap** for an animal (140:5). They worked in secret to bring him down.

140:6-8 No matter what the wicked did to him, David continues to declare his trust in the Lord, his **strong Savior**. As the king, David no doubt had the best of armor. But, ultimately, he knew that God himself was his **shield . . . on the day of battle**—especially when it came to maintaining peace of mind (140:7). He prays that God would thwart **the wicked** in **their goals** and short-circuit their pride (140:8).

140:9-11 David asks that the plans of these evildoers would backfire on them (140:9). He petitions God to judge them with **hot coals**

and **fire** so that their evil deeds would come to an end (140:10).

140:12-13 Just as David knows that the Lord would judge the wicked in righteousness, he also knows that the Lord would render **justice** to the **poor** and **needy** (140:12). God will intervene on behalf of the downtrodden—either in this life or in the life to come. One day, God will set all things right, and **the upright will live in [his] presence** (140:13).

➢ Psalm 141 ≪

141:1-2 David petitions with urgency and desperation, asking God to **hurry** to his aid (141:1). He describes his **prayer** in terms of priestly sacrifices: **incense** or an **offering** burned for the Lord (141:2). In other words, David didn't consider his entreaty as only a plea for help. It was an act of worship.

141:3-4 David understood his own sinfulness and longed for righteousness. Therefore, he asks the Lord to keep him from wickedness—in his speech, in his **heart**, and in his actions (141:3-4). He did not want to be lured into sin by the **delicacies** of the wicked (141:4)—that is, by anything that would appeal to his sinful desires and draw him away from the Lord.

Similarly, believers today are exhorted to beware of the desires of the world: "the lust of the flesh, the lust of the eyes, and the pride in one's possessions" (1 John 2:16). Indulging in such "delicacies" does not ultimately satisfy our spiritual hunger. It causes us to lose fellowship with God.

141:5-7 David welcomes the **rebuke** of the **righteous**. If words of correction were delivered to him in **faithful love**, David would **not refuse** them but would consider them like healing **oil for [his] head** (141:5). Yet, he still hoped that God would judge the wicked in light of their treatment of his people (141:6-7).

141:8-10 David affirms that his focus is on the Lord: **My eyes look to you. . . . I seek refuge in you** (141:8). He asks that God

would protect him from death and let his enemies **fall into their own nets** that they had set for him (141:10). When troubles surround you, keep your eyes on the one who can deliver you from them or through them.

➢ Psalm 142 ≪

142:1-3a David displays his great need for God in the midst of his desperate circumstances. He implores God to listen to his concerns: **I cry aloud . . . plead aloud . . . pour out my complaint . . . reveal my trouble** (141:1-2). Though David himself was **weak within**, his God is omnipotent and knows the **way** he should take (142:3).

If you have wrongly assumed that all prayer should be dignified and employ only theological jargon in your petitions to God, you have not understood prayer rightly. Let David be your model. He approaches God honestly, pleading emotionally for deliverance. As a troubled child depends on his or her daddy, go to your heavenly Father in your turmoil and open your heart to him.

142:3b-4 Whether David was actually alone, he certainly felt alone. He mourns, **No one stands up for me . . . no one cares about me.** That's why he fell on his knees before the Lord. David needed a **refuge** that only God could provide (142:4). Even when you have fellow believers standing by you, no one has the wisdom and power to care for you like God does.

142:5-7 David pleads with God because he was **weak** and his enemies were **too strong** (142:5-6). He asks for God to **free** him from the **prison** of his circumstances. Notice the purpose for this request: **so that I can praise your name**. It means David longs for deliverance in part so that he would have another reason to worship. He concludes with confidence that God would **deal generously with [him]**. As a result, **the righteous [would] gather around him** (142:7). Through divine intervention, then, the man who was alone would be alone no longer.

❧ Psalm 143 ❧

143:1-4 Because of God's **faithfulness** and **righteousness**, David calls on the Lord to save him from divine **judgment** (143:1). He acknowledges his own sinfulness, **for no one alive is righteous in [God's] sight** (143:2). But, his enemies were persecuting him unjustly (143:3), and David didn't have the spiritual or emotional strength to overcome them (143:4).

143:5-6 David finds solace and hope in remembering former **days**, when he had experienced God's mighty works (143:5). He longs for God's intervention to restore his spiritually thirsty soul (143:6).

143:7-10 David wants to **experience** the **faithful love** of God so that he might understand **the way [he] should go** for **protection** from his **enemies** (143:8-9). In addition, David wanted to walk in God's ways. He prays, **Teach me to do your will** (143:10). It wasn't enough to be saved from his troubles. David wants fellowship with God and his direction and guidance as he obeyed his commands.

143:11-12 He looks to the Lord's **righteousness** and **faithful love** to both **deliver** him and **destroy [his] enemies**. He appeals to the fact that he was God's **servant**. When we come under God's covenant covering and submit to his will, we can have confidence that he will work for our good and his glory.

❧ Psalm 144 ❧

144:1-2 David's descriptions of God show us two things clearly. First, he considers God the definitive source of security. The Lord is a **rock** . . . **fortress** . . . **stronghold** . . . **deliverer** . . . **shield**, and **refuge**. To put this in football terminology, we would say that God is the ultimate defensive line. No opposition

can break through. No other source of protection is as reliable.

Second, David expresses the depth of his personal relationship with the Lord through his repeated use of the pronoun **my** before these descriptions. Not only is God a fortress, but he is also *David's* fortress.

God was, is, and always will be almighty. The question is this: are you appropriating the divine King's power in your own life? Do you have access to his heavenly strength through faith and submission to his kingdom agenda?

144:3-4 David is overwhelmed that God would **care** for **human** beings in general and him in particular (144:3; see also 8:4). What amazing grace that God would condescend to enter into intimate fellowship with humanity! And how (even more) amazing is it that the divine Son of God would take on human nature so that he might redeem us (see Heb 2:1-18)?

144:5-8 David affirms God's control over the **heavens** . . . **mountains**, and **lightning** (144:5-6). He is their Creator; therefore, they do his bidding. With such sovereignty, the Lord could certainly **rescue** David **from the grasp of** those who sought him harm (144:7).

144:9-11 David sings **a new song** of praise to God, knowing that he is **the one who gives victory to kings** (144:9-10). In the end, the size of a king's army is irrelevant. The size of his God is what matters. As David testifies elsewhere, chariots and horses, symbols of ancient military power, are no match for the Lord (see 20:7). So, again, he pleads with God to **rescue** him from his **deceptive** enemies (144:11).

144:12-15 With God's deliverance of his people, David knows that blessings would follow. Israel's **sons** and **daughters** would flourish (144:12). The people would experience great productivity from crops and livestock (144:13). And their land would be secure (144:14). How should one respond to **such blessings** sent by God's hand? With joy! **Happy are the people whose God is the Lord** (144:15).

❧ Psalm 145 ❧

145:1-3 Because of God's unfathomable greatness, David commits himself to praising him **every day** (145:1-2). Such a commitment is not unreasonable, for God deserves endless worship. **His greatness is unsearchable** (145:3).

145:4-7 The knowledge and exaltation of God is to be passed down from **one generation . . . to the next** (145:4). David commits to doing his part to declare the **splendor . . . majesty . . . wondrous works**, and **greatness** of God to others (145:5-6).

Are you likewise committed to exalting God so that his kingdom expands? Do you regularly teach your children about the Lord? Do you share the gospel and your own personal testimony with unbelievers in your circle of influence? Are you discipling others so that the church may mature in Christ?

145:8-13 David recites what God himself had revealed to Moses (see Exod 34:6): **The LORD is gracious and compassionate, slow to anger and great in faithful love** (145:8). His glorious character and actions toward his people elicit their thanks and blessings (145:10). Those who have experienced the goodness of God, in fact, can't help but **declare** his **kingdom** and **mighty acts** to **all people** (145:11-12), because **[his] kingdom is an everlasting kingdom** (145:13). Because God's rule will endure forever, God's people ought to proclaim it and urge everyone everywhere to submit to the King.

145:14-20 David extols the gracious provision of God, who **helps** the **oppressed** and provides **food** for all humanity (145:14-15). He hears those **who call out to him with integrity** (145:18). He delivers **those who fear him** (145:19). He **guards all those who love him** (145:20). Thus, we see a clear picture of what God expects of us if he is to act on our behalf: we are to pray to him with integrity, live as those who takes him seriously, and love him with all that we are.

145:21 Like David, let us commit ourselves to vocal, public devotion to God. May we **declare** his **praise** so that **every living thing** might know and **bless** him **forever**.

❧ Psalm 146 ❧

146:1-4 The psalmist vows to **praise the LORD all [his] life** (146:2). This is eminently wise because the Lord is everlasting and able to save all who come to him. In contrast, **nobles**—no matter how powerful or glorious they are—**cannot save** (146:3). Moreover, a nobleman's days are numbered. He will die, and his **plans** with him (146:4).

146:5-6 The person who looks to the Lord—**the Maker of heaven and earth**—for his **help** is **happy** or blessed (the Hebrew word can be translated either way), because the Lord is **faithful forever**. He has no limitations and is eternally trustworthy.

146:7-9 God's resume is impeccable. He provides justice and care for **the exploited . . . the hungry . . . prisoners . . . the blind**, the **oppressed**, the **resident aliens . . . the fatherless and the widow**. There is no category of abused, broken, burdened, or underprivileged people on whom the Lord does not have compassion. The same should be true of God's people; the church is called to emulate its Savior and care for the downtrodden, renewing their hope and lightening their loads.

146:10 The psalmist concludes with an affirmation that **the LORD reigns forever**. No matter how difficult your trials, they will not last forever. But, God's kingdom will. **Hallelujah!** Praise the Lord!

❧ Psalm 147 ❧

147:1-6 The psalmist declares **how good** and **lovely** it is to give **praise** to God (147:1). Worship of God is always justified because of his **vast power** over his creation: he **counts** all **the stars** and **gives** them **names** (147:4-5). Worship is also right because of the amazing grace he demonstrates to his covenant people. Though his people were **brokenhearted**

and **oppressed** (either due to their sins or life circumstances), the Lord punished **the wicked**, gathered the exiles together, and granted them to rebuild **Jerusalem** (147:2-3, 6).

147:7-9 Another reason to praise God is his providential care of his world. He (not "Mother Nature") sends **rain** and **causes grass to grow** (147:8). All **animals** receive their sustenance from the Lord's gracious hand (147:9). This is God's common grace upon all of his creation.

147:10-14 What impresses God? What does he value? Not the things that typically capture the attention of humans. Powerful warriors and armies, for instance, are nothing to him (147:10). Rather, God cherishes **those who fear him** and **hope in his faithful love** (147:11). In other words, if you humbly submit to his kingdom agenda and live in dependence on him, you can rest assured that God will be crazy about you. He loves to bless his people (147:12-14).

147:15-20 The psalmist exalts God for his word. For by his **word**, he exercises control over the elements of nature (147:15-18). But, even more, he is to be praised for the word that he revealed specifically to his people. Only **Israel** personally received this gracious **word**—not any other **nation** (147:19-20). God's new covenant people should similarly exalt him for the special revelation of both the written Word and the living Word, our Lord Jesus Christ.

⁂ Psalm 148 ⁂

148:1-6 The psalmist invites **the heavens**, as well as the **heavenly** beings, to praise their Creator as they fulfill their created purposes (148:1-4). **For he commanded, and they were created** (148:5). The Maker deserves the worship of all he has made.

148:7-14 The psalmist also calls on everyone and everything that fills **the earth** to render **praise** to God (148:7). Creatures and inanimate objects, **kings** and **peoples**, **young** and **old** (148:7-12)—all should exalt him because he is the Creator, Sustainer, and Ruler of all. He demonstrated faithfulness to **the Israelites** (148:14), the people of Abraham. And through them, he blessed all peoples of the earth (see Gen 12:3; Gal 3:7-18).

⁂ Psalm 149 ⁂

149:1-5 This psalm calls God's people to praise him with fresh singing and **dancing** because he is both their **Maker** and their **King** (149:1-3). He showers his people with salvation because of his love for them. So, **the faithful**, those who look to him alone as their source, should **celebrate** and **shout for joy** (149:4-5).

149:6-9 Israel is called to have **exaltation of God . . . in their mouths** and a **sword in their hands** to carry out his **vengeance on the nations** (149:6-7). In other words, praise is to be accompanied by action. They were to honor God with their lips and also wage war against wickedness. The Lord honored his people by letting them carry out his own **judgment**, based on his word, against evildoers (149:9). He is to be praised both for his grace and for his justice.

⁂ Psalm 150 ⁂

150:1-6 The psalmist gives a final doxological call for **praise** to God—both **in his sanctuary** (the tabernacle or temple) and **in his mighty expanse** (heaven)—**for his abundant greatness** (that is, for who he is) and **for his powerful acts** (what he has done) (150:1-2). No instrument is to remain silent (150:3-5). And neither is any voice: **everything that breathes** is to render praise. Thus, the Psalter ends with a call to worship: **Hallelujah! Praise the Lord!** (150:6).

PROVERBS

INTRODUCTION

Author

SOLOMON IS CREDITED WITH THE proverbs of chapters 1–29 of the book. Scripture attests to Solomon's wisdom and that he was a collector of wise sayings (see 1 Kgs 3:5-14; 4:29-34; 5:7, 12; 10:2-3, 23-24). Chapters 1–24 may have been written down during his reign, while chapters 25–29 contain Solomon's proverbs collected later by King Hezekiah. The final two chapters are credited to Agur and Lemuel, about whom we know nothing. An editor was inspired to collect all of these sayings into the book we now have.

Historical Background

Solomon's reign as king represented the peak of prosperity for the nation of Israel. This period witnessed the greatest extent of the nation's territory and saw peace and international trade (see 1 Kgs 4:20-25; 10:21-29). Solomon was likely familiar with the ancient wisdom tradition in Egypt, but through God's inspiration and gift of great wisdom, he composed superior sayings. While he addressed his teachings to his son(s), they are applicable to all people.

Message and Purpose

Proverbs is one of the most neglected books in the Bible, yet it is a key piece of Scripture. It is a book about wisdom—the ability to take biblical truth and apply it to life's realities. It contrasts the person who does this with the fool, the person who refuses to live by God's standards. According to Proverbs, you become wise when you apply God's principles to your practical decision-making. And when you do, you can live life the way God meant it to be lived.

Life is full of choices. We've all made good choices and bad choices, wise ones and foolish ones. The good news is that with insight from the book of Proverbs in mind, you can begin applying its wisdom to all the scenarios of your life. Proverbs covers everything from parenting, marriage, money, and friends, to how to relate to God. If you will use the wisdom of Proverbs as you make future decisions, then it will save you time, grief, regret, and even money so that you can experience the benefits of kingdom living here and now.

VIDEO INTRO

www.bhpublishinggroup.com/qr/te/20_00

Outline

PROVERBS

I. INTRODUCTION AND PURPOSE (1:1-7)

1:1-7 In these introductory verses of Proverbs, **Solomon son of David, king of Israel** (1:1) explains the purpose of the book. Proverbs is intended to make us wise. To be wise is to be disciplined, understanding, just, shrewd, and discerning (1:2-6). It's the ability to take God's perspective and turn it into functional application. It's spiritual understanding applied to earthly living; it's the God-given ability to make good decisions.

Living wisely doesn't require a PhD. In fact, you can be a brilliant fool—someone who has a lot of book sense but no common sense. Information is not the only key to good decision-making, then; we need wisdom—the ability to apply the knowledge we have.

Wisdom is to truth as a shoe is to shoe leather. And lest we think we can have wisdom apart from the truth about God, Solomon hangs the key to the book right at the front door: **The fear of the LORD is the beginning of knowledge** (1:7).

To have true knowledge is to perceive the right nature of a thing, and it is not possible to be truly wise without fearing the Lord. This doesn't mean walking around feeling terrified of God. It means holding him in reverence, taking him seriously. Proverbs teaches that all true wisdom and knowledge is rooted in God and his Word, and it urges us to cultivate a fear of God through a relationship with him. The apostle Paul prayed for the Christians in Ephesus that God would give them a spirit of "wisdom and revelation in the knowledge of him" (Eph 1:17), further suggesting that being wise means knowing and fearing God.

Proverbs teaches that the knowledge of God opens the door to wisdom. By contrast, **fools despise wisdom and discipline** (1:7). A fool is a self-centered person who lives life without regard to wisdom and moral values. A fool rejects God's perspective. The Bible (and Proverbs in particular) commands us to become wise and condemns us if we don't.

II. A FATHER'S APPEAL: BECOME WISE (1:8–9:18)

1:8 Nearly the first third of Proverbs is a series of lectures from father to son:

Listen . . . to your father's instruction, and don't reject your mother's teaching. This fact is a reminder that instruction on how to be wise begins in the home. Parents have the responsibility to teach their children to know God, to see the world from his

perspective, and to live in accordance with his agenda. And children have the responsibility to listen.

1:9 Solomon says the teachings of one's parents **will be a garland of favor on [the] head.** It is important to God that children—and young adults living under the authority of their parents—obey their mothers and fathers unless they tell them to do something in clear disobedience to God's Word. That doesn't go down too well with a lot of kids today, especially when they reach the age at which they are confident they know more than their moms and dads and think they can do better. But Solomon says listening to your parents' advice is like storing up gold.

1:10-16 Plenty of voices give advice. All of us are subject to many influences, and we often become like those with whom we associate. Solomon tells his son, **If sinners entice you** saying, **come with us**, encouraging you to commit wickedness and promising reward (1:10-14), **don't travel that road with them** (1:15). Stay away from them **because their feet run toward evil** (1:16). To put this in modern terms, if you don't want to be a drug addict, don't hang out with drug addicts. If you don't want to be a gang member, don't let gang members be your running buddies. "Bad company corrupts good morals" (1 Cor 15:33)—that is, when you associate with people of impure character, they're going to rub off on you.

1:17-19 These verses provide a warning to parents; we must make sure we know our kids' companions. If they are going out with friends, find out where they'll be. When they tell you they're just going to hang out, ask them where they'll be hanging out—in case you want to join them. Don't be a wishy-washy parent: help your child. If they're living under your roof, they're under your authority. You have a right to know what they're up to, and you're responsible for knowing. Make sure your kids understand this: when foolish people look for trouble, they are simply setting a trap for themselves (1:17-19). What goes around comes around.

1:20-21 Sinners call for others to follow them, but wisdom is calling too. Solomon says wisdom—often personified in Proverbs—**calls out in the street ... makes her voice heard in the public squares ... cries out above the commotion.** Everybody has an idea or opinion, but there are only two answers to any issue: God's answer and everybody else's. And everybody else is wrong. Wisdom is crying

out for someone to pay attention to truth. Are you listening?

1:22-33 Only **inexperienced ones** and **mockers** would ignore, hate, refuse, and neglect God's wisdom, **knowledge, counsel,** and **correction** (1:22, 25, 29-30). In fact, Solomon warns that it's disastrous to miss wisdom. Those who reject God's counsel will fall into calamity one day, and then it will be too late (1:24-32). You do *not* want to hear God declare to you, **I . . . will laugh at your calamity. I will mock when terror strikes you** (1:26), so remember Galatians 6:7: "Don't be deceived: God is not mocked. For whatever a man sows he will also reap." When fools reject counsel, correction, and the fear of the Lord (1:29-30), they won't get off scot-free. Since they don't take God seriously, **they will eat the fruit of their way and be glutted with their own schemes** (1:31). In other words, a fool will be stuffed with his own stupidity to his own detriment. On the other hand, **whoever listens to [the LORD] will live securely** (1:33). The choice is yours.

2:1-5 Godly wisdom doesn't just fall into your lap. It requires diligent pursuit. Finding it requires digging into God's Word the way a miner digs into the ground for **silver** and other **hidden treasure** (2:4). Why hasn't God made it easy? Why not leave it on top of the ground for you to pick up? Because it's too valuable. People don't mind digging for gold; it's worth their efforts. If there's a vein of gold under their feet, they know their labor to unearth it will be richly rewarded. Wisdom is *a treasure* found in God's Word. Make it your quest to dig for it, and you will **discover the knowledge of God** (2:5).

2:6-19 God wants to know how serious we are about him. Many people rise early to exercise because they're serious about getting in shape, but they're too tired to rise early to spend time in God's Word. Others set aside time for their favorite TV show, but God can't get a slot on their schedules. The Lord is the one who **gives wisdom** (2:6). You can't obtain it anywhere else. **For those who live with integrity,** he's a **shield to guard and protect the way of his faithful followers** (2:7-8). But how serious are you to have his wisdom **enter** your mind and knowledge **delight** your **heart** (2:10)? How eager are you to have **discretion** and **understanding ... guard you** and **rescue you from the way of evil** (2:11-12)? How desperate are you to be protected from **those who enjoy doing evil ... whose paths are crooked ...** whose **house sinks down to death** (2:14-18)? God only feeds hungry people. If you are not spiritually hungry, ask God to give you a new spiritual appetite (see Ps 42:1; Matt 5:6).

2:20-22 Smart hikers know to stick to the trail. God has prepared a spiritual path from which we shouldn't deviate. We must **keep to the paths of the righteous** (2:20) because **the upright will inhabit the land** while **the wicked will be cut off** from it and **ripped out of it** (2:21-22). Those who reject God's wisdom in order to pursue wickedness and foolishness may seem to flourish for a while, but eventually they'll be pulled up like weeds.

3:1-4 Solomon pleads with his son to remember his **teaching** and store his **commands** in his heart (3:1). Why? What's the payoff? Doing so **will bring ... many days, a full life, and well-being** (3:2). While many Christians say they trust Christ to get them to heaven, their lives demonstrate a lack of trust in Christ to navigate their day-to-day journeys on earth. But the Lord knows how to deliver. If you inscribe **loyalty and faithfulness** on **your heart**, he will grant you favor with himself and people (3:3-4).

3:5-6 Chapter 3 contains one of the most beloved, quoted, and memorized passages in the Bible. It's a reminder that the knowledge of who God is should make us willing to trust him. Solomon says, **Trust in the LORD with all your heart, and do not rely on your own understanding; in all your ways know him, and he will make your paths straight.**

The Hebrew word for *trust* means to lie down on—to put your entire weight on something. When you go to sleep at night, you lie down on your bed because you believe it is strong enough to hold you up. "With all your heart" means entirely, without exception. So in essence God says, "Trust me

completely; I can sustain you. Your own understanding won't support you."

God doesn't want us coming to crucial crossroads in our lives with nothing to guide us but faulty human signposts. He wants us to know his ways, his divine perspective, so we don't take the wrong road.

The proof that we're not trusting God—even when we say we do—is when we turn to other sources first to address life's problems. If you want to know where your trust is, ask yourself, "Where do I turn *first* when I need help?" God is omniscient and his wisdom is infinite. He has the ability to coagulate and coordinate the events of history throughout eternity. Based on that impressive résumé and experience, there's no question that we should seek him first. Remember James's exhortation: "If any of you lacks wisdom, he should ask God—who gives generously and ungrudgingly—and it will be given to him" (Jas 1:5). But will we?

"In all your ways know him" is an umbrella statement covering anything having to do with your life. Pleasing God in all things is to become your goal. When you write a check, you need to be certain that you have the resources on deposit in the bank to cover the purchase. Otherwise, the check is going to bounce. A responsible adult, then, regularly keeps his bank account in mind when making purchases to be sure he can cover the charges. When it comes to negotiating life, God should be the source of your resources. You need to draw on an account that can support your decisions. Unfortunately, we often make life decisions that our spiritual account can't support and we wonder why our checks keep bouncing. Know God in all your ways by prayerfully consulting his Word.

When you rely on God in all you do, "he will make your paths straight." Life is crooked. It doesn't take long to figure that out. But God can remove the obstacles and cut a path through the woods. He will make sure your road reaches the right destination. An old axiom says, "The shortest distance between two points is a straight line." But when you are walking in the will of God, your life heads in a straight line no matter how the road curves. Jesus Christ knows the end from the beginning, the start from the finish. He knows where you need to be, how you are supposed to get there, and what route you should take. God wants you to trust him so you can start living.

3:7-10 Solomon cautions us: **Don't be wise in your own eyes.** Unless you **fear the Lord and turn away from evil,** you shouldn't count yourself a wise person (3:7). You can't just talk about trusting the Lord without walking the talk.

One of the ways God calls you to "trust him with all your heart" and "think about him in all your ways" as 3:5-6 says is to **honor the Lord with your possessions and with the first produce of your entire harvest** (3:9). Giving to the work of the Lord and honoring him with how you spend your money is crucial because it's a tangible expression of your faith. It demonstrates how much you value him. We must recognize God as the source of all we have and as the one who will provide for all our needs (3:10).

3:11-18 Sometimes God leads you backward to take you forward. No matter how hard the lesson is to learn, **do not despise the Lord's instruction** (3:11). The difficult path is always meant for our good. **For the Lord disciplines the one he loves, just as a father disciplines the son in whom he delights** (3:12). Godly parents don't withhold loving discipline from their children. The more you love, in fact, the more you correct what is wrong and train in what is right. So endure the hard times. For the one **who finds wisdom** will be truly **happy** (3:13, 18). Why? Because nothing of value in this world is more **profitable** or **precious** (3:14-15). What do you desire in this world? Whatever it is, it doesn't compare to what wisdom offers you. Money can't buy life, peace, or happiness. But wisdom can deliver them all (3:16-18).

3:19-20 God created the heavens and the earth **by wisdom** (3:19-20)—in other words, wisdom is part of the fabric of the universe. Reject wisdom, and you're rejecting the reason for your existence. See 8:22-31.

3:21-26 Do you want to be safe (3:23)? Do you want to get a good night's **sleep** (3:24)? Do you want to be free from anxiety (3:25)? Then **maintain sound wisdom and**

discretion (3:21). Exercise sound, biblical judgment in your day-to-day life, and God himself **will be your confidence** and watch over you (3:26).

3:27-30 The way of wisdom is not a solitary road. In fact, Solomon will repeatedly point out that wisdom is demonstrated by how we respond to and interact with others. **When it is in your power,** then, **don't withhold good from the one to whom it belongs. Don't say to your neighbor, "Go away! Come back later. I'll give it tomorrow"**—when it is there with you (3:27-28). **Don't plan any harm against your neighbor** or **accuse anyone** who **has done you no harm** (3:29-30). These admonitions, at their core, are really just another way of saying, "Love your neighbor as yourself" (Lev 19:18; Mark 12:31). Treat others the way you want to be treated. Love God and love your neighbor; you can't have one without the other.

3:31-35 When we see evil people prosper, we're tempted to **envy** them (3:31). But we need to make sure we're wearing our spiritual spectacles so that we get the complete picture. The Lord curses, **mocks,** and dishonors the wicked and the fool (3:33-35). Yet the one who is **righteous, humble,** and **wise** receives God's blessing, grace, and honor (3:33-35). God detests the **devious,** but **he is a friend to the upright** (3:32). Which would you rather be?

4:1-4 Again Solomon calls on his **sons** to **listen** (4:1-2), but since God inspired Solomon to write Proverbs as Scripture, then through these verses the Holy Spirit is calling on children everywhere to listen. Interestingly, Solomon shows the progression of godly instruction and obedience from one generation to the next: **When I was a son with my father, tender and precious to my mother, he taught me and said: "Your heart must hold on to my words. Keep my commands and live"** (4:3-4). It's clear, then, that Solomon expects parents to be the dominant moral influencers and instructors of children. Their role is critical because nobody can replace them. Proverbs is a blueprint for skillfully constructing the life of a child. It's a parenting manual.

4:5-9 Notice how Solomon urges his son to pursue wisdom and not **abandon** it (4:5-6). **Wisdom is supreme,** he says, **so get wisdom** (4:7). Solomon would also say, if asked, that the process of becoming wise starts with *wanting* to be wise.

Remember when cereal boxes came with prizes inside? They were at the bottom of the box, and your mom wouldn't let you shove your hand in to search for them. If you wanted the prizes, you had to eat your way to them. Similarly, if you want the rest of your life to be better than the part you've already lived, wisdom is there for the taking. But you must desire it and earnestly pursue it. **Cherish** wisdom like a husband is to cherish his wife, and wisdom **will honor you** (4:8-9).

4:10-13 Solomon doesn't stop pleading with his **son** to **listen** (4:10) because he knows there are very practical consequences to heeding that advice. Accepting godly wisdom from one's parents can help you **live** longer (4:10), and I never met anyone who didn't want to live a few extra years! **When you walk** the paths of life, wisdom can even keep you from getting tripped up (4:12). It helps you see things the way they really are—with spiritual insight. So if you know what's good for you, you'll **hold on to instruction** as if it were your life. Because, after all, it *is* **your life** (4:13). See 3:21-26.

4:14-15 Parents must exhort their children to pursue wisdom *and* **avoid** evil. Young people need to know the proper route to take, but they also need to recognize the telltale warning signs of a path that leads to destruction. They must **keep off the path of the wicked** and **pass it by.** When you see the highway leading to hell, turn your car the other way.

4:16-19 Practicing evil is woven into the daily life of the wicked—sleeping, eating, and walking. They even suffer from insomnia if they fail to **make someone stumble** (4:16). Just as Jesus considered obeying God to be his "food" (see John 4:34), those who reject God feast on a diet of **wickedness** (4:17). The path they walk is **the darkest gloom** so that they don't even know why they do what they do (4:19).

4:20-27 The repetitiveness of Solomon's call for his son to **pay attention** and **listen** (4:20) is intentional. It's a reminder that parents can't offer their children wise instructions one time and suppose their job is done—mission accomplished. No, instructing our children is an ongoing responsibility. Moms and dads must urge their children to **keep** wise words **within [their] heart** and **guard [their] heart above all else** (4:21, 23).

Why is the heart so important? Because **it is the source of life** (4:23). Jesus even said good and evil are produced from what is "stored up in" it (see Luke 6:45), so nothing in your life deserves more constant care and attention than your heart. Whatever is stored up inside it will dictate what you **speak** (4:24), what you **look** at (4:25), and where your **feet** take you (4:26-27). Keep your heart under lock and key.

5:1-14 Solomon tells his son to **pay attention** if he wants to be a man of **discretion** (5:1-2). He speaks plainly about the deadly lure a young man faces in the seduction of a **forbidden woman** (5:3). Whether the temptation is fornication, adultery, or pornography, fathers must warn their sons that though the promise made by such things is sweet, following such a path leads **to death** (5:3-6). **Keep your way far from her** (5:8) is a reminder not to walk near the edge of the cliff. Sexual indiscretion will affect your wealth (e.g., alimony payments), your health (e.g., sexually transmitted diseases), and your reputation (5:10, 14). The man who doesn't guard his heart but lets his untamed sexual desires lead the way is repeatedly shown by Solomon to be a fool who is walking to his own funeral (5:7-14; 6:20-35; 7:6-27). In the end, he inevitably admits that he **hated discipline**, and it led to his **complete ruin** (5:12, 14).

5:15-19 Many think the Bible is negative about sex, but it's difficult to reach that conclusion after reading passages like this one as well as Song of Solomon. In fact, God invented sex! But he designed it to take place between one man and one woman in the context of the marriage covenant. God is the one who commands, **Take pleasure in the wife of your youth** (5:18). Under the covering of

God's covenant, in the environment of a life-long commitment between a husband and wife, sex is a good gift of God intended to be enjoyed (5:19).

5:20-23 Because God grants the kindness of sexual intimacy to couples within the covenant of marriage, **why would you lose yourself with a forbidden woman** (5:20)? Make no mistake: nothing is truly done "in secret." We live under the gaze of an omnipresent God (5:21). You may think no one sees what you do in the dark. You might be good at covering your tracks. But the God whose opinion really matters sees all. Blessing and judgment are in his hands. So if you prefer stupidity to discipline on the matter of purity (5:23), you'll find yourself ensnared by your **own** sexual sin (5:22). Dads, be like Paul and warn your sons to "flee sexual immorality" (1 Cor 6:18).

6:1-5 Another recurring theme in Proverbs is financial responsibility. Solomon warns his son not to **put up security for [his] neighbor** (6:1). We would refer to this as being a cosigner for someone else's debts. If the borrow defaults, guess who's left holding the bag? Don't trap yourself into assuming another person's financial obligations. And if you've trapped yourself by agreeing to such an arrangement, **free yourself** from **your neighbor's power!** (6:2-3). Don't rest until you escape the mess (6:4-5).

6:6-11 Men and women of God's kingdom have the responsibility to rule faithfully over the domain God has entrusted to them. Laziness has no place among God's people. When Solomon wanted to show his son an example of diligent labor, he pointed to one of the smallest visible creatures in creation: **the ant** (6:6). Ants are self-starters. They don't need someone breathing down their necks, nagging them to be productive (6:7). Understanding how God's universe works is second nature to them: if you want to eat, you have to work (6:8). The **slacker**, by contrast, prefers getting his beauty rest: a **little sleep** here and a **little slumber** there (6:9-10). What he doesn't realize is that **poverty will** jump a shiftless man like a mugger in a dark alley (6:11). See 10:4; 12:24; 18:9.

6:12-15 God's Word says the person who speaks **dishonestly, plots evil,** and **stirs up trouble** is **worthless** (6:12-14). There's no value in his character or in his actions. Such a person doesn't even consider his own future. He never asks himself, "Where is this path taking me?" As a result, **calamity will strike him suddenly** (6:15). In Proverbs, the foolish person is always ultimately overtaken by the consequences of his own actions.

6:16-19 We know that God **hates** all sin. But Solomon says there are **seven** things that are especially **detestable to him** (6:16); interestingly, all of them have to do with how we relate to others (6:17-19). Pride, or **arrogant eyes** (6:17), is first on God's list. It's the sin that led Satan to rebel against God and set up a rival kingdom (see Isa 14:12-14). And if that's not reason enough to avoid it, know that "God resists the proud but gives grace to the humble" (Jas 4:6).

Pride is typically the headwaters of other sins. When we think too highly of ourselves, we are tempted to commit the other six things that are detestable to God, stirring up **trouble among brothers** (6:19). This is no minor matter because God responds to the unity of his people. That's why the devil loves to split believers apart, knowing that the power of God among them will be hindered.

6:20-23 In chapter 5, Solomon pleaded with his son to avoid sexual immorality, and he returns to the subject here. Dads must not assume they can have "the talk" one time with their boys and then forget the whole thing. Your son needs ongoing warning and exhortation if he is to avoid giving in to the sexual corruption that everyone around him is indulging in. Tell him to wear your instruction like a necklace so that it will always be a present source of guidance (6:20-22).

6:24-35 When temptation strikes, you have to be prepared. What do you do, man, when **an evil woman** speaks **flattering** words and bats her **eyelashes** at you (6:24-25)? **Don't lust in your heart for her beauty** (6:25). Why? Because the outcome for doing so is ugly: it's like embracing **fire** (6:27). You simply can't snuggle up to a flame and not be scorched! Make no mistake: **the one who sleeps with another man's wife** will not **go unpunished** (6:29). This is the Galatians 6:7 principle at work again, a reminder that you reap what you sow. If you adopt a baby dragon for a pet, don't be shocked when it grows up to eat you. **The one who commits adultery**—who pursues pleasure outside the cover of the marriage covenant—**lacks sense** because he **destroys himself** (6:32). As we also saw in 5:10-14, it will cost him his **wealth** (6:31) and bring **dishonor** and **disgrace** (6:33). And he just might **get a beating**, or worse, if a jealous husband **takes revenge** (6:33-34).

7:1-3 The wisdom of God must become not just our top priority, but part of who we are and what we do. Solomon advised his son, **Keep my commands and live, and guard my instructions as you would the pupil of your eye** (7:1-2). Tying God's commands **to your fingers** and writing them **on the tablet of your heart** (7:3) reminds us that the Israelites were commanded to make God's Word an inextricable part of their everyday lives (Deut 6:4-9).

7:4-27 Warnings to flee sexual sin continue through Proverbs 7. So parents, if the space Solomon devotes to this topic doesn't convince you to invest recurring time talking to your children—especially your sons—about it, you're missing the obvious. According to the Bible, sex education is the responsibility of parents—not the public schools.

In 7:6-27, sexual immorality is personified as a woman on the prowl. And make no mistake: she's seeking your sons. In every corner of our culture, in fact, immorality is poised to entrap new victims. Today, whether they want it or not, most people possess the easy ability to access pornography on the mobile devices they carry everywhere with them. But the one who impulsively pursues a woman who is not his wife—whether she is single, married to another, or beckoning from a digital screen—**doesn't know** intuitively that **it will cost him his life** (7:23). He must be warned. Too many men—including Christian men—are suffering the far-reaching consequences of sexual sin.

8:1-4 Wisdom is personified in Proverbs as a woman. The seductress mentioned in 7:10-21 walks the streets and entices young men to follow, and Lady **Wisdom** also stands in the streets and cries out for people to follow her (8:1-4). But that's where the similarities end. The forbidden woman has "a hidden agenda" (7:10). But Wisdom takes her message out into the open and offers her gift to everyone because her agenda is God's agenda. Therefore she stands in the middle of the street and calls out, freely offering a spiritual view of life.

Parents, God has given you the responsibility to instill wisdom in your children, and there are lots of noises competing for their attention. So since wisdom doesn't whisper or mumble, make sure you don't either. Your children need to hear you.

8:5-21 These verses spell out the virtues and rewards for those who will listen to Wisdom. What she offers is better than **silver**, **gold**, or **jewels** (8:10-11, 19). We should not be satisfied with pursuing merely the socially acceptable approach to life, then, for God has something better planned for those who do life his way. Whoever listens to Wisdom becomes **shrewd** and develops **common sense** (8:5), receiving **good advice** (8:14). Unfortunately, these qualities are in short supply today, so whoever possesses them will not go unnoticed. **Love** Wisdom, and she will **love** you; **search** for her, and you'll **find** her (8:17). If you heed God's "seek and find" commands, he always promises to deliver what you're looking for (see Jer 29:13; Matt 7:7-8).

8:22-36 Wisdom isn't some Johnny-come-lately. **Before the earth began**, before the **watery depths** were poured out, before **the mountains** were raised, before **the fields** were laid out, **the Lord acquired [wisdom] at the beginning** (8:22-26). From **the heavens** above to **the foundations of the earth** below, God made his world through wisdom (8:27-29). And wisdom wasn't a mere tool that God used; it was **his delight every day** (8:30).

What do we learn from this? First, if not for wisdom, you wouldn't be here. Wisdom is woven into creation; therefore, you can't escape the consequences of rejecting it.

Second, your Creator has given you an example to follow. God accomplished his glorious work with wisdom. So why attempt your own work without it? Third, wisdom brings joy. If you want to be truly happy in God's kingdom, pursuing wisdom guarantees God will bless you with rejoicing. And that's how Solomon concludes chapter 8—with an appeal to his sons to see wisdom as the door that leads to happiness (8:32-34). Finding wisdom is the difference between **life** and **death** (8:35-36).

9:1-6 If you don't feel hungry for wisdom, it's a good sign that you're actually starving for it. Wisdom has prepared a mind-blowing banquet of blessing for those who will accept her invitation (9:1-5), and rejecting her offer is like rejecting the only source of food. We desperately need God's wisdom, so we need to RSVP immediately and partake of the feast offered. Wisdom says, **come** and **you will live** (9:5-6).

9:7-9 Humans don't typically enjoy being rebuked, but Proverbs insists that the difference between **a mocker** and **the wise** lies in an individual's willingness to be corrected. Solomon says, if you **rebuke a mocker . . . he will hate you**—and maybe even **hurt** you (9:7-8). But a wise and righteous man knows that whatever wisdom he possesses is not

enough. He wants to **be wiser still** (9:9), so he's open to correction. He's not satisfied with making a few good choices in life. He wants to make them all the time.

9:10 Lest we forget what this discussion of wisdom is all about, Solomon repeats the theme he began with (1:7): **The fear of the LORD is the beginning of wisdom, and the knowledge of the Holy One is understanding.** Wisdom, the ability to understand the divine perspective and apply it to life, comes from God. He's the only source. If you're going to become wise, you have to get to know God through his Word and take him seriously.

9:11-12 You can't purchase years to add to your lifespan. But, if you accept Wisdom's banquet invitation (9:1-5), she'll keep you from dying an untimely death through foolishness (9:11).

9:13-18 Don't miss that there's another party going on, distracting people from the pursuit of wisdom. The devil has a banquet prepared too, hosted by **Folly**. But this hostess is **rowdy**; she's **gullible and knows nothing** (9:13). Her meal may be **sweet** and **tasty** (9:17), but it'll kill you (9:18). Her guests are in the grave. You won't come home from this party.

III. PROVERBS OF SOLOMON (10:1–22:16)

10:1 Solomon's proverbs begin here. A *proverb* is a pithy statement about how to make the best possible decision with regard to a particular scenario. Solomon's proverbs in the Bible offer godly wisdom for making choices about everything: marriage, parenting, work, money, friends, and more.

Because Proverbs is an essential manual that helps parents teach their children wisdom, it's not surprising that this first proverb speaks to how the presence or absence of wisdom in a child's heart affects his relationship to his parents. **A wise son brings joy to his father, but a foolish son, heartache to his mother.** When children walk in godliness, they bring joy to their moms and dads. Foolish sons and daughters, however,

cause their parents grief. You cannot control the decisions your children will make. But you can, from the beginning, teach them a divine perspective of life so they're equipped to make decisions that glorify God.

10:2-5 These verses address principles of hard work and prosperity. Those who are lazy or who use illicit means to obtain money will not prosper. Ultimately, the Lord **denies the wicked what they crave**, and the **idle** become **poor** (10:3-4). Obtain money illegally, and God will oppose you. Sit around playing video games all day, and you'll go hungry. But know God takes care of those who embrace righteousness and work with diligence. See 6:6-11; 12:24; 18:9.

10:6-7 To be blessed is to be happy, and I've never met anyone who didn't want to be happy. The problem is that human beings have messed-up ideas about how to become so. In God's economy, **blessings** come upon **the righteous**—that is, on those who seek to live in conformity to God's character.

10:8-10 Sadly, integrity is hard to come by in today's culture. But God promises security to the one **who lives with integrity** (10:9). The one who acts honestly and honorably, even when no one is watching, receives divine protection. No such safety net exists for the one who **perverts his ways.**

10:11 That **the mouth of the righteous is a fountain of life, but the mouth of the wicked conceals violence** is a reminder that growing up in Christ means using our tongues to refresh others. That, however, goes against the natural perversity of the human heart and requires the power of the Holy Spirit. Regardless of how much we shoot off our mouths and say, "But I just can't help it," we *can* control our tongues.

10:12 It's one thing to quote a passage like, **Hatred stirs up conflicts, but love covers all offenses,** but it's another to put it into practice. We must realize that our likes and personal preferences are irrelevant. The Bible doesn't command us to like one another; it commands us to "love one another" (John 13:34). In the Bible, love is not a giddy feeling or butterflies in the stomach. Love cannot be defined by how we feel, then. Biblical love is measured in sacrificing for the good of others.

10:13-14 It's amazing how much the Bible says about our speech. If you want to do a study that will challenge and change you, explore what God's Word says about your words. Observe a wise man, and you'll find God's wisdom on his lips and a storeroom of **knowledge** in his heart. Observe a fool, and you'll see someone who's going to take a beating and be destroyed by his own **mouth.**

10:15-16 Wealth provides protection that **poverty** can't (10:15). Throwing money away, then, will only lead to your ruin. But let your

bank account—whether large or small—be supplied by honest labor and not wicked gain (10:16).

10:17 If one has a choice between following a **path to life** and being lost, who would willingly choose the latter? Yet, countless people do this every day when they reject **correction** instead of following **instruction.**

10:18 The person whose heart is filled with hatred experiences a catch-22. Either he **conceals** his **hatred** and is a liar, or he **spreads [his] slander** and is **a fool.**

10:19-21 When there are many words, sin is unavoidable, but the one who controls his lips is prudent (10:19). In other words, if you don't know how to keep your mouth shut, you can expect sin to flow repeatedly from it. But **the tongue of the righteous is pure silver,** and his lips **feed many** (10:20-21)—that is, his mouth is valuable to those around him because it builds them up and dispenses God's viewpoint like a rich meal.

10:22 The LORD's blessing enriches, and he adds no painful effort to it. A blessing in this instance is a God-given capacity to enjoy his goodness in your life. Money and good health are certainly nice things to have, but they are not necessarily blessings in the biblical sense. Many people have such things but don't enjoy them and aren't blessed by them. They have no sense of God's peace or satisfaction in their hearts; thus, even "good" things can become a source of unhappiness or discontentment. When God pours out his goodness to you, he gives you joy and peace and satisfaction with it, regardless of your particular situation.

10:23-25 What's a telltale sign of a fool? **Shameful conduct is pleasure** to him. Evil has stopped being evil for the one who rejects God. It moves under the heading of entertainment. But **a person of understanding** finds pleasure and enjoyment in a life lived wisely (10:23). And, in the end, both **the wicked** and **the righteous** will reap the just consequences of the conflicting pleasures they sought (10:24-25).

10:26 See 6:6-11; 10:2-5; 12:24; 18:9; 26:13-16.

10:27-30 Our graveyards are filled with young people whose lives were **cut short** as a result of foolish choices. If you don't want to die before your time, **fear the LORD**—take God seriously (10:27). Verses 28-30 repeat this theme. The righteous have **hope** in the midst of trouble because God is a mighty fortress that can't be shaken. The wicked, however, avail themselves of no protection and can expect nothing but **destruction** (10:28-29).

10:31-32 You can tell the difference between the righteous and the wicked simply by listening to them talk (see 10:11, 13-14, 18-21). Jesus said, "The mouth speaks from the overflow of the heart" (Matt 12:34).

11:1 The Lord hates dishonesty in the marketplace. His delight and blessing are on those who do business with integrity—regardless of how others operate.

11:2 God stands ready to grant us wisdom in abundance, but we have to admit our need. **When arrogance comes, disgrace follows, but with humility comes wisdom.** We've got to humble ourselves and admit that we don't know everything. We need to stop flying blind and start communicating with the one in the control tower who can see everything and lead us to our destination.

11:3 Walk in the **integrity** that comes from being in alignment with God's priorities, and it will guide you.

11:4-10 Whatever success and profit the wicked have in this life will eventually come to ruin: **When the wicked person dies, his expectation comes to nothing** (11:7). At a wicked man's death, people don't even grieve; they celebrate (11:10). After death, he is consigned to a joyless eternity separated from God. There is no fulfillment in hell, no dreams, only bitter regrets. It's important to remember that **wealth** can't protect the wicked from judgment (11:4, 7); you can't buy off God. **The righteous**, though, will be **rescued** (11:4, 6, 8-9).

11:11 **A city is built up by the blessing of the upright**; thus, God's kingdom agenda is to be lived out by Christians as they interact with their world. We must align our lives with his game plan as we love God, love our neighbors, and influence our society. When Christians live with righteousness and justice, unbelievers will see God's truth in action and be blessed by it.

11:12-13 Wisdom is demonstrated by what does and does not come out of a person's mouth. Here, Solomon emphasizes what should *not* come out. **A person with understanding keeps silent** and does not show **contempt for his neighbor** by spewing out hatred (11:12).

How do you identify **a trustworthy person**? See if they can keep a secret. If they prefer spilling the beans in **gossip**, they don't deserve your **confidence** (11:13). See 17:9; 26:20-22.

11:14 Don't be a Lone Ranger Christian. Don't think you can succeed apart from the help of a community of believers in a local church. Instead, seek **guidance** from **many counselors** who will speak the divine viewpoint into your life.

11:15 See 6:1-5.

11:16-21 These verses are examples that describe the practical outcomes of two opposing mindsets, righteousness and wickedness. An evil person may gain **riches** temporarily (11:16). But, in the end, he brings disaster, punishment, and **death** upon himself (11:17, 19, 21) and is **detestable to the LORD** (11:20). In contrast, the righteous person gains **honor**, benefit, and **reward** (11:16-18); such a person is God's **delight** (11:20).

11:22 Nothing is more attractive than a wise woman who makes God's agenda her own (see 31:10-31). But, if a physically beautiful woman **rejects good sense**, at heart she's no more attractive than **a pig's snout** adorned with **a gold ring**. In other words, it doesn't matter how you try to dress up foolishness. Put lipstick on a pig, and it's still a pig.

11:23 See 11:4-9.

11:24-26 These verses emphasize the importance of generosity. Giving is an act of worship to God. It reveals who comes first in our lives (see 3:9). When we use our money and resources to promote God's agenda—building up the saints, spreading the gospel, helping those in need—he promises blessing, which is the capacity to enjoy and extend his goodness (see 10:22).

11:27 "The one who seeks finds," Jesus said in Matthew 7:8. Thus, whoever **searches for what is good** won't be disappointed (see 8:17). But this same principle applies to those who go hunting for evil. Look **for trouble,** and **it will come** find you.

11:28 God may provide riches or not. Regardless, **anyone trusting in his riches will fall.** As Solomon has said, "Trust in the LORD with all your heart" (3:5). Nothing else can support you. See 30:7-9.

11:29-30 If you prefer to be **a fool,** be prepared to spend your life doing what other people tell you (11:29). Righteous living, on the other hand, is like **a tree of life. A wise person captivates people** (11:30).

11:31 Sometimes it seems the wicked have it made in life, but that's an illusion. **If the righteous will be repaid on earth, how much more the wicked and sinful.** God may choose to demonstrate his righteous judgment on sin while a sinner is still living. But even if an evildoer escapes condemnation in this life, all his glittering gold means nothing in the end.

12:1 See 3:11-12; 9:7-9.

12:2-3 No one can be made secure by wickedness, but the root of the righteous is immovable (12:3). In other words, no **schemes** or plans of the wicked will succeed, nor will they give them safety or security (12:2). The righteous, on the other hand, need not worry about securing themselves or establishing a support system. Their roots go down deep; they will never be moved because the Lord secures them (12:3).

12:4 That **a wife of noble character is her husband's crown** foreshadows the book's closing praise of a capable wife (31:10-31).

Her husband is proud of her and lets her know it. On the other hand, **a wife who causes shame is like rottenness in** her husband's **bones.** Even if a man is healthy and fit, a shameful wife makes him miserable on the inside.

12:5 At conversion, the Christian receives a new mind: "the mind of Christ" (1 Cor 2:16). But too many believers slump into their old ways of thinking. Instead, we must be in tune with the Spirit of God so that our **thoughts** are **just.** Righteous living can only proceed from righteous thinking.

12:6 See 10:11, 18-21, 31-32.

12:7 This proverb calls to mind Jesus's parable of the two builders in Matthew 7:24-27. **The house of the righteous will stand** because everything they do is built on a foundation of trusting in God's view of things as revealed in his Word. By contrast, **the wicked are overthrown** because their lives are built on a foundation of shifting sand. Their choices and decisions have nothing of substance to back them up.

12:8 One either has a mind operating from the divine viewpoint or a **twisted mind.** The former produces **insight** that will earn praise. But the twisted mind produces corruption that will only be **despised.**

12:9 Better to be a nobody and have some measure of prosperity **than to act important but have no food.** So don't be something special in your own eyes. God's opinion is what matters.

12:10 When God created Adam and Eve, he gave them dominion over the world, including the animals. A Christian who is committed to God's rule knows that animals are part of God's creation and deserve our compassionate care.

12:11 See 10:4-5.

12:12 Not only is **the root of the righteous** immovable (12:7), it's also **productive** (12:12). Those who align themselves under God, then, are both secure from danger and able to accomplish good works that bring blessings to others.

12:13-14 Jesus told his listeners that they would be judged by their own words (see Matt 12:37). Be careful what you say, then; don't be hasty to speak. You will either be **trapped** by your words (12:13) or **satisfied** by them (12:14).

12:15 We need a divine perspective. We need the opinion of the one who can see things for what they really are. **A fool's way is right in his own eyes.** The fool's underlying problem is he can't see that his spiritual eyesight is blurred. As a result, he never **listens to counsel.** He just listens to himself tell himself that he's okay.

12:16-22 Remember what James says about the tongue: it's "a restless evil, full of deadly poison" (Jas 3:8). This is the principle at work behind the **fool's displeasure** (12:16) when he **speaks rashly** (12:18). It's a reminder that when we are quick to speak—often out of anger—good results rarely follow. We must engage our minds before we speak.

Of all the sins involving our speech, lying is one of the most disastrous. The wicked have **deceit** in their **hearts** (12:20). And, inevitably, deceit escapes the heart through a mouth that tells lies (12:17, 19, 22). But **lying lips are detestable to the LORD** (12:22). When he prayed to the Father, Jesus said, "Your word is truth" (John 17:17), and he told his disciples, "I am the way, the truth, and the life" (John 14:6). Lying, then, is contrary to God's own character and behavior. Therefore, let faithfulness fill your heart, and truth will come out of your mouth—because **truthful lips endure forever** (12:19).

12:23 That **a foolish heart publicizes stupidity** is a reminder that what we are on the inside will ultimately be on display for everyone to see. If you reject wisdom, the thoughts of your foolish heart will eventually go public. Stupidity isn't smart enough to stay hidden.

12:24 Kingdom men and women **will rule** with diligence over the realm God grants them. Lazy men and women only work when someone forces them. See 6:6-11; 10:2-5; 18:9; 26:13-16.

12:25 Throughout Scripture, we're called by God to practice the "one anothers" (see Rom 12:10; Gal 6:2; Eph 4:32; Col 3:9; 1 Thess 4:18; Heb 10:24; 1 Pet 1:22; 1 John 3:11). All Christians are susceptible to **anxiety** because of the trials of life. A practical way to love and bless one another is to offer a **good word** that **cheers** the heart of a struggling believer. See 17:22.

12:26 It doesn't matter which of **the ways of the wicked** a person chooses to follow. All will take him off course.

12:27 See 6:6-11; 10:2-5; 12:24; 18:9; 26:13-16.

12:28 This is a good summary of much of what Solomon is teaching his sons—and what parents need to impress on their children. There are two paths in life: the path of **life** and the path of **death.** You only get one go-around in history to make your choice.

13:1 Discipline should be both instructive and corrective—that is, it should include both teaching and rebuke. **A wise son responds to his father's discipline.** Parents have significantly more experience than their kids, and wise kids know it. Teenagers who want to grow in wisdom will humbly receive instruction and admonishment from their moms and dads. **But a mocker doesn't listen to rebuke.** His ears are closed. Convinced that he knows all he needs to know, he has preempted his own learning.

13:2-3 See 10:11, 13-14, 18-21, 31-32; 11:12-13; 12:13-14, 16-22; 16:21-24; 25:11-12.

13:4 See 6:6-11; 10:2-5; 12:24; 18:9; 26:13-16.

13:5 See 12:16-22.

13:6 Righteousness and **wickedness:** only one of them delivers what it promises.

13:7 See 12:9.

13:8 Wealth is not a blessing in and of itself. It has its own temptations, sorrows, and limitations (see 11:4, 7, 28). Wealth makes the rich a target for thieves, yet no one holds a **poor person** for **ransom**.

13:9 The Lord expects his people to live under his rule and let his glory shine through their good works (see Matt 5:14-16; Eph 5:8; Phil 2:15). **But the lamp of the wicked** will be snuffed out.

13:10 Arrogance is another word for pride. It's Satan's sin of choice (see Isa 14:13-14) and is number one on God's hate list (6:16-17).

13:11 See 10:2.

13:12 See 13:19.

13:13 See 1:22-33.

13:14 See 10:11.

13:15-16 Either we will learn to make decisions with **good sense**, winning **favor** with God and man, or we will follow a **treacherous** course (13:15). There are two agendas at work all around us: the way of the world and the way of God. Our decisions will be based on whichever agenda we're following. The truth is revealed by the decisions we make and the lifestyles we live, because **every sensible person acts knowledgeably, but a fool displays his stupidity** (13:16).

13:17 The **wicked** person bears troublesome news. The **trustworthy** person bears **healing** news. "How beautiful on the mountains are the feet of the herald . . . who brings news of good things . . . who says to Zion, 'Your God reigns!'" (Isa 52:7).

13:18 See 1:22-33; 3:11-12; 9:7-9; 10:17; 25:11-12; 29:1.

13:19 Everyone has desires; everyone wants something. Unfulfilled desires lead to sorrow (13:12), but having your desires met is **sweet** and life-giving. In Proverbs, Solomon urges us to desire wisdom above all else because it can actually deliver on the sweet promises it makes.

13:20-21 Here's the principle of 1 Corinthians 15:33 again: you become like your companions. Spend time with wise people, and you will learn from them. Hang out with fools, and their corrupt moral values will rub off on you so that you **suffer harm** (13:20). You see, fools don't offer correction. So if your thinking is self-centered and your decisions lack good judgment, a fool will simply make you feel good about the path you're already on. **Disaster** or **rewards**: which do you prefer (13:21)?

13:22 This verse states a key principle for the development of a kingdom-minded economic agenda: **the sinner's wealth is stored up for the righteous.** Although wicked people may accumulate much, God has a way of transferring the resources of the wicked to be used and developed for kingdom purposes. For example, after God judged Egypt with plagues, he told the Israelites to ask their Egyptian neighbors for silver and gold (see Exod 11:1-2). The Egyptians were only too glad to give God's people anything they asked (see Exod 12:35-36). God then had the Israelites take that wealth and build a tabernacle where they could worship him. Later, he told Israel to take the land of Canaan, then inhabited by unrighteous people, and do his kingdom business within it (see Ps 105:43-45). God knows how to make theological transactions in favor of the righteous to accomplish his purposes.

13:23 God hates injustice. He opposes those who take advantage of **the poor**—and his people should too. When he saw his rich countrymen exploiting their neighbors, Nehemiah raised his voice and called out for justice (see Neh 5:1-13). See 17:5.

13:24 If we love our children, we will be diligent to discipline them. This verse is not a license for abuse. A **rod** refers to any reasonable discipline inflicting sufficient pain that discourages the bad and encourages the good. When our children become teenagers, for instance, appropriate discipline may be the loss of a privilege—that can certainly be painful.

We must realize that lack of loving discipline can lead to a rebellious lifestyle that could cost our children their reputations or their lives. God's kingdom works through the family. Many of our society's problems, in fact, can be traced to a failure of parents to discipline their kids. See 19:18; 22:15.

13:25 Although poverty can result from injustice (13:23), it can also result from laziness (19:15). Refuse to work, and you'll end up with an empty **stomach** (see 2 Thess 3:10).

14:1-3 The actions of the wise bring success and protection; the actions of fools bring ruin and punishment. So what's the difference between the two kinds of people? The one **fears the Lord**; the other **despises him** (14:2). Your attitude toward God dictates how you live.

14:4 Use your resources wisely. Invest your money in that from which you can expect **an abundant harvest.**

14:5-7 See 10:11, 13-14, 18-21, 31-32; 11:12-13; 12:13-14, 16-22; 16:21-24; 25:11-12.

14:8-10 See 14:13-15.

14:11 See 12:7.

14:12 Make no mistake: God means every word he says. This, then, is one of the most sobering verses of Scripture: **There is a way that seems right to a person, but its end is the way to death.** In the book of Judges, Israel was in a dark and disastrous period because "everyone did whatever seemed right to him" (Judg 21:25). This highlights the problem with worldly, human wisdom: it *seems right!* And without comparison to the divine perspective, it looks pretty good. Human strategies and philosophies about life, in fact, have a bunch of people convinced because they appeal to our own self-centered notions of what's best. But those who won't seek God's opinion regarding the right path will pay a high price in the end. Rely solely on human logic to chart the course of your life, and it will lead you on a path to hell. See 12:15.

14:13-15 If we're not careful, we can be easily taken in, easily deceived by what we see or don't see. This is what 14:12 emphasizes. A fool is deceived by his own stupidity (14:8), mocks what he doesn't understand (14:9), and ultimately gets **what his conduct deserves** (14:14). In other words, a fool is easily duped. By contrast, we must beware external appearances. Things are not always what they seem. A person may look outwardly happy yet be inwardly **sad** and bitter (14:10, 13). Don't accept everything based on how it appears (14:15).

14:16-17 See 29:11.

14:18-24 These verses highlight the truth that the wise will ultimately be **crowned** for their godly deeds (14:18). Not so with fools: **don't those who plan evil go astray** (14:22)? Joseph is a prime biblical example of this principle. His jealous brothers sold him as a slave. He was unjustly accused of adultery and thrown in prison. Yet, through it all, he maintained his integrity and "the Lord was with Joseph" (see Gen 37:26-28; 39:6-21). In the end, he was elevated to prominence, and his wicked brothers bowed before him (see Gen 42:6)—just as he had dreamed they would (see Gen 37:5-11). Indeed, those who follow God are **crowned** (14:18), and **the evil bow before those who are good** (14:19).

14:25 See 12:22.

14:26-27 The man or woman who takes God seriously—whose life is characterized by **the fear of the Lord**—is a source of **refuge** (14:26). Why? Because that person is able to see things from God's point of view. Wearing divine glasses in a sense, he or she can turn people away **from the snares of death** (14:27). That individual can see Satan's traps and warn the inexperienced, "Don't step there!"

14:28-35 God's Word forms the standard not only for personal righteousness but also for national obedience: **Righteousness exalts a nation, but sin is a disgrace to any people** (14:34). There are principles God has established that will benefit a society if they are followed—even if the leaders themselves don't know God. As Paul later urged Timothy to pray for governmental leaders "so that we may lead a tranquil and quiet life in all godliness and dignity" (1 Tim 2:2), so we should pray for leaders to be sensitive to God's way of doing things.

Pray that your leaders will be **patient** (14:29), content and not power-hungry (14:30), **kind to the poor** (14:31), **righteous** (14:32), wise (14:33), and will surround themselves with wise administrators (14:35). When biblical principles infiltrate society, their restraining influence is felt as an expression of God's grace that he makes available to all. See 16:10-15; 19:12.

15:1-2 See 10:11, 13-14, 18-21, 31-32; 11:12-13; 12:13-14, 16-22; 16:21-24; 25:11-12.

15:3 God is omnipresent and omniscient. That's the theological way of saying God is everywhere, sees all, and knows all. And God's comprehensive knowledge includes a moral element: **The eyes of the Lord are everywhere, observing the wicked and the good.** No sin is overlooked—and neither is any righteous deed. That's comprehensive knowledge. And the amazing thing is that God invites us to tap into his wisdom for daily living.

15:4 See 10:11, 13-14, 18-21, 31-32; 11:12-13; 12:13-14, 16-22; 16:21-24; 25:11-12.

15:5 See 1:8-9; 4:10-13; 13:1.

15:6 See 10:2-4.

15:7 See 10:11, 13-14, 18-21, 31-32; 11:12-13; 12:13-14, 16-22; 16:21-24; 25:11-12.

15:8-9 The Lord **detests** both the **way of the wicked** (15:9) and their **sacrifice** (15:8). Neither an evil person's life nor religion, then, has value.

15:10 See 1:22-33; 3:11-12; 9:7-9; 10:17; 25:11-12; 29:1.

15:11 See 15:3.

15:12 See 1:22-33; 3:11-12; 9:7-9; 10:17; 25:11-12; 29:1.

15:13 See 12:25; 17:22.

15:14 See 10:11, 13-14, 18-21, 31-32; 11:12-13; 12:13-14, 16-22; 16:21-24; 25:11-12.

15:15 See 12:25; 17:22.

15:16-17 See 19:1; 22:1-5.

15:18 See 29:11.

15:19 See 6:6-11; 10:2-5; 12:24; 18:9; 26:13-16.

15:20 See 10:1.

15:21 Don't find **joy** in that which should bring shame. See 10:23-25.

15:22 See 11:14; 20:18.

15:23 See 12:25.

15:24 There are two ways to live, two paths to take. Each has a very different destination. See 2:20-22; 11:4-10, 16-21; 12:28; 14:12; 15:24.

15:25 "God resists the proud" (Jas 4:6), but Scripture declares that he looks with compassion on the orphan and widow in their humble circumstances (Deut 10:18; Ps 68:5). He expects his people to do the same (Jas 1:27).

15:26-27 To hate is not necessarily a sin. It depends on the object of your hatred. **The Lord detests the plans of the one who is evil** (15:26). So God's people ought to hate evil too—such as **bribes** that cause the wicked to profit **dishonestly** (15:27).

15:28 See 12:16, 18.

15:29 Prayer is like a key, and the secret to having the key work is Jesus Christ. The Lord **hears the prayer of the righteous.** But **the wicked** have no such access.

15:30 See 13:17.

15:31-33 See 1:22-33; 3:11-12; 9:7-9; 10:17; 25:11-12; 29:1.

16:1 Humans are responsible for the **reflections** and plans of their hearts, but they do nothing that falls outside of the sovereignty of God (16:1, 9). He is in control; his purposes will be accomplished; his kingdom will come. Align your agenda with his. See 16:4.

16:2 See 21:2.

16:3 If you truly **commit your activities to the LORD**, it means your will is in submission to his. When that happens, **your plans will be** achieved, because you're inviting his will to be done "on earth as it is in heaven" (Matt 6:10-11).

16:4 This is a wonderful declaration of God's sovereignty: **The LORD has prepared everything for his purpose—even the wicked for the day of disaster.** God exercises his prerogative to do whatever he pleases with his creation. Why? Because "the earth and everything in it, the world and its inhabitants, belong to the LORD" (Ps 24:1).

Suppose you came into my home and told me you didn't like how I had arranged and decorated everything. I would have one response for you: "When you start buying the furniture and paying the bills, we can entertain your viewpoint. But as long as I'm spending the money, your viewpoint carries no clout in my house."

When we start creating planets and giving life, perhaps then we can start dictating how God ought to run the universe. But unless we get that divine clout, we cannot exercise that divine prerogative. It always belongs to God, and he does whatever he chooses. This teaching does not just appear as a fleeting thought in the Bible, but as an overwhelming doctrine (see Job 42:2; Ps 115:3; Eph 1:11). Not even evil and unrighteousness can escape the all-controlling hand of the God who has even made wicked people for his own purposes.

16:5 See 6:16-17.

16:6 **One turns from evil** by ceasing to take God casually—that is, through exercising **the fear of the LORD.** Electricity is a good thing. But it's not something to take lightly. It's not something to play around with. God is your Creator, Sustainer, and Redeemer. Take him seriously.

16:7 When you align yourself under God's program, it leads to blessing. Most of those blessings are reserved for eternity. But, God can cause the most extraordinary things to happen in history when our **ways please** him.

16:8 See 19:1; 22:1-5.

16:9 See 16:1, 4.

16:10-15 God is the Creator and, therefore, the sovereign King over all. "He removes kings and establishes kings" (Dan 2:21). Rightly administered, government "is God's servant for your good" (Rom 13:4), so followers of God ought to "submit to the governing authorities" (Rom 13:1). As servants of the true King, human kings should render righteous judgments and hate wickedness. When human government is unrighteous, it is the responsibility of God's people to interpose themselves to defend innocent victims and to stand up in obedience to God (e.g., Exod 1:16-20; Esth 4; Dan 3; Acts 4:18-20). See 14:28-35; 24:10-12.

16:16 See 3:13-15.

16:17 See 2:11; 12:28.

16:18-19 See 6:16-17.

16:20 See 3:13, 18; 10:6-7; 29:18.

16:21-24 The one with **a wise heart** (16:21) thinks carefully about his words, so he may teach others with **speech** that **increases learning** (16:21, 23), gives **life** (16:22), and is **pleasant** to hear (16:21, 24).

16:25 See 14:12.

16:26 See 6:6-11; 10:2-5; 12:24; 18:9; 26:13-16.

16:27-30 Whether by deceiving (16:30), spreading **conflict** (16:28), or performing violence (16:29), wicked men cause harm to others. If you don't want to become like them, keep your distance! The righteous dig up wisdom "like hidden treasure" (2:4), but **a worthless person digs up evil** (16:27).

16:31 Young people who embrace foolishness typically despise the elderly as being out of touch and easily dismiss them. But they do so to their own peril. God's viewpoint is clear:

you are to "honor the old" out of the fear of the Lord (Lev 19:32). He grants **gray hair** as **a glorious crown.**

16:32 See 29:11.

16:33 See 16:1, 4.

17:1 See 19:1; 22:1-5.

17:2-3 If you embrace wisdom, God can miraculously reverse your circumstances. Servants become rulers (17:2) because **the LORD is the tester of hearts** (17:3). He sees what is internal and unseen (see 1 Sam 16:7).

17:4 See 10:11, 13-14, 18-21, 31-32; 11:12-13; 12:13-14, 16-22; 16:21-24; 25:11-12.

17:5 God cares for the poor (see Lev 19:10; Ps 35:10) and expects the same from his people (see Ps 41:1; Jas 2:1-7). Therefore, **the one who mocks the poor insults his Maker.** See 13:23.

17:6 This verse strikes a special chord with me. Now I don't claim the title "elderly," but I can testify that **grandchildren are the crown** of those in their senior years. What a blessing when God lets you enjoy the children of your own children in whom you've invested!

17:7 See 10:11, 13-14, 18-21, 31-32; 11:12-13; 12:13-14, 16-22; 16:21-24; 25:11-12.

17:8 See 15:27.

17:9 Whoever conceals an offense promotes love, but whoever gossips about it separates friends. Do you know what a friend is? A friend is someone to whom you can bare your soul and know it will go no further. Now, to "conceal an offense" doesn't mean to excuse sin; rather, it means a person isn't out to destroy you by using your transparency against you. A godly friend wants to lift you out of the mud—not leave you in it. See 11:13; 26:20-22.

17:10 A single **rebuke** is more effective in bringing about a change of heart in a wise man than **a hundred lashes** accomplishes on **a fool.** How easy is it for God to lead *you* to repent and learn?

17:11 See 14:28-35; 16:10-15.

17:12 Avoid the **fool!** How dangerous is it to pal around with foolish people? Solomon says you're better off facing a grizzly **bear** mama who's been **robbed of her cubs.**

17:13 See 25:21-22.

17:14 It only takes one harsh word to open the floodgates of **conflict.** "Don't give the devil an opportunity" (Eph 4:26-27) to hinder God's work among his people. **Stop a dispute** before it starts. See 29:11.

17:15 See 14:28-35; 16:10-15.

17:16 An old saying warns, "A fool and his money are soon parted." Unfortunately for him, he has no intention to put it to good use by **buying wisdom.** When all is said and done, a fool's money will be gone, and he'll still be stupid.

17:17 I can testify to the value of godly friends and brothers who have walked through life with me: **A friend loves at all times, and a brother is born for a difficult time.** Difficult times can test our relationships, to be sure. But if you want to be a kingdom man or woman who perseveres when you feel like throwing in the towel, you need fellow kingdom people who will hold you up when you grow weary. After all, when do you need a friend the most? Not when you're on top. A true friend stays with you when you're heading downhill, when times are rough. Sometimes you don't know who your friends are, in fact, until you're in trouble.

Too many of us are Lone Ranger Christians. We're trying to make it by ourselves when God's plan is for us to grow, serve, and love in community. You can't fulfill the "one another" commands of Scripture by yourself (see, e.g., John 15:12; Gal 6:2; Eph 4:32; 1 Thess 5:11). See 27:17.

17:18 See 6:1-5.

17:19 See 17:14; 29:11.

17:20 See 10:11, 13-14, 18-21, 31-32; 11:12-13; 12:13-14, 16-22; 16:21-24; 25:11-12.

17:21 See 10:1.

17:22 Speak "the truth in love" (see Eph 4:15) because God has given us the ability to turn **a broken spirit** into **a joyful heart** with our words. So whether we're offering loving admonishment to those in sin or tender comfort to those who are discouraged, we should speak with the knowledge that our mouths have power—and it's best used to declare God's perspective into a person's life. See 12:25.

17:23 See 15:27.

17:24 The **perceptive** seek out and **focus** on one thing: **wisdom**. Their chief desire is to apply the divine viewpoint to every area of life.

17:25 See 10:1.

17:26 See 14:28-35; 16:10-15.

17:27 See 17:14; 29:11.

17:28 There is a time when we must speak (see 17:22). On the other hand, the one who opens his mouth too much (usually to hear himself talk) is likely to stick his foot in it (see 10:19). Sometimes wisdom involves simply keeping your trap shut.

18:1 See 11:14; 17:17.

18:2 See 10:19; 17:28.

18:3 See 1:17-19; 13:20-21.

18:4 See 16:21-24; 17:22.

18:5 See 14:28-35; 16:10-15.

18:6-8 See 10:11, 13-14, 18-21, 31-32; 11:12-13; 12:13-14, 16-22; 16:21-24; 25:11-12.

18:9 That the **lazy** man **is brother to a vandal** indicates that to accept a paycheck without accomplishing the work agreed upon is stealing. See 6:6-11; 10:2-5; 12:24; 26:13-16.

18:10-12 When inevitable difficulties come, where will you turn? The rich man thinks his **wealth** is his **fortified city**. But Solomon says that's only true in his **imagination** (18:11). Solomon should know; he had more riches than he could ever want. But money is no silver bullet. The only sure refuge in times of tribulation is the Lord God. His name **is a strong tower; the righteous run to it and are protected** (18:10). Pride in one's own resources leads to **downfall** (18:12).

18:13 See 12:13-14, 16, 18.

18:14 See 12:25; 17:22.

18:15 See 2:1-19.

18:16 Solomon has condemned bribes—evil gifts that pervert justice (15:27; 17:23). But that's not what he's talking about here. He's simply acknowledging the fact that expressions of kindness can **open doors** that are otherwise closed.

18:17 Paul Harvey was famous for his radio program "The Rest of the Story." When hearing a **case**, that should be our motto. We should always be determined to hear both sides of a dispute before we come to any conclusions about the matter.

18:18 **Casting the lot** was a practice that acknowledged the sovereignty of God (see 16:33). It was similar to rolling dice to discern his will. Today God gives believers his indwelling Holy Spirit to guide us.

18:19 See 17:14.

18:20-21 See 10:11, 13-14, 18-21, 31-32; 11:12-13; 12:13-14, 16-22; 16:21-24; 25:11-12.

18:22 A man's decision to marry is one of the most important of his life. God gave Eve to Adam as a "helper"—a complement (see Gen 2:18). When a kingdom man finds a kingdom woman for a **wife**, he **finds a good thing and obtains favor from the Lord**.

18:23 See 17:5.

18:24 One with many friends may be harmed, but there is a friend who stays closer than a brother. Solomon isn't saying it's bad to have a lot of friends. But if everyone is your friend, something may be wrong. Everybody wants to be your friend when times are good for you—especially if you're wealthy (19:4). But if you make these hangers-on your constant and only source of companionship, you're not choosing wisely. We see illustrations of this all around us. Probably the most obvious is the politician who's a friend to everybody who will contribute to his campaign, regardless of their views. See 17:17; 27:6, 17.

19:1 Money frequently leads people astray and can distract us from the more valuable things of the Lord. Seeking success and recognition from the culture is tempting, but **better a poor person who lives with integrity than someone who has deceitful lips and is a fool**. It's obvious that in God's kingdom economy, it's better to be dirt poor with honorable character than to be insanely rich without also having spiritual wisdom. The plans that God gives us are far more valuable than anything we could obtain for ourselves.

19:2 See 12:16, 18.

19:3 See 14:1-3.

19:4 See 18:24.

19:5 See 12:17, 19, 22; 25:18-19.

19:6-7 The rich have the ability to influence others (19:6), yet the **friends** of the **poor** abandon him altogether (19:7). But remember 19:1.

19:8 The person who indulges in foolish living isn't doing himself any favors. In reality, he hates himself because foolishness leads to ruin and, perhaps, an early grave (see 4:10-13). But whoever **acquires good sense loves himself**. He seeks God's thoughts on life, receives God's blessing, and **finds success**.

19:9 12:17, 19, 22; 25:18-19.

19:10 See 17:16.

19:11 See 29:11.

19:12 When government is acting justly, the only person who needs to fear **a king's rage** is the one who does wrong (see Rom 13:4).

19:13-14 See 10:1; 18:22.

19:15 See 10:4-5; 13:25.

19:16 See 2:20-22; 11:4-10, 16-21; 12:28; 14:12; 15:24.

19:17 See 13:23; 17:5; 31:20.

19:18 If you fail to **discipline your son** in the home, he'll pay for his lack of self-control outside the home—maybe even by his death. Don't hate your child by neglecting to intervene in his life and to rebuke him when he strays. See 13:24.

19:19 See 17:14; 29:11.

19:20 See 1:22-33; 3:11-12; 9:7-9; 10:17; 25:11-12; 29:1.

19:21 Many plans are in a person's heart, but above all else, we must believe the value of seeking God and his mind on all things. We can plan our schedules as much as we want, but only what God has declared is guaranteed to take place. God did not create us and redeem us to live a plotless, purposeless existence. And that's good news! I don't know many people who are content to live and die and have on their tombstone, "Joe was here." We were made for greater things than to occupy space on the planet. God has a calling for you and me, and the beauty of it is that our callings are tailor-made for each of us. In the same way that we have unique fingerprints and DNA, we all have unique callings. Don't settle for a paycheck, a house, and two cars. That may be the American dream, but God has a dream for you that is bigger. **The LORD's decree will prevail**, so seek him and his calling for your life.

19:22 See 19:1.

19:23 See 3:21-26.

19:24 See 26:13-16.

19:25 See 17:10.

19:26 Young people need to know that their parents have a God-ordained role. A child's first obligation is to his parent—not his buddies. God considers it a disgrace to turn against one's own father and mother. See 10:1.

19:27 See 1:22-33; 3:11-12; 9:7-9; 10:17; 25:11-12; 29:1.

19:28-29 See 1:22-33.

20:1 Wine is a mocker, beer is a brawler; whoever goes astray because of them is not wise. Alcohol consumption is not completely condemned in the Bible. Wine is often featured in the Old and New Testaments during times of celebration. It was also a common beverage because of the lack of water purification systems in ancient times. Drunkenness, however, is condemned soundly in Scripture. Alcohol dulls the senses and can produce foolish decisions. Be wary of those who push drinks in front of you, then. The staggering statistics surrounding alcoholism and drunk driving are other sufficient reasons to be cautious of it.

20:2 See 19:12.

20:3 See 17:14; 18:17; 29:11.

20:4 See 10:4-5; 26:13-16.

20:5 God has a customized plan for each of us, and the wise person makes discovering that plan a priority. **Counsel in a person's heart is deep water; but a person of understanding draws it out.** When the Holy Spirit connects with the human spirit, he brings illumination to the mind concerning the plan and will of God.

20:6 See 11:12-13; 27:6.

20:7 A **righteous** man blesses his **children** by acting **with integrity.** So Dad, know that the choices you make every day—both small and large—affect your kids. What legacy do you want to leave them?

20:8 See 14:28-35; 16:10-15.

20:9 Who can say, "I have kept my heart pure"? Solomon's rhetorical question is a reminder that his exhortations in Proverbs regarding righteousness are not blind to the reality of human sinfulness. Ultimately, no one is righteous but one (see Luke 18:19; Rom 3:10). But by trusting in the righteousness of Jesus Christ and being led by the Holy Spirit, we can pursue lives in alignment with God's standards.

20:10 See 11:1.

20:11 Parents need to convince their teenagers that wisdom is something to pursue now—not once they become adults, for **even a young man is known by his actions.** Your reputation doesn't wait to develop until you reach a certain age; it is cultivated over time.

20:12-14 God has given you a **hearing ear** and a **seeing eye**—the ability to observe the world and grow in wisdom (20:12), so use Proverbs' observations about how the world works and the influence of the Holy Spirit to help you make sensible decisions. Two examples of what this looks like follow in 20:13-14. The lazy person loves **sleep** and thus goes hungry, so **open your eyes** if you don't want to be **poor** (20:13). Similarly, don't believe everything you hear. If someone is trying to work a deal to his own advantage, he may say something that doesn't match reality. Be discerning (20:14).

20:15 See 8:5-21.

20:16 See 6:1-5.

20:17 Sin never delivers what it promises. A little taste of it seems **sweet,** but indulging in it always leads to self-destruction.

20:18 An old saying warns, "If you fail to plan, you are planning to fail." Don't engage in an activity, then, without doing wise planning by obtaining **sound guidance.** If you seek no advice but your own, the results will be as limited as the input. See 11:14.

20:19 See 11:12-13; 17:9; 26:20.

20:20 Curse your parents—whom God has ordained to train you in wisdom—and get ready for the spiritual lights to go out.

20:21 This proverb brings to mind Jesus's parable of the prodigal son (see Luke 15:11-32). In that case **prematurely** obtaining **inheritance** did indeed result in ruin. When someone unskilled at financial management acquires money quickly, he's likely to lose it quickly too.

20:22 Don't seek vengeance when you are wronged. Trust in the one who sees all, knows all, and can do all to **rescue you.** Moses and Paul agree that the best course of action is leaving vengeance in the hands of God (see Deut 32:35; Rom 12:19).

20:23 See 11:1.

20:24 See 16:1, 4.

20:25 Don't make a rash commitment to the Lord and later change your mind. Jesus challenged those who listened to him to consider the cost of being his disciple (see Luke 14:27-30). Being a kingdom man or woman brings blessing, but it requires steadfast dedication to the divine purpose.

20:26 See 14:28-35; 16:10-15; 19:12.

20:27 The LORD's lamp sheds light on a person's life, searching the innermost parts. God uses his Holy Spirit and our own spirits to show us his will. The Holy Spirit illumines our spiritual eyes so we begin to see our circumstances through God's perspective. This functions as a satellite dish that enables us to tune in to the things of God. It's why your spirit needs to stay closely linked with the Holy Spirit.

20:28 See 14:28-35; 16:10-15.

20:29 See 16:31.

20:30 Governments are ordained by God to punish criminals (see Rom 13:4). Just rulers therefore protect their citizens and chastise wrongdoers.

21:1 A king's heart is like channeled water in the LORD's hand: He directs it wherever He chooses. Since God is the sovereign over his universe, he is intimately concerned with the affairs of nations. In fact, Psalm 22:28 declares that "kingship belongs to the LORD; he rules over the nations." No matter how powerful the rulers of this world are, they cannot prevent God from fulfilling his purposes—whether they acknowledge him or not.

21:2-3 All a person's ways seem right to him, but the LORD weighs hearts (21:2). This proverb will make you think twice before making an important decision without consulting the Lord! Motives are tricky things. In fact, even we don't always know why we do what we do, and at times we can fool ourselves into thinking that our reasons are God's reasons. The Lord looks right through to the very center of who we are, and he knows exactly what drives us. Doing what is righteous and just is more acceptable to the LORD than sacrifice (21:3). Remember the example of King Saul (see 1 Sam 15:1-29).

21:4 See 6:16-17; 13:10; 27:1.

21:5-7 God expects us to earn through honest and **diligent** labor (21:5), not through **lying** (21:6) or **violence** (21:7). This is a kingdom standard.

21:8 This verse encapsulates much of what Solomon has said. Whether we embrace our own agenda or God's agenda will be revealed by either **crooked** or **upright** behavior. It can't be hidden.

21:9 See 12:4.

21:10-13 These verses remind us of the differences between **the wicked** and the righteous. The wicked shows no mercy **for his neighbor** and receives no mercy himself (21:10, 13). The righteous loves others as himself (see 3:27-30; 10:11, 12; Lev 19:18; Mark 12:31). And while the wicked learn nothing from their ways, the righteous observe and learn (21:11-12).

21:14 See 18:16.

21:15 See 14:28-35; 16:10-15; 19:12.

21:16 See 2:20-22; 11:4-10, 21; 12:28; 14:12; 15:24.

21:17 See 6:6-11; 10:2-5; 12:24; 26:13-16.

21:18 The wicked will pay for their sins.

21:19 See 12:4.

21:20 See 6:6-11; 10:2-5; 12:24; 18:9; 26:13-16.

21:21 It's simple. If you pursue **righteousness**, you will find righteousness. "Seek, and you will find" (Matt 7:7). See 2:1-5; 11:27.

21:22 See 11:14; 20:18.

21:23 See 10:11, 13-14, 18-21, 31-32; 11:12-13; 12:13-14, 16-22; 16:21-24; 25:11-12.

21:24 See 6:16-17; 13:10; 27:1.

21:25-26 See 10:4-5.

21:27 Remember: God looks at the heart. Worshiping the Lord with wicked **motives** is detestable to him. We are to worship him because he deserves it—not simply because we selfishly want something from him.

21:28 See 12:17, 19, 22; 25:18-19.

21:29 A **bold face** doesn't replace sound decision-making. A confident attitude that's not informed by wisdom will lead to disaster. You can't bluff your way through life.

21:30-31 We mustn't forget that true wisdom comes from knowing and fearing God (1:7; 9:10). Try to be wise without bowing to him, and you will lose (21:30). Align yourself with God's agenda, and you will win (21:31).

22:1-5 The Lord has made both the **rich** man and the **poor** one (22:2), and both are accountable to him for how they live. If you follow a **crooked** path, riches will not protect you from punishment or the snares of life (22:3, 5). On the other hand, having **a good**

name—a good reputation—is far more valuable than **wealth** (22:1). The one who lives in the **fear of the LORD** will be blessed by him (22:4).

22:6 A vital way that biblical authority is made manifest in God's kingdom is through the family. That reality, in fact, stands behind one of the most well-known verses in the Bible: **Start a youth out on his way; even when he grows old he will not depart from it.** Child training involves making our teaching understandable so kids can differentiate between wisdom and foolishness as early as possible. We shouldn't soft-pedal the truth or only say what our children want to hear. And we shouldn't bulldoze them or beat them over the head with the truth either. Another way to translate "on his way" is "according to his way"—that is, according to each child's unique personality or bent. The way you deal with each child under your authority, then, should differ so that every one benefits from the kind of training most likely to leave a positive impact.

Proverbs has much to say about the necessity of training children in wisdom. The repeated refrain is that foolish children bring grief and sorrow to their parents, while a wise son or daughter brings them joy (10:1; 15:20; 17:21, 25; 19:13; 23:24; 29:3, 15). The obedience of a child is no small thing to God. Children living at home under the authority of their parents are called to obey their moms and dads, unless their parents lead them to disobey God. Yet not only are children commanded to receive their parents' wisdom and instruction, parents are commanded to intentionally train their children. We must be purposeful and take advantage of every opportunity to point them down the wise path. Tragically, the failure of many parents to teach and discipline their children is at the heart of many of society's problems today. God's kingdom works through the family.

22:7 Avoid excessive debt. If you don't want to be a **slave to the lender**, learn sound financial principles and live within your means.

22:8-11 If you plant tomatoes, you won't get pumpkins. You harvest what you plant; you reap what you sow. Sow **injustice** and **reap disaster** (22:8); sow generosity and reap a blessing (22:9). Mocking lips reap **conflict** (22:10); **gracious lips** reap the king's attention (22:11). See 1:22-33; 6:24-35.

22:12 See 15:3.

22:13 In other words, **the slacker** makes excuses to avoid working. See 10:2-5; 26:13-16.

22:14 See 5:1-23; 6:20–7:27.

22:15 Foolishness is bound to the heart of a youth; a rod of discipline will separate it

from him (see 13:24; 29:15, 17). Solomon is talking about willful foolishness—not just childishness and silliness. Many kids who are now reaching adulthood were never disciplined by their parents. Unfortunately, because they didn't receive loving discipline at home, society is forced to correct them through the police and the government. They weren't taught that their actions come with consequences. Disciplining your children requires courage and commitment. But, when done with love, it bears fruit that benefits everyone.

22:16 See 13:23; 17:5.

IV. WORDS OF THE WISE AND SAYINGS OF THE WISE
(22:17–24:34)

22:17-21 Proverbs continues with **the words of the wise** (22:17) and "sayings" that "belong to the wise" (24:23), which Solomon apparently collected. They are **true and reliable** (22:21). You can bank on them. Moreover, they are **pleasing** when they are **within you** and **on your lips** (22:18). God's wisdom satisfies whether it's going in or coming out.

Receiving wise instruction is essential **so that your confidence may be in the LORD** (22:19)—not in people. The wise therefore exhort you: **apply your mind** to **knowledge** (22:17). This is the process by which the Word of God gets off the page and into our lives. A disciple of Jesus Christ is one for whom regular interaction with the Word of God is as necessary and desirable as obtaining food for the body. Scripture equips us to live the Christian life.

If you've got a messed-up mind, you're going to have a messed-up life, which is why our minds need to be renewed so our lives can be transformed (see Rom 12:2). When you try to change your actions without changing your thinking, you only do a temporary, patchwork job. If you want to fix what you do, you must first fix how you think about what you do. A transformed mind comes through the study and application of the Word of God.

22:22-23 See 13:23; 17:5.

22:24-25 See 29:11.

22:26-27 See 6:1-5.

22:28 To **move an ancient boundary marker** was an attempt to acquire land dishonestly. But God sees when no one else does. Nothing is truly done in secret. See 15:3.

22:29 Because they represent the Lord Jesus Christ, Christians should be known as those who work with excellence at whatever they do (see Col 3:23). "Good enough" doesn't cut it. Whoever does quality labor will be recognized.

23:1-3 Beware of indebting yourself to the rich and powerful. Their extravagant gifts are often motivated by a desire to get more from you than they give.

23:4-5 Riches are hard to come by. If you give all your attention to generating wealth (23:4), you'll forsake relationship with the Lord and your riches will easily disappear (23:5).

23:6-8 Like the rich man (23:1-3), the **stingy** man may also have ulterior motives for his gifts. Be discerning.

23:9 See 9:7-9.

23:10-11 See 22:28.

23:12 Apply yourself to discipline and listen to words of knowledge. Many believers suffer from spiritual Alzheimer's. This malady manifests itself in a deterioration of the proper application of the mind of Christ—a kingdom mind—that should be operating in every believer's life. A Christian who suffers from spiritual Alzheimer's loses the ability to apply a spiritual mind to his daily interactions. He or she forgets how to think in terms of God's kingdom agenda. Such believers default to a secular way of thinking. Often our greatest problem is not what we do; it's the way we think. In order to transform what we do, we must transform our thought patterns and discipline our minds to focus on the realm of the Spirit.

23:13-14 See 13:24; 22:15; 29:15, 17.

23:15-16 Wisdom in children brings joy to their parents. See 10:1; 22:6.

23:17-18 See 3:31-35; 24:1-2.

23:19-21 See 20:1.

23:22-25 See 10:1; 22:6.

23:26-28 See 5:1-23; 6:20–7:27.

23:29-35 See 20:1.

24:1-2 Choosing friends will lead us down either the wise or the foolish path. Relationships are critical to our walks with God; the people in our lives can encourage wise, kingdom living or be a stumbling block to it. Solomon is thus very straightforward on this matter: **Don't envy the evil or desire to be with them, for their hearts plan violence, and their words stir up trouble.** The righteous and the wicked have two very different futures set out for them, so we can't expect to hang out with evil people without suffering the consequences.

24:3-4 The family was God's idea and invention, so he knows how it ought to function. If your family is built upon **wisdom, understanding,** and **knowledge,** your home will be filled with **beautiful treasure** regardless of your income. Such a family is prepared to extend God's kingdom rule into the world.

24:5-6 See 11:14; 20:18.

24:7 At the city gate, leaders gathered to discuss important matters. The **fool** has nothing to offer, and no one wants to hear from him; thus, he has no business there.

24:8-9 A good reputation can't be purchased, but it's worth its weight in gold (see 22:1). **The one who plots evil** and mocks wisdom, however, is known by his deeds (24:8) and hated for them (24:9).

24:10-12 Kingdom men and women do not sit by and **do nothing** in difficult times (24:10). To love your neighbor doesn't merely mean to avoid doing him harm; it means to intentionally do him good—especially when he's in distress or danger. God's people are called to **rescue those being** led to **death** and **slaughter** (24:11). One example of how this principle can be applied regards the wickedness of abortion. For Christians to say, **But we didn't know about this** (24:12) is to be like the priest and Levite in Jesus's parable of the good Samaritan who essentially stuck their heads in the sand to avoid helping their neighbor (see Luke 10:25-37). God will **repay a person according to his work** (24:12). So do what you can to help fight such wickedness and love those around you.

24:13-14 God doesn't command us to become wise simply because it's the right thing to do. Just as people eat **honey** because it's **sweet** (24:13), so we should choose wisely in life because doing so brings pleasure. When you access and act on divine wisdom, **you will have a future, and your hope will never fade** (24:14).

24:15-16 Though a righteous person falls **seven times, he will get up, but the wicked will stumble into ruin.** The foolish and wicked are stumbling through life without hope. God's people stumble too, but he helps them up (24:16)—often with the aid of the godly people we have gathered around us. Though the wicked seek to harm the righteous, they will not ultimately succeed (24:15).

24:17-18 Don't gloat when your enemy falls. In other word, as Jesus said, "Love your enemies and pray for those who persecute you" (Matt 5:44).

24:19-20 See 3:31-35; 24:1-2.

24:21-22 See 19:12; 20:30.

24:23-25 See 14:28-35; 16:10-15; 19:12.

24:26 Giving **an honest answer**—making sure your words match reality—is an act of kindness and love.

24:27 See 20:18.

24:28-29 See 12:17, 19, 22; 24:17-18; 25:18-19.

24:30-34 See 6:6-11; 10:2-5; 12:24; 18:9; 26:13-16.

V. PROVERBS OF SOLOMON COPIED BY HEZEKIAH'S MEN
(25:1–29:27)

25:1-3 These chapters contain more **proverbs of Solomon** that were collected by **King Hezekiah of Judah** (25:1). God has concealed his wisdom in the world, and it is **the glory of kings to investigate** and discover that wisdom (25:2). That is what Solomon and Hezekiah did. By contrast, **the hearts of kings cannot be investigated** (25:3); this means rulers keep close counsel.

25:4-5 As **a silversmith** must **remove impurities from silver** (25:4), so a king must **remove the wicked** from his **presence** (25:5). This implies that just government requires just officials. See 14:28-35; 16:10-15; 19:12.

25:6-7 As Solomon will say in 27:2, "let another praise you, and not your own mouth." No one likes to hear a braggart. Jesus told a parable that similarly condemns pride and praises humility (see Luke 14:7-11), so let the Lord exalt you. See 6:16-17; 13:10; 27:1.

25:8-10 Don't be quick to sue someone. You might be overestimating your chances of winning the case and end up humiliated. Make every effort to settle out of court.

25:11-12 Most of us don't like to be corrected, or have to correct someone else, even when such is needed. One reason may be that we don't know what to say, or we're afraid our words will be taken in the wrong way. But for our encouragement, Solomon reminds us, A **word spoken at the right time is like gold apples in silver settings. A wise correction**

to **a receptive ear is like a gold ring.** Even a wise word spoken at the wrong time can stir up flames of anger and cause pain, but the right word at the right time brings healing.

25:13-14 Few things are as highly valued as being **trustworthy.** Employers want employees whom they can trust to work diligently and with integrity. People want friends whom they can confide in without risk of betrayal. Add trustworthiness to your character, then, and watch your usefulness to God expand. You'll be **like the coolness of snow on a harvest day** (25:13). By contrast, **the one who boasts** is like **clouds and wind without rain** (25:14)—all hot air and empty promises.

25:15 This proverb reminds us of Jesus's parable of the persistent widow (see Luke 18:1-8). Patient persistence pays off.

25:16-17 It's possible to have too much of a good thing. A sweet treat tastes great, but overindulgence will make you **sick** (25:16). In the same way, it's good to be a friendly neighbor. But if you darken your neighbor's door too often, **he'll get sick of you** (25:17). Don't be high-maintenance.

25:18-19 Solomon has praised trustworthiness. So to what does he compare an unreliable person? A **club, a sword,** or **a sharp arrow . . . a rotten tooth,** and **a faltering foot.** In other words, a person whose words are **false** inevitably brings harm to others.

25:20 If we want to bless others with our words, we need to discern not only *what* is appropriate to say but also *when* it's appropriate to say it. **A troubled heart** needs somber comfort, not lightheartedness. See 25:11-12.

25:21-22 **If your enemy is hungry, give him food to eat, and if he is thirsty, give him water to drink; for you will heap burning coals on his head, and the LORD will reward you.** Solomon gives us another dose of godly advice that runs contrary to worldly thinking. Paul drew on this passage in Romans 12:19-21 to remind believers to conquer evil with good. Do good to those who hate you and leave their judgment to God.

25:23-28 These verses graphically demonstrate that our actions can either bless others or wear them out. Solomon condemns the **backbiting tongue** (25:23), the **nagging wife** (25:24), the **glory** seeker (25:27), and the **person who does not control his temper** (25:28). Do any of these describe you? If so, it's time to change course. Do you want people to think of you as **cold water to a parched throat** (25:25) or as **a polluted well** (25:26)?

26:1-3 A fool's mouth spews **an undeserved curse** rather than a gracious blessing (26:2). Clearly, **honor** is not fit for him (26:1). The only thing he earns for himself is punishment (26:3).

26:4-5 Sometimes, when dealing with a fool, the best policy is to ignore him so that you don't entangle yourself in his ways (26:4). At other times, the wiser choice may be to respond to the fool using his own argument to demonstrate how silly he is (26:5). Paul followed the latter course in 2 Corinthians (see 2 Cor 11:16-27). The false apostles boasted in themselves. Paul did too—but he "boasted" in his weakness so that God got all the glory.

26:6-12 Solomon makes clear that **a fool**— the one who rejects the wisdom God offers—has no redeeming value. He's pathetic and has nothing to offer. Why would anyone choose his way? Yet young people do so every day. Parents, love your children enough to teach them—and model for them—that life

lived from the divine point of view will bring them blessing and joy.

26:13-16 Lazy people who refuse to work were around in Solomon's time too. Avoiding labor is the slacker's priority, so he's never lacking for excuses—no matter how preposterous they are (26:13). **A door turns on its hinges, and a slacker, on his bed. The slacker buries his hand in the bowl; he is too weary to bring it to his mouth!** (26:14-16). Some of Solomon's descriptions of the lazy man are quite humorous—anything to get out of honest work. But there's nothing funny about Paul's prescription for the lazy in God's kingdom: "If anyone isn't willing to work, he should not eat" (2 Thess 3:10).

26:17 Solomon isn't talking about someone who's trying to bring reconciliation to those at odds with each other. He's talking about a busybody who's sticking his nose where it doesn't belong.

26:18-19 Harmless humor is one thing. But don't assume you can deceive others, claim you were **only joking**, and escape the consequence of people hating you for it in the end.

26:20-22 Some people love to gossip and quarrel like they're eating **choice food** (26:22). But gossip and quarreling are sins that plague our world and, unfortunately, many churches. Both serve as **wood** for the **fire** of conflict (26:20-21). Some have started gossip fires that burned up another's reputation entirely. Remember, a person who will gossip to you will certainly gossip about you. It's not the things that go in one ear and out the other that do the harm, but the things that go in one ear, get all mixed up, and come out of the mouth. When gossip is eliminated, conflict is snuffed out. See 11:13; 17:9.

26:23-28 See 12:17, 19, 22; 25:18-19.

27:1 We don't know what tomorrow holds, the Bible says, but too many people strut around talking boldly about what they're going to do with it. What does God say about such arrogance? **Don't boast about tomorrow, for you don't know what a day might bring.** It's a sin, then, to brag about all the deals we are going to cut without a thought to what God's mind is on the subject. The hospital emergency room is full of people who had plans for tomorrow. So is the cemetery.

27:2 See 25:6-7.

27:3 See 26:6-12.

27:4 Solomon says **jealousy** is more relentless than anger. Don't foolishly make yourself its target (see 6:32-35).

27:5 Don't claim to love your Christian brother or sister if you won't demonstrate your love by your actions. **Concealed love** is worthless. Better to speak the truth in love and give a straying brother or sister an **open reprimand** when needed.

27:6 The wounds of a friend are trustworthy, but the kisses of an enemy are excessive. In other words, better the friend who will, with love, wound us for our good, than someone who excessively kisses up to us and never tells it like it is. After all, didn't Judas betray Jesus with a kiss? A true friend corrects you when you're wrong. A legitimate friend will never absolve you of the evil you do.

27:7 Don't take the things you have for granted. Someone, somewhere would be grateful to have them.

27:8 The **wandering** man Solomon describes is not merely out for a stroll. He's wandering away from responsibility and into trouble. **Like a bird wandering from its nest**, he's abandoning his own protection.

27:9-10 Few things bring joy and blessing like a trustworthy **friend**. A faithful friend will speak godly counsel into your life (27:9) and is always willing to come when needed (27:10). Seek out such a friend and become such a friend.

27:11 See 10:1.

27:12 Avoid **danger** and punishment; be **sensible** and take **cover** within God's covenant and agenda.

27:13 See 6:1-5.

27:14 Being a morning person can be a blessing—unless you force it upon others until they curse you!

27:15-16 The **nagging wife** needs to spend some time with the "wife of noble character" described in 31:10-31. See 12:4; 25:24.

27:17 Friends can make us better Christians. We need friends who will challenge and sharpen our thinking, help us make good decisions, and help us hone our spiritual lives until they are razor-sharp: **Iron sharpens iron, and one person sharpens another.** Good friends work to rub off dull edges and make each other better. That's why we need ministries and churches that are full of men and women talking about more than work, the weather, and sports. See 17:17.

27:18 Be a faithful employee. A wise employer will recognize your value and honor you.

27:19 What's in your **heart reflects** who you are. See 10:31-32; 12:16-23.

27:20 A heart controlled by greed will never have pleasure. Just as the grave is never satisfied but always claims more and more corpses, so also the greedy person never has enough. The cure for the cycle is a heart that regularly expresses gratitude to God.

27:21-22 When trying circumstances shake a person up, what's inside him will inevitably spill out (see 27:19). When an honorable man is placed in the **crucible** of life, the godliness stored up in his heart will be seen, and people will **praise** him (27:21). Likewise, when hard times **grind a fool**, you'll see the **foolishness** that was within him all along (27:22).

27:23-27 Some people think financial planning is pointless because they have no money. But often the lack of planning *is* the problem. **Know** where you are; **pay attention to** what you have (27:23). Then plan for where you want to go. Wealth is not forever (27:24)—especially when you make no plans for it to grow. Look after what is placed in your care, though, and it **will provide** for you (27:25-27).

28:1 A **wicked** person has a guilty conscience and is always looking over his shoulder. **The righteous** can live with godly boldness.

28:2-5 See 14:28-35; 16:10-15; 19:12.

28:6 See 19:1; 22:1-5.

28:7 See 10:1.

28:8 See 13:23; 17:5.

28:9 See 15:8-9; 21:2-3.

28:10 Whoever **leads** others into **evil** won't escape judgment. He'll **fall into** the **pit** he himself dug.

28:11 Proverbs reminds us that things on earth are not always as they seem. Sometimes people see things the way they want to see them. Solomon speaks to the self-deception to which we are all prone. The person who is **wise in his own eyes,** which is an easy trap to fall into—especially when the person fooling himself has all the outward markings of success—can be completely *without* wisdom. The **discernment** spoken of here is a valuable tool because the Holy Spirit helps us see things clearly.

28:12 See 14:28-35; 16:10-15.

28:13-14 "Confess your sins," James says, so that "you may be healed" (Jas 5:16). Solomon agrees (28:13). But the one who **hardens his heart** against God—like Pharaoh (see Exod 8:15, 32; 9:34)—**falls into trouble** (28:14).

28:15-16 See 14:28-35; 16:10-15; 19:12.

28:17-18 The murderer has **no one to help him** (28:17), but the man of integrity **will be helped** (28:18). Your treatment of others will either bless you or curse you.

28:19 See 6:6-11; 10:2-5; 12:24; 18:9; 26:13-16.

28:20 The typical route to wealth is to earn it little by little, through honest labor.

Participating in a get-rich-quick scheme is the fastest route to ruin.

28:21 Some people can be bought cheaply, but bribes are wicked. See 15:27.

28:22 See 28:20.

28:23 Although rebukes sting while flattery praises, the former offers truth while the latter offers deceit. A loving rebuke is always better than empty flattery.

28:24 See 19:26.

28:25 See 27:20.

28:26 The one who trusts in himself is a fool, but one who walks in wisdom will be safe. The question we need to ask ourselves is this: "In whom do I really trust?" If we trust God, we're kept safe from the pitfalls the world and the devil put in our paths. And while this is no guarantee that misfortune won't befall us Christians, it is a promise that God will watch over us no matter our circumstances.

28:27 See 13:23; 17:5.

28:28 See 14:28-35; 16:10-15.

29:1 The fool is not open to learning from God, from others, or even from his own mistakes. He plunges straight ahead, trusts in himself, and heads for ruin. **One who becomes stiff-necked, after many reprimands will be shattered instantly—beyond recovery,** so we need to develop a humble spirit that enables us to receive warning, correction, and discipline. Falling into ruin because of your own foolishness is pitiful. But how much worse is it to fall into ruin *after* you've received many warnings to change your course? See 1:22-33; 3:11-12; 9:7-9; 10:17; 25:11-12.

29:2 See 14:28-35; 16:10-15.

29:3 See 10:1; also 5:1-23; 6:20−7:27.

29:4 See 14:28-35; 16:10-15.

29:5 See 28:23.

29:6 Sin promises freedom and then enslaves the one **caught by** it.

29:7 See 13:23; 17:5.

29:8 See 29:11.

29:9 Avoid a dispute with a fool. He'll rant and rave, but you'll go nowhere except in circles.

29:10 Do you love those who honor God? When we see people operating with honesty and integrity, our attitude toward them reveals the condition of our own hearts.

29:11 Controlling your anger is one of the most valuable expressions of self-discipline. **A fool gives full vent to his anger, but a wise person holds it in check.** It takes discipline to hold our anger in, and training a person to do this has to start in childhood. How many times do we utter words in a rage only to wish later that we could reel them in? A wise man guards his mouth, knowing that he can bring endless grief upon himself if he doesn't.

29:12-14 See 14:28-35; 16:10-15.

29:15-17 As discussed earlier, applying loving, biblical discipline to children imparts life to them. Solomon speaks to this and to the disaster looming ahead if children are left to figure out life on their own: **A rod of correction imparts wisdom, but a youth left to himself is a disgrace to his mother. . . . Discipline your child, and it will bring you peace of mind and give you delight** (29:15, 17). It's easy to wimp out, be passive, and withhold discipline. But doing so will eventually bring you sorrow and disgrace. So if you don't want to see your children join the ranks of the rebellious, discipline them for

their own good, for eventually the wicked will experience **downfall** (29:16). See 13:24; 22:15.

29:18 Why do we need wisdom and discipline? Because **without revelation people run wild, but one who follows divine instruction will be happy.** Without the wisdom God's Word gives, people are prone to throw off all restraint. This, in fact, is a description of our culture today: people are running into walls and down blind alleys for lack of truth. The remedy to the problem is found in receiving biblical instruction. The one who does this is happy, and true happiness is a result of God's blessing.

29:19-22 Just as one must properly govern his servants (29:19, 21), so also one must learn to properly govern himself (29:20, 22). Speaking too hastily or giving vent to a hot temper can be irresistible urges, but indulging them brings nothing but grief.

29:23 . See 6:16-17; 13:10; 27:1.

29:24 Beware whom you take as a **partner.** See 1:17-19.

29:25 Repeatedly in Proverbs, Solomon urges us to fear the Lord. Doing so is the gateway to wisdom. **The fear of mankind,** however, is a trap. If you live your life as a people-pleaser, you're not pleasing the Lord.

29:26 This verse is a reminder that although rulers are responsible for administering justice in the world, ultimately **justice** comes from a sovereign God.

29:27 An old saying points out that birds of a feather flock together. **The righteous** and **the wicked** are like oil and water; they don't mix. Each hates the actions of the other.

VI. WORDS OF AGUR AND LEMUEL (30:1–31:9)

30:1 We don't know anything about either **Agur** or King Lemuel (31:1), but the inclusion of their words in Proverbs is an example of the way the Holy Spirit oversaw and superintended the inspiration of Scripture.

30:2-4 Agur declares himself **more stupid than any other person,** lacking **ability to understand,** and having no **wisdom** (30:2-3), yet he knew the source of wisdom. His attitude toward himself, then, is similar to Paul's personal declaration that he was the chief of all sinners (see 1 Tim 1:15). Indeed, the one who spends much time with a holy God comes to see just how sinful his own heart is.

Similarly, the one who seeks divine wisdom comes to see just how foolish he is without God's instruction. **Who has gathered the wind in his hands? ... Who has established all the ends of the earth?** (30:4). The obvious answer is "God." So why do we humans arrogantly think we can navigate life without learning from him?

30:5-6 Agur gives us one of the best expressions of the Bible's inspiration anywhere in Scripture—and adds a warning to those who try to add to God's Word. **Every word of God is pure; he is a shield to those who take refuge in him. Don't add to his words, or he will rebuke you, and you will be proved a liar.** God has weighed and examined every word of the Bible to get just the ones he wanted. Our job is to believe and obey his Word, not to put our own words on par with his.

30:7-9 Here's a kingdom-minded attitude that will spare you a lifetime of worry: **Give me neither poverty nor wealth; feed me with the food I need. Otherwise, I might have too much and deny you, saying, "Who is the LORD?" or I might have nothing and steal, profaning the name of my God** (30:8-9). Neither poverty nor wealth offers safety from sin. We need to keep material things in their proper perspective and ask God to meet our needs so we can keep our focus where it ought to be.

30:10 **Slander** is one of the many sins of the tongue that the Bible condemns. James tells us that praising and cursing mustn't come from the same mouth (Jas 3:9-10), but it's easy to play fast and loose with our words when it comes to deriding others. Instead, develop a habit of praising good works so that others may be encouraged and so that you may give glory to the God who stands behind the good works.

30:11-14 Sadly, the **generation** Solomon describes could be the young people of our own time. They curse their parents (30:11), assume they are guiltless, indulge in wickedness

(30:12), think highly of themselves (30:13), wound with their speech, and withhold mercy (30:14). Turning the tide must begin in the context of the family. Kids need fathers who are kingdom-minded men—men who make it a priority to spend time with their children, teach them the ways of the Lord, discipline them with love, and model godliness.

30:15-16 See 27:20.

30:17 See 20:20.

30:18-20 **An eagle, a snake,** and **a ship** leave no long-term trace of their journeys (30:19). Similarly, the **adulteress** assumes she leaves no lasting trace of her liaisons and thus feels no guilt (30:20). But an omniscient God is always watching. See 5:1-23; 6:20–7:27.

30:21-23 These verses describe people no one wants to encounter. Be a blessing to others— not the kind of person others hope to avoid.

30:24-28 Size is irrelevant. Influence is what matters. God is immense and can accomplish mind-blowing things through you. Maximize your faith in him and you will be **extremely wise.**

30:29-31 If these **beasts** are **stately** (30:29-30), how much more grand is a mighty **king at the head of his army** (30:31)? And if a magnificent human king deserves our awe, what should our response be to the divine King who reigns from heaven with the earth as his footstool (see Isa 66:1)?

30:32-33 More people need to heed Solomon's advice to avoid **stirring up anger** and producing **strife** (30:33): **put your hand over your mouth** (30:32). Sometimes the best solution is just to stop talking. Nothing reveals a foolish heart like an open mouth.

31:1-2 Proverbs 31 begins with a mother's advice to her son. Even as a mighty ruler, Lemuel commended the teachings of **his mother** (31:1). To kids, **King Lemuel** would say, "Listen to your mama." To mothers he would say, "Keep doing what you're doing; teach them the way they should go; your faithful deeds do not go unnoticed."

31:3-9 A kingdom man doesn't spend all his energy playing the field (31:3). Instead he finds a godly woman (see 31:10-31), marries her, and cherishes her. He also doesn't waste all his time on drinking **wine** and **beer** so that his head is fogged and he forgets to do **justice** (31:4-5). Rather, he speaks up **for those who have no voice** (31:8) and defends **the cause of the oppressed** (31:9). A kingdom man goes into battle as God's soldier to serve others.

VII. THE WISE WIFE AND MOTHER (31:10-31)

31:10 The final passage of Proverbs is one of the best known in Scripture. King Lemuel's mother gave him a portrait of what a wise wife and mother looks like. **Who can find a wife of noble character?** This question opens a tribute to a capable wife, a woman of excellence in her being and character. An excellent woman is one who knows how to grab heaven and apply it to earth so life becomes better for everyone under her influence.

31:11-12 This woman is wise in her ways as well as in her words. Therefore, **her husband trusts in her** (31:11) and is blessed by her (31:12). If seeking a wife, you can find a pretty woman. You can find a rich woman. But many a man has been disappointed when he discovered that the elegance he saw on the outside didn't match what was on the inside. So find a wise woman of noble character who loves God, and don't let her go.

31:13-27 Notice that this woman prioritizes her family. God has given a woman the unique responsibility of watching **over the activities of her household** (31:27). The word *household* shows up three times in this section (31:15, 21, 27), indicating the attention a woman of real excellence gives to her family and its needs. In all of her endeavors, she's making sure the home is run effectively and efficiently. She understands the central place that the home plays in the kingdom of God. And while the husband's role is to be the head of the home, the wife is the chief operating officer—the internal home manager. She **is never idle** (31:27). Rather than bored, she's industrious.

What we have here is one amazing person. **She is like the merchant ships, bringing her food from far away** (31:14). She has business acumen. She spends money wisely and uses it in the best way to get maximum productivity for the benefit of her family. That's what's happening when **she evaluates a field and buys it** and **plants a vineyard with her earnings** (31:16). When Paul encourages women to be "workers at home" (Titus 2:5) and to "manage their households" (1 Tim 5:14), he doesn't mean they have to stay inside the four walls of a house twenty-four hours a day. He means that everything a woman does outside the home complements what goes on inside the home; it doesn't compete with it.

She also has a ministry: **Her hands reach out to the poor, and she extends her hands to the needy** (31:20). In other words, she's not talking on the phone or engaging on social media all day. She's not gossiping. She's too busy to do things like that. Instead, she's helping others who are less fortunate. She's busy making money, making a difference, and investing in others. When she does speak, she **speaks wisdom, and loving instruction is on her tongue** (31:26). When she talks, she has something worth saying. She has the ability to use the right words at the right time as she encounters real-life situations. **Her husband** benefits from the fact that he's married to such a rare lady (31:23).

31:28-29 What's her reward? **Her children rise up and call her blessed; her husband also praises her.** They rightly value her and make a big deal of her. They know she's worth her weight in gold.

31:30 In summary, **charm is deceptive and beauty is fleeting, but a woman who fears the Lord will be praised.** Time has a way of erasing beauty. No matter how physically attractive you are when young, that face in your mirror is going to change. The years and the decades guarantee that for all of us. What will last, though, is the inward person being renewed day by day even while the outward person is perishing (see 2 Cor 4:17). Ideally, a woman's internal class and her divine fear of God will shine, and those are beauty indicators that time can't erase.

The secret to this lady's *modus operandi* is found in her fear of the Lord. The reason she was wise, the reason she could prioritize her family, the reason she had everything in order is because she took God seriously. She had a divine worldview. The marketplace didn't control her; her friends didn't control her; the television didn't control her. God controlled her, and so her decisions were divinely authored.

31:31 Therefore, the writer concludes, **give her the reward of her labor, and let her works praise her.** Since she's a woman who goes the extra mile, let what she does bring her praise. The reason we forget to praise women of excellence in our marriages and homes is that we get used to them. We take them for granted. But offering praise is like watering a flower, thus allowing its buds to open up. So praise the godly women in your life and watch them blossom. This is the way God designed life to be lived, so let's be wise and live accordingly.

ECCLESIASTES

INTRODUCTION

Author

THE AUTHOR STATES THAT HE was "son of David" and "king over Israel in Jerusalem" (1:1, 12). He was also an explorer of proverbs (12:9). Solomon, then, is the likely author. Many scholars think the book was written too late in Israel's history to come from Solomon, so they date it to at least five hundred years after him. However, strong evidence attests that the book does indeed come from Solomon's time.

For example, the book displays knowledge of literature from Mesopotamia and Egypt. Solomon had close contacts with Egypt, and his empire stretched to the Euphrates River. Therefore, it makes sense that he would have known and reflected upon such texts. Moreover, it is unlikely that a Jew writing five hundred or more years later, when Egyptian and Mesopotamian glory was finished and when Israel was a backwater nation, would have had access to such texts or been so familiar with them. Importantly, the book shows no similarities with the Greek philosophy that flourished five hundred years after Solomon. Thus, the traditional view that Solomon is the author is best.

Historical Background

Ecclesiastes is identified as part of the Wisdom literature of the Bible. Ancient Egypt and Babylon produced their own wisdom writings as well. Books like Proverbs and Ecclesiastes help readers grapple with the practical and philosophical issues of life. Ecclesiastes goes further though, engaging the question of the "futility" of life lived "under the sun."

Message and Purpose

Ecclesiastes is one of my favorite books in the Old Testament because it deals with what life is all about and shows how real the Bible is. It was written by a very wealthy and wise man who described life as a puzzle he couldn't quite put together despite his vast riches and wisdom. So he went on a pilgrimage to find out the meaning of life, taking his readers along on his binges of the pleasures of the flesh, the accumulation of wealth, and the reality of death. He discovered that living independently of God was "a pursuit of the wind" (1:14, 17; 2:11, 17; 4:4; 6:9), or what Solomon calls "absolute futility" (1:2; 12:8).

This book is a big deal because in it we find a man who made huge mistakes that would eventually split his entire kingdom. It's important for us to grab hold of this book and learn from Solomon's mistakes as we build our families and apply God's kingdom principles to our lives today. That, in fact, was what Solomon wanted his readers to do because he finishes the book by talking about the importance of getting God into the picture early in life (12:1-7).

Outline

ECCLESIASTES

What is this thing called life? And is it even worth it? One moment it looks like you've scored a touchdown, only to have a whistle blower call back the play. Some days it's like a wild goose chase without the geese, as if you're doomed to chase something that's impossible to find.

The Book of Ecclesiastes is a book about life—and how not to waste it.

I. NOTHING NEW UNDER THE SUN (1:1-18)

1:1 In the following **words of the Teacher, son of David, king in Jerusalem,** Solomon is going to tell you plainly how life is to be viewed and understood—not based on a theoretical view but based on his experiences. Solomon can truly say, "Been there, done that."

What's the framework for understanding his thinking? At Solomon's request, God had granted him incredible wisdom (see 1 Kgs 3). But fast forward many years, and we find that he took seven hundred foreign wives and three hundred concubines who "turned his heart away" from God (1 Kgs 11:3). Importantly, in Ecclesiastes, we're reading about Solomon's perspective on his life experiences after he had returned to the Lord.

Solomon is highly qualified to be the author of this book because he had it all and tried it all. He experienced everything life could offer, yet he's going to say that a life perspective that's disconnected from God is not truly living. It's a saccharin existence, a sugary substitute for the real deal. Without God, life is empty. It's nothing more than the temporary things you use to fill it up.

1:2-3 Solomon begins with a summary of the book: **Absolute futility. Everything is futile** (1:2). In other words, he opens by telling you he doesn't have anything to talk about!

Everything is empty and meaningless, at least from a merely human perspective. The phrase **under the sun** (1:3) is a reference to living life from an earthly perspective because "under the sun" is where people live, work, play, and raise their families. **What does a person gain for all his efforts . . . under the sun?** (1:3) is the same as asking, What's the lasting benefit of what I do? Am I just spinning my wheels?

1:4-10 Generations come and go; **the sun rises** and **sets**; the **wind** blows here and there; rivers **flow to the sea** (1:4-7). As sure as the world works in set ways, so it seems that life is predictable. And thus, **all things are wearisome** (1:8).

What has been is what will be . . . there is nothing new under the sun (1:9). This brings to mind fashion trends. Styles will come back. Just give them time. And because that tends to be the way of things, can anyone truly say, **Look, this is new?** (1:10). Although advertisers may claim something is "new and improved," they are really just working with the same raw materials—just reconfigured.

1:11 No one wants to be forgotten, which is why a popular fundraising strategy is to invite people to donate to a project so it can be named after them. But the cold reality is this:

everyone is forgotten eventually. **There is no remembrance** of anyone.

1:12-16 When Solomon says, **I applied my mind . . . I have seen all the things that are done under the sun . . . I have amassed wisdom far beyond all those . . . before me** (1:13, 14, 16), he draws attention to the fact that he's tried it all. He's studied it all. But what did he conclude from those amazing experiences? Everything is **futile, a pursuit of the wind** (1:14). Try grabbing a breeze when it blows by; try to grasp a gust. As

soon as you think you have it, it has slipped through your fingers. Men at their best are striving after something they can't obtain.

1:17-18 Solomon studied **wisdom and knowledge, madness and folly** (1:17). He knew what it was to be smart and to be stupid, leading him to conclude that **with much wisdom is much sorrow; as knowledge increases, grief increases** (1:18). Indeed, most of us find that there are some things in life we wish we didn't know. Sometimes, as knowledge increases, pain increases.

II. THE FUTILITY OF LIFE APART FROM GOD (2:1-26)

2:1-3 It seems Solomon looked at his empire and experiences and said, "There's got to be more than this." And what we'll see in the chapters to come is that if you look for the meaning of life *in life*, you'll never find it. Nevertheless, Solomon began a tour of discovery, testing himself **with pleasure.** He decided to maximize life and **enjoy what is good** (2:1). Let the good times roll. It's party time!

But although he explored how to satisfy himself with fun and enjoyment (2:3), **it turned out to be futile** (2:1). It wasn't anymore fulfilling than an amusement park ride, which is exciting for two minutes, and then it's over. He was like a kid who gets every toy he wants for his birthday—only to be bored after a week. Solomon eventually said of pleasure, **What does this accomplish?** (2:2). It was fun while it lasted. But it didn't provide permanent meaning.

2:4-10 So he went on to increase his **achievements** and to accumulate things for himself. Solomon had all the necessary resources at his disposal. He **built houses and planted vineyards . . . made gardens and . . . constructed reservoirs . . . acquired male and female servants . . . amassed silver and gold and gathered . . . many concubines** (2:4-8). He **surpassed all who were before him** (2:9). He wasn't just one of the guys. He beat them all. And he didn't **refuse** himself **any pleasure** (2:10).

Have you ever gotten depressed and gone shopping? Have you ever envied the guy with

the nice car, fancy clothes, and female companions and set out to close the gap between you? Solomon knew the feeling. If he wanted it, he went after it.

2:11 How did all of this material indulgence work out for him? He **found everything to be futile** and decided **there was nothing to be gained under the sun.** Yes, accumulating was pleasurable for a while. But it didn't answer the deepest questions; it didn't provide meaning. Solomon had it all, but that left him empty.

2:12-13 In considering **wisdom, madness, and folly** (2:12), Solomon **realized that there is an advantage to wisdom** (2:13). After all, if you want a good job and decent income, it's better to be a college graduate than a kindergarten dropout. We've all made wise and foolish decisions, and most of us—like this king—conclude that it's better to be wise than foolish.

2:14-17 In spite of wisdom's benefits, however, Solomon is troubled that **one fate comes to . . . both** the wise person and the fool (2:14). As far as life "under the sun" is concerned, the fool and I will end up in the same place: the grave (2:15). My degree won't make me better off there. And whether you're buried in a crude wooden box or a stylish bronze casket transported by a limousine, dead is dead. Moreover, a dead dummy and a dead genius are equally deceased. Therefore, Solomon **hated life** (2:17).

2:18-23 But wait. It gets worse: **I hated all my work that I labored at under the sun because I must leave it to the man who comes after me. And who knows whether he will be wise or a fool?** (2:18-19). Solomon built an extraordinary kingdom, but he knew that one day someone would assume control of his empire and might ruin everything. That knowledge led to depression (2:20). Eventually the fruit of your labor, too, will be left to someone who hasn't worked for it and who might wreck it all. And there's nothing you can do about it (2:21-23).

2:24 Suddenly, at this point, we see a ray of light. Solomon comes to a refrain that he'll repeat throughout the book: **There is nothing better for a person than to eat, drink, and enjoy his work.... This is from God's hand** (2:24). He has spoken about the depressing realities of life "under the sun," but here he begins interjecting God strategically along the way.

God doesn't mind your enjoyment of legitimate pleasures. He isn't upset that you like your job, food, possessions, or relationships; in fact, these are gifts from him. The problem comes when you look for *meaning* in these things—because at that point you're trying to find in them something that they weren't designed to provide.

2:25-26 The question, then, is this: Is God included in your pleasure? After all, **who can enjoy life apart from him?** (2:25). Make sure you are looking to God to give you meaning. It's a sobering truth that **to the sinner**, God **gives the task of gathering and accumulating** for others. But to the person who is pleasing to God, **he gives wisdom, knowledge, and joy** (2:26).

III. THE REPETITIONS AND INJUSTICES OF LIFE (3:1-22)

3:1 Life can become miserably predictable. The same old you, wearing the same old clothes, driving the same old car, working the same old job, eating the same old food, returning to the same old house, sitting in the same old chair, watching the same old shows, and climbing into the same old bed—day-in and day-out. That frustration with routine reflects Solomon's mood here through verse 8. He's not merely saying there's a time for everything. He's saying, "We're trapped."

3:2-9 Solomon describes the repetitive nature of life in all its contrasts. There's **a time to give birth and a time to die; a time to plant and a time to uproot; a time to kill and a time to heal; a time to tear down and a time to build; a time to weep and a time to laugh** (3:2-4). In other words, we're trapped between competing realities. A person can experience the extremes of life—the highest joy and the deepest sorrow—in the same week, even in the same day.

What does the worker gain from his struggles? (3:9). Solomon highlights the reality that we are like hamsters running on a wheel. Their little legs do a lot of running, but they finish right where they started. So things often seem for us.

3:10-11 Here Solomon says something curious: **I have seen the task that God has given the children of Adam to keep them occupied. He has made everything appropriate in its time** (3:10-11). As we realize that God did this routine and repetition thing that we exist in on purpose, it can make us wonder why God has locked us in this cage called life between the ups and downs, between the good days and bad.

But perhaps life's rhythms are designed to point us to another reality. Indeed, God has **put eternity in their hearts** (3:11). We long for more. Solomon is saying, then, that God has created time in such a way that it cannot bring fulfillment. Rather, it reveals a vacuum in the human heart that can only be filled by the transcendent—by him. Humanity is in tension: we live in the routine of time, but our hearts are designed to long for something eternal.

3:12-13 Although we cannot find ultimate meaning in our time-bound lives, we can experience legitimate enjoyment (3:12). In fact, it is **the gift of God whenever anyone eats, drinks, and enjoys all his efforts** (3:13). So don't merely work for money; do something you like. Appropriate pleasures are a gift of God; enjoy them. But don't expect to discover ultimate meaning in these things. God has intentionally created dissatisfaction in life to drive us to him.

3:14-15 **Everything God does will last forever; there is no adding to it or taking from it. God works so that people will be in awe of him.** You can't change what God has made, so stop fighting the routine, the repetition, and the extremes of life. He's made both life and you this way so you'll seek him.

3:16-20 Here Solomon considers injustice and death **under the sun.** Miscarriages of justice are frequent in the world (3:16). The wicked prosper; the righteous suffer. As a result, life seems unfair. Moreover, **the fate of the children of Adam and the fate of animals is the same:** both die and their bodies **return to dust** (3:19-20). People unjustly treat each other like beasts, and then they join beasts in the grave.

3:22 Before he returns to his discussion of the futility of the world, Solomon encourages the responsible enjoyment of the life God has granted. Thus, he says, **there is nothing better than for a person to enjoy his activities because that is his reward.**

IV. FUTILITY IN RELATIONSHIPS (4:1-16)

4:1-3 Solomon has seen **oppression** and the misuse of **power** in situations in which there is **no one to comfort** the oppressed (4:1). Therefore, he concludes, the **dead** are better off **than the living** (4:2). But then he says no, wait—actually, it would be better if I'd never been born (4:3).

If we're honest with ourselves, most of us have felt the same way at one time or another. Oppression wasn't confined to Solomon's time. Cruelty and coercion are realities today: political corruption, racial discrimination, religious persecution, sex trafficking, domestic violence, child abuse, and the list goes on. Evil is everywhere, and its existence leads to skepticism.

4:4-6 Solomon's own skepticism continues: **All labor and all skillful work is due to one person's jealousy of another.** In other words, it's a dog-eat-dog world. **This too,** he says, **is futile and a pursuit of the wind** (4:4). But that doesn't mean you should just sit back and do nothing with your life: after all, **the fool folds his arms and consumes his own flesh** (4:5). This means that if you refuse to work, you'll go hungry. That it's better to have **one handful with rest than two handfuls with effort** (4:6) means it's better to earn only what you need and get rest, than to be a miserable workaholic keeping up with the Joneses.

4:8-12 **Without a companion** and with **no end to...struggles,** we start to ask, **who am I struggling for?** (4:8). It's better not to be alone; it's best to have someone walking beside you who cares for you. **Two are better than one** for many reasons (4:9). If one falls, the other **can lift him up** (4:10). **If two lie down together, they can keep warm** (4:11). If someone attacks, **two can resist.** There's obvious power in numbers. **A cord of three strands is not easily broken** (4:12). But **pity** the one who is alone. He has no one to pick him up, no one to keep him warm, no one to help him (4:10-12).

4:13-14 Don't ever get too old and self-important to learn. **Better is a poor but wise youth than an old but foolish king who no longer pays attention to warnings** (4:13). We all know people who've reached the top and yet are fools.

4:16 Solomon is frustrated as he thinks of all the successive generations that populate the earth and realizes again that trying to establish oneself for the long term **is futile and a pursuit of the wind** (4:16). That's why you need the interjection of the divine in your life, as Solomon will tell you throughout the book. Indeed, you need the God factor because life under the sun, if done without him, is meaningless.

V. THE FEAR OF GOD AND THE HAZARDS OF WEALTH
(5:1–6:12)

5:1-3 Guard your steps when you go to the house of God. . . . approach in obedience, not as fools do (5:1). Solomon considers the religious side of life. Do not be hasty to speak . . . before God. God is in heaven and you are on earth, so let your words be few (5:2) is advice accompanying the note that fools do a lot of talking (5:3). This is a reminder that you're a fool if you go to church to tell God what to do. He's up there, and you're down here. Your brain doesn't have as much to offer him as you might think it does. So be wise. Be quick to hear from God's divine perspective and slow to speak your mind.

5:4-7 Fulfill what you vow to God—or don't vow at all. You want God working for you, not against you (5:4-6). Don't take your spiritual commitment casually, then. You need God's supernatural intervention. You need him to pierce the average with the above average. And that doesn't happen everyday. Therefore, let your words be few, and **fear God** (5:7). Don't resist him by failing to take him seriously.

5:8-9 Solomon continues with his analysis of life under the sun. **Oppression of the poor and perversion of justice and righteousness** ought not astonish us. In a fallen world, those in power often do evil things. It was true then, and it's true today. One corrupt government official **protects another**, and justice is denied (5:8). But Scripture reminds us elsewhere that the wicked will not always prosper. A day of reckoning is coming (see Ps 73).

5:10-12 Solomon also condemns the love of money: **The one who loves silver is never satisfied with silver** (5:10). It's not wrong to have money, but it's wrong to *love* it—to consider the material more important than the spiritual. The accumulation of wealth usually means the accumulation of stuff, resulting in a lack of **sleep** (5:11-12). When you hoard, you become a slave to your stuff.

5:13-17 Another **tragedy** involving money is **wealth kept by its owner to his harm** (5:13). If it's **lost in a bad venture**, there is nothing for his offspring (5:14). This is a reminder that poor decisions about money affect the next generation. Money is a tool to be used, not a god to be worshipped. You can be buried with your possessions if you want, but you'll take nothing into eternity (5:15-16). And when your priorities are wrong, you will be miserable even with riches (5:17). In fact, I've seen many people die miserable although they possessed all the world had to offer.

In the end, the number of suits or dresses in your closet won't matter. On your deathbed, you won't be bragging about all of your cars. What's going to matter is the spiritual legacy you left behind for others and the heavenly investments you forwarded ahead. The spiritual must always trump the material. The fool "stores up treasure for himself" but isn't "rich toward God" (see Luke 12:21). It's far better to seek that which lasts forever: the kingdom of God (see Matt 6:33).

5:18-20 Solomon has seen the good, the bad, and the ugly of life. He assesses it and declares, "It's futility." Yet he also concludes that one should **eat, drink, and experience good . . . during the few days of his life God has given him** (5:18). **This is a gift of God** (5:19). So, with this perspective in mind, keep God at the forefront of your life and enjoy his gifts with gratitude. It's not wrong to want your circumstances to change, but it's wrong to be ungrateful while waiting for a change. So maintain a joyful **heart** (5:20) that comes from a spirit of thanksgiving as you benefit from the everyday blessings you enjoy. I might want steak and potatoes tomorrow, but I'm going to thank the Lord that I'm not starving as I settle for pork and beans today.

6:1-5 Solomon observes another **tragedy** (6:1). A man has **riches . . . but God does not allow him to enjoy them** (6:2). In other words, he notices that you can have it all but wind up with nothing.

The *quality* of our lives is better than the *quantity* of our lives. I've seen people who accumulated mountains of stuff who never got around to enjoying it. If you exclude God from your life equation, you may never experience pleasure from your wealth either (see Luke 12:19-20). Even long life and a houseful of children are no guarantee of happiness if one is not **satisfied** with the good he has (6:3-6). How awful to live your life in such a way that you wish you'd never been born (6:3-5)! The antidote for that tendency is a day-by-day grateful attitude toward God. Under the sun, we're all marching to the grave. How, then, are you going to live your days? Don't wait until retirement to live a thankful life. You may not make it to retirement.

6:7-9 It's possible to **labor** and strive but **never** be **satisfied** (6:7). Whether one yearns for wealth or wisdom or knowing **how to** conduct oneself, we must not be ruled by desire. In fact, **better what the eyes see than wandering desire** (6:9). Be content with what God gives you. Kids want toys; adults just want bigger and more expensive toys. But if you chase after physical pleasures, your soul will become anemic. Pursue what your soul needs to be truly satisfied.

6:10-12 We must know our limitations and our priorities. A man **is not able to contend with the one stronger than he** (6:10). **Many words** are futile (6:11). And our **few days** of life are **like a shadow** (6:12).

God has appointed a day for each of us to die (see Heb 9:27). You might be late for a lot of events in life, but you won't miss that one! So, under the sun, maximize the days you've been given, not contending with God, but looking to him to punctuate life with his presence.

VI. WISDOM AND ITS LIMITATIONS (7:1–9:18)

7:1 A good name is better than fine perfume. And whether it's a woman wearing the latest fragrance or a man wearing cologne, people take notice when a person smells good and ask, "What's that you have on?" It's far better, though, that people take notice of you because of the pleasant scent of your dignity and character. After all, no matter how sweet-smelling your perfume, it can't make up for a foul-smelling reputation. Work on your character so you'll have a fragrant reputation.

7:2-4 We might be tempted to raise our eyebrows at this passage: **It is better to go to a house of mourning** rather than **a house of feasting** (7:2). Really? After all, nobody goes to a funeral because they *want* to but because they *have* to. We put parties on our schedules—not funerals. Yet Solomon reminds us that if we're looking for the real deal, we need to attend a funeral rather than a party. Why? Because everything is camouflaged at a party. People at parties are usually just playing parts; they're escaping the realities of life. You won't get the truth. At a funeral, though, you're forced to remember that life under the sun doesn't go on forever. Death eventually comes to everyone. At the funeral home, therefore, things get real. You're obliged to stare at a casket and admit to yourself, "One day, that's going to be me in there." A visit to a funeral will remind you of what's important and that your days are numbered. It will help you live with an eternal perspective.

7:5-6 Being wise isn't tied to academic accomplishment: a fool can have a PhD. Wisdom is the ability to make spiritually informed decisions. It's applying the divine truth of God's kingdom rule to every area of life. If someone with a divine perspective rebukes you, let him speak into your life so you can become wise. No one likes to be rebuked, but a wise rebuke is far more valuable than a fool singing your praises.

7:8-9 A wise person knows that **the end of a matter is better than its beginning** (7:8). Regardless of how you begin, you want to make sure you finish strong. Don't be in a **rush to be angry** because anger lives in a fool's **heart** (7:9). Many people commit foolish mistakes because they were hasty in their outrage.

7:10 There's nothing wrong with reminiscing with friends and family. It's good to remember where you came from. But don't live in yesterday. Don't waste all your time gabbing about and longing for the good ol' days. If you choose to live in yesterday, you won't make forward progress and will fail to achieve what God wants you to be tomorrow.

7:11-12 Whatever financial **inheritance** you leave behind for your children, make certain that you also leave them some **wisdom** (7:11). We know money can offer some protection from the uncertainties of life. That's why we have insurance. But we need this same view regarding wisdom because it **preserves the life of its owner** (7:12). Financial security is tenuous. But wisdom provides the security of God's perspective.

7:13-15 Deuteronomy 29:29 reminds us that "the hidden things belong to the LORD." In the same vein, Solomon invites us to consider God's works and ask ourselves **who can straighten out what he has made crooked?** (7:13). If you consume yourself with trying to figure out what God doesn't explain, you'll only get a headache. As sure as we don't always answer our kids' "why?" questions because we know it wouldn't be appropriate to do so or because they wouldn't understand anyway, God often does not reveal his ways to us. That he has made the **day of prosperity** and the **day of adversity** (7:14) is a reminder that he's sovereign. When things are out of your control, thank God that they are in his control. From a purely earthly viewpoint, life often seems unfair (7:15). Therefore, you must develop a spiritual viewpoint for living life.

7:16-20 Don't be excessively righteous, and don't be overly wise (7:16). What? Now before you get the wrong idea, understand that Solomon is talking about going *beyond* what God requires. That approach is exactly what the Pharisees did. They added their own standards to God's standards, and in the name of righteousness became self-righteous. Wise in their own eyes. Of course, you don't want to **be excessively wicked** either (7:17). We all fall short; everyone **sins** (7:20)—but that doesn't give us license to persist in wickedness. Instead we are to live a balanced life, avoid excess, and take God seriously (7:18).

7:23–8:1 Whatever your life experiences, they don't match Solomon's. And as someone whom God blessed with profound wisdom, he can truly say, **I have tested all this by wisdom** (7:23). Yet all his study, all his investigation, didn't secure for him the answers to life's ultimate questions (7:24, 28). The answer to life can't be discovered in life. Under the sun, it's best to live wisely. **Folly is madness** (7:25). Although **God made people upright**, they **pursued many schemes** and mischief (7:29). Humanity wandered from God, evil proliferated, and the world suffers. But **a person's wisdom brightens his face** (8:1). All things being equal, wise living delivers happiness resulting from good life decisions.

8:2-5 The apostle Paul commands Christians to "submit to the governing authorities" (Rom 13:1). So, also, Solomon urges us to obey legitimate governmental authorities and to be careful how we relate to those authorities because of the power they exercise over us.

8:6 The wise person knows that **for every activity there is a right time and procedure.** Timing matters. *When* you do something is often as important as *what* you do. In other words, it's possible to do a good thing but at the wrong time. Certain comments are not appropriate when someone is grieving. And when in mixed company, it's sometimes best to save your thoughts for a private conversation later.

8:8-9 The concept of authority is a good thing. God exercises authority over humanity. He ordains rulers to have authority over people. Husbands are called to exercise godly authority in their homes. The problem is that **under the sun** a person often **has authority over another to his harm** (8:9). And the one thing that no one has any authority over is the one thing coming for us all: **the day of death** (8:8).

8:11-13 When a **sentence against an evil act is not carried out quickly, the heart of**

people is filled with the desire to commit evil (8:11). In other words, if justice doesn't come immediately, some people think it isn't coming at all. **God-fearing people**, however, know better (8:12). Eternal judgment may be delayed, but it's certain. One day the books will be opened. There will be a day of reckoning to determine the reward for believers and a judgment to punish unbelievers. **It will not go well with the wicked** (8:13). In the end, a price will be paid.

8:14-17 But that price doesn't always get paid on the earth. And in this Solomon sees more futility: Sometimes the righteous get what **the wicked deserve** and the wicked get what **the righteous deserve** (8:14). Life is filled with inequities and injustices. So if the under-the-sun perspective is all you have, you're going to experience frustration and despair. The way the world works is ultimately incomprehensible to man. **Even if a wise person claims to know it, he is unable to discover it** (8:17). On your best day, you're still human and not God. You need his perspective.

9:2-3 The divine perspective on life is essential because under the sun, **everything is the same for everyone: There is one fate for the righteous and the wicked** (9:2). Life is unpredictable, and death is inevitable for all (9:2-3). That's the one common denominator for every person.

9:4-6 The next twenty-four hours can lift you up or do you in. But **a live dog is better than a dead lion** (9:4). This is a reminder that

as far as our earthly existence is concerned, life—even when filled with struggles and disappointments—is preferable to death (9:5-6).

9:7-10 In light of this reality, Solomon returns to his repeated exhortation (see 2:24; 3:12-13; 5:18; 8:15): **Eat ... with pleasure, and drink ... with a cheerful heart ... Enjoy life ... Whatever your hands find to do, do with all your strength.** Whatever life God gives you, live it to the max. You don't need to chase misery; it knows where you live. And since you don't know what tomorrow will bring, enjoy the legitimate pleasures of each day, because God "richly provides us with all things to enjoy" (1 Tim 6:17). Don't, however, seek enjoyment independent of him.

9:11-12 Our existence under the sun often looks like a roll of the dice. And regardless of whatever strength, wisdom, riches, or skill a person has, **time and chance happen to all** (9:11). Life appears to be random. **Certainly no one knows his time** (9:12). Yet we must live with an eternal perspective. Remember Psalm 73 and remind yourself that it's not over yet.

9:13-18 **Wisdom** is not always rewarded by the world, but the good news is that you don't have to be a rich and powerful ruler to have it (9:13-16). Although no one may remember him in the end, a **poor man** can deliver a **city** from danger by his wisdom (9:15). It is **better than strength** and **weapons of war** (9:16, 18). Wisdom is bringing God's perspective to bear on life.

VII. LIFE IS SHORT; BE WISE (10:1–11:10)

As the author of the book of Proverbs, Solomon had vast experience in thinking about life and composing wise sayings. It's not surprising, then, that as he moves toward his conclusion to Ecclesiastes, he includes a string of proverbial statements about life and futility, wisdom and folly.

10:1-3 What Solomon is saying in these verses is that fools make their folly known;

there's no hiding it. Just as **dead flies make a perfumer's oil ferment and stink, so a little folly outweighs wisdom and honor** (10:1). It only takes a little foolishness, in fact, to contaminate an otherwise sweet reputation and stink it up. **A wise person's heart goes to the right, but a fool's heart to the left. Even when the fool walks along the road ... he shows everyone he is a fool** (10:2-3). This too is a way of saying that fools inevitably go public. Whichever way a wise man goes, you can count on a fool heading in the opposite direction. Although a man's wisdom may be unseen or even forgotten by everyone but God (9:15), a fool's actions are visible to all.

10:6-10 Wisdom is far better than foolishness. But let's not be naïve. Wisdom doesn't guarantee a perfect life; it doesn't prevent accidents. Great reversals happen: **The fool is appointed to great heights, but the rich remain in lowly positions** (10:6). The wise person needs to know that wisdom doesn't eliminate all negative contingencies (10:8-9); nevertheless, wisdom gives a person great **advantage**. It gives you an **edge** that you don't want to be without (10:10).

10:12-14 The wise and the foolish are known by their words. **The words from the mouth of a wise person are gracious** (10:12). They're pleasing to hear, filled with grace. But a fool's words start with **folly** and end in **madness** (10:13). One way to know fools, in fact, is by how much they talk because **the fool multiplies words** (10:14). Elsewhere, Solomon reminds us, "When there are many words, sin is unavoidable" (Prov 10:19).

10:16-17 Woe to the **land** that has an immature, irresponsible leader (10:16); **blessed** is that nation whose leader is responsible and not indulgent (10:17). The character of a nation's rulers is crucial since its citizens will inevitably be blessed or suffer as a result of their leadership.

10:18 Because of laziness the roof caves in. This is an illustration of what scientists call the second law of thermodynamics. Things left unattended will tend toward decay, decline, and disorder. You don't have to intentionally break something; just fail to take care of it. This can be applied to the physical realm as well as to the spiritual. Neglect your spiritual life, and it will deteriorate.

10:20 Watch the words you say. **Do not curse the king**—even in private. **For a bird of the sky may carry the message and . . . report the matter.** This advice sounds like Solomon was anticipating our age of YouTube and social media! And indeed, things said in secret often have a way of getting out. Be discerning.

11:1-6 At issue here is the need to practice fiscal responsibility. Give your investments time to grow (11:1) and diversify, **for you don't know what disaster may happen** (11:2). In other words, don't put all your eggs in one basket. Practice occupational responsibility, too. **One who watches the wind will not sow** (11:4), meaning that if you procrastinate because of circumstances, you won't accomplish anything. And because you **don't know the work of God who makes everything** (11:5), don't ever put God in a box based on your limited perspective and framework of thinking (see Isa 55:9). He'll blow up your box every time. Instead, be industrious even as you trust him. **In the morning sow your seed, and at evening do not let your hand rest** (11:6).

11:8-10 Youth and the prime of life are fleeting (11:10). Whether you live **many years** or few, your life is passing away before your eyes. So **rejoice** in all your days and **let your heart be glad** (11:8-9). Maximize your life while you can because you can't go back and do it over. Today is the tomorrow that you were looking for yesterday. But remember: **For all of these things God will bring you to judgment** (11:9). You and God are going to talk about your choices one day, so live with the end in view.

VIII. FEAR GOD AND KEEP HIS COMMANDS (12:1-14)

There's nothing like the thrill of a roller coaster ride. But when it ends, you return to standing in the next line, longing for a few more moments of exhilaration. Fireworks are captivating and exciting. But it doesn't take long before the show concludes and the sky turns dark once more. In Ecclesiastes, Solomon has considered the ups and downs of life, noting that even a good today can be quickly forgotten with a bad tomorrow. "Under the sun," life is unpredictable. Our real, physical world is filled with real people, real problems, and real pain. It's an uncertain reality in which we live, work, play, raise families, and die.

Yet, throughout the book, Solomon highlights the greater spiritual truth and meaning that only God can provide. Solomon wants us to see that life's ultimate meaning can only be found in him—not in the continually changing circumstances of life. To avoid living futile and meaningless lives, we need to make an awareness of God's kingdom rule a regular, ongoing, and strategic part of how we define, observe, and engage life.

12:1 The key to developing this divine perspective is to start early: **Remember your Creator in the days of your youth.** Children, then, should be urged to start looking at the world through the lens of God's Word while they're young, so sow the seeds of God consciousness into your children. Exhort them to make their Creator—the source and sustainer of life—their reference point. Why? Because **the days of adversity** are coming. In other words, old age and its frustrations are approaching all of us.

12:2-6 Solomon uses a variety of metaphors to talk about the aging process and what inevitably follows it: **The sun and the light are darkened** (12:2); **strong men stoop** (12:3); **the sound of the mill fades** (12:4); man **is headed to his eternal home** (12:5); **the silver cord is snapped** (12:6); **the wheel is broken** (12:6). He's talking about the body's operating systems breaking down. Given enough time, the aging process will take away your vigor and vitality. Sickness and weariness will become routine. Bones turn brittle; hands tremble; muscles weaken; disease invades. Therefore, before the gloom of old age sets in, make God's viewpoint your own. While you still have strength, remember your Creator. Adopt a God-perspective. If while you're young you're always "dying to do this" and "dying to do that," one day you'll be old and discover that you're just dying.

12:7-8 The dust returns to the earth as it once was, and the spirit returns to God who gave it (12:7). We began as dust, and we return to dust (see Gen 2:7). Therefore, Solomon ends where he started (1:2): **everything is futile** (12:8). He is certain that life under the sun is meaningless. While you can find some occasional enjoyment in it, it's mixed with disappointment. So if this is all you have to look forward to, it's empty. There's no ultimate meaning in it. To find true meaning, you have to bring God to bear on your life and let him bring perspective and higher purpose into this emptiness.

12:9-11 Solomon **taught the people knowledge; he weighed, explored, and arranged many proverbs** (12:9). God graciously gave Solomon wisdom so that he might teach us, and Solomon composed this wisdom into **delightful sayings** (12:10). His descriptions and illustrations are vital because they grab our attention, help us understand truth, and emphasize its relevance to our lives. (Preachers, take note!) He communicates in such a way that readers can't miss his points.

In a sense, Solomon's wise sayings **are like cattle prods** used to poke and motivate an ox; they provoke us and push us to a response. They provide a divine frame of reference and enable us to discern the best choices to make in life. When read and digested, they work **like firmly embedded nails** driven into our hearts and minds.

Ultimately, **the sayings** we find in this book **are given by one Shepherd** (12:11). The Lord Jesus Christ works through them to prick our consciences and apply them to our hearts.

12:12 There is no end to the making of many books, so while we should read what God has given us through Solomon and other biblical writers, we should also study other good books faithfully based on Scripture too. There's a seemingly endless supply of resources based on this one book. That's because the Bible is so deep that theologians can't touch the bottom, but it's so shallow that babies won't drown. Nevertheless, we must remember that **much study wearies the body.** There comes a time when you must put down the books and choose wisely.

12:13-14 Here Solomon says in essence, Let's bring it all home: **The conclusion of the matter is this: fear God and keep his commands, because this is for all humanity** (12:13). This truth applies to everyone. You are not an exception. **For God will bring every act to judgment, including every hidden thing, whether good or evil** (12:14).

Life isn't over when it's over. The actions of humanity—good and evil—are all on tape. And while you can't erase what's on your tape, you can create new and better footage. As long as you draw breath, the recorder is still running. Therefore, don't waste your days. Take God seriously and conform your will to his. Maximize the time God has given you, enjoy the legitimate pleasures he provides, and thank him in both good times and bad. Seek his divine perspective for your day-to-day decisions and make your life count toward the fulfillment of his kingdom agenda.

SONG OF SONGS

INTRODUCTION

Author

THIS BOOK CALLS ITSELF "THE Song of Songs, which is Solomon's" (1:1), but the phrasing reflects the ambiguity of the Hebrew words. It could be understood as claiming that King Solomon is the author, or it could indicate that it was written for Solomon. The traditional position of the church is that Solomon authored the book.

Some critical Bible scholars believe Solomon's authorship impossible, pointing to words that reflect Greek and Persian influence—which would be problematic because those kingdoms didn't arise for hundreds of years after his death. They claim that these words demonstrate that the book was written after the exile—not during the time of the monarchy of Solomon's day. The "evidence" to which they point, though, is inconclusive. Other scholars have shown that these words may actually come from other Semitic languages contemporary with Solomon's day, and many words and descriptions in the book actually favor a date during Israel's monarchy. Thus, we are on good ground to believe that 1:1 refers to Solomon as the writer.

True, Solomon strayed significantly from the biblical ideal for marriage, having hundreds of wives and concubines (see 1 Kgs 11:3). His sin, however, did not prevent God from graciously using him to reveal divine truth.

Historical Background

The book is an example of an ancient Near Eastern love song. The closest parallel to it is the Egyptian love poetry that existed during Solomon's time. Given his extensive knowledge, Solomon would have been familiar with such literature (see 1 Kgs 4:29-34).

The various place names mentioned in Song of Songs were located in the northern part of Solomon's kingdom (e.g., Damascus, Shunem, Tirzah, and Mount Hermon). After the division of the kingdom into north (Israel) and south (Judah), a poem about a king in Jerusalem likely would not have included these locations.

Message and Purpose

Song of Songs is a book that is often misunderstood, misapplied, or simply unread. It is the lover's song, a story about God's love applied to human relationships. God wants that love expressed in romantic relationships; therefore, Solomon is allowed to bring in a man and a woman on their journey to and into their marriage. His telling includes the physical part of their union—which is something that God himself endorses.

The Song of Songs is a very tender, touching—and, yes, sensual—book given to us so that we can understand not only how we can relate to God, but how he wants us to relate to one another within the context of marriage. God doesn't shy away from these matters. So because God gave us this book, let's find out what he has to say about tenderness, care, and love as a reflection of his kingdom relationship with us.

www.bhpublishinggroup.com/qr/te/22_00

SONG OF SONGS

I. COURTSHIP (1:1–3:5)

1:1 Given what we know of King Solomon, it might seem strange that he would be the author of **the Song of Songs**, a love poem about a monogamous romance. After all, someone who had seven hundred wives and three hundred concubines by the end of his life should hardly be offering marital advice! Moreover, his lack of self-control led to his downfall. His many wives turned his heart away from the Lord and led him into idolatry (see 1 Kgs 11:1-10). Nevertheless, God sovereignly used this man to give us a divine perspective on what real romance ought to look like.

1:2-4 The storyline of this book is presented as a poetic exchange between a man ("**the king**," 1:4) and a woman (the "Shulammite," 6:13), although a few other characters make appearances along the way. It begins with their courtship, leading up to their wedding.

The woman speaks first. She is captivated by her man and by the **fragrance** of his **perfume**. Yet, even better than how he smells is the kind of man he is: **your name is perfume poured out** (1:3). In this sense, "name" refers to character, to reputation. His has a pleasing aroma; therefore, the **young women adore** him and rightly so (1:3-4). Regardless of how appealing a man is on the outside, he's of little worth if his character is flawed.

1:5-7 Twice the woman describes her complexion as **dark** (1:5-6). Of special note here is the spirit of legitimate pride associated with her recognition of her color: **I am dark like the tents of Kedar, yet lovely** (1:5). She saw herself as black and beautiful.

Importantly, she is not like **one who veils herself**—a reference to a prostitute. So not only does she admire her man's character, she also has her own standards that she won't compromise. She is a woman of dignity. "Charm is deceptive and beauty is fleeting, but a woman who fears the LORD will be praised" (Prov 31:30).

1:8-17 The man's character is revealed in his response. Regardless of what she thinks of her own beauty, he affirms her as the **most beautiful of women** (1:8), comparing her loveliness to amazing creatures that God has made (1:9, 15). He says, **How beautiful you are, my darling** (1:15). Men have power to build women up or tear them down. So, husband, when was the last time you told your wife how beautiful she is?

2:1-3 As a result of his praise, the woman sees herself through his eyes: **I am a wildflower of Sharon, a lily of the valleys** (2:1). She can consider herself a lily because that's what she is to him (2:2). He is her **apricot tree**, and she delights to be **in his shade** (2:3). No matter how difficult her circumstances, she trusts that with him there is rest and refreshment.

2:4-5 **He looked on me with love** can be translated, "His banner over me is love" (2:4; see CSB note). I like that phrasing because banners are used to promote our allegiance. They advertise for all what we value. Solomon, then, makes no secret of his love. He wants everyone to know the woman is his treasure. She is his, and he is hers. In fact, his love for her is so powerful that her knees are weak, and she needs to be sustained because of how **lovesick** he makes her (2:5).

2:6-7 That she longs for **his left hand** to be **under** her **head** and **his right arm** to **embrace** her (2:6) means she desires the deepest of intimacy with him, sexual intimacy. But they are not yet married. Therefore, she tells the **young women of Jerusalem** (and herself), **do not stir up or awaken love until the appropriate time** (2:7). She's willing to be patient. The consummation of their love must await their wedding, when the time will be right.

2:8-9 He also longs to be with her. He is **leaping over the mountains** and moving **like a gazelle** because nothing will stand in his way or delay him. After all, *she* is waiting at the end of his journey.

2:10-14 He **calls** her to join him. It's springtime. **The winter is past**, and everything is **blossoming** (2:10-13). Husband, you are to be the spring to your woman's winter. The wife in Psalm 128:3 is "a fruitful vine" within the home. So if you want a summer wife who

consistently bears good fruit, don't bring home winter weather! As springtime brings new life, so this man brought new joy to his **darling** (2:13).

2:15-17 Catch the foxes for us ... that ruin the vineyards (2:15). This is a vivid way of addressing the fact that little things can wreck a relationship. Marriages aren't usually destroyed by major issues or events. Rather, they are harmed by the little things that go unaddressed. Over time, they will grow and cause a relationship to decay. So deal with them early. Seek counseling together, if necessary, to identify and catch your own "foxes" before it's too late.

3:1-5 The woman's longing caused her to dream of her love in her **bed at night**. Her intoxication with him drove her to envision herself searching for him **through the streets** (3:1-3). When she found him, she **would not let him go** (3:4). Once again (see 2:7), though, she urges the **young women** not to **awaken** sexual desires until they can be legitimately enjoyed in the marriage bed (3:5). So single men and women, don't play with fire. God created sex, but he means for us to delight in it within the covenant bonds of marriage. Avoid immorality so that you may honor your Creator and enjoy his gift as he intended.

II. WEDDING DAY (3:6–5:1)

3:6-11 Who is this coming? The groom, **King Solomon**, in all his splendor. The wedding processional is luxurious (3:6-10). **The day of his heart's rejoicing** has finally arrived: one man and one woman are coming together in holy matrimony (3:11).

4:1-7 The wedding ceremony is complete; the wedding night has begun. The new husband lavishes his new bride with admiration for her attractiveness. To him, she is **beautiful.** No—**very beautiful!** (4:1). She has **no imperfection** (4:7). Her **eyes**, **hair**, **teeth**, **lips**, and **neck** are all described with poetic praise (4:1-4). And although these could

have been adored before the wedding day, now even her **breasts** receive her husband's praise (4:5-6). This couple is naked and not ashamed.

4:8-11 She has **captured** his **heart**—a truth that's spoken twice for emphasis (4:9). And thus, they enter into the joy of consummating their marriage. Their lovemaking involves all their senses (4:9-11).

4:12-5:1 Solomon describes his new **bride** as a **locked garden** (4:12), which means she came to him as a virgin. She had been "locked" until the appropriate time. But now, on her wedding night, she is open for her husband's enjoyment. She invites him in because she's **his garden** (4:16). He accepts her invitation, and his delight in her is depicted as enjoyment of the choicest of pleasures: **myrrh**, **spices**, **honey**, **wine**, and **milk** (5:1).

Then, another person speaks: a **narrator**, someone with access to the couple's bedroom. Who could this be but God? His exhortation to the husband and wife is **Eat,** **friends! Drink, be intoxicated with caresses!** (5:1). This interruption is a reminder that God himself is pleased that the pair is pleased.

The Bible is not prudish about sex. Yes, sexual intimacy is reserved for marriage, but it is not something to be ashamed of or avoided by a husband and wife. God intends married couples to adore one another sexually. It's his gift to them.

III. RELUCTANCE AND ROMANCE (5:2–7:13)

5:2-8 In spite of a rapturous honeymoon, this marriage—like all others—experiences conflict. The husband comes home after a time away and longs to be with his wife (5:2). But, for whatever reason, she spurns his sexual advances (5:3). Instead of becoming angry that she's not in the mood, he responds with tenderness. As a result, her **feelings [are] stirred for him** (5:4). But by the time she reacts, his desires have subsided (5:5-6). When she searches for him in the night, she is mistaken for a prostitute and punished (5:6-7). Now she is the one who is **lovesick** (5:8).

The passions of husbands and wives are not always in sync. Our emotions and desires can be adversely affected by the littlest thing. We do well, then, to remember Paul's words: "Love is patient, love is kind. . . . [It] is not irritable, and does not keep a record of wrongs" (1 Cor 13:4-5).

5:9-16 At this point in the story, other young women want to know what's so special about Solomon: **What makes him better** **than another?** (5:9). Why go to such great lengths to be reconciled to him? The bride's answer describes her husband in the most exalted terms. As he delighted in her physical attractiveness, so she delights in him (5:10-16). Nevertheless, he is not merely good looking. He is her **love**, her **friend** (5:16). He's her intimate companion; he's a kingdom man.

6:1-3 The couple's lovemaking resumes (6:2), and the wife declares, **I am my love's and** **my love is mine** (6:3). In other words, she knows they are intimately bound together.

The two have "become one" (see Gen 2:24). As Paul explains, "A wife does not have the right over her own body, but her husband does. In the same way, a husband does not have the right over his own body, but his wife does" (1 Cor 7:4). Marriage partners belong to each other.

6:4-10 The husband again gives a detailed description of his wife's beauty. Although there are many other **women** in the world, his love **is unique** in his sight (6:8-9). None can compare to her.

6:11-12 Nature's readiness for spring is an illustration of his wife's readiness for lovemaking (6:11). Intimacy with her husband is compared to riding **in a chariot with a** **nobleman** (6:12). She's on cloud nine at the thought.

6:14–7:8 Solomon cannot get enough of his Shulammite bride. He is enraptured by her entire body: **feet**, **thighs**, **navel**, **belly**, **breasts**, **neck**, **eyes**, **nose**, **head**, and **hair** (7:1-5). Husband, do you affirm your wife? Let her know that she is your treasure.

7:9-13 Again, when she hears her man's praise, it arouses the woman's desire. She summons her **love** to **spend the night** enjoying **every delicacy** with her, for she has **treasured them up** for him (7:10-13). In a world in which promiscuity is rampant and exalted, our culture needs to see the joy and pleasure found in an exclusive relationship. Monogamy is holy, beautiful, and exciting.

IV. PERMANENCE AND PURITY (8:1-14)

8:1-5 That the Shulammite wishes she could **treat** her husband **like** her **brother** (8:1) means she wants to show affection to him in public—something that husbands and wives couldn't do appropriately. After that, she wanted to **lead** him home and be engulfed in his embrace (8:2-3). Such privacy for more romantic displays of affection was necessary so that other **young women** would not be stirred up until they could experience intimacy with their own husbands (8:4).

8:6-7 What these two share is no fling. She wants him always: **Set me as a seal on your heart**. Marriage demands commitment, **for love is as strong as death** (8:6). Like death, the love between a married man and woman is to be a given. Self-serving "love" won't survive. True love says, "I'm not simply in this partnership to feel good; I'm here to build a lasting relationship." Only this kind of love is enduring. Flood waters **cannot extinguish** it, and **wealth** cannot buy it (8:7).

8:8-10 Here we find advice regarding those who are not yet married. A group of **brothers** consider their **sister**, who **has no breasts** (8:8)—that is, she is still young and undeveloped. They discuss how they can help prepare her for marriage, deciding to **build a silver barricade on her** (8:9). In other words, they choose to help her protect herself as they can and to reward her for being steadfast in her commitment to purity. Let your daughters know, moms and dads, that you're proud of them when they demand that men respect them. Guide them in setting boundaries.

These brothers are also prepared to **enclose** their sister **with cedar planks** should she prove to be willing to compromise with sexual sin (8:9). This is a reminder that when your children abuse their freedoms, it's clear they're not ready for those freedoms. So don't give them more liberty than they're prepared to handle. Teach your daughters to have enough self-respect to stand tall and strong, regardless of cultural pressures.

A real man—a kingdom man—admires and longs for a woman who is **a wall** (8:10), a kingdom woman. Our culture does everything it can to encourage sexual freedom, especially among young people. So make sure your kids hear what God has to say on the matter of sexual purity.

8:11-14 Just as **Solomon** had the prerogative to lease his **vineyard to tenants** (8:11), so his wife had the prerogative to lease her **vineyard**, her body, to him (8:12). She gave herself willingly. As Song of Songs ends, their love and desire for each other continues (8:13-14).

Although this book is a rich celebration of the beauty of human love and intimacy between a husband and wife, it also points to the wonder of divine love. God gives us gifts in the physical world to teach us spiritual realities. The intimacy possible in marriage points us to the greatest intimacy of all: our eternal relationship with our Savior. In fact, Paul says the mystery of a one-flesh union between a man and a woman is meant to preview the union of Christ and the church (see Eph 5:29-31). John even describes the final joining together of the Lord Jesus and his people as the marriage feast of the Lamb and his bride (see Rev 19:7-9). The beautiful declaration of the lover, "I am my love's and my love is mine" (6:3), is but a pale reflection of the more glorious divine declaration: "I will be their God, and they will be my people" (Jer 31:33).

ISAIAH

INTRODUCTION

Author

ACCORDING TO ISAIAH 1:1, THE book is the vision of "Isaiah son of Amoz," who ministered in the eighth century BC during the reigns of "Uzziah, Jotham, Ahaz, and Hezekiah"—kings of Judah. Although Isaiah's authorship was accepted for centuries, it has been challenged by modern critical scholars. Many of them argue that Isaiah couldn't have written chapters 40–66, because these chapters detail Judah's defeat by Babylon, exile, and return to the land. These scholars believe a prophet in the eighth century BC couldn't possibly know about future events. And this is true—unless the Creator God who knows the future revealed them to him. Because God can make the future known to his servants, then there is no reason to reject that Isaiah wrote chapters 40–66 and is, therefore, the author of the entire book.

Historical Background

According to Isaiah 6:1, the prophet received his call from God to ministry "in the year that King Uzziah died" (ca. 742 BC). During this glorious vision of the Lord seated on his throne, Isaiah responded to the Lord's question, "Who will go for us?" with, "Here I am. Send me" (6:8).

Uzziah's reign was a prosperous time for Judah, but the nation of Assyria was rising to power. In 722 BC, the northern kingdom of Israel fell to Assyrian domination. Although the Lord would supernaturally protect Judah from Assyrian aggression, another superpower was on the horizon: Babylon. Isaiah would not live to see the Babylonians assail Judah. But he warned sinful Judah that they were coming. Nevertheless, God's judgment would be followed by God's grace, for Isaiah prophesied that the Lord would bring his people back from exile when their punishment was complete.

Message and Purpose

Isaiah, a great prophet to the southern kingdom of Judah, blazed onto the scene to describe the condition of this kingdom that was going down spiritually and headed toward disaster. He calls on the people to repent and get right with God, telling them, "Though your sins are scarlet, they will be as white as snow" (1:18).

The classic passage in this book is found in chapter 6, describing Isaiah's official call to his prophetic task when he saw the Lord in all of his majestic holiness. That call came in a bad year, when good King Uzziah died. That meant Judah's human hope to set things right was gone, but Isaiah learned that even in times like that, the Lord was still on his throne and still in control.

Isaiah is a long book because it deals with two great sweeps of time—the days in which the prophet lived and the time yet to come when the Messiah returns and establishes his kingdom of righteousness. That's why Isaiah 53 is such a precious chapter, telling us of the Messiah, the Suffering Servant, who would bear our sins and someday rule as King. The message of Isaiah to us today is to adjust the way we live so that when the King returns, we can enter into the kingdom full speed ahead because we have prepared ourselves by living according to God's righteous standards.

VIDEO INTRO

www.bhpublishinggroup.com/qr/te/23_00

Outline

ISAIAH

I. THE JUDGMENT OF GOD (1:1–39:8)

❧ A. God's Judgment on Judah (1:1–5:30) ❧

1:1 God called **Isaiah son of Amoz** to be a prophet **during the reigns of Kings Uzziah, Jotham, Ahaz, and Hezekiah** of the southern kingdom of **Judah.** Isaiah's prophetic ministry, then, occurred many years before the ministry of Jeremiah that ended with the nation's exile in Babylon. But even during Isaiah's ministry well over one hundred years before Jerusalem's destruction in 586 BC, the tone is one of God's great displeasure with his people and determination to judge them for their sin.

1:2-9 God put Judah on trial, calling the **heavens** and **earth** as witnesses (1:2) against his people, whom he described as a **sinful nation, people weighed down with iniquity, [a] brood of evildoers, depraved children!** (1:4). Judah's insistence on rebelling against the Lord was ridiculous in light of the chastisements God had already laid on them. The nation is pictured as a body so covered with **wounds, welts, and festering sores** that there's no healthy place to land another blow (1:6). And yet, Judah wouldn't throw in the towel and submit to God's agenda. She persisted in her sin, even though her enemies were already besieging her cities. Isaiah likened Judah to **Sodom** and **Gomorrah** (1:9), the epitome of God's judgment on sinful people. Yet God had gracious future plans for Judah, unlike those cities.

1:10-15 That assurance did not minimize the seriousness of Judah's sin, though. The tone of 1:10-23 is straightforward regarding the evil practices of the people and how God viewed them. Judah's citizens did all of the right things outwardly: they brought **offerings** to the temple and observed the religious **festivals** (1:13-14). Thus, they thought they were fine in God's eyes. But the Lord brushed all of their outward acts aside: **What are all your sacrifices to me? . . . I have had enough of burnt offerings. . . . I have no desire for the blood of bulls, lambs, or male goats** (1:11). And it only goes downhill from there. Every sacrifice and act of worship had become abhorrent to God because the people performed them with evil hearts. Even Judah's **prayers** went unheeded because their **hands [were] covered with blood** (1:15). Judah was a place where injustice and treachery flourished, and the helpless were mistreated by the powerful. Things were so bad that the people's hypocritical acts of religious observance made God sick.

1:16-17 The only remedy for Judah's sin was repentance and cleansing. True repentance, which is the inner resolve and determination to turn from sin and return to God, would be obvious in the nation's treatment of the oppressed, the orphan, and the widow—the weakest members of society (1:17). True religion is not selfish. It helps those who can do nothing in return for what is offered them. The charity giving of false religion, by contrast, is more of a business deal than it is faith in action.

In Isaiah's day, orphans and widows were the poorest of the poor. They needed help. And because they were basically powerless, they were often the victims of injustice. So God warned his people to make sure they defended the helpless. To live out a faith that is valuable to God, we must reach out to those who can't help themselves. Why? Because that's what our heavenly Father did for us. When we were sinners and could do nothing for God, God in Christ became sin for us that we might become the righteousness of God in him (2 Cor 5:21). God wants his children to act like their Father.

1:18-31 Judah was called to cleansing and repentance, and God promised that if they were **willing and obedient** (1:19), if they turned from their wickedness and embraced his agenda, their **crimson** sins would be made **white as snow** (1:18). But they wouldn't listen. Unfortunately, repentance would only come after the severest of judgment at the hands of the Babylonians. It would **burn** away Judah's **dross** and **impurities** (1:25), leaving behind a righteous remnant that would one day enjoy God's favor.

2:1-4 This passage is a magnificent prophetic look ahead to the millennial reign of Christ, when God will restore righteous rule to the world. The headquarters of his one-thousand-year rule will be Jerusalem on **the mountain of the LORD** in the holy city of **Jerusalem** (2:3). As glorious as the millennium will be for us as the church in general, it will have very special meaning for believing Israel. Christ's kingdom reign will mean the fulfillment of God's purposes for Israel. Jewish believers in Christ will finally live in real peace, as will all **the nations** (2:4), and Israel will occupy all of the land God gave to Abraham.

Israel will also have its rightful King in the millennium. Initially, Jesus was rejected when he presented himself to the Jews as their King. They even cried, "We have no king but Caesar!" (John 19:15), scorning Christ. But God promised David that his Son would rule on his throne forever. Jesus is that Son of David, and he will one day take the throne in Jerusalem. And make no mistake, his rule will be a righteous dictatorship. He will not share either his throne or his glory with another. The kingdom will be Israel's

golden age of restoration and the realization of all God's purposes.

2:5-8 As Isaiah was writing, though, the southern kingdom of Judah was in such desperate spiritual condition that he said God had **abandoned** his **people** (2:6). This was strong language telling Isaiah's readers that in reality, it wasn't God who had moved; they were the ones who had walked away from him by practicing idolatry. It must have stung to be told that in God's sight, they weren't any better than their arch enemies, **the Philistines** (2:6), because of their pagan practices. Yes, Judah's **land** was **full of silver and gold**, but it was also **full of idols** (2:7-8). Judah likely concluded its wealth was the fruit of worshiping idols.

2:9-22 It's no wonder Isaiah cried out, **Do not forgive them!** (2:9). Then in 2:10-21, he delivered a message of judgment that looked beyond the coming devastation of Judah to the end-time judgment God will bring on the whole earth during the great tribulation. He said, **Go into the rocks and hide in the dust from the terror of the LORD and from his majestic splendor** (2:10; see also 2:19, 21). This will not be finally fulfilled until God pours out his final judgments on an unbelieving world (see Rev 6:15-17). On that day, **idols** will finally be thrown away (2:20).

This section thus illustrates how the Old Testament prophets wrote not just of things relatively near but also of things further away. It is doubtful that Isaiah even knew he was writing about the last days when Israel's Messiah would return in glory. The prophet probably did not see the long valley between the two mountain peaks of Judah's judgment and the judgments of the tribulation. He just faithfully recorded what the Holy Spirit inspired him to write. This section speaks of the humbling of all of mankind's sinful pride, ending with this universal warning: **Put no more trust in a mere human, who has only the breath in his nostrils. What is he really worth?** (2:22).

3:1-8 Isaiah answered that question in chapter 3 by saying that God would **remove** from Judah the daily necessities of life and every category of leader and counselor the people trusted in—**heroes and warriors, fortune-tellers**, and **necromancers** (3:1-3).

That pagan occultists, whose penalty under the law was death, were included in this list gives a clear picture of how depraved God's people had become. Instead of wise, strong, and spiritually minded leaders, then, the nation would be ruled by **unstable**, oppressive, and foolish people (3:4-7). In other words, Judah would be led by those wholly inadequate to lead.

Unfortunately, we see this happening too often in our own times as leaders who know nothing of true leadership rise to power. As homes and families unravel, it tragically produces leaders who lack spiritual foundation. And this trend, of course, has to be addressed in our homes, because no government or school system alone can develop spiritual leaders when the home is lacking God's leadership.

Too often, when children leave their homes each day, there are forces at work to unravel everything good their parents try to teach them. The competition is great. The world will give your kids a different story than you give them. So while good families were important in Isaiah's day, remember that they're still desperately important today, and see your own home as a training ground for producing godly seed. We need to teach and live God's Word at home if we want to see godly leadership in our neighborhoods, schools, and government.

3:9 The people of Judah in Isaiah's time had failed miserably at the parenting assignment, and they would reap the bitter fruit of inept and ungodly leadership at the very time of crisis when they needed a word and direction from God the most. But Isaiah didn't feel sorry for them. After all, instead of seeking God in repentance and restoration, Judah paraded its sin **like Sodom**, whose men flaunted their homosexuality in God's face (see Gen 19). As a result, God's people **brought disaster on themselves**.

3:10-15 The good news was that there was a promise of rescue and blessing for **the righteous** amid this chaos (3:10): God would not destroy forever the people of his covenant. But this promise did nothing to ease the judgment due to **the wicked** (3:11). The rich and the powerful were so cruel and corrupt that

God called a special session of his heavenly court to denounce them for plundering **the poor** (3:14). They had crushed those less fortunate than them. But they weren't counting on **the Lord God of Armies** (3:15) who avenges the weak and levels justice upon their oppressors to address their behavior.

3:16–4:1 The **daughters of Zion**, who were elaborately adorned with all manner of jewelry and garments, obviously benefited from this ill-gotten wealth (3:16, 18-23). They were arrogant and **haughty** (3:16). In response to their shameful displays of finery, the Lord decreed, **Instead of perfume there will be a stench; instead of a belt, a rope; instead of beautifully styled hair, baldness; instead of fine clothes, sackcloth; instead of beauty, branding** (3:24). As Judah's men would fall in battle, slaughtered by the Babylonian invasion, Judah's surviving women—the ones not taken away as captives—would go to desperate lengths to try and ease their **disgrace** (4:1).

4:2-6 In the remaining verses of chapter 4, the Lord broke through the darkness with a prophecy of Israel's future glory in the millennial reign of Jesus Christ. While Isaiah may have only understood this as speaking of the nation's future return from captivity in Babylon, the term **Branch of the Lord** (4:2) is a reference to Christ as the righteous descendant of King David who springs out of David's roots (see 11:1). This will be ultimately fulfilled at Christ's return to reign as the true King of Israel. And just as God's glory was visible to Israel during the exodus, so the visible **glory** of God will be seen over **Mount Zion** (4:5). Despite severe judgment of Judah, there would be a remnant of God's people whom he would preserve, restore, and rebuild according to his promises.

5:1-7 Because the righteous remnant's restoration was still future, though, God had to return to the work of judgment. He pictured unfaithful Judah in terms of a **vineyard** that he had planted to be fruitful and produce joy (5:1-2). God lovingly tended his vineyard, but instead of **good grapes**, all **it yielded** was **worthless grapes** (5:2). He had done all that could have been done **for** his vineyard (5:4), yet when he looked for **justice** and **righteousness** there, all he discovered was **injustice** and **cries of despair** (5:7). Thus, God would allow the vineyard of his people to be destroyed.

One day, Jesus would allude to this metaphor (see Matt 21:33-46). In his retelling of the story of the vineyard owner, not only would his servants reject him but they would also kill his son (see Matt 21:38-39).

5:8-23 Woe to Judah, God said in response to his complete disappointment in his people (5:8). There are two meanings for this terminology in Scripture. One is that of sorrow for what has happened to the unfortunate, while the second is a warning of coming disaster. This woe is of the latter variety; it is followed by five more pronouncements of woe for various sins (5:11, 18, 20-22).

In the midst of these denunciations, God made a declaration that is relevant to our day. Because Judah disregarded God and his righteous requirements, he said, **My people will go into exile because they lack knowledge** (5:13)—that is, they lacked a God-centered worldview. It is inextricably clear that one major reason the people of Judah would be judged and sent into exile was that they didn't know—and hadn't bothered to learn—God's views on life. They didn't know (and didn't care) how God expected them to live. God meant for them to be learning and growing in him even as they were surrounded by pagan cultures, but they simply ignored him and his Word.

God meant for his entire people to be a light of his knowledge and a reflection of his glory, teaching their neighbors his truth. But instead of influencing the world around them, they had become imitators of the world. Even Judah's prophets and priests, who should have taught and led the nation to know God, were corrupt and self-serving. Thus, the people were wilting away like an unwatered and neglected vineyard.

This issue of worldview is relevant today because the church should be the primary university for the culture. It should be leading the way in educating the masses since it is the one entity that can interject a God-centered perspective, his kingdom agenda, into any discussion. Our culture looks at the world through the eyes of man rather than through the eyes of God. The church, therefore, must educate and encourage people to consider life from a divine kingdom perspective. It must provide a divine orientation on every subject. Everything the Bible speaks about, it speaks about authoritatively. And it speaks to every issue of life. So through all of the church's ministries, people ought to be encountering a God-centered worldview. The church is charged with imparting the knowledge and wisdom of God, executing his kingdom agenda in history.

Judah had sadly failed in this responsibility. They indulged every sinful desire imaginable. They even proudly challenged the Creator of the universe to execute his **plan** on his own so that they could **see it** (5:19). In other words, they mocked him! They called **evil good and good evil** (5:20), advocating a complete reversal of God's moral order. They considered themselves **wise** and **clever** (5:21), but their opinion was far too exalted.

5:24-30 Judah would pay a terrible price for their blasphemies. When **the Lord's anger burned**, their **corpses** would be **like garbage in the streets** (5:25). God would use the unnamed armies of **distant nations** to judge his people (5:26-29). The land would be left in **darkness and distress** (5:30).

➤ B. The Commissioning of Isaiah
(6:1-13) ❦

6:1 After five introductory chapters that set the stage for what is to come, Isaiah takes us to his backstory. Here we see the prophet's life-changing vision of God's overwhelming holiness and his call to ministry. It was a very crucial point in the history of Judah. **In the year that King Uzziah died, I saw the Lord seated on a high and lofty throne, and the hem of his robe filled the temple.** So although Judah was experiencing turmoil at the death of its king, the true King was seated on his throne in sovereign glory. Isaiah thus learned that the kingdom of God operates according to his will, not according to outward circumstances. If you embrace this kingdom principle, it will change your life.

That God was still in charge was crucial for Isaiah to grasp because the death of Uzziah was a personal tragedy for the prophet, as well as for the southern kingdom of Judah. Although he certainly wasn't perfect (see 2 Chr 26:16-21), Uzziah had been a good king who had brought Judah a long way back toward God (see 2 Chr 26:3-5). It would have been easy for Isaiah to pin his hopes on Uzziah for a national revival that would perhaps forestall God's judgment, but God had another plan. And to make it real to Isaiah, the Lord gave him an incredible vision. Of course, Isaiah knew the Lord before Uzziah died. But the point is that Isaiah didn't really *see* the Lord until Uzziah died. Isaiah needed to learn that although *a* king was dead, *the* King was alive and well. Judah had definitely flourished during Uzziah's reign. It had become a power to be reckoned with. And yet, times were changing.

Sometimes it takes a tragedy in our lives, or other negative circumstances, for us to truly see God. We may know him as our Savior but not be growing in a day-by-day experience of adopting his perspective of the world and living in obedience to it. In fact, that's one reason God sometimes allows difficult situations to come into our lives. They help shift our focus off the created things and onto the Creator. Until we adjust our vision from the temporal to the eternal, we may miss out on seeing the eternal altogether. God is not merely interested in getting us to heaven. He wants us to see and experience him here. Sometimes God is most clearly seen in the midst of painful situations.

6:2-3 What did Isaiah see? He saw a God who is holy to the third power: **Holy, holy, holy is the Lord of Armies** (6:3). The angelic beings who called out these words weren't stuttering; the triple repetition was for emphasis. God is holy—that is, he is separate or distinct. "God is light, and there is absolutely no darkness in him" (1 John 1:5). He is perfect, pure, and righteous. God's holiness is the centerpiece of his character. All of his other attributes flow from it. His wrath against sin, then, is a *holy* wrath. His sovereignty over the universe is a *holy* sovereignty. His love for the world is a *holy* love. If God is anything, he is holy.

The prophet saw a God who rules over all the situations of life. The **seraphim** who were calling out eternal praise had **six wings** (6:2): four were for worship, and two were for working. To me, this indicates that when we prioritize worship over working, our work will be more fruitful. Spending time in God's holy presence will enable us to understand his kingdom perspective so that we may live it out.

6:4-5 This was a terrifying sight for Isaiah as the foundations **shook** with the power of the angels' **voices** and **the temple was filled with smoke** (6:4)—a reference to the glory of God. Isaiah was so overcome that he cried out, **Woe is me for I am ruined** (6:5). The word *ruined* means "coming undone," so Isaiah felt like he was falling apart, unraveling before a holy God. The prophet was thus in despair: **I am a man of unclean lips** (6:5). Despite being a significant and prominent prophet dedicated to the service of God, Isaiah fully felt his own inadequacy and sinfulness in God's holy presence. And in that reality, Isaiah confessed his uncleanness.

6:6-7 Because of this, Isaiah experienced God's grace. **One of the seraphim flew** over to him with **a glowing coal that he had taken from the altar with tongs** (6:6). He touched Isaiah's lips with it and said, **Now that this has touched your lips, your iniquity is removed and your sin is atoned for** (6:7). The lips are the most sensitive part of the human face, so when the angel touched Isaiah's with a burning coal, there must have been pain. This was necessary because, in order for Isaiah to experience cleansing, he had to embrace the pain of the past that had gotten him there.

6:8-9 Isaiah discovered more than the purifying searing of the coal. He discovered his purpose. He **heard the voice of the Lord asking: Who should I send? Who will go for us?** The God of the universe was calling for kingdom volunteers. Isaiah didn't hesitate. He said, **Here I am. Send me** (6:8).

Isaiah came to know the revealed will of God and received the power to do that will when he saw God. The prophet got plugged into God's kingdom agenda when, in a broken and painful situation, he saw God for himself. Isaiah needed this powerful revelation, because the people to whom Isaiah was being sent were a rebellious and sinful crowd who had already signaled their lack of interest in what God had to tell them. But Isaiah was ready for service after his cleansing, and he knew that Judah needed the same purging of sin and forgiveness that he had experienced.

6:10-13 For the most part, the people of Judah were not going to listen, and God alerted Isaiah to that fact. **Their eyes** were **blind** to their sin and to spiritual reality; **their ears** were deaf to God's call for repentance; and **their minds** were dulled lest they **understand** and **be healed** (6:10). Understandably, then, Isaiah asked how long he would have to speak to a spiritually dead nation. Unfortunately, he learned, their defiant state would continue until Judah was destroyed (6:11-12). Isaiah would not live to see the Babylonian captivity; nevertheless, Isaiah would prophesy to Judah the rest of his life. But lest he become too discouraged, the Lord ended Isaiah's commissioning with a promise that a **holy seed** would remain as a remnant (6:13). In spite of the coming judgment, God was not finished with his people.

➣ C. The Coming Messiah (7:1–12:6) ❧

7:1-2 Isaiah's ministry began in a spectacular fashion with the announcement of a prophecy that would ultimately be fulfilled in the virgin birth of Jesus Christ (see 7:14), although it would also have a nearer fulfillment prefiguring that greater end. This message was delivered to the wicked King **Ahaz** of **Judah**, Uzziah's son (7:1).

The historical context explained here occurred while the northern kingdom of Israel was still intact, as it was during the early years of Isaiah's prophecy. The king of Israel and **King Rezin** of Aram (that is, Syria) allied themselves to wage war against Judah, which caused the hearts of Judah's people to tremble in fear. Notice that Isaiah referred to the kingdom of Judah as **the house of David** (7:2). This was a way of telling Isaiah's

readers that God had not forgotten or abandoned his promise that a ruler would come from David's line to fulfill all his promises to his people (see 2 Sam 7:1-17).

7:3-8 Isaiah went to Ahaz with the Lord's message that the king should not fear the alliance of Israel and Aram, or their plan to depose Ahaz and replace him with a king of their choice (7:3-6). God said this regarding their plot: **It will not happen; it will not occur** (7:7). In fact, God said that Israel, here referred to as **Ephraim** (one of the leading tribes there), would be devastated **within sixty-five years** (7:8). Not only would their threat come to nothing, but they wouldn't be around long.

7:9-13 God invited Ahaz to ask him for **a sign** to validate the prophecy (7:10-11), but the king answered with mock piety: **I will not ask. I will not test the LORD** (7:12). Isaiah's angry reaction shows that Ahaz's refusal was the result of his unbelief (7:13). Such lack of faith in God, in fact, would be Ahaz's downfall, for God made it clear: **If you do not stand firm in your faith, then you will not stand at all** (7:9). Those are words we all need to hear.

7:14-19 Isaiah responded to the king, **The Lord himself will give you a sign: See, the virgin will conceive, have a son, and name him Immanuel** (7:14). *Immanuel* means "God with us." While Isaiah's words would have ultimate fulfillment in Jesus Christ, as the Gospel of Matthew makes clear (see Matt 1:22-23), they had a more immediate application, too.

Importantly, the birth prophesied was to be "a sign" to King Ahaz specifically, but his lifetime unfolded hundreds of years before the birth of Christ. In fact, it's possible that Isaiah himself did not understand the full import of what he was writing. So the child, who was to be a sign that Judah would not be conquered by the Israel-Aram alliance, was most likely the son soon to be born to Isaiah and "the prophetess" (8:3). This son would have the God-given name **Maher-shalal-hash-baz**, which means "Speeding to the Plunder, Hurrying to the Spoil" (8:1). This child was the sign to Ahaz personally because, **before the boy [knew] to reject what is bad and choose what is good, the land of the two kings** whom Ahaz dreaded would **be abandoned** (7:16). And indeed, this happened about three years later when Aram was crushed by the Assyrians (7:17-19). The name Immanuel, when applied to Isaiah's son, indicated that God had not abandoned his promises to the house of David.

It is noteworthy that "the prophetess," Isaiah's wife, may well have been a virgin when Isaiah made this prophecy to Ahaz. If so, the meaning for the immediate context of 7:14 would then be, "An unmarried young woman who is a virgin now will get married and bear a son"—which was fulfilled when Isaiah married her and she gave birth.

7:20-25 The good news of Judah's escape from conquest by Israel and Aram was tempered by the bad news of God's judgment on Ahaz and Judah's unfaithful people. The prophecy that Isaiah's son would be eating "curds and honey" (see 7:15) was not encouraging, since these were foods of nomadic people—indicating that Judah would be desolated (see 7:21-25). **The king of Assyria**, Tiglath-pileser III, got Aram off Judah's back. But then he invaded Judah and exacted a heavy tribute. God called him **a razor hired from beyond the Euphrates River** who would **shave** all the hair off of Judah (7:20). Such was the ultimate humiliation for a Jewish man in that day.

Why was God so angry with Ahaz and Judah? In 2 Kings 16:7-14, we learn that Ahaz begged Tiglath-pileser III to save him from Aram and Israel, and he gave him silver and gold from the Lord's temple as incentive. Not only this, but Ahaz also liked Tiglath-pileser's pagan altar so much that he had one made just like it in Jerusalem! Looking to a pagan king for deliverance and worshiping his false gods will accomplish only one thing: arousing the anger of the living God.

8:1-10 Despite Judah's faithlessness, though, God promised that he had not forgotten his people and would deliver them. As happened so often in the prophets' writings, this assurance was given in the midst of God's pronouncements of judgment. Chapter 8 begins with the prophecy of Judah's deliverance

from Israel and Aram (8:1-4; see commentary on 7:14-19). But because this mercy from God did not lead Judah to repentance, the same Assyrian army would pour into Judah like **mighty rushing water** (8:7), reaching up the nation's **neck** (8:7-8). In other words, God's people would almost, but not quite, drown because of their sin. Yet Isaiah used the name **Immanuel**, and its meaning, **God is with us** (8:8, 10; see 7:14 above)—offering reminders that God would not completely abandon his people.

8:11-14 God cautioned the people not to **fear** their human enemies (8:12). Only the **Lord of Armies is holy. Only he should be feared** and **held in awe** (8:13). For those who will not fear him—that is, take him seriously, **he will be a stone to stumble over and a rock to trip over** (8:14). Interestingly, Paul and Peter apply this text to Jesus Christ (see Rom 9:33; 1 Pet 2:8). The Son of God shares the same divine nature as the Father, so the New Testament writers often read passages of Scripture that originally referred to God and apply them to God the Son. Just as the unfaithful in Israel stumbled over the Lord in Isaiah's day, so unbelieving Jews would stumble over the Lord Jesus in his.

8:15-22 The unrighteous would be **snared and captured**, but the faithful were to **wait for the Lord** as he went about his hard work of judgment (8:15, 17). Sadly, instead of seeking God through his appointed prophet, unfaithful Judah sought advice through **mediums** and **spiritists**. Isaiah's question cut to the heart of the matter: **Should they inquire of the dead on behalf of the living?** (8:18-19). Nobody, after all, calls the morgue for help when they're in trouble! So why seek counsel from those who have died rather than from the living God? While the righteous would flee to the safe haven of God and his Word, those who persisted in sin would perish (8:20-22).

9:1-5 Chapter 9 brings both a promise of future blessing and the reality of then-present judgment. The reference to **the land of Zebulun and the land of Naphtali** points to the northern kingdom of Israel. At this time, it was already a vassal state of Assyria and headed for destruction because of the people's sins. Yet God would one day **bring honor to** this land, for his Son would live and minister there (9:1). There would come a day when **the people walking in darkness** would see **a great light** (9:2), and the kingdom of heaven would come near (see Matt 4:15-17). Indeed, in the future the Messiah will reverse the humiliation and bondage of Israel and usher in an era of peace in which the **garments of war** will be no more (9:5).

9:6 Here we see another messianic prophecy. Its language is very precise. Isaiah said **a child will be** *born* **for us, a son will be** *given* **to us** (emphasis added). This tells us that Jesus had to be *born* as a child to come to us, but he is also the preexistent Son of God who was *given* to us. The child would be born in time and space in Bethlehem, but the Son has existed from all eternity. And since **the government will be on his shoulders**, which is a reference to Jesus's coming rule in the millennial kingdom, he rightly bears the great names ascribed to him: **Wonderful Counselor, Mighty God, Eternal Father, Prince of Peace.**

Here again we see the "near" and "far" aspects that frequently occur in Old Testament prophecy because Jesus was born two thousand years ago as a child, but the government of the universe has yet to be placed "on his shoulders." This will happen at his coronation as King of kings and Lord of lords in the millennium.

9:7 Notice the description of Jesus's kingdom rule: **He will reign on the throne of David and over his kingdom, to establish and sustain it with justice and righteousness.** In other words, his reign will have social and political aspects as much it will have spiritual aspects. This detail has implications for the church today as we seek to live in accordance with God's perspective.

Many Christians misunderstand these aspects of the kingdom, thereby marginalizing its authority and influence in their lives and in the land. Some have so spiritualized the kingdom, in fact, that its sociopolitical features have become little more than an ideology lacking modern application. This has led to a sad reduction of the vast socioethical implications of the church, creating an organism that offers little power toward transforming society.

The multifaceted nature of the kingdom of God is very real, biblically substantiated, and relevant to the manifestation of the church's greatest and true potential. Our kingdom activity today should be reflective of, and point to, the ultimate kingdom of Jesus Christ in which he will execute justice for the oppressed and rule righteously over his subjects (see 10:1-2).

9:8-21 Isaiah's turn to judgment in 9:8 is stark. But such alternating style between coming judgment and promised blessing is a common characteristic of the prophetic books. Although Isaiah was primarily a prophet to the southern kingdom of Judah, he also delivered God's message to **Jacob**— that is, to the people of Israel (9:8). They had arrogantly vowed to recover from the calamity that had fallen upon them and come out even stronger (9:9-10). But God had another plan—they'd be destroyed at the hands of their enemies. A recurring refrain here is God's anger: **In all this, his anger has not turned away, and his hand is still raised to strike** (9:12, 17, 21).

Because Israel refused to turn back to the Lord, he would **cut off Israel's head and tail.** In other words, Israel's wicked leaders, the elders and the prophets who led the whole nation astray, would be punished (9:14-16). God's fury against his faithless people would not be quenched until their destruction was complete. The **people** were **like fuel for the fire** (9:19).

10:1-2 The proclamation of judgment continued with a dire warning of **Woe.** God declared a curse on Israel's leaders for their **oppressive laws** (10:1) that deprived **the poor** and **the needy** of justice (10:2). God expects his people to demonstrate righteousness and justice in their lives. This was true in ancient Israel, and it's true today. The church of Jesus Christ should lead the way in caring for the poor and advocating for the oppressed. Isaiah condemned the mistreatment of **widows** and **the fatherless** (10:2); later, James tells Christians "to look after orphans and widows in their distress" (Jas 1:27).

10:3-4 Because of Israel's sin and social injustices, God's hand of judgment would not be lifted until Assyria had finished off the northern kingdom. Isaiah's readers in Judah should have taken warning, since their nation was heading down the same path. But they also refused to listen. When God's **anger** will not turn away (10:4), **who will you run to for help?** (10:3).

10:5-7 Here we see God's finger of judgment pointed to the Assyrians. As he often did with pagan powers, God used Assyria as a **rod** of his judgment to strike Israel, **a godless nation** (10:5-6). The Assyrian king was a tool in God's righteous hands to chastise his people. The Assyrian king, however, didn't see it the same way. His plan was **to destroy and to cut off many nations** (10:7). The king wasn't intentionally serving the Lord; he was serving himself. In fact, he wasn't even trying to punish the wicked; he was trying to conquer the world. But although the king of Assyria had evil intentions when he assaulted Israel, God worked through him to punish Israel for its disloyalty to his covenant.

    This is an example of the mysterious mingling of divine sovereignty and human responsibility that we often see in the Bible. Perhaps the most famous example is when Joseph told his brothers who had sold him into slavery, "You planned evil against me; God planned it for good to bring about the present result—the survival of many people" (Gen 50:20). So remember, regardless of what wickedness human beings have planned, God is always working behind the scenes to accomplish his purposes.

10:8-19 Assyria itself would not escape divine wrath. The arrogance of Assyria's king displeased God and invited his judgment. The Assyrians assumed that just as they had marched through and conquered other lands (including Israel), they could easily sweep on south and take **Jerusalem** (10:8-11). But Judah's day for chastisement and defeat had not yet come. So the Assyrians were stopped. God also declared through his prophet, **I will punish the king of Assyria for his arrogant acts and the proud look in his eyes** (10:12). The Lord, **Israel's Light**, would consume Assyria like a raging **fire** (10:17).

10:20-34 Although the northern kingdom of Israel would fall as a result of the **destruction** that God had **decreed** (10:22), he would spare a **remnant** (10:20). The southern kingdom of Judah need **not fear Assyria** (10:24). The Assyrians would strike at **Zion** (that is, Jerusalem), but they would meet with the **wrath** of the LORD of Armies (10:24-26). The Lord would level the pagan nation as if he were clearing a **forest** with an **ax** (10:33-34). The bigger they are, the harder they fall.

11:1-5 Although the evil "forest" would be chopped down (10:34), God's kingdom would grow. **A shoot** would sprout up **from the stump of Jesse** (11:1). Jesse was the father of King David, so God is proclaiming through Isaiah that he hasn't abandoned the Davidic dynasty. Although this line of kings was experiencing hard times—and worse ones were to come—a better descendant of David was coming. Clearly, this is a reference to the promised Messiah, who possesses the fullness of God's **Spirit**, endowing him with **wisdom**, **strength**, and **the fear of the LORD** (11:2). He will rule in perfect **justice** and **righteousness**, delivering the **oppressed** and slaying **the wicked** (11:4-5). Today, we have a difficult time finding leaders with integrity to occupy government offices. That will not be a problem when the Lord Jesus Christ takes the reins of government.

11:6-16 Even the animal kingdom will be renewed in Christ's millennial kingdom, and creatures now considered predator and prey will be at peace with one another (11:6-9). Also, God will initiate a "second exodus," bringing the Jews back to Israel from their lands of exile (11:11-12). All of this will take place in that day because **the land will be as full of the knowledge of the LORD as the sea is filled with water** (11:9). Given the hostility between Judah and Israel in Isaiah's day, this prophecy of reunification must have sounded impossible to Isaiah's readers. Nevertheless, the reestablished nation will appear in the kingdom age and defeat its enemies (11:13-14). God will **divide the Gulf of Suez** and **wave his hand over the Euphrates** (11:15) so that his people can return easily, just as he dried up the Red Sea when the Israelites departed **Egypt** (11:16).

12:1-6 The final chapter in this section is a song of praise for what God will do when Israel meets her King and acknowledges him at his second coming when he establishes his kingdom. On that day, the Lord's **anger** will be turned away as he becomes the **salvation** of his chosen people (12:1-3). There will be singing and rejoicing when the **Holy One of Israel** lives among and rules over them (12:6).

➤ D. God's Judgment on the Nations
(13:1–23:18) ❦

This section of eleven chapters includes pronouncements of judgment against the nations. The prophecies are open to several interpretations, which I will unpack.

13:1-22 Isaiah's **pronouncement against Babylon** (13:1) makes it clear that Babylon was going to be judged and destroyed because of its **pride** (13:19). The mention of **the Medes** (13:17) leads some to believe that Isaiah was describing Babylon's defeat in 539 BC, but the desolation described in 13:20-22 does not fit this later conquest because the city of Babylon was not destroyed and rendered unlivable by the Medes and Persians. More likely, Isaiah was prophesying the sack of Babylon by the Assyrian king, Sennacherib, in 689 BC. He ransacked the great city whose pride was an offense to God.

Interestingly, these chapters also have an element of eschatological prophecy, since the book of Revelation describes a rebuilt and revived Babylon that will be finally judged by God in the tribulation (see Rev 17-18). The Babylonian kingdom that conquered Judah under Nebuchadnezzar was a later kingdom, sometimes referred to as Neo-Babylon; it helped the Medes defeat and destroy the Assyrian Empire in 612 BC.

Whichever Babylonian kingdom is in view here, Babylon stood throughout Scripture for everything that was arrogant, evil, and opposed to God. Thus, the **Lord of Armies**, the name of God that signifies his power (13:4), would bring judgment upon this **jewel of** a kingdom (13:19). In the end, Babylon would be **like Sodom and Gomorrah when God overthrew them** (13:19).

14:1-23 At this defeat, Jacob and Israel would taunt the proud king of Babylon with **contempt** (14:1, 3-4). God would bring their arrogant earthly tormentor down to the dust, even to the grave (14:11). But notice the change of tone in 14:12-14. The ruler is described in language that could not be attributed to any mere human ruler. It's best, then, to see Isaiah speaking here of the original fall of Satan and applying it to the king of Babylon.

The devil was originally the **shining morning star**, a beautiful angelic being who fell **from the heavens** (14:12). He rebelled against God and thus became Satan, God's ultimate adversary. Satan's **I will** statements in these verses describe his rebellion when he tried to usurp God's throne (14:13-14). But he was judged, cast from heaven, and destined for eternal punishment (see Matt 25:41)—a sentence that will be carried out as the last stages of God's prophetic plan are unveiled (see Rev 20:10). Satan's future defeat at the end of the millennium was typified in history by the crushing of Babylon, a symbol of rebellion against God ever since the founding of the city of Babylon (or Babel; see Gen 11:1-9).

Appropriately, **the Lord of Armies** made several **I will** declarations of his own to describe Babylon's defeat and decimation. At the hands of God, the city would lose its **reputation** and **offspring** and become a **swampland** (14:22-23). Because the Lord carries a **broom** called **destruction**, wicked Babylon would be swept away (14:23).

14:24-27 These verses are a summary of God's judgment upon Assyria and Sennacherib, its king. When Assyria attacked Jerusalem, God delivered the city by decimating the Assyrian army and even taking out Sennacherib himself (see Isa 37:36-38). **The Lord of Armies himself . . . planned it** (14:27). This brings to mind the fact that it's okay to make plans, as long as you allow God room to overrule you with his own. Anyone—from the mightiest king to the lowliest citizen—who thinks his plans will stand is in for a rude awakening when his agenda bumps up against God's. His agenda always wins.

14:28-32 The Philistines were one of Israel's oldest and fiercest enemies. They felt secure in their land along the coast, but their confidence would be shattered when the Assyrians came like **a cloud of dust . . . from the north** to ransack **Philistia**, at the end of the eighth century BC (14:31). Those in **Zion** would be safe from this conflict because the Lord was their **refuge** (14:32).

15:1-9 The kingdom of **Moab** was also ripe for God's judgment (15:1). The Moabites should have been Israel's friends and allies, since they were kin. The Moabites descended from Moab, the son of Lot, who was the nephew of Abraham (see Gen 11:27; 19:36-37). But Moab was one of Israel's cruelest enemies, and they rejected the true God for idol worship. The various Moabite cities Isaiah catalogued in 15:1-4 would all be destroyed by an Assyrian invasion. And unlike Judah, Moab would receive no deliverance. Its army could do nothing to stop the destruction (15:4). The refugees who fled the onslaught would go as far as the southern end of the Dead Sea, but **their wailing** would echo far and wide (15:8).

16:1-14 In desperation, the Moabite refugees would **send lambs to the ruler of the land . . . to the mountain of Daughter Zion** (16:1), a reference to Jerusalem, in hopes that they could find asylum there (16:1). This plea was answered by a prophecy that **the aggressor**, Sennacherib, would be destroyed himself (16:4). Nevertheless, Moab would not be spared judgment. Moab's **haughtiness, pride, arrogance**, and **empty boasting** would be its undoing (16:6). The only cure was Moab's complete destruction for its prideful rejection of the Lord and reliance on its own power. The final blow would come soon, within **three years** (16:14). The Assyrians did come, and Moab was swept into the dustbin of history.

In the midst of this prophecy, there is another messianic reference. It looks beyond the immediate situation to the day when **a throne will be established in love, and one will sit on it faithfully in the tent of David,**

judging and pursuing what is right (16:5). This is an announcement of the coming kingdom of Jesus Christ.

17:1-3 Damascus was a major city in Aram (modern-day Syria; 17:1). The city appeared in Isaiah 7, when the kings of Aram and Israel made an ill-fated alliance to ward off the threat posed by the Assyrians. God prophesied their ruin then, and this chapter is a restatement of that disaster which left Damascus **a ruined heap** (17:1). The Assyrians defeated Aram in 732 BC and destroyed Israel in 722 BC, carrying its people into exile and repopulating the land with foreigners.

17:4-14 Isaiah drew a graphic picture of Israel's demise, likening it to a **healthy** person whose **body** slowly wastes away (17:4). Once the assault started, the Israelites would realize that their idols were powerless to save them, and they would turn to their **Maker . . . the Holy One of Israel** (17:7). Although individual Israelites may have been restored to a right relationship with God, it was too late to prevent the northern kingdom's defeat. There would be **desolation**, because the people had **forgotten the God of [their] salvation** (17:9-10). But this does not mean that the pagan nations that spurn God will flourish. No matter how powerful, the nations are nothing before God. **He rebukes them, and they flee** (17:13).

18:1-7 The biblical land of Cush encompassed parts of modern Sudan, Egypt, and Ethiopia, although it is usually identified with the latter. Rather than being "a pronouncement" (see 15:1; 17:1; 19:1), the Lord's message to **Cush** was a **woe** (18:1). It appears they had sent **envoys** to Judah, perhaps seeking to form an alliance against Assyria (18:2). But Isaiah said to send word back to Cush that God would judge Assyria in his own time (18:2-5). When his work with them was done, God would **cut off** the Assyrian Empire and leave it desolate (18:5). Interestingly, the chapter ends with a prophecy that the people of Cush would one day come to Jerusalem to worship the Lord (18:7), a possible reference to Christ's millennial kingdom when people of all the nations will worship him.

19:1-4 From early in the biblical storyline, the nation of **Egypt** figures prominently in the story of God's people. By the end of Genesis, Egypt was a source of protection from famine for the descendants of Jacob. By the beginning of Exodus, Egypt was their enemy and persecutor. At one time it was the greatest power in the ancient world. But by Isaiah's day, Egypt too was threatened by Assyria. Neither Egypt's power nor its wisdom would be able to deliver the nation, because God had decreed its judgment.

This would start internally, with God provoking **Egyptians against Egyptians** (19:2). The turmoil would cause distress and frustration; nevertheless, instead of turning to the Lord, the Egyptians would futilely seek their **idols, ghosts, and spiritists** for help (19:3). It would be of no use, though, because God would hand the Egyptians over to **a strong king** (19:4). Indeed, King Esarhaddon of Assyria conquered Egypt in 671 BC.

19:5-15 The conquest under God's judgment would wreak havoc on a land whose livelihood depended on the Nile River. The Lord would **dry up** Egypt's **water** source (19:5). **Fishermen** and **flax** workers would be unable to ply their trades, since both depended on the Nile being full (19:8-9). In fact, **all [Egypt's] wage earners will be demoralized** (19:10). Egypt's pride in its wise counselors would be crushed. Even the **wisest** of Pharaoh's **advisers** would **give stupid advice** (19:11). God would give Egypt **a spirit of confusion** to make their **leaders** like fools (19:13-14). The smartest and brightest are no match for the one who is the source of all wisdom.

19:16-25 Suddenly the pronouncement for Egypt took a different turn, one that Judah may not have believed possible. Once God's work of judgment against Egypt was complete, this pagan nation would **swear loyalty to the Lord of Armies** (19:18). **The Lord will strike Egypt**, but then heal them. **They will turn to the Lord and he will be receptive to their prayers and heal them** (19:22). God is always ready to show grace and mercy to those who will repent.

This amazing turnaround will come **on that day** (19:19), which in this case is a reference to the future kingdom of Christ. Not only will Egyptians become worshipers of the true God, but so also will Assyrians. This will occur in what Isaiah called **a triple alliance**. Egypt, Assyria, and Israel will all faithfully worship the Lord (19:23-25). God's plan is to win worshipers from all nations, not only from Israel.

20:1-6 Chapter 20 reverts to further explanation about Egypt's judgment, this time including Cush also. The people of Judah wanted to form alliances with the surrounding nations against the power of Assyria, but God continually warned them against that plan. Judah needed to understand that neither foreign power could protect them from the Assyrians. Their only protection was found in the Lord. They, however, didn't heed the warning, and both Cush and Egypt fell to the invaders. And as a result, Judah would learn a hard lesson: **Those who made Cush their hope and Egypt their boast will be dismayed and ashamed** (20:5). If these powers failed to stop the Assyrians, what chance did Judah have without relying on God? Rely on God, and you have nothing to fear—regardless of the outcome. Rely on man, and you have everything to lose—regardless of the promise.

21:1-10 Some Bible interpreters believe this passage refers to Babylon's defeat by the Assyrian king, Sennacherib, in 689 BC (see 13:1-22). Others believe it refers to the Persian Empire's conquest of Babylon in 539 BC (see Dan 5). Regardless, Isaiah's **troubling vision** of the destruction was so horrific that it caused the prophet to be **filled with anguish** and **with sheer terror** (21:2-4). God told Isaiah to **post a lookout** watching for news from the battle (21:6), but not until several verses later do we learn who the victim of this conquest is: **Babylon has fallen** (21:9). This judgment upon the nation would be a judgment upon her false **gods**—a pathetic defense against **the Lord of Armies** (21:9-10).

21:11-12 It is not clear what **Dumah** refers to. There was a Dumah in Arabia that was conquered by Assyria in the seventh century BC, but **Seir** was located in Edom (21:11).

Whichever location the prophet intended, the Lord's judgment upon them would come like nightfall.

21:13-17 The desert tribes in **Arabia** would also suffer at the hands of the Assyrians. **Tema** was an oasis whose water would be needed for the **thirsty . . . refugees** from the battle when Assyria attacked (21:13-14). This would happen **within one year** because the Lord had **spoken**, and nothing could change his decree (21:16-17).

22:1-14 In the midst of this series of pronouncements of judgment on the nations (13:1–23:18), there is **a pronouncement** against Jerusalem. Unfortunately, Judah was as unfaithful as any of her pagan neighbors. The siege of the great city by Assyria was a terrifying time for Jerusalem's inhabitants. They could go **up to the rooftops** of their houses and see the Assyrian army massed against the city and building siege ramps against its wall (22:1). But instead of turning to the Lord in repentance and seeking his protection, the people actually resorted to partying! (22:2, 13). There was a fatalistic tone to the festivities, though, because the people said, **Let us eat and drink, for tomorrow we die!** (22:13). The apostle Paul quotes this verse as an appropriate response to life if there is no resurrection—no hope in God beyond the grave (see 1 Cor 15:32).

Yet there would also be **confusion** and **crying** in **the Valley of Vision**, an expression for Jerusalem (22:5). The city was besieged and the people were helpless because God had **removed the defenses of Judah** (22:8). In spite of this, they scrambled to defend themselves anyway. They tried to **fortify** the **breaches in the walls** (22:9-10). They stored **water** to prepare for the siege. But their fatal mistake was not turning to the Lord, **the one who made** the water (22:11). All of Judah's planning and partying wouldn't help them. God **revealed** to Isaiah, **This iniquity will not be wiped out for you people as long as you live** (22:14).

22:15-19 The remainder of the chapter addressed two men in Judah, one who would experience God's curse and one who would experience God's blessing. The first was **Shebna**, the **steward . . . of the palace** (22:15). The reason for God's judgment on him is not stated, but he was a high official in Judah. He certainly must have been wicked to warrant mention among all the divine judgments in these chapters! Shebna's pride is evident in his grand plan to have a burial spot in Jerusalem that was so prominent that his name would be remembered for generations to come (22:16). God hates pride, so his plans for Shebna were the exact opposite of the steward's own. He would be **ousted from [his] position**, dragged off to **a wide land**, and **die** there (22:18-19).

22:20-25 In contrast to Shebna, **Eliakim** was a faithful **servant** of the Lord, who would provide wise counsel and a steadying hand in Jerusalem (22:20). God would grant him Shebna's **authority**, and he would serve Jerusalem in godliness (22:21). While Shebna sought glory and was denied, Eliakim sought nothing but would find **honor** from the Lord (22:23). Whereas Shebna would be plucked out of the land, Eliakim would be a firm leader in the land (22:22-24). Nevertheless, he would be unable to prevent Judah's inevitable collapse (22:25). Nations need godly leaders, yet godly leaders alone can't protect citizens who refuse to repent of their wickedness.

23:1-9 **Tyre**, a commercial giant whose people depended on sea trade for their wealth, was one of the most famous cities of the ancient world (21:1). In the Bible, Tyre is often linked with the city of **Sidon** because they were two major seaports of Phoenicia (21:4). Tyre and Sidon benefited greatly from their international trading, and the nations they traded with also prospered. The two cities' wealth had been made so quickly from trading that the sea could speak as if it were a person, noting, **I have not been in labor or given birth. I have not raised young men or brought up young women** (21:4). In other words, Tyre and Sidon had the benefits of "children" without having to go through the discomfort of delivery and the frustrations of being raised.

But Tyre was also menaced by Assyria, and God called on trading partners like **Tarshish** to **wail** over Tyre's demise—which meant great economic losses for them, too (23:1). Tyre's **merchants** were **the honored ones of the earth** (22:8), but that meant nothing because the Lord had **planned** to **disgrace all the honored ones** (22:9). This is a sobering reminder that to be honored in the eyes of people means nothing if you earn God's displeasure. By contrast, those who are "persecuted because of righteousness" will be honored by God, because "the kingdom of heaven is theirs" (Matt 5:10).

23:10-18 Tyre was not actually destroyed until several hundred years later, but in God's sight the judgment was as good as done. They would be like the **Chaldeans** (the Babylonians) who also fell under the Assyrian onslaught (23:13). The exact time frame in which Tyre would be **forgotten for seventy years** is unclear (23:15). The length suggests the seventy years of the Babylonian captivity of Judah, but that was much later. Thus, some suggest it refers to a period when Assyria ruled Tyre and limited its trade. In any case, the important message from God's perspective was that it did not lead to repentance. Tyre would **go back into business**, returning to its old ways like a prostitute returning to her sin (23:17). There would, however, be a difference this time: **Her profits and wages** would be **dedicated to the Lord**. And although Tyre didn't intend it, her wealth would **go to those who live in the Lord's presence, to provide them with ample food and sacred clothing** (23:18). God knows how to take the wealth of the wicked and use it for kingdom purposes. Tyre's final demise came in 332 BC when Alexander the Great destroyed the city.

➢ E. Isaiah's Prophecy of the End Times (24:1–27:13) ❧

In this section, the prophet turned from pronouncing judgment on various nations to address God's judgment during the great tribulation and the glorious kingdom of the Messiah that will follow. Thus, chapters 24–27 are often referred to as "Isaiah's apocalypse." As often happens in the Bible, judgment precedes blessing. In the last days,

God must remove the wicked from the earth before he pours out the universal blessings of Christ's millennial kingdom.

24:1-6 The descriptions of the coming judgment make it clear that Isaiah is referring to something far larger than the judgments of his day. In view here is universal judgment, set in motion directly by God. In that day, **the earth will be stripped completely bare and will be totally plundered**, because of humanity's rebellion against God (24:3). **They have transgressed teachings, overstepped decrees, and broken the permanent covenant**. Such blatant disregard for God's law causes the earth to be **polluted by its inhabitants** (24:5). The "permanent covenant" probably refers to God's universal laws of righteousness that all people are obliged to obey. Because of mankind's sin and rebellion, **only a few** will **survive** the awful judgments of the tribulation (24:6).

24:7-16 Isaiah then pictured a sinful humanity groaning under the weight of God's wrath (24:7-13). All of their joy, festivities, and drinking? Gone. **Only desolation** will be left behind (24:12). But in the midst of the gloom and destruction, something else was heard: **They raise their voices . . . they proclaim in the west the majesty of the Lord** (24:14). These were evidently the righteous praising God for his glory and his righteous judgment on sin. They sing because they are spared the wrath of God, which is the best reason of all to sing! And their song has one subject: **the Splendor of the Righteous One** (24:16). This great chorus of voices will be heard in Christ's millennial kingdom when he returns to judge and rule the earth for a thousand years. Yet even though Isaiah was one of the righteous who could sing of God's greatness, he was distressed when he saw the coming wrath against mankind. This tells us he was a sensitive soul who reflected the heart of his Lord who asked, "Do I take any pleasure in the death of the wicked? . . . Instead, don't I take pleasure when he turns from his ways and lives?" (Ezek 18:23). That truth about the Lord, in fact, is why Jesus said there is "more joy in heaven over one sinner who repents than over ninety-nine righteous people who don't need repentance" (Luke 15:7).

24:17-23 When the Son of God comes in his fiery wrath to execute his justice, it will be futile to run. **Whoever flees ... will fall into a pit, and whoever escapes from the pit will be caught in a trap** (24:18). They will call to the mountains, "Fall on us and hide us ... from the wrath of the Lamb!" (Rev 6:16). But the wicked won't escape. This group will include both God's earthly enemies and the heavenly ones too: **The Lord will punish the army of the heights in the heights and the kings of the ground on the ground** (24:21). The angelic forces that rebelled with Satan, then, will meet their doom. Moreover, the world's mighty leaders who defy God will be treated as **prisoners** in the great tribulation (24:22). When Jesus comes to take his rightful throne, there will be no doubt about who is earth's rightful King.

25:1-2 Isaiah recorded the reaction of the righteous to the announcement of Christ's coming millennial kingdom. The **Lord** is praised because his program of judgment on the wicked and salvation for the righteous are all part of **plans formed long ago**, and are executed **with perfect faithfulness** (25:1). Politicians make promises, especially when they're running for office. Frequently, though, their promises are never realized. But the faithful God has never made a promise he will not keep. He will turn the **fortified city**, here representing all the nations and kingdoms of earth, **into ruins** (25:2).

25:3-5 But after his judgment, all of the world will worship God. He will bring about a complete reversal of status for **the poor** and **the needy**. While God levels the strongholds of the mighty nations that do not honor him, he himself will become a **stronghold** for the destitute and the oppressed (25:4). He will rescue them, as sure as **the shade of a cloud cools the heat of the day** (25:5).

25:6-9 Still speaking of the future kingdom, Isaiah says, **On this mountain, the Lord of Armies will prepare for all the peoples a feast** (25:6). This promise emphasizes both God's care for his people and the worldwide reach of Christ's rule as the Lord of all the earth. This is not the marriage supper of the Lamb (Rev 19), which occurs before the kingdom is established, but a millennial banquet celebrating Christ's victory over all the forces of earth. And it gets even better. God will **destroy death forever** and **wipe away the tears from every face** (25:8). Those are promises you can bank on. And what a joy and privilege it will be to stand among those who declare, **Look, this is our God; we have waited for him, and he has saved us. ... Let us rejoice and be glad** (25:9)! Those who trust him now will see the vindication of their hope and the fulfillment of God's Word.

25:10-12 God will also deal with his enemies in the kingdom age. That Christ will rule **on this mountain** refers to Jerusalem where his throne will be established. **Moab** is used here probably as a representative of all of God's enemies—none of whom will be able to stand before him. The image of rebellious nations swimming **in a dung pile** could not be more graphic (25:10). Those who, like Moab, proudly shake their fist at God will experience complete humiliation.

26:1-4 Here Isaiah continues the praise of God's people for delivering them from the hands of their enemies. In fact, this chapter is actually a **song** that will be sung **on that day** when Christ establishes his kingdom. Although God will tear down the strongholds of wicked nations, in the kingdom the redeemed will **have a strong city** (26:1). This is Jerusalem, the capital city of the King. Believers can claim this promise: **You will keep the mind that is dependent on you in perfect peace** (26:3). This peace is not only valid in the kingdom age, but also for all those who tune their minds to God's spiritual realities. So while this was a message of hope and consolation to the people of Judah to whom Isaiah was writing, it also applies to us. The ambitions of selfish sinners will crumble, but **the Lord himself is an everlasting rock!** (26:4).

26:5-9 The reversal of earthly fortunes in Christ's kingdom continues with the picture of the proud and mighty **who live in lofty places** (26:5). They're convinced that they're out of reach, only to find themselves trampled by **the feet of the humble** and **the poor** (26:6). By contrast, although God's people may have trials, he will smooth out the path of the righteous (26:7). Those who desire and long for his agenda will see good results (26:8-9).

26:10-11 Tragically, the wicked do **not learn righteousness** even if God should show them his **favor** (26:10). God's kindness is intended to lead us to repentance (see Rom 2:4), but many refuse to follow where kindness leads.

These verses were probably written as a warning to Isaiah's contemporaries in Judah, many of whom fit this description. One of the recurring messages of the prophetic books is that Israel and Judah continued to plow ahead in every form of sin, even though God continually sent messengers to warn them. It takes a special kind of blindness not to recognize the work of God when it is all around us, but Judah did not turn back to the Lord because they stubbornly refused to give up their evil ways. They would not be saved from judgment because they didn't *want* to be saved. And so they would fall to God's consuming **fire** (26:11; see Heb 12:29).

26:12-15 The theme of praise returns as the redeemed in the kingdom exalt God for the **peace** they enjoy and the deliverance from earthly **lords** who oppressively ruled over them (26:12-13). Such oppression will never happen again because these evil rulers are **dead** (26:14). They will not even be remembered, but the righteous will flourish and grow under the kingdom rule of Christ (26:14-15).

26:16-21 The judgment of evil that precedes the kingdom will be a cause of great distress to the unrighteous in Judah. Isaiah likened them to **a pregnant woman about to give birth** (26:17). Instead of bringing forth something joyous, though, Judah **gave birth to wind** (26:18). This note is followed by a clear promise of resurrection for the righteous: **Your dead will live; their bodies will rise** (26:19). God's people need only to go into their **rooms** and wait **for a little while** as God completes his **wrath** on the earth (26:20). This should have been a strong encouragement to Isaiah's readers to stay true to the Lord. No rebellion will go unpunished; God will set the records straight.

27:1-6 On that day—that is, at Christ's return to defeat his foes and establish his kingdom—he will strike down Israel's enemies, represented here by **Leviathan, the fleeing serpent** (27:1). There was a myth in the ancient Near East about this creature. Isaiah was not endorsing it as fact; he simply borrowed the imagery to depict God's enemies. God's people, by contrast, purged of their sins, will finally become the fruitful **vineyard** that God always desired them to be (27:2-6).

This description of Israel as the Lord's vineyard in the kingdom contrasts sharply with the depiction of Israel as a vineyard in 5:1-7. The return of the vineyard imagery highlights the dramatic turn that will come about for God's people. In Isaiah's day, Israel was an unfruitful kingdom, producing worthless grapes. But in the kingdom to come, redeemed Israel will thrive under God's tending and protection. The Lord will care for the vineyard and bring forth produce. His anger against his people will be satisfied, and he will defend them against any enemy (27:4). God's judgment will be supplanted by his deliverance as the new vineyard prospers under his care. The vineyard of Israel will flourish in those days. And as often promised in the Old Testament, Israel will bless the whole world: **Israel will blossom and bloom and fill the whole world with fruit** (27:6). The assurances given in 27:2-6 underscore the coming restoration of Israel and set Israel's situation into relief with that of the nations.

27:7-13 But before the glories of the kingdom, Judah would be judged. Her sins had to be dealt with. Although God would not judge Judah in the way he had judged other nations (27:7), her punishment would still be severe, as God purged her **by banishing and driving her away** (27:8). One sign of Judah's repentance would be the complete **removal** and destruction of all evidence of her idolatry (27:9). But it would take severe chastisement for that to happen. **The fortified city** (Jerusalem) **will be desolate**, a place where animals graze (27:10). And even though God loved his people with a covenant love, he had to turn his back on them. **Their Maker will not have compassion**

on them or **be gracious to them** (27:11). What a sad reality for the people whom God had chosen "out of all the peoples" of the earth "to be his own possession" (Deut 7:6)! However, the chapter closes with a prophecy of Israel's future ingathering when King Jesus reigns in Jerusalem and Israel returns to the land God covenanted to give them (27:12-13).

↦ F. Woes and Blessings on Israel and Judah (28:1–35:10) ↤

This section begins with a series of woes on the disobedient and arrogant people of both Israel and Judah—particularly on their leaders but also on Assyria, which was ready to crush the northern kingdom and was menacing the southern one. We noted in Isaiah 5 that the word "woe" can mean either sorrow for what has happened to the unfortunate, or can be used as a strong word of warning for a coming disaster. The following woes are clearly warnings of coming evil days for God's sinful people; nevertheless, they are sprinkled with a message of hope for the future.

28:1-4 Although Isaiah's primary message was to Judah, God also used him to speak to the northern kingdom in the last years before its decimation by the Assyrians. The first **woe** is pronounced against the leaders of Israel, who lived in a disgraceful condition. God pronounced judgment on **the majestic crown of Ephraim's drunkards** and **the fading flower of its beautiful splendor**. The former tells us that although the fall of Israel was imminent, Israel's leaders were **overcome with wine** (28:1). Importantly, Ephraim was a common name for the northern kingdom, since it was the most prominent of its ten tribes. The fury with which Assyria would slam into the nation was described in unmistakable terms: it would come **like a devastating hail storm, like a storm with strong flooding water** (28:2). Such a warning made it inextricably clear that God was the one bringing this judgment, using the Assyrians as "the rod of" his punishment (see 10:5-6).

28:5-8 There was a word of comfort for the faithful, though. As the nation faded like a flower, God would be **a crown of beauty and a diadem of splendor** to those who kept faith with him (28:5). But the **priest and prophet**, Israel's pitiful spiritual leaders, were nothing more than drunks. They staggered in a dazed stupor so heavy they couldn't possibly serve as God's messengers and worship leaders for the people (28:7). They had been chosen to minister in God's holy temple and magnify his glory; instead, **all their tables [were] covered with vomit; there [was] no place without a stench** (28:8). Those who were to represent the Holy One had sunken to an almost unspeakable low.

28:9-13 And yet, in their arrogance these false leaders scorned Isaiah and made fun of his message! They mocked the prophet by speaking gibberish, being offended that he would talk to them as though they were little children who could take only **a little here, a little there** (28:9-10). But God turned the mocking of Israel's prophets and priests back on them (28:11-13). Isaiah said, in effect, "All right, if you don't want to listen to God's spokesman delivering his message of warning and judgment, then you will hear it from a people whose language you do not know." In fact, they would hear it from the Assyrians.

28:14-15 Although the warnings in this chapter were directed against the northern kingdom, the Lord also had a word for Judah, particularly those who ruled **in Jerusalem** (28:14). They had made a very strange boast: **We have made a covenant with Death, and we have an agreement with Sheol; when the overwhelming catastrophe passes through, it will not touch us, because we have made falsehood our refuge and have hidden behind treachery** (28:15). Evidently, and foolishly, these corrupt leaders were affirming their confidence in their alliance with Egypt to save them from the Assyrian invasion. The statement may also reflect their belief in false gods, since "Death" was often personified as a god in the pagan religions practiced around them.

28:16 Whatever its meaning, the boast the leaders made was an insult to God. Yet he would have the last word because he had set **a precious cornerstone** in **Zion**, the only **sure foundation** for deliverance. Indeed, the word of the Lord is the only sure foundation, and **the one who believes will be unshakable.** The apostle Paul saw this fulfilled in the Lord Jesus Christ, the "stone in Zion." Though many would "stumble over" him, "the one who believes on him will not be put to shame" (Rom 9:33).

28:17-22 The Lord announced to Judah, **Your covenant with Death will be dissolved, and your agreement with Sheol will not last** (28:18; see commentary on 28:14-15). In other words, the nation had zero hope of escaping judgment. Instead of avoiding the flood coming their way, the people would be swept away by it. God would sweep down on his rebellious people **to do his work, his unexpected work, and to perform his task, his unfamiliar task** of severe judgment (28:21).

28:23-29 Both Israel and Judah needed to listen to what God was telling them—including this word of hope. Just as a farmer knows how to plant and reap his various crops to bring about the best harvest, so God knows how to bring about restoration for his people. They needed his **wondrous advice** and **great wisdom** (28:29).

29:1-4 Even though the Assyrian army was occupied with the northern kingdom, Judah was also in the enemy's crosshairs. Sennacherib's army marched to **Ariel**, another name for Jerusalem, **the city where David camped** (29:1). The Assyrians besieged it, but it was not yet Judah's time for judgment. The Assyrian enemy would be destroyed by God's supernatural intervention (see ch. 37). However, Judah's pride would still **be brought low** (29:2-4).

29:5-8 The nation's deliverance is described in these verses, yet they also seem to have the end days in view. Isaiah speaks of a massive attack **against Ariel** (that is, Jerusalem) by **many nations** whom the Lord would defeat with a spectacular display of his power (29:5-7). This prophecy seems to go beyond

Assyria's assault on Jerusalem in Isaiah's day. So once again, God's prophetic word blends nearer events with the distant future.

29:9-12 In spite of God's miraculous rescue, the people of Judah soon fell back into their spiritually insensitive condition. These verses illustrate a principle of spiritual receptivity and blindness that we see throughout Scripture (29:9-11). When people refuse to listen to God and reject his Word by deliberately closing their ears and eyes to it, God confirms their rebellious decision by sending them blindness and deafness. That's what happened to Pharaoh: He hardened his heart (see Exod 7:22; 8:15, 32); then God hardened it for him (Exod 9:12). The people of Judah blinded themselves, yet God also covered the eyes of the **prophets** and **seers** (29:10). This brings to mind the fact that Jesus said on more than one occasion that his teaching was meant to veil spiritual truth from those who had already made up their minds to reject it. The result for Judah was that God's message was **like the words of a sealed document** that no one could understand (29:11).

29:13 Nevertheless, Judah continued to go through the motions of worshiping God. So God spoke of the futility of Judah's worship: **These people approach me with their speeches to honor me with lip-service—yet their hearts are far from me.** This is a reminder that prayer and praise have to come from within, from a heart in tune with God, to be valid. It's not enough merely to let words fall from our lips. Years later, these same words of condemnation would be fulfilled by the Jewish religious leaders of Jesus's day (see Matt 15:7-9).

29:14-16 Judah's people not only thought they could get away with insincere worship, but they even fooled themselves into believing that they could plot their evil **in the dark** without God's knowledge: **Who sees us? Who knows?** (29:15). But if you try to hide from God, you're like an ostrich sticking his head in the sand. You're only fooling yourself.

29:17-21 In the future, the spiritual blindness of God's people will be reversed forever. These verses point forward to the kingdom age, which from God's point of view will come in just a little while (29:17). On that day, when Jesus Christ reigns in righteous glory, the deaf will hear and the eyes of the blind will see (29:18). God's kingdom will also be characterized by complete justice for the humble and the poor, who will no longer be oppressed (29:19). The joys of the kingdom will teach God's people about his faithfulness, and we will worship him with pure hearts.

Isaiah's reference to the justice that will prevail in the millennial kingdom is not the first time we have encountered this aspect of God's righteous administration. Justice will be perfect when God's kingdom fully comes to earth, but we as believers are not to ignore the importance of justice today as we seek to live out God's kingdom agenda now. Biblical justice is not a human-made, socially imposed, top-down system ultimately leading to the negation of freedom. Instead, it promotes freedom by emphasizing accountability, equality, and responsibility in providing a spiritual underpinning in the social realms. Biblical justice is the equitable and impartial application of God's moral law in society.

Each of the four jurisdictions in God's kingdom—individual, family, church, and state—is called to promote justice and responsibility under God in its own distinct way. His Word is the standard by which the aspects of his law, reflected in truth and righteousness, govern what we do. God's justice is therefore predictable because his standard does not change. In the kingdom to come, this attribute of God will be on full display. But we can reflect his justice today, too.

30:1-5 Isaiah's next woe was pronounced on Judah's foolish and futile attempt to form an alliance with Egypt to ward off the threat from Assyria (30:1-2). A strong faction, the "pro-Egypt" party, was lobbying hard for Judah to reach out to Egypt for help. But seeking aid from that place made no sense on any level. Egypt was a fading power by this time, so politically and militarily the Egyptians had nothing to offer Judah. In fact, Egypt itself was headed for defeat at the hands of the Assyrians! But worst of all was that God had expressly forbidden his people to make alliances with Egypt, or even to go back to

that place of their slavery (see Deut 17:16). Relying on Egypt sent a clear signal that Judah was depending on Egypt's gods instead of the true God. The result of such a treaty would be only shame and humiliation (30:3). Egypt would be no help (30:5).

30:6-11 Nevertheless, the pro-Egypt party prevailed, so Judah sent caravans loaded with riches to Egypt to buy protection (30:6). The travelers even had to go through a dangerous part of the desert to avoid the Assyrians and reach Egypt, but they plowed on ahead. They even told their seers (prophets), Do not prophesy the truth to us (30:10). So they were like people who say, "I've made up my mind; don't confuse me with the facts." What comes through again and again in the book of Isaiah is the incredible stubborn rebellion of Judah. They didn't want to hear from the Holy One of Israel (30:11). They had their fingers in their ears.

30:12-17 Although the people of Judah didn't want another message from God, they got one—a powerful word of judgment. Their sin would crumble like a weak wall collapsing suddenly (30:13). And as in Humpty Dumpty's case, there would be no way to put the shattered pieces of their supposed strength back together again (30:14). While the people insisted on trusting in fast horses, a biblical image for military strength, God would deal with it by making the Assyrians' horses faster still (30:16). Their enemies would be so fearsome that one thousand of God's rebellious people would flee at the threat of one Assyrian (30:17).

30:18-33 But immediately after this prophecy of disaster, Isaiah turned again to a message of ultimate hope, a description of Israel's blessing in the millennial kingdom (30:18-26). Your Teacher will not hide any longer. Your eyes will see your Teacher (30:20) is clearly a messianic prophecy: no human could fulfill this role as perfectly as is described in verse 21 (see Ps 32:8). Even though God's people were then limited to bread and water, the rain of God's blessing (literally and figuratively) will pour down on them in the kingdom (30:20, 23). To assure his people of their future deliverance in the final days, God predicted Assyria's destruction even though its army was at the gates of Jerusalem (30:27-33). As powerful as the Assyrian force was, they would be wiped out by the mere **breath of the LORD** (30:33).

31:1-3 Isaiah again directed a **woe** against Judah's misguided attempt to seek an alliance with Egypt against Assyria. The arguments against this plan were ironclad. On the human level, it was a bad idea because Egypt was weak and had nothing to offer Judah in terms of any real military support. But far more important was the misguided motive behind the plan—a deliberate attempt to avoid obeying God and trusting in his deliverance. **They do not seek the LORD** (31:1). And how pitiful that they relied on **men, not God** (31:3)! It was only by God's grace, then, that he did not allow the Assyrians to wipe Judah off the map. The Egyptians were so weak that when Judah leaned on them for help, they would both **fall** together (31:3).

31:4-9 God could promise deliverance because he is like a ferocious **lion** that has no fear of **a band of shepherds** (31:4). He would **protect Jerusalem**—not because they deserved his protection—but because God remained faithful to his covenant (31:5). Through Isaiah, God told his people to **return to** him in repentance and faith (31:6). **On that day**, when their Messiah comes to reign over Israel in the future, they will throw away their **idols** (31:7). To this Judah might object, "But what about the Assyrians at our gates?" But they were no problem for the God of Israel. The Assyrians, in fact, would be taken out in one night (see ch. 37)—not by the armies of Judah, but by the angel of the Lord. God's people could depend on his promise: **This is the LORD's declaration** (31:9). When God declares it, it's as good as done.

32:1 God's protection of Jerusalem in Isaiah's day points forward to a time when he will be Israel's ruler through his Messiah, Jesus Christ. This description of Christ's reign in his millennial kingdom is unlike any Israel has seen. Not only will Christ rule **righteously**, but the **rulers** under him **will rule justly**. What a huge contrast to the way Judah's leaders in Isaiah's day ran things! One of God's

repeated indictments of their political and spiritual leadership was that they deprived the poor and defenseless of justice. Under the rule of heaven on earth, Christ's administrators will be a protection for those in need.

32:2-8 The people who enter the millennial kingdom will be believers who survived the great tribulation as well as the saints who return with Jesus. There will be births in the kingdom age, and these people will also see and understand spiritual truth clearly. It will be an age for which God's people have longed but have never fully experienced (32:3-8). Truth will be universally accepted, taught, and understood so that even **the reckless mind will gain knowledge, and the stammering tongue will speak clearly and fluently** (32:4). Our age has been marked by spiritual blindness. The truth is denied and twisted by those who don't know the Lord. But in the kingdom, the one who **speaks foolishness** and **plots iniquity** will no longer hold power or influence over others (32:6).

32:9-14 Isaiah then addressed the **complacent women** of Judah who thought they would continue in luxury and self-indulgence without interruption (32:9; see 3:16–4:1). **In a little more than a year**, when Sennacherib and his Assyrian army came against Jerusalem, their overconfidence would be overturned (32:9-11). Widespread destruction would occur throughout Judah (32:12-14)—even though Jerusalem would be spared. The abandonment of **the busy city** may imply that dozens of other Judean cities would be captured and ransacked by the Assyrians, too (32:14).

32:15-20 In verse 15, Isaiah turned to the distant future again with a further prophecy about the blessedness of the kingdom age. One of the blessings we enjoy today as believers under the new covenant is the indwelling presence of the Holy Spirit. The righteous in the kingdom will enjoy the same. Christ's rule will put down all attempts at rebellion and injustice so that the kingdom will be marked by perfect **justice** and **righteousness** (32:16-17). Israel will also be a place of true **peace** as her people live **in safe and**

secure dwellings (32:17-18). After centuries of conflict and persecution by her enemies, Israel will enjoy a thousand years of peace and security.

33:1-6 The final woe Isaiah pronounced was against Assyria, Israel's conqueror and Judah's then-current threat. God was using this powerful enemy to discipline his people—but Assyria's days were numbered, thus the warning, **woe, you destroyer never destroyed, you traitor never betrayed** (33:1). The Assyrian army was a destruction machine that would, in the end, be annihilated itself when God's wrath against his rebellious children had been satisfied. Assyria would experience the destruction it had wreaked on other kingdoms. In contrast, those in Judah who were living righteous lives cried out to God for **strength** and **salvation** in a **time of trouble** (33:2). The answer they received had to be tremendously comforting. God would be **a storehouse of salvation, wisdom, and knowledge** to those who were faithful in the middle of a faithless Judah (33:6).

33:7-12 Isaiah then described the Assyrian invasion, showing how futile were Judah's attempts to ally itself with other nations for protection. The invaders would cause even the **warriors** to **cry**. The **messengers of peace** could refer to those failed alliances that Judah had hoped would bring deliverance (33:7). It may also refer to the fact that even though King Sennacherib of Assyria had agreed to leave Jerusalem alone in return for the payment of tribute (see 2 Kgs 18:13-15), he attacked the city anyway. That betrayal (see 33:1) left King Hezekiah and the people of Judah without any place to turn. When the king called out to the Lord, however, Jerusalem was spared (see ch. 37).

33:13-24 Don't miss that even in this time of extreme distress when a brutal enemy was at Jerusalem's gates, the righteous would be delivered (33:13-16), and the day would soon come when the Assyrians who caused such dread would be gone forever. This deliverance, in fact, caused Isaiah to look ahead and prophesy the day when all of God's enemies will be defeated and Jerusalem will finally be

the city of peace God intended it to be (33:17-24). In the millennial kingdom, they will see **the King in his beauty** (33:17). Christ will rule from there in perfect peace and righteousness. Those who dwell in Jerusalem **will be forgiven their iniquity** (33:20, 24).

Isaiah 33:22 is an important testimony to God's kingdom agenda, both for the future reign of Jesus Christ and for our lives today. Isaiah said that **the LORD is our Judge, the LORD is our Lawgiver, the LORD is our King**. Man was created in the image of God, and God established government. Therefore, it stands to reason that human governments should pattern themselves after God's government, as they live under and reflect his rule. This should be manifested and modeled through the diversity of our own governmental institutions: legislative, executive, and judicial.

When Jesus Christ rules in his kingdom, he will exercise each of these areas of authority himself. But in a fallen world, God's kingdom agenda is accomplished through decentralized institutions. In other words, multiple governing authorities with distinct spheres of responsibility ought to rule under his divine authority. God is the only centralized Governor in the universe. He is the only one who can claim absolute power. All other authorities ought to have checks and balances.

In every area of our lives, we must recognize that the authority under which we operate goes far beyond any human authority. God operates his kingdom by his Word. The Bible is the divine blueprint by which all of life is to be lived. It is the benchmark by which all decisions should be made. If we are going to advance God's kingdom, we must recognize and submit to the divine authority of his Word.

Christians who are committed to living out God's kingdom agenda have a great future. The invisible kingdom of which we are a part will become universally visible the day when Jesus Christ returns to earth and establishes his reign, and that event gets closer daily (see Rev 20:1-6). Jesus will rule the world the way God intended it to be run when he created the first Adam. When Jesus returns as the last Adam (see 1 Cor 15:45-49), he will do what the first Adam did not do: he will serve as a just and righteous Judge,

Lawgiver, and King. Those who submit to his kingdom agenda now will have the privilege of ruling with him in the kingdom. Right now, God is selecting his prime ministers, governors, mayors, city council members, and so forth—faithful people who will rule with him in his earthly kingdom. Will you be among them?

34:1-4 Here God's judgment on Assyria expanded into a larger prophecy in which Isaiah looked ahead and described God's ultimate day of wrath and judgment on all **nations** (34:1). The universal nature of this judgment is clear: **The Lord is angry with all the nations, furious with all their armies** (34:2). The problem is that they have opposed God and his people, filling up the cup of God's righteous wrath to be poured out in fury against them during this last great rebellion against heaven. The reference to **the stars in the sky** (34:4) may be literal, in which case Isaiah could be describing the eternal state following the millennium: "The [New Jerusalem] does not need the sun or the moon to shine on it, because the glory of God illuminates it, and its lamp is the Lamb" (Rev 21:23). It's also possible that Isaiah was speaking metaphorically of worldly leaders whose powers will be stripped when Christ returns to defeat Satan and establish his kingdom.

34:5-7 **Edom** was an example of the ungodly nations God would judge and destroy. The Edomites were Israel's relatives, descendants of Jacob's brother Esau. Here they are held up as an example of nations that forget God. The New Testament similarly used Esau as an example of a godless person in order to warn believers: "Make sure that there isn't any immoral or irreverent person like Esau, who sold his birthright in exchange for a single meal" (Heb 12:16). Isaiah described Edom's judgment as **a sacrifice**, God's holy work (34:6).

34:8-17 Edom's destruction would be **a time of paying back Edom for its hostility against Zion** (34:8). Although the Edomites should have supported Israel on its journey through the desert from Egypt to Canaan, for instance, they turned against the Israelites

and made their journey harder (see Num 20:14-21). God would not let such sin go unpunished, so the land of Edom was turned into a heap of burning rubble, never to be inhabited again. Edom's fate is even described in terms of a fire whose **smoke will go up forever** (34:10). The same expression is used of the judgment on those who worship the Antichrist during the tribulation: "the smoke of their torment will go up forever and ever" (Rev 14:11). So Edom would fall, never to rise again. Wild animals would replace Edom's leaders and people as its only inhabitants (34:11-17).

35:1-2 As often happens in the prophetic books, a declaration of fierce judgment is followed by a promise of God's blessing on his people. After the judgments of the tribulation will follow the joys of Christ's millennial kingdom. The promises here are especially for Israel. **The desert will rejoice and blossom like a wildflower** (35:1). (This is a promise that is particularly meaningful to anyone who has been to the Holy Land and seen the vast expanses of dry, desert land.) The beauty of the land in the kingdom will not just be agricultural, though. All will see **the glory of the Lord, the splendor of our God** as he reigns in Jerusalem in the person of his Son (35:2).

35:3 The certainty of God's promise of Israel's future blessing also had immediate relevance to the people of Isaiah's day who held to their faith in God as they faced the terrifying menace of the Assyrian army. These believers needed to remain strong and continue to trust God, knowing that he would fulfill his promises. Isaiah's exhortation to the faithful was direct: **Strengthen the weak hands, steady the shaking knees!** There must have been palpable fear among the people as the Assyrian army commander stood outside the gates of Jerusalem. But the faithful remnant in Judah did not need to fear, for God knew who they were and how to preserve them.

The author of Hebrews similarly urges his Christian readers by using this same language: "Strengthen your tired hands and weakened knees" (Heb 12:12). God's people throughout the ages need encouragement to persevere in the midst of a sinful world that entices and threatens them. Yet, if you align yourself with the King, you need not fear. Though the gates of hell rise against you, Satan can't prevail against Christ's church (see Matt 16:18). Therefore, look to the Lord. If you focus on his will for you, it will bring you much joy. This, in turn, will strengthen you to keep fighting the good fight, because "the joy of the LORD is your strength" (Neh 8:10).

35:4 Isaiah exhorted God's faithful to say to those among them who cowered in fear, **Be strong. . . . Here is your God; vengeance is coming. God's retribution is coming; he will save you.** In their case, God's salvation was not a future kingdom promise. They saw it firsthand as he destroyed the Assyrians before their eyes.

35:5-10 Returning to the theme of kingdom blessing, Isaiah notes that both the people and the land of Israel would experience healing from the Lord (35:5-7). Those with any physical defect would be made whole, and the land itself would be changed from a desert to a well-watered paradise. In addition, God will make **a road** to Jerusalem, **called the Holy Way**, on which the righteous will travel to worship the Lord (35:8). The joys of the kingdom are unimaginable to us today. We experience the joy of the Lord as we sing to and worship him, but life also contains trials and sadness. In that day, however, we will know **unending joy** and the complete absence of **sorrow and sighing** (35:10).

✒ G. Historical Interlude: Sennacherib and Hezekiah
(36:1–39:8) ❧

36:1-3 Chapters 36 and 37 detail the fulfillment of Isaiah's prophetic word that Judah would be invaded by King Sennacherib and the Assyrians, but that Jerusalem would be delivered. The enemy invasion of Judah came in **the fourteenth year of King Hezekiah**, which was 701 BC (36:1). Hezekiah was being put to the test to see if he would trust in God's promises in the face of an Assyrian threat against his capital (36:2). The king

and his people certainly had reason to fear the Assyrians, who had already overrun and destroyed dozens of towns in Judah.

36:4-7 The royal spokesman for King Sennacherib announced his threat and offer with great authority (36:4). His speech to the leaders and people of Jerusalem was designed to intimidate them, instill fear, and cause them to lose heart at the seeming impossibility of being able to avoid defeat. Ironically, his first reason for demanding Jerusalem's surrender was what Isaiah had been telling his people. Judah's desperate hope that an alliance with Egypt would somehow bring victory was absolutely futile (36:6). But then the spokesman proceeded to insult **the LORD** by saying that Judah's hope in him was also pointless. After all, hadn't Hezekiah removed his **high places and altars**? (36:7). Of course, these were actually pagan locations for idol worship, and Hezekiah had done the right thing in destroying them. The Assyrian commander thus revealed his complete ignorance of God and the proper worship that he required.

36:8-10 The royal spokesman continued by ridiculing Judah's military abilities. **I'll give you two thousand horses if you're able to supply riders for them** (36:8) was the ancient equivalent of saying, "Beating you will be so easy that I'll fight you with one hand tied behind my back." Clearly this was not merely an announcement of terms of surrender, then. This was taunting and disdain for Jerusalem and her king. The spokesman even claimed that God had sent the Assyrians and given his hearty **approval** for them to **destroy** Judah (36:10). Actually, God *had* sent the Assyrians, wielding them as a rod of anger to chastise his people for their sin (10:5-6). But Isaiah made it clear that Assyria had not come on this quest in submission to the Lord. Assyria's intent was to conquer Israel and Judah as it had conquered other nations—for its own gain (10:7-11). Although God would use Assyria to discipline his people, he would also thrash Assyria for its pride (10:12).

36:11-20 The officials Hezekiah sent to deal with the Assyrian spokesman attempted to get him to speak to them in **Aramaic**, a trade language of the day similar to **Hebrew** because they didn't want the citizens **on the wall** to hear the threats (36:11). But the spokesman refused. He wanted everyone in Jerusalem—not just the king—to hear the Assyrian intimidations and to grasp what they were facing.

Based on the spokesman's warnings, it's clear that Hezekiah (to his great credit) had been assuring his people of God's ability to deliver them. In saying, **Don't let Hezekiah deceive you** (36:14), **Don't let Hezekiah persuade you** (36:15), **Don't listen to Hezekiah** (36:16), **Beware that Hezekiah does not mislead you** (36:18), the spokesman implied that their king was a fool who would get them all killed. And in case Jerusalem's king really was confident of withstanding the onslaught, the Assyrian spokesman wanted the population of Jerusalem to shudder at what they were in for. Even if they settled in for a prolonged siege, in time their only food and drink options would be horrifying (36:12). Thus, there was only one sane thing they could do, according to the Assyrian: **Make peace with me and surrender** (36:16). Interestingly, when life becomes hard, these are words that Satan will whisper to you. But although the "father of lies" (John 8:44) promises peace, he only delivers slavery.

The Assyrian spokesman concluded by mocking the ability of Jerusalem's God to deliver them. He pointed to the gods of the nations that Assyria had conquered: **Who among all the gods of these lands ever rescued his land from my power? So will the Lord rescue Jerusalem?** (36:20). In other words, he said, "No god has been able to stop us, and neither will yours." But Assyria would soon learn the difference between the gods of the nations and the one true, living God.

36:21-22 Hezekiah's officials didn't even dignify the commander's rant with an answer, since the king had ordered them to keep **silent** (36:21). But the reality of the mighty Assyrian army at the gates of Jerusalem caused Hezekiah's officials to tear their clothing as a sign of distress and despair (36:22).

37:1-4 When the officials reported Assyria's threat to **King Hezekiah**, the king did the right thing: **he tore his clothes, put on sackcloth, and went to the Lord's temple** (37:1). This is a reminder that, when there seems to be no hope, you too should humble yourself before the Lord and seek his face. Hezekiah's actions were an acknowledgment that Judah's only hope lay in the power and promises of God. The king also sent men to **Isaiah** for a word from the Lord (36:2). So although Israel and Judah were often filled with false, self-seeking prophets, Hezekiah sought counsel from a true prophet: one who spoke God's word without deviation. Hezekiah's message to him revealed the deep **distress** of the king and his people (37:3-4).

Hezekiah's use of the word **perhaps** in his message to Isaiah was not a sign of doubt in the Lord's ability to hear and answer (36:4). Instead, it was a sign of humility, showing that Hezekiah would wait for the divine King's answer instead of assuming he knew what it was. Hezekiah realized the Lord had heard the mocking words of the Assyrian commander, and he had faith that God would defend his people and vindicate his great name. The king also asked Isaiah to **offer a prayer for the surviving remnant** (36:4). So although Isaiah had endured repeated rejection and abuse as Judah's evil leaders refused to listen to his message, Hezekiah was a godly king who acknowledged before everyone that Isaiah was God's true spokesman.

37:5-7 The men the king sent to the prophet didn't have to wait long for a word from the Lord. While they were still in his presence, Isaiah gave them God's answer: **Don't be afraid** (37:6). That divine command is repeated multiple times throughout Scripture. It's an exhortation to those who trust in the Lord. If you place yourself under the umbrella of God's covenantal protection, you have no need to fear. Those in Jerusalem who submitted their lives to God certainly had nothing to fear from the Assyrians. He would judge King Sennacherib for his blasphemy by having him assassinated in **his own land** (37:6-7).

37:8-13 The fulfillment of this prophecy unfolded immediately. **The royal spokesman** left Jerusalem because **the king of Assyria had pulled out of Lachish** and was **fighting** at **Libnah**, a town about twenty-five miles southwest of Jerusalem (37:8). This change necessitated what the Assyrians no doubt thought was merely a temporary withdrawal from Jerusalem. The sight of enemy forces pulling back, however, must have been a tremendous relief to the people of Jerusalem; nevertheless, Sennacherib wanted them to know he had not abandoned his plan to attack and destroy their city. So **he sent messengers** to Hezekiah with a letter, repeating the previous threats (37:9-13).

37:14-20 Hezekiah responded once again in faith by taking the enemy's **letter** to the **temple** and offering a tremendous prayer that glorified the Lord as the only Creator and Sovereign of the world (37:14-19). Although Isaiah had promised deliverance, Hezekiah did not presume upon God's grace. Instead, he prayed. Furthermore, the king asked God to judge the Assyrians for the right reason: **Now, LORD our God, save us from his power so that all the kingdoms of the earth may know that you, LORD, are God** (37:20).

37:21-29 God's answer through Isaiah is a magnificent, poetic review of the situation and reminder of God's abundant power to deal with Sennacherib's blasphemous pride. **Who is it you have mocked?** (37:23). The king of Assyria had mocked Judah. But, ultimately, he had **mocked the LORD** (37:24), whom Sennacherib thought was no different from the gods of the nations. Importantly, the conquests Sennacherib bragged about were only possible because God had used him as a tool of his judgment on other nations (37:24-27). The king of Assyria thought he was the master of his own fate, but God was aware of the king's slightest daily activities (37:28). The king, in fact, couldn't make a move that God didn't know about ahead of time. So far from continuing as a world conqueror, Sennacherib would be guided **back** home like a farm animal under God's sovereignty (37:29).

37:30-38 God assured Hezekiah that life would continue in Judah despite the momentary Assyrian threat (36:30-32). Crops would be planted and harvested, even though the Assyrians had ravaged much of Judah. By **the third year**, the harvest would be plentiful (37:30). Then God said in no uncertain terms that Sennacherib wouldn't set foot in

Jerusalem, much less attack it, again (37:33-35). The Lord had earlier declared that the Assyrian king would return home and be killed there (37:7). All that remained was for the prophecy to be fulfilled. **The angel of the LORD** killed thousands of Assyrian soldiers in their own camp (37:36)! And as a result, Sennacherib returned to his **home**, where he was eventually slain by his own **sons** while **worshiping** his **god** (37:37-38). No matter how devotedly you serve them, idols can't deliver you either.

38:1-8 The actual chronological order of events recorded in chapters 36–39 is different than how they appear in Isaiah. According to 38:6, Hezekiah's illness preceded the siege of Jerusalem by the Assyrian army. The visit by representatives of Merodach-baladan, king of Babylon (39:1), must also have preceded the siege of chapters 36–37, since it is highly unlikely that these messengers would have been able to enter Jerusalem with the Assyrians surrounding the city.

When **Hezekiah became terminally ill**, God sent **Isaiah** to the king with the announcement of his impending death (38:1). The king **prayed** that God would remember his faithfulness and **wept bitterly** (38:2-3). In response, God had mercy on him and granted another **fifteen years** of life (38:5). It could be that this was a test of Hezekiah's faith, since God knew all along that he would heal him. If this was a faith test, Hezekiah passed. And he got a tremendous bonus. God said, **I will rescue you and this city from the grasp of the king of Assyria; I will defend [Jerusalem]** (38:6). Hezekiah would receive a **sign** to affirm that God would fulfill his promise: the sun's shadow would **go back by ten steps**, a miracle that Hezekiah could observe (38:7-8).

38:9-20 After he **recovered from his illness**, King Hezekiah penned **a poem**, giving God the glory for hearing and answering his prayer (38:9). The king spoke honestly of his anguish at the prospect of dying at a young age: **In the prime of my life I must go to the gates of Sheol; I am deprived of the rest of my years** (38:10). That's a gut-level emotional response that almost any human would experience in the same situation. Hezekiah wanted to live. "Sheol" was the name for the place of the dead. Though Hezekiah recorded his initial despair (38:11-15), his poem ends with praise to God for his mercy and **love** (38:16-20).

38:21-22 The final verses look back to Isaiah's prescription for Hezekiah's healing and the king's request for a **sign** that he would be healed and would worship at the **temple** again (38:22). Hezekiah was to have **a lump of pressed figs** applied to his infection—a simple act of faith (38:21).

39:1-2 Isaiah's inclusion of historical events from the reign of Hezekiah continues here. After Hezekiah's recovery, **Mero-dach-baladan**, the Babylonian **king**, sent Hezekiah **a gift** and congratulated him on that recovery (39:1). Babylon would be the next great world power in the years to come, but in Isaiah's day it was another vassal state

under Assyria. Hezekiah welcomed the envoys and, in a display of pride, the king of Judah **showed the envoys his treasure house . . . There was nothing in his palace and in all his realm that Hezekiah did not show them** (39:2). He was evidently trying to impress his Babylonian visitors.

39:3-8 God's response to this arrogance was immediate: He sent **Isaiah** to the king with a devastating prophecy of Judah's future destruction and captivity by **Babylon** (39:3-7). This tragic turn of events, however, must have seemed like a remote prospect to Hezekiah. After all, in his day more than a century before these events, Babylon was just another nation trying desperately to hold back the Assyrians. So selfishly, Hezekiah breathed a sigh of relief that this would not be fulfilled in his **lifetime** (39:8). Isaiah's prophecy is a foreboding hint of what is to follow in his book.

II. THE BLESSING OF GOD (40:1–66:24)

✸ A. God's Deliverance of His People
(40:1–48:22) ✺

There is no denying that a dramatic change of theme begins in Isaiah 40. Almost every Bible commentator acknowledges this. In fact, many critical Bible scholars believe this dramatic shift—combined with Isaiah's prophecy that Judah would suffer exile in Babylon—points to two different authors for the book of Isaiah. They suggest one author wrote chapters 1–39; then another author wrote chapters 40–66 after Judah's exile and put the two parts together. But the most significant evidence given for this argument is that Isaiah couldn't possibly have predicted a future Jewish exile in Babylon, which assumes that God could not supernaturally reveal this to him. If, however, one does not automatically rule out the possibility that God can reveal future events to his servants, then there is no compelling evidence to reject that all sixty-six chapters are the work of Isaiah having written under the inspiration of the Holy Spirit.

In the second half of Isaiah, the prophet looks ahead to the Babylonian captivity of Judah—about a century away—and her eventual return to the land. Furthermore, chapters 40–66 look far ahead to the suffering of Jesus the Messiah and his subsequent return to reign in his millennial kingdom.

40:1-2 Isaiah shares God's words of **comfort** for his **people: Speak tenderly to Jerusalem, and announce to her that her time of forced labor is over, her iniquity has been pardoned, and she has received from the LORD's hand double for all her sins.** Clearly, these words were meant to comfort the Jews after their exile in Babylon—which was still many years in the future as Isaiah wrote. Judah's "forced labor" there would end when the people had experienced the full measure of discipline for their many sins.

40:3-5 The **way of the LORD in the wilderness** that would be prepared was a reference to how God would providentially provide a smooth path for the Jews to return to Jerusalem from Babylon. Interestingly, the Gospel writers saw this as ultimately fulfilled in John the Baptist (see Matt 3:1-3; Mark 1:1:1-4; Luke 3:1-6). He would be the **voice . . . crying out** to **prepare the way of the LORD** (40:3). Through his prophetic ministry, John would pave the way for the ministry of Jesus and point others to "the Lamb of God, who takes away the sin of the world" (John 1:29).

40:6-11 God commanded Isaiah to **cry out** (40:6). The words given to him contrast transitory and frail human life with the eternal word of God. **The grass withers . . . when the breath of the LORD blows** (40:7). However, Isaiah isn't talking about mere grass but about **humanity** (40:6). The strongest man, then, is still just a man. God gives human life, and he sovereignly takes it away. But **the word of our God remains forever** (40:8). This was an assurance from God to his people that his promises are trustworthy. He will fulfill them. His people, therefore, should **not be afraid**, because the Lord has the **strength** to accomplish his will and cares for his people **like a shepherd** overseeing his flock (40:9-11).

To the people of Judah in Isaiah's day, this was a reminder to trust God's promises especially when times are hard. To the Jews in Babylon who read these words years later, this was a reminder of God's never-failing faithfulness to his covenant. And Peter uses it to remind us as Christians of the enduring power of the word of the gospel that we believed (see 1 Pet 1:23-25). Indeed, because "the word of our God remains forever," we can't lose the salvation Christ won for us.

40:12-26 The remainder of the chapter exalts the incomparable greatness of God. He dwarfs everyone and everything in his creation. God asks question after question, demonstrating his unrivaled sovereignty over the nations—which are a mere **drop in a bucket** by comparison (40:15). **Who has . . . weighed the mountains on a balance?** (40:12). Answer: No one. God alone spoke the world into existence and **calls all of them by name** (40:26). **Who has directed the Spirit of the LORD, or who gave him counsel?** (40:13). Answer: No one. The omniscient God possesses all knowledge; he doesn't need to ask advice or consult Google. **With**

whom will you compare God? ... Who is my equal? (40:18, 25). Answer: No one. He is the unique, one-and-only Lord of creation. And if humans are not worthy to be compared to him, how much less worthy is an inanimate **idol?** (40:18-20).

40:27-30 The LORD is the everlasting God, the Creator of the whole earth (40:28). This means his power is unlimited. Do you live as if this is true? The Lord **gives strength to the faint and strengthens the powerless** (40:29). Make no mistake: The words "faint" and "powerless" describe us all. So, when was the last time you asked the one who **never becomes faint or weary** (40:28) to renew your strength?

40:31 Whom does God bless in this way? Who are the recipients of God's gracious strengthening? **Those who trust in the LORD.** You see, not everyone gets strengthened by God's power. Not everyone is enabled to **soar on wings like eagles**, when God swoops down and lifts them out of bad situations. Only those who trust God's perspective on their situations **will run and not become weary** as God provides a second wind to make it through challenges. Only those who believe his Word and submit to it can expect to experience his spiritual power for daily life. You **will walk and not faint** as God changes you, whether or not he changes your situation.

41:1-4 This chapter continues unfolding the implications of who God is: **I am the LORD, the first and with the last—I am he** (41:4). God calls the nations to gather before him, but not for a committee meeting where all attendees voice their input. God calls a meeting like a lawyer prosecuting a **trial** (40:1), but the difference is that God is also the Judge. He is a committee of one. The world is firmly in his hands, and no one can stop him.

Who is this **someone from the east** whom God has **stirred up**? To whom will **the LORD** hand over **nations**? (41:2). This is a reference to Cyrus the Great, the leader of the (then-future) Persian Empire that would conquer Babylon in 539 BC, a hundred and fifty years into the future. Isaiah does not mention Cyrus by name until 44:28 and 45:1. But at this point, God is hinting that he has something up his sleeve. He begins to announce his long-range plan for Judah. This plan includes raising up a leader to smash the Babylonian Empire, releasing the Jews from captivity, and permitting them to return home (see 2 Chr 36:22-23).

41:5-7 God was also using his ability to act sovereignly in history to mock those who look to idols for deliverance. **The craftsman who constructs a god fastens it with nails so that it will not fall over** (41:7). So while God is raising up a world leader to overthrow an empire, the one who trusts an idol needs to nail it down so it won't tip over while he's praying to it!

41:8-29 Things were far different, however, for God's **servant, Jacob, whom** he had **chosen** (41:8). Israel was unique among the nations as God's chosen people. They were to worship him and be his light to the world. God set Israel apart and promised by covenant to be her protector. Kingdoms and empires that not only refused to recognize and bow before Israel's God, but also attacked and abused his people, would be tossed into the dustbin of history (41:11-16). They would be ground into dust so fine that **a wind will carry them away** (41:16). God's people, meanwhile, **will rejoice** and **boast in the Holy One of Israel** (40:16). He promised abundant care for them and will provide (41:17-20).

Once the nations were informed of God's incomparable ability to bring about his will in history, he invited them to call on their useless gods to predict the future (41:21-24). Knowing how that futile exercise would go, God repeated his plan to raise up Cyrus to liberate his captive people from Babylon: **I have stirred up one from the north** (41:25). Although in 41:2, it is said that Cyrus comes from the *east*, both are correct. Persia lay to the east, but it would attack Babylon from the north. God brings **good news** on behalf of his people; the gods of the nations perform **nonexistent** works for theirs (40:27, 29).

42:1 In the near future, King Cyrus of Persia would serve God as the human instrument of freedom to the Jews in bondage. But who is the ultimate preeminent servant of the Lord, the **chosen one**? Who is this one upon whom God will place his **Spirit** so that he may bring **justice to the nations**? Isaiah spoke of him earlier. "He will reign on the throne of David . . . with *justice*" (9:7). "The *Spirit* of the LORD will rest on him" (11:2). This is God's Messiah, his anointed one. The passage, then, is fulfilled in Jesus Christ (see Matt 12:15-21).

42:2-4 Both advents of Christ are in view in these verses. **He will not cry out or shout or make his voice heard in the streets. He will not break a bruised reed, and he will not put out a smoldering wick; he will faithfully bring justice** (42:2-3). In Christ's earthly ministry, he was humble and lowly, dealing gently with broken and sinful people. But when he comes a second time to defeat his foes and establish his kingdom, Jesus **will not grow weak or be discouraged.** He will establish **justice on earth** (32:4). For one thousand years, King Jesus will deal swiftly and surely from his throne in Jerusalem. He will be as strong at the end of his reign as at the beginning.

42:5-8 God always had **a righteous purpose** for his Messiah (42:6). He would be **a light to the nations** so that he might **open blind eyes**, extending God's offer of salvation to all people (42:6-7). Jesus purchased salvation from sin on the cross so that all who trust in him would have the righteousness God requires. This would be brought about by **the LORD**, the true God who alone is able to **announce** future **events** and bring them to pass (42:8-9). He **will not give [his] glory to another** (42:8). Only God is all glorious; he alone deserves praise. When it comes to his glory, he doesn't share.

42:10-17 The only appropriate response to this good news of salvation is for people everywhere to **sing his praise** and **give glory to the LORD** (42:10, 12), and those who will not have him for their King will have him for their enemy. There's no middle ground. **Like a warrior**, God wages war against **his enemies** (42:13). Therefore, those who foolishly say to idols, **You are our gods!** are urged to turn back (42:17). If they do, God **will turn darkness to light in front of them** (42:16).

There's only one cure for spiritual blindness: you must go to the one who can turn on the lights. "For God who said, 'Let light shine out of darkness,' has shone in our hearts to give the light of the knowledge of God's glory in the face of Jesus Christ" (2 Cor 4:6).

42:18-25 Unfortunately, there was no one so **blind** as God's **servant** Israel (42:19) because in spite of all the privileges Israel had received, in spite of all they had seen, they paid **no attention** (42:20). That is why Israel (and Judah) would suffer such strong judgment. **Who gave Jacob to the robber, and Israel to the plunderers?** It was **the Lord** because the people had **sinned against him**. Sadly, they **would not listen to his instruction** (42:24), so God **poured out his furious anger** on them (42:25). They had a choice between God's rich blessings and exile. They chose exile.

43:1-7 God repeatedly followed messages of judgment on Israel with promises of her future and ultimate redemption. Even though he had to judge his people, he reminded them, **I have called you by your name; you are mine** (43:1). God dealt differently with Israel than he did with any other people because of their special, covenantal relationship with him. The promise to give **Egypt as a ransom for** Israel, along with **Cush and Seba** (43:3), evidently refers to Cyrus as the Jews' liberator (see 44:28; 45:1). These nations were examples of God's promise: **I will give people in exchange for you and nations instead of your life** (43:4). Israel's enemies would be taken down, never to rise again. But God's people had a glorious future because of their glorious, merciful God. These verses teach a principle that is still true today: God adjusts his dealings with people based on their relationship to him.

43:8-13 The Lord returned to a theme we see repeatedly in Isaiah—God's ability to know the future because he is the one true God. His call for **witnesses** evokes the imagery of a courtroom (43:9-10). He called on the nations to testify about the ability of their gods to declare **former things** (43:9). Could their idols predict future events? Of course not. But Israel, his **servant**, was also called

to testify; his people were also to function as **witnesses** (4:10, 12). They could truly say that the Lord—**and not some foreign god**—had **alone . . . saved** (43:12). That's because **no god was formed before me, and there will be none after me** (43:10). Israel knew this, and their very existence proved God's declaration. God is the only Savior—for Israel and for the world: **Besides [him], there is no Savior** (43:11). To look anywhere else for salvation is to look in vain.

43:14-21 Isaiah repeated God's promise to bring his people out of captivity in **Babylon** and return them to the land of Israel (43:14). It is clear that this would be an act of God's covenant faithfulness and mercy, not a result of his people's merits. The promise of 43:18-19 must have reminded Isaiah's readers of the exodus from Egypt, when God saved their forefathers from bondage and led them through the wilderness. But this exodus from Babylon would be even better, since it would restore the Jews to their homeland from which they had been expelled because of their sins. **Look, I am about to do something new; even now it is coming. Do you not see it? Indeed, I will make a way in the wilderness, rivers in the desert** (43:19) implies that even though the trip from Babylon back to Israel would lead through treacherous territory, God would go ahead of the people and make a way.

43:22-28 Lest any doubt remain about God's justice in punishing his people so severely, God invited Israel to try to disprove his case: **Let's argue the case together** (43:26). God's charge was twofold. First, Israel had **become weary** of God and failed to honor him with the required **sacrifices** (43:22-23). Second, Israel had **burdened** God with their **sins**. *They* had **wearied** *him* (43:24).

In the end, God planned to rescue his people. He would **sweep away [their] transgressions** and **remember [their] sins no more**. But the reason he would do so was not because of their righteousness or their faithfulness to the covenant they'd made with him. (In this, they were complete and total failures.) He would save them **for [his] own sake** (43:25). Although Israel was unfaithful to the covenant, God would be faithful.

44:1-5 God's message of judgment on Israel is never the last word because of his eternal plan for his chosen people. Israel is God's **servant** whom he has **chosen** and **formed** (44:1-2). God promised to **pour out** his **Spirit** and **blessing** on their **offspring** (44:3). This national future blessing will be fulfilled completely during Christ's millennial kingdom, when Israel will be delivered from her unbelief. Then they will declare, I am the LORD's (44:5).

44:6-20 What follows is another of Isaiah's powerful declarations of God's uniqueness in contrast to lifeless and worthless idols. As for the Lord, **I am the first and . . . the last. There is no [other] God** (44:6). But those who insist on crafting **idols** are as **nothing** (44:9). Isaiah provides a detailed account of the efforts to make an idol (44:12-17). A man designs one, cuts down some wood, uses part of it for warmth and cooking, and carves a "god" out of the rest (44:13-17). Astoundingly, the man then **bows down to** his own carving and prays, **Save me, for you are my god** (44:17). Thus Isaiah shows how ludicrous the whole idea of idolatry is. Unfortunately, though, the idolater doesn't come **to his senses** to ask himself, **Should I bow down to a block of wood?** (44:19).

God's indictment argues against a common view that says pagan practices are simply the efforts of innocent, ignorant people trying their best to worship whoever they believe to be in control. Isaiah's account leaves us no room to conclude that those practicing idolatry are anything less than rebellious sinners who have allowed themselves to be deceived by the evil one. The apostle Paul adds the helpful insight that when people "suppress the truth" about God, they will believe anything. But they are "without excuse" (see Rom 1:18-23).

44:21-28 What a contrast to Israel's God, the only true God who **formed** and **redeemed** his people (44:21-22), are idols! They are blind, deaf, and mute, but the Lord **stretched out the heavens** by himself (44:24). Moreover, he was able to prophesy that he would use a future world leader to restore his people from captivity. While he pointed to this earlier (41:2, 25), here he identifies

him by name: **Cyrus** (44:28). This Persian king would rise and defeat the Babylonian Empire, and God announced it more than a century before it happened. Imagine the comfort and hope the book of Isaiah was to later readers exiled in Babylon, when a ruler named Cyrus came to power and challenged Babylon! This would be confirmation to them that **Jerusalem** and its **temple**— razed by the Babylonian army—would **be rebuilt** (44:28).

45:1-8 God continued the prophecy of **Cyrus** (45:1). God describes himself as the all-powerful Creator and Ruler of nations who will go before Cyrus as his point man, so to speak. He will providentially clear all obstacles before this pagan king and hand over earthly kingdoms to him. Babylon would crumble before Cyrus, who would liberate **Israel**, even though Cyrus himself did **not know** God (45:4-5). Ironically, this unredeemed, idol-worshiping king would do such a work by God's power that all would **know from the rising of the sun to its setting that there is no** god but the LORD (45:6).

45:9-13 It's foolish for anyone to argue **with his Maker** (45:9). After all, a **pot** can't question the one who formed it; children don't get to criticize Mom and Dad for giving them **birth** (45:9-10). God is the Creator of all things (45:12). He's the author of the story. We are his, and he gets to decide how the game is played. No one in Israel, then, could question why God did what he did in the way he chose to do it. If he wanted to use an unrighteous king like Cyrus to accomplish his righteous purposes, that's what he would do (45:13).

45:14-19 Because the Gentile nations surrounding Israel were also part of God's creation and under his sovereign rule, the Lord spoke of a day when these people would also bow before God and say to Israel, **God is indeed with you, and there is no other; there is no other God** (45:14). This can only describe conditions during Christ's millennial reign, when he will return in glory and power, purging Israel of her unbelief as she acknowledges her Messiah and Savior. This will be Israel's true golden age, when the nation **will be saved by the LORD with an everlasting salvation** and **will not be put to shame** (45:17). Furthermore, God will remake the **heavens** and the **earth**, another feat only he can accomplish (45:18).

45:20-25 In light of this, the wisest thing the Gentile nations could do was throw away their useless **wooden idols** that **cannot save** and turn to the Lord as **Savior** (45:20-21). For those who would listen, God had a wonderful invitation: **Turn to me and be saved, all the ends of the earth. For I am God, and there is no other** (45:22). It really is futile to resist him. There is nowhere else to turn. And one day, **every knee will bow to [him], every tongue will swear allegiance** (45:23). Paul applies these words to Jesus, demonstrating that he is truly God (see Phil 2:10-11). Thus, all people have two choices: either bow willingly in faith and confess Jesus Christ as the only Savior, or be broken by his wrath and forced to bow as an object of his judgment.

46:1-4 The contrast between the true God and the false gods of the nations continues with God's announcement of the certain destruction of Babylon. The Babylonian gods **Bel** and **Nebo**, possibly also known as the god Marduk and his son, were lifeless idols (46:1). They had to be carried on carts because they couldn't do anything for themselves (46:1-2). But, while the Babylonians had to carry their gods, the true God of Israel carried his people from **womb** to grave (46:3-4). Whom would you prefer to worship and serve?

46:5-10 God continued to mock the nations and their gods: **Who will you compare me or make me equal to?** (46:5). Again, Isaiah laid out the differences between the so-called gods and God. A pagan god is formed from **gold** or **silver** and carried by others. Then, when its worshipers **cry out** for help, **it saves no one** (45:6-7). The God of Israel, by contrast, can announce the future and bring it to pass as proof of his sovereign power and glory: **I am God, and no one is like me. I declare the end from the beginning, and from long ago what is not yet done, saying: my plan will take place, and I will do all my will** (46:9-10).

Because God will accomplish his will, his people ought to ask: What is God's will for us? Discovering and obeying the will of God—through his Word and in the power of his Holy Spirit—should be our chief concern. Whatever God plans, he accomplishes. His will can never be outwitted or thwarted. God was not caught off guard by human sin; his plan for the universe was drawn up and nailed down in eternity past. But God's sovereignty does not relieve us of our human responsibility. We are obligated to live righteously, and God will use our obedience to help accomplish his plan. There is plenty of mystery here because God's knowledge of the future includes not only everything that actually happens but also everything that could potentially happen.

46:11-13 The Lord can do whatever he wants whenever he chooses. In this case, he would call **a bird of prey from the east**, King Cyrus of Persia, **a man for my purpose from a far country** to punish Babylon and liberate the Jewish people (46:11). The **hardhearted** can't escape his **justice**, and his **salvation** won't **delay** (46:12-13).

47:1-7 Although she assumed she would be **queen forever** (47:7), **Virgin Daughter Babylon** would sit **in the dust** of defeat and humiliation, stripped bare of her pride and glory (47:1-3). Although God **was angry** with his people and would use Babylon to chastise them, Babylon's goal was domination and cruelty, showing **no mercy** (47:6). So God had already prepared Babylon's punishment: **I will take vengeance; I will spare no one** (47:3).

47:8-15 This pagan empire boasted: **I am, and there is no one else** (47:8). But this was a statement of deity reserved for God alone (see 43:10-11; 44:6; 45:21-22)! Babylon's pagan, demonically inspired worship included **spells** and **sorceries** and evil **astrologers** (47:12-13). But none of these could deliver them. And ominously, the only one who could save promised Babylon: **no one can save you** (47:15). These chapters provide significant insight into why the name "Babylon" became synonymous in Scripture with arrogant humanity rising up in fierce rebellion against God (see Rev 17).

48:1-9 Unfortunately, Babylon was not the only stubborn, rebellious, and unrighteous people with whom God had to deal. The **house of Jacob . . . Israel** was unbelieving as well, refusing to heed God's warnings prior to the captivity in Babylon. While the Jews took oaths before God, they didn't do so **in truth or righteousness** (48:1). God had told them ahead of time, through prophets like Isaiah, what would happen (48:3), demonstrating that he alone was God and worthy of worship. But Israel had ignored God's warnings about persisting in idolatry, so now he would reveal **new things** to them—things they had **never heard** (48:6-9).

Importantly, the prophecy of Israel's captivity and return was not new. As far back as Deuteronomy, God had told Israel that if they disobeyed him, he would scatter them in judgment and then regather them when their chastisement was complete (see Deut 30:1-5). The things God spoke through Isaiah were "new" in that until God revealed and named Cyrus as Israel's liberator, the people did not know how God would accomplish their release from captivity.

48:10-16 This judgment was imposed to refine Israel **in the furnace of affliction** (48:10). The Lord wanted to burn the idolatry out of them because idols have no place in his kingdom. He will share his throne with no one: **I will not give my glory to another** (48:11). Idols can't declare the end from the beginning. But God can—because he was there in the beginning, and he'll be there in the end (48:12-16). He is **the first** and **also the last** (48:12). Interestingly, the risen and glorified Lord Jesus Christ makes this same claim: "I am the Alpha and the Omega, the first and the last, the beginning and the end" (Rev 22:13).

48:17-22 If only the Israelites had listened to and obeyed God, the horrors of the Babylonian captivity would not have happened. Instead, they would have known **peace** and **righteousness** (48:18). But **there is no peace for the wicked** (48:22). If you sow wickedness, it is impossible to reap peace. In the world God has made, this simply isn't possible. The God they had rejected, however, is the God who mercifully proclaims freedom: **Leave**

Babylon, flee from the Chaldeans! (48:20). The Jews in Babylon, therefore, were to imitate their ancestors who had fled Egypt years ago, depending on God to sustain them (48:21).

B. Salvation through the Servant
(49:1–57:21)

This section of Isaiah includes some of the most profound passages in the Bible. Isaiah's picture of the suffering and triumphant Servant-Messiah clearly points to the ministry of Jesus Christ. He either has fulfilled, or will fulfill, all of these amazing prophecies.

49:1-7 The "servant" of the following chapters speaks in 49:1-5. Although he is called **Israel** in verse 3, he can't be the nation itself because the passage says that his mission is to bring **Jacob/Israel** back to the Lord (49:5). So what's going on? He is Christ who confirmed his calling as God's instrument of salvation: **The Lord called me before I was born** (49:1). This tells us that before the foundation of the world, in eternity past, the persons of the Godhead had determined the plan of salvation.

At the start of his ministry, Jesus was baptized—but not because he needed to repent. After all, he was without sin (see 2 Cor 5:21; Heb 4:15; 1 Pet 2:22). Through his baptism, he intended to identify with sinful humanity on whose behalf he would perfectly fulfill the demands of God (see Matt 3:13-15). In Isaiah, then, the Son of God is identified with the people of God, because he will succeed where Israel failed.

The servant laments, **I have labored in vain, I have spent my strength for nothing and futility** (49:4). This could be a reference to Israel's rejection of Christ at his first coming (see John 1:11). This makes sense because God promises the servant, **I will also make you a light for the nations, to be my salvation to the ends of the earth** (49:6). Jesus fulfilled this in his ministry (see Matt 4:14-16). Furthermore, God also said of the servant that he would be **despised** and **abhorred by people** (49:7). But, at his second coming, he will be triumphant, and all will **bow down** to him (49:7).

49:8-13 God promised victory and glory to his servant **in a time of favor** and **in the day of salvation**, a reference to Christ's millennial kingdom when the land of Israel will be restored to welcome back Israel's captives and exiles (49:8-9). Isaiah called on all the **earth** to praise God for fulfilling all his promises to Israel (49:13).

49:14-21 How could the people of Israel complain, "**The LORD has abandoned me; the Lord has forgotten me!**" (49:14)? This was the cry of captives, who were reassured that God's love for his people was greater than a mother's love for her **child** (49:15). Isaiah's later readers in captivity in Babylon would identify with this complaint, but they would also read of God's deliverance as their captors disappeared in a flood of God's judgment (49:17). The people of God will swell in number as they return to the land (49:18-21). The captives from Judah would be freed by Cyrus and return home. But these verses look especially to the nation's ultimate salvation. Israel's glorious prosperity and joy can only be fully accomplished by the Servant-Messiah in his millennial kingdom.

49:22-26 In that glorious day, the Gentile nations will help the Jews return to their land (49:22). Furthermore, the nations will **bow down** in humility before Israel and her Messiah (49:23). The Lord promises on their behalf, **I will contend with the one who contends with you, and I will save your children** (49:25). This brings to mind God's promise to Abraham: "I will curse anyone who treats you with contempt" (Gen 12:3). He will defeat all of Israel's enemies, and **all people will know** that the LORD is Israel's Savior (49:26).

50:1-4 God's faithful Servant-Messiah stands in stark contrast to the faithless nation of Israel, which was also intended by God to be his servant. Israel proved so unfaithful that she had to be **sent away**, divorced like a wife who had violated her marriage covenant (50:1). Israel had no excuse for her sinful rebellion, since God had the **power to rescue** his people (50:2). God's Servant-Messiah, by contrast, let his **ear** be **opened** by God. He was willing to be **instructed** (50:4-5)

50:5-9 Isaiah speaks of part of the suffering that the Servant-Messiah would endure (see 53:3-10). His **back** would be beaten, his **beard** would be torn out, and his **face** would be spat upon. The Gospel writers affirm that this humiliation was fulfilled in Jesus Christ (see Matt 26:67; 27:30; John 19:1). In spite of the disgraceful treatment, though, the servant expressed his confidence that God would vindicate him: **The LORD God will help me . . . I have set my face like flint, and I know I will not be put to shame. . . . The one who vindicates me is near. . . . The Lord GOD will help me** (49:7-9). In contrast, those who accused and condemned God's Suffering Servant would **wear out like a garment** (47:9). God will turn the tables, and this servant will become a judge. All who reject Christ will one day stand condemned at his judgment throne.

50:10-11 Given the servant's obedience in the midst of great suffering, Isaiah exhorted his readers, everyone who **fears the LORD**, to remain faithful in spite of their suffering (50:10). The same exhortation applies to us today. Christians are called to share in Christ's sufferings so that we may share in his joy (see 1 Pet 2:21; 4:13-14). While those who oppose him seem to prosper now, they **will lie down in a place of torment** if they remain unrepentant (50:11).

51:1-3 Since the Servant-Messiah would ultimately prevail, the Lord could encourage the faithful remnant, those **who pursue righteousness** and **seek the LORD** (51:1). Although in captivity, the faithful in Babylon were exhorted to remember their heritage by looking back **to Abraham your father, and to Sarah who gave birth to you** (51:2). This would have reminded the Jewish captives that their nation was born out of God's eternal covenant with Abraham, a promise of blessing they could cling to during their present suffering. The promise of future restoration was a reminder that God would remember his covenant (51:3).

51:4-8 Only when Christ reigns in his millennial kingdom will we see his **justice** shine as **a light to the nations** (51:4). In that glorious day, God's **arms**—that is, his power—will bring justice to all, including **the coasts and islands**, which is a figure of speech for the farthest corners of the world (51:5). Christ's second coming will also bring about the end of the present **heavens** and **earth**, which **will vanish like smoke** and **wear out like a garment** to make way for the new heavens and new earth (51:6; cp. 65:17; 66:22). The enemies of God, no matter how powerful they seem, **will die like gnats** (51:6). **But my righteousness will last forever, and my salvation for all generations** (51:8). Christ's glory will be magnified "forever and ever" (Eph 3:21), or as the KJV translators rendered it, "world without end."

51:9-11 The remnant's response to this good news was to pray for a "second exodus" from bondage that would be like the first exodus from Egypt under Moses (51:9-10). Because God had **dried up the sea** so the children of Israel could cross over to the promised land (51:10), he could similarly redeem his people again. And in that day, **the ransomed of the LORD will return** and rejoice (51:11).

51:12-23 But the captives of Judah had **forgotten the LORD**, so they lived **in constant dread all day long because of the fury of the oppressor**, the Babylonians (51:13). Nevertheless, **the prisoner** would **soon ... be set free** because they were in the loving **hand** of God (51:14, 16). He urged those who had experienced his **fury** to **wake** up (51:17). Though they had endured **devastation and destruction, famine and sword**, his judgment had ended (51:19-22). God would turn the tables and bring his fury upon their **tormentors** (51:23).

52:1-4 With this good news about to be realized, God's people were exhorted again, **Wake up, wake up** (52:1). But these verses speak of an even greater redemption than freedom from Babylon—or even from **Egypt** or **Assyria** (52:4) The day when **the unclean** will not be allowed in **Jerusalem, the Holy City**, can only be when the Servant-Messiah, Jesus Christ, reigns in his millennial kingdom (52:1).

52:5-6 Because of their gross unfaithfulness, God's people—who were supposed to

be a light to their pagan neighbors—caused God's **name** to be **continually blasphemed** (52:5). This could not stand. So in redeeming Israel, the Lord would display his glorious power and holiness. His **people will know** [his] name—that is, his righteous character (52:6).

52:7-12 This joyful announcement of **news of good things ... when the LORD returns to Zion** and **all the ends of the earth will see the salvation of our God** will also be fully and finally realized for Israel when Christ returns to reign (52:7-10). The warning to the righteous to separate themselves from the unrighteous (52:11-12) could have been addressed to the captives in Babylon, telling them not to stay behind once Cyrus set them free. Or it may be a yet future warning to the faithful in Israel to separate themselves from the ungodly in the kingdom age.

52:13-15 In this section of Isaiah's Servant Songs, we are on holy ground. The following verses (52:13–53:12) testify to the coming suffering, death, and resurrection of Jesus Christ. His exaltation and universal recognition as Lord is still future, but in God's eternal plan it is as good as accomplished. The Gentile nations will see Christ in his glory and be speechless (52:13, 15).

53:1-6 The great sin of Israel's leaders and people was their failure to recognize their Messiah when he came. A relative few in Israel **believed** (53:1). Most of the Jews in Jesus's day, though, did not even regard him as a person of importance. There was nothing **impressive** about Jesus's physical **appearance** (53:2). **He was despised and rejected.** People **turned away from** him in his **suffering** (53:3). These verses couldn't more clearly depict what Jesus Christ endured. The use of language is precise regarding the kind of death he would die: **he was pierced** (53:5). But God also makes clear through Isaiah the reason that the Servant-Messiah would die: **because of our rebellion ... because of our iniquities ... the LORD ... punished him for the iniquity of us all** (53:5-6). Hundreds of years before it would happen, the prophet testified to the substitutionary atonement of Christ on the cross.

53:7-9 Although he died for sinners, it is clear that the Messiah himself is innocent: **He had done no violence and had not spoken deceitfully** (53:7, 9). Jesus was tried, condemned, and led away by wicked people in what was clearly a miscarriage of justice. But this innocent one had to die—the righteous for the unrighteous—**because of . . . people's rebellion** (53:8).

Again, the accuracy of the details provided is jaw-dropping. For instance, **like a sheep silent before her shearers, he did not open his mouth** (53:7). The Gospel writers testify to Jesus's silence before those who falsely accused him (see Matt 27:13-14; Mark 14:60-61; 15:4-5; Luke 23:8-9). Also, **he was with a rich man at his death** (53:9). Matthew tells us that "a rich man from Arimathea named Joseph" asked Pilate for Jesus's body and buried him in his own tomb (Matt 27:57-60). The fulfillment of all these prophecies is testimony to the divine inspiration and truthfulness of the Bible.

53:10-12 The Father and Son had been in loving communion from eternity past, yet **the LORD was pleased to crush him severely.** Why? Because the Son's death as **a guilt offering** (53:10)—a reference to the Old Testament sacrifices for sin (see Lev 5:14–6:7)—was the only way to bring about our salvation. God "gave his one and only Son" because he "loved the world" (John 3:16). Nowhere is the amazing love of God for unworthy sinners on full display like in the cross of Christ, where Jesus **bore the sin of many** (53:12). And through the death of the **righteous servant**, he **will justify many** (53:11). The apostle Paul understood this: "For all have sinned and fall short of the glory of God. They are justified freely by his grace through the redemption that is in Christ Jesus" (Rom 3:23-24).

Isaiah doesn't stop there, though. Because of the obedience of the Servant-Messiah, God does not abandon him to the grave. **After his anguish . . . he will see light and be satisfied** (53:11). This refers to the fact that God the Father raised God the Son from the dead. He is now the resurrected Lord. But it gets better still: **Therefore [God] will give him the many as a portion, and he will receive the mighty as spoil** (53:12). The Father has

exalted the Son to a place of supremacy, "seating him at his right hand in the heavens" (Eph 1:20), and all those who trust in Christ are seated with him, having access to his spiritual blessings (see Eph 1:3-14; 2:4-6).

54:1-3 Because of the redeeming work of the Servant-Messiah, God could offer full salvation and restoration to Israel. The nation was described as **childless** (54:1), a situation that was considered a disgrace for a woman of that time. But although under God's hand of judgment, Israel had experienced a time of desolation, Israel will be restored when Messiah comes to reign in the millennial kingdom. She will have so many children that her people will have to expand their tents to accommodate everyone (54:2)! In the coming time of Israel's salvation and restoration, the nation **will dispossess nations and inhabit the desolate cities** (54:3).

54:4-7 In that day of salvation, Israel will no longer have to feel the **shame** of her **youth** and the **disgrace** of her **widowhood** (54:4). Israel was like **a wife deserted and wounded in spirit**, but not because her husband was cruel to her (54:6). Israel's husband was the Lord, who had to reject his wife for **a brief moment** because of her sin and uncleanness (54:7). His promise, though, has always been to take her back to cleanse and restore her.

54:8-10 The captives from Judah in Babylon must have wondered more than once if they had gone too far in their sin and alienated God forever, but God assured them of his **everlasting love** (54:8). To illustrate this, God compared their situation to **the days of Noah**, when God judged the earth in his righteous anger (54:9). Yet once the judgment was over, God's anger subsided and he gave Noah the promise that he would never again destroy the whole earth with a flood (see Gen 7:5–9:17). In the same way, God promised that he would never again forsake Israel: **My love will not be removed from you** (54:10). This refers ultimately to the millennial kingdom.

54:11-17 God could also assure his chosen people that **poor Jerusalem**, the **storm-tossed** city would not only be rebuilt but her people would also live there in perfect peace and security (54:11). The **precious** stones God will use to adorn his holy city (54:12) are described in detail in Rev 21:9-27. But the true beauty of the city will be the glorious presence of God, who himself will teach Israel's **children** and protect them (53:13-17).

55:1-5 Having laid out every blessing prepared for God's people, the only thing left to do was to invite Israel to receive the Lord's healing and salvation from sin, along with millennial and eternal blessings. The astounding thing was that God offered all of this **without silver and without cost**, a powerful Old Testament affirmation of God's free gift of grace (55:1). Israel's people had spent far too many years wasting their time on things that did not satisfy—which cost them dearly (54:2). But in the kingdom age and beyond, God's people will enjoy his best as the fruit of his **permanent covenant** (55:3). The statements of 55:4-5 are about Jesus the King of Israel, who will rule not only his own people, but also Gentile nations that did **not know** him (55:5). Christ's kingdom reign will extend to every corner of the earth.

55:6-9 God's invitation was gracious, but there was an urgency to it. **The wicked** were warned to abandon their evil ways and **thoughts** and **return to the LORD** for forgiveness and restoration to his favor (55:7). God can forgive even the worst of sinners because, as he told Israel, **My thoughts are not your thoughts, and your ways are not my ways. . . . For as heaven is higher than earth, so my ways are higher than your ways, and my thoughts than your thoughts** (55:8-9).

If we're honest, grace does not make sense to us because it does not reflect how people treat one another on earth. But God's perspective is not our perspective. That's why we need a divine translator. We need the Holy Spirit to enable us to have a heavenly perspective; we need "the mind of Christ" (1 Cor 2:16).

55:10-11 These verses offer rich encouragement regarding the power of God's Word. **Rain** falls **from heaven**, waters the earth, and causes plants to grow (55:10). Even children understand this truth about how God made the world. But God says his Word

works the same way. It proceeds from his **mouth** and does **not return . . . empty. It will accomplish what [he pleases]** (55:11). Humans often make grand plans. They plot and scheme. Sometimes they succeed; often they fail. That's because they lack the power to guarantee their plans. Power is the ability to effect change or produce a desired result, and God's Word alone has that kind of guaranteed power. The unstoppable power of God's Word to accomplish all of his purposes, in fact, sets it apart in a class by itself. God's Word is always purposeful, and his purposes are always achieved. The Bible can be trusted.

55:12-13 The greatness of God's salvation and grace will have tremendous effects on the earth in the millennial kingdom. These verses describe briefly the new earth God has promised in his reversal of the curse of Eden. The **thornbush** and **brier**, which began to plague the world after Adam and Eve sinned (see Gen 3:17-18), will be replaced by plants of beauty and usefulness (55:13).

56:1-8 The appeal to **preserve justice and do what is right** was addressed to Israel because God's **salvation** was near (56:1). There was also good news for every **foreigner who has joined himself to the LORD**, because in the millennial kingdom righteous non-Jews will also share in the blessings of Christ's rule (56:3). Gentiles who believed in the God of Israel and bound themselves to him had a place within his covenant community in the Old Testament dispensation. Here they were assured that they would also share in the kingdom with Israel, including sharing in Israel's regathering to enjoy God's salvation and blessings under Christ's righteous rule. God also promises a special blessing and kingdom position to those who maintain their sexual purity (1 Cor 6:9-19).

56:9-12 The joys and blessings of God's salvation and his millennial kingdom form a stark contrast to the close of this section (56:9–57:21), in which God turned his attention to the sinfulness of his people in Isaiah's day. Things were so bad that God invited the **animals** to devour them (56:9). The Babylonian destroyers of Judah are probably in view here. The nation's spiritual leaders, who should have been alert **watchmen** and caring **shepherds**, were like **mute dogs** who cared only for themselves and their own appetites (56:10-12).

57:1-3 The evil hearts of God's people were also apparent in another way—in their lack of care for their fellow righteous citizens: **The righteous person perishes, and no one takes it to heart** (57:1). Isaiah thus minced no words. He called such people **offspring of an adulterer and a prostitute**, which was a stinging rebuke of their unfaithfulness to the Lord by worshiping idols (57:3). The ugliness and depravity of their worship is a vivid example of how human beings become like the gods they worship.

57:4-10 It wasn't enough for the people in Isaiah's day to engage in pagan worship; they also mocked the righteous who remained faithful to God (57:4). The idolaters burned **with lust** and fed their sexual depravity with rituals that included every form of moral degeneration imaginable. This was combined with the unimaginable horror of sacrificing their **children** (57:5), possibly to Molech, the god of the Ammonites who demanded child sacrifice. Their debauchery knew no bounds (57:7-9).

57:11-13 In light of this mess, God questions them: **Who was it you dreaded and feared, so that you lied and didn't remember me or take it to heart?** The people might have argued in their defense that God had been **silent for a long time** (57:11)—which was not true. But even if he had been, they should have realized it was because of their sin and not because God didn't care about them. Because God's people chose to forget him and put their trust in idols, he gave them over to them. He said, **When you cry out, let your collection of idols rescue you!** Gods of wood, however, are a futile hope. **The wind will carry all of them off** (57:13). Even in the midst of such sin among the populace, though, there remained a promise of deliverance for the person who made God his **refuge** (57:13).

57:14-21 The rest of the chapter turns to the Lord's promise to **remove every obstacle**

from the road his faithful ones were taking to come to him. The righteous were encouraged to remember that even though the God of Israel is the **High and Exalted One**, he delights to dwell with **the lowly** (57:15). God's people were also assured that his wrath against them would not last **forever** (57:16). But lest they misunderstand, God reminded them that he had good reason for his anger (57:17). Nevertheless, anyone who repented and returned to the Lord would enjoy his **peace** and healing (57:19). However, **there is no peace for the wicked** (57:21).

➤ C. God's Restoration of Israel and the World (58:1–66:24) ᵜ

58:1-5 The last section of Isaiah's book puts the final pieces in place for God's work of salvation and restoration both for Israel and for all of creation. The beginning of that restoration, from God's standpoint, is the reestablishment of proper worship. Israel failed miserably at worshiping rightly and needed someone shouting to them with a **voice like a trumpet** the way an ancient herald would do (58:1) because though they wanted God's blessings, they had abandoned true worship and failed to perform what was right and just. While they sought to keep the fasts associated with Israel's worship and wondered why God wasn't answering their prayers, their fasting was a classic example of empty ritual: **You do as you please on the day of your fast.** Moreover, they were oppressing all their **workers** at the same time (58:3). Their fasting even involved hostility (58:4)!

58:6-7 What God wanted was religious practice offered from truly humble hearts. Seeking to worship with false motives and with no concern for righteousness is not true worship. So what does true religion look like? What is proper behavior for subjects of the King? Believers are to help **the oppressed**, give food to **the hungry**, provide shelter to the **homeless**, and **clothe the naked** (58:6-7). And lest any Christian thinks this was simply for Old Testament Israel, James offers similar counsel: "Pure and undefiled religion before God the Father is this: to look after orphans and widows in their distress and to keep oneself unstained in the world" (Jas 1:27). Kingdom people do these things.

58:8-14 If they followed through on God's agenda, spiritual blessings would flow: Their **recovery** would **come quickly** (58:8); when they call, **the LORD will answer** (58:9); their **light will shine in the darkness** (58:10); **the LORD will always lead** (58:11). But these things hinged on God's people restoring his proper worship, symbolized by fasting, coupled with just and charitable outreach to the poor and the oppressed.

Fasting is a spiritual discipline that continues to be proper for believers when we want to make our "voice heard on high" (58:4). When we fast with the proper motivation, our voices are heard in heaven—that is, we come into God's presence in a powerful way. So imagine the voice the church can have in heaven today, if we come together across class, ethnic, and denominational boundaries to collectively fast and call on God to intervene. We could perhaps be **the repairer of broken walls, the restorer of streets where people live** (58:12).

59:1-2 In spite of what the people of Judah may have thought, **the LORD's arm [was] not too weak to save, and his ear [was] not too deaf to hear** (59:1). God had not suddenly become impotent, nor did he get thrashed by the Babylonian god. It was the **iniquities** of the people that separated them from God; this was why he had refused to **listen** to their prayers (59:2). He was unwilling to bless them regardless of their actions. They were the problem, not him.

59:3-8 The catalog of sins in 59:3-4 includes murder, **lies**, evil thoughts, and **injustice**. It's no wonder that God was unimpressed by the people's insincere worship. (Given the list, I can't believe they had the nerve to wonder why God wasn't hearing and answering their prayers!) But in God's eyes, his people's sins were like **spiders' webs** that a person can easily see through, which means they **cannot become clothing** (59:5-6)—in this case, spiritual clothing to try and **cover** their works from God's sight (59:8).

59:9-15 Notice the words *us* and *we* and *our* here. Like other Old Testament prophets who denounced Israel's sins, Isaiah identified with his people in confessing Israel's sins. God sent prophet after prophet and calamity after calamity to wake his people to their need for repentance, leading Isaiah to lament that **righteousness does not reach us** (59:9). While God's hand of salvation was capable of reaching the people, Judah's citizens had convinced themselves that they were innocent and didn't need it. The truth was that they were **like the blind**; they were **like the dead among those who are healthy** (59:10).

59:16 God was **amazed that** no one among his people was capable of steering the nation in a righteous path. Where were the prophets, priests, and kings? Although there were exceptions (such as Isaiah, of course), most leaders had become corrupt. Instead of leading the nation in righteousness, they had led them in wickedness. So **there was no one interceding** on behalf of the people. What, then, would this faithful, covenant-keeping God do? **His own arm brought salvation.** He himself would intercede. No one could bring salvation except the Lord alone.

59:17-21 So God put on the **armor** of **righteousness** and the **helmet of salvation** to avenge, judge, and save (59:17). The following verses are a picture of Christ's second coming, when he will crush all of his **enemies** and reign in righteousness (59:18-20). To the enemies of God, Christ comes as a terrifying conqueror who will sweep them away **like a rushing stream** (59:19). But to those **who turn from transgression**, Christ will come as **Redeemer** (59:20).

60:1-3 Through God's redeeming power and his eternal covenant of blessing on Israel, the nation will experience unending joy and blessing as the world capital and centerpiece of Christ's reign in his millennial kingdom. Israel will be a light to the nations because **the glory of the LORD** will shine both in her and from her to the corners of the earth (60:1). God's light will overcome the **total darkness** that has covered the world since the fall and kept countless millions in spiritual darkness (60:2). But in the millennium, entire **nations** and their **kings** will be drawn to Israel to learn the truth about God and his salvation (60:3). This is necessary because many people will be born during this one-thousand-year paradise on earth, and they will need to learn of Christ.

60:4 The millennial age will also be the time of Israel's prophesied ingathering. This is a common theme in Isaiah, which pictures Israel's **sons** and **daughters** coming **from far away** (see also 49:22; 60:9). Although many Jews have returned to Israel from many countries in recent times, most do not believe in Jesus as their Messiah. Many Bible teachers, then, do not identify this modern return with the prophecies of Israel's regathering. More likely, passages such as Isaiah 60 refer to the reign of Christ on earth when the Jewish people will embrace him as Messiah.

60:5-14 This golden age will also be marked by **the wealth of the nations** coming into Israel (60:5). They will bring **gold** to beautify Jerusalem and enrich the nation. Moreover, they will **proclaim the praises of the LORD** (60:6). In fact, Jerusalem's **gates will always be open**, and **they will never be shut** so that the nations' **wealth** and **their kings** may come at all times to bring gifts and pay homage to Christ (60:11). We know from Revelation 20:7-9 that Satan will deceive and lead Gentile nations in a brief rebellion at the end of the millennial age, but this uprising will be immediately crushed and the rebels **annihilated** (60:12).

60:15-22 When Christ returns, Israel will be **an object of eternal pride, a joy from age to age**, with Jerusalem as the crown jewel (60:15). God's promise, **I will appoint peace as your government and righteousness as your overseers**, will signal the end of centuries of war and **destruction** against Israel and Jerusalem (60:17-18). Because of the light of God's presence in the person of Jesus the Messiah, Israel will shine like a welcoming beacon for the world. All of her **people will be righteous** in the millennial age, when Israel will finally fulfill her role as a witness to the nations, pointing them to the true God (60:21). We can be sure this will happen

because **the LORD** promises to **accomplish it quickly in its time** (60:22).

61:1-2 We know from Luke 4:16-21 that at least part of this passage opening with the words, **The Spirit of the LORD GOD is on me, because the LORD has anointed me . . .**, was fulfilled in Jesus Christ. The Hebrew word "Messiah" and the Greek word "Christ" mean "anointed one." Jesus was anointed by God the Father to redeem his world and reign over his kingdom. The people of Israel longed for the coming of God's Messiah to save them and be their king.

When Jesus read Isaiah 61:1-2 in the synagogue in Nazareth and proclaimed, "Today as you listen, this Scripture has been fulfilled," the people knew he was claiming to be the Messiah. And they weren't happy about it. After all, Jesus was one of them. Nazareth was his hometown, and he was thought to be the son of the local carpenter (Luke 4:21-22). They wanted a Messiah with might and power. And as Isaiah said about the Servant-Messiah, "He didn't have an impressive form or majesty . . . no appearance that we should desire him" (53:2). So Jesus wasn't the Messiah they were expecting. In fact, they were so enraged with him that they tried to toss him off a cliff (see Luke 4:28-30).

But Jesus was right. His earthly ministry did fulfill this messianic prophecy—at least part of it. He came **to bring good news**, to **heal**, and to proclaim **freedom** from Satan (61:1). He came **to proclaim the year of the LORD's favor** (61:2). But that's where Jesus stopped when he read from Isaiah (see Luke 4:18-19). At his first advent, he brought salvation. At his second advent, though, he will bring **the day of our God's vengeance** (61:2). God's judgment awaits the second coming of Christ, when he will crush his enemies and restore Israel to a place of glory.

61:3-6 Israel will go from being despised among the nations to becoming the head of the nations—a rebuilt and resplendent land that will be fitting as the place from which Messiah will rule (61:4-5). As the Gentiles enrich and serve Israel, God's people will finally be what they were always meant to be—a nation in which all of the people will be called **the LORD's priests** (60:6; see Exod

19:6), ministering his grace to all the world. This is why **they will speak of** Israel **as ministers of our God** (60:6).

61:7-9 Israel will receive **a double portion** of inheritance as the first born of the Lord (61:7; see Exod 4:22; Deut 21:17). This is in contrast to Israel having received "double for all her sins" (40:2). The Lord will make a **permanent covenant** with Israel (61:8). This is a reference to the "new covenant" (see Jer 31:31-34), which Jesus established when he "poured out" his blood on the cross for the forgiveness of sins (see Luke 22:20; Heb 8:7-13). Christians live under the new covenant, but one day Israel will too when Jesus comes to rule on the throne of David in his millennial kingdom and Israel receives him as their Messiah. In that day, all people will know **that they are a people the Lord has blessed** (61:9).

61:10-11 The Lord's Servant-Messiah will give praise to God for his luxurious **garments of salvation** and his **robe of righteousness** (61:10). Endowed with these, he will accomplish God's purposes for Israel and for the world. Therefore, God **will cause righteousness and praise to spring up before all the nations** (61:11).

62:1-3 This chapter is one of the crown jewels of prophecy in terms of the glorious future awaiting Israel when Jesus Christ returns and establishes his kingdom. In that bright future, Israel's **righteousness** will shine **like a bright light and her salvation, like a flaming torch** (62:1). God will also give his chosen nation a new name. In the Bible, a person's name signified his character or served as declaration about the future. God himself **will announce** this **new name** (61:2); therefore, we can trust that what it proclaims will certainly happen.

62:4-5 This power of God to give a new name to a person or a nation is nothing new (see Gen 17:3-5, 15-16; 32:27-28; Hos 1:4-7). In Isaiah's day, God called Israel **Deserted** (possibly referring specifically to Jerusalem) and **Desolate** (62:4). But the day is coming when God will say of Israel **My Delight Is in Her**, and the land of Israel will no longer be like a forlorn person but **will be married** (62:4). That is, his chosen people will once again be worthy of being called the Lord's **bride**, and **God will rejoice** (62:5).

62:6-9 These verses are an encouragement to God's people in any age to be persistent in prayer. We're to pray with expectancy, like **watchmen on [the] walls** of a city who are always on alert for whatever news comes (62:6). The immediate context is God's call to his people to pray persistently and expectantly for his salvation and deliverance to come in the person of the Messiah. **There is no rest for you, who remind the Lord** of his promises and ask him to fulfill them (62:6) could be called the Old Testament equivalent of Paul's command to "pray constantly" (1 Thess 5:17). We're even called to wear God out with our prayers: **Do not give him rest** (62:7). Jesus agreed and told his disciples "to pray always and not give up" (Luke 18:1).

62:10-12 The Lord will answer the prayers of his people, in this case for Jerusalem and all of Israel to be restored and thrive in the kingdom age. Because this is true, the Lord can make this announcement: **Say to Daughter Zion: Look, your salvation is coming, his wages are with him, and his reward accompanies him** (62:11). The new names God gave to his people (62:4-5) are not enough. He has a few more: **the Holy People, the Lord's Redeemed . . . Cared For, A City Not Deserted** (62:12). Those are names that guarantee a glorious future.

63:1 The vengeance God will wreak on his enemies at Christ's second coming is terrifying. **Edom** serves as an example of what will happen to the nations that reject Christ (**Bozrah** was one of its capital cities). The Edomites were the descendants of Esau, which means the Israelites were their brothers. Nevertheless, the Edomites were especially cruel to the Israelites on their journey from Egypt to the promised land (see Num 20:14-21).

63:2-6 The nations God will judge at Christ's return are pictured metaphorically as trampled in God's **winepress** until they are **crushed** (63:2, 6). Christ will grind them **underfoot** and spatter their **blood** on his garments (63:3). Indeed, when the sins of the nations are ripe, they will be judged in the "winepress of God's wrath" (Rev 14:19). Now is the day of repentance; now is the time for second chances. In that day, there will be no second chances, and there will be no escape.

63:7-10 Here the focus shifts dramatically to the declarations of God's people as they remember **the many good things he has done for the house of Israel.** Isaiah leads the nation in praising God for his **faithful love** and **praiseworthy acts** (63:7). **The angel of his presence saved them,** most notably in the exodus under Moses (63:9). But since that was true, the exiles in Babylon might ask, "Why are we in this mess in Babylon?" Isaiah answers on God's behalf: **they rebelled and grieved his Holy Spirit** (63:10)—a statement that Paul echoes in Ephesians 4:30. Therefore, God **fought against them** (63:10).

63:11-15 But Isaiah remembers how God had shown mercy to his people in the past when he delivered them from the Egyptians and brought them to the promised land. He **put his Holy Spirit among** them, **divided the water,** and **gave them rest** (63:11-14). Continuing the comparison to the days of Moses, Isaiah prays on behalf of the people for God to **look down from heaven and see**—a plea for God to come down and act on what he saw (63:15). The faithful ones knew their history. When God came to Moses in the burning bush, he said, "I have observed the misery of my people in Egypt, and have heard them crying out because of their oppressors. I know about their sufferings, and I have come down to rescue them" (Exod 3:7-8). He had done it before; he would do it again.

63:16-19 They asked for this deliverance even though they had to admit with embarrassment that they were so sinful that their ancestors **Abraham** and **Israel** (Jacob) would not **recognize** them (63:16). That's quite a statement considering what a deceiver Jacob was—until God straightened out his act. God's people had gotten so bad that they had become like Pharaoh, who rejected God's demands to let his people go and hardened his own heart (see Exod 8:32). Eventually, God confirmed Pharaoh's choice and hardened

his heart too (Exod 9:12). The people of Israel and Judah rejected the Lord repeatedly. No matter how many times God urged them through his prophets to repent, they pressed on in their idolatry. So he hardened their **hearts** and judged them through the nations that conquered them (63:17).

64:1-4 Because God's people were either heading for or in exile when they read the book of Isaiah, they cried out for him to **tear the heavens open** like a piece of cloth and **come down** to rescue them. They asked the Lord to act as he had acted before. They wanted **mountains** to **quake** at his **presence** (64:1)—just as the **mountains quaked** when he performed his **awesome works** in the past (64:3). This is one of the keys for God's people even today. We need to remember how God has come through in our past circumstances so that we can have faith to call on him in our time of need, for he **acts on behalf of the one who waits for him** (64:4). To "wait" for God doesn't mean to sit and do nothing. It means to live faithfully according to the agenda of God's Word as we patiently expect him to answer in his own time and way.

64:5-7 The people acknowledged the reason for God's apparent lack of intervention to prevent his land from being destroyed: **we have sinned, and you were angry** (64:5). No amount of worship and prayers for deliverance will help if we continue to live by our own agenda and for our own glory. Therefore, the people had to say, **All of us have become like something unclean, and all our righteous acts are like a polluted garment** (64:6). As the old saying goes, confession is good for the soul.

64:8-12 Because God is faithful to his promises, Israel could say, **Yet Lord, you are our Father** and plead once again for his help (64:8). The end of this long prayer is a good example of what it means to remind God that we as his people are frail and sinful humans, and that he needs to intervene because of what he values so much—his people and his holy land. Finally, the people asked, **Lord, after all this, will you restrain yourself? Will you keep silent and afflict us severely?** (64:12).

This was an urgent request for God to make his power manifest to his enemies, remember his people's afflictions, and rescue them before they were beyond recovery.

65:1-7 God had responded to his people with grace: **I was sought by those who did not ask; I was found by those who did not seek me** (65:1). But Israel rejected God's kindness. Although he **spread out [his] hands** to them, they followed **their own thoughts** (65:2). And, of course, their thoughts led to their actions: **sacrificing in gardens** (practicing idolatry), **sitting among the graves** (talking to the dead), and **eating the meat of pigs** (rejecting God's holiness laws). They **anger me to my face**, God declared (65:3-4). **I will repay them fully for [their] iniquities** (65:6-7).

Our actions are determined by our thinking. If you want to experience spiritual victory, you need a kingdom mind. You need to adopt God's thinking about the issues of life. You must be "transformed by the renewing of your mind" (Rom 12:2). By tending to the soil of our minds and sowing our thoughts with the Word of God, we will make it possible to bear good fruit in what we say and in what we do.

65:8-16 Even during judgment, though, God promised to spare his righteous remnant, those who were faithful to him in the midst of perverse generations (65:8-10). The wicked, on the other hand, will not be spared: **you did what was evil in my sight and chose what I did not delight in** (65:12). God then presented a stark contrast between the fate of the wicked and the fate of his **servants**. The wicked would experience hunger, thirst, shame, anguish, lament, cursing, and death. But God's servants will **eat**, **drink**, **rejoice**, and **shout for joy** (65:13-16). Given the two options, there's simply no contest. Regardless of the hardships one may face in life by following the Lord, the end result is worth it: **the former troubles will be forgotten** (65:16).

65:17-25 Several of the most well-known characteristics of Christ's kingdom are found in this description of that golden age, including **a new heaven and a new earth** (65:17), the end of **weeping** (65:19), and a redeemed animal kingdom (65:25). One of the painful aspects of Israel and Judah's exile was that their homes and lands were lived in and consumed by others. In the kingdom age, God's people will enjoy his complete blessing (65:22-24).

66:1-6 Isaiah's final call to faithfulness and rebuke of hypocrisy is fitting in light of all that the prophet had written. Those among the Israelites who could read the prophet's entire message and still reject their God were to be left to themselves, because they **have chosen their ways and delight in their abhorrent practices** (66:3). But God would choose too; he would **choose their punishment** (66:4). There will come a time when the grace of God will end and those who reject him will be confirmed in their choices. When the Lord **[pays] back his enemies what they deserve** (66:6), no one will stand, no one will escape.

66:7-17 Yet the fate of the wicked will not spoil the rejoicing of those who enter Christ's kingdom. Israel's restoration in the kingdom age will be accomplished so quickly it will be like a woman delivering her baby before she **was in labor** (66:7). Israel's rebirth is certain because God never begins what he doesn't finish (66:9). God's people will **be comforted**, but his **enemies** will receive his **wrath** (66:13-14). They will perish in **flames of fire** (66:15).

66:18-21 There will be no escape. You can't hide from an all-knowing God. He knows all of our **works** and **thoughts** (66:18). And as much as this is a terror to the wicked, it is also a comfort to the righteous. Those who trust in Christ can know that their sinful deeds and thoughts are forgiven, and they can also know that every deed and thought that they bring into submission to Christ will be remembered by him.

God will **gather** together all **nations and languages** who submit to him, and they will **see** his **glory** (66:18). When Jesus Christ returns to rule the earth, people in the farthest corners of the world will know of his salvation. Verse 19 may refer to believing Jews who will go to other **nations** to **proclaim**

God's **glory** (66:19), resulting in salvation for Israel's Gentile **brothers** as a gift to the Lord (66:20).

66:22-24 When God makes everything **new** in his eternal kingdom, the old distinctions and divisions won't apply anymore: **All mankind will come to worship** (66:22-23). Knowing that God is building his kingdom today, and that his kingdom will come fully and finally at the return of Christ, the best thing believers can do is to understand the requirements of his kingdom agenda and get on with the task of fulfilling them.

JEREMIAH

INTRODUCTION

Author

BEFORE HE WAS CALLED AS A prophet of the Lord, Jeremiah was a priest "living in Anathoth in the territory of Benjamin" (1:1). He began prophesying "in the thirteenth year of the reign of" Judah's King Josiah and continued into Judah's exile in Babylon (1:2-3). Thus, Jeremiah's ministry started in about 626 BC and continued for several years after 586 BC. Jeremiah saw the downfall of Judah, the destruction of Jerusalem, and the exile of God's people. Because of the tremendous sorrow this caused him (9:1), he is often referred to as "the weeping prophet."

Historical Background

Jeremiah's ministry began during the reign of King Josiah of Judah. Unlike his wicked father Amon and grandfather Manasseh, Josiah followed the Lord (see 2 Kgs 22:2). He even led the people to renew their covenant with God. He also brought about many reforms in Judah, including repairing the temple, removing pagan idolatry from the land, and observing the Passover. Although Josiah did much good, he could not ultimately overcome the great evils done by the kings who had gone before him—especially Manasseh's. Therefore, God was determined to bring his anger down on Judah and Jerusalem (see 2 Kgs 23:26-27).

Josiah died in a battle with Pharaoh Neco of Egypt in 609 BC. His son Jehoahaz was king for only three months before Neco imprisoned him and made Josiah's son Jehoiakim king in his place. In 605 BC, Neco was defeated by the Babylonians, and Judah fell into the hands of Babylon by the next year. When Jehoiakim rebelled against Babylon's King Nebuchadnezzar in about 600 BC, Nebuchadnezzar invaded Judah and besieged Jerusalem. He deposed Jehoiakim in 598 BC, carried his son Jehoiachin into exile in 597 BC, and made Zedekiah—another of Josiah's sons—king of Judah. Then, in 588 BC, Zedekiah rebelled against Babylon. And as a result, Nebuchadnezzar ravaged Jerusalem, destroyed the temple, and carried many of Judah's inhabitants (including Zedekiah) into exile in 587–586 BC.

Message and Purpose

Jeremiah brought a lot of emotion to his prophetic role, earning him the name "the weeping prophet." As judgment was being prepared for the sinful kingdom of Judah through the Babylonian Empire, Jeremiah was called to announce the rightness of that judgment because of Judah's great sin against God. His daunting task was to bring this message of rejection to God's people. But in the midst of that, Jeremiah also issued a call to the people to repent so that their situation might be reversed, and another call to the people who would not be taken into captivity in Babylon to repent so that things wouldn't become worse but better.

God commanded Jeremiah not to marry as an illustration of the isolation God was feeling from his sinful people. And yet, it is in Jeremiah that God reveals a new kingdom covenant he would make with his people to cleanse them, give them new hearts, and restore them to himself. The good news of Jeremiah is that despite our sin, God offers us restoration if we will repent and return to him.

VIDEO INTRO

www.bhpublishinggroup.com/qr/te/24_00

JEREMIAH

I. JEREMIAH'S CALL TO MINISTRY (1:1-19)

1:1-3 Jeremiah is a sad book. You don't want to read it if you are feeling down because "the weeping prophet" will have you crying with him (see 9:1) at the depths of unfaithfulness to which God's people sank and the severe judgment that God delivered.

Jeremiah was a priest from the town of **Anathoth in the territory of Benjamin** (1:1), located about three miles northeast of Jerusalem. He was called to deliver God's message of judgment to the southern kingdom of Judah. The northern kingdom of Israel had already been swept away by the Assyrians in 722 BC. The time stamp on his ministry covers a period of forty-plus years, beginning **in the thirteenth year of the reign of Josiah** (1:2), the last of the good kings of Judah, and continuing through the destruction of Jerusalem and the people's **exile** into Babylon in about 586 BC.

1:4-7 The Lord announced to Jeremiah that he had **appointed** him **a prophet to the nations** (1:5). Like Moses before him (see Exod 4:10), Jeremiah **protested** God's call on his life because he didn't **know how to speak** (1:6). But God had decided before Jeremiah was even born that he would use him this way (1:5), for he delights in demonstrating his great power in human weakness (see 2 Cor 12:9).

1:8-10 Happy times were not ahead for Jeremiah. When the Lord tells you, **Do not be afraid of anyone, for I will be with you to rescue you** (1:8), you know you're in for some hard days. Nevertheless, God fortified

Jeremiah and promised the prophet his divine protection. Jeremiah was going to need it, given his assigned role: **I [the LORD] have appointed you today over nations and kingdoms to uproot and tear down, to destroy and demolish, to build and plant** (1:10). Jeremiah's message was not one of complete despair and destruction: after the people had experienced seventy years of exile in Babylon, God was going to bring them back to the land and rebuild his temple. Still, it wouldn't be popular.

1:11-12 God gave Jeremiah two visions to confirm both his close involvement in the prophet's ministry and the basic message of that ministry. The first thing Jeremiah saw was the **branch of an almond tree** (1:11). The almond was one of the first trees in Israel to blossom in the spring. The Lord said he would **watch over [his] word to accomplish it** (1:12). The Hebrew words for "almond" and "watch" sound alike in Hebrew. Thus, God would see to it that every word he gave Jeremiah to deliver would blossom and come to pass.

1:13-16 Jeremiah then saw **a boiling pot**, its **lip tilted from the north to the south** (1:13), an unmistakable picture of the **disaster** coming upon Judah **from the north** (1:14) when the armies of King Nebuchadnezzar of Babylon would swoop down on Jerusalem. The accuracy of God's Word is amazing. Babylon was actually east of Judah, but its armies invaded from the north, following the trade routes that took travelers around the

Arabian Desert instead of through it. Babylon would execute God's **judgments** upon Judah for her idolatry (1:16).

1:17-19 Now, get ready. **Stand up and tell them everything that I command you** (1:17). If you have bad news to deliver that people need to hear, there's no use delaying it or dancing around it. God had already warned Jeremiah of fierce opposition and persecution, but he added, **I am the one who has made you a fortified city, an iron pillar, and bronze walls against the whole land [of Judah]** (1:18). Jeremiah would need all of these defenses for his years of ministry that lay ahead.

II. PROPHECIES ABOUT JUDAH AND ITS FALL (2:1–45:5)

⮞ A. Judah's Sin and Faithlessness (2:1–3:5) ⮜

2:1-3 That **the word of the LORD came** (2:1) is an all-important statement occurring many times throughout the prophetic books. Jeremiah was the recorder and deliverer of what he would share, but this opening denunciation of Judah's people came directly from God's mouth. Like the betrayed husband of a wayward bride, God recalls the days when his people were faithful. **Israel** (meaning the entire nation, not merely the northern kingdom) **was holy to the LORD** (2:3). Of all the nations of the world, Israel was set apart by God to be his chosen people.

2:4-8 But that was then, and so the Lord's indictment begins. And it isn't pretty. His people had turned away from the one who had delivered them from slavery and taken them **through the wilderness** and to the promised **land** (2:6-7). Everyone who should have known better was guilty of this betrayal: the **priests, experts in the law, rulers**, and **prophets** (2:8). To whom did they turn when they rejected God? **Worthless . . . useless idols** (2:5, 8). And this wasn't because God had somehow let them down (2:5).

2:9-13 God knew the people had no good answer for their behavior, so here he presents his indictment **against** Judah (2:9). Even pagan nations did not switch out their idol **gods** for others (2:10-11), yet God's **people have exchanged their Glory for useless idols** (2:11). The Lord describes this ridiculous exchange as **a double evil**—they had **abandoned** God, **the fountain of living water**, and dug cisterns for themselves—**cracked cisterns that cannot hold water** (2:13). Thirsty people trading a flowing fountain for empty holes. It doesn't get much more absurd than that.

2:14-25 Because of these **apostasies** (2:19), Judah had gone from freedom to slavery. And they **brought** it on themselves (2:17). Their so-called solution to the problem was not to turn back to the Lord, however, but to turn to **Egypt** and **Assyria** to fix the mess by playing the game of political intrigue and power brokering (2:18).

God considered Judah's idolatry with foreign gods to be spiritual adultery. She acted like **a prostitute**, offering sacrifices to idols **on every high hill** (2:20). She was like **a wild donkey . . . in the heat of her desire** (2:24). She had God for a husband, but instead Judah said, **I love strangers** (2:25).

2:27-37 When **disaster** struck, the people begged God to **save** them (2:27), but he pointed them to their false **gods** so they could see whether their idols of wood and stone could help (2:28). The people were so spiritually hardened that they actually thought they could bring **a case against** God (2:29). They were hopelessly mired in sin with no intention of repenting. Judah refused to **accept** God's **discipline** (2:30) and declared instead, **I have not sinned** (2:35). To deny your sin, though, is to call God a liar (see 1 John 1:10).

3:1-5 The Lord closes this first indictment by saying he cannot take Judah back because she left him **to marry another**. Actually, it was worse than that. She had **prostituted** herself **with many partners** (3:1)! What a picture of Judah's spiritual wickedness, forsaking her position as the Lord's bride to be a **brazen . . . prostitute** (3:3).

✥ B. Call to Repentance in Light of Coming Judgment (3:6–6:30) ✥

3:6-10 Jeremiah begins his next message by speaking of the northern kingdom of **Israel**, which had already been taken into captivity by the Assyrians. When Israel was judged for her spiritual adulteries (3:6), Judah should have taken note and avoided her ways. But **Judah** proved to be even more **treacherous** than her sister Israel (3:7-8)! And while Judah made a **pretense** of repenting, God saw right through it (3:10). We should take care because it's possible to show up at church on Sunday and sing praises to the Lord—but have a heart that is rock hard.

3:11-25 God issued a call to Israel to repent and be restored, an invitation to **return** and **acknowledge [her] guilt** (3:12-13). What follows is an ideal picture of a united nation (Israel and Judah) returning to the true worship of God; it would be so glorious that even the **ark of the LORD's covenant** would not be missed (3:14-18). God longs to welcome back his wayward people (3:19). He thus repeats his invitation to repentance (3:22), and Jeremiah pictures the nation **weeping and begging for mercy** (3:21). But such a turnaround would not happen in the days of Jeremiah. Rather, what we see here is a picture of Israel's future repentance when her Messiah Jesus Christ returns for his millennial kingdom. **The salvation of Israel is only in the LORD our God** (3:23).

4:1-4 Using a metaphor from farming, God calls Judah to repentance: **Break up the unplowed ground; do not sow among the thorns** (4:3). You need to cultivate good soil if you expect to grow a crop. While the Jews were circumcised in body, they were not set apart in their **hearts**. And unless something changed, God's **wrath** was going to **break out** on them like a **fire** that no one could **extinguish** (4:4). Tragically, though, they

refused to heed God's warning; they rejected his invitation to be forgiven. So, in 4:5–6:30, Jeremiah focuses on the coming judgment—the Babylonian invasion.

4:5-9 God makes it clear that he is using Babylon to accomplish his purposes: **I am bringing disaster from the north** (4:6). The picture he paints of the coming invasion leaves no doubt about the terror in store for Judah. Even **the king and the officials will lose their courage. The priests will tremble in fear, and the prophets will be scared speechless** (4:9). In other words, the leaders from every sphere, who should have led the people to the Lord, will be incapable of leading. This is a perfect illustration of the chaos that ensues when a nation's religious, political, and civil leaders are not following God's kingdom agenda. With both Judah's governmental and spiritual leadership in a mess, the people had little hope of repairing their lives and homes.

4:10 Jeremiah's anguish and horror at the destruction coming upon his nation and people is one of the central themes of the book. In response to God's declaration of judgment, he cries, **Oh no, Lord GOD, you have certainly deceived this people and Jerusalem, by announcing, "You will have peace," while a sword is at our throats.**

The best way to understand this is to see it as Jeremiah's complaint that God had *allowed* the false prophets of Judah to prophesy peace and prosperity when catastrophe was at the door. But we need to remember that God does not deceive or lie; that is contrary to his nature. His apparent deception only comes to people who have already welcomed deception and refuse to repent. God's hard work of judgment in this case was a confirming act to the hard-hearted, not a con of the innocent.

4:11-18 The Babylonian army would sweep across the land like the harsh desert wind, which blew so hard that it parched and cracked the ground. The advancing horses and chariots of Nebuchadnezzar's hordes would stir up **clouds** like those in a coming **storm** (4:13). But in spite of the people's anguish at the terrifying invaders, God leaves no doubt that they had brought this **bitter** judgment on themselves (4:18).

4:19-22 The prophet can taste the same bitterness: **My anguish, my anguish! I writhe in agony! Oh, the pain in my heart!** (4:19). He thus calls the people of Judah **fools** for ignoring God's warnings. They walked headlong into disaster like a bunch of **children** who play in the midst of danger. They were **skilled in doing what is evil, but they [did] not know how to do what is good** (4:22). Experts at wickedness; novices at righteousness. This is the exact opposite of God's will for his children, as Paul writes, "I want you to be wise about what is good, and yet innocent about what is evil" (Rom 16:19).

4:23-26 Jeremiah was so distraught that the only way he could adequately describe what he was hearing was by comparing Judah's judgment to a reversal of God's work in creation (4:23-26). Jeremiah describes **the earth** as **formless and empty** (4:23) to compare Judah's situation to the condition of the world before God began shaping and filling it (see Gen 1:2). Instead of putting **light** in **the heavens**, God had turned it off (4:23). The humans and animals God had created were gone (4:25). All that remained was a **wilderness** because of his **burning anger** (4:26). Creation was being undone.

4:27-31 Knowing the grief of his prophet, God adds a gracious promise. Although the **land** would experience **desolation**, he would **not finish it off** (4:27). He lets Jeremiah know that there would be a future hope. But for the people of Judah in Jeremiah's day, God would not **turn back from** his punishment (4:28). Judah's **lovers**—the foreign nations she had relied upon for aid—would **reject** her (4:30). And **like a woman in labor**, Judah would **cry** in **anguish** when the murderous Babylonians got hold of her (4:31). Normally the cries of a woman about to give birth signal that there is joy ahead, despite the pain. But for the people of Judah, labor would end in a spiritual miscarriage.

5:1 In chapter 5, Jeremiah shines the spotlight on the reasons for Jerusalem's judgment. To open the section, the Lord gives

Jeremiah what would seem like an easy assignment: **If you find one person, any who acts justly, who pursues faithfulness, then I will forgive** Jerusalem. Now, that's a better deal than God granted to Abraham, who received God's promise that Sodom would not be destroyed if there were ten righteous people in it (see Gen 18:32). But Jeremiah couldn't dig up even one person in **the streets of Jerusalem** who followed the Lord. The holy city, then, was worse than Sodom!

5:2-9 Jeremiah was so upset by the thought of his nation's utter destruction that he became convinced the problem was that he was looking on the wrong side of town. He had gone to the **poor** on the other side of the tracks (5:4) and then decided to go to **the powerful**, to the leaders. **Surely they know the way of the LORD** (5:5). But Judah's leaders were no better. Although God had **satisfied their needs**, the people **gashed themselves**—cutting their bodies in pagan rituals (see 1 Kgs 18:28). They committed spiritual **adultery** against the Lord and behaved like prostitutes with idols (5:7).

5:10-11 The house of Israel and the house of Judah were God's **vineyard** (see Isa 5:1-7), but the people had become so unfaithful that God decrees its branches are to be cut back. Yet even in severe judgment, God plants another seed of future hope by saying **do not finish them off** (5:10). The nation would survive in Babylon and eventually be replanted in the land, but that was a long way off.

5:12-19 The false **prophets** gave the people false hope: **Harm won't come to us; we won't see sword or famine** (5:12-13). It was all a lie. The Babylonian army was going to **destroy** everyone and everything in Judah (5:14-17). The devastation would be so great that God had to issue another assurance that he would not wipe his people completely off the map (5:18). Their judgment, however, matched their sin: **Just as you abandoned me and served foreign gods in your land, so will you serve strangers in a land that is not yours** (5:19). If you choose to serve the devil, God will let you do it. But it won't provide the pleasure and freedom you're expecting.

5:20-31 Although God is the Creator of land and **sea** (5:22), and he provided **seasonal rains** to guarantee **the harvest** (5:24), the people had **stubborn and rebellious hearts** (5:23). They didn't **fear** the Lord (5:22)—that is, they didn't take him seriously. The **powerful and rich** became even more so at the expense of others (5:26-27). They failed to defend **the fatherless** and **the needy** (5:28). And where were the spiritual leaders? Verse 31 answers that mystery: **The prophets prophesy falsely, and the priests rule by their own authority.** Jeremiah is right; the situation was **appalling** (5:30). But it gets even worse: **My people love it like this** (5:31). A culture cannot long stand when worship has become corrupted and the worshipers love the corruption.

6:1-12 Fearsome judgment was certain. It was so sure that the only hope of escape was to get **out of Jerusalem** (6:1), which meant running into the arms of the Babylonians. Jeremiah would eventually tell King Zedekiah to do just that, in fact—surrender to the Babylonians so that they might survive (38:17-18). But the king and the people would refuse to listen: **The word of the Lord has become contemptible to them** (6:10). They hated God's Word, which promised them life and blessing. And in rejecting it, they'd run headlong into his **wrath** (6:11).

6:13-15 From prophet to priest, everyone **deals falsely** (6:13) tells us that if the people were sinning, the religious leaders were giving them the example to follow. Those responsible to proclaim God's word and offer sacrifices for sins were leading the way in wickedness! They dealt **superficially** with the **brokenness** of God's people, **claiming, "Peace, peace," when there is no peace** (6:14). They had abdicated their responsibilities and were sugar-coating Judah's situation. Yet they were unashamed (6:15). We can't ignore problems or dance around them. Sin must be confronted.

6:16-30 The people of Judah hadn't merely stumbled into disobedience. They'd boldly **protested, "We won't listen!"** (6:17), and they **paid no attention to** God's words (6:19). Therefore, God pronounced their sacrifices

unacceptable (6:20). As the prophet Samuel had told Israel's first king years before, "To obey is better than sacrifice" (1 Sam 15:22) because when offered from sin-stained hands, offerings to the Lord are detestable. Given Judah's stubborn refusal to repent, the **cruel** Babylonians were coming, and they would **show no mercy** (6:23). God's people **are called rejected silver** (6:30) because they had become corrupted with impurities and could no longer be refined to be of any real worth.

❧ C. Jeremiah's Temple Sermon
(7:1–10:25) ❧

7:1-4 The title of this section comes from God's puncturing the balloon of the people's vain trust in the temple to spare them from judgment. It wasn't that the people weren't worshiping in the Jerusalem temple; rather, they were engaging in hypocritical worship there (7:2). They assumed that the mere presence of the temple in their nation would keep them safe. They even chanted about **the temple of the Lord** (7:4), showing that it was little more than a good-luck charm to them. Therefore, God told Jeremiah to **stand in the gate** of his **house** to announce his judgment (7:2).

7:5-10 God was into true repentance, not magical chants. He thus commanded the people through Jeremiah: **Correct your ways and your actions** (7:5). But he didn't leave that open to interpretation; he gave examples of what he expected. They were not to **oppress** the weak, **shed innocent blood . . . or follow other gods** (7:6). But Jeremiah's exhortations fell on deaf ears. The people just continued to arrogantly break every one of God's commands and then march into the temple with straight faces, saying, **We are rescued, so we can continue doing all these detestable acts** (7:10). They were like children playing tag, treating the temple like a base where they would be safe from harm.

7:11 In essence, God's response was, "Are you serious? You think you can act like that and then come before me for blessing as if I don't know what you're doing?" God's people had so corrupted themselves that they had turned his holy temple into a **den of robbers** (7:11). Later, Jesus took up Jeremiah's words against the people of Israel in his own day; they were also guilty of desecrating God's "house of prayer" (see Matt 21:13).

7:12-15 The Lord then gave Judah a history lesson. The tabernacle was first set up **at Shiloh** (7:12; see Josh 18:1) and remained there for years (see Judg 21:19; 1 Sam 4:3). The Bible doesn't describe what eventually happened to Shiloh (though see Ps 78:60), but archaeological evidence suggests that the Philistines destroyed it in about 1050 BC. The presence of the tabernacle, then, did not save Shiloh from God's judgment (7:12). What happened there would happen in Jeremiah's day: **What I did to Shiloh I will do to the house that bears my name** (7:14). And as he had **banished . . . the descendants of Ephraim** (that is, Israel) through the Assyrians, so God would banish Judah through the Babylonians.

7:16-26 God's wrath was so certain that he even told Jeremiah not to waste his breath praying for Judah (7:16). All of the people, from children to parents, eagerly worshiped **the queen of heaven** (7:18), probably the Assyrian-Babylonian goddess Ishtar who represented love and fertility. Their idolatry provoked God to fierce anger, but this was nothing new. All the way back to the exodus from Egypt and their birth as a nation, Israel had been rebellious and stubborn. God had given them one basic command: **Obey me, and then I will be your God, and you will be my people** (7:23). Yet they **followed their own advice** (7:24).

7:27-34 There was nothing left but to take up a lament for Judah. Jeremiah was ordered to **cut off [his] hair** and sing a funeral **dirge** for the terrible destruction that was coming (7:29). The people had built **high places** to worship false gods and **burn their sons and daughters in the fire** as a sacrifice. Not only had God not commanded this, but he **never entertained the thought** (7:31). Such

horrific crimes against children would not go unpunished.

8:1-7 God's judgment on Judah would be so complete that even the dead would not escape. Their **bones** would be dug up and left to parch, **exposed to the sun, the moon, and all the stars in the sky, which they have loved, served, followed, consulted, and worshiped** (8:1-2). Things would not be any better for the living, who would prefer **death** to life as captives (8:3). Even birds know where to go during various seasons (8:7), but the people of Judah had no sense to turn around when they had gone the wrong way (8:4-5). They lacked the sense to repent of their evil.

8:8-13 Once again, God pointed to the false security of those who thought they were **wise** simply because they had his **law** (8:8). God's word was corrupted by **the lying pen of scribes** (8:8) and the false claims of **prophet** and **priest** (8:10). No one among God's servants charged with teaching his word was speaking the truth. Jeremiah 8:10-12 repeats 6:13-15.

8:14-17 Their refusal to acknowledge what was coming would be rudely interrupted when the reality of the Babylonian invasion could no longer be denied. The people would realize their sin and repent, but it would be too late. Their hopes for peace would turn to **terror** (8:15) as the sound of the Babylonians' **horses** coming **from Dan** in the north echoed (8:16). Their doom was certain, and lest anyone misunderstand the source, Jeremiah made it clear: **This is the LORD's declaration** (8:17). The destruction coming upon them was the judgment God had warned them about through his prophets for years.

8:18-22 Jeremiah's intense pain over the suffering of his people led him into another lament. He asks God to **listen to the cry** of his **people** in captivity who wondered if God was still there (8:19). Their suffering was the result of their sin, but Jeremiah was still **broken by the brokenness** of his countrymen (8:21) and longed for God to apply the healing **balm in Gilead** to their wounds (8:22). May the church of Jesus Christ have the same concern and compassion for the suffering among God's people.

9:1-11 Jeremiah's declaration here shows why he is known as "the weeping prophet": **If my head were a flowing spring, my eyes a fountain of tears, I would weep day and night over the slain of my dear people** (9:1). But Jeremiah was not oblivious to the reason for Judah's judgment. In fact, his righteous soul was offended by their sin, so much so that he wanted to get away from them. They were **all adulterers, a solemn assembly of treacherous** folks (9:2). In a society where lying was commonplace, nobody could trust anyone—not even family (9:3-6). God had every right to judge these people, as Jeremiah well knew (9:9), but that didn't stop the prophet from **weeping** over the land he loved (9:10).

9:17-24 God calls upon professional mourners, who could teach the exiles of Judah to **lament** their fate, too (9:17-19). The picture he gives of the severe massacre of the people of Judah (9:21) is followed by two of the most well-known verses in Scripture: **The wise person should not boast in his wisdom; the strong should not boast in his strength; the wealthy should not boast in his wealth. But the one who boasts should boast in this: that he understands and knows me—that I am the Lord, showing faithful love, justice, and righteousness on the earth, for I delight in these things** (9:23-24).

These are timeless, universal truths—but they take on extra power for us when we see that this invitation from God to know him intimately, and reap the blessings of his covenant faithfulness, was made to a people who called themselves by God's name but refused to surrender their pride and bow before him. It's amazing what we tend to brag about: educational achievements, employment accomplishments, financial successes, physical prowess, and the list goes on. But God says here, "If you're going to brag, if you really want something to shout about, brag that you know me. If you can't talk about that, you don't have much to boast about." We need this lesson today. To know God (not merely to know *about* God) in intimate fellowship is the most meaningful pursuit of life.

9:25-26 Judah refused God's offer to brag on him instead of themselves, so their doom was sealed. The Jews trusted in their special place in God's sight by their confidence in the covenant sign of circumcision. They considered it as another good-luck charm or "get out of jail free" card, protecting them from God's wrath. But God reminds them that circumcision was to be an outward sign of an inner reality: a heart that loved God. He declares that **the whole house of Israel is uncircumcised in heart** (9:26), which in the end is the only circumcision that really counts. In the words of the apostle Paul, "A person is a Jew who is one inwardly, and circumcision is of the heart—by the Spirit, not the letter" (Rom 2:29).

10:1-5 These verses offer a powerful contrast between the God of Israel and **worthless** idols (10:3). Where does an idol come from? If made from wood, it's carved from **a tree**, decorated **with silver and gold**, and held together with **nails** (10:3-4). The futility of worshiping such a thing is unmistakable since those who worship them made them in the first place! Idols are as lifeless as **scarecrows in a cucumber patch**. They can't even move unless someone carries them. So why would anyone be afraid of them (10:5)? Idols are to be mocked, not feared!

10:6-10 In contrast to useless idols, Jeremiah declares, **Lord, there is no one like you. You are great; your name is great in power** (10:6). This is the God whom people should fear—the **King of the nations** who created all things, not an idol created and even dressed by human hands (10:7-10). Scripture teaches that those who make idols and trust in them "are just like them" (Pss 115:8; 135:18). Jeremiah would've agreed. To be **instructed by worthless idols** is to be **both stupid and foolish** (10:8).

10:11 Interestingly, Jeremiah 10:11 is written in Aramaic (a language similar to Hebrew), and is the only such verse in the book. Aramaic was the trade language of Jeremiah's day. So the verse is probably in this language so that the craftsmen and goldsmiths who made the idols (10:9, 14) could understand that **the gods that did not make the heavens and the earth will perish . . . from under these heavens.**

10:12-22 In contrast, the God of Israel is the Creator and Judge of **the earth** who is nothing like the false gods of the nations (10:12-13). Here God calls himself **Jacob's Portion** (10:16), a name that had to encourage Jeremiah. It was a reminder that God would not wipe out Israel forever. But in the immediate future, terrible destruction was ahead for Judah. God's announcement of judgment (10:17-18) again sent Jeremiah into grief and lament on behalf of Judah (10:19-22).

10:23-25 As the prophet's temple sermon concludes, he prays. Speaking as one who identifies with his people, Jeremiah acknowledges that he **is not his own** (10:23). He is a creature in the hands of his Creator; God's agenda, then, is Jeremiah's agenda. He also asks for the Lord to **discipline** him—but not in **anger** (10:24). God's discipline is for our good, if we are willing to receive it. It may be painful. But for those who are trained by it, "it yields the peaceful fruit of righteousness" (Heb 12:11). Finally, Jeremiah asks that God would **pour out [his] wrath on the nations** who don't acknowledge the Lord and who **have consumed** his people (10:25).

➢ D. Judah's Covenant Violations
(11:1–13:27) ❧

11:1-5 We are reminded **that this is the word that came to Jeremiah from the LORD** (11:1). It can be easy to skip over such statements, but this is here because we need the reminder. God is speaking to Jeremiah and, through Jeremiah, to us. In this case, God's message was a restatement of the basic terms of the Mosaic covenant. These were not hard to understand: **obey** God and be blessed, or disobey him and be cursed (11:2-5).

11:6-10 Judah was following an obvious path, so the Lord gave them another history lesson. Their **ancestors** whom God delivered out of

Egypt were given the same commands and the same warning (11:7). **Yet they would not obey**, so God unleashed on them **all the curses of this covenant** (11:8). In spite of hundreds of years of history showing what happened when the Israelites disobeyed God, the people **of Judah** plunged headlong into idolatry and other sins (11:9-10), bringing to mind the old cliché, "like father like son." And this wasn't an innocent oversight or mere childish foolishness. The people of Judah had conspired to disobey God (11:9)—that is, they were very deliberate in their sin.

11:11-23 Your gods are indeed as numerous as your cities, Judah. That's quite an accusation! They had **altars** to **Baal** everywhere (11:13). God was so angry that, once again, he told Jeremiah not to bother praying for Judah to be spared (11:14). The people had shoved Baal worship in God's face, so to speak, and he wasn't going to put up with them anymore. Their reaction to Jeremiah was a classic sinful response: We don't like the message, so let's kill the messenger (11:18-23). Shockingly, the conspirators were **the people of Anathoth,** Jeremiah's home boys (11:21, 23; see 1:1). But God assured the prophet their plot would fail.

12:1-4 This news apparently shook Jeremiah because he responded by complaining about what appeared to him to be the prosperity **of the wicked** (12:1). Jeremiah isn't accusing God of being unjust here, but at the same time he was upset about the way God was handling things. Why wicked people prosper is an age-old question (see Ps 73), but God didn't try to explain himself to Jeremiah because he doesn't have to defend his righteousness or the wisdom of his ways.

12:5-6 Instead, God asked Jeremiah two rhetorical questions (12:5). His point was this: If Jeremiah couldn't handle the present, he'd really have a tough time in the days ahead. There was no one Jeremiah could trust—no one but God.

12:7-17 While Jeremiah was absorbing that warning, God continued pronouncing doom on Judah (12:7-13). The reader of Jeremiah is familiar by now with God's use of a variety of illustrations to describe both the wicked nature of his people and the judgment he intends for them. One of the most powerful is his description of the invading Babylonians as **a sword [of the LORD] that devours** so completely that no one can escape (12:12). This chapter ends with a promise of judgment and restoration—not for Israel this time, but for any Gentile nation that will turn from its rebellion and follow the Lord (12:14-17). This will be fulfilled during Jesus Christ's millennial kingdom.

13:1-5 Judah wasn't responding to Jeremiah's message, so God turned to two object lessons to get his point across. He first ordered Jeremiah to buy **a linen undergarment** (13:1) and wear it. Then the prophet was to go **to the Euphrates and hide it in a rocky crevice** (13:4). The reference here is probably not to the Euphrates River, which would have required a 700-mile round trip for Jeremiah. More likely, it refers to another place a few miles from the prophet's home of Anathoth. In Hebrew, "Euphrates" is spelled "Perath." The site near Anathoth was spelled the same way.

13:6-11 When Jeremiah returned and **dug up** the garment, **it was ruined—of no use at all** (13:7). Similarly, God would **ruin the great pride** of Judah and Jerusalem (13:9). Because of their **stubbornness** and their worship of **other gods**, God's people were now **of no use at all** to him (13:10). They were like a tattered and rotted undergarment. God wanted to "wear" his people close to himself, but they wouldn't have it (13:11). Judah preferred a hole in the ground.

13:12-14 Jeremiah's second object lesson was to point to a **jar . . . filled with wine** (13:12). What was normally a sign of blessing and meant for refreshment thus became a symbol of God's curse on Judah. The people would stagger around like drunks when the Babylonians came. They would **smash** into each other in confusion and terror. But nothing would prevent the Lord from bringing judgment: **I will allow no mercy** (13:14).

13:15-20 The Lord's judgment is pictured here as **darkness** and **darkest gloom** (13:16), and Jeremiah continues to **weep** over the

destruction of his people (13:17). He was told to speak judgment to the eighteen-year-old **king**, Jehoiachin (Jeconiah), and **the queen mother**, Nahushta (13:18; see 2 Kgs 24:8). Jehoiachin reigned in Jerusalem for only three months before the Babylonian captivity. They were exhorted to humble themselves in light of the coming invasion, but they did not.

13:21-27 Jeremiah delivers yet another prophecy of certain doom against a people who were so proud and defiant in their sin. To set up a comparison, he makes a proverbial observation by asking, **Can the Cushite change his skin, or a leopard his spots?** (13:23). In this, Jeremiah was saying that black skin color was as basic to the Cushite/Ethiopian as unrighteous behavior was to the nation of Israel. In other words, it was a permanent characteristic. These people were experts at sinning because it's all they knew. They were like a prostitute who gave herself to anyone who solicited her. But instead of receiving favors and rewards from her "partners," the prostitute Judah would be exposed in **shame**. The only thing left to say was, **Woe to you, Jerusalem!** (13:26-27).

❧ E. Judah's Drought and Jeremiah's Response (14:1–15:21) ❧

14:1-9 One of the covenant curses God sent upon the rebellious people of Judah was **drought** (14:1; see Deut 28:22-24)—so severe that both man and animal alike were in severe distress (14:2-6). The people moaned in thirst and pain, the **cisterns** were **empty**, and the **ground** was **cracked** from lack of moisture (14:2-4). The people began to cry out to God in their suffering and expressed what sounded like genuine repentance (14:7-9). They admitted that they had been very sinful and rebellious, and called God the **Hope of Israel** and their **Savior** (14:8). They reminded God that they carried his **name** (14:9) and pled with him to save them on that basis if for no other reason.

14:10-12 God responded to this apparent confession by saying, in effect, "I hear what these people are saying, but it's all a sham. They are still wandering away from me as fast as **their feet** will carry them. So I will judge them." He was determined to **finish them off by sword, famine, and plague** (14:12). Those who survived these horrors would go into **captivity** (see 15:2).

14:13-16 Jeremiah was greatly distressed because the lying **prophets** of Judah were prophesying relief and **peace** instead of calling on the people to repent (14:13, 15). God denied that any of these prophets spoke on his behalf. Rather than prophesying from a divine perspective, they proclaimed **the deceit of their own minds** (14:14). Therefore, God had determined their fate. Any prophet who denied the approaching sword and famine would himself die by **sword and famine** (14:15). This is a warning that if you refuse to get on board with God's kingdom agenda, you'll be swallowed up by it.

14:17-22 Jeremiah's pain burst out again as he saw the ravages of war and famine around him (14:17-18). The people of Judah then spoke again, confessing their sins and pleading with God to forgive and restore them (14:19-22). Ironically, they became the ones referring to God's **covenant** with Israel, asking *him* to keep it, and freely admitting that the false gods they worshiped were **worthless idols** that had no power (14:21-22). Again, this *sounds* like a broken and contrite people who were ready to return to the Lord who was their true and only hope, but their pleadings were too little, too late. They were trying to make a foxhole deal with God so that he would get them out of their mess.

15:1 God's next answer was even more firm in slamming the door on Judah's insincere repentance. God chose two of the greatest intercessors in Israel's history, **Moses** and **Samuel**, to illustrate the impossibility of anyone changing his mind about his judgment of Judah (15:1). Moses had interceded for Israel after their idolatry with the golden calf (see Exod 32-33). Samuel interceded when they were being threatened by the Philistines (see 1 Sam 7:5-11) and again when the people sinned by asking for a human king (see 1 Sam 12:19-25).

15:2-4 It was too late to intercede on Judah's behalf. Her people were already destined for **death, sword, famine, and captivity** (15:2). The Lord had spoken. To make sure the message was not missed, God added gruesome detail to his pronouncement by saying that the bodies of the Jews who were killed by the invading Babylonians would be devoured by **birds** and **wild animals** (15:3). Because of the horrific acts committed by King **Manasseh** of Judah during his fifty-five-year reign that plunged Judah into the grossest sins imaginable (see 2 Kgs 21:1-16), God was not turning back (15:4).

15:5-7 Then God asked Jerusalem a painful and pointed question: **Who will have pity on you?** Historically, the Lord was the only one who had showed them **sympathy** and was concerned for their **well-being** (15:5). Time and again, though, they had **turned [their] back** on him (15:5-6). So who was left to mourn their pain? Answer: no one.

If human beings show you no concern or pity when you're suffering, you've got a problem. But if God becomes **tired of showing compassion** to you (15:6), you are without hope! That's why the good news of the gospel is so good. In it, God shows his overflowing compassion. Those who repent of their sin and trust in Jesus Christ have the sure hope of forgiveness and eternal life.

15:8-9 This was Judah's situation—and when God began unleashing his judgment, there was no place to hide. As a result of Judah's men being killed in battle, **widows** would become **more numerous than the sand of the seas** (15:8). A **mother of seven** was usually considered greatly blessed, but not in Judah, because her children were gone (15:9).

15:10-14 Here Jeremiah sinks further into despair: **Woe is me, my mother, that you gave birth to me.** In other words, he wishes he had never been born. It's hard to sink lower than that. He lamented his birth because he was the object of Judah's scorn, even though he had done nothing wrong and had been faithful in delivering God's message. That he **did not lend or borrow** means he had engaged in no activity that would give him an opportunity to take financial advantage of others (15:10). Yet, in spite of this, Judah's coming destruction and captivity were inevitable (15:12-14).

15:15-18 Jeremiah returns the conversation to his troubles: I suffer disgrace for your honor (15:15). God's words were a delight to him—he considered them his food (15:16). The prophet had also separated himself from the band of revelers (15:17) who were polluting Judah and Jerusalem with their sins. He sat alone, without friends or anyone to comfort him in his pain. God had become like a mirage to him (15:17-18).

15:19 But it seems the prophet went too far in his self-pity, because the chapter closes with God telling Jeremiah to repent so that he might continue serving God. Rather than sinking to the level of the people and their worthless words, which may refer to their worthless statements of false repentance, Jeremiah was recommissioned to speak the pure words of God. But he warned Jeremiah again not to expect to receive the "Citizen of the Year" award from the Jerusalem Chamber of Commerce for his faithful service. If Jeremiah served God faithfully, he would inevitably be hated by those who hated God.

15:20-21 The people of Judah would continue to fight against God's prophet but would not overcome him. God would make him a fortified wall of bronze against their attacks (15:20). Greater suffering was ahead for Jeremiah; however, he would endure—not because of his strength or will power—but because the Lord would rescue and redeem him (15:21).

Christian, take note. The power of evil people is not ultimate. It is nothing compared to the strong arm of God. Trust him with all your heart and remember his words: I am with you to save you and rescue you (15:20).

☞ F. Jeremiah's Restrictions and Judah's Sins (16:1–17:27) ☜

16:1-4 Next, God called Jeremiah to celibacy. He could not marry or have sons or daughters (16:2). Prohibiting the prophet from taking a wife and having children had

a purpose. Like the prophet Hosea's marriage to the prostitute Gomer (see Hos 1:2-3), Jeremiah's home situation was to be a sign to Judah—a sign of judgment upon God's people. The absence of children in Jeremiah's house was a warning that any children born in the land would die from deadly diseases or be finished off by sword and famine (16:3-4).

16:5-9 Jeremiah was also strictly prohibited from having any personal or social interaction with the people of Judah, whether they were mourning the loss of a loved one or feasting at an occasion for celebration (16:5, 8). Between having no family and not participating in social gatherings, Jeremiah would be a social pariah.

The reason for God's command was important, though: He had so given up on this rebellious and hard-hearted people that he had disowned them. He would no longer lament or rejoice with them, so Jeremiah couldn't either. This was another sign to Judah that the normal activities of life would soon end. The Lord had removed [his] peace . . . as well as [his] faithful love and compassion (16:5). The sound of joy and gladness was being eliminated (16:9).

16:10-13 God told Jeremiah that Judah's spiritually blind people would look him in the face and ask, Why has the LORD declared all this terrible disaster against us? What is our iniquity? What is our sin that we have committed against the LORD our God? (16:10). They were like a child standing over a broken jar with a cookie in each hand, asking his mother, "What cookies?" God told Jeremiah how to answer them (16:11-13). Not only had Judah failed to learn from their stubborn and idolatrous ancestors, but the current generation was even worse: You did more evil than your fathers (16:12). Often the reason we have to repeat history is because we weren't listening the first time.

16:14-15 Once again, even in his severe wrath, God remembered mercy. After announcing his people's impending exile, he added that one day there would be a second exodus. The defining moment in the history of the Jewish nation was exodus from Egypt, but God promised that in the future he would be known—not as the one who brought them out of Egypt—but as the one **who brought the Israelites from the land of the north and from all the other lands where he had banished them** (16:15). Although many Jews would eventually return to their homeland from Babylon, this regathering will be fully realized when Jesus Christ returns to establish his millennial kingdom.

16:16-20 In the meantime, Judah was still doomed to exile for her sins (16:16-18). Since they had filled God's land **with the carcasses** of their sacrificial offerings to **detestable idols**, the Lord would **repay them double for their iniquity** (16:18). The people's wickedness is contrasted with God's kingdom man, Jeremiah, who proclaims the Lord as his **strength, stronghold**, and **refuge**. He knows that one day—not only will Israel abandon her idols—but **the nations** will too (16:19).

17:1-4 Judah's people were such hard-hearted idolaters that even **their children** participated in false worship using **Asherah poles**, idols set up to the Canaanite goddess of fertility (17:2). These evil symbols appeared and disappeared at various times throughout Israel's history. The low point probably came when King Manasseh erected one in the temple, although he later removed it (see 2 Kgs 21:7; 2 Chr 33:15). This was significant because, as we saw above (15:4), God laid a large part of the blame for Judah's pitiful spiritual condition at Manasseh's feet. But as God said, the people of Jeremiah's day had far outdone their ancestors in their disobedience. They had set God's **anger on fire** (17:4). That's a blaze you don't want to be caught in.

17:5-8 Judah was facing the consuming fire of God when her people could have been experiencing his cool refreshment. These verses reveal the stark contrast between two ways of life—either to trust in the strength of mankind and be **cursed**, or to trust in the Lord and be **blessed** (17:5, 7). The picture of a bush in the **Arabah**, the desert portion of Israel, brings to mind the ultimate in dryness and scorching heat; it's **a salt land where no one lives** (17:6). This is probably a reference to the area around the Dead Sea, which is filled with salt and so many other minerals that nothing can survive in it. But the person who trusts the Lord **will be like a tree planted by water** (17:8), which is language reminiscent of the blessed man of Psalm 1.

17:9 One of the most famous verses in Jeremiah comes in this context of people who could sin greatly while asking naïvely, "What sins are we committing?" So God states, **The heart is more deceitful than anything else, and incurable—who can understand it?** Our human capacity to deceive ourselves and to function in rebellion against God is endless. We don't know ourselves as well as we think we do.

17:10-13 But 17:9 also has an important context on the other side. If our only hope for understanding the human heart is other humans, we're in big trouble. So here God adds that he examines **the mind** and tests **the heart** (17:10). This explains why people testify that when they read the Bible, they feel as if it is looking into the deepest recesses of their minds and hearts. They feel this because God's Word is alive and powerful, constantly probing us. It's a good thing to be probed and exposed by the incision that God makes in our lives by his Word (see Heb 4:12), because that's when we really deal with deep-rooted sin and begin to grow. The God who tests and knows the heart is also able to give sinners what they deserve—judgment for abandoning **the LORD, the fountain of living water** (17:13).

17:14-18 Jeremiah ends this message with another plea for God to protect and vindicate him as a faithful spokesman who neither ran from his tough assignment nor wished ill on Judah. And yet he had generated bitter opposition and persecution (17:14-17). Jeremiah prayed that his tormenters would be **put to shame** (17:18)—not out of personal bitterness or revenge but because they had scorned the Lord and his word.

17:19-27 The prophet was then sent on another assignment with a specific message, this one to be delivered to the people face-to-face as they entered **the gates of Jerusalem** (17:19). This word was a warning not to violate the Lord's **Sabbath** as their ancestors had done (17:21-23). But there was a promise in the midst of the warning: If God's people would keep his Sabbath, Israel would enjoy untold blessing, peace, and prosperity (17:24-26). Refusal to obey, however, would result in **fire** consuming **the gates** and **the citadels of Jerusalem** (17:27).

⇝ G. The Potter's Jar and Jeremiah's Persecution (18:1–20:18) ⇜

18:1-4 God sent Jeremiah to **the potter's house** to watch him form pottery from clay. God intended to **reveal [his] words** to Jeremiah through another object lesson (18:2). As the potter molded **the clay** into a **jar**, it **became flawed**. So he remade the jar, **as it seemed right for him to do** (18:4). This illustrated the message of judgment and restoration that Jeremiah was to take to God's people.

18:5-10 God's message to Judah was inextricably clear. Just as a potter has freedom to make what he chooses from his clay, so the sovereign Lord has freedom to save or destroy any nation based on its response to his pronouncement of doom or blessing. Nineveh comes to mind as an example of God relenting in judgment when the Ninevites humbled themselves with repentance in response to Jonah's preaching (see Jonah 3:5-10). The people of Jesus's day were an example of rejecting God's word—in this case the incarnate Word—and turning blessing into cursing (see Matt 12:41).

18:11-12 Jeremiah was to deliver the message and spell out the options (12:11), but God warned him ahead of time what the people's response would be (12:12). They would continue following their stubborn hearts as long as possible.

18:13-17 Judah's rebellion against God was so shocking that even those in **the nations** around her had never heard of such a thing as a people refusing to worship and follow their god (18:13). Judah's wanderings had made her people **stumble** on the well-marked path

of obedience to God (18:15). His destruction of Judah would be so complete that any traveler who passed by would be horrified and **shake** his head (18:16). Worst of all, God would turn his **back** and not his **face** to his people (18:17). Punishment is one thing; the absence of God's presence is everything.

18:18 Yet in spite of God's warnings and in spite of Jeremiah's weeping for them, certain people conspired against the prophet: **Come, let's make plans against Jeremiah.... Come, let's denounce him and pay no attention to all his words.** The prophet's enemies launched a slander campaign against him, hoping to smear Jeremiah's reputation so that no one would take his message seriously.

18:19-23 Here the prophet offers a prayer for God's vengeance on his enemies. They had **repaid** good **with evil** (18:20), and it was time for judgment. Jeremiah had heard God say time and again that Judah was beyond redemption in terms of warding off the coming invasion and captivity. Here he steps back, so to speak, and says, "God, pour out your judgment on my enemies, who are also your enemies. I've done all I can for them. Judge them as their sins deserve."

19:1-2 The Lord sent Jeremiah shopping for **a potter's clay jar.** The jar became another object lesson of God's determination to break Judah. To make the message even more emphatic, Jeremiah delivered it to a group of Judah's civil leaders and **priests** by leading them out to the **Hinnom Valley** near the entrance of **the Potsherd Gate** (19:1-2). The gate was so named because it was the passage through which potters took their potsherds (broken pieces of pottery) to be discarded. The valley mentioned was where the Judeans had previously sacrificed their children to idols (see 7:31). So if ever there was an unholy place, this was it.

19:3-9 Jeremiah delivered another in his series of condemnations on Judah. The people had **burned incense** in Jerusalem to false gods and even offered their children **in the fire as burnt offerings to Baal**, a pagan worship practice so abhorrent to God that he said such things had never entered his mind (19:4-5). As a result of these disgusting practices, God said Hinnom would be called **Slaughter Valley** because the dead bodies of Judah's slain people would pile up and become **food for the birds** and **wild animals** (19:6-7). The nations would gasp in horror at Jerusalem and ridicule its people because of the terrible judgment Judah had brought upon itself (19:8). And in a chilling prophecy, God also warned that the people would resort to cannibalism as the **siege** by the Babylonians cut off Jerusalem's food supply (19:9).

19:10-15 While Jeremiah's listeners were absorbing this grim message, the prophet was to smash the clay **jar** to drive home his point. As one shatters pottery, so the Lord would **shatter** the **people** and the **city** (19:10-11). Jeremiah delivered his message at **Topheth** (19:14), the place in the Hinnom Valley where the people had built high places and offered their child sacrifices (see 7:31). God vowed that they would **bury** their **dead** in that **impure** place (19:11-13). The pieces of the shattered jar lay at Jeremiah's feet as he left Topheth and went back into the city to deliver the same message of disaster to all the people (19:14-15).

20:1-6 Jeremiah had been ridiculed and persecuted previously because of his message, but this time it got physical. He was ordered **beaten** by a man named **Pashhur the priest**, the **chief official in the temple** (20:1-2). Pashhur also put Jeremiah in **stocks** at one of the gates of the temple to publicly humiliate him (20:3).

Jeremiah was let out the next day, but the flogging didn't dampen his commitment to share God's message. He even told Pashhur that the Lord had decided on a new name for him: **Terror Is on Every Side** (20:3), a reference to what this man and his family would experience when God handed **Judah over to the king of Babylon** (20:4). Pashhur and his family would be deported to **Babylon** and **die** there, in part because Pashhur had **prophesied lies** of his own—perhaps in an attempt to discredit Jeremiah's message (20:6).

20:7-10 The remainder of the chapter records Jeremiah's reaction to these events. It starts with complaint against his enemies. Jeremiah had never been shy about expressing his

emotions, and he also complains that God had **deceived** him by calling him into a ministry in which he experienced so much abuse and emotional pain (20:7). But Jeremiah is not charging God with being unfair or dishonest. He knew his message was from the Lord, and even when he tried to hold it back, God's word was like a **fire burning in** Jeremiah's **heart** that couldn't be contained (20:9). He had no choice but to speak what God gave him—even though everyone sought **vengeance on him** (20:10).

20:11-13 Then the prophet looked upward and broke out in praise to the God who was **like a violent warrior** on his side, able to bring down on the heads of Jeremiah's enemies the **vengeance** they had planned for him (20:11-12). Even though he was probably still in pain from his beating (20:2), Jeremiah found his voice to offer a song of praise to the Lord (20:13). This calls to mind Paul and Silas praying and singing praises to God in the Philippian jail after being beaten and put in stocks (see Acts 16:22-25).

20:14-18 In spite of his song of praise, Jeremiah's lament here is as strong as anything he wrote even at his worst times. He wishes he had never been **born** rather than to witness the destruction around him (20:14, 18). This is like the prayers of Job who suffered as much as any person ever has. Clearly Jeremiah's emotions are fluctuating in the midst of his distress—as anyone's would.

H. Final Messages of Judah's Judgment (21:1–25:38)

In 21:1-7, Jeremiah has a response for King Zedekiah, the last king of Judah before the nation's fall to Babylon. Chapter 22, however, addresses the three kings who immediately preceded Zedekiah. This demonstrates that Jeremiah's book does not always follow a neat chronological order.

21:1-2 With the Babylonian armies besieging Jerusalem, **King Zedekiah** was hoping for a word of deliverance from God. So he sent to Jeremiah two of his officials, **Pashhur**

(not the Pashhur of 20:1) and **Zephaniah** (21:1). The king wanted the Lord to **perform . . . something like all his past wondrous works so that Nebuchadnezzar** would **withdraw** (21:2). Zedekiah was probably referring to the days of King Hezekiah, when the Lord supernaturally routed the Assyrians (see 2 Kgs 18–19).

21:3-7 But that was then, and this is now. Jeremiah had no such message of rescue for Zedekiah—and this evil king should not have expected one. Instead of delivering the city, God himself would fight against it with **a strong arm**—a metaphorical way of referring to his omnipotent power (21:5). Many would die from **the plague, the sword, and** the **famine** (21:7). Zedekiah himself, in fact, would be handed over to **King Nebuchadnezzar of Babylon** who would not **show pity or compassion** (21:7). While that wasn't the response Zedekiah was looking for, it's a reminder that God acts in accordance with his agenda, not ours. We are to conform to his kingdom plans, not expect him to bless our programs.

21:8-10 This message of doom to Judah's leaders was followed by a plea to the people of Jerusalem to choose **life** or **death** (21:8). Through Jeremiah, God spelled out the consequences of each choice in the clearest terms. He had already decreed that Jerusalem would be handed over to the Babylonians and destroyed, in spite of futile hopes of deliverance or military victory. Those who held out in Jerusalem would die by God's three familiar forms of judgment: **the sword, famine, and plague.** Those who surrendered to the Babylonians (**Chaldeans**) would save their lives—although they'd be led into captivity (21:9). Because anyone who went over to the enemy was considered a traitor, this was not an easy choice to make. But the Lord of heaven and earth insisted there was no other hope.

21:11-14 The rest of the chapter makes clear that a large portion of the blame for Judah's sins could be laid at the foot of the throne in Jerusalem, where the kings had failed in the spiritual leadership role. The kings of Judah were part of no ordinary royal house;

they were the descendants of David, the one through whom Messiah would come. If any kings should have practiced righteousness and justice, then, it was the kings of the **House of David** (21:12).

David was "a man after [God's] own heart" (1 Sam 13:14), so it must have been painful for God to address such a sorry bunch as Zedekiah and his predecessors as part of the Davidic line. If Zedekiah thought that being David's successor gave him an insider advantage with God, he was sorely mistaken. Being David's descendent gave one no advantage unless it was accompanied by obedience. The Lord's message was, **Beware! I am against you** (21:13). The Babylonian siege ramps being built outside the walls of Jerusalem should have driven Zedekiah and his officials to their knees.

22:1-9 Jeremiah was told to take a message from God to **the king of Judah** (22:1). God's demand was straightforward: **Administer justice and righteousness** (22:3). Such was the burden on the shoulders of the Lord's king. This included treating fairly those who were being oppressed, such as **the resident alien, the fatherless, [and] the widow** (22:3). Obedience to God's commands would bring blessing and the continuance of David's line ruling in Jerusalem, but disobedience from **the house of the king of Judah** would turn Judah and its cities into **a wilderness** (22:6). The people of other nations would ask how that could happen to such a **great city** as Jerusalem (22:8), and those who had been their pagan neighbors would answer: God's people **abandoned the covenant of the LORD their God and bowed in worship to other gods and served them** (22:9). Make no mistake: your spiritual commitments have significant consequences for you and for those around you.

22:10-12 In the rest of the chapter, the Lord addressed Zedekiah's three predecessors: Shallum (Jehoahaz), Jehoiakim, and Coniah (Jehoiachin). The actions of these kings, and their corresponding judgment by the Lord, should have served as object lessons for Zedekiah not to follow their destructive and evil ways. But the lessons were lost on Judah's final king. The first of these three rulers was **Shallum** (22:11), also known as Jehoahaz. He was a son of good King Josiah. God didn't have much to say to Shallum. He was doomed to **die** in Egypt and **never return** to the Holy Land (22:11-12). Shallum's reign had lasted only three months before Pharaoh Neco deposed him and took him into captivity in Egypt.

22:13-17 Jehoiakim succeeded Shallum on the throne in Jerusalem, but he was spiritually bankrupt. He was a puppet king installed by the Egyptians and was so self-serving and corrupt that he made his subjects work for him **without pay** to build him **a massive palace** of cedar (22:13-14). Tragically, he too was a son of Josiah, one of Judah's most righteous kings who led a much-needed revival and cared deeply about his people. Josiah administered **justice and righteousness** and **took up the case of the poor and needy** (22:15-16). But his son only cared about making **dishonest profit**. Moreover, he was not above **shedding innocent blood and committing extortion and oppression** (22:17) to get what he wanted.

22:18-23 Jehoiakim was so despised that no one would **mourn for** him at his death; instead, his body would be **dragged off and thrown outside Jerusalem's gates** (22:18-19). Meanwhile, the people of Jerusalem would wail and lament when their captivity came. **Like a woman in labor**, they would **groan** in pain (22:23).

22:24-30 The third king addressed in Jeremiah's series of messages was Jehoiachin, also known as **Coniah** or Jeconiah (22:24; see Matt 1:11). God's word to this man was filled with judgment and even contempt, calling him **a despised, shattered pot** (22:28). Coniah was so useless to the Lord that he placed a severe curse on this king and his family, saying none of Coniah's descendants would sit **on the throne of David** (22:30).

This curse has serious messianic implications, for the Messiah was to come from David's line. And surprisingly, Coniah appears in Jesus's genealogy in Matthew (as Jeconiah; see Matt 1:11). Had Jesus been Joseph's biological son, then, he would have been prevented from sitting on the throne of David by this curse. But of course, Jesus was not conceived by Joseph but by the Holy Spirit. So since Joseph was Jesus's legal father, but not his biological father, Jesus was not contaminated by the curse on Jeconiah's descendants.

The Messiah, though, still had to have a biological tie to David, which Jesus had—as demonstrated in Luke's genealogy (see Luke 3:23-38). Luke traced Jesus's lineage back to David through Solomon's son Nathan, in what many commentators agree was the genealogical line of Mary, who *was* Jesus's biological mother.

23:1-4 The Lord declared **woe** on **the shepherds** who had destroyed and scattered **the sheep of [his] pasture** (23:1). These uncaring, faithless leaders of Judah would be destroyed and the people would go into exile. But the day will come when God will regather his flock and **raise up shepherds over them who will tend them** (23:4). In those days, his people will be cared for and have nothing to fear.

23:5-8 If 23:3-4 sounded good to Jeremiah's first readers, they hadn't heard anything yet. Through his prophet, the Lord here declares that he will **raise up a Righteous Branch for David**—signaling new growth from the Davidic tree (23:5; see 33:15; Isa 11:1; Zech 3:8). Unlike Zedekiah and his predecessors, this king will **administer justice and righteousness** (23:5). During his reign, **Judah ... and Israel will dwell securely**. Who is this king? What is his name? **He will be called: The Lord Is Our Righteousness** (23:6). God is predicting the coming of his Son, the Messiah, the Lord Jesus Christ. He will rule in righteousness for a thousand years in his millennial kingdom. And he will have the nation of Israel to govern, when God gathers the Jews and returns them to the land of Israel from all the **countries** where they had been **banished** (23:8).

23:9-14 But in the immediate context of Jeremiah's day, God still had false prophets to deal with. These were the liars who denied Jeremiah's message and lulled the people of Judah into a false security even as the Babylonians marched toward Jerusalem: **Both**

prophet and priest are ungodly, even in my house I have found their evil (23:11). They polluted the temple with their sins and idolatry. The false prophets preached peace to the people, and the priests led them in serving their idols. Just as the prophets of Samaria in the northern kingdom led . . . Israel astray (23:13), so the prophets of Judah were so gross in their immorality that the Lord compared them to Sodom and Gomorrah (23:14). Their judgment was certain.

23:15-32 God's counsel to the people of Judah and Jerusalem was simple: Do not listen to the words of the prophets because their visions come from their own minds, not from [my] mouth (23:16). In other words, God had not sent them; they had not stood in his presence; they were not communicating his word; he, in fact, was against them (23:21-22, 31-32). God couldn't have spoken more clearly.

The prophets' assurances of peace and safety to Judah were diametrically opposed to God's commands to repent (25:17-18). If God's Word clearly condemns your actions and someone assures you that no harm will come to you (23:17), you'd better find a new counselor. Otherwise, prepare to meet the wrath and anger of God (23:19-20). His word is like fire; it's like a hammer that pulverizes rock (23:29). If you play a game of chicken with God's Word on any matter, there's only one possible outcome for you: getting pulverized.

23:33-40 It's also clear that God was tired of hearing the lying prophets try to authenticate their messages by saying, The burden of the LORD (23:34), as if it were a magic formula. God holds his Word in high esteem. David said of the Lord, "You have exalted your name and your promise above everything else" (Ps 138:2). So it's not surprising that God told the false prophets of Judah to quit misusing his name and pretending to speak on his behalf. Those who disobeyed faced everlasting disgrace and humiliation (23:40).

24:1-10 Jeremiah's next prophecy to the rebellious leaders and people of Judah began with a vision that once again turned the false prophecies of the false prophets

on their heads. This vision was given after Nebuchadnezzar had sent Jeconiah (Jehoiachin), his officials, and Judah's craftsmen and metalsmiths to Babylon. The two baskets of figs Jeremiah saw couldn't have differed from one another more: there were ripe, edible figs and rotten, disgusting ones (24:1-2). They represented two groups of people: those who had gone into captivity and those who stayed in Judah or fled to Egypt (24:5, 8).

One might think the exiles were the bad figs and the latter were the good figs, but not so. The exiles who went to Babylon actually were sent away by the Lord (24:5). They went with his promise of restoration once their hearts had turned fully back to him (24:6-7). "Seventy years" in exile would finally get their attention (see 25:1-14).

King Zedekiah, Judah's final king, and those with him were the bad figs (24:8). They continued to disobey God and would experience his curse (24:9-10). Jeremiah warned Zedekiah to surrender to Nebuchadnezzar, but he wouldn't listen (see 38:14-28). He also advised those who rebelled against Nebuchadnezzar not to flee to Egypt, but they rejected his counsel (see 42:1–44:14). Therefore, God condemned them to be an object of scorn, ridicule, and cursing (24:9). Those who are determined to act like rotten fruit can't complain when they're treated like rotten fruit.

25:1-7 Chapter 25 marks the end of Jeremiah's prophecies of doom for Judah as far as the arrangement of the book is concerned. The date for this chapter places it even earlier than the previous message, around 604 BC, at the beginning of Nebuchadnezzar's reign (25:1). But the topical way the book is arranged makes this message the climax of Jeremiah's warnings to Judah. God's faithful prophet had been at it for twenty-three years (25:3), and more suffering lay ahead.

I don't know any pastor who would have wanted the flock Jeremiah oversaw. After all those years of delivering God's word to them, Jeremiah could probably have counted his "converts" on one hand, with fingers left over. He himself said, I have spoken to you time and time again, but you have not obeyed . . . or even paid attention

(25:3-4). As a result, God declared that the people of Judah had **brought disaster on** themselves (25:7).

25:8-14 Because of this disobedience, there would be **seventy years** of captivity in **Babylon** (25:11). But God immediately added that when he was finished using Babylon as his instrument of judgment, he would **punish the king of Babylon and that nation** and **make it a ruin forever** (25:12). The prophet Daniel was probably reading this portion of Jeremiah's prophecy when he realized that "the number of years for the desolation of Jerusalem would be seventy" and prayed for God to end the exile and restore his people to their land (Dan 9:2-3).

The number "seventy" wasn't chosen out of thin air. Over the years, Israel had failed to obey the law of Sabbath rest for the land, which required it to lie fallow every seventh year (see Lev 25:1-7). The people hadn't failed to do this once or twice—but for 490 years! That equates to a total of seventy missed Sabbath years. God would see to it that his land received its rest—with his people's obedience or without it. According to the Chronicler, the seventy-year exile "fulfilled the word of the LORD through Jeremiah, and the land enjoyed its Sabbath rest . . . until seventy years were fulfilled" (2 Chr 36:21). The Lord is "slow to anger" (Exod 34:6), but that doesn't mean he forgets.

25:15-26 The **cup of the wine of [God's] wrath** (25:15) is a familiar biblical image for the stored-up judgment of a holy God against sin. Jeremiah was to make many **nations** drink from it (25:15, 17). Sadly, **Jerusalem and the other cities of Judah** were to be the first ones to do so (25:18). But all the surrounding nations and cities that had provoked the Lord to anger were also ripe for judgment (25:18-26).

25:27-29 An important principle of biblical justice is embedded in this prophecy. If God was going to righteously judge the people and the city that were called by his **name** (25:29), then those who did not acknowledge him could not expect to avoid judgment for their sins. And one of the sins for which Judah was repeatedly condemned was mistreatment of

the poor and defenseless among her people. Also, one of the things that angered God most about the nations mentioned earlier in the chapter is that even though they were Israel's relatives, they harassed the Jews on their journey to the promised land and picked off the weak and defenseless.

Old Testament prophets like Jeremiah regularly condemned the people of Israel for their social injustices as well as their idolatry. Injustices were not merely viewed as secular affronts to communities, but also as a spiritual affront to God (see Zech 7:9-12). God's people were specifically instructed to seek the welfare of the secular city in which they were living and to pray for its well-being so that it would become a better place to live, work, and raise their families—as we will see in Jeremiah 29.

Therefore, the role of the church today, and of believers who comprise the church, is to execute divine justice on behalf of the defenseless, poor, and oppressed. Scripture relates biblical justice distinctly to these groups as a primary concern because they most often bear the brunt of injustices. We are not to mistreat the poor (see Jas 2:15-16) or have class and racial prejudice (see Gal 2:11-14). Rather, the church is commissioned to meet the physical needs of the "have nots" within it and in society.

This is not, however, to be confused with subsidizing irresponsibility, which the Bible strictly prohibits (see Prov 6:9-11; 10:4; 13:18; 24:30-34; 2 Thess 3:10). Even in the biblical practice of gleaning—leaving behind portions of a harvest for the poor to collect— the poor needed to exercise responsibility in gathering what had been left behind (see Lev 23:22). The amount of work that was put forth resulted in the amount of food obtained. The church is to work for conditions under which all people have the same opportunity to provide for themselves and their families. That's also the job of our governmental leaders in their spheres of responsibility.

25:30-38 Jeremiah was commanded to relay the Lord's judgment against the nations. Like a lion ready to pounce, God **roars** against them (25:30). The nations of Jeremiah's day were cruel and oppressive, so fierce judgment was coming that would bring **disaster**

(25:32). The **leaders** of the nations were warned: The lion **has left his den.** The LORD's **burning anger** would not be quenched (25:36-38).

This is where the prophetic section of Jeremiah comes to an end. He had warned and pled for repentance, but Judah would have none of the Lord's fatherly discipline. The only thing left was to experience his righteous wrath.

✧ I. Jeremiah's Conflict with Judah
(26:1–29:32) ✧

26:1-6 The message recorded here was actually delivered earlier, **at the beginning of the reign of Jehoiakim son of Josiah** (26:1), probably in 609–608 BC. It contained the same warning of God's judgment and offer to spare Judah if the people repented that Jeremiah proclaimed throughout his ministry. But this time the response to it was recorded.

26:7-11 Who responded? **The priests, the prophets, and all the people** (26:7-8). And rather than repenting, they were so furious at Jeremiah for his prophecy of doom for the **temple** and Jerusalem that they wanted to kill him (26:8-9). They even grabbed the prophet and dragged him to the temple for a trial! The city officials gathered at the **New Gate of the LORD's temple**, where the priests and prophets themselves called for the **death** penalty on God's spokesman—another indication of how far Judah had sunk into sin (26:10-11).

26:12-15 Jeremiah's defense was simple but powerful. He had not spoken on his own, but God had sent him **to prophesy all the words** he had shared (26:12). In fact, Jeremiah began and ended his defense with a plea to God's authority on him and his message (26:12, 15). Remember, then, that when you faithfully proclaim God's truth, it's backed by his authority, not yours.

Jeremiah also reminded the court that even though his word from the Lord contained a message of judgment on Judah, there was also the offer of forgiveness. In other words, Jeremiah was not simply bashing his people or giving them no chance to turn away God's wrath. God was willing to **relent concerning the disaster he had pronounced** (26:13). However, if these rulers put God's prophet to death, they would **bring innocent blood** upon their own heads and upon the city (26:15).

26:16 Wiser heads prevailed, and Jeremiah was spared execution. Interestingly, **all the people**, the same crowd that had helped drag him away to trial in the first place, changed their minds. They agreed with **the officials** and **told the priest and prophets, "This man doesn't deserve the death sentence, for he has spoken to us in the name of the LORD our God!"** The wicked priests and prophets, however, obviously didn't agree (26:7-8)—which made for a sorry picture of Judah's spiritual condition.

Here we see the kingdom agenda in reverse. The secular officials and the people did what the nation's spiritual leaders should have done—that is, recognize and authenticate God's true word spoken by his true prophet, and then lead the way in repentance.

26:17-24 Some of the wisest **elders of the land** cited a precedent for listening to, rather than executing, Jeremiah: the case of the prophet **Micah**, who brought a similar message during the reign of **Hezekiah** (26:17-18). That **king** listened to God's prophet and led Judah in repentance that delayed God's hand of judgment (26:19). Their input helped Jeremiah win his release (26:24).

The text includes a historical note about an otherwise unknown prophet of Jeremiah's time named **Uriah son of Shemaiah** (26:20). His message of judgment so infuriated the evil **King Jehoiakim** that he sent men to Egypt to extradite Uriah back to Judah after he had fled for his life. Uriah was **executed** (26:21-23), so Jeremiah had plenty of cause to be on edge.

27:1-11 Jehoiakim's successor **Zedekiah**, the last **king of Judah** before its fall, learned nothing from the experiences of his predecessors when it came to obeying God's word. Through Jeremiah, the Lord told Zedekiah to submit to Nebuchadnezzar and live, rather than resist and be crushed. But Zedekiah refused (see 38:14-28).

The kings of five other nations sent **messengers** (27:3) to Jerusalem asking Zedekiah to join them in a rebellion against Babylon, but Jeremiah was waiting for these envoys with a stark message of the futility of their plans. The prophet went to the court in Jerusalem with **chains and yoke bars** hanging around his neck as a warning not to try what they were planning, but to allow **Nebuchadnezzar** to put his yoke on them and take them away to Babylon (27:2-7).

Since these representatives were from pagan countries, it was time to identify the true God—**the LORD of Armies, the God of Israel** (27:4). There was no time for messing around. Jeremiah's word to them came from the Creator of the universe, who held all the nations in his hands and could do with them whatever he pleased (27:5). God had decreed that **all** lands would have to submit to **Babylon** until that great kingdom's own time of judgment and collapse came (27:6-7). Any nation that rejected the Lord's command, then, would be devastated by his threefold messengers of suffering: **sword, famine, and plague** (27:8). God also added a warning for these pagan envoys: **You should not listen to your prophets, diviners, dreamers, fortune-tellers, or sorcerers who say to you, "Don't serve the king of Babylon!" They are prophesying a lie** (27:9-10).

27:12-15 The sad thing is that God had to give **Zedekiah** the same warning through Jeremiah about the lying **prophets** of Judah (27:12, 14). The king was putting his hopes in these false preachers who were assuring him Judah would never be taken (27:14-15)! However, Zedekiah desperately needed to understand that submitting to Babylon was the only hope he and the people had if they wanted to live.

27:16-22 Then Jeremiah **spoke to the priests and ... people** with the same warning not to believe their false **prophets** (27:16). Here we learn one specific way in which they were lying. When Nebuchadnezzar deported the first exiles from Judah in about 609 BC, including Daniel and his three friends, he took some of the "vessels" from the temple to Babylon (see

Dan 1:1-7). Now it was about sixteen years past that time (the message of chapter 27 was probably given about 593 BC, judging by the time stamp of 28:1). Those temple **articles** were still in Babylon, but the false prophets boldly predicted that these items would be soon returned (27:16). According to Jeremiah, though, not only would the stolen articles remain in Babylon, but even the items currently in the temple would be carried off (27:17-22).

28:1-4 One of the false prophets who continually preached a prosperity gospel of success and restoration for Judah was **Hananiah** (28:1). He insisted that the nation's trouble with Babylon was just a two-year problem, not a seventy-year captivity (28:3). All would soon be resolved. Hananiah wasn't bashful about his lies either, spouting them to Jeremiah **in the temple** in front of **the priests and all the people** (28:1). His prophecy announced the return of the exiled king **Jeconiah**, the exiles, and the temple treasures to Jerusalem (28:3-4). Hananiah even stole Jeremiah's signature phrase: **This is the LORD's declaration** (28:4). Speaking lies is one thing; putting them in the mouth of the Lord is a whole other matter. Such audacity would cost Hananiah his life.

28:5-9 Surprisingly, Jeremiah declared, **Amen! May the LORD do that.** He did this not because Hananiah's words were true but because Jeremiah *wished* that this optimistic message could be true (28:6). Unfortunately, it was contrary to what God had revealed to Jeremiah and other true prophets in times past (28:8). Then Jeremiah stated the test of a true prophet: **Only when the word of the prophet comes true will the prophet be recognized as one the LORD has truly sent** (28:9; see Deut 18:20-22). Hananiah's prophecy wouldn't meet the standard.

28:10-17 This all happened as Jeremiah was still wearing **the yoke** God had commanded him to make as an object lesson (28:10; see 27:2). Hananiah dramatically snatched the yoke from Jeremiah's neck, broke it, and repeated his false prophecy about Babylon's doom (28:10-11). But God was not impressed. He simply issued a new word through

Jeremiah to Hananiah: I have put an iron yoke on the neck of all these nations that they might serve King Nebuchadnezzar of Babylon (28:14). And as for Hananiah, he died the same year (18:15-17).

Hananiah's lying and strutting were pointless. The Lord God, the King of the universe, is sovereign. Any attempt to oppose his agenda will fail. He will always accomplish his purposes—with or without you. Will you join his kingdom work and experience blessing, then, or oppose him and be put to shame?

29:1-3 Chapter 29 includes **the text of the letter** that Jeremiah sent to those **deported from Jerusalem to Babylon** (29:1). As a result of the damaging lies spread by false prophets like Hananiah, the exiles had been encouraged to become passive in their captivity, sitting around waiting for a quick release that wasn't coming (see 29:8-9). Jeremiah's letter offered a reliable ray of light to them, but it also includes a critically important message for believers today. It teaches the foundational principle that society is transformed when God's people execute his agenda in history. Through Jeremiah, God laid out his strategy for the Israelites in Babylon, explaining how to live and prosper in a pagan land.

29:4 The first thing the exiles needed to learn was that the Babylonians were not to blame for their captivity. In the grand scheme of things, *God* had **deported** them **to Babylon**. Nebuchadnezzar was merely the instrument God used to punish them for their sins. God's message through Jeremiah here was essentially this: "You're in this mess because I sent you there. And I sent you there because you forgot me." It was their failure to be God's distinct people who worshiped him alone that caused God to judge them.

29:5-6 God's agenda for the exiles covered everything from their employment to building their families. Hananiah had led the people to believe they would return home soon (28:11), as if they didn't need to do anything. But God told them, **Build houses and live in them. Plant gardens and eat their produce. Find wives for yourselves, and have sons and daughters. Find wives for your sons and give your daughters to men in marriage so that they may bear sons and daughters. Multiply there; do not decrease.**

As it was with the Babylonian exiles, so it is with Christians today. We need to prepare to do life because we might be here for a while. God wanted his people to establish a kingdom presence in exile. Building houses and planting gardens suggests ownership, a key element of a kingdom economic strategy. And ownership always requires some sort of investment. God told the exiles that while they were waiting for a better *tomorrow*, they were to be industrious *today*.

The exiles of Judah needed to understand that the Babylonians were not their problem; God was. And if God is your problem, then God is your only solution. It doesn't matter whom we elect or what programs we start if we lose our spiritual perspective. We have to see that God put us here for a reason. Earth is not merely a place to wait for a ride to heaven. It's where we live out God's kingdom agenda in history.

29:7-9 Pursue the well-being of the city I have deported you to. Pray to the Lord on its behalf, for when it thrives, you will thrive implies that God didn't want the Jews to build walls around their homes and create a Jewish subculture within Babylon to shield themselves from the pagans. One reason the wheels are coming off of our culture morally, in fact, is that for too many years, Christians have secluded themselves within churches. We have abandoned the culture to Satan. But God's message is to pursue the good of the culture in which we live—not necessarily the so-called good that the culture wants but the good it needs. We are to pursue the social and spiritual wellbeing of the community where we live, work, and raise families, which will result in improved lives for us.

29:10-14 God promised to **restore** his people when the **seventy years** of captivity ended (29:14, 10). Many Christians are familiar with Jeremiah 29:11, but they don't know its context. **For I know the plans I have for you . . . plans for your well-being, not for disaster, to give you a future and a hope** (29:11). This is God's promise to bless his people in the midst of a pagan culture. And it takes on greater significance when it's seen in the context of exile with no apparent hope (29:11).

Notice, though, that this promise was conditioned on God's people seeking him in a new way: **You will . . . find me when you search for me with all your heart** (29:13). The economic titans and power brokers of the world can't help us like God can, but enjoying this kind of blessing requires seeking God wholeheartedly. This demands more than attending church on Sunday, tapping our feet to the music, hearing a sermon, and saying, "Amen." Unless we commit our hearts to the Lord 24/7, we will be no different twelve months from now. But when we worship and obey the Lord through our day-to-day walk with him, he's ready to communicate with us and even reverse our circumstances.

29:15-19 Despite God's strategy and promises for the welfare of his people in exile, they were deceived initially by false prophets telling them not to unpack their bags in Babylon (see 29:8-9). They had begun to listen to these fake messengers and longed to be back in Jerusalem. But the Lord reveals through Jeremiah what awaits those in Jerusalem—from **the king sitting on David's throne** to **all the people** in the city (29:16). They will meet with **sword, famine, and plague** (29:17-18).

29:20-32 Jeremiah's letter punctured the fantasy spread by the false prophets. God even called out several of them by name, including **Ahab son of Kolaiah** and **Zedekiah son of Maaseiah** (29:21). Not only had they spoken lies in God's name, but they had also committed **adultery with their neighbors' wives**—a reminder that wicked theology is often accompanied by a wicked lifestyle (29:23). What price did they pay for their wickedness? **The king of Babylon roasted [them] in the fire** (29:22). God also condemned **Shemaiah**, another false prophet who wrote letters to the people and the priests that they should confine Jeremiah **in the stocks and an iron collar** for being a **madman who acts like a prophet** (29:24-26). God assured the exiles that **Shemaiah** would be wiped out for his **rebellion** (29:32).

ᴊ. *Judah's Hope of Future Restoration* (30:1–33:26)

30:1-3 These chapters illustrate a common biblical prophetic technique in which a prophet speaks of two events—events that may be widely separated in fulfillment—as if they immediately followed each other. It's as if the prophet were seeing and describing two distant mountain peaks—one behind the other—without describing the long valley between them. Often, in fact, the prophet himself didn't see the valley because God didn't reveal all the details to him. The most obvious examples of such prophecies are those that speak of Christ's first and second coming in the same breath, as in Isaiah 61:1-3. Some of Jeremiah's prophecies of Judah's restoration occurred in history, while others can only be accomplished when Christ returns.

God promises that **the days are coming . . . when [he] will restore the fortunes of . . . Israel and Judah** (30:3). This looks forward to the end of time, because the northern kingdom of Israel was not impacted by Judah's captivity, having gone into captivity itself well over a century earlier. This promise gave hope to the people of Judah, who were on the verge of defeat and captivity at the hands of the Babylonians. And there was hope for Israel too, as God prophesied a day when the two kingdoms would again join together as one in the promised land.

30:4-7 But first, the nation would have to undergo intense suffering: **a time of trouble for Jacob** (30:7). The language here is so strong that it seems to go beyond Judah's defeat by Babylon—as terrifying and destructive as that was. The Hebrew phrase translated "time of trouble" is the same phrase translated in Daniel 12:1 as "time of distress." Both passages speak of this time period as worse than any the world has ever seen: **There will be no other like it** (30:7); "such as never has occurred since nations came into being until that time" (Dan 12:1).

This is a picture of the coming seven-year great tribulation immediately preceding Christ's return. Matthew describes it in language similar to that of the Old Testament prophets: "For at that time there will be great distress, the kind that hasn't taken place from the beginning of the world until now and never will again" (Matt 24:21; see commentary on Dan 9:24-27; Matt 24). It will be a time of unparalleled suffering for Israel until Jesus appears to judge her enemies and rescue her. Jeremiah compared this time of dread to the pain experienced by **a woman in labor** (30:6). Matthew also described these end time events as "labor pains" (Matt 24:8).

30:8-11 The promise of Israel's deliverance at the end of 30:7 leads to a further prophecy of blessing and restoration. **Strangers will never again enslave** Israel, and God will raise up **David their king** (30:8-9) to rule over them. Christ, the Messiah from the line of David, will rescue and restore his people. In the meantime, they had no reason to **be afraid** because he promised to **save** them, return them from **captivity**, and **bring destruction** on their enemies (30:10-11).

30:12-17 This led to a restatement of Judah's current desperate, sinful condition that left the nation with gaping wounds that no one could heal (30:12-15). Yet, "what is impossible with man is possible with God" (Luke 18:27). The Lord would intervene. Judah's enemies would **be devoured**, and God would **heal** her **wounds** (30:16-17).

30:18-24 This promise included a glorious restoration of the people in the promised land (30:18). Even though Israel has been back in her territory since the rebirth of the nation in 1948, most of the Jewish people continue to disbelieve the gospel of Jesus Christ. In that day, Israel's leader **will be one of them** (30:21), instead of a foreign tyrant like Nebuchadnezzar. When many Jews embrace Jesus as their Messiah during his millennial kingdom (see Rom 11:25-27), God will again gladly identify with Israel (30:22). Until then, however, **the LORD's burning anger** would not be quenched until he had finished his hard work of judgment. But **in time to come**, they **will understand** (30:24).

31:1-30 Jeremiah 31 is one of the greatest mountain peaks of the Old Testament, encompassing both the glorious restoration of Israel under Jesus her Messiah and the prophecy of the new covenant that was inaugurated in his death and resurrection. The bulk of the chapter (31:1-30) is a beautiful prophecy of God's Father-love for Israel and his tenderness in restoring the nation both to her land and to himself. Jeremiah received this prophecy as he slept (31:26).

Israel **will be rebuilt** and praise the Lord their God (31:4-6). He will **gather them from the nations** (31:8, 10), and they will be filled with **joy** (31:12-13). As the Lord was the one **to uproot and to tear them down**, so he will be the one **to build and to plant them** (31:28). Jeremiah depicts **Rachel**, the wife of Jacob (see Gen 29:28), **weeping for her children**, the people of Israel who had gone into exile. But God promises future joy, for the **children will return. . . . There is hope** (31:15-17). Similarly, Matthew sees "Rachel weeping" at Herod's massacre of the children as he sought to slay the young Jesus (see Matt 2:16-18). But, again, this grief will one day turn to joy when many Jewish people receive their Messiah during his millennial reign (see Rom 11:25-27).

31:31-34 This section includes the glorious promise of the new covenant. This **new covenant** that God will make **with the house of Israel and the house of Judah** will be unlike the one he **made with their ancestors**, a reference to the Mosaic covenant (31:31-32). The blessings of the Mosaic covenant were conditioned on Israel's obedience, but Israel failed to keep its side of the agreement: they **broke** the covenant (32:32). Therefore, God brought down curses on the people.

But under the new covenant, God will put his **teaching within them and write it on their hearts** (31:33). Israel broke God's law—not because there was something wrong with the law—but because there was something wrong with their hearts. The law revealed their sinfulness and their inability to keep it. It showed their desperate need to have renewed hearts. God promised a new relationship with him that was so rich and dynamic that the people wouldn't need to have his law written on stone tablets. It will be inscribed on their hearts.

The church partakes of the benefits of the new covenant. The author of Hebrews quotes this passage from Jeremiah and points to its fulfillment in Christ (see Heb 8:7-13). On the night he was betrayed, Jesus gave the cup to his disciples and said, "This cup is the new covenant in my blood; which is poured out for you" (Luke 22:20). The cup represented his blood, poured out on the cross, for the forgiveness of sins. By means of Jesus's sacrifice, God is able to say, **I will forgive their iniquity and never again remember their sin** (31:34). In the Communion ceremony, Christians are told to partake of the cup "in remembrance of" Christ and the new covenant instituted by his atoning death (see 1 Cor 11:25-26).

We as believers are living under the new covenant. But the day is coming when the people of Israel will also follow their Messiah, Jesus Christ (see 31:31). From their standpoint, the provisions of this covenant are still future, to be fulfilled when Jesus returns. When he comes to rule on David's throne in his millennial kingdom, their hearts will turn to him (see Rom 11:25-27).

31:35-40 The Lord is the one who established the **sun**, the **moon**, and **stars**. Only if their **fixed order** can be undone **will Israel's descendants cease to be a nation before** him (31:35-36). This covenant is unilateral, depending only on God, and is therefore unbreakable. It also includes the establishment of a new Jerusalem that will stand as the throne of Christ in his millennial reign (31:38-40).

32:1-5 Chapter 32 begins by telling us that it was **the tenth year of King Zedekiah of Judah** and **the eighteenth year of Nebuchadnezzar** (32:1)—about a year before Jerusalem fell. Jerusalem was under siege by Babylon, and Zedekiah had **imprisoned** Jeremiah for prophesying that God would give over the city and its king to Nebuchadnezzar (32:2-5). The clueless Zedekiah demanded, **Why are you prophesying as you do?** (32:3). He couldn't understand why Jeremiah would predict disaster on his own people and king. He felt the prophet was a traitor! It never occurred to him that Jeremiah might actually be speaking on behalf of the Lord—serving as a *true* prophet.

32:6-15 Once again, however, God remembered mercy in the midst of wrath and gave Jeremiah another vivid object lesson of his assurance that he would not destroy his people completely. Even with the Babylonians at the gates of Jerusalem, God told Jeremiah to redeem a plot of his family's land in his hometown of **Anathoth** (32:6-12; see Lev 25:25-28), which was already under Babylonian control. God knew Jeremiah wouldn't buy the field on his own initiative. Who would? It would be like buying a car that the owner no longer possessed because it had been stolen! So God revealed ahead of time to Jeremiah that his **cousin Hanamel** would ask him to do this unusual thing (32:8).

Jeremiah obeyed God and bought the land, although it seemed to make about as much sense as arranging deck chairs on the sinking *Titanic*. But he duly recorded the deed and had his secretary Baruch put the two copies in a **jar** where they would **last a long time** (32:14). Then Jeremiah learned from **the LORD of Armies, the God of Israel** what this meant: **Houses, fields, and vineyards will again be bought in this land** (32:15). God's people would one day return home.

32:16-25 Jeremiah then prayed, expressing his faith and confidence in God—and his perplexity at how God was working out his plan. Jeremiah had a very high view of God's greatness (32:16-19). He affirmed the Lord's mighty works in bringing Israel from bondage in **Egypt** into their own **land**—where, tragically, they **failed** to obey him (32:20-23). Jeremiah knew God's sovereignty and his people's history. He knew that God had **handed over** Jerusalem **to the Chaldeans** (the Babylonians) because of Judah's sins (32:24). But Jeremiah still expressed bewilderment at what God was doing. Why tell him to buy a piece of land in a country that was about to be overrun and its inhabitants deported? (32:25).

32:26-44 In his response to Jeremiah's prayer, God first established some ground rules: **I am the LORD, the God over every creature. Is anything too difficult for me?** (32:27). Jeremiah himself had declared that nothing is too difficult for the Lord (32:17), so he knew this was not a multiple-choice question. Why, then, did God profess his omnipotence? Because he was about to tell Jeremiah that after Judah's punishment was complete (32:28-35), God would bring the nation back to its land and the people would enjoy prosperity again (32:36-44). Jeremiah's redemption of the field (32:6-15) was meaningful. It was a promise that God hadn't abandoned his people. **This is the LORD's declaration** (32:44) implies that you can count on it.

33:1-13 Chapter 33 contains further details about the ultimate restoration of God's people after the devastating judgment of the Babylonian captivity. Neither Jeremiah nor anyone else could ever have put these two things together on his own. They had to be revealed by the God who said, **Call to me and I will answer you and tell you great and incomprehensible things you do not know** (33:3). Those things included Judah's imminent judgment, but also the coming of the day when God **will restore the fortunes of Judah and of Israel and will rebuild them as in former times** (33:7). The picture that followed of a restored people in a restored land where there was **joy and gladness** (33:11) must have been an encouragement to Jeremiah as he heard the clanging of the Babylonians' tools as they built siege ramps against Jerusalem's walls.

33:14-16 As in 23:5-6 and 30:8-9, God reaffirms the Davidic covenant with its promise that a descendant of **David** will rule on his throne forever (33:15; see 2 Sam 7:12-17). The prophets often use tree imagery to speak of this Messiah who rises from the family of David. For instance, Isaiah says, "A shoot will grow from the stump of Jesse [the father of David]" (Isa 11:1). In other words, although God has chopped down the Davidic family tree—the royal dynasty of David—because of its sin, a new growth will sprout up from it. Isaiah calls him, "the Branch of the LORD" and "the root of Jesse" (Isa 4:2; 11:10). Zechariah refers to him as "the Branch" (Zech 3:8). In Revelation he is the "root of David" (see Rev 5:5; 22:16).

Using this same language, Jeremiah calls the coming king a **Righteous Branch** (33:15) whose reign would be so great that even **Jerusalem** herself **will be named: The LORD**

Is Our Righteousness (33:16). The Davidic covenant did not promise an unbroken monarchy because the exiles who returned from Babylon did not reestablish Israel's monarchy. Instead, God promised that a righteous king would arise from David's line to rule. Jesus fulfilled this promise, as we see in the genealogies of Matthew and Luke (see Matt 1:1-16; Luke 3:23-38).

33:17-22 God further promised that **David** would not **fail to have a man sitting on the throne** and that **the Levitical priests** would not **fail to have a man always before [the Lord]** (33:17-22). This is all fulfilled in Jesus Christ who is *both* king *and* priest (Ps 110:1, 4). In Old Testament Israel, these offices were kept distinct, but the New Testament reveals that they come together in Christ. Jesus is the true heir to the throne of David. He is also the true priest—not a Levitical priest—but a superior one, "a priest forever according to the order of Melchizedek" (Heb 5:6; 6:20; 7:17; see commentary on Heb 7:1-28). In Christ, the great priest-king, God's promise through Jeremiah has become a reality.

33:23-26 But some still questioned either God's ability or willingness to save his people, or maybe both. So the Lord gave Jeremiah a further reassurance regarding his promises: **If I do not keep my covenant with the day and with the night, and if I fail to establish the fixed order of heaven and earth, then I might also reject the descendants of Jacob** (33:25-26). Earlier he said that if "day and night cease to come at their regular time," then his covenant with David "may be broken" (33:20-21). So in other words, God says, "Bank on me coming through as promised." God has tied himself to his promises; the only way they can fail is if he ceases to be God.

⇒ *K. Events Surrounding the Fall of Jerusalem (34:1–45:5)* ⇐

34:1-7 Much of the book of Jeremiah focuses on the events surrounding the reign of **King Zedekiah** (34:2), ruler of Judah when Jerusalem fell, the temple was burned, and the people were led into captivity. He was a stubborn, rebellious leader who desperately clung to his futile hope that somehow he could escape defeat by the Babylonians. But through Jeremiah, God continually warned Zedekiah to stop resisting and accept God's severe discipline of his sinful children (34:1-3).

It's interesting that God said Zedekiah would **meet the king of Babylon eye to eye** (34:3), given that when they did meet, Nebuchadnezzar had Zedekiah blinded (see 52:11). But there was also grace for the king of Judah in God's promise that he would **die peacefully**, suggesting a full life, and be honored at death (34:5). Zedekiah should have obeyed.

34:8-16 But Zedekiah was desperately looking for any edge. So he reached back into the Mosaic law and revived the stipulation that any Jew who was enslaved to a fellow Jew in a form of indentured service was to be freed after six years (34:8-10, 13-14; see Exod 21:2). The people had not been obeying this statute, but Zedekiah called the entire city of Jerusalem together to make a covenant before the Lord, releasing all their slaves (34:8, 14-15). **All the officials and people who entered into covenant to let their male and female slaves go free . . . obeyed and let them go** (34:10).

Yet afterward they **changed their minds** and reenslaved their fellow Jews (34:11, 16)! Why? Apparently because the Babylonians had suddenly withdrawn from the siege of Jerusalem to deal with the Egyptian army that had marched out to engage them (see 34:21; 37:5). In other words, with things seemingly back to normal, they saw no need to become so spiritual. These actions demonstrated the insincerity of their pledge to the Lord. The people of Judah took the Babylonian withdrawal as a sign that their scheme had worked and that God had delivered Jerusalem, but their false spirituality simply increased the Lord's anger. Their actions initially **pleased** him, but reneging on their covenant **profaned [his] name** (34:15-16).

34:17-22 Thus, God had a bitterly ironic form of "freedom" in store for Judah: **I hereby proclaim freedom for you . . . to the sword, to plague, and to famine!** (34:17). All the people had ratified the slave-releasing covenant by

passing between the two halves of the sacrificial animal—so God said **their corpses** would be treated in the same way (34:18-20). As for the withdrawal of the Babylonian army, that was only temporary. God assured them: **I will bring them back** to Jerusalem to **fight against . . . capture . . . and burn it** (34:22). Zedekiah and the people could run, but they couldn't hide. As Paul told the Galatians, "God is not mocked. For whatever a person sows he will also reap" (Gal 6:7).

35:1-5 Previously, God sent the prophet to visit a Jewish clan called the **Rechabites**, nomads who were forced to move to Jerusalem when the Babylonians marched into Judah. The story in this chapter is actually a flashback to the years before Zedekiah came to the throne and faced the siege. Jeremiah was instructed by God to invite several Rechabite leaders to a side room in the **temple** and offer them **wine** (35:2). Jeremiah obeyed the Lord and encouraged them to **drink** up (35:3-5).

35:6-11 But the Rechabites' leaders kindly rejected the offer. They were under a long-standing family covenant not to drink wine or even live in permanent homes. **Jonadab, son of [their] ancestor Rechab**, had given them this command, and they were determined to keep it—they and their entire families (3:6-10).

35:12-16 Therein was the lesson God wanted Jeremiah to deliver to Judah. For generations, the Rechabites had remained faithful to their promises, although there was nothing inherently spiritual about living as they did. But the point was not the particular prohibition they had chosen to obey, but their unswerving faithfulness to their covenant.

In this instance God used an argument from "the lesser to the greater"—that which is true in a small matter is surely true in a similar, more significant matter. The Rechabites had obeyed Jonadab their ancestor even though he was a mere man. If these nomads could be so obedient to a man's words, why could the people of Judah not bring themselves to obey the word of **the LORD of Armies, the God of Israel** (35:13)? We don't know the reasons behind Jonadab's commands, yet the Rechabites heeded him. God commanded his people **time and time again** for their own good—so they could live and enjoy his blessing—but they **did not pay attention** to him (35:15-16).

35:17-19 The outcome for Judah and Jerusalem, therefore, was inevitable: **Disaster.** Why? **Because I have spoken to them, but they have not obeyed** (35:17). Meanwhile, the Rechabites were rewarded for their obedience. The Lord promised them a continuing line of descendants to **stand before** him (35:19). Make no mistake: Rebellion against God has consequences. But so does a life of faithfulness.

36:1-3 Jeremiah turned from being a speaking prophet to becoming a writing prophet when God commanded him to **take a scroll** and record all of his prophecies **from the time** he **first spoke** to him **during Josiah's reign until** that day (36:2). **Perhaps** if these warnings and judgments were read to the leaders and people of Judah, they would come back to the Lord, be forgiven, and be spared the fate that awaited them (36:3).

36:4-8 While Jeremiah dictated, his secretary **Baruch** faithfully wrote down **all the words the Lord had spoken** to him (36:4). However, Jeremiah was **restricted** from entering the **temple** (36:5). Imagine that. Jeremiah had been faithful to God's word, but the spiritual leaders who rejected it barred this prophet from God's house of worship. So he sent Baruch to **read from the scroll** to the **people at the temple** and to **all the Judeans who are coming from their cities** (36:6).

36:9-20 In the fifth year of Jehoiakim the king, Baruch read **the scroll** in the **temple** (36:9-10). Listening to Baruch was **Micaiah.** He reported what he heard to a group of **officials** who invited Baruch to **read** it to them (36:10-15). So, for the second time that day, he read God's words through Jeremiah, this time to some of Jerusalem's top officials (36:15). When he finished, **they turned to each other in fear**. Jerusalem was doomed. They knew they must **tell the king** (36:16). Yet the officials also knew King Jehoiakim was not likely to be happy about this news condemning Judah, its king, and its people.

So they told Baruch and Jeremiah to hide while they approached him about the scroll (36:19-20).

36:21-26 When Jehoiakim requested that the scroll be read, the officials knew their fears were justified. The king revealed his lack of concern for God's word and Judah's sin. Piece by piece, he sliced up the **scroll** with a **knife** and tossed it into a **fire** until it was **consumed** (36:22-23). His officials begged him not to do it, but the king refused to **listen** (36:25). His heart was so calloused that neither he nor his servants were **terrified or [tore] their clothes** upon hearing God's words of judgment (36:24). Then he ordered Jeremiah and Baruch arrested. **But the Lord hid them** away safely (36:26).

36:27-32 Jehoiakim's actions did nothing to stop God's program. If you receive an eviction notice, burning it won't keep you from being evicted. The judgment of God continued to roll unhindered toward Judah. The Lord told Jeremiah to dictate everything to **Baruch** again (36:27-28). But this time God added specific judgments against Jehoiakim: **He will have no one to sit on David's throne** (36:30). His son Jehoiachin would rule for only three months before the Babylonians carried him into exile. In addition, Jehoiakim's **corpse [would] be thrown out to be exposed to the heat of day and the frost of night** (36:30; see 22:18-19). This was the price Jehoiakim paid for rejecting the Lord.

37:1-2 The events of chapters 37–39 are in chronological order, focusing on the final days of King Zedekiah and Judah before it fell to the Babylonians. Like his predecessors, **Zedekiah** paid no heed to the Lord's warnings through Jeremiah. Zedekiah was a puppet king put on the throne by **Nebuchadnezzar**. Still, if he had listened to the Lord, he could have prevented disaster. But Zedekiah rebelled. Therefore, Nebuchadnezzar would swoop in for the final blow.

37:3-10 There was a deceptive lull in the siege of Jerusalem when the Babylonian army (**the Chaldeans**) temporarily withdrew to fight the armies of Pharaoh coming up from **Egypt** (37:5). The king asked Jeremiah to **pray**—probably for a victory by Egypt, so that the Babylonians would leave Judah standing (37:3). But it was not to be. God told Jeremiah to tell Zedekiah in no uncertain terms that Babylon would destroy Judah (37:6-9). It didn't depend on human ability but on God's sovereign judgment. Even if the invaders had only **badly wounded men** left, God was determined to see the wicked city burnt to the ground (37:10).

37:11-16 When the Babylonian army withdrew, the pressure on Jerusalem eased, for a while at least. So Jeremiah tried to leave the city to go to his home in **the land of Benjamin** on family business (37:11-12). But at the gate, the prophet was grabbed by **an officer of the guard** named **Irijah** (37:13), who accused him of deserting to the enemy. Despite the prophet's protests, Irijah **took him to the officials**, who **beat** Jeremiah and tossed him into a **dungeon** where he languished for **many days** (37:14-16).

37:17-21 Zedekiah weakly allowed the prophet to be mistreated. This was typical of the king's wishy-washy nature, which would be on display again with regard to Jeremiah in 38:5. But the king seemed to know in his heart that Jeremiah was speaking a true **word from the LORD**, so he sent for the prophet to see what God's latest word was.

Unfortunately for Zedekiah, the message had not changed: **You will be handed over to the king of Babylon** (37:17). Jeremiah knew this was not what Zedekiah wanted to hear, but he also knew that he had a case when it came to pleading for better treatment. The false **prophets** who had told Judah that Babylon was no threat were suddenly nowhere to be found, while Jeremiah had fearlessly and faithfully stood his ground (37:18-20). The king saw the point, and brought the aging Jeremiah to a place where he could care for him (37:21). This helped spare Jeremiah undue suffering in the dungeon, but it did not mean his enemies had gone away or given up on their desire to kill him.

38:1-6 Jeremiah had a powerful array of enemies, government officials in the court of the puppet king Zedekiah who pulled his strings.

They didn't like that the prophet was urging the people to avoid death by surrendering to the enemy (38:1-3). To them, Jeremiah's words were treason. So the leaders told the king that Jeremiah **ought to die** because he was **weakening the morale of the warriors . . . and of all the people** (38:4). Zedekiah's sniveling reply was pathetic: **Here he is; he's in your hands since [I] can't do anything against you** (38:5). That's all they needed to hear. They lowered Jeremiah into a deep **cistern** filled with **mud**. You may sometimes feel like your life is so bad that you're metaphorically "sinking in mud," but for Jeremiah, this was reality (38:6).

38:7-13 But, by God's grace, Jeremiah had friends too. The bravest of them was an African named **Ebed-melech, a Cushite court official in the king's palace** (38:7). This man obviously feared God, so he courageously approached Zedekiah and told him what Jeremiah's enemies had done to him (38:8-9). Zedekiah gave Ebed-melech permission to rescue Jeremiah from the pit, although he went back to being under house arrest (38:10-13).

38:14-16 Jeremiah was summoned by King Zedekiah (38:14). The king's vacillation was really on display as he arranged a secret meeting for fear of his own officials. He wanted to hear what Jeremiah had to say, but he lacked the courage and spiritual commitment to make the right call. Jeremiah was wary of speaking to Zedekiah; he knew his life was hanging by a thread. But the prophet didn't pull any punches: **If I give you advice, you won't listen to me** (38:15). The king, desperate to hear from the prophet, promised to keep him safe (38:16).

38:17-28 Jeremiah delivered God's message to the king: **surrender**. Only by submitting to defeat at the hands of Babylon would the king and the city **survive** (38:17-18). Then Zedekiah revealed the real reason he was afraid to follow Jeremiah's advice. The king was **worried about the Judeans who have defected to the Chaldeans. They may hand me over to the Judeans to abuse me** (38:19). Jeremiah assured the king this would not happen if he would only **obey the LORD**

(38:20). Refusal to obey, however, would result in mocking, capture, and destruction (38:22-23). Zedekiah warned Jeremiah to say nothing of their **conversation** (38:24-26) and still couldn't find the courage to do what was right. Jeremiah was kept in custody until the day Jerusalem fell (38:28).

39:1-10 The bottom fell out for Judah when the Babylonians breached Jerusalem's walls and entered the city in 587–586 BC (39:1-2). The **officials** of Babylon **sat at the Middle Gate** to demonstrate that they were now in charge and to judge those still in the city who had resisted them (39:3). Zedekiah attempted to escape, but it was not to be. He was brought before **Nebuchadnezzar** (39:4-5). Judah's king was made to watch the execution of his own **sons** and **Judah's nobles.** Then he was **blinded** and led in **chains** to Babylon (see 39:6-7). The southern kingdom had fallen, with only a handful of **poor people** permitted to stay behind (39:10).

39:11-18 But God had his eye on Jeremiah. Nebuchadnezzar gave orders for Jeremiah to be treated kindly (39:11-12). The prophet was entrusted to the care of a man named **Gedaliah** (39:14), whom the Babylonians had appointed as governor of the few people who were left behind in Judah (40:5, 7). Gedaliah took Jeremiah back to his **home**, which must have seemed a little surreal to the prophet with his nation in ruins. The Lord also preserved the life of **Ebed-melech** (39:15-18), the brave man who had saved Jeremiah's life (see 38:7-13).

40:1-6 In a crowning ironic rebuke to Judah, the Babylonian **captain of the guards** named **Nebuzaradan** (40:1) repeated God's judgment against Judah and verified its truth (40:1-3). Under orders from Nebuchadnezzar himself, Nebuzaradan gave Jeremiah the choice to come with him to Babylon or stay in Judah. Jeremiah's desire must have been reflected in his face, because even before he **turned to go** back to his people, the Babylonian advised him to go to the new governor **Gedaliah** for protection and provision (40:5-6). Knowing how many enemies he used to have in Judah, Jeremiah went to join Gedaliah in **Mizpah** (40:6), a town a few miles

north of Jerusalem, which became the new administrative center following the total destruction of Jerusalem.

40:7-10 Yet even amid the devastation, rebellion still lingered in some of the Jews left behind. **The commanders of the armies that were in the countryside** that had survived the Babylonian invasion heard about Gedaliah's appointment. These men and their leaders, most notably **Ishmael** (40:7-8), who was a relative of Zedekiah (see 41:1), came to Gedaliah at Mizpah to find out what was going on. The governor gave them the ground rules the Babylonians had established. They needed to **serve the king of Babylon**—which is what God had been telling the people of Judah to do for years. Then it would **go well** for everyone (40:9). Gedaliah also assured his visitors that he would represent them to the Babylonians (40:10).

40:11-14 The news of this arrangement spread quickly, and Jews who had fled to neighboring lands started pouring into Judah (40:11-12). These refugees helped bring in a great harvest (40:12), and things seemed to be looking up. But trouble was brewing. The army commanders, led by **Johanan** came to Gedaliah with disturbing news that Ishmael's earlier visit was part of a plot against the governor and the new government in Judah, masterminded by **Baalis, king of the Ammonites** (40:13-14).

There were political reasons for this scheme—good ones, from Ammon's point of view. Ammon was on Nebuchadnezzar's list of places to conquer, so it may be that this plot against Gedaliah was concocted to keep the Babylonians occupied with Judah and to preserve Ammon. It's also likely that Ishmael and his followers didn't want to submit to the Babylonians.

40:15-16 Whatever the reasons for this assassination plot, Gedaliah dismissed it. Johanan privately offered to **kill Ishmael** to avoid having the Babylonians come down on the people of Judah again (40:15). But the governor was indignant: **Don't do that! What you're saying about Ishmael is a lie!** (40:16). Although Gedaliah may have been a good man, he was blind to the danger ahead.

41:1-10 Gedaliah's naïve approach to the danger around him cost him his life and the lives of many others. Ishmael and his men killed the new governor, as well as the Judeans and the Chaldean soldiers **at Mizpah** (41:2-3). The news of the assassination had not yet gotten out when **eighty men came from Shechem, Shiloh, and Samaria**— that is, from what had been the northern kingdom of Israel. They had come grieving, hoping to make offerings to the Lord at the temple (41:5). Inexplicably, Ishmael lured them to Mizpah and almost killed them all (41:6-7)! However, ten men bribed him with supplies, so Ishmael let them live (41:8). As if this mass murder wasn't bad enough, **Ishmael took captive all the rest of the people of Mizpah** and fled to **the Ammonites** (41:10), where they would presumably be out of the Babylonians' reach.

We are not told Ishmael's motives for his actions. Perhaps in his twisted mind, Ishmael thought he was rescuing his people from the "Babylonian collaborator" Gedaliah and his accomplices. All we know is that Ishmael was a brutal murderer who made a difficult situation much worse. What happens in the upcoming chapters must be weighed against the Lord's repeated warning to those who survived the destruction of Jerusalem to submit to the Babylonians and be protected.

41:11-18 Johanan, the army commander who had warned Gedaliah about the danger Ishmael posed, heard the news, rallied his troops, and pursued him (41:11-12). Johanan and his men liberated the captives, but Ishmael **escaped** to Ammon (41:13-15). If the freed people had returned to Mizpah and resumed their lives, they might have been fine, despite the expected reprisals from Babylon. God had promised them his overseeing care. But fear dominated them. They were convinced that the Babylonians would return and slaughter them for Ishmael's deeds. They decided **to make their way into Egypt** (41:17), determined to put as many miles between themselves and Babylon as possible.

God had warned his people not to trust in the Egyptians, but these survivors had witnessed the horror of Jerusalem's destruction and the slaughter of thousands of Jews.

That's all they could see in their own future since Ishmael had messed everything up. But the people of Judah were looking in the wrong direction. Instead of looking north for the next attack from Nebuchadnezzar, or looking south for deliverance from Egypt, they should have been looking up to God for deliverance.

42:1-6 This straggly band of Israelites got together and decided it would be a good idea to get God's rubber stamp of approval for their plans, so they went en masse to Jeremiah with a very pious-sounding request. They wanted the prophet to inquire of the Lord about the best course of action (42:1-3). Jeremiah had heard empty statements like theirs before; nevertheless, he promised to **pray** and tell them **every word** God revealed to him (42:4). In response, the people promised that whether the news was good or bad, they would **certainly obey the Lord** (42:5-6).

42:7-12 It took **ten days**, but the **word of the Lord** came to Jeremiah (42:7). It included both blessings for obedience and curses for disobedience. If the people would **stay in [their] land**, God assured them of their welfare. He promised to **rebuild** and **plant** them after the disaster of Jerusalem's destruction and the captivity (42:9-10). God even said, I **relent concerning the disaster that I have brought on you** (42:10). Part of that relenting included giving Nebuchadnezzar **compassion** (42:12) so that he wouldn't take reprisals on them because of Ishmael's murders. Now that was quite a deal God was offering: recovery and prosperity in their own land and protection from their feared enemy! All the people had to do was stay home and enjoy God's blessings.

42:13-17 But Johanan and the people also needed to know the consequences of failing to obey the Lord. God knew exactly what they were thinking: "If we stay here, we've got a ravaged country to try and rebuild. And even if we get crops in the ground, we'll live in constant fear of an attack from Babylon in punishment for what Ishmael did. Besides, we've seen enough of war, hunger, and all that mess." And sure enough, the people made their decision: **No, instead we'll go**

to . . . Egypt (42:14). This was the equivalent of saying, "Thanks for your advice, God. But we've got a better plan." Besides, they thought, their stay in Egypt would only be **for a while** (42:17). Once the coast was clear, they could return to Judah. But, through Jeremiah, God declared that everything they feared—**sword, famine, and plague**—would **follow** them **to Egypt**. There they would **die** (42:16-17).

42:18-22 Don't go to Egypt (42:19) indicated that escape wasn't God's will for his people. Their plan to lie low there until things cooled off in Judah would backfire. God warned them that if they persisted in their plan, **You will never see this place** (Judah) **again** (42:18). If they abandoned their homeland, it would be for the last time. Jeremiah knew what the people's reaction would be, which is why he told them, **You have gone astray at the cost of your lives** (42:20). While they'd claimed that they wanted the truth from God, in reality they had no intention of obeying him (42:20-21). If they were to return to Egypt, they'd be dead people walking. Don't presume to ask for the King's direction in your life if you aren't truly prepared to follow in obedience.

43:1-7 Neither the Lord's promise nor his warning could convince this band of survivors to stay in Judah and enjoy God's blessings. In their arrogance, they claimed Jeremiah was a liar (43:2). They even went so far as to accuse **Baruch**, Jeremiah's secretary, of **inciting** Jeremiah against them **to hand [them] over to the Chaldeans** (43:3). **So Johanan** and his fellow **commanders** (43:4) led the people on a trek down to Egypt—it included Jeremiah and Baruch, who must have been taken against their will (43:4-7). Interestingly, **Tahpanhes** (43:7) means "palace of the Negro."

43:8-13 Once the group arrived in Egypt, God sent Jeremiah with a sign for the men of Judah, another object lesson of judgment for his disobedient people. Jeremiah told them he had a word from **the LORD of Armies** (43:10), one of the prophet's favorite names for God. Frequently in the book of Jeremiah, in fact, God is either summoning or defeating

great armies. The rebellious people of Judah—who feared the Babylonian army and ran to the Egyptian army for protection—needed to know that they had not outrun the reach of the God who controlled all the forces of earth.

Jeremiah's sign was simple. He **embedded** some stones in the **pavement** leading to **Pharaoh's palace at Tahpanhes** in northern Egypt (43:9-10). In this place where the people of Judah must have been feeling safe, Jeremiah then prophesied that they would see the Babylonian army invade Egypt to do there what they'd done in Judah (43:10-13). Where Jeremiah had placed the stones, Nebuchadnezzar would set up his headquarters (43:10)! A few hundred miles and a national border would be no problem for God to overcome when he stretched out his hand of judgment.

44:1-6 A popular proverb goes something like this: "Those who do not learn from history are doomed to repeat it." In other words, if you fail to learn from the mistakes of those who failed in the past, be prepared to follow in their footsteps. This seems to be God's message to the people of Judah who had disobediently run off to Egypt. Through Jeremiah, the Lord reminds the Jews of the idolatry of Judah and the **disaster** that resulted (44:2-6). It's unavoidable: Serving false gods and rejecting God is a sure path to ruin. The history of Israel and Judah demonstrates this vividly.

44:7-10 In light of the disastrous results of Judah's sin, God asked the Jews in Egypt, **Why are you doing such terrible harm to yourselves?** (44:7). The people refused to heed God's command to remain in Judah and receive his blessing. And not only did they flee to Egypt but—incredibly!—they angered God by **burning incense to other gods** there (44:8). Could they not anticipate what would happen? This is called a self-inflicted wound! They had **forgotten the evils** that they, their ancestors, and their kings had committed (44:9). They had learned *nothing*. **They [had] not become humble** (44:10).

When God takes a swat at your pride, it's meant to lead you to repentance and humility. "God resists the proud, but gives grace to the humble" (Jas 4:6). One of the purposes for Jeremiah's book was to teach subsequent generations the lessons about faithfulness to God that the Jews of his day failed to learn—and the price they paid.

44:11-19 The lessons of history were lost on the Jews who defiantly fled to Egypt. So Jeremiah repeated God's words of judgment against them for their foolishness (44:11-14; see 42:15-22). In defiance, the people proclaimed, **We are not going to listen to you!** (44:16). The depths of their depravity became even more clear when they claimed that their problems began when they **ceased to burn incense to the queen of heaven** (44:18). This means they actually credited a pagan goddess with the prosperity and blessings they had enjoyed in Judah! The unspoken assumption was that worshiping the Lord had gotten them nowhere. Serving him instead of their idols, they reasoned, was the reason for their disaster. They couldn't have been more wrong.

44:20-25 This blasphemy was so incredible that God essentially said, "Enough!" Jeremiah first corrected their twisted view of their history and the disastrous loyalty to pagan gods as the source of their well-being (44:20-23). Then God pulled down the curtain on this crowd. He had endured enough of their arrogance. If lies and destruction was what they demanded, lies and destruction is what they would receive: **Go ahead, confirm your vows! Keep your vows!** (44:25)—that is, "Have it your way. Worship and plead with the queen of heaven. See where that gets you."

44:26-30 Then God made an even more ominous statement: **My name will never again be invoked by anyone of Judah in all the** land of Egypt.... I am watching over them for disaster and not for good ... until they are finished off (44:26-27). God also said he would confirm his word of disaster and death by handing over **Pharaoh Hophra, Egypt's king**, to his enemies (44:30). The leader to whom the Jews fled for protection, then, wouldn't even be able to protect himself. This was fulfilled in 570–569 BC when Hophra was deposed in an army coup and eventually assassinated. When these things came to pass, the rebellious Jews would finally see, although it would be too late: **[They] will know whose word stands, mine or theirs!** (44:28).

45:1-5 As with other portions of the book of Jeremiah, the events of this chapter are out of sequence historically, since they occurred around 604 BC, years before Judah fell. Chapter 45 provides a short record of how God ministered through Jeremiah to the prophet's faithful secretary, **Baruch**. The event that triggered Baruch's lament (45:3) was writing Jeremiah's words on a scroll—only to have King **Jehoiakim** cut it into pieces, burn it, and swear out a warrant for the arrest of the prophet and his scribe (45:1; see 36:1-26).

Baruch took a cue from his master in pouring out his grief and complaint to God (45:3). Apparently, Baruch thought serving alongside a great prophet like Jeremiah would bring him **great things**, like prominence and respect (45:5). But God made it clear to Baruch that his dream of the bright lights would go unfulfilled. By the time God finished destroying Judah, there wouldn't be any nation left in which Baruch could realize his hopes of greatness (45:4). Instead, God gave him the best gift he could ask for in the midst of the destruction around him: his **life** (45:5).

III. PROPHECIES AGAINST VARIOUS NATIONS (46:1–51:64)

46:1-9 It's interesting that Egypt was first on Jeremiah's list of prophecies against the nations. Egypt was the very place from which God had rescued his people in bondage and birthed the nation of Israel on the night of Passover. Tragically, the people of Judah had willingly chosen to put themselves back under bondage to their enemies by disobeying God. But because God still had a future for his chosen people, he would deal in judgment with the nations that had oppressed and mistreated them. And so Egypt was brought into the divine court to have its sentence pronounced.

The execution of God's wrath against **Egypt** was fulfilled when **the army of Pharaoh Neco . . . was defeated at Carchemish on the Euphrates River by King Nebuchadnezzar of Babylon in the fourth year of Judah's King Jehoiakim** (46:2). This took place in 605 BC. Egypt was filled with pride. The Pharaoh had unlimited confidence in his army, and he had grand plans for Egypt to conquer the world and spread its influence like the Nile River overflowing its banks (46:7-8). But God had other plans. Here he sarcastically urges the Egyptian army to call out its forces and prepare for battle against Nebuchadnezzar (46:3-4, 9). Egypt's army did all this, but the battle turned into such a rout that Egypt's panic-stricken warriors stumbled over each other trying to get away from the slaughter (46:5-6).

46:10-12 The Babylonians may have thought they had conquered by their own strength, but the victory belonged to **the Lord, the GOD of Armies** (46:10). There would be **no healing** for the once great Egypt, no remedy for their **dishonor** (46:11-12).

46:13-19 There is a significant gap in time between the prophecy of Egypt's defeat at Carchemish in 605 BC (46:2) and the events prophesied beginning in 46:13. The latter was a prophecy of Nebuchadnezzar's invasion of Egypt, which occurred in about 568 BC. In between these events, Nebuchadnezzar's father died, so he returned to Babylon to secure his throne. When he resumed his attack on Egypt, Pharaoh Hophra was king. Now instead of fighting the Babylonians by the Euphrates River, the Egyptians would see them coming against their own land, ravaging as they went. **Pharaoh king of Egypt was all noise; he let the opportune moment pass** (46:17). And since Pharaoh was all talk and no action, Egypt's cities were destined for **ruins** (46:19).

46:20-28 God's word against Egypt is a powerful, poetic description of the nation's former glory and total defeat. Egypt is called **a beautiful young cow** (possibly a reference to the Egyptian bull-god Apis), and the mercenaries in their ranks are compared to **stall-fed calves** fattened up for slaughter (46:20-21). Egypt might **hiss like a slithering snake** (46:22), but that's about all it could do in the face of the Babylonian horde (46:22-23). The nation's doom at the hands of Nebuchadnezzar was sealed (46:26). God's judgment would fall on **Pharaoh, Egypt, her gods, and her kings** (46:25).

This prophecy against Egypt ends with an intriguing statement: **But after this, Egypt will be inhabited again as in ancient times** (46:26). Egypt was promised a place in the future. In Isaiah 19, we also learn that Egypt will one day be redeemed and worship the true God. In the meantime, God assures **Israel** that his ultimate plan is for her restoration and redemption, even though she had to undergo **discipline** for her sins (46:27-28).

47:1-7 The Philistines were longtime enemies of Israel. One of the most well-known Bible stories recounts the battle between a young Israelite named David and a Philistine giant (see 1 Sam 17:1-58). The Philistines were seafaring people who lived along Israel's coast and tried to push inland when they were strong. This prophecy pictures Babylon as **water . . . rising from the north** that would **overflow the land** (47:2). Through them, the Lord would **destroy all the Philistines** (47:4). This happened in 604 BC when Nebuchadnezzar's armies destroyed **Ashkelon**, one of Philistia's principal cities (47:5).

God's cup of wrath on the nations that opposed Israel included a long drink for the Philistines. They would be so terrified, fleeing from the Babylonian army, that **fathers** would **not turn back for their sons** (47:3)! Shaving one's head and cutting oneself were signs of mourning (47:5). Such displays of horror and grief would be appropriate because the Philistines would be reduced to nothing when God was finished with them. The **sword of the LORD** would not rest until it had carried out his **command** (47:6-7).

48:1-10 Moab was located east of the Dead Sea between Edom and Ammon. The Moabites should have been allies of Israel, since they were the descendants of Lot and, therefore, of Abraham. But Israel's history showed that the Moabites harassed and attacked the Israelites at various times—especially when they were weak. So Moab came up next in the court of heaven to have sentence pronounced on its people.

The Moabites trusted in their god **Chemosh**. In his unfaithfulness, Solomon had worshiped this false deity who was abhorrent to the Lord (see 1 Kgs 11:7). But this idol would topple, along with **his priests and officials** (48:7). The extent of God's anger against the Moabites was such that he even warns her destroyers to be diligent in their work: **The one who does the LORD's business deceitfully is cursed, and the one who withholds his sword from bloodshed is cursed** (48:10).

48:11-13 One reason for Moab's sin was her complacency, since the nation had never really experienced hardship or exile. He had been **left quiet since his youth**. But all that was about to change; Moab would experience devastation from God. Though they hadn't **been poured from one container to another** and gone **into exile** as other nations had, God was going to **send pourers** to **pour him out** (48:11-12). The Moabites had failed to learn an important lesson from their cousins in Israel. Moab would be **put to shame because of Chemosh, just as the house of Israel was put to shame** for their idolatry at Bethel (48:13; see 1 Kgs 12:25-33).

48:14-28 When God unleashed his judgment, Moab's **warriors** in whom the people gloried would be of no use in stopping the **slaughter** (48:14-15). Even people in the distant town of **Aroer** would see the people of Moab running past and ask **what happened** (48:19). The chilling answer would be this: **Moab is destroyed** (48:20). This prophecy picturing the completeness of Moab's destruction uses two familiar Old Testament metaphors for power: **Moab's horn is chopped off; his arm is shattered** (48:25). They had scorned the Lord by scorning his people: Israel's downfall was a **laughingstock** to Moab (48:26-27), so Moab's people are warned to flee from their cities and hide in caves to escape God's wrath (48:28).

48:29-39 Moab's problem was **pride**. The nation was known for **insolence, arrogance, pride, and haughty heart** (48:29). But all

of Moab's boasting was just **empty** words (48:30). The nation had been secure and well off, and the people no doubt attributed their good fortune to their gods. But neither Moab's gods nor its army could stop its destruction when God unleashed his fury. And yet, God says he will **wail, cry out**, and **weep** over Moab's fall (48:31-32). His **heart moans** for Moab (48:36). God takes no pleasure in judgment. Nevertheless, his holy character demands it. Because of Moab's arrogance, the nation would be made a **laughingstock and a shock** to all who saw it (48:38-39).

48:40-47 Changing the imagery, God says he will swoop down on Moab **like an eagle** (48:40) with such fury that even the **warriors** would become as helpless as a pregnant woman (48:41). Why? Moab **has exalted himself against the LORD** (48:42). Thus, though they try to run, those who flee **will fall in the pit, and he who climbs from the pit will be captured** (48:44). When you make yourself God's enemy, then, there is no escape. Yet there is also a word of future hope for Moab, just as there was for Egypt (see 46:26). God declares, **I will restore the fortunes of Moab in the last days** (48:47)— most likely a reference to the millennial kingdom of Christ.

49:1-6 Ammon was Moab's first cousin, the other son born to Lot's daughters in their incestuous relationship with their father (see Gen 19:36-38). The reasons for Ammon's judgment largely paralleled those of Moab: mistreatment of Israel, idolatry, and pride (49:1, 4). The Ammonite god **Milcom** (49:1), also known as Molech, was detestable to the Lord. His worship included child sacrifice, a horrific practice that Israel sometimes engaged in (see Lev 20:1-5; 2 Kgs 23:10; Jer 7:31). Ammon had **dispossessed** the tribe of **Gad** from their land, but God pronounced that Israel would **dispossess their dispossessors** (49:1-2). Yet, as in the case of other nations under his wrath, God promises to one day **restore the fortunes of the Ammonites** (49:6; see 46:26; 48:47).

49:7-22 Edom was next in line for judgment. The Edomites were the descendants of Esau, Jacob's brother. The **wisdom in Teman** was well known (49:7); "Eliphaz the Temanite" was one of the elders who counseled Job (Job 2:11). But their wisdom failed the Edomites as they fell under God's condemnation.

Jeremiah describes the completeness of Edom's destruction. **Grape harvesters** would typically leave behind **some gleanings**, and even **thieves** would only take **what they wanted** (49:9). But Esau would not be so fortunate. **He [would] exist no longer** (49:10). Ominously, there was no word of future restoration for Edom, as there was for Egypt, Moab, and Ammon. The Edomites felt secure because of their geographic location (49:16), but it would offer no protection from the Lord who would swoop down **like an eagle** to devastate them (49:22).

49:23-27 Damascus was the capital of Aram (modern Syria), another kingdom in Jeremiah's day that came under God's judgment. Even though God calls it **the town that brings me joy** here, her **warriors** were destined to **perish** (49:25-26). With **the Lord of Armies** directing their actions (49:26), the Babylonian army would not be stopped.

49:28-33 Kedar and **Hazor** were nomadic tribes of Arabia, which also experienced the fury of **Nebuchadnezzar** (49:28). They lived **at ease** and **in security**—or so they thought. They didn't bother with **doors** or **even a gate bar** (49:31). In other words, they didn't live in a walled city, which made them much easier prey. The devastation would be so great in their territory that **no one** would **live there**, not **even temporarily** (49:33).

49:34-39 Elam was a kingdom east of Babylon in modern-day Iran (49:34). God's judgments against the nations were often described in terms appropriate to each country, and so it was with Elam. Her soldiers were well-known as archers, so God would **shatter Elam's bow** in which they trusted (49:35). God declares, **I will set my throne in Elam** (49:38), so again, although Babylon would be the weapon in his hand, the Lord ultimately is the one who oversees the destruction. And yet, God also left Elam with a promise for the future: **In the last days, I will restore the fortunes of Elam** (49:39; see also 46:26; 48:47; 49:6).

50:1-3 Finally, **Babylon** was hauled into the divine courtroom for sentencing (50:1). Although God used Babylon to carry out his punishment of his people and the nations, Babylon was not a righteous servant of the Lord. While God's intention was to exercise his holy justice upon wicked nations, Babylon's intention was to vanquish and dominate others for the sake of its own pride and power.

The initial descriptions of judgment reflect the familiar prophetic technique of blending the immediate with the far-off, since the great devastation outlined in 50:2-3 did not happen when the Medes and Persians conquered the city and killed King Belshazzar (see Dan 5:30-31). There is a future destruction of Babylon in Revelation 17–18 during the end of the tribulation, when this proud empire that came to stand for the worst in resistance to the Lord will be crushed. This may be what is in view here in Jeremiah.

50:4-7 Similarly, the prophecy that **the Israelites and Judeans will come together, weeping as they come, and will seek the Lord their God** (50:4) awaits Christ's return in the millennium. At that time, his **lost sheep** (50:6) will recognize and bow before him as Savior and Messiah.

50:8-20 Turning back to Babylon's judgment, the Lord describes a day when he would **bring against Babylon an assembly of great nations from the north country** (50:9). God was angered at Babylon's joy and arrogance while plundering Judah, his **inheritance** (50:11). God's judgment against Babylon would not be satisfied until **every bit of her** had become desolate (50:13). **Assyria** was the first to devour God's people (the northern kingdom of Israel); **Babylon** was the next to crush them (the southern kingdom of Judah). But the Lord planned to **punish** Babylon just as he had punished Assyria (50:17-18). Then he would **return** his people to their land and **forgive** their sins (50:19-20).

50:21-32 Merathaim and **Pekod** were two districts in Babylon. The Lord would **completely destroy them** (50:21). Babylon's power in the ancient world was illustrated by its description as **the hammer of the whole earth** that smashed everything in its path. But when it **pitted** itself **against the LORD,** the hammer would itself be **smashed** (50:23-27). Babylon's arrogance **against the Holy One of Israel** and his people would be fully avenged (50:29-32).

In an amazing prophecy of God's vindication of his people, the Lord speaks of **fugitives** from Babylon escaping the destruction and coming to the land of Israel to announce the execution of God's **vengeance** on Babylon for destroying his holy **temple** (50:28).

50:33-40 The **Israelites and Judeans** had been **oppressed** by strong **captors** who refused **to release them** (50:33). But their safety and return to their land would be guaranteed by an infinitely stronger power, **the LORD of Armies** (50:34). This announcement is followed immediately by a fivefold prophecy of the ways that God's **sword** would assure Babylon's destruction (50:35-37). More imagery of judgment followed, illustrating a nation so devastated that it would become the haunt of wild animals (50:39-40).

50:41-46 The chapter ends with a prophecy that seems to point to the final destruction of a rebuilt Babylon in the end times: **At the sound of Babylon's conquest the earth will quake; a cry will be heard among the nations** (50:46). If this is yet future, it could refer to the wailing of Revelation 18:9-19, which ends with this cry of horror at Babylon's complete destruction: "Woe, woe, the great city, where all those who have ships on the sea became rich from her wealth; for in a single hour she was destroyed" (Rev 18:19).

51:1-5 The prophecy of Babylon's destruction continues in chapter 51. God's people **Israel and Judah** had brought judgment on themselves, to be sure, because their land was **full of guilt against the Holy One of Israel** (51:5). So he summoned the Assyrians and the Babylonians as his agents to execute his wrath on them. But now it is Babylon's turn to pay for her own idolatry and arrogance.

51:6-19 The warning to **leave Babylon** and avoid **her guilt** contains end-time imagery

reflected in the book of Revelation (51:6-9). God proclaims that he will pour his wrath on Babylon during the tribulation: "Come out of her, my people, so that you will not share in her sins or receive any of her plagues" (Rev 18:4; see also 51:45-46). According to Jeremiah, Babylon's destruction **extends to the sky and reaches as far as the clouds** (51:9). This reference to the sky is picked up by the apostle John in his recorded vision of an **angel** flying through the air, announcing, "It has fallen, Babylon the Great has fallen. She made all the nations drink the wine of her sexual immorality, which brings wrath" (Rev 14:8). To the one who is **rich in treasures** the **end has come** (51:13). Her **carved** images will be **destroyed** (50:17-18). No idol can deliver those under God's wrath.

51:20-32 The reference to God's **war club** that he used to **smash** nations (51:20-23) could refer to King Cyrus of Persia, who was Babylon's conqueror. Just as the Lord used Nebuchadnezzar as his hammer of judgment against other lands, so he would use Cyrus to rout the Babylonians. God uses pagan powers to accomplish his will, but he still holds them responsible for their sins. His devastation of Babylon would be total (51:24-32).

51:33-58 The city of **Jerusalem** is pictured as the spokesman for God's people, lamenting the devastation that **Nebuchadnezzar** brought upon the inhabitants of Judah (51:34-35). God vowed to hear his people's cry, take up their **cause,** and bring **vengeance on** Babylon (51:36). The people and the temple of God figured prominently among the reasons for his fury against Babylon (51:49-51).

51:59-64 At the end of Jeremiah's prophecy of Babylon's destruction, we learn of his command to **Seriah,** the brother of Baruch, Jeremiah's faithful secretary (51:59). Jeremiah wrote the prophecies of chapters 50–51 on a **scroll** for Seriah **when he went to Babylon with King Zedekiah of Judah in the fourth year of Zedekiah's reign,** which was possibly a move by Nebuchadnezzar to ensure Zedekiah's loyalty (51:59-60). Seriah was to **read all these words aloud,** tie a stone to the scroll, throw it in the Euphrates River, and declare, In the same way, Babylon will sink and never rise again (51:61-64). Such a prophecy hardly seemed possible at the time—except for those with eyes of faith to trust God's sovereign promises.

IV. CONCLUSION AND HISTORICAL SUPPLEMENT (52:1-34)

52:1-30 The words of Jeremiah end in 51:64. Chapter 52 is a historical supplement added about twenty-five years later as a further confirmation that Jeremiah's prophecies did come to pass. The fate of **Jerusalem** and **Zedekiah** (52:1-11) have already been discussed (see 39:1-7). Zedekiah was a humiliated king, **blinded** and **bound** in **bronze chains**, destined to spend the rest of his life in prison (52:11). Verses 12-30 review the fall of Jerusalem, destruction of the temple, plundering of its treasures, and deportation of the people to Babylon—just as Jeremiah had prophesied.

52:31-34 The fate of Jehoiachin is explained in these final verses. In God's providence, **King Evil-merodach**, Nebuchadnezzar's son, **pardoned King Jehoiachin of Judah and released him from prison** (52:31). Then he set Jehoiachin's **throne above the thrones of the kings who were with him in Babylon** (52:32). Jehoiachin had reigned only three months in Jerusalem before being deposed by Nebuchadnezzar and taken to Babylon (see 2 Kgs 24:8-12), but he was on the throne long enough to be identified as a king who did evil before the Lord. So why did Jehoiachin receive such favor from the Babylonians—and ultimately, from the Lord?

The explanation may lie in two realities that have to do with the purpose of the book of Jeremiah and the certainty of both God's judgments and his promises. The long life of Jehoiachin in exile had to be another reminder to his fellow exiles that God was executing his fierce judgment on his people. But at the same time, Jehoiachin's long survival in Babylon and his restoration to a place of honor also served to remind the exiles that God had not completely abandoned them and would one day restore them to their land.

Despite his unfaithfulness, Jehoiachin was, after all, a Davidic king, a symbol of hope to the people of Judah that God had a future of blessing for them. And even though Jehoiachin himself was judged and cursed by having no descendant "on the throne of David" (see 22:30), the Davidic line through whom Jesus would come did not end.

To bypass the curse on Jehoiachin, the last of Solomon's descendants, the line of succession transferred to David's son Nathan. The importance of this can be seen in the genealogy of Jesus through Mary, whose ancestors were of Nathan's line (see Luke 3:31). Thus the messianic line was preserved and Jesus's claim to the throne of David legitimized.

The subsequent generations of Israelites who would read the book of Jeremiah would find, even amid its judgments, the hope of fulfillment of God's ultimate promise—the coming of David's greater son, the Lord Jesus Christ, to bring together all of God's promises to his people.

LAMENTATIONS

INTRODUCTION

Author

THOUGH THE AUTHOR'S NAME IS nowhere listed in the book, ancient Jewish tradition holds that the prophet Jeremiah wrote Lamentations.

Historical Background

As the title of the book suggests, it is about pain and suffering—but not without hope in God. Jeremiah wrote in light of the fall of Jerusalem to the Babylonians in 587–586 BC. He includes references to the siege of Jerusalem (2:20-22; 3:5, 7), the devastation of the city (2:3-5; 4:11; 5:18), and the exile of the people (1:1, 4-5, 18; 2:9, 14; 3:2, 19; 4:22; 5:2). These events were cause for great sorrow, so Jeremiah has often been called "the weeping prophet."

The five chapters in the book are five poems of lament. Each one, except chapter 5, is an "alphabetic acrostic"—that means it is broken into twenty-two verses or stanzas that begin with the twenty-two letters of the Hebrew alphabet, in alphabetical order.

Message and Purpose

This is a sad book written by "the weeping prophet" Jeremiah during a sad time. The Babylonians had attacked Jerusalem and brought an end to the southern kingdom of Judah. Many of the people had been taken into captivity, while others had fled.

Lamentations is a poetic expression of the pain of sin's consequences. What we hear and read in it reflects the tears of the prophet who saw destruction all around him. Yet in the middle of all the pain and sorrow, Jeremiah highlights the faithfulness of God. First, there was God's faithfulness to his warning that if his people departed from him, he would bring judgment on them. But Lamentations is also about hope (3:21-23), because God's mercies are seen even in the midst of judgment. If his people will return to him in repentance, God will return to them and limit, or even reverse, the consequences of their disobedience.

Lamentations is a reminder of God's kingdom, covenantal sanctions—namely, that sin brings pain and tears, but God is always ready to show mercy when we repent and return to him.

Outline

www.bhpublishinggroup.com/qr/te/25_00

I. The Devastation and Lament of Jerusalem (1:1-22)

II. God's Judgment on Jerusalem (2:1-22)

III. Words of Anguish, Words of Hope (3:1-66)

IV. The Devastated People of Jerusalem (4:1-22)

V. The Prayer of Judah's People (5:1-22)

LAMENTATIONS

I. THE DEVASTATION AND LAMENT OF JERUSALEM (1:1-22)

1:1-4 Lamentations calls to mind the image of a desolate man of God sitting amid the ashes of the once-great and once-holy city of Jerusalem, weeping over its destruction and the exile of his people who had ignored decades of warnings and calls for repentance from the Lord. This opening chapter is littered with vivid descriptions of Jerusalem's terrible condition following the application of the terrifying judgments proclaimed through Jeremiah.

Whereas Jerusalem had been a **princess**, now the holy city is a **widow**, the epitome of poverty and destitution (1:1). **She weeps bitterly during the night** with no one to **comfort** her because Judah's false gods, **her lovers**, had turned on her and became **her enemies** as her people were dragged away in chains to Babylon (1:2). Now in **exile**, she has **been put to forced labor** and **harsh slavery** (1:1, 3).

1:5-11 All the splendor has vanished is a sobering statement (1:6). Jerusalem was a sight to behold in the **days of old** (1:7), but **all her precious belongings** are gone now—taken by the enemy or traded for food (1:7, 10-11). **All who honored her now despise her**, and **she herself groans** (1:8). Jeremiah was in deep agony over all this, but he knew the reason for the judgment received: **The Lord has made her suffer because of her many transgressions** (1:5). **Jerusalem has sinned grievously**, in spite of repeated warning from numerous prophets (1:8). **Her downfall was astonishing** (1:9)—both

to the Jews who'd assumed they were right with God and to the surrounding nations.

The picture of **Jerusalem** lying in the gutter is appropriate for a people who had been prostituting themselves with foreign gods for many years. God's people had turned from the well-lighted way of his word to follow evil down a dark backstreet. And now the city is like a discarded lady of the night whose lovers have tired of her and pushed her aside (1:8-9).

1:12-22 The second half of this poetic chapter personifies the city of Jerusalem and gives her a voice. The city calls to the nations around her for some measure of pity over her astonishing destruction (1:12). Yet, as she says repeatedly, **no one** will **comfort** her (1:16-17, 21). Among several metaphors regarding Jerusalem's judgment, one stands out: **My transgressions have been formed into a yoke, fastened together by his hand** (1:14). This word picture is the fulfillment of Jeremiah's "yoke of . . . Babylon" prophecy (see Jer 27:1-11), warning King Zedekiah that the people of Judah would serve Nebuchadnezzar and have their necks "under the yoke of the king of Babylon" (Jer 27:8).

Jerusalem acknowledges that **the Lord is just** and that she has **rebelled against his command** (1:18). Everything that had come upon her was deserved **because of all [her] transgressions** (1:22). All that she can do now is plead for God's mercy and vindication on her ungodly foes who were gloating at her devastation (1:20-21).

II. GOD'S JUDGMENT ON JERUSALEM (2:1-22)

2:1-5 With great grief, Jeremiah describes the total ruin of Jerusalem by the Babylonians. But the invaders are barely mentioned because the point is that God **overshadowed ... swallowed up ... demolished ... cut off ... and destroyed** Judah as a result of his **wrath** and **burning anger** against his people (2:1-5). That the Lord **cut off every horn of Israel** (2:3) refers to every symbol of strength—including **fortified cities** and **leaders** (2:2). God made them as helpless as children against the enemy.

2:6-10 Perhaps most disturbing of all, God had even **wrecked his temple** (2:6)! Although this was the place he had chosen for his name, he had warned, "I will banish [the temple] from my presence" if Israel turned to other gods (2 Chr 7:16, 19-20). And so he did.

With this rejection of Jerusalem's holy place of worship, God had **abolished appointed festivals and Sabbaths in Zion** and **despised king and priest** alike (2:6). The festivals had been ignored or conducted with hypocrisy anyway, and many of the kings and priests had demonstrated no spiritual leadership. That **even her prophets receive no vision from the LORD** (2:9) means that in Judah all three levels of leadership—king, priest, and prophet—had failed. All that the people could do was silently mourn while wearing **sackcloth** and putting **dust on their heads** (2:10)—symbolic acts of great grief (see Job 16:15; Neh 9:1).

2:11-14 As a witness to **the destruction of [his] dear people**, Jeremiah cannot stop **weeping** as he watches hungry children

cry out to their mothers, who are unable to feed their starving little ones (2:11-12). But as painful as it was to witness this, Jeremiah did not lose sight of the reason his people were suffering: they'd earned God's judgment for their sin. They needed to know this, in fact, so they could repent and not repeat their foolish decisions.

Jeremiah had chastised Judah's lying **prophets** who'd failed to point out the people's **iniquity** but instead told kings and people what they wanted to hear (2:14), thus contributing to their demise. Examples of false prophets from Jeremiah's day include Pashhur, Hananiah, Ahab, Zedekiah, and Shemaiah (see Jer 20:1-6; 28:1-17; 29:21-32).

2:15-22 Judah's enemies heaped scorn upon the people (2:15-16), but they weren't their primary foe. The Babylonians, after all, were merely the bows, arrows, and spears in God's hand used to accomplish what he had **planned** and **ordained** (2:17). Centuries before, when he'd established his covenant with Israel, he'd threatened judgment for their disobedience (see Deut 28:15-68). Then, after years of observing their idolatry, he specifically warned that he would use the Babylonians to punish his people (see 2 Kgs 20:17-18; Hab 1:6). Therefore, instead of simply moaning about their fate, God's people needed to **cry out** in repentance and beg him for mercy (2:19-20).

When God is your biggest problem, he is also your only hope. His holiness is unchanging. So when it confronts you, you must do the adjusting.

III. WORDS OF ANGUISH, WORDS OF HOPE (3:1-66)

3:1 Not only were things dark for the nation, but also for Jeremiah. **I am the man who has seen affliction under the rod of God's wrath** is a reminder that he had experienced a double load of grief. In addition to the pain of Jerusalem's destruction, Jeremiah had physical and emotional scars from decades

of prophetic ministry to people who'd refused to listen. He was the most hated man in Judah, the person everyone wanted gone.

3:2-20 Yet, Jeremiah sees his suffering as coming from the Lord. It was God who had appointed him as a prophet (see Jer 1:1-10), and it was God who'd told him that the people would "not listen to" him (Jer 7:27). God had set him on his path, and he had forced the prophet to walk in darkness (3:2), pounced on him like a bear waiting in ambush (3:10), made him a laughingstock among the people (3:14), and filled him with bitterness (3:15). Thus, Jeremiah is depressed (3:20). This detail brings us to the low point of the book, but it also leads us to a springboard for Jeremiah's great testimony of God's faithfulness: verses 21-23.

3:21-23 In 3:18 Jeremiah confessed that his hope was lost, but in 3:21 he declares, I have hope. So where did he find hope in the midst of his affliction? What caused the sudden reversal? Hope returned when he took control of his mind and turned his thoughts in a Godward direction (3:21). I call this to mind . . . Because of the LORD's faithful love we do not perish, for his mercies never end. They are new every morning; great is your faithfulness! Interestingly, the magnificent hymn, "Great Is Thy Faithfulness," takes its title from Lamentations 3:23. The lyrics are a testimony to the constancy of God's love and mercy.

The Lord is *faithful*. His character is unchanging, and he keeps his promises. As Scripture proclaims repeatedly, he is compassionate and gracious, slow to anger and abounding in faithful love (see Exod 34:6; Num 14:18; Ps 103:8; Neh 9:17). So though his people rejected him, God remains faithful to his covenant with them. Therefore, his mercies are new every morning (3:22-23).

God could be merciful because he knew what he would do through his Son. Jesus Christ satisfied God's wrath against sin so that he can deal with us in mercy—which is exactly what we need. When you're guilty,

you don't demand justice; you throw yourself on the mercy of the court.

Against the dark background of a lost nation and Jeremiah's personal agony, the light of God's faithfulness to his covenant and his people gave Jeremiah new hope. He didn't deny his pain, yet he was assured that despair never has the last word when God is our hope.

3:24-42 God's mercies are real, but they are only mine if I appropriate them, as Jeremiah did: The LORD is my portion, therefore I will put my hope in him (3:24). Putting your hope in God isn't passive—it's active. Those who hope in God wait for him, seek him, and receive his discipline (3:25-30).

Jeremiah knew of God's covenant love; he knew God would not reject [his people] forever. Although he causes suffering if necessary, he will show compassion according to the abundance of his faithful love (3:31-32). God did not approve of the injustices of the Babylonians, but he used them for his purposes—to punish his people for their sins (3:34-39). God's people are to hope in his mercy by examining their ways, confessing their sins, and turning back to him (3:40-42).

3:43-66 Jeremiah returns to lament in these verses, serving as a spokesman for Judah's devastated people who realize their agony is the Lord's doing (3:43-47). Then the prophet switches to the first person to describe his own suffering and rejection (3:48-54). His reference to being tossed in a pit by his enemies and almost drowning acknowledges a low point of his life, the moment he thought he would die (3:53; see Jer 38:1-6). But Jeremiah's distress turned to a prayer for deliverance and God answered (3:55-66).

IV. THE DEVASTATED PEOPLE OF JERUSALEM (4:1-22)

4:1-12 The story of Jerusalem under siege by the Babylonians is a gruesome one of suffering and death. No one thought Jerusalem could be conquered (4:12). Jeremiah makes the scene even more graphic by employing a series of illustrations contrasting the people's former health, security, and comforts

of life with their pitiful condition after the enemy finished with them (4:1-5). The people of Jerusalem were once worth their weight in pure gold, but now are as common and worthless as clay jars (4:2).

Even the members of Jerusalem's royal house are reduced to lying on trash heaps

(4:5), their bodies so wasted from hunger and thirst that they are unrecognizable. Things are so unbearable that those who die rather than waste away **are better off** (4:9). And in what may have been the worst development of all, innocent children suffer terribly because of their elders' sins. Intense hunger during the city's long siege by the Babylonian army turned normal human emotions into twisted attempts at self-survival. Not only did Jerusalem's children languish in hunger and thirst that their parents couldn't satisfy, but some families actually engaged in the horrific practice of cannibalism on their children (4:10)! These sufferings were a reminder that they had brought all these consequences upon themselves by their sin (4:11).

4:13-22 Because God was their problem, God alone was the solution for Judah's people. Yet they tried everyone and everything else. Prior to Jerusalem's fall, they listened to their lying **prophets** and corrupt **priests** (4:13-16), who assured them they were in good standing before the Lord and would never suffer defeat and exile. The nation kept looking in **vain** to foreign powers for help (4:17). But even their hope in King Zedekiah, **the LORD's anointed**, proved useless. The Davidic king who should have been the example to his people of godliness and justice repeatedly refused to listen to God through Jeremiah. As a result, he was **captured** by the enemy (4:20). But once more, amid the ruins, God promises to restore **Zion** from **exile** (4:22).

V. THE PRAYER OF JUDAH'S PEOPLE (5:1-22)

5:1-8 Now that the worst has happened, the people of Judah finally began looking up and acknowledging that their condition is the result of both their own sin and the ungodly actions of their ancestors in failing to trust God. Their lives are so miserable they even have to pay for **water** and the **wood** they need for cooking and warmth (5:4). The real tragedy of their foreign alliances was that in turning to nations like **Egypt** and **Assyria** for help, their **fathers** had disobeyed God and put his people at the mercy of the ungodly (5:6-8).

5:9-18 Every segment of society had been devastated by Judah's sin and judgment. Jeremiah had already told of the incredible suffering Judah's children underwent (4:4). But the **women ... princes ... elders ...** and **young men** suffered terrible fates as

well (5:11-13). It took all of this suffering for the people to utter the confession God had been waiting to hear: **Woe to us, for we have sinned** (5:16).

5:19-22 God had been waiting for his people to admit their sin so he could act on their behalf. Their confession was the first step in their restoration.

Verse 20, **Why do you continually forget us, abandon us for our entire lives?**, is a plea for God to remember his covenant. And importantly, the only way God would turn away from them forever was if he **completely rejected** them (5:22). That, however, would have required God to be unfaithful to his promises. And since that could never happen—see 3:23—the book of Lamentations ends with hope that God will bring them back and **renew** their days (5:21).

EZEKIEL

INTRODUCTION

Author

The writer of the book bearing his name is Ezekiel son of Buzi. This priest, along with thousands of other residents of Judah, had been deported to Babylon. He began prophesying when he was thirty years old (1:1-3). Some critical scholars have rejected the claim that the historical prophet Ezekiel could have served as the author of the entire book. However, the book is written with a unified and consistent style. It is reasonable, then, to accept Ezekiel as the author.

Historical Background

In 598–597 BC, King Nebuchadnezzar deported ten thousand people from Judah to Babylon (see 2 Kgs 24:10-14), including Ezekiel. Judah's King Jehoiachin was taken to Babylon as well (2 Kgs 24:15). It was during "the fifth year of Jehoiachin's exile" (593 BC), when Ezekiel was thirty, that the word of the Lord first came to him in Babylon (Ezek 1:1-3). The prophet's messages were intended primarily for the Jewish exiles there. Interestingly, many of Ezekiel's prophetic oracles include date references (e.g., 8:1; 20:1; 24:1; 26:1). The last date is found in 29:17; it refers to "the twenty-seventh year" of Jehoiachin's exile (571 BC). Thus, Ezekiel's prophetic ministry lasted at least twenty-two years.

Message and Purpose

The book of Ezekiel records the prophet's message to the people of the southern kingdom of Judah, now incarcerated in Babylon because of their rebellion against God. The theme of the book is the glory of God, which departed from the temple in Jerusalem because of the people's sin. Thus, his manifest presence was no longer in their midst.

Ezekiel also prophesied, in chapters 40–48, of a coming restoration. The regathering of God's people would occur with the coming of Messiah to establish his kingdom, which we know as the future one-thousand-year reign of Jesus Christ called the millennial kingdom. The prophet wanted God's people to know that as bad as things were during their captivity, God still had a plan and would keep his covenant promises despite their rebellion and the consequences they were enduring. Ezekiel thus called on the people to have faith in God even in the discipline of captivity.

He also foretold that the glory of God would return when Messiah reigns. We learn from this book that God's glorification is his greatest purpose. And when we too live for his kingdom purposes, his glory—his manifest presence—is made real to us and to the world.

VIDEO · INTRO

www.bhpublishinggroup.com/qr/te/26_00

EZEKIEL

I. GOD'S APPEARANCE TO AND COMMISSIONING OF EZEKIEL (1:1–3:27)

❧ A. Ezekiel's Vision of God (1:1-28) ❧

1:1-3 God called **the priest Ezekiel** (1:3) into his service as a prophet with one of the most spectacular, and most complex, visions recorded in Scripture. Ezekiel's reference to **the thirtieth year** (1:1) most likely reveals his age, which was the point at which a man from the tribe of Levi could become a priest (see Num 4:2-3, 22-23, 29-30). As one of the earliest captives taken from Jerusalem to Babylon by Nebuchadnezzar in 598–597 BC, Ezekiel was **among the exiles** of Judah when he **saw visions of God** and **the word of the LORD came directly to** him (1:1, 3). What he saw was *astounding*. His ministry was under divine mandate and authority.

1:4-14 Ezekiel's vision began with **a whirlwind coming from the north**, a brilliant **cloud** of flashing **fire** (1:4). But what really captured his attention were **four living creatures** in the middle of the whirlwind. These were awesome heavenly beings with **four faces and four wings** each, with **feet** that were **like the hooves of a calf** and **human hands under their wings on their four sides** (1:5-8). Later identified as cherubim, who are bearers of God's throne and protectors of his glory, **each of the four had the face of** a **human**, a **lion**, an **ox**, and an **eagle**; their faces were connected so they could move **without turning** (1:9-10, 12). As angelic beings who minister in God's holy presence (see also Isa 6:1-3), the cherubim had an appearance that seemed to Ezekiel **like the appearance of blazing coals of fire or like torches** as they darted **back and forth like flashes of lightning** (1:13-14)—a detail that perhaps indicates the burning judgments Ezekiel would be called to deliver.

1:15-21 As the prophet was still gazing in awe at the four living creatures, he saw four gleaming wheels under the four cherubim. These appeared to Ezekiel as **a wheel within a wheel**, intersecting in a way that allowed the wheels to move in any direction the cherubim moved **without turning as they** did so (1:15-17). That the **rims** of the wheels were **full of eyes all around** (1:18) suggests the all-seeing omniscience of God. What becomes clear in the rest of this chapter is that the cherubim were on God's throne, which was not a stationary object but a moving platform—like a chariot—that moved **wherever the Spirit wanted to go** (1:20). This was a picture of Israel's all-knowing, all-present God who could follow his people wherever they went, both in judgment and in restoration. His presence is inescapable.

1:22-28 Ezekiel saw and heard a brilliant display of God's glory that overwhelmed him. The **expanse** mentioned is translated from the same Hebrew word used in Genesis 1:6 to describe God's creation of the sky in order to separate the waters above the earth from the waters on it. Here the term describes an "expanse" surrounding God's throne, or at least **the likeness of** it (1:22). Throughout this vision Ezekiel used terms like this one in an attempt to find adequate language to describe what he was seeing.

Ezekiel saw **something like a throne**, on which was **someone who looked like a human** (1:26). The **brilliant light all around** him made Ezekiel realize that he was seeing **the appearance of the likeness of the LORD's glory**, and he **fell facedown** as he **heard a voice speaking** (1:28). The only appropriate response to the glory of God is worship and obedience. This position opens the door for God to speak to us personally.

➢ B. God's Call and Commission to Ezekiel (2:1–3:27) ⬿

2:1-5 God called Ezekiel to a prophetic ministry that would begin with scathing denunciations of Judah's sins and warnings of worse judgments to come. His prophetic career ended, however, with prophecies of restoration and kingdom blessing. Importantly, the cancer of sin had to be removed before the healing could begin. Repentance is God's requirement for restoration.

Ezekiel's humility before God was appropriate, but God had a work for him to do, so **the Spirit** enabled the prophet to **stand up** so he could hear what God wanted to tell him (2:1-2). It was not a pretty message. God's people were **rebellious pagans who . . . rebelled against** him (2:3). They were **a rebellious house** (2:5). The rebelliousness of the Israelites, in fact, is a common theme in this book as God moved in judgment against a people who were **obstinate and hardhearted** (2:4). His people even refused to repent when undergoing divine discipline!

Ezekiel's job was not to be "successful" as humans define success; rather, he was to be faithful in declaring, **This is what the Lord GOD says** (2:4). The compound name "Lord GOD," or Adonai Yahweh, was one of Ezekiel's favorite titles for God. He used it over two hundred times, though it appears just over one hundred times in the rest of the Old Testament. It's a powerful combination that emphasizes God's sovereign authority and covenant-keeping faithfulness: these are two themes of the prophet's ministry.

2:6-7 Ezekiel would need the strengthening of his sovereign and faithful God because in a sense he was being sent into a patch of **briers** and a nest of **scorpions**. God told him three times not to be **afraid of** the **words** or the scornful **look** (2:6) he would receive from the **rebellious** (2:7) people, though. He was to give them God's message regardless of their response.

2:8–3:3 That message was contained in the **scroll** that Ezekiel was given (2:9). Even though the scroll had writing **on the front and back** with **words of lamentation, mourning, and woe**, Ezekiel was told to **eat** it and then deliver its message to **the house of Israel** (2:10–3:1). In other words, Ezekiel was to "digest" the Word of God—to read it and make it a part of himself.

Despite its words of severe judgment, the prophet found the scroll to be **as sweet as honey in** his **mouth** (3:3). This indicates that even though a specific message from God can be hard to hear, nevertheless it is still sweet to the believer who appropriates it because it is the Word of God.

3:4-9 Once Ezekiel was fortified with the content of his prophecy, God reinforced Israel's rebellious nature to Ezekiel by saying that if he were sent to a foreign people whose **language** he didn't understand, they would believe him and repent (3:4-6)! But not **Israel** (or in Ezekiel's case specifically, the surviving kingdom of Judah); they didn't want to hear from Ezekiel because they didn't want to hear from God. The people to whom Ezekiel was being sent were **hardheaded and hardhearted**, so God told Ezekiel that he was going to make him just as tough so he could speak to them without being **discouraged** (3:7-9).

3:10-15 Now it was time for Ezekiel to be returned to the place where his ministry would begin, and it was quite a ride. He had started out **among the exiles . . . by the Chebar Canal** (3:15; see 1:1), and—don't miss this—the **Spirit . . . lifted** him **up** to take him back there (3:12). But suddenly he heard **a loud rumbling sound** and found himself being transported on God's chariot-throne by the four cherubim and the **wheels** (3:13).

So why did Ezekiel leave that glorious vision **in bitterness and in an angry spirit** (3:14)? Because the sin of Judah's people angered him as much as it angered the Lord. The prophet was so overwhelmed by all that had happened and the gravity of his message, in fact, that he **sat there among** the exiles **stunned for seven days** (3:15). This is a reminder that true spirituality is manifested when we feel the way God feels about unrighteousness.

3:16-21 At the end of that week, it was God who spoke, not Ezekiel. The prophet's commission as **a watchman over the house of Israel** (3:17) involved a two-fold principle: the individual's responsibility to turn from his own sin and the responsibility of God's spokesman to deliver his message faithfully. God would hold Ezekiel guilty of the **blood** of a **wicked person** if he failed to warn him of his sinfulness (3:18, 20). There was also the promise of vindication for Ezekiel should a **righteous person** heed his message and avoid sin (3:21).

Believers in Jesus Christ bear the responsibility to proclaim the good news so that sinners may believe, be saved, and follow him in godliness. After all, how can we keep silent when we know how people can escape the wrath of God?

3:22-27 Ezekiel's commissioning for service continued with a second appearance of God's **glory** that was similar to the first vision and brought the same response: the prophet **fell facedown** (3:23). God ordered him to confine himself to his **house** lest his fellow exiles in Babylon tie him up with **ropes** to keep him there (3:24-25). There doesn't seem to be any evidence that this was a physical threat; instead, it seems God intended to create an object lesson for the people about their refusal to hear Ezekiel's message. The same can be said for Ezekiel's **tongue** sticking **to the roof of** his **mouth** (3:26). It suggests that he wouldn't have anything to say to the rebellious Israelites unless it was the message God had given him. Whether the people heard and repented, or rejected and plunged into ruin, the prophet was only to say, **This is what the Lord God says** (3:27), letting the chips fall where they may. In fact, this should be the posture of every preacher who speaks for God.

II. PROPHECIES AGAINST JUDAH (4:1–24:27)

❧ A. The Necessity of Judah's Judgment and Exile (4:1–11:25) ❦

4:1-3 Since Ezekiel was confined to his house and the courtyard around it, God directed him to use signs in the form of visuals and certain actions to convey his message. There are four such signs in chapters 4 and 5, beginning with the depiction of the coming siege against Jerusalem by Nebuchadnezzar's armies when the city would finally fall around 587–586 BC.

Ezekiel gained the attention of his neighbors by drawing the easily recognizable outline of **Jerusalem** on a clay **brick** and then laying **siege** against it with a **wall** . . . **ramp** . . . **military camps** and **battering rams** . . . **on all sides** (4:1-2). The exiles observing this knew what these military devices meant, but they must have been in disbelief to think that the holy city would ever come under such a devastating attack (after all, the actual fall of Jerusalem was still about six years away). Jerusalem was the place of God's presence and, presumably, his protection. But it was exactly that kind of thinking that Ezekiel had to dislodge from the people's minds. Their sins had already doomed Jerusalem. God had set his face against the city and its people to such an extent that he was like an **iron plate** against them (4:3). The point of this sign would be hard to miss.

4:4-8 It is harder to interpret what Ezekiel did next. God required him to **lie down on** his sides for a specific number of days, **390** and **forty** respectively (4:4-6). It seems to be agreed upon that since Ezekiel would have been facing north when lying on his left side, God had the northern kingdom of Israel in mind with that action; Israel had been destroyed long before by the Assyrians in 722 BC. So, the "390" referred to the years of Israel's **iniquity according to the number of days** God told Ezekiel to **lie down** facing north (4:4).

As a priest, Ezekiel was also to **bear the iniquity** of his people (4:4-5). Israel's priests bore the people's sins as their representatives and carried them away, which Ezekiel could not do in this situation without an atoning sacrifice. Besides, God had already consigned the people of Judah to judgment (notice the lack of a call to repentance here). Ezekiel was to lie on his **right side** facing south toward **Jerusalem** to **bear the iniquity of the house of Judah**, which in this interpretation had accumulated forty years of sin before its judgment (4:6-7).

4:9-13 Part of the third sign God asked Ezekiel to act out was so repugnant to him as a priest that Ezekiel objected. He was told to take a number of grains that were common in Israel and bake them together **into bread** and eat them for the entire **390 days** he lay on his side (4:9). The meager size of the daily loaves, **eight ounces**, and rations of water, **a sixth of a gallon**, symbolized the extreme scarcity that the people of Jerusalem would experience during the coming Babylonian siege (4:10-11; see v. 16). Then God told Ezekiel to bake these cakes **over dried human excrement** in the **sight** of his fellow exiles to illustrate how the people in Jerusalem would have to eat **ceremonially unclean** food when God banished them from the land (4:12-13).

4:14-17 Ezekiel's entire life had been dedicated to keeping God's laws, including his dietary restrictions. So he strongly objected to using **human excrement** as fuel, and God granted his request to use the common fuel of **cow dung** (4:14-15). Nonetheless, God's point was made. The Jews of Jerusalem would face terrible famine and thirst as the Babylonians laid siege to the city. They would be reduced to taking desperate measures that they would never have imagined in their worst nightmares. The entire population would **be devastated . . . because of their iniquity** (4:16-17).

Again, no offer of repentance and restoration was made. The judgment of ruin and captivity would be fully carried out.

5:1-4 Ezekiel's signs were designed to call attention to the message he had for these first exiles in Babylon. This next sign required using **a sharp sword** to **shave** his **head and beard** (5:1), no doubt while his fellow exiles watched.

God provides us with an interpretation of what each part of this sign meant to Ezekiel's audience. He was told to weigh his hair and separate it into three equal parts, each pile symbolizing a judgment against Jerusalem and its people (5:2-4). The prophet was told to burn **a third** of his hair on the clay model of Jerusalem he had made, take the second **third** around the city **and slash it with the sword**, and **scatter a third to the wind** (5:2). But Ezekiel was to save **a few strands** and tuck them in his **robe** (5:3). This last action makes it sound like the people represented by the strands would be shielded from judgment, but even some of them would be thrown in the fire that would **spread . . . to the whole house of Israel** (5:3-4).

5:5-6 Fire, sword, and scattering to the wind. Those were three actions against the people of Jerusalem who had not yet experienced the full wrath of God's judgment against their gross sins and idolatry. And they all came to pass for one reason. God had **set . . . Jerusalem in the center of the nations** as a city on a hill, populated by his chosen people, to be a witness to his holiness by their love and devotion to him. But Israel had **rebelled** against his **ordinances** and **statutes** and had become more wicked **than the countries that surround her** (5:6).

5:7-10 Israel had committed disgraceful sins in the sight of all her neighbors, so God said, **I will execute judgments within you in the sight of the nations**, even decreeing a judgment so shocking that he promised he would **never do** it again—the horror of cannibalism **within Jerusalem** as the siege grew worse (5:8-10). Neither would there be mercy for the **survivors** of the famine and slaughter when the Babylonians finally breached Jerusalem's walls; they would be lost in exile (5:10). The principle at work here is this: The greater the sin, the greater the consequence.

5:11-13 The relentless judgments of this chapter give us another insight into how hard Ezekiel's ministry must have been. God swore by his own living character that he would have **no pity** on Israel because of the way its people had **defiled** his **sanctuary** (5:11). God provides in 5:12 the interpretation of the symbolic acts Ezekiel performed with the three parts of his hair (5:2). The few hairs hidden in his robe represent a righteous remnant preserved from immediate judgment. (Both 5:4 and the final verses of this chapter argue against their total safety.) Likely, God chose to deliver some so they would be a witness to the awfulness of Judah's sin and the righteousness of God's judgment, as indicated in 6:8-10.

5:14-17 The terrifying judgments are cataloged here. Notice the repetition of the phrase **I, the Lord, have spoken** (5:15, 17). It's a reminder that Judah's fate wasn't about the hotheaded vengeance of an angry sovereign flying off the handle at his subjects. Rather, these are the pronouncements of Israel's perfectly just and holy God whose righteous standards had been dragged through the dirt by the same people who had promised to uphold them in loving obedience. We must never extol the love of God at the expense of his just wrath against sin.

6:1 In chapters 6 and 7 Ezekiel turns from acting out signs to preaching (though note the clapping and stamping in 6:11). Nevertheless, the message of doom and destruction remained the same for the people of Jerusalem and the land of Judah. Ezekiel often used the name Israel to refer to the chosen nation, even though the northern kingdom which was known by that name was long gone. Both of these sermons begin with the prophetic formula, **The word of the Lord came to me** (see 7:1).

6:2-4 This first sermon is addressed to **the mountains of Israel**, and to **the hills, to the ravines and the valleys** (6:3). God spoke this way because these were the places where

idolatry was flourishing among the people of Judah. The **high places** (6:3) were worship centers set up in the mountains because it was believed they brought the worshiper closer to the false gods to whom they were bowing down and offering sacrifices. Canaanite high places had been in the land long before the Israelites arrived, and God had ordered his people to destroy them. But during the days of the monarchy, the bad kings rebuilt them, leaving the good ones to eradicate them all over again. Unfortunately, by the time of Ezekiel, idol worship at these pagan **altars** and **shrines** was active (6:4), and God was ready to take decisive action.

6:5-10 He vowed to kill the idolaters and **scatter** their **bones** on their ruined worship sites so that the nation would **know that I am the Lord** (6:5-7), a phrase that appears over sixty times in Ezekiel. By using the name "Lord" (Yahweh), the name of his covenant faithfulness, God was reminding his faithless people that he was no mere offended deity. He was a grieved, loving husband whose fidelity to his covenant promises had been met by his people's **promiscuous hearts**, which committed adultery and **lusted after . . . idols** (6:9). An idol is any person, place, thing, or thought that you look to as your source. Idolatry leads to divine discipline.

Yet in the middle of this sermon there is a promise: **I will leave a remnant when you are scattered among the nations** (6:8). Those in view in this statement were represented by the few strands of hair (5:3) that God told Ezekiel to hide in the folds of his robe, symbolizing those who would escape the **sword**, famine, and plague that he was bringing on Jerusalem through the Babylonians. These **survivors** were to serve as witnesses of two facts: the horrible nature of their nation's sins in turning away from God, and that he had every right and **reason** to bring disaster on them (6:9-10).

6:11-13 After this brief interlude, Ezekiel returns to his message of God's judgment without mercy or pity. The Lord instructed Ezekiel, **Clap your hands** and **stamp your feet** as signs of derision against **the house of Israel** for all of its sins. God made it clear that none of them would be **spared** from the disasters of **sword, famine, and plague** (6:11-12). He would not relent but would **exhaust** his **wrath on them** so that **their slain** would **lie among their idols** (6:12-13). Though God's justice is often delayed, it is not to be disregarded.

6:14 The people's sin was so complete and so widespread that God vowed not to stop until he had wiped out the idolaters **from the wilderness to Diblah**, which some Old Testament manuscripts read as "Riblah" (see CSB note), a northern city in the land of Israel. To date, there is no record of a city named "Diblah," and the letters *d* and *r* in Hebrew are very similar, so a scribe could easily have substituted one for the other. The reading "Riblah" fits the context, giving the meaning, "from the south [the wilderness] to the north [Riblah]," the entire land. Regardless, the judgment would cause the people to know that the Lord was their true God.

7:1-7 Ezekiel's second sermon drove the nail into Judah's coffin: **An end! The end has come on the four corners of the earth. The end is now upon you** (7:2-3). In other words, there would be no relenting. God's fierce **anger** would **judge** and **punish** his people for their **detestable practices** without **pity**, until they came to know that Yahweh was their true God (7:3-4).

The suddenness of Judah's judgment is pictured as a herald running to unsuspecting people with an announcement of imminent **disaster** (7:5) that is so close it would cause **panic on the mountains** among the idolaters (7:7). They had been celebrating in their idolatry amid a false sense of ease and security. They thought God didn't see them or wouldn't act because they were still his people, doing their religious duty at the temple (alongside their false worship). Besides, there was prosperity in Jerusalem and they had false prophets telling them that everything was fine.

7:8-14 That illusion was about to be shattered—**very soon**. God promises a second time in this sermon to **exhaust** his anger by punishing them for their sins without **pity** until they learned that he was the one who was judging them and that their misfortunes weren't just terrible coincidences (7:8-9).

God uses the imagery of a budding plant to illustrate this message, much like when Jeremiah spoke of an almond tree in bloom (Jer 1:11-12) to illustrate coming judgment. So here the message was the same, except that in this case the blossom was Judah's **arrogance** producing the **violence** that would come upon the people to punish their **wickedness** (7:10-11).

Interestingly, God uses the term **crowd** four times in 7:10-14 as a term of derision for people who are considered hopeless, those about whom little that's positive can be said. **That crowd** in Jerusalem included those of **wealth, the eminent**—the merchants who had accumulated a lot of gold and silver by their transactions (7:11). God's judgment, then, would also have economic consequences, which will always happen when his people ignore his kingdom agenda and misuse wealth for their own greed and self-satisfaction. When the Babylonians began to attack and besiege Jerusalem, both **the buyer** and **the seller** would suffer loss, for all of their commerce and profit would mean nothing: all would be lost (7:12-13). And the city would find no help in its army, because it was part of the **whole crowd**, which was utterly useless in the day of Jerusalem's disaster (7:14).

7:15-21 In fact, there was simply no place to go to escape. Those who tried to run away would find **the sword** of the Babylonians waiting to kill them; those who stayed inside Jerusalem would face **plague and famine**; and those who hid in the **mountains** would wail and **moan** at the catastrophe (7:15-16). If the rest of this sermon points back to Jerusalem, it pictures a people shaking so hard in terror that they literally wet themselves and try in vain to show some repentance by wearing **sackcloth** and shaving their heads **bald** (7:17-18). The **silver** and **gold** they valued so highly gets discarded in disgust as they realize it **will not satisfy their appetites**. After all, these things **were the stumbling blocks that brought about their iniquity**. They would become **plunder** for the Babylonians (7:19-21).

7:22-27 Most shocking of all is that God would allow the Babylonians to **profane** his holy temple (7:22). At this revelation, the exiles listening to Ezekiel in Babylon and the recipients of his prophecies back in Jerusalem knew the full horrors of God's coming judgment. Jerusalem would no longer be the city of peace, but the place from which they would be led in chains. Though the people would listen frantically to all kinds of rumors coming out of Babylon and other places that spoke of rescue or relief, they would all prove false. Nothing would hold back God's hand until his sinful people had learned that he alone is God (7:25-27).

8:1-6 The variety of means God gave Ezekiel to express his judgment on his people continues with a series of visions in chapters 8–11. Ezekiel was transported **in visions of God to Jerusalem** as he sat in his house with **the elders of Judah**, who were no doubt there seeking a word from the Lord (8:1-3). Ezekiel describes all of his visions before telling the elders what God had shown him (see 11:25).

The importance of these visions was made known to him from the start by the glorious appearance of a figure comprised of **fire** from the **waist down** who gleamed **of amber** from the **waist up** (8:2). He carried Ezekiel to **the inner gate that faces north** at the temple, where he saw a **statue** that provoked God to **jealousy** (8:3). Ezekiel must have been appalled at the sight of this pagan idol (perhaps an Asherah pole used in sexually degrading worship) defiling God's temple, where **the glory of the God of Israel** alone was to reside (8:4). But this scene marked only the beginning of Judah's detestable practices that caused God to ask Ezekiel essentially, "Can you believe what you are seeing? Do you understand now why I have to leave my temple? And you haven't seen anything yet!" (8:5-6).

8:7-12 Indeed, the state of affairs in Ezekiel's homeland were much worse. In his vision Ezekiel dug through **a hole in the wall** of the inner court and went through **a doorway** (8:7-9). There he found a room with a wall on which was **engraved . . . every kind of abhorrent thing—crawling creatures and beasts—as well as all the idols of the house of Israel** (8:10). **Seventy elders**, representing the leaders of Jerusalem, were worshiping these images, including a man

Ezekiel knew, **Jaazaniah son of Shaphan**. The men were offering incense in idolatrous worship, without any fear or remorse because they had concluded that God had **abandoned the land** and no longer saw or cared what they did (8:12).

8:13-15 God warned the prophet to be prepared for the next shock: **You will see even more detestable acts that they are committing** (8:13). Then Ezekiel was transported to the outer court where he saw a group of women **weeping for Tammuz** (8:14), the Babylonian god who was believed to provide vegetation. He supposedly died in the summer, as the hot Middle Eastern climate dried up the plants, and descended into the underworld as his worshipers mourned for him. He'd emerge in the spring, bringing new life and vegetation. His worship included all manner of immorality, yet these women of Judah were worshiping this degrading deity instead of the God of Israel who provided them with all the bounty of their land.

8:16-17 The Lord had one more disgusting practice within the temple to show Ezekiel. The **twenty-five men** the prophet saw must have been priests, based on their location **between the portico and the altar**. They were standing in that holy place, not interceding with God for the people, but **with their backs to the LORD's temple and their faces turned to the east . . . bowing . . . in worship of the sun** (8:16). This is exactly the kind of thing Paul describes when writing to the church in Rome: "They exchanged the truth of God for a lie, and worshiped and served what has been created instead of the Creator" (Rom 1:25). It was an act of deliberate contempt toward God. Such things always result in degrading lifestyles and the deterioration of the culture (see Rom 1:18-32).

8:18 Though these priests had departed from the Lord to worship a false deity in his temple, they probably kept up the pretense of serving the Lord by going through their priestly rituals when the people came to do their religious duty. But God had drawn the line and said, "Enough!" His faithless people had angered him beyond the point of restoration. God was entirely just in judging his people without **pity** despite their last-minute cries for mercy.

9:1-2 Ezekiel's visions contained so many images of God's righteous wrath poured out on the people of Jerusalem that Ezekiel feared the house of Israel would be wiped out completely (see 9:8). God **called loudly**, suggesting urgency, for Jerusalem's **executioners** to line up, **each . . . with a destructive weapon in his hand** (9:1). This was a group of **six men** coming from the **north** with **war** clubs. A seventh man, a scribe, also came at God's command, **carrying writing equipment**.

9:3 But before these men were told what to do, Ezekiel watched as **the glory of the God of Israel** began to depart from his people; his presence left the holy of holies in the innermost part of the temple and moved to the building's **threshold**. It was only the first step in a sad journey of abandonment by a holy God who could no longer live among a sinful people. But of all the judgments God would inflict on Israel, this was the most crushing. God's people had turned their backs on him, and in response he was turning his back on them. Believers today can forfeit the fellowship of God's active presence operating in their lives when they live with unaddressed sin (see 1 John 1:5-9).

9:4 As God's presence, symbolized by his glory, was moving through and out of the temple, he commanded the scribe to go **throughout** Jerusalem and **put a mark on the foreheads** of everyone who grieved over the **detestable practices** they saw being **committed in** (what was supposed to be) God's holy city. This is a reference to the righteous remnant, the ones who shared God's view of sin. God has always had his faithful ones, even when the majority of his people are at their worst. In the days of Ahab and Jezebel, for instance, when the prophet Elijah complained that he was the only faithful one left in Israel, the Lord told him that there were "seven thousand" others who had "not bowed to Baal" (see 1 Kgs 19:18).

9:5-7 We're not told how many righteous people were marked, but everyone else in Jerusalem was to be consigned to death—young and old, male and female, without **pity** (9:5; for more on God's lack of pity on them, see 5:11; 7:4, 9; 8:18; 9:10). The killings were to begin **with the elders** (the priests) whom Ezekiel saw in **the temple** with their backs turned to God (9:6; see 8:16). Their corpses in the house of God would **defile** it (9:7), but it had already been defiled by the idols and the false worship.

9:8-11 So the men God ordered to kill Jerusalem's inhabitants began carrying out their orders, to Ezekiel's horror: **Are you going to destroy the entire remnant of Israel?** (9:8). God's greater concern was the overwhelming **iniquity of the house of Israel and Judah**. His people had grown so spiritually calloused that they thought he had **abandoned the land** (9:9), which in their warped minds meant they could do anything they wanted without fear of reprisal. In one way, though, they were right: God's presence was in the process of departing from Jerusalem—but not because he no longer cared for his inheritance. The people's sins had brought disaster on them, while the righteous remnant had been marked out for God's mercy amid his wrath (9:11).

10:1-2 Ezekiel signals a new part of his vision by saying he **looked** again and saw **something like a throne**, the throne of God from which he **spoke to the man clothed in linen** who had been marking the faithful remnant in Jerusalem. This time, as Ezekiel **watched**, God ordered the angelic figure to scoop his hands full of **blazing coals** from the altar in the temple and **scatter them over** Jerusalem to purify the city in burning judgment. Indeed, Jerusalem would be cleansed by destruction as the Babylonians burned the city and temple to the ground.

10:3-8 Ezekiel's vision also included the reappearance of **the cherubim** (10:3) and the four wheels (see 10:9) that the prophet had seen at the beginning of his calling (1:4-28). Earlier, these were called "four living creatures" (1:5), but now they are clearly identified as the cherubim who are continually in God's presence (see also 10:20). They were standing next to the temple when the angelic figure entered it, and **the cloud filled the**

inner court (10:3), signifying God's glorious presence.

But instead of inhabiting his temple, which had been defiled by idol worship, God was in the process of departing his house and the now unholy city. That's why Ezekiel saw **the glory of the LORD** move **to the threshold of the temple**, as the courtyard where Ezekiel was standing was illuminated by **the brightness of the LORD's glory** (10:4-5). Ezekiel was once again in the middle of a vision of overwhelming glory and magnificence, but it was also a vision of judgment. He watched as the angelic being **clothed in linen** obeyed God's command and took the fiery coals from the hand of a **cherub** and **went out** to fulfill his mission (10:6-7).

10:9-14 Ezekiel's description of his second vision of the **four wheels** and **cherubim** matches his first one (1:4-28) in most details (10:9-11) except for a couple of additions. Here the bodies of all these figures are described as **full of eyes all around** (10:12), which suggests God's all-seeing omniscience. The wheels are also called **the wheelwork** (10:13), as if spinning in readiness to carry God's presence and glory on his chariot-throne out of the temple and away from Jerusalem.

10:15-20 The final part of Ezekiel's vision in this chapter must have been heartbreaking for him. Ezekiel had pled for God to spare his sinful people, but now he had the unhappy responsibility of recording for his fellow exiles in Babylon—and for the Israelites back in Jerusalem who thought God was still with them—news of the departure of God's presence from the temple and the city where he had chosen to put his name.

As Ezekiel watched, no doubt in anguish, the **cherubim ascended** and **the wheels moved beside them** as God's chariot-throne lifted up from the temple and prepared for lift-off (10:15-16). These cherubim were the same **living creatures** he has seen by the Chebar Canal in chapter 1 (10:20). For one moment, as God **moved away from the threshold of the temple**, his **glory** paused at **the entrance to the eastern gate of the LORD's house** (10:18-19). But this was it, the last stop on the way out of the temple

and the city. God's glory was departing. And the absence of God's presence leaves his people in a hopeless situation.

11:1-4 In the last portion of Ezekiel's vision, he was carried by **the Spirit** to the **eastern gate** of the temple, where he saw **twenty-five men**, probably the same ones who were earlier worshiping the sun in the temple (11:1; see 8:16). He recognized two of these men who were leading the people of Jerusalem into sin by plotting **evil** and giving **wicked advice** (11:2). They were telling the inhabitants of Jerusalem to ignore Ezekiel's warnings of judgment, **build houses**, and settle down. They compared Jerusalem to a strong iron **pot** that would keep its people, **the meat** in the pot, safe from the fire (11:3). That kind of blind arrogance aroused God's righteous anger, and he thundered, **Prophesy against them. Prophesy, son of man!** (11:4). The wording here is important. In Ezekiel, we see God regularly use the expression "son of man" to refer to the prophet as a term for the frailty of mankind in contrast to God.

11:5-11 The Spirit of the LORD came to Ezekiel with a serious dose of reality for the leaders and people of Jerusalem. God knew what they were **thinking**, and he also knew of their violence (11:5). They had filled Jerusalem's **streets** with those they had **slain**, the righteous in the city (11:6). Therefore, God said he would reverse the leaders' imagery of the safe **pot**, dumping Jerusalem's people out of it and bringing **the sword** of the Babylonians against them (11:7-8). He would hand the city and its people **over to foreigners** who would **judge** them **at the border of Israel** (11:9-10). Here we see, then, that God uses evil people, places, and things to judge the sin and rebellion among his own people.

This prophecy was fulfilled when those captured in Jerusalem by Nebuchadnezzar's army were brought to him at his army headquarters in Riblah in northern Israel to be either executed or sent into exile (see 2 Kgs 25:18-21). In another six years or so, Ezekiel and his fellow exiles in Babylon would be mourning the deaths of thousands more of their fellow Jews and watching the survivors join them in captivity.

11:12-15 This judgment did not come from Babylon. Ultimately, it came from the one **whose statutes** they'd ignored (11:12). Judah's secret sins on earth were an open scandal in heaven. But Ezekiel was still so distressed at the judgments coming on his people that when **Pelatiah** (one of the twenty-five evil leaders in 11:1) died, the prophet **fell facedown** to plead with God not to wipe out the house of Israel completely (11:13). Meanwhile, **the residents of Jerusalem** scoffed at the relatives of the exiles in Babylon. Though the **relatives** had **the right to redeem** the **property** of their exiled families, the wicked people of Jerusalem told them that the **land** had **been given to** *them* as a **possession** (11:15).

11:16-20 The selfish people mentioned in verse 15 were using geography to determine God's favor, but he was using an entirely different, spiritual standard. Ezekiel was told that he and his fellow exiles were actually the remnant of Israel whom God had said he would preserve—the first promise of restoration in the book of Ezekiel.

This prophecy has a near and a far fulfillment, which is true of so many Old Testament prophecies. God did reassemble his people from **the countries where** they were **scattered**, and he has given them **the land of Israel** again today (11:16-17). But, importantly, they do not have the **new spirit** that God said he would give them, replacing **their heart of stone** with **a heart of flesh** (11:19). These promises await the time when Israel collectively recognizes Jesus Christ as her Messiah (see Zech 12:10), and Christ establishes his millennial kingdom with his throne in Jerusalem. It's doubtful if Ezekiel understood everything he wrote, but he recorded it under the Spirit's inspiration for our encouragement as we wait for Christ's return.

11:21-25 Ezekiel's visions ended with a return to the reality of Jerusalem's sin and the Spirit's final departure from the city, leaving the people without God's presence and protection (11:21-23). The departure of God's glory had happened once before at the tabernacle, in the days of Eli the priest when the ark of the covenant was captured and

Eli was judged for failing to restrain his two evil sons, Hophni and Phinehas (1 Sam 3-4). In recognition of God's judgment, Phinehas's wife named her son "Ichabod," which means, "no glory." Maybe no one thought such a thing would ever happen again. Regardless, the warning of Ichabod even applies to the church: when it abandons Christ, its lampstand is removed (see Rev 2:5).

At this point, Ezekiel's **vision** of Jerusalem ended and he returned to **Chaldea** (11:24). There he **spoke to the exiles about all the things the LORD had shown** him (11:25).

➢ B. The Hopelessness of Judah's False Optimism (12:1–19:14) ☞

12:1-2 The people of Jerusalem certainly thought they were in no danger of having God's glory depart from their midst again. They couldn't see or hear any trouble coming their way from God, but they were a **house** full of rebels who had willfully chosen to make themselves blind and deaf to God's Word (12:2). Everything looked great to them because their leaders and false prophets were telling them to relax, but the nation's optimism would be blown away like smoke when the Babylonians returned.

12:3-6 God commanded Ezekiel to perform two more sign actions to deliver his next message. He was to pack his **bags** and **go into exile** as his fellow exiles in Babylon watched (12:3). Ezekiel was to do this twice, once in the daytime while the people looked on, and a second time at night by digging **through the wall** and taking **the bags out through it**. This second time he was to **cover** his **face** to symbolize that those going into exile would never see the land of Israel again (12:4-6).

12:7-16 Ezekiel obeyed (12:7). Before much longer, the people back in Judah and Jerusalem would know, as Ezekiel and the first exiles knew, what it was like to pack their bags, sling them over their shoulders, and leave their homeland to go **into captivity** (12:10-11). The prophecy was even more ominous for Zedekiah, the puppet king whom Nebuchadnezzar had placed on the throne in

Jerusalem (12:12-14). He tried to escape the city at night, but the Babylonians overtook him and brought him to Nebuchadnezzar, who killed Zedekiah's sons before his eyes and then gouged them out so that he never saw **Babylon** even though he was taken there (12:13; see 2 Kgs 25:1-7). What was the reason for all of this tragedy? People needed to **know that** God is **the Lord** (12:15-16). And this is a sobering reminder that if people will not respond to God voluntarily, they will be forced to do so by his judgment.

12:17-20 Ezekiel's second sign was brief, but also telling. God told him to **eat** and **drink** with **trembling** and **anxious shaking** (12:17-18). The display of nervousness reinforced the word the Lord had delivered to Jerusalem and Judah earlier (see 4:16). Indeed, the people would **eat their bread with anxiety and drink their water in dread** as God **stripped** the land bare and destroyed its cities because of the inhabitants' **violence** (12:19). This was the only way these spiritually blind and deaf rebels could be brought to see and understand that the Lord alone was their God.

12:21-25 Following these two signs, Ezekiel delivered a series of messages announcing certain judgment (12:21–14:23). The first one begins with God's view of the sinful people of Judah, who thought they had an answer for everything. They even had a proverb that basically said, "Ezekiel keeps insisting doom is coming. But nothing has happened yet!" (12:22). To this God replied, **I will put a stop to this proverb. . . . For in your days, rebellious house, I will . . . bring it to pass** (12:23-25). In other words, he'd heard enough of their nonsense. Every word he had spoken would happen—not in the distant future—but in their lifetime.

12:26-28 Part of the people's false optimism was tied to their belief that Ezekiel was prophesying **about distant times**. His vision, they reasoned, was related to **concerns many years from now** (12:27). Thus, they assumed they could live at ease and let the next generation worry about things. Yet God promised them that they themselves would experience the disaster

of his judgment: **None of my words will be delayed any longer** (12:28).

Sometimes people today think similarly. Since they see no divine judgment looming on the horizon, they assume all is well. But the fact that God does not immediately punish us for our sins doesn't mean he takes no notice of them or isn't offended by them. The reason that judgment is delayed is because God is giving people time to repent and put their faith in his Son. Nevertheless, death can take anyone at any time, and "It is appointed for people to die once—and after this, judgment" (Heb 9:27). We must urge people not to think that they have plenty of time to "get right with God." Our message should be the same as Paul's message: "See, now is the acceptable time; now is the day of salvation!" (2 Cor 6:2).

13:1-3 Judah's false perception of reality was partially driven by the lying prophets in its midst. These men claimed to speak for God but spoke **out of their own imagination** (13:1-2). In other words, they were "yes men" who no doubt said whatever the nation's political leaders wanted to hear—for their own profit. The damage they were doing was made even worse because the prophetic office was Judah's last hope for a true word from God. After all, the civil leaders were mostly corrupt, and the priests were worshiping the sun in God's temple (8:16). The prophets should have stepped into the gap; instead, they proclaimed visions from the Lord though they had actually **seen nothing** (13:3).

13:4-12 The **prophets** were **like jackals** feeding on the **ruins** of the people (13:4). Instead of restoring **the wall around the house of Israel** to keep out the enemy (13:5), they **saw false visions** and spread lies **when the Lord did not send them** (13:5-6). The only word that would be fulfilled concerning these lying prophets, then, would be God's pronouncement of judgment against them (13:8-9). They led the people astray, making a false promise of **peace** when there was **no peace** to be found. They uttered deception, covering up their **flimsy** position before God by whitewashing over the truth with lies, the way a poor builder would try to hide his defective work (13:10). But God would expose their lies, leaving the people to wonder, too late, what happened to all the false prophets' glowing promises (13:11-12).

13:13-16 The prophets would be exposed when God unleashed the **fury** of his judgment on Judah and Jerusalem at the hands of the Babylonians (13:13). At that time the white-washed **wall** of lies they had built would collapse, and the city of Jerusalem would be laid open to the invaders who would destroy it. As a result, the people would come to know that the Lord alone is God, and the false prophets would be **no more** (13:14-16).

13:17-19 God's anger was also stirred against Judah's prophetesses, who in this case were more like sorceresses or spiritists. Like their male counterparts, they were also speaking **out of their own imagination** (13:17), using pagan occult objects such as **magic bands** to trick the gullible into believing they warded off evil spirits or brought good luck. In fact, these women ensnared **lives** by their trickery (13:18), even using their evil powers to cause people **who should not die** to be put to death (13:19).

13:20-23 If God's people were where they should have been spiritually, these sorceresses would have been executed for their evil. But they were tolerated and patronized for their abilities. Therefore, God would take it upon himself to deal with them when he brought an end to Jerusalem and Judah.

14:1-4 Ezekiel also had a message for the hypocritical **elders** among the exiles in Babylon. They were harboring **idols in their hearts** and had placed **sinful stumbling blocks** before themselves, while pretending to seek a word from God (14:1-3). Maybe they wanted to hear when their captivity would end or some other good news, but God had a very different word for them in Ezekiel's fourth message of certain judgment (14:1-11). It began with the elders sitting in front of him but broadened to **anyone from the house of Israel** who turned to **idols** and then presumed to come **to the prophet** for a word from God (14:4).

14:5-8 Anyone who would inquire of God while secretly worshiping idols would indeed get an answer from him, but not the answer desired. God's answer would be a word of judgment: **I will turn against that one and make him a sign and a proverb; I will cut him off from among my people** (14:8). He would make the idolater an example to others so that they understood what would happen to those who make a pretense of following God but whose hearts are far from him. There are many people today who follow the same path, and it remains a dangerous route.

The Lord didn't want to judge his people; instead, he wanted them to see the folly of their ways and turn back to him. He wanted to recapture their hearts, so he urged them through Ezekiel, **Repent and turn away from your idols** (14:6). God has the same message for people today. Unbelievers are urged to turn from their idols to trust in Jesus Christ. And even Christians are urged to guard themselves from idols (1 John 5:21). This is the only way to experience true blessing from God, in fact. Since God is a jealous God, there is no room for competing deities in our lives (see Exod 20:5; 34:14; Jas 4:5).

14:9-11 If a **prophet** was **deceived** and answered an idolater, he was clearly a false prophet whom God himself had **deceived** for the purpose of exercising his judgment (14:9). Both the prophet and the idolater would **bear their punishment** (14:10). God's goal was to prevent his people from straying and defiling themselves. He desired to see them restored: **Then they will be my people and I will be their God** (14:11).

14:12-20 Ezekiel's fifth and final message was an unusual affirmation of Judah's inevitable judgment regardless of who prayed for its deliverance. The Bible is filled with examples of the power of intercessory prayer, but here God declares the futility of such prayer in this case—not because of any lack of power within prayer, but because of Judah's hopeless descent into sin. It had exhausted God's patience—"exhausted" is a fitting word here since God said at least five times in Ezekiel that Judah's people were so sinful that he was going to "exhaust" his anger against them (see 6:12; 7:8; 13:15; 20:8, 21).

So, how bad was it for Judah? Through Ezekiel, the Lord proposed a hypothetical situation in which a nation sinned against him **by acting faithlessly**, causing him to **stretch out** his **hand** in judgment (14:13). It doesn't require a genius to understand who this hypothetical nation was. But God didn't identify it yet. The focal question was, could such a faithless nation be spared? As it turned out, **even if these three men— Noah, Daniel, and Job—were in it, they would rescue only themselves by their righteousness** (14:14). Regardless of the destruction that the Lord was to bring upon such a faithless land—**famine** (14:13), **dangerous animals** (14:15), **sword** (14:17), or **plague** (14:19)—even these three couldn't rescue anyone but themselves (14:16, 18, 20). Clearly, Noah, Daniel, and Job had accomplished much for God by faith. But they couldn't pull this one off. They were three of the greatest examples of faith and godly favor; nevertheless, their righteousness could not protect such a wicked land.

Contrast this with the Lord Jesus Christ. He alone is able to save all sinners by his own righteousness. Anyone who trusts in Christ as his sin-bearer, in fact, is granted a righteousness that is not his own—"the righteousness from God based on faith" (Phil 3:9).

14:21-23 These **four devastating judgments—sword, famine, dangerous animals, and plague**—are what God vowed to send **against Jerusalem** (14:21). They foreshadow the four horsemen that God will unleash on an unbelieving world during the great tribulation (see Rev 6:1-8). Importantly, not every person in Judah would die. There would be **survivors** who would be taken to Babylon so Ezekiel and the other exiles could **be consoled about the devastation . . . on Jerusalem** (14:22). The consolation, however, wasn't based on the righteousness of these survivors. Rather, the people exiled previously would see the newcomers' unrighteous **conduct and actions**, and Ezekiel would know that **it was not without cause** that God brought destruction on Jerusalem (14:23). That God was just in his judgment.

15:1-8 God used Ezekiel's pen and person in numerous ways to convey his message of judgment. In chapters 15–17 the prophet tells three parables to deliver his indictment: the stories of a useless vine (15:1-8), an adulterous wife (16:1-63), and two eagles (17:1-24).

The parable of the useless vine is quite simple. God did not create **the wood of the vine** to be made into furniture or some other **useful** item requiring strength (15:2-3). Its job was to hold the fruit it was designed to produce, and then become **fuel** to be devoured in the fire (15:4-5). The message for **the residents of Jerusalem** was clear. They had **escaped** the **fire** of Babylon when the enemy first came in 597 BC, but the reprieve was only temporary. The fire would still **consume them** and **make the land desolate** when God brought down the final curtain of judgment (15:6-8).

16:1-5 The second parable is an extended story of Jerusalem's unfaithfulness and ingratitude to God for all of his goodness and provision, with the city serving as a representative of the Jewish people. Jerusalem's sins had become so **detestable** that it was as if her people had become the offspring of an **Amorite** and **Hethite**. These were two pagan peoples **in the land of the Canaanites** whose practices the Jews had adopted (16:2-3). Against this background, God pictured Jerusalem as an abandoned and uncared for infant **thrown** into **the open field** because no one wanted her (16:4-5).

16:6-14 God himself took pity on the **thrashing** baby and selected her as his own, providing her with everything necessary to make her **thrive** and mature into a young woman of beauty (16:6-7). Then, when Jerusalem became of marriageable age, God **spread the edge of** his **garment over** her in **a covenant** of marriage, pledging protection and provision, and she became his beloved (16:8). God described in great detail how he dressed his bride in the finest of clothing and jewels, giving her everything fit for a queen and even providing her with a queen's food (16:9-13). She **became extremely beautiful and attained royalty** under all this attention (16:13). Jerusalem's **fame spread among the**

nations because of the way her great God had blessed her and **bestowed** his **splendor** on her (16:14).

16:15 Shockingly, though, instead of praise and obedience to God, the Lord's bride (his people) **trusted** in her own **beauty**—the very thing with which God had blessed her. She let her looks and fame go to her head and turned from her Provider to **prostitute** herself to idols in the most degrading ways possible! Jerusalem's idolatry is described in terms of adultery. Ezekiel 16:5-34 contains sexually graphic imagery to depict the nation's idolatrous sins.

16:16-26 Jerusalem used the beautiful **clothing** God had given her to make **high places** for idols, and she used his gifts of **beautiful jewelry** to make sexually degrading **male images** (16:16-17). She even offered God's **oil**, **incense**, and **food** in worship to the idols (16:18-19). Worse, she also killed her **sons and daughters** as sacrifices to the pagan gods of the nations around her (16:20)! This was a particular outrage to God, for his bride who had been left to die in infancy was now killing the **children** he himself had given her (16:21-22).

So brazen was she about her actions that she wasn't even embarrassed to bring her idolatry from the high places right into the streets of Jerusalem, practicing it **in every square** and **at the head of every street**, essentially becoming like a shameless prostitute who offered her body to any man who passed (16:23-25). The reference to her dalliances with **Egyptian men** in particular (16:26; see also the Assyrians and Babylonians ["Chaldea"] in 16:28-29) may refer to the Israelites' foreign alliances as well as their searching for new pagan gods to worship.

16:27-34 God didn't simply watch while his bride chose unfaithfulness. He **gave** her **over** to her enemies, including the Philistines who attacked Israel at various times. And even these pagan nations were **embarrassed by** the depths of Jerusalem's **indecent conduct** (16:27)! God also made sure there was no satisfaction for Jerusalem in her lewdness, even as she continually lusted for more (16:29-30).

She became so desperate to satisfy herself that she offered her services to her foreign lovers without **payment**, even bribing them to be with her (16:31-34)!

16:35-43 Considering the evidence before him, God had no recourse but to pronounce judgment on his promiscuous bride. First, he read the charges against her (16:35-36). Then he pronounced his verdict with the reasons for it (16:37-43). The irony of Jerusalem's prostitution with her pagan lovers is that they, unlike the spiritual husband she'd scorned had done throughout her history, would not rally to her defense because they cared nothing for her. They would be her executioners! These verses describe the desolation the city of Jerusalem and its people would suffer under the final Babylonian assault to come.

Jerusalem's leaders had tried to please the invaders earlier to stave off destruction, but it was to no avail. God had already pronounced sentence. Even though he had been a loving and faithful husband, his bride had broken covenant with him. The Babylonians would **burn** the **houses** in Jerusalem and **execute judgments . . . in the sight of many women**—no doubt referring to atrocities—because that was the only way to **stop** Jerusalem **from being a prostitute**. It was the only way to calm God's anger (16:41-42). They had brought their judgment on themselves (16:43). And it all happened because God's people had forgotten what he had done for them.

16:44-47 God had more evidence to present regarding the justice of his harsh judgment against Jerusalem. Here the analogy turns from the city being a wife to a **daughter** (14:44-45). Jerusalem was compared to her two **sisters**: **Samaria** in the **north** and **Sodom** in the **south** (16:46). Both cities had committed **detestable practices**, but Jerusalem had become even more **corrupt** than they (16:47).

16:48-52 Sodom was legendary for its sin, revealed here to be a lack of concern for the poor along with its **detestable acts** (homosexuality, rape, and violence) (16:48-50). **Samaria**, the capital of the northern kingdom of Israel, had long since been destroyed by the Assyrians for its idolatry, but even its people **did not commit even half** the sins of Jerusalem (16:51). Both of these wicked cities, in fact, appeared **more righteous than** Jerusalem (16:52). This is an incredible statement of the extent of the city's sin, which was committed despite its people having the greatest of spiritual advantages—including the temple and the manifest presence of God.

16:53-58 Nevertheless, destruction was not the last word because God had not written off his sinful people. The closing verses of this long parable begin with the surprising prophecy that **Sodom** and **Samaria** will be rebuilt in Christ's millennial kingdom along with Jerusalem (16:53). But first Jerusalem, still being pictured as a disgraceful sister, would have to **bear** her shame (16:54)—even though in her former pride she had scorned her **sister Sodom** (16:56). Jerusalem would later feel the same scorn by the nations **around her** as she had to **bear the consequences of** her **depravity and detestable practices** (16:57-58).

16:59-63 In spite of all this, God would remain faithful to his covenants. **The oath** Israel made refers to the Mosaic **covenant** (16:59), the only one established by oath. The covenant **made with you in the days of your youth** refers to the Abrahamic covenant, and the **permanent covenant** speaks of the new covenant of Jeremiah 31:31-34, which also includes believers in Christ (16:60). In his millennial kingdom Jesus Christ will rule over all, and Israel will be fully redeemed and will know the Lord as it experiences the new covenant nationally (16:62).

17:1-2 Ezekiel's third and final parable in this section uses the imagery of two eagles and a tree. The Lord told the prophet to **pose a riddle and speak a parable to the house of Israel** (17:2). A riddle in the Bible is a puzzle, an enigma to be solved—as in the case of Samson's riddle to the Philistines (see Judg 14:12-14). It's hard to know how far to press the distinction in this chapter; perhaps the actions of the first eagle were intended as a riddle and those of the second were meant to be a parable.

17:3-21 At any rate, this chapter is best understood by pairing the actions of the eagles with their interpretations. In this first instance, that means reading 17:3-4 and 17:11-12 together. The **huge eagle** who **came to Lebanon** and **plucked off its topmost shoot** to take it to another land was clearly Nebuchadnezzar, which means that Lebanon stood for Jerusalem (17:3-4, cp. 17:12). This referred to the king's first invasion of Judah in 597 BC when he took King Jehoiachin, "the topmost shoot," to Babylon and installed Zedekiah in his place.

Nebuchadnezzar left Judah and Jerusalem intact, though weakened (17:5-6; explained in 17:13-14). It was **low in height**, humbled by Babylon with **its branches turned toward** Nebuchadnezzar in subjugation (17:6). When Nebuchadnezzar put Zedekiah on the throne in Jerusalem, he **made a covenant with him**, **putting him under oath** to be faithful to his Babylonian overlord (7:13). Nebuchadnezzar further weakened Judah by taking away **the leading men of the land**, but the **kingdom** of Judah would survive if Zedekiah would keep **covenant** (17:13-14).

Since Judah's people were faithless and had broken their solemn promise to keep their covenant with God, however, Zedekiah wouldn't think twice about breaking his promise to Nebuchadnezzar. Instead of keeping his pact with Babylon, **this vine** (Zedekiah) **bent its roots toward** the other **huge eagle** in Ezekiel's parable—that is, he revolted by going to the king of Egypt for military help in breaking Babylon's grip on Jerusalem (17:7-8, explained in 17:15).

Go back to 17:5-6 to recall how Nebuchadnezzar planted Zedekiah in Jerusalem as a vine whose branches were bent toward him—which was God's will and part of his judgment on his people. This was stated again in 17:8 to reinforce the deceit and futility of Zedekiah's revolt, which failed completely because he found no aid in **Egypt**. The **king**, acting foolishly, had broken his **covenant** and would find no **escape** (17:15). **Pharaoh with his mighty army** would provide no help when Jerusalem was attacked (17:17).

Think of Ezekiel's immediate readers here, his fellow exiles and the people still in the land of Judah who thought they were fine and needed no repentance. If he wrote chapter 17 about 592-591 BC, he was writing somewhere between five or six years before the final invasion and destruction of Jerusalem and Zedekiah's horrible fate. There were plenty of false prophets around in those days, both in Babylon and in Jerusalem, telling the people what they wanted to hear. Even after the final exile to Babylon, in fact, when Jerusalem was in ruins and the temple was gone, they were saying the exile would be brief. Thus, the early exiles may have said to one another, "We don't believe what Ezekiel has been saying. We're rooting for Zedekiah and the Egyptians to whip these Babylonians and bring us back home. We can't believe God will let his holy city and temple be destroyed." And when the rest of the people joined them in exile with their horror stories of the ruin of Jerusalem, they still had false prophets in their midst who told them they would be there for a short time—surely not seventy years. The truth was that it would take a long time for God to bring his people to their knees.

The parable continued with the ruin of Zedekiah (17:9-10, explained in 17:16, 18-21). Nebuchadnezzar would **tear out** his **roots** (17:9), using the imagery of Zedekiah and Jerusalem as a vine. He would **wither completely** (17:10), an image that God made clear in that Zedekiah would **die in Babylon** (17:16). Why? Because **he despised the oath by breaking the covenant** (17:18). Now, that's a statement that we need to read carefully. God hates covenant-breakers, even those who made a covenant with a pagan king! In 17:19-21 Ezekiel provides a detailed prophecy of what happened to Zedekiah and his army when they tried to escape out the back gate as the Babylonians broke into Jerusalem (see 2 Kgs 25:1-10).

17:22-24 This chapter of destruction, desolation, and judgment ends with a prophecy not only of restoration and hope for the faithful remnant, but also of the coming of the Messiah who will establish his glorious kingdom. The phrase **tender sprig** (17:22) alludes to another prophecy regarding Messiah: "A shoot will grow from the stump of Jesse, and a branch from his roots will bear fruit" (Isa 11:1). Although the nation was reduced to a stump by the judgments Ezekiel was

announcing, there was grace. These verses also picture other nations that will come under Messiah's reign as he rules the world from his throne in Jerusalem. This promise may have seemed remote to the people of Ezekiel's day, especially with judgment impending; nevertheless, God sealed it with his word.

18:1-2 In chapter 18 the people's twisted view of the situation brought about by their spiritual myopia reached a new low: they blamed God for judging them unfairly. So God put aside the visuals and the parables to deliver a hard-hitting message about personal responsibility for sin. At the time, a **proverb** was going around that excused the people from facing their sins: **The fathers eat sour grapes, and the children's teeth are set on edge** (18:2). The saying was so well known that Jeremiah, who also wrote to the Jews in exile, quoted it (see Jer 31:29-30). And the idea behind it was that those in the land under Babylon's heel were suffering, not because they had sinned, but because their parents had. They were confusing the cumulative effects of sin with each person's responsibility for his or her personal sins.

18:3-20 But God had had enough of that nonsense. He clarified that **the person who sins is the one who will die** (18:4). Then he presented three hypothetical cases to illustrate the principle. A **righteous** man will **live** by his righteousness (18:5-9); but if he has **a violent son**, that son will **certainly die** for his own evil (18:10-13). If this evil man in turn has a son who does not follow his father but does what is right, **he will certainly live** (18:14-17). His rotten father, however, **will die for his own iniquity** (18:18). Then the principle is restated: **The person who sins is the one who will die** (18:20). God wanted to make it clear that he judges people for their own sins—not for the sins of their parents.

18:21-24 Don't miss the news of hope for the person willing to abandon his sin. This chapter is not teaching that salvation is attained through works. The good or evil these hypothetical men, and the people of Jerusalem, were practicing was the outflow of hearts that were or were not in right standing before God. Therefore, God's plea here was for the people to recognize and repent of their sin and turn to him for forgiveness.

18:25-30 Yet Judah insisted on blaming God for being unfair in his judgments, so he turned their argument on its head. It was their way that was **unfair** (18:25). They had the common (and wrong) view that God weighed actions and if the good outweighed the bad, a person was okay in his sight. But God proved that salvation was a matter of where you end up, not where you start. That's why he told Judah in essence, "If you repent I will judge you based on your repentance, not your wickedness." That's good news. But he also reversed it and said, "If you don't repent, I will judge you on your wickedness, not how good you were before you turned to wickedness."

18:31-32 We know God was talking about the condition of a person's heart and not works salvation because of his second call to repentance: **Throw off all the transgressions you have committed, and get yourselves a new heart and a new spirit. . . . For I take no pleasure in anyone's death. . . . So repent and live!** (18:31-32). Ultimately, the only way to be saved is by getting a new heart. And the only way to get a new heart is to repent, trust Jesus Christ, and receive a transformed heart through the work of the Holy Spirit (see Ezek 36:26-27; cp. Jer 31:31-34).

19:1-4 To cap off this section (12:1–19:14), thus putting to rest any false hope the people of Judah and Jerusalem had of escaping God's judgment and the prophecies of exile, Ezekiel was commanded to **take up a lament for the princes of Israel** (19:1). A *lament* was normally a dirge or funeral song honoring someone who had died, although the three kings alluded to in this chapter deserved none.

The **lioness** who gave birth and **reared her cubs** (19:2) was Israel, the nation that had produced so many great kings. But the first one referenced here is generally agreed to be Jehoahaz, an evil king who came to the throne in Jerusalem after the early death of his father, good King Josiah (see 2 Kgs 23:31-32). Jehoahaz **devoured people** through his

bad decisions during his three-month reign, but he was captured by Pharaoh Neco of Egypt who **led him away with hooks** (Ezek 19:3-4; see 2 Kgs 23:33).

19:5-9 Then came another bad king, Jehoiachin. He also reigned just three months in Jerusalem, causing great suffering, before Nebuchadnezzar captured him and took him to Babylon (see 2 Kgs 23:34–24:6). Jehoiachin never returned home, **so his roar could no longer be heard on the mountains of Israel** (Ezek 19:9).

19:10-14 The third and last king is lamented here, King Zedekiah. Nebuchadnezzar left Zedekiah on the throne and left Jerusalem intact like a **vineyard**, still **planted** in the holy land to flourish if the king would only keep his covenant (19:10-11). But when Zedekiah broke his word, the Babylonian army came and **uprooted** Jerusalem **in fury** as **fire consumed** the holy city (19:12; see 2 Kgs 24:18-7). Its people were deported to **a dry and thirsty land** (19:13). With the Babylonian exile, the last Davidic king was removed from the throne. There was **no longer . . . a strong branch, a scepter for ruling** (19:14). Nevertheless, that branch and scepter will be restored in Jesus Christ when he comes to rule on his millennial throne. He is "the Son of David" (Matt 1:1), "the King of Israel" (John 1:49), and "the Lion from the tribe of Judah, the Root of David" (Rev 5:5).

❧ C. The History of Judah's Sins
(20:1–24:27) ❧

20:1 If the people of Judah retained any optimism that God would somehow come down at the last minute and rescue their nation from destruction, that bubble was about to pop. Ezekiel dates the event here to **the seventh year, in the fifth month, on the tenth day of the month.** That puts it in 591 BC, about the seventh year of Zedekiah's doomed rule in Jerusalem. **Some of Israel's elders** approached Ezekiel **to inquire of the LORD**—that is, to seek an oracle from God for them. Their inquiry isn't recorded, but judging from the response to it they had not come in humble repentance and with hearts fully devoted to God. They wanted good news from God without having a willingness to follow God.

20:2-4 As I live, I will not let you inquire of me. God flatly refused to speak to these elders because of their sins and those of Judah's people, whom they represented (20:3-4). His repeated question to Ezekiel, Will you pass judgment against them, will you pass judgment, son of man? is like a command in Hebrew: "Judge these people! Judge these people!" That's why God told the prophet to explain the detestable practices of their fathers to them (20:4). That is the outline of 20:1-32 in a nutshell. It has the force of a legal indictment.

20:5-9 Ezekiel obeyed and reviewed Israel's history from the nation's beginning to his own day. The reference to God choosing Israel during the days of Moses was not a denial of his choice of Abraham and his descendants to be his people. It was a recognition that Israel was born as a nation when God sent Moses to lead them out of the land of Egypt (20:5). God also searched out the land of Canaan for them and called them to get rid of any idols they had worshiped in Egypt (20:6-7). But they rebelled against him, and he considered pouring out his wrath on them (20:8). He did not do it so that his holy name would not be profaned in the eyes of the nations (20:9).

20:10-17 Then Ezekiel reviewed the nation's travels from Egypt to Mount Sinai, where God gave them his statutes and explained his ordinances to them (20:10-11). From there he led them into the wilderness where they rebelled against him (20:13). He would have destroyed them then, but he stayed his hand for the sake of his name (20:13-14). Nevertheless, Moses's generation had died in the wilderness because the Lord refused to bring them into the land he had given them (20:15). Their hearts went after their idols instead of the God who redeemed them (20:16). He could have brought the nation to an end in the wilderness; instead, he spared them from destruction (20:17). Their children would live to enter the promised land.

20:18-31 God gave the same commands and the same offer of blessing and land to the children of the exodus generation (20:18-20), but they too rebelled (20:21). Once again, he could have wiped the nation out. But he withheld his hand and acted for the sake of his name (20:22). Though God's people cared nothing for his glory, God himself is always zealous for it. He warned them that if they turned to idols, he would drive them out of the land (20:23). But it made no difference. They just turned to idolatry with such abandon and passion that they practiced a level of vileness and degradation their ancestors would never have imagined: child sacrifice (20:26). Their punishment, then, was richly deserved.

Ezekiel wrapped up his review and said that his generation was no better than their fathers (20:30), which was why God refused to have anything to do with the elders who had come to inquire of him (20:31; see 20:1-4).

20:32-44 Still, in keeping with God's eternal purposes, the Lord also had a message of hope and restoration for Israel (20:33-44). The language in these verses cannot be matched to the return from exile in Babylon, or to any era in Israel's history. This gathering, then, is yet in the future, when God reclaims Israel from the countries where it was scattered (20:34). Israel will then be led into the wilderness for the purpose of judgment, as God did after the exodus from Egypt (20:35-36). But this time all the rebels will be weeded out and only true believers will enter the land, which is a picture of Israel's purging in the tribulation and their worship of Messiah Jesus in his millennial kingdom. At that time, Israel's worship will be accepted and the nation will repent of all its unfaithfulness and idolatry (20:44).

20:45-49 In the meantime, the fire of judgment was going to be released on Judah. Even though the Babylonians would come from the north, the destructive fire they would ignite would burn from south (the Negev) to north and would not be extinguished (20:46-48). But the people's stubborn unbelief was such that even then they mocked Ezekiel, saying, Isn't he just composing parables? (20:49). In other words, they said, "He's merely making up stories. All is well."

21:1-7 Since the people of Judah refused to listen to Ezekiel's message about the fire in the south, God decided to make it inextricably clear by giving them this word: **Son of man, face Jerusalem and preach against the sanctuaries. Prophesy against the land of Israel** (21:2). Then he changed the imagery of judgment to a **sword** that would devour without mercy through the land of Judah, also moving **from the south to the north** (21:3-4). At this revelation, Ezekiel was told to **groan bitterly**. When the people asked him why, he was to tell them it was **because of the** terrible **news** of the approaching judgment (21:6-7).

21:8-17 The message of this section has several parts, beginning with the picture of **a sword** of God being **sharpened** and **polished** to prepare for a great **slaughter** (21:8-11). Ezekiel was again told to **cry out and wail** for the extent of this judgment that would leave no one on the throne of David in Jerusalem (21:12-13). The sword would strike again and again until God had satisfied his great **wrath** (21:14-17).

21:18-22 The next part of the message concerns the way God would lead Nebuchadnezzar against Jerusalem when he arrived to put down Zedekiah's revolt and destroy Jerusalem. **The Ammonites**, whose capital was **Rabbah** (modern-day Jordan with its capital of Amman), had also rebelled against Babylon. Nebuchadnezzar reached a crossroads and had to decide whether to attack Jerusalem or Rabbah (21:19-20). He consulted all of his pagan objects and rites, but God intervened and *led* him to **Jerusalem** where he set up his siege ramps and walls (21:21-22).

21:23-32 Yet even as Babylon was building these siege works, some in Jerusalem thought Nebuchadnezzar's actions were the result of **false divination** and would fail (21:23). So God made it known that he had given over Zedekiah, that **profane and wicked prince of Israel**, to judgment (21:24-25). Jerusalem would be **a ruin** (21:27).

What about the **Ammonites**? God had a **sword** of **slaughter** poised for them as well (21:28). Ammon was the first on a list of nations that were to be judged for their mistreatment of Israel, with God indicating it would be invaded and destroyed by "the people of the east" (see 25:1-5).

22:1-5 The indictment against Judah and her people continued with a repeat of the question/indictment that began in 20:4: **son of man, will you pass judgment?** (22:2). The new emphasis here is Jerusalem's shedding of **blood** (22:2-4; also 22:6, 9, 12-13, 27). It referred to the violence in the city that was a sin against one's fellow man (22:3-4).

22:6-16 The leaders of Judah led the people in breaking God's laws, one by one. **Father and mother** were mistreated; the **resident alien** was **exploited**; the **fatherless and widow** were **oppressed** (22:7). They profaned God's **holy things** and Sabbaths (22:8). There was also every form of depravity within the nation: **sexual** sin, bribery, and brutal extortion—all at the hands of a people who had **forgotten** their holy God (22:9-12). Therefore, God would **clap** his **hands** in derision against his **dishonest** people **and against the blood shed among** them. Their **courage** would melt when judgment came and they were scattered (22:13-15).

22:17-22 The images of fierce judgment kept coming. God next gave Ezekiel a word picture of Jerusalem as his **furnace** of judgment (22:20-21). He would consume the city and its people until there was nothing left but the **dross** or scum that is scraped away after metal is refined. **Because all of you have become dross**, he said, **I am about to gather you into Jerusalem** (22:19). There the Babylonians could burn them in **the fire of** God's **fury** (22:21). Then his sinful people would know that he is **the Lord** as his **wrath** was **poured out on** them (22:22). How much better it is for God to confirm his sovereignty in our lives by blessing our obedience than by punishing our disobedience!

22:23-29 The people came under specific indictment in groups for this catastrophe, beginning with the **prophets** who conspired to **seize wealth** from the populace **by seeing false visions and lying divinations** (22:25, 28). The **priests** failed to teach God's law and profaned his **holy things,** closing **their eyes** to even the **Sabbaths** (22:26). They were the (intentionally) blind leading the blind. The **officials,** meanwhile, were nothing but greedy bureaucrats, **destroying lives in order to make profit dishonestly** (22:27). Even the **people of the land** were corrupt and deserved judgment (29:29).

Here we get a picture of a society in complete chaos and breakdown. Every sphere of authority in God's kingdom program—from the religious leaders, to the civil government, and even the family unit—was failing in its responsibility to carry out God's kingdom agenda.

22:30-31 Not one person could be found to **stand in the gap** on God's behalf and stop his hand of judgment from falling on everyone (22:30). This is the principle of representation that allows God to hold back his judgment if he has sufficient intermediaries whose righteousness can be credited to the benefit of the unrighteous. When such representatives are absent and the people do not repent, then judgment falls (see Gen 18:22-33; 1 Cor 7:13-14).

23:1-4 To further illustrate Judah's unfaithfulness, God gave Ezekiel another parable to tell his listeners and to record for his readers. This one, like the parable of Sodom and Samaria (see 16:44-59), concerned **two** sinful **women,** sisters (23:1). They **acted like prostitutes in Egypt, behaving promiscuously** (23:3). Together these "sisters" represented the entire nation of Israel, which spent its youth in Egypt where its people first succumbed to idol worship. **Oholah** represented **Samaria,** the capital of the northern kingdom of Israel (which by this time had been destroyed), and **Oholibah** represented **Jerusalem** in the southern kingdom of Judah (23:4). Their sexual promiscuity was metaphorical for their idolatry—their spiritual adultery— against the Lord. They worshiped false gods and made alliances with the surrounding nations.

23:5-10 The parable unfolds as **Oholah** (Samaria) sought out **her lovers, the Assyrians** (23:5), as the rulers of the northern kingdom prostituted themselves to that pagan nation. Because God's people did not give up their **promiscuity that began in Egypt** (23:8), God handed them over to the Assyrians to be oppressed and eventually **killed** by them. Israel was destroyed in 722 BC (23:10).

23:11-13 Unbelievably, **Oholibah** (Jerusalem) watched all this unfold, yet became **even more depraved in her lust than Oholah** (23:11). Her lusting **after the Assyrians** (23:12) probably refers to the actions of King Ahaz of Judah, who sought an alliance with Assyria to beat back an invasion from Israel (the northern kingdom) and Aram (see 2 Kgs 16). In doing so, he made Judah a vassal state of Assyria for the next century. King Josiah freed Judah for a while, but he was killed and Judah came under Egyptian power.

23:14-21 To throw off Egypt, King Jehoiakim turned to the **Babylonians** and willingly made Judah its vassal state (23:14-17). But when Babylon proved to be a harsh taskmaster, God's nation came full circle and turned to **Egypt** for aid. Thus she **revisited the depravity of** her **youth** and turned to the country that had originally enslaved her (23:19-21). But her attempt to be rescued by Egypt proved futile. In God's sight the spiritual promiscuity of Oholibah / Jerusalem was as vulgar as actual prostitution. Instead of turning back to God for help and protection, Judah multiplied its unfaithfulness by continually turning to new pagan "lovers" for the same.

23:22-27 Therefore, there was nothing left for **Oholibah** but judgment at the hands of her **lovers,** whom God would **incite** against her **in disgust** (23:22). This is a reminder that God sometimes uses the unrighteous to judge his people (see Hab 1:12-13).

Ezekiel declared God's condemnation in horrific terms. The armies of the entire Babylonian kingdom would come against Jerusalem with devastating effect (23:23). They would inflict punishment similar to the mutilation that was often carried out in that part of the ancient world against a prostitute to ruin her beauty (23:24-27). When the Babylonians were finished with Jerusalem, she would no longer be attractive to anyone.

23:28-35 Ezekiel declared that Jerusalem would be left **stark naked**, exposing the **debauchery** of God's faithless people for all to see (23:28-29). The people of Judah **acted like a prostitute with the nations**, as did the people of Israel, so they would **drink** from the **cup** of Israel's punishment (23:30-34). The Lord stated clearly the reason for Jerusalem's judgment: **Because you have forgotten me and cast me behind your back, you must bear the consequences of your indecency and promiscuity** (23:35). The leaders and people of Jerusalem would pay the price for their betrayal of their covenant God.

23:36-39 This chapter concludes with a side-by-side comparison of the two sisters' sins and judgments. Both **Oholah and Oholibah**, the northern and southern kingdoms, engaged in **detestable** idolatry of the most disturbing kind (23:36). They **sacrificed** their children **in the fire as food for the idols** (23:37) and **on the same day** went into God's **sanctuary to profane it** (23:37-39). Our theology matters. Worship and obedience to the true God will result in righteousness and justice, but worship and obedience to idols results in the worst kinds of immorality and violence against the helpless.

23:40-49 The adulterous way both kingdoms lured other nations into alliances is graphically portrayed as a prostitute adorning herself to lure her lovers into her room (23:40-41). God said his people went for the lowest dregs of society, **drunkards from the desert**, along with **common men** (23:42). **But righteous men**, probably a reference to God's prophets like Ezekiel, would pronounce judgments on these **adulteresses** (23:45). The penalty for adultery was stoning, and their enemies would **cut them down with their swords . . . kill their sons and daughters and burn their houses** (23:47)—all of which happened when both Samaria and Jerusalem fell to invaders. In this way God made an end of their **depravity** (23:49).

24:1-3 This section (Ezek 20-24) concludes with one last parable and message. **The word of the LORD came to** Ezekiel on a specific and important day (24:1). That's why God commanded the prophet to **write down today's date, this very day. The king of Babylon has laid siege to Jerusalem** (24:2). This date was the same as is recorded in 2 Kings 25:1. It occurred in 588 BC when King Nebuchadnezzar and his army came against Jerusalem to begin the final siege. In other words, the collapse of the city of Jerusalem and the kingdom of Judah was near. So the **parable** of a boiling **pot** that God told Ezekiel to deliver to that **rebellious house** was extremely timely (24:3).

24:4-14 Some of Jerusalem's leaders had given its people false assurance by using the imagery of Jerusalem as a strong "pot" in which its inhabitants were safe inside, like "meat" (see 11:3). But that was far from the truth. Jerusalem was a rusty pot that was about to be set on fire and brought to a boil by the Babylonians, consuming everyone and everything in it. Jerusalem had become a **city of bloodshed**, and the **blood she shed** was still present **within her**—she didn't even try to cover up her crimes (24:6-7). So God would expose them when he himself piled up the **kindling** for the fire under the pot of her judgment until it was **empty** (24:9-11). Judah's people had **frustrated** God's **every effort** to **purify** them of their **uncleanness**, so he had no recourse but to bring judgment (24:12-14).

24:15-19 Ezekiel had delivered his distressing message again and again, but now it would take a heartbreaking turn for him. The Lord was taking away his wife, **the delight of** his **eyes**, and forbidding him to **lament or weep or let** his **tears flow** at her death (24:16-17). It was a hard command, and Ezekiel had little time to prepare for the blow. That may be why the people were especially surprised at Ezekiel's lack of outward mourning and wanted to know what it meant—sensing it was a prophetic message to them (23:18-19).

24:20-27 Ezekiel obliged them with a word from God. The prophet's message was of overwhelming loss for his fellow exiles, who were about to lose their beloved city and many loved ones when Jerusalem was destroyed and her people slaughtered. But the exiles, like Ezekiel, would be unable to grieve because of the draining effect of God's judgment (23:20-24). Once again, Ezekiel stated the purpose of God's judgment: When this happens, you will know that I am the Lord God (24:24). And when the news of the disaster came, Ezekiel's mouth would be opened to talk with the messenger (24:27), since he had previously been forbidden to speak except what God told him to say (see 3:25-27).

III. PROPHECIES AGAINST GENTILE NATIONS (25:1–32:32)

25:1-7 The sword of God's judgment turned next toward seven Gentile nations that had despised and mistreated his people, Israel. The first four of these judgments follow the same pattern. Here in chapter 25, God stated the sins of Ammon, Moab, Edom, and Philistia, and then announced judgment that fit their sins. The basis for these was the Abrahamic covenant, which included this promise to Abraham and a warning to his enemies: "I will bless those who bless you, I will curse anyone who treats you with contempt" (Gen 12:3).

The sin of the **Ammonites** was gloating over the fall of Jerusalem and the destruction of the temple (25:2-3). They gleefully said Aha! in derision when Israel was laid waste and the people of Judah ... went into exile (25:3). Therefore, their own land would be invaded and Ammon too would fall (25:4-5, 7). The judgment on Ammon was pronounced in 21:28-32.

25:8-10 Moab's people were close relatives of the Ammonites, since their two ancestors were the sons of Lot's incestuous relationships with his daughters (see Gen 19:30-38). Moab's sin was treating the house of Judah, representing all of God's chosen people, like all the other nations (25:8). Moab acted on that mistaken idea by becoming a perpetual enemy of Israel. God would judge Moab by turning over its land to the same people of the east who were going to conquer Ammon (25:10; see 25:4).

25:12-14 The judgment on Edom is the first for this nation in Ezekiel. Edom was mentioned in 16:57 as one of the peoples who despised the Israelites. The Edomites refused to allow Israel to cross their land after leaving Egypt, so they had a long history of hostility. Because **Edom** treated Israel as just another enemy and **acted vengefully against the house of Judah** by trying to help bring about its downfall during the years of Babylon's invasions, God decreed Edom's downfall (25:12-13; see the book of Obadiah).

25:15-17 Then Ezekiel addressed the Philistines. These longtime enemies of God's people lived along the Mediterranean coast. The conflict started with the conquest of the promised land when the Israelites failed to dislodge the Philistines and paid the price. David defeated them repeatedly during his reign, but the Philistines had for generations acted in vengeance and took revenge with deep contempt on Israel because of their perpetual hatred of God's people (25:15). So God announced destruction on the **Cherethites**, a synonym for Philistines, teaching them once and for all: I am the Lord (25:16-17).

26:1-6 The last two nations coming under God's judgment comprise the bulk of this section. Tyre (26:2) was actually a city on the seacoast, but it was a very powerful force in the ancient world. Ezekiel 26–28 is devoted to its prophesied demise. There are four messages or oracles against Tyre, each introduced by Ezekiel's familiar statement, the word of the Lord came to me (26:1; 27:1; 28:1, 11). The date of the prophecy places it just before Jerusalem's fall, which makes God's condemnation of Tyre very timely. It was a city on the Mediterranean coast that became wealthy and powerful through its navy and seafaring trade. Since God's prophetic word was certain of fulfillment, he could speak of future events as if they had already happened.

Tyre was being judged for gloating over Jerusalem's fall, saying **Aha!** in derision just as Ammon did (26:2; see 25:3). Tyre's joy was prompted by greed. With Judah out of the way, the lucrative overland trade routes between Mesopotamia and Egypt were open. Tyre hoped to control them as it controlled the sea trade routes (26:2). But God had other plans. Because Tyre rejoiced over the fall of his people, God would **raise up many nations against** Tyre that would crash into it like sea waves and **destroy the walls of Tyre and demolish her towers** (26:3-4). The city's defense would become **a bare rock** on which fishermen would **spread nets** to dry, and **her villages on the mainland** would **be slaughtered** (26:5-6).

26:7-14 This occurred when **King Nebuchadnezzar of Babylon** turned his fury on Tyre after destroying Jerusalem (26:7-11). History tells us that Nebuchadnezzar besieged Tyre for thirteen years, and although the island fortress survived, he destroyed all the mainland parts as noted above. The nouns changed to the plural in 26:12-14, possibly referring to later forces that came against Tyre, most notably Alexander the Great in 332 BC. He used the rubble from the destroyed mainland city to build a causeway to the island fortress, destroying it too. The ancient site of Tyre has never been **rebuilt**, as the Lord said (26:14).

26:15-21 Tyre's trading partners in the seafaring world that depended on the city for their own prosperity would shudder at its complete **downfall** and **sit on the ground** in mourning, taking up a funeral lament for her **demise** (26:15-18). God confirmed the completeness of Tyre's judgment, saying its people had descended **to the Pit** (26:20), the place of death which people in the ancient world feared as the place of no return. That was, in fact, the fate of Tyre; it would **no longer exist** as a sea power by the **declaration of the Lord God** (26:21). While there was a city of Tyre in Jesus's day, it was a greatly weakened place.

27:1-9 God had a **lament** of his own **for Tyre**, but it was very different than that of its trading partners (27:2). The first part of the lament describes Tyre's former greatness by comparing the city to its beautiful ships. They were made **with pine trees from Senir . . . cedar from Lebanon . . . oaks from Bashan . . . cypress wood from the coasts of Cyprus**, and **ivory** (27:5-6)—all products legendary in the ancient world for their strength and beauty. And the sails of Tyre's ships were made of **fine embroidered linen from Egypt**, with awnings of **blue and purple fabric** (27:7). They were also manned by the best **rowers**, **captains**, and repairmen (27:8-9).

27:10-25 This still doesn't sound like a lament so far, but Ezekiel was building toward a climax that describes Tyre's crushing fall from its height. It was well protected by an army including mercenaries from other lands (27:10-11), and its trading partners included nations from all over the known world carrying every kind of merchandise imaginable (27:12-25).

27:26-36 But it would all come crashing down when God's **east wind** of judgment blew on Tyre (27:26). Then everything and everyone which had made this city great would be lost: its **wealth, merchandise, and goods**, its **sailors and captains . . . those who barter for [its] goods**, all the warriors on board, and **all the other people within** Tyre would **sink into the heart of the sea on the day** of its **downfall** (27:27). This is the way God's lament began. And when Tyre fell, her **sailors** would cry out in their own **lament** and perform the acts of mourning for their great city that had come to such terrible ruin. And they would be joined in their grief by Tyre's trading partners who would **shudder** at the great city's utter destruction (27:28-36).

28:1-10 Ezekiel's third oracle describes the downfall of the **ruler of Tyre** (28:2). We find (to no surprise) that the leader of this proud city was a **proud** king who said, **I am a god**. God's rebuttal was, **Yet you are a man and not a god, though you have regarded your heart as that of a god** (28:2). This king thought he was **wiser than Daniel** because he had gained so much wealth for his kingdom by great skill in trading (28:3-5). But God had a very un-godlike end awaiting this prideful ruler. Like the people of Tyre, its king would also be brought down to **the Pit** (28:8) when the city fell, and he would **die the death of the uncircumcised** like all of God's enemies (28:9-10).

28:11-13 The fourth and last oracle against **the king of Tyre** has been the focus of much attention from commentators. Many see Ezekiel 28 as reaching far beyond the king of Tyre to address Satan himself. Indeed, the statements of 28:12-19 cannot be applied to any human ruler alone—especially one whom God had just taken pains to condemn as a mere man who had divine pretensions. The being we're introduced to in these verses, then, is the power behind this king. This being is Lucifer, whose pride led him to rebel against God in heaven and become Satan. He was **full of wisdom and perfect in beauty**; he was **in Eden, the garden of God** (28:12-13).

28:14-15 Satan wasn't just any angel, either. He was **an anointed guardian cherub** (28:14), the highest of God's created beings. As God's fire blazed in eternity past, Lucifer was right in the middle of it. He stood in the very presence of God as the highest-ranking angel (28:14). He was assigned to lead the entire angelic host in the worship and service of Yahweh. So how could **wickedness** be found in this exalted angel (28:15)? Because God gave this perfect being the right of choice—that is, to serve him by choice, not simply by mandate. God was not going to force Lucifer to worship him, because God wants willing worship. Lucifer exercised his choice to rebel against God and tried to usurp his rule.

28:16-19 As a result of his rebellion, he was **expelled . . . in disgrace** from heaven and thrown down to the earth because of his pride (28:16-17). One day he will be judged and "thrown into the lake of fire and sulfur . . . tormented day and night forever" (Rev 20:10).

Hell was created for Satan and the angels who joined him in rebellion (see Matt 25:41). People go to hell because they also choose to join Satan in his rebellion against God by refusing to accept God's means of salvation in Christ (see John 3:18-21).

28:20-26 After this long judgment on Tyre and Satan, the oracle against Tyre's neighbor **Sidon** (28:20-26) seems like an anti-climax. Sidon's sins are not listed, probably because it was so closely identified with Tyre. But the judgment against the city was certain. God's **glory** would be displayed when this pagan center was also brought down in judgment, and its people would be forced to acknowledge his **holiness** (28:22-23). Sidon was one of Israel's neighbors and treated God's people **with contempt** (28:24); thus, Sidon's demise would give Israel relief. God broadened that to a promise that someday, when he regathers Israel in the millennial kingdom, the nation will enjoy true peace and rest from all its enemies (28:25-26).

29:1-3 Another longtime nemesis of Israel, the land of Egypt (and its allies), came into focus for God's judgment in an extended oracle (chapters 29–32). This **word of the LORD** to Ezekiel came almost a year after Nebuchadnezzar's siege of Jerusalem began (29:1). **Pharaoh** was another **king** who considered himself to be a god and the master of the **Nile** River (29:2-3).

29:4-9 The Pharaoh at the time of Judah's servitude to Babylon was Hophra. When Zedekiah reached out to Egypt for help in his attempt to break his word to Nebuchadnezzar and throw off Babylon's rule, Hophra said he would assist Zedekiah. But Zedekiah was leaning on a useless ally (see 29:6-7). Hophra's half-hearted attempt didn't help, and he withdrew, leaving Zedekiah and Judah to face Nebuchadnezzar's wrath. Egypt would be judged for this and dragged away from her place of safety by the Lord putting **hooks** in her **jaws** and leaving the nation abandoned **in the desert** (29:4-5). Its false promises of support for Israel led it to become a **desolate ruin** (29:7-9).

29:10-16 The prophecy expanded on Egypt's desolation by referring to a period of exile when Egypt would be such **a desolate waste** that neither a **human** nor an **animal** would **pass through it** because the land would be **uninhabited for forty years** (29:10-11). This would be followed by a regathering and restoration of Egypt's **fortunes** (29:13-14), but the nation would be **the lowliest of kingdoms and** would **never again exalt itself over the nations** (29:15). Israel would **never again** rely on Egypt (29:16).

29:17-20 The **twenty-seventh year** is in view in these verses—a time after the other events Ezekiel described. It is included here because of its logical connection to the previous events discussed. Nebuchadnezzar's long siege of Tyre had been financially unprofitable. His army had fought so long that the men had become **bald** from wearing their helmets and **chafed** from their armor (29:18). So God decided to **give the land of Egypt to King Nebuchadnezzar** both as judgment against the land of Israel's original enslavement and as Nebuchadnezzar's **pay** since **he labored for** the Lord (29:19-20). This is an amazing statement of how God's work intertwines with human events as he raises up and puts down rulers. God is sovereign over nations and their leaders (see Prov 21:1).

29:21 The final verse of this chapter refers to Ezekiel being able to **speak out among** the people of Israel when all these things happened and Israel was restored to the land. It's not likely that this refers to Ezekiel speaking himself, since he would have been about eighty-three years old by this time. It could mean that when his prophecies came to pass, the people of Israel would see that he had faithfully and clearly declared God's word to them.

30:1-5 Ezekiel's messages of judgment against Egypt continue in chapter 30 with prophecies of how this ancient power would be brought to complete ruin at the hands of Nebuchadnezzar and the Babylonians. The prophecy divides into four sections, each beginning with a declaration of **what** the Lord **says** (30:2, 6, 10, 13). God's wrath on Egypt would be severe, a time **of clouds**, suggesting doom, when a **sword will come against Egypt** (30:3-4). The **anguish** would reach to **Cush**, encompassing southern Egypt, Sudan, and northern Ethiopia. Egypt's very **foundations** would be **demolished** as its massive army, filled with foreign mercenaries, would **fall by the sword** (30:4-5).

30:6-9 The second part of this prophecy continues the description of the anguish of Egypt's allies. **From Migdol to Syene**, the far northern to the far southern borders of Egypt, those who supported the nation would also **fall within it by the sword**, because the Lord declared it (30:6). Egypt's cities would be **desolate** and **ruined** in a complete collapse of this once proud and mighty power, after which the Egyptians and their allies would **know** that God alone is **the Lord** (30:7-8). The fires blazing across Egypt would bear witness to his power when he unleashed his judgment that spread terror **on the day of Egypt's doom** (30:9).

30:10-12 God again revealed the instrument of his judgment: **the hand of King Nebuchadnezzar of Babylon** (30:10). He led a **ruthless** army that would **destroy the land** of Egypt (30:11).

30:13-19 In the fourth and final section of this prophecy, God names a number of Egypt's major cities that lay in the path of Babylon's destructive forces, because none of the nation's important centers would escape God's hand of retribution. Several of these cities are worth noting. **Memphis** was an important religious center with many temples and idols (30:13). According to Jeremiah 44:1, there were also Jews from Judah living there (see 25:18). They had fled to Memphis in an attempt to escape Nebuchadnezzar's assault on Jerusalem, despite Jeremiah's clear warning not to leave the land (see Jer 42:19-22). Now they would be caught up in Egypt's disastrous judgment: "the men of the covenant land will fall by the sword along with them." (30:5). God promised to **put an end to [its] false gods** and bring the city's enemies against it **in broad daylight** (30:13, 16).

Thebes (30:14-16) was another major Egyptian city that was its longtime capital, destroyed by the Assyrians in 663 BC, but later rebuilt. Its **hordes** of people would be wiped out when the city was breached by the Babylonians, a destruction also prophesied by Jeremiah (30:15; see Jer 46:25, where the focus was on judging the god of Thebes). **Tehaphnehes** was the location of one of Pharaoh's palaces, a symbol of Egypt's **proud strength** that God would bring to an end. The people of Tehaphnehes would also **go into captivity** (30:18). And then Egypt also would have to bow on its knees in acknowledging that God alone is Lord (30:19).

30:20-26 The final verses of this chapter describe a separate prophecy against Egypt, using the imagery of broken and strengthened arms that shows once more the outworking of God's sovereign will and control in and through human events and rulers. Speaking as if the judgment on Egypt were already accomplished, God said he had **broken the arm of Pharaoh king of Egypt**, first the one and then the other, until he had no strength to **handle a sword** (30:21-22). But he'd also **strengthen[ed] the arms of Babylon's king** (30:24-25) to defeat and destroy Egypt until the Egyptians knew the truth: **I am the Lord** (30:26). God uses judgment to bring glory to his name.

31:1-9 Fewer than two months after the previous prophecy (31:1; cp. 30:20), **the word of the Lord came to** Ezekiel again with a further message of judgment directed to **Pharaoh** Hophra **of Egypt**, who was convinced there was no one like him in his **greatness** (31:2). This time, Ezekiel used an allegory about Assyria, a former invader of Egypt, to underscore Egypt's downfall. The reference to Assyria would remind Hophra not only that the Assyrians had once defeated his kingdom, but also that they themselves had been crushed later by the Babylonians under Nebuchadnezzar in 609 BC—the same nation and king whom God was going to use to topple Egypt.

The allegory about **Assyria** compares it to **a cedar in Lebanon** (31:3). These trees were legendary in the ancient world for their stately height and unmatched beauty, making them the perfect symbol of a proud king who believed he stood head and shoulders above all the other rulers of the world. Assyria was described as growing from the **waters** of the Tigris River (31:4). The **underground springs** nourished it, causing it to become greater **than all the trees of the field**—that is, all the other nations (31:4-5). Assyria grew so great that even those nations around it that considered themselves great **lived in its shade** (31:6). Ezekiel even

resorted to hyperbole to say that the **cedars in God's garden ... Eden**, could not **compare** to Assyria and **envied it** (31:8-9).

The picture Ezekiel drew of Assyria's greatness could not be denied because it was a matter of historical record. The Assyrian Empire dominated the ancient world from the ninth to the seventh centuries BC before it was conquered by Babylon. From God's perspective, Pharaoh Hophra fancied himself as the next great thing in world leaders (a reminder of how little things have changed), but this ruler of mighty Egypt was in for a rude awakening. God had brought down mightier thrones than his.

31:10-14 That's where the allegory of Assyria as a cedar of Lebanon takes us next, to the fall of this great empire. Assyria's **stature** as top dog among the nations caused it to grow **proud** (31:10). In this context, that refers to puffing oneself up in God's sight instead of humbly bowing before him and acknowledging him as the one true God. Assyria was also filled with **wickedness**, which caused God to hand it over to **ruthless men**, the Babylonians, who **cut it down and left it lying** in ruins as an object lesson to other nations not to exalt themselves as Assyria had done (31:11-14). Instead, they needed to learn that they were destined for the grave, **the Pit**, not for glory (31:14).

31:15-17 Unfortunately, Egypt completely ignored this lesson. The other nations that had lived in the shade of Assyria's greatness grieved her downfall. They **fainted** at the thought that such a great empire could be destroyed and quaked **at the sound of its downfall** (31:15-16). The idea of other nations already in **Sheol** (the grave or **underworld**) being **comforted** by Assyria's fall (31:16-17) may mean that they were "relieved," so to speak, that even the great Assyria could be taken down and suffer the same fate they had.

31:18 Egypt should have quaked too, because it was Assyria's ally in the years before its defeat by Babylon. Egypt would also be **brought down to the underworld** by Babylon. To make the point plain, Ezekiel closed this prophecy with, **This is Pharaoh and all his hordes**, bringing the allegory full circle (see 31:2). Pharaoh depended on his vast army, but it would do him no good when Babylon invaded.

32:1-2 The final two of Ezekiel's seven prophecies against Egypt come in chapter 32. Ezekiel dated this prophecy as occurring **in the twelfth year, in the twelfth month** (32:1)— that is, March of 585 BC. This was about a year and seven months after the fall of Jerusalem, and two months after the news of the disaster reached the exiles in Babylon. God told Ezekiel to write down a **lament**—not for Judah, which he had already done (see Ezek 19)—but for **Pharaoh king of Egypt** (32:2).

Ezekiel's fellow exiles may have been too deep in shock and mourning over the judgment of their fellow Jews in Jerusalem to grasp the importance of this lament against Egypt, but God wanted these messages recorded so that future generations would know that he judges evil nations, no matter how powerful. Egypt's people believed their Pharaoh was like a crocodile, **a monster** thrashing and churning up the **waters** in the Nile River, who was so powerful that he could not be overcome (32:2).

32:3-8 Pharaoh's crocodile-like power was no problem for God. He would **spread** his **net** over Pharaoh by the armies of Babylon, **haul** the king up on **the land**, and **throw** him out in an **open field** where the earth's scavengers could feed on his **carcass** (32:3-5). The mention of **blood** flowing through the land of Egypt and thick **darkness** covering it suggest two of the exodus plagues when God judged Egypt the first time (32:6-8).

32:9-10 The lament continues with the shattering effect that Egypt's fall would have on the other Gentile nations. The people in many nations would **be appalled** at Egypt's collapse, and **their kings** would **shudder with fear** when they realized that if this could happen to Egypt, it could happen to them. They would **tremble** at the thought of this possibility for the rest of their lives.

32:11-16 In this last stanza of the lament God lays aside the figurative language of a crocodile being caught in a net and plainly states that he would bring **the sword of Babylon's**

king against Egypt, overwhelming its **hordes** by the **swords** of Babylon's **ruthless** army (32:11-12). Even the animals in Egypt would suffer as the land was decimated (32:13). God also said the Nile and its streams would be placid and **flow like oil**, instead of being churned up and muddied by humans and animals moving through them, when he made an end of Egypt (32:14-15). Then he invited **the daughters of the nations** to take up this lament **over Egypt and all its hordes** (32:16).

32:17-20 The seventh and final prophecy against Egypt views the nation's demise from the perspective of the underworld, an expansion of what had been said earlier about Assyria. Using poetry, God depicts Egypt's arrival in **the underworld**, where it finds itself among many other ungodly nations that had already gone down **to the Pit** (32:18). There Egypt would discover that it was no better than any other nation that defied God, but would also **rest with the uncircumcised** (32:19). This term "uncircumcised" was used ten times in this section (32:19, 21, 24-30, 32) and always described a death of shame.

32:21-23 Those nations already in the grave would mock Egypt, saying in effect, "Well, look who has come to join the rest of us lowly warriors to lie here shamed in the afterlife! If it isn't mighty Egypt, who thought he was better than everyone else!" (32:21). The fact that Egypt would have plenty of company in **Sheol** was not in doubt. Assyria was there with its army, all of them **slain, fallen by the sword** (32:21-22) after its defeat by Babylon. God repeated that the **graves** of Assyria's soldiers were **all around her burial place**, despite the fact that Assyria had **once spread terror in the land of the living** (32:23).

32:24-32 Other nations are also mentioned, each suffering the same fate (32:24-30). Last of all, Egypt comes up for one final word of condemnation from the Lord. When **Pharaoh** Hophra and the **hordes** of his armies reached the grave, he would be able to take some perverse comfort from the fact that at least he and his army weren't the only ones to die **by the sword** in the same humiliating defeat that these other nations had suffered (32:30-31).

IV. PROPHECIES OF ISRAEL'S RESTORATION (33:1-39:29)

33:1-9 Ezekiel had been speaking words of judgment for seven years, otherwise keeping silent in obedience to God's command (see 3:26-27) as part of his original commission to his prophetic office (beginning at 3:16). He had proclaimed that the people of Judah, the only ones who remained of Israel, would be punished for their sins (chapters 1–24), as would the nations around them (chapters 25–32). But from here to the end of the book, the message to Israel becomes one of restoration, because God did not intend to abandon his covenant people forever. The nation of Israel was going to be brought back to him (and these messages spoke to the entire nation, not just to Judah).

Since Ezekiel's message was going to change, it was appropriate that God recommission him to his ministry. For seven years prior to the fall of Jerusalem, Ezekiel had remained mute when not delivering a prophetic oracle from God. But when news arrived that Jerusalem had fallen, God lifted that restriction and Ezekiel was free to speak (see 33:21-22).

This chapter may not sound like good news to God's people, but he had to do some spadework before he could begin rebuilding. The people of Judah who stayed behind in the land, and all of the Israelites, still needed to understand that they were personally responsible before God for their actions. God brought this point home by appointing Ezekiel as Israel's **watchman**, with the responsibility to blow his **trumpet** to **warn** of coming danger (33:2-3). Anyone who ignored a faithful watchman's warning and lost his life would be solely responsible for his own death. But if the watchman failed to give the warning and people died, the watchman would be held accountable for their deaths (33:4-9). In this way God stressed the personal responsibility of both the watchman (Ezekiel) and those who heard his message of repentance that was to follow.

Similarly, it is the role of spiritual leaders today to warn God's people of his just judgment against sin and call them to repentance.

Leaders who fail to fully carry out this sacred duty are accountable.

33:10-11 That message finally penetrated the hearts of his fellow Israelites. For the first time, they acknowledged that it was because of their **transgressions** and **sins** that they were **wasting away**, and they asked in despair, **How then can we survive?** (33:10). God told Ezekiel to give them words of comfort: God did not take **pleasure in the death of the wicked**, and their sin could be forgiven (33:11).

33:12-16 God's declaration that a person is righteous—in right standing before him— is always based on faith that expresses itself in right actions. That's the message Ezekiel delivered here. It was an invitation for the people to repent of sin and do **what is just and right** (33:14). It was a message that all the people of Israel desperately needed to hear and heed. One of the problems of the exiles, in fact, was that they loved to hear Ezekiel speak, but they didn't put his words into action (see 33:31). In today's terms, they shouted "Amen!" on Sunday, but lived as they pleased on Monday through Saturday. They voted for God's kingdom agenda with their mouths but voted for their own agenda with their hands and feet.

33:17-20 One way we know the Israelites of Ezekiel's day needed his preaching of personal responsibility was that they were still blaming God for being unfair in the way he dealt with them. This was the height of blasphemy, an instance of the creature accusing the Creator. But God turned their accusations around and reminded them that it was their ways that brought them into judgment, certainly not any unfairness on his part.

33:21-23 Verse 21 is a huge turning point in the book and in Israel's history. Jerusalem was destroyed and the temple burned in August 586 BC, but news of that didn't reach the exile community in Babylon until January 585 when a survivor reported it to

Ezekiel. The prophet knew something major was coming, since the Lord had **opened** his **mouth** the **evening before** (33:22). The **word of the LORD** (33:23) that God gave Ezekiel to deliver involved more of the spadework God needed to do in removing the rubble of Israel's sinful attitudes before its people were ready for healing and restoration. Both groups, those who remained in the land after Jerusalem's fall and the exiles in Babylon, were the recipients of God's word through Ezekiel.

33:24 The first group addressed here was hiding among **the ruins in the land of Israel**, having escaped death at the hands of the Babylonians. Incredibly, they were claiming to be a righteous remnant, the true sons and daughters of **Abraham** to whom God had given **the land** by an eternal covenant based on his faith. Their argument sounded like this: "Sure, things are bad for us now, but we're 'naming and claiming' our inheritance and expect God to restore our fortunes."

33:25-29 God's reply to them was this: "You have broken my covenant, relied on yourselves instead of on me, and **committed detestable acts**. And then you appeal to me on the grounds of my covenant with righteous Abraham? I don't think so." (33:25-26). The bad news for these survivors was that they had only temporarily escaped judgment. The same disasters that took down the other people of Jerusalem would catch up to them (33:27-29).

33:30-33 Ezekiel's message to his fellow exiles was different, but their fundamental problem was the same—failure to put God's Word into practice. In contrast to the obstinate refusal of those back in Judah to pay any attention to Ezekiel's messages, his "congregation" in Babylon had grown large. They were passing the word along that this preacher who was silent for most of the past seven years was speaking freely now and had a **message . . . from the LORD** (33:30). People came **in crowds** to **hear** God's **words** through Ezekiel, but they didn't **obey them** (33:31). Yet a day of reckoning was coming, probably referring to the day when all people will stand before God

to be judged by him, when Ezekiel's hearers would know he had spoken the truth.

34:1-4 Even though God had severely judged his people for their sins, they were still the sheep of his pasture that he loved. And now, with his sheep scattered all over the hills and in the caves of Israel and far away in Babylon, it was time to call their **shepherds**, their leaders, to account for their complete failure to lead his flock righteously. What was God's message to these rulers of his people? **Woe to the shepherds of Israel, who have been feeding themselves!** (34:2). Shepherds are to care for their sheep, but the nation's leaders preferred to feed themselves rather than to **tend the flock** (34:3). They did not care for the poor or meet other legitimate needs of their people. Yet, their sin was not mere neglect. They also treated the weakest members of society **with violence and cruelty** (34:4).

34:5-10 It's little wonder the people were **scattered for lack of a shepherd** with **no one searching or seeking for them**, because their false leaders didn't care (34:5-6). When government and religious leaders fail to fulfill their God-ordained calling in his kingdom program to uphold justice, keep the peace, and punish evil, then chaos, loss of freedom, and tyranny follow. That, in fact, is exactly what happened in Israel. Its bad kings, false prophets, and faithless priests had failed to carry out God's agenda. Therefore, God called them into his courtroom to hear the charges against them and their sentence. He read the indictment in 34:7-8 and the sentence in 34:9-10. The **flock** of Israel would be taken away from these greedy shepherds, who would never again be allowed to fatten themselves at the expense of God's people (34:10). This warning applies to church leaders today (see Acts 20:28-35).

34:11-16 Nevertheless, God's people were still scattered and leaderless, so God said he would become their shepherd himself. These promises of his care were not fulfilled completely when the people returned from exile in Babylon. These verses describe Israel in Christ's millennial kingdom when Israel is fully regathered and restored under its good shepherd. The nation's false leaders had allowed the people to be scattered, but Christ will **bring them out from the peoples, gather them from the countries, and bring them to their own soil** (34:13). Instead of taking advantage of the weak, he will **strengthen** them. In place of exploitation, there will be **justice** (34:16).

34:17-24 Before Christ establishes his kingdom, a judgment must be held to separate the righteous from the wicked—that is, the sheep from the goats (Matt 25:31-46)—because these two groups will still exist in that day as they did in Ezekiel's. The wicked are those who not only devour the **good pasture** and the **clear water** for themselves, but also ruin it for the **weak ones** so that they have to subsist on leftovers (34:17-19, 21). God promised to establish his true shepherd over his people: his **servant David**, Jesus Christ, the Son of David, who will be Israel's perfect shepherd and **prince** (34:23-24). As David was a faithful shepherd (see 1 Sam 17:34-37), so the Lord Jesus will be even more so (see John 10:11-18).

34:25-31 Since Christ will rule Israel, God said, **I will make a covenant of peace with** Israel (34:25). These verses echo other Old Testament prophecies that speak of Israel's safety in the land from both dangerous animals and human enemies. The land of Israel itself will also be perpetually productive during the kingdom age. Most important of all, the people of Israel will recognize their true Messiah, their shepherd. They will bow in worship to Jesus Christ. The Lord has declared it.

35:1-4 A declaration of judgment on Edom (35:1-15) might seem out of place in this section on Israel's restoration. But on closer examination, this chapter fits the theme because Edom stood for all of Israel's enemies that God would judge when he restored the fortunes of his chosen people. This was Ezekiel's second prophecy of judgment on Edom (see 25:12-14), but the current passage is more detailed. Even though the Edomites and Israelites were closely related (they were the descendants of Esau and Jacob, the sons of Isaac, respectively), **Mount Seir**, the range south of the Dead Sea where the Edomites

lived, was under God's judgment. When this judgment fell, God said Edom would **know that I am the LORD** (35:3-4; see also 35:9, 15).

35:5-9 One reason for Edom's judgment was its people's **perpetual hatred** against **the Israelites**. The Edomites gave them **over to the power of the sword in the time of their disaster** (35:5) as an ally of the Babylonians when they destroyed Jerusalem. Therefore, because of the Edomites' actions, God would **destine** them **for bloodshed** until **Mount Seir** was filled with **those slain by the sword** (35:6-8).

35:10-15 Edom would also come under God's wrath because when the **two nations** (Israel and Judah) fell, Edom greedily desired to take their **two lands** for itself, even though they were promised to the Jews (35:10). The Edomites hated God's people, blasphemed him, **rejoiced** when he judged **the mountains of Israel**, and **boasted against** God (35:11-13). Since Edom **rejoiced** when Israel was made **a desolation**, God would make Edom **a desolation** (35:14-15).

36:1-5 Ezekiel 36 is a tremendous picture of Israel's restoration to favor in both God's eyes and among the nations that had formerly ridiculed and attacked it. Coming on the heels of Judah's downfall, this prophecy might have sounded too good to be true to the exiles in Babylon. So God tied his promises to his character, not to Israel's present circumstances in captivity. No fewer than ten times in this chapter, God sealed his promise by saying, **This is what the LORD God says** (36:2-7, 13, 22, 33, 37). Israel's future restoration was as good as done in God's mind.

Notice how God also tied Israel's future blessing to the judgment he pronounced on Edom as the representative of all the nation's enemies (36:5). Edom's mountain, Mount Seir, would be destroyed because, in part, Edom thought it could seize the land of Israel after God had punished his people for their sins. Israel's enemies gathered around like vultures, saying, **Aha! The ancient heights have become our possession** as Israel became **an object of people's gossip and slander** after its conquest (36:2-4). Of course, this meant that Israel's enemies were really slandering the Lord, the true God, who would not let their cruelty toward his people and blasphemy toward him go unpunished.

36:6-12 God's **burning zeal** (36:6) would bring about blessing, fruitfulness, and salvation for Israel (36:8-15). In the prophets, God's "zeal" (or "jealousy") speaks of his exclusive covenant love for Israel and determination to act on his people's behalf (e.g., Isa 42:13; 63:15; Zech 1:14; 8:2). In this case, the land will produce abundantly, the people will flourish, and the ruined cities will be **rebuilt** (36:8-10). Israel will be **better off than** ever **before**, and the people will never again be driven off their land or suffer loss (36:11-12). These promises clearly await Christ's millennial kingdom for their fulfillment.

36:13-15 In the kingdom age, God will also take away Israel's reproach when her Messiah rules the nations. Israel's enemies had a saying: **You devour people and deprive your nation of children** (36:13), an insult that God said would no longer **be heard against** his people because there would no longer be any truth in it (36:15).

36:16-21 The bulk of this chapter is devoted to prophecies about the regathering of Israel's people that will be accomplished as God brings the tribulation period to an end and ushers in the millennium with Christ's second coming. Ezekiel received this message from God, which begins with a review of the people's sinful conduct. His audience was painfully aware of this because Jerusalem's destruction and the exile gave God's enemies the opportunity to profane his **holy name** (36:20).

36:22-23 But God would still act to restore his people and land. However, they needed to understand that it was not their merit or righteousness that moved him but zeal for his **holy name** (36:22). They had **profaned** it, but he would **honor** it again in the **sight** of the nations (36:22-23). This restoration is a further promise of blessing in the millennial kingdom, when Israel's rejection of its Messiah will end and Jesus Christ will reign as King and Savior on the Davidic throne in Jerusalem. These verses include Israel's spiritual restoration.

36:24-30 Israel's blessing in the kingdom will definitely include a return to the land God has given the nation by an eternal covenant. And with his people in their homeland, God will proceed to restore them spiritually. He will **sprinkle clean water on** them, give them **a new heart and put a new spirit within** them (36:25-26). He will also put his **Spirit within** his people (36:27), a description of the "new covenant" (see Jer 31:31-34) that was inaugurated with the death of Jesus Christ and that will be applied to Israel when he returns and his people confess him.

36:31-37 When Israel experiences God's grace in Christ, its people **will loathe** their sins and realize that God has saved them because of his grace and mercy (33:31-32). Israel's inward cleansing will be accompanied by the restoration of the land to a beauty and fruitfulness that will make the land **like the garden of Eden** (36:35). Israel's splendor in the kingdom will be such that everyone will know God has fulfilled all his promises to his covenant people.

37:1-3 Chapters 37–39 are probably the most well known and highly debated chapters in Ezekiel. Chapter 37 is known as "the dry bones" chapter, and chapters 38–39 discuss Gog and Magog.

The prophet received two signs in chapter 37. The **valley** filled with **very dry** bones was the first (37:1-2). God asked Ezekiel, **Son of man, can these bones live?** Ezekiel cautiously answered, **Lord God, only you know** (37:3). Ezekiel may have been reluctant to speak more confidently given that Israel was in ruins and the bones of Jerusalem's people were still lying in the city's rubble.

37:4-14 Since Ezekiel wouldn't answer, God completed the vision for him and then gave him the explanation. How was he going to revive the disconnected, lifeless bones of Israel? He would do it through two key words: Word and Spirit.

Ezekiel was told, **Prophesy concerning these bones and say to them: Dry bones, hear the word of the Lord!** (37:4). Then, as

Ezekiel obeyed, God caused the bones to begin knitting themselves together as **tendons, flesh,** and **skin** gave them shape again (37:7-8). But the Word had to be accompanied by the giving of the Spirit as **breath entered** these bodies **and they came to life** (37:10), providing a classic illustration of spiritual revival. Chapter 36 had already revealed that Israel's receiving the Spirit of God will occur in the kingdom when Jesus Christ returns and God's chosen people are given a new heart as promised in the new covenant. In that day, God said, **I will put my Spirit in you,** and Israel will be settled in its land (37:14). The dry bones will become a new nation.

Similarly, the Word and the Spirit bring spiritual revival to God's church today. When one or both are absent, then God's people have no living experience of his reality in their midst (see 2 Cor 3:17-18).

37:15-17 Ezekiel was then told to perform another visible sign or object lesson in front of his fellow exiles; it's the last one in the book. He was to take two sticks and **write on** them the names of the two most prominent tribes of the divided kingdom. **Judah** was the dominant tribe in the southern kingdom, while **Ephraim,** whose patriarch was one of Joseph's sons, was the largest tribe in the northern kingdom (37:16-17). But with both kingdoms gone, the future of Israel would be one of unity, not division.

37:18-24 The people watched Ezekiel write on the sticks, and they knew what the names meant. But in their seemingly hopeless circumstances, they couldn't grasp what he was trying to tell them. So he made it plain: God was going to reunite Israel by his mighty **hand** (37:18-19). Moreover, the people would one day be regathered from exile and live in their land, where **one king will rule over all of them** (37:20-22). God's interest was not merely physical restoration but spiritual revival and salvation. His people would be cleansed of their sins and become the holy people he had designed them to be. This will be possible because they will have new hearts ruled by Jesus Christ, the **one shepherd for all of them** (37:23-24), when he returns to reign.

37:25-28 Then God's people will live in the land forever under an eternal **covenant of peace,** worshiping God in his **sanctuary** (anticipating the prophecy of the rebuilt temple in Ezek 40–43), where he will be **among them forever.** Then, he declared, **I will be their God, and they will be my people** (37:25-27).

38:1-6 The identities of **Gog** and **Magog** (38:2) are key to understanding the cataclysmic battle described in the next two chapters and God's judgment on Israel's enemies. "Gog" is a person, and the ancient Jewish historian Josephus identified "Magog" as the land from which the Scythians descended around the Black Sea and Caspian Sea in an area now occupied by Russia and several other nations of the former Soviet Union. Gog was called **the chief prince of Meshech and Tubal** (38:2), areas located in modern-day Turkey. Ezekiel named these and other nations because God is going to draw them into battle against Israel at a strategic time in history, when his and Israel's enemies will be massed against them (38:4). The armies aligned against Israel will include **Persia . . . Cush . . . Put . . . Gomer . . . Beth-togarmah** (38:5-6).

38:7-9 The time of this attack has been debated. Some identify it with an attack at the end of the millennium (see Rev 20:7-9), but the details between the passages are vastly different, and in the latter case these names are probably used symbolically of God's worldwide enemies. The best choice for Ezekiel's battle seems to be around the middle of the tribulation, when Israel is **regathered** and is living in peace (38:8), but this peace may be that of its false covenant of peace with the Antichrist (see Dan 9:27; Matt 24:15-22), which he will violate. Israel at this point has not recognized its Messiah, and has more purging to undergo. Thus, Gog's **troops** will mass against Israel **like a cloud covering the land** (38:9).

38:10-16 Gog will think this is his own plan; therefore, he will be confident of success because he assumes Israel is undefended and will be easy pickings for spoil (38:10-13). But Gog and his allies do not know that God is gathering them to his land for another purpose entirely. Gog won't know that he and his massive army are heading straight into God's trap, **so that the nations may know** who the true God is when he shows himself **holy** to the whole world (38:14-16).

38:17-23 This judgment is then elaborated on. When Gog and his armies reach Israel, God's **wrath will flare up**. In his **zeal and fiery rage**, he will send a **great earthquake** to Israel that will make every living creature **tremble** and will demolish natural and man-made objects (38:18-20). Gog's troops will be so panicked and confused that they will begin fighting and killing each other, and the slaughter will be helped along by other natural, God-sent disasters (38:21-22). Gog's invasion will be crushed as the world watches God display his **greatness and holiness**, leaving no doubt to the unbelieving world during the tribulation that he alone is God (38:23).

39:1-8 God's judgment against Gog continues in chapter 39. After God has driven Gog's armies into the land of Israel **from the remotest parts of the north**, God will weaken these forces and they will **fall in battle on the mountains of Israel**, becoming food for the birds and **wild animals** (39:2-4). God will also punish **Magog**, the homeland of Gog, and all the people who sent their armies to attack Israel (39:6). Israel's people themselves will come to regard God's name as **holy**, and the nations will know that he is **the Holy One in Israel** (39:7).

39:9-13 The slaughter of this battle will be so great that its description almost defies the imagination. Many commentators have a hard time seeing a literal burning of the **weapons**, which would suggest they are like ancient wooden weapons that could be easily burned. But this is what the text says, and 39:10 is even clearer, stating that during this period of **seven years** (39:9) Israel would not need any other source of firewood. The burial time for Gog's troops also suggests the extent of the slaughter—**seven months** of burials **in order to cleanse the land** as the surrounding nations hear of the great victory God gave Israel and see his **glory** on display (39:12-13).

39:14-20 The importance in Israel of burying every bone so as not to defile the land with unburied corpses will lead to a **full-time** cadre of men searching for remains for **seven months**, during which they will find so many that the gravediggers will live in their own city until the job is done (39:14-16). God will also announce a "feast" to the creatures of Israel to fatten themselves on the corpses of Gog's troops, which is a reversal of God's usual **sacrificial feast** in which people eat the flesh of animals. This time, God will prepare the meal (39:17-20).

39:21-29 Two results of this stunning defeat of Gog will be that the **nations will see** God's **glory** manifested, as noted above, and Israel will turn back to God after experiencing his judgment (39:21-24). If this battle occurs during the tribulation, it will help prepare for Israel's restoration in Christ's millennial kingdom when God will **restore the fortunes of Jacob** by bringing his people back to their land where they will **live securely ... with no one to frighten them** (39:25-26). Not one Israelite will be left **behind** when Jesus Christ returns and institutes the new covenant of salvation and restoration with his people (39:27-28).

V. PROPHECIES OF ISRAEL IN THE MILLENNIAL KINGDOM (40:1–48:35)

⋙ *A. The New Temple (40:1–43:27)* ⋘

40:1-2 In the history of the world, many leaders—good and bad—have promised that their rule would bring a new order of things. But there is only one legitimate new order, and it will arrive when Jesus Christ establishes his millennial kingdom at his second coming. When that glorious day arrives, there will be a new order for his chosen people Israel in fulfillment of his covenant promises to them. Nowhere is that more clear than in Ezekiel 40–48, as the prophet describes a new temple, a new order of worship, and a new division of the land of Israel that will take effect in the kingdom age.

Ezekiel dated his final prophecies in **the twenty-fifth year of . . . exile, at the beginning of the year, on the tenth day of the month in the fourteenth year after Jerusalem had been captured** (40:1), which places them in 573 BC. The message God gave Ezekiel to deliver was in the form of **visions** in which the Lord **took** the prophet to **Israel** (40:2)—but a far different version of it than Ezekiel would have seen in his own day after the Babylonian conquest.

40:3-4 In his vision Ezekiel was taken to a "very high mountain" (40:2) where he saw a brilliant figure, no doubt an angel, **whose appearance was like bronze.** He was holding a **measuring rod** and commanding the prophet to write down everything he was about to hear and see for **the house of Israel** (40:3-4). In these words is a clear statement of the purpose for this entire book, not just the concluding chapters; nevertheless, it's hard for us to grasp what the message of Ezekiel must have meant to his immediate hearers and readers. They were reminded of God's perfect holiness and intolerance of sin—and yet also his unfailing love for the people he had set apart for himself.

40:5-16 The future revealed to Ezekiel includes a rebuilt **temple** where God's people will worship him in spirit and in truth under the rule of Jesus Christ. Ezekiel soon discovered that in his vision, he was standing at its entrance. This millennial temple will serve in the midst of God's people as a visible symbol of the new covenant he promised to establish.

The angel guiding Ezekiel measured the **wall surrounding the outside of the temple**, then the eastern **gate** with its various dimensions and decorations (40:5-16). This gate was listed first because in God's plan during the millennial kingdom it is the most important gate (see commentary on 44:1-3).

40:17-47 The angel then took Ezekiel to the temple's **outer court**, where he saw **thirty chambers** (40:17), rooms which might be used for storage or for meeting places when

the people celebrate their feasts. Ezekiel was then led from the east gate of the outer court to the north and south gates, with the angel measuring and the prophet recording each detail as they went. The tour continued with the temple's **inner court** and its gates and measurements (40:27-37), after which Ezekiel saw **eight tables . . . on which the slaughtering was to be done** (40:41).

This suggestion that animal sacrifices will be resumed in the millennial kingdom does not imply a reversion to the Levitical sacrificial system. After all, such sacrifices could never ultimately take away sins (see Heb 10:4, 11) and were fulfilled in Christ's once and for all atoning death on the cross (Heb 10:12-18). These sacrifices, however, will be offered not to cover sins, but as memorials to and reminders of the sacrifice of the Messiah that took away sin forever (see Acts 21:26). They will serve to commemorate what he did, just as the Lord's Supper does today. Millennial worship (Ezek 44–46) will include these sacrifices, properly understood.

Ezekiel was also shown two rooms in the inner court, one for **the singers** and one for the **priests** who will be on duty in their turn (40:44-47).

40:48–41:4 The vision shifted as Ezekiel, still in the inner court, stepped back to view the entire temple as the angel measured the **portico** or entrance to the temple, a vestibule much like a porch with **pillars on each side** (40:48). He had to climb a flight of stairs (40:49) to reach the **great hall** or outer sanctuary, which the angel also measured as he did each part of the temple (41:1-2). But he did not enter **the room adjacent to the great hall**, which the angel entered and measured (41:3-4). The angel explained why Ezekiel was barred from this smaller room: **This is the most holy place** (41:4).

41:5-26 Ezekiel was also told that **the wall** surrounding the temple was 10½ **feet thick,** and that the temple had three levels of **side rooms all around**, a total of **three stories** with **thirty rooms each** (41:5-6). The reason for these rooms is not stated, but they are probably storage rooms for temple equipment or are used to store the people's tithes and offering. These side rooms were supported by a **raised platform** serving as a **foundation**, which was 10 ½ **feet high**, with the **outer wall** of the rooms themselves measuring at 8 ¾ **feet** in thickness (41:8-9)—built to last! Ezekiel also saw a large building west of the temple that was left unexplained except for its dimensions (41:12), while the temple itself measured 175 **feet long** and the same width to the east. The temple's length **to the west** was the same (41:13-15).

Ezekiel also saw that the interior of the temple was **overlaid with wood on all sides**, etched with **carved . . . cherubim and palm trees** (41:16-18). The carved figures represent the guardians of God's presence, as Ezekiel had seen in his initial vision; the "palm trees" stand for God's blessing and fruitfulness.

There was also a wooden altar just outside, which the angel described as **the table that stands before the Lord** (41:22), indicating that it stands just outside the most holy place. This may be the altar of incense, or the one that holds the bread of the presence—both of which were in the original tabernacle (see Exod 30:1-3; 25:23-30). The angel did not explain the altar's purpose, and Ezekiel went on to describe the double doors of both the outer sanctuary and most holy place (41:23-26).

42:1-12 Ezekiel's angelic guide then took him to **the outer court** of the temple to see a **group of chambers** or rooms (42:1). These were connected to the **inner court** with entrances from the outer court. The complex was **in three tiers**, or three stories, with each one being **narrower** than the one below it (42:3-5). The first row of rooms Ezekiel saw, those next to the outer court, were 87 ½ **feet long**, while the row of rooms facing the **great hall** or sanctuary were 175 **feet long** (42:7-8). There was an identical group of rooms on the **south side** of the temple (42:10-12).

42:13-14 As Ezekiel viewed these **northern and southern chambers** and recorded their dimensions, the angel explained their purposes. First, they will serve as **holy chambers where the priests who approach the Lord will eat the most holy offerings** they have deposited from the sacrifices the people bring (42:13). The law of Moses made

provision for the priests to eat a portion of the Israelites' offerings as part of their means of support, and this will be the case again in the millennial temple. A second purpose for these rooms is to give the priests a place to change out of their holy garments and into their "street clothes" before leaving the **holy area** of the temple (42:14). This will keep the special garments within the temple.

42:15-20 When the angel finished taking Ezekiel through the entire **temple complex**, he led the prophet outside to measure the temple's external dimensions. It was a square, measuring **875 feet** long on each side (42:15-19). The wall around it had the same dimensions, which Ezekiel explained was for the purpose of separating **the holy from the common** (42:20).

This last statement emphasized what Ezekiel's vision of the temple—and in truth his entire prophecy was all about—preserving the holiness of God. The temple's design enforced that message with its doors and passages limiting access to the holy areas, culminating in the veil covering the most holy place in Solomon's temple and the doors to it in the millennial temple. But there was also access to God in the temple, either directly in the outer areas or through his appointed representatives, culminating in the sacrifice and ministry of his great high priest, Jesus Christ. He ministers today in the heavenly sanctuary, and will do so forever as our eternal high priest.

43:1-5 Ezekiel 43 is one of the most exciting chapters in the Bible. Here we see the departed glory of God coming back into his house in an awesome display of majesty. Ezekiel heard God's voice roaring **like the roar of a huge torrent, and the earth shone with his glory** when he **entered the temple** through the eastern **gate** and the temple was **filled** with his **glory** (43:2, 4-5).

43:6-9 God told Ezekiel to tell the people that this new indwelling of his new temple in the millennial kingdom would last **forever**. There would be no more of the defiling of his **holy name** by the **religious prostitution** of the people and their **kings** who dared to place their thrones and idols in God's house

(43:7-8). Political leaders and systems must never be allowed to make themselves equal to God, nor should God's people allow politics and political parties to compete with the kingdom of God.

43:10-12 God also told Ezekiel to **describe the temple to the house of Israel** (43:10) to remind them of the shameful acts they committed that caused the magnificent temple of Solomon in Jerusalem to be destroyed and to motivate them to obedience in the future.

43:13-27 When the millennial temple is built, before the redeemed people of Israel will be able to begin their daily worship of God in it, the altar of burnt offering must be consecrated. The altar's dimensions were given in great detail (43:13-17), with the expectation that they will be followed precisely when the altar is built in the kingdom age. Its completion will be followed by a seven-day period of consecration (43:18-27). This will involve many **burnt offerings** and a **sin offering** to be given **to the Levitical priests who are from the offspring of Zadok**, who will **apply** the **blood** in much the same way as it was applied in the sacrifices under the law of Moses (43:18-20). Once these seven days of consecration are complete, **on the eighth day and afterward, the priests will offer … burnt offerings and fellowship offerings on the altar** (43:27). The millennial worship of Israel will begin in earnest.

✦ *B. The New Worship (44:1–46:24)* ✦

44:1-3 But there will be one gate leading into the millennial Jerusalem through which Israel's worshipers will not come. Ezekiel had seen God's glory come back into the temple through the **gate that faced east**, which God ordered to be **closed** and **remain closed** because his glory and holy presence had **entered through it** (44:1-2). But **the prince himself** will be allowed to enter this gate (see also 46:2) **to eat a meal before the Lord**, possibly the fellowship offerings (44:3).

There is some debate about this prince's identity. One suggestion is that he is Christ himself, the only one worthy to enter a gate

that God sanctified by his holy presence. But elsewhere in Ezekiel this prince is said to offer a sin offering for himself (see 45:22), have children (see 46:16), and possess an allotment of land in Israel (see 46:18)—all of which are inappropriate descriptions of Christ.

In 34:24, God himself said, speaking of the kingdom age, "I, the Lord, will be their God, and my servant David will be a prince among them." God repeated this prophecy later by saying, "My servant David will be king over them … and [he] will be their prince forever" (37:24-25). Based on these passages, the prince Ezekiel mentions is none other than the resurrected King David, leading God's people again in a role under the lordship of the Messiah. There is a lot to commend this view, since David was a type of Christ and Jesus was called the Son of David.

44:4-8 Ezekiel assumed his usual position, **facedown**, when he entered the temple and saw **the glory of the Lord** as it **filled** it (44:4).

God's stern exhortation to Ezekiel's audience is a reminder that even though the prophet was seeing glorious visions of a restored Israel and a magnificent rebuilt temple in the kingdom age to come, he was ministering to a sinful people who had been devastated by judgment and exile. By the time the word came that Jerusalem was destroyed and the survivors of the slaughter reached Babylon in chains, even the most stubborn and rebellious among the Israelites could hardly deny that this catastrophe was the result of their sins.

God told Ezekiel to pay close attention to his holy laws regarding the temple. Then he could teach them to his fellow exiles and record them for future generations so that they wouldn't commit the same sins of their ancestors and fall under the same judgment (44:5). He said, **I have had enough of all your detestable practices, house of Israel** (44:6).

One of the sins practiced in the land was bringing **foreigners, uncircumcised in both heart and flesh**, into the temple for the wrong reasons (44:7). These were not Gentiles who wanted to sincerely worship the God of Israel but idolaters who corrupted God's worship and his people. Yet the Israelites gave these people **charge of** his **sanctuary** (44:8)!

44:9-14 The Levites weren't much help either. During the days of Israel's apostasy, these men who were supposed to be guardians of God's holiness and who handled his holy things also **strayed** into idolatry (44:10). As a result of their sin, they will have a diminished role in the millennial age, **serving as guards at the temple gates and ministering at the temple** in lesser roles (44:11-12). No longer will they be **priests** or handle **any of** the **holy things or the most holy things** as part of their reduced temple assignments (44:13-14).

44:15-23 It was a different story with the **Levitical priests descended from Zadok** (44:15), the chief priest during Solomon's reign who had remained faithful to God while the Israelites were turning away from him. These priests will be honored by their appointment to serve God in the priestly role in the millennial temple (44:16). They will follow Mosaic regulations such as wearing linen garments when they minister, changing their clothes before going back among the people, not adopting the common signs of mourning, not drinking wine before they go in to do their priestly duties, and not marrying women who have previously been married (44:17-23). Such regulations were restrictive, but that was the point. Those set apart to serve God were to demonstrate that they were wholly his in every area of their lives.

44:24-31 The priests will also serve as judges in Israel and will be allowed to mourn the death of a close relative, although death will be a rare occurrence in Christ's kingdom (44:24-27). And as in the days of the Old Testament priests, these servants of God will not have an allotment in the land of Israel, which will be divided again by God (see Ezek 48). God said, **I am their inheritance. . . . I am their possession** (44:28). One way he will provide for his servants is by the **best of all the firstfruits of every kind and contribution of every kind** brought to him at the temple (44:30).

45:1-5 Ezekiel 48 deals with the allotment of Israel's land by tribes. God gave directions on how Jerusalem and the area will be arranged in the kingdom, both as a place for the millennial temple and as places of residence for the priests and Levites close to it. They are to **set aside a donation to the LORD, a holy portion of the land** (45:1) for the obvious reason that it will contain God's holy house and servants (45:4-5).

45:6-8 This area is a rectangle, 8 ⅓ **miles long and 6 ⅔ miles wide** (45:1), further divided width-wise into two equal sections that are 3 ⅓ **miles wide** (45:3). The first section will contain both the temple and the priests' houses, with the Levites' houses being in the second rectangle. The rectangle will become a square when another area is added, which will be the dimensions of Jerusalem itself (45:6), along with an area **on each side of the holy donation of land and the city's property** for the **prince** to occupy (45:7-8).

45:9-12 Ezekiel 45:9 was a jarring return to reality for Ezekiel's readers after his extended description of the glories of the kingdom age. God turned his attention from the nation's future, righteous prince to the present, unrighteous **princes** who were in exile with Ezekiel. His rebuke of their evil that led to Judah's downfall was stinging: **You have gone too far, princes of Israel!** These coldhearted leaders had used **violence** and **oppression** to fuel their greed, using dishonest business practices to cheat their people (45:9-10). But God warned them to start using honest measures and reminded them what these were (45:11-12). Even in exile, the Israelite community needed leaders, and God wanted Israel's to know that he was watching and would weigh their actions in his scales.

45:13-25 Here the subject returns to the sacrificial system in the millennial temple when, unlike the unrighteous princes of Ezekiel's day, the kingdom **prince in Israel** will honestly weigh out and provide the **offerings** for **all the appointed times of the house of Israel** (45:16-17). Ezekiel was referring to the nation's feasts, from the first feast of the year, **Passover** followed by the **seven days** of **unleavened bread**, to the last of Israel's annual feasts, the feast of Tabernacles or Booths, which began **on the fifteenth day of the seventh month** and also lasted **seven**

days (45:21, 25). Clearly, in the millennial age, observances such as Passover will not be held to provide an animal sacrifice to cover the people's sins for another year; they will be a celebration of Christ's once-for-all sacrifice for sin.

46:1-11 God's instructions for Israel's worship in the millennial temple continue with instructions for the weekly Sabbath, monthly New Moon, feast days, and daily sacrifices. Ezekiel was still in his visionary state as he received these commands (see 40:1-2), being shown the new temple by the angelic figure who was leading him. He saw once again that the temple's eastern gate was to remain **closed** during the week, but **opened on the Sabbath day** and on **the New Moon** so **the prince** could **sacrifice his . . . offerings** and **bow in worship** (46:1-2), bringing what God prescribed (46:4-8). Instructions are also provided to show how **the people** are to **enter** and **leave** the temple when they come to present their sacrifices in worship to the Lord (46:9-11).

46:12-15 The eastern gate is to be opened on one other occasion, **when the prince makes a freewill offering** (46:12). By definition there is no set time for this offering, so the regulations for keeping the eastern gate closed will be set aside so that this leader can bring an offering expressing his love for God. As soon as his offering is done, the gate will be closed again. The regulations for worship in the millennial temple end with instructions for the daily sacrifice (46:13-15), which is appropriate because it is by its nature the most frequent way in which God's people will be reminded of their relationship to him and will have the opportunity to express their devotion.

46:16-18 Remarkably, even in the kingdom age the ownership of the new land of Israel will be governed by the ancient law of the Year of Jubilee (see Lev 25:8-13). Any land **the prince gives . . . to each of his sons** will stay in the family, but any land he gives to a servant **will revert to the prince** in the jubilee year (46:16-17). Unlike the evil princes of Ezekiel's day (see 45:8-9), the righteous prince of the millennial age will never take the people's land by force (46:18).

46:19-24 Ezekiel's angelic guide showed him a series of **kitchens** where the priests will cook their own portions of the sacrifices and the portions the worshipers are allowed to eat (46:24). These kitchens will be in distinct parts of the temple complex, keeping the priests separate from the people as they eat their sacrificial portions that have been made holy before the Lord. When the Israelites brought fellowship offerings to God at the temple, they were allowed to eat a part of them with their families and friends in a joyful meal. It will be that way again in the kingdom temple.

⇒ C. The New Land (47:1–48:35) ⇐

47:1-12 This vision of water flowing east from **the threshold of the temple** (47:1) began with a trickle and increased dramatically in depth every **third of a mile** (47:3, 4-5). This river will flow all the way to the Dead Sea, miraculously giving it life. Its **water will become fresh**, and **there will be life everywhere the river goes**, even along its banks (47:9, 12).

In Scripture, water is often tied to life and to the work of the Holy Spirit (see John 7:37-39), so the river that will flow from the millennial temple is further evidence that the Spirit of God has returned to his house. It's another way of testifying to God's people that he is in the place and that his blessing is flowing from him to the entire land. There's a kingdom lesson here for us today because the church is supposed to model the kingdom of God. We are supposed to be a living illustration of the flowing, deepening, and growing life that happens when the Holy Spirit manifests his growing presence in a community of believers (see Eph 2:19-22).

The book of Ezekiel is about a nation that was not just in religious decline, but also in governmental and family decline because none of the designated spheres of authority in God's kingdom program—the temple (think the church in our day), the government, and the family unit—were following God's statutes and commands. There was plenty of blame to share, but God started in Ezekiel's day where he always starts when his people descend into chaos. He started with judgment at his house, not at the courthouse downtown or at the White House, so to speak. Until we as God's people get our kingdom agenda priorities in order, he will not skip our failings to fix what's wrong with our culture either. "The time has come for judgment to begin with God's household, and if it begins with us, what will the outcome be for those who disobey the gospel of God?" (1 Pet 4:17).

The reason our culture is drying up is because there's no spiritual water flowing out of the sanctuary into the world. But we aren't going to get the water flowing down the streets of our communities, bringing life where there is death, until it begins to flow down the aisles of our churches. If God's presence doesn't show up among his people, how will it show up in our neighborhoods, in the nation, and in the world?

47:13-20 The rest of Ezekiel deals with the borders and divisions of Israel's land in the millennial kingdom. God wanted to remind his people that he had not forgotten the promise he **swore** to their **ancestors**—to Abraham, Isaac, and Jacob—to give them **this land . . . as an inheritance** (47:14). The borders outlined here are similar to those originally given to Moses (see Num 34:1-12), but Israel never fully occupied them at any time in its history.

The division of the land to the twelve tribes of Israel includes the note that **Joseph will receive two shares** (47:13), which is a reference to his two sons, Ephraim and Manasseh. There are different listings of the tribes throughout the Old Testament, depending on the reason for the listings. And that's the case even here in the millennium age, because the subject is the land allotments. The tribe of Levi did not have a portion of the land given to them since they were set apart to the Lord. He was to be their inheritance.

That doesn't mean, of course, that the Levites didn't have homes or anything to pass on to their descendants. They were provided for in Israel's history, and Ezekiel's vision showed

that they would have residences within the temple complex during the kingdom age, too. So there was no need to list them with the tribes. That takes care of one of the tribes that Ephraim and Manasseh replaced. But the other one was Joseph himself. This brings us to twelve allotments in Ezekiel 48, with the other ten of Jacob's sons being named.

47:21-23 Even **the aliens residing among** the Israelites in the kingdom, a reference to those Gentiles who believe in and worship the Messiah, will have special privileges (47:22-23). Aliens who wanted to follow the God of Israel were always allowed to live among his people and were treated kindly by them, but these people will also be **allotted an inheritance among the tribes of Israel** (47:22).

48:1-29 The division of the land will begin from the north and move to the south, with seven tribes receiving their allotments in the northern areas (48:1-7). The central part of the land will include Jerusalem and the area around it, which Ezekiel had already described in detail as the part that the people were to **donate to the LORD** (48:8). Its dimensions are repeated and specified as being for the use of **the consecrated priests, the sons of Zadok** and **the Levites** (48:11, 13). Also worth noting is the land belonging to **the prince** (48:21-22). The lower part of the land will be divided among the five remaining **tribes** (48:23-29).

48:30-35 The new Jerusalem will have twelve **gates**, three on each side of the city (48:30-34), but the most important thing Ezekiel could say about the city under the perfect, righteous rule of its rightful King was the new name it will bear: **The LORD Is There** (48:35). The holy city had become unholy and doomed to destruction. God's glory had departed in judgment. But in the glorious future, it will be restored when King Jesus returns to claim his rightful place as King and Lord and establishes his millennial kingdom reign.

DANIEL

INTRODUCTION

Author

U NTIL MODERN TIMES, IT WAS broadly accepted that Daniel authored the book that bears his name. Modern critical scholars, however, usually reject that the historical Daniel wrote it—as they do in the cases of a number of other prophetic biblical books. This is mostly based on a denial of the possibility of predictive prophecy. Yet, unless one assumes that God is unable to reveal the future to his prophets, then there is no good reason to deny the traditional view that Daniel wrote the book. Moreover, the discovery of a portion of a Daniel manuscript among the Dead Sea Scrolls testifies to an older date of writing than most critical scholars are willing to affirm. Thus, it is likely that Daniel wrote sometime after the end of the Babylonian captivity in the sixth century BC.

Daniel claims to have received visions from God, which he subsequently recorded (e.g., 2:19; 7:2; 8:1; 10:7). In Matthew 24:15, Jesus attributes the prophecy about the "abomination of desolation" (9:27; 11:31; 12:11) to Daniel. This confirms that our Lord believes the historical Daniel authored the book.

Historical Background

King Nebuchadnezzar of Babylon besieged Judah three times: once in 605 BC, again in 597 BC, and again in 586 BC. During the last of these, he destroyed Jerusalem and razed the temple. But, it was after the first invasion that Daniel and his friends were taken to Babylon in captivity (1:1-7). Daniel's service to Nebuchadnezzar began after his arrival there and continued into the reign of Cyrus, the Medo-Persian king who defeated the Babylonians (1:21; 10:1).

Message and Purpose

The book of Daniel is about how God's people are to live during the times of the Gentiles. Daniel was one of the first exiles to Babylon, where the Jews fell under Gentile domination because of their sin and rebellion against God.

Daniel's book is designed to teach how the entire period of Gentile rule—from Daniel's day to the second coming of the Messiah to set up his kingdom—should be viewed. God used the nations to bring judgment and discipline to Israel. In his own life, Daniel also illustrated how the people of God were to live, showing what faithfulness to God and his kingdom agenda looked like even when undergoing his discipline.

This book includes prophecy, as well as prayer, apocalyptic visions, and insight into spiritual warfare—all of which teach that God's people are under his sovereignty even when circumstances on earth do not appear to be in their favor. Daniel shows that the God of heaven rules on earth, even when earth seems to be out of control.

VIDEO INTRO

www.bhpublishinggroup.com/qr/te/27_oo

Outline

DANIEL

I. DANIEL'S DEPORTATION AND HIS FAITHFULNESS TO GOD (1:1-21)

1:1-7 Nebuchadnezzar's invasion of Judah in 605 BC was the first of his three invasions and deportations that ended in the exile of Judah. This early invasion resulted in his taking back to Babylon **some of the vessels from the house of God** (1:2), probably to show his dominance over Judah, and also some young men **from the royal family and from the nobility** (1:3). Among these was Daniel. He and his three friends (1:6-7) were perhaps teenagers at the time, which makes Daniel's story all the more remarkable. He was a person of exceptional character and capability. The royal plan was to train him and the others to be Nebuchadnezzar's court advisers (1:4). But, along the way, Daniel would face a crisis of worldview and truth that would pit him against the most powerful human king and kingdom on earth.

It's important for our overall study of Daniel—especially for the later chapters when Daniel reveals his great prophetic themes—to pause here and note that the conquest and destruction of Jerusalem by the Babylonians under King Nebuchadnezzar and the deportation of the people to exile in Babylon began what Jesus called "the times of the Gentiles" (Luke 21:24). This period beginning with the Babylonian exile is still in effect today, and will continue until Jesus Christ returns at the end of the great tribulation, frees Israel from its Gentile oppressors, and establishes his millennial kingdom. God revealed much of this coming history to Daniel, so this will become prominent later in the book.

For his new role in Babylon, Daniel was to learn **the Chaldean language and literature** and receive a Babylonian name: **Belteshazzar** (1:4, 7). His name and the names of his three friends, then, were changed to reflect the names of Babylonian gods. This detail is important because a name in the ancient world was more than a designation. Frequently in Scripture, God tied the name of someone to the character or even to the legacy of that person.

When the leaders of Babylon sought to alter Daniel's worldview, they knew they needed to begin with his identity. So, they removed from him any reference to the God of Israel. Thus, he was no longer to be called Daniel—"God is My Judge"—but Belteshazzar—"Bel Protect Him." Every aspect of Daniel's education and identity, in fact, was designed to remind him that he needed to operate from a Babylonian worldview. But, while Daniel could do nothing about his outward circumstances or the name forced upon him, in the integrity of his heart he knew that he served only one King and held to one worldview. And Daniel would find many opportunities to demonstrate his allegiance to a kingdom agenda that didn't come from Nebuchadnezzar.

1:8 It didn't take long before Daniel had his first opportunity to follow God in the midst of a pagan culture. He **determined that he would not defile himself with the king's food.** This decision was made to avoid violating the law of Moses regarding the foods the Jews were not to eat. The law explicitly taught, for instance, that they could not eat foods offered to idols (see Exod 34:15). Though he was serving a pagan king, Daniel resolved not to disobey God.

1:9-13 There were risks to Daniel's desire not to defile himself. The **chief eunuch** (named Ashpenaz, 1:3) worried that it would cost him his life if Daniel and his friends didn't eat the assigned food and became unhealthy. Daniel, therefore, appealed to **the guard** who was responsible for him and proposed a **test** (1:11-12). Daniel asked that he and his friends be given a diet of **vegetables** and **water** and that their health be observed (1:12-13). Note that God did not show up for Daniel until *after* he made this decision to obey.

1:14-16 God granted Daniel favor with the guard, who agreed to the conditions for a period of **ten days** (1:14). When the test was over, Daniel and his friends were not merely healthy, they were **healthier than all the young men who were eating the king's food** (1:15)! Round one went to Daniel and his friends (1:16). God had honored their faithfulness to him. This is the first of many occasions in the book of Daniel when he was blessed and rewarded for being true to God in a pagan society.

There was a lesson here for Daniel's earliest readers. Israel had disobeyed God and

suffered for it in exile, but God stood ready to bless his people when they obeyed and trusted him. There's a lesson here for Christians, too. We live in a fallen world, and we're called to be good citizens in it. Often, though, being good citizens requires rejecting the world's way of doing things and honoring God instead. What we need today are godly people who will offer society divine alternatives. Daniel did more than just refuse the king's food. He offered the chief eunuch another option in the matter—God's kingdom alternative.

1:17-21 God gave these four men knowledge and understanding in every kind of literature and wisdom (1:17). Though these Jewish men were the ones in exile, God would show himself to be superior through them. When the Babylonian **king interviewed them . . . no one was found equal to Daniel, Hananiah, Mishael, and Azariah.** They were the cream of the crop, the best of the best. They attended the **king**, and he **consulted them** in matters of **wisdom and understanding**. As a result, Nebuchadnezzar didn't merely find their counsel helpful, **he found them ten times better than** anyone else in his kingdom (1:19-20). In terms of ability, they stood head and shoulders above all of the so-called wise men of Babylon. That's because, even though they were living in an earthly kingdom, their allegiance was to a heavenly King.

II. NEBUCHADNEZZAR'S DREAM OF A GREAT IMAGE (2:1-49)

2:1 It wasn't long before **Nebuchadnezzar had dreams that troubled him**. Faithful readers of the Old Testament will recall an earlier biblical story—that of Pharaoh and Joseph—in which a pagan ruler had troubling dreams and turned to a spokesman of the one true God for counsel (Gen 41:1-45). Indeed, history was about to repeat itself.

2:2-4 The king was **anxious to understand** his dream (2:3). He was so disturbed by it that he called all his **magicians, mediums, sorcerers, and Chaldeans** (influential

Babylonian wise men) to interpret it for him (2:2). Therefore, the king's men praised him, invited him to explain the dream to them, and confidently assured him that they could **give the interpretation** (2:4)—or at least come up with something that sounded good!

The parenthetical note in 2:4 that **Aramaic begins here** refers to the fact that Daniel 2:4–7:28 was written in Aramaic (rather than Hebrew). Aramaic was the language of the Aramaeans, an ancient Mesopotamian people. It was similar to Hebrew and was used as a trade language (see 2 Kgs 18:26).

2:5-6 Nebuchadnezzar's response was the kind of outrageous demand ancient kings could make—illustrating the fury they could generate if their whims weren't met. The king was shrewd in saying, **my word is final** (2:5). It meant, "I shouldn't have to say another word. If you're so smart, you figure out what the dream was." The king may have been suspicious of his court wizards when he demanded they tell him what it was. The good news was that if they got it right, their **reward** would be extravagant (2:6). But, if they couldn't, they would all be put to death—**torn limb from limb**. And for good measure, he'd have their **houses** made into junkyards (2:5). It was a bad time to be a wise man in Babylon.

2:7-9 The wise men tried **a second time** to get Nebuchadnezzar to reveal his dream (2:7). But, the king wasn't buying it; he felt they were trying to pull a fast one so they could easily concoct an interpretation (2:8). So, he repeated his demands: **tell me the dream and I will know you can give me its interpretation** (2:9). Or else.

2:10-11 The Chaldeans insisted his idea was impossible. As diplomatically as they could, they informed the king that he was crazy: **No one on earth can make known what the king requests. . . . No one can make it known to him except the gods**. Now, they were partly correct because no one on earth could make it known. There is one in heaven, however, who can do anything. The Chaldeans were right to look for a divine answer, but there is only one capable deity.

2:12-16 Nebuchadnezzar **became violently angry** (2:12). He wasn't going to let his wise men tell him he didn't know what he was talking about. By attempting to smooth talk the king, then, they had simply signed their death warrant. **The decree was issued that the wise men were to be executed** (2:13), and that death order extended to Daniel and his three friends. Once Daniel learned the details of it (2:14-15), he boldly went to the king and asked for more **time** to make the **interpretation** known (2:16).

2:17-23 Daniel and his three Hebrew friends went to the only one who could deliver them; they prayed to **the God of the heavens** (2:17-18). And, **in a vision at night**, God graciously revealed **the mystery** to Daniel. But, before Daniel went public with the information, he first **praised the God of the heavens** (2:19). Why? Because when we're experiencing chaos, we need to remind ourselves that there's a God in heaven who reigns over the confusion on earth—and give him thanks. Daniel praised God for his **wisdom and power** (2:20). Even though this young man and his friends had been sentenced to death by a king, they gave glory to the one who **removes kings and establishes kings** (2:21). Their God is the one who **reveals . . . the hidden things** (2:22). By revealing what no one else could, God had given Daniel **wisdom and power** to fulfill the king's impossible request and shock Babylon (2:23).

2:24-30 Daniel confidently told **Arioch**, the king's captain of the guard (see 2:14), to stay the deadly order (2:24). He took Daniel to the king and made the announcement Nebuchadnezzar had been waiting for (2:25). When asked if he could tell **the dream** and **its interpretation** (2:26), Daniel didn't fail to give glory to **God** for the revelation (2:28). He confessed that the **mystery** was *not* revealed to him because he had **more wisdom than anyone living** (2:30), which indicates that even though Daniel was the only person on earth who knew the answer, he was humble. Indeed, God hadn't revealed the truth to Daniel to show how smart Daniel was; he'd revealed it so that the king would glorify God (see 2:45-47).

2:31-35 Daniel informed the king that he had dreamed of **a colossal statue** that had a **head** of **pure gold . . . chest and arms** of **silver . . . stomach and thighs** of **bronze . . . legs** of **iron**, and **feet** of partly iron and partly fired clay (2:31-33). Then **a stone . . . struck the statue on its feet of iron and fired clay, and crushed them** (2:34). After that, the entire statue **shattered**, and the metals were blown away **like chaff** never to be seen again. **But the stone that struck the statue became a great mountain and filled the whole earth** (2:35). Nebuchadnezzar must have been in shock as such details were recited.

2:36-38 After explaining what *the king alone* knew—the basic details of the **dream**, Daniel explained what *no one* knew—the dream's **interpretation** (2:36). Nebuchadnezzar himself was the **head of gold** because as far as earthly powers were concerned, he was currently **king of kings** (2:37-38). This power, however, had not originated with Nebuchadnezzar. On the contrary, this Hebrew exile boldly told the king that **the God of the heavens**—the God of Israel—had granted the king of Babylon **sovereignty, power, strength, and glory** (2:37).

2:39 Moreover, Babylon's rule wouldn't last forever. The eventual demise of the Babylonian Empire was illustrated in the destruction of the rest of the statue, which stood for the three great Gentile kingdoms that followed Babylon in history. The kingdom illustrated by a chest and arms of silver was the Medo-Persian Empire that overthrew Babylon decades later when Daniel was serving the Babylonian king named Belshazzar (see 5:20-31). The **third kingdom** of **bronze** was Greece under Alexander the Great, who destroyed the Medo-Persian Empire.

2:40-43 It's obvious that when Daniel came to the **fourth kingdom**, something was different because it occupied more of the vision than any of the others. In view here is the great Roman Empire, **as strong as iron**, which crushed Greece and became the most dominant empire in the ancient world. It was still in power when Jesus was born. But, even though Rome's might was unmatched and it would **crush and smash all the** other empires, it had a flaw, a weakness (2:40). From God's perspective, the thing that distinguished Rome was its **feet** and **toes** comprised of **iron** and **clay**, a mixture of two substances that **will not hold together** (2:41-43). And indeed, something would cause this kingdom to come apart from the inside. The Roman Empire fell not by military conquest but by decay from within as immorality, wanton luxury, and loose living collided with Rome's governmental structures to weaken the kingdom's moral will and desire to rule effectively.

Daniel's prophecy of these four major Gentile empires of the ancient world is so accurate that many critics claim this had to have been written after the fact. But, Daniel wrote in the sixth century BC, hundreds of years before the rise of the Greek or Roman Empires. The King whose heavenly kingdom rules over the world knows all earthly kingdoms that will come to pass. After all, as Daniel prayed, "He removes kings and establishes kings" (2:21).

2:44-45 The revelation of these four worldly kingdoms was followed by the revelation of another kingdom—that of the eternal kingdom of God. This kingdom's reign is future, to be fulfilled when Jesus Christ returns to set up his millennial rule. He is the "stone broke off without a hand touching it" (2:34), which means he is from God, and Jesus is called a stone throughout Scripture (e.g., 1 Pet 2:4-8). In Nebuchadnezzar's dream, the stone became a **mountain**—that is, a kingdom—that will **crush all these kingdoms** and **endure forever**.

2:46-49 Nebuchadnezzar received exactly what he'd demanded: someone told him his dream and its interpretation. He had made lavish promises to anyone who could (2:6), and now he fell **facedown** before Daniel and conferred all these promises on him (2:46, 48). The king even admitted that the God of Daniel was superior to all the gods of Babylon: **Your God is indeed God of gods, Lord of kings** (2:47). The greatest king on earth was made to confess the dominance of the true God.

Nebuchadnezzar made Daniel **ruler over the entire province of Babylon and chief governor over all the wise men** (2:48). Like Joseph before him (Gen 41:37-45), then, Daniel went from the bottom to the top—which is a reminder that God knows how to grant authority to those who submit themselves to his authority. Throughout his long career, Daniel continued to bring praise and honor to God by his faithfulness in the middle of a pagan empire. He also remembered his friends, who were promoted along with him (2:49) and would soon have their own opportunity to prove their faithfulness to God in the face of a deadly threat.

III. A TEST OF FAITH IN A FIERY FURNACE (3:1-30)

3:1-7 Clearly, Daniel was God's kingdom man, and the actions of Shadrach, Meshach, and Abednego in chapter 3 illustrate another type of kingdom response, one that is common to our era: protest through civil disobedience. This involves deliberate personal resistance to a government decree that violates God's standards.

The **gold statue** that Nebuchadnezzar ordered to be built must have been awe-inspiring: it was **ninety feet high** (3:1). The king may have set it up with the intent of consolidating his power, gathering all the classes of his officials to a great ceremony. These rulers were **to attend the dedication of the statue King Nebuchadnezzar had set up** (3:2) and to **fall facedown** in **worship** of it (3:5). Anyone who rejected this command would do so on pain of death by being **thrown into a furnace of blazing fire** (3:6). Nebuchadnezzar intended to establish himself as the supreme religious authority in Babylon as well as the undisputed political ruler, so everyone did as told (3:7). Or, at least, almost everyone.

3:8-12 Because **Shadrach, Meshach, and Abednego** were among the officials present for this huge gathering, a confrontation was unavoidable. When all the people who were gathered bowed down, these three men did not (3:12). But, like children in church looking around during prayer time to see whose eyes are open, **some Chaldeans** saw the three Hebrew boys standing tall among all those who'd prostrated themselves and ran to Nebuchadnezzar to tattle (3:8-12). Jealousy drips from their accusation against the three Jews who'd attained high positions despite their status as captives. These petty court officials saw their chance to destroy Shadrach, Meshach, and Abednego because their faith forbade them to worship any god but the true God of Israel, and they didn't miss it.

3:13-15 Nebuchadnezzar flew into **a furious rage** at the report (3:13). It's surprising that he gave the accused an opportunity to

answer the charges against them (3:14-15). That he did may indicate the esteem he had for them. But, make no mistake, the king would only accept one response: complete capitulation. They'd worship the giant idol of gold or be burned alive. Despite his previous praise of the Hebrew God (2:47), Nebuchadnezzar added, **who is the god who can rescue you from my power?** (3:15). As before, the king's question would eventually be answered.

3:16-18 These courageous Jewish men refused the king's direct order and placed themselves in God's hands. Their answer is impressive: **If the God we serve exists, then he can rescue us from the furnace of blazing fire. . . . But even if he does not rescue us, we want you as king to know that we will not serve your gods or worship the gold statue** (3:17-18). In other words, they declared, "We'll fear our God rather than your furnace any day. But, even if he sovereignly decides to let us burn, we'll still serve the living God rather than bow to your dead idol." Priceless! They preferred death over unfaithfulness to God and had no doubt prepared themselves for the possibility of this day far in advance.

3:19-23 Nebuchadnezzar's level of **rage** when his authority was defied is difficult to imagine, but apparently his **face** was livid. **He gave orders to heat the furnace seven times more than was customary** to match his fury (3:19). When **Shadrach, Meshach, and Abednego** were tossed into the flames, the radiant heat was so great that the men carrying them were **killed** (3:22). No doubt wearing flammable clothing (3:21), the faithful Hebrews had no hope—unless hope itself intervened.

3:24-27 Nebuchadnezzar stood amazed because he could see that not only were the men **walking around in the fire unharmed**, but there were **four** of them! The **fourth** looked like **a son of the gods** (3:25), which suggests that he was either the pre-incarnate Christ or an angel. When the king realized that the men he'd condemned had been divinely rescued, he called for them to **come out** (3:26), and **not a hair of their heads was singed** (3:27). Getting thrown into Nebuchadnezzar's deadly fire had proved to be nothing but a walk in the park.

3:28-30 The king exclaimed, **Praise to the God of Shadrach, Meshach, and Abednego! He sent his angel and rescued his servants who trusted in him** (3:28). Believers today should take note of the actions of these young men and the glory God received as a result. **They violated the king's command and risked their lives rather than serve or worship any god except their own God** (3:28). Are you prepared to do the same?

Following a familiar pattern (see 2:48-49), the king **rewarded** the three Hebrew boys and honored their God (3:30). But, this was not Nebuchadnezzar's last encounter with **the Most High** (3:26). Once again, the king would forget God and exalt himself. And, once again, the living God would humble him.

IV. NEBUCHADNEZZAR'S VISION, HUMILIATION, AND RESTORATION (4:1-37)

4:1-3 Chapter 4 begins with a remarkable testimony by the great King Nebuchadnezzar of **the miracles and wonders the Most High God** accomplished in his life (4:2). This pagan king had been made to see that the Lord's **kingdom is an eternal kingdom, and his dominion is from generation to generation** (4:3). This, in fact, is the second time the king had referred to God as "the Most High God" (see 3:26). This name, or the variation "the Most High," appears thirteen times in Daniel (3:26; 4:2, 17, 24-25, 32, 34; 5:18, 21; 7:18, 22, 25, 27). The title refers to God's ability to overrule man's kingdoms and his superiority over all so-called gods. As Nebuchadnezzar is about to explain, he learned this the hard way. God taught Nebuchadnezzar that his kingdom agenda sovereignly rules over all.

4:4-9 Nebuchadnezzar's life-changing experience began with another troubling **dream** (4:5). The king told his **magicians, mediums, Chaldeans, and diviners** about it, but they couldn't figure interpret it (4:7). When everyone else had failed, the king sent for **Daniel** (4:8). It's strange that Nebuchadnezzar asked his wise men instead of seeking out Daniel first—given Daniel's past experience with dreams (2:31-45). But, apparently, Nebuchadnezzar was a slow learner. Nebuchadnezzar had **named** Daniel **Belteshazzar** after the name of his

Babylonian god Bel. The man clung to his pagan idols (4:8).

4:10-18 Nebuchadnezzar's dream started out well. The **tree** he saw **grew large and strong** and was so fruitful that every kind of creature was provided for by it (4:10-12). But then, the dream turned dark. A **holy one**, perhaps an angel, gave the order to **cut down the tree** and **strip** it bare, leaving nothing but a **stump**. Then the stump was to have **a band of iron and bronze around it** (4:13, 15). **Let him be drenched with dew** suggests the "tree" was actually a man (4:15). He was to be driven mad and **given the mind of an animal for** seven years (4:16). What was the purpose of this decree? **So that the living will know that the Most High is ruler over human kingdoms** (4:17).

4:19-27 God apparently revealed to Daniel what the dream meant as soon as Nebuchadnezzar had finished telling it, because the interpretation left Daniel **stunned for a moment** (4:19). He didn't wish ill for the king; he wanted to see him come to repentance before God and forestall this awful judgment against the king. Daniel gave the king the good news, followed by the bad. Nebuchadnezzar was not only the tree, but would also be the stump (4:20-27). The last word in Daniel's visit was his heartfelt plea for Nebuchadnezzar to repent and throw himself on the mercy of God (4:27). But, interestingly, there was no response from the king at all.

4:28-33 Time passed and Nebuchadnezzar apparently forgot God's warning of judgment on his arrogance. God's extension of grace, which lasted **twelve months**, did not move the king to repent (4:29). If anything, the delay probably made him think he had dodged the bullet.

One day, he looked out from his palace and exclaimed, **Is this not Babylon the Great that I have built . . . by my vast power and for my majestic glory?** (4:30). In other words, his pride had reached its peak and he congratulated himself for the splendor of the kingdom he had established. But, at that very moment, a voice came from heaven declaring the judgment Nebuchadnezzar had seen foretold in his dream (4:31-32). Immediately, he was struck with a form of madness, causing him to behave and live like an animal (4:33).

4:34-37 Some time later, after his long punishment had ended, Nebuchadnezzar made a declaration very different from his previous one (4:30). He **praised the Most High**, saying **his dominion is an everlasting dominion. . . . He does what he wants. . . . No one can block his hand** (4:34-35). The Babylonian king had learned, through his humbling, who was truly in charge. With his **sanity returned**, he was **reestablished** over his **kingdom** (4:34, 36).

Nebuchadnezzar's last recorded words in the Bible are these: **[God] is able to humble those who walk in pride** (4:37)—a truth we all need to embrace and live in accordance with. Don't make God teach you like he taught Nebuchadnezzar. Remember, pride still comes before a fall (see Prov 16:18).

There is only one King who reigns in power over the universe. God sits in judgment on kings and nations. God judged the unrighteousness of Nebuchadnezzar's government because he sought to usurp the authority that belongs to God alone. And in the end, Nebuchadnezzar wound up making the very confession God decreed he would make—"Heaven rules" (4:34-37; see 4:26). This story is a reminder that the further a government drifts from God and seeks to become its own god, the more it sets itself up for heavenly political action.

V. BELSHAZZAR'S FEAST AND THE DESTRUCTION OF BABYLON (5:1-31)

5:1-4 The events of Daniel 5 occurred in 539 BC, the year—the very night, in fact—that the great Babylonian kingdom founded by Nebuchadnezzar fell to a coalition of the Medes and the Persians. By this time, **Belshazzar** was king (5:1). **Nebuchadnezzar** is called Belshazzar's **predecessor**, which some translations render as "father" because the ancient world often used this term to refer to a man's ancestors (5:2). In truth, Belshazzar was probably Nebuchadnezzar's grandson. But, in any case, he was an unworthy heir to the throne. Even as Persian troops were besieging Babylon, Belshazzar threw a great feast, and in the process he took **the gold vessels** that had been seized by Babylon from the **temple in Jerusalem** and gave them to his party guests (5:2-3). The guests **drank from them** and **praised their gods** as they did (5:3-4).

5:5-9 Assuming Belshazzar knew of Nebuchadnezzar's humiliation at the hands of God (see Dan 4), he certainly hadn't learned from it. Rather, he showed his contempt for God's holy vessels by treating them like bar mugs. From God's perspective, this move was the last straw—both for the foolish king and his empire. The Lord began to write about Belshazzar's doom on the **palace wall**, and the king literally lost control of his bowels out of fear (5:5-6). Like Nebuchadnezzar before him, though, the king promised reward to anyone who could interpret **the inscription** (5:7). But, his so-called wise men were fools (5:8).

5:10-16 By this time, the **queen** had come out from her chamber to calm the king (5:10). She knew what to do because she remembered Daniel's past service to Nebuchadnezzar (5:11-12), so Daniel was summoned and offered a lavish reward (5:13-16).

5:17-21 Daniel knew Belshazzar was a wicked king whom God had handed over to be judged, and Daniel wanted no part of his rewards (5:17). Nevertheless, Daniel had a message of judgment to deliver, preceded by a refresher course on the life of Nebuchadnezzar. He recounted how God had given Nebuchadnezzar **sovereignty, greatness, glory, and majesty** (5:18). But, when Nebuchadnezzar had become puffed up with pride, God humbled him **until he acknowledged that the Most High God is ruler over human kingdoms** (5:20-21).

5:22-24 The problem was, according to Daniel, that Belshazzar **knew all this** yet had **not humbled [his] heart** (5:22). Instead of praising the God who gave him breath and controlled his life, Belshazzar **exalted [himself] against the Lord** and **praised** lifeless idols (5:23). So, rather than repenting of the very things that had gotten his predecessor in trouble,

Belshazzar had simply shaken his fist in God's face.

5:25-31 After reviewing the king's crimes against God, Daniel interpreted **the writing** on the wall (5:25). The words meant that Belshazzar's reign had come **to an end** (5:26), he was **deficient** in God's sight (5:27), and his kingdom had been **given to the Medes and Persians** (5:28). Belshazzar rewarded and honored Daniel as he promised (5:29). But, we soon learn that honoring a servant of the Most High God was the last official act of this king. The fulfillment of the words was not long in coming. **That very night Belshazzar . . . was killed, and Darius the Mede received the kingdom** (5:30-31).

This story is so famous that the expression, "he can see the writing on the wall," has become a proverb meaning that a person can see what's coming in his future, that he understands his fate. And while it was too late for Belshazzar to change course, it's not too late for you. If you have a heart filled with pride, turn to the Lord in repentance, for "God resists the proud, but gives grace to the humble (Jas 4:6).

VI. DANIEL IN THE LIONS' DEN (6:1-28)

6:1-3 Daniel was a godly and capable leader because his first allegiance was to his heavenly King. He wasn't primarily serving human rulers, but rather serving God (see Col 3:23). King **Darius** had the good sense to make Daniel one of the top **three administrators** (6:1-2), and Daniel proved to be so exceptional that **the king planned to set him over the whole realm** (6:3). Yet, neither Daniel nor the king realized what lay ahead for this faithful kingdom man.

6:4-5 Daniel's faithfulness stirred up jealousy against him among the other government officials. They hated him—not because he was evil—but because he was good. This is often the response of the wicked toward the righteous. Why did Cain murder Abel? "Because [Cain's] deeds were evil, and his brother's were righteous" (1 John 3:12).

The officials tried **to find a charge against Daniel** (6:4), but he had been serving in the Babylonian government for almost forty years by this point, and his ethical record was spotless. So, what was plan B? They tried to **find something against him concerning the law of his God** (6:5). Consider yourself blessed if the only thing your enemies can say about you is that you're too faithful to God.

6:6-9 It's interesting that Daniel's life had been such a consistent testimony to his faith in God that these officials apparently knew about his prayer routine. We can assume this because of the suggestion they made to Darius (6:7). It was a brilliant scheme in that it appealed to the king's ego. They essentially said, "Your Majesty, we think it would be a great idea for you to declare yourself 'God for a month,' having all petitions directed to you." And when **Darius signed the written edict**, it became an **irrevocable** law (6:8-9).

6:10 Daniel didn't disappoint his enemies. They knew he would be true to his God, and he was. Notice that Daniel didn't make a big deal out of his opposition to the unfair edict or flaunt his prayers. He simply went home and prayed **just as he had done before**, with his windows **opened toward Jerusalem**. No earthly commands could prevent him from fulfilling his heavenly duties. His attitude was the same as that of the apostles many years later: "We must obey God rather than people" (Acts 5:29). Daniel was unflappable in his faith.

6:11-18 Daniel's accusers may have been cowardly plotters, but they had the powerful **law of the Medes and the Persians** behind them (6:12). They informed the king about Daniel, and the king immediately realized he'd been set up (6:13-14). Though he **made every effort** to set Daniel free, he could not break his own law (6:14-15). He'd been duped into executing his best administrator!

Beaten, Darius had Daniel thrown into **the lions' den** (6:16). Then, he spent a sleepless **night fasting** (6:18). Like Nebuchadnezzar, Darius even paid homage to the true God and declared to the prisoner, **May your God, whom you continually serve, rescue you!** (6:16). A pagan king who had never worshiped the Lord before was suddenly giving him glory in hopes that he would deliver his servant.

6:19-22 The next morning, nobody was happier over Daniel's survival than King Darius. At the miracle, he clearly realized that Daniel's God was wholly unlike gods of wood and stone. Daniel's God was not to be messed with. Daniel replied to him that God's **angel** had **shut the lions' mouths** because he was **innocent**. Then Daniel reminded the king, **Before you . . . I have not done harm** (6:22), essentially saying, "Your Majesty, the only thing I was 'guilty' of was being faithful to my God."

6:23-28 Darius was deeply relieved to have **Daniel out of the den**, and he vented his displeasure against **those men who had maliciously accused Daniel** (6:23-24). His gruesome judgment was typical of the vengeance taken by kings in the ancient world.

Darius's **decree** honoring the true God is a theological gem that sounds like it could have been written by one of the psalmists. Once again, as Nebuchadnezzar had (3:29; 4:3, 34-35), this Gentile ruler gave glory to **the living God** who **rescues and delivers** and whose **kingdom will never be destroyed** (6:26-27). The Jewish people may have been in exile, but God had not abandoned them; moreover, he was determined to receive praise from their captors. Thus, Daniel continued to prosper under Gentile rulers (6:28)—a reminder to the Jewish readers of his book to be faithful to God while Israel was under Gentile domination.

VII. DANIEL'S VISIONS AND THEIR INTERPRETATION (7:1-28)

7:1-3 It's important to note that the events in Daniel are not always presented in chronological order. This particular vision is said to have occurred **in the first year of King Belshazzar** (7:1), who was dethroned at the end of chapter 5. Later, in chapter 9, we will return to the time period of Darius.

In the first half of the book, Daniel interpreted the visions of others. In the second half, Daniel's own visions needed interpreting. Years after addressing King Nebuchadnezzar's dream concerning the four great world powers (see chapter 2), Daniel had a vision related to these same four kingdoms. It's fascinating to see the difference in perspective between the dream of a pagan king and the vision given to God's servant. While the sequence of the kingdoms and their eventual destruction are the same, there's an extraordinary difference in the way they are presented. In Nebuchadnezzar's dream, these powers were represented by a glorious, awe-inspiring statue (2:31). But, in Daniel's **dream** (7:1), these Gentile kingdoms were **huge beasts** coming **up from the sea** (7:3), bent on dominion.

7:4-5 The first beast represents Babylon, portrayed as a lion with eagle's wings. But, the wings were torn off this beast (7:4)—which is perhaps a reference to God reducing Nebuchadnezzar to madness until he learned to humbly give God glory (see 4:28-37). The second beast represents the Medo-Persian Empire, pictured as a bear that was told to gorge itself on flesh. Why was the bear raised up on one side (7:5)? Probably because the Persians defeated the Medes and absorbed them into the empire. Combined, their forces were able to defeat Babylon. The three ribs in the bear's mouth (7:5) symbolize the three great enemies that Persia defeated in its conquest: Egypt, Assyria, and Babylon. All of them were gobbled up by the Medo-Persian Empire, which ruled for some two hundred years.

7:6 The Greek Empire established by Alexander the Great is represented by the third beast—a leopard. Leopards are incredibly fast, but this one had four wings, thus indicating it could move with lightning speed. The Greeks under Alexander defeated the Medo-Persians in a matter of a few months in 334 BC, and Alexander had conquered the world by the time he was thirty years old. The four heads that Daniel saw refer to the four kingdoms into which Alexander's domain was split after his death.

7:7-8 The fourth beast of Daniel's vision corresponds to the Roman Empire. God gave Daniel a much more complete picture of it than received in Nebuchadnezzar's day, because we find that the Roman Empire will appear in history again, except in a different form—during the great tribulation. This beast was frightening and dreadful, and out of it came ten horns (7:7)—that is, ten kings or kingdoms. Daniel noticed that a little horn appeared among them, obviously of great importance. The key to identifying this figure is that it has the eyes of a human and a mouth that was speaking arrogantly (7:8). This figure is the Antichrist, called "a beast" in Revelation 13:1. He is the final world ruler whose reign of terror during the tribulation will bring to completion the times of the Gentiles, when Israel is trodden down by the nations.

7:9-14 Two other persons appear in Daniel 7, putting everything else in eternal perspective. There is hope for God's people in every age because the Ancient of Days (7:9) and the son of man (7:13), God the Father and God the Son, have everything under control. Until these two have acted, the story isn't over. God is called "the Ancient of Days" here because he is the timeless one. As chaos occurs on earth, he is seated on his throne. Daniel was shown a scene from the great tribulation, particularly the final three-and-a-half years when the Antichrist will break his covenant with Israel and demand that the world worship him on pain of death. The tribulation chaos will end when Jesus Christ returns in glory with his saints, defeats the Antichrist and his armies, and consigns all of his enemies to the burning fire (7:11).

That Daniel saw one like a son of man ... coming with the clouds of heaven is certainly a reference to God the Son because Jesus applied this passage to himself during his ministry (7:13; see Matt 26:64; Mark 14:62; Luke 21:27). Daniel saw him approach the Ancient of Days, who presented the Son with an everlasting dominion (7:13-14). This is a prophetic picture of God the Father handing over the kingdoms of this world for the Lord Jesus Christ to rule in fulfillment of the dominion mandate given to man (see Ps 8:3-8).

7:15-28 The visions were so overwhelming and troubling that Daniel was unable to interpret them. Therefore, he asked one of those who were standing by, probably an angel, to let him know the interpretation (7:15-16). The four beasts were in fact the four kings/kingdoms (7:17; see 2:39-40) that Nebuchadnezzar had seen in his dream. But, Daniel was especially distressed by the fourth beast, which was different from all the others and extremely terrifying (7:19). He was right to ask, because the Roman Empire did not fade away into history as did the other three kingdoms. The angel revealed to Daniel that a future form of the Roman Empire would emerge, characterized by ten horns (7:20): ten kings ... will rise from this kingdom (7:24).

At that time, the other horn (7:20), the Antichrist, will arise, wage war, and subdue

three kings in his march to power (7:24). Once he has seized world power, he will blaspheme **the Most High** and **oppress** the saints for his allotted three-and-one-half years—**time, times, and half a time** (7:25). Nevertheless, Christ will return in triumph, crush the Antichrist and his armies, and receive his **everlasting kingdom** (7:26-27). In spite of the trials to come, God reigns over his creation and will end rebellion once and for all. Daily we can rejoice because we know how the story ends.

VIII. ISRAEL'S PROPHETIC HISTORY DURING THE TIMES OF THE GENTILES (8:1–11:35)

8:1-8 Daniel's prophetic vision in chapter 8 is incredibly accurate in its historical fulfillment. This is one of the reasons why biblical critics, who dismiss the possibility of predictive prophecy, insist that this must have been written in the second century BC rather than in the sixth century. For believers, this is further evidence of the inspiration and inerrancy of God's Word.

Daniel had another vision during **King Belshazzar's reign** (8:1; see 7:1). In this dream, he saw a **ram** with **two horns** standing in **the fortress city of Susa** (8:2-3), which was in the eastern part of the Medo-Persian Empire. The ram was charging to the **west . . . north . . . south**, and no other power was able to stop him (8:4). But then, **a male goat appeared, coming from the west . . . without touching the ground**, a detail symbolizing lightning speed of movement and conquest. This goat had great power—**a conspicuous horn** (8:5). As Daniel watched, the goat smashed the ram to the ground and became the new world power (8:6-7). This is another picture of the Greek Empire under Alexander the Great, the "third king/kingdom" of the earlier visions in the book (see 2:39; 7:6). But, at the height of its power, the goat's **large horn was broken**, and out of it came **four** other **horns** (8:8). Indeed, when Alexander died, his kingdom was divided among four other men.

8:9-11 Daniel's attention was directed to **a little horn** (8:9). It emerged from the four, became great, and turned its fury against Israel—even trying to make itself as great as **the Prince of the heavenly army**, God himself (8:9-11). This figure sounds like the little horn of 7:8 and 24-26 (the Antichrist), but given the details here (and those later in

Daniel), this appears to be a picture of the brutal and infamous Seleucid ruler Antiochus IV. Also called Epiphanes, he was one of the four rulers who emerged from the divided Greek Empire after Alexander's death.

8:12-14 Antiochus Epiphanes invaded Israel with the purpose of "Hellenizing" the Jews, trying to force them to accept Greek dress, customs, and religion. He stopped the sacrifices from 168-165 BC—**2,300 evenings and mornings** or 1,150 days (8:13-14). He also slaughtered thousands of Jews and desecrated the temple in Jerusalem by erecting a statue of the Greek god Zeus and sacrificing a pig on the altar.

Eventually, a band of Jews led by Judas Maccabeus defeated the Seleucid forces and cleansed the temple (as described in the Jewish book of 1 Maccabees). The rededication of the temple is still celebrated by Jews today during the Jewish festival of Hanukkah (meaning, "dedication"). Antiochus appears here not only because he was a prominent figure in Israel's prophetic future, but because he was also a mirror image of the still-future little horn of Daniel 7, the Antichrist.

8:15-17 Daniel had a powerful interpreter to help him understand the meaning of his vision, an angel named **Gabriel** (8:16). This is the first time in Scripture that an angel is mentioned by name. Gabriel appears again in the Gospel of Luke, where he announces to the priest Zechariah the coming of John the Baptist, and to Mary the coming of Jesus Christ (Luke 1:19, 26). Gabriel was told to **explain the vision** to Daniel, who was **terrified** (8:16-17). In fact, humans in Scripture are frequently filled with awe and fear when knowingly in the presence of angels (see, e.g., Dan 10:8-9; Luke 1:12; Rev 19:10; 22:8).

8:18-27 The key to the vision's interpretation is that it was for **the conclusion of the time of wrath, because it refers to the appointed time of the end** (8:19). Thus, this is the span of time opening with the entry of the times of the Gentiles and ending with Christ's second coming. **The two-horned ram ... represents the kings of Media and Persia**, while the **shaggy goat** represents **the king of Greece** (Alexander the Great). Theirs are the second and third empires revealed in the book of Daniel (8:20-21). The **four horns** (8:22) represent the four leaders, including Antiochus Epiphanes (see 8:9-14), who divided Alexander's kingdom. Antiochus's demonic reign is prophesied again in 8:23-26 and once again mirrors the coming Antichrist.

9:1-2 Daniel was elderly by **the first year of Darius** (9:1)—having been in captivity for about sixty-seven years. One day, while reading **the word of the Lord**, Daniel realized that **the number of years for the desolation of Jerusalem would be seventy** (9:2). The Lord had revealed to Jeremiah (which Jeremiah subsequently communicated to the Jewish exiles), "When seventy years for Babylon are complete, I . . . will confirm my promise concerning you to restore you to this place" (Jer 29:10; see Jer 25:11-12). In other words, God's people would soon be returning to their land!

9:3-19 Like Nehemiah after him would do (Neh 1:4-11), Daniel immediately **prayed to the Lord** on behalf of the people (9:4). Though he knew what God had said, Daniel wasn't going to presume on God's promise. Rather, he decided to *ask* God to forgive the wickedness of his people and deliver them. Daniel confessed the people's sins and rebellion (9:4-10), acknowledged that God was righteous to judge them (9:11-14), and begged God for mercy on the people and city called by his **name** (9:15-19).

9:20-23 Though Daniel did not mention the future of Israel and especially Jerusalem—**the holy mountain of my God** (9:20)—by name in his prayer, it was evidently on his heart

because of the answer **Gabriel** brought him from heaven (9:21-23). Because Daniel was **treasured by God**, God was going to give him **understanding** about what would happen at the close of Babylonian captivity (9:22-23).

9:24 Gabriel declared that **seventy weeks are decreed about** Daniel's **people and . . . city**. "Seventy weeks" is literally "seventy sevens" in Hebrew. Here Gabriel is not talking in terms of days, though; he's talking in terms of years. In context, Daniel had just been praying with regard to the seventy *years* that Israel would be in captivity according to Jeremiah's prophecy. So, "seventy sevens" means seventy times seven years, or 490 years.

What will God accomplish during this 490-year period? Well, for starters, he will bring an **end** to the **rebellion** of Israel, **put a stop to sin** in Israel through the new covenant, **atone for iniquity** through his Son Jesus Christ, and **bring in everlasting righteousness** through the millennial reign of Christ. That's a pretty incredible to-do list!

9:25 Gabriel said this period would begin with **the issuing of the decree to restore and rebuild Jerusalem**. The reference is most likely to 444 BC, when Persian King Artaxerxes sent Nehemiah to begin rebuilding the walls in Jerusalem (see Neh 2:1-8). We know the date because Nehemiah tells us it happened "in the twentieth year of" Artaxerxes's reign (Neh 2:1). From that point until an **Anointed One** came, there would be **seven weeks and sixty-two weeks**. Again, remember that the "weeks" are periods of seven years. That's a total of sixty-nine (seven plus sixty-two) times seven years, or 483 years.

During the first "seven weeks" (or "seven sevens")—forty-nine years—Jerusalem was rebuilt. Nehemiah experienced these **difficult times** when his enemies wished to kill him and put an end to the work (see Neh 4:1-23; 6:1-14).

After the next time segment, the "sixty-two sevens" (434 years), the "Anointed One" would appear. This is the translation of the Hebrew word *Messiah*—in Greek, *Christ*. So, from the decree to rebuild Jerusalem (444 BC) to the coming of the Messiah would be 49 plus 434, equaling 483 years. However, we must keep in mind that these are *prophetic* years, not necessarily our modern *calendar* years. Nevertheless, if we compare Daniel's three and a half years (see 9:27 below) with the 1,260 days of Revelation 11:3 (also Rev 12:6) and the forty-two months of Revelation 11:2 (also Rev 13:5), we see that all three are talking about the same time period—the last half of the seven-year great tribulation period. Forty-two months of 1,260 days works out to thirty days per month. That results in a *prophetic* year of 360 days. When the calculations are made, 483 prophetic years from 444 BC causes us to arrive at AD 33, the year of Christ's crucifixion and resurrection. Our God is precise.

9:26 After those sixty-two weeks the Anointed One will be cut off refers to the crucifixion of Christ. But clearly, there is a break between Daniel's sixty-ninth and seventieth weeks. After the sixty-ninth week, the prophetic clock stopped ticking. The events of 9:26-27 refer to the seven-year tribulation period that is to come. Therefore, a gap of time began at the conclusion of the sixty-ninth week and continues today. This interlude between weeks sixty-nine and seventy is the church age, which Daniel did not foresee. **The coming ruler** is the Antichrist, who will arise at the beginning of Daniel's seventieth week (the tribulation) and wreak havoc.

9:27 When Daniel's final "week" (seven years) begins, the Antichrist **will make a firm covenant with many**. He will be a world leader pretending to bring peace to Israel. But, **in the middle of the week**—halfway through the tribulation—**he will put a stop to sacrifice and offering**. So, while the Jews will apparently be offering sacrifices again in a rebuilt temple during this time, the Antichrist will break his covenant and put a stop to it. Moreover, he will set up **the abomination of desolation . . . on a wing of the temple**. He will set himself up as a god in Israel's temple, demanding worship and finally revealing himself as the wicked beast that he is (see Rev 13:4-8). Yet, at the end of the tribulation, the Lord Jesus Christ will pour out his judgment on this **desolator**.

10:1-9 Once again, Daniel was being prepared to receive a **vision** and prophetic revelation from an angel. This time it would be a sweeping panorama of prophecy involving **King Cyrus of Persia** and even the establishment of God's kingdom on earth (10:1). Daniel knew something awe-inspiring was coming because he mourned and fasted for **three full weeks** beforehand (10:2-3). The angel who appeared to him was dazzling in appearance (10:5-6). The men with Daniel did not see the vision, but **a great terror fell on them** nonetheless (10:7). Meanwhile, Daniel was weakened by holy fear and **fell into a deep sleep** (10:8-9).

10:10-14 Here we are given insight into the warfare that takes place in the spiritual realm. Daniel had been praying and fasting for three weeks, and the angel had been sent **from the first day** in response (10:12). However, the angel had been hindered by a figure called **the prince of the kingdom of Persia** who opposed him **for twenty-one days**—for the full period during which Daniel had been fasting and praying (10:13; see 10:2-3)! This was clearly a high-ranking demon assigned to the nation of Persia to represent the devil's kingdom and fight against God's.

Scripture frequently says that Satan exercises a level of control and rule in this fallen world (see 2 Cor 4:4; Eph 2:2; 1 John 5:19). Thus, the messenger who had come to Daniel had been engaging in angelic warfare. In fact, the power of this demonic prince of Persia was so great that **Michael, one of the chief princes**, was sent to his aid (10:13). We learn in Jude 9 that Michael is an "archangel." By virtue of his strength, the angel prevailed and reached Daniel (10:14).

10:15-21 Though Daniel was overwhelmed with anguish and weakness, the angel strengthened him to receive the revelation that follows in chapters 11 and 12 (10:15-19). But, there was more angelic struggle ahead. The angel had to **return at once to fight against the prince of Persia**. Then he told Daniel that **the prince of Greece** would **come** (10:20). This indicates that the demons of Satan's kingdom are always at war against God's kingdom and servants. It's this warfare that you can't see—the war in the spiritual realm—that you must be prepared to wage (see Eph 6:10-18).

11:1-20 These verses contain some of the most detailed prophecy in Scripture. The angel first mentions the rise and fall of a succession of **kings . . . in Persia** (11:2). Then he focuses at length on the Greek Empire of Alexander the Great, the **warrior king** (11:3). Indeed, after he died, his empire was **divided** (11:4). It was the kingdoms of two of Alexander's generals who divided his domain that were important to the future of Israel. These were the kingdoms of the Ptolemies of Egypt and the Seleucids of Syria. Daniel called them **the king of the South** and **the king of the North** (10:5-6), referring to their geographical locations in relation to Israel. Here the angel provides an account of the continual conflict between these kingdoms (10:6-20), during which Israel would often be invaded by one or the other power.

11:21-35 The great enemy of the Jews, Antiochus Epiphanes (whom we saw earlier in 8:9-14), appears again in a prophecy of his abominations (11:21-35). This **despised person** was not even the rightful ruler of his kingdom, but seized it **by intrigue** (11:21). He invaded Egypt but did not get all he wanted. When the Romans opposed him on a second attempt to invade Egypt, Antiochus withdrew in humiliation and took out his rage on the Jews on his way back to Syria (11:29-30). It was then that he set up his own **abomination of desolation** (11:31; see 9:27), and thousands of faithful Jews who resisted him were martyred (11:33). **But the people who know their God will be strong and take action** (11:32). Life's circumstances will not keep them down.

IV. THE PROPHECY OF DANIEL'S SEVENTIETH WEEK (11:36–12:13)

11:36 The change in focus of this prophecy may not be readily apparent, but it is clear from what follows that the angel stops talking about Antiochus at this point. This is where Antiochus's role as the model or type of the "little horn" of 7:8 ends, because here, the antichrist himself steps onto the scene as the seventieth "week" of seven years in the prophecy in Daniel 9 is unfolded and the seven years of the tribulation to come are discussed. The antichrist's true character as a monstrous beast is revealed: **He will exalt and magnify himself above every god, and he will say outrageous things against the God of gods**, desiring to be worshiped personally.

11:37-45 But, the antichrist's world reign in the tribulation will not be without opposition, as these verses describe. The attack against him by **the king of the South** and **the king of the North** (11:40) almost certainly refers to a larger coalition of forces than simply Egypt and Syria, as was the case in the days of Antiochus. The fact that this conflict results in the antichrist meeting his end (11:45), which happens when Jesus Christ returns and defeats him, suggests that this battle occurs near the end of the tribulation.

12:1-3 These verses are the follow-up to the antichrist's destruction. The archangel **Michael**, Israel's protector, will see to it that Satan's attempts to annihilate the nation during the horrific suffering of the tribulation are not successful (12:1). All of the enemy's schemes will fail. Those Jews who believe in Jesus the Messiah will be resurrected at the beginning of Christ's millennial kingdom to enjoy the eternal benefits of God's covenant promises to his people (12:2).

12:4-11 The prophet had seen and heard things no human ever had, and he was told to **seal** his prophecy (12:4). But then, after asking for more information regarding what **the outcome** of all these prophecies would be (12:8), he was told that the second half of the tribulation would be **1,290 days** (12:11). This is a period of three-and-a-half *prophetic* years, 1,260 days, plus an extra thirty days (see the discussion of prophetic years in the commentary on 9:25). This, then, could be the time between the announcement that **the abomination of desolation** (12:11) is going to be **set up** and its actual erection, or it could allow for the cleansing of the temple after this sacrilege is removed.

12:12 Here we have another puzzling set of numbers, tied to a blessing: **Happy is the one who waits for and reaches 1,335 days**. This extends the time after the tribulation for another forty-five days, yet those who persevere to the end of this period are clearly blessed. This extra time could allow for the gathering and judgment of the Gentile nations (see Matt 25:31-46).

12:13 These final words from heaven are for Daniel personally: **you will rest, and then you will stand to receive your allotted inheritance at the end of the days**. Daniel had demonstrated extraordinary faithfulness throughout his life. He served God as an exile in a pagan world (1:3-6). He obeyed God's law regardless of the outcome (1:8-16) and delivered God's message loyally (2:31-45). He stood up to kings (5:13-29) and withstood persecution from those who wanted to take his life (6:1-28). He was a student of God's Word (9:2) and a man of prayer and fasting (9:3-19; 10:2-3, 12). Daniel served many kings and saw many kingdoms rise and fall, but his ultimate allegiance was to the agenda of only one King. A kingdom man like that will certainly not lose his reward.

HOSEA

INTRODUCTION

Author

HOSEA EXERCISED HIS PROPHET-ic ministry during the reigns of several kings (1:1), indicating that his career spanned at least forty years. It began sometime during the reign of Jeroboam II of Israel, who ruled the northern kingdom as co-regent with his father, Jehoash, from 793 to 782 BC. Then he ruled independently until 753 BC. Hosea's ministry ended during the reign of Hezekiah, who ruled the southern kingdom of Judah from 716 to 685 BC.

Of all the prophetic books, Hosea is perhaps the most autobiographical. His own marriage and family form a vital part of his unique message. Though Hosea did not neglect Judah in his prophecy, his messages were primarily directed toward the northern kingdom of Israel, often spoken of as "Ephraim" and represented by the royal city of Samaria. Hosea likely lived and worked in or around Samaria and probably moved to Jerusalem by the time Samaria fell to the Assyrians in 722 BC.

Historical Background

During the reign of Jeroboam II, the northern kingdom experienced a time of general affluence, military strength, and national stability. The economy was strong, and the mood was optimistic—at least among the upper class. During a time of Assyrian weakness (the time of the prophet Jonah), Israel and Judah

expanded. But, after Jeroboam's death in 753 BC, Israel experienced anarchy, going through six kings in thirty years—four of whom were assassinated: Zechariah, Shallum, Pekahiah, and Pekah. Assyria gained power at this time, so Israel's days were numbered. God would use Assyria to punish Israel for their sins against him, as Hosea made clear.

Message and Purpose

Hosea is a book of six cycles that involve sin, salvation, judgment, and restoration. It is set against the backdrop of a covenantal marriage between Hosea and his wife, Gomer, who broke that covenant. God used their relationship to illustrate the fact that Israel, the people with whom he had entered into a sacred covenant, had also broken faith by committing spiritual adultery with false gods. Their actions broke God's heart.

Israel's sin brought judgment, just as Hosea's wife suffered for her waywardness. But, this book also demonstrates God's heart for forgiveness and reconciliation as Hosea was told to welcome his wife back even though she had been unfaithful to him. Through his prophet's actions, then, God was saying to Israel, "I will welcome you back if you will re-covenant yourselves to me." Under God's kingdom plan, he would forgive his people's sins and restore their relationship.

Hosea teaches that God will not allow his people to become unfaithful to him without consequences. Just as a husband and wife expect faithfulness of one another in marriage, God expects the full-time commitment of his people.

www.bhpublishinggroup.com/qr/te/28_00

HOSEA

I. GOD'S TENACIOUS LOVE (1:1–3:5)

1:1 The name **Hosea** comes from the Hebrew verb meaning "to save or deliver." Hosea's message is an offer of salvation and deliverance to those in Israel and Judah who would receive it. Unfortunately, that message fell on deaf ears in Hosea's day.

1:2 When God called Hosea, he not only *gave* him a message, he also called him to *be* a message: **Go and marry a woman of promiscuity, and have children**. This, of course, was definitely not your typical calling to prophetic ministry! Given the Lord's stance toward sexual immorality, adultery, and prostitution (Exod 20:14; Lev 19:29; 1 Cor 6:12-19), this is a shocking command. But, there was a serious reason for God's directive: **the land is committing blatant acts of promiscuity by abandoning the Lord**, and people needed to see things from God's perspective.

Frequently in the Old Testament, "adultery" and "prostitution" are used as metaphors for Israel's idolatry (e.g., Deut 31:16; Judg 2:17; Jer 3:6; Ezek 16:15). The Lord was Israel's husband, and they were his bride. For Israel to worship false gods and bow to worthless idols, then, was to commit sexual immorality against their husband who had saved them. God called Hosea to be a living example to the people of their spiritual adultery. So, because God's bride was unfaithful, Hosea was to take an unfaithful bride for himself.

1:3 He went and married Gomer . . . and she conceived and bore him a son. Don't overlook Hosea's response of full obedience. He submitted himself and his family to be an object lesson for Israel and would experience firsthand what it means and how it feels to love someone who is unfaithful. In the long run, he'd become more passionate for God and Israel as a result.

1:4-5 God told Hosea to **name** his son **Jezreel**, a term symbolic of the judgment that would come upon Israel. Just as Jehu put the family members of the house of Ahab to death in Jezreel (see 2 Kgs 10:1-17), God was going to **put an end to the kingdom of the house of Israel**. The name of Hosea's son was to be a banner of this coming judgment.

1:6-7 The second child, a **daughter**, was to be given a name that meant "No Compassion." That's definitely a name that will make people do a double take. It indicated that God would **no longer have compassion on the house of Israel** because of their sin. For those who participate in it, sin has consequences. Unlike Israel, though, **Judah** would experience compassion and deliverance—not from the hand of man—but from the hand of God (1:7). Israel's mistake was failing to understand the source of their past deliverance.

1:8-9 Hosea's third and final child was given a name that meant "Not My People." Here, God rejects Israel as his people because they had rejected him (1:9). After delivering Israel from slavery in Egypt, God had made a covenant with them. He promised that if they would keep his commands, they would be his own special "possession" (Exod 19:5). But, Israel had forgotten that the blessings under

God's covenant were conditioned on their obedience.

1:10-11 With this revelation, Hosea immediately turns to a message of hope. Though the present circumstances are bleak, Hosea looks to a future day when the number of Israelites will be countless. Instead of being told, **You are not my people, they will be called: Sons of the living God** (1:10). Not only that, but Israel and Judah will be united under **a single ruler** (1:11). This suggests that God brings judgment in part so he can bring blessing. He wounds so he can heal.

2:1-4 Here the Lord tells the people of Israel to **rebuke [their] mother**—that is, their leadership. God declares, **She is not my wife and I am not her husband**. In other words, the marriage is over and divorce proceedings have begun. If Israel will not turn from their **promiscuous** and idolatrous ways, God will make them weak and desolate (2:2-3). All their people will suffer (2:4).

2:5-8 As a prostitute has **lovers** who meet her economic needs, Israel worshiped false gods that they assumed were meeting their own (2:5). But, God would prevent them from pursuing their idols so that they might return to him (2:6-7). They didn't realize that God was the one meeting their needs all along. He lavished produce and wealth on his people, but they turned around and offered those blessings to **Baal!** (2:8).

2:9-13 By following after Baal, in fact, Israel had thanked and worshiped the wrong god. Thus, the Lord would end their plentiful harvests (2:9). No more **celebrations**; no more parties (2:11). Israel would beg their idols to turn the blessings back on, but there would be no answer (2:10, 12). They enjoyed an illicit affair and **forgot** the husband who provided them with every comfort, so the day of reckoning was coming (2:13).

2:14-17 Once again, though, God expresses love and compassion toward his people through Hosea. He stands ready to forgive. He will **persuade her** and **speak tenderly to her** (2:14). He'll restore their fortunes and take them back to the days when they were first married—when **they came out of the land of Egypt** (2:15)—and rejoiced in the God who saved them. They will come to their senses, repent, and call the Lord, **My husband** (2:16). The names of false gods **will no longer be remembered** (2:17). You can't outrun the tenacious love of God.

2:18-23 On that day, the Lord will protect his people and enable them **to rest securely** (2:18). **I will take you to be my wife forever**, he says (2:19). What a glorious promise! Then the land will again yield its harvest (2:21-22). God **will have compassion** on those named "No Compassion," and he will say to those named "Not My People," **You are my people** (2:23). Don't ever think you can't experience a reversal of fortune. God delights in welcoming back his wayward children (consider the parable of the Prodigal Son; Luke 15:11-32).

3:1-5 We don't know how long Hosea and Gomer had been married, yet she had obviously forsaken her marriage vows by this point. God directs Hosea to **go again** and **show love to** this **woman who is loved by another man and is an adulteress**. How could God expect Hosea to pursue the wife who had betrayed him? Because **the LORD loves the Israelites though they turn to other gods** (3:1). So, despite his humiliation and pain, Hosea played the obedient kingdom man and paid to restore Gomer from whatever bondage she had sold herself into (3:2). He then brought her home again on the condition of faithfulness (3:3).

Imagine the anguish of buying back your own wife who had willingly left you! Yet, in this action is a picture of the unfailing, persistent love of God. Moreover, it is what God does for us through Jesus Christ, who bought us—not with money—but with his own blood: "He gave himself for us to redeem us from all lawlessness and to cleanse for himself a people for his own possession, eager to do good works" (Titus 2:14).

Hosea was telling Israel that God was pursuing his people—his bride. Through his chastisement, they would experience loss and realize the worthlessness of **idols** (3:4). **Afterward, the people of Israel will return and seek the LORD their God and David their king** (3:5). God's love wins.

II. THE CHARGE AGAINST ISRAEL
AND THEIR LEADERS (4:1–5:15)

4:1-3 Like a prosecuting attorney, **the LORD has a case against the inhabitants of the land.** What are his indictments? In Israel, **there is no truth, no faithful love, and no knowledge of God** (4:1). That sounds like charges against a pagan people! "Truth" is the objective standard of reality by which we measure our experiences and opinions, yet Israel was full of lies. Likewise, they lacked "faithful love." Though they may have expressed love in words, it didn't materialize in deeds. To cap it all off, there was no "knowledge of God." Regard for God didn't cross their minds on a daily basis; therefore, it's not surprising that the Ten Commandments were completely ignored (4:2). Even **the land** suffered under the weight of their sin (4:3; see Rom 8:20-21).

4:4-6 Though the people were guilty, God was especially angry with the **priests** and **prophet** because of their sin (4:4-5). They ought to have been examples to the people, leading them to worship and honor the Lord; instead, they **rejected knowledge.** As a result, God's **people [were] destroyed for lack of knowledge** (4:6). When leaders pursue their own selfish agenda, people almost inevitably follow.

4:7-14 Don't miss the tragedy behind this passage: **The more they multiplied, the more they sinned against me** (4:7) God had commanded humanity to "be fruitful and multiply" (see Gen 1:28; 9:7). He "multiplied" the people of Israel (Exod 1:7) and promised to multiply them further (see Lev 26:9). But, there was a condition for this blessing from God: their obedience (Deut 30:16). Thus, God would **repay them for their deeds** (4:9): **they will be promiscuous but not multiply** (4:10).

Nations surrounding Israel engaged in cult prostitution (4:14), committing sexual immorality as "worship" so the gods would bless them with children. Israel had become infected with this fertility religion (4:12-13), but it would not provide what they wanted. The blessing of children comes from God alone (see Ps 127:3). Those who follow destructive

thinking will come to ruin. **People without discernment are doomed** (4:14).

4:15-19 Here God warns Judah, **Do not go to Gilgal**—one of Israel's centers of false religion. In other words, he exhorts **Judah** not to follow the example of Israel, who was like **a stubborn cow** (4:15-16). Hosea refers to Israel as **Ephraim** many times in his prophecy (4:17). "Ephraim" was one of Joseph's sons (Gen 41:52), and the tribe called by his name lived within the northern kingdom. Though **Israel's leaders** loved **disgrace**, God would strike their consciences so they would be **ashamed** (4:18-19). Be open to the conviction of the Holy Spirit so that you don't develop a stubborn spirit and fail to experience shame when you should.

5:1-7 Now Hosea attacks the source of Israel's problems—its leadership (**priests** and the **royal house**). They're a **snare** and a **net** (5:1), trapping the people in idolatry. As a result of their sin, they have led Israel astray.

That Israel's **actions do not allow them to return to their God** (5:4) is a reminder that you can't have fellowship with God while walking in darkness. If you want to return to God and know his favor, you have to forsake the disobedience that led you away from him in the first place. On the other hand, if you persist in walking in darkness, you will inevitably **stumble** (5:5). When this happens, you won't **find** the Lord (5:6).

5:8-15 **Ephraim** and his cities think they are safe and secure, but Hosea foresees **war** and **desolation** (5:8-9). Nevertheless, Ephraim was **determined to follow what is worthless** (5:11). Instead of turning to God for help, **Ephraim** (and even **Judah**) sought help from Assyria (5:13). But, an alliance with Assyria cannot **rescue** them from the awesome power of God (5:14). Their only hope of restoration is to **recognize their guilt and seek [his] face** (5:15). God's favor, blessings, and fellowship are only accessible when we submit to the road of repentance.

III. ISRAEL'S WICKEDNESS AND GOD'S CALL TO REPENTANCE (6:1–7:16)

6:1-3 In these verses, Hosea reminds the people that God is always ready to receive and forgive. If you **return to the LORD** and submit yourself to his program, he will intervene in your situation (6:1). **He will revive... after two days, and on the third day he will raise us up** (6:2). Sometimes, the prophets provided more insight into spiritual matters than they could've realized. Though Hosea was saying this to Israel, it is supremely true of Jesus Christ, whom God "raised on the third day according to the Scriptures" (1 Cor 15:4).

6:4-6 What am I going to do with you, Ephraim? What am I going to do with you, Judah? (6:4). God sounds like an exasperated parent who loves his children but is grieved by their behavior. He had sent his **prophets** to chastise them and urge them to repent (6:5).

I desire faithful love and not sacrifice, the knowledge of God rather than burnt offerings (6:6) sounds like God's words to faithless King Saul (see 1 Sam 15:22). This is not a rejection of the sacrificial system. After all, God instituted it. Rather, God is telling Israel, "Don't think you can live as you please, reject my word, and then come offer a sacrifice to make everything OK."

Do we sin and need God's forgiveness? Of course. But, that doesn't grant us freedom to do whatever we choose. To quote the apostle Paul, "Should we continue in sin so that grace may multiply? Absolutely not!" (Rom 6:1-2).

6:7–7:2 Israel wasn't merely naughty. They had been wicked and **violated** God's gracious **covenant** with them (6:7). Even the **priests** were guilty of murder (6:9)! What God saw is **horrible**: promiscuity, fraud, theft, and pillaging (6:10; 7:1). Nothing can be hidden from an omniscient (all-knowing) and omnipresent (everywhere-present) God.

Whatever they did was done **right in front of [his] face** (7:2).

7:3-7 The wickedness of the nation went all the way to the top. **The king** and **the princes** were pleased with **evil** (7:3). They were guilty of **adultery**, drunkenness, and **anger** (7:4-6). Our sin affects other people, but the sin of rulers can be even more devastating than that of most because their unrighteous actions distress and influence the people of the nation: "When the wicked rule, people groan" (Prov 29:2). Yet, no matter how many kings fell as a result of their foolishness, **not one of them** called on God (7:7).

7:8-12 Have you ever had food on your plate that looked wonderful only to find that the bottom was burnt to a crisp? That's the idea behind, **Ephraim is unturned bread baked on a griddle.** They had gotten mixed up with foreign nations and didn't realize they were getting burned (7:8-9), and their people refused to return to God (7:10). Ephraim, therefore, is also pictured as **a silly, senseless dove.** They flit over to **Egypt** and then flutter over to **Assyria**, looking for a safe place to land. But, the Lord will bring them down (7:11-12).

7:13-16 You can sense the anguish God experienced from his people's rejection of him: **they fled from me ... they rebelled against me ... they do not cry to me from their hearts ... they plot evil against me** (7:13-15). Though he **trained and strengthened** them, they slashed themselves (7:14-15)—probably in a pagan ritual pleading for divine help (see 1 Kgs 18:27-29). And while the people turned to idols and other nations, they didn't turn **to what is above** (7:16). If you look for counsel or aid from anywhere other than the heavenly realm, you're wasting your time. You will only **fall** and **be ridiculed** (7:16).

IV. IDOLATRY AND EXILE (8:1–10:15)

8:1-3 Because Israel placed their trust in the strength of other nations, Hosea tells his countrymen that an enemy will come against them, and there is little point in crying, **My God, we know you**, when all of Israel's actions proved the opposite (8:1-2). **Israel** had **rejected** what was **good**, so judgment was coming (8:3).

8:4-10 They acted in their own interests without seeking God's guidance. They **installed kings** and **appointed leaders**—all without God's **approval**. They made **idols** that would lead to their **destruction**—not their salvation (8:4). The Lord's anger burned regarding the idolatry of **Samaria**, the capital of the northern kingdom (8:5-6). Ephraim ran after foreign nations (like **Assyria**) as an adulteress pursues **lovers** (8:9-10).

There's little difference between people then and people today. Israel put their hopes in earthly things that couldn't save them. Today, people are tempted to pursue the same poor bargains—trusting in money, power, the government, technology, etc., rather than trusting in the God who inhabits eternity.

8:11-14 Though I were to write out for him **ten thousand points of my instruction, they would be regarded as something strange** (8:12). This is just sad. But indeed, the person who refuses to listen to reason is determined to do what he wants no matter what anyone says. And, that's Ephraim. No matter what God said, they would be set in their ways and consider God's words "strange." **Israel** had **forgotten his Maker**, but God won't forget to punish (8:14).

9:1-6 Hosea exhorts **Israel** not to **rejoice jubilantly as the nations do**. They had **acted promiscuously** by engaging in pagan practices. **The wages of a prostitute on every grain-threshing floor** is another way of saying that Israel is participating in the Canaanite fertility rites, a sexual type of worship committed in the presence of an idol (9:1). Their promiscuous acts were evidence of departure from God's covenant. However, God would not let them prosper with a bountiful harvest, but rather would send them into exile instead (9:2-6).

Expulsion from the land is what happened to the previous occupants because of their sins (see Exod 23:24-33), and it is what was prophesied to happen to Israel if they followed in those footsteps (see Deut 4:25-27). Israel abandoned the covenant lifestyle, with all of its blessings, in favor of a promiscuous lifestyle identical to that of the surrounding nations. They wanted to be *like* everyone else; as a result, they would be *with* everyone else.

9:7-9 God repeatedly sent prophets to warn his people, but Israel considered **the prophet** a **fool** and **insane** (9:7). If you're faithful to God's Word, be prepared for people to think you're crazy, too. The **watchman**—a biblical term for prophet (Jer 6:17; Ezek 3:17)—met with **hostility** from a corrupt people (9:8-9).

9:10-17 At first, God was pleased with Israel, but they soon worshiped pagan gods (see Num 25:1-9). That they **became abhorrent like the thing they loved** (9:10) is a principle you can take to the bank. You will become like that which you worship (see Ps 115:4-8)—whether an idol or Christ. **Ephraim's glory** would end (9:11): they had sought fertility from lifeless idols, but they would lose their children (9:14). Because of their **evil, wicked actions** (9:15), God would reject them and make them **wanderers among the nations** (9:17). Turning away from the King and kingdom principles leaves you with some of the world—but all of nothing.

10:1-8 Hosea argues that God's blessings upon Israel actually made them worse. **The more his fruit increased, the more he increased the altars. The better his land produced, the better they made the sacred pillars** (10:1). They attributed the blessings of God to false gods. They neither acknowledged the king's authority nor feared the Lord (10:3). Instead, they **will have anxiety** over their **calf**-god and **mourn over it** when it is taken away **to Assyria** (10:5-6). When their places of pagan worship are **destroyed**, they will cry out in despair (10:8).

10:9-10 As proof of Israel's sin heritage, Hosea first calls Israel to remember **the days of Gibeah** (10:9; see Judg 19:1-30; 20:1-10). The gang rape and death of a Levite's concubine there is Hosea's historical point of reference. God did not allow the perverted men to go unpunished then, and he will not allow Israel to go unpunished now (10:10).

10:11-15 God compares Ephraim to **a well-trained calf that loves to thresh.** Sometimes calves were permitted to walk on grain stalks, separating the grain from the chaff. The calf could then eat freely without doing any real labor. But, God says such easy days are over. In response to Israel's sin, he will now **yoke** her for hard **plowing** (10:11). Instead of plowing **wickedness** and reaping **injustice** (10:13), though, the Lord calls Israel to **sow righteousness** and **reap faithful love** (10:12). But, he knows they won't listen. As a result of their wickedness, **the roar of battle will rise against [them].** War will bring devastation on both king and people (10:14-15).

V. GOD'S COMPASSION AND JUDGMENT (II:I–I4:9)

11:1 Chapter 11 includes an emotional description of God's love for Israel: **When Israel was a child, I loved him.** Israel's "childhood" refers to its journey into Egypt in obedience to God when they were less than a hundred people (see Gen 46:3-27). Israel arrived in Egypt as a family with the promise from God of becoming a great nation. **Out of Egypt I called my son** was another point of history taught to all Jewish children; it's a reference to the exodus when God brought his people out of slavery. When he wrote his Gospel, Matthew saw this as ultimately fulfilled in Jesus Christ—God's true Son who also came out of Egypt (see Matt 2:15).

11:2-7 In spite of God's loving care and deliverance, they departed from him. **They kept sacrificing to the Baals and burning offerings to idols** (11:2). Like a devoted father with a beloved child, God **taught** them **to walk, healed them** (11:3), **led them . . . with ropes of love** (11:4), and gave them **food** (11:4). But, Israel **refused to repent** (11:5). Punishment and captivity were unavoidable (11:6)—not because God has a bad temper—but because his people were **bent on turning from** him (11:7). Holy justice would have to be carried out.

11:8-9 Here again, God's heart turns toward mercy and compassion: **How can I give you up, Ephraim? How can I surrender you,** Israel? If you're a parent, those questions ought to put a lump in your throat. What mom or dad doesn't grieve over the thought of losing a child?

The average Bible reader probably cruises right past **Admah** and **Zeboiim** without recognizing the names; however, most readers recognize the names of their sister cities, Sodom and Gomorrah. Yet, the Lord actually destroyed all four places in his anger over their wickedness (see Deut 29:23). The thought of such destruction coming upon God's beloved people makes his heart ache and stirs up his **compassion.** The Lord declares, **I have had a change of heart** (11:8). That is grace in action. Israel had been thoroughly wicked and deserved judgment, but God's grace on sinners is a result of his own unmerited kindness and love. He vows, **I will not vent the full fury of my anger**—not because they didn't deserve it, but because he is gracious. He promises not to thoroughly wipe out his people. Why? **For I am God and not man** (11:9). His ways are higher than our ways (Isa 55:8-9).

11:10-12 Elsewhere, Hosea compares God to a lion who would attack Israel for their sins (5:14; 13:7). Here the comparison is positive. He will **roar like a lion** calling his cubs, and they **will come trembling** in submission (11:10). Though he will punish his people because of their faithlessness (11:12), he will bring a remnant back from exile and **settle them in their homes** (11:11).

12:1-6 Israel repeatedly pursued alliances with foreign nations (12:1), leading to idolatry and further failure to rely on the Lord. Though **Judah** had generally been more faithful, God had **a dispute** with them, too, and would **repay him based on his actions** (12:2). He reminds Judah of how **Jacob** had **wrestled with God** and **sought his favor** (12:3-4). Judah must also look to God for his blessing and not to foreign nations or false gods.

Return to your God. Maintain love and justice, and always put your hope in God (12:6). That's solid advice for the believer who has strayed from the path. God stands ready to receive those who make God's agenda of love and justice their own.

12:7-14 Israel, on the other hand, lacked love and justice. Judah only needed to look at Israel's practice of dishonest scales, that is, making things to be heavier than what they were in order to make a greater profit. Their scales lied, and they thought no one observed their deception: **No one can find any iniquity in me that I can be punished for** (12:8). This is the height of arrogance and ignorance. The God who brought Israel out of **Egypt** (12:9), spoke **through the prophets**, and gave them **visions** (12:10) knew Israel's crimes and would punish them for them. Their pagan **altars** at **Gilead** and **Gilgal** would be turned into **piles of rocks** (12:11). The Lord would **repay** Ephraim **for his contempt** (12:14).

13:1-3 When Ephraim spoke, there was trembling (13:1) is another way of saying there was great respect. Idolatry and rejection of the living God, however, had since ruined them (13:1-3). This is what sin does to a person. No matter a person's strength, ability, social status, or economic capability, moral degeneration and foolishness are cancers that eat away at character. Such people become like the **morning mist . . . chaff . . . smoke** (13:3); they are blown away.

13:4-13 God rescued Israel from slavery in Egypt and became their **Savior** (13:4). He

provided for them and satisfied them when they had nothing. But, when you become **satisfied**, you are tempted to take the credit for yourself. Then your heart becomes **proud**, and you forget God (13:5-6). So, you must constantly nurture a humble heart that looks to God's Word and power as your source of strength and sustenance. Otherwise, there's no telling what God may have to do (13:8) to prove that **you have no help but [him]** (13:9). In Ephraim's case, the **king** they'd demanded (see 1 Sam 8:1-22) did not deliver them, but rather led them into sin and foolishness (13:10-13).

13:14-16 Once again, the Lord, through Hosea, offers a ray of shining light: **I will ransom them from the power of Sheol. I will redeem them from death** (13:14). If salvation is to come, it has to come from God's hand. Death does not have the final word, so the Lord taunts death and the grave: **Where are your barbs? . . . Where is your sting?** (13:14)

The apostle Paul quotes from this text to demonstrate God's victory over death and the law through the resurrection power of Jesus Christ (see 1 Cor 15:54-57). Yet, this does not mean that God will not chasten Israel. In the near term, **compassion is hidden** (13:14), and God will deliver judgment (13:15-16).

14:1-8 What's the only appropriate response to God's anger against sin? **Repentance**— that is, **return to the LORD** (14:1-2). Do an "about face"; change your ways. Plead with him to **forgive** your sin and **praise** him (14:2), knowing that no one saves but the Lord (14:3). For the Israelites who will repent and trust in God, he promises to **heal** them, **love** them, and turn away his **anger** (14:4). His blessings will return (14:5-7).

14:9 Let whoever is wise understand these things, and whoever is insightful recognize them. Hosea is saying, "There's only one real option here. There's only one legitimate path to take if you want to experience life and blessing." **The ways of the LORD are right**.

Because the Lord's ways are right, you need to transform your thoughts to match his. In other words, you need a kingdom mind. A kingdom mind views life from the divine viewpoint (found in his Word) and lives accordingly. In fact, having a kingdom mindset is the difference between **the righteous** who **walk** in God's ways and **the rebellious** who **stumble in them**.

Hosea loved promiscuous Gomer even though she didn't deserve it. And God loves promiscuous you even though you don't deserve it. Praise him for his grace, turn to him in repentance, and live for his glory.

JOEL

INTRODUCTION

Author

THE OLD TESTAMENT INCLUDES A number of people named Joel (see 1 Sam 8:2; 1 Chr 4:35; 6:33; 11:38; 15:7; Ezra 10:43; Neh 11:9), but none of these can be identified with the author of this book. Unfortunately, we know nothing about Joel other than his father's name, Pethuel (1:1).

Background

It is impossible to determine the exact date of Joel's book. He does not introduce his prophetic work by mentioning who was on the throne in Israel or Judah at the time, unlike many other Old Testament prophets (see Isaiah, Jeremiah, Daniel, Hosea, Amos, Micah, Zephaniah, Haggai, and Zechariah). And Joel also doesn't indicate the specific sins of the people. He doesn't explicitly say what behavior needed changing. Rather, he was concerned mainly with motivating repentance by proclaiming the coming "day of the Lord" (1:15).

Message and Purpose

The prophet Joel speaks to God's people about their desperate need of repentance in order to experience restoration. They were under judgment because they continually rebelled against God, leading to exile and all manner of other repercussions. Joel's message was that it was no longer business as usual because of a catastrophic event they were facing, called the day of the Lord. This phrase refers to a time of judgment that precedes restoration, a time when God recalibrates to make right what is wrong. With the day of the Lord looming before the nation of Israel, Joel told the people to cease all normal activity. He urged them to call a solemn assembly to get right before God so he would remove the locusts that were ravaging the land—a sign of his judgment.

If the people would repent, Joel had a powerful message of blessing from God. Not only would he remove the locusts, but he would also restore the years the locusts had eaten. Joel wanted the people of God (then and now) to know that God is holy, demands repentance, and will judge. But when repentance occurs, he can restore what rebellion has destroyed and turn cursing into kingdom blessing.

www.bhpublishinggroup.com/qr/te/29_00

Outline

I. The Foreshadowing of Devastation (1:1-20)

II. The Day of The Lord and the Call to Repentance (2:1-32)

III. Judgment on the Nations and Blessing on Israel (3:1-21)

JOEL

I. THE FORESHADOW OF DEVASTATION (1:1-20)

1:1 Joel begins his prophecy by authenticating his prophetic office: **The word of the LORD that came to Joel**. The words that follow, then, have their source in God. Joel didn't seek this message. He was called by God—not vice versa. The King came to a servant and commanded the servant to comply.

1:2-3 Joel calls on the **elders** and **inhabitants of the land** to listen: **Has anything like this ever happened in your days or in the days of your ancestors?** (1:2). Nothing arrests one's attention quicker than an intriguing question, so Joel is drawing his audience in. By saying, **Tell your children about it, and let your children tell their children, and their children the next generation** (1:3), Joel builds the tension further to make the reader ask, "Well, what is it?"

1:4-7 What the devouring locust has left, the swarming locust has eaten; what the swarming locust has left, the young locust has eaten; and what the young locust has left, the destroying locust has eaten (1:4). In other words, massive locust swarms had stripped the land bare. Their destruction of the crops had reached epic proportions; the pestilence was historic. Joel even compares the locusts to **a nation** that had **invaded** the **land** (1:6). Indeed, a foreign army couldn't have left the country more devastated. The **grapevine** and the **fig tree**—two principle producers of food for the land—were left barren (1:7).

1:8-12 Joel tells the people to mourn **in sackcloth** (1:8). Internal grief was symbolized by wearing this rough, scratchy fabric. With the crops destroyed, grief comes upon **priests** and **farmers** alike (1:9-12). The former could receive no **grain** or **drink offerings**, which means there was no portion for them to eat (1:9). And the farming economy would be ruined without a **harvest** (1:11). For an agrarian culture like Joel's, it's not surprising that **human joy . . . dried up** at such a calamity (1:12).

1:13-14 Such a disastrous event calls for **a sacred fast**, a solemn **assembly**. In fact, Joel calls everyone to **lament**, gather at **the house of the LORD**, and **cry out to** him. The locust destruction was bad, but something worse was coming. Their work was only a prelude prefiguring something bigger.

1:15 Woe because of the day! For the day of the LORD is near and will come as devastation from the Almighty signals a significant theme in the book of Joel. The phrase "day of the LORD" also occurs in many other prophetic books of the Old Testament (see Isa 13:6, 9; Ezek 13:5; Amos 5:18, 20; Obad 15; Zeph 1:7, 14). It often refers to a time of God's judgment in history on the sins of Israel or of other nations. It can also refer to the ultimate day of the Lord, when his judgment will be carried out on unbelievers at the end of time (see 1 Thess 5:1-5).

1:16-20 Joel declares that the judgment is coming upon Israel. The locust plague **cut**

off their **food**, which cut off their **joy and gladness** (1:16). **Storehouses** and **granaries** were ruined, and **animals** groaned for lack of food (1:17-18). But this was only the beginning, foreshadowing what was to come.

II. THE DAY OF THE LORD AND THE CALL TO REPENTANCE (2:1-32)

2:1-2 The prophet urges the watchmen on the wall in Jerusalem to **blow the horn in Zion; sound the alarm on my holy mountain!** . . . **For the day of the LORD is coming; in fact, it is near** (2:1). And it isn't the kind of day you look forward to. It's **a day of darkness and gloom** that brings with it **a great and strong people** (2:2).

2:3-9 Who are they? This could be either a metaphorical description of the locusts from chapter 1 or a human army. One thing is clear: there's no stopping them. They ravage the land (2:3), make a deafening noise (2:5), and horrify those in their path (2:6). Their approach is comprehensive—all areas are covered; all exits are sealed; no escapes are left (2:7-9)

2:10-11 That **the earth quakes** . . . **the sky shakes** . . . **the sun and moon grow dark** and **the stars cease their shining** (2:10) means this is ultimately the work of God. The power of heaven was about to be unleashed on the earthly realm. It's *his* **army** in view, ready to bring *his* judgment. **Indeed, the day of the LORD is terrible and dreadful—who can endure it?** (2:11). Joel wants the people of Israel to know that God's anger is waiting at the door. Things won't end well.

2:12 Suddenly, the Lord, through the prophet, offers a message of hope: **turn to me with all your heart**. In other words, he says, repent! To repent is to change one's mind in order to reverse direction. When you realize you've taken the wrong road, the only right response is to turn around and go the other way. Such a spiritual turnaround requires an outward manifestation of actions that matches the inward attitude, including **fasting, weeping, and mourning**.

2:13-14 When you turn away from sin, you also must **return to the LORD your God**. Why? Because God **is gracious and compassionate, slow to anger, abounding in faithful love** (2:13). If you've held to prolonged unrighteous attitudes against God, you've made him your enemy. But, don't run from him because he's also your only hope. **He relents from sending disaster** and is the only source of true **blessing** (2:13-14).

2:15-17 Again, Joel urges all of the people to gather for a sacred **assembly**, intent on repentance (2:15-16). Crucial to genuine repentance is heartfelt prayer: **Have pity on your people, LORD.** Indeed, we too, should cultivate a desire to see God glorified and praised among all: **Why should it be said among the peoples, Where is their God?**

2:18 Apparently, the prophet's plea was successful, and God's people displayed the fruit of repentance (not every Old Testament prophet was so fortunate). For **the LORD became jealous** . . . **and spared his people**. Importantly, this is not the kind of sinful jealousy or envy that God condemns in us (as in Rom 13:13; 2 Cor 12:20; Gal 5:20). Instead, this is the jealousy of a faithful husband who prizes his bride and won't let anyone harm her.

2:19-27 The harvest and blessings God previously withheld (1:16-20), he would restore in abundance (2:19-26). As a result, they would be **satiated** (2:19) and **satisfied** (2:26)—stuffed full. God knows how to deliver blessings to those who align themselves with him.

The description of **the northerner** in 2:20 seems to indicate that those described in 2:2-9 were people and not locusts. Therefore, this is likely a reference to an eschatological event when God will protect Israel from invading armies (see, for example, Dan 11:36-45). When all this happens, God says, **you will know that I am present in Israel and that**

I am the LORD your God, and there is no other. Only God can cause such reversals of fortune. One day, his people will never again be put to shame (2:27).

2:28-32 The apostle Peter quotes this passage in his great sermon delivered on the first Pentecost following Christ's ascension (see Acts 2:17-21). It's a fitting mention in Acts because there, the Lord began to fulfill this promise to **pour out [his] Spirit on all humanity** (2:28). Moses had desired that God might do such a thing (see Num 11:29), and here Joel prophesies that this is God's plan. Indeed, on Pentecost, the initial fulfillment began among the Jews and then spread as Gentiles were brought into the church (see Acts 10:44-48).

The Holy Spirit is not reserved only for the Jews or for a select group of believers. There are no second-class Christians who receive only partial membership in the church. God's Spirit is available to all who receive Christ as their Savior.

III. JUDGMENT ON THE NATIONS AND BLESSING ON ISRAEL (3:1-21)

3:1-16 When God restores **the fortunes of Judah and Jerusalem**, he will **enter into judgment** with the godless nations (3:1-2). Because of how they treated the Lord's people, he **will bring retribution on [their] heads** (3:7). He will gather them in **the Valley of Jehoshaphat** (3:2, 12), which means "the Lord judges." Because there is no known valley with this name and it's also referred to as **the valley of decision** (3:14), it's likely the site of the end-time battle of Armageddon (see Rev 16:16), meaning "hill or mount of Megiddo." Megiddo was in the Valley of Jezreel, the site of many significant battles (e.g., Judg 5:19; 2 Kgs 9:27; 23:29-30). God will go to war with the nations, and he will triumph easily.

3:17-21 In contrast to the fate of the nations, Joel describes the exaltation of Israel **in that day** when **Jerusalem will be holy, and foreigners will never overrun it again**, and the blessings of the Lord will be on the land (3:17-18). They will be in full fellowship with the Lord. **Judah will be inhabited forever**, and their sins will be **pardoned** (3:20-21). Thus, the day of the Lord will bring judgment and destruction on God's enemies but blessing and deliverance for his people. The rider on the white horse, Jesus Christ, will come and set all things right (see Rev 19:11). Come, Lord Jesus.

AMOS

INTRODUCTION

Author

AMOS WAS NOT A PROPHET BY vocation; he was a sheep breeder (1:1). God took him from the flock and commanded him to prophesy to Israel (7:15). Thus, he ministered to the northern kingdom, even though Amos himself was from Judah. His hometown was Tekoa (1:1), a village located about ten miles south of Jerusalem. Tekoa was hill country, a rugged area that required its citizens to be just as rugged in order to make the land work for them. According to 2 Chronicles 11:5-11, Tekoa was fortified by Rehoboam, king of Judah, as a defense city for Jerusalem. Amos prophesied in the eighth century BC, during the reigns of King Uzziah (792–740 BC) of Judah and King Jeroboam II (793–753 BC) of Israel.

Historical Background

The time period during the reigns of Uzziah and Jeroboam II was one of prosperity and military success for both Israel and Judah. Samaria, the capital city of Israel, for instance, experienced wealth and luxury; however, this was accompanied by idolatry and moral decline. As a result, Amos cried out against Samaria's wickedness and self-indulgence (3:9; 4:1; 6:1; 8:14). Though its leaders experienced prosperity, the poor were exploited (2:6; 3:10; 4:1; 5:11; 8:4-6). It was against this nation—bereft of righteousness and full of corruption and idolatry—that Amos was sent to prophesy, "Let justice flow like water, and righteousness, like an unfailing stream" (5:24).

Message and Purpose

The prophecy of Amos was delivered to the people in the northern kingdom of Israel who appeared to be experiencing kingdom blessings. But God had a message for them: prosperity does not imply kingdom blessing when it is mixed with rebellion against him. Amos's readers were actually living under God's displeasure because they enjoyed the benefits of prosperity while ignoring the disenfranchised among them. They celebrated their affluence while being unjust to those who didn't enjoy the same economic and social status.

Amos was very direct in telling the people they could not enjoy kingdom benefits without living kingdom lives. God expects his people to be a blessing; we should not simply use his blessings for selfish indulgence. The people needed to learn that living under God's kingdom rule was to be done in an obedient and generous way.

Amos also prophesied about the day when a restored remnant of Israel would be the means through whom God would bring blessing to all people. Amos shows how God uses those living under his kingdom plan to accomplish his promises of blessing.

VIDEO INTRO

www.bhpublishinggroup.com/qr/te/30_00

Outline

AMOS

I. JUDGMENTS AGAINST THE NATIONS (1:3–2:16)

1:1 Here we are introduced to Amos as **one of the sheep breeders from Tekoa.** God called him to a prophetic ministry (7:14-15). Amos (1:1) tells what he saw **regarding Israel in the days of . . . Jeroboam . . . two years before the earthquake.** While most of the prophets date their ministries relative to the reigns of kings, as Amos does, he provides further historical context. Apparently, this particular earthquake was so significant that people knew exactly what he was referring to.

1:2 Sharing a message of doom during a time of plenty is not the way to inspire people and win friends, yet this is what Amos was to do. A kingdom man can speak with boldness when he knows the source of his message. **He said: The LORD roars from Zion and makes his voice heard from Jerusalem.** When you have a roaring lion backing you up, you have no need to fear either. God's voice can make the land **mourn** and a mountain wither. And two years before an earthquake shook the land (1:1), God shook things up with the power of his word.

1:3-5 Amos launches into a series of judgments against Israel's neighbors in 1:3–2:3: Damascus, Gaza, Tyre, Edom, Ammon, and Moab receive notice. But Judah and Israel he saves for last (2:4-16).

Each vision begins with, **I will not relent from punishing _____ for three crimes, even four** (1:3, 6, 9, 11, 13; 2:1, 4, 6). Bible scholars debate what this expression means. Some think the numbers are to be added together, totaling seven, the number of

completion. Thus, these nations had "maxed out" on their sins. Wickedness had reached its full measure, and they were ripe for judgment. Regardless of how the expression is to be interpreted, the time for judgment had come.

Damascus was the capital city of Aram (modern Syria), which bordered Israel to the north. Their sin concerned their treatment of **Gilead,** a city in northern Israel (1:3). Damascus was about to experience the kingdom principle of reaping what you sow (see Gal 6:7). Because of the harm Aram had done to Gilead, **the gates of Damascus** would be smashed, the rulers' **citadels** destroyed, and the people **exiled** (1:4-5).

1:6-8 Gaza, Ashdod, Ashkelon, and Ekron were major Philistine cities on the west side of Judah along the Mediterranean Coast. The Philistine armies had raided communities, captured the people, and sold them as slaves **to Edom** (1:6). God condemns kidnapping and selling humans into slavery (see Exod 21:16). Moreover, he promised to curse those who cursed his people (see Gen 12:3). Thus, **fire** would descend on the Philistine cities, and the people would **perish** (Amos 1:7-8).

1:9-10 Amos's message to **Tyre,** a Phoenician city on the Mediterranean Coast, is similar to the one given to Gaza. Tyre had **handed over a whole community of exiles to Edom and broke a treaty of brotherhood** (1:9). King David and Hiram, a former king of Tyre, had established a peaceful working trade relationship between their two countries (see

2 Sam 5:11), but Tyre eventually broke the treaty through war with Israel and turning their captives over to Edom. So, as with Gaza, Tyre's **walls** would be consumed with fire (1:10).

1:11-12 The fourth proclamation of judgment is against **Edom**. Its people lived south of the Dead Sea and were the descendants of Esau, Jacob's brother. Unfortunately, the relationship between Edom and Israel wasn't all that brotherly. Edom **pursued his brother with the sword** and **stifled his compassion** (1:11); therefore, its major cites—**Teman** and **Bozrah**—would be destroyed (1:12).

1:13-15 The Ammonites were also related to the Israelites. They were descendants of Lot, Abraham's nephew, through his youngest daughter. The Ammonites had a long history of fighting against Israel (see Judg 10:9) and Judah (see 2 Chr 26:6-9). Amos highlights a particularly horrifying war crime of the Ammonites: **They ripped open the pregnant women of Gilead in order to enlarge their territory** (1:13). It's unbelievable that human beings are capable of this kind of wickedness! And as with the others that Amos condemned (1:3-10), Ammon's capital city of **Rabbah** would be destroyed, and its leaders would be carried **into exile** (1:14-15).

2:1-3 The Moabites, too, were descendants of Lot (through his oldest daughter). Interpreters are uncertain why Moab **burned the bones of the king of Edom to lime** (2:1), but some believe they used this lime to make plaster for their walls. Whether this was the case or not, it was a severe act of violence. Thus, the same **fire** that God was sending against the rest of Israel's neighbors (1:4, 7, 10, 12, 14) would **consume** Moab (2:2). Importantly, God judges the nations by his standards—not by theirs. The world is his kingdom, and he operates by his agenda.

2:4-5 In response to Amos's condemnations of the nations around them (1:3–2:3), God's people may have been feeling self-assured and thinking, "They deserve it. Bring it on!" But then Amos turned his prophetic arsenal in Judah's direction; God does not show partiality toward them because of their position of privilege. **Because they have rejected the instruction of the LORD and have not kept his statutes**, God's **fire** will be unleashed on Judah too.

2:6-16 And because Israel wanted to act like those who don't know God, they would be treated like those who don't know God. Amos's prophecy against Israel is longer than any that came before. If anyone should have known better than to do the kind of things listed here, it was those who had received God's holy Word. However, Israel was selling people into slavery (2:6), just as the surrounding nations had done (1:6, 9). The **poor** and **needy** were being trampled, and sexual immorality infected homes (2:7). They had forgotten what God did for them when they were slaves in **Egypt** (2:10). There was no gratitude toward the One who had redeemed them. Therefore, God says, **I am about to crush you** (2:13). The **strong**, the **swift**, and the **courageous** will not be strong, swift, or courageous enough when the wrath of God comes to town (2:14-16).

II. MESSAGES OF JUDGMENT (3:1–5:17)

3:1-2 Israel's relationship to God makes their wicked behavior astounding. God had rescued them from **Egypt** and entered into a covenant with them. Here God even declares that of all the nations on earth, he has **known only** them. How much worse, then, was Israel's sin? Their **iniquities** could not be excused. Their rejection of the God who saved them couldn't go unpunished.

3:3-8 Amos asks a series of rhetorical questions in verses 3 through 6. Each assumes that the outcome of a particular scenario is assured. **Does a lion roar in the forest when it has no prey?** (3:4). No. **Does a bird land in a trap on the ground if there is no bait for it?** (3:5). Of course not. **If a ram's horn is blown in a city** [a warning of approaching disaster], **aren't people afraid?**

(3:6). Absolutely. Therefore, **if a disaster occurs in a city, hasn't the LORD done it?** (3:6). Well, yes, he has. The point here is that when disaster comes upon Israel, they can rest assured that it is the Lord's judgment on their sin. For he has revealed his will to his **prophets** (3:7)—namely, kingdom-minded prophets like Amos. **Fear** is the only appropriate response when the **lion has roared** (3:8; see 1:2).

3:9-15 The people are incapable of doing right (3:10). What an accusation! Such inability was the manifestation of the will of the people. They had persisted in sin for so long that it became second nature to them. Because **violence and destruction** were what they understood, violence and destruction were what they would get (3:10-11). Indeed, **an enemy will surround the land,** their **strongholds** and **citadels** will be plundered (3:11), the people will be devastated (3:12), pagan **altars** will be cut down (3:14), and the **houses** of the wealthy will be demolished (3:15). This prophecy came to pass when the Assyrians captured Samaria in 722 BC and carried the people into captivity (see 2 Kgs 17:6).

4:1 Amos had some choice words for the wealthy, indulgent women of Samaria: **Listen to this message, you cows of Bashan.** Bashan was an area east of the Sea of Galilee; it had flourishing pastures and plump livestock. Like spoiled cows, these women demanded luxury and pleasure. They oppressed the **poor** and **needy** and made demands on their **husbands.** What a contrast to the "wife of noble character" in Proverbs 31; she feared the Lord, served her family, and ministered to the poor (see Prov 31:10-31).

4:2-3 These women of Samaria, who snubbed God and committed social injustice against his people, would suffer humiliation, and be carried into exile in foreign lands. The Lord swore **by his holiness** that he would bring this about (4:2). There's no better guarantee than that.

4:4-5 Here Amos turns to sarcasm as he prosecutes his case on God's behalf: **Come to Bethel and rebel.... Bring your sacrifices ... for that is what you Israelites love to do!** When the nation split into northern and southern kingdoms, King Jeroboam of Israel built an altar at Bethel and made two golden calves for the people to worship in order to prevent them from traveling to Judah and the temple in Jerusalem (see 1 Kgs 12:25-33). This was in direct violation of the Mosaic law. Thus, Amos sarcastically encourages them to continue in the idolatry they love so that they can see where devotion to false gods ends.

4:6-13 This wasn't the first time God had responded to Israel's idolatry. Previous acts of discipline from God included food shortages, drought, withered crops, locusts, plagues, death, and destruction (4:6-11). But in spite of all this, God declared repeatedly that their response was the same: **You did not return to me** (4:6, 8, 9, 10, 11). Israel had been given chance after chance to repent. Now, the gloves were coming off: **Prepare to meet your God!** (4:12). **The one who forms the mountains** and **creates the wind** isn't making a social call here. He's coming in wrath (4:13).

5:1-3 Amos painfully sings a song of **lament** (5:1). Israel **has fallen,** and **no one** will **raise her up** (5:2). They turned away from the only one who could've helped them. If "the God of Armies" (4:13) doesn't march out with the soldiers, they'll be wiped out by the enemy no matter how strong they are (5:3; see Ps 108:11). So don't put confidence in yourself. Without "the full armor of God," you will not stand against your enemy, the devil (Eph 6:11).

5:4-12 Turning to worthless idols at **Bethel** and other sacrificial locations in Israel would **come to nothing** (5:5). What could the people do instead? **Seek the LORD and live** (5:6). Or, as Jesus put it, "Seek first the kingdom of God and his righteousness" (Matt 6:33). This, in fact, is the only path to blessing.

Seeking God and his kingdom is not a one-day-a-week activity, though. It's a daily attempt to adopt God's perspective on life as revealed in his Word. And it includes living out that perspective. But this is exactly what Israel refused to do. They hated **the one who convicts the guilty** and despised **the one who speaks with integrity** (5:10).

Their social injustices against the poor were innumerable (5:11-12).

5:13-17 God's promise was plain for all who would hear: Pursue good and not evil so that you may live, and the LORD, the God of Armies will be with you (5:14). But Israel wouldn't listen. Instead, their future would include wailing, cries of anguish, and mourning (5:16-17).

III. WOES OF JUDGMENT (5:18–6:14)

5:18-20 Amos proclaims woe twice in the following verses (5:18; 6:1). "Woe" was a declaration of sorrow and despair (e.g., Isa 6:5; Jer 4:13). Interestingly, the first woe is against those who long for the day of the LORD (5:18). The "day of the LORD" is a theme that occurs in many of the prophetic books (see Isa 13:6, 9; Ezek 13:5; Joel 1:15; Obad 15; Zeph 1:7, 14). Frequently, it refers to times in history when God carried out acts of judgment. The phrase "day of the LORD" also describes the day of God's ultimate judgment at the end of history (see 1 Thess 5:1-5).

Some Israelites looked forward to the day when God's vengeance would be unleashed on the pagan nations, but the problem was that Israel themselves had become a pagan nation! Thus, the thing they anticipated would not be a day of light and blessing but a day of darkness and judgment (5:18, 20). Its arrival would be akin to narrowly escaping the jaws of a lion only to be mauled by a bear (5:19).

5:21-27 God hated the religious practices of Israel and refused to accept them (5:21-23). Why? Justice was absent from Israelite society (5:24), a reminder that you can't worship God on Sunday and despise your neighbor on Monday. You can't read your Bible in private and then oppress your brother in public. The Lord therefore calls his people to let justice flow like water, and righteousness, like an unfailing stream (5:24). Martin Luther King Jr. underscored the connection between having faith in God and doing works of righteousness when he quoted Amos 5:24 in his "I Have a Dream" speech.

6:1-7 The second woe is for those who were at ease and felt secure (6:1). They enjoyed luxury (6:4-6)—clearly at the expense of the poor (see 2:7; 4:1; 5:11),convinced that nothing would happen to them because they were part of the house of Israel. But to these Amos says, "Think again." He names other nations that had been conquered by the Assyrians and asks, Are you better than these kingdoms? (6:2). Definitely not. Israel had done everything they could to look just like everyone else. Therefore, they would be carried into captivity by the same instrument of God's power (Assyria) that had destroyed all these others. The only thing standing between Israel and Assyria, in fact, was God. And he was about to get out of the way. Those who were at ease, sprawled out on their couches, making up songs, and gulping down bowls of wine would be the first to go into exile (6:4-7).

6:8-14 God hates all sin, but he especially hates pride. That was the sin of Satan, who wanted to set his throne in the heavens and be like God (see Isa 14:12-14). It's not surprising, then, for God to say, I loathe Jacob's pride (6:8). God's people are to reflect his character—not the devil's. And because this group had rejected their God, he would smash their homes to pieces (6:11) and raise up a nation against them (6:14).

IV. VISIONS OF JUDGMENT (7:1–9:10)

7:1-6 God showed his prophet Amos three visions (7:1-9). The first was a swarm of locusts and the second was a judgment by fire (7:1, 4). Both would be utterly devastating to the land.

Though understanding the reason for judgment, Amos pleads with God to forgive: How will Jacob survive since he is so small? (7:2, 5). In response to Amos's prayers,

the LORD relented (7:3, 6). So again, just as he did with Abraham (Gen 18:16-33), God shares his plans with a kingdom man. And just as Abraham did, Amos—this kingdom man—intercedes so that God might be merciful. The Lord is not quick-tempered but "slow to anger" (Ps 103:8).

7:7-9 Then God showed a vision of **a plumb line**. A plumb lines had weights tied to one end, and by holding the device, one could determine whether a wall was vertically straight. When the Lord told Amos, **I am setting a plumb line among my people Israel**, he was implying that Israel was crooked (7:8). Their continued idolatry, injustice, lying, and disloyalty were too much to overlook. With their third strike, they were out: **I will no longer spare them**, God said (7:8).

7:10-17 Crooked Israel was unwilling to be straightened. Instead of heeding the warnings of God's prophet, **Amaziah the priest** even told Israel's **King Jeroboam** that Amos had **conspired against** him (7:10)! So—no doubt under the king's orders—Amaziah commanded Amos to quit preaching and take his prophecies to **Judah** instead (7:12-13, 16). But Amos knew whose agenda he was called to follow. He had been content to look after his **figs** and **flocks**, until God told him, **Go, prophesy to my people Israel** (7:15). So like the apostles who knew they had to "obey God rather than people" (Acts 5:29), Amos rejected Amaziah's words and gave him God's words: **You yourself will die on pagan soil, and Israel will certainly go into exile** (7:17).

8:1-14 The **basket of summer fruit** represents the completion of a full cycle from growth to harvest to consumption. Israel's sins had come to completion and, like fruit removed from the trees when they are ripe, Israel was ripe for judgment (8:2-3). Israel trampled **the needy** and cheated **with dishonest scales** (8:4-5). Therefore, the judgment coming upon them would be devastating (8:8-13). Those who swore by false gods would **fall, never to rise again** (8:14).

9:1-10 There will be no escape from God's wrath when it comes. There will be nowhere to hide (9:1-3). The Lord is the maker and sustainer of the **earth** and **the heavens** (9:5-6). How can anyone escape his judgment? His **eyes** are **on the sinful kingdom** of Israel (9:8). All **who say: "Disaster will never overtake or confront us," will die by the sword** (9:10).

    The Cushites / Ethiopians were descended from Cush, the son of Ham, the son of Noah (see Gen 9:18; 10:6). Amos 9:7, therefore, is another reminder of how strong the Jewish-African link was in biblical times (see commentary on Gen 9:18—10:1-32).

V. PROMISES OF RESTORATION (9:11-15)

9:11-14 In spite of the judgment, though, God will not forget his people. **In that day I will restore the fallen shelter of David** (9:11) is a reference to the Davidic monarchy. In the future millennial kingdom, Jesus Christ will sit on David's throne. **The days are coming** when God's rich blessings will be upon Israel. The land will be filled with abundance (9:13), and God will **restore** their **fortunes** (9:14). Peace and prosperity will be established God's way and maintained according to his kingdom agenda.

9:15 I will plant them on their land, and they will never again be uprooted from the land I have given them tells us that, in the millennial kingdom, God will restore Israel to their land, never to be removed again. They will be permanent residents. And following this promise, Amos seals his prophecy with the following words to guarantee their truthfulness: **The LORD your God has spoken**.

OBADIAH

INTRODUCTION

Author

NOTHING IS KNOWN ABOUT OBA-diah. His common Hebrew name means "servant of the Lord."

Historical Background

Scholars are uncertain when Obadiah was written. The most likely option is that it was penned shortly after the final destruction of Jerusalem by the Babylonians in 586 BC. Verses 10-14 mention Edom's participation in the downfall and plundering of Jerusalem (see also Ezek 35:15).

Message and Purpose

Obadiah, the shortest book in the Old Testament, is a prophetic condemnation of Edom for its treatment of the people of Judah. Theirs was a conflict dating back to the twins in Rebekah's womb, who were their patriarchs. The Edomites were descendants of her elder son Esau, and the people of Judah were the descendants of Jacob.

Just as there was conflict in the womb between Jacob and Esau (see Gen 25:21-26), there was conflict between their peoples. The Edomites had closed their borders and their hearts to the people of Israel on their way to the promised land. They also reveled in the judgment and destruction of Judah years later by the Babylonians, picking off some stragglers and returning others to their captors. They even looted Jerusalem after its fall.

God's judgment against Edom, therefore, was harsh: the nation would be destroyed with no possibility of recovery. It tells us God is opposed to piling additional troubles on those who are suffering, even if they are being disciplined by him. Obadiah, in fact, teaches the vital lesson that God's treatment of us is based in part on the way we treat others in his kingdom family.

www.bhpublishinggroup.com/qr/te/31_00

Outline

I. The Judgment against Edom (1-9)
II. Edom's Sins against Judah (10-14)
III. The Day of the Lord (15-21)

OBADIAH

I. THE JUDGMENT AGAINST EDOM (1-9)

1 The prophet **Obadiah** received a vision from God **about Edom**, the descendants of Esau, who was Jacob's brother (see Gen 25:19-26). Edom was a hostile neighbor of Judah on its southeast border and fought with Israel and Judah on a number of occasions (e.g., 1 Sam 14:47; 1 Kgs 11:15-17; 2 Chr 20:22; 21:8-11). Obadiah was charged with delivering **a message from the LORD** about Edom. The Warrior in the heavens had summoned his armies and declared: **Let us go to war against her.**

2-4 The Edomites apparently thought they were big stuff, because here God vows to make them **insignificant** (verse 2). They had an **arrogant heart** (verse 3)—that is, they were proud. Pride is the chief sin, the one that led Satan to rebel against God (see Ezek 28:17), and humans have followed in Satan's footsteps. We puff out our chests like we're somebody, but God isn't impressed.

Edom seemed to **soar like an eagle**, asking, **Who can bring me down to the ground?** But their arrogant hearts had **deceived** them,

and God was going to **bring [them] down** hard (verses 3-4).

5-7 When **thieves** come to a house, they don't typically show up in a moving van. They usually creep in at night and **steal only what they** want, but Edom (**Esau**) would be **pillaged** and all **his hidden treasures** boldly taken (verses 5-6) until *nothing* was left! Worse, every surrounding nation that has **a treaty** with Edom would **deceive and conquer** them, which is a reminder that international **peace** negotiations are fragile and untrustworthy for a nation that rejects the Lord (verse 7).

8-9 Even **the wise ones of Edom** couldn't spare the populace from their coming doom (verse 8). The **warriors** of **Teman** (a region in Edom) would turn tail and run so that everyone was **destroyed** (verse 9). Notice Obadiah doesn't encourage Edom to repent to avoid God's judgment. The just Judge of the nations had rendered a verdict with no appeal.

II. EDOM'S SINS AGAINST JUDAH (10-14)

10-14 Why was God outraged with Edom? **Because of violence done to [their] brother Jacob** (verse 10). Because the Edomites had descended from Esau, the brother of Jacob, Scripture refers to their nations as brothers. But, there was bad blood in the family (see, e.g., 1 Sam 14:47-48; 2 Sam 8:13-14;

1 Kgs 11:14-22). And when Judah and **Jerusalem** were **captured** by Babylon, Edom acted like the rest of the nations (verse 11). In the day of his brother's **calamity**, Esau's descendants offered neither help nor compassion to **the people of Judah.** They could have blessed Israel and been blessed by God

(see Gen 12:3); instead, they chose to **gloat ... rejoice ... and mock** (verse 12). They took advantage of their brother in his **day of distress** (verses 13-14).

III. THE DAY OF THE LORD (15-21)

15 Edom rejected an opportunity to receive God's blessing by blessing his people so they would experience the terror of **the day of the Lord** instead. The prophets often spoke of "the day of the Lord" to refer to specific times of God's judgment on wicked **nations**—either in history or at its end.

As you have done, it will be done to you brings to mind the guy we've all known who got what he had coming to him. The hammer he dropped on other people finally fell on his own head. Here, God tells Edom they will receive exactly what they had dealt to others. And this is what all humanity deserves: just retribution for our sins. But that's what makes God's grace so amazing. Grace means giving someone what they *don't* deserve. And, as believers in Jesus Christ, that's what we receive. But for those, like Edom, who oppose God's agenda, **what they deserve will return on** their **own head.**

16 The Edomites had **drunk on [God's] holy mountain** in Jerusalem, perhaps celebrating Judah's downfall. So the Lord promised that **all the nations**—including Edom—would **drink continually**. But not at a party. The Bible often uses the metaphor of drinking to speak of God's judgment (e.g., Job 21:20; Isa 51:17; Jer 49:12-13; Rev 14:10). The unrighteous will **gulp down** God's wrath.

17-18 The day of the Lord will bring judgment to God's enemies but **deliverance** to his people, reversing fortunes (verse 17). **Esau will be stubble**, and **Jacob will be a blazing fire.** Given these insights, it doesn't take much imagination to figure out that **no survivor will remain of the house of Esau** (verse 18).

19-21 Those who live in southern Israel, the **people from the Negev**, will **possess** the land of Esau (verse 19). But, though the people will possess the land, **the kingdom will be the Lord's** (verse 21).

God has an agenda for his kingdom. Embrace your place in the King's plan.

JONAH

INTRODUCTION

Author

THE BOOK OF JONAH IS ANONY-mous. But if Jonah did not write it, he was presumably the source of the story.

Historical Background

Jonah son of Amittai was an eighth-century-BC prophet from Gath-hepher in the land of Zebulun (1:1; see 2 Kgs 14:25). According to 2 Kings 14:25, he predicted that King Jeroboam II (793–753 BC) of the northern kingdom would restore Israel's northern border.

The city of Nineveh, to which Jonah preached, was a major city of the Assyrian Empire; it was located in northeastern Mesopotamia on the east bank of the Tigris River (about 220 miles north of modern Baghdad, Iraq). Longtime enemies of Israel, the Assyrians were cruel in battle. Ancient Assyrian artwork, in fact, depicts horrific scenes of their treatment of those whom they conquered, and Israel would eventually fall to Assyria in 722 BC. During the days of King Sennacherib of Assyria, his palace was located in Nineveh (see 2 Kgs 19:36). The prophet Nahum prophesied the eventual destruction of Nineveh (Nah 3:7), which was overthrown by the Medes and Chaldeans in 612 BC.

Message and Purpose

Jonah ministered during the reign of King Jeroboam II. He was called by God to go to the wicked city of Nineveh and tell its people to repent. While it's easy to miss the concern of this book by focusing on Jonah, it is really about the character of God. It begins with God and ends with God. He is the one who initiates all the action.

The message of the book for Israel related to what was happening to Jonah. That message was that God loves all people, Jews and Gentiles. Though Israel's sins put them in the same scenario for judgment that the Ninevites were in, Jonah showed the Israelites that God's love is for all who repent. The book of Jonah, in fact, is a message of grace because God gave the Ninevites a forty-day window in which to repent. It reveals to us the heart of God to see people across all racial, social, class, and cultural lines repent and be saved. And our hearts should reflect the same desire. Jonah was a reluctant prophet who God used to teach us the kingdom perspective God's people are to have toward all people.

www.bhpublishinggroup.com/qr/te/32_00

Outline

I. The Prophet's Rebellion (1:1-17)
II. The Prophet's Prayer (2:1-10)
III. The Prophet's Preaching (3:1-10)
IV. The Prophet's Anger (4:1-11)

JONAH

I. THE PROPHET'S REBELLION (1:1-17)

1:1-3 One day during the eighth century BC, God reached down into the school of the prophets—which included Jonah, Amos, and Hosea in the northern kingdom of Israel—and told Jonah to **go to the great city of Nineveh and preach against it because** of **their evil** (1:1-2). Instead, Jonah went to **Joppa**, looking for a boat to **Tarshish** (1:3). So, rather than buying a ticket for Nineveh, he was heading in the opposite direction. Jonah was a rebel, a man who didn't like what God told him to do.

There are a couple of reasons why Jonah didn't want to obey God. First, the Ninevites were a wicked, violent people who showed their enemies no mercy. They would torture you, kill you, put your corpse on display, and later paint pictures to document their atrocities. "I'm not going to Nineveh. They slaughter people there," may have seemed the practical choice from Jonah's perspective (see the book of Nahum). The second reason Jonah disobeyed God is made clear in 4:1-2. He didn't want to preach to these people because he was afraid they might actually repent and be forgiven! Nineveh was a major city of the Assyrian Empire, and if its citizens were to escape God's judgment, they could eventually conquer Israel. So Jonah preferred to let God rain fiery wrath on them. He wanted them destroyed.

Do you have any "Ninevites" in your life— someone with whom God would want you to share the gospel, but to whom you refuse to go? Is there anyone who has done you wrong so that you'd prefer to see him judged rather than forgiven? That's how Jonah felt.

That Jonah fled **from the LORD's presence** (1:3) is interesting. Clearly, Jonah was no theological fool. He was a prophet, and he knew that God is everywhere. No one can flee from his presence really. But Jonah didn't want to submit to God's will because he didn't like God's plan. Therefore, he was *fleeing from God's demands*, which meant he was breaking fellowship with God.

If you're in God's will, he always supplies what he demands—that is, he picks up the tab and provides what's needed. But, when Jonah ran from the will of God, he **paid the fare** himself (1:3). Running from God's agenda can cost you time, money, health, peace, and joy. But make no mistake: it will cost you.

1:4 These days we hear much about "Mother Nature" but little about Father God. He's the one who **threw a great wind** against Jonah. When you're running from God and things get windy, that's not a chance event. If you're a Christian and rebelling against God, he's coming after you. And one of the ways he does this is through circumstances. The negative circumstances in your life may be a storm with your name on it.

1:5 The **sailors were afraid** and **threw the ship's cargo into the sea to lighten the load**. When Jonah disobeyed God, he not only messed up his own life but also the lives of those around him. If you think your sin only affects you, you're wrong. When we run from God, the same storms we cause hit the people in our vicinities.

1:6 Jonah was **asleep** in the midst of the storm. You can get so far out of the will of God that you sleep through a storm designed to discipline you. The **captain** roused him from his slumber and urged him to call on his **god** so that they wouldn't **perish**. Notice the irony: the pagan sailor was telling the preacher to pray! When Jonah wouldn't respond to discipline, the Lord rebuked him through an unbeliever.

1:7-10 **The sailors** decided to **cast lots** (a practice like rolling dice) to see who was the cause of their problems. In God's providence, this led them to Jonah. The prophet told them that he was **a Hebrew** who worshiped **the Lord, the God of the heavens, who made the sea and the dry land** (1:9). And when they heard that, they were terrified. It was clear to them that Jonah had made his God, the one who was apparently trying to kill them with the power of his sea, unhappy by **fleeing** (1:10).

1:11-17 Though they attempted to avoid Jonah's counsel at first (1:11-13), eventually they gave in and **threw him into the sea**. As a result, it **stopped its raging** (1:15). The problem that was causing

their trouble was spiritual, not merely meteorological or social. And the same is true for many of your problems. Often, solutions have to be based on a spiritual perspective.

These sailors, who earlier were praying to their false gods (1:5), suddenly **called out to the Lord . . . offered a sacrifice** to him, and **made vows** (1:14, 16). Within their actions is a reminder that God is sovereign—even when you are out of his will. Your disobedience doesn't stop his agenda; he will accomplish his purposes. The Lord used Jonah's disobedience to make these sinning sailors pray to him. So, even in our rebellion, God can accomplish his work. Ultimately, you don't determine what God accomplishes; you only determine where you fit in the plan.

Jonah was still unwilling to submit to God. He was willing to choose death instead (1:12, 15). But, once again, God wouldn't let him escape: **The Lord appointed a great fish to swallow Jonah** (1:17). When you're running from a particular aspect of your calling, God will send circumstances, and they will find you. The wind obeyed, the sea obeyed, and the fish obeyed. But there was still a problem with the preacher.

II. THE PROPHET'S PRAYER (2:1-10)

2:1 When God called Jonah to obedience, when the storm threatened destruction, when sinners criticized his rebellion, nothing changed in Jonah's attitude. But, when he was swallowed by a fish, **Jonah prayed**. Some of us don't get right with God until circumstances are so adverse that they swallow us whole, but God knows what it takes to teach us to repent and pray.

2:2-3 **You threw me into the depths** (2:3). Ultimately, it wasn't the sailors but God who was responsible for tossing the prophet overboard. Jonah recognized that they had only done to him what God wanted done. Then, God sent a whale-a-gram and trapped his fleeing prophet. In his glorious sovereignty, he brought Jonah to a place that drove him to call on the Lord.

2:4-6 Jonah had been **banished from** God's **sight** (2:4). He was out of fellowship with God. But then Jonah declared, **you raised my life from the Pit** (2:6).

Have you ever been in the Pit? Are you there now? If so, there's good news: The Pit is not a bad place to be if it gets you back into the will of God. When a visit to that place is what it takes to nudge you back on track spiritually, you can thank God for the Pit.

2:7-9 When my son was young, I told him to empty the trash. He told me that he didn't feel like it, but I assured him I could change the way he felt. And I did. God changed the way Jonah felt because God loved him enough to track him down. As a result, Jonah **remembered the Lord** (2:7). He remembered that **Salvation belongs to the Lord**;

therefore, he was ready to **fulfill** what he had previously **vowed** (2:9). The prophet was ready to fulfill his obligation to speak the words of God.

2:10 Many of us want *God* to act before *we* have acted, but notice that God didn't command change until Jonah got right with him. Then, the fish **vomited Jonah onto dry land**.

You can go straight to your own Nineveh to begin with, or you can let God get you there the hard way. But be warned: it can get messy if the "Hound of heaven" has to pursue you because of rebellion. He *will* track you down.

III. THE PROPHET'S PREACHING (3:1-10)

3:1-2 In saying, **Go to the great city of Nineveh and preach the message that I tell you** (3:1), God told Jonah the same thing he'd told him the first time. This time, Jonah **went to Nineveh** (3:2).

It's important to note that Jonah still had to choose to obey God and go. The fish didn't drop him off at Nineveh. Instead, he was taken to the place of his disobedience and given a second chance to make a right decision. Valuable time and energy had been wasted, and the prophet was no doubt stinky and sticky from his ordeal. When God calls you to obedience, you need to understand this: he's not going to change. So it's best to do things his way from the start.

3:3-4 Jonah went to Nineveh and proclaimed the Lord's message: **In forty days Nineveh will be demolished!** (3:4). There are two parts to this summary of his sermon: Nineveh would be judged for its sin, and the Ninevites had a forty-day window to fix the problem. God had every right to destroy this wicked city. But, in this case, he graciously gave them a chance to come clean and repent. To repent is to give God the opportunity to limit or reverse his judgment. And when repentance happens, you have revival: as people turn, so God turns. And if you're still alive, there's still time to repent.

3:5-9 In response to this message from the Lord, the people—the entire city!—repented. They **believed God**, but they also **proclaimed** a fast (3:5). Furthermore, **the king of Nineveh** urged **everyone** to **call out earnestly to God** and **turn from his evil ways and from his wrongdoing**, so that God might **turn from his burning anger** (3:6-9). In other words, the people put their money where their mouths were. Their actions were a visible demonstration of a heart change. They assumed a posture of repentance.

3:10 That **God relented from the disaster** is a reminder that God never changes, but he can adjust to the changes in humans. While he doesn't change his holy standards, he will alter his intended outcome in response to our actions. In this case, repentance produced something for his grace and mercy to respond to. Not only had God shown grace to the sailors and to Jonah, but he also showed mercy to some of the wickedest people on the planet. He has enough grace and mercy for everyone—including people whom you have given up on. God can get through when you can't.

Jonah reluctantly preached one sermon, and it resulted in the greatest revival in human history. That's the grace of God. But Jonah almost missed the privilege of participating in this great evangelistic event because he didn't like what God told him to do. So remember: if you run from God's will, you might miss out on one of the most significant moves of God in your life. God doesn't always explain himself in advance. We have to walk by faith to see what he's up to.

IV. THE PROPHET'S ANGER (4:1-11)

4:1 That Jonah was **greatly displeased** and **furious** when Nineveh repented means only one thing: Jonah was a fool. Everyone was turning to the Lord and renouncing their sinful ways. God had conquered the hearts of thousands in one of the mightiest cities of the Assyrian Empire! But Jonah was ticked off about it.

4:2-3 Jonah laid his cards on the table: **I fled toward Tarshish in the first place** because **I knew that you are a gracious and compassionate God . . . one who relents from sending disaster. And now, LORD . . . it is better for me to die than to live.** In short, Jonah didn't want to see God's grace fall on a wicked people. He knew God's character, and he knew that if Nineveh genuinely repented, God would forgive them.

When a person truly repents, God's heart melts. Isn't that good news? He loves to restore repentant sinners! All of us need a God who will reverse his decision of judgment, but we are often so unlike God that we are unwilling to reverse our own judgmental decisions. Are there people in your life whose salvation would make you angry? Would it disappoint you to learn that a certain person had become a Christian because you would then have to treat them as a brother or sister? Think about it. How would you fare before God, if he were as angry and unrelenting as you?

4:4-5 Here God raises a psychological question: **Is it right for you to be angry?** (4:4). This is a question we should ask ourselves more often. In every case, we must determine whether our anger is legitimate or illegitimate.

Interestingly, Jonah didn't answer the question. Instead, he **left the city** and sat down to watch **what would happen to it** (4:5). No doubt he was rooting for the Ninevites' zeal to fade so that God's judgment could fall.

4:6-8 But as Jonah was watching and hoping that God would still pull a Sodom and Gomorrah on Nineveh (see Gen 19:24-25, 28), God

was at work on the prophet. He **appointed a plant** to grow and **provide shade for** Jonah from the heat. That made Jonah happy (4:6). But then, God **appointed a worm** to wither the plant and **appointed a scorching east wind** to wither Jonah. That made Jonah want to **die** (4:7-8).

Clearly this man had issues. The wind obeyed, the fish obeyed, the Ninevites obeyed, the plant obeyed, and the worm obeyed. But the prophet still wasn't getting it. Jonah was spiritually immature, and God wanted to teach him a lesson to provoke him to spiritual maturity. Yet, even as God worked on behalf of his heart, Jonah couldn't see God: he simply saw negative circumstances that infuriated him.

When you're having a bad day, have you ever asked yourself if the things happening to you might be God's sovereign appointments designed for your good? Perhaps that irritating co-worker is meant to serve as a divine appointment to help you grow spiritually.

4:9-11 God asked, **Is it right for you to be angry about the plant?** Jonah retorted that he was not only **angry** that his shade was gone, but that he was ready to **die** over it (4:9). That's when the Lord unloaded on Jonah with a dose of divine wisdom: **You cared about the plant, which you did not labor over and did not grow. . . . But may I not care about the great city of Nineveh, which has more than a hundred and twenty thousand people . . . ?** (4:10-11).

In other words, while Jonah was miserable over the loss of a twenty-four hour *plant* that he had absolutely nothing to do with, he was willing to watch thousands of *people* created in God's image die and go to hell. And, though Jonah liked it when God cared for him and provided him with shade from the heat, when God wanted to care for sinners who couldn't **distinguish between their right and their left** (4:11)—that is, young children—Jonah got bent out of shape. God's prophet may have had God's words, but he didn't have God's heart.

Do you have God's heart for others? You cannot desire God's goodness for yourself but refuse to minister his goodness to others who need it, too. You cannot be a recipient of God's grace but not a dispenser of it.

The book ends abruptly, leaving us to wonder what happened to Jonah. Did he die in his bitterness? Did he return to God in repentance? Why does the story end here? It closes where it does because God is asking the readers of the book what he's asking Jonah: How can you be heartless toward sinners when you know what you have been saved from? After all, if not for God's providential work in your life, you would never have come to Christ. So will you be transformed by the grace of God and serve as his instrument of grace?

In Matthew's Gospel, we learn that the unbelieving scribes and Pharisees were demanding a sign from Jesus. He told them that they would be given "the sign of the prophet Jonah" (Matt 12:38-39). "For as Jonah was in the belly of the huge fish three days and three nights, so the Son of Man will be in the heart of the earth three days and three nights" (Matt 12:40).

When Jonah came out of the fish, he carried a message of repentance to Nineveh. God showed compassion on Nineveh through the symbolic death and resurrection of a prophet. But in Jesus Christ, he showed mercy on you and me by the actual death and resurrection of the Son of God. Indeed, then, "Something greater than Jonah is here" (Matt 12:41). If a rebel prophet could turn Nineveh around, Jesus Christ can certainly turn around the circumstances in our lives. This, as Paul calls it, is "the surpassing grace of God" (2 Cor 9:14).

MICAH

INTRODUCTION

Author

MICAH WAS A NATIVE OF MORE-sheth, a small town on the border of the city of Gath (1:1, 14). He ministered to both the northern kingdom of Israel and the southern kingdom of Judah, prophesying the destruction of Samaria (1:5-9) and Jerusalem (1:8-16). He also foresaw the birth of the Messiah in Bethlehem (5:2). Micah ministered "in the days of Jotham, Ahaz, and Hezekiah, kings of Judah" (1:1). And because he saw Samaria's future judgment, which occurred in 722 BC, the likely time period for his ministry is between 730 and 690 BC.

Historical Background

In Micah's day, the kingdoms of Judah and Israel were in the midst of positive economic changes. New wealth in the cities, primarily because of a long period of peace, allowed the rich to expand their wealth to the detriment of the lower class. This led to privileges being extended to one group while being denied to the other. With more wealth, people had the wherewithal to indulge other appetites—which sometimes manifested themselves in sin and moral degradation. In both kingdoms, the greater the wealth, the greater the distance there was between the people and their God. Micah called Samaria and Judah to repent and turn back to the Lord.

Message and Purpose

The message of Micah is that God is displeased with social injustice, declining morality, and living without a view to the Messiah's kingdom reign. Micah wanted his own people in the southern kingdom of Judah to know that God was just as upset with them as he

was with the rebellious northern kingdom of Israel. He condemned the social inequities of his day that did not reflect God's kingdom principles that they were to be living out until the Messiah came. Those in power were practicing bribery, confiscating the fields of the people, oppressing the poor, and abusing women and children. They were disregarding the Mosaic law and its protections for the vulnerable. Personal holiness was also absent as the people lived in decadence.

Micah directly connects the Messiah's reign with the everyday living of his people. God would not ignore the people's insensitivity, unrighteousness, and oppression. There is to be a direct connection between our faith and our social concerns. Micah's message is that the spiritual must not become disconnected from the social. When the spiritual is applied to the social in righteous ways, God blesses.

www.bhpublishinggroup.com/qr/te/33_00

Outline

I. The Approaching Punishment of Israel and Judah (1:1–2:13)

II. Punishment of Leaders and False Prophets (3:1-12)

III. The Coming Kingdom and King (4:1–5:15)

IV. The Lawsuit against Judah (6:1-16)

V. Spiritual Ruin, Renewal, and Restoration (7:1-20)

MICAH

I. THE APPROACHING PUNISHMENT OF ISRAEL AND JUDAH (1:1–2:13)

1:1 Micah introduces himself as one who received **the word of the LORD**. God **came to** him. Micah may have lived under the rule of three earthly kings—**Jotham, Ahaz, and Hezekiah**—but he was in service to the one whose kingdom rules over all.

Micah was a **Moreshite**, a native of Moresheth, which lay southwest of Jerusalem and under the control of the city of Gath. Moresheth was by no means a significant city. The calling of Micah, in fact, is proof that a kingdom man can be found in any place where the word of God can go, and God can use anyone from anywhere who yields to his call. Micah's vision centers on two representative cities—**Samaria**, the capital of Israel, and **Jerusalem**, the capital of Judah.

1:2-7 Listen, all you peoples; pay attention, earth and everyone in it is a reminder that when God has something to say, the whole earth is to give its undivided attention. Micah alerts his Jewish brethren that there is a case **against** them, and the Creator of the universe is the primary **witness** (1:2). The idolatry of **Samaria** and **Jerusalem**—the capital cities of the southern and northern kingdoms—had become so great that God was coming down to the **earth** to address it (1:3-5). As a result of their **rebellion** and **sins** against God's covenant (1:5), **Samaria** would become **a heap of ruins**, and her idols would **be smashed** (1:6-7).

Israel had entered into a covenant with the Lord. Through his prophets, God often spoke of it as a marriage covenant. He was the husband, and Israel was his bride (see Isa 54:5). Thus, when Israel engaged in idolatry, worshiping false gods, God considered it spiritual "adultery" (see Jer 13:27; Ezek 23:37). Israel had "prostituted" themselves with foreign nations and their false gods (Jer 3:1). That's why Micah says that Samaria had **collected the wages of a prostitute**. Yet, all her wealth would be carried off by another prostitute, another idol-worshiping nation (Mic 1:7).

1:8-16 Micah responds to his own message with weeping (1:8). He feels the pain of seeing the people of the kingdom being removed from the land—many under the threat of death. **Even Judah** would suffer from the influence of idolatry and the resulting scorn when the surrounding nations rejoiced over its demise (1:9). Micah grieves over the Judean towns that would be laid waste—including his hometown of **Moresheth-gath** (1:11-15). He calls on his countrymen to **shave** themselves **bald**, a sign of intense mourning (1:16).

2:1-5 Even though the prophet would prefer to see God's people blessed, he clearly sees the reason for judgment: **Woe to those who dream up wickedness and prepare evil plans on their beds! At morning light they accomplish it because the power is in their hands** (2:1). In addition, the rich and powerful leaders prepare plans to take farms, homes, and inheritances (2:2). But, God has plans for those who carry out such injustice.

Because the leaders deprive the innocent of their land, they will be removed from the land themselves (2:3-5).

2:6-11 What does Micah hear in response to his faithful proclamation of God's word? **Quit your preaching**. When a kingdom man speaks God's truth, the unrighteous don't want to hear it (see the response to Stephen in Acts 7:57). Therefore, like ostriches with their heads in the sand, Micah's audience insisted that none of these judgments would come upon them (2:6). They preferred a **preacher** who would preach **about wine and beer**—indulgence and pleasure (2:11).

2:12-13 Even though most of the people had rejected him, God would **collect a remnant** of his people. Like a faithful shepherd, he would gather his lost **sheep** (2:12)—just as the good shepherd, Jesus Christ, would do one day (see John 10:11-18). God himself will save his people: **Their King will pass through before them, the LORD as their leader** (12:13).

II. PUNISHMENT OF LEADERS AND FALSE PROPHETS (3:1-12)

3:1 Here, Micah points to the sin of those in leadership. Even when the average person of the kingdom strays from practicing truth, it is expected that those in leadership will stand fast and do what is right. Micah says, **Now listen, leaders of Jacob, you rulers of the house of Israel. Aren't you supposed to know what is just?** The obvious answer is yes.

3:2-3 Micah highlights the leaders' spiritual and moral weakness. They **hate good and love evil** (3:2). It doesn't matter what stellar competencies a leader possesses. If he hates what is good, he is disqualified. Regarding their treatment of the people, Micah compares these leaders with wild beasts or cannibals. Instead of protecting the people they are supposed to lead, they devour them! They **tear off people's skin and strip their flesh from their bones**. Then they **chop them up like flesh for the cooking pot**. This type of injustice brings God's wrath.

3:4 God's response is to **hide his face from** these evildoers. Therefore, when their time of trouble came (and it would come sooner than they thought), the leaders would **cry out to the LORD, but he** would **not answer them**.

3:5 Micah also indicts the false **prophets who lead [his] people astray**. They are supposed to be the heralds of the kingdom of God. But, like the leaders, these prophets were looking out for themselves. That they **proclaim peace when they have food to sink their teeth into but declare war against the one who puts nothing in their mouths** means they could be bought. You could guarantee a good word from them by filling their stomachs or pockets. If you were poor with nothing to offer, however, the prophets only had harsh words for you. They were charlatans. The only vision they could see was one of money flowing from someone else's pocket into their own. This state of affairs would make it hard for the poor to trust God, and it would give the rich a false sense of security.

3:6-7 The punishment for giving false light is experiencing darkness: **It will be night for you—without visions** (3:6). So, because these prophets were a discredit to God, God would discredit them and halt their prostitution of the office of prophet. Because they used their gifts (Micah never questions their power, just their motives) for debased purposes, God would debase them by cutting off their ability to communicate with him: **There will be no answer** (3:7). Those who refuse to speak God's word will be abandoned by God.

3:8 In contrast to these profiteering prophets, Micah asserts the weight of his credentials. He is a genuine prophet of the kingdom. What's his proof? **I am filled with power**

by the Spirit of the LORD, with justice and courage to proclaim to his Jewish brothers and sisters their **rebellion** and **sin**. A kingdom man relies on the Spirit's power (not his own) and is willing to speak boldly, calling sin what it is. Micah knew that he was called by and accountable to God; therefore, God's opinion was the only one that mattered.

3:9-12 Micah presses the issue of injustice once more, condemning all three levels of spiritual leadership: **leaders . . . priests . . .** and **prophets**. They exercised their roles in exchange for cash (3:11). "The love of money," the apostle Paul says, "is a root of all kinds of evil" (1 Tim 6:10). The leaders were corrupt, perverting **everything that is right** (3:9). Nonetheless, they assumed God was on their side and concluded that **no disaster** would **overtake [them]** (3:11). They couldn't be more misguided: **Jerusalem** would **become ruins** (3:12).

III. THE COMING KINGDOM AND KING (4:1–5:15)

4:1-2 In the midst of this bad news, Micah has glorious good news. A restored kingdom will come to **Jerusalem**: the future millennial kingdom of the Messiah. When it is established, the nations will say, **Come, let us go up to the mountain of the LORD**. They'll go there—not so they can merely know about God—but so that they may be taught to **walk in his paths** (4:2). Doing so is what it means to be kingdom people.

4:3-8 People will come to the Lord to settle their **disputes**. **War** will be a thing of the past, and there will be **no one to frighten** the righteous (4:3-4). Christ's millennial kingdom will bring the peace and security everyone has been dreaming of. When **the LORD of Armies** speaks, conflict comes to an end (4:4). And he **will reign over them in Mount Zion** (4:7).

In light of this future glory for the people of God, Micah and those who sided with him declare their convictions. Though they may be surrounded by idolatrous people who **walk in the name of their gods**, kingdom men and women **will walk in the name of the LORD . . . forever** (4:5). Such people wear their commitment to God on their sleeves each day.

4:9-13 Like **a woman in labor**, the people of Judah would cry out in pain. They would have no **king** or **counselor** to help them when **Babylon** carried them away (4:9-10). Yet the Lord would rescue them from their **enemies** (4:10). The plunderer would become the plundered (4:12).

5:1-2 A kingdom must have a king, but the one who will set all things right isn't just any king; he's *the* King. Like his ancestor David, this King would come from **Bethlehem** (5:2). Hundreds of years later, God would sovereignly ensure the fulfillment of this prophecy through a Roman census that took Joseph and his pregnant bride, Mary, to his ancestral home of Bethlehem. There, in the humblest of circumstances, Mary gave birth to the one who would one day rule the world (see Luke 2:1-7). Clearly, this would be no ordinary king: **His origin is from antiquity, from ancient times** (5:2). Micah thus affirms this King's preexistence. Conceived by the Holy Spirit in the womb of a virgin, this King is the Son of God (see Luke 1:26-37).

5:3-15 When the Messiah rules, his people **will live securely**. He will be their **shepherd** and their **peace** (5:4-5). **Then the remnant** of God's people will be **like a lion among** the nations, their **enemies will be destroyed**, and the Lord will remove all idolatry from the land (5:7-15). In the midst of a prophecy of decadence, doom, and destruction, Micah proclaims a vision of victory for the people of God.

IV. THE LAWSUIT AGAINST JUDAH (6:1-16)

6:1-3 After giving Israel a picture of their future hope, Micah returns to the issue at hand, namely, Israel's spiritual and moral decline: **Listen to the LORD's lawsuit, you mountains and enduring foundations of the earth, because the LORD has a case against his people, and he will argue it against Israel** (6:2). The Lord presents his lawsuit before all creation, and his point is solid.

6:4-5 The Lord's multipoint argument, in fact, goes to the core of his relationship with Israel. First, he says, **I brought you up out of Egypt and redeemed you from that place of slavery** (6:4). The exodus was the most significant historical event in the history of Israel. Nothing could compare with God's powerful work to deliver Israel from Egypt. Second, God gave Israel great leaders: **Moses, Aaron, and Miriam** have a place of prominence in Israel's history (6:4). Third, God provided protection in their journey to the promised land when he intervened in the matter of **King Balak of Moab** and **Balaam son of Beor** (6:5). Balak wanted Balaam to pronounce a curse upon Israel. Instead, God commanded Balaam to pronounce a blessing on them (see Num 22-24).

6:6-8 In every case, God acted faithfully toward his chosen people. They, on the other hand, couldn't say the same. So, how could they please the Lord? By bringing **burnt offerings?** By offering their **firstborn?** (6:6-7). No. God is not interested in mere religious rituals.

What God wants is your heart and mind. He wants your love and obedience. He's a personal God and expects a personal relationship. He also expects you to love your neighbors by doing them good and ministering to their needs. The answer to what it is that **the LORD requires** is simple. Every person is **to act justly, to love faithfulness, and to walk humbly with . . . God** (6:8). Religion becomes authentic when it demonstrates itself in the equitable application of biblical truth in order to meet the needs of people in God's name (see Jas 1:27).

6:9-16 Micah says God's people should **pay attention to the rod** of discipline **and the one who ordained it** (6:9). But they're like children disciplined by their father only to remain foolishly unwilling to change their ways. Micah knows, in fact, that these people are not going to subscribe to God's requirements. The evidence is against them. **Wickedness** and **violence** abound among them (6:10-12). Therefore, God's punishment will be unleashed. Regardless of what they have or acquire, they will **not be satisfied** with it (6:14).

It's possible to get everything you want—but not be satisfied. True satisfaction is found in God. By rejecting him and following Israel into idolatry, the people of Judah would face **contempt** and **scorn** (6:16).

V. SPIRITUAL RUIN, RENEWAL, AND RESTORATION (7:1-20)

7:1-7 Micah laments the problem he sees. Faithful people have vanished from the land; **there is no one upright** (7:2). Leaders take bribes; friends betray one another; families are dysfunctional (7:3-6). Punishment is the only thing that can correct this issue, and the only hope for the land is **salvation** from the Lord (7:7).

7:8-13 Here Micah gives voice to Jerusalem who confesses, **I have sinned** and **I must endure the LORD's rage.** But, in the end, Zion will be established again and **will see his salvation** (7:9). Then, the enemies of God and of his people will be put to **shame** (7:10). Jerusalem's **walls** will be rebuilt, and Israel will be renewed (7:11-13).

7:14 As a true prophet, Micah desired the best for the kingdom and its people. Micah's compassion and care is seen in his request to God: **Shepherd your people with your staff** (7:14). Scripture testifies to the loving care of God for his people in terms of a shepherd and his sheep (see Ps 23). Micah longs for Judah to know the peace and protection that comes from having God for a shepherd.

7:15-20 The prayer of this righteous prophet is answered by a loving God's promise to **perform miracles** and shame the **nations** who oppose his people (7:15-17). **His anger** is for a moment, but **he delights in faithful love** (7:18). The Lord is a covenant-keeping God who **will cast all our sins into the depths of the sea** (7:19). What a beautiful picture: our sins completely removed forever! The suffering and death of the sinless Son of God on our behalf made this possible. Israel *will* see all of the promises of **Jacob**, **Abraham**, and Isaac fulfilled (7:20).

NAHUM

INTRODUCTION

Author

THE AUTHOR OF THE BOOK OF NAhum is the only person with that name in the Old Testament. Except for the name of his hometown of Elkosh (1:1), nothing certain is known about him.

Background

Nahum's prophetic book is a declaration of judgment on the Assyrian city of Nineveh, which was located about twenty miles north of the modern Iraqi capital of Baghdad. The Ninevites had responded with repentance when Jonah preached to them many years prior, but by the time of Nahum's book, their leaders had returned to wickedness.

Two events help determine the earliest and latest possible dates for the composition of Nahum's writing. The first is the capture and downfall of Thebes in about 663 BC. The second is Nineveh's ultimate destruction, which occurred in 612 BC. Nahum's emphasis on the seemingly recent fall of Thebes (3:8) favors a date shortly after 663 BC, during the reign of wicked King Manasseh (686–642 BC) or his evil son Amon (642–640 BC). This likely coincided with the reign of the cruel Assyrian king named Ashurbanipal (ca. 668–627 BC); if so, Assyria was at the height of its power.

Message and Purpose

The book of Nahum is God's announcement of judgment on the kingdom of Assyria, specifically on its capital city, Nineveh. God had used the Assyrians as the agents of judgment against his people for their rebellion and disobedience: Assyria had destroyed the northern kingdom of Israel and carried the inhabitants into captivity. But through Nahum, God was declaring that the cruel, evil Assyrian Empire would fall, too.

The book also has a second purpose. The prophet wanted to assure God's people that he would restore them according to his kingdom promises if they would repent and return to him. Though God had allowed Israel's painful, crushing defeat because of their sin, he would not let his people's sins cancel out his promises.

Nahum's name means "to console" or "consolation." And through this prophet, God was consoling his people in the midst of their painful judgment and also letting Nineveh know that he would not ignore their evil. Nahum informs us that God is loving, yet he is also just. We must not allow one aspect of his character to cancel out the other in our minds.

www.bhpublishinggroup.com/qr/te/34_00

Outline

I.   The Declaration of Judgment (1:1-15)
II. The Power of Judgment (2:1-13)
III. The Finality of Judgment (3:1-19)

NAHUM

I. THE DECLARATION OF JUDGMENT (1:1-15)

1:1 The prophet **Nahum** was given a **vision** from the Lord **concerning Nineveh.** Of course, this was not the first time one of Israel's prophets delivered God's message to that Assyrian city. Previously, Jonah had warned that God would destroy it, and the Ninevites repented. But, by the time of Nahum, the people and their leaders had returned to wickedness.

1:2-6 This passage focuses on the attribute of God that no one wants to talk about: his **wrath.** Nahum describes the LORD as **a jealous and avenging God** (1:2). In view here is not the kind of wicked jealousy or envy that the Bible condemns in sinners (e.g., Rom 13:13; 2 Cor 12:20; Gal 5:20). Rather, this is the jealousy of a husband who sees some chump brazenly hitting on his wife and wants to protect her. As Israel's husband, the Lord would tolerate no rival gods or nations that abused his people. And though he is **slow to anger,** he is **furious with his enemies** (1:2-3). And when God gets angry, **rivers run dry... mountains quake... the earth trembles... and rocks are shattered** (1:4-6).

1:7-8 Don't miss this. After a terrifying description of God's wrath, Nahum says, **The LORD is good.** This is no contradiction—unless you assume *good* means "weak" or "apathetic." Rather, because God is good, he will be a **stronghold** and a **refuge** for those who align themselves with him (1:7). Because he's good, however, he must also address evil; he

can't let it go unanswered. Thus, he promises to **completely destroy Nineveh** (1:8).

1:9-11 Whatever you plot against the LORD, **he will bring it to complete destruction** (1:9). It's hard to imagine anyone plotting against an all-knowing, all-powerful being. Yet, to reject God's word and mistreat his people is to plot against him. So, because the Assyrians had besieged Israel and Judah (see 2 Kgs 17–19), they would **be consumed** (1:10).

1:12-14 Here the Lord promises to deliver Judah from the hand of Assyria. He had previously used the Assyrians as a tool to punish his people for their sin (see Isa 10:5-6), but he would **punish** Judah **no longer** (1:12) and would turn his vengeance on Assyria instead (1:13). The divine lawn mower was ready: **They** would **be mowed down** (1:12). The Lord's threat directed toward the Assyrian king showed how weak he really was in the grand scheme of things. The king would have **no offspring,** and the Lord himself would **prepare** his **grave** (1:14).

1:15 Look to the mountains—the feet of the herald, who proclaims peace. This verse is similar to Isaiah 40:9 and 52:7, which are quoted in Romans 10:15. When the news of victory is announced, Judah is to **celebrate.** But, more than this, God's people must **fulfill** the **vows** they made. Many people in Israel probably declared, "Lord, if you'll deliver us, I will do such-and-such." Time to make good on those pledges!

II. THE POWER OF JUDGMENT (2:1-13)

2:1-6 Nahum taunts Nineveh like the Assyrians used to taunt other nations (see 2 Kgs 18:30-35): **Man the fortifications! Watch the road! Brace yourself! Summon all your strength!** (2:1). He eggs them on with sarcasm, knowing full well that none of those actions will do them any good. They're like a ninety-eight-pound weakling facing a heavyweight boxer. They can man their chariots and fortify their walls, but it will all prove futile (2:3-5). For **the Lord will restore the majesty of Jacob, yes, the majesty of Israel** (2:2). Israel has a champion, and he has no equal.

2:7-13 Assyria was the big kid on the block. Nations trembled at its approach. But all of the **beauty** of Nineveh would be **stripped** away (2:7). All of its **silver** and **gold** would be plundered (2:9). **Desolation, decimation,** and **devastation** would be left in their place (2:10). While Judah's messenger would announce good news (1:15), Assyria's **messengers** would **never be heard again** (2:13).

III. THE FINALITY OF JUDGMENT (3:1-19)

3:1-15 Nahum tallies up the violent wickedness of Nineveh. They were murderous and **deceitful** conquerors (3:1). Their disregard for human life was horrifying (3:3). Nineveh is even described as a **prostitute** engaged in **sorcery** (3:4). They trusted in false gods; therefore, here the Lord declares: **I am against you** (3:5). These are not words that you want to hear from God.

As Assyria had exhibited cruelty and brought shame upon the nations, God would **shame** it before the **kingdoms** of the world (3:5). Everyone who saw its devastation, in fact, would **recoil** in horror (3:7). As it had sent others into exile, it would become an **exile** itself (3:10). Its **gates** are described as being **wide open** to its **enemies** (3:13),

and **the sword** would **cut [it] down** (3:15). Judgment may seem slow in coming. But it always comes. What goes around comes around.

3:16-19 Here the defeated **King of Assyria** is addressed by the prophet of the Lord: **Your people are scattered across the mountains with no one to gather them together** (3:18). Assyria's end, then, was like the end of the nations she defeated. **There** would be **no remedy for [its] injury** (3:19) because no power can turn back the hand of God. Indeed, Assyria's destruction came in 612 BC.

Of this you can be certain: A god-forsaken life of wickedness and injustice will lead to calamity and judgment. God always wins.

HABAKKUK

INTRODUCTION

Author

HABAKKUK WAS A PROPHET (1:1); otherwise, nothing is known about him. Though most prophets spoke to the people on behalf of God, Habakkuk spoke to God on behalf of the people.

Historical Background

The northern kingdom of Israel fell to the Assyrians in 722 BC. These conquerors subsequently fell to the Babylonians in 612 BC. The Babylonians, or "Chaldeans" (1:6), would also eventually bring Jerusalem and the whole southern kingdom of Judah to ruin.

In 609 BC, King Josiah of Judah was killed in battle by Pharaoh Neco of Egypt, and Judah came under Egyptian control. Neco was subsequently defeated by the Babylonians four years later, and Judah fell into the hands of Babylon by 604 BC. Jehoiakim, the king whom Neco had placed on Judah's throne, rebelled against Babylon in about 600 BC. In response, Nebuchadnezzar, the Babylonian king, besieged Jerusalem. He deposed Jehoiakim in 598 BC and carried his son Jehoiachin into exile the next year. But, that was not the end of Judah's misery. Zedekiah, Judah's final king, also rebelled against Babylon in 588 BC. As a result, Nebuchadnezzar descended on Jerusalem with a vengeance, ravaged the city, destroyed the temple, and carried many of Judah's inhabitants (including Zedekiah) into exile in 587–586 BC.

Habakkuk probably wrote in 609–605 BC, after the death of King Josiah but before Judah fell under Babylonian control.

Message and Purpose

Habakkuk was a perplexed prophet who lived in the last days of the southern kingdom of Judah, before the Babylonians invaded it and took the people into captivity. The prophet struggled because God used the evil Babylonians to judge his people; in other words, he used the clearly unrighteous to judge the more righteous, and Habakkuk wrestled with whether God was fair for doing so. While we all struggle with this issue at times, the book of Habakkuk serves as an invitation to look at the "who" when we don't understand the "why." It prompts us to trust God's sovereignty over his kingdom purposes even when we don't comprehend them.

Habakkuk invites us to draw near to God even when we don't get all of our questions answered—and even when it seems that God is working against us! The book teaches that we can take our stand and praise God even when we don't grasp what he's doing. Habakkuk both encourages us with his doxology at the end of the book (3:16-19) and with his declaration, "The righteous one will live by his faith" (2:4).

VIDEO INTRO

www.bhpublishinggroup.com/qr/te/35_00

HABAKKUK

I. HABAKKUK'S DIALOGUE WITH GOD (1:1–2:20)

A. Habakkuk's First Question (1:1-4)

1:1-3 Most prophets spoke to the people what they heard from God. Habakkuk spoke to God about what he **saw** (1:1). And what he witnessed caused him no small amount of consternation. All around him, he saw **injustice ... wrongdoing ... oppression ... violence ... strife ... and conflict** (1:3). Godly King Josiah had loved the Lord and his law (2 Kgs 23:1-27), but Josiah had been killed and replaced by his wicked son Jehoiakim who "did what was evil in the LORD's sight" (2 Kgs 23:36-37). And Judah's citizens followed his example.

So Habakkuk did something about it. He was a praying man and cried out to God. But his prayers seemed to go unanswered: **How long, LORD, must I call for help and you do not listen** (1:2). In time, Habakkuk decided God was taking too long to come through. He asked, **Why do you tolerate wrongdoing?** (1:3).

Have you ever felt alone in standing for justice in the world, while God seemed to be indifferent? This happens when we forget that God alone can see the whole picture, and he is working out his sovereign plan in the midst of the chaos. The Lord decides when to answer our prayers and how best to answer them. When you realize that he is omniscient (all knowing), omnipotent (all powerful), and holy (perfectly righteous in all he does), then you'll realize he knows how to run things better than we do.

1:4 Here, Habakkuk argues that when justice does not emerge, the **law is ineffective**. In order for laws to have teeth, there needs to be some form of enforcement behind them. Habakkuk wondered why God didn't do something about the wickedness in Judah.

B. God's First Response (1:5-11)

1:5-11 God was listening to his prophet, and now he answers. Indeed, he plans to do something about the injustice in Judah—and it will leave Habakkuk **utterly astounded** (1:5). God will punish Judah, and he names his minister of punishment: **the Chaldeans, that bitter, impetuous nation that marches across the earth's open spaces to seize territories** (1:6). *Chaldeans* is another name for the Babylonians. These people were **fierce and terrifying** and unleashed **violence** like animals (1:7-9). They **mock** and **laugh at** the rulers and lands that stand in their way (1:10). The nation God will use to finally punish his people, then, does not acknowledge the Lord; rather, **their strength is their god** (1:11).

C. Habakkuk's Second Question (1:12–2:1)

1:12-17 While Habakkuk got his answer, it wasn't the response he was looking for. How could a holy God **tolerate those who**

are **treacherous** (1:13)? How could God be **silent** while a **wicked** people swallowed those who were **more righteous** (1:13)? Sure, Judah was bad, but **the Chaldeans** were even worse! All the nations were like **fish** in their **net**, just waiting to be slaughtered **without mercy** (1:14-17). Habakkuk cannot comprehend that God, who is righteous and pure, gives free reign to an evil nation that does not give him glory.

2:1 In Habakkuk's mind, it's not fair that God is using an ally of Satan to judge the people of his kingdom. So, he registers his frustration and says, **I will watch to see what he will say to me . . . about my complaint.**

➤ D. God's Second Response (2:2-20) ✺

2:2-3 Though God is the Creator and Judge of the universe, he takes the time to respond to his servant and let him in on what he's doing. He commands Habakkuk to **write down this vision . . . so one may easily read it** (2:2). History would be a witness to God's revelation. The Babylonians would surely invade at **the appointed time** (2:3).

2:4-5 Yes, Habakkuk is exactly right about the Babylonian king. His **ego is inflated.** He is **without integrity . . . arrogant . . .** and **never satisfied** (2:5). **But**—and this is what Habakkuk and all those who follow God need to know above all else—**the righteous one will live by his faith** (2:4). So, Habakkuk

did not get a ten-point answer to his concerns. Nor did he receive a long, drawn out discussion of God's ways. God simply told him in essence, "Trust me and follow my instructions."

We, too, can operate in the knowledge that God has everything under control. God's agenda may be mysterious, but it's perfect. Everything he does will bring him glory and is ultimately for the good of his people (see Rom 8:28).

2:6-8 God would use the wicked Babylonians to punish Judah, but that didn't mean Babylon would get off scot-free. The Chaldeans, too, would be judged. The mocker would be mocked. The one who had **plundered many nations** (2:8) would himself be plundered. God's principles of righteousness and justice can be flouted—but not without consequence.

2:12-20 God reminds his prophet that the king of Babylon is nothing compared to him, **the LORD of Armies** (2:13). Though Babylon **will be filled with disgrace** (2:16), **the earth will be filled with the knowledge of the LORD's glory** (2:14). Those who worship an **idol** worship what is lifeless and **cannot speak** (2:18), but **the LORD** is alive and **in his holy temple** (2:20).

God has a track record of consistency, and persistent sin always brings about his judgment. Even the wicked who escape judgment in this earthly life will face it in eternity. All human sin will either be judged in hell or at the cross of Christ.

II. HABAKKUK'S PRAYER (3:1-19)

3:1-2 With his perspective righted, Habakkuk stands **in awe** of God. As he considers God's **deeds**—what he has done in the past and what he will do in the future—Habakkuk asks God to **remember mercy** even as he justly pours out his **wrath** (3:2). This kind of intercession on behalf of others, in fact, is what godly people do. It's what Moses did (see Exod 32:11-14), and it's what Daniel did (see Dan 9:1-19). So, remind God of his promises and plead for mercy.

3:3-19 Habakkuk praises God for his **splendor, brilliance,** and **power** (3:3-4). No one can stand before him; he makes the earth **tremble** (3:5-15). In time, he will **save [his] people** (3:13). But, in the meantime, Habakkuk would have to **quietly wait for the day of distress to come against the** invaders (3:16).

Sometimes, in the midst of trouble, we, too, must be patient, trusting God's promises and following his agenda for us. That, in fact, was the posture behind Habakkuk's declaration, **Though the fig tree does not bud . . . the flocks disappear . . . yet I will celebrate in the Lord; I will rejoice in the God of my salvation** (3:17-18). In other words, whatever happens to me, I'll praise the God who saves me because he **is my strength** (3:19). When you know God's character (who he is) and his works (what he has done), you'll know that you can trust him—even in the dark.

ZEPHANIAH

INTRODUCTION

Author

ZEPHANIAH'S NAME MEANS "YAHweh has hidden or protected." He was a prophet of royal lineage, and his genealogy in 1:1 reaches back four generations to King Hezekiah. (Most other prophets listed only two generations; see Zech 1:1). Zephaniah prophesied in the days of King Josiah.

Historical Background

King Josiah's father Amon (1:1) was a wicked man—so was his grandfather Manasseh. That heritage of wicked kings helps explain the rampant idolatry that plagued the land of Judah when Josiah inherited its throne in 640 BC.

Throughout his reign, Josiah struggled to squelch idolatry. Things were so bad that Judah's priests, along with pagan priests, led worship of Yahweh while also bowing before pagan gods (1:4-6)! It was the public reading of the book of the law that finally helped spawn reforms in the land: false priests were abolished, people repented, and pagan altars and idols were destroyed (see 2 Kgs 23:1-14). The existence of Judah's idolatrous practices in Zephaniah 1:4-6 implies that Zephaniah probably prophesied before Josiah's reforms began (ca. 621 BC).

Message and Purpose

The theme of Zephaniah is the day of the Lord—a time of darkness, gloom, and pain as God's response to people's sin, whether that of unbelievers or that of his people.

Nevertheless, the day of the Lord also has a positive side. It is a time of restoration after judgment, like the construction of new buildings in place of the condemned ones that were torn down.

Zephaniah not only wrote about the day of the Lord in his time, but also about the day of the Lord yet to come in the seven-year tribulation at the end of history. Then, God will judge the world and prepare the nation of Israel for Christ's second coming to establish his millennial kingdom.

Today, we experience glimpses of the day of the Lord as he judges us for our sins, with the hope of restoration. Society at large will see it in the days to come as God judges the world for its rejection of Christ. The character of God demands that this day must come, so place yourself in a posture of repentance.

www.bhpublishinggroup.com/qr/te/36_00

Outline

I. Introduction (1:1)
II. Judgment for Judah and a Call to Repentance (1:2–2:3)
III. Judgment for the Nations and Jerusalem (2:4–3:8)
IV. Hope for Israel and the Nations (3:9-20)

ZEPHANIAH

I. INTRODUCTION (1:1)

1:1 The word of the LORD . . . came to Zephaniah, God's man for God's message to God's place for God's people. He was of Hamitic origin, having descended from the lineage of Cush. This is implied in the name of his father, **Cushi** (see Gen 10:6). He was also a descendent of King **Hezekiah**. And, as a man of royal lineage, he had insider knowledge of how a righteous kingdom should be managed and what happens when unrighteousness runs rampant throughout a land.

Zephaniah had undoubtedly witnessed wicked King Manasseh's reign and observed how he led the people into idolatry. So, when God gave Zephaniah his message during **the days of Josiah . . . king of Judah**, Zephaniah fulfilled the role of a kingdom man. He knew whom he believed in and did not have a problem delivering the true King's message of judgment and restoration to a rebellious people.

II. JUDGMENT FOR JUDAH AND A CALL TO REPENTANCE (1:2–2:3)

1:2-3 The LORD's **declaration** of destruction is stunning, leaving no doubt that worldwide judgment will come. Indeed, God will **sweep away everything from the face of the earth** (1:2)—an insight that likely reminded Zephaniah's hearers of a time in the past when God spoke similarly to Noah before the flood (see Gen 6:7). This destruction will be comprehensive: **people and animals . . . the birds of the sky and the fish of the sea** (1:3). And not even a cruise liner could rescue those destined to perish.

1:4-6 God's judgment is coming **against Judah and against all the residents of Jerusalem**. He's going to clean up the land, and he's starting inside his own house. Not only were there **priests** of the Lord in Jerusalem, but there were also **pagan priests** (1:4). What's more, all of them bowed **in worship . . . to**

the stars in the sky—the heavenly bodies that God created. While they pledged **loyalty to the LORD**, they **also** pledged **loyalty to Milcom** to cover their bases (1:5).

The Lord, however, is a jealous God; he does not share worship with idols. The temple was intended to be his house and was designed to bear his name alone; therefore, he served notice: **Baal** is being evicted (1:4). Double-minded worshipers would be shown the door (1:4-5)—along with any **who do not seek the LORD** (1:6). Because they wanted to worship the gods they made rather than the God who made them, they would meet the same fate as their idols. God would turn the place upside down and wash the filth from the land.

1:7 Scripture frequently speaks of the **day of the LORD**, a time of judgment for God's enemies (1:7-18) and a time of hope for God's people (3:9-20). Sometimes, it refers to God's intervention in history (e.g., Joel 2:1-11); at other times, it refers to his intervention at the end of history (e.g., 1 Thess 5:1-5). Zephaniah warns Judah to repent (2:1) before the wrath of the day overtakes them (1:15).

1:8-9 Once the political leaders heard that there was a whole lot of shaking going on at the temple and that God was the cause of it, they knew he would be coming for them. **The king's sons** and his **officials** were going to be punished for their **violence and deceit** because the politicians were operating by their agenda and not by God's.

The Lord does not ride on the backs of politicians; he rides on his own glory and righteousness.

1:10-13 The business leaders and merchants who profited from the avarice behind the perverse worship at the temple and the corruption of the administration were going to be the recipients of the Lord's wrath, too. Nothing of their world would be spared. From the entry into the business area (**the Fish Gate**) to the business area itself (**the Second District**) to the **houses** and **vineyards** and **wealth** of the business owners, nothing would be left (1:10, 13). The writing was on the wall; their place would become **ruin** (1:13).

1:14-18 The wrath that God unleashed on the Egyptians leading up to the exodus and the awesome power of God displayed at Mount Sinai thereafter was coming to Judah and its capitol city, Jerusalem. Back then, God had told the Israelites through Moses what would happen if they broke their covenant with him (see Deut 28:15-68). Here, with vivid language, Zephaniah gives terrifying insight into the full scope of the **day of the** LORD (1:14). When **the LORD's wrath** comes, even **silver** and **gold** won't be able to rescue anyone. God will make **a horrifying end of all the inhabitants of the earth** (1:18).

2:1-3 God has an agenda for nations, cities, families, and individuals; and he holds everyone accountable to it. Judah had heard Zephaniah's basic message preached to them by many prophets previously, but they hadn't taken heed. Yet, even at this point in the nation's history, the divine King offers a call to repentance. He tells the **humble**—those who **carry out what he commands** that they can be protected from his **anger** if they'll **seek the** LORD . . . **righteousness** . . . and **humility** (2:3). They can be like the children of Israel in the exodus generation and accept the Lord's protection, or they can be like the Egyptians of that time and reject the message of judgment to their own destruction.

III. JUDGMENT FOR THE NATIONS AND JERUSALEM (2:4–3:8)

2:4-7 God the King's judgment was straightforward for the nation of Philistia in general and for four of its cities in particular. There is a "you will be" edict for each city—**abandoned** for **Gaza**, **ruin** for **Ashkelon**, **driven out** for **Ashdod** (and at **noon** no less, so they better have their bags packed!), and **uprooted** for **Ekron** (2:4). The **Philistines**, longtime enemies of Israel, would soon be no more: **I will destroy you until there is no one left** (2:5). Their land would be given to the **remnant** of God's people (2:7).

2:8-11 Because of their unrelenting **taunting** and **insults** against God's people, **Moab** and **the Ammonites** will become **like Sodom**

and **Gomorrah** (2:8-9). The mere mention of those two cities is enough to send chills down your spine in light of the judgment that God brought on them (see Gen 19:1-29). To oppose the Lord's chosen people has always been a bad idea. All people **will bow** before him in the end (2:11; see Phil 2:10-11). Better to do it in the joy of salvation than in the terror of judgment.

2:12 The King's message to the **Cushites** was short but not sweet: you **will also be slain by my sword**. Along with many other nations, they would be taken into captivity by Nebuchadnezzar in only a few years (see Jer 46:2, 9; Ezek 30:4-5).

2:13-15 Because **Assyria** took the ten tribes of the northern kingdom into captivity, they also receive a message of destruction. The Lord sends his message directly to the seat of Assyrian power, the city of **Nineveh** (2:13). It had thought to itself, **I exist, and there is no one else** (2:15), but this is God-talk reserved for the Lord alone (see Isa 46:9). When infinite power speaks to finite power, finite power loses the argument.

3:1-7 At this point, Zephaniah returns focus to Jerusalem, the **rebellious . . . defiled . . .** and **oppressive city** (3:1). In spite of God's **discipline**, they haven't repented (3:2). Instead, **princes, prophets,** and **priests**— all the civil and religious leaders—do harm to the people and know **no shame**. But **the righteous LORD** will not tolerate it (3:3-5). Jerusalem's God had judged wicked **nations** before her eyes (3:6), which should have made her take notice and **fear** the Lord. Instead, her people **became more corrupt** (3:7).

3:8 In the end, God will **gather nations** and **pour out [his] indignation on them**, a reminder that a final day of the Lord is coming. The only way to escape his judgment is to trust in him for salvation.

IV. HOPE FOR ISRAEL AND THE NATIONS (3:9-20)

3:9-12 As jaw-dropping as God's judgment is, so much more is his grace. Though he vows to judge Jerusalem and the nations, he also promises to **restore** (3:9). He **will remove . . . arrogant people** and **leave a meek and humble people** (3:11-12).

Satan fell because of pride (see Isa 14:12-15; Ezek 28:17). He wanted the glory that was God's alone. And he's been leading humanity in the same direction ever since. But, we must remember that God "resists the proud and gives grace to the humble" (Jas 4:6; 1 Pet 5:5). There's room for only one deity, and the role is taken.

3:13-20 The **remnant** that places trust in God and his plan of salvation will find safety and security (3:13). They will **sing for joy** and **celebrate** because the Lord **removed** their **punishment** (3:14-15). There is no greater joy than knowing the sins that condemned you have been forgiven!

If you are God's child, not only will *you* rejoice and shout for joy, but *God himself* will **rejoice over you** and **delight in you with singing** (3:17). God doesn't merely save repentant sinners from destruction; he makes them his own. Moreover, **those who were disgraced** will receive **praise** and **fame** (3:19-20). That's an agenda you want to be part of.

May the church of Jesus Christ live before the world as if **the King of Israel . . . is among** us (3:15). Live all of life under God because he **has spoken** (3:20).

HAGGAI

INTRODUCTION

Author

THIS BOOK STATES THAT ITS prophecies came from the Lord to the prophet Haggai (1:1, 3).

Historical Background

After years of rejecting the warnings of prophets, Judah was devastated by King Nebuchadnezzar, and Judah's people were taken into captivity to Babylon for seventy years. After that, God graciously allowed them to return home. At the time Haggai wrote, those who'd returned had been back in the promised land for sixteen years. They'd laid the foundation for a new temple, but no further work had been accomplished.

Message and Purpose

The book of Haggai was written to the Jewish remnant that had returned to their homeland after the Babylonian captivity. Unfortunately, they were suffering from spiritual insensitivity and inertia. God had been put on their back burner, and his kingdom priorities had become secondary to their personal priorities. So though the people were supposed to put God first by rebuilding the temple, they were letting it lay in ruins while they built their own houses. At the same time, however, they wanted God to prioritize them.

One of the kingdom principles seen throughout Scripture is that we must seek God's kingdom and glory above all. God will not allow himself to be in second place in the lives of his people. His message through Haggai was that if the people would put his kingdom agenda before their own agenda, then they would have his help. He wanted them to know what Jesus would tell his disciples many years later: "Seek first the kingdom of God and his righteousness, and all these things will be provided for you" (Matt 6:33).

www.bhpublishinggroup.com/qr/te/37_00

Outline

HAGGAI

I. THE WAKE-UP CALL (1:1-11)

1:1-2 The word of the LORD came through the prophet Haggai to the leaders of God's people (1:1). Prophets were God's alarm clocks in a sense. And, in the same way that our alarm clocks are often not appreciated when they interrupt our rest, biblical prophets were not appreciated when they sounded the divine alarm that a spiritual wake-up was needed. While the people of Haggai's day were saying **the time has not come for the house of the LORD to be rebuilt**, they needed to be shaken out of their lethargy. The Israelites had been back home for sixteen years, and they had not rebuilt the temple that the Babylonians destroyed many years earlier. It was still in ruins.

Keeping that structure in such a state was a significant decision because the temple was where the manifest presence of God was, where the glory of God came, and where God sat in the midst of his people. So, in neglecting to rebuild it, the people were saying that it was not important to have God in their midst. We, unfortunately, are often the same in our attitudes toward God: We are happy to have God *in our vicinity* even though he is not *in our midst*. We like to have God in *general*, but we think we don't need God in *specific*.

A *general* kind of God is omnipotent, omniscient, omnipresent, full of truth, and full of grace, mercy, and peace. But having *specific* God in our midst means we can say of these attributes, "I've experienced it! I know for myself." God *in our vicinity* is good. But God *in our midst* is what leads us to say, "He's been good *to me*! He came through *for me*. He answered *my* prayer."

As Haggai was prophesying in Jerusalem, Zechariah was prophesying, too. He said to the same people, "This is what the LORD of Armies says: Return to me" (Zech 1:3). Haggai's message called for a manifestation of what Zechariah was saying. Not rebuilding the temple was an indicator that they hadn't returned to God. Building it would indicate that they had.

We have indicator lights in our vehicles. When one illuminates, it means something's wrong—something deeper than a mere flashing light. If you ignore the light, the problem will only get worse. A lot of people come to church to address personal indicator lights flashing in their lives, but they often don't want to explore what those lights are indicating—that they need to return to God. They need to repent, to get right with him.

Repentance is turning *from* something and turning *to* something else. It's not enough to stop going the wrong way; you've also got to start going the right way. We put a lot of emphasis on what we want to stop doing, and that's correct. But, we also need to start doing: we need to pursue a relationship with God. The prodigal son, after all, didn't just leave the pigpen; he also returned to his father (see Luke 15:17-21).

1:3-4 Is it a time . . . to live in your paneled houses, while this house lies in ruins? That they had time to repair their own houses says their failure to erect the temple wasn't a time problem; it was a priority problem.

People make time for what they think is important. At three o'clock on Sunday afternoon, for instance, everybody makes time to watch football. For three hours, people will sit and observe a game. Yet, most routinely claim they've no time to read the Bible, pray, meditate, or go to church. People want God in a 9-1-1 situation, but then they don't want him between the invocation and benediction.

We know we are repenting and returning when we put God first. Israel was to give the first of its produce to the Lord (see Deut 26:2). Jesus is to have "first place in everything" (Col 1:18). When we give God priority, we are calling God down into our midst.

1:5-6 Think carefully about your ways: You have planted much but harvested little. One way to know you've not returned to God fully is if you find yourself living an unsatisfied life. To get our attention, God can make sure our hard work does not satisfy. But, if we're following his agenda—seeking first his kingdom (see Matt 6:33)—we can find satisfaction even when we don't have much. That's how Paul could write, "I have learned to be content . . . through him who strengthens me" (Phil 4:11, 13).

1:7-8 God's advice to his people to **go up into the hills, bring down lumber, and build the house; and I will be pleased with it and be glorified** (1:8) is a reminder that we can please him through actions. So, if you want God to make you happy, make him happy first. Don't just think about it and talk about it: do it.

1:9-11 You expected much, but then it amounted to little (1:9) is the Lord's way of saying, you wanted me to give you something, but I blew it away to remind you that **my house still lies in ruins** (1:11). You need to get to work on remedying the problem.

Sometimes, Christians call the negative circumstances in their lives "bad luck," but don't disconnect God from your mess. If there is calamity in your world, it didn't happen because of impersonal forces operating on the universe. God called for it. When you return to God, and invite him to operate in your midst, it won't stress you out when trials come. You'll know this truth firsthand: God "is able to do above and beyond all that we ask or think" (Eph 3:20).

II. THE PEOPLE'S RESPONSE (1:12-15)

1:12-15 Haggai reports the rapid response to his message. The leaders and people accepted it as a message from God, and they **feared the LORD** and began to reorganize their priorities (1:12). And in this response

of obedience, they were becoming what the remnant of God's people should be. Thus, God assured them of his presence to guide and empower them as they obeyed his Word: **I am with you** (1:13).

III. THE SHAKE-UP CALL (2:1-9)

2:1-4 Haggai addressed the people's comparison of the **house** of God they were constructing with Solomon's temple. His series of questions acknowledges their disappointment (2:3). Nevertheless, he called them to **be strong** and to proceed with the work of rebuilding for the Lord, for God would be **with** them (2:4).

2:5 God made a **promise** to Israel when he brought them **out of Egypt** that he would bring them to a place of blessing. And, indeed,

he had. They'd since been removed from that place and returned to it, but in spite of all that had happened, God's **Spirit** was still **among** his people. He'd not forgotten them.

2:6-7 God declares, **Once more, in a little while, I am going to shake the heavens and the earth** (2:6). Shaking refers to God's intentional interruption of the natural order of things. And, in this case, he intended to shake things up to turn things around so that **glory** would come to his **house** (2:7). In chapter 1,

God shook things up so that Israel would put him first. And often once we learn to do that, he'll shake things up "once more" to remind us that we are in an unshakeable kingdom. When Jesus had two fish and five barley loaves to feed thousands of people, the disciples said it was an unresolvable situation. Jesus took the bread and the fish, looked up to heaven, and gave thanks, because Jesus was looking at his unshakable kingdom (see Matt 14:13-21).

God often puts people in uncomfortable situations just before he does something that has never been done before. There is, in fact, a worldwide shake-up taking place now. The tragedy is that while we see the things going on, we don't make a spiritual connection— we don't realize that God is at work to take us to another place.

Before you go to church, you iron your clothes because you want to look nice. You see something crooked and wrinkly and straighten it out. You apply heat and steam to accomplish the desired result. And similarly, God will apply heat to your situation just long enough to straighten your thinking. He wants to look good in you when you represent him.

2:8-9 The people were advancing God's kingdom program, giving God a central place of worship. Thus, the temple they built would be a precursor to the millennial temple that will stand when the Messiah rules the world from Jerusalem. God has inexhaustible resources, including **silver and gold** from the nations (2:8), that he can use to beautify it. The restored temple of the future will have a **greater** glory than Solomon's (2:9) because of the presence of Jesus.

IV. THE LORD'S DECLARATION (2:10-23)

2:10-14 Haggai got the priest to give **a ruling** on a ceremonial matter (2:11) clarifying that defilement is transferable, just like a contagious disease (2:13). Disobedience by God's people, then, renders sacrifices unacceptable (2:14). Obedience is necessary for worship to be accepted.

2:15-19 Haggai reminded the people of the economic disaster that came on them because of their disobedience (2:15-17). Because they'd shifted priorities and obeyed, however, God would turn their curses into blessings.

2:20-23 Haggai addressed **Zerubbabel, governor of Judah**, directly to encourage him (2:21). God would accomplish his kingdom program by bringing judgment on the nations that opposed him (2:22). Zerubbabel was God's appointed leader for the temple rebuilding task and was a prototype of the Messiah as he led the people to do the kingdom work of prioritizing God. Indeed, the true Messiah would come in the Davidic line through Zerubbabel and will ultimately lead the nation from the temple in Jerusalem.

ZECHARIAH

INTRODUCTION

Author

ZECHARIAH, SON OF BERECHIAH and grandson of Iddo (1:1), was a prophet to the Jewish people who returned home from the Babylonian captivity. Apparently, he was also a priest (see Neh 12:12, 16). He and the prophet Haggai prophesied to Zerubbabel and the other leaders, encouraging them as they rebuilt the temple in Jerusalem (Ezra 5:1-2; 6:14), which was completed in 515/516 BC (Ezra 6:14-15). Zechariah dates the start of his prophetic ministry to "the eighth month, in the second year of Darius" (1:1), which was 520 BC.

Historical Background

In 538/539 BC, Cyrus the Persian king issued a decree for the Jewish people to rebuild their temple (Ezra 1:1-4). Though their homeland and capital city had been devastated, they began reconstructing the temple in earnest. But, opposition from surrounding enemies caused the project to come to a halt (Ezra 4:1-5). In 520 BC, during the reign of Cyrus's successor King Darius, Zechariah began his prophetic ministry and called God's discouraged people to continue the task of rebuilding the temple (Zech 1:1; Ezra 4:24—5:1-2).

Message and Purpose

Zechariah's prophetic book is filled with eschatological visions and symbols designed to show that God has a plan to bring about his kingdom through his coming Messiah. Zechariah called God's people to be faithful while God demonstrated his faithfulness to them. The Messiah's rule would come, but until then God's people had to prepare themselves for it. Zechariah teaches that, while God's promises are sure, the implementation of his kingdom program requires our involvement through repentance and obedience.

Zechariah, whose name means "the Lord remembers," called the people to remember God's promises. He also reassured them that God would establish his rule on earth through the union of the roles of king and priest in the Messiah. And he would exercise these roles not only for Israel, but also for the whole world. Thus, although the people had been sent into captivity because of their rebellion, God had not forgotten them and would restore them if they would repent.

Zechariah is also important for its prophetic accuracy, foretelling Jesus's triumphal entry into Jerusalem hundreds of years before it occurred.

VIDEO INTRO

www.bhpublishinggroup.com/qr/te/38_00

Outline

ZECHARIAH

I. THE KINGDOM IS COMING (1:1–8:23)

⮞ A. Kingdom Repentance (1:1-6) ⮜

1:1 To a people crushed and demoralized by years of captivity, oppression, and occupation, **the prophet Zechariah** offered a message of inspiration and encouragement so that his people might continue the reconstruction of God's temple. It had ceased years before due to enemy opposition (see Ezra 4:1-5; 5:1-2; 6:14).

Zechariah dates his ministry to **the second year of Darius**, king of the Persian Empire. All the Jews, of course, knew Darius because the Persian Empire was the world superpower that ruled over Judah.

Zechariah reminds his readers that the true King is in heaven when he says **the word of the LORD came to** him. When you're at the end of your rope, what you need more than anything else is the word of the Lord. With God's word comes God's presence, and with God's presence comes God's power, and with God's power comes God's deliverance.

1:2-3 Zechariah opens by reminding his audience how they got into their mess: **The LORD was extremely angry with** their **ancestors** (1:2). After years of rebellion and idolatry, the Lord had cast his people out of the land and sent them into exile. The destructive situation the people faced was directly related to the actions of their forefathers. They had no control over their ancestors' choices; however, they could respond to the Lord themselves. Thus, God urges them through his prophet: **Return to me . . . and I will return to you**

(1:3). Even today, God calls us to repentance and faith. If we respond to him, we can count on him to show himself mighty on our behalf.

1:4-6 God had commanded their **ancestors** to **turn from** their **evil ways and evil deeds**. In spite of God's incredible patience and continued threats of judgment through his prophets, though, Israel and Judah **did not listen** (1:4). And they paid a severe penalty. So, God asks the people, **Where are your ancestors now?** (1:5). That's an easy one: they were dead. **Didn't my words and my statutes . . . overtake your ancestors?** (1:6). While their ancestors thought they could despise God and get away with it, they'd been proven wrong. As Isaiah says, "People are grass. The grass withers, the flowers fade, but the word of our God remains forever" (Isa 40:7-8). So don't play chicken with God's word. There will be only one winner, and it won't be you.

The people to whom Zechariah was preaching learned what their ancestors had not. Thus, they **repented** of their own personal sins and accepted the circumstances that God had **dealt** them (1:6). The first step to following God's kingdom agenda is kingdom repentance.

⮞ B. Kingdom Visions (1:7–6:15) ⮜

1:7-9 The next time **the word of the LORD came to the prophet Zechariah** three months later, it was to deliver a series of eight visions. In the first vision, he **looked out in the night and saw a man riding on a chestnut horse ... Behind him** were other horses (1:8). In response to Zechariah's inquiry, an **angel** told him he would explain what he was seeing (1:9). The prophet was given a glimpse into the angelic activity transpiring behind the scenes. The hidden spiritual world that affects the visible physical world, therefore, is briefly laid open before our eyes. It's a reminder that when we think nothing is happening, God is always at work.

1:10-11 These riders **are the ones the LORD has sent to patrol the earth** (1:10). Having completed their patrol, **they reported to the angel of the LORD** that all was **calm and quiet** (1:11). The all-knowing God, of course, does not need angels to inform him of the state of the earth. Nevertheless, he has created them to serve him and to help humanity (see Heb 1:7, 13-14), and they must report to him. If angels must give an account of their work to the Lord, how much more will the followers of Jesus Christ have to give an account one day of their service to the King and his kingdom?

1:12-13 The angel asked the Lord **how long** he would **withhold mercy from Jerusalem**, the city with which he had been **angry** for **seventy years** (1:12). The **comforting words** from the Lord no doubt indicate that his anger was complete (1:13). After all, the Lord had promised through the prophet Jeremiah, "When seventy years for Babylon are complete, I ... will confirm my promise concerning you to restore you to this place" (Jer 29:10). The time of exile had come to an end.

1:14-17 That **the LORD** was **extremely jealous for Jerusalem** indicates his intense love for his people (1:14). Though he was **a little angry** with them, **the nations** he'd used to punish them had arrogantly **made the destruction worse** (1:15). So God promised to build his **house** (1:16). With this promise, Zechariah could encourage those in Jerusalem to persevere in their work on the temple, for God would be with them.

That was great news, but there's more here than a quick reading will reveal. According to the CSB, the Lord declares, **I have returned**

to Jerusalem (1:16). But, the original Hebrew from which this is translated can also be rendered as a future verb: "I *will return* to Jerusalem." The Lord's future return to Jerusalem is a reference to the coming of the Messiah to rule on his throne in the millennial kingdom. Zechariah is to proclaim that the cities of Judah **will again overflow with prosperity**, and they will be the recipients of God's **mercy** (1:16-17).

1:18-21 In the second vision, Zechariah saw **four horns** and **four craftsman** (1:18-20). The horns are the nations **that scattered Judah, Israel, and Jerusalem** (1:19). The craftsmen are the nations that would come **to cut off the horns** that attacked **the land** (1:21). God had given a promise regarding the nations of the world and their relationship to his people: "I will bless those who bless you, I will curse anyone who treats you with contempt" (Gen 12:3). These nations experienced the power of God's curse.

2:1-2 In Zechariah's third vision, he saw a man **with a measuring line** whose job was **to measure Jerusalem to determine its width and length**. Such dimensions could be determined by measuring the city's walls. In previous years, Jerusalem had formidable walls to provide defense against enemies. But, the fact that the Jews had been exiled was proof that the walls could be—and had been—breached (see 2 Chr 36:19).

2:3-5 In the future, though, **Jerusalem will be inhabited without walls because of the number of people and livestock in it** (2:4). The city will be bursting with people in the Messiah's coming kingdom. In that day, there will be no need for walls, for Jerusalem will have something indestructible and everlasting for its protection: God himself **will be a wall of fire around it, and ... the glory within it** (2:5).

The idea of a wall of fire protecting God's people is reminiscent of the pillar of fire God used to protect Moses and the children of Israel as they left Egypt (see Exod 14:24). The Egyptian army was a major earthly superpower, but it was nothing before the God of creation. Similarly, the Lord guarantees the safety of his city in the millennium. Though

Jerusalem will be swelling with people, they will have no need to fear because God himself will be their wall of protection.

2:6-9 Next, the Lord exhorts those Jews remaining in Babylon to return to Jerusalem: **Flee from the land of the north.... Escape, you who are living with Daughter Babylon** (2:6-7). Why? Those who'd plundered Judah would be the object of God's wrath: **I am raising my hand against them, and they will become plunder for their own servants** (2:9). God welcomes his people home and promises vengeance on their enemies.

2:10-13 Daughter Zion, shout for joy and be glad, for I am coming to dwell among you (2:10). Jerusalem will be glorified when the Messiah comes to dwell within the city during his millennial kingdom. At that time, Gentiles will join with believing Jews to worship the Messiah: **Many nations will join themselves to the Lord on that day and become** his **people** (2:11). Then, Israel will be **the Holy Land** it was created to be (2:12). All humanity will submit to the Messiah's authority when he returns to earth to rule his kingdom (2:13). Those who saw their nation in a state of destruction heard a promise of a glorious coming kingdom that would provide hope, encouragement, and comfort.

3:1 The fourth vision involved **Joshua**, who served as **high priest** in Jerusalem after the return from exile (see Hag 1:1, 12, 14; 2:2, 4). Zechariah saw Joshua **standing before the angel of the LORD, with Satan standing at his right side to accuse him.**

Satan is the Hebrew word that means "adversary." It is also used as a proper name to refer to the one known in Scripture as "the evil one" (Matt 6:13; 2 Thess 3:3), "the devil," "the ancient serpent," and "the great dragon" (Rev 12:9). Satan was once a righteous angel, but he rebelled against the Lord and fell from grace (see commentary on Isa 14:1-23). As the chief demon, he has set up a rival "kingdom" in opposition to God (Matt 12:26). He is "the god of this age" (2 Cor 4:4), "the ruler of the power of the air" (Eph 2:2), and "the one who deceives the whole world" (Rev 12:9). He tempted Adam and Eve to reject God's word (see Gen 3:1-5) and still tempts us today. He

seeks to hinder the work of God's kingdom in the world (see Mark 4:15; 1 Thess 2:18).

One of the chief ways Satan opposes God's kingdom is by acting as "the accuser of our brothers and sisters" whom he "accuses . . . before our God day and night" (Rev 12:10). We see Satan's accusing work in the life of Job (Job 1:9-11; 2:4-5), and we see it here in Zechariah.

3:2-7 But, when Satan stood by Joshua to accuse him, the Lord came to Joshua's defense with a **rebuke** for **Satan** (3:2). Joshua's **filthy clothes** represented his sins before God (3:3), but **the angel of the LORD** removed the high priest's **iniquity** and clothed him **with festive robes** and a **clean turban** (3:4-5)—that is, he took away his sin. With this cleansing work of God accomplished, he charged Joshua to **walk** in his **ways, keep** his **mandates**, and **rule** his **house** (that is, the temple) (3:7).

Though Satan is "a liar and the father of lies" (John 8:44), sometimes—when he points out our sin—his accusations are correct. Enter the redeeming work of Jesus Christ on the cross to forgive believers and set them free from slavery to sin. In spite of Satan's continual accusations, Christians have "conquered him by the blood of the Lamb" (Rev 12:10-11). And, in light of the cleansing power of Christ's blood, we can accomplish the kingdom tasks that God puts before us. In order for him to **grant you access** to his kingdom power and restore you to your kingdom position and purpose, he calls you to repent and walk in his ways and keep his mandates (3:7). This is the appropriate response to God's grace (see Luke 22:31-32; cf. John 21:15-17).

3:8 The cleansing of the **High Priest Joshua** and his fellow priests was **a sign** that God was **about to bring** his **servant, the Branch** (see also 6:2). The careful reader of the Old Testament knows that this is a messianic reference. God had promised David that a dynasty of kings would descend from him, leading to a King who would have an eternal throne and kingdom (see 2 Sam 7:11-16; 1 Chr 17:10-14). But, most of the Davidic kings rebelled against the Lord; therefore, they experienced God's judgment when Judah was carried into exile by Babylon.

Nevertheless, God promised, "A shoot will grow from the stump of Jesse [David's father], and a branch from his roots will bear fruit" (Isa 11:1). Though the Davidic dynasty had experienced the ax of God's judgment, the stump and its roots were still there, and a branch would grow—"the Branch of the LORD" (Isa 4:2), the Messiah.

3:9-10 According to Zechariah, the fact that the priests had returned from exile and were serving before the Lord again was a physical sign that the Branch, the messianic King, would come. When he establishes his kingdom on earth, he **will take away the iniquity** of Israel and grant it peace and prosperity.

4:1-5 The fifth vision was of a **gold lampstand with a bowl at the top**. It had **seven lamps**, each having **seven spouts** (4:2). Clearly, this lampstand could hold a tremendous amount of oil; it had a total of forty-nine lit wicks. That's one amazingly bright lampstand! On either side of it were **two olive trees** (4:3), but the prophet was at a loss to understand the significance of any of it (4:4-5).

4:6-7 The angel interpreted the vision for Zechariah by giving him a **word of the LORD** for **Zerubbabel**, the governor of Judah and descendant of David who was overseeing the rebuilding of the temple (see 1 Chr 3:17-19; Ezra 3:2, 8; Hag 1:1): **Not by strength or by might, but by my Spirit** (4:6). The Jews in Jerusalem had faced much opposition and discouragement (see Ezra 4:1-23); therefore, if Zerubbabel were to complete the temple, it would not be the result of mere human strength but through the supernatural empowering of the Holy Spirit. Thus, the abundant oil supplying the brilliant lampstand represented the overflowing power of God's Spirit.

4:8-10 Given the divine enablement of his Spirit, the Lord promised that just as **Zerubbabel's hands** had **laid the foundation** of the temple, so **his hands** would **complete it** (4:9). The angel assured Zechariah that the **seven eyes of the LORD, which scan throughout the whole earth, will rejoice when they see the ceremonial stone in Zerubbabel's hands** (4:10). The Lord had not

providentially brought the Jews back from exile simply to see them fail. He would ensure that the work would be accomplished. With that knowledge, Zechariah could confidently encourage Zerubbabel and the Jews to continue the task God had given them (see Ezra 4:24–5:2).

As you seek to engage in God's kingdom work in the world, you, too, should have the words of God to Zechariah ringing in your ears: "Not by strength or by might, but by my Spirit" (4:6). Human effort will only get you so far. The empowerment to do the work of God comes only through the Spirit of God.

4:11-14 When Zechariah asked about **the two olive trees** from the vision, the angel informed him that these were **the two anointed ones . . . who stand by the LORD of the whole earth** (4:11, 14). Who are they? Kings and priests were anointed in the Old Testament (see Lev 8:10-12; 1 Sam 16:13); therefore, in the days of Zechariah, the anointed ones would be Joshua, the high priest, and Zerubbabel, the (Davidic) governor (because Jerusalem was ruled by Persia and could not have its own king). The lampstand empowered by the Holy Spirit, then, would represent Israel itself.

However, the angel also seems to be pointing Zechariah to a yet future time. For these two anointed ones "stand by the LORD of the whole earth" (4:14). In the messianic kingdom, Israel will rebuild the millennial temple (see Ezek 40–48). Then, they will fulfill their role as a light to the nations as the Messiah (who is both King and priest) rules all on behalf of the Lord of the earth.

5:1-4 Zechariah's sixth vision was of **a flying scroll . . . thirty feet long and fifteen feet wide** (5:1-2). The scroll **is the curse that is going out over the whole land** (5:3). It represents the judgment of God's Word symbolically covering Israel. It will **enter the house of the thief and the house of the one who swears falsely. . . . It will stay inside his house and destroy it** (5:4). In others words, the Lord's judgment is all-encompassing and does not allow for any to escape. He *will* deal once and for all with the sinful transgression of his law when the Messiah comes and establishes his kingdom.

5:5-11 Zechariah then saw a seventh vision: **a measuring basket** with **a lead cover**, which represented Israel's **iniquity**. Inside it was a **woman** called **Wickedness** (5:5-8). Two other women with wings were carrying the basket **to build a shrine for it in the land of Shinar** to **be placed there on its pedestal.** When God's judgment comes on the sins of Israel (5:11), then, the nation's wickedness will be removed to the place of destruction: "Shinar"—that is, Babylon (see Gen 11:2; Rev 18:2, 21). In the coming kingdom ruled by the Messiah, there will be no room for wickedness.

6:1-8 The eighth vision of Zechariah involved **four chariots coming from between two mountains . . . made of bronze** (6:1). Mountains carry the idea of strength and power (see Isa 2:2; Dan 2:35); thus, these bronze mountains may represent heaven, because the chariots were **the four spirits of heaven going out after presenting themselves to the Lord of the whole earth** (6:5). Some went to **the north** and some to **the south** so that they might **patrol** as God commanded (6:6-7).

These spirits patrol the earth, keeping watch on the Lord's behalf for anything that opposes the King's agenda. To know that the God of heaven is always watching over his creation is a comfort to the people of God throughout the ages.

6:9-15 Having shown Zechariah some previews of the coming kingdom, the Lord then showed him a preview of a preview. This **word of the Lord** was like a taste of frosting just before it's placed on the cake (6:9). God commanded him to **take an offering from the exiles** (6:10). With this **silver and gold**, they were to **make a crown** to be placed on **Joshua . . . the high priest** (6:11). Then, Joshua was to be called by the **name** of **Branch** because he would **branch out from his place and build the Lord's temple** (6:12). Not only that, but he would also **sit on his throne and rule** (6:13).

The making of the crown symbolizes the unification of the office of priest and king. Joshua prefigured this, but it would ultimately be fulfilled in the Messiah, who will rebuild the temple and rule over his kingdom in the millennium. He will be **a priest on his** **throne** (6:13). **The crown** being **in the Lord's temple** was a reminder of their future Messiah and their obligation to **fully obey the Lord** (6:14-15). When the Messiah comes in his kingdom, Gentiles will join in and contribute to the building of the **temple** (6:15).

⇨ C. Kingdom Fast (7:1–8:23) ⇦

7:1-3 The next **word of the Lord** that Zechariah received came **in the fourth year of King Darius** (7:1) or about two years after the eight visions (1:7). This prophecy came in response to **the people of Bethel** inquiring of **the priests** about whether they should continue to **mourn and fast** at an appointed time as they had done in the past (7:2-3). Apparently, now that they were back in the land and the temple was nearly built, they wanted to know whether this mourning and fasting was still necessary.

7:4-6 God's answer makes it clear that they had not asked an innocent question: **When you fasted and lamented . . . for these seventy years, did you really fast for me?** (7:5). God knew their hearts and saw that they had gone through the rituals, but not out of love and reverence for him. **When you eat and drink** (for the annual feasts and festivals), **don't you eat and drink simply for yourselves?** (7:6). Rather than rejoicing in God's deeds and provisions at such time, they had been merely eating and drinking.

7:7 Aren't these the words that the Lord proclaimed through the earlier prophets when Jerusalem was inhabited and secure? This third question suggests the people's actions were nothing new. In fact, they were repeating some of the same sins for which the prophets had chastised the people before the exile! As Isaiah said prior to that event and as Jesus would say many years later, "This people honors me with their lips, but their heart is far from me" (Matt 15:8, quoting from Isa 29:13).

7:8-9 The people were walking on thin ice. If they weren't careful, they'd repeat the failures of their ancestors. God had given the prior generations of Israelites several benchmarks for their behavior, including the admonition to **show faithful love and compassion to one another** (7:9). Biblical love isn't a sentimental feeling. To love your neighbor is to righteously desire his good and to meet his needs in a way that glorifies God.

7:10 Do not oppress the widow or the fatherless, the resident alien or the poor brings to my mind James's teaching to the Christians to whom he was writing: "Pure and undefiled religion before God the Father is this: to look after orphans and widows in their distress and to keep oneself unstained from the world" (Jas 1:27). God champions the cause of the weak and oppressed. He expects the same of his people, if they expect to be in fellowship with him.

Do not plot evil in your hearts against one another. You can't plot evil in your heart against others if you're focused on showing "love and compassion to one another" as expected (7:9). Physical evil (whether through words or actions) starts in the heart and mind. The external and visible is driven by the internal and spiritual. Life transformation comes through "the renewing of your mind" (Rom 12:2).

7:11-14 Unfortunately, the previous generations had **refused to pay attention** to God. **They closed their ears** and **made their hearts like a rock** so that they wouldn't listen to God's **prophets** (7:11-12). In other words, they had not been merely passive but had actively opposed God's law. Nevertheless, you can't mock God and expect no consequences. And the consequences for Israel and Judah had been disastrous. Because of his **intense anger**, God **scattered them . . . over all the nations . . . and the land was left desolate behind them** (7:12-14).

To prevent the generation of Zechariah's day from repeating the problems of the previous generations, a history lesson was in order. Actions have consequences. Those who had returned from exile needed to know that. And so do you. The only way to remedy the violation of kingdom principles is to put in place kingdom practices.

8:1-3 At the close of their history lesson in chapter 7, God reminded the Judeans that the land was desolate because of the actions of their ancestors. But, that didn't mean that God's love for his people and their land had failed: **I am extremely jealous for Zion; I am jealous for her with great wrath** (8:2). In fact, God's love for Zion is so great that he made a promise: **I will return to Zion and live in Jerusalem. Then Jerusalem will be called the Faithful City; the mountain of the Lord of Armies will be called the Holy Mountain** (8:3).

The Jerusalem that existed prior to the captivity cannot compare with the Jerusalem of the future; they are as different as day and night. Zechariah's vision of the coming messianic kingdom when Jesus Christ will dwell in the midst of the city is a beautiful reminder that through his righteous reign and protective care, Jerusalem will be a place of faithfulness and security.

8:4-8 A people whose city had been destroyed and who had been oppressed and killed by their enemies will one day see a complete reversal of circumstances for Jerusalem. **Old men and women will again sit along the streets**, which **will be filled with boys and girls playing** (8:4-5). The Jews will return and once again **live in** their land (8:7-8). Those to whom Zechariah was preaching may have thought all this **impossible** (8:6), but "With God all things are possible" (Matt 19:26).

8:9-15 With Israel's punishment behind them, God exhorts the people through Zechariah to **let** their **hands be strong** so that they can finish the work of rebuilding (8:9, 13). Just as he had **resolved** to bring retribution on their ancestors, so now he had **resolved . . . to do what is good to Jerusalem** (8:14-15).

8:16-17 In view of this, their hearts should have been inspired and ready to continue the work on the temple. Nevertheless, that didn't mean they could cast aside God's kingdom principles. If they wanted the blessings that their ancestors had lost, they **must do** the kingdom agenda that their ancestors had rejected: **Speak truth to one another; make true and sound decisions within**

your city gates. Do not plot evil in your hearts against your neighbor, and do not love perjury.

8:18-19 After highlighting the motives of the people of Bethel, explaining his expectations, rehearsing the history of Israel's failure, and declaring the promises of the messianic kingdom (7:4–8:17), the Lord finally answers the question initially raised by them in 7:3. The appointed fasts **will become times of joy, gladness, and cheerful festivals for the house of Judah** (8:19).

Times of fasting honor the Lord and bring joy when they are set in the context of a relationship with him. Moreover, fasting must not be divorced from a life that loves **truth**

and peace (8:19). To fulfill religious duties while ignoring kingdom principles is to embrace empty ritual rather than kingdom relationship.

8:20-23 At this point, Zechariah returns to a vision of the millennial kingdom. In that day, peoples from all over the world will go to **Jerusalem** to **seek the LORD** due to their supernatural transformation as a result of their acceptance of the Messiah (8:20-22).

In that day, God's favor to his people will be so great that individuals **from nations of every language will grab the robe of a Jewish man tightly, urging: Let us go with you, for we have heard that God is with you** (8:23).

II. THE KING IS COMING (9:1–14:21)

In this section, Zechariah's good news of the coming kingdom is expanded to include the good news of the coming King. A future King will destroy Judah's enemies, protect the nation, and bring peace and prosperity. His glorious kingdom will have a champion who will make the house of Judah the preeminent empire on the planet. Zechariah reveals the agenda of the King.

✥ A. Judgment on Enemies and the Coming of the Shepherd (9:1–11:17) ✥

9:1-4 Israel and Judah had many enemies throughout their history. In every direction—north, south, east, and west—there were nations wishing for their demise. The prophetic promise of Zechariah is that there will come a time when the enemies of God's people will be permanently removed. That news would've captured the hearts and minds of the former exiles.

Zechariah mentions several cities and nation states that would be punished because of their mistreatment of Judah. And their judgment was certain because who can come to your defense if **the word of the LORD is against** you? This was the case for **Hadrach**

and **Damascus** (in modern Syria); they were longtime enemies of Israel (9:1). The list of names also includes **Hamath . . . Tyre and Sidon** (9:2-3). They would end up being **consumed by fire** (9:4).

9:5-8 Ashkelon . . . Gaza . . . Ekron were cities **of the Philistines**—arch enemies of God's people from before the time of King David (9:5-6). Soon, their atrocities would be repaid. Nevertheless, in spite of his judgment on the Philistines, God promised that **they, too**, would **become a remnant for our God** (9:7). There will one day be "a vast multitude from every nation, tribe, people, and language" worshipping the Lamb (Rev 7:9)— even from among those who were some of the greatest enemies of his people.

9:9 Then Zechariah exhorts **Jerusalem** to **rejoice** and **shout in triumph** because their **King is coming**. Of course, in Zechariah's day, Jerusalem had no king but was ruled over by foreign powers. But, Zechariah was looking to the future. On that day, the **righteous and victorious** Messiah would enter Jerusalem, **humble and riding on a donkey, on a colt, the foal of a donkey**.

This was fulfilled in part when Jesus rode into Jerusalem on a donkey days before he was crucified as an atoning substitute for sinners and rose from the dead (see Matt 21:1-11). When he returns, he will again enter Jerusalem—this time as a triumphant King establishing his kingdom.

9:10 The dominion of the King will cover the entire earth; it will **extend from sea to sea, from the Euphrates River to the ends of the earth**. The entire planet will submit to the reign of God's Messiah!

9:11-17 According to Isaiah, Jerusalem had received "double for all her sins" (Isa 40:2). But, in the days to come, God declares, **I will restore double to you** (9:12). They will conquer their enemies with the Lord providing defense (9:13-15). In the last days, in fact, God will deliver Israel and cause his people to sparkle **like jewels in a crown** (9:16). How does Zechariah respond to this glorious prophecy? He exclaims, **How lovely and beautiful!** (9:17).

10:1-7 Not only would the Lord judge the external enemies of his people (9:1-8), but he would also judge the enemies among them. They **wander like sheep . . . because there is no shepherd** (10:2)—that is, their leaders had failed to follow God and care for his people. Therefore, the Lord declares, **My anger burns against the shepherds** (10:3). In the last days, God will **strengthen . . . deliver . . .** and **restore** Judah. His **compassion** will be so great that it will be **as though** he **never rejected them** (10:6).

10:8-12 In the last days, God will draw Israel together. He will **whistle and gather them** from **the distant lands** (10:8-9). Any who oppose them will be brought **to an end** (10:11). But Israel will be strengthened by God (10:12). The Messiah will reunite and restore his people under his kingdom rule, and they will walk in his ways.

11:1-11 Next, Zechariah moves past the overtones of the greatness of the kingdom under the King to the pronouncement of judgment on Israel because their leaders would reject the King and his teachings. The shepherds cared only about profiting from the sheep. They had **no compassion for** the people (11:5). In view of that the Lord says, **I will no longer have compassion on the inhabitants of the land** (11:6).

The Lord called Zechariah to stand in for the good **shepherd** (11:4), so the prophet shepherded the flock with his **two staffs** named **Favor** and **Union** (11:7). Zechariah foresaw a time when the leadership would not respond to the Lord as they should and would go their own way just as their forefathers had done. That the leaders, **three shepherds** (probably representative of prophets, priests, and kings), **detested** the good shepherd (11:7-8) most likely refers prophetically to the rejection of the Messiah at his first coming. Thus, the prophet declares, **I will no longer shepherd you** (11:9). This might refer to the "partial hardening" that would come upon Israel for spurning her Messiah (Rom 11:25).

11:12-14 When the good shepherd, Zechariah in this case, asked for his wages, Israel **valued** him at **thirty pieces of silver**—the price of a slave (11:12-13; see Exod 21:32). So, as instructed by God, he **threw** the silver pieces **into the house of the LORD, to the potter**, demonstrating how insulting this cheap amount was (11:13). This rejection would lead to internal strife and division in Israel (11:14).

This prophecy would be fulfilled when the true good shepherd came. Judas Iscariot, one of Jesus's twelve disciples, agreed to betray him to the chief priests for "thirty pieces of silver" (Matt 26:14-16). When Judas felt remorse after this, he returned the money and hanged himself (Matt 27:1-5). The chief priests took the returned money and "bought the potter's field with it" (Matt 27:6-7).

11:15-17 After representing the "good shepherd" (11:4-14), Zechariah was called by God to represent **a foolish shepherd** (11:15). This so-called shepherd would be ruthless. He wouldn't **care for** the **perishing** or **seek the lost**. Instead, **he** would **devour the . . . sheep** (11:16). The **worthless shepherd** in view is likely the Antichrist (11:17). Everything he'll do is the opposite of what the good shepherd would (see John 10:11-16). In the end, the foolish shepherd will be vanquished (11:17).

⇝ B. The Messiah and His Kingdom
(12:1–14:21) ⇜

12:1 Zechariah prefaces this next **word of the LORD** by describing him as the one **who stretched out the heavens, laid the foundation of the earth, and formed the spirit of man**. In other words, the Creator of the universe is powerful enough to accomplish all of his will. If he declares something, it's as good as done.

12:2-9 In the final days, **Jerusalem** will be surrounded by their enemies. But, the Lord will make them **a cup that causes staggering for the peoples who surround** them (12:2). The image of a cup brings to mind other prophetic passages describing the "cup" of the wrath of God (see, e.g., Isa 51:17; Jer 25:15-16). Those who attempt to attack the Messiah's capital city, then, will experience God's fury. God will make his people **a flaming torch** that **will consume all the peoples around them** (12:6). He will deliver Israel from her enemies and **defend the inhabitants of Jerusalem**. The **weakest** of Jerusalem's inhabitants **will be like David**, the warrior king (12:8).

12:10-14 Not only will it be a time of deliverance for Jerusalem but also a time of repentance. God **will pour out a spirit of grace and prayer on** them. Then they will look on the one **whom they pierced**—Jesus Christ—and they will recognize their Messiah (12:10). There will be great weeping and mourning throughout the land, as individual and corporate repentance takes place (12:10-14).

13:1-6 On that day a **fountain will be opened for the house of David and for the residents of Jerusalem, to wash away sin and impurity** (13:1). After their repentance, God will cleanse the nation from its sinfulness, and the land will be purged from its evil and idolatry (13:2). False **prophets** will be removed from the land; they will no longer be able to fake being something they are not (13:2-6). False sheep will not be able to find any covering or hiding place in the kingdom.

13:7 Then, Zechariah returns to the Messiah's first coming, speaking a prophecy from the Lord that announces the Messiah's rejection and death: **Sword, awake against my shepherd ... Strike the shepherd, and the sheep will be scattered**. The Jews did, indeed, reject the shepherd when he came to them. In fact, on the night he was betrayed, during his final meal with his disciples, Jesus quoted from this passage and told them, "Tonight all of you will fall away because of me" (Matt 26:31).

13:8-9 This leads to the dispersion of Israel and, eventually, to the future tribulation that will result in Israel's persecution and ultimate purification when they call on the name of the Lord in repentance and faith: **They will call on my name, and I will answer them. I will say: They are my people, and they will say: The LORD is our God** (13:9). Then, God's people will experience his kingdom promises.

14:1-5 Zechariah 14:1 refers to the day of the Lord, a time of divine judgment and restoration. It will be a time of judgment for God's enemies and deliverance for his followers—judgment in the tribulation and restoration in the millennial kingdom. **Nations will gather ... against** Israel for her destruction (14:2), but God will use this gathering as the occasion to **fight** for them and rescue them (14:3). The Messiah will come to **the Mount of Olives** to judge the nations, and the mountain will **split** and provide a way of escape for those trapped in Jerusalem (14:4-5).

14:6-19 God will transform the entire environment and topography of Jerusalem (14:6-8, 10-11). **King** Jesus will reign **over the whole earth** from that place (14:9). Those who **warred against Jerusalem** and the Messiah will suffer a plague of judgment (14:12), but **all the survivors from the nations** will come to Jerusalem **to worship the King** who will reign in prominence and dominance (14:16). They will celebrate **the Festival of Shelters**, and if any nation refuses to celebrate, God will withhold **rain** from them (14:16-19). Though there will be some rebellion in the messianic kingdom before the eternal state is ushered in, the general nature of the kingdom will involve the exultation of the Lord. Any open rebellion against the Messiah will be quickly crushed, because he will be ruling with an iron rod.

14:20-21 In that day, everything will be sacred, and the whole earth will be permeated by the holiness of the Lord. This knowledge of God's glorious future for his people should motivate believers of every age to endure and obey. Let us joyfully worship the one who will bring history to its divinely ordained conclusion.

MALACHI

INTRODUCTION

Author

WE KNOW NOTHING ABOUT the author of the book bearing his name other than that Malachi means "my messenger." Because God is the one speaking in the vast majority of the verses, it's clear that the book's emphasis is on the message rather than the messenger.

Historical Background

There's nothing in the book to allow us to date it with certainty, but certain bits of evidence favor a date after the Babylonian exile. The mention of a governor in 1:8 points to the Persian period when Judah was a province or sub-province of the Persian Empire. In 515 BC, the Jerusalem temple had been rebuilt and worship reestablished (1:6-11; 2:1-3; 3:1, 10). But, the enthusiasm inspired by the ministries of Haggai and Zechariah had waned. The social and religious problems that Malachi addresses reflect the situation portrayed in Ezra 9 and 10 and Nehemiah 5 and 13. This suggests a date not long before Ezra's return to Judah (ca. 460 BC) or Nehemiah's second term as governor of Judah (Neh 13:6-7; ca. 435 BC).

Message and Purpose

Malachi is the in-your-face prophet who has one simple message: Take God seriously. The priests of his day were playing religious games, going through religious motions, and leading God's people to worship casually. Malachi was called to confront God's people with who he really is. When you understand who God is and how much he loves his people, you don't treat him carelessly.

God was insulted by the sloppy worship of Malachi's time: people were bringing him animals for sacrifice that they wouldn't serve to their human leaders. They didn't esteem God as the great King that he is. Moreover, they were divorcing without cause because they didn't take God's covenant of marriage seriously, and they were robbing him of the tithes due to him. God's people were acknowledging his name without engaging his person.

As a result, things were falling apart. Locusts were destroying the agriculture. Yet, through it all, the people acted as if they'd done nothing wrong. The book of Malachi is a call to all of us that, while God is a loving Father, he is not to be taken lightly. His kingdom demands our total allegiance.

VIDEO | INTRO

www.bhpublishinggroup.com/qr/te/39_00

Outline

MALACHI

I. INTRODUCTION (1:1)

1:1 The word of the LORD came to Israel through Malachi, whose name means "my messenger." The theme of Malachi's message is simple: take God seriously.

II. TAKING GOD'S LOVE SERIOUSLY (1:2-5)

1:2-3 The Lord's message through Malachi begins with **I have loved you** (1:2). Now that's good news. But, things go downhill from there. To it, the people respond, **How have you loved us?** (1:2). In other words, "We hear what you're saying, God, but we're not seeing what you're talking about." In light of their day-to-day experiences, it didn't look like God loved them. So, to their question God replies by reminding them of Isaac's sons, Esau and Jacob: **I loved Jacob, but I hated Esau**. These two brothers gave birth to two nations (see Gen 25:23), Israel descending from Jacob and Edom descending from Esau.

In the Bible, this love/hate contrast has to do with *selection*—choosing something. For instance, Jesus tells his followers they cannot be his disciples unless they "hate" their own parents (Luke 14:26). Jesus isn't contradicting the Ten Commandments with that statement (see Exod 20:12). Rather, he's saying that if you have to choose between your family on the one hand and God on the other, you should choose God. Likewise,

Christians must choose Christ over any competing claims. God chose Jacob—that is, Israel—to establish a covenantal relationship with him and receive his blessings. He selected them for a purpose: to be a light to the nations.

1:4-5 Esau was rejected because he rejected his birthright (see Gen 25:27-34). Similarly, the wickedness and violence of the nation of Edom was well-known (e.g., 2 Chr 20:1-2; Joel 3:19; Obad 1-4). The Lord's response was to make Edom "a wasteland" (Mal 1:3). Though the wicked Edomites vowed to **rebuild**, the Lord would **demolish** them, knocking them back down should they try to get up.

And how does God love Israel? Though they (like Edom) sinned and rebelled against him, God still had mercy on them. Though he **cursed** Edom (1:4), the Lord continued to pursue, love, and forgive Israel. Though he sent his people into exile, he brought them back. Israel, though, had forgotten the Lord's love and mercy.

III. TAKING WORSHIP SERIOUSLY (1:6-14)

1:6 God continues his case against Israel: **A son honors his father, and a servant his master**. So, the Lord asks, **Where is my honor? . . . Where is your fear of me?** To fear the Lord is to honor him, to take him seriously. Instead, his **priests** despised his name—that is, his character and position. They thought little of him.

1:7-9 How had they done this? After all, they'd been regularly coming to worship and bringing their sacrifices. But, they'd been **presenting defiled food on [his] altar** (1:7). Their chosen sacrifices were blind, lame, and sick animals (1:8). Instead of giving God their best, they gave him their junk, their leftovers. If the President of the United States were coming over for dinner, you wouldn't dream of serving him leftovers! And, as if to make the same point, God says that the Israelites wouldn't present such gifts to their **governor** (1:8). In spite of being quick to give God so little, the people still expected his blessings (1:9).

Do you want a first-class God while offering second-class worship? Do you give him your leftover time, talents, and treasures after you have little or nothing left? Are you unwilling to be inconvenienced by involvement in the church? Do you avoid sacrificing for fellow believers? You don't have to say you despise the Lord: to convey the same point, all you have to do is give him your leftovers while also asking for his blessings.

1:10-11 There's nothing impressive about dunking a basketball after you've lowered the rim from ten feet to six, yet Israel had lowered the standard of worship—and they were excited about dunking the worship ball. But God wasn't impressed: **I am not pleased with you . . . and I will accept no offering from your hands** (1:10). He is no ordinary king; he is in a class by himself: **My name will be great among the nations** (1:11).

1:12-14 The Israelites said **the LORD's table is defiled** and called it a **nuisance** (1:12). Sacrificing those lambs and spilling their blood was a messy, smelly business. It made them weary. But, they had forgotten that the sacrificial system was God's gracious means of dealing with their sin so he could give them the provisions of his covenant. They were despising that which was the source of their life and blessing!

Paul dealt with a similar defiling of the Lord's table when some of the Corinthians took Communion in an unworthy way and died (see 1 Cor 11:20-22, 27-31). So, how do you approach the Lord's Supper? Do you consider it a boring ritual? Remember, it's not a matter of merely eating and drinking. Through worshipfully participating in it, you're actually preaching a sermon: "You proclaim the Lord's death until he comes" (1 Cor 11:26).

On Sunday afternoon, many people will devote themselves to watching a one-hour spectacle that will last at least three hours. But no one will ask for early dismissal. They have decided that a football game warrants their prolonged and undivided attention. How much more is the unique God of the universe worthy of your undivided attention and devotion? He is **a great King**, and his **name will be feared among the nations** (1:14). Don't give him your leftovers. Give him your best so you can experience his favor.

IV. TAKING COVENANTS SERIOUSLY (2:1-9)

The first half of Malachi 2 is dominated by the word *covenant*. Few biblical words are more significant. The National Football League is approximately a nine-billion-dollar a year business. That's a lot of people, jobs, media, and logistics linked to a pigskin, the centerpiece of the game. Without the football, in fact, there is no game. And, without the game, the entire system is irrelevant and collapses. *Covenant* is a word often neglected and misunderstood, but it, too, is a centerpiece. Your relationship to God's covenant will govern everything else in your life.

2:1-9 God established many covenants in the Bible, such as the covenant with Noah (Gen 9:1-17), the covenant with Abraham (Gen 12:1-3; 15:1-21), the covenant with Moses (Exod 19-34), the covenant with David (2 Sam 7), and the new covenant through Christ (Luke 22:20; Heb 8). In Malachi 2, God speaks of his **covenant with Levi** (2:4)—that is, the covenant made with the descendants of Levi who were to perform priestly duties and to care for the tabernacle/temple under the umbrella of the Mosaic covenant that governed the sacrificial system.

A covenant is no mere contract. It's a spiritually binding, relational agreement between God and his people. Covenants are the means by which God administers and governs his kingdom. A divine covenant provides covering. It's like a divine umbrella. There is protection and provision under it. Through covenants, God works out his kingdom agenda for the benefit of his people. The covenant of Levi **was one of life and peace** (2:5).

But, though covenants were intended to bring blessing, they also included sanctions if the responsibilities and guidelines of the covenant were not followed. Malachi delivers a warning from the Lord to the **priests** who were failing to **honor [his] name** (2:1-2). He declares, **I will send a curse among you** because they did not take **it to heart** (2:2). They ought to have **revered** the Lord, walked with him in **peace** and fairness, **turned many from** sin, and instructed the people (2:5-7). Instead, they had **turned from the way** and **caused many to stumble by [their] instruction**. Put simply, they had **violated the covenant of Levi** (2:8). In response, the Lord **despised and humiliated** them (2:9). The flow of covenantal blessings was hindered, and the hammer of covenantal sanctions was falling.

Under the new covenant, we have a better and eternal high priest. The author of Hebrews tells us our mediator, Jesus Christ, can save those who come to God through him (see Heb 7:25). He's not talking here about initial conversion; he's writing to those who are already Christians. He's using the word "save" to speak of deliverance in history. The Levitical priests failed, but the high priest of the new covenant can bring God's promises to you. God has already blessed those who trust in Christ with every spiritual blessing (Eph 1:3). Your relationship to this mediator grants you access to these benefits.

V. TAKING MARRIAGE SERIOUSLY (2:10-16)

We're living in a day when divorce has lost its stigma. It is recognized as acceptable and often unavoidable—even among many Christians. As a result, couples often hedge their bets with prenuptial agreements or simply live together instead of marrying. In addition, some Christians fail to see the spiritual dimension of marriage and, as a result, marry unbelievers. Given our modern cultural context, we need to know God's view on marriage, and Malachi gives it to us without holding back.

2:10-13 Even though they have **one Father** and **one God**, the Israelites **act treacherously**

against one another, profaning the covenant (2:10). Judah has even profaned the Lord's sanctuary. How? By marrying the daughter of a foreign god (2:11). In other words, Jewish men were marrying non-Jewish women who worshiped pagan deities and brought their foreign gods into the Lord's sanctuary. As a result, the Lord threatened to cut off from the tents of Jacob any man who did so (2:12). Moreover, though they covered his altar with tears, with weeping and groaning, he did not respect their offerings or receive them (2:13). Because they disregarded the marriage covenant, God wasn't answering their prayers (see 1 Pet 3:7).

Paul tells Christians not to be mismatched with unbelievers (see 2 Cor 6:14-16), which would certainly apply to marriage. Marriage is a spiritual and covenantal matter. When a Christian marries a non-Christian, there will be a clash of gods and covenants. Malachi and Paul agree: don't partner with someone who doesn't share your faith because you're going in two different directions.

2:14 The people were in shock, wondering **why** God would not receive their offerings and hear their prayers. Because, the Lord tells the husbands, **you have acted treacherously against** your wife, though **she was your marriage partner . . . by covenant.** There's that word again: *covenant.* Marriage between a man and a woman is a covenant before God. It's not merely a social institution; it's a spiritual issue.

2:15 What does the Lord seek through the marriage covenant? Too many people think the purpose of marriage is happiness. But happiness is a *benefit* of marriage, not its *purpose.* The purpose of God's covenants is always the expansion of his kingdom in history. Through marriage, in particular, God seeks **godly offspring.** That means that having a child isn't about gaining a "mini-me." God wants us to have and raise children in the knowledge of the Lord so that his image is spread worldwide for his glory.

2:16 Not only were the men marrying daughters of foreign gods, but they were divorcing their wives to do it. The CSB reads, **If he hates and divorces his wife . . . he covers his garment with injustice.** Other translations think the Hebrew is better translated as God declaring, "I hate divorce." Whichever is correct, it's clear that divorce is not to be a norm. God permits divorce in certain cases (see Matt 19:9; 1 Cor 7:15), but it's not what he intended from the beginning (see Matt 19:8). Moreover, it's clear that the men Malachi is confronting were divorcing for *illegitimate* reasons and, therefore, committing injustice. So, call it what you like, but getting a "no-fault" divorce and separating for "irreconcilable differences" is not a covenantal option. In God's eyes, it's a treacherous act with spiritual consequences.

VI. TAKING GOD'S JUSTICE SERIOUSLY (2:17–3:6)

2:17 The Lord continues, telling the people they have **wearied him.** How? They complained that he was unfair: **Everyone who does what is evil is good in the LORD's sight, and he is pleased with them.** In their eyes, God was blessing the sinners and afflicting the saints. Thus, they asked, **Where is the God of justice?** Because unbelievers prospered while God's people struggled, they protested: God is unjust.

If we are honest, most of us have thought something similar from time to time. In this particular case, God turns the tables on his accusers. As the entire book of Malachi shows, the people were participating in religious exercises while neglecting a genuine relationship with the Lord. They wanted the covering of the covenant—the blessings—without being properly "aligned" under God. How fair is that?

3:1 God declares, **I am going to send my messenger, and he will clear the way before me. Then the LORD you seek will suddenly come to his temple.** This text is quoted in Mark 1:2 and applied to John the Baptist, who prepared the way for Jesus and called people to repent. A clear path must be made by cutting down the mountains of human pride to make a humble plain for God's glory to land on.

3:2-5 But who can endure the day of his coming? Indeed, when he comes, Malachi says, it will be **like a refiner's fire** (3:2). That is, the Lord first has to bring judgment in order to bring blessing. Just as the **refiner** puts **gold and silver** in the flame to burn off the dross (3:3), God has to refine and purify his people. He must remove what doesn't belong so they can receive his covenantal benefits. Similarly, the author of Hebrews insists that God disciplines his children for their good (see Heb 12:3-11). The Lord will come **in judgment** against those who demonstrate in a variety of ways that they think they can go to church on Sunday and treat others with injustice and contempt the rest of the week (3:5).

3:6 Though they thought God was being unfair, he reminded them of one of the greatest truths: the Lord has **not changed**. Therefore they had **not been destroyed**. In theology, this unchangeableness of God's essential nature and character is called the *immutability* of God. People change, but God is consistent and faithful. He is "compassionate and gracious, slow to anger and abounding in faithful love and truth" (Exod 34:6). Therefore, his people receive grace rather than what they deserve.

VII. TAKING GIVING SERIOUSLY (3:7-12)

The Lord's next grievance against his people has to do with something that continues to own the affections of humanity today: money. Just as there is an indicator light in my car that tells me when there's a hidden mechanical problem, so, too, an attitude toward money often serves as an indicator light revealing spiritual problems. Your level of spiritual seriousness and development will always show up in your checkbook.

3:7-8 God offers his people hope: **Return to me, and I will return to you** (3:7). But, the proof is in the pudding. Genuine repentance is known by its fruit. So, what must they do? He asks them, **Will a man rob God? Yet you are robbing me!** How? **By not making the payments of the tenth and the contributions** (3:8). Of all attempted robberies, surely robbing *God* must be considered the most ludicrous.

God commanded the Israelites to tithe—to give a tenth of what he gave to them (Lev 27:30, 32; Num 18:21-24; Deut 12:6; 14:22-23). By giving back to God ten percent of what he had provided, his people acknowledged his sovereignty, expressed gratitude to him, and demonstrated faith that he would continue to provide. When they did that, they came under the cover of his covenant. This practice and purpose of the tithe continued in the New Testament (see Heb 7:8), because Jesus continues the priesthood of Melchizedek who received a tithe (see Gen 14:18-20; Heb 5:5).

Statistics typically report that the average local church is supported by twenty percent of its members and that the average Christian gives less than three percent of his or her income to God. Many Christians, then, suffer from what I call "cirrhosis of the giver." And, while general paralysis sets in when reaching for the wallet or purse to support the ministry of one's church, the disease—amazingly—disappears at the mall. And at the movies. And at restaurants. We cannot accomplish kingdom work when we steal from the kingdom.

3:9-12 Even while **suffering**, the people were **still robbing** God (3:9). So, God challenges them. **Test me**, he says. **Bring the full tenth** and **see if I will not . . . pour out a blessing for you without measure** (3:10). **Then all the nations will consider you fortunate** (3:12).

Now, those who preach a "prosperity gospel" misuse passages like this one. Understand: God does not promise to give you earthly wealth when you give generously to the kingdom. He's not a slot machine. What is a "blessing" from God? It's experiencing, enjoying, and extending the goodness of God in your life. After all, you can have money and not be blessed. You can be wealthy and have no joy or peace.

God has already blessed believers in Jesus Christ with every spiritual blessing (see Eph 1:3). But, to access those blessings, he calls us to come under the cover of his covenant. He calls us to align ourselves with his kingdom agenda. When we do, we'll realize that what we already have is worth far more than anything we've been withholding (stealing) from the collection plate. Then, unbelievers will take notice and **consider** us **fortunate** (3:12), because it will be obvious that God is with us.

VIII. TAKING REVERENCE FOR GOD SERIOUSLY (3:13-18)

The fear of the LORD is the beginning of both knowledge and wisdom (Prov 1:7; 9:10). It leads to life and away from evil (Prov 16:6; 19:23). To fear the Lord is not to be terrified of him, but to hold him in reverence. Think about electricity. We don't go about our days frightened of electricity, but neither do we stick a screwdriver in an electrical outlet. We have an appropriate "fear" and respect for it. Taking God seriously is the key difference between the two groups described in Malachi 3:13-18.

3:13-15 This first group takes God casually. For them, God is like a spare tire—someone to turn to when circumstances go flat. When he bails them out, they put him back in the spiritual trunk. **Your words against me are harsh**, the Lord tells them. But they don't know what he's talking about (3:13). So, he spells it out for them. They have said, **It is useless to serve God. What have we gained by keeping his requirements?** (3:14). **We consider the arrogant to be fortunate** because they **prosper** (3:15). So, in other words, they feel they are doing a lot of religious activity for God and getting nothing out of it. The wicked, they believe, are thus better off than they.

The problem we've seen repeatedly in Malachi is that he's addressing a group of people who are fulfilling religious duty with no concern for a relationship. In a sense, they just want to come to church and get their cut. But the vital principle of covenant is *relationship*. The way to unlock the door to a new level of experience with God is to pursue a relationship with him—to pursue him for who he is, not just for what we want him to give us.

3:16-18 This second group is described as **those who feared the LORD**. They took God seriously. And, don't miss this: **The LORD took notice and listened** (3:16). And how does he respond to their faith? He says, **They will be mine . . . my own possession . . . I will have compassion on them** (3:17). In the end, people will look at these two groups and be able to see the difference **between one who serves God and one who does not** (3:18).

An appraiser is someone who examines something and sets a value on it. You and I must appraise God and see what he is worth. If we examine him honestly and see him as he has truly revealed himself in Scripture, we will find that he's absolutely worthy of all our love and reverence and service.

IX. TAKING GOD'S SOVEREIGNTY SERIOUSLY (4:1-6)

The concluding verses of Malachi remind us of the sovereignty of God over his creation. *Sovereignty* is a theological term that simply means that God rules, controls, and governs all things. There is absolutely nothing that happens anywhere, anytime, anyhow that God does not either cause or allow. He's not only God of the big stuff but also of the tiny details, as well. In fact, there is not a single hair that falls from your head of which he is not intimately aware (see Matt 10:30).

4:1a Scripture often speaks of "the day" or "the day of the Lord." It has both a temporal meaning and an eschatological one.

Temporally, the day refers to God's intervention in history to reverse circumstances. It is the day when heaven intervenes—such as when the Lord struck down the Assyrians as they threatened Jerusalem (see 2 Kgs 18:19–19:37). When things are headed in the wrong way, God can turn events on a dime to accomplish his purposes.

Malachi is talking here about the eschatological day. *Eschatology* is the study of the last things. **The day is coming** refers to the moment when Jesus Christ brings history to a climax (see 1 Thess 5:1-5). God always exercises his sovereignty. But, on that final day of Christ's coming, he'll display his sovereignty for all to see. When the day of the Lord arrives, it has a two-fold effect: the bringing down of the wicked and the lifting up of the righteous.

4:1b-2 The arrogant and everyone who commits wickedness will become stubble. The coming day will consume them (4:1) means that those who do not trust in Jesus Christ will experience eternal judgment, forever separated from the goodness and grace of God. For those **who fear [God's] name,** however, **the sun of righteousness will rise with healing in its wings, and** his people **will go out and playfully jump like calves from the stall** (4:2). So, whereas the calves have been cooped up and locked down, they're going to go skipping with joy when God opens the stall through Christ to set them free.

4:4-6 The admonition to **remember the instruction of Moses** (4:4) is a reminder to remember God's Word. In essence, he says,

"Don't give up—because the day is coming when I'm going to break through and separate the righteous from the wicked as promised."

Before the great and terrible day of the LORD comes, God will **send the prophet Elijah to turn the hearts of fathers to their children and the hearts of children to their fathers** (4:5-6). Jesus says this promise was fulfilled in John the Baptist (Matt 11:14). John called people to repentance in order to prepare the way for the Lord. This repentance would not only restore people's relationship to God but also their relationships to one another. The angel Gabriel told Zechariah that his son John would go before the Lord "in the Spirit and power of Elijah" and quoted from this passage in Malachi (Luke 1:17). God's messengers are responsible for restoring relationships—both the relationships between people and God and those between individuals.

With this, the final prophet of the Old Testament falls silent.

NEW TESTAMENT

MATTHEW

INTRODUCTION

Author

ALTHOUGH THE AUTHOR DIDN'T identify himself by name in the text, the title of this Gospel includes the name "Matthew" in the earliest existing manuscripts. In addition, several early church fathers (including Papias, Irenaeus, and Origen) attributed authorship to Matthew. Papias also said that Matthew originally wrote the Gospel in Hebrew (what we have today is in Greek).

Many critical scholars today deny that Matthew is the author. They claim that the Greek Matthew that we have does not look like it was translated from Hebrew. If Papias was wrong about that, they argue, he was probably wrong about who wrote it. But there are other scholars who think Matthew could be a Greek translation from Hebrew. Regardless, it wouldn't necessarily mean Papias was wrong about authorship. The early church unanimously claimed that the apostle Matthew penned the Gospel that bears his name.

There is also internal evidence to support this—that is, evidence within the Gospel itself. Mark 2:14 and Luke 5:27 call the tax collector who became a disciple "Levi." In Matthew 9:9-13, this man is named "Matthew." Also, in 10:3, the apostle Matthew is identified as a tax collector, and it may be that he had two names like Simon / Peter.

Though we can't be absolutely certain, it is best to trust the testimony of the early church and affirm that Matthew wrote this Gospel.

Background

Most—though not all—scholars today think that Matthew used Mark's Gospel as one of his sources when composing his own Gospel. If this is true, Matthew must have been written after Mark. It is likely that Mark's Gospel was written sometime in the 50s (see Background discussion on Mark's Gospel). Matthew, then, could have been written any time beginning in the mid to late 50s. The church father Irenaeus, who wrote in the late second century, claimed that Matthew wrote his Gospel while Paul and Peter were preaching in Rome. This would have been in the early 60s.

Message and Purpose

Matthew was a tax collector, which means he was unpopular. He left everything to follow Jesus after he concluded that Jesus was the Messiah. Matthew was authorized to write the Gospel that bears his name, and its subject is very simple: it's about the King and his kingdom. Matthew was introducing, especially to Jews, the message that God has sent his King, his Messiah, who would rule as his regent on earth by offering the kingdom to his people. In this sense Matthew is the culmination of all the Old Testament's anticipation of the Messiah who would come.

The apostle's concern was giving convincing proof that Jesus was the messianic King whom the Jews were anticipating and whom the world needs so desperately. That's why he began with Jesus's genealogy to establish his lineage through David. Matthew also presented Jesus's kingdom discourses, teaching, and miracles as proof of his messianic claim.

The book winds to a disquieting moment, the crucifixion. If Jesus is the Messiah, how could he be put to death? Thankfully, the scene is followed by the resurrection and the announcement that the King is alive and coming back, and that his kingdom is in this world today. Jesus's Great Commission at the end of Matthew's Gospel (28:18-20) means that the book of Matthew is relevant for us as believers today.

VIDEO   INTRO

www.bhpublishinggroup.com/qr/te/40_00

MATTHEW

I. GENEALOGY, BIRTH, AND CHILDHOOD (1:1–2:23)

1:1 The apostle Matthew opens his Gospel account with a **genealogy of Jesus Christ, the son of David, the Son of Abraham.** Many people tend to skip over this record and the one in Luke, but that's a mistake. These genealogies demonstrate that Jesus had a legitimate legal claim to be the Messiah—the Son of David and heir to the throne (see 2 Sam 7:12-16; Isa 11:1-10). Though Jewish genealogical records would be destroyed in AD 70 when Jerusalem fell to the Romans, Jesus's genealogy was supernaturally preserved in the Gospels.

1:2-17 Matthew's genealogy reaches back to **Abraham** (1:2) and proceeds through **King David** (1:6) to reach Jesus's assumed father, **Joseph** (1:16). There's a problem, though, with **Jeconiah** (1:11)—also known as Jehoiachin and Coniah (see 1 Chr 3:16; 2 Chr 36:8-9; and Jer 22:24). According to Jeremiah, Jeconiah would not have a biological descendent sitting on David's throne because of his own sins (Jer 22:30).

So, although Joseph had a legal right to the throne, because of Jeremiah's prophecy, it would never happen biologically. Thus, Matthew makes it clear that Joseph is not Jesus's *biological* father but his *adoptive* father, who was **the husband of Mary** (1:16). Interestingly, Luke provides Jesus's genealogy through her (Luke 3:23-38). This shows that Jesus is related to David biologically through David's son Nathan (Luke 3:31). Therefore, he's related to David on both sides of the family tree. And because his biological relationship is through Nathan

and not through Jeconiah, he can sit on the throne.

Notice that Jesus's genealogy is filled with imperfect people. **Jacob** (1:2) was a deceiver. **David** (1:6) committed adultery and murder. **Solomon** (1:7) took an abundance of wives and concubines. **Manasseh** (1:10) was one of Judah's most wicked kings. Moreover, and while women do not normally show up in genealogies, the women in Jesus's line were particularly questionable. **Tamar** (1:3) was a Canaanite who posed as a prostitute. **Rahab** was a prostitute; **Ruth** was from Moab, a non-Israelite people that worshiped false gods (1:5). Another observation about Jesus's genealogy is that it is mixed racially, including both Jews and Gentiles and indicating that Jesus's kingdom identity and rule includes all races of people.

All of this points to God's sovereign grace. He accomplishes his glorious purposes in spite of difficult circumstances and the character of the people involved. If he can use the people listed in 1:2-16 to bring the Christ into the world, God can surely use you too.

Notice also that of the five women mentioned in Matthew's genealogy, four are of Hamitic descent: Tamar, Rahab, Bathsheba, and Ruth. That doesn't mean that Jesus was black. To assert such, as some black theologians and religious leaders do, is to fall into the exclusionist perspective of many whites, who would make Jesus an Anglo-European, blue-eyed blond with little relevance to people of color. It would also fail to respect the distinct Jewish heritage of Christ. Jesus was a person of mixed ancestry.

It blesses me to know that Jesus had black in his blood because this destroys any perception of black inferiority once and for all. In Christ we find perfect man and sinless Savior. This knowledge frees blacks from an inferiority complex, and at the same time it frees whites from the superiority myth. In Christ, we all have our heritage.

Black people, as all other people, can find a place of historical, cultural, and racial identity in him. As Savior of all mankind, he can relate to all people, in every situation. In him, any person from any background can find comfort, understanding, direction, and affinity—as long as Christ is revered as the Son of God, a designation that transcends every culture and race and one to which all nations of people must pay homage.

1:18-19 In biblical times, a marriage in the Orient included several stages. The betrothal or engagement period was not like our modern engagements. The engagement of **Joseph** and **Mary** was a legal contract, as binding as marriage. So when Joseph **discovered** that Mary **was pregnant**, he **decided to divorce her secretly**. He was **a righteous man** and thought she had committed adultery, but **he** didn't want **to disgrace her publicly** (1:19).

1:20 Before Joseph could carry out his plans, though, **an angel of the Lord appeared to him in a dream**. Angels are divine messengers, and one of the ways they carry out their role in Scripture is by faithfully delivering God's message to humans. This angel told Joseph to take Mary for his **wife** because the child **conceived in her** was **from the Holy Spirit**.

God has created laws (such as the law of gravity) that govern the universe. When he intervenes in the regular course of events, interrupts those laws, and demonstrates his power over creation, a *miracle* takes place. This would be the most unique birth in history because Mary had never been touched by a man. A virgin would miraculously give birth because of the activity of the Holy Spirit.

Even so, this miracle involved more, for hers wasn't just any baby. The greatest miracle in human history occurred when God became man. The eternal Son of God took on human flesh, combining full deity and full humanity in one person. Jesus Christ is the God-man.

1:21-23 They were to call their son **Jesus**, a Greek name corresponding to the Hebrew name *Joshua*, which means "the Lord saves." Thus, according to the angel, the child's name was to indicate the reason he had come into the world—that is, **he will save his people from their sins** (1:21).

Matthew doesn't want his readers to think these are unexpected events; instead, they are a fulfillment of Old Testament prophecy (1:22). Mary was part of a plan that God had been orchestrating for centuries. Long before, Isaiah had prophesied, **The virgin will . . . give birth to a son, and they will name him Immanuel**. And Immanuel, Matthew tells us, means, **God is with us** (1:23). That is the essence of Christmas. The baby in the manger was God himself in the person of his Son. He was deity in a diaper. Heaven was coming down to earth; eternity was invading time. The King of the universe had come to be with us (see John 1:14) and save sinners (Matt 1:21).

All the problems in this world can be traced back to sin, and the Son of God came to save you from your sins because you couldn't save yourself. Jesus Christ entered the world to identify our sins, forgive us for our sins, give us victory over our sins, and give us an eternal home free from sin. That truth is what Christmas is all about. If you miss that, you've missed the point.

1:24-25 When Joseph awoke, he did as the **angel had commanded him** (1:24). Again, he was a righteous man (1:19). So, when he understood what God was doing, he complied in full obedience. He **did not have sexual relations with** Mary **until she gave birth**: Jesus was to be born of a virgin (1:25).

2:1-2 After Jesus was born in Bethlehem . . . wise men arrived. There are two common misconceptions to clear up about these visitors. First, according to legend, there were three wise men. However, we only know that they brought three specific gifts (2:11). We don't know how many men there were.

Second, contrary to how the scene is often portrayed, the wise men weren't present at the nativity. They weren't there for Jesus's birth. By the time they arrived, Joseph and Mary were living in a house (2:11). In addition, as we'll see, Herod sought to kill all the male children two years old and younger (2:16); therefore, Jesus was a toddler when the wise men saw him, not a baby.

Matthew tells us their origin was **from the east** (2:1)—perhaps Babylonia or Persia. They were looking for the **king of the Jews**, had seen **his star**, and had come **to worship him** (2:2). The Greek term for these men is *magi*. They were astrologers—students of the heavenly bodies. Whatever religious practices they'd engaged in previously, when they saw the manifestation of God's glory in the heavens, they responded and traveled to worship the true King.

2:3-8 They entered **Jerusalem** (the obvious place to find a king) and went to the palace of **King Herod**, also known as Herod the Great. Herod wasn't a Jew. He was an Idumean whom the Romans had made a ruler of the Jews. So when he heard what the wise men had to say, **he was deeply disturbed** (2:3). As far as he was concerned, there was no room for any king but him.

Herod asked **the chief priests and scribes** to tell him **where the Christ would be born** (2:4). And while these leaders clearly knew the Scriptures, they never pursued the Savior (see John 5:39-40). They didn't act on what they studied. Nevertheless, when Herod learned that Scripture foretold that the Messiah would be born **in Bethlehem** (2:5-6; see Mic 5:2), he **secretly summoned the wise men** (2:7). He told them he also desired to **worship** and asked them to **search carefully for the child** and **report back** (2:8). But Herod had ulterior motives. He wasn't about to let anyone take away his kingdom.

2:9-11 The wise men continued their search, following **the star** until it **stopped above the place where the child was** (2:9). Whereas Herod was deeply distressed over the news of a new king, the wise men **were overwhelmed with joy** to see him (2:10). They fell on **their knees** before the child and gave him gifts of **gold, frankincense, and myrrh** (2:11).

True worship can't be contained. These men had traveled an incredible distance for perhaps as long as two years to worship this King, but they knew he was worth the journey. How much are you willing to be inconvenienced to worship the King of kings? How badly do you want him?

2:12-13 Since they had faithfully sought the Savior, the wise men received inside information. They were **warned in a dream** about **Herod** and **returned** home **by another route** (2:12). Joseph also—since he had obeyed the Lord's word (1:24-25)—received further information and understanding. **An angel** warned him to **flee to Egypt** with Mary and Jesus for safety from **Herod** (2:13). When you obey God's revelation you get further divine illumination for your destination.

2:14-15 Joseph **took the child and his mother** and **escaped to Egypt** where they'd be safe until Herod died (2:14). Matthew tells his readers that this was to fulfill **what was spoken by the Lord** through the prophet Hosea: **Out of Egypt I called my Son** (2:15).

In his prophecy, Hosea was talking about Israel, whom God called his son and delivered from Egypt (see Hos 11:1), but Matthew understood that Israel was a type of God's Son who was yet to come. A *type* is a historical person, institution, or event that pre-figures a future corresponding reality. Thus, as God called his son Israel out of Egypt, so he would call his true Son out of Egypt. Matthew knew that many Old Testament texts point forward to Jesus.

2:16-18 When he realized that he had **been outwitted by the wise men**, Herod displayed his true, murderous colors. He ordered the massacre of **all the boys in and around Bethlehem who were two years old and under.** He used the information **learned from the wise men**—which they had learned by divine illumination—to slaughter innocent children (2:16). Matthew recognized this as another fulfillment of prophecy—this time from **Jeremiah** (2:17). Here too there is a connection between Israel and their Messiah. As Israel wept in

Jeremiah's day for their children in exile (see Jer 31:15-16), so they wept again in Matthew's day for their children who were persecuted in connection to Jesus.

2:19-22 After Herod's death, God once again communicated to **Joseph** in a **dream** to **take the child and his mother** back to **Israel** (2:19-21). When Joseph heard that **Archelaus,** Herod's son, **was ruling over Judea** in his father's place, **he was afraid to go to there.** But God addressed his fears and sent him to **Galilee** (2:22).

2:23 There the family settled in the town of **Nazareth** and thus it was fulfilled that Jesus **would be called a Nazarene.** Actually, though, such a statement is not found in any of the Old Testament prophets. So likely Matthew was thinking of statements like Isaiah 53:3: "He was despised and rejected by men" (see also Ps 22:6; Isa 49:7), because Nazareth was viewed as a despised community from which no good thing could come (see John 1:46). God sovereignly wove his plan in history to bring the Messiah into the world.

II. BAPTISM, TEMPTATION, AND THE START OF MINISTRY (3:1–4:25)

3:1-3 All four Gospels testify to the ministry of **John the Baptist** (3:1). He was the front man for Jesus, the one who came to prepare his way. John came **preaching in the wilderness of Judea** and calling people to **repent** (3:1-2). Here Matthew quotes Isaiah who prophesied that this **voice . . . in the wilderness** would come to **prepare the way for the Lord** (3:3).

The wilderness (then and now) is not a place of comfort and excitement. It's a barren place of preparation and development for what God is planning to do. John preached a revival in the wilderness, essentially telling the people, "The Messiah is coming, so you'd better get ready!" *Repentance* is essential for experiencing the presence and grace of God. It involves changing the mind in order to reverse direction. It is the inner resolve and determination to turn from sin and turn to God. So what's the motivation for repenting? **The kingdom of heaven has come near** (3:2). John wanted people to know that the King had arrived, and his promised earthly kingdom was ready to burst on the scene. Heaven had come to visit earth.

3:4-6 John's austere lifestyle, odd wardrobe, and confrontational preaching were reminiscent of another of God's messengers: Elijah (see, for example, 2 Kgs 1:3-17). As the **people from Jerusalem** and **Judea** heard John's message, they **were baptized by him** and confessed **their sins** (3:5-6). To

confess means to agree with. So by confessing their sins and being baptized, the people were making a public declaration that they had changed their minds and agreed with what God said about their sins. If you want to experience heaven's visitation in your history, true repentance can get you there.

3:7-10 The Jewish religious leaders, **the Pharisees and Sadducees**, also came to hear John. But they got an earful when he called them a bunch of venomous snakes (3:7)! Why did John accept other people but not this group? Because, although they were OK with listening to his message, they wanted their lives left alone. Like some people today, they didn't mind attending a church service as long as it didn't affect how they were running their own affairs. They wanted information, but not transformation. That's why John challenged them to **produce fruit consistent with repentance** (3:8).

Genuine repentance is confirmed by actions. When I travel, I tell the airline agent, "I'm Tony Evans, and I have a reservation." The agent then asks, "Can I see your proof identification?" They don't want mere communication that I am who I claim to be; they want authentication. Therefore, they want to see something that verifies what I affirm. Similarly, shouting, "Hallelujah! Amen! Praise the Lord!" is fine but insufficient. Repentance shows up in your hands and feet, not just in your lips. Without the fruit, the visible proof of true heart repentance, judgment is coming (3:10).

3:11 In light of the people's repentance, John baptized them **with water**. But **the one . . . coming** after him would baptize them **with the Holy Spirit**. John's declaration corresponds to the promise of the prophets (see Ezek 36:27; Joel 2:28), and the confirmation of Jesus (see John 14:16-17; 15:26; Acts 1:4-5), and the fulfillment in the early church (see Acts 2:1-4; 10:44-45).

The triune God is one God in three persons. The person at work on earth today is the Holy Spirit. Without a relationship to God the Holy Spirit, in fact, there is no relationship to God the Son. And without a relationship to God the Son, there is no relationship to God the Father. It is your relationship to the Holy Spirit that determines how much of Jesus the Son and God the Father you experience today.

3:12 John described the Messiah as having a **winnowing shovel . . . in his hand**. Such an implement was used to separate **wheat** from **chaff**. A farmer would winnow the grain by tossing it in the air. The wind would blow away the chaff—the useless husks—while the wheat would fall to the **threshing floor**. The wheat would then be gathered up, and the chaff would be burned. Those who will not repent and receive Jesus will experience the eternal wrath of God for their sins **with fire that never goes out**.

3:13-15 When **Jesus came from Galilee to John at the Jordan** River, **John tried to stop him** (3:13-14). Since John's message was about repentance, he considered it inappropriate and inconceivable that he would baptize the Messiah, because Jesus had nothing to repent of. Instead, John told him, **I need to be baptized by you** (3:14). But Jesus insisted on being baptized because doing so was **the way . . . to fulfill all righteousness** (3:15).

In his substitutionary death on the cross, Jesus would bear the transgressions of sinners and credit them with his perfect righteousness (see 2 Cor 5:21). So as his ministry began, he intended to identify with sinful

humanity on whose behalf he would perfectly fulfill all the demands of God's law. This baptism would also identify Jesus with John and affirm his kingdom message.

3:16-17 At Jesus's baptism, we see a Trinitarian affirmation. All three members of the Godhead inaugurated Jesus's public ministry. As Jesus rose from the water, **the Spirit of God** descended on him **like a dove** (3:16), and the **voice** of God the Father proclaimed, **This is my beloved Son, with whom I am well-pleased** (3:17). No other ministry commissioning service can compare to this one. The Father and the Spirit publicly endorsed the Son for his kingdom mission. Thus, he was prepared for battle with the enemy (4:1-11).

4:1 The first thing to notice about the temptation of Jesus in Matthew 4:1-11 is that it was God's idea: **Jesus was led up by the Spirit into the wilderness to be tempted by the devil**. This tells us God was not on the defensive in this matter. He was on the offensive, demonstrating the superiority of his Son over Satan.

In fact, this is why God allows us to be tempted by the devil—so he can demonstrate the superiority of Jesus Christ. God created humanity constitutionally lower than the angels (see Heb 2:7)—including fallen angels like the devil—to show what he could do with less (humans) when that less is committed to him, than he could with more (angels) when that more is in rebellion to him. Temptation, then, provides you with an opportunity to validate this truth: "the one who is in you is greater than the one who is in the world" (1 John 4:4).

Why did God test his Son this way? The Bible describes Jesus as the "second Adam" or "last Adam" (1 Cor 15:45, 47). The first Adam was tested in the garden, gave in to Satan, and got the human race kicked into the wilderness. The second Adam went into the wilderness to defeat Satan so that he can escort us back to the garden.

4:2 Jesus **had fasted forty days and forty nights**. To fast is to give up a physical craving to fulfill a greater spiritual need. It involves a switching of priorities. Fasting prioritizes prayer and fellowship with God to feed the spirit instead of the stomach. After forty days, Jesus **was hungry**—and ready for battle.

4:3 The tempter began by saying, **If you are the Son of God, tell these stones to become bread.** This tells us the devil had been watching Jesus go without food. He knows what you're up to, too, and directs his temptations accordingly. In this situation, Satan questioned the provision of God: Jesus was hungry. God hadn't fed him. Why shouldn't Jesus just make what was needed?

4:4 How did Jesus respond? By quoting Scripture: **It is written.** If Jesus, the living Word, needed to use the written Word to deal with the enemy of the Word, how much more do you? He gave you the Bible so you could wield it like a sword (see Eph 6:17).

Jesus quoted from Deuteronomy 8:3: **Man must not live on bread alone but on every word that comes from the mouth of God.** In this passage, Moses explained to Israel how they survived through the wilderness: by God's provision. They didn't survive merely because of the manna but because of the one who provided it. Was Jesus hungry? Yes. But he was willing to trust God to provide rather than to act independently of him.

4:5-6 Then the devil took him to Jerusalem to the **pinnacle of the temple** and said, **If you are the Son of God, throw yourself down** (4:5-6). Challenging Jesus to jump to his death doesn't sound like much of a temptation. But notice that he supported his appeal by quoting God's promise of angelic protection in Psalm 91:11-12 (4:6). Jesus, then, had an opportunity to demonstrate he was the Messiah for all Jerusalem to see. The problem was that doing so ignored God's plan. Satan urged Jesus to fulfill God's will for his life in a way that would bypass the cross.

Oh, yes—the devil knows the Bible, and he uses it. If he can't convince you to act independently of God, he'll work through your religion. But God doesn't need Satan's help to get you where he wants you to go.

4:7 Jesus quoted Deuteronomy 6:16: **Do not test the Lord your God.** In other words, he knew we are never to use disobedience to

back God into a corner in order to force him to fulfill his plan.

4:8-9 Finally, the devil showed Jesus **all the kingdoms of the world and their splendor** (4:8). Then he quit playing around and got to the bottom line: **I will give you all these things if you will fall down and worship me** (4:9). In the end, Satan wants your worship; he wants you to bow. That's what he got from Adam and Eve in the garden, and that's what he seeks from you. He'll make nice offers to get you to do so, but it's never worth the price.

4:10 Jesus had finally had enough: **Go away, Satan!** His absolute authority is on display in this command. Then Jesus quoted once again from Deuteronomy: **Worship the Lord your God, and serve only him** (Deut 6:13). Worship is reserved for the one true and living God.

If you're a Christian, you have no obligation to the devil, and you have Jesus's delegated authority against Satan. "Resist the devil [with the word and in obedience to God], and he will flee from you [as he fled from Christ]" (James 4:7). Too often we come to worship God on Sunday and then serve lesser agendas and gods the rest of the week. But if Jesus is the ultimate authority in the universe, he deserves your exclusive worship and service.

4:11 How did this battle end? **The devil left him, and angels came and began to serve him.** Satan is unable to handle a righteous life that consistently confronts him with God's Word. The true King has all authority and perfectly obeyed God. So the usurper had to retreat. When the fallen angel left, faithful angels came and fulfilled their rightful role: serving Christ and giving him the worship he deserved.

4:12-17 John the Baptist was **arrested** by Herod Antipas (see Matt 14:1-12), so Jesus **withdrew into Galilee** and lived **in Capernaum . . . in the region of Zebulun and Naphtali** (4:12-13). This fulfilled Isaiah 9:1-2, which said that those living **in darkness** in **Galilee** would see **a great light** (4:14-16). That's when Jesus's public ministry officially began, and he preached in continuity with the kingdom message of John: **Repent, because the kingdom of heaven has come near** (4:17; see 3:2).

4:18-22 In these verses we have the calling of the first disciples: **Peter** and **his brother Andrew** (4:18-20), and **James** and **his brother John**, the sons of Zebedee (4:21-22). All four men were fishermen. And when Jesus called them to follow him, he said, **I will make you fish for people** (4:19).

There's an important principle here. If you're not fishing, you're not following. If your Christian life does not involve evangelizing the lost, you're not functioning like the disciple Jesus intends you to be. Evangelism includes sharing the gospel and intentionally seeking to convert the hearer to faith in Jesus Christ.

When called, Peter, Andrew, James, and John **immediately** left their jobs and followed Jesus (4:20, 22). Not every believer is called to a full-time Christian vocation, but every believer is called to be a full-time Christian. That means that following Christ must be your number one priority.

4:23-25 Matthew tells us the hallmarks of Jesus ministry as he traveled throughout Galilee: **teaching in their synagogues, preaching the good news of the kingdom, and healing every disease and sickness among the people** (4:23). *Teaching* involves clearly articulating the content of the message. *Preaching* includes calling for a response to what is taught. *Healing* consists of a visible demonstration of the power of the message. As Jesus did these things, **the news about him spread**, and **large crowds followed him** (4:24-25). When he taught, preached, and healed, there was standing room only.

III. THE SERMON ON THE MOUNT (5:1–7:29)

5:1-2 When **the crowds** came to Jesus, **he went up on the mountain, sat down**, and **began to teach.** Matthew 5–7 is known as the Sermon on the Mount. It's Jesus's kingdom manifesto. In this sermon, he explained what the kingdom is, how it works, and what it ought to look like.

The first few verses of the Sermon on the Mount are known as the Beatitudes (5:3-10); they set forth the character of kingdom men and women. Jesus spoke primarily to those who were his disciples in order to take them to the next level. We could call the Beatitudes antibiotics from God's pharmacy that can aid life transformation. Each one includes a blessing, which is the God-given capacity to enjoy his goodness in your life and to extend that goodness to others.

Jesus pronounced these blessings on people with a kingdom mindset—those who consciously and unapologetically align their lives under the rule of God. The blessings are for those who reject religious externalism. Jesus is primarily concerned with what's happening on your inside, which should be the basis of what you're showing on the outside.

5:3 Blessed are the poor in spirit, for the kingdom of heaven is theirs. To be "poor in spirit" is to be in spiritual poverty, to be conscious of one's continual dependence on God. Kingdom people recognize their own inadequacy and insufficiency apart from him. As long as you think you are rich in spirit, you'll actually be independent and proud. So become a spiritual beggar.

God's *kingdom* refers to God's *rule*. If you are poor in spirit, you will get to see God's heavenly rule in your earthly life. Only by being desperately dependent on God can you become what he created you to be.

5:4 Blessed are those who mourn, for they will be comforted refers to being saddened by the things that sadden God. God grieves over the sin and wretchedness of the world (see Gen 6:5-6). Jesus lamented the disobedience of Jerusalem (Matt 23:37) and wept over the existence of death, which sin had produced (John 11:35). We must not laugh at or excuse that which causes God to mourn. Sin and its consequences surround us, so that we are tempted to become numb. Instead, we must pray that God would give us the emotions of his heart, so that we can experience the comfort of God to encourage and strengthen us.

5:5 Blessed are the humble, for they will inherit the earth. Some translations render "the humble" as "the meek." It's important to understand that meekness doesn't mean weakness. Consider, for example, the process of breaking a horse. The idea is not to break the horse of its strength or speed; rather, the goal is to break the horse of its self-will. As long as you remain independent and "wild," you will never maximize God's intention for you. To be meek is to learn to submit your will to God's. Those who do will inherit what God has allotted for them.

5:6 Blessed are those who hunger and thirst for righteousness, for they will be filled. This blessing is about having the right spiritual appetite. Far too many of God's children are malnourished—not because they don't eat, but because they eat the wrong things. Donuts taste good, but they have no nutritional value. You can't have a donut-level spiritual diet and then wonder why you don't experience God's blessings. To hunger for righteousness is to apply the righteous standard of God to your life. You need to be hungry for that which pleases God. If you train your appetite in this way you will be filled—that is, you'll be satisfied with divine contentment. Discontentment will give way to satisfaction in God.

5:7 Blessed are the merciful, for they will be shown mercy. To receive mercy is to not get what you deserve, to receive pity instead of just condemnation. Rather, when you're guilty, mercy removes the misery you ought to receive. There's a blessing for those who extend it, because you can bank on the fact that a time is coming when you'll need mercy. This is the Golden Rule in action: "Whatever you want others to do for you, do also the same for them" (Matt 7:12).

5:8 Blessed are the pure in heart, for they will see God. Purity of heart involves being authentic, and this begins with honesty before God. Prayer for many people is a stale practice because there is no raw

conversation with God—respectful but raw. We must go to God with our hearts completely open because we're not hiding anything from him; he knows everything already. So come clean with him about the good, the bad, and the ugly, and you'll see him operating powerfully in your life.

5:9 Blessed are the peacemakers, for they will be called sons of God. To be at peace is to be in harmony. To be a peacemaker is to be a mediator and resolve conflicts between estranged parties—whether individuals or groups. You make peace by identifying the truth, addressing the sin, and constructing a bridge between those who are at odds with one another. Peacemaking can be difficult work. But, if we persevere in it, we will be called "sons of God" because we will resemble our Daddy. He sent *the* Son of God to be our mediator, bridging the gap created by our sin and granting us peace with him.

5:10 Blessed are those who are persecuted because of righteousness, for the kingdom of heaven is theirs isn't about being persecuted because of wickedness. Instead it's about being mistreated because you display the kingdom characteristics described in 5:3-9, and some people won't like you for doing so. Persecution may take a variety of forms and come from a variety of sources (family, an employer, the culture, the government). But in receiving it you'll be in the company of a class of people (see Heb 11) of whom the world is not worthy (Heb 11:38). If you're willing to be rejected by men to be accepted by God, the kingdom of heaven is yours.

5:11-12 These verses expand on the idea in 5:10. It's hard to believe that undergoing persecution is a blessing, but Jesus wanted his disciples to know that he was serious. Notice that the persecution that brings blessing is directly tied to Jesus. **When they insult you** and tell lies about you **because of** Jesus, **you are blessed** (5:11). Since essentially the same thing happened to the Old Testament **prophets**, you're in good company. But how can you **be glad and rejoice** in the midst of the mess? You can remember that **your reward is great** (5:12). God knows how to deliver. And as Paul told the Romans, "The sufferings of this present time are not worth comparing with the glory that is going to be revealed to us" (Rom 8:18).

5:13 After describing the character of kingdom people, Jesus described the impact and influence of kingdom people. He told his disciples, **You are the salt of the earth.** Before the advent of refrigeration, people used salt to preserve food. Salting down a piece of meat slowed the decaying process. Notice that Jesus didn't tell them, "You are the salt of the shaker." Since it's under the curse of sin, the earth is like a decaying piece of meat. And salt can't preserve meat if it stays in the shaker.

For salt to **lose its taste** is to lose its uniqueness. Christians are to be salt in a decaying world. But if you become too mixed up with the world and allow its values to affect you, you will lose your uniqueness as a Christian and your ability to make a kingdom difference. Remember, Sodom and Gomorrah were destroyed—not only because of wicked people—but also because there weren't enough righteous people there to prevent God's judgment (see Gen 18:16–19:29).

5:14 You are the light of the world. Light has only one job: to shine. In Scripture, the world is pictured as a dark place that requires illumination (see John 1:5; 3:19). Jesus is "the light of the world" (John 8:12), so he expects his followers to be lights too.

5:15-16 A city situated on a hill cannot be hidden. No one lights a lamp and puts it under a basket (5:15). In other words, you're not to be a private Christian. Your faith must go public. There are to be no covert, secret agent Christians in the church. Are you a light among your family and acquaintances? Are you a light at work and at the gym? Are you a light in your culture and in your community? To hide a light is contradictory to its purpose. **Let your light shine** (5:16).

You must shine so that people **may see your good works and give glory to your Father in heaven** (5:16). Non-Christians are capable of doing good things, so what does Jesus mean by "good works"? Good works are connected to the kingdom work of God

(see Eph 2:10). A good work is a righteous and biblically authorized action that is beneficial to others and for which God gets the credit. So, unless God is a part of it, it's not a good work. It's merely a good thing. Our good works are accomplished so that we may glorify—that is, highlight, put on display, and make a big deal of—God.

5:17-20 Jesus did not come in opposition to **the Law or the Prophets** (which is a way of referring to the Old Testament); he came **to fulfill** them (5:17). The Old Testament was intended to point to Christ, who'd bring it to its God-intended consummation. He, in fact, is the theme of the Old Testament Scriptures (see Luke 24:27, 44; John 5:39-40). In order to provide us with righteousness, making us acceptable before God, he had to live a life of complete obedience to God's law. Not only is each letter of the Bible vital, but so is each part (or **stroke**) of each **letter** (5:18). God's Word is entirely authoritative, and Jesus submitted to it perfectly, allowing him to impart perfect righteousness to those who place personal faith in him (see 2 Cor 5:21). Christ calls them to follow him in obedience to the law—not for salvation but for sanctification, so they may see the kingdom rule of God in their lives.

Unless, as a disciple of Jesus, you are committed to growing in righteousness, the heavenly kingdom will not be expressed in your earthly history. As we will see, **the scribes and Pharisees** were concerned only with external righteousness (5:19-20).

5:21-22 After addressing God's commands in general, Jesus spoke about some specific commands. Six times in this chapter he said, **You have heard that it was said … but I tell you . . .** (5:21-22, 27-28, 31-32, 33-34, 38-39, 43-44) so that he might offer a corrective to some misunderstandings.

Do not murder was one of the Ten Commandments that all Jews knew (5:21). But Jesus said if you are **angry with [your] brother or sister** or use vicious words toward them, you are guilty of breaking the law (5:22). That takes God's standards to a whole new level. It tells us God not only considers our actions but also our thoughts and words, and it provides us a deeper understanding of the law. Jesus demonstrated that God is concerned with the motives of the heart.

5:23-26 So if you come to worship and remember that you are at odds with your brother, **go and be reconciled with** him (5:23-24). Jesus emphasized the connection between the vertical and the horizontal. In order to have a healthy vertical relationship—intimacy and fellowship with God—you must maintain your horizontal relationships with others. Make peace with your adversary inasmuch as it depends on you. Be reconciled before he takes legal action or the consequences of your dispute become worse (5:25-26).

5:27-30 Sexual purity involves more than avoiding a physical act. It too involves the heart. **Do not commit adultery** (5:27) was another of the Ten Commandments that many Jews probably assumed they could check on a list of sins successfully dodged. But Jesus said that looking **at a woman lustfully** is to commit **adultery with her in [your] heart** (5:28). Immoral actions, then, begin with immoral thoughts—and the immoral thoughts are evil too. You can't address sin by only dealing with external actions.

In today's world, pornography is a huge stumbling block to moral purity and a clear example of the kind of sin that Jesus warned against. Jesus wants his disciples to be so radical for moral purity that they're willing to **cut ... off** anything that draws them to sin (5:29-30). He's not calling for physical mutilation (again, sin is a matter of the heart and not merely the eyes and hands); instead, he's calling for a radical approach to avoiding sin.

5:31-32 The Jewish religious leaders had varying understandings of divorce. Some thought you could divorce for any reason. But Jesus limited divorce. He said, a man who **divorces his wife, except in a case of sexual immorality, causes her to commit adultery** because such an action would drive her to marry another. (In the first century, marriage provided a woman with necessary economic support.) Moreover, the one who **marries** such a **woman commits adultery** (5:32). Why? Because hers was an illegitimate divorce unsanctioned by God. Marriage

vows are to be viewed as sacred and permanent. Notice that it is the person seeking the illegitimate divorce who is blamed for the sin—not the woman who remarries.

5:33-37 Jesus didn't deny the legitimacy of all oath-taking. We find oaths in the Old Testament, as when covenant relationships were established. Jesus, then, was warning against careless, profane, and flippant uses of oaths in everyday speech. An oath shouldn't be used to convince someone of the truthfulness of what you're saying; that might only be a cover-up for deception. Remember, anything in creation that you swear by is under God's authority. So speak with truthfulness. **Let your 'yes' mean 'yes,' and your 'no' mean 'no'** (5:37).

5:38-42 Kingdom people think and live differently than those in the culture around them. The Old Testament principle **an eye for an eye and a tooth for a tooth** (5:38; see Lev 24:20) was intended to keep justice fair and limited. Punishment was to be in proportion to the crime. But Jesus wanted his followers to develop a servant mindset. He thus presented several scenarios with the same emphasis (5:39-42): Your spirit of servanthood must go beyond what is required and extend even to those who mistreat you.

If anyone forces you to go one mile, go with him two (5:41). This example refers to the practice of Roman soldiers forcing civilians to carry their packs for up to a mile. According to Jesus, servanthood should be such a dominant orientation in kingdom people that we are willing to go the extra mile even for people who don't like us. This doesn't involve placing yourself into an abusive situation, however. Nor does it mean there are no limitations. Instead, as Paul says, it means not repaying "evil for evil ... but [conquering] evil with good" (Rom 12:17, 21).

5:43-48 God's law commanded, **Love your neighbor** (see Lev 19:18). The natural conclusion for many Jews, though, was that you could **hate your enemy** (5:43). Jesus turned that thinking on its head. Instead, he said, you must **love your enemies** (5:44). To do so is a simple reflection of the character of **your Father in heaven**. It's a reminder that God doesn't show kindness only to believers. He extends common grace to all, meaning that there are certain blessings that he gives to all people. For instance, **he causes his sun to rise on the evil and the good** (5:45). You don't have to be a Christian to feel the sun shine and to breathe oxygen.

Jesus expects the behavior of his disciples to stand out in a sinful world. Even wicked people will look out for those who look out for them (5:46). So, if you love only those in your circle who like you, **what are you doing out of the ordinary?** (5:47).

To **be perfect** as God is perfect (5:48) does not mean to be sinless; rather, it means to love others—in the power of the Holy Spirit—by seeking their best interests as a reflection of God's character. To do this even for people you don't like. Loving your neighbor doesn't require having warm and fuzzy feelings for him; it means seeking his well-being.

6:1-4 Jesus wanted his followers to be kingdom people, but he didn't want them to do kingdom activities in order to be praised by others: **Be careful not to practice your righteousness . . . to be seen** (6:1). He gives three examples of practicing righteousness: giving to the poor (6:2-4), praying (6:5-8), and fasting (6:16-18). These are all good, legitimate practices. But we mustn't do them for public recognition.

To do so is to be a hypocrite (6:2, 5, 16)— that is, to be a play actor, giving an external appearance of spirituality without an accompanying internal reality. In the old western movies, they would create a town that appeared to be full of buildings. But each structure was a façade. A building might look like a saloon from the front, but there was nothing on the other side of its door. Such a movie set gave a false impression.

When you give money to those in need (whether directly or through your church or another ministry), **don't sound a trumpet** and **don't let your left hand know what your right hand is doing** (6:2-3). In other words, don't brag about your giving to let others know how generous you are. Those who announce their giving **have their reward** (6:2) and receive nothing from God (6:1). So, if you're playing for the applause of people, you have all you're going to get.

But give **in secret**, and then **your Father** will **reward you** (6:4).

6:5-8 Likewise, when **you pray**, don't do it for the applause of people (6:5). The hypocritical religious leaders would pray in public to be seen. Sometimes you're going to be called upon to pray in public. But, if you do it to put on a show, that's a problem.

Do you pray in public while God never hears from you in private? **Go into your private room, shut your door, and pray to your Father** (6:6). And **don't babble like the Gentiles**, using meaningless repetition and uttering chants, thinking that God hears you because of your **many words** (6:7).

6:9 When Jesus said, "whenever/when you pray" (6:5-7), he assumed that disciples pray. What is prayer? You don't need to attend seminary to understand it. Put simply, prayer is talking with God; it's communication with him. The religious leaders sounded fancy when they prayed, but they did it to impress others (6:5). You don't have to use fancy theological words.

How, then, should a disciple pray? Jesus showed them: **You should pray like this.** He wasn't giving them a prayer to repeat but guidelines to provide prayer categories—a prayer template, if you will.

Opening with **our Father in heaven** reminds us that when Christians pray, they're addressing their Daddy, their heavenly Father. Some people have had bad fathers and say they can't relate to God as Father, but we are not to measure our heavenly Father by the standard of our earthly ones. Rather, we are to measure our earthly fathers by the standard of our heavenly Father—who is perfect. He is the ultimate definition of what a father is. Notice also that he is *our* Father (so you're not the only kid in the family), and he is in heaven (a reminder that heaven overrules earth).

What should we ask of our heavenly Father? First, we must pray that his **name** would be **honored as holy**. When Scripture talks about God's "name," it's referring to who he is, his character. To honor him as "holy" is to treat him as unique—in a class by himself. He is the Creator of all and the only one deserving of worship.

6:10 In the phrase **your kingdom come**, Jesus calls his disciples to make a pledge of allegiance to the kingdom of God—to God's rule over his creation. But, if you want to know his kingdom purpose for your life, you must be committed to *his* kingdom agenda. When the U.S. Olympic athletes are awarded gold medals, they don't get to choose the songs they hear at the accompanying ceremony. They are representatives of our nation, so the song played is the national anthem of the U.S. Similarly, you are called to march to *God's* tune.

Your will be done on earth as it is in heaven suggests that if we're following God's agenda, we'll want his heavenly will to be done in our earthly history. So, what is God's "will"? God's will is what God wants—when, where, and how he wants it. Those who are part of God's family are to follow God's rules. He's sovereign, and he'll accomplish his purposes with you or without you. The question is, Will you get to take part in it? Remember, he's not limited to our obedience.

6:11 Once we align ourselves to God's program, that's where our requests come in. **Give us today our daily bread.** First, you ask God to meet your daily needs so you can fulfill his plan. God doesn't establish a program that he doesn't fund. Nevertheless, our requests for his provision are to be "daily." This is a reminder that you are dependent on him all day, every day. Just as the Israelites relied on God to provide manna regularly in the wilderness, so you are to live your life in dependence on God—one day at a time.

6:12 Forgive us our debts, as we also have forgiven our debtors relates to sins. When God forgives, he no longer credits sin to your account. And as we have been forgiven by God, so we are to forgive the sins others commit against us.

Some people have been seriously sinned against. They have endured horrific cruelty. Nevertheless, the Bible teaches that anything that comes a believer's way—the good, the bad, and the ugly—has to come through God's fingers. God is sovereign, and he permits things for the good of his children—even when we don't understand. Just as in the story of Joseph, human beings may

intend to do evil against us, but God intends even that for good (see Gen 50:20).

6:13 Do not bring us into temptation requires that we face facts. Satan is smarter than us and has centuries of experience ruining human lives. So ask God to keep you from getting into situations that detour you from the kingdom road. Pray that he would deliver you from temptations that you're not ready to handle.

6:14-15 Though Jesus emphasized forgiveness in the Lord's Prayer (6:12), he returns to it here. Don't miss that God's forgiveness is conditioned on your forgiveness of others. Jesus isn't talking about salvation here, though, but about our fellowship with God after we're saved, as a part of our discipleship. To forgive is to hold a grudge no longer, not to seek retribution. Since we all need God's forgiveness regularly, we must not withhold it from others. If we do, we'll lose out on fellowship with God.

6:16-18 As with giving and praying, Jesus exhorted his followers not to fast for public recognition. The fact that he says, **Whenever you fast** (6:16), tells us he considers fasting a legitimate spiritual discipline. To fast is to temporarily give up a bodily craving—typically food—because of a spiritual need. Instead of eating, then, you devote yourself to prayer **in secret** (6:18), seeking God's kingdom intervention. But, if your goal in avoiding food is for other people to celebrate how spiritual you look, then their approval will be your **reward** (6:16).

6:19-24 In these verses, Jesus emphasizes the spiritual over the physical. Everyone collects **treasures on earth.** But they don't last (6:19). Heavenly treasures are a far better investment. They're eternal and imperishable (6:20). **For where your treasure is, there your heart will be also** (6:21). Store your treasure where you want your heart to be. Your heart will follow your treasure.

In order to focus on heaven and store treasure there, you have to see clearly. **The eye is the lamp of the body** (6:22). Either you let light in through your eyes, or you remain in darkness. It's that simple. And unless your spiritual perspective is directed by God, you'll wander in the dark.

Few things can distract our spiritual focus and fill us with darkness as effectively as becoming a slave to **money**. Note that having money is not the problem, though. The danger is when money has you—that's when the physical becomes more important to you than the spiritual. You can't **serve two masters** (5:24). God must have your devotion if you are to receive his kingdom direction.

6:25-30 For many of us, the admonition not to **worry about your life** (6:25) sounds just as impossible to obey as, "Don't breathe." Worry and anxiety over life are commonplace. But to this Jesus said in effect, "When was the last time you saw a bird with an ulcer?" **Birds** don't worry about where they're going to get their next meal, and yet the **heavenly Father feeds them** (6:26). Flowers don't agonize over looking pretty, but not even **Solomon in all his splendor** could match the beauty in the fields of God's creation (6:28-29). If God gives this kind of attention to birds and flowers, **won't he do much more for you** (6:30)?

6:31-32 Don't worry about life's needs (6:31); after all, idolaters seek after things and become anxious. They plead with their false gods for help, but you have a **heavenly Father**—the true and living God—who **knows** what you **need** (6:32). It's not wrong to plan and work hard. We should do these things. Our error is when we remove God from the equation or fail to give him priority.

6:33 What, then, is the antidote for worry? **Seek first the kingdom of God and his righteousness.** This statement is the centerpiece of Jesus's Sermon on the Mount. If you get this right, everything else falls into place. God demands that his kingdom rule be first in your life. When it's missing, you've identified the key to your problems. *Righteousness* is the standard God requires in order for his people to rightly relate to him. To *seek* his *kingdom* is to seek to live in accordance with his standards, his guidelines.

Of course, prioritizing God's kingdom in this way doesn't mean you won't experience challenges and suffering, but your life will

be aligned under his kingdom authority so you can experience his provision. In baseball, you can step on second base, third base, and home plate without being tagged. But, if you miss first base on the way, nothing else matters. You're out.

God cannot be second. So, how do you know if you're putting God's kingdom first? Ask yourself this question: When I need guidance to make decisions, where do I go first? For many Christians, God is like a spare tire. He's where they run when all else fails. So, do you seek God's perspective first (through his Word and godly counsel), or do you seek the world's perspective? Kingdom Christians appeal to God's view and his righteous standards first. Do this, and **all these things will be provided for you.** Align yourself with his agenda, and your Daddy will take responsibility for meeting your needs.

6:34 So take care of today's concerns, and **don't worry about tomorrow, because tomorrow will worry about itself.** Today is the tomorrow you were worried about yesterday. Focusing on living for God's kingdom today is the antidote to worry.

7:1-2 Do not judge (7:1). That's one thing that most people seem to do very well. To illegitimately judge is to create your own standard of what is acceptable and measure everyone against it, hypocritically critiquing them. Not surprisingly, people who do this typically find no problems with their own behavior. That's because when a sinner creates a standard, he becomes the standard. When my son was eleven years old, he wanted to show me how he could dunk a basketball in the gym. The problem was that he had asked a janitor to lower the rim so that he could dunk it. Those who hypocritically judge others use a standard, but it isn't God's. It's been lowered.

Judgmental people lose sight of the fact that they too will be judged. And the same measuring stick they use will be used against them (7:2). Pass judgment on others, and your standard will be used to judge you. It's a boomerang effect.

7:3-5 Jesus compared having a judgmental attitude to noticing a tiny **splinter in your brother's eye** while being unaware of the beam of wood in your own (7:3-4). Imagine straining to see a nearly invisible speck but being oblivious to the board protruding from your eyeball!

Notice Jesus's remedy to the situation. He didn't say you shouldn't help the brother with the speck in his eye. He says, **First take the beam of wood out of your eye** (7:5). It'll hurt, but you'll see clearly. Instead of being judgmental toward others, allow God's standard to be applied to your own life. If you're honest, you'll discover that you fall short. When you've addressed your own sin, you'll be more understanding, compassionate, and righteous in your assessments and better able to help a brother address his own sin.

7:6 Jesus's instructions in 7:1-5 don't preclude all judgments. There are numerous places in the Bible in which God instructs his people to make judgment calls. Here is one of them: **Don't give what is holy to dogs or toss your pearls before pigs.** These are references to those who despise spiritual things, but you can't obey this command unless you can discern who the "dogs" and "pigs" are.

The difference between judgmentalism and what Jesus calls us to do here is the standard we use. When you sinfully judge, you use your own standard and condemn others. When you obey Jesus's words in 7:6, you use wisdom, refusing to give what is precious in God's sight to those who refuse to value spiritual things.

7:7-8 Prayer is an earthly request for heavenly intervention. It doesn't make God do what's outside his will but releases him to do what is inside his will. God has determined that he will not do certain things until asked. So we are to **ask, seek,** and **knock** for what we need (7:7). When you pursue and request those things that are in his will, he promises to deliver (7:8). The question is this: How long should you ask, seek, and knock? *Until you get an answer.* There are three answers to prayer: yes, no, or wait. If you haven't heard yes or no, then you keep asking.

7:9-11 Children will ask their parents repeatedly for things until they receive a reply. And God doesn't give harmful things in response to prayer—any more than a loving father would give harmful things to his kids when they ask (7:9-10). If even sinful dads know how to **give good gifts to [their] children, how much more will** your perfect **Father in heaven** give what is beneficial to you when you ask (7:11)?

7:12 In the context of this discussion of judging others and prayer, Jesus utters this boomerang principle: **Whatever you want others to do for you, do also the same for them.** We call this the Golden Rule. In short, it means to love others: to practice the "one anothers" of Scripture (e.g., John 15:12; Gal 6:2; Eph 4:32; 1 Thess 5:11). Do for the people around you what you want God to do for you, and watch how he delivers.

7:13-14 There's a **wide** gate and **broad** road that many people follow, seeking to have a relationship with God (7:13). It's called religion. *Religion* is man's attempt to make himself acceptable to a holy God. But the **narrow** gate that **leads to life** is Jesus; he makes us acceptable (7:14). Few find this road because few are willing to accept God's way to obtain eternal life. The only legitimate way to a relationship with God is *his* way: through his Son and his cross.

7:15-18 Often people follow the wide gate and the broad road because they've been given faulty directions. That's why people need to **be on . . . guard against false prophets.** They claim to speak for God, but they're liars. They come camouflaged, looking like sheep when they're actually **wolves** (7:15). How will you know them when you see them? **You'll recognize them by their fruit** (7:16). In saying this, Jesus used an agricultural illustration that makes perfect sense. If a **tree** is healthy, it will **produce good fruit.** If the fruit is bad, it's because the tree itself is **bad** (7:17-18).

The lesson here is that you need to examine the evidence of a teacher's life and ministry. Is that person's teaching and doctrine consistent with God's Word? Does his lifestyle display holiness and love for the Lord? If either answer is no, don't be deceived. Watch out for the counterfeit.

7:19-23 False teachers will experience God's judgment because their actions will demonstrate they never had a spiritual relationship with Jesus Christ (7:19-20). Someone can call Jesus, **Lord, Lord**, and have a ministry that *appears* to be authentic (7:21-22). Nevertheless, a lack of good fruit will expose them. The King of kings will thus respond, **Depart from me, you lawbreakers** (7:23).

7:24-27 I once had a crack on a wall of my house. No matter how many times I had it fixed, the crack came back. Finally, I learned the problem wasn't with the wall; the problem was a shifting foundation. Many of us have "cracks" in our lives—emotional, relational, financial—but we address the symptoms and not the source of the problem.

Jesus concluded the Sermon on the Mount with a story about two men who had three things in common. Each man **built a house** (7:24, 26); both heard the **words of** Jesus (7:24, 26); and both encountered a violent storm (7:25, 27). That's where the similarities end and the contrast begins. One of these men was wise and the other foolish. *Wisdom* is the ability and willingness to apply spiritual truth to life's circumstances. In contrast, *foolishness* is the inability and unwillingness to apply spiritual truth to life's realities.

The wise man heard Jesus's words and acted on them—that is, he built on a **foundation** of **rock** (7:24-25). To do so is harder and more time consuming. The fool built on sand. This is easier, cheaper, and faster to do. But the choice of approaches raises a question: How long do you want your house to stand? You cannot build a skyscraper life on a chicken coop's foundation. If you want stability in your personal life, your family, your ministry, and your community, you need the strong, sturdy foundation of God's Word—which includes both knowledge of the Bible and applying it to life.

The storm revealed which man was wise and which one was foolish. The trials of life will expose what your foundation is made of.

7:28-29 When Jesus had finished his Sermon on the Mount (Matthew 5–7), **the crowds were astonished at his teaching** (7:28) because he taught **like one who had authority, and not like their scribes** (7:29). The Jewish scribes had their traditions and opinions, but Jesus spoke with the authority of the voice of God. And we have his words in the Bible.

IV. HEALINGS AND MIRACLES (8:1–9:38)

8:1-2 Three accounts of healing appear in 8:1-17. Whether or not God heals sickness and disease today is a controversial subject. On the one side are those who say God will always heal if you have enough faith. On the other side are those who insist that God does not heal miraculously today and that healing must be left to the doctors. The Bible's teaching is between these two extremes.

Jesus **came down from the mountain**, and **a man with leprosy** approached him, seeking healing. Matthew makes it clear that Jesus's authority over disease is sovereignly exercised. The man acknowledged this ability to heal but did not presume upon him. He said, **If you are willing** (8:2). God is not your flunky. He is not required to do your bidding. He sovereignly decides what he will and won't do.

8:3-4 To the leper, Jesus responded, **I am willing; be made clean** (8:3). So, *can* the all-powerful Son of God heal? Of course! *Must* he heal? No. But notice: The man had to approach Jesus and ask to be healed. If you don't believe God can heal you, then you may never see that he will. You must be willing to go to him and say, "Lord, I know you can. Will you?" There's nothing wrong with seeking a doctor's help when you're sick. The problem is in neglecting to seek God's help and treating the doctor as if he's a god.

8:5-7 Another healing incident follows on the heels of 8:1-4. A Roman **centurion** pleaded with Jesus to heal his **servant** who was **paralyzed** and suffering (8:5-6). When Jesus spoke of going to the centurion's home to heal him (8:7), the centurion made a shocking reply.

8:8-9 This Roman officer understood how **authority** works. He had men under his command, and he didn't need to be present for his soldiers to obey his orders—any more than he needed Caesar to visit him personally to tell him to jump. A subordinate only needs to know that a superior has issued an order (8:9). The centurion knew that Jesus possessed authority to heal. Therefore, he trusted that Jesus didn't have to be physically present but only **say the word** for his servant to **be healed** (8:8).

8:10-13 Jesus marveled at the centurion's faith. When his own disciples panicked during a storm, he rebuked them for their "little faith" (8:23-27). Yet before him stood a Gentile about whom Jesus said, **I have not found anyone in Israel with so great a faith** (8:10). His kingdom authority and power are available to anyone who puts their trust in him (8:11), but what made the centurion's faith so great was his total confidence in Jesus's word.

The **sons of the kingdom** (8:12) refers to regenerate Jews. Unfaithful believers will lose rewards in Jesus's millennial kingdom rule while faithful believers will be rewarded with rich inheritance. **Outer darkness** and **weeping and gnashing of teeth** (8:12) are a picture of profound regret due to loss of rewards at the judgment seat of Christ because of their unfaithfulness. The context determines whether this phrase is referring to believers (see 25:29-30) or to unbelievers (see 13:47-50).

You don't need to be a spiritual giant, a person of prominence, or a member of a certain class of people. You only need to know who Jesus is and the authority of his Word. Great faith comes when we truly understand the greatness of the object of our faith. The **centurion** had great faith, and Jesus **healed** his **servant** (8:13).

8:14-15 The third healing account concerns Peter's **mother-in-law**, who was **in bed with a fever** (8:14). With a mere touch of Jesus's hand, **the fever left her**, and **she got up and began to serve him** (8:15). Observe her

response to God's work in her life. When the Lord ministers to you, it should be reflected in your service to him.

8:16-17 Many more people were **brought to** Jesus to be healed, including those who were **demon-possessed** and those **who were sick** (8:16). According to Matthew, this **fulfilled** what **Isaiah** spoke: **He himself took our weaknesses and carried our diseases** (8:17; see Isa 53:4). Jesus's healing ministry, then, validated prophecy regarding the Messiah.

Jesus's ability to heal doesn't guarantee all healing (that would deny the reality of death!), but it allows for the possibility of healing. Moreover, because of his death on the cross, sickness, pain, and death will be abolished forever (see Isa 53:5; Rev 21:4).

8:18-20 To be a disciple is to be a fully-devoted, verbal and visible follower of Jesus Christ. Jesus would often preach to crowds and then interact with individuals to see who was serious about discipleship. Once a scribe told him, **Teacher, I will follow you wherever you go** (8:19). But Jesus said **the Son of Man** had **no place to lay his head** (8:20). In other words, he asked, "Are you sure you understand what you're getting yourself into? Will you follow me when there's no Hilton, no Holiday Inn?" Are you committed to him, even when times are hard?

8:21-22 Another person wanted to follow Jesus but said, **First let me go bury my father** (8:21). That's another way of saying he wanted to receive his inheritance before he committed himself to discipleship. Once his father died and left him sufficient funds, he'd be all in. But Jesus permitted no postponement: **Follow me, and let the dead bury their own dead** (8:22)—that is, let those who are spiritually dead worry about such things. Are you willing to risk discipleship even when it doesn't fit with your economic plans?

8:23-25 Jesus used a storm to move his disciples from fear of circumstances to faith in him. While they were traveling by **boat**, a **violent storm arose** but Jesus was **sleeping** (8:23-24). Their circumstances looked bleak so they panicked: **Lord, save us! We're going to die!** (8:25).

8:26-27 Jesus **rebuked the winds and the sea** to calm the storm, and he rebuked the disciples for their **little faith** (8:26). He wanted to expand their understanding of him and their trust in him. As a result of what he did, the disciples were **amazed** at Jesus's lordship over creation (8:27), suggesting they hadn't *fully* known who was in the boat with them.

The storms and trials of life are designed to give you a bigger view of God and a more precise understanding of who Jesus is. The size of your faith is ultimately tied to the size of your God.

8:28-29 Upon reaching their destination, Jesus encountered **two demon-possessed men** coming **out of the tombs** (8:28). That's where demons operate—in the realm of death. The demons recognized Jesus as the **Son of God** and shouted, **Have you come here to torment us before the time?** (8:29). Demons, then, clearly know that a day of judgment is coming. But they refuse to live in light of it. People do that too (see Rom 1:32).

8:30-34 Acknowledging Jesus's authority and power, **the demons begged him** to send them into a **herd of pigs** (8:31). So he sent the demons into the swine, which subsequently plunged **into the sea and perished** (8:32). Pigs were unclean animals, which is likely why the demons chose to be cast into them: demons produce both destruction and death in environments that are unclean. Did the Gentile herdsmen rejoice that two men had been miraculously set free of their oppression? No. Instead, they **reported** the news so that **the whole town . . . begged** Jesus **to leave their region** (8:33-34). Jesus was responsible for a negative impact on their livelihood. So, sadly, financial loss took priority over spiritual gain.

9:1-3 When he left the region of the Gadarenes (8:28), Jesus again crossed the Sea of Galilee and **came to his own town** (9:1), Capernaum (see 4:13). There **some men brought to him a paralytic lying on a stretcher** to be healed. When Jesus saw this, he knew the man had a spiritual need that outweighed his physical one. So he forgave his **sins** (9:2). That move, however, sent the scribes into an uproar. They **said to themselves** that Jesus was guilty of blasphemy because only God has authority to forgive sins (9:3). They were right on the authority matter. By his words, Jesus affirmed his own deity by doing what only God could do.

9:4-8 Using his divine heart-monitor, Jesus perceived **the thoughts** of his critics (9:4) and asked which was easier to say: **Your sins are forgiven** or **Get up and walk** (9:5). Clearly it was easier to claim to be able to forgive sins than to heal, but in order to demonstrate his **authority** in the spiritual realm (**to forgive sins**), he also demonstrated his authority in the physical realm (to heal lame legs). When Jesus **told the paralytic** to **get up** and **go home**, he obeyed his Creator on legs that worked (9:6-7).

The **crowds** were **awestruck** and glorified God (9:8). That's an appropriate response. This Son of Man who has the authority to deal with the physical has the same clout to deal with the spiritual. We should be awestruck by him, too.

9:9 One day Jesus saw **Matthew** (also known as Levi; see Mark 2:14) **sitting at the toll booth** and said, **Follow me.** It wasn't merely that Jesus essentially invited an I.R.S. agent to be his disciple that would soon make people upset. It was worse than that. Jewish tax collectors were considered traitors. They collected taxes from their own people on behalf of the Roman Empire. Moreover, tax collectors would stick their own surcharge onto the tax so that they could make a nice profit off of their fellow Jews. Needless to say, tax collectors were hated. But when Matthew received an invitation from this itinerant teacher and miracle worker, he followed him.

9:10 Once Matthew became a disciple, he had a party and invited his friends to meet Jesus. Now, as a tax collector, whom would Matthew have for friends? **Tax collectors**, of course—as well as other unsavory people. Matthew had found grace and refused to keep it to himself because he knew others needed the same thing.

9:11 When the Pharisees saw this, they were appalled. They couldn't conceive of upstanding, religious Jews socializing and eating with **tax collectors and sinners.** They were resentful that Jesus would be fraternizing with the enemy. Tragically, like the Pharisees, many modern believers turn all of their focus inward to their Christian club and forget the reason Jesus came to earth: to invite new members into the family.

9:12-13 It is not those who are well who need a doctor, but those who are sick (9:12). Jesus observed the obvious: True doctors go where sick people are. Jesus was on a rescue mission. He didn't come to save the secure, but the perishing. He **didn't come to call the righteous, but sinners.** So, he essentially told the Pharisees to go back and study their Bibles by quoting Hosea 6:6: **I desire mercy and not sacrifice** (9:13). The Pharisees offered plenty of religious sacrifices, but their hearts weren't merciful. Similarly, if your praise and worship isn't making you more compassionate toward the lost, you've missed the point of church.

Many Christians get too comfortable in their holy huddles and forget that Jesus Christ invites all believers to be a part of his mission to rescue people from eternal disaster. We need to be like flowing water, not a stagnant pool. To avoid a stagnant spiritual experience, we need our faith to flow toward others. So ask yourself, Have I become too comfortable hanging out with saints? When was the last time I connected a sinner with my Savior?

9:14-17 The disciples of John the Baptist were concerned by what they saw. They wanted to know why Jesus's **disciples** didn't **fast** like they did (9:14). Jesus's simple answer was, "Because it's a party." The kingdom of God had come near because the King of the kingdom—the Messiah—had arrived. A time for fasting would come later when the **groom** (King Jesus) was taken from them. As sure as you don't grieve at a **wedding** feast (9:15), you don't fast at a celebration. Moreover, as a new patch is incompatible with old clothes, **new wine** is incompatible with **old wineskins** (9:16-17).

The newness of the King and his kingdom was incompatible with their religious practices.

9:18-21 A leader whose **daughter** had **just died** knelt before Jesus and begged him for her life (9:18). On the way, a woman who had **suffered from bleeding for twelve years approached** Jesus, believing if she could only touch his clothes she'd **be made well** (9:20-21). Her illness made her ceremonially unclean (see Lev 15:25-27), socially unacceptable, and an outcast as she lived with ongoing physical pain.

She touched one or more of the four ritual tassels that hung from each of the four corners of a rabbi's garment (see Num 15:37-41). They were designed to remind God's people to be faithful to him and seek him for divine intervention. Thus she was making a spiritual commitment (see Zech 8:22-23). Notice that even as Jesus was on his way to help someone else, he wasn't too busy to help this poor woman who came to him in faith. He has enough power to go around.

9:22 Your faith has saved you. The woman's flow of blood would've made her and anything she touched ceremonially unclean. But instead of uncleanness flowing to Jesus through her touch, healing flowed to her.

9:23-26 When Jesus finally arrived at **the leader's house**, the funeral music had begun (9:23). The girl was dead, but death is no match for the Lord of life (9:24). He **took her by the hand, and the girl got up** (9:25). Thus, the **news** of Jesus's power and authority **spread** like wildfire (9:26).

9:27 Two blind men started tailing Jesus, shouting, **Have mercy on us, Son of David!** The prophet Isaiah had much to say about the Messiah, God's Servant, the King who was to come. He would be a descendant of David ("stump of Jesse," Isa 11:1), and he would bring healing ("open blind eyes," Isa 42:7). These men, recognizing Jesus as the Messiah, knew what Jesus could do.

9:28-31 Before he healed them, Jesus asked the men if they believed he could do it (9:28). It's not enough to have faith: that faith must be declared publicly. When they confessed their **faith** in his power, he healed them and **warned them** not to tell anyone (9:29-30). Nevertheless, they **spread the news** (9:31).

9:32-34 A demon-possessed man who was unable to speak was brought to Jesus (9:32). When the Lord drove out the demon, **the man who had been mute** could speak (9:33). This tells us that in the realm of God's kingdom, Satan's power is restrained; thus, you want to be living under God's kingdom rule. **The Pharisees**, though, claimed Jesus was operating under Satan's authority (9:34). This wasn't the last time they would make this accusation. The next time, Jesus would respond (see 12:22-32).

9:35-37 As he did earlier (4:23), Matthew emphasizes Jesus's ministry of **teaching ... preaching ... healing** throughout the towns (9:35). Jesus had deep sympathy for the spiritual condition of the people. They had no spiritual guidance. They were **sheep without a shepherd** (9:36). There was a need for spiritual workers. While the **harvest** of souls was **abundant**, few workers were available to do anything about it. Therefore, he called his disciples—including us—to **pray** for the recruitment of kingdom-minded workers (9:37).

V. SENDING OUT THE TWELVE (10:1-42)

10:1-4 Jesus gathered **his twelve disciples** together and commissioned them to extend his work, giving them **authority** and power to perform what he himself had been doing (10:1). They had been promoted from disciples to **apostles** (10:2). Matthew then lists the Twelve by name, including the one who **betrayed him** (10:2-4).

10:5-10 As he sent them out, he instructed them to take their message only to the Jews, the people **of Israel** (10:5-6). Later, through the ministry of the Holy Spirit, the message of Jesus would spread to the Gentiles (see, for example, Acts 1:8; 10:34-48; 11:1-18). Their message was to be his message: **The kingdom of heaven has come near** (10:7). And they were to validate the power of the kingdom by their miraculous deeds (10:8). They were not to charge money for their ministry, but they could accept support (10:8-10).

10:11-15 They were to extend **peace** to towns and households that welcomed them and the kingdom message they proclaimed (10:11-13). But for **unworthy** households and towns, they were to **shake the dust off [their] feet**—a sign of disdain for rejecting God's kingdom (10:13-14). The **day of judgment** will be more bearable for the wicked Old Testament towns **of Sodom and Gomorrah than** it will be for those who reject the message of Jesus (10:15).

10:16-20 Jesus made clear to the Twelve that persecution from kingdom opponents would accompany message proclamation (10:17), so they were to be **shrewd** but **innocent**—that is, to minister with wisdom and grace (10:16). Jesus predicted that they would stand **before governors and kings** because they were his followers. They were to use such instances to testify, through the power of **the Spirit**, about the King and the kingdom (10:18-20).

10:21-25 Even family members will turn against believers. Christians will be **hated** because of the **name** of Jesus (10:21-22). This persecution will become especially intense during the tribulation period, about which Jesus will have more to say (see Matt 24). The goal of a **disciple** is **to become like his teacher** (10:24-25). So if they call Jesus **Beelzebul**, the ruler of demons (Satan), his followers shouldn't expect to receive better treatment from the world (10:25).

10:26-31 Don't be afraid of them. What motivation does Jesus offer to enable them to become fearless? First, there is **nothing hidden that won't be made known** (10:26). No persecution of God's people, then, will remain secret forever. God *will* turn the tables. Second, there's no need to **fear those who** have temporary power in history; believers rightly fear the one who has limitless power in eternity (10:28). Third, God the Father has great love for his children. He's sovereign over the events of your life. Nothing comes to you that hasn't first passed through his fingers. His children are valuable to him (10:29-31).

10:32-33 Everyone who will acknowledge me before others, I will also acknowledge him before my Father in heaven (10:32). The Greek word translated "acknowledge" can also be rendered as "confess." To confess something is to publicly affirm it—to declare it openly and plainly. Jesus isn't talking about salvation here. His words are set in the context of a discussion about being a disciple (10:24-25). You can be saved but fail to publicly acknowledge your relationship with Jesus. But if you're a secret agent Christian, you're not a disciple.

If you confess Jesus—go public with your Christian faith—Jesus will confess you before the Father and intercede for you. He'll run interference for you. But if you deny him before men, he will **deny** you **before [the] Father** (10:33). Again, this is not referring to salvation in eternity but deliverance in history. If you're a covert follower of Jesus, there will be negative repercussions; you can expect prayer requests to be denied in history and loss of kingdom rewards in eternity.

10:34-37 Don't assume that I came to bring peace on the earth (10:34). Peace on earth is coming, but not yet. Association with Jesus can introduce problems in your relationships—even within your own family (10:35-36). Some people, in fact, will be placed in situations in which they will have to choose love of Christ over love of **father** and **mother** as their parents demand that they renounce Christ (10:37).

10:38 A disciple of Jesus must **take up his cross and follow** him. The cross of Christ became relevant to you the day you accepted Jesus as your Savior, but you don't leave it behind after the moment of salvation. Instead, you're to carry it with you.

Your "cross" has to do with your public identification with Jesus. To bear your cross is to endure hardship specifically because you're a visible and verbal follower of him. If you're unwilling to do that, you're unworthy of Christ—that is, your relationship is distant.

10:39 In order to experience the life you're looking for, you must be willing to lose the life you have. This is one of Jesus's paradoxical statements. Give your life over to Christ, and he'll give it back to you. Try to live your life on your own terms, and you'll **lose** what you think you have.

10:40-42 A disciple of Jesus Christ is his representative. As Paul would later say, "We are ambassadors for Christ" (2 Cor 5:20). In fact, Jesus said the association is so close that when people welcome his disciples, they welcome him (10:40). This brings to mind another teaching of Paul: Christians "are the body of Christ" (1 Cor 12:27). When people show kindness to Jesus's disciples because of their public affiliation with him, Jesus takes notice and will **reward** such generosity (10:42).

VI. CONFUSION AND OPPOSITION (11:1–12:50)

11:1-3 As his **twelve disciples** departed on their mission, Jesus continued **to teach . . . in their towns** (11:1). When John the Baptist **heard in prison what the Christ was doing, he sent a message** (11:2). Matthew doesn't tell us until later about John's arrest (14:3-5), but he tells us now about John's confusion. John asked Jesus, **Are you the one?** (11:3). John had believed that Jesus was the Christ (3:14). But as he languished in prison, he began to have doubts. Wasn't the Christ supposed to separate the "wheat" from "the chaff" (see 3:12)? Jesus's miracles and healings were fine, but when would he judge God's enemies?

11:4-6 We all need reassurance at times, and John was no different. So Jesus reminded him of what he had been doing. His healing ministry and his proclamation of **the good news** matched the expectations of the Messiah (11:4-5; see Isa 61:1). His words and deeds validated who he was. The judgment of the wicked would come in the future. Now was a time of good news and grace.

11:7-15 A As these men were leaving, Jesus spoke **to the crowds about John.** He was no **reed swaying in the wind** (11:7). John was a kingdom man, urging sinners to repent (3:1-12). He was **a prophet** (11:9) who wasn't intimidated by the religious leaders or the king (3:7-10; 14:3-5). Moreover, he was God's chosen **messenger**, as foretold in the Old Testament, who would **prepare** the **way** for Christ (11:10; see Mal 3:1). Like the great Old Testament prophet **Elijah**, he boldly proclaimed God's word and faced violent opposition (11:12-14; see 1 Kgs 19:1-5; Matt 14:6-12). As John himself confessed, he was not the Messiah but a signpost pointing the way (John 1:19-23).

11:16-19 Jesus compared the **generation** that was rejecting his message to a group of fussy **children** who were never satisfied (11:16-17). John the Baptist lived an ascetic lifestyle, and they called him **demon**-possessed (11:18). **The Son of Man** ate and drank, and they called him **a glutton and a drunkard, a friend of tax collectors and sinners.** There's just no pleasing some people, **yet wisdom is vindicated by her deeds** (11:19)—that is, your ability to apply spiritual truth will be demonstrated by what you do. Those who scorned John and Jesus proved that their wisdom tanks were on empty.

11:20-24 Then Jesus got angry and named names. He denounced towns that had seen **his miracles** but **did not repent: Chorazin ... Bethsaida ... Capernaum** (11:20-21, 23). How bad would it be for them? Wicked Old Testament cities that incurred God's wrath will find **the day of judgment** more **tolerable** than will those cities that rejected Jesus (11:22, 24). These Galilean cities had heard the word and seen the power of the King of kings, the God-man. Therefore, their actions would be weightier. The greater the

knowledge of God's revelation, the greater the accountability for those who reject it.

11:25-27 Few would claim to have burden-free lives. In 11:28-30, Jesus tells his disciples how to release the burdens they're carrying. But first he lets them eavesdrop on a prayer pertinent to the topic: **I praise you, Father, ... because you have hidden these things from the wise and intelligent and revealed them to infants** (11:25). That statement isn't meant to disparage education. He's referring to those who think they can figure out life without God.

The answers to life's questions aren't discovered in graduate school, where you can obtain information without spiritual illumination. That's why Jesus said, in effect, "Thank you, Father, that you keep secrets from people who think they're smart enough to figure out life independent of you." God is happy to hide answers from those who don't think they need him (11:25-26).

The answer to life's burdens isn't found via human wisdom but through accepting the divine viewpoint. We must become like **infants** that trust their daddy (11:25). And the only way to know and have access to our **Father** who hides things from self-sufficient people is through knowing and trusting his **Son** Jesus Christ (11:27).

11:28 Come to me, all of you who are weary and burdened,. If life is weighing you down—if the burden you're carrying is too much to bear—come to Jesus. Why? Because only he can **give you rest.** In view here is the invitation to salvation. To rest is to put your burdens in God's hands and enjoy his provision of forgiveness and eternal life.

11:29 Take up my yoke and learn from me. Once you've come to Jesus, he invites you to hook up to him as a disciple. A yoke is a wooden bar harnessed to the necks of a pair of oxen to bring them under submission and enable them to do the work that the farmer has for them. To train younger oxen, farmers would yoke them to older, experienced oxen. It provided maturation and development.

Hooking to Jesus's "yoke" enables you to **learn** how to live. Therein **you will find rest.**

When you come to Jesus, he *gives* you rest in terms of your salvation. When you accept the yoke of discipleship, you *find* rest and experience it in your daily life.

11:30 My yoke is easy and my burden is light. Following Jesus won't make every problem in your life disappear. Jesus didn't say you would no longer have burdens if you hitched to him. He said their weight would decrease. A suitcase packed full may be too heavy to carry. But, if the case has wheels, your burden will become lighter though your circumstances haven't changed. God can put wheels on your burdens so that you can deal with them more easily.

12:1-2 The Pharisees were known for their knowledge of Scripture and their love of rules. When they saw Jesus's **disciples** picking and eating **grain** on **the Sabbath** (12:1), they said, "They're breaking the law!" (12:2). According to the Mosaic law, you couldn't work on the Sabbath, but the Pharisees had created so many additional regulations and introduced so many scenarios to the way the Sabbath was handled that they considered the disciples' actions equivalent to working in the grain fields.

12:3-4 Notice Jesus's response to the judgmental Pharisees: **Haven't you read what David did?** (12:3)—that is to say, "Don't you know your Bibles?" To mention David was to mention a Jewish hero. When David and his men were running from Saul, he took **the bread of the Presence** from **the house of God**—the tabernacle—for them to eat, even though it was **only for the priests** (12:4). Scripture itself, then, testifies that God's laws were never meant to get in the way of taking care of the necessities of life. The Sabbath was for the benefit of man, not for his destruction (see Mark 2:27).

12:5-8 Jesus also reminded them that **the priests . . . violate the Sabbath** all the time! They have to do God's work on **the Sabbath** (12:5). The Pharisees were legalists, serving to remind us that whenever the commands of God prevent you from loving and serving God, you're using his commands inappropriately. Jesus quoted from Hosea 6:6 to

show that the Lord is a God of **mercy**, not judgmentalism (12:7). He's not impressed if you know your Bible but have a heart of stone.

Finally, Jesus finished with the clincher: **Something greater than the temple is here** (12:6). The *only* thing greater than God's house is God; therefore, Jesus was letting them know who he was. Then he added, **The Son of Man is Lord of the Sabbath** (12:8). And since it's his show, he gets to decide how the Sabbath is honored.

12:9-10 On another occasion, Jesus saw a man with **a shriveled hand** in a **synagogue**, and the Pharisees asked if it was **lawful to heal on the Sabbath**. However, they weren't asking an honest question but looking for an opportunity to **accuse him** (12:10).

12:11-14 So Jesus turned the tables on them—as he so often did. Who wouldn't help his **sheep** if it **fell into a pit on the Sabbath**? (12:11). No one, of course. The Pharisees, then, were willing to do for a sheep what they wouldn't do for a hurting man! Jesus reasoned that acts of mercy don't dishonor the Sabbath—especially since people are more valuable than animals (12:12). Then he mercifully healed the man (12:13), while the **Pharisees** showed their true colors by plotting to **kill** Jesus (12:14).

12:15-21 Though his crowds were growing as **he healed them all** (12:15), Jesus **warned them not to make him known** (12:16). He wasn't seeking public notoriety. He wasn't seeking to be a superstar. As Matthew says, he wanted to fulfill God's Word as written in Isaiah 42:1-4, demonstrating the Messiah's compassion (12:17-21).

12:22-24 Attacking Jesus for his Sabbath observance wasn't enough for the Pharisees. When he healed **a demon-possessed man** and the **crowds** went wild (12:22-23), the Pharisees accused Jesus of driving out **demons** by the power of **Beelzebul**—that is, by Satan—**the ruler of the demons** (12:24).

12:25-29 Jesus observed how illogical their accusation was: **If Satan drives out Satan, he is divided against himself** (12:26). Satan may be thoroughly evil, but he's more clever than that. He doesn't work against his own plan, and the Pharisees knew it. The only alternative was the truth: Jesus had driven out demons **by the Spirit of God** (12:28). To illustrate, he spoke about tying up a **strong man** in order to steal from him (12:29). Jesus was saying that he could plunder Satan because he's stronger than Satan. His kingdom power over the forces of darkness had been displayed before their eyes.

12:30-32 Jesus's power over the devil was evident, and he told the Pharisees that **every sin and blasphemy** could **be forgiven.** That's why he came. But **the blasphemy against the Spirit will not be** (12:31). God revealed the reality of who Jesus is through his mighty words and works. If anyone rejects this demonstration of the Holy Spirit's power and attributes it to the devil, he is rejecting salvation.

To say from your heart (see 12:34) that the clear manifestation of Jesus Christ is the work of Satan reveals a hardened heart. If a person is worried that he has committed the sin of blasphemy against the Holy Spirit, then he clearly has not done so yet. He must show repentance (see 12:33-35) and come to Jesus by faith for forgiveness and the free gift of eternal life. Jesus even gave this opportunity to the leaders who were accusing him and invited them to take their stand with him (12:30).

12:33-37 Jesus returned to the illustration of a tree and its fruit used in 7:15-20: **A tree is known by its fruit** (12:33). The quality of its produce reflects the character of the tree. And considering displays of the Pharisees' fruit (12:1-32), Jesus called them what they were: a **brood of vipers** (12:34). The words the Pharisees spoke were windows into their hearts.

When you open your mouth, you reveal what's deep down inside—whether good or evil. So you've got to watch your mouth. God is tape-recording our words, and we will **have to account for every careless** one (12:36). The way to tame your tongue is to address your heart. And the way to address your heart is to devote it to the King's agenda.

12:38 Some of the scribes and Pharisees hadn't had enough. They pushed Jesus further: **We want to see a sign from you.** In other words, give us proof that you are who you claim to be. Yet, he'd given them plenty of demonstrations of his power and authority, and they'd said he was doing the devil's work (12:24)! Only spiritually stubborn and blind people request a sign in the face of overwhelming evidence.

12:39-40 The only sign Jesus would give them was **the sign of the prophet Jonah** (12:39), who was **in the belly of the huge fish three days and three nights.** Jesus would similarly spend **three days and three nights** in the earth (12:40). His resurrection from the dead would be the crowning demonstration that he is the Son of God.

12:41-42 On the day of **judgment**, many Gentiles will stand and condemn the wicked generation of Israelites who rejected Jesus. After all, the citizens of **Nineveh** repented at the preaching of **Jonah**, who had no great sign to show (12:41). **The queen of the south** traveled far to hear the wisdom of Solomon, who was a mere earthly king. But **something greater** than Jonah and Solomon had arrived (12:42). The heavenly King had come working miraculous signs, so they were without excuse for not repenting and believing in him.

12:43-45 Jesus compared the **evil generation** (12:45) that refused to receive him with a man who has **an unclean spirit.** The spirit comes out of the man, wanders, and decides to return (12:43-44). When it arrives, the spirit finds its old home **swept** and **put in order** (12:44), so it brings along **seven other spirits more evil than itself** so that the man's **condition is worse than** it was (12:45). If you try to clean up your life with self-righteousness and religious activity, you'll only make yourself worse. Without submission to the Lord and the presence of the Holy Spirit to fill the void, you're simply opening yourself to greater demonic influence.

12:46-47 As Jesus spoke to **the crowds,** someone informed him that **his mother**

and brothers wanted to speak with him. The Gospel of John says Jesus's brothers didn't believe in him during his ministry (John 7:1-5), so perhaps they'd come to take him home quietly. Regardless, this gave Jesus another opportunity to explain what true commitment to him is all about.

12:48-50 Whoever does the will of my Father in heaven is my brother and sister and mother (12:50). True belonging in the family of God, then, transcends biological family relations. Our blood relationships—whether by family or race—are outweighed by our relationship to other Christians through Jesus's blood. When you trust in Christ, you have a new family. This doesn't mean you ignore your physical family. It means your obedience as a child of your heavenly Father takes priority.

VII. PARABLES ABOUT THE KINGDOM (13:1-58)

13:1-9 Jesus began using parables to teach about the kingdom. A *parable* is a story used as an analogy to explain a spiritual truth. The first parable describes a **sower** who scattered seed on various kinds of soils (13:3). Each piece of **ground** produced a different result (13:4-8). As Jesus explains in 13:18-23, this story illustrates the different ways people respond when they hear the word of God. It's crucial that you not only hear Jesus, but have a heart that's willing to receive his words in order to benefit from them.

13:10-17 Why did Jesus speak **in parables** (13:10)? The disciples had been granted understanding of **the secrets of the kingdom**, but those who rejected him were not given such understanding (13:11). The "secrets," or "mysteries," of the kingdom refer to those things that were hidden in the Old Testament and are revealed in the New, with the coming of Christ. When you respond to the spiritual light you've been given, you'll receive more light—more understanding. But when you reject the light, the opposite happens (13:12).

Jesus spoke in parables to give understanding to the disciples while also confounding those who refused to believe (13:13). This fulfilled Isaiah's prophecy (see Isa 6:9-10), which spoke of those who would **listen** and not **understand** spiritual truth because of their **callous** hearts (13:14-15). Disciples, by contrast, are **blessed** because they **see** and **hear** (with understanding) the very Messiah (13:16) whom **many prophets and righteous people longed** for (13:17).

13:18-23 Jesus interpreted **the parable of the sower** (13:2-9), which has to do with one's response to the word of God—that is, living under the rule of God's kingdom. For some, **the evil one** snatches away the word before it can penetrate the heart so that they can be converted to faith in Christ (13:19). Others receive the word with joy (i.e., get converted), but they fail to grow in Christ because of the cares and pressures of the world (13:20-21). Still other believers aren't able to bear fruit because the word becomes choked out by worldliness and wealth (13:22). But the good soil represents the kingdom disciple who **hears** the word, **understands** it, and produces **fruit** (13:23). Fruit that results from faithful discipleship is always visible and benefits others. The parable's point is clear: It is the condition of the heart in its openness to receive and respond to God's word that will determine the word's effectiveness in a person's life.

13:24-30 In Jesus's parable about weeds and wheat, **the kingdom** is **compared to a man who sowed good seed in his field**, while **his enemy** snuck in and **sowed weeds among the wheat** (13:24-25). The farmer refuses to let his **servants** uproot the **weeds** since the **wheat** might also be ripped out in the process (13:27-29). Therefore, he tells the servants to **let both grow together.** The **reapers** will separate them **at harvest time** (13:30). Matthew includes Jesus's explanation of the parable in 13:36-43.

13:31-33 The kingdom is also **like a mustard seed** (13:31). Though it's smaller than other seeds, it grows to become **taller than** other **plants** (13:32). Though God's kingdom rule began in a seemingly insignificant way with a few Galilean fishermen and a tax collector, it would grow tremendously with the blessings of God. Christianity would become a significant worldwide movement in spite of its humble beginnings. Similarly, Jesus's parable of the **leaven** (13:33) reminds us that though the kingdom started out small, it will continue to expand and spread throughout the world by the power of the Holy Spirit.

13:34-35 Matthew frequently observes how Jesus's life, words, and deeds fulfilled the Old Testament (e.g., 2:15; 4:14-16; 8:17; 12:17-21). Even his ministry of teaching **in parables** was a fulfillment of Scripture (see Ps 78:2).

13:36-43 When the **crowds** left, the **disciples** asked Jesus privately to **explain** the meaning **of the parable of the weeds** to them (13:36; see 13:24-30). Jesus identified all the characters in the story (13:37-39), revealing that it's about the battle between the Son of Man and the devil. Both Christ and Satan sow their children in the world—those who do their will. But such won't go on forever. The Lord will send **his angels** to reap the **harvest** at the **end of the age** (13:39-41). Those who follow Satan will be cast **into the blazing furnace** to be punished. Here **weeping and gnashing of teeth** (13:42) refers to the profound regret of unbelievers who are cast into hell since they enter eternity without imputed righteousness (see 2 Cor 5:21). Those who follow the Son **will shine** in **their Father's kingdom** (13:43).

Self-righteous religion will grow in the world alongside true Christianity. There will be those who appear to be saved. They use spiritual-sounding language and get involved in church programs, but their Christianity is only an imitation. They may camouflage themselves among true believers, but God can't be deceived.

13:44-46 **The kingdom of heaven is like treasure, buried in a field** (13:44) and like a **priceless pearl** (13:46). Discoverers are willing to give up everything they possess in order to gain their prizes because they recognize their incalculable value (13:44, 46). Similarly,

men and women who discover and recognize the worth of living life under the rule of God will sacrifice anything of earthly value for participation in his kingdom. Life holds no greater treasure.

13:47-50 **The kingdom of heaven is like a large net thrown into the sea** that **collected every kind of fish** (13:47). What do good fishermen do? They gather the **good fish** and throw out **the worthless ones** (13:48). So also, **at the end of the age**, God's **angels** will **separate the evil people from the righteous**, throwing the evil **into the blazing furnace** (13:49-50). Like the parable of the weeds and wheat (13:24-30, 36-43), this illustration of fish in a net describes the final judgment when those who persist in unrepentance and unbelief will be cast into hell. Here again **weeping and gnashing of teeth** (13:50) refers to the profound regret of unbelievers who have rejected salvation.

Hell is an uncomfortable topic. But when you're dying of cancer and need drastic medical treatment, the doctor isn't concerned about making you comfortable. He tells you about the plan that might save your life. Sin is worse than cancer. Christians need to share the truth about Jesus, so that unbelievers have a chance to undergo gospel surgery and avoid the blazing furnace of God's judgment.

13:51-53 Jesus concluded his parables (13:53) by comparing **every teacher of the law who has become a disciple** to an **owner of a house who brings out of his storeroom treasures new and old** (13:52). He wasn't talking about a special class of Christians. All believers are called to be disciples of Jesus and students of the Word. As you grow in understanding the Bible—both *the new* (the teachings of Jesus and the apostles in the New Testament) and *the old* (the law and the prophets of the Old Testament)—you are to help the world know the King and follow his kingdom rule.

13:54-58 After this, Jesus **went to his hometown** of Nazareth and taught in **their synagogue**. But he didn't exactly receive a warm homecoming there. Though **they were astonished** at his **wisdom** and **miraculous powers** (11:54), **they were offended** when they realized he was one of them: "We know his family. How could this common man have this uncommon wisdom and power? He's no better than us!" (11:54-57). And as a result of **their unbelief**, he **did not do many miracles there** (11:58).

Unbelief can stop the miraculous. God will choose not to do things that he wants to do when you don't take seriously what he has to say. Don't be a hindrance to God's work in your life. Believe his word. Trust his promises. Follow in obedience.

VIII. SPREADING MINISTRY AND GROWING OPPOSITION (14:1–17:27)

14:1-2 Matthew previously mentioned the ministry of John the Baptist (3:1-16), his arrest by Herod Antipas (4:12), and his question about Jesus's identity (11:1-6). Here we learn the details of his arrest and martyrdom. **Herod the tetrarch** (14:1)—also known as Herod Antipas—was the son of Herod the Great, who'd sought to kill the infant Jesus (2:1-23). As we'll see, the apple didn't fall far from the tree. When Herod learned about Jesus's ministry, he panicked: **This is John the Baptist. . . . He has been raised from the dead** (14:2).

14:3-12 John had condemned Herod for having an illicit relationship with his own sister-in-law, **Herodias** (14:3-4). Herod wanted to execute him, but he was afraid of **the crowd** who considered John **a prophet** (14:5), so he simply locked John up. But Herodias wanted revenge. On **Herod's birthday**, he recklessly promised **Herodias's daughter** that he would give her anything (14:6-7). **Prompted by her mother**, she callously asked for John's **head** (14:8)! Herod reluctantly agreed and ordered John's death (14:9-12).

Herodias couldn't stand to hear John the Baptist call attention to her sin, so she wanted him dead. Herod's guilty conscience plagued him so much that he killed John and thought he'd come back to haunt him. The rejection of God by unbelievers will often lead them to hate his followers and their righteous lives (see 1 John 3:12-13).

14:13-17 When Jesus heard about John's death, **he withdrew . . . to a remote place.** Yet **the crowds** followed, and he continued to minister to them (14:13-14). Since they were in a **deserted** area, **the disciples** pressured Jesus to **send** the people to **the villages** to

buy food for themselves (14:15). But Jesus would have none of that: **You give them something to eat** (14:16). So the disciples threw up their arms and said, **But we only have five loaves and two fish** (14:17).

14:18-21 With the problem identified and his followers at a loss for how to fix it, Jesus went into action. He said in effect, **"Bring your 'not-enough' to me,"** and he **blessed** what they had (14:18-19). Miraculously, the disciples were able to give enough food to feed **five thousand men, besides women and children**—perhaps 15,000–20,000 people (14:19-21). Not only that, but the disciples also **picked up twelve baskets full of leftover pieces** (14:20). In other words, each of the Twelve got a doggy bag to remind them of what Jesus could do.

"Not-enough" can become "more-than-enough" when two things happen. First, rather than dismissing it, bring what little you have to Jesus. Second, believe that Jesus can intercede in your situation, bringing abundance out of deficiency. Put him first and see what he can do. He can demonstrate the supernatural in the midst of your natural problem.

14:22 Immediately, the **disciples** moved from a scene of miraculous provision from God (14:15-21) to a terrifying encounter (14:24-26). Yet notice that the circumstances that brought them fear fell under the Lord's sovereign control: Jesus **made the disciples get into the boat and go ahead of him.** They were in God's perfect will and about to enter a perfect storm, indicating that obeying God can sometimes lead to rough sailing. Nevertheless, it can only reach you by divine design and permission.

14:23-24 When the boat was far from shore, they were **battered by the waves, because the wind was against them** (14:24). And where was Jesus? He'd gone up **the mountain by himself to pray** (14:23). Though Jesus was absent from them, he wasn't unmindful of their needs. Paul told the Romans that Jesus intercedes for believers (Rom 8:34). His fulltime job is serving as the intercessor between you and God. And he's the perfect one to do it because he's fully God and fully human. He understands God, and he understands you.

14:25-27 In the midst of the disciples' distress, **Jesus came toward them walking on the sea** (11:25). The battering waves were their problem, and that's exactly what Jesus walked on. He came to them in an unexpected way so they could understand and experience him as never before. As he'd done previously (8:23-27), Jesus demonstrated his divine authority over the world that he himself created (see John 1:3; Col 1:16; Heb 1:2). When the disciples panicked, thinking him **a ghost**, he comforted them with his word before he addressed their circumstances (14:26-27).

14:28-32 That's when **Peter** did what no one else would. He asked Jesus to permit him to join him (11:28). Peter didn't want to merely be protected from trouble; he wanted to experience something with Jesus that he'd never dreamed possible. So Jesus invited Peter forward, and this bold disciple **started walking on the water** (11:29). When he lost focus on Jesus and gave attention to the **strength of the wind**, however, he became **afraid**, started **to sink**, and cried to Jesus to **save** him (14:30).

Matthew wants readers to know that this miracle was made possible by Jesus's power, not Peter's. Before you look down your nose at Peter, though, keep in mind that he was the only one who got out of the boat to attempt the impossible. The other disciples just stared as Peter stepped out in faith. Remember, Jesus rebuked him for having *little* **faith**— not for having *no* faith (14:31). Moreover, when Peter began to sink, he knew where to turn. In response to Peter's cry, Jesus **caught hold of him**, took him **into the boat**, and **the wind ceased** (14:31-32).

14:33 Why would Jesus intentionally let his followers go through such a fearful situation? Look what happened when he saved them. The disciples **worshiped him** and declared, **Truly you are the Son of God!** You may be wondering, Didn't they know this already? Yes, they did. But with each new encounter, Jesus increased their understanding and deepened their experience of him. By God's grace, they had been given an opportunity, through fearful circumstances, to come to know Jesus at a deeper level and worship him. He is the sovereign Son of God who exercises power over all things, wants you to discover that he's bigger than your fears, and invites you to praise him.

14:34-36 When they landed the boat **at Gennesaret**, the **whole vicinity** flooded Jesus with **sick** people who **begged** him to make them well (14:34-35). Those who just touched **the end of his robe . . . were healed** (14:36)! The power of the kingdom emanated from Jesus Christ. One day that power will rid the universe of pain and death forever (see Rev 21:4).

15:1-2 Jesus's sparring with the **Pharisees and scribes** continued (15:1; see 12:1-45). After observing his disciples, these religious leaders had an objection. Jesus's **disciples** were breaking **the tradition of the elders** because they didn't **wash their hands when** they ate (15:2). This wasn't a matter of proper hygiene. Washing hands before meals was a purely ritualistic exercise that had no basis in the Old Testament Scriptures. Nevertheless, they considered it a religious duty signaling spiritual purity.

15:3-9 Jesus didn't let this one slip by. Jesus had some objections of his own for them: **Why do you break God's commandment because of your tradition?** (15:3). Furthermore, he accused them of **teaching as doctrines human commands** (15:9).

Traditions aren't necessarily bad. They typically involve passing on some custom, practice, or belief to subsequent generations. Families can enjoy traditions. God provided Israel with many traditions to follow as part of his law and sacrificial system. But the problem with traditions comes in when they invalidate, cover up, camouflage, or negate the Word of God. And that's what had happened. The Pharisees taught and practiced traditions that they elevated to the level of Scripture, and that actually allowed them to ignore Scripture.

Jesus called them out for their traditionalism. Then he gave an example. The Old Testament commanded Israel to **honor your father and your mother** and mandated the death penalty for Israelites who spoke evil of their parents (15:4; see Exod 20:12; 21:17). But the Pharisees had a tradition that allowed them to bypass caring for their elderly parents by instead giving **a gift committed to the temple** (15:5). The practice allowed them to say, "Sorry, Mom and Dad, I can't offer you financial assistance. I'm giving to God instead." By means of their **tradition**, they had invalidated God's **word** (15:6).

Hypocrites! Jesus called it like it was. They were pretenders, preaching one thing but doing another. Jesus said **Isaiah prophesied correctly about** them: **This people honors me with their lips, but their heart is far from me. They worship me in vain** (15:7-8). When you replace Scripture with something of your own invention, you're wasting your time in worship on Sunday.

15:10-11 In light of his confrontation with the Pharisees and scribes, Jesus gathered the crowd to explain where true defilement comes from (15:10). The Pharisees ritualistically washed their hands before meals as a means of keeping themselves pure and undefiled. To be "defiled" religiously is to become dirty or polluted by sin. But Jesus turned wrong thinking about the topic on its head: **It's not what goes into the mouth that defiles a person, but what comes out of the mouth** (15:11).

Moral pollution, then, comes from the *inside*, not the *outside*. Your unwashed hands are not your problem. Your dirty heart is. We tend to justify our sinful words and actions by pointing to what others did that caused our responses, but our circumstances don't cause our sin. They just provide the context and the opportunity for the sinful desires ruling our hearts to express themselves. Defilement is an internal matter, and external activity can't change a heart.

15:12-14 The disciples asked Jesus if he realized that **the Pharisees** were offended by what he said (15:12). We can be confident that Jesus wasn't concerned with offending the Pharisees, given his response: **They are blind guides.** Unless you want to **fall into a pit,** don't follow them (15:14).

15:15-20 Jesus was more concerned with clearing up his disciples' **lack** of **understanding** (15:16) than with offending the Pharisees. When Peter asked him to **explain** his comments about being defiled (15:15), Jesus answered. When you eat food, it goes **into the mouth**, through **the stomach**, and is **eliminated** (15:17). No harm done. **Eating with unwashed hands** might make you sick, but it can't **defile** you (15:20).

What comes out of the mouth comes from the heart, and this defiles a person (15:18). Jesus spoke of the heart to refer to our inner spiritual selves. The heart is where sin and defilement arise. It's responsible for **evil thoughts, murders, adulteries, sexual immoralities, thefts, false testimonies, slander** (15:19).

You can engage in endless religious habits, but these don't have the power to make you a better man or woman because following external traditions can't change a wicked heart. But Jesus can, because he's a heart specialist. Through a relationship with him, your heart can be transformed so that you love God and love people.

15:21-24 Jesus left there and went **to the area of Tyre and Sidon** (15:21). The Old Testament prophets denounced these Gentile cities on the Mediterranean Coast for their wickedness (see Isa 23; Ezek 28; Joel 3:4-8). While he was there, **a Canaanite woman** pleaded with him to heal her **daughter** who was **severely tormented by a demon** (15:22). She was a pagan whose child was suffering severely, yet that was only her first problem.

The second problem was that in spite of the fact that she acknowledged him as the Jewish Messiah, the **Son of David** (15:22), **Jesus did not say a word to her** (15:23). Has that ever happened to you? Have you prayed repeatedly only to feel like heaven's answer was a busy signal?

Her third problem was the response of **his disciples.** As she continued to make a spectacle of herself, they **urged** Jesus to **send her away** because of the racket (15:23). So not only did Jesus not respond to her pleas, but his followers were trying to shut her up.

Jesus's spoken response was her fourth problem: **I was sent only to the lost sheep of the house of Israel** (15:24). In other words, he'd been sent on a mission to the Jews—not the Gentiles. Now, we know from the rest of Matthew (e.g., 8:5-13), and the rest of the Bible (e.g., Rom 1:16), that Jesus brought God's grace to all people, Jew and Gentile alike. But the focus of his earthly ministry was on the children of Abraham, Isaac, and Jacob. After his death and resurrection, he would command his disciples to take his message to "all nations" (Matt 28:19) and to "the ends of the earth" (Acts 1:8).

15:25 Would you have given up after hearing Jesus's response in verse 24? Most readers wouldn't be surprised if Matthew said the woman turned and walked away. But she didn't. Instead, she **knelt before him** and cried, **Lord, help me!** (15:25). Like Jacob wrestling with God, this Canaanite woman wouldn't "let go" unless Jesus blessed her (see Gen 32:24-26). Remember: when God doesn't answer your prayers about a specific need, it's likely he's trying to deepen your faith. So be persistent in prayer.

15:26-27 To the woman's persistence Jesus replied, **It isn't right to take the children's bread and throw it to the dogs** (15:26). The Greek word for "dogs" typically referred to little house-dogs or lap dogs. So Jesus wasn't insulting the woman but saying he had to feed the Jews first, just as a parent is obliged to feed the children before the house pets. Nevertheless, she wasn't giving up. **Even the dogs eat the crumbs that fall from their masters' table** (15:27)—that is, "Even though the puppies don't eat first, they still get to eat! I'm willing to settle for your leftovers, Jesus." That's desperate humility.

15:28 This woman needed the Lord's grace and wouldn't let anything stand in the way— not her race, not Jesus's silence, not her pride. And that's exactly where Jesus wanted her

to be. **Woman, your faith is great,** he told her, and then he healed **her daughter.** This Canaanite started with *faith.* Then, by persevering through a series of difficulties intended by God to take her deeper, she ended up with *great faith.*

15:29-31 Near **the Sea of Galilee, Jesus went up on a mountain,** and the **crowds** brought him **the lame, the blind, the crippled, those unable to speak, and many others** (15:29-30). **He healed them,** and they marveled at his kingdom power, giving **glory to the God of Israel** (15:30-31).

15:32-39 Then Jesus had **compassion on the crowd.** They had been with him for **days,** and he didn't want to **send them away hungry** (15:32). He was concerned for their physical and social well-being. But the disciples pointed out that they only had seven **loaves** of bread and **a few small fish** (15:34). So Jesus commanded the crowds to sit down, took the loaves and fish, and did an amazing thing: He **gave thanks** for insufficiency (15:35-36). When you have a need, give thanks for what you have, and let God multiply it to what you need. Jesus miraculously gave enough food to feed the crowds—**four thousand men ... besides women and children** (15:37-38).

Notice, though, that the food didn't supernaturally appear in the hands of the crowd. Rather, he used his **disciples** to distribute it (15:36). Jesus is at the center of his kingdom rule, and he calls his disciples to be distributors—on his behalf—of the blessings, provisions, power, and message of the kingdom.

16:1 The **Pharisees** had confronted Jesus previously. Now **the Sadducees** joined them. Though both were Jewish religious groups, they had little in common. They disagreed on significant theological matters, but their mutual disdain for Jesus brought them together to test him and ask him **to show them a sign from heaven.** Often in the Gospels, miracles are referred to as signs. So these religious leaders wanted Jesus to prove himself with a supernatural sign.

16:2-3 Jesus responded with a meteorological lesson. You don't have to be a genius to make an educated guess about the weather.

You don't have to see rain falling to know that it's about to rain (16:2-3). The men confronting him knew **how to read the appearance of the sky**, but they missed the open and obvious signs that the kingdom of God had appeared in Jesus Christ. They couldn't **read the signs of the times** (16:3), though Jesus had presented clear evidence. If they were really interested in who he was, the signs of the times would've convinced them of the truth.

16:4 Their pursuit of a **sign** was **evil** because they stubbornly rejected what God had already done through Jesus and demanded a custom-tailored command performance. **No sign**, therefore, would be given to them **except the sign of Jonah**. As Jonah spent three days "in the belly of the fish" (Jonah 1:17), Jesus Christ would spend three days in the belly of the earth (see 12:39-40). In effect, Jesus said, "You want a sign? I'm going to give you a whopper."

Jesus was going to rise from the dead. His resurrection would be the sign of signs, the supreme miracle demonstrating his identity. To reject what happened on the first Easter is to reject the greatest sign God could provide. As Paul would later tell the Corinthians, Christianity stands or falls with the resurrection of Jesus Christ from the dead (see 1 Cor 15:12-19). Unfortunately, most of the Jewish religious leaders prodding Jesus for a sign would refuse to believe even this (28:11-15).

16:5-7 Jesus and his disciples departed in a boat. When they **reached the other shore**, the **disciples** realized **they had forgotten to take bread** (16:5). So when Jesus warned them to **beware of the leaven** (yeast) **of the Pharisees and Sadducees** (16:6), their absent-mindedness and hunger left them confused (16:7). Clearly, they weren't on the same page as Jesus.

16:8-10 Jesus chastens his muddled disciples for their **little faith**. Had they forgotten so quickly how he'd miraculously fed thousands on two occasions (16:9-10; see 14:13-21; 15:32-39)? A lack of food isn't a problem when you're with the Son of God.

16:11-12 The disciples were thinking of literal **bread**, but Jesus wasn't talking about food at all when he spoke of yeast (16:11). **Leaven** is an essential ingredient in bread that must permeate the dough. Jesus was metaphorically comparing the **teaching of the Pharisees and Sadducees** to it (16:12). It permeated and influenced the Jewish people, resulting in unbelief. Watch out, then, for those who pursue self-righteous religion and teach others to do the same. A relationship with God through Christ is what's needed.

16:13 Jesus then took his disciples to **Caesarea Philippi**, a city about twenty-five miles north of the Sea of Galilee where there was a temple honoring the Roman emperor Caesar Augustus. Perhaps the reverence for a mortal man is what prompted Jesus to ask his followers, **Who do people say that the Son of Man is?**

16:14-15 Apparently, there was a lot of speculation among the crowds about Jesus. Like Herod Antipas (14:1-2), some thought he was **John the Baptist** back from the dead—or one of the Old Testament **prophets** (16:14). But after his disciples relayed all the gossip concerning Jesus, he got to his real question: **Who do you say that I am?** (16:15). The "you" here is plural, so the question was addressed to the entire group.

16:16-18 **Simon Peter** quickly and correctly answered: **You are the Messiah, the Son of the living God** (16:16). Jesus affirmed this great confession of faith by praising God the **Father** for revealing this truth to Peter and blessing him (16:17). That opened the door for an announcement from Jesus. Something so awesome that hell itself can't **overpower it** was coming: the **church** (16:18).

No matter how much Satan attacks, the church will win, and hell will lose. The offensive advance of the church exercising kingdom authority overrides hell's attempts to stop it.

But how would Jesus accomplish his building program? Since Peter confessed Jesus as the Christ, Jesus used his name in a word play. In Greek, Peter's name is *petros*, which means "stone." But when Jesus said, **On this rock I will build my church** (16:18), he used the Greek word *petra*, which was a collection of rocks knitted together to form a larger slab. Jesus's church, then, would be comprised of his unified followers who confess him as the Christ, the Son of the living God, as Peter did.

The Greek word for "church" is *ekklēsia*, a term used to refer to an assembly or gathering of people, especially for legal purposes (see Acts 19:39-41). The church is like an embassy. The U.S. has embassies throughout the world, and the people working at an embassy are to live out the values and laws of the U.S. as they represent their homeland in a foreign country. Each embassy, then, is a little bit of America a long way from home. Similarly, the church of the Lord Jesus is to adopt the agenda of its heavenly King and enact it on earth. Christ's church is a little bit of heaven a long way from home, designed to withstand the authority of hell (its **gates**) (16:18). Hell's attempt to stop the church's progress in history is thwarted as the church executes heaven's authority on earth.

16:19-20 Jesus then promised his disciples that he would give them **the keys of the kingdom** (6:19). God doesn't leave his church powerless. The problem is that we frequently don't understand who we are and don't access the resources available. Even though an American embassy is a small outpost surrounded by a foreign nation, it can be confident that America stands behind it because it's connected to something that exerts a powerful influence. And though the church often seems small and weak, it's connected to the ultimate power in the universe.

What are these "keys of the kingdom of heaven"? They're divinely authorized resources that grant us authority and access (see Isa 22:22). Christians, through the church, have access to heaven's kingdom rule. Your world isn't supposed to be ruling you; you are supposed to be ruling your world. You're supposed to be regularly utilizing heaven to help you live on earth—not merely visiting church on Sunday mornings. Believers are to study the Bible and gather with the church for a reason: to learn how to access the divine viewpoint and live out God's kingdom rule in the world. You will never rule your world of relationships, emotions, employment, or

finances if you continue to employ the keys the world offers you, or if you're not connected to a local church that possesses and operates with the keys of the kingdom.

Note that the word *keys* is plural in this passage; that's because the word *gates* is plural (16:18). For every hellish gate (the exercise of Satanic authority), there is a corresponding kingdom key designed to give the church access to heaven's kingdom authority.

Whatever you bind on earth will have been bound in heaven, and whatever you loose on earth will have been loosed in heaven (16:19). To "bind" and "loose" is to restrain and to set free. The church is to use heaven's keys (heaven's viewpoint and spiritual resources on a matter), operate according to that perspective, and then call on heaven's authority to bind and loose. It's critical to understand that heaven is waiting on the church to act in the matter of permitting and releasing before heaven's authority gets activated in history.

Binding and loosing doesn't imply you can make God do whatever you want. First, it must be in accordance with God's will. You can only bind and loose what "will have been" already bound and loosed in heaven. Second, know that answers to prayer are not for your sole benefit. They're to benefit others. God calls his people to be a blessing.

16:21 Having clearly affirmed his identity to his disciples (16:16-17), Jesus explained his mission. He told them **it was necessary for him to go to Jerusalem and suffer** at the hands of the religious leaders, **be killed, and be raised the third day**. In other words, Jesus gave them the foundation for the gospel in summary form (see 1 Cor 15:3-4).

16:22-23 Peter took him aside and rebuked him: **This will never happen to you!** (16:22). Peter had just confessed Jesus to be the Christ, the Son of God (16:16). Unfortunately, though, when he opened his mouth this time, things went downhill. Not days later, but only a few minutes later, Peter had gone from being blessed (16:17) to being reprimanded as Jesus said, **Get behind me, Satan!** (16:23).

Jesus knew something wicked was operating behind Peter's statement. His confession of Jesus as the Messiah was the work of

God (16:17). His attempt to protect Jesus was the work of the devil. Any attempt to make Jesus King without the cross (remember Satan's temptations in 4:2-10?) is an attempt to thwart God's plan of salvation. Instead of being a *stone* (see 16:18), Peter had become **a hindrance**, which can also be translated "stumbling block."

You're not thinking about God's concerns but human concerns means Peter's viewpoint was warped (16:23). He was seeing things from a merely human perspective, not a divine perspective. His words were flawed because his thinking was flawed. He had aligned himself with Satan's program without realizing it.

16:24 After explaining his mission (his death and resurrection), Jesus explained the mission of his followers, discipleship: **If anyone wants to follow after me, let him deny himself, take up his cross, and follow me.** That's a zinger to get your attention because denying yourself isn't fun. People don't typically wake in the morning and say, "I can't wait to deny myself today!" But, in order to experience the lordship and provision of Christ on earth, you must be willing to say "no" to yourself.

16:25-26 **Whoever wants to save his life will lose it, but whoever loses his life because of me will find it** (16:25). Many people misread, thinking Jesus is speaking of salvation. But remember, Peter is already a believer here. Thus, Jesus spoke about the daily commitment of being a disciple. If you want to run your own life, you'll find that you lose the life you were looking for. But if you totally identify with Jesus and live according to his agenda, you'll find the abundant life you never knew was possible (see John 10:10). What good is it to gain worldly stuff while losing spiritual blessings and the peace that make life worthwhile (16:26)?

16:27 One day **the Son of Man** will come in his **glory** and **reward** everyone according to what they've done. If you make the shift from self-interest to kingdom-interest, it doesn't mean you will have no trouble in the world. In fact, you can count on experiencing suffering. But, as sure as Jesus "conquered the world" (John 16:33), he will reward those who choose his way.

16:28 **There are some standing here who will not taste death until they see the Son of Man coming in his kingdom.** This was fulfilled when Peter, James, and John witnessed Jesus's transfiguration (see 17:1-9). They saw his humanity peeled back and got a glimpse of his glorious deity.

17:1-2 After this significant encounter with his disciples, discussing his identity, his mission, and the cost of discipleship (16:13-28), **Jesus took Peter, James, and his brother John** up **on a high mountain** (17:1). At that moment, he was supernaturally **transfigured.** These three Jewish fishermen were given a glimpse of the glory of the coming King and his kingdom (17:2).

17:3 As if this wasn't enough, two eminent Old Testament figures—**Moses and Elijah**—appeared and talked with Jesus. This scene informs us that those who experience death (e.g., Moses) have cognitive understanding and an ability to communicate. Together, they symbolize all those who make up God's kingdom—those who will be raptured and not see death (like Elijah) and those who will die and go to be with the Lord (like Moses).

Moreover, Moses represented the Law, and Elijah represented the Prophets. Together they represented the complete Old Testament. Along with the disciples, they represent both the Old and New Testaments centered on Jesus.

17:4-6 Always quick with a word when no one else knew what to say, Peter said, **Lord, it's good for us to be here.** He offered to build **three shelters**, one for each of them. **While he** still **was speaking, suddenly a bright cloud covered them** and **a voice** spoke: **This is my beloved Son, with whom I am well-pleased. Listen to him!** (17:4-5). God the Father interrupted Peter to give a verbal and visual validation of his one and only Son, the King of kings. How did the disciples respond? **They fell facedown and were terrified** (17:6). They had enough sense to take the holy and omnipotent God of heaven and earth seriously.

17:7-8 When Jesus **touched them** and told them not to **be afraid**, the three disciples looked and saw no one but him. Why? Because Jesus isn't merely one among many faithful servants of God. He is superior to them all. The ministries of Moses and Elijah ultimately pointed toward Christ. All of Scripture has him as its focus (see Luke 24:27).

17:9 As they descended the mountain, he told them not to **tell anyone about the vision until** he was **raised from the dead.** If the crowds heard about it, the story would likely create confusion and cause them to forcibly make him king. Instead, it was to be part of the kingdom message that they would proclaim, calling sinners to place their faith in the risen King.

17:10-13 The vision of Moses and Elijah prompted the disciples to ask Jesus why **the scribes say that Elijah must come first** (17:10). Jesus pointed out the reality that **Elijah** had **already come** (17:12). As he'd told them previously, John the Baptist "is the Elijah who is to come" (11:14). In the Gospel of Luke, the angel told John's father Zechariah that his son would go before the Lord "in the Spirit and power of Elijah" (Luke 1:17). The problem was that the leaders **didn't recognize** John in this way. Instead, they persecuted him and would do the same to **the Son of Man** (17:12).

17:14-16 When they'd descended the mountain and **reached the crowd**, a man **knelt down before** Jesus and begged him to heal his son. The boy had **seizures** and often fell into **fire** and **water** (17:14-15). We know from the parallel account in Mark's Gospel that the father also said his son had a demon (Mark 9:14-18). His physical impairments had a spiritual cause, and the disciples **couldn't heal him** (17:16). Though Jesus had deputized and empowered them to do supernatural kingdom work on his behalf (see 10:5-8), they were powerless this time.

17:17-18 Importantly, this wasn't merely a failure of power; it was a failure of faith, a failure to trust in the power of God. So Jesus rebuked them for it (17:17), and then he **rebuked the demon**, so that **the boy was healed** (17:18).

17:19-20 This was an embarrassing moment for the disciples, so they went to Jesus privately and asked in effect, "What happened?" **Why couldn't we drive it out?** (17:19). Jesus answered, **Because of your little faith** (17:20). Though Jesus had authorized them to drive out demons (10:8), their trust in God's power was insufficient in this instance. Regardless of your past success, then, you need a present faith.

What does such faith need to look like? In order to **move** a **mountain**, it must be **the size of a mustard seed** (17:20). But have you ever seen mustard seeds? They're tiny! So apparently, the disciples' faith was microscopic. But with even a small trust in an omnipotent God, the **impossible** becomes possible (17:20).

17:22-23 For a second time (see 16:21), Matthew describes how Jesus informed his disciples that **the Son of Man** would be **betrayed into the hands of men**, killed, and **raised up** three days later. Jesus understood the direction his life would take; he knew his fate. It was no surprise but under his sovereign control. However, his disciples **were deeply distressed** over it (17:23).

17:24-26 When they returned **to Capernaum**, tax collectors approached Peter and asked if his teacher paid **the temple tax** (17:24). This tax was used for the upkeep of the temple. Though this confrontation was probably another attempt to catch Jesus at being a lawbreaker, Peter answered, **Yes** (17:25).

In private, Jesus posed a question to Peter: **From whom do earthly kings collect tariffs or taxes? From their sons or from strangers?** The answer to Jesus's question is obvious. Kings collect taxes **from strangers**—their subjects—not from their own sons. **The sons are free,** Jesus said (11:26). In other words, if those running things at the temple understood who Jesus was, they wouldn't be asking him to pay a temple tax. After all, he's the King, and it's *his* temple. Likewise, to be sons and daughters of the kingdom is to be a privileged people who benefit from their relationship to the King.

17:27 Jesus didn't want to enter into unnecessary conflict—and you shouldn't either. Though the government and unbelievers don't recognize Christ or his kingdom, that's no reason to cause needless offense. So Jesus temporarily sent Peter back to his old fishing job for a supernatural moment. Soon, in the **mouth** of a **fish**, Peter found a **coin** to pay their tax.

IX. GREATNESS, RESTORATION, AND FORGIVENESS (18:1-35)

18:1 So who is the greatest in the kingdom of heaven? That's an unexpected question. Yet, notice that in 18:2-5 Jesus didn't condemn **the disciples** for asking it or for desiring to be great. Instead, he challenged worldly assumptions about the methods used to become great.

18:2-4 Jesus drew attention to **a child** to teach these grown men a lesson about greatness (18:2). He said, **Unless you . . . become like children, you will never enter the kingdom of heaven** (18:3). So what quality in children is Jesus looking for? **Whoever humbles himself like this child . . . is the greatest in the kingdom of heaven.**

True greatness, then, comes through humility and a childlike faith that trusts God completely. In the Roman world, children had no rights and were completely dependent on others to care for them. Therefore, believers in Jesus Christ are to be humbly dependent on their heaven Father. The Lord of heaven and earth doesn't ascribe to the world's criteria for determining greatness.

18:5-6 Jesus also highlighted the importance of treating children and those with childlike faith well. To welcome them and serve them is to welcome Jesus (18:5). So if you want fellowship with Jesus, you need to be in fellowship with the humble. In fact, this principle of caring for children and those who are childlike is so significant that Jesus warned of the serious danger of causing one of them **to fall away** (18:6). To trip up children spiritually is to incur greater judgment. How bad will this judgment be? According to Jesus, drowning in the sea with a heavy rock hung around your neck would be preferable!

18:7-9 It's one thing to be a stumbling block to yourself. It's far worse to be a spiritual stumbling block to others. Jesus pronounced **woe**—judgment—upon those who cause **offenses**, those who make people spiritually stumble (18:7).

If your hand . . . causes you to fall away, cut it off. . . . If your eye causes you to fall away, gouge it out (18:8-9). Jesus wasn't calling for self-mutilation. Sin ultimately begins in the heart and mind (see 5:21-30). Jesus, then, called for radical efforts to avoid **hell-fire** (18:9). The spiritual is vastly superior to the physical. People must be willing to avoid eternal judgment at any and all costs.

18:10-14 In no case are we to **despise** children and those who are humble, because God is their advocate and assigns **angels** to watch over them (18:10). He goes to great lengths to rescue them, as Jesus's story about the great love of God illustrates. If a shepherd with **a hundred sheep** loses one, he'll **search** high and low to find it (18:12). When he finds the lost sheep, **he rejoices over** it (18:13). Similarly, **it is not the will of your Father in heaven that one of these little ones perish** (18:14). Jesus's mission is to save the lost, and he wants nothing to hinder the fulfillment of that mission.

18:15 In 18:15-20 Jesus addressed the matter of church discipline. He clearly considered it a weighty issue, since he provided principles for disciplining church members before the church officially came into existence. Though these verses represent the foundational text for guiding churches through the disciplinary process, there are a number of other relevant passages as well (e.g., 1 Cor 5:1-13; 2 Cor 2:5-8; Gal 6:1; 2 Thess 3:14-15; 1 Tim 5:19-20; Jas 5:19-20).

To be a member of a local church is to live under the authority of Jesus Christ in fellowship with and accountability to other believers. The church is called to bring honor to God in all she does. So the purpose of church discipline is always to glorify God and lovingly restore wayward church members.

If your brother sins against you, go and rebuke him in private. If he listens to you, you have won your brother. Notice first that the matter involves "a brother"—a fellow believer. We're not talking about non-Christians, then. This is a matter for the family of God.

Second, the concern is your brother's "sin." It has nothing to do with a clash of personal preferences. The issue is a violation of God's standards. And importantly, we're not talking about rebuking a brother or sister for any and every offense. We all fall short, and Proverbs 19:11 reminds us that it's virtuous to "overlook an offense." The passages cited above make it clear that Jesus has in mind flagrant sin that is reflected in persistent, unrepentant spiritual rebellion.

Third, according to Jesus, such behavior calls for a "rebuke" in "private." Parents are to discipline their children out of love to keep them from harmful foolishness; so too are we to care enough about fellow believers that we're willing to correct them—with humility, patience, and love. Yet, Jesus calls us to do this privately. Matters should be dealt with quietly to help, not publicly to gossip.

"If he listens to you, you have won your brother." The end goal of confrontation isn't punishment or embarrassment or harassment. The end goal is to win him over—to come alongside a brother going in the wrong direction and help him turn back to God.

18:16 But if he won't listen, take one or two others with you. If the sinning saint refuses to repent, Jesus said to invoke the Old Testament principle of establishing **every fact** through **two or three witnesses** (see Deut 19:15). This helps to ensure that the matter isn't a mere personal squabble, a false accusation, or an overreaction—but a refusal to repent over sin. Notice, too, that this small group of witnesses must be able to testify to the truthfulness of the charge. It's a serious accountability process. The church is about more than sermons and songs. It's about holiness, grace, and tough love.

18:17 If he doesn't pay attention to them, tell the church. If a persistent sinner has been confronted—in patience and love—by several spiritually mature believers and still rejects the Lord, the congregation is to become involved. When a member of the church at Corinth was guilty of sexual immorality that was public knowledge, Paul commanded the entire church there to take action (see 1 Cor 5:1-5). The church is the final court of appeal, but it's also a family. This is the time for brothers and sisters in the Lord to rally around a brother so he might be restored.

If he fails to listen even to the church, though, the unrepentant member is to **be like a Gentile and a tax collector.** In other words, if he insists on living like an unbeliever, it's time to treat him like one unless and until he repents. This is the sober and unfortunate step of excommunication in which the person is no longer considered a member of the congregation and is removed from fellowship. The church is no longer to associate with him as they would a brother in Christ (see 1 Cor 5:3-5, 9-13; 2 Thess 3:14-15). One of the primary ways this discipline is carried out is around the Communion table. The Lord's Supper is a meal for believers, not unbelievers.

All the while, the church should pray for the straying sinner, holding out hope that the Lord might lead him to repentance. If he rejects his sinful lifestyle, the church should welcome him with forgiveness and an affirmation of love (see 2 Cor 2:5-8).

18:18-20 Jesus repeated the promise he gave to the disciples in 16:19 about binding and loosing (18:18). When a congregation acts in accordance with Scripture to promote God's glory and the good of an erring member, heaven backs up the church. If **two or three** under the umbrella of the church gather, **agree,** and **pray** about a matter—based on the application of God's Word—the Son of God will show up and validate it (18:19-20). Anything God has authorized to be bound or loosed in heaven will be bound and loosed when the church makes an earthly request for heavenly intervention.

18:21-22 Jewish rabbis taught that forgiveness need only be extended three times.

So **Peter** may have thought he was being generous by suggesting that he **forgive** his brother **seven times** (18:21). By saying, **seventy times seven**, though, Jesus insisted that forgiveness has no limits (18:22).

18:23-24 After emphasizing that his followers must always be prepared to forgive, Jesus illustrated with a story. He compared **the kingdom of heaven** to **a king** settling accounts with **his servants** (18:23). One **owed** his master **ten thousand talents** (18:24). A talent was the largest unit of currency. Ten thousand talents would be equivalent to an unfathomable amount of money today. If he were telling the story to modern U.S. listeners, Jesus would have said "millions of dollars." The point was the servant owed a debt that was impossible to pay—just like the sin debt we owe to God.

18:25-27 Since there was no chance the servant could ever repay the debt, the **master commanded that he**, his family, and his property **be sold** (18:25). So the servant did the only thing he could do: he begged for mercy (18:26). As a result, his master **had compassion** and **forgave him** the debt (18:27).

18:28 Here's the twist in the story. That same servant went to **one of his fellow servants who owed him a hundred denarii** (that is,

about a hundred days' wages). He **grabbed him, started choking him**, and demanded that he **pay** back what was no small amount (18:28). However, the amount was child's play compared to what he'd owed the king.

18:29-34 The second servant begged for mercy—just as the first had done (18:29). But this lender was unwilling to show the same compassion he'd been granted and **threw** his fellow servant **into prison** (18:30). **When the other servants** found out, they were grieved and told **their master** (18:31). The king denounced him as a **wicked servant** and asked the obvious question: **Shouldn't you also have had mercy on your fellow servant, as I had mercy on you?** (18:32-33). Then he threw him in prison **to be tortured until** he paid his debt (18:34).

18:35 **So also my heavenly Father will do to you unless every one of you forgives his brother or sister.** If God cancels our sin debts, we must do the same for those who sin against us. We cannot expect or demand mercy that we're unwilling to give. According to Jesus, we should offer forgiveness in the same way and to the same degree that we desire it from God. Why? Our debt to God is infinitely greater than our brother's debt to us. Recognizing that positions us to receive from God the very thing that others desire from us.

X. MINISTRY ON THE WAY TO JERUSALEM (19:1–20:34)

19:1-3 After a time of performing miraculous healings, Jesus was approached by the **Pharisees** with a theological question. However, they weren't interested in having a sincere discussion; they wanted **to test him.** They asked, **Is it lawful for a man to divorce his wife on any grounds?** (19:3). In other words, can a man quit his marriage when he gets tired of his wife? Is it OK for a couple to get divorced for "irreconcilable differences"?

Divorce is a difficult subject—and one that has affected virtually every American, either directly or indirectly. Today, divorce is easily attainable, and since so many marriages end in it, many couples hedge their bets by

signing a prenuptial agreement to protect themselves. Jesus's response to the Pharisees was not easy for the **disciples** to hear (19:10), nor is it popular in today's culture—even among many Christians. But the question is this: Are you willing to listen to what the Son of God has to say on this subject?

19:4 Among the Israelites of Jesus's day, there were both conservative and liberal views of divorce taught by the rabbis. The liberal perspective said a man could divorce his wife for almost any reason—including if she burned his dinner. The Pharisees wanted Jesus to take a side to stir up controversy.

Jesus didn't offer a mere opinion, though. He pointed them to God's Word: **Haven't you read?** He hit the Pharisees right between the eyes by essentially asking, "Don't you know your Bible?" He showed them that the only reason they were posing a question about divorce is because they didn't understand marriage. Before we can talk about divorce, then, we need to understand what marriage is. What does Scripture say? **In the beginning** God **made them male and female** (see Gen 2:24). At the dawn of creation, God made one man for one woman, with no escape hatch.

19:5 Jesus also said this meant that a man would **leave his father and mother and be joined to his wife.** As a result, the **two** would **become one flesh.** In marriage, a man and woman come together to make a new reality that God calls "one flesh." Thus, human relationships outside of the marriage bond are to be considered secondary—including the couple's relationships with their parents. Unfortunately, too many couples never get around to becoming one flesh in this sense. They're stuck together by cheap glue rather than divine cement.

Numerous husbands and wives spend too much time protecting their own turf: my career versus your career, my money versus your money, my dreams versus your dreams. Yet, the purpose of marriage is to advance *God's* kingdom rule on earth for his glory. This doesn't mean losing individuality. Rather, it means working together with your spouse for a joint goal. Husbands and wives need a bigger agenda that unites them: God's agenda. However, following it takes time, energy, humility, and sacrifice.

19:6 Since **they are no longer two, but one flesh**, man shouldn't destroy what God created: **What God has joined together, let no one separate.** God intended marriage as a permanent relationship between one man and one woman. And since marriage was created by God, only he can sanction divorce.

19:7-8 The Pharisees didn't give up. They wanted him to explain why Moses would **command** Israelite men **to give divorce papers** to their wives (19:7; see Deut 24:1-4). Jesus answered: **Moses permitted . . . divorce . . . because of**

the hardness of your hearts, but it was not like that from the beginning (19:8). Here Jesus emphasized two things. First, Moses *permitted* divorce; he did not *command* it. Second, the place to start is in the beginning— with God's creation of marriage, not with Moses's discussion of divorce.

19:9 Given the permanence of marriage, **whoever divorces his wife, except for sexual immorality, and marries another commits adultery.** So, if a husband or wife commits adultery (or abandons their mate; see 1 Cor 7:15), the spouse has a permissible reason for divorce—though this doesn't mean that divorce is *required*. Paul lays out in 1 Corinthians 6:1-6 the principle of having the church adjudicate legal disputes among believers; therefore, the church ought to determine the biblical permissibility of divorce for its members.

The Bible knows nothing of "no-fault" divorce—only "major-fault" divorce. If God's Word gives you permission to divorce, then you have permission to remarry another Christian. According to Jesus, though, if a divorce is illegitimate, it leads to an illegitimate remarriage. To remarry after an unbiblical divorce is to commit adultery.

Christian couples should never let the word *divorce* enter into their conversations. They ought to view the marriage bond as sacred, sacrifice as necessary to make it work, and seek godly counsel from the church.

19:10-12 Upon hearing Jesus's teaching, the disciples concluded, **It's better not to marry** (19:10). But Jesus insisted that **not everyone can accept this**—that is, only certain people can remain unmarried (19:11). First, there are those who are **eunuchs . . . from their mother's womb.** It's natural for those born with diminished sexual desire to remain unmarried. Second, **there are eunuchs who were made by men**—a reference to those who in ancient times were literally made eunuchs to guard a king's harem. Third, **there are eunuchs who have made themselves that way because of the kingdom of heaven** (19:12). In other words, God has given to these individuals the gift of celibacy. They are so committed to the Lord's work that it overrides desire for sexual fulfillment. Thus, not marrying is intended for those who are able to abstain from it. Otherwise we should not deny ourselves marriage and the fulfillment of sexual desire in marriage.

19:13-15 When **children were brought** to Jesus so he might bless and **pray** for them, his **disciples rebuked** the parents (19:13). But Jesus rebuked the disciples right back: **Leave the children alone.** Why? He doesn't want anyone to stand between him and children. That **the kingdom of heaven belongs to such as these** (19:14) implies you have to be willing to humble yourself like a little child to come to Jesus as your Savior and experience his kingdom rule as Lord.

19:16-19 A man who wanted to earn a standing with God came to Jesus, viewing him merely as a good teacher, and asked, **What good must I do to have eternal life?** (19:16). But Jesus wanted to clarify things. He asked, **Why do you ask me about what is good? . . . There is only one who is good** (19:17). In other words, to be good Jesus would have to be God. And since he is God incarnate, he has the authority to answer the man's question.

If he wanted to **enter into life**, Jesus told him to **keep the commandments** of God (19:17-19). God's laws represent his perfect, holy standard. If a person can perfectly keep the commandments, he will indeed merit eternal life. The problem is that we are all sinners unable to meet the standards of a righteous God (see Rom 3:23). God gave us his laws, in fact, to show us we couldn't keep them and to drive us to the Savior.

19:20-22 The man naively claimed to have **kept** them all (19:20). So Jesus pushed a little further and told him to **sell** his **belongings, give to the poor**, and **follow** him (19:21). At that point, the young man realized he didn't meet God's standard of perfection. In essence, Jesus had told him, "Love your neighbor as yourself" (19:19), but the man **had many possessions** and was unwilling to part with them for the sake of a neighbor in need, thus revealing that he was indeed a sinner. And rather than acknowledge his sinfulness and come to Christ for salvation, **he went away** (19:22).

19:23-24 When the rich young man departed, Jesus observed, **It will be hard for a rich person to enter the kingdom of heaven** (19:23). Why? The rich often trust in and are attached to their wealth. People who focus on storing up riches in this world easily allow this world to distract them from thoughts of the world to come. As Jesus said, we should collect "treasures in heaven," for they cannot be destroyed, stolen, or lost (6:20). Spiritual wealth is eternal, so be rich toward God. Disciples are not to pursue the things that unbelievers treasure. Doing so will keep them from getting their full rewards.

19:25-27 The disciples were shocked, asking, **Then who can be saved?** (19:25). Jesus reminded them that the **impossible** is **possible** for God (19:26). He is able to overrule harmful attachments in our lives when we place our faith in him. Peter, ever the bold disciple, reminded Jesus that they had **left everything** to follow him (19:27). Peter himself had set aside his perhaps prosperous fishing business (see 4:18-20). **So what will there be for us?** (19:27)—that is, "What's the payoff for our commitment to you?"

19:28-29 Jesus assured his disciples that in the **renewal of all things**—that is, during his millennial reign—they would hold positions of authority, **judging the twelve tribes of Israel** (19:28). Moreover, this is true of **everyone who has left houses or brothers or sisters or father or mother or children or fields** for Jesus's sake. Thus, all Christians who truly identify with Christ and forsake worldly gain to obtain heavenly gain through serving him, **will receive a hundred times more and will inherit eternal life** (19:29). To "inherit eternal life" is not only to enter eternal life but also to receive its benefits.

19:30 But **many who are first will be last, and the last first** means there will be a great reversal in the kingdom. Many who are viewed as successful in this world will be paupers there, while many of the paupers in this world will be granted greater authority in the kingdom. So don't let earthly success or worldly gain prevent you from sacrificing as necessary to serve the Lord in light of the rewards to be received in the world to come.

20:1-9 In 20:1-16, Jesus told a parable about a landowner and the laborers who work in **his vineyard.** Early one morning, he hired a group of **workers** for a **denarius**—one day's wage (20:1-2). Later that day, he obtained some more workers without giving them a contract but simply promising to pay them what was **right** (20:3-4). He did the same thing several more times, even hiring a group at **five** o'clock (20:5-7). When the day was done, he paid everyone the same amount, **starting with the last and ending with the first** (20:8-9).

20:10-16 Those hired in the morning were upset because those hired late in the day received the same pay (20:10-12). They felt they'd been treated unjustly, but the vineyard owner insisted he had treated them fairly. He'd paid them what was promised. However, while he had been fair with them, he had been **generous** with others (20:13-15). He asked, **Don't I have the right to do what I want with what is mine? . . . The last will be first, and the first last** (20:15-16).

Through this story Jesus was teaching that God is both fair and generous. We should rejoice when God is gracious toward others and not resent it. While the Jews expected better treatment from God because of their background as God's people, the Gentiles would be objects of his compassion as well.

20:17-19 Jesus predicted for the third time his suffering, **death**, and resurrection **on the third day** (20:18-19; see 16:21; 17:22-23). He wanted his disciples to understand it as his mission—the reason he had come. And this would be the basis for their future ministry and message. When Paul later summed up the gospel, this was what it was all about (see 1 Cor 15:3-4).

20:20-21 Christian discipleship is to be expressed by humbly identifying with Jesus Christ and serving others, but the disciples still hadn't learned this lesson. It seems that after hearing Jesus's promise that they would "sit on twelve thrones" in the messianic age (19:28), two of the disciples tried to work out an even better deal for themselves. **The mother of Zebedee's sons**, James and John, asked Jesus to let her boys sit on his **right** and **left** in his **kingdom** (20:20-21).

Now, in Mark's Gospel (Mark 10:35-45), he describes John and James asking Jesus. It appears, then, that this request was their idea, and their mother was simply asking on their behalf. Also, it's important to understand that the seats to the right and left of a king were reserved for those in positions of special authority. The New Testament describes Jesus sitting at God's right hand (see Rom 8:34; Eph 1:20; Col 3:1: Heb 1:3; 8:1; 1 Pet 3:22).

20:22-23 The disciples were a lot like many of us. The brothers' request suggests they wanted privilege and power without service and commitment. Jesus knew they didn't understand what they were asking: **Are you able to drink the cup that I am about to drink?** By this he meant the suffering he was about to endure. They said they could, and Jesus agreed that they would. James would be martyred (see Acts 12:1-2), and John would experience exile (see Rev 1:9). But the seats at Jesus's **right and left** are reserved **for those** sovereignly appointed by his **Father.**

20:24-27 When the other **ten disciples heard this** discussion, **they became indignant with the two brothers** (20:24). Maybe this was righteous indignation. Or maybe they were simply upset that they didn't come up with the same idea first! Regardless, Jesus saw it as another opportunity to teach about discipleship.

Among **the Gentiles**, people in positions of authority **lord it over** others and **act as tyrants** (20:25). But there is a fundamental difference in how the church is to view power and authority: **Whoever wants to become great among you must be your servant** (20:26). In the dog-eat-dog world of earthly success, you reach greatness by stepping on others. In the kingdom of God, you reach greatness by serving others in love.

Notice that Jesus didn't rebuke their desire to be great ("Whoever wants to become great"; 20:26). Sometimes people think being a Christian means having no aspirations, but Jesus didn't condemn the aspiration for greatness. Rather, he condemned the worldly method for achieving it. So dream big. Ask God how you can use your skills and talents to make the biggest possible kingdom impact. But realize that when it comes to the people of God, servants—not celebrities—are on top.

20:28 God's Son didn't merely demand servanthood, he demonstrated it: **[Jesus] did not come to be served, but to serve, and to give his life as a ransom for many.** God exalted Jesus and gave him the name above all names, but Jesus attained this greatness by humbling himself as a servant and suffering unto death to save others (see Phil 2:5-11). The Son of God chose the way of sacrificial service, so why would you expect a different path for yourself?

20:29-34 As Jesus traveled from **Jericho** to Jerusalem, **two blind men sitting by the road** began crying out, **Lord, have mercy on us, Son of David!** (20:29-30). Clearly, these men recognized his messianic authority, and with that authority came the supernatural right to heal. So though the crowd told them to **keep quiet**, they wouldn't be distracted (20:31). No one could keep them from Jesus. When he asked them what they wanted, they displayed bold faith by requesting their sight (20:32-33). Jesus healed them, **and they followed him** (20:34).

Don't let others keep you from crying out to the Lord either. Pursue him until you hear a word from him, in spite of voices that try to keep you quiet. And when he comes through, follow him in even deeper faith and greater service.

XI. MINISTRY IN JERUSALEM (21:1–23:39)

21:1-7 As he approached Jerusalem, Jesus **sent two disciples** to **find a donkey** and its **colt**, untie them, and deliver them to him (21:1-3). Matthew then tells us that this **fulfilled** the prophecy of Zechariah, declaring to Jerusalem that her **King** would come riding **on a donkey** (21:4-5; see Zech 9:9). His disciples obeyed, and Jesus saddled up (21:6-7).

21:8-11 When the **crowd** saw him, they **spread** tree **branches** and their **clothes** for his mount to walk on and shouted, **Hosanna to the Son of David!** (21:8-9). By calling Jesus the Son of David, they weren't merely acknowledging who his great, great grandfather was. They recognized this itinerant preacher from Nazareth as the Messiah, the promised King. **The whole city** of Jerusalem **was in an uproar** (21:10). Everyone was talking about him.

21:12-13 In **the temple** in Jerusalem, pilgrims who'd come to offer sacrifices could buy animals from those selling them, as well as exchange currency with the money changers. When Jesus entered the temple, he **threw out all those buying and selling** and **overturned the tables of the money changers** (21:12). Why? Because God's house

was to be **a house of prayer**, but they had made it **a den of thieves** (21:13). Instead of a place focused on worship of the one true and living God, the temple had become a place of materialism and commercialism. When the temple was dedicated, Solomon prayed that God would hear the prayers of his people from the temple and forgive, heal, defend, and bless them (2 Chr 6:14-42). Yet these "thieves" were using God's house to rob the people and reap a financial reward.

Religious materialism often appears among God's people today as a result of "prosperity theology." It's easy to find so-called preachers on the radio and television whose essential message is that God exists to bless you, as if the Creator and ruler of the universe is your personal, spiritual Santa Claus. Moreover, they seek their own financial "blessing" from God by using you to foot the bill. It doesn't matter who a preacher is, if you have to pay for his blessing, his ministry's a racket.

Jesus pronounced judgment on those misusing the temple and disrupted their program. And his actions didn't merely offend the businessmen in the temple, but also the religious leaders who would ask him, in effect, "Just who do you think you are?" (21:23).

21:14-17 Jesus healed the blind and the lame (21:14), and two different responses resulted. The children shouted, **Hosanna to the Son of David!** (21:15) just as the crowds had done (21:9). But **the chief priests and the scribes**, in spite of actually witnessing **the wonders** Jesus accomplished, **were indignant** (21:15). They couldn't believe this Galilean would allow children to hail him as the Messiah. But Jesus once again questioned the Jewish leaders' lack of Bible knowledge. He defended the children's **praise** by insisting that it was a fulfillment of Scripture (21:16; see Ps 8:2).

21:18-19 The next morning, Jesus saw a **fig tree** with **nothing on it except leaves.** Hungry, he cursed it, and it **withered** (21:19). While the tree had given the impression of having fruit, it was barren. This condition was true of Israel. With all its religious practices, it gave an appearance of godliness but bore no authentic fruit.

21:20-22 The disciples were **amazed** by how **quickly** the fig tree withered (21:20), so Jesus took the opportunity to teach them about faith. What he did to the fig tree was a small thing. By **faith**, they could move a **mountain**—an impossible circumstance (21:21). He wanted them to understand the power of **prayer** (21:22). God wants followers of great faith, as opposed to the faithless Jewish leaders.

21:23-27 While Jesus taught in **the temple**, **the chief priests and the elders** came to him to ask **by what authority** he was **doing these things** (21:23). He agreed to answer—if they answered his question first: **Did John's baptism come from heaven, or was it of human origin?** (21:24-25). Since they wanted to know the source of Jesus's authority, he asked them the source of John's authority.

This put them in a catch-22. If they said, **from heaven**, the obvious question would be, **Then why didn't you believe him?** If they said, **of human origin**, they would be in trouble with the crowds who considered **John to be a prophet** (21:25-26). Since they were concerned with appearance more than anything, they were in a no-win situation. So they answered, **We don't know** (21:27). They

punted the football, so to speak. Jesus had laid the perfect trap. They demonstrated by their response that they weren't really interested in the truth, so he refused to answer their question (21:27).

21:28-30 Instead of answering the question posed by the chief priests and elders, he told them a parable. **A man had two sons** whom he instructed to go and **work in the vineyard.** The first son refused but later **changed his mind** and obeyed. The second son said he would work but **didn't go.**

21:31-32 Jesus then asked, **Which of the two did his father's will?** (21:31). By answering correctly, the Jewish leaders condemned themselves. For the **tax collectors and prostitutes** refused to obey God but later repented. The leaders, on the other hand, claimed to follow God but didn't have the actions to back it up. And even when they saw the tax collectors and prostitutes repent and believe, they still didn't **change** their **minds** (21:32). Lips that say, "Amen," mean nothing without hands and feet backing them up.

21:33-39 Jesus then launched into another **parable** about a **landowner who planted a vineyard** and **leased it to tenant farmers and went away** (21:33). At harvest time, he sent his servants to the farmers to **collect his fruit**, but they rebelliously **beat** and **killed** them (21:34-36)! So the landowner **sent his son**, expecting them to **respect** him, yet the wicked farmers **killed** the son too (21:37-39).

21:40-42 Jesus asked, **What will** the vineyard owner **do to those farmers?** (21:40). There's only one possible answer, and the religious leaders gave it: **He will completely destroy those terrible men** (21:41). Again, the leaders' failure to understand the Bible was actually a fulfillment of the Bible. Jesus claimed that he was **the stone that the builders rejected**, as described in Psalm 118:22-23 (21:42). Thus, he was the "son" in the parable—scorned and (soon-to-be) killed—and they were the wicked tenant farmers.

21:43-46 As a result, **the kingdom of God** would be **taken away from** them (21:43).

The one they rejected would be their Judge. Realizing that **he was speaking about them,** they wanted to seize him, but **they feared** the people who regarded Jesus **as a prophet** (21:45-46).

22:1-7 Once more **Jesus** told them a parable (22:1). This time he compared **the kingdom of heaven** to **a king who gave a wedding banquet for his son** (22:2). The king made plans, invited guests, but no one would **come** (22:3-4). In fact, they **mistreated** his servants and **killed them** (22:6). **The king was enraged,** so he **burned down their city** (22:7).

This describes the response of the nation of Israel to God's messianic plan—a response reflected primarily in its leaders. They rejected God's Son and his kingdom, and God would bring fiery judgment on them with Rome's destruction of Jerusalem in AD 70.

22:8-14 The king had **his servants** invite all kinds of people until guests **filled** the **wedding banquet** (22:8-10)—an image that I understand to refer to the millennial reign of Christ. However, the guests who were invited and accepted the invitations had a personal responsibility to get **dressed** in **wedding clothes** appropriate for the banquet (22:11-12). Since the people had been invited off the streets (22:10), it's likely the king provided them with wedding clothes to wear. But one man refused to dress for the **wedding** (22:11-12). The king, therefore, had his attendants **throw him** out.

Many interpreters see this ejection as a description of final judgment. However, this language of **weeping and gnashing of teeth** (22:13) is a picture of "sons of the kingdom" losing rewards in the millennial period (see 8:12). While they have accepted an invitation to enter the banquet, the messianic kingdom, those who do not utilize what God has provided and fail to be faithful servants will lose out on full participation in the millennial kingdom. As a result, they will experience profound regret. Many are called to salvation because of their faith in Christ, but few are chosen to rule with him in his millennial reign because of their unfaithfulness (see Luke 19:12-27; 1 Cor 3:12-15; 9:26-29; 2 Tim 2:12).

22:15-17 Matthew tells us that **the Pharisees** and **the Herodians** plotted together **to trap** Jesus (22:15-16). So we know from the outset that their question in verse 17 was a trick. What's amazing is that the Pharisees and Herodians were working together. The Pharisees were the conservative religious movement of the day. The Herodians were not a religious group at all, but a political party that supported the dynasty of Herod. The only thing they had in common was their mutual hatred of Jesus.

Nevertheless, the groups came to Jesus full of compliments: **You are truthful . . . teach truthfully . . . don't care what anyone thinks nor do you show partiality** (22:16). Hearing such words from such people would raise a few eyebrows. The alert listener would suspect something was up. "Give us your opinion," the plotters told Jesus in essence. **Is it lawful to pay taxes to Caesar or not?** (22:17).

This may seem like an easy question to answer, but the men were attempting to put Jesus in a no-win situation. Israel was under Roman rule, so Jews were required to pay taxes to Rome. To be an advocate for paying taxes, then, would put Jesus at odds with the people who hated being subject to the pagan Romans. But to publicly denounce paying taxes would put him at odds with the Roman authorities. No doubt the Pharisees and Herodians were thinking, "Whichever way he answers, we'll win."

22:18-20 Jesus wasn't fazed: **Why are you testing me, hypocrites?** (22:18). He knew what they were up to. They claimed to be interested in Jesus's answer, but all they really wanted was to see him destroy himself. He asked them to **show** him **the coin used for the tax,** which was **a denarius,** a Roman coin that was the equivalent of one day's wage. Then he asked whose **image and inscription** was on it.

22:21 The coin bore the image of the Roman emperor, Tiberius Caesar. So Jesus gave his answer: **Give, then, to Caesar the things that are Caesar's, and to God the things that are God's.** This Roman coin had Caesar's image on it, so, Jesus concluded, it made sense to give Caesar what belonged to him. Moreover, since human beings bear God's "image," they naturally belong to God (Gen 1:26-27). So as sure as Jesus affirmed paying taxes to Caesar, he also said they should give themselves in total obedience to God. By opposing Jesus, they were opposing God.

It's proper to pay taxes to a government for the services it provides, including defense and roads. These are legitimate realms of government activity and must be supported. However, everything falls within God's realm. The government may give you highways, but God gives you oxygen. You owe him more than a weekly visit on Sundays. Give him total obedience in honor of the daily benefits he gives you.

22:22 The Pharisees and Herodians were **amazed** at Jesus's clever answer and **left.** Jesus will leave you speechless.

22:23-28 Next it was the Sadducees' turn to test Jesus with a question. The **Sadducees** were a powerful religious sect associated with the high priests and aristocratic families. They rejected many of the theological views of the Pharisees—including belief in the **resurrection** (22:23). Pointing to the law that required a deceased man's brother to marry his wife in order to continue his brother's family line (22:24; see Deut 25:5-6), they proposed a hypothetical scenario in order to make a mockery of the doctrine of the resurrection of the dead. If **seven brothers** had the same woman for a wife after each one died, **whose wife** would she be **in the resurrection?** (22:25-28).

22:29-33 They thought they'd tripped him up, but they were **mistaken** because they didn't **know the Scriptures or the power of God** (22:29). First, Jesus explained that people don't **marry** in the resurrection, but are eternal **like angels** (22:30). Second, Jesus quoted God's words to Moses: **I am the God of Abraham and the God of Isaac and the God of Jacob** (22:32; see Exod 3:6). In other words, though Abraham, Isaac, and Jacob were physically dead even back in Moses's day, he was still their God. Spiritually speaking, they are very much alive: God **is not the God of the dead, but of the**

living (22:32). Once again, **the crowds** were **astonished** (22:33).

22:34-36 Jesus's opponents weren't ready to give up yet. **He had silenced the Sadducees**, so **the Pharisees** decided to have another go (22:34). **One of them** who happened to be **an expert in the law** asked, **Teacher, which command in the law is the greatest?** (22:35-36).

22:37-38 Jesus wasted no time identifying **the greatest and most important command** by quoting from Deuteronomy 6:5: **Love the Lord your God with all your heart, with all your soul, and with all your mind** (22:37-38). God's entire law, in fact, can be reduced to this. At their core, the Ten Commandments are really a command to love God. While we frequently associate love with a *feeling*, it must be more than that because it's something that can be *commanded*.

God wants a relationship with you. He wants you to love him, to passionately and righteously pursue his glory. So what does loving God look like? It requires *all* of your heart, soul, and mind—in other words, your entire being. Some of us Christians love God with *some* rather than with *all*, yet we want all of God. But you can't love God some and love the world some because these two are antithetical to one another (see 1 John 2:15). God will not share you with anyone. Your love for him must be comprehensive.

It's easy to say, "I love God," but words can be cheap. So remember, love for God is consistently expressed when you obey his commands (see John 14:15; 1 John 5:3). Align your decisions with his expectations.

22:39 Then Jesus answered a question the Pharisee didn't ask. The command that ranks **second is** this: **Love your neighbor as yourself** (see Lev 19:18). Why does Jesus mention this command? Because you can't obey number one without obeying number two and vice-versa. To love your neighbor is the decision to compassionately and righteously pursue his or her well-being. The two commands, then, are inseparable (see 1 John 4:20–5:2).

Do you want to draw closer to God? Help someone else draw closer to God. When you love others, God will boomerang it back to you and provide you with a deeper experience of him.

22:40 All the Law and the Prophets depend on these two commands means all of God's commands are included in the first and second greatest commands. Fulfill these, through Christ, and you'll fulfill them all.

22:41-46 After a barrage of questions from different religious leaders, Jesus had a question of his own for **the Pharisees** about **the Messiah: Whose son is he?** They rightly replied that Messiah would come from the line of David (22:41-42). However, Jesus pointed out that in Psalm 110:1 David calls the Messiah, **Lord** (22:43-44). If the Messiah was merely David's descendant, why would David refer to him as his Lord—as his Master? The opposite would be expected.

Inspired by the Spirit when he wrote the Psalm (22:43), David confessed that the Messiah would be more than **his son** (22:45). He would be divine. Though he would be fully human, a descendant of King David, he would also be fully God. The view of the Jewish leaders, though, was that the Messiah would be merely human—not divine. It was Jesus's claim of deity that would lead to his rejection and crucifixion (26:57-68). The Pharisees were obviously stunned by Jesus's words, unable to understand, and unable to answer. So **no one dared to question him** further (22:46).

23:1-4 When all those who tried to trick him with their questions were gone, **Jesus spoke to the crowds and his disciples** to warn them about **the scribes and the Pharisees** (23:1-2). They were good at telling others what to do but not good at carrying those instructions out themselves: **They don't practice what they teach** (23:3). They were hypocrites. Instead of helping to relieve the burdens of others, the Pharisees weighed them down with burdens (23:4).

23:5 Everything the Pharisees did was for show; they wanted to **be seen by others.** They wanted observers to see how holy they looked regardless of how dirty and ugly they were on the inside. **Phylacteries**

were small boxes containing copies of Scripture verses that were tied to the arm or the head and were worn as reminders to pray. **Tassels** were on the edges of prayer shawls. The Pharisees wore super-sized versions of these items to impress people. They were like walking religious billboards, proclaiming to everyone, "Look how holy I am!"

23:6-7 The Pharisees didn't want to practice their righteous deeds (such as giving to the poor, praying, and fasting) "in secret" (6:1-6; 16-18). They wanted people to see them in action. **The front seats in the synagogues** allowed them to be the focus of attention at gatherings and being **called, Rabbi**, stroked their egos.

It's not wrong to honor others. Paul said to give honor to whom honor is owed (Rom 13:7) and to "give recognition to those who labor among you . . . in the Lord" (1 Thess 5:12). But it's another thing altogether to love being honored and to seek it for yourself. The scribes and Pharisees thought too highly of themselves (see Rom 12:3).

23:8-10 In light of the Pharisees' behavior, Jesus told his followers not to get wrapped up in being called by titles of honor, for we **are all brothers and sisters** of one another. There is **one Father** and one **Messiah** to whom we owe all honor (23:8, 10). We have different roles and job descriptions, but we're all equal in value before the Lord.

No matter the position a brother in Christ holds, he's still your brother. You can take a one-hundred-dollar bill, crumple it up, and rub it in the dirt. When you're finished, it may not look attractive but it's still worth the same as when you started.

23:11-12 There is to be no elitism in the family of God, and the cure for elitism is servanthood (23:11). When was the last time you served someone—someone who couldn't do anything for you in return? That's what Jesus did. The eternal Son of God became a servant to save those who couldn't save themselves (see Phil 2:5-8). As a result, God the Father exalted him (Phil 2:9-11). And that's what Jesus promises his disciples: **Whoever exalts himself will be humbled,**

and whoever humbles himself will be exalted (23:12).

23:13-15 In 23:13-36, Matthew presents Jesus's declarations of judgment to the scribes and Pharisees. To say, **Woe to you, scribes and Pharisees** is to pronounce condemnation on them. These men had rejected **the kingdom of heaven** through Jesus Christ, and, as a result, they were preventing others from receiving him too (23:13). They were blocking the way of salvation. Now, that doesn't mean they weren't religious. In fact, they were extremely zealous about their religious practices and would travel far and wide to make Pharisee converts. But by exhorting others to practice external religion without internal spirituality, they hindered them from true salvation and simply made them **fit for hell** (23:15).

23:16-22 Jesus explained how the Pharisees made false distinctions between different kinds of oaths. They considered some oaths binding and some not, but any oath made before God should be kept. Whether someone swore by the sanctuary or the **altar, the temple** was all God's house. The Pharisees were deceptive and served as **blind guides** to all who followed them (23:16).

23:23-24 The **scribes and Pharisees** proudly paid **a tenth of** their possessions—even of tiny things like spices. However, while focusing on these minute details, they would neglect **the more important matters of the law**—**justice, mercy, and faithfulness** (23:23). They would major on the minors, and minor on the majors. Jesus's illustration is vivid: **You strain out a gnat, but gulp down a camel** (23:24).

23:25-26 The men were consumed with external appearances and rituals but not with the internal condition of their hearts. They cleaned their outsides, but inside they were **full of greed and self-indulgence** (23:25). Be warned: when your chief concern is being seen and accepted by men, you'll concentrate on making a good outward impression while ignoring the corruption inside of you. But if you seek to please God above all by cleaning

the dirt from your heart, clean actions will follow (23:26).

23:27-28 Whitewashed tombs refers to the practice of painting tombs white so that they looked **beautiful.** On the inside, though, pretty tombs were still **full of . . . bones** (23:27). No matter how much you decorate the exterior of a grave, the interior still contains death. Similarly, the Pharisees seemed **righteous to people** on the outside, but on the inside they had wicked motives and desires (23:28).

23:29-32 The **scribes and Pharisees** were **hypocrites.** They built **tombs of the prophets** and decorated **the graves of the righteous** (23:29), quickly claiming that they wouldn't have joined with their forefathers who killed the Old Testament-era prophets (23:30). Yet, at the same time, they were rejecting the Messiah and planning to murder him! In truth, they were *just like* those who had gone before them and **murdered the prophets** (23:31).

23:33-36 In spite of all that he'd said against the scribes and Pharisees, Jesus wasn't done: **Snakes! Brood of vipers! How can you escape being condemned to hell?** (23:33). Since the scribes and Pharisees continued to reject the truth, their destiny would be eternal judgment. Jesus predicted that they would **kill** those whom he would send. In the same way that **Abel** and **Zechariah** were martyred by unbelievers, so the Pharisees would martyr the righteous believers in Jesus Christ (23:34-35).

23:37-39 After his outburst of righteous anger against the religious leaders (23:13-36), Jesus lamented over **Jerusalem,** the capital city of Israel and home of God's temple. Though it ought to have been a holy city devoted to the Lord, those within her gates slayed the servants of God **sent to her** (23:37).

Unlike **chicks** that naturally run to a hen during times of danger, the religious leaders were not running to their Messiah (23:37). Eventually the city and temple would be besieged and destroyed by the Romans. However, Jesus would return one day. Quoting Psalm 118:26 (23:39), Jesus announced that he would depart but promised he would come back. This moment was the time of his rejection. On that day, however, he will come to establish his millennial kingdom.

XII. THE OLIVET DISCOURSE (24:1–25:46)

24:1-2 Chapters 24–25 are often referred to as the Olivet Discourse because they include a lengthy section of Jesus's teaching to his disciples while **on the Mount of Olives** (24:3).

As Jesus departed **the temple**, the **disciples** observed the splendor of **its buildings** constructed by Herod the Great (24:1). Knowing what was to happen in the future, Jesus shocked them by revealing that the temple they so admired would be completely destroyed. **Not one stone will be left here on another**, he said (24:2). This would be the result of Israel's rejection of her Messiah.

24:3 When [would] these things happen? The disciples wanted to know the timing of the temple's destruction, which they connected to Jesus's return and **the end of the age**. While the Romans would overrun Jerusalem and decimate the temple in AD 70 under the Roman general Titus, the messianic age was yet future. So in chapter 24 Jesus described the tribulation period that will precede his millennial kingdom. The tribulation will begin with the seventieth of Daniel's "seventy weeks" (see commentary on Dan 9:24-27).

24:4-8 Here Jesus speaks of the first half of the seven-year tribulation period. He used the imagery of **the beginning of labor pains** to describe the events of this time, which would be characterized by worldwide grief and agony (24:8). The first half of the tribulation will be characterized by **wars and rumors of wars** (24:6). Messianic pretenders will arise to deceive (24:5). **Nation will rise up against nation**, and **famines and earthquakes** will be common (24:7). **But the end is not yet** (24:6). The tribulation will be a time of sorrow and unexpected pain, which will eventually lead to the end of the age, the return of Christ, and the birth of the messianic kingdom.

24:9-14 More severe trials will characterize the second half of the tribulation. Those who come to faith in Christ during this period will **be persecuted** (24:9). Betrayal and deception will be rampant (24:10-11). Nevertheless, **the one who endures to the end will be saved** (24:13)—which is not a reference to salvation but physical deliverance. So, in other words, believers who endure to the end of the tribulation will be spared physical death and enter the millennium. In spite of the horror on earth during the tribulation, the **good news of the kingdom will be proclaimed** (24:14). Many will be saved when they believe the good news of Jesus's coming kingdom rule.

24:15 The second half of the great tribulation will commence with what Jesus called **the abomination of desolation, spoken of by the prophet Daniel**. According to Daniel, the Antichrist "will make a firm covenant with many for one week" (Dan 9:27)—that is, for the seven-year tribulation period. He will be a world leader who will bring peace to the Middle East.

The Jews will be permitted to rebuild their temple and once again offer sacrifices. However, "in the middle of the week" (at the midpoint of the tribulation), the Antichrist "will put a stop to sacrifice and offering" and set up "the abomination of desolation" in the temple (Dan 9:27; see commentary on Dan 9:24-27). He will finally be revealed for the evil beast that he is (see Rev 13:4-8). This "abomination" will be an image of the Antichrist as he profanes the temple, sets himself up as God, and demands worship.

24:16-22 Those who will not bow down to the Antichrist will have to **flee**, leaving their property and possessions behind if they are to escape death (24:16-20; cf. Rev 13:15). It will be a time of **great distress** unlike any the world has ever seen (24:21). If not for the fact that God will limit those days so that the time is cut short, **no one would be saved.** But for the sake **of the elect**—those who will be saved during the tribulation—**those days will be cut short** (24:22).

24:23-28 Jesus warned that many **false messiahs and false prophets will arise** to lead people astray (24:24). Even today there are those who claim to speak for God but whose words stray from Scripture: **Do not believe it** (24:26). There will be no uncertainty when Christ returns at the end of the tribulation. No one can miss a bolt of **lightning** when it **flashes.** Neither will they miss **the coming of the Son of Man** (24:27).

24:29-31 **After the distress**, spectacular signs will appear in the heavens as predicted in the Old Testament (24:29; see Isa 13:10; 34:4; Joel 2:31). The glory of Christ's return will be revealed to all. **The peoples of the earth** who have not turned to Christ in repentance and faith **will mourn** when they **see the Son of Man coming** in **power and great glory** (24:30). But the Lord will **send out his angels** to **gather his elect** from throughout the earth—to gather those saved during the tribulation as well as the Old Testament saints who will be raised from the dead (24:31).

24:32-35 Following this revelation of the future to his disciples, Jesus applied the principles of the tribulation and his second coming. When a **fig tree . . . sprouts leaves**, any Israelite knows that **summer** is on the horizon (24:32). It's an obvious sign that's not difficult to interpret. In the same way, when those living during the great tribulation witness the signs taking place (24:29-30), they can be certain that the Messiah is quickly returning (24:33). These are the people Jesus spoke of when he referred to **this generation** (24:34). They will see everything take place exactly as Jesus foretold. Though **heaven and earth will pass away**, the words of Jesus **will never pass away** (24:35).

24:36-41 Apart from these signs, it will not be known exactly when Christ will return. Only **the Father** knows the timing. From the perspective of his humanity, not

even **the Son** knows (24:36). As in **the days of Noah** before the judgment of the flood came, so it will be before **the Son of Man** returns (24:37). Before **Noah boarded the ark**, people were enjoying the normal pursuits of life (24:38). Then **the flood came and swept them all away.** This is what it will be like prior to Christ's second coming (24:39). Some **will be taken** in judgment, and others will be **left** to enter into Christ's millennial kingdom (24:40-41).

24:42-44 In the meantime, Jesus wanted his followers to be watchful so they would be ready for the *rapture*. This is the event at which believers will be caught up in the air to be taken by Jesus to be with him (see commentary on 1 Thess 4:13-18). I believe Scripture teaches that the rapture will take place prior to the events of the tribulation.

Be alert, since you don't know what day your Lord is coming (24:42) is reminder that Christians must always be watching—like a **homeowner** on alert for a **thief** to break in—because the timing of the rapture is unknown. We must **be ready** (24:43-44).

24:45-51 As believers waiting with anticipation for our Lord, we must be wise and trustworthy until he returns. Jesus told a story of servants who were **put in charge of** their master's household while he was away (24:45). Those whom the master found diligently working when he returned were rewarded (24:46-47), but the servant who was lazy and unfaithful because the master was **delayed** was judged **with the hypocrites** when he returned (24:48-51).

When he comes for his church, Jesus will expect to find you busy serving him so he can reward you for faithfulness. As I noted earlier (see commentary on 22:13), I think the language of **weeping and gnashing of teeth** (24:51) is a description not of eternal judgment but of the grief experienced by believers who will lose out on rewards in the millennial kingdom. Since they didn't take the return of Christ seriously by serving faithfully, they will face profound regret and loss of rewards before their Lord. So as we await the rapture, let us serve God with gladness and devotion, knowing his promises are certain.

25:1 In chapter 25, Matthew recounts several parables that Jesus told related to his discussion of the future events foretold in chapter 24. First is the parable of the **ten virgins** (25:1-13). As was the custom of the day for wedding ceremonies, the groom would go to the bride's home and take her to the marriage feast. A great procession would accompany them, and then all would enter into the feast. The "ten virgins" were bridesmaids waiting for the groom to arrive.

25:2-5 According to Jesus, **five of them were foolish and five were wise** (25:2). This was demonstrated by their preparation (or lack of it). The foolish had no **oil** for **their lamps**, while the **wise** had **oil** (25:3-4). When the groom's arrival **was delayed**, all of them **fell asleep** (25:5).

25:6-13 Every person in the procession would have been expected to have his or her own lamp, but when the groom's appearance was announced **in the middle of the night**, the foolish virgins begged the wise to give them some oil because their lamps were **going out** (25:6-8). The wise, however, had only enough oil for themselves (25:9). So when the foolish virgins went to **buy** oil, they missed the groom and were locked out of **the wedding banquet** no matter how they cried to be let in (25:10-12). Therefore, Jesus said, **be alert** (25:13).

Jesus's parable is a description of Jewish believers during the great tribulation. The wise will be spiritually prepared so that when "the abomination of desolation" takes place (24:15), they will be ready and sustained by the Lord until his kingdom reign begins. However, the foolish will make no such spiritual preparations. As a result, they won't enter into the blessedness of the kingdom and its rewards. Though the parable speaks of those during the tribulation, it serves as a warning to all. Don't wait until the last minute to be spiritually prepared, because then it will be too late.

25:14 Then Jesus told a parable about the kingdom principle of stewardship. To be a steward is to protect and expand the assets of another on his behalf. When you put your money in the bank, you're asking the bank to act as a steward. You want it to *protect* your funds and to *expand* them by paying you interest.

In this parable, **a man** gave **his possessions** to each of his three **servants** before he went away **on a journey** so that they might manage them for him in his absence. This is a picture of what Jesus has done. Though he has gone away, he will return. In the meantime, he has given us his possessions to steward. Importantly, a steward is not an owner but one who manages the owner's possessions. We are stewards of what God has given us—not owners. The Bible makes clear that God owns "everything" (Ps 24:1; 50:10-12). And he expects us to protect and expand his possessions for the advancement of his kingdom in history.

25:15-18 To each of his servants, the man gave **talents**. A *talent* was a unit of currency. Notice the servants didn't receive the same amounts. The first received **five talents**, the second received **two**, and the third received **one**—**depending on each one's ability** (25:15). In other words, the servants received based on their capacity. The master didn't give any of them more than they could handle.

When their master departed, the servants with five and two talents went out and doubled what they'd been given (25:16-17). **But the man who had received one talent went off, dug a hole in the ground, and hid his master's money** (25:18).

If you're a Christian, God has given you three things to steward. First, until Jesus returns, you have *time*, the day-to-day context in which kingdom opportunities arise. Second, every believer has *talents* (abilities or skills) that are gifts from God to develop and use for his kingdom purposes. Third, you have *treasures* (financial resources). Your money isn't merely for your enjoyment but for kingdom advancement.

Much like the servants in the parable, no two of us have the exact same time, abilities, or treasures. The Lord has distributed what we have to us based on his perfect will and knowledge of our capacities. The question is not what or how much you have. The question is, What will you do with what you've been given?

25:19 After a long time the master ... came and settled accounts with his servants. Similarly, one day all Christians will stand before God to give an account. Scripture calls this the "tribunal [or "judgment seat"] of Christ" (2 Cor 5:10; cf. 1 Cor 3:12-15). Unbelievers will experience judgment too—the white throne judgment after the millennial kingdom (see Rev 20:11-15). But if you are a believer in Jesus Christ, your Lord is going to have a separate conversation with you about your stewardship of all that he put at your disposal. What will he say?

25:20-23 When his master returned, the man with **five talents** and the man with **two** explained how they had doubled what he had given them (25:20, 22). To both of them, the master said, **Well done ... You were faithful over a few things; I will put you in charge of many things. Share your master's joy** (25:21, 23). Notice that even though the one with five had more than the one with two, both received the same blessing. The master gave to each according to his abilities; they were faithful with what they'd been given and were rewarded.

25:24-27 The man with **one talent** told his master that he was **a harsh man** who had high expectations (25:24). Since he was **afraid** of him, the servant **hid [his] talent in the ground** so he wouldn't risk losing it (25:25). Thus, he returned what he had been given. But the master had no praise for this man. Instead he called him **evil** and **lazy** (25:26). The least he could've done, he pointed out, was to deposit the **money with the bankers** and earn some **interest** (25:27).

While the first two servants were concerned with their master's affairs, this man was solely concerned with himself. He didn't want to be bothered with caring for his master's resources, and putting the talent in the bank involved records and management. So he hid it in the ground. If his master didn't come back, he could keep it for himself. And if his master returned, he could just return it to him. But the master didn't merely want his money back. That wasn't the stewardship he demanded.

Jesus is your King, and he expects you to live faithfully with a kingdom agenda. Live today with a future orientation, knowing that one day he will call you by name to settle accounts.

25:28-30 In the end, the master gave his talent **to the one who [had] ten** (25:28). To those who are faithful, **more will be given**. To those who do nothing with their time, talents, or treasure for the sake of the kingdom of God, **what** they have **will be taken away** (25:29). Finally, the master had **this good-for-nothing servant** cast out where he would experience **weeping and gnashing of teeth** (25:30).

As with the earlier passages (22:13; 24:51), this text uses graphic language to speak—not of eternal judgment (as some interpreters argue)—but of the profound regret that many believers will experience when they receive no rewards because of their unfaithfulness in stewarding God's resources. Those who were saved but whose earthly lives were useless to the King will lose out on full participation in and the benefits of Christ's millennial kingdom. Don't let this be you—making time for your personal priorities but giving no time for the kingdom. Don't live for decades as a believer on earth and have nothing eternal to show for it.

25:31-40 Finally, Jesus explained what would happen **when the Son of Man comes in his glory** (25:31). This is a picture of Christ's second coming at the end of the great tribulation when he judges the **nations** who will be **gathered before him.** He will separate them—**the sheep from the goats** (25:32). The sheep will be **on his right**, the place of honor, and will be ushered into his millennial **kingdom** (25:34). The basis for their division from the goats will be the practical love and service they rendered during the tribulation to Jesus's **brothers and sisters**, the Jewish people, as an expression of their faith (25:35-40). Jesus will consider service rendered to his Jewish siblings as service rendered to him and as a demonstration of faith in him (25:40; see Joel 3:1-14).

25:41-46 Jesus will tell the goats to **depart** into **the eternal fire prepared for the devil and his angels** (25:41). For they refused to minister to the Jewish people during the tribulation period (25:42-45). Thus, Jesus will indict them for their indifference. This will be in keeping with the Abrahamic covenant in which God promised Abraham, "I will bless those who bless you," and "I will curse those who treat you with contempt" (Gen 12:3). Thus, the unrighteous of the nations will be sent **away into eternal punishment** (25:46).

XIII. SUFFERING, CRUCIFIXION, AND DEATH (26:1–27:66)

26:1-5 Again Jesus predicted to his disciples that he would soon **be handed over to be crucified** (26:1-2; see 16:21; 17:22-23; 20:17-19). It would be a **treacherous** act by the Jewish **chief priests and the elders of the people**, led by **Caiaphas** the **high priest** (26:3-4). They were determined to **kill** Jesus, so **they conspired to arrest** him (26:4). But they wanted to avoid the Passover **festival** to avoid **rioting among the people** (26:5). They hatched their plot in secret, thinking they were in control. But clearly this was no surprise to Jesus. It was part of God the Father's plan to save sinners.

26:6-9 Jesus was staying **in Bethany**, which was less than two miles southeast of Jerusalem on the road to Jericho, in the house of a man named **Simon** (26:6). While he was there, **a woman**, whom we know to be Mary the sister of Lazarus (see John 12:3), approached him. She took **expensive perfume** worth about a year's wages (see John 12:5) and **poured it on his head** (26:7). This upset **the disciples** who thought it should have been **sold** and **given to the poor** (26:8-9). John tells us in his Gospel that it was primarily Judas who was angry. Actually, he cared nothing for the poor but used to steal from the money-bag (see John 12:4-6).

26:10-13 Jesus came to the woman's defense and called her actions **noble** (26:10). Though believers are called to minister to and care for **the poor**, our allegiance to and worship of Jesus Christ has primacy (26:11). This act of devotion to Jesus symbolically **prepared** him for **burial** (26:12). The Messiah—"the Anointed One"—was being anointed in preparation for his death on the cross. Jesus predicted that Mary would be remembered for her actions **wherever this gospel is proclaimed in the whole world** (26:13). Since this story is in our Bibles, clearly his words have been fulfilled.

26:14-16 **Judas Iscariot**, one of **the Twelve** disciples, was so angered by this "waste" (26:8) that he **went to the chief priests** and agreed to betray Jesus for **thirty pieces of silver**. After that, he started looking for the right **opportunity** to hand him over (26:14-16).

26:17 Matthew next recounts the events of **the first day of Unleavened Bread**, the seven-day festival celebrated in connection with **the Passover**. The Passover commemorates God's deliverance of the Israelites from slavery in Egypt (see Exod 12). The Lord's final plague on the Egyptians claimed the life of every Egyptian firstborn, while the Israelites were spared by sacrificing a lamb and smearing its blood on their doorposts so that the Lord would "pass over" them. During the following seven days, they were to eat bread without leaven in memory of their hurried departure from Egypt (Exod 12:15-20; 13:6-8; 23:15). Jesus Christ is "our Passover lamb" (1 Cor 5:7).

26:18-21 Jesus told his disciples to meet **a certain man** in the city at whose place they would celebrate **the Passover** and to make preparations there (26:18). In the days leading up to this, he had predicted that he would suffer and be killed in Jerusalem (16:21; 17:22-23; 20:17-19; 26:1-2). During the Passover meal, he revealed that one of them would **betray** him (26:21).

26:22-25 All of them were **deeply distressed** at Jesus's words (26:22). The divine judgment for betraying **the Son of Man**

would be so great that **it would** be **better for the betrayer if he had not been born** (26:24). Judas had already agreed to hand over Jesus to the religious leaders (26:14-16); nevertheless, he deceptively played along with the others who were saying in shock, **Surely not I** (26:22, 25). Jesus not only knew he would be betrayed, but he knew his betrayer (26:25).

26:26-30 Then Jesus instituted what would become an ordinance of the church: Communion or the Lord's Supper (see 1 Cor 11:23-26). The **bread** represents his **body** and the **cup** represents his **blood**, which was about to be **poured out for many for the forgiveness of sins** (26:26-28).

Jesus's **blood** would establish the new **covenant** (26:28), the special agreement that God made with the church through the sacrificial death and resurrection of his Son. Jesus vowed that he would not **drink** with his disciples again until his earthly millennial **kingdom** (26:29). Until then, the church is to commemorate the work and spiritual presence of the true Passover lamb by remembering him and proclaiming him through Communion (see 1 Cor 5:7; 11:26).

26:31-35 Not only would one of them betray him (26:21-25), but **all of** them would **fall away** just as Scripture foretold (26:31; see Zech 13:7). When Peter forcefully vowed to stick with Jesus until the end (26:33), Jesus zeroed in on Peter's approaching fall. He would **deny** Jesus that night before the **rooster** crowed **three times** (26:34). Peter didn't believe such a thing could happen (26:35), but he clearly didn't know himself very well. The omniscience of Jesus saw where the dangerous pride of Peter would lead. "Pride comes before destruction, and an arrogant spirit before a fall" (Prov 16:18).

26:36-38 When they had arrived at **Gethsemane**, a garden at the foot of the Mount of Olives east of Jerusalem, Jesus told **Peter and the two sons of Zebedee** (James and John) that he was **deeply grieved** (26:36-38). He was in anguish as he considered the wrath of God that would be poured out on him as he bore the sins of the world on the cross.

Since the first Adam's fall occurred in a garden (see Gen 2–3), the last Adam entered into a garden to bring fallen man back into God's garden of fellowship through his substitutionary atonement. Since the first Adam brought sin into the world by means of a tree, the last Adam would be crucified on a tree to bring salvation (see Rom 5:15-19; 1 Cor 15:21-22, 45)

26:39-46 In his distress, he **prayed** three times to his **Father** (26:39, 42, 44). Though in his humanity, he preferred that the **cup** of suffering might **pass**, he voluntarily submitted himself to his Father's **will** (26:39, 42). "For the joy that lay before him" he was willing to endure the cross (Heb 12:2).

In spite of Jesus's urging, the disciples were unable to **stay awake with** him (26:38, 40). Though he exhorted them to **pray** that they might not **enter into temptation**, their **flesh** was **weak** (26:41). When the **betrayer** arrived (26:45-46), they were unprepared for the spiritual danger and would flee (26:56).

26:47-56 **Judas** arrived with **a large mob** armed **with swords and clubs**. They had come **from the chief priests and elders** to do their dirty work under the cover of night (26:47). When Judas betrayed Jesus with a **kiss** and the mob **arrested him** (26:48-50), Peter jumped into action like a vigilante (26:48-51; see John 18:10). But Jesus corrected him for taking matters into his own hands. If it had been part of God's plan, Jesus could have summoned **twelve legions of angels** to deliver him (26:53). But these awful events had to happen. Though the cowardly mob treated him like **a criminal** (26:55), everything in **the writings of the prophets** had to be **fulfilled** (26:54, 56).

26:57-64 **Jesus** was taken before **Caiaphas the high priest** and the **Sanhedrin** (26:57-59), the Jewish council of religious leaders that exercised authority under the Romans. Matthew forthrightly declares their evil intentions. They **were looking for false testimony** so they could condemn Jesus **to death** (26:59). **Many false witnesses came forward** (26:60), but their testimonies didn't agree (see Mark 14:56). Jesus refused to answer them.

Finally, **the high priest** placed Jesus under a sacred **oath** and demanded that he tell them if he was **the Messiah, the Son of God** (26:63). Jesus's response affirmed it. But he went even further and declared that they would **see the Son of Man seated at the right hand of Power and coming on the clouds of heaven** (26:64).

The "Son of Man" on the "clouds of heaven" is a reference to the glorious heavenly king of Daniel 7:13-14, whose kingdom would have no end. Being "seated at the right hand of Power" was a reference to the Messiah taken from Psalm 110:1. Jesus had earlier used the passage to argue that Messiah was a divine King (see 22:41-46).

26:65-68 Clearly, **the high priest** understood that Jesus was affirming both his messiahship and his deity, for he accused him of **blasphemy.** In outrage, **the high priest** even **tore his robes**, which he was forbidden to do (26:65; see Lev 21:10). Jesus's accusers felt they had all the evidence they needed to drag him before the Roman authorities and charge him as deserving **death** (26:66).

Jesus didn't object to their understanding about his identity; they had gotten it right. But instead of worshiping him as they should have, they wickedly mocked and abused him (26:67-68). The Son of God, who could have destroyed them with the mere breath of his mouth (see 2 Thess 2:8), submitted obediently to his Father's will for an important reason: he was winning your salvation. "Consider him who endured such hostility from sinners against himself, so that you won't grow weary and give up" (Heb 12:3).

26:69-75 Meanwhile, Peter had cautiously followed "at a distance" and sat in the high priest's **courtyard** to await the outcome (26:58, 69). There he had three opportunities to affirm his commitment to the Lord. First, **a servant** accused him of being associated **with Jesus** (26:69). Then **another woman** claimed he was one of his followers (26:71). Lastly, several other people indicted him as being a disciple of Jesus. On each occasion, Peter's courage collapsed as he vehemently **denied it** with curses and oaths (26:70, 72, 74).

Immediately a rooster crowed, and Peter remembered Jesus's prediction (26:74-75; see 26:33-35). Knowing he had failed the Lord, he broke down and **wept bitterly** (26:75). Though Peter had boasted of his willingness to die for Jesus (26:35), God mercifully revealed to him the true condition of his heart. And Peter responded with tears of repentance.

27:1-2 At **daybreak** after their trial, **the chief priests and the elders** led Jesus to Pontius **Pilate** who was the Roman **governor** of Judea from AD 26–36 (27:1-2). He was a brutal man with no love for the Jews. His residence was in Caesarea Maritima on the Mediterranean Sea. But given the Jewish crowds and potential for unrest, he was in Jerusalem during the Passover. Since Pilate had the power of execution, the Jewish leaders sought to convince him to put Jesus to death.

27:3-4 When **Judas** saw **that Jesus had been condemned**, he **was full of remorse** and returned the money he'd been paid to betray an **innocent** man (27:3-4). But though he felt the sting of guilt for his actions, he didn't turn to God in repentance (like Peter; see John 21:17). Repentance includes sorrow, but it's more than just sorrow. Repentance involves a change of mind—turning from sin and toward the God you have offended.

27:5-10 Instead, Judas resorted to suicide and **hanged himself** (27:5). Guilt is real, and the only true remedy for your guilt before God is the cross of Christ. Don't miss that **the chief priests took the silver** Judas had returned and bought a **field** with the money **as a burial place** (7:6-8). Matthew highlights this as another fulfillment of Old Testament prophecy (27:9-10).

27:11-14 When asked by Pilate if he was **the King of the Jews**, Jesus affirmed it (27:11-12). But he refused to answer the accusations leveled at him by **the chief priests and elders** (fulfilling Isa 53:7), so Pilate was **amazed** (27:13-14).

27:15-19 Pilate had a **custom** of releasing a **prisoner** to the people **at the festival** (27:15). He knew the Jewish leaders had handed over Jesus **because of envy** (27:18). The Galilean rabbi was getting all the attention of the people, and the leaders wanted him out of the way. Pilate therefore gave the people the option of having **Barabbas** (a rebel and a murderer; see Luke 23:19) or **Jesus** released, assuming they would ask for Jesus (27:16-17). Interestingly, Pilate's **wife** warned him to **have nothing to do with that righteous man** because she'd had a nightmare about Jesus (27:19). Undoubtedly, Pilate was eager to be finished with the case of the Jewish Messiah.

27:20-24 The chief priests were *determined* to kill Jesus. They **persuaded the crowds** to demand the release of **Barabbas** and the crucifixion of Jesus (27:20-23). To avoid **a riot** over the matter, Pilate **washed his hands in front of the crowd** to symbolize that he had nothing to do with Jesus's condemnation and was **innocent** of his **blood** (27:24). Some people today try to follow a similar course. They attempt to withhold judgment about Jesus, thinking they can take a middle road. But Jesus said, "Anyone who is not with me is against me" (12:30). There is no neutral choice regarding the Messiah. There are only two eternal destinies, and each is based on acceptance or rejection of Jesus Christ.

27:25-26 In response to Pilate's actions, the Jews in the crowd accepted the blame for Jesus's execution (27:25). Therefore, Pilate **released Barabbas**, had **Jesus flogged**, and **handed him over to be crucified** (27:26). Flogging or scourging involved the use of a whip of leather strips with bits of bone or metal tied to their ends. A cruel beating with this weapon would rip the skin from the victim's back, exposing tissue and bones. Flogging alone could result in death.

27:27-31 When **the governor's soldiers took Jesus**, they made a mockery of him (27:27). They abused him as a pretend king, putting **a scarlet robe** around him, **a crown of thorns** on his head, and **a staff** in his hand to serve as a scepter (27:28-29). Then **they knelt down before him and mocked him** by shouting, **Hail, King of the Jews!** (27:29). Little did they know as they viciously beat and spit on him that every human being (including them!) will bow one day before this God-man and confess, "Jesus Christ is Lord" (Phil 2:10-11).

Through all of their brutality, the prophecy of Isaiah 50:6 was fulfilled.

27:32-33 The Romans typically made crucifixion victims carry their crosses to the execution site. But in this case, the soldiers forced a man **named Simon** to **carry** Jesus's **cross** (probably its crossbeam), because he was so weakened by the flogging (27:32). Interestingly, as a **Cyrenian**, Simon was of African descent: Cyrene was in North Africa. He carried the cross to a location called **Place of the Skull**. In Aramaic the name is **Golgotha**. In Latin, it is Calvary (27:33).

27:34-37 They gave Jesus **wine mixed with gall** to help deaden the pain of crucifixion, but **he refused to drink it** (27:34). He was resolved to endure the suffering. Then they crucified him (27:35). Crucifixion was an extremely cruel form of execution. Victims were typically naked and either tied or nailed to their crosses. Their torture could last for days before death claimed them. While many people were crucified at the hands of the Romans, only Jesus was "pierced because of our rebellion" (Isa 53:5) so he might atone for the sins of the world.

In fulfillment of Psalm 22:18, the soldiers gambled for his clothes **by casting lots**, the ancient equivalent of rolling dice or flipping a coin (27:35). Above his head on the cross, they placed a sign with this accusation: **This is Jesus, the King of the Jews** (27:37). In an ironic sense, this is the full revelation of the theme that Matthew has pursued throughout his Gospel: on the cross Jesus was named "King."

27:38-44 **Two criminals were crucified** on either side of him—perhaps they were companions of Barabbas (27:38). **Those who passed by** showed no pity, but mocked Jesus. The people, as well as the **chief priests**, the **scribes**, and the **elders**, taunted him and told him to **come down from the cross** (27:39-42). Because of his deity, he could have done it, but his mission would have failed if he did. So while they ridiculed his trust in God and his claim that he was **the Son of God** (27:43), Jesus Christ steadfastly hung on that cross in obedience to his Father for your salvation.

27:45-49 From noon until three in the afternoon darkness covered the land (27:45). Then Jesus cried out loudly in despair: **My God, my God, why have you abandoned me?** (27:46), thus quoting and fulfilling Psalm 22:1. Though he had previously known only unbroken divine fellowship from all eternity, Jesus experienced the horrible abandonment of his Father as God poured out his wrath on his Son as he bore the sins of the world.

27:50-51 Finally, Jesus **gave up his spirit** and died (27:50). At that moment, **the curtain of the sanctuary was torn in two** (27:51). This refers to the veil separating the holy place from the most holy place (see Exod 26:33). Since the curtain was torn **from top to bottom**, clearly God did the tearing. In an instant, full access to God's holy presence, through Jesus Christ, was granted. No further sacrifices were necessary. Truly, as Jesus declared, "It is finished" (John 19:30).

27:52-53 Matthew also provides an aside here, telling us some **saints** were **raised** from the dead and **came out of the tombs after** Christ's **resurrection**. Why? Well, Jesus had defeated death. So this was a small picture of the future resurrection that will take place when Christ resurrects the bodies of *all* deceased believers to live forevermore (see 1 Thess 4:16; 1 Cor 15:20-23).

27:54-56 **The centurion and those with him** saw the things that happened and confessed, **Truly this man was the Son of God!** (27:54). So, though the Jewish religious leaders rejected him, these Gentiles believed Jesus was exactly who he'd claimed to be. **Many women** who were followers of Jesus were there too, **watching from a distance** (27:55). Though they wanted to be there for their Lord, they no doubt were horrified by his death.

27:57-61 That **evening, a rich man from Arimathea named Joseph** asked **Pilate** if he could bury **Jesus's body** (27:57-58). Joseph was a prominent member of the Sanhedrin who had objected to their denunciation of Jesus (see Mark 15:43; Luke 23:50-51). He **had also become a disciple** and wanted to honor his Lord with a proper burial (27:57). Though the Romans would typically leave the victims' bodies to rot on the crosses, Pilate respected his request (27:58). Joseph then placed the body **in his new tomb** (thus fulfilling Isa 53:9) and rolled a **great stone against the entrance** (27:59-60).

27:62-66 The following day, **the chief priests and the Pharisees** met with **Pilate** (27:62). The Jewish leaders were aware of Jesus's claims that he would **rise again** (27:63) and were fearful that Jesus's **disciples** would **steal** the body, announce that he was **raised from the dead**, and deceive the people (27:64). So Pilate granted a **guard of soldiers** and the sealing of the **tomb** (27:65-66).

XIV. RESURRECTION AND GREAT COMMISSION (28:1-20)

28:1-4 Early on Sunday, **the first day of the week**, some of the women who followed Jesus went to **the tomb** so they could anoint his body with spices (28:1; Mark 16:1). But there they encountered more than they were expecting. **An angel** in snowy white clothes, whose **appearance was like lightning**, came down, **rolled back the stone**, and perched on top of it (16:2-3). This was no cute little cherub. He was so astonishing and fearsome that **the guards** who saw him were terrified and passed out (16:4).

28:5-6 **The angel** announced to **the women** shocking news. **Jesus who was crucified** was not in the tomb. He'd **risen** as promised! (see 12:40; 16:21; 17:9, 22; 20:19). Even Jesus's enemies knew he'd claimed he would rise again from the dead. That's why they wanted a guard posted at his grave (27:62-66), but Jesus's disciples—and apparently these visitors—had been slow to understand and believe. The angel invited them to **see** the empty tomb, a glorious sight.

28:7-10 Then the angel commissioned the women to proclaim Jesus's resurrection to the **disciples** (28:7). So they left **quickly** with **fear and great joy** to tell them, trying to make sense of all that had happened (28:8). On their way, they met **Jesus**, their risen Lord. The only proper response to that miraculous sight was to fall down and worship him (28:9). He calmed their fears and sent them to tell the disciples they'd soon see him, too (28:10).

28:11-15 The soldiers who had been guarding the tomb **reported to the chief priests** what had happened (28:11). Knowing they had to come up with an explanation, the chief priests **gave the soldiers a large sum of money** to spread a lie (28:12-13). They were to claim that Jesus's disciples **stole** his body in **the night** as they slept (28:13). Not only did the priests promise the guards cash, but also protection from Pilate when he heard the news (28:14).

Notice the fatal flaw in the story the soldiers were to spread. How could they know what had happened if they'd been sound asleep? And, even if they had been awake, how could a small band of civilians overpower armed and trained Roman soldiers?

Here we see an attempt to deny a supernatural event by replacing it with a natural explanation. Jesus *really* rose from the dead! The resurrection is the greatest event of human history and is proof that Christianity is true. Without it, we have nothing. With it, we have hope in history and for eternity (see 1 Cor 15:12-19).

28:16-17 The **disciples traveled to Galilee** to meet with **Jesus** just as they'd been instructed (28:16; see 28:10). **When they saw him, they worshiped, but some doubted** (28:17). So, even while they fell at the feet of the Son of God, they had lingering questions. Is this for real? Can I bank on this? The good news is that their doubts didn't keep them from him. God is not afraid of your questions either. But don't let them keep you away.

28:18-20 These final words of Jesus in Matthew's Gospel have become known as the Great Commission. In them we find the church's marching orders. Jesus declared to his disciples that **all authority ... in heaven and on earth** had been given to him (20:18). In other words, he said, "I'm in charge." Indeed, the Father has given the Son all authority up there and down here, in heaven and in history, in eternity and in time. Christianity, then, is no generic religion tied to a generic god. Authority over the universe is in the hands of the Son of God, Jesus Christ.

On any football field, the players are more powerful than anyone else. But the referees have the authority. No matter how strong and fast the players are, referees can stop their whole show. The devil is far more powerful than you, but Jesus has all authority. That's why your association with Jesus is the ultimate determining factor in your life.

In light of Jesus's all-encompassing authority, he commands his disciples to **make disciples** (28:19). This is a command, not a suggestion or request. A *disciple* is a learner who seeks to become like the one whom he is following. The goal of discipleship, then, is to help people become progressively like Christ in character and conduct, in attitudes and actions. Jesus shares his authority only with disciples so that they may see the rule of God in and through their lives.

Discipleship is the key element of God's kingdom agenda; it's the visible manifestation of God's comprehensive rule over every area of life. The effectiveness of a church is therefore evaluated—not in the number of its members—but by its disciple-making. It's the absence of discipleship that keeps a church impotent and ineffective, because by not taking up Christ's mission of discipleship, its people cannot draw on Christ's authority.

We accomplish disciple-making by *going*, *baptizing*, and *teaching*. To make disciples, then, you must *go*: leave your holy huddle, take your witness with you into the world, and share the gospel.

Next, Jesus commanded them to *baptize* **in the name of the Father and of the Son and of the Holy Spirit** (28:19). The presence of the three titles with the singular "name" affirms the Trinity. To be baptized is to commit a covenantal act by which you are publicly identified with the triune God. As sure as wearing a wedding ring identifies you as married, it should be clear to all that you are under Jesus's authority.

Jesus said to *teach* would-be disciples **to observe everything** he had commanded (28:20). The goal of this is not merely to impart knowledge—it's to help people apply knowledge. Taking notes and memorizing verses is good, but until a learner also obeys God's Word, teaching has not produced a disciple.

King Jesus closed the meeting with a powerful promise: **I am with you always, to the end of the age** (28:20). The second Person of the Trinity promises to uniquely engage and be involved with believers and churches that are making disciples. The church's mission in history, in fact, is possible because of Jesus's heavenly presence. The one who is called Immanuel—"God is with us" (1:23)—will be with us until the end. Therefore, we are to live our lives as disciples and equip others to do the same. Importantly, Jesus does not have the same level of commitment to believers who refuse discipleship (see John 2:23-25).

MARK

INTRODUCTION

Author

LIKE THE OTHER GOSPELS, THE Gospel of Mark is anonymous; it names no author. Nevertheless, the earliest existing copies (dating perhaps to the late first century BC) include the name "Mark" in the title. Moreover, the early church father Papias claimed that Mark wrote his Gospel based on Peter's preaching. Indeed, Peter mentions Mark as his companion (see 1 Pet 5:12-13), and this is the same "John Mark" from the book of Acts who also traveled with Paul on his missionary journeys (see Acts 12:12, 25; 13:5, 13; 15:36-39; Col 4:10; 2 Tim 4:11). This early evidence gives us good reason to believe that John Mark was the author of the Gospel bearing his name and that the apostle Peter provided him with eyewitness testimony of Jesus. Some interpreters have suggested that the unidentified young man who fled the night Jesus was betrayed (14:50-52) was John Mark himself.

Historical Background

Many Bible scholars believe Mark's Gospel was written first, most likely during the 50s, and was used as a source by Matthew and Luke when they wrote their Gospels. It seems likely that Mark wrote primarily for a Gentile audience because he often explains Hebrew/Aramaic words and Jewish customs (e.g., 3:17; 5:41; 7:3-4, 11, 34; 15:34,

42). According to early church tradition, Mark wrote in Rome; therefore, his audience may have been Gentile churches in that city.

Message and Purpose

The book of Mark is written to disciples. It blends the two main topics of leadership and service. Mark unfolds what it means to serve as a kingdom leader and to lead as a servant, because both of these elements are included in what it means to be a follower of Jesus Christ. Discipleship, in fact, is that process whereby we progressively learn what it means to bring every area of life under his lordship. The Gospel of Mark takes us on a pilgrimage as Jesus teaches his first disciples who he is, what he is about, and what it means to follow him.

The disciples had much to learn: they actually argued about which of them would be the greatest in the kingdom. Jesus had to turn their thinking upside down, so he showed them that leadership comes through service. He demonstrated this himself, for indeed he had come "to serve" (10:45). He is called both Son of God and Son of Man because Jesus is both divine and human. He serves the purposes of God, yet he does so by meeting the needs of people. Our challenge in studying Mark is to learn from Jesus's example how to lead and how to serve.

VIDEO INTRO

www.bhpublishinggroup.com/qr/te/41_00

Outline

MARK

I. PREPARATION FOR MINISTRY (1:1-13)

1:1 Mark opens **the gospel**—the good news—by pointing out that it is **of Jesus Christ, the Son of God.** In obedience to an angel's command, the promised child's parents gave him the name "Jesus" (Matt 1:21). "Jesus" is the Greek rendering of the Hebrew name *Joshua*, which means, "the Lord saves." "Christ" is the Greek word for the Hebrew "Messiah," which means, "Anointed One." This was the title of the promised King, the descendant of David who would rule the kingdom and deliver his people. The title "Son of God" tells us Jesus is more than a mere man. He is fully divine; he's the God-Man.

1:2-5 Typically kings would send envoys ahead of them to prepare their way. Mark tells us that God did the same for his Son, sending an envoy to **prepare the way** for the King (1:2). Christ's ambassador was a man named John whose mission was foretold many years before by Isaiah (see Isa 40:3). The prophet said **a voice** would cry out **in the wilderness,** instructing people to **prepare** for the Lord's coming (1:3). This was fulfilled when John started **baptizing in the wilderness** of Judea. He proclaimed the need for spiritual cleansing in preparation for the Messiah and his kingdom. This would require **repentance**—turning from sin. John urged his hearers to be baptized and confess **their sins** as an outward sign of their inward willingness to repent (1:4-5). By "confessing" their sins, they were agreeing with heaven's evaluation of their sins; by "repenting" they were adopting heaven's perspective on their sins.

1:6-8 John's plain lifestyle was reflected in his clothing (**a camel-hair garment with a leather belt**) and his food (**locusts and wild honey**) (1:6). He was a simple, unworthy man pointing to someone **more powerful than** he (1:7). This Coming One would **baptize** his followers **with the Holy Spirit** (1:8). God had promised it long ago (Joel 2:28), and in time Jesus would deliver (see John 14:16-17; Acts 2:1-4).

1:9-11 When **Jesus** arrived at the **Jordan** River, he **was baptized . . . by John** (1:9). He did this to identify with sinners, whom he'd come to save (see commentary at Matt 3:13-15), and so that he might be distinguished as the Messiah, the Son of God (see John 1:29-34). As he rose from the water, **the Spirit** descended on him from heaven (1:10). Thus, though he was truly God, Jesus's humanity would be empowered by the Holy Spirit. Then the Father exalted his **beloved Son** (1:11). Thus, we see the Trinity at work at this crucial kingdom moment: The ministry of God the Son begins with the loving affirmation of God the Father and the empowering presence of God the Spirit.

1:12-13 In preparation for his mission, Jesus was compelled by **the Spirit** to go **into the wilderness** (1:12). As Israel had spent forty years in the wilderness, so Jesus spent **forty days,** identifying with God's people. There he was isolated from civilization, among **wild animals,** and **tempted by Satan** (1:13). And whereas Israel repeatedly failed to obey God during its time in the wilderness, Jesus was victorious. He demonstrated the power of God over the devil when led by the Holy Spirit. This is why the apostle Paul urges Christians to be "led by the Spirit" and to "keep in step with the Spirit" (Gal 5:18, 25).

II. INITIAL MINISTRY IN GALILEE (1:14–3:6)

1:14-15 John, the Messiah's forerunner, **was arrested** (1:14; see Matt 14:3-5). After this, Jesus began his public ministry in **Galilee** and proclaimed, **The time is fulfilled** (1:14-15). **The kingdom of God** had **come near** in the person of the King. Here at the beginning of Jesus's preaching ministry, then, he highlights that the focus of his mission is to declare and manifest the kingdom of God—the visible manifestation of the comprehensive rule of God over every area of life. How should people respond to this message? We should **repent** (change our minds about sin) **and believe** the saving message of Christ so the promise of the kingdom can come (1:15).

1:16-20 Jesus then called his first disciples, two sets of brothers. He used the occupation of **Simon** (Peter) **and Andrew** to challenge them to follow him: **I will make you fish for people** (1:16-17). God will often do something similar when he calls us to become disciples; he'll link our backgrounds and experiences to his purposes for our lives.

Jesus also called **James** and **John** (1:19). Though they had much to learn (see 10:35-45; Luke 9:51-56), they knew that God's kingdom was to overrule every other thing and relationship in their lives. Thus, **they left** everything **and followed** (1:20).

1:21-22 In 1:21-34, Mark presents examples of Jesus's public ministry: **teaching** with prophetic authority (1:21-22), exercising power over the forces of darkness (1:23-28), and performing miraculous healing (1:29-34). When Jesus entered **Capernaum**, a village on the north side of the Sea of Galilee, and **began to teach** in **the synagogue** (1:21), those who heard him were overwhelmed. **The scribes** who normally taught them were nothing like Jesus. He taught with **authority** (1:22), making God's Word powerfully clear.

1:23-24 Jesus followed the authority of his words with the authority of his actions. In the synagogue was **a man with an unclean spirit**—that is, a demon. The demon rightly saw Jesus as a threat to his ongoing destructive work in the man's life. The kingdom of God had come near in the person of the King, and it meant bad news for Satan's forces. **I know who you are**—**the Holy One of God**, the demon said (1:24). Demons have the insight to know who Jesus is, but they're unwilling to worship him. As James says, it's possible to believe in God yet be unwilling to follow him (Jas 2:18-20). This demon acknowledged Jesus's ability to **destroy** him (Mark 1:24).

1:25-28 Though the demon spoke the truth, Jesus had no intention of letting a follower of Satan be his spokesman to fuel the accusation that he was in league with the devil. So with an authoritative command, Jesus banished the spirit from the man (1:25-26). This caused his growing fame to soar even higher and **spread** even wider (1:27-28).

1:29-31 Still in Capernaum, Jesus and his four new disciples visited Simon Peter's **mother-in-law** who was sick **in bed with a fever** (1:29-30). Jesus miraculously **raised her up** and cured her. What's equally important to Mark is that she served Jesus as a result (1:31). The only appropriate response to God's goodness in your life, in fact, is gratitude and service.

1:32-34 When news got out about Jesus's ability to heal, people started bringing all of their **sick and demon-possessed** loved ones to him. **After the sun had set** (1:32), the Sabbath was over (see 1:21), so people had the freedom to carry burdens such as stretchers. He mercifully **healed** the **sick** and **drove out many demons**, not letting the agents of evil testify about his identity (1:34).

1:35 In spite of his exhausting ministry, Jesus woke **very early in the morning, while it was still dark**, and went **to a deserted place** to pray. He sought the fellowship of his heavenly Father—away from the distractions of the world. If the Son of God considered uninterrupted prayer such a priority, why do so many Christians consider it an afterthought?

1:36-38 When his disciples found him, they were annoyed, saying, **Everyone is looking for you** (1:36-37). Apparently they thought he wasn't capitalizing on the opportunities his popularity afforded him. Jesus, though, had not come merely to please the masses with miracles. He came to **preach** the good news and prepare people for God's kingdom (1:38).

1:39-41 Moving on from Capernaum, Jesus traveled and ministered throughout **Galilee** (1:39). On one occasion, **a man with leprosy . . . begged him** to **make** his body **clean** (1:40). With this scene Mark wants his readers to know that Jesus's healing ministry wasn't perfunctory. When he heard and saw the man, he was **moved with compassion** (1:41). The sinless Son of God is able to sympathize with our weaknesses, so let us approach [his] throne of grace with boldness (Heb 4:15-16).

Jesus's compassion was displayed not only by his willingness to heal the man, but also by the manner in which he healed him: **Jesus reached out . . . and touched him** (1:41). Understand: No one touched a leper. Doing so risked infection and made Jews unclean according to the Mosaic law. But the Son of God fears no uncleanness. He cannot be contaminated; he can only purify.

1:42-45 When he cleansed the man, Jesus **warned him** to **say nothing to anyone** but to **show** himself **to the priest** and **offer** the appropriate sacrifice for his **cleansing** (1:42-44). Nevertheless, the man **spread the news** everywhere about what Jesus had done. As a result of his disobedience, the man hindered Jesus's ministry because he **could no longer enter a town openly** (1:45).

2:1-2 Jesus returned to **Capernaum again** (2:1). Once the people discovered where he was staying, the place where he taught God's Word grew so full that no one could stand **even in the doorway** (2:2). When Jesus Christ preached, he drew a crowd.

2:3-4 While he was there, **four** men brought him **a paralytic**, carrying him on a mat (2:3). The paralyzed man could not seek out Jesus on his own, but these four friends cared enough to take him where he needed to go. The problem was that they couldn't approach Jesus about him **because of the crowd** (2:4). The sermon listeners were actually blocking access to Jesus. Undaunted, the man's four friends carried him to the roof of the house. The homes in Galilee were built with outside staircases you could ascend to access their flat tops. Once there, they dug up the mud and thatch **roof** and lowered the man through the hole (2:4).

Some Christians will invite friends to church but not invite them to Jesus. They'll invite them to hear sermons, choir concerts, and to see special programs, but they won't tell them about the life-changing power of Jesus Christ. These four men knew that getting their friend to a building wasn't the goal. Getting him to the Master was.

2:5 Jesus saw **their faith**. He witnessed *collective* faith. We weren't meant to be Lone Ranger Christians. We need one another. Sometimes our circumstances can be so overpowering, in fact, that we even need to piggyback on the faith of others. Have you gathered people around you who will carry your burdens (see Gal 6:2) when your faith is dull?

When he saw his friends' faith in action, Jesus told the paralyzed man, **Son, your sins are forgiven**. Now, these men had not brought their friend to Jesus because of a sin problem but because his leg muscles didn't work. Yet Jesus knew there was a deeper issue beyond the problem they could see. Similarly, no matter how poor your physical condition, your spiritual condition must take priority. Unforgiven sins are more detrimental than unhealed limbs. Spiritual sickness is worse than broken circumstances. And spiritual healing can reverse sin's physical consequences.

2:6-8 Some in the crowd weren't excited about what Jesus said. **Some of the scribes**

were **questioning** his words **in their hearts** (2:6) While they hadn't spoken out loud, **Jesus perceived** supernaturally what they were pondering (2:8). This is a reminder that there isn't a moment that goes by that Jesus doesn't know exactly what you're thinking.

What was it that concerned the scribes? **He's blaspheming! Who can forgive sins but God alone?** (2:8). While they were right that God alone could forgive sins, they had Jesus all wrong. He possessed divine authority because of his divine nature. And he was about to demonstrate that authority for all to see.

2:9-10 Jesus asked the skeptical religious leaders which was **easier**—to tell a lame man that he was **forgiven** or to tell him to **get up** and **walk** (2:9). Only God could accomplish either, but only one action produced physical results. So Jesus told them he would validate his authority to do the one (**forgive sins**) by demonstrating his authority to do the other (make a **paralytic** walk). His ability to accomplish a visible miracle would confirm his ability to accomplish an invisible spiritual one (2:10).

2:11-12 Jesus commanded a man with *lame* legs to **get up**—and a man with *healthy* legs **got up!** Then he **went out in front of everyone.** Mark doesn't tell us how the scribes responded to this miracle, but we know how the crowds did. They were **astounded** and **gave glory to God** (2:12). Don't go to Jesus for help with your physical circumstances unless you're willing for him to deal with your spiritual circumstances. And when he does, testify about it to others so that you and they can give God the glory.

2:13-14 Jesus's ministry was growing; many people flocked to hear him teach (2:13). One day he approached a man named **Levi** (also known as Matthew; see Matt 9:9), a tax collector **sitting at the toll booth.** As he did with the others (1:16-20), Jesus told Levi to **follow** him (2:14). It was one thing to enlist fishermen as his disciples; it was another to enlist a tax collector. Jews who served as tax collectors were considered unclean because they worked for Gentiles. Moreover, they typically charged extra taxes to keep

for themselves (see Luke 19:1-10). Having a thieving tax collector as a disciple wouldn't improve Jesus's reputation among the religious elite.

2:15-16 Showing his level of commitment to Jesus, Levi invited him and his disciples to his home to eat with **many tax collectors and sinners** (2:15). This was too much for **the scribes** and **Pharisees** who kept themselves physically separated from unclean types. So they harassed Jesus's **disciples**, wanting to know why a "holy" man would hang out with such people (2:16).

2:17 Obviously, the religious leaders had misunderstood Jesus's mission—and so have some church-goers today. It's the **sick** who **need a doctor.** It's the bad who need good news (see 1:15). Jesus **didn't come to call the righteous** to enter into fellowship with God, nor the self-righteous (like the scribes and Pharisees) who didn't perceive a need for spiritual help. Rather, he came to call **sinners**, those who are spiritually bankrupt and know it. So when was the last time you spent time with a sinner—not so you could share in sin but so you could point him to your Savior? If engaging with the lost is repulsive to you, you've lost sight of Jesus's mission and the calling on the church.

2:18-22 When people observed the followers of Jesus, they noticed something different. Though **John's disciples and the Pharisees** fasted, the disciples of Jesus didn't (2:18). The Old Testament certainly expected God's people to fast periodically, but Jesus said the circumstances in his day were different. The presence of the Messiah was a time for rejoicing and celebration. It would be no more appropriate for his followers to fast in his presence than for friends of a **groom** to **fast** at his **wedding** (2:19). Fasting would come later—when the groom was **taken away** (2:20). After Jesus's death, resurrection, and ascension, the legitimacy of fasting would resume for his people. You can't put **a patch of unshrunk cloth on an old garment** (2:21) and you can't put **new wine into old wineskins** (2:22). In other words, the newness of the Messiah and his kingdom wasn't compatible with their expectations.

2:23-24 The Jewish religious leaders had accused Jesus of blasphemy (2:1-12) and fraternizing with sinners (2:12-17). Here they accuse him of violating the Mosaic law. One **Sabbath** day while Jesus **and his disciples** walked through **grainfields**, they picked **heads of grain** to eat (2:23). But **the Pharisees** would have none of that (2:24). In their view, picking grain was tantamount to harvesting, harvesting was work, and work was forbidden on the Sabbath. Therefore, they labeled Jesus a lawbreaker.

2:25-28 Jesus replied to the charge against him by emphasizing how deficient these "experts" in the law were in their knowledge of Scripture: **Have you never read . . . ?** (2:25). His first example was **David**, who took **the bread of the Presence** for himself and his hungry men when he was on the run from King Saul (2:25-26; see 1 Sam 21:1-6). If the Lord's anointed could eat the sacred bread when in need and be innocent, how much more could the Anointed One do the same? **The Sabbath was made for man** (2:27), to meet people's needs and benefit them. It was not to be a mere religious observance, absent of all compassion. Furthermore, **the Son of Man is Lord even of the Sabbath** (2:28), which was another claim to deity. As God, Jesus had established the Sabbath; therefore, he knew its proper function. Once again, his reasoning silenced the Pharisees, but their hatred grew. This wouldn't be the last time Jesus offended their Sabbath sensibilities.

3:1-2 On another occasion Jesus, a man with **a shriveled hand**, and the Pharisees were together in a **synagogue** (3:1). It was a perfect storm because Mark makes it clear that the Pharisees weren't there to learn from Jesus. Instead, **they were watching him closely** to see if he would **heal** the man **on the Sabbath.** If so, they would have cause for accusing him of defiling the Sabbath (3:2).

3:3-4 Jesus had no intention of backing down from this public confrontation. He had **the man with the shriveled hand** stand before everyone in the synagogue (3:3). Then he posed a question to the Pharisees in order to make their motives clear: **Is it lawful to do good on the Sabbath or to do evil, to save life or to kill?** The answer was obvious. Failure to do good and save life would actually be a violation of the law. But they were unrepentant, remaining **silent** (3:4). They had no intention of answering the questions of this upstart rabbi, nor did they have an adequate response to give.

3:5-6 Jesus was filled with both **anger** and grief over **the hardness of their hearts.** They were zealous for religious tradition but remained insensitive to the poor man's need. Once again, Jesus healed by commanding a person to do what he was incapable of doing without divine help (see 2:10-12). He told the man to **stretch out** his **hand**, and in an instant **his hand was restored** (3:5). This miraculous act was exactly what **the Pharisees** were looking for. They began **plotting with the Herodians**—political supporters of Herod Antipas, the tetrarch of Galilee—to **kill** Jesus (3:6). Religion and politics joined forces against the true King.

III. MINISTRY AROUND THE SEA OF GALILEE (3:7–6:6)

3:7-12 Jesus's ministry continued to grow. **A large crowd followed him from Galilee** (3:7). People from **Judea** and **Jerusalem** followed him, but they also traveled from the outskirts: **Idumea** to the south, **beyond the Jordan** to the east, **and around Tyre and Sidon** in the northwest (2:7-8). His healing ministry had become so well known that people with **diseases were pressing toward him to touch him** (2:10). The demons had become familiar with him too, and they often shouted, **You are the Son of God!** (3:11). But Jesus warned them to keep quiet (3:12; see 1:25-26).

3:13-19 Jesus took **twelve** of those who'd been following him and **named** them **apostles** (3:13-14). Their role was **to be with him** (to have a relationship to Jesus), to **preach** (to proclaim the message of Jesus), and to **drive**

out demons (to exercise the authority of Jesus) (3:14-15). In the Gospels these men are known as the Twelve. Mark names them all (3:16-19), beginning with Peter, who functioned as something of a leader among them (3:16). Next come James and John, called the Sons of Thunder because of their intense personalities (3:17; see 10:35-45; Luke 9:51-56). These three—Peter, James, and John—made up Jesus's inner circle and were often with him apart from the other apostles (see 5:37; 9:2; 14:33). Mark identifies Judas Iscariot as the apostle who betrayed him (3:19); it's a hint to the reader that the opposition to Jesus arose even among his companions. Judas was the only non-Galilean among the Twelve.

3:20-21 Opposition to Jesus came from the Jewish religious leaders (2:6-7, 16, 24; 3:6), one of his apostles (3:19), and even from his own family members. When his family heard that he was drawing huge crowds, were they proud? Excited? No. They told others, He's out of his mind (3:21). In light of everything he was doing, they thought he'd gone crazy. His brothers didn't believe in him during his ministry (see John 7:3-4), and even from an early age his parents misunderstood him (see Luke 2:41-50).

All of this would change, however, after Jesus's resurrection. His mother and brothers would be counted among the first Christians in the early church (see Acts 1:14). His brothers James and Jude, in fact, would even write the Holy-Spirit-inspired New Testament books now bearing their names, and James would be a leader in the Jerusalem church (see Acts 12:17; 15:13; see 1 Cor 15:7).

3:22 Though during his ministry his family thought Jesus was insane, the scribes went a step further—a step too far. They couldn't refute the fact that he was driving out demons. So they accused Jesus of being possessed by Beelzebul—another name for Satan, the ruler of the demons. They claimed the devil was the source of his power.

3:23-26 Jesus demonstrated how ridiculous this claim was with a parable: How can Satan drive out Satan? If a kingdom is divided against itself, that kingdom cannot stand (3:23-24). Satan is the enemy of God, but he's not stupid. He's cunning like a serpent (see Gen 3:1) and prowls "like a roaring lion" (1 Pet 5:8). Why would he attack his own kingdom? Indeed, if Satan opposes himself and is divided, he . . . is finished (Mark 3:26). Why undermine his own authority? His kingdom would topple without God's interference.

3:27 Satan's kingdom hadn't been assaulted from the inside, but it had been assaulted from outside. Jesus had entered the strong man's house, tied him up, and plundered his possessions. And no one could render a strong man helpless unless he was stronger—in this case, unless his power was divine.

3:28-30 Jesus then explained to the scribes where they were headed by accusing him of being in league with the devil (3:30). All sins and blasphemies can be forgiven by God (3:28). But whoever blasphemes against the Holy Spirit never has forgiveness (3:29).

Empowered by the Holy Spirit, Jesus had overpowered Satan. Yet, in spite of irrefutable evidence of that fact, the scribes had attributed the deeds of the Holy Spirit to the ruler of demons. The work of Christ on the cross can atone for terrible sins, but one must believe in Christ to receive forgiveness. To claim that the authority and power behind Jesus is actually the authority and power of the devil is to reject God's salvation in light of clear revelation. The one who rejects what the Holy Spirit makes clear, then, is guilty of an eternal sin (3:29).

If you come to King Jesus and receive him as your Savior, he promises to forgive all. But if you spurn the King, call him the devil, and reject the Holy Spirit's testimony, you have no other option for salvation. As Jesus said, "I am the way, the truth, and the life. No one comes to the Father except through me." (John 14:6).

3:31-35 As Jesus was inside the house teaching, his mother and his brothers arrived outside, wanting to talk to him (3:31). Mark has already told us that his family didn't believe in him (see 3:20-21). Apparently, they wanted him to stop making a fool of himself. But Jesus pointed to those around him who had devoted themselves to his teaching and said, **Here are my mother and my brothers**—that is to say, **whoever does the will of God** is my family (3:34-35).

Jesus prioritized his relationship with those who submit themselves to God's will. If you want to experience more of Jesus and have a deeper relationship with him, respond to God's agenda for your life.

4:1-2 Once, the **crowd** was so **large** that Jesus climbed **into a boat on the sea** and began to teach as people listened from **shore** (4:1). He frequently **taught** using **parables** (4:2), stories used to convey spiritual truths. Mark provides several of these (4:3-32), beginning with the parable of the sower.

4:3-9 In an agrarian society, listeners would immediately relate to a parable about a man planting seed. As **the sower** walked, he dropped **seed** on various kinds of soil. Seed that **fell** on the hardened **path** was **devoured** by **birds** (4:3-4). **On rocky ground** where **the soil** was shallow, the seeds sprouted **quickly**. But without deep roots, they **withered** in **the sun** (4:5-6). **Other seed fell among thorns**, which **choked** the plant (4:7). But some **seed fell on good ground** and produced a bounty of **fruit** (4:8). As he concluded, Jesus explained to the crowd that understanding his story required spiritual insight: **Let anyone who has ears to hear listen** (4:9).

4:10-12 Later, in private, his disciples asked him to explain his **parables** to them (4:10). Jesus said that **the secret** or "mystery" **of the kingdom of God** had **been given to** them. Those things that had been hidden in the Old Testament about God's kingdom were being revealed to them through Christ. But for **those outside** who rejected Jesus's authority, the **parables** actually concealed truths (4:11). He then quoted Isaiah 6:9-10, in which the prophet pronounced God's judgment on Israel because of their failure to repent. The same was true for those who heard Jesus. Unless they responded to the truth they had been given, they would not be given further insight to lead them to repentance (see also Matt 13:10-12).

4:13-14 If they were to **understand all of the parables** about the kingdom, the disciples needed to **understand this parable** (4:13). The seed in the parable represents **the word** (4:14). The way one responds to God's Word has significant effects on one's life. To receive the Word is to live under the rule of the King. The parable of the sower shows what it looks like when different kinds of hearts encounter God's Word.

4:15-20 The hardened **path** represents a hardened heart. People with such hearts refuse to believe; therefore, **Satan** easily removes the Word from them (4:15). The seed that grows in **rocky ground** and **among thorns** represents believers who, either through spiritual immaturity or attachments to worldliness (such as **wealth**), fail to yield fruit (4:16-19). Spiritual growth cannot happen when God's kingdom is marginalized in a life. But the **good ground** represents hearts that are receptive to God's Word. They **welcome it**—that is, they believe and obey it. As a result, they **produce** abundant spiritual **fruit** because of the kingdom impact their lives have on others (4:20).

4:21-22 No one lights **a lamp** and then puts it **under a basket**. Instead, a lamp is put **on a lampstand** to light up a room and reveal its contents (4:21). In the same way, the lamp of God's Word is to shine into people's hearts in order to bring **to light** that which is **hidden** (4:22).

4:23-25 Disciples must heed the Word of God (4:23). To the degree that you welcome the Word in your life, you will bear fruit. The more believers accept God's kingdom agenda, the more fruitfulness God will entrust to them. But disobedience brings spiritual barrenness (4:24-25).

4:26-29 Jesus compared **the kingdom of God** to **seed** that a man planted (4:26). As he went about his life, the seed sprouted and grew, though he didn't understand how (4:27). Over time, a crop was produced that was ready for the harvesters (4:28-29). Similarly, the disciple of Jesus Christ who faithfully proclaims God's Word can have confidence that it will accomplish its work (see Isa 55:10-11). The

Word has life within itself, so God will ensure growth and harvest as people respond to his Word when it is rightly explained.

4:30-32 Jesus also compared God's kingdom to **a mustard seed** (4:31). Although it was **the smallest of all the seeds** that farmers planted, it would grow into a large shrub, in which **birds** could nest (4:31-32). In the same way, God's kingdom was starting small, with just a few disciples. But it would grow tremendously in spite of its inauspicious beginning so that the operation of the kingdom in history would spread blessings everywhere.

4:33-34 Thus, Jesus spoke in **parables** to communicate the truth of the kingdom (4:33). But to his **disciples**, he **explained everything** (see 4:10-12).

4:35-37 At the end of the day, Jesus said to his disciples, **Let's cross over to the other side of the sea** (4:35). Climbing into their boat, they **left the crowd** and their stressful day behind (4:36). Or so they thought.

Lying nearly seven hundred feet below sea level, the Sea of Galilee is surrounded by mountains and highlands. As a result of this geography, it is predisposed to violent windstorms, which is exactly what the disciples encountered. Not only were they being tossed about, but **waves were breaking over the boat** and filling it with water (4:37). Several of the disciples were hardened, lifelong fishermen. They had experienced storms on the Sea of Galilee before. But this one was different.

Notice that the disciples hadn't done anything wrong. Jesus had commanded them to get into the boat, and they were in the perfect center of God's will. Yet they were also in the center of a situation that was threatening their lives. Life is like that sometimes. It's true that our sinful choices often bring difficulties our way. Frequently, though, heartbreaking trials come when you're following God and experiencing intimate fellowship with him. So, remember to "consider it a great joy . . . whenever you experience various trials, because you know that the testing of your faith produces endurance" (Jas 1:2-3).

4:38 Where was Jesus while the storm raged and the disciples panicked? **He was in the stern, sleeping on the cushion.** He hadn't just inadvertently fallen asleep wherever he happened to be sitting. He'd curled up on *a cushion*, so this was planned snoozing! This was intentional. And the disciples didn't like it: **Teacher! Don't you care that we're going to die?** They were rocked by the storm outside, the storm of inner terror, and the theological storm of wrongly assuming Jesus didn't care. The last storm was the worst.

When God lets us go through ordeals, it often feels like he doesn't care. The fear and pain lead to confusion ("Why would God let this happen?"). But in such moments, you must know your Bible and trust in the King of creation. There are no storms that come into your life that do not first pass through his sovereign and loving fingers. If you know his character, you'll know that he does nothing that is not for your good and for his glory (see Rom 8:28).

4:39-40 When Jesus woke, he didn't speak to the disciples but to their surroundings. He **rebuked the wind** and told **the sea to be still** (4:39). Immediately, the creation obeyed its Creator. The wind stopped blowing, and the sea stopped churning. Then Jesus asked his disciples a startling question: **Why are you afraid?** His query implied that they shouldn't have been fearful. Then he rebuked them for having **no faith** (4:40).

Fear and faith: these two correspond to one another. An increase in one leads to a decrease in the other. The disciples had every reason to trust Jesus. They had *seen* his miraculous deeds; they *knew* God was with him. But it's easy to forget what Jesus did yesterday when we're going through a storm today. Furthermore, before the storm arose, Jesus had told them, "Let's cross over to the other side" (4:35). He had let them know in advance that they would make it to their destination. Our faith fails only when we allow our circumstances to override God's Word.

4:41 Moments before, the disciples had been afraid of their situation. Yet when they witnessed the power of Jesus, they became terrified *of him*. They feared the one whom they should have feared all along. Why does God put you in frightful circumstances? So that you'll learn to fear him more than your own circumstances. If you fear him above all else, you'll trust his Word above all else.

5:1-5 Once they arrived on **the other side of the sea**, another **man with an unclean spirit** approached Jesus (5:1-2). Mark has already told us about Jesus's encounters with demon-possessed people (1:23-26; 1:32-34; 3:11), but this account gets personal. Mark tells us what life was like for this particular man. First, **he lived in the tombs** (5:3). He was an utter social outcast. It's not that he had no human companions, but all of his human companions were dead! Second, he was out of control. Though people attempted to tie him up **with shackles and chains**, he would simply break them. Because of his demonically inspired strength, **no one** could **subdue him** (5:4). Third, he endured self-inflicted agony. He was awake at all hours, **crying out and cutting himself with stones** (5:5).

5:6-8 All of the man's external torture was due to internal turmoil. He wasn't merely crazy; he was under demonic influence (5:2). Like previous demons Jesus dealt with (1:23-24), the demon inhabiting this man recognized Jesus for who he truly is: **Son of the Most High God** (5:7). Moreover, he recognized Jesus's power and authority. Though the Son of God wanted the demon out (5:8), the demon begged, **Don't torment me!** (5:7).

5:9-13 Since Jesus demanded to know the demon's **name**, we learn that the demon who had been talking was only a spokesman. He wasn't alone. **My name is Legion ... because we are many** (5:9). In other words, his demonic aunts, uncles, cousins, and more had moved in with him. They **begged** Jesus to give them permission to relocate to a new home: a **herd of pigs** (5:11-12). So Jesus let **the unclean spirits** enter the unclean animals, which promptly **rushed ... into the sea and drowned** (5:13).

5:14-17 When the people from the nearby **town** and surrounding **countryside** heard about it, they came and saw the former **demon-possessed** man **in his right mind** (5:14-15). No more living among the tombs; no more hands and feet shackled; no more bleeding at his own hands. Yet how did these people respond to such a glorious healing? They begged Jesus **to leave their region** (5:17). Why? Mark says they responded this way after learning about the man and **about the pigs** (5:16). *Two thousand* pigs to be exact (5:13). All that pork represented a lot of money. Were Jesus to continue doing similar things, he'd ruin the local economy. Notice that their livelihood was more important to them than a human being delivered from demonic oppression. They valued the material over the spiritual.

5:18 There has been a lot of begging in this chapter. The demons begged Jesus not to torment them or send them out of the region (5:7, 10). Then they begged to enter a herd of pigs (5:12). The locals begged Jesus to go away (5:17). But here we see some begging that's God-honoring. The man who had been demon possessed **begged** Jesus **that he might remain with him** (5:18). He knew that Jesus had delivered him, and he didn't want to leave his side.

5:19-20 Jesus had other plans for the man. **Go home to your own people, and report to them how much the Lord has done for you** (5:19). In other words, "Go home to the people who knew what you were like and give God the glory for what you are now." And so the man did, all throughout the tencity region of Decapolis. He told everyone **how much Jesus had done for him, and they were all amazed** (5:20). Given his past, he was probably a fairly well-known person. Those who knew him needed to hear his testimony to know what happens when the kingdom of God invades a person's life. If you're a Christian, the people in your life need to hear what Jesus has done for you.

5:21-24 Again, Jesus and his disciples **crossed** the sea, and a **crowd gathered around him** (5:21). A **synagogue** leader named **Jairus** pleaded with him to heal his **little daughter** who was **dying** (5:22-23).

There's probably not a dad of young children who can't sympathize with how desperate this man was. He was surely relieved when Jesus agreed to go **with him** (5:24). But he was about to experience a delay in getting Jesus to his little girl.

5:25-26 As they made their way through the jam-packed crowd, there was **a woman** with a severe *medical* problem. She had suffered from **bleeding for twelve years** (5:25). But she also had a severe *financial* problem. **She had spent everything she had** on **doctors** who were unable to help (5:26). Though Mark doesn't mention it, she also had a severe *religious* problem. Leviticus 15:25-27 indicates that the woman would have been ceremonially unclean during the course of her illness. Therefore, she was defiled, destitute, and desperate.

5:27-29 She had **heard about Jesus** (5:27), had been told stories of this miracle-working teacher. The lame were made to walk; the blind were made to see; the leprous were made clean; the demon-possessed were made free. Jesus could heal her; he was her last hope. But there was a thick crowd, and Jesus was on a mission to heal someone else. She didn't want to stop him or call his name. She wanted to go unseen. **If I just touch his clothes**, she told herself, **I'll be made well** (5:28). So that's what she did. **Instantly her flow of blood ceased**, and she knew **she was healed** (5:29). It had worked! But her actions didn't go unnoticed.

5:30-31 Jesus knew **power had gone out from him**. Someone had accessed his kingdom power by desperate faith, and he wasn't going to ignore it. So he asked, **Who touched my clothes?** (5:30). The **disciples** were stunned by the question. **The crowd** was **pressing** on him from all directions, and he wanted to know who touched him (5:31)? But Jesus can distinguish between people bumping against him and those touching him in faith.

5:32-34 Why did Jesus want to single this woman out in front of the crowd? In Psalm 50:15, God says, "Call on me in a day of trouble; I will rescue you, and you will honor me."

It would seem, then, that Jesus was determined to see that God was glorified publicly in this healing.

How did the woman respond to being called out? With worship: **With fear and trembling** she **came and fell down before him** (3:33). When the Lord comes through in your life and no one knows about it but you, you need to declare his deeds and give him glory. "Let the redeemed of the LORD proclaim that he has redeemed them from the power of the foe" (Ps 107:2). When the woman honored God publicly, Jesus told her, **Your faith has saved you. Go in peace and be healed from your affliction** (5:34).

5:35 Jairus, the synagogue leader, had come to Jesus begging that he heal his daughter (5:21-24). But after the delay with the crowd and the woman, **people came from** Jairus's **house** to deliver heartbreaking news: **Your daughter is dead** (5:35). For a moment he probably thought, "If only the crowd had let Jesus through; if only that woman hadn't stopped him." But though we often think that God has mismanaged our circumstances, his plan is perfect and brings him more glory than our plans would.

5:36-37 The people had seen Jesus accomplish miraculous healing. But it would seem that some among them thought death was beyond his power. Jesus didn't respond to the crowd, but to the father: **Don't be afraid. Only believe** (5:36). Then he took only his inner circle of disciples (see commentary on 3:13-19) with him to see to the little girl (5:37).

5:38-40 The **people weeping and wailing loudly** (5:38) probably included professional mourners, who were paid to attend funerals and express grief over the loss of a loved one. Jesus questioned their **weeping** (5:39)—not because mourning isn't appropriate in such cases, but because it signaled unbelief. The King, after all, had come to heal; Jesus's arrival was cause for hope. Though the girl was dead from a human perspective, that was only a temporary condition. She was only **asleep** (5:39). Nevertheless, they continued to demonstrate their unbelief by laughing at him (5:40).

5:41-43 When Jesus, his three disciples, and the parents were alone with **the child**, he took her **by the hand** and told her to **get up** (5:41). There are parents who have more difficulty waking their children in the morning for school than the Son of God had raising this little girl from the dead. **She was twelve years old** (5:42), which is particularly interesting given that the woman Jesus had just healed had been "bleeding for twelve years" (5:25). This miracle was for the family of the little girl, so Jesus commanded them to keep silent about it (5:43). The people outside had already been given enough evidence to generate faith.

6:1-3 Sometime later, Jesus returned to his **hometown** of Nazareth and taught **in the synagogue** (6:1-2). Given his reputation, one would expect a hero's welcome for him. But, even though the townspeople were **astonished**, they were also **offended by him** (6:2-3). Likely they said, "Who does Jesus think he is? We know his brothers and sisters. He grew up here. How could he be performing miracles? He's nothing special." Since

Jesus's own family thought he was "out of his mind" (3:21), it's not surprising his former neighbors thought the same.

6:4-5 Like the Old Testament prophets, Jesus received no **honor . . . in his hometown** and **among his relatives** (6:4). They focused on his humanity and failed to recognize the supernatural nature of his words and works. As a result, they limited what God would do through Jesus (6:5). Understand, Christ did not lack power; rather, the absence of faith caused God to withhold supernatural work. The Messiah was in their midst, but they missed his work in their lives because they refused to believe. Don't hinder the work of God. His power is unlimited. But if you refuse to trust him, don't be surprised when eternity doesn't show up in your history.

6:6 Even Jesus was shocked **at their unbelief.** They'd seen what everyone else had seen, yet still they didn't believe. So he left and continued to proclaim his kingdom message in the surrounding **villages.**

IV. MINISTRY IN GALILEE AND BEYOND (6:7–8:30)

6:7-13 Jesus gathered the **Twelve** together (see 3:14-19) and authorized these apostles to engage in an expansion of his ministry (6:7). As his ambassadors, they were to do what he'd been doing: preaching the kingdom, casting out **demons**, and healing the **sick** (6:7, 12-13). They were to take no extra provisions (6:8-9) because God would provide for them through the hospitality of those who'd submit to his kingdom agenda. Yet just as Jesus experienced rejection, his representatives would as well. If a **place** refused to **welcome** them and their message, they were to **shake the dust off [their] feet as a testimony against them** (6:11). This is a reference to the Jewish practice of shaking the dust off one's feet upon returning to Israel from a Gentile region. If people would not receive the King's message, his ambassadors were to symbolically proclaim their coming judgment.

6:14-16 Herod Antipas, the tetrarch who ruled Galilee and Perea, **heard** of Jesus's growing fame (6:14). He was the son of Herod the Great, who'd tried to kill Jesus when he heard that a rival king had been born (see Matt 2:1-23). Superstitious man that he was, this Herod thought that Jesus was **John the Baptist . . . raised from the dead**, coming back to haunt him (6:14). **Others** believed Jesus was **Elijah** (whom God took away in a chariot to heaven; 2 Kgs 2:11) or **one of the prophets** (6:15; see 8:28). But Herod became convinced that **John**, whom he had **beheaded**, was back from the grave (6:16).

6:17-20 The mention of John's execution causes Mark to give his readers a flashback to explain what had happened to this man who hasn't been mentioned since he baptized Jesus in 1:9. Herod had arrested John to please his wife **Herodias**, who'd divorced Herod's **brother** Philip to marry Herod (6:17).

The divorce and remarriage had been unlawful, and John had the holy audacity to tell Herod so (6:18). As a result, Herodias hated John and wanted him dead (6:19). Herod, on the other hand, **feared John**, believed he was a **holy man**, enjoyed listening to him, and **protected him** from death by locking him in prison (6:20).

6:21-29 During Herod's **birthday** party, **Herodias's own daughter . . . danced** for him—probably in a sexually suggestive manner (6:21-22). The ruler foolishly **promised her** in front of his important **guests** that she could have whatever she wanted (6:22-23). Then daughter helped **mother** plot to obtain what she wanted: **John the Baptist's head** (6:24-25). Herod didn't want to embarrass himself in front of everyone. He feared John, his wife, and his party guests—but he didn't fear God. So he had John executed (6:26-28). Then **John's disciples** buried their revered teacher (6:29).

6:30-31 After their mission to proclaim the kingdom in word and deed (see 6:7-13), **the apostles** returned to Jesus and **reported to him** everything that had happened (6:30). So Jesus commanded them to go away with him to **rest** and **eat** (6:31). Sometimes, the most spiritual thing you can do is get some sleep. We need the reminder that we are created beings; we're not God. The fact that we need rest is a reminder that we are dependent on the one who "does not slumber or sleep" (Ps 121:4).

6:32-34 Many people saw Jesus and his disciples departing in a **boat** (6:32). His popularity was at a fever pitch. Folks were so anxious to see him that **they ran on foot** to arrive at Jesus's destination **ahead of** the boat (6:32-33). That's dedication. When Jesus saw the **large crowd**, he **had compassion** on them. To him **they were like sheep without a shepherd** (6:34).

There are three things to know about sheep. They are dumb, defenseless, and directionless. Sheep lack the knowledge to make the right choices, are vulnerable to attack from predators, and struggle with decision-making. But the Lord is "like a shepherd" who "gathers the lambs in his arms" (Isa 40:11). So Jesus was moved **to teach them** (6:34).

6:35-36 As it became **late**, the disciples became worried. They were in a **deserted** area, so they urged Jesus to **send** the people **away** to **buy** food (6:35-36). From a purely human perspective, the disciples' concerns were justified. Mark tells us there were "five thousand men" present (6:44). Were women and children also counted, there could've been a total of fifteen to twenty thousand people. The disciples were probably thinking, "Jesus, we've got some hungry people on our hands. We know you like to teach, but it's time to bring this sermon to a conclusion. Send these folks into the villages to boost the local economies, and let's get out of here."

6:37 Imagine seeing the expressions on the disciples' faces when Jesus told them, **You give them something to eat.** All they could say was, "It's not in the budget!" They didn't have the means to feed such a large crowd. Or did they? They had overlooked the fact that the kingdom power that had fed hundreds of thousands of Israelites in the wilderness for forty years (Exod 16:1-36) was the same kingdom power available to them through Jesus.

6:38-44 The Twelve informed Jesus that they had **five** loaves of bread and **two fish**—barely enough to feed the thirteen of their party (6:38). But God never lacks resources; he can always afford what he chooses to provide. So Jesus **instructed them to have all the people sit** and get ready for the meal (6:39). Then he **blessed** the **loaves** and **fish** and gave them to the disciples to distribute (6:41). And the food just kept on coming! Miraculously, enough was provided for everyone. And it's not because everyone had a mere nibble or a few crumbs. **Everyone ate and was satisfied** (6:42). **Five thousand men** (6:44), plus women and children, were stuffed like Thanksgiving turkeys. And there were still leftovers (6:43).

You may not have much. But, whatever you have, you have enough to accomplish the kingdom mission God has for you. We are called to give God whatever we have—our time, our money, our abilities. If you have the compassionate Christ who has access to the all-powerful Father, you have everything you need.

6:45 After this, Jesus **made his disciples get into the boat** and go without him **to the** lake's **other side.** They were about to enter a trial—that is, adverse circumstances allowed by God to deepen their experience of him. Unfortunately, the disciples were going to struggle with this trial because they hadn't learned from the previous one.

6:46 As his disciples departed, Jesus went **to pray.** They didn't know what was coming, but Jesus did. And he was already interceding for them. Because of his resurrection from the dead, Jesus "always lives to intercede for" you, too (Heb 7:25).

6:47-48 As they reached **the middle of the sea,** the disciples were struggling because of the fierce **wind** that **was against them.** They were in the middle of God's will (Jesus had sent them on their journey), yet they were also in the middle of threatening circumstances. If you're earnestly and faithfully seeking to follow God, don't be surprised when trials come. God grants these so that "your faith—more valuable than gold" may be refined and bring glory to Christ (1 Pet 1:7).

Jesus **saw them straining at the oars,** so though God may seem to be absent in your circumstances, rest assured that he sees you. Then Jesus **came toward them walking on the sea** (6:48). The very thing that was causing their problems was under his feet.

6:49-51 They became **terrified,** assuming that he was **a ghost** (6:49-50). The CSB's "very early in the morning" (6:48) is literally "around the fourth watch of the night." So this encounter occurred between three and six a.m. Jesus exhorted them: **Have courage! It is I. Don't be afraid** (6:50). Then he climbed **into the boat,** and **the wind ceased** (6:51). He gave them his word, then he gave them his presence, and then their circumstances changed.

6:52 The disciples were shocked by these events **because they had not understood**

about the loaves. Something had happened the previous day (see 6:30-44) that should've affected how they reacted this day. They didn't recognize Jesus because they weren't looking for him in the midst of their trial. And they weren't looking for him in this problem because they'd failed to see that Jesus was the answer to the previous problem.

6:53-56 Jesus's reputation continued to grow. Upon arriving at his destination, he was **recognized** by everyone (6:54). So they brought all who were **sick** to him, and anyone who merely touched **the end of his robe . . . was healed** (6:55-56; see 5:25-34).

7:1-5 As the common people grew in their excitement about Jesus, **the Pharisees** and **scribes** grew in their hatred of him. They wanted him destroyed (see 3:6). They were willing to travel to Galilee **from Jerusalem** to find further fault with him (7:1). They noticed the disciples **eating with unclean— that is, unwashed—hands** (7:2), which doesn't mean they were failing to practice good hygiene. Rather, they were failing to practice **ceremonial washing,** which was something that **the Pharisees and . . . Jews** practiced. This was not an Old Testament requirement from God, but a **tradition of the elders** (7:3, 5). Mark tells us that there were **many other** such **customs** that they practiced and expected others to practice (7:4).

7:6-9 Jesus didn't pull any punches. He called them **hypocrites.** They were the kind of leaders whom Isaiah talked about: those who say the right things but whose **hearts** are not in sync with God (7:6-7). They exalted **human tradition** while ignoring **the command of God** (7:8). They were professionals at trumping God's Word with their own preferences (7:9).

7:10-13 As an example, he pointed to two Old Testament texts: the command to **honor** one's parents and the threat of **death** for those who curse their parents (7:10; see Exod 20:12; 21:17; Lev 20:9; Deut 5:16). Clearly, God expects children, young and old, to respect their parents. But, in order to avoid giving financial help to parents who were in need, these hypocrites would declare their money to be *corban*, which was **an offering devoted to God**, so that they could give it to the temple instead (7:11-12). In this way, they would appear to be generous supporters of God's work, when actually they were cheapskates who avoided their obligation to their parents and nullified **the word of God** (7:13). Paul makes it clear that "if anyone does not provide for his own family . . . he has denied the faith and is worse than an unbeliever" (1 Tim 5:8).

7:14-23 Turning from the Pharisees and scribes to the crowd, Jesus told them the truth. People aren't defiled by what goes into them but by what comes out of them (7:14-15). Yet, when he was alone with his disciples, they still didn't understand, so he had to give them remedial instruction (7:17-18). Bad food might make you sick, but it can't make you spiritually unclean. God had given Israel commands about unclean animals they couldn't eat to teach them about holiness and unholiness (see Lev 11). But, ultimately, we are not defiled by **foods**; we are defiled by **what comes out of our hearts** (7:19-23). The Pharisees were concerned about making themselves look good on the outside, but wickedness came from within them.

Following customs and traditions can't fix your sinful heart. Only Jesus Christ, through his atoning work on the cross, can grant you forgiveness of sins and a transformed heart (see Heb 10:16-18) that is in sync with God, enabling you to love him and others.

7:24-26 From there, Jesus went **to the region of Tyre**, an area northwest of Galilee on the coast of the Mediterranean Sea (7:24). Previously, people from this region had come because they heard about his miraculous works (see 3:7-8). So even in this distant region, **he could not escape notice** (7:24). While he was there, **a woman** who was **a Gentile** pleaded with him **to cast the demon out of her daughter** (7:25-26).

7:27-28 Jesus responded by telling her that **it isn't right to take the children's bread and throw it to the dogs** (7:27). He was comparing the Jews to "children" and the

Gentiles to "dogs"—the Greek word referred to house-dogs or lap-dogs. Matthew reports that Jesus told her he was sent to "the lost sheep of the house of Israel" (Matt 15:24). Though his message of salvation would be for all people (Matt 28:19), his earthly ministry was primarily directed to the Jews. Nevertheless, this Gentile woman was humble and desperate. Picking up on Jesus's illustration, she told him that **even the dogs under the table eat the children's crumbs** (Mark 7:28). She didn't want to detract from his mission or prevent him from ministering to the people of Israel. All she wanted were some miracle leftovers to heal her daughter.

7:29-30 For this response—a response of faith in Jesus (Matt 15:28)—he healed her **daughter.** The Jewish religious leaders were seeking to kill Jesus, but this poor Gentile woman had more faith than all of them put together. And Jesus rewarded it. Faith is the qualification for experiencing the kingdom of God.

7:31-33 Jesus returned **to the Sea of Galilee, through the region of the Decapolis** (7:31). This is where the man who had been possessed by the "legion" of demons went to proclaim how much Jesus had done for him (see 5:1-20). The people of the region brought Jesus a man who was **deaf** and **had difficulty speaking** (7:32). Jesus took him aside. Often his miracles were performed in public, but this one was to be **private** (7:33).

Though Jesus could work the miraculous with mere words (e.g., 2:10-12; 3:5; 4:39; 7:29-30), frequently his miracles involved physical touch, demonstrating his compassion and confirming that he was the author of the deed (e.g., 1:31, 41-42; 5:27-29, 41-42; 6:56). On this occasion, Jesus put **his fingers in the man's ears** and **touched his tongue**, since his ability to hear and speak were the problems. Interpreters debate the purpose of the **spitting** (7:33), but this isn't the only time that spittle was involved in Jesus's healing miracles (see 8:23; John 9:6). Even Jesus's saliva was used for God's glory.

7:34-37 Jesus demonstrated his genuine humanity and emotional involvement in the lives of those to whom he ministered. He looked **to heaven** in dependence on the Father and **sighed deeply** in sorrow over the man's broken condition (7:34). Similarly, Jesus wept before he raised Lazarus from the dead (John 11:35). Once the man was healed, Jesus **ordered them** not to tell anyone (7:35-36), yet the people were **extremely astonished** and **proclaimed it** (7:36-37).

8:1-3 We've seen what happens in this chapter before (see 6:30-44). **A large crowd** gathered to hear Jesus for **three days**, but they had **nothing to eat** (8:1-2). This provides a small glimpse of how powerful Jesus's ministry was. People were willing to go without food to hear him proclaim the kingdom of God. But Jesus was concerned for their well-being. Some had traveled **a long distance** (8:2-3), and they needed physical nourishment.

8:4 He gathered his **disciples** together to address the problem. Unfortunately, none of them thought to say, "Lord, remember that time when you fed thousands with only five loaves and two fish? Surely you can do that again!" Instead, they were perplexed, having no idea where the food would come from. When you forget God's past deeds in your life, you will forget the kingdom power available to you. You'll fail to believe that "all things are possible with God" (10:27).

8:5-10 As before, Jesus took the only food that was available—**seven loaves** of bread and **a few small fish**—and **gave thanks** (8:5-7). He had *thousands* of mouths to feed, and only seven loaves to do it with; nevertheless, he gave thanks for what God had provided. Miraculously, they had enough to feed everyone and had more **leftover** food than they'd started with (8:8-9).

As God fed the Israelite multitude in a wilderness with manna and quail, so Jesus Christ fed the Israelite multitude in a "desolate place" (8:4) with bread and fish. Like Father, like Son. Jesus's gratefulness in the midst of insufficiency is also a lesson to us. Giving thanks for what God has provided opens the door for him to respond with abundance.

8:11-13 Mark records yet another encounter with **the Pharisees**. They had no other intent but to seek out conflict with Jesus about his identity. They **began to argue with him, demanding of him a sign from heaven** (8:11) because they wanted to invalidate his messianic claims. But Jesus had already given more than sufficient proof. He had performed a massive number of a variety of miracles before multiple witnesses. The Pharisees, then, had all of the "signs" they needed and had rejected them all. And Jesus had no intention of putting on a performance for these jealous, obstinate leaders who didn't really want proof. He refused their demand and departed with his disciples (8:12-13).

8:14-16 After that last encounter with the Pharisees, Jesus warned his disciples of how dangerous they were. The Pharisees were in league with the Herodians, political supporters of Herod Antipas (see 3:6). So Jesus described their harmful influence and teaching as **the leaven of the Pharisees and the leaven of Herod** (8:15). As Paul writes, "A little leaven leavens the whole batch" (Gal 5:9). In other words, it only takes a small amount of leaven, or yeast, to work through and affect an entire batch of dough. So, though they were few, the Pharisees and Herodians had a tremendous ability to influence the people with their human traditions and lead them away from God.

Unfortunately, the disciples weren't tracking with Jesus. They **had forgotten to take bread** with them, except for **one loaf** (8:14). **They were discussing** this (8:16), thinking that Jesus's comments about leaven were literal and assumed he was correcting their carelessness for forgetting to pack lunch. Jesus's metaphor had gone right over their heads.

8:17-21 The disciples' misunderstanding wasn't their only problem. Their worry about insufficient food demonstrated a lack of faith in Jesus. They had **hardened hearts** and failed to **remember** what he'd done (8:17-18)! Jesus had miraculously fed thousands on two different occasions using only a few loaves and fish (8:19-20; see 6:30-44; 8:1-10). His apostles' unbelief and inability to **understand** (8:21) was a result of forgetting what Jesus had already done. Don't overlook how God worked in your life yesterday; you'll need that knowledge for the trials you'll face tomorrow.

8:22-26 On the northern coast of the Sea of Galilee, they came to the village of **Bethsaida** (8:22), the hometown of Philip, Andrew, and Peter (see John 1:44). The people there brought Jesus **a blind man** to heal, but Jesus—to avoid publicity—took him **out of the village** (8:22-23, 26). Jesus then put spit on the man's eyes, touched them, and asked him what he saw (8:23). The man responded, **I see people—they look like trees walking** (8:24). So although he was no longer blind, he still wasn't seeing clearly. After a second touch from Jesus, the man's **sight was restored** and he saw **clearly** (8:25).

In a similar way, Peter was about to demonstrate spiritual insight (8:29), but he did not yet see clearly enough. Though he believed that Jesus was the Messiah, Peter would also have to embrace everything that meant—including Jesus's suffering and death (8:31-33).

8:27-28 Caesarea Philippi was located about twenty-five miles north of the Sea of Galilee. The city had been rebuilt by Philip, the son of Herod, and named after its builder and Caesar Augustus. Given Jesus's popularity, there had been plenty of speculation about his identity. So he asked **his disciples** to tell him what they'd heard (8:27). Since he had preached repentance, some thought he was **John the Baptist**. Since he had performed numerous miracles, some thought he was **Elijah**. Since he made prophetic proclamations, some thought he was **one of the prophets** (8:28).

8:29-30 Having heard enough speculation, Jesus asked, **Who do you say that I am?** Peter gave the right answer: **You are the Messiah** (8:29). Indeed, Jesus is the Christ, the Anointed One, the Son of David, the coming King. But he **warned them to tell no one** (8:30) because he didn't want people openly proclaiming him as the Messiah yet. There was still too much confusion about what the Messiah was to do, and that problem was about to be demonstrated by Peter himself.

V. MINISTRY ON THE WAY TO JERUSALEM (8:31–10:52)

8:31 For the first time, Jesus told his disciples what being the Messiah involved. He would **suffer** and **be rejected**—not merely by the Gentile rulers—but by the Jewish **elders, chief priests, and scribes.** Then he would **be killed**—but would **rise after three days** (8:31). Rejection and death certainly were not what the disciples were expecting for the Messiah. They were looking for victory, not defeat. Nevertheless, they had been with Jesus for a long time. They had heard his teaching; they'd seen his marvelous deeds. So if these difficult things were what Jesus said must happen, then they should've believed him.

8:32-33 Peter had been quick to pronounce Jesus as the Messiah. Unfortunately, he was also quick to **rebuke** Jesus for misunderstanding what the Messiah was all about—or so Peter thought (8:32). Jesus therefore spoke a quick and harsh word of rebuke to

Peter: **Get behind me Satan! You are not thinking about God's concerns but human concerns** (8:33).

Peter had not been merely confused. He'd adopted Satan's way of thinking, which involved rejecting God's revealed truth for mere human logic. Jesus was indeed the Messiah, the King. But there could be no kingly glory without the suffering of the cross. Without the death and resurrection of Jesus, there could be no atonement for sin and, thus, no salvation. To oppose the true understanding of the Messiah is to oppose God.

8:34 Jesus wanted to make it clear to **his disciples** and to **the crowd** that this principle of suffering would apply to his followers too. If you want to be a disciple of Jesus—you must **deny** yourself, **take up** your **cross**, and **follow** him. It's easy to say you're a follower of Jesus—until the going gets hard.

But Jesus expects you to identify with him, even if that means experiencing rejection and suffering.

8:35 In saying, **Whoever wants to save his life will lose it**, Jesus wasn't speaking to unbelievers. He was addressing those who had already decided to follow him. He wanted them to know what being a disciple would look like. If you seek to preserve yourself from inconveniences and difficulties that come from identifying with Jesus, you will lose out on the abundant life that Christ promises—that is, the experience of a relationship with him now and an eternal reward later.

On the other hand, **whoever loses his life because of [Jesus] and the gospel will save it**. So if you are willing to deny yourself (telling your desires "no" when they come in conflict with the kingdom), to pursue God's kingdom agenda in his Word, and to publicly identify with Jesus Christ, you will gain true life (that is, intimate experience with God) in history and even greater reward in eternity.

8:36-38 How **does it benefit** a believer to amass great wealth, notoriety, and power if he loses out on the abundant life God promises and his eternal rewards later? (8:36). Such a life is worthless. And we only get one chance to decide what kind of life we'll lead. As missionary C. T. Studd wrote, "Only one life, 'twill soon be past, / Only what's done for Christ will last." So don't let the pleasures this world has to offer replace the true meaning of life. Don't **be ashamed of** Christ and his words. Let his return be an experience of true joy, not of shame (8:38).

9:1-3 Jesus told his listeners that **some standing** among them would not experience **death until** they saw a powerful display of **the kingdom of God** (9:1). It would be a preview of coming attractions. About a week later, Jesus was on **a high mountain** with **Peter, James, and John.** They saw the Son of God's heavenly glory manifested before them. Jesus **was transfigured**—transformed (9:2). **His clothes became** so **white** that **no launderer** could compete (9:3). The deity of Jesus broke through his humanity so that it was undeniably visible. This glimpse

of glory was a sneak peek of the glory of the coming kingdom.

9:4 Not only was Jesus transfigured, but **Elijah** and **Moses**—both long deceased—appeared with him! Moses represented the Law, and Elijah represented the Prophets. The Old Testament ("the Law and the Prophets," Matt 5:17; 22:40) points to Jesus.

9:5-7 Have you ever known people who can't stop talking when they become nervous or afraid? That was Peter. He was **terrified** of what he saw and **did not know what to say** (9:6). So he suggested building **three shelters**, one for each of them (9:5), in fulfillment of Zechariah 14:16-19. However, by his affirmation of his **beloved Son**, God the Father made it clear that the disciples' focus was to be on Jesus alone (9:7).

9:8-10 After the voice spoke, the disciples found that they were alone with Jesus (9:8). Before they rejoined the others, Jesus told **them to tell no one** about what had happened **until the Son of Man had risen from the dead** (9:9). They did indeed keep it **to themselves**, but it was because they couldn't understand what he meant when he spoke of resurrection (9:10). Seeing would be believing.

9:11-13 Having seen Elijah, the disciples were prompted to ask why **the scribes say that Elijah must come first** (9:11)—that is, why must he come prior to the Messiah? The scribes were probably thinking of Malachi 4:5, in which God promised to send "the prophet Elijah before the great and terrible day of the Lord comes." Jesus agreed that **Elijah does come first and restores all things** (9:12). In fact, he said, Elijah had already **come, and they did whatever they pleased to him** (9:13).

In his account of this incident, Matthew makes it clear that Jesus was speaking about John the Baptist (Matt 17:13). On another occasion, Jesus said that John the Baptist "is the Elijah who is to come" (Matt 11:14). As Elijah is a messenger for God in the Old Testament, John is a messenger in the New Testament. John came to "restore all things" by calling Israel to repentance to prepare the way for the Messiah. But, the religious leaders "did whatever they pleased to him" by rejecting him (Matt 3:7-10; Mark 11:29-31), and ultimately Herod had him executed (6:25-29).

9:14-18 Upon their return, Jesus and the three disciples found the other **disciples** engulfed in a controversy with the **scribes** (9:14). When he inquired what it was all about, a father said that he had brought his demon-possessed **son** to the disciples, but they couldn't heal him (9:16-18). The evil spirit often brought great physical and emotional turmoil on the boy (9:18). The inability of the disciples to cast out the demon apparently led to dispute with the scribes, who questioned their legitimacy.

9:19-22 Jesus called them an **unbelieving generation** (9:19), no doubt including the disciples' lack of spiritual receptivity. In light of the signs Jesus had already demonstrated, they wanted the results of faith, without exercising faith. When the evil **spirit** inside **the boy** saw Jesus, he caused the boy to fall into **convulsions** (9:20). It's not clear how old the boy was, but apparently this had been happening to him **from childhood** (9:21). The father was in such despair that he wondered if even Jesus could **do anything**. After all, his disciples had failed (9:22).

9:23-24 Jesus offered encouragement: **Everything is possible for the one who believes** (9:23). The problem was that the man's faith was weak and mixed with doubt. He said, **I do believe; help my unbelief** (9:24). If you find yourself doubting God, let this man's cry be your prayer. Be honest with God about your doubts and proceed in faith. God will honor your faith and strengthen it in spite of your doubt.

9:25-27 Jesus ordered the **unclean spirit** to **come out of** the boy (9:25). Though the demon departed, it did so with such violence that it appeared the boy was **dead** (9:26). Yet all it took was a touch from Jesus, and the boy arose (9:27).

9:28-29 A bit humiliated, the disciples asked Jesus privately why they'd failed (9:28). Some demons are worse and more powerful than others, he told them. Some require greater dependence on divine intervention that is only accessed through **prayer** (9:29). Past spiritual victory does not necessarily fuel today's spiritual battles. Today's battles require fresh dependency on and communication with God.

9:30-32 They traveled from there **through Galilee**, but Jesus was keeping a low profile (9:30). He was focused on **teaching his disciples**. Again, he told them that he would be **betrayed**, killed, and would **rise three days later** (9:31). However, they were just as confused about this second prediction (9:32) as they were about the first (8:31-33).

9:33-34 Upon their arrival in **Capernaum** on the north side of the Sea of Galilee, Jesus asked his disciples to explain their argument he had overheard while they were traveling (9:33). Obviously, they hadn't realized that the Master had been listening because they all fell **silent**. They were ashamed to admit that they'd been arguing about which of them **was the greatest** (9:34).

9:35 It's interesting to note Jesus's response. He didn't correct them for having a desire to be great; rather, he corrected them with regard to the manner of becoming great. Greatness comes by being a servant to others—not by exalting yourself above others. You must believe that God will honor your servanthood in history and in eternity.

9:36-37 Jesus illustrated his point with a **child** (9:36). To show kindness to a child—who can offer nothing in return—is to serve God (9:37). Greatness is not achieved through marvelous actions that all see. It's often achieved through lowly and unseen acts of service toward those who cannot repay. But God sees, and God repays.

9:38-41 **John** was spokesman for the disciples this time. They were offended when they saw an exorcist casting out **demons** in Jesus's **name** because, they said, **He wasn't following us** (9:38). They considered themselves part of an exclusive team. After all, they were the only ones who'd been deputized by Jesus to minister in his name. So who did that guy think he was? Jesus made it clear that someone cannot work for him and against him at the same time (9:39): **Whoever is not against us is for us** (9:40). Then he broadened the scope of that principle beyond exorcisms. Not only would God reward the man for casting out demons in Jesus's name, but he will also **reward** all kind deeds done in Jesus's name—even giving a fellow disciple of Christ **a cup of water** (9:41). God sees and remembers all things done for his glory and for the good of others, especially those who belong to the household of faith (cf. Gal 6:10).

9:42 If anyone causes **one of these little ones**—like the child in 9:36-37 or the man in 9:38-39—who **believe in** Jesus to be led astray, he would be better off having a **millstone** wrapped around **his neck** and tossed **into the sea.** A millstone was used to grind grain, and it was so heavy that a donkey was typically used to move it. Thus, the consequences are grave for leading a follower of Christ astray through deception or false teaching. God's severe judgment will fall.

9:43-47 There are a variety of things that can keep a person from coming to Christ, including the **hand . . . foot . . .** and **eye.** Of course, you can cut off your hand, hack off your foot, and gouge out your eye and still fail to believe in Christ. But Jesus's point was that the hand (representing things you handle), the foot (representing the places you go), and the eye (symbolizing the things you look at) can open doors to sin; thus, an unbeliever must take drastic measures to remove sinful hindrances from coming to faith. Inconveniencing oneself and forgoing pleasure are far preferable to being **thrown into hell. The kingdom of God** is worth any sacrifice (9:47).

9:48 Quoting from Isaiah 66:24, Jesus described hell as a place **where their worm does not die, and the fire is not quenched.** There are several things we learn about hell from this brief statement. First, it's clear that Jesus considered it a real place. So though many today deny the existence of hell, their claims run contrary to Jesus's. Second, hell is a place of intense suffering, both external and internal. The "fire" represents the source

of external suffering. The "worm" represents the source of internal suffering—the gnawing from within. Third, hell is eternal. Some today argue that unbelievers are "annihilated" after death, but Jesus says the worm doesn't die and the fire isn't quenched. The suffering of hell, then, is never-ending. The good news of Jesus Christ is so good because the bad news of hell is so bad.

9:49-50 Even believers (signified by the word **everyone**) will have to deal with the salt of trial in their lives (9:49). As Old Testament sacrifices were offered with salt (Lev 2:13), so believers must live their lives with sacrifice in mind. Salt had a variety of helpful uses in New Testament times: it was a medicine, a seasoning, and a preservative. Similarly, believers are to be like **salt** in promoting peace among fellow believers (9:50). This demonstrates the preserving power of God.

10:1-2 After spending so much time in the north, in the region of Galilee, Jesus came to the south, **to the region of Judea,** in order to teach (10:1). As they'd done previously, **the Pharisees came** merely **to test him.** They asked him a controversial question—whether or not it was lawful **for a man to divorce his wife** (10:2).

There were two views about divorce held by first-century Jewish scholars. According to one view, a man could divorce his wife if she committed sexual immorality. According to the other, a man could divorce his wife for any reason. The Pharisees wanted Jesus to take sides and, thus, alienate some of his listeners.

10:3-5 Jesus, however, refused to enter their debate. Instead, he appealed solely to God's Word. He asked them what **Moses** had commanded, and the Pharisees pointed to Deuteronomy 24:1-4 (10:3-4). But this permission from Moses to divorce had only been granted **because of the hardness** of their **hearts** (10:5). It wasn't God's ideal. So instead of starting with divorce, Jesus insisted that they must start with marriage.

10:6-9 God's design for marriage is clear **from the beginning of creation.** First, marriage is to involve a **male and female**

(10:6)—that rules out a lot of what goes by the name of "marriage" in our culture. Second, marriage was intended as a permanent bond. Therefore, **what God has joined together , let no one separate** (10:7-9). People, including civil judges, are not to overrule God. The Pharisees had become so consumed with the question of divorce that they'd forgotten God's design for marriage as revealed in God's Word.

10:10-12 When they were alone, **the disciples** asked Jesus about the same issue (10:10). He explained that the one who illegitimately initiates divorce **and marries another** has entered an adulterous relationship (10:11-12) because God has not canceled the first marriage (see commentary on Matt 19:1-9).

10:13-16 Parents **were bringing little children to** Jesus so that he touched **and blessed them** (10:13, 16). For some reason, **the disciples rebuked them** (10:13). But you don't want to be the one to come between Jesus and children. Children held a low status in this ancient society, and Jesus was displeased by the marginalization of these precious ones. **He was indignant** and told people to **let the little children come** to him. He prioritized children **because the kingdom of God belongs to such as these** (10:14).

The reason Jesus valued children so highly is because they are a model of what it takes for someone to come to God. Little children know what it is to have a low and dependent status. When they put their trust in someone, they do it wholeheartedly and with humility. To trust in God is to **receive** his **kingdom ... like a little child** (10:15). We are not to be like the Pharisees, having pride in ourselves and in our own righteousness. We are to humble ourselves, acknowledging our sin, and put our whole trust and dependence in God.

10:17 A man approached Jesus with a question. Matthew adds he was a "young man" (Matt 19:20). Luke says he was "a ruler" (Luke 18:18). All three Synoptic Gospels note that he was wealthy (Matt 19:22; Mark 10:22; Luke 18:23). Thus, he is often described as the "rich young ruler." He asked Jesus, **Good teacher, what must I do to inherit eternal life?** This man, then, not only wanted to know how to

enter heaven but also how to gain inheritance rewards there.

10:18 First, Jesus wanted to deal with the matter of his own identity. The man called him "good" teacher. But **no one is good except God alone** (10:18). All are sinners before a holy God. So, the only way Jesus could truly be called good was if he was the Son of God.

10:19-20 Jesus reviewed God's **commandments** (10:19). These are divine standards of righteousness by which men can measure themselves. If someone could perfectly keep God's law, he or she would indeed be righteous before him. Yet we are all sinners. Our only hope of a righteous standing before God is to have a righteousness imputed or credited to us (Rom 4:22-25). Naively, the man claimed to have **kept all** of the commandments (10:20). But he was self-deceived. Our sinful hearts have a habit of appraising us as better than we are.

10:21-22 Yet, in spite of the man's self-deception, **Jesus loved him.** The glorious good news is that Jesus loves sinners. He therefore sought to enlighten the man and expose his spiritual blindness. The clear problem in this man's life was that his love for money prevented him from loving his neighbor, proving that he was not as righteous as he perceived himself to be. So Jesus called him to **sell** his possessions and **give to the poor** so that he might **have treasure in heaven.** Then, Jesus said, **follow me** (10:21). Sadly, the man was not the commandment-keeper that he thought he was. He was unwilling to part with his riches so that he could come to Christ to have eternal life and the rewards that would accompany following him. He departed in grief (10:22).

10:23-25 When the rich young ruler was gone, Jesus expressed a spiritual principle to his disciples: **How hard it is for those who have wealth to enter the kingdom of God!** (10:23). When they heard this, **the disciples were astonished,** but Jesus drove the point home with an illustration. You'd have better success stuffing **a camel ... through the eye of a needle than ... a rich person** would have entering **the kingdom** (10:24-25).

The problem is not wealth itself; the problem is a wealthy person who trusts in his wealth. An unhealthy dependence on worldly riches will obscure focus on kingdom values and eternal spiritual riches. And rich people can have a distorted picture of God's view of them, assuming that their wealth is proof of divine acceptance and blessing.

10:26-27 The disciples assumed that wealth was a sign of divine approval. And if this was not true, **then who can be saved?** (10:26). Jesus had the answer: Salvation is only **possible with God** (10:27). God can save and provide a heavenly inheritance for anyone who does not let wealth get in the way of relationship with Jesus Christ.

10:28 In contrast with the man who let riches stand between him and the kingdom, **Peter** spoke on behalf of the disciples and said, **Look, we have left everything and followed you.** His words are an indicator that if you intend to be the visible, vocal follower that Jesus calls you to be, it will cost you. You cannot grow as a disciple without paying a price. Peter testified that he and his comrades had given up much in their commitment to Jesus. His successful fishing business, for instance, had been left behind. So Peter was asking, "What's in it for us, Jesus? What's the payoff for our willingness to be committed disciples?"

10:29-30 Notice that Jesus didn't chastise Peter for his question, so it was a legitimate inquiry. Jesus told them **there is no one who has** made significant sacrifices **for the sake of the gospel** who will not be rewarded **now at this time** and **in the age to come** (10:29-30).

Observe six things: *First,* Jesus's pronouncement is true for all who associate with him as kingdom disciples. There are no exceptions ("there is no one," 10:29). *Second,* being a public disciple will cost you: maybe a location (**house**), relationships (**brothers or sisters or mother or father or children**), or even your business or means of employment (**fields**) (10:29). Jesus is not talking about abdicating one's responsibilities. A man does not become a Christian and stop providing for his children. But we must always give our

relationship with Jesus priority. We are not to compromise our commitment to Christ for the sake of anything. *Third,* these prices are paid "for the sake of the gospel"—that is, for the purpose of following Jesus and giving allegiance to his kingdom. *Fourth,* the very things that were left behind are what you receive. You don't truly lose anything; you make a trade. *Fifth,* you will also receive **persecutions** (10:30). The more committed you are to Christ, the more resistance there will be to the presence of Christ in your life. *Sixth,* a disciple's reward is divided between the ages: the present age and the age to come. Don't expect to receive all of your blessings now. Most of your reward is stored up and kept for you—and it's **a hundred times more** than anything you leave behind (10:30).

10:31 Many who are first will be last, and the last first. Believers whom God has blessed in the present life but who have been less than faithful with those blessings will find that God flips the script in the age to come. Don't desire all of your inheritance now. Let your motivation be for the reward that lies before you in the millennial kingdom and the new heaven and new earth.

10:32-34 As Jesus and his disciples made their way toward **Jerusalem**, he predicted his forthcoming death and resurrection a third time. Because of the mounting hostility from the religious leaders, **those who followed him were afraid.** Jesus therefore explained exactly what **would happen** (10:32). Nothing would take him by surprise. The Jewish **chief priests** and **scribes** would condemn him; however, they didn't have the authority to execute anyone. Thus, they would have to **hand him over to** the Romans—**the Gentiles** (10:33). Jesus knew what awaited him, down to the smallest detail: mocking, spitting, flogging. But he also knew that victory was waiting. He would **rise** again (10:34).

10:35-37 James and John wanted Jesus to do whatever they asked of him—to write them a blank check in a sense (10:35). In his future kingdom, they wanted to **sit** on the King's **right** and **left** (10:37)—positions of significant honor and authority. Jesus did not question their desire to be great, but he did question their assumptions about what it takes to get there.

10:38-40 He asked if they were prepared to suffer as Jesus himself would suffer—that is, to **drink the cup** he would **drink** or **be baptized with** his **baptism** (10:38), metaphors for enduring suffering. James and John committed themselves to suffering for Christ's kingdom, and Jesus admitted that they would (10:39). We know from Scripture that because of their faith in Christ, James was executed (Acts 12:1-2) and John was exiled (see Rev 1:9). In spite of this, sitting on King Jesus's **right or left** was not something that he would grant them. Those honors would go to whomever they'd been **prepared** for (10:40).

10:41-44 The other **ten disciples** were upset with **James and John** (10:41), leaving Jesus with a dozen followers battling over who would be top dog in the kingdom. So he explained how kingdom greatness contrasts with earthly greatness. Among **the Gentiles**, greatness is attained by **those in high positions** who **lord it over** others and **act as tyrants** (10:42). For most people, pursuing power, prestige, and possessions leads to "greatness." **But it is not so among you**—this is not the path Christians are to take (10:43).

His use of the phrase **whoever wants to become great** indicates Jesus didn't quench his disciples' desire for greatness. Instead, he explained that you can't use the standards of the unrighteous to attain true greatness. To be great, you must be a **servant** (10:43). According to Paul, believers are called to "serve one another through love" (Gal 5:13). God saves us by grace apart from good "works," but in Christ we are created "for good works" (Eph 2:8-10). So once we are saved, it's time to get to work! To practice servanthood among the people of God is to serve others with no strings attached for the glory of God. The church of Jesus Christ is a family, and as brothers and sisters in Christ we are called to serve each other (see 1 Pet 4:10).

10:45 For even the Son of Man did not come to be served, but to serve, and to give his life as a ransom for many. Jesus didn't call his disciples to walk a path that he wouldn't walk. "To serve" was the reason he came into the world. When Paul exhorts the Philippians to reject "selfish ambition," live with "humility," and be concerned for "the interests of others" (Phil 2:3-4), in fact, he puts Christ forward as the perfect example of selfless, loving, God-honoring service. As John put it, "The one who says he remains in [Christ] should walk just as he walked" (1 John 2:6).

10:46-52 Outside **Jericho**, a **blind beggar** named **Bartimaeus** heard that Jesus was passing by, hailed him as the **Son of David** (a messianic title), and pleaded with him to **have mercy on** him (10:46-47). Though he was physically blind, Bartimaeus could see better spiritually than the religious leaders could. The people tried to make him **keep quiet.** But the more they tried to silence him, the noisier he became (10:48). Jesus wasn't about to allow such a bold proclamation of **faith** to go unacknowledged. At the man's request, Jesus restored his vision so that his physical sight matched his spiritual sight. Then, he **began to follow** Jesus (10:52).

VI. MINISTRY IN JERUSALEM (11:1–13:37)

11:1-6 As they drew near to **Jerusalem**, Jesus **sent two of his disciples** to enter a **village** on the way and **untie** the **colt** they found there (11:1-2). All they would need to do is say, **The Lord needs it** (11:3). The disciples obeyed him, and everything happened **just as** he said (11:4-6). The colt would be one **on which no one** had **ever sat** (11:2). That it was unused would make it naturally unwilling to receive a rider, but its submission demonstrated Jesus's authority over creation.

11:7-11 While Jesus rode on **the colt**, people honored him by spreading **clothes** and **leafy branches** before him **on the road.** Matthew makes it clear that Jesus's actions in this scene were a fulfillment of messianic prophecy (see Zech 9:9). Welcoming Jesus as the Messiah, the coming King, they cried out, **Hosanna! Blessed is he who comes in the name of the Lord! Blessed is the coming kingdom of our father David!** (11:7-10). "Hosanna" is the Greek transliteration of a Hebrew phrase that means, "Please save!" (see Ps 118:25). Passover week was beginning. Thousands of Jewish pilgrims were arriving in Jerusalem, and already things were becoming chaotic because of how people were responding to Jesus. When Jesus entered **the temple**, he observed some matters he would need to address the following day (11:11).

11:12-14 Jesus's group didn't spend the night in Jerusalem but in **Bethany** (11:12), a village less than two miles to the east (see John 11:18). Near there Jesus attempted to get some **figs** for breakfast, but there were none on the **fig tree** even though it had **leaves**. Though **it was not the season for figs** yet, the presence of early leaves was an indication that fruit should've been appearing (11:13). Jesus cursed the tree so it might never bear **fruit** again (11:14).

Ultimately, Jesus's actions in this instance were symbolic. Though the tree showed signs of life and productivity, in reality it was barren. The same was true of Israel— especially in the case of its religious leaders. They looked righteous and godly on the outside, but on the inside they were corrupt. Their lack of faith meant that they were also barren—producing no fruit for God. Many people today are like that too. They attend church regularly, carry fancy Bibles, and shout "Amen!" But there's a lack of spiritual vitality inside them; thus, there's no kingdom fruit in their lives.

11:15-16 Arriving in **Jerusalem**, Jesus immediately returned to **the temple** (see 11:11) and went into action. He threw out those who were **buying and selling**, turned over the money-changer **tables**, and forbade people from carrying **goods through the temple** (11:15-16). The business activities themselves were not necessarily a problem since pilgrims coming to worship needed to buy animals to make sacrifices. The problem was that these activities were taking place *in*

the temple, hindering worship. Moreover, the businessmen themselves engaged in corrupt practices, cheating their customers.

11:17 In Old Testament times, wicked kings and priests in Jerusalem allowed God's temple to fall into disrepair and to be used for unrighteous purposes, but Jesus was zealous for his Father's temple. He couldn't let a materialistic use of God's house go unaddressed. He quoted from Isaiah 56:7 and Jeremiah 7:11 to condemn misuse of the temple, which was to be **a house of prayer for all nations.** Commerce had trumped communion with God.

11:18-19 The chief priests and **scribes** hated Jesus. They were looking for opportunities to use against him. Their problem was **the whole crowd.** They were **astonished by** Jesus, so naturally the religious leaders **were afraid** (11:18) because they didn't want Jesus leading an uprising of the people against them. At **evening**, Jesus and his followers stayed outside **of the city** (11:19).

11:20-23 The next day they passed by the fig tree that Jesus had cursed (see 11:12-14). In twenty-four hours, it had dried up from root to branch (11:20)! **Peter** was stunned (11:21). How could this have happened—and so quickly? The answer, according to Jesus, boiled down to **faith in God** (11:22). Then he took the lesson a step further. He said, **If anyone** has faith and tells **this mountain** (the Mount of Olives) to jump **into the sea . . . it will be done for him** (11:23). Since Peter thought the withered fig tree was impressive, this concept must've really blown his mind! Faith's authority allows the believer to speak directly to the obstacles of life (i.e., "mountains") and get them to move.

It's important to note that Jesus is not commending an extraordinary faith. After all, on one occasion he told his disciples something similar and said faith needed to be no larger than a tiny "mustard seed" (Matt 17:20). The most important aspect of faith, then, is the worthiness of its object. You must be trusting in the right thing. You can place tremendous faith in the tooth fairy or Santa Claus, but you'll be disappointed. If, however, you have true, vibrant faith in the God of the Bible, you have spiritual authority to access divine power. God has already blessed you "with every spiritual blessing in the heavens in Christ" (Eph 1:3). Through faith in Jesus, you have access to divine power. It's like having a contract with the electric company. Since you have a legal relationship with them, they provide you with electricity. Nevertheless, you must access that power yourself by flipping the light switch.

11:24-25 Exercising your spiritual authority comes by taking responsibility to do what God has told you to do. This comes through prayer and through repenting of sin—such as the sin of unforgiveness. Prayer enables us to access God's power in our lives, but unrepentant sin blocks God's power.

11:27-30 The religious leaders were furious with Jesus about the temple-cleansing incident (see 11:15-19). They wanted to know who authorized him to **do** such **things** (11:27-28). So Jesus answered their question with a question. If they would answer his inquiry, he'd answer theirs (11:29): **Was John's baptism from heaven or of human origin?** (11:30). In other words, he said, "You want to know if I'm legitimate, if I'm operating on God's authority? Tell me: Was John the Baptist legitimate? Did he minister on God's authority?"

11:31-32 Even before they answered, it was obvious the leaders weren't interested in the truth. They had to huddle together to discuss their response options. If they admitted that John's authority was **from heaven**, then Jesus would ask them, **why didn't you believe him?** (11:31). After all, John himself testified that Jesus was the Messiah. But they were also reluctant to reject John and his ministry because **they were afraid** of all the people who thought **John was truly a prophet** (11:32). If they denigrated John, the crowd might stone them!

11:33 Given their dilemma, the religious leaders chose to avoid the question by throwing in the towel: **We don't know.** They were self-serving hypocrites. They demanded that Jesus answer their questions truthfully, but they had no interest in the truth—only

in advancing their own agenda. Therefore, Jesus refused to answer them.

12:1 Jesus often used parables to teach about the kingdom of God. On this occasion (12:1-12), he used one to expose the evil intentions of the religious leaders. **A man planted a vineyard,** a very elaborate one with a **fence, a winepress,** and a **watchtower.** Then the man **leased** the vineyard **to tenant farmers and went away.** As becomes clear, the vineyard owner represents God, the vineyard is Israel, and the tenant farmers are Israel's leaders. God was the source, provider, and protector of his people. He entrusted his vineyard to leaders who were to care for it on his behalf.

Those listening to Jesus would've been familiar with these details. Isaiah the prophet told a similar story about a vineyard that represented Israel (Isa 5:1-7, esp. 5:7). Instead of producing good grapes, it yielded worthless ones, so the Lord threatened to destroy it (Isa 5:2, 5-6). In Jesus's parable, he added an important character: the vineyard owner's son.

12:2-5 At **harvest time,** the owner sent servants **to collect some of the fruit of the vineyard** (12:2). But on each occasion when the servants were sent, **the farmers** treated them shamefully, brutally beating and even killing them. This is a vivid description of how the leaders of Israel had abused God's prophets in the past. Though he sent them to warn his people to keep his covenant with them by pursuing righteousness, they refused. They owed God "fruit"—their obedience. But they scornfully mistreated and killed God's prophets, demonstrating their scorn for God himself.

12:6-8 **Finally** the owner sent his **son** to the farmers (12:6). Surely, they would honor their master's own son (12:6)! But instead, the wicked **farmers** saw killing the owner's **heir** as their opportunity to win **the inheritance** (12:7-8). Thus, Jesus revealed the intentions of the Jewish leaders to rule Israel without the Messiah.

12:9-12 The farmers, though, were foolish to think the owner would sit idly by and do nothing. He would justly execute them and give the vineyard to others (12:9). This speaks of God's coming judgment on the leaders and the temporary shifting of his kingdom program from Israel to the church. Jesus then quoted Psalm 118:22-23, identifying himself with the **rejected** stone that will ultimately be the preeminent **stone** in God's kingdom work—**the cornerstone** (12:10-11). Their rejection of God's agenda couldn't prevent him from accomplishing his plan. The leaders knew Jesus was talking about them, but because they **feared the crowd**—who held Jesus in such high esteem—the leaders **left him** alone and continued their plotting (12:12).

12:13 Since the crowds were amazed at Jesus, the leaders wanted to find a way to put him at odds with them. They wanted to force Jesus to say something that would turn the people against him, so **they sent some of the Pharisees and the Herodians to** him. The Pharisees were conservative religious Jews. The Herodians were political supporters of King Herod. They had little in common except a shared desire to take down Jesus. Mark tells us their intentions were wicked; they wanted **to trap** Jesus.

12:14 The Pharisees and Herodians began with flattery. They praised Jesus for his truthfulness and for the fact that he would give an unbiased answer. They weren't going to catch the Son of God off guard by sweet-talking him, but they tried. Then they posed their question: **Is it lawful to pay taxes to Caesar or not?** They were no doubt gleeful, assuming they had placed Jesus in a no-win situation. If he answered, "Yes," the crowd would be furious: They hated their Roman overlords. But if he said, "No," the Pharisees and Herodians could announce that Jesus was promoting sedition, since the Jews were required to pay taxes to Rome.

12:15-17 Jesus saw right through them. Though they feigned interest in hearing his answer, he knew it was all **hypocrisy**. They were merely **testing** him for their own gain. So he told them to show him **a denarius** (12:15), the Roman coin used for paying the tax. The **image** on the **coin** was that of Tiberius Caesar, the Roman emperor (12:16). So

Jesus answered them, **Give to Caesar the things that are Caesar's, and to God the things that are God's** (12:17).

It's appropriate to give to Caesar—that is, to the government—what belongs to him. As Paul told the Romans, "Let everyone submit to the governing authorities" (Rom 13:1). When government is functioning legitimately, it provides beneficial services to those living under its rule. So citizens rightly pay taxes to fund government services like police protection and adequate roads. Jesus makes it clear, though, that our commitment to the state is not our only commitment. We also have a commitment to God, since we bear his image. And our commitment to God is greater because, though the state's authority is limited, God's authority is comprehensive. So the key question is not, "Should we pay taxes?" Rather, the key question is, "Am I submitting to God's comprehensive rule over every area of my life?"

By attempting to entrap Jesus, the Pharisees and Herodians demonstrated that they were not pursuing God's agenda but their own. **They were utterly amazed** that he had outsmarted them again (12:17).

12:18 The **Sadducees** were a powerful Jewish group, but they had some faulty beliefs. For one, they said there was **no resurrection**, no physical life after death. Moreover, they only held the first five books of the Bible (the Pentateuch) as sacred Scripture.

12:19-23 On this occasion, the Sadducees wanted to confound Jesus and show how ridiculous the idea of resurrection from the dead was. The law of Moses required that if a man died and had no children, his brother was to marry his widow and **raise up offspring for his brother** (12:19; see Deut 25:5-6). With this in mind, they proposed a scenario. Each of **seven brothers** successively married a woman, had no children, and then died. Then **the woman died** (12:20-22). Their question was this: **In the resurrection ... whose wife will she be?** After all, **seven** men **had married her** (12:23). The Sadducees assumed that their hypothetical situation proved the resurrection concept absurd. If it were true, they reasoned, it would result in mass confusion.

12:24-27 But their question didn't panic Jesus. The Sadducees were **mistaken** because of their faulty belief system. He pinpointed their problem: **you don't know the Scriptures or the power of God** (12:24). First, in the resurrection, people will be **like angels** in that there will be no **marriage** or procreation (12:25). All believers will be one big extended family. Second, the Lord **is not the God of the dead but of the living** (12:27). Jesus demonstrated this by pointing to Exodus 3:6, which the Sadducees accepted as God's Word (see commentary on 12:18). God told Moses that he was (still) **the God of Abraham . . . Isaac . . . Jacob** (12:26) even though they had physically died. The point was that they were spiritually alive.

12:28-30 Apparently impressed when he **heard** Jesus **debating**, a scribe asked him, **Which command is the most important?** (12:28). Jesus answered him from Deuteronomy 6:5, which affirms that **the Lord is one** (12:29). He is the only God and the one to whom we owe our undying loyalty and affection. The passage goes on to call God's people to **love** him with all their **heart . . . soul . . . mind . . . strength** (12:30). In other words, we are to love God with the totality of our being. It's one thing to claim that you love God. It's another thing to demonstrate it through everything you think, say, and do.

12:31 Jesus answered the man's question, but he didn't stop there. He had quoted the greatest command in Scripture. Then he added **the second** greatest: **Love your neighbor as yourself.** Thus, Jesus connected the vertical (love of God) with the horizontal (love of others). To claim to love God while not loving people (or vice versa) is a contradiction. The two necessarily go together. To love God is to passionately pursue his glory with your total being. To love your neighbor is to decide to compassionately and righteously seek his or her well-being.

12:32-33 Recognizing that Jesus had answered well, the scribe commended him (12:32). To love God and love one's neighbor **is far more important than all the burnt offerings and sacrifices** (12:33). Mere religious observance is worthless. Conforming to external religious regulations and practices—without love—will not get you close to God.

12:34 Jesus affirmed this particular scribe. His understanding of God and the true purpose of the law had brought him near to the Messiah and salvation—**not far from the kingdom of God.** At that point, the religious leaders stopped asking him questions.

12:35-37 Since Jesus had silenced all of their questions, he now had a question of his own. The Jews believed and rightly taught that the Messiah would be descended from King David. So Jesus asked them how **the Messiah** could be **the son of David** when David himself (in Ps 110:1) called the Messiah **Lord** (12:35-36). A son, after all, would give honor to his father—not the other way around. So if David called his descendant "my Lord," clearly he was more than merely David's "son." Jesus was using the Scriptures to show that the Messiah would indeed be a human descendant of David, but he would also be far more. He would be divine. The Son of David is also the Lord of David. Jesus is fully man and fully God.

12:38-40 As he taught the crowds, Jesus warned them to be wary **of the scribes,** who were thought to be experts in and teachers of the law. They should've been examples of godliness and humility; instead, they frequently sought public **honor** and recognition (12:38-39). As if shamelessly seeking notoriety were not bad enough, they also defrauded vulnerable **widows.** Such leaders were not to serve as models for the people. Those who misuse others and display false piety **will receive harsher judgment** (12:40).

12:41-44 Jesus had just commented on how the scribes took advantage of and plundered poor widows (12:40). Then he took the opportunity to praise a widow for her sacrificial giving. While watching people put offerings in **the temple treasury,** Jesus noticed as the **rich** gave **large sums** of money (12:41). But then a poor widow, probably unnoticed by anyone else, **dropped in two tiny coins worth very little** (12:42). Jesus couldn't let such a teaching moment pass, so he called **his disciples** over (12:43).

When compared to the wealthy, the widow had contributed next to nothing. But when compared to what she had available, she had given **more . . . than all the others** (12:43). The reason is because the rich had given **out of their surplus**, out of their leftovers. After they had paid all of their expenses, they gave an offering—and still had money left. The widow, however, gave **out of her poverty** (12:44).

Stewardship is a matter of the heart. In your car, a light comes on to indicate when you are running low on fuel. Similarly, the way you relate to money is an indicator of your heart's state. The widow gave sacrificially from what little she had, because she loved God. Her giving provides a window into her heart. When God considers our Christian stewardship, he looks not merely at the amount of our gifts but at our motives.

13:1-2 As they left **the temple**, the **disciples** marveled at its **impressive buildings** (13:1). It was truly magnificent. But Jesus revealed to them what would happen to its stones in the future: **all [would] be thrown down.** The destruction would be so great that **not one** would be **left upon another** (13:2). Jesus's prediction became a reality in AD 70 when the Romans invaded Jerusalem under Titus, decimating the city.

13:3-4 Later, as Jesus and his disciples sat on **the Mount of Olives**, overlooking the **temple**, they asked him **when** these events would **happen** and about the **sign** of their accomplishment. They connected the events with the end of the age and the beginning of the messianic kingdom (see Matt 24:3), but they didn't understand that there would be an interval of time between the temple's destruction and Christ's millennial reign. In answering the disciples' questions, Jesus directed their attention beyond the coming destruction to the future events in God's prophetic timetable that would proceed Christ's second coming to set up his millennial kingdom.

13:5-8 Jesus warned them that many false Messiahs would come to **deceive.** Moreover, there would be various **wars . . . earthquakes . . . famines** (13:7-8). The disciples had asked what "sign" would precede his coming (13:4). Jesus warned them not to **be alarmed** about various conflicts and catastrophes that many might perceive to be signs of the end (13:7), for these were just **the beginning of birth pains** (13:8). The prophets spoke of labor or birth pains as a symbol of God's outpouring of judgment (see Jer 30:5-7), so Jesus uses this symbol to refer to the beginning of the tribulation period prophesied by Daniel (see commentary on Dan 9:24-27). This will be a time of sorrow and pain like a woman in labor. But it will eventually lead to the end of the age, the return of Christ, and the "birth" of the messianic kingdom.

13:9-13 Though this will be a time of judgment on the earth, the gospel will still be preached and a multitude of Jews and Gentiles will be saved (see Rev 7:4-17). Those who come to faith in Christ during this period of the tribulation will experience intense persecution, but they should have confidence. Jesus reminded the disciples that when they stood **before governors and kings**, it would be as his witnesses, preaching **the gospel** to the **nations** (Mark 13:9-10). They would not need to **worry** about what to say, for **the Holy Spirit** would speak through them (13:11). They would be opposed even by family members (13:12). These believers will be **hated** because of their witness for Christ, **but the one who endures to the end**—a reference to the end of the great tribulation period—**will be saved** (13:13). In this instance, "saved" does not refer to spiritual salvation but to preservation from physical death. In other words, believers who endure to the end of the tribulation will be spared physical death and enter the millennium.

13:14-20 The second half of the great tribulation period will begin with **the abomination of desolation** (13:14), prophesied by Daniel (see commentary on Dan 2:24-27). The Antichrist will arise during the seven-year tribulation period as a world ruler. At the midpoint of those seven years, he will break a covenant of peace made with Israel and set up an "abomination" in a rebuilt Jewish temple (see Dan 9:27). This will be an image in which he sets himself up as a god, revealing himself to be "the beast" who demands to be worshiped by all the people of earth (Rev 13:5-8).

This abomination will coincide with an intense persecution of anyone who refuses to worship the beast. Those who will not bow down will have to **flee to the mountains**, leaving their property and possessions behind if they are to escape death (Mark 13:14-16). Travel for **pregnant women** will be especially hard, and **winter** weather will make escape difficult (13:17-18). It will be the worst time of trouble and suffering in human history (13:19). If not for the Lord's divine intervention to shorten the days of tribulation, none of his people would survive (13:20).

13:21-23 The tribulation period will see more **Messiah** pretenders than any other time. God's people are not to **believe** them—even though they **perform signs and wonders** (13:21-22). Believers must be vigilant and discerning. Our theology has life-and-death consequences.

13:24-27 God will not abandon his people. Though the great **tribulation** will be a time of great distress, the Lord Jesus will come and set all things right. Amazing signs will appear in the heavens (13:24-25; see Isa 13:10; 34:4; Joel 2:31). When they witness these celestial abnormalities, people will know that the Lord is coming soon. Then **the Son of Man** will appear **in clouds with great power and glory** (Mark 13:26), in fulfillment of Daniel's prophecy (Dan 7:13-14). It will be an event visible to all. He will **send out the angels** who will **gather** all of the Jewish believers and those martyred during the tribulation

so that they may enter into his millennial kingdom (13:27).

13:28-32 Jesus told a parable to illustrate these truths. When a **fig tree . . . sprouts leaves, you know that summer is near** (13:28). Similarly, when believers during the tribulation see the things that Jesus predicted (13:24-25), they can be assured that his return is near (13:29). Christ's disciples can depend on his prophecies because his authoritative **words** are more reliable than **heaven and earth**, which **will pass away** (13:31). **This generation**—those believers living during the great tribulation—will **not pass away** until all of these prophecies come true (13:30). **Only the Father** knew the exact **day** and **hour**. In his humanity, the Son did not know because of his submission to the will of his Father (13:32).

13:33-37 Since no one will know the timing of these events, believers must be on the **alert** in light of Jesus's prophecies (13:33). He likened himself to **a man** who went away **on a journey**, leaving **his servants** with **authority** to watch over things while he was gone (13:34). After his resurrection, Jesus would ascend into heaven and give his church authority to minister in the world on his behalf. Christ's disciples, then, must not become spiritually lethargic but remain watchful and prepared for him to return at any time (13:35). The rapture of the church (see commentary on Matt 24:42-44; 1 Thess 4:13-18) will occur before the tribulation period begins. It has no preconditions and, therefore, could happen at any time. So believers must live constantly in light of Jesus's immanent return. **Be alert**, church! (13:37).

VII. BETRAYAL, SUFFERING, DEATH, AND RESURRECTION (14:1–16:20)

14:1-2 The Jewish leaders were determined to destroy Jesus, but they didn't want to do anything during **the Passover and the Festival of Unleavened Bread.** They feared **a riot among the people** because of Jesus's notoriety. They wanted things to proceed according to their timetable, but they were naïve. Jesus

had predicted that he would be crucified and rise from the dead in Jerusalem (8:31; 9:30-31; 10:32-34). God is sovereign; everything proceeds according to his timetable.

14:3-4 While they were in a home **in Bethany,** less than two miles from Jerusalem, a woman—Mary the sister of Lazarus (see John 12:3)—**poured** a **jar of very expensive perfume** on Jesus's **head** (14:3). Some of those present were angry. It could have **sold for more than three hundred denarii**—about a year's wages—and the money **given to the poor** (14:4). Thus, they scolded her for wasting it on Jesus (14:4).

14:5-9 That's when Jesus came to her defense. No service to Jesus is wasted. She had **done a noble thing** and **anointed** his **body in advance for burial** (14:6, 8). Mary knew about death and resurrection. It was a very real thing for her. Mary's brother Lazarus had died, and she saw Jesus raise him back to life (see John 11:1-44). So she sought to honor Jesus by sacrificially anointing him. In response, Jesus honored her. He said, **Wherever the gospel is proclaimed in the whole world, what she has done will also be told in memory of her** (14:9). The Lord says, "Those who honor me I will honor" (1 Sam 2:30).

14:10-11 This was apparently the last straw for **Judas Iscariot** (14:10). Mark has already informed his readers that Judas would betray his master (see 3:19). Now, motivated by financial gain (14:11), he went to **the chief priests** and offered **to betray Jesus to them** (14:10).

14:12 As **the Passover** celebration was about to begin, the **disciples asked** Jesus where they should go to **prepare** for him to **eat** the related meal. Of all the festivals in the Jewish calendar, Passover was preeminent. It commemorated the long-ago night in Egypt when God brought his judgment on that nation, killing every firstborn, so that Pharaoh would set the Israelites free. God had instructed his people to slay unblemished lambs, wipe their blood on their doorposts, roast the lambs, and eat them. When he saw the blood on the doorposts of the Israelites, God would "pass over" them. A reminder of God's deliverance from slavery, the Passover festival ultimately points to Jesus, "our Passover lamb" (1 Cor 5:7) who sets us free from sin (John 8:34-36).

14:13-16 Jesus told his disciples that upon entering Jerusalem they would meet a certain

man carrying a jar of water (14:13). They were to ask him to prepare a room for Jesus to **eat the Passover with** his disciples (14:14-15). Everything happened exactly as Jesus had said, so the disciples **prepared the Passover** (14:16).

14:17-21 As the Passover meal began, Jesus delivered a shocking revelation to his disciples: **one of you will betray me** (14:18). The reader of Mark's Gospel has known this (3:19; 14:10-11), but the apostles wondered who it could be. Each asked, **Surely not I?** (14:19). Jesus made it clear that his betrayer was **one of the Twelve**, one of his companions who had traveled with him and learned from him. It was one of those **dipping bread in the bowl** (14:20), a common bowl of sauce shared by all. To share a meal together is an act of friendship and trust, making Judas's betrayal especially despicable. Yet, he would not escape divine judgment for his actions (14:21).

14:22-24 Jesus took the bread and wine, common elements during the Passover, and gave them new significance. He explained them in light of the new **covenant**. The **bread** represented his **body**, and the **cup** represented the **blood** that would be **poured out for many**. The sacrificial death of Jesus Christ on the cross would accomplish what the old covenant had anticipated. It would atone for sins and make it possible for people to be forgiven and have a relationship with God. The church is to celebrate this Lord's Supper regularly by eating the bread and drinking the cup together. As often as we do this, we "proclaim the Lord's death until he comes" (1 Cor 11:26). It's a visible proclamation of the gospel.

14:25-26 Jesus vowed that he would not **drink of the fruit of the vine** until he shared it with them in his millennial **kingdom** (14:25). Then they sang **a hymn** (probably a psalm), left the city, and went to **the Mount of Olives** for the night (14:26).

14:27-28 Jesus had delivered much shocking news to his disciples, and he wasn't finished yet. He prophesied that **all** of them would **fall away** and abandon him, fulfilling the words of Zechariah 13:7 (14:27). Nevertheless, there was hope, for he also prophesied of their reunion and restoration after he had **risen** from the dead (14:28; see 8:31; 9:31; 10:34 for earlier predictions of his resurrection).

14:29-31 Finally, Peter spoke up: **Even if everyone falls away, I will not** (14:29). But Jesus informed Peter that not only would he fall away like the rest, he would also **deny** he even knew Jesus **three times** that **very night** (14:30). Though his motives may have been good, Peter was not as spiritual as he thought he was. His pride and spiritual weakness would give Satan something to take advantage of. When we pridefully exalt our abilities and fail to depend on God, we become bait for the evil one.

14:32-36 They arrived at **Gethsemane** at the foot of the Mount of Olives, and Jesus asked his disciples to wait while he went away to **pray** (14:32). Then **he took Peter, James, and John with him**, asking them to **stay awake** with him because he was so **distressed and troubled** (14:33-34). Jesus knew what lay ahead—not only a wretched execution but, even worse, separation from God the Father as he bore the sins of the world. The true and full humanity of the Son of God is on display here. He asked that the **cup** of God's wrath might be taken away if it were **possible**; nevertheless, he was fully prepared to submit to his Father's **will** (14:36).

14:37-42 Jesus returned to find his disciples **sleeping**. Even **Peter**, who had boasted of his commitment (14:29), had succumbed to weariness in spite of his Master's plea that he **stay awake** with him (14:37). Jesus challenged them to watch and **pray** so that they might have strength to deal with the **temptation** that was approaching. **The spirit is willing, but the flesh is weak** indicates that they had an inner desire to follow Jesus, but their physical exhaustion would make them susceptible to the devil (14:38). They needed to seek the strengthening that only God could provide, yet twice more Jesus returned to find them **sleeping** (14:40-41). Finally, the time was at hand. His betrayer had arrived (14:42).

14:43-46 **Judas** arrived with **a mob** carrying **swords and clubs. The chief priests, the scribes, and the elders** had sent them under cover of darkness to carry out their wicked desires (14:43). But the mob needed to know which man to grab, so Judas had given them a sign: whomever he kissed would be the one to **arrest** (14:44). To the very end, then, Judas's act of betrayal was vile. With a kiss—an act of kindness, friendship, intimacy—he handed over the Son of God to those who hated him (14:45-46).

14:47-49 We know from the other Gospels that it was Peter who **struck** the **servant** with violence and that Jesus rebuked him (14:47; see Matt 26:52-54; John 18:10). Then Jesus rebuked the mob for treating him like a common **criminal** (14:48). He had been **teaching in the temple** daily, where they could've arrested him (14:49). But their evil plans had to be carried out at night because they feared the daytime crowds (see 11:32; 14:1-2). Nevertheless, God used their wicked choices to fulfill **the Scriptures** and accomplish his will (14:49).

14:50-52 All the disciples **ran away** (14:50), just as Jesus had predicted (14:27). But Mark tells about a **young man** who was apparently caught sleeping, since he was only wearing **a linen cloth**. When they tried to seize him, he fled (14:51-52). Some interpreters believe this to be a veiled reference by the author (Mark) to himself.

14:53-59 When the mob **led Jesus away to the high priest**, Peter secretly followed them to the high priest's courtyard, **warming himself by the fire** (14:53-54). He assumed he wouldn't be noticed; he was wrong (see 14:66-72).

As Jesus had prophesied, he appeared before the Jewish religious leaders in a mock trial (14:53; see 8:31; 10:33). Acting with evil motives, they had already decided that they wanted him put to **death**. But though many gave **testimony** against Jesus, none of the witnesses were credible or consistent (14:56-59).

14:60-62 All the while, Jesus remained **silent**. So **the high priest** confronted him, asking him how he could remain quiet regarding all of the charges being made against him (14:60-61). Jesus had no obligation to answer the charges of witnesses who couldn't even agree with one another, so finally the high priest demanded that Jesus confess: **Are you the Messiah, the Son of the Blessed One?** (14:61). To this, he responded, **I am**. But Jesus didn't stop there. He attributed to himself the language of Psalm 110:1 and Daniel 7:13 (14:62), passages that prophesy of the glorious Messiah, human yet divine. Though the high priest was presiding over Jesus's "trial," one day all humanity will stand before Christ's judgment throne.

14:63-65 There can be no doubt that Jesus was affirming his deity as the Son of God, for **the high priest tore his robes** and accused him of **blasphemy** (14:63-64). No further witnesses were needed as far as the leaders were concerned. In their opinion, this Galilean rabbi had condemned himself (14:64). At that point, the floodgates were opened. They **spit on him . . . beat him . . .** mocked him as a prophet, and **slapped him** (14:65). "He was oppressed and afflicted, yet he did not open his mouth" (Isa 53:7). Don't skim over how the Son of God suffered for you.

14:66-72 Meanwhile, outside in the courtyard, one of the high priest's maidservants recognized Peter as a companion of Jesus (14:66-67). Immediately, **he denied it**, and **a rooster crowed** (14:68). Though Peter didn't realize it, Jesus's prediction was coming to pass (see 14:29-31). **When the maidservant** told others, Peter again **denied it**, probably fearing for his life (14:69-70). After being accused a third time, Peter resorted to cursing and swearing in order to convince everyone that he had nothing to do with Jesus of Nazareth (14:70-71). That's when the **rooster crowed** again, and **Peter remembered**. Filled with grief and guilt, the once-bold disciple **broke down and wept** (14:72).

Peter had brashly vowed to stand with Jesus, even if everyone else ran away. But he had placed his confidence in himself. Our flesh, no matter how sincere, cannot achieve

righteousness apart from yielding to and depending on the Lord.

15:1 In the morning, the **Sanhedrin**, the Jewish council over which the high priest presided, met and determined to hand Jesus over to Pontius **Pilate**, the Roman governor of Judea (from AD 26–36). Since the Jews were under Roman rule, they couldn't carry out the death penalty (see John 18:31); they would need the Roman governor's help. Pilate was a cruel man who was more than willing to execute enemies of Rome. Normally he would've been in Caesarea Maritima on the Mediterranean Sea, but given the number of Jewish pilgrims who traveled to Jerusalem for Passover, he was present in the holy city to maintain order.

15:2 In order for Pilate to be willing to execute Jesus, he would need to be guilty of a crime against Rome—like sedition. Since he claimed to be the Messiah, a Jewish King, this was the charge the Sanhedrin brought against him. The Jews were to have no king but Caesar. So Pilate asked, **Are you the King of the Jews?** Jesus's answer, **You say so**, is an affirmation. After all, this was the basis for his crucifixion (15:18, 26, 32). But Jesus didn't share Pilate's conception about what it meant to be the King of the Jews (see John 18:36).

15:3-14 As **the chief priests** leveled many accusations at Jesus, he refused to respond, and his silence annoyed and **amazed** Pilate (15:3-5). But Pilate knew how to deal with the situation. Each year during the Passover **festival**, he had a **custom** of releasing a **prisoner** that the Jews **requested** as a way of placating them (15:6, 8). He was aware that the Jewish leaders wanted Jesus killed simply because they were jealous of him (15:10).

So Pilate asked the crowd if they wanted him to release the popular teacher, the **King of the Jews** (15:9). However, **the chief priests stirred up the crowd** to ask instead for **Barabbas**, a murderer who had been part of a **rebellion** against Roman rule (15:7, 11). When Pilate asked what they wanted him to do with Jesus, the people demanded that he be crucified (15:12-13). Pilate was no kindhearted man, but he recognized that their demand made no sense. **What has he done wrong?** Yet the people had been worked into a frenzy and wanted blood (15:14). Incited by their religious leaders, the very ones who had been celebrating Jesus's teaching and miracles only a few days before were now calling for his death.

15:15 In the end, Pilate wasn't concerned about justice. He simply wanted to avoid a riot. In order **to satisfy the crowd,** he released a murderer and handed over the sinless Son of God **to be crucified.** Before that, Jesus was **flogged.** This was a brutal means of punishment in which a whip, with pieces of bone or metal tied into its ends, was applied to the back of a person until his flesh was ripped to shreds.

15:16-20 Soldiers led Jesus away for his execution, but not before mocking him in front of **the whole company** (15:16). They faked homage to him by putting a **purple robe** on him, pressing **a crown of thorns** into his head, crying out, **Hail, King of the Jews,** and bowing before him (15:17-19). They also beat him **with a stick** and spat on him (15:19). Then they took him away **to crucify him** (15:20). Hear the words of the author of Hebrews, fellow Christian: "Consider him who endured such hostility from sinners against himself, so that you won't grow weary and give up" (Heb 12:3).

15:21-22 After intense suffering in prayer, enduring an all-night trial, and being ruthlessly beaten, Jesus was too weak to carry his cross. So the soldiers had it carried by a passerby: **Simon,** a man from **Cyrene,** which was the capital city of the Roman district of Cyrenaica in northern Africa (15:21). The place of crucifixion was **called** *Golgotha,* an Aramaic name meaning **Place of the Skull** (15:22). Our English word *Calvary* is derived from the Latin translation, *Calvaria.* Scripture does not tell us why it had this name. Maybe people called it this because it was a customary place for executions, or perhaps it was because the place actually looked like a skull. What we do know is that it was near Jerusalem, outside the city walls (see John 19:20; Heb 13:12).

15:23-27 They offered Jesus **wine mixed with myrrh** to help dull the intense pain he was experiencing, but he refused it (15:23). He was determined not to lessen the suffering that he had voluntarily submitted to. Once they had **crucified him** between **two criminals,** the soldiers cast lots (a practice like rolling dice) for **his clothes**—all in fulfillment of Psalm 22:16-18 (15:24, 27). The **charge** against him was posted on his cross: **The King of the Jews** (15:26). Ironically, the charge was true. Below it hung the divine King, atoning for the sins of the world.

15:29-32 A few days prior, Jesus was praised as the coming King (11:1-10). Now everyone who **passed by** hurled **insults at him** (15:29). This included **the chief priests** and **the scribes** (15:31). Seeing Jesus put to death wasn't enough for them; they also wanted to mock him in his agony. They challenged him to **come down . . . from the cross** if he was truly **the Messiah, the King of Israel** (15:32). But remaining on the cross until death was exactly what the Messiah had to do.

15:33-34 At **noon** an unnatural **darkness came over the whole land** (15:33), signifying God's judgment on sin. Then Jesus cried out, **My God, my God, why have you abandoned me?** (15:34)—once again fulfilling the words of Psalm 22 (Ps 22:1). Though the Trinitarian nature of God remained unbroken, yet the Son experienced a judicial separation from the Father as he suffered for the sins of the world.

15:35-38 Some misunderstood Jesus's cry and thought he was **calling for Elijah** (15:35). In jest they mocked him, **offered him a drink** of **sour wine,** and said, **Let's see if Elijah comes to take him down** (15:36). Finally, Jesus cried in a loud voice and **breathed his last** (15:37). His willing sacrificial death had been accomplished. And at that moment, **the curtain of the temple was torn in two from top to bottom** (15:38). This symbolized that he had achieved what he came to do—granting human beings access to God. Indeed, by atoning for sin, Jesus made it possible for people to come into God's presence. We have no need for a mere human high priest to offer sacrifices repeatedly so that we can be right with God. Jesus Christ, the God-Man, is our great high priest who offered himself for sin once and for all (see Heb 4:14; 7:27; 10:10, 12).

15:39-41 When Jesus died, **the centurion** standing at the cross said, **Truly this man was the Son of God!** (15:39). In the midst of judgment on sin, then, salvation came to a Gentile centurion who confessed the truth. Jesus's disciples were nowhere to be seen, but the **women** who'd **followed him and took care of him** were there (15:40-41). Whereas the men had fled, these women stood faithfully by Jesus in his dying moments.

15:42-47 It was **the day before the Sabbath**, so Jesus would need to be buried before sunset (15:42). Therefore, **Joseph of Arimathea ... went to Pilate and asked for Jesus's body** (15:43). This took great courage because Joseph was a member of the Sanhedrin, which had condemned Jesus. However, he "had not agreed with their plan and action" (Luke 23:50-51) but **was himself looking forward to the kingdom of God** (15:43). He identified with Jesus's kingdom message and wanted to honor him. Once **Pilate** had obtained verification **from the centurion** that Jesus was indeed dead, he allowed Joseph **the corpse.** Then Joseph buried him in his own **tomb** (15:44-46; see Matt 27:59-60). Two of the women who'd followed Jesus, **Mary Magdalene and Mary the mother of Joses,** saw where he was buried (15:47), planning to visit the tomb after the Sabbath.

16:1-4 On the first of the week—Sunday—the women went to the tomb to **anoint** Jesus's body (16:1-2). They were discussing the fact that they needed someone to **roll away the stone** that covered **the entrance to the tomb** (16:3). But when they arrived, they saw that the **large** stone had already been moved (16:4). What had happened? Who rolled the stone away?

16:5-6 As the women stepped into the tomb, they expected to see a dead body—not a live one. **A young man dressed in a white robe** was **sitting** inside. Entering a dark tomb to find someone speaking to you is enough to alarm anyone, but this man immediately told them, **Don't be alarmed.** We know from Matthew's Gospel that the man was actually an angel (Matt 28:5), so his words come with divine authority: **You are looking for Jesus of Nazareth, who was crucified. He has risen!** (Mark 16:6). Jesus had told his disciples in advance, again and again, that it would happen (8:31; 9:31; 10:34). Now it had come to pass. Jesus Christ had risen from the dead.

16:7-8 The divine messenger told the women that they themselves were to be messengers, informing the **disciples and Peter** that he would meet them in **Galilee** (16:7). Peter, the one who had denied Jesus, was perhaps singled out to reassure him of the Lord's forgiveness. The women were so initially **overwhelmed** at what they had seen that they **ran** in fear and delayed carrying out the instructions (16:8), but they soon obeyed the angel and told the disciples the good news (see Matt 28:8; Luke 24:9-10).

16:9-20 Some of the earliest existing ancient manuscripts of the Gospel of Mark do not contain this section. Therefore, many scholars believe that Mark originally concluded at 16:8 and that these verses were added later by someone other than the author. Most of what appears in these verses is reported in the other Gospels.

Mary Magdalene was the first person who saw the risen Lord Jesus and informed the disciples (16:9-11; see Matt 28:1, 8-10; Luke 24:10-11; John 20:1-3, 11-18). The **two** to whom Jesus **appeared** while they were **walking** seem to be the two disciples who were on their way to Emmaus (16:12-13; see Luke 24:13-35). Later, Jesus appeared to all of the disciples and commissioned them to **preach the gospel** of the kingdom throughout the world (16:14-16; see Matt 28:16-20; Luke 24:36-49; John 20:19-22). Those who believe in Christ for the forgiveness of sins and eternal life will be delivered in eternity. Those who are baptized will be delivered (i.e., "saved") in history through their public identification with Christ (i.e., discipleship). He also promised them that they would perform miraculous **signs** as apostolic confirmation of the truth of their message (16:17-18; see esp. Heb 2:3-4; also Acts 2:1-13; 3:1-10; 5:12-16; 20:7-12; 28:1-6). Then **the Lord Jesus** ascended to **heaven** to **the right hand of God** the Father, and the disciples began their ministry (16:19-20; see Luke 24:50-53; Acts 1:9).

LUKE

INTRODUCTION

Author

ALL FOUR OF THE GOSPELS ARE anonymous, including the one attributed to Luke. However, we have good evidence for believing that Luke has been correctly identified as the author of the book bearing his name. First, the earliest manuscripts that exist include the name "Luke" in the title. Second, New Testament scholars agree that Luke and Acts are two works by the same author, and both are addressed to "Theophilus" (see Luke 1:1-4; Acts 1:1-3). In Acts 16:10-17, during Paul's second missionary journey, the narrative changes from third person, "they," to first person, "we" (see also Acts 20:5-15; 21:1-18; 27:1-37; 28:1-16). Thus, the author of Acts—and Luke—was one of Paul's traveling companions. Third, early Christian writers (e.g., Papias, Irenaeus, Justin Martyr, the Muratorian Canon, and Tertullian) unanimously affirm that Luke, the physician and companion of Paul (see Col 4:14; Phlm 24; 2 Tim 4:11), was the author. Granted, the writer could have been a different companion of Paul's. But since the early church didn't propose any other names, this is unlikely.

Identifying Luke as the author makes sense of features in the Gospel. For example, the author claims that he learned about the life and teaching of Jesus from "eyewitnesses" (Luke 1:2). Therefore, he was not himself an eyewitness to Jesus. In addition, Paul indicates that Luke was not "of the circumcised," that is, a Jew (see Col 4:10-14). In other words, he was a Gentile. This would explain the emphasis on Gentiles in both Luke and Acts.

Historical Background

Many scholars believe Mark's Gospel was written first and that Matthew and Luke made use of it when they authored their Gospels. If this is the case, Luke would have been written after Mark, which probably dates to the 50s. But Luke would also have been written prior to Acts. Acts, which refers to the Gospel of Luke as "the first narrative" (Acts 1:1), was apparently written prior to Paul's release from prison in Rome (see Acts 28:16-31). After his release around AD 60, Paul continued his missionary work and was later imprisoned again and martyred about AD 66/67. So if Acts was completed around AD 60, then Luke would've been written in the late 50s.

Luke addressed his Gospel and Acts to "most honorable Theophilus" (Luke 1:3; Acts 1:1). Since Luke addressed him in this way, he was apparently a person of high social status and perhaps wealthy too. Many scholars believe Theophilus may have served as Luke's patron, funding the production of his work.

Message and Purpose

Luke wrote his Gospel to provide a well-documented account of the life of Jesus Christ. Luke shows Jesus—fully God and fully man—moving among the people in compassion to free them from the myriad of things oppressing them. The disregarded, the outcast, the forgotten, and the marginalized got to see and experience the love of Christ— even if Jesus had to confront the Jewish leaders to do it. Luke reveals to us that God is no respecter of persons; he opened his heart to the needy through the kingdom ministry of his Son. The Son of Man who heals the sick, raises the dead, and calls the prodigal back is also the transcendent God who calls all people to himself in salvation.

Luke also demonstrates through the genealogy and birth of Jesus that he has the right to claim the title of Son of David, the Messiah and King. Throughout the book, Jesus used the Word of God to open people's minds and hearts to who he is—just as he did on the road to Emmaus after his resurrection. The God of Luke is touchable and knowable!

VIDEO INTRO

www.bhpublishinggroup.com/qr/te/42_00

LUKE

I. PROLOGUE, BIRTH, AND CHILDHOOD (1:1–2:51)

1:1-4 These first four verses serve as a preamble to Luke's work. He addresses his Gospel to the **most honorable Theophilus** (1:3), apparently a man of high social standing who perhaps served as Luke's patron, funding the production of his Gospel, as well as the book of Acts (Acts 1:1). Luke wants Theophilus to be certain of **the things about which** he had **been instructed** (1:4), indicating that Theophilus may have been a new convert to Christianity.

Luke sought to **compile a narrative about the events** that were **fulfilled** in the life of Jesus Christ (1:1). He had not been a firsthand follower of Jesus, but had learned everything from **eyewitnesses**—those (no doubt including the apostles) who heard and saw Jesus in person (1:2). Like a diligent historian or reporter, Luke had **carefully investigated everything** and wrote it down **in an orderly sequence** so that Theophilus and others might read and believe (1:3-4).

1:5 The Gospel opens **in the days of King Herod of Judea.** Luke frequently emphasizes the historicity of his account by mentioning the rulers who were in power at the time (see 2:1-2; 3:1-2). This is no fairy tale. Also known as "Herod the Great," King Herod ruled over Judea, Samaria, Galilee, and portions of Perea and Syria from 37 to 4 BC. He was not a Jew but an Idumean whom the Roman emperor had put in power.

Luke introduces his readers to **Zechariah** and his wife **Elizabeth** who were from the tribe of Levi and descended from Moses's brother **Aaron.** Thus, Zechariah **was a priest.** According to 1 Chronicles 24:7-18, the temple priests were divided into twenty-four divisions. Each division would serve for two weeks a year at the temple in Jerusalem.

1:6-7 Zechariah and Elizabeth were faithful, elderly followers of God (1:6). Nevertheless, they were childless because Elizabeth had never been able to **conceive** (1:7). This detail reminds us we must never assume that trials and difficulties only come our way because of our disobedience. God often brings or allows suffering into the lives of his people for his glorious purposes and for our sanctification.

1:8-9 On one occasion when Zechariah's **division was on duty** in Jerusalem, he was **chosen by lot**—and thus "at random"—to **burn incense** in **the sanctuary.** Remember: "The lot is cast into the lap, but its every decision is from the LORD" (Prov 16:33). God is sovereign in human affairs. He works through seemingly random processes to accomplish his will. Since God is sovereign, there is no such thing as luck.

1:10-15 While **the people** outside were **praying,** Zechariah went inside the temple to offer **incense** on the **altar** and was **terrified** to encounter **an angel of the Lord** (1:10-12). The divine messenger declared that **Elizabeth** would have **a son** whom they were to name **John** (1:13). Given their age, this would be miraculous. But God's purposes involved more than simply blessing an elderly couple with a child. This boy would grow to play a special role in God's kingdom plans. He would **be filled with the Holy Spirit** even **in his mother's womb** (1:15).

1:16-17 In his ministry to **the children of Israel**, John would **turn many** back to God and prepare the people for the Lord. The angel's words show that John would be the fulfillment of Malachi 4:5-6, in which the Lord promised to send **Elijah, to turn the hearts of fathers to their children**. John, then, would preach **in the spirit and power** of his Old Testament predecessor (1:17). Jesus later confirmed this when he told his disciples that John was "the Elijah . . . to come" (Matt 11:14; see also Matt 17:12).

1:18-20 In spite of the angel's words, Zechariah didn't believe. How could it be possible? **For I am an old man**, he said, **and my wife is well along in years** (1:18). In response, the angel identified himself: **I am Gabriel, who stands in the presence of God, and I was sent to speak to you and tell you this good news** (1:19). So, in other words, the visitor said, "I'm no third-rate heavenly messenger. I'm an angelic spokesman who serves in the divine presence. God himself sent me! And yet you don't believe me?" Importantly, Zechariah and other faithful Jews would've been familiar with Gabriel's name. He appears in the book of Daniel, where he explains the prophet's visions to him (see Dan 8:16; 9:21). Thus, this was no ordinary angel. Since Zechariah **did not believe**, he would be mute until the prophecy was **fulfilled**—as a sign that God would bring it to pass (1:20). Zechariah was disciplined for his unbelief.

1:21-25 When Zechariah finally emerged from **the sanctuary**, he was unable to talk. Because of this and the **signs he was making** to the people, they knew **he had seen a vision** (1:21-22). He returned **home**, and eventually Elizabeth became pregnant (1:23-24). She realized that **the Lord** had shown **favor** to her, removing the **disgrace** associated with being childless (1:25).

1:26-30 When Elizabeth was six months pregnant, **Gabriel** paid another visit. This time he went to the **town** of **Nazareth** in **Galilee**

and appeared **to a virgin** named **Mary** who was **engaged** to **Joseph**, a man who was descended from King **David** (1:26-27). Gabriel conveyed the Lord's **favor** to Mary, but she **was deeply troubled** (1:28-30). Why would a heavenly being come to see her?

1:31-33 The visitor told Mary she would **conceive** and **give birth to a son**, whom she was to name **Jesus** (1:31), the Greek version of the Hebrew name Joshua, which means "the Lord saves." He would be no ordinary child. He would be **called the Son of the Most High**—a carbon copy of his Father, bearing the divine nature. God would grant him **the throne of his father David**, and he will **reign . . . forever** in his **kingdom** (1:32-33). Thus, Jesus would be the fulfillment of the Old Testament promises of the coming Son of David, the Messiah, who would rule forever (see 2 Sam 7:12-16).

1:34-35 Mary, of course, was stunned. She was a virgin, asking, **How can this be?** (1:34). The child would be conceived by **the Holy Spirit**. Therefore, Jesus would be both divine and human—the God-Man. Theologians describe this as the *hypostatic union*, the combining of a divine nature and a human nature perfectly into one person. "Hypostatic" comes from the Greek word *hypostasis*, meaning "being" or "person." The union of two natures in one being. God in the flesh. Thus, he would **be called the Son of God** (1:35).

1:36-38 Moreover, Mary's **relative Elizabeth** had **conceived a son in her old age** (1:36). All of this could happen because **nothing will be impossible with God** (1:37). Mary didn't understand all of the implications for her life, but she humbly submitted to the will of God: **I am the Lord's servant** (1:38).

1:39-45 After this, Mary **hurried** off to visit Elizabeth (1:39). When Elizabeth heard Mary's voice, she was **filled with the Holy Spirit** and her **baby leaped inside her** (thus the unborn possesses personhood) (1:41). Elizabeth pronounced blessings on Mary (1:42, 45) and referred to her as **the mother of my Lord** (1:43)—confirming what Mary had heard from the angel.

1:46-56 **Mary** responded to all of this by praising God in song for his **favor** and for his **mighty deed** on behalf of his people (1:46-55). Mary's song is referred to as the *Magnificat*, which is the Latin translation of the Greek word rendered in English Bibles as **praises** or "magnifies" (1:46). Through his Messiah, God would extend **mercy** toward **those who fear him** (1:50). Those who recognize their need can expect good things from the Messiah. But he would also bring judgment, scattering **the proud** and toppling **the mighty** (1:51-52). God remembered his covenant with and promises to his people, and he would fulfill them (1:54-55).

1:57-66 When Elizabeth gave **birth** to John, **her neighbors and relatives** celebrated the Lord's mercy with her (1:57-58). Everyone assumed that the child would be named **after his father**, but Elizabeth insisted that he would **be called John** (1:59-60). When they asked Zechariah, who was still unable to speak, he confirmed it in writing: **His name is John** (1:62-63). At that moment, his ability **to speak** was restored, and he began **praising God** (1:64). **Fear** and awe came on everyone as they began to wonder, **What then will this child become?** (1:65-66).

1:67-80 **Zechariah** was then **filled with the Holy Spirit** and answered the question that everyone was asking (1:67). His prophecy of praise is called the *Benedictus*, which is the first word of the Latin rendering of **Blessed is the Lord, the God of Israel** (1:68): *Benedictus Dominus Deus Israel*. He worshiped God for the **redemption** and **salvation** he was providing for his people through the Messiah, just as he had promised long ago (1:68-75). As for Zechariah's son John, he would be **a prophet of the Most High** who would **go before the Lord to prepare his ways** as the Old Testament prophets foretold (see Isa 40:3; Mal 3:1). He would introduce Israel to her Messiah (see John 1:29-36). John **grew up and became spiritually strong**, spending much time **in the wilderness** and being prepared for his future public ministry (Luke 1:80).

2:1-2 As the time approached for Mary's baby to be born, the Roman emperor, **Caesar**

Augustus gave orders for the **empire** to be **registered** (2:1)—that is, a census was to be taken for taxation purposes. Augustus ruled from 31 BC to AD 14. This was **the first registration** that **took place while Quirinius was governing Syria**. Thus, Luke places the birth of Jesus squarely in the middle of Roman and Jewish history.

2:3-7 As a result of the emperor's decree, everyone traveled to his **town** to **be registered** (2:3). Since **Joseph** was **of the house and family line of David**, he had to travel from his home in **Nazareth** to **Bethlehem** (2:4), David's hometown (see 1 Sam 16:1). The distance between the two places was about ninety miles. **Mary** traveled with him, and while they were in Bethlehem **she gave birth to** Jesus (2:5-7) in fulfillment of Micah 5:2. Given the number of travelers, there was **no guest room available for them**, so she resorted to laying her baby **in a manger**, a feeding trough for animals (3:7). The King of creation, who deserved all honor and glory, had been born into the humblest of circumstances.

2:8-11 Luke reports another angelic visit, this time to nearby **shepherds** watching **their flock** at **night** (2:8). These were shepherds who cared for lambs used as sacrifices in the temple in Jerusalem. The unexpected and glorious appearance of the divine visitor **terrified** the shepherds (2:9), yet he brought **good news of great joy** (2:10). Not only was the visit unexpected, but the message was too: **Today in the city of David** (Bethlehem) **a Savior was born for you, who is the Messiah, the Lord** (2:11). Israel's Messiah, her anointed and appointed King, had finally come. And God chose to announce his Son's birth—not to the political or religious leaders of the day—but to a group of humble shepherds. He would be a Messiah **for all the people** (2:10) and offered as a sacrificial lamb like those cared for by the shepherds. He was born, the angel told them, "for you."

2:12 To confirm his words, the angel told the shepherds where they would find the Christ child. This infant King wasn't lying in a palace but **in a manger**. The shepherds were responsible for making sure that newborn lambs had no defects since the sacrificial animals had to be without spot or wrinkle. So the shepherds would tightly wrap the lambs in cloth to keep them from becoming blemished and injuring themselves. This explains why Luke makes the point that Jesus was **wrapped tightly in cloth**, since at his birth he was the sinless Lamb of God whose substitutionary sacrifice would take away the sin of the entire world (see John 1:29; 2 Cor 5:21; 1 Pet 1:19-20; 1 John 2:2).

2:13-15 Yet even though the circumstances of his entrance into the world were lowly, his birth announcement was anything but. **Suddenly** the **angel** was joined by a **multitude** of angels! The army of **heaven** came together to praise the Lord (2:13). They gave **glory to God** and announced **peace on earth to people he favors** (2:15)—to all those who would submit themselves to the Messiah.

The angelic announcement of "peace on earth" repeated so often at Christmastime is not about quiet tranquility or merely the absence of animosity between people. It is a declaration of the coming end of hostilities between a holy God and sinful humanity through the atoning work of the Messiah: peace with God. The Son of God came to pay the penalty for our sin and impute to us his righteousness. Only when "we have been declared righteous by faith," can "we have peace with God through our Lord Jesus Christ" (Rom 5:1). Peace among people is only possible when humanity is living at peace with God and submitting to his kingdom rule.

2:16-20 After an announcement like that, it's no surprise that the shepherds **hurried off** to find **the baby . . . in the manger** (2:16). They wanted to see this wonderful truth for themselves! And afterwards, they became the first human heralds of the good news of the Messiah, amazing **all who heard it** (2:17-18). The shepherds went back to work as changed men, **glorifying and praising God** (2:20). Mary, however, quietly reflected on the events (2:19). Of all the women in Israel, God had chosen this ordinary, humble young woman to bring the Messiah into the world. God regularly works through the lowly to fulfill his kingdom program (see 1 Cor 1:26-29).

2:21-24 Joseph and Mary fulfilled the law by circumcising their son "on the eighth day" (Lev 12:3). In obedience to the angel's instruction, they named him **Jesus**, meaning, "the Lord saves" (2:21; see 1:31). No one was ever more appropriately named! As faithful Jewish parents, they further kept God's commands by presenting Jesus to the Lord in fulfillment of Exodus 13:2 and 12, and by offering a sacrifice in fulfillment of Leviticus 12:6-8. The kind of animals they offered indicates that Joseph and Mary were poor (see Lev 12:8).

2:25-32 Luke mentions two more humble Israelites who gave thanks to God for Jesus. The first is a **righteous** man named **Simeon** who'd received special revelation from the Lord (2:25). **The Holy Spirit** had promised him that he wouldn't die until **he saw the Lord's Messiah** with his own eyes (2:26). **Guided by the Spirit**, he **entered the temple** just as Jesus's **parents** brought him in (2:27). Praising God, Simeon took the child in his arms. The Lord had fulfilled his promise, allowing him to *see* the one who would bring **salvation** (2:29-30). He would bring **light** and **glory** to peoples everywhere—to **the Gentiles** and **Israel** (2:31-32).

2:33-35 Simeon also **blessed** the parents. Then he informed **Mary** of the effect Jesus would have on **many in Israel**. Some would **fall** by rejecting him, and others would put their faith in him and **rise** (2:34). Though he would **be opposed**, the **hearts** of many would **be revealed** (2:34-35): True colors would be exposed. Unfortunately, there would be more than blessing for Mary: **A sword will pierce your own soul** (2:35). She would misunderstand her son (2:41-50), think he was "out of his mind" (Mark 3:21), and experience the grief of his crucifixion (John 19:25-27). But later, after his resurrection, she would know joy (Acts 1:14).

2:36-38 The second person Joseph and Mary encountered that day was an elderly **prophetess** named **Anna** (2:36-37). She had devoted her life to the Lord's service in **the temple** (2:37). When Simeon concluded his prophecy, Anna began. She thanked God and announced to everyone who was **looking**

forward to the redemption of Jerusalem that the Messiah had come (2:38).

2:39-40 Having faithfully accomplished **everything** that **the law of the Lord** required, Joseph and Mary **returned** with Jesus to **Nazareth** (2:39). **The boy grew up and became strong, filled with wisdom, and God's grace was on him** (2:40). In every way—physically, spiritually, and intellectually—Jesus matured in his humanity as God intended.

2:41-42 Jesus grew up in a godly Jewish home, demonstrated by the family's regular observance of **the Passover Festival** in Jerusalem (2:41). Luke describes an occasion in which Jesus's wisdom and grace (see 2:40) was evident even when he was **twelve years old** (2:42).

2:43-51 When the festival days were over in Jerusalem, Jesus lingered behind, while his parents assumed he was in **the traveling party** returning to Galilee. They would've been in a caravan with many **relatives and friends** (2:43-44), so it would have been easy to assume Jesus was among the group somewhere. When they realized he was missing, **they returned to Jerusalem** and found him **after three days** of searching (2:45-46). He was **in the temple**, interacting with **the teachers** and amazing them with **his understanding** (2:46-47). When his parents asked why he had worried them, Jesus replied, **Didn't you know that it was necessary for me to be in my Father's house?** (2:48-49). They **did not understand** that he had a unique kingdom mission from his heavenly Father (2:50). Nevertheless, he also had a responsibility to honor his earthly father and mother (see Exod 20:12), so he obeyed and **went** home with them (Luke 2:51).

Though her young son confused her, Mary **kept all these things in her heart** (2:51). One day, she would understand. Meanwhile, **Jesus increased in wisdom and stature, and in favor with God and people** (2:52). This demonstrates his true humanity. He wasn't simply God disguised as a man. He had both a perfect divine nature and a genuine human nature that matured as he grew.

II. BAPTISM, GENEALOGY, AND TEMPTATION (3:1-4:13)

3:1 Here Luke fast-forwards to the future. **Tiberius** had replaced Augustus as Roman emperor. When Herod the Great died in 4 BC, his territory was divided among his three sons: **Herod** Antipas, who ruled over **Galilee**; **Philip**, who ruled over **Iturea and Trachonitus** (areas in the northeastern part of Herod's kingdom beyond the Jordan); and Archelaus, who ruled over Judea. Archelaus was banished by Rome in AD 6 and replaced by a Roman governor. Thus, at this point in Luke's narrative, **Pontius Pilate** had been appointed the Roman **governor of Judea**. The Roman tetrarch ruling **Abilene** (an area northwest of Damascus in Syria) was **Lysanias**. It's uncertain why Luke mentions him. Some early church fathers claim that Luke was from Antioch in Syria, which would explain his interest in that area.

3:2 Having mentioned those ruling over Palestine in 3:1, Luke now mentions the Jewish religious rulers: **Annas and Caiaphas**. Caiaphas was the actual high priest at the time. Annas was Caiaphas's father-in-law and the former high priest, but he still retained the title.

During the historical period when the various men in 3:1-2 ruled over Palestine, the **word** of God **came to John . . . in the wilderness** of Judea. The Jewish people were oppressed by Gentile rulers and longed for deliverance, and John was going to prepare the way for their deliverer. But Jesus wouldn't be the kind of deliverer they were looking for. They wanted deliverance from Rome; Jesus would deliver them from sin and judgment, which is the prerequisite for social and political freedom. They needed the latter before they could have the former.

3:3 As John began his public ministry, he proclaimed **a baptism of repentance for the forgiveness of sins**. He was calling Israel back to God, which begins with repentance: sorrow over sin and an inner resolve to turn from it. Water baptism would be a visible declaration of their repentance. A right attitude and disposition toward their sin was necessary to prepare them for the Messiah's arrival.

3:4-6 John's ministry fulfilled the words of Isaiah 40:3-5. **The wilderness** in which he cried out reflected Israel's barren spiritual condition (3:4). True repentance would knock down **every mountain** of pride that kept the people from God. John's proclamation and baptism would make a **straight** path for the Messiah to bring **salvation** and all of his kingdom promises to them.

3:7-9 For those unwilling to acknowledge their sin and need for repentance, John pulled no punches: **Brood of vipers! . . . Produce fruit consistent with repentance** (3:7). In other words, if you claim you're not a sinner who needs to repent, then demonstrate your professed faith in God by bearing righteous fruit in your life. John also warned his hearers not to assume they were safe merely because they were descendants of **Abraham** (3:8). God had brought judgment on the people of Israel before because of their sins. That they were currently under foreign rule, in fact, was an indication that the nation had forsaken God in the past. That **the ax is already at the root of the trees** (3:9) meant judgment was right around the corner—a reference to the destruction of Jerusalem by the Romans in AD 70.

3:10-14 Those among **the crowds** who were convicted over their sins asked, **What then should we do?** (3:10). How could they meet the spiritual conditions John was setting forth? He told them to practice generosity, honesty, and contentment in their daily lives (3:11-14). Repentance is validated by how we relate to others. In the words of Paul, "The whole law is fulfilled in one statement: Love your neighbor as yourself" (Gal 5:14).

3:15-17 In light of everything John was saying and doing, many began to wonder if he **might be the Messiah** (3:15). But John made it clear that the differences between him and

the Messiah were so vast that he didn't even qualify to unfasten the coming King's **sandals**. John's water baptism was inferior to the baptism of **the Holy Spirit and fire** that the Messiah would bring (3:16), a reference to the fact that Jesus would send the Holy Spirit at Pentecost (see Acts 2:1-4). Fire is used in the Bible as a metaphor of both purification and judgment. Here John emphasized judgment: **the chaff he will burn with fire that never goes out** (Luke 3:17).

3:18-20 John exhorted the people to repentance and proclaimed to them the **good news** of the coming kingdom of God (3:18). But John was no coward. He spoke truth to power. Not only did he rebuke the masses, but he **rebuked** the rulers. **Herod** Antipas, for instance, had married **Herodias**, the **wife** of his brother Philip (see Lev 18:16). Herodias had unlawfully divorced Philip, so John reproved Herod for this and for **all the evil things he had done** (3:19). As a result, Herod arrested John and threw him **in prison** (3:20). Thus ended the public ministry of the greatest prophet prior to the coming of Jesus Christ (7:28).

3:21-22 Before John was locked up, he **baptized** Jesus (3:21). Jesus had not come for baptism to repent for his own sin but to identify with and represent the people whom he had come to save. At the moment of his baptism, **the Holy Spirit descended on him in a physical appearance like a dove**, and the Father announced from heaven his great pleasure in his **beloved Son** (3:22).

Scripture clearly teaches the Trinitarian nature of God. He is one (Deut 6:4), yet he exists in three co-equal persons: Father, Son, and Holy Spirit (see Matt 28:19). The Father is not the Son, and the Son is not the Spirit. Here Luke describes the actions of all three persons of the Godhead as the public ministry of Jesus began.

3:23-38 The genealogies of Luke and Matthew (Matt 1:1-16) demonstrate that Jesus was a legitimate heir to David's throne. The differences between the two lists have to do with the fact that Matthew provides Jesus's legal genealogy through Joseph, his adoptive father, and Luke provides Jesus's biological genealogy. Since he **was thought to be** Joseph's son (2:23), he is related to David on both sides of his family tree. He was qualified to be the Messiah, legally through Joseph and physically through Mary. Luke also traces Jesus's genealogy back to **Adam** through Nathan (3:38) because Jesus is the promised "offspring" who would strike Satan's head in fulfillment of God's promise (Gen 3:15).

4:1-2 After his baptism, Jesus, **full of the Holy Spirit, was led by the Spirit into the wilderness for forty days to be tempted by the devil.** Don't miss that when Jesus's ministry began, he was "full of the Holy Spirit." We should not be surprised, then, that Christians are exhorted to be "filled by the Spirit" (Eph 5:18). Paul contrasts this to being filled with wine. We are not to be intoxicated with alcohol but intoxicated with the Spirit, coming under the influence and governance of God in our daily lives. This will not happen if Christians merely sip from the Spirit on Sundays. Such limited engagement will not lead to changed lives.

Notice also that the Spirit led Jesus "into the wilderness . . . to be tempted by the devil." Evidently being under the influence of the Spirit does not mean uninterrupted peace and tranquility. Jesus was in the middle of the Judean wilderness, a completely barren place. **He was hungry,** having not eaten for forty days (4:2). And he was under spiritual attack by Satan. No one would volunteer for this assignment. Nevertheless, he was full of the Spirit. You cannot measure your spiritual condition by your circumstances, then. Jesus's circumstances were bleak, but he was in the center of God's will for him. Likewise, just because your external circumstances appear to be smooth, it doesn't necessarily mean you are spiritually healthy.

But why was Jesus in the wilderness? He was the "second" or "last" Adam (1 Cor 15:45, 47). The devil tempted the first Adam and succeeded in having him kicked out of the garden into the wilderness (Gen 3:1-24). The first Adam was on defense and lost, but the second Adam played offense. Empowered by the Holy Spirit, he went into the wilderness to face the devil so that he might bring humanity back to the garden. Though he was physically hungry from a lack of food, he was spiritually nourished for a spiritual battle.

4:3 Satan spoke three temptations to Jesus, but they were all driving at the same point. Would Jesus act independently of God? This is also the question that we face in each wilderness experience we encounter: Will I act independently of God?

The devil urged him, **If you are the Son of God, tell this stone to become bread.** The "if" clause doesn't mean he was tempting Jesus to *prove* that he was the Son of God. He was *not* saying, "If you're the Son of God (because I'm not sure that you are), then do this." The devil knows who Jesus is. Satan was well aware of Jesus's unique eternal relationship to the Father (10:18; see also Matt 3:17). The "if" clause assumes the reality of the statement. In other words, he was saying, "*Since* you are the Son of God, here's what the Son of God should do."

Satan had been watching Jesus, and he knew his weak spot: hunger. Therefore, Satan attacked at his point of crisis, at his point of need. He will do the same to you. You need to be aware of your weaknesses and vulnerabilities because you can be sure that Satan is aware of them.

4:4 Though Satan had identified a genuine need in Jesus's life, he tempted him to fill that need in an illegitimate way. He questioned God's willingness to provide for him. But Jesus wasn't fooled. He responded by quoting Scripture: **Man must not live on bread alone.** If the Son of God faced the devil while full of the Spirit and armed with the Word, why would you do otherwise? Jesus quoted Deuteronomy 8:3, in which Moses reminded the Israelites—who were in the wilderness—that they hadn't survived merely because they ate manna. They survived because of the source of the manna. Jesus refused to act independently of his Father; he trusted in his provision. We must not seek to meet legitimate needs in illegitimate ways.

4:5-7 Next the devil **showed** Jesus **all the kingdoms of the world** (4:5). He claimed that **all this authority** had been given to him, and he could **give it to anyone.** Therefore, he offered it to Jesus if he would **worship** him

(4:6-7). This raises questions. How did Satan obtain this authority? Who gave it to him?

Adam was called to rule the world on God's behalf (Gen 1:26, 28). By rebelling against God, he abdicated his role and handed it over to Satan, who is now the "god of this age [or 'world']" (2 Cor 4:4) and "the ruler of the power of the air" (Eph 2:2). Thus, the devil offered Jesus what he had come into the world to claim. He had come to be a King over a kingdom. And, if he listened to Satan, he wouldn't have to work so hard. All Jesus had to do was worship the one who could give it to him immediately.

4:8 Again, however, Jesus answered with the Bible: **Worship the Lord your God, and serve him only** (see Deut 6:13). Jesus didn't need Satan's offer. The Father had already promised his Son all of the kingdoms of the earth: "I will make the nations your inheritance and the ends of the earth your possession" (Ps 2:8). But obtaining that would require the fulfillment of a mission that included perfect obedience to the Father and a sacrificial atoning death for sinners. Anything less would result not in the redemption of the world but would deliver Satan a victory. Jesus was destined to be King, but he would only pursue it in submission to the Father. Worship is reserved for the one true God.

4:9-11 Finally, the devil **took him to Jerusalem**, stood him **on the pinnacle of the temple**, and tempted him to jump (4:9). Since Jesus liked using Scripture, Satan decided, "I can play that game too." Be warned: the Bible has been used many times throughout the centuries to lead people astray. Satan knows the Bible better than many Christians, and he uses it. He quoted Psalm 91:11-12, assuring Jesus that if he threw himself off the temple, God would send **his angels** to **protect** him (4:10-11). This would be a spectacular, supernatural way to convince the Jews that Jesus was the Messiah, and it would result in a safe landing. No suffering required. And no cross.

4:12-13 Once again, Jesus relied on God's Word: **Do not test the Lord your God** (see Deut 6:16). To say it another way, don't back God into a corner. We are not to intentionally create the need for a miracle. God will create miracle opportunities on his own.

Jesus was determined to be God's Messiah, in God's way, according to God's timetable, for the glory of God. After this, the devil **departed from him** (4:13). This demonstrates a very important principle for waging spiritual warfare. Satan is allergic to the proper use of Scripture. Three strikes, and he's out.

III. MINISTRY IN GALILEE (4:14–9:50)

A. Beginning Ministry and Calling Disciples (4:14–6:16)

4:14-15 Having spent time at the Jordan River for his baptism and in the Judean wilderness for his temptation, **Jesus returned to Galilee**. His battle with the devil had not left him spiritually drained but full of **the power of the Spirit** (4:14). As a result, his public ministry began and his popularity grew (4:15).

4:16 Then Jesus went **to Nazareth**, his hometown where he'd been raised. **On the Sabbath**, he went into **the synagogue** so that he could **read** Scripture. Luke says this was his **usual** activity. So whereas Jesus's public ministry had just begun, his spiritual practice of engaging with God, God's Word, and God's people had always been a regular pattern of his life.

4:17-21 The synagogue attendant handed him **the scroll of the prophet Isaiah**, and Jesus chose to read from Isaiah 61:1-2 (4:17). When he finished, he informed **everyone in the synagogue** that the passage had **been fulfilled** as they listened (4:20-21). He was claiming that the words were about him.

What did the words say? **The Spirit of the Lord** had **anointed** him (4:18). At Jesus's baptism, the Holy Spirit had descended on him (3:21-22). From that moment, he had been "full of the Holy Spirit" (4:1), "led by the

Spirit" (4:1), and ministering "in the power of the Spirit" (4:14). Jesus was claiming to be the Lord's "Anointed One"—in Hebrew, "Messiah"—in Greek, "Christ." The King whom Israel had been longing for had finally come.

His mission was **to preach the good news** of God's kingdom **to the poor.** He had come to set **captives** free, open **blind** eyes, **set free the oppressed,** and **proclaim the year of the Lord's favor** (4:18-19). "The year of the Lord's favor" is another name for the Year of Jubilee (every fifty years; see Lev 25:8-12) when Israel was instructed to set slaves free and release people from their debts, as well as allowing them to return to their family property. Jubilee is a symbol of the social and economic liberation of God's people. The key, however, to understanding the Year of Jubilee is that it was inaugurated by the Day of Atonement, when the issue of sin was addressed. Thus spiritual transformation is the foundation for the legitimate social, political, and economic restructuring of society.

Jesus's preaching, then, addresses both the content of the gospel (Jesus's coming death, burial, and resurrection for the forgiveness of sins) and the scope of the gospel (the impact this good news should make on issues of biblical justice—the equitable and impartial application of God's moral law in society). This is good news for those in economic crises (the poor), in political crises (the captives), and social crises (the oppressed). The gospel of the kingdom that Jesus preaches saves us *from* hell, but it should also save us *for* making a kingdom impact on this world through our "good works" that bring glory to God and benefit to people (see Matt 5:16). Jesus, then, is offering his people and us a new Jubilee.

4:22-24 Initially, people responded positively to **the gracious words** that he spoke. But then someone said, **Isn't this Joseph's son?** (4:22), meaning, "Hey, this is the carpenter's kid. He's a local. Who does he think he is?" Anticipating their unbelief, Jesus quoted a proverbial saying: **Doctor, heal yourself** (4:23). In other words, "If you really think you're the Messiah, give us some proof. Do something messianic." He knew they were unwilling to receive him: **Truly I tell you, no prophet is accepted in his hometown**

(4:24). You see, these people thought they knew him. He was, to them, nothing special. He couldn't possibly be the Messiah.

4:25-27 Jesus knew that performing a miracle to "prove" he was the Messiah would not help those who were inclined to skepticism and unbelief. He cited two Old Testament examples, **Elijah** and **Elisha,** who were rejected by Israelites in spite of the miracles they performed. As a result, Gentiles received God's benefits instead, because they were willing to act in faith at the word of God given them through the prophets. Elijah provided for the **widow at Zarephath**, and Elisha healed **Naaman the Syrian** of **leprosy** (see 1 Kgs 17:8-16; 2 Kgs 5:1-19).

4:28-30 The people became **enraged** (4:28) since Jesus was implying that God's grace would be withheld from them and given to the Gentiles. They **drove him out of town** and were intent on killing him by tossing him off a **cliff** (4:29). Yet he miraculously escaped what would have been a premature death (4:30). It was not yet his time. His death would be at the time and place of his choosing.

4:31-32 Jesus traveled **to Capernaum**, on the north side of the Sea of **Galilee** (4:31). The people there marveled at his **teaching because his message had authority** (4:32). He wasn't merely conveying information. He was proclaiming the kingdom of God and the effect of God's kingdom agenda on every area of life. One couldn't be indifferent to Jesus's authoritative message. It had to be believed and obeyed—or rejected and defied.

4:33-37 In the **synagogue** at Capernaum, a demon-possessed man identified Jesus as **the Holy One of God** and asked if he had **come to destroy** them (4:33-34). The demons recognized Jesus as the Son of God, and they feared him. (They know their days are numbered.) **Jesus rebuked** the evil spirit and told him to **be silent.** Though the devil's forces understood Jesus's true identity, he wasn't going to let them handle his public relations campaign. So he commanded the demon to **come out.** With one last act of defiance, the demon threw the man down and left him. But Jesus supernaturally protected the man from being hurt (4:35). Again, Jesus turned heads and left **amazement** in his wake (4:36). Soon everyone in Galilee was talking about him (4:37).

4:38-39 After he left the synagogue, Jesus **entered** the **house** of Simon—that is, Simon Peter (4:38). Jesus healed Peter's ailing **mother-in-law**, and she responded by serving him (4:39). Her actions are a reminder that when the Lord meets a need in your life, it should always provoke you to greater service.

Peter witnessed Jesus's miraculous power firsthand. But it would be during a later supernatural encounter with Jesus that Peter's life would be forever changed (see 5:4-11).

4:40-41 Everyone who had heard about his miracles brought to him people with **diseases** and those who were demon-possessed. They came to him **when the sun was setting**—that is, when the Sabbath was over and they were free to travel (4:40). The **demons** were **shouting** out, **You are the Son of God!** But he refused to let them **speak** (4:41). Jesus didn't want acknowledgment from demons; he wants praise from people.

4:42-44 After an all-night healing session, Jesus departed in the morning to **a deserted place**. The **crowds** pursued him and **tried to keep him from leaving** (4:42), but his ministry wasn't for them alone. And he wasn't a mere healer. He had come **to proclaim the good news about the kingdom of God** (4:43). His miracles authenticated his message, but he didn't want to be known simply as a miracle worker. He had a message to announce.

5:1-3 Crowds of people were **pressing in** while Jesus was teaching them **by Lake Gennesaret**, another name for the Sea of Galilee (5:1). **Simon** Peter's fishing boat was nearby, so Jesus got in it and **asked him to put out a little from the land**, so that he had a platform from which to teach the people and not be smothered by them (5:2-3).

5:4 At the conclusion of his sermon to everyone, Jesus gave a directive to an individual. Having taught about spiritual matters, he gave Peter fishing instructions: **Put out

into deep water and let down your nets for a catch.

Peter had probably been fishing his whole life. He had a business partnership with James and John (5:10). Jesus, on the other hand, was an itinerant preacher who had probably spent much of his life doing carpentry work like his dad (see Matt 13:55). But those things didn't stop him from advising a professional fisherman how to do his job.

5:5 Peter's answer shows that he didn't think too highly of Jesus's counsel. They had **worked hard all night long and caught nothing.** To land a major catch on the Sea of Galilee, you had to fish at night near the land—not during the day in deep water. So, here it's as if Peter were saying, "Jesus, I don't tell you how to preach, do I? Your instructions simply don't match with my years of experience." Nevertheless, he told him, **I'll let down the nets.**

How often does a similar situation happen to you? Through his Word, God calls you to action in your specific circumstances, but your instincts and experience tell you that it won't work. We have to remember that our instincts and experience have been distorted by sin. We can't see things perfectly. We lack information. Our understanding is flawed. That's why we depend on an almighty God who is all knowing and can accomplish the impossible.

5:6-7 Peter reluctantly obeyed Jesus, and then the unexpected happened. The catch of **fish** was so tremendous that **their nets began to tear** (5:6). This wasn't flimsy fishing gear; these were professional nets made to hold a lot of fish, and Peter and his partners had never encountered anything like this before. Moreover, the haul was so huge that **both boats** started **to sink** (5:7). Jesus had blessed his followers with more than they could handle. In the same way, his Word will often contradict your natural reasoning. But if you will obey him in faith, then your vision of him, praise for him, trust in him, and experience of blessings from him will grow.

5:8-9 After this display of Jesus's knowledge and power, Peter was **amazed** and saw him in a different way. He **fell** before Jesus and said, **Go away from me, because I'm a sinful man, Lord!** Peter knew that Jesus was no mere miracle-working preacher. He realized that, just as the demons had declared, he was "the Holy One of God" (see 4:34). When human beings are confronted with the holiness of God, their sinfulness is exposed. Isaiah was a godly man. But when he saw God on his throne in all his glory and the heavenly beings describing him as, "Holy, holy, holy," Isaiah said, "Woe is me for I am ruined because I am a man of unclean lips" (Isa 6:1-5). Peter saw Jesus for who he really was, and he saw himself for who he really was. The huge catch of fish was nice, but the real blessing was having his eyes opened to his own sin. You won't understand your need for Jesus Christ unless you understand that you're a sinner before a holy God.

5:10-11 Jesus told Simon Peter, **Don't be afraid.** Peter's response was understandable. The Son of God was the only one who could rightly calm his fears. Then he pronounced his new vocation: **From now on you will be catching people** (5:10). Previously he had caught fish for a living. Now he would fish for people as a kingdom ambassador so that they might become followers of Jesus. Peter, James, and John **left everything** and **followed him** (5:11).

Jesus had blessed Peter, opening his eyes to his sinful condition and need for God. But this blessing wasn't for Peter's own sake. It was so that Peter could extend that blessing to others. The same is true for you. Regardless of the blessings God brings into your life—physical, spiritual, financial, relational—they are not meant for your benefit and enjoyment alone. He has blessed you so that you may bless others as you follow him.

5:12 As he traveled, Jesus encountered a man with **leprosy all over** his body. He came to Jesus and acknowledged his power to cleanse him: **you can make me clean.** What he didn't know was whether he was **willing** to cleanse him. He recognized both Jesus's sovereignty and his prerogative to heal.

5:13-16 The Mosaic law required those with such skin conditions to separate from others. However, when **Jesus touched** the man,

contamination didn't flow in; cleansing flowed out (5:13). Then Jesus told him **to tell no one.** Instead, he was to show **the priest** that God had cleansed him, and he was to give an offering as **Moses** had **commanded** (5:14). Nevertheless, as **news about him spread**, the **crowds** flocked to Jesus for healing (5:15). So **he often withdrew to deserted places and prayed** (5:16). The greater the demand on him, the more Jesus in his humanity depended on God the Father.

5:17-19 As Jesus's reputation spread, he attracted the attention of the Jewish religious leaders: **Pharisees and teachers of the law** (5:17). One day they were listening and watching as he taught, and **some men** brought a **paralyzed** man to him (5:18). This was nothing new. Many had been coming to Jesus for healing. But on this occasion, the men couldn't get their friend to Jesus because of the size of the **crowd.** So they carried him on top of the house in which he was teaching, made a hole in the **roof**, and **lowered** the man's **stretcher** to the front row (5:19).

5:20 Luke tells us that Jesus saw **their faith.** How do you see faith? You see it by what it produces. Jesus saw their actions on behalf of their friend. But he also saw what no one else could. They saw a paralyzed man who needed healing. Jesus saw a sinner who needed forgiveness. The men had brought their friend for physical restoration. Jesus knew he needed spiritual restoration. So he said to him, **Friend, your sins are forgiven.** Forgiveness came first. Getting right with God takes priority over getting your circumstances right. This incident also shows the importance of having fellow believers in your life on whose faith you can piggyback in times of your own spiritual and physical weakness.

5:21 When this happened, **the scribes and the Pharisees** started thinking. Since **God alone** can **forgive sins**, then this man **speaks blasphemies.** They started with the (correct) assumption that God alone could forgive sins, and they arrived at the (correct) conclusion that Jesus was making himself equal to God. For any other man, this would indeed be blasphemy. But not for the Son of God.

5:22-24 Jesus supernaturally perceived **their thoughts** (5:22). Notice that he didn't contradict their conclusion that he'd made himself equal to God. Rather, he contradicted their conclusion that he'd committed blasphemy. Forgiving sins and healing a paralytic are equally impossible for mere human beings. But Jesus validated his divine **authority** to **forgive sins** in the spiritual realm by demonstrating his divine authority to heal lame legs in the physical realm (5:23-24).

5:25-26 The former paralytic **got up** and walked away (5:25). If Jesus were a blasphemer, he could not have healed him. But since he healed him, he showed that he could also forgive sins. And since he could forgive sins, he should be acknowledged as the Son of Man, the Messiah. The **incredible things** they witnessed caused awe among the masses and led them to give **glory to God** (5:26).

5:27-29 Jesus had already called several fishermen to be his disciples (5:1-11). Now he called someone whom the Pharisees and scribes would really dislike. **Levi** (also known as Matthew; see Matt 9:9) was **a tax collector**. Jews who served as tax collectors for the Roman government were considered traitors by their countrymen. Moreover, they often padded their own pockets by collecting more than necessary. But rather than avoid such a sinner, Jesus told him, **Follow me**, and Levi obeyed (5:27-28). Then the man further demonstrated his repentant heart by hosting **a grand banquet** for Jesus at his house and inviting his fellow **tax collectors and others** to meet him (5:29). When you truly encounter Jesus, it's not enough to follow him. You want others to know the joy of following him too.

5:30 The religious leaders were disgusted and complained, **Why do you eat and drink with tax collectors and sinners?** They questioned the propriety of Jesus's association and fellowship with sinful people. But their concern confirmed that they didn't understand Jesus's mission—nor did they understand their own duty as supposed servants of God.

5:31-32 Jesus stated the obvious: **sick** people need doctors, not the **healthy** (5:31). Then he

applied this truth to his ministry: **I have not come to call the righteous, but sinners to repentance** (5:32). Jesus's mission was to invite the spiritually sick to repent and experience a restored relationship with God. He hadn't come to simply hang out with religious people. The scribes and Pharisees, on the other hand, were the religious leaders. Yet they didn't have enough concern for sinners to show them compassion and point them to God.

5:33 Some were observing that while **John's disciples** and **those of the Pharisees** fasted **often**, Jesus's disciples did not. The implication was that Jesus was not encouraging his disciples to practice piety toward God.

5:34-35 Jesus informed them that there is a legitimate time for fasting. Often fasting in the Old Testament was a solemn occasion that involved sorrow over sins or an urgent request for divine intervention (see, e.g., 1 Sam 7:6; 2 Sam 12:16; Neh 1:4; Esth 4:15-16; Ps 35:13). But this wasn't a somber occasion; it was a time of celebration. Jesus compared it to a **wedding** and himself to **the groom** (5:34). When you attend a wedding, you don't fast, because it's an event of merriment and rejoicing. The Messiah had finally come; it was party time! Later, though, when the **groom** was **taken away from them**—after his resurrection and ascension—his disciples would have legitimate opportunities for fasting (5:35).

5:36-39 To illustrate what he was explaining to them, Jesus used **a parable**, a word picture. You can't take a **patch** that's **new** and put it on **an old garment**. Not only will the two **not match**, but the new patch will shrink and tear the garment (5:36). Similarly, you can't put **new wine into old wineskins** (3:37). The brittle containers will burst, and you will lose both the wineskins and the wine.

Jesus was bringing a new covenant. As the author of Hebrews says, Jesus has a "superior ministry" and is the "mediator of a better covenant, which has been established on better promises" (Heb 8:6). Everything about him is superior. The scribes and Pharisees wanted their old ways to stay the same. They scorned the "newness" of Jesus and the kingdom he was proclaiming. But **no one** who truly welcomes the King and his teaching—who tastes and sees "that the LORD is good" (Ps 34:8)—would say, **The old is better** (5:39).

6:1-2 The criticism of Jesus by the Pharisees continued. When he and his disciples passed through **grainfields** on a **Sabbath** day, the Pharisees saw them plucking the **heads of grain** to eat, and they became furious, accusing them of breaking the law of Moses about the Sabbath. The law permitted the Israelites to pick some of their neighbor's grain for a bite to eat when they were hungry (see Deut 23:25). But the Pharisees weren't questioning this practice. Instead, they were questioning the fact that they were doing it on a Sabbath.

God had commanded Israel to remember the Sabbath as a time of rest, spiritual refreshment, and no labor (see Exod 20:8-11). But the Pharisees were extra-scrupulous. They added numerous laws to God's law about what kind of activities constituted "labor." As far as they were concerned, Jesus and his disciples were "harvesting" and, thus, breaking the law.

6:3-5 Jesus informed them that not only did they not understand the intention of the law, but they also didn't understand their Bibles very well. He pointed to an Old Testament passage (1 Sam 21:1-9) in which **David** and his men **ate the bread of the Presence**, even though it was only intended for **the priests** (6:3-4). As God's anointed one, David was authorized to eat the bread because of his extreme need. If this was true in David's case, it was even more so in the case of God's true Anointed One (Messiah). For Jesus was **Lord of the Sabbath** (6:5). By saying this, Jesus indicated that he knew better than they how the Sabbath was to properly function. He also was making a not-so-subtle affirmation of his deity. Since God had given the Sabbath command, Jesus would have to be equal to God to consider himself "Lord of the Sabbath."

6:6-8 The Sabbath was a frequent matter of contention between Jesus and the religious leaders. **On another Sabbath**, he **was teaching** when he saw a man with a **shriveled hand** (6:6). There were **scribes and Pharisees**

present, and Jesus knew they were watching to see if he would "break" the Sabbath so that they could pounce on him (6:7-8). But Jesus wasn't one to back down from a fight.

6:9-11 He challenged them, asking whether one should **do good on the Sabbath** or **do evil** (6:9). His point was that if one chose not to do good to someone by alleviating his suffering, it was evil. Then Jesus **restored** the man's **hand** (6:10). This should have resulted in rejoicing by anyone who witnessed the miracle; instead, these leaders were **filled with rage**, and they conspired to do away with him (6:11).

6:12-13 Luke has previously described how Jesus called some of his disciples (see 5:4-11, 27-28). Now he describes how he **chose twelve of them** to be his **apostles** (6:13). Prior to this he **spent all night in prayer to God** (6:12). Given this significant moment and the mounting hostility to his ministry, Jesus sought time with his Father. This was how the Son of God approached critical moments. How do you approach them?

6:14-16 Luke names the twelve men whom Jesus designated as apostles—including the one who would become **a traitor** (6:16). These handpicked men would travel with Jesus, learn from him, and be granted special authority to share in the responsibility of proclaiming his kingdom message.

⇾ B. Teaching and Miracles
(6:17–8:56) ⇽

6:17-19 Having been on a mountain (6:12), Jesus descended and **stood on a level place** with a great **crowd** of people who had traveled from far and wide to **hear him** teach and **be healed** (6:17-18).

6:20-23 Jesus's teaching in 6:20-49 is parallel to what we find in Matthew's "Sermon on the Mount" (Matthew 5–7), though Luke's version is shorter. Although Jesus taught the material on a mountain in Matthew, in Luke he came down from a mountain and taught on a level place (16:17). Thus, Bible interpreters often refer to this passage in Luke as the "Sermon on the Plain." It's likely that Jesus taught the same material multiple times to different audiences in different locations.

The blessings or "beatitudes" in these verses are expressions of divine favor and kingdom benefits that would come to Jesus's followers. Those **who are poor**—that is, those who recognize their spiritual bankruptcy—will see the authority of **the kingdom of God** overruling life's challenges (6:20). Those **who are now hungry** with a passionate spiritual appetite for a relationship with God will receive satisfaction in their souls. Those **who weep** and mourn over their sin will have their sorrow replaced with joy (6:21). Those who are persecuted and treated spitefully for the sake of their witness to Christ will receive a **reward** in **heaven** that is greater than they can imagine (6:22-23).

6:24-26 In addition to pronouncing blessings on those who receive him as Messiah, Jesus also pronounced woes on those who reject him. Those **who are rich** in the physical world but have no spiritual wealth toward God will ultimately lose their riches and find that it was meaningless (6:24). Those who let this present age fill them will experience spiritual lack in the age to come. Those who laugh and find all their enjoyment in this present age will be spiritual mourners in the age to come (6:25). Jesus's followers are not to regard complimentary words from the unrighteous as indicators of God's approval. The ungodly spoke well of **false prophets** during Old Testament times (6:26). God's people must remember that divine approval is more important than human praise.

6:27-36 In 6:27-38, Jesus differentiated between his disciples and those who did not heed his words. Christ's followers will have different values and will thus be distinguishable from the rest of the world. They will **love** their **enemies**, do **good** to those who **hate** them, and **pray** for those who **mistreat** them (6:27-28). They will respond with blessing and generosity rather than cursing and retaliation (6:29-30). They will demonstrate **love** to those who do not love them (6:31-35) with a view toward bringing such detractors to

the knowledge of God's love in Jesus Christ. For those who treat people this way will reflect the love and mercy of their **Father** in heaven (6:35-36).

6:37-38 Kingdom people won't **judge** and **condemn** others according to their own standards. Those who do so will find their own standards used against them as they are **judged** and **condemned** by God (6:37). **Give, and it will be given to you** (6:38) implies kingdom men and women will give generously in time, prayer, finances, and service. They'll realize that they are not their own source. All that they have has been given to them—on loan from heaven—so that they may bless others. God will reward such sacrificial generosity done in his name with overflowing spiritual and physical blessings (6:38). The key is to give to others the very thing ("it") that you want God to give to you. God's principle of reciprocity is activated when we minister to the needs of others with the result that he raises up people to minister in return to us in that same area of need (e.g., the widow of Zarephath, 1 Kgs 17:8-16).

6:39-40 Jesus told them a simple **parable** to contrast his teaching with that of the religious leaders. If the **blind** try to **guide the blind**, then **both** will **fall into a pit** (6:39). What is true in the physical world is true spiritually too. Those who reject God's Messiah and teach others to do so will lead them to destruction. In contrast, **a disciple** of Jesus is to **be like his teacher** in his attitudes and actions (6:40). The character and conduct of their Master should shine through, because discipleship is a reflection of the life of Christ.

6:41-42 The lives of Christ's followers should have no hint of hypocrisy. A hypocrite says one thing and does another. It's easy to talk a big game and give an impression of being a spiritual person, but the proof is in the pudding. A truly spiritual person has an internal reality that overflows into external actions. Such a person will not complain about **the splinter** in his **brother's eye** (a minor fault) while doing nothing about **the beam of wood** in his **own eye** (a grievous sin) (6:41). We must address the larger issues in our own hearts before we seek to address the small issues in the lives of our brothers and sisters in Christ (6:42).

6:43-45 People identify fruit trees based on the kind of **fruit** they **produce** (6:43-44). Apple trees bear only apples. Orange trees bear only oranges. In the same way, you can identify people who follow God based on what they say and do. Righteousness is produced in a person's life only as a result of righteousness in the heart. For we speak and act **from the overflow of the heart** (6:45).

6:46-49 A fruitful disciple will do what Jesus says. Jesus illustrated this principle by telling a story of two men. One **man** laid the **foundation** of his home on a **rock**. When **flood** waters **came**, it withstood the onslaught (6:48). The other **man** built his home **without a foundation**. As a result, the flood swept his **house** away (6:49). Jesus said that the first man is like the person who **acts** on his **words**, and the second man is like the person who **hears** but **does not act** (6:47, 49).

Hearing and reading God's Word are absolutely essential. But if you stop there, disaster will result. The Bible wasn't meant to be merely studied and memorized; it was meant to be believed and obeyed. We are to "be doers of the word and not hearers only" (Jas 1:22). Failure to obey Jesus's words will lead to ruin. When the storms of life come, it's not merely what you hear but what you do with what you hear that determines how much of Jesus you will experience. The foundation of God's Word operating in your life will determine the stability of your future—especially when serious trials come your way.

7:1-5 In most cases, the Jews hated Roman occupation and rule of their land. But this particular Roman was different. He was a **centurion**, an army officer commanding about one hundred men. He had practically demonstrated love for the Jewish people by building their **synagogue** in **Capernaum** (7:1, 3, 5). Many Gentiles were drawn to the Jewish religion because of its monotheism (belief in one God) and moral teachings. They were known as "God fearers" and participated in much of the Jewish religious life (see,

e.g., Acts 10:1-2). However, they did not fully convert to Judaism—perhaps to avoid circumcision or certain other practices.

This particular centurion was beloved by the Jews of the town. So when he sent a request to Jesus, the **Jewish elders** urged Jesus to **grant** it (7:3-4). He had a **servant** whom he **valued** greatly, but, unfortunately, the servant **was sick and about to die** (7:2). The centurion believed that Jesus could heal him. But since he was uncertain whether Jesus would respond to a Gentile's request, he sent the message through some Jewish leaders.

7:6-8 Upon hearing the centurion's request and the positive testimony about him, Jesus set off for his house. As he drew near, the centurion sent word to him: **Lord . . . I am not worthy to have you come under my roof** (7:6). Clearly, his self-perception was quite different from that of the various Jewish religious leaders who had been critical of Jesus. This man had a high view of Jesus ("Lord") and a humble view of himself ("I am not worthy"). He considered himself unworthy of inviting Jesus into his home or even meeting him in person.

Not only did he view himself with humility, the centurion viewed Jesus as possessing extreme authority: **Say the word, and my servant will be healed** (7:7). He knew that Jesus didn't have to be in the presence of a sick man in order to command his healing—any more than the centurion had to personally visit a subordinate in order to command him to action (7:8). When Caesar issued an order, he didn't need to speak it to every soldier in his army. His authority ensured that his wishes were carried out. Likewise, the centurion believed that Jesus's spiritual authority allowed him to simply speak, and the servant would be healed.

7:9-10 Repeatedly, we have seen the crowds amazed at Jesus. But on this occasion, **Jesus** himself **was amazed**. This Gentile had more **faith** than anyone Jesus had met **in Israel** (7:9). When the messengers returned home, **they found the servant in good health** (7:10). Jesus healed the servant from a distance, rewarding the centurion's faith by doing exactly what he had believed Jesus could do. The centurion had "great" faith (7:9). The key to having truly great faith is to believe that the object of your faith is great. In the same way, Jesus does not have to be physically present for his Word to work when we are operating under his kingdom authority:

7:11-17 Jesus, **his disciples**, and **a large crowd** neared the Galilean town of **Nain** and encountered a funeral procession (7:11). The **dead man** was an **only son**, and his mother was a **widow** (7:12). With no husband or grown children to care for her, the woman would have no means of support, no hope. The scene moved Jesus to **compassion**. He gently commanded the woman to stop weeping, and then he commanded her dead son to **get up** (7:13-14). Instantly, the son woke from death, **sat up** in his coffin, **and began to speak** (7:15). Jesus had performed many miracles, but this is the first time (reported in Luke's Gospel) that he raised someone from the dead. When they saw it, **fear came over everyone**—that is, the crowds were in awe and **glorified God** (7:16). This miracle was a small foretaste of a greater resurrection miracle that was to come (24:1-53).

7:18-20 John the Baptist had been locked up in prison by Herod Antipas (see 3:19-20). Prior to that, he had prepared the way for the Messiah to begin his mission. He had urged his listeners to repent, warned of God's coming wrath, and foretold of the baptism of fire that the Messiah would bring (3:2-18). Receiving word about all that Jesus was doing, John was beginning to wonder if he had been wrong. He asked **his disciples** to ask Jesus, **Are you the one who is to come, or should we expect someone else?** John was expecting the kingdom of God to come. Yet now he was in prison with no kingdom.

7:21-23 Jesus told John's disciples to report back to John all the miracles that they had **seen and heard**. The miraculous works he was performing were fulfilling Isaiah 61:1, which foretold of the Messiah's deeds (7:21-22). Jesus wanted John to be encouraged to continue to have faith in him, despite his circumstances. When experiencing suffering, even strong believers sometimes need reassurance and reaffirmation about Jesus and the gospel.

7:24-28 Jesus then proceeded to speak to the crowd about John's character and ministry. Lest they think John weak, given his current misgivings, Jesus wanted to assure them that John was a man of strong conviction. He was no **reed swaying in the wind** (7:24). Nor was he living **in luxury** (7:25). Instead, the king who was living in luxury had locked John up. In fact, John was a **prophet** and the fulfillment of Malachi 3:1—the **messenger** who prepared the Messiah's **way** (7:26-27). Thus John was a very great man, **but the least in the kingdom of God is greater than he** (7:28). The new covenant, which Jesus would bring about through his atoning death on the cross, was greater than the old covenant. Thus, the citizens in the kingdom operating under the new covenant will have a greater spiritual capacity than John, who had been operating under the old.

7:29-30 The people responded positively to Jesus's message about John. **They had been baptized** by him and received him as the forerunner of the Christ (7:29). In contrast, the religious leaders had rejected John, rejected the one to whom John pointed, and thus **rejected the plan of God for themselves** (7:30). Such rejection would continue until Israel's leaders led the people in condemning their Messiah.

7:31-35 Jesus told a parable to explain the treatment that he and John had received from the Jewish leadership (7:31). The leaders were behaving like cranky **children** singing a silly song (7:32). They could not be pleased by the somberness of the kingdom, represented by John's ascetic lifestyle and call to repentance (7:33). Nor could they be pleased by the joy of the kingdom, represented by Jesus's gracious fellowship with sinners (7:34). The scribes and Pharisees couldn't be satisfied. They saw John as demonic and Jesus as liberal. **Yet wisdom is vindicated by all her children** (7:35). In other words, those with spiritual insight validate it by their actions—their "children." The crowds who had received both John and Jesus demonstrated that they were wiser than Israel's religious leaders.

7:36-38 A Pharisee named Simon had **invited** Jesus over for a dinner party (7:36). Jesus had been generating a lot of curiosity, so the man apparently wanted a closer look at this controversial rabbi. During the dinner, however, an unexpected guest showed up: **a woman in the town who was a sinner** (7:37). Understand that all people are sinners. To call a particular woman a sinner was to say something about her lifestyle. She was probably either a loose woman or a prostitute.

The woman's uninvited appearance was bad enough. But things really became awkward when she took out **an alabaster jar of perfume**, anointed Jesus's **feet**, wept on his feet, kissed his feet, and wiped his feet with her hair (7:37-38). She was breaking all of the rules of decency and polite society—and she didn't care. Obviously, she wanted to show love for Jesus and honor him for bringing the grace of God into her life.

7:39 But **the Pharisee who** was hosting the meal was more disgusted with Jesus than with the woman. He didn't speak out loud but thought **to himself** that if Jesus were **a prophet**, he would know the truth about the woman. If he were all he was cracked up to be, he would have told her, "Please don't touch me. I can't be associated with you."

7:40-43 Luke tells us that **Jesus replied to him** (7:40). Don't miss that. The Pharisee hadn't spoken to Jesus. He had been talking to himself (7:39), meaning he had muttered under his breath or merely entertained a thought. But all our deepest beliefs, feelings, and judgments are an open book before Jesus (see 5:21-22). You can't have a private reflection without Jesus knowing about it.

Jesus had a question for Simon (7:40), but it was a setup. He was going to have Simon dig a hole and then watch him fall into it. He described a scenario in which **two debtors** owed money to **a creditor**. One **owed five hundred denarii, and the other fifty** (7:41). A denarius was the daily wage for the average laborer. Neither debtor could **pay** the **debt**, but one clearly owed considerably more than the other. Nevertheless, the creditor **graciously forgave them both** and cancelled the debts. **So, which of them will love him more?** (7:42). Jesus's question implies that there's a direct correlation between the amount of debt cancelled and the resulting

love that's shown—a direct correlation between forgiveness and gratitude. Simon took the bait and gave the obvious answer: **I suppose the one he forgave more** (7:43). Jesus told him he had aced the test, and then he moved in for the kill.

7:44-46 In response to **Do you see this woman?**, Simon probably thought, "How could I miss her?" But Jesus wasn't questioning the Pharisee's eyesight. He was questioning his discernment. In those days of walking through dusty streets in sandals, feet would become filthy. To provide a guest with **water** to wash his **feet** was common hospitality. Moreover, greeting a guest with a **kiss** and **oil** for his **head** were signs of warmth and friendliness. Simon hadn't shown any of these courtesies to Jesus. But the woman had washed his dirty feet **with her tears** and **hair**. She had kissed his feet and **anointed** them **with perfume**. It took an uninvited, sinful woman to show hospitality to Jesus in this Pharisee's home. Simon must have been squirming in his seat.

7:47 Then Jesus really lowered the boom: **Her many sins are forgiven; that's why she loved much.** The adoration and honor the woman showed to Jesus were proof that she realized she was a great sinner who had been forgiven many sins. By contrast, **the one who is forgiven little, loves little.** Simon was self-righteous. He saw little in his life that needed to be forgiven. He assumed he had it all together, and as a result he felt no need for the grace of God that Jesus was proclaiming.

What drives your time with, devotion to, and experience of Jesus? Do you go to church for social connection? Do you read your Bible out of duty? Do you pray in boredom? Do you serve others for what you can get in return? If so, you have forgotten your sin before God and the cross of Christ that cancels all debt (see Col 2:14). Don't lose sight of how much you've been forgiven. Drink in the truth of the gospel, and it will drive you to a deep love for Jesus that spurs you to worship him with passion and serve others sacrificially.

7:48-50 **Your sins are forgiven** is a glorious thing to hear your Savior say (7:48). If you are putting your faith in Christ as your substitutionary sacrifice, then he says those same words to you. Those who heard him questioned how he could do such a thing (7:49), and the answer is that he can't—unless he is more than a mere man. Then the Son of God commended the woman for her **faith** and sent her away **in peace** (7:50).

8:1-3 Jesus didn't remain in one place long. He was constantly **traveling from one town and village to another** so that he could preach **the good news of the kingdom of God.** Many followed him, but there was a core group that went with him everywhere. This included **the Twelve** (8:1), the disciples whom he chose and named as his apostles (see 6:12-16). Additionally, there were several women who accompanied him. One of these was Mary **Magdalene**, from whom Jesus had cast out **seven demons** (8:2). As Jesus told Simon the Pharisee, whoever is forgiven much loves much (see 7:47). Mary had been set free from overwhelming demonic oppression. Therefore, her devotion to Jesus was significant. Along with the other women, she was **supporting** his needs from her **possessions** (8:3).

8:4 People were coming from everywhere to hear Jesus. So, as he often did, he told them **a parable.** Jesus's parables were earthly stories with heavenly meanings. He took ordinary, everyday people or activities, put them into a story's format, and taught his listeners a valuable kingdom principle that used the familiar to explain the unfamiliar.

8:5-8 This parable was about **a sower** who **went out to sow his seed** (8:5). Though such imagery may be unfamiliar to modern readers, it was very familiar to Jesus's listeners who lived in an agrarian society. After the furrows were dug, the farmer would "sow" or plant his seed by scattering them, perhaps from the back of a donkey. The seed would fall into the furrows, but some would not, since he was scattering by hand without the scope-limiting assistance of modern technology.

As the farmer **sowed**, some seed **fell** on a **path** where it was **trampled** and **devoured by birds** (8:5). Some **fell on rock**, where it

sprouted up and then **withered** for lack of **moisture** (8:6). Some fell among **thorns** that **choked** the plant as it grew (8:7). Some **fell on good ground** and produced abundant **fruit: a hundred times what was sown.** Then Jesus concluded with, **Let anyone who has ears to hear listen** (8:8). Teachers sometimes signal to students that something is especially important (and will probably appear on a test!) by saying, "Make sure you write this down." Jesus told the people to "listen" because what he said was critically important. It would come up again.

8:9-10 The disciples were confused, so they asked Jesus to explain the meaning of **this parable** (8:9). He responded by quoting from Isaiah 6:9. The **secrets of the kingdom**— that is, things concealed in the Old Testament but revealed in the New Testament—were being made known to Jesus's followers. But to others his **parables** would make no sense because, though they had ears, they refused to "listen" (8:10; see 8:8). Although a large crowd heard Jesus, most would not understand. Only a small group would get it. (See commentary on Matt 13:10-17.)

8:11 When Jesus interpreted the parable for his disciples, he explained that **the seed** represented **the word of God**, and the different soils represented different kinds of people, different kinds of hearts. He made it clear that the success of the seed had nothing to do with the seed itself; rather, it had everything to do with where it landed. It's the soil that determines whether or not there will be a crop. So, if God's Word is not "working" in a person's life, we need to check the "ground" that it landed on. The soil of your heart needs to be receptive to the seed in order for you to experience spiritual change and growth in your life.

8:12 The path on which **seed** fell represents the person whose heart is hard. Just as seed cannot penetrate a hardened patch of ground, so God's Word cannot penetrate into the hearts of those who have hardened themselves against it. If people set themselves against receiving God's Word, **the devil . . . takes away the word from their hearts** like the birds devoured the seeds. The devil does this **so that they may not believe and be saved.**

This has two applications. The word *saved* can have two meanings: "salvation" in eternity and "deliverance" in history. When an unbeliever hardens his heart against the gospel, Satan removes the Word that he's heard, lest he believe the good news about Christ and be saved—that is, become a Christian. When a believer hardens his heart against a specific truth of God's Word, he is susceptible to satanic deception. As a result of failing to embrace God's truth, a believer can fail to experience God's deliverance in his earthly struggles—that is, growing and overcoming persistent sin.

8:13-14 The ground with rocks represents the person who initially receives the word joyfully, but has **no root.** He will **believe for a while and fall away in a time of testing** (8:13). Such believers, who lack the discipline of spending time with God, living in obedience to his Word, and serving his people, are unable to stand up under the pressure when difficulties come their way. And thus, they become unproductive.

The ground with **thorns** represents the person whose spiritual growth is **choked with worries, riches, and pleasures.** As a result, he or she will **produce no mature fruit** (8:14). Remember this: If the devil can't hinder you with difficulties, he'll choke you with distractions. Regardless of the impediment, your growth will stall, and your life will be void of righteous fruit.

8:15 The good ground represents those who **heard the word with an honest and good heart,** held on to it, endured, and produced **fruit** in their lives. This kind of believer gladly receives God's Word honestly. This person holds or embraces the Word tightly and perseveres in obedience with it. In other words, he or she is no fair weather Christian, happy to shout "amen" on Sunday but living according to a personal agenda on Monday. The "good-ground" Christian consistently endures and bears fruit as his character and conduct are transformed as he lives in obedience to God's Word. To be one, you must come clean with God, confessing sin and seeking change.

8:16-18 Jesus made clear to his listeners that if one understands the Word of God, then his lifestyle should reflect that knowledge. Just as a person does not light **a lamp** in order to hide it, so also one is not given access to the secrets of the kingdom in order to keep them secret (8:16-17). When we respond in faith to God's truth, more truth will be given. The one who refuses to respond to the truth will be lost (8:18).

8:19-21 Jesus's **mother and brothers** tried to **meet with him** but could not because **the crowd** was so large (8:19). We learn in the other Gospels that his family thought he was "out of his mind" during his ministry and didn't believe in him (Mark 3:20-21; John 7:1-5). When he was notified that his family was trying to reach him (8:20), Jesus used the opportunity to teach his listeners a kingdom lesson. Intimacy with Christ is tied to obedience to **the word of God.** Such intimacy transcends earthly family relationships. Those who not only **hear** but also **do** the Word will know true spiritual intimacy with Jesus (8:21).

8:22 One day Jesus had **his disciples** climb **into a boat** to cross the Sea of Galilee. This was something they had done many times before. Several of the disciples who had been professional fishermen, in fact, had sailed this sea more times than they could count. But this occasion would test the limits of their faith and expand their view of Jesus.

Notice two things. First, they had not done anything wrong by getting into the boat. They had obeyed Jesus by doing so and were thus in the middle of God's will for them. When trials come, then, it is not necessarily because we are outside of God's will. Sometimes he tests us when we are in the center of his will because he has something bigger for us to experience. Second, as the following verses show, the disciples soon forgot Jesus's word. He told them, **Let's cross over to the other side of the lake.** Thus, whatever happened along the way, they were going to reach the other side.

8:23-24 On the way across the sea, Jesus **fell asleep.** Had they paid attention to him and trusted his assurance that they would reach their destination, the disciples could have slept too. But when a vicious **windstorm** swept down on them, they feared that they would sink and drown (8:23). They woke Jesus in a panic, but he simply scolded the **wind** and **waves**. Unlike the disciples, the elements of creation heeded the words of their Maker and calmed (8:24).

8:25 Having rebuked nature, he now turned to rebuke the Twelve: **Where is your faith?** The storm had been a test of whether they believed him. Instead of focusing on his word, though, they focused on their circumstances. If they had rightly feared Jesus, they wouldn't have had to fear this storm. Clearly, the storms of life need not paralyze us either—if we keep God's Word ever before us. When they saw his command of nature, the storm was instantly forgotten, and the disciples were in awe of Jesus. Their Messiah was bigger than they'd thought. Their fear of their circumstances diminished as their righteous fear of Jesus increased.

8:26-29 They disembarked from the boat in **the region of the Gerasenes** on the other side of the sea **opposite Galilee** (8:26). There Jesus encountered a man who was **demon-possessed**, naked, dwelling among **the tombs**, and often **bound by chains** (8:27, 29). His condition was truly dire: spiritually oppressed, weak, homeless, and isolated. Jesus commanded the **spirit to come out of** him. But the man **fell down before him**, and the demon within him cried out in terror, fearing the **Son of the Most High God** would **torment** him (8:28-29). Whatever power they possess over human beings, Satan's minions must bow to the authority of Jesus Christ.

8:30-33 As Jesus talked to the demon, he learned that there was actually a whole **legion** of them inhabiting the poor man (8:30). They feared Jesus would **banish them**, so they **begged him** to let them **enter** some nearby **pigs** (8:31-32). When he permitted them, they left the man, entered the pigs, and caused the crazed swine to rush into the lake and drown (8:32-33).

8:34-37 Once word got out about what had happened, the people from the **town** and **countryside** implored Jesus to **leave them**

(8:34, 37). It didn't matter that a pitiful man had finally been set free from his captivity and suffering (8:35). The death of the pigs had affected the local economy. It signaled a significant loss of revenue. Were Jesus to linger and cast out more demons, it would affect everyone—and the locals weren't interested in making such sacrifices.

8:38-39 Though the people wanted Jesus to go away, the man whom he had delivered from spiritual bondage **begged him earnestly** to take him with him (8:38). He valued what Jesus had done for him and was willing to devote himself to following him. But Jesus had other plans. He wanted the man to be his follower not by joining him in the boat but by returning to his **home** and telling everyone what God had done for him (8:39). He was to be a witness, then, spreading the good news to the very people who wished Jesus to go away. Our Lord calls us to do the same—to proclaim what he has done for us to those who have rejected him, in hope that they might believe.

8:40-42 When they **returned** to the other side of the Sea of Galilee, crowds surrounded Jesus again (8:40). One of those who approached him was a man named **Jairus**, a **leader** in the local **synagogue**. Falling at **Jesus's feet**, he **pleaded with him** to heal his twelve-year-old **daughter** (8:41-42). Though many of the Jewish religious leaders were opposed to Jesus and his ministry, Jairus wasn't one of them. His story is a reminder that when we encounter desperate circumstances, they can cause us to exercise a desperate faith.

8:43 As Jesus followed Jairus to help his dying daughter, another desperate person approached him. But this one did so stealthily. A woman who had suffered **from bleeding for twelve years** was there. She was financially ruined, having spent every penny on **doctors** who couldn't help her. Moreover, her medical condition would've made her ceremonially unclean (see Lev 15:25-27), affecting her ability to worship at the temple and to have contact with people. Thus, her physical problem led to financial, spiritual, and social problems.

8:44-48 Jesus was on a mission, but so was this woman. She had heard about Jesus, believed he had the power to heal her, and was not going to let this opportunity pass. All she wanted to do was touch **his robe**. As she did, a condition that had plagued her for over a decade **stopped** in an instant (8:44). But in spite of her desire to be healed secretly, Jesus wasn't going to let it go unnoticed. When he asked who had **touched** him, Peter was astonished (8:45). Jesus was being accosted from every side. *Everyone* was touching him! But the Son of God knows when someone has reached out to him in faith (8:46). And he was calling the woman out so that she could bear witness and glorify God. Knowing she couldn't hide, the woman **fell down before him** and confessed everything (8:47). She went public with her testimony, and Jesus told her, **Your faith has saved you. Go in peace** (8:48).

8:49-56 In the midst of this joy, a messenger arrived from Jairus's house with tragic news. His **daughter** was **dead** (8:49). Nevertheless, Jesus challenged Jairus to act in faith, regardless of how things appeared, and his little girl would **be saved** (8:50). So, by faith, Jairus took Jesus into his home (8:51), and Jesus commanded the mourners to stop weeping because the girl was only **asleep** (8:52). So they **laughed at him** (8:53). Their cloud of unbelief set the stage for Jesus to demonstrate his supernatural power in spite of it. He held the girl's **hand** and told her lifeless corpse to **get up** (8:54). At that moment, **her spirit returned** and **she got up** as if she had been napping (8:55). Then Jesus told her astonished parents **to tell no one** of this (8:56). The formal acknowledgment of his messiahship awaited his entry into Jerusalem.

⮞ C. *Preparing the Twelve* (9:1-50) ⮜

9:1-2 Jesus's small band of disciples whom he had named apostles (6:12-16), often referred to in the Gospels as "the Twelve," had been with him everywhere. They heard him proclaim God's kingdom, watched him heal the sick, and observed as he rescued many from demonic oppression. Now it was their turn.

He transferred his **power and authority** to them so that they might go out in his name and do the same.

9:3-6 Jesus instructed them to take no provisions on their journey (9:3); rather, they were to accept hospitality from whoever would welcome them (9:4). Those who welcomed Jesus's kingdom message would welcome his ambassadors, but those who rejected Jesus's disciples were spurning him and placing themselves in a position of judgment. To **shake off the dust** of a town **from your feet** was to separate oneself from those who separated themselves from God (9:5).

9:7-9 Herod Antipas was tetrarch over Galilee. His father, Herod the Great, had been appointed by Rome to rule over Israel and had tried to kill Jesus when he heard that a new king had been born (see Matt 2:16-18). Though Herod Antipas couldn't have known that Jesus was the same person whom his father had tried to murder, he was vexed by him. Many rumors were spreading concerning Jesus. Some said he was one of the Old Testament **prophets**, and some said he was **John** the Baptist back **from the dead**. Herod was confused, but **he wanted to see** this man he was hearing so much about. Jesus's reputation had reached every level of society, including those in political power. Interestingly, one day Herod would have his opportunity to see Jesus (23:6-12), but it would be according to Jesus's timetable.

9:10-11 The apostles returned from their mission (see 9:1-6) and told Jesus all that had happened. **He took them** to a private place, but **the crowds** still discovered him. Nevertheless, Jesus wasn't impatient with the masses but **welcomed them**, taught them, and **healed** them.

9:12-17 As the day drew to a close, **the Twelve** urged Jesus to **send the crowds away** to **find food and lodging** because they were **in a deserted place** (9:12). Jesus suggested that they should feed the crowds. But as the disciples surveyed their supplies, they found that they had only **five loaves and two fish**—hardly enough to feed **five thousand men** (plus women and children) (9:13-14). By making them assess their situation, then, Jesus had shown them that their resources were insufficient. Feeding the crowd was humanly impossible; it required divine assistance.

So Jesus had the crowds sit in groups for ease of distribution (9:14). Then he gave thanks for their inadequate food and passed it to the disciples, who served as waiters (9:15-16). When the disciples started handing out the bread and fish, it miraculously lasted until **everyone ate and was filled.** There were even leftovers (9:16-17)! Jesus proved himself to be the source for the peoples' needs. He is a sufficient King who has an abundant supply.

9:18-20 After a time of **private** prayer, Jesus turned to his disciples and asked the question that was on everyone's mind: **Who do the crowds say that I am?** (9:18). They reported to him the same things that Herod had been hearing (see 9:7-9). People were saying that he was **John the Baptist** or **Elijah** or **one of the ancient prophets** (9:19). But then Jesus turned it into a personal question: **Who do you say that I am?** And **Peter**, speaking on behalf of them all, responded, **God's Messiah** (9:20)—that is, the anointed one who is both King of the Jews and Savior of the world.

9:21-22 This correct appraisal of his identity opened the door for Jesus to reveal further truth about himself. After warning them **to tell this to no one** (9:21), he explained what kind of Messiah he would be. It was God's plan that he **suffer . . . be rejected by** Israel's religious leaders . . . **be killed, and then be raised the third day** (9:22).

9:23 In light of the path he must take as the Messiah, he informed them of what it would look like for believers to identify with him on the path of true discipleship. The one who wants to follow God's Messiah must **deny himself**—that is, place Jesus's glory ahead of his own. He must also **take up his cross daily.** This is a clear allusion to crucifixion. People condemned to it were required to carry their crosses to the place of execution. Likewise, true disciples must daily submit to Christ's authority over their lives, even to the point of suffering and death. To **follow** King Jesus is to live according to God's kingdom

agenda, which is the visible manifestation of the comprehensive rule of God over every area of life.

9:24-26 The paradox of Christian discipleship is this: **Whoever wants to save his life will lose it, but whoever loses his life because of [Christ] will save it** (9:24). Radical commitment to Christ will result in the experience of God's abundant life in history and even greater reward in eternity. Jesus made it clear that in God's economy, true profit comes from giving away your life for God's purposes. Those who strive after this world's power, wealth, success, and values to the neglect of their spiritual lives will forfeit their experience of God's reality now and his kingdom reward at Christ's return (9:25). Those who reject the call of true discipleship—who are **ashamed of** Jesus—will lose out on the glorious recognition given to true disciples in glory (9:26).

9:27 In saying **some standing** there would **not taste death** before seeing **the kingdom of God**, Jesus was speaking of three of his disciples who, in a few days, would experience a foretaste of the glory of the kingdom.

9:28-31 Eight days later, Jesus took **Peter, John, and James** on a **mountain to pray** (9:28) These three were his inner circle of disciples, often accompanying him without the others (see 8:51; Mark 14:33).

When Jesus prayed, he was transformed. Not only did his **clothes** become **dazzling white**, but his **face** was also **changed** (9:29). And as if that weren't startling enough, two Old Testament visitors appeared: **Moses and Elijah** (9:30). These men represented the Law and the Prophets. Peter, James, and John represented the New Testament. Thus, the Old and New Testaments both are centered on Jesus. The visitors spoke with Jesus about the **departure** he would **accomplish in Jerusalem** (9:31)—his death, resurrection, and ascension, which would open the door to salvation.

9:32-33 The disciples had been **in a deep sleep.** When they woke, they were confronted with this spectacular display (9:32). Then Peter suggested that they build **three shelters**—one for each of them—in fulfillment of Zechariah 14:16-19, because he thought it was time to inaugurate the kingdom (9:33). But Peter didn't understand God's plan.

9:34-36 At that moment, another visitor spoke, this one unseen. God the Father declared, **This is my Son, the Chosen One; listen to him!** (9:35). They had seen Jesus's glory. Next came confirmation as the Father praised his unique Son, the one who was to be King and have all authority. Then, suddenly, they were alone again with Jesus. They **told no one what they had seen** (9:36) in obedience to Jesus's instructions (see Mark 9:9). After his resurrection, they would describe the glory that they had witnessed and heard (see 2 Pet 1:16-18).

9:37-41 Upon descending **the mountain**, they found **a large crowd** gathered around the other disciples. A father emerged from the mass of people and begged Jesus to deliver his demon-possessed **son**, who was routinely tortured and injured (9:38-39). Though the **disciples** had tried **to drive** the evil spirit **out** of him, they failed (9:40). Jesus rebuked the **unbelieving** crowd and told the father to **bring** his **son** to him (9:41).

9:42-45 When **the boy** was brought forward, **the demon** sent him into **convulsions**, but Jesus supernaturally healed him by merely rebuking the spirit (9:42). As everyone marveled at Jesus's power, he again predicted to his disciples his impending betrayal and death (9:44; see 9:21-22). **But they did not understand** how he could exercise such extraordinary authority one moment and be killed the next. So, being **afraid to ask him about it**, they remained silent (9:45).

9:46-48 The disciples had **an argument** about **who was the greatest of them** (9:46). Though they tried to keep their disagreement from Jesus, he knew **their inner thoughts** (9:47), which is a reminder that the wisest thing to do with our concerns, emotions, thoughts, and desires is to come clean in prayer. Whether we speak about them or not, he already knows about them the moment they enter our minds. Trying to hide them from him is pointless.

Importantly, Jesus didn't rebuke his followers for desiring to be great, but he did want them to understand what true greatness looks like. Kingdom greatness is not obtained in the way the world obtains greatness. To illustrate this, Jesus stood **a child** in front of them (9:47). Kingdom greatness, he then implied, is achieved through service (see Mark 9:35-37). This includes caring for and valuing those with the lowest social standing in culture because they can do nothing for you in return. (Children were a prime example of this social tier in the first century.) To welcome a child would be to welcome Christ and the Father (9:48). This humble mindset is the road to greatness.

9:49-50 When **John** and the other disciples **saw someone driving out demons** in Jesus's **name**, they **tried to stop** his unsanctioned ministry since he wasn't part of the Twelve (9:49). But Jesus corrected their thinking: **Whoever is not against you is for you** (9:50). The Twelve were not to think of themselves as an exclusive body of representatives; they were to rejoice that God's kingdom power was being manifested by others too. God's people ought to celebrate the ministries of fellow Christians when they are carried out in a spirit of love and faithfulness to God and his Word.

IV. MINISTRY ON THE WAY TO JERUSALEM (9:51–19:27)

❧ A. Belief and Unbelief (9:51–11:54) ❧

9:51-56 As the time drew near **for him to be taken up**—a reference to his death, resurrection, and ascension—Jesus resolutely made his way toward **Jerusalem** (9:51). On

the way, he would pass through Samaritan territory, so **he sent messengers ahead** in order that **the Samaritans** might **make preparations for him** (9:52). But since he was going to Jerusalem, the Samaritans **did not welcome him** (9:53). This passage reflects the racial and theological divide that existed between the Jews and the Samaritans (see, e.g., John 4:9, 20). When **James and John saw** how the Samaritans responded, they asked Jesus if they should **call down fire from heaven** to destroy them (9:54). But Jesus **rebuked them** for their animosity (9:55). The Son of God had not come to destroy but to save, to deliver, to heal (see John 3:17). Such should be the attitude of his followers as well.

9:57-58 As Jesus traveled during his ministry, he encountered a number of would-be followers. They made a show of wanting to be his disciples, but in the end they weren't willing to make a commitment. God's goal is not merely your salvation but your discipleship. He doesn't want you to just show up for church on Sunday; he wants you to be a visible, verbal follower of Jesus Christ every day of the week.

Luke provides three examples of people who talked a good game but who were unwilling to get off the bench. The first man told Jesus, **I will follow you wherever you go** (9:57). That sounded good, but Jesus has a way of going beneath your words to discover your motives. He told the man that **foxes** know where they'll sleep at night, and **birds** know where they'll nest for the evening. **But the Son of Man has no place to lay his head** (9:58). What he meant was that following his call to become a disciple will become hard at times. There will be uncertainties. In fact, "All who want to live a godly life in Christ Jesus," Paul says, "will be persecuted" (2 Tim 3:12). Will you follow him no matter what the cost?

9:59-60 When Jesus urged another man to follow him, the man pleaded, **First let me go bury my father** (9:59). This sounds like a reasonable request, but he wasn't asking to go to a funeral. He was referring to the *future* death of his father. He wanted to make sure that he received his father's inheritance. Then, when his circumstances were secure, he'd be equipped to be a disciple.

Jesus challenged him: **Let the dead bury their own dead, but you go and spread the news of the kingdom of God** (9:60). In other words, he said, let those who are *spiritually* dead worry about such things. You can't delay the calling of the kingdom. It's

God's comprehensive rule over every area of life. Indeed, he calls you to be his follower right now, where you are, with whatever you have—not later, somewhere else, with a little bit more.

9:61-62 A third man responded in the affirmative but asked to **say good-bye to those at his house** (9:61). To this, Jesus insisted that anyone **who puts his hand to the plow and looks back** is not **fit for the kingdom of God** (9:62). In other words, Jesus considered this man double-minded. He compared him to someone plowing a field while looking behind himself, and such farming will result in nothing but a crooked field. The man's mention of his family left the door open for them to persuade him to rethink his decision. To all who want to have it both ways—being the Lord's disciple *and* maintaining control of their own lives—Jesus insists, "You have to get off the fence to follow me. You must not allow even family relationships to trump loyalty to me."

10:1-4 Jesus **appointed seventy-two** other disciples to carry out the mission of proclaiming the kingdom of God in word and deed. They were to travel **ahead of him** two-by-two to the towns that he would be visiting (10:1). He gave them instructions similar to those he gave to the Twelve when he sent them out (see 9:1-2). There was much to do— **the harvest** was **abundant**—but those willing to do the kingdom work were **few** (10:2). Moreover, they would face much hostility; they would be **like lambs among wolves** (10:3). The mission required haste. They were not to carry supplies that one would normally take on a journey, and they were to avoid unnecessary distractions (10:4). There was no time to waste. But God would provide for all of their mission needs. The disciples were to be completely focused on their calling and not be deterred from it. Living God's kingdom agenda isn't easy. But since the King is sovereign, the outcome is sure.

10:5-12 The people they encountered who accepted the kingdom message would support them by demonstrating hospitality (10:5-8). The disciples would be granted authority to perform miracles as a way to authenticate their message about **the kingdom of God** and of the coming Messiah (10:9). Even those who rejected the message were to be informed of the nearness of the kingdom, but the disciples were to wipe **the dust** off of their **feet** as a **witness against** the unbelieving towns (10:10-11). That **it will be more tolerable for Sodom than for that town** (10:12) is a reference to the wicked Old Testament city destroyed by burning sulfur that rained from heaven (see Gen 19:24-25). Those who reject the clear revelation of God's kingdom message through his emissaries, then, will incur a more severe judgment than they. The rejection of greater light brings greater judgment.

10:13-15 Jesus then pronounced judgment against three Galilean cities that had rejected his past ministry: **Chorazin ... Bethsaida ... Capernaum** (10:13, 15). Bethsaida was the hometown of Peter, Andrew, and Philip (see John 1:44). Capernaum was Jesus's home during his ministry (Matt 4:13). The condemnation of the towns would be based on the revelation they'd received. The principle is this: the greater the level of revelation, the greater the judgment for rejecting that revelation. Jesus declared that the coastal cities of **Tyre and Sidon** north of Israel **would have repented long ago** if they had seen and heard what these Galilean cities had (10:14-15). Capernaum, in particular, had witnessed many of Jesus's miraculous works (4:31-41; 7:1-10), yet the majority of its inhabitants rejected him.

10:16 Whoever listens to you listens to me When Christ's disciples speak his Word, the listeners hear Christ; therefore, **whoever rejects** them **rejects** Jesus. And to reject Christ is to reject **the one who sent** him—God the Father. That chain reaction of rejection will lead to eternal damnation.

10:17-20 When **the seventy-two returned**, they were full of **joy**. Jesus's powerful **name**, even without his physical presence, was enough to give them authority over **demons** (10:17). To this, Jesus testified that he'd **watched Satan fall from heaven like lightning** (10:18)—a reference to the judgment on Satan when he rebelled against God and

was kicked out of heaven (see Isa 14:12-14). Not only does this affirm the pre-existence of Jesus and that he was involved in Satan's judgment, but it gives insight into how the devil was sentenced to earth, setting the stage for the angelic conflict and the creation of mankind (see Eph 6:12; Heb 2:6-8). It also shows that the spiritual warfare ministry of the seventy-two was a continuation of the defeat of Satan. Yet as special as this spiritual authority was, it was not to be the followers' primary source of joy. More important than having wicked **spirits** submitting to them was having their **names ... written in heaven** (10:20). To have a relationship with God—to be citizens of the kingdom and headed toward glory—is to be our supreme source of joy. Everything else is a bonus.

10:21-22 Jesus **rejoiced in the Holy Spirit** that God's will was being fully accomplished in his ministry, and he praised the **Father** for the spiritually inspired success of the seventy-two. His prayer demonstrates the unique, intimate relationship he shared with the Father, as well as his exclusive prerogative to **reveal** the Father to others who trusted in his words and works through childlike faith.

10:23-24 Jesus then said **privately** to his **disciples** that they belonged to that spiritual category of trusting children that he had just spoken of. They had seen and heard what many Old Testament saints had longed to **see** and **hear**: the coming of the Messiah and his kingdom.

10:25-27 An expert in the law came to **test** Jesus, asking him how one could **inherit eternal life** (10:25). This concept of inheritance involves not merely entering the kingdom, which is by faith alone in Christ alone, but receiving the rewards and quality of life associated with following God. When Jesus asked the man how he read **the law**, the man answered by quoting two passages of Scripture (10:26-27): Deuteronomy 6:5, **Love the Lord your God with all your heart, with all your soul, with all your strength, and with all your mind** and Leviticus 19:18, **Love your neighbor as yourself.**

Jesus identified these as the two greatest commands from the Old Testament (see

Matt 22:34-40). To love God is to passionately pursue his glory; to love your neighbor is to compassionately, righteously, and responsibly seek his or her well-being. The two are inseparable.

10:28-29 Jesus affirmed the man's answer (10:28). But the man wanted **to justify himself**, so he asked, **And who is my neighbor?** (10:29). The question implied that he had no objective way to determine whom he should be loving. His assumption was that some people didn't qualify to be his neighbor and were therefore undeserving of his love, so he wanted to know how Jesus would define a neighbor.

10:30-32 Jesus answered by telling a parable. A man was traveling **from Jerusalem to Jericho**, a distance of seventeen miles that involved a 3,000-foot drop in elevation. It was a dangerous journey. On the way, he fell among **robbers** who **beat him** and left him **half dead** (10:30). The first two travelers to pass by the crime scene were **a priest** and **a Levite**. Now, priests were responsible for interpreting the law and officiating in the temple. The Levites (the tribe from which the priests came) assisted the priests in their duties.

Perhaps these men had fulfilled their religious obligations in Jerusalem and wanted to get home, or perhaps they were on their way to Jerusalem and didn't want to be late. Maybe they thought contact with the man would contaminate them or were afraid of being robbed themselves should they stop. Regardless, they didn't want to be bothered with this stricken man, so they **passed by on the other side** of the road (10:31-32).

The priest and Levite are, unfortunately, like many religious people today who hold tenaciously to their theology but ignore those around them who are suffering. Broken people need someone to show them compassion and give them life—not merely talk to them and pray for them. This priest and Levite had run into an unplanned ministry opportunity, and they ignored it.

10:33-35 Then **a Samaritan** came along. The Jews' hatred of the Samaritans had historical roots (see 9:51-56; John 4:9, 20). When Assyria conquered the northern kingdom of Israel, many Israelites were exiled from the land, but some were left behind. Then the Assyrians brought many captives from other lands to Israel. As a result, many Jews intermarried with these peoples. The Samaritans of Jesus's day were descendants of those intermarriages, and the animosity between Jew and Samaritan was strong. Nevertheless, this Samaritan **saw the man** and **had compassion** on him, bandaging **his wounds**, taking him to **an inn**, and paying for his care.

Jesus chose to use a despised and rejected person to make his point. And our neighbors, too, are found in any and every racial and ethnic group. The care demonstrated by the Samaritan reflects the care that should be demonstrated by God's people. The church of Jesus Christ ought to be a place where wounded people can come to receive love and life.

10:36-37 The man had asked Jesus, "Who is my neighbor?" (10:29). But Jesus turned the question around and asked, **Which of these three do you think proved to be a neighbor?** (10:36). In other words, he pressed, what kind of neighbor are you? Tellingly, the expert in the law couldn't even bring himself to utter the words, "The Samaritan." He simply said, **The one who showed mercy to him.** So Jesus exhorted him, **Go and do the same** (10:37).

Your neighbor is the person whose need you see, feel, and are able to meet. Mercy is compassion to a person in need. When you see a legitimate need with which you emotionally connect, and which is within your capacity to address, you are called in the name of Christ to demonstrate compassion. Love is not abstract and theoretical. It is concrete and requires action toward those who are hurting. Our devotion to God must be seen. To experience the life, blessing, and reward that the kingdom has to offer, we are to reflect our vertical love for God through our horizontal love to others.

10:38-39 Martha and Mary were intimate friends of Jesus. We see these sisters several times in the Gospels—the most well-known occasion being when Jesus raised their brother Lazarus from the dead (John 11:1-44).

On this day, **Martha** had invited Jesus **into her home** for dinner (Luke 10:38). But while she was making preparations for her honored guest, her sister **sat at the Lord's feet . . . listening to what he said** (10:39). Every time we see Mary, in fact, she's at Jesus's feet. In John 11:32, she fell at Jesus's feet. In John 12:3, she anointed Jesus's feet. Here in Luke, she's listening at Jesus's feet. To sit at one's feet was the position of a learner in submission to a teacher. Mary loved Jesus and wanted to absorb everything he had to say.

10:40 But Martha was distracted by her many tasks. And somewhere in the midst of her preparations, it dawned on Martha that she was preparing alone. Her sister was listening to a sermon, and Martha was becoming fed up with fixing the Messiah's dinner all by herself. So she stormed out of the kitchen, ignored her sister, and said to Jesus, **Lord, don't you care that my sister has left me to serve alone? So tell her to give me a hand.** Just like that, Martha went from welcoming Jesus as her guest to blaming him for not caring about her. Notice her inference: Jesus, if you really cared, you wouldn't be talking right now. You'd do things my way. Martha was so upset with her sister Mary that she refused to address her directly but asked Jesus to do so for her.

Martha had become so focused on what she was doing for Jesus that she'd become frustrated with Jesus. Luke says she was "distracted by her many tasks." It's easy for us to be distracted from God when we think we're ministering to him. So remember that when your service to God affects your relationship with God and your fellowship with other believers, there's a problem.

10:41-42 Jesus told Martha that she was **worried and upset about many things, but** only **one** was **necessary.** Martha had become so distracted by all of her service that she had forgotten the main thing. **Mary,** Jesus said, **has made the right choice, and it will not be taken away from her** (10:42). Jesus wasn't suggesting to Martha that there was no work to be done. Rather, he was saying that when your work for the Lord damages your relationship with him, you need to reassess the amount of work and motivation for

your service. Mary had chosen what matters most: relationship. She wasn't going to miss an opportunity to sit in Jesus's presence and humbly hear him teach. Mary understood that "man does not live on bread alone but on every word that comes from the mouth of the LORD" (Deut 8:3).

God wants you to serve him—but not at the expense of your relationship with him. If lately you are doing more for God but are colder toward God, if you are working harder but praying less, you need to do a spiritual reassessment.

11:1 The disciples witnessed Jesus's intimate prayer to the Father on many occasions (3:21-22; 5:16; 6:12; 10:21-22). After **he finished** this time, **one of his disciples** asked him to **teach** them how **to pray.** They had observed his commitment to and the results of his prayer, and they wanted to have the same experience.

11:2 So Jesus spoke a model prayer for the disciples. He opened it this way: **Father, your name be honored as holy.** Prayer begins with our orientation to God. You must know the one to whom you are praying. Many of us have a mere thimble full of prayer because we have a thimble full of knowledge about God. If you know little about God, you won't have much to say.

We begin by addressing him as "Father." Regardless of what your earthly father was like, your heavenly Father is perfect. And he is "holy"—that is, he is separate from and transcendent over his creation. Holiness, in fact, is God's chief characteristic. It's the attribute that ties all of his other attributes together. His love is holy; his justice is holy; his mercy is holy. He is "holy, holy, holy" (Isa 6:3). We are to honor his name (i.e., his character and reputation) as holy, recognizing him as pure and distinct. He alone is to be worshiped and obeyed.

In light of this, we are to pray that his **kingdom** would **come.** God's people are to be about God's program. The people of the King are called to follow his kingdom agenda. As the Creator, God rules over the world, and his priorities are to be our priorities. No aspect of life falls outside of his kingdom rule. Our allegiance is to be total.

11:3 To accomplish God's program, we depend on his provision. So we must pray that he would **give us each day our daily bread.** If we occupy ourselves with kingdom business, we can count on God supplying our needs (see Phil 4:19); nevertheless, we must ask for those provisions. Notice also that we must ask "each day." We want to receive enough provision to last for years, but he will supply *today* everything that we need to accomplish his will *today.* This keeps us in daily dependence on him.

11:4 Disciples are to pray that God would **forgive us our sins.** Forgiveness is the cancellation of a debt. You cannot have dynamic fellowship with God if you are not dealing seriously with your sin. As the Holy Spirit reveals sin in our lives, we are to address it. We don't deal with last week's sins today; we deal with today's sins today. "If we confess our sins, he is faithful and righteous to forgive us our sins and to cleanse us from all unrighteousness" (1 John 1:9). But we also must **forgive everyone in debt to us.** Just as God in Christ forgave us, so we are called to forgive one another (see Eph 4:32).

    Do not bring us into temptation is a request for God to keep or protect us from any situation that we can't handle. Every Christian will experience trials. What we need is God's help in the midst of trial so we can say no to temptation. The purpose of prayer is to prepare you for a trial so that you can face the trial, honor God, and grow spiritually as a result.

11:5-8 To encourage his disciples to petition God boldly in prayer in spite of their circumstances, Jesus told them a story of two friends. One **friend** went to the home of the other **at midnight,** asking for **bread** to feed a visitor who'd come to stay with him (11:5-6). Yet, even though the time was inconvenient and his family was in bed, the man met his need **because of his friend's shameless boldness** (11:7-8). Bold persistence in a relationship with God leads to needs being met.

11:9-13 Jesus follows this story with an invitation to his disciples to seek God in prayer with boldness. We are not to sit back and wait for things to happen. Jesus calls us to

ask . . . seek . . . knock in prayer (11:9), and his followers can expect a positive response from the Father if they come to him boldly (11:10). Human fathers, though sinful, intuitively give food to their children rather than something that will harm them (11:11-12). How much more, then, will our perfect, holy, and righteous **heavenly Father** discriminate and **give good gifts** to his children? The best heavenly gift that God gives to those who ask is **the Holy Spirit** (11:13), who in the new covenant delivers God's will to his children. Thus, the Holy Spirit is available to operate on God's behalf through our prayers for our benefit and through us for the benefit of others.

11:14-16 Jesus continued to perform miraculous works that confirmed his identity. Once when he cast **a demon** from a **mute** man so that the man **spoke,** some of his opponents accused him of driving out demons under the authority of **Beelzebul, the ruler of the demons**—that is, Satan (11:14-15). Others demanded he give them **a sign from heaven** to prove his authority (11:16)—as if his miracles weren't sign enough.

11:17-19 Jesus responded by explaining how ridiculous their accusations were. **If Satan** were driving out his own demons, he would be counteracting his own purposes (11:17-18). The devil will one day be defeated, but it won't be because he defeats himself. He'll be vanquished at the hands of King Jesus (see Rev 20:10). Furthermore, if Jesus were driving out spirits by the hand of Satan, then by whose power were the followers of the religious leaders driving them out? They couldn't condemn Jesus without condemning themselves (11:19).

11:20-23 On the other hand, if he cast **out demons by the finger**—that is, the power—**of God,** then he must be Messiah bringing his **kingdom** (11:20). Jesus affirmed that he is the one with power over Satan, the **strong man** (11:21). Though Satan had bound people, Jesus demonstrated that he was **stronger** by overpowering his evil forces, setting captives free, and dividing up Satan's **plunder** (11:22). The refusal of Jesus's accusers to gather fellow Israelites to follow him as Messiah made them complicit in the eventual destruction of the nation (11:23). There can be no neutrality when it comes to Jesus Christ. He is either the Messiah or he is Satan, but he cannot be a mere teacher or miracle worker.

11:24-26 Jesus explained what happens **when an unclean spirit** leaves the person it had possessed and returns (11:24). When it finds its former "home" **put in order**, it returns with a whole host of demons **more evil than itself**. Then **that person's last condition is worse than the first** (11:25-26). It's not enough, then, to be rid of demonic activity in one's life. The emptiness must be replaced by the Holy Spirit. There is no neutral position. We must not create a comfortable lodging place for the demonic realm to call home.

11:27-28 A woman pronounced a blessing on Jesus based on the blessedness of his mother Mary (11:27), but Jesus made it plain that admiration of him does not replace obedience to him (11:28). Attending church, praising God, and carrying a Bible are worthless when there is disobedience in one's life.

11:29-32 Jesus condemned those demanding **a sign** of him (11:29; see 11:16). Gentiles in **Nineveh** believed **Jonah**, though he performed no miracles (11:30). **The queen of the south** traveled from far away **to hear** Solomon's God-given **wisdom**, though he offered no heavenly signs (11:31). How much more should the crowds believe the Son of Man who is far **greater than** either Jonah or Solomon? (11:32). The only sign they would receive was **the sign of Jonah** (11:29), who had spent three days and nights in the belly of a huge fish, leading to the repentance of the Gentiles (see Matt 12:40). Similarly, Jesus would spend three days and nights in the earth—dead and buried. Then he would rise again as proof of his identity as the Messiah, leading also to the repentance of the Gentiles.

11:33-36 To listen and respond to Jesus is to receive light. When a person's **eye** reacts properly to **light**, he can function normally. Jesus keeps you from operating in **darkness** and deception (11:34-35). When you respond to God's truth, you are enabled to live an authentic life (11:36). You will clearly see your life's path and make wise decisions.

11:37-41 Jesus accepted the invitation of **a Pharisee** to join him for lunch (11:37). When Jesus didn't engage in the **ritual** cleansing that was the Pharisees' custom before a meal, the Pharisee was shocked (11:38). So Jesus used the opportunity to show the Jewish leaders that their spiritual focus was wrongly placed and dishonoring to God. They were scrupulous to cleanse **the outside of the cup and dish**, but they weren't concerned with cleansing the **greed and evil** within their own hearts (11:39). Since God made the external and the internal aspects of man, obedience needs to be both internal and external. Proof that one is clean on the inside is demonstrated through service to others, particularly charitable giving to those who can do nothing in return (11:41). How you handle possessions reveals major truth about your inner life.

11:42-44 The encounter in 11:37-41 set off a chain reaction in which Jesus pronounced "woes" of condemnation on the Pharisees and experts in the law. He criticized them for their commitment to externals and the appearance of righteousness. They diligently tithed garden herbs and loved **the front seat in the synagogues**, but they failed to show **justice** to their neighbors and **love for God** (11:42-43). Instead of serving as safe spiritual guides for people, the Pharisees caused others to be contaminated—just as a Jew would become defiled by walking on an **unmarked** grave without knowing it (11:44; see Num 19:16).

11:45-46 Hearing this, **one of the experts in the law** told Jesus that he was insulting them too by saying such things (11:45). Thus, Jesus turned his sights on them. He pronounced woe on these experts in the Mosaic law because their legal prescriptions went far beyond the Old Testament commandments so that they loaded people down with **burdens** too heavy to bear (11:46). They neglected the very law that they studied and contributed to moving people further from God rather than closer to him.

11:47-52 While these men were happy to build **monuments** for dead **prophets**, it was the live ones they had a problem with (11:47-51). As their ancestors killed the Old Testament prophets, so the Jewish religious leaders wanted to kill the Messiah. In reality, these **experts in the law** were anything but experts. They had **taken away the key to knowledge** (11:52). They lacked true knowledge of God, and they denied others access to the truth as well.

11:53-54 The **scribes** and **Pharisees** didn't take this lying down. They vigorously opposed him. They constantly questioned him, plotted against him, and sought **to trap him** in his answers. Jesus was their archenemy.

⤞ B. Discipleship and Opposition
(12:1–15:32) ⬳

12:1-3 Jesus was getting national exposure. **Many thousands** were flocking to him. After his recent conflict with the religious leadership (11:37-54), Jesus warned his disciples about **the leaven of the Pharisees, which is hypocrisy** (12:1). Leaven or yeast slowly and imperceptibly permeates a batch of dough, and similarly the undetected wicked influence of the Pharisees could spread to many—even the disciples—if not guarded against. Nevertheless, Jesus promised that nothing would remain **hidden** forever. Secret motives and **whispered** words would one day be public knowledge (12:2-3). Nothing can be hidden from God.

12:4-7 Knowing his disciples were fearful of the Pharisees' power and threats, Jesus comforted his **friends.** In light of their intimate connection with him, he urged them, **Don't fear.** Though some of them would experience martyrdom at the hands of their opponents (see, e.g., Acts 12:1-2), such enemies of God could **kill the body** and **do nothing more** (Luke 12:4). The one to truly **fear** is God, **who has authority to throw people into hell** (12:5). In the grand scheme of things, birds are insignificant and of very little value, yet God cares for them. How much greater is his care for his children who trust him (12:6-7)?

12:8-10 When Jesus's followers acknowledge him, even in a hostile context, God will **acknowledge** and honor them. They also will experience access to the Father in prayer as the Son confesses them before the Father (12:8). Conversely, the believer who does not publicly acknowledge association with Jesus will not receive recognition by the Father. He will lose rewards and experience unanswered prayer, since he won't be endorsed by the Son (12:9).

Jesus gave two examples of negative responses—words spoken against him and blasphemy **against the Holy Spirit.** Words spoken against Jesus could **be forgiven.** But blasphemy against the Holy Spirit **will not be** (12:10). Why? Because it is deliberate, willful rejection of Christ whom the Holy Spirit reveals. To reject the Holy Spirit's testimony of Christ is to reject the only means God has provided for salvation.

12:11-12 God would not abandon his disciples. When they appeared before **synagogues and rulers and authorities** in Jesus's name, **the Holy Spirit** would give them the words to say. An example of the fulfillment of this promise is seen in Peter's testimony in Acts 4:8-12.

12:13-14 The more things change, the more things stay the same. Greed, covetousness, the desire to be rich—such cravings transcend time and culture. Jesus was confronted by a man who wanted his **brother to divide the inheritance with** him (12:13). But Jesus answered, **Who appointed me a judge or arbitrator over you?** (12:14). Jesus was on a spiritual mission. He had just finished teaching about the Holy Spirit (12:10, 12) and was talking about eternal, heavenly matters. But this man wanted to distract Jesus with temporal, earthly matters.

12:15 So Jesus used this as an opportunity to teach the crowds (note that he spoke to **them** not merely to "him") about material strongholds in a person's life. He said, **Watch out and be on guard against all greed.** Greed comes in all shapes and sizes. It appeals to people from all walks of life, regardless of income or social status. No one is immune to the attacks of covetousness. It is when the material takes priority over the spiritual. The man who spoke in 12:13 was as greedy as his brother whom he was complaining about. Therefore, we must have our defenses up at all times **because one's life is not in the abundance of his possessions.** What you possess has nothing to do with what life is all about. Life does not consist of stuff.

12:16-19 Jesus illustrated with **a parable.** A **rich** man had a bumper crop. Having nowhere to store his harvest, he tore down his **barns** and built **bigger ones** (12:16-18). Once he solved the problem of what to do with all his stuff, he kicked back and said to himself, **Take it easy; eat, drink, and enjoy yourself** (12:19). At no point did he say, "God has blessed me with an abundance. I have more than I need. Whom can I serve with what I have?" There was no room in this man's life for anyone else. God doesn't bless you just so you can build bigger storage spaces. He blesses you so that you can also bless others.

12:20-21 What was God's assessment of this man and his materialism (i.e., prioritizing the physical over the spiritual)? **You fool!** Why was he a fool? After all, he had invested well; his retirement was secure. The problem was that his **life** was about to be **demanded of** him. **And the things** he'd **prepared** would go to someone else (12:20). The man saw gain; God saw loss. The man saw life; God saw death. According to Jesus, this man is what a person is like **who stores up treasure for himself and is not rich toward God** (12:21). The man's wealth is not the issue here; it's that he hoarded it for himself with no thought of God or the temporal nature of life. Though he was physically rich, he was spiritually poor. He had everything except God—which means he had nothing.

12:22-26 Jesus explained **to his disciples** that it's foolish to be anxious about **food** and **clothing** because **life** consists of **more than** these things (12:22-23). The disciples were more valuable than unclean **birds** that **God feeds** and cares for. How much more will he take care of his own children who trust him? (12:24). Worrying is foolish because it cannot bring about change to your situation. Think of it as a rocking chair: it will get you moving, but it can't take you anywhere. You

can't add a single second to your **life-span by worrying** (12:25). If you can't accomplish something so minuscule, **why worry about** the big stuff (12:26)?

12:27-32 Like the birds of the air (12:24), **wildflowers** don't worry. Yet God cares for this simple aspect of his creation. And he is much more inclined to care for you (12:27-28). Another reason that worrying is foolish is because the Gentiles are **anxious** about the things of life. It's one thing for unbelievers to worry, but believers who trust in a heavenly **Father** should not by filled with anxiety (12:29-30). Instead, Christ's disciples have access to the spiritual realm when they prioritize the **kingdom** of God (12:31), with its promises and provisions, because the kingdom is the divine rule. As defenseless as his children are in the world, it would be the Father's joy to give them (the **little flock**) kingdom covering (12:32).

12:33-34 The disciples were to divest themselves of anything that would prohibit the pursuit of the kingdom and its priorities (12:33). They were to pursue spiritual treasures above physical ones. When we value heaven more than earth, we build and protect true wealth that's unlike **treasure** accumulated here that is subject to decay and theft (12:33). The heart follows treasures and not vice versa. So wherever you want your **heart** to be, put your **treasure** there; your heart will follow it (12:34).

12:35-40 As the disciples waited for Christ to return (that is, for his second coming), they were to **be ready for service** (12:35). He compared them to servants **waiting for their master to return** (12:36). They were to be **alert** and ready to receive him (12:37). Christ's disciples today are also to **be ready** always, for his return could come at any time (12:40). During the darkness of this present age, followers of Jesus are to be ready and active. Our witness must be visible and clear. We must live with a sense of expectancy as we wait for our master's appearing.

12:41-44 Peter wondered whether this teaching was for the Twelve only or for the crowd in general (12:41). Jesus's response demonstrated that his teaching was for anyone who would receive and apply it. He introduced an illustration with the question, **Who then is the faithful and sensible manager his master will put in charge?** (12:42). The answer is **that servant whom the master finds doing his job when he comes** (12:43). The faithful servant of Jesus is the one who is given a task, performs it, and is blessed by it. The reward that Jesus will give to the faithful steward will be far greater than the challenges encountered in this service. Faithful believers will receive greater responsibility at the return of Christ (12:44).

12:45-48 Conversely, if one is not expecting his master to return and is, therefore, unfaithful and foolish, that person will be judged (12:45-46). Unfaithful believers will be weighed based on the level of their knowledge and responsibility, which means leaders will receive greater judgment than those who didn't have that level of responsibility (12:48).

12:49-53 Jesus would bring **division** and not **peace** (12:51) because some would accept him, while others would reject him. In fulfillment of Scripture, in fact, he would bring division even within the same **household** (12:52; see Mic 7:6). His ministry would be **fire** that devours (12:49), but the goal of that blazing fire is national purification. This would involve Jesus's **baptism** (12:50)—which is not a reference to his baptism by John, but a metaphorical reference to his coming death and resurrection to bring about redemption for those who respond to him.

12:54-56 Jesus acknowledged that **the crowds** knew how to interpret the natural signs of clouds and wind and make correct weather predictions (12:54-55). However, they couldn't interpret the signs of the **time** (12:56). They couldn't understand spiritual signs. Though many of them had seen the signs of his ministry, they refused to conclude that Jesus was the promised Messiah. They couldn't see what was right in front of their eyes.

12:57-59 Jesus compared their failure to discern the signs before them (12:54-56) with someone settling a legal dispute. Rather than waiting to address a matter in court, a person should seek to settle out of court to avoid prison time and to decrease the penalty that has to be paid (12:58-59). Likewise, those who continue to reject Messiah, while the day of opportunity to be reconciled to God is available, will in the end face a more severe judgment.

13:1-5 Pontius Pilate was a ruthless ruler. Even before he confronts Jesus at the end of Luke's Gospel, readers learn of the Roman governor's violent nature. **Some people** told Jesus that **Pilate** had killed some **Galileans** and **mixed** their **blood** with **their sacrifices** (13:1). Perhaps they wanted to hear Jesus condemn Pilate for that; instead, Jesus used the opportunity to urge his listeners to **repent** (13:3).

Repentance is the inner resolve and determination to turn from sin and toward the Lord. The goal of repentance is to reverse, avoid, limit, or cancel divine judgment and the consequences of sin. That **eighteen** people were **killed** when a **tower in Siloam fell** on them (13:4) is a sobering reminder that regardless of the circumstances, death can come when we least expect it—on the righteous and the unrighteous. Unless we as believers repent of sin, we are subject to temporal judgment, including physical death. **Unless** the lost **repent**, they will **perish** eternally in hell (13:5).

13:6-9 Jesus told a parable of **a fig tree** that bore no **fruit** (13:6). The owner ordered his **worker** to **cut it down** (13:7). But the worker asked that the owner let him **fertilize** the tree. If it still bore no **fruit next year**, then he would **cut it** (13:8-9). A fig tree's well-being is dependent on its bearing fruit, and this parable follows Jesus's exhortation that people repent of sin (13:1-5). If good fruit is absent from a person's life, some kind of judgment is certain. Inner repentance leads to an external demonstration of righteousness. Without visible fruit, professions of repentance are as genuine as a barren fig tree pretending to be healthy.

13:10-13 On another occasion, Jesus **was teaching** in a synagogue **on the Sabbath** when a woman came in **who had been**

disabled by a spirit for over eighteen years (13:10-11) Her disability caused her to be **bent over** and unable to **straighten up at all** (13:11). For almost two decades, then, she saw nothing but the ground. But this day, Jesus set her **free** (13:12). She was instantly healed and **began to glorify God** (13:13) when she accepted his invitation to come to him.

Though she had a physical ailment, Luke tells us twice that it was not the real source of her problem. She had been "disabled by a spirit" (13:11) and "bound" by "Satan" (13:16). Thus, she was under demonic attack. The evil spirit was the root, and her physical deformity was the fruit. But Jesus was able to see what no one else could and took care of the spiritual issue.

13:14 Unfortunately, **the leader of the synagogue** was not happy. He had an order of service, and Jesus deviated from it. The Sabbath was for worship alone, not for **work**. He thus told the crowd to come on the other **six days** of the week to get **healed**, but **not on the Sabbath** (13:14). But if the man had known what fury Jesus was about to unleash, he perhaps would've kept his mouth shut.

13:15-17 Hypocrites! The synagogue leader and his companions didn't practice what they preached. Even **on the Sabbath**, they would **untie** their **ox or donkey** and **lead it to water** (13:15). Such care for an animal is expected and not the kind of work that God had prohibited by the Sabbath command. So, if an animal is worthy of such mercy, shouldn't **a daughter of Abraham**—a member of the covenant and its promises—be **untied** from her **bondage on the Sabbath day?** (13:16). With that stinging criticism from Jesus, **all his adversaries** in the synagogue **were humiliated**, and the **crowd was rejoicing** (13:17).

13:18-21 Jesus offered two parables to describe God's work in bringing his **kingdom** (13:18). The kingdom is like a small **mustard seed** that grows large so that **birds** can nest **in its branches** (13:19). While God's kingdom work began small and with seemingly insignificant people (fishermen and tax collectors), it would grow significantly and accommodate all of its citizens. The kingdom is also **like leaven**, which **a woman** mixed throughout a large batch **of flour** (13:20-21). Over time, God's kingdom would continue to expand and work its way throughout the world.

13:22-30 As Jesus continued his ministry en route **to Jerusalem**, a person asked—in light of the opposition and rejection he was experiencing—if **only a few people** were **going to be saved** (13:22-23). Jesus made it clear that to enter the kingdom, one would have to accept him and his words. No other option was possible. He illustrated this by describing a **homeowner** shutting **the door** to his home, representing the kingdom. Once the entrance is closed, no one will be able to enter. Those who cry out for entry after it's too late will face the consequences (13:24-27). Meanwhile, the godly will be saved. **Some who are last will be first, and some who are first will be last** (13:30) implies a great reversal. For example, though many Jews would reject Jesus, Gentiles would receive him. Gentiles would be among the first to enter, while Jews would be the last.

13:31-33 Some **Pharisees** approached Jesus and warned him to leave because **Herod** wanted **to kill** him (13:31). Herod Antipas was the tetrarch over Galilee, appointed by the Romans. This warning was presumably a pretext to get Jesus out of their area. But even though it meant traveling through Herod's district, Jesus had to reach **Jerusalem**. That's where he would **complete** his **work** (13:32-33). He had a mission to fulfill and a schedule to meet, and neither Herod nor the Pharisees could thwart him.

13:34-35 At the thought of **Jerusalem**, the city that housed the temple, Jesus lamented over its centuries of rejecting God and his **prophets**. As a **hen** desires to protect her **chicks**, Jesus longed to do the same for Jerusalem (13:34). But since the holy city was rejecting its Messiah, he would have to reject her. After his death and resurrection, Jerusalem would **not see** him again until his return to reign as King in his kingdom when believing Jews call out, **Blessed is he who come in the name of the Lord!** (13:35).

14:1-6 Jesus was invited to eat at the home of one of the leading Pharisees (14:1). One of those present was a man suffering from dropsy, a condition that resulted in his **body being swollen with fluid** (14:2). Knowing that they were watching to see what he would do, Jesus asked them if it was **lawful to heal on the Sabbath** (14:3). No doubt they felt the same as the synagogue leader in 13:10-17, believing that it was unlawful to do so. But they were unwilling to answer and remained **silent**, so Jesus **healed** the man (14:4). Then he asked a question that showed they were hypocrites. Any one of them would help a **son** or an **ox** on **the Sabbath** if it fell into **a well** (14:5). So why was it wrong in their eyes to do good to a man by healing him? They were twisting God's law to suit themselves.

14:7-11 When he noticed how the invited guests chose places of honor closer to the host, Jesus exhorted them to do otherwise. Rather than choosing the **best** seat, only to be asked to give it up to a **more distinguished person**, they should instead choose **the lowest place.** This would give the host an opportunity to move them up to a better seat (14:8-10). Notice that the first scenario results in humiliation, but the latter results in honor. **Everyone who exalts himself will be humbled, and the one who humbles himself will be exalted** (14:11).

The Pharisees exalted themselves, assuming that they held important positions in the kingdom. But Jesus sought to teach them the relationship between humility and exaltation. We are to live with an eternal perspective in mind—not with a desire for notoriety. Followers of Christ are not to exalt themselves by presumptuously seeking positions of greatness; rather, they are to assume lower positions of service and allow God to exalt them. Humility is the true path to glory.

14:12-14 Having spoken to the guests, Jesus then addressed the host. He encouraged him not to **invite** merely his **friends** and **relatives** to share meals with him (14:12) but to invite the **poor** and **lame**—those who could not **repay** him (14:13-14). Inviting the outcasts of society would indicate that he had an eternal perspective, since repayment for such would come at the resurrection (14:14).

14:15-24 One of the guests with him at the meal declared, **Blessed is the one who will eat bread in the kingdom of God!** (14:15). So Jesus told a parable emphasizing that many who expected to be there would be excluded from the kingdom. The **man** in the parable **invited** a large number of people to a **banquet** (14:16-17), but they all gave excuses explaining why they could not come (14:18-20). Angry at this, the man sent his **servant** to gather the rejected of society—**the poor, maimed, blind, and lame** (14:21). Even after this, there was **still room** for more (14:22). So the host insisted that others be brought in, since those originally **invited** had rejected it (14:23-24). Since most of the Jews rejected Jesus, his kingdom message would be declared and received by others—by the Gentiles. There's no excuse for rejecting Jesus. The King and his kingdom must have priority.

14:25-26 Tremendous **crowds** were following Jesus (14:25). But he knew that many of them were merely following him for the show he was providing: the miracles, the healings, the exorcisms, the teachings. So he wanted them to understand that to truly be his disciple was costly and said that unless one were to **hate his own father and mother, wife and children, brothers and sisters,** he could not be a disciple (14:26). Now, that's a pretty tall order. Aren't children called to love and honor their parents (see Exod 20:12)? Aren't husbands called to love their wives as Christ loved the church (see Eph 5:25)? What did Jesus mean?

The parallel passage in Matthew helps explain. In Matthew 10:37, Jesus said, "The one who loves a father or mother more than me is not worthy of me; the one who loves a son or daughter more than me is not worthy of me." The point is that Jesus deserves priority over every other relationship. If you must choose between Jesus and a family member, then, Jesus wins. Our love for him must be so strong that unbelieving family members think our love for them might as well be *hate*, because we chose to obey Jesus rather than do what they want. This is the call to and cost of discipleship.

14:27 The cost of discipleship doesn't end there. **Whoever does not bear his own**

cross and come after Jesus cannot be his disciple. Crucifixion was the Roman execution of choice for heinous criminals. And a condemned person had to carry his cross to his crucifixion site. So Jesus's listeners knew what he was talking about. Many had seen it happen. Jesus was telling them that becoming his disciple would involve some form of suffering. Not every Christian disciple's suffering is the same, but every Christian disciple will suffer. This is because to bear your cross and follow Jesus means to identify with him. And as Jesus told his disciples, "If they persecuted me, they will also persecute you" (John 15:20).

14:28-33 Continuing his discussion of the cost of discipleship, Jesus described two scenarios. In the first, a man decided to **build a tower.** Before beginning, a wise builder would naturally **calculate the cost** to ensure that he could **complete** the work (14:28-30). The second scenario involved a **king** going to **war.** Long before battle begins, a king must make sure that he has sufficient forces to defeat his enemy; otherwise, he should seek **terms of peace** (14:31-32). The follower of Christ must similarly count the cost of what it means to truly be his disciple. In particular, a disciple must **renounce all his possessions** (14:33). That means recognizing that you are a *steward* of all you have; you are not an *owner.* God has given you possessions to manage. You are to thank him for them, use them for his glory, and bless others with them. What you must *not* do is claim ownership.

14:34-35 Jesus concluded his discourse on the costly nature of discipleship with an observation about the nature of salt: **Salt is good.** That statement meant more to Jesus's hearers than to most of us. To them salt not only flavored food but preserved it (there were no refrigerators!). **But if salt loses its taste, how will it be made salty?** (14:34). The obvious answer is that it won't be. The saltiness of salt is what makes it salt! Without that, **it isn't fit for . . . the manure pile.** Likewise, unless a Christian is willing to endure the costly nature of being a disciple, he is useless to the kingdom of God. **Let anyone who has ears to hear listen** (14:35) is Jesus's

way of saying, "Though everyone has ears, not everyone listens. You'd better pay close attention."

15:1-2 One of the things **the Pharisees and scribes** hated about Jesus was that he spent time and ate with those whom they despised: **tax collectors and sinners.** As far as the religious leaders were concerned, such people were to be avoided—not welcomed. They thought Jesus should be hanging out with religious people who were serious about keeping the law.

15:3-6 Aware of this, Jesus told them a **parable** about a shepherd who owned **a hundred sheep** and lost **one** (15:3-4). Wouldn't the man **leave the ninety-nine** and search for the missing one (15:4)? The way Jesus asked the question implies that the answer he expected was "yes." Of course the shepherd would search for his lost sheep. Once it was found, he'd even hold a party and call everyone to **rejoice with** him over it (15:5-6). Jesus clearly considered this to be the most natural response to finding a lost lamb.

15:7 **In the same way,** the host of **heaven** party more **over one sinner who repents than over ninety-nine righteous people who don't need repentance.** Hanging out with safe sheep when one is lost is as absurd as hanging out with only righteous people when you want to urge lost people to repent or to encourage erring believers to be restored to the Father. If you want to rescue the lost, you've got to go where they are. Sinners who repent, and erring saints who return, experience restored fellowship with God, and heaven rejoices. The Pharisees and scribes should have rejoiced too.

15:8-10 Jesus's second parable was similar to the first. **A woman** lost **one** of her **ten silver coins.** Wasting no time, she went to great lengths to find it, lighting **a lamp,** sweeping **the house,** and looking everywhere (15:8). **When she** found **it, she** called **her friends and neighbors** to **rejoice with** her (15:9). The principle is the same as the previous parable. Heaven gets excited to see **one sinner** who repairs his relationship with God through repentance (15:10). The Lord goes to great lengths to see salvation and restoration take place in a sinner's life. Do we?

15:11-13 The third parable continues the same emphasis as the first two (15:3-10). All three parables tell one story. They were prompted by the religious leaders' anger at Jesus for welcoming and eating with tax collectors and sinners (15:1-2). Why would Jesus spend time with dirty sinners rather than righteous folks?

Jesus's third story is usually called "The Parable of the Prodigal Son." However, the prodigal son—the reckless and wasteful son who got himself lost—is not the focus of the story. He's an essential character, but ultimately the parable is about the older brother because Jesus was speaking to the Pharisees and scribes (15:1-3). Jesus wanted these self-righteous leaders who had no compassion on the lost to see themselves in him.

The story opens on **a man** with **two sons** (15:11). **The younger** of the two had become tired of the restrictions of living at home. He wanted to spread his wings; he wanted his freedom. So he asked **his father** to give him his portion of the inheritance. It would not be normal, of course, for a father to divide his estate before his death. But this one did it (15:12). In requesting his inheritance, it was tantamount to wishing his father were dead. The younger son was thus independent, unencumbered, and well-funded. And it soon became clear why he wanted to leave: **He squandered his estate in foolish living** (15:13). You can always find out what a person cares about when you look at how he spends his money. A person's heart is revealed by his credit card statement. "Where your treasure is, there your heart will be also" (12:34).

15:14-16 Then the bottom fell out. When all his money was gone, **a severe famine struck that country** (15:14). The young man became so desperate that he accepted a job feeding **pigs** (15:15). Don't miss that. This is a Jewish man accepting a job to feed unclean animals. Furthermore, he had nothing to eat: **He longed to eat his fill from the pods that the pigs were eating.** The "pods" were carob pods, the fruit of the carob tree, which were used to feed animals. Since no one gave him

anything to eat (15:16), the pigs were doing better than he was. His newly acquired "freedom" had come at a high cost.

15:17-19 Then **he came to his senses**. Sometimes God lets us experience a tremendous fall because that's what it takes to open our eyes. It took life on a pig farm to bring this young man to his senses. He finally saw things as they really were and realized he should never have left home. His **father's hired workers** were doing better than he was (15:17). So he resolved to return, confess his sin against God and his father, declare his unworthiness, and ask to be treated like the **hired** help (15:18-19).

15:20-22 While the son was still a long way off, his father saw him. What does that imply? The father had been looking for him. When he saw his son, he was overwhelmed **with compassion, ran** to him, and embraced him (15:20). The son tried to say his rehearsed confession, but the father cut him off, commanding his servants to dress his boy with a **robe**, a **ring**, and **sandals** (15:21-22).

That's a beautiful picture of salvation and the restoration of erring saints. A destitute sinner comes to a holy God in repentance and faith with nothing to offer but desperate need. God the Father responds with love and compassion, granting the sinner all the privileges of sonship in the family and showers him with blessings—"every spiritual blessing in the heavens in Christ" (Eph 1:3).

15:23-24 Yet all of this wasn't enough. The father told his servants, "Let's have a party." He had them kill **the fattened calf** and prepare a **feast** (15:23). For his **dead** son was **alive again**; his **lost** son was **found** (15:24).

15:25-30 Finally, Jesus introduced his listeners to the **older son**. Since he's telling this parable to the Pharisees and scribes (15:1-3), everything in the story leads us to the response of the older son. He was coming in from **the field**—which means he had been working—when **he heard music and dancing** (15:25). That meant there was a party going on that he didn't know about. When he learned that the celebration was for his brother, **he became angry** and refused to go inside (15:26-28). The young fool had run off, wasted his inheritance, and wrecked his life. Then he came home to be treated like a king?

When his father tried to plead with him, the older son pointed to his years of service and obedience (15:28-29). In spite of all his hard work, he never even received **a goat** to **celebrate with** his **friends** (15:29). **But when this son of yours came** (Notice that he didn't refer to him as "my brother" but as "this son of yours") **who has devoured your assets with prostitutes, you slaughtered the fattened calf for him** (15:30). In other words, "I slave for you all these years and get nothing. But he blows your money on decadence and gets a bash."

15:31-32 But the older son didn't understand. He was **always with** his father (15:31). Safe, secure, provided for, loved. His brother, meanwhile, had been **lost** and as good as **dead.** Given that he was **found** and **alive**, it was only natural **to celebrate** (15:32).

What makes a shepherd rejoice? When a straying sheep is found. What gives a woman joy? When she finds her lost coin. What causes a father to celebrate? The return of his lost son whom he loves. The Pharisees and scribes were angry with Jesus for welcoming tax collectors and sinners (15:1-2) because they had failed to understand the heart of God. He longs for the lost to be found. He's filled with joy when a single sinner repents and comes home. He rejoices when a relationship is restored.

Notice the abrupt ending of the parable. We don't know how the older brother responded. Did he return to the house with his father to celebrate his younger brother's repentance? Or did he walk away in disgust and jealousy? There's no answer because Jesus intended the religious leaders to ask themselves these questions. Were their hearts where God's heart is? Is yours?

⌖ C. Living in Light of the Kingdom
(16:1–19:27) ⌖

16:1-4 Jesus told a parable to remind his disciples to live and use earthly resources from an eternal perspective. **A rich man** had a **manager** who handled his business transactions, but the manager was found to be corrupt. He had been **squandering** his boss's **possessions** (16:1). So the rich man **called** in his manager to fire him (16:2). As we'll see, the manager may have been dishonest, but he wasn't stupid. Immediately, the wheels of his mind started spinning: **What will I do? . . . I'm not strong enough to dig; I'm ashamed to beg** (16:3). He didn't have the physique to be a ditch digger, and he was too proud to stand on the street with a tin cup. He was a white-collar guy who didn't want to give up his lifestyle. He needed a plan so that when his job was gone, **people** would **welcome** him **into their homes** and provide for him (16:4).

16:5-9 So he went to every person who owed his **master** money and cut deals with them. To one who owed **a hundred measures of olive oil**, he had him **write fifty** on his **invoice** (16:5-6). To another who owed **a hundred measures of wheat**, he had him **write eighty** on his **invoice** (16:7). Clearly he was being dishonest toward his employer, but he wasn't trying to get his job back. He was trying to ingratiate himself with his boss's debtors so that they might take him in or give him a job. Later, his **master praised the unrighteous manager**—not because he was faithful—but **because he had acted shrewdly** (16:8). Though he was out of a job, he cleverly found a way to provide for his future.

Jesus then told his disciples the lesson behind the parable: **The children of this age are more shrewd than the children of light** (16:8). In other words, unbelievers are often sharper than believers are. Though the manager had messed up his past, the man cunningly set things in motion to secure his future. So what should believers do? **Make friends for yourselves by means of worldly wealth so that when it fails, they may welcome you into eternal dwellings** (16:9).

Jesus reminded his disciples that they were stewards of their earthly resources, not owners. So they should use their possessions with eternity in mind. Christians ought to use their earthly resources wisely and generously for kingdom purposes. In this way, lives will be changed and people saved by the gospel. Such shrewd kingdom people will be greeted in eternity by a welcoming committee of friends whose lives were forever transformed by their righteous use of worldly wealth.

16:10-13 Jesus spoke a principle that we often see demonstrated in life. **Whoever is faithful in very little is also faithful in much.** Likewise, the one who **is unrighteous in very little is also unrighteous in much** (16:10). If you aren't dependable in small things, you're not likely to be dependable in more significant ones. So if you're unfaithful in your use of **worldly wealth, who will trust you with what is genuine?** (16:11). You must be trustworthy with what God has loaned you in this life if you expect to receive anything of true value in eternity. And the only way to properly use money and possessions is to use them in service to God. You cannot have **two masters. . . . You cannot serve both God and money** (16:13). Either your money will serve God, or you will ask God to serve your money. Live your life and use your resources with eternity in mind.

16:14-15 After Jesus concluded this weighty teaching about money, **the Pharisees** scoffed at him because they **were lovers of money** (16:14). Jesus pointed out that God knew their **hearts**, regardless of how they justified themselves before others. They were self-deceived hypocrites, using their wealth to camouflage their greedy hearts. But **what is highly admired by people is revolting in God's sight** (16:15).

16:16-17 **The Law and the Prophets**, which is a shorthand way of referring to the Old Testament, teach about the kingdom of God—the rule or reign of God. This was an unbroken message up until the coming of John the Baptist. **Since then, the good news of the kingdom of God has been proclaimed** (16:16)—that is, the good news that the King of the kingdom, Jesus Christ, had come. God's Word is more reliable than creation; it will last forever and not fail (16:17).

16:18 Jesus gave an example of the abiding authority of God's Word: **Everyone who divorces his wife and marries another woman commits adultery.** Marriage was God's idea. In the beginning he declared that a man and woman who came together as husband and wife are "one flesh" (Gen 2:24). Therefore, divorce and remarriage without a biblically authorized reason (see commentary on Matt 5:31-32; 19:1-9)—ignores the authority of Scripture and results in adultery, since God has not cancelled the original marriage. Some of the Pharisees would permit divorce for virtually any reason, so they were not the law keepers they claimed to be.

16:19-21 Jesus had just finished teaching about having the right perspective on money (16:1-13) and condemning the Pharisees for loving money (16:14-15) when he told a story about **a rich man**—who was meant to illustrate the Pharisees—and **a poor man named Lazarus** (16:19-20). This wealthy man had access to every good thing life had to offer (16:19). Lazarus, on the other hand, was not only destitute but also **covered with sores** (16:20). **He longed** to eat the crumbs that **fell from the rich man's table**, but all he received were **dogs** licking **his sores** (16:21). The contrast between the two men couldn't be starker. From a purely earthly perspective, the rich man was the clear winner. But Jesus was about to provide a heavenly perspective.

16:22-24 Although the two men had virtually nothing in common in life, one day both suffered an event common to all human beings: death. However, after death, each experienced a complete reversal of fortune. When **the poor man died**, the **angels** took him **to Abraham's side** or bosom (an idiom for heaven), but when **the rich man** died, he suffered **torment in Hades** (16:22-23). In the Greek translation of the Old Testament, the Greek word *hades* was used to translate the Hebrew word *sheol*—the grave, the realm of the dead. In the New Testament, the unrighteous are tormented in Hades (see 10:15). Thus, it is synonymous with hell.

Many people believe there is no afterlife. They argue that those who die simply cease to exist. But Scripture claims otherwise. The two men had different destinations: the poor man went up; the rich man went down. But both continued to exist. Some Christians prefer to believe that the unrighteous experience annihilation after death rather than conscious, eternal punishment. But Jesus disagrees. The rich man was *not* annihilated. Not only did he undergo torment, but he could also see Lazarus in comfort **a long way off**, speak to Abraham of his **agony**, and cry out for **mercy** (16:23-24). His faculties were intact.

16:25-26 In response to the rich man's plea for mercy, Abraham gave him two answers. First, the man was receiving the just consequences of a life that had rejected God. While they lived, the rich man **received** his **good things**, and **Lazarus received bad things.** Yet, the rich man neither acknowledged God nor sought to care for his neighbor Lazarus with the wealth God had given him. Therefore, while **Lazarus** was **comforted**, the rich man was justly punished with **agony** (16:25). Second, Abraham told him that the reversal was permanent. **A great chasm** was **fixed between** them so that no one could **cross over** from one side to the other (16:26). The judgment of hell is so awful because it is forever. There is no escape.

16:27-28 Even though his destiny was permanent, the rich man had another request. His reference to Abraham as **Father** (16:27; cf. 16:24) shows that the rich man was Jewish, a descendent of Abraham, a member of the covenant people of Israel. Thus, he reflects the Pharisees who thought they were right with God simply because of their ancestry. He asked Abraham to send Lazarus back from the dead to his **five brothers** so that they didn't end up in the same **place of torment** (16:28).

16:29-30 Abraham stated the obvious: **They have Moses and the prophets; they should listen to them** (16:29). In other words, he said, "Your brothers have God's Word. Let them heed it. If they believe God's promise of eternal life like their father Abraham did, they will be saved." But that wasn't good enough for the rich man. After all, *he* had access to God's Word, but he hadn't believed it. So, from his perspective, his brothers needed something more: **If someone from the dead goes to them, they will repent** (16:30). "Give them a tremendous miracle—a resurrection from the dead," he reasoned, "and then they'll believe and turn to God."

16:31 That's when Abraham ended the conversation: **If they don't listen to Moses and the prophets, they will not be persuaded if someone rises from the dead.** If one will not believe God's Word, a miracle will not convince him. Though Jesus had performed countless miracles, still the Pharisees refused to believe he was the Messiah. And while he would rise from the dead, even that miracle would not persuade them (see Acts 5:30-33). Their hearts were hard. They were unwilling to believe.

Death comes for all. There is a heaven to be embraced and a hell to be shunned. All human beings will experience one or the other for eternity. This is what makes the church's gospel mission so vital. We must do all we can to win people to faith in Christ. For at the grave, it will be too late.

17:1-2 Divine judgment for sin is bad. Divine judgment for causing others to sin is worse. Jesus warned against causing **little ones**—defenseless, vulnerable believers—**to stumble**, to fall into sin. At the final judgment, the one who leads them to sin will prefer to have a huge rock **hung around his neck** before being dropped in the ocean to drown (17:2). That's how severe God's retribution against such a person will be.

17:3-4 Christ's disciple is to counteract sin in the life of a **brother** or sister Christian with a loving **rebuke** and forgiveness—not once but repeatedly: **If he sins against you seven times in a day**, you are to **forgive him** seven times. The number seven doesn't denote a limit to forgiveness. In the Bible, seven is the number of completion. Thus, our forgiveness of one another is to be complete. We are always to be ready to forgive our brothers and sisters when they repent.

17:5-6 How did Jesus's **apostles** respond to being commanded to forgive someone who sinned against them repeatedly in one day? **Increase our faith.** Fundamentally, they were telling him, "What you're expecting isn't normal. It would require superhuman faith to be able to do that. Please, supersize our faith!" Often we think that God's asking for something that's out of our reach, as if he wants the impossible.

But Jesus corrected their perspective: **If you have faith the size of a mustard seed**, you can command a tree to **be uprooted and planted in the sea** (17:6). In other words, such faith can cause the impossible to happen. The apostles wanted Jesus to give them a supersized faith, but Jesus said, "You only need a mustard-seed-sized faith." The *size* of the faith, then, isn't the issue. The *right kind* of faith is. That's because the right kind of faith packs a powerful punch. A mustard seed is incredibly small. So, you don't need big faith; you need true faith. Don't be concerned with how big your faith is; be concerned with how big *the object of your faith* is. We don't require tremendous faith. All we need is genuine faith in our tremendous God.

17:7-10 Jesus explained a scenario to his disciples. He wasn't changing the subject. He was explaining what it looks like to have a mustard-seed **faith** that can do the impossible (17:6), like enabling a believer to forgive someone "seven times in a day" (17:3-4). If **a servant** went inside after working in **the field**, his master wouldn't tell him **sit down** and **eat** (17:7). Instead, the master would expect the servant to finish his work by feeding him. Only then would the servant sit down to his own meal (17:8). Moreover, the master wouldn't **thank** the **servant** for doing his job. To work in the field and prepare his master's meal was what was expected of him (17:9).

There was nothing surprising about this master-servant relationship that Jesus described. He simply wanted his disciples to apply the concept to their relationship with God. True faith, mustard-seed faith, submits to divine authority. The duty of a servant is to honor and obey his master. The reason why many Christians lack the faith to forgive (see 17:3-5) is because they're out of spiritual alignment. They make demands of God, and they're unwilling to submit to him. If you are out of alignment with your Master, you're not acting with mustard-seed faith. Trust God and obey him in the little things. Then you won't need him to "increase your faith" because you'll have the right kind of faith to do what seems impossible.

17:11-13 On his way to **Jerusalem**, Jesus **passed between Samaria and Galilee** (17:11). In **a village** he encountered **ten men** with the same problem: **leprosy**. Upon learning that Jesus was visiting their town, they cried out, **Jesus, Master, have mercy on us!** (17:12-13). Not only were they suffering from the dreaded physical skin condition, but it also affected them relationally and psychologically. Lepers had to identify themselves by yelling, "Unclean! Unclean!" so that people would not get close enough to be contaminated by them. Furthermore, they had to live apart from others and could not participate in communal life (see Lev 13:45-46). Their condition was incurable from an earthly perspective. They needed heavenly intervention.

17:14 They asked for mercy, and Jesus demonstrated it. He commanded them to **show** themselves **to the priests**. As they went, **they were cleansed**. This instruction about going to the priests wasn't pulled out of thin air. According to Leviticus 13-14, the priests were responsible for examining those with skin diseases and pronouncing them either clean or unclean. Once they were declared "clean," they could return to full participation in the covenant community under the blessing of God.

17:15-16 When he noticed that he was cleansed, one of them **returned and, with a loud voice, gave glory to God** (17:15). He didn't care what anyone thought: he was not ashamed to give God vocal praise for intervening in his life. In addition, he wanted to identify with Jesus. He knew where his blessing had come from. So **he fell facedown at his feet** and thanked him. But Luke tells us that this man **was a Samaritan** (17:16; see commentary at 10:33-35 on Samaritans).

17:17-19 Seeing only one of the **ten** return to praise God, Jesus wanted to know what happened to the rest (17:17). Nine Jews and one Samaritan were healed, but only the **foreigner** returned to **give glory to God** (17:18). So Jesus said to him, **Get up and go on your way. Your faith has saved you** (17:19). The word translated "saved" can also mean "deliver" or "make well," depending on the context. Though all ten had been healed of their leprosy, clearly the Samaritan received something more as a result of his praise. The nine experienced external blessing, but only one experienced an internal spiritual blessing in response to his visible and vocal faith and gratitude to God. Many people, even believers, only want physical blessings from the Lord and lose out on the true spiritual blessings that come through worship, praise, and thanksgiving.

17:20-21 The Pharisees asked Jesus **when the kingdom of God would come.** They wanted dates and times. But Jesus told them it was not **something observable** (17:20). The kingdom was not coming as they expected. They couldn't point to it. The reason was because **the kingdom of God** was in their **midst** (17:21). The King was standing in front of them. He was the one who would usher in his kingdom, yet they didn't recognize him.

17:22-25 Turning from the antagonistic religious leaders, Jesus taught his **disciples** about the coming kingdom. He urged them not to **follow** after false teachers with their deceitful claims (17:22-23). The coming of the Son of Man will be clear to all. It will not be done in secret (17:24). **But first it [was] necessary that he suffer many things and be rejected** (17:25). The disciples still didn't understand that Jesus had come to suffer and die as an atoning sacrifice for sin. His return to rule on his throne in his millennial kingdom is still future.

17:26-29 He compared his future coming to **the days of Noah** (17:26). Back then, there was both deliverance and destruction— deliverance for Noah and his family, and destruction for everyone else. **People went** about their daily lives, giving no attention to God, until **the flood came** and his judgment fell (17:27). Similarly, it will be like **the days of Lot** (17:28). People were absorbed in the normal activities of life so that they failed to take God seriously. But when **Lot left Sodom,** God's retribution fell on the city (17:29). The rapture will introduce **the days of the Son of Man** (17:26).

17:30-33 Christ's future return and God's accompanying judgment will follow a pattern similar to these Old Testament times of deliverance and judgment (17:30). So people must be prepared. We must not be attached to material possessions like **Lot's wife** was (17:31-32). Judgment will be swift and comprehensive. There will be no time to reclaim anything. Those who fail to take God's Word seriously and disobey will bear the consequences.

17:34-37 A great separation of humanity will take place. No matter where they are or the time of day, some **will be taken** in judgment, and some **will be left** to enter into the kingdom (17:34-35). People will be split apart based on their relationship to God. Where will this happen? **Where the corpse is, there also the vultures will be gathered** (11:37). Judgment, then, will come wherever death reigns. Just as a dead body draws vultures, those who are spiritually dead will draw divine punishment.

18:1-3 Jesus told parables for various reasons and to explain diverse spiritual principles. On this occasion, he told **a parable** to his disciples **on the need to pray always and not give up** (18:1). The story included two characters: **a judge** who had neither **fear** for **God** nor **respect** for **people** (18:2) and **a widow** who wanted **justice against** an unnamed **adversary** (18:3). From the outset, this doesn't look good for the widow. Since the judge cared nothing for God or people, what could persuade him to rule in her favor? Moreover, in those days, if a widow didn't remarry or had no family to care for her, she could easily end up destitute.

18:4-5 The widow needed action from the judge, but **he was unwilling.** He despised justice. She was too insignificant for him to trifle with. The problem for him was that she wouldn't give up! In spite of his rejection of her case, the widow kept **pestering** him. So **even though** he didn't **fear God or respect people,** he eventually gave the woman **justice.** Why? So that she wouldn't **wear** him **out.** The Greek word translated "wear out" can also mean to "ruin one's reputation." Either way, he finally ruled in her favor against her opponent. The key to the widow's persistence was her legal right to justice.

18:6-8 Having concluded the parable, Jesus asked his disciples a question: **Will not God grant justice to his elect who cry out to him day and night?** (18:7). If an unjust judge who doesn't fear God will rule justly in a poor woman's favor because of her persistence based on the law, won't a holy God give justice to his people who pray to him with perseverance based on his Word? **Nevertheless, when the Son of Man comes, will he find faith on earth?** (18:8). The question isn't about God's willingness to be just. The question is about our willingness to persevere by faith in prayer based on God's Word. Believers have a legal right to answered prayer.

18:9-10 He told another **parable to some who trusted in themselves that they were righteous and looked down on everyone else** (18:9). A lot of people fall into that category. **A Pharisee** and **a tax collector** went **to the temple to pray** (18:10). Most of Jesus's listeners would have assumed that they knew who the hero and the villain were in this story (but things are not always as they appear). The Pharisees were strict adherents to God's law. The common people considered them the epitome of orthodoxy and godliness. Meanwhile, the tax collectors were considered vile sinners. They were Jews who collected taxes from their own countrymen on behalf of the Roman Empire, and they often took extra to line their own pockets (see 19:1-10).

18:11-12 The Pharisee spent his prayer praising himself. He thanked God that he was generous, fulfilled his religious obligations, and was **not like other** depraved **people**—especially the **tax collector**. He used other people as his standard of righteousness. And since he surpassed all of them, he celebrated his own virtue. Since he was "better" than everyone else, he assumed that God must be pleased with him.

18:13 Meanwhile, **the tax collector** stood **far off** at the outer edges of the temple, ashamed to approach God or even **raise his eyes to**

him. Unlike the Pharisee, he didn't praise himself but struck **his chest** and begged for God's **mercy**. He recognized that he was **a sinner**. Since God himself is the standard of righteousness, the tax collector knew that he fell far short. His only hope was God's grace.

18:14 Many of Jesus's parables feature surprising reversals or shocking endings (see 10:25-37; 12:13-21; 14:16-24; 15:11-32), and this one is no exception. Jesus said that the tax collector—not the Pharisee—went home **justified** (declared righteous) before God. He understood that he was a sinful man before a holy God, and he humbled himself in God's sight, pleading for mercy so that he might find salvation and restoration. The Pharisee, on the other hand, was self-righteous and self-sufficient. He was elevated in his own eyes because he compared himself to other sinners. Had he looked at himself in light of God's character, he would have realized that he—like the tax collector—was a sinner. Grace will only be given to the humble, not to the proud (see Jas 4:6).

18:15-17 As parents brought their **infants** to Jesus **so he might touch** and bless them, the disciples **rebuked them** (18:15). But Jesus rebuked the disciples right back: **Let the little children come to me** (18:16). Then he used the opportunity to illustrate the disposition one must have to enter the kingdom and receive kingdom rewards. God's **kingdom** is only available to those who **receive** it **like a little child** (18:17). In a parent-child relationship, children bring nothing to the table but their own weakness, need, and dependency. In the same way, we come to God through Jesus Christ, entirely dependent on him for both kingdom entry and kingdom blessing. These verses also support the importance of bringing children to Christ while they are young.

18:18 A man approached Jesus and asked, **Good teacher, what must I do to inherit eternal life?** In Matthew, he's described as a "young man" (Matt 19:20). Luke says here that he was **a ruler**. All three Synoptic Gospels tell us he was rich (Matt 19:22; Mark 10:22; Luke 18:23). Thus, he is typically referred to as the "rich young ruler."

18:19 Jesus asked the man, **Why do you call me good? . . . No one is good except God alone.** Before talking to him about how to get to heaven and to receive the rewards of inheritance, Jesus wanted to make sure he understood what it meant to be good. Furthermore, the only way Jesus could be called good is if he were in fact the Son of God.

18:20-23 When Jesus recited several of the Ten **Commandments** that address our relations with other people, the man assured him that he had **kept** them **all** since childhood (18:20-21). The man was either a bold liar or self-deceived. But rather than challenge this claim of perfect righteousness, Jesus appealed to the one thing that he knew the man lacked: love for his neighbor. So he told him to **sell** everything and give it **to the poor** so that he would **have treasure in heaven. Then come, follow me** (18:22). Upon hearing this, the man **became extremely sad, because he was very rich.** His love for his wealth superseded his love for people.

18:24-27 Jesus used his encounter with the rich young ruler to warn his disciples about the dangers of wealth. It is **hard** for the rich **to enter the kingdom of God** (18:24). In fact, squeezing **a camel . . . through the eye of a needle** would be easier (18:25) because the rich think that they are self-sufficient and that their wealth makes them acceptable before God. The disciples were shocked: **Then who can be saved?** (18:26). Jesus answered, **What is impossible with man is possible with God** (18:27). In other words, anyone can be saved—rich or poor. All are sinners, and all deserve eternal judgment. It's not possible for a single person to receive salvation apart from God's grace. God can work in the hearts and minds of even the wealthy to humble them so that they look to him, rather than to their riches, as their source of eternal life.

18:28-30 Since the rich young ruler was unwilling to sacrifice his wealth for the kingdom of God, **Peter** wanted to know what would happen to those believers who actually responded faithfully, who were willing to leave everything for Jesus (18:28). Jesus promised that a true commitment of discipleship would be rewarded. No sacrifice made for God's kingdom agenda gets overlooked or forgotten. Faithful kingdom disciples will be repaid, sometimes in history but ultimately in eternity (18:29-30).

18:31-34 Jesus had predicted his approaching sacrificial death twice already (9:21-22; 9:43-45). As they neared **Jerusalem**, he once again clearly explained to them what was about to happen. **Everything** that was **written** concerning **the Son of Man** in **the prophets**—the Old Testament Scriptures—would be fulfilled (18:31). He would be **handed over to the Gentiles** (i.e., the Romans). They would mock him, **spit on** him, **flog** (beat) **him**, and **kill him** (18:32-33). Yet as unbelievable as this was, the last part was even more confusing: **he** would **rise on the third day** (18:33). The disciples were baffled; they couldn't **grasp** it (18:34). They couldn't understand how the Messiah could be killed in Jerusalem—the place where he was to be enthroned. They would need the Holy Spirit to provide full spiritual clarity.

18:35-39 As Jesus and his disciples **approached Jericho**, a **blind** beggar asked what the commotion was all about (18:35-36). When he learned that **Jesus** was **passing by**, he knew he couldn't miss this opportunity (18:37). He had heard of Jesus's healing ministry, so he cried out, **Jesus, Son of David, have mercy on me!** (18:38). Though the crowds tried to shut him up, **he kept crying out all the more** (18:39). He knew that if this man were the Messiah, he could transform his helpless situation. How desperate are you for Jesus to intervene in your circumstances?

18:40-43 Though Jesus had planned to walk right by, he **stopped** in response to this cry of faith and asked the blind man what he wanted (18:40-41). Did Jesus really have to ask? Could the man's need be more obvious? But Jesus wanted the man to make his request for all to hear. **Lord . . . I want to see** (18:41). With the blind man's verbal proclamation of faith in Jesus's ability to restore sight, Jesus healed him **instantly**. As soon as he had regained his sight, he became a disciple, following Jesus and **glorifying God**. This is the only appropriate response to the work of God in your life. As a result, the people who witnessed it gave praise to God (18:43).

This served as a spiritual lesson to the nation of Israel. If they would respond to the Messiah and acknowledge their spiritual blindness, God would grant them spiritual life and entrance into the kingdom that Jesus was offering. But would they humble themselves and receive him?

19:1-2 The blind man wasn't the only person in Jericho to experience God's grace that day. A wealthy **chief tax collector** named **Zacchaeus** had heard that Jesus was **passing through**. Since the Jews were subjugated by Rome, they paid taxes to the Roman Empire. Rome would employ Jews to collect taxes from their own people. However, tax collectors would often collect extra for themselves. So, needless to say, the Jews weren't fond of Jewish tax collectors. In fact, they considered them traitors. That's why in the New Testament you typically see tax collectors mentioned alongside prostitutes and sinners (e.g., Matt 11:19; 21:31; Luke 15:1). As a chief tax collector, Zacchaeus would have had a lot of money and few friends.

19:3-5 Though Zacchaeus wanted **to see** Jesus, he couldn't because **the crowd** was so big and **he was a short man** (19:3). So he resorted to the only option left: **he climbed up a sycamore tree** (19:4). His desperation caused him to do something a bit below his dignity. But Zacchaeus was willing to endure some public scorn to see the one everyone had been talking about. When Jesus saw him, he said, **Come down because today it is necessary for me to stay at your house** (19:5). Notice, he didn't say, "I'd like to stay at your house." No, this was a divine appointment: "it is necessary."

19:6-7 Zacchaeus was thrilled. He **welcomed** Jesus **joyfully** (19:6). But the crowd was in shock: **He's gone to stay with a sinful man** (19:7). Some people in the crowd were probably hoping to have Jesus as their own dinner guest. Why had he chosen this sinner instead? Because sinners were the reason he had come in the first place (19:10).

19:8-10 Knowing that he was a sinner and knowing the grace that Jesus was showing to him, Zacchaeus said, **I'll give half of my possessions to the poor, Lord. And if I have extorted anything from anyone, I'll pay back four times as much** (19:8). That's what repentance looks like. Repentance doesn't merely say, "I'm sorry," it makes amends for wrongdoing. The crowds had complained that Jesus went to this wicked man's home. But after Jesus got through with him, Zacchaeus would be a better man for the community and restore what he had taken from them. Jesus observed, **Salvation has come to this house** (19:9). Zacchaeus's outward actions were testimony of an inward transformation. This was why Jesus came—**to seek and to save the lost** (19:10).

19:11-12 Once again Luke gives us the reason why Jesus told one of his parables. The people **thought the kingdom of God was going to appear right away** (19:11). Jesus proceeded to tell a story of **a nobleman** who **traveled to a far country to receive ... authority to be king** (19:12). Jesus wanted his hearers to understand that his kingdom reign was not coming immediately. He would depart and return at a later time.

19:13-14 In the meantime, God would expect his followers (i.e., believers) to manage what he gave them until the King returned to be enthroned in Jerusalem. The nobleman commanded his servants to **engage in business** on his behalf **until** he returned. To **ten of his servants**, he gave **ten minas**, one to each (19:13). A mina was a coin worth about a hundred days' wages. The nobleman's **subjects hated him**, though, and declared that they didn't want him **to rule over** them (19:14). God's servants are called to follow him in obedience, even though the world rejects the King and his kingdom.

19:15-19 When the nobleman returned, he **summoned** his **servants** so he could learn how they had managed his **money** (19:15). The **first** servant had proved faithful with his master's resources and **earned ten more minas** (19:16). For this stewardship, the master rewarded him with **authority over ten towns** (19:17). The **second** servant was also faithful (19:18). He didn't earn as much as the first, but he earned in accordance with his ability. So the master similarly rewarded him (19:19).

Everything we have is a gift from God. We must recognize that we are stewards of our resources, not owners. God will call us to give an account for how we have managed our money, our possessions, our spiritual gifts, our relationships, and our time—and will reward or judge his people accordingly.

19:20-27 The next servant simply returned his master's mina to him. He considered his master **a harsh man** so he did nothing with his money (19:20-21). His lack of stewardship was fueled by a lack of relationship and the failure to take seriously the knowledge of his master's expectations and the fact that he would return. When the master heard the servant's testimony, he chastised him. He could have at least put the **money in the bank** to earn a minimal amount of **interest** (19:22-23). But even this was too much for him. This servant (an unfaithful believer) wanted nothing to do with the responsibilities of stewardship. Unfaithful believers will experience negative consequences at the judgment seat of Christ (see 1 Cor 3:15). So his money was given instead to one of the servants who had been faithful (19:24). Don't miss out on the eternal rewards that God has for faithful stewards who manage well what he has given them. Faithfulness results in kingdom reward; unfaithfulness results in lack and loss of reward (19:26). But worst of all are the consequences that await those who make themselves God's **enemies** (19:27; see 19:14). These will experience eternal judgment.

V. MINISTRY IN JERUSALEM (19:28–21:38)

19:28-35 As Jesus and his disciples drew near to **Jerusalem**, he had **two of his disciples** go into a **village**. There they would find a colt ... **on which no one [had] ever sat** (19:28-30). If anyone were to ask them why they were taking the colt, all they needed to say was **The Lord needs it** (19:31). As the disciples obeyed, everything happened exactly as the Lord told them (19:32-34). Then Jesus climbed on the animal and rode toward his destination (19:35).

Three things are clear from these events. First, Matthew informs his readers that these actions fulfilled the prophecy of Zechariah 9:9 (see Matt 21:4-5). Jesus was publicly presenting himself as the Messiah. Second, Jesus's knowledge of what would happen demonstrated his omniscience to his disciples. Third, a colt that had never been ridden would not accept a rider easily. But Jesus showed himself to be the Master over creation. He came not on a horse as an emerging military king but as a humble servant of peace, represented by the colt.

19:36-40 As Jesus made his way on the colt, people spread **their clothes on the road** in honor of him (19:36). The crowd also began to **praise God joyfully** and shouted, **Blessed is the King who comes in the name of the Lord** (19:37-38), quoting from Psalm 118. The people openly acknowledged Jesus as the Messiah, and he received their praise. But this was too much for **the Pharisees.** They demanded that Jesus **rebuke** his **disciples** (19:39). It was their way of saying, "Surely you don't believe this yourself, do you? Stop them!" But Jesus assured the Pharisees that if the crowd remained **silent, the stones would cry out** (19:40). God's long-waited Messiah had finally come, and he deserved all honor and glory. If the Jewish leadership and the nation refused to accept him (see Matt 23:37), God would bring to life those who had died (indicated by the visible gravestones that surrounded the Mount of Olives) to bear testimony to Jesus (19:37-40).

19:41-44 When **the city** of Jerusalem finally came into view, Jesus **wept for it** (19:41). If its inhabitants would have accepted him nationally, they could have known **peace** (19:42). But they would soon reject him. As a result, God would hand the city over to judgment. Jerusalem's **enemies** would **surround** her (19:43). This would be fulfilled in AD 70 when the Romans decimated the city. Jerusalem failed to **recognize** her Messiah, even when he was in her **midst** (19:44).

19:45-46 Upon his arrival in the city, Jesus entered **the temple** and was filled with anger. Business activities were taking place inside, hindering worship and taking advantage of the people. So Jesus threw out the sellers and condemned them for making God's **house of prayer** into a **den of thieves**. Communicating with God had been replaced by religious activity for profit. The absence of the priority of prayer in the church is a significant indication that it has abandoned its primary calling.

19:47-48 **Every day** after this, Jesus taught the people **in the temple**. This provoked even greater opposition from the religious leaders who wanted **to kill him** (19:47). But they were unable to do anything since the crowds were **captivated by** him and constantly surrounded him (19:48). Ultimately, Jesus's enemies would resort to using a traitor and the cover of darkness to accomplish their wicked plans (22:47-48, 52-53).

20:1-4 During one occasion as he was **teaching** in **the temple**, the religious leaders demanded to know the source of Jesus's **authority** for everything he was doing (20:1-2). He had received messianic praise from the crowds (19:36-38) and cleansed the temple as if it were his own (19:45-46). Who authorized him to do such things? Jesus answered their question with a **question** (20:3). He would respond to their query if they answered his: **Was the baptism of John from heaven or of human origin?** (20:4). In other words, did John act on God's authority or on his own?

20:5-6 Before they would respond, though, **they discussed it among themselves**—a good indication that responding truthfully wasn't high on their priority list. They laid out their options and the possible repercussions of their answers. If they said that John's baptism was authorized by **heaven**, Jesus would ask, **Why didn't you believe him?** (20:5). After all, John had called all Israel to repent and be baptized—something the religious leaders didn't do. John had also pointed

to Jesus as the Messiah (see John 1:29-33)—something the religious leaders refused to believe. On the other hand, if they said John's baptism was **of human origin**, they would probably be stoned to death by **the people**, since they believed **John** was a true **prophet** of God (20:6).

20:7-8 Thus, as far as the religious leaders were concerned, Jesus's question was one that they couldn't prudently answer. So instead they replied, "No comment" (20:7). That was exactly what Jesus had anticipated. They weren't interested in the truth. All they wanted was incriminating evidence so that they had cause to condemn him. Therefore, he wouldn't answer their question either (20:8). If you won't speak the truth, don't expect to receive the truth.

20:9 Jesus followed this encounter with the religious leaders with a parable about a vineyard owner. As Israel's leaders moved steadily toward rejecting their Messiah, Jesus wanted to make clear to them what they were doing. In the parable, **a man planted a vineyard, leased it to tenant farmers, and went away for a long time.** The vineyard owner represented God, and his vineyard was Israel. Isaiah the prophet had spoken of Israel as a vineyard too (Isa 5:1-7), so this would have sounded familiar to Jesus's listeners. In Isaiah's song, the vineyard produced worthless grapes. In Jesus's parable, the vineyard doesn't fare much better.

20:10-12 At **harvest time**, the owner sent servants to the tenant farmers to **give** their master **fruit from** his vineyard. **But the farmers** simply **beat** them (20:10). They assumed they had nothing to fear: the owner was far away and probably wouldn't return. The vineyard owner continued to send servants, but each time they **treated** them **shamefully**, assaulted them, and sent them **away empty-handed** (20:11-12). Over the centuries, God had sent his servants the prophets to warn his people to bear fruit—to keep his covenant and to live righteously. But Israel repeatedly rejected God's Word spoken by his messengers.

20:13-16 Finally, the **owner** sent his own **beloved son**, expecting him to be respected and obeyed (20:13). But the tenant farmers saw this as their chance to be rid of the owner forever. The son was the **heir**. With him out of the way, **the inheritance** would be theirs (20:14). So they **killed** the owner's son (20:15).

Jesus asked his listeners, **What then will the owner of the vineyard do to them?** (20:15). Then he answered his own question: **He will come and kill those farmers and give the vineyard to others.** This declaration of judgment on Israel for her rebellion against God was too much for the religious leaders. They rejected his story and shouted, **That must never happen!** (20:16). They were unwilling to entertain the possibility that they had been unfaithful to God and were rejecting his Son.

20:17-18 Jesus made it clear to them that their rejection of him was a rejection of God and a fulfillment of **Scripture.** He quoted from Psalm 118:22: **The stone that the builders rejected has become the cornerstone** (20:17). Though the religious leaders scorned Jesus as a worthless stone, he was the most important part of the building, the key element of the kingdom. One cannot reject him and go unharmed (20:18). Reject the cornerstone, and your building falls to ruin. Reject the Messiah, and your eternal condemnation is certain.

20:19 The scribes and the chief priests knew that this story was about them. They were the villains in Jesus's tale, and they hated him for it. So they plotted a way **to get their hands on him.** But they were still incapable of seizing him because **they feared the people.**

20:20 Their hatred for Jesus kept the religious leaders going. They weren't willing to give up. This time they **sent spies who pretended to be righteous** to attempt to trip him in his words. Perhaps if they could trick him into saying something treasonous, they could **hand him over** to the Roman **governor** to be tried.

20:21-23 The "spies" approached Jesus under the guise of desiring a truthful answer from a God-honoring **teacher** on a complex, controversial subject (20:21). They asked, **Is it lawful for us to pay taxes to Caesar or not?** (20:22). But, as we've seen before, you can't hide anything from Jesus because he can see the motives of your heart (see 5:22). He could see **their craftiness** (20:23). If he answered, "Yes," the crowds (who hated the Romans) would be angry with him. But if he answered, "No," the religious leaders would have reason to accuse him of treason against Rome.

20:24-25 Jesus requested **a denarius**, the Roman coin used to pay taxes. When someone produced one, he asked them whose **image and inscription** were on it. Everyone knew the answer: **Caesar's** (20:24). **Well then**, Jesus told them, **give to Caesar the things that are Caesar's, and to God the things that are God's** (20:25). They had expected a yes or no answer, but Jesus had a better one. The coin with Caesar's image on it belonged to Rome, so it was right to give Caesar what belonged to him for the services the empire provided. On the other hand, human beings bear God's "image" (Gen 1:26-27), so they are to give themselves in humble obedience to him. Thus, Jesus affirmed both the civil and religious obligations of people.

20:26 Once again Jesus had outsmarted the religious hypocrites, and once again they had failed **to catch him in** his words. **Amazed at** out how he had answered them, they fell **silent.**

20:27 The Sadducees were a group with a lot of power since they were associated with aristocratic families and the high priests. They differed from the Pharisees on a number of theological issues. For example, they rejected belief in the **resurrection** and only believed in the first five books of the Bible (the Pentateuch) as Scripture.

20:28-33 Since everyone else had failed to trap Jesus, the Sadducees decided to give it a try. They reminded Jesus of the law of **Moses** in Deuteronomy 25:5-6, which required that if a Jewish man died, **his brother** was to marry his widow and raise up a son **for his brother**, in order to carry on his brother's name (20:28). Given this law, they proposed a scenario. A woman married **seven brothers**, each one of them dying successively.

None of them had any **children** (20:29-31). When the **woman died, whose wife** would she be **in the resurrection** because she had been married to all of them? (20:32-33). The Sadducees believed that their hypothetical situation proved how ridiculous the idea of the resurrection was.

20:34-36 But their scenario only proved one thing to Jesus: the Sadducees were foolish, and they didn't know their Bibles well. First, he explained that those who experience **the resurrection** in the **age** to come do not **marry** (20:34-35). Though marriage is part of God's design for his creation, it will not be a feature of the new creation. So questions like, "Whose wife will the woman be?" are irrelevant. Resurrected believers will **no longer die** (20:36). So there will be no need for procreation.

20:37-38 Second, Jesus pointed to God's declaration to **Moses** in Exodus 3:6 that he was **the God of Abraham and the God of Isaac and the God of Jacob**. To say that he was still their God—after they had died—indicates that **the dead are raised** (20:37). Existence does not end with physical death.

20:39-40 Hearing Jesus respond to the Sadducees, **the scribes** said, **Teacher, you have spoken well** (20:39). After that, no one **dared to ask him anything** (20:40). Jesus had proven himself a formidable adversary. His understanding of the Scriptures and teaching authority were vastly superior to that of these religious leaders. They finally realized that challenging him in such ways wasn't working.

20:41-44 Once his opponents were silenced, Jesus had a question for them: **How can they say that the Christ is the son of David?** (20:41). This was a universally accepted notion. Then he quoted from Psalm 110:1, a passage in which **David** (the author and highly revered king), speaking of the Messiah sitting at God's **right hand**, calls him **my Lord** (20:42-44). A son would honor his father, but a father wouldn't call his descendant "Lord."

Jesus wasn't denying the fact that the Christ would be descended from David. The Old Testament makes that clear in many places. Rather, Jesus was emphasizing the fact that the Christ was *much more* than merely the son of David. Though he would be human, he wouldn't be merely human. He would also be God.

20:45-47 Jesus warned **his disciples** to **beware** of the hypocrisy **of the scribes** (20:45-46). They loved to exalt themselves and attempted to look spiritual in public. But their wickedness—in light of their privileged position as religious leaders—would earn them a **harsher judgment** (20:47). Thus, just as there will be degrees of rewards for believers, there will be degrees of punishment for unbelievers.

21:1-4 Jesus had just censured the scribes for devouring "widows' houses" (20:47). Now he would further condemn their greed by contrasting it with one particular widow's virtue. As **the rich** were **dropping their offerings into the temple treasury**, a **poor widow** put in **two tiny coins** (21:1-2). To the casual observer, it appeared that the widow had given next to nothing. But Jesus said she had **put in more than all of them** (21:3). They gave **out of their surplus**; she gave **out of her poverty**. The percentage of what she gave, in relation to what she had, exceeded all the rest. The wealthy showed little dependence on God, since they gave out of their excess. But the widow's willingness to give her livelihood demonstrated her great reliance on God as her source of blessing and provision.

21:5-6 The temple, which had been rebuilt and expanded by Herod the Great, was grand and **beautiful** (21:5). The disciples admired it. But Jesus stunned them with his prediction that this magnificent structure would be destroyed—**not one stone** would be **left on another** (21:6). This prediction would come true a few decades later in AD 70 when the Roman general (and later emperor) Titus conquered Jerusalem and leveled the temple.

21:7 The disciples couldn't believe it. They wanted to know **when** these events concerning the destruction of the temple would **happen** and what **sign** would precede them. They believed the temple's destruction was linked to the start of the messianic kingdom (see Matt 24:3). They didn't yet realize that there would be a gap of time between these events. So Jesus began to explain to them the signs and events that would precede his return.

21:8-19 Many momentous happenings would take place in the years to come. But Christ's followers are not to be **deceived** by them. False christs will appear, and **wars** will take place. **But the end won't come right away** (21:8-9). Many disturbing events will occur (21:10-11). Here Jesus began to describe the first half of the seven-year tribulation period prophesied by Daniel (see commentary on Dan 9:24-27). Followers of Christ will experience severe persecution—even at the hands of **relatives** and **friends** (21:12, 16). But this will provide **an opportunity to bear witness** to the truth (21:12-13). Yet, through God's sovereign protection and provision, they will be able to endure (21:17-19). While many of Christ's followers throughout history have experienced persecution and death, Jesus spoke here primarily of the suffering of those who become believers during the tribulation.

21:20-24 When he mentioned **Jerusalem surrounded by armies**, Jesus returned to the disciples' question about the destruction of Jerusalem (21:20). At that sign, those in Jerusalem **must flee**, and those outside **must not enter it** (21:21). It would be a time of **great distress in the land**, resulting in many Jews being **killed** and **Jerusalem** being **trampled by the Gentiles** (21:23-24), resulting in the times of the Gentiles when Israel would no longer possess or live in peace in their homeland and the Messiah would not yet sit on the throne of David. Such could have been averted by the nation's repentance and acceptance of the Messiah.

Jesus had the destruction of Jerusalem in AD 70 in view here, but he also extends this to the future "abomination of desolation" (21:20) mentioned in Daniel 9:27, when the antichrist will set up his image in the Jerusalem temple and require everyone to worship that image (see Rev 13:4-8). Anyone who does not worship it will be persecuted (see Rev 13:15).

21:25-28 Next Jesus described events prior to his second coming to set up his millennial kingdom. Distressing **signs** will be evident to all—both cosmic signs and terrestrial signs (21:25). Great upheaval will take place in the natural world. The enemies of God will be overcome by **fear** at all these things and especially when they **see the Son of Man coming in a cloud with power and glory** (21:26-27; see Dan 7:13-14). When these things occur, the end of evil will be close at hand. **Redemption** and the deliverance of God's people and the promised kingdom blessings will be **near** (21:28).

21:29-33 Jesus used a common agrarian feature of the region—**the fig tree**—to illustrate the need to be watchful (21:29). When **leaves** sprout on the fig tree, **summer is already near** (21:30). One doesn't have to be a farmer to reach this conclusion. Nearly anyone can interpret this sign. **In the same way**, Jesus told them, when his followers see the signs he described, they need to **recognize that the kingdom of God**, the earthly rule of Jesus's messianic reign in the millennium, **is near** (21:31). Such events will continue uninterrupted till the conclusion of Christ's second coming. **This generation** is a reference to those who will be alive during the great tribulation. They can be certain that **all** these **things** will **take place**. Though **heaven and earth will pass away**, Jesus's **words will never pass away** (21:32). He claimed absolute sovereignty and authority over the fulfillment of his prophetic words.

21:34-36 Jesus warned that his followers would need to be ready at all times in light of the coming day of God's judgment. They were not to become entangled in the desires and affairs of the world so that the day comes on them **unexpectedly** (21:34). Rather, believers must be ready for the kingdom when it arrives. **For it will come on all who live on the face of the whole earth** (21:35). The coming of the kingdom of God and the judgment that precedes it will have a universal affect. No one will escape. And those not prepared for God's judgment will not enter the peace and joy of Christ's millennial reign. Believers need to **be alert at all times, praying** for **strength** to be prepared for his second coming (21:36). What will be true for believers in that day is still true for his disciples today. We must be alert, ready, and living in anticipation of the coming rapture that will precede the period of the tribulation (see 1 Thess 4:13-18), when Christ will come in the clouds to summon believers to "always be with the Lord" (1 Thess 4:17).

21:37-38 During the day, Jesus continued to experience the favor of the people as he taught **in the temple.** He would **spend the night,** though, outside the city on **the Mount of Olives** (21:37). Eventually, the religious leaders would find out where Jesus was staying each night—led there by a traitor (22:47-53).

VI. BETRAYAL, SUFFERING, DEATH, AND RESURRECTION (22:1–24:53)

22:1-6 As the **Festival of Unleavened Bread, which is called Passover** (see Exod 12:1-28) approached, the plot to kill Jesus began to unfold (22:1). **The chief priests and the scribes** could not figure out a way to seize him without causing a riot among **the people** (22:2). That's when **Satan entered Judas,** one of **the Twelve,** and inspired him to betray Jesus for money (22:3-5). The religious leaders accepted his offer. They were leery of the crowd's enthusiasm for Jesus, so they wanted Judas to betray him to them **when the crowd was not present** (22:6).

22:7-13 On the day that **the Passover lamb** was **to be sacrificed,** the Lord **sent Peter and John** to make preparations (22:7-8). He gave them detailed instructions regarding where they were to go, what they would find, and what they should do. Upon entering **the city,** they would find **a man carrying a water jug** and **follow him** to a **house** (22:10). This guy would be easy to spot because such a task was typically carried out by women. Then they were to **tell the owner of the house** that **the Teacher** wanted a **guest room** where he could share **the Passover** with his **disciples** (22:11). The man, probably a follower of Jesus, would oblige and show them a **furnished room upstairs** that they could use (22:12). Everything happened **just as he had told them** (22:13). Thus, Jesus demonstrated his supernatural, detailed knowledge of the future.

22:14-20 The hour came (22:14). The time had come for the passion of the Christ. His suffering and death was linked to the **Passover** because he would be its fulfillment

(22:15). Jesus Christ is "our Passover lamb," sacrificed for us (1 Cor 5:7). He informed the disciples that he would **not eat** this meal **again until** he reigned in his **kingdom** (22:16). Then he took the **bread** and the **cup** and instituted a meal (22:17-20) that the church has partaken of together ever since: Communion or the Lord's Supper.

He **broke** the **bread** and **gave it to them,** symbolizing his broken body offered up for them. Just as these first disciples did, the church today eats this bread together **in remembrance of** him (22:19). **The cup** symbolizes **the new covenant** that he was establishing in his **blood,** which has been **poured out for** our sins (22:20). As the church partakes of this meal together, we affirm our common faith in Christ's substitutionary atoning sacrifice, our new covenantal, unified relationship with him, and his ongoing spiritual presence in our lives. As the apostle Paul told the church in Corinth, "As often as you eat this bread and drink the cup, you proclaim the Lord's death until he comes" (1 Cor 11:26). We remember his death for us in the *past* and utilize its power and provisions for us in the *present,* until he returns for us in the *future.*

22:21-23 Jesus announced that one of the Twelve, one of those sitting **at the table with** him, would betray him (22:21). This no doubt shocked them. They had no idea who the betrayer could be, and **they began to argue among themselves** (22:23). Thus, Jesus demonstrated his omniscience by announcing what would happen beforehand.

But he also made it clear that his betrayal involved both divine sovereignty and human responsibility. **The Son of Man** would **go away** (be killed) **as . . . determined** (22:22). In other words, what was about to happen had been foretold long ago in Scripture. It was God's predetermined plan to sacrifice his Son—the Suffering Servant—to atone for sin (see Isa 53:5-6). Christ's death on the cross was a fulfillment of God's Word. But, at the same time, **woe to that man by whom he is betrayed** (22:22) meant Judas was accountable for his actions. He was no puppet being forced to do something against his will. He chose to betray Christ for profit and was responsible for his sin.

22:24-30 Jesus had just informed the disciples of his own impending suffering and death (22:14-20). Then he added that one of them—his closest companions—would betray him (22:21-22). Yet, surprisingly, they started to **dispute** with one another about which one of them **should be considered the greatest** (22:24). At that point, Jesus rebuked them for talking like unbelievers. Among the **Gentiles, kings** would **lord it over** their subjects, exalting themselves and expecting their people to serve and honor them (22:25). But this was not to be the path to greatness for Christ's disciples: **It is not to be like that among you.** Instead, their focus should have been on a mindset of servanthood. **Serving** was the road to true **greatness** and was what Jesus himself had modeled for them (22:26-27). Their greatness would come in the kingdom because of their faithfulness in Christ's **trials** (22:28). They would attain high **kingdom** privilege—ruling with Christ and enjoying fellowship with him (22:29-30)—not as a result of exalting themselves, but as a result of serving God and others.

22:31 Not only did Jesus foretell his approaching betrayal and death (22:14-22), but he also foretold the disciples' failure—especially Peter's: **Simon, Simon, look out. Satan has asked to sift you like wheat.** The "you" in Greek is plural, so Satan wanted to wreak havoc on all of the disciples. Yet, Jesus addressed Simon Peter. That's because Peter served as the de facto leader of the group. His failure would be the worst and could lead to the defeat and defection of the rest of the

disciples. But Jesus intended to use him to restore the others.

Notice that Satan needed permission. If you are a child of God, then, Satan has no power over you unless God grants it. The devil is powerful, but he's God's devil. He operates under the sovereign hand of God. Why would God grant a satanic request? Though Satan simply wants to harm and destroy, God uses Satan's activity for his own holy purposes. The Lord sometimes allows Satan to tempt us in order to draw out the evil that's in us—evil of which we may not even be aware. By doing this, he reveals to us our sinful tendencies and weaknesses so that he might lead us to repent. We are not as strong as we think we are.

22:32 But I have prayed for you that your faith may not fail. Jesus didn't pray that Peter would not fail. He prayed that Peter's *faith* would not fail. He prayed for his faith to be strengthened and not shattered. Then he said, **When you have turned back, strengthen your brothers.** According to Matthew, Jesus foretold that "all" of the disciples would run away that night, and they did (Matt 26:31, 56). So Jesus exhorted Peter to encourage and help them afterwards.

Notice that Jesus didn't tell Peter, "*If* you turn back," but "*When* you have turned back." Jesus told Peter that he had prayed for him, and then he assured him that his prayer was effectual. As a result, Peter would be a humbler and more effective tool in the hands of his Master. Jesus prophesied Peter's failure, his repentance, and his usefulness. This gives hope to believers who have fallen. Jesus offers a road to spiritual recovery and future ministry usefulness when they repent (see John 21:15-17).

22:33-34 Peter was full of confidence in himself and not yet ready to believe that he could fail so significantly: **I'm ready to go with you both to prison and to death** (22:33). In other words, he assured Jesus, "You can count on me to endure jail time and execution alongside you. I'm your man!" But Peter didn't realize how frail he was. It would only take the accusations of a servant girl to cause him to fall to pieces (22:56-57; cf. Matt 26:69-70). In just a few hours, he would **deny three times**

that he even knew who Jesus was (Luke 22:34). This is a clear illustration of Proverbs 16:18: "Pride comes before destruction, and an arrogant spirit before a fall." What happened to Peter can happen to you, if you're long on pride and short on humility. "Whoever thinks he stands must be careful not to fall" (1 Cor 10:12).

22:35-38 Previously, Jesus had **sent** the disciples to do ministry without supplies, and their needs were met (22:35; see 10:1-12). But at this point he urged them to make preparations and take supplies, even a **sword** for self-defense (22:36), for the environment was about to become hostile. Jesus would be **counted** as a **lawless** man in **fulfillment** of Scripture (22:37).

Notice that when they told him that they already had **two swords**, he said that was **enough** (22:38). Jesus's goal was not a military overthrow. They were not to become a militia.

22:39-42 **As usual** they went **to the Mount of Olives** where they spent the night (22:39; see 21:37). Once there, he admonished his disciples to **pray** that they might not fold under the pressure of the **temptation** they were about to face (22:40). They would need strength and divine assistance. Then Jesus **withdrew from them** for a time of private prayer (22:41): **Father, if you are willing, take this cup away from me.** These words tell us Jesus knew the suffering he was about to face. In his humanity, he wanted to avoid the intense physical and spiritual anguish if it were possible. Yet, he wanted even more to do the will of his Father: **Nevertheless, not my will, but yours, be done** (22:42).

22:43-46 In response to his prayer, **an angel from heaven appeared** and strengthened him (22:43). His **anguish** was so great and his prayers so fervent that **his sweat became like drops of blood** (22:44).

After such intense personal prayer, Jesus found his disciples fast asleep, heedless of his warning to pray for themselves (22:45). He rebuked them for seeking physical rest when what they needed more than anything was spiritual strength (22:46). Most of us are willing to prepare ourselves to meet physical

threats. Few of us, however, are willing to engage in the deep spiritual preparation necessary to meet spiritual threats. Why? We do not recognize the danger.

22:47-48 As Jesus was trying to rouse his disciples from their spiritual lethargy, **a mob** arrived. It was led by **Judas**, who approached his Master and kissed him (22:47). This was the sign to let everyone know whom to arrest. Judas used an act of love as a weapon! He betrayed his Creator **with a kiss** (22:48).

22:49-51 As they realized what was happening, the disciples asked if it was time to use **the sword** (22:49; see 22:36-38). Peter didn't wait for an answer, taking a sword and cutting off the **ear** of **the high priest's servant** (22:50; see John 18:10). But Jesus rebuked him. The Scripture had to be fulfilled. The divine plan had to be accomplished. Sin had to be atoned for. So he touched the servant's **ear** and **healed him** (22:51).

22:52-53 Jesus condemned **the chief priests, temple police, and the elders** for their hypocrisy. They arrested him at night like **a criminal** (22:52) rather than publicly during the day **in the temple** so that the crowds could witness it. They didn't want anyone to see the injustice of their actions because they were cowards, under demonic influence, and operating in **the dominion of darkness** (22:53).

22:54-62 Once the mob **seized** Jesus, they took him to **the high priest's house** for a mock trial. **At a distance**, so he wouldn't be seen, **Peter** followed (22:54). As he waited in **the courtyard** outside the high priest's home, **a servant** looked at him, recognized him, and accused Peter of being an associate of Jesus (22:55-56). This was Peter's opportunity to make good on his promise to his Lord: "I'm ready to go with you both to prison and to death" (22:33). Instead, he caved: **Woman, I don't know him** (22:57). Before long, in fact, he'd been granted three opportunities to boldly acknowledge his discipleship, and he made three vehement denials that he knew who they were talking about (22:56-60). Thus, he failed just as Jesus had predicted: three denials **before the rooster** crowed. And as soon as he heard it, Peter's eyes met Jesus's.

Then Peter **remembered**, went away, **and wept bitterly** (22:61-62). It's easy to forget our spiritual commitment in a crisis.

22:63-65 While at the high priest's house, Jesus was mistreated brutally. They mocked him and beat him (22:63). This was no arrest and trial of a dangerous man; this was the illegal and cruel treatment of a righteous man whom they hated. They blindfolded him and taunted him to **prophesy** by declaring which of his captors had **hit** him (22:64). Luke recognized their words and actions as **blasphemous** (22:65). They treated the Son of God with disgrace and humiliation rather than with praise and worship.

22:66-69 At **daylight**, Jesus was taken before the council of elders over which the high priest presided; the body of Jewish religious leaders was known as the **Sanhedrin** (22:66). They interrogated him directly, demanding that he confess whether or not he believed himself to be **the Messiah** (22:67). Jesus highlighted their hypocrisy. They had already dismissed his claims as false, no matter the evidence he produced by his teaching and miracles. They would **not believe** that he was the Messiah if he confessed it, and if he asked them what they thought, they would refuse to **answer** (22:67-68). They had only one agenda: to condemn him and put him to death. But Jesus had a word for them: **From now on, the Son of Man will be seated at the right hand of the power of God** (22:69; see Ps 110:1). Though the religious leaders thought they were about to be rid of him, Jesus knew that he would soon be seated in glory at the right hand of his Father.

22:70-71 They asked if he was **the Son of God** and clearly understood Jesus's answer in the affirmative, for they declared, **We've heard it ourselves from his mouth**. He had not recanted anything but claimed to be the one who would sit at God's right hand. The council was satisfied that they had sufficient incriminating evidence from Jesus's own lips to move forward with their plans.

23:1-5 Since the Jews were unable to execute anyone themselves, they led Jesus **before Pilate**, the Roman governor (23:1). They accused Jesus of **misleading** the **nation**, opposing paying **taxes to Caesar** (which was a lie; see 20:20-26), and claiming to be **the Messiah, a king** (23:2). They wanted to make Jesus appear to be an insurrectionist, someone who was a threat to Roman rule. If he was proclaiming himself to be a king and opposing Caesar, then Pilate would have to take action. Yet Pilate found **no grounds for charging** the man with a crime. Jesus was clearly no threat (23:3-4). Nevertheless, the Jews continued to insist that he caused problems among the people—from **Judea** to **Galilee** (23:5).

23:6-7 When he learned that Jesus **was a Galilean**, he sent him to **Herod** Antipas, the son of Herod the Great and the tetrarch who ruled over Galilee. Herod had put John the Baptist in prison and later beheaded him (3:18-20; 9:7-9). He had heard of Jesus's ministry and was concerned about him (9:7-9), but he had not yet had a chance to meet him face-to-face. Thanks to Pilate, he now had that opportunity.

23:8-12 For a **long time**, Herod had been **hoping** to see Jesus perform a **miracle** (23:8). But if he thought Jesus was going to do tricks for him, he was sorely mistaken. Herod asked him **questions**, and **the chief priests** shouted accusations at him. **But Jesus did not answer** (23:9-10). Since Jesus wouldn't act like a performing seal, **Herod** and **his soldiers** made a mockery of him instead. They **dressed him in bright clothing** like a false king and **sent him back to Pilate** (23:11). Ironically, these circumstances brought **Herod and Pilate** together. **Previously, they had been enemies**; their roles in the drama led them to become **friends** (23:12).

23:13-16 When he had gathered all of the Jewish religious leaders together, Pilate once again declared Jesus innocent. He **found no grounds to charge** him with a crime—and **neither** had **Herod**. Jesus **clearly** did not **deserve** the **death** penalty (23:13-15). But since he wanted to appease the Jewish leaders, Pilate planned to have Jesus **whipped** before releasing him (23:16). Pilate was not ultimately concerned with justice but with maintaining order.

23:17-19 But the Jewish leaders refused to be pacified so easily. They would only be satisfied with blood. They shouted, **Take this man away! Release Barabbas to us!** (23:18). Pilate would customarily perform an act of clemency during the Passover and set a Jewish prisoner free. Though he wanted to release Jesus, the leaders demanded Barabbas, a rebel and murderer, instead (23:19). This sheds light on how great their hatred of Jesus was. He had committed no sin. Yet he had won the adoration of the crowds, challenged the leaders' sacred traditions, and made them look like fools. Their jealousy and anger drove them to petition for the release of a murderer and to condemn a righteous man.

23:20-25 In spite of Pilate's attempts to set Jesus free, the religious leaders demanded that he **crucify him** (23:20-21). What's more, they stirred up the crowds of Jews who were in Jerusalem for the Passover so that Pilate was soon facing an angry mob (see Mark 15:11). The people demanded that Barabbas be set free, indicating that they preferred a murderer to their Messiah. After a third attempt to release Jesus and declare his innocence, Pilate gave in to **their demand** (23:22-24). He set Barabbas loose and surrendered Jesus **to their will** (23:25). He preferred public order to justice—expediency to righteousness.

23:26 The other Gospels make it clear that Jesus had endured a brutal beating and scourging by this point (see Matt 27:26-31; Mark 15:16-20; John 19:1-3). So, even though a condemned man was typically forced to carry his cross to the place of crucifixion, Jesus was apparently too weakened to bear the burden. So the soldiers forced someone else to **carry** the **cross**: an African man named **Simon** who was from Cyrene, on the coast of what is now Libya.

23:27-31 A large **crowd of people followed him, including** sympathetic **women** who were **mourning** for **him** (23:27). Yet even in the midst of his suffering, he warned them **not** to **weep** for him but for themselves and their **children** (23:28), in light of the judgment that was coming on the nation for rejecting the Messiah. When the catastrophe came, those **without children** would be

called **blessed** because they would not have to endure watching the suffering of their offspring (23:29). Quoting from Hosea 10:8, Jesus described this coming day as a time when people would prefer a horrendous death to divine judgment (23:30). **If they do these things when the wood is green** (that is, when the Messiah is with them), **what will happen when it is dry** (after he is gone)? (23:31). Israel could not reject her Messiah without experiencing severe consequences.

23:32-34 Crucifixion was a common method of execution that the Romans inflicted on heinous criminals, so it's not surprising that **two others** were to be put to death along with Jesus (23:32). The soldiers took them to the execution site, a foreboding **place called The Skull**. There **they crucified** Jesus between the others (23:33). Don't miss that even as he was being tortured to death, Jesus remembered the purpose for which he came— to open the door of divine forgiveness for all who would receive him. He prayed that the Father would **forgive** even his executioners, because they did not **know what they [were] doing**. Yet, even as he pleaded for mercy for them, they gambled for **his clothes** (23:34), fulfilling prophecy from Psalm 22:18 (see John 19:23-24). Behold our Savior: As sinners mocked him, he interceded for them so that they might repent and be saved.

23:35 The Jewish religious leaders who had longed for this day stood **scoffing** at Jesus as he suffered on the cross. They scornfully urged him to **save himself** if he were truly **God's Messiah**. They observed that he had **saved others** yet was unable to do the same for himself. However, only by remaining on the cross and sacrificing his own life could he provide salvation. The religious leaders reveled in their "victory," but they had failed to grasp his mission. Even as he hung dying, the Son was winning the victory for which the Father had sent him.

23:36-38 The soldiers also mocked him. They knew nothing of Jesus's teaching or ministry. They probably jeered at every criminal they were ordered to execute. But in this case, their ridicule reflected the **inscription** that Pilate had commanded to be placed on the cross: THIS IS THE KING OF THE JEWS (23:37-38; see John 19:19-22). Yet, ironically, the very thing they mocked was true. Before them hung the King of the Jews—and the King of all creation. One day, they will stand before him again. But on that day he will be seated on a throne pronouncing their judgment.

23:39-42 When Matthew and Mark mention the criminals crucified with Jesus, they report that these two taunted him (Matt 27:44; Mark 15:32). But Luke tells us something more. Though both criminals started down the same road that day, at some point one of them chose a different path. Both heard and saw the same things, but they reached different conclusions.

The criminals' words here reveal the differences between the men. First, they reached different conclusions about who the man in the middle was. The rebellious criminal joined the crowd. He hurled **insults at** Jesus, ridiculing the idea that he was **the Messiah** (23:39). But the repentant one recognized that Jesus was both an innocent man who had **done nothing wrong** and a King about to enter his heavenly **kingdom** (23:41-42). Your eternal destiny is necessarily connected to your understanding of who Jesus is.

Second, they reached different conclusions regarding their own guilt. The first criminal failed to come to grips with his own sinfulness. There was no admission of blame, no **fear of God** (20:40). But his companion rebuked him. He rightly concluded that they were being **punished justly** for their crimes (20:40-41). Without the comprehension that you are a sinner in rebellion against and separated from a holy God, you cannot be saved.

Third, the two men reached different conclusions about what they needed to be delivered from. The unrepentant criminal simply wanted deliverance from his present earthly circumstances. **Save yourself and us**, he demanded of Jesus, meaning, "Keep us from dying!" (23:39). But the second criminal understood that there was something beyond their present trouble. No matter how bad things were on earth, a much more serious concern awaited. One day, we all must face

eternity and—unless we have a mediator—the wrath of God. With a repentant heart, this man recognized Jesus as the mediator he needed: **Jesus, remember me when you come into your kingdom** (23:42). Hearing Jesus call his Father to forgive his executioners (23:34) was sufficient for this man to change his opinion about Jesus and place saving faith in him.

23:43 In response to the man's repentance and faith, Jesus told him, **Truly I tell you, today you will be with me in paradise.** According to the New Testament, all believers are called to obey the Lord by being baptized, locking arms with Christian brothers and sisters in a local church, and growing as disciples by seeking to love God and neighbor. But none of these things can save a person. They are acts of obedience in response to the saving work of God in our lives through Jesus Christ. Salvation comes when we put our faith alone in Christ alone. And that's what this criminal did. He didn't have an opportunity to follow the Lord in a life of obedience—though if he had lived he surely would have. Nevertheless, he did exactly what was required in order to be reconciled to God. And later that day, though his physical body died, his spirit and soul went to paradise with King Jesus, awaiting his future bodily resurrection from the dead. This affirms that believers go immediately into God's presence at death.

23:44-46 As Christ's death approached, a number of events took place. From **about noon . . . until three** there was **darkness on the land . . . because the sun's light** had **failed** (23:44). It wasn't possible for the Son of God to be rejected and killed without it causing an ominous reaction from his creation. When Jesus finally yielded up his life and **breathed his last**, he entrusted himself to his **Father**, quoting Psalm 31:5 (23:46).

At that moment, **the curtain of the sanctuary**, which separated the holy place from the most holy place, **was split down the middle** (23:45; see Exod 26:33). The curtain symbolized the separation that existed between a holy God and sinful people. Only the high priest could enter the most holy place to make atonement for Israel's sins. But through the perfect atoning sacrifice of our "great high priest" Jesus Christ (see Heb 4:14; 7:27; 10:10, 12), human beings everywhere have access to God through him. The way to God is open. You no longer need the Old Testament sacrificial system; you only need Jesus and faith in his work.

23:47-49 Though many who witnessed the crucifixion were unbelievers who insulted Jesus, many others were sorrowful and realized that a miscarriage of justice had taken place. The Roman **centurion** who oversaw the execution of the three men began to **glorify God** by declaring Jesus to be a **righteous man** (23:47). **The crowds that had gathered** to watch the event went away **striking their chests** in grief (23:48). Those **who knew him**, including **the women who had followed him from Galilee, stood at a distance** and watched (23:49). They were anxious to know where he would be buried so that they could later anoint his body (see 23:55-56).

23:50-53 Though most of the Jewish religious leaders had opposed Jesus, there were notable exceptions. One of these was **a member of the Sanhedrin who was named Joseph.** He was **a good and righteous man** from the **Judean town** of **Arimathea** who was **looking forward to the kingdom of God** (23:50-51). He boldly demonstrated his faith in Jesus by going publicly to **Pilate** and asking for **Jesus's body** so that he might bury him (23:52). Helped by Nicodemus, another Jewish leader who had opposed the Sanhedrin's plan (see John 3:1-2; 7:50-51; 19:39-40), Joseph **wrapped** and buried the body **in a tomb** that had never been used, one **cut** out of **rock** (Luke 23:53).

23:54-56 Jesus was crucified, died, and was buried on Friday. The next day was **the Sabbath**, which began at sundown on Friday (23:54). **The women** who had **followed** Jesus **from Galilee** saw **the tomb** where he was buried so that they could return on Sunday, after the Sabbath, and anoint his body with **spices and perfumes** (23:55-56).

24:1-3 On the **first day of the week**—Sunday—**early in the morning**, the women **came to the tomb** with their **spices** (24:1).

The **stone** covering the opening to the tomb had been **rolled away**, but Jesus's **body** was not there (24:2-3).

24:4-8 As the women puzzled over what had happened, **suddenly** they realized they weren't alone. **Two** others were there. They appeared to be **men** (24:4), but they were angels (see 24:23; Matt 28:5). Their **clothes** were **dazzling**, and the women **bowed down** in fear (Luke 24:4-5). The angels asked perhaps the most glorious question ever: **Why are you looking for the living among the dead?** (24:5). Jesus had truly died, but he had **risen** from the dead as he'd predicted when telling them he would be **crucified** and **rise on the third day** (24:6-7; see 9:21-22; 18:31-33). The heavenly rebuke helped the women remember (24:8).

24:9-12 They ran to find **the Eleven** and **all the rest** to tell them what had happened (24:9). These weren't nameless, fictional women but real people: **Mary Magdalene, Joanna, Mary the mother of James** (24:10). Women played a prominent role in Jesus's ministry, supporting him from their own possessions (8:1-3), so they were given the privilege of being the first to learn of the resurrection and to communicate it. Initially, the others disbelieved the women's testimony (24:11), yet it prompted **Peter** to run **to the tomb** to see for himself. When he saw nothing there except **the linen cloths** that had wrapped Jesus's body, **he went away, amazed** and trying to make sense of what had happened (24:12).

24:13-17 Luke cuts to another resurrection account featuring two disciples, one of whom was named Cleopas (see 24:18). These **two** were traveling to **Emmaus**, a town located **about seven miles from Jerusalem** (24:13). As **they were discussing** what had happened that weekend, the risen **Jesus** began walking alongside them (24:14-15). However, they didn't know who he was, for **they were prevented from recognizing him** (24:16). So he asked them what they were discussing, and **they stopped walking and looked discouraged** (24:17). Their unbelief prevented them from recognizing him.

24:18-21 Cleopas was stunned: **Are you the only visitor in Jerusalem who doesn't know the things that happened there in these days?** In other words, he said, "Where have you been, Mister? Don't you know what's occurred?" Then they proceeded to explain who **Jesus of Nazareth** was—to *Jesus*!

Though he was a mighty **prophet** of God, **the chief priests and leaders** saw to it that he was **sentenced to death** (24:19-20). Yet it wasn't just the miscarriage of justice that discouraged them; they were discouraged because their hopes had been dashed: **We were hoping that he was the one who was about to redeem Israel** (24:21). This implies they had expected him to redeem them from Roman rule and set them free. They had put all of their eggs in the Jesus basket. But their dreams had been destroyed; their hearts had been broken.

24:22-24 As if that weren't enough, **some women from** their **group** had gone to **the tomb** that morning but **didn't find his body** (24:22-23). Instead, **angels** testified that **he was alive** (24:23). **Some** of their friends **went to the tomb** and **found it just as the women had said** (24:24). "We don't know where he is," was essentially the complaint these men made to the very man they were looking for! How wonderful that the one they couldn't find was walking alongside them. "They were prevented from recognizing him" (24:16) because of their disheartening circumstances.

24:25-26 Though they were discouraged, Jesus rebuked them: **How foolish you are and how slow.** That was not exactly a compliment! Rather than try to encourage them, he first wanted to take them to the truth. When we see the truth rightly, our emotions will follow. He told them they had not believed **all that prophets have spoken.** Their reading of Scripture had been selective. They needed to be taken back to see *all* that the prophets had said. **It was necessary for the Messiah to suffer these things and enter into his glory** (2:26).

Jesus is the Son of God, sitting now at the right hand of the Father, crowned with honor and glory. But he had to endure great

suffering to get there. The disciples had missed what Scripture said about the Messiah. Likewise, many people today are excited about the promises and blessings of the Bible, but they avoid those passages that talk about trials and pain. However, you can't have one without the other. We must be willing to accept the total package.

24:27 So what did Jesus do? **Beginning with Moses and all the Prophets** (that is, the entire Old Testament), **he interpreted for them the things concerning himself in all the Scriptures.** There was no New Testament yet; Jesus *was* the New Testament. So he helped them to see the Messiah in the Old Testament. Similarly, whether we're reading about Adam, Abraham, Moses, David, or Isaiah, we must always be looking for Jesus in the Old Testament Scriptures because they were written with him in mind. As the saying goes, Jesus is in the Old Testament concealed but in the New Testament revealed.

24:28-30 As **they came near** Emmaus, their destination, Jesus **gave the impression** that he was going to continue on his way (24:28). But they **urged him** to **stay,** and he accepted their invitation (24:29). They went from Bible study to personal fellowship, from information to relationship. And as they sat down to eat, **he took the bread, blessed and broke it, and gave it to them** (29:30). Notice what happened. The guest became the host. They invited him in, and he fed them.

24:31-35 At that moment, **their eyes were opened, and they recognized him, but he disappeared** (24:31). Their **hearts** had been **burning** when he explained **the Scriptures** to them and the truth of God's Word had transformed their discouraged hearts. But it was during **the breaking of the bread**—when they saw the nail prints in his hands—that they realized who he was (24:35). The purpose of the written Word is always to lead us to an experience with the living Word.

Once Jesus disappeared, they hurried off to **Jerusalem,** making the same seven-mile journey in reverse! They told **the Eleven** everything that had happened and learned that **the Lord** had also **appeared to Simon** (24:33-34).

24:36-43 As they were all standing around sharing their resurrection stories, Jesus **himself stood in their midst** and greeted them (24:36). At first they were **terrified**, thinking him a **ghost** (24:37). But he assured them that he had a real physical body. He encouraged them to **touch** him and see that he had **flesh and bones** (24:38-39). Then he **showed them his hands and feet** with their nail scars (24:40). Finally, he **ate a piece of broiled fish** to give further proof that he was no apparition but had a resurrected body (24:41-43).

24:44-48 Then he reminded them of what he had told them—**that everything written** about him **in the Law of Moses, the Prophets, and the Psalms** (i.e., the Old Testament) had to **be fulfilled** (24:44). He had taught them previously, but at this point **he opened their minds** so that they could fully **understand the Scriptures** (24:45). As eyewitnesses of Jesus and his resurrection, they were to proclaim the good news **to all the nations**—that **the Messiah would suffer and rise from the dead the third day** and that **repentance for forgiveness of sins** comes through believing **in his name** (24:46-48). This gospel was what the apostles preached and is what the New Testament declares.

24:49-51 Jesus commanded them to stay in Jerusalem and wait for what his **Father** had **promised**—the Holy Spirit, so that they would be **empowered from on high** (24:49). Then he **led them** near **Bethany** (less than two miles from Jerusalem). As he **blessed them**, they watched as he ascended **into heaven** (24:50-51).

24:52-53 After **worshiping** Christ, they went back to **Jerusalem**, filled with **joy**, and **continually** went to **the temple praising God**. Worship, joy, praise—that's where our faith in the risen Lord Jesus Christ should lead us.

Thus ends the first part of Luke's two-part narrative (see 1:1-4; Acts 1:1-3). The stage is set for its sequel, the book of Acts.

JOHN

INTRODUCTION

Author

THE TITLE OF THIS GOSPEL (ALSO frequently called "the Fourth Gospel") indicates that its author was John. Early church fathers like Irenaeus and Clement of Alexandria attributed authorship to the apostle John, the son of Zebedee. Some modern critical scholars have attempted to argue that the Fourth Gospel was penned by a different John (or someone else entirely), but this is speculation lacking genuine proof.

In addition to the testimony of the early church, the internal evidence from the Gospel itself supports the idea that it was written by John the son of Zebedee. Not only was the author an eyewitness to Jesus (1:14; 19:35), but he also identifies himself in 21:20 as "the disciple Jesus loved" (see 13:23; 19:26; 20:2). This disciple was present at the Last Supper (13:23), a meal that Jesus shared with the Twelve (see Matt 26:20; Mark 14:17; Luke 22:14). Moreover, since this disciple is not named in the Fourth Gospel, he can't be any of the disciples who are named (Andrew, Nathanael, Peter, Philip, Thomas, Judas Iscariot, or Judas the son of James). We also see that this disciple whom Jesus loved was one of those present when the resurrected Jesus appeared to Peter, Thomas, Nathanael, Zebedee's sons (James and John), and two other disciples (see 21:2; 21:20). That means he must be James, John, or one of the two unnamed disciples. James, however, died an early martyr's death in AD 42—a date too early for him to have written the Gospel. And there's no historical support for the Gospel being written by any of the remaining disciples. We thus have good reasons for believing that John the son of Zebedee authored the Fourth Gospel.

Historical Background

The author is aware of Peter's martyrdom (21:19), which happened in AD 65/66. The church historian Jerome claims that John died in about AD 98; thus, the Gospel was written sometime between these dates. Many evangelical scholars think a date in the 80s is most likely. Testimony from the church fathers indicates that the apostle John ministered in Ephesus during the latter years of his life. Therefore, he likely wrote it from there.

Message and Purpose

John was the beloved disciple of Jesus, with whom he had a close relationship. He wanted the readers of his Gospel to know Jesus Christ and become intimate with him as well. To only know Jesus for heaven tomorrow is to miss the joy of heaven on earth in a growing, living relationship with Christ today.

John brings both of these concepts together in his book. He says Jesus is the divine Messiah—God dwelling in our midst—who has a kingdom that is not of this world. John records eight miracles to show that Jesus is no ordinary man. He is a man, to be sure, but he is the God-Man, the Word who became flesh (1:14). He wept at a grave one moment, and raised Lazarus from the dead the next.

John also records seven "I am" statements of Jesus, showing him to be the one who revealed himself to Moses at the burning bush. John conclusively demonstrates that Jesus is the Christ so that by believing in him you may have eternal life (20:31). But the Gospel of John is also about how to have abundant life (10:10), the fruitful, fulfilling, kingdom life that Jesus offers those who follow him.

VIDEO   INTRO

www.bhpublishinggroup.com/qr/te/43_00

JOHN

I. PROLOGUE: THE WORD BECAME FLESH (1:1-18)

1:1-2 When we read the Gospels of Matthew and Luke, the story begins in history with Jesus Christ conceived by the Holy Spirit and born to Joseph and Mary. But in the Fourth Gospel, John reaches back even further—into eternity. We are given access to the prequel, so to speak.

With the phrase, **In the beginning**, John alludes to Genesis 1:1: "In the beginning God created the heavens and the earth." Thus, in eternity past, **the Word** (the Son of God, the eternal expression of God who "became flesh"; see 1:14) **was with God** (1:2). From before the creation of the world, God the Son shared an eternal, intimate father-son relationship with God the Father. Starting in Genesis 1:3, God spoke his word and the universe came into existence. According to the New Testament, the Father made the world through the divine Word, his Son (see Col 1:16; Heb 1:2). In light of the Spirit's involvement as well (see Gen 1:2), we see that each person of the triune God was unified in the work of creation.

Not only was the Word *with* God, but also **the Word was God** (1:1). In other words, the Father and Son are not two distinct gods. Rather, the Son shares the divine nature. Theologically speaking, the Father, Son, and Spirit are co-equal members of the Trinity. Our one God (see Deut 6:4; 1 Cor 8:6) exists in three co-equal persons (see Matt 28:19).

1:3-5 **All things were created through** the Word (1:3), a truth taught elsewhere in the New Testament (see Col 1:16; Heb 1:2). Nothing in creation exists outside of the sovereign power of Jesus. **Not one thing** was made **apart from him** (1:3). He is the Creator and Sustainer of all things, including life. Since **in him** there is divine **life**, he is able to create **life**—both physical and spiritual (see 3:16). The existence of life in creation is proof that the created order is not the result of impersonal chance events, as atheistic evolutionists assert.

Jesus gives life that provides **light** to **men** (1:4). **Light** is needed because **darkness** exists (1:5). Because of the temptation of Satan, humankind has fallen into the darkness of sin (see Gen 3). He has blinded the minds of people to keep them from seeing the glory of Christ (see 2 Cor 4:4). But Jesus has come to bring illumination so that people can see things as they truly are. John's Gospel shows us how Jesus was continually rejected; nevertheless, the darkness **did not overcome** his light (1:5). Though his enemies crucified him, he was actually glorified in his death on the cross (see 13:31-32) and victorious in his resurrection, resulting in the provision of salvation for all people (see John 3:16; Rom 5:18; 1 Tim 2:6; Heb 2:9; 1 John 2:2).

1:6-7 John, the apostle and author of the Gospel, introduces us to **John** the Baptist, **sent** on a mission **from God** (1:6). **He came as a witness to testify about the light** of Jesus Christ **so that all might believe through him** (1:7; see 1:29-36). Though he was the first to bear witness to Christ, he is not to be the last. All Christians have the responsibility to "testify about" him, to declare the truth of Jesus Christ "so that all might believe" in him. That's the foundation of evangelism and missions.

1:8-11 John the Baptist **was not** himself **the light**, though many were confused about his identity (see 1:19-22). As foretold in the Old Testament (see 1:23), John **came to testify about the light**—**the true light**, the Son of God (1:8-9). Though the Son **created** the world, **the world did not recognize him** (1:10). Sin blinds people so that they do not know their own Creator. Even **his own people**—the Jews, those who were waiting for the Messiah, those who should have recognized him—**did not receive him** (1:11). Of course, the first believers, including the apostles, were Jews. But by and large, the Jewish leadership and people rejected Jesus during his earthly ministry.

1:12-13 But to everyone who received him **he gave them the right to be children of God**. To **receive** Christ is not like passively receiving a letter in your mailbox. Instead, it means to welcome him (based on his substitutionary atonement), like one welcomes a guest into his home. Those who do so are adopted into the family of God as his children. To **believe** in Jesus's **name** is to believe in his person (who he is) and work (what he has done) (1:12). When someone receives and believes in Jesus for the free gift of eternal life, he undergoes a supernatural birth, the impartation of spiritual life. He is **born . . . of God** (1:13)—what Jesus would call being "born again" (3:3).

1:14 The Word became flesh and dwelt among us. This verse testifies to the glory of the incarnation. Conceived by the Holy Spirit in the womb of Mary (see Matt 1:20), the divine Son of God became a man. He is thus the God-Man—not half man and half God, but one person with a fully divine nature and a fully human nature. He is deity poured into humanity. He is fully human so he cried as an infant, but he is fully divine and gave life to his mother! He is fully human so he had to sleep, but he is fully divine and can raise the dead back to life. Our God fully experienced what it is to be human—yet without sinning (see Heb 4:15). He faced hunger, pain,

temptation, grief, hardship, and rejection. You face no category of human experience that your Savior has not endured.

We beheld his glory. An obvious example of this is when Peter, James, and John saw Jesus transfigured before their eyes (see Matt 17:1-2). But according to John, Jesus was also glorified through his miracles and ultimately in his cross and resurrection (see 2:11; 7:39; 11:4; 12:16, 23; 13:31-32).

1:15 John the Baptist affirmed the superiority of Jesus. Though Jesus's ministry came **after** John's, he **ranks ahead of** John **because he existed before** him. Though John was born before Jesus (see Luke 1:57-58; 2:1-7), he recognized that Jesus preceded him in eternity.

1:16-17 What does it mean to receive **grace upon grace** (1:16)? John explains: **The law was given through Moses.** This was a good gift to Israel, revealing God's righteous character and his will for their lives. The problem was that the law couldn't enable people to keep it. It highlighted their sin but couldn't transform their sinful hearts. But **grace and truth came through Jesus Christ** (1:17).

When we personally receive the substitutionary atoning death of Christ on the cross, our sins are forgiven and eternal life is imparted. That's amazing grace! The gospel, then, does what the law couldn't do. Through Jesus, we have access to the unmerited and unlimited favor of God. In eternity he will "display the immeasurable riches of his grace" to us without interruption (Eph 2:7). Grace is the inexhaustible supply of God's goodness that continuously brings his favor to his people, doing for us what we can't do for ourselves. God will provide believers with a never-ending supply of "grace upon grace" through Christ, like waves crashing on the seashore.

1:18 John concludes the prologue to his Gospel by explaining that **no one has ever seen God.** In our sinfulness, to see God in unfiltered glory and holiness would result in our obliteration. Even Moses saw only the backside of God's glory. No one can see God's face on this side of eternity and live (see Exod 33:18-23). But **the one and only** (i.e., unique) **Son who is himself God and is**

at the Father's side—he has revealed him. In other words, the divine nature of the Father is fully expressed in the Son. Since Jesus is fully God, to know Jesus is to know God.

As Jesus himself told his disciples, "The one who has seen me has seen the Father" (14:9). He has perfectly revealed him. The only way to God is through the Son (14:6).

II. JESUS CHRIST, THE LAMB OF GOD (1:19-51)

1:19-22 The apostle John's narrative begins with John the Baptist confronted by **priests and Levites** sent by the Jewish leaders to ask, **Who are you?** (1:19). John had been preaching and baptizing, so they wondered if he thought he was the Messiah, the coming King. But he denied it: **I am not the Messiah** (1:20). They continued to interrogate him, asking if he was **Elijah** or **the Prophet** (1:21), referring to the prophecy that Elijah would return (Mal 4:5-6) and Moses's prophecy that God would raise up a great prophet like him (see Deut 18:15-18). But he denied these possibilities as well.

1:23-28 John confessed that he was the **voice of one crying out in the wilderness** that Isaiah had predicted—the one who would prepare **the way of the Lord** (1:23; see Isa 40:3). The word *Lord* in this quotation from Isaiah refers to God, thus identifying the deity of Jesus. Though John was not the King, he was getting things ready for him by calling people to be baptized and confess their sins (see Matt 3:5-6). John recognized his inferiority to the **one coming after** him. He wasn't even **worthy to untie** his sandals, which was the most menial role of a slave (1:27).

1:29 The next day, the moment finally came. **John saw Jesus** and announced, **Here is the Lamb of God, who takes away the sin of the world!** Behind this statement is the Old Testament practice of animal sacrifice in general and the Passover offering of a lamb in particular. God had commanded Israel to sacrifice a lamb so that he might rescue them from Pharaoh before instituting the sacrificial system to atone for their sins. But ultimately the blood of these animals couldn't "take away sins" (Heb 10:4). It was a temporary measure (a layaway plan!) that pointed to a permanent means of salvation. Only the sacrifice of Jesus could truly address the sin

"of the whole world" (1 John 2:2). For unbelievers, the problem is not that their sin hasn't been atoned for; the problem is that they are unwilling to *receive* the atonement that Jesus has already made (see 1:12). The sacrificial death of Jesus Christ removes the judicial barrier caused by sin so that all people are savable.

1:30-34 How did John recognize Jesus as the Messiah? Divine revelation. Without that, he confessed, **I didn't know him** (1:31). But the Lord revealed to John that when he saw **the Spirit descending from heaven like a dove**, he could be certain that the one upon whom **the Spirit** rested was the one (1:32-33). Jesus is the **Son of God** who would baptize people **with the Holy Spirit** (1:33-34).

1:35-42 On the following day, **John** pointed out Jesus to **two of his** own **disciples** and again identified him as **the Lamb of God** (1:35-36). So they **followed Jesus** (1:37). One of the two men was **Andrew, Simon Peter's brother** (1:40). He located his brother and told him that they had **found the Messiah** and **brought Simon to Jesus** (1:41-42).

A Christian's testimony ought to accomplish what John the Baptist's testimony did: pointing people to Jesus so that they want to follow him. Notice the domino effect in this passage. Having encountered Jesus, Andrew wanted his brother to experience him too. When you understand who Jesus is, you'll want others to know him.

1:43-45 Upon finding **Philip**, Jesus told him, **Follow me** (1:43). An invitation to follow Jesus is an invitation to become his disciple. As with Andrew and Peter (1:35-42), meeting Jesus had an effect on Philip. He immediately went out, **found** his friend **Nathanael**, and told him he'd met the Messiah, **the one Moses wrote about** (1:45). When you're serious about Jesus, it doesn't take long to become a witness for him.

1:46 Learning that Jesus was from **Nazareth**, Nathanael was appalled. Nazareth, a town in Galilee, had a poor reputation. Besides, the Messiah was supposed to hail from Bethlehem (see Mic 5:2). In fact, Jesus had been born in Bethlehem, but he'd been raised in Nazareth (see Matt 2:1, 23).

1:47-51 When Jesus and Nathanael met—before Nathanael uttered a word—Jesus called him **an Israelite in whom there is no deceit** (1:47). Nathanael was stunned. He'd only just met the guy, so how could he know anything about him? Then Jesus told him where he'd been (**under the fig tree**) when Philip had found him (1:48). That was too much for Nathanael. He hailed Jesus as **the Son of God . . . the King of Israel** (1:49). Jesus responded to Nathanael by telling him that, because he believed, he'd **see greater things than this** (1:50). When we exercise faith in what God reveals to us, he will grant us an even greater experience of himself.

Jesus had displayed his omniscience, his supernatural knowledge of all things. Not only did he know about Nathanael's character and where he was when Philip found him, but he also knew what Nathanael had been thinking about. Notice that Jesus told Nathanael that he, along with the other disciples (the "you" is plural), would **see heaven opened and the angels of God ascending and descending on the Son of Man** (1:51). This statement is a reference to Jacob's experience of dreaming about a stairway reaching from earth to heaven with angels "going up and down on it" (Gen 28:10-12). This Old Testament account is what Nathanael had been thinking about under the fig tree. How do I know? Because not only did Jesus make explicit reference to this story, but he also told Nathanael that he was "an Israelite in whom there is no deceit" (1:47). Being a deceiver was exactly what Jacob was known for (see Gen 27:1-36). So by these two comments, Jesus was making Nathanael aware that he knew what he was thinking.

We should not miss the fact that Jesus replaced the image of a stairway in Jacob's dream with "the Son of Man" (a reference to himself). Thus, Jesus Christ is the bridge between heaven and earth. He grants access to eternity. As he would tell his disciples later, "No one comes to the Father except through me" (14:6). Jesus also brings the supernatural into history for believers who exercise faith in his Word.

III. EARLY MINISTRY AND SIGNS (2:1–4:54)

2:1-3 Jesus, his mother, and his disciples **were invited** to a **wedding** in **Cana of Galilee** (2:1-2). But as the festivities were proceeding, his **mother** informed him that they had run out of **wine** (2:3). Wedding celebrations often lasted for several days, so this was indeed an embarrassing problem. Though the Old Testament condemns drunkenness (e.g., Deut 21:20-21; Prov 20:1; 23:19-21; 31:4-5), wine is often spoken of in terms of celebration, blessing, and joy (e.g., Ps 4:7; 104:15; Prov 3:9-10; Songs 1:2; Isa 25:6; 55:1).

2:4-8 Mary knew Jesus was able to solve the problem. But Jesus said, **What does that have to do with you and me? . . . My hour has not yet come** (2:4). Apparently she thought this was the perfect opportunity for him to publicly reveal his identity, but Jesus didn't agree. It was not yet the time to publicly manifest his supernatural activity for all to see. Nevertheless, he solved the dilemma without advertising his identity. His mother told the servants, **Do whatever he tells you** (2:5). Jesus had the servants fill **six stone water jars** (able to hold **twenty or thirty gallons** each) **with water**, and then **draw some out and take it to the headwaiter** (2:6-8).

Mary's words ought to ring in our ears. The Lord wants us to "do whatever he tells" us. He often doesn't describe the path that he's taking us on. He doesn't explain how he intends to deal with our problems. He simply calls us to obey his revealed Word. Only after we've obeyed will we have the opportunity to experience him at a deeper level.

2:9-10 The headwaiter . . . did not know where [the wine] came from, but he knew it was good stuff. The practice in those days was to supply guests with **fine wine** followed by wine of **inferior** quality. But the headwaiter praised **the groom** for unexpectedly providing them with excellent wine at that point in the celebration (2:10). This was a miracle of transformation that illustrates the change in people's lives that takes place when they believe in Jesus and obey his Word.

What does that tell us about Jesus? Well, when he moves in your life, you can count on it being the best thing for you. If you position yourself rightly through obedient submission to his agenda, he can flip the script and give you his best—even when you thought his best was a thing of the past. Jesus *is* the new wine, and some of his best work comes in the midst of our emptiness.

2:11-12 This was **the first of his** miracles—or **signs** as John refers to them (see, e.g., 4:54; 6:2, 14). While Jesus was not yet ready to manifest his identity to the crowd (see 2:4-8), who had no idea where the wine came from, he performed this sign to reveal his **glory** to **his disciples** so that their faith would be strengthened (2:11).

2:13-14 During the **Passover** celebration, **Jesus went up to Jerusalem** (2:13), as did many Jewish pilgrims. When Jesus saw what was happening in the temple, he was infuriated. There were people **selling** animals. In and of itself, this was fine. After all, those who had traveled from far away would need to purchase animals to offer as sacrifices. But sales were taking place in the outermost court of the temple—the court of the Gentiles. Thus, non-Jews who came to worship the God of Israel were prevented from doing so. Moreover, the Synoptic Gospels make clear that the sellers were charging an exorbitant amount because Jesus said they had turned it into a "den of thieves." They were lining their pockets at the expense of the worshipers (cf. Matt 21:12-13). The prophet Malachi also predicted that one would come to purify the temple (see Mal 3:1-5).

2:15-17 So Jesus made **a whip** and **drove** all of them **out of the temple** (2:15). Legitimate business is one thing. But these people had taken a place intended for worship and turned it into **a marketplace** (2:16). **His disciples** saw in Jesus's deeds the fulfillment of Psalm 69:9: **Zeal for your house will consume me** (2:17).

2:18-22 When the Jews saw the ruckus he had caused, they demanded, **What sign will you show us for doing these things?** (2:18). In other words, "Who died and left you in charge? What right do you have to do this?" Jesus replied, **Destroy this temple, and I will raise it up in three days** (2:19). They assumed he was talking about the **temple** complex; this one was constructed by Herod the Great and had taken **forty-six years to build** (2:20). They thought he was crazy, **but he was speaking about the temple of his body** (2:21). And though they couldn't understand him, he was right. The Jewish leaders would deliver Jesus over to the Romans to be put to death. Then, in three days, he would rise from the grave. His resurrection would indeed demonstrate his authority for cleansing the temple. Interestingly, the **disciples** didn't comprehend everything he said either. It would require Jesus's resurrection for them to grow in their faith and understanding (2:22).

2:23-25 Though **many** people **believed** in him (were converted) **when they saw [his] signs**, Jesus **would not entrust himself to them** (2:23-24)—that is, he wasn't ready to reveal more of himself to them because of their spiritual immaturity. They were not yet ready for full commitment to discipleship and public identification with him. Jesus **knew what was in man** (2:25). He could see into their hearts. And he can see into yours too. So don't miss this truth: Spiritual growth is important because it expands our capacity to experience more of God. Jesus does not relate to all believers the same way.

3:1-2 The Pharisees were a group of conservative Jews devoted to keeping the law (and often adding to it). One of them, a man **named Nicodemus**, approached Jesus **at night**. Why at night? After all, Nicodemus clearly thought well of Jesus. He called him **Rabbi** and considered him **a teacher**

who [had] come from God, who was able to **perform** miraculous **signs** because **God [was] with him**. But we'll see that most of his colleagues didn't feel the same way. They would grow in their opposition and hatred of Jesus (see, e.g., 7:32, 47-48; 8:3-6; 11:45-57). Therefore, Nicodemus went to Jesus under cover of darkness so that he could avoid the scorn of his fellow Pharisees—especially in light of Jesus's cleansing of the temple. He didn't want to admit to his admiration of Jesus during the daytime!

3:3 Jesus prefaced his response with **Truly I tell you**. Some translations render it, "Truly, truly." He frequently began important statements with this phrase, emphasizing the spiritual significance of what he was about to say.

Nicodemus had just paid Jesus a compliment. But Jesus didn't beat around the bush. He told him, **Unless someone is born again, he cannot see the kingdom of God**. So though essentially Nicodemus had come to tell Jesus, "I approve of you," Jesus, rather than being flattered, told this Jewish teacher, "You need to be born again." The Greek word translated "again" can also mean "from above." Probably both ideas are intended. Indeed, we need to be born again (to have a spiritual birth in contrast to our physical birth), and that new birth comes only from heaven above.

All of the Jews were longing for the kingdom of God, for that day when the Messiah would come, vanquish Israel's enemies, and bless God's people. Jesus's first disciples recognized him as the "Messiah" and the "King of Israel" (1:41, 49), but Jesus wanted Nicodemus to understand that entering into the kingdom required an individual to be spiritually reborn. As the apostle Paul explains it, all people are dead in their trespasses and sins, and only God can give us spiritual life (Eph 2:1-5). Nicodemus needed a spiritual rebirth; simply being a religious leader wouldn't cut it.

3:4-8 Nicodemus was confused. How could he climb back into his **mother's womb** for a **second** birth (3:4)? But Jesus was speaking spiritually. He told him that it was necessary for a person to be **born of water** (a reference

to physical birth) **and the Spirit to enter the kingdom** (3:5). Since Nicodemus's question involved the issue of human birth (3:4) and since the contrast was between **flesh** and **Spirit** (3:6), Jesus was contrasting physical birth with spiritual birth. To enter God's kingdom, you must not only be born physically (of water and flesh) but also supernaturally (of the Spirit). Human birth and physical ancestry are insufficient for obtaining eternal life.

The only way to experience spiritual life is to be **born of the Spirit** (3:6). It's like **the wind**. You **hear** it, but you don't see it. You can't control it; all you can do is see its effects. It's the same way with being **born of the Spirit** (3:8) God's Spirit invisibly does its work inside the human heart. We can't see it happening. All we see are the results.

3:9-13 Nicodemus was perplexed: **How can these things be?** (3:9). Jesus's reply probably stung: **Are you a teacher of Israel and don't know these things?** (3:10). The concept that Nicodemus couldn't understand concerning the new kingdom age of the working of the Spirit was clearly taught in the Old Testament (see Isa 32:15; Ezek 36:25-27; Joel 2:28-29). As a teacher and leader, Nicodemus should have known that. If he could not grasp **earthly things** that were plainly taught in the Scriptures, how could he grasp the **heavenly things** that only Jesus could reveal (3:12)— that is, that God in grace can give people a new heart (see 1 Sam 10:6; Jer 31:33)? Jesus could truly reveal deep heavenly truths since only he had **descended from heaven** (3:13).

3:14-15 The mention of **Moses [lifting] up the snake in the wilderness** is a reference to an incident recorded in the book of Numbers (3:14; see Num 21:4-9). On one occasion, when the people of Israel were complaining that God and Moses had only brought them out of Egypt to die in the wilderness, the Lord sent venomous snakes that bit and killed many. But God provided a means of deliverance. He had Moses make a bronze snake and tell the people to look at it. If anyone bitten trusted God and looked at the bronze snake, he would be healed. Similarly, **the Son of Man** would also be **lifted up** (on a cross), **so that everyone who believes in him may have eternal life**. Trusting Christ and his substitutionary atonement is God's provision for addressing his righteous judgment on sin.

3:16 Here we have perhaps the most well-known verse in the Bible. **God loved the world** of people, and his love was not merely sentimental. Rather, it prompted him to take action. God the Father **gave his one and only Son** as a substitute for sinful human beings. He would die in their place, bearing their sins. But salvation from sin through the Son requires faith: **Everyone who believes in him will not perish but have eternal life.** When you trust in Jesus alone as your personal sin-bearer, divine judgment is removed and eternal life is freely given.

3:17-18 The Father's purpose in sending **his Son into the world** was to bring salvation, not condemnation (3:17). Motivated by love (3:16), God acted **to save the world** (3:17). Condemnation only comes to the one **who does not believe** in the **one and only Son of God** (3:18). Salvation from sin and judgment is free for the taking. But if you reject the miracle cure that the doctor offers you, don't blame him when you succumb to your fatal illness.

3:19-21 Those who love **darkness rather than the light**, so that they can try (in vain) to hide their sinful **deeds** (3:19-20), will experience eternal judgment for rejecting the free gift of God. Those who receive **the truth** and live their lives in accordance with it come **to the light** in order to show that their good **works** have been **accomplished by God** (3:21). Unbelievers are responsible for their evil deeds, but believers know that God gets the glory for their good ones. Nicodemus was being challenged to come out of the darkness and into the light (see 3:1-2).

3:22-26 At this time both Jesus and John the Baptist were engaged in ministry (3:22-23). John (the apostle and author) notes that **John** (the Baptist) **had not yet been thrown into prison** (3:24; on John's imprisonment and execution, see Matt 14:3-12; Mark 6:17-29; Luke 3:18-20). **John's disciples** had become concerned because **everyone [was] going to** Jesus (3:25-26). Thus, they essentially told

their master, "Wait a minute, this Jesus fella is moving in on your ministry. Now fewer people are coming to you."

3:27-30 But John's pride was not wounded like his disciples' was. First, he acknowledged that **no one can receive anything unless it has been given to him from heaven** (3:27). John knew that his job had been assigned to him by God; therefore, he was content to receive no more than what God wanted him to have. Second, John confessed his secondary role in relationship to Jesus. John was **not the Messiah.** Rather, he had **been sent ahead of him** to prepare his way (3:28). He wasn't **the groom** but **the groom's friend.** The groom gets **the bride,** and the groom's friend is glad for him (3:29). Third, John said, **He must increase, but I must decrease** (3:30). John was simply the opening act, expected to warm up the crowd and then get off the stage. Jesus was the main event, the star attraction.

John's job was to point to and glorify the Messiah. And that's our job too. John was content with and grateful for his role. Are you?

3:31-36 Jesus has superiority. He **comes from above . . . from heaven.** He is no mere man speaking from an **earthly** viewpoint (3:31). He is the Son of God speaking from a heavenly perspective. His **testimony is true,** whether someone **accepts** it or not (3:32-33). To reject the Son's testimony is to call God a liar since the Son speaks the very **words** of God and **the Father . . . has given all things into his hands** (3:34-35). He will one day rule the world as King. Thus, the matter is simple. Believe in **the Son** to receive **eternal life.** Reject him and experience divine **wrath** (3:36).

4:1-4 The **Pharisees had heard** about the ministry of **Jesus** and his **disciples.** Now that Jesus was making **more disciples than John,** the Jewish leaders focused their attention on him (4:1). So Jesus **left Judea** in the south and went to **Galilee** in the north (4:3). But to get there, **he had to travel through Samaria** (4:4).

The Jews disliked the Samaritans, considering them an unclean race. Originally, the name *Samaria* applied to the capital city of the northern kingdom of Israel, which was founded by King Omri (see 1 Kgs 16:23-24). But eventually the entire northern kingdom was referred to by this name. When the Assyrians conquered it, they deported many Israelites, but left others in the land. Then the Assyrians settled other conquered peoples there, who intermarried with the remaining Israelites. This mixture of peoples also involved the worship of various false gods (see 2 Kgs 17:24-41). The Samaritans of Jesus's day were their descendants, a people of mixed ancestry and syncretistic religious practices. Thus, the Jews despised them.

It is also important to note that Jesus had to go through Samaria (4:4). This would not be the normal route for orthodox Jews, who sought to avoid contact with Samaritans. Thus, Jesus prioritized meeting spiritual needs over facilitating, endorsing, and practicing ungodly social and racial divisions.

4:5-6 Jesus stopped at a Samaritan **town** where **Jacob's well** was. The well is not mentioned in the Old Testament, but **the property that Jacob** purchased and **had given his son Joseph** was in Shechem (see Gen 33:18-19; Josh 24:32). Jesus **sat down** to rest because he was **worn out from his journey** (4:6).

Notice that John emphasizes the full deity ("the Word was God," 1:1) and the full humanity (he was "worn out," 4:6) of Jesus. In theological terminology, the uniting of two distinct natures (divine and human) in one person (Jesus Christ) is known as the hypostatic union. Jesus Christ was, is, and ever will be the God-Man (see Phil 2:6-11). It is also important to note that Jacob's well represents common ground, since both Jews and Samaritans revered Jacob.

4:7-10 Jesus was alone because **his disciples had gone into town to buy** groceries (4:8). Their absence implies that Jesus knew he couldn't effectively minister to the woman with the presence of the racial and gender biases of the disciples. He sat down at the well at "about noon" (4:6) when a Samaritan **woman . . . came to draw water** (4:7). Typically people wouldn't draw water during the heat of the day. So, why would she arrive at a time when no one would be

around? We'll soon see that she was a woman of questionable character.

The woman was shocked when Jesus asked her for **a drink**, since **Jews [did] not associate with Samaritans** (4:7, 9; see commentary on 4:1-4). Jesus told her that if she understood who he was, she would have been asking him for **a drink** of **living water**—that is, spiritual life (4:10). Thus, he used a conversation about something physical to introduce her to a spiritual reality. Notice too that Jesus did not give up his cultural and racial identity to minister to someone of a different race and culture. His willingness to engage her socially by drinking water from her cup opened the door for him to reach her spiritually. We should never ignore or reject the humanity of different people as we seek to share with them the good news of the gospel.

4:11-14 But she didn't grasp the transition. She was still stuck thinking about physical water, wondering where and how Jesus was going to get it. This well was good enough for Jacob (4:11-12). Did this strange Jew think he was better than his own patriarch? So **Jesus** proceeded further down the spiritual road. Anyone who **drinks from this water** would be **thirsty again**, he told her, but anyone who drinks the water that only he could provide would have a **well** within, **springing up . . . for eternal life** (4:13-14). If you receive a drink from Jesus, you don't have to come back for another. His living water becomes its own everlasting well. Thirst no more.

4:15-18 Apparently still not grasping the point, **the woman** smugly asked for some of this water so that she'd no longer **get thirsty** and have to keep coming out to **draw water** every day (4:15). So Jesus made the conversation a little more personal: **Go call your husband** (4:16). Her testimony that she had no **husband** was only half true, and Jesus knew it (4:17). She'd been married **five** times, and **the man** she currently lived with was **not** her **husband** (4:18). Because Jesus was willing to drink from her cup, he could now address her sin.

4:19-21 The Samaritan woman acknowledged Jesus's divine insight by calling him **a prophet** since he accurately pinpointed her unrighteous lifestyle (4:19). Then (perhaps since his comments hit a little too close to home!) she changed the subject to the topic of worship. The Samaritans worshiped on Mount Gerizim, while the Jews worshiped at the temple **in Jerusalem** (4:20). So who was right? Jesus explained that **an hour was coming** when true **worship** of **the Father** wouldn't involve a specific location (4:21). In John's Gospel, Jesus's "hour" is usually associated with his crucifixion and resurrection (see 2:4; 7:30; 8:20; 12:23, 27; 13:1; 16:32; 17:1). So through his death on the cross and resurrection from the grave, Jesus would transform worship for God's people.

4:22-24 Jesus insisted that her ancestral understanding of worship was flawed and that **salvation is from the Jews** (4:22) because the Messiah would be of Jewish lineage, descended from the tribe of Judah. Jesus made it clear that truth trumps race and culture. **An hour is coming** (after his resurrection) **and is now here** (because the Messiah was present with her at that moment) **when the true worshipers will worship the Father in Spirit and in truth** (4:23). To "worship the Father in Spirit" is to have a heart that is in pursuit of an intimate spiritual relationship with the **God** who **is Spirit** (4:24). To worship God "in truth" is to worship him in a biblically accurate way— through the one who *is* the truth (see 14:6). **The Father wants such people to worship him** (4:23). God is on the hunt for those who will worship him spiritually through Jesus Christ based on the truth of his Word.

4:25-26 The woman was in an immoral relationship and theologically confused. Nevertheless, she had a genuine messianic expectation: when **the Messiah . . . comes, he will explain everything to us** (4:25). Their conversation, then, had reached the destination Jesus had intended. He introduced himself: **I, the one speaking to you, am he** (4:26).

Jesus can deal with your sin (that's why he came), and he can straighten out your confusion. What's needed is an openness to receive him.

4:27-30 At that moment, the disciples returned from their food run (see 4:8) and were

bewildered that Jesus **was talking with a woman** (4:27)—in particular with a Samaritan one (see commentary on 4:1-4). But the woman **went into town**, told everyone about Jesus, and asked, **Could this be the Messiah?** (4:28-29). Her testimony was so effective that the locals turned out in droves to see Jesus (4:30).

Notice this: The woman hadn't attended seminary; she'd had no theological training. She had simply met Jesus. In fact, she'd only *just* met him. But she knew enough to want to share him with others. New believers should be encouraged to share their faith as soon as possible.

4:31-34 Having returned with lunch, **the disciples** urged Jesus to **eat something** (4:31). But he had **food to eat** that they knew nothing about (4:32). For Jesus, the spiritual trumped the physical: **My food is to do the will of him who sent me and to finish his work** (4:34). His greatest satisfaction and fulfillment, then, was not in filling his belly but in obeying God. To him, doing the will of God was not drudgery but joy. For us too, the spiritual must always take precedence over the physical (see Matt 4:3-4; 6:31-33).

4:35 Jesus repeated a proverb that was probably well known in such an agrarian society: **There are still four months, and then comes the harvest**. Crops take time to grow. But Jesus had a ministry harvest ready for them to reap. As he pointed to the crowd of Samaritan men who had heard the woman's testimony and who were coming to see him, Jesus said, **Open your eyes and look at the fields, because they are ready for harvest**.

How often do we postpone sharing the gospel with others? How often do we put God's kingdom second, when Jesus commands us to seek it first (see Matt 6:33)? If we pay close attention, we will see God at work all around us and discover ministry opportunities right before our eyes—if we have spiritual sight to see them.

4:36-38 Jesus compared gospel ministry to sowing seeds and reaping a harvest. Sometimes **one sows and another reaps** (4:37)— that is, it may take several encounters with the gospel delivered through more than one messenger before a person believes it. One Christian explains the gospel to an unbeliever, and later another Christian eventually leads that unbeliever to Christ. Seeds are sown by one believer, and a harvest is reaped by another (4:38). Such shared ministry allows us to share in the blessings of God's kingdom with one another.

4:39-42 Though her faith in Jesus was brand new, the Samaritan woman **testified**, and **many Samaritans from that town believed in** Jesus (4:39). They came to Jesus because of the woman's witness; they stayed because they encountered Jesus personally (4:42). There's no telling what God can do with your passionate, genuine testimony about how the grace of God transformed your life.

John indicated earlier that "Jews [did] not associate with Samaritans" (4:9; see commentary on 4:1-4). Nevertheless, **the Samaritans . . . asked [Jesus] to stay with them.** So he and his disciples hung out with them for **two days** (4:40). So, is racial reconciliation possible? If you're operating spiritually and united in Jesus, the answer is a resounding, "Yes!" And it doesn't take long when people are right with Jesus.

4:43-45 After his brief sojourn in Samaria, Jesus went to **Galilee,** the region where he had grown up (4:43). **The Galileans welcomed him because they had seen everything he did in Jerusalem** (4:45); nevertheless, John

lets the reader know that rejection is coming because **Jesus himself had testified that a prophet has no honor in his own country** (4:44). Not only would those from his hometown reject him, but they'd even seek to kill him (see Luke 4:16-30).

4:46-50 Jesus went **to Cana of Galilee, where he had turned the water into wine** (see 2:1-2). There a **royal official** begged Jesus to heal his dying **son** (4:46-47). But Jesus rebuked **him** and the other **people** who had gathered. Apparently, though they wanted to **see** and experience the benefits of Jesus's miraculous **signs and wonders**, they were unwilling to **believe** that he was the Messiah based on his word, as the Samaritans did (4:48). In spite of this, Jesus mercifully healed the official's son from a distance and told him, **Go . . . your son will live.** At that moment, **the man believed.** How do we know? Because his faith went into action: He obeyed Jesus and **departed** for his home (4:50).

4:51-54 As the official was on his way, **his servants met him** and said that his son had recovered—at **the very hour** that Jesus had spoken to him (4:51-53). (When Jesus is ready to move, don't blink, or you may miss his work.) As a result, the official shared what happened with **his whole household**, and they all **believed** in Jesus as the Messiah and not just as a miracle worker (4:53).

IV. MORE SIGNS AND OPPOSITION (5:1–10:42)

A. Healing the Disabled, Feeding the Hungry, Walking on Water (5:1–6:71)

5:1-6 Jesus went up to Jerusalem for a Jewish festival (5:1). Near the **pool, called Bethesda,** there were many **blind, lame, and paralyzed** people waiting for a supernatural healing (5:2-3). **Jesus saw a man** there who had been disabled **for thirty-eight years** and asked him an interesting question: **Do you want to get well?** (5:5-6). It suggests that some people have been stuck in their

negative circumstances for so long that they have given up hope that things can ever change. God's work occurs in cooperation with our will.

5:7 In response, the man told Jesus that every time there was a healing opportunity he never had anyone to help him **into the pool.** The healing was so near and yet so far away. The man's situation was hopeless, and he had no one to offer him aid.

5:8-9 So Jesus told the man, **Get up . . . pick up your mat and walk** (5:8). Wherever your bed is, that's where your home is. Thus, this man would no longer be sleeping in a place of despair. His home was changing. **Instantly the man got well, picked up his mat, and started to walk** (5:9).

5:10 In spite of Jesus's miraculous healing, there was a problem: **that day was the Sabbath.** It wasn't a problem for Jesus, but it was for the Jewish religious leaders. They considered picking up a mat to be work (!) and, therefore, prohibited on the Sabbath, so they rebuked the man. They had taken a divine command that provided physical rest for God's people and erroneously turned it into a human restriction on acts of mercy.

5:11-13 The man who made me well told me to **pick up** my **mat** (5:11) indicates that the healed man preferred to listen to the one with the miraculous power, not leaders who were just practicing religion! He had lain there for thirty-eight years, and the religious leaders had never aided in his healing. So when an unknown healer fixed his legs and commanded him to carry his mat, there was no question about whom he would listen to. The leaders wanted to know who this miraculous healer was, but **Jesus had slipped away** (5:12-13).

5:14 Later **Jesus found** the man **in the temple** and said, **See, you are well. Do not sin anymore, so that something worse doesn't happen to you.** It's possible, then, that the man had been stuck because of unaddressed sin in his life. Sin carries long-term consequences.

5:15-16 Having encountered Jesus again, the man who had been healed found the Jewish religious leaders and pointed out to them the man who had done the healing (5:15). One would think that they would have been excited to meet Jesus. Instead, they **began persecuting Jesus because he was doing these things on the Sabbath** (5:16).

While Jesus was changing lives, the leaders were playing religion. No matter how much religious activity you are engaged in, if you're not in the business of changing lives, then you're not in the business of Jesus.

5:17-18 Jesus justified his activity on the Sabbath by telling them, **My Father is still working, and I am working also** (5:17). God the Father was engaged in kingdom business, and so was his Son. When they heard this, the Jewish leaders wanted to kill Jesus—**not only** because he was **breaking the Sabbath,** but because he was **calling God his own Father, making himself equal to God** (5:18).

They hadn't misunderstood Jesus; they knew exactly what he was saying. The Son shared the Father's divine nature. He had the DNA of deity. As John himself has already said, "The Word was with God, and the Word was God" (1:1). But as far as the leaders were concerned, Jesus's claims were blasphemy.

5:19 But Jesus wasn't committing blasphemy. He was acting in perfect harmony and solidarity with the Father. **The Son does only what he sees the Father doing.** Their relationship is so close that they function simultaneously. So whatever Jesus was doing, the Father was doing. Thus, healing the man on the Sabbath was not blasphemy but an act of God.

5:20-21 The Father loves the Son. The Godhead is united in perfect love, transparency, and intimacy. This line, then, is a subtle warning to the religious leaders. The one whom they wanted to kill (5:18) was dearly loved by God the Father. And because of that, the Father would **show him greater works than these** so that they would **be amazed** (5:20); these works included raising **the dead** (5:21). So in a way, Jesus was telling them, "You think you're upset now because I healed a paralytic? You haven't seen anything yet. Wait until you see what I do with Lazarus!" (see 11:1-44).

5:22-23 God the Father has also turned over **all judgment to the Son** (5:22). Jesus Christ has been made the final Judge of all mankind. Why? **So that all people may honor the Son just as they honor the Father.** Those words from Jesus are another clear and explicit claim to his deity. To be honored as God is to be God. In fact, Jesus told them, **Anyone who does not honor the Son does not honor the Father who sent him** (5:23). It's a family matter. To reject Jesus is to reject God altogether. There's no true religion without Jesus Christ.

5:24 If Jesus is the Judge of humanity, how does one escape divine **judgment** on sin? Jesus gives the answer: **Anyone who hears my word and believes him who sent me has eternal life.** To believe in the Son, then, is to pass **from death** (eternal separation from God) **to life** (eternal relationship with God). That's eternal security. Faith in God's promise through Jesus Christ guarantees eternal life to all who believe in him for it. Assurance is the essence of saving faith.

5:25-29 The dead will hear the voice of the **Son of God** and **live** because **the Father** is the source of **life** and has given **the Son** the right to grant life (5:25-26). Eternal, spiritual life is available through Jesus. To him, the Father **has granted . . . the right to pass judgment** (5:27). One day, **all who are in the graves will hear** the Son's **voice and come out**— either **to the resurrection of life** or **to the resurrection of condemnation** (8:28-29). There will be no exceptions. Whether people experience eternal life or condemnation after the resurrection will depend entirely on their response to Jesus in this life. If they believed in Jesus, they will **have done good things** because of the eternal life in them. If they did not believe in Jesus, they will **have done wicked things** because of the lack of life in them (5:29).

5:30 Everything Jesus did, he did at the initiative of his Father. He did **not seek [his] own will** but the Father's. That, in fact, is what a life looks like when it is completely yielded to God.

5:31-35 Jesus wasn't merely speaking on his own behalf. In fulfillment of Scripture, **John** the Baptist **testified to the truth** about him (5:32; see 1:19-36). **John was a . . . shining lamp**, bearing **testimony** so that they might **be saved** (5:34-35). Though they listened to John at first, eventually they rejected him (5:35).

5:36-40 But there was a **greater** witness than John that testified to Jesus's identity. That witness was Jesus's **works** (5:36). The miraculous signs he performed were evidence that he was the Messiah **sent** from the Father. So in essence, Jesus told them,

"My deeds are my validation." Everything had been done before their eyes. Moreover, **the Father** also **testified** about Jesus, but the religious leaders had rejected this too. They didn't have God's **word residing in [them]** because they didn't **believe** in his Son (5:37-38). They thought they had **eternal life** because they studied **the Scriptures.** Yet those very Scriptures pointed to Jesus, and they refused to go to him to **have life** (5:39-40).

A person can diligently study the Bible (the written Word) and still miss Jesus (the living Word). Knowing God's written Word is absolutely essential, but if your knowledge of it doesn't lead you to the living Word, then you have completely missed the point. This sad fact was illustrated when Jewish leaders told the wise men that Scripture foretold the Messiah's birth in Bethlehem, but they never bothered to make the trip to worship him (see Matt 2:1-6).

5:41-43 Jesus confronted the religious leaders with hard truth: **You have no love for God within you** (5:42). Why? Because Jesus had come in his **Father's name**, but they wouldn't **accept** him (5:43). They thought they loved God, claimed they loved God, boasted that they loved God. But they were unwilling to accept Jesus. Therefore, their professed love for God was a fraud. You simply can't have the Father without the Son. You can't have God without Jesus Christ.

5:44 What was keeping them from Jesus? Rather than seeking **glory that comes from the only God**, they were accepting **glory from one another**. In other words, they enjoyed being popular. Unconcerned with pleasing God, they sought to please each other.

5:45-47 Jesus told the religious leaders that he wouldn't be their accuser. Instead Moses, the very person whose words they were reading in the Old Testament, would accuse them before God because they hadn't learned from him (5:45). **Moses**, Jesus told them, **wrote about me** (5:46). For example, Moses (who authored the books of Genesis–Deuteronomy) wrote about the Passover lamb (see Exod 12:1-28), and John the Baptist had identified Jesus as "the Lamb of God" (1:29,

36). Moses wrote that God would "raise up … a prophet" like him from among God's people (Deut 18:15; see 1:14; Acts 7:37). But the religious leaders were unwilling to accept that Jesus spoke for God. They had read Moses; they just weren't paying attention to him. So, if they wouldn't believe Moses, they weren't going to **believe** Jesus (5:47).

6:1-6 Jesus had been ministering in **Galilee**, and **a huge crowd** followed him because of the miraculous **signs** he performed (6:2). **The Passover** was **near**; therefore, many people were gathering and would be making their journey to Jerusalem (6:4). Jesus saw the **crowd** and **asked Philip** where they could **buy bread** for everyone to **eat** (6:5). But he knew what he intended to do and was saying this **to test** Philip (6:6).

Teachers give students tests to allow them to apply what they have learned. When God tests us, he grants us opportunity to apply spiritual truth to the challenging circumstances we face. With thousands of hungry people gathering, Jesus gave Philip a pop quiz he'd never forget.

6:7-9 Philip responded that **two hundred denarii** (over six months' wages) **wouldn't be enough** to feed the crowd (6:7). And he was right. But Jesus wasn't asking about the cost; he was asking where the food would come from. **Andrew** at least pointed to a food source: **a boy** with **five barley loaves and two fish** (6:8-9). However, he observed, **What are they for so many?** (6:9). Neither man could see a solution to the dilemma.

6:10-11 Jesus had **the people sit down.** The number of **men** was **five thousand** (6:10). Thus, were women and children included (see Matt 14:21), there could have been over fifteen thousand people present. Then, taking the **loaves** and the **fish**, Jesus gave **thanks**—thanking God for what was not nearly enough! After that, **he distributed** the food and, miraculously, everyone ate **as much as they wanted** (6:11). Jesus took insufficiency, thanked God for it, and provided more than enough. Don't let your lack of resources limit what God can do. Offer prayers of thanksgiving even in the midst of your insufficiency.

6:12-13 When everyone was **full**, Jesus had the disciples collect the leftovers, which **filled twelve baskets.** That's one doggy bag per disciple, each a reminder of God's supernatural provision for each disciple.

6:14-15 When they **saw the sign**, the people exclaimed, **This truly is the Prophet who is to come into the world** (6:14; see Deut 18:15-18). They recognized that Jesus's miracles pointed to his identity. So far, so good. But **when Jesus realized** that they wanted to **take him by force to make him king, he withdrew again to the mountain by himself** (6:15). As we'll see in 6:26-27, they only wanted the physical benefits he offered. They wanted the blessings without the blesser.

6:16-19 While Jesus was still on the mountain, the **disciples** got into their **boat** and **started across the sea** since he **had not yet** arrived (6:16-17). **A high wind** started to blow, and the waves **began to churn** (6:18). As if that weren't bad enough, **they saw Jesus walking on the sea**, and the sight terrified them (6:19). They feared he was a ghost (see Matt 14:26).

6:20-21 Jesus calmed their fears and assured them that he was no specter (6:20). So **they were willing to take him on board.** Then, **at once the boat was at the shore where they were heading** (6:21). So, one moment they were in the middle of a stormy sea; the next moment they had miraculously reached their destination! Don't miss that once they were willing to receive Jesus into the boat, he dealt with their problem and delivered them where they needed to go. When believers recognize and respond to the presence of Jesus in the midst of their struggles, they invite the supernatural into their negative circumstances.

6:22-25 The next day, the crowd that had been left behind was puzzled. The **disciples** had departed in a **boat**, but Jesus hadn't been with them. Yet **Jesus** was nowhere to be found (6:22-24). So they sailed to **Capernaum** and **found [Jesus] on the other side of the sea** (6:24-25). How was that possible? He hadn't left in the boat. So they asked him,

When did you get here? (6:25). They suspected Jesus had arrived in some supernatural way.

6:26 In spite of their pursuit of him, Jesus could see the motivation of their hearts: **You are looking for me, not because you saw the signs, but because you ate the loaves and were filled.** They hadn't sought him for who he was, then. They sought him for what he could give them. They didn't want him, but his blessings.

God isn't opposed to blessing people. He is opposed, however, to people who simply want to use him for his blessings—people who only want him for the stuff he can provide. He's looking for those who don't want his blessings without him.

When the Israelites sinned against the Lord by constructing a golden calf, he told Moses that though he would give them the land of Canaan, he himself would not accompany them (see Exod 33:1-3). But Moses would have none of that. He didn't want the promised land unless God would go with them (Exod 33:15). When you want God more than you want his blessings, you will receive him—as well as whatever he graciously plans to give you. We are to pursue more *of* God not just more *from* God.

6:27 Jesus urged them to give the spiritual priority over the physical: **Don't work for the food that perishes but for the food that lasts for eternal life, which the Son of Man will give you.** They were striving for miraculous physical food (like the prioritization of the material over the spiritual in prosperity theology), when the Son was offering the free gift of spiritual food—that is, eternal life.

6:28-29 They wanted to know what **works** God required of them (6:28). So Jesus clarified: **This is the work of God—that you believe in the one he has sent** (6:29). The only thing God demands of those wanting to receive the free gift of eternal life is belief in his Son, Jesus Christ.

6:30-35 That wasn't good enough for them. If they were to **believe in** him, they wanted to know **what sign** he would **perform** (6:30). They pointed to the Old Testament miracle

when Moses supplied Israel with **manna— bread from heaven**—in the wilderness (6:31). But Jesus corrected them. **Moses** hadn't given them any **bread**. God was their source, not Moses (6:32).

In fact, God was offering them something greater than mere bread. He offered them **true bread—the one who comes down from heaven and gives life to the world** (6:32-33). But the crowd was still thinking about food. **Give us this bread always,** they said (6:34), which may as well have been the cry, "We're hungry!" So, once again, Jesus made himself clear: **I am the bread of life ... No one who comes to me will ever be hungry, and no one who believes in me will ever be thirsty again** (6:35). That's Jesus's way of describing the gift of eternal life.

We must consider Jesus our source of life. If we "feed" on him (i.e., "believe in" him, 6:29) as **the bread of God** (6:33), we will never go hungry again (i.e., we "will never die," 11:26). This eternal life is permanent, secure, and irrevocable.

6:36-40 Though the people had seen Jesus's works, they refused to **believe** (6:36). They desired physical blessings over spiritual ones. But Jesus assured them, **Everyone the Father gives me will come to me.** So, just whom does the Father give to the Son? All those who believe in him. Whoever believes in the Son is a gift from the Father to the Son. They come to Jesus, and he will **never cast** them **out** (6:37). It's God's **will** that the Son **lose none of those** whom the Father gives to him (6:39). This means that when you trust in Jesus Christ, you are eternally secure. If you come to him for salvation, you cannot be lost again. Not only does the Son vow not to lose you, but he also promises to give you **eternal life** and **raise** you **up on the last day** (6:40). As Jesus was raised from the dead (20:1-29), believers will also be raised.

6:41-42 Rather than believe in him, though, **the Jews started complaining.** How could this guy call himself **bread that came down from heaven?** (6:41). They said to one another, **Isn't this Jesus the son of Joseph?** (6:42). That is to say, "We know him. He's not from heaven; he's from Nazareth!"

6:43-46 But Jesus rebuked them for their complaints (6:43) and spoke of God's ministry of drawing people to himself: **No one can come to [the Son] unless the Father . . . draws him** (6:44). Jesus is "the true light that gives light to everyone" (1:9). It's what a person does with that light, then, that determines whether or not he will come to Jesus, who is the only one who **has seen the Father** (6:46). This drawing is universal (see 12:32; 16:7-11) and can be rejected (see Acts 7:51).

6:47-51 The beautiful promise of the gospel is that **anyone who believes** in Jesus **has eternal life** (6:47). When Jesus said, **I am the bread of life** (6:48), it was the first of his seven "I am" statements recorded in John's Gospel (see also 8:12; 10:7, 11; 11:25; 14:6; 15:1). He would also say "I am" in an absolute sense to emphasize his divine identity (see 8:58).

The Jews wanted Jesus to give them physical bread like the manna God had given to their ancestors in the wilderness (see 6:30-31, 34), but Jesus reminded them that physical bread would only keep them alive for so long (6:49). Those who come to him— **the bread that comes down from heaven**—as their spiritual sustenance, however, will **not die** (6:50). In the same way that we eat bread to sustain our physical lives, we must eat **the living bread** (that is, believe in Jesus) to **live forever** (6:51).

The bread I will give for the life of the world is my flesh (6:51). Jesus was speaking of the sacrifice of his body (his life) on the cross for the sins of the world (see 1:29; 19:18). On the basis of this sacrifice, those who trust in Jesus as the atoning sacrifice for their sins will receive eternal life.

6:52-59 Since the people hadn't made the mental jump from the physical to the spiritual, they thought Jesus was talking nonsense (6:52). Nevertheless, Jesus insisted on the necessity of eating his **flesh** and drinking his **blood** to have **eternal life** (6:53-56). He wasn't talking about cannibalism, of course! He was using a rich metaphor to emphasize that believing in him is essential. Just as you will die without physical food, so also you can't have spiritual life apart from Jesus. You must **eat** him—that is, *receive* him, *trust* him,

believe in him, *have faith* in him, *partake* of him. **The one who feeds on [him] will live because of [him]** (6:53, 57).

Also, it is the believer's continuous act of faith through partaking spiritually of the body and blood of Christ in Communion that the benefits, power, and blessings of the new covenant are increasingly accessed (see 1 Cor 10:16, 17; 11:23-20).

6:60-62 Many of his disciples were confused and couldn't comprehend what he was talking about (6:60). Jesus asked them, **Does this offend you?** (6:61)—that is, "Is this teaching tripping you up?" What would they think if they saw him returning to heaven (6:62)? Would that change their minds?

6:63 The flesh doesn't give life. Only the Holy **Spirit . . . gives life**. Jesus's **words** are spiritual and life-giving. The Holy Spirit takes a person's belief in Jesus's words and activates Jesus's life in that person to give him spiritual life. Salvation cannot be attained through human effort.

6:64-65 Given his deity, Jesus knew **those who did not believe** in him, as well as **the one who would betray him**: Judas (6:64). Therefore, he said, **No one can come to me unless it is granted to him by the Father** (6:65). In other words, God only grants to Jesus those who are willing to respond to him. The Father cooperates with a person's decision to believe in his Son.

6:66-69 After this, many of those who had been following Jesus **no longer accompanied him** (6:66). When he asked **the Twelve** if they planned to leave him as well, Peter spoke up and expressed his faith: **Lord, to whom will we go? You have the words of eternal life** (6:68). He recognized what those who departed did not: Jesus's words "are spirit and life" (6:63). He alone is **the Holy One of God** (6:69). Only those who continue with Christ in the school of discipleship will receive more understanding from him. Those who drop out will not.

6:70-71 Jesus had chosen these twelve followers to travel and minister with him. Yet he chose one of them, knowing that he was a devil—an unbeliever who would hand him over to his enemies for money (6:70). John lets his readers know in advance that Jesus was talking about **Judas, Simon Iscariot's son**. He would **betray him** (6:71; see 13:21-30; 18:1-5). But none of this would take Jesus by surprise, and God's plan would be fulfilled even though it involved using Satan and his followers to accomplish it.

⤳ B. Living Water, the Light of the World, and the Good Shepherd
(7:1–10:42) ⤳

7:1-5 Since **Jews** in **Judea** were seeking **to kill him**, Jesus remained **in Galilee** (7:1). However, it was time for **the Jewish Festival of Shelters** (7:2), when Jews would travel to Jerusalem (in Judea). So Jesus's **brothers** (sons of Mary and Joseph who were younger than Jesus) tried to convince him to go there so that everyone could see the miraculous **works** that he was performing (7:3). They wanted him to go put on a **public** show and make front-page headlines (7:4). But ultimately, John tells us, **not even his brothers believed in him** (7:5). In fact, they thought he was crazy (see Mark 3:21).

Like many others who encountered Jesus, his brothers got excited about miraculous signs but were unwilling to embrace his true identity. The same is still true today. Many only want what Jesus can do for them, but they are unwilling to believe in him for eternal life and follow him as disciples.

Matthew 13:55 identifies Jesus's brothers as "James, Joseph, Simon, and Judas." James believed in Jesus after his resurrection, became a leader in the early church, and authored the New Testament letter that bears his name (see, e.g., Acts 15:13; 21:18; 1 Cor 15:7; Gal 1:19; Jas 1:1). Judas (better known as Jude) is the author of the New Testament letter that bears his (see Jude 1).

7:6-7 In spite of his brothers' pleas, Jesus told them, **My time has not yet arrived** (7:6). It was not yet the moment for his public presentation as the Messiah (see 12:12-19). Jesus knew that his death would follow soon after this open acknowledgment. **The world**

didn't **hate** his brothers; after all, they were still a part of the world system. But it did **hate** Jesus because he testified to the world's **evil** deeds (7:7).

7:8-10 Since his time had **not yet fully come**, he told his brothers to go to **the festival** without him (7:8). Later, though, he went **secretly** to the festival (7:10). Jesus does things according to his Father's timetable, not ours. And God's timing is perfect (see Gal 4:4-5).

7:11-12 During the festival, people **were looking for** Jesus and **murmuring about him** (7:11-12). Yet **nobody was talking publicly about him** because they were afraid of the Jewish leaders who hated Jesus (7:13). When a man eventually did speak favorably of Jesus in public, the religious leaders banned him from the synagogue (see 9:13-34).

7:13-16 When the festival was already half over, Jesus started teaching in **the temple** (7:14). When they heard him, the people were puzzled that he was so **learned** since he hadn't been **trained** by the religious leaders (7:15). But Jesus made clear who the source of his teaching was: **My teaching isn't mine but is from the one who sent me** (7:16). He accurately represented the Father in everything he said.

7:17 Jesus also made clear what was necessary for true spiritual insight: **If anyone wants to do [God's] will, he will know whether the teaching is from God.** A willingness to receive God's words and obey them must precede understanding. God does not want to waste his truth.

If we approach God with a mindset of obedience, he will give us clarity into his Word and discernment. I have been in counseling situations in which I have asked, "Are you willing to do what God says? Because if not, it's a waste of your time and mine to continue to talk about the next steps." Clarity comes through commitment.

7:18-20 Jesus sought God's **glory** alone and confessed that there is **no unrighteousness in him** (7:18). He is perfect and sinless. Nevertheless, even though the Jews had **the law**, they didn't keep it and yet wanted to **kill**

Jesus (7:19). The **crowd** denied this and accused him of being **demon** possessed (7:20).

7:21-24 Many of the Jews had become **angry** with Jesus because he healed a lame man **on the Sabbath** (7:22-23; see 5:1-13). Yet Jesus pointed out their inconsistency. The Jews obeyed the law of **Moses** by performing **circumcision** on "the Sabbath" (7:22). So if the act of circumcision didn't break the law, how could making **a man entirely well** break it? (7:23). Jesus exhorted them to **judge** rightly and not by **outward appearances** (7:24)—that is, they were to use God's standards for judgments and not their personal preferences.

7:25-29 More speculation arose concerning Jesus's identity. They wondered why the Jewish **authorities** weren't trying to stop him and whether the leaders had concluded that Jesus was **the Messiah** (7:26). Others assumed he couldn't be **the Messiah** since they knew where Jesus had come **from** (7:27). At least, they *thought* they knew. But Jesus told them that he had come on behalf of the one who had **sent** him—that is, he'd come from God (7:28-29). Though they thought he was merely a preacher from Nazareth, he was much more. He was the Son of God from heaven.

7:30-32 This kind of talk from Jesus was apparently the last straw, so **they tried to seize him.** But notice this: **No one laid a hand on him because his hour had not yet come.** An angry mob wanted to lay their hands on Jesus. He stood before them, alone and defenseless. But nothing happened, because it wasn't in God's sovereign schedule. When **the Pharisees** heard that **many from the crowd believed in [Jesus]**, they **sent servants to arrest him** (7:31-32). Apparently, they didn't realize that seizing Jesus wasn't working out too well! (No matter how bad your circumstances appear, nothing can harm you outside of God's will and timing.)

7:33-36 Jesus told those listening that he would only be with them for a little while longer. They'd **look for** him but be unable to **find** or follow him (7:33-34). Though Jesus

was talking about his return to heaven at his ascension (see Acts 1:9), **the Jews** were still thinking on the physical level rather than the spiritual, and they wondered where he was planning **to go** (7:35-36). Approaching God's Word at the purely physical level will inevitably result in confusion. We need our antennae tuned to God's heavenly broadcast.

7:37-39 On the last . . . day of the festival (7:37), the Jews engaged in a water-pouring ritual. While this was happening, Jesus called out, **If anyone is thirsty, let him come to me and drink.** There is only one oasis for those who are in a spiritual desert. If you're spiritually parched, go to Jesus. He won't merely quench your thirst, he'll provide internal **streams of living water** (7:38). But it gets better. His is no impersonal water supply; this *living* water is actually the Holy **Spirit**, the person of the Godhead who comes to dwell within believers to give them eternal life. Yet Jesus would first have to be **glorified**—that is, crucified and resurrected (7:39).

7:40-43 As happened previously (see 7:25-29), **the crowd was divided because of him** (7:43). Some thought he was the great **Prophet** who was to come (7:40; see Deut 18:15-18). Others argued that Jesus couldn't be **the Messiah**, since the Messiah wasn't supposed to hail from **Galilee** but from King **David's offspring** in **Bethlehem** (7:41-42).

Of course, they didn't realize that Jesus actually *was* born from the line of David (see Matt 1:1-17) in Bethlehem as Scripture had foretold (see Mic 5:2; Matt 2:1; Luke 2:1-7) but grew up and ministered in Galilee—which Scripture had also foretold (see Isa 9:1-2; Matt 2:19-23; 4:14-15).

7:44-46 Though **some of them wanted to seize him . . . no one laid hands on him.** Trying and failing to arrest Jesus, then, was becoming a habit (see 7:30-32). Frustrated with **the servants** whom they had sent to seize him, **the chief priests and Pharisees asked, Why didn't you bring him?** (7:45). All the servants could respond with was, **No man ever spoke like this!** (7:46). In other words, they said, "We intended to grab him, but then we heard him talk and changed our minds!"

Jesus's sermon was so mesmerizing that it prevented them from obeying wicked men.

7:47-53 The Pharisees rebuked the servants: **Have any of the rulers or Pharisees believed in him?** (7:48). Well, actually, there was a Pharisee named Nicodemus who had been captivated by Jesus's teaching. But he had kept his interest under wraps by only visiting Jesus at night (see 3:1-13). Interestingly, though, when he heard these words, **Nicodemus** spoke up: **Our law doesn't judge a man before it hears from him and knows what he's doing, does it?** (7:51). Thus, he wisely sought to calm everyone down and to urge them against condemning someone without proper investigation. But the Pharisees had no need for investigation since they knew **that no prophet arises from Galilee** (7:53). Not only were they wrong about Jesus's birthplace (see 7:40-43), though, but they also were wrong about no prophets coming from Galilee. Jonah's hometown of Gath-hepher was located there (see 2 Kgs 14:25).

8:1-5 While Jesus was in **the temple** teaching, **the scribes and the Pharisees brought** before him **a woman caught in adultery** (8:2-3). The law of Moses said **to stone** her, but they wanted to know what Jesus thought they should do (8:4-5). They assumed they had Jesus in a catch-22. If he opposed stoning her, he would be opposing the law of Moses (see Deut 22:22). But if he advocated her death, he would be in trouble with the Romans because the Jews (under Roman rule) weren't permitted to execute anyone (see 18:31).

8:6 Clearly, they had no interest in a righteous application of the law. As the author tells us, they were deceitfully trying **to trap** Jesus so that **they might have evidence to accuse him.** Moreover, if the woman was "caught in adultery" (8:3), where was the man? The law required that both the man and the woman were to be judged (see Lev 20:10; Deut 22:22). This, therefore, smells like a setup. But they didn't realize whom they were dealing with.

Jesus stooped down and started writing on the ground with his finger. Just as the Ten Commandments had been "inscribed by the finger of God" (Exod 31:18), whatever

Jesus was writing was a subtle way of communicating to them that he himself was the divine author of the law. Writing on the dirt was also an allusion to the fact that the law had been given to mankind who had been created out of dust and were therefore vulnerable to weakness and sin.

8:7-8 When they persisted in questioning him, Jesus proposed a test of his own: **The one without sin among you should be the first to throw a stone at her** (8:7). He wanted to know which of them was qualified to judge her. The obvious answer? None of them were. Their hypocrisy was revealed because they had failed to produce the man, since she was "caught in the act" (8:4). **Then he stooped down** a second time to write with his finger (8:8), just as God had written the Ten Commandments on two tablets a second time after the Israelites had sinned and Moses smashed the first ones (see Exod 34:1). The second giving of the law meant God was giving his people a second chance just as he was about to do with this woman; something these hypocritical leaders were unwilling to do.

8:9-11 Each man knew that he himself was guilty of the same or similar sin, which disqualified him from acting as a legitimate judge (see Matt 7:1-6). Because of their malicious intent, they would be subject to the same judgment they were seeking to impose on the woman (see Deut 19:16-19).

They all walked away. When only Jesus **was left**, he asked the **woman** if any accusers remained (8:9-10). Once she said, **No,** Jesus made a staggering statement: **Neither do I condemn you. . . . Go, and from now on do not sin anymore** (8:11). Notice that he demonstrated grace and mercy to her (removing her condemnation) *before* he told her to start living right. A true understanding of grace and mercy does not endorse or promote sin; rather, it's designed to produce gratitude and holiness (see Rom 6:1-7).

We do not obey God in order to earn forgiveness. Rather, grace and mercy are to motivate our obedience. When we truly understand God's amazing grace, we do not go out and merely sin *less*—we go out and seek to sin *no more.*

8:12-16 Jesus declared the second of his seven "I am" metaphors (see also 6:48; 10:7, 11; 11:25; 14:6; 15:1): **I am the light of the world.** Those who follow him (i.e., his true disciples) **will never walk in the darkness** (8:12). In response to this invitation to discipleship, **the Pharisees** accused him of simply bragging on himself; therefore, his **testimony [was] not valid** (8:13). On the contrary, Jesus told them, **My testimony is true, because I know where I came from** (heaven) **and where I'm going** (heaven) (8:14). The divine Son of God isn't capable of giving false testimony. Nor is he capable of rendering false **judgment** (8:16). The Pharisees, on the other hand, lacked spiritual perception, judging Jesus according to **human standards** (8:15).

8:17-18 Jesus pointed to the **law** of Moses, which declared **the testimony of two witnesses** to be **true** (8:17). Jesus's words passed this requirement. He testified about himself through his messianic claims, **and the Father** also testified about him through his miraculous deeds (8:18; see also commentary on 5:36-40).

8:19-20 When they asked about his **Father**, Jesus said, **You know neither me nor my Father.** Thus, he publicly condemned them: the religious leaders of Israel did not know God. Then he explained that knowledge of the Father is intertwined with knowledge of the Son: **If you knew me, you would also know my Father** (8:19). Anyone who rejects Jesus cannot know God because the former provides access to the latter (see 14:6). On 8:20, see the commentary on 7:30-32 and 44-46.

8:21-24 Once again (see 7:33-34), Jesus told them that he would be going somewhere they couldn't go. Instead, they would **die in their sin** because of their rejection of him (8:21). When they heard this, the religious leaders assumed that Jesus was talking about suicide (8:22), demonstrating that their spiritual insight hadn't improved. So Jesus got straight to the point: **You are from below. . . . I am from above** (8:23). He and his interlocutors were approaching their debate from two different realms, the physical and the spiritual. Unless the Jewish leaders could see Jesus from a heavenly perspective, they would experience

eternal judgment. Unless they believed that Jesus was the Messiah and received his payment for their sins, they would **die in [their] sins** (8:24).

8:25-27 When they asked Jesus, **Who are you?**, he responded, **Exactly what I've been telling you from the very beginning** (8:25). In essence he said, "You keep asking me the same old question. I answer it. And you refuse to listen." He had been speaking the Father's word, but they didn't even **know he was speaking to them about the Father** (8:26-27).

These people weren't making a spiritual connection because they were rejecting what had already been revealed. This is an important spiritual principle. When you reject what God has revealed, spiritual truth becomes even more difficult to understand. On the other hand, when you are willing to receive what God has revealed, he provides further spiritual clarity.

8:28-30 Though the Father had **sent** the Son into the world, he had **not left [him] alone.** Jesus affirmed that the Father was **with** him because he **always [does] what pleases him** (8:29). In response to these words, **many believed in him** (8:30). Those who likewise place their faith in Jesus can have confidence that God will receive them—not because of their perfect faith but because of Jesus's perfect obedience. He *always* does what pleases the Father.

8:31 To those **who had believed in him**, Jesus said, **If you continue in my word, you really are my disciples.** So notice that you can believe in Jesus but not continue in his word and, thus, not function as a true disciple. Justification does not automatically result in continuous discipleship.

8:32 You will know the truth, and the truth will set you free. Note two things. First, there is such a thing as *truth*. Truth is the absolute standard by which reality is measured. We live in a relativistic society that denies absolute truth, claiming, "What's true for you may not be true for me." But truth is not based on our feelings, experiences, or desires. Truth is God's viewpoint on every matter, and it is not subject to redefinition. Pilate would ask, "What is truth?" (18:38), and the answer to that question is "Jesus" (see 14:6).

Second, knowing the truth results in genuine freedom. Don't be confused. Truth alone doesn't liberate; rather, the *knowledge* of the truth liberates. Deliverance comes when we know the truth—that is, when we hang out in what God says. When this happens, we will experience the truth setting us free from illegitimate bondage.

8:33-36 Hearing him, the Jews appealed to their lineage from **Abraham** and denied that they needed to **become free** (8:33). They were basing their spiritual status on their physical link to Abraham. However, Jesus corrected them: **Everyone who commits sin is a slave of sin** (8:34). But **if the Son sets you free, you really will be free** (8:36)—that is, delivered experientially. Only the Son can set a person free from enslavement to sin. But remember what the Son requires for freedom: "continue in my word" (8:31).

For true freedom, we need the living Word and the written Word. The *living* Word (Jesus) provides us with legal freedom from sin through his atoning death on the cross; thus, we no longer stand condemned before God. But we must continue in his *written* Word (Scripture) in order to enjoy freedom from the sin to which we can be enslaved in our daily lives.

8:37-43 Jesus and the Jews who opposed him engaged in a paternity dispute. Because they were **trying to kill** him, Jesus said they were following the counsel of their **father** (8:37-38). They claimed that **Abraham** was their father (8:39). However, Jesus insisted that they weren't behaving like him but like their **father** (8:39-41). What "father" did Jesus have in mind?

Next the Jews claimed that **God** was their **Father** and also jabbed at Jesus with a low blow: **We weren't born of sexual immorality** (8:41). In other words, they said, "We know all about your illegitimate birth, Jesus! Your mother was pregnant before she was married" (see Matt 1:18). But Jesus said, **If God were your Father, you would love me, because I came from God** (8:42). Thus, he denied their accusation; his birth wasn't immoral but

supernatural. Moreover, he denied that God was their Father. God had **sent** Jesus, yet they refused to **listen to [his] word** (8:42-43).

8:44-47 But if Abraham wasn't their father, and God wasn't their Father, who *was*? Jesus didn't pull any punches: **You are of your father the devil, and you want to carry out your father's desires** (8:44). These Jews had lied about Jesus's mama (8:41), but he was telling the truth about their daddy!

The devil **was a murderer from the beginning** (8:44), and *they* wanted to kill Jesus (8:37). The devil is **the father of lies** (8:44), and *they* rejected Jesus because he told **the truth** (8:45). In other words, their opposition to Jesus was Satanic in origin. They wanted to do whatever their father did. Like father, like children. This explained all of their actions. Their religion was a fiction, and their allegiance was to the wrong kingdom. They were **not from God** (8:47).

8:48-50 Instead of repenting, **the Jews** fired more insults at Jesus, claiming that he was **a Samaritan** and **demon** possessed (8:48; see commentary on 4:1-4). While they dishonored the Son, the Son steadfastly honored his **Father**, and the Father glorified the Son (8:49-50).

8:51 **If anyone keeps my word, he will never see death.** Every person who believes in Jesus Christ as his Savior will escape death. When a Christian dies, he or she is immediately ushered into the presence of the Lord. Have no fear. Physical death is merely a transition into eternity.

8:52-55 Still thinking purely from the perspective of the physical rather than the spiritual, they were now certain that Jesus was crazy. How could he say that those who keep his word won't die? After all, **Abraham died** and **the prophets died**. Did he think he was **greater than** them (8:52-53)? Again, Jesus denied that they knew the one whom they claimed as their **God** (8:54-55).

8:56-58 Then, since they brought up Abraham, Jesus made an amazing claim: **Abraham rejoiced to see my day; he saw it and was glad** (8:56; see Gen 22:1-4; Heb 11:19).

What?! That sent the Jews reeling. How could Abraham have encountered Jesus? They said, **You aren't fifty years old yet, and you've seen Abraham?** (8:57). If that statement upset them, his follow-up would really send them over the edge: **Truly I tell you, before Abraham was, I am** (8:58).

This is one of Jesus's most profound claims to deity in the Gospels. He didn't say, "Before Abraham was, I *was*," but "I *am*." The former wording could be ambiguous and misunderstood, but not the latter. Not only was he claiming to have existed in Abraham's day, but he was also claiming divine identity.

When Moses asked God his name so that he could tell the Israelites who had sent him to them, God responded, "I AM WHO I AM. This is what you are to say to the Israelites: I AM has sent me to you" (Exod 3:14). Thus, Jesus identified himself as the God who had spoken to Moses. That is an astounding assertion. But it simply confirms what John has already said: "The Word was with God, and the Word was God" (John 1:1).

8:59 The Jews understood exactly what Jesus was saying. They thought he was speaking blasphemy (see commentary on 5:17-18). That's why **they picked up stones to throw at him**. But, once again, it wasn't Jesus's time, so he **was hidden** from them and **went out of the temple.**

9:1-5 Jesus spotted **a man** who had been **blind from birth** (9:1). Many at that time believed such serious birth defects were the product of personal sin. Therefore, **his disciples** wondered whether it was the man's sin or his parents' sin that had resulted in his condition (9:2). But Jesus corrected their thinking: **Neither this man nor his parents sinned. . . . This came about that God's works might be displayed in him** (9:3). Sickness, disease, and defect are not necessarily the result of personal sin (consider Job!). Sometimes God allows negative conditions and circumstances in our lives in order to accomplish positive goals: our good, his glory, and bringing benefit to others (see Gen 50:19-20; Rom 8:28). God had granted blindness to this man so that he could do amazing works in his life. As **the light of the world**, Jesus had come to **do the works** of God (9:4-5).

9:6 Jesus **spit** in the dirt (the substance from which man was made; see Gen 2:7), **made some mud** from it, and put it on the blind man's **eyes**. Thus the word of God (i.e., spit from Jesus's mouth) mixed with humanity (i.e., dirt from which man was created) provided the basis for the miracle. By using his saliva, Jesus was imparting divine DNA to the human defect in order to bring about a supernatural transformation of his humanity. This was to serve as a physical illustration of the supernatural spiritual transformation Jesus came to bring (see Isa 35:4-5)

9:7 Then he told the man to **wash.** Thus, his healing required an act of faith on his part. Jesus gave the man something to do, and the man did it. When his face was washed, he could see for the first time in his life.

9:8-13 At first **his neighbors** didn't believe this was the same man they knew (9:8-9). So he had to keep saying, "It's me!" (9:9). They pelted him with more questions. Though he gave credit to **the man called Jesus** for healing him, he didn't know where he had gone (9:10-12). After all, he had never seen him! So the crowd took the man **to the Pharisees** (9:13), where the moment of rejoicing would turn sour.

9:14-16 As it turns out, Jesus had healed the man on the **Sabbath** (9:14). The Pharisees had already tangled with Jesus previously regarding his healing activity on a Sabbath day (see 5:1-19). So it's really not surprising that they were unwilling to celebrate. Instead of rejoicing over the miraculous healing of a man who had been born blind, in fact, the Pharisees complained about the day of the week on which he'd been healed. After the man explained what happened, some of the Pharisees scoffed: **This man is not from God, because he doesn't keep the Sabbath** (9:15-16). Others insisted that a sinner couldn't **perform such signs.** So they were divided over Jesus (9:16).

9:17-23 They asked the man who had been healed what he thought, and he hailed Jesus as **a prophet** (9:17). But, since they were unwilling to accept this praise of Jesus, they tried to obtain evidence to deny that the miracle even happened. So they **summoned [his] parents** and **asked them** (9:18-19). But the **parents** were too interested in self-preservation. **They were afraid** because they'd heard that **the Jews** planned to ban **from the synagogue** anyone who **confessed [Jesus] as the Messiah** (9:22). They acknowledged that their **son** was previously **blind**. But they claimed to know nothing else and instead said, **Ask him** (9:20-21).

Nothing much has changed today. If you publicly confess Christ, you will likely experience some form of ridicule or ostracism. Believing in a generic "God" is safe; confessing Christ will earn you mockery.

9:24-25 The Pharisees turned again to the man who had been healed. They urged him to **give glory to God** because they were convinced that Jesus was **a sinner**, and they wanted the man to agree (9:24). Given the man's limited experience with Jesus, he simply confessed the **one thing** he knew to be true: **I was blind, and now I can see!** (9:25).

9:26-29 When they asked him to give another account of his healing, it was clear that they hadn't believed him the first time (9:26). So the man was blunt: **I already told you . . . and you didn't listen.** He wondered whether they wanted to hear his story **again** in order to become Jesus's **disciples** (9:27). That riled them up! **They ridiculed** the man, claimed to be followers of **Moses**, and said they didn't even know where **this man** (Jesus) had come from (9:28-29).

9:30-34 This is an amazing thing! (9:30). Though the man's parents may have feared the religious leaders (9:22), he himself boldly challenged the illogical thinking of the Pharisees. He laid out the facts: They didn't know where Jesus was from; Jesus had granted sight to a blind man; **God doesn't listen to sinners** but to those who do his will; no one has heard of someone **opening the eyes of the blind** (9:30-32). How do you explain such supernatural activity, if it's not from God? The man could only reach one conclusion: **If this man were not from God, he wouldn't be able to do anything** (9:33). In going toe-to-toe with the Jewish religious leaders, he

had bested them. Humiliated by this humble, once-blind beggar, they told him he was **born entirely in sin**, rebuked him for **trying to teach** them, and kicked him out of the synagogue to limit his influence on others (9:34).

9:35-38 When Jesus heard that the man had been persecuted in this way, he showed up. Whatever negative consequences you experience for confessing Christ are not the last word. He knows what you've been through. Jesus was aware of the blind man's circumstances, and he tracked him down.

Then Jesus asked him, **Do you believe in the Son of Man?** (9:35). Remember: the man had never even seen Jesus. He wanted to believe in the Son of Man, but he didn't know who he was (9:36). That's when Jesus introduced himself: **You have seen him; in fact, he is the one speaking with you** (9:37). So the man confessed, **I believe, Lord**, and **worshiped him** (9:38). There's only one being in the universe worthy of worship, and Jesus didn't stop the man. As John says at the beginning of his Gospel, "The Word was God" (1:1). Accepting worship was a declaration of deity. Were Jesus not divine, it would be an endorsement of idolatry.

9:39 Jesus articulates his purpose for coming **into this world**: so that **those who do not see will see and those who do see will become blind**. But he wasn't primarily talking about physical blindness. He used the man's physical blindness to teach a spiritual truth. Jesus had come into the world to give spiritual sight to those who desperately acknowledge their spiritual blindness. But to those who claimed to be spiritual know-it-alls, Jesus promised the **judgment** of becoming even more spiritually blind. Humility brings sight; pride leads to darkness.

9:40-41 When **the Pharisees** heard this, they smugly asked Jesus in essence, "Are you calling us **blind**?" (9:40). If they had been willing to admit their blindness—their lostness, their sinfulness—Jesus would have shown them grace. But since they claimed to **see**, their **sin** remained (9:41). Their treatment of the Son of God confirmed their lack of sight. When you think that nothing is wrong with you (see 1 John 1:8), everything is wrong.

10:1-5 After highlighting the spiritual blindness of the Jewish religious leaders—those who should have been Israel's spiritual shepherds—Jesus explained the difference between shepherds and thieves. The one who **climbs** the fence of **the sheep pen** is **a thief and robber**, but **the one who enters by the gate is the shepherd** (10:1-2). Satan and his followers have no concern for the well-being of the sheep. They enter the sheep pen for their own gain. But a true shepherd **calls his own sheep by name** and **leads them** (10:3-4). In return, the sheep **follow** their shepherd only and flee from **strangers** (10:5). Jesus was using this imagery to describe himself and to emphasize the importance of his followers (his sheep) having a personal knowledge of and relationship with him (their shepherd).

10:6-10 Since the people couldn't grasp the meaning of Jesus's illustration, he made it plain: **Truly I tell you, I am the gate for the sheep** (10:7). To enter the safety of the pen or to **go out and find pasture**, the sheep have to go through the gate (10:9). Jesus is "the way" to safety and life (14:6). We must go through him to **be saved** (10:9). Thieves come to **destroy**, but Jesus came to give **life** and to give it **in abundance** (10:10).

Jesus doesn't want you *merely* to posses eternal life but also to possess the full experience of life. Following the shepherd leads to blessing and joy and a growing experience of eternal life. It allows him to rebuke and reverse the enemy's attempts at blocking the blessings, purpose, and spiritual fulfillment God has for your life (see Joel 2:25; Mal 3:11).

10:11-15 Not only is Jesus the gate for the sheep to pass through, but he is the one who protects and provides for them: **I am the good shepherd**. Notice he's no mere shepherd but a *good* one. What does a good shepherd do? He **lays down his life for the sheep** (10:11). A **hired hand**, by contrast, is only there to earn a living. He **doesn't care about the sheep** because they aren't his. So when a **wolf** attacks, the hired hand **runs away**, while the wolf **snatches and scatters** the sheep (10:12-13). But **the good shepherd** knows his sheep, and they **know** him (10:14). Jesus confessed, **I lay down my life for the sheep** (10:15).

Though it wouldn't have been clear to his listeners at that moment, Jesus was speaking of his substitutionary atonement when he would sacrifice his life on the cross for the sins of the world. As he would tell his disciples later, "No one has greater love than this: to lay down his life for his friends" (15:13). Though the Pharisees cared only for themselves, Jesus was prepared to sacrifice everything to save the sheep he loved.

10:16 Jesus did not come to give his life for Jews only. God the Father gave his one and only Son because he loved *the world*—all mankind, without exception (see John 3:16; Heb 2:9; 1 Tim 2:6; 1 John 2:2). The **other sheep** that Jesus would save are Gentiles who would believe in him so that the church would consist of both Jewish and Gentile believers (see Eph 2:11-22). **There will be one flock, one shepherd.**

10:17-18 I **lay down my life . . . No one takes it from me** (10:17-18). Notice two things in this statement. First, Jesus was under no obligation to sacrifice himself for sinners. That's why it's called *grace*. Second, though the Jews would hand him over and the Romans would crucify him, this was only possible because he let them (see 19:10-11). No one *takes* the life of the Son of God. He lays it down voluntarily. And **this is why the Father loves [him]**—because he is willing to give his life in obedience to the Father's **command** and in love for sinners (10:17-18). Believers benefit from this divine love between Father and Son, as we live in obedience.

10:19-21 **The Jews** continued to be **divided** over him (10:19). Some thought he was **demon-possessed** and **crazy**; others thought his miracles proved that he was the genuine article (10:20-21). But no one was on the fence about him.

10:22-26 Today **the Festival of Dedication** is commonly known as Hanukkah, which celebrates the rededication of the temple in 165 BC after its desecration by Antiochus IV Epiphanes in 168 BC. During this particular festival, a group of Jews accosted Jesus and demanded, **If you are the Messiah, tell us**

plainly (10:22-24). Yet, he had already told them in word and deed, and they refused to **believe.** The **works** he did in the **Father's name** were his proof (10:25). They had all the evidence they needed, but they had no interest in listening to him because they had no interest in being his **sheep** (10:26).

10:27-29 What happens to those who *do* want to be Jesus's **sheep**? He gives them **eternal life** so that **they will never perish.** How secure are those who receive eternal life through Jesus? **No one** can **snatch them** out of Jesus's **hand** (10:28) or **the Father's** (10:29). Thus, believers are not eternally secure because of their grip on God but because of his grip on them. If you come to Jesus by faith, he's got you. When you're too weak and your hands go limp, he'll still be hanging on to you.

10:30-33 I and the Father are one—in essence and in purpose (10:30). You don't get a clearer claim to deity than that. And **the Jews** knew it. So they **picked up rocks to stone him** for what they considered **blasphemy** (10:31, 33). This **man** was claiming to be **God** (10:33). But, though they couldn't accept it, he was telling the truth. Our Creator is one God in three persons: Father, Son, and Holy Spirit. And Jesus Christ is one person with two natures (divine and human).

10:34-38 Jesus pointed to Psalm 82:6: **I said, you are gods** (10:34). In this psalm, God referred to human rulers, who were made in God's image and responsible to imitate God's character, as "gods." So if sinful men in honored positions could be called "gods," what about a perfect man?

If Jesus was doing the **Father's works**— and clearly he had been—how could they accuse him of blasphemy (10:35-37)? If they had trouble with his words, all they had to do was look at his works. Where had he fallen short? Why hadn't they believed him? Jesus declares that **Scripture cannot be broken**—that is, canceled or annulled (10:35). This means that Scripture is inerrant, authoritative, and binding.

10:39 They were trying again to seize him, but he eluded their grasp. You'd think that by this point they would realize that seizing Jesus is a dead end street (see 7:30-32, 44-46; 8:20). No one could take his life from him (see 10:18). But soon he would lay it down. Jesus was sovereign over his own death.

10:40-42 Given the hostility directed against him in Jerusalem, Jesus **departed again across the Jordan** (10:40). But that didn't put a damper on his ministry. The crowds simply followed him there, **and many believed in him** (10:41-42).

V. THE RESURRECTION OF LAZARUS AND THE APPROACHING DEATH OF JESUS (11:1–12:50)

11:1-3 A certain man named **Lazarus** and his two sisters, **Mary** and **Martha**, were followers of Jesus. They appear several times in the Gospels (11:1-2; see Luke 10:38-42; John 12:1-8). But on this occasion, there was a problem. Lazarus was **sick** and dying (11:2). Knowing that Jesus had power to heal their brother, Mary and Martha **sent a message to** Jesus, urging him to come (11:3).

11:4 When he received the message, Jesus vowed that the **sickness [would] not end in death** but would end in **the glory of God.** As in the case of the blind man (see 9:1-3), these

negative circumstances were not the result of sin; they were for the purpose of glorifying Jesus. If someone says that a Christian walking with the Lord can't become ill or contract a disease, that person is simply wrong. Lazarus's sickness was not a means of punishment, not a sign of rebellion. Rather, it had a spiritual purpose.

11:5-6 John tells us that **Jesus loved Martha, her sister, and Lazarus** (11:5), and they knew of his love for them (see 11:3). They shared an intimate relationship with him. But, in spite of this, Jesus **stayed two more days in**

the place where he was (11:6). His delay appeared to contradict his promise of healing. However, it was *because* he loved them that he delayed his arrival.

This passage demonstrates an important theological truth regarding prayer. In our times of struggle, we want God to respond immediately. When he doesn't, we're tempted to assume he doesn't care. But the reality is that we don't understand his timing or his purposes because his ways are not our ways (see Isa 55:8-9). There's a method to his (apparent) contradictions. He responds as he does because he loves us and because he's seeking his glory. Trust him in his delays.

11:7-8 Finally, Jesus said, **Let's go to Judea again** (11:7). His disciples looked at one another and wondered if their **Rabbi** was losing it. Judea was where people had wanted to kill him (11:8). But, though one can understand their concern, the disciples apparently hadn't noticed that a lot of folks were having trouble seizing Jesus (see 7:30-32, 44-46; 8:20; 10:39). The Son of God—not the angry religious leaders—was sovereign over his ministry timetable.

11:9-10 Jesus told them that **the day**—the time of his public, earthly ministry—was the opportunity for action. While Jesus, **the light of this world**, was with them, they could walk and not **stumble** (11:9). Later, they would have the light of the Holy Spirit's presence. But to function apart from Jesus is like walking around at **night** (11:10). Operating without his illumination will cause you to trip and wind up on your face.

11:11 The reason they needed to return to Judea was because **Lazarus [had] fallen asleep** and needed waking. For those who trust in the Lord, the Bible describes death as sleep (i.e., a new level of spiritual consciousness), from which we will one day be physically raised (see 1 Thess 4:13).

11:12-15 The disciples were confused, thinking that Jesus **was speaking about natural sleep** (11:12-13). So he said, **Lazarus has died** (11:14). But the most startling thing he said was that he was **glad** (11:15)! However, Jesus

was not glad concerning Lazarus's death but glad concerning what he was about to do. Sometimes God will let things get worse before they get better. That's often because he has something in mind that's even better than what we requested.

11:16 Later, **Thomas** would express doubt over Jesus's resurrection (20:24-29). But for now, he was ready to **die with [Jesus]**. Those who are spiritually confident today may find themselves in the depths of despair and doubt tomorrow.

11:17-22 When Jesus and his disciples **arrived** in Bethany, **Lazarus** had been dead and buried for **four days**. Though the funeral was over, many friends were present who **had come to Martha and Mary to comfort them** (11:17-19). Martha met Jesus and said, **Lord, if you had been here, my brother wouldn't have died** (11:21-22). Translation: "This is all your fault, Jesus! I called you, but you didn't come. If you had listened to me, none of this would have happened." Yet this doesn't mean she had lost all hope, because she adds, **Even now I know that whatever you ask from God, God will give you** (11:22). Thus, Martha was filled with both faith and doubt. She is like the man who cried out to Jesus in desperation, "I do believe; help my unbelief! (Mark 9:24).

Sometimes doubt comes when we least expect it. When it does, bring your doubts to God in prayer (he's omniscient and knows about them anyway!). Believe that he can deal with your disappointment and spiritual struggle.

11:23-26 Jesus responded to Martha's faith in spite of her doubts: **Your brother will rise again** (11:23). Martha's theology was sound. She knew that her brother would be raised **in the resurrection at the last day** (11:24). But Jesus wanted her to know that the resurrection isn't just an event; the resurrection is a person. He told her, **I am the resurrection and the life** (11:25). The Son of God has "life in himself" (5:26) and can give life so that a person may "live forever" (6:51). He himself is the basis of eternal life. That's how he can say that the one who **believes in me will never die** (11:26)—that is, he will pass from physical life immediately into eternal life (see Phil 1:23). The present tense ("lives and believes in me") also shows that Jesus is a right now deliverer, not just a future one.

11:27-31 Though she still didn't comprehend everything or know what exactly was going to happen, Martha trusted Jesus and confessed him as **the Messiah, the Son of God** (11:27). Then she went to call **her sister Mary** (11:28). Whereas Martha's sorrow and disappointment had driven her to Jesus, Mary's had kept her from him. But when she heard that Jesus was **calling for [her]**, she immediately **went to him** (11:28-29).

11:31-35 The first words out of Mary's mouth were the same as her sister's: **Lord, if you had been here, my brother would not have died!** (11:32; see 11:21). Jesus was **deeply moved** by **her crying** and asked to see the tomb (11:33-34). Then, we read the shortest, yet one of the most profound, verses in all of the Bible: **Jesus wept** (11:35).

Jesus is fully God, but he is also fully human. Two natures in one person, unmixed forever. Even though he knew he was about to perform the miracle, he grieved with the pain and sorrow as well as the death-dealing effects of sin on those he loves. "We do not have a high priest who is unable to sympathize with our weaknesses, but one who has been tempted in every way as we are, yet without sin" (Heb 4:15). Jesus was agitated as he stirred up the work of the Spirit within him for the miracle he was about to perform.

11:36-37 Those with Mary and Martha could see how much Jesus **loved** Lazarus (11:36). **But some** were confused, wondering why a man who could give sight to the **blind** couldn't keep a sick **man from dying** (11:37). If they thought keeping a man from dying would be spectacular, they were in for the shock of their lives.

11:38-40 Jesus commanded them to **remove the stone** from the mouth of the burial **cave** (11:38-39). At this, **Martha** objected. After all, Lazarus had been **dead four days**. She no doubt appreciated Jesus's desire to pay his last respects to her deceased brother, but the **stench** of decay would be awful (11:39). Jesus replied by telling her that she hadn't been paying attention: **Didn't I tell you that if you believed you would see the glory of God?** (11:40). He called her to demonstrate her faith in him by her action—allowing the stone to be removed. Jesus didn't want her explanations about bodily decay; he wanted her to walk by faith, putting one foot in front of the other. Faith is acting like God is telling the truth. Then, demonstrating the "glory of God" would be up to Jesus. Faith must precede sight if we want to see God's supernatural intervention in our circumstances. We can never know what God plans to do in secret until we obey what he has clearly revealed.

11:41-42 When **the stone** was **removed**, Jesus looked to heaven and prayed. He thanked the **Father** that he always hears him (11:41). He acknowledged the reason that the Son had delayed coming to see Lazarus in the first place: so that **the crowd standing** there might **believe** that the Father had **sent** Jesus (11:42).

He could've showed up on time and conducted a private miracle to heal Lazarus. Instead, he arrived late to put on a public, supernatural display, validating his messianic identity and sparking faith in a mass gathering of people. The latter, though it resulted in temporary grief, would produce tremendous spiritual impact and bring God greater glory. Jesus's prayer for his Father's supernatural intervention also illustrates his current intercessory work of deliverance for believers when we respond in faith and obedience (see Heb 7:25). This is why we pray to the Father in the name of Jesus. The Father responds to what the Son endorses.

11:43-44 Jesus addressed the dead man and called, **Lazarus, come out!** (11:43). Then, from out of the tomb, a living man walked, still **bound** and **wrapped in** burial cloths (11:44). The dead had been raised to life! This is a foretaste of what is to come. One day, Lazarus would physically die again. But those who believe in Jesus will take part in the everlasting resurrection and live forever.

11:45-48 As a result, **many of the Jews . . . believed in him** (11:45). One would think that there couldn't possibly be any other response! But, unfortunately, **some of them went** and tattled to the **Pharisees** (11:46). When the news reached them, **the chief priests and the Pharisees convened the Sanhedrin**, the council of the Jewish religious leaders. Notice that they didn't deny his miraculous **signs** (11:47). Rather, they lamented them. Instead of cheering his raising of the dead, they worried that his winning of followers would cause **the Romans** to think there was an insurrection, thus bringing the Roman hammer down on their **nation** (11:48).

11:49-53 Caiaphas the **high priest** had a solution. He said it was better that **one man should die** than that **the whole nation perish** (11:50). In other words, he wanted to ensure that Jesus was silenced once and for all. That would solve their problem. But John tells us that, unknown to Caiaphas, he had actually **prophesied**. This wicked **high priest** was merely thinking on the physical level, but his words providentially foretold a spiritual reality. Indeed, the one man would die for the sins of the many. **Jesus was going to die for the nation** (11:51). And not only for Israel, but for Gentiles too (11:52). So **they plotted to kill him** (11:53). But what they planned for evil, God planned for good (see Gen 50:20).

11:54-57 Since the religious leaders were conspiring to kill him, Jesus stopped walking **openly among the Jews** (11:54). **The chief priests and Pharisees had given orders** to **arrest him** if anyone spotted him (11:57). But everything would happen according to God's sovereign timing. **Jerusalem** began filling with people because it was time for **the Passover** celebrating God's deliverance of Israel from Egyptian slavery (11:55; see Exod 12:1-28). Soon God would provide a new and ultimate means of deliverance from slavery to sin.

12:1-3 Less than a week **before the Passover, Jesus** and his disciples were in **Bethany** again, having **dinner** with **Martha, Mary**, and **Lazarus**, who had recently been **raised from the dead**. While Martha served, Mary **anointed Jesus's feet** with costly **perfume** and **wiped his feet with her hair**. This was an act of amazing devotion and love. But, as we'll see, some didn't appreciate such extravagant sacrifice for Jesus. The same is true today.

12:4-6 **Judas Iscariot**, the disciple who would **betray** Jesus (12:4), was indignant regarding Mary's gift. He chastised her for wasting **perfume** that could have been **sold for three hundred denarii** (about a year's wages) and donated **to the poor** (12:5). But John tells his readers the truth, something that the disciples apparently didn't know until after the fact: Judas didn't care about the poor. **He was a thief.** He was in charge of the disciples' **money-bag** and used to **steal** from it (12:6). Adding three hundred denarii to the piggybank would've meant more cash in Judas's pocket.

12:7-8 Jesus rebuked Judas, telling him to **leave** Mary **alone.** Her actions had prepared his body for **burial** (12:7), which was only a few days away. **For you always have the poor with you, but you do not always have me.** Providing for the poor is a biblical mandate for God's people (see Lev 19:9-10; Deut 15:10; Prov 14:31; 19:17; 28:27; 2 Cor 9:7; Eph 4:28). (Of course, the Bible is talking about those who are legitimately poor, not those who are poor through their own laziness; see 2 Thess 3:10.) But Jesus reminded them that dealing with poverty is an unending reality in this sinful, fallen world. And this reality was not to prevent them from honoring their long-awaited Lord and Messiah who would only be with them a short while longer.

12:9-11 When they learned that Jesus had **raised** Lazarus **from the dead**, crowds of people wanted to get a glimpse of the ex-corpse (12:9). Because of Jesus's miraculous deed, **many of the Jews were deserting** the Jewish religious leaders **and believing in Jesus** (12:11). How did **the chief priests** respond to this? They **decided to kill Lazarus** too (12:10)! Their wickedness knew no bounds.

12:12-13 **A large crowd . . . heard that Jesus was** about to enter **Jerusalem** (12:12). With palm branches in hand, they met him, shouting in language from Psalm 118:25-26: Hosanna! Blessed is he who comes in the name of the Lord—the King of Israel! (12:13). *Hosanna* is Hebrew for "save us"—it's a cry of deliverance. By applying the psalm to Jesus and identifying him as their King, they were hailing Jesus as the Messiah who would deliver them from Roman domination.

12:14-16 In fulfillment of the messianic prophecy written hundreds of years before in Zechariah 9:9, Jesus rode into Jerusalem on a young donkey (12:14). The prophet "saw" Zion's King . . . coming . . . on a donkey's colt (12:15). Jesus fulfilled Scripture and entered Jerusalem in exactly the manner foretold. His disciples did not understand what he was doing. But after he was glorified, they remembered and understood (12:16).

Fulfilled prophecies like this one testify to the divine inspiration and inerrancy of Scripture. The many Old Testament prophecies about the Messiah were written hundreds of years before his birth, yet they were fulfilled in his life accurately and in detail. This should encourage all believers to trust that the Bible is indeed the authoritative Word of God.

12:17-19 Those who had witnessed Jesus raise Lazarus from the dead were testifying to the rest of the crowds, so Jesus's following grew even larger (12:17-18). All of this made the Pharisees furious (12:19). More followers for Jesus meant fewer followers for them! The Gospels make clear that the religious leaders in Jerusalem were motivated in their hatred of Jesus by jealousy (see Matt 27:18; Mark 15:10).

12:20-21 Also in Jerusalem for the Passover were some Greeks—that is, Gentile proselytes who worshiped the God of Israel (12:20). Earlier Jesus had said, "I have other sheep that are not from this sheep pen; I must bring them also" (10:16). By "other sheep" he meant Gentiles. Jesus came to be the Savior of the world (see 3:16). And now the world was starting to come to him, saying, We want to see Jesus (12:21).

12:22-23 We've seen repeatedly in John's Gospel that it was not Jesus's time or that his hour had not yet come (see 2:4; 7:6, 8, 30; 8:20). Jesus operated on a divine clock. But when his disciples told him that these Greeks wanted to see him, Jesus finally said, "It's time"—the hour has come for the Son of Man to be glorified (12:23). The Son's glorification involves his death, resurrection, and ascension back to the Father.

12:24 Jesus used an agricultural illustration to teach a spiritual principle: Unless a grain of wheat falls to the ground and dies, it remains by itself. But if it dies, it produces much fruit. Jesus had come into the world to die, to give his life as a substitutionary atonement for sinners. In the same way that a single grain produces much wheat, Jesus's death would yield much spiritual fruit—salvation and eternal life for all who will trust him.

12:25 The one who loves his life will lose it, and the one who hates his life in this world will keep it for eternal life. Thus, if you live a self-centered existence, you will lose the very thing you are trying to hold on to. If your life is all about you and finding yourself, you will not find the "you" that you're looking for. To hate your life means *not* living in a self-centered way but being a servant of others. The one who lives a life of service in the name of the Lord Jesus will be rewarded in this life and in the life to come.

12:26 If anyone serves me, he must follow me. . . . If anyone serves me, the Father will honor him. To serve the King, we must follow the King. If he serves, we must serve (see Mark 10:45). The first responsibility of a follower of Christ is to his people. We are to love those whom he loves and gave himself for. And if we love and serve sacrificially, the Father promises to honor us with a reward—some of which may come in this life, though most will come in eternity.

12:27-28 Jesus's soul was troubled because he knew the suffering that would be required. He would die for the sins of the world, enduring separation from his Father. Nevertheless, his grief didn't cause him to flee from his task. To suffer and die for sinners is **why [Jesus] came** (12:27). He was committed to the will of God, so he prayed aloud: **Father, glorify your name.** After this, **a voice** responded **from heaven: I have glorified it, and I will glorify it again** (12:28). Throughout the Son's ministry, the Father had been glorified through the miraculous signs. But the ultimate glorification was coming in the cross and resurrection.

12:29-30 The crowds had been divided over Jesus before (7:25-27, 40-43). Now they were even divided over the voice from heaven. Some thought it was **an angel**; others claimed it was only **thunder** (12:29). Jesus told them that **this voice** was for their sake, not his (12:30). The Father validated the Son so that they might believe.

12:31 Jesus's death on the cross would be an act of **judgment** on the devil, **the ruler of this world.** In the garden, Adam and Eve were given the responsibility to rule the world on God's behalf. Instead, they chose to sin against God and thereby granted rule of the world to Satan (see 2 Cor 4:4; Eph 2:2; 1 John 5:19). So the Son of God became a man to defeat the devil. The cross guarantees the enemy's defeat because Satan achieves victory through accusing sinners. But through the cross, Jesus Christ would deal with sin once and for all (see Heb 7:26-27; 9:12; 10:10).

12:32-33 The cross drew all judgment for all people to Jesus Christ as the Savior of the world (1 John 2:2). The death of Christ saved all humankind from the consequences of original sin (Rom 5:18) and made all people savable for their personal sin when they place personal faith in him. This is why we are to share the gospel with everyone in the world.

12:34-36 Still **the crowd** was confused (12:34). Their minds needed enlightening. So Jesus encouraged them to receive **the light** and **walk in the light** while it was still with them (12:35), for Jesus himself is the light (see 1:9; 8:12). If you reject him, your life will

consist of **darkness** (12:35). This, in fact, is why we live in such a dark and sin-scarred world. But if you **believe in the light** (that is, trust in Jesus Christ), you will **become a child of light** (12:36). God will grant you understanding so that you may walk in his ways.

12:37-41 In spite of all the miraculous **signs** Jesus performed, many people **did not believe in him** (12:37). This fulfilled the words spoken by **Isaiah the prophet,** which John quotes in 12:38 (see Isa 53:1) and 12:40 (see Isa 6:10). Isaiah said that God **blinded their eyes and hardened their hearts** (12:40). Why? Because they had rejected the light (see 12:35-36). When Pharaoh repeatedly and willfully hardened his heart against God, the Lord eventually cooperated with Pharaoh and hardened his heart further (see commentary on Exod 4:21). If a person persists in pursuing darkness, eventually God will confirm his desire. Be careful what you wish for.

12:42-43 Nevertheless, many did believe in him even among the rulers. However, these rulers **did not confess** Jesus because **the Pharisees** had threatened to kick Jesus's followers out of **the synagogue** (12:42). They were unwilling to go public with their belief in Jesus because **they loved human praise more than praise from God** (12:43). We must not remain silent about our faith (see commentary on Matt 10:32-33).

12:44-50 In these verses, Jesus summarizes why he came into the world. He **did not come to judge the world but to save** it (12:47). Those who reject him will experience judgment **on the last day** (12:48). To reject Jesus Christ, the Son of God, is to reject the Father who sent him. And the opposite is also true: **The one who believes in [him] believes** in the one **who sent [him]** (12:44). It's a package deal. You cannot say you believe in God while simultaneously rejecting Jesus. We only truly come to God through the Son, for he has truly **spoken** the words of **the Father,** words that lead to **eternal life** (12:49-50).

VI. THE FAREWELL DISCOURSE (13:1–17:26)

A. The Last Supper, Foot Washing, and Jesus's Betrayer (13:1-30)

13:1-2 Jesus's **hour** had finally **come**; it was time for him to be glorified and **depart from this world to the Father** (13:1; see 2:4; 7:30; 8:20; 12:23, 27; 16:32; 17:1). John tells us that Jesus **loved his own**—his disciples—**to the end** (13:1). He had spent three years with the Twelve—teaching them, leading them, praying for them, loving them. He had done everything for them that he had come to do. Yet one of the men, **Judas** Iscariot, was going to betray him. In intending to do this, he had opened the door for **the devil** to put a specific idea **into [his] heart** (13:2).

13:3-5 Knowing that he, the Son of God, **had come from God** and **was going back to God**, Jesus **took a towel** and a **basin** and **began to wash his disciples' feet**. Notice that Jesus understood his identity and where he'd come from. He himself is God, the Creator of the universe (see 1:1-3). He is the King of kings, having legions of angels standing poised to do his bidding (see 18:36). And yet, as the apostle Paul would write, Jesus "did not consider equality with God as something to be exploited. Instead he emptied himself by assuming the form of a servant" (Phil 2:6-7). He took that humble role to wash the dirty feet of those who should have been washing his, because he came to serve (see Mark 10:45). To this servanthood mindset, the Lord calls each one of us.

13:6-9 The Lord made it clear that though they didn't understand what he was doing, later they would (13:7). However, **Peter** would have none of it: **You will never wash my feet**. But unless Jesus washed him, he could have no fellowship with him (13:8). "In that case," Peter essentially said, "forget the foot wash. Give me a shower!" (13:9). With this statement, Peter revealed his heart. He was willing to do anything to show Jesus that he didn't want to be disconnected from him.

13:10-11 Jesus assured Peter that if one **has bathed**, he only needs to **wash his feet** (13:10). In other words, if you're already saved, you don't need to be saved again. You just need to address the dirty areas in your life so that you can stay clean. To maintain fellowship with the Lord, we must regularly come to him in confession and repentance. "If we confess our sins, he is faithful and righteous to forgive us our sins and to cleanse us from all unrighteousness" (1 John 1:9).

All of Jesus's disciples were **completely clean** except one (13:10). That one disciple was Judas (see 13:2). Jesus **knew who would betray him** (13:11). Nothing takes him by surprise.

13:12-17 After he **had washed their feet** (13:12), he exhorted his disciples to do the same. He should serve as their **example**. If he, their **Lord and Teacher**, washed their feet, then they should **wash one another's** (that is, serve one another; see 1 Tim 5:10), because **a servant is not greater than his master** (13:14-16).

Our Lord Jesus is a model of servanthood, and one that we should follow. How does Jesus's foot-washing command apply in our modern context? To put it simply, we are to serve people in the family of God—especially by helping them when things get dirty. Our service is most needed in the messiness of life where people are hurting and suffering.

13:18-19 **I'm not speaking about all of you.** Once again, the reader is reminded that Jesus knew which of his disciples was about to betray him, all in fulfillment of **Scripture**. Importantly, those he had **chosen** (13:18) is a reference to those chosen for service, not for salvation. The Scripture Jesus quotes is from Psalm 41:9. Just as David was betrayed, so also the Messiah—the Son of David—would be betrayed. Jesus wanted them to know that he knew the future and was in control. When everything happened just as he foretold, it would be further evidence of his divine identity (13:19).

13:20 Whoever receives anyone I send receives me, and the one who receives me receives him who sent me. The one who receives the Son of God receives God the Father because the Son is the way to the Father (see 14:6). But Jesus added, "Whoever receives anyone I send receives me." When we go into the world in the name of Jesus and proclaim his gospel and his teachings, we go as his and the Father's authorized representatives.

13:21-30 Jesus became **troubled**, knowing what was about to occur. Then he prophesied: **Truly I tell you, one of you will betray me** (13:21). Thus, something that the readers of John's Gospel have been told for some time (see 6:66-71; 12:4; 13:2) was finally revealed to the disciples. And they were in shock, **looking at one another** in bewilderment (13:22). **Peter** told John, the author of this Gospel and **the one Jesus loved** (see the introduction), to ask Jesus who this betrayer was (13:23-25). So Jesus told John that it was the disciple to whom he would give a **piece of bread.** Then he handed bread **to Judas** (13:26).

To offer food was a sign of friendship; therefore, Jesus was extending a final offer of grace and mercy to the one who was about to betray him. Judas took the bread, but he rejected the offer of friendship: **Satan entered him** (13:27). Yet Satan only entered him because Judas had invited him by rejecting Jesus and intending to betray him (see commentary on 13:1-2).

Essentially, Jesus told Judas, "What you're planning to do—get it over with" (13:27). The other disciples were confused by the exchange, thinking that Jesus was telling Judas to make preparations for the Passover feast (12:28-29). They didn't realize that Judas would not only betray their Master, but would do so that very night. So Judas **left** to carry out his evil deed (13:30).

☙ B. Final Teaching *(13:31-16:33)* ☙

13:31-32 With the betrayal set in motion, the events leading up to the crucifixion had begun. **Now the Son of Man is glorified** (13:31) refers to why Jesus had come into the world.

He would offer himself as a substitutionary atonement and then be raised from the dead. The Son would glorify the Father, and the Father would glorify the Son (13:32); they would mutually advertise one another's glory. Highlighting the greatness of God, in fact, is what Christians are called to as well. Everything we do—in thought, word, and deed—is to be done for the glory of God (see 1 Cor 10:31).

13:33-34 In **a little while**, Jesus would be gone and ascend to God the Father (13:33; see Acts 1:9). In light of this impending departure, he gave them **a new command: Love one another** (13:34). It was new because it related to what was about to happen within the family of God.

Biblical love is the decision to compassionately, responsibly, and righteously pursue the well-being of another person. It's not the same as *liking* someone. To like someone or something is to express a feeling. By contrast, loving someone may or may not have feelings connected to it. Love is a decision to seek another's best, regardless of your feelings.

13:35 Through loving one another, Jesus told them, **everyone will know that you are my disciples.** Notice that he didn't say everyone would recognize his disciples by how much of the Bible they knew. Knowing the Bible is essential, but knowledge means nothing without love (see 1 Cor 13:1-3). A loveless Christian actually undermines the gospel. Why? Because, as John says elsewhere, "God is love" (1 John 4:8). How can people come to know the God who perfectly expresses love—both within the Trinity and to humanity—if his representatives don't demonstrate love?

13:36-38 In response to Jesus's comments about leaving them (13:33), **Peter** asked, **Where are you going?** When Jesus told him that he couldn't **follow** (13:36), Peter decided to set him straight. The rest of the disciples might not be ready to follow, but Peter was confident that he was prepared: **I will lay down my life for you** (13:37). But that's when Jesus poured cold water on this fiery disciple. He said, **A rooster will not crow until you have denied me three times**

(13:38). Jesus wanted Peter to put his pride to death. He was talking a good game, but he wouldn't be able to back it up with action (see 18:15-18, 25-27).

Too often we're exactly like Peter. In our minds we envision ourselves as better disciples than we actually are. Pride will cause us to think too highly of ourselves and then fall flat on our faces.

14:1-2 Don't let your heart be troubled. Jesus compassionately sought to calm his disciples' fears over his impending departure. What words of comfort did he offer to give them confidence? First, he said, **Believe in God; believe also in me** (14:1). In other words, "Place your full trust in me, just as you trust in the Father. We are unified, sharing the same divine nature and the same divine purpose." Second, he told them that they had heavenly real estate waiting on them: **In my Father's house are many rooms . . . I am going away to prepare a place for you** (14:2). According to Jewish wedding custom, the father would add rooms onto his house for his newly married son. Jesus wasn't abandoning them but heading out to get their eternal home ready. When your time comes, have no fear. Heaven has been prepared for you.

14:3 Jesus promised them, **I will come again and take you to myself.** This return of which Jesus prophesied is what we call the *rapture*, the time when he will return to receive his saints and take them to heaven (see 1 Thess 4:16-17). This will happen prior to his return to earth to establish his millennial kingdom.

14:4-7 Jesus promised his disciples that they knew **the way to where** he was going (14:4). However, **Thomas** wasn't so sure: **How can we know the way?** (14:5). It was as if he said, "You haven't given us a map, Lord!" But Thomas had misunderstood. "The way" isn't a path; it's a person: **I am the way, the truth, and the life. No one comes to the Father except through me** (14:6). The Lord Jesus Christ is the universal point of access to God. There is no other entrance into heaven. If you want to know the Father, you must come to him through his Son. Jesus assured

Thomas that if he knew the Son, he knew the Father (14:7).

14:8-9 Then it was Philip's turn to sound dissatisfied: **Show us the Father, and that's enough for us** (14:8). Philip wanted to be like Moses, who got to catch a glimpse of God (see Exod 33:12–34:9). But he didn't understand that fully revealing God the Father was exactly what Jesus had come to do. "No one has ever seen God. The one and only Son, who is himself God and is at the Father's side—he has revealed him" (1:18). Whereas Moses only saw a hint of the glory of the invisible God, Jesus said, **The one who has seen me has seen the Father** (14:9). Jesus Christ is God incarnate, the God-Man.

14:10-11 I am in the Father and the Father is in me (14:11). Jesus emphasized the unity of Father and Son. As he'd told the Jews previously, "I and the Father are one" (10:30). He is one God in three persons: Father, Son, and Holy Spirit.

14:12 Jesus's works confirmed his divine identity (see 10:11). But he affirmed to his followers, **The one who believes in me will also do the works that I do. And he will do even greater works than these.** Now, obviously, he's not saying that his followers will do every work that he did. We aren't God and never will be. Rather, Jesus was talking about scope of impact. His travels were limited, as were the number of people who heard his voice. But in the years since, the church has carried his message to billions all over the world.

14:13-15 When we are rightly connected to **the Father** through **the Son**, more prayers **in [Jesus's] name** get answered (14:13-14). How do we ensure that we are rightly connected to the Trinitarian God? Jesus provided the answer: **If you love me, you will keep my commands** (14:15). You can talk all day about your love for God. But, according to Jesus, obedience is the proof of love. If we truly love him, we will seek to obey him. Why? Because love is first and foremost a decision, not an emotion. Our relationship with him drives our desire to please him. God wants your obedience, but he wants it to be motivated by love—not law.

14:16-17 Where would the disciples look for help when Jesus was gone? Jesus told them: **I will ask the Father, and he will give you another Counselor to be with you forever. He is the Spirit of truth.** In Greek there are two words that could be used to mean "another." One means "another of a different kind"; the other means "another of the same kind." The latter is used here. The Holy Spirit is another Counselor, but one who shares in the divine nature. Therefore, God would still be with them in the person of God the Holy Spirit. The same sovereign love and power they enjoyed in Jesus, then, would be present in their lives.

As a "Counselor" or "Helper," the Holy Spirit enables believers to pull off the will of God in their lives. He is "the Spirit of truth" because he only deals in truth (like Jesus; see 14:6); as God, he operates according to divine, holy standards. **The world is unable to receive [the Holy Spirit] because it doesn't … know him.** The only way to know and receive the Spirit of God, in fact, is through knowing and receiving the Son of God, Jesus Christ. And when the Spirit comes, **he remains with you** forever—not merely alongside you, but **in you** (14:17).

Importantly, this promise wasn't simply for those first disciples: it's for everyone who calls on the name of Jesus. When you trust in Christ to take away your sins and give you eternal life, the Holy Spirit comes to dwell within you, ministering the presence of God to you.

14:18 Jesus comforted his disciples with the promise, **I will not leave you as orphans.** He would send the Holy Spirit to be with them. And one day the Son will return to take his followers to the place prepared for them (see 14:2-4).

14:19-20 In a little while **the world will no longer see me, but you will** (14:19). Though he would be executed on a Roman cross, Jesus would rise bodily from the grave and show himself to his disciples (see 20:1-29). **Because I live, you will live too** (14:19). Jesus shares his resurrection life with his followers through the Holy Spirit, who connects us to the Trinitarian God: **I am in my Father, you are in me, and I am in you** (14:20).

14:21 Again, Jesus explained that love is the motivation for keeping his **commands** (see 14:15). If you want to know whether someone really **loves** Jesus, watch to see whether he does what Jesus said. When you are connected to the love of the Father and Son in obedience, Jesus promises to **reveal** more of himself to you.

If you listen to a radio station in your car, you know that the further you get from the broadcast station, the worse your reception of the signal gets. Many people have difficulty connecting with God because they've wandered too far away to pick up his signal. But if you come back home in obedience, relating to God through Christ in love, he will disclose more of himself to you.

14:22-25 Judas **(not Iscariot)** wanted to know why he promised to **reveal** himself to them but **not to the world** (14:22; see 14:21). But Jesus insisted that his love is available to all: **If anyone loves me, he will keep my word.** And those willing to come to Jesus in love and obedience will find **the Father** and Son coming to make their **home** with them (14:23). It's **the one who doesn't love** Jesus or his **words** who will lose out on a relationship with him (14:24).

14:26 When Jesus returned to heaven, **the Father** would send **the Counselor, the Holy Spirit** to be with his disciples (see 14:16-17). Jesus said that the Spirit would come **in [his] name** because he would represent Jesus and testify about him (see 15:26). He also said that the Holy Spirit would **teach** them **all things and remind** them **of everything** he told them. This applies to the first disciples because the Holy Spirit helped them to recall Jesus's words, sharing them with others and recording them in the pages of Scripture (see 2 Pet 1:21). But the Spirit also helps believers today, enabling us to recall Scripture at the appropriate time and helping us to understand its meaning and its application to our lives, as he activates "the mind of Christ" in us (1 Cor 2:10-16).

14:27 Jesus promised, **Peace I leave you. My peace I give to you.** Please understand what Jesus is and is not promising here. He is *not* promising the absence of a storm. Anyone can be at peace when nothing is wrong. Rather, he promises peace *in the midst of* a storm. He's talking about peace in the midst of tribulation—at a time when you shouldn't have any peace. This, of course, doesn't come from **the world**. It's the peace *of God*, "which surpasses all understanding, [and guards] your hearts and minds in Christ Jesus" (Phil 4:7).

Next Jesus said, **Don't let your heart be troubled or fearful**. In the coming hours, the disciples would have good reason to be troubled. Likewise, you will have experiences that prompt you to fear. But with a sovereign God ruling the world and "the peace of Christ" ruling in your heart (see Col 3:15), you can overcome trouble and fear.

14:28-29 Rather than being fearful, the disciples should have been filled with joy over the fact that Jesus was **going to the Father** (14:28). For Jesus loves the Father, and his imminent departure to be with him meant that his mission—the reason for which he'd come into the world—was almost complete. Jesus was explaining all these things to them in advance so that when the time of suffering arrived, they would **believe** that he was truly the Messiah, the Son of God (14:29).

14:30-31 The ruler of the world is coming (14:30). When Adam and Eve sinned, they gave up their role as king and queen, ruling creation on God's behalf, and turned it over to Satan. Therefore, the devil is appropriately called "the ruler of this world," "the god of this age" (2 Cor 4:4), and "the ruler of the power of the air" (Eph 2:2). He holds "the power of death" and keeps people in slavery by "the fear of death" (see Heb 2:14-15). But Satan had **no power over** Jesus (14:30) because Jesus is without sin. The Son of God became a man so that he might defeat the devil as a man and restore God's kingdom rule. And this he would do through his **love** for **the Father** and his obedience to what **the Father commanded** (14:31).

15:1 Jesus frequently used agricultural imagery in his teaching. On this occasion he told his disciples, **I am the true vine, and my Father is the gardener**. But he didn't pull this imagery out of thin air. The prophet Isaiah had spoken of Israel as the Lord's vineyard. God expected his vineyard to bear fruit, but it produced nothing but worthless grapes (see Isa 5:1-7). In contrast, the Son of God came as the authentic vine, perfectly obeying the Father and revealing his will to the people.

15:2 Every branch in [Jesus] that does not produce fruit [the Father] removes. And **every branch that produces fruit** the Father **prunes . . . so that it will produce more**. "Every branch" refers to Christians because they are *in* Jesus. The vine (the Son) feeds the branches, and the gardener (the Father) tends the branches. God's goal for every Christian is to increase in fruit bearing. We are to progress from producing *no fruit* (15:2) to some *fruit* (15:2) to *more fruit* (15:2) to *much fruit* (15:5) to *remaining fruit* (15:16). Fruitfulness is a life of spiritual usefulness and productivity for the good of others and the glory of God. It's the proof of true discipleship (15:8).

Fruit has three characteristics. First, it reflects the character of its tree. Apples come from apple trees; oranges grow on orange trees. The fruit in your life should reflect Christ—his attitudes and actions, his character and conduct. Second, fruit is visible. The presence of fruit lets you identify a tree's kind and whether it's healthy. An authentic follower of Christ is a visible follower of Christ, not a secret-agent saint. Third, fruit is always for the benefit of others. If you're always serving yourself instead of others, your fruit is going to rot on the tree.

The Greek verb translated "removes" in this verse can also be rendered "takes away" or "lifts up." The branches in a vineyard could become large and drag on the ground easily. So God the gardener "takes them away" from the ground by lifting them up. God will, therefore, seek to make you fruitful by lifting you up, encouraging you, and motivating you—for example, through his Word and through the people of God. Those who are fruitful God also prunes so that they bear more fruit. Sometimes God will bring challenges and trials into our lives to enable us to grow in our faith and cast off anything hindering full productivity.

15:3-5 The disciples were **clean** through the washing of Christ's **word** (15:3; see Eph 5:26). This is how we stay clean too; nevertheless, we must **remain in** Jesus. A **branch** that's disconnected from the **vine** is useless. So also we can't **produce fruit** unless we remain in Jesus (15:4). The idea of "remaining" or "abiding" in Christ has to do with intimacy and relationship. Jesus Christ is our source, the only one who can provide the spiritual sustenance and vitality we need to be useful believers. Thus, we need to hang out with him. You can't avoid Jesus all week and then show up on Sunday morning expecting growth. We only produce **much fruit** when we remain in him (15:5).

15:6 If someone chooses **not** to **remain in** Jesus, **he is thrown aside like a branch and he withers.** Such branches are gathered and **burned.** This is not a description of hell and cannot refer to loss of salvation since believers are eternally secure. We've already seen that everyone who comes to Jesus will never be cast out. If you could lose eternal life, then it wasn't eternal to begin with (see commentary on 6:36-40). So instead, the burning is a reference to the consequences of a loss of both fellowship with God and rewards from him. If you disconnect from the vine for too long, don't be surprised to find yourself experiencing divine discipline, getting burned, and seeing your spiritual life withering. Such a believer is useless to himself, God, and others. So, if you find such things happening to you, repent! "Draw near to God, and he will draw near to you" (Jas 4:8).

15:7 To have Jesus's **words remain** (or "abide") **in you** requires more than merely reading or listening to them. You must internalize them. Another way to describe this is *meditating* on God's Word, rolling it around in your mind to grasp what it means and how to apply it to your specific circumstances. We must chew and swallow Scripture, so to speak, so that it becomes part of us. When you do this, you can **ask whatever you want and it will be done for you.** In other words, prayers get answered when we maintain intimate fellowship with God through his Word. That's because you'll find your will aligning with his.

15:8 My Father is glorified by this: that **you produce much fruit and prove to be my disciples.** The more useful you become to

the kingdom, the more glory God will receive and the more people will recognize you as a serious saint (rather than a casual Christian). The Lord wants followers, not mere fans.

15:9-10 Jesus told his disciples, **Remain in my love** (15:9). How do we do that? Jesus said, **If you keep my commands you will remain in my love.** Love for Jesus results in obedience. And obedience produces a deeper relationship with him. The Son wants us to enjoy the intimate kind of loving relationship that he enjoys with the **Father** (15:10).

15:11 Jesus's goal in teaching his disciples things was that their **joy** would **be complete.** *Joy* is internal stability in spite of external circumstances because of the knowledge that God is in control. It is a settled assurance and quiet confidence in God's sovereignty that results in the decision to praise him. Notice that Jesus offered them his own joy. So, if your joy container is empty, Jesus will let you borrow some of his.

15:12-14 Jesus repeated the command he gave them earlier (see 13:34): **Love one another as I have loved you** (15:12). Biblical love involves more than mere emotions and personal preferences. *Love* is the decision to compassionately, righteously, responsibly, and sacrificially seek the well-being of another. You can love people whom you may not necessarily like because love is not dependent on your feelings. That's why Jesus can command you to "love your enemies" (Matt 5:44). It's true that love may include feelings of affection, and such feelings may develop over time. But it's not driven by them. Love is driven by sacrifice for the welfare of others. And the greatest expression of love is to **lay down** one's **life for . . . friends** (15:13). That's the kind of love Jesus modeled for us.

15:15 Jesus told his disciples that they were not mere **servants** to him. They were his **friends.** A master doesn't reveal things to a servant, but friends do. Jesus had **made known to** his disciples **everything** he had **heard from** his **Father.**

15:16-17 When the Bible refers to God's choice (or election) of people, it's a choosing for service, not salvation. Jesus **chose** his disciples so that they would **produce fruit** that would be useful to his kingdom and reflect God's character. He didn't simply save them for heaven only; he **appointed** them to a mission on earth that would involve winning people to Christ and growing them in the faith (15:16)—a mission that involves keeping his commands, loving him, and loving one another (15:9-15). When that happens, **the Father** answers prayer (15:16).

15:18-21 The world system headed by Satan (see commentary on 12:31; 14:30-31) **hates** Jesus. Therefore, followers of Jesus who identify with his person and character will face hatred and opposition from the world (15:18-19). As servants of Christ, we should not expect to be treated better than he was. **If they persecuted [him], they will also persecute you.** But, similarly, **if they kept [his] word, they will also keep** the word spoken by his disciples (15:20). When you faithfully represent Jesus, the world will relate to you as it related to him.

15:22-25 The Son of God came personally into the world to reveal the Father, so those who rejected him **have no excuse for their sin** (15:22). **The one who hates me**, he told them, **also hates my Father** (15:23). That's strong language, but there's no way around it. People can't talk about their love for God while simultaneously rejecting his Son. In spite of all Jesus's words and **works**, many refused to believe in him, thus demonstrating their hatred for the Father and the Son (15:24). They **fulfilled** the Scripture spoken by David in Psalm 69:4: **They hated me for no reason** (15:25). As the wicked showed their disdain for King David, so they showed disdain for the Son of David.

15:26-27 Again Jesus told his disciples about the Holy Spirit, **the Counselor, the Spirit of truth** (15:26; see 14:16-17, 26). Jesus said that when the Spirit comes, **he will testify about** Jesus (15:26). Since the role of the Holy Spirit is to testify about the Son of God, the Spirit has a Christocentric ministry. He does not merely draw attention to himself; he draws attention to Jesus. Therefore, we should be wary of those who claim the Spirit's involvement in a ministry that ignores Jesus. If the

Spirit makes much of Jesus, then his disciples should too (15:27).

16:1-4 Jesus had told his disciples **these things to keep [them] from stumbling** (16:1)—that is, to keep them from abandoning the faith due to persecution. In the days to come, followers of Jesus would face being banned **from the synagogues** and put to death—often by those who would think they were serving God by doing so (16:2). However, such people **haven't known the Father or [Jesus]** (16:3).

Jesus wanted them—and us—to be prepared. We should not be shocked when we experience some form of rejection or censure for our Christian beliefs and standards. This could come from family, friends, employers, customers, coworkers, the government—and the list goes on. As Paul told Timothy, "All who want to live a godly life in Christ Jesus will be persecuted" (2 Tim 3:12). But the Holy Spirit is available to empower us in our time of need.

16:5-7 Jesus told them he was **going away** and **sorrow** had **filled** his disciples' hearts (16:5-6). They had been with him for three years of ministry. They wanted to see him reign as King; they wanted to be with him. But he assured them that his departure was for their **benefit**. How could that be possible? Well, unless he left, **the Counselor [would] not come** (16:6-7)—that is, the Holy Spirit (see 14:16-17, 26; 15:26). The Father sent the Son into the world (see 3:17), and the Son would **send** the Spirit into the world (16:7). Thus, the Trinitarian God is at work, each Person carrying out the next phase of his kingdom program.

The coming of the Holy Spirit would benefit the disciples because his presence would not be physically limited (as Jesus's was). He would dwell within each of them (14:17) and go with them wherever they traveled (see Eph 1:22, 23). If you have trusted Jesus Christ and received the Holy Spirit, you are never alone.

16:8-11 The role of the Holy Spirit would be to **convict** (that is, convince concerning the truth) **the world about sin, righteousness, and judgment** (16:8). People would be convicted **about sin** because of their failure to **believe in** Jesus for forgiveness and the gift of eternal life (16:9). They would be convicted **about righteousness** because Jesus would no longer be physically present (16:10). The resurrection and ascension are proof of the righteousness of Christ because he was crucified as one who was unrighteous. With Jesus gone, people would think that his righteous standard no longer applied, but the Spirit would demonstrate otherwise. Finally, the world would be convicted **about judgment, because the ruler of this world**—Satan—**has been judged** (16:11). Therefore, his followers (see 8:44) will also be judged. The death of Christ condemned and defeated Satan (see Col 2:15), and—like a condemned criminal—he is waiting for his coming execution (see Rev 20:2, 7-10).

16:12-13 Though Jesus yet had **many things to tell** his disciples, he knew they were unable to **bear them** (16:12). But when **the Spirit of truth** came, he would help them and **guide [them] into all the truth.** He would **declare to** them things that were yet **to come** (such as the prophecies in Revelation) (16:13). The Spirit would ensure that the apostles' writings were true, guaranteeing that they wrote Scripture, the very words of God.

16:14-15 The Holy Spirit's role is to **glorify** the Son, receiving the Son's words and disclosing them to his followers (16:14). Once again we see the Trinity in action in that the Son took revelation from **the Father** and would **declare it** to his disciples through the Holy Spirit (16:15).

Though the Spirit provided the apostles with perfect revelation in order that they might write Scripture, this does not mean that we are excluded from his ministry. This text applies to us in two ways. First, we are recipients of the Scriptural revelation that the apostles received. Second, the Holy Spirit provides us with personal illumination, enabling us to understand Scripture and to see how it applies in the details of our lives. This work of the Spirit in the life of the believer is called "the anointing" (see 1 John 2:20, 27).

16:16-19 The time of Jesus's crucifixion was drawing near. In **a little while**, the disciples would **no longer see** him because he would be dead and buried. But in another **little while**, they would see him **again** when he rose from the grave (16:16). However, the disciples weren't getting it (16:17). They said quietly to one another, **We don't know what he's talking about** (16:18). Yet Jesus knew they were confused (16:19). They couldn't hide anything from him. He knows your private conversations and thoughts, too.

Don't be upset when you don't understand what Jesus is doing in your life. After all, Jesus's first disciples were confused, and they had Jesus right there with them! Choose to pursue him in the midst of your confusion.

16:20-22 Jesus foretold the great **sorrow** that they would soon experience at his crucifixion (while **the world** rejoiced), but he also foretold that their grief would **turn to joy** at his resurrection (16:20). To explain how they could go from mourning to elation in such a brief span of time, he gave them an illustration. **A woman** experiencing **labor** goes through great **pain.** But when her **child** is born, her suffering is forgotten and replaced by rejoicing (16:21). In the same way, the disciples' pain would lead to joy. And, Jesus told them, **No one will take away your joy from you** (16:22). Why? Because it is rooted in the presence and work of Christ on the inside—not on the ever-changing circumstances of life (i.e., happiness).

16:23-24 Once again, Jesus told them, **Anything you ask the Father in my name, he will give you** (16:23; see 14:13-14; 15:16). No matter what sorrow you experience, remain in Jesus because God is still in the prayer-answering business when we love and seek to honor the Son. In fact, Jesus encouraged his disciples to take advantage of the opportunity to **ask** of him so that they might experience **joy** (16:24). There's nothing like the joy that comes when the Creator of the universe answers your personal prayer. This joy does not depend on what happens; rather, it can be chosen based on our confidence in and commitment to God.

16:25 Jesus had been using **figures of speech** with them (e.g., the vine, 15:1-8; the woman in labor, 16:21). But in time, he would **tell [them]**

plainly about the Father. There is a principle at work here for believers in Christ: God only explains what you are ready and able to handle. You may not understand the circumstances that you're experiencing, but God loves you and is taking you through a growth process. He calls for your trust and obedience now. Further understanding will come later, when you're prepared to receive it.

16:26-28 On that day when the disciples would **ask the Father** in Jesus's name, they would not need Jesus to ask on their behalf. Why? Because the Father himself loved *them* due to their relationship to his Son (16:26-27).

16:29-32 After this, the disciples affirmed their belief in Jesus. He had known and answered their private questions (see 16:16-19). They were certain that he was the Messiah who had come **from God** (16:30). However, Jesus knew them better than they knew themselves. He said, **Do you now believe? Indeed, an hour is coming, and has come, when each of you will be scattered . . . and you will leave me alone** (16:31-32). Translation: "You don't believe as strongly as you think you do. Now, while all is quiet and safe, this is easy for you to say. But very soon you're going to forget your fragile faith and run for your lives."

Have you ever made a vow to God during a church service only to back away from it later—perhaps as quickly as when you left the church parking lot? It's easy to boast about our faith; it's harder to live it, as Peter would soon discover (18:15-18, 25-27). This is one of the reasons why God causes us to experience challenges. Through them, we come to see how brittle our faith is and how mighty our Savior is, and thus our faith is made a little stronger.

Though the disciples would abandon him, Jesus was **not alone.** His **Father** was with him (16:32). He was "sent" from the Father (3:17), is "in the Father" (14:11), and would return "to the Father" (14:28). The Son and the Father "are one" (10:30).

16:33 Jesus revealed all of these things to his disciples, not to fill them with fear, but so that they might **have peace** in him. Peace is not mere serenity and the absence of crisis. The peace that Jesus was talking about is something that only he can give, and it's something that believers can experience *in* a crisis (see commentary on 14:27). In reality, you can't know if you truly have peace until conflict strikes. A Christian's peace is found in his or her connection to Jesus Christ based on his Word.

No matter what **suffering** you endure in this life, Jesus exhorts you to **be courageous.** How can we have courage to pursue God's agenda in the midst of tribulation? Jesus gave us the answer: **I have conquered the world.** Regardless of how the world beats you down, you have reason to live with bold faith because Jesus is the sovereign King over the world. He has defeated sin, Satan, and death. If you're a believer, your eternity is secure. And Jesus has the power to overrule your earthly circumstances. Knowing this truth and maintaining an intimate relationship with the Lord (**in me**) will radically change your perspective as you face whatever obstacles come your way. His peace gives you peace in the midst of life's crises.

❧ C. Jesus's Prayer (17:1-26) ❧

17:1 In chapters 13–16, John presents Jesus's "Farewell Discourse," the final teachings and exhortations he gave to his disciples in the upper room after the Passover supper. In chapter 17, John records the prayer Jesus spoke at the conclusion of their time together—just before his betrayal.

Jesus recognized that **the hour** had **come** for **the Son** and **the Father** to **glorify** each other (see 2:4; 7:30; 8:20; 12:23, 27; 13:1). The Father and Son love one another and desire to make much of one another before a watching world. Those who come to God through Jesus Christ are called to participate in this intra-Trinitarian love, bringing glory to God through our faith in and obedience to the Son.

17:2 As John has already made clear, everyone who believes in Jesus receives **eternal life** (see 3:16). The Father loves the Son so much that he desired to give this redeemed humanity to him as a gift. The Father gave the Son **authority over all flesh** and then gave us to him so that the King would have a people to rule.

17:3 In his prayer, Jesus gave a definition of **eternal life.** This is important because it does not merely refer to an existence that lasts forever. After all, everyone will live eternally, either in heaven or in hell. Eternal life, then, is not merely the continuation of life but the experience of God's reality. **This is eternal life: that they may know you, the only true God, and the one you have sent—Jesus Christ.** To receive eternal life is to enter into the divine realm with the goal of experiencing an intimate relationship with God through Jesus, a relationship that will grow throughout eternity. It is the uninterrupted, deepening knowledge and experience of God. This is the purpose for which we were created.

17:4 Jesus **glorified** the Father **on the earth by completing the work** he gave him to accomplish. Jesus said, "My food is to do the will of him who sent me and to finish his work" (4:34). We bring glory to God in the same way—by pursuing his will for our lives. Do you consider doing the will of God to be as desirous and life-sustaining as eating?

17:5 Jesus prayed the **Father** would **glorify** him **in [his] presence with that glory** he had with the Father **before the world existed.** Notice that Jesus clearly affirmed his pre-existence. Before the incarnation, before Jesus was conceived by the Holy Spirit in the womb of Mary, before the creation week even began, God the Son eternally existed in the glorious presence of God the Father. And to this glory he would soon return.

17:6-8 Jesus confessed that he had faithfully **revealed** the Father to his disciples, those who had **kept [his] word** (17:6). As a result, they believed that Jesus had been **sent** by God (17:7-8). He really was the Messiah, just as he claimed.

17:9-11 Next Jesus prayed, **not . . . for the world,** but for his disciples whom the Father had **given** him (17:9; see 17:2). Jesus was **glorified in them** because they had received **everything** he revealed to them (17:10). As

Jesus prepared to leave the world, he prayed that the Father would protect his disciples by his **name** (17:11)—that is, by the Father's name. In Scripture, names do not merely identify people but speak of their character. Therefore, Jesus was asking that God would protect them by keeping them connected to their holy and righteous Father. Specifically, he asked that God would grant that Jesus's followers might **be one,** as the Father and Son **are.** In other words, he prayed for the unity of his disciples—that they'd be unified in love in the same way that the persons of the Godhead are unified in love.

17:12 While Jesus was with his disciples, he protected them. None of them was **lost, except the son of destruction, so that the Scripture** could **be fulfilled.** God knew far in advance that Judas would betray the Messiah (see commentary on 13:18-19). Nevertheless, Judas's rebellion could not thwart the divine plan. On the contrary, it facilitated it. Understand that even wickedness falls under the sovereignty of God—not because God prescribes it, but because he uses it. How much better would it be for you to fulfill God's purposes through your obedience than through your rebellion?

17:13-16 Jesus spoke these things to his disciples so that they would have his **joy completed in them** (17:13). Notice that it's *his* joy. To experience peace in the midst of suffering is for Jesus to share his joy with you, and this comes by means of confidence in his **word** (17:14). But when one receives God's word through Jesus, one also receives the hatred of the world. The world hates the followers of Jesus because **they are not of the world, just as [Jesus] is not** (17:16). Yet Jesus does not pray that the Father would **take them out of the world** but that he would **protect them from the evil one** (17:15).

Christians must function in this world—in our families, neighborhoods, schools, workplaces, marketplaces, and civic arenas. Yet, we are not to adopt the world's perspective or let it dictate our values. We must operate on earth from a heavenly perspective, God's perspective. God's Word is to determine our understanding of right and wrong. Though we are *in* the world, we must not be *of* it.

17:17 Then Jesus prayed, **Sanctify them by the truth; your word is truth.** To be *sanctified* is to be set apart for God's purposes. This process happens through internalizing the eternal truth of God's Word. Think of the Word like food. You can chew it all day, but unless you swallow it, you receive no health benefits from it. You internalize God's Word, not by merely hearing or reading it, but by trusting and obeying it. Then its work of spiritual transformation is activated in your life (see 2 Cor 3:17-18).

17:18-19 Jesus was sending his disciples **into the world** (17:18)—that is, sending them on a mission. They would not be cloistered in a monastery but making their God-glorifying presence known in the culture. He said, **I sanctify myself for them, so that they also may be sanctified by the truth** (17:19). In other words, Jesus had set himself apart to God's will so that he might enable his followers to do the same.

17:20 Not only did Jesus pray for the eleven disciples in front of him, **but also for those who believe in [him] through their word.** The disciples / apostles with him that night would proclaim the gospel through their preaching and through their Holy-Spirit-inspired writings, which would become the New Testament. Therefore, "those who believe in [him] through their word" includes all those who have trusted in Christ down through the ages. This means that Jesus was praying here for you and me.

17:21 He prayed that all believers would **all be one**—that is, experience unity. Legitimate unity is not uniformity or sameness. Rather, Jesus was talking about being unified in God and his purposes. That's why he prayed, **May**

they also be in us, so that the world may believe you sent me.

A football team consists of different players filling different positions with different roles. But the entire team has one purpose: reaching the goal line. Their unity consists of pursuing that one goal according to the rules of the game. The church of Jesus Christ is composed of people from every race, ethnicity, gender, and walk of life. But we have the common purpose of proclaiming the gospel and pursuing God's kingdom agenda. Our effectiveness is determined by our unity. That's why Satan works so hard at causing division among Christians and within churches. Unity in truth is critical to experiencing the presence and power of God (see Acts 2:1-2, 43-44; 4:24-31). Illegitimate disunity disconnects us from God and causes us to be ineffective in our lives and in our prayers (see 1 Pet 3:7).

17:22-23 When legitimate unity is present, God's **glory** is manifested (17:22)—that is, he advertises himself to the world through us, so that even more people might come to know, love, and serve him. Our unity makes it possible for **the world** to **know** that God the Father **loved** and **sent** Jesus (17:23). Our involvement in the church is not trivial, then. We are caught up in something much bigger than us. We are called to serve the Lord in unity so that the love and glory of our Trinitarian God is visibly and powerfully manifested to a watching world.

17:24-26 Jesus concluded his prayer, acknowledging that **the world** had **not known** God. That's why the Father **sent** the Son (17:25), and that's why the Son came. Jesus Christ **made** the **name** of God **known** so that God's intra-Trinitarian **love** might be known and experienced by the world (17:26).

VII. BETRAYAL, TRIAL, CRUCIFIXION, AND DEATH (18:1–19:42)

18:1-2 At the conclusion of Jesus's discourse and prayer, **he** and **his disciples** went **across the Kidron Valley** (which lay between Jerusalem and the Mount of Olives) to **a garden** (18:1). But **Judas, who betrayed him, also**

knew the place (18:2). So, clearly, Jesus wasn't hiding from his enemies. He went to a location where he knew Judas could find him. Jesus was ready to complete his mission in obedience to the Father.

18:3 Judas showed up with **a company of soldiers and some officials** from the Jewish religious leaders. The latter were willing to work together with their Roman overlords to deal with Jesus.

18:4-6 Once again, John makes clear to his readers that nothing caught Jesus by surprise. He knew **everything that was about to happen to him**. After all, he's the Son of God. When Jesus asked whom they were looking for, they said, **Jesus of Nazareth** (18:4-5). (His disciples had fallen asleep; see Luke 22:45-46.) When he merely replied, **I am he**, they all **fell to the ground** (18:5-6). Jesus's words sure do pack a punch!

The Greek words behind the translation "I am he" can simply be rendered as "I am"—the divine name, the self-designation that God revealed to Moses (see commentary on 8:56-58). Jesus is no mere man. He's the God-Man. He's the Word who was with God, was God, and became flesh (1:1, 14). Jesus spoke the divine name using the same voice that had spoken the world into existence. And it knocked the betrayer and his accomplices off their feet.

18:7-9 When **he asked them again** and they gave the same reply, Jesus again said, **I am he**, and told them to let the disciples **go** (18:7-8). John tells us that Jesus said this to **fulfill the words** he had just prayed: **I have not lost one of those you have given me** (18:9; see 17:12). When Jesus intervenes to protect you, his intervention is always effective.

18:10-11 At that moment, **Simon Peter** took his **sword** and **cut off** the **right ear** of the **high priest's servant** (18:10). Yet Jesus didn't praise Peter for his zeal but rebuked him for stepping between Jesus and God's will: **Am I not to drink the cup the Father has given me?** (18:11). Though John doesn't tell us anything further about the servant's injury, we learn in Luke's Gospel that Jesus healed his ear before they led him away (see Luke 22:51).

18:12-14 Since the **soldiers** and **Jewish officials** (18:12) had been knocked over by Jesus's mere words and then watched him reattach a severed ear, you might assume that they would be rethinking their plans

to arrest him. But apparently they were so determined to do evil that it didn't matter. **They led him to Annas.** Though **Caiaphas** was the high priest, Annas was Caiaphas's **father-in-law** and the former high priest (so he retained the title) (18:13). John reminds us that **Caiaphas was the one who had advised the Jews** on the expediency of killing Jesus so that the Romans wouldn't punish them for the disturbance Jesus was causing (18:14; see 11:49-53).

18:15-18 **Simon Peter was following** at a distance, along with **another disciple.** This unnamed disciple was John, the author of the Gospel. John never identifies himself by name but typically calls himself "the disciple Jesus loved" (see 13:23; 19:26; 20:2; also see the introduction). Since John knew **the high priest**, he was able to get himself and Peter **into the high priest's courtyard** (18:15-16). Earlier, Peter had declared emphatically that he would lay down his life for Jesus but Jesus predicted that he would, in fact, deny him (see 13:36-38). This was the time of reckoning. **A servant girl** saw **Peter** and asked if he was one of Jesus's **disciples** (18:17). He denied it. John then tells us that **the servants** in the courtyard were **warming themselves** by **a charcoal fire** (18:18). The Greek word translated "charcoal fire" appears only one other time in John's Gospel. When it shows up in 21:9, it will be significant.

18:19-21 The scene switches to Jesus standing before **the high priest** Annas, who asked him **about his disciples and about his teaching** (18:19). He wanted Jesus to tell him what he had been doing to get everyone so riled up. But Jesus wasn't about to recount everything he'd done and said. He had **spoken openly** both **in the synagogue and in the temple**. He had done nothing **in secret**, nor did he lead any secret organization (18:20). Why didn't the high priest simply ask the people **who heard** him (18:21)?

18:22-24 For his response to **the high priest**, Jesus received a slap in the face (18:22). But he was unfazed. If he had **spoken wrongly**, he demanded that they **give evidence about the wrong**. Otherwise, the slap was an unjust assault (18:23).

If this trial were to be legitimate, they would have to bring forward witnesses to testify about what he had done wrong. Jesus requested that the high priest do so. Instead, someone simply hit him! When they refused to answer his query and instead **sent him bound to Caiaphas** (18:24), they merely confirmed that they had no interest in justice. They wanted blood.

18:25-27 The scene returns to **Peter** outside in the courtyard **warming himself** by the fire (18:25). He had denied a direct question about whether he was a disciple of Jesus (see 18:17). Here he denies twice more having any relationship with Jesus. One of those who accused him of being with Jesus was **a relative of the man whose ear Peter had cut off** (18:26; see 18:10). Surrounded by the stares of an inquisitive crowd, Peter was asked in essence, "Aren't you the one who drew my kin's blood?" In spite of his former boasting that he would die for Jesus, Peter wasn't ready to put his life on the line. And **immediately** after his third denial, **a rooster crowed** (18:27)— just as Jesus had predicted (see 13:38).

18:28 Next **they led Jesus from Caiaphas to the governor's headquarters.** However, the Jewish officials refused to enter this Gentile arena because it would make them unclean and **unable to eat the Passover.** They had rejected God's Messiah and were seeking to put to death an innocent man, but they were worried about being ceremonially unclean! They couldn't see that their wicked actions had already made them filthy.

18:29-31 Pontius **Pilate** (18:29) was the Roman governor over Judea. Typically, he governed in Caesarea Maritima on the Mediterranean Sea. But during the Passover when large crowds were present in Jerusalem, Pilate was on the scene to squelch any Jewish disturbances. He was a ruthless man with no affection for the Jews, and they had no fondness for him either. But since the Romans alone had the power of execution, the Jewish leaders needed Pilate to condemn Jesus. When Pilate insisted that they judge Jesus themselves **according to** their own law, they made their intentions clear: **It's not legal for us to put anyone to death** (18:31).

Importantly, it was necessary for the Romans to be involved so that the Gentiles would be included in the guilt of the matter (see Acts 2:23; 4:27).

18:32 Again John interrupts his narrative (see 18:9) to let us know that these actions were fulfilling **Jesus's words.** He had foretold the **kind of death he was going to die.** Previously, Jesus had spoken of being "lifted up" to indicate the kind of death he would die (see 12:32-33). The Old Testament teaches that a person under God's curse was to be displayed by hanging on a tree as a sign of divine judgment on sin (see Deut 21:23; Gal 3:13). Clearly, Jesus was not a victim of fate; he is the sovereign Lord who proceeded toward his death according to plan.

18:33-35 Apparently, the Jews had told **Pilate** that Jesus was claiming to be the Messiah and a king in opposition to Caesar, because when Jesus stood before him, he asked, **Are you the King of the Jews?** (18:33). Jesus asked Pilate if he wanted to know the answer himself or if he were asking because his accusers put him up to it (18:34). Pilate sounds disgusted with the whole thing: **I'm not a Jew, am I? . . . Your . . . chief priests handed you over to me. What have you done?** (18:35). He wasn't interested in this religious squabble. He just wanted to get the case over with.

18:36 So Jesus answered Pilate's question about whether he was a king: **My kingdom is not of this world.** Or, "Yes, I'm a King. But not from here." Was he the King of the Jews? Of course. He was also King of the Romans. In fact, he is King of the entire world. But the *source* of his kingship and authority is in heaven.

If my kingdom were of this world, my servants would fight. Actually, one of them (Peter) tried! And Jesus scolded him and healed the man he attacked (18:10-11; Luke 22:51). But those were earthly methods—not the methods of Jesus's kingdom. This is a good reminder that if you're going to be a kingdom disciple, you've got to use kingdom methods—not the methods of this world. Earthly means won't work when your source is spiritual.

18:37-39 Pilate followed the logic. If Jesus claimed to have a kingdom, then he must be claiming to be a **king**. Jesus affirmed his response: **I was born for this**. Indeed, he had come **into the world . . . to testify to the truth**. In fact, he said, **Everyone who is of the truth listens to** me (18:37). This was Jesus's way of saying, "If you want the truth—if you care about the truth—then you'll listen to me, too." But **Pilate** brushed Jesus's assertion aside by asking, **What is truth?** (18:38).

Sadly, Pilate's question is repeated by this fallen postmodern world today. Many in our culture reject the notion of absolute truth. "Truth" to them is relative—that is, what's true for one person isn't necessarily true for another. But this is preposterous. *Truth* is the absolute standard by which reality is measured. It's not something that changes based on feelings or perspective. A person can deny that gravity is true, but if he decides to jump off a building to prove it, he's going to find that truth doesn't care about his feelings or perspective. Truth exists whether you embrace it or not.

So Pilate told **the Jews** that he found **no grounds for charging** Jesus with a crime (18:38). The Roman governor concluded that he wasn't worthy of death, so he reminded them of the **custom** in which he would **release one prisoner** during **the Passover**. Then he proposed releasing **the King of the Jews** (18:39).

18:40 But the Jewish leaders would have none of it: **Not this man, but Barabbas!** As it turned out, **Barabbas was a revolutionary**. He was an insurrectionist who had created havoc for Rome because he wanted the Jews out from under Roman rule. Whatever his specific crime was, he had earned the death penalty.

Don't miss that the leaders preferred a criminal who had fought for physical deliverance from Rome because that's all they cared about. They wanted political deliverance from Gentile rule, when what they needed was spiritual deliverance from sin.

19:1-3 Seeking to pacify the Jewish leaders, **Pilate** had Jesus **flogged** (19:1). Flogging involved the use of a whip of leather strips with bits of bone or metal tied to the ends.

The resulting vicious beating would rip the skin from the victim's back. **The soldiers** then mocked Christ's claim to be a king by putting **a crown of thorns** on his head, dressing him **in a purple robe**, and shouting, **Hail, King of the Jews!** (19:2-3). Then they slapped him in the **face** (19:3). Though Pilate and the soldiers no doubt thought they were merely exercising the might of Rome over a simple Jew, they were actually fulfilling biblical prophecy about the Messiah in detail (see Isa 50:6; 53:5).

19:4-6 Pilate then put Jesus on display for the Jews to see. He had found **no grounds for charging him** (19:4). Nevertheless, he had thoroughly humiliated him and inflicted great pain on him. **Here is the man**, he said (19:5). Pilate surely thought they would be satisfied with the brutality and humiliation that Jesus had experienced. But only one thing would satisfy them. **The chief priests and the temple servants** called out, **Crucify! Crucify!** (19:6).

19:7 Jesus had done more than claim to be a mere human Messiah. He had made claims that only God could make. The Jews therefore accused him of blasphemy, saying, "You—being a man—make yourself God" (10:33). They demanded death and gave their reasoning: **He ought to die, because he made himself the Son of God.**

19:8 Hearing this, Pilate **was more afraid than ever**. What would make Pilate fearful? Jesus had told Pilate that he ruled a kingdom that was "not of this world" (see 18:36). Now the Jews were telling Pilate that Jesus claimed to be the Son of God. In Matthew 27:19 we learn that Pilate's wife told him she had dreamed about this "righteous man" and that he should have nothing to do with him. Pilate was a brutal ruler, but he was probably also a superstitious pagan who feared the gods. He was perhaps thinking, "Who is this guy standing before me?"

19:9-10 Pilate asked Jesus, **Where are you from?** Now clearly Pilate knew the answer to that question; Jesus was "from Galilee" (see Luke 23:5-7). But, given Pilate's rising fear, he was essentially saying, "Where are you from, *really*?" However, Jesus refused to **answer** (19:9), fulfilling Scripture yet again (see Isa 53:7). Pilate, probably with a mixture of anger and dread, demanded that Jesus say something: **Don't you know that I have the authority to release you and the authority to crucify you?** (19:10). But when someone insists on shouting, "Don't you know that I'm in charge here?," it usually means he's uncertain himself.

19:11 Finally, Jesus spoke. Pilate had **no authority** except what had been **given** to him **from above.** God grants authority and takes it away. Two important truths are wrapped up in Jesus's statement. First, if a person exercises any authority on earth, ultimately that authority has been granted by God. So, will that authority be wielded for his kingdom purposes or not? How you answer that question has serious consequences because you will one day be called to give an account for your own use of authority. Second, remember to maintain a heavenly perspective: God is your ultimate authority. Anyone who seeks to rule over you illegitimately will not have the final say. He may be *a* boss, but he isn't *the* boss.

The one who handed me over to you has the greater sin. God would hold Pilate accountable for his gross violation of justice. Like a coward, he delivered Jesus over to be crucified. But at least Pilate acknowledged that Jesus wasn't guilty. The sin of the Jewish high priest was much worse since he had the Scriptures available to him and was aware of Jesus's teachings and miracles, yet closed his eyes to the truth.

19:12 Pilate **kept trying to release** Jesus. Pilate was nervous (see 19:8). But the Jews wouldn't let him off the hook: **If you release this man, you are not Caesar's friend. Anyone who makes himself a king opposes Caesar.** With that statement, the Jewish leaders had won because they had pitted Pilate against the Roman emperor. What would Caesar think if he heard one of his governors was setting free some would-be revolutionary who claimed to be a rival king in the Roman Empire? Caesar didn't mind religion—as long as it didn't compete with his absolute authority.

19:13 So Pilate **sat down on the judge's seat** to proclaim his verdict. One day every Christian will stand before the judgment seat of Christ so that he may render a verdict, not regarding salvation, but regarding each person's service and faithfulness to him. What will he say to you?

19:14-15 It was the preparation day for the Passover (19:14). When the Israelites were slaves in Egypt, God had commanded them to slaughter a lamb and place its blood on the doorposts of their homes. Then, when he struck down the firstborn of Egypt, he "passed over" the homes with a blood covering. By means of this, God rescued his people from slavery (see Exod 12:1-28). Jesus, "the Lamb of God, who takes away the sin of the world" (1:29) was about to shed his blood so that all those who believe in him would be saved from slavery to sin. His death at this particular moment wasn't due to chance, then, but due to the sovereign timing of God.

Though the Jewish leaders had gotten their way, Pilate got in one last dig at them: **Here is your king!** (19:14). But they wanted nothing to do with Jesus: **Take him away! Crucify him!** Again Pilate referred to Jesus as *their* king. But they rejected any such notion: **We have no king but Caesar** (19:15). Notice that they didn't say, "We have no king but God." Their hatred of Jesus was so great that they were willing to disregard their divine ruler and align themselves with a pagan king. Placing human government above God never ends well.

19:16-18 Pilate **handed him over to be crucified** (19:16). Crucifixion was a horrific form of execution that the Romans had perfected. It was typical for the condemned to carry the crossbar for his own **cross,** as Jesus was made to do. The place of crucifixion was **called Place of the Skull,** which meant *Golgotha* in **Aramaic** (19:17). The Latin translation is *Calvaria,* from which we get the English rendering *Calvary.* There they crucified him between **two others** (19:18), criminals according to Luke (see 23:33).

19:19-22 Pilate had **a sign** hung on Jesus's cross that said, **Jesus of Nazareth, the King of the Jews.** It was **written in Aramaic,**

Latin, and Greek, so that everyone could read it (19:19-20). Thus, the sign displayed the charge for which he was put to death. But it made the chief priests furious. Pilate had made the sign read as a title, a fact. The Jewish leaders wanted it to clearly indicate that this was merely Jesus's claim (19:21). But Pilate rebuffed them, saying, What I have written, I have written (19:22). He meant for the sign to sting the Jews. But, in his sovereignty, God meant it to declare to the world the truth about his Son.

19:23-24 As Jesus writhed in agony above them, the soldiers pitilessly divided his clothes among them and gambled to see which of them would get to keep his tunic. John tells us that this too fulfilled Scripture, quoting Psalm 22:18 (19:24).

19:25-27 Standing by the cross were four women who had followed Jesus, including his mother Mary (19:25). Jesus saw the disciple he loved—that is, John the son of Zebedee, the author of the Gospel (see the introduction), and told his mother that John was now her son, and he told John that Mary was now his mother (19:26-27). And from that hour the disciple took her into his home (19:27). Even as he hung dying on a cross, then, Jesus fulfilled his obligation to care for his widowed mother.

Jesus entrusted the well-being of his mother to John rather than to one of her biological sons because they had not yet believed in him (see 7:5). Spiritual relationships are to take precedence over biological and physical relationships (see Matt 12:46-50).

19:28-30 When Jesus knew that his mission was complete, that everything was now finished that the Scripture might be fulfilled, that he had endured the wrath of God and fully atoned for the sins of the world, he said, I'm thirsty (19:28). So they put a sponge full of sour wine on a hyssop branch and held it up to his mouth (19:29). Hyssop was the very plant used to brush lamb's blood on the doorposts during the Passover (see Exod 12:21-23). As the apostle Paul says, "Christ our Passover lamb has been sacrificed" (1 Cor 5:7). Then Jesus declared, It is finished (19:30). His work of

atonement for sin was done. The demands of the law had been met. The debt for sin had been paid in full.

Jesus had proclaimed, "No one takes [my life] from me, but I lay it down on my own" (10:18). Here the truth of that claim was verified: Bowing his head, he gave up his spirit (19:30). Jesus was not robbed of his life; he voluntarily laid it down. "No one has greater love than this: to lay down his life for his friends" (15:13).

19:31 It sometimes took crucifixion victims days to die. Normally, then, the Romans would have left the men on the crosses. But since it was the preparation day for the Passover, the Jews did not want the bodies to remain on the cross on the Sabbath. Moreover, for a cursed man to remain hanging on a tree overnight would defile the land (see Deut 21:22-23). So they requested that Pilate have the men's legs broken so that they would die and could be buried. Victims hanging on a cross had to put weight on their legs in order to lift themselves to breathe. Without the use of their legs, they would die of asphyxiation.

19:32-37 When the soldiers arrived to break Jesus's legs, they found him already dead (19:33). Therefore, a soldier pierced his side with a spear, and blood and water flowed out (19:34). This indicated that his heart was no longer beating.

In the early years of the church, a heresy arose claiming that Jesus was totally divine and only pretended to be human (see 1 John 4:1-2). But John wants his readers to know that such talk is a complete lie. As sure as Jesus was fully God, he was fully human: he bled and died on a Roman cross. In fact, John himself was an eyewitness to this, and his testimony is true (19:35). All that happened, John tells us, was fulfillment of biblical prophecy. He quotes from Psalm 34:20 and Zechariah 12:10, proving it was no accident that Jesus was pierced rather than having his legs broken. Our sovereign God was fulfilling his Word.

19:38-42 Joseph of Arimathea was a secret disciple of Jesus because he feared the Jews. The other Gospels inform us that he was wealthy and a prominent member of the Jewish Sanhedrin (see Matt 27:57; Mark 15:43). In spite of his fears, he boldly went forward to ask Pilate if he could bury **Jesus's body** (19:38). Joining Joseph was **Nicodemus**, another secret disciple **who had previously** spoken with Jesus **at night** (19:39; see 3:1-13). He also came into the light to assist Joseph with his task.

They prepared the **body** and laid it in **a new tomb** in a **garden** near the place of his crucifixion (19:39-41). **No one had yet been placed** in the tomb (19:41). This is a very significant detail because later, when Jesus's body was gone, no one was able to point to any bones in the tomb to claim them as Jesus's remains. His was the first corpse to lie there.

VIII. THE RESURRECTION (20:1-21)

20:1-2 On the first day of the week—Sunday—**Mary Magdalene** went **to the tomb early** in the morning (20:1). Jesus had cast seven demons from her (see Luke 8:2), so she was a devoted follower. The Synoptic Gospels inform us that Mary had gone to the tomb with other women to anoint Jesus's body (see Mark 16:1; Luke 23:55–24:1). She saw that the large **stone** sealing the tomb **had been removed** (20:1), and she had also seen an angel (see Mark 16:5). So she ran to tell **Simon Peter** and John (the **disciple . . . Jesus loved**) that the Lord's body had been **taken** (20:2).

20:3-7 Thus, Peter and John ran **for the tomb** (20:3). John was faster and arrived there **first**, but Peter **entered the tomb** ahead of him (20:4-6). They **saw the linen cloths lying there**, which had been used to wrap Jesus's body (20:5-6; see 19:40). And **the wrapping that had been on his head** was **folded** and set aside **by itself** (20:7).

One of the many theories that men have concocted to explain away the resurrection is that Jesus was merely resuscitated. This theory proposes that after enduring the intense brutality of being beaten and crucified, Jesus was revived by the cool interior of the tomb. But this doesn't explain why a half-dead man would remove his head cloth, neatly fold it, and place it separate from his intact linen wrappings! Nor does it explain how he could have had the strength to move the heavy stone blocking the entrance. As with other attempts by unbelievers to deny the resurrection, this one fails to adequately explain the evidence. One thing is clear: When the disciples saw Jesus later (see

20:19-23), he didn't look like a man who had been merely resuscitated from a near death experience!

20:8-10 John **believed** (20:8). Previously he had believed in Jesus's identity. Now he believed in the resurrection. Though Jesus had predicted his resurrection (see Luke 9:21-22; 18:31-34), and Scripture foretold that the Messiah must rise from the dead (see Acts 2:24-31), the disciples had not understood (20:9). They **returned to the place where they were staying** (20:10), no doubt still trying to piece things together and figure out exactly what had happened.

20:11-13 But **Mary** was still standing there crying (20:11). She couldn't grasp what had happened. Then inside the tomb **she saw two angels . . . sitting where Jesus's body had been lying**, asking her **why** she was **crying** (20:12-13). The only thing she could conclude was that someone had **taken away** Jesus's body, and it had broken her heart (20:13). Resurrection was not an option she had considered.

20:14-16 Then she saw another person—only this one turned out to be **Jesus** (20:14)! He also asked her **why** she was **crying** (20:15). But she didn't recognize him and supposed **he was the gardener** (since the tomb was in a garden, 19:41). She even wondered if he'd moved the body (20:15). The Son of God, the King of creation, had risen from the dead. And he was mistaken for a gardener! But when she heard the man say, **Mary**, she finally knew this was her **Teacher** (20:16). She hadn't recognized him. But when he spoke her name, her eyes were opened. "The sheep follow [the shepherd] because they know his voice" (10:4).

20:17-18 Once Mary had Jesus, she didn't want to let him go. But he told her not to **cling to** him because he **had not yet ascended to the Father.** In other words, he said, "I haven't gone anywhere yet. There's no need to hang on to me." Instead, he wanted her to go **tell** the good news to his disciples (20:17). The risen Lord Jesus gave Mary Magdalene the privilege of going to his disciples on that first resurrection morning and telling them, **I have seen the Lord!** (20:18).

Don't overlook that the resurrection of Jesus Christ was first announced by a woman. In first-century Judaism, a woman's testimony wasn't considered credible. So if the disciples were going to invent a resurrection story, they wouldn't choose women to be the first to see and declare it. Such testimonies would have been rejected by the Jews. Thus, the fact that the first witnesses were women (see Matt 28:1-10) provides evidence for the historicity of the resurrection. It also affirms the communication gifting of women as long as the gift is exercised under the legitimately authorized spiritual authority and covering of the home and the church (see 1 Cor 11:5, 10).

20:19 That **evening . . . the disciples were gathered together with the doors locked.** They were in hiding because they were afraid of what **the Jews** might do to them. But at that moment, **Jesus came** and **stood among them.** Don't miss what John tells us: the doors were shut and locked. Nevertheless, Jesus joined them.

Now, clearly, Jesus had a physical body. Mary touched him (20:17); Thomas would touch him (20:27); later he would eat with his disciples (21:12-13). He was no mere phantom (see Luke 24:39). He had risen bodily from the grave. But his resurrected body no longer had material limitations. Apparently, he could pass through locked doors if he wanted. And later he would ascend on a cloud into heaven (see Acts 1:9). The apostles tell us that our resurrection bodies will be like his (see 1 Cor 15:45-57; Phil 3:21; 1 John 3:2).

20:20 The disciples were surely reeling as Jesus stood before them alive. But **he showed them his hands,** with nail wounds, and his **side,** which had been pierced by a Roman spear (see 19:34). Those scars had not been removed from his resurrection body. One day, then, all believers will see them. They will serve as eternal reminders of the cost of our redemption, and they will forever give us reason to praise him. Jesus will be the only scarred person in eternity, a perpetual reminder of the price paid for our redemption.

20:21 He said, **Peace be with you.** Why? Because they were terrified of the Jews. That's why they had locked the doors (20:19). Yet Jesus gave them his peace. Notice that their situation hadn't changed. The Jewish leaders would still oppose them in the days ahead (see Acts 4:1-24; 5:17-42). But Jesus can speak peace into trouble. Though your circumstances are unstable, he can provide the internal stability your heart needs.

As the Father has sent me, I also send you. The Father had sent the Son on a kingdom mission to atone for the sins of the world so that all who believe would receive eternal life. Now the Son was sending his disciples on a kingdom mission to proclaim that message and make other disciples throughout the world (see Matt 28:16-20).

20:22-23 Jesus **breathed on** his disciples and said, **Receive the Holy Spirit** (20:22). Most interpreters recognize this as an anticipatory act. The Holy Spirit would come to dwell within the apostles on the day of Pentecost (see Acts 2:1-21), enabling them to accomplish the mission on which Jesus was sending them. Here, then, Jesus was visibly and physically preparing them for what was spiritually to come. They would be granted kingdom authority, so he told them, **If you forgive the sins of any, they are forgiven; if you retain the sins of any, they are retained** (20:23). The Holy Spirit would enable them to authoritatively declare that God had indeed forgiven the sins of any who believe in Jesus.

20:24-25 One of the disciples, **Thomas,** had not been present on that evening (20:24). When they told him about what happened, he refused to believe unless he could **put** his finger into the mark of the nails and put his **hand into** Jesus's **side** (20:25). This is why, in church history, he earned the nickname "Doubting Thomas." But this isn't a fair appraisal of his character. Previously, Thomas was prepared to go into hostile territory and die with Jesus (see 11:7-8, 16). So it's clear that a believer can be spiritually strong one moment and spiritually deflated the next.

20:26-28 Jesus responded to Thomas's unbelief with grace. He gave the struggling disciple the opportunity to do exactly what he had wanted: to touch the wounds of his risen Savior (20:26-27). Then Thomas made a profound confession: **My Lord and my God!** (20:28). He acknowledged Jesus's deity. As John says at the beginning of his Gospel, "The Word was God" (1:1).

20:29 Notice that Jesus did not correct Thomas but accepted his worship, saying, **Because you have seen me, you have believed. Blessed are those who have not seen and yet believe.** God wants you to believe in him before you see him work in your life.

20:30-31 Jesus performed many other signs . . . that are not written in this book (20:30). In other words, John tells his readers that the things he has written down in his Gospel are merely the highlights! Nevertheless, **these are written so that you may believe that Jesus is the Messiah, the Son of God, and that by believing you may have life in his name** (20:31).

Here John gives us the evangelistic purpose for his book. He wrote it "so that" readers might believe that Jesus is the Messiah—the God-Man—who died as a substitutionary atonement for sins and that, by believing, they will receive eternal life—that is, an eternal relationship with God and an ever-expanding experience of his reality in our lives (see 17:3). That's what salvation is all about.

IX. EPILOGUE (21:1-25)

21:1-3 In the final chapter, John describes how **Jesus revealed himself again to his disciples by the Sea of Tiberias** (21:1), another name for the Sea of Galilee. Seven of the disciples were together: **Simon Peter, Thomas, Nathanael, Zebedee's sons** (James and John), **and two others** (21:2). **Simon Peter** told them, **I'm going fishing.** He had a family to support, and he was still reeling from his denial of the Lord. They joined him for an all-**night** fishing expedition but **caught nothing** (21:3). Before Jesus had called them, Peter and the Zebedee brothers had been fishermen. With Jesus gone, Peter returned to his old line of work. But he was proving to be unsuccessful.

21:4-6 Jesus was standing **on the shore**, but they didn't recognize him because it was only **daybreak** and they were still some distance away. He called to them to **cast the net on the right side of the boat**, and they caught so many **fish** that they were **unable to haul** them (21:4-6).

Peter had been a fisherman all his life. Nevertheless, he had failed without the Lord's enablement—something that Jesus had shown him previously (see Luke 5:4-11). Peter was not ultimately self-sufficient but entirely dependent on God, even to accomplish work that had been his whole life. As Jesus told his disciples, "You can do nothing without me" (15:5).

21:7-8 This miraculous catch of fish opened the eyes of John, **the disciple** whom **Jesus loved.** When he said, **It is the Lord!**, Peter **plunged into the sea** and headed for shore (21:7). The impetuous disciple couldn't wait. Then the rest of the disciples followed, **dragging the net full of fish** behind them (21:8).

21:9-11 When they arrived on the beach, they saw that Jesus had cooked a breakfast of **fish** and **bread** on a **charcoal fire** (21:9). The Greek word for "charcoal fire" appears two times in John's Gospel: here and at 18:18, when Peter was warming himself by another such blaze. On that occasion, Peter had denied three times that he knew Jesus. Thus, the Lord was reminding Peter of his recent past. We can be certain of this because of the conversation that follows in 21:15-19. Peter never forgot this meal; he even mentioned it in his preaching (see Acts 10:41).

21:12-14 Jesus invited them to join him for **breakfast**. John tells us that **the disciples** didn't ask, **Who are you?** They all recognized that this was their risen **Lord** (21:12). **This was now the third time Jesus appeared to his disciples after he was raised from the dead** (21:14). John describes the first time in 20:19-23 and the second in 20:24-29. The resurrection of Jesus Christ was neither a fairytale nor a hallucination. He "presented himself alive to [his disciples] by many convincing proofs ... over a period of forty days" (Acts 1:3). As Jesus himself told them, "It is I myself! Touch me and see, because a ghost does not have flesh and bones as you can see I have" (Luke 24:39).

21:15 After **breakfast**, Jesus had a talk with Simon Peter. He asked him, **Simon, son of John, do you love me more than these?**— that is, "more than these other disciples do?" Why would Jesus ask this? Because when he had predicted that the disciples would fall away, Peter had vowed, "Even if everyone falls away because of you, I will never fall away" (Matt 26:31-33). Peter had wanted Jesus to know that though the devotion of the other disciples might waver, he could count on Peter remaining steadfast. He would be the one disciple that Jesus could trust. But here, after Peter had shamefully denied Jesus three times, Jesus basically asked Peter, "Are you still the most committed disciple?"

Yes, Lord . . . you know that I love you. When Jesus asked Peter if he loved him, the Greek verb used is *agapaō*, often used to describe self-sacrificial love. But when Peter affirmed his love for Jesus, the Greek verb is *phileō*, a brotherly kind of love and affection—a love between good friends. Previously, Peter had claimed that his love for and commitment to Jesus was superior to that of the others. But after his failure and denial, he wasn't willing to arrogantly say that he loved Jesus with a sacrificial love. In light of this humble response, Jesus told him, **Feed my lambs.** In other words, "Since you're not thinking so highly of yourself anymore, I can use you to lead and care for my people."

21:16-17 A second time, Jesus asked, **Simon, son of John, do you love me?** (using *agapaō*). Peter responded again, **Yes, Lord ... you know that I love you** (using *phileō*). And again Jesus commanded him to look after his people: **Shepherd my sheep** (21:16). Then, for a third time, Jesus asked, **Simon, son of John, do you love me?** This time the verb is *phileō*. So, seeing Peter humbled, Jesus came down to Peter's level and met him where he was. **Peter was grieved.** His three denials of his Lord had now been matched by a question from his Lord repeated three times: "Do you love me?" It broke Peter's heart. All he could do was say, **Lord, you know everything; you know that I love you** (21:17).

When Peter was proudly self-assured about his ability to stand fast at a critical moment, Jesus knew that he would actually crack under pressure (see 13:37-38). He knew Peter's heart better than Peter did. The grieving disciple understood that now. And since Jesus knew all things, Peter was convinced that Jesus also knew that Peter loved him in spite of his prior failure.

Again, Jesus told him, **Feed my sheep.** Thus, Jesus was restoring his humbled disciple to ministry. Peter's repentance allowed for restoration. Though Peter had previously thought highly of himself, he had come to adopt Jesus's view of leadership in ministry. Peter understood that being a leader of God's people is not about arrogantly exercising power. Therefore, he could later write to other church leaders, "Shepherd God's flock among you ... not lording it over those entrusted to you, but being examples to the flock" (1 Pet 5:2-3). Peter had taken to heart Jesus's command, "Shepherd my sheep." Sometimes God lets his people fail in order to develop them spiritually and prepare them for greater usefulness (see Luke 22:31-32).

21:18-19 After this restoration, Jesus prophesied about Peter's future: **When you grow old, you will stretch out your hands and someone else will tie you and carry you where you don't want to go** (21:18). John explains Jesus's mysterious prophecy: **He said this to indicate by what kind of death Peter would glorify God.** According to tradition passed down in the early church, Peter was martyred in Rome under Emperor Nero for his faith in Jesus Christ: he was crucified upside down. In spite of what was to come, Jesus urged Peter, **Follow me** (21:19). And the New Testament shows that Peter did indeed humbly follow his Lord and devote himself to gospel ministry. Are you prepared to follow Jesus in good times and bad, at whatever the cost?

21:20-22 Peter turned around and saw John, **the disciple Jesus loved** (see the introduction) **following them** (21:20). So Peter asked Jesus, **What about him?** (21:21). Peter accepted that he had a martyr's death awaiting him, but he wanted to know what Jesus's plans were for John. Jesus's response was short and to the point: **If I want him to remain until I come ... what is that to you? As for you, follow me** (21:22). So in essence, Jesus said, "That's none of your business, Peter. If I want him to remain alive until my second coming, what difference does that make to you? You worry about yourself, and follow me."

God has a *general will* for all of his people. This is expressed in his biblical commands for all of his followers. But he also has a specific will for each individual Christian. Jesus graciously revealed to Peter his will for him. But he wasn't about to tell Peter his specific will for John.

We are called to follow Jesus *corporately* as the church and *personally* as individuals. Each of us is to have a personal relationship with God through Jesus and seek to discern how he wants us to serve and glorify him. You are not to use God's specific will for you to measure anyone else, nor are you to take his specific will for another and use it to measure your own circumstances. We are not to sit as judges regarding how God chooses to use other believers.

21:23 As a result of Jesus saying this, **rumor spread ... that this disciple would not die.** But this was a misinterpretation. Jesus was being hyperbolic in order to make a point. He wasn't saying that John would remain alive until his second coming. He was simply saying, "Whatever my specific will is for John, it doesn't concern you." We must read and interpret the Bible carefully. Poor interpretation leads to erroneous conclusions!

21:24-25 This **disciple**—the one Jesus loved—is the one **who testifies to these things and who wrote them down.** The Gospel of the apostle John, then, is based on his eyewitness testimony. And **we know that his testimony is true** (21:24). But this Gospel contains only a small sample of what Jesus did and taught. **There are also many other things** that could have been written. **If every one of them were written down, I suppose not even the world itself could contain the books that would be written** (21:25).

The apostle John has only given us a highlight reel! But God providentially determined that what we have in Scripture is enough. You don't need to know *everything* that Jesus did and said. But, John says, you *do* need to "believe that Jesus is the Messiah, the Son of God, and that by believing you may have life in his name" (20:31). Amen.

ACTS

INTRODUCTION

Author

IF LUKE WAS THE AUTHOR OF THE Gospel that bears his name (and we have good reason for believing that; see the introduction to Luke), then he was also the author of the book of Acts. First, the two books are clearly connected and written to the same man, Theophilus (see Luke 1:1-4; Acts 1:1-3). Second, the author was one of Paul's traveling companions, because during Paul's second missionary journey, the narrative changes from third person, "they," to first person, "we" (16:10-17; see also 20:5-15; 21:1-18; 27:1-37; 28:1-16), indicating that the author had joined Paul. And we know from Paul's letters that Luke the physician was one of Paul's companions (see Col 4:14; Phlm 24; 2 Tim 4:11). Third, beginning in the second century, early Christian writers affirm that Luke was the author of Acts.

Historical Background

Acts is the second volume of Luke's two-volume work. He refers to his Gospel as "the first narrative" that described "all that Jesus began to do and teach until the day he was taken up" (1:1-2). In Acts the narrative continues with the Holy Spirit coming to empower the disciples in proclaiming Jesus to both Jews and Gentiles.

Theophilus, to whom Luke wrote, was most likely his patron—that is, a wealthy person who funded Luke's research and writing of his two books (notice that he calls him "most honorable Theophilus" in Luke 1:3).

Acts appears to have been written before Paul was released from prison in Rome (see Acts 28:16-31). The Gospel of Luke was probably written in the late 50s, and Paul was released from his first Roman imprisonment about AD 60. Since the Gospel was written first (see 1:1), Acts would have been completed around that time.

Message and Purpose

Acts is unique because it links the Gospels with the Epistles by recording the birth and early history of the church, the expression of God's kingdom for this age. When the disciples asked Jesus if the kingdom was coming at that moment, he told them it was not for them to know, but that they would see a manifestation of the kingdom's power in the work of the church through the power of the Holy Spirit (1:6-8).

The rest of Acts records what happened when the Holy Spirit's power infused the church. That makes the book critical because it is the blueprint for the church today. It reveals how the church functions when not filled with the Spirit and what happens when the Spirit fills the church so that it explodes with power and kingdom authority. We see what we are supposed to be and do today as the church of the Lord Jesus.

Acts is a kingdom book: Jesus spoke about the kingdom of God at the beginning (1:3), and Paul proclaims the kingdom of God at the end (28:30-31). That's crucial because the whole Bible wraps around this theme of the kingdom agenda, the visible manifestation of the comprehensive rule of God over every area of life. And that rule is to be reflected in and through the church.

www.bhpublishinggroup.com/qr/te/44_00

Outline

I. The Holy Spirit's Empowerment of the Church for Kingdom Witness (1:1–2:47)

II. Kingdom Witness in Jerusalem (3:1–7:60)

III. Kingdom Witness beyond Jerusalem (8:1–20:38)

   A. Kingdom Witness in Judea and Samaria, and the Conversion of Paul (8:1–9:43)

   B. Peter's Kingdom Witness to the Gentiles and Escape from Prison (10:1–12:25)

   C. Paul's First Missionary Journey (13:1–14:28)

   D. The Jerusalem Council (15:1-35)

   E. Paul's Second Missionary Journey (15:36–18:21)

   F. Paul's Third Missionary Journey (18:22–20:38)

IV. Paul's Arrest, Trial, and Kingdom Witness in Rome (21:1–28:31)

ACTS

I. THE HOLY SPIRIT'S EMPOWERMENT OF THE CHURCH FOR KINGDOM WITNESS (1:1–2:47)

1:1-2 In the prologue to the book of Acts, Luke reminds **Theophilus** (probably Luke's patron who funded his work) that **the first narrative** he **wrote** (the Gospel of Luke) told **about all that Jesus began to do and teach until he was taken up**—that is, until he ascended into heaven. It is at this point that the two books overlap. Luke ends with the ascension of Jesus (see Luke 24:50-52), and Acts opens with it (1:9-11).

1:3 Jesus had **presented himself alive to [his disciples] by many convincing proofs.** The disciples didn't have a corporate delusion. Nor did they see a ghost. Jesus proved to them that he was the same flesh and blood man who had been crucified and buried—though he'd since gained a glorified body (see Luke 24:36-43).

What did Jesus talk to his disciples about between his resurrection and his ascension? During this **forty days** of intensive teaching, his focus was on **the kingdom of God.** The Bible reveals that God has an agenda, and that agenda is the advancement of his kingdom in the world. This is the unifying theme of Scripture. God's kingdom agenda is the visible manifestation of the comprehensive rule of God in every area of life. Not only does Acts begin by telling us that Jesus focused on the kingdom before his departure, but the book also ends by telling us that Paul focused on the kingdom in his preaching. While he was in a Roman prison, he was "proclaiming the kingdom of God and teaching about the Lord Jesus Christ" (28:31). Thus, the church

exists to serve King Jesus and his kingdom— that is, his rule over every area of life.

1:4-5 Jesus **commanded** his disciples to stay in **Jerusalem** until they received the Holy Spirit whom the Father had promised (1:4). He compared this to baptism. **John** had **baptized with water,** but the disciples would **be baptized with the Holy Spirit** (1:5). The Greek word *baptizō* means "to immerse." Just as new Christians are immersed in the waters of baptism, Jesus promised that his disciples would be immersed in the Holy Spirit so that they would be empowered to obey their King and proclaim his kingdom.

1:6-8 All of Jesus's talk about the kingdom of God and the soon-to-arrive Holy Spirit prompted the disciples to ask him if he was **restoring the kingdom to Israel at this time** (1:6). Was it finally time for Israel to be delivered from the yoke of Rome? But Jesus told them that the timing for Israel's earthly promised messianic kingdom was not for them to know. **The Father** would determine that by **his own authority** (1:7). Nevertheless, they would soon **receive power when the Holy Spirit** came upon them so that they would be his **witnesses in Jerusalem, in all Judea and Samaria, and to the ends of the earth** (1:8).

It was not yet time for Christ's millennial kingdom in which he will rule over the entire earth from Jerusalem on David's throne. But it *was* time for the Holy Spirit's arrival. The disciples were not permitted to know the timing of the establishment of the kingdom, but they would not need to wait much longer to experience the power of the kingdom. The Old Testament had promised the Spirit (see Ezek 36:26-27; Joel 2:28-29). Jesus had promised the Spirit (see John 14:16-17, 26; 15:26-27; 16:13-15). Finally, the Spirit's coming was near at hand.

Empowered by the Holy Spirit, the disciples would go as Jesus's witnesses to proclaim him and make kingdom disciples in Jerusalem in obedience to the Great Commission (see Matt 28:16-20). From there the gospel would expand to "all Judea and Samaria" and then "to the ends of the earth." This is what we see in the book of Acts, as the gospel incorporates Jews and Gentiles into the church. And this kingdom work continues today, as the church goes to the ends of the earth to proclaim King Jesus with kingdom authority in the power of the Holy Spirit.

1:9-11 Finally, it was time for Jesus's departure. After he finished speaking to his disciples, they watched as **he was taken up**, and **a cloud took him out of their sight** (1:9). Jesus ascended into heaven, and one day he will return in the same way. This is exactly what the **two** angels who appeared to the disciples told them: **This same Jesus, who has been taken from you into heaven, will come in the same way that you have seen him going into heaven** (1:10-11).

1:12-14 They **returned to Jerusalem from the Mount of Olives** and gathered in **the room upstairs where they were staying** (1:12-13). The eleven disciples were present **along with the women** who had followed Jesus, **Mary the mother of Jesus, and his brothers** (1:14). While he had been alive, Jesus's brothers were skeptical of him (see John 7:1-5). But after the resurrection, they believed.

All of the disciples **were continually united in prayer** (1:14). Prayer is the mechanism that God has given to his people so that we may communicate with him. Prayer is our link between earth and heaven. The Holy Spirit uses it to deliver our requests to heaven and to bring heaven's deliverance to earth. Their unity in prayer was critical for experiencing God's divine intervention.

1:15-19 Peter **stood up among the brothers and sisters** who numbered **about a hundred and twenty** and explained how **the Scripture** had been **fulfilled** regarding **Judas** (1:15-16). He had been one of the Twelve and had **shared** in their **ministry** (1:17). But Judas had been a wolf in sheep's clothing. For betraying Jesus to the chief priests, Judas had received payment and **acquired a field** (1:18).

Comparing this passage with what we read in Matthew's Gospel, we obtain a more complete picture of what happened. Realizing that he had sinned by betraying Jesus—but unwilling to repent—Judas threw the money he received from the chief priests into the temple and hanged himself (see Matt 27:3-9). Thus, unrepentant sin can lead to suicide. Refusing to take back Judas's "blood money," the chief priests used it to buy the field in which Judas hanged himself. There, Judas's decaying body eventually **fell** and **burst open and his intestines spilled out** (1:18). Therefore, they named the place **Field of Blood** (1:19; see Matt 27:8).

1:20 Peter quotes from Psalms 69:25 and 109:8. In both passages, David prays that the wicked man would be removed from his **position** and that someone else would replace him. If those who betrayed King David should have been judged and replaced, how much more should the one who betrayed the Son of David experience judgment and be replaced?

1:21-23 In light of this, Peter concluded that they should replace Judas with another man—one who had been with them from Jesus's **baptism** by **John** until his ascension into heaven, so that he could serve as a fellow **witness . . . of his resurrection** (1:21-22). So **they proposed two** men: **Joseph** (who was also **called Barsabbas** and **Justus**—three names!) **and Matthias** (1:23).

1:24-26 Notice what they did next: **they prayed**, asking God whom he wanted to serve **in this apostolic ministry** (1:24-25). Both men were *good* choices, so they needed the Lord's guidance to make the *right* choice. **They cast lots** (a practice analogous to throwing dice), **and the lot fell to Matthias**, who became an apostle (1:26).

According to Proverbs, "The lot is cast into the lap, but its every decision is from the LORD" (Prov 16:33). In other words, nothing happens according to chance when a sovereign God is running the universe. The disciples knew that God directed the lot. Nevertheless, it's interesting to note that after the coming of the Holy Spirit to dwell within them, the apostles never again made a decision by casting lots. Instead, they depended on the Holy Spirit through prayer.

2:1-4 The day of Pentecost, which occurred fifty days after Passover, was a Jewish holiday marking the time of the wheat harvest and also commemorating the giving of the law on Mount Sinai. In the Old Testament, it is called "the Festival of Weeks" (Exod 34:22; Deut 16:10). Jews would travel to Jerusalem for Pentecost or else stay there after Passover to await it.

On Pentecost the apostles **were all together** when they heard what sounded like **a violent rushing wind . . . from heaven** that **filled the whole house** (2:1-2). Here again, then, an important emphasis is made connecting unity and obedience in order to experience the presence, power, and influence of the work of the Holy Spirit. The wind was invisible, but its work wouldn't be (see John 3:8). Those present **saw tongues like flames of fire that separated and rested on each one of them** (2:3). These were an indication that **the Holy Spirit** had come to dwell within them. As a result, they were enabled by **the Spirit** to begin speaking **in different tongues** (2:4; see further below).

2:5-11 Many **Jews** had come **from every nation** to **Jerusalem** for Pentecost (2:5). When they heard the apostles speaking, they were both **confused** and **amazed**, because each person **heard them speaking in his own language** (2:6-7). Though the apostles were **Galileans**, each of these **Jews and converts** to Judaism who had come from throughout the Roman Empire heard them speaking in his **own native language** and **declaring the magnificent acts of God in [their] own tongues** (2:7-11). According to 1 Corinthians 14:20-22, tongues were a sign to the Jews of God's power and his willingness to overcome the effects of their dispersion.

Thus, the "tongues" (2:4, 11) in which the apostles were enabled to speak were the various native "languages" (2:6, 8) of the visitors to Jerusalem (not some unintelligible heavenly language). This was the fulfillment of Jesus's promise that they would receive power from the Holy Spirit to be his witnesses to the world (1:8).

2:12-13 How was this possible? Galilean Jews would have known Aramaic (the language of the Jews) and perhaps also Greek (the lingua franca of the Roman Empire). But how could they have known all of the other languages? That's what these visiting Jews and converts wanted to know. Imagine never having studied French and suddenly you're able to speak it fluently. They asked one another, **What does this mean?** (2:12). Some mockingly concluded, **They're drunk** (2:13).

2:14-21 Peter stood up with the Eleven and took advantage of the opportunity to address both the visiting **Jews** and the **residents of Jerusalem** (2:14). The combination of divine activity and human confusion was a perfect occasion for proclaiming the truth of what God had done through Christ and what he was now doing among them.

First, Peter dismissed the ridiculous notion that they were **drunk** (2:15). The only thing they were "drunk" with was the Holy Spirit (see Eph 5:18). What they were witnessing was actually the fulfillment of Old Testament prophecy. Peter quoted **the prophet Joel** (2:16), who foretold of the day when God would **pour out [his] Spirit on [his] servants** without distinction—both **young** and **old** . . . **both men and women** when repentance occurred (2:17-18; see Joel 2:28-32).

Calling **on the name of the Lord** (Acts 2:21) is a specific act of Christians appealing to a higher court for divine intervention in human affairs (see 1 Cor 1:2). Through the Holy Spirit all believers have access to divine illumination (see 1 Cor 2:9-16) and divine enablement for ministry (see 1 Cor 12:7).

2:22-23 This outpouring of the Holy Spirit had to do with **Jesus of Nazareth** (2:22). Jesus himself had promised to send the Holy Spirit, whose role was to witness to and glorify him (1:8; see John 14:16-17; 15:26-27;

16:13-14). So if you are unwilling to bear witness to Jesus, you can forget about experiencing the power of the Holy Spirit in your life. The Spirit's task on earth is to make much of Jesus.

Importantly, Jesus was not unknown to the Jews who were listening to Peter. They had witnessed his **miracles, wonders, and signs** (2:22). With this connection made, Peter got personal: **Though he was delivered up according to God's determined plan and foreknowledge, you used lawless people to nail him to a cross and kill him** (2:23). In these words we see both divine sovereignty and human responsibility in action. God had a sovereign plan to sacrifice his Son for sinners, but that did not absolve these free moral agents of their sinful actions. Some of those listening to Peter had joined together with the mob on that day, crying out, "Crucify! Crucify him!" (see Luke 23:13-25). Jews and Gentiles joined together to kill Jesus.

2:24-31 Nevertheless, **God raised him up** from the dead. **Death** could not hold him (2:24). Then Peter quoted **David** from Psalm 16:8-11; he spoke of **the Lord** not abandoning him to the grave or allowing **his holy one to see decay** (2:25, 27). But Peter made it clear that David wasn't speaking about himself. He was speaking about Jesus (2:25). Peter could say **confidently** that **David** was **dead and buried** (2:29). None of his listeners would disagree with that! So David was talking about someone else, one of David's **descendants** whom **God had sworn ... to seat** on David's **throne** (2:30; see Ps 110:1). That descendant was none other than **the Messiah**, who was raised from the dead so that **his flesh did not experience decay** (2:31).

2:32 God has raised this Jesus; we are all witnesses of this. The frightened disciples (see John 20:19) had been transformed by the Holy Spirit to risk their lives by boldly and publicly proclaiming the resurrection of Jesus. How could they have done that unless they were telling the truth? If they were intentionally fabricating the whole story, what explains their transformation and willingness to face persecution and death? The only sane answer is that they

were truly witnesses to the resurrected Jesus.

2:33-36 This risen Messiah who had been **exalted to the right hand of God** had poured out the promised Holy Spirit. *That*, Peter told them, is what they were seeing and hearing (2:33). He then quoted David (from Psalm 110:1), who overheard God the Father telling the Messiah, **Sit at my right hand until I make your enemies your footstool** (2:34-35; see commentary on Ps 110). That Scripture had been fulfilled in Jesus. **God [had] made this Jesus ... both Lord and Messiah** (2:36).

2:37-39 When the crowd **heard** Peter's words, **they were pierced to the heart.** They were convicted of their sin and asked, **What should we do?** (2:37). That was exactly what Peter wanted to hear, and he was quick with the answer: **Repent and be baptized ... in the name of Jesus Christ for the forgiveness of your sins, and you will receive the gift of the Holy Spirit** (2:38).

Now don't misunderstand this. The New Testament is clear that we are saved by grace through faith in Jesus Christ apart from works (see Eph 2:8-9; Rom 4:4-5). But repentance and baptism are to accompany faith. To repent is to turn from sin to God. As Paul will later tell the Ephesian elders, he preached "repentance toward God and faith in our Lord Jesus" (Acts 20:21). And to be baptized in the name of Jesus is to obediently go public with a profession of faith in him. But baptism doesn't save, as Paul makes clear in 1 Corinthians 1:17.

Since the goal of repentance is to reduce or remove the consequences of sin, Peter was calling on the Jews who had witnessed and endorsed the crucifixion of Jesus (in identification with their Jewish leaders), to publicly renounce their actions via baptism. By doing this, they would disconnect themselves from the perverse generation that was about to experience the temporal wrath of God when Rome destroyed the city of Jerusalem and the Jewish temple in AD 70.

2:40-41 With this sermon and Peter's exhortation to **be saved** (2:40), the church age began. This evangelistic campaign resulted in **three thousand** new believers (2:41)! The church of Jesus Christ was off to an amazing start.

2:42-47 So what did the fledgling church do? Luke says the early church was known for four activities that should be foundational for every kingdom-minded local church. First, there was devotion to **the apostles' teaching** (2:42). The church was learning divine truth from God's Word (only the Old Testament was written at this point, but in the years to come the apostles would be inspired by the Holy Spirit to write what would become the New Testament). You cannot grow beyond what you know. The teaching of the apostles was to give believers God's perspective on every matter so that they could learn, obey, and experience spiritual growth and make kingdom impact.

Second, they devoted themselves to **fellowship** (2:42)—mutually sharing the life of Christ within the family of God. We are not to live as Lone Ranger Christians but to engage in the life of faith together. We are called to "love one another" (John 15:12), to "carry one another's burdens" (Gal 6:2), to forgive one another (Eph 4:32), to "encourage one another" (1 Thess 5:11), and the list

goes on. A disconnected Christian is a disobedient and unfruitful Christian. Each of us is an integral part of the body of Christ (see 1 Cor 12:12-26; Heb 10:23-25).

Third, the church regularly prioritized worship, reflected in **the breaking of bread** (i.e., Communion or the Lord's Supper) and **prayer** (2:42). Worship is the recognition and celebration of who God is, what he has done, and what we are trusting him to do. The church is called to make a big deal about God because this is what he deserves.

Fourth, the church was clearly engaged in outreach because **every day the Lord added to their number those who were being saved** (2:47). Everyone was involved in evangelism. They weren't merely letting the apostles take care of it. All of the believers were living out their faith publicly (2:44-47). Such public love, devotion, joy, ministry, and testimony convinced unbelievers to trust in Jesus Christ.

As a result of these activities, **everyone** in the church **was filled with awe** and experiencing **wonders and signs . . . performed through the apostles** (2:43). The Holy Spirit will cause amazing things to happen when the church is unified in its devotion to God and to its members in fulfillment of God's kingdom program.

II. KINGDOM WITNESS IN JERUSALEM (3:1–7:60)

3:1-6 Peter and John encountered **a man who was lame from birth** (he was over forty years old; see 4:22). He regularly begged outside **the temple gate** (3:1-2) and was without help and without hope. Simply hanging out at the temple had not made a difference. When he **asked** them **for money**, Peter told him to **look at** them (3:3-4). The beggar obviously expected **to get something from them** (3:5), but he had no idea what was coming! Peter had no **silver or gold** to give; instead, he had something much better. **In the name of Jesus Christ of Nazareth**, Peter said, **get up and walk!** (3:6).

The lame man asked for what he *wanted*; he was about to receive what he *needed*. Don't settle for what you want from God. When God meets your needs, he may not

give you what you asked for, but what he provides will always be greater than what you wanted.

3:7-10 After pronouncing the man's healing, Peter took the initiative and **raised him up**; therefore, the church must *both* speak hope into a broken life *and* extend practical help. Immediately, the lame man's **feet and ankles became strong** (3:7). He **started to walk**, but soon he was **leaping** and **praising God** (3:8). His response to God's work in his life was visible and vocal. The man went from limping to leaping. **All the people saw** what had happened to the beggar who had always been lame (3:9-10). As a result, **they were filled with awe and astonishment at what had happened** (3:10).

When God does something amazing in an individual's life, he usually has a greater purpose in mind than that individual's benefit. He wants to do something even more amazing *through* that individual. The Holy Spirit worked in this lame man's life and then worked through him so that the truth might be proclaimed to a large crowd of people (3:11-26) and to the Jewish leaders (4:1-22). His transformation ultimately led to the salvation of many souls (see 4:4). All of this took place because God acted in the life of a simple beggar who responded with public praise.

3:11-16 With a large attentive crowd observing the miraculous healing, **Peter** seized the opportunity to bear testimony to Jesus again (3:11-12). Peter didn't take credit for the miracle but pointed to the one true God: **the God of Abraham, Isaac, and Jacob** (3:12-13). He had **glorified his servant Jesus**, even though the people standing there had **handed** him **over, denied** him, and **asked** for a **murderer** (Barabbas) to be **released** instead (3:13-14). They were so blinded by their own sin that they couldn't see they had put to death **the Holy and Righteous One . . . the source of life** (3:14-15). But, Peter declared, **God raised** him **from the dead; we are witnesses of this** (3:15; see 1:8). It was through **faith in the name** of the resurrected Lord Jesus that this lame man had been made well (3:16). Peter exercised faith when he told the man to walk, and the lame man exercised faith when he allowed himself to be seized and responded to the spiritual help that enabled him to get up and start walking.

3:17-18 Peter explained what God had accomplished through Jesus and how the man had been healed (3:11-16). Next he turned his attention to the listening crowd: **I know that you acted in ignorance** (3:17). Though they were still accountable for their sin, they hadn't truly realized that they had been dealing with **the Messiah** whom **the prophets** had **predicted** (3:18).

3:19-24 What could they do? **Repent and turn back** (3:19)—turn away from sin and back to God. This was necessary so that

seasons of refreshing could **come** and so that God would **send Jesus**—a reference to the coming millennial reign of **the Messiah** (3:20). He has gone to **heaven . . . until the time of the restoration of all things**, the time when Israel will repent and receive her Messiah as predicted by the **prophets** (3:21-24; see Rom 11:25-27). The coming of the earthly messianic kingdom is directly connected to the repentance of the Jewish nation (see Matt 23:39; Zech 12:10).

3:25-26 Though the national restoration of Israel under King Jesus is yet future, Peter called the Israelites standing before him—**these sons of the prophets and of the covenant that God made with [their] ancestors**—to place their faith in Jesus so that God could **bless** them **by turning** them from their wickedness.

4:1-4 Jesus had told his disciples, "If they persecuted me, they will also persecute you" (John 15:20). That persecution was about to begin. **While** Peter and John **were speaking to the people**, the Jewish religious leaders got ticked off because they were **proclaiming in Jesus the resurrection of the dead** (4:1-2). **The Sadducees** didn't believe in the resurrection of the dead, so clearly **they were annoyed** (4:2). They seized Peter and John and threw them in jail **until the next day since it was already evening** (the Jewish council, the Sanhedrin, didn't meet at night) (4:3). But **many . . . who heard the message believed** and were saved.

Beginning in the life of one lame man (3:1-10), God brought **five thousand men** to Christ—in spite of the opposition of powerful unbelievers (4:4). There's no stopping the kingdom of God manifested through the power of the Holy Spirit when Jesus is being glorified.

4:5-8 The next day **the high priest** and all of the Jewish leadership—basically every leader that had been aligned against Jesus at his mock trial—brought **Peter and John** to **stand before them** for questioning (4:5-7).

By what power or in what name have you done this? (4:7). In other words, "Who authorized you to say and do these things?" (Unless they truly wanted to hear the answer, they shouldn't have asked the question.) Notice that the Peter who boldly answered them was the same Peter who, when previously asked about Jesus, said, "I don't know him" (Luke 22:57). What had changed him? He was **filled with the Holy Spirit** (4:8). Giving himself over to the influence of the Spirit's power enabled him (and will enable us) to confidently bear witness to Christ.

4:9-11 If they wanted to know how a lame man had been healed, Peter made it clear: **By the name of Jesus Christ of Nazareth, whom you crucified and whom God raised from the dead—by him this man is standing here before you healthy** (4:9-10). Jesus is the fulfillment of Psalm 118:22; he is **the stone** that the Jewish leaders had **rejected**, which became **the cornerstone**, the stone upon which the rest of the building depends (4:11). The only way to avoid the implications of what they had done was to repent and turn to the risen Lord Jesus, the one whom they had killed.

4:12 Peter concluded by telling the leaders that **salvation** is found **in no one else. There is no other name under heaven given to people by which we must be saved.** Names in the Bible are not mere titles; they reflect the person. The name *Jesus* is the Greek version of the Hebrew name *Joshua*, which means, "The Lord saves." Jesus's name, then, speaks to who he is, what he has done, and what he can do. Salvation from sin, death, and hell is found in him alone.

4:13 The Jewish leaders **observed** Peter and John's **boldness**, as well as the fact that **they were uneducated and untrained men.** Now that doesn't mean they had received no training whatsoever. It means they had received no formal rabbinical training, the ancient equivalent of seminary. The leaders **recognized that these men had been with Jesus.** *That's* where they got their training. Over the course of three years, the Son of God had taught these former fishermen everything they knew.

You can receive extensive, formal, theological education and have degrees after your name. But if you've never "been with Jesus" in a spiritual relationship and enrolled in his school of discipleship, you'll make no lasting spiritual effect on others.

4:14-18 They couldn't deny the reality of the **healed** man **standing with them,** so they put Peter and John outside and **conferred among themselves** (4:14-15). They didn't know what to do. On the one hand, a clear miraculous **sign** had been publicly performed **through them** and couldn't be denied (4:16). On the other hand, if they didn't do something to stop them, the message they were preaching would **spread . . . among the people** (4:17). The hearts of the Jewish leaders were so hard that they decided to **threaten** them **not to speak or teach at all in the name of Jesus** (4:17-18). They didn't care about truth; they cared only about preserving their own religious authority.

4:19-20 How did Peter and John respond to the Sanhedrin's order? Was it better **to listen** to human rulers **rather than to God?** They answered, **You decide.** In other words, "We'll let you debate whether people should obey you instead of obeying God. That's a no brainer for us!" **For we are unable to stop speaking about what we have seen and heard** (4:20).

Christians are called to "submit to the governing authorities" (Rom 13:1) and "to every human authority" (1 Pet 2:13). We are to be model citizens. But when the commands of the government conflict with the clearly revealed commands of God, our allegiance must be to the King of creation and his kingdom.

4:21-22 With all of **the people** glorifying God over the miracle that had been done, the Sanhedrin didn't want **to punish** the apostles and start a riot (4:21). After all, this man who was now walking had been lame for **forty years** (4:22). His healing couldn't have been faked. Therefore, they threatened them again and **released them** (4:21).

4:23-28 Returning to the rest of the believers, Peter and John **reported everything** that had happened. The apostles had experienced their first opposition—from those who had delivered Jesus to the Romans to be crucified. So what did they do next? Cower in fear? Leave town? They prayed to the Maker of **heaven, the earth, and the sea, and everything in them** (4:24). They did not fear the Sanhedrin: they feared God. They saw the opposition of Jewish and Gentile leaders to God's **holy servant Jesus** as the fulfillment of Psalm 2 (4:25-27).

Again we see divine sovereignty and human responsibility brought together (see commentary on 2:22-23). The leaders had **assembled together against** Jesus **to do whatever [God's] hand and [God's] will had predestined to take place** (4:27-28). These wicked rulers were doing exactly what they wanted to do. Nevertheless, God used their actions to accomplish his holy purposes. God can take humanity's worst and accomplish his best. Through the killing of Jesus at the hands of sinners, God was providing a way to save sinners.

4:29-31 Having praised God for his marvelous wisdom and salvation, here the apostles make their request of God: **Consider their threats, and grant that your servants may speak your word with all boldness** (4:29). They didn't want the threats to shut them up; rather, they wanted even more confidence to speak in Jesus's name. So God responded to their prayer by shaking **the place where they were assembled** and filling them **with the Holy Spirit ... to speak the word of God boldly** (4:31).

They had already received the Holy Spirit (2:1-4), but a Christian who is indwelt by the Spirit can be powerfully filled by (i.e., under the control of) the Spirit for bold proclamation. This is the kind of boldness the church needs; this is the kind of boldness we ought to pray for; this is the kind of boldness that God makes available to you. The absence of such boldness indicates the absence of the Spirit's filling.

4:32-35 Notice how the early church is described: They **were of one heart and mind** (4:32). Unity among the people of God is critical for the revealing of the visible manifestation of his glory (see 2 Chr 5:1-14). It's what Jesus prayed for (see John 17:20-23), and it's

what these first believers demonstrated and what the apostle Paul insisted on (see Eph 4:3). When there is disunity, the Spirit does not work.

No one claimed that any of his possessions was his own (4:32)—that is, they were generous and met one another's needs. **The apostles were** powerfully **giving testimony to the resurrection of the Lord Jesus**, and everyone was caring for one another (4:33-34). It was not a selfish environment. Believers were voluntarily (not by compulsion!) selling possessions and laying **the proceeds ... at the apostles' feet** in order to serve the needy (4:34-35). They were unified spiritually and materially.

4:36-37 Luke then gives his readers an example of one of these generous believers: **a Levite from Cyprus** named **Barnabas**, whose name meant **Son of Encouragement** (4:36). He demonstrated the appropriateness of his name by selling **a field he owned** and giving **the money** to the apostles (4:37). Barnabas's generosity is set in stark contrast to the couple that Luke describes next.

5:1-2 A man named Ananias, with his wife **Sapphira, sold** some **property**—just like Barnabas did (5:1). However, Ananias **kept back part of the proceeds with his wife's knowledge.** When he **laid** the money **at the apostles' feet**, he gave the impression that he was giving it all (5:2).

5:3-4 But the Holy Spirit wasn't fooled. Peter confronted Ananias, who had allowed **Satan** to fill his **heart** with deception and had lied to **the Holy Spirit** about the **proceeds of the land** (5:3). Thus, believers can allow Satan to manipulate them. Peter asked some key questions: **Wasn't it yours while you possessed it? And after it was sold, wasn't it at your disposal?** (5:4).

In other words, Ananias owned the land, and he hadn't been forced to sell it. Even when he did sell it, he wasn't required to give the church the money. His sin was that he made a *commitment* to give all of the proceeds to meet the needs of others (like Barnabas did) and then deceptively kept back some for himself—to the detriment of those in need. Thus, he **lied ... to God** (5:4) by not providing for his brothers and sisters as he'd claimed he would. It was a lie that damaged the family of God. Such deceit incurs greater judgment (see 1 Cor 3:17).

5:5-10 For this, **Ananias dropped dead**, and he was **buried** (5:5-6). Later, when Sapphira **came in**, Peter asked her if they sold **the land** for a certain **price** (the amount that they gave the apostles). She condemned herself by following her husband into sin and telling the same lie (5:7-8). She had agreed **to test the Spirit of God** (to do so is to see how much you can get away with) and, as a result, **dropped dead** just like Ananias (5:9-10).

The marriage bond ought to be the strongest of human relationships. Yet it must never trump a relationship with God. Though a husband is to love his wife sacrificially and a wife is to submit to the leadership of her husband, neither is to follow the other into sin. Our relationship with and commitment to God must always be primary.

5:11 As a result of what happened to Ananias and Sapphira, **great fear came on the whole church and on all who heard these things.** It was obvious to everyone that the supernatural work of God was operating in the apostles' ministry; therefore, people who hadn't been taking God seriously before were definitely taking him seriously after that. Church discipline, in fact, is designed to encourage believers to take God seriously with regard to sin.

5:12-14 The apostles were performing **many signs and wonders.** Because of this and the judgment on Ananias and Sapphira, unbelievers kept their distance but **spoke well of them** (5:12-13). They respected the apostles and realized that they were engaged in serious business. Yet those who genuinely believed the gospel—**both men and women**—continued to be **added to the Lord in increasing numbers** (5:14). The Holy-Spirit-empowered witness of the church was causing all people to hold them in high esteem and drawing many to faith in Christ.

5:15-16 Luke gives examples of the supernatural activity that surrounded the apostles' ministry. People were laying the **sick** on cots in the **streets** so that Peter's **shadow might fall on** them and heal them (5:15). Residents from **the towns surrounding Jerusalem** brought **the sick** and demon-possessed into the city so that they might be **healed** (5:16). Jesus had promised his disciples that they would do miraculous works like him (see John 14:12), and they were doing so with gusto.

5:17-21 Unfortunately, when God starts working, the devil does too. **The high priest** and **the Sadducees** began to oppose the apostles. Were the Jewish leaders concerned that the apostles were teaching bad theology? No. They **were filled with jealousy** (5:17). They cared nothing for God's glory, only for their own. So they threw **the apostles** in **jail** (5:18). But a locked cell was hardly capable of stopping the supernatural. In the middle of **the night**, an **angel of the Lord opened the doors of the jail** and sent the apostles to **stand in the temple** and preach (5:19-20)—not to go hide from their enemies, but to stand in public and preach!

5:22-24 The next morning, **the high priest** and others **convened the Sanhedrin** so that they could deal with the apostles. But **the servants** reported that **the jail** was **securely locked**, the **guards** were on duty, and the apostles were gone (5:22-23). The Jewish leaders were **baffled** and wondered **what would come of this** (5:24). One can imagine the comical picture of all of them staring at one another with puzzled looks.

5:25-26 Then **someone** announced that the men who had been locked up were **in the temple . . . teaching the people** (5:25). They were doing the very thing they had been locked up for in the first place! So **the commander** of the temple police and his **servants** rounded up the apostles **without force, because they were afraid the people might stone them** (5:26). Don't miss the fact that the captors, instead of the captives, were cowering.

5:27-28 Notice that they weren't even willing to say Jesus's name nor act under his authority: **Didn't we strictly order you not to**

teach in this name? Not only had the apostles continued **teaching**, but they were holding the Jewish leadership **guilty of** Jesus's **blood** (5:28)! These powerful men who had condemned Jesus to death (and who could do the same to the apostles) wanted to know why they weren't being obeyed.

5:29-32 Let the church take note of Peter's answer: **We must obey God rather than people** (5:29). Then, consistent with his preaching to this point in Acts, Peter emphasized the apostles' role as Holy-Spirit-empowered witnesses to the resurrected Jesus (5:30, 32; see 2:32; 3:15). Our chief authority is not merely *a* king. He is *the* King. Therefore, human beings must never have the last word in our lives. When a human command contradicts a divine one, our obligation to God is supreme.

5:33-40 The high priest and those with him **were enraged and wanted to kill** the apostles (5:33). But **a Pharisee named Gamaliel**, who was **respected** by everyone, had the apostles **taken outside** so that he could speak privately to the **Sanhedrin** (5:34). He reminded them of two other would-be leaders who had gathered supporters around them: **Theudas** and **Judas the Galilean**. These men were eventually **killed**, their **followers were scattered**, and their movements **came to nothing** (5:36-37). Therefore, he advised the men to **leave** the apostles **alone**. If their activity was **of human origin**, it would fizzle out just like the others (5:38). But if it was of divine origin, they could **be found fighting against God** (5:39). Thus, Gamaliel **persuaded** them. So they **flogged** the apostles, threatened them, and set them free (5:39-40).

5:41-42 When the apostles left **the Sanhedrin**, they went out **rejoicing that they were counted worthy to be treated shamefully on behalf of the Name** (5:41). Then they went right back to **proclaiming the good news that Jesus is the Messiah** (5:42). Consider their response. They didn't depart in fear or grief. They departed with joy! And not only did they walk away from their beating rejoicing, but they rejoiced that they were deemed worthy to suffer for the name of Jesus. As Peter would later write to Christians experiencing persecution, "Rejoice as you share in the sufferings of Christ" (1 Pet 4:13; see also 2:18-21; 3:17). Suffering for Jesus is far better than living at ease without him. He won't forget what you do for his name.

6:1-4 The disciples were increasing in number (6:1; see 2:41, 47; 4:4; 5:14). A kingdom disciple is a believer in Christ who takes part in the spiritual developmental process of progressively learning to live all of life in submission to the lordship of Jesus Christ. The goal of the church is not merely for people to become Christians, but for them to develop into fully committed disciples.

But this growth in number led to a problem. **The Hellenistic Jews** (those who spoke Greek) and **the Hebraic Jews** (those who spoke Aramaic) began to argue, the former complaining that **their widows were being overlooked** in charitable distributions (6:1). While they were racially the same, they were culturally different. This clash of cultures and accusations of unfair treatment led **the Twelve** to gather **the disciples** to address the concerns (6:2). Since their primary responsibilities were **preaching the word of God** and **prayer**, the apostles had the community of believers choose **seven men of good reputation** to deal with the issue (6:2-4)

Many interpreters understand this passage to describe the selection of the first deacons, who would serve the physical needs of God's people, while the apostles (and, eventually, the elders / overseers) addressed the spiritual needs.

6:5-7 The whole company of disciples agreed with **this proposal**. They chose seven spiritual men, all of whom had Greek names (6:5). That's an important point because they wanted men who could relate to the Hellenistic Jews so that they could address their specific needs and concerns. So the apostles **laid their hands on them** and **prayed** for them, commissioning them for their work (6:6). Then **the word of God spread**, and **the disciples** grew **in number** (6:7). A legitimate need was not ignored but addressed with wisdom—and God blessed their faithfulness.

6:8-10 One of these men, **Stephen**, receives high praise from Luke. He was "full of faith and the Holy Spirit" (6:5), **full of grace and power**, and **was performing great wonders and signs among the people** (6:8). That's quite a resume. Clearly, then, Stephen was no spiritual slouch. When **opposition arose** from various unbelieving Jews, they were no match for **his wisdom** or for **the Spirit** who empowered his **speaking** (6:9-10).

6:11-14 Since they couldn't best Stephen in legitimate argument, they sought to destroy him by deception. They **persuaded some men** to lie about him, claiming that he had spoken **blasphemous words against Moses and God** (6:11). Those accusations were enough to get **the Sanhedrin** to take notice (6:12). When Stephen was taken before the Jewish leaders, more **false witnesses** alleged that he was preaching **against** the temple and **the law**, and that he was claiming **Jesus** was going to **destroy** the temple and **change** their **customs** (6:13-14). They considered Stephen a threat to Judaism.

6:15 –7:1 The Jewish leaders hated Stephen and lied about him. But when they **looked** at him, **his face was like the face of an angel** (6:15). The man whom they wanted to kill had the appearance of one who had been in the holy presence of God. When **the high priest** asked whether the accusations made were **true**, he opened the door for Stephen to launch into a history lesson (7:1-53) that they'd never forget. His words demonstrate that the Jewish leaders had misunderstood the Old Testament Scriptures and, thus, misunderstood Jesus.

7:2-5 Stephen began with God's call of **Abraham** to **leave** his **country** and family in order to journey to an unknown **land** God would **show** him (7:2-3). So Abraham traveled and eventually arrived in **the land** in which Stephen and the Jewish leaders were living (7:4). But Abraham never inherited the land himself; God **promised to give it . . . to his descendants** (7:5).

The Jewish leaders of Stephen's day had become so focused on their religion—encapsulated in the law, the land, and the temple—that they had forgotten the fact that God wanted relationship. While the land was a benefit received by Abraham's descendants, the main idea here is that Abraham's relationship with God was key.

7:6-7 God predicted that Abraham's **descendants** would be enslaved in **a foreign country** for **four hundred years** (7:6). Yet he would deliver them so that they could **worship** him **in this place**—that is, in the land of Israel (7:7). The land was to be the geographical context for knowing and worshiping God. Being God's people, however, was about more than living in the land.

7:8-16 From **Abraham, Isaac, and Jacob** descended **the twelve patriarchs**, eleven of whom **sold** their brother **Joseph** into Egyptian slavery out of jealousy (7:8-9). Nevertheless, **God was with** Joseph (7:9)—even though he was no longer living in the promised land. Then God **rescued** Joseph, **gave him favor** with **Pharaoh**, and used him to deliver **his relatives** from a **famine** (7:10-15). This highlights another theme from Stephen's sermon. Unbelieving Israelites often rejected those whom God chose. God exalted Joseph and used him, even though his brothers rejected and persecuted him. In a similar way, the Jewish leaders rejected and persecuted Jesus.

7:17-28 In fulfillment of what God told Abraham (see 7:6-7), the people **multiplied** and eventually a new Pharaoh **oppressed** and enslaved them (7:17-19). Though the Egyptians sought to kill the infant sons of the Israelites, **Moses** was preserved and raised by **Pharaoh's** own **daughter** so that he became wise and **powerful** (7:19-22). Later, when Moses tried to help his brother **Israelites**, his attempts at leadership were rejected (7:23-28).

7:29-33 Fleeing to **Midian**, Moses encountered God, who **appeared to him in the wilderness of Mount Sinai** (7:29-32). Again, then, the Lord initiated a relationship outside the promised land. Moreover, the land where God appeared to Moses was **holy ground** because of God's presence (7:33). Land is only holy if God is present; a church is only holy if Jesus is in its midst.

7:34-36 God sent Moses to return to **Egypt** and deliver his people from bondage (7:34). This man whom the Israelites had **rejected** was God's chosen **deliverer** to lead them out of Egypt and **in the wilderness for forty years** (7:35-36). Thus, when the Jewish leaders rejected Jesus whom God had sent, they were following in the footsteps of their ancestors.

7:37-43 **Moses** told the Israelites that **God** would **raise up** another **prophet like** him from among the people (7:37)—a prophecy that was fulfilled in Jesus (see Deut 18:15-18; John 1:21; 6:14; Acts 3:22). The Jewish **ancestors were unwilling to obey** Moses and turned to idolatry, scorning God (7:39-43). In the same way, their descendants in Stephen's day were unwilling to obey Jesus. And by scorning Jesus, their Messiah, they too had scorned God.

7:44-50 Their **ancestors had the tabernacle** that God **commanded** Moses to make (7:44). Then **Joshua brought it** into the promised land when **God drove out** their enemies **before them** (7:45). Then **Solomon** constructed God's temple in Jerusalem (7:47). But, ultimately, God doesn't **dwell** in a manmade structure because **heaven is [his] throne and the earth [his] footstool** (7:48-49). The Jewish leaders of Stephen's day were devoted to the temple (see 6:13-14), but they had lost sight of the God to whom the temple pointed.

7:51 With the history lesson complete, Stephen brought his message home: **You stiff-necked people! . . . You are always resisting the Holy Spirit. As your ancestors did, you do also.** It wasn't that the Holy Spirit had not spoken to them. The problem was that, just like their ancestors, they had **uncircumcised hearts and ears** that refused to listen.

Don't miss that the Holy Spirit can be resisted. Though the Spirit brings the truth to bear on a heart and mind, a person can be stubborn and unwilling to respond. Don't be obstinate to what God says through his Word and by his Spirit. The consequences can be disastrous.

7:52-53 The **ancestors** of those to whom Stephen was speaking had persecuted **the prophets**, even killing **those who foretold the coming of the Righteous One**, the Messiah. And Stephen's listeners had followed in their footsteps, betraying and murdering Jesus Christ when he came (7:52)! Though they professed to treasure God's **law** as law keepers, they demonstrated by their actions that their hearts were actually lawless (7:53).

7:54-56 Stephen was a man **full of the Holy Spirit** and spoke by means of the Spirit's power (7:55; see also 6:5, 10). So when his listeners **were enraged** at him (7:54), they actually were enraged at God himself and the truth that was spoken about them.

As their animosity reached a fever pitch, Stephen looked **into heaven** and saw **Jesus standing at the right hand of God** (7:55-56). His Lord and Savior, about whom he had faithfully testified, was ready to receive him into glory with a standing ovation! This is the way our Lord wants to receive all of his faithful servants. He received a glimpse of heaven before he died, one of the glorious privileges God gives to faithful believers as they transition from earth to heaven.

7:57-58 The Jewish leaders couldn't stand to listen to him any longer. They **covered their ears** and **dragged him out of the city**, and stoned Stephen to death (7:57-58). And it's at this point in the narrative that Luke introduces us to the man who would become one of the most significant persons in the book of Acts and who would write more New Testament Letters than any other: **Saul** (eventually known as Paul) (7:58). At this moment, however, Saul was united with those putting Stephen to death. Stephen became the first martyr of the church.

7:59-60 Before he died, Stephen followed in Jesus's footsteps, commending his **spirit** to the **Lord** and praying that God would forgive his attackers (see Luke 23:34, 46). That kind of response is impossible without supernatural enabling.

III. KINGDOM WITNESS BEYOND JERUSALEM (8:1–20:38)

✎ A. Kingdom Witness in Judea and Samaria, and the Conversion of Paul
(8:1–9:43) ✎

8:1 **Saul** had watched the garments of those who stoned Stephen (see 7:58) and **agreed with putting him to death**. The murder set off a chain reaction of **persecution...against the church**. All of the disciples **except the apostles were scattered throughout the land of Judea and Samaria**. Nevertheless, the Jewish leaders were playing right into God's hands, though they didn't realize it. Jesus had promised his disciples that they would be his witnesses in Jerusalem and "in all Judea and Samaria" (1:8). Thus, God was using this persecution to send his people out to spread the gospel and grow the church.

Remember this when hardship comes into your own life because of your faith in Christ. Your circumstances are not outside of God's sovereign control and care. He can use your adversity to glorify himself, accomplish his purposes, bring others to Christ, and strengthen you in your faith.

8:2 **Devout men buried Stephen and mourned deeply over him**. The loss of a beloved Christian friend or family member can bring great pain and sorrow, but the apostle Paul reminds us that, though we grieve, we don't do so like unbelievers "who have no hope" (1 Thess 4:13). At the moment of his death, Stephen was with his Lord in heaven. That transition is called falling asleep (see the CSB note on 7:60).

8:3 **Saul**, on the other hand, **was ravaging the church**. He began to **enter** the houses of Christians and **drag off men and women** to **prison**. He was making it his personal agenda to stamp out Christianity before it spread any further. But God had other plans for him. Soon he would be pursuing another agenda, a kingdom agenda.

Saul hated Christianity, rejected Jesus, and persecuted Christians. So, in light of what happens to him in Acts 9, don't ever

tell yourself that an unbeliever you know could never become a Christian. Saul was as opposed to Christ as a person can be. But God converted him, and he became the greatest missionary the world has ever known.

8:4-8 The Christians **who were scattered** as a result of the persecution **went on their way preaching the word** (8:4; see 8:1). The persecutors certainly didn't intend this consequence, but God used their wicked actions to fulfill his purposes.

One of those who left Jerusalem for **Samaria** was **Philip** (who had been chosen along with Stephen and several others to serve; see 6:1-6). He **proclaimed the Messiah**, cast out **unclean spirits**, **healed** the sick, and spread **great joy** (8:5-7). The miracles served to give visible validity to the gospel message.

8:9-13 In the Samaritan **city** where Philip was preaching and ministering, there was **a man named Simon** practicing **sorcery** and making quite a name for himself among the people who called him **the Great Power of God** (8:9-10). But when Philip preached **the good news about the kingdom of God and the name of Jesus Christ**, many people **believed** and **were baptized**, including **Simon** (8:12-13). Afterwards, he **followed Philip everywhere** and watched him perform **signs**. This former magician was **amazed** when he saw genuine **miracles** accomplished by a follower of the true God (8:13).

8:14-17 Once **the apostles** heard that Samaritans had believed the gospel, **they sent Peter and John** for a visit (8:14). The Samaritan believers had not yet received the Holy Spirit, so Peter and John **prayed for them** and **laid their hands on them, and they** did (8:15-17).

Today, when a person trusts in Christ, he receives the Holy Spirit at that moment (see 1 Cor 12:13). But this Holy Spirit activity in the book of Acts represented a unique moment in the early church. As each new group came to believe the gospel (Samaritans, Gentiles, etc.), they received the Holy

Spirit when the apostles were present. This demonstrated the unity of the believers and that all were embracing the same faith (see 10:44-46; 19:1-7).

8:18-20 When he observed that **the Spirit** was bestowed **through the laying on of the apostles' hands,** Simon's old sorcerer's ways kicked in (8:18). He wanted to be able to do the same thing. So **he offered them money,** thinking he could purchase and exercise **this power** of God (8:18-19). But Peter condemned his attitude: **May your silver be destroyed with you!** God's **gift** cannot be acquired **with money** but is sovereignly and freely given. (8:20). The Holy Spirit cannot be bought.

8:21-24 Peter urged Simon to **repent of this wickedness** so that he might **be forgiven,** because his **heart [was] not right before God** (8:21-22). Simon then asked Peter to **pray** for him, so that he wouldn't be destroyed (8:24). Repentance is God's means to limit or reverse the consequences of sin.

It is clear that Simon was a believer (see 8:13)—though one in extreme error. Years of practicing magic and claiming to have divine power (see 8:9-11) had resulted in **bitterness** and **wickedness** in his heart (8:23). Repentance and prayer were needed (8:22) to root out the evil ways and desires that had so long been a part of his life. God is not a slot machine to be used to fulfill our carnal desires.

8:25 On the way **back to Jerusalem,** the apostles proclaimed **the gospel** in other Samaritan **villages.** The good news of Jesus Christ and the kingdom of God was being preached across racial lines, and barriers were falling.

8:26-29 After his successful ministry in Samaria (8:4-13), **Philip** received a message from **an angel of the Lord,** telling him to go **to the road** between **Jerusalem** and **Gaza** (8:26). There he encountered **an Ethiopian man.** He was **a eunuch and high official of Candace, queen of the Ethiopians, who was in charge of her entire treasury** (8:27). In ancient times, a eunuch was a castrated man—usually a slave who was used to watch over a harem or a treasury. However, the practice of a eunuch serving as a treasurer

became so common that frequently the title "eunuch" was used even for treasurers who were not physical eunuchs. So it may be that the term simply denotes his high position in the queen's administration. Regardless, he had obviously come to believe in the God of Israel because he was returning home after worshiping **in Jerusalem** (8:27-28).

When he saw the **chariot,** Philip heard two voices: the Ethiopian man's as he read from **the prophet Isaiah** and the Holy Spirit's, telling him to **join** the man (8:28-29). Philip didn't have to be told twice. He sprang into action.

8:30-35 When Philip asked the man if he understood the passage he was reading, the Ethiopian confessed his ignorance and **invited Philip** into his chariot to explain it to him (8:30-31). The passage was from Isaiah 53:7-8, speaking of the Suffering Servant of the Lord who would be **led like a sheep to the slaughter** (8:32). The man asked, **Who is the prophet saying this about?** (8:34). You don't get a much better opportunity to share **the good news about Jesus** than that. And that's exactly what **Philip** did (8:35).

This story is a good reminder to us to be ready to share the gospel with those whom we encounter and to be open to the prompting of the Holy Spirit. Pray regularly for God to bring someone across your path with whom you can share the love of God in Jesus Christ. There are people out there whom the Spirit has prepared. Like the Ethiopian man, they're asking themselves, "**How can I** understand **unless someone guides me?**" (8:31). Believers are to know the Scriptures so that they are prepared to help unbelievers properly understand and respond to the gospel, as well as to help fellow believers grow in their faith (see 1 Pet 3:15).

8:36-40 The eunuch had become a believer in Jesus. Seeing some **water,** he asked Philip about **being baptized.** So they stopped, and Philip **baptized him** (8:36-38), thus identifying him as a public follower of Christ (see Rom 6:1-7). Then the Spirit supernaturally **carried** Philip away to preach **the gospel** in more **towns** (8:39-40). But the eunuch continued home to Ethiopia, carrying his faith with him and **rejoicing** (8:39).

This account of the Ethiopian official is significant for three reasons. First, it acknowledges the existence of a royal kingdom of dark-skinned people at the time of first-century Christianity. Second, it records the continuation of Christianity in Africa after having been initiated through the first African-Jewish proselytes who were converts at Pentecost (see Acts 2:10). Third, it verifies God's promise in Zephaniah 3:9-10 about followers of God who would come from Cush (that is, Ethiopia). God desired to call to himself peoples from the African continent to serve him in brotherhood with all men.

9:1-2 Last we heard of Saul, he had approved of the death of the first Christian martyr and was dragging Christian men and women off to prison (8:1-3). Here we see that he received **letters** from **the high priest** to go to **the synagogues in Damascus** (a city about one hundred and fifty miles north of Jerusalem in Syria) to find Jews **who belonged to the Way** and **bring them as prisoners to Jerusalem** (9:1-2). "The Way" was an early name referring to Christianity (see, e.g., 19:9, 23; 24:14, 22), because Jesus was "the way" (see John 14:6). "The Way" also represented the new life of believers as they followed the pattern of their Messiah. The gospel was expanding outside of Judea (see 1:8), and Saul had become a religious bounty hunter to put a stop to it.

9:3-5 On his way to Damascus, Saul had an unexpected encounter. A bright **light from heaven . . . flashed**, a light more brilliant "than the sun" (26:13), and the **voice** of **Jesus** said, **Saul, why are you persecuting me?** Please don't miss this. Jesus so identifies with his people that to persecute them is to persecute him. The church is "the body of Christ" (1 Cor 12:27). So anyone who attacks God's people is attacking the one who loved them, died for them, and united them to himself.

9:6-8 Jesus commanded Saul to go to Damascus to learn **what [he] must do** (9:6). Though his companions heard a **sound**, they couldn't see anyone (9:7). The resurrected Lord Jesus was revealing himself to Saul alone. But the encounter left him blind, a physical reflection of his spiritual blindness, so that the men had to lead him **by the hand.** And **for three days** he couldn't **see** and refused to **eat or drink** (9:8) as he reflected on his supernatural encounter. The Lord Jesus wasn't happy with what Saul had been doing to the church, his body. Saul had good reason to be uneasy. Jesus was taking his actions personally.

9:9-14 While this was happening, **the Lord** spoke to **a disciple in Damascus named Ananias**, told him **in a vision** where he could find Saul, and commanded him to go and heal **his sight** (9:9-12). But Ananias wasn't exactly ready to jump at the opportunity. He had **heard** that Saul was causing **much harm** to the **saints in Jerusalem** and had come to Damascus **to arrest** others (9:13-14). Ananias was probably thinking, "You want me to go talk to the man who's in town to arrest believers—like me?" But even when it looks like obedience could result in trouble, God calls us to trust and obey. He is usually up to something much bigger than we realize.

9:15-19 The Lord revealed to Ananias that Saul was his **chosen instrument** to speak about him **to Gentiles, kings, and Israelites** (9:15). Here is another indication, then, that divine election is to service and not eternal life. Saul would **suffer for** the **name** of Jesus (9:16). So Ananias went to Saul, explained that he had been **sent** by the same **Lord Jesus** who had **appeared** to him, and put **his hands on him** so that he would be healed and **filled with the Holy Spirit** (9:17). Then Saul **regained his sight** and **was baptized** (9:18).

God used a faithful (though frightened!) disciple to launch Saul into a sudden new direction in life. A menace was about to become a missionary. If you know someone whom you think could never be converted, don't forget what the grace and mercy of God accomplished in the life of a wicked man named Saul.

9:20 What did Saul do after a supernatural encounter with Jesus? **Immediately he began proclaiming Jesus in the synagogues**, saying, **He is the Son of God.** He didn't waste any time. So, once again, we see the fulfillment of Jesus's words (see 1:8).

Saul was filled with the Spirit and became a vocal and formidable witness for Jesus. Anyone who walks around bragging about being filled with the Spirit, but who does not bear testimony to Jesus Christ, is a walking contradiction.

9:21-22 Everyone who heard Saul was shocked, asking, "Isn't this the man who's been making **prisoners** of Christians?" (9:21). He was **confounding the Jews . . . by proving that Jesus is the Messiah** (9:22). Saul was a Pharisee (see Phil 3:5), and he knew his Old Testament well. His encounter with Jesus made the Scriptures come together for him. Everything made sense.

9:23-25 Saul's zeal, however, wasn't winning him any friends among **the Jews.** They wanted **to kill him** (9:23). Their star persecutor of Christians had switched his allegiance, and now he was a liability to them. **So they were watching** for him to pass through the **gates,** which would have been the only way in or out of the walled city of Damascus (9:24). But Saul's **disciples** helped Saul escape **through an opening in the** city **wall** (9:25; cf. 1 Cor 4:7-12). Those whom he had previously come to imprison were saving his life.

9:26-27 When Saul **arrived in Jerusalem,** he couldn't find any **disciples** willing to take him in. **They did not believe he was a disciple** (9:26)! Everyone feared him—everyone except Barnabas, whose name meant "Son of Encouragement" (see 4:36-37): that name described him well. He took **[Saul] to the apostles,** described his conversion, and testified to his gospel ministry **in Damascus** (2:27). Barnabas was willing to embrace the work of grace that God was doing in Saul's life.

9:28-30 As Saul began **speaking boldly** in Jerusalem, the **Jews** there wanted **to kill him** too (9:28-29). So **the brothers . . . sent him off to Tarsus** (9:30), Saul's hometown (see 9:11). It was located in the Roman province of Cilicia (in modern south-central Turkey).

9:31 Luke tells us that **the church throughout all Judea, Galilee, and Samaria had peace and was strengthened.** As believers lived **in the fear of the Lord** and received

encouragement from **the Holy Spirit,** the church **increased in numbers.** But wait a minute. What about the "severe persecution" (8:1) that had broken out against the church? How could things be going so well for Christ's followers when their external circumstances were so bad? In God's sovereignty, the period of persecution actually caused the church to increase and grow stronger. True Christianity, in fact, prospers in spite of outward pressure when believers depend on God's peace that "surpasses all understanding" (Phil 4:7), receive comfort that only the Holy Spirit can provide, and take God and his Word seriously.

In many places in the world today, Christians are persecuted and even killed for their faith. Though believers in many places may not face such severity, they can still undergo persecution in other forms: rejection, mocking, ostracism, and discrimination by employers to name a few. Paul writes, "All who want to live a godly life in Christ Jesus will be persecuted" (2 Tim 3:12). However, if a believer experiences no form of persecution, it may mean that he doesn't have a faith worth persecuting. Don't be a secret agent Christian: go public with your trust in Christ.

9:32-35 As **Peter was traveling,** he encountered **a man named Aeneas** who had been **paralyzed** for **eight years** (9:32-33). Peter told him that **Jesus Christ** had healed him, and Aeneas stood **up** (9:34-35). As a result of this public miracle, many people in that region **turned to the Lord** (9:35). Obviously, the miracles the apostles were performing were not merely for shock and awe. Their purpose was to draw people to Christ.

9:36-43 In **Joppa,** northwest of Jerusalem on the Mediterranean Coast, a faithful believer named **Tabitha,** who was known for her **good works, became sick and died** (9:36-37). Since the disciples in Joppa knew that **Peter** was nearby, they **urged** him to come (9:38). When Peter arrived, there was much **weeping** over this generous saint (9:39). So he **prayed,** told Tabitha to **get up,** and her life was restored (9:40-41). As a result, **many believed in the Lord** (9:42).

This was the first time that one of the apostles, like Jesus, had raised the dead back to life (see Luke 7:11-15; 8:50-56; John 11:1-44).

But it wouldn't be the last (see 20:7-12). Once again, a miracle served as confirmation of the gospel and brought many to saving faith. In addition, God brought Tabitha's good works back to her. She had sacrificially served others, and here God showed mercy to her. Our God is a God of reciprocity (see Luke 6:38).

☞ B. Peter's Kingdom Witness to the Gentiles and Escape from Prison
(10:1–12:25) ☜

10:1-8 Luke introduces us to a key figure: **Cornelius**, a Roman **centurion** (10:1). He was a Gentile "God fearer"—that is, he believed in the God of Israel. But he was not a Jewish proselyte—that is, he was not circumcised as a full-fledged convert to Judaism. He engaged in **charitable deeds for the Jewish people and always prayed to God** (10:2). One day, he had **a vision** in which **an angel** commended him for his devotion and told him to send for a man named **Peter** in **Joppa** (10:3-6). It's not every day that someone receives a visit from a heavenly being, so Cornelius didn't waste time obeying! Representatives were soon on their way to find Peter (10:7-8).

10:9-16 Here the scene cuts to **Peter** in Joppa, praying **on the roof about noon** (10:9). **Hungry** and waiting for lunch to be prepared, **he fell into a trance** (10:10). He saw **a large sheet . . . lowered** from **heaven** to **earth** with all kinds of **animals** in it that were unclean for Jews to eat (10:11-12). When he heard **a voice** tell him to **eat**, he refused (10:13-14). Peter was a good, faithful Jew who had always obeyed the Jewish food laws (10:14). But the voice said, **What God has made clean, do not call impure** (10:15). After seeing two reruns of this message (two or three witnesses are God's method of divine confirmation; see, e.g., Deut 17:6; 19:15; Matt 18:16; 2 Cor 13:1; 1 Tim 5:19), Peter woke up.

Peter had been faithful to the dietary restrictions God had given Israel under the old covenant (see Lev 11:1-47). But during his ministry Jesus had "declared all foods clean" (Mark 7:19). The previous standards

Peter had learned, then, were irrelevant in light of what God had done and was doing. The Lord was getting ready to teach Peter about more than mere changes to his diet. He was about to break down racial divides and signal the dawning of a new day.

10:17-23 At that moment, Cornelius's **men** showed up (10:17-20). They explained that **a holy angel** had commanded Cornelius to send for Peter and **hear a message from** him (10:22). So he agreed to go **with them** (10:23). Though Cornelius was a Gentile, Peter wasn't going to ignore the combination of the two messages from heaven. He knew God was trying to tell him something (see 10:28-29).

10:24-29 When they arrived, **Cornelius** was waiting along with **his relatives and close friends**, and he **fell** down and **worshiped** Peter (10:24-25). **But Peter** would have none of that: he **lifted him up** and addressed the **large gathering** (10:26-27). He got right to the point: **It's forbidden for a Jewish man to . . . visit a foreigner.** Indeed, Jews didn't associate with those who lived on the other side of the tracks, so to speak. But God had just revealed to him that he shouldn't **call any person impure or unclean**, and that's why he was willing to go into this Gentile's home **without objection** (10:28).

At a clear word from God, Peter had changed his convictions on a matter and obeyed at once. Given the Bible's clear teaching on racial equality, since all people come from one source (see 17:26) it doesn't require years of training and seminars to embrace the truth. It simply requires a quick willingness to take God at his Word. We must see people as God sees them.

10:30-33 Cornelius explained his own heavenly revelation that had prompted him to send for Peter. Then he concluded, **So now we are all in the presence of God to hear everything you have been commanded by the Lord** to share (10:33). What other message could God possibly want Peter to proclaim to this crowd but the message of the gospel? God had sovereignly orchestrated events so that Peter had been invited to his own evangelistic crusade with a crowd ready and willing to listen.

10:34-35 Now I truly understand that God doesn't show favoritism. Peter had come to understand what Paul would later write: "Is God the God of Jews only? Is he not the God of Gentiles too? Yes, of Gentiles too" (Rom 3:29). No ethnic or racial group is superior to another or gets preferential treatment from God. He accepts all who come to him on his terms (10:35).

10:36-43 Then Peter launched into **the good news of peace through Jesus Christ**, who is **Lord of all** (not of Jews only) (10:36). He began with the **baptism** of **John**, reviewed the details of Jesus's miraculous life and ministry, and culminated with his crucifixion and resurrection—to which many (including Peter) were eyewitnesses (10:37-41). This is what Peter and the other apostles had been **commanded . . . to preach**, because the risen Lord Jesus is coming back one day to judge **the living and the dead** (10:42). **Forgiveness of sins** is available to **everyone who believes in him** (10:43).

10:44-48 At that moment, **the Holy Spirit came down on all** of the Gentiles **who heard the message** (10:44). And the Jewish Christians **with Peter were amazed** as they heard them **speaking in other tongues** (10:45-46)—just as Peter and the other apostles had done on the day of Pentecost (see commentary on 2:1-11). Since they had **received the Holy Spirit** just as the Jewish believers had, Peter knew they could do nothing other than baptize them **in the name of Jesus Christ** (10:47-48). This was a Gentile Pentecost, an event bringing Jews and Gentiles together into the family of God.

When an Olympic athlete wins a gold medal, they do not ask the athlete what song he or she would like to hear played at the award ceremony. They play the anthem of the country that the athlete represents. No matter how diverse the athletes are from a given country, they compete under the same flag. Similarly, believers in Jesus Christ come from every tribe, tongue, nation, race, and gender. These different aspects of humanity are part of God's creation and, therefore, are not obliterated by the gospel. But they are not the most important things about us. We do not primarily represent our race;

we represent God's kingdom. We live, work, and worship together under *his* banner, not our own.

11:1-18 All the believers in Judea **heard that the Gentiles had also received the word of God** (11:1). But those who were members of **the circumcision party criticized** Peter for fellowshipping and eating with Gentiles without having required their circumcision first (11:2). So Peter explained everything that had happened, including a detailed account of his heavenly trance, the angel's message to Cornelius, and the Holy Spirit's baptism of the new Gentile believers (11:3-16). He concluded, **If, then, God gave them the same gift that he also gave to us when we believed in the Lord Jesus Christ, how could I possibly hinder God?** (11:17). In other words, Peter was saying, illegitimate racial divisions stand in God's way and oppose the truth of the gospel (see Gal 2:11-14). To oppose something that so clearly had a divine stamp of approval on it would be to oppose God. Peter's explanation caused the other Jewish believers to give glory to God for granting **repentance resulting in life even to the Gentiles** (11:18).

11:19-21 The persecution that began **because of Stephen** caused believers to be **scattered . . . as far as Phoenicia** (on the Mediterranean Coast in Syria), **Cyprus** (an island south of Asia Minor), **and Antioch** (in southeast Turkey). Antioch would become a dominant church, sending missionaries (including Paul) throughout the Roman Empire. Up to this point, the Jewish believers who been scattered to these places had only preached **the word** to Jews (11:19). But now believers began **speaking to the Greeks** about **the Lord Jesus**, resulting in many conversions (11:20-21).

11:22-26 The church in Jerusalem heard about these Gentile conversions and sent **Barnabas** to **Antioch** (11:22). As he saw evidence of the work of God and people being saved, he **encouraged** them to follow God **with devoted hearts** (11:23). Then Barnabas sought out **Saul** in **Tarsus** and took him to minister to the **church** in **Antioch** (11:25-26). This was the second time that Barnabas had served as a bridge to help Saul get connected to other believers (see 9:26-30). Do you make opportunities to facilitate and encourage the ministries of others?

It was in Antioch that **disciples** of Jesus Christ **were first called Christians** (11:26); they were named for the one whom they worshiped and obeyed. If we are going to bear his name in the world, then we must likewise bear his attitudes and actions, his character and conduct.

11:27-30 During this time, a prophet **named Agabus** came **from Jerusalem to Antioch** predicting an empire-wide **famine** while **Claudius** was the Roman emperor (11:27-28). So each believer in Antioch, **according to his ability**, set aside funds to be delivered by **Barnabas and Saul** to relieve the suffering saints in **Judea** (11:29-30).

Initially, the Jewish believers were reluctant to have anything to do with the Gentiles (see 11:1-3). Then, prompted by divine initiative, Peter proclaimed the gospel to Gentiles and watched them receive the Holy Spirit just as Jewish believers had (see 11:4-17). Now, recognizing that they were all part of the same family of God, Gentile believers in Antioch provided loving support to Jewish believers in need. Regardless of past divisions, these people saw Christians from another race as their brothers and sisters, and they acted accordingly. Do you?

12:1-5 Wherever the Holy Spirit is at work and believers are living in faithfulness to God, ungodly resistance will eventually rear its ugly head. On this occasion, resistance manifested itself as **King Herod violently attacked some who belonged to the church** (12:1). This man was Herod Agrippa I (grandson of Herod the Great; see Matt 2:1-23). He ruled over Judea from AD 41–44. He leveled persecution at the church and **executed** the apostle **James**, the **brother** of John (12:2). Since this made the unbelieving **Jews** happy, Herod also tossed **Peter** in jail **during the Festival of Unleavened Bread** (12:3). The wicked ruler's plan was to hold a public trial **after the Passover** and execute Peter too (12:4). In response, **the church** prayed **fervently** for **Peter** in prison (12:5).

As we'll see in the following verses, their prayers for Peter were answered. But what about James? Why wasn't he delivered? Such difficult questions still arise today. Why does one believer undergo intense suffering, while another believer does not? Though the Bible does not enable us to answer such questions, Scripture does assure us that all suffering falls under the sovereign purposes of God (see, e.g., Rom 8:28-39). We can be certain that whatever he does or allows to happen is ultimately for our good and his glory. We can trust him to do what is right.

God's purposes are not the same for each Christian. That's why we must never compare our circumstances to those of others (see John 21:21-23). Rather, we ought to ask ourselves, "Am I, to the best of my ability, following the Word of God and the leading of the Holy Spirit in determining God's will for my life?" James and Peter were both operating in the will of God, but God had different plans for how each would bring him glory on earth.

12:6-10 Clearly, Peter was securely imprisoned. He was **bound with two chains**, asleep **between two soldiers**, and behind a **door guarded** by **sentries** (12:6). He wasn't going anywhere. Yet "the church was praying fervently" (12:5). Prayer is the divinely authorized method for accessing heavenly authority for earthly intervention. And heaven certainly intervened here. **An angel of the Lord** showed up, **woke** Peter, and caused his **chains** to fall off (12:7). As he followed the angel, Peter assumed he was **seeing a vision** (12:9). Surely attaining freedom couldn't be this easy! But after they had miraculously passed the **guards** and gotten into the streets, **the angel** departed, and Peter realized that he wasn't dreaming (12:10). He was free.

12:11-14 Realizing that he had just benefited from a divine rescue mission, Peter went to the home of **the mother of John Mark** (author of the Gospel of Mark), where he knew that the believers were gathered to pray for him (12:11-12). **He knocked at the door**, and a **servant named Rhoda** answered (12:13). But she was so full of **joy** when she saw him that she left poor Peter in the cold and **ran back inside to tell** everyone that he was knocking (12:14)!

12:15 Notice the church's response. They had been "praying fervently to God" for Peter (12:5). But when God miraculously answered, they couldn't believe it and told Rhoda, **You're out of your mind!** They assumed that it was just **his** guardian **angel.**

Do you ever pray because you know you're supposed to, but you don't actually expect God to answer? Don't put God in a box. Believe that he "is able to do above and beyond all that we ask or think according to the power that works in us" (Eph 3:20).

12:16-17 Meanwhile, as the church responded with skepticism (and told Rhoda she was crazy!), **Peter . . . kept on knocking,** wishing someone would let him in! Finally, **they opened the door** and **were amazed** (12:16). Then Peter explained what had happened, urged them to **tell** everything **to James** (the brother of Jesus; see 15:13; 1 Cor 15:7; Gal 1:19) **and the brothers,** and departed (12:17). When the Lord answers your prayers, be sure to give testimony about it so that others are encouraged and God receives the glory he deserves.

12:18-19 Imagine the surprise of **the soldiers** when they found **Peter** missing in the morning (12:18)! But their consternation was nothing compared to Herod's. After his search for Peter turned up empty, he had **the guards** executed and then left town for a change of scenery at his palace in **Caesarea** (12:19). Yet, this despot would soon give an account to God for his arrogance.

12:20-23 We learn that **Herod had been very angry with the people of Tyre and Sidon,** Phoenician cities north of Caesarea on the Mediterranean Coast that he **supplied with food** (12:20). But **they asked** Herod **for peace,** so he **delivered a speech to them** (12:20-21). No doubt seeking to flatter the king, the **people** shouted, **It's the voice of a god and not of a man!** (12:22). But when Herod received this blasphemous praise and failed to **give the glory to God,** he was **struck** by **an angel** and **died** (12:23).

When King Nebuchadnezzar arrogantly claimed credit for the glory of Babylon, God made him insane and caused him to live with animals, until the king was willing to humbly praise and honor the Lord who alone deserves glory (see Dan 4:28-37). God declared through Isaiah, "I will not give my glory to another" (Isa 42:8). Pride is an ugly sin and will come under the Lord's just condemnation—perhaps in this life, but definitely in eternity. When you are tempted to think more highly of yourself than you ought, remember that you have nothing which has not been given to you by God. Humble yourself before him.

12:24-25 Contrast the downfall of Herod with the flourishing and growth of **the word of God** (12:24). This narcissistic king had attempted to stop the spread of the gospel by murdering and imprisoning the church's leaders (see 12:1-4). Instead, Herod had become worm food (12:23), the gospel continued to spread (12:24), and the church's leaders were successfully serving God and his people (12:25).

❧ C. Paul's First Missionary Journey
(13:1–14:28) ❧

13:1-3 The church at Antioch had several **prophets** (who carried on an itinerant ministry) **and teachers** (who instructed in the local churches) serving in leadership. In addition to **Barnabas** and **Saul,** there were two black leaders. Their names were **Simeon who was called Niger** (meaning "black" or "dark") and **Lucius of Cyrene** (a city in North Africa). When **the Holy Spirit** told the church to **set apart . . . Barnabas and Saul** for mission work, these two black men assisted in their ordination and commissioning (13:2-3). Clearly, then, black people were not only leaders in the culture of the New Testament era, but they were also leaders in the church itself. The church of Jesus Christ was becoming the racially mixed group that it was intended and destined to be (see Rev 7:9). Note that the Holy Spirit spoke in the context of corporate worship and fasting. The laying on of **hands** gave official recognition of the Spirit's ministry call and endorsement (13:3).

13:4-5 Barnabas and Saul went to **Seleucia** on the Mediterranean Coast, **and from there they sailed to** the island of **Cyprus** (13:4), Barnabas's home territory (see 4:36). After they arrived, they began preaching about Jesus **in the Jewish synagogues** (13:5)—something that would become their standard practice.

13:6-8 When they reached **Paphos** on the western side of the island, they encountered a man named **Bar-Jesus** (meaning "son of Jesus)," who was also known as **Elymas** (13:6, 8). He was **a sorcerer** and **Jewish false prophet**, having mixed Jewish religion with pagan practices (13:6). Elymas was hanging out with the island's intelligent **proconsul** (a governor of the province under Roman authority), **Sergius Paulus**. He was trying to keep him from listening to **the word of God** spoken by Barnabas and Saul (13:7-8).

13:9-11 Saul was a Hebrew name, and **Paul** was a Roman name (13:9). From this point forward in Acts (and in all of his letters), the man who would become known as the "apostle to the Gentiles" (Rom 11:13) is called Paul.

Filled with the Holy Spirit, Paul saw that **Elymas** was operating in sync with the **devil** (13:9-10; just as Jesus had detected in Peter; see Matt 16:23). Therefore, the apostle took action and pronounced blindness on Elymas. Since he had embraced *spiritual* blindness, he would now be *physically* **blind** (13:11).

13:12 When he saw this, **the proconsul believed.** Although Elymas had tried to prevent Sergius Paulus from becoming a Christian, God used **what happened** to Elymas to bring the proconsul to faith. There is no doubt that the Lord will fulfill all of his sovereign purposes. The question is this: Will he accomplish his will through your obedience resulting in your blessing, or in spite of your rebellion resulting in your shame? It's your choice.

13:13 From Cyprus, **Paul and his companions** sailed **to Perga** in Asia Minor (modern Turkey). **John** (that is, John Mark, author of the Gospel of Mark) had been accompanying them. But at this point he returned **to Jerusalem.** Apparently, the intense mission work had proven to be too much for him. In the future, Paul and Barnabas would go their separate ways because Barnabas wanted to give John Mark a second chance and Paul did not (see 15:36-40). Eventually, though, Paul would be reconciled to John Mark and find his ministry helpful (see 2 Tim 4:11).

13:14-15 In **Pisidian Antioch** (not to be confused with Syrian Antioch where their sending church was located; see 13:1), they entered the Jewish **synagogue** on **the Sabbath** and were invited by the **leaders** to speak.

13:16-25 Paul wasn't about to pass up an invitation to proclaim the gospel, so he started with the Old Testament and worked his way to Jesus. Along the way, he emphasized the sovereign hand of God in Israel's history. He reminded his Jewish listeners of how God made the Israelites into a prosperous nation in **Egypt** and rescued them from slavery there (13:17). He destroyed wicked **nations** in **Canaan**, gave his people the land, and appointed for them leaders—**judges** and later kings (13:18-22). From the **descendants** of King David, **God brought Israel the Savior, Jesus,** just **as he promised** David (13:23; see 2 Sam 7:11-16). Jesus is the fulfillment of God's Old Testament promises to send a Messiah.

13:26-37 Though God had **sent** Israel **salvation** through Jesus, **the residents of Jerusalem and their rulers** rejected him and handed him over to the Romans to be put to death on a cross (13:26-29). **But God raised him from the dead,** and **he appeared** to many **witnesses**—including Paul (13:30-31). The Lord had prophesied through David of the resurrection. However, **David** had not been speaking about himself rising from the dead but about his descendant, the Messiah, God's Holy One (13:34-35; see commentary on 2:24-31). David **decayed** in his tomb; Jesus **did not decay** and walked out of his (13:35-37).

13:38-41 Having explained how Jesus fulfilled the Old Testament, Paul applied his message to his Jewish listeners. **Through**

[Jesus] forgiveness of sins is being proclaimed (13:38). If a person believes in Jesus as the one who died for his sins, he **is justified through him from everything that one could not be justified from through the law of Moses** (13:39). The law was unable to set anyone free. All it could do was show people the problem of sin in their hearts. Only the gospel of Jesus Christ can justify—make us right before God.

Paul concluded by warning them not to scoff at what God was doing, like many of the Jews in Jerusalem had done (13:40-41).

13:42-45 Those who heard Paul **urged** him and his companions to come and speak again on **the following Sabbath** (13:42). You didn't have to tell Paul twice. The next week **almost the whole town** showed up at the synagogue **to hear the word of the Lord** (13:44). Paul's message had earned him quite an audience. But just as the Jewish leaders had been jealous of Jesus (see Mark 15:10), these Jews were jealous when they observed Paul drawing larger crowds than they ever had. So they contradicted Paul's message and insulted him (13:45).

13:46-47 That was the last straw for Paul. He had delivered the gospel message to the Jews **first** (13:46) because God had made a covenant with them, given them his Word, and brought the Messiah into the world through Israel. But since they considered themselves **unworthy of eternal life** by rejecting God's offer, Paul determined to take the gospel straight to the **Gentiles** (13:46). It had always been God's plan to bring his **salvation** to all people (13:47; see Isa 49:6). And here, through the apostle Paul, the Gentile mission was about to start in earnest.

13:48-52 The Gentiles were overjoyed (13:48). Even though **the Jews incited** people to persecute **Paul and Barnabas** and kick them out, **the word of the Lord spread throughout the whole region** (13:49-50). Don't miss that the gospel prevails in spite of opposition. No matter how much unbelievers seek to silence Jesus's followers, God's Word can't be stopped. So **Paul and Barnabas shook the dust off their feet**—a sign of the coming judgment against these unbelievers because of their rebellion—and departed (13:51). The new **disciples**, however, **were filled with joy**. When **the Holy Spirit** is doing his work within you, you can experience internal peace and joy regardless of your external circumstances (13:52).

14:1-7 In Iconium they once again spoke in the **synagogue**, leading to the conversion of many **Jews and Greeks** (14:1). When **unbelieving Jews** opposed them, Paul and his companions **spoke boldly for the Lord** and were enabled to perform **signs and wonders** (14:2-3). God, then, backed up their preaching with supernatural authority to verify the truth of their message. As a result, **the city** was **divided**, some backing **the Jews** and some backing **the apostles** (14:4). When the believers learned of a plot to **stone them**, they **fled** to nearby **towns** and preached **the gospel** there (14:5-7).

Knowing when to stay in spite of persecution (see 14:2-3) and when to leave to escape it requires wisdom. There's no one-size-fits-all answer. We need to follow the Spirit's leading.

14:8-10 In Lystra, as Paul was preaching, there was a man listening who **had been lame from birth**, and Paul saw **that he had faith to be healed** (14:8-9). It's one thing to believe God is able to do amazing works; it's another to believe that he is willing to do them in and through you. Aware of the man's faith, **Paul** called him to his **feet**, and the man stood and walked for the first time in his life (14:10). As you follow Jesus in discipleship, believe the truth that "with God all things are possible" (Matt 19:26)—even and especially in your own life.

14:11-13 When the inhabitants of the city saw this supernatural display, they thought the Greek **gods** had **come down . . . in human form** (14:11). They assumed **Barnabas** was **Zeus** (the king of the gods) and **Paul** was **Hermes** (the messenger of the gods), **because he was the chief speaker** (14:12). They intended **to offer sacrifice** to them (14:13) because their superstitious, pagan worldview left them with no alternative way to interpret and respond to this miracle.

14:14-18 Unlike Herod, who foolishly embraced being treated like a god (and paid the price for it; see 12:20-23), Paul and Barnabas were horrified at being mistaken for gods. They **tore their robes** in grief and shouted, **We are people also, just like you** (14:14-15). While the crowd wanted to glorify these two men, Paul and Barnabas deflected the glory to God. They told them to **turn from these worthless things** (their polytheistic worship) and turn to **the living God** who created all things (14:15). As David explains in Psalm 19:1, God testifies to his own existence through the world he made: "The heavens declare the glory of God." **He did not leave himself without a witness** (14:17). Nevertheless, **they barely** talked the people out of offering sacrifices to them (14:18).

14:19-20 Notice the fickleness of sinful human hearts. When **Jews** from the previous cities followed Paul and Barnabas **to Iconium**, they turned this crowd against them until **they stoned Paul and dragged him out of the city** (14:19). Human devotion can quickly turn to animosity when it's not tethered to truth. The crowds that hailed Jesus as the Messiah (see Matt 21:8-11) were shouting for his crucifixion a few days later (see Matt 27:20-23).

Though Paul was presumed **dead**, he got up, moved on to the next town (**Derbe**), and preached the gospel again (14:19-20). There was no stopping him. Paul had been a vile persecutor of the church, but when the Lord shook him to his senses and poured out his mercy on him, there wasn't anything he wouldn't endure for the sake of the gospel. What about you?

14:21-22 After making **many disciples** in Derbe, Paul and Barnabas retraced their steps, passing back through the towns they had visited, **strengthening the disciples by encouraging them to continue in the faith.** God doesn't merely want to punch our tickets to heaven; he wants us to "continue in the faith," following his kingdom agenda while we're on earth. Walking as a kingdom disciple of Jesus, however, is challenging because **it is necessary to go through many hardships to enter the kingdom of God** (14:22).

Although not all believers will experience the same kinds of problems or the same level of persecution, "all who want to live a godly life in Christ Jesus will be persecuted" (2 Tim 3:12). So we need the encouragement of a community of disciples to help us "continue in the faith" and spiritually grow as kingdom disciples.

14:23-28 Paul and Barnabas **appointed elders for them in every church** they founded. Jesus's church polity calls for a plurality of elders (governing body of male spiritual leaders; see 1 Tim 3:1) in each local church. Then they **prayed**, fasted, and **committed** these new believers **to the Lord** (14:23). Eventually, they made their way back to where they had started, the church in **Antioch** (14:24-26). There they reported to all the believers how God **had opened the door of faith to the Gentiles** (14:27). Just as God had promised, he was bringing his blessing to all peoples of the earth through the offspring of Abraham, Jesus Christ (see Gen 12:3; Gal 3:16). Paul had completed his first missionary journey proclaiming this truth; it wouldn't be his last.

⤞ D. The Jerusalem Council
(15:1-35) ⤝

15:1-3 **Some men came down** to Antioch **from Judea** and were teaching that **unless** men were **circumcised according** to the law of **Moses**, they couldn't **be saved** (15:1). Thus, they were making this requirement a part of the gospel. To be saved, they argued, one had to believe in Jesus *and* be circumcised. **After Paul and Barnabas had engaged** these men **in serious argument and debate**, the church sent them to meet with the church leaders **in Jerusalem** (15:2). This controversy would be the basis of Paul writing his letter to the Galatians.

In this fallen world, the church won't be free of controversy. When theological controversies arise, godly church leaders need to come together in submission to Scripture and openness to the Holy Spirit's direction. Many times throughout history, church councils have assembled to address difficult theological issues. The first of these met in Jerusalem.

15:4-5 The church in Jerusalem welcomed Paul and Barnabas and listened as **they reported all that God had done with them** on their mission work to the Gentiles (15:4). But members of **the party of the Pharisees** insisted that the Gentiles would have to be circumcised and **keep the law of Moses** (15:5), thus placing a burden on the Gentiles that God had not placed on them. We are not saved by trusting in Christ *and* keeping the law. The message of the gospel calls people to believe in Christ and his substitutionary atonement alone to be saved.

15:6-11 The apostles and the elders debated the matter extensively. Then **Peter stood up** to remind them of what God had done through him (15:6-7; see 10:1-48). God had chosen Peter to preach the gospel to a group of Gentiles—all of whom believed and received **the Holy Spirit** without being circumcised or keeping the law (15:7-8). God **made no distinction between us** (the Jews) **and them** (the Gentiles), Peter said (15:9). Ethnic distinctions should not matter within the body of Christ (see Gal 3:28; Eph 2:11-22). If God had not made an additional requirement of the Gentiles, **why** were these men **testing God by putting a yoke on** their **necks** that the Jewish **ancestors** themselves couldn't **bear**? (15:10). The Jews had been unable to keep the law, so what made them think the Gentiles could? "The law," Paul writes, "was our guardian until Christ, so that we could be justified by faith" (Gal 3:24). With this, Peter agreed: **We believe that we are saved through the grace of the Lord Jesus in the same way that [Gentiles] are** (15:11). We are saved by grace through faith in Christ—not through law-keeping.

15:12-18 Next **Barnabas and Paul** described their missionary journey and how God had performed **signs and wonders ... through them among the Gentiles** (15:12). Then **James** stood up to speak (15:13). This James was the half brother of the Lord Jesus. He became a believer after the resurrection, rose to leadership in the Jerusalem church, and wrote the New Testament letter that bears

his name (see Matt 13:55; Acts 12:17; 21:18; 1 Cor 15:7; Gal 1:19; Jas 1:1).

James reminded them that God had **intervened** to save the **Gentiles** through **Simeon** (Peter), just as the prophets had promised long before (15:14-18). He quoted from Amos 9:11-12 to show that Scripture testified to God's comprehensive plan of redemption for all people. James sets a good example for us all. Many of our questions would be answered if we would look to the Bible more than we look to human opinions.

15:19-21 James's **judgment** was that the church **should not cause difficulties** for **the Gentiles** who were turning to God by requiring them to keep the law. Instead, he advised that they write a letter to send to the Gentile churches, urging them **to abstain from things polluted by idols ... from eating anything that has been strangled, and from blood** (15:20). These were all things forbidden to Jews in the law of Moses and were also linked to Gentile idolatry (see 1 Cor 10:19-20). Abstaining from these actions would not save the Gentile Christians or cause them to break fellowship with God (see 1 Cor 10:28-32), but it would prevent them from unnecessarily offending Jewish Christians and would facilitate fellowship with them. The directive to abstain **from sexual immorality** (15:20) is a natural outworking of the gospel. Many Gentiles would have had low standards regarding sexual purity, so James knew they needed exhortation on this matter.

15:22-35 The apostles and the elders agreed with James's proposal, so they wrote a letter along the lines outlined by James (15:23-29) and sent it **to Antioch** by means of **Paul and Barnabas**, accompanied by representatives from the Jerusalem church: **Judas and Silas** (15:22). When they **delivered the letter** to the believers in Antioch, they responded with great rejoicing and **encouragement** (15:30-31). **Judas and Silas** taught and **strengthened** the Christians there and then returned to Jerusalem **in peace** (15:32-33).

What had started as controversy ended in unity, edification, and joy. This is what happens when godly leaders address problems in obedience to God's Word, recognizing how

God's Spirit has been at work, and encouraging God's people to seek one another's well-being.

➣ E. Paul's Second Missionary Journey
(15:36–18:21) ᴄ

15:36-38 After some time passed, Paul suggested to **Barnabas** that they **visit** all of the churches they had started to see how they were getting along (15:36). **Barnabas wanted to take along John Mark . . . but Paul** disagreed since he **had deserted them** on their previous missionary journey (15:37-38; see 13:13). The work had apparently been too much for John Mark, and he had thrown in the towel. Ministry is hard business because it necessarily involves people and their problems. For the missionary serving in a foreign culture and away from family and friends, the difficulties are compounded.

15:39-41 Paul wanted a reliable and effective missionary team, and he didn't have confidence that John Mark wouldn't bail out on them again. So he and Barnabas had **such a sharp disagreement** over this issue that they decided to go their separate ways. **Barnabas took Mark** and left for **Cyprus** (15:39). **But Paul chose** a Christian brother named **Silas** and went **through Syria and Cilicia** (15:40-41).

Notice how God used the conflict that arose between these two godly leaders. Paul rightly concluded that John Mark had failed, so he didn't want to take the risk that he might quit again. But Barnabas, the "Son of Encouragement" (see 4:36), saw potential in Mark and wanted to give him another chance. Both men had a point and neither was wrong, yet they couldn't convince one another. Therefore, they split into two missionary teams. God took their disagreement, then, and used it to expand their gospel reach. In spite of their dispute, more ground would be covered and more lives transformed for Christ. Though Paul and Barnabas would part ways, in God's providence their gospel impact would be doubled. God knows how to take a mess and make a miracle.

16:1 While ministering in **Lystra**, Paul met a believer **named Timothy.** His mother was a **Jewish** Christian, and **his father was a Greek**. Thus, Timothy was the son of what might be called an interracial marriage. We learn elsewhere that his mother and grandmother had a significant influence on him, teaching him the Scriptures from childhood (see 2 Tim 1:5; 3:14-15). Paul would come to call Timothy his "true son in the faith" (1 Tim 1:2) and his "dearly loved son" (2 Tim 1:2); therefore, it's likely that Timothy had been converted during Paul's first visit to Lystra (see Acts 14:8-20; also 1 Cor 4:17). The men would serve together for years, and Paul would frequently mention Timothy in his correspondence to churches (see Rom 16:21; 1 Cor 4:17; 16:10; 2 Cor 1:19; Phil 2:19-22; 1 Thess 3:2, 6). In time, Paul would assign Timothy to lead the church in Ephesus under difficult circumstances because of his trust in and respect for him (see 1 Tim 1:3-4; 4:11-16).

16:2-3 As Paul got to know Timothy and saw how everyone **spoke highly of him**, he wanted to take him along on his missionary team. So Paul **circumcised him because of the Jews** (16:3). Now wait a minute. We just read the outcome of the Jerusalem Council (see 15:1-35). They (including Paul) concluded that Gentiles did not need to be circumcised and keep the law of Moses in order to be saved. So why would Paul have Timothy circumcised?

Paul didn't do this so that Timothy could be saved but so that he could effectively minister among the Jews. He didn't want Timothy to be a stumbling block to them. Having an uncircumcised man as part of his team would have distracted Jews from the gospel; therefore, Paul was willing to be flexible on non-essential issues for the sake of his gospel ministry: "I have become all things to all people, so that I may by every possible means save some" (1 Cor 9:22; see 9:19-23). Paul didn't want to hinder the message of Christ. Do you put any roadblocks in front of unbelievers that prevent them from coming to Jesus? Adopt Paul's attitude and flexibility (apart from sin).

16:4-5 As they went from town to town, Paul faithfully **delivered the decisions reached by** the leaders in **Jerusalem** (16:4;

see 15:23-29), and the churches were edified and **grew** larger, both numerically and spiritually (16:5).

16:6-7 A strange thing happened after they had traveled through **Phrygia and Galatia. The Holy Spirit** forbade them **to speak the word in Asia** (16:6). When **they tried to go to Bithynia . . . the Spirit of Jesus did not allow them** (16:7). (Notice an implicit affirmation of the Trinity here: the Holy Spirit is also "the Spirit of Jesus.") Why wouldn't God want them to proclaim the gospel in these places? Because he had other plans for them.

We ought to seek to be open to the Holy Spirit's leadership in our lives. One of the primary ways the Holy Spirit guides believers is by his ministry of illumination, enabling us to understand and apply biblical truth in our lives. The more Scripture we know, the more material the Spirit has to work with in our hearts and minds. The Spirit also provides guidance by stirring up inner convictions about decisions we need to make. He will never lead us to do anything contrary to Scripture. But within the framework of God's moral will, he can place within us a burden that doesn't go away. If this happens, slow down, get quiet with God, and ask him to help you understand how he's trying to guide you. One primary way the Holy Spirit provides guidance is through the confirmation of two or three witnesses (see Deut 19:15; 2 Cor 13:1). Notice Paul was twice forbidden to more forward.

16:8-10 As they spent **the night** in the port city of **Troas** (in modern Turkey), **Paul had a vision of a Macedonian man . . . pleading with him** to come **to Macedonia** (across the Aegean Sea) to **help** (16:8-9). After the Holy Spirit had communicated where they were *not* to go, then, God gave Paul a clear vision that directed them to their destination. They knew that **God** wanted them **to preach the gospel** there, so they **immediately** sailed **for Macedonia** (16:10). The gospel moved westward, connecting Asia and Europe.

Notice that this is the first instance in which the author of the book—Luke—uses the pronoun **we.** Thus, Luke had obviously joined Paul in his mission work at this point

(see the authorship discussion in the Introduction).

16:11-15 They sailed **from Troas** and eventually arrived in **Philippi, a Roman colony and a leading city of the district of Macedonia** (16:11-12). The church in Philippi would be the first one Paul would start in Europe, and he would pen his letter to the Philippians about a decade or so later.

On the Sabbath, Paul and his companions **went outside the city . . . to find a place of prayer** (16:13). They met a God-fearer (a Gentile believer in the God of Israel who had not become a proselyte—that is, a convert to Judaism) **named Lydia.** She was **a dealer in purple cloth** and, thus, a businesswoman of some means. As she listened to Paul talk about Jesus, **the Lord opened her heart** and she believed, along with **her** whole **household** (16:14-15). They were all **baptized,** and then she invited Paul and the other disciples to **stay at [her] house** (16:15). Clearly her business had produced some wealth if she had a home large enough to house all of the missionaries in Paul's group.

16:16-18 Then they encountered another woman—**a slave girl** inhabited by **a spirit** that enabled her to tell fortunes and make large sums of money **for her owners** (16:16). For days she **followed Paul** around the city, telling everyone that **these men** were **servants of the Most High God** who were **proclaiming . . . the way of salvation** (16:17-18). But Paul was **greatly annoyed**; he didn't want a demonic, fortune-telling spirit shouting about his work and marketing the gospel in such a manner. So he commanded the spirit **to come out of her** (16:18).

16:19-24 The poor slave girl was set free, but **her owners** were not happy when they **realized that their hope of profit was gone.** So they **dragged** Paul before **the chief magistrates** and accused him and the others of creating a disturbance and advocating **customs** that were illegal for **Romans** (16:19-21). Notice that they were unconcerned with their religious message. Instead, they were trying to pit the disciples against Rome. Without giving them a trial, the **chief magistrates** had them **stripped** and **beaten with rods**

(16:22). Then they **threw them** in prison and put **their feet in . . . stocks** (16:23-24). Paul would later write that they "were treated outrageously in Philippi" (1 Thess 2:2). Little did the Philippian magistrates realize that they were in for a shock.

16:25 How would you have responded if you were treated this way? **About midnight Paul and Silas were praying and singing hymns to God.** So, at their dark moment (physically and figuratively), Paul and Silas weren't weeping or complaining or feeling sorry for themselves. In the middle of their pain and difficulty, they were praising! Their external circumstances did not dictate their internal disposition. Moreover, the other **prisoners were listening to them.** Such peace and hope coming from the mouths of those with bloody backs in a jail cell wasn't natural! Paul and Silas were demonstrating to those around them that King Jesus wasn't just ruling their message; he was also ruling their lives. As you encounter troubling times, pray for God to help you bring him glory as you praise him in the midst of your pain. The world is watching.

16:26-27 At that moment, there was **a violent earthquake** that rocked **the jail**, opened **the doors**, and loosed their **chains** (16:26). **When the jailer** saw what had happened, he prepared to fall on **his sword** because he thought they **had escaped** (16:27). If prisoners escaped in that era, the one guarding them was subject to capital punishment. Remember the fate of the soldiers who had been guarding Peter when Herod locked him up (see 12:6-10, 18-19).

16:28-34 Paul immediately urged him not to **harm** himself, saying, **We're all here!** (16:28). And in that instant, Paul's prison time turned into an evangelistic opportunity because the man on the verge of suicide was looking for salvation. **The jailer . . . fell down trembling** before them and said, **Sirs, what must I do to be saved?** (16:29-30). Paul and Silas didn't waste time: **Believe in the Lord Jesus, and you will be saved—you and your household** (16:31). Typically, when the leader of the household believed, the family would follow.

That's what happened here, as the jailer and his whole **family** became disciples of Jesus Christ and **were baptized** (16:33).

Afterwards, the jailer, his heart transformed, **washed** Paul and Silas's **wounds** and served them **a meal** in **his house** (16:33-34). A hardnosed man had been changed by the love of God and **rejoiced** over the salvation of his family (16:34).

16:35-37 The next morning, **the chief magistrates** gave orders for Paul and Silas to be **released** (16:35-36). But Paul would have none of it. These city officials had beaten **Roman citizens** publicly **without a trial**, put them **in jail**, and were now trying to **secretly** get rid of them. The believers hadn't broken Roman law; government leaders had. So, since they had been unjustly and publicly humiliated, Paul insisted that things be publicly made right. They demanded that the magistrates **come** and **escort** them **out** of the jail to demonstrate their innocence (16:37). Having just established a new church in Philippi, Paul didn't want the citizens to think that its founders were disreputable men. This illustrates the legitimacy of righteous social protest; Paul essentially conducted a sit-in against injustice.

16:38-40 When **the magistrates** learned that **Paul and Silas were Roman citizens**, they **were afraid** (16:38). They went from being arrogant authorities to humble beggars, **escorting them from prison** and urging **them to leave town** (16:39). With the disciples vindicated and the reputation of Christianity cleared, they **encouraged the brothers and sisters** further and then **departed** (16:40).

17:1-4 The next missionary stop was **Thessalonica**, the capital of Macedonia. The city had **a Jewish synagogue** (17:1), so Paul began there, according to his custom. Since the Jews believed in the Old Testament, he could start there and show them how Jesus fulfilled the Scriptures. He went to the synagogue on the **Sabbath** and **reasoned with them from the Scriptures** that Jesus was **the Messiah** and that he had **to suffer and rise from the dead** (17:2-3). As a result, **some** Jews and **a large number of God-fearing Greeks** believed (17:4).

17:5-9 But the Jews didn't like this. Out of jealousy, they gathered **some wicked men, started a riot**, and **dragged** a man named **Jason and some** other Christian **brothers before the city officials** (17:5-6). **Jason** had **welcomed** Paul and the others into his home, so the Jews were holding him responsible. Like the antagonists in Philippi (see 16:19-21), they tried to make the Christians political opponents of Rome by claiming that they were **acting contrary to Caesar's decrees** and following **another king—Jesus—**who was proclaiming another kingdom (17:7). They wanted to discredit Christianity by politicizing it. So they made **Jason** post a **security bond** (17:9), probably agreeing to send Paul and Silas away.

Similar attempts to discredit the Christian faith happen today—not on religious grounds but for political expediency. Traditional Christianity is deemed unacceptable because its adherents' moral views prevent them from affirming, for example, abortion and homosexual marriage. Thus, followers of Christ can find themselves running afoul of the law for standing true to their Christian convictions. Here we must follow the apostle Peter's counsel by regarding Christ as holy and giving a defense for our faith "with gentleness and respect" (1 Pet 3:15-16). "For it is better to suffer for doing good, if that should be God's will, than for doing evil" (1 Pet 3:17).

17:10-11 This time, Paul and Silas went to the city of **Berea** and, again, began preaching in **the synagogue of the Jews** (17:10). After their difficult experience in Thessalonica, Berea surely seemed like a breath of fresh air. The Bereans **were of more noble character**; they were willing to hear the disciples out and evaluate their message objectively. **They received the word with eagerness and examined the Scripture daily to see if these things were so** (17:11).

How a person receives the Word of God will determine the effect that the Word has on him. God will not hide the truth from the one who honestly seeks it (see Jer 29:12-13). All believers, then, should seek to be like the Bereans, welcoming God's Word with anticipation and regularly mining it for God's truth in order to be transformed by it through obedience.

17:12-15 As a result of this attitude toward Scripture, many were saved, including **prominent** men and women (17:12). But the opponents from **Thessalonica** couldn't leave well enough alone. They came and stirred up the Berean crowds against them so that the Christians there had to send Paul away. While **Silas and Timothy stayed** behind for a while, Paul journeyed on to **Athens** (17:13-15), always ready to proclaim the truth of Christ in places where he had never been named.

17:16-18 In Athens (located in modern Greece), **Paul** became **deeply distressed** because of the **idols** filling **the city** (17:16). So whether in the Jewish **synagogue** or in the city **marketplace**, the apostle **reasoned** with anyone **who happened to be there** (17:17). He considered no location off limits for sharing **the good news about Jesus and the resurrection**. So **Epicurean and Stoic philosophers** decided to debate with him, thinking he was an **ignorant show-off** (17:18).

Epicureanism and Stoicism were two popular schools of philosophical thought. The former was founded by Epicurus, who did not believe in the afterlife and emphasized the pursuit of pleasure and freedom from pain. Founded by Zeno, Stoicism was pantheistic and emphasized the pursuit of virtue.

17:19-21 They led Paul **to the Areopagus**, meaning "Mars Hill," a place where philosophical and religious beliefs were debated and discussed, and they asked him to explain his **strange** teaching to a wider audience (17:19-20). Those who came loved to spend **time on nothing else but telling or hearing something new**.

Some things never change. There will always be people who love to debate theology and spirituality but who are never willing to commit. They like to know about new religious and philosophical ideas. But God wants us to know *him* (see John 17:3).

17:22-23 Paul began by observing how **extremely religious** they were (today, he might say, "spiritual") based on their **objects** of **worship**. They even had an **altar** honoring **an Unknown God**, just to make sure they had all of their bases covered! So Paul took this as an open-door opportunity. That which was unknown to them, Paul would be happy to explain (17:23).

17:24-29 Paul proclaimed God as the Creator of all things in **heaven and earth** (17:24). He is the source, ruler, and sustainer of life. He neither dwells in temples nor depends on humans to serve him because he is transcendent—above, beyond, and independent of the physical universe that he made. God needs nothing (17:25). **From one man** (Adam), he created all people **so that they might seek God** (17:26-27).

This affirms that the human race exists because of a personal Creator, not some random, impersonal evolutionary process. It also affirms the historicity of Adam and the essential unity and dignity of the human race, leaving no basis for racial superiority.

Paul said, **In him we live and move and have our being** (17:28). Thus, God is not only transcendent, he is immanent—he is present within and interacts with the world he has made. He exists outside of time and space yet is closer to you than your own breath. Since God is the sum total of all of life, it is in getting to know him intimately that you truly come to know who you are and what you were created to be.

Paul even quoted one of their **poets** to make his point that God is our Creator (17:28). Given this role, we shouldn't represent **the divine nature** using **gold or silver or stone** (17:29). Idols are any nouns (person, place, thing, or thought) that you look to as your source. They misrepresent and diminish the glory of the living and true God.

17:30-31 Such idolatry must be put aside because **God now commands all people everywhere to repent**—to turn from sin (in this case, the particular sin of idolatry) and turn toward God (17:30). Why? Because judgment day is coming, the day when God will **judge the world . . . by the man he has appointed.** Who is he? God has confirmed his identity **by raising him from the dead** (17:31). Having begun with the truth of God's nature and work, Paul made a beeline to Jesus Christ.

When evangelizing Jews, Paul sought to show them from Scripture that Jesus is the Messiah. When evangelizing Gentiles who didn't know the Bible, Paul started with their general interest in religion, moved to the living and true God who created the world, explained human sin and accountability before God, and then made his way to Christ. His approach serves as a good model for our own evangelism efforts. We must tailor our methods to meet our listeners where they are and take them to what they need—the gospel, the free gift of eternal life through faith alone in Christ alone.

17:32-34 Paul received varied responses to his preaching: some **believed**, some mocked him with **ridicule**, and some wanted **to hear more** (17:32, 34). As we share the gospel, then, we can expect the same kinds of reactions. Whenever and wherever you have opportunity, be faithful to make Jesus known and invite people to place their faith in him for the gift of eternal life. Then leave the rest in God's hands as the Holy Spirit works in their hearts.

18:1-4 From **Athens**, Paul traveled **to Corinth** in the Roman province of Achaia in the southern region of ancient Greece (18:1). Corinth was a significant city located along important trade routes with close access to port cities. It also had multiple pagan temples and was known for its immorality. Paul obviously saw the city as strategic for his ministry since he remained there for "a year and a half" (18:11).

In Corinth Paul met **Aquila** and **Priscilla**, Jews **who had recently come from Italy.** The Roman emperor **Claudius had ordered all the Jews to leave Rome** in AD 49 (18:2). According to Roman historical sources, the expulsion was because of riots over someone named "Chrestus," probably a garbled reference to "Christos," the Greek rendering of "Christ." Either Aquila and Priscilla were Christians when they left Rome, or they became believers through Paul's ministry. Regardless, they shared his **trade** as **tentmakers, worked** together (18:3), and eventually became ministry partners (see 18:19, 26; 1 Cor 16:19; 2 Tim 4:19). Thus, Paul made tents to pay the bills so that he could engage in his primary work: trying **to persuade both Jews and Greeks** to believe in and follow Christ (18:4).

18:5-6 When Silas and Timothy arrived from Macedonia (Paul had left them in Berea; see 17:14-15), Paul was able to devote himself full time **to preaching the word** and convincing **Jews that Jesus is the Messiah** (18:5). Yet, finally, after he encountered much resistance, **he shook out his clothes.** This was a symbolic gesture like brushing the dust from his garment (cf. 13:51). By it Paul was communicating that he was **innocent** of responsibility for the judgment they would incur for scorning God's Messiah. **From now on** he would focus on **the Gentiles** (18:6).

18:7-11 So Paul stayed in the home of a Gentile convert **named Titius Justus**, who lived **next door to the synagogue** (18:7). In addition, **the leader of the synagogue** became a believer, followed by many others (18:8). So though the Jews as a whole had rejected Paul's message, the Lord saw to it that Paul's base of operations moved right next to their gathering place. Not only did God deal with Paul's external problems, but he also addressed his internal struggles. In a night vision, he told Paul, **Don't be afraid, but keep on speaking**, and he promised to be **with** him (18:9-10). Fortified by God's encouragement, Paul ministered in Corinth for **a year and a half** (18:11).

Modern-day believers sometimes think of Paul as a missionary superman, but he was as human as the rest of us. Yes, he faithfully served God. But, if the Lord had to tell him not to be fearful, apparently Paul struggled with fear. When you similarly find your emotions getting the better of you, heed God's Word and go to him in prayer, accessing his heavenly resources for your earthly circumstances so that "the peace of God, which surpasses all understanding, [can] guard your hearts and minds in Christ Jesus" (Phil 4:6-7).

18:12-13 The Jews made a concerted effort to **attack** Paul when **Gallio was proconsul in Achaia** (the Roman province in which Corinth was located). Archeological evidence verifies that Gallio became proconsul in AD 51. As a result of this Jewish assault, Paul was taken before **the tribunal** to face charges of **persuading people to worship God in ways contrary to the law.**

"Tribunal" translates the Greek word *bēma*. It refers to the seat on which an authority figure sat to render judicial judgments (see, e.g., Matt 27:19; John 19:13). Archeological excavations have unearthed the Corinthian *bēma* in the marketplace; this is probably the site at which Paul's encounter with Gallio took place. Regardless, Paul would later tell the Corinthians that all believers will "appear before the judgment seat [*bēma*] of Christ," so that he may judge our work on earth to determine our rewards (see 2 Cor 5:10).

18:14-17 As before, there was an attempt to put Christianity at odds with secular authorities (see commentary on 16:19-24; 17:5-9). But if the unbelieving Jews thought they were going to receive a sympathetic hearing from Gallio, they were sadly mistaken. Had they brought Paul to the proconsul on charges **of wrongdoing or of a serious crime**, he would have taken their concerns seriously (18:14). But since they were simply riled up about their **own** religious **law**, he wanted nothing to do with it and **drove** them away (18:15-16). In other words, Gallio said, "This man has committed no crime against Rome. So quit pestering me with your religious squabbles!" Then the **leader of the synagogue** received a beating for good measure (18:17). And once again Paul was vindicated and freed.

18:18-21 Eventually, Paul set sail for **Syria, accompanied by Priscilla and Aquila**, so that he might return to his home church in Antioch. In **Cenchreae** (a port city near Corinth) Paul **shaved his head . . . because of a vow**, which is probably a reference to a Nazirite vow (see Num 6:1-21). In **Ephesus**, he **debated with the Jews** for a time. Then he left Priscilla and Aquila there, told the believers he would return **if God wills**, and departed (18:19-21).

Notice Paul's phrase, "if God wills." It was no mere pious sentiment but Paul's humble acknowledgment that his life and plans were in God's hands. Similarly, James warns his readers not to boast arrogantly about their intentions, schedules, and efforts. Instead, he urges them to say, "If the Lord wills, we will live and do this or that" (see Jas 4:13-17). It wasn't to be merely a religious saying

Christians were to quote, but a heart philosophy they were to adopt. The same is true of us. It's okay to make plans; in fact, we ought to make wise plans (see Prov 16:9; 19:21). But we must allow for divine flexibility, welcoming God to disturb our plans when he has other purposes for us.

☞ F. Paul's Third Missionary Journey
(18:22–20:38) ☜

18:22-23 When Paul landed at the port city of **Caesarea**, he traveled **to Jerusalem** to greet **the church**, and finally returned **to Antioch**—thus completing his second missionary journey (18:22). Yet, Paul was not the kind to stay at home when churches needed strengthening and the lost needed the gospel. So, after **some time**, he began his third missionary journey, **traveling through** . . . **Galatia and Phrygia** in Asia Minor (18:23).

18:24-26 Before picking up again with Paul in chapter 19, Luke tells us about **a Jew named Apollos** who came to **Ephesus** (where Paul had left Priscilla and Aquila; see 18:18-19). He was both **an eloquent** speaker and very **competent in the use of the Scriptures** (18:24). He **had been instructed** well **about Jesus** but was only familiar with **John's baptism**—that is, he had not yet heard about the coming of and baptism of the Holy Spirit (18:25).

When **Priscilla and Aquila heard him** speak, **they took him aside** and filled in the blanks for him, explaining **the way of God** . . . **more accurately** (18:26). Thus, men and women in the body of Christ can discuss and explain Scripture to one other. This is distinct from the restriction on women serving in the office of elder / pastor (see commentary on 1 Tim 2:11-12). Notice also that they didn't embarrass Apollos by correcting him publicly; they addressed him privately.

18:27-28 As a result of Priscilla and Aquila's teamwork, Apollos was better equipped. So the church sent him to Corinth in **Achaia** (see 19:1) where he helped believers and **refuted the Jews** . . . **demonstrating through the Scriptures that Jesus is the Messiah.**

Believers today should likewise seek to be equipped to explain the Scriptures. How sad it is to see Christians who are unable to use their Bibles to explain the gospel to an unbeliever! All of us who claim the name of Christ should have a growing knowledge of God's Word and an ability to defend what we say we believe (see 1 Pet 3:15).

19:1-7 As **Paul traveled through the interior regions** of Asia Minor (see 18:23), he eventually **came to Ephesus**. There **he found some disciples** who had not yet received **the Holy Spirit** (19:1-2). Paul had expected all Christians to receive the Spirit (notice he said, **when you believed**). But, we must remember that the books of Acts chronicles a unique transition stage after the death and resurrection of Jesus (see commentary on 8:14-17). As different groups came to believe the gospel, their reception of the Spirit came later when an apostle was present: this showed the unity of their faith.

This particular group was comprised of those who had only received the **baptism** of **John** (the Baptist) (19:3-4). So Paul provided a full explanation of **Jesus**, the one to whom John had pointed, and he **baptized** them **into** Jesus's **name** (19:4-5). Then when he **laid his hands on them**, they received **the Holy Spirit, began to speak in other tongues** (i.e., languages) **and to prophesy** (19:6)—just as had happened to the apostles on the day of Pentecost (see commentary on 2:5-11). Thus, another band of disciples was brought fully into the new covenant age.

19:8 While in Ephesus, Paul spent **three months** in **the synagogue** trying to persuade them concerning **the kingdom of God**. The kingdom was the constant focus of Jesus's teaching, from the start of his ministry (Mark 1:14-15) to after his resurrection (Acts 1:3). Therefore, we shouldn't be surprised that it was the focus of Paul's preaching through the book of Acts (see 28:30-31). The goal of redemption is that believers in Jesus Christ would live their entire lives under God's sovereign rule as kingdom disciples.

19:9-10 As happened in the past, some unbelieving Jews **became hardened** and slandered **the Way.** "The Way" was an early title for Christianity (see, e.g., 9:2, 19:23; 24:14, 22). Believers in Christ were to follow a new way of life because Jesus is "the way" (see John 14:6; Rom 6:1-7). So Paul moved his teaching and **discussions** from the synagogue to **the lecture hall of Tyrannus** (19:9). How effective was that? He taught there **every day** (19:9) for a period of **two years, so that all the residents of Asia, both Jews and Greeks, heard the word of the Lord** (19:9-10). Paul was incredible!

Notice that the opposition to the gospel drove Paul to a different setting that resulted in more ministry fruit than the original location. God knows how to take the actions of wicked men and use them to accomplish his good purposes.

19:11-12 The **miracles** that the Holy Spirit had enabled Paul to perform were indeed **extraordinary** (19:11). He healed **the sick** and cast out **evil spirits**. People even took the **aprons** he used in his tent-making trade to heal others of **diseases** (19:12). Paul was so devoted to the Lord that after a hard day's work, he had sanctified sweat!

19:13-17 Some **itinerant Jewish exorcists** had seen the amazing power Paul displayed, and they wanted in on it. They decided to imitate him, using Jesus's **name** like a magical formula to wield power against **evil spirits** (19:13). They didn't believe Jesus was the Messiah, but they didn't mind using his name for their benefit. But understand this: Jesus won't be used for our selfish ends. **Seven sons** of **a Jewish high priest** tried this approach (19:14). However, after they pronounced the name of Jesus over a demon-possessed man, **the evil spirit** answered, **I know Jesus, and I recognize Paul—but who are you?** (19:15). Then, as these exorcists were probably staring wide-eyed at each other, **the man** with the **evil spirit** attacked them (which was not the response they were anticipating!) until they fled **naked and wounded** (19:16). When news of this spread, people held **the name of the Lord Jesus . . . in high esteem** (19:17). God was using even fools to magnify his Son.

19:18-20 Many of those who **practiced magic** like these men became **believers**, confessed their sins, and **burned** their sorcery **books** (19:18-19). They no longer wanted to be associated with false and deceptive spirituality. Such idolatrous practices were good for nothing. When they rid their lives of these things, **the word** of God **flourished and prevailed** even more (19:20).

Christian, are you dabbling with horoscopes? Tarot cards? Palm reading? God doesn't work through superstitious practices. The only way for the power of God to be present in your life is for you to leave them behind. "Little children, guard yourselves from idols" (1 John 5:21).

19:21-23 Paul had determined **to pass through Macedonia and Achaia** again (the territory he covered during his second missionary journey; see 16:9–18:22) and then **go to Jerusalem**. After that, his goal was to visit and proclaim the gospel in **Rome**, the capital of the Roman Empire (19:21). But before he departed, **a major disturbance** occurred **about the Way** (19:23; on "the Way," see above on 19:9-10). Wherever Paul preached, two things would regularly happen: people got saved, and people got mad. That pattern was about to repeat itself.

19:24-27 Demetrius, a silversmith who made silver shrines of Artemis, and his fellow **craftsmen** were annoyed. Artemis was a Greek goddess (known among the Romans as "Diana"), and Ephesus was home to the great temple of Artemis—one of the Seven Wonders of the Ancient World. It was the major Ephesian tourist attraction; people from all over Asia visited it to worship. But a problem arose, an economic one. As a result of Paul preaching that **gods made by hand are not gods**, many people had stopped buying the idolatrous trinkets produced by Demetrius and his comrades (19:25-26). People were coming to Christ and tossing their Artemis statues in the trash. Thus, these craftsmen were watching their religion suffer and their **business** flat line—and they weren't happy (19:27).

19:28-34 Demetrius worked the crowd into a frenzy so that they began shouting, **Great is Artemis of the Ephesians!** (19:28). This created much **confusion** in **the city.** People wanted to know what was going on. So they started streaming into **the amphitheater**, which seated approximately 24,000, and dragged **along** two of **Paul's traveling companions** (19:29). When Paul wanted to **go in** with them, other believers restrained him (19:30-31). The townspeople had lost it! The atmosphere was no longer safe. Confused **shouting** continued, and many people didn't even **know why they** were there (19:32). They were just going with the flow. When a Jewish believer named **Alexander** attempted to talk, they simply shouted him down (19:33). They didn't want to hear about this Jewish Messiah who was a rival to their goddess. Instead, they shouted about Artemis's greatness for **two hours** (19:34).

19:35-41 Finally **the city clerk**, who was responsible for keeping the city records and managing the temple funds, appeared before **the crowd** in an attempt to pacify them. First, he was conciliatory. He said, in essence, "Of course Artemis is great. Everyone is on the same page about this, so please chill!" (19:35-36). Next he urged Demetrius and any others who had **a case against anyone** to bring it to **the courts** and follow the **legal** process (19:37-39). Finally, he told them that if they wanted to worry about something, he could give them something to worry about: **We run a risk of being charged** (by Rome) **with rioting** (19:40). Nobody wanted Roman legions coming against the city! So with these words, the city clerk calmed **the assembly** and **dismissed** them (19:41).

The word translated "assembly" here is the Greek word *ekklēsia*. When it refers to the assembly of believers, it's translated "church." So when Jesus and the apostles started speaking of the *church*, they were not coining a new term. It was a common word used to speak of a gathering of people to address an issue, especially one legal in nature. The church of Jesus Christ is God's legally authorized assembly on earth to draw down heaven to execute the will of God in history (see commentary on Matt 16:16-20).

20:1-6 After these events, Paul **departed** as planned (see 19:21) for **Macedonia** (20:1). He stayed in **Greece** for **three months** and then had to reroute his travel plans because of a Jewish plot **against him** (20:2-3). **From**

Philippi in Macedonia, he **sailed** to **Troas** on the coast of Asia Minor. Notice the first-person plural **we** appears again (20:6). Therefore, Luke, the author of Acts, had once again joined Paul (see commentary on 16:8-10).

20:7-12 One Sunday, they had gathered **to break bread** together. It must have been an evening service because **Paul . . . kept on talking until midnight** (20:7). About that time, **a young man named Eutychus** was about to suffer the consequences of choosing a back row seat for the church service! He **was sitting on the window sill**, fell **into a deep sleep**, and dropped **from the third story**. But Paul **embraced** the **dead** boy and raised him back to life (20:9-10). Then they returned to the room and Paul talked **until dawn** (20:11). Just as Jesus had done before them, both Peter and Paul raised the dead through the power of the Holy Spirit (see 9:36-43).

20:13-17 From Troas he sailed on, making multiple pit stops, until he **came to Miletus**, the port city for **Ephesus**, which was about thirty miles to the north. Paul was afraid that traveling to Ephesus would delay his journey to **Jerusalem** because he wanted to arrive by **Pentecost** (20:13-16), so he **summoned the elders of** the Ephesian **church** to come to him at **Miletus** (20:17).

20:18-21 The remainder of chapter 20 relates Paul's visit with and farewell address to the Ephesian elders. It was an emotional time. Paul was on his way to Jerusalem, opposition awaited, and he realized he might never see the Ephesians again. Therefore, he wanted to give them a final exhortation so that they might continue the work to which God had called them, teaching and leading his people.

Paul began by reminding them of how he had served the Lord among them with **humility**, **with tears**, and in spite of Jewish **plots** against his life (20:18-19). He taught them everything **profitable** from Scripture, both **publicly and from house to house** (20:20). What did he proclaim? **Repentance toward God and faith in our Lord Jesus** (20:21). *Repentance* is an internal decision and determination to turn from sin. To have *faith* in Jesus is to trust in Christ alone for the gift of eternal life.

20:22-24 After describing his past ministry, Paul explained his present circumstances. He was traveling **to Jerusalem, compelled by the Spirit** (this is when God puts a vice grip on your soul, confirming his purpose for you and urging you in a particular direction) (20:22). He was unaware of exactly what lay ahead, but he knew it would involve **chains and afflictions** (20:23). Yet, despite his trials and uncertainties, Paul had an eternal perspective: **I consider my life of no value to myself.** Instead, what he valued above all things was **the ministry** he had **received from the Lord Jesus, to testify to the gospel of God's grace.** Therefore, Paul wanted to faithfully **finish** his **course**, to reach the finish line (20:24).

Are you prepared to live the rest of your life the same way? Or is your testimony instead, "I haven't even tried to determine God's will for my life"? Don't let your days pass you by. Pursue God and his plans for you. Whatever the future held, Paul wanted to complete his life, saying in essence, "I have done what God put me on earth to do" (see 2 Tim 4:6-8).

20:25-27 Paul was confident that the Ephesian elders would never see him again, given the doubts surrounding his own future. Nevertheless, he knew he had faithfully proclaimed **the kingdom**—the rule of God—among them (20:25). Therefore, he was **innocent** of their **blood** (20:26), like the "watchman" the prophet Ezekiel spoke of (see Ezek 3:16-27). Paul had never failed to take advantage of a gospel opportunity. If someone needed to hear truth from God's Word, he avoided nothing and exhorted everyone (20:27). No one could blame Paul for failing to talk about Jesus.

What about you? Do you have family members, friends, or co-workers with whom you've never shared the gospel? Take advantage of God-given opportunities to make Christ known to people in your circle of influence. Don't shrink back from helping someone understand how to know God and escape eternal judgment, as well as how to live under his rule as a kingdom disciple.

20:28 Paul warned the elders, **Be on guard for yourselves and for all the flock. The Holy Spirit** had **appointed** them as **overseers, to shepherd** or pastor **the church of God.** It is a pastoral duty to guide the people of God in biblical truth and protect them from error—to provide spiritual direction and warn against dangerous spiritual influences. To fail at this is to fail as a spiritual shepherd.

Notice that Paul says God **purchased** the church **with his own blood.** This is a clear affirmation of the deity of Jesus Christ. God the Father is spirit (see John 4:24); he has no body and therefore no blood. So this is obviously a reference to God the Son, who "became flesh" (John 1:14)—that is, became incarnate. Jesus is the God-Man, fully divine and fully human.

20:29-31 Paul urged this obligation on them because he knew that when he departed **savage wolves** would enter the church, **not sparing the flock** (20:29). Some would even **rise up** among their **own number**—that is, among the elders—to **distort the truth** and **to lure the disciples** away (20:30). So Paul admonished the elders to **be on the alert** and remember the example he had set for them, as he warned them **night and day for three years . . . with tears** (20:31). Paul cried over the people in the church at Ephesus. He wasn't in the ministry for power or glory. He genuinely cared about the well-being of those under his care.

Protecting the flock sometimes means confronting wolves, people who don't have the best interests of others in mind but only care to satisfy their own desires. They might be people who are not grounded in Scripture and are simply looking for attention. Or they may be those propagating false teaching, preying on people in the church who have genuine needs and are too trusting. That's why the church needs spiritual men to serve as pastors who know God's Word, can discern negative influences, and will step in to guard the flock that God has entrusted to them. These leaders should also be motivated by a deep love for God's people.

20:32 As he prepared to leave them, Paul committed the Ephesian elders **to God** and his **word**, which was able to **build** them **up.**

Pastors, don't sacrifice the ministry of the Word. No matter how eloquent you are as a preacher, dynamic as a leader, or competent as an administrator, never forget that you are nothing without the Word of God. The church is founded on and edified through the Bible. Let it be at the center of your ministry.

20:33-35 Paul had neither **coveted** nor taken anything from the Ephesian church. He had supported himself (20:33-34). He didn't simply talk a good game; he labored hard among them (20:35). Beware of those who seek to use the church merely to line their pockets. A faithful pastor / elder is worthy of his wages (see 1 Tim 5:17-18), but that's quite different from someone who is fleecing the flock for personal gain.

Paul reminded them, **It is more blessed to give than to receive** (20:35). Indeed, in God's economy you will be more blessed if you're a spiritual conduit rather than a spiritual cul-de-sac. God wants to work through you so that you will be a blessing to others. If you have the capacity to address a need (with your money, your time, or your encouragement), be used by God to give to and meet that need. God will return the favor (see Luke 6:38).

20:36-38 When he had finished addressing the elders, Paul **knelt down and prayed with all of them** (20:36). This was an emotional time. They wept over, **embraced**, and **kissed** him, knowing that they would probably **never see his face again** (20:37-38). Paul had the heart of a shepherd; that truth was reflected in the response to his departure.

IV. PAUL'S ARREST, TRIAL, AND KINGDOM WITNESS IN ROME (21:1–28:31)

21:1-6 Paul and his companions journeyed by **ship** from port to port until they finally arrived in **Tyre** on the Mediterranean Coast (21:1-3). There they visited with the local believers for seven days. **The Spirit** had revealed to them what was awaiting Paul in **Jerusalem**, so out of fear they kept telling him **not to go** (21:4). Yet when it was time for him to depart, they all went outside **the city** and prayed with him (21:5). There was no stopping Paul. He was "compelled by the Spirit" to go to Jerusalem (20:22).

21:7-9 From **Tyre** they sailed to **Ptolemais** and then to **Caesarea**, where they **stayed** with **Philip the evangelist** (21:7-8) who had zeal for spreading the gospel (see 8:4-8, 26-40). Philip was **one of the Seven**—that is, one of the first seven deacons appointed by the church (see 6:1-6)—and he shared the gospel with the Ethiopian eunuch (see 8:26-40). He **had four virgin daughters who prophesied** (21:9).

Notice that the gift of prophecy was bestowed by the Spirit without gender distinction. Though women are restricted from the office of elder / overseer / pastor (see 1 Tim 2:11-13), the Spirit makes no gender distinction in the distribution of spiritual gifts.

21:10-13 A prophet named **Agabus** visited them and let Paul know what he could expect in Jerusalem. They would **bind** his **hands** and **feet** and **deliver him over to the Gentiles** (21:10-11). When Paul's companions and the **local** believers heard this, they **pleaded with him not to go** (21:12). This was too much for Paul; it was a very emotional moment. They were **breaking** his **heart**. Nevertheless, he was determined to go to Jerusalem, **ready . . . to be bound** and even **to die . . . for the name of the Lord Jesus** (21:13).

When eternity is that real in your heart, whether you live or die doesn't make a difference as long as the Lord is glorified. As Paul told the Philippians, "For me, to live is Christ and to die is gain" (Phil 1:21).

21:14 Since they couldn't change his mind, they concluded, **The Lord's will be done**. We will frequently be unable to understand the reason God allows certain circumstances in our lives. Nevertheless, like Paul and the Lord Jesus himself (see Luke 22:42), we must have hearts that submit to our King's will for our lives.

21:15-21 Arriving in **Jerusalem**, Paul and his companions were greeted **warmly** by the

Christian **brothers and sisters** (21:15-17). When he met with **James** (the Lord's brother) and **the elders**, they were overjoyed to hear about **what God had done among the Gentiles through** the **ministry** of this former persecutor of the church (21:18-20). However, some had been reporting to the Jewish believers in Jerusalem that Paul was telling **Jews** who lived **among the Gentiles . . . not to circumcise their children** or follow Jewish **customs** (21:21).

In other words, some were saying Paul was telling Jews to forget about their Jewish heritage when they came to Christ. But that wasn't true. Though Paul clearly told all people (Jew and Gentile) that salvation came through faith in Christ alone, he didn't argue that Jewish customs couldn't be practiced. After all, Paul had Timothy circumcised to make it easier for the two of them to conduct ministry among the Jews (see 16:1-3). Circumcision is not a problem as long as one doesn't rely on it for salvation or sanctification (see Gal 5:1-6).

21:22-25 To deal with this problem, the Christian elders encouraged Paul to **pay** for **four men** who had taken **a vow** to have their **heads shaved** (21:23-24). This was probably a reference to the Nazirite vow (see Num 6:1-21), something Paul had done himself (see Acts 18:18). Once the other Jews saw Paul do this, they would realize that the rumors they had heard about him rejecting Jewish customs amounted to **nothing** (21:24). Then they reminded Paul of the **letter** to the **Gentiles** that had been written as a result of the Jerusalem council (21:25; see 15:22-29). As long as the gospel message wasn't compromised, they didn't want anything to unnecessarily offend Jews and hinder them from believing in Christ.

21:26-30 Paul did as the elders recommended, but when some Jews **saw him in the temple**, they flew into a rage, grabbing Paul and telling everyone that he was guilty of speaking against the Jewish **people**, the **law**, and **temple** (21:26-28). To top it off, they accused him of bringing **Greeks into the temple** because they had seen Paul walking around the city with a Gentile man from Ephesus and assumed he **had brought him** inside it

(21:28-29). So **the whole city was** upset and **dragged** Paul **out of the temple** (21:30).

Thus, the warnings and prophecies from the Holy Spirit were coming true (see 20:23; 21:4, 10). But Paul had prepared himself. The Spirit had compelled him to go, and he was determined to follow through in obedience (see 20:22; 21:13).

21:31-36 Paul was rescued from death by a Roman **commander** and his **soldiers**. They ended the **chaos**, stopped the people from **beating** Paul, and chained him up—assuming he was some kind of criminal (21:31-33). Unable to get to the bottom of things, the commander had his **soldiers** carry Paul (because **the crowd** wouldn't stop attacking him!) to **the barracks** (21:34-36).

21:37-40 The average person would have left well enough alone and allowed himself to be carried off safe from harm! But not Paul. He wanted to speak (21:37). The Roman commander had misidentified the apostle, thinking he was an **Egyptian who started a revolt some time ago** (21:38). But once Paul informed him of his true identity as **a citizen of an important city** in the Roman Empire, he was **given permission** to address the crowd (21:39-40).

When we read Paul's letters, we might be tempted to think that he was just a heady theologian. But actually Paul wrote from an incredible Christian experience that included genuine love for people, intense emotional and physical suffering, and active pursuit of his King's agenda.

22:1-5 Paul began to address the crowd that only moments before had been beating him to a pulp. They had become angry with him based on false pretenses, so Paul wanted to clarify who he was and what he had been doing. He began by explaining how much they had in common. He was **a Jew**, spoke **Aramaic**, had been **educated** by the great Pharisee **Gamaliel**, and had been **zealous** for the **law** (22:2-3). How zealous? He had **persecuted this Way to the death** (22:4), "the Way" being an early title given to Christianity (see 9:2; 19:9, 23; 24:14, 22). He had been concerned with nothing other than **arresting**, punishing, and jailing believers (21:4-5). If anyone had wanted to destroy the Christian faith, it was Paul. If they doubted him, the Jewish **high priest** and **council of elders** could verify it all (21:5).

22:6-16 One day, though, while he was pursuing the followers of Jesus, Paul ran right into Jesus himself! The risen and glorified Lord asked Paul, **Why are you persecuting me?** (21:7; see commentary on 9:1-19; 26:12-18). To persecute Christ's people, then, is to persecute Christ because the church is his body. Yet Jesus hadn't come to punish Paul; he had come to draft him into service to take his gospel message throughout the empire. Paul didn't learn this, though, until he obeyed God and went to **Damascus** to meet a believer named **Ananias** who healed him and gave him his marching orders to **be a witness for [Christ] to all people** (21:11-15).

Paul was saved for a purpose, and the same is true of all believers. Christians are God's "workmanship, created in Christ Jesus for good works, which God prepared ahead of time for us to do" (Eph 2:10). The Lord didn't inform Paul about his purpose until he went to Damascus as commanded. Many Christians want to know God's purposes for their lives, but they're unwilling to obey the clear commands that he's already given. But God hits a moving target. Follow God in faith; do what you already know you're supposed to do. By doing so, you'll show him that you're serious about pursuing him so that he can begin guiding, directing, and ordering your steps.

22:17-21 Upon Paul's return **to Jerusalem**, God commanded Paul to leave because he knew the Jews there wouldn't **accept** his **testimony** (22:17-18). In fact, they would seek to kill him (see 9:28-30). But Paul thought he had a compelling testimony to share, since he had formerly **imprisoned** believers and approved of Stephen's death (22:19-20; see 7:54–8:3). Nevertheless, God had other plans for Paul: He would take the gospel **to the Gentiles** (22:21).

What Paul said about the Ephesian church was also once true of most of us: "Remember that at one time you were Gentiles . . . without Christ, excluded from the citizenship of Israel, and foreigners to the covenants of

promise, without hope and without God in the world" (Eph 2:11-12). But praise God for his grace to Gentiles and for Paul's faithfulness to his Gentile mission.

22:22-24 When the Jewish listeners heard Paul mention "Gentiles," they'd had enough. They wanted him dead (22:22). So the Roman **commander** ordered Paul to be taken to the barracks—not to protect him—but to whip him **with the scourge to discover** why everyone was so angry with him (22:24). Clearly, then, the commander wasn't concerned with justice.

22:25-29 As they stretched him out for **the lash,** Paul asked, **Is it legal for you to scourge a man who is a Roman citizen and is uncondemned?** (22:25). The clear answer was "No." Paul, therefore, was shrewd. He used his citizenship to his advantage. He had legal protection, and he utilized it. When the commander learned that Paul had been born a Roman **citizen** (and had not purchased his **citizenship** like he had), he and those with him became **alarmed** (22:28-29). If they punished a Roman citizen without a trial, they'd be in for severe punishment themselves.

Paul wasn't afraid to be beaten for Christ. But he also wasn't afraid to exercise his legal rights to escape illegitimate punishment and to take his case and message to a higher governmental authority—ultimately to Caesar (see 25:11-12).

22:30–23:5 The Roman commander **released** Paul and had **the chief priests** and the Jewish **Sanhedrin** gather together so that he could try to find out what they were accusing him of (22:30). So Paul began speaking, testifying that he had **lived . . . before God in all good conscience,** yet **the high priest** had him slapped to shut him up (23:1-2). In response to this unjust treatment, Paul called the high priest a **whitewashed wall** (that is, a thing made to look clean on the outside though it is actually dirty on the inside) and condemned his unlawful actions (23:3).

When challenged for daring to **revile** the **high priest,** Paul said he **did not know** Ananias **was the high priest** (23:4-5). Some interpreters think Paul truly didn't know to whom he was speaking. Others think Paul's eyesight was bad. But more likely, Paul considered him an illegitimate high priest because of his unjust actions in conducting the trial (see Lev 19:15). In other words, he took this stance: "He may be your high priest, but he's not my high priest." In any case, by quoting Exodus 22:28, Paul was acknowledging respect for the leader's office but saying, "This is a fake leader."

23:6-9 It was clear to Paul that he wasn't going to get a fair hearing. So when he **realized that some of those gathered were Sadducees** (a group that denied the resurrection of the dead) and some were Pharisees (a group that believed in the resurrection of the dead), he told them he was **a Pharisee** on trial **because of the hope of the resurrection** (23:6, 8). That was another shrewd move because technically, he was right. His message was the proclamation that Jesus was the Messiah who had risen from the dead. But he used that truth to highlight the theological conflict that existed between the two groups, winning sympathy for himself from the Pharisees. Eventually they declared, **We find nothing evil in this man** (23:9). Mission accomplished. The Jewish Sanhedrin wouldn't be condemning Paul that day.

23:10-11 As fists started flying, **the commander** had his **troops** whisk **Paul** away to **the barracks** again (23:10). **The following night, the Lord** appeared to Paul to encourage him. Just as Paul had **testified about** Jesus **in Jerusalem**, it was the Lord's will that he **testify in Rome** (23:11). It wouldn't be a smooth ride, but God would ultimately take Paul to the heart of the Roman Empire. Sometimes, in his providence, God will take you on a long and difficult road to get you where he wants you. Trust God, maintain your kingdom perspective, and (as the Lord told Paul) **have courage** (23:11).

23:12-22 The Jews who hated Paul weren't going to give up that easily. **Forty** of them had vowed **not to eat or drink until they had killed** him (23:12-13). So they told the religious leaders to ask the Roman commander to have Paul appear before him again so he could be questioned. But as he was being delivered, they would lie in wait **to kill him**

(23:14-15). Somehow, however, Paul's nephew heard about the **ambush** and **reported it** to Uncle Paul! So Paul had a centurion take his nephew **to the commander** and inform him of the secret plot (23:17-22). God's providence had intervened again. The Lord knows how to have a nephew at the right place at the right time to foil the plans of a band of killers.

23:23-30 The commander took word of this plot very seriously. He was under obligation to look after this Roman citizen in his charge. Nothing was going to happen to Paul on his watch. So he gathered **two hundred soldiers ... with seventy cavalry and two hundred spearmen** (470 armed Romans against 40 fasting Jews sound like pretty good odds!) to transport Paul by night **to Felix the governor** in **Caesarea** (23:23-24). Not only was Paul being delivered safely from the hands of those who wanted to kill him, he was getting a massive, armed escort. The commander also sent a **letter** to the **governor**, explaining the circumstances and making it clear that he had been doing his job well (23:25-30).

23:31-35 Paul was taken to Caesarea on the Mediterranean Coast to see Marcus Antonius Felix, the Roman governor (or procurator) of Judea from AD 52–58. According to historical sources, Felix was a lousy and brutal ruler. He learned that Paul **was from Cilicia**, a Roman **province** (23:34) on the coast of modern day Turkey. That's where Paul's home city of Tarsus was located (see 9:11; 21:39; 22:3). Then Felix agreed to **give** Paul **a hearing** when his **accusers** arrived from Jerusalem. Though Paul was **kept under guard** (23:35), Luke makes it clear throughout the narrative that Paul is ultimately in God's hands—not in the hands of Rome.

24:1-9 In a few days, **Ananias the high priest** and **some elders** showed up with **a lawyer named Tertullus** (24:1). They were determined to have Paul legally condemned to death. Tertullus thus began by flattering Felix and then getting down to business, arguing that Paul was **an agitator** and **ringleader of the sect of the Nazarenes**—a reference to the fact that Jesus grew up in Nazareth (24:2-5). Then he accused Paul of trying **to desecrate the temple** (24:6). This was plainly untrue, but they knew they had to make Paul guilty of something that would concern a Roman ruler. If Paul were disturbing the peace and causing riots, Rome would need to do something.

24:10-15 When given opportunity to respond, Paul did not hesitate to speak the truth and seek to address his illegitimate incarceration through the legal means available to him. He agreed that he had been **in Jerusalem** but denied the accusation that he had caused **a disturbance**, whether **in the temple** or anywhere **in the city** (24:11-12). None of **the charges** they made could be proved (24:13). The only thing to which Paul would **admit** was being a worshiper of God **according to the Way**—that is, Christianity (see 9:2; 19:9, 23; 22:4), which these Jews rejected as **a sect** but which was nonetheless a fulfillment of **the law** and **the prophets** (24:14). Paul pointed out the **hope** that he had in common with **these men**: a belief in the **resurrection** of the dead, which had happened in Jesus Christ (24:15).

24:16-21 Paul also highlighted the fact that he had brought **charitable gifts** to his fellow Jews (24:17)—hardly something he'd do if he despised them. It was while he was delivering this offering that some hostile **Jews from Asia** found Paul **in the temple**, but he had been **without a crowd and without any uproar** (24:18). Then he raised a significant point: Where were those men who had seized him in the temple and accused him of wrongdoing? They hadn't even shown up for his trial! (24:19). Moreover, the men who *were* there couldn't explain what Paul had done wrong when he had **stood before the Sanhedrin**, except that he affirmed **the resurrection of the dead** (24:20-21)—something which the Pharisees in the Sanhedrin agreed with (see 23:6-8).

24:22-27 Felix refused to render a judgment until **Lysias the commander**—the one who had sent Paul to Felix—arrived in Caesarea (24:22; see 23:23-30). Then he had **Paul** kept **under guard** but allowed **his friends** to visit and provide for him (24:23). Later, Felix and his Jewish **wife Drusilla . . . listened to** Paul talk about **faith in Christ Jesus** (24:24). But when Paul **spoke about** the subjects of

righteousness, self-control, and the judgment to come, Felix became afraid (24:25). Why? Because someone who is unrighteous and lacking self-control doesn't want to hear how divine judgment will be poured out. Felix was **well informed about** Christianity (24:22). He was apparently interested in religious matters. But when the conversation turned to his own sins and his accountability before God, Felix squirmed in his seat.

Therefore, Felix sent Paul away, but regularly invited him back to talk, always hoping that **Paul would offer him** a bribe to let him go (24:25-26). It's clear Felix knew that Paul was innocent of all charges, but he was unwilling to upset the Jews by setting him free. So **to do the Jews a favor, he left Paul in prison** for **two years** until he was **succeeded** by the new governor, **Porcius Festus** (24:27). Paul was unjustly imprisoned. But God providentially used this injustice to move him toward the goal of proclaiming the gospel in Rome, the center of earthly power in Paul's day.

25:1-5 When the new governor arrived in **Jerusalem**, the Jewish religious leaders **appealed** to **Festus** to grant them **a favor**: transfer **Paul** to Jerusalem (25:1-3). Their secret plan was to **ambush** and **kill** Paul when he was moved—a plot they had devised two years ago that had resulted in Paul being transferred to Caesarea in the first place (see 23:12-30). But Festus denied their request and told them to send representatives to accompany him to Caesarea to **accuse** Paul of any wrongdoing (25:4-5).

Once again, then, God was working behind the scenes to protect Paul from the murderous plans of the Jewish leaders. They were scheming to have Paul returned to Jerusalem. But God was working to take Paul far from their grasp—to stand before Caesar. No matter how grim your circumstances appear, do not forget the glorious truth that God is in control, whether directly or indirectly. Submit to his kingdom agenda in Scripture and trust him to accomplish his will for your life as he sovereignly directs your path.

25:6-9 In **Caesarea** Festus had **Paul** brought before him (25:6). **The Jews** also came forward and accused Paul of **serious charges**

that they were not able to prove (25:7). As he had been in the habit of doing, Paul denied the unsubstantiated charges. He was not guilty of anything against the **Jewish law**, the Jewish **temple**, or **Caesar** (25:8). Like his predecessor, Festus could find no reason to condemn Paul. Nevertheless, he had a province to run, and he wanted his constituents to be peaceable citizens. So as **a favor** to **the Jews**, he asked Paul if he'd be willing to stand trial in **Jerusalem** (25:9).

25:10-12 But Paul had had enough. He had not wronged the Jews, so he argued that he shouldn't be given over to them (25:10-11). The question before Festus was, "Is Paul guilty of wrongdoing against Rome?" Although Paul was **standing at Caesar's tribunal**, being tried before Caesar's representative, Felix was unwilling to render a verdict (25:10). As a Roman citizen, Paul had the full right of appeal, so he declared, **I appeal to Caesar**, and Festus consented (25:11-12).

Paul had been exercising every legal right available to him. He wanted to make it clear to all that neither he nor Christianity was guilty of subverting the empire. Moreover, he wanted to go to Rome, the highest level of earthly authority, with a message from the supreme authority: Believe in the Lord Jesus and submit to his kingdom agenda.

25:13-14 King Agrippa (Herod Agrippa II) was the son of Herod Agrippa I (see 12:1-5, 20-23) and the last member of the Herodian dynasty to rule. (The Romans had put him in charge of a few territories that did not include Judea). When he paid a visit to **Festus**, the Roman governor presented Paul's case to the king. Since Agrippa was Jewish, Festus hoped he could help him make sense of Paul's case so that he would know what to communicate to Caesar when he sent him.

25:15-22 Festus laid out the sequence of events for Agrippa. The governor had expected accusations of horrific **evils** against Paul, but instead the case against him turned out to be one of religious disagreement **about a certain Jesus, a dead man Paul claimed to be alive** (25:18-19). Not being familiar with Jewish religious teachings, Festus confessed, **I was at a loss** (25:20). But when he **asked**

Paul **if he wanted to** be **tried** in **Jerusalem**, he instead **appealed** to **Caesar** (25:20-21). After listening to the explanation, Agrippa said, **I would like to hear the man myself** (25:22). Paul was about to have an opportunity to talk to a human king about King Jesus.

25:23-27 The next day, Paul appeared before **Festus, Agrippa**, and **Bernice** (25:23). (Bernice was Agrippa's sister, with whom he was rumored to be in an incestuous relationship.) Festus explained that the **Jewish community** wanted Paul dead, that he (Festus) had not found him guilty of anything, and that Paul had **appealed to the Emperor** (25:24-25). Then Festus described his dilemma: **I have nothing definite to write to my lord** (Caesar) **about him**. That's why he wanted Agrippa to listen to Paul and to offer some advice (25:26). Festus was understandably embarrassed **to send a prisoner** to Caesar **without indicating the charges against him** (25:27). Doing so was no small matter. In essence Festus was saying, "Help me out, Agrippa. Don't let me look like a fool in front of the emperor!"

26:1-3 When given a chance to speak, Paul **stretched out his hand** as a show of respect and expressed his gratefulness for the opportunity to address King Agrippa. In his letter to the church in Rome, Paul writes, "Let everyone submit to the governing authorities, since there is no authority except from God, and the authorities that exist are instituted by God" (Rom 13:1). Paul knew that a government office is to be respected—even if the person holding the office isn't worthy of respect—because such governmental authorities were established by the Lord.

26:4-8 Paul began by telling the king that none of **the Jews** could deny—that **from [his] youth** he had been zealous for the Jewish **religion** and **lived as a Pharisee** (26:4-5). The reason he was on trial, though, was for believing in something that had been **promised** to the Jewish people in the Old Testament Scriptures: the **hope** of the resurrection of the dead (26:6-7). Paul knew he wasn't merely bearing witness to his own innocence; ultimately he was bearing witness to Christ. Having raised the topic of resurrection, he wanted his listeners to consider the reality of Jesus's resurrection and press it on their consciences: **Why do any of you consider it incredible that God raises the dead?** (26:8).

26:9-11 Paul confessed that he had opposed Christianity vigorously. He had sought to have Christians locked up and put to death. So, what was his point? Paul wanted Agrippa to know that if anything could transform him from being the chief persecutor of Christianity to its chief advocate, it would have to be miraculous. And it was.

26:12-18 Paul recounted his conversion on the **Damascus** road when the Lord Jesus appeared to him (see commentary on 9:1-19; 22:6-16). At the moment when he encountered the supernatural vision, he had been on his way—with no intentions of repenting—to arrest believers (26:12). The **light from heaven** that struck him **at midday** was **brighter than the sun**, and then the crucified one whom Paul thought was dead spoke to him (26:13-15)!

Jesus brought both salvation and a **purpose** to Paul. His mission would be to serve as a **witness of what he [had] seen and [would] see of** the Lord (26:16). In particular he would take the gospel to **the Gentiles**, turning them **from the power of Satan to God** (26:17-18).

Formerly, Paul was an aggressive opponent of Christ; he'd become an aggressive soldier for Christ. Instead of keeping people *from* the kingdom, Paul's energies would be redirected toward bringing them *into* the kingdom.

26:19-23 So then, King Agrippa, **I was not disobedient to the heavenly vision** (28:19). In other words, Paul said, "What did you expect me to do? Say 'No' to God?" Paul immediately began preaching, wherever he was, that the Gentiles **should repent and turn to God, and do works worthy of repentance** (26:20). That's why **the Jews seized** him and tried **to kill** him (26:21). They were outraged by his message of salvation for the Gentiles, but Paul hadn't invented it or pulled it out of thin air. Everything he had preached was consistent with and in fulfillment of **what**

the prophets and Moses said would take place (26:22; see Ps 16:10; Isa 52:13–53:12). Then Paul highlighted the heart of the gospel: the suffering of **the Messiah**, his resurrection **from the dead**, and the proclamation in his name of **light** and forgiveness to Jews and **Gentiles** alike (26:23).

26:24-25 Divine visions? A voice from heaven? A dead man raised to life? This was too much for **Festus**, who thought **Paul** had gone crazy: **Too much study is driving you mad** (26:24). But Paul was unfazed by Festus's insult. Far from being **out of [his] mind**, Paul was **speaking words of truth and good judgment** (26:25). He would have been crazy *not* to submit to King Jesus.

26:26-29 Then Paul turned his attention to the king, knowing that none of this had **escaped his notice** (26:26). Agrippa was well aware of both the message about Jesus and the fact that Paul had been publicly vocal about it. Putting the Jewish king on the spot, Paul asked, **Do you believe the prophets? I know you believe** (26:27). So although Paul was the one on trial, he turned the tables on Agrippa and played the prosecutor.

The king wondered if Paul thought he could **persuade** him **to become a Christian so easily**, and the apostle admitted that he wanted everyone to be saved (26:28-29). **Whether** someone came to know Jesus **easily or with difficulty**, it was worth it as far as Paul was concerned. The only thing he didn't want them to experience was the **chains** that he had endured (26:29).

To Paul, no one was beyond the reach of the gospel. He was willing to talk to anyone about Jesus, regardless of their social status: government officials (13:7, 12), the lame (14:8-10), women (16:13-15), a jailer (16:25-34), and intellectuals (17:16-34). What about you? Are you willing to step outside of your comfort zone to share the good news with those whom others might avoid?

26:30-32 When Agrippa, Festus, and Bernice conferred privately afterward, they concluded that Paul was innocent (26:30-31). He had certainly committed no crime against Rome. If not for his appeal **to Caesar**, Paul **could have been released** (26:32). Yet, more than his freedom, Paul wanted to testify about Jesus to the Roman emperor. And God was going to give him that opportunity.

27:1-8 Eventually, **Paul and some other prisoners** were placed into the custody of a centurion named **Julius**, and they set **sail** for **Italy**. The use of the first person plural (**we**) once again indicates that the author, Luke, and a believer from **Thessalonica** named **Aristarchus** were with Paul (27:1-2; see 16:8-10; 20:1-6). Julius was kind to Paul and allowed **his friends to** tend to his needs (27:3). From Caesarea, they sailed north to **Sidon**, then around the island of **Cyprus** to land at **Myra** in Asia Minor. There they transferred to another **ship** (27:2-6). They had great difficulty reaching the island of **Crete**, eventually stopping at a port called **Fair Havens** (27:7-8).

27:9-12 The sailing had been slow going due to the winds, and the voyage had become **dangerous. The Day of Atonement was already over**, meaning it was late in the year (27:9). So Paul thought it advisable to spend the winter there, foreseeing disaster if they continued—loss of **the cargo**, the **ship**, and their **lives** (27:10). But **the centurion** listened to the counsel of **the captain and the owner of the ship** instead of **Paul** (27:11). They preferred to **winter** in **Phoenix**, a **harbor** that was further west on the coast of **Crete** (27:12). But listening to the "professional" rather than the man with a connection to God would prove costly.

Notice that Paul was not outside of God's will. He had been obedient to the Lord, seeking to take his case to Rome, which was exactly where God wanted him to go (see 23:11). Paul gave good advice to the centurion, but it was rejected. As a result, the crew and passengers of the ship were about to enter a terrible storm. So, clearly, being in a storm does not mean you're out of God's will. Sometimes, it's exactly where he wants you to be so that he can accomplish his purposes in you and through you (see commentary on Mark 4:35-37).

27:13-20 Although they set out with **a gentle south wind**, soon they encountered **a fierce wind** and **were driven along** (27:13-15).

Having difficulty controlling the heavy ship, the crew tried everything to keep it from running **aground** (27:16-17). Eventually, they started tossing **the cargo** and **the ship's tackle** (the rigging and equipment) **overboard** to lighten the load (27:18-19). The **storm** raged **for many days**, and **finally all hope was fading** (27:20).

27:21-26 In the midst of this bleak situation, Paul told them, **You men should have followed my advice** (27:21)—that is, "I told you so!" But after this slap on the wrist, he urged them **to take courage** because no **lives** would be lost, only **the ship** (27:22). How did he know? **God** had sent **an angel** to assure Paul of two things (27:23). First, it was **necessary** for the apostle **to appear before Caesar**. God had a mission for Paul, and he wouldn't die before that mission was accomplished. Second, all of those **sailing with** Paul would be divinely protected (27:24). They needed no better assurance than that. Paul exhorted them again to have **courage** because **God** is faithful to keep his promises (27:25).

27:27-32 During the night, **the sailors** feared that **they were approaching land** and might crash **on the rocks** (27:27-29). So **they dropped four anchors** to try and keep the ship from running **aground** (27:29). Panicking, **some sailors** pretended to let down a smaller boat in order to drop more **anchors**. But actually they were planning to flee (27:30). When Paul realized what was happening, he warned the centurion that the way to **be saved** was to remain **in the ship**, not to abandon it (27:31). So the centurion and his **soldiers** put a stop to the sailors' escape plans (27:32). They had finally learned to start listening to Paul.

27:33-38 Two weeks into their ordeal, Paul urged them to eat something, promising them that no one would be harmed (27:33-34). Then he set an example for them by eating **some bread** himself. Notice that in the midst of their affliction Paul **gave thanks to God** for the bread **in the presence of all of them** (27:35). Then **they were all encouraged** to eat as well (27:36).

When times are hard and you don't know what God is up to, do you continue to thank him for his provision in your life (see Phil 4:6-7)? Not only will you remind yourself of the goodness of God, but you may also be a witness to those around you that God is worthy of our trust in difficult times. This is why Jesus could give thanks in spite of insufficiency when he fed the five thousand (see John 6:1-14).

27:39-44 At daybreak, they saw **a beach**, cut **loose the anchors**, and ran aground on **a sandbar** (27:39-41). Unfortunately, **the stern** of the ship **began to break up** because **of the waves**, so they would have to swim for shore (27:41). When they realized this, the soldiers wanted **to kill the prisoners** so that they couldn't **swim away and escape** (27:42). After all, a soldier or guard who allowed a prisoner to get away would forfeit his own life (see 12:6-10, 18-19; 16:26-27). But God providentially protected Paul through **the centurion** who **wanted to save** him (27:43). So **everyone** made it to land **safely**, either by swimming or floating **on debris** (27:43-44).

28:1-10 They **learned** that they had arrived on **Malta**, an **island** south of Sicily (28:1). The locals were kind and cared for the castaways (28:2). But when they saw a venomous **snake** bite **Paul**, the superstitious people were convinced that he must be **a murderer** because, although he had **escaped the sea**, **Justice** (a Greek goddess) had **not allowed him to live** (28:3-4). However, when Paul didn't become sick or die, **they changed their minds and said he was a god** (28:5-6). (How fickle is the human heart!) When Paul miraculously **healed** the **father** of **the leading man of the island**, everyone started bringing those with sickness and disease so that Paul might heal them (28:7-9). As a result, when their visitors sailed away, the natives **heaped many honors on** them and gave them all the supplies they **needed** (28:10).

God provided for all of the men's needs through the island's inhabitants. Don't overlook the fact, though, that their admiration for Paul began when he was bitten by a snake. God's providence sometimes requires that we pass through painful experiences so that he can give us—and even others—his blessing.

28:11-16 From Malta they climbed aboard a ship that took them to **Syracuse** on the island of Sicily (28:11-12). From there they reached the Italian **coast**, stopping first at **Rhegium** and then at **Puteoli** (28:13). After spending some time with Christian **brothers and sisters**, they eventually arrived in **Rome** where **Paul was allowed to live by himself with a soldier who guarded him** (28:14-16).

28:17-22 Paul gathered the local Jewish **leaders** and explained all of the events surrounding the circumstances of his case. He wanted them to know that he bore no animosity against his fellow **Jews** in Jerusalem but instead wanted to talk to the Jews in Rome about why he was in chains (28:17-20). He had been imprisoned because of his belief in **the hope of Israel**, the resurrection of the dead (28:20; see 23:6; 24:15; 26:23). Although the Jewish leaders hadn't **received any letters** from Jerusalem about Paul, they were willing to listen to him because everyone **everywhere** was talking about this new **sect** called Christianity (28:21-22).

28:23-24 When the Jewish leaders met with him, Paul talked to them **from dawn to dusk**, testifying **about the kingdom of God** and seeking **to persuade them** that **Jesus** is the Messiah in fulfillment of **the Law** and **the Prophets** (28:23). The Old Testament anticipated Jesus and pointed to him. Rightly interpreted, it leads people to the King who came to establish God's kingdom. **Some** of the Jews believed, **but others did not** (28:24).

28:25-28 Those who refused to believe departed in anger when they heard Paul say that **the Holy Spirit was right** about their **ancestors** when he chastised them **through the prophet Isaiah** for failing to believe the Word of God (28:25-27; see Isa 6:6-19). In other words, Paul was telling them, "Don't be like your foolish forefathers. Believe the Scriptures—all of which point to Jesus as the Messiah." But since they were unwilling to repent of their stubborn unbelief, the apostle told them that **God** had **sent** this message of **salvation** to **the Gentiles**, who would **listen** (28:28). God's gift of grace will not go unappreciated. If some reject it, there are others who will gladly accept it.

28:30-31 Paul remained in Rome for **two whole years in his own rented house**, receiving visitors. During that time he engaged in **proclaiming** (preaching) **the kingdom of God** and **teaching** people **about the Lord Jesus Christ**. Biblical *preaching* focuses on persuading people with kingdom truth in order to bring about an obedient response. Biblical *teaching* focuses on delivering a clear understanding of the King. This dual emphasis of the kingdom and its King should dominate every pulpit of every church that truly understands, accepts, and is committed to fulfilling its kingdom calling.

Thus, the book of Acts closes as it opened (see 1:3)—with the proclamation of "the kingdom of God." Though Paul was a prisoner, the Word of God was unhindered and flourishing through his ministry (see 2 Tim 2:9). Throughout Acts, we have seen the fulfillment of Jesus's promise that the Holy Spirit would enable his servants to be his "witnesses" to all people everywhere (1:8).

The Holy Spirit will do his greatest work in your life when you bear witness to Jesus Christ and live in submission to his kingdom rule. When you live under the umbrella of God's kingdom agenda, the Holy Spirit is free to take you on your own life's journey—sometimes it will be frustrating; sometimes it will prove frightening; but God will always fulfill his purposes for you.

ROMANS

INTRODUCTION

Author

THE APOSTLE PAUL CLAIMS TO BE the author of the letter (1:1), and no serious objections have been made to suggest otherwise. According to 16:22, Paul used Tertius as his *amanuensis*, or secretary, to write it—a common first-century practice.

Historical Background

Paul addressed his letter to Christians living in Rome (1:7), the capital of the vast Roman Empire. The people living there in the first century represented the empire's various cultures and religions and included many Jews. The Christian churches in Rome were not founded by Paul, though he was anxious to visit them (1:13-15). The first Christians there were probably those "visitors from Rome (both Jews and converts)" who came to Jerusalem at Pentecost (Acts 2:10), were converted under the gospel preaching of Peter (see Acts 2:14-41), and later returned to the capital city to begin churches.

According to Acts, Aquila and Priscilla were two Jewish Christians from Rome whom Paul met during his ministry in Corinth. This husband and wife had to leave their home because the Roman emperor, Claudius, "had ordered all the Jews to leave Rome" (Acts 18:2)—which happened in AD 49. A first-century Roman historian named Suetonius reports that Claudius did this because of Jewish unrest over "Chrestus"—which is most likely a reference to Christ. Given all of the quarreling in Rome between Jews who had embraced Jesus as the Messiah and Jews who had not, the Roman emperor simply kicked out all of the Jews. This exit of Jewish Christians would have left local church leadership in the hands of Gentile Christians. When Claudius's decree expired at his death, many Jewish Christians returned to Rome. The cultural diversity between Jewish and Gentile Christians would have caused tensions between the groups—a fact evident in Paul's letter to the Romans (e.g., Rom 2, 11, 14–15).

Paul wrote the letter most likely in AD 57 during his third missionary journey while in Corinth (in Greece). He was on his way to Jerusalem to deliver a contribution from Gentile churches to the poor Jewish Christians in Jerusalem. After this, he planned to visit Rome (Acts 19:21; 20:3, 16; Rom 15:25-29).

Message and Purpose

Romans is the constitution of the church. Its major theme is the righteousness of God. Paul wanted the Romans to understand this great truth both theologically and practically—what it means and how it is to be lived out. He began by teaching that all human beings have failed to meet God's standards of righteousness. They have been turned over to the passive wrath of God—yet, instead of destroying them instantly, God made provision for redemption.

The apostle continues by teaching that God, recognizing we had a problem we could not fix, freely provided a way we could be made righteous. Faith in the sacrifice of Jesus Christ on the cross and his resurrection results in his righteousness being applied to our accounts in payment for our sins. But this great transaction was only the beginning, because now we can have a relationship with Jesus Christ because we have a new identity. That doesn't mean we sin no longer. Even though Christians are saved, we still struggle with our flesh, as Paul related very honestly about himself.

Romans also tells us what God is going to do about his people Israel. Though they rejected him, God still has a plan for them. The book ends with a celebration of the faith we have in Christ and the power it gives us for victorious living as his kingdom representatives, individually and in community.

VIDEO INTRO

www.bhpublishinggroup.com/qr/te/45_00

ROMANS

I. NOT ASHAMED OF THE GOSPEL (1:1–17)

1:1-2 The book of Romans is the clearest and most beautiful explanation of **the gospel** ever written. So it is no surprise that Paul begins, in the first verse, by talking about it. The word *gospel* means "good news" and is a translation of the Greek word *euangelion*. Throughout Romans it refers to the entirety of salvation: justification (salvation past), sanctification (salvation present), and glorification (salvation future).

This gospel—this good news—however, does not belong to Paul. Paul is **a servant of Christ Jesus** (1:1), whose gospel it truly is. In fact, this message long preceded Paul, for it had been **promised beforehand through [God's] prophets in the Holy Scriptures** (1:2). The Old Testament gave signs of what the Messiah—the Christ—would be like, what he would bring, and what he would accomplish.

1:3-4 This Messiah **was a descendant of David** (1:3), which was no surprise to the Jews of Paul's day. But what shocked them was the revelation that the Messiah was also **the powerful Son of God** (1:4). The Jews had expected a coming Messiah who would reign on David's throne; they had not anticipated him to also be divine. Yet Paul could not deny that Jesus was both God and man, since **by the resurrection of the dead** (1:4) God the Father had established the uniqueness of Jesus Christ. The resurrection served as a demonstration and validation of Jesus's divinity.

1:5-6 Paul was called by God **to bring about the obedience of faith for the sake of his name among all the Gentiles** (1:5). In other words, he was not to focus on taking the gospel to his fellow Jews (though he began there), but to the Gentiles.

1:7 Everything prior to this verse is, technically, a lengthy introduction to who Paul is. Beginning here, Paul greets the Roman Christians in his characteristic way: **Grace to you and peace from God our Father and the Lord Jesus Christ**. The grace of God our Father *leads* to peace with Jesus Christ. We can't have one without the other.

1:8 Paul gives thanks to **God through Jesus Christ** for the Roman church **because the news of [their] faith [was] being reported in all the world**. These, then, were not secret agent Christians; these people went public with their allegiance to God's kingdom agenda. They were open in their testimony, just as all churches and believers should be. The result of that public confession was obvious: the gospel spread.

1:9-11 Paul deeply desired to go to Rome, so much so that he was **always asking in [his] prayers** for God to allow it (1:10). Why was Paul so insistent on seeing the Roman believers? He wanted to **impart to [them] some spiritual gift to strengthen** them (1:11). He wanted to have a spiritual impact on them and bring them spiritual benefit so that their ministry would be even stronger and their growth even deeper.

1:12-13 Paul's brief words here model a healthy relationship between minister and church. He wants them **to be mutually encouraged by each other's faith** (1:12). Ideally, we encourage the one who ministers to us *while* he ministers to and encourages us. The Christian life is one of giving in every direction, always seeking to encourage and enrich others.

1:14-15 All of Paul's ministry, his life, his every action, point toward one thing—the gospel. So Paul says, **I am obligated** to preach that gospel (1:14). He doesn't have a choice. The cost of *not* sharing the gospel is too high. If you see your neighbor's house on fire, do you shrug and say, "Glad that's not my home"? No! You feel an obligation to act, because something valuable is at stake, and doing nothing is too costly.

Paul feels that kind of obligation to everyone. He is **eager to preach the gospel** (1:15) to people of every race, creed, culture, education level, and economic status—to **Greeks and barbarians**, to **the wise and the foolish** (1:14). Paul has one mission concerning all of them: get the gospel to them, because the price tag of not embracing it is so high and the gift to us is too great to miss.

1:16 Paul knows how to keep first things first: **I am not ashamed of the gospel.** That should convict us. Though we say we believe the gospel, in truth many of us *are* ashamed of it. Why? Because we don't really believe what Paul believed, that the gospel **is the power of God for salvation.** This salvation is not merely for deliverance from hell but also for the deliverance of believers from the temporal wrath of God against sin (1:18). If we're ashamed to share the gospel, it's because we do not understand the power embedded in it. But how can you be ashamed of something with so much firepower? If you believe that the gospel has power not only to save sinners but also to give victory to saints, you won't be ashamed of it.

1:17 Another reason Paul had confidence in the gospel was that **in it the righteousness of God is revealed.** The word *righteousness* means "to be right." Not "better than others," or "good enough," but *right*, as in, *right with God.* Our problem is that we mentally dumb down God, reducing him to our level so that our sin doesn't seem so bad. The gospel, though, makes God's righteousness the standard. So it doesn't matter how nice of a sinner you are, you are still a sinner.

The gospel, however, doesn't just reveal the standard. It also gives us a provision: **The righteous will live by faith.** If we appeal to our relative goodness, we'll always fall short. But if we appeal to God by faith, then the gospel has already saved us. Think of it this way. If I can't afford a house, but a generous oil baron puts up his bankroll for me, does it matter that I have eighty-five dollars in my bank account? No! My finances are irrelevant. He bought the house *for me.* I am dependent on his resources, and he can afford it. That's what the gospel is like: God has resources available for every believer who lives by faith. The act of faith in the finished work of Christ justifies us, and it is the lifestyle of faith that sanctifies and transforms us.

II. REJECTING THE GOSPEL: THE WRATH OF GOD (1:18–2:11)

1:18 Paul shifts to talk about what necessitates the gospel—God's wrath. **God's wrath is revealed from heaven,** meaning he's not hiding it. His wrath is his righteous and just retribution against sin. He does not apologize for his righteous anger, like we often try to do. Rather, he publishes it for all to see. Sinful human beings, conversely, would rather **suppress the truth.** *Suppress* means "to hold down." It's like holding a beach ball under water. The beach ball resists that and wants to pop back up; so if you want to keep the ball under, you have to suppress it, to force it down. That's what we do with the truth about God's righteousness: we humans tend to force it down because we don't want to deal with it.

1:19-20 Though they may suppress the truth, **people are without excuse.** Whether a man lives in Timbuktu or Dallas, he knows something about God because God's **invisible attributes, that is, his eternal power and divine nature, have been clearly seen** (1:20) Human beings cannot see God, but we can see God's effects. Consider the wind: even though we cannot see the wind, we know it's there because its effects are obvious. Creation testifies to the existence, greatness, power, and glory of God (see Ps 19:1-6).

1:21-23 Suppressing the truth results in a vicious cycle of idolatry. Because humanity **did not glorify him as God . . . their thinking became worthless** (1:21). We humans decided to exchange God for something we thought would be more satisfying, so we swapped **the glory of the immortal God** for all manner of earthly things—**images resembling mortal man, birds, four-footed animals**, and cars and houses and money and sex (1:23). An idol is any person, place, thing, or thought that you look to in order to get your needs met apart from God. It's the worst exchange imaginable, as Paul plainly says: **Claiming to be wise, they became fools** (1:22).

1:24-25 What is God's response to this nonsense? **God delivered them over** (1:24). That phrase appears here three times (1:24, 26, 28), and it shows God taking his hand of restraint off, essentially saying, "You want to do life without me? You've got it." This is the passive wrath of God at work in history. He lets you experience the built-in negative consequences of living independent of him. But when we **[exchange] the truth of God for a lie** (1:25), we end up **degraded among [ourselves]** (1:24).

1:26-27 Sex has always been one of humanity's favorite idols. But when sex becomes a god, lust reigns. So we find men and women exchanging **natural sexual relations for unnatural ones** (1:26). God, then, allows us to come up with all kinds of sexual lusts, but the result is a mess. Broken homes, broken hearts, sexually transmitted diseases—all are the fallout of letting lust rule. Moral degradation is the result of the abandonment of God and his righteous standards in both an individual's life and in society.

1:28-32 It gets worse. When people reject God, God delivers **them over to a corrupt mind** (1:28). Thus, instead of acting sane, they act like people who have gone stark raving mad. The worst part is that they still assume they are thinking clearly.

You can know a person or a culture has descended into ultimate corruption when people give public and legal approval to sin. Paul lists twenty-four ways godlessness leads to madness. This is a catalogue of societal breakdown, filled with **greed, murder**, and **deceit** (1:29). We look around at our culture and say, "How did things get so crazy?" Paul answers: as a society, you asked to be free from God. This is what you get.

2:1-3 At this point in Paul's argument, his Jewish listeners would be nodding their heads in agreement: "Get those pagans, Paul!" We may likewise be tempted to cheer Paul on, thinking that he is talking about someone else. Certainly we are not godless and immoral like other people out there. But Paul turns the tables, showing the impartiality of God when it comes to judgment. The moralistic Jews were practicing the same things for which they judged others. Paul's response? **When you judge another, you condemn yourself** (2:1). God's judgment is not based on our self-evaluation of our morals, but **is based on the truth** (2:2). It is complete foolishness to pass judgment on others for what you are doing and to think that **you will escape God's judgment** (2:3).

2:4-5 The Jews, you see, had made the same mistake we often do: they mistook God's patience for his absence. They assumed that if God had not judged them yet, he would not judge at all. But Paul says that **God's kindness is intended to lead . . . to repentance** (2:4). He waits to pour out his wrath—not because his wrath is a myth, but because he knows that once it begins, there is no reprieve. Those who do not repent **are storing up wrath for** themselves (2:5). This should encourage us when people seem to get away with evil. Their account is enlarging, and the bill will come due in eternity. We should never envy the wicked because all they are accumulating is a greater degree of divine judgment.

2:6-8 God **will repay each one according to his works** (2:6), not for salvation, but to address the level of **wrath and anger** (2:8) and **affliction and distress** his works have earned (2:9)—or, for those who persevere in doing good, for the level of **glory, honor, and immortality** (2:7). Paul's point here is not that we can be saved by works (the rest of Romans makes that obvious), but that God is an impartial Judge. He does not reward people based on their ethnic background. He looks at each individual specifically.

2:9-11 Lest Paul's Jewish readers miss his point, he makes it clear: salvation can come **to the Jew, and also to the Greek** (2:9-10). But so can judgment. After all, **there is no favoritism with God** (2:11). As he says in the next chapter, *all* have sinned and *all* are justified by God's grace (3:23-24).

III. EVERYONE NEEDS THE GOSPEL (2:12–3:18)

2:12-16 God will judge people according to the light they have. Thus, those who sinned **without the law** (2:12)—that is, the Gentiles—will be judged according to **the law** that **is written on their hearts.** Although the Gentiles may not have had the Jewish law, they had their conscience, which was sufficient to **either accuse or even excuse them** (2:15). Gentiles have ignored their conscience and acted wickedly. But Paul highlights the opposite possibility, saying that the ability of the Gentiles to **do what the law demands** (2:14)—not perfectly, of course—even without God's law, was meant to put the Jews to shame. The Gentiles' obedience was an authentic witness to the Jews, who were often **hearers of the law** but not **doers of the law** (2:13).

2:17-22 As you might imagine, Paul's claim that the Gentiles were often more faithful than the Jews would have bothered them. The Jews felt that they knew God's will, **being instructed from the law** (2:18). They thought of themselves as **a guide for the blind, a light to those in darkness** (2:19). They were the teachers **of the immature**, the ones who had **truth in the law** (2:20). The Jews felt that because they had the law, they were superior. But having the law only made them more self-righteous and hypocritical.

2:23 The Jews assumed that God wanted external, religious conformity. So they said all the right things and boasted **in the law.** But external religion without internal conversion has absolutely no value to God. He never intended for his people to simply memorize his law. He intends for us to keep it, and we can only do that when we are changed from the inside out.

2:24 Perhaps the most tragic result of the Jews dishonoring God was their terrible witness to the world. Instead of being "a light for the nations" (Isa 49:6) as God intended, the Jews caused **the name of God** to be **blasphemed among the Gentiles.** The hypocrisy of the saved kept the gospel from getting to the lost!

2:25-29 Paul uses circumcision to illustrate his point about religion: **If you are a lawbreaker, your circumcision has become uncircumcision** (2:25). The Jews' external circumcision was supposed to be matched by a circumcision **of the heart—by the Spirit** (2:29). To be outwardly circumcised without such inward transformation, in fact, was worthless. Circumcision was never about externals: **true circumcision is not something visible in the flesh** (2:28). Those who were authentic Jews were not those who had merely performed external rituals, but those who followed God in obedient relationship. External religion can never replace authentic relationship. When religion trumps relationship, God is not present.

3:1-2 Paul continues his hypothetical dialogue with his Jewish objector in chapter 3: **So what advantage does the Jew have?** If Gentiles can be circumcised in spirit without being circumcised in the flesh, **what is the benefit of circumcision?** (3:1). Why go through the painful procedure at all? More importantly, why go through the trouble of keeping the law if, as it seems, the law doesn't really matter? Paul quickly corrects this line of thinking, pointing out that having the law was a unique privilege for the Jews—not a burden (3:2).

3:3-4 Paul's objector fires back: If **some** (of the Jews) **were unfaithful, will their unfaithfulness nullify God's faithfulness?** (3:3). The Jews were supposed to be a "light for the nations" (Isa 49:6), as Paul hinted at already (2:19). But if that light goes out, what hope is left? Isn't God's plan dead in the water? To this Paul responds with the most adamant denial possible in the Greek language: **Absolutely not!** (3:4). God's faithfulness is not overcome by our faithlessness, however great it may be. As Paul puts it, **Let God be true, even though everyone is a liar** (3:4). Our very unrighteousness demonstrates God's righteousness.

3:5-8 Paul's objector retorts, **But if our unrighteousness highlights God's righteousness**, how can that be fair? (3:5). **If by my lie God's truth abounds to his glory, why am I also still being judged as a sinner?** (3:7). Don't miss the indignation that these questions ignite in Paul (3:8); it shows that people really were asking them. Their attitude is the pinnacle of proud humanity: when God turns

our evil toward his good plan, we ask to be let off for our evil. But just because God uses our unrighteousness to reveal his righteousness does not negate the fact that we broke the law.

3:9 Paul finally leaves his objector behind and returns to his main theme for this section—the impartiality of God. Before the impartial Judge, **both Jews and Gentiles are all under sin.** The Jews may have sinned by ignoring the law, but the Gentiles sinned by ignoring their conscience. We started on different paths, but we ended up in the same hopeless place.

3:10-18 None of us like to hear that our case is hopeless. The Jews certainly didn't. So Paul has to prove it to them, using a parade of their own oracles to show that the whole world is guilty before God. He intentionally uses six body parts to illustrate his point: the **throat is an open grave** (3:13); there is deceit on **their tongues** (3:13); there is venom **under their lips** (3:13); the **mouth is full of cursing** (3:14); the **feet are swift to shed blood** (3:15); and **there is no fear of God before their eyes** (3:18). People use every part of their bodies, their minds, and their hearts to rebel against the Word and will of God. Paul could not be clearer: **there is no one who seeks God** (3:11). All of us stand under condemnation; all of us need salvation.

IV. THE GOSPEL OF GOD IN THE CROSS OF CHRIST (3:19-31)

3:19-20 The law was never given to make people righteous. In fact, **the knowledge of sin comes through the law** (3:20). Think of the law as a mirror that shows you who you really are. While a mirror reveals your messed-up hair, you don't pull it off the wall and brush your hair with it! Mirrors don't fix anything; they show us what needs fixing. The law was not designed to fix you, but to reveal what needs fixing.

3:21-22 If the law was primarily meant to reveal our unrighteousness, we've got a problem because we need righteousness if we're going to see God. **The righteousness of God has been revealed**, Paul says, **apart from**

the law (3:21). What we need, then, is apart from what we can do, apart from our human standards, apart from our abilities. There is nothing we can do to satisfy the perfect standard of a holy God.

3:23 When Paul says that **all have sinned and fall short of the glory of God**, he means *all*. No exceptions. And when the standard is God's glory, God's righteousness, it makes no difference if we miss by an inch or a mile. If two men are running to catch a plane, and one man is an hour late, while the other is one minute late, who is in a worse situation? After all, they both missed the flight! It doesn't matter if you are "better" than your neighbor. Your neighbor is not the standard. God is the standard, and we all fall short.

3:24 The cross answers our problem, for through it we **are justified freely by his grace.** Justification is a legal concept meaning that in God's courtroom, he pronounced us innocent of all charges. He does this through what theologians call "imputation"—taking Jesus's perfect record and crediting it to our accounts. **The redemption that is in Christ Jesus** released us from spiritual bondage through the paying of a price, one that was too high for us to pay (and was continually gaining interest!).

3:25 The cross also acts as our **atoning sacrifice**, providing forgiveness through shed blood—in this case, Christ's. Throughout the Old Testament, we see that God requires a blood payment for sin. It's even how Israel escaped Egypt—when God saw lambs' blood on their doorframes, his judgment "passed over" them. The **blood** sacrifice of Christ propitiated, or satisfied, the righteous demands of a holy God.

Forgiveness *always* comes at a cost. A man once owned a Rolls-Royce that started to give him trouble. At his call, the company sent an expert to repair the car. Over time, the man noticed that he never got billed. And when he called Rolls-Royce to check on the matter, they said, "Sir, there is no recorded problem with any Rolls Royce." So what happened to the repair bill? Rolls-Royce absorbed it. Likewise, God sent Jesus to repair our sin problem, but he didn't leave a bill behind because he absorbed the cost himself.

3:26-27 God gets all the glory for saving us. God sent Jesus **to demonstrate his righteousness** (3:26), not to show us how to earn our way to heaven. That's the economy of grace. God gave the grace, so God gets the glory. **Where, then, is boasting?** (3:27). In an economy of grace, boasting **is excluded** (3:27).

3:28-31 Paul's objector has come back in this section, asking if grace and faith make people become bolder sinners. **Do we then nullify the law through faith?** To this Paul again says, **Absolutely not!** (3:31). When you understand grace, you find that it's exactly the opposite. You do the right thing, not because you're driven to (as under the law), but because you're grateful. If you really get grace, you can't help but worship God, give to him, and love other people. Grace isn't license to sin; it's God's supply of goodness. And it's always more than enough.

V. JUSTIFICATION'S ROOTS IN ABRAHAM (4:1-25)

4:1-2 Paul reaches back to **Abraham** to illustrate the way that justification in the gospel functions. Abraham was not **justified by works**, because if he were, he would have **something to boast about.** This, in fact, is always the problem with works: they can't save us because they give us something to brag about. As long as we're boasting, we aren't clinging to God's grace.

4:3 How did Abraham become righteous? Not by circumcision or the law. **Abraham believed God**, and because of that, he was **credited** with **righteousness.** God told Abraham something, and Abraham took him at his word. That's the essence of faith.

Abraham wasn't saved simply by believing something, but by believing *God*. Faith is merely a channel to get to its object. It doesn't matter how sincere or passionate your faith is if the object is wrong. Back in the 1980s, there was a tragic case in Chicago where some Tylenol had become laced with cyanide. Seven people died. Those involved believed they were just getting pain medicine, but their belief was insufficient: the contents of the bottles couldn't be trusted. It is the *object* of our faith, and not our faith itself, that matters.

4:4-5 Salvation is not a transaction; it comes **to the one who does not work**, the one who **believes on him who declares the ungodly to be righteous** (4:5). It's a gift, plain and simple. If you just reach out your hand and take it, then it's yours. But if you work for it, you dismiss the gift and treat it as a wage that is earned.

Many people will stand before God and list their credentials: I worked my head off; I went to church every Sunday; I helped the needy; I read my Bible. But God will not grant salvation **as something owed** (4:4; see Eph 2:8-9).

4:6-8 The Jews revered Abraham as the father of their faith, but Paul brings in an additional witness to solidify his case. David, Israel's greatest king, also wrote about **God** crediting **righteousness apart from works** (4:6). Quoting from the Psalms, Paul shows that assurance of salvation comes from the knowledge that **lawless acts are forgiven** and **sins are covered** (4:7). Sins are not overcome by hard work, and lawless acts are not outweighed by good deeds. God does the forgiving; God does the covering; we simply believe it and receive it.

4:9-12 Paul returns to the idea of circumcision to further his point. When was Abraham credited with righteousness—**while he was circumcised, or uncircumcised** (4:10)? Any Jew would have known the answer to that. Abraham believed God's promise back in Genesis 15, which took place *before* **the sign of circumcision.** Circumcision acted **as a seal of the righteousness that he had by faith.** It was a confirmation of Abraham's faith, not the cause of it.

The timing of Abraham's circumcision was not a historical accident, but an intentional orchestration of God. Since Abraham believed before circumcision, he could become **the father of all who believe**— Gentile as well as Jew, **circumcised** and **uncircumcised** (4:11-12). Again, we see the radical equality of all people before God. Jew and Gentile come to God on the same basis—faith.

4:13-17 All the law can do is reveal our sin. Without it, we wouldn't know that we had fallen short of the standard. But as it is, **the law produces wrath** (4:15). This is why faith is so essential: **those who are of the law** (4:16) are under a just penalty of condemnation *because* of the law. Trying to escape the penalty of the law by works of the law is like trying to quench your thirst by drinking salt water. You only make the problem worse.

4:18-19 Abraham's great act of faith actually didn't have anything to do with circumcision or the law at all. It had to do with God's promise to give Abraham and Sarah a son, even though Abraham **was about a hundred years old** and **Sarah's womb** was barren (4:19). Trusting that God would make Abraham **the father of many nations** (4:18) in that circumstance required more than optimism. It required a supernatural level of hope.

4:20-21 Here we see how Abraham could have such incredible hope and faith. Abraham **was strengthened in his faith** (4:20) because **he was fully convinced that what God had promised, he was also able to do** (4:21). That's the best definition of faith ever. Did God say it? Can God pull off what God said? To doubt him is to question whether he tells the truth.

4:22-25 Paul returns to the primary theme of this chapter again: Abraham's faith **was credited to him for righteousness** (4:22). Similarly, righteousness **will be credited to us** (4:24) like it was credited to Abraham— on the basis of faith. But what Abraham only saw in shadows and hints, we see fully. We know that the object of our faith is **Jesus our Lord,** who was raised **from the dead** (4:24). Abraham trusted the power of God to bring life from a seemingly dead situation (barrenness). We have seen the power of God bring life from the literal death of the Son.

VI. RECONCILIATION AND THE LAST ADAM (5:1-21)

5:1 In chapter 5, Paul begins to talk not only about the *process* of salvation, but the *results* of salvation. The process, as he has said before, is that **we have been declared**

righteous by faith. While faith leads to righteousness, it also leads to **peace with God.** Previously, we were God's enemies. We were at war with him. Now, through

Jesus, he has drawn us close and made us his friends.

5:2-5 Faith accesses the grace that God wants to dispense in our lives, not just in salvation and sanctification, but also in tribulation. If we are in Christ, **we also rejoice in our afflictions** (5:3) because God is working in those afflictions for our good. Through affliction, God intends to create in us **endurance**, which **produces proven character, and proven character produces hope** (5:4). Hope, like faith, is only as good as its object. Just as our faith can only lead to salvation if it is faith *in God*, our **hope will not disappoint us** because it is the hope of **God's love . . . poured out in our hearts through the Holy Spirit** (5:5). Even in our suffering, God's Spirit provides a fresh experience of God's love to us and for us.

5:6 We know love by its price tag. Authentic love is costly and sacrifices for its beloved. What, then, does it say about God's love that in order to save us, he was willing to pay with his own Son's life? **Christ died for the ungodly** because he loved us with an everlasting love. And this love is unconditional because it came **while we were still helpless.** He loved us when there was nothing lovely about us; we were totally unable to save ourselves.

5:7-8 In the United States, on occasions like Memorial Day, we honor the sacrifices of people who died so that others might live. Remembering these heroes brings to my mind what Paul says here, that **for a good person perhaps someone might even dare to die** (5:7). It's rare for someone to lay his life down for others. It's tremendously courageous and loving and worthy of honor. But God's love is even bigger and more worthy of recognition than this. Jesus died, but not for friends; God proved **his own love for us** by dying for us while we were his enemies (5:8)! It's as if he says to unbelievers, "I know you're rebelling against me. But I still love you so much that I'll go to the cross for you." The world has never seen a love like this.

5:9-11 Paul broadens the idea of salvation by drawing on the resurrection: If **the death of [God's] Son** made us **reconciled to God**, then

how much more . . . will we be saved by his life (5:10)? The death of Jesus reconciled us to God, but Jesus didn't stay dead. He's alive right now. And he's interceding for us (see Heb 7:25) in order to give us victory over the power of sin and its consequences. Think about it. If Jesus could take you from hell to heaven by dying, what he can do for you by living is even more exciting. Many believers who have accepted the saving death of Christ have yet to understand and access the saving life of Christ, which gives us victory in history.

5:12-14 By mentioning Jesus's life, Paul reminds himself of another comparison between Jesus and the Old Testament—the connection to Adam. Adam **is a type of the Coming One** (5:14), a foreshadow of Jesus. We got our physical life from Adam, and we get our spiritual life from the second Adam, Christ. Both Adams give life, but only the second Adam can give us life that never ends.

There is another important commonality to point out here. Adam gave us sin through imputation. He deposited sin into our accounts so that we were born with it. Because he was our representative, when sin and death entered Adam, **death spread to all people, because all sinned** (5:12). The way out of death and into life is similar: Christ imputes righteousness and life into us. He is our representative, and in his righteousness we find our righteousness.

5:15 Adam may have given us life, but his main legacy is that **by the one man's trespass the many died.** He left the legacy of death for us, but we don't have any grounds to complain, because we prove every time we sin that we wouldn't have chosen any better than he did. God's **gift** of grace is **not like the trespass.** Unlike Adam, who gave us life and death, Jesus gives us only life. And while we *earned* Adam's penalty of death, we *receive* **the grace of God** as a **gift.**

5:16-17 You can group the human race under two people—Adam or Christ. Every person you meet is either in Adam or in Christ, and that's a difference with eternal consequences. The path of Adam leads to **judgment, resulting in condemnation.** But the path of

Christ results **in justification** (5:16). God saves us so that we reign in life—that is, live lives of spiritual victory rather than spiritual defeat.

5:18 The sin we inherited from Adam—called *original sin*—is overridden by the death of Christ because **through one righteous act there is justification leading to life for everyone.** By "everyone," Paul means everyone. Thus, even though we are all born sinners, Christ's blood covers us until we reach an age of accountability, that time when a person is capable of choosing to transgress and reject his revelation. So while **there is condemnation for everyone**, there is divine covering through Christ for those who have not yet chosen to rebel against God's law. This explains how babies or people born with mental handicaps are saved by Christ's death, since original sin is no longer the issue in those cases.

5:19 We are saved by works—just not our own works. We are saved by the works of Christ. Through Christ's **obedience the many will be made righteous.** Because he lived the perfect life we should have, we can share in his perfect record.

5:20-21 The law came along to multiply the trespass (5:20), which would be a tragedy without God's intervention. But the beauty of the gospel is that **where sin multiplied, grace multiplied even more** (5:20). Indeed, anyone who has a deep understanding of his own sin knows this from experience: the more we see our sin as a violation of God's perfect law, the more we stand in awe of God's grace toward us. God's grace, Paul says, is stronger than our sin. Sin may have **reigned in death**, but through Christ **grace will reign through righteousness** (5:21). Sin is simply not strong enough to overpower grace. Between sin and grace, in fact, grace wins every time. This is why it is essential for all believers to grow in their understanding and appreciation of the magnificent grace of God (see Titus 2:11-14; 2 Pet 3:18).

VII. DEAD TO SIN, ALIVE TO CHRIST (6:1-23)

6:1 Paul anticipates a misunderstanding: **Should we continue in sin so that grace may multiply?** People often make the mistake of seeing grace as license to do whatever they want: If more sin means more grace, why not just sin on purpose? Why not just live it up? This is why some people come to Communion on Sunday, hoping to get just enough of God to cover their debauchery on Monday. But no judge shows mercy to a criminal so that he can go out and commit more crimes.

6:2 Paul had absolutely zero patience with this kind of nonsense. "Keep sinning *because* of grace?" **Absolutely not! How can we who died to sin still live in it?** The fundamental issue here is one of identity. Anyone who says that salvation makes him free to sin has totally misunderstood his new identity in Christ. When we battle sin, we usually try to do it in our own power, fighting the flesh with the flesh. But Paul knows that won't work. So instead of giving us principles for stomping on the flesh, Paul reminds us we are dead to what once controlled us.

6:3-5 Who are we, as Christians? We are the people who were co-baptized with Christ, co-buried with him, and co-resurrected with him. So when **all of us . . . were baptized into Christ Jesus**, we **were baptized into his death** (6:3). When he died two thousand years ago, we died two thousand years ago. When he was buried, **we were buried with him** (6:4). What is true of Jesus physically is true of us spiritually.

Paul uses baptism to illustrate how this works. In Greek, the word translated **baptism** meant to plunge or dip (6:4). It was the word used for dying clothes. You would dip a cloth in purple dye, let it soak (or be "baptized"), and it would absorb the color. The properties of the dye became part of the cloth. That's what happens to Christians: we are dipped in the blood of Jesus, so that the properties of Jesus become a part of us (see Gal 2:20).

Paul again reminds us that we've been united to Jesus. Why? Because unity fuels power. We **walk in newness of life** (6:4) only when we intimately know that **we have been united with** Christ. The same power that led to **his resurrection** (6:5) is available to us—not by working for it, but by steeping ourselves in our Christian identity.

6:6-8 This raises a question: if the Christian has the resurrection power of Jesus to overcome sin, why is it so hard to do? If **our old self was crucified with him** (6:6), why does that old self still have such power?

I've heard that cadavers can do some odd things. A mortician I know says that their muscles sometimes twitch. He even saw a twitch that actually catapulted the cadaver off the table! (One reason why I will never be a mortician.) But after sharing that insight, he told me, "That stuff doesn't bother me, because I know that *dead* is *dead*, even when it acts alive." Indeed, it's the same with our body of sin. Yes, it's moving around like it's still in charge. Yes, we'll still sin. But previously we *had* to, because we were sin's slaves. Now we **no longer** need to **be enslaved to sin** (6:6). If we continue to sin, it's because we've forgotten our true identity.

6:9-10 Our main problem with sin is not a lack of willpower, but a lack of vision. We take our eyes off of the cross, and Paul wants us to look back there. He can't talk about it enough. Jesus **died to sin once for all** (6:10), which removes any power sin has over our lives. He was **raised from the dead**, proving that sin and death **no longer [rule]** (6:9). Before you and I were saved, we were like radios with only one frequency. When we came to Christ, he added a new one. The problem is that many of us are still tuning in to the old frequency. But as sure as Jesus **lives to God** (6:10), he can live in us and through us.

6:11 That one little word "consider" is the key to the entire passage. It means, "calculate" or "reckon." Count it to be so. To experience

victory over sin, you must **consider yourselves dead to sin and alive to God in Christ Jesus.** That is, you need to buy into the new identity bought for you at the cross. Jesus died to sin in our place; we don't have to die too.

During the Civil War, it was legal for men who wanted to avoid the draft to pay for personal replacements. In one particular instance, a man paid for another to go into battle for him, and that individual was killed. A few months later, the man who paid for the replacement received a second draft notice. But he took the legal agreement to the draft board, saying, "The second draft is invalid. Someone already went to war and died in my place." This is a picture of the Christian's situation. When Satan wants to re-draft us into sin, we must oppose him by pointing to Jesus's victory: "Satan, you can't force me to that old life anymore. The payment has already been paid. Jesus died in my place."

6:12-14 After *understanding* your identity in Christ and *reckoning* that identity to your account, you must also *yield* to it. You have a choice before you, either to **let sin reign in your mortal body** (6:12) or to **offer yourselves to God** (6:13). Sin wants to boss you around, using your passions and lusts as **weapons for unrighteousness** (6:13). And though we usually wish that God would just take the desires of the flesh away at the point of salvation, he doesn't. Those desires remain with us, but since he gives us the Spirit, we now have the power to say, "No." The key to enjoying this power is a recognition that we as believers are under a different authority. When we realize and submit to Christ's rule over us, regardless of our emotions, the flesh progressively loses its domination, and the grace of God is activated in our lives. We then obey because of our relationship. We are no longer bound to the fleshly based legalistic rule of law.

6:15 Some carnal Christians might think that living **under grace** means they can go on sinning. But Paul shoots that down. If you are living under grace, you will actually keep the law. And if you don't keep the law, it only proves you're not operating under the grace of God. Christians obey the standard, but the motivation isn't the standard. The motivation is God's grace.

6:16-18 Paul shows Christians a choice: we can be slaves of **sin leading to death** or servants **of obedience leading to righteousness** (6:16). There is no third choice where we choose not to serve anyone. Every one of us serves somebody. The sobering danger is that people may be Christians and still offering their bodies up to sin.

In January of 1863, President Lincoln issued his famous Emancipation Proclamation, freeing all slaves throughout the Confederacy. But even years later, there were certain places where that announcement had been kept secret. Thus, even after being declared free, African Americans were still acting like slaves. No one had told them the truth of their situation! How foolish is it for those of us who *know* we're free in Christ to keep saying "yes" to sin?

6:19-22 Paul brings up the issue of life and death to amplify his point. Serving sin leads **to greater and greater lawlessness** (6:19).

And while serving sin means **you were free with regard to righteousness** (6:20), what did it really gain you? Sure, you were free from righteousness. But **the outcome of those things is death** (6:21). If you become a slave of sin, you get some short-term pleasure, but that pleasure led to death. What kind of a trade-off is that? If, however, you become a slave of God, you get sanctification and righteousness—both of which lead to life (6:22).

6:23 Another way to put this is to say that **the wages of sin is death.** Although we like to quote this to non-Christians, Paul is writing to Christians. And whether physical death or a spiritual separation from the enjoyment of the eternal life of God is in view—since believers can't lose their salvation—the payment of sin is always the same. Indeed, Christians can lose their joy because sin separates us from fellowship with God. They can also lose out on the will of God. The point is that believers can still choose sin, but when they do, they collect their rightful wages: weakness, sickness, meaninglessness, and death.

VIII. SLAVES OF GOD (7:1-25)

7:1-4 Paul uses the analogy of marriage to illustrate our freedom from the law. If a married woman remarries, whether or not she is an adulteress depends on whether her husband is still alive. **If she is married to another man while her husband is living, she will be called an adulteress** (7:3). But a married woman is only **legally bound to her husband while he lives.** When he passes away, she is **released from the law** (7:2). Marrying as a widow is completely legal because her obligation to the first contract ended with her husband's death. The law was our "husband," and **through the body of Christ** (7:4), that relationship is dead. We are thus free to enjoy a new union with Christ.

7:5 Because the law is designed to reveal sin, it actually aroused **the sinful passions . . . in us to bear fruit for death.** But having

come to Christ, we're no longer under the authority of the law. If it reveals our sin (which it still does), we have a new righteousness in Christ that overrides our sin.

7:7 Importantly, just because the law instigated our sinful passions doesn't mean something is wrong with the law. It is like a mirror; it shows us what's wrong, but it's not designed to fix it. Without it, we **would not have known sin.** As Paul says, **I would not have known what it is to covet if the law had not said, Do not covet.** The law, then, is also like a speed limit sign that reads, "Speed Limit 55," which may or may not slow us down. Nevertheless, that sign validates the police officer who pulls us over when we're driving 80! Without the sign, he would have no authority to stop us. With the sign, our "sin" is revealed, and we're without excuse.

7:8-11 Paul addresses the problem of legalism here. Legalism expects a set of rules to keep us from sinning. But the more we try to meet God's standard by ourselves, the worse we become. Without the commandment, we were breaking God's laws. But once the commandment was revealed, **sin sprang to life** (7:9). The law is good, but sin always seizes **an opportunity through the commandment** to produce more sin (7:8).

Have you ever seen a "Don't Touch" sign? The sign itself makes you want to reach out your hand! Likewise, sin conjures up the desire to do the opposite of what the law says, so the more law (apart from the gospel), the more sin.

7:12-13 Is the law good or bad? Paul reminds us that **the commandment is holy and just and good** (7:12). It came from God and represents his holy character. The main issue here isn't the law at all, but sin. The power of indwelling sin, even for believers, is so strong that it can take **what is good** and twist it to **become sinful beyond measure** (7:13). Sin keeps us locked in a struggle.

7:14-15 It's encouraging for us as believers to know that Paul suffered from the same struggles we do. We all have had candid moments in which we stepped back and said, I **do not understand what I am doing.** Haven't we all asked, "What's wrong with me?" There is a war within us, and like Paul, we often say, **I do not practice what I want to do, but I do what I hate** (7:15).

7:16 Even worse, Paul knows he can't claim ignorance. He recognizes the internal struggle as a validation of the law: **I agree with the law that it is good.** He agrees that he is doing wrong. He simply can't break free. Was this because Paul was especially sinful? Probably not. The closer you get to God, the more sensitive you are about your own moral failure. Show me a Christian who does not feel the pain of his sin, and I'll show you someone who isn't close to God.

7:17-18 Here we get to the heart of the problem. Paul struggles because he is still in the **flesh, and nothing good lives** in him (7:18). Even though our old self was crucified with Christ (6:6), the flesh was not. Our sin nature was put to death, but our flesh remains active. Our sin nature was like a factory that produced unrighteousness, evil, and sin. When we came to Christ, however, God shut that factory down. That solved the problem of future production, but it didn't address what was already produced. Existing sin from that factory found a new home, and that home is called our flesh.

7:19-23 When you come to Christ, your identity changes. But your location stays the same. There is now a distinction between who you are and where you live. You are totally redeemed, totally sanctified, totally brand new in Christ, but you live in a body contaminated by flesh. Thus, when we as Christians sin, we are no longer the ones doing it: **it is the sin that lives in [us]** (7:20). In saying this, Paul is not excusing our sin. He is reminding us that our true identity is no longer found in our actions, even if we keep sinning.

When I want to do what is good, evil is present with me (7:21). Note that it's *with* me, it doesn't define *me*. My "I" has changed from sinner to saint. Therefore, when sin wants me to define myself by what I've done wrong, I remember that God defines me by who I am in Christ.

7:24-25 Paul recognizes what many Christians miss—that he is helpless to resolve his own problem: **Who will rescue me from this body of death?** (7:24). All throughout this chapter he has been struggling to pull himself out of his inner war, but as if battling quicksand, he found that the more he struggled, the deeper he sank. The power of positive thinking did nothing for him. Until he finally lifted his eyes to the only one who could rescue him, his situation was hopeless. Then, like a bolt of lightning, he finally shouts, **thanks be to God through Jesus Christ our Lord!** (7:25). And all of chapter 8 shows us just what lifted Paul out of the muck and mire.

IX. THE SPIRIT LEADS US TO GLORY (8:1-39)

8:1 Paul's **therefore** in this verse is tied to the "thanks be to God" in 7:25. In light of what God did through his Son, there is "therefore" **no condemnation for those in Christ Jesus.** If you are a believer in Jesus, it does not matter what your heart tells you; God says you stand before him with zero condemnation.

8:2-3 Until now, Paul has been talking about the law of Moses. Here he introduces a new law—**the law of the Spirit of life.** Unlike Moses's law, this one can **set you free from . . . sin and death** (8:2).

Which law you operate by determines whether you live in victory or defeat. The law of sin and death is like gravity. It inherently pulls you down, no matter how high you jump. But the law of the Spirit overrides gravity. It's like climbing aboard an airplane, where the laws of aerodynamics apply. You cannot get rid of the law of gravity, but you can transcend it. The Spirit's law transcends the law of sin so that sin no longer controls the agenda.

8:4 For the Spirit's law to apply, we must **not walk according to the flesh but according to the Spirit.** The word "walk" refers to our entire way of life, and it has three concepts imbedded in it. First, it implies a destination: you must point your life toward the will and glory of God. Second, it implies dependence: when you walk, you place one foot in front of another, putting all your weight on that foot for that step. You must rest all of the weight of your soul on God's power, not your own. Third, walking implies dedication: you must continually take steps, perpetually calling on God to do in you what you could never do alone.

8:5-8 If we have a problem with our walk, the problem is not in our feet. It's in our minds. If we **have [our] minds set on the things of the flesh**, we will **live according to the flesh** (8:5). Conversely, if we set our minds on **the things of the Spirit**, we will **live according to the Spirit** (8:5). If our minds are set on the wrong things, our feet will automatically go the wrong way. Setting your mind is like choosing a television station. You can watch channel 5 or channel 8, but you can't watch channel "5-and-8." You have two different channels—one that leads to **death** and one that leads to **life and peace** (8:6). God says, "Choose life!"

8:9-10 When you became a Christian, **the Spirit of God** came to live **in you** (8:9). The Spirit cannot dwell with sin, so he kicked sin out of its place of authority in your life. Where did it go? It took up residence in your **body**, which still **is dead because of sin** (8:10). It's dead, unresponsive. When you try to "be better" for God by getting more religious, you are kicking that dead body and trying to get it moving. It won't move.

8:11 We become alive, not by telling our dead bodies to live, but by letting the Spirit do to us what he did for Jesus—raising him from the dead. If **his Spirit . . . lives in you**, then **he who raised Christ from the dead will also bring your mortal [body] to life.** We have a new power within us: the Spirit is like an engine in a car that can take us where God wants us to go. Too many of us are trying to push the car of life around, when God wants us to let the engine do the work.

8:12-13 Paul wants us to kick the flesh to the curb so that we can experience the abundant life God has promised. If we **put to death the deeds of the body, [we] will live** (8:13). We can overcome the discouragement of a bad marriage, or singleness, or financial stress because he who is in us is "greater than the one who is in the world" (1 John 4:4)! Jesus promised that we would have trouble (see John 16:33), but he also promised to give us overflowing life in the midst of it.

8:14-15 If we walk according to the Spirit as God desires, we prove ourselves to be **God's sons** (8:14). Not only are we sons (and daughters), but we are *adopted* children (8:15). If a person was adopted in Paul's time, that individual immediately received all of the rights of an adult heir. The chief right that Paul mentions here is intimacy with God. We therefore can pray, **Abba, Father** (8:15). *Abba* is a term of intimacy meaning "Papa" or "Daddy." We can say it with complete assurance that God is listening.

8:16-17 Being adopted as **God's children** (8:16) may come with extreme benefits, but it also carries with it intense responsibility. Yes, we are already **heirs of God**, but we can only become **coheirs with Christ** if we **suffer with him** (8:17). If we do suffer, we will **be glorified with him** (8:17). If we shrink back in the day of trial, we'll lose something valuable. We cannot lose our salvation, but we can certainly lose some of the reward God intends to give us.

8:18 If we focus exclusively on our suffering, we may be tempted to lose heart. Paul therefore reminds us that **the sufferings of this present time** are not even **worth comparing with the glory that is going to be revealed to us**. For believers, the glory ahead is not only greater than our present suffering. It is *so much greater* that should we look back on our earthly existence from the joys of eternity, our only response will be, "Suffering? *What* suffering?"

8:19-21 Our present suffering, though small in the context of eternity, actually gives us a window into what God is doing cosmically. Our suffering mirrors that of the rest of creation, which **eagerly waits with anticipation for God's sons to be revealed** (8:19). God has tied the sanctification of believers together with the perfection of the created order so that creation will only **be set free from the bondage to decay** when **God's children** experience their own **glorious freedom** (8:21). Human sin corrupted creation and dragged it down into the messes we see today. It brought about things like earthquakes, volcanoes, and disease. But our righteousness, bought and perfected by Christ, will act as the agent of change in creation. When the sons of God are ruling, the earth will once again have order, perfection, and untarnished beauty.

8:22-23 In the meantime, we share with creation in painful anticipation, groaning **within ourselves, eagerly waiting for . . . the redemption of our bodies** (8:23). But this anticipation is colored with hope, because the creation groans **with labor pains** (8:22), a fact proving that the present suffering is not meaningless. It may be difficult, but our groaning *now* is leading to life *then*. And just as a mother forgets the pain of childbirth once her baby is born, we too will forget our pains in the world to come.

8:24-25 This context of suffering and anticipation requires hope. *Hope* is a joyful expectation about the future, a trust that our tomorrows will be greater than our yesterdays. But **hope that is seen is not hope** (8:24). Real hope combines a radical trust in God with the candid admission that we don't know the details about our own futures. What we *do* know, however, outweighs what we do *not*. We know that what awaits us is salvation, which gives us the confidence to **eagerly wait for it with patience** (8:25).

8:26 We have a helper as we wait for our sanctification. The Spirit **helps us in our weakness**, and he helps by praying for us, interceding **for us with unspoken groanings**. I'm glad the Spirit is praying for us because **we do not know what to pray for as we should**. That is, we don't know the language of prayer like God does. We're like foreigners, wandering around a country completely helpless. But in this unknown territory, the Spirit of God translates for us.

8:27 The Greek word for "intercede" that Paul uses means "to appeal." In our weakness, we may simply be groaning, but the Spirit translates that into an appeal that is **according to the will of God**. If we pray from the heart—even if our prayers are only groans—they are exactly as they should be by the time they reach God.

8:28-29 Everybody likes the first part of 8:28, where **all things work together for the good of those who love God**. Most people, though, ignore the second part—which is even more important. God is working in our lives for our good, but not so that we'll live on Easy Street. Rather, he works for our good **according to his purpose.**

So, what exactly is God's purpose for our lives? God desires to conform us **to the image of his Son** (8:29). He wants to make us clones of Christ, people who mirror Christ's character and conduct. Sure, he wants to give us "all things," but we can only receive them if we are conformed to Christ. Therefore, the promise of 8:28 is a conditional one. If believers are not loving God and progressively being "conformed to the image of" Christ, they will not see things working together for good. Unfortunately, not all Christians steadfastly remain in God's love (see Jude 21).

8:30 God always finishes what he starts. It's an unbroken chain. Note that all who are **called** reach glorification, which guarantees the eternal security of all believers. This should give us tremendous assurance.

8:31-34 The staggering promise of 8:30 launches Paul into the most beautiful and victorious passage in the book. He asks, **What then are we to say about these things?** (8:31). If God has done all of this for us, what could possibly overrule it? If God **did not even spare his own Son** (8:32), why would we ever doubt his goodness and generosity toward us? And **if God is for us** (8:31), then who could **bring an accusation against God's elect?** (8:33). If God says you're not guilty (and he does!) then charges against you are irrelevant.

8:35-39 Paul ends this chapter with another eternal security question: **Who can separate us from the love of Christ?** (8:35). The answer, at this point, should be obvious: *no one.* But Paul wants us to feel that answer, so he piles up problem after problem. Will **affliction or distress or persecution or famine or nakedness or danger or sword?** (8:35). In other words, can the worst circumstances on earth separate us from God's love? What about **death . . . rulers . . . things present . . . things to come?** (8:38). Will the spiritual powers of the invisible world divorce us from God? Will one's past, present, or future do it? Will **any other created thing** (8:39)? Paul covers *every* possibility with that phrase. That's as "everything" as "everything" gets.

Paul's answer to every possible objection is, "No!" Of course these things can't separate us from God's love! Nothing can. In fact, even in the midst of terrible situations, we emerge **more than conquerors** (8:37). With God's love, we don't just get by. We overwhelmingly conquer.

X. GOD'S SOVEREIGNTY (9:1-29)

Chapters 9–11 are like a parenthesis in Paul's overall argument. Normally, we would expect a rich theological section like chapter 8 to flow seamlessly into the practical commands of chapter 12. This is Paul's usual pattern—teach theology, then give application. But here Paul pauses to address a pertinent question: If God loves his chosen people and keeps his promises, how is it that he seems to have forgotten both his people and his Old Testament promises? The answer is that even though God has temporarily set Israel aside, he has decidedly *not* cancelled his promises to them. In fact, God's promises are more certain than we realize. His sovereignty, illustrated through the history of Israel, provides a bedrock foundation for our trust in his unchanging plan.

9:1-3 Nowhere does Paul so vehemently assert his truthfulness as he does here. Three times he underscores it: **I speak the truth in Christ—I am not lying; my conscience testifies to me through the Holy Spirit** (9:1). Why the repetition? Paul knows that what he says next is so outrageous that many people would take it as exaggeration: **I could wish that I myself were cursed and cut off from Christ** for the sake of Israel (9:3). Like the Lord whom he followed, then, Paul was willing to experience divine judgment so that others might be saved. Do you have the same **sorrow and unceasing anguish** (9:2) in your heart for those who don't know Jesus?

9:4-5 The nation of Israel received special privileges, including **the glory, the**

covenants, the giving of the law, the unique opportunity to worship God in the temple service, and the promises of the Savior (9:4). By the drawing of Gentiles into the people of God, Israel was not diminished in the least. They had been favored by God in a way no other nation had.

9:6-7 It seemed, though, as if the word of God to Israel had failed. The Jews were supposed to welcome their Messiah; instead, many (in fact, most) of them rejected Jesus. So Paul reminds us of an Old Testament idea known as "the remnant" (e.g., Isa 10:21). He says that not all who are descended from Israel are Israel (9:6). There had *always* been a true people of God within the nation, a spiritual Israel within the physical Israel. So it is today. Only those who accept Christ are truly Abraham's children and his descendants (9:7).

9:8 Israel fell into the same temptation we often fall into, assuming that children by physical descent . . . are God's children. Don't we similarly assume that our kids, because they grow up in church, are all right—even if everything in their lives says otherwise? God has a lot of *children*, but he doesn't have any *grandchildren*. Each one of our kids must accept the promise personally, because only the children of the promise are considered . . . offspring.

9:9 Paul uses an example to further his point. Abraham had more than one child, but the promise only stayed with the one that God planned supernaturally. Ishmael (Hagar's son) was born out of the will of man, but Isaac (Sarah's son) was born by God's sovereign plan, as he promised Abraham: At this time I will come, and Sarah will have a son. God's plan doesn't need our manmade solutions. That only gets us "Ishmaels." God's plan is supernatural. If he promised it, he'll see it through.

9:10-13 God's election is not for personal, eternal salvation, but for blessing, service, and usefulness. Abraham was called not so that God would save him, but because God would use him to bless all the families of the earth (see Gen 12:3). That line of blessing

skipped over Isaac's older son Esau, even though he had not been born yet, passing to the younger, Jacob. Why? Not because they had done anything good or bad, but that God's purpose according to election might stand (9:11). By withholding the blessing from Esau, God effectively hated Esau (9:13)—not out of preference or from an emotional motivation, but in order to display his sovereignty in going against the cultural norms so that the older [would] serve the younger (9:12). Paul clearly states that this election was about service, not eternal salvation. Jacob—not Esau—was chosen to be the Messiah's ancestor even though both were Abraham's descendants.

In saying, I have loved Jacob, but I have hated Esau (9:13), Paul switches from individual to national election by quoting Malachi 1:2-3, where the two sons represent nations (see Gen 25:23) as Esau's descendants (the Edomites) served Jacob (Israel). The concepts of *love* and *hate* refer to God's decision to bestow inheritance, blessings, and kingdom responsibility on Jacob's descendants rather than on Esau's. Although Esau never served Jacob personally, Jacob called himself Esau's servant (see Gen 33:3, 5, 8, 14). God was pointing to his favor of Israel (Jacob's descendants) over the Edomites (Esau's descendants). God has the sovereign right to choose whom he will use to accomplish his kingdom purposes.

9:14-16 Choosing Jacob over Esau raises the question of God's fairness: Is there injustice with God? Paul shouts back, once again, Absolutely not! (9:14). God has the sovereign right to show mercy to whom [he] will (9:15). This mercy is given for the purpose of receiving blessing to accomplish and advance his kingdom program, not for individual salvation. He can accomplish his purposes with our assistance, or over our resistance.

9:17-18 Pharaoh's actions prove a perfect picture of God's sovereign plan at work. God told Pharaoh, I raised you up for this reason so that I may display my power . . . and that my name may be proclaimed (9:17). God, then, was the one raising up Pharaoh. But he was also the one hardening Pharaoh's heart (9:18). Importantly, God does not harden the hearts of people until they reject him. It was only after Pharaoh hardened his own heart (see Exod 7:22; 8:15, 32) that God hardened it further (Exod 9:12). He may harden your heart, too, but he won't do it without your help.

This hardening is not predestination to damnation; it's an expression of God's prerogative to choose whom he will use to serve his purposes and how he will use them (see Jer 18:1-13). God punishes the wicked by using their wickedness to accomplish his purposes. God uses obedience and disobedience to accomplish his kingdom agenda while holding people responsible for their own decisions.

9:19-24 All this "hardening" talk doesn't seem to be helping Paul's case. After all, if God is doing the hardening, **Why then does he still find fault** (9:19)? If God's will isn't on the basis of human behavior, why are we blamed? Paul offers two responses. The first is to remind his objector that he's talking back to *God*, the very one who formed him

like a **potter** forming a piece of **clay** (9:20-21). The Creator has rights over his creation, plain and simple.

But Paul's second response reminds us that our behavior still matters. The example of Pharaoh is still fresh in his mind when Paul mentions **objects of wrath** (9:22) and **objects of mercy** (9:23). "Wrath" refers to the present consequences of sin (as we've seen earlier in the writing of Paul), not to eternal destiny. And that wrath is tied to rejection or acceptance of the will of God. But whether God is acting in wrath or in mercy, he is accomplishing his plan. The big difference is in how *we* experience that plan—as willing sons and daughters, or as unwilling slaves.

9:25-29 Between wrath and mercy, God leans toward mercy, as the example of Hosea reminds us. Even though Israel was subjected to God's wrath in history, their remnant will return as God's **Beloved** and **People** (9:25). God has always kept his promises, but as the quotations in 9:27-29 show us, their fulfillment is often unexpected and surprising.

XI. OUR RESPONSIBILITY (9:30–10:21)

9:30-33 Paul turns a corner as he begins to examine the other side of the equation—our responsibility. From one perspective, it was God's sovereign will to extend grace to the Gentiles. From another perspective, though, the Gentiles **have obtained righteousness** because they pursued it the right way, by faith (9:30). Israel, on the other hand, failed to achieve **the law of righteousness** (9:31) because **they did not pursue it by faith** (9:32). As long as anyone pursues salvation by works, as Israel did, the grace of Jesus will act like a **stumbling stone** (9:32). Jesus is either the stone we trip over in our self-righteousness, or he's the rock we build our lives upon.

10:1-2 The problem with Israel, Paul points out, is not a lack of passion. He testifies **that they have zeal for God**. They are dead serious. They are incredibly religious. They believe in God and think they are running

God's race. But their zeal is **not according to knowledge** (10:2). So, although they're running a race, it's the race of religion—the Jewish equivalent of going to church and trying to be a good person. Paul knew this race well, because he too had been running it for years.

10:3 There are two approaches to getting to heaven: God's approach and yours. If we **are ignorant of the righteousness of God**, the automatic tendency is to **establish [our] own righteousness.** We'll naturally submit to God's way or we'll create our own. Those are the only two choices, but they'll lead us to very different ends.

Society may tell us there are dozens of ways to get to heaven, but in the end, there's just one. Think of it like the game of basketball. Two guys take shots to win the game: the first guy misses the rim and backboard completely, an air ball; the second guy puts up a shot that rattles around, *nearly* goes in, but still misses. Which shot is of greater value? Neither. There's a set standard for scoring (the ball must go through the hoop), and both guys missed it. The worst thing in the world is thinking that just because your ball went around the rim, spiritually speaking, it went in.

10:4 Paul calls Jesus **the end of the law for righteousness**, meaning he's the termination point, the goal. In other words, the point of the law wasn't the law; the point of the law was to point us to Jesus. And for **everyone who believes**, we get the record of Jesus's perfect righteousness in our place.

10:5 We can choose to pursue our own **righteousness that is from the law**, of course. As Paul says, referencing Mosaic law, **The one who does these things will live by them.** So if you want the law to judge you, fine. Have it your way. God will judge you by the law. But it won't be a pretty sight. God demands absolute perfection, so if you're hoping to be justified by the law, you had better live a life without sin. And history tells us there's only been one such life.

10:6-8 The **righteousness that comes from faith** (10:6) may be supernatural, but it's not difficult or complicated. The righteousness of the law is hard, always making us wonder if we've done enough. It makes us ask, **Who will go up to heaven?** (10:6) or **Who will go down into the abyss?** (10:7), because we want to have some assurance from beyond the grave. But somebody has already come from heaven and somebody has already gotten up from the grave. In Jesus you have a gospel message that is as close as the person next to you, **in your mouth and in your heart** (10:8). It's accessible and available for the justification of sinners and the sanctification of saints.

10:9-10 The whole book of Romans, and arguably the entire Bible, comes down to this: **If you confess with your mouth, "Jesus is Lord," and believe in your heart that God raised him from the dead, you will be saved.** That word "confess" means "agree." You have to agree with God about Jesus's identity, that he's the eternal Son of God.

The concern of this passage is not primarily establishing the conditions for justification but establishing the conditions for deliverance from temporal wrath (see 1:18, 24, 26, 28) and the consequences of sin (i.e., salvation) and for divine help that is available to all who are justified through faith in Christ. When a person believes, he receives justification. But in order to receive deliverance from temporal wrath, a believer must confess, or publicly acknowledge, the lordship of Jesus Christ and call on him for divine assistance. This is why "confess" and "believe" are flipped in 10:9-10. When a person believes, he receives God's righteousness (i.e., he is born again). But when he publicly acknowledges identification with Christ, he receives temporal divine intervention (i.e., deliverance; see Matt 10:32-33).

10:11-13 The result of this belief, for both **Jew and Greek** (10:12), is that they **will not be put to shame** (10:11). We often think of coming to Jesus as a chance for our sins to be wiped away. And Jesus certainly does that. But he also removes our shame, delivering us in our everyday circumstances. If we call on Jesus, though the consequences may be difficult, we will never regret it. Calling on the name of the Lord for deliverance is a practice and provision for believers only (see Acts 7:59; 1 Cor 1:2; 1 Pet 1:17).

10:14-15 Before a person can **call on** Jesus for deliverance from temporal wrath and the consequences of sin, he or she must first **believe** through the **hearing** of the gospel. Thus, the person is already a believer when calling for divine intervention.

10:16-17 Many people, of course, don't believe *even though* they've been told about Jesus. In fact, from Isaiah's time down to Paul's, the normal response to the Word of the Lord is rejection. So Paul says that **not all obeyed the gospel.** And Isaiah goes so far as to say, **Lord, who has believed our message?** (10:16). The faithful will always be in the minority.

10:18 The word of God has gone out to every individual, whether they know Jesus's name or not. The voice of God, as Paul quotes from the Psalms, **has gone out to . . . the ends of the world.** We call that *general revelation*, the idea that in the beauty and majesty of nature, people are confronted with the reality and power of God. The problem, as Paul brought up in the first chapter of Romans, is that they reject and suppress this knowledge of God. Thus, *special revelation* is necessary for people to be reconciled to God.

10:19-20 Paul returns to the idea of Gentile salvation here to remind his Jewish readers of God's purpose: by extending grace to the Gentiles, **who were not looking for** or **asking for** him (10:20), God's goal was to make Israel **jealous of those who are not a nation** (10:19).

10:21 Why would God want his people to be jealous? Not to mistreat them or to punish them, but to provoke them and drive them back to him. He often does the same with us. In our pain, God is not trying to pay us back as much as to bring us back. So what he says to Israel he says to us: **All day long I have held out my hands to a disobedient and defiant people.** Nobody is more heartbroken by your disobedience than God. And nobody but God will show you more patience as you return to him.

XII. GOD AND ISRAEL (11:1-36)

11:1 God's promises to Israel have not been cancelled just because most of Israel is disobedient. Paul himself is proof, for he is **an Israelite, a descendant of Abraham.** God's grace toward Paul illustrates the kind of compassion God will show to Israel as a whole.

11:2-6 Here again we see the idea of the "remnant," which Paul introduced in 9:6 (though without the specific word). The nation of Israel was always a mixed group, a combination of faithful and faithless people. And while those who remained faithful, like Elijah, often felt completely alone, God reminds the remnant that they are not (see 1 Kgs 19:14-18). For Elijah, God had preserved **seven thousand** (11:4); for Paul, **there is also . . . a remnant chosen by grace** (11:5); and for us, too, God keeps a remnant of faithful believers to remind us that we are never alone. This remnant was chosen **by grace** because they believed on Christ for eternal life apart from **works** (11:6; cf. 4:4-6).

11:7-10 Just as Pharaoh's heart was hardened because he rejected God's command (9:17-18), Israel's heart was hardened because they rejected God's Son. Thus **God gave them . . . eyes that cannot see and ears that cannot hear** (11:8) so that they would **not find what [they] were looking for** (11:7)—namely, salvation, because they sought it by works.

11:11 Israel may have been hardened like Pharaoh, but they are not beyond recovery. They have **stumbled,** but not so badly **as to fall** away from God forever. In fact, God planned on their rejection as the vehicle for delivering salvation to the Gentiles. Paul himself saw this in his own life: when the Jews rejected his message, it led him to take his ministry to the Gentiles. By rejecting the gospel, the nation of Israel allowed **salvation to come to the Gentiles.**

11:12-15 When Christ returns, the **failure** of Israel will be reversed to **their fullness** (11:12) because they will believe on Jesus as their Messiah. Not only will this reversal lead to the salvation of Israel, but it will lead to **riches for the world** (11:12) and **life from the dead** (11:15). God's salvation has always been tied to Israel; so if their *stumbling* brought salvation to the rest of the world, how much more will their *strengthening!*

11:16 As if to anticipate any objections to the certainty of Israel's redemption, Paul compares the remnant to **the firstfruits.** If the firstfruits of a particular crop are healthy and sweet, that's a guarantee that the rest of the crop will follow suit. God's promises to Abraham form **the root,** and that root produces the fruit: the remnant of Israel. Through this remnant, God will be able to fulfill his promises to Abraham and restore Israel as a nation.

11:17-21 At this point, Paul's Gentile readers might be tempted to respond in arrogance. "After all," they might think, "Israel rejected God's message, but we didn't!" Paul warns them to avoid this attitude at all costs: **Do not be arrogant** (11:20) and **do not boast that you are better than those branches** (11:18)—that is, the nation of Israel. After all, Israel was cut off **because of unbelief** (11:20), and God may just as readily cut off Gentile branches as Israelite ones (11:21). All who remain grafted into God's tree of salvation **stand by faith** (11:20), and faith cannot coexist with arrogant pride.

11:22-24 Many people feel like they have to choose between **God's kindness and severity** (11:22), as if God could only be tough *or* loving, strong *or* compassionate. But Paul knows the two go together: God is severe toward our sin, but kind enough to cover it in Christ. We only know the kindness of God *because* that kindness saves us from his severity.

11:25-27 God will fulfill his promises to Israel. Even though **a partial hardening has come upon** them (11:25), they will experience future salvation. Once **the fullness of the Gentiles has come** (11:25), God will pick up his program with Israel again. All of this will happen during the tumultuous end times, when Jesus returns as **the Deliverer** to eliminate all **godlessness**. In that day, all Israel that survives the great tribulation **will be saved** (11:26).

11:28-29 Paul winds down his argument by summarizing what he's been saying throughout the entire chapter, that God's **election** of Israel makes them beloved of God (11:28). God can be depended on to keep his **gracious gifts and calling** (11:29)

to them, even though they've been set aside for a time. *Election*, then, is the selection of a people through whom God would fulfill his kingdom purpose and program. It is not an election to individual, eternal salvation.

11:30-32 Because of Israel's rejection, the Gentiles **have received mercy** (11:30). Yet that mercy was not for the Gentiles alone, because God still desires **that [Israel] also may now receive mercy** (11:31). That has been God's masterful plan all along: taking the rejection of one and causing it to be a blessing to others before returning to those who rejected and having them accept. Only in this way could God **have mercy on all** (11:32), magnifying his awesome plan and his wisdom.

11:33-36 In contemplating **the wisdom** and **the knowledge of God** (11:33) through the process of salvation, Paul is overcome with God's **glory** (11:36). The word *glory* comes from a word meaning "weighty" or "heavy." Those who grew up in the 1960s may remember that back then we would say, "That dude is heavy." The expression meant that a person was deep; there was a lot to him. It was our way of saying someone had "glory." Thus, Paul stops here to say, in essence, that God is the weightiest, heaviest, deepest being in the universe. His glory is unmatched: no one can even outline his actions (11:33); no one can get inside his head to know what he's thinking (11:34); no one can offer something to God that puts him in their debt (11:35). His glory is beyond comprehension. Whatever you think about God, he is much more than that.

Then Paul adds an **Amen** (11:36). *Amen* means, "That's it." We don't have to add to God's glory because there's nothing to add. What else could there be? **For from him and through him and to him are all things**, not just now, but **forever** (11:36).

XIII. LOVE IN THE FAMILY OF GOD (12:1-21)

Chapter 12 begins the next major section of the book of Romans. The first four chapters dealt with condemnation and justification; chapters 5–8 dealt with sanctification; then chapters 9–11 were a parenthetical discussion about Israel's unique position in the program of God. Beginning in chapter 12 (and running to the end of the book), Paul makes a transition to his pragmatic section, his section of application. It was Paul's habit to discuss theology and then applicability.

12:1 Throughout chapter 12, Paul discusses what our faith looks like with "one another," a phrase he uses four times here. But before we can have a dynamic, personal involvement with one another, we need a dynamic involvement with God. Step one is responding to the mercies of God (explained in chapters 1–11) by presenting our **bodies as a living sacrifice, holy and pleasing to God.** That means complete and total surrender. It's the difference between what a chicken and a pig bring to a bacon-and-egg breakfast. The chicken makes a contribution; the pig gives everything. What we often try to do with God is give an egg here and an egg there, but God wants sacrifice—the ham and bacon. Only total surrender can be called **true worship.**

12:2 Once we offer ourselves to God, our relationship to the world is altered. Paul urges us not to **be conformed to this age**, meaning the world system that leaves God out, but to **be transformed by the renewing of [our] mind.** Notice that both commands are passive. We aren't conforming or transforming our minds. Someone else is. When God has all of us, and when the world has none of us, God does the work of renewing our confused minds. He brings our thoughts in line with his own so that we think God's thoughts after him (see 1 Cor 2:16).

God has a goal in renewing our minds. This renewal allows him to merge his thoughts with our thoughts so that he can bring his plans into our lives. He calls it **the good, pleasing, and perfect will of God.** God has a purpose and a plan for each of our lives— one that finds us when we are fully surrendered. But as we'll see in the following verses, that purpose isn't just about us.

12:3 If we understand **the grace given to us**, our worship will overflow in service to others. Whatever abilities, skills, or resources we have, they are the grace of God. They are gifts. So Paul says, nobody should **think** of himself **more highly than he should**, because everything we have is a gift. You don't brag about a birthday present as if you made it and paid for it. Don't brag about the God-given gifts you have, either. On the flip side, don't disparage yourself as if God has given you nothing. **God has distributed a measure of faith to each one**, including you. Don't think too highly of yourself, but don't think too low either.

12:4 Paul compares the local church to a human body, in which **all the parts do not have the same function**, but every part *does* function for the good of the whole. If I cut my finger off and put it in a jar, it's still technically a part of my body, but it's worthless. I'll say my point bluntly: any Christian who is not a functioning, serving member of a local church is living outside the will of God.

12:5 There are no Lone Rangers in the Christian life, because though **we . . . are many**, God has put us together as **one body in Christ**. We are members of that body, not for ourselves, but for **one another**. Because you're a part of the body, you matter. But because you're only one part, it's not all about you.

12:6a We serve one another because of **the grace given to us.** The more you understand grace, the easier it is to serve others. Imagine a boy leaving his mother a note, saying, "For mowing the lawn, a dollar. For washing the dishes, a dollar. For making the bed, a dollar. You owe me, Mother, three dollars." That's works-based service in a nutshell. Now, imagine a mother leaving her own note: "For being in labor with you for sixteen hours, no charge. For staying up with you all night when you were sick, no charge. For buying you clothing and food, no charge." That's grace-based service.

12:6b-8 In the body of Christ, like the human body, each member has **different gifts** (12:6). Paul lists seven gifts here: **prophecy** (12:6), **service, teaching** (12:7), **exhortation, giving, leading,** and **mercy** (12:8). We know from other lists of spiritual gifts that these are just a handful of the ways God's people exercise their gifts. We also know that every

Christian has at least one. If you aren't sure what yours is, start ministering, because God only hits a moving target.

12:9 Contrary to what our culture says, love is not primarily a feeling. Love is an action, meeting the need of someone else, even at personal expense. Thus, Paul says our **love** for one another must **be without hypocrisy.** The Greek word for "hypocrite" was used of an actor who wore a mask. Some of the best actors and actresses I know come to church with their masks on. They fake it when people ask them, "How you doing?" They fake it because they're worried that people won't love them unless they wear a mask. So to all of us Paul says, be the kind of community where it's safe for people to take their masks off.

12:10 We can **love one another deeply** once we recognize that we don't have to like someone to love them well. Love is associated with emotion, but it starts with a decision to compassionately and righteously seek the well-being of others. That decision is founded in the truth that fellow believers are our **brothers and sisters.** We are a family. God even says that we can gauge our love for the Father based on our love for our brothers and sisters (see 1 John 4:20). Just like the small gauge on a boiler indicates how full the vessel is, our love for one another indicates how full our hearts are with the love of Jesus.

12:11-12 Behind the Greek word translated **fervent** is the idea of boiling water. If you're **fervent in the Spirit,** you're boiling for the kingdom of God; you're fired up to **serve the Lord** (12:11). Have you ever noticed how kids, who otherwise might seem tired, get a sudden burst of energy if you offer to play some game they love? They boil over with enthusiasm because they love it.

12:13 One way we can serve God and love one another is to **share with the saints in their needs** and to **pursue hospitality.** God gave you a job, which brings you money, which pays for your house. Grace got you the house. Grace got you your car. And grace wants you to use them to help the saints. If all of

the doors in your life stay closed, you don't understand hospitality—or grace.

12:14 It's one thing to love our family in the church. To love our enemies, however, requires a special kind of power. Only Jesus could say something so bold as to **bless those who persecute you.** But isn't that what Jesus did for us? Our sins put Jesus on the cross, yet he said, "Father, forgive them, because they do not know what they are doing" (Luke 23:34). If he forgave you when you were his enemy (after all, your sins put him on the cross), shouldn't that change the way you view your enemies?

12:15-16 Just as we serve and love one another in the church, we must **live in harmony.** Unity is the most important aspect of the church. Paul shows us one of the most obvious ways to live that out: **associate with the humble** (12:16). If you want to keep from thinking too highly of yourself, make it a regular part of your agenda to connect with people who have nothing to give back. And you won't have to look far. Look for people in the church who are without designer clothes, high school degrees, or even steady jobs. They may be nobodies in the world's eyes, but in the church, they ought to feel like somebodies. If you see that they are rejoicing, **rejoice** with them; if you see that they are weeping, **weep** with them (12:15)—especially when you have no stake in the matter. Do it simply out of love.

12:17 When reading Paul's reminder to the Romans not to **repay anyone evil for evil,** it's important to remember that he's still talking to the church here! The church is a family, and as the family grows, people grate on each other. Remember, though: the church is also a body. So if your sister is grating on you, she's a sprained ankle. If a brother is giving you trouble, he's a dislocated finger. Don't attack the hurting parts of your body; they're part of you. If you repay evil for evil, you'll end up hurting yourself.

12:18 Many misinterpret this verse to say, in essence, "Be patient for as long as you can, but once your patience runs out, get ready to throw down." This verse is actually saying, **as**

far as it depends on you, that is, on your side of the relationship, **live at peace with everyone.** Do everything you can to get along with people, and if they should still harbor a grudge, that's on them.

12:19-20 A question naturally follows Paul's exhortations to love and forgive our enemies: "If I keep loving my enemies and they never change, isn't that unfair?" God has an answer. You should never **avenge yourselves** (12:19), not because God doesn't care (he does), but because he wants to handle things himself. So when **your enemy is hungry**, you **feed him** (12:20), and **if he is thirsty**, you **give him something to drink** (12:20)—not only because God commands it, but because by

doing this we **leave room for God's wrath** (12:19). And he promises to pay in full. It could be that one of the reasons God hasn't dealt with your enemy yet is that you are still in the way!

12:21 The only way to **conquer evil** is **with good.** You don't overcome evil by being evil too, as natural as that approach feels. Remember: God made Jesus, who knew no sin, "to be sin for" you and me. He did it so that we could "become the righteousness of God," sharing in his forgiveness (2 Cor 5:21). As Dr. Martin Luther King Jr. once said, "Darkness cannot drive out darkness; only light can do that. Hate cannot drive out hate; only love can do that."

XIV. GOD'S KINGDOM IN SOCIETY (13:1-14)

13:1 God has ordered human history to operate according to a system of covenants, with the husband as the head of his wife, the parents as the head of their children, elders as the head of their congregations, and the government as the head of its citizenry. These heads are not to be dictatorial or to "lord it over" those whom God has placed under their authority (see, e.g., Matt 20:25). Rather, they are to exercise their headship for the good of those who submit to their legitimate authority. Since God has placed governmental rulers over us, we should **submit to the governing authorities**, recognizing them as God's agents. Still, Paul offers a radical political statement in saying that our governments stand under *another* authority—that of God. While there is an institutional separation between church and state, there must never be a separation between God and government. The closer God is to a government and its citizens, the more ordered the society will be. The further God is from a government and its citizens, the more chaotic the society will become.

13:2 In light of Paul's statement that even governments are under God's authority, we see that this verse applies to individuals and governments equally. **The one who resists**

the authority of God—whether that's a person rebelling against the government or the government rebelling against God—**is opposing God's command** and **will bring judgment on themselves.**

13:3 This is a concise definition and summary of the role of civil government: resist evil and promote good. The problem lies in defining *evil* and *good.* Much of the time, what the government promotes as good aligns with the Bible. But when it doesn't, we must **do what is good** before God and trust him with the political results. God and his Word give us the definitive standard of what should be viewed as right and wrong. The biblical responsibility of civil government is to maintain a safe, just, righteous, and compassionately responsible environment in which freedom can flourish.

13:4-5 Twice in this passage Paul calls the governing authorities **God's servant**, which reinforces their role (13:4). Whenever God is removed from government, a vacuum is created in which government seeks to be God. In a democratic republic like ours, we citizens get the honor of choosing many of God's servants; thus, part of the responsibility of governing lies with us. We the people can be servants to God's servants, pointing them to truth. If we don't, then "one nation under God" will become "one nation under chaos."

13:6-7 As Paul closes this brief section on government, his words intentionally echo those of Jesus. Paul commands us: Pay **taxes to those you owe taxes**, and give **honor to those you owe honor** (13:7). Jesus said, "Give, then, to Caesar the things that are Caesar's, and to God the things that are God's" (Matt 22:21). We owe government leaders our taxes. We owe them earthly honor. But both Paul and Jesus remind us that we must never give them our hearts. They cannot have our ultimate allegiance, since we are created in the image of God and not in the image of government rulers. God is above all.

13:8-10 All of our debts should be repaid. Well, all but one: the debt that can never be fully paid is our debt **to love one another** (13:8). Biblical love, as Paul showed in chapter 12, is the decision to compassionately and righteously seek the benefit and well-being of another. We owe that to others without end, because that kind of love is the underlying factor in all of God's horizontal commandments: **Do not commit adultery; do not murder; do not steal; do not covet** (13:9). This is why Paul, again echoing Jesus, calls the command to **love your neighbor as yourself . . . the fulfillment of the law** (13:9-10). The way Jesus put it was to say that "all the Law and the Prophets depend" on two commands: (1) Love God with all of your heart, soul, and mind; (2) love your neighbor as yourself (Matt 22:37-40).

13:11 We must live in light of Jesus's imminent return, which **is nearer than when we first believed**. Doing so means we **wake up from sleep**, the spiritual lethargy that plagues so many people in our churches. God didn't save us just for heaven after we die, but to experience his salvation in history. To experience that salvation is to be spared from the consequences of our sins.

13:12-13 Too many Christians trust God enough to take them to heaven, but not enough to guide their lives daily. Thus, their lives look like the darkness around them, filled with **drunkenness** and **sexual impurity** and **quarreling and jealousy** (13:13). Paul reminds us that Jesus is returning quickly, and when he does, both the darkness and **the deeds of darkness** will be judged without mercy. So stop being spiritually sleepy, and **put on the armor of light** (13:12).

13:14 We put on the armor of light in two ways—one positive and one negative. Positively, we **put on the Lord Jesus Christ**, living by faith in him, studying his Word, and seeking to reflect him in our actions. Negatively, we **don't make plans to gratify the desires of the flesh**, which would counteract being clothed in Christ. Imagine you just put on your best suit or dress for church. As you're walking to service, you notice a shortcut—but it's through a back alley and involves climbing through two dumpsters. Do you take that route? No! That dirty environment would foul your pristine clothes. Put on the purity of Christ and don't climb through the dumpsters of sin.

XV. LOVE AND LIBERTY (14:1-23)

14:1 There are two ways to judge others. We can judge them critically or charitably, to hurt or to help. God intends us to judge other people's actions according to God's principles, but to do so with love. Here Paul addresses the idea of judging others based on our own personal preferences and opinions. These are the **disputed matters** on which Christians should be able to disagree. Many manmade rules address things that

aren't clearly spelled out in Scripture. When we talk about human rules as if they're God's ideas, we harm those who are **weak in faith**.

14:2 Paul names a couple of the manmade rules that were tripping up these particular believers. The first regards diet. On one side, some believers thought eating meat was sinful, so they would **eat only vegetables**.

Other believers thought it was okay to **eat anything**. The first group didn't become vegetarian for dietary reasons, but convictional ones. The meat in Rome had been offered to idols; therefore, many people felt it was tainted with the demonic. The second group, however, thought, "Well, what's an idol, anyway? It's not a real god, and I don't believe in them, so whatever happens to the meat before it arrives on my table is fine." These differences of opinion created conflict.

14:3 Paul offers his input on eating, saying to *both* groups that **God has accepted** them. The problem was that the believers weren't accepting each other. They were looking **down on** each other. We don't usually argue over meat in the church today, but we do similar things by saying, "If you were really saved, you wouldn't go to the movies. God's people don't go to places where secular music is played." It's fine to have personal convictions, but if the Bible hasn't condemned a thing, we should give space to believers whose convictions differ on matters that Scripture does not address plainly.

14:4 Suppose you think movies and dancing are okay. That's great: you're free in Christ. But please don't **judge another's household servant** based on your house rules. Remember, he answers to God, and it is **before his own Lord** that **he stands or falls.** God's Word gives a standard, and we are all called to meet it. But once we meet that standard, we can differ on the kind of bags we carry along the way.

14:5 Paul introduces another example regarding the same concept. Some people were celebrating special holidays, while others thought **every day** was **the same.** This discussion resonates with me because my father-in-law didn't celebrate Christmas: he thought our culture had taken it over with commercialism. My wife, my kids, and I, however, do. The Bible says that I would be wrong to condemn him for what he was doing, just as he would've been wrong to condemn us. If **each one** is **fully convinced in his own mind** that he's honoring God regarding a matter on which Scripture isn't

crystal clear, we need to let our brothers and sisters exercise liberty.

14:6-9 It's uncomfortable for people at different levels of faith and maturity to coexist without judging each other on matters of preference. Paul gives us both a reason to respect others' freedom and a motivation: *you aren't their master.* In these verses, the phrase **for the Lord** shows up seven times. If a brother eats, let him eat **for the Lord** (14:6). If he doesn't, let him *not* eat for *the Lord.* If he celebrates a day, he does it *for the Lord*; if not, he's still doing it *for the Lord.* If he **lives** or **dies**, he's doing it **for the Lord**—not for you (14:7-8). Many of our churches are drowning in legalism, and we're putting a leash around the necks of other Christians with our manmade preferences. Moreover, we're keeping rules for Brother Tom or for Sister Dana! We've got to stop trying to please each other and focus on pleasing the one who **died and returned to life** for this: **that he might be Lord over both the dead and the living** (14:9). There is one Lord, and you're not him.

14:10-12 The more we police the behavior of others, the more dangerous our own position becomes. Jesus said that is foolishness to point out a speck of sawdust in your brother's eye if you have a two-by-four in your own (see Matt 7:3). Paul is getting at the same idea here: **Why do you judge your brother or sister** (14:10), when you know that **each of us will give an account of himself to God** (14:12)? God won't be asking you about the opinions and preferences of your brother. He'll be looking into your account. So don't worry about your neighbor so much; keep a better, closer eye on yourself. Get out of his business and tend to your own.

14:13 Just because our focus is on pleasing God doesn't mean we aren't thinking of others at all. Instead of judging **one another**, we **decide never to put a stumbling block or pitfall** in their way. We think of others all the time, but our first question is not, "What faults can I find in their lives?" Instead, it is, "How will my actions affect them?" Yes, you are free to enjoy what God gives you the freedom to enjoy. But don't use that freedom to hurt others. Don't flaunt it.

14:14 Freedom is related to knowledge. Paul says, **I know and am persuaded in the Lord Jesus that nothing is unclean in itself.** Because he *knows*, he *grows* in freedom. Think of a baby: when you have a baby in the house, certain freedoms go away. The scissors have to be put up high; the cabinets have to be locked. Why? Because the baby is too young to know how to use these things without hurting himself. As he gets older, you can relax the restrictions. God often prevents us from enjoying certain things, not because the actions themselves are wrong, but because we are too immature to enjoy them the right way. God wants us to know and to grow, and then he'll expand our freedom.

14:15 Knowledge, by itself, is never enough. Knowledge must be used **according to love.** If your daughter wakes up terrified, telling you there's a ghost in her room, you don't just shout at her that ghosts aren't real. She needs that knowledge, of course, but she also needs you in the room, hugging her. Love without knowledge is sentimental religion. Knowledge without love is cold religion. You've got to have *both* love *and* knowledge for a balanced faith.

14:16-18 This is the heart of this issue. **The kingdom of God** is not primarily about externals like **eating and drinking.** It's about what happens internally, through the Spirit—**righteousness, peace, and joy** (14:17). Deep down, we all know that happiness is more about personal relationships than external circumstances. Give me beans and bread with a happy family rather than a T-bone steak with my wife refusing to speak to me (see Prov 17:1). The kingdom of God is not about the food you eat, but the relationships you have.

14:19-21 The goal of the kingdom is not to keep other people in line with our preferences, but to **pursue what promotes peace** (14:19). We can use our freedom in two ways: either we **tear down God's work** (14:20) in people's lives by flaunting our liberty, or we build **up one another** (14:19) by being sensitive to our weaker brothers and sisters. The irony is that while we may have the freedom to do something, if we continue to do it knowing it will make our brother stumble, that action suddenly becomes evil. On the contrary, **it is a good thing not to . . . do anything that makes your brother or sister stumble** (14:21). We are given freedom to build up the body of Christ, not to tear it down.

14:22-23 Throughout the entire conversation about freedom, Paul presupposes that we are following our conscience. A helpful way to summarize this is to say that **everything that is not from faith is sin** (14:23). So when in doubt about something, don't do it. Your conscience is like a metal detector: it beeps when you approach something God hasn't freed you to do. You may watch a dozen people walk through that metaphorical gate without the beep going off. Don't bother about them. If your conscience beeps, don't follow.

XVI. UNITY AND MISSION (15:1–16:27)

15:1-4 Paul is still musing on the idea of weakness and strength (the theme of chapter 14) as he begins chapter 15. But now he includes an example to help bolster his case. **Each one of us is to please his neighbor** (15:2) because **even Christ did not please himself** (15:3). If Jesus used his strength to bear with our weaknesses, how much more should **we who are strong . . . bear the weaknesses of those without strength** (15:1)? Patience for others should flow from our understanding of how patient Jesus has been toward us.

15:5 God's desire is for believers **to live in harmony with one another.** He wants us to be united around our common Savior and toward a common kingdom agenda. Unity means oneness of purpose. Just as in an orchestra each instrument makes a unique sound but plays the same song, so also each believer possesses unique traits, but moves in a common direction. Unity embraces uniqueness—as long as the goal of the uniqueness is one purpose.

15:6 When we are united, we **glorify the God and Father of our Lord Jesus Christ**, not by being identical in every way, but by sharing **one mind and one voice**. Paul chooses the word "one" intentionally. Note that he doesn't say we have the *same* mind and the *same* voice. Unity is not a matter of sameness, but of oneness. Like a quilt with various colors and patterns blended into a beautiful whole, the body of Christ blends different people together into a beautiful array of redeemed lives. Unity doesn't wash out our differences; it combines them to form something greater.

15:7 As wide as we imagine the gap to be between ourselves and our most disliked enemies, Paul reminds us that there was never a gap wider than the one between us and God. If **Christ . . . accepted you** when you were weak and ungodly, certainly you can accept others when they differ from you in much less significant ways.

15:8-9a The unified body of Christ becomes a reflection of God's intended mission. **Christ became a servant of the circumcised** (15:8)—that is, the Jews—not merely to save them, but also **so that Gentiles may glorify God for his mercy** (15:9). Together, a united fellowship of Jews and Gentiles carries the gospel of reconciliation to the rest of the world. After all, a message of reconciliation could only be communicated through a reconciled community.

15:9b-12 As if to remind his audience that God had this multi-ethnic unity in mind all along, Paul quotes from a number of Old Testament prophets who all preach the same message: God has always desired for **all the peoples** to **praise him** together (15:11).

15:13 In the midst of dark times, when it seems that the church will never achieve the unity God desires, or when the world seems immune to our message, we desperately need hope. This only comes **by the power of the Holy Spirit** of God, because he is **the God of hope**. Without him, we can make resolutions,

try to fix our relationships, and seek all the best advice. But great advice without the power of the Spirit is like a ladder resting on a shaky foundation: we can only climb so high before we come crashing down.

15:14 The Greek word Paul uses when he tells us **to instruct one another** means "to admonish" or "to counsel." Every mature believer has a responsibility to be a counselor to his brother and sister. To do this, we need two things. First, we must be **full of goodness**. If you aren't seeking to please the Lord, don't try leading other folks to please him. You can only lead someone where you're traveling yourself. Second, we must be **filled with all knowledge**. This refers to the knowledge of God, the knowledge of the Scriptures. Biblical counseling comes from the overflow of the Word of God in you—not from your own thoughts and opinions.

15:15-16 Paul talks about something here that a lot of Christians have never experienced: a personal passion and call. **My purpose**, he says, **is that the Gentiles may be an acceptable offering, sanctified by the Holy Spirit** (15:16). Paul had found what made his bones burn within him. And even though he endured incredible hardships, that passion in his heart kept him moving. Passion is the motivation that compels you to take action.

15:17-19 One reason many Christians lack passion to fulfill God's call is that they are seeking that calling from the perspective of time rather than the perspective of eternity. It's no wonder when they quickly run out of steam because their goal in life is not **what pertains to God** (15:17). If we boast in anything other than Jesus Christ, then there is a large neon sign over our lives that flashes this message: "Temporary." But if we **boast in Christ Jesus** (15:17), not only will our calling last; we will find that Jesus himself does the work through us. As Paul says, **I would not dare say anything except what Christ has accomplished through me by word and deed** (15:18). Paul had done **miraculous signs and wonders**, not because he knew special techniques, but because he relied deeply on **God's Spirit** and trusted him to guide him (15:19). He was able to do miraculous things precisely because he was aware that he couldn't do miraculous things on his own.

15:20-22 At a moment's notice, Paul was able to offer up his mission statement in a single line. Paul's **aim** was **to preach the gospel where Christ has not been named** (15:20). I wonder how many of us have the same confidence about God's call on our lives. It may be that we have not, as James would say, because we ask not (see Jas 4:2). Have you asked God to show you your role in his mission? Have you prayed, "God, it's all yours. I won't tell you 'never.' I'm here to do whatever you ask"? Ask God to ignite his fire in you and to direct you to his mission. I promise you: it's worth it.

15:23-24 Paul does not just preach about the importance of Christian community. He lives it out. As he discusses his travel plans with the Roman believers, he candidly admits that he has **strongly desired for many years to come to** them (15:23), and that he hopes **to be assisted by** them for his **journey** to Spain (15:24). Paul may have been the greatest missionary of his—or any—generation, but he knew he needed help. Even the strongest saints need each other, to enjoy the **company** of other believers **for a while** (15:24).

15:25-29 One of the many tasks Paul undertook during his travels was collecting money for the poor. On his way to Jerusalem, he had with him **a contribution for the poor among the saints** there. It had been generously given by the churches in **Macedonia and Achaia** (15:25-26).

Churches always have been, and always should be, the primary organization for alleviating poverty in communities. When we assume that someone else should take care of the poor, not only do we harm those in poverty, but we also send out a terrible false message about our Lord, who "though he was rich, for [our] sake he became poor" (2 Cor 8:9).

15:30-33 Paul had a keen sense of God's unique call on his life; he had a vision of the united church; he had a passion burning in his bones to be a minister of the gospel. But even Paul knew that the power for ministry comes through prayer. He thus appeals to his Roman **brothers and sisters . . . to strive together with [him] in fervent prayers to God on [his] behalf** (15:30). This is not false modesty. Paul knows that he will fail if not sustained by prayer. We have the same need Paul did. Do we have the same conviction?

16:1-2 Paul begins his greetings with mention of **Phoebe**, called **a servant of the church** (16:1). The word Paul uses for "servant" is the same root word that is translated "deacon" in other parts of Scripture. Therefore, Phoebe—whose name means "bright" or "radiant"—had an official capacity as a deaconess in the Roman church, showing that women have critical roles to play in church leadership under male authority. They too work toward accomplishing God's kingdom program. Those women among us who serve the church are to be welcomed **in the Lord** and assisted **in whatever matter [they] may require . . . help** (16:2).

16:3-16 We don't know much about most of the people in this list, yet what we see here is an example of unity within diversity. There is ethnic diversity: **Prisca and Aquila** (16:3), **Andronicus and Junia** (16:7), and **Herodion** (16:11) are all Jewish believers; they are included in this list right alongside the many Gentile believers. There is diversity of gender, as several prominent women are named—**Phoebe** (16:1), **Prisca** (16:3), **Mary** (16:6), **Junia** (16:7), **Tryphaena and Tryphosa** (16:12), and **Julia** (16:15). There is even a diversity of class: **Aristobulus** (16:10) and **Narcissus** (16:11) are called heads of "households," indicating a high position in society; they are in this list with others who probably owned nothing at all. While diverse in their backgrounds, origins, and skills, all of these people co-labored with Paul in the ministry of the gospel. As Paul says repeatedly, they **worked very hard in the Lord** (16:12).

16:17-18 Unity in the church, however beautiful, is fragile. Even as Paul delightfully sends greetings to his unified brothers and sisters in Rome, he knows that a threat lurks. Thus, he warns them **to watch out for those who create divisions and obstacles** (16:17).

"Keep your eyes open," he says, "for those who are actively seeking to split people up instead of bringing them together. You can recognize them by what they say and whom they serve." Indeed, they speak words that are **contrary to the teaching that you learned** (16:17), and they **do not serve our Lord Christ but their own appetites** (16:18). Even though they have **smooth talk and flattering words** (16:18), they are deceivers who will destroy the unity of the body of Christ.

16:19-20 Deceivers in the church are not merely annoyances. As Paul hints here, they are tools of Satan. The good news is that Satan loses: **The God of peace will soon crush Satan under your feet** (16:20). The more the Word of God goes out and the church is built up, the harder God drives his heel down on Satan's neck.

16:21-27 The book of Romans began with a declaration that Paul's message was not his own, but is the gospel of God, promised in the Scriptures. It ends in much the same way, as Paul prays that God would **strengthen . . . according to [the] gospel** (16:25), a gospel that was **revealed and made known through the prophetic Scriptures** (16:26). This is part of Paul's closing benediction, in which he points everything back **to the only wise God, through Jesus Christ.** In other words, history is *his* story, and our lives exist to bring him **glory forever** (16:27).

1 CORINTHIANS

INTRODUCTION

Author

THE LETTER IDENTIFIES THE apostle Paul as its author (1:1; 16:21). Though critical scholars often question the authenticity of several other Pauline letters, most biblical scholars are unanimous in affirming that Paul wrote 1 Corinthians.

Historical Background

Paul visited Corinth in the Roman province of Achaia in about AD 50 during his second missionary journey and ministered there for a year and a half (see Acts 18:1-18). While there, he met a Jewish couple named Aquila and Priscilla. Since he shared their tent-making trade, he stayed with them (Acts 18:2-3). He also preached in the Jewish synagogue in Corinth, but when the Jews resisted him, he began teaching in a house next door to the synagogue and saw many Corinthians place faith in Christ (Acts 18:4-8).

Paul probably wrote 1 Corinthians around AD 54 while he ministered in Ephesus for about three years during his third missionary journey (1 Cor 16:8; see Acts 19:1–20:1, 31). This was actually the second letter that Paul wrote to the Corinthians, the first having been lost to history (see 1 Cor 5:9). A number of problems had arisen in the church that Paul felt the need to address. He learned of these issues from "members of Chloe's people" (1:11; cf. 5:1; 11:18) and from a letter the Corinthians had sent him (7:1; cf. 7:25; 8:1; 12:1; 16:1).

Message and Purpose

The apostle Paul wrote this letter to deal with the worldliness that had entered the church in Corinth. It was full of divisions, as well as gross immorality that was tolerated and even approved by the church.

Paul addressed a variety of topics in his letter. He explained the importance and purpose of marriage. He wanted the Corinthians to understand the principle of spiritual freedom because some of them were holding fellow believers hostage to rules that no longer apply in the church age. Paul addressed the Lord's Supper, which the church was abusing. He was also concerned about the people's excitement over spiritual gifts alongside their lack of love for one another and their misunderstanding of the resurrection.

Paul had first visited the Corinthians several years prior; therefore, they should have been more spiritually mature than reports suggested. Sadly, the people were carnal, at times living like unbelievers rather than as servants of Jesus Christ. They needed to allow the Holy Spirit to bring them to maturity so that they could have a godly influence on their world and advance God's kingdom agenda.

VIDEO INTRO

www.bhpublishinggroup.com/qr/te/46_00

1 CORINTHIANS

I. INTRODUCTION (1:1-9)

1:1-3 Paul begins his letter to the **church** in **Corinth** by affirming his calling **as an apostle of Christ Jesus**. And that appointment came by the **will** of God (1:1-2), when the resurrected Lord appeared to Paul and made him his chosen instrument to proclaim his name (see Acts 9:1-30).

Paul writes along with a Christian **brother** named **Sosthenes** (1:1). Clearly, though, the letter expresses the thoughts of Paul himself (see the repeated uses of "I" throughout). So it's possible that Sosthenes served as Paul's *amanuensis*—that is, his secretary who wrote down his words (as Tertius did in Paul's letter to the Romans; see Rom 16:22). Paul would have signed the letter's end with a greeting in his own hand (see 1 Cor 16:21).

Paul calls the Corinthians **saints . . . who call on the name of Jesus Christ** (1:2). Believers have the unique privilege of appealing to their Savior for divine intervention in their lives (see Acts 7:59; Rom 10:9-14; 2 Tim 2:21-22). Although the church at Corinth had become quite carnal, as reflected in their actions, Paul knew they were saved and had been **sanctified** through their faith **in Christ Jesus** (1:2). Thus, it is possible (though detrimental!) to be an immature Christian whose life reflects more worldly thinking and living than heavenly. That's why we need

to be transformed "by the renewing of" our minds (Rom 12:2) so that we experience the realities and benefits of our salvation. To this earthly-minded church, Paul extends the **grace** and **peace** of **God** and **Christ** (1:3).

1:4-8 In spite of the church's many problems, Paul actually gave thanks for the believers because he was confident they had experienced God's **grace**, the basis of salvation (1:4). Because they had been saved, they had been **enriched** by God **in every way**, particularly in the **spiritual [gifts]** they had received, which gave **testimony about** the validity of Christ's work in their midst (1:5-7). So even though they had misused their spiritual gifts (something that would be addressed later; see 12:1–14:40), Paul was confident that they would stand **blameless** on judgment day because of the finished work of **Jesus Christ** for them (1:8).

1:9 God is faithful to keep his promises to save us through our faith in Christ. As a result of our salvation, we have access to **fellowship with** Christ. But we are called to live out our fellowship with our Savior through fellowship with his saints. Sadly, the prevalent sins in the church were hindering such fellowship. And this is why Paul needed to write to them.

II. RESPONSE TO REPORTS FROM WITHIN THE CHURCH (1:10–6:20)

➢ A. Divisions in the Church
(1:10–4:21) ❧

1:10-12 The first problem Paul addresses is the discord that was widespread in the Corinthian church. He exhorts them to reject **divisions among** them and to pursue unity (1:10). They had set up illegitimate criteria for separating themselves from one another. Reports had reached Paul that rivalries existed among the church members based on allegiance to a favorite ministry leader (1:11). As he explains in 1:12, some followed **Paul** (probably those who'd been around since the church's founding) or **Apollos** (likely those who preferred a more eloquent and sophisticated speaker; see Acts 18:24-28) or **Cephas**/Peter (probably Jewish believers who lamented the loss of their traditions)—or even **Christ** (likely the super spiritual ones!).

Perhaps you've seen factions rear their ugly heads in a local church as personal preferences took priority over unity, so let's be clear. *Unity* does not equate with sameness or uniformity. Paul wasn't urging the Corinthian believers to disregard their differences. Rather, he wanted this group of believers—consisting of Jews and Gentiles, men and women, and young and old from different walks of life—to be united in their **understanding** and **conviction** about Jesus (1:10). They had been called by God to a *oneness of purpose* in the midst of their diversity. Unity is critical because of God's unified Trinitarian nature. While there is a *legitimate* form of disunity—that is, we are not to be unified in the endorsement of sin, *illegitimate* disunity can negate the active presence of God in our midst.

A football team is unified—not because everyone plays the same position—but because everyone is straining for the same goal line. An orchestra is unified—not because everyone performs on the same instrument—but because everyone harmoniously plays the same song under the direction of one conductor. Likewise, the church is to be unified—not because every Christian is exactly alike—but because we all pledge allegiance to the same Lord.

1:13-17 Paul asks some rhetorical questions to shame them over their divisive factions. **Is Christ divided? Was Paul crucified for you? Were you baptized in Paul's name?** (1:13). The answer to all of these is a resounding "No!" Christ alone is the one to whom we owe our loyalty. Paul is grateful that his primary mission wasn't to **baptize** so that no one could claim he'd been simply dunking personal supporters (thus, water baptism is not a requirement for salvation). Rather, Paul had been sent **to preach the gospel**—a message about **Christ**, not about himself (1:14-17). The apostle didn't seek to impress people with his **eloquent wisdom**; rather, he wanted them to be overwhelmed by **the cross of Christ** (1:17). For Paul, gospel ministry wasn't about winning a following for anyone but for Jesus.

1:18 **The word** (the message) **of the cross is foolishness to** unbelievers—**to those who are perishing.** But to Christians—those **who are being saved**—the cross's message **is the power of God.** Notice that the latter group consists of those who are already saved. But having been delivered from hell, they're now "being saved"—delivered from the power and effects of sin in history. How do Christians who are being saved access the power of God? Through the cross of Christ.

Some believers (like the Corinthians), short-circuit God's power in their lives. They know the cross is the power of God for heaven, but by their actions they seem to consider the cross foolishness for daily living on earth. How? What do they do to disrupt God's work in their lives? Paul continues.

1:19-25 He quotes from Isaiah 29:14, in which the Lord rejects worldly **wisdom** (1:19). Why? Because **the world's wisdom** is **foolish** (1:20); it lacks the divine point of view and considers life from a merely human perspective. The Corinthians were aligning themselves with human teachers and against one another. As a result of their pursuing such a worldly way of thinking, sin was running rampant among them and they lacked God's power. Human **wisdom** considers the word of the cross to be **foolishness**, but God uses this so-called foolishness to save people (1:21). Moreover, though **Jews** sought **signs** (power) and **Greeks** sought man's **wisdom**, the "foolish" message of **Christ crucified** grants believers access to both **the power** and **wisdom of God**, which far exceed **human wisdom** and **strength** (1:22-25).

God's *wisdom* enables us to see things from a divine perspective, make wise choices, and open ourselves to his intervention in our circumstances. God's *power* enables us to identify sin problems in our lives and to be delivered from them. So why would anyone prefer human wisdom and strength, which are incapable of delivering results?

1:26-29 The Corinthians were looking at things from the wrong perspective. They were busy trying to identify with the right people (see 1:11-12). But Paul reminds them that notoriety was never part of God's criteria for saving and using people. He didn't go searching for impressive people to save either. The Corinthians, for example, hadn't been **wise** or **powerful** or **noble** (1:26). Instead, God brought his saving message of the cross of Christ to ordinary sinners. He chose **insignificant and despised** people like fishermen and tax collectors to do his kingdom work so that those from the upper crust of society would be put **to shame** (1:27-28). That way, **no one**—no matter how esteemed in the world's eyes—gets to **boast in his presence** (1:29).

If you have low self-esteem, come from humble beginnings, have experienced significant struggles, or are despised by the in crowd, then you're a choice candidate to be used by God for his kingdom program. If you are a child of God through Jesus Christ, it's not because of who you are but in spite of it.

1:30-31 As a believer, everything you need comes from Jesus Christ; he is your sufficiency. Aligning yourself with notable people will get you rivalries, divisions, and disappointment. But aligning yourself with King Jesus and his agenda will get you **righteousness, sanctification, and redemption** (1:30). Therefore, **let the one who boasts, boast in the Lord** (1:31). Only one person deserves any credit—and all of it. Worldly wisdom gets you nothing in the end. But the so-called foolishness of God gives you access to all you need and more.

2:1-5 Paul emphasizes the futility of mere human wisdom by considering the example of his own ministry and preaching. As a result of the influence of Greek rhetoric in Paul's day, a heavy emphasis was placed on a speaker's mastery of philosophy and oratorical skills. However, when Paul preached to the Corinthians, it wasn't **with brilliance of speech or wisdom** (2:1)—that is, he didn't speak with eloquence because his goal wasn't to impress people. On the contrary, he acknowledges that he actually preached **in weakness** and **fear** (2:3). More than his delivery, Paul was focused on the content of his message: **Jesus Christ and him crucified** (2:2). His confidence was not in his own intellect, training, abilities, or background. Rather, Paul was confident in **the Spirit's power** that accompanied his message so that the Corinthians' **faith** would be in **God's power** and not **human wisdom** (2:4-5).

Paul placed his entire dependence on the message itself (which was from God) and the power of the Holy Spirit to make that message effective. Where do you place your confidence when you share Christ with others? Is it in your own rhetorical and persuasive abilities? Or does your confidence rest solely in the power of God to bring salvation and life transformation? No matter how brilliant the spokesperson, he or she cannot achieve what only divine sovereignty can accomplish.

2:6 To be sure, Paul wasn't rejecting wisdom or suggesting that God despises it. After all, the Lord doesn't celebrate ignorance! Instead, the issue has to do with one's source of **wisdom**. Do we pursue divine wisdom, or do we pursue the **wisdom of this age**, which will come **to nothing**? Believers whose life perspectives have been nurtured by the Spirit of God are **mature**; on the other hand, **the**

rulers of this age do not use divine truth as the reference point for their lives.

2:7-8 Paul's message was based on **God's hidden wisdom in a mystery**—that is, something that was previously unknown but which God had since revealed. God's plan to bring salvation to humanity **for our glory** had been established **before** the world began (2:7) because he knew what would be needed in history to redeem sinners. But **the rulers of this age** didn't comprehend God's wisdom; otherwise, **they would not have crucified** Jesus Christ (2:8). In their attempt to destroy this Jewish rabbi, they were actually furthering God's plan of redemption.

In his glorious sovereignty and providence, the Lord is able to use unbelievers to achieve his purposes. Don't put God in a box. His infinite wisdom is more than we can grasp through our finite human logic and understanding.

2:9-10 Spiritual wisdom is made possible by means of the personalized work of God in our lives. Quoting from the prophet Isaiah, Paul explains that **for those who love** God, he is able to make known things that **no eye has seen, no ear has heard, and no human heart has conceived** (2:9). This is not a reference to heaven but to God's work in the life of the believer. It indicates that God can help believers understand things that they cannot learn through natural means. How does he do this? He reveals **these things to us by the Spirit** (2:10). This is called *illumination*.

Though God has revealed to us his inspired, written Word, believers need illumination to give us understanding. This is the work of the Holy Spirit, through the Word of God, within the mind of a Christian that causes him to supernaturally learn, understand, and apply the things of God. It is the voice of God through the Word by means of the Holy Spirit becoming personalized to you. Illumination does not involve new revelation; rather, it involves God giving a believer understanding of the meaning and application of Scripture in the midst of his own experiences.

2:11 No one knows my thoughts better than I do; no one knows your thoughts better than

you. **In the same way**, then, **no one knows the thoughts of God except the Spirit.** Therefore, we are dependent on the Spirit to enable us to make a spiritual connection with God. When this happens, God illuminates his Word so that it becomes relevant to specific circumstances.

2:12-15 The spirit of the world can't help you, for spiritual truth isn't **taught by human wisdom** (2:12-13). Worldly thinking doesn't have access to the things of God. Using it to discern them is like trying to connect your television to a signal when you don't have the right equipment. All you get is static. Similarly, a **person without the Spirit** (an unbeliever) cannot **receive** what comes from God. It appears to be **foolishness to him** because it can only be **evaluated spiritually** (2:14).

The great news is that this divine insight is **freely given to us** who believe (2:12). God earnestly wants to personalize his revelation to you through his spiritual illumination. Yet it requires being a **spiritual person** so that you may **evaluate everything** from a spiritual perspective (2:15). Though all believers have received the Holy Spirit, not every believer operates as a "spiritual person" because it requires evaluating things in accordance with Scripture and with openness to the Spirit's illuminating work. Such a person **cannot be evaluated by anyone** (2:15)—that is, it will be obvious to those who don't know God that a spiritual person doesn't approach life like everyone else does.

2:16 Paul poses a rhetorical question (quoting again from Isaiah): **Who has known the Lord's mind, that he may instruct him?** The answer is obvious: no one! God doesn't need an education; he certainly doesn't need human counsel. On the other hand, we definitely need his instruction and perspective. That's why he's given believers **the mind of Christ**, the capacity to think Christ's thoughts after him, so that we will live life as we ought.

3:1-4 Unfortunately, the Corinthians hadn't been operating like **spiritual people** but like **people of the flesh** (3:1). Rather than living from a spiritual perspective, they continued to live in accordance with their pre-salvation worldview. In a word, they were **worldly** (3:3; or, as the KJV translates it, "carnal"). They were saved, but not living in light of the spiritual realm into which they had been adopted.

They were like **babies in Christ**. They couldn't eat the **solid food**—that is, acquire the spiritual discernment based on Scripture—that Paul wanted to give them. Instead they could only handle spiritual **milk** (3:1-2)—that is, the gospel message and the doctrinal ABCs of the faith (see Heb 5:11-14). Since there had been approximately a five-year gap between Paul's visit to Corinth and this letter, we can conclude that a new believer can attain a basic level of spiritual maturity in five years, if he or she prioritizes spiritual development.

Babies need milk. However, if a five-year-old is still consuming nothing but milk, there's a problem. Christian maturation is required to avoid stagnation. Without spiritual growth, believers will continue to live as they did before coming to Christ. They will operate from a worldly and earthly perspective and behave **like mere humans** (i.e., unbelievers), rather than spiritual people. How did Paul know that the Corinthians were **acting** this way? Because they were dividing themselves into factions behind various leaders (**Paul**, **Apollos**, etc.), causing nothing but **envy and strife** among themselves (2:3-4; see 1:10-13). This is worldliness at its worst!

A spiritual person seeks to think about a matter as Christ would think (see 2:16)—he or she is biblically informed and spiritually illumined—and then applies that perspective to life decisions. Without such an orientation, life will lead to chaos at the personal, family, and church levels.

3:5-9 Although the Corinthians were aligning themselves with personalities in the church, Paul explains the futility of such an outlook. **Apollos** and **Paul** and all the other teachers were mere **servants**, each exercising **the role** that **the Lord [had] given** him (3:5). Paul's task had been to plant a spiritual seed, while Apollos's job was to water. But **God** was the one who **gave the growth** (3:6). If believers were to align themselves with anyone, then, it should have been with the Lord—not with his servants. Paul and

Apollos were **coworkers** with legitimate **labor** from God, but they were not the Corinthian church's source (3:8-9). Their source of spiritual life and growth was God.

3:10-11 Living as a Christian is like constructing a building. Paul was **a skilled master builder** in his spiritual construction work among the Corinthians (3:10). By preaching the gospel to them, Paul had laid the necessary **foundation**—that is, **Jesus Christ** himself (3:11). But he warns the Corinthians (and us) that each must also **be careful how he builds on** that foundation (3:10).

A sturdy foundation is essential. And spiritually speaking, the only one you want to build on is Jesus because he paid top dollar, so to speak, to save you from your sins so that you might have eternal life and fellowship with God. If you have trusted in him, beware what you build. For God will call you to give an account for it.

3:12-15 Continuing his construction metaphor, Paul mentions two different kinds of building material. On the one hand, there are valuable and lasting materials: **gold, silver, costly stones**. On the other, there are inferior and feeble materials: **wood, hay, or straw** (3:12). Whichever a person decides to use, the results **will become obvious** (3:13). To seek to obey God's Word and be faithful with what he has given you is to build wisely using precious metals and stones. But to disregard his Word and live for yourself is to build foolishly using worthless materials. Such work just won't stand the test.

The day will disclose everyone's work (3:13)—that is, "the day" when Christians stand before the judgment seat of Christ (see 2 Cor 5:10). Under the revealing gaze of the Lord Jesus, the **quality of** our **work** will be tested **by fire** to determine our level of loss or rewards (3:13). Those whose deeds and faithfulness withstand the flames will **receive a reward** (3:14). But anyone whose work is **burned up . . . will experience loss** before Christ. Though **he himself will be saved . . . as through** the **fire** of Christ's judgment seat, he will receive nothing to show for a life that should have been lived for God. Don't give God your leftovers; give him the best you've got to offer. This passage affirms the eternal security of unfaithful believers who enter heaven with little or nothing to show in terms of service to God and his kingdom.

3:16-17 Paul wants the Corinthians to take seriously what they were doing (the **you** here is plural in the original Greek text). They were not their own. As the church of Jesus Christ, they were in fact **God's temple**, indwelt by **the Spirit of God** (3:16). To bring harm upon the church through illegitimate division or false doctrine would result in God's temporal judgment because God manifests his **holy** presence among his people (3:17). It is no small thing in God's eyes to bring destruction upon his church (see Acts 5:1-11).

3:18-20 Paul wants **no one** to **deceive himself** by operating according to mere human wisdom. Better to **become a fool** in the world's eyes in order to **become wise** in God's (3:18). **The wisdom of the world**, which considers everything from an earthly perspective and has no place for a supernatural view of reality, **is foolishness with God** (3:19). You can call it "wisdom," if you like, but if a worldview disagrees with God's view of things, it's nothing but folly.

Paul points to Job 5:13 and Psalm 94:11, which articulate the truth that our infinite Creator's thoughts are far superior to the **craftiness** and **reasonings** of those whom the world considers wise (3:19-20). The Lord is able to turn their supposed wisdom on its head and use it against them. True wisdom is in God's hands alone.

3:21-23 In light of these truths, Paul urges the Corinthians to cease boasting in **human leaders** (3:21). They shouldn't exalt one leader over another because God had given all of these teachers to them for their good. They **belong to Christ, and Christ belongs to God** (3:23). Therefore, as Paul says earlier, "Let the one who boasts, boast in the Lord" (1:31).

4:1-2 Paul encourages the church to think of these teachers **as servants of Christ and managers of the mysteries of God** (4:1) rather than placing them on pedestals. After all, they're accountable to the Lord Jesus for all they do. If all **managers** must **be found faithful** (4:2), how much more true is it that

managers of the gospel message must be faithful proclaimers of that message and representatives of their Master?

Regardless of whether or not you serve in full-time Christian ministry, if you have believed in Jesus as the atoning sacrifice for your sins, you are to live as a full-time Christian and, therefore, as a servant of Christ. You are called to operate under his authority, to be faithful to your King's agenda.

4:3-5 Since Paul was ultimately accountable to God, it mattered little to him how he was **judged by** the Corinthians or by some **human court**. God has higher standards than people do! Paul didn't even attempt to judge himself (4:3). Although he did not detect any selfish motives on his own part, that fact was irrelevant because **the Lord** is the one **who judges** (4:4). At the judgment seat of Christ, he will **bring to light what is hidden in darkness**; he will **reveal the intentions of the hearts**. Therefore, premature judgment must be set aside (4:5). Sin-scarred human beings can't perfectly assess the motives of others (or even their own!). Only God knows all of the facts and can render a perfect and righteous judgment.

4:6 Paul had spoken of himself and Apollos as "managers" and "servants" (4:1) so that the Corinthians could **learn from** them. He didn't want them **favoring one leader** or minister **over another** as they had been doing. Instead, they were not to go **beyond what is written**—that is, everything they thought, said, and did was to be rooted in and derived from God's authoritative, inerrant Word. Scripture is sufficient; worldly opinions are not.

4:7 The Corinthians had been acting arrogantly. But Paul confronts their attitude: **Who makes you so superior? What do you have that you didn't receive?** Mere human wisdom had led them to exalt themselves over one another. But they had blinded themselves to the truth that everything they had was from God. So why would they **boast** as if they had achieved anything on their own? God's stewards and managers must never think or act like owners. Kingdom stewards faithfully manage the time, talents, and treasures that God has given them to oversee on his behalf.

4:8 Believers in Jesus Christ are to be marked by humility; exaltation comes from the Lord when we humble ourselves (see Jas 4:10). But the Corinthians insisted on immediate exaltation—without humility, trials, or pain. They wanted **to reign as kings** who needed nothing, when actually they were behaving foolishly. Those who live in pride and self-sufficiency do not submit to the divine King who requires that we live in dependence on him to experience his blessing.

4:9-13 Paul contrasts himself and other apostles with the Corinthians. Though the apostles had lived in meekness and been treated shamefully, the Corinthians acted like they owned the world. They had forgotten what Jesus told his disciples: "A servant is not greater than his master. If they persecuted me, they will also persecute you" (John 15:20). Jesus himself experienced suffering and rejection. Similarly, Paul and his coworkers were treated **like the scum of the earth** by the world (4:13). Yet the Corinthians expected nothing but the best for themselves.

Is your assessment of what it means to live as a disciple of Christ based on the Bible? Or is it based on worldly assumptions and viewpoints? Are you willing to be **dishonored** for Christ? Or do you expect to be **distinguished** and admired (4:10)? If you are **reviled** or **slandered** for your Christian faith, do you **respond graciously** (4:12-13), or do you repay evil with evil?

4:14-15 Although his words likely stung them, Paul wasn't seeking to **shame** them. Rather, he had been motivated by love. As a father to his **children**, he wanted to **warn** the Corinthian Christians of the spiritual danger in which they had put themselves (4:14). Sometimes parents must speak hard and painful truth into their kids' hearts to awaken them out of their lethargy and point them to wisdom. And Paul wasn't merely pretending to be a father figure. He had actually served as their spiritual **father**, preaching **the gospel** to them so that they had experienced the new birth and eternal life through **Jesus Christ** (see Acts 18:1-11). So regardless

of how many Christian **instructors** had taught them since, there was only one man who had brought the Corinthians to faith in Christ through his ministry, and he had their best interests and their spiritual development at heart (4:15).

4:16-17 Therefore, Paul urges them to **imitate** him (4:16). In him, they had a good model of what it looks like to submit to God's kingdom agenda. It was for this reason that Paul had **sent Timothy to** the Corinthians (4:17). Like them, Timothy had Paul as a spiritual father (see commentary on Acts 16:1). So if anyone could serve as a visible reminder and validator of the humble life and ministry of Paul, it was Timothy.

Are you able to encourage others to imitate your Christian life? Do you place faithfulness to God above your personal satisfaction so that in essence you can say to others (perhaps to your children), "Follow me and, inasmuch as I follow Christ, do what I do"?

4:18-21 Paul recognizes that **some** individuals in the Corinthian church were **arrogant** and acting like Paul was all talk and no action (4:18-19). Yet he assured them that he would go to them, not merely for a chat, but to demonstrate **the kingdom of God** (4:20), which is accompanied by visible **power** and authority, not merely verbal declarations (see Matt 16:19). Paul understood that a loving father must correct his children. As the spiritual father of this church and an apostle of Jesus Christ, he was obliged to visit them with **a rod** of discipline if they refused to repent. However, he much preferred to go to them in **a spirit of gentleness** (4:21). He desired that they would be convinced by the truth of his words and the conviction of the Holy Spirit so that he didn't have to resort to extreme measures.

❧ B. Immorality and Settling Disputes in the Church (5:1–6:20) ❧

5:1 The attitude of arrogance in the Corinthian church was unfounded. And Paul points to "exhibit A" to explain why: It was **reported** to him that there was **sexual immorality**

among them. Moreover, it was a level of sexual sin that was **not even tolerated among the Gentiles** (that is, among unbelievers). So, even as depraved as the city of Corinth often was, the non-Christians there would at least draw the line at the kind of immorality taking place in the church! **A man** from their congregation was **sleeping with his father's wife.** Paul doesn't say that it was the man's mother, so the implication is that she was his stepmother. We know that the woman was unsaved and not a part of the church because Paul only concerns himself with the actions of the man.

5:2 Not only was Paul shocked by the sin, but he was also shocked by the fact that the Corinthians were **arrogant** instead of grieved. The church was bragging about all its supposed greatness instead of mourning over its sin. They were like a person who goes to the doctor, learns that he has a malignant cancer, and then proceeds to boast about his good looks, personality, and bank balance. In view of such a diagnosis, what matters is removing the cancerous tumor from the body, and that's what Paul urges: **remove from your congregation the one who did this.**

One of the marks of a true and spiritually healthy church is how it deals with sin—particularly, an ongoing pattern of rebellious behavior against God. When you hear about a fellow Christian entrapped in a web of sin, does it break your heart and cause you to seek to rescue them (see Jas 5:19-20)? Or does it prompt you to pick up your phone and gossip? As Paul explains later in the letter, members of the church are part of the body of Christ and should "have . . . concern for each other" (see 1 Cor 12:25).

5:3 Frequently, people quote Jesus's words: "Do not judge" (Matt 7:1). But when Jesus said this, he wasn't saying that his followers were never to judge. He was warning them not to use a self-imposed standard to judge others; such people will find that their hypocritical standard will be used against them (see Matt 7:2). Paul tells the Corinthians that he had **already pronounced judgment on** this particular man. Why? Because his was a serious and public sin that required

public judgment. Not only did everyone in the church know about it, but also people outside the church. And while the believers weren't called to judge anyone's motives, they were to judge this man's actions.

Some people might say, "What a man does is his own business." No, what a professing believer does is God's business because it's his church. And it's the church's business because we are a family. If a member of your family is physically sick or injured, you wouldn't simply say, "That's his business." Rather, the problem is family business.

5:4-5 What was the Corinthian church to do? They were to gather **in the name of our Lord Jesus** and **with the power of our Lord Jesus** (5:4). That means they were to act on Jesus's behalf, under his authority, to exercise his kingdom power. Then they were to **hand over** this man **to Satan**—that is, excommunicate him from the church, so that God's covenant protection was removed from his life. With that umbrella gone, the man would have no defense against the devil's schemes. But the goal of this move was not punitive. Rather, the goal was **for the destruction of the flesh, so that his spirit may be saved in the day of the Lord** (5:5). In other words, Paul wants the man to be driven to repentance and even allows the devil to be used as the instrument to accomplish this so that the man could be delivered from this sin before facing Christ's judgment seat.

5:6 Paul uses a baking metaphor to explain the consequences of not dealing with serious sin in the church: **Don't you know that a little leaven leavens the whole batch of dough?** To put it another way, one bad apple will spoil the whole barrelful. Or, to use another analogy, you need to treat cancer before it metastasizes and spreads throughout the body. Paul was telling them that sin, left unchecked, would harm the entire congregation. Consider the account of Israel at the battle of Ai (see Josh 7:1-26). The sin of one man (Achan), who lived among God's people, cost other men their lives and resulted in the temporary loss of victory for the entire congregation.

5:7-8 The mention of leaven leads Paul to point to Israel's exodus experience as an illustration. The Israelites were commanded to sacrifice a lamb and put its blood on their doorframes so that the angel of death would pass over them when the Lord brought judgment on Egypt's firstborn. In addition, the Israelites were to remove leaven from their homes and eat unleavened bread for seven days as a reminder of their hurried departure from Egypt (see Exod 12:1-28).

Paul tells the Corinthians that **Christ** is the fulfillment of the **Passover lamb.** He was **sacrificed** to protect them from judgment. Furthermore, leaven is symbolic of sin. So just as the Israelites were to rid their homes of all leaven, so the Corinthians must **clean out the old leaven so that** they might **be a new unleavened batch** (5:7). In other words, sin—the old way of life—must be left behind so that the church can live as the new people we are in Christ and not as the old people we were. One person's sin (leaven) can hinder or stop God's blessing for everyone. Therefore, we must discard **the leaven of malice and evil** so that we may live **with the unleavened bread of sincerity and truth** (5:8).

5:9-11 The Corinthians should have known better than to ignore this church member's sexual immorality (5:1). For Paul reminds them of a previous **letter** he had written in which he told them **not to associate with sexually immoral people** (5:9). By this he **did not mean the immoral people of this world**—that is, unbelievers. After all, we all have to together live in the world. We will inevitably encounter sinners—those who are **greedy and swindlers or idolaters.** We can't **leave the world** (5:10). Rather, Paul says, Christians are **not to associate with** an unrepentant person engaged in these sins **who claims to be a** Christian **brother or sister** (5:11).

Unbelievers are expected to live as unbelievers. But those who consider themselves part of God's people are expected to live as God's people. This doesn't mean that Christians never sin. Instead, it means that clear patterns of sin are not acceptable and must be confronted. To call oneself a child of God and live like a child of the devil is a contradiction.

If a so-called brother refuses to repent of such actions, Paul insists that the church must put him out (excommunication; 5:4-5) and not associate with him—that is, engage in intimate social fellowship with him. They're **not even** to **eat** with him (5:11). This doesn't mean you can't speak to the person, or that you are to treat him cruelly. Instead, it means you are not to treat him like a fellow Christian when he is showing contempt for God and for his people by ignoring the divinely prescribed process of church discipline (see Matt 18:15-18). In other words, we must not treat someone who is sick as if he is well. To do so is unloving.

5:12-13 It is not the church's business **to judge outsiders**—unbelievers (5:12). **God** will deal with them (5:13). But the church is called to judge its own, to **judge those who are inside** (5:12; see 1 Pet 4:17), for the good of the sinning member, the purity of the church, and the glory of God. Churches that refuse to lovingly and clearly address unrepentant sin are not functioning as biblically centered, New Testament churches. Therefore, they are limiting or negating God's powerful presence in their midst.

The local church is to be a hospital for the sick, a place where sinners can come to be healed. Indeed, we must welcome the sick and never keep them away. But what the church must *not* do is allow the sick to be content with being sick. When we do that, we cease to be a hospital and devolve into a hospice that simply makes people comfortable in their sin.

6:1-3 Paul next addresses the issue of how Christians should handle disputes with one another. The Corinthians were taking their disputes to the local courts to be tried **before the unrighteous** rather than **before the saints** in the church (6:1). But Paul insists that such problems should be settled among the church family; after all, Christians are not to live as adversaries. He reminds them that believers will one day **judge the world** when they reign with Christ (see Rev 20:4-6). If Christians will participate in worldwide judgment—including judging (fallen) **angels**—then surely they can handle **trivial cases** among themselves (6:2-3).

6:4-6 Rather than Christian brothers taking one another to a secular court **before unbelievers** with **no standing in the church** (6:4, 6), every local church should have a church court of sorts. **Wise**, spiritual church leaders should **arbitrate between fellow believers** (6:5). This enables a body of believers to bring God's point of view to bear on specific situations in order to settle disputes between members and provide resolution. To do otherwise brings **shame** on God's people (6:5). To call on unbelievers to arbitrate disputes between Christians—those who have been reconciled to God and to one another—hinders the proclamation of the gospel and reputation of the church before the world.

6:7-8 As far as Paul was concerned, when believers engage in **legal disputes against one another** before the world, they've already lost. Better to **be wronged** than to experience spiritual loss by engaging in such shameful behavior (6:7). **Instead**, they were wronging and cheating their **brothers and sisters** (6:8). Their actions did not bring God glory in the eyes of unbelievers but brought division to the church.

6:9-11 Paul reminds them that **the unrighteous will not inherit God's kingdom**, as he lists various sinful lifestyles (6:9-10). To *inherit* God's kingdom is more than *entering* it, the latter being by faith alone in Christ alone. Inheritance has to do with the kingdom rewards and blessings to be received or lost by believers at the judgment seat of Christ based on our obedience and faithfulness (see 2 Tim 2:12; Heb 12:16-17). Paul further reminds the Corinthians that some of them once practiced these things (**some of you used to be like this**). But, by the grace of God, they had been **washed** (cleansed of guilt by the blood of Jesus), **sanctified** (spiritually set apart to God), and **justified** (declared righteous before God) **in the name of the Lord Jesus Christ and by the Spirit of God** (6:11). Thus, they were called to live in a way reflecting the reality of what God had done for them.

6:12 Everything is permissible for me was a slogan spoken by the Corinthians that they used to justify and rationalize their immorality. Paul counters it by telling them that "permissible" things aren't necessarily **beneficial**. Christian freedom should never be used to sin or harm fellow believers. Moreover, there's a danger of being **mastered by** such things—that is, becoming slaves to them. Liberty becomes detrimental when it negates the law of love—whether to another person or to yourself by bringing you into bondage.

6:13-17 Like the statement in 6:12, this one was probably also a Corinthian slogan: **Food is for the stomach and the stomach for food.** It conveys the idea, "I've got a bodily appetite, so I need to satisfy it." The problem was that the Corinthians extended this argument beyond just eating. Some were arguing that *sexual* cravings also needed to be satisfied—even by visiting pagan temple prostitutes (6:15)! However, Paul would have none of that kind of thinking: **The body is not for sexual immorality.** God created sex for procreation and intimacy between a husband and wife within the covenant bond of marriage. Our bodies are not our own to do with as we please but are **for the Lord** (6:13). What we do with them, then, is not irrelevant and is to be determined by the Lord. After all, **God raised up** the body of **the Lord** Jesus and will one day **raise** the bodies of believers **by his power** (6:14).

Furthermore, our **bodies are a part of Christ's body**—that is, the church is in spiritual union with him. To sexually unite with a prostitute is to be illegitimately **one body with her.** According to Genesis 2:24, when a man and woman are joined sexually in marriage, they legitimately **become one flesh** (6:16). Thus, to engage in prostitution or any other sexually immoral relationship is to make Christ and his **body** (the church) part of an illegitimate union (6:15). And that's exactly what happens when a person is both **joined to a prostitute** *and* **joined to the Lord** (6:16-17). We should never make our Savior part of such an unrighteous union!

6:18 Paul's exhortation is brief and to the point: **Flee sexual immorality!** Sexual sin is unique because by joining sexually to someone other than one's spouse, a person enters into an illegitimate one-flesh union (see 6:16) and **sins against his own body**. This, in fact, is why people experience emotional, psychological, and spiritual scars as a result of sexual sin.

6:19-20 Then Paul comes to the capstone of his argument: **Don't you know that your body is a temple of the Holy Spirit who is in you?** (6:19). A Christian's body is a house of worship; therefore, sexual immorality brings such sin directly into God's presence! When you have sex, you are going to church. The Lord is present when a husband and wife

experience physical intimacy too (see commentary on Songs 5:1), but sexual pleasure within marriage brings God glory because it honors his design for sex. Sexual immorality, in whatever form it takes (adultery, fornication, homosexuality, pornography, etc.), makes a mockery of God's design.

Since, then, your body is a temple of the Holy Spirit, **you are not your own**, but Jesus Christ **bought** you with his own blood. We are not owners but stewards of our bodies. God will call everyone to account for how they manage their sexuality. So, **glorify God with your body** (6:20).

III. RESPONSE TO THE CORINTHIANS' LETTER (7:1–16:4)

A. Sex and Marriage (7:1-40)

7:1 Paul begins to address **matters** that the Corinthians **wrote** to him **about**. A literal rendering of the Greek text into English is, "It is good for a man not to touch a woman." Touching a woman is a euphemism for engaging in sexual activity with her. Thus, for those who are single, abstinence is God's good plan until marriage. God created sex for marriage between one man and one woman. He designed it and knows best how it is to be expressed. Pursuing it outside of the covenant bond of marriage is sin and will not bring the fulfillment that God intends.

7:2 Since **sexual immorality** (fornication, adultery, homosexuality, pornography, etc.) **is so common**, Paul encourages men and women to pursue marriage so that **each man** may **have sexual relations with his own wife**, and **a woman . . . with her own husband.** Of course, a Christian isn't to marry just anyone, but to marry "in the Lord" (7:39)—that is, to marry a fellow believer who is likewise submitting to Christ and pursuing his kingdom. But Paul's main point is to emphasize that sexual expression within marriage is *not* immorality.

7:3-4 Since marriage is God's answer to preventing sexual immorality, husbands and

wives must fulfill their **marital** duties to one another (7:3). This isn't to say that having sex is a "duty"; rather, it emphasizes that husbands and wives should not be selfish and should focus on the needs of their spouses.

Husband, if you're really serious about meeting your wife's needs, you'll talk with her more, listen better, compliment her more, and serve her. You'll regularly show her that you value and esteem her—and not just after the sun goes down. Strong marital relationships foster true intimacy. And true intimacy involves vulnerability with your spouse, selfless giving to one another (7:4; see commentary on Songs 4:1–5:1).

7:5-6 Husbands and wives are to protect one another from sin by not depriving one another. The only exception to regular sexual intimacy is when the couple agrees to a limited **time** period in which they **devote** themselves **to prayer** (7:5). We might refer to this as "sexual fasting." To fast is to temporarily give up satisfying a craving of the body in order to focus and give extra attention to a spiritual need. If a husband and wife need God to intervene in a situation, a sexual fast for the purpose of prayer is in order; nevertheless, Paul offers this **as a concession, not as a command** (7:6). But, as the apostle reminds them, they must **come together again** in sexual intimacy so that they don't fall prey to Satan's temptations to sexual immorality (7:5).

7:7-9 Paul says, **I wish that all people were as I am**—that is, single (7:7). For those who were **unmarried** or **widows**, he recognizes the benefit of remaining unmarried (7:8; see 7:32-35). Nevertheless, if people lack **self-control . . . it is better to marry than burn with** sexual **desire** (7:9). Unless God has granted the gift of celibacy, marriage is a wise and legitimate pursuit.

7:10-11 Paul tells Christians in the Corinthian church that they are **not to leave**—that is, divorce—one another (7:10). Instead, if a **husband** or **wife** does leave, he or she must **remain unmarried or be reconciled** to his or her spouse (7:11). When two people marry, there will always be struggles and challenges. But, even when there are difficult problems, Paul urges the pursuit of reconciliation—not divorce. Thus, Paul stands in agreement with Jesus (see commentary on Matt 19:1-9) and the Father (see commentary on Mal 2:10-16).

7:12-14 Believers are to marry "in the Lord" (7:39) and not to partner together with unbelievers (see 2 Cor 6:14-15). But what happens when a Christian is married to an unbeliever? Perhaps a woman comes to faith in Christ after marriage and finds that her spouse refuses to believe. Some of the Corinthians were apparently experiencing things like this, because Paul gives counsel for such scenarios. By saying that his instructions are from himself and **not the Lord** (7:12), Paul means that Jesus never spoke directly on this subject during his earthly ministry. Nevertheless, as an inspired apostle, Paul provides guidance from the Holy Spirit.

A believing spouse is **not** to **divorce** an **unbelieving wife** or **husband** (7:12-13). Why? Because the **unbelieving** spouse **is made holy by** the believing spouse (7:14). In other words, the Christian husband or wife serves as a channel of grace in the marriage. Not only can the believing spouse share the gospel with the unbelieving spouse and their children, but he or she also brings a covering of God's blessing to the marriage and family. Consider Rahab's situation (see Josh 2:8-14). When she confessed faith in the Lord and sheltered his people, she and her unbelieving family were delivered from the destruction that God brought upon Jericho.

7:15 Paul recognizes that an unbelieving husband or wife may not want to stay married to a Christian. So **if the unbeliever leaves**, the believer **is not bound.** Thus, abandonment (like adultery; see Matt 19:9) is an exception to the biblical prohibition against divorce. Sometimes abandonment happens when a spouse physically leaves the home, or it can happen when a spouse abandons his or her divinely ordained role. For example, if a husband becomes physically abusive toward his wife, that would be a form of abandonment of his role as husband. In such a case, the wife "is not bound" to the marriage because **God has called** us **to live in peace.** Thus, if a Christian spouse has done everything possible to preserve the marriage but the unbeliever still leaves home or his divinely ordained role, Scripture considers such a situation legitimate grounds for divorce (and, thus, the believing spouse would be free to remarry). Importantly, accusations of abandonment must be validated by the church.

7:16 Why should a Christian seek to remain married to an unbelieving spouse? Because the believing spouse just **might save** the unbeliever through the gospel witness he or she brings to the relationship. Daily exposure to the verbal and visual message of the gospel is a powerful testimony that God might use to bring someone to faith in Christ.

7:17-19 Paul's counsel for believers to remain married to unbelievers (7:12-16) is an application of his overall principle that every Christian should **live his life in the situation the Lord assigned when God called him** (7:17). Whether one is **circumcised** or **uncircumcised** before becoming a believer **does not matter** (7:18-19). Externals are non-essential. **What matters** is internalizing **God's commands** and **keeping** them (7:19).

7:20-24 This also applies to those who were slaves. If they could avail themselves of their freedom, Paul encourages them to do so (7:21). But if unable to gain it, Paul tells them that they can still serve Christ. For even one **who is called by the Lord as a slave is the Lord's freedman.** Believers have been **bought at a price** by the blood of Christ, so regardless of our status in life, we are to serve as **Christ's slave** (7:22-23). Christian, no matter your vocation, you are called first and foremost to render faithful service to the Lord who saved you.

7:25 Having spoken about a kingdom view of marriage, Paul also addresses what it means to live as a kingdom single. A *kingdom single* is an unmarried Christian who is committed to fully and freely maximizing his or her life under the rule of God and the lordship of Jesus Christ. An unmarried believer is to approach life as a follower of the King. Paul's instructions here follow the same principle he just outlined in 7:17, 20, and 24: Believers ought to remain in the situation in which they were called to Christ. He applies this to single believers, whom he refers to as **virgins** because according to a biblical worldview unmarried believers are not to be sexually active. Paul says he has **no command from the Lord** about this situation but provides his own **opinion** (or decision). What he means is that the Lord Jesus didn't teach on this matter during his earthly ministry, so Paul gives Holy-Spirit-inspired instruction (see 7:12).

7:26-28 Paul argues that **it is good for a man to remain as he is** (7:26). Given the **distress** and **trouble** that believers will have **in this life** (7:26, 28), both marriage and singlehood will include difficulties; thus, he encourages single and married Christians to remain as they are (7:26-27). Nevertheless, if a single person gets **married**, he or she has **not sinned**; Paul is simply **trying to spare** them trouble (7:28). Marriage, even Christian marriage, has unique challenges because it's the uniting of two imperfect people. So no one should go running about in a flippant search for a spouse. That will inevitably bring some level of trouble, so Paul wants them to give the matter careful investigation.

7:29-31 Time is limited, so we need to be wise about how we live in the present world (7:29). **The world in its current form is passing away**; therefore, we must not live with a temporal mindset as if this world is all there is (7:31). We must not lose sight

of heaven by maximizing the time spent in earthly pursuits. Make decisions based on an eternal perspective and not based on earthly pressures.

7:32-35 Paul wants single Christians to know that there can be kingdom benefit to singlehood. An **unmarried** believer is free to be **concerned about the things of the Lord** in a way that a married believer cannot (7:32). The **married** believer has obligations to his spouse, so **his interests are divided** (7:33-34). But, sadly, many Christian singles are divided as well—consumed with finding spouses when they could be using their singlehood to serve the Lord without hindrance, to maximize their kingdom calling, and to enjoy the completeness of being fully free. Again, Paul is not trying to **put a restraint on** the Corinthians and prevent them from marrying but to help them **be devoted to the Lord without distraction** (7:35).

Adam was consumed with his calling until God gave him Eve. Likewise, every Christian single should maximize the freedom of his or her single status until God brings a mate. It is okay to have the desire for a mate; it is not okay to allow the desire to become a spiritual distraction.

7:36-38 Paul is saying that fathers who have made a pledge to dedicate their **virgin** daughters to the Lord are free to break such pledges when their daughters reach marriageable age and desire to **marry** (7:36; see CSB notes on 7:36-38). However, if a daughter is not pressing the issue, a man does well to keep his desire for her to be fully devoted to the Lord. The issue is not a matter of right or wrong (7:37-38; cf. 7:28).

7:39-40 Before leaving the topic of marriage, Paul considers the inevitable situation in which a spouse dies. A Christian husband or **wife is bound as long as** the spouse is **living**. But if the spouse dies, a believer is **free to** remarry **anyone . . . only in the Lord** (7:39). In other words, a believer in Jesus Christ must marry a fellow believer. Many people talk about finding a *soul*-mate, but the Lord wants us to find a *spirit*-mate. Within that context, there is freedom of choice. As

Paul writes to the Corinthians later, "Don't become partners with those who do not believe. . . . What fellowship does light have with darkness?" (2 Cor 6:14).

Though marriage is permissible in this case, Paul concludes by again providing Spirit-inspired counsel: If a believer has lost a spouse, Paul believes he or she is happier remaining unmarried (7:40).

⮞ B. Food Sacrificed to Idols
(8:1–11:1) ⮜

8:1-3 The next topic that the Corinthians had asked Paul about is **food sacrificed to idols** (8:1; see 7:1). But before addressing the issue, Paul exhorts them to do everything with love. Whatever **knowledge** they have, it must not be exercised without love. *Biblical love* is the decision to compassionately, righteously, and responsibly seek the well-being of another. **Knowledge puffs up, but love builds up** (8:1)—that is, knowledge can lead to pride if it's not accompanied by love to strengthen others. Such a person assumes **he knows** but doesn't **know** at the level **he ought** (7:2). Better to love God and be **known by him** (8:3). When a person uses knowledge with love, it becomes a ministry and reflects favorably on God.

8:4-6 Paul makes it clear that **idols are nothing**, for **there is no God but one** (8:4). No matter how many so-called **gods** and **lords** the Greeks and Romans revered, for Christians there is **one God, the Father**, the source of all things (8:5-6). **And there is one Lord, Jesus Christ**, the agent of creation (8:6). We know these things to be true. But, Paul goes on to tell the Corinthians that this knowledge must be accompanied by love.

8:7 Since there is no God but one, then food that unbelievers sacrificed to idols means nothing, right? Why worry about the issue? Paul explains: **Not everyone has this knowledge. Some** new believers had been **so used to idolatry** before their conversion that to **eat food sacrificed to idols** would defile **their conscience.** They wanted nothing to do with it.

8:8-11 Paul acknowledges that **food** in and off itself can't **bring us close to God**, regardless of whether we eat it (8:8). At issue here is not harming brothers and sisters in Christ by practicing something that is a **stumbling block** to them (8:9). After all, we don't want to do something that causes a fellow Christian to fail to move forward in his or her faith. Some of the Corinthians rightly recognized that idols are nothing and, so, had no problem eating food sacrificed to idols. But, if their liberty **encouraged** a believer with a **weak conscience** to also **eat the food**, the latter would experience spiritual harm. We must not ruin the faith of a **brother or sister for whom Christ died** (8:10-11).

Paul is talking about believers who are seeking to honor God and grow in their faith, but are not yet at a spiritual level where they can exercise the full spiritual freedom they have in Christ. We should not intentionally do anything to harm the spiritual progress of such fellow Christians. We don't want to exercise our knowledge and freedom in such a way that we cause them to stumble. Our Christian liberty may be legitimate in and of itself, but if it causes a weaker brother or sister to fall, we have sinned against them. So let's act in love toward such individuals so that their faith is strengthened and not undermined.

8:12-13 Paul takes this matter a step further. To insist on exercising our liberty at the expense of weaker Christians is not only to sin against them but to sin **against Christ** (8:12). As Paul himself learned, Jesus takes sins against his church (his "body") seriously (see commentary on Acts 9:3-5). Therefore, if eating meat sacrificed to idols caused spiritual harm to other believers, Paul would **never again eat** it (8:13). He would go out of his way to avoid hindering the spiritual development of another Christian. Love for one another must come first.

Are you willing to let your freedom be subordinated to love? Let us not use our knowledge to hurt someone else who does not yet have our knowledge. Don't trip up others in their spiritual progress; rather, help them on their journey to know, love, and obey God.

9:1-6 Having encouraged the Corinthians to set aside their rights for the sake of the gospel and the body of Christ, Paul explains how he himself had engaged in such sacrificial behavior as an example to them. He asks four rhetorical questions that assume an affirmative answer, highlighting his authority as an **apostle** of the risen **Lord** Jesus (9:1-2). Of those who wonder if he practices what he preaches, Paul asks further questions to show that he has rights as an apostle. These rights included eating and drinking whatever he chose, taking a spouse, and ceasing his tent-making vocation to support himself (9:3-6). But Paul was willing to forego his freedoms for the benefit of the church and the advancement of the gospel.

9:7 Paul illustrates his entitlement to these rights with several examples. **A soldier** doesn't go to war **at his own expense.** The one who **plants a vineyard** and the one who **shepherds a flock** each have the prerogative to enjoy some of the **fruit** and **milk** associated with their labor. Similarly, an apostle of Jesus Christ is certainly entitled to receive remuneration for his work. Nevertheless, Paul chose not to exercise this right so the gospel wouldn't be hindered.

9:8-10 Even the Old Testament **law** supports Paul's argument: **Do not muzzle an ox while it treads out grain** (9:8-9). Ultimately, this command was not written for the sake of the oxen but for the **sake** of God's people. If an ox has the right to eat of the fruit of his labor, do people not have the same right (9:10)? Thus, those who engage in Christian ministry have the right to receive compensation for their work.

9:11-12 Paul had invested heavily in the Corinthian believers. His spiritual ministry was significant and, thus, he had a right to expect **material benefits** from them (9:11). If the Corinthians had been willing to support other Christian ministers who had followed Paul, surely they should have been willing to support the one who had first brought them to Christ and founded the church. Yet, though Paul had a right to compensation, he never exercised it among them. He didn't want to be falsely accused of engaging

in ministry for profit and, thus, **hinder the gospel of Christ** (9:12). He didn't want to risk staining the credibility of the gospel or be the cause of anyone rejecting the message of Christ, so he had relinquished his right to financial support while among the Corinthians.

9:13-14 Paul once again points to the Old Testament. The priests who served in the **temple** had the right to receive the sacrificial **offerings** as their **food** (9:13; see, e.g., Num 18:8-32). **In the same way, the Lord** Jesus had **commanded that those who preach the gospel should earn their living by the gospel** (9:14; see Matt 10:8-10; Luke 10:7).

9:15-18 Clearly, then, Paul had every right to receive financial support for his missionary work, but he refused to exercise those rights so that he couldn't be accused of acting from wrong motives (9:15). The apostle wasn't motivated by money but **compelled** by God **to preach** (9:16). He had been **entrusted with a commission** from the Lord Jesus to serve as his ambassador, proclaiming the gospel to the world (9:17 see Acts 26:12-18). So he was willing to give up compensation and relinquish the **full use of** his **rights in the gospel** and **offer it free of charge.** Paul's **reward** was seeing lives transformed by God (9:18); therefore, he preferred to secure his own financial support rather than lose out on that joy.

9:19-22 Even though Paul was **free** and no man's **slave**, he **made** himself **a slave to everyone**, serving all people so that he might **win** them to Christ (9:19). In non-essential matters, he was willing to adopt the ways of either Jews or Gentiles so that he might gain a hearing among them for the sake of the gospel. Since Paul was himself a Jew, he was willing to engage in Jewish practices and live **like one under the law**—even though he was free from the law—so that he might **win Jews** to Christ (9:20; see commentary on Acts 16:3). Similarly, he was willing to live **like one without God's law** in order to win Gentiles—though, of course, Paul was still **under the law of Christ** (9:21). In other words, through Paul was free from the Old Testament law, he wasn't free to sin. As a Christian, he was obligated to God's moral law in accordance with God's character. Thus, Paul was willing to **become all things to all people, so that ... by every possible means** he might **save some** (9:22). Because of God's call on his life, Paul would do whatever he had to do to fulfill it.

What motivates you? Is it money or power or notoriety? None of these things will ultimately satisfy, and none of them deserve your allegiance. Instead, following your Savior and adjusting your life as necessary to make him known ought to be your highest ambitions. When we truly grasp his great love for us, we come to see that serving him and winning others to him should be our passion. After all, "God proves his own love for us in that while we were still sinners, Christ died for us" (Rom 5:8). Let that be your motivation, and resolve to let nothing prevent you from exalting your Savior and making the good news known to others.

9:23-24 Paul subjugated his personal preferences to **the gospel, so that [he might] share in the blessings** (9:23). The apostle knew that payday was coming. One day God will reward us for our sacrificial service to and love for him. Therefore, Paul was motivated to receive God's blessing. Using athletic imagery, he asks the Corinthians, **Don't you know that the runners in a stadium all race, but only one receives the prize? Run in such a way to win the prize** (9:24). In the race of the Christian life, Paul wasn't content to receive a participation ribbon. He wanted to obtain the gold.

True athletes don't compete for mere exercise; they compete to win. Followers of Christ shouldn't merely go through the motions either. Instead, we should run the Christian race for the prize. There is nothing wrong with wanting to climb the ladder to reach the top. Just ensure that your ladder is leaning against the right wall. You want to scale the ladder that has Christ at its top. You should long to hear him say, "Well done, good and faithful servant!" (Matt 25:23).

9:25 Paul again uses athletic games to illustrate his point. Those who compete know they must exercise **self-control in everything** if they are to win. Without maintaining

strict control over eating habits, sleeping habits, and training routines, an athlete can't expect to be in the running for the prize. That's why athletes must discipline themselves and focus all their energy on the end goal. In ancient times, they competed to **receive a perishable crown**. In other words, they labored long and hard to obtain something that lacked long-term value.

Paul tips his hat to such devotion but nevertheless says, in effect, "That's not our plan. We aim higher. We strive from an eternal perspective." We seek **an imperishable crown**. God's rewards do not fade, rust, or perish.

For what are you living your life? All Christians will stand before the judgment seat of Christ to be "repaid for" our service to our Master (2 Cor 5:10). He has seen everything since your conversion, the good and the bad. Nothing has been missed. So, how will you fare when the day comes? Maintain a kingdom perspective and strive for the imperishable reward.

9:26-27 Whatever the Corinthians decided to do, Paul's mind was made up. He says he has no intention of running **aimlessly** or flailing his arms like a boxer who doesn't know his purpose (9:26). Rather, he disciplines himself **so that after preaching to others**, he's **not** himself **disqualified** (9:27). Paul's mission was to fulfill his King's agenda. No matter what happened, he was not going to let anything prevent him from maintaining that focus and receiving Christ's approval.

Only one passion in your life is worth your total commitment and pursuit: Loving Christ and serving him. Don't disqualify yourself for the prize by quitting the race, running in the wrong direction, or breaking the rules. Run to win.

10:1-4 Having spoken about the possibility of being disqualified (9:27), Paul exhorts the Corinthians to serve the Lord. He points to the negative example of the Israelites in the wilderness. In speaking of the Israelites' experiences, Paul repeatedly uses the word **all** to emphasize the fact that every one of them experienced the supernatural benefits of the deliverance, guidance, and provision of God. The Lord guided them by his glory **cloud** and delivered them through the Red Sea (10:1). They were **baptized into** their spiritual leader **Moses, ate the same spiritual food** (manna) that God provided, and **drank** from the **spiritual rock that followed them**—which **was Christ** (10:2-4). This is another indicator that the Son of God was active in Old Testament times before his incarnation.

10:5 In spite of this, **God was not pleased with most of them**, disciplining them severely. Because of their perpetual disobedience and ungratefulness, God **struck** them **down in the wilderness** (see Num 14:1-38). Thus, being recipients of God's kindness is no guarantee of avoiding his disciplining hand for our rebellion.

10:6-11 The worldliness in the Corinthian church was putting them in danger of divine chastisement. Therefore, Paul warns them to consider the example of the Israelites and not to **desire evil things as they did** (10:6). Specifically, he urges them to avoid idolatry (10:7), **sexual immorality** (10:8), and complaining (10:10). These sins led to the downfall of the Israelites (see, e.g., Exod 32:1-6; Num 16:41-50; 25:1-15), and they can lead to ours. Paul tells his readers, **These things happened to them as examples, and they were written for our instruction**. The apostle didn't want lessons of old to be lost on the Corinthians. What happened to Israel was included in the pages of Scripture as a warning for their benefit—and for ours.

Christians are those **on whom the ends of the ages have come** (10:11). The consequences are high for any believers in the church age who choose to follow the sinful example of Israel's wilderness generation. Remember God's warning to the Galatians: "God is not mocked. For whatever a person sows he will also reap" (Gal 6:7).

10:12-13 Paul didn't want the Corinthians **to fall** like Israel had done in the past, so they needed to **be careful** (10:12). Temptations to sin and trials to develop us come to all Christians alike. No matter what **temptation** confronts you, know for certain that you are not alone. You have encountered nothing **except what is common to humanity** (10:13). None of us can claim to have experienced a

temptation worse than anyone else's. Just as Israel's path from Egypt to the promised land took them through the wilderness, the same is true for all of God's people. To get where God wants you, he will test and develop you through wilderness experiences.

Take heart, though. **God is faithful; he will not allow you to be tempted beyond what you are able.** No temptation or trial will prove overpowering because Christians are no longer slaves to sin; we have the freedom to choose what is good. God will **provide a way out**; he will grant you the strength so that you may say "no" to sinful **temptation** (10:13). Through the power of the Holy Spirit, we have the ability to withstand the temptation and pass the test.

10:14-22 In light of the help that God provides in the midst of temptation and trials, Paul urges them to **flee from idolatry** (10:14). He reminds them of the intimacy Christians are able to share with Christ through Communion. **The cup** represents **the blood of Christ**, and **the bread** represents **the body of Christ**. When we partake of it together, we are **sharing in** a special time of spiritual intimacy with Christ (10:16-17). But some of the Corinthians were apparently attempting to **share in the Lord's table and the table of demons** (10:21) by partaking of Communion and also eating with unbelievers who were sacrificing to idols in pagan temples. Though **idols** are not truly gods, Paul contends that **demons** stand behind them (10:19-20). A sacrifice offered to a false god, then, has actually been offered to a demon. You **cannot** draw closer in intimacy with Christ and experience his kingdom blessings, while at the same time drawing closer to demonic activity (10:21).

These believers were attempting to have it both ways by participating in both meals. But, Paul contends, they would only succeed in **provoking the Lord to jealousy**, causing him to discipline them and withhold his blessings.

10:23-24 Paul gives the proper balance and understanding of Christian liberty by saying that the exercise of freedom must be tempered and regulated by the principle of love. Paul insists that what **is permissible** may not be **beneficial** or edifying to fellow believers (10:23). We are called to seek **the good of** others, not our own good (10:24).

10:25-29 Paul insists that they may **eat** any food **sold in the meat market**, for everything in creation **is the Lord's** (10:25-26). The point is that Corinthian believers didn't need to research whether or not a piece of meat had been part of a pagan sacrifice prior to being delivered to the market. Moreover, if **unbelievers** invited them into their homes, they were free to go and eat what was set before them (10:27). However, if a host told them that the food had been sacrificed to an idol, Christians were to abstain from the meal—not because it would bring harm to the mature believer's conscience but to the unbeliever's **conscience** (10:28-29). If a believer knowingly eats food sacrificed to idols, someone might interpret it as a compromise of their faith and a participation in idolatry. This could hinder some from coming to Christ, and it could injure a weak believer's conscience.

10:30 Paul didn't want believers being judged by non-Christians because of what they ate. Thus, believers are not to participate in meals in pagan temples (10:19-22), nor should they eat meat sacrificed to idols if it's offered to them by unbelievers (10:25-29). Our Christian freedom must be exercised in such a way that we do not bring spiritual harm to ourselves or other believers, nor set up a stumbling block that prevents unbelievers from coming to faith in Christ.

10:31–11:1 Everything a believer does—whether a significant task or something as mundane as eating and drinking—ought to be carried out with a heartfelt desire to bring **glory** to **God** (10:31). Paul exhorts the Corinthians to **imitate** his example as he imitates **Christ**, giving no unnecessary **offense to Jews or Greeks or the church** (10:32; 11:1). Why? Because God's reputation is more important than our personal preferences! The gospel is at stake. Eternity hangs in the balance! Let us not seek our **own benefit** but seek to compassionately, righteously, and responsibly seek the well-being of others **so that they may be saved**

(10:33). Let's live such faithful lives that people see our King on display and marvel at how glorious he is.

➤ C. Proper Order, Love, and Spiritual Gifts in the Church (11:2–14:40) ⬳

11:2 Paul praises the Corinthians for remembering the traditions that he had **delivered** to **them**. Nevertheless, in the next several chapters he addresses matters that were causing them significant problems.

11:3 Paul raises the first topic with a thesis statement that lays out God's chain of command, so to speak: **Christ is the head of every man, and the man is the head of woman, and God is the head of Christ.** The description of one person as "the head of" another introduces the concept of headship. Just as the head provides guidance and leadership to the human body, one who is the head in a relationship serves in a leadership role as a governing authority (like a head of state, for instance). This, however, does not imply inferiority on the part of those under the headship. Rather, in the orderly nature of God's design, headship provides a covering under which people are to function and flourish.

Let's start where Paul concludes: "God is the head of Christ." According to the New Testament, Jesus Christ is himself God, sharing the Father's divine nature (see John 1:1; 10:30). Yet, the Son is also distinct in person from the Father and functioned in a subordinate role to the Father during his earthly ministry (see John 8:29; 14:28). So he is equal in essence to the Father but subordinate in role and function.

So when the apostle says, "the man is the head of woman," Paul is not saying that every man is the head of every woman. Here he is speaking of the headship of the husband over the wife (see also Eph 5:22-33; Col 3:18-19). Paul is also not saying that the husband is superior to the wife. As the Father and Son are equal in essence while different in function, so the husband and wife are equal as human beings and in their spiritual standing before God (see Gal 3:28-29) but different in their roles in marriage. The wife is called to submit to her husband's spiritual leadership—though, of course, she is never to follow her husband into sin or to submit to abuse, since her commitment to Christ is to transcend her commitment to her husband (see commentary on Eph 5:22-33; 1 Pet 3:1-7). Refusal to submit to her husband's legitimate authority can result in the loss of God's spiritual covering.

Importantly, the man is not autonomous. He is also called to submit: "Christ is the head of every man." He is not free to lead his wife and children as he deems fit; rather, he is to lead in full submission to the lordship of Christ. When God's people operate within this divine order, there is covering and protection. But, like a car, we're in danger of crashing when we get out of alignment.

11:4-6 Paul moves from this general statement of divine order to specific matters of worship. It was an accepted custom that whenever a **man** prayed or prophesied in the church, he was not to cover his physical **head**; otherwise, he would dishonor his (spiritual) **head**, Christ (11:4). On the other hand, a **woman** was to pray or prophesy with her physical **head** covered; otherwise, she would dishonor her (spiritual) **head**, her husband (11:5), and violate the prescribed church order. This is the exception to Paul's prohibition against women speaking in the public worship of the church (see 1 Tim 2:11-14). A woman is permitted to do so if she is operating under the approval of the legitimate male authority of her husband and church leadership.

Paul's comments in verse 5 reflect the first-century practice of a woman wearing a head covering. He argues that if either the husband or wife rejected these common distinctions between men and women, it would signal a rejection of God's design and order for men and women. But apparently, women in the Corinthian church were expressing their own version of women's liberation, rebelling against any sense of submission to their husbands' spiritual authority by refusing to wear a head covering during worship. Paul said if a woman disregarded this male-female role distinction by uncovering her head, she might as well go all the way and

shave **her head** (11:5-6)—and thus look like a man! To reject submission to authority is to reject God's prescribed order.

11:7-10 Here Paul is not talking about a distinction in essence between men and women but a distinction in function. The husband glorifies God through his kingdom role as head, and the wife glorifies God by fulfilling her kingdom role to help her husband (11:7-9; see commentary on Gen 2:18-25). **This is why a woman should have a symbol of authority on her head, because of the angels** (11:10). In that culture at that time, the head covering was a visible symbol of the woman's submission to her God-given role. "Because of the angels" is Paul's way of saying that if a woman operates out of alignment with God's will (uncovered), either in the home or in the church (see 14:34-35; 1 Tim 2:11-14), she will lose angelic assistance. Angels serve as God's heavenly messengers, helping to bring about his will in our lives. But when a wife rebels against his revealed will, she will lose divine support. The same is true for the husband (see 1 Pet 3:7).

11:11-12 Men and women should view themselves as mutually dependent. They certainly are not **independent of** one another (11:11). The first **woman** (Eve) **came from** the first **man** (Adam), but every other **man** is born of a **woman** (11:12). Thus, God has demonstrated through his creation design that neither can do without the other, and neither is superior. Men and women need each other to fulfill God's kingdom agenda.

11:13-16 Even nature itself, Paul argues, confirms the distinction between men and women. In his day, women wore **long hair**, and men wore short hair. To do otherwise was disgraceful (11:14-15) because men ought to be distinguished from women. We should not do anything to blur the lines between the two. God designed and created men and women equal, yet different. And as he concludes this topic, Paul maintains that this is not merely his own opinion. All of **the churches of God** submit to this teaching. Gender distinctions are to be evidenced visibly, although Paul did not require every church to abide by the external symbols.

Though the wearing of a head covering was tied to a particular culture at a particular time (since Paul acknowledges it was a **custom**; 11:16), it was nevertheless an expression of a biblical principle that transcends culture and time. Even as Christ submitted to the Father, so also wives are to submit to the legitimate authority of their husbands, husbands are to submit to Christ, and both are to submit to the Lord and to the leadership of their church in a visibly clear way. Our humble submission to divine design and the theological, covenantal kingdom principle of headship frees God to accomplish his work in our lives.

11:17-22 Turning to Communion, or the Lord's Supper, Paul describes the shameful behavior that had been reported to him. What was supposed to be an intimate time of worship and remembrance had turned into a circus. The church was to come together as one, but there were **divisions** among them instead (11:17-18). For instance, they weren't partaking of **the Lord's Supper** together (11:20). Instead some ate their **own supper**, others went **hungry**, and still others got **drunk** (11:21-22)! Their actions showed disdain for **the church of God** and humiliation to those who had **nothing** to eat. There was nothing about the warped way the Corinthians celebrated the sacrificial death of Christ that Paul could **praise** (11:22).

11:23-25 Given the chaos surrounding the Corinthian practice, Paul gets back to basics, reminding them of what he had **passed on to** them when he was with them. He recounts for them the final Passover meal that **the Lord Jesus** shared with his disciples **on the night when he was betrayed** (11:23). Jesus infused the meal with new significance. The **bread** represents his **body**, and **the cup is the new covenant in** his **blood**. The disciples were to eat the bread and drink the cup **in remembrance of** him (11:24-25; cf. Luke 22:19-20). This was the institution of the church ordinance of the Lord's Supper.

A *covenant* is a divinely created bond through which God administers his kingdom program. Those who operate under a covenant receive its intended blessings. "The

new covenant" refers to the new relationship that God established through the death, burial, and resurrection of Jesus Christ, the Son of God. If you are a Christian, one who has trusted in Jesus as the substitutionary atoning sacrifice for your sins, you are a member of the new covenant—along with the rest of the people of God.

Remembering ("in remembrance of") is not just recalling. The Lord's Supper offers a uniquely powerful time of spiritual intimacy with the Lord in the same way that physical intimacy in marriage serves as a special time of intimacy between a couple. This is why we are encouraged to partake of Communion as often as possible. It is a special sharing with Christ beyond the normal relationship, enabling access to heaven at a deeper level. Communion is also designed to demonstrate the unity of the church at a common meal with the Savior.

11:26 When the church of Christ gathers to partake of the Lord's Supper, Paul says we **proclaim the Lord's death until he comes.** We evangelistically proclaim it to the world to invite them to trust in Christ for forgiveness and eternal life. We triumphantly proclaim it to the devil and the demonic realm (see Col 2:15; 1 Pet 3:18-19) to remind them of their defeat and their coming judgment. And we gloriously proclaim it to one another to recognize anew the victory over sin and the spiritual authority that Christ won for us on the cross.

11:27 Having once again explained the significance of the Lord's Supper and the sacrifice to which it points, Paul here returns to how the Corinthians had been making a mockery of the meal (see 11:20-22): **So, then, whoever eats the bread or drinks the cup of the Lord in an unworthy manner will be guilty of sin against the body and blood of the Lord.** By "unworthy" Paul isn't referring to personal worthiness. We are all sinful; no person is worthy of salvation. That's why we need God's grace. Rather, Paul is talking about the illegitimate *manner* in which they participated in Communion. They were taking something sacred and treating it as common. This special moment of remembrance and intimacy with the Lord and his people had lost its solemn significance because of the self-centered way they engaged in it.

We are not required to come to the Lord's Supper without any sin in our lives. If we had to be perfect, we'd never be able to partake. But we must take it seriously, recognizing its significance and the principle of the unity of his body (the church), which this ordinance is designed to encourage. We must not sin against the Lord by showing contempt for his sacrifice.

11:28-29 Therefore, Paul says, **let a person examine himself** so that he may partake of this holy meal in a worthy manner (11:28). In view here is not only the addressing of personal sin but the way in which believers relate to one another. The absence of unity and the presence of racial, social, and class division are to be avoided. How we relate to Christ's body affects how God relates to us. To treat it with anything other than respect is to eat and drink **judgment on** oneself (11:29), which brings to mind the case of Ananias and Sapphira (see Acts 5:1-11). Unless you recognize that the Lord's Supper represents Christ's victory on the cross, through which he transfers spiritual victory to your life, and unless you are also in fellowship with his spiritual family, the Communion moment that's intended to bless you could actually hurt you.

11:30-32 Paul explains that the Corinthian believers had been experiencing such divine judgment. Their selfish actions around the Lord's Table had resulted in **many** of them becoming **ill** or falling **asleep** (i.e., dying). Since they had not **judged** their own actions **properly**, God had severely **disciplined** them.

The Bible is clear that suffering and poor health are not necessarily a result of personal sin. Job, for instance, was a righteous man who suffered much. A man whom Jesus healed was not born blind because of anyone's sin but "so that God's works might be displayed in him" (John 9:3). Nevertheless, sin *can* result in suffering, sickness, and even death. That's what had happened to many of the Christians in Corinth. So examine yourself before you partake of the Lord's Supper. Ask, Do I recognize that it points to the judgment of God, the forgiveness of sin,

the defeat of Satan, the victory of grace, and the unity of the church? Do I expect God's blessings to flow to me through Communion, while I ignore known sin and disunity in my life? This will allow repentant believers to access the healing benefits of the cross (Isa 53:5; Jas 5:15-16)

11:33-34 Paul concludes the matter by urging them to eat and drink at the Lord's Supper in a worthy manner. When you **gather together** with Christian **brothers and sisters**, show love and hospitality. If you're **hungry**, **eat at home** before Communion. Approach the Lord's table with reverence—not only reverence for the Lord but also for his spiritual family—and receive his blessing.

12:1-3 Next Paul takes up a lengthy discussion of **spiritual gifts** (12:1). The essential feature of all those who have trusted in Jesus Christ is that they are indwelt by the Holy Spirit. Before coming to faith in Christ, the Corinthian believers were **pagans . . . enticed and led astray by mute idols** (12:2). But by the power of the Spirit, they were enabled to turn to God and say, **Jesus is Lord** (12:3).

12:4-7 Before discussing the multiplicity of gifts that the Spirit provides to believers, Paul wants to emphasize the unity believers ought to have. The **different gifts** Christians receive equip them for **different ministries** and **different activities**. Yet making all of this possible is their triune God: **the same** Holy **Spirit . . . the same Lord** Jesus . . . **the same God** (12:4-6). Though our God exists in three persons, yet he is one God (see Deut 6:4). And since the one God stands behind **each gift** received by every Christian, then he intends for them to work **for the common good** (12:6-7).

Not only is the church of Jesus Christ made up of a variety of people of both genders and of different ethnicities, nationalities, languages, and ages, but all those individuals receive from God a variety of spiritual gifts. Our physical and spiritual variety is good. But we were all created—and recreated in Christ (see 2 Cor 5:17)—by the same God who saved us for a single purpose: service in his kingdom. A *spiritual gift* is a God-given and empowered ability to serve him in ways that benefit others. Our variety is to be unified in submission to our King's agenda for the good of all. We must not use our spiritual gifts for selfish ends, promoting division among God's people.

12:8-11 Next Paul mentions some of the various spiritual gifts that **the same Spirit** makes available to believers (see also Rom 12:6-8; Eph 4:11). Notice that **one** Christian is given this gift, and **another** Christian is given that gift (12:8-10); thus, no one obtains a spiritual monopoly. Rather, within the church, we are dependent on one another for the exercise of all these different gifts. Furthermore, **one and the same Spirit** distributes **to each person as he wills** (12:11). You don't choose the spiritual gift of your preference. The Spirit gives as he sees fit. He knows what you and his kingdom need better than you do, so trust him to supply you with the spiritual ability with which you can best serve him and bless others.

12:12-14 Paul uses the analogy of a human **body** to describe how the church—the body of **Christ**—ought to function. Indeed, a body best illustrates what the church is: **many parts** that are **one** (12:12). Not only does the body consist of a variety of external parts but also many complex internal systems, including the circulatory, respiratory, nervous, skeletal, and digestive systems. Nevertheless (when working properly!) all of the parts and systems function together for the good of the whole. **Indeed, the body is not one part but many** (12:14).

Though the Corinthians consisted of **Jews or Greeks . . . slaves or free**, they were all made a part of the same body. Paul elaborates, noting that believers are **baptized by one Spirit into one body** (12:13). The Greek verb *baptizō* means "to immerse." It could be used to describe the action of immersing a cloth into a dye to change its color. The baptism of the cloth in such a case brings about a transformation that changes its visible identity. In the same way, the Spirit transforms all believers for a new way of life that is to be done together. They are baptized "into one body"—the body of Christ, the family of God.

12:15-16 What happens when Christians operate on their own, when they disconnect

from the church and do not benefit others? Paul describes the absurdity of this by again using the human body analogy. If **a hand** or an **ear** says, **I don't belong to the body**, breakdown results. Because of the loss of use of the hand or ear, the body is left incomplete. Moreover, the severed hand or ear does not benefit from the rest of the body.

Too many believers are detached from the church, unwilling to commit to being fully functioning members. As a result, both the believer and the church lose out on the blessings God intends. A light bulb may be in a light socket, but if there's no light coming through, it's just taking up space and providing no benefit. Similarly, believers who are disconnected from active involvement in the local church are living outside of the will of God.

12:17-20 No single person in the church is more valuable than any other. After all, Paul asks, **If the whole body were an eye, where would the hearing be?** (12:17). We must not expect everyone to be exactly like us. Without the multiplicity of spiritual gifts operating within the church, we lose out on essential functions. No single body part is more important than all the rest. But while you are a critical part of the body of Christ, you are only one part. You're not the whole thing; it's not all about you. Nor should you expect everyone to be just like you. If every part of the body were the same, it would cease to be a **body** (12:19)!

In the same way that God designed the human body with each part functioning exactly as he intended, so also **God has arranged each** part of **the body** of Christ **just as he wanted** (12:18). The one who created you gave you the spiritual gift that he wanted you to have. To insist that you want to serve the church in a different capacity than what God intended is like an ear insisting on being an eye. Not only is such a stance futile, but it is also a prideful rejection of your King's wise and perfect plan for you.

12:21-22 No part of the body can say to another part, **I don't need you!** (12:21). Every part is necessary. We may not always be aware of how a certain part is contributing or visibly observe its contribution, but that doesn't mean it's pointless. As Paul says, **those parts**

of the body that are weaker are indispensable (10:22). For instance, the internal parts of our bodies that we cannot see are incredibly significant! Without their functions, the external parts could not function.

Often we place too much emphasis on members and ministries that are visible. But this wrongly equates visibility with value. Not every member has the same gift, the same role, or the same level of responsibility. But every member matters. Those whose ministries go on behind the scenes are vital to the health of the church.

12:23-24 Paul notes that we give **greater honor** to the **less honorable** parts of our bodies (that is, our private parts). We treat **unrespectable parts . . . with greater respect** (12:23). Though they are not displayed for the world to see, they perform indispensable functions. So it is in the body of Christ.

12:25 In light of the necessity of every body part, there should **be no division** in the church so that every member has **the same concern for each other.** If every member is needed, then we ought to be concerned if any one member is suffering or experiencing dysfunction. This, in fact, is why Scripture places such emphasis on caring for one another (see, e.g., John 15:12; Gal 6:2; Eph 4:32; 1 Thess 5:11). We are responsible to and accountable for one another because we all share in the same body.

12:26 A little toe may seem fairly insignificant. But if you stub yours, it will shut you down! The pain affects the whole body. Indeed, **if one member** of the body **suffers, all the members suffer with it.** Therefore, don't be concerned only for your own needs within Christ's body. As Paul says elsewhere, "Rejoice with those who rejoice; weep with those who weep" (Rom 12:15). This is simply an application of the second greatest commandment: "Love your neighbor as yourself" (Matt 22:39).

12:27-31 The church in Corinth (and every other local church) is an expression of **the body of Christ**, and all Christians are **individual members of it** (12:27). Paul mentions several offices within the church for which

individuals are spiritually equipped. Their ranking (**first . . . second . . . third**) has to do with the level of the office. The **apostles** were those who had seen the risen Jesus and were appointed by him as foundational leaders to teach doctrine to the church. The **prophets** communicate God's revelation to God's people. **Teachers** explain the meaning of God's truth (12:28).

Notice that **various kinds of tongues** are mentioned last on the list (12:28). Though more is said about this topic in chapter 14, given how controversial the issue of speaking in tongues is today, note two important things. First, since it comes last in the list, it should not be given such supreme importance as some have assigned it. Second, observe that Paul asks, **Do all speak in other tongues?** (12:30). This question implies that not all Christians have been given this gift; therefore, it is not a super-Christian status indicator or the only sign that someone has been baptized by the Holy Spirit. Paul's instruction regarding tongues is written to a carnal, divided church (see 3:1-3). Thus, the exercise of the gift of tongues is not necessarily a sign of spiritual maturity.

Paul's questions in 12:29-30 indicate that no one receives every gift. But each receives the gift that God intends him to receive. Nevertheless, Paul says it is not wrong to **desire the greater gifts** to be manifested in the church (12:31)—that is, the higher-ranking gifts (if God chooses to grant them)—in order to provide the broadest edification to the church.

13:1-3 Paul insists that love is critical to any understanding and application of spiritual gifts. If love is absent, spiritual gifts do not edify. No matter what language one speaks (angels only spoke human languages in Scripture), without love the sound is nothing more than **a noisy gong or a clanging cymbal** (13:1). No matter how visible and effective my **gift** or ministry may be, if I **do not have love** for my fellow Christians, **I am nothing** and **I gain nothing** because spiritual gifts are for the benefit of others (13:2-3). The gift does not matter when love is missing.

13:4-7 What does love look like? Paul explains what love does and what it does not do. Biblical love is the decision (not merely a feeling) to compassionately (out of concern for someone else), righteously (based on God's standards), and sacrificially (giving to meet a need) seek the well-being of another. Notice each of the characteristics of love: it is **patient . . . kind . . . not [envious] . . . not arrogant . . . not irritable.** These things are only possible when we put others before ourselves (13:4-5). Love does not affirm someone in their sin or their false beliefs because **love finds no joy in unrighteousness but rejoices in the truth** (13:6). Love does not quit; it endures through thick and thin (13:7).

13:8-10 One day when we experience the joyous intimacy of God's presence, spiritual gifts will come to an end because we will no longer need them. But not love. **Love never ends** (13:8). **When the perfect comes**, though, **the partial will come to an end** (13:10). By "perfect," Paul is referring to spiritual maturity. The more a person grows in spiritual maturity, the less dependent one is on the particular gifts of **prophecy** and **tongues** (13:8).

13:11-12 A **child** speaks, thinks, and reasons **like a child.** But **a man** has grown in maturity and **put aside childish things** (13:11). Our Christian goal is spiritual maturity. Full maturity will only finally occur in God's glorious presence, but we are to progressively mature now. Currently, our experience is like looking at our **reflection** in a dim **mirror**, but eventually we will see **face to face.** Even **as I am fully known** to God now, one day I **will know fully** reality as God meant me to know it (13:12). All will be made clear.

13:13 These three remain: faith, hope, and love—but the greatest of these is love. In eternity, you will no longer need faith because you will have sight. You will no longer need hope because your expectations and anticipations will all have been met and exceeded. But the love that will characterize our eternal relationship with God will continue since "God is love" (1 John 4:8).

14:1-5 Since love is critical and eternal, Paul exhorts them to **pursue love.** Love is superior to spiritual gifts and enables one to

understand and utilize spiritual gifts rightly. Though he wanted them to **desire spiritual gifts** (14:1), exercising them was not for the purpose of self-exaltation because that would be contrary to love.

Apparently, the Corinthians were using the gift of other tongues to show off; thus, Paul confronts them. He prefers that they **prophesy** because the one who does so brings a clear word from God to everyone, edifying and encouraging the gathered body of believers (14:1, 3). But the one who **speaks in another tongue** speaks only **to God.** Unless someone is able to interpret the tongue, **no one understands**, and the church is not **built up** (14:2, 5). Since the person **who speaks in tongues** only edifies **himself**, while the person **who prophesies** edifies **the church**, prophecy is clearly the **greater** gift of the two (14:4-5). Paul wishes they all **spoke in other tongues** (14:5) so that someone was always available to interpret. But, of course, as he already said, God doesn't give the gift of tongues to everyone (see 12:30).

It's important to understand what Paul means regarding the gift of speaking "in another tongue." Though some interpret this to mean "a heavenly language," the New Testament evidence favors the meaning "human language." Note the key passage in Acts 2:4-11 when the apostles had been "filled with the Holy Spirit and began to speak in different tongues" (2:4). The context makes clear that these "tongues" (2:4, 11) were actually various native languages (2:6, 8) spoken by those who had come to Jerusalem for Pentecost.

14:6-12 In these verses, Paul emphasizes how important it is that all believers understand what is spoken when they gather together. Even if the apostle Paul himself came to a meeting **speaking in other tongues**, the church could not **benefit** if he communicated something that no one could understand (14:6). After all, if someone plays a musical instrument—a **flute** or **harp** or **bugle**— without playing clear notes, the result will be incoherent noise (14:7-8). **In the same way**, an uninterpreted tongue is unintelligible to anyone who hears it (14:9). It's nothing but hot air. Without an understanding of the **meaning** of the words spoken, members of the church will be like foreigners to one another (14:10-11). Shared understanding is necessary for communication to be meaningful. Thus, Paul wants their zeal **for spiritual gifts** to be matched by an equal zeal for **building up the church** (14:12) so that the Spirit could do his work among them.

How do you view the spiritual gift that you have received from the Holy Spirit? Is it a tool for winning attention, admiration, and praise from others? Or do you consider your gift to be an opportunity to glorify God and lovingly build up your brothers and sisters in Christ? It could be that you need to reread 13:1-7. In any case, don't misunderstand the purpose of spiritual gifts, and don't forget the chief element of exercising them: love.

14:13-17 In light of Paul's concerns, he urges those who do have the gift of **another tongue** to **pray** for the gift to **interpret** (14:13). For to **pray in another** language without **understanding is unfruitful** (14:14). Prayer and **praise** must be accompanied by **understanding** if anyone is to hear and say, **Amen** (14:15-16). How can you affirm what someone has spoken if it's unintelligible gibberish to you?

14:18-19 Though Paul himself spoke **in other tongues more than all** the Corinthians, he didn't consider it a badge of honor to be flaunted (14:18). He preferred to utter **five** comprehensible **words** that edified others, **than ten thousand** incoherent **words** that benefited no one (14:19). May God grant that our convictions be the same as Paul's.

14:20 The only case in which its beneficial to **be childish** and immature is with regard to **evil**: we do not want to be experienced in wickedness. Otherwise, we want to be **adult** and mature in our **thinking**. Excitement about exercising exotic spiritual gifts that no one can understand is immature. A more mature stance is to exercise gifts for the good of others.

14:21-22 Paul quotes from Isaiah 28:11-12, which recounts the defeat of the rebellious and unbelieving Israelites at the hands of the Assyrian army which spoke a language the people couldn't understand. Based on this, he says, **speaking in other tongues . . . is**

intended as a sign . . . for unbelievers— that is, a sign of judgment—while **prophecy** is **for believers**.

14:23-25 If the **church** is gathered and the members speak **in other tongues** when unbelievers are present, the **unbelievers** will think the Christians are crazy since they hear what they can't understand (14:23). But if the unbelieving visitor hears prophecy, he can be **convicted by** the truth of the gospel, be saved, and acknowledge God's presence **among** them (14:24-25). Thus, Paul desires the meaningful use of spiritual gifts.

14:26-28 Still concerned that the church be edified, Paul next moves to the issue of orderliness in the gathered church. If **each** person **has a hymn, a teaching, a revelation, another tongue, or an interpretation**, Paul insists that **everything is to be done for building up** and in an ordered manner (14:26). A coherent process should be followed. At **most** there should be **three** people speaking **in another tongue**; however, **if there is no interpreter** people should remain **silent**, speaking only to themselves **and God** (14:27-28; see 14:13).

14:29-33 Prophecy should likewise be regulated, Paul insists. Only **two or three prophets** are to **speak** at one gathering, and those prophecies are to be evaluated to determine that they are true, as the Word of God is applied to a particular circumstance in the life of the church (14:29). Thus, the exercise of prophecy has to be orderly. One can't irrationally begin spouting off a prophecy; rather, people are to **prophesy one by one** so that all can **learn** and **be encouraged** (14:30-31). **The prophets' spirits are subject to the prophets**—meaning they must exercise self-control in giving prophecy because **God is not a God of disorder but of peace** (14:32-33).

These last words are important for both individual believers and the church as a whole to apply. Since "God is not a God of disorder" (since he is unified in his triune nature), then he expects his people to do everything in a proper and orderly way (see 14:40). Such behavior promotes understanding, edification, and harmony.

14:34-35 When Paul says **women should be silent in the churches** (11:34), he's not forbidding a woman from praying and prophesying when the church gathers. After all, he has already made clear that a woman can do so if she submits to the spiritual authority of her husband and the church's leadership (see 11:5). Apparently, though, some of the women in Corinth were being disruptive during the church service and not submitting themselves to their husbands (11:34; see commentary on 11:4-6). Rather than engaging in disorderly and distracting conduct when prophesies were being given, they were **to ask their own husbands at home** (11:35) to preserve order and peace in the gathering.

14:36-38 For those who might become disgruntled and oppose Paul's instructions on these matters, comes this reminder: **the word of God** did not **originate from** them (11:36). Rather, Paul had proclaimed it. Furthermore, he maintains that anyone who claims to be **a prophet** or a **spiritual** person will **recognize that** he wasn't offering mere personal opinion but **the Lord's command** (14:37). Thus, to reject this teaching is to reject the Lord. Such a person will **be ignored** by the Lord (14:38).

14:39-40 Paul concludes the topic with an exhortation to engage in these spiritual gifts—**prophecy** and **speaking in other tongues**—in accordance with his instructions so that everything is carried out **decently and in order**. Obedience to this invites the blessing of God who "is not a God of disorder but of peace" (14:33). Righteous unity is critical for the church to experience God's presence in its midst.

❧ D. The Resurrection (15:1-58) ☙

15:1-2 Paul seeks to make clear for the Corinthians the gospel—the good news—that he had preached to them on his previous visit, which they had received, and on which they had taken their stand (15:1) In other words, he was repeating to them the same thing he had told them then. The gospel they had received had kept them standing thus

far—and would continue to do so. Paul also affirms that the same gospel that justifies sinners, giving them eternal life, also sanctifies them as saints (**being saved** here refers to present tense salvation for deliverance from the power of sin). But they must continually abide (i.e., **hold** fast) in the knowledge and application of God's Word (15:2).

15:3 There were many things that Paul could have spoken about to the Corinthians when he first visited them. What did he tell them? What had he himself **received** and **passed on to** them? What was it that he considered **most important**?

First, **that Christ died for our sins according to the Scriptures**. The reason these facts are so significant is because of who Christ is and what his death accomplished. Jesus Christ is the God-man. He is the Word of God who became flesh (John 1:14). He is the Son of God, the second Person of the Godhead, who became a man without giving up his deity (see Phil 2:5-8). He is the one and only person with both a divine nature and a human nature, unmixed forever. Therefore, he could serve as a perfect substitutionary sacrifice for sinners because as God he is without sin, and as a man he could die in our place. By bearing our sins on the cross, he suffered the wrath of God that we deserved so that we might be forgiven, receive eternal life, and be saved (see, e.g., 2 Cor 5:21; 1 Pet 2:24).

15:4 Second, **he was buried**. Jesus didn't merely swoon on the cross; he died. The Old Testament predicted that the Messiah would give his life as a sacrificial offering (see Isa 53:4-12), and the New Testament record assures us that this was indeed true of Jesus (see John 19:33-42; Phil 2:8).

Third, **he was raised on the third day according to the Scriptures**. Jesus suffered and died on our behalf; he made payment for our sins. Was this payment accepted? We can be certain that it was because God raised him from the dead. This is the clear and consistent testimony of the early church (see, e.g., Acts 2:24-32; 3:15; 5:30; 10:39-41; 13:29-37; 17:31). Jesus has risen from the grave, and the apostles and many others were eyewitnesses to this. The resurrection, then, is your receipt that God accepted Christ's payment for your sins and mine. And all of this happened "according to the Scriptures." The Old Testament not only foretold the Messiah's death but also his resurrection (see Ps 16:10). As Paul essentially says later in this chapter, without the resurrection of Jesus Christ, there is no Christianity (see 1 Cor 15:13-19).

15:5-8 The risen Lord Jesus wasn't seen by merely one or two people. On the contrary, Paul assures the Corinthians that there were numerous eyewitnesses to the resurrection. **He appeared to Cephas** (Peter) and **the Twelve** (the apostles) (15:5). One of the qualifications of being an apostle was to have seen the risen Christ (see Acts 1:21-22). Besides this, **he appeared to over five hundred brothers and sisters at one time—most** of whom were **still alive** and could verify this claim. This was no conspiracy concocted by a small band of people, then. *Hundreds* saw him! He also **appeared to James** (15:7), the Lord's own half-brother. Though he didn't believe in Jesus during his earthly ministry (see John 7:3-5), when he witnessed the resurrection, James believed, became a leader in the early church (see Acts 12:17; 15:13; 21:18), and wrote the New Testament letter bearing his name. Finally, Paul says, **he also appeared to me** (15:8). The persecutor of the church had been called by the risen Lord Jesus himself to be an apostle (see Acts 9:1-22).

These are the essential truths of the gospel. Through the sacrificial substitutionary death and resurrection of the God-man Jesus Christ, all those who place their faith in him are forgiven of their sins, reconciled to God, adopted as his children, and receive eternal life. Sinners can be saved. This is the good news that the church is called to proclaim to the world.

15:9-11 With his typical humility (see 1 Tim 1:15), Paul declares that he is **the least of the apostles** and **not worthy to** bear the title of **apostle** since he had been a violent persecutor of **the church** (15:9). He never forgot the horrific actions he had taken against God's people when he was an unbeliever. But **the grace of God** bore fruit in his life; it was **not in vain** (15:10). Paul's understanding of and appreciation for God's grace through Christ inspired his labor and love.

This appreciation for grace is what should empower and motivate Christians for service. Paul didn't care whether he or others received the credit for the spread of the gospel, as long as the good news was proclaimed and sinners were saved for God's kingdom (15:11).

15:12-14 Some of the Corinthians were claiming that there was **no resurrection of the dead** (15:12). Whether the teaching had come from within the church or from outside is unknown. Perhaps they thought Christ had risen spiritually to heaven but not bodily from the grave. Whatever the origin or the particulars of this heresy, Paul confronts it because it strikes at the heart of the gospel. The resurrection is essential. **If Christ has not been raised,** Paul's preaching—and the Christian message—would be empty and meaningless. Moreover, the Corinthians' **faith** was wasted because you can't have a living faith in a dead Savior (15:14).

Our salvation depends on the truth that Jesus Christ is the sinless Son of God whose death paid for our sins and whom God vindicated by raising him from the grave. Without this, we have no sinless Savior, no high priest who always lives to intercede for us (see Heb 7:25), no forgiveness, no hope of being raised from the dead ourselves.

15:15-18 Paul continues stating the implications of a denial of Christ's resurrection. It would mean that Paul and the other apostles were **false witnesses,** lying to Jews and Gentiles about what **God** had accomplished through **Christ** (15:15). **If Christ has not been raised,** then their **faith** was **worthless.** Instead of being alive with Christ (see Eph 2:4-5), the Corinthians were still dead **in [their] sins** (15:17; see Eph 2:1). A dead Savior is no Savior at all. Therefore, believers who have died would be lost forever (15:18).

15:19 Then Paul sums things up: **If we have put our hope in Christ for this life only, we should be pitied more than anyone.** Indeed, if our belief in the resurrection is something that does not extend beyond the grave—that is, if it's not true—then we have no hope of eternal life after death, are living a lie, and ought to be pitied by the world.

15:20 Contrary to what some Corinthians were claiming, though, Paul insists that **Christ has been raised from the dead.** He is the **firstfruits of those who have fallen asleep**—that is, of those who have died. The use of "firstfruits" here calls to mind Leviticus 23:10-14. In that passage, the Israelites were to bring the first portion of their harvests to the priest as an offering to the Lord. This was done in anticipation of the full harvest that was to come, as they trusted in God to provide. Thus, Christ's resurrection is the promise that believers will one day be raised.

15:21-22 Adam disobeyed God and brought both spiritual and physical **death** to the human race. But through his own **resurrection, Christ**—the second Adam (see 15:47)—has made eternal life available to all.

15:23-28 God has a plan and an order to his resurrection process. **Christ, the firstfruits,** was the first to rise. **At his next coming,** all those who belong to Christ will receive resurrection bodies (15:23; see 1 Thess 4:13-18). At the end, after his millennial reign, he will hand **over the kingdom to God the Father,** and abolish all his enemies—including **death**—putting **everything under his feet** (15:24-27; see Ps 110:1). With everything else **subjected** to him, **the Son** will in turn **be subject** to the Father (15:28).

The Son will have succeeded where Adam failed and fulfilled the created kingdom destiny of man to rule (see Ps 8:4-6). He will have established a kingdom to defeat Satan's kingdom, ruling on behalf of humanity for God. When he hands over the kingdom to the Father at the end of his millennial reign, his earthly mission in history will be complete, ushering in eternity. And God will be **all in all** (15:28).

15:29 Paul mentions a practice that some in Corinth were engaging in: **being baptized for the dead.** It appears that some were being baptized by proxy on behalf of those who had died before they could be baptized. Paul isn't advocating this practice; rather, he's pointing out its absurdity if there's no resurrection. Why be **baptized for** the dead **if the dead are not raised?**

15:30-32 Paul speaks about how the truth of the resurrection affected him personally. He was in mortal **danger** on a regular basis because of his gospel ministry (15:30-31). Both Jews and Gentiles had tried to kill him. He contended with **wild beasts in Ephesus**—which may be a reference to those who opposed God's kingdom. Yet, what was the point **if the dead are not raised?** If there's no resurrection, Paul says, quoting the self-indulgent attitude of the Israelites in Isaiah 22:13, **Let us eat and drink, for tomorrow we die** (15:32).

15:33-34 The apostle argues, **Bad company corrupts.** The Corinthian believers needed to stop hanging out with those who were promoting false doctrine, denying the resurrection, and living unrighteously. You cannot make unbelievers your constant, intimate companions and think you will escape unscathed. Cozying up to heretical teachings and lifestyles is dangerous. Thus, Paul tells the Corinthian believers point blank, **Come to your senses and stop sinning** (15:34).

15:35-44 To those naysayers who ask, **How are the dead raised?** and, **What kind of body will they have?** Paul exclaims, **You fool!** (15:35-36). In their attempts to ridicule the resurrection, they forgot that **what you sow does not come to life unless it dies** (15:36). What is sown is **only a seed** (15:37). God **gives** us bodies as he pleases. In fact, there are **bodies** for **humans, animals,** planets, and **stars** (15:38-41). The human body is like a seed. It is **sown in corruption** and **weakness,** but **raised in glory** and **power** (15:42-43). Just as seeds are transformed, so our bodies will be transformed. A dead **natural body** will be raised as an eternal **spiritual body** (15:44).

15:45-49 Paul compares Adam to Christ; he discusses the first Adam and the last Adam. *Adam* is Hebrew for "man." **The first man,** made **of dust, became a living being** through the power of God. But **the second man,** who has come **from heaven, became a life-giving spirit** (15:45, 47). **The natural** man could only die; **the spiritual** man can give life (15:46). **We have** all **borne the image of the man of dust.** What we need is to **bear**

the image of the man of heaven (15:49). From birth, all human beings are "in Adam," but through faith in the gospel we are "in Christ" and granted the hope of resurrection to life (see 15:22).

15:50-57 One day we will all be changed . . . in the twinkling of an eye (15:51-52). Our corruptible bodies will be clothed with incorruptibility; our mortal bodies clothed with immortality (15:53-54). Pain, sickness, disease, disability, and suffering of every kind will be gone. Our resurrection bodies will be indestructible and incorruptible. For all those who are in Christ Jesus, there is no sting to death, for death will be swallowed up in victory (15:54-55). Death is the result of sin (see also Rom 6:23), and sin gets power from the law (15:56). When God's law commands, "Do not," the sinful human heart desires the opposite (see Rom 7:7-11). But because of his faithfulness to perfectly keep the law and bear our sins, our Lord Jesus Christ has given us the victory (15:57).

15:58 Therefore, Paul concludes at the end of this glorious chapter on the resurrection, be steadfast, immovable, always excelling in the Lord's work, because you know that your labor in the Lord is not in vain. The salvation Christ accomplished through his cross and resurrection is the gracious gift of God for sinners. We can't earn it. But after we've received it, we're not to sit back and do nothing. In light of our victory over sin and death due to our faith in King Jesus, believers are encouraged to labor for their Lord.

So make God's kingdom agenda your own. Don't become weary or give up because your labor "is not in vain." It's not wasted. You're not spinning your wheels when you engage in faithful kingdom service. God sees your work for him, and he has a reward in store for you that will exceed your wildest expectations.

❧ E. Collection for the Church in Jerusalem (16:1-4) ❧

16:1 Following his exhortation in 15:58 to do "the Lord's work," Paul encourages them to apply this principle by taking up a collection for the saints. Though Paul doesn't say explicitly whom the collection is for, references elsewhere make it clear that he's talking about a relief gift for the impoverished believers in Jerusalem (see Acts 24:17; Rom 15:25-26; 2 Cor 8:1–9:15).

16:2 He asks them to take up the collection on the first day of the week (Sunday) as a part of their weekly worship gathering. Paul desires that each person set something aside in accordance with how he is prospering. Thus, giving was to be planned—not haphazard—and based on one's personal means. Moreover, setting aside the offerings in advance would prevent Paul from having to chide or browbeat them when he visited, avoiding embarrassment for everyone.

16:3-4 Paul had a burden for the poor in Jerusalem. He greatly desired that the Gentile believers might bless Jewish believers in their time of distress. As he told the Christians in Rome, "If the Gentiles have shared in [the Jewish believers'] spiritual benefits, then they are obligated to minister to them in material needs" (Rom 15:27). His plan was to send the gift to Jerusalem through trusted representatives whom the Corinthians selected (16:3).

IV. CONCLUSION (16:5-24)

16:5-9 Paul intends to travel through Macedonia and then visit Corinth, perhaps—if the Lord allows—spending the winter with them since travel by sea would be too hazardous (16:5-7). Meanwhile, he would remain in Ephesus until Pentecost (16:8) because he had an opportunity for ministry. Notice how Paul describes it: A wide door for effective ministry (16:9). Knowing that God had provided a significant opening for the gospel, Paul was willing to trust him and be faithful no matter the opposition he faced from unbelievers.

16:10-12 Paul was sending **Timothy** to them and therefore urges the church to receive him well. He wanted the Corinthians to know that Timothy shared Paul's love and concerns and that he expected them to treat him with respect and **peace** (16:10-11). **Apollos** would also visit them when he had the **opportunity** (16:12; see Acts 18:24-28).

16:13-14 Paul has addressed many problems in the letter. Since the church was beset with self-centeredness, arrogance, and division, he wants to move them to a love-centered mentality (see 13:1-13). He thus urges them to **stand firm in the faith, be courageous,** and **be strong**—but to wrap all of this **in love.**

16:15-18 Describing **the household of Stephanas** as **the firstfruits of Achaia** (the Roman province in which Corinth was located) means that they were among the first Christian converts in Corinth (16:15). Stephanas and others had personally ministered to Paul on the Corinthians' behalf (16:17-18), and Paul praises them for their **devoted** service **to the saints** and urges his audience **to submit to such people** (16:15-16). Just as "bad company corrupts good morals" (15:33), hanging out with godly people will encourage you to follow their example of faith, love, and service.

16:19-21 Paul sends greetings from **the churches of Asia,** as well from **Aquila and Priscilla** whom Paul had first met in Corinth and whom the Corinthians knew well (16:19; see Acts 18:1–19:1). The apostle then adds a **greeting** in **[his] own hand** (16:21). Paul probably dictated the letter to a secretary (see Rom 16:22) and then added a personal greeting, as was his custom (see 2 Thess 3:17).

16:22-24 If anyone does not love the Lord, a curse be on him (16:22). With this statement, Paul announces divine chastisement on believers who do not love the Lord, which is demonstrated by promoting dissension and division in the church. Lack of affection for God's people is proof of a lack of affection for God, which results in being outside of his divine covering (see 1 John 4:11, 20-21). Paul then concludes with a prayer for **the Lord** to **come,** a benediction of **grace,** and a personal expression of his **love** for this troubled church (16:23-24).

2 CORINTHIANS

INTRODUCTION

Author

VIRTUALLY NO BIBLICAL SCHOLar questions the authenticity of 2 Corinthians as a Pauline letter. It contains more personal information about him than any of his other letters.

Historical Background

On Paul's initial ministry among the Corinthians, see the discussion of historical background for 1 Corinthians. It appears that Paul wrote at least four letters to the church in Corinth: (1) a letter that has been lost (see 1 Cor 5:9), (2) 1 Corinthians, (3) a tearful letter (see 2 Cor 2:3-4, 9; 7:8, 12), and (4) 2 Corinthians.

Between the penning of 1 and 2 Corinthians, Paul made a visit to Corinth that proved to be "painful" (2 Cor 2:1; 13:2). Perhaps this was because Timothy, who had visited the church (see 1 Cor 16:10-11), had reported to him that they didn't respond well to 1 Corinthians. Later Paul sent his tearful letter (2 Cor 2:3-4, 9; 7:8, 12), probably by means of Titus, who returned and reported that the majority had corrected someone in the church who had sinned against Paul (2:6; 7:6-16). At some point, some "super-apostles"—better known as "false apostles"—had infiltrated the church in Corinth, seeking to undermine Paul (11:5, 12-15, 20-23). In 2 Corinthians, Paul defends his ministry and encourages the Corinthians to complete their collection for the relief of the believers in Jerusalem.

Message and Purpose

This is Paul's most intimate letter to a church; it expresses his heart and his passion. False teachers had entered the church in Corinth, and they were receiving a hearing even though they were undermining Paul's message. They also questioned his kingdom calling and responsibility as an apostle of Jesus Christ. So Paul offered a defense of his ministry because the gospel was being undermined by Jewish teachers who were trying to put Christians back under the law of Moses.

Paul also called the Corinthians to show concern for the poor. He wanted the Jewish and Gentile Christians to understand that they are one people in Christ. What better way to show this than for Gentile believers to help Jewish believers in need?

The apostle appealed to the Corinthians' hearts and minds, showing them that truth without love is damaging, while love without truth is deceptive. Paul even spoke of his personal experience of a heavenly vision. If Paul could humble himself after receiving such a privilege, surely the Corinthians could see that he was not operating with pride but with a servant's heart.

VIDEO | INTRO

www.bhpublishinggroup.com/qr/te/47_00

Outline

2 CORINTHIANS

I. INTRODUCTION (1:1-11)

1:1 Paul identifies himself as **an apostle of Christ Jesus.** This was not because Paul had volunteered for the job but because God had called him to service (see Acts 9:1-22). He was an apostle **by God's will.** Paul's co-laborer **Timothy** is also listed, but the first person pronouns throughout the letter make clear that it is primarily from Paul. The city of **Corinth** was located in the Roman province of **Achaia,** in modern Greece.

1:2 Paul greets them with **grace** and **peace,** which can only come **from God our Father and the Lord Jesus Christ.**

1:3-7 The apostle praises **God** who provides **comfort** when we are in **affliction** (1:3-4). It's clear from the following verses that Paul had been in a painful situation. He speaks of affliction (1:4, 6, 8), suffering (1:5-7), despair (1:8), and death (1:9-10). Thus, Paul was able to validate Jesus's promise to his disciples: "You will have suffering in this world" (John 16:33).

If anyone assures you that you can avoid suffering like health problems, mental anguish, relational difficulties, or financial straits—provided that you have enough faith—they're not telling you the truth. Paul was a visible and verbal follower of Christ who stood head and shoulders above other Christians in terms of faithfulness. And he suffered greatly—not in spite of his faith but because of his faith in and obedience to Christ. Paul's suffering and ours is directly related to God's purpose of using us to minister to others. So if you're suffering, read on.

In addition to the words of pain, there's another word repeated in these verses with which we need to come to grips: *comfort.* God is **the God of all comfort** who **comforts us in all our affliction** (1:3-4). We must not be so overcome by our suffering that we miss the unlimited comfort that God makes available in every circumstance.

Notice two things. First, God is sovereign over our suffering. Christians follow in their Master's footsteps, sharing in **the sufferings of Christ** that **overflow to us** (1:5). Our trials and tribulations don't catch God off guard. Nothing happens to you that hasn't first passed through his fingers. Remember that "all things work together for the good of those who love God" (Rom 8:28). When Jesus promised his disciples that they would undergo suffering, he also told them, "Be courageous! I have conquered the world" (John 16:33). Don't run from the Lord when suffering strikes. Run to him and let him work in you so that you may be comforted.

Second, there is an important purpose for our affliction: it equips us **to comfort those who are in any kind of affliction, through the comfort we ourselves receive from God** (1:4). Paul knew that he was **afflicted** and **comforted** so that he could bring **comfort** to the Corinthians (1:6). God often lets us experience difficult circumstances so that he can use us to experientially minister to others, since they empower us to empathize with their pain. When you offer comfort to a fellow believer, you serve as a conduit for the comfort of God, and you open yourself up to experience a deeper level of his reality at work in your life.

1:8-11 How bad had it gotten for Paul? He and his ministry companions **were completely overwhelmed**, enduring situations that were **beyond** their **strength** (1:8). It was like they had **received the sentence of death**. But Paul realized the reason they had been besieged by suffering: It was **so that** they **would not trust** in themselves **but in God who raises the dead** (1:9). Paul and his partners had the opportunity to experience God's deliverance so that they might **hope in him** to **deliver** them **again** (1:10). Therefore, God will place on us what seems more than we

can bear when he is preparing us for a special ministry to others and when he wants to give us a deeper manifestation of his presence and power in our lives.

One of the important truths of Scripture is that God must remove our attitude of self-sufficiency. When you encounter a seemingly hopeless situation, it opens your eyes to the reality that you cannot depend on and deliver yourself. Allow personal brokenness that strips you of your self-sufficiency to move you to a deeper level of trust in and dependency on our all-sufficient God. The one who is able to raise the dead can surely breathe life into your seemingly impossible circumstances.

II. PAUL'S EXPLANATION OF HIS APOSTOLIC MINISTRY (1:12–7:16)

1:12-21 Paul had intended **to visit** the Corinthians, but events caused him to change his plans (1:15-16). Apparently some had criticized the apostle for this, accusing him of operating **by human wisdom** (1:12) or in a worldly fashion (1:17). But Paul explained his conduct, insisting that his **conscience** was clear and that he had acted with **godly sincerity and purity** toward them (1:12). Paul wasn't the fickle type. He didn't indecisively say **yes** and **no** simultaneously (1:17-18). Instead, he sought to follow God's will; therefore, the answer was always **yes** in Christ. Furthermore, **Jesus Christ—whom** Paul **proclaimed—**is the fulfillment (the **yes**) of all **God's promises** (1:19-20). Paul's message and ministry were characterized by consistency and a Christ-centered focus.

1:22-24 Paul and his ministry partners had not operated in a worldly way but in accordance with the Holy **Spirit**, who was God's **seal on** them (1:22). Far from being fickle, Paul had changed his mind about visiting **Corinth** because he wanted to **spare** them. He didn't want to **lord it over** their **faith**, forcing them to submit to his apostolic authority, but wanted to come to them in **joy** (1:23-24). He desired to minister effectively to them rather than simply exercising authority over them.

2:1-4 Someone in the Corinthian church had publicly opposed and sinned against Paul (see 2:5-10), so he wanted to avoid a **painful visit** like his previous one (2:1). Therefore, Paul had written a tearful letter to them from an **anguished heart** so that they could deal with the sin, have their **joy** restored, and know of Paul's **abundant love** for them (2:3-4).

2:5-8 Paul insists that the person had caused harm not so much to him but to the whole church (2:5). But he acknowledges that the Corinthians had exercised church discipline (**punishment**) against the **person**, so apparently the man had repented (2:6). Now it was time to restore this repentant brother by comforting him, forgiving him, and reaffirming their **love** for him so that he wouldn't **be overwhelmed by excessive grief** (2:7-8).

Biblical instructions on church discipline are crucial for dealing with sin in the church (see commentary on Matt 18:15-17; 1 Cor 5:3). But it's also crucial that the church forgive when a sinning believer repents. For the health of the church, sin must be addressed, but love and forgiveness must be shown in response to repentance. We must never put a limit on God's grace and mercy to sinners. Rather, we must seek to lead them out of sin to a place of spiritual restoration (see Gal 6:1; Jas 5:19-20).

2:9-11 Rather than visit, cause pain, and exercise apostolic authority, Paul had written his letter **to test** the church's **character** in this matter and prompt them to obedience (2:9). He made it clear that he too had **forgiven** the man, desiring nothing but their **benefit** (2:10). Satan's goal is to incite disunity in the church, and this was a perfect opportunity for him to take advantage of them. Don't be **ignorant of his schemes** (2:11). He'll tempt you both to ignore sin and to refuse to forgive.

2:12-13 Paul had been so anxious about this problem in the church that it had become a distraction to his ministry. When he reached **Troas**, a city on the Aegean Sea in Asia Minor (modern Turkey), he had an open **door** to **preach the gospel** (2:12). However, since he had not yet linked up with **Titus**—who had visited the Corinthians and would be bringing news from them—Paul had **no rest in** his **spirit**. So he departed **for Macedonia** (2:13). Thus, the problems in the Corinthian church had unnecessarily prevented his ministry from moving forward.

2:14 After a victorious battle, a Roman general would engage in a parade that included those whom he had conquered. In addition, incense was burned along the parade route, providing a sweet aroma of victory. Here Paul compares Jesus Christ to a conquering general who **leads** the apostle and other believers in **triumphal procession** and in spreading **the aroma of the knowledge of** Christ everywhere they go. The imagery also reminds us of Old Testament sacrifices that offered pleasing aromas to God (see, e.g., Lev 1:13). Believers are to live in a manner that pleases God so that our lives are "a sacrificial and fragrant offering to" him (Eph 5:2).

2:15-17 Paul and his companions were **the fragrance of Christ** among those to whom they preached. The message they proclaimed had paradoxical results. To those who believed and were **being saved**, they were **an aroma of life**. But to those who rejected the message and were **perishing**, they were **an aroma of death** (2:15-16). This is a reminder that a person's response to the gospel has eternal consequences. When you share the good news of Jesus Christ with someone,

eternity hangs in the balance. It's for this reason that Paul was engaged with a high degree of integrity in authentic ministry. This is no game; heaven and hell are on the line. And he didn't peddle **the word of God** for financial gain. Paul acted from authentic motives, knowing that he spoke a message **from God** and ministered **before God** for the well-being of the church and for God's glory (2:17). That should be the motivation of every Christian.

3:1-3 Paul makes it clear that he needs no human validation for his ministry, like some false teachers sought. They praised themselves with **letters of recommendation**, but Paul didn't need to engage in self-promotion (3:1). His ministry had received divine validation. The Corinthians themselves—won to the gospel from pagan idolatry—were Paul's **letter** of recommendation. This evidence was available for **everyone** to read (3:2). Just as the new covenant was greater than the old covenant (with God's law written on **human hearts** rather than **on tablets of stone**; see Heb 8:8-10), so Paul's commendation is greater than any false teacher's because of the visible effect **the Spirit of the living God** had on the lives of the Corinthians through Paul's ministry (3:3).

If no one's life is being changed at a local church, then the "ministry" taking place there lacks validation. A church's goal is not the installation of nice carpets and comfortable pews, but the life-transforming work of producing kingdom disciples. Our goal is to facilitate God's extreme makeovers and the spiritual transformation of his children.

3:4-6 Though his gospel ministry had been effective, Paul understood his own inadequacy. His full **confidence** was in **God** who is able to make us adequate to accomplish his kingdom purposes (3:4-5). The Lord had made Paul a **competent** minister of the **new covenant**. The **letter** of the law reveals our sinful inability to keep it and condemns us. But through Christ's new covenant sacrifice, **the Spirit gives life** and transformation to those who believe (3:6).

Replace your self-confidence with God-confidence. Regardless of your personal abilities and competencies, you are incapable of producing spiritual results via earthly means. Submit to your omni-competent King and humbly depend on the power of the Holy Spirit so that he can accomplish his kingdom agenda through you.

3:7-11 The old covenant **ministry . . . brought death** because the sinful hearts of the people were unable to keep the law. Nevertheless, **glory** accompanied the old covenant when God's glory rubbed off on **Moses's face** as he spent time in his presence (3:7; see Exod 34:29-32). So if a **ministry** that ultimately brought **condemnation** was glorious, how much **more glorious** must new covenant ministry be since it brings **righteousness** (3:8-9)? In fact, the glorious ministry of Jesus Christ so far **surpasses** the old covenant that the latter is not even **glorious** by **comparison** (3:10). Thus, any attempt to return to the law and the old covenant for righteousness and transformation is a spiritually backwards step. By contrast, the new covenant transforms sinners into saints and **endures** forever (3:11).

3:12-13 Paul had **great boldness** in the power of the gospel to change lives (3:12). Again he mentions the example of **Moses**, whose **face** shone with **glory** after spending time in God's presence. But the moment he left God's presence, the glory began to fade, so he wore a veil **to prevent the Israelites** from seeing that (3:13). Paul uses this incident to introduce a discussion of the transformation God wanted in the lives of the Corinthians (and in our lives), producing a glory that increases and doesn't fade.

3:14-18 The transforming work that God accomplished through Christ is intended for *all* believers—not merely for a small subset of super saints—so that we live in spiritual victory and freedom (see John 8:31-32, 36). Notice that Paul says, **We all . . . are being transformed** (3:18). So it applies to every Christian, and we all undergo this transformation in the same way.

First, let's be clear about what transformation is *not*. It's not the mere accumulation of information. You can attend church and acquire a tremendous amount of Bible knowledge—both of which are important things. But these actions in and of themselves won't

change you. Moreover, transformation is not simply behavior modification. If parents tell their son to take out the trash and he refuses, they can threaten punishment to get him to conform to their instructions. But this won't necessarily produce internal transformation and a change of character. In fact, as the son takes out the trash, he may be boiling with rebellion on the inside.

What, then, is true *spiritual transformation*? It's an internal change that reflects the character of Christ and brings about a corresponding external change. Moreover, though it requires your involvement, you don't actually transform yourself. Notice that Paul says we are "being transformed." God accomplishes the transformation. But as Moses climbed the mountain to go where he could access God's glow, we must position ourselves so that the Lord can do his work in us. We are transformed as the Holy Spirit uses our exposure, openness, and obedience to the Word of God (i.e., the **mirror**, 3:18; see Jas 1:21-25) to grow us from one level of spiritual development to the next (i.e., "from glory to glory"; see below).

Into what are believers to be transformed? **Into the same image from glory to glory** (3:18). With this phrase Paul is speaking about being made to resemble and reflect Jesus who is "the image of the invisible God" (Col 1:15). God doesn't intend that we look like Jesus physically, of course, but that we look like him in our attitudes and actions, in our character and conduct. Spiritual transformation is the development of Christlikeness within the believer that grows from one level of glory to another so that it expresses itself externally in righteous words and deeds.

This is only made possible by the work of **the Spirit** in our lives (note that "Spirit" is repeated three times in 3:17-18) as we look **at the glory of the Lord** (3:18). When we look to the Lord through his glorious Word, transformation is inevitable. But we must approach him with honesty and integrity, turning to the Lord with no **veil** of unbelief over our faces, as Paul says (3:16). In Paul's day, many who were still looking to the old covenant of law were coming to God's Word with a veil **over their hearts** (3:15)—that is, they were not pursuing an intimate relationship like Moses did. But not to expose yourself to the glory of the Word will result in no change. We must approach God's Word with unveiled faces as we obediently welcome his truth into our lives (see Jas 1:19-25), giving the Holy Spirit permission to do his transforming work from one level of spiritual development to the next. "Glory to glory" (3:18) is the stage of spiritual development that is usually introduced by a trial (see Jas 1:2-4).

4:1-2 Since Paul had been **shown mercy** by God and received his new covenant **ministry** directly from Christ, he would **not give up** in spite of the struggles he had faced with the Corinthian church (4:1). No matter what other would-be teachers might do, Paul and his companions had no intention of **acting deceitfully or distorting the word of God.** Though some had attributed false motives to Paul, he engaged in **an open display of the truth** and commended himself **to everyone's conscience** (4:2). No one had a shred of evidence to substantiate an accusation against him. Let the same be true of you.

4:3-6 When people reject the **gospel**, the truth **is veiled** from their view (4:3). Their spiritual darkness is facilitated by the devil—**the god of this age**—who **has blinded the minds of the unbelievers** to prevent them from believing **the gospel of the glory of Christ** (4:4). This is a reminder that we do not struggle "against flesh and blood" but "against evil, spiritual forces in the heavens" (Eph 6:12). Therefore, Paul knew he couldn't wage this battle by **proclaiming** himself **but** instead **Jesus Christ as Lord** (4:5). Only **God** can cause **light** to **shine out of darkness.** Just as he created visible light at the dawn of creation, so also he shines spiritual light into darkened **hearts to give** sinners **the light of the knowledge of God's glory in the face of Jesus** (4:6).

4:7 The **treasure** Paul is talking about is the knowledge of God experienced through Christ that he just mentioned in 4:6. Only through Jesus do we have access to this experiential knowledge, and the closer you get to Jesus, the more of God you experience. "For the entire fullness of God's nature

dwells bodily in Christ" (Col 2:9), and "in him are hidden all the treasures of wisdom and knowledge" (Col 2:3).

What's even more amazing is that this treasure is inside every Christian. Paul speaks of our bodies as **clay jars**, fragile containers made from earth (see Gen 2:7). On our best days, then, we're just dignified dirt. But the weakness of such humble vessels is set in sharp contrast to their valuable and supernatural contents. And the purpose is **so that this extraordinary power may be from God and not from us.** In other words, this experience of the knowledge of God cannot be manifested by your own strength but only by God's power. Thus, it's not who you are, but whom you know.

4:8-9 To demonstrate how the glory and power of God are manifested in and through such frail clay jars, Paul describes the trials he and his companions had endured. They had been **afflicted . . . perplexed . . . persecuted . . . struck down.** Yet in spite of this, they were **not crushed . . . not in despair . . . not abandoned . . . not destroyed.** How is that possible? Only by means of the sustaining hand of Jesus. Such perseverance in troubles is a clear indicator of God's power.

4:10-12 Paul adds, **We always carry the death of Jesus in our body, so that the life of Jesus may also be displayed in our body** (4:10). God lets us experience problems so that the divine life of Jesus is manifested **in our mortal flesh** (4:11). It couldn't be more clear, then: Those who claim that faithfully following Jesus brings only blessings and never complications are dead wrong. God will allow the circumstances of 4:9 into your life to force you to rely on Jesus. So how will you know when you're truly connecting with Christ and allowing him to work in and through you? As Paul says, you'll be afflicted but not crushed—that is, in the midst of life's turmoil, you won't sink into despair.

4:13 What do you do when you're experiencing such hardship? Paul says, **I believed, therefore I spoke.** So, speak God's Word into your situation. Don't let your words contradict what you claim to believe. Instead, speak and pray only what is biblical.

For example, when experiencing difficulties, remember what James says: "Let the brother of humble circumstances boast in his exaltation" (Jas 1:9). This doesn't mean that you deny your earthly circumstances but that you praise God who has blessed you "with every spiritual blessing in the heavens in Christ" (Eph 1:3). Furthermore, whatever the outcome of your trial, you can pray Paul's promise that God "will supply all your needs according to his riches in glory in Christ Jesus" (Phil 4:19). Through your trial, God may be trying to accomplish something within you (such as the strengthening of your faith, your growth in godliness, or the transformation of your character), or he may want to use you to have a spiritual impact on the lives of others. He knows what you need better than you do.

4:14-15 Paul has confidence (and so can we) **that the one who raised the Lord Jesus** from the dead **will also raise us with Jesus** (4:14). Our earthly ordeals are temporary: a glorious eternity awaits! When we truly acknowledge this provision of **grace**, it will lead to increased **thanksgiving** and bring **glory** to **God** (4:15).

4:16 Therefore—in light of the power of God at work on our behalf—**we do not give up.** We can keep going since we know the truth: **Even though our outer person is being destroyed, our inner person is being renewed day by day.** If you have not yet experienced signs of aging, be patient. You will! But there's good news. Though our bodies grow older and decay, we believers are becoming strengthened in "our inner person," which is where our treasure is (4:7). Believers should be growing spiritually younger (i.e., healthier) as they grow physical older. We are being made fit for our future heavenly home, and this happens through a process that comes "day by day." As when the Israelites received the manna in the wilderness, the Lord provides you with the grace you need for today. Next week's grace must wait until next week.

4:17-18 Paul calls his troubles **momentary light affliction.** How can he possibly refer to such intense, prolonged suffering this

way? First, he understands that negative circumstances have a positive effect when we trust and obey God through them. They are **producing for us an absolutely incomparable eternal weight of glory** (4:17). The pain and suffering of this life can be truly awful. But when the input of affliction is compared to the output of glory that Christ is accomplishing on your behalf, Paul insists that the difference between them is like night and day.

Second, Paul can call his affliction "momentary" and "light" because he does **not focus on what is seen, but on what is unseen. For what is seen is temporary, but what is unseen is eternal** (4:18). So if your tribulations seem long and heavy, you're looking at the wrong thing. To put it another way, if all you see is what you see, then you do not see all there is to be seen! Paul is not saying we must close our eyes to the reality of our suffering; he's saying we need to open our eyes by faith to unseen realities that will last forever. An eternal perspective gives the believer the ability to handle the struggles of this life.

5:1 When Paul speaks of **our earthly tent**, he's talking about our physical bodies. When this life on earth is over, and our bodies return to dust, life has only just begun. Eternity awaits! And for those who trust in Christ, God has **an eternal dwelling** prepared for our incorruptible resurrection bodies—something Paul had previously explained to the Corinthians (see 1 Cor 15:35-57).

5:2-5 In fact, Paul says **we groan in** our present **tent**, because we long for **our heavenly dwelling** (5:2). According to Ecclesiastes 3:11, God has "put eternity in [our] hearts." Though we operate in time, we ache for what is everlasting because God created us to last forever. He made us **for this very purpose** (5:5). **We do not want to be unclothed but clothed** is Paul's way of saying we don't want life to end but desire our **mortality** to be **swallowed up by life** (5:4). How do we know God will follow through on his promise to grant believers eternal life? Because he has given us the Holy **Spirit as a down payment** guaranteeing what is to come (5:5).

Every human being is rapidly headed for eternity, whether he or she realizes it or not. So, are you living your temporal days in light of your eternal destiny? Approach your every decision and maximize your earthly time by living from an eternal perspective.

5:6-8 While we live in our earthly bodies, **we are away from the Lord** (5:6) and have not yet realized the fullness of the glory that will be revealed to us when we are taken into God's presence. Paul's preference was to be **at home with the Lord** (5:8). But until that day, he exhorted the Corinthian believers, **we walk by faith, not by sight** (5:7).

As the apostle said previously, "We do not focus on what is seen, but on what is unseen. For what is seen is temporary, but what is unseen is eternal" (4:18). Thus, we must live based on what God's Word teaches us to believe instead of on what we can see. We walk by faith, trusting that God is telling the truth. Though we can't see the eternal realities that he has promised, we act—living heavenly in a hellish world—because we are confident in him.

5:9-10 Regardless of his circumstances, Paul's **aim** was **to be pleasing to** the Lord in all aspects of his life (5:9). For he knew he would have to give an account for his life as a believer. Indeed, **we must all appear before the judgment seat of Christ, so that each one may be repaid for what he has done in the body, whether good or evil** (5:10). The Greek word translated "judgment seat" is *bēma*. In the ancient world, it was on a *bēma* that a ruler or person with authority would sit to render judicial decisions. Paul, for example, stood before the judgment seat (or "tribunal") of Gallio in Achaia when the Jews made charges against him (see Acts 12–13).

One day every Christian will have to stand before Christ's *bēma* to have his or her faithfulness (or lack thereof) evaluated and recompensed. Believers will be granted or denied rewards based on whether or not they have lived for Christ. There will be no hiding on that day. And there will be no actions in your Christian life that will be overlooked. Therefore, knowing that everything "good or evil" will be repaid, how do you want to spend the few days allotted to you?

5:11 Given that he would appear before the judgment seat of Christ, Paul lived in **the fear of the Lord**—that is, he took God seriously. He was earnest about the ministry God had given him, so he sought **to persuade people** to believe in King Jesus and submit their lives to his kingdom agenda. He was confident that the integrity of his ministry was plain to God, and he hoped that his method and motivation were **also plain** to the **consciences** of the Corinthians.

5:12-13 Paul insists that he is not **commending** himself to the Corinthians but instead **giving** them the **opportunity to be proud of** the authentic nature of the ministry he and his companions were carrying out on behalf of the church. Some among the Corinthians were boasting **in outward** appearances, but Paul made it clear that one's **heart** motivation is what matters (5:12). Whatever Paul was accused of, he assures them that his actions were for God's glory and their edification (5:13).

5:14-15 Paul is compelled by **the love of Christ** for sinners. Since Christ **died for all** people (a reference to unlimited atonement), **then all died**—that is, the penalty for all sin has been paid by Christ's sacrifice (5:14). Thus, the barrier between God and people has been removed, and Paul wants all people to hear, believe, and receive that good news of forgiveness of sins and reconciliation to God. Further, if Christ gave his life for us, then our lives are no longer our own. Rather than living for ourselves, then, we ought to live **for the one who died for [us] and was raised** (5:15).

This is what Paul was doing, what he wanted the Corinthians to do, and what is missing in the lives of many Christians today. The Son of God suffered the wrath of God to purchase our eternal destiny in glory. What greater privilege is there than serving him during our brief pilgrimages on earth as our loving response to his overwhelming love for us?

5:16 In light of these eternal realities, Paul confesses that he no longer knows **anyone from a worldly perspective**. In other words, Christians are not to evaluate people based on mere physical appearances like age, gender, or ethnicity but based on their eternal destinies. Similarly, we don't evaluate **Christ from a worldly perspective.** He is no mere crucified first-century Jewish man; rather, he is the risen Savior and King who is seated at the right hand of the Father. We must see and evaluate things according to their heavenly, spiritual realities—not their mere earthly, physical, racial, and temporal appearances.

5:17 If anyone is in Christ, he is a new creation. If you are a Christian, you have been born again of imperishable seed and share in the divine nature (see John 3:3; 1 Pet 1:23; 2 Pet 1:4). God has brought about a spiritual transformation inside of you, and your identity is tied to your new birth. You are no longer who you once were: **the old has passed away.** Therefore, you are called to live in accordance with your new identity.

5:18-20 All of this newness **is from God, who has reconciled us to himself through Christ.** And as those who have been reconciled to God, we have been given **the ministry of reconciliation** (5:18). In other words, every believer has a mission—the same mission—to tell others of the good news of Jesus Christ. Thus, **we are ambassadors for Christ.** An *ambassador* is an officially designated representative who is authorized to speak in a foreign land on behalf of the country by which he was sent. Therefore, we must speak faithfully for the one who sent us. Since we are Christ's ambassadors, **God is making his appeal through us** (5:20). We are to share **the message of reconciliation,** urging all sinners to **be reconciled to God** because, through the atoning work of Christ, he is **not counting their trespasses against them** (5:19-20). There is no more glorious news to be proclaimed!

Scripture declares that God wants "everyone to be saved and to come to the knowledge of the truth" (1 Tim 2:4). God the Father desires that all people would hear and understand the gospel so that they may have the opportunity to believe for eternal life. The Son of God died on the cross to make this possible. But he isn't coming down from heaven to do the witnessing directly. Instead, he has committed the message to

us. Our job as his ambassadors is to carry out that mission and proclaim that message to the world.

5:21 God the Father **made** his Son Jesus Christ **who did not know sin to be sin for us, so that in him we might become the righteousness of God.** By his glorious grace, God offers human beings the deal of a lifetime. As a result of our sin, every human being owes a debt to God that he or she can't repay. Our sin demands God's eternal judgment. Yet, "because of his great love that he had for us" (Eph 2:4), God acted on our behalf. As Paul says, "The one who did not know sin became sin for us." The sinless Son of God became our substitute on the cross: "He himself bore our sins in his body on the tree" (1 Pet 2:24).

Yet that's only half the story. Although that addresses our sins, we still have a lack of righteousness to commend us to God. So, in exchange for our sins, Jesus offers to give us his perfect righteousness—that is, when we place our faith in him, he credits our spiritual bank accounts with his own perfection. The theological term for this transaction is *imputation*. When you believe in Jesus as your substitutionary atonement, your sin is imputed (or credited) to Christ, and his righteousness is imputed to you. This is the glorious exchange that the gospel offers to everyone who will receive it. And this is the good news of which we are ambassadors.

6:1-2 The false apostles who were leading some astray in Corinth had been preaching "another Jesus" (11:4) and were Jews (11:22). So they may have been affiliated with the "Judaizers" that Paul addressed in Galatians, those who were telling Gentile Christians that they had to keep the Mosaic law in addition to believing in Jesus. Since Paul urges the Corinthians not to **receive the grace of God in vain** (6:1), it may be that these false teachers were telling them to focus on keeping the law by their own self-effort, rather than relying on God's gracious provision to live the Christian life (see Gal 3:1-5). Paul quotes from Isaiah 49:8 to emphasize that **the day of salvation** has arrived (6:2). Today, we must operate in light of God's grace if we are to maximize the salvation we have received.

6:3-5 Paul puts himself forward as an example for the Corinthians to follow. He didn't worry about protecting himself but sought to protect his **ministry** from accusations (6:3). **As God's ministers**, he and his coworkers were representatives of the Lord. So Paul wants to **commend** his ministry (6:4) and avoid anything that would compromise it and bring spiritual ruin to the lives of others—as many false teachers were doing. Paul lists a series of hardships that he had endured on behalf of his ministry (6:4-5), demonstrating that he was willing to suffer many intense afflictions to honor Christ and see lives transformed for his kingdom.

6:6-10 After listing the adversities he faced, Paul lists the qualities necessary for this kind of faithful ministry. Paul's service to the Lord and his people was marked by **purity . . . patience . . . sincere love**, and was fueled **by the Holy Spirit . . . the word of truth . . . the power of God** (6:6-7). Next Paul lists nine pairs of paradoxes that he experienced. These include **glory and dishonor . . . unknown, yet recognized . . . having nothing, yet possessing everything** (6:8-10). Through his personal character, the divine affirmation of his work, and his spiritual successes in spite of adversity, Paul's apostleship was validated.

6:11-13 Paul had not operated in secret among the **Corinthians**. He had kept nothing from them but had always **spoken openly** with a **heart** like an open book (6:11). His ministry was nothing if not authentic and characterized by **affection**. In contrast, the Corinthians were the ones **withholding** affection from Paul. So, like a father to his **children** (they were, in fact, his spiritual children, having been converted under his preaching), he pleads with them to display the same commitment to him that he had to them (6:13).

Paul is an authentic and powerful example not only for all church leaders but for all church members as well. Those who serve in positions of leadership ought to have a deep love for those under their spiritual care. Likewise, the congregation should have warm affection and respect for their leaders who will one day "give an account" to God for the souls of those whom they serve (Heb 13:17). Without this two-way openness, it's difficult for those within a church to care for and protect one another spiritually.

6:14-18 Quoting from several Old Testament passages for support (6:16-18), Paul exhorts them not to have intimate fellowship with unbelievers. Some of the Corinthians were doing this with the Jewish false teachers who were opposing Paul and sowing discord in the church. To **become partners with** can also be translated "be unequally yoked" (6:14). The idea comes from Deuteronomy 22:10, in which the Israelites were commanded not to have "an ox and a donkey" plowing together. What's true among animals is true among humans. Close relationships or partnerships between believers and unbelievers result in an unholy union. After all, **what does a believer have in common with an unbeliever?** (6:15).

Whether it's a romantic relationship, intimate friendship, or a business partnership, such compromise negatively affects your intimacy with God. When you align yourself with those whose beliefs and lives are far from God, you'll find God distancing himself from you too.

7:1 Therefore, in light of the **promises** of God's nearness—"we are the temple of the living God" (6:16)—Paul urges them to cleanse themselves of impurity (through illegitimate partnerships with unbelievers) that may have hindered their sanctification process. Instead, they should be serious about their relationship with the Lord by living **in the fear of God**.

7:2-4 Regarding any accusations or rumors that the false apostles had made against him, Paul reiterates that he has not **wronged** or **taken advantage of** anyone and pleads with them to open their **hearts** to him (7:2). He quickly explains that he and his coworkers are not attempting to **condemn** the Corinthians. Their **hearts** are filled with affection, **pride**, and **joy** over them in spite of the **afflictions** suffered (7:3-4). The false apostles were to blame for the unrest they had caused.

7:5-11 Paul had experienced turmoil, unrest, and **fears** when he arrived in **Macedonia** because he had still not heard from Titus regarding his previous letter to the Corinthians (7:5; see 2:12-13). **But God** provided him with great **comfort** by **the arrival of Titus**, who brought good news of how the Corinthians had repented of their previous attitude and had disciplined the man who'd opposed Paul (7:5-7; see 2:1-8).

God often comforts his children through their fellow believers (see 1:3-7). In his providence, he will bring people alongside those experiencing conflict who can offer a sympathetic ear and speak words of truth and encouragement. So when you see a brother or sister in Christ suffering, don't pass up the opportunity to be used of God to bring them comfort that perhaps only you can provide.

Even if Paul had **grieved** the Corinthians with his **letter**, he knew it had been worth it because of the positive spiritual results (7:8). Their **grief led to repentance** followed by a godly **zeal** for Paul (7:7, 9). Paul distinguishes between **godly grief** and **worldly grief**— the former leads to **repentance** while the latter leads to **death** (7:10). Worldly grief is what Judas experienced after he betrayed Jesus. He knew he had sinned and was filled with remorse, but he was unwilling to repent (see Matt 27:3-5). In contrast, Peter experienced godly grief after denying Christ. This led to his repentance and recommitment to the Lord, resulting in his spiritual restoration (see Matt 26:75; John 21:15-19).

7:12-16 The Corinthians' response to what Paul **wrote** provided them with the opportunity to demonstrate their own **devotion to** him **in the sight of God** (7:12). This, in turn, **comforted** Paul and his companions (7:13) because it validated the Corinthians' faith and their desire to walk faithfully before God.

Titus had been a key player in bringing harmony between the Corinthian church and Paul. The apostle had boasted of his confidence in the Corinthian believers, and he was not **disappointed** by the results (7:14). Titus had been **refreshed** by them and grew in **affection toward** them because of their **obedience**, and this brought much rejoicing to them all (7:13, 15-16).

Notice how both Paul and Titus experienced joy over, encouragement from, and affection for other believers because of their obedience to God. How does the obedience or disobedience of your fellow believers affect you? Are you grieved when they stray from the Lord? Are you willing to intervene as Paul did and have a difficult conversation so that they might be moved to godly grief and repentance? When they honor God through their obedience, do you rejoice and praise God? Kingdom disciples care deeply about the reputation of their King and the welfare of his people.

III. THE COLLECTION FOR THE SAINTS AND THE IMPORTANCE OF GENEROSITY (8:1–9:15)

8:1-2 From Paul's other letters, we know that he had taken up a collection among the Gentile churches on behalf of the poor believers in Jerusalem (see Rom 15:25-28; Gal 2:9-10). He had previously urged the Corinthians to take up an offering of their own that he could deliver when he traveled to Jerusalem (see 1 Cor 16:1-4). In this chapter, he makes an appeal for them to complete their collection.

Paul begins by highlighting **the churches of Macedonia** (this would have included the churches in Philippi, Thessalonica, and Berea; see Acts 16:6–17:15) as an example of generosity to motivate the Corinthians' own giving. Although the Macedonian believers had experienced **a severe trial**, this did not prevent them from expressing **generosity** that **overflowed** from their internal **joy** in the Lord.

8:3-5 Not only did the Macedonians give, but they **even** went **beyond their ability**, begging for the opportunity to contribute to believers in need whom they had never even met. By giving to a legitimate need through legitimate ministers, they had **the privilege of sharing in the ministry** (8:3-4). Thus, they opened themselves to experiencing the spiritual blessings and benefits that accrue as a result of sacrificially giving to the Lord's work with the right attitude. Their submission **to the Lord** Jesus had prompted them to commit their financial resources through these God-ordained leaders (8:5).

Why do you give to gospel ministry? Is it because you feel guilty? Is it because you're trying to cut a deal with God? Or is it because you know and have experienced the unmerited goodness of God in your life? When you are characterized by spiritual satisfaction and a true understanding and appreciation of grace, giving to the Lord's work will be something you are excited to do.

8:6-7 In light of the evident grace of God in the response of the Macedonians, how could the Corinthians do less? So just as **Titus** had **begun** the collection among the Corinthians, Paul dispatched him again to bring it to completion (8:6). The apostle longs to see them **excel in** giving to the poor Jewish Christians, just as they have excelled in other ways—**in faith, speech, knowledge, and in all diligence** (8:7). When we respond to God's grace in our lives with a willingness to give to others, his grace to us and through us is magnified all the more. The Corinthians had the chance to make God look good.

8:8-9 Paul wants them to be motivated by **love**, however, not by external pressure. He was not giving them **a command** but pleading with them to follow in their Lord's footsteps (8:8). Though **Jesus Christ ... was rich, for [our] sake he became poor, so that by his poverty [we] might become rich** (8:9). The eternal Son of God had enjoyed heavenly glory and fellowship with the Father from all eternity. But "he emptied himself" and took "on the likeness of humanity" (Phil 2:7). Then he gave "his life as a ransom for many" (Mark 10:45). Christ exemplified the spirit and attitude that Paul longs to see from the Corinthian church. It wasn't asking too much to prompt them to honor what Christ did for them by meeting the needs of fellow saints.

8:10-14 Paul encourages them to fulfill the commitment that they had made a **year** ago, for this would be spiritually **profitable for** them (8:10-11). Moreover, as long as the right attitude is present (**eagerness**), what is given **is acceptable** in God's eyes **according to what a person has, not what he does not** (8:12). God looks at the heart of the giver, not at the size of the gift. Paul does not expect the Corinthians to relieve the Jewish Christians by bringing **hardship** on themselves (8:13). Rather, he wants the current Corinthian **surplus** to meet the needs of those in Jerusalem (8:14).

8:15 To provide an illustration, Paul quotes from Exodus 16:18. God provided a sufficient supply of manna to the Israelites in the wilderness so that everyone had enough. In the same way, he wanted the church in Corinth (and churches today) to help other saints when it was in their capacity to do so. The church of Jesus Christ is the means by which God meets needs.

8:16-22 Paul was blessed with a like-minded coworker in **Titus**, who wished to visit the Corinthians of his own volition to make this **appeal** (8:16-17). In addition, Paul **sent** an unnamed **brother . . . praised among the churches for his gospel ministry**, who would assist in delivering the gift to Jerusalem (8:18-19). Paul also mentions a third **brother** who also accompanying the group. He had been **tested** and found **diligent** (8:22). The apostle was taking every **precaution** because he wanted to honor **the Lord** and avoid the appearance of any wrongdoing, given the **large sum** that was being collected and delivered (8:20-21). Local churches should similarly ensure that financial matters are handled in a manner that is above reproach. Our Christian testimony is at stake, as well as the Lord's reputation.

8:23-24 **Titus** and these **brothers** had come to the Corinthians as **the messengers of the churches, the glory of Christ** (8:23). As far as Paul was concerned, there was no more trustworthy assembly of ambassadors for this task. **Therefore**, he implores the Corinthians to validate **before all the**

churches that their **love** was genuine and that Paul's **boasting** in them was not in vain (8:24).

9:1-5 Having said all this (8:1-24), Paul did not need to provide any further justification for the need to give **to the saints** in Jerusalem (9:1). He had boasted about the churches in **Achaia** (where Corinth was located) **to the Macedonians**, saying that they had been eager for a **year** to give and that the example of the Macedonians only made them more exited to contribute (9:2). Therefore, Paul was **sending** this delegation **in advance** to receive **the generous gift** they had **promised** so that neither Paul nor the Corinthians would be embarrassed because of a failure to follow through on their commitment (9:3-5). Moreover, he wants their giving to be a genuine gift from true motives and not a result of compulsion (9:5).

9:6 Paul finally arrives at his main **point** in his exhortation on giving: **The person who sows sparingly will also reap sparingly, and the person who sows generously will also reap generously.** In other words, a cheap giver will be a cheap receiver, and a generous giver will be a generous receiver. Paul uses a simple farming illustration. A farmer's harvest is dependent on what he sows. Unless seeds are planted, there will be no crop. The seed deposited in the ground is an investment made in faithful expectation of reaping something much more significant.

In spite of what some health-and-wealth gospel advocates may say, Paul is not promising that giving generously to gospel ministry will result in earthly, material prosperity and the elimination of all your problems. Anyone who says that doesn't know what he's talking about and is claiming biblical support for false teaching.

But clearly there's a principle of sowing and reaping here that's not to be ignored. If you give generously to a legitimate need from sincere gospel motives when it is in your capacity to do so, God will give you his blessing. A *blessing* is the God-given capacity to experience, enjoy, and extend the goodness and favor of God in your life. Regardless of what God provides to you, he will bless you

with his presence and the ability to use what he provides.

9:7 All giving should be done willingly and not **out of compulsion.** Why? Because **God loves a cheerful giver.** Thus, giving is not only about the gift but also about the attitude behind it. We are to be cheerful in our giving because of an understanding that our capacity to give is determined by God and not by ourselves. When you know that God is your source, you can be cheerful in giving since you understand there would be no possibility of giving if he hadn't given to you first. "The earth and everything in it . . . belong to the LORD" (Ps 24:1). Thus, one of the ways you know you are growing in your faith is when you give with a glad heart in response to the goodness of God. Giving should be a joy not a job.

9:8-9 Paul's next statement applies to all cheerful givers: **God is able to make every grace overflow to you.** God's super abundant grace includes all that he can do for you that you are unable to do for yourself. He can guide you when you're lost and provide for you when you're in need. He can heal a relationship that's broken and grant peace where there's conflict.

When we have stingy hearts and are reluctant to give to a legitimate need, though, we restrict the flow of God's grace. It's cheerful generosity that causes his grace to comprehensively "overflow" **so that in every way** you have **everything you need** to **excel in every good work** (9:8). As Paul's quotation from Psalm 112:9 shows, when God gives **freely** to those in need, his righteous character is magnified (9:9).

When God's kingdom is given priority in your life, you open yourself to waves of grace that are bigger than your gift. History and eternity have more grace available than we could ever access (see Eph 2:7). As a result, the fruit that comes through your service to his kingdom multiplies into greater benefit to you, greater blessings to others, and greater glory to God.

9:10-12 Paul assures the Corinthians that **the one who provides seed** will **multiply** seed, and the one who provides **bread** will increase the harvest of . . . righteousness (9:10). The emphasis here is that God is both the source of what is planted and also the source of what is harvested. Truly acknowledging this rightly produces **thanksgiving to God** (9:11)—in other words, it causes internal transformation that is expressed in external praise. Thus, there is a twofold effect from this **ministry: supplying the needs of the saints** and **expressions of thanks to God** (9:12). God's goal is that both giver and receiver obtain his blessing as he himself is exalted.

9:13-14 This **ministry** to the poor saints in Jerusalem was **proof** of God's goodness and provision. As a result, Paul explains that the recipients **will glorify God** for the generous gift and lovingly **pray** for the Corinthians for being willing conduits of the **grace of God.** Cheerful and willing contributions to legitimate needs result in an overabundance of grace and blessing, leading to increased prayer and praise to God, which lead to more giving and grace. Those who refuse to give, or who give from mere compulsion, short-circuit this chain of blessing before it can even begin.

9:15 The only way Paul can respond to this amazing grace of God is to say, **Thanks be to God for his indescribable gift!** The "surpassing grace of God" (9:14) so overwhelms Paul that he doesn't have a vocabulary capable of describing it. It is, in fact, beyond description. That's the kind of grace you need. That's the kind of grace you want operating in your life. Don't cut yourself off from it.

IV. TRUE APOSTLESHIP VERSUS FALSE APOSTLESHIP
(10:1–13:10)

10:1-2 Some of the Corinthians were being influenced by false teachers who had infiltrated the church. So Paul pleads with the believers in a spirit of **meekness and gentleness** to listen to him to avoid his having to boldly confront those who were **behaving according to the flesh** and had accused Paul of being self-serving.

10:3-5 The apostle Paul is willing to go to battle against false apostles because he does **not wage war according to the flesh** (10:3). He recognizes that the **warfare** in which he is engaged is spiritual and requires spiritual **weapons** that are **powerful through God for the demolition of strongholds** (10:4). By "strongholds," Paul isn't talking about physical fortresses, of course, but about destructive patterns of thought that lead people astray and hold them hostage to sinful, harmful and addictive behavior. We know Paul is concerned with the mind because he is demolishing **arguments and every proud thing that is raised up against the knowledge of God**, and he wants to help believers **take every thought captive to obey Christ** (10:4-5). Satan's strategy is to block the knowledge and/or application of God's Word in the thinking of believers so that they can be held hostage by his lies, which are communicated through false teaching.

If addictive behavior is present in a person's life, that behavior is not the stronghold but merely its fruit. Strongholds can only be demolished by the knowledge of God—that is, by truth. As Jesus told his disciples, "The truth will set you free" (John 8:32). When your relationship to the living Word connects to the written Word, "you really will be free" (John 8:36). If you're not taking every thought captive to obey Christ and are instead succumbing to a stronghold, it's because you either don't know the truth or aren't making use of the truth you know

10:6 Paul warns that he and his coworkers **are ready to punish any disobedience, once** the Corinthians' **obedience is complete.** In order for Paul to deal effectively with the disobedience of the false apostles, the Corinthians would need to be unified in their commitment to the Lord and to Paul by complete—not partial—obedience. If a minority of the Corinthians still allowed themselves to be influenced by heretical teachers, it would affect the entire church.

10:7-8 Whatever the false apostles claimed about being authoritative ambassadors for Christ, Paul had greater confidence in his **authority** as an apostle, which he'd received from the Lord Jesus himself. But he reminds them that he had used his authority **for building** the church in Corinth **up**, not **for tearing** them **down** as the false apostles had (10:8).

10:9-11 Paul had no intention of frightening the Corinthians with his forceful **letters** (10:9) but sought to be forthright and bold to lead them to obey Christ. He preferred to do this by written correspondence so that there would be no need for confrontation in person. This had led some to accuse him of being a vacillating person whose **letters** were **powerful** but who was **weak** in person (10:10). But Paul assures them that they would find him to be the same in his **letters** as he would be in his **actions when** he visited them (10:11). There would be no inconsistency in his message. He had only been trying to deal with them in a manner that would cause the least amount of pain and embarrassment.

10:12-16 The false teachers to whom some of the Corinthians were listening had a faulty view of themselves. They were **measuring themselves by themselves and comparing themselves to themselves** (10:12). In other words, they served as their own standard. This is the epitome of human wisdom and pride. Paul, however, refused to **boast beyond measure** (10:13; cf. 10:15)—that is, to boast and operate outside of the God-designed boundaries in which he had been placed. He knew what Christ had equipped and called him to do, unlike these false apostles who exalted themselves and criticized Paul.

We too must realize that we can't serve as our own standard because sin has contaminated us. Our only legitimate standard is Scripture. Furthermore, we must be content with the boundaries in which God has placed us. To live within God-given boundaries is freedom; it maximizes your uniqueness and abilities. To try to function outside of those boundaries will produce frustration and often leads to sin.

10:17-18 Paul quotes the wisdom of the prophet Jeremiah: **So let the one who boasts, boast in the Lord** (10:17). How do you know you're operating in the right spot and for the right reasons? Because you find that you're consciously doing what you do for the glory of God—that is, you're making God look good by how you live. Boasting in yourself, your abilities, and your accomplishments is a dead-end street because it's a lie (the Lord is your source, not you) and it ultimately won't satisfy. Remember, **it is not the one commending himself who is approved, but the one the Lord commends** (10:18).

Self-approval carries no weight, no legitimacy. But when you boast in God rather than in yourself, you will align yourself with God's kingdom agenda. And when you do, you'll obtain the only approval that matters, the approval of the King.

11:1 In order to respond to his opponents and try to win back those among the Corinthians who had embraced them, Paul feels compelled to engage in the very thing that he hates: the **foolishness** of boasting.

11:2-4 He had a **godly jealousy** for them, which made him zealous to silence once and for all the false teachers who were misleading them. Paul was their spiritual father in the gospel, and the Corinthians were like **a pure virgin** whom he had **promised** to a **husband**, Jesus **Christ** (11:2). But Paul was afraid that they were in danger of being **deceived** by the devil (**the serpent**) and led astray from a **pure devotion to Christ** (11:3) because they were willing to **put up with** false teaching, which amounted to **another Jesus . . . a different spirit . . . a different gospel** (11:4).

11:5-6 The false teachers had promoted themselves as being superior to Paul, but he knew he was not **inferior** to these so-called **super-apostles** (11:5). They had accused him of being **untrained in public speaking.** Yet Paul knew that his **knowledge** of the true gospel and the content of his message were far more important that oratorical skill (11:6).

You may be a dynamic and persuasive public speaker. Nevertheless, if you're not proclaiming, "Jesus Christ and him cruci-fied" (1 Cor 2:2), your message is insufficient and will be devoid of the spiritual power that comes only from the Word of God.

11:7-12 Paul always subordinated himself to the gospel. Instead of exalting himself and having the Corinthians pay for his services, he had received financial support from **other churches** and **preached the gospel** to them **free of charge** (11:7-8). He describes this as having **robbed** believers **from Macedonia** (11:8-9), meaning other Christians paid for his ministry when he could rightly have expected the Corinthians to support him themselves. But Paul hadn't wanted to **burden** them and hinder the work of the gospel among them (11:9). This kind of **boasting** Paul was willing to engage in—that is, boasting about how he had sacrificed for them and about his great **love** for them (11:10-11). The false apostles wouldn't boast in these kinds of humble attitudes and actions; thus, they were clearly not Paul's **equals** (11:12).

11:13-15 Paul calls these opponents exactly what they were: **false apostles** and **deceitful workers** (11:13). They weren't Christians but devilish imposters. Just as **Satan disguises himself as an angel of light** in order to deceive and corrupt, so these false teachers pretended to be **servants of righteousness** (11:14-15). But Paul promises that God will judge them **according to their works** (11:15).

Don't assume that Satan's temptations and tactics will always be obvious. He's a liar and deceiver, and he's been plying his trade for millennia. He's familiar with your weaknesses, just like a coach who studies the game films of his opponents in order to exploit theirs. The enemy knows how to make succumbing to his temptations appear like good and right things to do. So, what can you do? "Put on the full armor of God so that you can stand against the schemes of the devil" (Eph 6:11), and "resist him, firm in the faith" (1 Pet 5:9).

11:16-21 Paul confesses to acting like **a fool** with his **boasting** because apparently that's what some of the Corinthians were responding to from the false apostles (11:16-18). They were willing to put up with those whom they

considered "super-apostles" (11:5), even if it meant they actually exploited and mistreated them (11:20)! Paul sarcastically admits, **We have been too weak for that!** (11:21). In other words, he says, "You're right. They're much better apostles than I. They take advantage of you and insult you. But me? All I do is sacrifice for you and love you!"

11:22-29 What did Paul boast in? First, he boasted in his Jewish credentials because apparently the false apostles had done the same (11:22). But then his boasting takes a different turn. Though the false teachers exalted themselves, Paul bragged (**like a madman**, he says) of his **labors . . . imprisonments . . . beatings . . . near death** experiences (11:23). Then he lists examples of all the trials and persecutions he endured throughout his missionary endeavors (11:24-27). On top of these physical ordeals, he experienced **the daily pressure** of leading and ministering to struggling **churches** (11:28). Even if he was physically separated from these churches, when he heard about their problems, Paul suffered right along with them because of his deep affection for them and for Christ (11:29).

Paul's point is this: suffering was not an indicator of his failure as an apostle; it was a sign of his superiority. His superior suffering on behalf of his Savior (who suffered!) demonstrated his superior service and commitment.

11:30-33 Since the Corinthians had put up with the boasting of the false apostles, Paul would boast too. But he would do so **about** his **weaknesses** (10:30). On one occasion **in Damascus**, he had been lowered down **in a basket through a window in the wall** of the city to escape those who wanted to kill him (11:32-33). He was willing to be weak and helpless for the sake of proclaiming the gospel.

12:1-5 Paul continues his boasting. He tells of **a man in Christ who was caught up to the third heaven fourteen years ago** (12:2). The first heaven refers to the earth's atmosphere, and the second heaven is the area that includes the sun, moon, planets, stars, and galaxies. The third heaven is the dwelling place of God. We know Paul is referring to himself because he's talking about his own **boasting** and **weaknesses** (12:1, 5). What happened was such an overwhelming experience that Paul doesn't **know** whether he was **in the body or out of the body** at the time (12:3). What he does know is that he alone had experienced a personal tour of heaven and came back to talk about it. Nevertheless, he speaks of his experience humbly in the third person (a man, he, this person) because ultimately he prefers to boast in his weakness (see 12:6-10) since this is where true strength lies and how God is most glorified.

12:6 If Paul had wanted **to boast** about his heavenly experiences like this (and more), he would have been **telling the truth**. The false apostles had nothing to compare with this! But he didn't want to boast in these things; rather, he wanted to speak only about what the Corinthians had seen or heard from him.

12:7 If anyone had reason to boast, it was Paul. No one else could say of heaven, "Been there. Done that!" So, to keep him from exalting himself concerning these **extraordinary revelations**, God gave him **a thorn in the flesh**. A "thorn" is something or someone that painfully nags or irritates one's humanity on a continuous basis.

Many interpreters have speculated about what Paul's particular thorn might be. That we're left to guess at exactly what it was gives us the freedom to apply any of our "thorns" to this passage, but Paul tells us several things about it. First, it was clearly painful. Thorns don't bring comfort! It brought him **torment**. Second, though God was the ultimate source of the thorn (see 12:8-9), **Satan** served as the delivery system, probably by means of the false teachers. As in Job's experience, God allowed Satan to bring suffering into Paul's life, but (unlike Satan) God had good purposes in mind. Third, God's intention was that Paul **not exalt** himself as a result of his astonishing experiences. The Lord wanted to keep Paul humble because removing his self-sufficiency would eliminate any stubborn pride, make him more useful, cause him to bear more fruit in ministry, and bring more glory to God.

If God gives you a "thorn in the flesh," you can be certain that it's for your good

and because he loves you. Such a thing is intended to unveil anything in your life (an actual or potential sin) that is not in sync with God's kingdom agenda. Your self-sufficient attitude stands in his way; he wants you to see him as your all-sufficient God. Thus, sometimes God acts like a recycling plant in our lives: He breaks us down so that he can re-use us and increase our anointing.

12:8 Notice what Paul *didn't* do in response. He didn't rebuke the devil. Why? Because the devil was only the messenger service. Paul knew that his sovereign God had permitted the devil's actions, so he prayed to **the Lord three times** that the thorn **would leave**. And this was no mere prayer: Paul **pleaded** repeatedly. He begged that God would take away the cause of his intense suffering.

12:9 God answered Paul's prayer, but it wasn't the response he was looking for: **My grace is sufficient for you, for my power is perfected in weakness.** We see in the example of Paul that when you suffer you should tell God what you want in prayer. Nevertheless, once you've said your piece, you have to be willing to listen to and accept God's answer. The Lord had determined not to remove Paul's thorn in the flesh. What he *did* do, however, was grant divine grace that was sufficient for Paul's needs (see 2 Cor 9:8).

God's *sufficient grace* is the inexhaustible supply of his goodness that we cannot earn and do not deserve—but that keeps on coming. No matter how bad Paul's thorn got, God promised that his grace was more than enough because his "power is perfected in weakness." Indeed, sometimes God gives us a second wind and turns an infirmity into a spiritual asset that allows us to see a fresh manifestation of his presence and power.

When I have a really bad headache, I take extra strength pain reliever because it has the power to address my problem. In other words, my weakness drives me to a pill so that its power may be demonstrated in my life. If not for the weaknesses that God allows us to endure, we would lack opportunities to seek his sufficient grace and experience his perfect power.

Once Paul was permitted to see his thorn in the flesh in light of God's glorious purposes, he chose an interesting response. He confesses, **I will most gladly boast all the more about my weaknesses, so that Christ's power may reside in me.** He doesn't complain about his weaknesses: he brags about them! Notice that Paul isn't sugar-coating his thorn. He calls it what it is: a painful weakness. Nevertheless, he boasts in it because he sees it as the doorway to experiencing the power of Christ in his life.

12:10 Paul's entire perspective had changed. No matter what he faced—**insults, hardships, persecutions,** or **difficulties**—he was willing to endure it all **for the sake of Christ.** Likewise, the Lord calls on you to look to him when your thorn—whatever it is—pricks you. For even if he doesn't take it away, he has grace and power to accomplish in your life only what is possible in the midst of your profound weakness. By God's grace, **take pleasure in** your **weaknesses** so that his power can be revealed. Then you will be able to say along with the apostle Paul, **When I am weak, then I am strong.**

12:11-12 The Corinthians had compelled Paul to act like **a fool** with his boasting. Rather than putting him in a situation in which he had to defend his ministry, they should have **commended** him. Though Paul may have been **nothing** by worldly standards, he was by no means **inferior** to the so-called **super-apostles** (12:11). Unlike those deceivers, Paul had his ministry validated by supernatural **signs and wonders and miracles** (12:12).

12:13 Some of the Corinthians, no doubt instigated by the false apostles, accused Paul of making them inferior to **other churches.** But given the divine affirmation that accompanied his ministry (see 12:12), the only thing they'd "suffered" was not being burdened by Paul (see 11:7-9). For this, Paul sarcastically begs, **Forgive me for this wrong!**

12:14-19 Paul had refused funds from the Corinthian church because he was concerned for their spiritual condition, not their money (12:14). Like a father, he felt responsible to care for his spiritual **children**—not to have them take care of him. Nevertheless, because of his **love** for them, he longed that they

would love him in return (12:15). Even Titus and those who had gone with him to visit the Corinthians had not taken **advantage of** them but had walked in Paul's **footsteps** (12:16-18). The apostle was not concerned for his own self-image but for **building** the church **up** (12:19).

12:20-21 Paul is worried that when he comes he will find the church full of strife and sin (12:20). He laments the fact that he might discover a lack of repentance among those who had **sinned** previously, insisting that this would bring him nothing but grief (12:21).

13:1-4 As his **third** visit to Corinth approached, Paul warns that he **will not be lenient** toward unrepentant sinners but will discipline them (13:1-2). If they want **proof of** his apostolic authority, he will demonstrate it, and they will see Christ's power working through him (13:3). Though Paul himself was **weak,** the risen Christ was operating in him, and **God's power** will be displayed unless the sin was addressed (13:4).

13:5-6 Paul urges them, **Test yourselves to see if you are in the faith. Examine yourselves.** This testing was not for the purpose of determining whether they were saved. Paul was confident that they had experienced God's saving grace in Christ (see, e.g., 1 Cor 1:4-9). Instead, he wants them to examine whether Christ's abiding presence was operating through them. They needed to test whether they were operating in sync with the true faith or with the heretical teachings of the false apostles. Were they progressing in the faith as disciples? Or were they regressing due to sin and error? Regardless, Paul knew that he and his co-workers would **not fail the test** (13:6).

13:7-10 Paul earnestly prays that the Corinthians would **do nothing wrong.** He had no desire to vindicate himself or to see God discipline them (13:7). The driving force behind Paul's ministry was nothing less than **the truth** of the gospel and its impact in the spiritual development of these believers (13:8). He was happy for them to become **strong** though he himself was **weak.** His longing was to see them continue their spiritual growth and **become fully mature** believers (13:9), so he wishes to avoid dealing **harshly** with them and disciplining them. Better

to have the privilege on the Lord's behalf of **building** them **up** rather than **tearing** them **down** (13:10).

V. CLOSING (13:11-13)

13:11-13 Paul closes the letter with exhortations that apply to all believers: **rejoice, become mature, be encouraged, be of the same mind, be at peace.** We are capable of all these actions because of the work of God in our lives. If the Corinthians followed

through, **the God of love and peace** would be with them and grant them his power (13:11).

The apostle extends **greetings** of love and concludes with a Trinitarian benediction of **grace, love,** and **fellowship** (13:12-13).

GALATIANS

INTRODUCTION

Author

THE WRITER IDENTIFIES HIMSELF as the apostle Paul (1:1), and even most critical New Testament scholars agree that he served as the author. Interpreters believe Galatians may be the earliest of his letters.

Historical Background

Paul wrote this letter "to the churches of Galatia" (1:2). In his day, the term *Galatia* could be used to refer to an ethic group or a province. If Paul was using the term ethnically, then Galatians was written to the people who lived in north central Asia Minor (modern-day Turkey). Alternatively, Paul could have been using the term to speak of the Roman province of Galatia in southern Asia Minor. New Testament scholars describe these two options as the North Galatian theory and the South Galatian theory.

Though certainty is impossible, the South Galatian theory seems most likely for at least two reasons. First, we know Paul ministered extensively in southern Asia Minor during his missionary journeys as described in the book of Acts. However, no clear evidence exists that Paul visited northern Asia Minor. The second reason has to do with when Paul wrote the letter. Those who argue for the South Galatian theory believe he wrote it after his first missionary journey to that region. Those who argue for the North Galatian theory believe Paul wrote later,

giving him time to visit that region at some point.

As a result of these two perspectives, interpreters disagree over how to identify Paul's visit to Jerusalem mentioned in 2:1-10. North Galatian interpreters believe the visit is identical with the Jerusalem Council visit of Acts 15:1-29. But, if so, it's strange that Paul didn't tell the Galatians about the letter that the leaders of the Jerusalem church wrote to Gentile believes after the council (Acts 15:22-29). Doing so would've made sense. After all, the Jerusalem Council dealt with the same problem that Paul seems to address in Galatians: Judaizers were telling Gentile Christians that they had to become circumcised to be saved (see Acts 15:1; Gal 5:1-6; 6:12-13). Thus, it seems more likely that Paul's visit to Jerusalem in 2:10 is the famine relief visit of Acts 11:27-30.

If "Galatians" refers to the churches Paul visited on his first missionary journey in AD 47–48 (the South Galatian theory), then Paul likely wrote it in AD 48 or 49, prior to the Jerusalem Council in AD 49. That would make Galatians Paul's earliest New Testament letter.

Message and Purpose

The Galatians were bewitched by false teachers known as Judaizers; these people were teaching a gospel that was no gospel at all. Paul wrote to the confused believers in Galatia to help them see that what they were being taught was a false gospel that depended on human efforts to make a person acceptable to God, which was completely contrary to the true gospel of salvation and sanctification by grace through the power of the Holy Spirit.

Throughout Galatians, the contrast between the flesh and the Spirit—between living by human perspective and living by God's perspective—is highlighted. Paul says it's impossible to live by both because they are diametrically opposed to one another. The flesh and the Spirit are at war. That's why Galatians teaches us that the only way to obtain victory over the flesh is to walk by the Spirit. God knows we need this truth because we will continue to battle with the flesh as long as we are in these imperfect bodies. If we are to experience the liberty, freedom, and victory that the true gospel offers, we must adopt a spiritual, kingdom-based mindset so that we live in the power of the Spirit and not in the defeat of the flesh.

VIDEO   INTRO

www.bhpublishinggroup.com/qr/te/48_00

Outline

I. Introduction: No Other Gospel (1:1–10)
II. Defense of Paul's Apostleship and of the Gospel (1:11–2:21)
III. Justified by Faith, Not by the Law (3:1–4:31)
IV. Freedom to Love, and Walking by the Spirit (5:1–6:10)
V. Conclusion: Only the Cross (6:11–18)

GALATIANS

I. INTRODUCTION: NO OTHER GOSPEL (1:1-10)

1:1-2 Paul wrote his letter **to the churches of Galatia** to counter a false gospel that was being preached to them. This was serious business. So he wanted to grab their attention right away. He immediately identifies himself as **an apostle**—not sent **from men or by a man**—but sent **by Jesus Christ and God the Father**. He was God's messenger carrying God's message. They couldn't reject what he had to say without serious consequences.

1:3-5 The central message of the gospel that Paul proclaimed was that **God the Father** offers **grace** and **peace** to all through his Son, the **Lord Jesus Christ** (1:3). Jesus **gave himself for our sins to rescue us from this present evil age** for the **glory** of God (1:4-5). The substitutionary sacrifice of Christ on the cross is the centerpiece of the gospel. A holy God cannot overlook humanity's sin and rebellion. He must punish it. But because of God's great love, he sent his Son—fully God and fully man—to suffer and die in our place, bearing the wrath of God against sin. Everyone who trusts in the free gift of Christ's sin-bearing sacrifice on his or her behalf will be saved. This rescue not only justifies sinners for heaven but also gives saints the ability to be delivered from the power of sin on earth ("this present evil age").

1:6 After greeting churches in his letters, Paul would typically bless God or give thanks to him for the work of the gospel in the recipients' lives (see Rom 1:8; 1 Cor 1:4; 2 Cor 1:3; Eph 1:3; Phil 1:3; Col 1:3; 1 Thess 1:2; 2 Thess 1:3). But we see none of that here. Instead, he immediately expressed how **amazed** he was—amazed not at God's grace but by how quickly the Galatians were turning away from it! They were **turning to a different gospel**.

The Galatians had been visited by false teachers after Paul's departure. These appear to be the same as the "Judaizers" mentioned in Acts who were telling Gentile Christians, "Unless you are circumcised according to the custom prescribed by Moses, you cannot be saved" (justified or sanctified) (Acts 15:1). They told the Galatians that they were required to keep the law and be circumcised (see, e.g., Gal 3:2, 10-11; 4:21; 5:1-6; 6:12-13) in order to truly receive salvation from God. But salvation cannot be earned by law-keeping. It is a free gift from God through **the grace of Christ**.

Grace is unmerited favor. It is the inexhaustible goodness of God that is not deserved, cannot be earned, and which we would never be able to repay. Grace is always free and apart from works (Rom 11:6). The good news of justification—being granted a righteous legal standing before God through faith in Jesus Christ—was being undermined by these Judaizers with the result that the Galatian believers would either question the authenticity of their salvation or return to law as a means for sanctification (the process of spiritual growth).

1:7 Though Paul calls the Judaizers' message "a different gospel" (1:6), he quickly clarifies that there is no such thing as **another**

gospel. The word *gospel* means "good news." And it is truly good news that sinners can be justified and forgiven through Christ. He is not merely *a way* to be saved; Jesus is the *only way* to be saved (see John 14:6). Therefore, any other message of salvation cannot be considered a gospel—good news. What was being urged upon the Galatians was an attempt **to distort the gospel of Christ** and to leave grace for the law, which equaled a loss in Christian liberty.

1:8-10 Since there is only one gospel Paul declares that if anyone—even **an angel from heaven**—preaches **contrary to** the true gospel they had heard, that person is under a divine **curse** (1:8). To make sure they didn't miss what he said, Paul repeats himself. Those proclaiming a false gospel are cursed (1:9). He wanted the Galatians to stop listening to the false teachers and not to welcome them into their churches. Paul's strong language made it clear that he was not **striving to please people.** A people-pleaser, after all, will say what people want to hear. But **a servant of Christ** speaks the truth no matter what people think and no matter the outcome (1:10).

The world we live in does not want to hear about a holy God who condemns sinners. But we must not soft-pedal the good news of salvation through faith in Jesus Christ. Let us, like Paul, desire the approval of God more than the approval of others. We must always be "speaking the truth in love" (Eph 4:15) and let the chips fall where they will. Obey God and love lost people enough to share the gospel with them. It is powerful enough to save us for eternity and to transform our lives in history.

II. DEFENSE OF PAUL'S APOSTLESHIP AND OF THE GOSPEL (1:11–2:21)

1:11-12 Paul emphasizes again (see 1:1) **that the gospel** he **preached** was **not of human origin** (1:11). He didn't **receive it from** another preacher or invent the message himself. **Jesus Christ** revealed the gospel message directly to Paul and called him to be his apostle to the Gentiles (1:12; see Acts 9:1-19; 26:12-23).

1:13-14 Paul goes on to give evidence to support his claim that he received the message directly from God. When Paul visited the Galatians on his missionary journey, he was not the same person he used to be. In his **former way of life in Judaism,** he **persecuted God's church** (1:13). When Stephen was martyred, Paul (Saul) "agreed with putting him to death" (Acts 8:1). He sought out Jewish Christians so that he might drag them off to prison (see Acts 8:3; 9:1-2). He wanted nothing more than to **destroy** the church (Gal 1:13), which he believed was corrupting his Jewish religion. Furthermore, Paul was a rising star in Judaism. He was surpassing his peers in his zeal for **the traditions of** his Jewish **ancestors** (1:14). When it came to Pharisaical law keepers, Paul was the cream of the crop (see Phil 3:4-6).

1:15-17 Given Paul's zeal as a superior Pharisee and his hatred for the church, it would take something spectacular to turn him around and make him a follower of Jesus. And "something spectacular" is exactly what he got. **God** graciously and miraculously revealed **his Son** to Paul on the road to Damascus (1:15-16; see Acts 9:3-9). Paul even talks of God planning this long ago when he was in his **mother's womb,** using the same kind of language used to describe Jeremiah's ministry calling from God (Gal 1:15; see Jer 1:4-5).

When God revealed Jesus to Paul and commissioned him to **preach him among the Gentiles,** Paul didn't **immediately consult with anyone**—not even with the other **apostles** (1:16-17). Why would he? He had received marching orders from the Lord Jesus himself when he **went to Arabia** for further instructions (1:17). He needed no confirmation from man. He went out right away to preach the gospel.

1:18-20 Three years later, he went to Jerusalem to get to know Cephas—that is, Peter—and stayed with him for two weeks (1:18; see John 1:42). The only other apostle he saw at that time was **James**, the Lord Jesus's **brother** (Gal 1:19). Paul insisted, **I am not lying** (1:20). He wanted the Galatians to know that his apostleship was not derivative from the other apostles. He had not been "ordained" by them. When he did finally meet the other apostles, he spent a short amount of time with only two of them—not to gain their apostolic approval but simply to get acquainted with them. Paul didn't get his gospel authority via Peter; he got it directly from Christ.

1:21-23 After this, Paul preached the gospel in **Syria** (north of Judea) **and Cilicia** (southern Asia Minor) (1:21). **The Judean churches** didn't even know Paul as an apostle because his God-ordained ministry was elsewhere (1:22). **They simply kept hearing** that this famous persecutor of the church was now preaching **the faith he once tried to destroy** (1:23). What a glorious testimony! It's a reminder that no one is beyond the grace of God. The vilest sinner can repent and believe. The heart that hates Christ can be softened and filled with love.

1:24 They glorified God because of me. When the churches in and around Jerusalem heard that Saul the persecutor had become Paul the evangelist, they gave glory to God. He had received an authentic apostolic calling from God and was preaching the authentic gospel of Christ. Though Paul was unknown to these churches personally, they were united with him by the joint mission to proclaim the same good news he'd once sought to destroy.

2:1-2 Fourteen years after his new birth in Christ, Paul made another visit **to Jerusalem.** This time, he went with two of his ministry partners, **Barnabas** and **Titus** (2:1). He met **privately** with the church **leaders** and **presented to them the gospel** that he preached to **the Gentiles** (2:2), a gospel of justification before God and of growth in sanctification.

2:3-5 False brothers who pretended to be true followers of Christ had **infiltrated** the church **to spy on** them. They wanted to take away the liberty they had as Christians that freed them from the Mosaic law to live under the rule of Christ (2:4). Though these

false brothers sought to enslave the church to legalism—the attempt to earn salvation and sanctification by keeping the law—Paul refused to yield to them. He **preserved** the **truth of the gospel**, insisting that salvation and sanctification come through faith and not through law keeping (2:5). Even **Titus**, a **Greek**, was not **compelled to be circumcised** (2:3). He knew submitting to it could add nothing to the standing Christ had obtained for him before God. Thus, Titus serves as an object lesson of Gentile salvation and ministry involvement apart from the law.

2:6 Those who were **recognized as important**, including the other apostles, didn't intimidate Paul. He knew that **God does not show favoritism.** These leaders **added nothing to** Paul (2:6). Though he had come to make clear to them the gospel he preached (2:2), he did not need their validation. God had revealed the message of the gospel directly to Paul through Christ. He needed no human endorsement or permission to preach it.

2:7-8 The church leaders in Jerusalem recognized Paul's apostolic authority. They recognized that just as **Peter** had been **entrusted** and empowered by God to preach **the gospel** to **the circumcised**, the same was true of Paul on behalf of **the uncircumcised.** Though each was ministering primarily to different audiences (Jews and Gentiles), their gospel was the same: circumcision was not required to be saved. Salvation is by grace apart from works (see Titus 3:5).

2:9-10 James, Cephas (Peter), **and John**— those who had been part of Jesus's original inner circle of apostles, the **pillars** of the Jerusalem church—fully **acknowledged** Paul's gospel ministry and extended **the right hand of fellowship to** Paul and Barnabas (2:9). Thus, they were all in full agreement on the gospel. James, Peter, and John only asked one thing of Paul—not that he would modify his message, but that he would **remember the poor.** To this Paul gladly agreed, for it was something he himself **made every effort to do** (1:10).

Not only should we observe the unity that the apostles had on the gospel message of salvation through faith in Christ apart from keeping the law, but we should also notice their unity in the outworking of the gospel in society. In the Old Testament, God regularly showed concern for the poor and oppressed. He commanded Israel to show compassion and care to the marginalized, including widows and orphans (see Exod 22:22; 23:6; Lev 19:10; Deut 10:18; 15:7-8; Prov 22:22-23; 28:27; Isa 1:17), and he commands the church to do the same (see Jas 1:27; 2:15-16; 1 John 3:17). His agenda should be our agenda. We should "remember the poor."

2:11 Unfortunately, the unity among the apostles was broken **when Cephas** (Peter) started going the wrong way down a one-way street. When that happened in **Antioch**, Paul **opposed** Peter **to his face.** When Peter was in the wrong, Paul loved God, Peter, and others enough to confront his fellow apostle and try to reverse his direction.

2:12-13 Peter **regularly ate with the Gentiles** (2:12), which is a detail that sounds rather mundane until we have a grasp of related historical and biblical background. Jews didn't eat with Gentiles for religious and racial reasons. Both Gentiles and their food were considered unclean, unholy. To fellowship with Gentiles over a meal would make Jews spiritually unclean before God. But one day God showed Peter a vision of various unclean animals and commanded him to eat (see Acts 10:9-13). Even though Jesus had "declared all foods clean" (Mark 7:19), Peter hadn't yet gotten the message. He refused the Lord's command (see Acts 10:14). As a faithful Jew, he had never eaten unclean foods and wasn't about to start. But to his hesitation God responded, "What God has made clean, do not call impure" (Acts 10:15).

God wasn't merely teaching Peter that he could eat any kind of food, but that he could eat with any kind of person. All are equal before God. Peter learned this when God directed him to the home of a Roman centurion who believed the gospel and received the Holy Spirit (see Acts 10:44-46). God was willing to give his Holy Spirit even to Gentiles who would repent and believe in the atoning sacrifice of Jesus. This, in fact, was the point of the vision. "Now I truly understand," Peter declared, "that God doesn't show favoritism" (Acts 10:34). Peter adjusted his agenda to God's.

That's why Peter "regularly ate with Gentiles." The gospel had broken down the racial barrier between Jew and Gentile. But then **certain men came,** those of **the circumcision party,** devout Jews. Whatever they said to Peter, they clearly found his behavior inappropriate. Perhaps they said, "Of course we 'accept' the Gentile Christians, Peter. But we need to maintain our Jewish identity. Sure we're all equal. But we need to be 'separate but equal.'" And at that moment, because **he feared** these Jews (2:12), Peter failed. He separated himself from his Gentile brothers in Christ, and **the rest of the Jews.** Even **Barnabas,** a Jew who had grown up in Cyprus among Gentiles (see Acts 4:36), **joined his hypocrisy** (2:13). They thus became hypocrites, preaching about the unifying nature of the gospel message but living contrary to that message.

2:14 Peter hadn't merely committed a social *faux pas.* He was **deviating from the truth of the gospel.** It had been undermined by his behavior. Through Christ's atoning work, he made peace between Jews and Gentiles, tearing down the wall that divided them and creating "one new man from the two" (Eph 2:14-15). But by his actions, Peter had built the wall again, because others started following his lead. Peter tripped, the rest of the Jewish Christians stumbled over him, and the reconciling truth of the gospel was put in jeopardy. Peter was their spiritual leader, and what happened in this case is a reminder that a mist in the pulpit will always result in a fog in the pew.

Paul swung into action. He confronted Peter **in front of everyone.** Why the public confrontation? Peter's sin had been public, and he had led others into sin. Therefore, the public harm to the gospel had to be put right publicly. Paul shone a light on Peter's hypocrisy. Though **a Jew,** Peter lived **like a Gentile**—that is, he didn't practice Judaism in order to be made right with God. Yet, by his recent actions he was compelling **Gentiles to live like Jews.** Gentiles watching Peter would have thought, "In order to fellowship with Jewish Christians, I guess we need to adopt Jewish practices like the food laws and circumcision." Such thinking would have convinced them that the gospel hadn't really worked and that racial unity and right standing before God would only result from keeping the law. This was the same danger that confronted the Galatians. Legalism leads to hypocrisy, disrupting the gospel's power to produce racial harmony

2:15-18 Paul couldn't ignore this. **A person is not justified**—declared righteous—**by the works of the law.** We are not made right with God by obedience to the law **but by faith in Jesus Christ**, whether we are Jews or Gentiles (2:16). Some of Paul's opponents argued that abolishing the law promoted sinful behavior. **Christ** would be **a promoter of sin**, since someone could **be justified** by faith and then live as he pleased (2:17). But Paul denied this. Rather, the real sin was turning back to the law after one had believed in Christ alone for justification—building up what had been torn down (2:18).

2:19-20 Paul makes clear what happened to him (and to us) at the moment of salvation: **Through the law I died to the law.** God's holy law required death for sinners, but Jesus Christ served as our substitute. He bore the wrath of God and died in our place so that we **might live for God**—not so that we would satisfy our own racial or religious biases (2:19).

Our ethnic identities are part of God's creation. We should acknowledge and celebrate the various expressions of our common humanity that God has made. The problem comes when our racial identity takes precedence over our identity in Christ. This was Peter's mistake. By virtue of the gospel, **I have been crucified with Christ**. Through faith in Christ, I am united with him—both in his death and in his resurrection. Therefore, **I no longer live, but Christ lives in me** (2:20). This is the substitutionary life of Christ, which is the key to victorious

Christian living (see Rom 5:10). My identity in Christ is the most important thing about me. Everything else is secondary. We must die to any identity we have that is *independent* of Christ.

When I place racial or ethnic identity above my identity in Christ (as Peter did), I forget God's amazing grace. I forget **the Son of God, who loved me and gave himself for me** so that I might be reconciled to God and reconciled to others. We have been called to **live by faith in** Christ (2:20)—to be visible and verbal followers of Christ in all we do. This kingdom identity in Christ puts my racial identity into proper perspective. The cross is not merely a historical event; it affects contemporary life, as well as social and racial relationships.

2:21 If obedience to the law is sufficient to make us righteous before God, to enable us to successfully live the Christian life, and to unite us as his people, **then Christ died for nothing.** In truth, the Son of God gave his life on the cross so that we might be justified—declared righteous—before God and become "one in Christ Jesus" (3:28). To claim that both **righteousness** and identity as God's people are obtainable **through the law** is to negate the work of **the grace of God.** Grace is sufficient for "every good work" (2 Cor 9:8).

By his actions, Peter had unwittingly negated God's grace. If the Galatians listened to the Judaizers and became law keepers, they would too. And that would be declaring the gospel irrelevant and cancelling the power of grace to work in their lives and ours. Spirituality, then, does not come from performing an external list of rules (this is at the heart of legalism); rather, it comes from the internal flow of grace in and through the life of the believer. In order to live under grace, we must die to the law (see Rom 7:1-4).

III. JUSTIFIED BY FAITH, NOT BY THE LAW (3:1–4:31)

3:1 You foolish Galatians! In the Bible, a *fool* isn't someone who lacks intelligence, formal education, or rational capacity. It's someone who lacks spiritual sense. The

Galatian church had been tricked; they'd been duped. It was as if someone had **cast a spell on** or hypnotized them. After all, they had clearly heard the gospel from Paul. They had come face-to-face with the reality that **Jesus Christ** was **crucified**, which made the law obsolete (Heb 8:13). This was central to the gospel. To believe the false teachers who were encouraging the Galatians to embrace circumcision was, in essence, to make Christ's death unnecessary (2:21). It showed a lack of spiritual sense.

3:2-4 Paul highlights their inconsistency by asking a series of questions. **Did you receive the Spirit by the works of the law or by believing what you heard?** (3:2) In other words, did you get saved and receive the Spirit by keeping the Ten Commandments? Clearly, the Galatians were saved and received the Holy Spirit when they put their faith in Christ alone. **After beginning by the Spirit, are you now finishing by the flesh?** (3:3). Are you justified (beginning) by the Spirit's application of the death of Christ to your life, but being sanctified (finishing) by your flesh—by your human effort apart from the work of the Spirit? No. Sanctification comes through the empowerment of the Spirit in our lives (see 2 Cor 3:17-18), not from our own will power, effort, or rule keeping.

3:5 Does God . . . work miracles among you by your doing the works of the law? Of course not. Miracles by definition involve the invasion of the supernatural world into the natural world. No matter how hard you work, you can't pull off the miraculous. This can only happen through faith in the power of the Holy Spirit.

3:6 What God requires is faith, complete trust that he can and will do as he promised. Paul quotes Genesis 15:6, citing as an example **Abraham who believed God.** Abraham's faith was **credited to him for righteousness.** When God promised Abraham numerous descendants, Abraham didn't try to earn that promise from God; he simply believed what God said. If, therefore, the great patriarch Abraham was declared righteous on account of his faith (and not because he was circumcised), why did the Galatians need to become circumcised?

3:7-9 Abraham's sons—his spiritual children, both Jews and Gentiles—are **those who have faith** in God, not those who seek to keep the law (3:7). The Judaizers were just plain wrong. **The gospel** was announced **ahead of time to Abraham** when God promised that **all the nations** would be **blessed** through him (3:8; Gen 12:3). They would be blessed through "the seed" of Abraham, Jesus Christ (Gal 3:16, 19). God's blessings come to **those who have faith** like **Abraham** (3:9), who exercised faith before the giving of the law. Trying to keep the law to earn acceptance from God is a dead-end street.

3:10 Blessing doesn't come through law keeping. If you depend on it to make you right with God, you're in for a shock because those **who rely on the works of the law** are actually **under a curse.** Why? Because Scripture says in Deuteronomy 27:26, **Everyone who does not do everything written in the book of the law is cursed.** When it comes to our standing before a holy God, only perfection is acceptable. But even on our best days, we're nowhere close to perfect. Unless you obey *everything* in God's law, you're under his judgment. His righteous nature demands it. As James says, "Whoever keeps the entire law, and yet stumbles at one point, is guilty of breaking it all" (Jas 2:10).

Consider two travelers who are running late. One misses his plane by one hour; the other misses the same plane by one minute. Which man is better off? Neither—they've both missed the flight! Regardless of your track record of attempting to obey God's commands, your efforts are not good enough because you're not perfect. To meet God's standard, you'd have to obey all the law, all the time, all your life—even in your thoughts and motivations. Ninety-nine percent won't cut it.

3:11-12 Paul continues to point to the Old Testament. Even there it was clear that justification comes through faith, not through the law. According to Habakkuk the prophet, **the righteous will live by faith** (3:11; see Hab 2:4). The same faith that saves also sanctifies believers who live their lives by faith. **The law,** on the other hand, says that the righteous **will live by** doing things (Gal 2:12; see Lev 18:5)—that is, by keeping the Mosaic law or any other set of fleshly performance-based rule keeping. But perfect obedience to the law is impossible. The law simply shows us that we are incapable of keeping it.

3:13 God, thankfully, stepped in. In the midst of our despair, while we were under his curse because of our sins against his law, **Christ redeemed us from the curse of the law.** Redemption is a beautiful picture of what Christ did for us. A slave could be redeemed for a price and set free (see Lev 25:47-49). God had redeemed Israel from Egyptian slavery (Deut 24:18), and Christ redeemed us from sin and death. How could he do this? **By becoming a curse for us.** On the cross, God took the sins of the whole world and credited them to Christ's account. Thus, he was cursed for us so that he might serve as a perfect substitute for us, and so that he might fulfill Scripture: **Cursed is everyone who is hung on a tree** (Deut 21:23).

3:14 Paul tells us God's **purpose** in all of this. It was **that the blessing of Abraham would come to the Gentiles by Christ Jesus.** Remember: God promised to bless all the nations (the Gentiles) through Abraham (3:8; see Gen 12:3). This blessing—justification by faith—comes to the world through the seed, the descendant of Abraham: Jesus Christ (Gal 3:16, 19). As a result of Christ's work, all people who have **faith** in him can **receive the promised** Holy **Spirit.** You cannot inherit, earn, or buy the Holy Spirit. You can only receive him as a free gift from God through his Son. It is the Spirit's role to activate the perfect righteousness of Christ, who has already fulfilled the law, in the life of the believer who lives by faith.

3:15 Paul uses an **illustration** of an earthly reality to help his readers understand a spiritual reality. **A validated human will** can't be altered. You can't make changes to it or supersede it. The Galatians would not have argued with this.

3:16-17 Having established this, he moves to the spiritual reality. First, he reminded them that God spoke his covenant **promises . . . to Abraham and to his seed**—not to multiple **seeds**, but to **one** seed, **Christ** (3:16). Jesus is the true seed of Abraham. And, as Paul will

explain, those who are united to Christ by faith inherit Abraham's covenant promises (3:19-26). Second, Paul makes it clear that **the law**—which came **430 years** after God's **covenant** with Abraham—could not **invalidate** that covenant (3:17). In fact, all the law could do was validate Israel's fellowship with God. It could not establish a relationship or empower their fellowship. It served as a measuring tool.

Just as a human will cannot be supplanted (3:15), so the Abrahamic covenant could not be supplanted by the Mosaic law. God's covenant with Abraham existed long before he gave Israel the law. And it was ratified unilaterally since it was solely dependent on God (see Gen 15:1-18).

3:18 By pushing the law as the basis for salvation, the Judaizers were essentially saying that God's law had eradicated God's promises to Abraham. But God unconditionally promised Abraham an **inheritance**—the blessing of all nations through justification by faith. Therefore, this inheritance is not **based on the law.** So keeping the law has nothing to do with being justified before God.

3:19-20 If the law can't justify (2:16), can't provide the Spirit (3:2), and only brings a curse (3:10), what was its point? **Why then was the law given?** What was God up to? Paul gives three answers. First, God gave the law because of Israel's **transgressions** (3:19). Their sin produced the need for the law, which served as a means of restraint. Sometimes parents establish a rule (which formerly didn't exist) to deal with behavior in their children that cannot be tolerated. The law identified the actions that were contrary to God's will and that would result in his wrath.

Second, the law was temporary. It was given **until the Seed to whom the promise was made would come** (3:19). Paul has already said that this Seed is Christ (3:16), the descendant of Abraham. God's promise to bless all the nations through Abraham has been fulfilled through Christ (3:8, 14). Through faith in him, we receive the blessing of justification, a righteous standing before God, and the power for sanctification through the work of the Holy Spirit. The coming of Christ issued in a new administration of grace, cancelling the old administration of the law (Eph 1:9-12).

Third, the law was second class. Why? God put it **into effect through angels by means of a mediator** (3:19). He used both divine intermediaries (angels; see Acts 7:53; Heb 2:2) and a human intermediary (Moses; see Exod 32:15-16) to establish the law. But when it came to God's covenant with Abraham, God spoke his promises *directly* to the patriarch. "A mediator" is used when two parties are involved. Such was the case with the law. God established the law, and Israel was obligated to keep it. In the case of the Abrahamic covenant, though, only **one** party was obligated: **God** (3:20). He alone would fulfill his promises.

3:21-23 In light of all this, one of Paul's readers might have concluded that **the law** was **contrary to God's promises**—that they were opposed to one another. Thus Paul exclaims, **Absolutely not!** God doesn't work against himself. One simply has to understand what the law *can do* and what it *cannot*. People couldn't become righteous **on the basis of the law** because people are sinners, incapable of keeping it. The law can't empower sinners to obey; it can't **give life** (3:21). Instead, the law served the promises by helping prepare the way. It revealed God's righteous standards and **imprisoned** everyone **under sin's power** so that people were positioned to receive **the promise** through **faith in Jesus Christ** (3:22).

The law is like a mirror. When you look in a mirror, it shows you that you need to brush your hair, wash your face, and straighten your clothes. But it can't do any of those things for you. The mirror shows your faults, but it can't fix them. That's what the law does for sinful people. It reveals our problem, our disobedience. But it can't enable us to obey.

3:24-26 The law served as **our guardian until Christ** (3:24). In ancient Greco-Roman society, the *paidagōgos* (translated in the CSB as "guardian") was a household slave who was responsible for looking after younger children, providing them with moral instruction and discipline. Thus, the law functioned in this temporary way, preparing

us to come to Christ **by faith**, not by works of the law. With the coming of **faith**, we **no longer** have need of **a guardian** (3:24-25). To become **sons of God** and to grow in our Christian lives requires only **faith** in **Christ Jesus** (3:26). The Judaizers were wrong. The Galatians didn't need anything else.

3:27 Those of you who were baptized into Christ have been clothed with Christ. Here Paul speaks of spiritual baptism, the baptism of the Holy Spirit, which is shared by all believers (see 1 Cor 12:13). Jesus himself baptizes believers "with the Holy Spirit" (Matt 3:11). Everyone who puts faith in Christ is baptized into his body and clothed with his righteousness. Spiritual growth is the ongoing process of the Holy Spirit making our condition equal to our position.

3:28-29 As a result, **there is no Jew or Greek, slave or free, male and female; since you are all one in Christ Jesus.** Paul is not saying that these distinctions cease to exist. He is saying that in spite of our human differences we are all unified because we are **one in Christ** (3:28). No one is superior to anyone else before God. We all share equally in our relationship with him through Jesus. Thus, the Galatians didn't have to keep the law and undergo circumcision as the Judaizers insisted. They didn't have to become Jews. The Galatians already belonged **to Christ** (3:29), since they were "clothed with" him (3:27) and were "one in" him (3:28). Since Christ is the true seed of Abraham (3:16, 19), then those united with him by faith are **heirs** with Christ and, by extension, **Abraham's seed** spiritually (3:29; since God still has a plan for the physical seed of Abraham, Rom 11:1).

If you trust in Jesus Christ as the perfect substitutionary sacrifice for your sins, then the same is true of you. You have been justified and have a righteous standing before God because he has clothed you with the righteousness of his Son. Through faith in Christ, you are adopted into God's family and receive the Holy Spirit, sharing in this relationship with all believers. You cannot earn salvation and grow properly in your walk with the Lord by keeping the law. It is the free gift of God.

4:1-3 Paul uses an illustration to further explain the role of the law. In Greco-Roman society, though **a child** was an **heir** who would inherit his father's estate and become **the owner of everything**, he was really no different than **a slave** (4:1). **Until the time set by his father**, the child wasn't free to leave and had no inheritance. Instead, he lived **under guardians and trustees** (4:2). **In the same way, we** (Jews and Gentiles) **when we were children** (before coming to faith in Christ) **were in slavery under the elements of the world** (4:3)—whether Jews under the law or Gentiles under false religion. Both systems were based on a philosophy that you have to perform to get God to accept you and to bless you. This perspective is the essence of legalism and has the effect of putting God in our debt—which, of course, he cannot be.

4:4-7 At the appropriate time, **God sent his Son** (4:4) This was the time prophesied by the prophet Daniel of an ascending fourth and final human kingdom that would be overcome by Messiah (Dan 2:40-45; 7:1-28). The Roman Empire serves as a miniature, visible illustration of the worldwide scope and dominance of the kingdom Messiah came to proclaim and offer.

He was **born of a woman, born under the law** (4:4). The Son of God had to become incarnate as a Jew, a member of the Mosaic covenant, so that he could perfectly obey and fulfill the law (Matt 5:17-18). Only then could he **redeem those under** it (4:5; see 3:13). By paying the price of redemption, Jesus makes the slave **no longer a slave but a son** and **an heir** (4:7) because he has been adopted into the family (4:5). Every member of the Trinity is at work in Christians, filling us with the full presence of God as we pray: Believers in the **Son** have the **Spirit** in their **hearts**, leading them to cry, **Abba, Father!** (4:6). Our former father, Satan (see Eph 2:3), has lost all rights over us, and we have no obligation to obey him or the flesh (see Rom 8:12). We have a brand new family under the stewardship of a new teacher and guide.

4:8-9 Previously, the Galatians had lived as idolaters. They **didn't know God** and **were enslaved to things** that **were not gods** (4:8).

After placing faith in Christ, they did **know God.** And, even better, they were **known by God.** Why, when they enjoyed this reality, this freedom, would they want to be **enslaved** once **again** by bringing themselves under the law? (4:9). Why return to something that binds you when Christ came to set you free?

4:10-12 The Judaizers had sought to convince the Galatians to observe the Jewish religious calendar as part of their law-keeping efforts to obtain acceptance from God (4:10). When he learned of this, Paul became concerned that his efforts at disciple-making were **wasted** on them (4:11). He therefore urges the Galatians to **become like** him because he had become **like** them (4:12)—that is, he was like a Gentile who was under no obligation to keep the law. They, on the other hand, were headed in the other direction, placing themselves back under the law.

4:13-16 Paul reminds them of his first visit with them when he **preached the gospel to** them. Though he suffered from a **physical condition** and **a weakness of the flesh**, they did not **despise** him but embraced him just the same (4:13-14). They had **received** him as **an angel**, as even **Jesus himself** (4:14). They would have done anything for him (4:15). So, what had happened? Why were they now turning against him and the gospel? He had spoken **the truth** to them. Why were they now treating him like an **enemy**? (4:16).

4:17-20 The Judaizers had been working against Paul, undermining him. They courted the Galatians, flattering them and seeking to disconnect them from Paul's ministry (4:17). They had disgraceful motives. They were false teachers who didn't want what was best for the churches; they wanted the Galatian believers to revere and honor them. In contrast, Paul had honorable intentions toward the Galatians. He even compares himself to a mother in **labor**. He was **suffering** on their behalf, wanting to deliver them from false doctrine and see them transformed into the image of **Christ** (4:19). But this could only happen if they lived by faith, not by the law. Paul longed to be with them (4:20). His confusion, pain, and sorrow for them demonstrate the great love he had for those he brought to Christ. This group was trading the freedom of a relationship of love for the slavery of the law.

4:21-23 It was clear to Paul that many of the Galatians had been deceived and desired **to be under the law** (4:21). So he wanted to make sure that they understood what the law was all about. Paul uses two of Abraham's **sons** and their mothers to make his appeal. Ishmael was born to Hagar, **a slave**. Isaac was born to Sarah, **a free woman** (4:22). Though Ishmael was born by natural means, Isaac was born through supernatural intervention to a woman past her child-bearing years—as a result of God's **promise** (4:23).

4:24-27 Paul explains that he is treating the women **figuratively** in order to contrast law and grace. This contrast is reflected in **two covenants** (4:24). **Hagar represents** the Mosaic covenant given at **Mount Sinai**. The Jews who remain under this covenant are, like Hagar, slaves—slaves to the law (4:25). Such was the earthly Jerusalem. **But the Jerusalem above is free** (4:26)—that is, "the new Jerusalem," which will come "down out of heaven from God" one day (Rev 21:2). This city corresponds to Sarah, who represents God's covenant of promise with Abraham, which was fulfilled in Christ and his new covenant sacrifice. The children of this covenant are free children of grace. Paul then

quotes from Isaiah 54:1, which likened Israel in Babylonian exile to a **childless woman**. Just as Israel would be released from captivity and blessed with **numerous** children (Gal 4:27), so Sarah—a once barren woman—received a promised son and numerous descendants.

4:28-31 In the same way, the Galatian believers were **like Isaac**, Abraham's son, **children of promise** (4:28). They were the recipients of God's promise to justify the Gentiles through faith in Christ (3:8-9). They were children of grace, of freedom (4:31). But just as Ishmael **persecuted** Isaac (4:29; Gen 21:9), so the Judaizers who promoted law keeping in order to be made right or remain right with God were persecuting believers with their false teaching (Gal 4:29). In the same way that Sarah cast out the slave woman and her son for mocking Isaac (Gen 21:10), so too the Galatians should cast out the Judaizers for their legalism.

The legalist, who functions under the law, has no inheritance alongside the believer who is under grace. Law and grace cannot co-exist in the same house (or in the same church). Salvation and spiritual development cannot take place when these two are under the same roof. Followers of Christ are not to live under the law but to live under grace, responding to the love of God by faith through obedience. Paul further explains what this life looks like in chapter 5.

IV. FREEDOM TO LOVE, AND WALKING BY THE SPIRIT (5:1–6:10)

5:1 Sometimes people miss the obvious, so Paul sums things up for the Galatians: **For freedom, Christ set us free.** Why did Christ set them free? So that they could *be free*! Spiritual freedom is deliverance from the power and bondage of sin so that we can serve the living God as well as his people. It is freedom from legalism and the control of the flesh so that we can experience the substitutionary, resurrected life of Christ. It's living a "thank you" life and a "want to" life (relationship), rather than a "have to" life (law). But to submit to the law as the Judaizers were telling

them to do—to live by a legalistic mentality of trying to be justified and/or sanctified by obedience to the law—was to **submit** to **slavery** or to seek to prove their justification by their works.

Freedom allows and enables the believer to obey, not to gain acceptance, but because of the acceptance we already know we have in Christ through grace. We are to seek to please God and gain approval for our obedience because of our acceptance—not to earn it. Grace is accessed by faith to both motivate and empower our service (see Eph 2:8-10; 1 Cor 15:10).

5:2-4 The Judaizers tried to compel the Galatians to be **circumcised.** But Paul explains that you can't pick and choose which laws you want to obey. If they insisted on getting circumcised, they would be obligating themselves **to do the entire law** (5:2-3; see 3:10). To attempt to keep that would cut them off from experiencing the power of the substitutionary life of Christ in their lives (see 2:20; Rom 5:10). For believers to be **alienated from Christ** and to **have fallen from grace** is (5:4) not a reference to losing salvation. The phrase refers to ceasing to operate from a grace standard and adopting a works-based mentality rather than a relationship-driven one. Doing so leads to nothing but a life of slavery and spiritual defeat—a life lacking joy, love, true obedience, spiritual intimacy, and the power that only grace can provide.

5:5 As a result of the Judaizers' deceptive teaching, the Galatians were being taught to obtain their own righteousness through the law, which is really the work of the flesh. But Paul has insisted that justification only comes by faith in Christ (2:16). Moreover, it was **by faith** that Paul and his fellow believers **eagerly** awaited **the hope of righteousness**—that time when righteousness will flow throughout the earth during the millennial reign of Christ. The life to which God calls us is by faith from beginning to end (see Rom 1:17).

5:6 The Judaizers had told the Galatians that they needed to be circumcised. But Paul counters: **neither circumcision nor uncircumcision accomplishes anything.** Such adherence to the Mosaic law has no value in the Christian life. The law had served a function, but its time was past (see 3:19-26). For those who are **in Christ Jesus . . . what matters is faith working through love.**

Love for God and for others is both the outgrowth of faith and God's method for our sanctification. God's love for us brought us to faith in Christ. Thus, love is to be the motivation that compels us to minister to fellow believers and meet their needs. God is not looking for obedience through law keeping; he's looking for obedience motivated by love that naturally comes from faith.

5:7-9 The Galatians had been **running well** after Paul had preached the gospel to them, taught them, and ministered to them. But they had encountered opposition from those who were opposed to **the truth** (5:7). Paul was trying to help get them back on course so that they didn't lose any of their reward. The negative influence on them had not come from God (**the one who calls you**) but from Satan working through the false teachers (5:8). **A little leaven leavens the whole batch of dough** (5:9) implies that small things can have a huge impact. The believers in the Galatian churches may have outnumbered the Judaizing teachers, but it only took a few people pushing false doctrine to produce destructive results among the flock. Legalistic teaching was permeating churches and turning people from faith to law.

5:10 In spite of how bad things looked, Paul was optimistic that ultimately they would **not accept any other view** but the right one. He believed the truth would prevail: the Galatians would adopt God's view of justification and sanctification by grace, and the false teachers would **pay the penalty**—that is, they'd be judged.

5:11 Paul was being **persecuted** by Jews because he didn't preach the need to keep the law, illustrated through **circumcision.** The fact of his persecution demonstrated that he was truly preaching the cross. The message **of the cross**—that we are justified by faith alone in Christ's substitutionary sacrifice alone—is an **offense** or stumbling block to those who proudly insist on pleasing God through their own efforts. It is also the cross that is the basis and foundation for believers to live the victorious Christian life, since it has broken the power of Satan, sin, and the world.

5:12 Paul's intense anger at the Judaizers' attempt to undermine the gospel causes him to use graphic language: **I wish those who are disturbing you might also let themselves be mutilated.** Since the Judaizers wanted the Galatians to be circumcised, Paul wishes that the troublemakers would just go ahead and emasculate themselves. It's as if he's saying, "You think circumcision is important, do you? Well, why not go all the way and complete the operation?" Paul wanted to see their heresy cut off so that they could no longer win followers to their false religion. As sure as emasculation would make a man unable to reproduce physically, Paul wanted the Judaizers to be unable to reproduce spiritually.

5:13 Though the Judaizers were trying to keep the Galatians in bondage, Paul tells his **brothers and sisters** in the faith that they **were called to be free.** Of course, "freedom" can be a slippery word. Many people think it means having the freedom to do whatever you want. But biblical freedom is liberty from illegitimate bondage so that you can enjoy the responsibilities of a new relationship with God and fulfill your divinely ordained purpose. Thus, the Galatians (and we) are not to **use** our **freedom as an opportunity for the flesh.** Fulfilling the desires of the flesh, after all, is what got us into our messes in the first place! To be a slave of sin is to be chained to your own selfish desires. Christ came to free us from this.

Spiritual freedom is not the absence of boundaries. Suppose a football player catches the ball and wants to play the game without restrictions. He proceeds to run out of bounds and into the stands to avoid being tackled. Eventually, he re-enters the stadium and crosses into the end zone from the opposite direction. He's no longer playing football but creating chaos. Football can only be football, in fact, when played within the boundaries of sidelines.

What, then, does Christian freedom look like? **Serve one another through love.** Remember: biblical love is the decision to compassionately, righteously, and sacrificially seek the well-being of another. Just as Jesus loved us, we are to love one another. For by such love everyone will know that we are his disciples (see John 13:34-35). In this way, we make Christ look good. We also foster our vertical fellowship with God when we show love in our horizontal relationship with fellow believers: "the one who remains in love remains in God" (1 John 4:16). And let's not forget that the supreme act of *service* was rendered by Jesus Christ (see Mark 10:45);

this was also the supreme act of *love* (see John 3:16). Therefore, since the Son of God served *us* through love, why would his disciples expect to do anything less?

5:14-15 Paul tells these Christians who were being tempted to submit to the law that **the whole law is fulfilled** in what Jesus identified as the second great commandment: **Love your neighbor as yourself** (5:14; see Matt 22:35-40, quoting Lev 19:18). But if instead of neighbor love they chose self-love—if they chose to **bite and devour one another**— they were not to be surprised to find themselves **consumed by one another** (5:15).

When crabs are cooked, they're placed in a pot of water. As the water temperature within the pot starts to rise, the crabs attempt to climb out, only to discover that their fellow crabs pull them back in as they likewise attempt to escape. When church members assume an "every-man-for-himself" mindset rather than a "serve-through-love" mindset, they will claw and grab one another until all are roasted in the pot.

5:16 What's Paul's counsel for living in freedom, serving one another in love, and loving your neighbor as yourself (5:13-15)? What's the fundamental principle for spiritual victory, maximizing your spiritual life in Christ, and bringing the most benefit to other believers? **Walk by the Spirit** (i.e., pleasing God over pleasing self) **and you will certainly not carry out the desire of the flesh** (i.e., pleasing self independently of God). The flesh and the Spirit are two different spheres. Just as you can't turn fat into muscle in the human body, you cannot use the flesh to live spiritually.

When Scripture talks about our "walk," it's talking about the conduct of our lives. To "carry out the desire of the flesh" is to live life based on a sinful human viewpoint. To "walk by the Spirit" is to *discover* God's view on a matter, *decide* to act on that divine perspective, and *depend* on the Holy Spirit to empower your obedience. Notice that walking by the Spirit doesn't mean resting while the Spirit does all the work. We're not to be passive but active. We are called to *walk* while trusting in the Spirit's empowerment. It's much like walking on a moving sidewalk at the airport.

You are walking in dependence on a power at work underneath you.

It's also important to note that Paul does not say we won't have desires of the flesh. It's just that walking by the Spirit keeps us from yielding to those desires. Notice that you don't seek to address the sinful desires of the flesh first. You focus on walking by the Spirit first, and he overrides—not necessarily cancels—the desires of the flesh. To flip that order is either to lose the battle or to settle for flesh management rather than true spiritual transformation.

5:17-18 Paul observes that there's a civil war happening in every Christian, a battle between **the flesh** and **the Spirit**. At times we may think that the flesh and the Spirit can work together in our lives, but Paul reminds us that this is impossible: they **are opposed to each other** (5:17). The two ways of living are based on different perspectives, have different goals, and will lead to different outcomes. The good news for the Galatians (and us) is that those **led by the Spirit** are **not under the law** (5:18).

The life of faith is the life of walking by the Spirit. Since in the Greek text there is no article before "law," Paul is not only speaking of the law of Moses but the "law principle," which is seeking to use our own strength (the flesh) to have victory or to motivate God to do something. While the law principle may temporarily work to manage the impulses of the flesh, it ultimately dooms us to failure and frustration because of the gravitational pull of sin. The difference between law and grace is the difference between utilizing a battery that you must keep recharging versus being continually plugged-in to an electrical outlet. Being led by the Spirit is like following the lead of a dance partner. You are moving, but you do so in response to what the Spirit is doing.

It is also important to recognize that the flesh urges us to do things contrary to what we wish. This wishing comes from the Spirit's urging us to yield to him. Our prayer, when we are challenged by the flesh, must be, "Lord, I'm trusting you to enable me to do what you want me to do because I want to please you." The Spirit automatically leads us when we are walking according to his urges, and we no longer have to depend on legalistic rule keeping in the flesh. Rather, we are empowered by our relationship with the Holy Spirit.

5:19-21 In these verses, Paul explains what **the works of the flesh** look like (5:19) so that he can contrast them with "the fruit of the Spirit" (5:22-23). No one has to guess at what the works of the flesh might be. They're **obvious** and observable (5:19). They don't reside only in the mind but demonstrate themselves in human deeds. They include sexual sins (summarized by **sexual immorality**), superstitious sins (like **sorcery**), and social sins (like **hatreds ... jealousy ... selfish ambitions**) (5:19-21). Paul doesn't provide an exhaustive list. Instead, after mentioning all of these sinful works, he adds, **and anything similar** (5:21). The point is that such sins are the natural result of living according to the flesh and are evidence we are not walking in the Spirit. Such is not freedom (see 5:1, 13), but slavery. Believers living in the flesh will face the consequences of a loss of their kingdom inheritance ("reward"), both in this life and at the judgment seat of Christ (Col 3:24).

5:22-23 In contrast to the works of the flesh is **the fruit of the Spirit**. Works are something that you do, motivated by your *flesh*. But fruit is something produced through you by the Spirit as you respond to his urging (see John 7:38-39). The sources are different, and their outcomes are different. But just as the works of the flesh are visible to all, so also is the fruit of the Spirit. You can't miss it. And make no mistake: fruit always bears the character of the tree that produces it. Apple trees don't produce oranges. You don't display **love, joy, peace, patience, kindness, goodness, faithfulness, gentleness, and self-control** (5:22-23) in your life without the Holy Spirit.

While the works of the flesh destroy, the fruit of the Spirit provides life and refreshment. It benefits others. To *love* is to seek another person's good—especially when that person can do nothing for you in return. *Joy* is the settled celebration of the soul within us, even when circumstances don't make us happy. *Peace* results when strife gives way to harmony. To exercise *patience* is to be long-suffering instead of short-tempered. We demonstrate *kindness* when we help rather than hurt. *Goodness* summarizes the virtuous acts and attitudes that advance the kingdom of God and benefit others. The fruit of *faithfulness* brings constancy, perseverance, and dependability. *Gentleness* is seen in the one who practices tenderness in submission to God. When we say "no" to sin and "yes" to God in the midst of temptation, we exhibit *self-control*. The fruit of the Spirit is primarily manifested in our relationships.

5:24-25 The Spirit bears fruit in your life when you **keep in step with** him (5:25). The verb for "keep in step" is different from the word for "walk" in 5:16. It means to march in step with your commander so that he can lead you, step-by-step. Therefore, the Holy Spirit must be included in every move we make if we truly want him to lead us. Live based on the divine perspective of God's Word and pray for the Spirit's empowerment. The result will be victory over the flesh, the production of spiritual fruit (5:22-23), and service through love (5:13).

5:26 But **let us not become conceited**. Remember: as you submit to the Spirit, he bears fruit through you. You can't take credit for it. To become arrogant regarding spiritual fruit in your life is to forget its source, and it will serve as a quick way to end the Spirit's fruit production in you. The same is true of **envying** the fruit bearing of another. To "love your neighbor as yourself" (5:14) is to celebrate the goodness in the lives of our spiritual brothers and sisters, just as we would desire them to do for us. Thus, the fruit of the Spirit is to be visibly lived out in the context of the community of the local church.

6:1 In chapter 6, Paul continues his exhortation to the Galatians that they should love their neighbor (see 5:14). Their submission to the law as a result of the Judaizers' false teachings had promoted selfishness and strife (5:15, 26). Instead, they were to walk by the Spirit (5:16) so that they might bear the fruit of the Spirit (5:22-23). They were to cultivate their relationship with God by cultivating their relationship to one another.

Lone Ranger Christians who are disconnected from the body of Christ are not walking in the Spirit. The New Testament frequently urges Christians to practice the "one anothers"; for example, we are to "love one another" (John 15:12), "serve one another" (Gal 5:13), "forgive one another" (Eph 4:32), and "encourage one another" (1 Thess 5:11). Such concern for each other promotes harmony in the church and ensures God's work on our behalf.

Paul calls on Christian **brothers and sisters** to watch for a fellow believer who is **overtaken in any wrongdoing**—that is, caught in a sin from which he can't free himself. Paul urges those **who are spiritual** to **restore such a person**. The word translated "restore" is used of setting a bone to its former usefulness. Since **you** is plural, it refers to more than one person being part of the restoration process.

If you are trapped in something that doesn't please God, you need help from someone who can work on God's behalf. This is one of the reasons, in fact, why believers are to be united with a local church. If you need help, a faithful church is where you can find those "who are spiritual." Think about it. When you're sick, you don't want a quack doctor prescribing bad medicine. Likewise, if you are "overtaken in any wrongdoing," you need someone who can provide God's assessment of the problem according to his Word and counsel you with God's solution.

When you help a fellow Christian in trouble due to a sin from which they can't free themselves, you must do so **with a gentle spirit**. Gentleness doesn't mean soft-pedaling the diagnosis or the prescription. We're not to compromise the truth. Instead, we are to treat the person as we'd want to be treated—with patience, care, and kindness, restoring him or her with the least amount of pain possible. But be careful. Watch out that you aren't **tempted** as well. The tempter who wreaked havoc in your brother's life has his eye on you too.

6:2 To restore a sinning brother or sister is an example of carrying **one another's burdens**. But burdens don't necessarily imply sin. The burdens of life can include all sorts of weighty problems: physical, relational, financial, and emotional. Believers are to serve one another like spotters serving those who are lifting weights. When the strain of a burden becomes more than an individual can bear, a spotter helps lift the weight off of his chest. Carrying the burden of another can take an unlimited number of forms, including prayer, making time for a person, providing practical assistance, giving financial assistance, and providing a listening ear. Such burden bearing **will fulfill the law of Christ**, the law of love (5:13-14; see John 13:34).

6:3-4 Any Christian who considers himself above the responsibility to serve others in this way is thinking too highly of himself. He **considers himself to be something when he is nothing** (6:3). He's self-deceived. No one is too good to serve and carry burdens. After all, the Lord Jesus served his disciples by washing their feet (see John 13:2-15). If the Master didn't consider himself above service, how can we? He gave us an example of how we ought to treat one another, so let us not **compare** ourselves with **someone else** (6:4). The only one to whom you should compare yourself is Jesus. Do that, and you'll never think more of yourself than you ought.

6:5 Though we are called to "carry one another's burdens" (6:2), Paul reminds believers that **each person will have to carry his own load.** Everyone needs help with his burdens from time to time, but this gives no one the right to absolve himself of responsibilities and shift them completely to others. Feeding those who are in need is commanded and expected. But, as Paul told the Thessalonians, "If anyone isn't willing to work, he should not eat" (2 Thess 3:10). Helping with burdens doesn't mean carrying someone's full load for them so that they are alleviated of all responsibility. Each must be willing to carry his own backpack.

6:6 Let the one who is taught the word share all his good things with the teacher. Paul places a high value on spiritual ministry because he knows that internalizing the Word of God is what makes a person "spiritual." Such a person is then able to "restore" someone "overtaken in any wrongdoing"

(6:1). It's right and good to invest materially in that which brings you spiritual life and growth. Reciprocity in ministry keeps believers from becoming selfish and self-centered.

6:7 God has established certain laws that govern the universe he has made. This is true in the physical world (e.g., the law of gravity). But it's true of the spiritual world as well. Paul articulates an important spiritual law or principle when he says, **Whatever a person sows he will also reap.** A farmer harvests exactly what he plants. If he sows potatoes, he won't be looking to harvest green beans. Decide what you want to harvest spiritually, and let that control what you decide to sow.

This law is universal (it applies to all people everywhere) and inviolable (it proves true without fail). Therefore, Paul warns, **Don't be deceived: God is not mocked.** We mustn't dupe ourselves into thinking that we can embrace sin without effect. Don't kid yourself into believing that you can rebel against God without consequence.

6:8-9 There are only two places where you can sow or invest spiritually: the flesh and the Spirit. **The one who sows to his flesh** (i.e., pleasing self over pleasing God) **will reap destruction from the flesh.** To sow to the flesh is to perform "the works of the flesh" that Paul has identified (5:19-21). Sooner or later, it will bring a harvest of destruction. **But the one who sows to the Spirit** (i.e., pleasing God over pleasing self)—walking by the Spirit (5:16) and bearing the fruit of the Spirit (5:22-23)—**will reap eternal life from the Spirit**, which is a reference to a higher quality of spiritual fulfillment and victory. The one who sows to the Spirit is living to please God. We must not grow weary of **doing good.** So be patient. **At the proper time**, the harvest will come. Keep sowing. Remember that there's an appropriate seasonal time gap for the purpose of development between sowing and reaping.

6:10 Therefore, Paul tells the Galatians, let's do **good** while **we have opportunity.** While we wait for our time of reaping, we are to sow in the Spirit by busily doing good works that benefit others in God's name. As he told the Ephesians, pay attention to how you live, "making the most of the time" (Eph 5:15-16). Don't throw in the towel. Reward is coming! So do good to everyone, but **especially . . .** **to the household of faith.** We are called to show love to all people, but we are to have a special love for the people of God.

V. CONCLUSION: ONLY THE CROSS (6:11-18)

6:11 Paul mentions his **own handwriting** here. It's possible that he may have used an amanuensis, a secretary, to write his letter (see Rom 16:22), before taking up the pen himself to write these final words. Regardless, Paul calls attention to the **large letters** he uses here to add emphasis to his argument as he concludes. Sometimes we use bold type, italics, or all capital letters for emphasis. This was the apostle's way of saying, "Don't miss what I'm telling you!"

6:12-13 Paul has argued strongly throughout the letter that the law cannot be added to the gospel. To do so results in "a different gospel" (1:6), which is really no gospel at all. The message of the Judaizers was false. Yet not only was their message corrupt, their motives were corrupt too. Paul already said that they wanted the Galatians to honor them (4:17). Now he adds that they pushed circumcision **to avoid being persecuted for the cross of Christ** (6:12). They were unwilling to accept the "stumbling block" of the cross (1 Cor 1:23). They knew it would lead to persecution from fellow Jews, so they adopted a false gospel instead. The Judaizers were also motivated by a desire **to boast about** the Galatians—that is, to boast in the fact that they had convinced them to become **circumcised** (Gal 6:13). Thus returning them to life under the law and removing them from life under grace.

6:14 Whatever the Judaizers boasted in, Paul wants everyone to know that he **will never boast about anything except the cross.** The atoning work of Jesus Christ is the only thing the apostle will brag about. Why? Because through the cross, **the world has been crucified** to Paul. The "world" is part of the "present evil age" from which Christ rescues us (1:4). Because of Jesus's work on our

behalf, the world no longer dictated how Paul lived his life; nor should it dictate to you. Paul also notes that he has been crucified **to the world.** He has been "crucified with Christ" so that he is united to and fully identified with the Son of God who loves him (2:19-20). Our lives should identify more with our Savior than with the world that is opposed to him. When the cross becomes our claim to fame, we will find ourselves fulfilling the law by the Spirit and not attempting to do so by the works of the flesh.

6:15-16 Neither **circumcision** nor **uncircumcision** means anything (6:15). Christianity is not about a set of rules (i.e., legalism) but about a growing dynamic relationship with the living God. As Paul said earlier, "There is no Jew or Greek" (3:28)—not that these distinctions don't exist but that they don't matter before God. Being made **a new creation** is what matters (6:15). "If anyone is in Christ, he is a new creation" (2 Cor 5:17). Your relationship with Christ is the most important thing about you. Those who recognize this and live according to **this standard** will experience God's **peace** and **mercy** (6:16) because they will be focusing on that which gets God's greatest attention.

6:17-18 Before Paul concludes with a blessing of **grace** (6:18), the theme of this letter, he offers a stern warning: **let no one** (especially the Judaizers!) **cause me trouble, because I bear on my body the marks of Jesus** (6:17). These "marks of Jesus" are probably visible wounds and scars that Paul carried with him as a result of his gospel ministry (see Acts 14:19; 16:22-23; 2 Cor 6:4-5; 11:23-25). Though the Judaizers preached a false gospel to avoid persecution (6:12), Paul embraced persecution for the sake of the true gospel.

EPHESIANS

INTRODUCTION

Author

THE AUTHOR OF EPHESIANS twice identifies himself as Paul (1:1; 3:1), and the early church accepted the book as being written by the apostle. Some scholars think the writing style, vocabulary, and even some teachings of the letter are not typical of Paul, but the objections are exaggerated. Furthermore, the evidence we have from the early church indicates that early Christians rejected letters known to be pseudonymous (falsely written under someone else's name). So there is no good reason to dispute that Paul authored Ephesians.

Historical Background

Paul stayed at Ephesus, the capital city of the province of Asia, for almost three years (see Acts 20:31)—probably from AD 51–54 or 52–55. He subsequently penned this letter while in prison (3:1; 4:1; 6:20). Disagreement exists concerning whether Paul wrote Ephesians while imprisoned in Caesarea (Acts 23:23, 33-35; 24:22-23, 27) around 57–59 or while held in Rome (Acts 28:30) in about 60–62, but Christian tradition suggests that Paul wrote Ephesians from Rome around 60–61. Paul was under house arrest in guarded rental quarters (Acts 28:30). He most likely wrote Colossians, Philemon, and Philippians during the same imprisonment.

Little is known about the Christian recipients of the letter. It was carried to its destination by Tychicus, who in Ephesians 6:21 and Colossians 4:7 is identified as Paul's emissary. The Ephesian and Colossian letters probably were delivered at the same time since the apostle noted in both that Tychicus would inform the churches concerning Paul's situation.

Message and Purpose

Central to the message of Ephesians is the re-creation of the human family according to God's original kingdom intention for mankind. Jews and Gentiles are brought together in Christ as one people. For those who trust in Jesus, the distinction between Jew and Gentile is abolished by his sacrificial death. No more hindrance remains to reuniting all humanity as the people of God with Christ as the head (1:22-23). The new body, the church, has been endowed by the power of the Holy Spirit to enable those comprising it to serve together in unity (1:3–2:10), to live new lives of faith and maturity for the fulfillment of God's kingdom program (4:1–6:9), and to access the spiritual blessings they have as those who are seated with Christ in the heavens (1:3, 20; 2:6).

Outline

EPHESIANS

I. GREETINGS (1:1-2)

1:1-2 In this letter magnifying God's grace, the apostle Paul appropriately greets the **faithful saints in Christ Jesus at Ephesus** with his trademark salutation: **Grace to you.**

II. EVERY SPIRITUAL BLESSING IN THE HEAVENLY PLACES (1:3-14)

1:3 Paul writes verses 3-12 as one long sentence in Greek (in English we'd call it a run-on sentence), and it's all about what believers possess because of the cross of Christ. He begins in verse 3 with worship: **Blessed is the God and Father of our Lord Jesus Christ.** To bless the name of God is to speak well of him, to praise him. *Worship* is the celebration of who God is, what he has done, and what we trust him to do. God is not interested in spectators. He invites you to praise him.

Why? Because, **in Christ**, he **has blessed us with every spiritual blessing in the heavens**— or we could translate it "heavenly places" (see 1:20; 2:6; 3:10; 6:12). What are heavenly places? This is a reference to the spiritual realm where God and Satan battle for our allegiance. We live in the physical realm with our problems, needs, struggles, and sins. But whatever happens in the physical realm originates in the spiritual realm. Conflict in our homes, then, is a spiritual problem. Although conflict is visible fruit, its root is spiritual in nature. Thus, we need a spiritual solution to our circumstances. That's why we must live with a spiritual worldview.

Paul says God has already done everything he is ever going to do for believers. He's

blessed them with **every spiritual blessing** in the heavenly places. And, as Paul will soon say, believers are "seated" there with Jesus (2:6). Think of this like a video teleconference in which you're in two places at once— seated physically in one place but operating in another. Believers are present in two places at the same time: we're physically located on earth but operate from heavenly places. God wants our position there to dictate our activity on earth. Only by operating from a spiritual perspective will you have access to God's kingdom power and provisions to deal victoriously with life in the physical realm.

1:4 Spiritual blessings are accessible because God **chose us**, drafted us, **before the foundation of the world, to be holy and blameless.** *Sinning* is failing to give God glory, attempting to make God revolve around us when we're supposed to be revolving around him. It's approaching things wrongly, like those who once thought the earth was the center of the solar system. But God created us for himself, for *his* happiness. He's chosen us "to be holy and blameless" so that the church will bring *him* pleasure. When we pursue his pleasure, we position ourselves to experience the blessings of God, which have already been preordained for us.

1:5-6 We can do this because **he predestined us to be adopted as sons through Jesus Christ** (1:5). Paul thus introduces us to the mysterious doctrine of election. God has predestined to save a people who will be trophies of his grace. Those who believe the gospel are chosen "in him" (1:4). Paul uses the phrase "in him," "in Christ," or "in the Beloved One" throughout the passage (1:3-4, 6-7, 9-10, 12-13). So God's election isn't abstract; it's centered in the person and work of Jesus.

The focus of the book of Ephesians is on the corporate church, not on individual Christian salvation (see 1:22-23; 2:14, 16, 22; 3:10, 21; 4:16; 5:32). Therefore, the choosing and election to which Paul refers is not for individuals to eternal life but regards God's choice to establish a group of people (that is, the body of Christ) **in the Beloved One** (1:5-6) whose purpose is to live godly lives and reflect his holy character in a sinful world. This election defines the corporate identity believers share because of their relationship to Christ (as in the case with Israel; see Rom 9:3-5). This is similar to family members sharing in the medical insurance benefits of the head of the household.

Those no longer "in Adam" but "in Christ" are predestined to be adopted by God. To be adopted in the ancient world meant receiving the same rights, privileges, and inheritance due to a natural-born adult son. In Christ, God adopts sons and daughters for himself for a specific purpose. Once you're adopted because of your faith in Christ, you are defined by your new Father. God gives all of his children access to every spiritual blessing—according to his **good pleasure** and **to the praise of his glorious grace** (1:5-6). So God predetermined to bring a group of people into his family, drafting them into his Son for the goal of receiving spiritual benefits and manifesting his heavenly rule in their lives and bringing him glory. Election is for service and spiritual benefit, not for individual, personal salvation.

1:7-8 For this to happen, God redeemed us from sin (1:7). In the ancient world, slaves could be redeemed, a price could be paid for their freedom. Redemption from sin comes through the price paid by Jesus Christ **through his blood** (1:7). Why blood? Because the judgment for sin is death (Rom 6:23), and shedding blood means taking life (see Deut 12:23). The sinless Son of God had to die to pay for our sins so we might have **forgiveness** (Eph 1:7)—God's grace **richly poured out on us** (1:8).

1:9-12 But God doesn't save people just so they can go to heaven when they die. He saves them so they transfer kingdoms—leaving the kingdom of darkness for the kingdom of Christ, their new King. Through God's "wisdom and understanding," he has planned **to bring everything together in Christ** (1:8-10), to bring all history under his rule. In Christ, **things in heaven and things on earth** are unified (1:10) so that we might be aligned under God's kingdom reign, living transformed lives for his pleasure. God works out everything in agreement with his purpose and will (1:11) to advance this Christ-centered philosophy of history. Nothing is left to chance. All is for the praise of his glory and the exaltation of his Son (1:12).

1:13-14 Whoever hears and believes the gospel of salvation in Jesus Christ is **sealed with the promised Holy Spirit** (1:13). Official documents were sealed in antiquity, implying protection and ownership. When you believe in Christ as your Savior, God puts you inside an envelope called Christ. You are "in Christ." But God also guarantees delivery. He registers the letter and seals it with the Holy Spirit—indicating that he is its owner and the only one qualified to open it.

Paul also says the Holy Spirit is God's pledge to us—**the down payment of our inheritance** (1:14), the guarantee that God will do for us everything he promised for his children. Like an engagement ring, the Holy Spirit is like a down payment on an eternal commitment. The Spirit is a heavenly first installment given in anticipation of eternal life, a life that is eternally secure. He's a foretaste of what's ahead.

III. UNDERSTANDING YOUR SPIRITUAL RESOURCES (1:15-23)

1:15-16 In the middle of Paul's excitement about what the Ephesians have through the cross of Christ, he tells them he has never stopped thanking God for them. Then he tells them the content of his prayer.

1:17 First, he prays God would give them **wisdom**. *Wisdom* is effectively applying divine truth to the twists, turns, and dangers of everyday life. But Paul correlates the ability to be wise with the **knowledge of** God. Knowing God and being wise are tied together. Trying to be wise without knowing God is like flying a plane without having a control tower to help you navigate. We all need the help of someone who can see what we can't.

1:18 Paul also prays that **the eyes of [their] heart may be enlightened so** they **may know what is the hope of [their] calling** and **what is the wealth of [God's] glorious inheritance.** When you are adopted into God's family, your life has a customized purpose. God himself has called you. Not only that, but you're also spiritually wealthy. There are no spiritually poor people in God's family. "Every spiritual blessing" (1:3) is banked in a deposit box with your name on it.

Because I'm a platinum flyer for an airline, I was given a booklet explaining the privileges of membership. But for a long time, I never read it. When I finally did, I found that I had privileges available to me that could make my life and travel much more convenient. A lack of awareness about what's available to those in the family of God similarly causes people to miss out, so Paul wants the Ephesians to be aware of their family privileges. Knowing who their Daddy is has *staggering* implications.

Many Christians are living spiritually poor lives, while sitting on a pile of spiritual wealth. While God holds most of your spiritual inheritance for eternity, he will give you what you need now to fulfill his purpose for you.

1:19 Finally, Paul prays the Ephesians would understand **what is the immeasurable**

greatness of his power toward us who believe. Notice he didn't say he wants them to know God's power—but the *immeasurable greatness* of his power. He wants them to know that God can flip, turn, and twist things in their lives. You're not supposed to be an average human being. If you're a believer in Jesus, you're a candidate to see the working of God's immeasurably great power in your life.

1:20-23 What does this power look like? It's the power God exercised in Christ **by raising him from the dead and seating him at his right hand in the heavens ... [subjecting] everything under his feet** (1:20-22). So, if your circumstances are bad, remember that God's immeasurably great power raised Jesus from the dead. You don't get worse circumstances than that! And that same resurrection power is available to you. Through your connection to Jesus, God can invade the circumstances of your life and demonstrate his sufficiency.

Jesus is now seated **above every ruler and authority, power and dominion** (1:21). You know someone who sits in "heavenly places" in the seat of highest authority, and you're seated right there with him (2:6)! Whatever you're dealing with, then, doesn't have final say; it doesn't have to define your life. Moreover, Christ has the right to override—veto—your decisions. Only if you align your life under his rule will you see his agenda demonstrated in your circumstances.

God the Father has appointed his Son **as head over everything for the church, which is his body.** Jesus Christ, the one who has dominion over all things (kingdom authority), has only been given to the church. So only the church, operating under Christ's kingdom authority (i.e., headship), can give the world a picture of what life under God's kingdom authority looks like. And as the church does this, Christ **fills** it with his powerful presence (1:22-23). The more the church fulfills Christ's kingdom mission, the more the church will experience his presence and power as it infiltrates every area of society as his kingdom representative.

IV. SAVED TO SERVE (2:1-10)

When displaying diamonds, a jeweler places them against a black cloth because diamonds shine more brilliantly against a dark backdrop. Before he describes God's grace, Paul wants the Ephesian Christians to know how dark things were without it. Paul thus places the diamond of grace against the backdrop of sin so that grace will glitter even more.

2:1-3 He begins with a coroner's report. Every person outside of Jesus Christ is spiritually **dead**—separated from God—and the name of the graveyard is **trespasses and sins** (2:1). In verses 2-3, Paul describes the three locks on the coffins that keep people there: the world (**the ways of this world**), the devil (**the ruler of the power of the air**), and the flesh (**our fleshly desires**). Our situation in that cemetery was so grim that there was no way we could create or find a way of escape. We were **children under wrath** (2:3)—subjects of Satan's kingdom and under God's judgment.

Being in Satan's kingdom is like being the living dead. In it, we had mobility, but no life—that is, no spiritual life. Indeed, those who are spiritually dead are unable to respond to spiritual stimuli. There is no capacity to relate to the spiritual realm. So while outside of Christ, you may have been pretty, educated, and rich, you were alienated from the life of God. No clever arrangement of bad eggs can result in a good omelet.

2:4 Then Paul introduces two words that change everything: **but God**. They remind us that salvation came at God's initiative. And why did he act? Because he **is rich in mercy** and **because of his great love that he had for us**. The reason God shows grace is because of how much he loves us. Motivated by love, he extends grace. And that's the gospel message.

2:5 What did God do? He **made us alive with Christ**; he gave us spiritual life. When you are dead, only a resurrection can help

you. God thus intervened at our gravesites and resurrected our corpses. Against the dark backdrop of death is the glory of resurrection life. **You are saved by grace!** *Grace* is the unmerited favor of God. It is the inexhaustible supply of God's goodness, based on the work of Christ, whereby he does for us what we do not deserve, could never earn, and would never be able to repay.

2:6 But that's not all. When God saved you, he relocated you: **He . . . raised us up with him and seated us with him in the heavens.** Paul said previously that Jesus was seated in the heavenly places with resurrection power and dominion (1:20-21). Now he says God relocated us there too **in Christ Jesus.** Believers are participants with Christ in this spiritual reality. We are linked with him, in union with him. This is how you have access to your spiritual privileges—to "every spiritual blessing" (1:3)—that God has placed in your account.

2:7 It is grace that makes Christianity different from every other religion. Other religions tell you what you must do to get to God. Christianity tells you what God has done to get to you. For all eternity God will **display the immeasurable riches of his grace through his kindness to us in Christ Jesus.** Or, to put it another way, you haven't seen anything yet! Eternity with God will be a nonstop, never-ending, blow-your-mind experience.

2:8-9 This grace is only available **through faith** (2:8). If grace is what God deposited for you, faith is the way you make a withdrawal. It is the means of withdrawing God's grace so that it is made manifest in history. Grace is **God's gift** (2:8)—received, not earned (see Rom 4:4-5; 11:6). It doesn't come by means of **works, so that no one can boast** (2:9). In other words, there will be no strutting like peacocks in heaven. You will only be able to brag about the magnificent grace of God. **You are saved by grace** (2:8).

2:10 Although you're not saved *by* good works, you are saved *for* good works. **We are his workmanship**, Paul says, **created in Christ Jesus for good works**. When it comes to your salvation, God is crafting your life into a piece of art. He is working on you and doing something with you. You are being re-created to do good works. A *good work* is a divinely prescribed action that benefits others in such a way that God is glorified (see Matt 5:16).

God saved you for his purposes and pleasure. Many Christians are unfulfilled and miserable because they've never gotten around to the work God has for them. When you understand the grace with which God saved you, gratitude will drive your response to it. The purpose for your life has already been designed. You don't have to come up with it. **God prepared ahead of time for us** to do good works. He will give you the desire for them and the ability to pull them off, but you must live them out. Remember, the canvas does not dictate to the painter; the painter dictates to the canvas.

V. HEAVEN'S NEW COMMUNITY: ONE NEW MAN (2:11-22)

The cross of Christ not only deals with our separation from God, but it also deals with our separation from one another. We are saved by grace "for good works" (2:10). And those works are to be lived out in the Christian dynamic called the church—heaven's kingdom community. Having discussed grace, Paul now discusses race.

2:11-12 He reminds the Ephesians of their prior separation from the people of God. The Gentiles were **called "the uncircumcised"** by Jews—**those called "the circumcised"** (2:11). They had no access to the Jewish **covenants of promise**. They were **without Christ . . . without hope . . . without God in the world** (2:12). Their sin had separated them from their Creator.

2:13-16 But . . . **in Christ Jesus** they have been drawn close. **The blood of Christ** not only brings people **near** to God, it brings Jews and Gentiles near to one another (2:13). Christ's atoning death **tore down the dividing wall of hostility**. A wall in the Jerusalem temple prevented Gentiles from entering, but the cross removes such barriers, granting Jews and Gentiles equal access to God. Jesus **made both groups one** (2:14). Why? **So that he might create in himself one new man from the two** (2:15). This new group—this "one new man"—that incorporates Jews and Gentiles is called the church. Heaven's new community is a new race, reconciled **to God in one body through the cross** (2:16).

2:17 The reason we have racial, ethnic, gender, and class divisions in the church is because we have not fully and properly understood the cross. Christians divided along illegitimate lines don't see themselves as part of the one new man. All barriers based on factors such as race and gender are obliterated by the cross. This doesn't mean these distinctions don't exist; instead, these legitimate distinctions are absorbed into something bigger. In terms of spiritual relationship and development, a white man has no advantage over a black man. A man has no spiritual advantage over a woman. We can embrace our differences with a common commitment to Christ because we are at peace with one another through our peace with God. We live in **the good news of peace**.

If you do not see yourself belonging to this new race, this one new man, you will follow the world's agenda. You will say things like, "Races don't mix, just like oil and water don't mix." But, you see, there is an exception. When you add an emulsifier, it allows two liquids to mix that normally don't. The atoning death of Jesus is God's emulsifier to bring into harmony those who wouldn't otherwise mix. In the midst of hostility, Jesus not only brings peace, **he is our peace** (2:14).

2:18-19 Through Christ we have unity. Not uniformity. We're not all the same. *Unity* is uniqueness working toward a common goal. This is possible because all Christians have access in one Spirit to the Father (2:18). Christian unity, then, is a spiritual issue. Where the Spirit is working, there is oneness. If there is disharmony and division for illegitimate criteria, the Spirit is not at work. Believers are **no longer foreigners and strangers** but have been made **fellow citizens** and **members of God's household** (2:19). The church is a family.

2:20-22 Paul's final illustration of unity is a building. The church is **built on the foundation of the apostles and prophets.** They laid the foundation by recording and proclaiming the Word of God. And this building has **Christ Jesus himself as the cornerstone** (2:20). When a building is constructed, its stones must be placed in alignment with the cornerstone. So, as God's building, we Christians must be in alignment with Christ. Every one of us must be properly positioned. After all, **in him the whole building . . . grows into a holy temple in the Lord** (2:21).

In the Old Testament, the glory of God was manifested in the temple. It was where God hung out. Today he's in the new temple, the church. Together we believers are the temple of God, **God's dwelling in the Spirit** (2:22), meant to display God's glory. But that glory isn't on display when we are not aligned with Christ.

God wants us to have a complete view of the cross. The cross that gets you to heaven is the same cross that led to the creation of something new on earth: the church, heaven's community, a new race of people. The church is united in Jesus Christ in spite of believers' individual differences. We are to practice the "one anothers" of Scripture (e.g., John 15:12; Gal 6:2; Eph 4:32; 1 Thess 5:11), developing spiritual relationships and growing spiritually together. The church is more than a corporate gathering on Sunday because when that corporate gathering is over, we as the church still march on.

VI. THE MULTIFACETED WISDOM OF GOD ON DISPLAY (3:1-13)

3:1 Paul begins to explain the application of what he has discussed in chapter 2. **For this reason**, he says. But then he pauses. It dawns on him that he hasn't milked his subject yet. He has more to say. In verse 14, he'll pick up where he left off when he repeats, "for this reason." Before that, though, verses 2-13 function as if in parenthesis. Paul is overwhelmed by this thing called the family of God made up of people from every background and every race. Before he discusses how spiritually rich believers are (3:14-21), he wants to make sure they know who they are (3:2-13).

3:2-6 Paul had been given **the administration of God's grace** (3:2). God gave Paul a stewardship, something to manage. Here that grace that God gave Paul for the Gentiles is called **the mystery of Christ**, which God had made known to Paul **by revelation** (3:3-4). This "mystery" is a sacred secret that was not understood previously but was made known to God's **holy apostles and prophets by the**

Spirit (3:5). The content of the mystery is this: **The Gentiles are coheirs, members of the same body, and partners in the promise in Christ Jesus through the gospel** (3:6).

God broke down the division between Jews and Gentiles, ending years of hostility. Through the gospel, both have been brought into one body of Christ, reconciled to one another. They are fellow partakers of grace, on equal footing before God. If you've been brought into God's family through the blood of Christ, the color of your skin doesn't matter. Regardless of your race, you get the same spiritual DNA given to every other believer planted within you by the Spirit as soon as you are born into the family of God. We have the same Father and sit at the same table. Once you come into the body of Christ, you come as an equal. There are no insignificant people in God's army.

3:7-8 Paul **was made a servant of this gospel** by **God's grace** and through **the working of his power** (2:7). That grace and power were so mighty that Paul, the former confident Pharisee (see Phil 3:4-6), considered himself **the least of all the saints** (Eph 3:8). When Mr. Big Stuff met Jesus, he shrunk in size. Here Paul calls himself a **prisoner of Christ Jesus** (3:1). But though writing from prison, Paul knows he is no prisoner of man. When you're in the will of God, the negative circumstances of your life happen with God's purposes in mind. And God's purpose was that "the least" of the saints would proclaim **the incalculable riches of Christ** (3:8).

3:9-10 These incalculable riches are made known as Paul exposes **the mystery hidden for ages in God** (3:9). Why reveal this mystery? **So that God's multi-faceted wisdom may now be made known through the church to the rulers and authorities in the heavens** (3:10). God's glorious wisdom is multicolored, multidimensional. And through the church, it's on display to the spiritual world order—for the beings in the heavenly places (and their human counterparts).

The church is like a prism displaying the rich colors of God's manifold wisdom. It's a microcosm of the kingdom, an expression in history of the glory of eternity. God is teaching the angelic realm—both good angels and demons, as well as their human representatives—his wisdom as he brings together

sinners from every tribe, tongue, and nation into one heavenly community called the church. And no doubt the righteous angels stare at this in wonder (see 1 Pet 1:12), awaiting instructions on what heaven wants done in history through the church.

3:11-13 This **eternal purpose** of God has been **accomplished in Christ** so that **in him we have boldness and confident access through faith in him** (Eph 3:11-12). You can't do that with human leaders. You can't stroll into the office of the President of the United States, but through Jesus Christ, all believers can boldly and confidently come into the presence of God the Father—the Creator and sustainer of the universe. Thus, the Ephesians ought not be **discouraged**. Paul's **afflictions** on their behalf are for their **glory** (3:13).

God is demonstrating the beauty of his program. He is stitching people from every race, every gender, and every ethnicity together into a beautiful work of art. The church, that masterpiece, is to demonstrate to the spiritual world and the physical world what God's kingdom looks like. It is a demonstration to the angelic realm of God's manifold wisdom. It is a demonstration to Satan of God's victory and Satan's defeat. It is a demonstration to the world of what it looks like when heavenly values operate in history.

VII. EXPERIENCING SPIRITUAL POWER (3:14-21)

These verses contain one of the greatest prayers in the New Testament. Now that Paul has explained the glorious reality of the body of Christ, he wants the Ephesians to be able to access the spiritual power available to them. So that's what he prays for.

3:14-15 Paul kneels before God the Father **from whom every family in heaven and on earth is named.** In doing so, he returns to the idea of family. Jews and Gentiles who believe in Christ are both part of "God's household" (2:18-19). Brothers and sisters in Christ bear the same family name and have equal access to the Father.

3:16 First, Paul prays for God to grant them **to be strengthened with power** in their **inner being through his Spirit.** He wants the Ephesians to have increased spiritual strength, and this is based on the internal work of the Holy Spirit. What you need primarily is not a change in your situation. You need an internal change. When my cell phone is out of power, no external alterations will make a difference. The problem is an uncharged battery. We need the internal strength that only the Spirit can provide.

3:17-19 Increased spiritual strength requires increased spiritual intimacy. Paul prays **that**

Christ may dwell in . . . hearts through faith (3:17). He's not talking about salvation; he's writing to Christians. The Greek word for "dwell" means to make yourself at home. That's what we tell people to do when they come to visit. Nevertheless, we don't mean that we want them roaming the entire house and rummaging through our closets. But if you want spiritual power, Jesus must be free to be fully at home in your heart. He must have access to every room. He wants to clean and straighten out the messy closets that you're hiding. If you want to realize all that God has for you, Christ must be Lord of your heart.

Next Paul prays they may be **rooted and firmly established in love** (3:17). He wants them to be like plants with deep roots, like a building with a solid foundation. He wants their love for others to go deep, so they **may be able to comprehend with all the saints what is the length and width, height and depth of God's love, and to know Christ's love that surpasses knowledge, so that [they] may be filled with all the fullness of God** (3:18-19). Paul wants them to have increased comprehension, increased understanding of God's love. But they can't comprehend it without "all the saints." Your individual experiences of God are limited. You need to be a part of the family of God and learn how God works in the lives of others to see how truly great he is.

Did you notice what Paul wants them to comprehend? This will blow your mind. He wants them to know "the length and width, height and depth" (3:18) of the love of God in Jesus Christ—a "love that surpasses knowledge" (3:19) That means he wants them to know something that is beyond their capacity to grasp! Even when you've been in God's presence for one hundred quadrillion years, you will have just been introduced to him. Those will be your introductory years. Because the God of the Bible is inexhaustible. There is no end to knowing God and the "great love that he [has] for us" (2:4).

Paul wants them to experience the reality of Christ, of God's working in their lives, which has no limits. He prays they will have an increased spiritual capacity, so they **may**

be filled with all the fullness of God (3:19). If you dip a thimble into the Pacific Ocean, you'll get a thimble's worth of ocean. That's it. Your container is at full capacity. While many Christians want a tanker full of blessing, they only have a thimble full of relationship with the Lord. Understand that God wants your spiritual capacity increased so you can comprehend God's love with other believers and be filled to capacity with his fullness. God will only give us as much of himself as we can handle. He will not waste the manifestation of his glory on vessels unprepared to handle it.

3:20 Paul concludes this prayer by pointing to the God **who is able to do above and beyond all that we ask or think.** What does Scripture say God is able to do? He is able to rescue from a fiery furnace (see Dan 3:17). He is able to deliver from lions' mouths (see Dan 6:20-22). He is able to give sight to the blind (see Matt 9:28-30). He is able to keep you from stumbling (see Jude 24). He is able to save completely (see Heb 7:25). He is able "to make every grace overflow to you" (2 Cor 9:8). He is able to do above and beyond all that you can ask or think.

God can work exceedingly abundantly beyond our wildest dreams. But it is **according to the power that works in us.** God's power works in accordance with a believer's spiritual strength, intimacy, and capacity—everything for which Paul prays an increase.

A fire hydrant is small, but it can gush water in volume and force that is out of proportion to its size. That's because the water isn't in the hydrant. The hydrant is connected to a reservoir that is always full. When the church is in sync with Jesus Christ, it has a connection to a reservoir that is always overflowing. When God's people's internal connection to him is tight, they will gush out the power of God in and through their lives individually and collectively.

3:21 To him be glory in the church and in Christ Jesus to all generations, forever. The greatest manifestation of God's glory is through the church, which is why it is absolutely critical for every believer to be an active part of a solid church family.

VIII. UNITY AND MATURITY IN THE BODY OF CHRIST (4:1-16)

4:1-2 Paul begins the second half of his letter with the word **therefore**. In light of the gracious riches they have in Christ and the glorious reality of this new community called the church, there are now accompanying responsibilities.

He urges them **to live worthy of [their] calling** (4:1). They must conduct themselves in a way that reflects their new status. There must be **humility and gentleness**—a willingness to submit to the lordship of Jesus Christ—among them. They must have **patience, bearing with one another in love** (4:2), showing tolerance for others and seeking their well-being.

4:3 By living this way, they will be able **to keep the unity of the Spirit**. Again, unity is not sameness. We Christians maintain our God-created uniqueness but share a common vision and goal. A football team includes players with different roles, but teammates work together for the same purpose.

Notice Paul commands them to "keep" this unity, not to "establish" it. This is God's program. The church didn't create the unity. God calls us to preserve what he's already created (see 2:11-22). This unity is tied to our Christian character (4:2) and is based on the work of the Holy Spirit. If your point of reference isn't the Spirit of God, you'll be operating from a merely human point of view. But when you relate to people based on God's point of view, the Spirit can override human differences and hold us together **through the bond of peace**. Peace—harmony where once there was conflict—will act like a belt to hold us together.

4:4-6 The operative word, Paul says, is "one." **There is one body and one Spirit . . . one hope . . . one Lord, one faith, one baptism, one God and Father**. The church is one body, united by one Spirit, called to one hope, worshiping one Lord, trusting with one faith, identified by one baptism, submitting to one God and Father. When we fail to keep the unity of the Spirit, we deny our oneness.

Cancer is a dreaded disease in which cells no longer want to unify with the body as a whole. Cancerous cells have their own independent vision and program. They want to stay in your body, but they want to do their own thing—and multiply. Their goal is to shut you down. Similarly, Satan wants to shut down God's people. And he knows nothing will shut us down like disunity, since God is a God of order (see 1 Cor 14:33).

4:7-10 To equip the church for unity and service, God graciously gives every believer a spiritual gift (4:7)—a spiritual ability to be used in service to God's people for the expansion of his kingdom. Paul quotes from the Old Testament (4:8) to explain that before Jesus **ascended far above all the heavens** (4:10), he **descended to the lower parts of the earth** (4:9). After defeating Satan on the cross, Jesus's spirit descended and declared victory to the demons (see 1 Pet 3:19). Then the conquering King **took the captives captive** and **gave gifts to people** (Eph 4:8). Behind those words is the picture of a Roman general who defeats the enemy and leads his captives in a triumphal procession. Those people who were formerly captives of Satan's kingdom are now captives of God's kingdom. And the victorious King distributes gifts to them.

4:11-12 These gifts include empowerment for the leaders: he **gave some to be apostles, some prophets, some evangelists, some pastors and teachers** (4:11). Their purpose is for **equipping the saints for the work of ministry, to build up the body of Christ** (4:12). Some people attend church only for their own benefit. But that's not what being a church member looks like; that's called being a leech. God saved and equipped *you* for the work of ministry, the work of service. Why? To build up the body.

To understand the church, all you have to do is understand your body. It's a living organism composed of many parts working in harmony to contribute to the whole. Paul says the church is Christ's body. And the church will only grow and mature when all the parts operate in harmony, in unity. If you have a Lone Ranger personality, you will be a feeble saint—and the body will suffer for it. Our relationship to the corporate body is crucial to our own spiritual development and the development of the church.

4:13-14 Only by **growing into maturity** will we **no longer be little children.** Children are unstable in their thinking, easily tossed to and fro. Christians need the right theological and spiritual foundation to keep from being **blown around by every wind of teaching, by human cunning.** We need to be stabilized by maturity, and maturity only comes when we're connected to each other.

4:15 To mature, to **grow in every way**, we must be in an environment of **speaking the truth in love.** Truth is what God says about a matter. Truth must reign, and sometimes it isn't pretty when the truth confronts our sin. That's why the truth can't be used like a destructive hammer. It must be spoken with love, which involves compassionately, righteously, and responsibly seeking the well-being of its recipient.

4:16 Paul says the body grows with **the proper working of each individual part** when it is **fitted and knit together.** The body is built up when the various parts contribute to the whole. California has some of the largest organisms on the planet: redwood trees. They grow massive in size and ancient in age. The secret to their stability and growth is that their roots intertwine. Underground, they're all interconnected. You can't mess with one without messing with the whole grove. When fierce winds blow, their connectedness allows them to borrow from one another and grow strong. So it is, Paul says, with the body of Christ.

IX. LIVING A NEW LIFE IN THE NEW COMMUNITY (4:17-32)

Paul's main point in verses 17-32 is that Christians are not to live the way they used to live because they're not the people they used to be. Understanding your new life affects how you live in the new community.

4:17-19 Paul says the Ephesians **should no longer live as the Gentiles live** (4:17). He's referring to those outside of Christ. Here and in several other verses in Ephesians, Paul uses the Greek word for "walk" (2:2; 4:1, 17; 5:2, 8, 15). Some translations render the term "walk" in English, but others use "live" because that's what it means. It's an expression that refers to your lifestyle, your conduct, the direction or course of your life. Those who are in Christ are no longer to conduct themselves like the mass of humanity surrounding them.

Describing unbelievers, Paul speaks of **the futility of their thoughts** (4:17). Their thinking has no aim or purpose. Although you can go to an airport to buy gum or a newspaper, doing so is ancillary to the main purpose for going to an airport: to catch a plane and reach a new destination. But since the **understanding** of unbelievers is **darkened** (4:18), they don't have a clear life purpose in mind.

They're **excluded from the life of God** (4:18), which means they have no divine perspective. Their hearts are hard, and they have become **callous**, leading to **every kind of impurity with a desire for more and more** (4:19). In other words, their consciences are dead. They have committed sins for so long that their consciences no longer feel. Things that might have shocked them once don't shock anymore.

4:20-21 But that is not how you came to know Christ (4:20). Here Paul is referring to a Christian's new relationship with Christ. Believers have **heard about him** and have been **taught by him** (4:21). To learn Christ is to learn *about* Christ but also—more than this—to enter a relationship *with* Christ. **The truth**, Paul says, **is in Jesus** (4:21). It isn't something abstract. Truth is personal. Jesus *is* the truth (John 14:6), and everyone who is of the truth "listens to" him (John 18:37). The better you know Jesus, the better you'll make sense of truth.

4:22-24 In this relationship with Christ, you have to change: **take off your former way of life, the old self** (4:22) and **put on the new self, the one created according to God's likeness in righteousness and purity** (4:24). When you were saved, you received a new wardrobe. But you've got to take off the old clothes to put on the new. When God makes your inside clean, you want your outside to match.

How do we make this happen? Speaking of unbelievers, Paul uses words like "thoughts," "understanding," and "ignorance" (4:17-18). The common denominator is their thinking. Your lifestyle too is controlled by your brain. So the key to taking off the old and putting on the new is **to be renewed in the spirit of your** mind (4:23). Christians must not go back to the worldview they had before Christ. To "put on the new self" requires a new way of thinking, a renewed mind.

4:25 In verses 25-32, Paul explains how to implement the new way of life that results from renewed thinking and that produces authentic community. Since the church is the body of Christ, **we are members of one another**. We're connected. So we must not lie but **speak the truth** to one another. Satan is "the father of lies" (John 8:44), so children of God the Father must speak truth. We can't be community unless we honestly address and admit our faults, failures, and weaknesses. We must speak truth, but that must be done with love (see Eph 4:15).

4:26-27 Be angry and do not sin (4:26). People are going to make each other mad in the community of faith. But Paul says control your anger, deal with it daily, and don't give the devil an opportunity to inflame it into something bigger. Anger is sinful when it attacks people and seeks revenge rather than addressing the problem.

4:28 The follower of Christ must not **steal** but **do honest work** so he can **share with anyone in need**. Not only is Satan the father of lies, but he's also a thief (John 10:10). Christians are not to rip each other off but be productive and serve one another. That includes putting in a full day's work and serving in ministry that blesses others for the advancement of God's kingdom.

4:29-31 In order to build authentic community, you have to build people up rather than tearing them down. What comes out of your mouth is part of your new wardrobe, and it doesn't include **foul language** (4:29), **bitterness, anger and wrath, shouting and slander** (4:31). We must say what is needed. And while we must deal with real life issues, our goal must always be to help and not hurt. Our words must minister **grace to those who hear** (4:29). **Don't grieve God's Holy Spirit** (4:30). The Spirit's joy, presence, and power will not be yours if you make him sad when you open your mouth.

4:32 Just as God also forgave you in Christ, so you must forgive. Some people say they can't forget what others did to them. And let's be clear. God hasn't forgotten your sins, or else he wouldn't be omniscient. Nevertheless, he's forgiven you through Christ—he's cancelled your debt and doesn't bill you for it. If your credit card company said they were cancelling your debt but continued sending you a bill every month, it would mean they hadn't really cancelled what you owed. So forgive, as you have been forgiven.

X. IMITATING GOD IN LOVE, LIGHT, AND WISDOM (5:1-21)

5:1 This section can be understood by Paul's opening statement: **be imitators of God, as dearly loved children**. In light of who we are in Christ, we are called to imitate God. As a child often mimics the characteristics and behavior of a parent, so God's children are to copy their heavenly Father. As beloved children, we have the same status as God's "beloved Son" (Matt 3:17), so Jesus Christ is the model by which to pattern ourselves. The

Son put the Father on display (see John 1:18). So if you don't know how to pattern yourself after God the Father, all you need to do is take a close look at God the Son.

5:2 We imitate God with lives characterized by love (5:2), light (5:8), and wisdom (5:15). So first, we must **walk in love, as Christ also loved us.** Christians are to reflect the nature of God's love by serving others rather than self. Christ's sacrifice on the cross is the supreme illustration of what it means to love. It was **a fragrant offering**—it was acceptable **to God.** Similarly, when we love others by seeking what is best for their lives, it smells good to God.

5:3-7 The flip side is living in **sexual immorality . . . impurity or greed.** These things **should not even be heard of among you, as is proper for saints** (5:3). The culture of Ephesus embraced all forms of immorality. But Paul told the church there not to let the culture set the standard for them. As saints or "holy ones," they were to be set apart for God. **Obscene and foolish talking or crude joking** didn't belong on their lips (5:4). Believers ought not laugh over things that should make us cry. You can't adopt a non-Christian lifestyle and think you will have **an inheritance in the kingdom** (i.e., rewards that will be given to faithful believers) (5:5). We must not be deceived. Because of these things, **God's wrath is coming,** so we must not be **partners** with unbelievers (5:6-7). Don't let their lifestyles be your own. God wants us to see sin the way he sees it.

5:8 Followers of Christ **were once darkness,** but now they **are light in the Lord.** So, second, Paul tells them, **live as children of light.** Jesus is "the light of the world" (John 8:12). His followers must reflect him the way the moon reflects the sun—not as crescent-moon Christians but as full-moon Christians. And we can't *reflect* his light unless we're *in* the light. So, if you want to reflect Christ, you have to be absorbing Christ through cultivating an intimate walk and relationship with him (see John 15:1-16).

5:9-14 If you do that, you will be fruitful. Light bears fruit: **goodness, righteousness, and truth** (5:9). But the **works of darkness**

are **fruitless** (5:11): they have no long-term benefits. The more you look like Jesus, the more darkness will be unhappy with you— and the more heaven *will* be happy with you. Remember, heaven's got your bank account—"every spiritual blessing" (1:3).

Instead of participating in works of darkness, **expose them** (5:11) because **everything exposed by the light is made visible** (5:13). Does that mean we go around telling on people? No. **What makes everything visible is light** (5:14). If cockroaches are in a room, all you have to do is turn on the light, and they scatter. If you live as children of light, shameful deeds will be exposed by your lifestyle and words that reflect God's standard. You know how Jesus got in trouble with the religious leaders? By being Jesus. He just showed up, speaking truth and living righteousness. So if you're spiritually sleeping, get up and **Christ will shine** (5:14).

5:15-17 Third, we must live **not as unwise people but as wise** (5:15). How? By **making the most of the time** (5:16). Don't miss opportunities by making the same choices you've always made. The only way to make right choices is to **understand what the Lord's will is** (5:17)—that is, to determine God's view on a matter. Most of us will watch the weather report to get an expert opinion on the weather. But then we follow mere human opinions about life rather than tuning to the heavenly channel to get God's viewpoint. **The days are evil** (5:16). Don't waste your life. What opportunity is God giving you to maximize your potential?

5:18 Instead of getting **drunk,** which is **reckless,** we should **be filled by the Spirit.** When you come to Christ, you are indwelt by the Spirit, and he will never leave you. But being *filled* by the Spirit is different. A drunk is under the influence of alcohol. A person filled by the Spirit is under the Spirit's influence. Since the Greek verb "filled" is plural, Paul is emphasizing that the church must collectively operate as a Spirit-controlled environment.

5:19-21 Paul says this happens by speaking and singing **to one another in psalms, hymns, and spiritual songs, . . . giving**

thanks always for everything to God . . . and **submitting to one another in the fear of Christ**. This is a reminder that we need spiritual input. We also need to speak God's perspective to one another so that we all become full of spiritual things. We need to worship and give thanks to God regularly,

being subject to one another. But not just on Sundays. After all, the moment your car leaves the filling station, you begin burning fuel. So let worship become a lifestyle and regularly fill the tanks of others with God's perspective. That way we will be filled by the Spirit—and not some cheap substitute.

XI. KINGDOM HUSBANDS AND WIVES (5:22-33)

In the final verses of chapter 5, Paul gives specific instructions to husbands and wives. Scripture makes clear that marriage is not for a person's happiness. Happiness and companionship are good and desirable *benefits* of marriage, but they're not its *purpose*. The purpose of marriage and family is to advance God's kingdom in history through replicating the image of God and exercising dominion over the earth (see Gen 1:28).

But even if the biblical purpose of family is acknowledged within a marriage, that household may not be organized according to God's structure. Paul tells the Ephesians that God works through the institution of marriage based on the structure he has designed. If the husband and wife are out of alignment with that, God's blessings will not flow and his kingdom will not advance.

5:22 Ephesians 5:32 summarizes the husband-wife relationship, showing that it is meant to mirror something much bigger: "This mystery is profound, but I am talking about Christ and the church." God intends marriage to model the love of Christ for the church and the response of the church to Christ for the world to see. Paul explains what this should look like.

Wives, he says, **submit to your husbands as to the Lord** (5:22). Wives are called to submit to—to voluntarily place themselves under the legitimate authority of—their husbands. This sounds like a difficult command, but we must keep two things in mind.

First, we must be absolutely clear that the passage is *not* talking about a distinction in value or personhood. God the Son is equal in essence to God the Father, but he is subordinate to him in function (see 1 Cor 11:3). Likewise, a wife is equal to her husband in

her being—both are made in God's "image" (Gen 1:27). But God has created a wife to function in a significant, but subordinate, role to her husband (see Gen 2:18).

Second, a wife's submission to her husband is not absolute. It is **as to the Lord**. The husband's authority has limitations, then. He cannot ask his wife to submit to anything outside of God's will. The wife submits within boundaries.

So, what if the wife is the "better" leader in the home or has greater intelligence or more ability than her spouse? Think of it this way. A merging tractor-trailer may be bigger, longer, and carry more cargo than a tiny car coming down the road. Nevertheless, the tractor-trailer doesn't have the right of way but must yield as instructed to avoid catastrophe. God as Creator has placed a husband on the highway and given his wife the yield sign within the will of God.

5:23-24 As the church submits to Christ, so also wives are to submit to their husbands in everything (5:24). If a husband is not asking his wife to sin, she is to yield to his authority **because the husband is the head of the wife as Christ is the head of the church** (5:23). This doesn't mean a wife can't disagree with her spouse, but it means God has placed husbands in a position that is to be honored. A kingdom wife "is to respect her husband" (5:33), even when expressing disagreement.

5:25-30 To **husbands**, Paul says, **love your wives, just as Christ loved the church and gave himself for her** (5:25). Far too many men think headship means playing dictator and telling everyone what to do. But *biblical* headship means being a responsible governing authority. The husband is responsible for leading his family in the advancement of God's kingdom in the context of love. Biblical love compassionately, righteously, and sacrificially pursues the well-being of another.

Husbands are to love according to Christ's standard. How did Christ love the church? To death! Love came in the shape of a cross. Therefore, a husband is to sacrifice for his wife and be her deliverer—protecting her and paying the price for her well-being. A kingdom husband is also to be his wife's sanctifier—taking her (and all her history) from where she is and helping her to where she ought to be, just as Christ sanctifies the church (5:26-27). A kingdom husband outserves his wife. Even as a **husband loves himself**, he is **to love his wife** (5:28, 33)—giving her his strength and encouragement. The goal is to facilitate transformation through the influence of love.

5:31-33 Paul then points back to creation and quotes from Genesis 2:24. God has created husbands to lead and wives to respond. The husband **will leave his father and mother and be joined to his wife, and the two will become one flesh** (5:31). The man, then, has got to move first. When a woman sees her man initiating, owning responsibility, treating her as special, and sacrificing for her well-being, she is apt to respond to him with heartfelt respect and submission.

When a car is out of alignment, your tires are going to wear unevenly, and getting new tires won't fix the problem. Many married people think that if they could just find a new mate, their problems would go away. But that's not the answer. If kingdom husbands and wives expect to draw on their heavenly blessings, they must align their roles in the family according to God's good design through love and respect.

XII. KINGDOM KIDS AND HEAVEN ON THE JOB (6:1-9)

6:1-3 The saga of a nation is the saga of its families magnified. Our culture is reaping the devastation of family disintegration. We need Paul's timeless words for children and parents. **Children** play their own role in God's kingdom agenda: they are to **obey** and **honor** their **parents** (6:1-2). In action and attitude, they are to submit to their parents' legitimate authority because their obedience is **in the Lord**. In other words, children are to respond to parents out of their response to God because parents are to lead them in the ways of God. Doing so **is right** (6:1), Paul says, because it reflects God's righteous character. Unless parents contradict God, children are to obey them.

Children must also "honor" their parents, showing respect and holding them in high regard. When adult children leave the home and are no longer dependent on their parents for provision and protection, they are not obligated to obey them. Nevertheless, no one outgrows the requirement to honor mother and father. This **is the first commandment with a promise** (6:2). If children want things to **go well** for them and want to **have a long**

life (i.e., live out their fully ordained days) (6:3), it is absolutely critical that they respond properly to their parents. Thus, however many years they live, they will experience the life and blessings God has for them.

6:4 Then Paul turns to **fathers**. As the head, the leader of the family, a father has primary responsibility for raising his children. Of course, mothers are not excluded from responsibility; children are called to obey and honor both (6:1-2). But the father has ultimate responsibility. In ancient Roman households, men had great authority over their children. They could even decide whether their newborns were to live or die. But Paul would have no such misuse of authority. He says in effect, "This is what to do, Christian men. Bring up your children (i.e., raise them righteously)."

He tells fathers, **Don't stir up anger in your children**. In other words, don't correct your kids in such a way that they become embittered. Be an encourager, not a discourager. Praise them and make sure they know you are proud to be their dad. Furthermore, **bring them up in the training and**

instruction of the Lord. To bring up children is to nurture and care for them. "The training and instruction" of which Paul speaks has to do with teaching and discipline. Thus, fathers who have been given the primary biblical role for childrearing (see Gen 18:19) should teach kids God's divine guidelines on their own level and break it down in such a way that they can grasp it. We must give them age-appropriate discipline—not in anger, but in love. Discipline isn't the same thing as venting. God disciplines us in love in order to correct our behavior (Heb 12:5-6). We owe our children the same.

6:5-9 Paul continues with commands for **slaves** and **masters.** When God created Adam, he gave him a job: to work and watch over the garden (Gen 2:15). Work, then, came *before* the fall. But when Adam sinned, work—like a lot of things—became corrupted. One corruption of work is slavery.

Most of what we know of slavery (especially American antebellum slavery) is condemned in the Bible: human beings were not to be kidnapped and sold (Exod 21:16); slaves were not to be abused (Exod 21:26-27); fugitive slaves were not to be returned to their masters (Deut 23:15-16).

In a Roman culture infused with an unrighteous institution of slavery, Paul writes to tell a church how to live with a heavenly perspective. We can apply Paul's principles here to our own workplaces. God wants to be an integral part of your daily nine-to-five. For Christian employees and employers to access their heavenly blessings, they must bring a heavenly perspective to bear on the job.

To slaves, he says, **obey your human masters . . . serve . . . as to the Lord** (6:5, 7). Ultimately, each of us works for the Lord in all we do. So to serve Christ in your job, obey your employer as long as he doesn't ask you to disobey Christ (work "as to the Lord," 6:7). Furthermore, you must work respectfully **(with fear and trembling,** 6:5), sincerely **(in the sincerity of your heart,** 6:5), and **with a good attitude** (6:7). **Don't work only while being watched** (6:6). Because whether or not the boss is around, God is always watching. And even if your boss doesn't appreciate your efforts or is unfair, your work will never go unnoticed or be in vain. **Whatever good each one does . . . he will receive this back from the Lord** (6:8). You work for an unseen employer who sees all and will reward you.

Masters, treat your slaves the same way. Why? Because **both their Master and yours is in heaven.** So, even if you're the boss, you're under divine authority too. Employees may be under you in position, but they are equal to you in value. They bear the image of God, so honor their dignity. And treat all your employees with equity, consistently applying righteous standards to them. Don't play favorites because **there is no favoritism with [God]** (6:9).

XIII. THE FULL ARMOR OF GOD (6:10-20)

6:10-13 After saying so much about how to live in these relationships, Paul wants to emphasize that people are not our ultimate problem. Humanity's true **struggle is not against flesh and blood** but **against evil, spiritual forces in the heavens** (6:12). What we call *spiritual warfare* is the conflict in the spiritual realm that affects the physical realm. The daily problems we face here are rooted there. But, importantly, the resources you need to fight the battle are there too.

Paul told the Ephesians that through Christ, God has given them every blessing they need in heavenly places (i.e., the spiritual realm) (1:3). The risen Christ is there at God's right hand (1:20), and Christians are spiritually there with him (2:6). But **the cosmic powers of this darkness** are also in the spiritual realm (6:12).

The battle Christians face every day is rooted in **the schemes of the devil** (6:11), in his efforts to deceive us. He is happy for you to picture him as a cartoon character wearing a red jumpsuit with horns and carrying a pitchfork so that you won't take him seriously. Meanwhile, like an opposing football team, his demonic realm watches your game film. They know your history, your weak spots, and your sin patterns. Their goal is to keep you from experiencing God's will for your life. You're not their first assignment. They're good at what they do.

You, then, have to fight the spiritual with the spiritual. Your human strength won't work. Your only hope is to **be strengthened by the Lord** and to **put on the full armor of God** (6:10-11). Through the cross and resurrection of Christ, victory is already won. The devil has lost. The only power he has is the power you give him. We are to stand firm in Christ's victory.

Paul tells the Ephesians over and over: **stand** (6:11, 13-14). In other words, stay in the area where victory has been achieved under the cover of God's armor. When you stand under an umbrella, it doesn't stop the rain. But it does stop you from getting wet. You have to dress for success in this thing called the Christian life. **In the evil day**, when your number comes up and you are under full-frontal Satanic attack, you must be wearing **the full armor of God** (6:13).

The six pieces of armor are divided into two categories of three each. The first three you have with you all of the time, but Christians are called to take and use the last three as needed.

6:14-15 Stand . . . with truth like a belt around your waist. When a Roman soldier went to war, he tucked his clothing into his belt and fastened it securely for mobility in battle. *Truth* is the objective standard by which reality is measured. God's Word is truth. To wear "truth like a belt" is to live in authenticity before God. Since the devil is a liar, you must start with truth to be ready for battle. He can't function in an environment of integrity.

You also need **righteousness like armor on your chest** (6:14). Remember, our righteousness is not our own. God *imputed* Christ's perfect righteousness to us (see 2 Cor 5:21). When Satan accuses you, then, protect your heart with the truth of your righteous standing in Christ that is to be reflected by righteous living based on the truth. Unrighteousness acts like an open invitation to Satan and his demonic forces to invade our hearts and lives in order to defeat us spiritually.

You also need **your feet sandaled with readiness for the gospel of peace** (6:15). Roman soldiers wore sandals with cleats built in to help them have firm footing and to stand their ground under attack. Regardless of external turmoil, let the peace from God that results from righteous living confirm that you are operating and moving in God's will.

6:16 Next, **take up the shield of faith to extinguish all the flaming arrows of the evil one.** What is faith? It's acting like God's telling the truth—being obedient to God's view on a matter. Whatever temptations the devil fires at you, you can overcome him by believing God's Word and acting on it. Acting in faith is like activating a divine fire extinguisher.

6:17 Take the helmet of salvation. A helmet protects the head, the mind, the control center of the body. Our spiritual standing in Christ must protect our thinking. If you don't clearly understand the gospel—that it is God's power "for salvation" (Rom 1:16)—you will not operate as one whom God promises to deliver from the power and penalty of sin. We are to think God's thoughts and not operate on human wisdom.

The last piece of armor is **the sword of the Spirit—which is the word of God.** This is the only offensive weapon in the ensemble. The term Paul uses does not describe a long sword but something more like a dagger intended for hand-to-hand combat. He's talking about the Word of God spoken, made effective by the Spirit, to cut through the devil's lies. When Jesus was tempted, he declared, "It is written" (Matt 4:1-11), defeating the devil by using the Word. And just as Jesus did when tempted in the wilderness, Christians must learn to use Bible study against the devil. He is allergic to the Word of God when it is consistently used against him.

6:18 Paul finishes with prayer—the divine means of putting on our spiritual armor, which is a reflection of the person and work of Jesus Christ on our behalf. A Christian's spiritual resources are accessed through relational communication with God. How often should prayer be offered, then? **At all times**

. . . with all perseverance and intercession for all the saints. Prayer must be woven into all of life. We need to stay in regular communication with God and pray **in the Spirit** in order to access heaven's authority for intervention on earth (6:18). In other words, we must be on the same page as the Spirit, utilizing spiritual wisdom. The most powerful way to do that is to pray God's Word back to him and apply it to your situation.

6:19-20 Even Paul knew he needed prayer, asking the Ephesians to pray for him—not merely for his own sake but for the sake of the gospel. We too need **boldness** to proclaim faithfully **the mystery of the gospel** (6:19-20).

XIV. CLOSING (6:21-24)

6:21-24 Paul closes by saying that **Tychicus**, who probably delivered the letter, will update them on Paul's situation and **encourage** their **hearts** (6:21-22). His benediction extends to the Ephesians the Christian triad of **peace . . . love . . .** and **grace** (6:23-24).

PHILIPPIANS

INTRODUCTION

Author

THE APOSTLE PAUL IDENTIFIES himself as the author of this letter, and even the most critical scholars agree that he is. Though the greeting mentions "Paul and Timothy" (1:1), Paul is simply noting Timothy's physical presence with him. The first person "I" used throughout the letter makes it clear that this is not a case of joint authorship.

Historical Background

Paul indicates that he was imprisoned at the time he wrote Philippians (1:7, 13). We cannot be certain which imprisonment this was. Bible scholars debate about the three most likely locations: Rome, Caesarea, or Ephesus. Paul experienced frequent troubles in Ephesus (see Acts 19:21-41; 1 Cor 15:32; 16:8-9), but though he indicates that he had been imprisoned many times (2 Cor 11:23), we don't have conclusive evidence of an Ephesian imprisonment. We know he was jailed in Caesarea from AD 57–59 (see Acts 24:22-27). But it's more likely that Philippians was written from Rome around AD 62. This would make sense of Paul's reference to the saints of "Caesar's household" sending greetings (Phil 4:22).

During his second missionary journey in AD 51, Paul received a vision of "a Macedonian man" (Acts 16:9-10). As a result, he traveled to Philippi and founded a church in that leading city in Macedonia (see Acts 16:11-15). He also experienced persecution and imprisonment there (see Acts 16:16-40). The congregation at Philippi was the first church in Europe.

Message and Purpose

Philippians is the book of joy. Paul wants God's saints to live in the joy of the Lord and his kingdom instead of just reacting to their circumstances. Joy consists of internal stability in spite of external circumstances. And Paul was particularly qualified to teach on the subject because he wrote this book from a prison cell.

Philippians is in part a thank-you letter to the saints at Philippi for sending Epaphroditus to comfort Paul and deliver him a financial gift when they heard of his arrest and dire straits. But Paul also used the occasion to send some correction to the Philippians. He wrote the famous passage in chapter 2 to instruct the church to bring the mindset of Christ into the church rather than conforming to the world's mindset. Since two prominent women were fighting within the church, Paul knew he had to challenge the prevailing mentality.

He went on to explain that the church affects the angelic realm when it is operating properly. But that requires unity, which is why Paul prays in chapter 3 that the church might be unified. His conclusion is an exhortation to victory, to prayer instead of worry, and to choosing the mind of Christ that brings peace and joy.

Outline

PHILIPPIANS

I. GREETING AND PRAYER (1:1-11)

1:1-2 Paul's letter to the Philippians is often called "the epistle of joy" due to its glad, vigorous, overcoming presentation of the Christian life. It starts off with an immediate ring of gratitude from the imprisoned apostle to the well-beloved church in Philippi. Paul describes himself and **Timothy** as **servants of Christ Jesus** (1:1). He will return to this theme of humble service in chapter 2 especially, but it's found throughout his letter. Paul includes Timothy, his son in the faith, in his greeting since Timothy had ministered with Paul in that region (see Acts 16:1-15).

Paul addresses his letter **to all the saints in Christ Jesus who are in Philippi, including the overseers and deacons** (1:1). While the letter was written to the whole congregation, Paul makes special mention of "the overseers and deacons" because they were responsible to lead the church in love and obedience. Then Paul offers a greeting that could be called a summary of the gospel: **Grace to you and peace from God our Father and the Lord Jesus Christ** (1:2).

1:3-4 Years after Paul's initial ministry to the Philippians (see Acts 16:11-40), the church was ever-present in his heart and mind: **I give thanks to my God for every remembrance of you** (1:3). He keeps them before God because of their value to him as a church and as brothers and sisters in Christ. He loves them deeply, misses them, and desires their welfare and blessing. His love is evidenced by his **always praying with joy** for all of them in his **every prayer** (1:4). All believers in Jesus Christ should follow Paul's lead.

Remembering fellow Christians provides opportunity to praise God for their faith and to seek God for their good.

1:5-6 Paul was devoted to joyfully praying for the Philippian believers because of their shared mission—their **partnership in the gospel from the first day** (1:5). He was supremely confident that their spiritual and material investment in him would result in God's continued work of sanctification in their lives. He thus assures them, **He who started a good work in you will carry it on to completion until the day of Christ Jesus** (1:6).

People often start projects with great enthusiasm. However, when their zeal fades, the work fizzles out. But God is not like us. He never undertakes anything that he doesn't finish. When he begins a good work in a believer's heart, it's as good as done.

1:7-8 Paul continues to express his deep affection for them because of their spiritual partnership with him in the gospel: **I have you in my heart** (1:7). He considers them **partners ... in grace.** Just how did the Philippians partner with the apostle in ministry? They supported him in his **imprisonment and in the defense and confirmation of the gospel** (1:7). They were not, then, fair-weather Christians. When the gospel was spreading powerfully, they supported him. And when the name of Jesus landed Paul in a jail cell, the Philippian believers still remained true to him. Therefore, Paul missed them **with the affection of Christ Jesus** (1:8).

1:9-11 Paul wants to make sure their love continues to grow for the Lord and for each other in a context of truth, which he describes as **knowledge and every kind of discernment** (1:9). Love must be more than sentimental emotion; it must conform with the truth of the Word of God. Our love must be authentic and whole, not merely emotional and full of cracks. Discerning love helps us **approve the things that are superior** so that we don't waste our lives on inferior things (1:10). And this kind of life is **filled with the fruit of righteousness that comes through Jesus Christ** (1:11).

II. THE PROGRESS OF THE GOSPEL (1:12-30)

1:12-14 Paul was experiencing difficult circumstances, but he wants the Philippians to know that God is using his suffering to promote the gospel. Other Christians were emboldened because they knew that Paul's **imprisonment** was for **Christ** (1:13). They **gained confidence** and spoke **the word fearlessly** because of him (1:14). This brings up an important point: The gospel is not hindered by struggle and persecution when they are tied to our faith and witness.

1:15-18 There were two responses to Paul's imprisonment and resulting gospel ministry. Some detractors were jealous of Paul's impact and giftedness. Such people proclaimed **Christ out of selfish ambition** (1:15). They wanted to see Paul even more troubled (1:17)! Thankfully, many others preached Christ **out of good will** and **love** (1:15-16). Either way, Paul was thankful to hear that **Christ** was **proclaimed.** It takes a radical kind of God-centeredness to **rejoice** in gospel proclamation—even when the preachers intend your harm (1:18). But as long as Jesus was exalted and people were believing in him, Paul was content.

1:19-20 Paul declares that he will be vindicated through the **prayers** of the saints and **help from the Spirit of Jesus Christ** despite those working against him (1:19). He says his **eager expectation and hope is that** he will **not be ashamed about anything** in his life and ministry but will proclaim Christ **with all courage.** Because of his love for and commitment to Christ, Paul's main concern is that **Christ will be highly honored . . . whether by life or by death** (1:20).

1:21-26 Without a hint of exaggeration or bravado, Paul writes, **For me, to live is Christ and to die is gain** (1:21). Paul's purpose was to glorify Christ, come what may. The Lord Jesus was his all-consuming focus. He even admits his desire **to depart and be with Christ— which is far better** than remaining alive in this fallen world (1:23). Nevertheless, he knows that **to remain in the flesh is more necessary** so that he might continue to minister to the Philippian believers (1:24). Ministry requires self-sacrifice, and Paul was pleased to contribute to the spiritual growth of others so that their **boasting in Christ Jesus** could **abound** (1:26). By willingly laying down his life for the Philippians, Paul was simply following in the footsteps of his Master, Jesus Christ.

1:27 Paul wants to make sure these Philippian believers will honor Christ no matter what happens to him—**whether I come and see you or am absent.** He doesn't know what the future holds for him, but he wants them to be strong and unified in the faith and in the gospel, living courageously for Christ and modeling faith to a watching world despite opposition. He summarizes their calling as living in a manner **worthy of the gospel of Christ.** Their unity is also crucial to Paul because division can hurt the spread of the gospel (see 2:1-4; 4:2-3). Paul's hope is to hear of them **standing firm in one spirit, in one accord, contending together for the faith of the gospel.**

1:28 Moreover, they were not to be **frightened in any way by [their] opponents.** Courage is crucial to our gospel witness. Paul says the Philippian Christians' unashamed witness **is a sign of destruction for** their opponents but one indicating their own **salvation.** Of course, all of this **is from God,**

the sovereign King who can embolden failing hearts and eradicate stumbling blocks.

1:29 Paul goes so far as to say that their suffering is a sign of God's favor: **For it has been granted to you on Christ's behalf not only to believe in him, but also to suffer for him.** Suffering may appear to be a strange gift, but it's not. Suffering for the sake of Christ is *purposeful*, not purposeless. He allows it for our good and for his glory—and that makes all the difference.

1:30 Believers in Jesus Christ are called to take a stand for the gospel in love and truth regardless of repercussions, knowing that some people will support us and others will oppose us. That's to be expected. The goal, whether it leads to life or death, is to make Christ look good and glorify his name. He takes note of everything and will not forget it.

The Philippians endured **the same struggle** as Paul. And we too are called to live for Christ despite struggle and opposition. Far from being a miserable existence, though, this is the only way to find true life and purpose. The one who lived for us, died for us, and rose to live again calls us to experience the only life that is truly life.

III. CHRISTIAN HUMILITY (2:1-11)

2:1-2 In the kingdom of God, you can measure greatness by looking at a service record. Paul thus urges the Philippian Christians to embrace a servant mindset, putting the mission of Christ and the good of others before themselves. **If then there is any encouragement in Christ,** he says, **make my joy complete by thinking the same way, having the same love, united in spirit, intent on one purpose.** Notice the word *same*. That has to do with harmony and unity. A servant thinks in terms of pulling things together, not tearing things apart. A servant asks, "Is what I'm about to do or say going to make things better, or is it going to make things worse?"

Paul isn't arguing for harmony and unity at all costs. Truth isn't to be compromised in the name of harmony. But neither is the truth set forth to the exclusion of love. In dealing with the truth, expressing the truth, and communicating the truth, the goal is still unity.

Consider an example from the sports world. A football team is unified, not because every player plays the same position—that would be *uniformity*. A football team is unified because they are operating in harmony to reach the same goal line. Each player is playing his position with the objective of either helping his team score or stopping the opposing team from scoring. Everyone is moving in the same direction.

Why is unity so important? Because the Spirit doesn't work in disunity. Where there is disunity, the spirit of God backs up. Conversely, where there is unity, the Spirit of God is at home. So, if we are going to have the mindset of a servant, which is the key to greatness in the kingdom of God, we must choose to pursue harmony and unity without losing uniqueness.

2:3 By definition a servant serves others, not himself. **Do nothing out of selfish ambition or conceit, but in humility consider others as more important than yourselves** is a radical statement. "Nothing" doesn't allow for exceptions. It would be a lot easier if Paul had said, "Don't do *most* things out of selfish ambition or conceit." That would allow us an escape clause. But "nothing" requires ongoing commitment to humility.

2:4 Though servants think in terms of the benefits others will receive, they too can benefit from serving. **Everyone should look out not only for his own interests, but also for the interests of others.** There's a win-win scenario behind Christian service being rendered.

2:5-7 If you want to have a servant mindset, you should look to the ultimate servant, Jesus Christ, and **adopt the same attitude** he had (2:5). If anyone deserved to be served, it was the Son of God. He existed **in the form of God**. But he didn't **consider** his **equality with God as something to be exploited** for his own gain (2:6). Instead, **he emptied himself by assuming the form of a servant** (2:7). What did Jesus give up to do that? Well, he didn't empty himself of deity; he didn't stop being God. Rather, he took on human flesh and became a servant. He didn't let his deity stop him from expressing humanity. Like pouring water into a container, Jesus poured the entirety of his deity into the container of his humanity, resulting in him being fully God and fully man. In theology, this is known as the *hypostatic union*—two natures in one person, unmixed forever.

So, how can we adopt Christ's mindset? Jesus could serve *because* he knew he was God. Service was never a threat to him because he never lost sight of who he was. He was never insecure in his identity. He knew his position with the Father. Similarly, when you know who you are—a saint and a son or daughter of God—rendering service won't be a problem. It's when you don't know who you are that serving becomes a problem. When you are unsure of your identity, you'll fear that serving is beneath you, that you'll somehow be taken advantage of if you serve.

2:8 What did Jesus's service look like? He became **obedient to the point of death . . . on a cross**. He died as a substitutionary sacrifice so that he might atone for sinners. He died the death we deserve. That's the ultimate

sacrifice; it's the ultimate act of service. But he could do it willingly because he kept the end in view (2:9-11).

2:9 A servant of Jesus thinks in terms of true greatness because that's what Jesus did. He understood true greatness, so he could serve. What was true greatness for him? Divine exaltation: **God highly exalted him and gave him the name that is above every name.** False greatness is human exaltation. People will pump you up, but they will also stick a pin in your balloon. Jesus was after something more than the praises of people; he lived for divine recognition.

2:10-11 When you aim to please people rather than glorify God, you may receive some applause for a time, and that will be your reward. Unfortunately, though, you won't receive the approval and exaltation of God. Some divine exaltation comes in this life, but most of it comes in eternity. So, if you want to be great, take advantage of every opportunity you can to serve others to the glory of God alone.

Jesus could sacrificially serve humanity because he knew that one day **every tongue will confess that Jesus Christ is Lord, to the glory of God the Father** (2:11). All of life is to be the supreme recognition of the comprehensive kingdom rule of Jesus Christ. This can now be done voluntarily, but one day all will do it mandatorily.

IV. CHRIST-LIKE CHARACTER (2:12-30)

2:12-13 Paul shifts the discussion from Christ's humility and lordship to our response to it. These verses are some of the most powerful in the New Testament in terms of our development and spiritual growth. They are often quoted, but often misunderstood.

Paul says to **work out your own salvation** (2:12). To interpret this correctly, we must note the little word used to translate what Paul said. We are not to work "for" our salvation but to work "out" our salvation. Salvation is by grace through faith in Jesus Christ. But

what we do with that salvation once we receive it is another matter. Paul encourages the church in Philippi to develop the salvation that has been deposited within them.

This they were to do **with fear and trembling** (2:12). To *fear God* is to take God seriously. We're to honor God in our decisions, regardless of the cost, so that he might be glorified. God brings circumstances into our lives, in fact, that will require us to "work out" our salvation, to gain an increasingly high reverence for God and to choose his will over our own. This allows us to have an ever-increasing experience of his saving work and kingdom purpose in and through us.

Where does the motivation to obey come from? **It is God who is working in you both to will and to work according to his good purpose** (2:13). The reason the Philippians could "work out" their salvation was because God had already been "working in" them. God had already deposited within them that which was to be worked out. He gives us the desire and ability to obey. Obedience is not based on our willpower, but on God's power working in us.

2:14 Practically speaking, they were to **do everything without grumbling and arguing.** *Grumbling* refers to any negative emotional response to something you don't like. We all know what arguing is. Both hinder obedience. If we want to see God at work, we shouldn't waste our time grumbling and arguing about his will.

2:15-18 Why is this point important? Paul clearly tells us the reason: it's **so that you may be blameless and pure, children of God who are faultless in a crooked and perverted generation, among whom you shine like stars in the world** (2:15). God takes us through a developmental process so that even though things are dark around us, we are light. He's not telling us to become light. Rather, if God is in us, we *are* light. We're to be unhindered light, shining forth. Because when we are, it becomes clear that we're different than the world surrounding us. So, how do we shine? **By holding firm to the word of life** (2:16). We reflect God's perspective to a watching world when we

hold tight to his Word through trust and obedience.

2:19-24 Timothy, Paul's protégé and "son in the faith" (1 Tim 1:2), was an example of humble servanthood. Paul hopes **to send Timothy** to Philippi because, he says, **I have no one else like-minded who will genuinely care about your interests** (2:19-20, 23). Timothy shared the same love for the Lord and love for the church that Paul did. Thus, Timothy could act as an extension of Paul himself. Paul reminds the Philippians of Timothy's **proven character** as demonstrated by his service with Paul **in the gospel ministry** (2:22). Timothy was an example worth emulating.

2:25-30 In the meantime, Paul **considered it necessary to send** back to them **Epaphroditus**—his **brother, coworker, and fellow soldier, as well as** their **messenger and minister to** his **need** (2:25). Paul wants the church to recognize and appreciate the great sacrifices Epaphroditus made—for Paul, for them, and for the gospel. He had become sick and almost **died** while serving the Lord and Paul on behalf of the Philippian church (2:26-27).

But Paul says, **God had mercy on him, and not only on him but also on me, so that I would not have sorrow upon sorrow** (2:27)—that is, emotional sorrow over losing a friend, and also ministry sorrow because the church would have lost Epaphroditus's gospel commitment to ministry. His great service is an example of the kind of commitment believers are to have to Christ and also to each other. The church ought to **hold people like him in honor** (2:29).

V. KNOWING CHRIST (3:1-11)

3:1 Paul begins chapter 3 with joy, not despair, urging the Philippians to **rejoice in the Lord.** Reminding them to do this is **no trouble for** him and **is a safeguard** for them. We can't be reminded too often to rejoice in Jesus. But how can we find joy in the Lord when our circumstances are bad? Paul is about to answer that question.

3:2 Paul opens by warning them to **watch out for the dogs . . . for the evil workers . . . for those who mutilate the flesh.** In biblical times, dogs were considered unclean animals; thus, Paul is saying to beware of false, "unclean" teachers. Paul had a perpetual problem with a group called the Judaizers. These Jews said one must keep the Old

Testament law to be saved and sanctified. They tried to combine faith and works as a way of getting right and staying right with God. In spreading that message, they were undermining the ministry of Paul and the truth of the gospel—a message of grace, not law keeping.

We must beware of any system of theology that says we must earn our standing with God. All the spiritual calisthenics we might do, including good things like going to church, reading our Bibles, praying, and giving will not help us earn right standing with him. Religion, in fact, only weighs us down. It never tells us when we've done enough because it allows no such end. The Judaizers highlighted circumcision, but that ritual—and all things similar— was made obsolete by the death of Christ. God gives us right standing with him only through the righteousness of his Son, Jesus Christ. This comes by grace, not by how hard we work. These religious teachers were relying on their works instead of on Jesus.

3:3 Paul contrasts these false teachers with followers of Jesus, saying **we are the circumcision, the ones who worship by the Spirit of God**. The true circumcision, then, is comprised of those who understand that a relationship with God under the new covenant occurs in the realm of the Spirit of God. To "worship by the Spirit" means to relate to God based on God's standard, not on standards we make up. That's why living in the Spirit is also living according to the Word.

Next, he says we are to **boast in Christ Jesus**. We are to make a big deal about Jesus. He must be the focus of our worship. If Jesus is not a big deal to us, we can't worship by the Spirit of God because the Spirit was sent to make much of Jesus.

Paul concludes with a huge point of emphasis—we are not to **put confidence in the flesh**. "Confidence in the flesh" refers to the conviction that I can do on my own what's necessary for me to become what I'm supposed to be as a Christian. But when you put confidence in yourself about your relationship with God, you nullify his work in your life.

3:4-6 Next Paul lists his impressive spiritual pedigree, saying he has **reasons for confidence in the flesh** if **anyone** does (3:4). Indeed, he had quite the spiritual record before becoming a Christian. His discussion of the topic culminates with the bold claim that **regarding the righteousness that is in the law**, he was **blameless** (3:6). Yet, as a believer, he puts *no* confidence in the flesh. If he had, he wouldn't have been able to rejoice in the Lord from a prison cell.

If we place our confidence in our accomplishments, or in anything other than Christ, we will find it impossible to rejoice in the Lord when things don't go well. When we struggle in our marriages or in our careers, we'll be miserable if we've placed our confidence in things. To be steady and joyful in all circumstances, we must place our confidence in Jesus.

3:7-8 Paul says, **Everything that was a gain to me, I have considered to be a loss because of Christ** (3:7). Then he gets even more radical, pointing out that he continues to consider **everything to be a loss in view of the surpassing value of knowing Christ Jesus** (3:8). Paul counts his past accomplishments and anything in the present or future as a "loss" compared to knowing Jesus. In fact, he considers them no better than **dung** (3:8). Things are worthless to Paul when compared to Christ. But the only way a person can view life from this perspective is to see how valuable Christ truly is.

3:9-11 Paul then returns to the necessity of finding his righteousness in Christ—**the righteousness from God based on faith** (3:9). If you have accepted Christ, he took up residence within you through the Spirit and gave you his righteousness. The key to the Christian life is not you living it, but Jesus living it through you. That's what makes Christianity unique. Christianity is not merely a religion; it is driven by a relationship. That's why Paul says his **goal is to know him** (3:10). Our passion, too, must be knowing Jesus. All the religious stuff we do only becomes valid if knowing Christ is the goal.

Paul wants to know **the power of his resurrection and the fellowship of his sufferings, being conformed to his death**

(3:10). When you are going through a rough time, then, remember that Jesus Christ invites you to get to know him better through it. He will hurt with you, and you will get to understand him better in the process. Suffering is a call to intimacy with Jesus. Walking through hard things with the Lord results in **resurrection from among the dead** (3:11).

Paul is not talking about rising from the dead when Jesus comes back, though that will happen. He's talking about experiencing Jesus's resurrection power in this life to joyously overcome every challenge. Paul desired an outside-the-box experience of the living Christ operating in and through his life. Do you?

VI. REACHING FORWARD TO GOD'S GOAL (3:12-21)

3:12-13 Paul says he hasn't arrived at full maturity, but he is pressing on toward knowing Christ more and maturing. Paul makes **every effort to take hold** of that goal because Christ has **taken hold of** him (3:12). He is striving to get closer to that for which Christ has grabbed him. He is not satisfied with where he is; he wants to keep growing. He has a holy discontent that keeps him pressing on. Therefore, Paul forgets **what is behind** and reaches for **what is ahead** (3:13).

To become an excellent Christian and fulfill your kingdom purpose, you too must have a short memory and a clear direction. So, what aspects of yesterday must you forget? All of them—the good, the bad, and the ugly. You've got to let go of your successes, your failures, and the ways others have hurt you. It's not that you don't remember the past; it's that you don't allow the past to be a controlling factor in your life. Don't spend too much time looking in the rearview mirror. A much bigger piece of glass called the windshield should have your focus because where you're going is a lot bigger than where you've been.

3:14 The way to get over yesterday is to have a forward focus, to press on. That's why Paul pursues as his goal **the prize promised by God's heavenly call in Christ Jesus.** Notice he's looking to the future, not the past.

3:15-17 According to Paul, **all of us who are mature** should **think this way,** and if we aren't thinking this way, **God will reveal this also** to us (3:15). If we have a mediocre attitude and a get-by mentality, we're not listening to God. **We should live up to**

whatever truth we have attained (3:16). We should practice what we know to do. And to this point he adds that we should imitate and **pay careful attention to those who live according to the example** of Paul and others who are pursuing Christ (3:17).

We will never ascend to an excellent life if we're constantly hanging out with get-by people who are thinking in a mediocre way. We can't be excellent if we follow the world's ways. Excellent people—spiritually minded people who want to excel in their walk with God—hang around excellent people. They spend time with others sharing that same goal.

3:18-19 Paul says, **with tears, that many live as enemies of the cross of Christ** (3:18). They live lives of physical gratification and self-centeredness. He says **their glory is in their shame.** They praise themselves, which is shameful, when they should be praising the Lord. They are **focused on earthly things** (3:19) rather than the pursuit of Christ.

3:20-21 He reminds the Philippian believers that **our citizenship is in heaven, and we eagerly wait for a Savior from there, the Lord Jesus Christ** (3:20). He did not want their earthly experience to crowd out the reality of their heavenly citizenship. They were to look forward to the return of Jesus Christ, who **will transform the body of our humble condition into the likeness of his glorious body, by the power that enables him to subject everything to himself** (3:21). We are to focus on the returning King and his kingdom, not on this world and its lesser kingdoms.

VII. PRACTICAL COUNSEL (4:1-9)

4:1 After issuing a strong challenge to the Philippians in chapter 3, Paul once again expresses his great affection for them, calling them **dearly loved and longed for brothers and sisters.** He urges them to **stand firm in the Lord** (4:1) and will explain how to do that. But first he addresses a division in the church that is a threat to their unity and joy.

4:2-3 Paul urges **Euodia** and **Syntyche to agree in the Lord** (4:2). And he calls the church **to help these women** get along; they **have contended for the gospel at [his] side** (4:3). These faithful women had lost sight of the big picture. Evidently, the dispute between them had spread throughout the church, so Paul tells them they need to agree in the Lord. To set aside their differences for the sake of the gospel.

4:4 The church faces opposition within and without, yet here is Paul, writing a letter about joy and telling the Philippians to rejoice. From a human perspective, it doesn't make sense. And yet the path to joy is to actually choose to rejoice, so Paul tells them to **rejoice in the Lord always.** And to drive home the point, he repeats himself: **I will say it again: Rejoice!**

Worldly happiness is not the same as godly happiness. Godly happiness is called joy. In the Bible, the word *joy* is a celebration term. Thus, Paul is calling for celebration. The difference between joy and secular happiness is that the latter depends on what happens; it is circumstantially driven. So, if things are going in an upward direction in life, you feel up, but if things are going down, you feel down. This keeps you on an emotional rollercoaster. Biblical joy, by contrast, has to do with stability and celebration on the inside regardless of circumstances on the outside. We must choose to rejoice in order to experience the joy God promises us.

4:5 The path to joy includes letting **your graciousness be known to everyone.** It means not spreading unhappiness to others. Being gracious means we don't use our ministries

to be vindictive or hateful when things aren't going well. Rather, we embrace a good attitude because we know **the Lord is near.** He's closer to us than we think. But if we refuse to rejoice and instead complain, we can make the very near God feel very far off indeed.

4:6 At this point in the letter, we come to some of the most helpful and well-loved verses in the Bible. Paul provides the antidote to worry: **Don't worry about anything, but in everything, through prayer and petition with thanksgiving, present your requests to God.** *Prayer* is relational communication with God. It seeks to draw resources from the invisible spiritual realm into visible, physical reality. Every time we begin to worry, we should see that as a call from God telling us that it's time to pray. This is an important principle: the more you worry, the less you pray. The more you pray, the less you worry.

Prayer is the umbrella word under which Paul includes "petition with thanksgiving." Our petitions must be specific. We need to tell God what we're worried about and ask for his help. A moment in which you are plagued by worry is not the time for one of those general prayers for God to bless the world. To deal with anxiety, make sure your petitions are precise. Get real with God.

Prayer can often feel frustrating—like when you go to a soda machine, put in your money, punch the button, and nothing comes out. But thinking of it in those terms causes us to miss how prayer works. God wants us to make requests "with thanksgiving." Of course, when you have a problem and it isn't going away, giving thanks is not at the top of your priorities list. But Paul's telling us to give thanks, not for the problem itself but for the God we are inviting into our specific problem. Offering thanks is a demonstration of faith in God's goodness and provision despite what we see.

4:7 What can you expect when you pray in this way? **The peace of God, which surpasses all understanding, will guard your hearts and minds in Christ Jesus.** In other words, you'll experience calm in the midst of chaos. You will know God heard your prayer, not necessarily because the problem is solved, but because of the peace that God gives you. Paul calls it a peace that "surpasses all understanding" because even we won't entirely understand how we are able to have peace in light of some of the troubles we experience. Nevertheless, this peace guards our "hearts and minds." It's as if God puts soldiers and sentries around our feelings and our thoughts.

4:8 God gives us peace, but we must hold onto it. We don't want to lose our peace in the next hour or the next day. So to prevent that, Paul says we're to dwell on **whatever is true . . . honorable . . . just . . . pure . . . lovely . . . commendable**, and **if there is any moral excellence and if there is anything praiseworthy**, we're to focus our attention there. One of the reasons we don't keep our peace is because we tend to dwell on the things that are set in opposition to the peace we're asking for. We mull over a lie or

over bad things that could happen. And if we continue to entertain messages that work against our peace, anxiety will soon return. We must, therefore, ask ourselves if we are able to praise God for the things that we are dwelling on. If we can't, then we'll soon lose the peace God has given us.

4:9 Paul gives one more step to living in God's peace: **Do what you have learned and received and heard from me, and seen in me.** The Philippians, then, were to handle things the way they had seen Paul handle things. He was in prison, but he was praising God instead of worrying. One of the purposes of the church is to connect people with other kingdom-minded people. We need support, and we need good examples.

Then Paul closes with the promise that **the God of peace will be with you.** When we're rejoicing and praying and dwelling on the right things and watching the right people, we don't just have the peace of God, we have "the God of peace." We get his peace, and we get his presence.

VIII. APPRECIATION OF SUPPORT (4:10-23)

4:10 Paul is grateful for the support he's received from the Philippians. He **rejoiced in the Lord greatly because once again** they expressed their care for him. Though they couldn't support him previously, now they could. Paul understands the providence of God. *Providence* is God arranging things beforehand for the fulfillment of his purposes. God is in control, and there's no such thing as luck, chance, or coincidence. If something doesn't work out, God must have another plan.

4:11-12 Paul had **learned to be content in whatever circumstances** he found himself (4:11). Whether he had much or little, he had **learned the secret of being content** (4:12). *Contentment* means being satisfied and at rest with where God has you, despite what's happening around you. It's not natural or automatic; it must be learned. God teaches us contentment through the ups and downs of changing circumstances. He wants us to

learn to depend on him and his divine enablement no matter what happens to us or around us. As we grow in our understanding and experience of his providence, we will also grow in our level of contentment.

4:13-14 Paul confesses, **I am able to do all things through him who strengthens me** (4:13). The secret of Paul's contentment, then, is the infusion of strength he gets when he can't go any further. Many times, it seems that God doesn't come through for us until we can't take one more step. Then he provides at just the right time—as he did for Paul through the generosity of the Philippians (4:14). The lesson of contentment is most effectively learned during times of suffering need.

4:15-18 Continuing to build on the themes of contentment and God's providence, Paul recounts the Philippians' faithfulness to him in the past (4:15-16). He desires to increase their **account** (4:17)—that is, their heavenly reward. Paul had received **an abundance** from them, **a fragrant offering, an acceptable sacrifice, pleasing to God** (4:18). These are Old Testament images that describe their service.

4:19-20 He then says that they will be blessed for their generosity, promising, **God will supply all your needs according to his riches in glory in Christ Jesus** (4:19). In other words, their generosity led to God's provision. God is concerned not only with our receiving from him; he also wants others to receive from us. In other words, God doesn't just want to give you a miracle; he wants you to become a miracle for someone else (see Luke 6:38). This brings to him greater **glory**, which brings to you greater blessing (4:20).

4:21-23 Paul concludes his joyous letter with a warm farewell and a final word of blessing: **the grace of the Lord Jesus Christ be with your spirit** (4:23). Like Paul, they (and we) need God's grace to continue to joyfully stand firm in the Lord.

COLOSSIANS

INTRODUCTION

Author

THE AUTHOR OF THE LETTER claims to be the apostle Paul (1:1). Many modern critical scholars, though, deny Pauline authorship. They believe Colossians differs in style and theology from Paul's undisputed letters and conclude that some later imitator of Paul wrote it in his name. But no theological truths in the letter contradict what Paul says elsewhere. Moreover, there are many stylistic and theological similarities between Colossians and Paul's other letters. Importantly, the early church—including church fathers Irenaeus, Tertullian, Clement of Alexandria, and Justin—believed that Paul was the author. Therefore, we are justified in believing the same.

Historical Background

Colossae was a city located in the Lycus River Valley in Phrygia—a part of what is now modern Turkey. The church in Colossae was not established by Paul but by his co-worker Epaphras (1:7; 4:12-13). It is clear that Paul was imprisoned while writing Colossians (4:3, 18). Many scholars agree that Paul most likely wrote Ephesians, Philippians, Colossians, and Philemon (the Prison Epistles) while he was imprisoned in Rome in AD 60–62 (see Acts 28:30). There are a number of links between these letters. Tychicus delivered both Colossians and Ephesians to their recipients (Eph 6:21-22; Col 4:7-8). Both the letter to the Colossians and the one to Philemon mention Onesimus, Archippus, and Epaphras (Col 4:9, 17; Phm 1-2, 9-10, 12, 23). It appears, then, that Philemon was a member of the Colossian church.

Message and Purpose

Paul wrote Colossians from jail to deal with some heresies that were circulating among the churches—particularly one false teaching about the uniqueness and deity of Jesus Christ. Such teachings involved a blending of Jewish and Greek ideas with a smattering of Christian perspective that resulted in a dumbing down of the truth about Christ. Paul counters this with a striking argument for the deity of Jesus—"he is the image of the invisible God" (1:15) who was responsible for creation and is the head of the church. He is King over all of his kingdom.

Paul calls for rejection of any so-called knowledge, religious or secular, that diminishes the uniqueness of Christ. But he didn't want believers' stance on the topic to be merely theoretical. He therefore calls the Colossian believers to reflect Christ's character in every area of their lives, to put the truth into practice. The key to doing this is to submit to Jesus as Lord, both because he is God and because he is the final word of authority in the life of every believer. In the book of Colossians, Paul exalts Christ and calls the church to display his glory and truth by the way we live for his kingdom.

VIDEO INTRO

www.bhpublishinggroup.com/qr/te/51_00

Outline

COLOSSIANS

I. GREETINGS AND PRAYER (1:1-12)

1:1-5 Paul and his "son in the faith" **Timothy** (see 1 Tim 1:2) greeted their **brothers and sisters** in Christ in **Colossae.** Paul wished them God's **grace** and **peace**—that is, God's favor and wellbeing in life (1:1-2). These believers had a vertical-horizontal connection: their **faith in Christ** (vertical) could intersect with their **love** for **the saints** (horizontal) because both came from the same **hope** that was waiting for them (1:4-5). The **gospel** not only offers the hope of eternal life but also rewards us in this life (1:5).

1:6 Paul saw the scope of the gospel as universal. God's good news in Jesus Christ isn't reserved for a privileged few—any person in the **world** may respond to the grace of God. It is also productive, since it was **bearing fruit and growing.** Truth will always bring change, development, and growth.

1:7-8 Epaphras was evidently the founder and teacher of the church at Colossae (1:7). He brought good news back to Paul that they were bearing fruit. It was a loving, caring, faith-filled congregation.

1:9-10 When God wanted to explain what knowing him would produce in the lives of Christians, he used the word *fruit.* Fruit has three characteristics: it is visible; it reflects the nature of the tree it grows on; and it exists for someone else's benefit. God is concerned that what we produce is in keeping with who he is—that the products of our lives are consistent with our biblically grounded experience with him. Sometimes, though, when we

look over our lives, we'll see rotten fruit. That should concern us, too.

Paul never **stopped praying for** the spiritual growth of the church in Colossae (1:9). He connects **bearing** good **fruit** with **the knowledge of God** (1:10). This is experiential knowledge, not just informational. When Adam *knew* Eve, she conceived; that intimacy produced fruit. Paul asks the Lord that the Colossians would have the **wisdom** to make biblically-based decisions that come from knowing God's **will** (1:9). Then he prays that the **walk** of their Christian life (how they live) would result **in every good work** (1:10). The product of all of this is *fruitfulness*, having a useful Christian life that positively affects the lives of others. On the basis of our experience with him, God produces something in our lives that is beautiful, enjoyable, and useful.

Most of us want to bear good fruit. The problem is that though many Christians hear about God and carry his book around, they're not really getting to know him, not really experiencing him. To bear fruit, which is contributing to the development of Christ-like character in the discipleship of others, we need to be grafted into "the true vine" (Christ), to be lifted up out of the dirt, to set aside our diversions, and to "remain" in Christ (John 15:1-8). You don't just visit God for two hours on Sunday; you talk to him all the time, threading the discussion through all of your activities. While you're walking or while you're driving, "whether you eat or drink, or whatever you do" (1 Cor 10:31), stay plugged in. You don't need a *microwave* experience with God; you need a *crockpot* experience with him. Simmer in his presence, and impact the lives of others with the impact the Lord has on you.

1:11-12 Paul prayed that they would **have great endurance** and be joyful (1:11). Endurance usually involves inconvenience and an unpleasant experience. A pregnant woman, for instance, endures significant inconveniences and unpleasant symptoms. But the joy of what awaits her at the end of her trial overrides any inconvenience. For Christians, God has a spiritual **inheritance** prepared (1:12). Most of that inheritance awaits us in eternity, but God grants access to enough of it now that you are spiritually equipped to fulfill his kingdom purposes for you.

II. THE PREEMINENCE OF CHRIST (1:13-20)

These verses include some of the most exalting statements about Christ contained in the New Testament. Paul emphasizes the *preeminence* of Christ, meaning he is superior in who he is and surpassing in all he does.

1:13-14 Jesus is preeminent in his *purchase*. God **rescued** believers **from the domain of darkness** and into the **kingdom of** his beloved **Son** (1:13). We were under the rule of the devil, but Jesus Christ provided **redemption** (1:14). A slave could be redeemed in the ancient world if a price was paid for his freedom. We were slaves to sin and Satan, but through his atoning death Christ purchased us off the slave block, granting us **forgiveness of sins** and transferring us into his glorious kingdom.

1:15-19 Jesus is preeminent in his *person*. **He is the image of the invisible God** (1:15). The word *image* means perfect replica. **God was pleased to have all his fullness dwell in him** (1:19). The one God exists in three persons—as a Trinity—Father, Son, and Holy Spirit. The Second Person of the Trinity took on human flesh; he is fully God and fully man. Every attribute of God is manifested in the Son; Jesus is God in bodily form (see 2:9). That's why we see in Scripture that one minute Jesus is thirsty because he's a man, and the next minute he calms the sea because he's the Son of God.

Jesus is preeminent in his *position*. First, he is **the firstborn over all creation** (1:15). This phrase has nothing to do with time but with rank. It's like the term *first lady*. The president's wife is not the first woman ever to live in the White House. She holds the rank of first lady because of her connection to the one in charge. By his divine connection to God the Father, Christ inherits creation and the right to rule: "God has appointed him heir of all things" (Heb 1:2). He is the rightful King of creation. Second, he is **the firstborn from the dead** (1:18)—the down payment on our resurrection. You can be raised from the dead because Jesus was raised from the dead. Third, he **is also the head of the body, the church**. The church isn't ours; it's his. He runs it. When it comes to the covenant people of God, then, Jesus is never to come in second place. He is to have **first place in everything** (1:18).

Jesus is preeminent in his *power*. **Everything was created by him** (1:16). Genesis 1:1 says, "God created the heavens and the earth." Yet Jesus is the uncreated Creator of all things (see John 1:1-4), and there is only one uncreated, eternal being. Thus, Jesus is God. What, then, should we make of the claim in Isaiah 9:6 that "A child will be born for us, a son will be given"? Well, the child (that is, Jesus) had to be *born* because the incarnation was a new thing, but the Son was *given* because he already existed. **By him all things hold together** (1:17). The planets stay in their orbits because Jesus holds them there. If he can do that, you can be confident that he can hold you too. If things are falling apart in your life, it might just be because Jesus doesn't hold the preeminent position in your heart.

1:20 Jesus is preeminent in his *provision*. **Through him** God reconciled **everything to himself**. Sin has separated us from God, and we need reconciliation to bring things back into proper harmony. Job spoke of needing someone to mediate between him and God—someone like him who understood his pain (see Job 9:32-33). Since Jesus is a man, he understands our problems; since he's God, he can fix them. Jesus experienced rejection, temptation, hunger, abuse, and death. He knows how you feel. But he's also an Advocate (see 1 John 2:1) who reconciles sinners to God **through his blood, shed on the cross.** Your bank statement of righteousness is reconciled by Jesus Christ; you have perfect righteousness because you received a credit from him.

III. THE MATURITY OF BELIEVERS (1:21–2:3)

1:21-23 The Colossians' former state of hostility toward God was manifest in their **evil actions** (1:21). They were reconciled, brought into relationship with God, based on the atoning work of Christ (1:22). The goal for every Christian is to be presented as a mature believer, though no one is perfect. Maturity requires responsibility on our part—we are not to be **shifted away from the hope of the gospel** (1:23).

1:24-29 Paul's motivation for his **sufferings** was that they would benefit **the church** (1:24). He wanted believers to be filled with what was necessary for their spiritual development, and that includes suffering. Paul's ministry and stewardship were to prepare the church for the judgment seat of Christ. He wanted to facilitate the spiritual development of its members and to expose them to **the mystery** (1:26)—that is, to the fact that Christ indwells every believer (1:27) so that they increasingly reflect his character, conduct, attitude, and actions as they use God's Word to deal with life (see Heb 5:11-14). As internal spiritual maturation is manifested externally in the action of believers, transformation takes place. Christ's indwelling presence functions within us like a new motor in an old car.

Paul's ministry centered on proclaiming this mystery, particularly to **the Gentiles**, so that they might be presented as mature in **glory** (1:27). His proclamation—with a call to response, with admonishment, and with guidance in the application of truth— required **all wisdom** (1:28). People are at various stages in their spiritual experience. Every minister should strive with God's **strength** (1:29) for the spiritual development of his entire congregation.

2:1-3 Paul's labor of love not only went to the Colossians, but it extended to people he'd never met (2:1). He wanted them to understand the fullness of the gospel. In Christ is found the secret to truth and to **knowledge** and to life; therefore, he wanted them to apprehend that truth so they could have **wisdom** (2:2-3). *Knowledge* is the apprehension of truth; *wisdom* is the application of that truth to life.

IV. THE VICTORY AND FREEDOM OF FAITH (2:4-23)

2:4-5 Paul's concern was that the Colossians would go to false teachers who were offering supposed insider, secret spiritual understanding that was inconsistent with Christ. Lies can **sound reasonable** (2:4), but they're still lies. Remember, the Bible is our standard for discerning truth from error. Only the full understanding of Christ can keep believers from being deceived by persuasive arguments. Paul was delighted in how these particular believers were standing fast on the truth even in his absence (2:5).

2:6-7 The Christian life is to **continue** as it began—with **faith** in the gospel message. Like mighty trees fed by strong roots, believers are to remain **rooted** in Jesus Christ, both in knowledge and in practice. That way, growth will occur and protection from false teachers will be provided.

2:8-10 We are not to be taken **captive through philosophy and empty deceit based on human tradition** (2:8). Rather, we are to be captive to **Christ** because **the entire fullness of God's nature dwells bodily in** him (2:9; see 1:19), and he **is the head over every ruler and authority** (2:10).

When Satan—the once glorious angel—rebelled, God judged him (see Isa 14:12-14; Ezek 28:12-16). Then God created man, a creature made "lower than the angels" and "subjected everything under his feet" (Heb 2:7-8). Man was to rule over creation on God's behalf (Gen 1:26-28). God planned to show what he could do with "less" (when less was devoted to him) in contrast to "more" (when more was in rebellion against him). But Adam abdicated his role as manager of creation (Gen 3:1-19), turning rule over to Satan—"the god of this age" (2 Cor 4:4) and "the ruler of the power of the air" (Eph 2:2).

But the "last Adam" (1 Cor 15:45), Jesus Christ, succeeded where the first Adam failed. He came to solve the problem. As the Second Person of the Trinity, he possesses "the entire fullness of God's nature" (Col 2:9). But he also became a man, because God the Father intended that man would rule over his kingdom on earth and defeat Satan. Through his sinless life, atoning death, and resurrection, Jesus defeated Satan's legal authority and reclaimed the earthly kingdom.

2:11-13 Since Jesus is "the head over every ruler and authority," we are called to realign ourselves to God under the rule of Christ and thus reverse the rule of the devil. As a believer, "you have been filled by" Jesus, so you are lacking nothing that you need (2:10). God **made you alive with** Christ. Spiritual death because of sin has been replaced with spiritual life. Though **you were dead**, you have been **made** spiritually **alive** (2:13). You have been **raised with him** (2:12) who is enthroned over all. Therefore, by your connection to Christ, God can overrule your difficult circumstances.

Note the recurring theme: "by him" (2:10), "in him" (2:11), "with him" (2:12[x2]; 2:13). Paul is expressing the great theological truth of our union with Christ. By faith, we are united

inseparably with him, like cream stirred into coffee. That means you don't have to be defined by your struggles. Align your life under his rule, and your King's agenda will be demonstrated in your situation.

If you watch a replay of yesterday's football game—and you already know the final score is in your team's favor—you won't get upset if your team falls behind. Knowing how the game ends will have a stabilizing effect. Scripture tells us where everything is going. Scripture tells us how everything is going to turn out. If you are trusting in Christ, you can have confidence whatever your struggles because you know how the story ends. Jesus is already victorious, and you are in union with him.

2:14-15 By means of his death on **the cross**, Christ **erased the certificate of debt, with its obligations, that was against us** (2:14). When a person was executed under Roman law, the sentence was attached to the accused's cross (see John 19:19). But Jesus took *our* sentence away, effectively nailing our certificates of debt to *his* cross. He paid our penalty; he died for our guilt. God "made the one who did not know sin to be sin for us, so that in him we might become the righteousness of God" (2 Cor 5:21). In doing so, he also **disarmed** the spiritual **rulers and authorities**—Satan and his forces—**disgraced them** and **triumphed over them** (2:15). A fallen angel is no match for the Son of God, who took away Satan's rulership.

Satan is actually the transliteration of a Hebrew word meaning "adversary" or "accuser." He is "the accuser of our brothers and sisters" whom he "accuses . . . before our God day and night" (Rev 12:10). He accused Job (see Job 1:9-11; 2:4-5) and Joshua the high priest (see Zech 3:1). But in light of the atoning sacrifice of Christ, Satan's accusations are empty.

If somebody has a gun pointed at you, whether or not it's loaded is a huge deal. The devil doesn't want you to know that his gun has been emptied by the cross of Christ. Now, if you don't know that, you're still going to cower and run, living in fear and shame. But you don't have to listen to him. Though he is right about your sin, your debt has been paid by Christ. You are free to live for God. Satan still has power, but he no longer possesses final authority in history.

2:16-17 Old Testament sacrifices were like a layaway plan. But ultimately, "it is impossible for the blood of bulls and goats to take away sins" (Heb 10:4). At the right time, God sent his Son to offer the perfect sacrifice for sin once and for all (see Gal 4:4: Heb 10:10-14).

Therefore, since the price has been paid and you have your spiritual reward, **don't let anyone** deceive you by saying that you must do this or that ritual (2:16). The **shadow** of the Old Testament was meant to point to the **substance** of **Christ** (2:17). Why would anyone want a mere shadow when they can have the thing that cast the shadow?

2:18-19 Don't let a puffed-up false prophet tell you that you are in trouble unless you know some secret information to which only he has access (2:18). What you need is to be part of the **body**, the church, which is connected by **ligaments and tendons** and vertebrae and nerves and muscles to **the head**, Jesus Christ. This is the *only* way to receive ongoing spiritual **growth from God** (2:19). Any unchurched Christian will be a spiritually malnourished one.

2:20-23 We don't belong to the kingdom **of this world** anymore, so we shouldn't act like we do. We have spiritual freedom in the kingdom of God, so we should not **submit to regulations** from the world (2:20). Adding to God's commands might sound wise and religious, but such **human commands** are going to be destroyed (2:22). They carry no authority, and they strip away your freedom in Christ. Add-on rules function like extra carry-on bags: they'll rob you of the freedom to fly. **Self-made religion** has no power to control **self-indulgence** (2:23). The world's decrees and precepts don't help a person to be truly spiritual. They are of no value in the eternal kingdom of God.

V. THE DEVELOPMENT AND APPLICATION OF THE CHRISTIAN MIND (3:1-17)

3:1-2 Unfortunately, many modern Christians are out of their minds. What do I mean? Well, if you have bad habits that you can't control, you have a mind problem. Actions originate in the thinking. You may assume you can just break your bad habit, but you must begin to pry it loose in your mind. If there is no change to how you think, there will be no substantive change in how you live. This is why Scripture calls for "the renewing of your mind" (Rom 12:2).

Paul wants us to understand that our minds will determine our well-being. The only source for a victorious new mind is **where Christ is, seated at the right hand of God** (3:1). Therefore, we are to **set [our] minds on things above, not on earthly things** (3:2). Believers must be tuned in to the Heavenly Broadcasting Network to receive the data needed for daily living. The problem is that too many of us frequently change the channel to faulty programming. Some embrace unbiblical data from the world and then wonder why their lives are a wreck.

We'll never become spiritual by using the world's methodology (2:20).

Victorious living requires a shift of focus. We must have a heavenly mindset for earthly action. Paul is not saying, "Think about heaven all day, so you will know how to live when you get there." Rather, he says in essence, "Take a good look at heaven's perspective on every issue, so you will know how to live on earth." We need a kingdom mentality if we expect to receive heavenly benefits.

3:3-4 To help the Colossians develop a new mentality, Paul reminds them of their new identity. First, he says, **you died**. Your old life has no more power over you. Second, **your life is hidden with Christ in God**. In fact, Christ is not merely to be in your life; he is to *be* the total sum of **your life** (3:4).

We have been "raised with Christ" and "seated" with him (2:13; 3:1). If Christ is your new identity (that is, if you're a Christian) and heaven is your new location (you're physically on earth but participating in the spiritual realm), then you're called to live from that new perspective. Decisions are to be informed by an eternal, heavenly perspective rather than an imperfect, earthly one. We need a Christian view of the world—a kingdom worldview.

3:5-7 Paul's words in 3:1-4 are crucial and essential. But we can't stop there. Though you have heavenly blessings available to you through faith in Christ, you must access them by taking heed to God's Word. Paul calls Christians to **put to death what belongs to [the] earthly nature** (cp. Rom 8:12-13)—to kick that earthly perspective out! Don't give it a chance to breathe or rear its ugly head. Paul then gives a sordid list of common sins that need to be dealt a deathblow (3:5). **Because of these** things, **God's wrath is coming** (3:6). **You once walked in** them (3:7), Paul says, but you've been saved and cleansed by Christ. You've been "raised" and "seated" with him (3:1). Your spiritual bank account is full (see Eph 1:18). Why go from the palace to the poorhouse spiritually? As Paul argues in Romans (see Rom 6:15-22), why offer yourself as a slave to those things from which you've been freed? Why continue to participate in things that you're ashamed of?

3:8-11 In 3:5, Paul says to "put to death" the sins of "your earthly nature." Here he says **put away** even **anger** and **filthy language** (3:8). They don't belong in your life. When you have taken a shower, you naturally put on clean clothes. They complement what the shower was designed to do. Jesus Christ cleansed you by his blood. Therefore, you must ask yourself concerning your actions, "Will those clothes match what Jesus did in my life? Or will they dirty up what Jesus made clean?" Instead of wearing the dirty grave clothes of **the old self**—by doing things like telling lies **to one another**—**put on** the clean clothes of **the new self** (3:9-10). Paul lists a variety of ways people sin with the **mouth** (3:8-9). But because Christ has set you free, your mouth no longer rules you. You're no longer a slave. You have a new, domesticated mouth as part of your "new self." So use it rightly. This is what it looks like to be **renewed in knowledge according to the image of your Creator** (3:10). And God does

not have favorites, because Christ has first place in everything (3:11).

3:12-14 What are some of the clothes of "the new self" that we need to wear (3:9-10)? Paul tells the Colossians what to put on: **compassion, kindness, humility, gentleness, and patience** (3:12). These are the counterparts to the dirty clothes of "the old self" (3:8-9). And over all of this, we are to **put on love, which is the perfect bond of unity** (3:14). If the qualities in 3:12 comprise the Christian's new wardrobe, love is the overcoat.

One way we manifest the characteristics of the new self is by **forgiving one another** (3:13). Some believers harbor unforgiveness, and it results in perpetual anger and bitterness. Why? Because, as far as they're concerned, offenses committed against them linger like unpaid bills, and they demand payment. However, they forget that our vertical relationship with God is linked with our horizontal relationships with one another.

Forgiveness does *not* mean approving a sin or excusing evil. Rather, forgiveness means releasing people from obligations incurred by their wrongs against you. This may come in the form of unilateral forgiveness—that is, forgiving someone who has not asked for forgiveness. Or it may come in the form of transactional forgiveness, which involves the confession of the offender, his repentance, and reconciliation.

What makes forgiveness possible is recognizing that **the Lord has forgiven you** (3:13). There is an inseparable link between forgiving and recognizing that you've been forgiven. To refuse to forgive, in fact, is to burn a bridge over which you must cross (see Matt 6:14-15). If you refuse to forgive, you have blocked God's operation in your life (see Matt 18:21-35). But when you forgive, you no longer "grieve" the Holy Spirit (Eph 4:30), and you imitate the one who has forgiven you.

3:15-16 Let the peace of Christ . . . rule your hearts. When you are committed to setting your mind "on things above" (3:2), God will give you the peace of Christ—inner calm despite trying circumstances to help confirm your decisions and the directions for your life. If you don't have that, something is out of alignment. So, in order for peace to rule, you must **let the word of Christ dwell richly** (3:16). The Word of God must be at home in you, welcome in every room of your heart.

When I visit with members of my church, they say, "Make yourself at home, pastor." But they don't want me going into every room and doing whatever I want! God's Word, by contrast, must have access to every inch of the house of your heart—every bedroom, closet, and attic. You may have junk and dirt in places that you don't want God to see. But rest assured: he already knows about it. And if you'll let him, he can clean it up.

Our **psalms, hymns, and spiritual songs** are to be directed toward God and toward one another. With them we worship our Lord **with gratitude**, and we also teach one another biblical truth.

3:17 Doing something **in the name of . . . Jesus** is like authorizing a contract with his signature. You are to **do everything** under the authority of Jesus, making sure he approves of your actions. Jesus's name signed at the bottom of your day means his power is behind your life. You are to do all things with his reputation in mind.

VI. KINGDOM PEOPLE IN THE HOME, ON THE JOB, AND IN THE CHURCH (3:18–4:1)

3:18 A Christian home is not just a place where some Christians reside; it's where the authority of Jesus Christ rules the participants of a family (see commentary on Eph 5:22–6:4).

Paul begins offering guidance about the kind of household in which kingdom families are made by telling **wives** to **submit** to their **husbands**. This is not a command of subservience. The husband serves as the "head" of the wife in a role of authority, just as God the Father is "the head of" God the Son (1 Cor 11:3). The Father and Son are equally God. Neither is greater in value; both share in the divine essence. Similarly, both a husband and wife are made in God's image (Gen 1:27). They are equal as human beings before God. But God has created them to operate with different functions in the home. Wives are to align themselves under the legitimate leadership of their husbands. This doesn't mean that wives have no input. A wise kingdom husband, in fact, will always value the input of the kingdom wife God has given him! But the point here is that the husband has the ultimate responsibility for making decisions under God that affect the well-being of the family.

Importantly, wives are not to submit to their husbands in just anything. Their submission is limited to what is **fitting in the Lord**—that is, to what falls within the boundaries of God's will. A wife owes her ultimate

allegiance to Jesus Christ—not her husband. If a husband asks his wife to sin, she does not owe him her submission.

3:19 Husbands are commanded to **love** their **wives**. A kingdom man, then, is not a dictator, ruling his home with a heavy hand and expecting his family to wait on him. Instead, he is a benevolent leader under the authority of God, acting with love and seeking the well-being of his wife and children. The husband's model is Christ, who sacrificially loved his bride—the church—to the point of death (see Eph 5:25).

Too many men marry because of what they expect to get out of marriage. They mistake the *benefits* of marriage for the *purpose* of marriage. Marriage's purpose is the advancement of God's kingdom in history through replicating his image and exercising dominion over the earth (see Gen 1:28).

3:20 Parents must be unified in their parenting, seeking to act as one, because it's hard for children to obey contradictory instructions. **Children** are to **obey** their **parents in everything**. Kids are only to disobey parents should those parents tell them to disobey God. The proper ordering of God's kingdom family requires children to be aligned under their parents, wives to be aligned under their husbands, and everyone to be aligned under the Son who is aligned under the Father. This glorifies God and allows his blessings to flow.

Furthermore, dads and moms need to teach their sons and daughters the spiritual motivation for their obedience: it **pleases the Lord**. This fact should be taught from an early age. Children who are taught to obey parents who love them will come to understand what it means to obey their loving heavenly Father.

3:21 Though children are to honor and obey both fathers and mothers (3:20; Eph 6:1; Prov 1:8; 6:20), fathers have the responsibility of taking the lead in disciplining their children. Biblical discipline is exercised in love for the recipient's well-being. As Solomon declares, "The LORD disciplines the one he loves, just as a father disciplines the son in whom he delights" (Prov 3:12).

Never does a loving father want to **exasperate [his] children** and cause them to **become discouraged**. When you correct your children, you want to break their will—their stubbornness—without breaking their spirit. The goal is to lead them to willing obedience and righteousness. God takes the same approach with us, reminding us that "No discipline seems enjoyable at the time, but painful. Later on, however, it yields the peaceful fruit of righteousness to those who have been trained by it" (Heb 12:11). We need to know of the value God places on us. Likewise, our children need to know that they are significant and important and that we as their parents will love them and not place demands on them that they can never satisfy. Remember, rules without relationship lead to rebellion.

3:22 Paul instructs **slaves** to **obey** their **human masters** (see commentary on Eph 6:5-9), which is a principle we can apply to our own vocations. Ultimately, regardless of our occupations, we all serve God and are accountable to him for the quality of our work (see 1 Cor 10:31; Eph 6:5-6). Therefore, we should serve our employers **wholeheartedly**, rather than being **people-pleasers** who work only when being watched. You live before a sovereign God who sees everything you do. His rewards for your faithfulness are better than any raise you can receive.

3:23-25 Work like it is **something done for the Lord** (3:23)—because it is. Let your motivation be spiritual. Since you work for God, you are to produce excellence. Since you produce excellence, you should satisfy your earthly employer and your customer. Make no mistake: with God, nothing goes unnoticed. As a result of your faithfulness, **you will receive the reward of an inheritance from the Lord** (3:24). But if you decide to be a **wrongdoer** instead, count on being **paid back** by the Lord for that too (3:25).

4:1 Masters, **deal with your slaves justly and fairly** (see commentary on Eph 6:5-9). As with 3:22, the principle is applicable today. Employers ought to treat their employees with dignity, justness, and fairness. That clearly excludes abuse and oppression. If you are an employer, remember that **you too have a Master in heaven**. And God will deal with your business and your life in accordance with how you deal with those who work for you. Your employment practices are to reflect the character of the God you serve.

VII. FINAL GREETINGS AND FAREWELL (4:2-18)

4:2 Paul urges the Colossians to pray. Christians must take **prayer** seriously and not casually. Like a lookout watching for the enemy, we must **stay alert** in prayer. A believer who is outfitted with "the full armor of God" (Eph 6:11-17) but refuses to "pray" (Eph 6:18) is like a front-line soldier outfitted with the best weapons technology and protective gear but who has no communication with his command authority. He won't last long.

4:3-6 Paul also requests prayer for the sake of his own gospel ministry (4:3). This is a reminder that Christians must pray for pastors, missionaries, and themselves—that God would **open** doors with unbelievers so that they will hear **the mystery of Christ**

(4:3). Behave **wisely** with regard to non-believers (4:5), and don't waste opportunities to share the gospel. Combine tact with spice. Our witness should be crafted for **each person** in his unique situation (4:6) so that the gospel message is applied rightly to those who need to know about the Christian faith.

4:7-9 Not wanting to deliver **all** of his **news** by letter, Paul placed it in the hands of **Tychicus** and **Onesimus**, each a trusted and **dearly loved brother** (4:7, 9). They could give the Colossian church a personal update and encouragement (4:8-9).

4:10-17 Paul sent **greetings** from six fellow workers, and then he asked the Colossians to send greetings to the believers in **Laodicea** (4:10-15)—located about ten miles from Colossae. He also wanted these churches to pass around the letters he had written, which shows how Paul's letters were first circulated (4:16). Though we do not have a copy of Paul's letter to the Laodiceans, we do have the risen Lord Jesus's letter to the church in Laodicea that the apostle John records in the book of Revelation (Rev 3:14-22).

4:18 Paul provided a handwritten **greeting** as a stamp of authenticity that the letter was indeed from him. He also made a final request to be remembered in prayer during his time of imprisonment.

1 THESSALONIANS

INTRODUCTION

Author

PAUL IDENTIFIES HIMSELF AS THE author of 1 and 2 Thessalonians (1 Thess 1:1; 2 Thess 1:1). No serious objections have been made about his authorship of the former, but some critical scholars have questioned his authorship of the latter. Some argue that the two letters are too different from one another to have been penned by the same author. Alleged differences, however, are overblown. We are fully justified in believing that the apostle Paul wrote both. And though he mentions Silvanus and Timothy in his initial greetings (1 Thess 1:1; 2 Thess 1:1), clearly Paul is the primary author.

Historical Background

Paul visited Thessalonica (the modern Greek city of Thessaloniki) during his second missionary journey. It was an important port city on the Aegean Sea, the capital of the Roman province of Macedonia, and was located at the crossroads of two major routes. Thus, it was significant culturally and economically.

Though a large number of Greeks in Thessalonica initially believed Paul's preaching, the Jews there stirred up persecution against him so that he had to flee to Berea (see Acts 17:1-10). Paul probably wrote 1 and 2 Thessalonians in AD 50–51 during his lengthy ministry in Corinth (see Acts 18:1-17).

Message and Purpose

Paul wrote to the believers in Thessalonica because false teachers had infiltrated and were threatening damage to the church. He also wanted to challenge the moral laxity that had penetrated the church and to correct confusion that had arisen concerning Christ's second coming. Some believers in Thessalonica were suffering for their commitment to Christ, so Paul also wrote to encourage them to remain faithful given that Christ could return at any moment. If these believers would live in light of Christ's immanent return, they would have lifestyles pleasing to the Lord.

The apostle balanced encouragement, correction, and challenge to call this church to remain faithful to Christ even though things were not going their way. He wanted them to operate with a kingdom mentality so that they would live out the values of God's kingdom in their daily lives.

www.bhpublishinggroup.com/qr/te/52_00

Outline

I. An Authentic Message for an Authentic Community (1:1-10)
II. Paul's Authentic Ministry (2:1-12)
III. The Authentic Testimony (2:13-20)
IV. The Authentic Touch (3:1-13)
V. The Authentic Walk (4:1-12)
VI. The Authentic Hope (4:13–5:11)
VII. An Authentic Farewell (5:12-28)

1 THESSALONIANS

I. AN AUTHENTIC MESSAGE FOR AN AUTHENTIC COMMUNITY (1:1-10)

1:1 Paul addresses his letter **to the church of the Thessalonians**, which is an important greeting. The word translated "church," *ekklēsia*, means a "called-out group." In the first century, any time people gathered for a common purpose, especially to address legal matters (as in a town hall meeting; see Acts 19:39-41) it was called an *ekklēsia*. Paul takes this everyday word and gives it new meaning: *we* as believers are the "called out ones"—called out from the agenda of hell to a kingdom agenda that executes the rule of heaven on earth. And the caller is none other than **God the Father**.

1:2-3 Immediately Paul begins to show us what this called-out community should be doing. We are to be characterized by **work produced by faith . . . labor motivated by love, and . . . endurance inspired by hope in** Christ (1:3). Faith, love, hope: these are the three Christian virtues that are the *product* of the gospel message. When people truly receive the grace and peace of Jesus (1:1), faith, hope, and love start radiating outward from them.

Understand: these are not merely feelings. You have a *working* faith, a *laboring* love, and an *enduring* hope. What will distinguish you in a cold, indifferent world is not how many Bible verses you quote, or how intense your emotions are, but how tangibly you serve others with your faith, hope, and love.

1:4 As **brothers and sisters loved by God**, we remember that our salvation happens because **[God] has chosen [us]**. God saved you—and all you can say is "thank you" because God certainly did not have to do it. You are saved to serve God by choice, not by chance. God found you before you found him. And that choice was for fulfilling a divinely ordained purpose on earth.

1:5 Even though the gospel reached you because of God's choice, it also came *through people.* Someone had the courage to have an awkward conversation with you—and thank God he or she did! But Paul says the **gospel did not come to you in word only** (though it certainly did come through words), **but also in power, in the Holy Spirit, and with full assurance.**

Don't miss Paul's statement, **You know how we lived among you.** His life was an open book. Just as our words tell people the good news about Jesus, our lives need to *show* them the good news too. Have you ever been to a movie when the picture turns off but the sound is still on? Audio alone proves insufficient, because you need both the sound and the picture to grasp the full scope of the film. The world needs to hear the gospel from our mouths and to see the gospel in our lives.

1:6 If you believe the gospel can transform you, then you believe it can transform others. That was happening in Thessalonica, because, as Paul says, the Thessalonians **became imitators of us and of the Lord.** This is no problem-free gospel or fairy-tale gospel in which believers just name and claim whatever they want and Jesus gives them miracle after miracle. This gospel may be accompanied by **severe persecution**. In fact, if you are an authentic Christian, you will experience tribulation (see 2 Tim 3:12). You are going to be resisted and rejected.

Nevertheless, even in tribulation, an authentic Christian community has **joy from the Holy Spirit**. In spite of rejection, in spite of difficulties, in spite of hard times, you have internal stability that external troubles can't touch because you have the Spirit.

1:7-8 You became an example to all the believers (1:7). The Thessalonians were an example—the Greek word *tupos* means "type" or "pattern"—allowing other people to see Jesus by looking at them.

If you want to show off a new clothing line, you put samples on a beautiful model. The model's role is to make the clothes look good. Similarly, the Thessalonians wore kingdom clothes—godly attitudes and actions—well. When they reacted to tragedy, they made Jesus look good. The language they used made Jesus look good. The way they conducted themselves at home made Jesus look good. Do you wear kingdom clothes well?

1:9 Paul mentions that the Thessalonians **turned to God from idols**. We might think this statement doesn't apply to us, but there are still idols today. An idol is any unauthorized person, place, thing, or thought that you look to as your source. An idol is anyone or anything, other than God, that holds your confidence, trust, and allegiance. While many American households lack idols of stone, many of us drive idols of steel. And though we don't have idols of wood, we stash idols of paper in our bank accounts. Further, even though we don't have idols of gold, we put all our hope into particular people in our lives. Everybody has a god. Everybody has a master. The only question is this: what (or who) is yours?

The alternative to serving idols is to **serve the living and true God**. Don't miss that word *serve*. Our footsteps, just as much as our mouths, show the world whether we believe in the God of the Bible.

1:10 We will see this theme come up again, but it is significant to note that already in this first chapter Paul brings up the second coming of Christ. We **wait for [God's] Son from heaven**. An authentic Christian community becomes an expectant community. And if we are truly waiting for him, we'll be about his kingdom work.

II. PAUL'S AUTHENTIC MINISTRY (2:1-12)

2:1-2 When Paul encourages the Thessalonians to stand firm in the midst of persecution, he does so as one familiar with trials. Paul **suffered** and was **treated outrageously in Philippi**—he was beaten and wrongly imprisoned; nevertheless, he still felt **emboldened by . . . God to speak the gospel** (2:2). Paul knows that the authentic Christian life is going to have tough times. He knows what it feels like to want to quit. But he also knows that an authentic minister never throws in the towel.

2:3-6 Apparently Paul was accused of having terrible motives. Some were saying that he was deceiving others, seeking the praise of people, and running after wealth. Thus, Paul spends this next section defending his actual motives.

Paul points out that his preaching did not, despite rumors, **come from error or impurity or an intent to deceive** (2:3). The Thessalonians knew better than that (cf. 2:5). In fact, when your preaching makes people want to stone you, beat you, and throw you in prison, it quickly becomes obvious that you are not a clever salesman trying to tickle people's ears. Paul was interested in one audience only—God. Therefore, Paul had one concern—**not to please people, but . . . God** (2:4). Since God was his only audience, he was able to say with confidence, **God is our witness** (2:5). That's a powerful thought. If you walk with God, God himself will testify on your behalf. No slanderous accusation of greed or self-interest or flattery will stick when God takes the witness stand for you.

2:7-12 As further proof of Paul's pure motives, he reminds the Thessalonians of his relationship with them. He was **gentle among [them], as a nurse nurtures her own children** (2:7), or, as he says later, **like a father with his own children** (2:11). Caring relationships—not merely sermons—were the key to his ministry. And that principle applies to everyone in the church, not just to the pastor. Lives touching lives is what makes a church. Individuals can't care for hundreds or thousands of people, but they can care for each other.

What does this sort of care look like? Paul shows us. We preach **God's gospel** to each other (2:9). We encourage and comfort each other by sharing burdens (2:12). Most of all, we **live worthy of God.** Only by walking with him will we have life to give to others.

III. THE AUTHENTIC TESTIMONY (2:13-20)

Authentic Christianity will lead to suffering and rejection. (If you haven't suffered yet, just wait!) Therefore, Paul teaches the Thessalonians how to hang on; he shows them what an authentic testimony looks like in tough times.

2:13 The first anchor of an authentic testimony is God's Word. Paul thanks God because the Thessalonians recognized his message for what it was—not **a human message** but **the word of God.** Only having Scripture within can sustain you when there is trouble without. If you don't have anything cooking on the inside, don't be surprised if you fall apart on the outside.

The Thessalonians knew Paul's teaching was God's Word, so they **received** and **welcomed it.** The Greek word translated "welcomed" means more than just hearing the Word and appreciating it. It means they respected, reverenced, embraced, and inculcated it. Like people enjoying a good meal, they not only tasted and chewed the Word but digested it. It does us no good merely to read a few Bible passages. We have to swallow and digest them by acting on what they say. Only then will we experience Scripture's work in our lives.

2:14-18 The second anchor of an authentic testimony is having fellowship with other believers. Paul points out that the Thessalonians **suffered the same things from people of [their] own country, just as** the Jewish churches **did from the Jews** (2:14). The Thessalonians' own people had turned on them! But, in the midst of that betrayal, the Thessalonians **became imitators of God's churches in Christ Jesus . . . in Judea** (2:14).

God created churches so that you would not have to be a Christian alone. You are part of a body (cf. 1 Cor 12), and no body part works unless it is attached to the whole.

The Thessalonians had problems with Gentiles. The Jewish churches had problems with Jews. But these churches could look to each other in tough times, offering support out of a shared understanding of what it is like to suffer for Christ. They had become family—Paul calls them **brothers and sisters** (2:17)—and we all know that blood is thicker than water.

2:19-20 The last anchor of an authentic testimony—that which will carry us through the difficult times—is a vision of the glory of God. Paul mentions **the presence of our Lord Jesus at his coming** yet again. But this time he adds a twist. The reward that Paul looks forward to when Jesus returns, Paul's **crown,** is the Thessalonians themselves. He can't contain himself and blurts out: **You are our glory and joy!** (2:20).

In light of Jesus's return, Paul's greatest joy was leading people to Jesus. He had a kingdom perspective, an *eternal* perspective. When I get to heaven, I want to see a welcoming committee there because of what I've done on earth. I want to look around and say, "I invested in her"; "I led him to Christ"; "I discipled and built them up." There is a deep, unshakable joy in saying, "Lord Jesus, let me deliver to you these other saints. They *are* my joy."

IV. THE AUTHENTIC TOUCH (3:1-13)

We live in a high tech world, but even the best technology is no replacement for relationship. We can be high tech, but we need high *touch* to grow spiritually. We in the church need real intimacy, and that only comes through authentic touch.

3:1-2 Paul was so devoted to authentic touch that he let his closest ministry partner go so that the Thessalonians could receive it. Long distance contact was just not enough. Paul **sent Timothy ... God's coworker in the gospel of Christ** (3:2), because Paul knew that the Thessalonians needed flesh and blood. They needed someone to **strengthen and encourage** them in person (3:2).

The Greek verb Paul uses for "encourage" is *parakaleō*. It shares a root with the noun (*paraklētos*) that describes the Holy Spirit in John 14:26 ("Counselor") and 1 John 2:1 ("advocate"). When God wants to encourage a believer, he uses his Holy Spirit to do it, but he often does that *through* another believer. You and I are to function like the Holy Spirit with skin on.

3:3 Why did Paul think authentic touch so important? Well, Paul knew something that we often forget: life is full of suffering. He wants us to have our eyes open to the reality of suffering **so that no one will be shaken by ... afflictions.** Paul was concerned that the Thessalonians' spiritual lives would prove fickle—going up and down, back and forth, just like a dog's tail. He wanted them to be consistent and unshaken when trouble came.

And Paul knew that trouble would come. Believers, in fact, **are appointed to this.** In other words, Christians are elected, chosen, destined *for trouble.* That's probably not what you were hoping for! But it's true. As soon as we start following Jesus, trouble starts following us. We don't have to find it. It knows our address; it will arrive (see John 16:33). But the good news is that God intends to use it for our good.

3:4-5 Trouble comes at us in myriad ways. Paul knew, for instance, that he was **going to experience affliction** (3:4). The only way to avoid affliction in this world, in fact, is to leave it. Everyone suffers. But when you come to Jesus, you get double trouble, because then you have a target on your back. You're a target for the world and for the devil.

Many of us think of the devil as a silly guy in a red jump suit with horns who carries a pitchfork. We aren't worried about him. But Paul was. When Paul thought of the devil, he didn't have in mind some ridiculous caricature. He knew that the devil is an evil spirit who hates God and seeks to tempt God's children and destroy their faith. Paul was concerned that **the tempter** might have **tempted** the Thessalonians and that his own **labor might be for nothing** (3:5). Satan is real, and he is after you and me. We need authentic touch to overcome his schemes.

3:7 Paul practiced what he preached. He starts off this chapter exhorting the Thessalonians to live high-touch lives of authenticity, and he lets them see that he's already doing it. In all of Paul's **distress and affliction,** what kept him going, he says, was their **faith.** Paul was going through trouble. Maybe he felt like he could not muster up enough of his own faith, so he borrowed some of the Thessalonians'. Indeed, we have to borrow each other's faith sometimes. Call it "faith on loan." Everybody loses faith. Everybody falls down. We need somebody to pick us up again. Paul had the Thessalonians. Whom do you have? Connectivity with a solid, biblically centered local church is indispensable for properly progressing in the Christian life.

3:8 What Paul says here is a statement about how inextricably connected we are in the church. **For now we live,** Paul says, **if you stand firm in the Lord.** This is staggering! Paul, the greatest missionary ever, says to the Thessalonians, "How *you* stand will determine how *we* live." In other words, he says, "I can't make it without you." Even apostles and pastors need encouragement in this vicious and divided world.

3:10 Here is the idea of borrowing faith again; this time it's seen in the phrase, **complete**

what is lacking in your faith. Faith needs community. I need you, and you need me. On our own, our faith is lacking. There are no Lone Ranger believers. If we believe all by ourselves, we will not believe for long. Any unchurched, uninvolved Christian is living outside the will of God.

3:12-13 Paul prays three things for the Thessalonian believers. First, he prays for spiritual growth. He wants the Thessalonians **to increase and overflow with love for one another** (3:12). Love is the hallmark of true spiritual growth. Love is a choice to serve someone for his or her good. It is a decision of the will, which is why we can—and should—love people even if we do not *like* them. We choose to love, and then we ask God to help our emotions catch up.

Second, Paul prays for spiritual unity. The Thessalonians needed to have love for each other, but also **for everyone** (3:12). Love and unity go hand-in-hand. If this were easy, Paul would not need to pray for it! Some of us need to take a hard look at our lives. If the only people we love are just like us, Paul may have some harsh words for us.

Third, Paul prays for their holiness. He asks that God would make their **hearts blameless in holiness** because Jesus is coming back (3:13). Paul simply cannot stop mentioning the return of Christ! He wants us all to live in light of Jesus's second coming, and that means living in holiness. If Jesus came back today—in the next hour—would he find you doing kingdom work? Would he say to you, "Well done, good and faithful servant" (Matt 25:23)?

V. THE AUTHENTIC WALK (4:1-12)

4:1 Almost all of Paul's letters follow a simple pattern. They begin with encouragement and prayer, and about halfway through, they turn to instruct and challenge readers. In chapter 4, we see that Paul is making this turn.

Specifically, Paul wants to see them **live and please God.** It can be easy to begin the Christian life well, but following Jesus is not just a single step. It's about putting one foot in front of the other for a lifetime. Thankfully for the Thessalonians, Paul sees little reason to rebuke them in this. He simply says, **as you are doing** this (pleasing God), **do this even more.** In other words, keep letting your life and words point toward Jesus.

4:2 Paul is about to give some ethical and moral guidance about what this walk looks like, but the details are slim. That's because the Thessalonians already **know what commands** he gave **through the Lord Jesus.** They do not need to hear a long discourse about right and wrong because they *know* right and wrong already.

I suspect we are like the Thessalonians, but we might say that we don't know enough to follow God's will. If we are honest, however, our problem is not that we don't know God's commands—it's that we are not obedient to

what we already know. To that Paul would say, "Remember what Jesus said? Don't ask me for the next lesson unless you're obeying *that.*"

4:3 What is **God's will** for the Thessalonians? Simple: their **sanctification,** which Paul connects to **sexual immorality.** Paul knows that believers need to be sanctified in a lot of areas, but he starts with the topic of sex on purpose. He knows that if Jesus can help us to win in this matter, we can win in any other. Indeed, if Jesus helps us to walk away from pornography or to stop sleeping around, then he's really the Master of our lives.

4:5 At the root of sexual strongholds is not sex itself. Our **lustful passions** are not just bodily passions, and overcoming them is not just a matter of better discipline. When we succumb to sexual strongholds, we are worshiping the wrong thing. In committing acts of sexual immorality, then, we are not just making a mistake. We are proving that we are **like the** unsaved **Gentiles, who don't know God.** Sexual immorality is a fruit of an idolatrous root—of the worship of pleasure over God, something that should not be true of believers who possess the Spirit. And if we worship our way into sin, the only solution is to worship our way out of it.

4:6 One of the most attractive lies about sexual immorality is that we can get away with the thrill and not experience negative consequences. But Paul reminds us that **the Lord is an avenger of all these offenses.** He sees what we are doing, even if no one else does.

4:7 Living an authentic kingdom life doesn't start with obeying commands. It starts with understanding who we are in Christ. God tells us who we are before telling us what he wants us to do. Thus, when Paul wants to give the Thessalonians motivation to stay sexually pure, he does not just say, "Watch out! God will get you!" He reminds them of their identity in Christ: **God has not called us to impurity but to live in holiness.** Though we do not stay pure to earn God's love, we are to stay pure *because* God loves us.

4:9-10 If the Thessalonians had avoided sexual immorality but were gossiping and back-biting, verses 3-7 would be much shorter and verses 9-10 would be much longer. But apparently Paul felt that the Thessalonians were demonstrating Christian love to each other well. **About brotherly love,** he says, **you don't need me to write you** (4:9). Paul's advice on the topic is therefore short and sweet: **do this even more** (4:10). Paul has nothing to say other than, "Keep walking that walk." Unlike most churches, the Thessalonian church seemed to have mastered the art of loving each other.

4:11 Evidently, some of the Thessalonians had gotten so excited about Jesus's return that they had quit their jobs. But Paul reminds them **to work with [their] own hands,** because their laziness had become a liability to their friends and neighbors. Waiting expectantly for Jesus's return does not mean that we stop working and sit around doing nothing, wasting time until the rapture. It means we work *differently,* looking to Jesus (and not our work) for our hope.

VI. THE AUTHENTIC HOPE (4:13–5:11)

4:13 Paul knows how dangerous ignorance can be; therefore, he doesn't want the Thessalonians **to be uninformed.** An ignorant Christian can become a hopeless Christian. And as sure as wrong doctrine leads to wrong beliefs, wrong beliefs lead to wrong living. To know the truth is to be set free from the hopelessness of ignorance. As Jesus said, the truth shall set us free (see John 8:32).

What kind of ignorance is Paul concerned with? Here he mentions **those who are asleep,** referring to people in the Thessalonian congregation who have died. Their living loved ones were afraid that they had missed the rapture. But Christians need not **grieve like the rest,** those **who have no hope** because they are uncertain what happens after death (if anything). Paul reminds us that for the Christian, death is not the end. It is the beginning of a brand new life.

4:14-15 There is a contrast here between our deaths and Jesus's. Note that **Jesus died and**

rose again (4:14), whereas we are described as having **fallen asleep.** If we believe in Jesus, what we call "death" is no more permanent or harmful than sleep. We need not fear it anymore than we'd fear a nap. Believers who perish will come back with Christ, which means that Christian loved ones who pass away remain alive in heaven with him, not trapped in the grave (see 2 Cor 5:8; Phil 1:22-23). At the rapture, they'll return with Christ to reclaim their resurrected, eternally glorified bodies.

4:16 Repeatedly in the letter, Paul has told the Thessalonians that Jesus is coming back (see John 14:1-3). Now we see *how* he is coming. Apparently it will be a loud event since **the Lord himself will descend from heaven with a shout.** Jesus came the first time like a whisper. Most people, in fact, missed him. But no believer will miss him the second time.

What will Jesus be shouting when he returns? There's another instance in Scripture when Jesus shouted—when he called the dead man Lazarus by name, and Lazarus walked out of the grave (see John 11:43-44). When Jesus comes back, he will do that again, many times over. I'm going to hear, "Evans, come forth!" And my old body, decayed in the grave, is going to jump back to life again and be united with my spirit and soul.

4:17 Many of us have heard the word *rapture*. And it is from this verse that we get the idea. Where Paul says that we **will be caught up together**, the Latin word for "caught up" is *rapturo*. At the rapture, those of us **who are still alive** will join other brothers and sisters in Christ, and we will meet **them in the clouds**. Our bodies will not have the same limitations that they do today. Not only will our busted bodies be put back together, but you and I will literally be able to walk on cloud nine since we will have a resurrected body like his (see 1 John 3:2). Since those alive will join those who are coming back with the Lord, this clearly proves that believers who die immediately go to be with the Lord (2 Cor 5:8).

4:18 What are we supposed to do with all of this information? Well, Paul's point is not just to teach eschatology or give us details about the rapture. Paul wants us to **encourage one another with these words.** As we saw earlier (3:2), we are to walk alongside other believers and encourage them, just as the Holy Spirit does. We are called to comfort others when they are hurting—in the same way we expect them to comfort us.

5:1 Paul knows the Thessalonians want to hear **about the times and the seasons**—that is, they want a timeline for Jesus's return. But the illustrations Paul uses here remind us that we will not get one. After all, if we're busily looking at dates on the calendar we'll fail to look for the Lord. Jesus's second coming is imminent—that is, we should expect him to return at any time. It could be tomorrow or it could be in a hundred years. One thing is certain: It will be a surprise for people who do not expect it.

5:2 The day of the Lord is the future time of judgment and blessing after the rapture through the conclusion of the millennial kingdom (see Isa 13:9-11; Joel 2:28-32; Zeph

1:14-18; 3:14-15). Paul says Jesus will return **like a thief in the night** (5:2). A thief does not send a note in advance. He doesn't say, "Tomorrow night, around 11:00 pm, I plan to break your back door with a sledgehammer and take your television." So, if you are not prepared for a thief to arrive at any hour, you are not prepared at all.

5:3 The other analogy Paul uses here is **labor pains** (5:3). Doctors can tell mothers when they *think* a particular baby will arrive, but mothers know that the baby will ultimately choose the time of his arrival. And when baby decides to come, Mom isn't going anywhere. In one moment, everything changes for her. The day of the Lord is that time after the rapture when God directly intervenes in world affairs for judgment during the tribulation and for blessings in Messiah's millennial reign.

5:4-5 Jesus's return will be a surprise for nonbelievers, but it should not be a surprise for Christians. You **are not in the dark, for this day to surprise you** (5:4). If you are a Christian, you should not be staggering through life like everyone else. You **do not belong to the night** because **you are all children of light and children of the day** (5:5). Therefore, you ought to be living with grateful assurance, knowing you are headed to glory and not to the wrath of the tribulation (5:9). Your knowledge of the future should grant you confidence in the present.

5:6-10 We must **stay awake and be self-controlled** (5:6), rather than **sleep** and **get drunk** (5:7)—which is a reference to spiritual soberness and spiritual drunkenness. To do this, we need three things: faith, hope, and love. We must put these on: **the armor of faith and love** and the **helmet of the hope of salvation** (5:8). Without these, we have no protection in this world. With them, however, we can be confident in our deliverance since God has not destined us for **wrath** (5:9).

5:11 Here is that command again: **encourage one another**. And this time Paul adds, **build each other up**. These theological truths are not for personal education alone but for our corporate edification. We stand or we fall—together.

VII. AN AUTHENTIC FAREWELL (5:12-28)

5:14 It takes great wisdom to shepherd God's people well. Part of that wisdom lies in being aware of the different seasons in which people live. For **those who are idle**, Paul says we should **warn** them. There comes a time we must, out of love for fellow believers, confront them when they are not walking with Jesus.

To those who are **discouraged**, Paul says we should offer **comfort**. Not every problem a person experiences in life is a result of their sin. When a fellow believer is lacking in courage, he or she needs you to believe for them, and to be their comfort.

To those who are **weak**, we should offer **help**. After all, as the old song says, we all need somebody to lean on. Today I may help you in your weakness, but tomorrow I will need you to help me in mine. That's how the body of Christ works.

Finally—and this is the most difficult part—we should **be patient with everyone.** We must be patient with people who are sinning and with people who are suffering, with people who want to change and with people who do not. Patience aims for every target. We must demonstrate compassion without compromise.

5:16-22 Here is Paul the preacher again. Though it almost seems as if he is nearing the end of his sermon, he has a lot more to say. He peppers the Thessalonians with short commands, trusting the Holy Spirit to put meat on those bones and help them apply the commands more specifically. **Rejoice always, pray constantly, give thanks in everything. . . . Don't stifle the Spirit. . . . Hold on to what is good. Stay away from every kind of evil.** The commands are simple, but following them certainly isn't! The only way we can constantly give thanks and rejoice is by knowing that God is working something out in our lives.

5:23-24 Not only is God working in our lives, but Paul is confident that **he who calls [us] is faithful** (5:24). God has never started a project he did not finish. And if he has started on you, you can be sure that he *will* **sanctify you completely** as you allow him to transform you from the inside out (spirit, soul, and body) (5:23).

5:25-28 Paul concludes by asking for prayer, sending greetings to all the church, and commanding that his letter **be read** to everyone (5:25-27). He began the letter with mention of grace (1:1) and ends it the same way: **the grace of our Lord Jesus Christ be with you** (5:28). From first to last, and every step along the way, the Christian life is lived by grace.

2 THESSALONIANS

INTRODUCTION

Author

See discussion in 1 Thessalonians.

Historical Background

See discussion in 1 Thessalonians.

Message and Purpose

Paul wrote this letter to correct doctrinal error because many of the Thessalonian Christians were confused. Their misunderstanding about the day of the Lord, the time of God's judgment preceded by the rapture (see 1 Thess 4:13-18), had caused some of the believers to live slothfully. They reasoned that since Christ's coming could happen any day, there was no point in working every day and dealing with daily burdens. Many were quitting their jobs and using prophecy as an excuse to be irresponsible, surviving off of the generosity of others.

Paul sought to correct the church's thinking and to explain how they should live responsibly in light of the truth about the day of the Lord. Paul was concerned that the Thessalonians understand right doctrine, but he also wanted them to engage in right living in light of it as part of God's kingdom people.

www.bhpublishinggroup.com/qr/te/53_00

Outline

I. Standing Firm in Suffering (1:1-12)
II. Standing Firm in Doctrine (2:1-12)
III. Standing Firm in Faithfulness (2:13-17)
IV. Standing Firm in Obedience (3:1-18)

2 THESSALONIANS

I. STANDING FIRM IN SUFFERING (1:1-12)

1:1-4 After greeting the Thessalonian church with **grace** and **peace** on behalf of himself, **Silvanus, and Timothy** (1:1-2), Paul encourages the church: **We ought to thank God always for you, brothers and sisters ... since your faith is flourishing** (1:3). Though the Thessalonians were experiencing difficult times, their faith was strong. Trials expand faith, just like exercise develops muscle. After all, how will you know God is bigger than your problems unless God gives you some you can't handle on your own—some "faith weights"?

Paul also says, **the love each one of you has for one another is increasing** (1:3). This is a reminder that in the midst of suffering, one of the greatest things you can do is serve. Why? Because God's power flows through his love! As faith reaches upward, love reaches outward. And as a result of the Thessalonians' growth in faith and love, Paul and his companions boasted about the Thessalonians **among God's churches**, about their **perseverance and faith in all** they were enduring (1:4). Other churches were being encouraged by the Thessalonians' spiritual commitment, patience, and love for one another, in spite of the persecution they were enduring.

Remember, you go to church not just for yourself, but also impact the lives of others through meaningful service. If you're ready to give up, I encourage you to stand firm. If you're too weak to move, call on somebody else to move you, but hang on to your faith. Don't disconnect. When believers suffer for the faith, they are gaining greater kingdom rewards and authority (see Rom 8:17).

1:5 You will be counted worthy of God's kingdom, for which you also are suffering. If you haven't suffered as a Christian, it's likely because nobody knows you are one. If this world order knows where you stand, it *will* resist you. Every believer, in fact, is going to have some kind of affliction. But remember this: When God finally establishes his kingdom, he's going to reward those who are worthy. None of us is worthy in and of ourselves, but when we have suffered, we will be co-reigners with Christ (see Rom 8:17).

1:6-10 Moreover, God will afflict **those who afflict you** (1:6). Count on it: there's a payday coming. God is going to take **vengeance ... on those who don't ... obey the gospel of our Lord Jesus. They will pay the penalty of eternal destruction** (1:8-9). What's the most frightening doctrine in the Bible? The doctrine of hell. If you don't know Christ, pay attention: a day of reckoning is coming! Eternal destruction means never-ending pain and regret. But if today you receive Christ as your deliverer, he will **give relief** (1:7).

The Bible gives peeks at both heaven and hell. Those who like to hang out with Satan in life will be away **from the Lord's presence and from his glorious strength** after death (1:9). There will be no answered prayers in hell. There will be no light and no peace, because God is light, and God is peace. Those who choose God, on the other hand, will experience glory unspeakable when they pass from this life (1:10). We should love heaven more than earth.

1:11-12 Life is like a machine, and prayer can recharge a person's batteries. If you keep up ongoing communication with the Lord, God will **fulfill your every desire to do good and your work produced by faith** (1:11). Paul knew that if the Thessalonian church was recharged by prayer, it would have an even more powerful witness: **The name of our Lord Jesus will be glorified by you . . .**

according to the grace of our God and the Lord Jesus (1:12).

If you go through a particularly difficult season and choose to lean on the Lord in prayer, somebody may look at you and ask, "How can you smile at a time like this? How are you standing when you ought to be stooping? How are you still worshiping when you ought to be complaining?" The answer will be that "those who trust in the LORD will renew their strength; they will soar on wings like eagles; they will run and not become weary, they will walk and not faint" (Isa 40:31).

II. STANDING FIRM IN DOCTRINE (2:1-12)

2:1-2 To build a doghouse, you don't need a foundation. But you do need one to build a house. And to build a skyscraper, you need a *deep* foundation. Many want to be skyscraper Christians, but don't want to pay the price of digging a foundation. Paul tells his readers **not to be easily upset or troubled** by false teaching (2:2). But if you're not grounded in the truth of Scripture, don't be surprised if you are unable to stand firm.

The Thessalonians were being told that **the day of the Lord [had] come**—that they had missed the rapture and were thus living in the tribulation! They were deceived in three ways. *First,* they were deceived by a **prophecy**—a spiritual or religious utterance. Paul told them previously, "Don't despise prophecies" (1 Thess 5:20), but the devil tries to talk in the name of God too. That's why John said we must "test the spirits" (1 John 4:1). Beware anyone who says, "God told me such-and-such," if it doesn't agree with God's Word.

Second, they were deceived by a **message**—hearsay. You might still be doing things merely because "Mama said." But the only legitimate messages we are to follow are those that agree with the message that comes from God.

Third, they were deceived by **a letter**— by things written down. Some of us need to change the books we're reading and skip looking at the newspaper horoscope. Rat poison is 90% food. But it's that last 10% that's

designed to kill. The standard of God's Word must provide our foundation.

2:3 Paul says they could not have missed the rapture and entered into the tribulation period (1 Thess 4:13-18; 5:1-3), because **the apostasy comes first and the man of lawlessness is revealed** before that. This is a good reminder that even new believers need to seek to understand prophecy because knowledge of the future will control decisions in the present. You don't need to study every religion in the world; you just need to know Christianity well. Then you'll be able to identify counterfeit religion. After all, federal agents learn to identify counterfeit dollars by studying the real thing.

2:4 Satan convinced Adam and Eve to rebel, to operate independently of God. That's what couples do who illegitimately give up on their marriages; that's what children do who disrespect their parents. The agenda of hell is to deceive people. Eventually, the human preference for lies through Satanic deception will lead to the appearance of "the lawless one" (2:3). He will be empowered to bring the rebellion against God to ultimate fruition. The lawless one will exalt himself as the supreme object of worship and proclaim himself to be God (see Rev 13:5-8). You have to listen carefully to what people say— learn to discern. Know what you believe and why you believe it to protect yourself from the enemy's lies.

2:5-8 The only reason the world is not as wicked as it could be is because something **currently restrains** the lawless one (2:6). **The mystery of lawlessness** is Satan's program of sin, and **the one now restraining** is the Holy Spirit working through the church (2:7). The Spirit sets himself up like a dam to hold back the full expression of evil until God removes his church out of the world at the rapture. The relationship of the church (and individual Christians) to the Holy Spirit affects the expansion or limitation of sin in our lives, our families, and the broader society.

2:9-10 Satan comes with **miracles, signs, and wonders**, but they are **false** (2:9). Satan is no ninety-pound weakling. He is a powerful spiritual being, and he can mimic supernatural wonders. **Deception** started with Satan's influence, and it continues as **those who are perishing** refuse to **accept the love of the truth** (2:10). When you reject truth, you invite lies into your life. The Word of God is truth; therefore, we should measure everything by Scripture.

2:11-12 If someone persists in hardening his heart and believing a lie, eventually God will give him what he wants (see commentary on Exod 4:21). That's the reality behind Paul's insight that **for this reason God sends them a strong delusion so that they will believe the lie** (2:11). Although you might believe you can get to heaven on your own—by living a good life, going to church, and doing your best—that's a lie. The only way to heaven is through God's channel, Jesus Christ. Those who allow themselves to believe anything else **will be condemned** (2:12). They will be judged for their decision to reject the truth. Delusion and deception will be greatly amplified during the tribulation (see Rev 13:11-18).

III. STANDING FIRM IN FAITHFULNESS (2:13-17)

2:13-14 Paul gives thanks for the Thessalonians and identifies four ways God has been active in their lives. *First*, they are **loved by the Lord** (2:13). God's love operates in cosmic proportions. In fact, you were loved "before the foundation of the world" (Eph 1:4-5). If he loved you that far in advance, just imagine how he feels about you now that you believe in Jesus for eternal life.

Second, Paul tells the believers, **God has chosen you** (2:13). In view here is the doctrine of election. The surrounding context makes it clear that this choosing does not refer to personal salvation but to deliverance from the tribulation through the rapture (2:1-4, 11-12; cp. 1 Thess 5:1-9). That ought to make you persevere when things become rough.

Third, God desires **sanctification** in his people (2:13). You were set apart for special use—to be holy. God sanctifies us **by the Spirit and through belief in the truth** (2:13)—that is, when the Holy Spirit works in us as we obediently trust his Word.

Fourth, God **called you** (2:14). God always calls people from *here* to *there*, and Satan's job is to keep us from getting *there*—to keep you from finding your purpose in life. And you certainly can't get *there* if you keep looking back at where you've been (see Phil 3:13-14).

God wants Christians to be partners with his Son, to **obtain the glory of our Lord Jesus** (2:14). God will eventually turn the whole universe over to Christ. That's why Jesus refused Satan's temptation to worship him in exchange for all the kingdoms of the world (see Matt 4:8-10). Jesus knew that he would one day rule the world anyway—through faithfulness to the Father. Some of us seek the things of this world through unrighteousness, but God already intends to give the world to his people, if we stand firm.

2:15 This is Paul's theme: **Stand firm.** You are to be like a member of the Queen's Guard in England—no matter what happens around you, you stand firm. While everybody else is waffling and buying into different worldviews, you hold onto the truth of Scripture.

Too many are fast-food Christians or spiritual hitchhikers, desiring convenience and a free ride. The Christian life is based on long-term perseverance. If you only follow Christ when he gives you good things, and not when you struggle, then you're not following Christ at all.

Paul told the Thessalonians to **hold to the traditions . . . taught** by apostolic authority, by the Word of God. Legitimate tradition does not contradict Christ. False traditions, the things you do because that's what you've always done, should be cast aside. Personal preference and cultural practice are not equal to the Word of God. Don't let human traditions enslave you; your Master is Christ (see Col 2:8).

2:16 The Christian life can be difficult as we try to hang on, try to toe the line, and wait for God to come through. But consider Paul: He said he was beaten, but he wasn't destroyed; he was downcast, but he wasn't obliterated (see 2 Cor 4:8-9). He got tired. But he reminds us that God has given us **eternal encouragement and good hope.**

God has already put on deposit in eternity all the comfort you need to deal with any situation you face. Think of it like having a well-supplied account at the bank; all you have to do is write a withdrawal slip.

And prayer is the slip. When David was depressed, he looked inside himself, and said, "Why, my soul, are you so dejected?" Then he told himself, "Put your hope in God." He knew that in doing so, he could keep praising God (Ps 42:5).

2:17 Encouragement comes from other people too. Paul prays for the Thessalonians, that God would **encourage [their] hearts and strengthen [them] in every good work and word.** Maybe you've been downcast, but then you go to church, and the sermon is exactly what you needed to hear. Maybe somebody called you at just the right moment when you were filled with despair. Such experiences aren't lucky coincidences. They are God's use of others to perform his supernatural encouragement and strengthening in our lives. That's why we need one another.

But how can you stand firm if you don't know how long it will be until deliverance comes? Well, imagine the teams rowing together in the Olympics. Eight men in the boat have their backs to the finish line, but they're looking at the coxswain. He's looking at the line and talking to them: "Row harder! The finish line is coming; don't give up!" Jesus is your coxswain. He knows where the end point is. You just watch him and row. Keep your eyes on "the source and perfecter of our faith" (Heb 12:2), and stand firm.

IV. STANDING FIRM IN OBEDIENCE (3:1-18)

3:1-2 Pray for us (3:1). Paul understood that he could not make it unless people prayed for him. If the apostle Paul needed prayer, how much more do we? The reason he asked for it was so that he might be **delivered from wicked and evil people, for not all have faith** (3:2).

Many people talk as if they're saved, but they're not truly saved. And their hypocrisy can rub off on us if we're not careful. One of the things God gives us when we pray is discernment. Paul reminds us elsewhere, "Our struggle is not against flesh and blood, but against the rulers, against the authorities, against the cosmic powers of

this darkness, against evil, spiritual forces in the heavens" (Eph 6:12). When you're in war, the enemy tries to cut off the communication lines. That's what Satan has done to many of us. Don't stop praying.

3:3-5 The Lord is faithful. There are a lot of people you can't count on, but you can count on God. **He will strengthen and guard you from the evil one** (3:3). That is why being with the people of God in the presence of God is critical. Paul is confident about what God will do for the Thessalonians. He will preserve them in obedience and **direct [their] hearts to God's love and Christ's**

endurance (3:5). Similarly, as you live in the presence of God, he will preserve you and you will stand firm.

3:6 Paul indicates the kind of people Christians ought to avoid and those they ought to hang around. He starts by saying, **in the name of the Lord**, to tell his readers that the matter he is about to address is serious: **Keep away from every brother or sister who is idle and does not live according to the tradition received from us.** Why? Well, just because people are members of your church doesn't mean they're spiritual. A church serves like a hospital: sick people go there to get better. Not every professing Christian, then, is somebody to follow—a person may be spiritually immature and still "sick," or just plain lazy and not concerned with growing in the Lord. Not everyone under a church's roof is exercising historical biblical faith. As the psalmist says, don't "walk in the advice of the wicked" (Ps 1:1).

3:7-9 So whom should you follow? Paul says, **you should imitate us: We were not idle among you** (3:7). And he uses a practical illustration about discipline: **we did not eat anyone's food free of charge; instead, we labored and toiled ... so that we would not be a burden to any of you** (3:8). Paul took responsibility for his well-being. If your theology makes you irresponsible, you're reading the Bible wrongly.

3:10 Then Paul gives a strong command: **If anyone is not willing to work, he should not eat.** Yes, according to James 2:15-16 and 1 John 3:17, believers are to feed those in need. But we must deal with the whole counsel of God on a topic and not simply pick verses for convenience. If somebody comes to you and says, "I'm not into working, but I'm hungry. If you don't feed me, I'll starve," Paul says it's okay to answer, "Starve." Of course, he's not talking about someone who *can't* work. He's talking about someone who can and should work—but who *won't*.

There are four tiers of responsibility. First is *personal* responsibility: you shouldn't expect anybody else to do for you what you ought and are able to do for yourself (see 3:6-8). The second tier is *family*

responsibility. Relatives are to care for each other: "If anyone does not provide for his own family, . . . [he] is worse than an unbeliever" (1 Tim 5:8). If the family can't help, then there's *church* responsibility (see 1 Tim 5:9-10, 16); after all, it's God's extended family. *State* responsibility is to be the very last tier. Unfortunately, for many, the state is tier number one in addressing human need. It is the primary role of civil government to maintain a safe, just, righteous, and compassionately responsible environment for freedom and personal responsibility to flourish (see Rom 13:1-7).

3:11-13 We hear that there are some **among you who are idle. They are not busy but busybodies** (3:11). This is a reminder that if you don't occupy your time with the right thing, you're going to occupy it with the wrong thing. Busybodies mind everyone's business but their own. Paul commands the Thessalonians **to work quietly and provide for themselves** (3:12). Ironically, it often takes more time and effort to avoid work than to work.

3:14-15 If anyone **does not obey our instruction . . . don't associate with him, so that he may be ashamed** (3:14). While we often assume we're not supposed to make people feel guilty or ashamed, understand that those who won't take personal responsibility and obey the Word of God need to experience legitimate guilt. We must **warn** them and, if necessary due to a refusal to repent, break our fellowship with them (3:15). Sometimes a brother needs a lesson.

3:16-18 Paul concludes with three characteristics of God that will enable you to stand firm in trials. *First*, God is **the Lord of peace.** You know you're where God wants you to be when you are objectively in his Word and he subjectively confirms it with his peace. *Peace* is harmony on the inside **always in every way**—that is, regardless of your circumstances.

Second, God is present: **The Lord be with . . . you** (3:16). God is everywhere; he has no limitations. He is equally present with you now and with a believer on the other side of the world.

The *third* characteristic is of God is **grace** (3:18). *Grace* is God doing for you what you don't deserve and can't earn (see Rom 11:6). It is his unmerited favor. You have an account in heaven, and God gives you the grace needed for today—but only for today. Nevertheless, it's more than you'll ever need.

1 TIMOTHY

INTRODUCTION

Author

THE LETTERS OF 1–2 TIMOTHY and Titus are often referred to as the Pastoral Epistles. Each indicates that Paul was its author (1 Tim 1:1; 2 Tim 1:1; Titus 1:1). Nine of Paul's thirteen letters were written to churches. Four were written to individuals. The three Pastoral Epistles were written to two of Paul's co-workers and sons in the ministry—Timothy and Titus—who were serving in pastoral roles within churches. Early church fathers such as Irenaeus identified Paul as the author as well.

It was not until critical scholars began to question Pauline authorship in the nineteenth century that these assertions were disputed. Many critical scholars today deny Pauline authorship because they claim that the Pastoral Epistles differ in style, vocabulary, and theology from Paul's other letters. However, some differences in style and vocabulary hardly demand different authors. One has to keep in mind the different audiences of Paul's letters: some were penned to individuals and others to whole churches. It's not unreasonable, then, to believe that Paul might express himself differently in style and vocabulary when writing to an entire church versus when writing to a colleague in ministry. Importantly, regarding the supposed differences in theology, none of the examples raised are actual contradictions. Rather, they involve different theological emphases

or topics. There are no serious objections, then, to believing that the letters were authored by the apostle Paul.

Historical Background

Timothy hailed from Lystra in Asia Minor (modern-day Turkey), a place Paul visited on his first missionary journey (see Acts 14:5-23). Timothy was the son of a believing Jewish woman and a Greek father (Acts 16:1), and he was likely converted under Paul's ministry (1 Cor 4:17; 1 Tim 1:2). During Paul's second missionary journey, he visited Lystra again and took Timothy with him as a co-worker (see Acts 16:2-3). Over time, the man served as a trusted companion and ministry ally of unquestionable commitment and character (see, e.g., Acts 17:14-15; 19:22; 20:4; Rom 16:21; 1 Cor 4:17; 16:10; 2 Cor 1:19; Phil 2:19-22; 1 Thess 3:2, 6). Titus was also a Gentile convert and co-worker of Paul. He accompanied Paul in his missionary work and was often sent on ministry missions (see, e.g., 2 Cor 7:6-7; 8:16-18, 23; 12:18; Gal 2:1, 3).

Paul probably wrote these letters after the time period covered in the book of Acts. Released from Roman imprisonment, Paul continued his missionary work. During this time, he left Timothy to minister in Ephesus (1 Tim 1:3-4). Paul also visited Crete and left Titus to minister there (Titus 1:5). Later Paul wrote 2 Timothy when he was again imprisoned in Rome (2 Tim 1:8, 16; 4:16)—that imprisonment would lead to his martyrdom (2 Tim 4:6-8).

Message and Purpose

This is the first of the Pastoral Epistles that instruct church leaders and members how to do church God's way. Having left Timothy behind in Ephesus to grow what Paul had himself established, Paul explained to him how the church should work. The key verse of the book is 3:15, in which Paul says, "I have written so that you will know how people ought to conduct themselves in God's household, which is the church of the living God."

Paul spends a lot of time explaining how to grow and develop church leadership, how leaders are to function, and what their responsibilities entail. Timothy was to study, learn, and grow himself from God's Word, and then preach what he was learning. The letter also points out that the quality of leaders affects the quality of the members. This, in fact, is why Paul was so concerned that Timothy develop the right kind of leaders. First Timothy can help pastors and church members maximize their potential in making their church all that God designed it to be in the ministry of his kingdom.

www.bhpublishinggroup.com/qr/te/54_00

Outline

1 TIMOTHY

I. FALSE TEACHING AND THE TRUE GOSPEL (1:1-20)

1:1-2 Paul was **an apostle of Christ Jesus.** This was not because of a letter of recommendation or Paul's job history. He was an apostle only **by the command of God** and **Christ.** God is **our Savior** because he sent his Son to save us, and Jesus is **our hope** because he secured our salvation (1:1). The apostle wrote to Timothy, his **son in the faith.** Paul served as a spiritual mentor to Timothy, who was perhaps converted under his ministry (see "Historical Background"). Paul greets this trusted ministry companion with **grace, mercy, and peace** (1:2).

1:3-4 Paul had left Timothy **in Ephesus** to continue some much needed, difficult ministry work. **Certain people** were spreading harmful **false doctrine,** and Timothy was to put a stop to it (1:3). These false teachers were following **myths** and **genealogies** that obscured the truth rather than promoting **God's** kingdom **plan** (1:4).

1:5 The goal of true biblical **instruction is love**—love for God (to love God is to passionately pursue his glory and submit to his will) and love for neighbor (to love people is the decision to compassionately, righteously, and responsibly seek the well-being of others). The absence of love means that teaching (no matter how accurate) has not fully accomplished its goal. Love arises when the Holy Spirit uses sound doctrine to produce in us **a pure heart, a good conscience, and a sincere faith.** When these aspects are rightly trained within a believer, they help keep us on the right path. For

example, the conscience is designed to serve as a megaphone directed at our souls to help us understand right from wrong and distinguish authentic Christian faith from false religion.

1:6 Some people—whether teachers or also their followers—had **turned aside** from sound teaching to lies. This resulted in **fruitless** talk and behavior that was not beneficial (1:6). This is a reminder that false doctrine never ends in ideas alone. What enters the mind comes out in the actions. Ideas have consequences. Beliefs—whether true or false—determine behavior.

1:7 These heretics wanted to be respected **teachers of the law** and were perhaps motivated by pride. They were **saying** and **insisting on** things that they didn't **understand.** When you act like an expert about spiritual and biblical subjects that you know little about, you're going to confuse and harm those who trust your expertise. Remember: "Where there are many words, sin is unavoidable" (Prov 10:19).

1:8-11 Paul emphasizes that he is not disparaging the law but those who misunderstand it and use it legalistically. **The law is good,** but it must be understood **legitimately** (1:8). The law shows us how sinful we are (see Rom 7:7-13). It was meant **for the lawless,** not for the **righteous** (1:9). It cannot make anyone good; it only reveals how incapable we are of keeping it. The law was intended to point us to our need for a Savior (see Gal 3:21-26).

Believers satisfy the demands of the law as they walk in the Spirit (see Rom 8:1-13; Gal 5:16-18). The law is for those who have not yet become convinced of their sin. The types of sinners Paul names in 1:9-10 point to those who break the Ten Commandments (Exod 20:1-17).

Paul's measuring stick for **sound teaching** was **the gospel**—the good news—of Jesus Christ (1:10-11). Only that which **conforms to** the gospel message and teaching of Christ is to be taught to and urged upon churches. This good news **was entrusted to** Paul (1:11). He taught in strict accordance with it and opposed anything that detracted from it.

1:12-14 Talking about "the gospel concerning the glory of the blessed God" (1:11) causes Paul to reflect on the grace of God in his own life. Even though Paul **was formerly a blasphemer, a persecutor** of the church, **and an arrogant man**, he **received mercy** from **Jesus**. Not only did Christ extend mercy to Paul in his **unbelief**, but he went further than that, **appointing** him **to the ministry** (1:12-13). **Grace**—God's unmerited favor—was not merely sprinkled on Paul. It **overflowed** into his life (1:14). God's grace is more than sufficient; it is greater than all your sin. And sufficient for all of life's needs (see 2 Cor 9:8).

Timothy had no doubt heard Paul's testimony before, but Paul apparently never tired of telling the story of the power of God's grace in his life. This is a reminder of two things. First, no one is beyond the reach of Christ. If Saul the persecutor could become Paul the evangelist, anyone else can be similarly transformed. Don't ever neglect to share the gospel. Second, like Paul, you should never forget the love and grace of God shown to you. No matter where you came from or what you did, if you trust in Jesus as your substitutionary sacrifice, you have a testimony of grace to proclaim.

1:15-16 Paul's personal testimony leads to a **trustworthy** declaration: **Christ Jesus came into the world to save sinners—and I am**

the worst of them (1:15). This statement includes both doctrine (the mission of Christ) and experience (the personal application of the gospel to Paul). He considered himself **an example** to others, an example of how **the worst of** sinners could be saved because of the **extraordinary patience** of Jesus (1:16). The apostle was grateful to serve as a testimony of hope and encouragement so that others might be motivated to believe the gospel as well.

1:17 Mentioning the glorious gospel (1:11) led Paul to talk about the amazing grace of God in his own life (1:12-16), which led to a Christological doxology of **honor and glory** to **the King eternal, immortal, invisible, the only God.** Jesus Christ *is* God. He is sovereign above all earthly and spiritual power. He deserves our worship and service because of who he is and what he has done.

1:18 After his digression in 1:12-17, Paul returns to exhorting Timothy. He reminds his **son** in the faith about **the prophecies** made concerning him so that he will be motivated to **fight the good fight.**

1:19-20 Paul opened his letter by reiterating the purpose for which he had left Timothy in Ephesus: to stop the work of false teachers (1:3). To encourage him in that work, Paul reminds Timothy that he's not telling him to do anything that he was unwilling to do himself. Paul had dealt with two false teachers named **Hymenaeus and Alexander** (1:20). In his second letter to Timothy, Paul explains that Hymenaeus was teaching that the resurrection had already happened (2 Tim 2:17-18). Such men had **shipwrecked** their own **faith** and were harming others (1 Tim 1:19). So Paul **delivered** them **to Satan** so that they might **be taught not to blaspheme** (1:20). By excommunicating them from the church, Paul put the men out from under God's kingdom covering and delivered them to the realm of Satan—with the hope that they would see the error of their deeds and be led to repentance.

II. THE PRIORITY OF PRAYER AND THE
REALITY OF GENDER ROLES (2:1-15)

2:1-2 Here Paul begins the heart of his letter. And at the top of the list is the topic of prayer. He wants **petitions . . . intercessions, and thanksgivings** to **be made** by the church **for everyone** (2:1). In other words, we should make all kinds of prayers for all kinds of people. But he especially asks prayers **for kings and all those who are in authority.** Why? **So that we may lead a tranquil and quiet life in all godliness and dignity** (2:2).

Paul wants Timothy and the Ephesian church to pray for secular leaders so that they will govern well and provide a peaceful environment that will provide Christians with the freedom to follow the true King's agenda. God expects us to submit to his rule regardless of the political environments in which we live, but in a culture of religious freedom, believers are able to have a more public witness and can share their faith in ways that they could not under an oppressive regime. An orderly, free society is a positive environment for the proliferation of the gospel.

2:3-4 It's **good** for Christians to live, work, and minister in such a peaceful environment. Why? Because **it pleases God our Savior, who wants everyone to be saved and to come to the knowledge of the truth.** This is the second of three times in the letter that Paul calls God our "Savior" (see also 1:1; 4:10). We rightly call the Son of God our "Savior" because of his sacrificial death on the cross (see, e.g., Luke 2:11; Acts 5:31; Eph 5:23; Phil 3:20; 2 Tim 1:10; Titus 3:6; 2 Pet 2:20; 1 John 4:14). But God was known by this title in the Old Testament (see, e.g., 2 Sam 22:3; Ps 17:7; 42:5; Isa 43:3; Jer 14:8; Hos 13:4). Besides, it was God the Father who loved the world and gave his Son to save those who will believe (see John 3:16). And it's God the Father **who wants everyone to be saved and to come to the knowledge of the truth** (2:4). This should be our goal as well.

When natural disasters strike, rescue units mobilize and enter the devastation so that they might help those who will surely perish

without them. God has a mobilized rescue unit; it's called the church. And the church's job is to enter this sin-scarred world and rescue the dying with the King's message of life. Notice that God's desire is universal: he wants "everyone to be saved." The gospel is not restricted to any race, gender, ethnicity, class, individual. "Red, yellow, black, and white—they are precious in his sight." Don't let anything prevent you from going to the lost: you have the message with the power to rescue them.

2:5-6 This saving message is so vital because it's the only one that is valid. **For there is** only **one mediator between God and humanity, the man Christ Jesus** (2:5). A *mediator* is someone who brings two estranged parties together. Sinful humanity stands condemned under the righteous wrath of a holy God. And only Jesus Christ, the God-Man, can reconcile them. Because of his divine nature, he is sinless. Because of his human nature, he can serve as a substitutionary sacrifice for sinful humans. Knowing this, he **gave himself as a ransom for all** (2:6)—that is, he paid the price for everyone (theologians call this *unlimited atonement*).

The judgment of God against rebellious humanity has been completely satisfied through Christ's sin-bearing work (see 1 John 2:2). But to receive the benefits of this sacrifice, you must personally receive Christ's payment by faith. To get to God, you must go through his Son.

2:7 Paul **was appointed a herald** of this good news, **an apostle** on behalf of Christ, and **a teacher of the Gentiles.** Whatever lies the false teachers were spreading (1:3-4), Paul was devoted to **telling the truth,** to proclaiming the standard of reality. Are you?

2:8 The purpose of prayer is to convey earthly permission for heavenly interference in history. Since prayer is so essential for accomplishing the King's agenda and proclaiming his gospel message, Paul specifies the kind of prayer God desires: **I want the men in every place to pray.** He addresses the men first because they are to take the lead in calling heaven down to earth. Men are called to be leaders in their homes and in their churches. And there's no more important way to lead among the people of God than by praying for divine intervention.

Lifting up holy hands refers to a common prayer stance (e.g., Exod 9:29; 1 Kgs 8:22; Ps 28:2). But this must be done in the context of purity and unity **without anger or argument.** When God's people are at odds with one another, we block heaven's involvement.

Jesus is not looking for spectators; he's looking for participants. He wants followers, not fans. He's looking for men who are willing to get in the game and get dirty on the field. Leading in prayer is frontline ministry.

2:9-10 Women in the church are called to prayer **also.** But just as men and women are different, so Paul's exhortation to the women is different. They are **to dress** modestly. Godly character is to be reflected outwardly in godly apparel. This doesn't mean women are to wear ugly rags. It means they aren't to let the world determine their fashion preferences. Worldly standards are often unacceptable—and this is sometimes true when it comes to clothing choices too. Do not dress in a way that brings inappropriate attention to yourself by either underdressing or overdressing

Importantly, Paul is not forbidding women to wear nice clothes; he's saying that nice clothes are not what Christian women should be known for. **Women who profess to worship Go**d should be known more for their **decency**, their **good sense**, and their **good works** than they are known for their **expensive apparel.** If you claim to be a Christ follower, proof should show up in your actions. So walk in godliness, dress with godliness, and be worthy of respect.

2:11-12 Having addressed men and women separately in 2:8-10, Paul continues in 2:11-15 to discuss gender role differences in the church. **A woman**, for instance, **is to learn quietly with full submission.** Paul says, **I do not allow a woman to teach or to have authority over a man.**

Understand that Paul is not calling for an absolute silence, nor is he forbidding women from using their gifts. Indeed, Paul allows women to speak in the church when it is under the proper covering of legitimate male authority (see 1 Cor 11:2-10). So what he's talking about here is the exercise of a role, an office. He's talking about *teaching* and *having authority.* An overseer / elder / pastor (these terms are interchangeable in the New Testament) is expected both to teach and to govern and lead the church (3:2, 5; 5:17; Titus 1:9; see 1 Thess 5:12; Heb 13:17). Women are restricted from serving in this role of final authority in the church, where teaching and exercising authority are combined (senior pastor, elder, bishop).

2:13 Some claim Paul's words in 2:11-12 are a mere artifact of an ancient male-chauvinist culture. But Paul gives a reason his restriction, and it has nothing to do with cultural norms: **Adam was formed first, then Eve.** In other words, the limitation on women serving in a role of final authority in the church is based on a creation principle. There was an order to God's creation of humanity. He made people, male and then female. He created the man first *not* because the man was superior to the woman, but because he was to be the positional leader. Scripture lays out a pattern of male leadership in the home and in the church.

The married couple was to function as an inseparable team, exercising dominion together over God's creation, with the man exhibiting godly servant leadership. The man's role as "head" (i.e., governing authority) over the woman (Eph 5:22-23) does not make him superior to her any more than God the Father's role as "head" makes him superior in essence to God the Son (see 1 Cor 11:3). They are co-equal members of the Trinity, though they have different functions. Likewise, the husband is to submit to Christ's headship over him and the wife is to submit to her husband's headship (Eph 5:24; Col 3:18; 1 Pet 3:1); nonetheless, they are unified in Christ (Gal 3:28) and "co-heirs of the grace of life" (1 Pet 3:7). There is no inferiority. Rather, there is a functional order. When this clearly defined covenantal order is breached, the door is opened for Satan to sow discord (see Gen 3:1-6) and limit the intervention of angels (see 1 Cor 11:10).

2:14 Paul provides further biblical support for the restriction on women serving as overseers / elders / pastors: **Adam was not deceived, but the woman was deceived and transgressed.** Satan caused their roles to be reversed, approaching Eve with his deception while Adam stood silently and watched. Though he was supposed to take an active role in watching over the garden and keeping God's command (Gen 2:15-17), Adam became passive, allowed the devil to tempt Eve, and then knowingly followed her into sin.

Importantly, though Eve was deceived, Scripture lays responsibility for humankind's fall into sin at the feet of Adam (see Rom 5:12; 1 Cor 15:21). As the "head," he should have defended both his wife and God's garden against the lying intruder. In the same way, God-called men are to serve as spiritual guardians and overseers in the church, leading God's people, teaching the truth, and equipping the church to guard against Satanic intrusion.

2:15 She will be saved through childbearing, if they continue in faith, love, and **holiness, with good sense.** After Adam and Eve rebelled against God, he promised that one day Eve's offspring would strike the serpent's head (Gen 3:15). This is the first biblical prophecy pointing to Jesus Christ. A descendent of Eve would defeat Satan and his power (see Heb 2:14).

What does this have to do with women bearing children today? Every time a believing woman has a baby and raises her child "in faith, love, and holiness," she's preparing another offspring to help put hell on the run. Only Jesus's work on the cross ultimately defeats the devil. But, as his body, we the church are promised that the devil will also be crushed under our feet (see Rom 16:20). Women are to influence their children to be agents of God's kingdom, battling the enemy through the power of the Holy Spirit. Such a faithful kingdom woman will be saved—that is, "delivered"—and experience spiritual victory. Godly childbearing and childrearing is payback against the devil for his deception in the garden; it provides women opportunity to experience spiritual significance and victory. Single women and those unable to bear children can share in this victory by teaching and discipling the next generation of kingdom warriors.

III. QUALIFICATIONS FOR LEADERS IN GOD'S HOUSEHOLD (3:1-16)

3:1 Having addressed the restriction of women from the office of final authority (2:11-15; see also Titus 1:5-9), Paul goes on to explain to Timothy the qualifications for appointing men as overseers. The term **overseer** is interchangeable in the New Testament with the term *elder* (see Acts 20:17, 28; Titus 1:5-7). It is also interchangeable with the office of *pastor*, because overseers and elders are charged with the pastoral duty of "shepherding" (see Acts 20:17; 1 Pet 5:1-2) and serving as the final human authority in the church. Paul tells Timothy that to desire to serve in this leadership role is a **noble** aspiration.

3:2-3 Paul then provides a list of qualifications for overseers. Most of these requirements have to do with the *character* of the man who aspires to exercise spiritual authority in the church. At the top of the list is that he **must be above reproach**—that is, he must be blameless. There should be no grounds for accusing him of improper behavior. He should also be **the husband of one wife**—a necessary stipulation in a culture in which men often took more than one wife (3:2).

Furthermore, an overseer must be **self-controlled** (not enslaved to the desires of the flesh), **sensible** (wise and balanced in his judgment), **respectable** (living an ordered and honorable life), **hospitable** (selflessly willing to share with others), **able to teach** (capable of communicating God's truth), **not an excessive drinker** (not addicted to alcohol), **not a bully but gentle** (characterized by tenderness), **not quarrelsome** (not given to starting fights), **not greedy** (free from the love of money).

3:4-5 As a husband and father, an overseer must be able to **manage his own household** and lead **his children** well. After all, if he can't **manage his own** home, **how will he take care of God's church?** (3:5). To competently manage one's home or church does not mean that no problems arise. It means that when they do, he takes responsibility for addressing them biblically and properly.

3:6-7 An overseer should **not be a new convert**, a babe in Christ; instead, he should exhibit maturity after having been a believer for a period of time. Otherwise he may be easily tempted to conceit and pride, which brought the devil's downfall (3:6). He should **have a good reputation** among those outside the church and not bring **disgrace** on Christ's name and his people (3:7). Though outsiders may not believe what the church teaches, they should be able to respect the overseer for his character and integrity.

3:8-10 After addressing overseers, Paul gives qualifications for **deacons** (3:8). The Greek word for this role is *diakonos*, which means "servant." The deacon is to execute the ministry for the well-being of the people by serving them under the leadership of the overseers / elders. The qualifications for deacon are similar to those of overseers, demanding high-quality character (3:8-9). The only differences are that deacons are not required to be able to teach or to manage the church (see 3:2, 4-5).

Nevertheless, a deacon is to hold **the mystery of the faith with a clear conscience** (3:9). That is, he must be well grounded in Christian doctrine. Furthermore, potential candidates for deacon should **be tested first**, demonstrating faithfulness and service in the life of the church before they assume the role.

3:11 The Greek word rendered **wives** in the CSB could also be rendered "women." Thus, it could be referring to the wives of deacons or to female deacons (deaconesses). Most likely, Paul speaks here of the latter (see Rom

16:1-2). First, the fact that he returns to deacon qualifications in 3:12 indicates that he is speaking throughout 3:11-13 of the requirements for male and female deacons. Second, it would be odd for Paul to provide qualifications for deacons' wives but say nothing about overseers' wives in 3:1-7.

3:12-13 Like overseers (3:2), **deacons** must be **husbands of one wife** and be able to manage their **children** and **households** well (3:12). Those who function faithfully as deacons and deaconesses have **a good standing** before God for their selfless service (3:13). He will reward them for their devotion and sacrifice.

3:14-16 When Paul went to Macedonia, he had to leave Timothy in Ephesus (1:3). Though he hoped to return to Ephesus **soon**, this letter was to provide Timothy with instruction if the apostle was **delayed** (3:14-15). It focuses on the church's motivation, Master, mission, and message (3:15-16).

As **God's household**, the **people** of God needed to know how **to conduct themselves** (3:15). Our *motivation* for gathering together is that we may learn how to live differently under God's kingdom rule as members of his family. This includes knowing how to raise up godly church leadership, as Paul has just described (3:1-13). The problem with many Christians is that they are out of kingdom alignment. As a result, they don't run straight. The job of the church is to bring people into alignment with God's character.

Paul also reminds Timothy of the *Master* of the household: it is **the church of the living God** (3:15). The church is no human institution. Man neither created it nor determines how it is run. The Lord Jesus purchased the church with his own blood (Acts 20:28), and he is the head of the church (Eph 1:22; Col 1:18). It's his house, and he decides the rules.

Next the apostle describes the church's *mission*: It is **the pillar and foundation of the truth** (1 Tim 3:15). *Truth* is the fixed standard by which reality is measured. It is God's perspective on every subject. Truth is absolute and non-negotiable. Jesus told his disciples, "I am the way, the truth, and the life" (John 14:6). The church is tasked with the mission of undergirding and upholding this reality.

Finally, in 3:16, we find the distinctive *message* or confession of the church—**the mystery of godliness**, something that was formerly unknown but which has now been revealed. This was a hymn sung by the church in Paul's day, affirming the good news about Jesus Christ. It sets forth the core beliefs about Christ that need to operate in a believer's life to promote godliness.

Manifested in the flesh is a reference to the incarnation of the Son of God. **Vindicated in the Spirit** means Jesus was declared by the Father as his beloved Son, empowered by the Spirit to perform supernatural works, and raised from the dead. **Seen by angels** reminds us that heavenly beings attended Jesus at his birth, temptation, resurrection, and ascension, signifying divine approval. **Preached among the nations** refers to the proclamation of the gospel to the world. **Believed on in the world** refers to faith in Christ for forgiveness of sins and eternal life. **Taken up in glory** references Christ's ascension into heaven.

IV. THE HARD BUT ESSENTIAL WORK OF MINISTRY (4:1–6:2)

4:1-2 The Spirit revealed to Paul that there would be those who would **depart from the faith**—false teachers who would listen to **deceitful spirits and the teachings of demons** (4:1). He thus describes these propagators of heresy as **liars whose consciences are seared** (4:2). The conscience, rightly trained, helps us to know right from wrong. But these false teachers had burned theirs to the point that they were numb; they could no longer discern goodness from wickedness.

4:3 As a result of their hardened hearts, the heretics were getting their doctrine from demons. What did their demonic teachings look like? Were they commanding animal sacrifices? Were they instructing people to commit murder and mayhem? No. They were forbidding divinely ordained institutions and provisions like **marriage** and certain **foods**—things that **God** had **created to be received with gratitude**.

We don't typically associate a lack of gratitude with demonic influence, but that's what this wicked teaching produced. Paul says in Romans 1 that though human beings knew something of God's great power from the world he created, they refused to show gratitude to him (Rom 1:19-21). Moses warned the Israelites not to forget how the Lord had provided them with everything they needed when they entered the land of Canaan, otherwise they would follow false gods (Deut 6:10-15). When we fail to thank God, acknowledging that all we have comes from him, we quickly forget him, which leads to idolatry.

4:4-5 Instead, we are to confess that **everything created by God is good, and nothing is to be rejected if it is received with thanksgiving** (4:4). There is nothing from which you receive godly enjoyment and benefit that cannot be traced back to God. Therefore, we are to give thanks to God "always" and "in everything" (Eph 5:20; 1 Thess 5:18). This should be one of the chief characteristics of a Christian. Anything that we receive from God is **sanctified**—rendered holy—**by the word of God** (which establishes the boundaries for our lives) and **prayer** (through which we express our gratitude).

4:6 How would Timothy prove himself to be **a good servant of Christ Jesus** as he provided leadership to the church at Ephesus? First, by taking the truths that Paul had taught him and pointing them **out to the brothers and sisters**. Shepherds of God's people are called to feed his Word to the flock. If they don't, the church will end up malnourished and useless. Second, Timothy was to himself be **nourished by the words of the faith** and **good teaching**. If pastors and teachers do not sustain their own spiritual development by feeding on Scripture, it will be impossible for them to provide spiritual sustenance to others.

4:7-8 Timothy was to **have nothing to do with pointless and silly myths**—that is, popular, speculative fables and unbiblical stories that have no basis in reality and no positive affect on one's life. Instead, he was to **train** himself **in godliness** (4:7). Godliness—becoming more like God in actions, attitudes, character, and conduct—should be the Christian's goal. Listening to silly myths produces nothing of value in a person's life, but the Word of God produces godliness when obeyed. This, however, requires training and hard work.

People are willing to pour extensive money and effort into physical **training of the body**, even though it **has limited benefit**. How much more, then, should we devote ourselves to training ourselves for **godliness**, which provides benefit **for the present life** and for **the life to come?** (4:8) Godliness provides a deeper experience of God's reality at work in our lives. Our passion for and pursuit of spiritual growth should be greater than our drive to be physically fit. Our souls need a regular workout program. You don't become godly by chance.

4:9-10 Given the value of the reward, Paul urges Timothy to **labor and strive** in the pursuit of godliness—both for himself and for those he serves. In fact, hard work with a heavenly focus is required because of our **hope in the living God**. He is **the Savior of all people** in that Christ's death removed the guilt of original sin so that everyone can come to him in repentance and faith. The cross made all mankind savable. But he is the Savior **especially of those who believe** (4:10)—those who have received the gift of eternal life through placing faith alone in Christ alone.

4:11-12 Command and teach these things (4:11). Pastors are to instruct the people of God in the truths of God, admonishing them to believe and obey so that they may properly respond. Paul counsels Timothy not to let anyone **despise** his **youth**. Though Timothy was young, he had demonstrated profound faithfulness—and that's the key. It's hard to disregard someone for their youth, when their character and conduct are impeccable. Therefore, he needed to serve as **an example**

for the believers in speech, in conduct, in love, in faith, and in purity (4:12). Teaching the truth is not enough; church leaders must model the truth they teach.

4:13-14 To what was Timothy to **give** his attention? To the **public reading** of Scripture, to **exhortation** to apply the truth to life, and to **teaching** how to understand and follow the Word (4:13). Passivity in ministry is sin. Timothy couldn't **neglect** the spiritual **gift** given to him by the Holy Spirit and affirmed **by the council of elders** (4:14).

You must not neglect the development and use of your spiritual gifts either. God gives gifts to be used for the benefit of others, not to be buried for safekeeping. You will be called to give an account of how you used the spiritual and physical blessings God entrusted to you.

4:15-16 Timothy was to devote himself fully to his ministry so that his spiritual **progress** would be **evident to all** (4:15). Gospel ministry should produce growth in the gospel minister, not only in those to whom he ministers. He does not serve others well, in fact, if he doesn't **pay close attention** to his own **life** and **teaching**. By persevering in spiritual development, both personally and professionally, he **will save**—in the sense of "deliver"—**both** himself and those under his care (4:16). Timothy had already experienced personal salvation through faith in Christ, but through the delivering and transforming power of God's Word, he and the church could experience daily victory over the power of sin.

5:1-2 Through Jesus Christ we have been adopted as sons and daughters of God. So the church is the family of God. Thus, Timothy was not to sharply **rebuke an older man**, but to **exhort him as a father** (5:1). Likewise, he was to treat **younger men as brothers, older women as mothers, and the younger women as sisters** (5:1-2). Such a family mindset transforms how we think about and respond to fellow believers.

5:3-8 The church is to **support widows who are genuinely in need** (5:3). The care of widows and orphans is a priority for the people of God (Jas 1:27). The church should recognize and support a **widow who is truly in need**, has no family support, and who serves God and his people with **prayers** and a life that is **above reproach** (1 Tim 3:5-7).

But those widows who have adult **children and grandchildren** should receive care from them. Children have an obligation to **practice godliness** toward **their parents** for the investment they made in their lives (5:4). No widow should be in want who has believing children. Importantly, **if anyone will not provide for his own family** members, **he has denied the faith and is worse than an unbeliever** (5:8). God calls parents, and especially husbands, to provide for their families. Men are to reflect the fatherhood of God. A man who will not take care of his wife and children lies about what God is like. Believing men should also care for widows in their families because God is "a champion of widows" (Ps 68:5). Believing men and women with widows in their families share this responsibility (1 Tim 5:16).

5:9-10 A **widow** without family assistance is eligible **for support** from the church if **she is at least sixty years old** and was **the wife of one husband** (5:9). She should also be **well known for good works**—that is, deeds that glorify God and benefit other people. This would include raising **children** and helping those in need, such as through offering **hospitality**, serving **the saints**, and caring for **the afflicted** (5:10). A widow who has demonstrated faithful service *to* the church deserves the faithful support *of* the church.

5:11-16 **Younger widows**, however, should not be enrolled. They might make a pledge to remain a widow, but they'll likely be **drawn away** and **desire** to get married again (5:11). Thus, they'll incur **condemnation** for renouncing **their original pledge** (5:12). Moreover, young women with nothing to do will be tempted to **be idle**, to act as **gossips and busybodies** (5:13). So, instead, Paul says the **younger women** should **marry, have children, manage their households.** Through this kind of noble service and productivity, they will **give the adversary no opportunity to accuse** the church of promoting sin (5:14).

Notice that Paul does not give cultural reasons for this directive. Rather, he provides a theological and spiritual reason. By devoting her primary focus to her home, a kingdom woman protects herself and her family from **Satan** (5:15).

5:17-18 In 5:17-25 Paul discusses the church's ministry to elders. The church is to be governed by elders (i.e., overseers; see 3:1-7), males designated as the spiritual leadership and final human authority of the church. They are to be **considered worthy of double honor.** Elders engaged in pastoral work, **preaching and teaching**, should not be expected to work without generous financial support (5:17). As Scripture says, if **an ox** is provided with food for his work (see Deut 25:4), how much more is a hard-working minister of the gospel **worthy of his wages** (5:18)?

5:19-21 An **accusation** of wrongdoing **against an elder** is serious business. It should not be easy for a disgruntled church member to falsely accuse an elder. Therefore, all accusations must be confirmed **by two or three witnesses** (5:19). If an elder is found guilty of unrepentantly continuing in **sin**, he must be rebuked **publicly, so that the rest** of the elders (and the congregation) will fear the consequences of sin (5:20). Paul delivers a solemn **charge** to Timothy that he carry out any cases of disciplines **without prejudice** or **favoritism** (5:21). God's people see that their leaders are held to the same standards as they are—and to an even higher level.

5:22 Churches should not be **too quick to appoint** someone as **an elder**. We don't want to unintentionally **share in the sins of others** because we fail to do the proper vetting of a candidate. We also do not want to fail to take the appropriate time to observe a man's life and spiritual condition, as outlined in 3:1-7.

5:23 Paul encourages Timothy to drink **a little wine** for his **stomach** and **frequent illnesses**. In a day before modern medicine, a moderate amount of wine provided medicinal benefits to those who needed them.

5:24-25 Paul reminds Timothy that, most of the time, **sins** and **good works are obvious.** Over time, then, he'll be able to evaluate candidates for leadership in the local church by observing their lifestyles. But even those who commit sin or good works unnoticed will not be able to keep them **hidden** forever. What we do—whether good or bad—will come to light.

6:1-2 On slavery in the Bible, see commentary on Ephesians 6:5-9. **Slaves** were to show **respect** for their **masters** and not, through ungodly behavior, cause **God's name** and **teaching** to be blasphemed (6:1). They were to protect the integrity of God's Word and character through their service. Those with **believing masters** were to **serve** them as **brothers**, since both slave and master are sons of God and one in Christ (Gal 3:26, 28). Their masters were **dearly loved** by God, so they should honor them (6:2). These principles apply to employer-employee relationships today.

V. THE GAIN OF GODLINESS AND THE DECEPTION OF GREED (6:3-21)

6:3-5 In the final verses of his first letter to Timothy, Paul draws a distinction between godliness and greed. **Godliness** (6:3) is a lifestyle that consistently pursues and reflects the character of God. It is a way of life. It's the way you should roll. All of God's people are called to godliness (2:2; 4:7-8; 5:4).

How does one grow in it? First, it comes through "the mystery of godliness" (3:16), the revelation of Jesus Christ, the God-Man, who died as a substitute for sinners, was raised from the dead, and ascended to God the Father. Godliness begins by believing the gospel message. Second, **the sound teaching** of God's Word **promotes godliness** (6:3). Third, you are called to obedience—to "train yourself in godliness" (4:7). Why? Because it's beneficial both for this life and the life to come (4:8). It's a wise investment.

Anyone who **teaches false doctrine and does not agree with . . . sound teaching** has disqualified himself for godliness (6:3). The reason Paul had left Timothy behind in Ephesus was so that he might deal with false teachers who were causing problems (1:3-4; see also 1:18-20). These men may have promoted themselves as superior instructors of deep doctrine. But Paul had a different appraisal of them. They were spreading "the teachings of demons" (4:1), were **conceited**, and understood **nothing.** They were known for their godlessness. They saw godliness as **a way of material gain** (6:4-5). Their motivation for ministry was money.

6:6 Though it is not to be viewed as a means of material gain, **godliness** is nevertheless a means of **great gain** when it is accompanied by **contentment.** *Contentment* is being at ease (inner sufficiency) where you are and being thankful for what you have. Contentment doesn't mean complacency; rather, it's learning to be satisfied until God gives you more (see Phil 4:11-13; Prov 30:8-9). Complaining is empirical proof of discontentment. But if you have contentment, you have inner sufficiency in spite of external circumstances. You have that which "is truly life" (6:19). A lack of contentment will stifle godliness, but content people know that God is acting on their behalf.

6:7-8 We brought nothing into this world, and we can take nothing out (6:7). We don't need to accumulate stuff, then, because we can't take it with us when life is over. So instead, **if we have food and clothing,** we should **be content** (6:8). Godliness with a full stomach, clothes on your back, and a roof over your head is enough for you to be content. Everything else is a bonus. Godly people are content with their needs being met (see Heb 13:5-6).

6:9-10 When Paul speaks of **those who want to be rich,** he's talking about those who pursue and prize riches as life's priority. When they deceive themselves in this way, they're subject to **temptation.** When riches become all important, people succumb to **foolish and**

harmful desires, prioritizing the material over the spiritual (6:9). **The love of money is a root of all kinds of evil** (6:10).

Notice that Paul didn't say that *money* leads to evil—rather, *the love of* money leads to evil. When we make time to grow our material lives, while allowing our spiritual lives to decline (cutting back on church participation, prayer, Bible study, and fellowship), then we are demonstrating that we love money.

King Solomon was once the wealthiest man in the world, and he said, "The one who loves silver is never satisfied with silver, and whoever loves wealth is never satisfied with income" (Eccl 5:10). One can be filled to overflowing with wealth and material possessions. But without an eternal perspective, such earthly focus will only result in **craving** for more and end in **many griefs** (6:10). On the other hand, one can be the steward of God-given wealth and yet find peace, purpose, and contentment in God when pursuing the spiritual over the material.

6:11 Having spoken of the benefits of godliness and the dangers of greed, what does Paul tell Timothy to do? **Flee from these things** (the pursuit of purpose in wealth) **and pursue righteousness, godliness** (surprise!), **faith, love, endurance, and gentleness.** We must do both: flee what harms and pursue what gives life. As the writer of Hebrews says, "Lay aside every hindrance . . . and run with endurance" (Heb 12:1). Leave sin behind and pursue spiritual development.

6:12-14 Timothy is to consider the life of **faith** as a **good** and worthwhile **fight** that he is to wage. In this fight, he must **take hold of eternal life**—not eternal salvation (for Timothy was already born again) but of the experiential knowledge of God through Christ. "This is eternal life: that they may know you, the only true God, and the one you have sent— Jesus Christ" (John 17:3). It was to this that Timothy had been **called** and about which he had **made a good confession**: to grow in the knowledge of God and help others to do the same (1 Tim 6:12). Paul charges the young minister **in the presence of God** and **Christ Jesus**—who made his own public **confession before Pontius Pilate** (6:13)—to be a faithful minister, doing nothing to dishonor his calling until the **Lord** appears (6:14).

6:15-16 Paul praises God for his sovereignty: **He is the blessed and only Sovereign, the King of kings, and the Lord of lords** (6:15). There is no one superior to him, no greater authority, no higher court of appeal. He is unique. God **alone is immortal** and **lives in unapproachable light** (6:16).

When trials and tribulations strike, remember that God is sovereign. When you think more highly of yourself than you ought, remember that God is sovereign. When your life hits rock bottom, remember that God is sovereign. The worst nightmare of the wicked is that God is sovereign. The overruling hope of the saint is that God is sovereign.

6:17 Paul has just warned Timothy of the dangers of greed, of loving money, of pursuing material blessing above godliness (6:3-10). Now he urges him to **instruct those** in the church **who are rich in the present age not to be arrogant or to set their hope on the uncertainty of wealth.** To be rich means to have an abundance beyond your needs (food, clothes, and shelter). In gauging whether or not you are wealthy, then, don't confuse wants with needs.

Paul highlights two threats or side effects of wealth without godliness. First, when you prioritize the material over the spiritual, you become arrogant and conceited—thinking more highly of yourself than others simply because you have more money than they. Thus, a dangerous potential side effect of wealth is pride.

A second threat or side effect is that you misplace your hope. If your hope is in the riches you possess "in the present age," you have forgotten that money can't deliver. "The uncertainty of wealth" means it cannot be depended upon, either in this age or the one to come. Instead, we must set our hope **on God.** We must not expect money to do what only God can. God **richly provides us with all things to enjoy.**

It is not a sin to be rich, but we must not let wealth blind us to the "great gain" of "godliness with contentment" (6:6). Riches were not meant to replace or compete with our trust in God and our pursuit of godliness. We must never lose sight of the fact that God is the only source of all that we enjoy and possess.

6:18 How can the rich safeguard their hearts? How does a Christian to whom God has given wealth position himself so that he is not taken captive by arrogance? Paul tells Timothy the antidote: **Instruct them to do what is good** (that is, to prioritize the pursuit of godliness), **to be rich in good works** (to let exceptional net worth be matched by exceptional service to benefit others), **to be generous and willing to share** (to acknowledge God as source and be characterized by generosity).

6:19 Living with this perspective will result in **treasure . . . for the coming age.** Earthly wealth is uncertain no matter how hard you strive (6:17). Spiritual wealth, stored up through "godliness with contentment" (6:6), is guaranteed. With this heavenly mindset, you will experience great gain—you will **take hold of what is truly life** in the spiritual fulfillment that God gives and the future kingdom rewards earned.

6:20-21 Paul closes by exhorting Timothy to **guard** the ministry of the gospel **entrusted to** him. Embracing **what is falsely called knowledge** had caused **some people**, false teachers and those who followed them, to stray **from the faith** (see 1:3-4, 18-20). By avoiding things that are a waste of time—whatever has no basis in Scripture and no spiritual benefit—Timothy would keep himself and those he shepherded on the road to godliness.

As God's **grace** was with Timothy, may it also **be with you all** (6:21).

2 TIMOTHY

INTRODUCTION

Author and Historical Background

SEE THE INTRODUCTION TO 1 TIMothy for a discussion of the author and historical background of the Pastoral Epistles (1 Timothy, 2 Timothy, and Titus).

Message and Purpose

Second Timothy is the apostle Paul's final letter, written to his beloved son in the faith. Paul gives clear indications in the book that he knows his departure is soon at hand, and therefore he wanted to encourage Timothy in his ministry. The aging apostle knew that Timothy was struggling. He had been having health problems, and it was easy for some people to write him off. This highly personal letter was meant to encourage him to step up to the plate, to take his ministry seriously, and to see it as a long-term commitment.

It was important for Timothy to gain right perspective in the face of the stresses and strains, demands and disappointments of ministry. Paul wanted to encourage him by his own testimony of having fought the good fight and finished his own race (4:7). Paul didn't throw in the towel when things got tough; he chose the right battles to fight and he won them. He desired Timothy do the same.

Paul also wanted Timothy to pass this message along to those coming behind him in ministry. And the apostle gave Timothy—and all of us—the best reason of all for being faithful: to receive the crown of righteousness from the Lord himself, which is available to all believers who faithfully serve the King and his kingdom.

www.bhpublishinggroup.com/qr/te/55_00

Outline

I. Persuaded by God's Power (1:1-18)
II. Persevering in Ministry (2:1-26)
III. Prepared for Perilous Times (3:1-17)
IV. Preaching the Word (4:1-22)

2 TIMOTHY

I. PERSUADED BY GOD'S POWER (1:1-18)

1:1-2 Paul identifies himself as **an apostle**—an authorized messenger—of Christ Jesus. Paul didn't apply for the job. He served in the role because it was **God's will**, allowing him to make known **the promise of life** that is **in Christ Jesus** (1:1). This is to be both the motivation and mission of all who are called into ministry. This is Paul's second letter **to Timothy** (1:2), his son in the ministry. It's also the last New Testament letter he wrote before his martyrdom.

1:3-4 Paul wants Timothy to know that he thanks **God** every time he remembers him in his **prayers** (1:3). Paul had a deep affection for this young man who had served with him so faithfully in ministry. He remembers Timothy's **tears**, perhaps shed during their last parting, and longs to see him so that sorrow can be replaced by **joy** (1:4).

1:5 Timothy had a strong and **sincere faith** in Jesus Christ inspired by his **grandmother Lois** and his **mother Eunice**. This serves as a reminder of how important a godly heritage is to a family. The family unit is God's first and foundational institution for the transfer of the faith. When the family fails, the culture is in trouble. This passage also shows the powerful influence women can have on the life of a young man should his father be either absent or spiritually inactive. It is critical that parents and grandparents pass on their faith, in word and deed, to the next generation (see Judg 2:10).

1:6 Paul urges Timothy **to rekindle** the spiritual **gift** that he had received and that was recognized when Paul laid **hands** on him and validated his ministry. Timothy could not be passive about his spiritual gift and neither can we. God intends that we develop—keep fresh and vibrant—the gifts he provides for the benefit of others. We will be held accountable for failure to do so.

1:7 Timothy struggled with **a spirit of fear**. His timidity probably resulted from a variety of factors, including his personality, persecution, false teachers, the burdens of ministry, and the lack of a strong male influence in his growing up years. But Paul assures him that fearfulness does not come from God. Rather, God's Holy Spirit provides **power, love, and sound judgment**—the necessary spiritual resources for fulfilling ministry and employing spiritual gifts. Such divine resources are available to all—that is, power for the use of our gifts, love for those who benefit from them, and good discernment in the application of our gifts.

1:8 Paul encourages Timothy not to **be ashamed** of identifying with Christ or with Paul, who was a **prisoner** in Rome because of **the gospel**. This could have added to Timothy's timidity. Instead, Paul calls him to join him **in suffering for the gospel**, something one can only do through **the power of God**, rather than human strength.

1:9-10 Why should we be willing to suffer for the gospel? Because through it, God **saved**

us—not according to our works—but in accordance with **his own purpose** and based on his **grace**, which he showed us through his Son, Jesus Christ. In his love, God planned this **before time began**, but it has **been made evident through the appearing** of the Son as **our Savior**. Through his sacrificial atoning death on the cross, Christ **abolished death** and **brought** us **life and immortality . . . through the gospel**. Even the possibility of death should not nullify an effective ministry since it is no longer an issue for the believer.

1:11-12 It was for the ministry of **this gospel** that Paul had been **appointed** by Christ himself as **a herald** (proclaiming the good news), an **apostle** (serving as God's authoritative leader and messenger), **and teacher** (instructing in the Word of God) (1:11). Because of his faithfulness to the message, Paul had been persecuted. Nevertheless, in spite of the pain and sorrow, suffering brought him no shame or regret. For the apostle was **persuaded that** God had the power to care for him and deliver him through any obstacles and trials **until that day** when he would call him home (1:12). He wanted Timothy (and all believers) to have that same confidence in God.

1:13 So Paul encourages Timothy to **hold** tightly **to the pattern of sound teaching that** he had **heard from** Paul, and to do so in **faith and love**. Thus, trusting confidently in God (1:12) is combined with serving God's people. The horizontal and the vertical must always go together in ministry.

1:14 Paul charges him to **guard the good deposit**, the good news of salvation and the good work of ministry to which he had been called. God had committed to him this sacred treasure. We carry the message of eternal salvation. We must recognize the gospel's value and not treat it casually. With the empowerment of **the Holy Spirit who lives in us**, we must guard the gospel, proclaiming it faithfully and defending it against error and ministering its truth to others for their spiritual development.

1:15-18 Paul reminds Timothy of the trials he endured. He was aware of those who had **deserted** him (1:15). But Paul also knew that God had provided for him in the midst of the negative treatment. A believer named **Onesiphorus** (1:16), unknown to us apart from this mention, is immortalized in the pages of Scripture because of his love and care for the aging apostle. Previously, he had **ministered** to Paul at **Ephesus** (1:18). But Onesiphorus was no fair-weather Christian. He sought Paul out and **refreshed** him even when he was a prisoner **in Rome**. Onesiphorus was **not ashamed of** the gospel or Paul, its spokesman. Therefore, Paul prayed for God's **mercy** on him and all his **household** (1:16-17). We too must pray for God's favor on those who support the ministry and its ministers.

Paul shared this with Timothy as a means of encouraging the young gospel minister. He could have focused solely on who had deserted him. Instead, Paul recognized how God had graciously provided support that offset the mistreatment received. In order to persevere through the struggles and difficulties of ministry, Timothy would have to do as Paul had done: see with eyes of faith and celebrate God's grace in his life. You need to do the same.

II. PERSEVERING IN MINISTRY (2:1-26)

2:1-2 Timothy was Paul's **son** in the faith. In light of the defection of others, he calls him to **be strong**—not merely in his own will power but in the **grace that is in Christ Jesus** (2:1). In spite of challenges, Timothy needed to move forward in his ministry. Moreover, he needed to take what he had learned from Paul and **commit** it to **faithful** believers so that they could **teach others**, ensuring its continuation in a dark world. Timothy couldn't bear the burden alone; he needed to pass the spiritual baton to faithful men and women who could transfer God's truth to others. (2:2).

2:3-7 Paul uses three illustrations in 2:3-6 to encourage Timothy in the work he was called to perform. By carefully considering Paul's analogies, Timothy could be sure that **the Lord** would grant him **understanding** (2:7).

First, he was to **share in suffering as a good soldier of Christ Jesus** (2:3). Paul thus presents the Christian life as warfare against Satan in a hostile world (see Eph 6:10-18). To be victorious in battle, no **soldier gets entangled** in **civilian** affairs but **seeks to please** his **commanding officer** (2 Tim 2:4). Military service places restrictions on personal liberty—so does Christian ministry. The *second* illustration involves an **athlete.** All of his efforts are wasted unless **he competes according to the rules**—that is, operates within biblical guidelines and does not yield to worldly pleasures. He cannot be **crowned** a victor otherwise (2:5). You cannot disobey God's Word in the pursuit of spiritual victory. To disregard God's boundaries is to disqualify yourself from receiving reward. *Third*, Paul compares Timothy's work to that of a **farmer.** Farmers must work long hours in all conditions. Laziness will fail to produce a harvest. Paul wants Timothy to be **hardworking**, knowing that when the **crops** are harvested, he will share in the reward (2:6). Faithfulness, then, takes work.

2:8-10 Above all, Timothy needed to keep before his eyes the truth about Jesus Christ: **Remember Jesus Christ, risen from the dead and descended from David** (2:8). Not only is he alive, but he is the legal heir to David's throne (see Luke 1:32-33). Timothy serves the risen King Jesus and his kingdom. One day, all creation will bow before him, whether willingly or by compulsion. There is intimate fellowship with him available now and the reward of meaningful participation in the kingdom that is to come. Therefore, Timothy has every reason to take courage, like Paul who suffered **to the point of being bound like a criminal.** Regardless of Paul's negative physical imprisonment, **the word of God is not bound** (2:9). God's Word will accomplish God's purposes (see Isa 55:11). That's why Paul was willing to **endure all things** for the sake of those who would become part of the family of God and **obtain salvation** through the gospel (2:10). This salvation is ruling with

Christ in his millennial kingdom. This should be the ministry goal of every pastor for himself and his flock.

2:11-13 To further encourage Timothy to persevere, Paul recites a **trustworthy** statement. This series of four couplets was perhaps a common **saying** among first-century Christians.

If we died with him, we will also live with him (2:11). This first couplet refers to our union with Christ. Through trusting in him as Savior, we are united with him by faith. Therefore, we have died with Christ (Gal 2:19-20) and are also raised with him (Eph 2:6). Your eternal future is secure through your connection to and identification with Christ.

The two middle couplets refer to our obedience to Christ. **If we endure, we will also reign with him** means that if we live a consistent Christian life, we will be rewarded with reigning with Christ in his millennial kingdom (see Rev 20:4). **If we deny him, he will also deny us** (2 Tim 2:12) means that if our Christian lives are more covert than public (see commentary on Matt 10:32-33), if we seek to please ourselves more than to please our Lord, we will lose the opportunity to partake in his millennial reign. This does not involve loss of salvation but loss of rewards and privileges.

The final couplet repeats the idea of the first in a different way: **If we are faithless, he remains faithful.** When our faith grows weak or even fails, God remains true to his promise to save us through Christ. To fail to keep his promise would be for him to **deny himself**, and that **he cannot** do (2:13). He is true to us because he is true to himself. Therefore, we must appeal to God's faithfulness even when we feel we are losing our faith.

2:14-15 Timothy's job was to **remind** the church in Ephesus not to engage in fights with false teachers **about words** because doing so was **useless** and harmful to listeners (2:14). Paul had originally left Timothy in Ephesus to deal with false teaching (1 Tim 1:3-4), but apparently the problem had continued. Stopping false teachers wasn't enough. Timothy also had to teach the true meaning of Scripture so that the Ephesian Christians would be equipped to understand it and to identify heresy when they heard it. In the same way that federal agents identify counterfeit currency through their intimate knowledge of the real thing, it is believers' knowledge of the truth that will enable them to identify error. So Timothy was to **be diligent** to be an **approved** expositor of the Scriptures, **correctly teaching the word of truth** (2 Tim 2:15). Local churches need pastors who know the Word and help God's people know and apply it.

2:16-19 Not only do believers need to avoid unbiblical teaching, but they must also **avoid irreverent and empty speech** that leads to godlessness (2:16). Paul mentions two of the false teachers: **Hymenaeus and Philetus** (2:17). The apostle had previously dealt with Hymenaeus himself (see 1 Tim 1:19-20). These men had **departed from the truth**, leading believers astray by telling them that **the resurrection** had **already taken place** and, thus, denying a future bodily resurrection from the dead (2 Tim 2:18). Paul assures Timothy that God is intimately acquainted with his children. Anyone who **calls on** God's **name** should pursue him and **turn away from wickedness**, which is where false teaching inevitably leads (2:19). Calling on God's name is the special privilege given to believers to invoke his supernatural intervention into the circumstances of life for his divine deliverance (see Rom 10:9, 13; 1 Cor 1:2).

2:20-21 In these verses, Paul talks about two kinds of **vessels** in a **house.** Common vessels (containers) would be made of **wood and clay.** These would be used for **dishonorable** purposes—that is, they were used for anything. Valuable vessels were made of **gold and silver.** These were special and used only for **honorable** purposes (2:20). Believers are to be vessels of honor, cleansing themselves from false teaching so that they will be **useful to** God's kingdom and prepared **for every good work** (2:21). By pursuing sanctification, growth in holiness, and obedience to God, you make yourself useful for his kingdom purposes.

2:22 Timothy was to encourage spiritual purification in the lives of believers. Paul gives him several commands to help the body of Christ put away sin and reflect God's character. They were to **flee from youthful passions** (whether lust, greed, or pride) **and pursue righteousness, faith, love, and peace.** Believers must understand that it's not enough to "run away" from the one; we must "go after" the other. If we remove our filthy rags, we must put on clean clothes.

2:23-26 Paul tells Timothy again (see 2:14, 16) to **reject . . . ignorant disputes** over **foolish** matters that only result in **quarrels** (2:23). As **the Lord's servant,** a believer is to be about *his* business. We should not be known for our quarreling but for our **gentleness** and patience. When someone errs through sin or unbiblical teaching, correct him gently, not cruelly. In this way, people will be lead to **repentance** and **the knowledge of the truth,** rather than to arguments and divisiveness (2:24-25). Our goal is to help people **come to their senses and escape the trap of the devil** (2:26). This happens through kindness, not harshness.

III. PREPARED FOR PERILOUS TIMES (3:1-17)

3:1-5 Hard times will come in the last days (3:1). "The last days" refers to the period of time between Christ's resurrection and the rapture (see Heb 1:2; 2 Pet 3:3). Paul lists the sinful attitudes and behaviors that will characterize these perilous times (2 Tim 3:2-5). Being **lovers of self** and **pleasure rather than lovers of God** (3:2, 4) will produce all manner of wickedness in people. They will be savage wolves, full of pride and brutality, while lacking love and concern for others. Nevertheless, they will operate under religious camouflage. They'll hold to **the form of godliness** but deny **its power.** Paul's warning to Timothy is a warning to us all: **Avoid these people** (3:5).

The false teachers whom Timothy was confronting projected an external display of religious devotion, but the power of God would not operate in them or through them. Theirs was a religion masquerading as godliness, a shadow without real substance. Religion without the presence and power of God is like wax fruit—it looks real but possesses no nutritional value. True godliness moves people from sin to righteousness.

3:6-9 The false teachers with whom Timothy had to contend preyed on **gullible women** whose **sins** made them vulnerable to being **led astray** (3:6). Rather than giving these women the gospel of true repentance and conversion, they took advantage of them in their weakness! The false teachers were very studious men, always learning. Yet because of their rejection of God and his Word, they were **never able to come to a knowledge of the truth** (3:7). In this way, they were similar to **Jannes and Jambres**, Pharaoh's magicians who had opposed **Moses** and **the truth** (see Exod 7:8-12). The **men** who opposed God in Paul and Timothy's day were **corrupt** and **worthless** (2 Tim 3:8). But as sure as God overruled the Egyptian magicians, he would also overrule the false teachers and make their folly evident **to all** (3:9).

3:10-11 Having reviewed the present circumstances and the dangers ahead, Paul encourages Timothy to continue to follow him. In contrast to the false teachers, Paul was known for his **faith, patience, love, endurance**, character and **conduct** that Timothy had adopted as his own (3:10). The true servant of God is others-centered, not self-centered. Paul maintained devotion to God and people in spite of **the persecutions sufferings** he had faced. His troubles were many and overwhelming, **yet the Lord rescued** him **from them all** (3:11). Timothy was not alone in his struggles. Paul had been through worse, and he could testify to the sustaining grace of God.

3:12-13 Notice the universal nature of this statement: **All who want to live a godly life in Christ Jesus will be persecuted.** Not everyone will suffer in the same way because persecution takes many forms, but if you seek to be a visible and verbal follower of Christ and give allegiance to his kingdom agenda in every area of your life, you will face significant opposition from the devil and the world. **Evil people** will only **become worse** (3:13). As Jesus told his disciples, "If they persecuted me, they will also persecute you" (John 15:20). Remember, we are not above our Master. But the good news is that whatever persecution you face, God can deliver you from it or through it.

3:14-15 What should Timothy do in light of this reality? **Continue in what you have learned and firmly believed.** Don't deviate from your present course. Continue to follow God through Jesus Christ. Keep to the truth of his Word. Timothy knew who had **taught** the Word to him initially (2:14): his mother and grandmother (1:5). He had known the sacred Scriptures from an early age. He knew firsthand that they alone could give him **wisdom for salvation through faith in Christ Jesus** (3:15).

3:16-17 All **Scripture is inspired by God** (3:16). What does this mean? The doctrine of inspiration refers to the process by which God oversaw the composition of Scripture, guiding the authors to write exactly what he wanted them to write without error. The Greek word translated "inspired" is literally "breathed out by God." Our God is unique in that he speaks—unlike other so-called "gods" (see Ps 115:4-5). Numerous times the Old Testament uses the phrase, "The Lord says." Our God communicates. And he has worked supernaturally through the Holy Spirit to communicate perfectly to us through *all* of Scripture, which is the Word of God. When we read the Bible, we are reading the very words of the living God. "No prophecy of Scripture comes from the prophet's own interpretation, because no prophecy ever came by the will of man; instead, men spoke from God as they were carried along by the Holy Spirit" (2 Pet 1:20-21).

If *all Scripture* is inspired by God, then *all Scripture* **is profitable for teaching** (instructing you in the truths that you need to know), **for rebuking** (reproving you for what you've done wrong), **for correcting** (showing you what is right), and **for training in**

righteousness (guiding you to approach life as God intended it to be lived) (3:16). Why are we to use the Bible in these ways? **So that the man of God may be complete, equipped for every good work** (3:17). To faithfully accomplish the difficult task ahead of him, all Timothy needed was the inerrant Word of God. Everything that you need in order to be what God wants you to be is already in Scripture.

IV. PREACHING THE WORD (4:1-22)

4:1 After emphasizing the divine source and purpose of Scripture, Paul directs a solemn **charge** to his faithful son in the faith, Timothy. It was not a private charge from apostle to young pastor. Rather, this was a public charge delivered before witnesses: **God and Christ Jesus**—the same Christ Jesus who will one day **judge** all humanity and reign as King in his glorious **kingdom.** The God who called Timothy into ministry was delivering a sacred command to him through his authoritative messenger Paul. And he directs that same sacred command to every man who takes up the mantle of pastor in a local church.

4:2 Preach the word. What should believers expect to be the standard of authority at their local churches? Feelings? Intellect? Tradition? Paul says there is only one standard by which a church is to properly function: God's Word. The Bible—and only the Bible—is the final authority for Christian individuals, families, churches, and even the broader culture. "The word of God is living and effective and sharper than any double-edged sword. . . . It is able to judge the thoughts and intentions of the heart" (Heb 4:12). Nothing else can do what Scripture does.

What was Timothy to do with the Word? "Preach" it. What does it mean to preach? The action calls to mind the role of a herald who was responsible for receiving the message of a king and delivering it the king's subjects. *To preach* is to declare what God has to say to his people and to exhort them to act on that word by believing and obeying it. Biblical preaching confronts us with God, through the Word, inspired by the Holy Spirit, through the personality of a preacher, so that we will understand and respond to God. Preaching includes reading the Word, explaining the Word, and applying it.

Be ready in season and out of season. When do you preach the Word? When it's convenient, and also when it's inconvenient. A pastor should preach when he knows he'll hear an "amen!" and when he knows he'll be reviled. He must preach the parts of Scripture that people like, and preach the parts they don't. He must use Scripture to **rebuke, correct, and encourage with great patience and teaching.** In other words, a preacher must use the Bible to do what Paul said it's "profitable" for (3:16). Preaching should teach and encourage. But preaching should also rebuke and correct. In a world that claims everything is relative, people ought to be able to hear the absolute truth of the Word of God (John 17:17) preached in "the church of the living God, the pillar and foundation of the truth" (1 Tim 3:15). Each person might have his or her own view. But when we come to church, we need to hear *God's* view. We need to know his agenda.

4:3-5 Why must the Word be preached? **For the time will come when people will not tolerate sound doctrine.** People will not want spiritual food that is healthy but simply something that tastes good. They'll even gather **teachers** who will satisfy their **desires,** who will address the **itch** they want scratched (4:3). They'll turn from the **truth** toward **myths** (4:4). Sinful people don't naturally run toward what is holy and righteous. They prefer what makes them feel good. That's why they need to hear the Word faithfully preached. Timothy couldn't control the response to his sermons. But he could commit himself to God's calling on his life. He could **exercise self-control** (letting the gospel transform his life), **endure hardship** (suffering for the gospel), **and do the work of an evangelist** (proclaiming the gospel). In this way, he would **fulfill his ministry.** He'd complete what he started (4:5).

4:6 Paul's words in 3:16–4:5 emphasize the priority of God's Word, and he solemnly charges Timothy to preach it faithfully. Why? Because these are the apostle's final words to this young man whom he dearly loves, and he saved this most important exhortation for the end.

Having delivered his charge, Paul now pens his own obituary: **I am already being poured out as a drink offering, and the time for my departure is close.** Paul uses Old Testament imagery to describe his impending death. Just as drink offerings were poured out to God on the altar, the apostle recognized that his life was being poured out, and **the time for [his] departure** was **close.** He was sitting in a Roman prison, awaiting his execution.

4:7 How did he evaluate the life he had lived as he reached its end? Paul knew that he had been a wicked man who was rescued only by God's grace. But he also knew that since then he had worked hard and been faithful to the task God gave him.

I have fought the good fight. Everyone gets into fights, and most of the fights in which we engage are not good ones. There are battles you shouldn't wage, motivated by pride and selfishness. And then there are things worth fighting for, things that truly matter. Paul fought the noblest battle of all: the battle for people's souls. He held nothing back. What about you? Have you given Christ your all? Do you have the scars to show for it?

I have finished the race. It's not enough to *start* the Christian race. It's not enough to *run* the race. You must *finish* the race. Your goal in life must be to finish well. Paul didn't reach the end of his days to contemplate the things he hadn't done. In fact, he had no sense of incompleteness. Christ can get you to the finish line, but you must focus your attention on him. Even if you have fallen, get up, and keep running. "Let us run with endurance the race that lies before us, keeping our eyes on Jesus, the source and perfecter of our faith" (Heb 12:1-2).

I have kept the faith. Paul had been faithful with the faith. Just as he had exhorted Timothy (2 Tim 1:14), Paul had also guarded "the good deposit," the good news of salvation. He recognized its great value, and he protected it as a treasure. To him, the gospel was worth any hardship. Indeed, the blessings of the faith outweigh any sufferings related to it.

4:8 There is reserved for me the crown of righteousness, which the Lord, the righteous Judge, will give me on that day. Paul knew he would soon die at Rome's hands. According to ancient tradition, he was beheaded. But that frightening fate made no difference to Paul. Not only would the Lord restore his head to his body, but he would also place a crown on it. And **not only** on *his* head, but on the heads of **all those who have loved** Christ's **appearing** through faithful living.

A football team can perform poorly during the first quarter—or even during the first half of the game. But what's most important is how they finish. Don't, then, look backward on the mess in your past. The grace of God can cover it. Instead, look forward. There's still time. Fight the good fight, finish the race, and keep the faith. Your reward is waiting.

4:9-12 Timothy had been a faithful companion and colleague of Paul. Therefore, the aging apostle longed for the young minister **to come to** him **soon** (4:9). Timothy's visit was needful because practically everyone else had left Paul. **Demas,** whom Paul mentions elsewhere as a co-worker (Col 4:14; Phlm 24), ultimately decided not to follow Paul's example in 4:7-8. Instead, **he loved this present world** more than the world to come and **deserted** him. Sadly, he had traded an eternal perspective for a mere earthly one. Others also left, but for more noble reasons. **Crescens** and **Titus** apparently departed to fulfill mission work (4:10). **Tychicus** left because Paul **sent** him **to Ephesus** (4:12). **Only Luke** (4:11), "the dearly loved physician" (Col 4:14), remained.

It's interesting to see that Paul asks Timothy to **bring Mark** with him. Mark (also called "John" or "John Mark") had traveled with Paul before (see Acts 13:5). But after Mark left Paul in the middle of his first missionary journey (Acts 13:13), Paul was unwilling to take him the next time around. Paul and Barnabas had such a sharp disagreement over Mark that they parted ways (Acts 15:36-40). But once the relationship was mended, Paul found Mark **useful** to his **ministry** (2 Tim 4:11).

4:13 Paul asks Timothy to **bring** his **cloak** and **the scrolls, especially the parchments.** The first request would address a practical, physical need: Paul was living in a cold Roman dungeon. The second request would address a ministry need. Most likely, the scrolls were copies of Scripture. Even to the very end, Paul was a diligent student of the Word.

4:14-15 Though Demas had merely deserted Paul, **Alexander the coppersmith did** him **great harm** (4:14). It's likely that this is the same Alexander in Ephesus who was a false teacher and whom Paul "delivered to Satan" (1 Tim 1:19-20) because Paul warns Timothy, who was ministering in Ephesus, to **watch out for him** and his opposition to sound teaching (2 Tim 4:15). Regardless, Paul knew that ultimately **the Lord** would **repay** Alexander for his deeds (4:14). "Don't be deceived:

God is not mocked. For whatever a person sows he will also reap" (Gal 6:7).

4:16-18 Paul didn't put his hope in people. After all, men and women fail. During his trial, at his **first defense**, he was **deserted** by everyone. Yet, he followed in the footsteps of the Lord Jesus and the first Christian martyr (Stephen) by asking the Lord to forgive them (4:16; see Luke 23:34; Acts 7:59-60). Regardless of who had abandoned Paul, **the Lord** had consistently **stood with** him **and strengthened** him throughout his ministry so that he could **fully preach the word** to **the Gentiles** (4:17). God had kept Paul from disaster time and again, and he knew that God would bring him **safely into his heavenly kingdom** (4:18).

The **lion's mouth** (4:17) may either refer metaphorically to evil people like Emperor Nero (see Ps 22:13, 19-21) or literally to the wild animals that killed Christians in the Roman coliseum (see Dan 6:22).

4:19-22 Paul closes his letter with greetings and additional news (4:19-21). Then he offers a benediction for Timothy and the church he served: **The Lord be with your spirit. Grace be with you all** (4:22).

TITUS

INTRODUCTION

Author and Historical Background

SEE THE INTRODUCTION TO 1 TIMothy for a discussion of the author and historical background of the Pastoral Epistles (1 Timothy, 2 Timothy, and Titus)

Message and Purpose

Titus was one of the apostle Paul's sons in the ministry. Paul sent him to lead the churches on the island of Crete, and then he wrote this brief letter to equip Titus to effectively lead them in serving the body of Christ. Paul explained to Titus the importance of leadership, noting that part of Titus's responsibility as a pastor and spiritual leader was to develop leaders who would help the church fulfill its role. This included encouraging the older men to disciple the younger men and the older women to disciple the younger women so that the members of the body of Christ could help one another grow.

Titus contains solid teaching on the importance of good works—those ministries that benefit the members of the church and others as well. It also includes instructions on the absolute necessity of teaching sound doctrine through the proclamation of God's Word with both love and clarity. Two words summarize Paul's message here: proclamation and coordination. Titus was to preach the Word and coordinate the ministry so that lives would be changed and God's kingdom expanded.

www.bhpublishinggroup.com/qr/te/56_00

Outline

I. Greetings (1:1-4)
II. Instructions for Leadership (1:5-16)
III. Virtues and Ethics for God's People (2:1-15)
IV. Christian Behavior and Good Works toward Others (3:1-11)
V. Final Words (3:12-15)

TITUS

I. GREETINGS (1:1-4)

1:1-4 Paul calls himself **a servant of God** and **apostle of Jesus Christ**. Thus, he's operating on God's agenda, not his own. Paul's goal is to build up **the faith** and **knowledge of** God's people. Why? To lead them to **godliness** (1:1) so that their lifestyle honors the God who gave them **eternal life** (1:2), which is one of the primary goals of election (see Eph 1:4-5).

God **promised** eternal life **before time began** (1:2) but brought it about **in his own time** (1:3). You can bank on God's promises. Anything he says in eternity is guaranteed in time. But you're dependent on his schedule. The timing for Jesus's entry into the world was perfect—and so is the timing for everything God does in your life.

Paul writes **to Titus**, his pastoral delegate on Crete. Paul either led Titus to Christ or nurtured him in the faith since he calls him his **true son** in their **common faith** (1:4). He wants Titus to help the churches conduct themselves properly, reflecting the values and behavior of their heavenly Father. When we live under our parents' roofs, we must submit to the rules and ethics of their houses. Similarly, God's people must conform to his guidelines that govern the church. Thus, the church needs to have its ministry coordinated effectively and sound doctrine firmly established.

II. INSTRUCTIONS FOR LEADERSHIP (1:5-16)

1:5-9 A task from God cannot be underestimated, and God carefully decides who will carry out his work. This is why Paul writes to Titus, not only to encourage him but also to help him pick out **elders** who can share in the divine task. We all know of things left undone in our lives, families, businesses, schools, and relationships. But when something of God's is left undone, it's a *big* deal. These leaders would serve Titus's need to **set right** things that were broken in the church so that the ministry would be healthy and operate effectively based on sound doctrine (1:5). Qualified spiritual leadership is critical for a church to function properly. Titus's twofold task was the identification of such leadership and the teaching of sound doctrine.

Titus wasn't left to wonder who should fill these kingdom positions because Paul provides a list of virtues and traits for elders (see also 1 Tim 3:1-7). And the criteria are quite stout! Notice that these are not descriptions of *performance* but of *character*. Paul wanted a certain kind of man to serve as an elder. An "elder," also called **an overseer** (1:7), is not necessarily an old man, but a mature man who knows and walks with God.

First, Paul provides the general traits of an elder / overseer, particularly with respect to his family. It is essential that an elder be the **husband of one wife** and have **faithful children** (1:6). Since he is the steward and caretaker of God's household, it only makes sense that he be able to take care of his own house (see 1 Tim 3:4-5).

Next the apostle highlights what an elder should *not* be like. Since he is doing God's work, he should not reflect poorly on his Lord. He cannot be **arrogant . . . hot-tempered . . . an excessive drinker . . . a bully . . . or greedy for money** (1:7). These traits don't make for a good employee in a secular job. They certainly shouldn't describe a shepherd of God's people.

Finally, Paul lists the positive characteristics. Elders should be **hospitable . . . sensible, righteous, holy, self-controlled.** They should hold tightly **to the faithful message** (1:8-9). These are high expectations, but God's elders / overseers / pastors must exhibit these virtues if they are going to faithfully shepherd the flock that belongs to the chief Shepherd (see 1 Pet 5:2-4).

All of these character traits come together in the final comment of 1:9. If elders do not live out these divine virtues, then they cannot **encourage with sound teaching** or **refute those who contradict it.** This is a weighty responsibility. It takes men of integrity to submit faithfully to their King's agenda, to teach others to do likewise, and to correct others who oppose it. That's why Paul gave Titus such high expectations for elder candidates. Character is everything.

1:10-11 Strong church leaders were needed in Crete because **rebellious people** were upsetting God's work and deceiving his people (1:10). Pastoring is difficult work; cowards need not apply. God loves his sheep, and he wants shepherds who will lovingly protect them. Deceitful men were overthrowing **households** by means of false **teaching** in order to obtain **money dishonestly** (1:11). Sadly, such wicked men are still with us today. Because false teachers are outside the church, elders must equip Christians with sound, biblical teaching to help them discern truth from lies. But should false teachers try to operate inside the church, elders must **silence them** (1:11).

1:12-14 Paul quotes a Cretan poet from the sixth century BC: **Cretans are always liars, evil beasts, lazy gluttons.** It's never good when someone describes his own countrymen like that. But unfortunately, Paul found the saying to be **true** of at least some of the Cretans. He thus urged Titus to **rebuke them sharply** (1:13). Of course, for Paul rebuke is never the end but only the means to an end. He wanted church members in Crete to be **sound in the faith** and to ignore those **who reject the truth** (1:13-14). Only by conforming your thinking to God's truth can you live a life that is pleasing to God.

1:15-16 On the other hand, those who persist in rebellion **are defiled and unbelieving.** Notice again the connection between *thinking* and *living.* Their **mind and conscience are defiled,** dirty (1:15). What kind of life is produced by minds that are dominated by such self-interest? Even though **they claim to know God . . . they deny him by their works.** And how does Paul characterize their works? They are **detestable, disobedient, and unfit** (and were, therefore, to be opposed) (1:16). That's a sobering description. Lips that claim to praise God mean nothing when they are combined with a lifestyle that denies him.

III. VIRTUES AND ETHICS FOR GOD'S PEOPLE (2:1-15)

Paul transitions to discuss what God's people should look like. Good character leads to good conduct. For Paul, this is how kingdom disciple-making is done and is the primary task of the church. We need a transformed and transferred faith, and this occurs as we all shape and sanctify each other in the church under healthy teaching from God's Word (i.e., sound doctrine). It is as if we pass the faith baton on to each other in an Olympic relay.

2:1-2 In 2:2-8, Paul gives Titus some clear examples regarding how various people should live as Christ-followers: he covers older men, older women, younger women, and younger men. **Older men**, for instance, should **be self-controlled, worthy of respect, sensible, and sound in faith, love, and endurance.** Such senior kingdom men serve as authentic models and spiritual mentors for young Christian men who are confronted by a very different kind of "manhood" on exhibit in the surrounding culture.

2:3-5 In a similar way, **older women** among God's people should model Christian virtues to the younger women in the congregation. Where can a young Christian wife find holy women to disciple her to live faithfully and build up her family? According to Paul, she ought to find such kingdom women in the church. By aligning their lives with God's principles for a kingdom wife (2:4-5; see also Eph 5:22-24, 33), young women will not only experience God's blessing but also prevent **God's word** from being **slandered** (2:5). When wives and mothers abandon the priority of the home, they bring shame and dishonor to the authority, truthfulness, and power of God's Word. They also call into question the seriousness of their spiritual commitment.

2:6-8 There are many qualities Paul could have encouraged in young men. But he sums up godliness for this group by telling Titus to exhort them **to be self-controlled in everything.** If young men today need any advice, surely that is it. In a culture that encourages men to indulge their every desire, self-control is a radical message. Paul urges Titus to be **an example of good works** (actions that glorify God and benefit others) and to engage in sound teaching so that young men have a worthy example to follow and so those who oppose the faith won't have **anything bad to say about** God's people (2:7-8). Gender-based discipleship should be a major part of every local church's ministry.

2:9-10 Paul also tells **slaves** to obey **their masters** (2:9). Scripture condemns most of what we know of slavery (especially American antebellum slavery). For example, human beings are not to be kidnapped and sold (Exod 21:16); slaves are not to be abused (Exod 21:26-27); and fugitive slaves are not to be returned to their masters (Deut 23:15-16).

But given the unrighteous institution of slavery as it existed in the Roman Empire, Paul tells Christian slaves how to live with a heavenly perspective.

How does this teaching affect us today? Paul's principles for slaves ought to be applied by believers in their workplaces. When employers think of their Christians employees, they ought to consider them **to be well-pleasing, not** given to **talking back or stealing, but demonstrating utter faithfulness.** Does that describe your approach to your daily nine-to-five?

We often segregate ourselves and mix only with people who are like us in age, interests, or even socio-economic level. But such divisions are out of place in the New Testament church. Paul wants Titus to have all of God's people mixing and mingling: the older with the younger, the free with the slaves. Otherwise, how can we learn from each other about loving and serving Christ and others better?

2:11-14 In light of what Paul wrote in 2:1-10, **all people** are within the hopeful reach of God's **salvation** (2:11). No one is beyond God's rescue, no matter who he or she is or what's been done. In fact, the "worst" people in society are exactly those whom God seeks for his rescue project. The **grace of God has appeared** (2:11)—that is, it has emerged out of the shadows of the law (see John 1:15-17). Grace is not just a doctrine; it's a person. And grace has a name: Jesus Christ, **our great God and Savior**, who says to all, "Come to me" (2:13). Grace grows us in godliness and increases our victory over sin.

Jesus **gave himself** on the cross **to redeem us from all lawlessness** (2:14). In other words, through his death, Jesus paid the price to free us from slavery to sin. So, how should redeemed people live? Though they wait for the return of Jesus (2:13), they wait actively and not passively. God's grace teaches and empowers us to **deny godlessness** and embrace the **godly way** (2:12). Only by adopting a godly perspective and being **eager to do good works** (2:14) can believers see the power of heaven at work in their earthly lives. *Good works* are the divinely approved acts that benefit people and bring glory to God.

God's grace is personified in the person and work of Jesus Christ and is the basis and foundation for both justification and sanctification, since it enables the good works we are commanded to do.

2:15 Encourage and rebuke with all authority. Let no one disregard you. Paul gave Titus some serious marching orders. The work of ministry is not for the faint of heart. It is to be exercised with loving but firm kingdom authority.

IV. CHRISTIAN BEHAVIOR AND GOOD WORKS TOWARD OTHERS (3:1-11)

3:1-3 The apostle urges the Christians in Crete **to submit to rulers and authorities.** This is a hard bit of instruction, but government officials, employers, and any other persons of authority should be the recipients of our **every good work** (3:1). In the end, Christians are serving God in all they do, and he is always watching our motives and actions. When we cheat the time clock at work, we are really cheating God himself—and giving the world a poor reflection of our Master.

As we live, Paul wants us to remember where we came from. We are to show **gentleness to all people** because God showed the same to us when we were **foolish, disobedient, deceived** (3:2-3). Believers are often tempted to look down their noses at unbelievers—forgetting that they too were once lost.

3:4-7 God displayed his **kindness** and **love** for us by giving us a merciful washing of **regeneration and renewal by the Holy Spirit** (3:4-5). We were soiled and stained, and God cleaned us up. None of this was due to our **works of righteousness** but simply **his mercy** (3:5). And mercy doesn't stop there. We are now **heirs,** sons and daughters of the King, **with the hope**

of eternal life (3:7). So live like a royal heir and make his kingdom vision your own.

3:8 Kingdom men and women are **to devote themselves to good works.** *Good works* are divinely prescribed actions that benefit others and glorify God (see Matt 5:16). Thus, they **are good and profitable for everyone.** They bless those in the church, and they bless those outside it by giving them an accurate picture of the love and grace of God and his offer of the free gift of salvation (see Eph 2:8-9).

3:9-11 Meanwhile, kingdom men and women are to **avoid foolish debates** and **quarrels** (3:9). Few things drive away seekers like church infighting. So Satan loves to encourage selfish strife and division among church members. What should churches do with **a divisive person** who quarrels about **unprofitable and worthless** matters? Warn him twice and then **reject** him (3:10-11).

In essence, Paul is saying, "Keep to the instructions I have given you and devote yourselves to good works toward all people. If it's not from the sacred Scriptures, then don't worry yourselves with it."

V. FINAL WORDS (3:12-15)

3:12-14 Paul wasn't the kind of person to take credit for all of the work of ministry. He gave honor where honor was due. **Artemas, Tychicus, Zenas,** and **Apollos** were his co-laborers who served the church well, and Paul wanted others to know it (3:12-13). He held them up as examples of good works and then added one final reminder for believers to **devote themselves to**

good works too (3:14). After all, trusting in Christ the King as your sin-bearer will get you from earth to heaven. But adopting his kingdom agenda will bring heaven's help to your earthly life.

3:15 Paul closes by extending his customary, priceless salutation: **Grace be with all of you.**

PHILEMON

INTRODUCTION

Author

PAUL WROTE HIS LETTER TO PHI-lemon while in prison (vv. 1, 9-10, 13). He most likely wrote Ephesians, Philippians, Colossians, and Philemon during the same imprisonment in Rome. In AD 60–61, he was under house arrest in guarded rental quarters (see Acts 28:30).

Historical Background

Paul addresses his letter to Apphia, Archippus, and the church that met in Philemon's home; nevertheless, his main addressee is Philemon who lived in Colossae (see the reference to Onesimus in Col 4:9). Apparently he was a wealthy man, since he owned slaves and a house large enough to accommodate church meetings. In any case, it appears Philemon had become a convert through the ministry of Paul himself (v. 19). Importantly, though this letter is a personal appeal to Philemon, it was not private. The rest of the church would have heard it read aloud and witnessed Philemon's response to Paul.

Message and Purpose

This is an intimate letter from the apostle Paul to his friend Philemon. This man had a slave named Onesimus, who stole from him, ran away to Rome, and through a series of circumstances encountered Paul. Not only did Paul lead Onesimus to Christ but discipled him to such an extent that Onesimus ministered back to Paul. Nevertheless, when the apostle learned about the circumstances that had brought Onesimus to Rome, Paul sent Onesimus back to Philemon to make things right. The theme of Paul's letter to Philemon is thus forgiveness and reconciliation. Philemon was in a position to forgive Onesimus and restore their relationship, showing Onesimus the same forgiveness that Philemon himself had received from God, since the two men had become brothers in Christ.

Here we see a very tender side of Paul as he pleads with his friend Philemon to forgive and reconcile with Onesimus. His words are a reminder that forgiveness is prerequisite to reconciliation, and reconciliation is prerequisite to restoration. The message of Philemon is desperately needed in our day of division and strife. As believers, we need to be kingdom agents of forgiveness and reconciliation in each other's lives and in the world.

VIDEO   INTRO

www.bhpublishinggroup.com/qr/te/57_00

Outline

I. Address and Greeting (1-3)
II. Thanksgiving for Philemon (4-7)
III. Paul's Appeal for Onesimus (8-16)
IV. Closing (17-25)

PHILEMON

I. ADDRESS AND GREETING (1-3)

1-3 Paul addresses his letter to **Apphia . . . Archippus . . .** and **the church that meets in your home** (v. 2). Apphia was probably Philemon's wife. Archippus was perhaps their son or maybe the pastor of the church. Regardless, it quickly becomes clear that Paul is writing primarily to Philemon. In the Greek language in which Paul wrote, the instances of "you" and "your" in the body of the letter (vv. 2, 4-21, 23) are singular, not plural. Nonetheless, since it was also addressed to the church that met in Philemon's house, the congregation would have been listening as it was read. Thus, the principles of forgiveness and reconciliation raised in this personal letter are applicable to the whole church.

II. THANKSGIVING FOR PHILEMON (4-7)

4-7 Philemon was a good man. Paul regularly remembers him in his prayers and thanks God for him (v. 4) because he was well known for his **love for all the saints and** his **faith . . . in the Lord Jesus** (v. 5). The only way to know that you have a working love for Jesus Christ is if you have a working love toward God's people. It is a contradiction to say you love God if you fail to love your fellow Christians (see 1 John 4:7-12, 20-21). Paul tells Philemon that his positive reputation is known all over the place. The apostle is filled with joy **because the hearts of the saints have been refreshed through** Philemon (v. 7). He was constantly encouraging, helping, and ministering to other Christians.

III. PAUL'S APPEAL FOR ONESIMUS (8-16)

It's at this point that Paul makes his transition. After praising Philemon for his faithfulness, Paul mentions the name he probably didn't want to hear: Onesimus. Previously, Philemon had a slave named Onesimus who wronged him by perhaps stealing from him (v. 18) and then running away. Somehow Onesimus came into contact with Paul in Rome and believed the gospel (v. 10). The runaway slave, then, had become a saint.

Everything changes when a person places faith in Christ. When a person comes to Jesus, he has a new status. When people enter the family of God, their relationships change. The question addressed in this passage is this: how do you relate to a person who has wronged you based on his new status with Jesus Christ?

8-11 Paul admits he could use his authority as an apostle and **command** Philemon **to do**

what is right (v. 8). But he cares about their relationship and makes an appeal, **instead, on the basis of love** (v. 9). Since the name "Onesimus" actually means "useful," Paul makes a play on words: the man who was formerly **useless to you** is now **useful both to you and to me** (v. 11). Paul has seen that Onesimus's new status in Christ matches his name.

12-16 Given his **imprisonment for the gospel**, Paul would like Onesimus to stay and **serve** him on Philemon's behalf. Philemon's runaway slave could become his representative to support God's premier missionary. But Paul doesn't want to obligate his friend

without his **consent** (v. 14), so he is **sending [Onesimus] back** (v. 12). Why? Because Onesimus needs to return and face up to what he's done. He has to go to Philemon and make things right. But, also, Paul is helping Philemon grow in love and forgiveness. Philemon has the opportunity to receive Onesimus back **no longer as a slave, but . . . as a dearly loved brother** (v. 16). Paul wants these men to deal with their problem, not to bypass it. That way, they can show the church what reconciliation looks like. Regardless of role differences, class distinctions, or economic disparities, the ground is level at the cross.

IV. CLOSING (17-25)

17 Then Paul takes his role as mediator a step further. He says, **If you consider me a partner, welcome him as you would me.** Thus, how Philemon treats Onesimus will reflect how Philemon feels about Paul. Jesus said, "Whatever you did for one of the least of these brothers and sisters of mine, you did for me" (Matt 25:40). The body of Christ is one: we're a family.

18 Then Paul tells Philemon, if he **wronged you** or **owes you anything, charge that to my account.** In other words, he says, "Charge Onesimus's debt to me. I love him so much that I will stand in his place. You can put what he owes on my tab." We need mediators in the church like Paul, who mirrored his Savior. After all, Jesus Christ took every sinful debt that we owed God and said, "Charge it to my account."

19-20 Paul reminds Philemon that he owes his own conversion to him (v. 19) and asks that Philemon **refresh [his] heart** (v. 20), just as Philemon had refreshed the hearts of other Christians (v. 7).

Though this letter is short, it demonstrates the great power of the gospel when it comes to interpersonal relationships. Whether we have done wrong like Onesimus, been wronged like Philemon, or need to mediate between two brothers like Paul, following Jesus Christ means submitting to his kingdom agenda for reconciliation. Forgiveness is a divine condition for experiencing and exercising kingdom authority in prayer (see Mark 11:22-26).

21-25 Paul concludes with confidence in Philemon's response (v. 21), hopefulness that he can visit soon (v. 22), and greetings from those with him (v. 23-24).

HEBREWS

INTRODUCTION

Author

THE LETTER TO THE HEBREWS does not identify its author; therefore, there has been much speculation as to his identity. Some argue for Paul, Luke, Barnabas, Apollos, Timothy, Silvanus, and others. But in the end, we cannot be certain. Regardless, the writer has an in-depth understanding of the Old Testament and the conventions of the religious life of Israel, including the priesthood (see 5:1-10; 7:1-28), the tabernacle/tent of meeting (see 9:1-14), and the sacrificial system (see 10:1-25). He also demonstrates a command of the Greek language. His range of vocabulary and the style in which he presented his arguments, in fact, resulted in what many have agreed is some of the most sophisticated writing in the New Testament.

Historically, many opted for either Paul or a missionary associate of his as the author of Hebrews because the writer was familiar with Paul's companion Timothy (see 13:23). But while Paul was identified as the author by the early Christian writer Clement (ca. AD 150–215), and he was followed by other prominent church fathers like Eusebius and Augustine, no definitive case can be made. The best position might be that of Origen who wrote, "Who wrote the epistle, in truth God knows." This uncertainty should not, however, trouble us. The early church received the letter as inspired and authoritative Scripture. It has unquestioned value for the Christian life.

Historical Background

The author presumably knew the Christian recipients of his letter well because he referred to them as "brothers and sisters" (3:12; 10:19; 13:22). Like him, they had heard about the gospel through the earliest followers of Jesus (2:3). They were Jewish Christians, having familiarity with the old covenant sacrificial system. Moreover, they were a group enduring various forms of persecution (10:32-34) under Emperor Nero prior to the destruction of the temple in AD 70. As a result, some among them had grown unwilling to grow spiritually and risked forfeiting—not their salvation—but the blessings and rewards God had in store for them. Thus, the author urges them to "go on to maturity" (6:1) and to hold fast to their commitment to Christ.

Message and Purpose

Hebrews is often considered one of the most difficult books in the New Testament to interpret, second only to Revelation. That's because Hebrews is very dependent on the Old Testament for much of what the author has to say to Jewish Christians who have come upon hard times and are considering bailing out on their Christian commitment to return to Judaism.

This letter's recipients were wondering whether following Christ was worth the persecution. In effect, the author of Hebrews urged them, "Yes it is! Keep going. Don't turn back. Jesus *is* worth the trouble." That's also the same message Hebrews offers to anyone today who is encountering opposition in the Christian faith and thinking of throwing in the towel. Some things are worth the struggle, and some things aren't. But Jesus definitely is!

The author has a lot to say about how Jesus is superior to the Old Testament sacrificial system. Hebrews will rev up your faith in Christ and his unshakeable kingdom. Following him is worth it.

www.bhpublishinggroup.com/qr/te/58_00

HEBREWS

I. THE SUPERIORITY OF THE SON OF GOD (1:1-14)

The recipients of Hebrews were Jewish Christians struggling to persevere in their commitment to Christ in the face of temptations and persecution. The author knew their situation was serious and thus functioned a bit like a parent with a child who is in danger and not paying attention. Out of love, he essentially grabbed these children in the faith to say, "You need to listen to me! This is serious."

1:1 He opens by explaining how **God spoke to the fathers** of the faith **long ago.** As our transcendent Creator, God is unknowable unless he reveals himself. And that's what he's done, pulling back the curtain on spiritual matters to disclose himself. The Bible is God's revelation to us. In times past, he communicated to his people **in different ways:** by **prophets,** angels (e.g., Josh 5:13-15), and even a donkey (Num 22:22-41).

1:2 In these last days, however, **he has spoken to us by his Son.** When the author mentions "these last days," he's talking about the New Testament days—everything that falls between the time of Christ's birth and his return. Jesus's goal was to put on flesh in order to make God known (see John 1:1, 14, 18). God used various means to reveal himself in the past. But now he's funneling everything through his Son, the incarnate revelation of God. He is God's final Word on every subject.

What else does the author tell us about this Son? Jesus is **heir of all things.** God has bequeathed creation to his Son. Moreover, he is the creative power of God: God **made the universe through him.** When God said, "Let there be light" (Gen 1:3), Jesus was the Word doing the action (John 1:1-3).

1:3 Furthermore, **the Son is the radiance of God's glory and the exact expression of his nature.** Jesus Christ possesses *all* of the divine attributes. And he couldn't be the "exact expression" of God without being God. The author of Hebrews, then, heartily agrees with John (John 1:1) and Paul (Phil 2:6): Jesus is God. And not only does he bear all the attributes of deity, he also sustains **all things by his powerful word.** He's the *creative* power of God as well as the *sustaining* power of God.

Many people feel like they're coming apart. But if Jesus Christ has the power to keep a universe from unraveling, he has the power to hold you together too! This is why believers must never give up.

After Christ completed his work of redemption, **making purification for sins, he sat down at the right hand of the Majesty on high.** When the high priest entered the most holy place in the tabernacle/temple to offer sacrifice for the sins of the people, there was no chair. He couldn't sit down because his work was never done. He had to repeat the work over and over.

The sacrificial system of the Old Testament was God's layaway plan. It couldn't deal with sin once and for all. It was God's temporary solution, pointing forward to something better. But when Jesus died on the cross for sin, he declared, "It is finished" (John 19:30)—that is, "The sin debt is paid in full." With his resurrection, his work was complete, and he sat down at God's right hand—in the seat of authority and power, which guarantees that final victory belongs to him. Thus, believers can have assurance of divine victory in their lives. This is an important theme we'll see repeated in Hebrews.

1:4 Jesus **became superior to the angels, just as the name he inherited is more excellent than theirs.** God made humans "lower than the angels," yet he crowned them "with glory and honor" (2:7; Ps 8:5). God created Adam constitutionally inferior to angelic beings, but he made him to rule the earth (Gen 1:28) and manifest God's rule in history. But when Adam listened to Satan and sinned, he relinquished control. In rebelling against God's rule, he submitted to Satan's. As a result, Satan became the "god of this age" (2 Cor 4:4), and the world needed to be reclaimed.

So, who could reclaim it? Well, it had to be a human being—that was God's plan from the beginning. But sinful humans were under the authority of the devil (Eph 2:2). The only answer, then, was "the last Adam" (1 Cor 15:45): Jesus Christ. He was perfectly righteous and not under Satan's authority. Nevertheless, he had to inherit a name. He had to become human. Jesus is the Son—both Son of God and Son of Man, divine and human.

1:5-14 The author quotes a number of Old Testament passages to support his statements in 1:2-4 and to demonstrate Christ's superiority to the angels. Many first-century Jewish Christian revered angels because they were a means of divine revelation. But God never said to an angel, **You are my Son** (1:5). Nor does an angel have the right to receive worship, which is for God alone (see Exod 20:3-5). Rather, **all God's angels worship** the Son (1:6). Not only that, but God calls the Son "**God**" (1:8-9)!

Unlike the rest of humanity, the Son consistently **loved righteousness and hated lawlessness** (1:9). He is the everlasting Creator of **the heavens** (1:10-12) who has been seated at God's **right hand** with his **enemies** under his feet (1:13; see Eph 1:20-22). Angels are merely **ministering spirits** who **serve those who are going to inherit salvation** (1:14).

So where do we fit into this discussion? The psalm quoted by the author in verse 9 speaks of Christ's **companions.** The idea of being a "companion" or "partner" of Christ shows up several times in Hebrews (e.g., 3:1, 14). What does it mean? Well, believers have the opportunity to be Christ's companions, his partners, who will rule with him as part of his inner circle. This honor is distinct from justification. Those who accept him as their sin-bearer gain entrance by grace into the kingdom of God as heirs. But your participation as Christ's *companion* or *partner* determines the level of your inheritance in the kingdom.

Christ himself had to inherit a name (1:4) even though he was appointed as an heir (1:2). You are an heir by grace. But your obedience and participation with Christ determines your benefits and privileges in the kingdom. If you are a Christian, you have been saved to become a partner and to rule with Christ. You can't lose your salvation, but God doesn't want you to lose out on partnership—the calling he has on your life. How important is this to God? He has assigned ministering angels to oversee you and make sure you receive your inheritance in time and in eternity (1:14). However, faithfulness to the King is the criteria to become part of Christ's administrative cabinet when he establishes his earthly millennial kingdom on his return (3:14; see Rom 8:17; 2 Tim 2:12; Rev 2:16-17).

II. THE SUPERIORITY OF THE SON IN HIS HUMANITY (2:1-18)

2:1-4 Here the author gives his first warning. He's concerned that the readers **not drift away.** He wants them to **pay attention,** and he exhorts them not to **neglect such a great salvation** (2:1-3). If God was serious about his **message** that came **through angels** (the

law), how much more serious is he about his message that came through his Son, **the Lord** (the gospel)? (2:2-3).

If you're bobbing along on the ocean and do nothing, you're going to drift. Similarly, if you're neglecting your spiritual life, you're going to drift from God and will inevitably find trouble. What do you do when times are hard and the waves are rough? Keep swimming. Don't give up.

2:5-9 The author has more to say about angels, humanity, and Jesus Christ. After Satan rebelled and took a host of fallen angels with him, God created humans—constitutionally inferior beings—and **subjected** the **world** to them instead of **angels** (2:5). Why? To demonstrate what he can do with less when less is dependent on him than he can do with more when more is in rebellion against him. According to Psalm 8, God made Adam **lower than the angels** but **crowned him with glory and honor and subjected everything under his feet** (2:7-8).

The problem is this: the first Adam failed and handed over ruling authority to Satan. That's why **we do not yet see everything subjected to [man]** (2:8). What did God do in response? He didn't change his strategy. Rather, he committed himself to bring about his kingdom rule on earth through a man. He even accomplished it himself through the person of his Son, Jesus Christ. The Son temporarily became **lower than the angels** to realign heaven and earth. He came down to **taste death for everyone** and was **crowned with glory and honor** (2:9). The Son became man and won the victory over Satan and sin through his obedience, sacrificial death, and resurrection.

Even in Christ's victory, though, we do not yet **see** the full results with our eyes (2:8). It's like what a person who wins the presidential election but whose presidency has not yet been fully experienced. We still await Christ's return to judge and rule on the earth. But make no mistake: Jesus is already in the victor's chair (2:9).

2:10-13 In the meantime, he's assembling his cabinet. You and I are his companions (1:9), so he has roles for us to play—in history and in eternity. You were saved to become Christ's companion, his partner. But he needs people he can trust.

To bring **many sons and daughters to glory**, God made **the source of their salvation perfect through sufferings** (2:10). Jesus was perfect in his deity. But he had to learn obedience as a man (5:8-9) so that he might

accomplish God's kingdom purposes. To do that, he had to suffer. He received glory and honor on Sunday, in fact, because of his obedient suffering and death on Friday.

The author of Hebrews says we are to look to Jesus not only as our Savior but also as our example as we endure suffering (12:2-3). To assume the place of honor God has for you in his kingdom will always require enduring something. This is God's process of helping Christ's followers to become **sanctified** (2:11), that is, "conformed to the image of" Christ (Rom 8:29). When you became a Christian, you entered into the family of God. He adopted you, and you became a brother or sister to Jesus. Now, he's working to sanctify you so that he's **not ashamed to call** you his brother and proclaim your name to the rest of the family (2:11-12). Remember that while this process involves varying levels of suffering, it's always for your good. Though both a criminal and a surgeon will seek to cut you, a surgeon will cut only to heal.

2:14-18 Since we're made of **flesh and blood**, the Son of God **shared in these.** Why? First, to defeat **the devil.** The Son became man to put the devil in his place. Christ came to render the devil powerless and take away his authority in fulfillment of God's dominion covenant for mankind to rule the earth on his behalf under his authority (see Gen 1:26-28; Ps 8:3-6). **Through his death**, Jesus conquered death to free people from **the fear of death** (2:14-15). If the Son has set you free, then, the only power the devil has over you is what you permit him.

Satan is "the father of lies" (John 8:44), so he'll try to trick you into giving him permission to exercise authority over you. But the devil no longer has **the power of death** (2:14). The gun he's been intimidating you with has no bullets. Jesus Christ emptied its chamber into himself. Thus, all Satan can do is deceive you into thinking the gun still has ammunition. But the fear of death should no longer make you a slave (see 1 Cor 15:51-57).

The second reason the Son took on flesh was so he could perfectly relate to us. God does not **help angels** but **Abraham's offspring** (2:16). Consider this. The fallen angels that rebelled against God had no opportunity for redemption. Yet God offers help to us—the children of Abraham. In fact, he graciously became like us **in every way, so that he could become a merciful and faithful high priest**. This enabled him to make atonement for our sins (2:17). But **since he himself . . . suffered when he was tempted**, it also enabled him to **help those who are tempted** (2:18). The Son of God experienced what you experience. In his earthly life, he faced the temptations and hardships that daily come your way. Being tempted isn't sin. Jesus was tempted, and he didn't sin (4:15). He understands what it's like, so he can help you.

When a woman is delivering a baby, a male doctor can sympathize with her to a point. Academically speaking, he knows the pain she's going through. But a female doctor who has actually experienced childbirth herself can truly empathize. As a mother, she's felt that pain. As a doctor, she can help others through it. Jesus is a merciful and faithful high priest. He has truly felt your pain, and he can empathize with you. Moreover, he can deliver you from sin and enable you to overcome your circumstances (see John 16:33).

III. FOLLOWING THE FAITHFUL SON BY FAITH (3:1-19)

3:1 Consider Jesus. Given who Jesus is and what he has done, you've got to look to him in the midst of your trials. The author calls the readers **holy brothers and sisters**, so he's clearly talking to Christians. And he reminds them (and us) that God didn't save them just so they could go to heaven. He saved them to partner with him in his kingdom agenda, to **share in a heavenly calling**—to be his companions in the messianic kingdom that is to come (see 11:16).

3:2-6 If you were a first-century Jew, Moses was your hero. Moses faithfully served God, delivered his word to Israel, and oversaw the establishment of the tabernacle and sacrificial system. These Jewish Christian readers, then, revered Moses. But Jesus is **worthy of more glory than Moses, just as the builder has more honor than the house** (3:3). Moses was an important part of the household, but Jesus built the house! Thus, the two cannot be fairly compared. Though **Moses was faithful as a servant in all God's household** (3:5), **Christ was faithful as a Son over [God's] household**. As the Son *over* the house, he has more say-so than a faithful servant. Keep going with Christ until you reach the finish line. We must **hold on to our confidence and the hope in which we boast** (3:6)—not to obtain salvation but to obtain the blessings of salvation.

3:7-11 Here the author quotes from Psalm 95 to provide an Old Testament illustration of his point. The warning is this: **do not harden your hearts** (3:8)—that is, don't tell God, "no." Psalm 95 refers to Israel's period of forty years in the wilderness after departing Egypt. Numbers 13–14 recounts how the Israelites refused to listen to God and enter the promised land of Canaan because they feared the inhabitants. As a result of that rebellion, God made them wander in the wilderness where they continued to rebel. **Therefore, I was provoked**, God said (3:10). He thus swore in his anger, **They will not enter my rest** (3:11).

This is an Old Testament principle for New Testament Christians. God was angry because his chosen people did not know his ways (3:10). The Bible teaches that God's ways with his people include three stages: deliverance, development, and destiny.

First, Israel experienced *deliverance* when God set them free from Egyptian bondage. Similarly, when he saved you—caused you to be born again in Christ—he delivered you. But his involvement in your life doesn't end there. The second stage is *development*, in which he brings you into a deeper relationship with himself. This includes the trials and tests of life; there's no development without these experiences. Most of the Israelites in the wilderness failed in the development stage because they wouldn't trust God to provide for them. Remember: it is only when God comes through for you in tough times that you experience the blessings of trusting him.

Finally, the developmental process leads to *destiny*. This is where God wants you to wind up. But you can't go from deliverance to destiny and skip development. God swore that the people would not enter his rest (3:11). The "rest" in view is a way of referring to their inheritance. He promised to give the people the land of Canaan. But because of their continual rebellion, they forfeited that inheritance.

3:12 Similarly, the author is telling his readers that if there is no development in their lives, they could miss out on their own inheritance—the spiritual blessings God has for them in history and in eternity. That's why he says, **Watch out.** You can be saved but refuse to develop. In other words, you can end up in the bleachers rather than on the playing field.

Don't waste the opportunities God gives you. How sad it would be not to be allowed to participate in his rule! Don't do what they did and miss out on your destiny. In terms of your spiritual progress and kingdom rewards, then, don't have **an evil, unbelieving heart** that allows sin to disconnect you from fellowship with God.

3:13-14 What's going to keep you persevering when times are hard? **Encourage each another daily . . . so that none of you is hardened by sin's deception.** One of the primary purposes of the local church is to create an environment in which believers can help

each other persevere. This is why the New Testament emphasizes (and why churches should emphasize) the "one anothers"— the exhortations to care for and encourage each other (e.g., John 15:12; Gal 6:2; Eph 4:32; 1 Thess 5:11). If we want to be Christ's companions, those who partner with him in his kingdom agenda, we must **hold firmly until the end** (3:14). To do that, we must help one another avoid sin's deception.

3:15-19 If you don't want to **harden your hearts** (3:15), you need regular exposure to God's Word. It's the only thing with the power to keep your heart soft (see 4:12-13). Those who **rebelled** against and angered God in the wilderness **disobeyed** him **because of unbelief** (3:16-19). They didn't reach their destination, Canaan, because of their lack of faith. Faith is acting like God is telling the truth. It's one thing to say, "I have faith." It's another thing to demonstrate your faith in God by acting on it.

This, of course, is not always easy. But even when you don't feel like it, you must keep following Jesus. You may fall down. If so, make sure you're close to someone who can pick you up. If you see a brother or sister fall, pick him or her up. To reach your destiny—to be a special companion with Jesus at a whole different level—you have to operate by faith and keep going.

IV. THE PROMISED REST AND THE GREAT HIGH PRIEST (4:1–5:10)

4:1 Therefore, the author says, in light of this Old Testament example, beware that you don't fall **short** of God's **rest** like they did. The unfaithful Israelites didn't miss out on heaven, but they missed out on the promised land. The "rest" God promises is participation in and enjoyment of the blessings he has planned.

Don't run the risk of falling short of your inheritance. If you're seriously living the Christian life, you will run into challenges and trials. In fact, the godlier you become, the more difficulties you're likely to face. The temptation is to acquiesce to your environment to ease the pressure. But if you follow

the route of least resistance, you will fail to be Christ's *companion* or *partner* (1:9; 3:1, 14). And while you won't lose your salvation, you will lose the opportunity to experience his plans for you in his kingdom. Don't squander your inheritance.

4:2 The Israelites received **good news**—not good news about heaven but about Canaan. **But the message** didn't **benefit them, since they were not united with those who heard it in faith.** Who were "those who heard it in faith"? Well, when God brought Israel to the edge of the promised land, twelve spies entered on a reconnaissance mission. Afterward, ten of them said, "We can't take Canaan. The job's too big for us." Only two—Joshua and Caleb—believed God and said, "Yes, we can do it with God's help." Unfortunately, the people of Israel believed the majority report. As a result, God refused to let anyone of that generation enter the land except Joshua and Caleb. Unbelief for the believer is the refusal to act like God is telling the truth.

It's easy to side with the majority. But if the majority rejects the will of God, they'll lead you to failure. Everyone knows the temptation to embellish personal problems. So get some Joshuas and Calebs in your life who will embellish the Lord when they hear you making much of your fears. When we embellish our problems, we make them bigger than they are. When we embellish the Lord, we remind ourselves that he's bigger than we think.

4:3-6 The author does something interesting here. He continues the theme of "rest" by mentioning God's rest **on the seventh day** when he **rested** after his work of creation (4:4). That doesn't mean he took a nap. It means he enjoyed his work, for he saw that it "was very good" (Gen 1:31). But the people of Israel failed to enter God's rest (i.e., the place of promised blessing) and find enjoyment **because of disobedience** (4:5-6).

In 3:19 they failed "because of *unbelief.*" In 4:6 they failed "because of *disobedience.*" He's saying the same thing in both. There must be a union between the Word you hear and the faith you have (4:2). When you install motion-detector lighting, the sensors perceive movement and activate the lights. But no power flows unless motion is detected. Many Christians want to experience God's power. But they aren't making any spiritual motions that he can detect! Faith in God's Word will result in movement—in obedience. When that happens, his power flows.

4:7 To **harden your hearts** is to tell God, "No" (4:7). When you do this, it's like constructing a wall of bricks around your heart. Instead, you need to expose yourself to godly people and principles that help chip away at whatever keeps the truth from getting through.

4:8-11 Just as God rested and enjoyed the completion of his work on the seventh day, he established in the Ten Commandments a **Sabbath** for Israel—the day of rest on which they were to enjoy the fruits of their labor (4:9). Moreover, for the generation that departed Egypt, entering the land of Canaan was to be their rest—their inheritance—their "Sabbath." The principle of Sabbath rest still operates today. Believers are called to enter the **rest** God has prepared for them (4:10) rather than following Israel's example of disobedience (4:11).

4:12-13 Like the Israelites, you will regularly find that your circumstances tempt you to disobey God. Focus on circumstances too long, and his Word will fail to influence your life.

The author reminds his audience that **the word of God is living and effective and sharper than any double-edged sword.** And indeed, Scripture isn't composed of dead words on a page; it's alive. It cuts deep and can separate the spiritual from the earthly. The Word can **judge the thoughts and intentions of the heart** (4:12). It lays us **naked and exposed** before God.

Have you ever had an experience with God's Word that made you feel "exposed"? Have you ever heard it preached and felt like it was directed right at you? Have you ever felt your soul sliced open by the Word? Remember, we have no private lives. We don't even get to have private thoughts. Everything is laid bare before the one **to whom we must give an account** (4:13).

4:14-16 After those terrifying comments, the author urges his readers to keep moving forward with Jesus (4:14) and offers sweet comfort: **For we do not have a high priest who is unable to sympathize with our weaknesses.** No, on the contrary, Jesus has been **tempted in every way as we are, yet without sin** (4:15). In one sense, he's like all of us—he has endured incredible temptation, suffering, and hardship. Yet, in another, he's like none of us—he has never sinned. Therefore, he is the perfect high priest. He can sympathize with you in your weakness and suffering. Yet, since he resisted completely, he can also help you.

So, what should you do? **Approach the throne of grace with boldness.** Prayer is the divinely authorized method of accessing heavenly authority for intervention on earth. It's the believer's passport into the spiritual realm. So, when you're tempted to give up, that *temptation* is actually an *invitation* to draw near to the King's throne so you **may receive mercy and find grace** (4:16). *Mercy* is not getting what you deserve; *grace* is getting what you don't deserve. But to lay claim to these wonderful gifts, you have to approach him. The King extends his invitation to you: "Don't stay away! Come get what you need."

5:1-3 The reference to Jesus as high priest in Hebrews 4:14-15 (see also 2:17; 3:1) opens the door to the author's discussion that will follow in much of the letter (7:1–10:18). Israel's **high priest** stood between God and the people. He entered the tabernacle / temple to offer **gifts and sacrifices** on their behalf to make atonement **for sins** (5:1). He was a go-between, a mediator. But, given that the high priest was also **clothed with weakness**, he could **deal gently** with those who were **going astray** (5:2). Since he was himself a sinner, the sin **offering** he made was **for his own sins as well as** theirs (5:3).

5:4-6 But a person didn't apply for the job. You didn't jump into the office of high priest and say, "Here I am!" Rather, a person had to be **called by God, just as Aaron was** (5:4). **In the same way, Christ did not exalt himself**, but the Father appointed the Son to his role as high priest (5:5). The author verifies this by quoting God's words from Psalm 110:4: **You are a priest forever according to the order of Melchizedek** (5:6). Jesus Christ, then, wasn't appointed to the priesthood of Aaron but to the priesthood of Melchizedek. The

author will return to discuss Melchizedek in chapter 7. It's a significant part of what he wants readers to understand.

5:7-10 We know that every high priest was appointed "from among men" (5:1). So, what kind of man was Jesus? The author focuses on the fact that **he offered prayers and appeals** to God **who was able to save him from death** (5:7) Jesus Christ is the great God-man, fully divine and fully human. In his humanity, he went through intense suffering and struggles—though without ever sinning (4:15). **Although he was the Son, he learned obedience** and **was perfected** (5:8-9). As the Son of God, he was perfectly obedient; but as the Son of Man, he had to learn obedience.

To be humanity's high priest, Jesus had to experience what we do. He had to learn to obey God when it hurts. Jesus did what the author tells us to do in 4:14-16—he drew near to God when he was struggling (5:7-8). As a result, **he became the source of eternal salvation for all who obey him** and was **declared by God a high priest according to the order of Melchizedek** (5:9-10).

The Greek verb and noun that we translate "saved" and "salvation" don't always refer to salvation from the penalty of sin and eternal judgment. Depending on the context, the words can be rendered "delivered" or "deliverance"—implying rescue from challenges or dangers in life, and from divine wrath in history (see, e.g., Matt 14:30; Acts 27:20; Rom 5:9-10). This is the meaning of the use of the word "saved" here, since the author's readers are already believers (3:1, 12; 10:19; 13:22). Having become our great high priest who endured suffering and remained faithful to God, Jesus Christ is the source of deliverance for all believers who obey him. How do you receive deliverance? The same way Jesus did: by crying out to God and obeying him.

V. WARNING AND ENCOURAGEMENT (5:11–6:20)

5:11-12 In spite of the author's desire to help his readers and teach them how Christ is a priest in the order of Melchizedek, they had **become too lazy to understand** (5:11). The Greek word translated "lazy" can mean "dull"

or "stubborn." So, in other words, they had become mule-headed and refused to grow spiritually. And even though they should've been **teachers** by the time the letter was penned, they needed someone to teach them the basic principles of God's revelation again (5:12). Sadly, they weren't experiencing Christ's deliverance because they were still in spiritual elementary school!

Something is wrong if a thirty-year-old is still eating baby food. Knowing the ABCs and 123s of the Bible is crucial, but there comes a time to build on this foundation with further understanding and growth. After all, if you don't advance beyond kindergarten, you never discover what lies ahead. Any believer who fails to move on from **milk** to **solid food** (5:12)—"milk" being the content of God's Word, while "solid food" is the spiritual application and use of God's Word to life—has some developmental issues and becomes stagnant in spiritual development.

5:13-14 Anyone **who lives on milk is inexperienced** (5:13). To be **mature**, you need **solid food.** Only in this way will your senses be **trained to distinguish between good and evil** so that you can live from a heavenly rather than an earthly perspective (5:14). This, in fact, is why God allows trials in our lives.

The only way you grow in most things is through training, through practice. It's true in sports, it's true in education, and it's true in spiritual growth. You may have experience listening to and memorizing the Word, but that's not sufficient. If you chew your food but don't swallow, you will starve. You have to internalize and put God's Word into practice (see Jas 1:21-25). Only then will you be equipped to make Word-driven decisions rather than circumstance-driven decisions. The recipients of the letter were becoming stagnant; they were refusing to grow.

6:1-3 Therefore, the writer says, let's leave kindergarten behind. **Let us . . . go on to maturity.** Laying the proper spiritual **foundation** is certainly necessary: you must repent of **dead works** and put your **faith in** the finished work of Christ (6:1). But there comes a time to build on the foundation and press on. **And we will do this if God permits,** he tells them (6:3). This is a reminder that God is the one who enables growth. He won't make the decision for you, however. You *decide* to grow; God *permits* the growth.

6:4-6 Now we come to a controversial passage. The author gives an example of people **who were once enlightened, who tasted the heavenly gift, who shared in the Holy Spirit, who tasted God's good word and the powers of the coming age** (6:4-5). Some interpreters feel this isn't a reference to believers. It's hard, though, to know what else the author would have to say to describe someone as a Christian. For example, some say that the people described here merely "*tasted* the heavenly gift." In other words, they didn't go all the way and eat it. But Hebrews also says that Jesus *tasted* death for everyone (2:9). You can be certain that he didn't just nibble death! He died. The people described in 6:4-5 are Christians.

So, what's going on here? The author says if such people **have fallen away** (6:6), it's **impossible to renew** them **to repentance** (6:4). Some interpreters think this means Christians can lose their salvation, but the rest of the Bible clearly teaches our eternal security in Christ (see, e.g., John 6:37-40; 10:26-29; Rom 8:28-39; Eph 1:13-14; 1 John 5:13). And if this text teaches that believers can lose their salvation, it also teaches that it's impossible for them to return to Christ. But no one claims that those who deny Jesus (like Peter; see Matt 26:69-75) can't repent and return to him.

The key, then, is to remember that the author has just urged the readers to "go on to maturity" (6:1). The problem is that they are in danger of having hardened, rebellious hearts because they refuse to press on in spiritual growth. To persist in this state is to forget what God has done for you, acting like those who crucified **the Son of God** and held **him up to contempt** (6:6). To stubbornly refuse to follow Christ in obedience is to mock him.

For such unfaithful believers, it's impossible to renew them to repentance. The question is: impossible for whom? After all, the angel told Mary, "Nothing will be impossible with God" (Luke 1:37), and Jesus said, "With God all things are possible" (Matt 19:26). The issue, then, is not God's inability to bring someone back to repentance; it's man's inability to do so. God has to directly intervene.

I have ministered to people who have slipped into sin, worldliness, and denial. Nothing I did could bring them to repentance.

When someone gets to such a point, it requires God bringing cataclysmic events into their lives as a wake-up call. When Peter denied Jesus (Luke 22:54-62), for example, it took the prayers of Jesus (in advance!) to bring him back around (Luke 22:31-34). When believers in the early church were involved in flagrant sin, sometimes the Lord even took them home early (e.g., the believers who had "fallen asleep" mentioned in 1 Cor 11:30). The Lord's discipline can be severe. That's why you want to have a sensitive, humble heart.

6:7-8 The author supports his argument with an illustration about a plot of **ground**. When land has been **cultivated** and experiences the goodness of God in the form of **rain** (6:7), it can produce either useful **vegetation** or **thorns and thistles**. What should a farmer do if the soil proves to be **worthless**? His field **will be burned**. The purpose of the burning isn't to destroy, however. The ground is burned to remove the thorns and thistles in order to make it productive again.

The author is not describing eternal judgment. The Bible speaks of fire in hell, but fire is also used to describe God's discipline of believers (see 1 Cor 3:11-15). At the judgment seat of Christ, then, a believer's faithless works will be burned up. "He himself will be saved—but only as through fire" (1 Cor 3:15). So don't give up. Persevere! If you're falling down, get back in the game. If you're too weak to get up, ask your fellow believers for help so that you can press on to maturity.

6:9-12 Even though the author spoke harshly, he is **confident** that God has **better** things in store for his hearers (6:9). He's like a parent who spanks a young child and then hugs him with the assurance, "I did this because I love you." The author is convinced that his readers are better than the poor ground in his illustration; he feels they'll continue in faith. Though God hasn't forgotten their past faithfulness when they had a passion for ministering to others (6:10), he wants them to demonstrate **diligence** and to imitate others who **inherit the promises through faith and perseverance** (6:11-12).

God's purpose in saving you was not merely so you could go to heaven when you die; he

wants to use you here until you die. and then reward you with your kingdom inheritance when he returns (see Luke 19:11-19). Your usefulness increases as you grow in spiritual maturity during your pilgrimage from earth to glory, from time to eternity. By developing in maturity and usefulness, you will obtain your full inheritance. This inheritance is not your salvation; rather, it's the good things God has in store for you in this life and in the life to come.

6:13-15 How did promise and perseverance play out in the life of Abraham, that great hero of the faith? Twenty-five years passed between God's promise of a son and the birth of Isaac. Then many further years passed before that fateful day when Abraham faithfully offered Isaac on the altar and God **swore by himself** (6:13) that he would **bless** and **multiply** Abraham (6:14). Long, patient waiting was required before **Abraham obtained the promise** (6:15).

6:16-19 To demonstrate his **unchangeable purpose**, God **guaranteed** his **promise** by swearing **an oath** (6:16-17). Now, of course, **it is impossible for God to lie**. To do so, he would have to cease being God. But by these **two unchangeable things**—the promise and the oath—he gives his children **strong encouragement to seize the hope set before** them (6:18-19). *Hope* is a confident expectation of God fulfilling his promises.

To put it simply, God's *promise* is his declaration of what he will do, and his *oath* is his announcement that he is ready to do it. God made a promise to Abraham in Genesis 12:1-3, but many years passed before he swore the oath in Genesis 22:16-17. In between, there was a long gap of preparation.

During gaps, God prepares the promise for the person and prepares the person for the promise. In the case of Israel, God made a promise to deliver the land of Canaan to them. But during their time of preparation, they refused to move forward. So the oath God swore to them was a negative one: "They will not enter my rest" (Heb 3:11). This is why persevering in faith is so important.

6:20 Here the author finally returns to the topic of Jesus as **a high priest ... according**

to the order of Melchizedek (see 5:10). Given their recent struggles, he needed to give them warning and encouragement to keep moving forward (5:11–6:20) before introducing them to the spiritually mature discussion about Melchizedek.

VI. THE MELCHIZEDEKIAN PRIEST WHO CAN DELIVER YOU (7:1-28)

7:1-3 Who is **Melchizedek**? He appears on the scene in Genesis 14:17-24. Then he's mentioned briefly in Psalm 110:4. That's it. However, here in Hebrews, he suddenly becomes a key figure in the Bible. He was **king of Salem** and **priest of God Most High** (that is, of the God who overrules every other power). When Abraham experienced God's provision and deliverance in a battle with several **kings**, Melchizedek **met Abraham and blessed him** (7:1). He also renewed Abraham's strength with bread and wine. In response, Abraham honored this priest-king with a tithe—**a tenth of everything** he had (7:2).

The author tells us that Melchizedek's **name** means **king of righteousness** (based on the Hebrew) and **king of peace** (*Salem* means "peace"). Who comes to mind when you consider those titles? Moreover, the Old Testament doesn't mention his **beginning** or **end**. Of course, the author of Hebrews isn't saying that he literally had no parents and never died. He's saying that there is no record of his birth or death. Thus, he **remains a priest forever** (7:3).

The point is that Melchizedek is a prototype of Jesus, the true King of righteousness and peace. As the divine Son of God, he had no beginning of days. And as the resurrected Lord, he has no end. Like Melchizedek, Jesus is both a priest and a King. Such a dual role was unheard of in Israel, where the offices of priest and king were intentionally distinct. The Levitical priests didn't rule, and the king didn't perform priestly duties. Nevertheless, **resembling the Son of God**, Melchizedek is an Old Testament illustration of what Jesus Christ would be like (7:3). Jesus has a unique priesthood that, like the priesthood of Melchizedek, brings blessing and renews the spiritual strength of his people with the bread and wine of Communion so that we can live in spiritual victory.

7:4-10 Not only is Jesus different from the Levitical priests (since he's both priest and king), but he's also superior to them. How so? Because he's a priest like Melchizedek. The author draws attention to the fact that Abraham paid a tithe to Melchizedek (7:4). The Levites also collected tithes. They received them from **the people** of Israel—Abraham's descendants (7:5). But, **without a doubt, the inferior is blessed by the superior** (7:7). In other words, as great as Abraham was as the father of Israel, he was inferior to Melchizedek because Melchizedek blessed him.

Abraham acknowledged his submission to Melchizedek and expressed his gratitude by giving him a tithe. And notice this: he didn't tithe to get a blessing; he tithed out of thankfulness for the blessing he received. In a sense, though, **Levi** *also* paid tithes to Melchizedek because **he was still within his ancestor** Abraham at the time (7:9-10). So Melchizedek's priesthood is superior because he blessed Abraham (and his descendants) and received tithes from them. Furthermore, his priesthood is superior because, though the Levitical priests died, **Scripture testifies that [Melchizedek] lives** (7:8).

It is because of Jesus's continuity with the Melchizedekian priesthood that it is legitimate for the church to receive tithes today. They are, in fact, a tangible indication of submission to our great high priest who has already "blessed us with every spiritual blessing in the heavens" (Eph 1:3). Jesus mediates the experience of these blessings to his people around Communion (1 Cor 10:16; 11:23-26).

What the author is saying is that the priesthood of Jesus (in the order of Melchizedek) is superior to the Levitical priesthood. Melchizedek is a prototype of Jesus Christ, who is an eternal priest-king with the spiritual responsibility to dispense blessings and the authority to authorize them.

7:11-12 Now if perfection came through the Levitical priesthood, why would we need another priest to appear . . . according to the order of Melchizedek? (7:11). To say it another way, if you could become all that God created you to be through the Old Testament system (which was administered through the Levitical priesthood), why would he declare his Son to be a Melchizedekian priest (5:6; Ps 110:4)? The point is that the coming of Christ made the Old Testament sacrificial system and the Levitical priests obsolete. The change of the priesthood meant a change of law as well (7:12). These Jewish Christians were tempted to return to Judaism, but they couldn't go back.

When a new coach comes to a team, he brings his own playbook. If you look back to the old coach and old playbook, you'll run the wrong plays and frustrate your new coach.

7:13-17 You can't mix Jesus with the Old Testament system. The Levites have been superseded. Jesus descended from the line of Judah, so the priesthood to whom believers owe allegiance has changed. His priesthood, though, isn't dependent on his lineage (no priests ever came from Judah); it's based on the power of an indestructible life (7:16). By virtue of his resurrection from the dead, Jesus is a priest forever (7:17).

7:18-22 The old system is annulled because the law perfected nothing (7:18-19). In other words, the law couldn't make you better. The Ten Commandments are good and righteous; they can inform you of God's standards. But they can't change you.

The Mosaic law is like a mirror. When you stare into a mirror, it tells the truth; it shows you how messed up you look. But it can't also wash your face, comb your hair, or brush your teeth. The law highlights your deficiencies; it can't correct them. To draw near to God, we needed something better than the law (7:19). And God delivered just what was necessary, establishing a better priest and guaranteeing it with an oath (7:20-21) so that Jesus has also become the guarantee of a better covenant (7:22).

7:23-25 Over the years, there were many Levitical priests for one simple reason: you can't remain in office when you're dead (7:23).

But since the Son of God remains forever, he holds his priesthood permanently (7:24). Therefore, he is able to save completely those who come to God through him, since he always lives to intercede for them (7:25).

As in 5:9, the author is not talking about being *saved* in terms of forgiveness of sin and eternal life in 7:25. He's talking to those who are already Christians. He's talking about being *delivered* from and through trials and circumstances in this life. Since Jesus Christ is a permanent priest who has no breaks in his schedule and no time off, he is always able to deliver. His full-time job is to intercede for believers and to rescue them from the power of sin, Satan, and adverse circumstances as they draw near to him (see 4:16).

However, your deliverance is tied to your obedience (5:9) and coming to God through him (7:25). If you "draw near to God," he "will draw near to you" (Jas 4:8). When you need deliverance, that's your invitation to go to "the throne of grace with boldness" so you can receive mercy and grace at the right time (Heb 4:16).

It's important to remember that there are two forms of deliverance. The first is deliverance *from* your trial. That's when God takes you out of the circumstances. The second kind is deliverance *through* a trial. Sometimes God does not remove you from your circumstances; instead, he walks you through them. For instance, God didn't deliver the young Hebrew men *from* Nebuchadnezzar's fiery furnace. He joined them and delivered them *through* it (Dan 3:1-30).

7:26-28 When you need deliverance from a difficult situation, draw near to God the Father through your eternal high priest Jesus Christ. He's on duty twenty-four hours, seven days a week. Sometimes he delivers you emotionally. Sometimes he calms you spiritually. Sometimes he changes your thinking. Sometimes he brings a person into your life to help. Regardless of your trouble, he can sympathize perfectly (4:15), and he can deliver perfectly (7:25). He is a unique, one-of-a-kind priest who is exalted above the heavens (7:26). Unlike the weak, sinful priests appointed by the law (7:27-28), the Son has been appointed by God's oath and has been perfected forever (7:28).

VII. THE NEW COVENANT AND ITS SUPERIOR HIGH PRIEST (8:1-13)

8:1 Due to the structure, content, style, and pastoral concerns of the Letter to the Hebrews, it's often compared to a sermon. And indeed the author sounds like a preacher as he talks about his **main point**. He wants readers to know that a better **high priest** necessarily brings a better ministry. Our high priest, Jesus, is seated at God's **right hand**—the place of power and authority. When he died on the cross and made a perfect offering for sin, his work was finished (John 19:30). Therefore, he's now in a "finished" position from which to intercede for you.

8:2-6 The author draws a contrast between the work of the former priests in the earthly tabernacle and the work of Jesus in the heavenly tabernacle (8:2-4). The Old Testament tabernacle, priests, and sacrifices were intended to point to the true tabernacle, priest, and sacrifice to come. The system that **Moses** established was good and done in obedience to God, but it was all preparatory. It was a **copy and shadow of the heavenly things** (8:5). It pointed forward to Jesus who **obtained a superior ministry**, mediating a **better covenant**, which is **established on better promises** (8:6).

The first readers of Hebrews were being tempted to quit moving forward and to stop maturing. But they couldn't go back because everything behind them was inferior to Jesus. Their only option was pursuing Christ.

8:7 The author emphasizes the superiority of the new covenant that Christ established. A *covenant* is a special agreement that God makes with his people. It is a divinely created, relational bond through which God reveals himself and administers his kingdom program. Through his covenants, God exercises his kingdom rule on earth and blesses his people. The old covenant made with the people of Israel was good, but it was

also temporary and weak because God had something better in store. If the **first covenant had been faultless**, we wouldn't have needed **a second one**.

8:8-13 Here the author quotes from Jeremiah 31:31-34 to support his argument. Through the prophet Jeremiah, God had explained that the law wasn't able to change a heart (see commentary on 7:18-22). Under the new covenant, however, he promised to **put [his] laws into their minds and write them on their hearts** (8:10).

When you became a Christian, you received a new heart and mind. You were born again. But like an infant's, your new heart and mind are underdeveloped; there's a lot of growth needed. Nevertheless, you received a new spiritual radar—a new ability to perceive spiritual things. You now have the capacity to experience God and obey him. But while every Christian has this ability, not every Christian has developed it (see 5:11-14; 1 Cor 3:1-3).

Through Jesus Christ, God has established this **new covenant**. Therefore, the old covenant **is obsolete** (8:13). The readers of Hebrews no longer needed to jump through the hoops of the old system and regulations because at the heart of the new covenant is this promise: **I will never again remember their sins** (8:12).

It's an unspeakable joy to know that the sins you've committed are forgiven. But God's promise doesn't stop there. Through Christ, tomorrow's sins are wiped away too. Everything you have done—past, present, and future—is covered by the cross. And if you really understand the greatness of that grace, you will be motivated to live to please the one who saved you. You will transfer from a "have to" life to a "thank you" life, leaving you free to experience and enjoy the power and privilege of your relationship with God.

VIII. THE OLD COVENANT AND
THE NEW COVENANT (9:1-28)

9:1-3 In chapter 9, the author speaks in more detail about the distinction between the two covenants. **The first covenant** had **regulations for ministry and an earthly sanctuary** (9:1). Israel's sanctuary was a **tabernacle.** Later, under God's direction, they built a permanent structure—a temple. But, until then, the tabernacle moved with the people wherever they went. It included two sections separated by a curtain: **the holy place** and **the most holy place** (9:2-3).

9:4-7 Each of these included various furnishings used to carry out the old covenant ministry (9:4-5). In the holy place, **the priests** entered **repeatedly**, performing their daily **ministry** (9:6). But once a year **the high priest alone** passed through the curtain and entered the most holy place (9:7). Why? This was where God manifested his holy presence above the **ark of the covenant** (9:4). Annually on the Day of Atonement, the high priest would enter with the **blood** of a sacrifice offered **for himself and for the sins the people had committed in ignorance** (9:7).

9:8-10 By means of these regulations **the Holy Spirit was making it clear that** the people didn't have unhindered access into God's presence in **the most holy place** (9:8). The sacrifices couldn't **perfect the worshiper's conscience** (9:9)—that is, the old covenant couldn't change them. God had prescribed external acts to deal temporarily with sin because of his holy nature. But following them couldn't bring about an internal change. Rather, the old covenant ministry consisted of **physical regulations** that God temporarily **imposed until the time of the new order** (9:10).

9:11-12 But now **Christ has appeared.** The **high priest of the** new covenant has also entered a tabernacle, but it's **not of this creation.** It's a **perfect tabernacle** where you enter into God's presence (9:11). Christ entered, **not by the blood of goats and calves, but by his own blood, having obtained**

eternal redemption (9:12). What the Old Testament high priest did every year with the blood of animals, Christ did once and for all with his own blood. The Old Testament sacrifices were not permanent. They only had a one-year warranty. But Christ's sacrifice was eternal and, therefore, obtained eternal redemption.

9:13-14 But wait—it gets better. The **blood of goats and bulls**, offered in accordance with divine regulations, could **sanctify** the **flesh.** In other words, the Old Testament sacrifices could cleanse the outside (9:13). **The blood of Christ**, though, can **cleanse our consciences from dead works so that we can serve the living God** (9:14). The blood of the holy Son of God can give you a bath on the inside; it can make your conscience clean. And if you're clean on the inside, it can work its way out so that dead works that seek to earn God's favor become good works that are the result of our response to God's favor.

9:15-22 Jesus Christ **is the mediator of a new covenant** so that you may receive **the eternal inheritance** (9:15). The author makes a comparison to a will. If you have **a will**, it's only **in effect** when you **die** (9:16-17). Your beneficiaries can't claim your belongings while you're still kicking. The whole point of such a document is to make provision for the stewardship of your resources after you're dead. Similarly, **the first covenant was inaugurated with blood** (9:18). For the provisions of the old covenant to go into effect and benefit the people, they had to shed the blood of animals (9:19-21). **Without the shedding of blood**, there was no cleansing and **no forgiveness** (9:22).

9:23-26 Therefore, **the heavenly things** had **to be purified with better sacrifices than these** (9:23). So Christ didn't enter an earthly sanctuary but **into heaven itself** to **appear in the presence of God for us** (9:24). In other words, Jesus didn't enter a man-made tabernacle that was "a copy and shadow of" God's presence (8:5) to offer an animal sacrifice that could only provide temporary external purification (9:13). This had been done. Every year. Over and over (9:25). Instead, Christ offered **the sacrifice of himself** to remove sin—internal and external—once and for all, so that he might appear in God's presence for you in **heaven** (9:24, 26). Jesus isn't the copy; he's the real thing. His sacrifice doesn't have limited application; it endures forever.

9:27-28 It is appointed for people to die once—and after this, judgment (9:27) reminds us that death isn't the end. Human beings, however, typically live as if death is the last word. Therefore, they want to do it all. They want to fulfill all their desires before they reach the end. Remember that death is a transition—not a conclusion. Judgment is coming.

Just as people die once, **Christ** also died once. But he's coming back. He came the first time **to bear the sins of many**. He's coming **a second time** to grab us. We're now living in the interim between Christ's death and return, **waiting for him** (9:28). So don't give up. Keep moving forward in faith. He's coming back.

IX. SANCTIFICATION AND FORGIVENESS ONCE AND FOR ALL (10:1-18)

10:1-4 To help his readers press on and keep following Christ, the author is going to great lengths to demonstrate the superiority of Christ's priesthood, his sacrifice, and the new covenant he mediates. After all, if you don't keep growing with Jesus, there's nowhere else to go. Christ's eternal Melchizedekian priesthood is better than the temporary Levitical priesthood (7:11, 28). The new covenant accomplished what the obsolete old covenant could not (8:6-13). Unlike the repeated sacrifices of the Old Testament system, Christ's sacrifice atoned for sin once and for all.

The law can't save you. It was **a shadow of the good things to come**. It can't **perfect the worshipers** through **sacrifices** repeated **year after year** (10:1). That doesn't mean the law was evil. The law was good. But we need to understand the purpose of the law. It reveals our sinfulness and weakness. The law can't fix you; it can only condemn. Have you ever had a police officer pull you over and congratulate you for obeying the speed limit? Of course not! His job is to reprimand you for breaking the law. The law's job was to prove that you and I are sinners based on the holy standard of God.

The sacrifices offered in accordance with the law couldn't purify your conscience (10:2). The law couldn't make you good, and the sacrifices couldn't take your sin away permanently. Instead, the annual sacrifices were a **reminder of sins** (10:3). **For it is impossible for the blood of bulls and goats to take away sins** (10:4). God didn't provide the law and the Old Testament sacrificial system to fully and finally address the problem of sin but to prepare and point the way to something better.

10:5-10 Jesus Christ came to accomplish what the old covenant, its priests, and its sacrifices could not. He was uniquely prepared to provide a once-and-for-all sacrifice to please God and satisfy the demands of his holiness. The quotation from Psalm 40:6-8 in 10:5-7 supports this. Jesus came to do the will of God perfectly. And by his perfect obedience, **we have been sanctified ... once for all time** (10:10).

Everything you have broken, he has kept. If you have trusted in Christ, he dwells in you; therefore, you have the fulfillment of God's standard within you. By Christ's death, you have been *sanctified*—that is, you've been set apart for God's purposes and glory. You've been set apart to be Christ's kingdom companion and to live your life in submission to his lordship and kingdom agenda.

10:11-12 The Levitical priests were fighting a losing battle. They offered **the same sacrifices time after time**, which could not **take away sins** (10:11). This, however, was all part of God's plan so that, at the right time, he could send **this man**—"the last Adam" (1 Cor 15:45)—to offer **one sacrifice for sins forever** and then sit down **at the right hand of God** (10:12). Israel's high priest never sat down because his work was never done. But Jesus finished the job. And when he sat, it was in the seat of authority to exercise his kingdom rule.

10:13-14 From his throne, this priest-king is **waiting until his enemies are made his footstool** (10:13). At Christ's return, everyone—those who submit to him now and those who don't—will be placed under his authority, and he will rule in his millennial kingdom. Let his righteous program, then, be what guides your decision-making and actions. **For by one offering he has perfected forever those who are sanctified** (10:14). By his grace, he accomplished God's purposes for you and set you apart for his use. He has defeated Satan and sin so that nothing separates you from God. He has

redeemed you forever: your salvation cannot be lost. Why give your life in service to anyone else?

10:15-18 Here the author quotes again from Jeremiah 31 (see Heb 8:8-12). Through the new covenant work of Christ, God puts his **laws** on your heart (10:16). That means God's standard is within you. That's why you experience conviction when you sin by breaking his law. Moreover, he has also given you the Holy Spirit to enable you to obey. As you grow in your Christian faith, you become more aware of the fact that you fall short of God's standard but increase in your desire to obey him.

At the heart of the new covenant is this beautiful promise: **I will never again remember their sins** (10:17). The sin debt is paid. There is complete **forgiveness**. No further **offering for sin** is needed (10:18). Thus, you are freed to walk with the Lord, to please him, and to pursue his purpose for your life.

X. EXHORTATION TO DRAW NEAR AND WARNING AGAINST REBELLION (10:19-39)

10:19-21 After his long and powerful discussion of the superiority of Jesus Christ and his work, the author returns to the matter at hand: the readers are struggling. They had encountered trials and had become complacent. They were neglecting their salvation (2:3) and refusing to "go on to maturity" (6:1). They thus needed a reminder of what they had in front of them.

In light of who Jesus is and what he has done (7:1–10:18), **we have boldness to enter the sanctuary through the blood of Jesus** (10:19). The author is again using the imagery of the tabernacle. You couldn't just go waltzing into God's presence in the most holy place. Only the high priest could enter and only once a year. But through the blood of Jesus our **great high priest**, the **curtain** between God and humanity has been removed (10:20-21). Access has been granted. You can now enter into the presence of God—and you can come with confidence. You don't have to be ashamed. You don't have to tip-toe.

10:22-25 Just **draw near with a true heart in full assurance of faith** (10:22). With this kind of access to God, we come into his presence boldly. Prayer becomes vibrant when we become real. Everything changes when you realize that Jesus has already dealt with the things you're ashamed to discuss. Have you ever heard someone beat around the bush because he is afraid to get to the point and address the problem? We never have to do that with the Lord! God knows our issues, and he's dealt with our problems. In fact, **our hearts [are] sprinkled clean** and **our bodies [are] washed in pure water** (10:22). He's just waiting for us to start a conversation; he's waiting for us to draw near to him. So, do it with confidence. Be real with the Father. Boldness in drawing near to God is critical for avoiding divine discipline associated with the willful sin the author is about to address.

Also, **let us hold on to the confession of our hope** (10:24). Don't persist in rebellion against God. Pursue Christ and grow in grace! And if you're wondering how to do that when times are hard, that's what the local church is for. Connecting to a vibrant, biblically based, loving church is a critical tool that can steer us away from disobedience so that we can avert sin's consequences and divine discipline. Believers who are not a functioning part of a local church are living outside of the will of God and limiting God's work in their lives.

Tragically, some of this letter's readers had started **neglecting to gather together** (10:25). They were avoiding the means God had provided to help them. Remember, when your "get-up-and-go" has gotten up and gone, you need someone who can lift you up. Furthermore, there's someone ready to throw in the towel who needs you to walk alongside him or her. That's why the writer of Hebrews says, **Let us watch out for one another to provoke love and good works** (10:24). It can be hard to be a Christian. We need to be practicing the "one-anothers," **encouraging each other . . . as [we] see the day approaching** (10:25).

10:26-27 But what if you refuse to let others help you? What if you intentionally choose to rebel against the Lord? Well, **if we deliberately go on sinning after receiving the knowledge of the truth**—that is, after hearing God's Word—**there no longer remains a sacrifice for sins** (10:26). What remains instead? **A terrifying expectation of judgment and the fury of a fire** (10:27).

The idea here is willful sin against God, a sin committed because a believer develops a defiant spirit. Think of a teenager who, when corrected for disobedience, becomes stubborn and says to his parents, "I don't care what you say."

Houston, we have a problem! This is rebellion. And it has to be dealt with because unaddressed rebellion only gets worse and can spread. What we see in this passage is not a description of a struggling believer who sins. This is willful rebellion. That's why the author uses the word "deliberately." This is a determined mindset to have one's own way.

When a believer continues in this kind of unrepentant rebellion, there are consequences: judgment and fire (10:27). This is

not, however, a reference to hell. As we saw earlier (see 6:7-8), Scripture sometimes uses fire to describe God's discipline of believers (see 1 Cor 3:11-15). We've seen throughout Hebrews that the author is speaking to Christians (e.g., "brothers and sisters" in 10:19) whose salvation is secure (e.g., 10:14), so the consequences he's describing refer to the stern discipline of God.

10:28-31 The most severe form of discipline for spiritual disobedience is physical death (see 1 John 5:16). This was the case in Israel for those **who disregarded** the Mosaic law (10:28). Their countrymen stoned them. The author says that for the Christian who defies God, there will be a **worse punishment** than even this. And while we don't see it happen very often, the very idea demonstrates how serious God is about his holiness. In Corinth, some believers became sick and even died because of their disobedience regarding the Lord's Supper (see 1 Cor 11:27-32). As Paul told the Corinthians: "When we are judged by the Lord, we are disciplined, so that we may not be condemned with the world" (1 Cor 11:32).

If you persist willfully in the very sin for which Christ died to set you free, you've **trampled on the Son of God . . . regarded as profane the blood of the covenant** and **insulted the Spirit of grace** (10:29). Such is the willful rebellion of believers who treat with contempt the high sacrificial price paid by God's Son to bring us our great salvation. God will not ignore this. The sacrifice that saves you from the eternal consequences of sin will not necessarily deliver you from the consequences of sin in history. The Lord vows to **judge his people** (10:30). This is not the side of God you want to see, because **it is a terrifying thing to fall into the hands of the living God** (10:31; see Rom 11:22).

10:32-34 Though he's delivered a stern warning to his readers so they might avoid indulging a rebellious heart, the author immediately follows it up with warm encouragement. He urges them to **remember the earlier days**—that is, to recall what it was like after they were first saved. Their passion for Christ and for the gospel was so strong that they **endured** intense **sufferings**, mistreatment, and the **confiscation** of their property. They didn't quit but **sympathized** with others who were similarly mistreated. "Persevere as you did before," the author tells them in essence. "Don't give up now!"

10:35-36 Not only is there severe discipline for those who rebel, but there is reward for those who obey: **Don't throw away your confidence, which has a great reward** (10:35). The author calls them to **endurance** so that they may do **God's will** and **receive what was promised.** God always keeps his promises. But notice what the writer says: you receive what was promised *after* you have done the Lord's will (10:36). The promise, the reward, the inheritance—some of which is granted in history and the rest in eternity—is attached to performing the will of God.

The longer the obedience takes, the longer it takes for the promise to be fulfilled.

Israel should have possessed the promised land in minimal time. However, it took them forty years to enter—not because the promise changed but because they refused to do God's will. And sadly, in the end, it required a new generation of Israelites to accomplish the work and receive the promise.

Remember the three-fold process discussed in the commentary on 3:7-11? Deliverance, development, and destiny are each parts of God's process. You never get to skip the development stage. God wants to change your character, not just your circumstances. He's working to make you more like Jesus.

10:37-39 Make no mistake: **the Coming One will come and not delay** (10:37). He will move on our behalf in history as we trust and obey him (Jas 5:7-8). If you want to experience his **pleasure** now and when he comes, then keep moving forward, press on to maturity, and **live by faith** (10:38). You became a Christian by faith, and you can only live the Christian life by faith. The author is confident that his readers are not like **those who draw back** but **those who have faith.** He's talking to believers, describing the difference between those who do and do not experience God's deliverance from or through circumstances.

Sometimes we need examples to follow. We need to look to the lives of heroes of the faith who endured tremendous struggles but continued to trust God. In the next chapter, the author will help the readers do just that, reminding them that they're not alone. He'll take them on a historical tour of fellow believers who lived by faith.

XI. THE HALL OF FAITH (11:1-40)

Canton, Ohio, is home to the Pro Football Hall of Fame. It is where those who excelled at the game are recognized for their achievements on the field. Hebrews 11 is home to the Hall of Faith. Here the champions of the Old Testament are recognized for their achievements as they followed God by faith. Success for them didn't bypass suffering. Instead they trusted God and ran the race to the end. To encourage his readers to keep going, the author of Hebrews reminds them that they're not the first to travel the faith road. Others have encountered the hardships of the race and crossed the finish line.

11:1-2 How does the writer of Hebrews define faith? **Faith is the reality of what is hoped for, the proof of what is not seen** (11:1). To exercise faith is to have confidence about an expectation without visible proof that it will happen. What makes this confidence possible? The trustworthiness of the object of faith. The question we must answer is this: Is God trustworthy? And as I like to say, faith is acting like God is telling the truth. If you want to increase your faith, grow in your understanding of God. Believers of the past trusted him by faith and **won God's approval** (11:2). Notice that each of the heroes of the faith mentioned in this chapter acted on what they believed.

11:3 A clear example of something Christians accept **by faith** is God's creation of the universe. We believe that **what is seen was made from things that are not visible** by a being who is not visible. We trust that the word of God created everything, in all its vastness and complexity. That should encourage us that God may be doing extraordinary things in our lives for our good even when we can't see what he's doing.

In the following "Hall of Faith," the author uses a repeated structure: he gives the name of an Old Testament believer, explains what he or she did, and uses the expression "by faith" to connect that person's actions with a belief system. This pattern is a reminder that faith is measured by the steps of one's feet—not by his feelings. Many faith-based decisions, in fact, go against feelings. We must, therefore, walk by faith in the integrity of God's Word rather than by gut instinct or emotionalism. Feelings are the caboose; they don't get to drive the train.

11:4 By faith Abel worshiped God based on God's standards and expectations: he offered shed blood as a sacrifice rather than just giving him something his own hands had produced. He offered God his best and **was approved as a righteous man**. In fact, **even though he is dead**—murdered by his brother—Abel's faith still speaks. It teaches us that access to God's presence is through the blood. That's the kind of legacy you want to leave. You want your life of faith to be a testimony to others, to point them to the truth.

11:5-6 Enoch is one of only two people who **did not experience death** (Elijah is the other; see 2 Kgs 2:1-12). Why? Hebrews says it's because he **pleased God** (11:5). That doesn't mean, of course, that if you're pleasing God you won't die! But it does mean that his departure from the world was a direct result of how he lived. He lived a godly life within the context of an evil and corrupt society. What he did mattered.

Do you want to live in a way that pleases God? Then you must know that **without faith it is impossible to please God**. You must **believe that he exists and rewards those who seek him** (11:6). You must operate by faith, even if you must do so alone and go against the accepted norms of the day. You must believe with expectation that God

responds—regarding his will for your life—when you seek to please him.

11:7 Though **Noah** was **warned about what was not yet seen**, he was **motivated by godly fear.** He couldn't even conceive of the flood God was going to bring on the earth. Nevertheless, Noah took God seriously and acted on what he said. Just consider the obstacles he faced: There was a 120-year gap between God's command to build the ark and the flood; Noah was instructed to build a tremendously huge boat on dry land; everyone who saw it no doubt called him crazy. But Noah believed God and obeyed, even though what he'd been asked to do didn't make sense since it had never rained a drop at that point in history. He thus **became an heir of the righteousness that comes by faith.** Be prepared to answer this wisely: When God's Word says something contrary to popular opinion, whom are you going to believe?

11:8-10 Abraham made a pilgrimage of faith. God called; he obeyed. That sounds simple until you realize that Abraham **did not know where he was going** (11:8). How did he do it? And how did he live **as a foreigner in the land of promise** without ever owning it? (11:9). The answer is that he had his heart set on another **city**—one **whose architect and builder is God** (11:10). He focused on the spiritual while looking for the physical.

Often in life, you won't know where God is taking you. And if you overlook the spiritual, you will become discouraged. God is the architect of the eternal city, and he's the architect of the opportunities in your life.

11:11-12 Sarah is an example of the power of God in a person's life. **She was unable to have children**, and Abraham was **as good as dead** in terms of ability to procreate. In fact, Hebrews only gives us the conclusion to the couple's infertility story. When God promised her a child, Sarah laughed (Gen 18:11-12). She thought it was a joke. Eventually, though, she had faith that **the one who had promised was faithful** (11:11). It took twenty-five years to get from promise to baby. Oftentimes God doesn't complete what he wants to do in your life until you're spiritually prepared.

11:13-16 At this point, the author pauses before continuing. He points out that all these believers **died in faith, although they had not received** all **the things that were promised** (11:13). They walked by faith, but God didn't plan to deliver the promise while they were on earth. Though they could have turned around and given up (11:15), they were **seeking a homeland** (11:14); they desired **a better place—a heavenly one** (11:16). Their approach to life, then, was based on an eternal perspective, a kingdom perspective. When you know the one who's preparing a better city for you, you can survive the wait. And when that's your mindset, **God is not ashamed to be called [your] God** (11:16).

11:17-19 After years of waiting, **Abraham** received his son **Isaac**. Thus, the promise was fulfilled and the testing began. God told him to sacrifice Isaac—the very son through whom Abraham was to become the father of a nation (11:17-18). Make no mistake. In one way or another, God will test how much you love him. Do you love the gift or the Giver more? So, how did Abraham cope when it seemed like God's command contradicted his promise? He considered that God was able to **raise** the **dead** (11:19). And why would he think that? Because Sarah was barren (11:11), and Abraham was "as good as dead" (11:12); nevertheless, it is God who gives life, and he had a promise to keep.

Don't forget what God did for you yesterday. The situation you face may be different than anything you've experienced before, but God is the same. The receiving back of Isaac is an illustration of the same type of divine intervention that God's people can expect today if they live by faith.

11:20-22 These verses illustrate a legacy of faith. **By faith Isaac blessed** his sons **concerning things to come** (11:20). **By faith Jacob, when he was dying, blessed** his grandsons while he **worshiped** (11:21). **By faith Joseph**, near the end of his life, told the Israelites to bury **his bones** in the promised land when they got there.

If you're a parent, you're going to pass on many things to your kids. Make sure that you pass them the baton of faith in God above all else. Let them pray with you about

things you're trusting God for so they can see your faith in action.

11:23-29 Here we see a summary of Moses's life: eighty years are covered in seven verses. His **parents** valued God instead of the evil culture and refused to let their baby be killed (11:23). When he grew up, Moses himself chose God over the surrounding culture. He opted **to suffer with the people of God** rather than **to be called the son of Pharaoh's daughter** (11:24-25). **By faith he left Egypt . . . instituted the Passover**, and **crossed the Red Sea** (11:27-29). Why? Because **he was looking ahead to the reward.** He considered suffering **reproach for the sake of Christ to be greater wealth** than Egypt's riches (11:26). Don't miss that Moses chose Christ in the Old Testament era! Though it doesn't always appear to be true on the front end, choosing Christ is never a losing deal.

11:30-40 The walls of Jericho fell as a result of the most bizarre military strategy enacted in history (11:30). And as a result of her willingness to align with God's people, **Rahab the prostitute**—the lowest of the low—got recognized alongside Abraham and Moses as a hero in the Hall of Faith (11:31). How can these things be? Simple. God tells us, "My thoughts are not your thoughts, and your ways are not my ways," declares the Lord (Isa 55:8).

Then, like a preacher, the author rolls through a list of even more Old Testament heroes of faith and how they lived. Some conquered; others perished. All lived by faith in God (11:32-37). When faith is inaugurated in your life and you keep on going, your circumstances don't have the final word. **The world was not worthy of them** (11:38), but they were **approved through their faith** (11:39). Did you catch that? The world didn't deserve them, but God applauded them. Whose approval are you seeking? You can't please both the world and God.

The author concludes the chapter by observing that God **provided something better for us** New Testament believers so that we can all **be made perfect** (11:40). Salvation in Christ is the culmination of God's plan of redemption for eternity and deliverance in history.

XII. FATHERLY DISCIPLINE AND AN
UNSHAKEABLE KINGDOM (12:1-29)

12:1 Chapter 11 is a long chain of testimonies about what faith can do. Then the author says, **Therefore, since we also have such a large cloud of witnesses surrounding us . . . let us run with endurance.** It's like parading a previous boxing champion through the ring before a title fight. He shakes the contestants' hands and says, "I've been through this, and I testify that you can endure and emerge as a victor." Clearly, the author wants his audience to **lay aside every hindrance and the sin that so easily ensnares.** Their spiritual immaturity and unwillingness to grow through living by faith had become an encumbrance.

An Olympic sprinter strips off his warm-up gear to eliminate extra weight and wind resistance. Similarly, we need to jettison unbelief and anything in our lives that might trip us up spiritually and prevent us from running the race well all the way to the finish line.

12:2-3 We also need to keep **our eyes on Jesus, the source and perfecter** (or "completer") **of our faith.** After all, we started with Jesus, and, if we keep our eyes on him, he will get us through the Christian journey.

Have you ever been running and felt like you wanted to quit? Then someone draws alongside you and encourages you to keep going, enabling you to go farther than you could have managed by yourself. When this happens, it shifts the focus from your pain to the person helping you, and you get a second wind. Similarly, if you keep your attention on him, Jesus will enable you to persevere through your *development* and reach your *destiny* (see commentary on 3:7-11).

How did Jesus himself reach the finish line? **For the joy that lay before him, he endured the cross, despising the shame.** The joy would come on Sunday, but the shame had to be endured on Friday. The Son of God made it through Friday by keeping his eyes on Sunday. We need no better example. When he ascended back to the Father in heaven, he **sat down at the right hand of the throne of God** (12:2). Regardless of the suffering and trials you're facing, know that resurrection day is coming. The author wants his readers to do what Jesus did **so that [they] won't grow weary and give up** (12:3).

12:4-7 He also reminds them of two things. First, they had not yet resisted to the point of bloodshed (12:4)—that is, they had experienced significant difficulties, but they were still living. And if you're still here, God isn't finished with you! Second, they had **forgotten the exhortation that addresses [them] as sons** (12:5). In 12:5-6 the author quotes from Proverbs 3:11-12 and encourages them to **endure suffering as discipline** because God is treating them **as sons** (12:7).

Discipline includes both positive and negative repercussions, instruction and correction. Parents are to instruct their children and train them to live with wisdom (see Prov 1:7-9). But when a child is disobedient, a loving father also disciplines him. Whether through instruction or correction, the end goal is the child's development. If a good parent takes this matter seriously, how much more does God? God is a perfect parent who disciplines his children perfectly.

12:8 If you are without discipline—which all receive—then you are illegitimate children and not sons. Illegitimate children in ancient Rome had no rights and could not be beneficiaries of an inheritance. "Which all receive" could be translated "of which all are partakers." The Greek term for "partaker" is the same word we saw earlier meaning "companion" or "partner" (1:9; 3:1, 14). Thus, the author is reminding them that if they want to be Christ's special "companions/partners/partakers" and receive the inheritance—his kingdom blessings in history and eternity—they must be willing to submit to his fatherly discipline and grow (see commentary on 1:5-14; 3:7-11; 4:1; 6:9-12; 10:35-36).

12:9-13 Godly fathers discipline their children as best they can, but our heavenly Father always disciplines us perfectly and for our good (12:9-10). **No discipline seems enjoyable at the time, but painful.** So don't expect otherwise! Few children enjoy being disciplined or thank their parents for it afterwards. But if you will humbly receive God's fatherly discipline, you will grow in holiness and **righteousness** (12:10-11). He wants you to be **trained by it** (12:11) so you can experience your relationship with him at another level. If your hands are tired and your knees are buckling, don't give up—keep walking the **straight** and narrow (12:12-13). As with any kind of training, regular submission to godly discipline leads to increased strength and righteousness.

12:14-15 The author exhorts them to pursue **peace** and **holiness**—that is, their sanctification (12:14). Keep striving in your spiritual development. And beware of any **root of bitterness** in your life (12:15). When you're experiencing troublesome circumstances, you're in danger of resenting what God is doing in your life. But resentment will only serve to compound the problems.

12:16-17 The author not only points to positive examples to emulate (the Old Testament saints in chapter 11 and Jesus in 12:2-3) but also to negative examples to avoid. Don't yield to transitory pleasure **like Esau, who sold his birthright** for a bowl of soup (12:16). Though he regretted it later, it was too late. He had forfeited his inheritance (12:17). God has blessings in store for you, an inheritance. Don't be like Esau and foolishly throw away your reward for fleeting, temporal gratification.

12:18-24 In these verses, the author contrasts Mount Sinai with Mount Zion. When the Lord appeared to Israel on Mount Sinai to deliver the law, the people were filled with terror (12:18-21). You won't find comfort in the Ten Commandments either. The law can only identify your weaknesses and indict you. So don't climb Sinai. That's not your mountain. Instead, **you have come to Mount Zion** (12:22). Zion represents the **new covenant** in Jesus Christ (12:24). Only through him are the

spirits of **righteous people made perfect** (12:23). Only Jesus can make you everything God wants you to be.

12:25-26 Therefore, **do not reject the one who speaks** (12:25). When he spoke at Sinai, God's **voice shook the earth** (12:26). When your world is shaking, then, it's because God is talking. We tend to focus our attention on our circumstances. But God wants your attention on him. He has something he wants to tell you, something he wants you to learn.

12:27 What's the goal of the shaking (i.e., the upsetting off the natural order of things)? **The removal of what can be shaken . . . so that what is not shaken might remain.** When things are shaking, God is trying to eliminate a hindrance in your life. He's attempting to loosen your grip on **created** physical **things** so that you'll grasp tightly onto eternal things instead. The shaking process isn't fun—especially when you don't want to let go. But, remember: God is treating you like his child (12:5-11) and not his enemy.

12:28-29 As a follower of Jesus Christ, you're part of his kingdom. That's great news because Christ's is **a kingdom that cannot be shaken**, and everything around you is subject to it. To accomplish his purposes for you, though, he's going to shake you loose from anything that's not part of his kingdom. So instead of clutching earthly things that are trembling and wobbling, **let us be thankful.**

When your world is shaking, **serve God acceptably, with reverence and awe** (12:28). Why? Because **our God is a consuming fire** (12:29). When animals were placed on the sacrificial altar in the Old Testament era, fire would consume them. The fire burned up the carcass with the positive intent of providing a sacrifice to the Lord.

Tomorrow you may press a hot iron to your wrinkled clothes. But your intent isn't to ruin them. Your goal will be to remove the wrinkles to make your garment fit to wear. Guess what. God wants to wear you and look good in you. So he will apply a consuming fire to you for your good. Even though there will be steam and heat, you're going to look good when he's through.

XIII. EXHORTATIONS AND BENEDICTION (13:1-25)

13:1 As he prepares to complete his letter, the author delivers a series of exhortations to empower his readers to keep going and pursue Christian maturity. What's at the top of the list? **Let brotherly love continue.**

You need to be connected to a loving fellowship of believers so you can help keep them going and they can do the same for you. Problems tempt us to be self-focused, but continuing in brotherly love helps shift our focus to the well-being of others. Biblical love is always others-focused.

13:2-3 Moreover, he encourages them to **show hospitality** (13:2). In this context of brotherly love, he's primarily thinking of showing it to fellow Christians. Sometimes God's answers to prayer will come from unexpected sources—even from strangers. The Greek word translated **"angels"** can also mean "messengers." Angels can be divine or human messengers. So whether the messenger God sends you is supernatural or not, remember that hospitality opens the door to those who are on a divine mission for your good.

We are also called to care for fellow believers who are being persecuted and incarcerated (13:3). Don't focus so much on your problems that you overlook those who are worse off than you. Most of our problems in the western world pale in comparison to the persecution our brothers and sisters are facing around the globe.

13:4-6 The next two subjects the author touches on are marriage and money. Most of the friction and frustration that people experience in life have to do with one or both of these issues. Therefore, believers should set themselves apart from the world through their marital unions and attitudes toward finances. For example, Christians are to respect and celebrate the institution of marriage between one man and one woman because it is God's creation order (see Matt 19:4-6). One way this is accomplished is through honoring **the marriage bed**—that is, through maintaining godly sexual morality and fidelity in marriage (13:4).

Furthermore, believers should seek to be **free from the love of money** (see 1 Tim 6:10). It's not that money itself is bad or that earning is bad. Rather, the *love* of money leads to character corruptions like greed, covetousness, and discontentment. Managing money is a theological issue. To **be satisfied with what you have** (13:5), you have to trust in the Lord's promise that he will **never leave you or abandon you.** When you believe that, you can declare boldly, **The Lord is my helper; I will not be afraid. What can man do to me?** (13:6). A Christian who fears the Lord and not people is free and unstoppable.

13:7-9 Remember your leaders who taught you Scripture and **imitate their faith** (13:7). Don't forget those who influenced you spiritually and keep their legacy alive. Yet, while you remember them, focus on **Jesus Christ**, who **is the same yesterday, today, and forever** (13:8). The people in your life may change, but King Jesus never will. If you do these things, you won't **be led astray** by **strange teachings** that distract you from growing in God's **grace** (13:9).

13:10-13 The priests in **the tabernacle** served at an altar. Yet, we have a better **altar**—Jesus Christ, who nourishes us with grace (13:10). After the priests sacrificed the **blood** of the **animals**, the animal **bodies** were **burned outside the camp** (13:11). Similarly, **Jesus also suffered.** But he did so **outside the gate** of Jerusalem (13:12). His blood was shed *outside*, not inside the tabernacle or temple.

There's no refuge in the old covenant sacrificial system. Jesus isn't there. Thus, we also need to go **outside** (i.e., away from dead religious activity) with him, identifying with him, and **bearing his disgrace** (13:13). Being a serious Christian will mean enduring ridicule and reproach at some level, even by the religious establishment. But take heart. You're in good company.

13:14-15 This fallen world is not our home; it's a temporary residence. **We seek the [city] to come** (13:14). As followers of Jesus

Christ, we must decisively leave that which draws us away from him and clearly align ourselves as kingdom disciples with an eternal focus. With this perspective and mission, you will be enabled to deal with life's ups and downs. So get your **praise** on: **confess the name** of the Lord. Let that be the **fruit of** your **lips** (13:15). Boldly identify yourself as a disciple of Jesus. Ask yourself, If I was accused of being a Christian, would there be sufficient evidence to convict me, or would I be found innocent of all charges?

13:16-18 Make sacrifices with your lips (13:15) but also make sacrifices with your life. Don't be all talk and no action. **Don't neglect to do what is good and to share.** When you reach out to benefit someone other than yourself, it pleases God (13:16). Moreover, **obey your** church **leaders** (when they're following Scripture) and **pray for** them. Allow them to do their work **with joy** because they're responsible to God to **watch over** you (13:17-18).

13:20-25 The author finishes with his benediction. God **brought up** our Lord Jesus **from the dead** (13:20). The resurrection verifies the truth of Christianity and sets it apart from all other religions. The grave is empty; our Savior and King is alive and reigning. **Through Jesus Christ**, God will **equip you . . . to do his will** (13:21). He will give you the spiritual tools you need to please him. So don't give up. Keep maturing in the faith. In the end, you'll see that it was all worth it.

The author concludes his **message of exhortation** with news of **Timothy**, greetings of farewell, and a blessing of **grace** (13:22-25).

JAMES

INTRODUCTION

Author

THE AUTHOR IDENTIFIES HIMSELF as James, but that's a name shared by several New Testament personalities. The first candidate, is James the son of Zebedee, brother of John. But he died in AD 44 (see Acts 12:1-2), a date which is too early for him to have written this letter. A second possibility is James the son of Alphaeus (see Mark 3:18). But no early Christian tradition acknowledges him as the author. Most likely, the writer is James the brother of Jesus (Mark 6:3; Acts 1:14; 12:17; 15:13; 21:18; 1 Cor 15:7; Gal 2:9).

Though not a follower of his brother during his earthly ministry (see John 7:3-5), James came to believe in Jesus after his resurrection (Acts 1:14; 1 Cor 15:7). He was a leader in the Jerusalem church and exerted significant influence.

Historical Background

Since James died in AD 62 or 66, his letter was written before this time. There are some similarities between themes in James's letter and the writings of Paul. If time is allowed for the events of Acts 15 and 21 to have occurred (these chapters recount events in which Paul and James were together), then a date between AD 48 and 52 seems the most likely time for the writing of the letter.

The reference "to the twelve tribes dispersed abroad" in 1:1 suggests that James was writing to Jewish Christians living in or around Palestine. The reference to a synagogue in 2:2 strengthens this view. Since James led the Jerusalem church, it's likely the audience lived in and around there.

Message and Purpose

James is the in-your-face, no-holds-barred apostle. He says in essence, "If you are going to be a Christian, be a real one." This book thus explains what practical Christianity looks like. It's about living out your faith in everyday situations with everyday people, and doing it victoriously.

James opens by talking about trials that affect every area of life. He then exhorts his readers to stop whining and keep going because there's a crown waiting for each of us, not only in heaven but here on earth. Then James tackles discrimination in the church and tells God's people to stop honoring the wrong folks. Some, for instance, had rewarded the rich and ignored the poor even as the ones they were honoring were awaiting their day of reckoning and the ones they were ignoring were God's kingdom priority. James also warns believers to watch their tongues and to quit living by earthly wisdom. He urges God's people to quit fighting and fussing with each other, to submit themselves to God. James says that if God's people will get right with God, they will have his power at their disposal. But if we aren't using our faith, it is dead (useless).

VIDEO INTRO

www.bhpublishinggroup.com/qr/te/59_00

JAMES

I. TRIALS, TEMPTATION, AND TRUE RELIGION (1:1-27)

1:1 James, the half brother of Jesus, greets his readers as **a servant of God and . . . Christ.** He wants them to know he's writing in submission to his Master's agenda.

1:2 Consider it a great joy . . . whenever you experience various trials. Notice James said "whenever," not "if." But regardless of the form your trials take (physical, emotional, relational, financial), God wants you to be joyful because one of the primary means he uses to make us like Christ is by sending trouble our way. A *trial* is a divinely ordained difficulty that God causes or permits so that he may grow us and conform us into the image of his Son (see Rom 8:28-29). Christians in crisis are actually undergoing extreme makeovers. Hardships can transform us into something beautiful. That is cause for unspeakable joy—not because of the *pain* but because of the *purpose* behind it. In God's providence, you have bad days on purpose. God uses trials to develop us spiritually.

1:3-4 The testing of your faith produces endurance (1:3). It's one thing to tell your teacher that you know the material; it's another thing to write the correct answers on a test. Similarly, you may claim to believe and follow God, but how do you respond when he tests your faith and pushes your buttons? God is working to produce endurance in you, so **let endurance have its full effect.** Don't try to short-circuit a trial by illegitimately seeking to exit it. God is trying to make you spiritually **mature and complete** (1:4). The

conflict you experience in the physical world is a means he uses to draw your attention to something in the spiritual world. God applies the iron of trials to the wrinkles of our lives so that Jesus Christ looks good wearing us.

1:5 What should you do when trouble begins? Pray. **Ask God** for *wisdom*, which is the ability to apply spiritual truth to life's circumstances. He promises to give you wisdom to respond to your trials with maximum spiritual benefit.

1:6-8 How does God communicate this wisdom? Primarily through his Word and secondarily through godly counsel. So, after you've prayed, go to the Scriptures and see what God says about your problem. Then ask him for help from spiritually minded people who can teach you how best to apply biblical truth to it. You must, however, approach with **faith** not **doubting**—or "double-mindedness"(1:6, 8). You can't go in two directions at once, responding to your problem from a divine perspective *and* a human one. The double-minded person **should not expect to receive** wisdom from God because he's **unstable**, mixing divine answers with conflicting human answers (1:7-8).

1:9-11 The poor and the rich offer examples of responding to life with wisdom. **The brother of humble circumstances** is a fellow who doesn't have much. James tells this person to **boast in his exaltation** (1:9)—that is, to glory in the fact that God is conforming him to Christ through his struggle. But the rich man is to **boast in his humiliation** (1:10). In other words, James reminds the rich man that nothing material he has will last. It will fade away like grass and flowers (1:11). There's more to life than stuff. Don't neglect the eternal.

1:12 Blessed is the one who endures trials, because when he has stood the test he will receive the crown of life, which is kingdom victory in history as a result of passing a test. Everyone is looking for a blessing. Unfortunately, what they often mean by "blessing" is a car, a house, a mate, a job, or a raise. A true *blessing*, however, is a God-given capacity to experience, enjoy, and extend his goodness in life. Regardless of whether God's blessings include external components, they are intended to bring about *internal* change so that our lives display his kingdom relationship and rule. Trials open the door to God's blessings. So receive them with joy, pray for wisdom, and grow in Christlikeness.

1:13 Christians must distinguish between trials and temptations. A *temptation* is a solicitation to do evil. And while the same Greek word is used here to speak of both trial and temptation, they differ in terms of source, purpose, and outcome. In the same event, God and the devil can be at work— one to test you and the other to tempt you. But let's be clear: God **doesn't tempt anyone.** And any temptation hatched by Satan must pass through God's fingers first even though God is not its source (see Job 1:6-12). Satan desires your downfall; God desires your development.

1:14-15 Temptation leads to sin when you yield to it. If you are a Christian, the devil cannot make you sin. But like an expert football coach, he studies your game films. He knows your distinctive weaknesses and tendencies. He knows how to appeal to your **evil desire** so that you'll be **drawn away** to sin (1:14). And **sin** leads to **death**—separation (1:15). When we sin, we break fellowship with God.

1:16-18 Don't be deceived (1:16). When faced with temptation, you must shift your focus.

Focus, first, on the goodness of God: **Every good and perfect gift is from** him. Look to all the kindness God has shown you rather than at the temptation confronting you.

Second, focus on the faithfulness of God's character: he's **the Father of lights, who does not change like shifting shadows** (1:17). God never changes and always shines. Why does a portion of the earth become dark even though the sun always shines? Because earth keeps turning. God is consistently shining forth his goodness, truth, and grace. Turn *to* him, not *away* from him.

Third, focus on God's Word: **he gave us birth by the word of truth** (1:18). For many, the Bible is like the queen of England. It's held in high esteem but wields no power over them personally. What Scripture accomplished for your salvation, though, it can accomplish for your sanctification. Face temptation, like Jesus (Matt 4:1-11), with the spiritual power of the Word. After all, if the living Word needed the written Word to defeat the enemy of the Word, you certainly do.

Finally, focus on God's plan: you are the **firstfruits of his creatures** (1:18). The Israelites gave God the firstfruits of their crops, flocks, and herds. They demonstrated how they valued him by giving him the first and best of what they owned. As God's "firstfruits," you are of highest value to him. You are a son or daughter of the living God. Don't succumb to temptation and lower your dignity.

1:19-21 If you are saved and sanctified by the Word of God, how should you approach it? **Be quick to listen** to God's thoughts on a matter, **slow to speak** your own point of view, and **slow to anger** (1:19) should you not like what God has to say in contrast to your own human perspective. God's Word will confront you, but getting angry with him will not achieve his righteous plan for your life (1:20). So instead, put aside **moral filth** and **evil** by confessing and repenting of your sin and **humbly receive the implanted word.** Through it, after all, God has implanted in you a new nature. You have everything you need for spiritual growth. But you have to receive it, humbly placing yourself under its authority so that it can

save you (1:21)—that is, deliver and transform you.

1:22-25 Without application, there can be no spiritual transformation. Therefore, we should **be doers of the word and not hearers only** (1:22). You can read the Bible and listen to sermons all day without it having effect. But to be a **hearer** and **not a doer** is **like someone looking at his own face in a mirror** only to go **away, and immediately** forget what he looks like (1:23-24). A mirror shows the reality. It exposes what you look like, but it can't change you. It won't comb your hair or brush your teeth. To look in a mirror is a call to action.

We must look **intently into the perfect law of freedom.** The Bible calls us to true freedom, which is submission to God's perfect Word. To live this way requires going to the Word intently—not casually—in prayer and meditation. The one who submits to transformation by the Word and is **a doer** will be **blessed** (1:25).

1:26-27 James is an in-your-face apostle. He doesn't want to know the words you heard on Sunday unless they resulted in action on Monday. **If anyone thinks he is religious**, his Christianity must be practical (1:26). Vertical worship must have horizontal expression. Your faith must be seen in your conversation, your compassion, and your conduct.

First, your *conversation* ought to demonstrate mastery of your **tongue** (1:26). Talk less and bless more. Second, if your religion is to be **pure and undefiled**, it must express itself in *compassion.* **Look after orphans and widows.** Provide for those who can do nothing for you in return because that's what your heavenly Father did for you. Third, practice an in-the-world-but-not-of-the-world religion (see John 17:15-16)—that is, in your *conduct*, keep yourself **unstained** (1:27). Don't let the world rub off on you. Instead, rub off on the world and leave behind a trace of grace.

II. THE FAILURE OF FAVORITISM AND USELESS FAITH (2:1-26)

2:1 One of the ways we become stained by the world (1:27) is by practicing the sin of discrimination. James has some choice words for his readers about showing partiality: **Do not show favoritism.** Doctrine wasn't this group's problem: they had faith in **our glorious Lord Jesus Christ**. But that wasn't affecting how they related to others. To illegitimately discriminate against people (we *are* to discriminate against evil) is to make a value judgment based on unbiblical criteria (such as race, class, or culture) and act inappropriately toward them.

2:2-4 James uses an example based on class difference. If a GQ-looking rich guy **in fine clothes** receives preferential treatment in your church because of his status and wealth, while a **poor person** is disregarded because he has nothing to offer (2:2-3), you have **made distinctions . . . with evil thoughts** (2:4). Regardless of the motivation for the favoritism—whether race, class, education, gender, or culture—we cannot blame

society or our upbringing for this tendency that James calls "evil." Understand: we're not talking about discriminating between right and wrong based on God's Word. We're talking about discriminating where God shows no partiality—looking at the outside to determine a person's worth.

2:5-7 James reminds them that God chose **the poor in this world to be rich in faith and heirs of the kingdom** (2:5). Meanwhile, **rich** unbelievers are often the ones who persecute Christians and **blaspheme** God (2:6-7). This doesn't mean all poor people are saved and all rich people are condemned. Rather, it's a simple acknowledgment that those who are destitute often recognize their need for a Savior. Likewise, those living proudly in wealth and comfort frequently miss their need for God.

2:8-9 If you **love your neighbor as yourself, you are doing well.** James learned faithfully from his Master. When asked about the greatest commandment, Jesus said the law has two sides to it: love God and love neighbor (Matt 22:34-40). You can't claim to love God while you hate your brother (1 John 4:20). But if **you show favoritism**, you don't merely do something socially unacceptable—**you commit sin** (2:9).

2:10-11 How serious is the sin of favoritism? James sets it alongside **adultery** and **murder**. The reason the church still suffers from sins of discrimination like racism is because we're not willing to acknowledge how serious and wretched it is. If you're condemned as a murderer, it does no good telling the judge that you're innocent of adultery (2:11). If you're hanging from a chain off the edge of a cliff, it doesn't matter which of the links breaks because they're all connected. The end result will be the same. If you practice discrimination against those made in the image of God, you're **guilty** no matter how many rules you follow (2:10).

2:12-13 Therefore, **speak and act** with the knowledge that you will stand before the judgment seat of Christ one day (2:12). Everyone who enters our churches should experience them as environments of mercy and hope. If you don't show mercy, don't expect mercy. If you don't offer hope, don't expect hope. Confess any partiality in your life and look for opportunities to show mercy, for **mercy triumphs over judgment** (2:13).

2:14 Indulging the sin of discrimination is but one example of living in contradiction to the faith you profess. James wants his readers to know that it's possible for a believer to have a useless faith—one that's devoid of good works. He asks, **What good is it** to claim to have **faith** but no **works? Can such faith save?** Some people think that James is contradicting Paul, who said, "A person is justified by faith apart from the works of the law" (Rom 3:28). But James and Paul aren't speaking about the same thing. Paul is talking about how a sinner becomes a saint. James is talking about how a saint brings heaven to earth. You cannot merit salvation; it is received by grace through faith in Christ alone (see Eph 2:8-9). Our

sanctification, however, requires that our faith express itself in works.

In Greek, the word for "save" can have different meanings based on the context. It can refer to being delivered or rescued from challenges or dangers in life (see, e.g., Matt 14:30; Acts 27:20). Here James is discussing a faith that can "save" or "deliver" from the power of sin's consequences in history (cf. 1:21). In order to grow in your faith and live with power, you have to connect your faith to works.

2:15-17 James offers a scenario. **A brother** comes to you **without clothes and lacks daily food** (2:15). So, what should you do? You may offer profound theological insight and assure him that God will supply his needs (Phil 4:9). Then you might pray with him and wish him well: **Go in peace, stay warm, and be well fed.** But what good have you done if **you don't give . . . what the body needs?** (2:16). James isn't deriding the spiritual; he's simply insisting that it's not enough. If a brother is hungry, he doesn't need a sermon. He needs a ham sandwich! Put your faith in action by helping those in need.

Faith, if it doesn't have works, is dead (2:17). It's possible to have a useless faith that's not accomplishing anything in life. If you say you trust God, it should affect your feet. Once you become a Christian by faith alone, your faith has to get married to works. Then, what you believe about eternity will become real in your history.

2:18-20 James provides the argument of a hypothetical skeptic. This person disagrees with James and says the validity of his faith is not connected to his works: **you have faith, and I have works** (2:18). This objector seeks to validate his premise by arguing that demons believe and tremble at their knowledge of God's reality yet have no supporting works to support their belief. According to James, such a person is **senseless** and missing the point entirely because saving **faith without works is useless**—that is, it has no spiritual value in history (2:20). It will only leave you feeling defeated.

If you want to understand the strength of your faith, look at *what you do*. In the Hall of Faith of Hebrews 11, the author repeatedly describes what various Old Testament figures *accomplished* "by faith." Belief was demonstrated by what they did.

2:21-24 Abraham is a perfect example of a biblical hero whose faith was married to his works. He was **justified by works in offering Isaac his son on the altar** (2:21). This activity didn't save the patriarch; after all, Abraham had already believed God and had his faith credited "as righteousness" in Genesis 15:6. It's in Genesis 22 that God called him to sacrifice his son. When Abraham obeyed, God confirmed his intent to bless him on earth and make a great nation of him (Gen 22:15-18). **By works**, his **faith was made complete** or matured (2:22). Faith must be demonstrated, not just discussed, to be beneficial in history. A person is *justified by faith* alone apart from works for heaven, but he is *justified by works* for usefulness on earth (2:24).

2:25 Rahab is another example. She was **justified by works** that others could see—she helped Israel's spies, evidencing the trust she'd already placed in God. This justification by works brought her deliverance and victory in history (see Josh 2:8-19; 6:22-23).

2:26 Just as the body without the spirit is dead, so also faith without works is dead. The faith of a believer can atrophy, and we can become orthodox corpses unless our faith is put to work. Many of us have spiritual life, yet we're spiritually sick. We attend church to hear what the Great Physician has to say and leave feeling good about his prescription. We remain spiritually unhealthy, though, because we don't swallow the medicine. Once we hear God's Word, we must act on it to be transformed by it.

III. THE UNTAMED TONGUE AND THE WAY OF WISDOM (3:1-18)

3:1-2 In the absence of good works, there's often an abundance of worthless words. So James addresses the necessity of controlling our tongues. This is practical, down-to-earth Christianity. He begins with teachers in the church: **not many should become teachers.** Why? Teachers influence the thinking of others and have the power to lead them astray. Therefore, teachers **will receive a stricter judgment** (3:1). Heaven notices what you say. **We all stumble in many ways**; none of us is perfect. But the one who controls his tongue **is mature** (3:2). The tongue is a crucial—and often deadly—part of the body. It's like a master switch. Take command of it, and you have the potential for bringing your spiritual life under control.

3:3-6 James delivers two insightful illustrations. When you **direct** the **bits** in the **mouths** of large **horses**, you control their movement (3:3). Similarly, steering a **small rudder** will direct the course of a large ship (3:4). As the bit is to the horse, and as the rudder is to the ship, so is the mouth to the saint. The **tongue** is **small**, but it can do great damage (3:5).

Some spouses have hurled insults that their mates have never forgotten. Some individuals started gossip fires years ago, and the flames are still burning. A mouth can set the whole **course of life on fire** (3:6). It can destroy self-esteem, devastate relationships, ruin a career, and kill a ministry. As sure as a tiny match can set a forest ablaze, the mouth causes harm that is out of proportion to its size.

3:7-8 Mankind has **tamed** every **kind of animal** (3:7). We have seals that clap, dolphins that talk, birds that flip, and dogs that jump through hoops. We can do with beasts what we can't do to the human mouth: **No one can tame the tongue** (3:8). The only successful tongue-tamer is God. Remember, whatever is inside will come out. This is why you need to be filled with Scripture and the Holy Spirit.

3:9-12 James isn't writing to the world. He's exhorting Christians. **Brothers and sisters**

(3:10), he says, the tongue is polluted. Our air and water become polluted when they include contaminants. It doesn't matter if a poisonous contaminant comprises only a small percentage of the whole. If you breathe polluted air or drink polluted water, you can become seriously ill or die. The mixture is deadly. With our tongues we can **bless our Lord** and also **curse people who are made in God's likeness. Blessing and cursing come out of the same mouth** (3:9-10). When this happens, our mouths have become polluted. After singing hallelujahs, some families start tearing each other down before they've even departed the church parking lot. But to verbally attack another human being is to attack God because people are made in his likeness.

A fig tree can't **produce olives.** A saltwater spring can't produce **fresh water** (3:12). Why? Because production is based on what's inside. Therefore, if criticizing, gossiping, and swearing come out of your mouth, the content of your heart needs to be addressed. So if you want to change the course of your life, you need to ask God to help steer that little rudder called your tongue.

3:13 When it comes to negotiating the twists and turns of this highway called life, wisdom gives us the ability to press the brake, flip the turn signal, turn the steering wheel, engage the accelerator, and navigate through heavy traffic. *Wisdom* is the application of heavenly knowledge to earthly living.

James asks his readers, **Who among you is wise and has understanding?** Notice what he *does not* answer. He doesn't say that it's the one who has read widely, attained advanced degrees, and can wax eloquently about any subject. Rather, the wise person shows **that his works are done in the gentleness that comes from wisdom.** In other words, wise deeds are the proof of a wise life.

Few believers need a change in their circumstances half as much as they need wisdom to *manage* their circumstances. For instance, a Christian man doesn't need a new spouse; he needs God's wisdom to love and live with the spouse he has.

3:14-15 The hearts of some people are characterized by **bitter envy and selfish ambition** (3:14). Such attitudes may enable them to go places in life, but this kind of "wisdom" **does not come down from above.** It's **demonic** and comes straight from hell (3:15). Remember, mere human wisdom is an expression of Satan's agenda. To convey heavenly wisdom, you must communicate with heaven.

3:17-18 Human wisdom is rooted in selfish ambition, and its fruit is bitter envy. Contrast that with the root and fruit of heavenly wisdom. True wisdom comes **from above**; the Lord is its source. What does it look like? It's **pure, then peace-loving, gentle, compliant, full of mercy and good fruits, unwavering, without pretense** (3:17). Whereas human wisdom tears others down, godly wisdom builds others up. It's authentic and leads to peace rather than strife. Do you want to bear **the fruit of righteousness?** Then you must sow and **cultivate peace** (3:18).

IV. HOSTILITY OR HUMILITY (4:1-17)

4:1 You can't have peace if you're constantly at war (3:18). According to James, his readers engaged in **fights among** themselves. What caused them? What was the **source?** Ask people why they're fighting, and they're likely to point their fingers at others. But James insists that wars **come from your passions that wage war within you.** Conflicts emerge from within.

4:2-3 The human heart manufactures desires, frequently selfish ones. These can range from the mundane ("I want a little peace and quiet") to the weighty ("I want power and significance"). When someone prevents you from satisfying a **desire**, you are tempted to view that person as an obstacle to be overcome, as an enemy to be defeated. Therefore, the natural tendency is to murder and covet. It's not necessarily that you intend to slay anyone physically. Jesus, after all, reminds us that murder begins in the heart with hatred (Matt 5:21-26). Thus, the believers James addressed were relating to one another as adversaries.

Importantly, James says one of the reasons they did not have what they wanted was because they didn't ask (4:2). How tragic to declare war against a friend or spouse about something that God may have granted if only asked! On the other hand, often it's the asking that's the problem. Many people don't receive what they want from God because they ask with wrong motives, so they may spend it on their pleasures (4:3). The kingdom of God and the needs of others don't factor into the equation. A helpful question to pose when we pray about something for ourselves is this: "How will God's program be advanced through the granting of my request?"

4:4 When we want the satisfaction of our own desires above all else, we commit idolatry and worship something other than God. Worldliness and godliness cannot coexist. When Israel strayed after other gods, the Lord accused them of adultery because he was Israel's husband (e.g., Jer 3:8). Therefore, it's not surprising that James calls these church members adulterous people. The church is the bride of Christ (see Eph 5:22-33). So friendship with the world is hostility toward God. If you cozy up to the world and pursue worldly desires, you make yourself the enemy of God. And when you put yourself in that position, you cannot expect your prayers to be answered.

4:5-6 God wants you. If you commit adultery with the world, then, he won't sit back and do nothing. The Holy Spirit who dwells in us envies intensely (4:5). The Lord is a jealous God (Exod 34:14) who won't share his bride with false gods. So, what does a holy, jealous God do when his people foolishly pursue the world and treat him like an enemy? Well, God resists the proud (4:6).

If you place yourself in opposition to God through your attachment to the world, he'll resist you. He'll oppose you because such pride imitates the king of pride, Satan, who exalted himself above God (see Isa 14:12-14).

The only solution is to humble yourself before him in order to experience the outpouring of his grace (4:6). Pride is like a beard. It grows without our cultivation, and we have to daily, humbly shave it off.

4:7-10 What does it look like to daily humble yourself before the Lord? First, you must submit to God and draw near to him (4:7-8). To submit to God is to recognize your weakness, to stop fighting, and to surrender to him as your ultimate and final authority (see Rom 12:1-2). If you had the power to live a transformed life on your own, you wouldn't need "greater grace" (4:6). To draw near to God is to come into his presence with prayer, praise, and obedience. However, if you reserve this for Sundays only, you won't draw near enough.

Second, you must resist the devil (4:7). Submitting to God is one side of the coin; resisting the devil is the other. In the spiritual war, we must surrender to the true King and join in opposition to the wicked usurper. Don't underestimate Satan. He's stronger than you, smarter than you, and has been practicing his craft for millennia. There's only one way to resist him: the same way the King of kings resisted him—by wielding Scripture (see Matt 4:1-11). When the devil whispers his lies to your conscience, proclaim the truth of the Word of God, and he will flee from you (Jas 4:7) as he fled from Christ (Matt 4:11). But you can't proclaim what you don't know.

Third, regularly repent of your sin: cleanse your hands and purify your hearts (4:8). Some people don't receive the help they need from God because they "don't sin." Rather, they "make mistakes." But Jesus didn't die for mistakes; he died for sins. We live in a culture that rejects personal responsibility and downplays sin. Those are symptoms of pride, which takes us right back to where James started (4:6) and where he ends: humble yourselves before the Lord, and he will exalt you (4:10). Admit your sin and eradicate pride. Riding God's elevator to the top always starts with a trip down.

4:11-12 In these verses, James gives an illustration of what humility requires. It demands a change in how you speak of others. Don't criticize. Don't speak about a fellow believer with the intent of doing harm rather than providing help. The one who **defames** and **judges** a brother or sister **defames** and **judges the law** (4:11). How? Jesus said the great commandments are love God and love your neighbor as yourself (see Mark 12:28-31). So if you judge your neighbor, you're judging the law that commands us to love others. You're saying to God, "I refuse to do that." But **there is one lawgiver and judge**, and you're not him! The Lord is the one who will pass judgment at the appropriate time. So **who are you to judge your neighbor?** (4:12). As the saying goes, "There but for the grace of God go I." That brother you criticize could have been you. As God has shown you grace and mercy, practice grace and mercy.

4:13 God hates pride; therefore, James continues to confront his readers' arrogance. If spoken in modern English the phrase **Come now** would be "You've got to be kidding me." These believers had plans for the future and had sketched in the details fairly specifically. They had a timetable (**today or tomorrow**), a location (**such and such a city**), a schedule (**a year**), a plan (**do business**), and a determined conclusion (**make a profit**).

4:14 Let's be clear: God is not against making plans. But it's one thing for a believer to make plans and another to think himself sovereign over them. After all, **you do not know what tomorrow will bring**. These people didn't allow for contingencies. They were definitive, had an air of self-sufficiency. But life has too many variables for you to guarantee your tomorrow. God's kingdom agenda is assured because he's an omniscient (all knowing) and omnipotent (all powerful) eternal King. Your agenda is uncertain at best. You're like **vapor** that **vanishes**. Here for a moment and then gone.

4:15-17 You must acknowledge that your plans fall within a larger, controlling reality: the will of God (4:15). So make your plans (see Prov 16:9), but then submit them to the Lord for approval. God is excellent at interrupting plans. To do something "if the Lord wills" is not a pious phrase but a philosophy of life. Jesus's "food" was doing the will of his Father (John 4:34), so put it on your menu. To accomplish his will in your life, God will interrupt your program. Will you humble yourself and accept it? Or will you **boast in your arrogance** about your future? (4:16-17).

V. PRIDE, PATIENCE, AND PRAYER (5:1-20)

5:1 At the heart of pride is often a love for money—that is, materialism. James isn't condemning money itself. Some of God's servants were wealthy (e.g., Abraham, Job), and money was not their problem. Condemned here is a mindset that turns gold into a god. James addressed riches previously (1:10-11; 2:1-4), but in 5:1-6, he rebukes the **rich people** among his readers whose hearts were devoted to materialism. Theirs is a sin that transcends time. If you live in modern America, you are tempted to be a materialist.

5:2-6 First, he warns the rich that wealth and possessions will pass away. They're unreliable. Riches can come to nothing in a day; expensive **clothes** become moth food (5:2). Then he reminds them that **stored up treasure** won't profit them **in the last days**

(5:3). Remember the rich young ruler of Matthew 19:16-22? Remember Jesus's story of the rich man and Lazarus (see Luke 16:19-31)? Clutching riches can cost you eternity. Materialism (when the physical and financial take precedence over the spiritual and the eternal) has a high price tag. Finally, he condemns the rich for how they treated others—especially those who worked for them. God greatly condemns economic injustice in the workplace. They **withheld** pay from their **workers** while they themselves lived **luxuriously** and **indulged** (5:4-5). They had **murdered the righteous**, which probably means they hated (murdered in their hearts; see 4:2) those less fortunate than they.

The key is to recall Jesus's teaching, "Don't store up for yourselves treasures on earth. . . . But store up for yourselves treasures in heaven.... For where your treasure is, there your heart will be also" (Matt 6:19-21). The stuff of earth is tied to earth. But that which is tied to eternity will have eternal repercussions.

5:7-9 To believers who are suffering, James says, **Be patient until the Lord's coming** (5:7). He isn't referring to Christ's return to rapture the church. He's exhorting them to be patient until the Lord comes to intervene in their historical circumstances. The problem is that many people don't know how to exercise patience. They equate patience with twiddling their thumbs. But that's not biblical patience.

James illustrates the concept using the **farmer**. When a farmer **waits for the precious fruit of the earth**, he doesn't sit on his porch in a rocker. He daily cares for his crops. He is responsible to be busy while he "waits." Nevertheless, he must exercise patience until **the early and the late rains** come (5:7). The farmer must fulfill his responsibilities on earth. That's a necessity—yet it's not enough. He knows he's dependent on heaven to send rain.

Similarly, Christians who need deliverance **must be patient ... strengthen [their] hearts** and **not complain about one another** (5:8-9). They must act responsibly and faithfully in history. Only heaven can bring rain. But have you fulfilled your responsibility as you wait for it?

5:10-11 James points to the Old Testament prophets as an example of suffering and patience. They endured unjust treatment for speaking **in the Lord's name** (5:10). What was the outcome? They were **blessed**. More specifically, James considers the example of **Job's endurance**. Few believers have suffered anything close to what Job did. He lost his wealth, his health, and—worst of all—his children. Yet in spite of missteps along the way, Job didn't turn away from God. He knew only the Lord could deliver him. At the end of his trial, **the Lord** proved himself to be **compassionate and merciful** (5:11).

5:12 James isn't implying that all oaths are bad. He is urging believers to be truth-tellers. Give a simple **yes** or **no** because if you have

to swear to convince someone that you're sincere, you have a reliability problem.

5:13 If you want to gauge your spiritual life, look at the thermostat setting on your prayer life. Your knee-jerk reaction to **suffering** should be to **pray**. Likewise, if life is smooth and you are **cheerful**, you **should sing praises** (5:13). These responses acknowledge that affliction and blessing both come from the Lord, who works through them to accomplish his purposes.

5:14 In these verses, James addresses one who is **sick**. The Greek word from which this is translated can mean "weak." Thus, it can refer to any kind of weakness, physical or otherwise. Those beaten down and struggling to pray, then, can seek help from **the elders**—the male spiritual leadership of the church. The **oil** would have been used for soothing or grooming the body (5:14; see Matt 6:17; Luke 10:34).

5:15 We must be careful here. The verse cannot be saying that *every* physical sickness will be healed. That would suggest we would never die. The application is wider. The elders were to express the love of Jesus tangibly through prayer, encouragement, and refreshment. The idea is that the church should have practical ministry in place to aid members who are weak. The **prayer** offered in **faith** will provide divine encouragement in the mist of problems (5:15).

5:16-18 Suffering and sickness do not necessarily result from sin. Job, for instance, was afflicted though he didn't sin (Job 1). Moreover, Jesus made it clear that a person can be stricken with an illness or condition that has no connection to wrongdoing (John 9:1-3). On the other hand, a sinful lifestyle *can* result in weakness and suffering. Therefore, if needed, **confess your sins to** a trusted, spiritually mature believer (5:16). If you will deal with your sin, you will see God work in your life.

God will do extraordinary things with an ordinary person who is **righteous** (walks with him by faith) and makes an energized **prayer** (5:16). Elijah not only prayed **earnestly** but persistently (see 1 Kgs 18:42-44), and God worked miraculously in response (5:17-18). Elijah **was a human being** like us (5:17), yet he knew he had a God who is sovereign and expects his people to pray to him. Do you?

5:19-20 As he closes, James reminds us that the church should be a spiritual hospital where believers are involved in each other's lives. One who **strays from the truth** from **among** the **brothers and sisters** is a backslider (5:19). He is not progressing in the faith but regressing. He has deviated from the right path. The most famous example of this is Peter, who denied his Lord (see Matt 26:69-75).

These verses are not so much about the backslider, though, as they are about those around him. Some believers aid the spiritual regression of fellow Christians by assuming it's none of their business. But if your child darted into the street in front of a car, would you say it's none of your business? Of course not! Though many believers fail to comprehend their responsibility to the family of faith, your Christianity is real when you see a brother in Christ backsliding and act in love. You cannot be a passive Christian.

The one who **turns a sinner from the error of his way will save his soul from death** (5:20). James is referring to a believer, so he's not talking about losing salvation. "Death" can have two meanings. First, it may mean untimely physical death. The New Testament describes instances in which Christians died early. Sometimes God takes a straying and unrepentant believer home (see 1 Cor 11:30). It can also refer metaphorically to the deterioration in circumstances because the intimate presence of God is no longer operating in a person's life.

God says you and I have the power to interpose ourselves into a situation and intercept straying Christians on the road to spiritual misery. By doing so, we **cover a multitude of sins** (5:20). James alludes here to Proverbs 10:12, which says, "Love covers all offenses." There may have been a vast number of decisions and choices that led a particular backslider astray. But with the sacrificial love of Christ, James says believers can be used of God to provide a covering for past sins and lead an erring brother to restoration. May we do so.

1 PETER

INTRODUCTION

Author

THE AUTHOR CLAIMS TO BE "PEter, an apostle of Jesus Christ" (1:1). He maintains he is an "elder and witness" to Christ's sufferings (5:1). Moreover, his exhortation to "shepherd God's flock" (5:2) is reminiscent of the charge Jesus gave to Peter in John 21:15-17. Several themes in 1 Peter appear in Peter's sermons in Acts, such as the God "who judges impartially" (1:17; cf. Acts 10:34); the idea that God "raised [Jesus] from the dead and gave him glory" (1:21; cf. Acts 2:32-36); and truth about "the stone that the builders rejected" being the cornerstone (2:7-8; cf. Acts 4:10-11).

Some critical scholars have disputed this claim of authorship, arguing that someone else wrote the letter in Peter's name. But their theories are inconclusive and cannot be proven. Several early church leaders—Irenaeus, Tertullian, and Clement of Alexandria—accepted 1 Peter as authentic. Furthermore, there are examples of the early church rejecting the practice of writing under an apostolic pseudonym as forgery. They likely would have dismissed the letter if they had believed it to be falsely attributed to Peter. In light of this, the book should be accepted as the apostle Peter's work.

Historical Background

Peter writes to Christians in various regions of Asia Minor, the area we know today as Turkey. The recipients of the letter were primarily Jewish believers (but included some Gentile believers) since Peter refers to them as sojourners of the *dispersion* ("dispersed abroad," 1:1). The Greek word *diaspora*, which is behind that phrase, referred to Jews who were separated from their homeland. Though they had earlier been involved in idolatry (4:3) and were ignorant (1:14) and empty (1:18) before coming to Christ, they had since been accepted as "God's people" (2:9-10). They were experiencing some form of persecution for their faith (1:6; 2:19; 3:16; 4:12-19).

The cryptic statement in 5:13 suggests that Peter probably wrote the letter from Rome. "Babylon" was used cryptically for the capital of the Roman Empire. Peter doesn't mention Paul's presence at the end of the letter, and Paul doesn't mention Peter's presence in the letters he wrote while under house arrest in Rome (AD 60–62). Therefore, Peter likely wrote 1 Peter in Rome after Paul was released and before 2 Peter was written—between AD 62–64.

Message and Purpose

Peter loved to lead, but he had to go through a lot of brokenness to learn how. He thus wrote this book to churches to encourage them to persevere in spite of their own suffering, trials, and persecution. Peter wanted believers to know that new birth in Christ gives hope that will aid perseverance in spite of what we go through. Peter blends doctrinal truth about our salvation with practical truth about how it is to be lived out in our various life situations—including in the relationship between husbands and wives.

Peter knew about suffering because he had experienced it as a disciple of Christ. But he also learned how to endure it with joy and victory rather than with sadness and defeat. This is a lesson we need today as our own culture grows increasingly hostile against the Christian faith. If we are going to be real kingdom citizens, our salvation has to become a visible reality that affects all we do. Peter tells us we need a Christianity that can be seen, even in a world that opposes and rejects us.

Outline

I. Greeting (1:1-2)
II. Praise for Salvation (1:3-12)
III. A Call to Holy Living and Spiritual Growth (1:13—2:3)
IV. A New Identity (2:4-10)
V. Good Works for God's Glory (2:11-17)
VI. Godly Submission and Suffering (2:18-25)
VII. Biblical Alignment in Marriage and in the Church (3:1-12)
VIII. Following Christ While Suffering (3:13—4:19)
IX. Final Exhortations and Conclusion (5:1-14)

VIDEO INTRO

www.bhpublishinggroup.com/qr/te/60_00

1 PETER

I. GREETING (1:1-2)

1:1-2 Peter's greeting highlights the saving work of each member of the Trinity. The Christian recipients were **chosen according to the foreknowledge of God the Father, through the sanctifying work of the Spirit, to be obedient and to be sprinkled with the blood of Jesus Christ.** Peter was writing to Jewish (and some Gentile) Christians who were dispersed among Gentile nations. He reminded them that like their forefathers in faith, they were sovereignly chosen to be a light to the Gentiles (see Deut 4:6; Matt 5:13-16). Having come to Christ, they were to fulfill their divinely authorized and preplanned kingdom mission.

Salvation is no small thing. It involves the actions of the whole Godhead, with the specific election goal of creating obedient pilgrims on earth who share in Christ's sufferings as we advance his kingdom agenda in the world.

Peter prays that **grace and peace** would **be multiplied** to them—that they will take advantage of the spiritual resources God has richly supplied so that his grace (i.e., his unmerited favor) may be exponentially expanded in their day-to-day lives.

II. PRAISE FOR SALVATION (1:3-12)

1:3 Peter enters into praise for **the God and Father of our Lord Jesus Christ** who saved us **because of his great mercy**, not because of our own worthiness. He describes this salvation as a **new birth into a living hope**, which is a positive expectation about the future. When you were born the first time, it was into a dead hope. You were born to die. But, **through the resurrection of Jesus**, there's a better future on the horizon. Jesus's resurrection guarantees our own (see 1 Cor 15:30-32). We have been "born again" (John 3:1-8).

1:4 Peter says Christians have **an inheritance** (which includes our rewards for faithfulness and fidelity to the King and his kingdom) **that is imperishable.** Have you ever made a hotel reservation only to discover that the hotel had no record of it when you showed up? That won't happen with this reservation because it is **kept in heaven.** No one can take it, lose it, or hack it out of God's heavenly computer.

1:5 Not only is your inheritance in safekeeping, but you are eternally secure. **You are being guarded by God's power** for the **salvation** that is to come. If you are truly born again, you're not going anywhere—not because of your power to hold on to God, but because God has an omnipotent grip on you (see John 10:27-29). And he won't let go.

1:6-7 You rejoice in this. Nothing should produce greater joy than knowing your security in Christ. That's true even if **you suffer grief in various trials** (1:6). Your ability to cope in the present is tied to your understanding of your inheritance in the future. If you cannot make the link between the "now" (trials and suffering) and the "not yet" (eternal glory), grace won't be multiplied in your life. God allows trials to refine your **faith** like **gold** so that it may **result in praise** of Jesus when he returns (1:7). All trials are designed to do three things: prove your faith, develop your faith, and glorify your Savior. You never know what you believe until you face a test. The heavenly goldsmith wants to refine your character.

1:8-9 How should we respond while living in time of trials? We need to **love** Christ, **believe in him**, and **rejoice** in him (1:8). You *love* Christ by seeking his glory, so determine how you can bring him the most glory in a given circumstance and do it. You *believe* Christ—or trust him—by obeying him.

Trusting Christ isn't a feeling; it's a decision to obey. *Rejoicing* in Christ means thanking and praising him **because you are receiving the goal of your faith, the salvation of your souls** (1:9). This is not a reference to eternal salvation; the first readers already had it (1:4). It's about the future rewards that await us.

1:10-12 The **prophets, who prophesied about** this coming salvation **searched** and **investigated** these things (1:10). They didn't understand all of the details about the coming of the Messiah that the Spirit revealed to them, but they did know that **they were not serving themselves** (1:12). Through Peter and his fellow apostles, this good news that they anticipated has now been preached even to us. The gospel is so incredible that even **angels long to catch a glimpse of these things** (1:12). They are observing the church to try and understand God's amazing grace.

III. A CALL TO HOLY LIVING AND SPIRITUAL GROWTH (1:13–2:3)

1:13-16 Becoming a Christian is a call to action. That's why Peter tells them to have their **minds ready for action** and to set their **hope** on the **grace** they will receive **at the revelation of Jesus Christ** (1:13). Notice that here too how these believers function *now* is determined by what they know about the *future*. If you don't want to live a defeated life, you must roll up the sleeves of your mind and determine to focus on Christ. God won't make up your mind for you. What action does Peter call them to take? They are not to follow their former desires when they were ignorant of Christ (1:14). Instead, they **are to be holy in all [their] conduct** (1:15) Why? Peter quotes God who said, **Be holy, because I am holy** (1:16; see Lev 11:44-45).

Indeed, God is *holy*, which means, "separate" or "set apart." He is distinct from his creation, unstained by sin, and is the standard of righteousness. Holiness is central to who God is. He is never described in the Bible as "love, love, love" or "sovereign, sovereign, sovereign." But the angelic beings emphasize

that he is "holy, holy, holy" (Isa 6:3; Rev 4:8). Therefore, his love is a *holy* love; his sovereignty is a *holy* sovereignty. God's perfect holiness is at the heart of his other attributes. Everything about him is in a class by itself. And he calls his people to pursue holiness by seeking to please him in every dimension of their lives.

1:17 Those who come to God through Jesus address him as **Father** and are to **conduct** themselves **in reverence** for God by taking him seriously. God expects his kingdom kids to look like him. Since he is holy, we are to be holy. Non-Christians should be viewing you as a little strange because you're seeking to conform to God's standards and not to the world's.

1:18-21 Peter urges Christ's followers to live in holiness and fear because the Lord has **redeemed** them (1:18-19). To *redeem* is to pay a price to set someone free. For instance, slaves could be redeemed (see, e.g., Lev 25:47-49).

God "redeemed" Israel from slavery in Egypt (Deut 24:18) and was called their "Redeemer" (Isa 41:14; 44:6; 47:4).

What did it cost to free you from slavery to sin? Not **silver or gold** but something much more valuable: **the precious blood of Christ** (1:18-19). Why? Well, if you and I are both stuck in a ditch, we can't help each other. We need someone who's not in the ditch. Sinners can't redeem other sinners. Under Israel's sacrificial system, to atone for sin you had to offer **an unblemished and spotless lamb** (1:19). But that was not a once-and-for-all offering. Jesus Christ, however, is the perfect Lamb of God (see John 1:29). He was without sin (see 1 Pet 2:22), so he could serve as a perfect Savior.

When the Bible talks about the shedding of blood, it means the losing of life because "the blood is the life" (Deut 12:23). Our holy God demanded a price for sin, and he met his own demands through the sacrificial death of his Son who redeemed us from slavery to sin.

If you've been redeemed, you're no longer your own. You have a new allegiance. This was God's plan **before the foundation of the world** (1:20). He redeemed sinners through Christ, **raised him from the dead and gave him glory.** We have been transferred from slavery to the glorious kingdom of Christ, so our **faith and hope are in God** (1:21). He will keep his word to deliver and reward his people.

1:22-25 Peter urges his audience to have **sincere brotherly love for** their Christian brothers and sisters (1:22). How can those who were formerly slaves to sin be holy, fear the Lord, and love others? Because they **have been born again.** If you have believed in Jesus Christ, you received a **seed** (i.e., the divine nature; see 2 Pet 1:4) that is **imperishable** (which means believers cannot

lose their salvation). God sparked life in you where once there was death, and he did it **through the living and enduring word** (1:23). As Isaiah said, **the grass withers** and dies, but **the word of the Lord endures forever** (1:24-25; see Isa 40:6-8).

2:1-3 Although this new life is imperishable, it requires growth. Our sinful self-centeredness will continue to rule if we let it, unless the seed of spiritual life is nourished. How do we ensure maturity? If we want to be physically healthy, we must feed our bodies what is nutritious, while avoiding what is unwholesome. The same principle is true in the spiritual realm.

Therefore, Peter says, **rid yourselves of all malice, all deceit, hypocrisy, envy, and all slander** (2:1). Such actions belong to the former life of sin, but they lead to death (i.e., separation from fellowship with God). Returning to the metaphor of new life ("born again," "seed" 1:23), he exhorts them to be **like newborn infants** and **desire the pure milk of the word** so they **may grow** for **salvation** (2:2). The Word that caused us to be born again is the same Word that causes growth (2:2). But, unfortunately, many Christians choose malnourishment.

You don't have to command babies to eat; they know when they're hungry. Christians must be reminded that they are spiritually hungry and must be fed. You also won't find infants consuming big meals on Sunday in order to last them the whole week. Babies eat regularly for day-to-day nourishment; Christians need the same. Some believers are consuming spiritual junk food that can't nourish and won't produce growth. They need a steady diet and application of God's Word instead of man's opinion. Once we taste for ourselves **that the Lord is good** (2:3), we'll know that nothing else will satisfy.

IV. A NEW IDENTITY (2:4-10)

2:4-8 In 2:4-10, Peter describes our identity as the people of God with support from several Old Testament passages. The overall metaphor here is the idea of stones being

fit together into a building. The chief stone on which all the others depend for proper alignment is Jesus Christ. By virtue of his resurrection from the dead, he is **a living stone.**

During his earthly ministry, he was **rejected by people** but **honored by God** (2:4).

As it was then, so it is today. You have only two choices with Jesus: accept him or reject him. Those who accept him know he is the Lord's **honored cornerstone**—the stone on which the whole house aligns. We are to live our lives with reference to him, and we **will never be put to shame** (2:6). But for those who reject him, he is **a stone to stumble over**; thus, they will **trip over** him right into judgment (2:7-8).

Notice that Peter is not just talking about each individual's coming to Jesus but to our corporate coming to him (2:4). God is taking **living stones**—that have life because of *the* living stone—and building **a spiritual house** (2:5). He's not building *houses* but a *house*. And he wants all of us stones to fit snugly into that building.

You can be a good brick, but you can't be the whole house. It takes all the bricks contributing together in the one house. We do not stand alone. All of us were dug out of the quarry of sin and cemented together by the grace of God

2:9-10 Peter describes Christians in a number of ways. They are **a royal priesthood** (also "a holy priesthood" in 2:5). Through Jesus Christ, we have access to God and need no other human priest to represent us or intercede for us.

Believers are **a chosen race** (2:9). As the last Adam (see Rom 5:12-21; 1 Cor 15:45-49), Jesus is the head of a new race of people. The first Adam brought sin and death, but the last Adam brought spiritual life. This new race includes believers from every ethnic group. All physical or cultural distinctions are subservient to this greater category: we are children of God.

The people of God are **a holy nation**—not a perfect people, but a people set apart with a passion to live corporately to please God. We are **a people for his possession**—we're not special because of who we are, but because of the one to whom we belong (2:9).

Along with this new identity, God's people are to live a new lifestyle. You are to **proclaim the praises of the one who called you out of darkness into his marvelous light.** In other words, you are to serve as an advertising agency tasked with sharing the message of his love. We were formerly not his people. Now we **are** and **have received mercy** (2:10). Therefore, as we live in this world—both as individuals and when we gather corporately—people ought to be able to *see* what our marvelous God is like.

V. GOOD WORKS FOR GOD'S GLORY (2:11-17)

2:11-12 In light of their new identity as God's people, Christ's followers should have a unique, influential presence. This only happens, though, if believers understand themselves **as strangers and exiles.** This fallen world is not your home. It's roughly a seventy- or eighty-year pit stop on the way to your eternal destination. The Christian's job in this interim period is to make a difference for God in the world. You are to **abstain from sinful desires that wage war against the soul** (2:11)—that is, don't do what everyone else is doing. You are to **conduct yourselves honorably among the Gentiles**, those who don't know God (2:12).

Jesus told his disciples to let their light shine before unbelievers so that they would see their good works and glorify God (Matt 5:14-16). Peter didn't forget his Master's teaching on this. Even those who **slander you** will **glorify God**, he says, when they **observe your good works** (2:12).

The problem is that too many Christians haven't listened to Jesus's command and have hidden their lights under a basket (see Matt 5:15). Consider a huddle in a football game. Fans don't pay money to go watch eleven grown men stand around in a circle. They don't mind the huddle—as long as the players don't stay in it. What they really want to know is whether the huddle will make a difference. Though the players huddle in private, can they score in public? The challenge for local churches is to break huddle, go public, and influence neighbors and communities for God.

2:13-17 Those who have come to Jesus Christ have transferred kingdoms and sworn allegiance to a new King. His agenda is theirs. But until Jesus returns, his followers must live in this world of nations, rulers, and laws. Christians have a responsibility to civil government. Jesus told his disciples to give "to Caesar the things that are Caesar's, and to God the things that are God's" (Matt 22:21).

Once again, Peter had been listening to his Lord. He tells his Christian readers to **submit to every** lawful **human authority** (2:13).

This is **God's will** (2:15) because he intends human rulers **to punish those who do what is evil** (2:14). Paul agreed (see Rom 13:1-7). Unfortunately, though, in a fallen world, governments can be unjust and act in ways that are contrary to God's rule. When that happens, we have a legitimate basis to protest (see, e.g., Acts 4:19-20; 5:29). But we are not to use our **freedom** as God's people **as a cover-up for evil** (2:16). The world should find Christians to be exemplary citizens who **honor** all people, **love** others, **fear God**, and respect ruling authorities (2:17).

VI. GODLY SUBMISSION AND SUFFERING (2:18-25)

2:18-20 Like Paul (see commentary on Eph 6:5-9), Peter urges Christian **household slaves** to **submit** to their **masters**. He thus takes the reality of an unrighteous institution in the Roman world and tells believers how to honor God within it. Whether their masters were **gentle** or **cruel**, Christian slaves were to shine the light of Christ by their service (2:18). Though this could result in **suffering unjustly** (2:19), Peter reminds them that it is better to do **good and suffer** for it than to do evil and suffer. If we **endure** suffering for doing what is right, **this brings favor with God** (2:20). Consider Joseph. Though he acted with integrity toward his master, he was treated unjustly (Gen 39:1-20). Nevertheless, he entrusted himself to the Lord who "extended kindness to him" and "granted him favor" (Gen 39:21). This does not, however, negate using just means to address unrighteous treatment.

2:21-23 One matter Peter addresses repeatedly in this letter is how Christians should understand and respond to suffering. Though he will have much to say on this, Peter's most important reminder is that we are **called to** suffer **because Christ also suffered for** us, giving us **an example** so we may **follow in his steps** (2:21). Jesus is the perfect example of someone enduring unjust suffering, since he alone is sinless (2:22). Rather than returning evil for evil, he **entrusted himself to the one who judges**

justly (2:23). In this way, Joseph foreshadowed the great Suffering Servant—Jesus Christ.

2:24-25 We must also remember that Christ's suffering was unique. He was more than a mere example. He suffered as our substitute to win our salvation. **He himself bore our sins** (2:24). Jesus not only died because we are sinners (we have a sin nature), but he also died for our sins—for every wrong we have committed or will commit: whether in thought, attitude, or action. Think of our sin nature as a car factory. When he died on the cross, Christ judged the factory. But he also judged the cars that came from the factory—our individual sins.

What was the purpose? **So that, having died to sins, we might live for righteousness** (2:24). Righteousness is the standard that God requires. If you're saved, Jesus gave you the ability to turn sin off and turn righteousness on. The devil doesn't want you to know you can make such a switch and definitely doesn't want you to do it. But we can say "no" to sin and "yes" to righteousness—"no" to Satan's agenda and "yes" to God's.

Peter then quotes from Isaiah 53:5-6: **By his wounds you have been healed. For you were like sheep going astray.** God is not promising that followers of Jesus never get sick (though some teach that false theology). There are various kinds of healing that we need. Yes, sometimes God grants physical healing, but we also need emotional healing and relational healing. And all healing is connected to Jesus's wounds, and Jesus's wounds are connected to his death for sin. So if you want healing in a relationship, you have to be willing to address the sins that brought about the relational problems. Jesus can bring such healing only if the root sins are dealt with (see Jas 5:14-16).

We were all like lost, dumb sheep. But by God's grace, we **have now returned to the Shepherd and Overseer of [our] souls** (2:25). We need him to govern and guide our sin-infected souls so that we live to please God.

VII. BIBLICAL ALIGNMENT IN MARRIAGE AND IN THE CHURCH (3:1-12)

3:1-2 Like Paul (see commentary on Eph 5:22-33; Col 3:18-19), Peter explains God's principles of biblical alignment within the home. He calls Christian **wives** to **submit** themselves to their **own husbands**.

The idea of a wife submitting is despised in today's culture, but part of the problem is that it's also misunderstood. First, though God commands it, submission is a voluntary act. You submit by choice, not by coercion. Second, submission has nothing to do with intrinsic value. Men and women are equal before God; both are created in his image. Neither is more significant. Third, submission is not passivity. A wife is not to give up who she is and become a doormat.

Submitting is about being in alignment under God and recognizing the God-given roles he assigned to husbands and wives. A kingdom husband, for instance, is to lead his family with love. A kingdom wife is to support that leadership with her gifts and abilities.

What if the wife is a better leader? To this I say that though a tractor-trailer is more powerful, it has to yield to even the smallest vehicle on the highway that has the right-of-way. Submission has nothing to do with limiting what a wife brings to the table. It's just an acknowledgment that God has given wives the yield sign. Biblical submission honors the husband's position even if the wife disagrees with his perspectives and decisions. Nevertheless, a wife is never obligated to compromise her greater commitment to God. Her submission is to be "as to the Lord" (Eph 5:22). Like the Proverbs 31 woman, a wife is to employ all her skills and talents serving her family. She manages the home and helps her husband make wise decisions. But in the end, a kingdom wife yields to her husband in making final calls after her perspective has been heard and valued.

What if the husband isn't obeying Christ? How can a wife follow him? Indeed, how can you follow a parked car? Understand that a man needs his wife to help him and encourage him to be the leader God appointed him to be. While a wife will not transform her husband by nagging, fussing, and complaining, God can transform a husband when he observes his wife's **pure, reverent** life (3:2). If some husbands **disobey the word**, wives may be able to win them over by honoring their God-given role without compromising their spiritual commitment (3:1).

3:3-4 Pure, reverent lives are characterized by an emphasis on the inward and spiritual rather than the outward and physical. There's nothing wrong with looking nice. But **don't let your beauty consist of outward things** alone (3:3); it should not be *merely* external. Don't, then, be captivated by store-bought beauty. Outward attractiveness can give a false impression about what someone is like on the inside. God wants internal beauty—**what is inside the heart**—to take precedence (3:4). Don't be gorgeous outside and ugly inside.

3:5-6 Peter calls wives to look to **the holy women** from the past as their models. Putting **their hope in God**, they **adorned themselves** by **submitting to their own husbands** (3:5). A wife's holiness before God is tied to her respect for her husband. An example of a holy woman is **Sarah**, who used her words to build up **Abraham** rather than tear him down—even though he was often a poor leader. As a result, she received the miracle of God opening her womb at the age of ninety. Peter expects Christian women to take their cues from Sarah (not their contemporary culture) in the way they honor their husbands. This way they too can see God's divine intervention in their lives. **Do what is good** and don't be frightened (3:6). God says, "I've got your back."

3:7 Paul commands husbands to love their wives sacrificially like Christ loved the church (Eph 5:25). Peter adds to that. He exhorts husbands to live with their wives with **understanding**. The Bible says in effect that if you're going to be God's kingdom man, you've got to spend time with your wife, listen to her, know what her needs are, and grow in understanding of her. You can't lead someone whom you don't understand. Wives may be physically **weaker**, but they are their husbands' **coheirs of the grace of life**. So **honor** your wife as an equal partner in the relationship; treat her as special **so that your prayers will not be hindered**. A husband who refuses to align himself under God's agenda and value, appreciate, and utilize the contributions of his wife cannot expect God to answer his requests.

3:8-12 Too many church congregations are characterized by attitudes and actions that are shameful. But Jesus told his followers the world would know they are his disciples if they "love one another" (John 13:35). Once again, Peter repeats his Lord's teaching, telling Christians to **love one another**. For God's power and blessings to flow to his people, the church must live in alignment under King Jesus. The church is like an embassy in a foreign land. It's where the rules and ethics of eternity operate within history.

Before the cross, we are all on equal footing. Therefore, we ought to be **like-minded and sympathetic . . . compassionate and humble** toward each other (3:8). When insulted, you are to bless **so that you may inherit a blessing** (3:9). God blesses believers "with every spiritual blessing in the heavens" (Eph 1:3). To access them and **see good days**, you must place yourself under his rule and authority. That means taming your **tongue**, turning **from evil**, doing **what is good**, and pursuing **peace** (3:10-11). For those who align themselves in this way, the Lord's **ears are open to their prayer** (see 3:7). But **those who do what is evil** will find him opposing them (3:12).

VIII. FOLLOWING CHRIST WHILE SUFFERING (3:13–4:19)

3:13-16 Peter lays down a principle for his readers: in general, **if you are devoted to what is good**, no one will harm you (3:13). But **even if you** suffer for doing what is right, **you are blessed**. God has you covered either way, so **do not fear** (3:14). Whatever response you receive from the world, be **ready at any time to give a defense to anyone who asks you for a reason for the hope that is in you** (3:15). Christians must be a strong witness for Jesus with their lives so that they have opportunity to be a strong witness for Jesus with their words. God is not looking for spectators but "players" who live for their King with righteousness and then give testimony about him **with gentleness and respect** (3:16).

3:17-22 In this fallen world, all people suffer. But **it is better to suffer for doing good**—if God wills it—**than for doing evil** (3:17; see 2:19-20). Again, Peter reminds them (see 2:21-25) that Christ is their supreme example of godly suffering. He **suffered for sins**—your sins and mine—to **bring [us] to God** (3:18). He visited the devil and his followers in the spiritual realm and proclaimed his victory over them (3:19). Then he was raised from the dead and seated **at the right hand of God with angels, authorities, and powers subject to him** (3:22). And if you know Christ, you were raised with him (see Eph 2:6). So your present suffering doesn't compare to the victory you have, and will have, through Christ.

Jesus spiritually spoke through **Noah** offering salvation to humanity as he built the ark, but only Noah and his family responded (3:20). The ark provided salvation and deliverance from judgment. Similarly, the believers to whom Peter was writing would be brought to safety through God's judgment by being united to Christ, the New Testament ark of safety. Deliverance does not come through water **baptism** but by testifying of entering the ark of safety (i.e., Jesus Christ), which is the basis of spiritual baptism (3:21; see Rom 6:1-7). Jesus now sits at the right hand of God where all authorities, human and divine, are subject to his control.

4:1-5 Therefore, believers are to have the same attitude toward suffering that Christ had. We are to live our remaining days **for God's will** and **no longer for human desires** (4:1-2). Peter lists the kinds of ungodly **behavior** that **unrestrained** humanity desires (4:3). Not only do unbelievers do these things, but they also **slander** Christians because they don't engage in such **wild living** with them (4:4). But they don't realize **they will give an account** one day to the one who will **judge the living and the dead** (4:5). Which is worse? Being slandered by the ungodly or judged by God?

4:6 Between Christ's crucifixion and resurrection, he **preached** to people who had died, proclaiming his salvation to Old Testament believers in preparation for his leading them to paradise (see Eph 4:8-10). It was also the victorious proclamation of the victory of the cross over sin and Satan's authority (see Col 2:14-15).

4:7 Time is short; **the end of all things is near.** You and I are on death row; we're fuses burning out. So, how should we live? From God's viewpoint, time is the boundary of opportunity. Peter explains how to make the most of the opportunity you've been given. At the top of the list is **prayer**. It replaces self-focus with a God-focus. It reminds us who we are and—more importantly—who we are not.

4:8-9 Then Peter encourages them to **love** each other (4:8). Biblical love is not defined by our feelings but by sacrificing for the good of others. What's a practical way we can do this? By being **hospitable to one another** (4:9). This is one of the many "one anothers" of Scripture. Biblical hospitality is an authentic welcoming and serving, especially toward those who can do nothing in return. Jesus reminds us that what we do for "the least of these" we do for him (Matt 25:40).

4:10-11 We are to **serve others** based on the spiritual **gift** we have **received**. Full-service gas stations are hard to find today. Most are self-service. Unfortunately, many attend church like a self-service station. They fill up on preaching and go home until they need more fuel. But God intends his church to be full service with each member providing for the well-being of others. We are **stewards** of God's **grace** (4:10). We manage something precious that we received but don't own. And since you are a receptor of grace, you ought to be a conduit for grace. So whatever your spiritual gift, it's all about God—not you. Whether you speak or serve, it should be done with **God's words** and **the strength God provides, so that God may be glorified through Jesus Christ in everything.** Do you serve your boss with more excellence than you serve God? Eternal **glory** and **power** belong to just one of them (4:11).

4:12-19 Peter again returns to the theme of suffering. No one looks forward to suffering. We want to reign with Christ, not suffer with him. But to reign with Christ in glory, we must suffer with him now. Whatever form of suffering God calls you to, **don't be surprised** but **rejoice** instead **so that you may also rejoice with great joy when** he returns (4:12-13). There is no virtue in suffering as a **murderer** or **thief** (4:15), but if we suffer **as a Christian** we are **blessed** (4:14, 16). For **judgment** begins **with God's household.** And if God's fatherly discipline is painful, how much worse will his judgment be on **the ungodly** (4:17-18)? So if it is **God's will** that we suffer while doing good, let us entrust our lives to our **faithful Creator** even as we entrust our eternal souls to him (4:19).

IX. FINAL EXHORTATIONS AND CONCLUSION (5:1-14)

5:1-4 As **a fellow elder** himself, Peter has an exhortation for **the elders** of the church, the church's leadership (5:1). They are part of God's chain of command. For God's blessings to flow through the church, the elders must faithfully exercise authority, and the congregation must faithfully follow. Elders are to **shepherd God's flock** (5:2). They must remember that they are "under-shepherds," caring for a flock that isn't theirs—a flock the Lord "purchased with his own blood" (Acts 20:28). Therefore, they are to do their work not **out of compulsion . . . not out of greed for money . . . not lording it over** the people (5:2-3). A shepherd's job is to preserve and protect the sheep.

I once saw a magazine advertisement for a mail-in ordination certificate. You could become a reverend by mail without even answering questions about doctrine, conduct, or character. The problem is that doctrine, conduct, and character are everything! It is only when pastors and elders serve as **examples to the flock** that they will be rewarded by the **chief Shepherd**, Jesus Christ (5:3-4; see John 10:7-11; Heb 13:20).

5:5-7 For the people of God to be in proper alignment, church congregations must be **subject to the elders** when they are exercising godly, biblical authority. This takes **humility**. But remember: **God resists the proud but gives grace to the humble** (5:5). If you want God to oppose you, press on with your stiff neck. But if you want **the mighty hand of God** to **exalt you**, you must **humble** yourself before him (5:6). Cast **all your cares on him**. Why? Because the Creator and ruler of the universe **cares about you** (5:7).

5:8-11 Peter closes with a warning: **be alert** and **resist** the devil. When you transferred out of Satan's realm and into Christ's kingdom, you became a target. **The devil** prowls **like a roaring lion** looking for food. He wants to keep you from advancing God's kingdom on earth, and don't think you can fly under his radar. He wants to destroy you. So be **firm in the faith**. Remember that you can conquer Satan, but only through your faith in and obedience to Jesus Christ (5:8-9). Through Christ, **the God of all grace . . . will himself restore, establish, strengthen, and support you** (5:10). All **dominion** belongs to him (5:11). You need no other security policy.

5:12-14 Peter concludes by commending **Silvanus**, who delivered the letter (5:12), and sending **greetings** of **love** and **peace** from his co-workers (5:13-14).

2 PETER

Author

THE AUTHOR OF THE LETTER identifies himself as "Simeon Peter, a servant and an apostle of Jesus" (1:1). Though Simeon is not the name typically used for Peter, it is a Semitic spelling of his name and does occur at Acts 15:14. The letter writer includes a reference to being personally present at the transfiguration of Jesus (1:16-18)—an event the Gospels say happened when Peter, James, and John were with him (see Matt 17:1-13; Mark 9:2-8; Luke 9:28-36). Moreover, the author is personally familiar with the apostle Paul, a truth we know from Acts 15 and Paul's own letter to the Galatians (Gal 2:9-14). Based on the letter itself, then, we have every reason to believe that it comes from the hand of Peter.

Many modern critical scholars, though, deny Peter's authorship. They believe the letter is pseudonymous—that is, written by someone else under Peter's name. They also argue that the style of writing is different from 1 Peter, and that 2 Peter copied from the letter of Jude—with which it shares common themes and language. But none of these arguments should prevent us from accepting Peter as the author. First, we know from testimony in the early church that the practice of people writing falsely under the name of an apostle was soundly rejected. Such writings were not accepted as Scripture. Second, two letters from the same author are not required to be exactly alike in style to be authentic. Furthermore, it may be that Peter used Silvanus as an amanuensis (secretary) to write 1 Peter (see 1 Pet 5:12). If so, this could easily account for stylistic differences. Finally, the fact that Peter may have borrowed from Jude, Jude may have borrowed from Peter, or both may have borrowed from another source is no stumbling block to authenticity. Therefore, we are justified in believing that the apostle Peter penned the letter.

Historical Background

Peter claims in 3:1 that this is "the second letter" he has written to his readers. But 2 Peter doesn't list any recipients, like 1 Peter does (1 Pet 1:1). So we cannot know for sure if he is writing to the same Christians, or if the statement in 3:1 refers to another letter that has been lost to history.

According to early church tradition, Peter was martyred during the rule of the Roman emperor Nero around AD 67. Since he acknowledges that his death is approaching ("I will soon lay aside my tent"; 1:14), it is likely that he wrote near the end of his life and, thus, probably from Rome.

The Christians to whom he wrote were obviously confronted by false teachers (see 2 Peter 2). So Peter warns them to reject false doctrine, urges them to be faithful to grow spiritually, and reminds them that certain judgment is coming on such teachers.

Message and Purpose

Shortly before his death, Peter desired to build up the faith of these believers so that they could recognize what was counterfeit by knowing what is true. He knew that if they increased in their understanding and application of Scripture, they would grow in their relationship with Jesus Christ. Believers have a new nature from God, but it needs to be fed and nurtured as they participate with Christ in their growth in grace.

Before concluding, Peter warns the churches under his charge against the influence of false teachers infiltrating the churches, denying the Scriptures and the Lord in an attempt to destroy the faith. Peter urges believers to hold tightly to their faith, to continue growing in grace, to keep alert for false teaching, to know the Word, and to be ready and watching for Christ's return when they will receive their kingdom reward. Patient waiting for Christ is not wasted faith.

www.bhpublishinggroup.com/qr/te/61_00

Outline

I. Greeting (1:1-2)
II. Growing in the Faith (1:3-15)
III. The Trustworthy Prophetic Word (1:16-21)
IV. False Teachers (2:1-22)
V. The Day of the Lord (3:1-13)
VI. Final Words (3:14-18)

2 PETER

I. GREETING (1:1-2)

1:1 The author of this epistle is Simon Peter, **a servant ... of Jesus Christ** (that is, one under his authority and lordship) and **an apostle** (a member of the team of Jews chosen and commissioned by Jesus to proclaim the gospel and plant churches). He identifies himself here, however, as **Simeon Peter**, which has led some to conclude incorrectly that someone other than Peter wrote the letter. A better explanation for the alternate spelling is that "Simeon" was a Semitic rendering, used especially in first-century Palestinian settings (cf. Acts 15:14).

The recipients of the letter are **those who have received a faith equal to ours through the righteousness of our God and Savior Jesus Christ.** They are born-again Christians.

In this letter, Peter is not concerned with winning the lost as much as he is with leading the saved into a deeper, experiential knowledge of God. Note also that he explicitly affirms the deity of Jesus—he is "our God and Savior."

1:2 Peter's purpose in fostering spiritual growth and a greater personal experience with God in this life is underscored by his prayer that **grace and peace** would be **multiplied to** them **through the knowledge of God and of Jesus our Lord.** Notice that this prayer turns the greeting in a Trinitarian direction by referring to God (the Father) and Jesus—who is called "God" in 1:1. There is only one God, but he exists in three persons: Father, Son, and Holy Spirit.

II. GROWING IN THE FAITH (1:3-15)

1:3 Spiritual growth can be a reality for every believer because God already **has given us everything required for life and godliness.** The spiritual blessings we need are already available to us (see Eph 1:3), but it's up to us to access them. These comprehensive blessings are appropriated **through the knowledge of God**—that is, through the specific knowledge of God's will for and blessings to believers. This knowledge is the difference between merely meeting the President of the United States and having a personal relationship with him.

1:4 A key to spiritual growth is sharing **in the divine nature**, which penetrates and

lives within every believer beginning at the moment of salvation through the Holy Spirit. Christians, in a manner of speaking, have God's nature woven into their DNA. This nature includes spiritual appetite and godly behavior.

Yet the divine nature is implanted in seed form (cf. 1 Pet 1:23) and doesn't immediately translate into mature, godly living. Rather, it gives every Christian the potential to escape **the corruption that is in the world because of evil desire**, much like a seed gives the person who possesses it the potential to grow a plant. When the seed is tended and grows, the life of the Spirit expands in a believer's soul, and the expansion is manifested in the body through righteous living.

1:5-7 For the divine nature to express itself manifestly in a believer's life, the believer must **make every effort to supplement** his or her **faith with** seven qualities (1:5)—the number *seven* signifying completeness. The new nature has already been programmed to respond to the right input, just like a baby has been programmed to respond to its mother's milk. The nutrients in the milk enable the baby's growth and development.

The seven supplemental qualities necessary for spiritual growth are **goodness** (living to glorify God), **knowledge** (responding to divine revelation), **self-control** (resisting sinful desires), **endurance** (not quitting until God releases you), **godliness** (seeking to please God with your choices), **brotherly affection** (caring for the well-being of other members of God's family), **love** (compassionately and righteously seeking the well-being of others, including nonbelievers). These qualities act like vitamin supplements, enabling believers to adopt God's kingdom perspective and live in accordance with it. As a packet of seeds instructs the gardener to add soil and water to his crop to see it yield fruit, God instructs believers to add these qualities to their saving faith in order to actualize the potential for maturity and godly living.

1:8 If believers **possess these qualities in increasing measure, they will** not be **useless or unfruitful in the knowledge of our Lord Jesus Christ.** A growing Christian produces spiritual fruit that God uses to bless others and bring joy. When you're growing in Christ, you don't have to strain to bear fruit. It will

emerge as naturally as apples develop on a healthy apple tree.

1:9-11 On the other hand, **the person who lacks** the qualities listed in 1:5-7 **is blind and shortsighted and has forgotten** the price Jesus paid on the cross to make spiritual growth and spiritual productivity possible (1:9). In this context, the admonition to **make every effort to confirm your calling and election** (1:10) is not about making sure we're saved. It's about making sure we are spiritually productive. God chose believers for the purpose of spiritual productivity (cf. 1 Pet 1:2, 15; 2:21). Therefore, we must ensure that the purpose for which God called us is being achieved. If we do, we **will never stumble** in this life (1:10) and **entry into the eternal kingdom** will be **richly provided** (1:11)—that is, with maximum rewards. It is possible to be saved yet enter heaven without rewards, but that is a destiny believers should strive to avoid.

1:12-14 Peter's purpose in writing this letter was to **remind** believers **about these things, even though** they knew them and were **established in the truth** (1:12). His urgency to issue the reminder stemmed not from any failure on the part of Christians but from the impending reality of his own death, about which Jesus **made** a **clear** prophecy (1:14; see John 21:18-19).

1:15 Just as believers are to "make every effort" to grow in their faith (1:5), Peter vowed to **make every effort** to teach God's people about spiritual growth **so that** they would be **able to recall these things at any time after [his] departure.**

III. THE TRUSTWORTHY PROPHETIC WORD (1:16-21)

1:16 Here Peter moves from the reason for his admonition to the authority behind it. He and his fellow apostles (see 1:1) could speak authoritatively about spiritual matters because they **were eyewitnesses of** Christ's majesty. They **did not follow cleverly contrived myths** but **made known . . . the power and coming of our Lord Jesus Christ.**

1:17-18 Peter saw Christ's majesty with particular clarity **on the holy mountain** (1:18)—that is, on the mount of transfiguration (see Matt 17:1-13; Mark 9:2-8; Luke 9:28-36)—**when the voice came to him from the Majestic Glory, saying, This is my beloved Son, with whom I am well-pleased** (1:17). One of Peter's goals for his readers was that they enjoy a glorious entrance to heaven and likewise behold Christ's unveiled magnificence. He also wanted them, like Jesus, to please the Father.

1:19 God's revelation of Christ's glory to Peter **strongly confirmed** the authority and truthfulness of the **prophetic word** Peter presented. Hence, believers **do well to pay attention to it.** God's Word, delivered through Peter, functions like **a lamp shining in a dark place**, sustaining believers in their spiritual walks until the divine seed in their souls blossoms to its full potential. Indeed, the entire Bible causes Christ (**the morning star**; see Rev 22:16) to come alive **in [our] hearts.**

1:20-21 Peter's prophetic word is to be understood in its proper context: as being on par with other **Scripture** (1:20). The defense of his authority is not boastful or proud, but is intended to help believers receive this letter appropriately and with full benefit. The authors of Scripture, he says, did not offer their **own interpretation** (1:20). Rather, they **spoke from God as they were carried along by the Holy Spirit** (1:21). Thus, the Bible is uncontaminated and completely without error in the same way that the Holy Spirit protected Jesus from sin in his conception and birth, even though it included human involvement. Thus, we can confidently say that Scripture's true author is God.

IV. FALSE TEACHERS (2:1-22)

2:1 In opposition to the prophets and apostles, who rightly convey the Word of God (cf. 1:16-21), **there were indeed false prophets among** God's **people** in former times, **just as there will be false teachers among** churches today and in days to come. Such teachers infiltrate the body of Christ with **destructive heresies**, false doctrines that lead to eternal destruction for those who believe them and for the false teachers. The assertion that such people deny **the Master who bought them** affirms an unlimited and universal *atonement*. But this doesn't imply a universal *salvation*. Christ's atoning work is available to all, but effective only for those who will receive it.

2:2-3 Peter warns against false teachers because **many** in the church **follow their depraved ways**, and pure Christianity is **maligned because of them** (2:2). What's more, they **exploit** the church **with made-up stories** (2:3) for wicked, self-centered, and self-serving purposes. The false teachers referenced here do not veer unknowingly into error but intentionally perpetuate lies. Therefore, they will receive **condemnation** and eternal **destruction** (2:3).

2:4-6 Peter gives three examples to demonstrate that God judges evil and that punishment, therefore, awaits false teachers. First,

God judged **the angels who sinned** and **cast them into hell** (2:4). This is a reference to the prehistoric rebellion of Satan and the angels who sided with him (see Isa 14:12-15). Second, God **didn't spare the ancient world . . . when he brought the flood on the world of the ungodly** (2:5; see Gen 6-8). This example highlights the fact that God preserves the godly even as he judges the wicked, a theme picked up again in 2:7-10. In the flood, the godly person spared was **Noah, a preacher of righteousness**, along with **seven** of his family members (2:5). Third, God **reduced the cities of Sodom and Gomorrah to ashes and condemned them to extinction, making them an example of what is coming to the ungodly** (2:6; see Gen 19:23-29). This example highlights the Lord's judgment of those who lead ungodly lifestyles and are unrepentant.

2:7-8 The God who judges also delivers. As he delivered Noah from the flood (2:5), he delivered Lot from Sodom, for Lot was a **righteous man** whose **righteous soul was tormented by the lawless deeds he saw and heard** (2:8). Even today, feeling tormented by wickedness is one indication of a person's desire for righteousness.

2:9-12 Here Peter brings the themes of judgment and deliverance together, noting that the Lord knows how to rescue the godly from trials and to keep the unrighteous under punishment for the day of judgment (2:9). Ultimate deliverance for believers will come at the rapture of the church (see 1 Thess 4:13-18), yet God also brings deliverance in history at times. For the wicked, there is no hope apart from repentance and faith in Christ, only the fearful expectation of eternal destruction in hell, especially for those who follow the polluting desires of the flesh and despise authority (2:10).

These verses begin a more detailed description of false teachers. Though such people identify with Christ's church publicly (2:1), they refuse to live under his lordship. They are bold and arrogant, mocking the spiritual power of Satan and demons—referenced here as glorious ones to denote their status as celestial beings, but not any moral goodness within them (2:10). In contrast, angels, who are greater in might and power than evil principalities, know better than to treat such beings flippantly (2:11). False teachers are like irrational animals in their lack of moral constraint and their reckless attack of powers they do not understand. Also like wild animals, the false teachers eventually will be captured and destroyed (2:12).

2:13-14 Such false teachers are not only evil at night when their deeds can be hidden. They are evil in broad daylight as well. They are flagrant with their unrighteousness, feasting at the Lord's Table and fellowshipping with the church while using their Christian veneers to hide evil intentions. In the end, they will be paid back with harm for the harm they have done (2:13). Such false teachers see women as tools to be used, preying particularly upon unstable people. They are greedy as well, like children (2:14).

2:15-16 The greed of false teachers is like that of the Old Testament false prophet Balaam . . . who loved the wages of wickedness (2:15). Peter sheds light on the narrative of Balaam in Numbers 22–24, clarifying that he attempted to curse Israel in hopes of financial gain. However, a rebuke from a speechless donkey illustrated that an animal had more spiritual insight than Balaam (see Num 22:28-30). So too with the false teachers.

2:17 Like springs without water and clouds without rain, the false teachers arrive with a pretense of offering refreshment but in reality offer nothing to sustain spiritual life. Thus, they are destined for the gloom of darkness, eternal hell.

2:18-19 Contrary to the way of spiritual growth, false teachers use their communication abilities to arouse the fleshly desires of recent converts to Christianity—referenced here as people who have barely escaped—and drag them backward into their old lifestyles rather than forward in righteousness (2:18). The false teachers promise . . . freedom to those who follow their counsel. But they deliver, and experience, slavery to corruption (2:19).

2:20-21 When Christians are tricked by false teachers into returning to their previous, unrighteous lifestyle that the knowledge of Christ had delivered them from, they will find themselves in a worse state since they now know better.

2:22 In the end, those believers who follow false teachers become like them in their lifestyles. They seek ultimately to satisfy their sinful desires above all else. That situation is depicted by appropriate proverbs, portraying such lifestyles as behaving like disgusting animals.

V. THE DAY OF THE LORD (3:1-13)

3:1-2 The original readers of this epistle were Peter's dear friends and the recipients of at least two letters from him (3:2). The other letter referenced could be either 1 Peter or a letter that has been lost. In either case, the purpose of both (3:1) was to remind believers of the words previously spoken by the holy prophets and the command of Jesus given through [his] apostles (3:2).

3:3-4 The specific reminder Peter sought to give was that **in the last days** before the return of Jesus, **scoffers** would make light of divine realities and not take seriously the things God said. The reason for their scoffing is that God's truth interferes with their immoral lifestyles. Such people want to follow **their own evil desires**, and doing so requires keeping God distant (3:3). This is a posture of deism more than atheism. The scoffers believe there is a God, but they claim he has little to do with daily reality. In particular, they deny that Jesus will return to earth. They argue that **all things continue as they have been since the beginning of creation** (3:4). The incorrect implication of their observation—which itself is inaccurate, as Peter will demonstrate—is that world affairs will always continue as they are, and God will not intervene in human history.

3:5-6 Those with a scoffing mentality **deliberately overlook** the fact that God has intervened in human history numerous times. For one, he intervened **long ago** by bringing **the heavens . . . into being** and bringing forth **the earth . . . from water** (Gen 1). This happened **by the word of God** (3:5)—that is, when God spoke at creation, things happened. Likewise today, when God speaks his authoritative Word over an individual's life, things happen. The scoffers also ignore Genesis 6–8, where **the world of that time perished when it was flooded** (3:6). Here is yet another example of God's obvious intervention in the affairs of humankind.

3:7 By the same word that created the world and brought the flood, God will intervene in human history again by destroying **the present heavens and earth** with **fire** and bringing a **day of judgment and destruction of the ungodly.** So don't scoff, saying, "I don't see God." Those who do so have forgotten what he has done. When God is ready to invade your situation, he can reorganize reality and bring the solution to your problem.

3:8-9 Shifting focus from the scoffers to the recipients of this letter, Peter tells his **dear friends** they must not **overlook** God's timetable. When it seems God's work is taking a long time, Christians should remember that

God can do in **one day** what it would take humans **a thousand years** to do (3:8). God's apparent slowness to intervene on some occasions is not a **delay** of **his promise, as some understand delay.** Rather, it is an opportunity for humans to fulfill their responsibilities. The supreme example of this principle is that God delays final judgment because he does not want **any to perish but all to come to repentance** and believe the gospel (3:9). When we fulfill our responsibilities, we'll see more of God's sovereign action. Many are waiting on God, when God is actually waiting on them.

3:10 The day of the Lord in Scripture is distinguished from the day of man. The former refers to instances when God intervenes in the affairs of man, and the latter refers to instances when sinful man appears to be in control of the world. The phrase "day of the Lord" denotes different divine interventions in different Scripture passages. Here it refers specifically to the coming great tribulation period when God will govern the affairs of man in a more direct and open way than he does at present. At the end of the tribulation, **the heavens will pass away with a loud noise, the elements will burn and be dissolved, and the earth and the works on it will be disclosed** (cf. 3:12).

3:11-12 Since the things this world values **are to be dissolved in this way,** believers should stop focusing on worldly success and achievement. Instead, they should focus on **holy conduct and godliness** (3:11). In other words, we must abandon what is temporary and embrace what is eternal. Doing so will **hasten** the **coming** of **the day of God** (3:12). Peter is not saying humans can change God's sovereign timetable. Rather, when a believer focuses every moment of life on pleasing God and doing his will, time seems to fly by like it does on a busy workday in which we hasten from one task to another.

3:13 Based on [God's] promise, his followers are to be active in their obedience as they wait for divine intervention in their lives, waiting ultimately **for new heavens and a new earth, where righteousness dwells**—a promise God made to his people long ago (see Isa 65:17; 66:22).

VI. FINAL WORDS (3:14-18)

3:14 This final section recaps some of the themes highlighted elsewhere in the letter. In light of the imminent return of Christ, believers are to **make every effort** (cf. 1:5, 15) to be holy and godly. As sacrificial animals in the Old Testament were to be **without spot or blemish in [God's] sight**, new covenant believers are to be without moral defect before the Lord, repenting when they do sin.

3:15 The Lord's delay in coming is designed to give men and women time to repent of their sin and come to **salvation**. Therefore, we must take advantage of his patience by repenting, rather than presuming upon his patience and living for unrighteous purposes. The apostle **Paul**, Peter says, **has written** similar admonitions in his epistles.

3:16 Paul's letters spoke often of godly living and the Lord's patience (e.g., Rom 2:4; 3:25; 9:22), but false teachers apparently distorted Paul's statements because they were **hard to understand**. The distortions did not reflect any fault in Paul's writings. Rather, the fault was with **the untaught and unstable** false teachers who **[twisted] them to their own destruction**. A passing comment acknowledges that Paul's letters already were regarded by the church as among **the Scriptures**.

3:17 Because false teachers are going to infiltrate the church, believers must **be on [their] guard** not to be **led away by the error of** men who talk like Christians but live rebellious, ungodly lives. Maintaining a **stable position** spiritually is a key to godly living.

3:18 The theme of spiritual growth bookends the letter, recurring here after its introduction in 1:1-15. Believers are to **grow** in their understanding of grace and their experiential **knowledge of our Lord and Savior Jesus Christ**. They should resist false teachers, focusing on growth and spiritual development in a way that glorifies God **both now and to the day of eternity**.

1 JOHN

INTRODUCTION

Author

ANCIENT MANUSCRIPTS UNANImously name the author of this letter as John, the son of Zebedee who also authored the Fourth Gospel. The style and vocabulary of 1–3 John and the Fourth Gospel are so similar that it seems they must have come from the same hand. Some scholars, however, believe a different John (that is, someone other than the apostle) is responsible for these New Testament books. Others claim they are a product of a "Johannine school"—the work of early followers of John. Nevertheless, the view with the best support is that John, the disciple of Jesus, is the author.

Historical Background

Second-century Christian sources report that John eventually relocated to Ephesus and ministered to churches there. He continued his pastoral work in that region until nearly AD 100. Thus, Ephesus is the likely location from which John penned 1–3 John. These letters could have been written at any time in the last quarter of the first century.

Message and Purpose

John is the apostle of intimacy. He's very concerned with our fellowship—that is, our closeness with the Lord. His epistles form a trilogy of intimacy. John wrote to Christians, whom he addressed in 1 John as "little children" (2:1, 28; 4:4; 5:21). He speaks of obedience, walking with God in righteousness, submission to the truth, and functioning together in love as being key elements of intimacy with God.

In 2 John 1:1, the apostle addresses the church as "the elect lady and her children," since the church is the bride of Christ. He writes about truth and love. *Truth* is the absolute standard by which reality is measured, and love is the expression of that truth in our care for others. John says that when the church operates in truth and love, we experience true intimacy with God

In 3 John, he addresses Gaius, a hospitable leader who loved to bring in outside teachers who presented the truth. But the church had a problem in the person of Diotrephes, who tried to reject these sound teachers. So John warned about this power-seeking man and the evil behind any attempt to stop true teachers of the Word.

All three epistles seek to promote intimacy with the King as well as with the fellow citizens of the kingdom.

VIDEO   INTRO

www.bhpublishinggroup.com/qr/te/62_00

Outline

I. Fellowship with God by Walking in the Light (1:1-10)

II. Obey, Remain, and Love (2:1-11)

III. Spiritual Maturity and the Enemies of Fellowship (2:12-29)

IV. Being a Child of God and Loving the Children of God (3:1-24)

V. The Spirit of Truth and the Love of God (4:1-19)

VI. Intimacy with God and Praying with Confidence (4:20–5:21)

1 JOHN

I. FELLOWSHIP WITH GOD BY WALKING IN THE LIGHT (1:1-10)

1:1-2 The apostle John wrote the Gospel of John to tell sinners how to become saints. He wrote 1 John to tell saints how to enjoy sainthood. The Gospel of John was written to explain how to enter into a relationship with God through faith alone in Christ alone for the forgiveness of sins and the free gift of eternal life. This first epistle of John was written to explain how to enjoy fellowship with God. The Gospel of John describes how to enter eternity; 1 John describes how to experience intimacy with God in history. Just as a marriage or parent-child relationship can be legally secure yet lack intimate fellowship, believers in Christ are legally declared righteous, but do not automatically enjoy intimate fellowship with the Lord. First John is about the test of intimacy, not the test of conversion.

What was from the beginning refers to Jesus Christ and the **life** he offers. When John talks about Jesus, he's not delivering second-hand information. He's communicating about what he saw and **observed** and **touched**. The Son of God **revealed** himself to John and the other apostles in person. Thus, John is essentially saying, "We were there; we know Jesus." And now **we testify and declare to you the eternal life that was with the Father.**

1:3 Why is John declaring this? What's the theme of his letter? **Fellowship.** The Greek word translated "fellowship" (*koinonia*) could be used to speak of a business venture or partnership. It means to share something in common. It's important, though, to understand what God means by biblical fellowship.

When you trusted in Christ as your Savior, you entered into a legal relationship with God. But it's possible to have a legal relationship with God en route to heaven without enjoying closeness with God on earth. John wrote this letter so that its readers could **have fellowship with us** [the apostles]; **and indeed our fellowship is with the Father and with his Son Jesus Christ.**

You can't have fellowship with God apart from the apostles. They experienced Jesus Christ firsthand (1:1-3). People who skip what the apostles have to say about him will invent their own false spirituality. But how can you, in the twenty-first century, hang out with the apostles so you can have fellowship with God that they enjoyed? This goes beyond the legal relationship of justification to intimate communion with the Savior that is available to all believers. The truth of the Bible, when applied to the life of the believer, enhances their fellowship and spiritual intimacy with God.

Cities establish high occupancy vehicle (HOV) lanes to prevent having too many cars clogging up the interstates. In a sense, they want you to be in fellowship while traveling to work. God wants you traveling a HOV lane in life, and he also wants to be your companion in the car.

1:4 John writes so that their **joy may be complete.** It's possible to be a Christian and lack joy. It's possible to merely go through the motions. But John wants his audience to know joy. And when you experience meaningful, intimate fellowship with God through Jesus Christ, you will experience true joy that is not dependent on your circumstances and that is available nowhere else. True joy transcends external circumstances. It is stability on the inside in spite of what is occurring on the outside.

1:5 After concluding the prologue to his letter in 1:1-4, John gets down to business: **This is the message we have heard from him and declare to you.** What is it? What does John want these Christians to know? **God is light, and there is absolutely no darkness in him.** This isn't a mere spiritual platitude. If you want to enjoy closeness with God, you must embrace the truth that *he is light* because it has significant implications for your life.

When John describes God as "light," he calls to mind Jesus's words as recorded in his Gospel: "The light has come into the world, and people loved darkness rather than the light because their deeds were evil" (John 3:19). The function of light is to reveal things as they truly are. Light exposes. If you shine a light down a city alley in the middle of night, you'll see cockroaches scatter because they want to do their dirty work in secret. If you want God's personal presence and activity in your life, you must be willing to allow his light to expose your sinful thoughts, attitudes, speech, and actions that are inconsistent with his character.

1:6-7 If you claim to have **fellowship with** God but **walk in darkness**, John says, "You're a liar" (1:6). Fellowship with God isn't validated by your lips; it's validated by your walk. Praising God and shouting "amen" have their place. But intimacy with God must be demonstrated through actions, not merely through vocabulary. We have fellowship with the Lord and fellow believers when **we walk in the light as he . . . is in the light** (1:7).

This, of course, doesn't mean you must live without sinning. Only God *is* light (1:5); you are called to *walk in* the light. You must be willing to let God expose the sin in you. Those who walk in the light aren't sinless. But the light enables them to see their sin so they may repent. When that happens, **the blood of Jesus . . . cleanses us** (1:7) so that we may grow in sanctification, spiritual maturity, and intimacy with the Lord. When holy people see themselves in God's light, they see their dirt. And when they see the dirt, they want God to deal with it—something he is delighted to do.

Only as we live fully exposed to the truth of God is the ongoing cleansing work of **the blood of Christ** activated to reveal, cleanse, and empower us to address the sin that has been exposed. Then fellowship with God is maintained and expanded. Failure to do this keeps God's work dormant in the life of the believer (see 2 Cor 3:17-18).

1:8-10 If you deny there is **sin** in your life, you're **deceiving** yourself (1:8) because you're certainly not deceiving anyone else. On our best days, we fall miles short of God's holy standard. But **if we confess our sins, he is faithful and righteous to forgive us our sins and to cleanse us** (1:9). Why? Well, when we confess our sins to God, we are agreeing with what God's Word reveals about us. We are admitting that what the light exposes is not just a mistake, a bad habit, or a mere product of our upbringing. It's sin. This allows forgiveness and cleansing power to flow. To deny your sin is to call God **a liar** and forfeit the hope of his **word** doing its transforming work in your life (1:10).

II. OBEY, REMAIN, AND LOVE (2:1-11)

2:1 John's love for these Christians is clear. He speaks as a father to his **little children**, as a pastor to his flock. He has just told them (more or less) that they're crazy if they deny their sin (1:8-10). And in fact, the closer you get to God, the more sinful stains his light will reveal in you. But this doesn't grant you license to sin! On the contrary, John says, **I am writing you these things so that you may not sin.** John wants his readers to know intimate and joy-filled fellowship with God, which requires confessing sin and turning from it.

The reason why confession and forgiveness are possible is because of the advocacy of Jesus: **if anyone does sin, we have an advocate with the Father—Jesus Christ**. The concept here is of a defense attorney in a court of law. If you are a believer, Jesus represents you before the bar of God's judgment. You were a bankrupt sinner who couldn't afford a lawyer, but the Father appointed his own Son in your defense. This advocate doesn't share your sin problem; he's the only **righteous one**. He paid your debt on the cross, and his shed blood continues to cleanse you today.

2:2 Not only is Jesus our advocate, but he's **the atoning sacrifice**—or the "propitiation"—**for our sins.** *Propitiation* is one of those ten-dollar theological words. It means Jesus has appeased God's just wrath against sin by his sacrificial death for the whole human race (i.e., unlimited atonement). He satisfied (i.e., propitiation) God's righteous demands so that the Creator is favorably disposed toward those who place faith in him for eternal life. God himself paid the price for a legal relationship and intimate fellowship with you.

2:3-5 How does our fellowship with God grow deeper? **This is how we know that we know him: if we keep his commands** (2:3). **Whoever keeps his word, truly in him the love of God is made complete** (2:5). Obedience rooted in love is the requirement for ongoing, deepening fellowship with God. To "know him" is a reference to intimate fellowship not justification, since John's readers are already believers (see 2:1, 28; 4:4; 5:21). We are saved by grace. But grace doesn't negate the commandments of God. Rather, grace grants you the ability to fulfill them and grow in love. When this happens, you will increase your experiential knowledge of closeness with God.

2:6 The one who says he remains in him should walk just as he walked. The Greek word for "remains" (or "abides") is a favorite of John (see John 15:4-7). In contemporary,

colloquial language it means to "hang out with." You can't hang out with Christ without him rubbing off on you.

When it comes to making tea, some people dip their teabags in and out of the hot water. Many Christians approach their relationship with Jesus like this—dipping in and out of church on Sunday mornings, with little change resulting. Other tea drinkers place their teabags in the water and let them remain. In time, the tea seeps into the water and transforms it. For Christ to influence and transform your life, you must remain in him.

2:7-8 A question naturally arises: to grow in intimacy with God, which commandments do I need to keep? John reduces the answer to one. As will be clear in 2:9-11, he's thinking specifically of the commandment to love one another. It summarizes the others. John says it's **old** and yet **new**. It's old because it's found in Leviticus 19:18, but it's also new because it's the governing commandment for the Christian life. Jesus said loving God and loving neighbor are the two great commandments (see Matt 22:36-40). If love has a fresh ongoing effect in your life, all the other commandments will fall into place.

2:9-11 Love has become watered down in our world. "I love chocolate cake." "I love this dress." "I love that TV show." For many people, love describes sentimental feelings. But John will tell his readers in 4:8 that "God is love." It is part of his inexhaustible nature for the good of the beloved and for his own glory.

When you love your **brother or sister**, you seek to comprehensively and righteously meet his or her need in a way that brings glory to God. It is no mere expression of feelings but an expression of something higher, something eternal. When this happens, you remain **in the light** and have **no cause for stumbling** (2:10). Love for God and neighbor allow you to see clearly and avoid falling into sin.

However, the one who **hates his brother or sister is in the darkness** (2:9, 11) and, thus, out of fellowship with the God of light. Such a person is **blinded** and **doesn't know where he's going** (2:11). Walking around in darkness never ends well.

III. SPIRITUAL MATURITY AND THE
ENEMIES OF FELLOWSHIP (2:12-29)

2:12-14 In these verses, John reminds his audience of who they are. He begins by telling them they are **little children** whose **sins have been forgiven** (2:12). All Christians enjoy God's judicial forgiveness and have been adopted as his children. Then, in 2:13-14, John divides believers into three categories: **fathers . . . young men . . . children** (this is a different Greek word for children than is used in 2:12). These three terms correspond to different stages of spiritual development. Their goal is maturity.

Children . . . have come to know the Father (2:14). We all begin as children—both physically and spiritually. And babies get to know their daddies. New Christians come to know God as Father. But we must not remain children. So, next are the **young men**, the spiritual adolescents. In the teen years, there are many battles and temptations. But John wants people to know that they need not listen to Satan's lies; they **have conquered the evil one** through Christ. Finally, there are the mature believers: **fathers.** They **have come to know the one who is from the beginning** (2:13, 14). They have persevered over the long haul. Circumstances do not dictate their actions. Their eyes are on the eternal. In which developmental stage are you?

2:15 When the moon shines, it's actually reflecting the light of the sun. Sometimes the earth gets in the way, though, so that the moon's light is diminished. Similarly, we have an enemy that prevents us from reflecting the *Son's* light on us. That enemy is called the world.

Do not love the world. When John talks about "the world," he's not talking about planet earth. He's talking about an organized system headed by Satan that draws us away from God's love and will. If you love the world, you lose intimate fellowship with God. You love the world when it owns your affections and governs your choices by getting you to exclude God.

2:16-17 What does the world offer you? First, it promises to satisfy legitimate desires in illegitimate ways (**the lust of the flesh**). Eating is legitimate; gluttony is worldly. Sex is legitimate; immorality is worldly. Second, the world tempts your mind through what your eyes see (**the lust of the eyes**). The biblical word for this is *covetousness*, which is desiring and pursuing that which is not legitimate for you to have. Third, there is **the pride in one's possessions** (2:16)—that is, living to impress others. What those in love with the world forget, however, is that **the world with its lust is passing away.** Worldliness makes the "now" more important than eternity. But you are passing through, and the world is passing by. It's transient. Only **the one who does the will of God remains forever** (2:17). The price tag for loving the world is the loss of personal intimacy with God.

2:18-19 John wants them to know the time: **It is the last hour.** He means the last segment of time, from the coming of Christ until his return. During this period of history, we know **antichrist is coming** but **even now many antichrists have come** (2:18). Though Antichrist will appear during the tribulation when the church is raptured (see Dan 9:26-27; 1 Thess 4:13-18; 2 Thess 2:3; Rev 11:2; 13:1-8), *little* antichrists are active already. An "antichrist" *opposes* and *replaces* Christ with the goal of distracting and derailing Christians from pursuing Christ. Some antichrists had been involved among the believers to whom John was writing. However, like Judas, they eventually demonstrated their true colors and agenda by departing (2:19). They tried **to deceive** Christians (2:26), but when the truth reigned, they left.

2:20-29 What did these antichrists teach? It was probably an early form of a second-century heresy called Gnosticism that imparted false views about Jesus. Regardless, John says they were liars who denied **that Jesus is the Christ** (2:22). And, importantly, **no one**

who denies the Son has the Father (2:23). John understands what the Lord Jesus himself taught when he said, "No one comes to the Father except through me" (John 14:6). Access to God is only found in his Son, Jesus Christ.

What power and protection do believers have against these liars? **The anointing and the truth** (2:20-21). "The anointing" is not some special gift shared by only elite clergy. John is addressing spiritual "children" (2:18). Every Christian has the anointing: the internal teaching ministry of the Holy Spirit who illuminates the believer's mind to understand and apply God's truth, as well as to detect deception. Paul refers to it as having the "mind of Christ" (1 Cor 2:16). Jesus told his disciples that the Holy Spirit would teach them and guide them into truth (John 14:26; 16:13). Indeed, **the anointing you received from him remains in you** and **teaches you** (2:27).

What you have heard from the beginning is to remain in you (2:24). John's point here is that the Holy Spirit's ministry always remains available to teach Christians, but the truth ("what you have heard from the beginning") *must* remain in us. Think of it like satellite TV. The satellite communicates, but your satellite dish must receive the signal. The power of the Holy Spirit is available to every believer, but many believers do not operate in a position of dependence on the Spirit because their satellite dishes only function on Sunday mornings.

So what should we do? **Remain in him** (2:28). Again, there's that word that John loves so much (2:6, 10, 27). If you remain or abide in Jesus, you will **have confidence and not be ashamed before him at his coming** (2:28). A Christian can be accepted but not "acceptable." A child who plays in the mud, for instance, is accepted by his parents; he is not, however, in an acceptable condition. Live everyday on high alert, looking for Jesus to return, and it will influence how you live.

IV. BEING A CHILD OF GOD AND LOVING THE CHILDREN OF GOD (3:1-24)

3:1 See what great love the Father has given us that we should be called God's children. Few verses in the Bible are more beautiful than this one. But to experience victory, you need to *know* who your Daddy is. This "Father" business isn't mere religious talk or an attempt to tap into the power of positive thinking. If you are a Christian, you have a perfect heavenly Father who loves you and who doesn't share any of the failures of your earthly father. What's more, he's the King of creation. You are royalty. Nevertheless, do not be surprised when the world rejects you; it rejected God's Son because **it didn't know him** either. You're in good company. On the other hand, if the world loves you, that's when you should worry.

3:2-3 We are God's children now, but **what we will be has not yet been revealed** (3:2). Your new spiritual life is currently invisible to the world. But at Christ's return, you will be miraculously changed, and it will be manifest to all. At his appearing, the graves will be robbed, and we will be transformed with resurrected bodies. So look to him with **this hope**, and he will purify you inwardly as you await your outward renewal (3:3).

3:4-5 Everyone who commits sin practices lawlessness (3:4). When you sin, you're a lawbreaker; it's an act of rebellion against God. It doesn't matter whether you sin one time or a thousand times. This is why the Son of God came: to **take away sins**. And only he is qualified for the job because **there is no sin in him** (3:5).

3:6-10 These verses have confused many, so let me be clear: If John is saying that Christians do not sin at all, then no one is saved. Even on your best Holy-Spirit led day, you still sin. In considering this passage, we need to remember that John is communicating to Christians about how to have intimacy with God.

Everyone who remains in him does not sin (3:6). John said "there is no sin in" Christ

(3:5). Therefore, whoever remains or abides in him does not sin either. We are called to remain in him (2:6; John 15:5-7). So, the problem is this: when we sin, it's because we're not remaining in Christ. In 3:9, John says, **Everyone who has been born of God does not sin.** The reason is because God's **seed remains in him** (3:9). "If anyone is in Christ," Paul says, "he is a new creation" (2 Cor 5:17). When you placed your faith in Jesus Christ, God gave you new life—which John describes as God's "seed." Every Christian is born again. This new spiritual life or seed is from God, so it is pure and sinless.

Why, then, do we still sin in thought, word, and deed even though we'd prefer not to? Because the old part of us (Paul calls our unredeemed humanity "the flesh") is still contaminated by sin. Paul wrestles with this in Romans 7:13-25. The new life of Christ is planted in us in seed form, but we still bear the damage of sin in our souls. When Christ returns, the flesh will be completely eradicated, and we will be without sin. Until then, we must continually repent of sin, submit to God's Word, and walk with the Spirit so that the seed of the new divine nature may grow (see 1 Pet 1:23; 2 Pet 1:4).

Don't be deceived. **The one who does what is right is righteous** (3:7). **The one who commits sin is of the devil** (3:8). How, then, can a believer do what is right *and* commit sin in the space of a few seconds? Consider Peter. He boldly confessed that Jesus is the Christ, and Jesus blessed him because God had revealed it to him (see Matt 16:13-17). However, in no time, Jesus told Peter, "Get behind me, Satan," when he denied that Christ must suffer (Matt 16:21-23).

Throughout each day, your actions will either be influenced by God or the devil. Satan can't make you sin, but he can entice you. So, to whom will you listen? Will you be "of the devil" so that he gets credit for your deeds? Or will you live by the truth, come to the light, and do works for which God gets the credit (see John 3:21)? Turn to Christ who can render powerless **the devil's works** in your life (1 John 3:8). To avoid living a life that is **not of God** takes more than merely carrying your Bible and saying, "hallelujah." It requires doing **what is right** and loving fellow believers in submission to the Holy Spirit (3:10).

3:11 How important is it to love your brothers and sisters in Christ? Imagine a patient claims to have the flu but has no symptoms. A doctor would say, "You don't have the flu." Similarly, the ultimate "symptom" or proof of your vertical intimacy with God is your horizontal love for his children. **We should love one another.** From the beginning, the apostles heard this message from Jesus himself (see John 13:35). Biblical love is not a mere emotion. *Love* is demonstrating selfless concern for our brothers and sisters in Christ in response to God's grace to us. It is the decision to compassionately, righteously, and responsibly seek the well-being of another.

3:12-13 John points to biological brothers to illustrate this point about spiritual brothers. **Cain . . . murdered his brother . . . because his deeds were evil, and his brother's were righteous** (3:12). Cain envied Abel's acceptance by God, and it led him into hatred. Therefore, **do not be surprised . . . if the world hates you** (3:13). As Cain hated his brother because of his righteousness, many in the world will hate you for living righteously and loving others.

3:14-15 **The one who does not love remains in death** (3:14). Remember, John is writing to Christians who are saved. It's possible, then, for a believer to operate in the realm of death. If a believer hates his brother, he is not remaining in Christ but remaining in death. **Everyone who hates his brother or sister is a murderer.** To hate is to murder in your heart, and **no murderer has eternal life residing in him** (3:15). Notice that "residing" is the same Greek word translated in John as "abiding." So again, he's not referring to salvation but to enjoyment of the Christian life and intimacy with God. If you hate your fellow believers, you will not experience the blessings and fellowship of God.

3:16-17 John gave his readers a negative example (3:12). His positive example is the ultimate expression of love. Jesus **laid down his life for us** (3:16). Observe the love of Christ. First, he "laid down his life." It was voluntary, a willing action. Second, it was "for us." It was vicarious. He sacrificed in our place.

What are the implications for us? **We should also lay down our lives for our brothers and sisters** (3:16). Now, few of us will ever be faced with a scenario that would call upon us to give up our lives for others. That's why John doesn't leave it there. But if you see **a fellow believer in need**, remember that love expresses itself by providing for him (3:17). Meeting the needs of fellow Christians—whether physical, emotional, or financial—is the most practical demonstration of love and the most telling symptom of fellowship with God.

3:18-24 Beware of merely declaring your love with your mouth. We must **not love in word or speech, but in action and in truth** (3:18). What your lips proclaim, your life must support. God promises two things. First, if we love in action and truth, we **will reassure our hearts ... whenever our hearts condemn us** (3:19-20). The idea here is that when your heart condemns you unjustifiably, God gives you peace or assurance. Biblical peace is inner tranquility regardless of external circumstances. When you serve other believers in love, God will calm your heart when you are in turmoil.

The second promise is that when **we keep his commands** (3:22)—that is, **believe** in **Jesus Christ** and **love one another** (3:23)—we will **have confidence before God and receive whatever we ask from him** (3:21-22). Lack of confidence is a tremendous stumbling block to prayer. But when you love others and act as an answer to their prayers, you can be confident that your Father will put things in motion to answer your prayer. To put this idea into an everyday expression: what goes around comes around. When this happens, you will remain in God, and he will remain in you by his **Spirit** (3:24). That's intimacy.

V. THE SPIRIT OF TRUTH AND THE LOVE OF GOD (4:1-19)

4:1-3 The evil one cannot sever your relationship with God, but he can disrupt your fellowship with him. Thus, John warns, **Do not believe every spirit.** In other words, be able to discern truth from error. You need to determine which spiritual claims **are from God**, for the world is full of **false prophets.** There are those who will deceive you, offering an unbiblical spiritual experience. They may even come in the name of Jesus. So if you watch Christian television, listen to Christian radio, or read Christian books, be discerning. "Satan disguises himself as an angel of light" (2 Cor 11:14).

How do you **test the spirits** (4:1)? Well, **every spirit who confesses that Jesus Christ has come in the flesh is from God** (4:2). The one who denies this is **the spirit of the antichrist** (4:3; see 2:18-23). According to early Christian tradition, a heresy circulated in John's day that distinguished between Jesus (a man) and Christ (a supernatural being). Proponents taught that Christ descended on Jesus at his baptism and departed at the crucifixion.

To this lie John says, "No." Jesus *is* the Christ (2:22), and Jesus Christ came "in the flesh" (4:2). He is the unique, eternal Son of God who offers salvation from sin only by grace through faith in him. He is the God-Man. He limited himself because he has a human body, but he is limitless because he's God. His mother gave birth to him because he's man, but he created her because he's God. He went to sleep because he's a man, but he commanded the wind and waves to go to sleep because he's God. The truth about the uniqueness of Jesus must be your spiritual foundation.

4:4-6 What resources are available to you? First, you have the Holy Spirit whom God gave you (3:24). **The one who is in you is greater than the one who is in the world** (4:4). Do not fear the devil and his false prophets, for you have "the Spirit of truth" (John 16:13).

The tremendous pressure in the ocean's depths can crush a human diver. But if you descend inside a pressurized diving bell, it exerts pressure *outward* to protect you from destruction. When Christians go into the world, they will experience extreme pressure—especially as they go deeper. We can't prevent it. But have no fear. The pressure inside of you is greater than the pressure on you.

Second, John tells his readers, **we are from God. Anyone who knows God listens to us** (4:6). The apostles were Jesus's chosen representatives. They witnessed his resurrection, and they composed the New Testament under the inspiration of the Holy Spirit. Read and know what they wrote. This is how **we know the Spirit of truth and the spirit of deception** (4:6). If someone teaches contrary to the objective truth of Scripture, he or she is a false prophet.

4:7-8 John continues through chapter 4 with a dominant theme in his letter. Fellowship with God is demonstrated and attained when Christians love each other. If **love is from God**, then there is no option. We *must* **love one another** (4:7). This is not rocket science. Since **God is love**, an absence of love in your life reveals an absence of fellowship with God. It indicates that you don't **know** him like you claim you do (4:8). As sure as the magnetic pull of the earth causes a compass to point north, the magnetic pull of God's love at work in your heart will always point you to other brothers and sisters who need love.

4:9-10 In these verses, John gives us one of the clearest definitions of love in the Bible. First, love is visible: **God's love was revealed.** Invisible love is no love at all. Second, love is an act of the will: God **sent his Son** (4:9). To love someone requires a decision to act on his behalf.

Third, love is sacrificial. It cost God **his one and only Son.** He didn't throw you his leftovers; he provided his best. Why? **So that we might live through him** (4:9). He saw our deepest need and gave of himself. If you profess love without also embracing inconvenience and being willing to give up your rights, you don't understand God's love.

Fourth, love serves the unlovable. It's **not that we loved God, but that he loved us.** We hated him. We were fools, rebelling against the King of the universe. Nevertheless, he set his love on us. You're going to love people who won't respond in kind. But they need your love nonetheless.

Fifth, love addresses sin. God **sent his Son to be the atoning sacrifice for our sins** (4:10; see 2:2). You can't ignore sin in the body of Christ. Only Jesus can atone for our sin. But we must, with humility and love, help those caught in it.

4:11-13 Considering the example of God's love, we **must love one another** (4:11). **No one has ever seen God.** But **if we love one another**, he **remains in us** and **his love is made complete in us**—it accomplishes its goal (4:10). You can't see the wind, but you can see its effects. People can't see God, but they should see the love of God operating through you. Love God's children, and he will grant his rich, intimate fellowship to you through **his Spirit** (4:13).

4:14-16 The **Son** of God is the **Savior** of the world (4:14). If you have trusted in him, he has delivered you from sin, Satan, and death. But he wants to use you to communicate that saving love to others. **Whoever confesses that Jesus is the Son of God** participates with God in his delivering activity (4:15). **The one who remains in love remains in God** (4:16). Remember, to "remain" is to "hang out" (see 2:6). Hang out with love—seek out opportunities to express God's definition of love (see 4:9-10)—and God will hang out with you. Living in the atmosphere of love means you are living in the atmosphere of God.

4:17-19 When **love is made complete** in you in this way, you can **have confidence in the day of judgment** (4:17). Every believer will stand before the judgment seat of Christ. Don't think of it as a trial to determine your salvation but as the Judge's opportunity to evaluate the Christian life you lived (see 2 Cor 5:10). In spite of your sins and failures, if you actively sought to minister in love to members of God's family, you will be able to stand with confidence on that day because "love covers a multitude of" offenses (1 Pet 4:8). You will have no reason to fear. Mature, **perfect love drives out fear** (4:18). Our capacity for love is only possible **because he first loved us** (4:19).

VI. INTIMACY WITH GOD AND PRAYING
WITH CONFIDENCE (4:20–5:21)

4:20-21 Too many Christians began their spiritual lives with excitement about Jesus only to become burdened and discouraged at some point. Their abundant life suddenly felt more like a back-bender. According to John, victory over this problem is achieved when faith in Christ leads to love of God's children.

Your love for God is not measured by what you say ("**I love God**") but what you do. You cannot claim to **love** the invisible **God** if you refuse to actively **love** the Christian **brother or sister** standing in front of you (4:20). Don't fool yourself. God has intertwined loving him and loving his children. You can't disconnect them (4:21).

5:1 So, exactly whom should you love? The one **who believes that Jesus is the Christ.** Your brother in Christ is not determined by his race, his level of education, his social status, the church he attends, or the Bible version he carries. If he trusts in Christ alone as his sin bearer, he's your brother.

5:2 So, how do **we know that we love God's children**? **When we love God and obey his commands** (2:3-4; John 14:15). As we've seen, the primary command John has in mind is love for fellow believers (3:23). You are not an only child in the family of God. To ignore your brother in Christ is to cut yourself off from intimacy with God.

5:3 If your Christian life is weighing you down, you're not living the real Christian life. How do I know? Because God's **commands are not a burden.** When obedience is driven by love, it loses its burden. Ask any mother of a newborn. A mother doesn't feed, change, clean, and comfort her baby because of a command—but because of love. Does she become tired and dirty? Of course. But the work isn't a burden per se because it's her baby she's attending. When you love others based on your love for Jesus, he says in effect, "Hitch up to me, and I'll do the pulling" (Matt 11:30).

5:4-5 If you have trusted in Christ by **faith,** you have already **conquered the world.** The faith that saved you, that gave you positional, spiritual victory at conversion, will continue to give you victory through what you do. Why? Because the faith that acts—that loves one's neighbor—is placed in the same **Jesus** (5:5).

5:6-8 Do you believe God? John tells his readers that (1) **Jesus Christ . . . came by water and blood**, and (2) **the Spirit** validates this (5:6). These **three** witnesses **testify** together: **the Spirit, the water, and the blood** (5:7-8). The *water* refers to Christ's baptism when the Father himself praised his Son and the Holy Spirit descended on him (see Matt 3:16-17). The *blood* refers to Christ's sacrificial death on the cross when darkness covered the land, the earth quaked, and the temple veil split in two (Matt 27:45, 51). In these events, God gave testimony to the truthfulness of his Son and his mission. The third witness is the *Spirit*, who validates on the inside what God does on the outside.

5:9-12 A basic principle of God's Word is that a "matter must be established by the testimony of two or three witnesses" (2 Cor 13:1; see Deut 19:15). The tragic truth is that in spite of the threefold testimony God has provided (5:6-8), too many believe man rather than God. That's equivalent to calling God **a liar** (5:10). However, **God's testimony is greater**—he's the only one who needs no margin of error (5:9).

What does God want you to believe? **God has given us eternal life** (5:11). In John's Gospel, Jesus defined eternal life this way: "that they may know you, the only true God, and the one you have sent—Jesus Christ" (John 17:3). *Eternal life* is the knowledge of God. You receive this at the moment of salvation, but that's only the beginning. You must grow in your knowledge and understanding, as sure as an infant must progress toward childhood. God wants us to grow in our knowledge of him—he wants us to deepen in our experience of eternal life. To do that, you must have intimacy with his Son, because **this life is in his Son. The one who has the Son has life** (5:11-12).

5:13 How important is assurance of salvation? John wants those who have trusted in **the Son of God** for salvation from sin to **know that [they] have eternal life.** Assurance is part of the essence of saving faith. If eternal life can be lost, it can't be *eternal.* God wants you to know that you have eternal life—not based on your fluctuating faith—but based on the object of your faith, Jesus.

5:14-15 Describing it as *eternal* life doesn't refer to *time* only but also to *quality.* John wants his readers to do more than live forever. Remember: this letter is about experiencing intimate fellowship with God. John wants his readers to experience a meaningful manifestation of the life of Christ. When our intimacy with him runs deep, we have a new **confidence** before him in prayer (5:14). Show me a person experiencing the life of Christ, and I'll show you someone who prays with power and confidence that God will come through (5:15).

How do we know that we're on the same wavelength with God and praying **according to his will?** (5:14). We begin with the Word of God. Pray the Bible with all of its promises and commands. Let it be in your heart and on your tongue. God wants his Word to be done, so pray for it to be done in your life and in the lives of others. Prayer is a toll-free number; the tab is picked up at the other end.

5:16-17 John offers a specific example of confident prayer that is according to God's will and that involves a horizontal expression of love. If you see a brother **committing a sin**, he needs a believer who is intimate with God to intercede for him (5:16). As a result of his own intimacy with God, Moses intervened on behalf of Israel (Exod 32:7-14). When the four men who carried the paralytic took him to Jesus, he forgave and

healed when he saw *their* faith (Mark 2:5). When we reach out in love to a brother or sister who is being defeated, God can allow that believer to piggyback on our faith to receive deliverance. That's what the family of God is about.

There is a more serious kind of sin, though—a **sin that leads to death.** This is sin that results in the physical death of a believer. We see examples of this in Scripture when God takes unrepentant believers home before their time (see 1 Cor 3:16-17; 11:30). These are typically gross sins against the body of Christ. In view here is not a believer struggling with sin (after all, the church is a hospital for sinners) but a hard-headed fool who adopts a harsh, unloving attitude toward God's people.

When someone wreaks havoc in the family of God, he may experience severe discipline from the Lord. John says, **I am not saying** that a believer walking with God **should pray about that.** Though he doesn't say we shouldn't pray in such cases, he is communicating that you cannot have confidence that God will answer such a prayer.

5:18-19 See the commentary on 3:6-10. Your victory over sin is determined by the degree to which you "walk by the Spirit" (Gal 5:16). When you live by the Spirit (not by willful determination, by keeping New Year's resolutions, or through the "power of positive thinking"), Satan cannot touch you (5:18)— even though **the whole world is under the sway of the evil one** (5:19; see Eph 2:3; 2 Cor 4:4).

5:20-21 Jesus is the Christ, **the Son of God**, who has come in the flesh (2:22; 4:2-3; 4:15). Spiritual life and intimate fellowship with God are found nowhere else. Knowing this, why would you look elsewhere?

Idols are false gods, cheap imitations. John urges you to pursue the real deal. Accept no imitations. Jesus **is the true God and eternal life** (5:20), so **guard yourselves from idols** (5:21).

2 JOHN

INTRODUCTION

Author

See discussion in 1 John.

Historical Background

See discussion in 1 John.

Message and Purpose

See discussion in 1 John.

Outline

I. Greetings (1-2)
II. Walking in Truth and Love (3-6)
III. Warning to Remain in Christ's Teaching (7-11)
IV. Farewell (12-13)

VIDEO   INTRO

www.bhpublishinggroup.com/qr/te/62_00

2 JOHN

I. GREETINGS (1-2)

1 The letters of 2–3 John are like brief postcards that the apostle John sent to believers until he was able to personally visit with them again. He addresses his letter **to the elect lady and her children.** John is using the term *lady* metaphorically. He's not writing to a *woman* but to a *church.* New Testament writers speak of the church using female terminology because the church is "the bride" of Christ (Rev 22:17; see also 2 Cor 11:2; Eph 5:22-33). Thus, John is writing to a congregation and its members, "her children."

John says this church is one whom he loves **in the truth.** Here two great biblical realities are combined: love and truth. They must be tied together because they balance each other and really cannot be separated. Truth without love is cold orthodoxy; love without truth is empty sentimentalism. *Love* is truth in action.

2 Truth is incredibly important to John. He mentions it five times in the first four verses. Though truth has fallen on hard times today, it is non-negotiable for the Christian. Many people say that truth is relative, but one plus one still equals two. Truth is that which corresponds to reality, and it finds its roots in God. He is the absolute standard against which truth is measured. In fact, *truth* is what God says about a matter. The revealed Word of God speaks truth about life and death, heaven and hell, money and parenting, marriage and sex, and every other topic relevant to life's big questions. Therefore, we don't have to wallow in a sea of relativity. On the contrary, we must stand for truth.

II. WALKING IN TRUTH AND LOVE (3-6)

3-6 Grace, mercy, and peace will be with us from God the Father and from Jesus Christ. These blessings are available nowhere else. But note that they only come in concert with the **truth and love** (v. 3). To experience more of God's grace, mercy, and peace, believers must be **walking in truth.** Seeing this behavior in Christians is what made John **glad** (v. 4). God never gives you his blessings when you contaminate his truth. We "walk in the truth"—that is, live in accordance with God's Word—by keeping the Father's commands. And the chief command, after loving God, is **that we love one another** (v. 5). What does God call us to do with our lives? **Walk in love** (v. 6).

The church is to be an incubator for the *truth.* We do not gather together to have our ears tickled but to preserve, hear, and speak the truth. The church is the family of God, and our heavenly Father has given his family a set of standards. As the family expands, there will be problems. The test of a true church is not whether or not it has problems, but whether or not it addresses those problems with God's standard of truth. Yet, all things must be done with *love*. We can't be "walking in the truth" (v. 4) if we don't "walk in love" (v. 6). We love others when we compassionately, righteously, and responsibly seek their well-being—that which God desires for them.

III. WARNING TO REMAIN IN CHRIST'S TEACHING (7-11)

7 One of the reasons that Christians need to know the truth is because **many deceivers have gone out into the world.** I love to watch magic shows. I'm amazed at how magicians can make things disappear or bend the laws of physics. How do they do it? They trick us! They create illusions, causing things to appear to contradict reality. John is warning his readers about "deceivers" who dupe people into believing what is not true. But John isn't concerned about someone claiming to pull a rabbit out of a hat. He's concerned about those **who do not confess the coming of Jesus Christ in the flesh.**

Truth is measured by what people conclude about Jesus Christ. He is in a class by himself. It doesn't matter how eloquently a person speaks or what social causes he advocates. If he suggests Jesus is anything less than the eternal Son of God who became a sinless man, died to atone for sins, and rose from the dead, he is **the deceiver and the antichrist.** As John has said previously in 1 John, *the* Antichrist is coming and will appear during the great tribulation (see Dan 9:26-27; 1 Thess 4:13-18; 2 Thess 2:3; Rev 11:2; 13:1-8), but *little* antichrists are active now (see 1 John 2:18). The category of *antichrist* applies to those who oppose and replace Christ. They were active in John's day, and they're active today.

8-9 God has rewards in store for his followers. Though you may receive some blessings on earth, no one obtains their full reward in history. Most is reserved for our heavenly eternity. But if you are unfaithful and allow yourself to be tricked regarding the truth, you can **lose** what God has in store and not **receive** your **full reward** (v. 8). What prevents this? Intimacy with God. You must **remain in Christ's teaching** (v. 9). The word "remain" can also be translated "stay" or "abide"; the idea is to "be in close proximity." You can't be close to Christ without being close to his teaching. Intimacy with God requires remaining or abiding in his Word.

10-11 What do you do about someone who teaches something contrary to what Scripture reveals about Jesus Christ? **Do not receive him into your home** (v. 10). Know that **the one who greets him shares in his evil works** (v. 11). Importantly, in the early church, believers didn't have church buildings but often met in each other's homes (see Acts 2:46; 5:42; 20:20; Rom 16:5; 1 Cor 16:19; Col 4:15). Thus, John warns the church to give no hearing or exposure to deceivers who do not hold to the truth of Christ. This doesn't mean you can't talk to unbelievers and try to evangelize them. Rather, it means the church must not give an audience to those who deny who Christ is. If someone's wrong on this point, it's a cataclysmic error.

IV. FAREWELL (12-13)

12-13 Though it was urgent that John **write to** these Christians with both warning and encouragement, he knew it was far better to visit them in person. The most effective form of ministry—the kind that brings the most **joy**—is that done **face to face** (v. 12). The apostle concludes with warm **greetings** from a **sister** church (v. 13).

3 JOHN

INTRODUCTION

Author

See the discussion in 1 John.

Historical Background

See the discussion in 1 John.

Message and Purpose

See the discussion in 1 John.

Outline

I. Greetings (1-4)
II. Being Coworkers with the Truth (5-8)
III. Good and Evil Leaders (9-12)
IV. Farewell (13-15)

VIDEO INTRO

www.bhpublishinggroup.com/qr/te/62_00

3 JOHN

I. GREETINGS (1-4)

1-2 Like 2 John, 3 John is more or less a brief postcard from the apostle. This one is written to his **dear friend Gaius** (v. 1), whom we can assume was probably a church leader. John prays that Gaius is **prospering in every way and . . . in good health, just as [his] whole life is going well** (v. 2). That latter phrase could also be translated "just as your soul prospers."

Some people have wrongly tried to advocate a "prosperity gospel" using these verses. Now, God is not necessarily against prosperity and health. There's nothing inherently evil in having money or being physically fit. Getting a raise at work and improving your fitness are fine. But these things are only beneficial "as your soul prospers." Without a prospering soul—that is, without spiritual development—your motivations will be misplaced, and your health and wealth will leave you hollow.

3-4 How did John know that Gaius's soul was prospering? Not because of any material benefits he had, but because **fellow believers . . . testified to** his **fidelity to the truth.** How do you measure your success in the Christian life? The measuring rod for your spiritual well-being is whether or not **you are walking in truth**—that is, whether you're living by the standard of God's Word (v. 3). Knowing that believers were **walking in truth** brought great **joy** to the apostle (v. 4), and it brings joy to God too.

II. BEING COWORKERS WITH THE TRUTH (5-8)

5-8 In 2 John 10-11, we see that the church must not support or give an audience to those who reject the truth about Jesus Christ. Instead, we should **support** those who **set out for the sake of the Name** of Jesus (vv. 7-8)—in other words, those who are doing the work of God as evangelists, teachers, church planters, and missionaries. By providing them with financial support, hospitality, encouragement, and prayer, **we can be coworkers with the truth** (v. 8). That's what Gaius did. He demonstrated **love** for **the brothers and sisters** who were engaging in ministry, even those who were **strangers** to him (vv. 5-6). When we support those who are faithful to the truth, God credits to our account the blessings that he gives to them because we are their coworkers, sharing in their ministry.

III. GOOD AND EVIL LEADERS (9-12)

9 Gaius was a faithful leader, committed to the truth. Sadly, we can encounter church leaders who don't share his commitment. John identified one of them by name: **Diotrephes.** What was wrong with him? He loved **to have first place.** He liked to be the center of attention, the king of the hill, the top dog. Diotrephes was full of pride, which demonstrated itself in a variety of ways. When John wrote to the church, Diotrephes refused to receive his **authority.** Understand that John had been chosen by the Son of God himself to serve as one of his apostles and to write Scripture. Nevertheless, Diotrephes wouldn't listen to him. You don't get a clearer rejection of the truth than that!

10 Diotrephes compounded his sin by **slandering** John and his coworkers **with malicious words** and kicking out of the church people who tried to **welcome fellow believers.** Gaius supported traveling believers who were doing the work of Christ (vv. 5-8), but Diotrephes slammed the door in their faces and excommunicated church members for helping them. In a word, Diotrephes was a despot. A leader submits himself to the truth and exercises godly authority for the good of those under him. A despot refuses to submit to the truth and rules over others for his own gain. The apostle John was not afraid to call him out.

11-12 John urges Gaius (and us): **do not imitate what is evil, but what is good** (v. 11). Diotrephes was an obvious example of evil to avoid. **Demetrius**, by contrast, was a good example to emulate. The church spoke well of him, the apostle and those with him spoke well of him, and **even the truth itself** spoke well of Demetrius (v. 12). There was consistency in the man's life. The way he lived matched the truth of Scripture. When you see this kind of pattern in a leader, you know you can follow him, because **the one who does good is of God** (v. 11).

IV. FAREWELL (13-15)

13-15 John concludes his letter by highlighting the limitation of using **pen and ink** (v. 13). This is a reminder that writing can be useful, but it can't replace talking **face to face** (v. 14). Whether someone needs warning or encouragement, emails and text messages don't compare to looking a brother or sister in the eye and "speaking the truth in love" (Eph 4:15).

JUDE

INTRODUCTION

Author

THE AUTHOR IDENTIFIES HIM-self as Jude, "brother of James" (v. 1). It's unlikely he would be referring to James the son of Zebedee, who was martyred at an early date (see Acts 12:1-2). Likely, he is referencing the well-known leader of the Jerusalem church (Acts 15:13-21; Gal 2:9) and brother of Jesus (Mark 6:3). Yet though Jude was also Jesus's brother, he humbly calls himself a "servant of Jesus Christ" instead (v. 1).

Historical Background

The first readers of Jude's letter were probably Jewish Christians because of his several references to Jewish history. He identifies them as "those who are the called, loved by God the Father and kept for Jesus Christ" (v. 1), which could be a general designation referring to believers anywhere. But in verse 3 he also calls them "dear friends" and goes on to address a specific situation; thus, he likely has a specific group in mind—perhaps several churches. Aside from this, we do not know who Jude's recipients were.

It's hard to determine the date of the letter. All we know is that it was written within Jude's lifetime, and the false teaching he addresses had time to develop. A reasonable date for it, then, would be between AD 65 and 80. Nothing in the letter points to a date beyond this period.

Message and Purpose

Jude had intended to write about the great salvation that believers share, but he had to adjust his message because false teachers had infiltrated the church. He wanted these troublemakers to be identified by their false teaching and false living because the former inevitably leads to the latter. It's imperative that believers learn to distinguish truth from error.

In a series of contrasts, Jude shows the difference between doctrinal error that manifests itself in corrupt living and the truth of God that leads to righteous living. Jude also warned about rebelling against God's ordained authorities; to do so is to rebel against God. Jude wanted believers to stand and fight for the truth—combining holy kingdom truth with holy kingdom living.

www.bhpublishinggroup.com/qr/te/65_00

Outline

I. Introduction and Purpose (1-4)
II. Illustrations of Past Rebels (5-11)
III. False Teachers and their Judgment (12-19)
IV. Exhortations for Believers (20-23)
V. Benediction (24-25)

JUDE

I. INTRODUCTION AND PURPOSE (1-4)

1-2 The author, **Jude**, was **a brother of James** (v. 1), and a half-brother of Jesus (see Mark 6:3). But like Paul (Rom 1:1; Phil 1:1), Jude saw himself as **a servant of Jesus Christ** and radically submitted to his lordship. He prays that God would give the readers his best: **mercy, peace, and love** (v. 2).

3 Why is Jude writing? He **was eager to write** to the recipients about their salvation, but changed his mind and instead wrote them **to contend for the faith that was delivered to the saints**. Jude, then, was open to the Holy Spirit's adjustment of his plans so he could address something urgent that came up. He wants believers to energetically "contend for the faith," that is, for the body of scripturally based doctrine that is to be the authoritative guide for our belief and practice. Christians

are to wage battle on behalf of the true faith as deposited in God's inerrant Word (see 2 Tim 3:14-17).

4 This is vital because **ungodly** men who were prophesied by Peter (see 2 Pet 2:1; 3:3) had **come in by stealth ... turning the grace of our God into sensuality and denying Jesus** (v. 4). False teachers had crept into the church, masquerading as authentic followers of Christ (2 Cor 11:14-15). But they were deceivers. They rebelled against Christ's lordship over their lifestyle (see Luke 6:46). If there is anything the New Testament emphasizes, it is that grace teaches us to live better than those in the world do, not worse (see Titus 2:11-12). Yet these false teachers turned grace into something it was never meant to be—an excuse for sin (see Rom 6:1-7; Titus 2:11-14).

II. ILLUSTRATIONS OF PAST REBELS (5-11)

5-7 So Jude provides some illustrations. He reminds the readers of past rebels who were like the false teachers, emphasizing what became of them. Though the Lord **saved a people out of Egypt**, only Joshua and Caleb entered the promised land. God **destroyed those who did not believe** (v. 5). He also points to the angelic rebellion. Lucifer led a *coup d'état* and was followed by **angels who ... abandoned their proper dwelling**. Now they're kept **in eternal chains** for judgment (v. 6). His third illustration is the **sexual immorality** of **Sodom and Gomorrah**. God's judgment on these cities is

an example of the **eternal fire** that will fall on those who legitimize evil (v. 7).

8-11 Scripture instructs us to obey the legitimate authorities appointed over us. But false teachers **reject authority**. In this case, they were accountable to no one but themselves. Moreover, the group would **slander glorious ones** (v. 8). Jude illustrates this with an account of a dispute over **Moses's body** between **the archangel** and **the devil**. Michael refused to **utter a slanderous condemnation** against Satan but said, **The Lord**

rebuke you! (v. 9). The false teachers, by contrast, didn't understand how spiritual warfare works. They lived in a dream world, out of touch with spiritual reality. They'd blaspheme rather than invoking the Lord like Michael did. Why? They didn't understand that Satan is not to be taken lightly. Instead, they were **like irrational animals** who only operate **by instinct** (v. 10). Jude compares them to **Cain** (who gave a bloodless offering), Balaam (who only ministered for money), and Korah (who rejected the authority of God's word). For rebelling against spiritual authority, all of them were judged (v. 11).

III. FALSE TEACHERS AND THEIR JUDGMENT (12-19)

12-13 Jude uses a variety of images to describe these heretics. These images are of nature in turmoil and distress. He says they are like **dangerous reefs**, which are hidden dangers to ships. They are **waterless clouds**, putting on a big show as if they will relieve the spiritually parched even though there's no substance behind what they say. They are like **fruitless** trees that produce nothing of spiritual value. They're also akin to **wild waves** that foam up **shameful deeds** and like **wandering stars** that lead others astray. God takes false teachers seriously, and eternal **darkness is reserved** for them (v. 13).

14 Jude says that **Enoch** prophesied about the Lord's coming judgment against them. Enoch was a man who walked with God in the midst of moral decay in the days of Noah and spoke of the coming judgment (see Gen 5:21-24).

15-16 Notice how many times Jude uses the word "ungodly." They will be judged for their ungodly acts and **ungodly way** because they are **ungodly sinners** (v. 15). They use their positions and their mouths to exploit others, **flattering people for their own advantage** (v. 16) and to satisfy their own lusts. Thus, believers have to be on guard. Scripture warns us to "test the Spirits" (1 John 4:1) to discern what is legitimate and what is not. If you are led by a blind teacher on spiritual matters, you'll wind up falling into a ditch with him.

17-19 Remember what was predicted by the apostles (v. 17). In other words, don't forget apostolic teaching (v. 17). For us, that means looking to the Word of God, which the apostles wrote. They warned that Christians will face **scoffers**, those who make a joke of the faith (v. 18). Such people don't view life from a spiritual perspective but **create divisions** (v. 19)—thus providing the devil with the opportunities he wants. All Satan needs is a crack to slither through so he can amplify problems, cause disunity, and hinder God's work.

IV. EXHORTATIONS FOR BELIEVERS (20-23)

20-21 What can Christians do to protect themselves? Jude makes several points. First, **build yourselves up in your most holy faith** (v. 20). That is, don't be a static Christian: grow. If your son finished sixth grade and said, "I'm done with school," you'd probably ask him if he had lost his mind! No matter what he had learned so far, it's insufficient to carry him through to the end of life successfully. We need to grow spiritually by continually learning what God says and acting on it.

Second, pray **in the Holy Spirit** (v. 20)—that is, pray with a spiritual mindset, in concert with God's desires and God's design based on God's Word.

Third, **keep yourselves in the love of God, waiting expectantly for the mercy of . . . Jesus . . . for eternal life** (v. 21). In other words, live with an eternal perspective and in a close relationship with the Lord.

22-23 Not only must we grow in relationship with the Lord, but we must also consider our relationships with the rest of God's family. We must **have mercy on those who waver** (v. 22). Some Christians struggle in their faith and need compassion. Others need to be aggressively snatched **from the fire** (v. 23), that is, redirected from a behavior or relationship that will burn them.

But helping the latter, be wise: hate **even the garment defiled by the flesh.** As sure as clothing contaminated by a leper's skin could infect you, helping others overcome their sinful tendencies could drag you down with them. Reject the sin; help the sinner.

V. BENEDICTION (24-25)

24 Jude concludes with a glorious doxology by pointing to the one who can **protect you from stumbling.** God is able to keep you from being duped by the deceptions of false teachers. He can keep you from being tripped up so that you stand before him **without blemish and with great joy.** No one is sinless. To be *blameless* means that whatever your failures, they are sufficiently covered. When you stand before

God, based on your commitment to the truth, he's going to declare that you look just right.

25 The closing, to him **be glory, majesty, power, and authority,** is a reminder that God has the attributes, the position, and the legitimate right to get you through whatever challenges confront you and the moral decay in the world around you.

REVELATION

INTRODUCTION

Author

THE TRADITIONAL VIEW IS THAT the apostle John, the son of Zebedee, wrote the book of Revelation. This position has been challenged by critical scholars; nevertheless, it is still the most defensible view. The writer identifies himself as "John" (1:1, 4, 9; 22:8)—presumably a well-known John among first-century Christians. The many allusions to the Old Testament found in the book, as well as the style of writing, suggest the author was a Jewish Christian from Palestine. According to early church tradition, the apostle John ministered from about AD 70–100 in Asia Minor—the location of the "seven churches in Asia" (1:4, 11; 2:1–3:22). Thus, these believers would have been well acquainted with him. Furthermore, all of the earliest Christian writers attributed the book to John the apostle.

Historical Background

John addressed Revelation to seven churches in Asia Minor (modern Turkey): the church in Ephesus, in Smyrna, in Pergamum, in Thyatira, in Sardis, in Philadelphia, and the one in Laodicea (1:4, 11). Conservative evangelical scholars have suggested various dates for the time of this writing. Some believe that the persecution experienced by these churches reflects the reign of Nero in the late-60s. But the majority favor a date in the mid-90s, during the reign of the Roman emperor Domitian who ruled from AD 81–96. Early church tradition attests that local persecution of Christians took place under Domitian and that John was exiled to the island of Patmos (1:9) during his reign. These early Christian writers support a mid-90s date for the writing of Revelation. Thus, the aged apostle wrote what Jesus Christ revealed to him while he endured exile for his faithful preaching ministry.

Message and Purpose

The book of Revelation is specifically designed to explain what happens before, during, and after the return of Jesus Christ. It can be summarized in one phrase: "Things to come." It explains what God's prophetic kingdom program is and how it works and offers the most comprehensive detail in all of Scripture.

This book has two goals: to encourage Christians to live righteous and holy lives in light of the prophetic timetable that is to come and to challenge unbelievers about the judgment ahead if they reject Christ.

The apostle John begins by telling the church how it ought to live. He tells each church the special reward believers will receive for living holy lives that are pleasing to the Lord. Then he enters into an extensive description of the tribulation that fulfills many Old Testament prophecies, as well as Jesus's Olivet discourse. This section also describes God's dealings with Israel after the church has been raptured and the times of the Gentiles have ended. This leads to Christ's millennial kingdom on earth, followed by the judgment of unbelievers and the transition into the new heaven and new earth—the eternal state in which believers will be with the Lord forever.

VIDEO INTRO

www.bhpublishinggroup.com/qr/te/66_00

Outline

I. Prologue and John's Vision of Jesus (1:1-20)

II. Letters to the Seven Churches (2:1–3:22)

 A. Letter to the Church in Ephesus (2:1-7)

 B. Letter to the Church in Smyrna (2:8-11)

 C. Letter to the Church in Pergamum (2:12-17)

 D. Letter to the Church in Thyatira (2:18-29)

 E. Letter to the Church in Sardis (3:1-6)

 F. Letter to the Church in Philadelphia (3:7-13)

 G. Letter to the Church in Laodicea (3:14-22)

III. The Throne Room of Heaven (4:1–5:14)

IV. The Seven Seals (6:1–8:1)

V. The Seven Trumpets (8:2–11:19)

VI. The Woman, the Dragon, the Beast, and the Lamb (12:1–15:8)

VII. The Seven Bowls (16:1-21)

VIII. The Fall of Babylon (17:1–19:21)

IX. The Millennium and the Final Judgment (20:1-15)

X. The New Creation and the New Jerusalem (21:1-27)

XI. The Source of Life and Conclusion (22:1-21)

REVELATION

I. PROLOGUE AND JOHN'S VISION OF JESUS (1:1-20)

Revelation is one of the most difficult biblical books to interpret. The subject matter and widespread symbolism can make it hard to determine what to take literally and what to take figuratively. But even though it's a challenge, it can't be ignored. The warning near the end of the book (22:18) makes it clear that God expects us to take it seriously.

1:1-2 The theme and title of the book are displayed in its opening phrase: **The revelation of Jesus Christ** refers to Christ's unveiling or disclosure of matters related to his second coming to earth. The recipient of this disclosure is **his servant John** (1:1). The apostles regularly refer to themselves as servants of God because being dependent upon and yielded to God is the best way to hear his voice. Indeed, as the Lord's servant, John received **the word of God** and **the testimony of Jesus Christ** (1:2).

1:3 Blessing comes from hearing and reading this book and then heeding the commands written in it. Knowing and obeying God's words in Revelation is particularly important **because the time is near.** That is, the return of Christ is imminent. It could happen at any time.

1:4-7 Speaking of **the seven churches in Asia** is a way of speaking of all churches because the number seven represents completion or fullness. These churches are representative of all Christian churches throughout history. Though written by John, the content of Revelation is **from the one who is, who was, and**

who is to come; and **from the seven spirits** (that is, from the completeness or fullness of the Holy Spirit; the number seven is the number of completeness); and **from Jesus Christ** (1:4-5). The Trinitarian reference here is clear, with the rule of God being linked to all three persons of the Godhead.

Jesus, John says, is **the firstborn from the dead**, the first of a whole company of people who will one day rise from the grave because they are **set free from [their] sins by his blood.** Jesus also is **the ruler of the kings of the earth**, though his personal earthly kingdom rule is not yet visible in history (1:5). It will become so at his second coming. As **priests** of God's kingdom, believers are to represent men to God and God to men (1:6). The long-term goal of this plan is to bring God glory and to establish his kingdom rule and agenda forever. When Christ returns, it is going to be a spectacle because **every eye will see him** (1:7) as he rotates around the sun at his return.

1:8 Alpha and **Omega** are the first and last letters of the Greek alphabet, signifying that God is the beginning and the end. He's the Creator of all things, and he'll bring history to its conclusion. He is **the one who is, who was, and who is to come.** God is yesterday, today, and tomorrow because he exists eternally. But later in the letter, it's Jesus who calls himself the "Alpha and Omega" (22:13), and clearly he is the coming one (22:7, 12, 20). This is not surprising, though, because Jesus is the Second Person of the Trinity and coequal with the Father (see John 1:1; Col 1:15).

1:9-11 John had been exiled to **the island called Patmos** in the Aegean Sea because of his Christian faith and his refusal to compromise **the word of God and the testimony of Jesus** (1:9). John was **in the Spirit**—that is, he was thinking and functioning spiritually, engulfed in a spiritual framework **on the Lord's day** (the first day of the week)—when he heard **a loud voice . . . like a trumpet** (1:10). The voice told him to **write** down what he saw **and send it** to **the seven churches** (1:11), a group representative of all churches (see 1:4).

1:12 The seven churches are represented by **seven golden lampstands** to signify the expression of divine life that should radiate through all churches. Indeed, churches are to illuminate their communities.

1:13-16 These verses present a picture of Jesus that contrasts with much of what we see in the four Gospels. He is no longer a baby in a manger with nowhere to lay his head. Instead, he is mighty and majestic as he will certainly be at his second coming as Judge and King of the earth. **His eyes** are **like a fiery flame**, his feet **like fine bronze . . . and his voice** is **like the sound of cascading waters.** There is a **sword** coming **from his mouth**, and his face is **shining like the sun at full strength** (1:14-15). This image assures us that when Christ returns, the rulership he has always possessed by virtue of his position as God's Son will be realized in practice.

Notably, Jesus in his might and power is situated **among the lampstands** to signify his visible rulership of the church as Judge and King, even before his second coming to personally and directly rule the entire world (1:13; see 1:20). In other words, before he returns to rule the world, he wants to rule the church. The church, then, cannot view Jesus merely as a gentle figure with long hair and a loving gaze. Christians must view him as a ruler, for there is a judgment side of Jesus along with the blessing side we love to talk about. He is the might and strength at the center of the church.

1:17-18 When John saw Jesus as the church's Judge and Ruler, he **fell at his feet like a dead man**, and the Lord had to raise him up with the admonition, **Don't be afraid** (1:17). The **keys** Jesus spoke of represent access to **death and Hades**, and by extension, access to heaven (1:18).

1:19 This verse presents an outline of the book of Revelation. John was commanded to write **what you have seen, what is, and what will take place after this.** After writing the vision he had just seen (chapter 1), John was to share about the present state of the seven churches (chapters 2–3), and then the future tribulation and eternal state (chapters 4–22).

1:20 The chapter closes with an explanation of the vision's symbolism. **The seven stars** (see 1:16) represent the seven **angels of the seven churches.** The Greek word translated "angel" in the CSB, *angelos*, means "messenger," and that's the intended sense here. The pastors who declare God's Word, then, are God's messengers to the churches. **The seven lampstands** represent the churches themselves, specifically the spiritual light they are to emit.

II. LETTERS TO THE SEVEN CHURCHES (2:1–3:22)

The return of Christ is imminent—it could happen at any time. And although we don't know when he will return, we do know how we are to function in the church in the meantime. Christ's message to each church in chapters 2–3 represents an aspect of his plan during the church age for every properly functioning church—represented by the numeral seven, the number of completion.

❧ A. Letter to the Church in Ephesus (2:1-7) ❧

2:1 Jesus reminds the pastor (*angelos*, "messenger"; see 1:20) **of the church in Ephesus** that he **holds** pastors **in his right hand** and **walks among** churches. Jesus knows what's going on.

2:2-3 Because of this, he could say, **I know your works, your labor, and your endurance.** He also knew they did not **tolerate evil people** (2:2). They tested everything by the Scriptures and rightly found that some so-called apostles did not teach pure doctrine. Moreover, the Ephesian believers **persevered** amid **hardships for the sake of** Christ's **name** (2:3). There were a lot of positive things happening in this church.

2:4 But Jesus shifts from patting them on the back to rebuke: **You have abandoned the love you had at first.** They had correct doctrine, but not a correct heart. The key word here is *first*, not *love*. As with romantic love between a man and a woman, first love always involves passion. Yet there was not passionate pursuit of an intimate relationship with Christ in the church. They were merely following a program. Duty had replaced devotion.

2:5-6 The remedy was to **remember** how it used to be when the church was excited about Jesus and return to that attitude. If the church failed to **repent**, Christ would **remove** its **lampstand** (2:5)—that is, put out its light. If our church's activity is about us rather than about Jesus, he'll remove his presence from it. The Ephesians hated the practices of evil people, but that positive did not outweigh their loss of passion for Christ (2:6). They needed to remember the primacy of relationship over performance, to repent of their spiritual departure, and to repeat prioritizing intimate fellowship with God (see Luke 10:38-42).

2:7 At the end of each letter, Jesus gets personal, directing his remarks to individuals in the church rather than the church as a collective. In each case, he addresses individual believers with the words **"to the one who conquers"** (2:7, 11, 17, 26; 3:5, 12, 21). The Greek verb translated as "conquers" is *nikaō*, and it means to be victorious in the midst of, over, in, or through whatever circumstances are illegitimately holding a believer hostage. In 1 John 5:5 we read, "Who is the one who conquers the world but the one who believes that Jesus is the Son of God?" If by believing in Jesus we are conquerors, then why in these letters to the churches are we still exhorted

to conquer? Well, John is addressing the contrast between our legal status (our declared position in Christ) and our experiential reality. We must work out this position of being a conqueror in the experiences of our everyday lives in order to have special intimacy with Christ in the kingdom.

In this message to the Christians at Ephesus, Christ appeals to **anyone who has ears**, referring to the person who heeds this spiritual principle being articulated. **The one who conquers** the temptation to push Christ to second place will be granted **to eat from the tree of life** in **the paradise of God.** The tree of life was a special tree in the garden of Eden (see Gen 2:9), and here it represents a special level of intimacy with God in heaven. All believers will go to heaven, but those who do not lose passion for Christ in this life will experience a special place of intimacy with the Lord.

☙ B. Letter to the Church in Smyrna
(2:8-11) ❧

2:8-10 Christ acknowledges that **the church in Smyrna** is a faithful congregation undergoing persecution. Some who claimed to be **Jews** were actually **a synagogue of Satan** because they were doing the devil's work, slandering believers (2:8-9). Christians at Smyrna would be thrown **into prison** as a **test** of their faith, and the church would be afflicted (2:10). While such circumstances might make them feel poor, they actually were **rich** due to the coming reward for their spiritual endurance (2:10). To those who refuse to compromise when faced with persecution, there is no condemnation. That's why Jesus says nothing negative about this church.

2:11 To **never be harmed by the second death** refers to enjoying a sense of full gain when Christ separates believers from unbelievers at the end of history. Because the recipients of this letter were already Christians, they could not be separated from God. Yet at the final judgment, some Christians will experience a sense of loss, despite their eternal salvation, when Jesus rebukes their unfaithfulness (see Matt 25:28-30; 1 Cor 3:15). The faithful at Smyrna, in contrast, would be untouched by any negative consequence on that day.

⟿ C. Letter to the Church in Pergamum (2:12-17) ⟵

2:12-16 The one who has the sharp, double-edged sword is Jesus speaking the Word of God. **The church in Pergamum** had some good things going. They were **holding on to** Jesus's **name and did not deny [their] faith** in him (2:12-13). Yet they tolerated those who, like Balaam in the Old Testament, claimed God's name (see Num 22–24) while also enticing his people to compromise (Num 25:1; 31:16). It's a big deal to God when we cause other people to stumble, especially when we do it knowingly and for profit like Balaam (2:14-15). That's why the Lord demanded that the Christians in Pergamum **repent** (2:16).

2:17 The reward is twofold for those who refuse to compromise or tempt others to do so. First, there is **hidden manna.** *Manna* was the supernatural food God rained down from heaven to sustain Israel in the wilderness (see Deut 8:16). This manna is "hidden" in that it is not available to all. It represents exclusive sustenance and kingdom fellowship with God for Christians who reject the way of Balaam (see commentary on 2:12-16).

Second, there is **a white stone** inscribed with **a new name.** In the Roman world, a white stone was used as an admission ticket for an event. A white stone with someone's name on it was a personalized, all-access pass. This image, then, reinforces the idea of exclusive, personal fellowship with God as the conquering Christian's reward. For the one who rises above being a nominal Christian, Jesus has special benefits. You get invited to the private reception.

⟿ D. Letter to the Church in Thyatira (2:18-29) ⟵

2:18-20 The description of Jesus here echoes 1:14-15, where he is positioned as the church's powerful Judge. **The church**

in Thyatira needed a judge because despite its **faithfulness, service, and endurance,** it tolerated the sin of a woman referred to as **Jezebel** (2:19-20). Though perhaps this was her real name, Jezebel also brings to mind the wife of Israel's King Ahab (see 1 Kgs 16:31; 2 Kgs 9) and represents an entire category of immoral and idolatrous women. This woman in Thyatira promoted **sexual immorality** and idolatry (2:20). Christ condemned both her and the church's tolerance of her.

2:21 Though Christ **gave her time to repent,** she refused. A refusal is different than a struggle. At times, believers fight sins but cannot stop committing them on their own power. Jezebel was unwilling to make any effort.

2:22-25 The **affliction** described here illustrates that one purpose of repentance is to limit or remove sin's consequences (2:22). Repentance allows Christians to regain fellowship with the Lord. Those not following the way of Jezebel did not have to worry about the burdens listed. They were to **hold on** until Christ returned (2:24-25).

2:26-27 The reward for obeying Christ is **authority over the nations,** a reference to the thousand-year reign of Jesus following his second coming. During that time, believers who exhibit purity in this life will help the Lord rule the world. That millennial reign, though, is merely a down payment on eternity.

2:28-29 Jesus himself is **the morning star** (see 22:16). Thus, the reward for a pure life is a greater experience of Jesus during his millennial reign and for eternity. Naturally, a co-ruler of the universe will have greater access to the King than a common citizen.

⟿ E. Letter to the Church in Sardis (3:1-6) ⟵

3:1-4 The seven spirits of God is a reference to the Holy Spirit (see commentary on 1:4-7). This church had a **reputation for being alive.** It was the kind of place about which people today might say, "They have great music and great preaching." Yet because Jesus knew their **works**, he saw there was no true spiritual life there (3:1-2). They were merely playing church. The believers in Sardis, then, were to stop the spiritual sleeping. The remedy included remembering **what you have received and heard**. Jesus warned that he was coming in judgment. But as he does repeatedly with his people, he gave the church in Sardis an opportunity to **repent** first (3:3). Notably, **a few** believers in this church were committed spiritually and not acquiescing to spiritual apathy (3:4).

3:5-6 White clothes for **the one who conquers** represent the garments required for a special event, like a gown or tuxedo of today. The promise to **never erase his name from the book of life** is not a reference to eternal life, because every believer has a secure place in heaven. Instead, the names in this book are invitees to special fellowship with God, to an exclusive party, so to speak, for those who persist in spiritual vitality. The special clothes and invitation list are two parts of the same metaphor: a banquet with God for those who conquer. At that banquet, Jesus will brag on the conquerors **before [his] Father and before his angels** (3:5).

➢ F. Letter to the Church in Philadelphia (3:7-13) ❦

3:7-9 The church in Philadelphia (3:7), although small and viewed by the world as insignificant, was spiritually serious. They were committed (3:8). Except for the church at Smyrna, this was the only church not to receive a rebuke from Jesus. Even though this church had **little** worldly **power**, Jesus promised to reward their faithfulness by overruling the satanic enemies that came against them. That act of divine defense, he said, would put wicked enemies on notice **that I have loved you** (3:8-9).

3:10 Within the premillennial view of eschatology, which this commentary adopts, there are at least four different views on *the rapture*—the return of Christ to remove his

church from the world. Some premillennialists believe the rapture will occur prior to a seven-year period of tribulation; some believe it will occur in the middle of that tribulation; some say it will happen two-thirds of the way through; and some insist it will come at the end. This verse suggests a pre-tribulational rapture because it says, **I will also keep you from the hour of testing that is going to come on the whole earth.** Jesus will not merely keep them from the test but from the period of the test—that is, the tribulation period.

3:11-13 The believer's **crown** is a symbol of his or her eternal reward. The admonition, **Hold on to what you have, so that no one takes your crown**, suggests eternal rewards can be lost (3:11). Christ's promise to make **the one who conquers** a **pillar in the temple of God** is a promise of public recognition (3:12). In the end, everyone will know the spiritually serious person is special to God because Jesus will publicly identify that person as set apart.

➢ G. Letter to the Church in Laodicea (3:14-22) ❦

3:14-16 The church in Laodicea can be labeled the carnal church (3:14). The key sentence here is this: **Because you are lukewarm, and neither hot nor cold, I am going to vomit you out of my mouth** (3:16). The Everyday English Tony Evans Translation puts it this way: "Y'all make me want to throw up!" Nobody orders a lukewarm drink. They want iced tea or hot coffee. In the spiritual realm, God finds tepidness unappealing as well.

3:17 Here Jesus debunks a prominent lie of prosperity theology: being materially successful means God has blessed you. Not so. The Laodiceans said, **I'm rich; I have become wealthy and need nothing.** But the external appearance of prosperity was not indicative of the condition of their hearts or their level of fellowship with God. They were spiritually uncommitted, carnal, and compromising. As Jesus put it, they were **wretched, pitiful, poor, blind, and naked** spiritually.

3:18-20 They needed to acquire from Jesus true wealth—those character traits, behaviors, and beliefs that have eternal value. Then they truly would **be rich** (3:18). By stating, **be zealous and repent,** Christ gave this carnal church an opportunity to get right with God (3:19). **See! I stand at the door and knock** was an invitation. Jesus will not force himself into a church. But if any member of a congregation will open the door by submitting to his will, he **will come in and**

eat (3:20)—that is, he will have intimate fellowship with believers who respond to his invitation.

3:21-22 To the one who conquers, Christ offers a high position of rulership and an elevated level of personal experience with him (3:21). He uses rewards here, as with the other six churches, as a motivation to conquer sin and slackness—not as a motivation to salvation.

III. THE THRONE ROOM OF HEAVEN (4:1–5:14)

4:1 The phrase **after this** marks a transition to the third section of the book, with the pronoun *this* referring to the church age—that is, the period of history between Christ's ascension and his rapture of believers. The first section of Revelation recounted a vision of Jesus (1:1-20) while the second depicted the present state of the church through letters to seven representative congregations (2:1–3:22). Now John begins describing events that will occur during the seven-year period of divine judgment on earth known as the tribulation. All events described in Revelation from this point forward will occur following the rapture. But not only has John shifted in the time period he is describing, the venue has shifted as well from earth to heaven.

4:2-3 A key phrase here is **in the Spirit** (4:2). The command to do anything "in the Spirit" is a command to enter the spiritual perspective. That is, to see things that physical eyes cannot see, as when believers are commanded to pray in the Spirit (Jude 20). Naturally, certain aspects of John's experience of being in the Spirit were unique and not repeatable since he was writing Holy Scripture. But much of it is repeatable. Believers today can abide in the Spirit, receiving understanding of God's will and work. Too often, though, we merely "visit" the Spirit, so to speak, without "living with him" in a condition of heightened spiritual awareness.

With the right spiritual perspective, John gets a view of God's **throne in heaven** (4:2); his is similar to the perspective depicted in Isaiah 6:1-8, in which the prophet "saw the

Lord seated on a high and lofty throne, and the hem of his robe filled the temple" as "seraphim" stood "above him" (Isa 6:1-2). The description of God as having **the appearance of** precious stones—**jasper and carnelian** (4:3)—refers to his value and elegance. The **rainbow** that **surrounded the throne** (4:3) harkens back to Genesis 9:12-17, where God designated the rainbow as a sign of his covenant with Noah never to destroy the earth with a flood again. Each time a rainbow appears in Scripture, it is a reminder of God's faithfulness.

4:4 Similar to the number seven, **twenty-four** has special significance in Scripture, pointing to people who stand out as spiritual leaders like the twenty-four priestly divisions among Aaron's descendants (see 1 Chr 24) and the twenty-four divisions of singers who led Israel in worship at the temple (see 1 Chr 25). Here, the **twenty-four elders** are believers who have overcome during the church age and are ruling with Christ, providing spiritual leadership through their faithful example. The **thrones, white clothes,** and **golden crowns** correspond to the rewards of 2:26; 3:5; and 3:10 for, respectively, "the one who conquers and who keeps [Christ's] works to the end," "the one who conquers," and the one who perseveres in faithfulness amid persecution.

4:5-7 Flashes of lightning and . . . peals of thunder (4:5) depict the power and majesty of God. The **seven spirits of God** signify the Holy Spirit present before God the Father on his **throne** (4:5). Also **before the throne** is an utterly calm and smooth body of water, described metaphorically as **a sea of glass.**

The **four living creatures** harken back to awesome angelic beings described in Ezekiel 1 and Isaiah 6. Like the angels in Ezekiel 1:5-11, they have appearances like **a lion, an ox, a man**, and an **eagle** as well as eyes facing multiple directions (4:6-7). The appearances of these four angels may symbolize the portraits of Jesus in the four Gospels. In Matthew, Jesus is King of the Jews, represented by a regal lion. In Mark, he is a servant, represented by an ox—a beast of burden. In Luke, he is the Son of Man, represented by the face of a man. And in John, he is the Son of God who gives eternal life, represented by a majestic eagle.

4:8 As in Isaiah 6:2-3, each creature has **six wings** and cries, **Holy, holy, holy** without stopping—**day and night.** In Isaiah, each creature covered its face with two wings, its feet with two wings, and flew with two wings. They called to one another, "Holy, holy, holy is the Lord of Armies; his glory fills the whole earth" (Isa 6:3).

4:9-11 Whenever the living creatures worship God (4:9), **the twenty-four elders** join them (4:10). The elders, in fact, appear inspired by the angelic worship and sing a song declaring God **worthy to receive glory and honor and power, because** he has **created all things** (4:11). The worship of God as Creator sets the stage for subsequent chapters in which God is depicted as moving into creation and setting it right from the effects of sin. This entire scene is a lead-up to chapter five, in which Jesus Christ is introduced.

5:1 The **seven seals** represent the first in a series of judgments to come on the earth that will also include seven trumpets (8:1-9:20; 11:15-19) and seven bowls (16:1-21) among metaphorical depictions of God's wrath. The **scroll** is like a title deed to the earth. It depicts God's ownership of all creation and right to hold accountable those who misuse it and thus dishonor him. Through judgment administered by Jesus, God once again will lay claim to his creation, which was plunged into sin by Adam in Genesis 3.

5:2-4 In response to the question of **a mighty angel—Who is worthy to open the scroll and break its seals?** (5:2)—**no one in heaven or on earth or under the earth** is found worthy (5:3). In fact, no one is worthy **even to look** at the Lord's plan for worldwide judgment, much less administer it, prompting John to weep (5:4).

5:5 One of the elders comforts John, telling him not to cry because Jesus—**the Lion from the tribe of Judah** and **the Root of David**—*is* worthy to open the scroll and administer the judgment of its seals. This scene reflects the fact that sinful people, even when they are redeemed, fall short of the qualifications necessary for one who could judge the earth. But Christ, by virtue of his full divinity, sinless humanity, and atoning death, is qualified. God the Father has granted judging authority to the Son (see John 5:22, 27). Jesus died to redeem humanity at his first coming. He will judge in order to redeem the entire creation at his second.

5:6-7 The depiction of Christ **like a slaughtered lamb** (5:6) contrasts with the lion metaphor of 5:5. Yet this is not a contradiction. Jesus is regal like a lion, and he was slain like a sacrificial lamb to atone for the sins of the whole world (cf. Isa 53:7; 1 John 2:2). The repetition of the number seven—**seven horns . . . seven eyes . . . seven spirits of God** (5:6)—signifies the completeness of Christ's atoning work. Because he "[fulfilled] all righteousness" (Matt 3:15), he is qualified to bring judgment on the earth. Hence, **he went and took the scroll out of the right hand of the one seated on the throne** (5:7).

5:8-9 Prayers of God's people for vindication are pictured as **incense** rising from **golden bowls** (5:8). Two implications of the metaphor are that prayer truly reaches God and pleases him. As the **living creatures** and **twenty-four elders** fall down before Christ, they cite his redemption of a diverse population as part of the reason he is worthy to judge the world.

The mention of redeemed people in heaven being **from every tribe and language and people and nation** (5:9; repeated in 7:9) portrays the ethnic, linguistic, and national diversity that will be present in eternity. This means that difference and diversity are not problems to be solved, but were part of God's plan from the very beginning. God delights in the variety and beauty of his creation. Here in this perfect, complete worship service around the throne we can see clearly that "red, yellow, black, and white" are all precious in God's sight. And this diverse community of saints is unified in their worship of the Lamb. Christian unity does not mean uniformity, but a shared focus on and worship of Christ Jesus.

5:10 The destiny of every believer is to **reign on the earth** as **priests to our God.** This will occur in the millennial kingdom (20:6) and in the new heavens and new earth (21:1). Of the millennium, John wrote specifically, "Blessed and holy is the one who shares in the first resurrection [salvation]! The second death [eternal judgment] has no power over them, but they will be priests of God and of Christ, and they will reign with him for a thousand years" (Rev 20:6). Previously, John recorded Christ's promise of "authority over the nations" for "the one who conquers" (2:26). You were redeemed to reign.

5:11-14 The chapter culminates in a magnificent scene of worship, involving **many angels, the living creatures,** and **the elders**—the total number of worshipers reaching **countless thousands, plus thousands of thousands** (5:11). Their song repeats the word **worthy** (5:12) for the fifth time since 4:11, over which span it first was applied to God the Father and then twice to the Son, emphasizing their coequality and divinity. The first two persons of the Trinity are worshiped together when **every creature in heaven, on earth, under the earth, on the sea, and everything in them** praises **the one seated on the throne** and **the Lamb, forever** (5:13). The worship is affirmed by **the four living creatures,** with **the elders** joining as well. (5:14). As when people clamor to see and cheer a celebrity, no prodding is required to incite this worship. When humans and angels behold Christ—the Lion and the Lamb—they cannot help but fall down and worship. In fact, Revelation is fundamentally a book about worship.

IV. THE SEVEN SEALS (6:1–8:1)

6:1-2 With the opening of the first seal, the tribulation period begins on earth—a seven-year span following the rapture of the church in which God brings judgment to earth in order to reclaim it. Once the church is in heaven and worshiping around God's throne, divinely wrought calamities will come upon the earth.

The **rider** on **a white horse** is a geopolitical leader; he's referenced elsewhere as the Antichrist (see 1 John 2:18; 4:3) who will insert himself in the world following the rapture and bring order out of chaos. This person will claim victory—represented by his white mount and **crown**—and gain world power. Notably, there is no mention of an arrow with his **bow,** indicating the bloodless nature of his coup (6:2). He will assume power through his strength, recognition, and substance, but without resorting to violence initially. The ensuing sense of peace throughout the world, though, will prove false.

6:3-4 The **fiery red** horse (6:4) of **the second seal** (6:3) represents chaos. Following initial peace to begin the tribulation, the world will devolve into violence, with people beginning to **slaughter one another** (6:4). Like Adolf Hitler before him, the Antichrist is going to transition from pretending to be peaceful to wielding **a large sword** (6:4), representative of his capacity to slay people. The parallel to Hitler is instructive because the German chancellor rose to power amid the turbulence of the Great Depression by building consensus and support before his administration devolved into violence and dictatorship.

6:5-6 The opening of **the third seal** heightens the world chaos, bringing economic instability to the tribulation period, a reality depicted by **a black horse** whose rider holds **a set of scales** (6:5). Inflation will be so severe that **a quart of wheat** and **three quarts of barley** each will cost a day's wage, which was **a denarius** in Roman currency (6:6). In addition to seizing control politically, the Antichrist will take over the world's economic order. Whether global economic instability sets the stage for his control or is the result of it is unclear.

6:7-8 The fourth seal (6:7), with its **pale green horse** and **rider . . . named Death** (6:8), brings an astonishingly severe judgment. In the aftermath of social conflict, **a fourth of the** earth's population will die from a combination of violence, **famine**, **plague**, and attacks by **wild animals** (6:8). If this occurred today, the fourth seal would bring the demise of approximately two billion people!

6:9-10 The fifth seal opens to reveal a prayer meeting in heaven involving **the souls of those . . . slaughtered** for their faith during the tribulation by the Antichrist (6:9). Obviously, then, people will come to faith in Jesus following the rapture because believers of the church age all will have been removed from earth. Notably, this is the first seal in which God's judgment comes in response to the cries of people. In effect, these believers ask God, **How long** will it be **until** you bring justice and judgment to the unrighteous people who persecuted us (6:10)?

6:11 The Lord's answer has two components, one explicit and the other implicit. First, they are **told to rest a little while longer** until God finishes unleashing his temporal judgments on the earth and **until the number would be completed of their fellow servants and their brothers and sisters, who were going to be killed just as they had been.** Second, they are reminded that even though God's justice is delayed at times, it always comes. He misses nothing and eventually will bring complete justice in response to every wrong committed.

6:12-14 The sixth seal brings disruption of nature: **a violent earthquake** (6:12); the sun's turning **black like sackcloth made of hair,**

which is likely because of volcanoes erupting and spewing ash that blocks sunlight; disruption of the **moon** (6:12) and **stars of heaven** (6:13); splitting of **the sky**; and the moving of mountains and islands (6:14). It will appear that God is undoing the created elements he formed in Genesis 1.

6:15-16 As people of all social classes—**kings** and **nobles** along with **every slave and free person** (6:15)—run for their lives, they'll *know* they are under God's judgment. This is evident from their cry **to the mountains and to the rocks, Fall on us and hide us from the face of the one seated on the throne and from the wrath of the Lamb** (6:16). But while it would be logical for individuals under judgment to call for mercy and salvation, these people's hearts have become so hardened that they prefer death to salvation! Notice that they know God's identity precisely: he is God the Father and God the Son. Nevertheless, they want nothing to do with him.

6:17 The great day of . . . wrath marks a transition point in the tribulation. Approximately three and a half years through the seven-year period, earth will experience what Jesus called the "great tribulation" (Matt 24:21; CSB: "great distress"). Though the CSB renders it as merely a description, it can also be taken as a proper name. The Old Testament prophet Jeremiah speaks of the great tribulation in stark terms: "How awful that day will be! There will be no other like it! It will be a time of trouble for Jacob, but he will be saved out of it" (Jer 30:7). The encouraging news, then, is that many people will be saved during this period; however, those still in rebellion against God will experience heightened judgment.

7:1 Chapter 7 marks an interlude in the judgments, with the seventh seal remaining unbroken until chapter 8. Up to this point, John's depictions of judgment have focused on events. Now, in describing this interlude, he focuses on the followers of Jesus who will be alive on earth during the tribulation, including 144,000 Jews and "a vast multitude" (7:9) of Jews and Gentiles.

Four angels hold back the wind during this interlude so it cannot serve as a force of destruction and judgment until the servants of God are sealed. **The four corners of the earth** represent north, south, east, and west. The overall picture here, then, is one of divine restraint of destructive weather patterns during a break in the judgment.

7:2-3 The four angels who were allowed to harm the earth and the sea—apparently a reference to powers they would exercise later—are the same four angels mentioned in 7:1. They are instructed by **another angel rising up from the east, who had the seal of the living God** (7:2). With the destructive forces of nature in check, the rising angel tells them, **Don't harm the earth or the sea or the trees until we seal the servants of God on their foreheads** (7:3). To "seal the servants of our God" is to designate them as subject to his ownership and protection.

7:4 The **144,000 sealed from every tribe of the Israelites** does not represent, as the Jehovah's Witnesses claim, an "anointed class" of people from the general population that will go to heaven immediately upon death to rule with Jesus. According to such theology, there will be another group of people known as "other sheep" or the "great crowd," who will lay in the ground in a form of soul-sleep at death, living forever in paradise on earth after the millennium. Such thinking, though, reflects a misunderstanding of this passage. Limiting the number of the anointed to 144,000 needlessly creates fear and apprehension.

On the contrary, these 144,000 sealed individuals are Jewish evangelists who will be God's witnesses during the tribulation. A reliance on the witness of Jewish evangelists is in keeping with Isaiah 49:6, in which Isaiah prophesied the Jews would become "a light for the nations" so that people "to the ends of the earth" might be saved. That promise remains largely unfulfilled during the church age because most Jews have rejected Jesus's claim to be the Messiah and have failed to become the light of the world (cf. Rom 9-11). However, God will resume his work with the Jewish people during the tribulation.

7:5-8 The 144,000 Jewish evangelists who proclaim the gospel during the tribulation

will be divided evenly among the twelve tribes of Israel: **Judah, Reuben, Gad, Asher, Naphtali, Manasseh, Simeon, Levi, Issachar, Zebulun, Joseph**, and **Benjamin**.

7:9-12 At this point, yet another great worship service occurs in heaven, the third such service in four chapters. The presence of **a vast multitude from every nation, tribe, people, and language** confirms the truthfulness of 5:9, where the Lamb is praised for redeeming such a diverse multitude. This indicates that racial distinctions and uniquenesses are retained in eternity. They appear wearing **white robes**, holding **palm branches**, standing before both God the Father and God the Son (7:9), and praising both: **Salvation belongs to our God . . . and to the Lamb** (7:10). **Angels**, the twenty-four **elders**, and **the four living creatures** (7:11) join the worship with a chorus attributing **blessing, glory, wisdom, thanksgiving, honor, power**, and **strength** to **God forever and ever** (7:12).

7:13-14 One of the elders asks about the identity of the multitude **in white robes** (7:13) only to answer the question himself when John replies, **Sir, you know**: they are people who come to salvation during the **tribulation** (7:14). This suggests the 144,000 Jewish evangelists will lead a large number of Jews and Gentiles to embrace Christ as their Lord and Savior. God wants everyone to know that even amid judgment, he offers abundant mercy and opportunity for pardon as well as abundant opportunity for turning from evil. Of course, that opportunity will close at Christ's second coming. Yet for the moment, men and women cannot claim God inhibited them from repenting and following him.

7:15-17 The phrase **for this reason** refers to the salvation described in 7:14. Because they have been "made . . . white in the blood of the Lamb," this multitude engages in a victory celebration that prefigures the final victory celebration at the end of history (cf. 21:1–22:5). The celebration is unending, and they **are before the throne of God** and **serve him day and night** (7:15). Their **hunger** and **thirst** will be satisfied forever, and forever they will be sheltered from harm (7:16). Each of these benefits is dispensed personally by **the Lamb**. He **is at the center of the throne** and **will shepherd them, guide them to springs of the waters of life**, and **wipe away every tear from their eyes** (7:17).

8:1 The **silence in heaven for about half an hour** upon the opening of **the seventh seal** is a pause to allow repentance before God unleashes the next round of judgment. The provision of such a pause underscores God's mercy. Its brevity highlights the need to repent quickly as opportunity remains.

V. THE SEVEN TRUMPETS (8:2–11:19)

8:2-3 **Seven angels who stand in the presence of God** are given **seven trumpets** (8:2) that will be used to release another series of judgments. In the meantime, **another angel** offers to the Lord **a large amount of incense** and **the prayers of all the saints** (8:3). These prayers are the petitions of martyrs from the tribulation who cried out previously for divine vengeance and justice and were told to wait (cf. 6:10-11). The fact that they rise with sweet smelling incense suggests it is a pleasant experience for God to receive the prayers of his people.

8:4-5 The martyrs' prayers were not in vain despite God's delayed response because now, as they go **up in the presence of God from the angel's hand** (8:4), they prompt an immediate response of angelic fire being **hurled . . . to the earth**. This brings about accompanying **peals of thunder, rumblings, flashes of lightning, and an earthquake** (8:5).

8:6-7 Within the seventh seal are **seven trumpets**, which depict a whole new round of judgments, **and the seven angels** prepare to administer them. The first trumpet's **hail and fire, mixed with blood** depicts a firestorm that dwarfs even the most gigantic contemporary wildfires. While wildfires in the western United States, for example, burn tens of thousands of acres, this firestorm will affect **a third** of the planet, consuming **a third of the trees** and **all the green grass**.

8:8-9 The **second** trumpet brings **something like a great mountain ablaze with fire** that is **hurled into the sea** (8:8), scorching **a third** of the sea **creatures** and destroying **a third of the ships** (8:9). This may be part of the same firestorm triggered by the

sounding of the first trumpet, or it could be a separate event.

8:10-11 The **great star** associated with the **third . . . trumpet** (8:10) appears to be a meteor or asteroid falling to earth. Science fiction works commonly have depicted the damage such a celestial body could cause were it to collide with earth, but in this instance the damage will be real. **Wormwood** (8:11) means bitter, referencing the effect this thing will have on **a third of the rivers and springs** (8:10). **Many . . . people** will die because of severely contaminated water that has **been made bitter** (8:11).

8:12 The **fourth . . . trumpet** brings a darkening of **a third of** the sunlight, **a third of** the moonlight, and **a third of the stars**. As a result, **a third of the day** will be **without light**, with **a third of the night** experiencing a similar effect. This means that normal cycles of daylight and darkness will be thrown off, perhaps somewhat resembling an Alaskan winter, whose lingering darkness has physical, emotional, and psychological effects.

8:13 Prior to the final three trumpets and their accompanying judgments, God sends **an eagle flying high overhead, crying out in a loud voice** to warn **those who live on the earth** regarding the coming judgments' severity. The warning has a twofold purpose. First, it suggests the remaining judgments will be harsh. That is because they are intended to purify and reclaim the earth. Second, it underscores the graciousness of God in offering an opportunity for humanity to repent before judgment falls. God the Father, like an earthly parent, takes two approaches with people—one of grace and another of wrath (cf. Rom 11:22). During the church age, he generally exhibits grace and mercy. He also exhibits a form of passive wrath by allowing people and nations to face the destructive consequences of their actions.

Romans 1 is a prime example of this, depicting idolatrous people whom "God delivered . . . over to degrading passions" (1:26)—that is, to homosexual passions. As recipients of this passive divine wrath, they "received in their own persons the appropriate penalty of their error" (1:27). As Paul explains, "Because they did not think it worthwhile to acknowledge God, God delivered them over to a corrupt mind so that they do what is not right" (1:28). When the tribulation begins, though, this passive form of God's wrath that merely declines to hold back the just dessert of human actions will yield to more active wrath. God's wrath will rain down as it did on Sodom and Gomorrah (cf. Gen 19:23-29).

9:1 Upon the **fifth** angel's **trumpet** blast, John saw **a star that had fallen from heaven to earth**. Notably, the star is not an inanimate object but has a personal identity, for John says a key was given **to him**. Specifically, the star represents Satan. In Isaiah 14:12, the prophet says the "shining morning star" had "fallen from the heavens." The subsequent description of that star in Isaiah 14:12-14 has led many Bible interpreters to conclude that the passage is describing Satan, in addition to its reference to King Nebuchadnezzar of Babylon. In other words, Isaiah spoke of Satan's original fall into rebellion and applied it to Babylon's prideful king.

Just as a key grants us access to a home, office, or car, this **key** grants Satan access to **the shaft to the abyss**. The *abyss* is the abode of the demons, according to Luke 8:31, in which demons begged Jesus "not to banish them." During the tribulation, Satan will be granted authority to unlock the pit. A principle illustrated in this verse is that Satan only has as much authority as God grants him. Nowhere in Scripture is that principle more prominently displayed than in Job 1:12 and 2:6, in which Satan cannot harm Job without God's permission. But what the devil intends for evil, God intends for good.

9:2-4 From **the abyss** comes **smoke . . . like smoke from a great furnace** (9:2). When it rises, **the sun and the air** will be **darkened** as though it were nighttime (9:2). **Locusts** will emerge from the smoke with scorpion-like powers (9:3) and will be **told not to harm the grass of the earth, or any green plant, or any tree, but only those people who do not have God's seal on their foreheads** (9:4). Interestingly, this marks a departure from the activity of normal locusts, which eat grass, plants, and trees. But as indicated by their origin in the abode of demons, these "locusts" are demons. The "seal" represents God's divine protection of believers. These demons will have to leave followers of Jesus alone.

9:5-6 These locusts will be permitted **to torment** nonbelievers on earth **for five months**, though they will not be **permitted to kill them**. We do not know the specific manner in which this demonic attack will be delivered, but it will be painful, **like the torment caused by a scorpion when it stings** (9:5). This will make people **long to die**, but **death will flee from them** (9:6). They will be forced to live through a period of prolonged, demonic suffering intended for those who do not know Jesus as their Savior.

9:7-8 The appearance of the locusts was like horses prepared for battle (9:7). This sentence emphasizes the ferociousness of the locusts and their intimidating looks. In the Old Testament, locusts were instruments of judgment, as in the eighth plague God brought upon the Egyptians (see Exod 10:1-20) and in the judgment envisioned by the prophet in Joel 1:2-12. The placement of **something like golden crowns . . . on their heads** signifies authority—in this case, authority from hell. The locusts' demonic origin is further underscored by their strange appearance: they have **faces . . . like human faces** and **hair like women's hair** (9:7). That they have **teeth like lions' teeth** (9:8) also points to their ferociousness.

9:9-11 Because the locusts have **chests like iron breastplates**, they will be protected from harm as they torment others. This second mention of **horses rushing into battle** (see 9:7) highlights the organization and the power of God's judgment on nonbelievers. Venomous **tails with stingers like scorpions** (9:10) are mentioned in addition to the locusts' teeth as another instrument of destruction. The harm they inflict will last **for five months** (9:10). The **angel of the abyss**, the **Hebrew** name **Abaddon**, and the **Greek** name **Apollyon** (9:11) are references to Satan. He is directing the entire locust attack.

9:12 Prior to the fifth trumpet's sounding, an eagle spoke a threefold "woe" (8:13). John tells readers the fifth seal represented only the first of those. So though the locust judgment may seem sufficient from a human vantage point, God says he is only getting started.

9:13-15 At the sounding of the **sixth . . . trumpet** (9:13), the command for further judgment comes from God, who orders the release of **four angels bound at the great river Euphrates** (9:14) to **kill a third of the human race**. Even the judgments directed by Satan are carried out under God's authority, but here God's role is explicit and direct. These angels of judgment **were prepared for** this specific **hour, day, month, and year** (9:15). The deaths noted here, combined with the fourth of the earth killed in 6:8, bring the death total during the first three and a half years of the tribulation to more than half of the world's population.

9:16-17 Two hundred million mounted **troops** probably refers to the same demons associated with the fifth trumpet (cf. 9:1-11). They will serve again as instruments of judgment. As with the fifth trumpet, the agents of judgment here are described in terms of **horses** (cf. 9:7) and lions (cf. 9:8). This time, their ferocious appearance is heightened by **mouths** emitting **fire, smoke, and sulfur.**

9:18-19 The mode of death is specified for the third of mankind mentioned in 9:15. They will be killed by **plagues** of **fire, smoke**, and **sulfur** (9:18). The description of

the horses (9:19) underscores the likelihood that the agents of judgment associated with the sixth trumpet are the same as those of the fifth trumpet, both having **mouths** and **tails** with destructive powers.

9:20-21 Why would God allow something as horrific as the judgments described in this chapter? A partial answer is that despite **these plagues**, mankind **did not repent of the works of their hands to stop worshiping demons and idols** (9:20). Moreover, **they did not repent of their murders, their sorceries, their sexual immorality, or their thefts** (9:21). This is a picture of utterly hardened hearts. Already, technology could allow every human on the planet to witness these catastrophic judgments; and as 6:16-17 explained, all will know that God is the source of them. Yet men and women will continue to harden their hearts.

The anti-God movement in America today is a harbinger of this tragic reality. It used to be that atheists were quiet about their beliefs, whispering here and there. Now, though, atheists and worshipers of false gods are becoming bolder. As Romans 1:21-25 explains, when people possess ample evidence of God's activity but fail to honor or give thanks to him, he gives them over to the just consequences of their actions. Those consequences come in the form of passive wrath during the church age, in which God's hand of restraint and protection are removed. But during the tribulation period, his wrath will be active. You can get a lot of stuff without God—money, popularity, notoriety. However, your soul will starve without him, and eventually you will face the Lord's judgment.

10:1 A majestic, **mighty angel** emerges **from heaven . . . with a rainbow over his head** and **a cloud** beneath it. The rainbow and cloud serve as a reminder of God's faithfulness to keep his promises. That was, after all, the stated purpose of the rainbow amid clouds when God pointed to it following the flood (see Gen 9:12-17), and that was likewise the rainbow's significance in 4:3, where it surrounded God's throne. The angel's **face . . . like the sun** and legs **. . . like pillars of fire** denote awesome majesty.

10:2-3 There is no mention of what is written on the **little scroll opened in his hand**, but context suggests it contains more prophecy of events to transpire during the tribulation. The presentation of this scroll is accompanied by a roaring in nature signified by the angel's **right foot on the sea** and **his left on the land** (10:2) as he cries out with a **voice like a roaring lion**. This suggests the judgments described in the scroll are awesome and powerful. To underscore this reality, **the seven thunders raised their voices** (10:3).

10:4 **Seven** is the number of completion in Scripture and denotes that all prophecy on the scroll had been revealed to John. Thus, John **was about to write** the prophecy when **a voice from heaven** stopped him: **Seal up what the seven thunders said, and do not write it down.** On many occasions in Revelation, an angel speaks for God. But here, God himself speaks and says he wants the scroll's prophecy to remain secret, at least for a time. For all the information Revelation tells about Christ's second coming, there are still some things God has opted not to disclose yet.

10:5-6 Upon hearing God's prohibition against revealing the scroll's prophecy, the mighty angel **raised his right hand to heaven** (10:5) and swore an oath that there would **no longer be a delay** (10:6). With the rapid pace at which descriptions of judgment have proceeded thus far, it may seem surprising that God's messenger would say there has been a delay! Yet what has been delayed to this point is the full and final outpouring of God's wrath. Through the judgment of the seven seals (6:1-17; 8:1-5) and the first six trumpets (8:6–9:21), God has been restraining his final judgment to allow continued opportunity for repentance. As Peter put it, the delay is not slowness but patience: "The Lord does not delay his promise, as some understand delay, but is patient with you, not wanting any to perish but all to come to repentance" (2 Pet 3:9).

10:7 This verse begins with a word of contrast—**but**—to signify a change from the delay referenced in 10:6. **When the seventh**

angel will blow his trumpet in 11:15, it will mark a shift to the end of the tribulation, when the seven bowls of God's wrath will be poured out on the earth (16:1-21). At that point, the narrative truly will begin rushing toward the return of Jesus to set up his throne on earth. It might seem puzzling that John would announce a rush to the second coming when there are still twelve chapters remaining in Revelation. However, some of those chapters will rehash from a different perspective events already described. Thus far, God has revealed events to come. Beginning in chapter 11, he will focus on personalities involved in those events. These include the two witnesses, the Antichrist, and the false prophet.

10:8-9 Following the angel's oath, the voice speaks once again and commands John to **go, take the scroll that lies open in the hand of the angel** (10:8). The angel's further command to **take and eat** the scroll is accompanied by this explanation: **It will be bitter in your stomach, but it will be as sweet as honey in your mouth** (10:9).

10:10 John's consumption of the scroll is reminiscent of events in Ezekiel 2:8–3:15, in which the prophet had a similar experience. God instructed Ezekiel to take a scroll from an extended hand and eat it. When Ezekiel obeyed, he reported the scroll to be "as sweet as honey in my mouth" (Ezek 3:3). Yet after learning the people of Israel would not listen to God, the prophet reported feeling "bitterness" and "an angry spirit" and that "the LORD's hand was on [him] powerfully" (Ezek 3:14).

Likewise in Revelation, God's words of prophecy are **sweet as honey** in John's mouth. But when he begins to digest them in his spirit, he reports, **My stomach became bitter.** The hard word of prophecy is pleasant to receive because it is, after all, the very word of God. Processing the prophecy internally, however, is a different matter that can prove difficult and even unpleasant.

10:11 Equipped with this harsh word from God, John is instructed by the angel and the voice from heaven: **You must prophecy**

again about many people, nations, languages, and kings. Even when the word of God is difficult, then, the man of God must continue to proclaim it.

11:1 John is **given a measuring reed like a rod** and told to **go measure the temple of God and the altar, and count those who worship there.** To measure a structure or piece of property in Scripture is a means of laying claim to it. You measure it because you own it. In this case, then, God is laying claim to the Jewish temple in Jerusalem that will be rebuilt during the tribulation. Today a Muslim mosque known as the Dome of the Rock sits on the temple site. Orthodox Jews, however, pray daily for the return of the temple at the Western Wall—the one remaining structure from the ancient Jewish temple complex that sits beneath the Dome of the Rock.

11:2 The measurement is not to include, according to these instructions, **the courtyard outside the temple . . . because it is given to the nations, and they will trample the holy city for forty-two months.** "Nations" is a translation of the Greek word that refers to Gentiles in this context. The outer court of the temple will be the only place in the complex that Gentiles are allowed to enter. "Forty-two months" correspond with three and a half years, indicating that the events described in this chapter will occur during the latter half of the seven-year tribulation.

11:3 During the tribulation, **two witnesses** will be granted **authority to prophesy 1,260 days**—three and a half years on the Jewish calendar of thirty-day months. One reason to be confident in the Bible's truth is its specificity in passages like this. It not only prophesies events, but precise details about their occurrence. The message of these two witnesses will be somber, for they will be **dressed in sackcloth.**

11:4 The two witnesses are pictured metaphorically as **two olive trees** and **two lampstands that stand before the Lord.** Olive trees stand for God's people in the Old and New Testaments (see Ps 52:8; Jer 11:16; Rom

11:24). The lampstands signify that God will provide spiritual illumination through these witnesses.

11:5 **If anyone** harms these two witnesses, **fire comes from their mouths and consumes their enemies.** These, then, are two extraordinary individuals. Yet that should not come as a surprise because the tribulation is not an ordinary period of history. To underscore the divine anointing on these witnesses, as well as the seriousness of coming against them, the death penalty is pronounced even upon **anyone** who **wants to harm them.**

11:6 **Authority to close up the sky so that it does not rain during the days of their prophecy** harkens back to Elijah, and **power over the waters to turn them into blood and to strike the earth with every plague** reminds of Moses. Elijah prophesied a drought (see 1 Kgs 17:1-7), and Moses pronounced a series of plagues on Egypt, including the water being turned into blood (see Exod 7–12). These realities may indicate that the two witnesses are Elijah and Moses—who have returned to earth at least once before at the Mount of Transfiguration (see Matt 17:1-13). What's more, Elijah did not die (see 2 Kgs 2:1-14) and Moses's body was hidden by God (Deut 34:6), possibly hinting at the Lord's intention to use both of their bodies on earth again.

Another reality underscored in this verse is that events connected with the Old Testament will occur again during the tribulation. The pattern of God's work operative in the church age will change because his relationship to the world will shift at the rapture of the church.

11:7 **The beast that comes up out of the abyss** is also known as the Antichrist. He was introduced in 6:1-11 as the rider of four horses, and he will be discussed at length in 13:1-10 as a "beast," the same appellation he is given here. By whatever name he is referenced, this figure is the chief antagonist of the tribulation. After the two witnesses **finish their testimony,** he **will make war on them, conquer them, and kill them.** No one will be able to stop these witnesses except the Antichrist. His power overrules theirs—but only temporarily.

11:8-9 It will be worldwide news when these two witnesses with supernatural powers die in Jerusalem and **their dead bodies . . . lie in the main street.** The wickedness of the city during the tribulation is highlighted by the reference to it as **Sodom and Egypt** (11:8). Some **peoples, tribes, languages, and nations** will not allow the two witnesses to be buried, viewing their corpses **for three and a half days** (11:9). Notably, just as some individuals from every "nation, tribe, people, and language" will be saved (6:9), some from every ethnic group also will harden their hearts against God. The beast will mastermind all this activity in an effort to show he is superior in power to God's two witnesses.

11:10 Those who live on the earth will celebrate not only the death of the two witnesses, but the triumph of the beast as well. This celebration will involve gifts, like those given at a Christmas or birthday party, because wicked men and women will delight in the death of two figures who **tormented** them with supernatural judgments and preaching of righteousness.

11:11-12 After three and a half days of gloating over the slain witnesses, the party will end for the beast and his followers. **The breath of life from God** will enter the two witnesses, bringing about a resurrection, and they will stand **on their feet**, causing **great fear** to come upon all who see them (11:11). The beast's bragging will be interrupted by God's voice calling, **Come up here.** At that, the witnesses will be raptured in a cloud **while their enemies** watch (11:12).

11:13 At the **moment** of their rapture, a **violent earthquake** will cause **a tenth** of Jerusalem to fall to the ground and **seven thousand people** to die. The survivors will be **terrified** and give **glory to the God of heaven.** As God often does, in this instance he will allow negative events to occur because those events will bring him greater glory.

11:14 With the passing of **the second woe**, it is appropriate to pause and note that these events could be disorienting at first glance. That is because chapter 11 occurs in the section of Revelation describing the events of the tribulation without focusing much on the personalities involved. When the focus turns to personalities in chapter 12, John moves back chronologically and fills in details.

11:15 The **seventh . . . trumpet** announces the imminent arrival of Christ's reign as **loud voices in heaven** declare, **The kingdom of the world has become the kingdom of our Lord and of his Christ, and he will reign forever.** This sequence depicts events strikingly close to the end of the tribulation and the coming of God's kingdom. Take note that the rapture is not synonymous with the second coming. The rapture is when Christ will come in the air to receive believers into heaven. He will not come all the way down to earth in the rapture. He will only do that at the second coming, when he will be accompanied by the saints.

11:16-18 In preparation for Jesus's coming, **the twenty-four elders** who were introduced in 4:4 fall down in worship (11:16). Their praise announces that God, in this **great power**, has **begun to reign** (11:17). Then they speak of another resurrection. This is not the resurrection of New Testament believers because that occurs at the rapture. This is the resurrection of Old Testament **saints**—God's **servants the prophets**, who will be given **the reward** they are due along with **those who fear [his] name, both small and great** (11:18). The Old Testament has a unique connection to the tribulation because it prophesies this seven-year period (cf. Jer 30:3-7; Dan 9:24-27). Therefore, Old Testament saints will receive their resurrection bodies following the tribulation.

11:19 The culminating preparation for Christ's return occurs with the opening of **the temple of God in heaven** and the appearance of the **ark of the covenant.** This is accompanied by **flashes of lightning, rumblings and peals of thunder, an earthquake, and severe hail.** Now the stage is fully set for Christ's return. But prior to highlighting that glorious moment, John rewinds the narrative to discuss characters in greater depth.

VI. THE WOMAN, THE DRAGON, THE BEAST, AND THE LAMB (12:1–15:8)

The rewind commences as John retells the story of the tribulation through the eyes of its dominant characters. This section of the book focuses on the second half of the tribulation period.

12:1-2 The first person to whom we're introduced is **a woman clothed with the sun, with the moon under her feet and a crown of twelve stars on her head** (12:1). The "twelve stars" symbolize the twelve tribes of Israel, and the "woman" is Israel. Her pregnancy denotes two realities. First, it symbolizes the fact that Jesus the Messiah came through Israel. At his first coming, Jesus was born of a Jewish woman. Second, it symbolizes the fact that Jesus's second coming must again originate with Israel. The purpose of the tribulation is for Israel to give birth, so to speak, to the Messiah once again. In other words, Jesus cannot return until Israel receives him. Most of the Jewish people currently reject him. Yet through the **labor and agony** (12:2) of the tribulation, overwhelming numbers of Israelites will receive Christ. Only after that occurs can he appear to the rest of the world.

12:3-4 The second character introduced in this scene is **a great fiery red dragon having seven heads and ten horns** and **seven crowns** on its heads (12:3). John states explicitly in 12:9 that this dragon is the devil. The sweeping **away** of **a third of the stars in heaven** (12:4) depicts Satan's control over a third of the angels, who have rebelled against God and help carry out Satan's evil schemes. Scripture suggests there are millions of angels, so the devil controls an extraordinary multitude.

During the tribulation, Satan will seek to destroy Israel and **devour her child** (12:4). That is, he wants to preclude the possibility that Christ will return to the world through Israel. If there is no Israel, there can be no triumphant return of Christ and Satan will rule the earth. He employed a similar strategy at Jesus's first coming, with King Herod's attempt to kill the Christ child (see Matt 2:1-18).

12:5-6 The **birth of a Son**, of course, is a reference to Jesus's advent as a baby in Bethlehem. His **rule of all nations with an iron rod** refers to the millennial kingdom, in which he will reign over the earth with his people for a thousand years. The child's being **caught up to God and to his throne** (12:5) pictures the ascension of Christ (see Acts 1:6-11). Israel's nourishment in **the wilderness** for 1,260 **days** (12:6) depicts God's protection of Israel during the second half of the tribulation—three and a half years. During that time, the Jewish people will receive Jesus as Messiah en masse and hasten his second coming.

12:7-8 To protect Israel, the archangel **Michael** and his fellow **angels** will fight **against the dragon** and his demons (12:7). The angels' manner of fighting will be similar to what they do on behalf of all believers today (see Heb 1:14). The accidents we narrowly avoid and the perfect timing of various life events are not coincidences, but heaven's orchestration of all things for our good. As Michael fought on Daniel's behalf against demons in the Old Testament era (see Dan 10:13), angels fight for believers today and will fight for Israel in the tribulation to come. Despite the devil's raging, he and his demons will **not prevail**. Indeed, there is **no place ... in heaven** for them **any longer** (12:8). In the end, they will neither thwart God's plan for Israel nor for the return of his Son.

12:9 Satan's expulsion from heaven is the same episode referenced in Isaiah 14:12-15 and Revelation 9:1, which occurred sometime before the fall of mankind (see Gen 3). At that time, Satan **was thrown to earth, and his** fallen **angels with him**. Since then, his chief strategy has been to act as **the one who deceives the whole world**. He cannot win spiritual battles by exerting authority because he has been defeated on the cross. He has to win by deception, influencing our thinking through spiritual and worldly means. We allow Satan to achieve victories in our lives when we act on that deception rather than rejecting it as a lie.

12:10 Another strategy of Satan's is to be **the accuser of** believers (see Zech 3:1-7), accusing **them before our God day and night.** This indicates, first, that God has allowed Satan access to his divine presence. Second, it indicates Satan uses that access to level accusations against God's people. He does that because he knows the Lord's righteous character and that human sin breaks their fellowship with God. If Satan cannot prevent a person from being saved, he at least wants to steal the joy that comes from walking in fellowship with God.

12:11 Those who conquer Satan in their lives do so **by the blood of the Lamb and by the word of their testimony.** Every Christian is saved from eternal condemnation by Christ's blood. Those who defeat Satan's schemes in this life and receive the reward of eternal authority do so by a godly public testimony. Secret agent Christians, those who are saved but operate undercover, so to speak, will receive no authority from Christ. Triumphant, conquering believers **do not love their lives** more than they love God. His kingdom agenda for their lives overrules all others.

12:12-13 During the final three and a half years of the tribulation, **the earth** will experience Satan's **great fury, because he knows his time is short** (12:12). The devil can read Revelation too, and he knows from 20:1-3 that he will be locked up for a thousand years following Christ's return. This reality will prompt him to take full advantage of his final forty-two months of freedom to wreak havoc in Israel and the world. His goal will be to destroy Israel and thus render God's Word false. As John puts it, **when the dragon saw that he had been thrown down to the earth, he persecuted the woman** (Israel) **who had given birth to the male child** (Jesus) (12:13).

12:14 During the same three and a half years—**a time, times, and half a time**—in which Satan comes against Israel with wild

fury, God will protect Israel supernaturally. This cosmic conflict of good and evil will eventuate in an epic battle known as Armageddon (16:16).

12:15-16 Satan will unleash a particularly severe attack on Israel at some point, depicted as water **spewed** from **the serpent . . . like a river flowing after the woman, to sweep her away with a flood** (12:15). To counter this diabolical attempt at Israel's destruction, God will activate a supernatural defense mechanism, pictured metaphorically as the earth's opening **its mouth** and swallowing **up the river that the dragon had spewed** (12:16). This prophecy illustrates a broader principle: We discover God most powerfully in the context of being overwhelmed. When believers are flooded with opposition, often they are able to watch God supernaturally suck up the flood of despair and avert Satan's plan for destruction.

12:17-18 This defeat will leave Satan **furious** with Israel and intent **to wage war** against men and women from every nation **who keep the commands of God and hold firmly to the testimony about Jesus** (12:17). The scene closes with **the dragon** standing **on the sand of the sea** (12:18).

13:1 Chapter 13 completes the description of an unholy trinity that John began in 12:3. The three members of this pseudo-trinity are the devil, depicted as a dragon; the Antichrist, depicted as a beast from the sea; and the false prophet, depicted as a beast from the earth.

The sea represents the Gentiles. So depicting the Antichrist as **a beast coming up out of the sea** signifies that he will be a Gentile. The Antichrist's **ten horns** represent a ten-nation confederacy that he will rule (see Dan 7:7-8). The setting of this chapter is the second half of the tribulation, during which time the Antichrist will oppose Israel after appearing to be its ally during the first half. This figure will blaspheme the names of God, signified by the **blasphemous names** on **its heads.**

13:2 The Antichrist will be a human monster. He is described as a predator **like a leopard** with **feet . . . like a bear's** and a mouth like

a lion's. History has known monsters in the persons of Hitler, Stalin, Lenin, and Mao among others. The reason we classify them this way is that they sought to exterminate people en masse. This is precisely what the Antichrist will seek to do with Israel. This man's **great authority** will come directly from Satan.

13:3-4 At some point, the Antichrist will appear **to be fatally wounded**, but the **fatal wound** will be **healed**. This will lead **the whole earth** to be **amazed** and to follow him (13:3). As they do, he will direct worship toward the devil. Mass worship of the devil may seem bizarre and even unthinkable to us, but it is not so absurd in a culture that has dismissed God. The Antichrist will seize upon the spiritual vacuum and inspire widespread worship of himself and of Satan (13:4).

13:5-7 The Antichrist's **authority** during the latter half of the tribulation will be significant. Not only will he be permitted to **utter boasts and blasphemies** against God for three and a half years (13:5), but he will also **blaspheme** the Lord's **dwelling** in heaven and **those who dwell in heaven** (13:6)—either believers there, or angels, or both. The Antichrist also will have authority **to wage war against** followers of Jesus living on earth **and to conquer them** (13:7). This evil power will touch **every tribe, people, language, and nation**—a familiar refrain by this point in Revelation.

If the thought of a world ruler with such sweeping authority seems farfetched, think of Hitler. If not for a series of providential interventions, he might have achieved the goal of world domination. For example, a snowstorm kept the Germans from conquering Russia, and America's entrance into World War II pushed them back on the western front. Hitler wasn't *the* Antichrist, but he was *an* antichrist. And his near conquest of the world makes an actual conquest by this future leader seem less implausible.

13:8 Only believers will refuse to worship the Antichrist. All others will bow—**everyone whose name was not written from the foundation of the world in the book of life of the Lamb who was slaughtered.** This

verse implies that God the Father reckoned the death of Jesus to humans as righteousness before the foundation of the world. Christ's death occurred at a specific point in history some two thousand years ago, but for God all moments are the present. Thus, even before creating the universe, he counted Christ's death as atoning for the sin each person inherits from Adam (cf. Rom 5:18).

Importantly, no one is condemned for original, inherited sin. The only cause for anyone's consignment to hell is his or her own personal sin, including rejection of Jesus as Savior. That's why children who die in infancy and people born with severe mental disabilities go to heaven. They have no conscience, personal sin, or spiritual rejection of the Savior for which to be condemned. Yet when a person knowingly sins and rejects the revelation of God in creation, his or her name is erased from the book of life and only reinserted should he or she place faith in Jesus as Savior.

13:9-10 The tribulation will be a rough period for followers of Jesus. All who refuse to worship the beast will be under a sentence of captivity and death, though not everyone who follows Jesus will die. The heightened cost of discipleship at that time will make it much less desirable to be saved then than it is now. Extreme persecution **calls for endurance and faithfulness from the saints** (13:10).

13:11 The earth is a reference to the promised land. Thus, the **beast coming up out of the earth** will be Jewish. He will have a gentle side **like a lamb** but will speak the very words of Satan **like a dragon.**

13:12 This second beast, the false prophet, completes the unholy trinity, which imitates the work of the Holy Trinity. Within the Godhead, the Father seeks worship; the Son gives glory to the Father; and the Holy Spirit gives glory to the Son. Here, Satan seeks worship for himself; the first beast glorifies Satan; and the second beast glorifies the first. Specifically, this second beast **compels the earth and those who live on it to worship the first beast.** Additionally, he will heal the Antichrist's fatal wound, imitating the Holy

Spirit's work of raising Christ from the dead (see Rom 8:11).

13:13-15 The false prophet will perform **great signs, even causing fire to come down from heaven to earth in front of people** (13:13). Many will be deceived **because of the signs**, the apex of which will be the Antichrist's resurrection (13:14). The false prophet also will animate a previously inanimate **image of the** Antichrist **so that the image of the beast [will] both speak and cause whoever [will] not worship the image to be killed** (13:15). Many people will assume a person doing such miracles is divine, but Scripture teaches otherwise. Just because someone can work a miracle doesn't make him worthy of following. God does miracles in a righteous way and in support of biblical truth. But even if someone can call down fire and raise the dead, he is an instrument of Satan if he does not also point people to Jesus.

13:16-18 Another role of the false prophet will be to force everyone on earth **to receive a mark on his right hand or on his forehead** to signify allegiance to the Antichrist (13:16). Without this mark, a person will not be permitted to engage in commerce of any kind (13:17). Such a mark may take the form of a chip embedded under the skin. The mark will contain **the number** of the Antichrist, which **is 666** (13:18). Six is the number of man; it contrasts with seven, which is the number of God. The numeral six is repeated three times, once each for Satan, the Antichrist, and the false prophet. Only by the grace of God will those without this mark be able to function in a world under their influence. Note that the centralized, governmental control of trade is the economics of the Antichrist (13:17).

14:1 Some religious groups, like the Jehovah's Witnesses, contend the **144,000** people with Jesus **on Mount Zion** with **his name and his Father's name written on their foreheads** are the sum total of all saved people. That's absolutely false. These are Jewish evangelists, whose job is to announce the gospel worldwide during the tribulation to lead many more to faith in Christ. These evangelists will prepare the way for the return of Jesus. The mark on their foreheads contrasts with the mark placed on nonbelievers by the false prophet (cf. 13:16).

14:2-3 John hears thunderous music in heaven **like harpists playing** (14:2) as the 144,000 evangelists sing **a new song before the throne and before the four living creatures and the elders**, a song which **no one could learn except them** (14:3). The privilege of sharing the gospel worldwide during this period of widespread Christian persecution will inspire worship among the Jewish evangelists.

14:4-5 Two key characteristics of the 144,000 are their moral purity and their status as **firstfruits** of God's saving work during the tribulation. Their purity is evident from their description as having **not defiled themselves with women** (14:4) and from the fact that **no lie was found in their mouths**. Indeed, **they are blameless** (14:5). Morally and spiritually, they **follow the Lamb wherever he goes** (14:4).

As Jesus is the firstfruits of the resurrection (see 1 Cor 15:23), the 144,000 Jewish evangelists are the "firstfruits" of those to be saved during the tribulation. There will be a multitude saved during the tribulation, but these 144,000 are presented to God the Father and God the Son as the initial harvest of those **redeemed from humanity** (14:4).

14:6 The message announced by these 144,000 evangelists also is heralded by an **angel flying high overhead**. It is **the eternal gospel** announced **to every nation, tribe, language, and people**. Even while judgment and persecution are being poured out on the earth, widespread evangelism will be occurring.

14:7 Multitudes will persist in rebellion against God, but multitudes will heed the call to **fear God and give him glory, because the hour of his judgment has come**. Worship of God as Maker of **heaven and earth, the sea and the springs** marks a contrast with the false worship of Satan and the Antichrist.

14:8 Babylon the Great is a metaphorical expression depicting the system of false religion and rebellion against God established by the devil and the two beasts (cf. 17:1-18). Unlike worship of God, which will endure, this false religion will prove temporary. Nevertheless, it will entice **all the nations** to indulge fleshly lusts such as the craving for **sexual immorality**, which will bring God's **wrath**.

14:9-10 Anyone who receives the **mark** of the beast **on his forehead or on his hand** (14:9) has positioned himself against God and thus **will also drink the wine of God's wrath**. Receiving the mark of 666 (13:18) may appear to be a harmless formality to enable commerce, but it designates its recipients for judgment at **full strength** in hell—a place where the wicked are **tormented with fire and sulfur in the sight of the holy angels and in the sight of the Lamb** (14:10).

14:11-12 Those who reject God's offer of mercy in Christ will not simply die and pass into unconsciousness. Rather, their conscious **torment** will go on **forever and ever**. One aspect of that torment is a lack of **rest** during the **day** and the **night** (14:11). Hell is separation from God, and God is the one who gives rest (see Matt 11:28). So picture the unpleasantness of battling insomnia for a week. Then extend that into eternity. Then contrast that potential future with heaven, which is depicted in Scripture as a place of eternal rest (Heb 3:7-4:11). Consignment to hell is a free choice, a penalty men and women bring on themselves, as when they elect to receive **the mark of** the beast (14:11). That reality should motivate followers of Jesus to endure in their obedience to **God's commandments and their faith** (14:12).

14:13 The dead who die in the Lord from now on is a reference to those who are persecuted for their faith in Christ during the tribulation. They will find **rest from their labors**, a fate which is the opposite of that experienced by those who receive the mark of the beast.

14:14-16 With the end of history rapidly approaching, **one like the Son of Man** appears **on the cloud, with a golden crown on his head and a sharp sickle in his hand** (14:14).

The sickle here is an instrument to inflict judgment and death on those who reject God. It is mentioned six times in five verses (14:14-18) to underscore the impending doom for those who reject God during the tribulation. In general, a sickle is a tool used to harvest crops, and that makes it an entirely appropriate metaphor for divine judgment because a **harvest** (14:15) of people's deeds during their earthly lives is in view. Thus, **the one seated on the cloud swung his sickle over the earth, and the earth was harvested** (14:16).

14:17-19 The number of divine messengers prepared to reap the harvest of judgment increases when **another angel who [has] a sharp sickle [comes] out of the temple in heaven** (14:17). Yet **another angel** calls to the one with the sharp sickle that the harvest has **ripened** (14:18). This phrase is a reminder that God does not pour out his wrath on people at the first hint of their sinful rebellion, though that would be entirely justified. Instead, he provides extended opportunity for repentance and strikes with the sickle of judgment when rebellion has matured into an unmistakable pattern. He is like the keeper of a cosmic vineyard, casting grapes **into the great winepress of [his] wrath** (14:19).

14:20 When God brings final judgment against the nations who attack him at Armageddon (cf. 16:14-16), the bloodletting will be so severe that blood will splatter up the level of a horse's bridle for approximately **180 miles**.

15:1 This chapter is a prelude to **seven last plagues**, which will be delivered by **seven angels**. With the delivery of these judgments, **God's wrath will be completed**. That is, there will be no more judgment to be poured out on earth during the tribulation. Final judgment will remain, in which the wicked and the righteous are consigned to their respective eternal destinies. In view here is the cessation of the temporal judgments of the tribulation. While all the judgments to this point have been catastrophic, John hints at the uniquely awesome nature of these last judgments by noting that the sight of the seven angels was **great and awe-inspiring**.

15:2 As in 4:6, John sees **something like a sea of glass.** In all likelihood, it is not actually made of glass but is a body of water that is utterly smooth. The calmness, however, does not indicate serenity, for the sea is **mixed with fire,** an indication that the calm is merely a dramatic pause before a display of God's burning wrath. **Standing on the sea** are **those who had won the victory over the beast** by refusing to worship **its image** or be marked by **the number of its name.** These believers presumably have been martyred because they are in heaven rather than on earth. They hold **harps from God.**

15:3 The song of these believers is **the song of God's servant Moses and the song of the Lamb.** As Moses sang in triumph after Israel's Egyptian enemies had been swallowed up by the Red Sea (see Exod 15:1-18), followers of Christ from the tribulation will sing at the prospect of Satan, the Antichrist, and the false prophet being overwhelmed with judgment. This song will be even more glorious than that of Moses, though, because the judgment will be carried out by the Lamb of God. Jesus was active in Moses's day, following Israel through the wilderness (see 1 Cor 10:1-4). But he was not yet openly identified as the incarnate Messiah and Redeemer, as he is here. The worship song celebrates God's **great and awe-inspiring works,** which are never capricious or unfair, but **just and true.**

15:4 The two specific reasons for which God is worshiped are his character and his works. He is to be feared because of his glorious **name** and utter holiness. His **acts** during the tribulation—both of judging the rebellious and of saving great multitudes—are

righteous and have drawn **all the nations** to **worship before** him.

15:5-6 The procession of **the seven angels** (15:6) out of **the heavenly temple** (15:5) indicates the judgments they are to bear come directly from God's presence, for in the Old Testament, the temple was where God's presence dwelled. The agents of judgment are dressed to highlight their glory and moral purity, with **pure, bright linen** and **golden sashes wrapped around their chests** (15:6).

15:7 One of **the four living creatures,** introduced in 4:6, gives **the seven angels seven golden bowls filled with the wrath of God.** The appearance of these elements in chapter 4 and again here bookends the judgments of the tribulation. As a worship service in heaven featuring the four living creatures inaugurated the tribulation, a worship service featuring the creatures will culminate it. While God's wrath against the earth will last only for a season, he lives **forever.**

15:8 The temple's filling **with smoke** harkens back to two Old Testament scenes. The first occurred in 1 Kings 8:10-11, in which Solomon dedicated the temple and God's presence was manifested as a cloud that filled the building. No one could stand to enter, and the priests could not carry out their assigned functions. The second scene occurred in Isaiah 6:4. There the temple "filled with smoke" as Isaiah beheld God's glorious presence seated on a throne, surrounded by angelic creatures. In both instances, the cloud/smoke signified God's manifest presence. That is the point of the smoke in Revelation as well. God wants all to recognize him as the source of the fierce judgments to ensue.

VII. THE SEVEN BOWLS (16:1-21)

16:1 The seven bowls represent God's final judgments during the latter three and a half years of the tribulation. Foreshadowed by the "song of Moses" (15:3), some of these judgments parallel the plagues God brought upon Egypt through Moses (Exod 7–12). At the command of **a loud voice from the**

temple, the seven angels of chapter 15 **pour out . . . God's wrath** in rapid succession on those who reject God.

16:2 At the pouring of the **first** bowl, those who have taken **the mark of the beast** during the tribulation break out in **severely**

painful sores. As noted previously, such judgments are an expression of God's active wrath on sinners. During the church age, sinners on earth primarily experience God's passive wrath, in which he lets people face the just consequences of their sin without actively punishing them.

16:3-4 The **second** and **third** bowls turn the **sea, rivers,** and **springs of water** into blood. **All life in the sea** dies (16:3), and the fresh water becomes useless.

16:5-7 Because God is **just,** as **the angel of the waters** puts it, judgment is always an expression of his righteous standard. Since God is eternal—the one **who is and who was** (16:5)—he never lowers that standard. We must either meet his standard or have a substitute, Jesus Christ, meet it in our place. When a person accepts Jesus as his Savior, God imputes his righteous life to the saved person's account; thus, that person is counted as having met the standard. Those who will not receive Jesus get what they deserve for their actions. Those who ally with the beast in his campaign to pour out **the blood of the saints and the prophets** receive **blood to drink** because **they deserve it** (16:6). The Lord's judgments are **true and just** (16:7).

16:8-9 When the **fourth** angel pours **out his bowl on the sun,** it scorches **people with fire** (16:8). This marks a supernatural departure from the sun's historic pattern of providing heat and light. Yet even as people are **scorched by the intense heat,** they blaspheme **the name of God** and refuse to **repent.** Those who take the mark of the beast have confirmed their allegiance to the forces of darkness and are hardened against the Lord and his gospel. They are set against turning to God even though he **has the power over these plagues** (16:9).

16:10-11 At the pouring of the **fifth . . . bowl,** the beast's **kingdom [is] plunged into darkness,** leading to such intense emotional anguish that people engage in self-mutilation by gnawing **their tongues** (16:10). All the while, they blaspheme **the God of heaven because of their pains and their sores** but do **not repent of their works** (16:11). As in

16:9, the scene is reminiscent of a child cursing his parent while he is being spanked. Such a reaction to punishment inevitably triggers more punishment.

16:12 As God carries out the **sixth** bowl judgment, he is providentially guiding history toward the battle of Armageddon. **The great river Euphrates** dries up and opens a travel route for armies of the orient (i.e., **kings from the east**) to converge on the Middle East with the forces of the Antichrist and other world armies.

16:13-14 The convergence of armies for history's final war will not be merely a geopolitical event. Rather, it will be a supernatural event because **demonic spirits performing signs** will **travel to the kings of the whole world to assemble them for battle** (16:14). John pictures these demonic spirits **like frogs coming from** Satan's **mouth, from the beast's mouth, and from the mouth of the false prophet** (16:13). These three evil figures will employ miraculous signs to rally the nations behind their cause.

16:15 During the lead-up to war, Jesus injects a personal warning that his return will be sudden and unexpected, **like** the coming of **a thief.** The only way to avoid **shame** on that day is to be spiritually **alert** and **clothed** with a righteous life.

16:16 Satan, the Antichrist, the false prophet, and their demonic cronies eventually assemble all **the kings** of the earth **at the place called in Hebrew, Armageddon.** This is a Greek transliteration of the Hebrew phrase "Har Megiddo," meaning "Mount of Megiddo." It is the name of an ancient hilltop settlement in northern Israel near Haifa. Near it is a staggeringly huge plain that has been the site of several historic battles, though the greatest battle on this site has yet to occur.

16:17-18 The **seventh** angel pours out **his bowl into the air,** and a **loud voice** announces the immanent end of history with the words, **It is done.** At that, **flashes of lightning, rumblings, and peals of thunder** materialize (16:17) along with **a severe earthquake . . . like no other** (16:18). Though the armies have gathered, the direct and mighty acts of God are what draw John's attention as the Lord begins to convulse nature in opposition to his enemies.

16:19 **The great city** referenced at the beginning of the verse is synonymous with **Babylon the Great** in the next sentence. Identified by the name of the wicked Old Testament kingdom that conquered Israel, "Babylon" represents the secular, worldly system of people and institutions opposed to God. Eventually, this system will be destroyed by **the wine of his fierce anger.**

16:20-21 When God releases his anger in judgment, **every island** flees and **the mountains** disappear (16:20). What's more, **enormous hailstones, each weighing about a hundred pounds, [fall] from the sky on people** (16:21). It is as though the creation, formed as an expression of God's love, is being undone as an expression of his wrath. As in 6:16-17, people know the source of their judgment, yet they refuse to repent or honor God. Instead, they blaspheme him, enraged at the severity of the hailstones plague. Their response is as irrational as it is immoral.

VIII. THE FALL OF BABYLON (17:1–19:21)

17:1-5 The identity of **the notorious prostitute who is seated on many waters** (17:1) is revealed in 17:5, when John calls her BABYLON THE GREAT, THE MOTHER OF PROSTITUTES AND OF THE DETESTABLE THINGS OF THE EARTH. The term *prostitute* is used as a metaphor for people who are unfaithful to God. What John calls the mother, or origin, of such unfaithfulness is the city of Babylon, introduced in Genesis 11:1-9. Led by a man named Nimrod (Gen 10:8-12), the people of Babylon rejected God's rule and put humankind at the center of their civilization. God dispersed that city in judgment by confusing its languages.

Throughout subsequent history, though, it spawned other civilizations in which man attempted to elevate himself to the role of deity—such as in the later kingdom of Babylon led by Nebuchadnezzar. After that, the Roman Empire embodied the values of ancient Babylon. Eventually, the term *Babylon* came to be used for any worldly system that attempted to replace God. Today, secularism and worldliness are children of this great mother of prostitutes.

The image of this prostitute **seated on many waters** (17:1) depicts worldliness and secularism dispersed among the many people groups and nations of the world (cf. 17:15) who have **become drunk**, so to speak, on **immorality** (17:2). The prostitute is riding **on a scarlet beast** (17:3), which is the Antichrist, because the Antichrist will carry godlessness

across his dominion. The materialism associated with worldly systems is depicted as the woman's clothing of **purple and scarlet** as well as her adornment of **gold, jewels, and pearls.** Perversion is depicted as the **detestable** content of a **golden cup** (17:4).

17:6 In the Antichrist's kingdom in particular, ungodliness will extend beyond mere secularism and worldliness to active persecution of Christians. Thus, the personification of worldliness, **the woman**, is said to be **drunk with the blood of the saints and with the blood of the witnesses to Jesus.** The persecution and immorality are so overwhelming that John is left **astonished.**

17:7-8 The angel who has been guiding John begins to **explain . . . the mystery of the woman and of the beast** (17:7). The description of the beast is similar to his description in 13:1, and the statement that he **was, and is not, and is about to come up from the abyss** refers to the reality described in 13:3: the Antichrist will receive a fatal wound only to rise from the dead and increase his following. This passage, however, adds a detail absent from chapter 13—that is, the Antichrist's ultimate end is **destruction.** Nonetheless, nonbelievers **will be astonished** temporarily at his apparent resurrection (17:8).

17:9-11 Key to understanding this scene is John's description of the beast's **seven heads**

as **seven mountains on which the woman is seated**. Historically, the Roman Empire has been described as a nation built on seven hills or seven mountains. Accordingly, John seems to be saying the Antichrist will lead a renewed Roman Empire. Worldliness and rebellion against God will spread across it, personified by the unfaithful woman seated on it.

The seven heads also represent **seven kings** (17:9) or world leaders. The presence of **five** kings who **have fallen** (17:10) indicates the Antichrist will depose some world leaders in order to increase his power. Nevertheless, he will leave some leaders in power and allow still others to rise to power. The Antichrist will govern alongside his political contemporaries, although eventually, as John repeats, he **is going to destruction** (17:11).

17:12-14 **The ten horns** represent ten kings, or world leaders, who **will receive authority** (17:12) for a short time and for one purpose: to **give their power and authority to the** Antichrist (17:13). There will be ten nations in the renewed Roman Empire that form an alliance under the Antichrist and **make war against the Lamb** at the battle of Armageddon. **But the Lamb will conquer them because he is Lord of lords and King of kings** (17:14).

17:15-17 **The waters**, as has been noted, symbolize the **peoples, multitudes, nations, and languages** (17:15) of the world, the majority of which embrace self-centeredness and ungodliness. The image of ten nations devouring **the prostitute** and burning **her up with fire** (17:16) serves as a reminder that the worldly system, which promises pleasure, will soon pass away. Those who embrace that system seek self-glorification and thrills. But in the end, their long-sought gratification will amount to nothing, and they will be given **to the beast** as his pawns (17:17).

17:18 Despite the fact that worldly systems and schemes ultimately leave their adherents empty handed, worldliness will exert **power over the kings of the earth** for a time, especially during the tribulation.

It's appropriate to pause here and note an important application: These events could

occur very soon indeed. Jesus said no one knows the "day or hour" of his coming (Mark 13:32), and we make no attempt to predict the precise timing of that glorious return. At the same time, we see chaos in the Middle East and what seems an increasing marginalization of God. The stage appears set for the Antichrist to arise out of chaos. Christians, then, must remain alert and devote their full energy, while there is still time, to God's agenda for themselves, their families, their churches, and their communities. Unbelievers would be wise to confess Jesus as their Savior immediately before it is too late.

18:1 The presence of **another angel with great authority coming down from heaven** underscores the importance of angels in Revelation. They are present and active in the church age as well, and indeed some followers of Christ "have welcomed angels as guests without knowing it" (Heb 13:2). But after the church is removed from the earth, angels will assume a more visible role to fill the spiritual void.

18:2-3 The angel proclaims that man-centered society **has fallen** (18:2) because **all the nations** became unfaithful to God, which is depicted metaphorically as society's drinking **the wine of** Babylon's **sexual immorality**. As a result of this wicked activity, **the merchants of the earth** are said to **have grown wealthy** (18:3). This passage, then, illustrates that all wealth does not come as a blessing from God. Satan can give wealth too, as is evident from his promise to give Jesus worldly kingdoms in exchange for worship (see Matt 4:9). It would be a mistake to assume that the presence of wealth in a particular life indicates God's blessing and his approval of that person's actions.

18:4-5 God's **people** are called to withdraw from worldly living in order to avoid the judgment to come upon godless society. In delivering that warning, a **voice from heaven** (18:4) refers to Babylon's sins as being **piled up** and triggering God's remembrance. God will delay judgment at times for the sins of the wicked. But when judgment comes, no sin will be passed over. All will receive their just recompense.

18:6-8 The members of the secular, godless society within the Antichrist's kingdom are sentenced to a **double portion** of judgment for their sins (18:6). The reason for such severe judgment is the arrogance and self-centeredness of those under the beast's rule. The society metaphorically called Babylon **glorified herself and indulged her sensual and excessive ways**, proclaiming, **I sit as a queen; I am not a widow, and I will never see grief** (18:7). God hates such brazen rejection of his ways and an accompanying view of oneself as indestructible. Therefore, he will send **death and grief and famine** and burning **with fire, because the Lord God who judges her is mighty** (18:8).

18:9-14 Judgment of the Antichrist's realm will be swift. Leading up to the moment of divine recompense, there will be many warnings and much display of God's patience. Yet when judgment finally falls, **the kings of the earth who have . . . shared her sensual and excessive ways will weep and mourn** (18:9) and say in amazement, **in a single hour, your judgment has come** (18:10). God's judgment will involve economic disruption. **The merchants of the earth will weep and mourn . . . because no one buys their cargo any longer** (18:11), including precious metals, cloth, spices, livestock, and produce (18:12-14).

Divine destruction of wealth in this instance should not be taken to indicate divine condemnation of wealth per se. There are many wealthy people in the Bible who walked with God—Abraham, Joseph, and Solomon to name a few. In Solomon's case, Scripture says explicitly that great wealth was a gift and reward from God (see 2 Chr 1:12). What the Lord condemns is a person being controlled by wealth. The more blessed you are, the more grateful and worshipful you should be. Yet in the case of Babylon, wealth led to self-centeredness and denial of God.

18:15-20 That wealth controlled the inhabitants of the Antichrist's kingdom is evident from the **torment, weeping and mourning** of **the merchants** upon the destruction of their material goods (18:15). They lament not the loss of life or swift removal of other people's livelihood, but that in a **single hour such fabulous wealth was destroyed**. The judgment's swiftness is underscored by the second and third repetitions of the phrase **a single hour** (18:17, 19; cf. 18:10 and "just one day" in 18:8). The severity of the economic disruption is emphasized by the threefold repetition of a double **woe** by the residents of Babylon (18:10, 16, 19). Lest anyone mistakenly think this economic destruction is mere happenstance, John makes its source clear: **Rejoice over her, heaven, and you saints, apostles, and prophets, because God has pronounced on her the judgment she passed on you** (18:20).

18:21 Not only will the destruction of godless, secular society be severe, but it will also be final. **A mighty angel** graphically illustrates that point when he picks up **a stone like a large millstone**, throws **it into the sea**, and declares: **In this way, Babylon the great city will be thrown down violently and never be found again**.

18:22-23 Commercial and social activity that is not in itself evil will be destroyed because secular society perverts it in service of a man-centered agenda. Thus, **the sound of harpists, musicians, flutists, and trumpeters** will be silenced, and skilled labor, industrial production, and weddings will cease. **This will happen because** people have been **deceived** by the lie that material wealth is all-satisfying in itself. God, in his infinite wisdom, will redirect human society to a better path.

18:24 Not surprisingly, worship of the wrong object (wealth) is accompanied by wrath misdirected at an improper target (Christians). In the Antichrist's kingdom, as with other godless societies throughout history, **the blood of prophets and saints** testifies to the slaughter of those who stand for God's values in opposition to the religion of materialism.

19:1 The scene shifts from earth to heaven as **something like the loud voice of a vast multitude** praises God with cries of **Hallelujah!** This Greek word is the transliteration of a Hebrew compound: *"hallal"* (praise) and *"Yah"* (an abbreviated form of Yahweh). Thus, the word means "praise Yahweh." *Praise* is the declaration of the glory, greatness, power, and majesty of God, and there is no such thing as silent praise. Unlike worship, which can occur quietly within a believer's heart, praise in Scripture often is tied to our lips (e.g., Pss 34:1; 51:15; 119:171). God is not untoward in demanding praise because he is worthy of it. Hundreds of thousands of people attend parades to celebrate championship sports teams, yet God is infinitely more worthy of celebration than any athlete. That's why the multitude in Scripture is found crying out, **Salvation, glory, and power belong to our God.**

19:2 The reasons for praising God are manifold, but here the praise comes specifically **because his judgments are true and righteous.** At Christ's second coming, he will judge those who are unfaithful to their Creator, and doing so will be entirely appropriate. During the tribulation, such people will corrupt **the earth with . . . sexual immorality** and inflict violence on the Lord's **servants.**

19:3-4 A second cry of **hallelujah** comes because **smoke ascends** from godless society **forever and ever** following God's judgment (19:3). Like God, his people are not to delight in the destruction of the wicked (see Ezek 33:11); however, worship is an entirely appropriate response to God's righteous judgments and his establishment of justice where there once was injustice. That is precisely why **the twenty-four elders,** who represent the church, **and the four living creatures,** who are angelic beings, worship **God, who is seated on the throne, saying, Amen! Hallelujah!** (19:4)—the third repetition of the latter term in four verses.

19:5-6 A voice . . . from the throne in heaven affirms the rightness of praise as a response to God's judgment. All believers—**both small and great**—are to render such praise (19:5). A **hallelujah** sounds for the fourth time, and with intense volume, when **a vast multitude, like the sound of**

cascading waters, and like the rumbling of loud thunder, worships God because he **reigns** (19:6). There are two ways in which God can reign: in blessing and in judgment. Either way, it is an awesome thing when the Lord manifests his presence and establishes his rule in an open and visible way. Here he is reigning in judgment.

19:7-9 The **marriage of the Lamb** (19:7) and the ensuing **marriage feast of the Lamb** (19:9) will occur on earth after Jesus returns. The feast will last for a thousand years during the millennial kingdom (cf. 20:1-6). This wedding imagery draws from the tradition of an ancient wedding, in which a formal betrothal was followed by a wedding ceremony that involved the bridegroom taking the bride to his father's house. Then, at a wedding party, guests celebrated the marriage.

In the church's spiritual marriage to Christ, the betrothal period is the church age, when Christians are pledged to Christ. The wedding will occur when Jesus returns to take his bride to his heavenly Father's house. The celebration will occur during the millennium, after the church **has prepared herself** (19:7) by adorning herself with **righteous acts** (19:8).

The marriage feast of the Lamb destroys the common caricature of heaven as a place where each believer simply sits on a cloud playing a harp. During this thousand-year party, believers' rewards and responsibilities will be determined by their levels of faithfulness to Christ on earth. Jesus will ensure the complete absence of disorder and discord.

19:10 The **he** in this verse and in 19:9 refers to the angel who began guiding John in 18:1. The glorious sight of the feast and reign of God leads John to fall at the angel's feet **to worship him.** But he corrects John: **Don't do that! I am a fellow servant with you and your brothers and sisters who hold firmly to the testimony of Jesus. Worship Jesus.**

19:11-12 Verse 11 takes the reader back in time to the second coming of Jesus, which will occur before the millennium. The public nature of the coming is depicted by heaven's visible opening. Jesus rides **a white horse**, the Roman symbol of victory. Christ's main task upon returning to earth is making **war** against the enemies of God (19:11). **His eyes** are pictured as glorious and intense, and he wears **many crowns** as a symbol of his vast authority. Even at the open manifestation of Christ in his glory, aspects of his person will remain beyond human comprehension. That reality is symbolized by **a name written** on him **that no one knows except himself** (19:12).

19:13-14 The meekness and mildness of Jesus at his first coming contrast with his disposition at his second coming. On that day, he will establish his reign on earth by force. Thus, he is pictured wearing **a robe dipped in blood** (19:13) and accompanied by **the armies that were in heaven**, who follow him **on white horses, wearing pure white linen** (19:14). Those armies are followers of Jesus from the church age and the tribulation who will rule on earth with him for a thousand years.

19:15-16 At his second coming, Jesus's weapon of choice will be his Word, pictured here as **a sharp sword** that **came from his mouth, so that he might strike the nations with it** (19:15). Because he is KING OF KINGS AND LORD OF LORDS (19:16), conquering every enemy on earth will be a matter of relative ease. It will be a matter of speaking.

This is nothing new, though. From Genesis to Revelation, Jesus is pictured as possessing an authoritative Word. John 1:1 says of Jesus, "In the beginning was the Word, and the Word was with God, and the Word was God." At creation Jesus spoke the words, "Let there be light" (Gen 1:3), and by his Word light came about. It was by that same authoritative Word that Jesus caused the devil to flee in the wilderness (see Matt 4:1-11) and sent a legion of demons out of a demon-possessed man and into a herd of pigs (see Mark 5:1-13). In each of these instances, the way he brought about powerful results was by speaking his Word. And so shall it be at the end of time.

Likewise, for followers of Jesus, we must not simply know God's Word or study it, but also verbally quote it. So, when was the last time you actually quoted God to another person or even to the devil in order to handle a specific situation? If you have truly received authority from God—which all believers have—and you quote the Word accurately to people or forces of Satan, it carries intrinsic authority to accomplish God's purposes. In some cases, it draws a person to salvation. In others, it causes a hardened sinner to be without excuse for his or her conduct. In no situation, however, will a child of God verbally quote and obey the Word of God and have that Word return empty (see Isa 55:11).

19:17-18 Vultures are summoned to **gather together for the great supper of God** so that they **may eat the flesh of kings, the flesh of military commanders, the flesh of horses and of their riders, and the flesh of everyone, both free and slave, small and great.** The context of this summons is that Satan, the Antichrist, and their allies will seek to destroy Jesus when he returns at the battle of Armageddon (16:12-16). Nevertheless, Jesus will utterly defeat them and leave their bodies to be eaten by birds of prey, a reality mentioned in Matthew 24:27-28 as well.

19:19 The active opposition of the Antichrist and his allies to Christ is made explicit here. Jesus will not return to bring capricious judgment against unsuspecting innocent parties. He will strike down the wicked who are **gathered to wage war against** him.

19:20 The **beast**, or Antichrist, and **the false prophet** are **taken prisoner** and **thrown alive into the lake of fire that burns with sulfur.** This makes it clear that there is no annihilation in store for those who reject Christ. Some have wrongly taught that the wicked are punished in hell for a time before simply ceasing to exist. It is clear from this verse (and others), however, that punishment is unending.

19:21 In addition to receiving eternal judgment in hell, which will be described further in 20:13-15, those who stand against Jesus at the battle of Armageddon will face a temporal judgment on earth: They will be **killed with the sword that [comes] from the mouth** of Jesus—his Word (see 19:15).

IX. THE MILLENNIUM AND THE
FINAL JUDGMENT (20:1-15)

20:1-2 The **abyss** (20:1) is a place of captivity and judgment. The **angel** who comes **down from heaven** has **the key** to this prison, symbolic of God's authority over it, as well as a **great chain**. The angel seizes **the dragon, that ancient serpent who is the devil and Satan, and [binds] him for a thousand years** (20:1). The word "thousand" is repeated six times in this chapter and marks a key theological concept in this section of the book. We derive the word *millennium* from the Latin words for "thousand years." Theologians use this term to reference various interpretations of the "thousand years" in Revelation 20.

Premillennialism, which is the position adopted in this commentary, teaches that Christ will return before his thousand-year reign on earth and Satan's thousand-year binding. *Postmillennialism* teaches that there will be a thousand-year period of peace and righteousness on earth preceding Christ's return. *Amillennialism* teaches that the "thousand years" is not a future era of earth's history, but a figurative designation for either Christ's present reign in the church or his eternal reign in the new heaven and new earth.

20:3 During Satan's thousand-year captivity in **the abyss**, he will **no longer** be able to **deceive the nations**. The sinfulness of humanity will not be removed during this period, but the devil's ability to exacerbate it through deception will be. After the thousand years, however, Satan **must be released for a short time.**

20:4 Immediately following the tribulation, at the opening of the millennium, God will judge all non-believers to come out of the tribulation, those who took the mark of the best and cast their allegiance with the Antichrist. This judgment is implied by the presence of **thrones** and the **people seated on them who were given authority to judge.** In contrast to the judgment of non-believers from the tribulation, all followers of Christ from all ages will reign **with Christ** during the millennium, including those from the tribulation **who had not worshiped the beast or his image, and who had not accepted the mark on their foreheads or their hands.**

20:5-6 Nonbelievers from all periods of history other than the tribulation will not be raised for judgment **until the thousand years [are] completed.** That post-millennial resurrection will be **the first resurrection** of that group (20:5). Importantly, in verse 6, the phrase **the first resurrection** is used with a different referent: the resurrection of believers at the beginning of the millennium to reign with Jesus. Over such people, **the second death** (i.e., eternal judgment) **has no power.**

The millennial reign of Christ and his followers is the utopia for which the world longs. There will be no war. The lion will lie down with the lamb. Lifespans will increase exponentially as in the early days of the Old Testament. The reason such utopia will be possible is that Jesus will be ruling with a rod of iron, and there will be no allowance for rebellion. Each believer will be a co-regent with Jesus, receiving rewards and responsibilities in accordance with his or her level of faithfulness in the present life. Because Christ's followers will have glorified, heavenly bodies, each person will be perfectly suited to carry out his or her responsibilities.

20:7-8 At the end of the millennium, **Satan will be released from his prison and will go out to deceive the nations** as he has been doing since the fall of mankind (see Gen 3). Surprisingly, even following a thousand years of utopia on earth under the reign of Christ, there will be people who rebel against him and fall for Satan's deception. These will be like people in the first century AD who followed Jesus and applauded his miracles but then yelled, "Crucify him!" before Pilate (Luke 23:21).

Such people follow Jesus outwardly but have experienced no heart transformation. When Satan is released from captivity, he will not force anyone to rebel against Christ. He simply will take advantage of what's already inside them.

The people Satan deceives are referred to as **Gog and Magog**, an evil man in Ezekiel 38-39 and the land over which he ruled, respectively. Here the terms are symbolic of the enemies of God in general. Such people will **gather . . . for battle** against Jesus, and their numbers will be vast, **like the sand of the sea** (20:8). Until the final judgment, there will always be people who choose to rebel against Jesus.

20:9 These allies of Satan will come **up across the breadth of the earth and [surround] the encampment of the saints, the beloved city**—that is, Jerusalem. But unlike the protracted battle God wages against his enemies during the tribulation, divine victory in this situation is going to come quickly. **Fire** will come **down from heaven and [consume] them**.

20:10 The judgment experienced by individuals in hell will not be identical. Rather, the judgment a person or demon receives will be in proportion to their sin. In this case, **the devil** is **thrown** straight **into** the same portion of hell as **the beast and the false prophet**. Second, punishment in hell lasts **forever and ever**. Third, as Matthew 25:41 teaches, hell was "prepared for" Satan and his demons. It was never prepared for people. The only way people go there is by actively choosing the way of Satan. No one goes to hell by chance.

20:11-12 The **great white throne** (20:11) is the site at which unbelievers from all ages of history will be judged by God. This judgment will involve the consultation of two heavenly records: the **books** and **the book of life**. The former are records of people's deeds, by which their levels of judgment will be determined, since their names will be shown not

to be in the book of life. Each nonbeliever's level of punishment will be **according to their works** (20:12)—that is, in proportion to their sins and good things committed while in the body. The book of life lists those who have trusted Jesus Christ as Savior and been credited with his imputed righteousness. No one will receive salvation based on what's written in a book of deeds because everyone has sinned and fallen short of God's perfect standard (see Rom 3:23; 6:23). Having one's name appear in the book of life is the only way of salvation.

20:13 Non-believers will appear at the judgment in a resurrected state, in which their souls are united with non-glorified bodies. John describes a bodily resurrection to judgment when he says **the sea gave up the dead that were in it, and death and Hades gave up the dead that were in them**. At death, the soul is separated from the body, with the soul going immediately into the presence of God (see Luke 23:43) or to a state of judgment (see Luke 16:22-24). At the rapture, believers' souls will be united with glorified bodies appropriate to their eternal existence in paradise. Here, nonbelievers' souls are united with bodies suited for their eternal location.

20:14-15 The **lake of fire** will be the final, eternal location of every human **whose name [is] not found written in the book of life** (20:15; see the commentary on 13:8). It is a place of eternal, conscious torment received in proportion to one's sins in the body. Those who receive this judgment have not necessarily committed worse sins than those who dwell with God in paradise. They simply are reaping the fruit of their sins rather than enjoying the benefits of having Christ's perfect record credited to their accounts. **The second death** (20:14) is another way of speaking of eternal judgment. The first death is the physical death of the body. The second death is eternal separation from the love, blessings, and benefits of God.

X. THE NEW CREATION AND THE
NEW JERUSALEM (21:1-27)

21:1 History as we know it is over at this point, and John begins to describe the eternal state in which believers will dwell. The eternal state in which unbelievers will exist has already been described (see 20:14-15). Believers will live in **a new heaven and a new earth** because the **first heaven and the first earth** will **pass away**.

God will un-create the universe because each part of it is affected by sin, and the eternal state must be completely free from sin's consequences. But that doesn't mean the end for planet earth. Every molecule, atom, proton, and neutron in existence today will disintegrate only to be replaced by a glorious new creation. In it, **the sea** will be **no more**. So while three-quarters of the planet on which we live is currently underwater, that entire vast expanse will be made habitable for God's people.

21:2-4 Right now, Christ dwells in a heavenly city with the souls of all believers who have died (see John 14:2-3). During the millennium, God's people will live and work on the earth we know now, with their capital in Jerusalem. But after God destroys and makes the earth new, he's going to send that heavenly city **down out of heaven** to the new earth, **prepared like a bride adorned for her husband.** That city will become the capital of the new creation and be known as **the new Jerusalem**. And there God will dwell in the midst of his new creation and **live with** his people (21:3). All sadness, hurt, and disappointment will be no more as we live alongside our Creator (21:4).

21:5-6 The idea that God will make **everything new** may seem too spectacular to be true, but he says this promise is indeed **faithful and true** (21:5). His people will experience complete satisfaction in the new creation, symbolized here by the metaphor of thirst being quenched **from the spring of the water of life** (21:6). The refreshing satisfaction of downing a cold glass of water when you're parched is nothing compared to the spectacular satisfaction to come.

21:7 Every saved person will live in the new creation, but the Christian who is fully committed—**the one who conquers**—will **inherit** an even greater reward, and God will dwell with him at an increased level of intimacy like a father with his **son**.

21:8 The description of heaven is interrupted with a brief reminder that those who persist in sin and rebellion against God will spend eternity **in the lake that burns with fire and sulfur, which is the second death.** Unbelievers, with their unglorified bodies and unredeemed souls, will enter a place where every problem from this life will be amplified without any hope of improvement. They will become locked at varying levels in the consequences of their sinfulness.

21:9-11 One of the seven angels, **who had held the seven bowls filled with the seven last plagues** (21:9; cf. 16:1-21), shows John the new **Jerusalem** (21:10). Although believers will dwell across the entire new creation, the angel focuses John's attention on the new earth's capital. Because it will be **arrayed with God's glory**, this city will be more radiant than a cut diamond (21:11).

21:12-14 The city's **massive high wall** (21:12) signifies the identity of its inhabitants. First, **the names of the twelve tribes of Israel's sons [are] inscribed on the gates** (21:12), signifying that believers from Old Testament Israel will be present within it. Second, **the city wall** is pictured with **twelve foundations** and **the twelve names of the twelve apostles of the Lamb** are written **on the foundations** (21:14). This signifies the presence of believers from the church, which was established in the New Testament era. Old and new covenant followers of the Lord will dwell together in the new creation.

21:15-17 The angel measures **the city, its gates, and its wall** (21:15) to reveal that the city is a cube of **12,000** *stadia* in **length, width, and height** (21:16). A *stadia* is approximately 600 feet, which means each dimension of the city is approximately 1,400 miles—about half the distance from New York to Los Angeles. The most mind-blowing aspect of these dimensions is the height. It's a multi-storied city that extends up—and this is just the capital of God's new creation! The wall encasing this city will be **144 cubits**, about 72 yards, thick.

21:18-21 The **wall** will be made of **jasper**, an opaque gemstone. The **city** itself will be **pure gold** (21:18). **The foundations of the city wall** are to be **adorned with every kind of jewel** (21:19). The list of them in 21:19-20 defies comment. Each of the **twelve gates** will be **a single pearl**, and **the main street of the city** will be **pure gold** (21:21). This is where we draw the idea that there are streets of gold in our eternal home—not of tar, not of cement, but of gold!

21:22 There will be a temple in Jerusalem during the tribulation and during the millennium. But there will be no **temple** in the new Jerusalem because a representation of God's presence will no longer be necessary. We will have his direct presence.

21:23-26 There will be no **sun** or **moon** needed in the city **because the glory of God illumines it, and its lamp is the Lamb** (21:23). Our sun is ninety-three million miles away, yet its power is sufficient to illumine the earth. God's presence, though, can replace the sun with ease because the Lord possesses an even greater degree of power and radiance. That **it will never be night there** suggests believers' glorified bodies will never get tired and need to sleep.

Moreover, we won't get bored. On the new earth, there will be **nations** and **kings** (21:24) functioning in a national context and bringing their **glory and honor** into the city (21:26). Everyone will come to the new Jerusalem as a highlight of their lives on the new earth. And why not, given its splendor?

21:27 While the invitation to dwell in this city is universal, the requirements to enter are specific: **Nothing unclean will ever enter it, nor anyone who does what is detestable or false, but only those written in the Lamb's book of life**, who have received Jesus as their Savior by faith.

XI. THE SOURCE OF LIFE AND CONCLUSION (22:1-21)

22:1-2 Since there is no sea on the new earth, water will be supplied by **the river of the water of life . . . flowing from the throne of God and of the Lamb**—a single throne shared by God the Father and God the Son (22:1). The new earth also will contain **the tree of life** (22:2), which first appeared in the garden of Eden (Gen 2:9) and from which humans were barred from eating after Adam and Eve sinned (Gen 3:22-24).

The leaves of the tree are for healing the nations. Why would healing be necessary in the new heaven and new earth? Because there is a group of people who have access to the heavenly Jerusalem but who do not live there (see 21:24-26). There is only one group of people left on earth to go into eternity in their physical bodies—those who were true to Jesus Christ and served him during his millennial reign. They go into eternity after the millennium with physically glorified bodies not spiritually glorified bodies (see 1 Cor 15:38-41)—that is, like Adam and Eve in the garden. These will make up the nations who do not live in the new Jerusalem but who will have access to the city. They will need the leaves of the tree for their continued health and well-being.

22:3-5 In the new heaven and new earth, **there will no longer be any curse.** Everything will be just as God intended it, and **his servants will worship him** (22:3). Use of the term "servants" implies that believers will be happily serving and working in the new creation, overseeing the planet to varying degrees corresponding to their rewards. In this environment, God's people **will see his face** (22:4), and there will no longer be a need for either **the light of a lamp or the light of the sun** because God's radiant presence will provide all necessary illumination.

22:6-7 The speaker in 22:6 is the angel who began guiding John in 21:9. He offers a reminder that every word spoken in Revelation is **true**. We don't know when these events will occur, but we are assured they will **soon take place** (22:6), a truth echoed by Jesus himself in 22:7. In response to the imminence of Christ's return, readers are commanded to take this book seriously and act on it.

22:8-9 Often, Revelation is portrayed as a book of prophecy, and this is certainly true. But, more fundamentally, it is a book about worship, a theme that recurs from chapters 1-22. Here, as he has before, John falls **down to worship at the feet of the angel** (22:8). The angel, however, corrects him: **Don't do that! I am a fellow servant with you ... and those who keep the words of this book. Worship God!** (22:9). Worship of God is the appropriate response to the words of Revelation.

22:10-11 The words of the book were not to be sealed up **because the time is near** (22:10). Rather, they are to be read—which will lead people to one of two responses. Some will not heed the admonitions and continue on a path of rebellion against God. As John puts it, **the filthy** will **still be filthy**. Others, however, will heed the warnings and move in the direction God wants them to go, namely, **righteousness** (22:11).

22:12-14 Jesus—**the Alpha and the Omega, the first and the last, the beginning and the end** (22:13)—is **coming soon** to **reward** each believer **according to his work** (22:12). The reward will include access **to the tree of life** and **the city** (22:14). The greater a person's faithfulness in earthly life, the greater his or her access will be to special blessings in the eternal state.

22:15 The wicked, those who never received Jesus as their Savior, will remain under the curse and be separated from the blessings described in this chapter. Among them will be those whose base, sensual living made them like **dogs, the sorcerers, the sexually immoral, the murderers, the idolaters, and everyone who loves and practices falsehood.**

22:16 Revelation was written specifically for believers. That's why Jesus declares, **I ... have sent my angel to attest these things to you for the churches.** It's about the future, but it's for the present-day church. **The bright morning star** is another way of referring to the sun. In the daytime, it is the one star sufficiently luminous and powerful to light the entire earth. Spiritually speaking, Jesus is "the bright morning star" because he is the most powerful source of spiritual illumination and is the sole source of eternal life.

22:17 John ends the book with an evangelistic invitation. The Holy **Spirit**, the church, and **anyone who hears** the message all beckon sinners to **come** to Christ. *Anyone* who is spiritually **thirsty** may have his or her thirst quenched by Jesus. And best of all, this spiritual satisfaction is free. **The water of life** is a gift. All that is required to possess eternal life in the paradise that has been described is to receive the free gift of salvation by placing your faith in Jesus Christ alone and his substitutionary death. Embrace the agenda of his eternal kingdom. No earthly agenda compares.

22:18-19 Don't mess with the Word. That's John's admonition in these verses, and it applies specifically to the book of Revelation. It has two components. First, do not add to **the prophecy of this book.** The penalty for doing so will be **the plagues that are written in** it (22:18). Second, do not take **away from the words of the book.** Those who do so will have their heavenly rewards taken away, namely, their **share of the tree of life and the holy city** (21:19).

22:20 Much of Revelation is difficult to understand because of its symbolism, but the book concludes by underscoring with notable simplicity two central themes. First, Jesus is **coming soon.** You can understand this even if details of the rapture, the tribulation, the second coming of Jesus, the millennium, and the eternal state remain unclear.

Second, the glorious future in store for followers of Jesus should inspire worship. John's response to all that was revealed to him was an exclamation of worshipful affirmation: **Amen! Come, Lord Jesus!** There is enough truth stated plainly in Revelation for you to thank God for your salvation, for your eternal future, and for God's grace. If reading Revelation makes you a better worshiper, it has achieved its goal.

22:21 The wrath to come on all who do not acknowledge Jesus as Savior contrasts with **the grace of the Lord Jesus** available to **everyone** during the church era. It is with a prayer for that saving grace to be broadly bestowed that John closes the book.